40TH ANNIVERSARY EDITION

KOVELS'
Antiques &
Collectibles
PRICE LIST 2008

BLACK DOG
& LEVENTHAL
PUBLISHERS
NEW YORK

Published by
Black Dog & Leventhal Publishers, Inc.
151 W. 19th Street
New York, NY 10011

Distributed by
Workman Publishing Company
225 Varick Street
New York, NY 10014

Designed by Sheila Hart Design, Inc.
Manufactured in the United States of America

ISBN-13: : 978-1-57912-745-9
Hardcover ISBN-13: 978-1-57912-742-8

Library of Congress Cataloging-in-Publication Data is available on file at
the offices of the publisher.

Paperback
b d f h g e c a

Hardcover
b d f h g e c a

BOOKS BY RALPH AND TERRY KOVEL

American Country Furniture, 1780-1875

A Directory of American Silver, Pewter, and Silver Plate

Kovels' Advertising Collectibles Price List

Kovels' American Antiques, 1750-1900

Kovels' American Art Pottery

Kovels' American Collectibles, 1900 – 2000

Kovels' American Silver Marks, 1650 to the Present

Kovels' Antiques & Collectibles Fix-It Source Book

Kovels' Antiques & Collectibles Price List

Kovels' Bid, Buy, and Sell Online

Kovels' Book of Antique Labels

Kovels' Bottles Price List

Kovels' Collector's Guide to American Art Pottery

Kovels' Collectors' Guide to Limited Editions

Kovels' Collectors' Source Book

Kovels' Depression Glass & Dinnerware Price List

Kovels' Dictionary of Marks—Pottery and Porcelain, 1650 to 1850

Kovels' Guide to Selling, Buying, and Fixing Your Antiques and Collectibles

Kovels' Guide to Selling Your Antiques & Collectibles

Kovels' Illustrated Price Guide to Royal Doulton

Kovels' Know Your Antiques

Kovels' Know Your Collectibles

Kovels' New Dictionary of Marks— Pottery and Porcelain, 1850 to the Present

Kovels' Organizer for Collectors

Kovels' Price Guide for Collector Plates, Figurines, Paperweights
and Other Limited Edition Items

Kovels' Quick Tips: 799 Helpful Hints on How to Care for your Collectibles

Kovels' Yellow Pages, A Resource Guide for Collectors

The Label Made Me Buy It: From Aunt Jemima to Zonkers—
The Best-Dressed Boxes, Bottles, and Cans from the Past

To Alan Mirken
Who worked with us through our many books
as everything changed, from the antiques market to the technologies of production.
His help and friendship made this book possible.

INTRODUCTION

This is the fortieth year *Kovels' Antiques & Collectibles Price List* has been published. The book is still written by its original authors, Ralph and Terry Kovel, and has the same reliable content. But this year it is very different, and thanks to suggestions from readers, a very improved book. There are five times as many color pictures, 2,500, plus sketches of product logos, about 45,000 prices, dozens of tips about care, and facts of interest. Each picture is shown with a complete caption that includes the price, a feature you asked for. The entire book has been redesigned. Each page is bigger, giving more room for text and pictures. It has color tabs and color-coded paragraphs that make it easier to find the listings you want. It even has a new, readable typestyle. There are seven hundred categories with introductory paragraphs. And, as always, all of the antiques and collectibles priced here were offered for sale in the American market during the past year.

READ THIS FIRST

This is a book for the collector. We check prices, visit shops, shows, and flea markets, read hundreds of publications and catalogs, check online services and the Internet, and decide which antiques and collectibles are of most interest to most collectors. We concentrate on the average pieces in any category. Sometimes high-priced items are included so you will realize that rarities are very valuable.

Examples of furniture, silver, Tiffany, art pottery, and some other items may sell for more than $40,000; we list a few. Most pieces cost less than $10,000. The highest price in this book is $464,000 for a copper Liberty and American flag weather vane. The lowest price is $1.00 for a Clover Leaf Dairy bottle cap. We also include the weird and the wonderful. This year you can find a 7½-inch-high cut glass toupee holder made by Libbey glass for $649 or an advertising pot scraper with the unexpected slogan "King Midas flour, highest priced flour in America," $375. A folk art coconut cup that is hoof shaped with carved flowers, an eagle, a coat of arms, and a silver hook brought $978. Macabre items sold well this year. A 24-inch toy truck marked "Milgrimm Mortuary" that held a tiny casket was $468. A pair of carved wooden hearse curtains sold for $690 and a begging bowl made from a Tibetan human skull set with precious stones brought $770. The smallest item in the book is a ½-inch gold-plated button from an Edwardian vest. It is made of abalone shell inset with brass and sold with the box for $85. The biggest item is a 20-foot Mississippi Riverboat gangplank for $920.

Prices are up in some categories: Art pottery, especially "monumental" vases over 24 inches high, have been setting records. But an 11-inch-tall Frederick Hurten Rhead designed Santa Barbara vase sold for the highest price of $516,000. Ceramic tiles have gone up from just a few dollars to the hundreds of dollars range, perhaps because other pottery is so expensive. French and English art pottery has become more popular and more expensive in the United States. Unusual Fifties studio silver and copper jewelry by famous designers sells for thousands of dollars. (There is a museum exhibit of this type of jewelry scheduled in 2007-08.) Modern and contemporary silver tableware, especially pitchers and bowls in organic shapes, are also up in price, perhaps because of a traveling museum exhibit of a collection in 2006 and 2007.

Decoys keep going up. It is said that several very, very wealthy collectors are battling for the very top examples. Name designer furniture made from the 1950s to 2007 brings astounding prices at the art shows as well as some of the top auctions. Rare, large advertising pieces used before World War I, modern textiles, and American Indian pieces of quality are still going up. Garden antiques and collectibles continue to interest collectors at all levels of the market, from $25 vintage clay pots to $2,000 cast-iron statues of dogs. Viktor Schreckengost, the Cowan artist who made the Jazz bowl, had 100 birthday exhibits for his 100th birthday and now anything he designed, from dinnerware to bicycles, is up in price. Less-than-perfect antiques and collectibles, like repaired bottles or art pottery, are selling at about 80 percent of the price of a perfect piece—if they are rare. Prices at large, well-advertised auctions look high when compared to presale estimates, but if you take a closer look you'll find that estimates are low to encourage bidders. Prices seem much the same for most collectibles. On eBay, opening bids are often very low because the seller pays an insertion fee to eBay based on the opening bid, not on the final price. In general, Internet-only auction prices are still dropping, and many items don't sell. However, many larger auction houses are selling on land and online at the same time, giving them a wider customer base and the expected prices.

This book seems to have gotten younger over the past forty years. Most items in our original book were made before 1860. Today we have pieces made as recently as the 1990s, and there is great interest in furniture, glass, and ceramics made since 1950.

The book is about 800 pages long, and crammed full of prices and pictures. We try to have a balanced format—not too many glass, pottery, or collectible items; furniture from the eighteenth through the twentieth centuries; and not too many items that sell for over $5,000. Prices are from the American market for the American market. Few European sales are reported. We take the editorial privilege of not including prices we think result from "auction fever." There is a computer-generated index. Use it often. It includes categories and much more. For example, there is a category for Celluloid. Most celluloid will be there, but a toy made of celluloid will be listed under Toy and also indexed under Celluloid. There are also cross-references in the listings and in the paragraphs. But some searching must be done. For example, Barbie dolls are in the Doll category; there is no Barbie category. And when you look at "doll, Barbie," you see a note that Barbie is under "doll, Mattel, Barbie" because most dolls are listed by maker. Where possible, we list the maker at the beginning of an entry, and the size and age at the end.

All photographs and prices are new. Antiques and collectibles pictured are items that were offered for sale. Whenever computer-generated spaces appear, we fill them with new tips about care of collections, security, and other useful information. Don't discard this book. Old Kovels' price books should be saved for future reference and for tax and appraisal information.

The prices in this book are reports of the general antiques market. Every price in the book is new. We do not estimate or "update" prices. Prices are asking prices; a buyer may have negotiated to a lower selling price. No price is an estimate. We do not pay dealers, collectors, or writers to estimate prices. Experience has shown us that estimated prices are usually high or low, but rarely an accurate report. If a price range is given, at least two identical items were offered for sale at different prices. Price ranges are found only in categories such as Pressed Glass, where identical items can be identified. If the price is from an auction, it includes the buyer's premium, but like all the prices, it does not include sales tax. Some prices in *Kovels' Antiques & Collectibles Price List* may seem high and some may seem low because of regional variations, but each price is one you could have paid for the object somewhere in the United States. Some Internet prices, carefully edited, are included, but we find prices there can be misleading. Because so many non-collectors sell online but know little about the objects they are describing, there are often inaccuracies in the descriptions.

If you are selling your collection, do not expect to get retail value unless you are a dealer. Wholesale prices for antiques are usually 50 percent of retail prices. The antiques dealer must make a profit or go out of business. Internet auction prices are less predictable. Because of the international audience and "auction fever," prices can be higher or lower than retail.

RECORD PRICES

Every year the media reports record prices because a million-dollar table makes a great story. They tend to ignore the everyday prices of collectibles. We report the records because it is always nice to dream that Grandma's vase *could* be worth a fortune. Just remember, it is as likely as winning the lottery. These are the prices for the rarest and the best this past year. We have chosen some record prices that will interest the average collector. We have omitted other records, especially many for paintings, photographs, and Asian art.

ADVERTISING

Diana cartridge box: $11,865 for an empty "Diana" cartridges shotgun shell box, manufactured by California Powder Works. Twenty-five 10-gauge shells, showing a huntress with bow & arrow, c.1908.

Leaded-glass sign: $19,800 for a California Steam Beer stained leaded glass sign. Multicolored glass panels, 74 x 21½ in.

Mr. Peanut display: $35,750 for a Planters three-dimensional Mr. Peanut store display figure. Standing, holding cane, wearing black top hat, papier-mâché, 1920s, 50 in.

Peters Quick Shot 12-gauge full box: $8,899 for a full box of Peters Quick Shot cartridges. Twelve-gauge PRIZE shells, 3½- 1½- 7 shot.

Reverse-on-glass sign: $28,600 for a C.A. Lammers Beer reverse-on-glass sign. Pictures couple at table, waiter and stagecoach in background, P.H. Zang Brewing Co., Denver, Colorado, Tuchfarber Mfg. Co., Cincinnati, Ohio, 1905. Frame, 41 x 33 in.

DECOYS

American decoy: $856,000 for a red-breasted merganser hen carved by Lothrop Holmes. Mid to late 19th century, branded on its underside "L.T. HOLMES."

Crowell black bellied plover decoy: $830,000 for the A. E. Crowell black bellied plover life-size decoy in spring plumage, carved in a feeding pose. From the collection of William J. Mackey, known as the missing "dust jacket" decoy pictured on the slip cover of *American Bird Decoys* by William Mackey.

Nathan Cobb and Virginia decoy: $390,000 for the Nathan Cobb large plump curlew with classic split-tail and original paint, marked with "N." From the collection of William J. Mackey.

New York decoy: $450,500 for the turned head Hudsonian curlew, Quoque, Long Island, carved by Thomas Gelston. From the collection of William J. Mackey.

FURNITURE

19th-century English furniture: $3,176,000 for the Hertford jewel cabinet, by John Webb, 3 spring-loaded secret drawers opens to reveal 18 small drawers, 3 spring-released frieze drawers, coat-of-arms of Marie-Josephine-Louise of Savoy on the crest, c.1787, 8 ft. 1¾ in. h. x 58 in. l. x 20⅝ in. w.

George Nakashima: $822,400 for George Nakashima furniture in the United States, an "Arlyn" table with redwood burl top and free-form edge, fissures and madrone burl butterflies. American black walnut base with butterflies of the same wood, East Indian laurel pegs, 26 x 89 x 91 in., 1988.

Greene & Greene: $2,144,000 for an 11-piece dining suite consisting of circular extending dining table, 2 armchairs and 8 side chairs with 4 extension leaves. Mahogany table with ebony pegs, various inlays, chair with original under upholstery.

Philadelphia Queen Anne armchair: $2,256,000 for the Philadelphia high-back Queen Anne walnut armchair, made c.1755, with Roman numeral V on its seat and seat rail, 45½ x 32½ x 16½ in.

Shaker furniture: $491,400 for a Shaker work stand from Mount Lebanon, Pennsylvania. Cherry, pine and poplar, dark stained finish with six small drawers on the upper portion and two full drawers below the work surface, 1870s, 42½ x 32½ x 22¾ in.

GLASS

Any piece of American Lily Pad glass: $55,000 for a Redford Crown Glass Works lily pad sugar bowl with lily pad cover. Aquamarine, c.1838, 8¾ in.

Canary example of this compote: $48,300 for a Sandwich glass canary yellow compote in Princess Feather Medallion & Basket of Flowers pattern.

Glass candy container: $15,400 for a Boob McNutt comic character glass candy container.

Glass target ball: $17,050 for a glass target ball made by Bogardus & Co. Medium to deep amber. Embossed on the bottom, "Bogardus & Company Shooting Gallery 158 South Clark St. Chicago/Bogardus Glass Ball Patd Apr 10 77 Embossed around Mouth Target Ball," 1877-1890, 2¾ in.

Lacy period covered salt: $34,100 for a Lyre pattern pressed Lacy salt, with original cover, opaque violet blue, four scrolled feet, pinecone finial and beaded rim, Boston & Sandwich Glass Co., 1840, 2 x 3⅛ in.

Lalique perfume presentation bottle: $216,000 for a 1939 presentation "Trésor de la Mer" (Treasure from the Sea) perfume bottle by Rene Lalique for Saks Fifth Avenue. Oyster shell-form box and pearl-form bottle, limited production of 100 examples, presentation box: 7½ x 8¼ x 5 in.

IRON

Any escutcheon/Pennsylvania wrought iron: $42,120 for a wrought-iron door escutcheon in the form of an Indian head with feathered headdress, 18th century, 8¼ in.

Halloween Girl doorstop: $72,800 for a Halloween Girl doorstop, figural whimsical girl in ghostly costume holding an over-sized Jack O' Lantern. Cast iron, with original Littco Products label on reverse side, 13⅞ in. h. x 8¾ in. w.

LAMPS

Emile-Jacques Ruhlmann lamp: $441,960 for an Emile-Jacques Ruhlmann (also known as Jacques-Emile Ruhlmann) table lamp, c.1925. Silvered bronze, glass, and ivory, domed shade with a curtain of hanging glass beads, 39⅜ in.

Fulper lamp: $36,000 for a Fulper mushroom-shaped lamp with crystalline glaze, 2-socket base, shade inset with leaded glass, and vertical mark, 17 x 17 in.

MISCELLANEOUS

American Indian object: $1,808,000 for a Tsimshian polychrome wood portrait mask. Chin slightly forward, down-turned mouth, high cheekbones, open eyes, and painted black, 7¾ x 7 x 4¾ in.

Rhinoceros horn vessel: $832,250 for a rhinoceros horn libation vessel. Carved with three elephant-head supports, main body carved in low relief with split-tailed dragons and topped by a nephrite serpent finial, 17th-18th century, 6 in.

Shaker oval carrier: $105,300 for a 19th-century Shaker oval carrier. Maple and pine, with 3 fingers, copper nails, chrome-yellow paint, and fixed carved handle, 7 in. h. to top of handle, 9⅛ in. l. x 6½ in. d.

Signed Beatles album: $115,228 for the signed album cover "Meet The Beatles," signed by all four Beatles as a gift for George Harrison's sister, Louise, in 1964.

Cane: (North American auction record) $45,920 for a 17th-century English cane with an elephant ivory handle, 3¾ x 1½ in. diameter. Decorated with piqué hollow dots, silvery string inlay, and silver overlay of a bird, cat, butterflies, flowers, and leaves. Silver scalloped collar and dark Malacca shaft with 4½-in. brass ferrule, cane length, 36¼ in.

Weather vane records: An October 2006 auction included four Indian-shaped weather vanes from a single collection. The almost-unbelievable record price was $5.8 million, for a molded copper Indian chief weather vane attributed to J.L. Mott Iron works, c.1900. The other Indian weather vanes sold for $72,000, $192,000, and $716,000. The $5.8 million Indian, the highest-priced piece of American folk art ever auctioned, was on top of an owner's house for years. Previous 2006 record prices for auctioned weather vanes were $1,080,000 in January for a Goddess of Liberty and $1,216,000 in August for a locomotive.

MUSIC

Musical instrument: $3,544,000 for a violin by Antonio Stradivari known as "The Hammer," made in Cremona, Italy, in 1707. (Its name, The Hammer, comes from Christian Hammer, a 19th-century Swedish collector.)

PAINTING & PRINTS

American Folk Art & Artist Edward Hicks: $6,176,000 for an oil-on-canvas painting by Pennsylvania Quaker Edward Hicks, "The Peaceable Kingdom," painted in 1849 for his daughter just before his death, 24¼ x 30¼ in.

Copley, John Singleton, painting, artist at auction: $3,376,000 for the signed and dated oil-on-canvas portrait titled Mrs. Theodore Atkinson, Jr. (Francis Deering Wentworth), by John Singleton Copley, 1765, 51 x 40 in.

Hiroshige print "Firefoxes on New Year's Eve at the Shozoku Hackberry Tree": $142,229 for this Japanese woodblock print by Ando Hiroshige.

Hiroshige print "Sudden Shower over the Ohashi Bridge, Atake": $156,870 for this Japanese woodblock print by Ando Hiroshige.

Mucha, Alphonse, oil-on-canvas: $1,472,000 for the 1920 painting "The Abolition of Serfdom in Russia," (reduced version), by Alphonse Mucha. Signed, inscribed, and dated "Mucha 1920 N.Y.," 40 x 57 in.

Painting from the Campbell Soup can series: $11,776,000 for the Andy Warhol painting "Small Torn Campbell's Soup Can (Pepper Pot)," hand painted, large soup can with a torn label, signed and dated "Andy Warhol/62," on the reverse. Gold paint, graphite on linen, 20 x 16 in.

Portrait by Ammi Phillips: $1,248,000 for the unsigned Ammi Phillips oil-on-canvas painting of a little girl in red with her cat, "Portrait of a Young Girl and Her Cat," c.1830-35, 36 x 28 in.

Rockwell, Norman, painting: $9,200,000 for Norman Rockwell's oil-on-canvas painting, "Homecoming Marine," commissioned for the cover of *The Saturday Evening Post* on October 13, 1945, signed "Norman Rockwell" in lower right corner, 46 x 42 in.

Wood, Grant, painting, artist at auction: $6,960,000 for the 1932 signed Grant Wood painting "Spring Plowing," picturing green hills, trimmed tracts of land, blue sky, oil-on-board, 18¼ x 22 in.

PAPER

Declaration of Independence official copy: $477,650 for an 1823 official copy of the Declaration of Independence—one of 200 commissioned by John Quincy Adams in 1820, printed by William Stone in 1823. The document was found in a thrift store encrusted with layers of shellac which helped preserve the color and clarity, priced at $2.48.

Edward McKnight Kauffer, poster: $5,060 for the 1947 poster by Edward McKnight Kauffer, "American Airlines to California," depicting a young woman on the beach & and a large beach ball, 40 x 30¼ in.

Houdini poster: $78,000 for a color lithograph poster, "Houdini, Europe's Eclipsing Sensation, The World's Handcuff King & Prison Breaker, Nothing On Earth Can Hold Houdini A Prisoner," picturing Houdini in hand restraints, and eight additional pictures of various other hand restraints. From the Fechner Collection, one of two copies known.

Montegue B. Black, poster: $12,650 for the Montague B. Black poster from 1911, "White Star Line," depicting the "Olympic" and the "Titanic" passing at sea (the Titanic in the distance), based on a painting by Black. Company overpainted the Titanic name, removing it from the caption, after Titanic's catastrophic maiden voyage. The caption read "White Star Line/Olympic 45,000 tons—Titanic 45,000 tons the Largest Steamers in the World," 29½ x 39½ in.

Original artwork from Spider-Man comic books: $101,700 for the original artwork from the cover of Spider-Man #43, drawn by John Romita, for the December 1966 issue. Depicting Spider-Man locked in mortal combat with his arch enemy, "The Rhino."

Santa hold-to-light postcard: $1,057 for a die cut hold-to-light Santa postcard. Image of old-fashioned Santa walking past village home, 2 children at open window, church in background, starry night.

Santa linen advertising postcard: $793 for a linen advertising postcard, "Atlas Snowfall Crystal Paperweights, Presents Santa Claus." Pictures Santa in a snow globe carrying sack.

Superman trading card set: $33,378 for a complete 72-card set of Superman cards from the 1940 trading card set by Gum, Inc.

Winsch Starry Halloween postcard: $1,495 for a Winsch Starry Halloween postcard, embossed series no. 382. Pictures 2 girls, black cat, and flying pumpkins on circular black background; on the right side is a witch on a broom and "A Starry Hallowe'en."

WPA poster: $9,000 for the WPA poster, "Grand Canyon National Park," c. 1938, U.S. Department of the Interior National Park Service, 19 x 14 in.

PHOTOGRAPHY

Ansel Adams photograph: $609,600 for the Ansel Adams photograph, "Moonrise, Hernandez, New Mexico." Mounted to Strathmore board, signed in pencil on the mount, matted, 1941, printed in 1948, 14⅜ x 19⅛ in.

Any 20th-century photograph at auction: $2,928,000 for the Edward Steichen photograph, "The Pond–Moonlight." Taken in the fall of 1904 of a moonlit pond on Long Island, 16¹¹⁄₁₆ x 19¹¹⁄₁₆ in.

Civil War officer photo: $44,812 for the ¼th plate tintype of Confederate Lt. Col. Walter H. Taylor, the only war-date hard image known.

Civil War soldier photo: $13,475 for the two Confederate ⅙th plate ambrotypes of Alabama brothers housed together in a double union case.

Leica M3 camera: $93,260 for a Leica M3 prototype of the pre-production (0-series) camera, serial no. 0016 including rare spool, with original Leitz lens "Summicron 2/50," c.1952.

POTTERY & PORCELAIN

19th-century European ceramics: $531,200 for a monumental Mintons exposition polychrome pâte-sur-pâte Jubilee vase, peacock-blue, with flaring neck, scrolling ribbon handles, and continuous scene of nymphs and warrior putti. Signed and dated L. Solon, 1888, gilt crowned globe mark and retail mark, 32 in. h.

American art pottery: $516,000 for a Santa Barbara vase made by Frederick Hurten Rhead, with stylized landscape and mirror black glaze. Stamped medallion of potter at kiln, c.1915, 11¼ x 6 in.

American stoneware water cooler: $88,000 for a stoneware water cooler impressed "Fenton & Hancock, St. Johnsbury, VT." Pictures Civil War General Asa Peabody Blunt and his wife, 4 gallon.

Denver Denaura vase: $9,600 for a Denver Denaura squat vase carved with fish, underwater flora, and cresting waves, covered in dark green vellum glaze. Considered the best-known example of Denaura and the only hand-signed piece by William Long, 11 x 5½ in.

Newcomb Pottery vase: 108,400 for a blue and white high glaze Newcomb pottery vase decorated in 1902 by Marie de Hoa LeBlanc. Incised birds (also called pukeko or purple gallinules or swamp hens) amongst bamboo, 12½ in. h.

Pennsylvania stoneware: $71,500 for a dome-shaped Pennsylvania stoneware birdhouse made in Newport, Pennsylvania. Cobalt blue decoration of a bust of a man, 2 birds in branches, and the inscription, "M & T Miller, New Port, Perry Co., Penn.," c.1870, 9 in.

Stoneware water cooler: $59,950 for a 5-gal. stoneware water cooler with original fitted lid by J. & E. Norton of Bennington, Vt. Decorated with houses, large reclining deer, basket of flowers, fences, hills, and dots, accented with incised lines above and below picture, 15 in., c.1855.

SPORTS

Hockey memorabilia: $179,655 for the Bobby Orr game-worn Boston Bruins hockey jersey from his second year in the NHL—the 1967-68 season.

Jim Thorpe autograph: $28,680 for a 1940s Jim Thorpe single-signed autographed baseball.

Non-Baseball sports item: $71,700 for Dr. James Naismith's (the inventor of the game of basketball) personal handwritten manuscript of the first basketball game played in 1891.

Postwar football card set: $59,750 for the 1952 complete set (144) of large Bowman football cards, high grade.

T206 baseball card set: $255,200 for a near-complete set of T206 "White Border" tobacco cards (520 of 524 cards), graded high by PSA.

Topps 1971 baseball trading cards: $19,613 for three Authentic Case Fresh 500-count unopened vending boxes of 1971 Topps Baseball trading cards (1,500 cards in total), 4th-6th Series, featuring Nolan Ryan, Willie Mays, Roberto Clemente, and Hank Aaron.

TEXTILES

Civil War flag: $956,000 for the personal battle flag of Confederate General JEB Stuart, hand-sewn by his wife Flora, made on a bunting field, 34 in. square, white border on all 4 sides, incorporates the 13-star design.

Civil War officer's uniform: $77,675 for the Confederate uniform of Cuban-born Officer Lt. Francisco Moreno, killed at the Battle of Shiloh wearing this uniform.

TOYS, DOLLS & GAMES

Chief Big Moon bank: $33,350 for a J. & E. Stevens cast-iron mechanical bank, Chief Big Moon. Red base, features a squaw sitting outside a teepee holding a fish, large frog emerges from nearby pond, c.1899, 10 in.

Game board: $57,360 for a 19th-century hand-drawn & painted Parcheesi board. Yellow & cream with borders painted red, green, blue, and brown on black ground, reverse side painted with checkerboard, 18½ x 16¾ in.

Hubley DO-X toy airplane: $9,200 for a Hubley DO-X toy airplane, painted gray with red wings, nickel-plated wheels, 6½ in.

Marklin Paterson train station: $40,250 for Marklin Paterson train station. Two-story building with 4 "Paterson" signs in black letters, 4 doors labeled baggage room, waiting room, ladies and gentleman, 2 windows labeled ticket office and telegraph office. Station is orange-yellow with red brick outline, green and black trim, and wood grain doors, c.1910-1912, 8½ in. w. x 16¼ in. l. x 10⅝ in. h.

Steiff monkey: $6,612 for a Steiff "60PB" monkey. Plush velvet hands, feet, ears, and face, and shoebutton eyes, string jointing with horizontal rod between his shoulders, bent arms, and voice box (inoperative), elephant button remains in ear, c.1903, 32 in.

WEAPONS

Civil War sword from Louisiana: $22,705 for the Confederate Foot Officer's Presentation Sword made by the Thomas Griswold Company, New Orleans.

Texas Civil War pistol: $77,675 for the Dance .44 Caliber Revolver with original holster.

A NOTE TO COLLECTORS

You already know this is a great overall price guide for antiques and collectibles. Each entry is current, every picture is new, and all prices are accurate.

Now there is another Kovel publication designed to keep you up-to-the-minute in the world of collecting. Things change quickly. Important sales produce new record prices. Fakes appear. Rarities are discovered. To keep up with developments, you can read *Kovels on Antiques and Collectibles*, our monthly newsletter. It is now available in two forms, a print edition that is mailed and an electronic edition. Both have the identical current information on collecting. They are filled with color photographs, about forty per issue. The newsletter reports prices, trends, auction results, Internet sales, and other news for collectors as it happens. For a free printed sample of *Kovels on Antiques and Collectibles*, see the last page of this book. Our website takes electronic subscriptions and also offers FREE pricing information, lists of publications and sources, news, and more. Visit www.Kovels.com to keep up on the buy-sell world of antiques.

HOW TO USE THIS BOOK

There are a few rules for using this book. Each listing is arranged in the following manner: CATEGORY (such as Pressed Glass), OBJECT (such as vase), DESCRIPTION (as much information as possible about size, age, color, and pattern). Some types of glass, pottery, and silver are exceptions to this rule. These are listed CATEGORY, PATTERN, OBJECT, DESCRIPTION. All items are presumed to be in good condition and undamaged, unless otherwise noted. In most sections, if a maker's name is easily recognized, like Gustav Stickley, we include it near the beginning of the entry. If the maker is obscure, the name may be at the end.

Many of the general glass entries are in special categories: Glass-Art, Glass-Blown, Glass-Bohemian, Glass-Contemporary, Glass-Midcentury, and Glass-Venetian. Major glass factories are listed under factory names. Well-known types of glass, such as Cut, Pressed, Depression, Carnival, etc., can be found in their own categories. You will find silver flatware in either Silver Flatware Plated or Silver Flatware Sterling. There is also a section for Silver Plate, which includes coffeepots, trays, and other plated pieces. Most solid or sterling silver is listed by country, so look for Silver-American, Silver-Danish, Silver-English, etc. Silver jewelry is listed under Jewelry. Most pottery and porcelain is listed by factory name, such as Weller; by item, such as Calendar Plate; in sections like Dinnerware or Kitchen; or in a special section, such as Pottery-Art, Pottery-Contemporary, Pottery-Midcentury, etc.

Sometimes we make arbitrary decisions. Fishing has its own category, but hunting is part of the larger category called Sports. We have omitted all guns except toys. It is not legal to sell weapons without a special license, so guns are not part of the general antiques market. Airguns, BB guns, rocket guns, and others are listed in the Toy section. Everything is listed according to the computer alphabetizing system. This means words such as "Mt." are alphabetized as "M-T," not as "M-O-U-N-T." All numerals are before all letters; thus "2" comes before "A."

We made several editorial decisions. A butter dish is a "butter." A salt dish is called a "salt" to differentiate it from a saltshaker. It is always "sugar and creamer," never "creamer and sugar." Political collectors often refer to "pinbacks," the round celluloid or tin pins decorated with candidates' names and faces. We use the word "button" instead of "pinback." The word "button" is also used when referring to fasteners on clothing. Where one dimension is given, it is the height; or if the object is round, the dimension is the diameter. The height of a picture is listed before width. Glass is clear unless a color is indicated.

Every entry is listed alphabetically, but idiosyncrasies of language remain. Some antiques terms, such as "Sheffield" or "Pratt," have two meanings. Read the paragraph headings to know the meaning used. All category headings are based on the language of the average person, and we use terms like "mud figures" even if not technically correct.

This book does *not* include price listings for fine art paintings, antiquities, stamps, coins, or most types of books. *Big Little Books* and similar children's books *are* included. Comic books are listed only in special categories like Superman, but original comic art and cels are listed in their own categories.

Prices for items pictured can be found in the appropriate category. Look for the matching entry with the abbreviation "Illus." The picture will be nearby. Pictures are not to to scale, but sizes are indicated.

Because of the computer, the book can be produced quickly. The last entries are added in June; the book is available in October. But human help finds prices and checks accuracy. We read everything at least three times, sometimes more. We edit more than 55,000 entries down to the approximately 45,000 entries found here. We correct spelling, remove incorrect data, write category paragraphs, and decide on new categories. We proofread copy and prices at least six times, but there will always be some misspelled words and other errors. Information in the paragraphs is updated each year and this year more than 15 updates and additions were made.

Prices are reported from all parts of the United States, Canada, and Europe, and converted to U.S. dollars at the time of the sale. The average rate of exchange between June 2006 and June 2007 was $1 U.S. to about $1.14 Canadian, .77 Euro, and .52 British Pound. Prices are from auctions, shops, Internet sales, and shows. Every price is checked for accuracy, but we are not responsible for errors.

We cannot answer your letters asking for price information, but please write if you have any requests for categories to be included in future editions or any corrections to the paragraphs or prices.

When you see us at shows and flea markets, stop and say hello. Don't be surprised if we ask for your suggestions. You can write to us at P.O. Box 22192, Beachwood, Ohio 44122, or visit us at our website, www.Kovels.com.

RALPH & TERRY KOVEL
July 2007

ACKNOWLEDGMENTS

This year, because of the new design of the 40th *Kovels' Antiques & Collectibles Price List*, we have asked for extra help from many dealers, collectors, and companies who are part of the wonderful world of antiques and collectibles. We give special thanks to those who helped us with pictures and deeds: Alderfer Auction Co.; Auction Team Köln; Belhorn Auction Services; Bertoia Auctions; Brunk Auctions; Cincinnati Art Galleries; Conestoga Auction Co.; Cowan's Auctions; Cripple Creek Auctions; CRN Auctions; DuMouchelles; Early American History Auctions; Early Auction Co.; Fellows & Sons Auctioneers; Fontaine's Auction Gallery; Garth's Auctions; Glass Works Auctions; Green Valley Auctions; Hake's Americana & Collectibles; Heritage Auction Galleries; Jackson's International Auctioneers & Appraisers; James D. Julia Auctioneers; James Measell; John Toomey Gallery; L.H. Selman Ltd; Lang's Sporting Collectables; Live Free or Die Antique Tool Auctions; Los Angeles Modern Auctions; Mastro Auctions; McMasters Harris Auction Co.; Morphy Auctions; Noel Barrett Auctions; Pook & Pook; Rago Arts and Auction Center; Randy Inman Auctions; Replacements, Ltd.; Rich Penn Auctions; Richard Opfer Auctioneering; Robert C. Eldred Co., RubyLane.com; Samuel T. Freeman & Co.; Showplace Antique Center; Showtime Auction Services; Skinner Inc.; Sloans and Kenyon; Sotheby's; Tom Harris Auctions; Treadway Gallery; Trocadero.com; Vectis Auctions Ltd.; Willis Henry Auctions; Woody Auction.

To the others in the antiques trade who knowingly or unknowingly contributed to this book, we say "thank you": Allard Auctions; American Antique Furniture; American Bottle Auctions; American Cut Glass Association; American Political Items Collectors; Anderson Auctions; Andre Ammelounx; Antique Bottle & Glass Collector; Antique Fan Collectors Association; Antique Phonograph Gallery Online; Antiques Journal; Antiques Marketplace; Ark Antiques; Aumann Auctions; Austin T. Miller American Antiques; Aux Belles Choses New Orleans; BBR Auctions; Beanpot Antiques; Be-hold; Bertolet House Antiques; The Best Things; Blyth's Auction Service; Bonhams & Butterfields; Bookend Collector's Club; Boyz Toyz Antiques; Brewery Collectibles Club of America; Canes Through the Ages; Carlson & Stevenson Antiques & Art; Carlton Antique Toys; Charles Gilbert; Charlton Hall Galleries; Christie's; Coffman's Antiques Market; Collect It Magazine; Collectors News; Cooper Owen; Copake Auction; Cordier Antiques & Fine Art; Cottone Auctions; Country Bear Antiques; Country Lane Antiques; Craftsman Antiques; Crocker Farm, Crown Jewels of the Wire; Cyberattic.com; Cyr Auction Gallery; Daguerreian Society; Dan Ripley's Antique Helper; Daniel Auction Co.; Dark Horse Antiques; Delmarva Acquisitions & Appraisals; Dovetail Antiques; Doyle New York; Ed's Toy Shop; Elm Bank Estate Show; Eloquence Antiques; Erie Canal Antiques; Faganarms; Federation of Historical Bottle Collectors; Fenton Art Glass Collectors of America; Finnegan Gallery; Forsythes' Auctions; Frank & Grace Zuest; Frank & Terri Martin; Frank H. Boos Gallery; Frankoma Family Collectors Association; Frank's Antiques & Auctions; G.K.S. Bush; Georgian Manor Antiques; Gil Leacock; Gisela Antiques; Gold Bug Antiques; Hearts & Roses Antiques; Heisey Collectors of America; Herrs Antiques; Hesse Galleries; Hillcrest Gallery; Hoosier Peddler; Hummel Collector's Club; International Institute of Antique Glass; Iron Man Toys; Ivey-Selkirk Auctioneers; J & P Antiques International; J.D. Querry; J.J. Keating Auction; Jack Eubanks Auctions; JHP Quilts & Antiques; Joan R. Brownstein; John F. Rinaldi Nautical Antiques & Related Items; John Moore Matchbox; John T. Roth American Antiques; Jones & Horan; Joy Luke Fine Arts Brokers & Auctioneers; Judd Gregory Fine Antiques; Ken Farmer Auctions; Keystone Toy Trader; King's Cross Antiques; Laura's Collectibles; Leighton House Antiques; Leslie Hindman Auctioneers; London Market Antiques; Loudonville Folk Art; Maine Antiques Digest; Manion's International Auction House; Margaret Lane Antiques; Master Auctions; McCoy Lovers' NMXpress; Metz Superlative Auction; Michael Ivankovich

Auction Co. Inc.; Monsen & Baer; National Association of Aladdin Lamp Collectors; National Association of Milk Bottle Collectors; National Cambridge Collectors; Neal Auction Co.; New Orleans Auction Galleries; Norman C. Heckler & Co.; North Country Bottle Shop; O.J. Club; Old Barn Auction; Old Sleepy Eye Collectors Club of America; Old Toy Town; Only Mint; Pamela D. Riesberg Antiques; Paper & Advertising Collectors' Marketplace; Parzow Auctions; Past Tyme Pleasures; Period Antiques; Petroleum Collectibles; Pewter Collectors Club of America; Phoenix Militaria Corporation; Pink Lemonade; Political Heritage; Port 'N Starboard Gallery; Potteries Specialists Auctions; R.O. Schmitt Fine Arts; Rachel Davis Fine Arts; Raccoon Creek Antiques; Rail Splitter; Random Treasures Auction; Red Baron's Antiques; Red's Candy Container Collection; RGL Antiques; Richard D. Hatch & Associates; Richard Norton; Robert Edward Auctions; Ron Smith; Russ Cochran's Comic Art Auction; Second Childhood NYC; Seeck Auctions; Serioustoyz.com; Simmons & Co. Auctioneers; Singer Antiques Galleries; Smith House Toys & Auction Co.; Stair Galleries; Steeplechase Antiques; Steve Butler; Strawser's Auction; Studio Antiques & Fine Art; Sunflowerauction.com; Susanin's Auctions; Swann Auction Galleries; Tea Leaf Club International; Team's Tiffany Treasures; Ted Kromer; The Internet Antique Shop; Theriault's; Thomas C. Campbell; Thomaston Place Auction Galleries; Tom Biskner; Toothpick Bulletin; Toy Shop; Trader Fred's Toys of Yore; Vicki & Bruce Waasdorp; Vintageweaponry.com; Waddington's; Webb Gallery; Weschler's; William Bunch Auctions; William Morford Auctions; Wooden Nickel Antiques; Yankee Picker; Yankee Toys.

We thank those at Black Dog and Leventhal, especially J.P. Leventhal and Laura Ross, for taking on the huge job of modernizing and redesigning this, our fortieth edition of *Kovels' Antiques & Collectibles Price List*. Their confidence and interest in our price book made this improved edition possible. Much has changed in the world of collecting since our first book was written in 1967 with the help of a giant room-filling computer and keypunch cards. Our newest look includes a larger size, thousands of color pictures, hundreds of marks, factoids, tips, and about 45,000 prices. To do this required working through new problems and still maintaining the unique way we write a price book. Thanks to True Sims, who was in charge of production, April Clark, who conquered the new computer programs and problems; and especially Sheila Hart, who coordinated all of the parts and supervised all of the editing, layouts, copy editing, art decisions, and more.

The details and hard work required to record prices, assemble photos and information, check accuracy, spelling, and solve many other problems are all done by our staff. We thank Carmie Amata, Lisa Bell, Grace DeFrancisco, Marcia Goldberg, Evelyn Hayes, Katie Karrick, Kim Kovel, Liz Lillis, Heidi Makela, Tina McBean, Nancy Saada, Julie Seaman, June Smith, and Cherrie Smrekar. Pictures come from many sources and they were all sized and digitally enhanced by Karen Kneisley, our picture editor. Gay Hunter, our book editor, has handled most of our problems of redesign and new thinking. She supervised the project, kept the records, and made sure all of us were on track and on schedule. Thanks to all of them, we have what we are sure is our best book ever. We know that the book is a group effort, even though it is our names that appear on the cover.

A. WALTER

A. WALTER made pate-de-verre glass under contract at the Daum glassworks from 1908 to 1914. He started his own firm in Nancy, France, in 1919. Pieces made before 1914 are signed *Daum, Nancy* with a cross. After 1919 the signature is *A. Walter Nancy*.

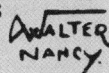

Ashtray, Triangular, Yellow & Orange, Fly On Green Pine Needle Branch, Signed, 3 In.	1035.00
Dish, Leaf Form, Mottled Orange & Yellow, Seashell Handle, Signed, 6½ In.	920.00
Dish, Stylized Vegetation, Blue Shaded To Purple Ground, Yellow Mottles, 3-Sided, 7 In. *illus*	2578.00
Paperweight, Cicada, Laurel Branch, Yellow & Emerald Green, Signed, Nancy, 1⅞ x 5 In. ..	1290.00
Paperweight, Sea Lion, On Boulder, Cadmium Yellow & Chestnut Brown, Signed, Nancy, 6⅝ In.	1400.00
Vase, Green & Turquoise, Square Windowpanes, Raised Prunts, Incised, 5½ In.	2300.00
Vase, Yellow Snails, Gold Trim, Green Flora, Blue Shaded Ground, Footed, Signed, 8 In. *illus*	6000.00

ABC

ABC plates, or children's alphabet plates, were most popular from 1780 to 1860, but are still being made. The letters on the plate were meant as teaching aids for children learning to read. The plates were made of pottery, porcelain, metal, or glass. Mugs and other items were also made with alphabet decorations.

Bowl, Baby Bunting, D.E. McNicol, East Liverpool, Ohio, c.1910, 8¼ x 2 In.	95.00
Plate, 2 Rabbits, Embossed Alphabet Rim, Aynsley China, England	440.00
Plate, Brownies, Verse, Up The Table See Them Climb, Ready For A Jolly Time, Tin, 9 In. *illus*	55.00
Plate, Children, Hard Paste, Germany, Deep, 6½ In. ....*illus*	138.00
Plate, Cock Robin, Tin, Who Killed Cock Robin, 8 In.	120.00
Plate, Hen & Chicks, Glass, 6 In.	55.00
Plate, Little Bo Peep, Amber Glass, Molded, 6½ In.	15.00
Plate, Mary Had A Little Lamb, Embossed Scene, Tin, 1870, 8 In.	55.00
Plate, Nursery, Decal Print Cartoon Animal, Lord Nelson, Staffordshire, England, 7 In.	35.00
Plate, Riddle On Front, Answer On Back, Pastry Cook, Soldier, Staffordshire, 1800s, 5 In. ...	250.00
Plate, Stork, Bundled Baby, Carnival Glass, Belmont Glass Co., 1800s, 7½ In.	105.00
Plate, Sunbonnet Chicken In Center, Decal, Wood & Sons, 7 In.	35.00
Plate, Vaseline Glass, Bee Mark, M In Shield, 6¼ In.	17.25
Plate, Vaseline Glass, Mosser Glass 20th Century, 6½ In.	45.00

ABINGDON POTTERY

ABINGDON POTTERY was established in 1908 by Raymond E. Bidwell as the Abingdon Sanitary Manufacturing Company. The company started making art pottery in 1934. The factory ceased production of art pottery in 1950.

Bookends, Horse Head, Black, Original Stickers, 6½ In.	100.00
Bookends, Ivory Honey Glaze, Gliding Sea Gulls, Felt Bottom, Pair, 6 In.	150.00
Bowl, Aster, Molded Shape, Leaves, Petals, 14 In.	69.00
Bowl, Shell, No. 533, Sea Green, Shell Embossed Inside, c.1948, 11¼ x 8 In.	35.00
Candlestick, Open Shell, Blue, 4 x 3½ In., Pair	42.00
Console, Multicolored Flowers, Gilt, 17 x 7 In.	50.00
Console, White Matte, Satin Finish, Embossed Feather Design, 17 x 7¼ x 4½ In.	48.00
Planter, Cornucopia, Yellow, 10 x 4½ x 5 In.	15.00
Planter, Window Box, Aqua Matte Glaze, c.1950, 10 x 3 x 3¾ In.	32.50
Vase, Blue & Gold, Handles, Blue Gloss Glaze, Gold Trim, Flowers, 8½ In.	38.00
Vase, Double Cornucopia, Cream, 5 x 11 In.	35.00

ADAMS

ADAMS china was made by William Adams and Sons of Staffordshire, England. The firm was founded in 1769 and became part of the Wedgwood Group in 1966. The name *Adams* appeared on various items through 1998. All types of tablewares and useful wares were made. Other pieces of Adams may be found listed under Flow Blue and Tea Leaf Ironstone.

Cup & Saucer, Adams' Rose, Yellow Spatter Border, Handleless	660.00
Pitcher, Adams' Rose, Scalloped Rim, Scroll Handle, 8¼ In.	523.00
Plate, Adams' Rose, Red, Green Leaves, Blue Spatter Border, Paneled, 7¼ In.	165.00
Washbowl & Pitcher, Adams' Rose, Blue Ground, Spatter, Paneled, 12¾-In. Pitcher	715.00

ADVERTISING

ADVERTISING containers and products sold in the old country store are now all collectibles. These stores, with the crackers in a barrel and a potbellied stove, are a symbol of an earlier, less hectic time. Listed here are many of the advertising items. Other similar pieces may be found under the product name, such as Planters Peanuts. We have tried to list items in the logical places, so large store fixtures will be found under the Architectural category, enameled tin dishes under Graniteware, paper items in the Paper category, etc. Store fixtures, cases, signs, and other items that have no advertising as part of the decoration are listed in the Store category. For more information, see *Kovels' Advertising Collectibles Price List*. The early Dr Pepper logo included a period after "Dr," but it was dropped in 1950. We list all Dr Pepper items without a period so they alphabetize together.

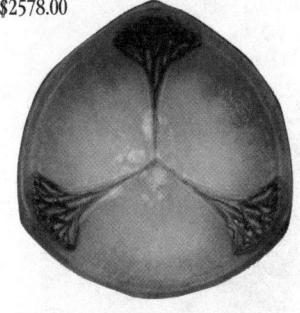

A. Walter, Dish, Stylized Vegetation, Blue Shaded To Purple Ground, Yellow Mottles, 3-Sided, 7 In. $2578.00

A. Walter, Vase, Yellow Snails, Gold Trim, Green Flora, Blue Shaded Ground, Footed, Signed, 8 In. $6000.00

ABC, Plate, Brownies, Verse, Up The Table See Them Climb, Ready For A Jolly Time, Tin, 9 In. $55.00

ABC, Plate, Children, Hard Paste, Germany, Deep, 6½ In. $138.00

Advertising, Bin,
Mistletoe Coffee,
Timothy Gay & Co.,
Children Pulling Wagon,
13 x 20 In.
$489.00

Advertising, Cabinet, Diamond Dyes,
Children With Balloon, Tin Panel,
24 x 14 x 8 In.
$3218.00

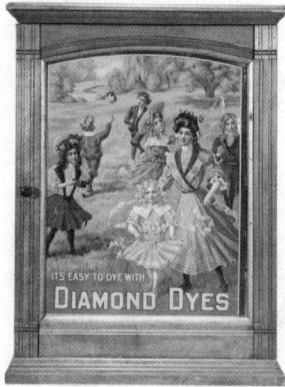

Advertising, Cabinet, Diamond Dyes,
Governess, Tin Panel, 30 x 22 x 10 In.
$2633.00

Ad, Dust Trap, Rexair Rainbow, c.1963, 5 x 5 In.	10.00
Ad, Star-Kist Tuna, On The Riviera With Gene Tierney, Recipe For Tuna, 1951, 5 x 13 In.	7.50
Ashtray, RCA Nipper, Brass, Gray Metal Base, 1930s	88.00
Ashtray, Wm. K. Hayes, Frogs, Porcelain, Marked, H. & Co., 5 x 5 In.	220.00
Backbar, Falls City Beer, Always A Winner, 2 Horses, Jockeys, Louisville, 11 x 17 In.	2027.00
Bag Holder, Display, Country Store, Cast Iron, 22 x 8¼ x 16 In.	1705.00
Banner, Bireley's, Natural Thing To Drink, Woman, Holding Bottle, Canvas, 1940-50, 60 In.	164.00
Banner, Clabber Girl Baking Powder, Cloth, c.1930, 18 x 36 In.	169.00 to 400.00
Banner, Farmer's Pride Coffee, Everything Good To Eat, Hulman & Co., Frame, 41 x 65 In.	275.00
Banner, Green Spot Orange-Ade, 5 Cents, Blue, Green, Orange, White, 27 x 36 In.	88.00
Banner, Remington UMC, Arms & Ammunition, Indians & Buffalo, Frame, 36 x 63 In.	6600.00
Barrel, Country Store, Paper Label For Monroe Taylor's Gold Medal Soda, 14 x 19 In.	315.00
Billhook, Breakfast Cheer Coffee, Woman, Box, Bell, Green, Red, Celluloid, Metal, 7 In.	187.00
Bin, Beech-Nut Chewing Tobacco, Quality Made It Famous, Tin Lithograph, 9 x 10 x 8 In.	440.00
Bin, Capital Coffee, Wood, Stenciled, 33 x 21 x 16½ In.	715.00
Bin, Coffee, Swain Earle & Co., Painted, Boston Harbor, Stenciled, 19 x 18 In.	588.00
Bin, Gladiator Coffee, Metal, Stenciled, Roll-Up Door, 21½ x 13¼ x 13¼ In.	1375.00
Bin, Mistletoe Coffee, Timothy Gay & Co., Children Pulling Wagon, 13 x 20 In. *illus*	489.00
Bin, Scotten, Dillon Co., Sweet Mist Tobacco, Children, Fountain, 11 x 8½ In.	330.00
Bin, Tiger Chewing Tobacco, Cardboard, Tin Top, 11⅛ x 8⅛ x 6⅜ In.	198.00
Booklet, Dr. Lesure's Veterinary, Illustrated, 7⅞ x 5⅜ In., 126 Pages	88.00
Booklet, Wrigley's Spearmint Gum Storybook, Mother Goose, 1915, 24 Pages	20.00
Books may be included in the Paper category.	
Bootjack, Mussleman's Tobacco, Embossed, Cast Iron, 9¾ x 3½ x 2⅜ In.	231.00
Bottle Openers are listed in their own category.	
Bottle Topper, Orange Crush, Refreshing As An Ocean Wave, 10¾ x 5½ In.	448.00
Bottle Topper, Red Wing Grape Juice, Girl & Boy, On Chair, Die Cut, Cardboard, 16 x 11 In.	232.00
Bottles are listed in their own category.	
Bowl, Cereal, Barclay Hotel, Embossed Gold Flower Band, Syracuse China, 6¼ In.	5.00
Bowl, Friends' Oats, Girl Holding Box, Porcelain, 5⅜ x 1¼ In.	253.00
Box, see also Box category.	
Box, 3 Stooges Candy & Toy, 1959, 2½ x 3⅝ x ⅞ In.	112.00
Box, Albers Flapjack Flour, Hotcakes Of The West, Cardboard, 4 x 2¾ x 1½ In.	132.00
Box, Albers Whole Wheat, 1 Lb. 4 Oz., 6½ x 4¼ x 2 In.	88.00
Box, Aunt Lydia's Button & Carpet Thread, Extra Strong, 4 Boxes, Wood	137.00
Box, Barber Ink Co., Wood, Black Letters, Dovetailed Corners, 11 x 13 x 11 In.	59.00
Box, Beech-Nut Chlorophyll Gum, For The Breath, 15 Cents, 12 Unopened Packs, 1940s	55.00
Box, Best Pal Candy, Child, Dog, Cardboard, 1930, 8⅝ x 9½ x 2¾ In.	55.00
Box, Buster Brown Black Pepper, Cardboard, Round, ½ Lb., 5⅜ x 3⅛ In.	242.00
Box, Castile Soap, 3 Teddy Bear Soap, On Toboggan, Paperboard, 1930s, 8 In.	95.00
Box, Cereal, Quaker Oats, Picturing Roy Rogers Microscope Ring, 1950s	95.00
Box, Collar, Drum Shape, Philadelphia Collar Co., Civil War Era, 3 x 4¼ In.	775.00
Box, D.M. Ferry & Co., Flower Seeds, Oak, 8½ x 16 x 4 In.	90.00
Box, Display, Adams Tutti Frutti Chewing Gum, L. Russel, Cardboard, Glass, 10 x 4 x 1 In.	60.00
Box, Display, Ellen's New Discovery Powder, Cardboard, 10 x 8¼ x 5½ In.	385.00
Box, Display, Esquire Boot Polish, Cat, 6½ x 9 x 3 In.	44.00
Box, Display, Francis H. Leggett & Co., Spices, Tiger, Wood, 4 x 19 x 12 In.	165.00
Box, Display, Hohner's Harmonicas, Wood, 3 Drawers, 14 x 10¼ In.	358.00
Box, Display, Johnson Robbins & Co., American Seed Gardens, 13 x 24 x 10 In.	2640.00
Box, Display, Royal Shaving Brush, 6 Brushes	59.00
Box, Display, Spice, Slade's, Sailing Ships, Wood, 14⅛ x 19⅛ x 12 In.	187.00
Box, DuPont Mascotte Toothbrush, 2 Girls, Cardboard, 3⅜ x 6½ In.	220.00
Box, Fairway Corn Flakes, Boy, Girl, Twin City Wholesale Grocer, Cardboard, 11 x 8 x 3 In.	1320.00
Box, Ferry Seeds, Flower Seeds, 4 Girls In Boat, Oak, Paper Label, 9 x 11 x 6¾ In.	275.00
Box, Gold Dust, Twins On Front, Gold & Blue, 1920s, 7 In.	700.00
Box, Grandma's Powdered Soap, Woman Washing, Cardboard, 8½ x 5¾ In.	99.00
Box, Griffin Shoe Polish, A B C, For That Famous Griffin, Blue, White, 9 Red Tins	27.00
Box, Hobson Dog & Veterinary, Soap, Pfeiffer Chemical Co., 2⅛ x 3¼ In.	220.00
Box, Home Brand Oats, Griggs, Cooper Co., Mansion, 9½ x 5½ In.	55.00
Box, Hoosier Poet Jar Rings, Red Lipped, Cardboard, 1 Doz., 3 x 3 x 1¼ In.	253.00
Box, Ice Cream Cone, Duble Heder, Cake Cones, 5 Cents, Contents, 1934, 20 x 7 In.	192.00
Box, Kleen Chief Handkerchiefs, Cardboard, Contents	55.00
Box, Mother Goose Popcorn, Washington Cracker Co., Cardboard, 6 x 2¾ x 2¾ In.	110.00
Box, Nabisco Log Cabin Brownies, Cardboard, Cabin Shape, Rope Handle, 3 x 3¾ x 3 In.	77.00
Box, Philadelphia Collar Co., Civil War Drum Form, Hard To Beat, c.1870, 2¾ x 4 In.	975.00
Box, Plantes Aviator, Woman Aviator Eating Nuts, Cardboard, 1940s, 2-Piece	825.00

Box, Priscilla Hexagon Crayons, Tin Lithograph, No. 37, 1937, 4½ x 5½ In.	50.00
Box, Rice's Seeds, Girl, Flowers, Wood, Paper Label, 9⅝ x 11 x 6⅝ In.	77.00
Box, Royal Crown Straws, Bottle, Best By Taste Test, Cardboard, 1930s, 11 x 4 x 4 In.	469.00
Box, Shirt, Levi Strauss & Co., Home Run, Baseball On Lid, 12¼ x 10⅛ x 1½ In.	110.00
Box, Soapine, Dirt Killer, Whale, 5 Cents, Kendall Mfg. Co., 8 Oz., 5 x 3½ x 1 In.	150.00
Box, Soapine, Soap Products, Wood, Whale, Ships, Children, 9 x 20 x 13 In.	187.00
Box, Tobacco, Seal Of NC Plug Cut Tobacco, Wood, 6⅛ x 6¾ x 4 In.	330.00
Box, Vanity Rolled Oats, Peacock, Kickbusch Grocery Co., Cardboard, 9½ x 5 In.	358.00
Broom Holder, Gold Medal Flour, Eventually, Why Not Now?, Red, Black, Wood, Tin, 42 x 20 In.	385.00
Broom Holder, Little Polly, Tin Lithograph, 6 x 2½ In.	121.00
Brush, Billiard Table Cleaning, Madison Billiard Academy, Celluloid, c.1910, 3½ In.	334.00
Brush, Clothes, Celluloid, Paper Manufacturers Co., Philadelphia Co., c.1920, 4 In.	41.00
Brush, Clothes, Gregertsen Brothers Co., Andy Gump, Celluloid, Round, 3½ In.	46.00
Bucket, Dwight's Baking Soda, Cow, Wood, Paper Label, Bail Handle, 10 Lb., 7½ x 8 In.	358.00
Bucket, Heinz, Apple Jelly, Howard Standard, Wood, Label, Bail Handle, 6½ In.	450.00
Bucket, Paint, Dutch Boy, Black, Yellow Letters, Metal, Handle, National Lead Co., 6⅜ In.	56.00
Cabinet, Ambergs Cabinet, Roll Top Slide Front, 4 Drawers, Oak, 27 x 16 In.	990.00
Cabinet, Diamond Dyes, Children, Evolution Of Woman, Color Spectrum, 30 x 22 x 10 In.	575.00 to 825.00
Cabinet, Diamond Dyes, Children, Red-Haired Fairy With Wand, 10 Cents, 30 x 22 x 10 In.	495.00
Cabinet, Diamond Dyes, Children Skipping Rope, 24½ x 14½ x 8 In.	1045.00
Cabinet, Diamond Dyes, Children With Balloon, Tin Panel, 24 x 14 x 8 In. *illus*	3218.00
Cabinet, Diamond Dyes, Court Jester, c.1890, 27 x 21 x 10 In.	880.00 to 1300.00
Cabinet, Diamond Dyes, Governess, Tin Panel, 30 x 22 x 10 In. *illus*	2633.00
Cabinet, Diamond Dyes, Little Girl, Rear Sliding Doors, 20 x 15 x 8 In. *illus*	1290.00
Cabinet, Diamond Dyes, Washer Woman, Green Ground, c.1910, 30 x 22 x 10 In.	1180.00
Cabinet, Dr. A.C. Daniels' Animal Medicines, Wood, Tin Panel, 25 x 19 x 5 In. *illus*	7605.00
Cabinet, Dr. Daniels' Veterinary Medicines, Wood, Tin, 29 x 19½ x 7 In. *illus*	3803.00
Cabinet, Dr. Daniels' Veterinary Medicines, Warranted, Wood, Glass, 29 x 20 x 8 In.	3920.00
Cabinet, Embroidery Floss, Oak Royal Society, 19 x 19 x 36 In.	110.00
Cabinet, Harper's Oval Eyed Redditch Needles, 4 Drawers, 19 x 13 x 23 In.	440.00
Cabinet, Humphreys' Homeopathic Specifics, Maple, Tin Panel, 28 x 21 In.	4025.00
Cabinet, Humphreys' Remedies, Divided Interior, Wood, Tin Panels, 20¾ x 18 x 6⅝ In.	825.00
Cabinet, Munyon's Homoeopathic Home Remedies, 3 Drawers, Packages, 14 x 12 In. *illus*	1170.00
Cabinet, Parker Lucky Curve Fountain Pen, Oak, Floor Model, 42 x 16 In.	230.00
Cabinet, Pearl Lustre Dyes, Tin, 22 x 16½ x 8 In.	1485.00
Cabinet, Pratts' Veterinary Remedies, Shelves, Wood, Tin Panel, 34 x 16 x 7 In. *illus*	1989.00
Cabinet, Rice's Seeds, Collapsible, 45 x 22 In. *illus*	1053.00
Cabinet, Sauer's Extract, Wood, 12 x 7 x 26 In.	358.00
Cabinet, Sauer's Flavoring Extracts, Decals On Side, Wood, 26 x 12 In.	495.00
Cabinet, Sauer's Flavoring Extracts, Reverse Painted Letters On Glass, Wood, 21 x 15 In.	1100.00
Cabinet, Sherwin Williams Paints, Lizard, Tree, 28 x 18½ x 4½ In.	532.00
Cabinet, Spool, Brainerd & Armstrong, 4 Glass Drawers, Butterfly Hardware, 15 x 20 x 9 In.	935.00
Cabinet, Spool, Brainerd & Armstrong, 28 Drawers, Cornucopia Hardware, Mirror, 36 x 29 x 16 In.	2700.00
Cabinet, Spool, Clark's, 6 Drawers, Ruby Glass, On White Spools, 22 x 29 In.	1320.00
Cabinet, Spool, Clark's, 6 Drawers, Ruby Glass, Sole Agent, George A. Clark, 29 x 22 x 17 In.	3015.00
Cabinet, Spool, Clark's, Walnut, 6 Drawers, Blue Glass, 30 x 22 x 18 In.	990.00
Cabinet, Spool, Clark's, Walnut, 6 Drawers, Reverse Painted Panels, 22 x 24 In.	1155.00
Cabinet, Spool, Clark's Mile-End, Best Six Cord, 4 Drawers, 14 x 23 x 16 In. *illus*	702.00
Cabinet, Spool, Clark's Mile-End, Cotton, 6 Drawers, Walnut, 30 x 22 x 18 In. *illus*	1053.00
Cabinet, Spool, Clark's O.N.T., No. 40, 23 In.	660.00
Cabinet, Spool, Clark's O.N.T., Oak, 6 Drawers, Wood Knobs, 24 x 34 x 14 In.	385.00
Cabinet, Spool, Clark's O.N.T., Spool Cotton, Paper Labels, 22½ x 15 x 16 In.	220.00
Cabinet, Spool, Clark's O.N.T., Walnut, 6 Drawers, Ruby Glass, 30 x 22 x 18 In. *illus*	3218.00
Cabinet, Spool, Clark's Spool Cotton, Elm, Slant Front, 6 Drawers, Early 1900s, 15 x 33 In.	153.00
Cabinet, Spool, J. & P. Coats', No. 40, Swivel Base, 24 In.	275.00
Cabinet, Spool, J. & P. Coats', No. 50, 22½ x 16 x 16 In.	825.00
Cabinet, Spool, J. & P. Coats', Oak, 6 Drawers	248.00
Cabinet, Spool, J. & P. Coats', Oak, Tambour Door, 16 x 21 x 23 In.	248.00
Cabinet, Spool, J. & P. Coats', Walnut, 6 Drawers, Embossed Front, 22 x 26 In.	330.00
Cabinet, Spool, Merrick's, Cotton, Glass, Stenciled, Cylindrical, 1897, 26 In.	770.00
Cabinet, Spool, Merrick's, Double, c.1900, 31 x 23 x 17 In.	3456.00
Cabinet, Spool, Merrick's, Six-Cord, Wood, Glass, Mirror, Stenciled, 1897, 24 x 33 In.	1045.00
Cabinet, Spool, Merrick's, Wood, Glass, Stenciled, Mirror, 1897, 24 x 33 In.	1430.00
Cabinet, Spool, Nun's Boilproof, Walnut, 7 Drawers, 21 x 25 x 18 In.	137.00
Cabinet, Spool, Willimantic, Walnut, 4 Drawers, Six-Cord, Spool Cotton, 16½ x 25 x 15 In.	2090.00
Calendars are listed in their own category.	

Advertising, Cabinet, Diamond Dyes, Little Girl, Rear Sliding Doors, 20 x 15 x 8 In. $1290.00

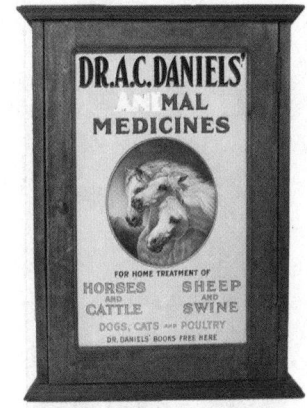

Advertising, Cabinet, Dr. A.C. Daniels' Animal Medicines, Wood, Tin Panel, 25 x 19 x 5 In. $7605.00

Advertising, Cabinet, Dr. Daniels' Veterinary Medicines, Wood, Tin, 29 x 19½ x 7 In. $3803.00

A

Advertising, Cabinet, Munyon's Homoeopathic Home Remedies, 3 Drawers, Packages, 14 x 12 In. $1170.00

Advertising, Cabinet, Pratts' Veterinary Remedies, Shelves, Wood, Tin Panel, 34 x 16 x 7 In. $1989.00

Advertising, Cabinet, Rice's Seeds, Collapsible, 45 x 22 In. $1053.00

Can, Castle Packing Co., Oysters, Wood, Red, Black Letters, Labels, 16 x 14 x 11 In.	79.00
Canisters, see introductory paragraph to Tins in this category.	
Cards are listed in the Card category	
Carrier, Kickapoo Joy Juice, Glass Bottles, 6-Pack, Cardboard, 10 In.	88.00
Carton, Chesterfield Cigarettes, Finest Turkish, Domestic Tobaccos, 20 Packs	192.00
Case, Display, Merricks, Oak, 6 Drawers, Inkwell, c.1900, 17 x 30 In.	294.00
Case, Display, Nestle Candy Bars, Labels, 4¾ x 10⅛ x 7⅜ In.	303.00
Case, Display, Sanford's Inks, Oak, Glass, 1890-1915, 23½ x 27 x 11¼ In.	896.00
Case, Display, Sauer's Flavoring Extracts, Reverse Painted, Oak, 20 x 15 x 11 In. .....*illus*	1345.00
Case, Display, Zeno Chewing Gum, Oak, 18 x 10½ x 8 In.	853.00
Case Opener, Wrigley's, Spearmint, Doublemint, Juicy Fruit, Wood, Beveled, 13½ In.	36.00
Chair, Duke Cameo Cigarettes, Wood, Folding, 31 x 16½ x 20 In.	440.00
Chair, Lone Jack Cigarettes, Image On Both Sides, Wood, Folding, 33 x 15 In.	1210.00
Change Receiver, see also Tip Tray in this category.	
Change Receiver, Hires Root Beer, Join Health & Cheer, Mettlach Glaze, 5 In. Diam.	3080.00
Change Receiver, Royal Princess Cigars, Indian Princess, Glass, Paper Lithograph, 6¾ In.	232.00
Change Receiver, Southern Pacific Passenger Steamships, Copper, Porcelain, 4 In. Diam.	291.00
Cigar Box, Buffalo Bill Cody, Wood, 5 Cents, 2½ x 8¾ In.	750.00
Cigar Box, Pony Post Cigars, Man Riding Horse, Wood, Paper Label, 7¾ x 9¾ x 2¾ In.	66.00
Cigar Box Lid, Mekosa Paper Makers Baseball Team, 5 x 8 In.	99.00
Cigar Cutter, Artie, Cast Iron, Mechanical, Nickel Plated, Windup, 10 x 6 x 7 In.	2970.00
Cigar Cutter, Betsy Ross 5 Cent Cigar, Cast Iron, A.S. Valentine & Son, 8 x 8 x 6 In.	825.00
Cigar Cutter, General Electric, Figural, Cast Bronze, Steel Door, 1899, 4 x 4½ In.	357.00
Cigar Cutter, Geo. W. Childs, Figure, Embossed Desk, Windup, Cast Iron, c.1877, 9 x 10 In.	2475.00
Cigar Cutter, Goldstein & Sons Havana Cigar, Donkey, Iron, Brass Plate, c.1897, 8¼ In.	5225.00
Cigar Cutter, John Gund Brewing Co., La Crosse, Wis., Barrel Form, 7 x 8½ In.	719.00
Cigar Cutter, Rocky Ford, Indian Warrior, Clockwork, Electroplated Iron, 6½ x 8 In.	1760.00
Cigar Cutter, Schlosse & Co. Handwerks, Boston, Iron, Nickeled, Glass, 2¾ x 6½ In.	1320.00
Cigar Cutter, Waitt & Bond's Little Lord Fauntleroy, 2¾ x 5½ In.	770.00
Cigarette Pack, Liggett & Myers Home Run, Ball Players, 2⅞ x 2⅛ x ⅞ In.	143.00
Cigarette Pack, Lucky Strike, Contents, 1953	55.00
Clicker, Chirper, Columbus Biggy Co., Wireless Telegraphy, Celluloid, c.1900, 1¼ In.	103.00
Clicker, PEZ, Girl, c.1970, 1½ In.	31.00
Clocks are listed in their own category.	
Coaster, Michelob Draught Beer, Keg Shape, Heavy Cardboard, 1941, 4 In.	9.00
Coaster, Virginia Brewing Co., Roanoke, Va., Green Lettering, 4¼ In.	499.00
Coaster, Worthburger, Texas Brewing Co., Fort Worth, 1 Side Red, Reverse Blue, 4 In.	621.00
Container, Bowey's Hot Chocolate, Porcelain, 6 x 8⅞ In.	110.00
Container, Figural, Spratt's Dog Biscuits, Glass Eyes, Removable Head, 1940s, 11 In.	196.00
Container, Franco-American Coffee, Red, White, Blue, Cardboard, Lid, 3 x 2⅜ x 1⅞ In.	242.00
Container, Talc, Gone With The Wind Scarlett, Purple Ground, Pinard, 4 Oz.	250.00
Container, Tarzan Casein Glue, Cardboard, Metal Lid, 5 Oz., 4⅛ x 2½ In.	168.00
Cooler, Dr Pepper, Good For Life, Red, Restored, 1960s	98.00
Cooler, Griesedieck Bros. Beer, Good Beer, Black, 19 x 13 x 17 In.	197.00
Cooler, Moxie Bottle, Figural, Hinged Doors, United Indurated Co., 1886, 35 In.	1670.00
Counter Felt, Barber's Pet Razors, Green, Keen Kutter	500.00
Counter Felt, Barber's Pet Razors, Red, Keen Kutter	1100.00
Counter Felt, Luden's Cough Drops, Green, Yellow, Red, c.1930, 11½ In. Diam.	40.00
Crayon Set, Dr Pepper, Pad & Eraser, 1982	13.00
Creamer, Regency Hotel, Gold Trim, Porcelain, c.1974	8.00
Crock, Cake, S.S. Pierce Co., Importers & Grocers, Blue Band, Lid, c.1900, 6 In.	633.00
Crock, Geo. W. Lillie, Butternuts, 3 Flower Design, Blue Accents, c.1870, 3 Gal., 11 In.	303.00
Crock, H.J. Heinz, Co., Salt Glaze, Blue Accents, ½ Gal., 5½ In.	209.00
Crock, Heinz, Apple Butter, Paper Label, Bail Handle, 7½ In.	658.00
Crock, Heinz, Apple Butter, Stoneware, Paper Label, 6 x 4¾ In.	469.00
Crock, Heinz, Blackberry Jelly, Howard Brand, Stoneware, Bail Handle, c.1890, 7⅜ In.	550.00
Crock, Heinz, Currant Jelly, Standard Quality, Lid, Bail Handle	191.00
Crock, Heinz, Grape Fruit Marmalade, Lid, Clasp, 9½ In.	717.00
Crock, Heinz, Mustard, Keystone Brand, Paper Label, Bail Handle, 11½ In.	155.00
Crock, Heinz, Preserved Blackberries, No Lid, 7½ x 7 In.	96.00
Crock, Heinz, Raspberry Jelly, Standard Quality, 8¾ In.	419.00
Crock, Heinz, Raspberry Preserves, Standard Quality, Lid, Bail Handle	480.00
Crock, Heinz Apple Butter, Standard Quality, Stoneware, 10½ x 7 In.	385.00
Crock, Heinz Peach Butter, White, Stoneware, Wire Bail, Wood Handle, 5¼ x 5 In.	1072.00
Cup, Clark's Zig Zag & Pepsin Gum, Tin Lithograph, 1½ x 1¼ In.	80.00
Cup, Dairy Queen Ice Cream, Waxed Paper, 1950, 1¾ In.	9.00

Cup, Ovaltine, House, Uncle Wiggily, Premium, Sebring Pottery Co., 1924	95.00
Cup & Saucer, Baker's Cocoa, Image Of Baker's Woman, Marked Dresden	495.00
Disc & Price Calculator, Wm. F. Helm Commission Co., Fruit, Celluloid, Round, 2½ In.	69.00
Dish, Cover, Baker's Cocoa, Porcelain, Baker's Lady, 2½ x 5 In.	358.00
Dispenser, Ad-Lee-Z Gum Ball, Columbus, Home Run Marquee, c.1930, 15½ In.	944.00
Dispenser, Booth's Unsweetened Gin, Glass, England, 1880-1910, 24¾ In.	728.00
Dispenser, Buckeye Root Beer Syrup, Black, White, Cleveland Fruit Juice Co., Oh., 16 In.	1760.00
Dispenser, Emerson's Ginger Mint Julep, Label Under Glass, Aluminum Cap, 12½ In.	330.00
Dispenser, Fowler's Cherry Smash, Ceramic, 15 x 9½ In.	3080.00
Dispenser, Hires Root Beer, Drink Hires, It's Pure, Hourglass, Red, Spigot, 12 x 7¾ In.	1430.00
Dispenser, Hy-Po, Milk Glass Base, Clear Top, 13 x 8 In.	220.00
Dispenser, Lime Rickey Syrup, Painted, Cast Iron, Pivots, 1915	660.00
Dispenser, Mission Orangeade, Orange Slices On Top, Spigot, Footed, 15½ In.	1121.00
Dispenser, Mission Rickey Lime, Lime Slices On Top, Spigot, Footed, 15½ In.	880.00
Dispenser, Paper Bag, Geo. S. Adams Wholesale, Wood, Willow, 1884, 19 In. *illus*	1170.00
Dispenser, Pau Cola Syrup, 5 Cents, Silver Plate, Patent 1908, 15 In.	770.00
Dispenser, Queen Dairy Co., Buttermilk, Churn Shape, Porcelain, 35 x 20 In.	5720.00
Dispenser, Ward's Lemon Crush, Figural, Lemon, Flowered Base, 1920s, 14 In. *illus*	1300.00
Dispenser, Ward's Lemon Crush, Lemon, Stoneware, Soda Fountain Lid, 14 x 11 x 7 In.	1320.00
Dispenser, Ward's Lemon Crush, Porcelain, Metal Pump, 11½ x 12 x 7½ In.	1150.00
Dispenser, Ward's Orange Crush, Orange, Porcelain, Flowered Base, Pump, 13 In. *illus*	1380.00
Dispenser, Ward's Orange Crush, Porcelain, Metal Pump, 13½ x 8½ In.	975.00
Display, Alka-Seltzer, Tape Dispenser, Liquid Quick Relief, Tin Lithograph, 1940-50	290.00
Display, Armstrong's Quaker Rug, Quaker Woman, Cardboard, Die Cut, 62 x 18½ In. *illus*	29.00
Display, B-Deks Decorative Confections, 12 Unopened Tubes Of Sprinkles	27.00
Display, Beach & Motor Hair Nets, Tin Lithograph, 1920, 10 x 6 x 5 In.	385.00
Display, Beech-Nut Chewing Gum, 5 Cents, Girl, Stand, Cardboard, 6 x 6 x 4 In.	500.00
Display, Beech-Nut Chewing Gum, Girl With Gum, 5 Cents, Holds 4 Cartons, Metal, 15 In.	1049.00
Display, Betsyette Hair Net, Wood, 2 Nets, 20 x 9 In.	137.00
Display, Blatz Beer, Barmaid Standing On Keg, Painted, Composition, 1935, 19 x 8 x 5½ In.	330.00
Display, Borden's, Elsie, Drink More Milk, 15 x 11 In.	110.00
Display, Brillo Soap Pads, Quick, Yellow, Red, Black, Cardboard, 1915, 13 x 10 In.	55.00
Display, Budde Dry Cleaners, Deliveryman, Figural, Bag Of Cleaning, 1940s, 19 In.	895.00
Display, Bunny, Easter Chocolate Candy, Basket On Back, Molded Rubber, 25 x 9 x 5 In.	330.00
Display, Camels' Hair, Wood, Glass, 7 x 15 x 7 In.	192.00
Display, Chiclets, 1 Cent, Exchange Your Pennies For Chiclets, 8 Packs, 8 x 7 In. *illus*	290.00
Display, Chiclets, Box, Gum, Glass Cardboard, 5 Cents The Ounce, 8 x 10 x 2 In.	105.00
Display, Chief Watta Pop, Painted, Early 20th Century, 9½ In.	176.00
Display, City Mills Pure Spices, House, Ship, Wood, Paper Label, c.1880, 12 x 19 x 10 In.	232.00
Display, Clark's Teaberry Pepsin Gum, It's On The Level, 5 Cents, Tin, Counter, 5 x 7 x 2 In.	170.00
Display, Collar, 26 Collars, Metal, Reverse Paint On Glass, Shelf, 47 x 24 In.	880.00
Display, Collar Case, Oak, 14 Collars, Buttons, Chicago, 25 x 13 x 7 In.	935.00
Display, Councilman's Cigar, Tin, Glass, Red, Yellow, 11 x 16 x 21 In.	165.00
Display, Cream Dove Peanuts, Whole, 10 Lb., 8½ x 9½ In.	110.00
Display, Curtiss Saf-T-Pops, Play Safe, Contents, Metal, 19 In.	192.00
Display, Dentyne Gum, Woman, Red & White Stripe Shirt, Tin Lithograph, 7 x 2⅞ x 3⅞ In.	440.00
Display, Dixon Pencils, American Graphite, 2 Pencils, Metal, Shonk Co., 11 x 9 x 3 In.	137.00
Display, Dr. Morse's Indian Root Pills, Indian, Cardboard, Trifold, Easel Back, 27 x 34 In.	522.00
Display, Dr. Pierce's Medicines, Window, Graphics, Cardboard, Trifold, 27 x 31 In.	633.00
Display, E & W Collars, Smart & Durable, 18 Collars, Wood, Glass, Electric, 37 x 26 x 12 In.	1870.00
Display, Eat-It-All, Ice Cream Cone, 21 In.	28.00
Display, Ever-Ready Shaving Brushes, Need Blades?, Wood, Glass, 1950s, 14 x 12½ In.	27.00
Display, Fairbank's Gold Dust Washing Powder, Kids, Die Cut, Cardboard, 12¾ x 15 In.	1680.00
Display, Faultless Nursing Bottle, Jar, Nipple, Embossed, Glass, 13 x 5⅞ In.	8140.00
Display, Freihofer's Quality Cakes, 3 Shelves, Tin Lithograph, c.1920, 27 x 15 x 17 In.	1870.00
Display, Frog In Your Throat, Cough Drops, Cardboard, 12 x 21 In.	4510.00
Display, Gem, Nail Clippers, Files, Tweezers, Contents, Cardboard	27.00
Display, Glory Cocoanut Oil Soap, Jar, Hinged Lid, 11 In.	550.00
Display, Goody Mints, Peppermint, Clove, Wintergreen, 5 Cents, Metal, Glass, 9 x 9 x 2 In.	297.00
Display, Heinz Tomato Head, Top Hat, Red, Black, White, Composition, 5½ x 3 In.	440.00
Display, Hennessy Cognac Brandy, St. Bernard, Composition, 12 x 13 x 4½ In.	50.00
Display, Hires Root Beer, Make At Home, 3-Tiered Rack, 3 Boxes, Contents, 14 x 5 In. *illus*	260.00
Display, His First Duck, Shotgun Shells, 24¾ x 45 In.	230.00
Display, Hood's Tires, Man, Sign, Flag, Outdoor Parking, 2-Sided, Tin, Iron, 48 x 15 In.	5170.00
Display, Ideal White Soap, Pug, J. D. Larkins & Co., Easel Back, 13 x 8½ In.	300.00
Display, Kellogg's Cereal, We Suggest Kellogg's Cereals, 4 Shelves, Metal, 26 x 18 In.	165.00

Advertising, Cabinet, Spool, Clark's Mile-End, Best Six Cord, 4 Drawers, 14 x 23 x 16 in.
$702.00

Advertising, Cabinet, Spool, Clark's Mile-End, Cotton, 6 Drawers, Walnut, 30 x 22 x 18 in.
$1053.00

Advertising, Cabinet, Spool, Clark's O.N.T., Walnut, 6 Drawers, Ruby Glass, 30 x 22 x 18 in.
$3218.00

Advertising, Case, Display, Sauer's Flavoring Extracts, Reverse Painted, Oak, 20 x 15 x 11 In.
$1345.00

Advertising, Dispenser, Paper Bag, Geo. S. Adams Wholesale, Wood, Willow, 1884, 19 In. $1170.00

Advertising, Dispenser, Ward's Lemon Crush, Figural, Lemon, Flowered Base, 1920s, 14 In. $1300.00

Advertising, Dispenser, Ward's Orange Crush, Orange, Porcelain, Flowered Base, Pump, 13 In. $1380.00

Display, Kleen Chief Hankies, Cardboard ....*illus*	58.00
Display, Kolynos Dental Cream, Figures, Fountain, Gazebo, Cardboard, Trifold, 28 x 34 In. ..	579.00
Display, Kurly Kate Pot Cleaners, Die Cut, Cardboard, 18 Potholders	220.00
Display, Kyanize Floor Finish, For All Woodwork, Metal, Wood, 5 Tins, 30 x 20 In.	440.00
Display, Las Vegas Cigars, Always Pleasing, Ladies, Cardboard, Trifold, 29 x 47 In. .....*illus*	470.00
Display, Life Savers Pep-O-Mint, 5 Cents, 2 Levels, Tin, Shonk, Chicago, 11 x 11 x 9½ In. ...	825.00
Display, Little Boy Blue Laundry Bluing, Tin Lithograph, Wall Hanging, 19 x 4 x 4 In.	264.00
Display, Mail Pouch Tobacco, Ship, Columbus Had His Troubles, Cardboard, Easel, 34 x 21 In. .	110.00
Display, Master Hasplock Locks, Lock, No Key, 7 In.	55.00
Display, Mentholatum, Girl Nurse, Jar, Feel It Heal, Chalkware, 13 In. ....*illus*	1989.00
Display, Nabisco Shredded Wheat, Straight Arrow, Standee, Cardboard, 1949, 10¼ In.	1008.00
Display, Old Crow Whiskey, Black Crow, Monocle, Wood, Stand-Up, 20¾ x 8½ x 5⅝ In.	385.00
Display, Orange Crush, Girl At Beach, Drink Orange Crush, Frame, 1930s, 21½ x 31½ In. ...	606.00
Display, Orange Crush, Window, Bathing Beauty, Pier Post, River, 1930s, 21 x 31 In.	615.00
Display, Paul Stanley Lone Star Beer, Monkey Turns, Dome, c.1960, 48 In.	2500.00
Display, Peters Shoes, Weatherbird, Accordion Folds, Tin Lithograph, 1930s, 20 x 15 In.	410.00
Display, Post Sugar Crisps Cereal, Leo Durocher, Cardboard, 1955, 20 x 30 In.	425.00
Display, RCA Radiotron, Look In The Book, Man Reading, Cardboard, c.1920, 12¾ x 13 In. ..	715.00
Display, Reich Bicycle Bell, Metal, 6 Bells, 17½ x 6½ In.	192.00
Display, Remington UMC, 22 Caliber, Boys, Fold-Out, Die Cut, Cardboard, 9¾ x 14 In.	1050.00
Display, Rice's Popular Flower Seeds, Wood, Folds, 19 Seed Packets, 17 x 19 In.	302.00
Display, Safe-T-Cup Ice Cream Cones, Ice Cream Cone, Figural, Papier-Mache, 21 In. 110.00 to 120.00	
Display, Sauer's Flavoring Extract, Oak, Reverse Paint On Glass, 20 x 15 x 11 In.	1210.00
Display, Sawyers Crystal Blue, Wood, 3 Doz. No. 5, 36 Cans, 11¼ x 16¼ In.	469.00
Display, Sir Walter Raleigh Tobacco, Tin, 12 x 12 In.	28.00
Display, Smith Bros. Cough Drops, 5 Cents, Tin Lithograph, Hinged Lid, 10 x 4 x 4 In.	525.00
Display, Smith Bros. Cough Drops, Holder, 10⅝ x 4⅛ x 3½ In.	468.00
Display, Star Cough Drop, Pug Dog, Kenyon Potter & Co., Tin, 7⅛ x 6 x 4¼ In.	1650.00
Display, Stonewall Jackson Cigars, Cardboard, Countertop	1230.00
Display, Sunshine Biscuits & Snakes, Chef Holding Box, Molded Styrofoam, 1960s	336.00
Display, Tennyson's Cigars, 5 Cents, Red, Yellow, White, Tin, Glass, 9½ x 12½ x 6 In.	207.00
Display, Topps Football Cards, 2-Box Tray, 1978	3109.00
Display, Topps Football Cards, 3-Box Tray, 1980	987.00
Display, Venida Woman's Hair Net, 10 Cents, 20 Hair Nets, 23 x 7 In.	165.00
Display, Victor Duck Decoys, Figural, White, Cardboard 6 x 6 x 4½ In.	187.00
Display, Vidor Batteries, Robot, For Super Power, Super Life, Cardboard, 14 x 9 In.	112.00
Display, Walter Baker & Co., Cocoa, Tin Lithograph, Stand-Up, Tray, 24 x 16 x 7 In.	4510.00
Display, Ward's Cakes, Children, Glass Top, Case, Tin Lithograph, 20 x 17 x 13 In.	1815.00
Display, Waterman's Ink, Fountain Pen Ink Bottles, Tin Lithograph, 21 x 14½ x 17 In.	2640.00
Display, Western Super X Mark 5, Stand-Up, Box, 34 In.	303.00
Display, Wilbur's Veterinary Stock Food, Salesman's Sample, Wood, 10 x 5 x 5 In.	2420.00
Display, Winchester Guns & Ammunition, 2 Men, Dog, Die Cut, c.1930, 37 x 33 In.	4400.00
Display, Woodbury Soap, Man & Woman, Facial Cocktail, Cardboard, 10 Bars, 18 In. ..*illus*	205.00
Display, Woodbury Soap, Man Kissing Woman, Cardboard, 10 Bars, 18 In.	192.00
Display, Wrigley's, 4-Box, Figural, Die Cut, 14 x 6 x 14 In.	715.00
Display, Wrigley's Chewing Gum, Cardboard, Dummy Package Inserts, 6 x 17 x 4 In.	523.00
Display, Zeno Gum, 1 Cent, Sliding Door, Etched, Glass, Brass, 10 x 30 x 8 In.	280.00
Display, Zeno Gum, Windmills, Boats, Tin Lithograph, 6¾ x 9⅝ x 4½ In.	99.00
Dolls are listed in their own category.	
Door, Colonial Bread, Door Push On Each Side, Wood, Screen, 80 x 39½ In.	165.00
Door Pull, Ex-Lax, Porcelain, 4 x 8 In.	264.00
Door Pull, Merita Bread, Porcelain, 4 x 8 In.	300.00
Door Push, Crescent Flour, Try A Snack, Blue, White, Tin Lithograph, 9⅝ x 3 In.	2035.00
Door Push, Domino Cigarettes, Tin Lithograph, 13¾ x 4 In.	77.00
Door Push, Dr. Caldwell's Syrup Pepsin, 6½ x 3⅞ In.	253.00
Door Push, Edgeworth Tobacco, Larus & Bro. Co., 14 x 4 In.	176.00
Door Push, Hoffman Bicycles, Please Close The Door, Best In The World, Tin, 9 x 3 In.	522.00
Door Push, Ken-L Meal, Ration & Biskit, Tin, 4 x 11 In.	220.00
Door Push, Majors Cement, Porcelain, 7½ x 3⅛ x ⅞ In.	385.00
Door Push, Munsingwear, Union Suits, Man Playing Tennis, Metal, 7 x 2¾ In.	330.00
Door Push, Orange Crush, Soda Bottle, Embossed, Tin Lithograph, 1920s, 12 x 3 In. 425.00 to 469.00	
Door Push, Red Rose Tea, Is Good Tea, Red, White, Porcelain, 9¼ x 3 In. .... 385.00 to 605.00	
Door Push, Spring Grove Farms, Milk Bottle, Cap, Label, Tin Lithograph, 11½ x 3½ In.	330.00
Door Push, Star Naphtha Washing Powder, Porcelain, 3½ x 6 In.	300.00
Door Push, Sweetheart Products, Flour, Corn Meal, Red, White, Heart Shape, Porcelain, c.1935 .	395.00
Door Push, Texas Punch, Tin, 4 x 10 In.	165.00

Door Push, Wise Potato Chips, Did You Buy Wise?, Tin Lithograph, 6⅝ x 3¼ In.	1925.00
Fan Hanger, Star Soap, Children On Swing, 2-Sided, Die Cut, Cardboard, 6 x 8 In.	546.00
Fans are listed in their own category.	
Festoon, Rice Krispies, Train, Snap, Crackle, Pop & Friends In Train, Die Cut, 60 In.	330.00
Figure, Budweiser, Spuds MacKenzie, Light-Up, c.1987, 9 x 16 x 16 In.	121.00
Figure, Eskimo Pie, Plastic, Beige & Brown, 1950s, 5 In.	195.00
Figure, Esky, Man, Composition, Painted, 1940s, 24 In.	1476.00
Figure, Esky, Man, Suit, You Saw It In Esquire, Painted, Composition, 1940s, 8½ In.	420.00
Figure, Jacquemaire Baby Food Bean, Bendable, Can, France, 1950s, 9 In.	280.00
Figure, Jiggs, I Smoke Edgeworth Tobacco, Painted, Plaster, c.1930, 10 In.	554.00
Figure, Kikkoman Soy Sauce, Cloth Over Wire, Painted Accents, 1960s, 10 In.	420.00
Figure, National Cash Register, Red Head Man, Blue Bowtie, 1941, 10½ In.	2285.00
Figure, Pfeiffer's Beer, Man Playing Flute, Plaster, Plasto, c.1950, 7¼ In.	135.00
Figure, Ram, Butcher Shop Display, Sheet Iron, c.1900, 28 x 32 In.	3800.00
Figure, RCA Dog, Papier-Mache, Painted, White, Brown, Black, 36 x 26 x 16 In.	863.00
Figure, RCA Nipper, Chalkware, 1920s, 4½ In.	29.00
Figure, Robin Hood Shoes, Fox As Robin Hood, 1950s, 26 In.	560.00
Figure, Roof, Dairy Queen, Fiberglass, Yellow, Black Hair, 87 In.	468.00
Figure, Ropp, Man, Extended Arms To Hold Ties, Composition, 1940s, 12½ In.	2177.00
Fire Extinguisher, B&O Railroad, Brass, Copper, 23½ In.	193.00
Foam Scraper, National Brewing Co., Syracuse, N.Y., Celluloid	405.00
Fold-Out, Jackson Wagon Sun Flower Band, At The Great Fairs Of 1884, 9 x 11 In.	263.00
Gambling Wheel, Old Mr. Boston, 16 In.	288.00
Game, Buy Star Soap, Mirror, Black Woman, Schultz & Co., Zanesville, Oh., 2 In. Diam. . . .	60.00
Game, Fine Cut Tobacco, Game Birds, Jno. J. Bagley & Co., 7½ x 11½ x 7¾ In.	1006.00
Globe, Alderney A Dairy, Bottle Form, Milk Glass, 20 x 8 In.	525.00
Globe, Colonel Sanders, Bucket Of Chicken, Milk Glass, c.1969, 9½ x 8½ In.	140.00
Hat, Oilzum, America's Finest Oil, Man's Face, Black, Gold, Oilcloth, 4 x 11 x 3½ In.	385.00
Holder, Soap, Eagle Lye, Purest & Best, Tin Lithograph, Hanging, 4¾ x 5¾ x 4 In.	495.00
Holder, Soap, Laurel Stoves & Ranges, Blue, White, Tin Lithograph, Wire, 4¾ x 5 x 4 In. . . .	550.00
Jar, Borden's Malted Milk, Glass, Fountain Counter, Lid, 9⅜ x 6½ In.	660.00
Jar, H.J. Heinz Co., Purveyors, Gherkins, Cylinder, Glass, Lid, 19½ In.	538.00
Jar, Heinz Apple Butter, Bristol Glaze, Lid, Stoneware, June 30, 1906, 8½ In.	690.00
Jar, Heinz, Pickling Vinegar, Put Up In, Glass, Lid, 19 In. 418.00 to 1016.00
Jar, Heinz, Prepared Mustard, Fluted, Glass, Lid, 4½ In.	215.00
Jar, Heinz Tomato Preserves, Standard Quality, Clamp & Lid, Stoneware, 8 x 4 In.	1045.00
Jar, Heinz's Lemon Jelly, Glass, Lid	155.00
Jar, Heinz's Pure Malt Vinegar, Glass, Lid, 15 In.	239.00
Jar, Heinz's Selected Queen Olives, Glass, Lid, 13¼ In.	203.00
Jar, Horlick's, Fruit, Stoneware, Large	33.00
Jar, Lutted's Cough Drops, Dakota Style, 11½ x 5¾ In.	1375.00
Jar, Meadow Gold Dairy Products, Brown Bands, Stencil, Yellowware, c.1910, 5¼ In.	209.00
Jar, Pepsin Chewing Gum, Walla Walla, Indian, Embossed, Glass, 13 x 4¾ x 4¾ In.	690.00
Jar, Tom's Toasted Peanuts, Glass, Clear, Red Knop, 9½ In.	22.00
Jigsaw Puzzle, Chase & Sanborn, People Picking Coffee Beans, Box, 6 x 8 In.	99.00
Jug, Geo. A. Dickel & Co., Cascade, Distillery, Blue, White Bands, c.1900, ½ Gal., 9 In.	220.00
Jug, Green River Whiskey, Brown Top, 3 Gal., 13 In.	385.00
Jug, Heinz, Pure Olive Oil, Sample, 2½ In.	120.00
Jug, Heinz Keystone Dressing, 3 In.	90.00
Jug, Heinz Tomato Ketchup, 2¾ In.	167.00
Jug, M.A. Ingalls, Liquor Dealer, Little Falls, 2 Handles, Stoneware, c.1870, 5 Gal., 19 In. . . .	330.00
Keg, DuPont Gun Powder, Tin Lithograph, 3¾ x 3⅜ In.	385.00
Keg, Kentucy Rifle Gunpowder, Wood, Hazard Powder Co., 8⅝ x 8½ In.	770.00
Keg, Oriental Powder Mill, Indian, Landscape, Texas Rifle, Wood, Red Paint, Label, 9 x 6 In. .	489.00
Kickplate, Squeeze Soda, 2 Children On Bench, Embossed, Tin, 1947, 10 x 28 In.	400.00
Knife Sharpener, Doyle Taxi, Cigars, Tobaccos, Magazines, Red, 1⅝ In.	81.00
Label, Food, Don't Cry Brand Sweet Potatoes, Black Boy Rolling Dice, 1950s, 9 x 9 In.	25.00
Label, Food, Ketch-Em Brand Lands' Em, Salmon Eggs, Fisherman, Astoria, 10 x 11 In.	100.00
Label, Food, Schooner Lemons, California Red Ball, Sailing Ship, 1930, 8 x 10 In.	8.00
Label, Miscellaneous, Coach-In Cotton, Black Man, Baby, Cart, Pulled By Rooster, 8⅜ x 10 In.	957.00
Label, Tobacco, Dan Patch Tobacco, 9 Piece	44.00
Lamps are listed in the Lamp category.	
Ledger Marker, National Fire Insurance Co., Woman, Flag, Eagle, Shield, Tin Litho, 12 x 3 In. .	400.00
Ledger Marker, Vaseline Toilet Soap, Somers Bros., Gold, Black, Tin Litho, 3 x 12⅜ In.	1100.00
Letter Opener, Fuller Brush, Salesman Carrying Sample Case, Brown, Plastic, 7⅜ In.	10.00
Letter Opener, Grundy Register, Dow Co., St. Paul, Metal, Embossed, Painted Handle, 10 In.	10.00

Advertising, Display, Armstrong's Quaker Rug, Quaker Woman, Cardboard, Die Cut, 62 x 18½ In.
$29.00

Advertising, Display, Chiclets, 1 Cent, Exchange Your Pennies For Chiclets, 8 Packs, 8 x 7 In.
$290.00

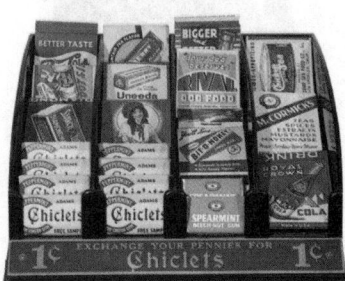

Hires History

Charles E. Hires, a Philadelphia druggist, became "The Father of Root Beer" in the early 1870s when he concocted a drink made of roots and herbs. He sold the syrup at his drugstore, at soda fountains, and at grocery stores for home use. He promoted the syrup through advertising pieces, such as mugs, signs, bottles, trays, and trade cards. Some of the most desirable early pieces feature the Hires boy, who was illustrated wearing a dress from 1891 to 1906, a bathrobe from 1907 to 1914, and a dinner jacket from 1915 to 1926.

Advertising, Display,
Hires Root Beer, Make At Home,
3-Tiered Rack, 3 Boxes, Contents,
14 x 5 In.
$260.00

Letter Opener, Highton Resisters & Grille, Female Head, Flowing Hair, 8¾ x 1 In.	82.00
Letter Opener, Kansas City Southern Railway, Heart Of America, Celluloid, 8 In.	59.00
Letter Opener, Mills Oil Co., Booker Texas, 7 In.	10.00
Letter Opener, Neighborhood News, Nordmann Printing Co., 9¾ In.	10.00
Letter Opener, Southwestern Life Insurance, Dallas, Plastic Blade, Leather Handle	13.00
Lipstick Tissues, Broadmoor Colorado Hotel, Kleenex, Contents, Parrish, 3 x 2 x ¼ In.	100.00
Lunch Box, Dixie Kid Cut Plug, Black Child, Nall & Williams Tob., Tin, 4 x 8 x 5 In.	385.00
Lunch Box, Pedro Smoking Tobacco, Cut Plug, Yellow, Red, Tin, 4½ x 8 x 5¼ In.	495.00
Lunch Box, Rainbow Cut Plug Tobacco, Yellow, Blue, Handle, 4 x 7¾ In.	209.00
Lunch Box, Winner Cut Plug, Smoke & Chew, Race Car Scene, Tin, 4¼ x 7⅞ In.	632.00
Lunch Boxes are also listed in their own category.	
Match Striker, Absinthe Dutruc, Ceramic, c.1900	176.00
Match Striker, Amer. Chinois Absinthe, Lescuras, Ceramic, Limoges, c.1900	214.00
Match Striker, Compliments Of Simmons Hardware, Holder	625.00
Match Striker, Mugnier Grande Absinthe, Ceramic, c.1900	349.00
Match Striker, Oxygenee Absinthe, Ceramic, c.1900	176.00
Match Striker, Pauvre-Homme Liqueur Exquise, Ceramic, c.1900	88.00
Match Striker, Soda-Indien Limonadiers, Ceramic, c.1900	214.00
Menu Board, Heinz Soups, 2 Minute Service, Have A Bowl, Wood, 13 x 26¾ In.	56.00
Menu Holder, American Can Co., National Paint, Oil, Varnish, Palette Form, Tin, 1903, 7 x 5 In.	198.00
Menu Holder, Drink Smile, Orange Smiling, Plaster, 7 x 5 x 4¾ In.	395.00

Advertising mirrors of all sizes are listed here. Pocket mirrors range in size from 1½ to 5 inches in diameter. Most of these mirrors were given away as advertising promotions and include the name of the company in the design.

Mirror, Arlington Hotel & Bar, Good For 12½ Cents In Trade, Girl, Celluloid, 2½ In.	1430.00
Mirror, Bailey's Pure Rye, 3 Scenes, 2¾ In.	506.00
Mirror, Berry Bros. Varnish, Boy, Pulling Dog In Wagon, Celluloid, Oval, 1¾ x 2¾ In.	176.00
Mirror, Bertsch & H.B. Hard Fan Shoes For Men & Boys, Girl, Flowers, Pocket, 2½ In.	145.00
Mirror, Campbell's Soup, 10 Cent Can, Celluloid, Pocket, 2¾ x 1¼ In.	143.00
Mirror, Cascarets Did It, Cherub On Potty, Early 1900s, 2½ In.	112.00
Mirror, C-Er-Lay Poultry Feed, Chicken, J. J. Badenoch Co., Celluloid, 2 In. Diam.	120.00
Mirror, Crawford Notch Cafe, Boston, Lake Scene, Celluloid, 2⅛ In. Diam.	33.00
Mirror, Creme Elcaya, William Jennings Bryan, Celluloid, Oval, 2¾ x 1¾ In.	465.00
Mirror, Dokash Stoves & Ranges, Scranto Stove Works, Black, White, Celluloid, 2½ In.	20.00
Mirror, Dr. Daniels' Dog & Puppy Bread, Celluloid, G.A. Quimby, 2½ In.	165.00
Mirror, Dr. Daniels' Veterinary Medicines, Woman, Horse, Dog, Celluloid, 2 In. Diam.	187.00
Mirror, Duffy's Malt Whiskey, Image Of Chemist, 2¾ In.	48.00
Mirror, Ferner Shoes, Woman, Brown Hair, Pocket, 2¾ In.	125.00
Mirror, Flynn Storage Warehouse, N.Y.C., Truck, Celluloid, c.1920, 3 In. Diam.	114.00
Mirror, Green Duck Co., Mark Of Quality, Celluloid, Round, 3 In.	33.00
Mirror, Heidelberger Sweets, Celluloid, 2¾ In. Diam.	29.00
Mirror, Lypsyl Vinolia, For The Lips, Woman At Dressing Table, Celluloid, Canada, 2¼ In.	66.00
Mirror, Magnolia Metal Company, Celluloid, 3 In. Diam.	94.00
Mirror, McCaffrey Bros., Good For 10 Cents In Trade, Celluloid, Pocket, c.1910, 3 In.	1450.00
Mirror, Nature's Remedy, Face, Tablet On Tongue, 2⅛ In.	55.00
Mirror, Ohio Farm Machinery, Celluloid, Pocket, 1¾ In.	715.00
Mirror, Osborn's Ice Cream Parlor, Purse, c.1910, 2⅛ In.	230.00
Mirror, Pacific Shoes, St. Louis, 2¼ In.	39.00
Mirror, Parisian Novelty Company, Chicago, Spirit Of Good Will, Celluloid, 3⅜ In.	80.00
Mirror, Pittsburgh Butcher & Packing Co., Celluloid, Pocket, 2¾ x 1¾ In.	468.00
Mirror, Portland Taxicab Co., Celluloid, c.1910, 1¾ In. Diam.	103.00
Mirror, Quaker Bread, Puzzle, Heissler & Junge Co., 1 Lb., 5 Cents, Tin Lithograph, 1½ In.	44.00
Mirror, S. Oppenheimer & Co., Sausage Casings, Clock, Celluloid, 4 In. Diam.	85.00
Mirror, Skeezix Shoes, Outgrown Before Outworn, 18 Months, Celluloid, 2½ In. Diam.	75.00
Mirror, Socony Motor Gasoline, Standard Oil, 3½ In. Diam.	110.00
Mirror, Standard Brwg. Co., New Orleans, Image Of Bottle, 2¾ In.	187.00
Mirror, State Firemen's Assoc., Meredith, N.H., Sept. 28, 1910, Celluloid, 2⅞ x 1¾ In.	132.00
Mirror, Stutz-Ideal Motor Car Co., Indianapolis, Indiana, 2½ In. Diam.	145.00
Mirror, Sunlight Soap, For Dainty Clothes, Hanging Laundry, Celluloid, 2¼ In.	550.00
Mirror, Tricofero Hair Tonic, Celluloid, Pocket, 2¾ x 1¾ In.	132.00
Mirror, W. Jones Brewing Co., Barrel, Granite State, Celluloid, 1¾ x 2¾ In.	176.00
Mirror, Wm. F. Murphy's Sons Company, Blank Book & Loose Leaf, c.1920, 3 In.	41.00
Mirror, Woolsey's Marine & Yacht Paint, Red, Green, Celluloid, 2¾ x 1¾ In.	165.00
Mug, Hausmann's Beer, Hausmann Brewing Co., Madison, Wis.	898.00

Mug, Hires Root Beer, Boy, Pointing, Bib, 4 x 3½ In.	144.00
Notebook, Berg's Guanos & Bone Manures, Celluloid, 5 x 3 In.	76.00
Notebook, Hoffman House Pure Rye, Celluloid, 4½ x 3 In.	275.00
Package, Nestle Colortint Hair Dye, 3 Week Hair Colour, 3 Packs, 1960s	5.00
Pail, 3 Pigs Candy, Nursery Rhyme Images, Tin Lithograph, 2¾ x 2⅞ In.	121.00
Pail, Aragon Coffee Co., Galaxy Coffee, Milk Can Shape, 8¾ x 5½ In.	1155.00
Pail, Argosy Braces, Nesting Containers, Men, Cue Stick, Enamel, Rack, c.1900	65.00
Pail, Armour's Peanut Butter, Nursery Rhymes, Yellow, Handle, Tin Lithograph, 3⅞ In.	176.00
Pail, Bayle Peanut Butter, Boy Scouts, 3¼ x 3¾ In.	99.00
Pail, Beaver Brand Peanut Butter, Tapered, Bail Handle, 3 x 4 In.	748.00
Pail, Calumet Lard, Indian, G.H. Hammond Co., Tin Lithograph, Handle, 6 x 5¾ In.	1595.00
Pail, Clark's Peanut Butter, Indian & Hunter In Canoe, Bail Handle, 3½ x 4 In.	460.00
Pail, Dixie Queen, Tobacco, Image Of Queen, Embossed, 6½ x 4¾ In.	600.00
Pail, Eatsum Peanut Butter, Child, Dog, Tin Lithograph, 2 Lb., 4⅝ x 5⅛ In.	44.00
Pail, Empire Axle Grease, Horse Drawn Wagon, Tin Lithograph, 1 Lb., 3½ In.	330.00
Pail, Fast Mail Chewing Tobacco, Ginna & Co., Bail Handle, 5¼ In.	330.00
Pail, Fenix Lard, Blue, Gold, Tin Lithograph, Handle, 4 Oz., 2⅞ In.	22.00
Pail, Foss & Deering Co., Mustard, Fruits, Vines, Ginna Lithograph, 2⅞ x 2½ In.	633.00
Pail, Garden Co. Ltd., Bakers & Confectioners, Children At Beach, Lid, 3 x 2¼ In.	195.00
Pail, Giant Salted Peanuts, Circus Images, Superior Peanut Co., Tin, 3½ x 3⅞ In.	580.00
Pail, Gillies Coffee Co., Girls At Seashore, Boys Playing Football, Tin, 4¾ x 5 In.	1320.00
Pail, Hoody's Famous Peanut Butter, Children On Seesaw, Swing Handle	385.00
Pail, Jackie Coogan Peanut Butter, Jackie C. Images, Handle, Kelly Co., 3½ x 3 In.	165.00 to 385.00
Pail, Jolly Time Popcorn, Guaranteed To Pop, American Popcorn, Iowa, 1925, 5 x 2½ In.	40.00
Pail, Jolly Time Popcorn, Lid, Bail Handle, 1927, 4½ In.	248.00
Pail, Mammy's Coffee, C.D. Kenney's, Tin Lithograph, 11 x 6⅛ In.	253.00
Pail, Mayo's Cut Plug Tobacco, For Smoking & Chewing, Tin, Expandable ....*illus*	330.00
Pail, Monadnock Peanut Butter, Holbrook Grocery, Handle, 1 Lb., 3⅜ x 3⅞ In.	242.00
Pail, Morris Supreme Peanut Butter, Children At Seashore, 3 x 3½ In.	550.00
Pail, Old Reliable Peanut Butter, Children Playing, Handle, 1 Lb., 3¾ x 3¼ In.	550.00
Pail, Pedro Tobacco, 8 x 4 x 5½ In.	295.00
Pail, Peter Cottontail Candy, Nursery Rhymes, Tin Litho, Lovell & Covel, 2¾ x 2⅞ In.	187.00
Pail, Peter Cottontail Candy, Pure Hard Candies, Lovell & Covel, 1920s, 2¾ In.	389.00
Pail, Peter Rabbit Candy, Story, Lovell & Covel, Handle, 2¾ x 2⅞ In.	209.00
Pail, Peter Rabbit Candy, Tin, Hinged Lid, Harrison Cady, 2½ x 3½ x 4½ In.	275.00
Pail, Pickaninny Peanut Butter, F.M. Hoyt's, Tin Lithograph, 3⅜ x 3⅞ In.	660.00
Pail, Potter-Parlan Co., Children Skating, Sledding, Tin Lithograph, 4½ x 5 In.	330.00
Pail, Red Riding Hood Candy, Nursery Rhyme, Lovell & Covel, Handle, 2¾ x 2⅞ In.	198.00 to 253.00
Pail, Rival Peanut Butter, 2 Girls, Tin Lithograph, 1 Lb., 3½ x 3⅞ In.	110.00
Pail, Teller Coffee Co., Milkmaid, Painted, Stenciled, Milkmaid Shape, 9 x 6⅝ In.	2850.00
Pail, Toyland Peanut Butter, Circus Image, Tin Lithograph, 1 Lb., 3¾ x 3½ In.	253.00
Pail, Woman's Club Peanut Butter, Girl With Wings, Tin, Red, 5 Lb., 6½ x 6 In.	154.00
Pails are also listed in the Lunch Box category.	
Paper Clip, Benito Rovira Co., Makers Of Good Cigars, Metal, 1920s, 2½ x 2½ In.	41.00
Patch Set, Rin Tin Tin, Nabisco, Mounted, 1958, 2½ x 2⅝ In., 7 Piece ....*illus*	180.00
Pencil Box, Red Goose, Tin Lithograph, 2⅜ x 7¾ x ¾ In.	132.00
Pennant, Minneapolis Brewing Co., Grain Belt, Felt, 11 x 28 In.	785.00
Picture, Pabst Extract, Woman, Basket Of Flowers, Milwaukee, 1920s, 36 x 7 In.	90.00
Pin, American Boy Bread, c.1940, 1⅜ In.	62.00
Pin, Bond Bread, Amelia Earhart, No. 5	30.00
Pin, Budweiser, Rocky III, Red, Black, Yellow Ground, Celluloid, 2¼ In.	10.00
Pin, Dr. LeGear, Giant Horse, 21 Hands Tall, 1¼ In.	49.00
Pin, Drink Dukehart's Ale, Duck, Fish, Crab, Oyster, 1901, ¹³⁄₁₆ In.	151.00
Pin, Drovers Telegram, Reglar Fellars, & Girls Too, Kansas, Celluloid, ⅞ In.	17.00
Pin, Experts Use Peters Cartridges, Gray Ground, ⅞ In.	73.00
Pin, Fleer Bubble Gum, Junior Salesmen, 1¼ In.	18.00
Pin, Gold Dust Washing Powder, Black Twins, In Tub, c.1896, ⅞ In.	67.00
Pin, Gold Dust Washing Powder, Black Twins, In Tub, c.1900, 1¼ In.	73.00
Pin, H.P. Hood & Sons, Milk, Celluloid, 1¼ In.	11.00
Pin, IC Baking Powder, Celluloid, 1¾ In.	22.00
Pin, Ivory Snow, Marilyn Chambers, Lithograph, ⅞ In.	69.00
Pin, Jim Nabors Hour, CBS, c.1970, 6 In.	45.00
Pin, Life Bread, Always Fresh, Celluloid, 1¼ In.	17.00
Pin, Long Beach Festival Of The Sea, California, Lapel, 1908, 2⅛ In.	506.00
Pin, Montgomery Ward, Horseless Carriage, 4 People In Carriage, Celluloid, 1 In.	31.00
Pin, Oliver Typewriter, Printype Man, Oval, Green Ground	191.00

Advertising, Display,
Kleen Chief Hankies, Cardboard
$58.00

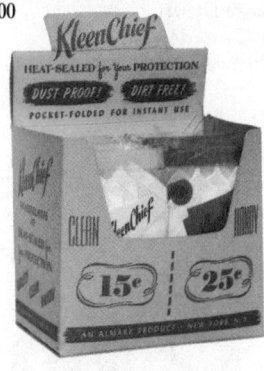

Advertising, Display, Las Vegas Cigars,
Always Pleasing, Ladies, Cardboard,
Trifold, 29 x 47 In.
$470.00

Advertising Collectible "Firsts"
Printed matchbook label:
"Percussion Matches Manufactured by P. Truesdell, Warsaw, New York. Warranted New Yorker Print" was printed on the first matchbook label, which was made from 1855 to 1857.

Cigarette cards: In 1885 Allen and Ginter of Richmond, Virginia, issued ten cigarettes in a box plus a picture card for five cents. These eventually inspired baseball cards.

Paper advertising fans: Paper fans were made in the eighteenth century. A Crystal Palace exhibition in New York in 1853 used advertising fans.

Paper napkins: The first paper napkins, which were plain tissue paper squares, were introduced at the Chicago World's Fair in 1893. The first printed paper napkin appeared in 1898.

Advertising, Display, Mentholatum, Girl Nurse, Jar, Feel It Heal, Chalkware, 13 In. $1989.00

Advertising, Display, Woodbury Soap, Man & Woman, Facial Cocktail, Cardboard, 10 Bars, 18 In. $205.00

Advertising, Pail, Mayo's Cut Plug Tobacco, For Smoking & Chewing, Tin, Expandable $330.00

Pin, Peerless Rubber Mfg. Co., Rainbow Packing, 225, Multicolored, Celluloid, 1 In.	26.00
Pin, Quaker Rolled Oats, Try Me, 30 Days, 1920s, 1¼ In.	34.00
Pin, Ralston Club, Members Around The World, 1930s, ⅞ In.	55.00
Pin, Reifsnyder & Sons Pianos, 2⅛ In.	22.00
Pin, Smith Typewriter, 1¼ In.	51.00
Pin, Southwestern Bell System, c.1910, 1¼ In.	91.00
Pin, Stoehmann's Sunbeam Bread, Lithograph, 1¼ In.	16.00
Pin, Swift Premium Co., Large S, Red, White, Black, Celluloid	11.00
Pin, Swift's Ham & Bacon, Cartoon, Celluloid, 1¼ In.	38.00
Pin, Swift's Meat Co., Little Cook Hanger, Celluloid, c.1900	46.00
Pin, Whitehead & Hoag, Black, Youngsters, Here Comes Da Parade, ⅞ In.	55.00
Pin, Wurlitzer, Cincinnati, His Master's Voice, Nipper, Victor, Celluloid, c.1910, 1⅛ In.	960.00
Pin Tray, Eye-Fix, Great Eye Remedy, Angel, Tin Lithograph, 4¼ In.	900.00
Pitcher, Friends Oats, Girl Holding Box & Sign, Gilt Trim, Porcelain, 2¾ x 1¾ In.	440.00
Plate, Dessert, Willard Hotel, Washington D.C., Winthrop, 7¼ In.	5.00
Platter, Oval, Keeler's State St., Syracuse China, 15¼ x 10½ In.	10.00
Pop Gun, Ladies Home Journal, Baseball Theme, Cardboard, 6 x 11½ In.	44.00
Pot Scraper, American-Maid Bread, Red, White, Blue, 1¾ x 3 In.	240.00
Pot Scraper, Babbitt's Cleanser, 5 Cents, Soap Bar, Boxes, Tin Lithograph, 3⅛ x 3⅝ In.	176.00
Pot Scraper, Babbitt's Cleanser, 5 Cents, Cleanse Any Good Utensil, 2-Sided, 3½ x 3 In.	325.00
Pot Scraper, Dove Brand Ham & Bacon, He Didn't Ask For It, Red, Green, c.1900, 3 x 2½ In.	1450.00
Pot Scraper, Fairmont Creamery Co., Your Cream, You Cannot Lose, 3½ x 2¾ In.	110.00
Pot Scraper, Henkel's Flour, Don't Take Untried Brands, 3½ x 2¾ In.	140.00 to 165.00
Pot Scraper, Junket, Makes Milk Into Desserts, 2-Sided, Little Falls, N.H., 3¼ x 2½ In.	100.00
Pot Scraper, King Midas Flour, Highest Priced Flour In America, 3¼ x 2¾ In.	375.00
Pot Scraper, Nesco, Royal Granite Enamel Ware, Boy, Red, White, Blue, 2-Sided, 3 x 3¼ In.	170.00
Pot Scraper, Penn, Stoves, Furnaces, Ranges, Clover, 3¼ x 2¾ In.	150.00
Pot Scraper, Red Wing Special Flour, Red Wing, Minn., 3¼ x 2¼ In.	600.00
Pot Scraper, Sharples Tubular Cream Separator, Lady Carrying Bucket, 2¾ x 2¼ In.	210.00
Pot Scraper, Ward's, Remedies, Extracts, Toilet Articles, Ground Spices, 2¾ x 3½ In.	135.00
Pouch, Piedmont Tobacco Co., Black Man Holding Hambone, Cloth, Paper Label, Sealed, 3 x 2 In.	950.00
Pouch, Tobacco, B. Leiserdof & Co., Great Puff, Man Smoking, Rolling Papers, Label, 3⅜ x 2 In.	440.00
Pouch, Tobacco, Old Virginia, Honey-Dew, Dancing Black Man, Cloth, Label, 6 x 1¾ In.	1430.00
Pouch, Tobacco, Victory Smoking Tobacco, Indian On Horse, Cloth, Label, 4 x 2½ In.	385.00
Print, Union Pacific Railroad Depot, Buffalo, Oak Frame, 23½ x 27½ In.	850.00
Punch Bowl, Bardwell's Root Beer, Embossed, Stoneware, White's, Utica, 18 x 10 In. *illus*	1150.00
Rack, Black Draught, Porcelain, 14 Full Product Boxes, 24 x 2⅞ x 1¾ In.	209.00
Rack, Boyers Vim Shoe Polish, Red, White, Blue, Metal, 12 x 8 In.	165.00
Rack, Economy Pretzels, Red, White, 2 Tins, Metal, 30 In.	27.00
Rack, French's Pure, Spices, Pepper, Cloves, Ginger, Red, Yellow, Tin, 25 x 17 In. *illus*	633.00
Rack, Hershey's, Milk Chocolate, 2 Cardboard Boxes, Metal, 13 x 10 In.	165.00
Rack, Lititz Spring Pretzels, Orange, Yellow, 2 Tins, Metal, 30 In.	385.00
Rack, Merkles Blu-J Brooms, Embossed, Tin Lithograph, 35 x 23 x 13½ In.	385.00
Rack, National Biscuit Company, Oak, 4 Shelves, 68 x 46½ In.	495.00
Rack, National Biscuit Company, Uneeda, 8 Bins, Wood, 48 x 62 x 11 In. *illus*	440.00
Rack, PEZ, Spinning, 6 Compartments, Metal, 3 Decals, Yellow, 1950s, 12½ In.	308.00
Rack, Sack, Samoa Island Coffee, Bement Seitz Grocers, Stringholder, c.1880	1600.00
Rack, Sir Walter Raleigh Smoking Tobacco, 6 Pocket Tins, Tin Lithograph, 7¾ x 6 x 3 In.	198.00
Ring, Jet Red Ball Sneakers, Super Space Ring, Secret Decoder, Whistle, Premium, 1950s	75.00
Rolling Pin, C.F. Brobeil, The Name Of Briardale Pure Food Products, Lytton, Ia., Rust Band	475.00
Rolling Pin, Central Block Grocery, Decorah, Iowa, Orange Band, Stoneware, 8 In.	470.00
Rolling Pin, Compliments Of Frank M. Hughes Groceries, Schuyler, Neb., Stoneware, 1916	650.00
Rolling Pin, Jacob Geiger Dealer, General Merchandise, Minden, Iowa, Rust Band, Stoneware	575.00
Rolling Pin, Klines Dep't. Store, La Porte City, Iowa, Orange Bands, Stoneware, 8 In.	588.00
Rolling Pin, White Swan Flour, Garrison, Iowa, Orange Bands, Stoneware, 8 In.	353.00
Ruler Guide, White Sewing Machine, Heavy Duty Cardboard, Made In USA, 6 In.	10.00
Salt & Pepper Shakers are listed in their own category.	
Saw, Winchester, No. 40, Old Trusty Old Trusty Design, Medallion, 26 In.	70.00
Scales are listed in their own category.	
Screen, Winchester Guns & Ammunition, Man, Boy, 5 Panels, Wood, Cardboard, 48 x 20 In.	605.00
Shaving Mug, Sunray For The Scalp & Skin, Sun, Red Letters, 1890-1930, 3½ In. *illus*	168.00
Sign, 3-Way, Steel Pens, Spencerian, Are The Best, Tin Lithograph, Chain, 4 x 18½ In.	1045.00
Sign, 75 Cents Cash & Carry $1.00, Shield Form, Green, White, 2-Sided, Wood, 17 x 19 In.	660.00
Sign, 7Up, Rotating, Light-Up, 18 x 26 In.	110.00
Sign, A No. 1, Tiny Chocolate Candy Dolls, 10 For 1 Cent, Girl, Blue Hat, Cardboard, 9 x 6 In.	2700.00
Sign, A&P Grocery Co., Red, Yellow, Tin, Embossed, 42 In. Diam.	88.00

Sign, Abdulla Superb Cigarettes, Tin, 1910s, 30 x 20 In.		416.00
Sign, Allen's Root Beer Extract, Cherubs, Girl, Paper Lithograph, 22 x 15 x 13 In.		3190.00
Sign, Alta Crest Certified Milk, Porcelain, 6 x 18 In.		1073.00
Sign, American Express, Money Orders, Blue, White, Red, 2-Sided, Porcelain, 13 x 18 In.		312.00
Sign, American Express, Money Orders For Sale Here, 2-Sided, Metal, 18 x 14 In.		121.00
Sign, American Radiator, 2 Girls Keeping Warm By Radiator, Paper, 21½ x 19¾ In.		357.00
Sign, Anheuser-Busch, Budweiser, St. Louis, Convex, Porcelain, Enamel, Metal, 13 x 13 In.		2124.00
Sign, Anheuser-Busch, Budweiser, Woman, Paper Lithograph, 39 x 24 x 14 In.		1320.00
Sign, Apollo Chocolates, Porcelain, 16 x 24 In.		675.00
Sign, Apothecary, Wood Mortar, Gold Paint, Iron Bracket, 20 x 19 In.	*illus*	1800.00
Sign, Aqua Crystal Eyeglasses, For Sale Here, Reverse Glass, Oak Frame, 5¼ x 15¼ In.		1265.00
Sign, Arm & Hammer Baking Soda, Fish Jumping At Lure, 25 x 16½ In.		240.00
Sign, Arm & Hammer Soda, Black Duck, Cardboard, Gustav Mus-Arnolt, 11 x 15 In.		50.00
Sign, Arm & Hammer Soda, Mallard Duck, Cardboard, Gustav Mus-Arnolt, 11 x 15 In.		50.00
Sign, Arm & Hammer Soda, Mongolian Pheasant, Cardboard, Gustav Mus-Arnolt, 11 x 15 In.		50.00
Sign, Arm & Hammer Soda, Purple Grackle, Cardboard, M.E. Eaton, 1915, 11 x 14 In.		50.00
Sign, Arm & Hammer Soda, Tin Lithograph, Orange, Black, White, 6½ x 13½ In.		110.00
Sign, Arm & Hammer Soda, Woodcock, Cardboard, Gustav Mus-Arnolt, 11 x 15 In.		50.00
Sign, Arrow Collars, Embossed Paper Inserts, Metal Frame, 43¼ x 7¼ In.		412.00
Sign, Artie Cigar, Tin Lithograph, Easel Back, 9⅞ x 6⅜ In.		1375.00
Sign, Ayer's Cathartic Pills, Black Figures, Die Cut, Cardboard, 12½ x 7¼ In.		660.00
Sign, Ayer's Hair Vigor, Nude Inside Flower, Reverse Glass, Frame, 12⅝ x 10¾ In.		1250.00
Sign, Ayer's Sarsaparilla, Man & Woman, Die Cut, Cardboard, 13¼ x 7 In.		330.00
Sign, Bagley's Clam Bake, Tobacco Hanger, 2-Sided, Cardboard, Ceiling String, 7 x 7½ In.		253.00
Sign, Baker's Cocoa, Pure, Delicious, Nutritious, Tin Lithograph, Frame, 22 x 17 In.		1165.00
Sign, Baker's Cocoa, Woman, Tin Lithograph Over Cardboard, 9⅜ x 6¼ In.		1265.00
Sign, Bakery, Eglomise, Pains Chaud, Brioches & Croissants, France, 76 x 17 In., Pair		11400.00
Sign, Ball's Health Preserving Corsets, Lady, Dog, Cardboard, 14 x 11 In.		1320.00
Sign, Band Boys Cigar, Vermont Marble Co. Store, Photo, Cardboard, 9¾ x 10⅞ In.		77.00
Sign, Barber Shop, It Pays To Look Well, Tin Over Cardboard, 6⅛ x 15 In.		121.00
Sign, Battle Creek Diet System, Lacto-Dextrin, Cardboard, Easel, 26¼ x 17 In.		198.00
Sign, Beech-Nut Cigarettes, You Can't Help But Like Them, Tin Lithograph, Frame, 20 x 14 In.		154.00
Sign, Beech-Nut Gum, Have You Had Your Beech-Nut Gum Today?, Cardboard, 16 x 44 In.		330.00
Sign, Beech-Nut Peanut Butter, It Tempts Them All, Boy, Ladder, Cardboard, Frame, 26 x 19 In.		121.00
Sign, Beech-Nut Tobacco, Depicting Package, Porcelain, 22 x 10 In.		176.00
Sign, Bevo Beverage, All Year Round Soft Drink, Fox, Bottle, Tin Lithograph, 6 x 27 In.		145.00
Sign, Bill Dugan Cigar, Glossy Cardboard, 24¼ x 20¼ In.		176.00
Sign, Black & White Cigars, Black Minstrel, Die Cut, Cardboard, 18½ x 7¾ In.		176.00
Sign, Bond Bread, Home-Like Loaf, Porcelain, 14 x 19 In.		165.00
Sign, Bottle Top, Gold-En Girl Cola, Red, White, 33 In. Diam.		100.00
Sign, Breyer's Ice Cream, Logo, 2-Sided, Porcelain, 20 x 28 In.		220.00
Sign, Brink's Express Co., Only Can Open Safe, Porcelain, 12½ In.		187.00
Sign, Bubble Balloon Chewing Gum, Boy Blowing Bubble, Paper, Frame, 4 x 14⅜ In.		264.00
Sign, Buckeye Beer, On Draught Here, Man Holding Hat & Sign, Tin, 1940s, 3 x 13 In.		100.00
Sign, Budweiser Girl, Pink Dress, Holding Bottle, Frame, 1904, 39 x 24 In.		2150.00
Sign, Buick Valve, In Head, Round, 2-Sided, Porcelain, 42 In.		1430.00
Sign, Bull Durham Smoking Tobacco, Lady, Cow, Prize Winners, Metal, Gilt Frame, 22 In.		1100.00
Sign, Bunny Bread, Bunny, Blue, Yellow, White, Enamel, 1968, 37 x 28 In.		392.00
Sign, Burma-Shave, Wood, Reverse Says Another Sitter, 40 x 17 In.		99.00
Sign, Burn's Detective Agency, Warning, Porcelain, 3 x 4 In.		88.00
Sign, C.D. Kenny Co., 2 Girls, Sitting, Mother Rabbit, Bunnies, Tin Lithograph, 12 x 8 In.		1100.00
Sign, C.W. Parker Co., Carousel, Paper Lithograph, 22¾ x 29¾ In.		2310.00
Sign, California Chew Gum, Victorian Children, Cardboard, Embossed, 13½ x 9¾ In.		330.00
Sign, Calumet Baking Powder, Embossed, Curved, Tin Lithograph, 23 x 17 In.		2310.00
Sign, Camark Pottery, Arkansas Shape, Melon Green Glaze, Pottery, 6⅜ In.		345.00
Sign, Campbell's Soup, Curved, Porcelain, 22½ x 14 In.		1430.00
Sign, Canada Dry's Spur Soda, 2-Sided, Tin, Flange, c.1940, 13⅝ x 15 In.		231.00
Sign, Cappuccino, Neon, Black Enamel Frame, 18½ x 68½ In.		239.00
Sign, Capt. Sigsbee 5 Cent Cigar, Captain, Eagle, Ship, Tin Lithograph, Frame, 28 x 22 In.		4100.00
Sign, Carmona Lawn Fertilizer, Makes Turf, Lawn Sport Scenes, Tin Lithograph, 13 x 19 In.		605.00
Sign, Cary's Liniment For Horses, Tin Lithograph, Embossed, 6⅝ x 13⅞ In.		908.00
Sign, Cat's Paw Non Slip Rubber Heels & Soles, Cat-Tex, 8-Sided, Light-Up, 26 x 19 In.		136.00
Sign, Charles Cuomo Cheese, Different Cheeses, Red, Brown, White, Tin On Cardboard, 18 x 13 In.		55.00
Sign, Chas. Goodall & Sons Playing Cards, Hand, Cards, Die Cut, Cardboard, 8 x 6 In.		1375.00
Sign, Chase & Sanborn, Teas & Coffees, Metal, 2-Sided, Flange, 16 x 8 In.		132.00
Sign, Checker Cab Co., Taxi, Dial 2-3434, Car, Green, Black, White, Cardboard, 7 x 11 In.		242.00

Value of Cans

Tin containers are judged by rarity, condition, and maker. Higher prices are paid for a three-dimensional shape like a book or a carriage, or for a can label picturing an animal, sports figure, Uncle Sam, flag, woman (especially nude), black person, car, train, or airplane.

A picture as part of the can design adds value for a collector. Any paper-labeled can made before 1875 is rare. A well-known maker's name also adds value.

Companies that manufactured cans in the United States before 1900 include Ginna and Company (1870s) of New York City; S.A. Ilsley and Company (1865) of Brooklyn, New York; Somers Brothers (1869) of Brooklyn, New York; and Hasker and Marcus Manufacturing Company (1891) of Richmond, Virginia.

Advertising, Rack, French's Pure, Spices, Pepper, Cloves, Ginger, Red, Yellow, Tin, 25 x 17 In.
$633.00

Advertising, Rack, National Biscuit Company, Uneeda, 8 Bins, Wood, 48 x 62 x 11 In.
$440.00

Advertising, Shaving Mug, Sunray For The Scalp & Skin, Sun, Red Letters, 1890-1930, 3½ In.
$168.00

Sign, Cherry Blush Soda, Tin Over Cardboard, 6¼ x 9¼ In.	825.00
Sign, Cherry's Ice Cream, We Serve, Red, White, Porcelain, Flange, 1930s, 12 x 16 In.	290.00
Sign, Chesterfield Cigarettes, Couple Celebrating New Year, 1927, 10 x 21 In.	275.00
Sign, Chesterfield Cigarettes, Like Your Pleasure Big?, Tin Litho, Embossed, Frame, 31 x 25 In.	165.00
Sign, Chesterfield Cigarettes, Smoke For Real, Tin Lithograph, Embossed, 31 x 25 In. _illus_	175.00
Sign, Chew Horse Shoe Tobacco, Yellow Ground, Tin, Embossed, 11½ x 17½ In.	880.00
Sign, Chilton Paint, Woman Painting, Tin, 7¼ x 11½ In.	143.00
Sign, Chocolate Cigarettes, Lithograph, 8¾ x 8½ In.	275.00
Sign, Chocolate-Crush, Rich Creamy Chocolate Soda In A Bottle, Tin, 14 x 19 In.	165.00
Sign, Clark's Mile-End Spool Cotton, Cardboard, Beveled, String Hung, 17¾ x 12¾ In.	90.00
Sign, Clark's O.N.T. Spool Cotton, Dog Sitting On Spool, Die Cut, 7 x 9½ In.	198.00
Sign, Clark's Thread, Cats, Spools Of Thread, Paper Lithograph, 16 x 23 In.	2035.00
Sign, Cletrac Crawler Tractors, Blue, White, Orange, 2-Sided, Porcelain, Flange	2450.00
Sign, Climax Plug Tobacco, Black Woman, White Woman, Cardboard, 1885, 19 x 18 In.	1072.00
Sign, Coburger Beer, Barmaid Holding Steins, Tin Lithograph, R. Naegelis Sons, 20 x 16 In.	330.00
Sign, Cole Brothers Circus, The Great Florenzo, Erie Litho Manufacturing Co., 19 x 28 In.	770.00
Sign, Colgate Cashmere Bouquet, Die Cut, Cardboard, Easel Back, 7¼ x 9¾ In.	198.00
Sign, Colonial Club Cigars, 5 Cents, Blue, Red, White, 2-Sided, Metal, Flange, 8¾ x 18⅝ In.	143.00
Sign, Columbia Fastener Co., Girl Wearing Star Crown, 15½ x 12 In.	308.00
Sign, Columbia Records, Hanging Record Center, Blue, White, Black, 2-Sided, Porcelain, 24 x 16 In.	770.00
Sign, Columbus Buggy, Scenic, Stone Lithograph, Frame, 36 x 23½ In.	2588.00
Sign, Common Sense Kettle, Self-Tilting, For Sale, Blue, White, Porcelain, c.1925, 11 x 13 In.	790.00
Sign, Continental Brewing Co., Soldier Carrying Musket, Gold Ground, Tin, 20 x 27 In.	675.00
Sign, Cook's Beer, Embossed, Tin, 28 x 14 In.	275.00
Sign, Cooks Imperial Wine Co, Woman, Glass Of Wine, Copyright 1896, 30 x 38 In.	9350.00
Sign, Copenhagen Snuff, Town Square, Weyman & Bros., c.1880, 23½ x 33½ In.	978.00
Sign, Copenhagen Tobacco, More Satisfying, Red, White, Porcelain, 6 x 22¾ In.	165.00
Sign, Corner, Andes Stoves & Ranges, Curved, Tin, Wood Frame, 20¼ x 20½ In.	523.00
Sign, Costeno Havana Cigar, 5 Cents, Tin, Yellow, Red, Black, Wood Frame, 16 x 46 In.	154.00
Sign, Cottolene, For Frying & Shortening, Embossed, Tin Lithograph, 19½ x 13⅞ In.	495.00
Sign, Cotton Candy, Tell & Sell, Motion, Light-Up, 31 x 4 x 13 In.	110.00
Sign, Curtiss Candies, Baby Ruth, Butterfinger, Cardboard, 11 x 29 In.	330.00
Sign, D & H Lackawanna Anthracite Coal, Red, Black, Porcelain, 12 In. Diam.	263.00
Sign, Damascus Ice Cream, 2-Sided, Porcelain, 18⅛ x 17⅜ In.	330.00
Sign, Dargai Cigar, Marconi & Pan-American, Canadian Tin Plate Co., 2-Sided, 9½ x 6½ In.	130.00
Sign, David's Cookies, Neon, 2-Sided, 23½ x 23¾ In.	418.00
Sign, Davy Crockett Cigar, Be Sure You're Right, Then Go Ahead, Tin, Frame, 19 x 27 In.	33000.00
Sign, De Soto Chewing Gum, Explorer, Indians, Paper, c.1880, 8¾ x 8¾ In.	525.00
Sign, Deadshot Smokeless Powder, Hunter, Duck, 22 x 12½ In.	550.00
Sign, DeLaval, Authorized Agency, Separator, Blue, 2-Sided, Porcelain, 26½ x 18 In.	1320.00
Sign, DeLaval, We Use The DeLaval Cream Separator, Blue, Yellow, Porcelain, 12 x 16 In.	80.00
Sign, DeLaval Cream Separator, Porcelain, Flange, 26½ x 18 In. _illus_	1404.00
Sign, DeLaval Cream Separator, Tin, Original Frame, 30 x 42 In.	1430.00
Sign, Diamond Dyes, Blond Fairy, Tin Lithograph, c.1890, 18 x 24. In.	460.00
Sign, Diamond Dyes, Busy Day In Dollville, Tin Over Cardboard, Frame, 11 x 17 In.	3190.00
Sign, Diamond Dyes, Domestic Fancy Dyeing, Fairy, Cherubs, People, Tin, Frame, 27 x 21 In.	385.00
Sign, Diehl's Condition Powders, Animals, We Are On Top, Moyer Bros., Tin, Chain, 10 x 14 In.	632.00
Sign, Ditto Quality Cigar, R & R, Indian Princess, Celluloid Over Cardboard, 12 x 8 In.	775.00
Sign, Dog Chains & Leads, Holes Along Side, Tin Lithograph, George Lawrence Co., 10 x 10 In.	198.00
Sign, Domino Sugar, Cardboard Lithograph, c.1910, 14 x 10½ In.	165.00
Sign, Donald Duck Soft Drinks, Celluloid Disc, Philadelphia Badge Co., 9 In.	220.00
Sign, Dr Pepper, Join Me, Cardboard, 19 x 32 In.	300.00
Sign, Dr Pepper, Soldier, In Tank, Cardboard, Frame, 21 x 27 In.	468.00
Sign, Dr. Caldwell Syrup Pepsin, Die Cut, Cardboard Lithograph, Easel, 15 x 6 In.	495.00
Sign, Dr. Daniels' Veterinary Remedies, Paper Lithograph, 15½ x 20 In.	633.00
Sign, Dr. Halle's Medicine, Old Injun, Indian, 13¾ x 20¾ In.	743.00
Sign, Dr. LeGear, Giant Horse, Tin Lithograph, 14¼ x 17⅝ In.	121.00
Sign, Dr. W.B. Caldwell's Syrup Pepsin, Women, Children, Cardboard, 28 x 19½ In.	385.00
Sign, Dr. White's Medicinal Cures, Lady, 3 Panels, Paper Lithograph, Frame, 28 x 36¼ In.	1794.00
Sign, Drewerys Ale & Beer, Canadian Ranger, Horse, Tin, Frame, 26½ x 21 In.	56.00
Sign, Drink Chocolate Crush, Embossed, Tin Lithograph, c.1920, 14 x 19½ In.	187.00
Sign, Drink Delaware Punch, Bottle, Embossed, Tin, Stout, St. Louis, 40 x 13 In.	277.00
Sign, Drink Green Spot, Orangeade, Bottle, Orange, Green, White, Tin Lithograph, 64 x 17 In.	110.00
Sign, Drink Krim's For Health, Yellow, Red, Black, Porcelain, 14 x 33 In.	247.00
Sign, Drink Squirt, Bottle, Yellow, Green, Red, Blue, Embossed, Tin, 1941, 4 x 17 In.	115.00
Sign, Duke & Sons Tobacco, Cameo Cigarettes, Woman, Frame, 23 x 10⅞ In.	1650.00

Sign, Duke's Cameo Cigarette, People Smoking, Cardboard, 1893, 28 x 14 In.	2350.00
Sign, DuPont Shoot Powders, Game Loads For The World, 31 x 20 In.	275.00
Sign, Dutch Boy Red Seal Paint, Die Cut, Tin, Flange, 2-Sided, 21 x 24 In.	863.00
Sign, Dutch Girl, Curved, Porcelain, 19 x 31 In.	675.00
Sign, E.R. Durkee & Co., Salad Dressing & Cold Meat Sauce, Couple, 1885, 28 x 13 In.	1650.00
Sign, Eagle, Shield, Enterta Inment, Wood, Wrought Iron, Painted, 2-Sided, 1802, 58 x 56 In.	6000.00
Sign, Economy Whiskey, Pure Rye & Malt, Reverse Painted, Pittsburg, Frame, 32 x 44 In.	4200.00
Sign, Edgeworth Tobacco, Ready Rub, Crystoglass, Whitehead & Hoag, 6 x 11 In.	280.00
Sign, Edison Mazda Lamps, Men In Purple Outfits, 2-Sided, Tin Lithograph, Frame, 28 x 71 In.	1980.00
Sign, El Lanos 10 Cent Cigar, Tin Lithograph Over Cardboard, 6 x 13¼ In.	77.00
Sign, Elgin Boy Wearing Watch, Oak, Frame, 18¼ x 25 In.	230.00
Sign, Emblem Cigarettes, Marked, Original Glass, Frame, 17 x 23 In.	220.00
Sign, Eveready, Radio Batteries, Cat, Die Cut, Porcelain, 18 x 24 In.	300.00
Sign, Eveready Flashlights, Batteries, Porcelain, 18 x 36 In.	468.00
Sign, Evinrude First In Outboards, Tin, 15 x 26 In.	110.00
Sign, Ex-Lax, Cardboard, 37¼ x 24¼ In.	440.00
Sign, Ex-Lax, Chocolate Laxative, Porcelain Over Steel, c.1930, 36 x 8 In.	395.00
Sign, Expert Hairdressing For Ladies & Gentlemen, Reverse Painted, Glass, Frame, 36 x 14 In.	192.00
Sign, F.W. Woolworth Co. 5 & 10 Cent Store, Reverse On Glass, Foil Back, 19 x 60 In.	550.00
Sign, Fairy Soap, 5 Cents, Blue, White, Porcelain, 3 x 20 In.	715.00
Sign, Fairy Soap, Have You A Little Fairy In Your Home?, Tin, Frame, 27¾ x 18 In.	1320.00
Sign, Farmer's Pride, Extra Quality Food Products, Paper, Cardboard, Frame, 20½ x 38 In.	110.00
Sign, Farrier, Horseshoe, Cloven Foot Ox Shoe, Iron, 19th Century, 17½ x 14¾ In.	1800.00
Sign, Favorite Stoves & Ranges, Base Burners, Family, Paper, Frame, 45 x 84 In., 3 Piece	2750.00
Sign, Federal Monark Shells, For Sale Here, Cardboard, 22 x 8 In.	440.00
Sign, Fehr's Malt Tonic, Topless Woman, Cherubs, Tin Lithograph, Frame, 28½ x 23 In.	990.00
Sign, Ferry Seeds, Jack & The Beanstalk Plant, Jack Holding Shovel, Parrish, c.1923, 25 x 20 In.	1595.00
Sign, Fish Bait, Tin, 9 In.	259.00
Sign, Fleck's Stock Food, Paper Lithograph, Frame, Glass, c.1915, 26 x 19½ In.	1300.00
Sign, Fleck's Beer, Age Purity, Bottle, Die Cut, Cardboard, 2-Piece, 9 x 6 In.	88.00
Sign, Fly TWA, Plane, Los Angeles, Palm Tree, Mission, Bob Smith, 1950s, 40 x 23¾ In.	1315.00
Sign, Foster Hose Supporters, Celluloid, 8 x 15 In.	770.00
Sign, Foster Rubber Co., Cat's Paw, Rubber Heels, 42 x 30 In.	990.00
Sign, Franco-American Soup, Paper Lithograph, 22 x 35 In.	2085.00
Sign, Frank Fehr Brewing Co., Bock Beer, Paper Lithograph, Louisville, Ky., 24 x 34 In.	1525.00
Sign, Franklin Fire Insurance Co., Olive Green, Logo, 17½ x 27½ In.	448.00
Sign, Free Land Overalls, World's Highest Standard, Red, White, Blue, Porcelain, 10 x 30 In.	580.00
Sign, Friedman Bros. Shoes, U.S. Shoe For Women, St. Louis, Paper, Frame, 20 x 13⅝ In.	857.00
Sign, Frigidaire, Cow, We Cool Our Milk, Blue, White, Porcelain, c.1935, 14 x 20 In.	1060.00
Sign, Frog In Your Throat, Girls In Frog Pond, Die Cut, Cardboard, 12 x 9 In.	468.00
Sign, Frostlene, For Perfect Frosting, Gypsy Woman, Embossed, Tin, c.1900, 27 x 19 In.	3500.00
Sign, Fruit Bowl, Drink, Bottle, Tin, Flange, 14 x 19 In.	248.00
Sign, Funk's Dairy, Butter, Delicious, Sweet Cream, Cow, Yellow, Brown, Porcelain, 6 x 10 In.	198.00
Sign, G.E., Red, White, Porcelain, 20 In. Diam.	209.00
Sign, Gail & Ax Tobacco, Vicar Pear, Tin Lithograph, c.1880, 12¾ x 12¾ In.	715.00
Sign, Germania Brewing Co., Buffalo, N.Y., Lager Beer, Porcelain, 22 x 15 In.	2247.00
Sign, Ghirardelli's Chocolate, Girl & Doll Having Hot Chocolate, 23 x 17 In.	10980.00
Sign, Gluek Beer, Vitrolite Corner, Minneapolis, 24 x 16 In.	2500.00
Sign, Gold Y Rock Draught Birch Beer, Clifton Bottling, Yellow, Black, Tin, 9 x 20 In.	70.00
Sign, Golden Grain Whiskey, Nude Woman, Celluloid, Frame, 20 x 24 In.	21240.00
Sign, Golden Lion Cigars, Demuth, 2 For 15 Cents, Red, Black, White, Tin, Cardboard, 9 x 13 In.	55.00
Sign, Golden Orangeade, 5 Cents, Gold, Black, Red, Rolled Edge, 5¾ x 9¾ In.	550.00
Sign, Goodyear Bicycle Tires, Paper Lithograph, Frame, 21 x 13 In.	550.00
Sign, Goodyear Tires, Wingfoot, Horizontal, Porcelain, Wood Frame, 66 x 24 In.	495.00
Sign, Gotham Gold Stripe, Countertop, Cardboard, 10½ In.	56.00
Sign, Gourmet Soups, 2-Sided, Bowl, Steam, 23½ x 23½ x 4½ In.	418.00
Sign, Grand Union Hotel, Porcelain, Busy Street Scene, Hotel, Black & White	440.00
Sign, Grand Union Hotel, Street Scene, Hotel, Rooms $1.00 Per Day, Black, White, Porcelain	440.00
Sign, Granger Tobacco, Johnny Mize, Cardboard, 1930s, 20 x 15 In.	616.00
Sign, Grapico, Refreshing, Sparkling, Naturally Good, Bottle, Embossed, Tin, 13 x 27 In.	185.00
Sign, Great Atlantic & Pacific Tea Co., Toung Taloung, Die Cut, 10½ x 8½ In.	40.00
Sign, Green River Whiskey, Black Man & Mule, Metal, 1900, 24 In. Diam.	1250.00 to 1450.00
Sign, Greenwich Insurance, Woman Crossing Creek, Cardboard, 10⅝ x 7⅞ In.	77.00
Sign, Greenwood Seed Corn, Tin, 18 x 24 In.	28.00
Sign, Greyhound, Ticket Office, Red, White, Blue, 2-Sided, Porcelain, 1920-30, 30 x 25 In.	7150.00
Sign, Groceries & Fruit, Red, Painted, 2-Sided, Wood, 16 x 72¼ In.	2200.00

Store Signs

Some old store signs were lithographed directly on tin and made to look like a picture with a wooden frame. The Grape Nuts sign picturing a girl and her St. Bernard is one of the best known examples.

Advertising, Sign, Apothecary, Wood Mortar, Gold Paint, Iron Bracket, 20 x 19 In. 1800.00

Advertising, Sign, Chesterfield Cigarettes, Smoke For Real, Tin Lithograph, Embossed, 31 x 25 In. $175.00

TIP
Don't open a collectible beer can from the top. Leave the pull tab intact and open the can from the bottom using a standard punch-type opener.

Advertising, Sign, DeLaval Cream
Separator, Porcelain, Flange,
26½ x 18 In.
$1404.00

Advertising, Sign, J. & F. Schroth
Packing Co., Victorian Mother,
Daughter, Fountain, Tin, 20 x 21 In.
$1868.00

Advertising, Sign, Lambertville
Snag-Proof Rubber Boots & Shoes,
Metal, Flange, 13½ x 18 In.
$3803.00

Sign, H.B. Cigar, 5 Cents, Woman, Black Hat, 23 x 17 In.	650.00
Sign, Hamilton Watch, Lady Of Quality, Young Girl, Tin Lithograph, Frame, c.1904, 19 x 13½ In.	990.00
Sign, Hamilton Watch, Railroad Timekeeper, Eglomise, Frame, Scroll Border, 22 x 26 In.	1650.00
Sign, Hamm's Beer, Land Of Sky Blue Waters, Motion, Canoe, Waterfall, Electric, 19 x 34 x 6 In.	840.00
Sign, Hamm's Beer, Smooth Mellow, Theo. Hamm Brewing Co., St. Paul, Tin, 23 x 18 In.	1025.00
Sign, Harding Cream Co., Milk Can Shape, 2-Sided, Porcelain, Flange, 27 x 15 In.	2750.00
Sign, Harkavy's Beverages, Porcelain, Raised Letters, 9¾ x 27½ In.	77.00
Sign, Harvester Cigar, Heart Of Havana, Tin Lithograph, Self-Framed, Oval, 13 x 9 In.	252.00
Sign, Heinz 57, Chili Sauce, Taste Is The Test, Steak, Corn, Cardboard, 14 x 23 In.	112.00
Sign, Heinz 57, Mince Meat, Holiday Desserts, Pie, Can, Jar, Cardboard, 13¾ x 23 In.	168.00
Sign, Heinz Peanut Butter, Delicious, Sandwiches, Jar, Cardboard, 12½ x 22½ In.	112.00
Sign, Heinz Vinegars, You Can Be Sure Of Them, 3 Bottles, Cardboard, 12½ x 22½ In.	168.00
Sign, Highland Steam Laundry, 2-Sided, Metal, Flange, Beaver Falls, Penn, 17 x 8 In.	88.00
Sign, Hinckel Brewing Co., Lager Beers, Woman, Owl Hat, Die Cut, Cardboard, 12 x 9 In.	700.00
Sign, Hires Root Beer, Courteous Service, Painted, Wood, 10 x 40 In.	176.00
Sign, Hires Root Beer, Delicious In Bottles, So We Suggest, 28 x 10 In.	220.00
Sign, Hires Root Beer, Die Cut, Tin, 8¼ x 12 In.	121.00
Sign, Hires Root Beer, Drink Hires, 2 Girls Sipping From Straws, Tin, Oval, 19 x 23 In.	168.00
Sign, Hires Root Beer, Enjoy Hires, Woman, Cardboard, Bradshaw Crandell, Frame, 11⅜ x 8 In.	850.00
Sign, Hires Root Beer, Josh Slinger, Window, Paper, 1914, 13 x 17 In.	413.00
Sign, Hires Root Beer, Porcelain, 11 x 28 In.	198.00
Sign, Hires Root Beer, R-J Root Beer, Real Root Juice, Tin Lithograph, 14 In. Diam.	84.00
Sign, Hires Root Beer, Round, Made With Real Root Juice, Embossed, Tin, 14 In.	358.00
Sign, Hires Root Beer, So Refreshing, Girl, Tin Lithograph, 1900s, 14 x 9¾ In.	2800.00
Sign, His Master's Voice, Oval, Porcelain, 18 x 24 In.	578.00
Sign, His Master's Voice Records, Record Shape, Porcelain, 24 In. Diam.	110.00
Sign, Hoosier Beer, Man Fishing On Boat, South Bend, In., 12½ x 15 In.	1180.00
Sign, Hoosier Drill Co., Horses Pulling Machine, Cardboard, Richmond, Ind., 20 x 24 In.	187.00
Sign, Hotel, Irma, Named For Buffalo Bill's Daughter, Cody, Wy., 1902, 37 x 118 In.	7800.00
Sign, Hyco Smoking Tobacco, Indian, C.R. Ayers, Paper, Frame, 12¼ x 15¼ In.	852.00
Sign, Ice Cold, Fountain Cup, Tin, 20 x 28 In.	1210.00
Sign, Ice Cold, Sold Here, Bottle, Black, Orange, White, 2-Sided, 14 In. Diam.	330.00
Sign, Ice Skates, Blades Only, Steel, 7 x 29 In., Pair	495.00
Sign, Ideal Ear Stopples, For Swimming, Woman, Umbrella, Beach, Cardboard, 8 x 7 In.	300.00
Sign, Imperial Club Cigar, Best For The Money, Embossed, Tin, 9⅞ x 13¾ In.	143.00
Sign, Infallible Smokeless Shotgun Powder, Woman, Dog, c.1920, 26 x 18 In.	1150.00
Sign, Ingersoll Dollar Watch, Guaranteed, Pocket Watch, Blue, Red, White, Wood, 60 x 36 In.	1760.00
Sign, Insurance Co. Of North America, Founded 1792, Philadelphia, Porcelain, 12 x 18 In.	880.00
Sign, Ivy Cigar, 5 Cents, Good All The Year Round, Frame, 23 x 18 In.	275.00
Sign, J. & F. Schroth Packing Co., Victorian Mother, Daughter, Fountain, Tin, 20 x 21 In. *illus*	1868.00
Sign, J. & P. Coats', Thread, Hand & Machine, Orange, Gold, Black, White, Tin, 14 x 19¾ In.	440.00
Sign, J.A. Doughertys Sons Pure Rye Whiskey, Philadelphia, Reverse On Glass, Frame	1120.00
Sign, J.E. Knowles, Foreign & Domestic Stationery, Painted, Wood, 1800s, 71 x 17 In.	6000.00
Sign, J.G. Dill's Best Tobacco, Smoke, Plug & Cut, Yellow, Black, Richmond, Va., 7 x 14 In.	577.00
Sign, J. Ruppert's Brewery Lager Bier, Tuchfarber Co., New York, Tin, 28 x 20 In.	3616.00
Sign, Jay-Bee, Drink Jay-Bee, No Sting, Nearest Beer, Yellow, Blue, Tin, 1920s, 6 In. Diam.	605.00
Sign, Job Cigarette Papers, Color Lithograph, Signed Alphonse Mucha, 1898, 61 x 41¼ In.	8912.00
Sign, Johnnie Walker, Born 1820, Still Going Strong, Man, Tin Lithograph, c.1930, 10 x 6 In.	110.00
Sign, Jolly Tar Tobacco, 2 Sailors, Cardboard, Finzer & Bros., 8 x 8 In.	742.00
Sign, Ju-C-Orange, Krim's, It's Fresh, Yellow, Red, Porcelain, Oval, 8 x 15 In.	385.00
Sign, Ju-C-Orange, Krim's, Real Juice For Health, Oranges, Embossed, Tin Lithograph	275.00
Sign, Kayo Soda, Tops In Taste, It's Real Chocolate Flavor, Embossed, Tin Litho, 27 x 14 In.	358.00
Sign, Keen Kutter, Die Cut, 37 x 29 In.	575.00
Sign, Kellogg's, Toasted Corn Flakes, Woman Cornstalks, Cardboard, c.1920, 41 x 22 In.	209.00
Sign, Kellogg's Corn Flakes, Bowl Of Cereal, Box, Paper Lithograph, c.1920, 28 x 23 In.	525.00
Sign, Kellogg's Corn Flakes, Campfire Girl, Paper Lithograph, c.1920, 28 x 23 In.	1100.00
Sign, Kemp's Medicine, Die Cut Cardboard, Little Girl Taking Medicine, 14 In.	165.00
Sign, Kemp's Balsam, For That Cough, Girl With Spoon, 2-Sided, Cardboard, 14 x 10 In.	176.00
Sign, Kendall's Veterinary Cures, Paper Lithograph, 34¾ x 28¾ In.	3190.00
Sign, Ken-L-Ration, Die Cut, Tin, Flange, 18 x 28 In.	275.00
Sign, Kerns Bread, Take Home, Red, Yellow, Black, White, Tin, Flange, 1950s, 14 x 18 In.	150.00
Sign, Kingfisher Fishing Tackle, Fisherman's Choice, Cardboard, Easel Back, 24 x 18½ In.	100.00
Sign, King's Candies, For American Queens, Green, Porcelain, 1910, 16 x 20 In.	2185.00
Sign, Kist Beverages, Drink Kist, Bottle, Orange, Black, Embossed, Tin Lithograph, 13 x 6 In.	475.00
Sign, Knudsen Milk, Red, White, Carton Shape, Embossed, Die Cut, Tin, 1940-50, 28 x 13 In.	165.00
Sign, Kodak, All Kodak Supplies, Verichrome Film, 2-Sided, Porcelain, 28 x 24 In.	450.00

Sign, Kodak, Orange, Red, Blue, Black, 2-Sided, Porcelain, 12 x 30 In. 522.00
Sign, Kodak, Take A Kodak With You, Girl, Boy, Luggage, Cardboard, c.1920, 33 x 25 In. 198.00
Sign, Kodak, Triangular Shape, 2-Sided, Tin, Hanging, 17 x 17 In. 605.00
Sign, Kodak Film, Die Cu, 2-Sided, Porcelain, 28 x 24 In. 248.00
Sign, Koppers Seaboard Coke, Horizontal, Red, White, Metal, 24 x 12 In. 77.00
Sign, Korbel Sec California Champagne, Woman, Grapes, Tin Over Cardboard, 13 x 19 In. .. 160.00
Sign, Kow Kare, Tin, Flange, 10 x 13 In. 413.00
Sign, L. Bacon Co., Cough Drops, Embossed, Die Cut, Cardboard, 9¼ x 7 In. 165.00
Sign, Lackawanna Anthracite Coal, D & H Railroad Coal, 12¼ In. 358.00
Sign, Lambertville Snag-Proof Rubber Boots & Shoes, Metal, Flange, 13½ x 18 In. .....*illus* 3803.00
Sign, Larrabees, Originators Of Low Spot Cash Prices, Blue, White, Wood, 11 x 47 In. 143.00
Sign, Lavine Laundry Soap, Woman Cleaning, Paper, Roll Down, 28½ x 13 In. 880.00
Sign, Le Mans Tourism, Golfer, Caddy, Ancient Buildings, 38¾ x 23½ In. 1071.00
Sign, Lee Union-Alls, For Comfort, Economy, Safety, 2 Men, Porcelain, 11 x 30 In. 1792.00
Sign, Lictonic Veterinary, Buy It By The Case, Embossed, Tin Lithograph, 9 x 20 In. 468.00
Sign, Lisk Self-Basting Roaster, Lady Holding Turkey, Die Cut, Cardboard, 33 x 22 In. 247.00
Sign, Little Barrister Cigar, 5 Cents, Child Attorney, Tin Lithograph, 13½ x 8½ In. 3520.00
Sign, Log Cabin Tobacco, Smoke Log Cabin, Cowboy, Paper, Frame, 26½ x 22 In. 1210.00
Sign, London Life Cigarettes, Tent, Cricket Player, Tin, Chromolithograph, Frame, 38 x 27 In. . 345.00
Sign, Louisville Slugger Bats, Ty Cobb, Hillerich & Bradsy Co., 17¾ x 13¼ In. 77.00
Sign, Luden's Cough Drops, 5 Cents, Tin, 20 x 36 In. 358.00
Sign, Luden's Menthol Cough Drops, Quick Relief, 5 Cents, Tin, c.1925, 20 x 36 In. 475.00
Sign, Lux For Fine, Laundry, Porcelain, 12 x 24 In. 154.00
Sign, M.E. Schanzenback, Watchmaker, Jeweler, Pocket Watch, Ring, Wood, 41 x 17¾ In. ... 402.00
Sign, Madame Grace, Foundation Garments Of Grace & Beauty, Light-Up, Frame, 12 In. ... 175.00
Sign, Magnet Cream Separator, Factory, Hand Separator, Tin Lithograph, 13½ x 19⅝ In. ... 440.00
Sign, Mail Pouch, Chew, Smoke, Blue, Yellow, White, Porcelain, 2¾ x 12 In. 302.00
Sign, Mandeville & Kings Superior Flower Seeds, Woman, c.1890, 29 x 14 In. 475.00
Sign, Marquette Club Pale Dry Ginger Ale, Woman, Ice Box, Paper, 26 x 19 In. 92.00
Sign, Maryland Beauty Brand Oysters, Fresh From Shell, Tin, R.E. Roberts Co., 10 x 14 In. .. 730.00
Sign, Mayo's Plug, Smoking Cock O' The Walk, Rooster, Porcelain, 13 x 6½ In. 1945.00
Sign, McFadden's Spices & Coffee Co., Tin Lithograph Over Cardboard, 19 x 13 In. 688.00
Sign, McIntosh & Zeiter, Blue Ground, Gold, Green, Michigan, 14 x 146 In. 1265.00
Sign, Mecca Cigarettes, Perfect Satisfaction, Woman, Cardboard, Frame, 1912, 19 x 11 In. .. 504.00
Sign, Milhen Eggs, Worth Crowing About, Rooster, 2-Sided, Cardboard, 12½ x 10½ In. 110.00
Sign, Mil-Kay, Black Waiter, Die Cut, Cardboard, Stand-Up, 18 x 28 In. 110.00
Sign, Miller & Co. Liverymen, Fashionable Lady, Terre Haute, Frame, 24 x 19 In. 425.00
Sign, Miller Bock Beer, Special Brew, Girl On Goat, Paper Lithograph, 23 x 17 In. 797.00
Sign, Millers Soda, With Delicious Flavors, Blue, White, Porcelain, 1890s, 24 x 18 In. 460.00
Sign, Mit-Che Soda, Ice Cold, New Refreshment, Embossed, Tin Litho, c.1930, 15 x 23⅜ In. . 242.00
Sign, Moehn Brewing Co. Beer, Burlington, Ia., Porcelain Enamel, 17½ In. Diam. 2500.00
Sign, Montauk Coffee, Indian, Tin Lithograph, Wood Finial On Lid, 6½ x 4⅜ In. 121.00
Sign, Moxie, Girl Holding Drink, Die Cut, Tin, 6½ x 6¾ In. ....*illus* 880.00
Sign, Moxie, Soda Syrups, 5 Cents, Cardboard, Frame, 18 x 13 In. 825.00
Sign, N.Y. City Subway Sign, No Smoking, Spitting, Porcelain, 20⅜ x 27 In. 330.00
Sign, Nabisco Biscuit Co., Uneeda, O-So-Gud Pretzels, Cardboard, Frame, 14 x 24 In. 742.00
Sign, National Bohemian Exit, Mr. Boh, Red, White, Black, Electric, 10 In. Diam. 784.00
Sign, National Cyclists Union, 2-Sided, 18 In. 475.00
Sign, Necco, Eat Necco Candies, Embossed, Tin Lithograph, Self-Framed, 27 x 9 In. 248.00
Sign, Nectar Tea, Cup Of Tea Shape, Die Cut, Porcelain, 21½ x 12½ In. 176.00
Sign, Nehi, Drink Nehi, Bottle, Yellow, Red, Black, Die Cut, Tin, Flange, c.1935, 18 x 31 In. .. 480.00
Sign, New York Giants, Neon Tubing, Logo, Blue, Red, 18 x 41½ In. 598.00
Sign, New York Mets, Neon, 35½ x 25¾ In. 1912.00
Sign, New York Jets, Neon, Logo, 15¼ x 50 In. 96.00
Sign, Nichol Cola, Bottle Cap, Red, White, Black, Embossed, Tin, 14 x 14 In. 50.00
Sign, Notary Public, Red, White, Blue, Porcelain, Chain, 8 In. Diam. 232.00
Sign, Nu Icy Soda, Assorted Flavors You Can't Forget, Tin Lithograph, c.1920, 19 x 9 In. 358.00
Sign, NuGrape Soda, A Flavor You Can't Forget, Hand, Bottle, Die Cut, Tin, 1940s, 13 x 20 In. . 610.00
Sign, Oakley's Queen Soap, Lady With Umbrella, Chair, Canvas Back, 28 x 13½ In. 310.00
Sign, Occident Flour, 6 Glass Domes, Tin Lithograph, Cardboard, 9 x 14 x ¾ In. 413.00
Sign, Odin Cigar, 5 Cents, Man With Brief Case, Cigar In Mouth, Embossed, Tin, 28 x 20 In. . 275.00
Sign, Old Coon Sour Mash, Coon Hunters, Tin, Self-Framed, 1900, 29 x 23 In. ..... 1750.00 to 1950.00
Sign, Old Dutch Cleanser, Curved, Porcelain, 20 x 32 In. 220.00
Sign, Old Gold Cigarettes, Woman Holding Opera Glasses, Smoking, 1952, 10 x 14 In. 7.00
Sign, Old Reading Beer, Traditionally Pennsylvania Dutch, Wood, Chain, 13 x 20 In. 55.00
Sign, Old Reliable Brand Fresh Oysters, Lord-Mott Co., Tin Lithograph, 10 x 14 In. 1650.00

Advertising, Sign, Moxie, Girl Holding Drink, Die Cut, Tin, 6½ x 6¾ In.
$880.00

Advertising, Sign, Pflueger Fishing Tackle, Die Cut, 1930, 16 In.
$1525.00

Advertising, Sign, Red Goose Shoes, Goose, Tin, Neon, Light-Up, 24 x 13 In.
$1525.00

Advertising, Sign, Rockford Watch, Incomparable, Victorian Woman, Watch, Tin Lithograph, 23 x 17 In. $819.00

Advertising, Sign, Squire's, Pig, Tin Lithograph, Oval, Self-Framed, 1906, 23 x 19 In. $2106.00

Item	Price
Sign, Old Reliable Coffee, Always Good, Old Russian Man Smoking, Tin, 6½ x 9 In.	55.00
Sign, Old Tucker Whiskey, Suspects His Master, Tin Lithograph, 9 x 13 In.	264.00
Sign, Omega Watch, Embossed, Tin, 9⅝ x 13½ In.	132.00
Sign, One-A-Day Vitamins, Biologically Standardized, Reverse Glass, Frame, 11 x 17 In.	187.00
Sign, Orange Crush, Drink Ward's Orange Crush, Bottle, Orange, Black, White, Tin, 9 x 20 In.	465.00
Sign, Orange Squeeze, It Has The Real Fruit Juice, Bottle, Oranges, Tin, 13 x 28 In.	151.00
Sign, Ottesen Millinery, Boy At Fence, Die Cut, 9 x 5 In.	50.00
Sign, P.H. Zang Brewing Co., People, Horse, Reverse On Glass, Frame, 41 x 33 In.	30680.00
Sign, Pages Tested Seeds, Sold Here, At Your Service, Flowers, Fruits & Vegetables, 15 x 28 In.	55.00
Sign, Pear's Soap, Embossed, View Of Woman, Red Hair, Stand-Up, 1885, 7 x 9 In.	40.00
Sign, Pear's Soap, Woman Wearing Shawl, Embossed, 1885, 9½ x 7 In.	40.00
Sign, Pearl Beer, Man Carrying Case Of Beer, Who Can Beat It, Wood, 27 x 22⅝ In.	413.00
Sign, Pearson Remedies, Base Ball Liniment, 12 x 26 In.	633.00
Sign, Pepper's Ginger Ale, Celluloid Over Cardboard, 4½ x 6½ In.	88.00
Sign, Peter Schuyler Cigar, Get Back Of, Porcelain Over Steel, c.1920-30, 12 x 30 In.	350.00
Sign, Peters Packs The Power, For Any Game, In Any Gun, 36 x 24 In.	100.00
Sign, Pflueger Fishing Tackle, Die Cut, 1930, 16 In. ....*illus*	1525.00
Sign, Phillies 5 Cent Cigar, Black Ground, White Letters, Cardboard, 14 x 42 In.	138.00
Sign, Phillip Morris, Call For Phillip Morris, Bellboy, Cardboard, 43 x 25¾ In.	112.00
Sign, Piedmont Cigarette, Woman, Feather In Hat, Frame, 24 x 16 In.	475.00
Sign, Polar Tobacco, Polar Bear, Always Best, Die Cut, Embossed, Tin, c.1910, 14 x 9½ In.	522.00
Sign, Poppers 8 Center Cigars, 2 For 15 Cents, Red, White, Black, Tin Lithograph, 11 x 35 In.	275.00
Sign, Popsicle, Refreshing, Easy To Eat, Red, Black, Yellow, Embossed, Tin, 1930s, 12 x 35 In.	175.00
Sign, Potomac Insurance Co., Capital Building, Black, Red Letters, Aluminum, 13 x 19 In.	224.00
Sign, Pratt's Vet, Embossed, Tin Lithograph, 5 x 13⅝ In.	605.00
Sign, Prince Albert, Tobacco, Metal, Flange, 17½ x 10¼ In.	633.00
Sign, Pub, Queen's Head, Queen Elizabeth I, Painted, c.1950, 42 x 32 In.	2125.00
Sign, Queen Quality & Gold Crumbs Tobacco, Tin Lithograph, 13½ x 19⅜ In.	385.00
Sign, Quencho, Gee!, It's Cool & Delicious, Couple, Embossed, Tin, 10 x 28 In.	385.00
Sign, R & G Corsets, Lady In Corset, Tin Lithograph, 1900s, 16 x 11¾ In.	2200.00
Sign, R & R Syrup Of White Pine Tar, Woman, Smelling Flower, Cardboard, 15 x 10 In.	469.00
Sign, R.G. Dun Quality Cigar, El Verso, Glass, Frame, 17 x 67 In.	27.00
Sign, Railway Express, 2-Sided, 18 x 15 In.	775.00
Sign, Rainbow Overalls, Built For Service, Glass, Mirror Around Edge, Cardboard, Light-Up	50.00
Sign, Reach Baseball Equipment, Keep Up Your Game, Die Cut, Cardboard, Easel, 10 x 8 In.	962.00
Sign, Red Goose Shoes, Goose, Tin, Neon, Light-Up, 24 x 13 In. ....*illus*	1525.00
Sign, Red Indian Tobacco, Indian In Headdress, Paper Lithograph, 33 x 25 x 21 In.	1210.00
Sign, Red Raven, Victorian Woman Holding Red Raven, Metal, c.1900, 26 In.	2750.00
Sign, Redwood Empire Tour, By Rail & Motor Coach, Southern Pacific, 1933, 23 x 16 In.	130.00
Sign, Remington Kleanbore Cartridges, Boy, Shotgun, Cardboard, Lynn Bogue Hunt, 26 x 16 In.	2100.00
Sign, Rev O Noc Fire Arms, Sporting Goods, Fishing Tackle, Tin Over Cardboard, 13 x 19 In.	3000.00
Sign, Richmond Straight Cut Cigarettes, Man Smoking, Allen & Genter, 19 In. Diam.	522.00
Sign, Richmond Straight Cut Cigarettes, Marked Frame, Original Glass, 14 x 17 In.	330.00
Sign, Rising Sun Stove Polish, Woman Cleans Stove, Die Cut, Cardboard, 9⅝ x 1½ In.	633.00
Sign, Rockford Watch, Incomparable, Victorian Woman, Watch, Tin Lithograph, 23 x 17 In. *illus*	819.00
Sign, Royal Token Cigar, Leading 10 Cent Cigar, Litho Poster Board, Gilt Frame, 20 In.	1540.00
Sign, Safe-T-Cup Ice Cream Cone, Ice Cream In Cone, 3-Dimensional, Paper, 20¾ In.	176.00
Sign, Schell's Beer, Deer Brand, Light-Up, Aug. Schell Brewing Co., New Ulm, 28 x 6½ In.	610.00
Sign, Schmidt Bros. Brew Co., Reverse On Glass, Frame, 36 x 27 In.	4425.00
Sign, Schuttler Wagon Co., Covered Wagons In Ute Pass, Paper, Frame, 27 x 33 In.	2970.00
Sign, Shaker Salt, Flows Freely, Metal, Chalkboard, 41 x 20 x 18 In.	403.00
Sign, Sherer, Shirk & Co., Git On, Black Man Riding Donkey, Frame, 11¾ x 11¾ In.	795.00
Sign, Sherwin Williams, 2-Sided, Porcelain, Flange, 33 x 48 In.	1350.00
Sign, Sherwin Williams, Paint Covering Globe, Enamel, 64 x 36 In.	86.00
Sign, Sherwin Williams, Paints & Varnishes, Blue, Red, White, Yellow, Tin, 51 x 36½ In.	137.00
Sign, Sherwin Williams Paint, Cover The Earth, Yellow, Red, Green, 3-Dimensional, 36 x 18 In.	840.00
Sign, Shine, Shoe, Enamel, 1930s, 52 x 7½ In.	611.00
Sign, Shlag's Pony Express Bread, Child, Horses, Embossed, Tin Lithograph, 14 x 20 In.	825.00
Sign, Shoney's Restaurant, Figural, Chef Hat, Carrying Hamburger, 5½ Ft.	320.00
Sign, Showroom, Dodge Builds Job Rated Trucks, Neon, Hanging, 42 x 22 In.	220.00
Sign, Sinclair Aircraft, Single-Engine Plane, Metal, 12 In. Diam.	1320.00
Sign, Singer Sewing Machine, Calendar, Green, White, Cardboard	137.00
Sign, Singer Sewing Machine, Woman Sewing, Red S, Embossed, Tin Lithograph, 23 x 35 In.	220.00
Sign, Sitckney & Poor Spice Co., Graphics, Wood, Frame, 32½ x 24½ In.	1100.00
Sign, Sloman's Diamond Wedding Rye, Essence Of Strength, Cherubs, Lithograph, 20 x 14 In.	1040.00
Sign, Sloman's Diamond Wedding Pure Rye, Woman On Chair, Baetzhold, 12 In. Diam.	875.00

Sign, Society Of American Florists, Say It With Flowers, Metal Globe, 16½ In.	110.00
Sign, Socony Aircraft Oils, Standard Oil, Airplane, Red, White, Blue, Porcelain, 20 x 30 In.	488.00
Sign, Solace Tobacco, Woman Climbing Ladder, 29 x 13 In.	525.00
Sign, Southern Pacific, Redwood Empire Tour By Rail & Mother Coach, 1933, 16 x 23 In.	775.00
Sign, Spear Head Chewing Tobacco, Porcelain, 6 x 14 In.	198.00
Sign, Sports Illustrated, Joe DiMaggio, How Will They Finish In 49?, May, Cardboard, 14 x 10 In.	121.00
Sign, Squire's, Pig, Tin Lithograph, Oval, Self-Framed, 1906, 23 x 19 In. ..... *illus*	2106.00
Sign, Star Shoes, Racing Car, Die Cut, Tin Lithograph, 4⅛ x 8½ In.	429.00
Sign, Star Tobacco, Sold Here, Yellow, Brown, Blue, White, Porcelain, 12 x 24 In.	385.00
Sign, Stransky Graniteware, The Ware That Wears, Tray Shape, Porcelain, 19 x 24 In.	495.00
Sign, Success Horse Collars, Horse Sitting At Desk, Paper Lithograph, 24 x 19 In.	3520.00
Sign, Sun Crest Soda, Bottle, Orange, Blue, White, Aluminum, 1949, 22 x 8 In.	465.00
Sign, Sun Drop Ma Cherie Cola, Refreshing As A Cup Of Coffee, Tin, Oval, 15 x 23 In.	190.00
Sign, Sunbeam Bread, Exploding Loaf, Die Cut, Tin, 31 x 58 In.	220.00
Sign, Sunbeam Bread, Girl Eating Bread, Embossed, Tin Lithograph, 54 x 19 In. ...... *illus*	527.00
Sign, Sunkist Navel Oranges, Big Buy Right Now, Man In Oranges, Paper, 34 x 26 In.	55.00
Sign, Superb Ink Pad, Leading Pad, Always Reliable, Tin Lithograph, Frame, 10 x 14 In.	143.00
Sign, Sweet Caporal Cigarettes, Please Shut Door, Woman, Cardboard, 14 x 5 In.	330.00
Sign, Sweet-Orr, Clothes To Work In, Overalls, Pants, Shirts, 8 x 29¾ In.	176.00
Sign, Sweet-Orr, Pants, Overalls, Shirts, Yellow, Red, White, Blue, Porcelain, 9½ x 27 In.	685.00
Sign, Sweet-Orr Overalls, Union Made, Image Of 6 Men Pulling On Pants, 14 x 20 In.	6200.00
Sign, Tavern, Banbury Way, Man On Horse, Square Frame, Iron, 30 x 33½ In.	1560.00
Sign, Texcell Cellophane Tape, 1957, 10 x 13 In.	10.00
Sign, Timken Hyatt Bearing, 2-Sided, Porcelain, 29 x 18 In.	875.00
Sign, Tin, Painted, 5 Cent Counter, Red, White Numbers, Letters, 5 x 27 In.	206.00
Sign, Tiolene, Pure Oil Co., 2-Sided, Porcelain, Round, 30 In.	468.00
Sign, Tom Hood Cigar, 5 Cents, Woman Leaning Over Man, Wolf & Co., 1915, 20 x 15 In.	325.00
Sign, Tootsie Rolls, Appetizingly Delicious, Tin, 11 x 22 In.	77.00
Sign, Tootsie Rolls, Chewy Candy, Tin, 11 x 22 In.	121.00
Sign, Toytown, Headquarters For Newest Toys & Gifts, 1930s, 27½ x 20 In.	739.00
Sign, Trade, Magnetic Healer, 10-Sided, Painted, Wood, 1800s, 15 x 27 In.	1645.00
Sign, Trade, N.M. Bean & Son, Pine, Applied Molding, Black, Red Paint, 87½ In.	1528.00
Sign, Trade, Optometrist, Forged Iron, Glass, 16 x 33 In.	690.00
Sign, Trade, Wheelwright Shop, Painted, Panel, Green & White, Frame, 103 x 11 In.	1880.00
Sign, Trolley, 4th Liberty Loan, German Swept Out Of France, Cardboard, 1940s, 12 x 22 In.	255.00
Sign, Trolley, Lime Life Savers, Amazing New Taste Sensation, Cardboard, 12 x 22 In. *illus*	275.00
Sign, True Fruit Syrup, Fruit On Tray, Tin, Self-Framed, 25 x 37½ In.	247.00
Sign, Turf & Sport Digest, Woman Reading, Painted On Board, Frame, 24 x 18 In.	84.00
Sign, Turkey Red Cigarettes, Cardboard, c.1930, 16½ x 13 In.	50.00
Sign, Tuttle's Elixir, For Man & Beast, Blue, White, Tin Lithograph, 4¼ x 19¾ In.	231.00
Sign, Tygert-Allen Fertilizer, Chestnut St., Buildings, Boats, Paper, Frame, 25 x 31 In.	252.00
Sign, US Ammunition, Hits Where You Aim, Man, Horse, Bear, Cardboard, Elwell, 16 x 12 In.	515.00
Sign, US Rubber Hunting Boots, Mallard Duck, Non-Slip Grip, Stand-Up, 2¼ In.	71.00
Sign, Utility & Atlas Numbering Machines, Tin Over Cardboard, 6¾ x 9¾ In.	198.00
Sign, Valley Forge Special, Ice Cold, Tin, Flange, Adam Scheidt Brewing Co., 18 x 14 In.	866.00
Sign, Van Heusen Shirts, Give Your Neck A Break, Wood, Particle Board, 1950s, 36 x 24 In.	112.00
Sign, Van Houten's Cocoa, Cardboard Lithograph, 24 x 35 In.	1925.00
Sign, Velvet Tobacco, Porcelain, Liggett & Myers, 39 x 12 In.	165.00
Sign, Venable Tobacco, Factory, Angels, Flowers, Paper, Petersburg, Va., Frame, 31 x 25 In.	302.00
Sign, Vet, International Stock Food Tonic, Red Ground, Animals On Corners, 9 In.	500.00
Sign, Virginia Cheroots, Woman Looking Forward, Paper, Self-Framed, 12 x 15¼ In.	220.00
Sign, Walsh-DeRoo Milling Co., Sunlight Flour, Stone Lithograph, 27¾ x 20 In.	231.00
Sign, Walter A. Wood Harvesting Machines, Blue, White, 2-Sided, Frame, 13½ x 31 In.	232.00
Sign, Washing, Green, Red, White, Porcelain, Self-Framed, 9 x 84 x 1 In.	192.00
Sign, Welch's Grape Juice, Drink A Bunch Of Grapes, Embossed, Tin Lithograph, 20 x 14 In.	413.00
Sign, Western Ammunition, Man, Saw, Hunters, Dog, William Eaton, 1928, 24 x 15 In.	775.00
Sign, Western Farms Dairy, Milk That Is Milk, Baby In Highchair, 4 x 13 In.	440.00
Sign, Western Union, Porcelain, 30 x 9 In.	475.00
Sign, Western Union, Telephone Your Telegrams From Here, Phone, Porcelain, Flange, 1930s	715.00
Sign, Western Union Telegraph & Cable Blanks, Blue, White, Porcelain, 4 x 9 In.	253.00
Sign, Western Union Telegraph Here, Porcelain, Flange, 11 x 18 In.	55.00
Sign, Western Winchester, Buck Jumping Over Rock, 40 x 26 In.	210.00
Sign, Western Winchester, Pheasant, 40 x 26 In.	60.00
Sign, Western Winchester, Squirrel, 40 x 26 In.	60.00
Sign, Western Winchester, Winter Rabbit, 40 x 26 In.	60.00
Sign, Westinghouse Generators, Black, Orange, White, Embossed, Tin, 24 x 22½ In.	98.00

Advertising, Sign,
Sunbeam Bread, Girl Eating Bread,
Embossed, Tin Lithograph,
54 x 19 In.
$527.00

Advertising, Sign, Trolley, Lime
Life Savers, Amazing New Taste
Sensation, Cardboard, 12 x 22 In.
$275.00

Popular Brands
Some brands are more
popular with collectors
than others. Coca-Cola,
McDonald's restaurants, and
M&Ms are tops. Others are
Planters Peanuts, Anheuser-
Busch, Budweiser, Kentucky
Fried Chicken, and soft
drinks like Pepsi-Cola,
Moxie, and Hires Root Beer.

Advertising, Stringholder, Heinz, Pickle Shape, Banner, Pure Foods, Chains, 15 x 14½ x 7 In. $6900.00

Sign, Wheat Bitters Co., Royal Appetizer Of The Age, Scrolled, Dowels, 1870s, 14 x 12 In. 325.00
Sign, Whistle, Thirsty?, Just Whistle, Certified Pure, Tin, 20 x 14 In. 275.00
Sign, Whistle, Thirsty?, Just Whistle, Morning, Noon, Night, Tin Lithograph, 1938, 12 x 27 In. . 330.00
Sign, Whistle, Thirsty?, Just Whistle, Wholesome & Delicious, Porcelain, 7 x 20 In. 990.00
Sign, Whistle, Thirsty?, Just Whistle, Elves Pushing Bottle, Tin, 26 x 30 In. .... 935.00 to 1705.00
Sign, White Label Cigars, Favorite Everywhere, 5 Cents, Embossed, Tin, 9⅞ x 13¾ In. 154.00
Sign, White Rock Table Water, Fairy On Rock, Tin Lithograph, 11 In. Diam. 525.00
Sign, Whites Excelsior Chewing Gum, Girl, Baby In Carriage, Die Cut, Cardboard, 7 x 8 In. .. 220.00
Sign, Wiedemanns Beer, Fine Bottled, Reverse Painted Glass, Electric, 10½ In. Diam. 500.00
Sign, Wilbur's Cocoa, Paper Lithograph, 13½ x 23½ In. 660.00
Sign, Wilbur's Stock Food, Mechtchilde, Cow, Paper, 21 x 14 In. 525.00
Sign, Wildroot, Barber Shop, Ask For Wild Root, Barber Pole, Embossed, Tin, 14 x 40 In. 357.00
Sign, Wildroot Hair Tonic, Cardboard, Easel Back, Stand-Up, 24 x 17¾ In. 330.00
Sign, William Conway's Pure Wood Ash Soap, Tin, 1878, 9⅞ x 13⅞ In. 385.00
Sign, Winchester Fishing Tackle, Striped Bass, Die Cut, Cardboard, Molded Frame, 21 In. ... 467.00
Sign, Wings Cigarettes, 10 Cents, Baseball Player, Cardboard, c.1930, 29 x 20 In. 325.00
Sign, Wink, Canada Dry Beverage, Horizontal, Embossed, Tin, 54 x 18 In. 248.00
Sign, Wirt's Exterminator Blood Purifier, Woman, Harp, Child, Roses, Cardboard, 12 x 6 In. . 44.00
Sign, Woco Pep, Drive Safely, Tag Topper, Tin, 6 x 10 In. 176.00
Sign, Wonder Bread, Here's Quick Energy, Football Player, Cardboard, c.1935, 32 x 43 In. ... 400.00
Sign, Won-Up Grapefruit Juice, For Your Health's Sake, 5 Cents, Tin, Cardboard, 9 x 13 In. .. 143.00
Sign, Wrigley's Chewing Gum, Boy Scout, Girl Scout, c.1960, 7½ x 23½ In. 136.00
Sign, Wrigley's Spearmint, Lunch, Black, Red, White, Porcelain, c.1925, 9 x 30 In. 2320.00
Sign, Wrigley's Spearmint Gum, Buy The Best, Calendar, Metal On Cardboard, 1917, 18 x 9 In. .. 385.00
Sign, Wrigley's Spearmint Pepsin Gum, Die Cut, Easel Back, Stand-Up, 7¾ x 8⅛ In. 385.00
Sign, Yellow Cab Cigar, Traffic Cop, Taxi, Embossed, Tin Lithograph, 6⅝ x 19⅞ In. 788.00
Sign, Zimmerman Jeweler, Watch Repairing, Stanley, Train, Tin, 12 x 48 In. 350.00
Slide, Intermission, Silent Movie, Mallory Hats, 1920, 3¼ x 4 In. 25.00
Spinner, Snyder's Garage, Chalmers Six, Celluloid, Chambersburg, Pa., 1¼ In. 51.00
Stickpin, Plymouth Twine, Wheat Sheaf, Early 1900s, 1-In. Pin, 2-In. Stem 64.00
Stirrers, Beverage, Pregnant Girl, Kilroy Was Here, Hartland, 5 Colors, Plastic, 9 In. 140.00
Stringholder, Heinz, Pickle Shape, Banner, Pure Foods, Chains, 15 x 14½ x 7 In. .....*illus* 6900.00
Stringholder, Helmar Turkish Cigarettes, Girl Holding Box, Tin, Hanging, 10 In. Diam. 385.00
Stringholder, King Midas, Tin Lithograph, 19¾ x 15 In. 2640.00
Stringholder, Olo Soap Powder, Advertising Novelty Co., 12 x 8 x 16 In. 440.00
Stringholder, Red Seal, White Lead, Dutch Boy, Bucket, Tin, Chain, 14 x 25 In. 4313.00
Stringholder, Use Jaxon Soap, Cast Iron, Kettle Form, Bail Handle, Footed, 4½ x 4½ In. 165.00
Tape Measure, Brick-Making Machine, J.C. Steele & Sons Mfg., Celluloid, 1½ In. 88.00
Thermometers are listed in their own category.

Advertising tin cans or canisters were first used commercially in the United States in 1819 and were called tins. Today the word *tin* is used by most collectors to describe many types of containers, including food tins, biscuit boxes, roly poly tobacco containers, gunpowder cans, talcum powder sprinkle-top cans, cigarette flat-fifty tins, and more. Beer Cans are listed in their own category. Things made of undecorated tin are listed under Tinware.

Tin, 3 Feathers Tobacco, Plug Cut, Choice Granulated, 4 x 3¼ x 1 In. 412.00
Tin, 3 States Tobacco Mixture, Harry Wessinger Co., Hinged Lid, 3 x 4½ x 2½ In. 112.00
Tin, 4 Roses Smoking Tobacco, Red, Green, Gold, Tin Lithograph, Flip Lid, 4 x 3 x 1 In. 66.00
Tin, 1775 Minute Men Coffee, Paper Label, 1 Lb. 193.00
Tin, Admiral Blend Coffee, Franklin MacVeagh, Lithograph, Handle, 7 x 4½ In. 560.00
Tin, Airfloat Borated Baby Powder, With Olive Oil, Baby, 5 x 2⅛ In. 88.00
Tin, All Nations Tobacco, Cleanest & Best, Yellow, Red, 7 x 11⅝ x 7⅞ In. 357.00
Tin, American Antiseptic Powder, Paper Over Tin, 3⅞ x 2⅛ In. 413.00
Tin, American Mills Coffee, Samson Brand, 5½ x 4¾ In. 605.00
Tin, Astor House Brand Coffee, Screw Top, 1 Lb., 6 x 4 In. 180.00
Tin, Atlantic Refining Co., Cream Separator, Oil, Lithograph, ½ Gal. 264.00
Tin, Azomis Baby Powder, Sharp & Dohme, c.1940, 5½ x 1¾ In. 100.00
Tin, Bagdad Smoking Tobacco, Man, Profile, Blue, Gold, Red, 3¾ x 3¼ x 2⅛ In. 100.00
Tin, Bagley's Game Cut Tobacco, Birds, Flowers, 7⅜ x 11½ x 8 In. 660.00
Tin, Bagley's Sweet Tips, Pocket, 4 x 2½ x 1⅜ In. 77.00
Tin, Bagley's Sweet Tips Smoking, Blue, White, Yellow, 4⅝ x 3 x ⅞ In. 44.00
Tin, Baker's Breakfast Cocoa, Woman Carrying Tray, Paper Label, 5½ x 3¼ x 3¼ In. 176.00
Tin, Barrus Mustard, Eagle On Globe, c.1880, 10 Lb., 11¼ x 7 x 7 In. 412.00
Tin, Battle Royal Tobacco, Cut Plug, Sailing Ship, 2¾ x 4⅝ In. 143.00
Tin, Beech-Nut Tobacco, Quality Made It Famous, Hinged Slant Lid, 8¾ x 10 x 8 In. ...*illus* 605.00

Tin, Biscuit, Bookcase Filled With Books, Lithograph, 6¼ x 5 In. 88.00
Tin, Biscuit, Female Figures, Classical Style, Faux Marble, Late 1800s, 7 x 5 In. 176.00
Tin, Black Chief Stove Polish, For Hot Stoves, 3 x 1⅛ In. 165.00
Tin, Black Sheep Cigar, Wallet Style, Lithograph, Hinged Lid, 5⅝ x 3¼ x ⅞ In. 143.00
Tin, Blanke's World's Fair Coffee, St. Louis Fair, Red, Lithograph, 11⅞ x 3¼ In. 688.00
Tin, Blue Bird Marsh Mallow, Tin Lithograph, Pry Lid, 4½ x 4⅜ In. 176.00
Tin, Brater's Asthma Powder, Lithograph, Trial Size, 1⅝ x 2⅞ x 1⅞ In. 55.00
Tin, Buckingham Smoking Tobacco, John J. Bagley & Co., 4⅜ x 3 x ¾ In. 176.00
Tin, Bulldog Cut Plug, De Luxe, Blue, Gold, Red, Green, Pocket, Unopened 825.00
Tin, Bunnies Peanut, Rabbit Holding Product, Small Rabbits, 10 Lb., 11 x 7⅞ In. 187.00
Tin, Bunte, Diana Stuft Confections, Girl, Dog, Yellow, Red, White, 10 In. 110.00
Tin, Bunte Marshmallows, Child, Factory Scene, Tin Lithograph, 5 Lb., 5⅜ x 12⅝ In. 440.00
Tin, Burkholder's Potato Chips, Red, White, Lititz, Pa. 27.00
Tin, Butler Boy Popcorn, Ray G. Redding, Mattoon, Ill., 8 Oz., 4 x 2½ In. 198.00
Tin, C.H. Peerless Co., June Peas, 4½ x 3⅜ In. 99.00
Tin, Cafe Savoy Coffee, White, Blue, 2 x 2¼ x 1½ In. 88.00
Tin, Campbell's Shag Tobacco, Man Smoking Pipe, Gold Ground, 1908, 4 x 3 In. 518.00
Tin, Carmen Brand Latex Condoms, Woman Holding Black Fan, ⅝ x 1½ In. 350.00
Tin, Carr & Co. Biscuit, Luggage Shape, Green, Handle, Marked, C.C.C., 4¾ x 5⅛ In. 121.00
Tin, City Club Tobacco, Crushed Cubes, Man Reading Paper, Red, White, Black, 4⅝ x 3 In. 358.00
Tin, Clabber Girl, Paper Label, 1931, 4 x 3 In. 12.00
Tin, Clark's Zig Zag, New Confection, Colonial Couple, 1½ x ¾ In. 40.00
Tin, Colgate's Baby Talc, Baby Holding Can, 2⅛ x 1¼ In. 176.00
Tin, College Town Spices, Always A Treat, 1½ Oz., 2¾ x 2½ In. 385.00
Tin, Comfort Powder, Nurse Holding Can, c.1890, 4 x 2½ In. 440.00
Tin, Continental Cubes Tobacco, George Washington, 3¾ x 3¼ In. 632.00
Tin, Cream Brand Coffee, Red, Gold Writing, Milk Pail Style, Bail Handle, 11½ In. 472.00
Tin, Crescent Club Tobacco, Turkish Girls, Hinged Lid, Lithograph, 3¼ x 4½ x 2 In. 132.00
Tin, Crossed Swords Plug Cut Tobacco, Square Corners, Richmond, Va., 4 x 3 In. 85.00
Tin, Cuticura Talcum Powder, Baby, Woman Holding Mirror, Potter Drug, 3½ x 2¼ In. 40.00
Tin, D.F. Stauffer Biscuit Co., Pretzels, 2 Boys Sitting On Steps, Black, Yellow, 5 In. 55.00
Tin, Dickinson's Little Buster White Popcorn, Contents, 10 Oz., 4¾ x 2½ In. 60.00
Tin, Dixie Queen Cut Plug Tobacco, Red, White, Black, 6 x 5 In. 300.00
Tin, Dixie Queen Cut Plug Tobacco, Small Top, 6½ x 5 In. 495.00
Tin, Dixie Queen Cut Plug Tobacco, Woman, Embossed, Paper Label, Handle, 6 x 4¾ In. 660.00
Tin, Dot Coffee, Dot's Good, Blue, Orange, White, 5 Cup, 2½ x 2 In. 253.00
Tin, Dr. Daniels' Antiseptic Dusting Powder, 6 Oz., 5⅛ x 2⅜ In. 121.00
Tin, Dr. Hess Medicated Powder, For Animals & Family, 25 Cents, 5 x 2½ In. 60.00
Tin, Dr. Hobbs Asparagus Kidney Pills, Drug Act Label, Lithograph, Lid, 1⅝ x 2¾ In. 121.00
Tin, Dunham's Cocoanut, Monkey Hitting Black Man, Paper Label, Twist Off Lid 275.00
Tin, DuPont Ballistite Smokeless Powder, Shotguns Only, Lithograph, 5 x 3 x 1 In. 95.00
Tin, DuPont Rifle Powder, Dead Stag, Trees, Smokeless, No. 1, Red, Paper Label, 3¾ x 3 In. 154.00
Tin, DuPont Schitzen Smokeless, Paper Label, 6 x 4 x 1¼ In. 155.00
Tin, Dusenberry's Moth Destroyer, Extra Strength, Yellow, Black, 6½ x 4½ In. 253.00
Tin, Dutch Maid Cigars, Beats 'Em All, Dutch Girl, Windmill, 25 Count, 5⅜ x 3⅜ In. 312.00
Tin, E.J. Hoadley's Chewing Gum, Tolu, Lithograph, 1 x 2¼ x ¾ In. 908.00
Tin, E.J. Oppelt Tobacco, Red Ground, Paper Label, 2½ x 3½ In. 518.00
Tin, Eagle Brand Coffee, George C. Buell & Co., Cylindrical, 1 Lb. 150.00
Tin, Edgeworth, Larus & Bros. Pipe Tobacco, Tin Lithograph, Pocket, 4½ x 3 x ⅞ In. 231.00
Tin, Empire Mills Coffee, Green, Tin Lithograph, 8¾ x 4⅛ In. 743.00
Tin, Ensign Perfection Cut Tobacco, Yale, 5 In. .... *illus* 825.00
Tin, Erminie Cigar, Straiton & Storms, 1879, 1½ x 4½ x 3½ In. 160.00
Tin, Every Day Coffee, Cups & Saucers, Red, White, Blue, 1 Lb., 4½ x 5¼ In. 143.00
Tin, F.W. Cough Drop, Graphics, Lithograph, Geo. Miller & Sons, 8 x 5 x 5 In. 2530.00
Tin, F.W. Hinz & Son Coffee, Eagle, Shield, Red, Gold, Milk Pail, 5 Lb., 10½ x 7⅜ In. 850.00
Tin, Fatima's Aroma Coffee, Silver Bros., Turkish Style, Label, Cleveland, Oh., 5 x 4 In. 200.00
Tin, Folgers Golden Gate Coffee, Boats, Paper Over Cardboard, Tin Lid, 6½ x 6 In. 522.00
Tin, Forest & Stream Tobacco, 2 Fishermen, Canoe, Red, Canada, 4 x 3 In. .... 374.00 to 632.00
Tin, Forest & Stream Tobacco, Fisherman, 4½ x 3 In. 345.00
Tin, Forest & Stream Tobacco, Fisherman, Canada, 3¼ x 3⅜ In. .... 187.00 to 270.00
Tin, Fountain Fine Cut Tobacco, 8½ x 8½ In. .... *illus* 220.00
Tin, Franklin Coffee, Columbus, Oh., 3 Lb., 9 x 6 In. 525.00
Tin, Full Dress, Man In Tuxedo, Top Hat, Lithograph, Flip Lid, 4¼ x 3 x 1 In. 143.00
Tin, Gallagher's Rich Dark Honeydew Tobacco, Pool Player, 3½ x 6½ In. 235.00
Tin, Game Fine Cut Tobacco, Quails, Hinged Lid, Jno. J. Bagley & Co., 7 x 11 x 8 In. 413.00
Tin, Gem Cutlery Co., Razor, Safety Razor, Tin Lithograph, Hinged Lid, 2 x 2 x 1 In. 330.00

Advertising, Tin, Beech-Nut Tobacco, Quality Made It Famous, Hinged Slant Lid, 8¾ x 10 x 8 In.
$605.00

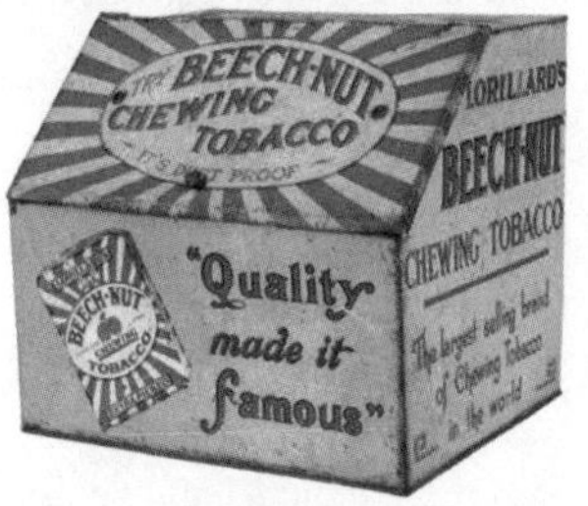

Advertising, Tin, Ensign Perfection Cut Tobacco, Yale, 5 In.
$825.00

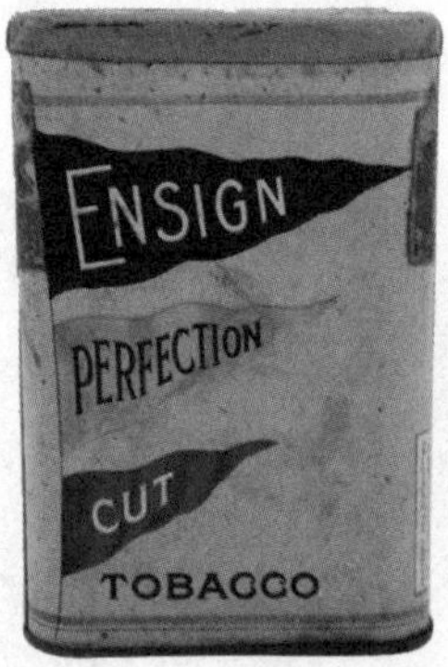

Advertising, Tin, Fountain Fine Cut Tobacco, 8½ x 8½ In.
$220.00

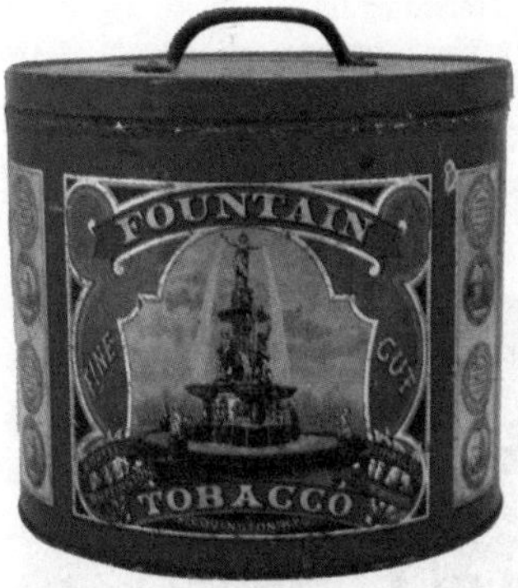

Mail Pouch Ads on Barns
Mail Pouch tobacco used signs painted on barns as huge ads from the beginning of the twentieth century until the 1990s.

Tobacco Cans

Tobacco can collectors prefer cans made to hold pipe tobacco. Other tins were made to hold chewing plugs, snuff, cigars, or cigarettes. There were large containers to dispense or display tobacco in stores. Tobacco was sold in cloth or paper bags until about 1880, when tobacco tins were made.

Advertising, Tin, Herold Smoked Sardines, Highest Quality, Book Shape, Hinged Lid, 10 x 11 In.
$29.00

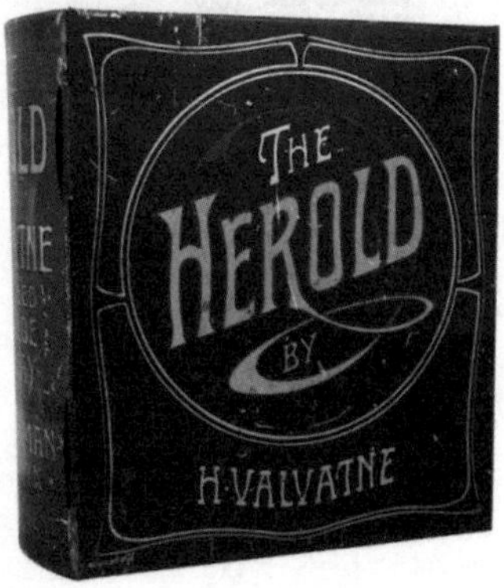

Advertising, Tin, Huntley & Palmers, Book Shape, Leather Strap, Marbleized Ends, 6 x 6 In.
$99.00

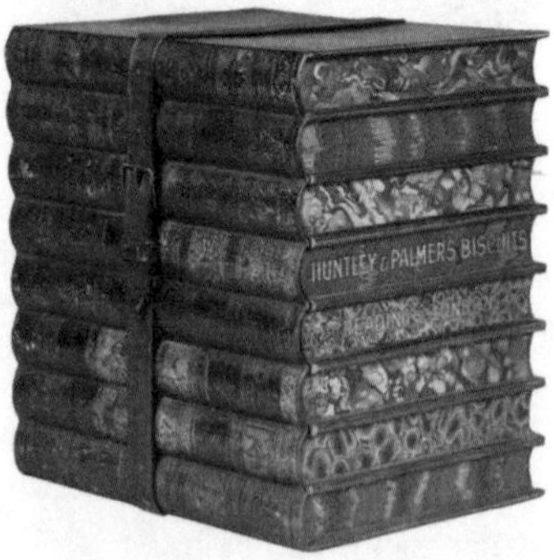

Tin, Gillies & Co. Tea, Stag In Woods, Teapot, Lake Scene, Ginna, 6 x 4 In. 495.00
Tin, Glendora Coffee, Gold, Blue, White, Paper Label, Sample, 3¼ x 2 In. 100.00
Tin, Gold Dust Scouring Powder, Fairbank Co., Sample, 2¾ x 2 In. 165.00
Tin, Golden West Coffee, Cowgirl Drinking Coffee, 1937, 3 Lb., 6 x 6½ In. 90.00
Tin, Golden West Coffee, Cowgirl Drinking Coffee, Red, White, Key Wind, 1 Lb., 3½ x 5 In. 60.00
Tin, Great Eagle Coffee, Vesey 39 Street, Sole Importer, Small Top, c.1880, 9 x 4¾ In. 605.00
Tin, Guide Pipe & Cigarette Tobacco, Your Way To Better Smoking, 4 x 3 x ⅞ In. 242.00
Tin, Gypsy Boy, Cream Of Tarter, Spice, Lithograph, 2 x 2¼ x 1½ In. 77.00
Tin, Handsome Dan Tobacco, Yale Dog Mascot, Hinged Lid, L.L. Stoddard, 5 x 6 x 2 In. 358.00
Tin, Hazard Smokeless Gunpowder, Lithograph, c.1890, 6 x 3½ x 1⅝ In. 440.00
Tin, Hercules Coffee, Red, Black, Lithograph, Winslow, Rand & Watson, 7 x 3½ x 3½ In. 210.00
Tin, Herold Smoked Sardines, Highest Quality, Book Shape, Hinged Lid, 10 x 11 In. .... *illus* 29.00
Tin, Hi Plane, Tobacco, Pocket, Lithograph, Twin Engine, Unopened, 4⅜ x 3 x ⅞ In. 242.00
Tin, Hoadley's Marshmallow Tablets, Gelatin, Green, Black, 5½ x 8½ x 3¼ In. 88.00
Tin, Home Brand, Tumeric, Yellow, Red, Black, Label, Griggs, Cooper & Co., 3 x 2 x 1 In. 40.00
Tin, Home Brand Coffee, More Cups Of Better Coffee, Drip, Key Wind, 1 Lb., 3½ x 5 In. 90.00
Tin, Home Oil Co., Pry Lid, 1 Lb., 4⅝ x 3⅜ In. 187.00
Tin, Honey Moon Tobacco, Couple On Moon, Red Ground, 4½ x 3 In. 748.00
Tin, Honey Moon Tobacco, Man Sitting On Moon, Penn Tobacco Co., 4⅜ x 3 In. .... 121.00 to 154.00
Tin, Huntley & Palmers, Book Shape, Leather Strap, Marbleized Ends, 6 x 6 In. .... *illus* 99.00
Tin, Huntley & Palmers, Toby Mug, Biscuit, Embossed, 6⅜ In. 88.00
Tin, Imperial Gun Powder, Fox & Hound, Paper Label, No Cap, 5 x 4 x 2 In. 135.00
Tin, International Stock Food, 3 Feeds For 1 Cent, Stock Food Tonic, 9¾ x 8 x 7 In. 550.00
Tin, Java & Mocha Coffee, Lithograph, 1 Lb., 8½ x 3¾ x 3⅛ In. 495.00
Tin, Jess Talcum, Image Of Woman, Talcum Powder, Green Ground, 5 x 3 In. 575.00
Tin, Jumbo Blanched Salted Peanuts, Peanut Specialty, Oval Brand, 10 Lb., 9 x 8 In. 95.00
Tin, Kampfe Safety Razor, Man Shaving, 2½ x 1¼ In. 88.00
Tin, Kaspers Timur Coffee, Arabian Man Riding Horse, 5¾ x 4¼ In. 450.00
Tin, Kenton's Baking Powder, Owl, Moon, Paper Label, 2⅞ x 1 In. 143.00
Tin, Killark Fuse, 30 Amps, 5 Fuses, Electric Mfg. Co. 7.50
Tin, King Dutch Stogies, 3 For 5 Cents, Made In Pittsburgh, Contents, 6 x 4⅜ x 4⅜ In. 176.00
Tin, King's Semi-Smokeless, Powder For Rifles & Shotguns, Paper Label, 6 x 4 In., 1 Lb. 90.00
Tin, Lady Esther Talcum Powder, Red & Gold Design, Chicago, Contents, 2 x 6 In. .. 40.00 to 50.00
Tin, Laflin & Rand Orange Extra Sporting FFG Powder, Hercules Powder Co., 5 x 4 In. 100.00
Tin, Larus's Gold Bond, Old Reliable Tobacco, Cross Cut, Gold, Blue, 4½ x 3⅜ x 1 In. 385.00
Tin, Little Elf Coffee, Elf Carrying Tray, Bursely & Co., Fort Wayner, 1 Lb. 670.00
Tin, Little Mozart Cigars, 5 Cents, Liberty, Can., Oval, Lithograph, 4½ x 6½ In. 190.00
Tin, Log Cabin Maple Syrup, Children Playing Cowboys, 2 Lb., 5 x 4⅝ x 2⅞ In. 132.00
Tin, Lorillard's Maccoboy Snuff, Man, Woman, Red, Black, 5 Lb., 6⅜ x 7½ x 5 In. 187.00
Tin, Maltby's Cocoanut, Patent, Prepared, 4-Sided, 1878, 6 x 3 x 3 In. 425.00
Tin, Mammy's Coffee, Favorite Brand, Orange, Black, Gold, C.D. Kenny Co., 4 Lb., 11 x 6 In. . 577.00
Tin, Master Mason Smoking Tobacco, A Square Deal, Man Smoking, 4½ x 3 In. 1380.00
Tin, Mathewson FFFF Gun Powder, Dog, Fox, Birds, Orange, Black, No Cap, 7 x 3¾ In. 90.00
Tin, McCormick Fruit Tablets, Yellow, Black, 5 Lb., 7¾ x 5⅛ x 5⅛ In. 690.00
Tin, Mellor & Rittenhouse, Licorice Cough Drops, Lithograph, Glass, 6⅞ x 5 In. 715.00
Tin, Miami Bouquet Talcum, Girl, Brown, Blue, White, 2⅛ x 1¼ In. 77.00
Tin, Milltown Cigar, Pittsburg's Best Stogies, Smokestack Skyline, 100 Count, 4 x 6 x 6 In. 660.00
Tin, Moses Cough Drops, Image On Both Sides, 2⅜ x 2¾ x 1⅝ In. 121.00
Tin, Moshier Bros. Spice, Gilt Edge, Hinged Lid, 11 x 7½ x 7½ In. 1320.00
Tin, Moxie Candy, 5 Cent, Pointing Druggist, Horse Driving Car 85.00
Tin, Mrs. Dinsmore's Cough Drops, Yellow, Somers Bros., 5 Lb., 8 x 5⅛ In. 330.00
Tin, N.L. Co. Lozenges, Glass Front, 5 Lb., 7¾ x 6 x 4 In. 88.00
Tin, Nelson's Baby Powder, Borated Talcum, Blue, White, Black, Lithograph, 5 x 2 In., 4 Oz. . 70.00
Tin, Nestle Milk Cocoa, Vince Lombardi, Football Offer, Red Ground, 28 Oz. 139.00
Tin, Newmark's Allspice, Highest Grade, Red, Blue, Yellow, White, 2 Oz., 3 x 2⅜ x 1 In. 121.00
Tin, Newton's Horse Remedy, Heave, Cough, Distemper, Compound, Yellow, Black, 7 x 3½ In. 80.00
Tin, Nonsuch Harness Oil Dressing, Horse Head, Canada, 5 In. Diam. 187.00
Tin, North Pole Cut Plug Tobacco, Polar Bears, 5 x 6 x 4 In. 316.00
Tin, North Pole Smoking Tobacco, North Pole Scene, Hinged Lid, Handle, 6 x 4 In. 770.00
Tin, Oilzum Co., Sample, Cleanzum Hand Cleaner, Buck Tooth Image, 1½ x ⅝ In. 798.00
Tin, Old Glory Tobacco, Eagle, Spalding & Merrick, Red, Hinged Lid, 2⅜ x 3¾ In. 143.00
Tin, Old Rip Tobacco, Allen & Ginter's, Rip Van Winkle, 4¾ x 3¼ x 2⅛ In. 1760.00
Tin, Old Statesmans Cut Plug Tobacco, Square Corners, Somers, Pre 1900, 4½ x 3¼ In. 236.00
Tin, Old Virginia Tobacco, Red Ground, 2½ x 3½ In. 201.00
Tin, Par After Shave Powder, Golfer, Nyal Co., 5⅝ x 2¼ In. 275.00
Tin, Patterson Bros., Whip, Horseman, Canister, 5½ x 5½ x 5½ In. 253.00

Tin, Patterson's Tuxedo Tobacco, Man In Tux, Green, Gold, 4⅜ x 2⅝ x 2⅝ In.	176.00
Tin, Peachy Tobacco, Double Cut, Peach, Leaves, Yellow, Orange, Green, 4⅛ x 2½ In.	187.00
Tin, Pedro Tobacco, Cut Plug, Hinged Lid, Yellow, Red, Handle, 4¼ x 7⅞ x 5¼ In.	132.00
Tin, Perfumed Violet Talcum Powder, Girl, 4⅛ x 1¾ In.	242.00
Tin, Peter Pan Peanut Butter, Improved By Hydrogenation, 10½ Oz., 2¾ x 3½ In.	60.00
Tin, Peter Pan Peanut Butter, Improved By Hydrogenation, Pry Lid, 2⅝ x 2⅝ In.	165.00
Tin, Philip Morris' Puritan Tobacco, Lithograph, Pocket, 4½ x 3 x ⅞ In.	330.00
Tin, Philips & Townsend Barbed Nails, Lithograph, Hinged Lid, 3 x 4½ x 1⅝ In.	143.00
Tin, Planters House Coffee, Steel Cut, Building, Red, White, Blue, Hanley & Kinsella, 1 Lb. ...	242.00
Tin, Polar Bear Coffee, Paper Label, 5¾ x 4⅛ In.	330.00
Tin, Popcorn, Dickinson's Little Buster, Blue, Buster Popping Corn Over Fire, 10 Oz.	75.00
Tin, Prince Hamlet Cigar, Havana, Embossed, Lithograph, 5½ x 5 In.	230.00
Tin, Prof. Serles Horse & Cattle Powder, Green, 3½ x 2¾ x 1⅝ In.	209.00
Tin, Puritan Tobacco, Pilgrim, Crushed Plug Mixture, Gray, Black, White, 4⅜ x 3 In.	154.00
Tin, Qboid Granulated Plug, Plantation, Larus & Bro., Co., Pocket, 4⅛ x 3½ x 1⅛ In.	358.00
Tin, Qboid Tobacco, Yellow, Brown, 4 x 3 x 1¼ In.	100.00
Tin, Rainbow Cut Plug Tobacco, 4½ x 5½ In.	605.00
Tin, Red Cough Drops, Bone, Eagle Co., Red, Yellow, Green, 5 Lb., 7¾ x 5¼ In.	154.00
Tin, Red Cross Foot Powder, Antiseptic, Red, White, Blue, 4 x 2½ x 1⅜ In.	44.00
Tin, Red Lodge Stringless Beans, Cut Green, Indians, Teepee, Paper Label, Montana, 4½ x 3¼ In.	160.00
Tin, Red Turkey Coffee, J.B. Maltby, Turkey, 5¾ x 4¼ In. .... 132.00 to 170.00	
Tin, Red Wolf Coffee, Steel Cut, Red Wolf, Bail Handle, 6 Lb.	115.00
Tin, Reed & Carnrick, Beef Peptonoids, Steer, Girl, Wheat Bundles, 4 x 2¾ In.	132.00
Tin, Reed & Carnrick, Beef Peptonoids, Lid, Sample, 1¾ x 2⅞ x ½ In.	143.00
Tin, Regal Smoking Tobacco, Cube Cut, Embossed, Foldover Lid, Canada, 4 x 3½ In.	522.00
Tin, Robinson Crusoe Peanut Butter, Lithograph, 10 Lb., 9¾ x 8⅜ In.	990.00
Tin, Rockwood's Pure Cocoa, Paper Label, 2 Lb., 9 x 4 In.	40.00
Tin, Round Trip Smoking Tobacco, Cut Plug, Ship In Rope Cartouche, 4 x 6½ x 5 In.	230.00
Tin, Rubon Cleaner & Polish, 2 Women Polishing Table, 4 Oz., 4 x 2 In.	40.00
Tin, Ruby Mocha & Java, Yellow, Handle, Depew & Co., 2¾ x 2¾ In.	132.00
Tin, Santa Fe Trail Coffee, Indians On Horseback, Stage Coach, Wagon Trail, 3½ x 5¼ In. ...	176.00
Tin, Sawyers Electric Cough Drops, Red, Black, 4¼ x 8½ x 7¼ In.	797.00
Tin, Schepp's Cocoanut, Monkey Juggling Coconuts, Yellow, Black, 5¾ x 3¾ x 3¾ In.	440.00
Tin, Seal Of Minnesota Coffee, Farmer Plowing, 1 Lb., 7¼ x 4¼ In.	4070.00
Tin, Seal Of North Carolina Tobacco, Man, Woman, 6¼ x 4⅞ In.	42.00
Tin, Senate Coffee, Screw Top, Newell & Truesdell Co., 1 Lb., 6 x 4 In.	170.00
Tin, Shotgun Smokeless Gunpowder, 3¼ x 5½ x 1½ In.	198.00
Tin, Slippery Elm Cough Drop, Henry There & Co.'s, Lithograph, 1 Lb., 3⅜ x 5 x 3 In.	66.00
Tin, Slussers Gall Powder, Horse, Yellow, Black, 3⅞ x 1½ In.	143.00
Tin, Smith Bros. Cough Drops, Blue, White, Tin Lithograph, Flip Lid, 2⅜ x 3⅝ In.	385.00
Tin, Sparkling Gems, Rodda Candy, Red, Gold, Black, 6½ In.	27.00
Tin, Spice, Premium Mills, Cloves, St. Bernard Dog, Lithograph, 3⅜ x 2⅜ In.	468.00
Tin, Squirrel Peanut Butter, Lithograph, 3⅜ x 3⅞ In.	385.00
Tin, Stag Tobacco, Stag, Hunt Scene, Riders On Horseback, 5½ x 4¾ In.	580.00
Tin, Startup's Gum, Buy Roz, Lithograph, 1½ x ½ In.	77.00
Tin, State House Coffee, Black Hawk Coffee Spice Co., Ia., Paper Label, 1 Lb.	385.00
Tin, Statler Bros., Tobacco, Guru Smoking, Lithograph, Pocket, 3⅝ x 3½ x 2 In.	385.00
Tin, Stauffer Biscuit Company Pretzels, 5 In. ....*illus*	58.00
Tin, Sterling Light Tobacco, Spaulding & Merrick, Canister, 11 x 8½ In.	173.00
Tin, Sterling Tobacco, Canister, 8 x 11 In.	525.00
Tin, Strong Heart Coffee, Charles Hewitt & Sons, Indian, 1 Lb., 5¾ x 4¼ In. .... 375.00 to 522.00	
Tin, Sturbrug's Golden Sceptre Tobacco, Sample, Lithograph, 1⅝ x 1⅝ x 1 In.	231.00
Tin, Sun-Kist Tobacco, Tobacco Plantation, Yellow, Brown, White, 5¼ x 4¼ In.	154.00
Tin, Sunset Trail Cigars, Cowboy & Cowgirl, Hinged Lid, 50 Count, 5⅜ x 6 x 4 In.	400.00
Tin, Sure Shot Chewing Tobacco, Indian, Hinged Lid, Porcelain Knob, 7 x 15 x 10 In.	1320.00
Tin, Sure Shot Chewing Tobacco, Touches The Spot, Indian, Bow, Arrow, 8 x 15 x 10 In.	825.00
Tin, Swansdown Coffee, Swan, High Grade, 1 Lb., 6¼ x 4 In.	210.00
Tin, Sweet Clover Tobacco, Lovell & Buffington, Lithograph, Pocket, 2⅜ x 3¾ x ⅝ In.	66.00
Tin, Sweet Cuba Fine Cut Tobacco, Pie Shape, Green, Red, Black, 1 Lb., 8¼ x 2 In.	88.00
Tin, Sykes Comfort Talc, Children, Nurse, Lithograph, 4¼ x 1⅜ x 1 In.	143.00
Tin, Tartan Brand, Lowrey Coffee Co., Sealed, Tin Lithograph, 1 Lb., 3⅝ x 5⅛ In.	154.00
Tin, Taylor's White Manor, Tobacco, Plantation, Trees, Lithograph, Pocket, 3⅛ x 3½ In.	143.00
Tin, Thayer & Co.'s, Slippery Elm Lozenges, Lithograph, 5 Lb., 7¾ x 7 x 4¾ In.	330.00
Tin, Thurber Importing Co., Tea, Eagle, Factory Street, Lithograph, 8¾ x 4¼ In.	633.00
Tin, Tiger Chewing Tobacco, Bright, Sweet, Tiger, 15 Cents, Lorillard Co., 2⅞ x 3 In.	412.00
Tin, Tiger Chewing Tobacco, Canister, 8 x 11 In.	475.00

Advertising, Tin, Stauffer Biscuit Company Pretzels, 5 In. $58.00

Advertising, Tin, Yellow Cab Cigar, Takes The Right Of Way, 50 Count, c.1920, 5⅝ x 5⅜ In. $962.00

Burma-Shave Ads

Remember Burma-Shave Signs? These sets of rectangular wooden signs advertising shaving cream first appeared by the side of roads in 1925. Each sign was one line of a limerick. They were put up about every hundred feet. They were no longer used after the 1960s. Typical signs were:

> WITHIN THIS VALE
> OF TOIL
> AND SIN
> YOUR HEAD GROWS
> BALD
> BUT NOT YOUR CHIN
> Burma-Shave

> BEFORE I TRIED IT
> THE KISSES
> I MISSED
> BUT AFTERWARD-BOY!
> THE MISSES I KISSED
> Burma-Shave

> IT WOULD BE MORE
> FUN
> TO GO BY AIR
> BUT WE CAN'T HANG
> THESE SIGNS UP THERE
> Burma-Shave

Advertising, Tip Tray,
American Line,
Ocean Liner On Water, 4¼ In.
$138.00

Tin, Times Square Smoking Mixture, Mellowed In Wood, 4½ x 3 x ⅞ In.	77.00
Tin, Totem Tobacco, Pocket, Red Ground, Indian Smoking Pipe, 1910, 4 x 3 In.	1975.00 to 2100.00
Tin, Trout Line Smoking Tobacco, Burley Cut, Man Fishing, Oval, Pocket, 3¼ x 2½ In.	546.00
Tin, Turkey Coffee, Lithograph, Wild Turkey, 3 Lb., 10 x 5½ In.	1018.00
Tin, Tuxedo Tobacco, Specially Prepared For Pipe Or Cigarette, Green, Gold, 4⅜ x 3 x 1 In.	99.00
Tin, Twin Oaks Tobacco, Acorns, Flip Lid, 2⅞ x 2¼ In.	77.00
Tin, Veteran Brand Spice, Civil War Officer, Brewster Gordon Co., 3 x 2⅜ x 1¼ In.	132.00
Tin, Virginity, Smoking Tobacco, Lithograph, Hinged Lid, c.1880, 3⅞ x 4½ x 7 In.	385.00
Tin, Walter Baker Best Cocoa, Woman Sipping From Cup, Paper Label, 3¾ x 3 In.	242.00
Tin, War Eagle Cigars, Eagle Logo, Lithograph, 5¼ x 3½ In.	358.00
Tin, War Eagle Cigars, Eagle, 2 For 5 Cents, 50 Count, 5 x 5 In.	176.00
Tin, Watkins Talc, Couple, Embossed, Lithograph, 5⅝ x 2⅝ x 1⅜ In.	132.00
Tin, Whalene Axle Grease, Whale, Contents, 3¼ x 3 x 3 In.	176.00
Tin, White House Coffee, Drip, Blue, White, Keywind, ½ Lb., 3 x 4 In.	100.00
Tin, White House Coffee, Tin, Paper Label, 1 Lb., 6 x 3¾ In.	110.00
Tin, Whiz Metal Polish, Paper Label, Soldered, Sample, 2 In.	385.00
Tin, Wilbur Cocoa, 10 Cents, Cherub Stirring Cocoa, Paper Label, 3¼ x 2¼ In.	100.00
Tin, Williams Russian Cough Drops, Polar Bears, Red, Black, 4⅛ x 8⅝ x 5⅝ In.	422.00
Tin, Woodbury & Latham Coffee, Ginna, 1 Lb., 7 x 3½ x 3½ In.	385.00
Tin, Yankee Boy Tobacco, Plug Cut, Boy Holding Bat, Red, White Checks, 4 x 3½ x 1 In.	412.00
Tin, Yellow Cab Cigar, Takes The Right Of Way, 50 Count, c.1920, 5⅝ x 5⅜ In. *illus*	962.00
Tin, Zeno Chewing Gum, Man Climbing Brick Wall, Hinged Lid, 6½ x 9⅜ x 4½ In.	143.00
Tin, Zeno Chewing Gum, Man Climbing Brick Wall, Windmills, 4½ x 9½ x 2 In.	105.00

Advertising tip trays are decorated metal trays less than 5 inches in diameter. They were placed on the table or counter to hold either the bill or the coins that were left as a tip. Change receivers could be made of glass, plastic, or metal. They were kept on the counter near the cash register and held the money passed back and forth by the cashier. Related items may be listed in the Advertising category under Change Receiver.

Tip Tray, Adam Scheidt Brewing Co., Valley Forge Special, Bottle, 4 In.	56.00
Tip Tray, America's Pride, Sailor, Soldier, Plane, 4¼ In.	308.00
Tip Tray, American Line, Ocean Liner On Water, 4¼ In. *illus*	138.00
Tip Tray, American Ship Line, Philadelphia, Queenstown, Liverpool, 4¼ In.	120.00
Tip Tray, Andrew D. White, Mild & Satisfying, Harkert Cigar Co., 4¼ In.	350.00
Tip Tray, Bartholomay Beers, Ales & Porter, Woman On Winged Wheel, Rochester, 4⅜ In.	280.00
Tip Tray, Beer Drivers Union Local 132, Submarine, Cherub, Philadelphia & Vicinity, 4¼ In.	280.00
Tip Tray, Brewers Local Union No. 5, 15th Anniversary, Philadelphia, Nov. 4, 1907, 4¼ In.	672.00
Tip Tray, Bromo-Seltzer, Cures All Headaches, Bottle, 4¼ In.	1000.00
Tip Tray, Buffalo Brewing Co., San Francisco Expo, People, 1915, 4¼ In.	375.00
Tip Tray, Bull Frog Ale, Frog On Lily Pad, Let Your Ashes Repose Here, 3¾ In. *illus*	770.00
Tip Tray, C. Worz Saloon & Restaurant, Meet Me Here, Liberty Bell, Phila., Pa., 4⅛ In.	168.00
Tip Tray, Cheon, For Iced Tea, Geisha Girl Holding Tray, 1900s, 4⅜ In.	125.00 to 140.00
Tip Tray, Columbia Brewing, Heidelberg, Old Pilsner, Woman, Eagle, Tin Lithograph, 4¼ In.	198.00
Tip Tray, Columbus Brewing Co., Select Pale Beer, Man, Brown Hat, 4⅛ In.	176.00
Tip Tray, Consumers Brewing Co., Factory Scene, Tin Lithograph, 4½ In.	1050.00
Tip Tray, Cottolene, Nature's Gift From The Sunny South, Cotton Picker, Child, 4 In.	242.00
Tip Tray, Cudahy's Diamond C Hams, Taste Tells, Pilgrim Holding Ham, Tin, 4¼ In.	120.00
Tip Tray, Day & Night Tobacco, Woman, Chewing & Smoking, 5 Cents, 3 Oz., 5¼ In.	300.00
Tip Tray, Demp & Burpee Mfg. Co., Manure Spreader, Tin Lithograph, 3⅜ x 4¾ In.	578.00
Tip Tray, Dorne's Carnation Gum, Taste The Smell, Tin Lithograph, 4¼ In.	105.00
Tip Tray, Dr. A.C. Daniels, Horse & Cattle Medicines, 3 Horses, Tin Lithograph, 4 In.	520.00
Tip Tray, Drink Beacon Brown, King Of Phosphates, Woman, Striped Shirt, 1911, 5 In.	1850.00
Tip Tray, Drink Modox, Made From Indian Herbs, Indian, Die Cut, Tin Lithograph, 4¾ In.	1550.00
Tip Tray, Drink Schlitz Beer, The Beer That Made Milwaukee Famous, 4½ In.	169.00
Tip Tray, Fairy Soap, Have You A Little Fairy In Your Home, Girl Sitting On Bar, 4¼ In.	28.00
Tip Tray, Finlay Brewing, Woman Holding Bottle, Toledo, Oh., 4¼ In.	325.00
Tip Tray, Goebel Malt Extract, Girl, Chalkboard, Tin Lithograph, 4½ In.	350.00
Tip Tray, Gottfried Krueger Brewing Co., High Grade Beer, Stein, 4⅜ In.	336.00
Tip Tray, Have Some Junket, Girl, Holding Spoon, Hansen Labs, Little Falls, N.H., 4¼ In.	300.00
Tip Tray, Heptol Splits, For Health's Sake, Cowboy On Bucking Horse, 1904, 4¼ In.	1500.00
Tip Tray, Hoffman House, Setter, Ducks, Scalloped, Tin Lithograph, Sunbury, Pa., 5 x 3 In.	44.00
Tip Tray, Home Sewing Machine, Grandma Sews Pants On Boy	150.00
Tip Tray, Intercolonial Railway Of Canada, Compliments Of Moose Head, 5½ In.	280.00
Tip Tray, Jap Rose Soap, Boy, Girl Washing Doll, Kirk, Chicago, 4¼ In.	180.00
Tip Tray, La Toco Havana Cigars, Woman, Cherubs, Tin Lithograph, 4¼ In.	77.00

Tip Tray, Liberty Beer, In Bottles Only, American Brew Co., 4¼ In.		308.00
Tip Tray, London Whiffs, Box Of Cigars, Marcus Feder Cigar Co., Cleveland, Oh., 4¼ In.		220.00
Tip Tray, Los Angeles Brewing Co., Home Of East Side Beer, Tin Lithograph, 5 In.		412.00
Tip Tray, Ludens Cough Drops, Give Instant Relief, Tin Lithograph, Reading, Pa., 3⅝ In.		490.00
Tip Tray, Maltosia Pure Food Beer, German American Brewing Co., 5⅛ In.		84.00
Tip Tray, Moxie, Girl Holding Cup, 1906, 6 In.		330.00
Tip Tray, Moxie, I Just Love Moxie Don't You, Victorian Woman, 1906, 6 In.		485.00
Tip Tray, Mr. Thomas 5 Cents Cigar, Black Cat, Shonk, Chicago, 4¼ In.		1500.00
Tip Tray, Muehlebach Pilsener Beer, Purest & Best, Bottle, 5⅛ In.		140.00
Tip Tray, National Brewing Co., Best In The West, Cowboy On Horse, Yellow, Black, 4½ In.		725.00
Tip Tray, Nittanus Chiefs Cigars, 6 Indian Chiefs, Dog, Embossed, Celluloid, 7 x 7 In.		1485.00
Tip Tray, Old Export Beer, People's Choice For 45 Years, Cumberland Brewing Co., 4⅛ In.		140.00
Tip Tray, Pennsy Select Beer, Quick A Glass Please, Our Mutual Friend, 4⅛ In.		725.00
Tip Tray, Pilsener Brewing Co., Bottle, Cup, Cleveland, Ohio, 4¼ In.		280.00
Tip Tray, Poinsetta, Drink Poinsetta, Woman, 1907, 4¼ In.		168.00
Tip Tray, Pulvers Cocoa, Purity Itself, Girl On Box, Tin Lithograph, 4½ In.		275.00
Tip Tray, Puritan Hams, First In The Land, Cudahay Packing Co., 4¼ In.		150.00
Tip Tray, Red Raven, Ask The Man, Girl, Great For Headache, Tin Lithograph, 4¼ In.		195.00
Tip Tray, Red Raven, Ask The Man, Pittsburg Exposition, 1905, 4⅜ In.		140.00
Tip Tray, Rienzi Beer, In Bottles Only, Bartholomay Brewery, Man On Horse, 4¼ In.		308.00
Tip Tray, Ruhstaller's Lager, Woman Holding Mugs, Gilt Edge, Sacramento, Cal., 4¼ In.		195.00
Tip Tray, Rupperts Beer, Woman Serving Turkey, 1940s, 4¼ In.		50.00
Tip Tray, Salaam Temple, Pilgrimage To New Orleans, Newark, N.J., 1910, 4⅜ In.		168.00
Tip Tray, Seitz Beer, Eagle, Brewers Since 1821, Easton, Pa., 6½ x 4½ In.		224.00
Tip Tray, Standard Ginger Ale & Root Beer, Tin Lithograph, c.1910, 5 In. ....*illus*		115.00
Tip Tray, Success Manure Spreader, Farmer, Horse Drawn Spreader, Kemp & Burpee, 5 x 3⅜ In.		308.00
Tip Tray, Taka-Kola, Every Hour, Take No Other, 5 Cents, Girl Holding Bottle, 4¼ In.		336.00
Tip Tray, Tech Beer, None Better, Bottle, Pittsburgh Brewing Co., 6½ x 4½ In.		112.00
Tip Tray, Tin, White House Ginger Ale, 1920s, 4½ In.		185.00
Tip Tray, Velvet Candy, See, Hear, Speak No Evil But Eat Velvet Candy, 1900s, 4⅜ In.		224.00
Tip Tray, White House Ginger Ale, Purity Guaranteed, Tin Lithograph, 4¼ In.		90.00
Tip Tray, White Rock, World's Best Table Water, Fairy On Rock, 4¼ In.		85.00
Tip Tray, Wrigley's Mineral Scouring Soap, 5 Cents, Black Cat, 3½ In.		400.00
Tobacco Cutter, Betsy Ross, A.S. Valentine & Son, Cast Iron, 8¾ x 8½ In.		605.00
Towel, Dorothy Hart Sunbrite Junior Nurse Corps, Cannon, c.1937, 16½ x 13½ In.		84.00
Tray, Bellmore Whiskey, Bernard Fischer, Man, Red Nightcap, Tin Lithograph, 12 In. Diam.		100.00
Tray, Campfire Marshmallows Supreme, People Roasting Marshmallows, Teepee, 8 In.		115.00
Tray, Central Brewing Co., Brewery, Boats, Cars, Oval, 13½ x 16½ In.		1980.00
Tray, Dixie's Ice Cream, Enjoy, Red, White, Blue, Tin, 10½ x 15 In.		28.00
Tray, Dobler Lager, Famous Brew, Horse Drawn Wagons, Tin Lithograph, Oval, 15 x 18½ In.		132.00
Tray, Dr Pepper, You'll Like It Too, Drink A Bite To Eat, 1930s		418.00
Tray, E. Robinson's Sons, Pilsener Bottled Beer, Lake Scene, 12 In.		616.00
Tray, Enterprise Brewing, Yosemite Lager, Tin Lithograph, 1905, 13¼ In.		775.00
Tray, Ever Welcome Beer, Party, People, Cherubs, Terre Haute Brewing, Tin, Oval, 15 x 12 In.		440.00
Tray, Fairmont's Ice Cream, Peak Of Quality, Yellow, Red, Tin, 10½ x 15 In.		33.00
Tray, Fearsons Ice Cream, Girl Eating Ice Cream, 15 x 10 In.		224.00
Tray, Galliker's Quality Ice Cream, Boy & Girl Under Umbrella, 1923, 13 In. ....*illus*		1540.00
Tray, Gateway Deluxe Ice Cream, Black, White, Tin, 10½ x 15 In.		40.00
Tray, German American Brewing Co., Equal To Best Imported, Bottles, Buffalo, 13 x 13 In.		392.00
Tray, Glencliff Ice Cream, That's New, Black, Yellow, Red, Tin, 10½ x 15 In.		55.00
Tray, Henry Weinhard City Brewery, Factory, Columbia Export, Tin, Oval, 13½ x 16 In.		275.00
Tray, Hires, Woman, Green Dress, Haskell Coffin		335.00
Tray, Hires Root Beer, American Beauty Coffin Girl, Drink Hires, 13 x 10 In.		240.00
Tray, Honey-Fruit Chewing Gum, Va., Red, White, Blue, Hanger, Franklin-Caro Co, 5½ x 9 In.		590.00
Tray, Jackson Brewing Co., Drink Jax, House, Trees, 10½ x 13½ In.		308.00
Tray, Justrite Ice Cream, Just Taste Its Richness, Red, Yellow, Tin, 10½ x 15 In.		55.00
Tray, Lakeside Grape Juice, From Selected Grapes, Early 1900s, 13½ In. Diam.		252.00
Tray, Menommee River Brewing Co., Dublin Stout, Golden Drop, Building, Oval, 13 x 16 In.		910.00
Tray, Mid-West Ice Cream, Kewpies On Mound Of Ice Cream, 13 x 13 In.		550.00
Tray, Murray Soda Water, 2 Gentlemen, Seated, Holding Cups, Tin, c.1920, 12 In. Diam.		115.00
Tray, New Life Beer, Woman On Moon, Goenner & Co., Johnstown, Pa., Round		1907.00
Tray, Orange Julep, Girl On Beach, 13 x 10½ In.		224.00
Tray, Quality Ice Cream, Ice Cream Of All Ice Creams, Taste Tells, 1913, 13 In. Diam.		196.00
Tray, Quincy Beer, Building, Dick & Bros., 10½ x 13½ In.		449.00
Tray, Red Ribbon Beer, Bear Digging In Box, Tin Lithograph, 13¼ x 13¼ In.		578.00
Tray, Robert H. Gaupners Brewery, Export Elfenweiss Porter & Ale, Building, 12 In.		728.00

Advertising, Tip Tray,
Bull Frog Ale,
Frog On Lily Pad,
Let Your Ashes Repose Here, 3¾ In.
$770.00

Advertising, Tip Tray,
Standard Ginger Ale & Root Beer,
Tin Lithograph, c.1910, 5 In.
$115.00

Advertising, Tray,
Galliker's Quality Ice Cream,
Boy & Girl Under Umbrella,
1923, 13 In.
$1540.00

Akro Agate
Glass marbles were made by
the Akro Agate Company
of Akron, Ohio, founded in
1911. Marbles were the only
thing the company made
until 1932. Then ashtrays,
figurines, bowls, garden pots,
and other pieces were added
to the line. The glass was
a mixture of two or more
opaque marbleized colors.
The factory made children's
glass tea sets and glassware
after 1942 but went out
of business in 1951, and
its molds, trademark, and
other assets were sold to the
Master Glass Company of
Clarksburg, West Virginia.

Akro Agate, Tea Set,
Doll's, Service For 4,
Green Crystal, 21 Piece
$106.00

Tray, Seiple & Son, Girl, White Dress, Flowers In Hair, Tin Lithograph, Easton, Pa., 13 In. ...	230.00
Tray, Sparks Kidney Liver, Ceramic, Picture Of Mrs. Grover Cleveland, 11 x 16 In.	880.00
Tray, Tip, see Tip Trays in this category.	
Tray, Tracy's Ice Cream, Yellow, Green, Tin, 10½ x 15 In.	66.00
Tray, White Label Guinness Stout, Horse Show, Thomas McMullen & Co., 10½ x 13 In.	110.00
Tray, Wieland's Extra Pale Lager, Indian Squaw, Tin Lithograph, 13 In. Diam.	850.00
Tray, Wrigley's Happy To Serve You, After Every Meal, 13¼ x 10½ In.	336.00
Tray, Yuengling Lager, Ale & Porter, Woman Holding Glass & Bottle, Pottsville, Pa.	1344.00
Wheel, Gambling, Lucky Strike, White, Decals, Outer Ring Numbers, 46½ In.	165.00
Wrapper, First Column Defenders Chewing Gum, Goudey, c.1940, 4¾ x 6 In.	224.00

AGATA glass was made by Joseph Locke of the New England Glass Company of Cambridge, Massachusetts, after 1885. A metallic stain was applied to New England Peachblow, which the company called Wild Rose, and the mottled design characteristic of agata appeared. There are a few known items made of opaque green with the mottled finish.

Cruet, Bulbous, Trifold Rim, Pink Stopper & Applied Handle, 6 In.	863.00
Cruet, Ruffled Rim, Cream Handle & Ball Stopper, 6 In.	403.00
Cuspidor, Peachblow, Purple Mottling, New England Glass Co., Lady's, 5 x 2½ In.	1550.00
Cuspidor, Peachblow, Lady's, 5 In.	1256.00
Figurine, Phoenix Bird, Red, White, Teakwood Base, 6 In.	66.00
Finger Bowl, Crimped Rim, Ground Pontil, 5½ x 2¾ In.	1050.00
Finger Bowl, Ruffled Rim, New England, 5 In., Pair	345.00
Punch Cup, Pink Reeded Handle, 2½ In.	316.00
Saltshaker, Mineral Stain, Pillar Shape, 4 In.	518.00
Toothpick, Crimped Rim, 2½ In.	489.00
Toothpick, Square Mouth, 2¼ In.	403.00
Tumbler, 3½ In., Pair	403.00
Tumbler, Green Opaque, Gold & Amethyst Mineral Stain Band, 3¾ In.	633.00
Tumbler, Juice, Peachblow, Mottled, 3⅞ x 2¼ In.	550.00
Tumbler, Mineral Stain, 3½ In.	489.00
Vase, Lily, Flower Form, Trifold Rim, Footed, 12 In.	863.00
Vase, Lily, Mineral Stain, Trifold Rim, Footed, 12 In.	978.00
Vase, Lily, Trifold Rim, 18 In.	1035.00
Vase, Lily, Trifold Rim, Disc Foot, 6 In.	546.00
Vase, Lily, Trifold Rim, Mineral Stain, 10½ In.	1265.00

AKRO AGATE glass was made in Clarksburg, West Virginia, from 1932 to 1951. Before that time, the firm made children's glass marbles, which are listed in this book in the Marble category. Most of the glass is marked with a crow flying through the letter *A*.

Bowl, Cereal, Transparent Topaz, Interior Panel, 3⅜ In.	30.00
Creamer, Amber, Herringbone, 2¼ In.	11.79
Creamer, Transparent Green, Interior Panel, 1¼ In.	75.00
Creamer, Transparent Topaz, Interior Panel, 1⅜ In.	40.00
Creamer, Transparent Topaz, Stippled Band, 1¼ In.	28.00
Creamer, Yellow, Concentric Ring, 1¼ In.	20.00
Cup, Green, Octagonal, 1½ In.	9.00
Cup, Transparent Blue, Concentric Ring, 1¼ In.	65.00
Cup, Transparent Topaz, Stippled Band, 1¼ In.	20.00
Cup & Saucer, Green, Concentric Rib, 3½-In. Saucer	14.00
Cup & Saucer, Green, Marbleized, Octagonal, Large	22.00
Cup & Saucer, Transparent Green, Interior Panel, 1¼-In. Cup	32.00
Cup & Saucer, Transparent Green, Stippled Band	30.00
Cup & Saucer, Transparent Topaz, Interior Panel, 1¼-In. Cup	32.00 to 40.00
Dish, Shell, Green, Marbleized, 3⅞ x 3¾ In.	7.50
Planter, Pumpkin Orange, Scalloped Top, 4½ x 8½ In.	28.00
Plate, Amber, Herringbone, 3¼ In.	7.29
Plate, Blue, Octagonal, 4¼ In.	8.25
Plate, Dark Blue, Concentric Ring, 3¼ In.	10.00
Plate, Green, Concentric Ring, 3¼ In.	6.00
Plate, Green, Marbleized, Octagonal, 4¼ In.	10.00
Plate, Green, Octagonal, Panel Pattern Rim, 4 In.	7.00
Plate, Transparent Green, Interior Panel, Child's	18.00
Plate, Transparent Topaz, Interior Panel, 4¼ In.	18.00
Saucer, Blue, Octagonal, 4¼ In.	16.00
Saucer, Pink, Octagonal, 3⅜ In.	4.25 to 10.00

Saucer, White, Concentric Ring, 2¾ In.	6.00 to 7.00
Sugar, Transparent Topaz, Stippled Band	50.00
Tea Set, Chiquita, Green, Box, 22 Piece	413.00
Tea Set, Chiquita, Prossa Fired On, Box, 8 Piece	220.00
Tea Set, Doll's, Service For 4, Green Crystal, 21 Piece ....*illus*	106.00
Tea Set, Little American Maid, Interior Panel, Lemonade & Oxblood Onyx, Box, 17 Piece *illus*	468.00
Tea Set, Little American Maid, Octagonal, Opaque Colors, Closed Handles, Box, 29 Piece *illus*	358.00
Tea Set, Little American Maid, Stippled Band, Box, 17 Piece	110.00 to 176.00
Tea Set, Play-Time, Concentric Ring, Box, 8 Piece	110.00
Tea Set, Play-Time, Interior Panel, Box, 16 Piece	220.00
Tea Set, Play-Time, Stippled Band, No Sugar & Creamer, Jade Trans-Optic, Box, 14 Piece *illus*	220.00
Teapot, Cover, Blue, Concentric Ring, 3 In.	40.00
Teapot, Cover, Dark Blue, Concentric Ring, 3 In.	38.00
Teapot, Cover, Transparent Green, Interior Panel, 2⅝ In.	95.00
Teapot, Cover, Transparent Topaz, Interior Panel, 2⅜ In.	95.00
Teapot, Green, Concentric Ring, 2⅜ In.	15.00
Teapot, Transparent Topaz, Stippled Band, 2⅜ In.	70.00
Tumbler, Ivory, Octagonal, 2 In.	20.00
Tumbler, Pink, Stacked Disc, Interior Panel, 2 In.	16.00
Tumbler, White, Stacked Disc, Interior Panel, 2 In.	16.00
Tumbler, Yellow, Octagonal, 2 In.	20.00
Vase, Daffodil Green, Slag, 4¼ x 4½ x 3 In.	20.00
Vase, Lily, Orange Marbleized, 4½ x 4¾ In.	14.00
Water Set, Play-Time, Interior Panel, Box, 7 Piece	143.00

ALABASTER is a very soft form of gypsum, a stone that resembles marble. It was often carved into vases or statues in Victorian times. There are alabaster carvings being made even today.

Box, Figural, Carved, Demilune, Adonis & Venus, Italy, 19th Century, 13 x 14 In.	761.00
Bust, Girl With Curly Hair, Wrapped In Bun In Back, E. Fiachi, 18 x 18 In.	1093.00
Column, Ionic, Octagonal Base, 3 Sections, 38½ In.	805.00
Compote, Stone Fruit, Assorted Fruits, Round, 19th Century, 2½ x 7¾ In.	823.00
Doorstop, Sheep, Lying Down, Carved, Pedestal Base, Peaked Ends, 5½ x 6 x 4¼ In.	495.00
Figurine, Girl, Bunny Resting On Open Book, 9½ In.	999.00
Figurine, Girl Carrying Hay, 2 Sheep, Continental, 19th Century, 18¼ In.	499.00
Figurine, Renaissance Woman Seated, Savonarola Chair, 18½ In.	288.00
Light Fixture, Ivory, Conch Shell Form, Reclining Nude Woman Inside, Italy, 20 In.	1680.00
Luminaire, Ribs, Cover, Ball Finial, Vase Form, Square Base, 17 In., Pair	600.00
Pedestal, Renaissance Style, Round, Turned, Square Top, Chamfered Corners, 37 x 12 In.	720.00
Statue, Venus With Cupid At Her Toilette, Signed, P. Barranti, Florence, 1800s, 30 In.	826.00
Statue, Woman, Holds Metal Crescent, Bronze Plaque On Base, 31½ In.	4485.00
Statue, Woman, Long Robe, Belt, Fringed Necklace, Italy, 25⅝ In.	2468.00

ALUMINUM was more expensive than gold or silver until the 1850s. Chemists learned how to refine bauxite to get aluminum. Jewelry and other small objects were made of the valuable metal until 1914, when an inexpensive smelting process was invented. The aluminum collected today dates from the 1930s through the 1950s. Hand-hammered pieces are the most popular.

Bowl, Flowers, Flared, Ruffled Top Edge, 11½ x 3½ In.	68.00
Bread Box, Slide Door, 17 x 6½ In.	50.00
Candleholder, Arts & Crafts Style, Hammered, 6½ x 2½ In., Pair	25.00
Coaster, Leaf Shape, Hammered, 1950s, 4 In., 7 Piece	35.00
Coaster Set, Ducks In Flight, Cattails, 3³⁄₁₆ In., 8 Piece	25.00
Coffee Server, Mayfair, Kensington, Lurelle Guild, Cherry Wood Handles, 1940s, 10 In.	60.00
Coffee Set, Chrysanthemum, Urn, Creamer, Sugar & Tray, Continental Silver Co.	150.00
Crumber, Flower Design, Hammered, Forged, Everlast, 8 x 4 In.	10.00
Ice Bucket, Flower Handles, Flower Knob, Marked Foreman Family, 7½ x 7 In.	27.00
Pan, Roasting, 11¼ x 6⅞ In.	25.00
Pitcher, Ice Lip, Hammered, Forged, Everlast, 9 In.	25.00
Serving Dish, 2 Tiers, Flower Designs, Wilson Specialties Co., Brooklyn, 11½ x 7 In.	19.95
Serving Dish, 3 Tiers, Marked, Gaistyn, 12½ x 13¼ In.	39.00
Spice Jar, Spun, Kromex, Cylindrical, Black Plastic Lid, Rack, 1950s, 3¼ x 2 In., 8 Piece	49.00
Teapot, 5 Cup, Black Plastic Handle, Lid Knob, Mirro	11.00
Tidbit, Embossed Dogwood Blossoms, Hammered, Handle, 6 x 5 In.	15.00
Tray, Engraved, Flowers, Fruit, Hand Wrought, Handles, Cromwell, 14½ In.	20.00

Akro Agate, Tea Set, Little American Maid, Interior Panel, Lemonade & Oxblood Onyx, Box, 17 Piece
$468.00

Akro Agate, Tea Set, Little American Maid, Octagonal, Opaque Colors, Closed Handles, Box, 29 Piece
$358.00

Akro Agate, Tea Set, Play-Time, Stippled Band, No Sugar & Creamer, Jade Trans-Optic, Box, 14 Piece
$220.00

Lurelle Guild

People sometimes are confused when reading the name Lurelle Guild. They think it is a group of designers, but it is a man. Lurelle is the designer's first name and Guild (rhymes with child) is his last. Lurelle Guild (1898–1985) was an industrial designer. He said "Beauty alone does not sell" and made designs for the average buyer—practical, up-to-date, never ahead or behind the styles. The sleek aluminum pieces created for Alcoa's Kensington division after 1934 and the 1937 Electrolux vacuum cleaner with sleigh feet are his best-known designs for today's collectors. Other important designs were cooking utensils for Wear-Ever Aluminum Company (1932), home accessories like lamps and candlesticks for Chase Brass and Copper, silverware for International Silver, air-conditioning units for Carrier Engineering Corporation, and a refrigerator for Norge.

Amber Glass, Salt, Scroll & Bearded Face, Medium Amber, France, 1¾ x 3⅛ x 2 In.
$1760.00

TIP

For a pollution-free glass cleaner, use a mixture of white vinegar and water.

Tray, Flowers, Hammered, Rodney Kent, 12¾ x 8 In.	85.00
Tray, Fruit Design, Hammered, 1960s, 21½ x 12 In.	85.00
Tray, Round, Savoy, Kensington, 1940s, 12¼ In.	30.00

AMBER, *see Jewelry category.*

AMBER GLASS is the name of any glassware with the proper yellow-brown shading. It was a popular color just after the Civil War and many pressed glass pieces were made of amber glass. Depression glass of the 1930s–50s was also made in shades of amber glass. Other pieces may be found in the Depression Glass, Pressed Glass, and other glass categories. All types are being reproduced.

Ashtray, Embossed Stag, 8 In.	20.00
Ashtray, Horse's Head Decal, Brown & White Bean Bag Base, 2 x 4 In.	25.00
Basket, Alternating Scalloped Panels, 6½ x 5 x 8 In.	28.00
Bell, Dinner, Tiara Exclusives, Sandwich Glass, Indiana Glass, 1978	15.00
Bookend, Figural, Young Girl, 2 Geese, 5¾ x 2½ x 4 In.	14.00
Bowl, Engraved, Flowers & Leaves, 4¾ x 7 In.	28.00
Box, Hinged Cover, Enameled, Orange Flowers, Swirled Ribs, Gold, Footed, 4⅜ x 4½ In.	350.00
Box, Hinged Cover, Various Motifs, Rabbit, Squirrel, Round, 3 x 8¼ In.	255.00
Cake Stand, 4½ x 10 In.	45.00
Candleholder, 3-Piece Mold, 4½ x 4 In., Pair	65.00
Compote, Inverted Thumbprint, Ruffled Edge, 6 In.	28.00
Compote, Pretzel, Pattern, Indiana, 1950s, 7 x 6½ In.	21.00
Cordial Set, Flower Decal, Spa, Lubiana, Italy, Carafe, Stopper, 6 Tumblers, Handles	39.00
Decanter, Teardrop Shape, Blown Flame Stopper, 1960s, 15 In.	70.00
Dish, Cover, Paneled, 7 x 5 In.	45.00
Dish, Ruffled Rim, Pastel Speckles, 2 x 7 In.	10.00
Dresser Set, Angular Half Moon Designs, Bagley Factory, England, 1939, 8 Piece	189.00
Dresser Set, Butterfly & Daffodil, 1920-30, 7 Piece	200.00
Figure, Hen On Nest, Oval Base, 7 x 5½ In.	15.00
Flower Frog, 11 Holes, 1½ x 2⅞ In.	40.00
Lamp Chimney, Oil, Embossed, Flowers, Leaf Design, 7 In.	6.00
Lamp Shade, Bullet Shape, Stippled Pattern, Bas Relief, 1930s, 5½ x 3 In.	22.00
Measuring Cup, Solid Spout, 1 Cup, ¼ Liter, 4 In.	15.00
Napkin Holder, Footed, Flowers, Stylized Leaves, Beaded Ground, 7¾ x 2½ In.	17.00
Pitcher, Enameled Flowers, Pink, Blue, White, Green Leaves, Applied Handle, 9¼ In.	42.00
Pitcher, Ice Lip, Diagonal Swirl Pattern, 8¼ In.	16.00
Salt, Scroll & Bearded Face, Medium Amber, France, 1¾ x 3⅛ x 2 In. ....*illus*	1760.00
Sugar Shaker, Screw Cap, USA Eagle Seal Relief On Front, 6 In., Pair	35.00
Tieback, Flower Shape, Bead Rows On Petals, Recessed Center Bead, 4¼ In., Pair	60.00
Vase, Art Deco, 3-Part Mold, 1920s, 8 x 4½ In.	35.00
Vase, Bulbous, Thumbprint, 7½ x 2½ In.	50.00
Vase, Fan Shape, Scalloped Edge, Fluting, Engraved, Diamonds, 11 In.	10.00
Vase, Swan Neck, Textured, 6-Sided, 15¾ In.	25.00
Vase, Zipper Pattern, Footed, 10 In.	29.00

AMBERINA, a two-toned glassware, was originally made from 1883 to about 1900. It was patented by Joseph Locke of the New England Glass Company, but was also made by other companies and is still being made. The glass shades from red to amber. Similar pieces of glass may be found in the Baccarat, Libbey, Plated Amberina, and other categories. Glass shaded from blue to amber is called Blue Amberina or Bluerina.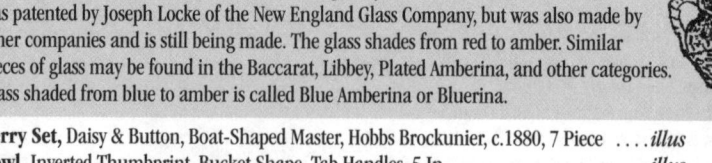

Berry Set, Daisy & Button, Boat-Shaped Master, Hobbs Brockunier, c.1880, 7 Piece ....*illus*	441.00
Bowl, Inverted Thumbprint, Bucket Shape, Tab Handles, 5 In. ....*illus*	147.00
Bowl, Leaf Shape, Cutout Handle, Satin, 8 x 8 x 2 In.	285.00
Butter, Daisy & Button Base, Inverted Thumbprint Cover, Applied Knop, 7 x 5 In.	86.00
Compote, Daisy & Button, 7 x 8 In.	45.00
Cup, Inverted Thumbprint, Applied Handles, Cupped Rim, 3 In., 6 Piece	316.00
Ewer, Flattened Oval Body, Diagonal Swirled Ribs, Applied Foot, 12 In.	60.00
Finger Bowl, Ruffled Edge, 5¼ In.	70.00
Goblet, Amber Stem, Red Bowl, Foot, 8½ In., Pair	518.00
Pickle Castor, Inverted Thumbprint, Silver Plated Lid, Tongs, 12 In.	200.00
Pitcher, Coin Spot Optic, Cambridge Glass Works, 7½ In.	259.00
Pitcher, Coin Spot Optic, Oval, Square Mouth, Applied Amber Handle, Hobbs Brockunier, 8 In.	230.00
Pitcher, Enameled, Flowers, c.1870, 11¼ In.	293.00
Pitcher, Inverted Thumbprint Pattern, Floral Prunt, Bulbous, 8½ In.	150.00

Pitcher, Tankard, Amber Reeded Handle, 9⅛ In. ....*illus*	230.00
Pitcher, Water, Optic Ribbed, Bulbous, Applied Amber Handle, 7¾ In.	144.00
Punch Cup, Coin Spot Optic, Scalloped Rim, Handle, 2½ In.	201.00
Punch Set, Bowl, Cover, Enameled, Flowers, Dragonflies, Ladle, 8 Cups	805.00
Salt & Pepper, Blue Flowers, Silver Plated Caddy, Sculptured Leaves, Twisted Handle	460.00
Toothpick, Daisy & Button, 3-Footed, 3 In.	144.00
Tumbler, Diamond-Quilted, 3¾ In.	50.00
Vase, Diamond-Quilted, Egg Shape, Tricornered Rim, 3 Reeded Feet, 6 In.	633.00
Vase, Inverted Thumbprint, 5 In.	110.00
Vase, Jack-In-The-Pulpit, Amber Foot Graduating To Ruby Rim, 10 In.	316.00
Vase, Jack-In-The-Pulpit, Coral Flowers, Footed, 11¾ In.	500.00
Vase, Lily, Disc Foot, Ruffled Edge, 8¼ In.	173.00
Vase, Lily, Ribbed Body, Tricornered Rim, 8¾ In.	120.00
Vase, Urn Shape, Swirled Ribs, Amber Rigaree Rim, Footed, 10 In.	173.00
Water Set, Coin Spot Optic, c.1900, 8½ In. Pitcher, 3¾-In. Tumblers, 7 Piece	323.00

AMERICAN DINNERWARE, *see Dinnerware.*

AMERICAN ENCAUSTIC TILING COMPANY was founded in Zanesville, Ohio, in 1875. The company planned to make a variety of tiles to compete with the English tiles that were selling in the United States for use in fireplaces and other architectural designs. The first glazed tiles were made in 1880, embossed tiles in 1881, faience tiles in the 1920s. The firm closed in 1935 and reopened in 1937 as the Shawnee Pottery.

Bookends, Putti, Rabbit, Pottery Cipher Mark, 4½ In., Pair	353.00
Fire Surround, Green Glaze, Urns, Daylilies, Flowers, 24½ x 66 In.	745.00
Fireplace Surround, Flowers, Mottled Cream, Brown, Green Glaze, 17 6-In. Tiles	150.00
Fireplace Surround, Man With Lyre, Woman, Brown Glaze, 36 x 42 In.	863.00
Frieze, Art Nouveau Nude Woman, Tan Glaze, Frame, 3 6-In. Tiles, Pair	805.00
Paperweight, Gazelle, c.1930, 5½ In.	113.00
Plaque, Autumn, 4 Seasons Series, Blue Glaze, 12 x 18 In. ....*illus*	1800.00
Tile, Woman Holding Leaf, Light Blue, Embossed, 2 x 4 In.	121.00

AMETHYST GLASS is any of the many glasswares made in the dark purple color of the gemstone amethyst. Included in this category are many pieces made in the nineteenth and twentieth centuries. Very dark pieces are called black amethyst and are listed under that heading.

Bowl, 3-Footed, 7¼ In.	20.00
Candlestick, 7 In., Pair	46.00
Cheese Dish, Flat Lid, Ribbed, Red, 6 x 5 In.	22.00
Compote, Ruffled Edge, Bubble, Swirled, Twisted Stem, 1930s, 5¾ x 6 In.	44.00
Cup, Whiskey Taster, Dark Swirls, Fluted, Molded, Smooth Base, 1860-90, 2½ In. Diam.	60.00
Decanter, 22⅔ In.	295.00
Lamp, Finger, Sandwich, Paneled Sides, Applied Loop Handle, 3½ In.	270.00
Pitcher, Ribbed, 6½ In.	23.00
Rose Bowl, 3½ In.	65.00
Vase, Crackle, 5 In.	85.00

AMPHORA *pieces are listed in the Teplitz category.*

ANDIRONS *and related fireplace items are included in the Fireplace category.*

ANIMAL TROPHIES, such as stuffed animals, rugs made of animal skins, and other similar collectibles made from animal, fish, or bird parts are listed in this category. Collectors should be aware of the endangered species laws that make it illegal to buy and sell some of these items. Any eagle feathers, many types of pelts or rugs (such as leopard), ivory, and many forms of tortoiseshell can be confiscated by the government. Related trophies may be found in the Fishing category. Ivory items may be found in the Scrimshaw or Ivory categories.

Antlers, Rocky Mountain Elk, 12-Point, Wooden Shield Mount	29.00
Bird Menagerie, Under Glass Globe, Wood Base, c.1880, 15½ x 13 x 8 In.	1638.00
Boar Skull, Tusks	132.00
Candlestick, Zebra Leg, Taxidermy, Brass, c.1900, 18 In., Pair	660.00
Capercaillie, On Rock, Naturalistic Setting, Taxidermy, Cased, 26 x 29 In.	708.00
Deer Rack, 10-Point, Iron Skull Plate, Rifle, Powder Horn, Hunting Bag, c.1891	226.00
Hide, Deerskin, Smoked, Scraped, c.1950, 68 x 64 In.	518.00

Amberina, Berry Set, Daisy & Button, Boat-Shaped Master, Hobbs Brockunier, c.1880, 7 Piece
$441.00

Amberina, Bowl, Inverted Thumbprint, Bucket Shape, Tab Handles, 5 In.
$147.00

Amberina, Pitcher, Tankard, Amber Reeded Handle, 9⅛ In.
$230.00

American Encaustic Tiling Company, Plaque, Autumn, 4 Seasons Series, Blue Glaze, 12 x 18 In.
$1800.00

Animation, Cel,
Jiminy Cricket,
Disney, c.1950, 7¼ x 3 In.
$248.00

TIP

Date Mickey Mouse
from his appearance.
He has changed in
the 60 years since
his introduction in
Steamboat Willie.
Originally, he didn't
have pupils in his eyes.
His legs were like pipe
cleaners, now they have
shape. He had a neck
and white inside his
ears in his middle years,
but none when young or
old. His nose has gotten
shorter and more tilted.

Animation, Cel,
Marvin The Martian & Bugs Bunny,
Numbered 56 Of 300,
Warner Brothers, 1988
$550.00

Lake Trout, Carved, Painted, Oval Painted Board, Lawrence C. Irvine, 39 x 16 In.	1553.00
Ostrich Egg, Wild Animals, Hand Painted, Wood Base, South Africa, 6½ In.	234.00
Panther Head, Wood, Carved, Open Mouth, Branch Motif Bracket, 17 x 13 In.	2703.00
Wild Boar, Snarling, Taxidermy Eyes, France, 17 In.	900.00

ANIMATION ART collectibles include cels that are painted drawings on celluloid needed to make animated cartoons shown in movie theaters or on TV. Hundreds of cels were made, then photographed in sequence to make a cartoon showing moving figures. Early examples made by the Walt Disney Studios are popular with collectors today. Original sketches used by the artists are also listed here. Modern animated cartoons are made using computer-generated pictures. Some of these are being produced as cels to be sold to collectors. Other cartoon art is listed in Comic Art and Disneyana.

Cel, Beauty & The Beast, Beauty & Lumiere, Enchanted Le, Frame, 1993, 21 x 18 In.	249.00
Cel, Bugs Bunny, 1970s	248.00
Cel, Jetsons, George & Astro, Frame, 24½ x 21 In.	300.00
Cel, Jiminy Cricket, Disney, c.1950, 7¼ x 3 In. .... *illus*	248.00
Cel, Lady & The Tramp, Cats Si & Am Pulling Fishbowl Off Piano, 1955, 6 x 8 In.	1430.00
Cel, Marvin The Martian & Bugs Bunny, Numbered 56 Of 300, Warner Brothers, 1988 ..*illus*	550.00
Cel, Mickey's Christmas Carol, Willie The Giant Holding Grapes, 1983	165.00
Cel, Peter Pan, Nana, Nurse Maid, Disney, 1953, 6 x 8 In. .... *illus*	495.00
Cel, Pink Panther, Snowdrift, 7 x 10 In.	150.00
Cel, Rescuers, Image Of Madame Medusa, 1977, 8½ x 12 In.	85.00
Cel, Sylvester & Pepe Le Pew, Warner Brothers, 1954 .... *illus*	1430.00
Cel, Wyle E. Coyote, Serving Up An Exploding Tennis Ball	715.00
Drawing, Dognappers, Mickey Mouse On Motorcycle, Officer Donald Duck, 1934	220.00
Drawing, Mickey's Gala Premiere, 1933, 6 x 11 In.	385.00
Drawing, Mickey's Service Station, Mickey, Goofy, Donald, 1935	1100.00
Drawing, Moth & The Flame, 1937	550.00
Drawing, Mother Goose Goes Hollywood, 1938	1320.00
Drawing, Pinocchio, Geppetto's Shelves Loaded With Toys, 1940	330.00
Drawing, Pinocchio, Stromboli Throws Pinocchio In Birdcage, 1940	1210.00
Drawing, Red Hot Riding Hood, 1943, 7½ x 3 In.	193.00
Drawing, Steeplechase, 1933	2200.00

APPLE PEELERS *are listed in the Kitchen category under Peeler, Apple.*

ARC-EN-CIEL is the French word for rainbow. A pottery factory named Arc-en-ciel was founded in Zanesville, Ohio, in 1903. The company made art pottery for a short time, then became the Brighton Pottery in 1905.

Vase, 4 Vignettes, Raised Figures, Gray, Green Matte Glaze, 4½ In.	179.00

ARCHITECTURAL antiques include a variety of collectibles, usually very large, that have been removed from buildings. Hardware, backbars, doors, paneling, and even old bathtubs are now wanted by collectors. Pieces of the Victorian, Art Nouveau, and Art Deco styles are in greatest demand.

Baluster, Iron, Guaranty Bldg., Buffalo, N.Y., Yale & Towne Mfg., 1896, 26 x 11 In.	1200.00
Birdhouse, Mailbox Shape, Bird Figure, Painted, Black, Red, Willie Massey, 12 x 10¾ In.	201.00
Bracket, Copper, Verdigris, Classical, Scroll Form, Acanthus Leaf, 31 x 17 In., Pair	1410.00
Bracket, Walnut, Carved Eagle, Glass Eye, 13½ x 14 In.	431.00
Bracket Shelf, Giltwood, French Regency, Carved, Stylized Scallop, Scrolls, 20 In.	1680.00
Corbel, Hardwood, Carved, Acrobat Standing On Head, Continental, 34 x 12 In.	793.00
Door, Leaded Glass, Early 20th Century, 32 x 86 In., Pair	644.00
Door, Leaded Glass, Wood, Jacques Gruber, c.1905, 112 x 98 In., Pair	21600.00
Door, Painted, North Europe, 19th Century, 39 x 10½ In.	92.00
Door Handle, Iron, Forged, Tulip End Plate, Scrolls, Incised Line, 11 In.	83.00
Doorknob, Black Glass, Brass Shank, c.1860	63.00
Doorknob, Bronze, Oval, Buffalo, 3 x 2 In.	1495.00
Doorknob, Cast Glass, Pewter Shank, Flower Sulphide, 1860s	92.00
Doorknob, Crystal, Brass Fittings, Cambridge Glass	50.00
Doorknob, Flower, Mid 1880s	167.00
Doorknob, Geisha, c.1885	662.00
Doorknob, Glass, Octagonal, c.1850	92.00
Doorknob, Porcelain, Multicolored	98.00
Doorknob, Red Bronze, Holly, c.1890	52.00
Doorknocker, Brass, Anchor, On Shield, 8 x 6 In.	195.00

Doorknocker, Brass, Boston Terrier In Wreath, Indian, Embossed, 3⅜ x 1⅞ In.	84.00
Doorknocker, Brass, Woman Gardener, Green Dress, Hand Painted, 3 In.	275.00
Doorknocker, Bronze, Backplate, Shaped, Mounted, Early 20th Century, 10 In.	206.00
Doorknocker, Iron, 3 Roses, Tied With Bow, Oval Spiral Twist Border, No. 626, Hubley, 4 In. .	330.00
Doorknocker, Iron, Bathing Beauty, Anne Fish, Hubley, 5⅛ x 2½ In.	715.00
Doorknocker, Iron, Bird Of Paradise, Bright Colors, Art Deco Style, Oval, 3½ In.	330.00
Doorknocker, Iron, Birdhouse, No. 228, 3¾ In.	110.00
Doorknocker, Iron, Bunch Of Cherries, Leaves, No. 607, Judd Co., 3¼ In.	110.00
Doorknocker, Iron, Butterfly, Blue, White & Purple, Pink Rose, 3½ x 2⅝ In.	385.00
Doorknocker, Iron, Butterfly, Pink Roses, Painted, Waverly Studios, 3½ x 2⅝ In.	248.00
Doorknocker, Iron, Cardinal, On Branch, Cherries, Oval Base, Hubley, 5 x 3 In. ... 220.00 to 275.00	
Doorknocker, Iron, Castle, 3 Towers, Scrolled Base, Oval Backplate, Hubley, No. 680, 4 In. ..	385.00
Doorknocker, Iron, Castle, In Woods, Hubley, 3½ In.	605.00
Doorknocker, Iron, Cherries, Painted, CJO Co., 3¼ In.	165.00
Doorknocker, Iron, Cherub, Roses, Blue Ribbon, Embossed, Painted, 4¼ x 3 In.	275.00
Doorknocker, Iron, Cockatoo, On Branch, Yellow Rose, Creations Co., 3¾ x 2½ In.	83.00
Doorknocker, Iron, Colonial Man, Medallion, Waverly Studio, 4⅜ x 2⅝ In.	392.00
Doorknocker, Iron, Colonial Woman, Medallion, Waverly Studio, 4⅜ x 2⅝ In.	168.00
Doorknocker, Iron, Cottage, In Forest, Judd Co., 3½ x 2⅜ In.	193.00
Doorknocker, Iron, Dachshund, In Doghouse, Feeding Dish, CJO, 4 x 3 In.	330.00
Doorknocker, Iron, Flamenco Dancer, Spanish Woman, Fan, Red Dress, 9¾ In.	575.00
Doorknocker, Iron, Flower Basket, Wicker Basket, Medallion, Hubley, 3¾ In.	110.00
Doorknocker, Iron, Flowers, Bulbous Vase, Hubley, 3¾ x 2¼ In.	392.00
Doorknocker, Iron, Flowers, In Bulbous Black Vase, Oval Base, Hubley, 3¾ x 2¼ In.	110.00
Doorknocker, Iron, Flowers, In Splint Basket, Bow On Top, Creations Co., 3¾ x 2⅝ In.	715.00
Doorknocker, Iron, Flowers, In Wall Pocket, Shaped Base, Hubley, 4 x 2 In.	28.00
Doorknocker, Iron, French Flower Basket, Oval Base, Hubley, 3½ In.	193.00
Doorknocker, Iron, Girl, Wearing Yellow Bonnet With Flowers, Judd Co., No. 616, 4¼ x 3 In.	330.00
Doorknocker, Iron, Grandpa Rabbit, In Formal Wear, 4 In.	303.00
Doorknocker, Iron, Hand Forged, Horseshoe, Stamped Rosettes, Scroll Supports, 8¾ In. ...	825.00
Doorknocker, Iron, Ivy, In Red Basket, Hubley, 4½ In.	220.00
Doorknocker, Iron, Little Girl, Knocking On Door, Painted, G. Raynor, Hubley, 1921, 3⅝ x 2 In. .	330.00
Doorknocker, Iron, Morning Glory, Leaves, Judd Co., 3¼ x 2¾ In.	138.00
Doorknocker, Iron, Parrot, Flying Through Ring, Bow, Hubley, 3¾ x 3 In.	138.00
Doorknocker, Iron, Parrot, Green & Yellow, Perched On Ring, 3¼ x 2¾ In.	220.00
Doorknocker, Iron, Parrot, Multicolored, Perched On Tree Branch, Hubley, 4⅝ x 3 In.	83.00
Doorknocker, Iron, Parrot, On Ring, Yellow, Green, Red, Judd Co., 3 x 2¾ In.	336.00
Doorknocker, Iron, Parrot, Painted, Multicolored, Hubley, Box, 4 x 3 In.	392.00
Doorknocker, Iron, Poinsettia, White Oval Base, Judd Co., 3¼ x 3 In.	385.00
Doorknocker, Iron, Rabbit, Orange Sweater, Eating Cabbage, Oval Base, Albany, 5 In.	770.00
Doorknocker, Iron, Rooster, On Branch, Crowing, 4 x 3 In.	385.00
Doorknocker, Iron, Rooster, On Ring, Crowing, Judd Co., 3¼ x 2¾ In.	220.00
Doorknocker, Iron, Rose, Pink, Thorns, Leaves, Hand Painted, 5 In.	77.00
Doorknocker, Iron, Rose, Yellow, 3 Buds, Green Leaves, 5 x 3 In.	495.00
Doorknocker, Iron, Ship, Full Sail, Oval Rope Twist Border, Hubley, 3½ In.	83.00
Doorknocker, Iron, Ship, On High Seas, Painted, 4 In.	300.00
Doorknocker, Iron, Smiling Boy, Knocker Hangs From Ears, Painted, 3⅜ x 3½ In.	385.00
Doorknocker, Iron, Spider With Fly, Web Base, Painted, 3⅝ x 1¾ In.	1430.00
Doorknocker, Iron, Woodpecker, On Tree Trunk, Hubley, 2¾ x 3¾ In.	138.00
Doorknocker, Patinated Bronze, English Regency, Flowerheads, Rings, 4 x 5½ In., Pair	558.00
Downspout, Tin, Funnel Top, Rope Twist Band Rim, Stars, Scalloped Brace, 42 x 10 In.	230.00
Drawer Pull, Round, Lion's Head, Brass, Early 19th Century, 1¾ In, 6 Piece	823.00
Fan, Over Door, Green Paint, 65 In.	1150.00
Fence, Iron, 19th Century, 24 In., 12 Piece	478.00
Finial, Zinc, Spread Eagle, Gold Repaint, M.J. Frand Co., Camden, N.J., 35 x 19 In.	805.00
Fireplace Surround, Duquesa Rosa Marble, Louis XVI, Panel Carved, 41½ x 45 In.	2280.00
Fireplace Surround, Pine, Carved Panels, Applied Pilasters, 55 x 42 In. ....*illus*	460.00
Fireplace Surround, Tile, Dawn, Midday, Twilight, Ruth Winterbotham, 18 x 6 In., 9 Piece .	3360.00
Fretwork, Oak, Stick & Ball, Original Finish, 22 x 60 In.	360.00
Gate, Iron, Mounted Panels, Scroll Decoration, 80 x 42 In., Pair	1150.00
Gate, Wood, Iron, Eagle Shape, Cutout, Iron Straps, 24 x 27 In.	3055.00
Hinge, Wrought Iron, Stylized Ends, 21¾ In., Pair	358.00
Letter Box, Iron, Steel, U.S. Mail, Padlock, Cutler Mail Chute Co., Rochester, N.Y., 21 x 36 In.	1770.00
Mantel, American Federal, Carved Dolphins & Angel Heads, White, 1800, 67 x 40 In.	4130.00
Mantel, Cherry, Federal, Stepped Cornice, Reeded Pilasters, Half Columns, 52 x 63 In.	920.00
Mantel, Louis XV Style, Canted Ends, Scrolling Shell Carved, 42 x 53 x 7½ In.	354.00

Animation, Cel, Peter Pan, Nana, Nurse Maid, Disney, 1953, 6 x 8 In. $495.00

Animation, Cel, Sylvester & Pepe Le Pew, Warner Brothers, 1954 $1430.00

Architectural, Fireplace Surround, Pine, Carved Panels, Applied Pilasters, 55 x 42 In. $460.00

Arequipa Pottery, Vase, Purple Matte Glaze, Squeezebag Decoration At Neck, 1913, 7½ x 4 In. $8400.00

William Morris

William Morris (1834–1896), British designer, writer, and artist, was the leader of the Arts and Crafts movement in England. He preached a return to medieval traditions of craftsmanship. In 1861 he and some associates started Morris, Marshall, Faulkner & Company, a store in London. It changed its name to Morris and Company and operated from 1874 to 1940. The company designed and made home furnishings ranging from textiles and wallpaper to furniture and stained glass. Traditional methods were favored, like using woodblocks for printing wallpaper and textiles. Morris and his ideas inspired the Arts and Crafts movement in the United States and Europe.

Mantel, Variegated Marble, Bronze, Black, Red, Green, Molded Top, 5 Panels, 33 x 61 In.	5290.00
Mount, Brass Federal, Eagle, Spread Wings, 13 Stars, 1¾ x 2½ In., 9 Piece	1058.00
Mount, Brass, Liberty Head, Cast, 1 Facing Left, Other Facing Right, Early 1800s, 2¾ In., Pair	411.00
Ornament, Brass, Phoenix Rising From Ashes, Igne Vivimus, Phila., 23 x 23 In.	920.00
Ornament, Bronze, Leaf Medallion, 2 Concentric Rings, c.1925, 15¾ In.	2390.00
Ornament, Iron, Bull's Head, Shaped Scrolled Plaque, Swags, 23 x 15 In.	646.00
Ornament, Iron, Eagle, Spread Wings, 37 x 73 In.	9000.00
Ornament, Limestone, Greek Soldier In Relief, 39 x 36 In.	6900.00
Overdoor, Iron, D Shape, Scrolling, Spear Tip Design, 32 x 64 In.	690.00
Overmantel Mirror, Gilt, Regency, Classical Frieze, 3 Part, 35 x 48 In.	259.00
Overmantel Mirror, Giltwood, Carved, Arched Strapwork Crest, 79 x 64 In.	6463.00
Overmantel Mirror, Giltwood, Chippendale Style, 3 Panels, 24 x 61 In.	748.00
Overmantel Mirror, Giltwood, Classical, Floral Moldings, Beaded, 54 x 85 In.	1880.00
Overmantel Mirror, Giltwood, Continental, Pierce Carved Frame, 46½ In.	1265.00
Overmantel Mirror, Giltwood, Louis XVI Style, Crest, Scrolled Shield, 75 x 56 In.	2938.00
Overmantel Mirror, Giltwood, Molded Frame, Leaves, Flowers, c.1900, 59 x 71 In.	1840.00
Overmantel Mirror, Giltwood, Neoclassical Style, 30½ x 73¼ In.	3840.00
Overmantel Mirror, Giltwood, Plaster, Napoleon III, Carved, Wreath, 72 x 38 In.	3360.00
Overmantel Mirror, Giltwood, Renaissance Revival, Carved Crest, 69 x 51 In.	1560.00
Panel, Applied Scroll Decoration, Bull's-Eye Rosettes, White Paint, 47 x 50 In.	550.00
Plinth, Wood, Faux Marble, Applied Molding, Shaped Panels, 29¾ x 9¾ In.	1998.00
Portico, Chinese Giltwood, Lacquer, Curved Panel, Faux Bamboo, 57 x 81 In.	940.00
Roof Finial, Iron, Fireman's Axe, Gilt Paint, Wood Block Mount, 20 In.	165.00
Shelf, Hanging, Pine, 2 Tiers, Cutout Scrolled Panels, Brown Paint, 16 x 10¾ In.	1410.00
Shutter, Arched Top, Green, 31 x 47 In.	690.00
Tieback, Iron, Daisy, Blue, Yellow, White, Hubley, 2½ x 4 In., Pair	140.00
Tieback, Iron, Daisy & Mixed Flower, Signed, WS, Waverly 3 x 5½ In., Pair	224.00
Tieback, Iron, Dogwood, Pink, Yellow, White, 2¾ x 3¼ In., Pair	392.00
Tieback, Iron, Mixed Flowers, Woven Basket, Painted, 1¾ x 1½ In., 2 Pair	28.00
Tieback, Iron, Zinnia, Yellow, Signed, LVL, Candlestick Co., 2½ x 2 In., Pair	196.00
Towel Bar, Walnut, Flower, Leaves Around Mirror, Victorian, 22 In.	147.00
Valance, Carved Gilt, Multicolored, Eagle Form, 11¾ x 54 In., Pair	7800.00
Valance, Napoleon III, Gilt Lacquered, Embossed Brass, Rococo Style, 11 x 55 In., Pair	780.00
Wall Bracket, Giltwood, Demilune, Continental, 19th Century, 13¾ In., Pair	1924.00
Wall Plate, Iron, Ribbons, Flowers, Hubley	250.00

AREQUIPA POTTERY was produced from 1911 to 1918 by the patients of the Arequipa Sanatorium in Marin County, north of San Francisco. The patients were trained by Frederick Hurten Rhead, who had worked at the Roseville Pottery.

Jardiniere, Acanthus Leaves, Blue, Gray Matte Glaze, Brown Clay, 4½ x 9 In.	1800.00
Vase, Carved, Organic Design, Thick Texture, Brown To Purple Matte Glaze, Marked, 3½ In.	850.00
Vase, Purple Matte Glaze, Squeezebag Decoration At Neck, 1913, 7½ x 4 In. ....*illus*	8400.00
Vase, Ribbed, Semi Sheer, Blue, Gray Glaze, 6 x 4 In.	1800.00
Vase, Squat, Slip Trails, Spade Shape Leaves, Brown, Green Ground, 1912, 2½ x 5½ In.	2520.00
Vase, Squeezebag, Scroll Design, Textured Purple Matte Glaze, Marked, 1913, 7½ x 4 In.	7000.00
Vase, Squeezebag, Spade Shape Leaves, Yellow, Green Matte Ground, c.1912, 8 x 4 In.	9600.00
Vase, Stylized Brown Blossoms, Gray Brown Ground, 3½ x 3 In.	1200.00

ARGY-ROUSSEAU, *see G. Argy-Rousseau category.*

ARITA is a port in Japan. Porcelain was made there from about 1616. Many types of decorations were used, including the popular Imari designs, which are listed under Imari in this book.

Charger, Fan, Cranes, Flowering Branches, Brocade, 18½ In. Diam	384.00
Charger, Multicolored Landscape, Blue Border, Early 1900s, 15¾ In.	73.00
Dish, Bird & Lion Design, Blue, White, 19th Century, 7¼ In.	192.00
Jardiniere, Birds, Flowers, Withing Lappet, Mollo Borders, Blue, White, 13 x 18 In.	174.00
Plate, Landscape Center, Chrysanthemum Form, Blue, White, c.1800, 7 In.	127.00
Vase, Shishi & Phoenix, Temple Form, Shaped Rim, Blue, White, Late 19th Century	270.00

ART DECO, or Art Moderne, a style started at the Paris Exposition of 1925, is characterized by linear, geometric designs. All types of furniture and decorative arts, jewelry, book bindings, and even games were designed in this style. Additional items may be found in the Furniture category or in various glass and pottery categories, etc.

Bowl, Footed, Blue Overlay, Blue To Clear, Overlapping Fan Pattern, c.1932, 8 In. 264.00
Bowl, Topaz Green, 2 Rows Of Faceted Panels, Polished Pontil, Marked, c.1937, 8 In. 353.00
Breakfast Set, Coz Rouge, France, 28 Piece 527.00
Cigarette Holder, 2 Women Holding Box, Green Glass, Metal Holder, 4 x 7 In. 504.00
Drink Bar, Metal, Enamel, Accessories, c.1930, 9 x 25 In. 234.00
Figurine, Dog, Lying Down, Green Glaze, Italy, 12 In. 96.00
Figurine, Woman, Dogs, Marble Plinth, Spelterware, 18 x 30 In. 1410.00
Table Set, Frost, Ribbon Ormolu Mounts, Cheekwood, Bowl, Candlesticks 200.00
Vase, Emerald Green, 14 Panel Sides, Inverted Foot, c.1915, 6⅝ In. 353.00
Vase, Frosted, Nude Woman In Relief, Marked, 11¾ x 7 In., Pair 805.00
Wall Plaque, Huntress, Great Dane, Carved Wood, Gesso, c.1935, 33 In. 478.00

ART GLASS, *see Glass-Art category.*

ART NOUVEAU is a style of design that was at its most popular from 1895 to 1905. Famous designers, including Rene Lalique and Emile Galle, produced furniture, glass, silver, metalwork, and buildings in the new style. Ladies with long flowing hair and elongated bodies were among the more easily recognized design elements. Copies of this style are being made today. Many modern pieces of jewelry can be found. Additional Art Nouveau pieces may be found in Furniture or in various glass categories.

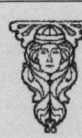

Bowl, Butterfly, Ruffled Edges, Butterfly Handles, c.1900, 5¾ x 4 In. 280.00
Plate, Stylized Gilt, 9¾ In., 12 Piece 96.00
Tray, Dried Butterfly Wings Mounted Under Glass, 10 x 18 In. 375.00
Vase, Bronzed Silver Plated, Lily Form, Trumpet Form, Pair, 14½ In. 143.00
Vase, Green, Sterling Silver Overlay, Flared, Footed, c.1910, 14 In. 890.00

ART POTTERY, *see Pottery-Art*

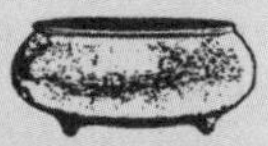

ARTS & CRAFTS was a design style popular in American decorative arts from 1894 to 1923. In the 1970s collectors began to rediscover Mission furniture, art pottery, metalwork, linens, and light fixtures from this period. The interest has continued. Today everything from this era is collectible, including jewelry, graphics, and silverware. Additional items may be found in the Furniture category and other categories.

Desk Set, Copper & Silver, Inkwell, Stamp Box, Blotter, c.1912, 3 Piece 206.00
Pitcher, Crimped Rim, Black Accent, Black Linework, Arthur Stone, 4¼ In. 294.00
Tray, Metal, Hammered Finish, Piecrust Edge, Incised Vine, Raised Buds, 18 In. 75.00
Vase, Bulbous, Red Clay, Stylized Design, Brown, Caramel, Matte Glaze, c.1925, 3 In. 382.00

AURENE

AURENE glass was made by Frederick Carder of New York about 1904. It is an iridescent gold, blue, green, or red glass, usually marked *Aurene* or *Steuben*.

Atomizer, Blue, Gold, 5⅝ In. 690.00
Bonbon, Gold, Footed, Scalloped Rim, 3 Reeded Feet, Steuben, Marked, 5 In. 690.00
Bonbon, Gold Iridescent, Scalloped Rim, Engraved, 1⅝ x 4⅞ In. 620.00
Bowl, Blue, Cupped, 8⅞ In. 633.00
Bowl, Floral, Gold, Oval, 8 Pinched-Loop Bud Holders At Rim, 6½ In. 945.00
Bowl, Gold, 10 In. 900.00
Bowl, Gold, Marked, 3¼ In. 850.00
Bowl, Gold, Rose, Marked, 2¼ x 5 In. 650.00
Bowl, Gold Over Calcite Glass, Ruffled Edge, Steuben, 9½ x 3¼ In. 1100.00
Candlestick, Blue, Twisted Stem, Flattened Rim, 8 In. 575.00
Cologne, Blue, Melon Ribbed, 3 Reeded Scrolled Feet, Flattened Stopper, 5 In. 2588.00
Compote, Gold, Magenta & Blue Interior Highlights, Inscribed, 1⅞ x 7¾ In. 164.00
Compote, Gold, Marked, 10 In. 450.00
Compote, Gold, Marked, 2½ In. 400.00
Cordial, Gold, Pinch-Sided, Steuben, 2¾ In. 230.00
Darner, Blue, 7 x 2½ In. 875.00
Dish, Gold, Footed, Marked, 5⅜ In. 675.00
Finger Bowl, Gold, 3 x 5 In. 450.00
Finger Bowl, Underplate, Gold, Iridescence, Marked Aurene 818, Steuben, 6 In. 995.00
Glass, Wine, Gold, Marked, 3¾ In. 375.00
Goblet, Gold, Twisted Stem, Marked, 6¼ In. 800.00
Jar, Potpourri, Blue, Marked, 6⅜ In. 2650.00
Nappy, Gold, Tricornered, Pinched Handle, 2⅜ x 3¾ In. .... *illus* 633.00
Perfume Bottle, Blue, c.1910, 3¼ In. 293.00

Arts and Crafts
The Arts and Crafts movement started in England. It encouraged hand crafts and simple construction. The English ideas influenced American designers from about 1875 to 1930, then went out of fashion. Collectors rediscovered the style in the 1970s.

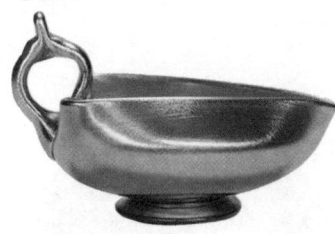

Aurene, Nappy, Gold, Tricornered, Pinched Handle, 2⅜ x 3¾ In.
$633.00

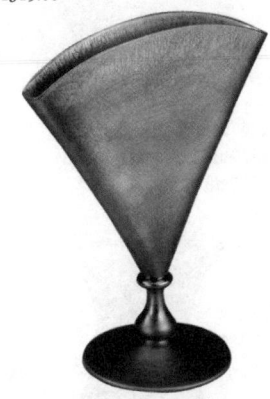

Aurene, Vase, Fan, Blue, Baluster Stem, Disc Foot, 1925, 11½ In.
$1315.00

TIP
Leave a small air space between the wall and the back of a painting to allow air to flow. 'Bumpers' to put on the back of pictures are available at frame shops.

Aurene, Vase, Gold, Ribbed, Ruffled Edge, Footed, 10¼ In. $978.00

Aurene, Vase, Gold, Shouldered, 12 In. $1955.00

Aurene, Vase, Green, Platinum Pulled Hearts & Flowers, Trailing Blue & Platinum Vines, 7½ In. $4025.00

Punch Cup, Booted, Gold, Marked, 3¼ In.	560.00
Vase, Fan, Blue, Baluster Stem, Disc Foot, 1925, 11½ In. ....*illus*	1315.00
Vase, Flower, Gold Over Calcite, Pink Highlights, 6¼ In.	975.00
Vase, Gold, Baluster, Polished Pontil, Marked, 14¼ In.	1528.00
Vase, Gold, Flared Rim, Narrow Neck, Tapered, 5⅝ In.	353.00
Vase, Gold, Ribbed, Ruffled Edge, Footed, 10¼ In. ....*illus*	978.00
Vase, Gold, Shouldered, 12 In. ....*illus*	1955.00
Vase, Gold Iridescent, Ribs, 4¼ In.	300.00
Vase, Green, Platinum Pulled Hearts & Flowers, Trailing Blue & Platinum Vines, 7½ In. *illus*	4025.00
Vase, Mold Blown, Cobalt Blue Aurene Flashed, Cased White Inside, 5½ x 3¾ In.	105.00
Vase, Red, White & Gold, Drag Loop & Feather, Marked, 9¾ In. ....*illus*	40250.00
Vase, Stump, Blue, 3 Prongs, Marked, 6⅛ x 4½ In.	1900.00
Vase, Trumpet, Calcite, Gold, 6¼ In.	750.00
Vase, Trumpet, Gold Iridescent, Marked, 8¼ In.	475.00

AUSTRIA *is a collecting term that covers pieces made by a wide variety of factories. They are listed in this book in categories such as Kauffmann, Royal Dux, or Porcelain.*

AUTO parts and accessories are collectors' items today. Gas pump globes and license plates are part of this specialty. Prices are determined by age, rarity, and condition. Signs and packaging related to automobiles may also be found in the Advertising category. Lalique hood ornaments will be listed in the Lalique category.

Ad, AC Fuel Pumps, Eddie Rickenbacker, c.1951, 5¼ x 12¼ In.	9.00
Air Pump, ECO, Air Meter	600.00
Ashtray, Champion Sparkplug, Sterling Silver, Square, 1930s	264.00
Badge, Texaco, Cap, Cloisonne, Enamel, Green, Red, White, Black, 2¾ x 2¼ In.	267.00
Badge, Texaco, Employee, Red Star, Cloisonne, Enamel, 2⅛ x 1¼ In.	165.00
Bank, Havoline, Countertop Display, Plastic, 20 In.	17.00
Clock, Ford, Aztec, Neon, 1946, 18 In.	1760.00
Clock, Mohawk Tires, Indian, Neon, 8-Sided, 19 x 19 In.	800.00
Clock, Quaker State Oil, Neon, Spinner, 22 In.	750.00
Clock, Wolf's Head Motor Oil, Neon, Rectangular	1750.00
Creamer, Mobiloil, Pegasus In Shield, 1960s, 3¼ In.	50.00
Dash Cluster, Chevrolet, 1957 Model, Die Cast, Cast Iron, 14½ In.	165.00
Display, AC Spark Plug, Countertop, Black, Red, Yellow, 18 In.	88.00
Display, AC Spark Plug, Birdcage, Pressed Steel, Original Spark Plugs, 15 In.	330.00
Display, ANCO, Windshield Wiper, Countertop, Original Booklets, Supplies, 17 In.	110.00
Display, Devil Grip, Tire Tube Patches, Red, Yellow, Tin, 24 x 10 In.	2640.00
Display, Firestone, Antifreeze, 21 x 21 In.	6.00
Display, Havoline Oil, Wire Carrier, Metal, 8 Bottles, Qt., 1926, 10 x 14½ x 19 In.	1066.00
Display, Mobiloil A, Red, Yellow, Metal, Tin, 4 Bottles, Gargoyle, 1920s, 10 x 19 x 21 In.	1120.00
Display, Oilzum Motor Oil, If Motors Could Speak, Orange, Black, Metal, 43 x 17 x 15 In.	1456.00
Display, Sunoco Motor Oil, Mercury Made, Yellow, Blue, 3 Carriers, 18 Bottles, Metal, 28 x 28 In.	3080.00
Display Rack, Packard, Battery Cable, Wall Mounted, 21 x 10 In.	99.00
Doll, Texaco, Buddy L, Station Attendant, Original Tin Case, 13 In.	143.00
Eco Tireflator, Texaco, 50 In.	990.00
End Table, Engine Block, Glass Top, Ceramic, Rubber Hoses, Spark Plug Wires, 26 In.	880.00
Gas Can, Sinclair, White, Embossed, 5 Gal.	28.00
Gas Can, Sunoco, Yellow, Blue, 10 Gal.	22.00
Gas Pump, Harley-Davidson, Black, Red, 74 In.	715.00
Gas Pump, Harley-Davidson, Glass Globe, Black, Orange, White, 60 x 26 In.	5244.00
Gas Pump, Mobilgas, National Model A38	2900.00
Gas Pump, Mobilgas Special, Martin & Schwartz, Computing Gas	2250.00
Gas Pump, Polly Gas, Pittsburgh, Small Clock Face, Parrot	4000.00
Gas Pump, Sinclair Dino, Bennett Co., 70 In.	1100.00
Gas Pump, Texaco Wayne, Model 576, 2-Sided, Milk Glass Globe, 1925, 80 In.	3735.00
Gas Pump, Wayne Roman, Column, Model 492	11000.00
Gas Pump Globe, American Glass, Red, White, Blue, Gill Body, 13⅝ In.	728.00
Gas Pump Globe, Buffalo Gasoline, Buffalo, 13½ In.	2250.00
Gas Pump Globe, Calso Gasoline, California Oil Co., Red, White, Blue, Plastic, 13⅝ In.	280.00
Gas Pump Globe, Clark Gas, Porcelain Glass, Wide Body, 13½ In.	121.00
Gas Pump Globe, Crown Oil Gas, Red, White, Blue, Gill Body, 13⅝ In. ....*illus*	392.00
Gas Pump Globe, D-X Diamond Motor Fuel, 13½ In., 3 Piece	121.00
Gas Pump Globe, Esta Motor Fuel, Red, White, Blue, Gill Body, 13⅝ In.	672.00
Gas Pump Globe, Fleet-Wing Golden, Bird, White, Red, Blue, Yellow, Red Hull, 13½ In.	1904.00

Gas Pump Globe, Galtex Pale Filtered Motor Oils, Etched	1300.00
Gas Pump Globe, Independent Home Gasoline, Green, White, 15 In.	10000.00
Gas Pump Globe, Mobilgas, Red, White, Blue, Metal Body, 17 In.	616.00
Gas Pump Globe, Shell, Red, White, Shell, 18 In.	336.00
Gas Pump Globe, Sinclair Diesel, Green, White, Plastic, 13⅝ In.	560.00
Gas Pump Globe, Sinclair Dino Gasoline, White, Red, Green, Glass, 13½ In. ....*illus*	392.00
Gas Pump Globe, Sinclair H-C Gasoline, White, Red, Green, Glass, 16½ x 14½ In.	392.00
Gas Pump Globe, Smith-O-Lene Ethyl Grade Gasoline, Airplane	5250.00
Gas Pump Globe, Speedway Gas & Oils, Better Gas, Car, 13 In.	1800.00
Gas Pump Globe, Standard Oil, Flame, Red, Yellow, 20½ In.	495.00
Gas Pump Globe, Standard Oil, Red Crown, 17 x 16 In.	660.00
Gas Pump Globe, Super Shell, Etched	2250.00
Gas Pump Globe, Texaco, Black T, Metal	5750.00
Gas Pump Globe, Texaco, Glass, 16 x 18 x 36 In.	578.00
Gas Pump Globe, Texaco, Star, Red, Green, Black, White, 13½ In.	560.00
Gas Pump Globe, Texaco Sky Chief, Green Globe, Black Band, Red, White, Gill Body, 14 In.	4200.00
Gas Pump Globe, Tydol Flying A Kerosene, Red, White, Black, 13⅝ In.	672.00
Gas Pump Globe, White Flash, Glass, Pressed Steel, Brass, 10 In.	3080.00
Gas Pump Globe, White Flash, Plastic, Pressed Steel, Wood Base, 21½ In.	17.00
Gas Pump Plate, Flying A Gasoline, Porcelain, Round, 10 In.	121.00
Gas Pump Plate, Gulf, Kerosene, 9 x 11 In.	39.00
Gas Pump Plate, Gulf Diesel, Porcelain, Round, 11 In.	121.00
Gas Pump Plate, Gulfpride Outboard Motor Oil, Porcelain, 10 x 8 In.	770.00
Gas Pump Plate, Sign, Gulf, Marine, Porcelain, 9 x 11 In.	110.00
Gauge, Gas Per Mile, 1960 Ford Falcon Test Drive, Cast Aluminum, Glass, Suction Cups	75.00
Grill, Rolls-Royce, Stainless Steel, Chrome Mascot, c.1950, 24 x 26 In.	1463.00
Hood Ornament, Nash, Chrome, Deco Woman Shape, Petty, 1951-55, 11 In.	108.00
License Plate, Arizona, 1933, Embossed Copper On Black Ground	55.00
License Plate, Arizona, 1933, PP43, Embossed, Copper, 5½ x 10¼ In.	55.00
License Plate, California, 1916, Blue On White Porcelain	300.00
License Plate, Holder, John F. Kennedy For President, White Ground, Green Letters, 1960	310.00
License Plate, Pennsylvania, 1907, Porcelain, White Letters, Orange Ground, 8 x 6½ In.	345.00
License Plate, Pennsylvania, 1932, Black On Yellow	45.00
License Plate, Puerto Rico, 1965, Yellow On Black	20.00
License Plate Attachment, Curtiss Wright, Gold, Blue, Embossed, 4¼ x 11 In.	312.00
License Plate Attachment, Smith Flying Service, Learn To Fly, Metal, 4½ x 10 In.	605.00
Matchbook, 1958 Buick, Red Convertible On Cover	12.00
Neon Light, BF Goodrich, Ford, 1932, Fiberglass Insert, 28 In.	303.00
Oil Can, Invincible, Ship, Lighthouse, Oil Well, Tin Lithograph, 9¼ x 6¼ In.	660.00
Oil Can, Iroquois Motor Oil, Pennsylvania, Red, Yellow, Tin Lithograph, Qt., 5½ x 4 In.	408.00
Oil Can, Mobiloil, Heavy Medium Grade Motor Oil, 5 Gal., 15 In.	66.00
Oil Can, Tankar Special Motor Oil, Railroad Tanker Car, Red, Black, White, 2 Gal.	143.00
Oil Pump, Texaco, Exterior Pump, Green Paint, Decal, 55 In.	121.00
Oil Tank, Harley-Davidson, Pressed Steel, Cast Iron, 59 x 29 In.	303.00
Ornament, Radiator Neck, Spirit Of St. Louis, 7 Flags, c.1927	750.00
Pail, Texaco, Barns, Farm Buildings, Factories, Tin Lithograph, 10 Lb., 5¾ x 7¾ In.	55.00
Pennant, Indianapolis 500 Auto Race, Red Border, Green Ground, Felt, 1914	300.00
Pin, Buick's The Buy, Anthony Buick, 1936, 2 In.	92.00
Pin, Chevrolet, Try It, Lithograph, 1930s, ⅞ In.	49.00
Pin, I Am A Buick Man, Celluloid, 1930s, 1½ In.	45.00
Pin, Ride The Green Lane Of Safety In A New Hudson, 1939, 1¼ In.	55.00
Playing Card Holder, Automobile Co., Locomobile, Cards, Celluloid, 1908, 1¼ x 2¼ In.	103.00
Rack, Comment Card, Amoco, Pressed Steel, Celluloid, Service Station Shape, 11½ In.	11.00
Rack, Map, Mobil Gas, Early Maps, Tour Guide, Iron, Rubber Coating, Tin, 13 In.	132.00
Rack, Mobiloil, World Best Known Quality Motor Oil, Pegasus, 12 Cans, Handle	500.00
Rack, Mobiloil Artic, Fil-Pruf, 5 Bottles, Handle	650.00
Rack, Ohio Oil Co., Metal, 16 Linco Marathon Bottles	600.00
Rack, Oil, Mobiloil, Pegasus Horse, Sidewalk, Pressed Steel, 26 In.	413.00
Rack, Richlube Motor Oil, Prolong The Life Of Your Engine, Sliding Door, Hold 28 Cans	500.00
Service Chart, Mobiloil, Gargoyle Graphic, 19½ x 38½ In.	523.00
Sign, AC Oil Filter Service, Tin, Flange, 12 x 13 In.	55.00
Sign, Amalie Motor Oil, 2-Sided, Porcelain, 20 x 28 In.	55.00
Sign, Amoco, Battery Cable, Pressed Steel, 17 In.	55.00
Sign, Atlantic, Metal, Atlantic White Flash, 13 x 17½ In.	248.00
Sign, Atlantic Refining Co., Porcelain, Automobile Gasoline For Sale Here, 30½ x 20 In.	385.00
Sign, Buick Authorized Service, Valve In Head, Porcelain, 2-Sided, 42 In. Diam.	8800.00

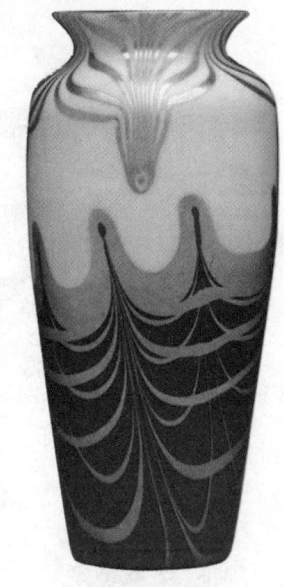

Aurene, Vase, Red,
White & Gold, Drag Loop & Feather,
Marked, 9¾ In.
$40250.00

Auto, Gas Pump Globe,
Crown Oil Gas, Red, White, Blue,
Gill Body, 13⅝ In.
$392.00

Auto, Gas Pump Globe,
Sinclair Dino Gasoline,
White, Red, Green, Glass, 13½ In.
$392.00

Auto, Sign, Mobiloil,
Flying Pegasus, Red,
White Trim, Cookie Cutter,
93 x 69 In.
$2970.00

Auto, Sign, Pennzoil,
Sidewalk, Lollipop Shape, 60 In.
$770.00

Auto, Sign, Sinclair,
H-C Gasoline, Porcelain,
2-Sided, 48 In.
$935.00

Sign, Cadillac, Authorized Service, 2-Sided, Porcelain, Round, 42 In.	3740.00
Sign, Chevrolet Corvette Roadster, 1958, Vinyl Mesh, 15 x 45 In.	598.00
Sign, Chevrolet Service, Porcelain, 1949, 80 x 36 In.	605.00
Sign, Chevrolet Superior Service, Neon, Blue, Yellow, White, Porcelain, 2-Sided, 42 x 48 In.	20900.00
Sign, Chevrolet Used Cars, Blue, White Letters, 2-Sided, Light-Up, 28 x 42 In.	7040.00
Sign, Conoco, Do Not Oil While In Motion, Porcelain, 15 x 8 In.	165.00
Sign, Defiance Spark Plugs, Engineered For Replacement, Red, Black, 2-Sided, 10 x 12½ In.	1210.00
Sign, Dynafuel, Yellow, Black, Die Cut, Porcelain, Diamond Shape, 12 x 8 In.	248.00
Sign, Esso, Elephant, Porcelain, 24 x 12 In.	231.00
Sign, Fleet-Wing Ethyl, Tin, Flange, 1930-40, 18 x 18 In.	550.00
Sign, Ford, Genuine Parts, 2-Sided, Porcelain, Oval, Bracket, 24 x 16 In.	715.00
Sign, Ford V-8 Genuine Parts, Porcelain, Die Cut, 2-Sided, 36 x 28 In.	6600.00
Sign, Francisco Auto Heater, Old Car In Landscape, Tin, 18 x 40 In.	1155.00
Sign, General Gasoline & Lubricants, Porcelain, 2-Sided, 30 In.	4500.00
Sign, Georgia-Carolina Oil Co., Tin, 24 x 48 In.	110.00
Sign, GMC Trucks, Neon, Porcelain, 2-Sided, 45 x 72 In.	14850.00
Sign, Goodyear Tire, They Cost No More, 2-Sided, Porcelain, 19½ x 10 In.	275.00
Sign, Goodyear Tire & Rubber Co., Embossed, Tin Plated, 1899, 27½ x 39½ In.	5963.00
Sign, Gulf Gasoline, Orange, Blue, Gray, Round, Porcelain, 2-Sided, 30 In.	523.00
Sign, Gulf Gasoline, That Good Gulf Gasoline, Red, White, Blue, Porcelain, c.1940, 10 In. Diam.	290.00
Sign, Havoline, Wax Free Oil, Die Cut, Porcelain, 30 x 16 In.	275.00
Sign, Havoline Motor Oil, Wax Free, Flange, Porcelain, Flange, 20 x 12 In.	1000.00
Sign, Hood, Tires & Tubes, 2-Sided, Die Cut, Tin, 31 x 43 In.	330.00
Sign, Invincible Motor Insurance, Car, Ship With Spotlight, Tin, Britain, 1930s, 9 x 20 In.	215.00
Sign, Jayhawk Oils, Jayhawk, Tin, 36 x 24 In.	1200.00
Sign, Kaiser Service, Kaiser Approved Service, Porcelain, 2 Sided, 58 x 42 In.	220.00
Sign, Kendall Motor Oil, Guaranteed 100% Pennsylvania, Metal, 2 Sided, 24 x 10 In.	110.00
Sign, Kool Motor, Refill With Cities Service Oils, Tin, Embossed, 2-Sided, 21 x 12 In.	220.00
Sign, Michelin, Michelin Man, Tire, Blue, White, Yellow, Black, Porcelain, 1970, 33 x 14 In.	115.00
Sign, Mobiloil, Pegasus Lubster, Porcelain, Round, c.1941, 9 In.	55.00
Sign, Mobiloil, Flying Pegasus, Red, White Trim, Cookie Cutter, 93 x 69 In. .... *illus*	2970.00
Sign, Mobilfuel Diesel, Winged Horse, Red, Blue, Porcelain, Shield Shape, c.1950, 12 x 12 In.	330.00
Sign, Mobilgas, Fill Up With Mobile Gas, Porcelain, 2-Sided, Round, 36 In.	303.00
Sign, Mobiloil, 60, Winged Horse, Red, White, Blue, Shield Shape, Porcelain, Germany, 6⅜ In.	176.00
Sign, Mobiloil, Ask For, Porcelain, Gargoyle Graphic, 19½ x 24 In.	385.00
Sign, Mustang Oil, Red Center, Blue Rim, Porcelain, 2-Sided, 72 In. Diam.	12100.00
Sign, Oak Motor Oil, Summer & Winter, For All Cars, Porcelain, 2-Sided, 1920s, 26 x 17 In.	1792.00
Sign, OK Used Cars, Porcelain, Round, 36 In.	110.00
Sign, Oldsmobile GM Hydra-Matic Drive, Neon, Porcelain, 2-Sided, 35 x 102 In.	17050.00
Sign, Packard, Approved Service, 2-Sided, Porcelain, Round, 42 In.	2860.00
Sign, Pennzoil, Sidewalk, Lollipop Shape, 60 In. .... *illus*	770.00
Sign, Polarine Motor Oil, Porcelain, 59 x 28 In.	550.00
Sign, Pontiac Trail, Indian, State Of Illinois, Red, White, Blue, 24 x 13 In.	3500.00
Sign, Purol, Pure Company, Round, 2-Sided, Porcelain, 26 In.	468.00
Sign, Rand McNally, Auto Road Maps, Lithograph On Canvas, 42 x 61 In.	2800.00
Sign, Red Crown Gasoline, Crown, 2-Sided, Porcelain, 1920-30, 41 In.	1100.00
Sign, Seagull Gasoline, Porcelain, 2-Sided, 30 In.	10500.00
Sign, Shell, Gas, With Arrow, Horizontal, Tin, 48 x 12 In.	413.00
Sign, Shell Gas, Shell, Yellow, Red, Embossed, Porcelain, 48 In.	1980.00
Sign, Shell Gasoline, Diecut, Porcelain, Clamshell Shape, 41 x 42 In.	880.00
Sign, Shell Gasoline, Symbol, Enamel, 12 x 12 In.	12.00
Sign, Signal Gasoline, Traffic Light, Porcelain Pump Tag, 12 In.	750.00
Sign, Sinclair, H-C Gasoline, Porcelain, 2-Sided, 48 In. .... *illus*	935.00
Sign, Skelly Oil Co., Tagolene, Shows All Grades Of Lubrication, Self-Framed, Tin, 28 x 22 In.	440.00
Sign, Sunoco, Blue Sunoco, Blue, Yellow, Red Arrow, Die Cut, Porcelain, 18 x 22 In.	248.00
Sign, Sunray D-X Petroleum Products, Octagon, 26 x 26 In.	5000.00
Sign, Texaco, 2-Sided, Wall Mount, 24 In.	385.00
Sign, Texaco, Filling Station, Motor Oils, Porcelain, Round, 42 In.	1100.00
Sign, Texaco, Porcelain, Horizontal, No Smoking, 23 x 4 In.	121.00
Sign, Texaco, Round, Porcelain, 24 In.	358.00
Sign, Texaco Gasoline Motor Oil, Red, Black, Green, Enamel, 2-Sided, 1930s, 41 In. Diam.	1344.00
Sign, Texaco Motor Oil, Free Crankcase Service, Refill With, Enamel, 1930s, 30 x 30 In.	1064.00
Sign, Texaco Motor Oil, Petroleum Products, Enamel, Flange, 2-Sided, 23 x 18 In.	1064.00
Sign, Tydol Gasoline, Round, Porcelain, Cast Iron, 48 In. .... *illus*	605.00
Sign, U.S. Tires, Vertical, Porcelain, Red, Black, 18 x 72 In.	468.00
Sign, Union Gas, 2-Sided, Porcelain, 32 x 26 In.	775.00

Sign, United Motors Service, Orange & Blue Neon, Porcelain, Oval, 22 x 38 In.	1760.00
Sign, United Motors Service, Porcelain, 1930s, 48 In.	999.00
Sign, Veedol Motor Oil, Ask For Veedol Motor Oils, Metal, 2-Sided, Dome Shape, 22 x 28 In.	198.00
Speaker Stand, Drivein Movie, Speakers, Die Cast Pressed Steel Base, 40 In.	413.00
Street Sign, Sears Automotive, Service Area Only, Yellow, Black, St. Paul, Minn., 59 In.	2420.00
Tape Measure, Hupmobile, F.E. Bucher Garage, Celluloid, Round, 1½ In.	447.00
Tape Measure, Sible's Garage, Chandler Cleveland & Dort Cars, Celluloid, Round, 1½ In.	51.00
Tape Measure, Texaco, Texas Company, Houston, Texas, Celluloid, Round, c.1913	368.00
Thermometer, Esso, Diamond Shape, Image Of Antifreeze & Batteries, Metal, 17 x 17 In.	275.00
Thermometer, Universal Batteries, Heart Of Your Car, Tin, Box	475.00
Tire Pump, Michelin Man Figure, R. Toussaint, France, c.1928	626.00
Tube Repair Kit, Handy Andy, 25 Cans, Original Boxes, 4½ In.	28.00
Wall Decoration, 1955 Chevrolet Front, Clip Wall Mount, Fiberglass, 6 In.	550.00
Wall Sconce, Sinclair Dino, Glass Globe, Cast Iron, Plastic Sleeve, 22 In.	358.00
Weather Vane, Mobil, Pegasus, Porcelain, 19 x 38 In.	2860.00

AUTUMN LEAF pattern china was made for the Jewel Tea Company beginning in 1933. Hall China Company of East Liverpool, Ohio, Crooksville China Company of Crooksville, Ohio, Harker Potteries of Chester, West Virginia, and Paden City Pottery, Paden City, West Virginia, made dishes with this design. Autumn Leaf has remained popular and was made by Hall China Company until 1978. Some other pieces in the Autumn Leaf pattern are still being made. For more information, see *Kovels' Depression Glass & Dinnerware Price List*.

Bowl, Cereal, 6½ In.	8.00 to 12.00
Bowl, Fruit, 5½ In.	7.00
Bowl, Nesting, 3⅜ In.	12.00
Bowl, Salad, 9 In.	29.00
Bowl, Vegetable, 9 In.	20.00 to 36.00
Cake Plate, 9½ In.	25.00
Cards, Playing, Pinochle, 2 Decks, Box	225.00
Casserole, Cover, 3 x 7 In.	40.00
Coffeepot, 9 In.	46.00
Coffeepot, Aluminum Dripper, 8 Cup	110.00
Coffeepot, Electric, 8 Cup	400.00
Cookie Jar, Eva Zeisel, 7½ In.	325.00
Cookie Jar, Tootsie	325.00
Creamer, 3½ x 4 In.	15.00
Cup & Saucer, Ruffle D	11.00
Dish, Divided	110.00
Gravy Boat, Hall, Underplate, 9½ x 3½ In.	30.00 to 75.00
Jug, Ball, Ice Lip, 5½ Pt.	50.00
Jug, Rayed, 2½ Pt.	40.00
Jug, Water, Donut, Collector Club, 1991 ....*illus*	200.00
Mixing Bowl, 6 In.	18.00 to 31.00
Mixing Bowl, 7½ In.	30.00 to 40.00
Mixing Bowl, 9 In.	35.00
Mixing Bowl, Nesting, 3 Piece	125.00
Mustard Set, 3 Piece	125.00
Pitcher, Beverage, 6 In.	26.00
Pitcher, Water, Round, 7 In.	67.00
Pitt Baker, Footed, Oval, 6¾ x 5 In.	255.00
Plate, Bread & Butter, 6 In.	8.00
Plate, Dinner, 10 In.	13.00 to 17.00
Plate, Luncheon, 8 In.	9.00
Platter, 11¼ x 8¾ In.	24.00
Platter, Oval, 13½ x 10½ In.	32.00
Salt & Pepper, 5 In.	125.00
Souffle, 7¾ In.	25.00 to 30.00
Sugar, Cover	25.00
Sugar & Creamer, Cover	36.00
Teapot, 10 Cup ....*illus*	20.00
Teapot, Aladdin	75.00 to 89.00
Tidbit, Handle, 3 Tiers	125.00
Tin, Fruit Cake, 7 In.	22.00
Tumbler, Iced Tea, Anchor Hocking, 16 Oz.	6.00
Vase, Bud, 5¾ In.	275.00

Auto, Sign, Tydol Gasoline, Round, Porcelain, Cast Iron, 48 In. $605.00

TIP
When starting a dirty job like cleaning metal or refinishing pewter, try this trick. Rub your nails into a bar of soap. At cleanup time the dirt will easily come out from under the nail tips.

Autumn Leaf, Jug, Water, Donut, Collector Club, 1991 $200.00

Autumn Leaf, Teapot, 10 Cup $20.00

A

Baccarat, Basket, Amethyst, Diagonal Ribs, Gold Birds, Insects, Flowers, Metal Base, 4-Footed, 9 In. $225.00

Baccarat, Bottle Set, Amberina, Spiral Swirl, Ball Stopper, 5½, 6¼, 7¼ In., 3 Piece $605.00

Baccarat, Paperweight, Clematis, Pansies, Primrose, Star Cane Center, 3½ In. $14950.00

Baccarat, Paperweight, Millefiori, Stars, Silhouettes, Hunter, Squirrel, Monkey, 1848, 2¾ In. $4025.00

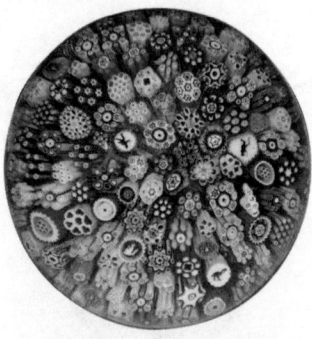

Warmer, Round	225.00
Wastebasket, 14½ x 13½ In.	275.00

AVON bottles are listed in the Bottle category under Avon.

AZALEA dinnerware was made for Larkin Company customers from 1918 to 1941. Larkin, the soap company, was in Buffalo, New York. The dishes were made by Noritake China Company of Japan. Each piece of the white china was decorated with pink azaleas.

Bonbon, 6⅝ In.	32.00
Bowl, 5¼ In.	9.00
Bowl, Fruit, Marked Noritake In Green, 5¼ In.	9.00
Bowl, Vegetable, Open Handles, 10 In.	40.00
Bowl, Vegetable, Oval, 2 Handles, 9⅜ In.	29.00
Bowl, Vegetable, Oval, 2 Handles, 10½ In.	31.00
Butter, Cover Only, Gold Finial	75.00
Butter Chip, c.1930	69.00
Butter Tub, Liner, 5⅛ In.	45.00 to 65.00
Cake Plate, Handles, 9¾ In.	45.00
Candy Jar, Cover, Gold Trim	60.00
Casserole, Cover, Gold Trim, Handles, Marked, 10 In.	50.00
Celery Dish, Open Handles, Red Stamp, 12½ In.	30.00
Cheese Dish, 6½ x 2½ In.	90.00
Creamer, 3½ In.	55.00
Cup & Saucer, Gold	20.00
Cup & Saucer, Marked Noritake, Hand Painted, Made In Japan	18.00
Dish, Mayonnaise, 3-Footed	22.00
Gravy Boat, Attached Underplate	40.00
Gravy Boat, Red M In Wreath, Tray 6 x 9 In., Boat 4 x 7½ In.	22.00
Plate, Bread & Butter, 6½ In.	9.00 to 10.00
Plate, Dinner, 9¾ In.	16.00 to 20.00
Plate, Luncheon, 8½ In., 6 Piece	54.00
Plate, Salad, 7⅞ In.	12.00
Plate, Tea, Gold, 7½ In.	10.00
Platter, Oval, 11¾ In.	24.00
Platter, Oval, 14 x 10½ In.	55.00
Relish, Divided, 1½ x 8½ x 5½ In.	65.00
Relish, Oval, 8¼ In.	20.00
Saltshaker, Gold Top, Bulbous	20.00
Saucer, Gold Trim, 5½ In.	4.00
Sugar, Lid, Gold, Green M Mark, No. 19322	13.00
Sugar & Creamer	65.00 to 135.00
Sugar Lid	20.00
Sugar Shaker, 6½ In.	137.00
Vase, Bud, Fan, Gold, Footed, 5½ In.	250.00
Whipped Cream Set, Footed, Ladle, Saucer, 5½ In., 3 Piece	60.00

BACCARAT glass was made in France by La Compagnie des Cristalleries de Baccarat, located 150 miles from Paris. The factory was started in 1765. The firm went bankrupt and began operating again about 1822. Cane and millefiori paperweights were made during the 1845 to 1880 period. The firm is still working near Paris making paperweights and glasswares.

Basket, Amethyst, Diagonal Ribs, Gold Birds, Insects, Flowers, Metal Base, 4-Footed, 9 In. *illus*	225.00
Basket, Sweetmeat, Rustic Style, Brass, Cranberry Glass, Gold Lacquer, 10¼ In.	450.00
Bottle Set, Amberina, Spiral Swirl, Ball Stopper, 5½, 6¼, 7¼ In., 3 Piece *illus*	605.00
Candelabrum, 2-Light, 13 x 9½ In.	410.00
Candelabrum, 4-Light, Silver Plated Brass, Sphere, 5 x 8¾ In., Pair	1554.00
Candelabrum, Lobed Circular Bobeches, Topaz Shaded To Garnet, Spiral, Prisms, 23½ In.	5875.00
Candlestick, Globe, Ruby Flashed, Late 19th Century, 19 In.	205.00
Decanter, Etched, Tangent Scroll Decoration, Oval, Flat Moon Stopper, Signed, 9¾ x 4 In., Pair	587.00
Figurine, Rabbit, 3 In.	117.00
Inkstand, Brilliant, Betjemanns, Star-Cut Bottom, Swirl Design, 1800s, 4½ x 5¼ In.	695.00
Inkwell, Silver Top, Swirl Star-Cut Bottom, c.1890, 3½ x 4¾ In.	375.00
Lamp, Cylinder, Stone Castle, Trees, Enameled, 9½ In.	1150.00
Paperweight, 1000-Petal Red Rose, Pansy, Purple, Yellow, Clematis, White, Faceted, 3 In.	14000.00
Paperweight, Clematis, Pansies, Primrose, Star Cane Center, 3½ In. *illus*	14950.00
Paperweight, Figural, Tortoise, Late 20th Century, 4 In.	146.00

Paperweight, Millefiori, Blue Star Carpet, Stars, Silhouettes, Dog, Deer, Goat, Swan, 1848 ..	21850.00
Paperweight, Millefiori, C-Scroll, Garlands, Red, White, Green, Blue, 3⅛ In.	600.00
Paperweight, Millefiori, Stars, Silhouettes, Hunter, Squirrel, Monkey, 1848, 2¾ In. .....*illus*	4025.00
Paperweight, Millefiori & Gridel Canes, Multicolored, Signed, B 1847, 3 In.	4250.00
Paperweight, Millefiori Mushroom & Torsade, Close Packed, 3¹⁄₁₆ In.	1600.00
Paperweight, Pansy, Bud, Leaves, White & Yellow Stardust Cane Center, 2¹³⁄₁₆ In. .....*illus*	633.00
Paperweight, Pansy, Purple & Yellow, Bud, Green Leaves & Stem, Star Cut Ground, 2¹³⁄₁₆ In.	1100.00
Paperweight, Primrose, Blue & White, Green Stem & Leaves, 3¼ In.	1150.00
Paperweight, Primrose, Red & White, Green Leaves & Stem, Faceted, 2⅞ In.	1400.00
Paperweight, Rose Cane, Pink, Trefoil Millefiori Garlands, 2⅝ In. ....*illus*	518.00
Paperweight, Strawberry, Green Stem & Leaves, Clear Star-Cut Ground, 2½ In. ....*illus*	978.00
Perfume Bottle, Guerlain Of Paris, 5¾ x 4⅛ In.	137.00
Perfume Bottle, Ybry, Desir Du Coeur, Pink Crystal, Lalique Pendant, c.1926, 4 In. ...*illus*	3960.00
Vase, Gray, White Opaline, Japanese Style, Birds On Branches, Signed, 10¼ In.	4800.00
Vase, Sauterelle, Grasshopper, Flowers, Pressed & Parcel-Satine, 8¼ x 4¾ In., Pair	1800.00
Vase, Textured, Gold Pond Lilies & Cattails, 4 Curved Sides, Cameo, Gold Foot, 11½ In. .*illus*	764.00

Baccarat, Paperweight, Pansy, Bud, Leaves, White & Yellow Stardust Cane Center, 2¹³⁄₁₆ In. $633.00

BADGES have been used since before the Civil War. Collectors search for examples of all types, including law enforcement and company identification badges. Well-known prison or law enforcement badges are most desirable. Most are made of nickel or brass. Many recent reproductions have been made.

Baggage Master, Stagecoach, 1880s, 1¾ In.	114.00
Employee, A&P, Red, 1930-40s	20.00
Identification, American Optical Co., Yellow Border, Photograph, Round, 1½ In.	29.00
Identification, Conn. Telephone & Electric, Meriden, Photograph, Round, 1940s, 1½ In. ...	51.00
Identification, International Silver Co., Black, Silver, Photograph, Round, 1940s, 1½ In. ...	29.00
Identification, Raymond Bag Co., Middletown, O., Oval, Photograph, Black Enamel Rim, 2 In. .	29.00
Police, Butte, 6-Point Star, Oro Y Plata, Metal, 1920s, 3½ In.	133.00
Police, Culver City, Captain, 6-Point Star Inside Circle, c.1920, 2½ In.	1021.00
Police, Supt. Of Traffic, Sacramento, 7-Point Star, Blue Letters, 3 In.	291.00
Taxi Driver, Red Cab Co., Boston, Metal, Cloisonne Enamel, 2¼ x 4⅛ In.	357.00
Taxi Driver, Yellow Cab Co., Shield Shape, 1920s, 2½ In.	56.00

Baccarat, Paperweight, Rose Cane, Pink, Trefoil Millefiori Garlands, 2⅝ In. $518.00

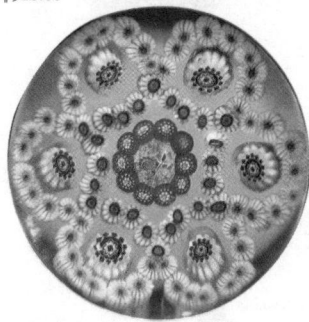

BANKS of metal have been made since 1868. There are still banks, mechanical banks, and registering banks (those that show the total money deposited on the face of the bank). Many old iron or tin banks have been reproduced since the 1950s in iron or plastic. Some old reproductions marked Book of Knowledge, John Wright, or Capron are listed. Pottery, glass, and plastic banks are also listed here. Mickey Mouse and other Disneyana banks are listed in Disneyana. We have added the M numbers based on *The Penny Bank Book: Collecting Still Banks* by Andy and Susan Moore and the R numbers based on *Coin Banks by Banthrico* by James L. Redwine.

Andy Gump, Cast Iron, Arcade, 1928, M 217, 4½ In.	385.00
Apple, Branch & Leaf, Cast Iron, Green, Brown, Kyser & Rex, M 1621, 5 x 5¼ x 3 In.	2128.00 to 3300.00
Aunt Jemima, Standing, Apron, Cast Iron, M 168	185.00
Bank Building, Eagle Finial, Cast Iron, Painted, 19th Century, 5¼ x 4¼ In.	2220.00
Bank Building, State, Cast Iron, Brown, Gold, Kenton, c.1900, M 1078, 8 x 7 x 5½ In.	1120.00
Baseball, Held Up By 3 Bats, Cast Iron, Silver & Red Paint, Hubley, M 1608, 5¼ In.	770.00
Baseball Player, Bat On Shoulder, Cast Iron, Red Cap, Gold Paint, A.C. Williams, M 18, 5¾ In. .	385.00
Beaky, At Barrel, Key, Metal, Moss, Box, M 296, 5¾ x 4⅛ In.	280.00
Beaky, At Tree, Key, Metal, Moss, Box, M 303, 5¾ x 4⅛ In.	336.00
Bear, Honey Pot, Cast Iron, Brown, White, Yellow, M 717, 6½ In.	224.00
Bear, Stealing Pig, Cast Iron, Gold Overall Paint, M 693, 5 In.	440.00
Beehive, Industry Shall Be, 6-Sided Base, Cast Iron, John Harper Ltd., England, M 686, 4⅛ In.	413.00
Billy Can, Cast Iron, Gold Paint Overall, M 79, c.1910, 5⅛ In.	715.00
Black Men Playing Baseball, J. & E. Stevens, 9¾ In.	5885.00
Boat, Battleship Maine, Cast Iron, Japanned, Grey Iron Casting, M 1440, 4⅝ x 4½ In. ..*illus*	316.00
Boat, Steamboat, Cast Iron, Arcade, M 1460, 1926, 7½ In.	187.00
Bugs Bunny, At Tree, Key, White Metal, Moss, Box, M 278, 5¾ x 5½ In.	280.00
Building, Belfry, Cast Iron, Japanned, Kenton, M 1233, 8 In. ....*illus*	1610.00
Building, Church, Bell Tower, Wood, Multicolored Paint, 9¼ In.	1176.00
Building, House, Penny, Cast Iron, Front Porch, Young Boy & Girl, 3¾ x 3⅜ In.	94.00
Building, House, Pewter, Impressed Roof, Ralph Long Warrington, 4¼ x 3½ In.	28.00
Building, House, Tin, Painted, Green, Silver Speckles, Stamped, H. Wagner, 4⅝ x 4 In.	22.00
Building, Independence Hall, Pressed Glass, Tin Base, M 1207, 7¼ x 3½ In.	253.00
Building, Independence Hall Tower, Cast Iron, Multicolored, Enterprise, M 1205, 9½ In.	5600.00

Baccarat, Paperweight, Strawberry, Green Stem & Leaves, Clear Star-Cut Ground, 2½ In. $978.00

Baccarat, Perfume Bottle, Ybry, Desir Du Coeur, Pink Crystal, Lalique Pendant, c.1926, 4 In. $3960.00

Baccarat, Vase, Textured,
Gold Pond Lilies & Cattails,
4 Curved Sides, Cameo,
Gold Foot, 11½ In.
$764.00

Bank, Boat, Battleship Maine,
Cast Iron, Japanned Finish,
Grey Iron Casting,
M 1440, 4⅝ x 4½ In.
$316.00

Bank, Building, Belfry,
Cast Iron, Japanned, Kenton,
M 1233, 8 In.
$1610.00

Building, Independence Hall Tower, Centennial, Cast Iron, Phila., Enterprise, M 1202, 9½ In.	382.00
Building, Palace, Painted, Key Lock Trap, Cast Iron, Ives, c.1885, M 1116, 7½ x 8 In.	8960.00
Building, State, Cast Iron, Arcade, M 1083, 3 In.	110.00
Cannon, Cast Iron, Green, Red Spoke Wheels, Hubley, c.1914, M 1425, 6⅞ In.	1320.00
Captain Kidd, Standing With Shovel By Stump, Cast Iron, Painted, M 38, 5 x 4 In. ...*illus*	288.00
Car, Armored, Cast Iron, Red, Gold Wheels, Cannons, A.C. Williams, M 1424, 6¹¹⁄₁₆ In.	5500.00
Car, Buick, Cast Iron, Nickel Driver, Green, White, Black, Original Tires, 8 In.	1344.00
Car, Packard, Cast Metal, Banthrico, 1953, R 401, 8 In.	169.00
Car, Yellow Cab, Driver, Cast Iron, Arcade, M 1489, 8 In.	960.00
Car, Yellow Cab, Driver, Yellow, Black, White, Steel Wheels, Sheet Metal Trap, M 1493, 7⅞ In.	2128.00
Car, Yellow Cab, Rexoline Oil Co., Cast Iron, Yellow, Black, White, Arcade	2800.00
Casper, Ceramic, Painted, Glazed, American Bisque Co., Early 1960s, 8 In.	185.00
Cat, Standing, Long Tail, Cast Iron, Black, M 369, 4½ In. ...*illus*	1210.00
Celluloid, Allentown Trust Co., Save A Coin A Day, Oval, 1940s	126.00
Cleveland Indians, Chief Wahoo, Hand Painted, Pottery, Marked, Stanford Pottery, 8 In.	198.00
Clock, World Time, Nickel, Paper Lithograph Insert, Arcade, 1926, M 1539, 4⅛ In.	220.00
Coronation, Silhouettes, Iron, Japanned, Sydenham & McOustra, M 1319, 6½ x 7½ In. ..*illus*	403.00
Cow, Holstein, Cast Iron, Arcade, 1931, M 544, 4½ In.	330.00
Daffy Duck, At Barrel, Metal, Key, Moss, M 285, 5¾ x 4¼ In.	252.00
Devil, 2 Faces, Cast Iron, Red & Black Paint, A.C. Williams, M 31, 4¼ In.	825.00
Dog, Boston Terrier, Cast Iron, M 421, 5 x 5 In.	147.00
Dog, Bulldog, Cast Iron, Arcade, 1926, 4 In.	248.00
Dog, Bulldog, Cast Iron, White, Pink, Blue, 4 In.	1568.00
Dog, Fido, On Flower Pillow, Cast Iron, White, Black, Red, Yellow, Green, Hubley, M 443, 7⅜ In.	784.00
Dog, Puppo, Cast Iron, Black & White, Painted Bee, Hubley, M 442, 5 In. ...*illus*	330.00
Dog, Spaniel, Cast Iron, White, Black, Trap, Hubley, M 418, 3¾ x 6 In.	560.00
Dog, Wirehaired Terrier, Cast Iron, White, Brown, Red Collar, Hubley, M 422, 5¾ x 4⅝ In.	308.00
Dordrecht, Angels On Rock, Hinged Door, Cast Iron, Holland, Late 1800s, 7¼ In.	358.00
Dower Chest, Brass, Decorated Arched Panels, A.B. Fenster, Lancaster, Penn., 2 x 3¾ In.	28.00
Duck, Key Locked Trap, Cast Iron, White, Yellow, Green, Hubley, M 624, 4¾ In.	392.00
Duck On Tub, Top Hat, Umbrella, Save For A Rainy Day, Cast Iron, Hubley, M 616, 5⅜ In.	280.00
Dutch Boy, On Barrel, Cast Iron, White, Yellow, Gray, Brown, Hubley, M 180, 5⅝ In.	168.00
Dutch Girl, Holding Flowers, Cast Iron, White, Pink, Yellow, Orange, Hubley, M 183, 5¼ In.	112.00
Eagle, Old Abe, Shield, Cast Iron, Silver Color, c.1880, M 676, 3⅞ In.	935.00
Elmer Fudd, At Barrel, White Metal, Moss, Box, M 306, 5¾ x 5½ In.	112.00
Elsie The Cow, White, Metal, 1950s, 6½ In.	168.00
Football Player, Football Tucked Under Arm, Cast Iron, Gold Paint, A.C. Williams, M 11, 5 In.	330.00
Fremlins Beers, Elephant, Red Blanket, Molded Plastic, Slot At Top, 1950s	115.00
Frowning Face, Cast Iron, Hanging, M 12, 5⅝ In.	715.00
Gas Pump, Cast Iron, Red, Gold, Arcade, M 1485, 5¹¹⁄₁₆ In.	330.00 to 504.00
General Sheridan, On Horse, Cast Iron, 1926, M 50, 6 In.	303.00
Give Me A Penny, Black Man, Cast Iron, Red Collar, Lips, Gold Suspenders, Hubley, M 166, 5½ In.	448.00
Give Me A Penny, Black Man, Cast Iron, Red Shirt, Lips, Turnpin, Hubley, M 167, 5½ In.	448.00
Globe, Cast Iron, Painted, Arcade, 1926, 4¾ In.	248.00
Globe, Hinged Door, Combination Lock, Claw Foot, Electroplated, Embossed, Kenton, M 812, 5 In.	193.00
Globe, On Arc, Cast Iron, Red, Grey Iron Casting, M 789, 5¼ In.	224.00
Globe, Tin, Gene Bosch, Chein, M 798, 4⅜ In.	95.00
Golliwog, Aluminum, John Harper, M 86, 6 In.	125.00
Golliwog, Cast Iron, Red Pants & Bow, Black Jacket, Face, England, c.1890, M 85, 6½ In.	303.00
Graf Zeppelin, Cast Iron, Silver, A.C. Williams, M 1428, 6½ In.	175.00
Horse, Beauty, Cast Iron, Arcade, c.1912, M 532, 4⅛ x 4¾ In.	125.00
Horse, Cast Iron, Arcade, 1923, 4½ In.	248.00
Horseshoe, Cast Iron, Pressed Steel, Horse Heads, Arcade, 1926, M 524, 3½ In.	121.00
Ice Box, Save For Ice, Cast Iron, Arcade, 1926, M 1337, 4¼ In.	275.00
Indian, With Tomahawk, Indian Echo Caves, Cast Iron, Hubley, M 228, 5⅞ In.	952.00
Jewel Chest, Cast Iron, Painted, Combination Lock Front, Footed, M 952, 6⅛ In.	385.00
Jug, Pottery, Bulbous, Knob Finial, Applied Handle, Brown Manganese, Copper Oxide Drip, 4⅛ In.	176.00
King Midas, Holding Gold Bag, Cast Iron, Painted, Embossed, Hubley, 4½ In.	6050.00
Lennox Aire Flo Gas Heating, Figural, Lennie Lennox, Coin Slot, 1949, 7½ In.	246.00
Mammy, Hands On Hips, Scarf, Dress, Apron, Cast Iron, Hubley, Box, M 176, 5¼ In.	336.00
Man In Barrel, Cast Iron, J. & E. Stevens, Late 1800s, M 282, 3⅝ In.	825.00
Man In Barrel, Outstretched Arms, Squatting, Cast Iron, J. & E. Stevens, 3½ In.	420.00
Man On Cotton Bale, Blue Jacket, Yellow Pants, Cast Iron, US Hardware, M 37, 4⅞ x 4 In.	935.00
Mary & Little Lamb, Cast Iron, White, Red Trim On Dress, Painted, U.S., M 164, 4⅜ In.	550.00
Mascot, Boy, Standing On Baseball, Cast Iron, Gold Paint, Red Cap & Socks, Hubley, M 3, 5¹³⁄₁₆ In.	2200.00

Mechanical banks were first made about 1870. Any bank with moving parts is considered mechanical. The metal banks made before World War I are the most desirable. Copies and new designs of mechanical banks have been made in metal or plastic since the 1920s. The condition of the paint on the old banks is important. Worn paint can lower a price by 90%.

Mechanical, Acrobat, Kicks Clown, Painted, Cast Iron, J. & E. Stevens, c.1883		4125.00
Mechanical, Archie Andrews, Painted, Aluminum, Starkie		448.00
Mechanical, Artillery, Rectangular Coin Trap, Iron, Bronze Plate, Shepard Hardware, 1900		450.00
Mechanical, Atlas, Globe On Shoulders, Spins, Lever, Cast Iron, White, Gold		15680.00
Mechanical, Atomic, Cast Metal, Duro Pattern & Mold Co., Box, 1950s, 8 In.		193.00
Mechanical, Bird, Comes Out For Money, Metal, Germany, 1950s		75.00
Mechanical, Bowling, Battery Operated, Daniel Imports, ASC, Japan, Box, 1960s, 10 In.		241.00
Mechanical, Boy & Bulldog, Brass Casting, Cast Iron, H.L. Judd, c.1870		7840.00
Mechanical, Boy On Trapeze, Cast Iron, J. Barton Smith, c.1891		19040.00
Mechanical, Boy Robbing Bird's Nest, Cast Iron, J. & E. Stevens, Box		77000.00
Mechanical, Boy Robbing Bird's Nest, Painted, Cast Iron, J. & E. Stevens, 1906		25200.00
Mechanical, Boy Scout Camp, Cast Iron, Charles A. Bailey, c.1915, 6 x 10 In.		3000.00 to 3700.00
Mechanical, Boys Stealing Watermelons, Cast Iron, Kyser & Rex		990.00
Mechanical, Bulldog, Cast Iron, Draped Base, J. & E. Stevens, c.1880, 8 x 6 In.		1528.00
Mechanical, Bulldog, Cast Iron, Key, Windup, Ives, 1878 Patent		15680.00
Mechanical, Bulldog, Coin On Nose, Pull Tail, Flips In Mouth, J. & E. Stevens, 1880		2240.00
Mechanical, Cabin, Black Man, Blue Shirt, Red Pants, Cast Iron, J. & E. Stevens, 1885 Patent		3920.00
Mechanical, Calumet Baking Powder, Boy Moves Back & Forth, Paper Over Tin, 1924		175.00
Mechanical, Canon Fires Coin Into Tank, Cast Iron, Starkie, 1919		1050.00
Mechanical, Carnival, Man Swings Hammer, Striking Bell, Painted, Cast Iron		13750.00
Mechanical, Carnival, Man Swings Hammer, Striking Bell, Painted, Aluminum		4400.00
Mechanical, Cat & Mouse, Cat Balancing, Cast Iron, J. & E. Stevens, 1891 Patent		13440.00
Mechanical, Chief Big Moon, Cast Iron, Silver Stripe, J. & E. Stevens, 1899 Patent		13440.00
Mechanical, Chief Big Moon, Frog Jumps After Fish, Cast Iron, J. & E. Stevens, 1899		1950.00
Mechanical, Circus, Clown & Cart, Painted, Cast Iron, Shepard Hardware, 1888		16500.00
Mechanical, Clown, Chein, 1949, 5 In.		142.00
Mechanical, Clown On Globe, Spins, Windup, Cast Iron, J. & E. Stevens, 9¼ In.		978.00
Mechanical, Creedmoor, Red Pants, Cast Iron, J. & E. Stevens, 1877 Patent		1344.00
Mechanical, Darktown, Battery, Baseball Players, Cast Iron, James Bowen, 1888, 7 x 10 In.		5100.00
Mechanical, Dentist, Patient Flips, Dentist Falls Back, Cast Iron, J. & E. Stevens, 1880-90		5500.00
Mechanical, Dinah, Black, Yellow, Long Sleeve, Cast Iron, John Harper		896.00
Mechanical, Dinah, Black, Yellow, Short Sleeve, Cast Iron, John Harper		560.00
Mechanical, Dog On Turntable, Cast Iron, Japanned, Judd, c.1870		3080.00
Mechanical, Dog On Turntable, Goes In & Out Of Bank, Cast Iron, H.L. Judd, 1870s		585.00
Mechanical, Dog Tray, Blue, Painted, Cast Iron, Kyser & Rex Co., c.1880		13400.00
Mechanical, Eagle & Eaglets, Cast Iron, J. & E. Stevens, 1883		880.00
Mechanical, Elephant, Lifts Trunk To Deposit Coin, Chein, 1950s, 5 In.		228.00
Mechanical, Elephant & 3 Clowns, Moves Trunk, Cast Iron, J. & E. Stevens, c.1883		5025.00
Mechanical, Ferris Wheel, Lever, Red, Yellow, Painted, Cast Iron, Hubley		24200.00
Mechanical, Football, Kicks Coin In Goal, Painted, Cast Iron, John Harper		11200.00
Mechanical, Fort Sumter, Canon Fires Coin Into Tower, Cast Iron, 1890		3500.00
Mechanical, Frog, On Round Base, Green Lattice, Cast Iron, J. & E. Stevens, 1872		6160.00
Mechanical, Frog, On Round Base, White Lattice, Cast Iron, J. & E. Stevens, 1872		2240.00
Mechanical, Frog, On Rock, Painted, Cast Iron, Kilgore, c.1920		1456.00
Mechanical, Giant In Tower, Red, Yellow, Black, Cast Iron, John Harper, 1892		42000.00
Mechanical, Girl Skipping Rope, Yellow Dress, Painted, Cast Iron, J. & E. Stevens, c.1890		72600.00
Mechanical, Hall's Excelsior, Light Blue, Cast Iron, J. & E. Stevens		3080.00
Mechanical, Hall's Liliput, Brown Steps, Green, Cast Iron, John D. Hall, 1877 Patent		1904.00
Mechanical, Hall's Liliput, Brown Steps, Yellow, Cast Iron, John D. Hall, 1877 Patent		6160.00
Mechanical, Harlequin, 2 Dancers, Cast Iron, J. & E. Stevens	*illus*	11000.00
Mechanical, Harold Lloyd, Tin, Germany, 1920s		715.00
Mechanical, Hen & Chick, Yellow, Green, Blue, Cast Iron, J. & E. Stevens, 1901 Patent		4400.00 to 6160.00
Mechanical, Horse Race, Straight Base, Yellow, Red, Blue, Brown, Iron, J. & E. Stevens, 1870		100800.00
Mechanical, I Always Did 'Spise A Mule, Jockey Over, Red Base, J. & E. Stevens, 1879		3080.00 to 4600.00
Mechanical, Indian & Bear, J. & E. Stevens, c.1883, 7½ x 11 In.		2750.00
Mechanical, Initiating Bank, 1st Degree, Cast Iron, Mechanical Novelty Works, 1880		42000.00
Mechanical, Initiating Bank, 2nd Degree, Cast Iron, Mechanical Novelty Works, 1880		12320.00
Mechanical, Jolly Nigger, Dark Blue Butterfly Tie, Red Lips, Cast Iron, John Harper		224.00
Mechanical, Jolly Nigger, Light Blue Butterfly Tie, Pink Lips, Cast Iron, John Harper, Box		728.00
Mechanical, Jolly Nigger, Red Shirt, Cast Iron, Shepard Hardware, Box		10640.00
Mechanical, Jolly Nigger, White Top Hat, Cast Iron, John Harper		672.00

Bank, Captain Kidd, Standing With Shovel By Stump, Cast Iron, Painted, M 38, 5 x 4 In. $288.00

Bank, Cat, Standing, Long Tail, Cast Iron, Black, M 369, 4½ In. $1210.00

Bank, Coronation, Silhouettes, Iron, Japanned, Sydenham & McOustra, M 1319, 6½ x 7½ In. $403.00

Bank, Dog, Puppo, Cast Iron, Black & White, Painted Bee, Hubley, M 442, 5 In. $330.00

Bank, Mechanical, Harlequin, 2 Dancers, Cast Iron, J. & E. Stevens $11000.00

Bank, Mechanical, Leap Frog, Cast Iron, Shepard Hardware, 1891 $4388.00

Bank, Mechanical, Novelty Bank, Cast Iron, J. & E. Stevens, 1873 $1345.00

Mechanical, Leap Frog, Cast Iron, Shepard Hardware, 1891 ....*illus*	4388.00
Mechanical, Lion & 2 Monkeys, Cast Iron, Kyser & Rex, 1883 Patent	2240.00
Mechanical, Lone Ranger, Silver Rearing Up, Plastic, Coin Slot, Box, 1940s, 5⅝ In.	1500.00
Mechanical, Lyons Toffee, Tin, Golliwog, Spring-Action Tongue Takes Coin, c.1920 .	7895.00
Mechanical, Mama Katzenjammer, Eyes Roll Up, Blue Dress, Cast Iron, Kenton, c.1908	67200.00
Mechanical, Mammy & Child, Cast Iron, Kyser & Rex, 1884	5225.00
Mechanical, Mason Bank, Cast Iron, Bricklayers, Shepard Hardware, 1887, 7 x 7 In.	4000.00
Mechanical, Memorial Money Bank, Bell, Lever, Cast Iron, Enterprise, c.1876	8960.00
Mechanical, Monkey, Organ Grinder, Cast Iron, Hubley, c.1906, 7¾ x 9 x 3 In. ..... 431.00 to	2016.00
Mechanical, Monkey, Tips Hat, Tin, Chein, 1950s, 5¼ In.	214.00
Mechanical, Monkey & Coconut, Cast Iron, J. & E. Stevens, 1886	10640.00
Mechanical, Monkey With Tray, Raises Arms, Opens Mouth, Tin, Germany, 1908	325.00
Mechanical, Mosque, Black, Blue Wash, Crank Handle, Cast Iron, H.L. Judd, c.1875	12320.00
Mechanical, Mule Entering Barn, Cast Iron, J. & E. Stevens, 1880 .... 1175.00 to	2240.00
Mechanical, National Bank, Cashier, Cast Iron, Paper, J. & E. Stevens, 1873 Patent	17920.00
Mechanical, North Pole, American Flag, Skiers, Dogsled, Cast Iron, J. & E. Stevens, c.1910 ..	39600.00
Mechanical, Novelty Bank, Cast Iron, J. & E. Stevens, 1873 ....*illus*	1345.00
Mechanical, Organ Bank, Blue Jacket, Yellow Hat, Cast Iron, Kyser & Rex, 1881 Patent	2016.00
Mechanical, Organ Bank, Red Jacket, Cast Iron, Kyser & Rex, c.1890, Miniature	2800.00
Mechanical, Organ Bank, Yellow Jacket, Cast Iron, Kyser & Rex, 1881 Patent	1120.00
Mechanical, Owl, Turns Head, Cast Iron, Glass Eyes, Gray Brown, J. & E. Stevens, 1880	1568.00
Mechanical, Owl, Turns Head, Iron, Glass Eyes, Paint, J. & E. Stevens, 7⅜ In. ...... 495.00 to	895.00
Mechanical, Paddy & The Pig, Blue Coat, Cast Iron, J. & E. Stevens, c.1882	2350.00
Mechanical, Paddy & The Pig, Brown Coat, Cast Iron, J. & E. Stevens, c.1882	4400.00
Mechanical, Paddy & The Pig, Green Coat, Cast Iron, J. & E. Stevens, c.1882	1430.00
Mechanical, Panorama, Blue Roof, White Sides, Red, Cast Iron, J. & E. Stevens, c.1876	17050.00
Mechanical, Patronize The Blind Man, Dog Grabs Coin From Man, J. & E. Stevens, 1878 ...	2875.00
Mechanical, Peg-Leg Beggar, Japanned, Off-White Face, Cast Iron, H.L. Judd, c.1875	10080.00
Mechanical, Pelican & Rabbit, Beak Opens, Rabbit Appears, J. & E. Stevens, 1878, 7¾ In.	1210.00
Mechanical, Picture Gallery, Red, Green, Cast Iron, Shepard Hardware, c.1885	67200.00
Mechanical, Pig In Highchair, Cast Iron, J. & E. Stevens, 1887 ....*illus*	1100.00
Mechanical, Pig Playing Drum, Tin, Windup, Felt Head & Body, Schuco, Germany, 5 In. 275.00 to	560.00
Mechanical, Pistol, Silver Finish, Cast Iron, Richard Elliot Co., 1909 Patent	4200.00
Mechanical, Professor Pug Frog's Great Bicycle Feat, Cast Iron, J. & E. Stevens, c.1886	7700.00
Mechanical, Punch & Judy, Cast Iron, Medium Letters, Shepard Hardware, 1884 ......*illus*	920.00
Mechanical, Punch & Judy, Large Letters, Cast Iron, Shepard Hardware, 1884 ....*illus*	1017.00
Mechanical, Rabbit, Standing, Bronze Paint, Japanned Base, Cast Iron, Lockwood, Small ..	1992.00
Mechanical, Reclining Chinaman, Blue Coat, Yellow Pants, J. & E. Stevens, c.1885	3500.00
Mechanical, Reclining Chinaman, Blue Pants, Cast Iron, J. & E. Stevens, c.1885	28000.00
Mechanical, Roller Skating Rink, Skaters, Cast Iron, Kyser & Rex, c.1880 ....*illus*	132000.00
Mechanical, Rooster, Painted, Cast Iron, Kyser & Rex, c.1880 .... 450.00 to	1904.00
Mechanical, Shell Service Station, Tin, Mechanic Pops Out Of Station, Germany, 5 In.	605.00
Mechanical, Speaking Dog, Girl & Dog, Cast Iron, John Harper, c.1902 ....*illus*	495.00
Mechanical, Springing Cat, Lead, Wood Base, Charles A. Bailey, 1882	24750.00
Mechanical, Stump Speaker, Cast Iron, Shepard Hardware, 1886	1430.00
Mechanical, Tammany, Brown Pants, Blue Coat, Cast Iron, J. & E. Stevens, 12-23-1873 *illus*	259.00
Mechanical, Tammany, Yellow Vest, Black Coat, Cast Iron, 1875, 5¾ x 4½ x 3 In. .. 240.00 to	345.00
Mechanical, Teddy & The Bear, Cast Iron, Book Of Knowledge, c.1950, 10 In.	71.00
Mechanical, Teddy & The Bear, Cast Iron, J. & E. Stevens, 1907	3700.00
Mechanical, Tennis Players, Man, Woman, Cast Iron, John Wright, 1975, 6 x 10½ x 9 In. ...	280.00
Mechanical, Thrifty Tom, Jigger, Tin, Windup, Ferdinand, Strauss, 1918	1450.00
Mechanical, Toad On Stump, Dark Green, Cast Iron, J. & E. Stevens, c.1880 .... 495.00 to	952.00
Mechanical, Trenton Trust, Cast Iron, Grey Iron Casting, Unopened Box, No. 56 Of 100	672.00
Mechanical, Trick Dog, 6-Part Base, Clown, Hoop, Dog, Barrel, Cast Iron, Hubley, 1896	650.00
Mechanical, Trick Dog, Solid Base, Clown, Hoop, Dog, Barrel, Cast Iron, Hubley, c.1906 *illus*	748.00
Mechanical, Trick Pony, Cast Iron, Shepard Hardware, 1885 ....*illus*	7020.00
Mechanical, Two Frogs, Cast Iron, J. & E. Stevens, Patented 1882, 9 In.	630.00
Mechanical, U.S. & Spain, Sand Finish Block Wall, Cast Iron, J. & E. Stevens, 1898 Patent ..	30500.00
Mechanical, U.S. Bank, Boy & Dog's Face Appear In Windows, J. & E. Stevens, c.1870	67100.00
Mechanical, Uncle Sam, Painted, Original Trap, Key, Cast Iron, Shepard Hardware, 1886 ...	3920.00
Mechanical, Uncle Wiggily, Tin Lithograph, Raises Carrot To Mouth, Graphics, Chein, 5 In. ..	308.00
Mechanical, Watchdog Safe, Dalmatian, Cast Iron, J. & E. Stevens, c.1880	3360.00
Mechanical, Weeden's, Plantation Darky Savings Bank, Tin, Japanned Ground, 1888	1450.00
Mechanical, William Tell, Cast Iron, J. & E. Stevens ....*illus*	660.00
Mechanical, Wimbledon, Rifleman Shooting, Original Flag, Cast Iron, John Harper, 1885 Patent ..	30800.00
Mechanical, Woodpecker, Tin, Musical, Crank, Gebruder Bing Co., Germany	1768.00

Mechanical, World's Fair, Columbus, Log, Indian, Cast Iron, J. & E. Stevens, 1893 .... 4200.00
Mechanical, Zoo, Monkey, Lion, Bear, Cast Iron, Kyser & Rex, c.1894 .... 4025.00 to 7840.00
Mother Embracing Children, Lead Alloy, Signed, Kodel, 1907, 11½ In. 935.00
Mulligan, Policeman, Cast Iron, Blue Overall, Flesh-Painted Face, A.C. Williams, M 177, 5¾ In. 358.00
Multiplying, Cast Iron, Mirrors, Green, Brown, J. & E. Stevens, c.1883, M 1184, 6½ In. 2800.00
Nesting Doves, Cast Iron, Copper Color, J.M. Harper, c.1907, M 647, 5½ In. 2750.00
Nursery Rhyme Figures, Tin Lithograph, Metal Package Corp., 1918, 4⅛ x 2½ In. 33.00
Old Doc Yak, Cast Iron, Red & White Paint, Arcade, M 30, 4½ In. 605.00
One Dime Saved Me, Buy A Chinese Baby, 1000 A Day Are Thrown Away, Celluloid, Round, 1930s . 226.00
Pig, Decker's Iowana, Cast Iron, Early 20th Century, M 603, 4½ In. 82.00
Pig, Laughing, Cast Iron, White, Blue, Pink, Hubley, M 640, 2½ x 5¼ In. 1008.00
Pig, Wise Pig, Thrifty, Cast Iron, White, Pink, Blue, Black, Hubley, Box, M 609, 6⅝ x 2⅞ In. .. 504.00
Policeman, Cast Iron, Blue Paint Overall, Embossed, Arcade, c.1920, M 182, 5½ In. 358.00 to 1100.00
Possum, Cast Iron, Arcade, 1926, M 561, 4⅜ In. 660.00
Rabbit, Seated, Cast Iron, White, Red Eyes, Hubley, M 570, 4⅝ x 4⅜ In. 840.00
Radio, Combination Door, Green, Cast Iron, Kenton, M 833, 4½ In. .... *illus* 345.00
Ray-O-Vac Man, Vinyl, Vinilos Romay S.A., 5½ In. 112.00
Red Goose Shoes, Brass Radiator Cap, Cast Iron, Arcade, M 611, 1926, 6 In. 605.00
Refrigerator, Cast Iron, Pressed Steel, Majestic, M 1332, 4½ In. 143.00
Refrigerator, Kelvinator, Cast Iron, White, Door Opens, M 1338, 3⅞ x 2½ In. 392.00
Register, Building, Opens At $5, Painted, Label, Kyser & Rex, c.1890 .... 28600.00
Register, Cash Register, Nickeled Cast Iron, Embossed Keys, Cash Drawer, M 931, J. & E. Stevens, 5 In. 138.00
Register, Dime Savings Bank, Clock, Cast Iron, Ives, 1890 Patent 5600.00
Register, Your Dream, Opens At $10.00, Tin Lithograph, Kalon Mfg., Brooklyn, 1950, 4¾ In. 143.00 to 168.00
Reindeer, Cast Iron, Turnpin, Arcade, 1928, M 736, 6¼ In. 385.00
Rhino, Cast Iron, Arcade, 1926, M 721, 5 In. .... 275.00 to 605.00
Royal Safe Deposit, Cast Iron, Painted, Decals, Baby, Girl, 19th Century, 6 In. 92.00
Safe, Burglar Proof, Cast Iron, Nickel Plated, J. & E. Stevens, 1897, 6 x 4 x 4¾ In. 978.00
Safe, Cast Iron, Keyless, Copper Luster, 2 Dials, 1920s 102.00
Safe, Horses, Fox Deer & Dog Decal, Cast Iron, Ives, 11 x 9 x 7 In. 1344.00
Safe, National, Cast Iron, Combination Lock, Early 20th Century, 5 In. 59.00
Safe, National, Nickel Plated, Arcade, 1928, 4¾ In. 50.00
Safe, Painted Cast Iron, Pressed Steel, Arcade, 1926, 2½ In. 330.00
Safe, Roller, Key, Kyser & Rex, 1882 .... 225.00
Safe, Security, Nickel Plated, Arcade, 1926, 6½ In. 495.00
Safe, State, Nickel Plated, Arcade, 1928, 4 In. 50.00
Santa Claus, Holding Tree, Cast Iron, Red, White, Gold, Green, Hubley, M 61, 5⅞ In. 715.00 to 1120.00
Santa Claus, Red Robe, Gold Boots, Cast Iron, Hubley, M 59, c.1900, 5⅞ In. 298.00
Santa Claus, Save & Smile, Black Paint, Red Hat, Embossed, Cast Iron, England, M 60, 7 In. 825.00
Satchel, Tippecanoe Loan & Trust Co., Brass, Moveable Handle, Embossed, 6 In. 220.00
Save & Smile, Cast Iron, Black Paint, Gold Trim, England, M 1641, 4 x 4 In. 138.00
Save & Smile, Cast Iron, Red & Black Paint, White & Blue Eyes, England, M 1641, 4 x 4 In. . 715.00
Seal On Rock, Cast Iron, Arcade, 1926, M 732, 4¼ In. 385.00
Sharecropper, Cast Iron, A.C. Williams, M 173, 5½ In. 195.00
Sniffles, At Barrel, Key, White Metal, Moss, Box, M 289, 5¾ x 5⅛ In. 224.00
Sniffles, At Tree, Key, White Metal, Moss, Box, M 293, 5¾ x 5⅛ In. 196.00
Speedy Alka-Seltzer, Vinyl, c.1960, 6 In. 370.00
Stag Brand Shirts, Celluloid, Round, 1930s 168.00
Standard Safe Deposit, Cast Iron, Painted, 2 Coin Slots, 20th Century, 7 In. 123.00
State Bank, Cast Iron, 1913, 4¼ x 2¾ x 2 In. 40.00
Stove, Hot Point, Porcelain Over Cast Iron, Arcade, 1935, 3⅞ In. 1045.00
Street Clock, Cast Iron, Red, Gold Face, A.C. Williams, M 1548, 6 In. 193.00
Tank, Plaster, Save For Victory, Box, 1942, 3 x 4¾ x 7½ In. 249.00
Thrift, Eagle Pencil Company, Eagle, Celluloid, Round, 1930s 62.00
Trolley, Cast Iron, Silver Paint, Wheels Roll, Kenton, M 1474, 5¼ In. 358.00
Two Kids, On Stump, Black & Silver Paint, Green Base, Cast Iron, Harper, M 594, 4½ In. 495.00
Victorian Recording, Cast Iron, Gold Paint, Glass Front, Embossed, M 1257, 6 In. 880.00
Watch Me Grow, Tin, 1930s, 9 In. Tall When Full 45.00
Wisconsin War Eagle, Gold Dollar Shape, Cast Iron, Embossed, M 678, 3 In. 1100.00
Wurlitzer Hi-Fi Stereo, Model 2400, Metal, Japan, Box, 1950s, 3⅛ In. 140.00

BANKO is a group of rustic Japanese wares made in the nineteenth and twentieth centuries. Some pieces are made of mosaics of colored clay; some are fanciful teapots. Redware and other materials were also used.

Bowl, Dragon, Around Reddish Brown Pottery Bowl, c.1900-20, 2 x 4½ In. 273.00

Bank, Mechanical, Pig In Highchair, Cast Iron, J. & E. Stevens, 1887
$1100.00

Bank, Mechanical, Punch & Judy, Cast Iron, Medium Letters, Shepard Hardware, 1884
$920.00

Bank, Mechanical, Punch & Judy, Large Letters, Cast Iron, Shepard Hardware, 1884
$1017.00

Bank, Mechanical, Roller Skating Rink, Skaters, Cast Iron, Kyser & Rex, c.1880
$132000.00

Bank, Mechanical, Speaking Dog, Girl & Dog, Cast Iron, John Harper, c.1902
$495.00

Bank, Mechanical, Tammany, Brown Pants, Blue Coat, Cast Iron, J. & E. Stevens, 12-23-1873
$259.00

Bank, Mechanical, Trick Dog, Solid Base, Clown, Hoop, Dog, Barrel, Cast Iron, Hubley, c.1906
$748.00

Bank, Mechanical, Trick Pony, Cast Iron, Shepard Hardware, 1885
$7020.00

Censer, Crane, Figural, 19th Century	600.00
Figurine, 3 Monkeys, Hear, See, Speak No Evil, 6 In.	125.00
Figurine, Fish Seller, Kneeling, Multicolored, 4½ x 3¾ In.	450.00
Incense Box, 2 Tsuru Cranes, Flowers, Hand Painted, 1920s	100.00
Nodder, Boy With Injured Arm, 1930s, 4⅜ x 4 In.	200.00
Nodder, Old Man & Wife, 7¾ x 2¾ In., Pair	700.00
Teapot, 5 Faces, c.1920, 4¾ x 6¾ In.	395.00
Teapot, Bird, Figural, Raffia, Handle, 2⅛ x 4½ In.	165.00
Teapot, Elephant, Figural, Gray, Floral Blanket On Back, Mid 20th Century, 5 x 8 In.	125.00

BARBER collectibles range from the popular red and white striped pole that used to be found in front of every shop to the small scissors and tools of the trade. Barber chairs are wanted, especially the older models with elaborate iron trim.

Chair, Airplane, Teddy Bear Pilot, Flying Lady Cafe, Red, White, Yellow, Child's, 44 x 46 In.	2542.00
Chair, Argyle, Walnut, Stick & Ball, Carving, Hydraulic, Upholstered, c.1890, 46 x 28 In.	8300.00
Chair, Horse Head, White, Black Mane, Wood, Porcelain, Theo A. Kochs Co., Child's, 42 In.	3025.00
Chair, Leather Seat & Back, Koken, 53 In. ....*illus*	117.00
Chair, Tiger Oak Frame, Carved, Congress Hydraulic Pedestal, Koken, Patented 1911	1400.00
Coat Rack, Mahogany, Porcelain Base, Ball Top, Koken, 90 In.	2310.00
Display, 3 Figures, Barber Pole, Fearless Fosdick, Got Wildroot Cream-Oil, Automaton, 48 x 34 In.	1210.00
Display, Pal Razor Blades, Man What A Blade, Red, White, Blue, Black, 13 x 9½ In.	44.00
Display, Sunbeam Shavemaster, Electric Razor Included, 24 x 9½ In.	283.00
Pole, Ball Finial, Red, Blue, White, Wood, Square	413.00
Pole, Massage, Barbershop, Hair Bobbing, Leaded Glass, Light-Up, Porcelain Base, Koken, 88 In.	7700.00
Pole, Pine, Painted, Ball Final, Faceted, Red, White, Blue, Block Base, 19th Century, 95 In.	7200.00
Pole, Red, White, Blue, Chrome, Aluminum, Glass, Electric, Marvy, 26 x 9 In.	80.00
Pole, Red, White, Blue, Chrome, Aluminum, Milk Glass Globe, Electric, Marvy, 35 x 9 In.	400.00
Pole, Red, White, Blue, Gold, Painted, Square Base, Ball Finial, 19th Century, 37 In.	203.00
Pole, Red, White Blue, Gold Stars, Barbershop Ball Top, Porcelain, Marvy, 96 In.	1888.00
Pole, Red, White, Green, Leaded Glass, Porcelain Top, Bottom, Wall, Koken, 33 x 11 In. .. 990.00 to 1210.00
Pole, Red & White, Gold Finial Ball, Polychrome, Square Block Mount, 22 In.	100.00
Pole, Red & White, Turned Shaft, Cut Down Center, 45 In.	220.00
Pole, Stained Glass, Floor Model, Koken, 84 x 16 In.	4000.00
Pole, Wood, Red, White, Blue, Polychrome, Red Ball Finial Over Block & Turned Column, 20 In.	660.00
Pole, Wood, Red & White Spiral Stripes, Blue Acorn Finial, 37 x 7 In.	690.00
Sanitizer, Towel, Copper, Brass, 4-Footed, 62 In.	1265.00
Sign, Barbershop, Red, White, Blue, Curved, Porcelain, Marvy, 24 x 15 In.	660.00
Sign, Look Better, Feel Better, Pole Form, Red, White, Blue, Porcelain, Marvy, 48 In.	165.00
Sign, Spike Straight Razor, Gets Them All The First Time, Green, Gold, Tin, Wood, 3½ x 8½ In.	590.00
Sign, Zepps & Noonans Hair Dressing, Red, White Blue, Porcelain, Flange, 2-Sided, 12 x 16 In.	531.00
Sterilizer, Straight Razor, Nickel Plated Steel, Glass, 5 Razors, 9½ x 7½ x 5 In.	113.00
Towel Steamer, Copper, Brass Faucet, Wood Handle, 1885-1925, 13½ x 11 In.	308.00
Work Station, Quartersawn Oak, 2 Drawers, Beveled Mirror, Light, Brass, 1890s, 37 x 37 In.	2775.00

BAROMETERS are used to forecast the weather. Antique barometers with elaborate wooden cases and brass trim are the most desirable. Mercury column barometers are also popular with collectors. It is difficult to find someone to repair a broken one, so be sure your barometer is in working condition.

Aneroid, Negretti & Zambra, Mahogany, Gilt Brass, Swan's Neck Pediment, London, 39 In.	1645.00
Antler & Tusk Surround, 3 Carved Deer On Antlers, Germany, 31 x 15 In.	358.00
Banjo, George III Style, Inlaid Mahogany, 4 Gauge, 42½ In.	531.00
Banjo, W.T. Ferrier Hull, Mahogany Over Pine, Open Mercury Tube, 39 In.	575.00
Banjo, Sheraton, Mahogany, Broken Arch Pediment, Brass Finial, c.1795, 38 x 10 In.	1652.00
Fortin Type, Portable, No. 335, Jas. Green, Silvered Scale, Engraved, Shackle, 36 In.	118.00
Giltwood, Painted Dial, Blue Ground, 8-Point Rose, Circular Gesso Case, 29 In.	1763.00
Holosteric, Chelsea, Silver Dial, Brass Case, 10 In. Diam.	460.00
Lyre Shape, Painted, Parcel Gilt, France, Early 19th Century, 39½ In.	2768.00
Nautical, Black Forest, Carved Plaque, Mounted Oak Leaves, Enameled Dial, 14 In.	204.00
Nautical, Rosewood Veneer, Pine, Thermometer, 2 Dials, Mercury Tube, 36 In.	316.00
Stick, D.E. Llest, Mercury, Ripple Mahogany Case, c.1865, 37 In.	1980.00
Stick, F. Pastorelli, Bowfront, Bone Register Plate, Rosewood Trunk, 38 In.	5288.00
Stick, R.N. Deterro, Brass, Hanging Loop, Gimbal, Weighted End, Lisbon, c.1875, 37 In.	1058.00
Stick, Simmons, Portable, Paper Scale, Silvered Alcohol Thermometer, Case, 38 In.	764.00
Thermometer, A. Frufs Hamburg, Porcelain, Ebonized Columns, Round, Germany, 19 x 9 In.	132.00
Thermometer, Mathews Warranted, Banjo, Mahogany, Silver Face, Hydrometer, Dials, 42 In.	805.00

Thermometer, George III Style, Inlaid Mahogany, Mid 19th Century, 36¾ In.		705.00
Weather Station, Tiffany & Co., Portable, Diamond Shape, Leather Case, 4½ x 8 In.		805.00
Wheel, Hygrometer, Thermometer, Mirror, Weather Dial, Mahogany, Inlaid, 38 x 10 In.		587.00

BASALT is a special type of ceramic invented by Josiah Wedgwood in the eighteenth century. It is a fine-grained, unglazed stoneware. Some pieces are listed in that section. The most common type is black, but many other colors were made. It was made by many factories. Some pieces are listed in the Wedgwood section.

Bowl, Black, Footed, Drapery Swags, High Relief, Acanthus Leaf Foot, 17¼ In.		5288.00
Bust, Jacques Necker, Black, Stepped Tapered Square Plinth Base, 19th Century, 7¼ In.		382.00
Bust, Tsar Alexander, Black, Wood & Caldwell, Flaring Base, Early 1800s, 11¼ In.		1058.00
Vase, Classical Relief, Leaf & Flower Border, Rosso Antico, Handles, Turner, 19th Century, 10 In.		2115.00
Vase, Cover, Palmer, Classical, Scrolled Handles, Medallions, Hercules, Late 1700s, 8¾ In.		999.00
Vase, Turner, 2 Handles, Rosso Antico, Classical Relief, Stiff Leaf, Leaf Border, 10½ In.		2115.00

BASEBALL collectibles are in the Sports category, except for baseball cards, which are listed under Baseball in the Card category.

BASKETS of all types are popular with collectors. American Indian, Japanese, African, Shaker, and many other kinds of baskets can be found. Of course, baskets are still being made, so the collector must learn to tell the age and style of the basket to determine the value.

Animal Carrier, Splint, Fixed Bentwood Handle, Melon Shape, God's-Eye Ends, 14 x 20 In.		138.00
Apple Picker, Swing Handle, Iron Hook, Leather Strap, Old Red Paint, 17¼ x 13¾ In.		2200.00
Art Deco, Wicker, Decorative Weaving, Diamond Pattern, Openwork, 1920s, 15 x 12 In.		165.00
Art Deco, Wood, Cane Wrapped Handle, Diamond Designs, 1920s, 18 x 21 In.		395.00
Bee Skep, Rye Straw, Flared Body, Center Door, Slide Closure, 13 x 13½ In.		193.00
Beehive, Coiled Straw, Bark Binding, Wood Frame Base, 20 x 19 x 16 In.		1265.00
Buttocks, 60 Ribs, Bentwood Handle, 12¼ x 5 In.		891.00
Buttocks, Bentwood Handle, 2 x 4 In.		115.00
Buttocks, Bentwood Handle, Copper Rivets With Embossed Stars, 16½ x 8¾ In.		460.00
Buttocks, Fixed Bentwood Handle, 10 x 11 In.		72.00
Buttocks, Fixed Bentwood Handle, Stained Bands, Geometric Design, 10 x 10½ In.		83.00
Buttocks, Hand Woven, Patina, Wide Handle, 19th Century, 6½ x 3½ x 4 In.		550.00
Buttocks, Splint, Fixed Bentwood Handle, God's-Eye Wrap, 4 x 4½ In.		413.00
Buttocks, Splint, Fixed Bentwood Handle, God's-Eye Wrap, 6½ x 8 In.		853.00
Buttocks, Splint, Fixed Bentwood Handle, God's-Eye Wrap, 10¼ x 12½ In.		94.00
Buttocks, Splint, Fixed Bentwood Handle, God's-Eye Wrap, 12 x 14½ In.		55.00 to 105.00
Buttocks, Splint, Fixed Bentwood Handle, God's-Eye Wrap, 13 x 16 In.		44.00 to 72.00
Buttocks, Splint, Fixed Bentwood Handle, God's-Eye Wrap, 18½ x 22½ In.		248.00
Buttocks, Splint, Fixed Bentwood Handle, Miniature, 2½ x 3 In.		385.00
Buttocks, Splint, Fixed Bentwood Handle, Painted Red Band, 5½ x 6½ In.		220.00
Buttocks, Splint, Fixed Handle, Miniature, 4½ x 5¼ In.		55.00
Buttocks, Splint, Oak, Fixed Handle, 5 x 4 In.		165.00
Buttocks, Splint, Oak, Fixed Handle, 9½ In.		110.00
Buttocks, Splint, Oak, Fixed Handle, 9¼ x 10¼ In.		121.00
Buttocks, Splint, Oak, Handle, Miniature, 4 x 5 In.	*illus*	187.00
Buttocks, Splint, Woven, Bentwood Handle, 8 x 16 In.		115.00
Coushatta, Pine Needle, Round, Coil Design, Red Stepped Rectangles, 4½ x 10½ In.		110.00
Crown Of Thorns, Chip Carved, Spear-Point Rim, Wood Floor, 5¼ x 10¾ In.		110.00
Curlicues, Arched Wrapped Handle, Braiding, Heywood, 1890s, 22 x 21 In.		550.00
Dog Carrier, Wicker, Wirework Door, Arched Shape, 21 x 17 x 24 In.	*illus*	345.00
Egg, Splint, Fixed Bentwood Handle, 8¼ x 11 In.		83.00
Eskimo, Bowl, Coil, Pictorial, Multicolored Flowers & Insects, 2 x 14 x 10 In.		167.00
Eskimo, Coil, Serrated Diamonds, Bulbous, Cone Shape Cover, Finial, 8¾ x 8½ In.		288.00
Field, Splint, Fixed Bentwood Loop Handles, 19 x 26 In.		83.00
Field, Splint, Openwork Side Handles, 14 x 22½ In.		193.00
Field, Splint, Openwork Side Handles, 14 x 27 In.		77.00
Gathering, Splint, Fixed Bentwood, God's-Eye Wrap, 9 x 13 In.		110.00
Gathering, Splint, Fixed Bentwood Handle, Dark Patina, 8½ x 8¾ In.		77.00
Gathering, Splint, Fixed Bentwood Swing Handle, 10 x 14½ In.		110.00
Gathering, Splint, Fixed Handle, God's-Eye Wrap, 11¼ x 22½ In.		55.00
Gathering, Splint, Oak, Fixed Handle, 15 In.		83.00
Gathering, Splint, Oak, Fixed Side Handles, 8¾ In.		132.00
Gathering, Splint, Oak, Old Green Paint, Fixed Side Handles, 13 x 23 In.		523.00
Gathering, Splint, Old Red Paint, Fixed Bentwood Handle, 9 x 10 In.		138.00

Bank, Mechanical, William Tell, Cast Iron, J. & E. Stevens
$660.00

Bank, Radio, Combination Door, Green, Cast Iron, Kenton, M 833, 4½ In.
$345.00

Barber, Chair, Leather Seat & Back, Koken, 53 In.
$117.00
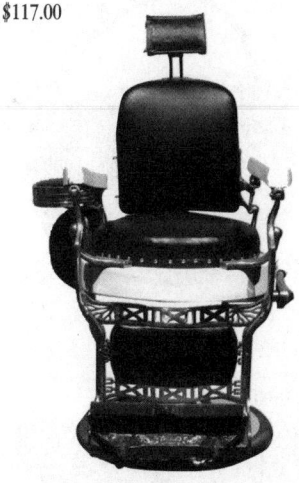

Basket, Buttocks, Splint, Oak, Handle, Miniature, 4 x 5 In.
$187.00

B

Basket, Dog Carrier, Wicker, Wirework Door, Arched Shape, 21 x 17 x 24 In. $345.00

Basket, Splint, Oriole, Oak, 10½ x 9½ In. $33.00

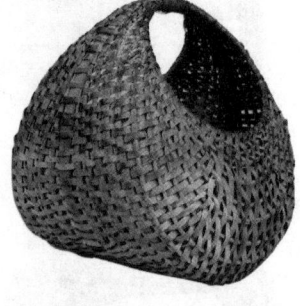

Basket, Splint, Wall, Woven, Half Melon Shape, 7½ x 7½ In. $575.00

Batman, Comic Book, No. 15, February 3, 1945 $291.00

Horsehair, Human Figure Border Holding Hands, Center Star Medallion, 8¾ In.	288.00
Leather, Multicolored, Punch Decorated Hearts, Stars, Leaves, 1800s, 7 x 7½ In.	12000.00
Loom, Splint, Woven, 3 Tiers, Stepped Crest, Pink, Green, Decorative Curls, 26 x 6 x 38 In.	345.00
Nantucket, Carved Handles, Turned Base, South Shoal Lighthouse, Andrew J. Sandsbury, 3 x 6⅜ In.	1195.00
Nantucket, Curly Maple, Swing Handle, Bottom Branded C, 4¼ x 10 In.	690.00
Nantucket, Lightship, Brass Pin Mount, Bentwood Handle, Thomas James, 1850-60, 12 In.	2760.00
Nantucket, Lightship, Purse, Swing Handle, Bone Whale & Latch Pin, Oval, 16¼ x 12½ In.	575.00
Nantucket, Lightship, Round, Squared Swing Handle, Robin A. Reyes, 11 x 9¼ In.	978.00
Nantucket, Lightship, Swing Handle, Brass Pins, Oval, Irving Burnside, c.1945, 10 x 6 x 7¾ In.	1380.00
Nantucket, Oval, Shaped Swing Handle, Marked, E.M.W., 7¾ x 4¾ In.	2390.00
Nantucket, Patina, Wooden Disk Base, Bentwood Handle, Brass Tabs, 14¼ In.	1265.00
Nantucket, Round, Honey Brown, Carved Swing Handle, 9 In.	661.00
Nantucket, Round, Swing Handle, Paper Label, Made By Ferdinand Sylvaro, 4 x 10¼ In.	978.00
Nantucket, Swing Handle, Wood Oval Bottom, Mitchell Ray, 13 x 14½ In.	4025.00
Oriole, Splint, Fixed Bentwood Handle, Shaped Bottom, 13½ x 8¼ In.	385.00
Painted Black Ash, Monumental, c.1990, 17 x 20⅛ In.	480.00
Picnic, Fitted Handle, Cover, Square Base, Support Shelves, Cup Holders, 14½ x 14 In.	80.00
Picnic, Rectangular, Wicker, Leather Handle, Abercrombie & Fitch, 17 x 16 x 7 In.	40.00
Rye, Coiled, Openwork Side Handles, Mellow Patina, 15 In.	83.00
Rye, Cover, Oval, 10 x 21½ In.	253.00
Rye, Oval, Openwork Sawtooth Band, Fixed Handle, 11¾ x 16¾ In.	176.00
Sailor's, Rope Work, Open Pattern, Scalloped Design, Varnished, 6 x 3½ In.	125.00
Splint, Ash, Rectangular, 9 x 18 In.	50.00
Splint, Bentwood Swing Handle, Copper Pins, 9½ In.	58.00
Splint, Carved Wood Swing Handle, Fine Weave, 12½ x 6½ In.	115.00
Splint, Divided Wall, Openwork Decorative Band, 12 x 5¼ In.	165.00
Splint, Fixed Bentwood Handle, 5½ In.	83.00 to 138.00
Splint, Fixed Handle, Interior Lining Spout, God's-Eye Wrap On Handle, 16 x 20 In.	22.00
Splint, Fixed Handle, Miniature, 4½ x 4½ In.	110.00
Splint, Gathering, Bentwood Swing Handle, 6¼ x 8½ In.	110.00
Splint, Hickory, Carved & Woven Handle, 19th Century, 15½ In.	59.00
Splint, Oak, Alternating Stained Bands, Openwork Side Handles, 5 In.	39.00
Splint, Oak, Bentwood Handle, Sled-Runner Base, White Paint, 17 In.	690.00
Splint, Oak, Fixed Handle, 3¼ x 3½ In.	220.00
Splint, Oak, Flower, Fixed Handle, 5 In.	66.00
Splint, Oak, Old Yellow Wash, 12 x 17½ In.	319.00
Splint, Oak, Openwork Handles, 28½ x 24 In.	115.00
Splint, Oak, Ribs, God's-Eye Wrap, 6⅝ x 8¼ In.	176.00
Splint, Oak, Woven, Bentwood Handle, Coker Creek Crafts, Tenn., 11 x 11½ x 7½ In.	144.00
Splint, Oriole, Oak, 10½ x 9½ In.	*illus* 33.00
Splint, Painted, Red, White, Blue, Yellow, Internal Basket, Bentwood Handles, 5 x 15½ In.	110.00
Splint, Round, Loop Side Handles, 4½ x 8½ In.	50.00
Splint, Wall, Curlicue Decorations, Early 20th Century, 19 x 12 In.	920.00
Splint, Wall, Fixed Bentwood Handle, Bulbous Body, 8½ x 8½ In.	77.00
Splint, Wall, Woven, Half Melon Shape, 7½ x 7½ In.	*illus* 575.00
String, Dyed Bands, Openwork Shoulder, Central Hole In Lid, Footed Base, 4¼ In.	22.00
Willow, Beaded, Footed Ring Base, Note Inside, North Dakota 1934, 4 x 5¼ In.	58.00
Wood, Cane Wrapped Handle, Legs, Brass Caps, Heywood Bros., 1880s	475.00
Wood, Cane Wrapped Posts, Handle, Wood Turned Finials, Lyre Design, 1890s	495.00
Wood, Wicker, Decorative Loop, Beadwork, Flat Weaving, 1890s, 21 x 20 In.	495.00

BATCHELDER products are made from California clay. Ernest Batchelder established a tile studio in Pasadena, California, in 1909 and expanded until 1916. Then he built a larger factory with a new partner. The Batchelder-Wilson Company made all types of architectural tiles, garden pots, and bookends. The plant closed in 1932. In 1936 Batchelder opened Batchelder Ceramics, also in Pasadena, and made bowls, vases, and earthenware pots. He retired in 1951 and died in 1957. Pieces are marked *Batchelder Pasadena* or *Batchelder Los Angeles*.

BATCHELDER LOS ANGELES

Tile, Modeled, Flowers, Blue Grounds, Arts & Crafts Frame, 6 x 6 In., 2 Piece	240.00

BATMAN and Robin are characters from a comic strip by Bob Kane that started in 1939. In 1966, the characters became part of a popular television series. There have been radio and movie serials that featured the pair. The first full-length movie was made in 1989.

Action Figure, Penguin, Mego, Box, 1973, 8 In.	140.00
Bath Towel, Poncho, Cap Graphic On Back, Chest On Front, 1976, 55 x 54 In.	110.00
Batmobile, Tin, Battery Operated, Mystery Action, Flashing Dome, Box, 9½ In.	220.00

Batmobile, Tin Lithograph, Friction, Marx, c.1966, 4 In.	493.00
Blanket, Thermal, Rayon & Acrylic, Comic Book Logo, Batman & Robin In Batmobile, 1966	750.00
Comic Book, No. 15, February 3, 1945 ....*illus*	291.00
Figure, Batman, Posable, Removable Cape, On Kresge Card, Mego, 1972, 8 In.	4312.00
Gun, Plastic, Spring Loaded, Ideal, 1966, 7½ In.	84.00
Lobby Card, Batman, Daka Is Batman's Prisoner, Doom Of Rising Sun, Chapter 15, Columbia, 1943	748.00
Lobby Card, Batman, Release Linda, Doom Of Rising Sun, Chapter 15, Columbia, 1943	805.00
Model, Batplane, Aurora, Box, Unused, 1966	154.00
Movie Poster, Batman, 20th Century Fox, Australia, 1966, 27 x 41 In.	431.00
Movie Poster, Phony Doctor, Re-Release, 1954, 27 x 41 In.	271.00
PEZ Dispenser, Plastic, Vinyl Head, Dc Comics Inc., 1978, 4¼ In.	139.00
Place Mat, Batman & Robin With Full Capes, Vinyl, Foam Back, NPP Inc., 1966, Pair	112.00
Place Mat, Robin, Vinyl, Foam Backs, Pair, 13 x 19 In.	112.00
Record, 45 RPM, Batman Theme, Nelson's Riddler, Photo Sleeve, NPP Inc., 1966, 7 x 7 In.	598.00

BAUER pottery is a California-made ware. J.A. Bauer bought Paducah Pottery in Paducah, Kentucky, in 1885. He moved the pottery to Los Angeles, California, in 1909. The company made art pottery after 1912 and dinnerwares marked *Bauer* in 1930. The factory went out of business in 1962. See also the Russel Wright category.

Bean Pot, Plainware, Brown, Handle, Marked 2, 2 Qt.	100.00
Bean Pot, Underplate, Whiteware, Flowers, Matt Carlton	495.00
Bean Pot, Yellow, Wheel Turned, Matt Carlton	55.00
Oil Jar, Indigo Glaze, 22 x 17 In., Pair	3240.00
Oil Jar, Indigo Glaze, 25½ x 17½ In. ....*illus*	2160.00
Oil Jar, Orange Glaze, 19½ x 13 In., Pair	2400.00
Pitcher, Flowers, White Matte, Wheel Thrown, 5¼ In.	495.00
Sugar & Creamer, Plainware, Wheel Thrown, Matt Carlton	75.00
Vase, Bean Pot, Whiteware, Flowers, Wheel Thrown, Matt Carlton, 4½ In.	500.00
Vase, Jade Glaze, Ruffled Rim, Matt Carlton, 7 x 10 In.	700.00

BAVARIA is a region in Europe where many types of porcelain were made. In the nineteenth century, the mark often included the word *Bavaria*. After 1871, the words *Bavaria, Germany*, were used. Listed here are pieces that include the name *Bavaria* in some form, but major porcelain makers, such as Rosenthal, are listed in their own categories.

Bowl, Vegetable, Cover, Aragon, Blue Flower Band, Knob, 8⅜ x 3 In.	55.00
Card Holder, Flowers, Yellow, Green, Gold Highlights, 3 x 4 In.	20.00
Plate Set, Bird Design, Transfer, P & M, 9 In., 5 Piece	94.00

BEADED BAGS *are included in the Purse category.*

BEATLES collectors search for any items picturing the four members of the famous music group or any of their recordings. Because these items are so new, the condition is very important and top prices are paid only for items in mint condition. The Beatles first appeared on American network television in 1964. The group disbanded in 1971. Ringo Starr and Paul McCartney are still performing. John Lennon died in 1980. George Harrison died in 2001.

Blanket, English Fiber, Wool, Drums, Guitars, Beatles, Signatures, 1964	325.00
Doll Set, With Instruments, Vinyl & Plastic, Remco, 1964, 4½ In., 4 Piece ....*illus*	290.00
Inflatable Doll Premium Offer, Lux Soap Box, Lever Bros., c.1966, 4 x 5 In. ....*illus*	354.00
Jacket, Authentic Mod Fashions, 3 Pockets, Tag, NEMS, 9th Street East Ltd., 1966, 30 In.	112.00
Lunch Box, Embossed Portraits, Aladdin, Thermos, 1965 ....*illus*	478.00
Lunch Box, John, Paul, George, Ringo, Blue, Steel, Thermos	495.00
Lunch Box, Yellow Submarine, Steel, Thermos, Nick Lobianco, 1968	880.00
Model Set, Ringo, Revell, Box, Unopened, 1964, 6¼ x 9½ x 2¼ In.	393.00
Nodder, Bobbin' Head Beatles, Plaster, Painted, Car Mascots Inc., Box, 1964, 9 x 11 In., 4 Piece ..	2240.00
Pin, Fabulous Beatles, Guitar, Group Photo, Plastic, On Card, 1964, 2½ x 5½ In.	451.00
Pin, Fabulous Beatles, Guitar, Individual Photos, Plastic, On Card, 1964, 2½ x 5½ In., 4 Piece	574.00
Pin, The 4 Beatles, Black & White Photos, c.1965, 3½ In.	256.00
Poster, Hard Day's Night, 6 Brand New Songs, United Artists, 1964, 41 x 27 In.	717.00
Poster, Hard Day's Night, United Artists, 1964, 81 x 40 In.	978.00
Poster, Help!, United Artists, 1965, 81 x 40 In.	748.00
Poster, Let It Be, United Artists, 1970, 81 x 40 In.	748.00
Poster, Yellow Submarine, Sgt. Pepper's Lonely Hearts Club Band, United Artists, 1968, 41 x 27 In. ..	1075.00
Scarf, Facsimile Signatures, Ulster, 1964, 31 In.	280.00

Bauer, Oil Jar, Indigo Glaze, 25½ x 17½ In. $2160.00

Beatles, Doll Set, With Instruments, Vinyl & Plastic, Remco, 1964, 4½ In., 4 Piece $290.00

Beatles, Inflatable Doll Premium Offer, Lux Soap Box, Lever Bros., c.1966, 4 x 5 In. $354.00

Beatles, Lunch Box, Embossed Portraits, Aladdin, Thermos, 1965 $478.00

Beatles, Scarf,
Portraits, With Love From Me To You,
Cloth, 1964, 14 x 14 In.
$29.00

Beatles, Sneakers,
Blue, Allover Faces & Signatures,
Wing Dings, Box, c.1964
$748.00

Beatles, Toy,
Yellow Submarine, Cast Metal, Plastic,
Corgi Toys, Box, 6 In.
$385.00

Scarf, Portraits, With Love From Me To You, Cloth, 1964, 14 x 14 In. .... *illus*	29.00
Sneakers, Blue, Allover Faces & Signatures, Wing Dings, Box, c.1964 .... *illus*	748.00
Toy, Yellow Submarine, Cast Metal, Plastic, Corgi Toys, Box, 6 In. .... *illus*	385.00
Wig, Authentic, Bag, Header Card, Lowell Toy Manufacturing, c.1964, 9¾ x 12 In.	172.00

BEEHIVE, Austria, or Beehive, Vienna, are terms used in English-speaking countries to refer to the many types of decorated porcelain bearing a mark that looks like a beehive. The mark is actually a shield, viewed upside down. It was first used in 1744 by the Royal Porcelain Manufactory of Vienna. The firm made what collectors call Royal Vienna porcelains until it closed in 1864. Many other German, Austrian, and Japanese factories have reproduced Royal Vienna wares, complete with the original shield or beehive mark. This listing includes the expensive, original Royal Vienna porcelains and many other types of beehive porcelain. The Royal Vienna pieces include that name in the description.

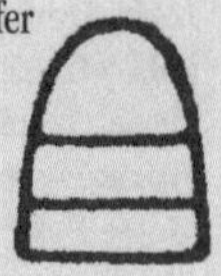

Box, Lid, Egg Shape, Cobalt Blue, Painted Design, Royal Vienna, Austria, 5½ x 7 In.	29.00
Chocolate Pot, Flowers, Snake Handle, White, Orange Band, 4-Sided, Germany, 10 In.	110.00
Compote, Painted Figures In Center, Geometric Reserves, Royal Vienna, c.1930, 5 x 8 In. ...	117.00
Cup, Scene, Flared Cylindrical, Scrolling Handle, Gilt, 1800s, 3¾ In.	288.00
Cup & Saucer, Jeweled, Alexander, Campocope, Apelless, Vienna, Late 1800s, 6 In.	475.00
Cup & Saucer, Portrait, Archbishop Writing In Book, 2½ x 5¼ In.	1175.00
Dish, Purple Rose, Green Trim, Royal Vienna, 4½ x 3¾ In.	8.00
Dresser Box, Cobalt Blue, Hand-Painted Scene, Royal Vienna, Austria, c.1920, 6¼ In.	35.00
Figurine, Greek Style Woman, Classical Pose, Chopsticks, Royal Vienna, 15½ x 6½ In.	250.00
Plate, Classical Scenes, Fired Gold Rim, Royal Vienna, 11 In., 12 Piece	761.00
Plate, Fired Gold, Royal Vienna, 9⅝ In.	234.00
Plate, Portrait, Clio, Royal Vienna, c.1900, 9½ In.	1305.00
Plate, Reticulated, Rose, Flowers, Green Band, Early 1800s, 9½ In., Pair	350.00
Stein, Man, Woman Seated, Wooded Landscape, Scrolls, Moss Green, Royal Vienna, 3¾ In. ..	1280.00
Tea Bowl, Saucer, Rosebuds, Royal Vienna, c.1791	185.00
Urn, Cover, Allegorical Figures, Fired Gold Designs, Royal Vienna, 20½ In.	2106.00
Urn, Cover, Romeo & Juliet Scene, Cobalt Blue, Gilt, Royal Vienna, c.1900, 17½ In.	650.00
Urn, Girls In Landscape, Signed, Drilled, Angelica Kauffman, Royal Vienna, 17¼ In., Pair ..	189.00
Urn, Women, Classical Setting, Electrified, Royal Vienna, 15¼ In.	207.00
Vase, Maiden, Grapes & Leaves On Head, Flowers, Vines, Purple Luster Ground, Royal Vienna, 9½ In.	1020.00
Vase, Portrait, Woman Wearing Cap, Peacock Blue Luster, Royal Vienna, 10⅜ In.	1035.00
Vase, Woman Putting Flowers In Vase, Cobalt Blue, Royal Vienna, Blue Beehive Mark, 9½ In. .	170.00

BEER BOTTLES *are listed in the Bottle category under Beer.*

BEER CANS are a twentieth-century idea. Beer was sold in kegs or returnable bottles until 1934. The first patent for a can was issued to the American Can Company in September of that year; and Gotfried Kruger Brewing Company, Newark, New Jersey, was the first to use the can. The cone-top can was first made in 1935, the aluminum pop-top in 1962. Collectors should look for cans in good condition, with no dents or rust. Serious collectors prefer cans that have been opened from the bottom.

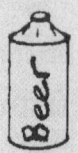

21 Century, Canadian Ace Brewing, Chicago, Ill.	41.00
49ers, Atlas Brewing, Chicago, Ill.	41.00
Badger, Whitewater Brewing Co.	183.00
Burger Sparkling Ale, Burger Brewing, Cincinnati, Oh., Cone Top	262.00
Clipper Pale, Grace Bros., Santa Rosa, Calif.	76.00
Drewrys Ale, Drewrys Ltd., South Bend, Ind.	81.00
Drut Super Premium, Lone Star Brewing, Gold & Red, Pull Tab, Steel, 1971, 12 Oz.	13.00
Eastside Sparkling Ale, Los Angeles Brewing	119.00
Excel Pale, Grace Bros., Santa Rosa, Calif.	31.00
Goebel Bock, Goebel Brewing, Detroit, Mich.	75.00
Gold Medal Extra Pale, Grace Bros., Santa Rosa, Calif.	53.00
Hopsburger Premium Lager, Pacific Brewing, Oakland, Calif.	100.00
Iron City, 1976 Steelers Super Bowl Champions, Pull Tab, Aluminum, 12 Oz.	15.00
John Courage Ale, Put Tabs In Can, Pull Tab, Courage Ltd, London, 12 Oz.	10.00
Kings Taste, Grace Bros., Santa Rosa, Calif.	821.00
Krug, San Francisco Brewing, Calif.	60.00
Kuebler Pilsner, Man, Kuebler Brewing, Cone Top, Easton, Pa., Qt.	258.00
Martins, Yakima Valley Brewing, Cone Top, Selah, Wash.	67.00
Old Dutch Brand, Old Dutch Brewing, Cone Top, Brooklyn, N.Y., Qt.	519.00
Old Reading, Old Reading Brewing, Cone Top, Reading, Pa.	259.00
Pabst Blue Ribbon, Big Cat Malt Liquor, Pull Tab, Please Don't Litter Big Cat, 12 Oz.	13.00

Playmate Premium Beer, Lady's Face, Zip-Top, Sunshine Brewing, Reading, Pa.	100.00
Red Top, Flat Top, Red Top Brewing Co., Cincinnati, Ohio	3550.00
Rheingold Extra Dry Lager, Lady, Liebmann Breweries, New York, N.Y.	306.00
Time Lager, Time Brewing, Cone Top, Dallas, Tex.	20.00
Tooheys Australian, Please Don't Litter Michigan, Flat Top, 10 Cent Refund	9.00

BELL collectors collect all types of bells. Favorites include glass bells, figural bells, school bells, and cowbells. Bells have been made of porcelain, china, or metal through the centuries.

Brass, Harness Set, Iron Frame, 20½ In., 4 Piece	132.00
Brass, Harness Set, Larger Center, Iron Frame, Contemporary Stand, 21½ In., 3 Piece	385.00
Brass, Hotel, Double Ender, 6 x 5 In.	120.00
Brass, Hotel, Hammered, 5 x 4¾ In.	190.00
Brass, Hotel, Top Plunger, 5 x 4 x 4 In.	150.00
Brass, Vine & Rose Trellis Handle, Flowers, Painted, Embossed, 4¼ In.	112.00
Bronze, Boy, Dust Pan, Russia, c.1900, 4½ In.	71.00
Bronze, Figural, Joan Of Arc, Nodding Head, Enameled Features, 4¼ In. ....*illus*	558.00
Bronze, Hemony Style, Embossed Inscription, Amor Vincit Omnia Ao 1647, 6 In. ......*illus*	71.00
Bronze, Napoleonic, Patinated, Figural Finial, Cast Battle Relief, 5½ x 2⅝ In.	88.00
Bronze, Plantation, Buckeye Bell Foundry, Wooden Harness, 30 x 28 In.	6463.00
Bronze, Ritual, Vaja Shape Finial, Khmer, 12th Century, 5½ In.	384.00
Bronze, Woman, Bustled Dress, 19th Century, 6¼ In.	147.00
Bronze, Woman, Medieval, Wearing Hennin, 19th Century, 6¼ In.	206.00
Glass, Wedding, Cobalt Blue, Clear Shaped Handle, 19th Century, 12½ In. ....*illus*	71.00
Glass, Wedding, Cranberry, Swirled Base, Clear Handle, 19th Century, 14 In.	71.00
Glass, Wedding, White, Ruby Rim, Clear Handle, 19th Century, 11¾ In.	12.00
Iron, Lady, In Hoop Skirt, White, Green, Purple, 3¾ In.	168.00
Iron, Parrot, Multicolored, Hubley	392.00
Iron, Plantation, Clapper, c.1780, 14½ x 17 In.	2400.00
Pressed Glass, Sunburst, Faceted Glass Ball Ringer, 4 In.	18.00
Ruby Red, Coralene, Holly Design, 1980, 6¾ In.	23.00
Silver, Ship, Eagle Finial, Stand, Plate, 24 x 12 In.	345.00
Sleigh, Leather Strap, 25 Graduated Bells	1200.00
Sterling Silver, Applied & Tooled Designs, Marked, Gorham, 4¼ x 2 In.	810.00
Sterling Silver, Decorative Finial, Etched Mark, Royal Danish, 3½ x 2 In.	170.00
Sterling Silver, Embossed Flowers, Impressed Mark, Shiebler, 3¼ x 2¼ In.	300.00
Sterling Silver, Hammered, Engraved Monogram, Impressed Mark, Lebolt, 3 x 2 In.	210.00
Sterling Silver, Hammered, Memorial, Tooled Design, 1911, 3½ x 2¼ In.	240.00
Sterling Silver, Hammered, No. 105A, Marked, Wood & Hughes, 4½ x 2¼ In.	405.00
Sterling Silver, Organic Design, No. 204A, Marked, Georg Jensen, 3½ x 2 In.	290.00
Sterling Silver, Organic Finial, Marked, Randahl, 2½ x 2 In.	60.00

BELLEEK china was made in Ireland, other European countries, and the United States. The glaze is creamy yellow and appears wet. The first Belleek was made in 1857. All pieces listed here are Irish Belleek. The mark changed through the years. The first mark, black, dates from 1863 to 1890. The second mark, black, dates from 1891 to 1926 and includes the words *Co. Fermanagh, Ireland*. The third mark, black, dates from 1926 to 1946 and has the words *Deanta in Eirinn*. The fourth mark, same as the third mark but green, dates from 1946 to 1955. The fifth mark, green, dates from 1955 to 1965 and has an R in a circle added in the upper right. The sixth mark, green, dates after 1965 and the words *Co. Fermanagh* have been omitted. The seventh mark, gold, was used from 1980 to 1993 and omits the words *Deanta in Eirinn*. The eighth mark, introduced in 1993, is similar to the second mark but is printed in blue. The word *Belleek* is now used only on the pieces made in Ireland even though earlier pieces from other countries were sometimes marked *Belleek*. These early pieces are listed by manufacturer, such as Ceramic Art Co., Ott & Brewer, and Willets.

Bust, Clytie, Socle, 1926-46, 10¾ In.	1069.00
Dinner Set, Shamrock Pattern, Pitcher, Cake Plate, 11 Piece Place Setting	255.00
Sugar & Creamer, Lily, Ivory, Parian, Ireland, c.1955-65	85.00
Sugar & Creamer, Lotus Blossoms, Ivory, Parian, Ireland, c.1926-46	115.00
Tankard, Nude Woman Dropping Petals, Dragon Handle, 1906, 15 x 8½ In.	2480.00
Tea Set, Exotic Birds, On Flowering Branch, Black Mark, 4½-In. Pot, 10 Piece ....*illus*	12075.00
Urn, Grape Clusters, Scalloped Rim, Hand Painted, W. Marsh, 10¾ x 12½ In., Pair	1560.00
Vase, 3 Tulips, c.1890, 9 In., Pair	1238.00
Vase, Calla Lily, 7½ In.	41.00
Vase, Nautilus Shell, Porcelain, Corals Supports, Round Base, Ireland, Late 1800s, 8 In.	470.00

Beer Trays

Beer trays illustrate over 100 years of brewery history. At the turn of the twentieth century, every brewery (and there were many) gave colored tin trays to the local taverns. The eye-catching serving pieces acted as point-of-purchase advertising for the brewery's product. Improved manufacturing methods assured that trays could be produced inexpensively and they are still given away to bars and restaurants.

Bell, Bronze, Figural, Joan Of Arc, Nodding Head, Enameled Features, 4¼ In. $558.00

Bell, Bronze, Hemony Style, Embossed Inscription, Amor Vincit Omnia Ao 1647, 6 In. $71.00

Bell, Glass, Wedding, Cobalt Blue, Clear Shaped Handle, 19th Century, 12½ In.
$71.00

Belleek, Tea Set, Exotic Birds, On Flowering Branch, Black Mark, 4½-In. Pot, 10 Piece
$12075.00

Bennington, Crock, Flowers, Cobalt Blue, Stoneware, J. Norton, 6 Gal., 13½ x 13¼ In.
$819.00

Vase, Red Rose, Green Tones, Hand Painted, 19 In.	950.00
Vase, Rose, Leaves, 3¾ In.	185.00
Vase, Sailing Ship, Cylindrical, 1910, 11¼ x 4 In.	495.00

BENNINGTON ware was the product of two factories working in Bennington, Vermont. Both the Norton Company and the Lyman Fenton Company were out of business by 1896. The wares include brown and yellow mottled pottery, Parian, scroddled ware, stoneware, graniteware, yellowware, and Staffordshire-type vases. The name is also a generic term for mottled brownware of the type made in Bennington.

Coffeepot, Lid, 8 Panels, Flint Enamel, Brown, Blue, Green Glaze, 12¾ In.	470.00
Crock, Cobalt Blue, Decorated, Stoneware, Norton, 4 Gal., 11¼ In.	588.00
Crock, Flowers, Cobalt Blue, Stoneware, J. Norton, 6 Gal., 13½ x 13¼ In. ....*illus*	819.00
Jar, Canning, Bird, Dotted Leaf, Blue, Stoneware, E. & L.P. Norton, 2 Gal., 11½ In.	3190.00
Jar, Cobalt Blue, Decoration, Norton Pottery, Stoneware, 3 Gal., 12¾ In.	9400.00
Pitcher, Hunting Scene, Deer, Rabbits, Rockingham Glaze, 9½ In. ....*illus*	129.00
Vase, Spill, Doe, Lying Down, Flint Enamel, Rock Base, 1849-58, 10½ In.	2160.00
Vase, Spill, Stag, Lying Down, Flint Enamel, Rock Base, 1855, 11 In.	2160.00

BERLIN, a German porcelain factory, was started in 1751 by Wilhelm Kaspar Wegely. In 1763, the factory was taken over by Frederick the Great and became the Royal Berlin Porcelain Manufactory. It is still in operation today. Pieces have been marked in a variety of ways.

Plaque, Reflection, Bust, Woman, Flowing Hair, Oval, Metal Frame, 3¾ x 2½ In.	230.00
Plaque, Ruth, Bust, Woman, Blue Dress, White Head Scarf, Reticulated, Metal Frame, 3 x 2 In.	518.00
Plaque, Woman, Candlestick, Gilt Wood Frame, Signed, Wagner, 6 x 4 In.	936.00

BESWICK started making earthenware in Staffordshire, England, in 1936. The company is now part of Royal Doulton Tableware, Ltd. Figurines of animals, especially dogs and horses, Beatrix Potter animals, and other wares are still being made.

Animal, Gamecock, No. 2059, 1966-75, 9½ In.	1084.00
Decanter, Whiskey, Osprey, Beneagles, 1977, 8 In.	46.00
Figurine, Aberdeen Angus Cow, Matte, No. 1563, 1985-89, 3 In.	110.00
Figurine, Angel On Horse Back, Thelwell, No. 2740B, 1982-89, 4½ In.	169.00
Figurine, Anna Maria, BP 38	192.00
Figurine, Appley Dapply, Bottle Out, BP 2	192.00
Figurine, Arab Bahram, Chestnut, No. 1771, 1961-67, 7½ In.	610.00
Figurine, Arab Xayal, Palomino, No. 1265, 1961-89, 6¼ In.	90.00
Figurine, Arab Xayal, Rocking Horse Gray, No. 1265, 1953-62, 6¼ In.	497.00
Figurine, Baltimore Oriole, Matte, No. 2183, 1970-72, 3½ In.	130.00
Figurine, Baltimore Orioles, No. 926, 1941-65, 5 In.	169.00
Figurine, Basset Hound, No. 2045A, 1965-94, 5 In.	74.00
Figurine, Bison, No. 1019, 1945-73, 5¾ In.	56.00
Figurine, Budgerigar, Yellow, No. 1216B, 1970-72, 7 In.	1016.00
Figurine, Canadian Mountie, No. 1375, 1955-76, 8¼ In.	1016.00
Figurine, Cancara, No. 3426, Box, 1994, 16½ In.	632.00
Figurine, Cantering Shire, Black, No. 975, 1996, 8¾ In.	452.00
Figurine, Charolais Bull, No. 2463A, 1975-79, 5½ In.	169.00
Figurine, Cheshire Cat, LC3, 1999, 3½ In.	93.00
Figurine, Chimpanzee With Pipe, No. 1049, 1946-69, 4¾ In.	90.00
Figurine, Christopher Robin & Pooh, 1996-97, 3¼ In.	158.00
Figurine, Cockatoo, Turquoise, Yellow, No. 1818, 1962-73, 11¼ In.	157.00
Figurine, Comical Fox, No. 1733, 1961-68, 3¼ In.	56.00 to 74.00
Figurine, Connemara, No. 1641, 1961-84, 7 In.	34.00
Figurine, Cuckoo, No. 2315, 1970-82, 5 In.	167.00
Figurine, Dales Pony, Maisie, No. 1671, 1961-82, 6½ In.	226.00 to 305.00
Figurine, Elephant, Trunk In Salute, Gloss, No. 1770, 1961-75, 12 In.	93.00
Figurine, Elephant & Tiger, No. 1720, 1960-75, 12 In.	452.00 to 655.00
Figurine, Exmoor Pony, Heatherman, No. 1645, 1961-83, 6½ In.	157.00 to 169.00
Figurine, Fell Pony, No. 1647, 1961-82, 6¾ In.	316.00
Figurine, Foal, White Paint, No. 997, 1961-67, 3¼ In.	632.00
Figurine, Fox, Standing, No. 1016A, 1945-97, 5½ In.	95.00
Figurine, Fresian Cow, Gloss, No. 1362A, 1954-97, 4½ In.	79.00
Figurine, Galloping Horse, Brown, No. 1374, 1955-75, 7½ In.	293.00
Figurine, Galloway Bull, Black, No. 1746A, 1962-69, 4½ In.	3388.00
Figurine, Gamecock, No. 2059, 1966-75, 9½ In. ....*illus*	150.00

Figurine, Girl, On Skewbald Pony, No. 1499, 1957-65, 5½ In.	429.00
Figurine, Goldeneye Duck, No. 1524, 1958-71, 3½ In.	185.00
Figurine, Goosander, Peter Scott, No. 1525	226.00
Figurine, Guernsey Bull, No. 1451, 1956-89, 4¾ In.	337.00
Figurine, Guernsey Cow, No. 1248A, 1952-53, 4¼ In.	147.00
Figurine, Guernsey Cow, No. 1248B, 1953-89, 4¼ In.	194.00
Figurine, H.M. Queen Elizabeth II, On Imperial, No. 1546, 1958-81, 10½ In.	452.00
Figurine, Hereford Bull, No. 1363A, c.1955, 4½ In.	130.00
Figurine, Highland Calf, No. 1827D, 1962-90, 3 In.	83.00
Figurine, Highland Snowman, DS 7, 1987-93, 5¼ In.	83.00
Figurine, Horse, Spirit Of Fire, Brown Matte, No. 2829, 1986-89, 8 In.	65.00 to 83.00
Figurine, Horse, Spirit Of Wind, Brown Gloss, No. 2688, c.1987, 8 In.	56.00
Figurine, Horse, Spirit Of Youth, Gray Matte, No. 2703, 1982-89, 7 In.	93.00
Figurine, Hunca Munca Sweeping, BP 6A, 1977-Present	19.00
Figurine, Hunter, Brown, Large, No. 1734, 1961-63, 11¼ In.	113.00
Figurine, Hunter, Gray, Large, No. 1734, 1961-63, 11¼ In.	169.00
Figurine, Huntsman, Brown Horse, No. 1501, 1957-95, 8¼ In.	339.00
Figurine, Huntsman, On Rearing Horse, Brown, No. 868, 2nd Version, 1940-52, 10 In.	316.00
Figurine, Huntsman, On Rearing Horse, White, No. 868, 2nd Version, 1965-71, 10 In.	1084.00
Figurine, Huntswoman, Gray Horse, No. 1730, 1960-95, 8¼ In.	790.00
Figurine, Huntswoman, No. 982, 1942-67, 10 In.	444.00
Figurine, Jay, No. 2417, 1972-82, 5 In.	147.00
Figurine, Jemima & Her Ducklings, BP 10A	79.00
Figurine, Jersey Bull, Matte, No. 1422, 1985-89, 4⅓ In.	130.00
Figurine, Kick Start, Thelwell, No. 2769B, 1983-89, 3½ In.	192.00
Figurine, King Eider Duck, Peter Scott, No. 1521, 1958-71, 4 In.	158.00
Figurine, Kookaburra, No. 1159, 1949-76, 5¾ In.	169.00
Figurine, Lady Mouse, BP 2	79.00
Figurine, Lapwing, Split Tail Feathers, No. 2416A, 1972, 5½ In.	185.00
Figurine, Lipizzaner, With Rider, No. 2467, 2nd Version, 1981, 10 In.	903.00
Figurine, Magpie, No. 2305, 1970-82, 5 In.	148.00
Figurine, Merino Ram, No. 1917, 1964-67, 4¼ In.	1855.00 to 2260.00
Figurine, Morgan Stallion, Tarryall Maestro, No. 2605, 1979-89, 11½ In.	277.00
Figurine, Mounted Indian, Skewbald, No. 1391, 1955-90, 8½ In.	320.00
Figurine, Mr. Alderman Ptolemy, No. 2424, 3½ In.	53.00
Figurine, Mr. Jeremy Fisher, Spotted Legs, BP 2	102.00
Figurine, Mrs. Rabbit, Umbrella Out, BP 2	124.00
Figurine, Mrs. Tiggy-Winkle, No. 1107, 1998	37.00
Figurine, Nijinsky, No. 2345, 1971-89, 11¼ In.	169.00
Figurine, Norwegian Fjord Horse, No. 2282, 1970-75, 6½ In.	632.00
Figurine, Paddington At The Station, Box, 1996-98, 4¼ In.	42.00
Figurine, Peter On His Book, No. 4217, 2002	37.00
Figurine, Pigeon, Blue, No. 1383, 1955-72, 5½ In.	148.00
Figurine, Pigeon, Red, No. 1383, 1955-72, 5½ In.	148.00
Figurine, Piglet, No. 2214, 1968-90, 2¾ In.	68.00
Figurine, Pigling Bland, BP 2	181.00
Figurine, Pinto Pony, Skewbaldno. 1373, 1st Version, 1st Edition, 1955, 6½ In.	181.00
Figurine, Pony Express, Thelwell, No. 2789A, 1983-89, 4½ In.	519.00
Figurine, Puppit Dog, No. 1002, 1944-69, 4¾ In.	56.00
Figurine, Red Setter, Lying, No. 1060, 1946-73, 3 In.	194.00
Figurine, Rough Collie, No. 3129, 1988-89, 5½ In.	83.00
Figurine, Sally Henny Penny, BP 3A	79.00
Figurine, Samuel Whiskers, BP 2	102.00
Figurine, Shetland Pony, Brown, No. 1033, 1945-89, 5¾ In.	45.00
Figurine, Shoveler, Peter Scott, No. 1528, 1958-71, 3½ In.	147.00
Figurine, Simpkin, No. 2508, 4 In.	284.00
Figurine, Songthrush, Matte, No. 2308, 1983-89, 5¾ In.	102.00
Figurine, Spirit Of Peace, White, No. 2916, 1986-89, 4¾ In.	45.00
Figurine, Steeplechaser, No. 2505, 1975-81, 8¾ In.	903.00
Figurine, Swish Tail Horse, Chestnut, No. 1182, 1958-67, 8¾ In.	316.00
Figurine, Tableau, Flopsy, Mopsy, Cottontail, Limited Edition	79.00
Figurine, Thoroughbred Stallion, Chestnut, No. 1772, 8 In.	700.00
Figurine, Tom Kitten, No. 1100, 1972-87, 3½ In. ....*illus*	106.00
Figurine, Tommy Brock, BP 2, 1st Version Spade, Handle Out	271.00
Figurine, Turkey, Brown, No. 1957, 1964-69, 7¼ In.	632.00 to 648.00
Figurine, Unicorn, Bronze, No. 3021, 1989-92, 9 In.	350.00

Bennington, Pitcher, Hunting Scene, Deer, Rabbits, Rockingham Glaze, 9½ In. $129.00

Beswick, Figurine, Gamecock, No. 2059, 1966-75, 9½ In. $150.00

Beswick, Figurine, Tom Kitten, No. 1100, 1972-87, 3½ In. $106.00

Betty Boop, Figurine Set,
Betty & Her Pals, Bisque, Box,
Fleischer Studios, 1930s, 4 Piece
$1075.00

Betty Boop, Nodder,
Celluloid, Tin Base, Windup,
Prewar Japan, 7 In.
$805.00

Bicycle, Postcard,
Photo, Excelsior
Auto Cycle, Rider, c.1909
$588.00

Figurine, Welsh Mountain Pony, No. 1643, 1961-89, 6¼ In.	339.00
Figurine, Wessex, Saddleback Boar, No. 1512, 1957-69, 2¾ In.	368.00
Figurine, Wessex, Saddleback Sow, No. 1511, 1957-69, 2¾ In.	245.00
Figurine, Wired Haired Terrier, No. 963, 1941-84, 5¾ In.	126.00
Figurine, Woodpecker, Lesser Spotted, No. 2420, 1972-82, 5½ In.	240.00
Jug, Double Diamond Man, No. 1517, 1958, 8 In.	181.00
Jug, Face, Midshipman, Toby, No. 1112, 1948-63, 5¼ In.	316.00
Plaque, Point Of Sale, Millennium, c.2000	215.00

BETTY BOOP, the cartoon figure, first appeared on the screen in 1931. Her face was modeled after the famous singer Helen Kane and her body after Mae West. In 1935, a comic strip was started. Her dog was named Bimbo. Although the Betty Boop cartoons ended by 1938, there was a revival of interest in the Betty Boop image in the 1980s and new pieces are being made.

Ashtray, Betty & Bimbo, Lustreware, 2 Cigarette Indents, 4 In.	29.00
Ashtray, Bimbo, Seated, 4 Snuffers, Lustreware, 3 In.	29.00
Dish, Betty Boop, Vandor Label, Marked, 1984, 4½ In.	3.00
Doll, Cloth, Felt, Straw Filled, Dog Look Face, Spain, c.1930, 10 In.	196.00
Doll, Composition, Cloth Dress & Shoes, Heart Decal, Cameo Doll Co., 1930s, 12 In.	4700.00
Figure, Blond, Cardboard, Movable, Brass Rivets, 1930s, 9½ In.	496.00
Figurine, Pink Dress, Jointed, Celluloid, Prewar Japan, 8 In.	392.00
Figurine Set, Betty & Her Pals, Bisque, Box, Fleischer Studios, 1930s, 4 Piece *illus*	1075.00
Nodder, Celluloid, Tin Base, Windup, Prewar Japan, 7 In. *illus*	805.00
Nodder, Pink Dress, Blue Base, Celluloid, Tin, Prewar, Japan, Marked, 7 In.	330.00
Nodder, Windup, Celluloid, Tin, Fleischer Studios, Prewar Japan, Box, 7 In.	952.00
Toy, Acrobat, Flag On Pole, Windup, Celluloid, Prewar Japan, Box, 9 In.	1232.00
Toy, Betty Boop, On Swing, Windup, Celluloid, Prewar	750.00
Wall Pocket, Betty & Bimbo, Lusterware, 1940s	217.00

BICYCLES were invented in 1839. The first manufactured bicycle was made in 1861. Special ladies' bicycles were made after 1874. The modern safety bicycle was not produced until 1885. Collectors search for all types of bicycles and tricycles. Bicycle-related items are also listed here.

Bike Plate, Iver Johnson Bicycles, Porcelain Insert, Fitchburg, Mass., 1890s, 3½ In.	59.00
Boneshaker, Wood, Horse, Leather Seat, T-Shape Handle, Horsehair Tail, c.1825, 69 In.	9227.00
Chris Craft, Fold-Away, Storage Bag, Oak, Pair	352.00
Clipper, Chainless, Drive Shaft, Maroon Paint, c.1900	1210.00
Columbia Clipper, Super Deluxe, Boy's, 1950s	330.00
Headlight, Wheel Driven, 121-6W Super Mini, MD612GD, Mitsuba	47.50
Hickory 2-Wheeler, Original Paint, Wooden Rims & Spokes, c.1890-1910	1000.00
High Wheel, Short Handlebars, Leather Seat, c.1890-95, 54-In. Front Wheel, 60 In.	2415.00
J.C. Higgins Colorflow, Silver & Black, Restored, 1950s	2090.00
Medal, Gold, Boston Wheelmen, Star Shape, 100 Mile Race, 1895, 2 x 1½ In.	72.00
Medal, Gold, Jacob Nicholsen, ½ Mile, Engraved, c.1892, 2¼ x 1¼ In.	127.00
Motor, Rollaway, Toledo, Box, c.1919	302.00
Pin, Iver Johnson Cycles, Bicycle Wheel, Woman's Head, c.1901, ⅞ In.	62.00
Pin, Major Taylor, Iver Johnson Cycles, 1901	160.00
Postcard, Photo, Excelsior Auto Cycle, Rider, c.1909 *illus*	588.00
Schwinn, Black Phantom, Pressed Steel, Cast Iron, Rubber Tires, Springer Front, 26 In.	550.00
Schwinn, Spitfire, Red & Cream Paint, 1950s, 16 In.	99.00
Schwinn, Wasp, 3-Wheeler, Rear Carrying Basket, Late 1940s	358.00
Scooter, 4 Spoked Wheels, Roll-About, Henley, 28 In. *illus*	527.00
Sears, GTO, Muscle Type, 1960s	88.00
Shelby, Donald Duck, Yellow, Donald Head Ornament In Front, Blue Accents, 1949	2630.00
Sign, Humber Cycles, Enamel, 19 x 28½ In.	157.00
Sign, Raleigh, Enamel, c.1920, 18½ x 28½ In.	458.00
Tray, Columbia Cycles, Brass, Enamel, c.1900, 4 x 3 In.	85.00
Tricycle, Columbia Boycycle, Wire Spokes, Leather Seat, Steinfeld Brothers, 35 x 37 In.	374.00
Tricycle, Steelcraft, Front Headlight, Back Wheel Fenders, Pressed Steel, 28 In. *illus*	527.00
Velocipede, 3 Spoked Wheels, Pedals, Upholstered Seat Cushions, 19th Century, 38 In. *illus*	323.00

BING & GRONDAHL is a famous Danish factory making fine porcelains from 1853 to the present. Underglaze blue decoration was started in 1886. The annual Christmas plate series was introduced in 1895. Dinnerwares, stoneware, and figurines are still being made today. The firm has used the initials B & G and a stylized castle as part of the mark since 1898. The company became part of Royal Copenhagen in 1987.

Bell, Christmas, 1981, Box, 3 In.	19.00
Bell, Church, Trees, Snow, Incised, Jule Aften, 1986, 3 x 2⅝ In.	18.00
Figurine, 3 Birds, No. 1670	275.00
Figurine, Boy, With Umbrella, Marked, 7¼ x 3¼ In.	116.00
Figurine, Boy & Girl Kissing, 7 In.	88.00
Figurine, Dickie, Boy Bending Down, No. 1636	140.00
Figurine, Dog, Boxer, Stamped, No. 2212	75.00
Figurine, Eagle, Painted, Glossy, 20th Century, 21½ In.	333.00
Figurine, Fish Girl, Signed, Kai Nielsen, 3 x 4 In.	250.00
Figurine, Girl, Touching Hem Of Skirt, No. 1995, 5 In.	185.00
Figurine, Girl Cradling Doll, 8 In.	47.00
Figurine, Goose, No. 1902, 1½ x 3½ In.	65.00
Plaque, Easter Song, Figure On Hill Watching Sunrise, Acton Friis, 1916, 8 In.	125.00
Plate, Christmas, 1895, Behind The Frozen Window	6000.00
Plate, Christmas, 1896, New Moon Over Snow-Covered Trees, 7 In.	2700.00
Plate, Christmas, 1897, Christmas Meal Of The Sparrows, 7 In.	1300.00
Plate, Christmas, 1898, Christmas Roses & Christmas Star, 7 In.	900.00
Plate, Christmas, 1899, Crows Enjoying Christmas, 7 In.	1350.00
Plate, Christmas, 1900, Church Bells Chiming In Christmas, 7 In.	1050.00
Plate, Christmas, 1901, 3 Wise Men From The East, 7 In.	400.00
Plate, Christmas, 1902, Interior Of Gothic Church, Jensen, 7 In.	340.00
Plate, Christmas, 1903, Happy Expectations Of The Children, 7 In.	340.00
Plate, Christmas, 1904, View Of Copenhagen From Frederiksberg Hill, 7 In.	150.00
Plate, Christmas, 1905, Anxiety Of The Coming Christmas Night, 7 In.	150.00
Plate, Christmas, 1906, Sleighing To Church On Christmas Eve, 7 In.	70.00
Plate, Christmas, 1909, Happiness Over The Yule Tree, 7 In.	110.00
Plate, Christmas, 1910, Old Organist, 7 In.	85.00
Plate, Christmas, 1911, First It Was Sung By The Angels To The Shepherds In The Field, 7 In.	70.00
Plate, Christmas, 1914, Royal Castle Amalienborg, Copenhagen, 7 In.	70.00
Plate, Christmas, 1915, Chained Dog Getting Double Meal Christmas Eve, 7 In.	110.00
Plate, Christmas, 1916, Christmas Prayer Of The Sparrows, 7 In.	70.00
Plate, Christmas, 1917, Arrival Of Christmas Boat, 7 In.	100.00
Plate, Christmas, 1919, Outside The Lighted Window, 7 In.	60.00
Plate, Christmas, 1920, Hare In The Snow, 7 In.	60.00
Plate, Christmas, 1921, Pigeons In Castle Court, 7 In.	60.00
Plate, Christmas, 1922, Star Of Bethlehem, 7 In.	60.00
Plate, Christmas, 1923, Royal Hunting Castle, Ermitage, 7 In.	60.00
Plate, Christmas, 1924, Lighthouse In Danish Waters, 7 In.	70.00
Plate, Christmas, 1925, Child's Christmas, 7 In.	60.00
Plate, Christmas, 1926, Churchgoers On Christmas Day, 7 In.	60.00
Plate, Christmas, 1927, Skating Couple, 7 In.	70.00 to 100.00
Plate, Christmas, 1929, Fox Outside On Christmas Eve, 7 In.	60.00
Plate, Christmas, 1930, Yule Tree In Town Hall Square Of Copenhagen, 7 In.	95.00
Plate, Christmas, 1931, Arrival Of The Christmas Train, 7 In.	60.00
Plate, Christmas, 1932, Lifeboat At Work, 7 In.	60.00
Plate, Christmas, 1933, Korsor-Nyborg Ferry, 7 In.	60.00
Plate, Christmas, 1934, Church Bell In Tower, 7 In.	60.00
Plate, Christmas, 1935, Lillebelt Bridge Connecting Funen With Jutland, 7 In.	60.00
Plate, Christmas, 1936, Royal Guard, Outside Amalienborg Castle, 7 In.	60.00
Plate, Christmas, 1950, Kronborg Castle At Elsinore, 7 In.	70.00
Plate, Christmas, 1951, Jens Bang, New Passenger Boat, 7 In.	60.00
Plate, Christmas, 1952, Old Copenhagen Canals At Wintertime, 7 In.	60.00
Plate, Christmas, 1954, Birthplace Of Han Christian Andersen, 7 In.	90.00
Plate, Christmas, 1955, Kalundborg Church, 7 In.	118.00
Plate, Christmas, 1961, Winter Harmony, 7 In.	70.00
Plate, Christmas, 1963, Christmas Elf, 7 In.	70.00
Plate, Christmas, 1966, Home For Christmas, 7 In.	13.50
Plate, Christmas, 1970, Pheasants In Snow At Christmas, 7 In.	40.00
Plate, Christmas, 1974, Christmas In Village, 7 In.	17.00
Plate, Christmas, 1990, Changing Of The Guard At Fredensborg, 7 In.	55.00
Plate, Christmas, 1991, Copenhagen Stock Exchange, 7 In.	55.00
Plate, Christmas, 1992, Pastor's Christmas, 7 In.	55.00
Plate, Christmas, 1993, Father Christmas In Copenhagen, 7 In.	60.00
Plate, Christmas, 1997, Country Christmas, 7 In.	55.00
Plate, Christmas, 1998, Santa Around The World	50.00
Plate, Christmas, 1999, Christmas Eve At Mt. Rushmore, 5 In.	38.00

Bicycle, Scooter,
4 Spoked Wheels,
Roll-About, Henley, 28 In.
$527.00

Bicycle, Tricycle,
Steelcraft, Front Headlight,
Back Wheel Fenders,
Pressed Steel, 28 In.
$527.00

Bicycle, Velocipede,
3 Spoked Wheels, Pedals,
Upholstered Seat Cushions,
19th Century, 38 In.
$323.00

TIP

*Your collectibles will live
best at the temperature
and humidity that is
comfortable for you.
Not too hot, cold, wet,
or dry.*

B

Bing & Grøndahl

When Bing & Grøndahl became part of Royal Copenhagen in 1987, some Bing & Grøndahl dinnerware, figurines, and vases were discontinued; some remained in production, but were marked with the Royal Copenhagen mark. The Bing & Grøndahl name was used only on commemorative and annual pieces and a few overglaze-decorated figurines.

Birdcage, French Chateau,
Tin Roof, Colored Glass Windows,
19th Century, 40 x 39 x 13 In.
$3335.00

Birdcage, Tin,
Painted, Domed Roof, 16½ In.
$732.00

Plate, Christmas, 2000, Santa Around The World		65.00
Plate, Christmas, 2001, Christmas Eve At The White House, 5½ In.		22.00
Plate, Christmas, 2002, Christmas Eve, 7 In.		65.00
Plate, Christmas, 2004, Christmas Tree, 7 In.		66.00
Plate, Easter, 1910, Empty Tomb		55.00
Plate, Easter, 1911, Angel & Mount Cavalry		55.00
Plate, Easter, 1912, Mount Cavalry & Crosses		55.00
Plate, Easter, 1913, Birds & Daffodils		55.00
Plate, Easter, 1915, Sheep Grazing		55.00
Plate, Easter, 1916, Country Church, The Coming Of Spring		55.00
Plate, Easter, 1919, Black Bird		55.00
Plate, Easter, 1920, Tomb		55.00
Plate, Easter, 1924, Man Sowing Seeds		55.00
Plate, Easter, 1926, Farmer		55.00
Plate, First Crush, Boy Gets Kiss, Kurt Ard, Box		30.00
Plate, Mother's Day, 1969, Cocker & Pups		225.00
Plate, Mother's Day, 1987, Sheep & Lambs		55.00
Plate, Mother's Day, 1988, Crested Plover & Young		55.00
Plate, Mother's Day, 1989, Cow & Calf		55.00
Plate, Mother's Day, 1990, Hen & Chicks		70.00
Plate, Mother's Day, 1992, Panda & Cubs		60.00
Plate, Mother's Day, 1993, St. Bernard Dog & Pups		72.00
Plate, Mother's Day, 1994, Cat & Kittens		75.00
Plate, Mother's Day, 1995, Hedgehog & Young		55.00
Plate, Mother's Day, 1996, Koala & Young		55.00
Plate, Mother's Day, 1998, Emperor Penguin & Family		55.00
Tray, Water Lily, Lily Pad Design, Blue, Green, Marked, 10½ In.		75.00

BINOCULARS of all types are wanted by collectors. Those made in the eighteenth and nineteenth centuries are favored by serious collectors. The small, attractive binoculars called opera glasses are listed in their own category.

Airguide Chicago, 4 x 32, Leather Case		55.00
Busch, Terlux, B 24 x 54, No. 165748, Leather Covered Barrels, Strap, Case		176.00
Civil War, Black Enamel, Sliding Eyeshades, Gutta-Percha Wheel, Baltimore		150.00
Civil War, Black Enameled Brass Body, Draw Tubes, Leatherette Caps, Case		195.00
Gun Sight, Ross, No. 122943, Coated Optics, Royal Navy, c.1947, 15 In.		1293.00
Kevin Kuhne, Wild 20 x 80, 8 Cm., No. 20012, 3 Degree Field, Tripod, 5 Ft.		2820.00
Sport, 4 x 30, Center Wheel Focus, Hinged Barrels, Neck Strap, Case		15.00
Tower, 3 x 33, Metal, Black Paint, Case, Plastic Strap		10.00
U.S. Signal Corp., Gutta-Percha, Leatherette Covers, Marchand, 1907, 8 In.		250.00
Westinghouse, 7 x 50, U.S. Military, M-15, No. 3803, Leather Case, 1944		225.00

BIRDCAGES are collected for use as homes for pet birds and as decorative objects of folk art. Elaborate wooden cages of the past centuries can still be found. The brass or wicker cages of the 1930s are popular with bird owners.

Ash, Wire, Bronzed, Conservatory Shape, Turned Posts & Finials, Germany, 42 x 29 In.		1800.00
Brass, Art Deco, Greek Key, Acid Etched, Glass Seed Guard, Perch, Slide-Out Tray		400.00
Brass, Perch, Glass Seed Guards, Victorian		250.00
Canary, Wire Scrolls, Looped, Perch, Slide-Out Tray, 4 Raised Feet, Victorian, Germany		400.00
Crown, Metal, 5 Cups, 1920-40, 14¼ x 13 x 9 In.		139.00
Crown, Metal, Light Green, 2 Springs, Perch, 2 Plastic Containers, Stand, Cast Iron Base, 63 In.		155.00
French Chateau, Tin Roof, Colored Glass Windows, 19th Century, 40 x 39 x 13 In.	*illus*	3335.00
Hendryx, Chrome, Swing, Perches, Seed Cups, 1920-40, 15 x 14 x 9 In.		129.00
Hendryx, Painted Red Flowers On Panels, Metal, 1930-40, 15½ x 14 x 9 In.		129.00
Metal, Ceramic Cup, 3 Bottom Clips, 1930s, 16 x 12½ In.		120.00
Tin, Painted, Domed Roof, 16½ In.	*illus*	732.00
Tin & Wire, Clock Tower, Belfry, Glass & Metal Watering Equipment, France, 40 x 40 In.		3335.00
Victorian, White, 3-Piece, 61 x 31½ x 14 In.		650.00
Wire, Wood, 2-Tower Top, Turned Finials, Painted Flowers On Sides, Gray Ground, 34 x 27 In.		690.00
Wood & Wire, 39 x 21 x 10 In.		146.00

BISQUE is an unglazed baked porcelain. Finished bisque has a slightly sandy texture with a dull finish. Some of it may be decorated with various colors. Bisque gained favor during the late Victorian era when thousands of bisque figurines were made. It is still being made. Additional bisque items may be listed under the factory name.

Bust, Sevres Style, Gilt Metal Plinth, 19th Century, 8 In.	529.00
Bust, Victorian Boy, Flower Shirt, Brown Hair, 9⅛ In.	44.00
Compote, Minton, Turquoise Ground, Reticulated Basket, Gilt, 12 In.	764.00
Figurine, Bust, Boy, Victorian, Blond Hair, Striped Shirt, Bowtie, 11½ In. ....*illus*	55.00
Figurine, Fisherman, A. Balcari, Italy, c.1980, 12 In.	41.00
Figurine, Gentleman Holding Hand Of Woman With Flower, 15¼ In.	176.00
Figurine, Girl & Dog, In Chair, Tray, Spoon & Plate, Putting Bib On Dog, 12½ In.	230.00
Figurine, Horses, France, c.1950, 8 x 10 In.	82.00
Figurine, Madonna, White, On Serpent, Domed Astral Globe, Italy, 19 In.	240.00
Figurine, Peasant Girl, Holding Pitcher, Beaker, Basket, Gardner, 8 In.	2233.00
Figurine, Peasant Girl, Holding Sheaf Of Wheat, Shielding Eyes, 9 In.	1145.00
Figurine, Peasant Woman, Feeding Baby, Child Seated, Gardner, 5¾ In.	1528.00
Group, Man, Clutching Bottle, Wife, Helping Him Up, Child Tugging At Skirt, 7 In.	3290.00
Group, Mother On Bench, Feeding Children, Gardner, 5½ In.	1175.00
Plaque, Multicolored, Relief, Courting Couple, Frame, 21 x 19 & 24 x 22 In., 2 Piece	293.00
Vase, Andrea, Hand Painted, Flowers, Putti, 10½ In., Pair	94.00
Vase, Painted, Flower, Gilt Bands, England, 10½ In., Pair	70.00
Vase, Victorian Girl Standing Next To Petal Form Vase, 6¼ In.	44.00

Bisque, Figurine,
Bust, Boy, Victorian,
Blond Hair, Striped Shirt,
Bowtie, 11½ In.
$55.00

BLACK memorabilia has become an important area of collecting since the 1970s. The best material dates from past centuries, but many recent items are also of interest. F & F is the mark used on plastic made by Fiedler & Fiedler Mold & Die Works, Inc. in the 1930s and 1940s. Objects that picture a black person may also be listed in this book under Advertising; Tin; Bank; Bottle Opener; Cookie Jar; Doll; Salt & Pepper; Sheet Music; Toy; etc.

Ashtray, Butler, Ashtray, Yellow & Salmon Coat, Green Striped Pants, Tin, Wood, 36 In.	550.00
Banner, Aunt Jemima Pancakes, Image Of Aunt Jemima, 2-Sided, Oilcloth, 1950s, 15 Ft.	250.00
Box, Recipe, Aunt Jemima, Plastic, Cardboard, Hinged Lid, 3¾ x 5¼ x 3½ In.	99.00
Cigar Box, Log Cabin Home, Blacks Dancing, Lithograph, 5½ x 8⅝ x 4⅞ In.	121.00
Cigar Vender, Tom Distributor, Coin-Operated, Black Jockey, Walnut Frame, 25½ In.	12100.00
Cookie Jars are listed in the Cookie Jar category.	
Doll, Bisque Socket Head, Mohair, Jointed Wood, Composition, Stick Leg Body, 17½ In.	201.00
Doll, Bisque Socket Head, Side Set Sleep Eyes, Curly Mohair, Composition, Baby, 12 In.	518.00
Doll, Child, Glass Eyes, Velveteen Construction, Norah Wellings, c.1930, 17 In.	118.00
Doll, Cloth, Bead Eyes, Striped Shirt, Overalls, 7½ In.	495.00
Doll, Cloth, Bottle, Sewn Facial Features, Cotton Wig, Holding 2 Small Cloth Dolls, 14 In.	660.00
Doll, Cloth, Cotton Head, Horsehair Stuffing, Attached Limbs, Stitched Fingers, Jointed, 30 In.	2070.00
Doll, Cloth, Flat Face, Painted Features, Gathered Ears, Open Mouth, Teeth, Woolly Wig, 21 In.	764.00
Doll, Cloth, Homemade Outfits, Embroidered Facial Features, Yarn Hair, 16 In., Pair	303.00
Doll, Cloth, Oil-Painted Face, 2-Piece Rounded Back Head, Jointed Shoulder, Knees, 12 In.	345.00
Doll, Cloth, Relief Facial Features, Gray Hair, Shoebutton Eyes, Red Print Dress, 19½ In.	990.00
Doll, Cloth, Sewn Facial Features, Pouty Mouth, Brown Hair, Dress, Striped Socks, 21 In.	2640.00
Doll, Girl, Bisque Socket Head, Black Complexion, Eyes, Mohair, Jointed, c.1900	7150.00
Doll, Mammy, Stockinet, Painted Eyes & Mouth, Original Clothes, c.1900, 20 In. ......*illus*	489.00
Doll, Man, Tuxedo, Cane, Top Hat, Holding Flowers, Celluloid, Japan, 1920s, 7½ In.	80.00
Doll, Rag, Made By Emily Stover, Brunswick, Maine, 1915	633.00
Doll, Sasha, Caleb, Vinyl, Jointed, c.1972-79, 16 In.	29.00
Doorknocker, Mammy, Clothesbasket On Head, Arms & Chest Are Clapper, Cast Iron, 7 x 4½ In.	2475.00
Figure, Old Jo, Wood, Metal, Clark Coe, Late 19th Century, 55 x 20¾ x 7¾ In.	36000.00
Figure, Preacher, Wood Podium, Lead Hands, Glass Eyes, Cast Iron, Windup, 9 In.	1380.00
Figure, Woman Behind Podium, Pounds Hand, Windup, 8 In.	6900.00
Figure, Zeke, Composition Bust, Black Man, Green Hat, Late 19th Century, 16 In.	283.00
Figurine, Black Boy Playing Concertina, Ceramic, Painted, c.1900, 9½ In.	478.00
Figurine, Hitchy-Koo Lady & Man, c.1920, 4¼ In., Pair	717.00
Figurine, Mr. Adam & Mrs. Eve, Bisque, c.1900, 7½ In., Pair	800.00
Hitching Post, Boy, Mottled, White Shirt, Blue Pants, Suspenders, Square Base, Iron, 44 x 15 In.	1140.00
Lawn Sprinkler, Black Man, In Overalls, Striped Shirt, Hat, Tin Lithograph, Mid 1900s, 36 In.	146.00
Marionette, Wood, Carved & Painted Head, Hinged Mouth, Jointed Body, Fabric Suit, 36 In.	1840.00
Mug, Golly Golliwog, Robertson's Jams & Marmalades, 1960s-70s, 3 In. ....*illus*	31.00
Pail, Aunt Jemima, Sugar Butter, Rigney & Co., 3½ x 4⅜ In.	825.00
Pail, Pickaninny Peanut Butter, Child, Doll, Yellow, Red, Tin Litho, Handle, 1 Lb., 3½ x 3¾ In.	358.00
Pipe, Pottery, Man's Head, Big Red Lips, Floppy Hat, Bandana, Carved Wood Stem, 2 x 6 In.	187.00
Postcard, J.J. Allen & Co., America's Largest Colored Owned Department Store, Buffalo	30.00
Poster, Field Minstrels, Emmett Miller, c.1925, 41 x 27 In.	2350.00
Salt & Pepper, Aunt Jemima, Uncle Moses, F & F Mold & Die Works, 5 In. ....*illus*	77.00
Sign, Aunt Jemima Pancake Flour, Perfect Pancakes, Cardboard, 1918, 12 x 22 In.	280.00

TIP
A good way to clean bisque is with a toothbrush and white toothpaste. Brush gently, then rinse completely in warm water.

Black, Doll,
Mammy, Stockinet,
Painted Eyes & Mouth, Original Clothes,
c.1900, 20 In.
$489.00

Black, Mug, Golly Golliwog, Robertson's Jams & Marmalades, 1960s-70s, 3 In. $31.00

Black, Salt & Pepper, Aunt Jemima, Uncle Moses, F & F Mold & Die Works, 5 In. $77.00

SECURITY TIP

Don't keep identification on your key ring. If it is lost, it's an invitation for burglars to visit.

Blenko Glass Company, Pitcher, Amberina, Paneled, Applied Amber Handle, 9 x 9¾ In. $71.00

Slave Anklet, Cast Iron, Oval Opening, 2 Wide Hollow Flanges, c.1800, 5¼ x 7½ In.	1770.00
Slave Identification Tag, Servant, Copper, Diamond Shape, South Carolina, 1838	3186.00
Slave Merchant Token, W.W. Wilbur, Charleston, S.C., c.1846	413.00
Slave Shackles, Leg, Wrought Iron, c.1750, 13 x 3½ In.	1298.00
Syrup, Aunt Jemima, Red Plastic, Impressed On Bottom F & F, 5½ In.	55.00
Tie Rack, Porter, Sirocco, 1920s, 8 x 10 In.	65.00
Tin, Aunt Jemima Pancakes, Quaker Limited Edition, 1983, 6 In.	13.00
Tobacco Jar, Black Boy On Watermelon, Blue Shirt, Red Hat, Stamped 9909, 9¼ In.	2011.00
Tobacco Jar, Man Holding Up Grinning Pig, Ceramic, Stamped, Austria	1868.00
Token, Slave Auctioneer, W.W. Wilbur, Copper, 1846	2714.00
Ventriloquist Dummy, Black Man, Composition Head, Original Clothing, 37 In.	7300.00
Ventriloquist Dummy, Man, Papier-Mache, Wood, Fabric, Hinged Mouth, Striped Clothing, 32 In.	1725.00
Ventriloquist Dummy, Sailor, Hinged Jaw, Big Eyes, Wood Stand, 45 In.	5520.00
Watercolor, Young Black Girl With Black Cat, Frame, Alice Scott, 4¼ x 3¼ In.	920.00
Wood Carving, Figure, Minstrel, Man, Green Coat, Woman, Striped Dress, 17 In., Pair	6600.00

BLACK AMETHYST glass appears black until it is held to the light, then a dark purple can be seen. It has been made in many factories from 1860 to the present.

Biscuit Jar, 6½ In.	155.00
Compote, Candy, 3-Footed	18.00
Tidbit, Center Handle, 8-Sided, 11 x 5 In.	35.00
Vase, 2 Silver Bands, 6¼ In.	29.00
Wine, Goblet, Black, 7 In.	4.00

BLENKO GLASS COMPANY is the 1930s successor to several glassworks founded by William John Blenko in Milton, West Virginia. In 1933, his son, William H. Blenko Sr. took charge. The company made a line of reproductions for Colonial Williamsburg. They are still in business and are best known today for their decorative wares and stained glass.

BLENKO — HANDCRAFT.

Apple, Ruby, 3½ In.	85.00
Ashtray, Orange Yellow Amber, 6 In.	9.60
Beaker, 3 Green Leaves, 7 In.	75.00
Beaker, Crackle, 4 Turquoise Blue Leafs, 6 x 9½ In.	135.00
Bottle, Stopper, Tangerine, 13 In.	140.00
Bottle, Water, Antique Green, Original Label, 8 In.	28.00
Bowl, Amethyst, Pedestal, 7 In.	45.00
Bowl, Antique Green, 12 In.	50.00
Bowl, Crackle, Green Stem & Foot, 7 In.	75.00
Bowl, Emerald Green, Ringed, 3¾ x 11 In.	125.00
Bowl, Nut, Cobalt Blue, 5½ In.	24.00
Decanter, Amethyst, 1950s, 22¾ In.	295.00
Decanter, Pinched Sides, 10 In.	60.00
Decanter, Tangerine Fish, 1962, 19 In.	30.00
Ewer, Ball Stopper, Tangerine Crackle, 11½ In.	95.00
Lighter, Metal Insert, Japanned, 7½ In.	85.00
Paperweight, Mushroom Shape, Green With Yellow Swirls, 4½ In.	31.50
Pitcher, Amberina, Paneled, Applied Amber Handle, 9 x 9¾ In. . . . . *illus*	71.00
Pitcher, Optic Tangerine, 10½ In.	95.00
Pitcher, Spout, Long Handle, Aqua, Blown Glass Bottom, 1950s, 12 In.	65.00
Tile, Amber, 8 x 8 In.	25.00
Tray, Ruby, Ruffled Edge, 11½ In.	25.00
Vase, 3 Rosettes, Crackle, 4½ In.	99.50
Vase, Applied Amber Leaves, 9 x 6 In.	125.00
Vase, Blue Spiral Threading, 10½ x 6¼ In.	50.00
Vase, Crackle, Rippled Fans, Blenko Blue, Winslow Anderson, Early 1950s, 7⅝ In.	45.00
Vase, Crystal, Rosette, 7½ In.	110.00
Vase, Emerald Green, Controlled Bubble, 3½ In.	15.00
Vase, Emerald Green, Pinched, 9 In.	119.00
Vase, Fire Red, Pulled, 33 In.	200.00
Vase, Fish, Figural, Amber, 1960s, 9 In.	95.00
Vase, Heart Shape, Original Sticker, 4¾ In.	33.00
Vase, Pulled Glass, Fire Red, Horizontal Waves, 33 In.	200.00
Vase, Red, Twisted, 20 x 8 In.	150.00
Vase, Rosette, Yellow, 7½ In.	110.00
Vase, Topaz, Cobalt Blue Handles, Original Label, 9 In.	41.00

Vase, Transparent Green Vase, Fluted Top, Footed Base, Foil Label, 8 x 7¼ In.		55.00
Vase, Trumpet, Amberina, 1950s, 14 In.		125.00

BLOWN GLASS, *see Glass-Blown category.*

BLUE GLASS, *see Cobalt Blue category.*

BLUE ONION, *see Onion category.*

BLUE WILLOW, *see Willow category.*

BOCH FRERES factory was founded in 1841 in La Louviere in eastern Belgium. The wares resemble the work of Villeroy & Boch. The factory is still in business.

Box, White, Blue, Turquoise, Charles Catteau, c.1925, 5½ In.	267.00
Vase, 5 Bats, Blue, Stylized Landscape, Gres Keramis, Ch. Cattiar, 10⅜ In.	8913.00
Vase, 5 Falcons, Blue Rocks, Matte Glaze, Egg Shape, Earthenware, 7⅛ In.	1380.00
Vase, Antelope, Flowers, Leaves, Blue, Turquoise, White, Crackled Glaze, Egg Shape, Keramis, 12 In.	1725.00
Vase, Antelope Grazing, Reverse Head High, Charles Catteau, Keramis, c.1925, 10 In.	1175.00
Vase, Black Elephants & Palm Trees, Red Ground, Flared Rim, C. Catteau, 10⅛ In.	920.00
Vase, Crackle Ground, Art Deco, 9 x 7 In.	300.00
Vase, Earthenware, Leaping Deer, Green Bands, Bulbous, Keramis, 11½ In. ....*illus*	2530.00
Vase, Earthenware, Matte Glaze, Doves, Leaves, Grass, Flared Rim, Charles Catteau, 16 In. *illus*	6900.00
Vase, Exotic Flowers & Leaves, Yellow, Orange, Green, Earthenware, Keramis, 11½ In.	633.00
Vase, Giraffes, Tree Fronds, Grasses, Brown, White, Crackled, Egg Shape, Keramis, 12 In.	4600.00
Vase, Gold Tone, Multicolored Flowers, 20th Century, 10 In.	206.00
Vase, Owls, Brown, Gray & Yellow Mottled Glazes, Rolled Rim, Gres Keramis, 12 In.	5060.00
Vase, Enameled Flowers, Green Crystalline Matte Glaze, Double Gourd Shape, 8⅝ In.	288.00
Vase, Squirrels With Acorns, Pine Needles, Brown Stylized Sun Borders, Ch. Catteau, 13½ In.	5060.00
Vase, Stoneware, 6 Panels, Floral Medallions, Gres Keramis Mark, 12⅛ In. ....*illus*	978.00
Vase, Stylized Dried Maize Leaves, Brown, Crackle Glaze Ground, Gres Keramis, 9⅝ In.	2185.00
Vase, Stylized Exotic Birds & Flowers, Green, Yellow, Orange, Brown, Matte Glaze, 10 In.	633.00
Vase, Swallows, Black, Turquoise, Blue, Crackle Ground, Oval, Earthenware, Keramis, 7½ In.	230.00
Vase, Wading Birds In Heavy Surf, Blue, Turquoise, White, Crackle Glaze Ground, 12 In.	805.00

BOEHM is the collector's name for the porcelains of Edward Marshall Boehm. In 1953 the Osso China Company was reorganized as Edward Marshall Boehm, Inc. The company is still working in England and New Jersey. In the early days of the factory, dishes were made, but the elaborate and lifelike bird figurines are the best-known ware. Edward Marshall Boehm, the founder, died in 1969, but the firm has continued to design and produce porcelain. Today, the firm makes both limited and unlimited editions of figurines and plates.

American Avocet, No. 206, 15½ In.	468.00
Arizona Queen Of The Night Cactus With Collard Lizard, c.1996, 10¼ x 6 In.	351.00
Asian Lion, No. 500-17, c.1980, 7¾ x 15½ In.	702.00
Baby Ocelot, No. 400-40, 5 x 9 In.	146.00
Baby Penguin, Bisque, 6 In.	117.00 to 146.00
Baby Robin, No. 437, 3¾ In.	35.00
Baby Wood Thrush, No. 444, 4½ In.	59.00
Bisque, Bushtit With Wall Flower, No. 100-39, No. 19, 1982, 7 x 7½ In.	146.00
Blue Grosbeak, 11½ x 8½ In.	351.00
Blue Jay, On Branch, Feeding Berry To 2 Chicks, Late 20th Century, 12 x 11 In.	805.00
Bonapart's Gulls, Bisque, 200-18, 6 x 6 In.	205.00
Boreal Owl, Bisque, No. 40172, No. 36, 12¼ x 13 In.	468.00
Dandelion, No. 20498, 1989, 5½ In.	146.00
Elephant, Gold Decorated, 7½ x 10 In.	527.00
Fledgling Brown Thrashers, Bisque, No. 400-72, 5½ In.	70.00
Fledgling Falcon, 6½ In.	59.00
Fledgling Magpie, No. 428, 5¼ In.	47.00
Fledgling Pilated Cleated Woodpecker, Bisque, No. 400-81, 6½ In.	234.00
Flower, 80th Birthday Her Majesty Queen Elizabeth, Queen Mother, c.1980, 7 x 10 In.	146.00
Flower, Alec's Red Rose, c.1980, No. 300-39, No. 114, 6½ x 8 In.	176.00
Flower, Begonia, 6 x 10½ In.	205.00
Flower, Royal Duet, Bisque, 19981, No. 330-68, No. 294	117.00
Frog, Bisque, No. 400-99, 2½ x 6 In.	146.00

Boch Freres, Vase, Earthenware, Leaping Deer, Green Bands, Bulbous, Keramis, 11½ In. $2530.00

Boch Freres, Vase, Earthenware, Matte Glaze, Doves, Leaves, Grass, Flared Rim, Charles Catteau, 16 In. $6900.00

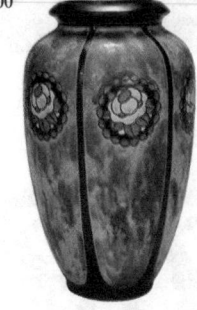

Boch Freres, Vase, Stoneware, 6 Panels, Floral Medallions, Gres Keramis Mark, 12⅛ In. $978.00

Boehm, Owl, Perched On Stump, Snails & Leaves, 8 In. $403.00

Bookends, Boy, Carrying Books, Art Deco Style, Anzengruber Keramik, Austria, 8½ In. **$69.00**

Bookends, Copper, Rivets, Walter Von Nessen, Chase Copper, c.1935, 6½ In. **$4500.00**

Bookends, Dutch Girl Carrying Pails, Cast Iron, Stepped Base, 6½ x 4½ In. **$29.00**

Bookends, Girl, Inside Wreath, Art Deco, Green, Cast Iron, 5 x 3½ In. **$165.00**

Bookends, Owl, Perched On Branch, Cast Iron, Octagonal Base, 5½ x 4⅝ In. **$220.00**

Giant Panda Cub, No. 400-47, 6 x 7¾ In.	527.00
Golden Crowned Kinglets, Bisque, 11 x 7 In.	351.00
Goldfinches, 11¾ x 4½ In.	410.00
Great Egret, Taking Flight, National Audubon Society, c.1982, 12 x 14 In.	575.00
Horse, Adios, Wood Base, Late 20th Century, 13¼ x 15½ In.	489.00
Indigo Bunting, No. 400-33, 10 In.	176.00
Kirkland's Warbler, Bisque, 1980, 8½ x 8 In.	410.00
Mandarin Duck, Bisque, No. 40106, 4 x 5 In.	117.00
Northern Water Thrush, Running Past Mushrooms & Ferns, Marked, 10 In.	1825.00
Owl, Perched, Limited Edition, No. 214, 10½ x 5 In.	351.00
Owl, Perched On Stump, Snails & Leaves, 8 In. *illus*	403.00
Owl, Standing On Books, Porcelain, Black Printed Mark, 9¼ In.	374.00
Painted Bunting, No. 420-38, 10½ In.	585.00
Quail, Stepping Over Log, Tail Up, Brown, Golden Tan Plumage, 11¾ In.	173.00
Screech Owl, Bisque, Signed, No. 40132, No. 85, 1980, 14 x 21½ In.	380.00
Slate Colored Junco, Marked Edward Marshall Boehm, c.2000, 11 x 11½ In.	115.00
Towhee, c.1969, 7½ x 8¼ In.	374.00
Tropical Rose, Bisque, No. 300-22, 1978, 10 In.	117.00

BONE includes those articles made of bone not listed elsewhere in this book.

Bodkin, Pierce Carved, Black Dot Decoration, Arched Top, 6½ In.	450.00
Pie Crimper, Crescent Notched Crimper, Crosshatched Handle, 5¼ In.	165.00
Pie Crimper, Crescent Notched Crimper, Shaped Handle, Pierced Heart Design, 6⅞ In.	275.00
Pie Crimper, Crescent Notched Crimper, Shaped Tulip Handle, 5 In.	220.00
Pie Crimper, Ivory Wheel, Turned, Shaped, Tapered, Ball Finial, c.1840, 1¾ x 7⅜ In.	625.00
Pie Crimper, Turned & Shaped Handle, Ivory Wheel, c.1835, 7⅜ In.	625.00
Snuffbox, Prisoner-Of-War, Relief Carved, Depicting Brittania, Dome Lid, c.1790	595.00
Spoon, Carved, Whale Shape, Harpoon, Inscribed, 1871	295.00

BOOKENDS have probably been used since books became inexpensive. Early libraries kept books in cupboards, not on open shelves. By the 1870s bookends appeared, especially homemade fret-carved wooden examples. Most bookends listed in this book date from the twentieth century. Bookends are also listed in other categories by manufacturer or material. All bookends listed here are pairs.

3 Dogs, Singing, Music Notes, Cast Iron, Hubley, 4¾ x 5 In.	392.00
Abraham Lincoln, Brass, Black Paint, Bradley & Hubbard, 5¼ x 3⅞ In.	129.00
Abraham Lincoln, Cast Metal, Black Patina, Strikalite Label, 6½ In.	35.00
Abraham Lincoln, Cast Metal, Bronze Finish, c.1930, 6½ In.	59.00
Aladdin's Lamp, Brick Wall, Cast Iron, Bradley & Hubbard, 5½ x 5 In.	66.00
Albany Bouquet, Painted, Iron, Albany Foundry, 1926, 5½ In.	295.00
Ballerina, Holding Blanket, Green, Gold, Brown, Cast Iron, 7¼ x 5 In.	112.00
Books By The Armful, Colonial Figure, Carrying Books, Metal, K & O, c.1930, 6½ In.	125.00
Bookworm, Monochrome & Polychrome, Metal, K & O, c.1930, 5¼ In.	125.00
Boy, Carrying Books, Art Deco Style, Anzengruber Keramik, Austria, 8½ In. *illus*	69.00
Burns & Armour, Iron, Shop Mark, Bradley & Hubbard, c.1925	100.00
Church, Horses & Coach, Lady, Multicolored, Cast Iron, c.1925, 5⅝ x 4⅜ x 2⅞ In.	265.00
Conestoga Covered Wagon, Horses, Painted, Cast Iron, Hubley, No. 378, 3⅝ x 6½ In.	252.00
Conestoga Covered Wagon, Oxen, Cast Iron, Arion Hardware, No. 1849, 1931, 3 x 6 In.	196.00
Constitution Ship, Cast Iron, Signed, U.S. Frigate, Greenblatt Studios, 6⅜ x 4⅝ In.	308.00
Copper, Rivets, Walter Von Nessen, Chase Copper, c.1935, 6½ In. *illus*	4500.00
Dog, Cat On Fence, Cast Iron, Wilton Products, 5¾ x 4¾ In.	616.00
Dog, Great Dane, Cast Iron, Hubley, No. 354, 6¼ x 6¾ In.	280.00
Dog, Pekingese, Cast Iron, Hubley, No. 366, 5 x 5¼ In.	385.00
Dog, Scottie, Cast Iron, 1929, 6 x 6 In.	176.00
Dog, Sealyham, White, Green, Cast Iron, Hubley, No. 52, 4¾ x 5⅛ In.	308.00
Dog & Cat, Soon To Be Friends, Bronze Clad, Armor Bronze, Shop Mark, c.1925, 6 In.	395.00
Doorway, Flower Frame, Painted, Cast Iron, Bradley & Hubbard, 5¾ In.	20.00
Draped Woman, Art Deco, Green, Cast Iron, Hubley, No. 73, 6 x 5¼ In.	252.00
Dream Girl, Iron, c.1930, 6 In.	225.00
Dutch Couple, Kissing, Cast Iron, Hubley, No. 332, 4¾ In.	140.00
Dutch Girl Carrying Pails, Cast Iron, Stepped Base, 6½ x 4½ In. *illus*	29.00
Elephant, Bronze, Trunk Up, Trunk Down, Wood Base, 11⅛ & 6⅞ In.	9600.00
Floral Arch, White Metal, Copper Patina, Bradley & Hubbard, 5¼ x 3¾ In.	165.00
Fossil Ivory, Gilt Copper Base, A. Berry, c.1915, 5¾ In.	2400.00

Girl, Inside Wreath, Art Deco, Green, Cast Iron, 5 x 3½ In. ....*illus*		165.00
Homer, Gray Metal, Weidlich Brothers, Shop Mark, No. 646, 1926, 5¾ In.		275.00
Horse, Jumping Over Fence, Iron, 6½ In.		82.00
Horse Head, Nodding, Porcelain, White, Lenox, c.1940, 7 x 5 In.		88.00
Lindy Over The Waves, Iron, c.1928, 5 In.		175.00
Log Cabin, Moonlight, Woodland Scene, Painted, Cast Iron, 6⅛ In.		220.00
Man, Woman Running, Under Blanket, Storm, Art Deco, Iron, Connecticut, 1928, 6 x 4 In. ..		280.00
Old Ironsides, Cast Iron, Signed, Bradley & Hubbard, 4 x 5⅜ In.		168.00
Owl, On Branch, Ivy, Embossed, Cast Iron, Judd Co., No. 9890, 5½ x 3½ In.		140.00
Owl, Perched In Archway, Cast Iron, Bradley & Hubbard, 6 x 5⅛ In.		83.00
Owl, Perched On Branch, Cast Iron, Octagonal Base, 5½ x 4⅝ In. ....*illus*		220.00
Penguins, Cast Iron, 5¾ x 3⅜ In. ....*illus*		935.00
Pilgrim Landing, Ship, Cast Iron, Bradley & Hubbard, c.1925, 6 x 4¼ In.		175.00
Raggedy Ann & Raggedy Andy, Cast Iron, P.F. Volland & Co., Copyright 1931, 6 In. ....*illus*		1430.00
Ship, On Rough Sea, Painted, Cast Iron, Signed, Albany Fdry. Co., 4 x 4 In.		196.00
Ship, Sailing, Cast Iron, 5⅜ x 5¼ In. ....*illus*		28.00
Ship, Signed, Bradley & Hubbard, 6 x 4⅛ In.		275.00
Sir Galahad, Standing Under Arch, Cast Iron, 5⅞ x 4⅜ In.		28.00
Sir Galahad With Horse, In Archway, Cast Iron, 6½ x 4½ In. ....*illus*		85.00
Soldiers, Art Deco, Red Jackets, Black Helmets, Brass, Marked, Chase, 7¼ In.		323.00
Sphinx, Cast Iron, Marked, 4¾ x 4⅝ x 2¾ In.		120.00
Spirit Of St. Louis, Painted, Cast Iron, 4⅞ x 4¾ In.		560.00
Stagecoach, Painted, Cast Iron, Hubley, No. 379, 4 x 7 In.		308.00
Study & Science, Cast Iron, Brass, Bradley & Hubbard, 6 x 5 In.		215.00
Victorian Lady, Layered Dress, Parasol, Flowers, Painted, Cast Iron, Bradley & Hubbard, 5 In. *illus*		248.00
Westward Ho, Bronze, c.1928, 6½ In.		300.00
Whittier & Holmes, Cast Iron, Bradley & Hubbard, 6¼ x 5 In.		135.00
Woman, Nude, Art Deco, Cast Iron, No. 15, 6½ x 4⅛ In.		252.00
Woman, Nude, In Ring, Dancing With Scarf, Art Deco, Copper Electroplated, Cast Iron, 5 x 5¾ In. ..		196.00
Woman, Nude, Kneeling, Cast Metal, Bronze Patina, c.1930, 6½ In.		106.00
Woman, Nude, With Drape, Art Deco, Cast Iron, Creations, 1930, 6 x 3¾ In.		252.00
Woman, Nude, With Swan, Art Deco, Copper Electroplated Cast Iron, 3⅞ x 7½ In.		252.00
Women, Nude, Kneeling, L-Shaped Support, Etched, Glass, France, 8¾ In.		529.00
Wood, Steer Head, Bronze, C.M. Russell, Early 1900s, 8½ x 7½ In.		633.00

BOOKMARKS were originally made of parchment, cloth, or leather. Soon woven silk ribbon, thin cardboard, celluloid, wood, silver, tortoiseshell, and metals were used. Examples made before 1850 are scarce, but there are many to be found dating before 1920.

Bone, Carved, Elephant Finial, 2½ In.		20.00
Elastica Floor Finish, Elastica Stands The Rocks, Girl On Horse, 5¾ x 2 In.		55.00
Flowers, Happy New Year, Early 1900s, 2 x 10 In.		16.00
Hoyt's German Cologne, Victorian, Ad On Reverse, Rubifoam For The Teeth		18.00
Lady Wearing Large Hat, Green Cloth, c.1911, 3 x 10 In.		18.00
Pacific Line, Royal Mail Steamers, Celluloid, 7 In.		153.00
Sterling Silver, Circle, Deer In Center, Marked AB, Made In Mexico		20.00
The Black Abbott, Edgar Wallace, Doubleday Page & Co., Brass, 1927, 4¼ In.		29.00
TV Guide, Television Set, Knobs For Channel Selection, On-Off		25.00

BOSSONS character wall masks (heads), plaques, figurines, and other decorative pieces are made by W.H. Bossons, Limited, of Congleton, England. The company was founded in 1946 and closed in 1996. Dates shown are the date the item was introduced.

BOSSONS

Plaque, Abdhul, Middle Eastern Face, Turban, c.1960, 8 In.		76.00
Wall Figure, Peon, 1963, 15½ In.		275.00
Wall Figure, Raccoon, 12½ In.		35.00
Wall Figure, Woodpecker, 12½ In.		35.00
Wall Mask, Chef, 6 x 3½ In.		30.00
Wall Mask, Coolie, 1963, 6½ In.		149.00
Wall Mask, Jock, 1969, 5½ In.		43.00
Wall Mask, Punjabi, 1964, 7 In.		25.00
Wall Mask, Saracen, 1960, 7 In.		165.00

BOSTON & SANDWICH CO. *pieces may be found in the Lutz, Paperweight, and Sandwich Glass categories.*

Bookends, Penguins, Cast Iron, 5¾ x 3⅜ In. $935.00

Bookends, Raggedy Ann & Raggedy Andy, Cast Iron, P.F. Volland & Co., Copyright 1931, 6 In. $1430.00

Bookends, Ship, Sailing, Cast Iron, 5⅜ x 5¼ In. $28.00

Bookends, Sir Galahad With Horse, In Archway, Cast Iron, 6½ x 4½ In. $85.00

Bookends, Victorian Lady, Layered Dress, Parasol, Flowers, Painted, Cast Iron, Bradley & Hubbard, 5 In. $248.00

Bottle, Barber, Amethyst, Mary Gregory Girl, Twig, Ribbed, Rolled Lip, Pontil, c.1900, 7⅞ In.
$168.00

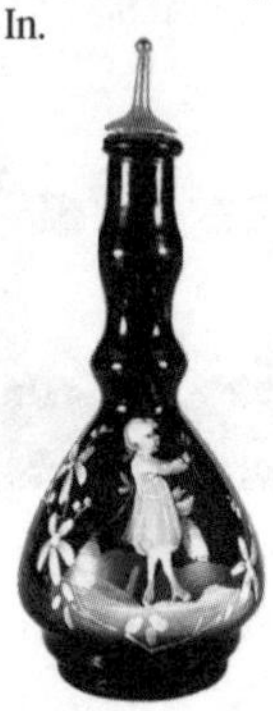

Bottle, Barber, Bay Rum, Milk Glass, Multicolored Tulips, Rolled Lip, 1885-1925, 9¼ In.
$78.00

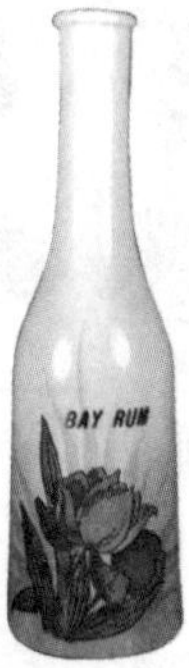

Barber Bottles

Barber bottles are available in all kinds of glass: pressed, carnival, milk, cut, opalescent, overlay, and other art glass. Many have enameled designs or acid-etched decorations. They are sometimes labeled with the customer's name, or with contents, such as "Bay Rum," or "Witch Hazel." They often come in pairs, and occasionally have a matching vase for shaving paper. The vases are rare today.

The era of barber bottles came to an end when the Pure Food and Drug Act of 1906 regulated the use of alcohol-based substances in refillable containers. Barbers stopped using them in their shops, but some bottles were made until the 1920s for home use.

BOTTLE collecting has become a major American hobby. There are several general categories of bottles, such as historic flasks, bitters, household, and figural. ABM means the bottle was made by an automatic bottle machine after 1903. Pyro is the shortened form of the word *pyroglaze,* an enameled lettering used on bottles after the mid-1930s. This form of decoration is also called ACL or applied color label. For more bottle prices, see the book *Kovels' Bottles Price List* by Ralph and Terry Kovel.

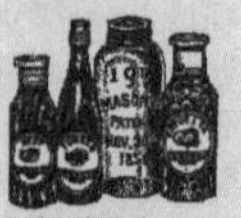

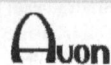

Avon started in 1886 as the California Perfume Company. It was not until 1929 that the name Avon was used. In 1939, it became Avon Products, Inc. Avon has made many figural bottles filled with cosmetic products. Ceramic, plastic, and glass bottles were made in limited editions.

Avon, Car, Solid Gold Cadillac, 1969, 6 Oz. 10.00
Avon, Car, Sterling 6, 1978, 7 Oz. 18.00
Avon, Car, Straight Eight Racer, Dark Green, 1969, 5 Oz. 10.00
Avon, Car, Sure Winner Racer, Cobalt Blue, 1972, 5½ Oz. 9.00
Avon, Car, Volkswagen, Spicy After-Shave, 1972, 4 Oz. 12.00
Avon, Cologne, Bird Of Paradise, 1970, 5 Oz. 8.00
Avon, Cologne, Candlestick Holder, Opalescent Stripes, 1976, 5 Oz. 24.00
Avon, Cologne, Pierrot, 1982, 1¾ Oz. 13.00
Avon, Cologne, Regal Peacock, 1973, 4 Oz. 20.00
Avon, Crystal Sons, Bell, Ruby Red, 1975, 4 Oz. 22.50
Avon, Decanter, 1910 Firefighter, 1975, 6 Oz. 11.00
Avon, Decanter, Bulldog Pipe, 1972, 6 Oz. 16.00
Avon, Decanter, Honey Bee, 1978, 1¼ Oz. 7.00
Avon, Decanter, Marine Binoculars, Tribute Cologne, Aftershave, Box, 1973-74, 4 Oz. 17.00
Avon, Decanter, Quail, Deep Woods Aftershave, 1973, 5½ Oz. 10.00
Avon, Decanter, Stagecoach, Oland Aftershave, 1970, 5 Oz. 5.00
Avon, Extract Set, Vanilla, Peppermint, Lemon, Almond, 1933 .... 99.00
Avon, Perfume, Christmas Bells, Sweet Honesty, Box, Oz. 12.00
Avon, Perfume, Moonwind, 1971, 4 Oz. 18.00
Avon, Perfume, Owl, Roses Roses Cream Sachet, 1972, ½ Oz. 9.00
Avon, Perfume, Pheasant, Leather Aftershave, 1972, 5 Oz. 22.50
Avon, Perfume, Rapture Cologne, 1964, 2 Oz. 12.00
Avon, Snail, 1968, ¼ Oz. 5.00
Avon, Teapot, Delft Blue Design, White Ground, Peaked Lid, Box, c.1972, 6 In. 15.00
Avon, Victorian Lady, Milk Glass, 1970, 8½ In. 14.00
Barber, Amethyst, Frosted, Ribs, White, Gold Enamel, Flowers, Art Nouveau, c.1900, 7⅞ In. .. 78.00
Barber, Amethyst, Mary Gregory Girl, Twig, Ribbed, Rolled Lip, Pontil, c.1900, 7⅞ In. .. *illus* 168.00
Barber, Bay Rum, Aqua, Cylinder, Pontil, Applied Mouth, Label, 1840-60, 9⅝ In. 90.00
Barber, Bay Rum, Flowers, Opalescent, Enamel, Pontil, Applied Mouth, 8⅞ In. 165.00
Barber, Bay Rum, Milk Glass, Enamel, Bird, Flowers, Rolled Lip, 1885-1925, 11 In. 476.00
Barber, Bay Rum, Milk Glass, Enamel, Flowers, Tooled Mouth, 1885-1925, 8¾ In. 235.00
Barber, Bay Rum, Milk Glass, Multicolored Tulips, Rolled Lip, 1885-1925, 9¼ In. ..... *illus* 78.00
Barber, Bay Rum, Opalescent, Twisted Swirl, Red Letters, Tooled Mouth, 1885-1925, 8 In. ... 220.00
Barber, Bay Rum, Purple Amethyst, Grist Mill, c.1900, 7⅝ In. .... 358.00 to 420.00
Barber, Bay Rum, Roses, Milk Glass, Enamel, Pontil, Tooled Mouth, 10⅜ In. 275.00
Barber, Clear, Ribs, Multicolored Enamel Flowers, Blue Ground, 1885-1925, 7⅝ In. 728.00
Barber, Cobalt Blue, White Mary Gregory Boy, Playing Tennis, Ribs, 1885-1925, 7 In. 179.00
Barber, Cobalt Blue, White Mary Gregory Girl, Playing Tennis, Pontil, Rolled Lip, c.1900, 8 In. . 213.00
Barber, Coin Spot, White Opalescent, Clear, Rolled Lip, 1885-1925, 7⅛ In. 176.00
Barber, Cranberry Opalescent, Ferns, Melon Sides, Rolled Lip, 1885-1925, 6⅞ In. 146.00
Barber, Cranberry Opalescent, White Swirled To Left, Pontil, Tooled Mouth, c.1900, 7 In. ... 495.00
Barber, Emerald Green, Gold Enamel, Flowers, Pontil, Art Nouveau, 1885-1925, 8 In. 190.00
Barber, Fiery Opalescent, Stars & Stripes, Pontil, Rolled Lip, 1885-1925, 7⅛ In. 415.00
Barber, Flowers, Yellow, Pink, Feather Mold, Keystone, Signed, 7 In. 45.00
Barber, Frosted Glass, Enamel Label, Bulbous, Shampoo, 6½ In. 59.00
Barber, Green, White & Gold Art Nouveau Flowers, Rolled Lip, Pontil, 7⅞ In. .... *illus* 168.00
Barber, Hair Tonic, Opalescent Milk Glass, Tulips, Enamel, Rolled Lip, 8⅝ In. 176.00
Barber, Hobnail, Canary Yellow Opalescent, Pontil, Rolled Lip, 1885-1925, 6¾ In. 55.00
Barber, Hobnail, Clear, Ruby Red Flashed Interior, Pontil, Rolled Lip, 1885-1925, 7½ In. ... 77.00
Barber, Hobnail, Turquoise Blue, Pontil, Rolled Lip, 1885-1925, 6⅞ In. 88.00
Barber, Hobnail, Yellow Amber, Pontil, Rolled Lip, 1885-1925, 6⅞ In. 77.00
Barber, Milk Glass, 2 Standing Cranes, Enamel, W.T. & Co., 9¼ In. 467.00
Barber, Milk Glass, Cherub, Rose Sprig, Blue Scarf, Blue & Yellow Ground, Pontil, 7¾ In. ... 220.00
Barber, Milk Glass, Cherub, Rose Sprig, Pink Scarf, Blue & Yellow Ground, Pontil, 7⅝ In. ... 220.00
Barber, Milk Glass, Deer Running Across Field, Screw Cap, J. Kaufmann, 10¼ In. 784.00

Barber, Milk Glass, Enamel, Bird, Branch, Tan Ground, W.T. & Co., 1885-1925, 9⅝ In. 364.00
Barber, Milk Glass, Enamel, Cottage On Lake, Pewter Cap, W.T. & Co., 1885-1925, 9¾ In. 336.00
Barber, Milk Glass, Enamel, Lighthouse, Ship, Pewter Cap, W.T. & Co., 1885-1925, 9⅝ In. 616.00
Barber, Milk Glass, Red, Black, Gold Label Under Glass, Tooled Mouth, 7⅞ In. 330.00
Barber, Milk Glass, Running Horse, Enamel, Ground Lip, Pewter Screw Cap, Thos. L. Kirk, 9 In. 467.00
Barber, Opalescent, White Ribs, Swirled To Left, Pontil, Rolled Lip, 1885-1925, 6⅞ In. 78.00
Barber, Opalescent, White Swirls, Applied Lip, 1860-80, 9 In. 112.00
Barber, Opalescent Milk Glass, Sea Foam, Swallows, Flowers, Enamel, Pontil, Applied Mouth, 8⅞ In. 209.00
Barber, Opalescent Milk Glass, Tulips, Enamel, Rolled Lip, Toilet Water, 8⅝ In. 110.00
Barber, Purple Amethyst, Multicolored Enamel Flowers, 1885-1925, 7¾ In. 101.00
Barber, Purple Amethyst, White, Gold Enamel Flowers, Art Nouveau, 1885-1925, 8⅛ In. 90.00
Barber, Purple Amethyst, Windmill, White Enamel, Pontil, Rolled Lip, Hair Tonic, 7⅝ In. 519.00
Barber, Topaz, Ribs, Pinched Waist, Pontil, Polished Lip, 1885-1925, 6½ In. 213.00
Barber, Turquoise, White Mary Gregory Girl, Holding Twig, Ribs, 1885-1925, 7 In. 246.00
Barber, Turquoise Opalescent, Coral Pattern, Pontil, 1885-1925, 6⅞ In. 246.00
Barber, Turquoise Opalescent, Stars & Stripes, Tooled Lip, 7 in. *illus* 190.00
Barber, Turquoise Opalescent, White Swirled To Left, Pontil, Tooled Mouth, 1885-1925, 6⅞ In. 415.00
Barber, Uno Tonique For The Hair, Opalescent Milk Glass, Mint Green Ground, 9⅜ In. 440.00
Barber, Vegederma, Lady's Bust, Long Hair, Bulbous, Amethyst, Flared Mouth, Pontil, 8 In. 336.00
Barber, Vegederma, Yellow Green, White Enamel, Woman, Long Hair, Open Pontil, c.1900, 7¾ In. 168.00
Barber, White Opalescent, Swirled To Left, Pontil, Tooled Mouth, 1885-1925, 6¾ In. 330.00
Barber, Yellow, Green, Frosted, Multicolored Enamel Rose, Pontil, Tooled Lip, 8⅛ In. 78.00
Barber, Yellow Green, White Mary Gregory Girl, Holding Twig, Ribs, 7⅞ In. 364.00
Barber, Zepps Lustrial Dandruff Condition, Label Under Glass, 7½ In. 138.00

Beam bottles were made to hold Kentucky Straight Bourbon, made by the James B. Beam Distilling Company. The Beam series of ceramic bottles began in 1953.

Beam, 1872 Grant Locomotive, 8 x 14 x 6 In. 11.00 to 20.00
Beam, Antique Clock, 1985, 11½ In. 19.00
Beam, Baseball's 100th Anniversary, 1869-1969 14.00
Beam, Car, 1909 Thomas Flyer, Ivory 29.00
Beam, Car, Chevrolet Bel Air, Blue & White, 1987 10.00
Beam, Car, Oldsmobile 75th Anniversary, 1897-1972 25.00
Beam, Covered Wagon, Harold's Club, Reno Or Bust, 1974, 7 x 11 In. 28.00
Beam, Cowboy, 1981, 14½ In. 58.00
Beam, Doe, Standing On Rocks, 1963, 13¾ In. 32.00
Beam, I Dream Of Jeannie, Smoky Green, 1964, 14 In. 41.00
Beam, Mt. St. Helen's Volcano, Eruption Is Stopper, 1980, 9 x 8 In. 20.00
Beam, Northern Pike, National Fresh Water Fishing Hall Of Fame, 1978, 9½ x 15½ In. 21.00
Beam, Olsonite Gurney Eagle Indy Racing Car, Box, 1975 78.00
Beam, Ponderosa Ranch, Nevada, 1969 8.00
Beam, Professional Football Hall Of Fame Building, 1972, 9½ x 8½ In. 10.00
Beam, Rocky Marciano, Face, Fight List, 1973 21.00
Beam, Seattle Space Needle,World's Fair, 1962, 12 In. 25.00
Beam, Slot Machine, Pull Handle, Harold's Club Casino, 1968 39.00
Beer, C.A. Cole & Co., Medium Cobalt Blue, Ten Pin, Applied Tapered Collar, 1850-60, 8⅜ In. 1344.00
Beer, C.A. Cole & Co., Medium Green, Ten Pin, Applied Tapered Collar, c.1855, 8¾ In. 2016.00
Beer, Carbutt & Hamilton, Blue Aqua, Applied Mouth, Ten Pin, c.1865, 7⅞ In. 616.00
Beer, F. & L. Schaum, Deep Olive Amber, Squat, Iron Pontil, Tapered Collar Mouth, c.1850, 7⅜ In. 2800.00
Beer, G. A. Kohl, Deep Cobalt Blue, Iron Pontil, Applied Mouth, c.1850, 7⅜ In. 896.00
Beer, Hutchinson's, Stoneware, Shaded Brown Glaze, 1850-70, 9½ In. 532.00
Beer, Kenmare Bottling Works, Aqua, Blob, 14 In., ½ Gal. 150.00
Beer, McKay & Clark, Medium Blue, Green, Iron Pontil, Applied Mouth, c.1850, 7⅝ In. 784.00
Beer, Moss & Graham, Blue, Aqua, Iron Pontil, Applied Blob Mouth, c.1850, 7⅜ In. 224.00
Beer, National Bottling Works, San Francisco, Embossed Eagle, Stopper, Amber, Qt. 130.00
Beer, Ogden's, Porter, Arched Panel, Blob Top, Iron Pontil, 7 In. *illus* 224.00
Beer, Phoenix Brewing Co., Pittsburg, Pa., Golden Yellow Amber, Qt., 11½ In. 79.00
Beer, Rainier, Seattle, Dark Amber, 5¼ In. 110.00
Beer, Schlitz, Milwaukee, Embossed, Tooled Top, 5¾ In. 33.00
Beer, Wunder Bottling Co., Orange Amber, Blob, Porcelain Top, Wire Bail, 11¾ In. 59.00
Bininger, A.M. & Co., 19 Broad St., N.Y., Yellow Amber, Double Collar, Jug, Handle, 8 In. *illus* 2240.00
Bininger, A.M. & Co., 375 Broadway, N.Y., Moss Green, Applied Mouth, c.1870, 9⅝ In. 1456.00
Bininger, A.M. & Co., 375 Broadway, N.Y., Topaz, Applied Mouth, c.1870, 9¾ In. 784.00
Bininger, A.M. & Co., Cannon, Golden, Amber 925.00
Bininger, A.M. & Co., Pink Puce, Square, Beveled Corners, Collared Mouth, 9¾ In. 1344.00

Bottle, Barber, Green, White & Gold Art Nouveau Flowers, Rolled Lip, Pontil, 7⅞ In.
$168.00

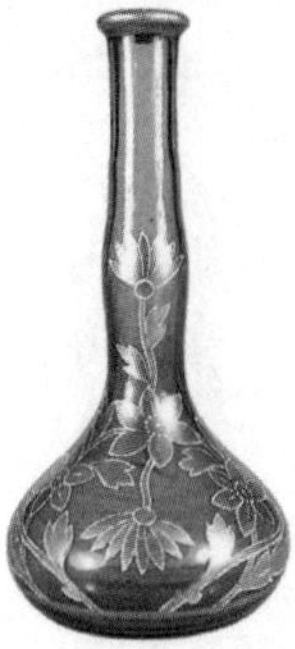

Bottle, Barber, Turquoise Opalescent, Stars & Stripes, Tooled Lip, 7 In.
$190.00

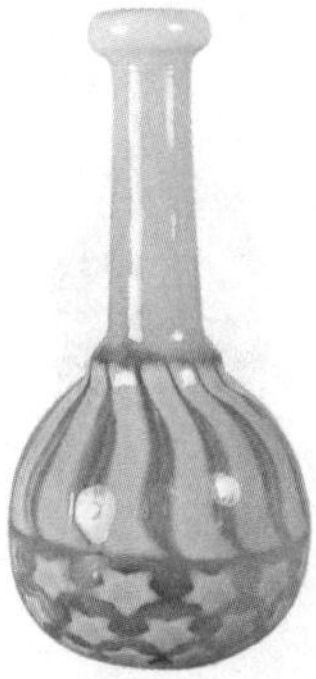

Bottle, Beer, Ogden's, Porter, Arched Panel, Blob Top, Iron Pontil, 7 In.
$224.00

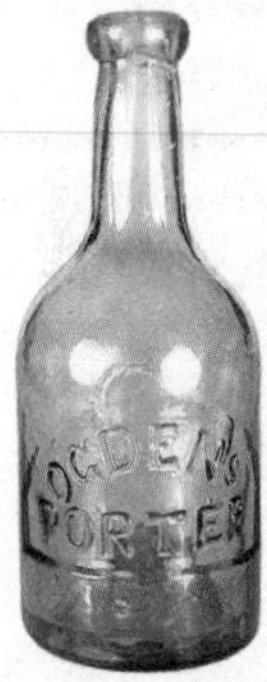

Bottle, Bininger, A.M. & Co., 19 Broad St., N.Y., Yellow Amber, Double Collar, Jug, Handle, 8 In.
$2240.00

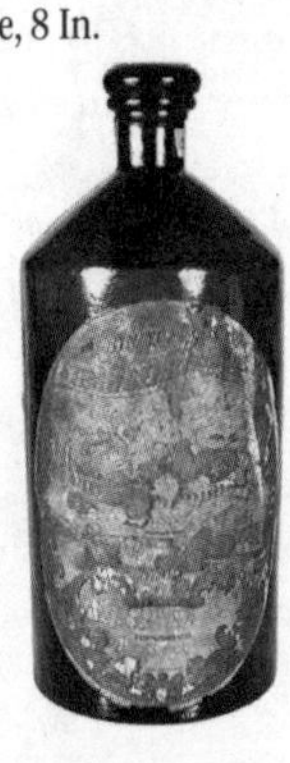

Bottle, Bitters, Brown's Celebrated Indian Herb, Patented Feb 1868, Yellow, Amber, Rolled Lip, 12 In. $1232.00

Bottle, Bitters, Drake's Plantation, 6 Log, Medium Strawberry Puce, Applied Sloping Collar, 10 In. $784.00

Bottles Glossary

Master ink: large bottles used for bulk ink.

Pontil mark or scar: scar of glass left on bottom of a bottle by the punty (pontil) rod that held the glass for the glass blower. Scar may be jagged or incomplete. It may have been ground or smoothed.

Iron pontil (IP): smooth black scar left on bottom of bottle from a heated iron rod.

Open pontil (OP): pontil scar that is a perfect circular ring.

Sheared lip: found on bottles made before 1840. The top of the bottle was cut from the blowpipe with shears.

Tooled lip or collar: shaped and smoothed with an iron

Bininger, A.M. & Co., Yellow Amber, Cannon Barrel, Roughly Ground Mouth, 12 In.	952.00
Bininger, Whiskey, Jug, Amber, Applied Mouth, Handle, 1860-75, 6½ In.	952.00
Bininger, Whiskey, Yellow, Amber, Urn, Sheared, Tooled Lip, Applied Handle, 9 In.	4760.00
Bitters, Amber, Log Shape, Embossed Canoe, Rochester, N.Y., Pat. Nov. 20, 1888, 9 In.	121.00
Bitters, Brophy's, Aqua, Tooled Lip, c.1885, 7⅜ In.	146.00
Bitters, Brown's Celebrated Indian Herb, Yellow, Topaz, Inward-Rolled Mouth, 12⅛ In.	2576.00
Bitters, Brown's Celebrated Indian Herb, Amber, Rolled Lip, Embossed, 1868-70, 12¼ In.	515.00
Bitters, Brown's Celebrated Indian Herb, Patented Feb 1868, Yellow, Amber, Rolled Lip, 12 In. *illus*	1232.00
Bitters, Brown's Celebrated Indian Herb, Yellow Amber, Tooled Lip, Dimple, 1868, 12 In.	605.00
Bitters, Brown's Iron, Tooled Top, Amber, 8½ In.	30.00
Bitters, Bryant's Stomach, Olive Green, Applied Top, Open Pontil, 12¼ In.	2420.00
Bitters, Castilian, Cannon, Amber, Applied Mouth, c.1870, 10⅛ In.	672.00
Bitters, Cotton's Stomach, Backbar, Black Olive, Amber, Ringed Mouth, Pewter Label, 11¾ In.	616.00
Bitters, Doyles Hop, 1872, Hop Cluster, Yellow Olive, Semi-Cabin, 1872-75, 9⅝ In.	392.00
Bitters, Dr. C. Parham, Cure Of Dyspepsia, Aqua, OP, Applied Ring Mouth, Embossed Panels, 6 In.	2530.00
Bitters, Dr. C.W. Roback's Stomach, Olive Yellow, Barrel Shape, Applied Collar	2464.00
Bitters, Dr. Caldwell's Herb, Great Tonic, Yellow Amber, Applied Mouth, c.1870, 12⅛ In.	336.00
Bitters, Dr. Fisch's, Fish Form, Yellow Olive, Applied Mouth, c.1870, 11⅝ In.	3095.00
Bitters, Dr. Fisch's, Medium Amber, Applied Rolled Lip, 1866, 11½ In.	209.00
Bitters, Dr. Geo Pierce's, Indian Restorative, Blue Aqua, Open Pontil, c.1850, 8 In.	392.00
Bitters, Dr. H.S. Flint's Quaker, Aquamarine, Applied Squared Lip, 9¼ In.	33.00
Bitters, Dr. Henley's Wild Grape Root, IXL, Blue Aqua, Applied Ring Mouth, c.1875, 12 In.	220.00
Bitters, Dr. Hoofland's German, C.M. Jackson, Philadelphia, Applied Top, Clear	70.00
Bitters, Dr. Huntington's Gold Tonic, Amber, Label	770.00
Bitters, Dr. Loew's Celebrated Stomach & Nerve Tonic, Lime Green, Fluted Neck, Tooled Lip, 4 In.	242.00
Bitters, Dr. Loew's Celebrated Stomach & Nerve Tonic, Lime Green, Fluted Neck, Tooled Lip, 9 In.	440.00
Bitters, Dr. Lovegood's, XX, Cabin, Amber, Applied Tapered Collar Mouth, 9⅜ In.	1100.00
Bitters, Dr. Renz's Herb, Applied Top, Amber, c.1880, 10 In.	1000.00
Bitters, Dr. Sawen's Life Invigorating, Amber Panel, Troy, N.Y.	30.00
Bitters, Dr. Skinner's Celebrated, Aqua, Applied Double Collar, Open Pontil, c.1850, 8¾ In.	336.00
Bitters, Dr. Tompkin's Vegetable, Green, Blue, Applied Collared, Beveled Corners, 8¾ In.	4200.00
Bitters, Drake's Plantation, 4 Log, Amber, Label, Applied Tapered Collar Mouth, 10⅜ In.	165.00
Bitters, Drake's Plantation, 4 Log, Yellow Amber, Applied Mouth, c.1865, 10⅛ In.	448.00
Bitters, Drake's Plantation, 4 Log, Yellow Amber, Applied Tapered Collar Mouth, 10 In.	121.00
Bitters, Drake's Plantation, 4 Log, Yellow Amber Olive, Applied Tapered Collar Mouth, 10 In.	469.00
Bitters, Drake's Plantation, 6 Log, Amber, Applied Tapered Lip, Embossed, 1860, 9⅝ In.	112.00
Bitters, Drake's Plantation, 6 Log, Copper Puce, Applied Mouth, c.1865, 10 In.	198.00
Bitters, Drake's Plantation, 6 Log, Medium Strawberry Puce, Applied Sloping Collar, 10 In. *illus*	784.00
Bitters, Drake's Plantation, 6 Log, Pink, Puce, Applied Mouth, 1860, 10 In.	616.00
Bitters, Drake's Plantation, 6 Log, Puce Topaz, Applied Sloping Collar, 10 In.	3080.00
Bitters, Drake's Plantation, 6 Log, Purple Amethyst, Applied Mouth, c.1870, 10⅛ In.	896.00
Bitters, Drake's Plantation, 6 Log, Strawberry Puce, Applied Tapered Collar Mouth, 9⅞ In.	825.00
Bitters, Drake's Plantation, 6 Log, Yellow Green, Sloping Collar, 9¾ In. *illus*	4760.00
Bitters, Drake's Plantation, 6 Log, Yellow Olive, Applied Tapered Collar Mouth, 10 In.	3095.00
Bitters, Fish, Yellow Amber Shaded To Yellow, Applied Ring Mouth, 1866, 11 In.	550.00
Bitters, Geo. Benz & Sons, Deep Amber, Tooled Lip, 1897-1900, 8⅛ In.	235.00
Bitters, Greeley's Bourbon, Applied Top, Smoky Amber, 9⅜ In.	425.00
Bitters, Greeley's Bourbon, Barrel, Olive Green, Applied Mouth, 9⅜ In.	385.00
Bitters, Greeley's Bourbon, Barrel, Pink Puce, Applied Mouth, 9⅜ In.	990.00
Bitters, Greeley's Bourbon, Smoky Olive Topaz, Barrel, Applied Mouth, c.1870, 9¼ In.	1232.00
Bitters, Greeley's Bourbon, Smoky Pink Puce, Barrel, Applied Mouth, c.1870, 9⅜ In.	1120.00
Bitters, Hall's, Barrel, Golden Yellow Amber, Applied Mouth, 9¼ In.	143.00
Bitters, Hall's, Barrel, Orange Amber, Applied Mouth, 9¼ In.	295.00
Bitters, Hall's, Barrel, Orange Amber, Label, Neck Foil, Applied Mouth, 9¼ In.	275.00
Bitters, Hart's Star, Clear, Fish, Tooled Lip, 1868, 9⅛ In.	616.00
Bitters, Harvey's Prairie, Amber Shaded To Yellow Amber, Corncob Dome Top, 9¾ In.	20900.00
Bitters, Herkules, 7Up Green, Tooled Lip, c.1885, 4⅛ In.	1792.00
Bitters, Holtzermann's Stomach, Cabin, Paper Label, Tooled Lip, 10 In.	143.00
Bitters, Indian Restorative, Applied Top, Open Pontil, Aqua, 7½ In.	300.00
Bitters, Indian Vegetable & Sarsaparilla, Aqua, Pontil, Geo. C. Goodwin, Boston, c.1850, 8 In.	1100.00
Bitters, John Moffat, Olive Amber, Applied Sloping Collar Mouth, Beveled Corners, 5⅛ In.	1792.00
Bitters, John Moffat, Phoenix, Blue Aqua, Open Pontil, Applied Ring Mouth, 5⅝ In.	100.00
Bitters, John Root's, Buffalo, N.Y., Blue Green, Semi-Cabin, 10¼ In. *illus*	2688.00
Bitters, Khoosh, Yellow Olive, Applied Double Collar Mouth, 8¼ In.	110.00
Bitters, Kimball's Jaundice, Olive Amber, Troy, N.H., Applied Collar, c.1845, 7 In.	1550.00
Bitters, Lediard's, Teal, Applied Sloping Double Collar Mouth, 1860-75, 10⅛ In.	1870.00

Bitters, Litthauer Stomach, Milk Glass, Gin Form, Josef Lowenthal, Berlin, 1864, 9½ In. 110.00
Bitters, Lutz's German Stomach, Reading, Pa., Amber, Label Under Glass, Tooled Lip, 7¾ In. ..*illus* 4760.00
Bitters, Malabac, Semi Lady's Leg, Yellow Amber, M. Cziner Chemist, 1870-80, 11¾ In. 770.00
Bitters, McKeever's Army, Cannonballs On Drum, Applied Tapered Collar, 10⅝ In. 3095.00
Bitters, Mishler's Herb, Tablespoon Graduation, Yellow Olive, Applied Collar Mouth, 9 In. ... 300.00
Bitters, Moulton's Olorosa, Blue Aqua, Fluted Neck, Applied Mouth, 1865-80, 11¼ In. 330.00
Bitters, National, Aqua Blue, Applied Top, 12⅝ In. 8800.00
Bitters, National, Ear Of Corn, Medium Amber, Applied Mouth, c.1870, 12⅜ In. 476.00
Bitters, National, Ear Of Corn, Yellow Amber, Applied Mouth, c.1870, 12¾ In. 990.00
Bitters, National, Ear Of Corn, Yellow Green, Applied Top, 1867, 12½ In. 2200.00
Bitters, Old Home, Laughlin, Golden Orange, Amber 2700.00
Bitters, Old Homestead Wild Cherry, Cabin, Yellow Amber, Tapered Collar, c.1870, 9¾ In. ... 990.00
Bitters, Old Homestead Wild Cherry, Semi-Cabin, Amber, Tapered Lip, Embossed, 1865-75, 9¾ In. .. 305.00
Bitters, Old Sachem & Wigwam Tonic, Barrel, Apricot Puce, Applied Square Collar, 9½ In. .*illus* 672.00
Bitters, Old Sachem & Wigwam Tonic, Barrel, Copper Puce, Applied Mouth, 9½ In. 660.00
Bitters, Old Sachem & Wigwam Tonic, Barrel, Pink Puce, Applied Mouth, 9¼ In. 3300.00
Bitters, Old Sachem & Wigwam Tonic, Barrel, Strawberry Puce, Applied Square Collar, 9¼ In. .*illus* 560.00
Bitters, Old Sachem & Wigwam Tonic, Barrel, Yellow Amber, Applied Mouth, c.1870, 9¼ In. . 448.00
Bitters, Old Sachem & Wigwam Tonic, Barrel, Yellow Olive, Applied Disc Lip, c.1860, 9½ In. . 1120.00
Bitters, Pineapple, Medium Olive Green, Embossed, W & Co., N.Y., c.1870, 5½ In. 3050.00
Bitters, Plantation, Amber, Applied Top 110.00
Bitters, Ramsay's Virginia, 8-Sided, Applied Top, Graphite Pontil, 8½ In. 1650.00
Bitters, Sanborn's Kidney & Liver, Amber, Tooled Lip, c.1895, 10 In. 90.00
Bitters, Sazerac Aromatic, Phd & Co., Milk Glass, Applied Ring Mouth, c.1875, 12¼ In. 336.00
Bitters, St. Drake's Plantation, 6 Log, Yellow Amber Olive, 10¼ In. 952.00
Bitters, Sunny Castle, Amber 145.00
Bitters, Wakefield's Strengthening, Blue Aqua, Olive Green Striations, 8 In. 69.00
Bitters, Weis Bros., Knickerbocker Stomach, Orange Amber, Lady's Leg, Seal, c.1880, 12 In. . 2688.00
Bitters, Wilder's, Semi-Cabin, Tapered Collar Lip, Embossed, Edw. Wilders, 10½ In. 264.00
Bitters, Zingari, F. Rahter, Amber, Lady's Leg, Applied Ring Mouth, c.1870, 12¼ In. 308.00
Bitters, Zoeller's Stomach, Orange, Amber, Pittsburgh, Pa. 325.00
Black Glass, Mallet, Olive Green, Squat, String Lip, Sheared Mouth, England, c.1760, 7 x 4⅜ In. ... 358.00
Black Glass, Olive Green, Applied Seal, ICC, Sheared Mouth, String Lip, Pontil, c.1775, 10 In. . 560.00
Black Glass, Onion, Blue Emerald Green, Pontil, Applied String Lip, Germany, c.1730, 7½ x 5⅝ In. . 100.00
Black Glass, Onion, Blue Green, Pontil, Applied String Lip, Germany, c.1740, 6½ x 5⅝ In. .. 165.00
Black Glass, Onion, Emerald Green, Pontil, Applied String Lip, Germany, c.1730, 6⅜ x 5⅝ In. 143.00
Black Glass, Onion, Emerald Green, Pontil, Applied String Lip, Germany, c.1730, 7⅝ x 5¾ In. 100.00
Black Glass, Onion, Olive Green, Pancake, Pontil, Applied String Lip, England, c.1700, 5 x 6⅜ In. .. 1100.00
Black Glass, Onion, Olive Green, Pontil, Applied String Lip, Dutch, c.1730, 7⅜ x 5¾ In. 110.00
Black Glass, Onion, Olive Green, Pontil, Applied String Lip, England, c.1730, 5⅞ x 4½ In. .. 495.00
Black Glass, Onion, Olive Green, Pontil, Applied String Lip, England, c.1735, 7 x 5¼ In. 385.00
Black Glass, Onion, Yellow Green, Pontil, Applied String Lip, England, c.1735, 5⅝ x 4⅝ In. . 415.00
Black Glass, Onion, Yellow Olive, Applied Lip, Sheared Mouth, Dutch, Pontil, c.1740, 7 x 5 In. 88.00
Black Glass, Onion, Yellow Olive Amber, Horse Hoof, Applied String Lip, Dutch, c.1730, 8⅜ x 5⅞ In. 176.00
Black Glass, Onion, Yellow Olive Amber, Applied String Lip, Sheared Lip, Dutch, c.1730, 7 x 5 In. 132.00
Black Glass, Onion, Yellow Olive Green, String Lip, Sheared Mouth, Dutch, c.1730, 7 x 5⅝ In. 77.00
Black Glass, Pale Olive Green, Seal, J.A. Willink, Applied Collared Lip, Pontil, c.1810, 10½ In. . 1400.00
Blown, 24 Ribs, Globular, Swirled To Left, Golden Amber, Rolled Collar Mouth, Pontil, 8 In. *illus* 748.00
Blown, 24 Ribs, Globular, Swirled To Left, Shaded Green, Outward-Rolled Lip, Pontil, 8 In. .*illus* 1456.00
Blown, 24 Ribs, Globular, Swirled To Left, Topaz, Green, Pontil, Midwestern, c.1825, 7½ In. . 2320.00
Blown, 24 Ribs, Swirled To Left, Blue, Green, Rolled Lip, 1825, 8 In. 1456.00
Blown, 24 Ribs, Swirled To Left, Cobalt Blue, Pontil, Blob Mouth, 1820, 8¼ In. 7840.00
Blown, 24 Ribs, Swirled To Right, Yellow Amber, Olive Tone, Blob Mouth, 8⅝ In. 5045.00
Blown, 30 Ribs, Vertical, Medium Olive Green, Tooled Lip, 1815, 6⅜ In. 1344.00
Blown, Globular, Amber, Applied String Lip, Pontil, Midwestern, c.1820, 8 In. 440.00
Blown, Globular, Green Aqua, Bulbous, Applied Donut Lip, Pontil, 1820-30, 8¼ In. 264.00
Coca-Cola bottles are listed in the Coca-Cola category.
Cordial, Enameled, Articulated Woman, German Verse, Pewter Collar, Screw Cap, 6 In. 440.00
Cordial, Enameled, Flowers, 4⅝ In. 44.00
Cordial, Enameled, Flowers, Pewter Cap, 5¼ In. 110.00
Cordial, Mrs. E. Kidder, Dysentery, Boston, Aqua, Oval, OP, 1840-60, 7½ In. 123.00
Cordial, Wishart's Pine Tree Tar, Phila., Patent 1859, Blue Green, 7⅞ In. ....*illus* 280.00
Cordial, Wishart's Pine Tree Tar, Phila., Patent 1859, Emerald Green, Square, Embossed, 8 In. .. 176.00
Cordial, Wishart's Pine Tree Tar, Phila., Patent 1859, Emerald Green, Square, Embossed, 9⅜ In. 253.00
Cordial, Wishart's Pine Tree Tar, Phila., Patent 1859, Teal Blue, Square, Embossed, 7⅝ In. .. 220.00
Cordial, Wishart's Pine Tree Tar, Phila., Patent 1859, Teal Blue, Square, Embossed, 10 In. .. 253.00

Bitters

Bitters was a mixture of herbs, roots, spices, and barks blended with alcohol. Some ingredients, like opium or marijuana, are dangerous and illegal today. Bitters was considered medicine and was taken by the spoonful or more. It was considered a wonder cure in the days before penicillin and other medicinal drugs.

Bottle, Bitters, Drake's Plantation, 6 Log, Yellow Green, Sloping Collar, 9¾ In.
$4760.00

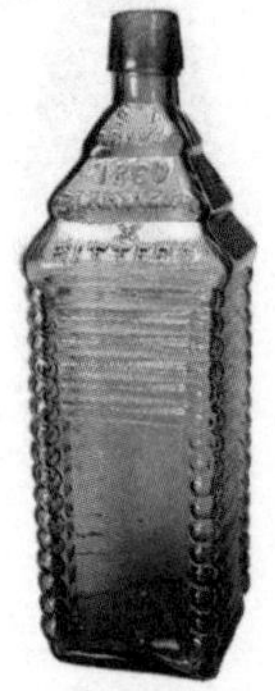

Bottle, Bitters, John Root's, Buffalo, N.Y., Blue Green, Semi-Cabin, 10¼ In.
$2688.00

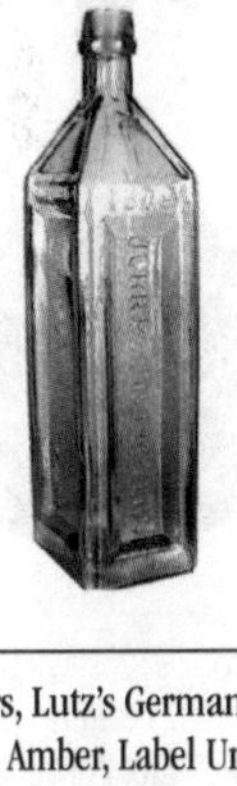

Bottle, Bitters, Lutz's German Stomach, Reading, Pa., Amber, Label Under Glass, Tooled Lip, 7¾ In.
$4760.00

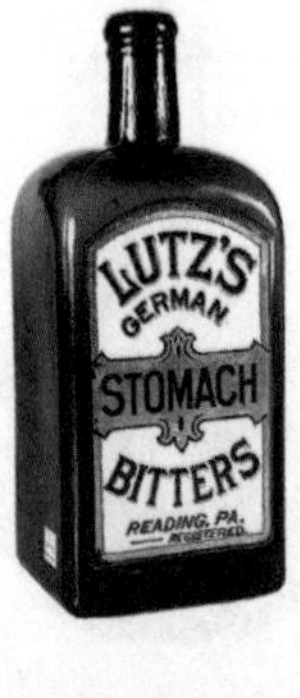

Bottle, Bitters, Old Sachem & Wigwam Tonic, Barrel, Apricot Puce, Applied Square Collar, 9½ In.
$672.00

Bottle, Bitters, Old Sachem & Wigwam Tonic, Barrel, Strawberry Puce, Applied Square Collar, 9¼ In.
$560.00

Bottle, Blown, 24 Ribs, Globular, Swirled To Left, Golden Amber, Rolled Collar Mouth, Pontil, 8 In.
$748.00

Bottle, Blown, 24 Ribs, Globular, Swirled To Left, Shaded Green, Outward-Rolled Lip, Pontil, 8 In.
$1456.00

Cosmetic, Agrandjean's, Clear, Wide Mouth, Pontil, Tool Flared Lip, c.1850, 3 In.	392.00
Cosmetic, Ayer's Hair Vigor, Sapphire Blue, Tooled Lip, c.1890, 2¾ In.	392.00
Cosmetic, Ayer's Hair Vigor, Sapphire Blue, Tooled Lip, Glass Stopper, 6½ In. *illus*	112.00
Cosmetic, Kickapoo Sage Hair Tonic, Cobalt Blue, Tooled Mouth, c.1890, 4½ In.	420.00
Cosmetic, Lyon's Indian Hair Dye No. 1, Aqua, Rolled Lip, Open Pontil, c.1850, 3¼ In.	448.00
Cosmetic, Mexican Hair Renewer, Cobalt Blue, Oval, 7 In.	69.00
Cosmetic, Mrs. S.A. Allen's World's Hair Restorer, N.Y., Shaded Amethyst, Double Collar, 7⅜ In. *illus*	202.00
Cosmetic, Rose Hair Oil, Milk Glass, Arched Shoulder, Labels, 5¼ In.	79.00
Cure, Coke Dandruff, Clear, Glass Stopper, Labels, 1906, 8 In.	59.00
Cure, Dr. Grave's Heart Regulator, For Heart Disease, Aqua, 7¾ In.	48.00
Cure, Dr. Seeley's, Magic Cough & Consumption, Aqua, Double Collar, c.1890, 7 In.	440.00 to 925.00
Cure, Dr. Seeley's, Magic Cough & Consumption, Aqua, Double Collar Mouth, c.1890, 9 In.	660.00
Cure, Tus Sano Cures Coughs, Sample, 2 In.	55.00
Cure, Warner's Safe Kidney, Dark Amber, 9½ In.	40.00
Cure, Warner's Safe Kidney & Liver, Chocolate, Amber	20.00
Decanter, Aqua, 3-Piece Mold, Flared Lip, Pontil, Keene, N.H., c.1820, 6¾ In.	940.00
Decanter, Aqua, Cone Shape, Flared Lip, 3-Piece Mold, Pontil, Midwestern, c.1820, 7¼ In.	3592.00
Decanter, Barrel, Yellow Green, Flared Mouth, Pontil, 3-Piece Mold, 1820-30, Pt.	4700.00
Decanter, Bristol Blue, Gilt, Stopper, England, 1780	250.00
Decanter, Bulbous, Light To Medium, Olive Yellow, 3-Piece Mold, Sheared Mouth, Pt.	672.00
Decanter, Clear, 3-Piece Mold, Matching Stopper, Pontil, c.1820, 10¾ In.	112.00
Decanter, Clear, Applied Annulated Rings, 3-Piece Mold, Pontil, Stopper, c.1820, 9 In.	204.00
Decanter, Clear, Flared Lip, 3-Piece Mold, Pontil, Matching Stopper, c.1820, 10½ In.	149.00
Decanter, Cone Shape, 3-Piece Mold, Stopper, Pontil, c.1820, 11 In.	340.00
Decanter, Dark Cobalt Blue, Corset Waist, 6-Sided, Applied Bar Lip, Pontil, c.1850, 10 In.	198.00
Decanter, Dark Forest Green, 3-Piece Mold, Pontil, c.1820, 7½ In.	720.00
Decanter, Dark Olive Green, 3-Piece Mold, Pontil, 9½ In.	1990.00
Decanter, Dark Olive Green, White Spots, Applied Rigaree, Pontil, c.1815, 8½ In.	1100.00
Decanter, Flared Lip, 3-Piece Mold, Stopper, Pontil, c.1820, 11 In.	150.00
Decanter, Lavender, Applied Bar Lip, Pontil, No Stopper, 1830-50, 6 In.	395.00
Decanter, Light To Medium Cobalt Blue, 3-Piece Mold, Flared Lip, New England, c.1820, 9 In.	1045.00
Decanter, Light Yellow Aqua, 3-Piece Mold, Flared Lip, Pontil, c.1820, 8½ In.	770.00
Decanter, Midwestern, Flared Lip, Mushroom Stopper, Pontil, 3-Piece Mold, c.1820, 9¼ In.	200.00
Decanter, Olive Amber, 3-Piece Mold, Sheared & Fire-Polished Lip, c.1820, 7¼ In.	615.00 to 650.00
Decanter, Olive Amber, Cone Shape, Flared Lip, Open Pontil, New England, 1810-30, 2½ In.	1490.00
Decanter, Olive Green, 3-Piece Mold, Sheared & Fire-Polished Lip, Pontil, c.1820, 7 In.	670.00
Decanter, Pale Aqua, 3-Piece Mold, Wheel Stopper, Pontil, 1820-30, 9¾ In.	153.00
Decanter, Purple Amethyst, White Inclusions, 12 Panels, Applied Bar Lip, Pontil, 1840-60, 10 In.	2200.00
Decanter, Square, Deep Emerald Green, Blown In Mold, 7⅛ x 2⅝ In.	7700.00
Decanter, Teal Green, Corset Waist, 6-Sided, Applied Bar Lip, Pontil, c.1850, 10 In.	3300.00
Decanter, Whiskey, Always Pure, Elk's Head, Lime Green, Ear Of Corn, c.1900, 8¾ In.	101.00
Demijohn, Black, Cylindrical, 14½ In., Gal.	48.00
Demijohn, Blue, Green, Heart Shape, Turnmold, Applied Top, 1860-70, 5 Gal., 20½ In.	129.00
Demijohn, Blue Green, Kidney Shape, Open Pontil, c.1850, 2 Gal., 15 In.	129.00
Demijohn, Bright Orange Amber, Kidney Shape, Qt., 8½ In.	89.00
Demijohn, Bright Yellow Green, Cylindrical, Bubbles, Applied Top, ½ Gal., 13 In.	79.00
Demijohn, Cornflower Blue, Cylindrical, Applied Collar, Pontil, 12½ In.	728.00
Demijohn, Dark Olive Green, Applied Top, Smooth Base, 11½ In.	66.00
Demijohn, Emerald Green, Cylindrical, Iron Pontil, Applied Lip, c.1845, 13 In.	109.00
Demijohn, Emerald Green, Cylindrical, Open Pontil, Squat, 2 Gal.	119.00
Demijohn, Lemon Yellow, Cylindrical, Applied Gloppy Top, 1860-70, 15 In., Gal.	99.00
Demijohn, Lemon Yellow, Squat, Qt., 9½ In.	59.00
Demijohn, Lime Green, Cylindrical, Kick-Up, Applied Top, 12½ In., ½ Gal.	79.00
Demijohn, Loaf Of Bread, Green, Applied Collar, Pontil, 1840-60, 8¼ x 9¾ x 6 In.	336.00
Demijohn, Medium Green, Pear Shape, Wide Mouth, 5 Gal., 7½ In.	139.00
Demijohn, Medium Sapphire Blue, Applied Tapered Mouth, 1870-80, 15¾ In.	616.00
Demijohn, Olive, Applied Top, Qt., 9¼ In.	39.00
Demijohn, Olive Green, Cylindrical, Dip Mold, Open Pontil, c.1820, 2 Gal.	79.00
Demijohn, Olive Yellow, Bulbous, Cylindrical, Tapered, Swirls, Gal., 14 In.	48.00
Demijohn, Pink Puce, Cylindrical, Whittled, Bubbles, Applied Top, 1860-70, 12 Gal.	500.00
Demijohn, Teal Blue, Green, Olive Yellow, Open Pontil, Whittled, 2 Gal., 17½ In.	119.00
Demijohn, Yellow, Olive Amber, Cylindrical, Stoddard Type, Applied Top, Qt., 9¼ In.	79.00
Demijohn, Yellow, Olive Green, Red Iron Pontil, Double Collar Mouth, 2-Piece Mold, c.1850, 15 In.	134.00
Demijohn, Yellow Amber, Whittled, Bubbles, Drippy Applied Top, c.1860, 3 Gal., 21 In.	89.00
Figural, Barrel, Deep Olive Green, Kick-Up, Applied Lip, 3¾ In.	45.00
Figural, Bear, Seated, Applied Face, Blue Aqua, Embossed A.A.T., 1890, 8¼ In. *illus*	112.00

B

Figural, Bear, Seated, Teal Blue, Sheared Mouth, Pontil, 10¾ In.	3080.00
Figural, Bear, Seated, Yellow Green, Sheared Mouth, 10¼ In.	280.00
Figural, Bear, Seated, Yellow Green, Sheared Mouth, 1860-70, 9 In.	840.00
Figural, Bellows, Clear, Applied Handles, Rigaree, Pontil, 6½ In.	22.00
Figural, Bird, Painted, Rosewater, 4-Bird Footed, Turkish, 8 In.	291.00
Figural, Boy, Ruffled Collar, Smock, Pants, Holding Instrument, Porcelain, Germany, 8 In.	118.00
Figural, Column, Milk Glass, Gold Christopher Columbus, Ground Lip, 1893-95, 18 In.	504.00
Figural, Dog, Aqua, 1860s, 8½ In.	100.00
Figural, Duck, Milk Glass, Sheared & Ground Lip, Patd. April 11th, 1871, 11 In.	300.00
Figural, Flask, Columbian Exposition, Bust Of Columbus, Yellow Amber, 1893, 6¾ In.	1265.00
Figural, Frog, Clear, Frosted, Sheared, Ground Lip, 1890-1915, 5½ In.	90.00
Figural, General DeBrigade, Porcelain, White Glaze, Robj, 10 In.	1410.00
Figural, Horse's Head, Light Aqua, Manhattan Bottling Co.	45.00
Figural, La Cantinere, Porcelain, Robj, 12½ In.	2585.00
Figural, Le Muscadin Ou L'Incroyable, Porcelain, Robj, 12½ In.	4406.00
Figural, Legionnaire, Porcelain, Robj, 9¾ In.	3055.00
Figural, Paysanne Revolutionnaire, Porcelain, Robj, 10½ In.	2468.00 to 3290.00
Figural, Pig, Drink While It Lasts, From This Hog's, Clear, Tooled Lip, c.1890, 6¾ In.	308.00
Figural, Pig, Embossed, Good Old Bourbon In A Hog's, 6¾ In.	145.00
Figural, Pig, Something Good, In A Hog's, Clear, Tooled Lip, 1885-1900, 4¼ In.	123.00
Figural, Shorebird, Milk Glass, Tooled Lip, Pontil, 1880-1900, 12½ In.	448.00
Flask, 13 Ribs, Broken Swirl, Applied Lip, Polished Pontil, 1820-40, 8 In.	186.00
Flask, 15 Diamonds, Medium Amethyst, Sheared Mouth, Pontil, 1800-40, 7 x 4½ In.	3360.00
Flask, 16 Ribs, Sapphire Blue, Flattened Coin Shape, Sheared Mouth, 6 In.	2464.00
Flask, 24 Diamonds, Green, Yellow Tone, Sheared Mouth, Pontil, 1800-30, 5⅛ In.	415.00
Flask, 24 Ribs, Swirled To Right, Apple Green, Globular, Pontil, Rolled Lip, c.1825, 9¼ In.	280.00
Flask, 29th National Encampment, Louisville, Ky., Label Under Glass, I.W. Harper's, 1895, 6 In. *illus*	358.00
Flask, 33rd National Encampment, Phila., Pa., Label Under Glass, 1899, 4½ In. *illus*	767.00
Flask, Admiral Dewey, Remember The Maine, Sepia Photo, Blue Ground, Metal Cap, 5 x 4 In.	250.00
Flask, Anchor, Embossed, Orange Amber, Strap, ½ Pt.	39.00
Flask, Anchor, Spring Garden Glassworks, Log Cabin & Tree, Aqua, Open Pontil, Pt.	109.00
Flask, Anchor & Spring Garden, Yellow, Olive, Applied Double-Collared Mouth, Pt.	1120.00
Flask, Aqua, 15 Diamonds, Broken Swirl Pattern, Sheared Lip, Pontil, 1810-30, 6¾ In.	505.00
Flask, Aqua, Sheared & Fire-Polished Lip, Open Pontil, c.1815, 5½ In.	58.00
Flask, Blue, Aqua, Open Pontil, Handle, Midwestern Type, 6¼ In.	2300.00
Flask, Captain Bragg, Grape Clusters, A Little More Grape, Light Aqua, Pt., 7 In.	382.00
Flask, Chestnut, 16 Ribs, Broken Swirl, Aquamarine, Sheared Lip, Pontil, 6⅝ x 4¾ In.	880.00
Flask, Chestnut, 23 Ribs, Clear, 5 Rows, 18 Hobnails, Applied Sloping Mouth, 5 x 4 In.	99.00
Flask, Chestnut, 24 Ribs, Swirled To Left, Blue Aqua, Open Pontil, Sheered Top, 8½ In.	160.00
Flask, Chestnut, 25 Ribs, Swirled To Right, Aquamarine, Applied Collar, Pontil, 8¾ In.	132.00
Flask, Chestnut, 28 Ribs, Swirled To Right, Aquamarine, Sloping Mouth, Pontil, 9⅞ In.	121.00
Flask, Chestnut, Amber, Ground Rim, Open Blister, 5 In.	288.00
Flask, Chestnut, Cobalt Blue, Flared Lip, Pontil, 5¼ In.	550.00
Flask, Chestnut, Free-Blown, Olive Green, Applied Mouth, Open Pontil, c.1790, 8 In.	560.00
Flask, Chestnut, Lion's Paw, String Glass, Green, Pontil, c.1780, 5½ In.	675.00
Flask, Chestnut, Olive Green, Bulbous, Long Narrow Neck, Open Pontil, c.1830, 6½ In.	403.00
Flask, Chestnut, Orange, Amber, Free-Blown, Applied Tapered Top, c.1820-40, 10¾ In.	339.00
Flask, Chestnut, Yellow Amber, Applied Lip, Open Pontil, 6¾ In. *illus*	308.00
Flask, Chestnut, Yellow Citron Green, Bulbous, Crude Applied Lip, Pontil, 1800-20, 6¾ In.	477.00
Flask, Chestnut, Yellow Green, Applied Lip, Pontil, 1800-30, 6 In.	340.00
Flask, Clear, Shared Lip, Applied Ring, Stitched Leather Cover, 6¾ In.	176.00
Flask, Coffin, Diamond, Clear, ½ Pt.	19.00
Flask, Coffin, Wood, Carved Schooner, Dinghy Stopper, c.1880	99.00
Flask, Corn For The World, Baltimore Monument, Golden Amber, c.1850, Qt.	1064.00
Flask, Cornucopia & Urn, Blue Green, Sheared, Tooled Lip, Open Pontil, c.1830, Pt.	728.00
Flask, Cornucopia & Urn, Medium Green, Sheared Lip, Pontil, ½ Pt., 5⅝ In.	231.00
Flask, Cornucopia & Urn, Medium Olive Green, Sheared Lip, Pontil, ½ Pt., 5½ In.	99.00
Flask, Cornucopia & Urn, Olive Green, Sheared Lip, Pontil, Pt., 7 In.	88.00
Flask, Diamond, Clear, Blue, Gold, Black, Label Under Glass, 1880-1910, 6 In.	840.00
Flask, Diamond, Sheared Lip, Pontil, c.1780, 6 In.	242.00
Flask, Diamond, Sheared Lip, Pontil, German Half-Post, 1785, 4½ In.	132.00
Flask, Double Eagle, Blue, Aqua, Pt.	99.00
Flask, Double Eagle, Emerald Green, Tooled Lip, Kensington Glassworks, c.1825, Pt.	2530.00
Flask, Double Eagle, Light To Medium Emerald Green, Whittled, Open Pontil, Qt.	359.00
Flask, Double Eagle, Pink, Tooled Collared Mouth, ½ Pt.	2016.00
Flask, Double Eagle, Shaded Amber, Applied Collar, Open Pontil, Pt. *illus*	6160.00

Bottle, Cordial, Wishart's Pine Tree Tar, Phila., Patent 1859, Blue Green, 7⅞ In.
$280.00

Bottle, Cosmetic, Ayer's Hair Vigor, Sapphire Blue, Tooled Lip, Glass Stopper, 6½ In.
$112.00

Bottle, Cosmetic, Mrs. S.A. Allen's World's Hair Restorer, N.Y., Shaded Amethyst, Double Collar, 7⅜ In.
$202.00

Bottle, Figural, Bear, Seated, Applied Face, Blue Aqua, Embossed A.A.T., 1890, 8¼ In.
$112.00

Bottle, Flask, 29th National
Encampment, Louisville, Ky.,
Label Under Glass, I.W. Harper's Whiskey,
1895, 6 In.
$358.00

Bottle, Flask, 33rd National
Encampment, Phila., Pa.,
Label Under Glass, Canteen Shape,
1899, 4½ In.
$767.00

Flasks Shapes

The *calabash flask* looks
like the calabash gourd, a
vegetable often hollowed out
to hold water.

The *chestnut flask* is almost
round. It is named for the
nut from the chestnut trees
that grow in Europe and the
United States.

The *Pitkin-type flask*
is named for the Pitkin
Glassworks of East Hartford,
Connecticut. The glass
blower added glass to make
the sides of the flask thicker.
The bottle was blown into
a ribbed mold. The finished
bottle could have vertical or
swirled ribs.

Flask, Eagle, Aquamarine, Embossed, Applied Ring Lip, Qt., 9⅛ In.	99.00
Flask, Eagle, Aquamarine, Embossed, Sheared Lip, Pontil, Pt., 6¾ In.	165.00
Flask, Eagle, Aquamarine, Sheared Lip, Pontil, Qt., 8¼ In.	132.00
Flask, Eagle, Medium Amber, Applied Ring Mouth, Louisville, Ky., c.1860, ½ Pt.	220.00
Flask, Eagle, Medium To Deep Olive Green, Embossed, Applied Lip, Collar, ½ Pt., 6 In.	275.00
Flask, Eagle, Olive Green, Sheared Lip, Pontil, Pt., 6¾ In.	143.00 to 154.00
Flask, Eagle, Yellow Olive Amber, Sheared Lip, Pontil, Pt., 7¼ In.	187.00
Flask, Eagle & Anchor, Aquamarine, Applied Sloping-Collar Mouth, c.1865, Qt.	784.00
Flask, Eagle & Cornucopia, Aqua, Open Pontil, Sheared & Tooled Lip, c.1825, ½ Pt.	264.00
Flask, Eagle & Cornucopia, Green, Aquamarine, Sheared Lip, Pontil, ½ Pt., 5½ In.	413.00 to 495.00
Flask, Eagle & Cornucopia, Olive Amber, Sheared Lip, Open Pontil, 1830-40, 7 In.	110.00
Flask, Eagle & Franklin, Frigate, Green, Aquamarine, Sheared Lip, Pontil, Pt., 6⅝ In.	330.00
Flask, Eagle & New London, Blue, Green, Sheared Mouth, Tubular Pontil, Pt.	1792.00
Flask, Eagle & New London, Yellow Amber, Topaz, Collared Mouth, 1860-66, Pt.	896.00
Flask, Eagle & Ravenna, Dark Olive Green, Tooled Lip, Iron Pontil, Pt. ....*illus*	1792.00
Flask, Eagle & Sunburst, Light Vaseline, Sheared Lip, Pontil, Pt.	5280.00
Flask, Eagle & Tree, Aqua, Sheared, Tooled Lip, Open Pontil, c.1830, Qt.	840.00
Flask, Eagle & Wilmington, Yellow Amber, Applied Double-Collar Mouth, Qt.	896.00
Flask, Flora Temple & Harness Trot, Copper Amber, Embossed, Applied Ring, Pt., 8½ In.	385.00
Flask, For Pike's Peak & Eagle, Aqua, Applied Band, Smooth Base, Pt.	99.00
Flask, Franklin & Dyott, Black Olive Amber, Embossed, Sheared Lip, Pontil, Pt., 6¾ In.	8250.00
Flask, Franklin & Dyott, Gray Tint, Open Pontil, c.1830, Pt.	1456.00
Flask, Green River Whiskey, Leather Cover, Telescopic Cup Lid, 7½ In.	59.00
Flask, Harvard Rye K.B., Clear, Rectangular, ½ Pt.	19.00
Flask, Horseman & Hound, Olive Yellow, 8¾ In.	1610.00
Flask, J.H. Kline & Co., Amber, Flattened Oval, Applied Mouth, Collar, 2⅞ x 5⅝ In.	176.00
Flask, J.P. Haddox, Winchester, Va., Label Under Glass, 5 In.	1650.00
Flask, Jenny Lind & Glasshouse, Calabash, Blue Aqua, Double Collar, Iron Pontil, 9¾ In. *illus*	336.00
Flask, Jenny Lind & Lyre, Blue, Aqua, Pontil, Sheared, Tooled Lip, 1850-55, Pt.	840.00
Flask, John P. Cooney, Providence, R.I., Yellow Olive, Double Collar, 1860-72, Pt.	850.00
Flask, Lafayette & DeWitt Clinton, Amber, 1820s, 7¼ x 3¾ In.	1619.00
Flask, Lafayette & De Witt Clinton, Olive Yellow, Sheared Mouth, Pontil, 1824-25, Pt.	2128.00
Flask, Lafayette & Liberty, Olive Yellow, Pontil, ½ Pt. ....*illus*	1064.00
Flask, Light Gray, White Squiggles, Bulbous, Pontil, 2¾ In.	160.00
Flask, Masonic, Blue Green, Smoky, Embossed, Oval, Rolled Lip, Pontil, Pt., 7¼ In.	1320.00
Flask, Masonic, Blue Green, Tooled Collar, Pontil, ½ Pt., 6⅝ In.	550.00
Flask, Masonic & Eagle, Blue Green, Pontil, c.1820, Pt.	532.00 to 672.00
Flask, Masonic & Eagle, Olive Green, Applied Top, Pontil, Pt.	1760.00
Flask, Masonic & Eagle, Sapphire Blue, Swirls, Tooled Lip, Pontil, Pt. ....*illus*	4200.00
Flask, Merry Christmas, Happy New Year, Clear, Label Under Glass, c.1900, 6 In.	224.00
Flask, Merry Christmas, Happy New Year, Label Under Glass, Clear, Diamonds, Cap, 6 In. *illus*	840.00
Flask, Milk Glass, Red Looping, Sheared & Fire-Polished Lip, Pontil, 8 In.	140.00
Flask, Nailsea, White Loop, Clear, Open Pontil, 8 In.	75.00
Flask, Olive Amber, Teardrop, Sheared Lip, Open Pontil, 1810-30, 6½ In.	165.00
Flask, Olive Amber, Westford Glass Co., ½ Pt.	139.00
Flask, P & W, Sunburst, Yellow, Olive Tone, Sheared Mouth, Pontil, 1820-30, ½ Pt.	952.00
Flask, Pike's Peak, Old Rye, Aquamarine, Embossed, Sheared Lip, Pontil, ½ Pt., 6 In.	143.00
Flask, Pitkin Type, 28 Ribs, Swirled To Left, Cobalt Blue, Tooled Square, Collar Mouth, 6⅜ In.	728.00
Flask, Pitkin Type, 30 Ribs, Swirled To Left, Olive Yellow, Sheared Mouth, Pontil, 6⅝ In.	784.00
Flask, Pitkin Type, 30 Ribs, Swirled To Left, Yellow Olive, Sheared Mouth, Pontil, c.1820, 5 In.	1090.00
Flask, Pitkin Type, 32 Broken Ribs, Blue Green, Pontil, Sheared, Tooled Lip, 1820, 6⅜ In.	784.00
Flask, Pitkin Type, 32 Ribs, Swirled To Right, Yellow Olive, Sheared Mouth, Pontil, 6¼ In.	728.00
Flask, Pitkin Type, 34 Broken Ribs, Swirled To Right, Clear, Sheared, Tooled, c.1800, 5 In.	364.00
Flask, Pitkin Type, 36 Broken Ribs, Swirled To Left, Dark Amber, Sheared Mouth, c.1820, 6 In.	1045.00
Flask, Pitkin Type, 36 Ribs, Swirled To Left, Forest Green, Sheared Mouth, Pontil, c.1820, 5 In.	1120.00
Flask, Pitkin Type, 36 Ribs, Swirled To Left, Golden Amber, Olive, Sheared Mouth, 4½ In.	840.00
Flask, Pitkin Type, 36 Ribs, Swirled To Left, Olive Green, Pontil, Paper Label, Cork, c.1820, 7 In.	4150.00
Flask, Pitkin Type, 36 Ribs, Swirled To Right, Amethyst, Sheared Mouth, Pontil, c.1820, 5⅝ In.	16500.00
Flask, Pitkin Type, 36 Ribs, Swirled To Right, Light Yellow Olive, Pontil, c.1800, 5 In.	920.00
Flask, Pitkin Type, 36 Ribs, Swirled To Right, Olive Green, Flattened Oval, Pt., 6½ In.	495.00
Flask, Pitkin Type, 36 Ribs, Swirled To Right, Olive Yellow, Sheared Mouth, 5½ x 3 In.	1232.00
Flask, Pitkin Type, 36 Ribs, Swirled To Right, Yellow, Green, Sheared Mouth, Open Pontil, 5 In.	892.00
Flask, Pitkin Type, 36 Ribs, Swirled To Right, Yellow Amber, Sheared Mouth, Pontil, c.1815, 6 In.	1240.00
Flask, Pitkin Type, Ribs, Swirled To Right, Olive Amber, Open Pontil, 7 In. ....*illus*	863.00
Flask, Pittsburgh Type, Double Eagle, Sheared Top, Blue Aqua, Open Pontil, ½ Pt.	99.00
Flask, Pocket Watch Shape, Here Is To You, Milk Glass, Gold Paint, c.1900, 4⅜ In.	280.00

Flask, Pumpkinseed, Hand Made Sour Mash, 7 Years Old, Embossed, ¼ Pt.	29.00
Flask, Railroad, Blue, Aquamarine, Embossed, Sheared, Tooled Lip, Pontil, Pt., 6¾ In.	330.00
Flask, S. Harrison, Lincoln, Stoneware, Cogwheel, Slab Seal, Handle, c.1850, 6½ In.	616.00
Flask, Scroll, Applied Top, Graphite Pontil, Deep Aqua, Pt.	90.00
Flask, Scroll, Aqua, Applied Lip, Graphite Pontil, 7¼ In., Pt.	209.00
Flask, Scroll, Aquamarine, Applied Rolled Lip, Iron Pontil, Qt., 8⅞ In.	88.00
Flask, Scroll, Ice Blue, Iron Pontil, ½ Pt.	109.00
Flask, Scroll, Moonstone, Pink Tone, Pontil, c.1850, Qt.	1456.00
Flask, Scroll, Yellow Green, Applied Ring Mouth, Iron Pontil, Pt. _illus_	280.00
Flask, Scroll, Yellow Green, Pontil, c.1850, Pt.	1064.00
Flask, Sheaf Of Grain, Yellow Amber, Embossed, Applied Lip, Collar, Pt., 7¾ In.	121.00
Flask, Spirits, Clear, Etched, Pontil, Sheared Lip, Pewter Neck Ring, Screw Cap, 5⅜ In.	213.00
Flask, Spirits, Clear, Enamel, Pontil, Tooled Lip, Pewter Neck Ring, Screw Cap, 1770-1810, 5⅝ In.	308.00
Flask, Stag Whiskey, Elk, Aqua, Label, ½ Pt.	29.00
Flask, Stoddard Type, Applied Double Collar, Yellow, Olive Amber, Pt.	59.00
Flask, Success To The Railroad, Moss Green, Tooled Lip, Open Pontil, Pt. _illus_	448.00
Flask, Success To The Railroad, Olive Green, Open Pontil, c.1830, Pt.	364.00
Flask, Summer & Winter, Blue Green, Top-Hat Mouth, Open Pontil, Qt.	420.00
Flask, Sunburst, Green, Sheared Lip, Pontil, c.1820, Pt.	896.00
Flask, Sunburst, Olive Yellow, Sheared Lip, Pontil, Pt., 7½ In.	715.00
Flask, Sunburst, Turquoise, Sheared Lip, Open Pontil, Pt.	605.00
Flask, Sunburst, Yellow Amber, Tooled Lip, Pontil, ½ Pt. _illus_	784.00
Flask, Taylor & Major Ringgold, Amethystine, Open Pontil, c.1850, Pt.	1344.00
Flask, Taylor & Ringgold, Clear, Pale Green Tint, Sheared Lip, Pontil, Pt., 6¾ In.	110.00
Flask, Theodore Roosevelt, Label Under Glass, 6½ In.	550.00
Flask, Traveler's Companion & Star, Golden Amber, c.1855, Pt.	840.00
Flask, Union, Clasped Hands & Eagle, Blue Aqua, Pt.	175.00
Flask, Union, Clasped Hands & Eagle, Medium Amber, Applied Ring, ½ Pt. _illus_	280.00
Flask, Union & Clasped Hands, Old Rye, Olive Yellow, Embossed, Flat Collar, Qt., 9 In.	825.00
Flask, Washington, Aquamarine, Applied Sloping Mouth, Collar, Pontil, Pt., 7¼ In.	66.00
Flask, Washington, Calabash, Aquamarine, Round Lip, Collar, Pontil, Qt., 8¾ In.	132.00
Flask, Washington, Father Of His Country, Cobalt Blue, Sheared Lip, Open Pontil, Pt. _illus_	5600.00
Flask, Washington, Fells Point, Aqua, Open Pontil, Qt.	140.00
Flask, Washington & Eagle, Amethystine, Open Pontil, c.1830, Qt.	1344.00
Flask, Washington & Eagle, Aqua, Open Pontil, Sheared, Tooled Lip, c.1825, Pt.	258.00
Flask, Washington & Eagle, Blue, Aqua, Open Pontil, Sheared, Tooled Lip, c.1835, Pt.	616.00
Flask, Washington & Eagle, Emerald Green, Sheared Lip, Open Pontil, Pt. _illus_	12320.00
Flask, Washington & Eagle, Green Aqua, Pontil, Sheared & Tooled Lip, c.1835, Pt.	784.00
Flask, Washington & Jackson, Deep Amber, Olive Tint, Sheared Lip, Pontil, ½ Pt.	220.00
Flask, Washington & Jackson, Olive Yellow, Embossed, Sheared Lip, Pontil, Pt., 6¾ In.	385.00
Flask, Washington & Jackson, Yellow Amber, Embossed, Sheared Lip, Pontil, Pt., 7 In.	143.00
Flask, Washington & Sheath Of Wheat, Blue, Aqua, ½ Pt.	109.00
Flask, Washington & Taylor, Aquamarine, Sheared Lip, Iron Pontil, Qt., 8½ In.	66.00
Flask, Washington & Taylor, Blue Aquamarine, Embossed, Sheared Lip, Pontil, Qt., 8 In.	99.00
Flask, Washington & Taylor, Blue Green, Embossed, Sheared Lip, Qt., 8 In.	300.00
Flask, Washington & Taylor, Emerald Green, Open Pontil, c.1850, Qt.	840.00
Flask, Washington & Taylor, Green, Yellow, Applied Sloping Mouth, Qt., 8¾ In.	935.00
Flask, Washington & Taylor, Green Aquamarine, Embossed, Sheared Lip, Pontil, Qt., 8 In.	77.00
Flask, Washington & Taylor, Pink Amethyst, Open Pontil, Sheared & Tooled Lip, Qt.	5225.00
Flask, Wharton's Whiskey, Amber, Sloping Mouth, 2⅞ x 5 In.	264.00
Flask, Wharton's Whiskey, Cobalt Blue, Sloping Mouth, 2⅞ x 5½ In.	413.00
Flask, Yellow, Amber, Blown, Globular, Outward-Rolled Lip, c.1795, 8½ In.	308.00
Food, Blueberry Preserves, Golden Amber, Olive, Cylindrical, Fluted Shoulders, Applied Collar, 11 In.	1232.00
Food, Gray Green, 11 Ribs, Outward-Folded Lip, Pontil, 1760, 2¾ In.	450.00
Food, H.J. Heinz Chili Sauce, Rope Design Edge, 8 In.	191.00
Food, Heinz Table Sauce, Wicker Cover, c.1900, 7½ In.	657.00
Food, Light To Medium Aqua, Globular, Applied String Lip, Pontil, 1810, 4 In.	605.00
Food, Olive Yellow, Applied Flared Lip, 1815, 12½ In.	235.00
Food, Raccoon Mountain Syrup, Car, Glass, 4⅞ In.	12.50
Food, Sea Green, Applied Lip, Iron Pontil, 1850, 8½ In.	105.00
Food, Storage, Aqua, Cylindrical, 3-Piece Mold, Double Collar, Applied Top, Open Pontil, 10½ In.	39.00
Food, Storage, Utility, Dark Teal, Drawn & Folded Lip, Pontil, 1840, 6½ In.	110.00
Food, Storage, Yellow, Olive Green, Sheared, Outward-Rolled Lip, 1870, 9 In.	48.00
Food, Syrup, Peacock Green, 8 Panels, Molded Neck Ring, Polished Metal Rim, 11 In.	1210.00
Food, Tea, Finley Acker Co., Green, Elephant, Tea Leaves, Square, Crown Stopper, 11 In.	439.00
Food, W.M. & P., Aqua, Rolled Lip, Open Pontil, 9 In.	121.00

Bottle, Flask, Chestnut, Yellow Amber, Applied Lip, Open Pontil, 6¾ In.
$308.00

Bottle, Flask, Double Eagle, Shaded Amber, Applied Collar, Open Pontil, Pt.
$6160.00

Bottle, Flask, Eagle & Ravenna, Dark Olive Green, Tooled Lip, Iron Pontil, Pt.
$1792.00

Bottle, Flask, Jenny Lind & Glasshouse, Calabash, Blue Aqua, Double Collar, Iron Pontil, 9¾ In.
$336.00

Bottle, Flask, Lafayette & Liberty, Olive Yellow, Pontil, ½ Pt.
$1064.00

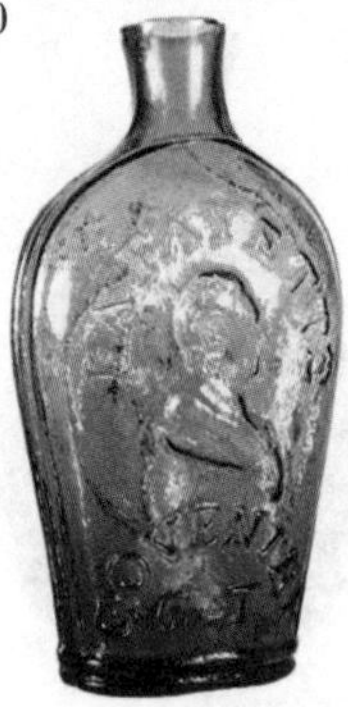

Bottle, Flask, Masonic & Eagle, Sapphire Blue, Swirls, Tooled Lip, Pontil, Pt.
$4200.00

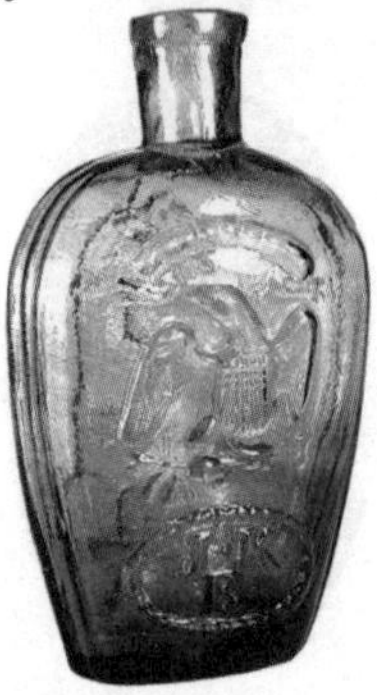

Bottle, Flask, Merry Christmas, Happy New Year, Label Under Glass, Clear, Diamonds, Cap, 6 In.
$840.00

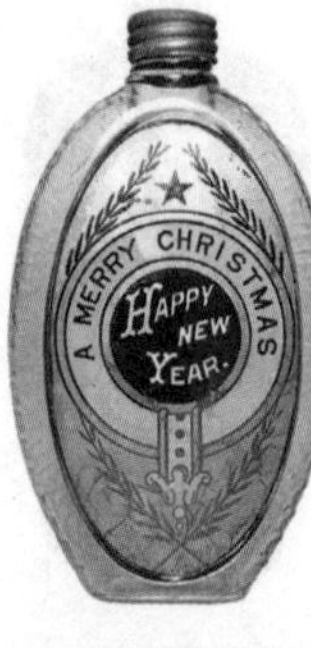

Bottle, Flask, Pitkin Type, Ribs, Swirled To Right, Olive Amber, Open Pontil, 7 In.
$863.00

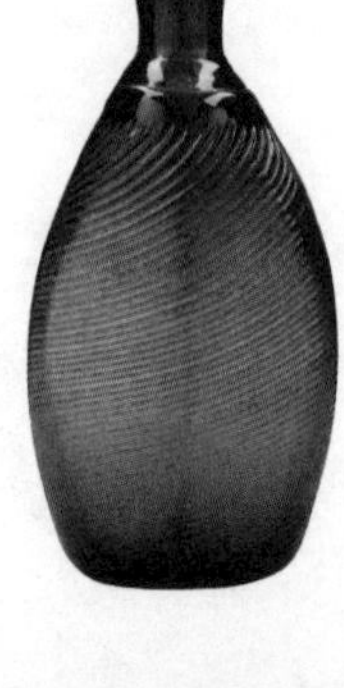

Food, Wendell Sauce, Applied Top, Open Pontil, Clear, 10 In. 50.00
Food, Yellow Amber, Applied String Lip, Pontil, Bubbles, 1790, 4 In. 55.00
Food, Yellow Olive, Flared Lip, Semi-Oval, Pontil, New England, 1810, 2¾ In. 1340.00
Fruit Jar, A. Stone & Co., Philada, Blue Aqua, Internal Screw Threads, Glass Lid, Pt. ... *illus* 1120.00
Fruit Jar, Aqua, Globe, Qt. 70.00
Fruit Jar, Aqua, Globe, Wide Mouth, 2 Qt. 70.00
Fruit Jar, Arthur Burnham & Gilroy, Pat. Jan. 2, 1855, Seal Top, 4¼ In. 2820.00
Fruit Jar, Belle, Patent Dec. 14th 1869, Aquamarine, Glass Lid, Tin Band, Wire Bale, 2 Qt. 2016.00
Fruit Jar, Bennetts, No. 1, Aquamarine, Cylindrical, Applied Collar Mouth, c.1870, Qt. 840.00
Fruit Jar, C. Burnham & Co., Aquamarine, Ground Mouth, Iron Lid, Cardboard Insert, Qt. 460.00
Fruit Jar, Commodore, Aquamarine, Cylindrical, c.1870, Qt. 952.00
Fruit Jar, Gregory's Patent, Aug 17th 1869, Common Sense, Aquamarine, Cylindrical, Qt. 1792.00
Fruit Jar, J.J. Squire, Aquamarine, Olive Amber Striations, 3 Pedestal Feet, c.1870, Qt. 1795.00
Fruit Jar, J.J. Squire 3, Patd Octr 18, 1864, Aquamarine, Ground Rim, Cylindrical, Qt. 784.00
Fruit Jar, Lafayette, Aquamarine, Cylindrical, Ground Mouth, 3-Piece Glass & Metal Stopper, Qt. 1232.00
Fruit Jar, Lafayette, Aquamarine, Cylindrical, Ground Mouth, Glass & Metal Stopper, c.1890, Pt. . 5000.00
Fruit Jar, Mason's, Cornflower Blue, Tin Lid, Bubbles, Qt. 25.00
Fruit Jar, Mason's Keystone Patent, Nov 30th. 1858, Yellow, Cylindrical, 1870-90, Pt. 2464.00
Fruit Jar, Mason's Patent, Nov 30th 58, Yellow, Cylindrical, Zinc Lid, 1870-90, Pt. 3360.00
Fruit Jar, Potter & Bodine's, Air-Tight, Aquamarine, Barrel, Wax Seal, Pontil, ½ Gal. 1340.00
Fruit Jar, Potter & Bodine's, Philadelphia, Aqua, Pontil 920.00
Fruit Jar, S.B. Dewey Jr., Buffalo, Blue, Aqua, Applied Mouth, Metal Stopper, Sealer, c.1865, Qt. 2016.00
Fruit Jar, Safety Valve, Cylindrical, Yellow Green, 2 Bands Greek Key, Metal Clamp, c.1895, ½ Gal. 370.00
Fruit Jar, Trademark Lightning, Putnam On Base, Citron, Qt. .... *illus* 448.00
Gemel, Free-Blown, Marbrie White Looping, Gray Clear, Baluster Form, Knop Stem, 8 In. 1760.00
Gemel, Marbrie White Looping, Gray, Green Aquamarine, Oval, 9 In. 99.00
Gemel, Marbrie White Looping, Gray & Clear, Oval, Cobalt Blue Lips, 8¼ In. 110.00
Gin, Booth & Sedgwick's Cordial, Green, Applied Top, Graphite Pontil, 8 In., Pt. 523.00
Gin, Case, Engraved, Flowers, 2-Handle Urn, Lattice, 10 In. 220.00
Gin, Case, Engraved, Flowers, 2-Handle Urn, Octagonal Body, Glass Screw Cap, 6¾ In. 50.00
Gin, Case, Engraved, Pewter Mounts, Floral, Leafy Scroll, Initial F, 8¾ In. 248.00
Gin, Case, Engraved, Tulip, Flowers, Shaped Stopper, 7 In. 33.00
Gin, Case, Yellow, Olive Green, Pontil, Tooled Lip, String Ring, c.1750, 18 In. 1232.00
Gin, Case, Yellow Olive, Rolled Lip, Open Pontil, 1770-1800, 10⅜ In. 213.00
Household, Boot Polish, Crockers Union, Blue Green, OP, Rolled Lip, Norwich, Conn., c.1850, 4 In. . 4950.00
Household, Larkin Soap Co., Emerald Green, Stopper 35.00
Ink, Aquamarine, Corset Waist, Iron Pontil, Blown, 1840, 2¾ In. 358.00
Ink, Boss Patent, Umbrella, 6-Sided, Aquamarine, Rolled Mouth, Pontil, 2⅝ In. 679.00
Ink, Butler's, 12-Sided, Aquamarine, Inward-Rolled Mouth, Pontil, c.1850, 2⅞ In. 465.00
Ink, Butler's, Cincinnati, 12-Sided, Blue Aqua, Rolled Lip, Open Pontil, 2¼ In. .... *illus* 202.00
Ink, Carter's, Cathedral, Cobalt Blue, Embossed, Tooled Lip, c.1915, 9¾ In. 94.00
Ink, Carter's, Cone, Blue Aqua, Tooled Lip, c.1880, 2⅜ In. 605.00
Ink, Carter's, No. 1, Cobalt Blue, Master, 32 Oz. 30.00
Ink, Cone, Emerald Green, Outward-Rolled Mouth, Pontil, c.1850, 2⅜ In. 1080.00
Ink, Dovell's Patent, Cone, Cloudy, Aqua 35.00
Ink, E. Waters, Troy, N.Y., Cylindrical, Green, Fluted Shoulders, Applied Collar, Pontil, 5½ In. 1075.00
Ink, Estes, N.Y., Aquamarine, Teepee, Inward-Rolled Mouth, Pontil, c.1850, 4 In. 489.00
Ink, Farley's, 8-Sided, Olive Amber, Sheared Mouth, Pontil, Stoddard, N.H., c.1850, 1¾ In. 1120.00
Ink, Geometric, Yellow Olive Green, 3-Piece Mold, Tooled Disc Mouth, 1½ In. .... *illus* 179.00
Ink, Harrison's Columbian, 6-Sided, Emerald Green, Rolled Mouth, Pontil, 1½ In. 1330.00
Ink, Harrison's Columbian, 8-Sided, Blue Green, Collared Mouth, Pontil, c.1950, 3¾ In. 395.00
Ink, Harrison's Columbian, 12-Sided, Aquamarine, Applied Flared Collar, Pontil, 9 In. 1500.00
Ink, Harrison's Columbian, 12-Sided, Aquamarine, Applied Flared Mouth, Paper Label, 4⅞ In. . 540.00
Ink, Harrison's Columbian, 12-Sided, Yellow Green, Applied Flared Collar, Pontil, 4½ In. 510.00
Ink, Harrison's Columbian, Cobalt Blue, Cylindrical, Open Pontil, Applied Mouth, c.1850, 5¾ In. 2090.00
Ink, Harrison's Columbian, Cobalt Blue, Cylindrical, Rolled Lip, Whittled, c.1850, 2 In. 1980.00
Ink, Harrison's Columbian, Cylindrical, Cobalt Blue, Applied Flared Mouth, Pontil, 4⅜ In. 1120.00
Ink, Harrison's Columbian, Cylindrical, Cobalt Blue, Inward-Rolled Lip, Open Pontil, 2 In. . *illus* 784.00
Ink, Harrison's Columbian, Cylindrical, Sapphire Blue, Rolled Mouth, Pontil, 1840-60, 2 In. 1350.00
Ink, Harrison's Columbian, Octagonal, Sapphire Blue, Outward-Rolled Mouth, Pontil, 2 In. . 2576.00
Ink, Hoffman's Carmine Chemical, Bridgeport, Conn., Emerald, Applied Lip, Label, c.1850, 9 In. . 112.00
Ink, House, Aquamarine, Milk Glass, Mansard Roof, Collared Mouth, 2 Piece 560.00
Ink, Hover, Phila., Cylindrical, Moss Green, Embossed, Tooled Flared Mouth, Pontil, 1840-60, 4½ In. 635.00
Ink, Inverted Cone, Olive Yellow, Outward-Rolled Mouth, 3 x 3⅛ In. 784.00
Ink, J & I.E.M., Turtle, 5-Sided, Aqua, 1⅞ x 2¼ In. 18.00
Ink, J.S. Dunham, 12-Sided, Aquamarine, Inward-Rolled Mouth, Pontil, c.1850, 2¼ In. 490.00

B

Ink, James S. Mason & Co., Umbrella, 8-Sided, Blue Green, Rolled Mouth, Pontil, 1850, 2½ In. ..	2110.00
Ink, M & P, Umbrella, 8-Sided, Blue Green, Rolled Mouth, Pontil, 1850, 2½ In.	1020.00
Ink, Pitkin Type, 36 Ribs, Swirled To Left, Dark Olive Green, Tooled Disc Mouth, OP, 1⅝ In. . *illus*	1008.00
Ink, Pitkin Type, 36 Ribs, Swirled To Left, Olive Green, 1¾ x 2⅛ In.	110.00
Ink, Redware, Cylindrical, Flared Rim, Sloping Shoulders, 6 In.	1763.00
Ink, S. Fine, Cylindrical, Blue Green, Inward-Rolled Mouth, Pontil, 1850, 3 In.	429.00
Ink, S. Fine, Emerald Green, Pontil, Rolled Lip, 1850, 3 In.	385.00
Ink, S.I. Comp., Barrelblue, Aqua, 2¼ In.	149.00
Ink, Stoddard, Cone, Olive, X Base	400.00
Ink, Superior Blue Ink, 12-Sided, Blue Green, Rolled Mouth, Pontil, Paper Label, 1850, 2 In.	1120.00
Ink, Teakettle, 6-Sided, Milk Glass, Raised Flowers, Brass Collar & Cap, 2⅜ In. ....*illus*	560.00
Ink, Teakettle, 11-Sided, Cobalt Blue, Ground Lip, Brass Collar & Cap, 2⅜ In. ....*illus*	224.00
Ink, Teakettle, Milk Glass, Powder Blue, Lobed, Brass Neck, Hinged Lid, 2¾ In.	476.00
Ink, Umbrella, 8-Sided, Aqua, Applied Lip, 2¾ In.	15.00
Ink, Umbrella, 8-Sided, Aqua, Rolled Lip, Label, Jet Black, For School Use, 2½ In. .....*illus*	101.00
Ink, Umbrella, 8-Sided, Blue Green, Inward-Rolled Lip, OP, 2⅝ In. ....*illus*	112.00
Ink, Umbrella, 8-Sided, Midnight Blue, Rolled Mouth, Pontil, 2¼ In.	1120.00
Ink, Umbrella, 8-Sided, Pink Amethyst, Pontil, Sheared & Tooled Mouth, 1⅞ In.	3300.00
Ink, Umbrella, 8-Sided, Sapphire Blue, Rolled Mouth, Pontil, 1850, 2⅜ In.	1380.00
Ink, Umbrella, 12-Sided, Aqua Stain, 3 x 2¼ In.	10.00
Ink, Umbrella, J. Gundry, 12-Sided, Aquamarine, Rolled Mouth, Pontil, 1850, 3 x 2⅜ In.	670.00
Ink, Water's, Umbrella, Pale Aquamarine, Rolled Mouth, Pontil, 1850, 2¾ In.	625.00
Jar, Blue Green, Flared Rim, Pontil, 1840-60, 12½ In.	275.00
Jar, Grease, Clambroth, Embossed Eugene Bize & Fricke, 3¾ In.	825.00
Jar, Storage, Blue Aqua, Open Pontil, Cylindrical, Dip Mold, 1815, Pt., 6¾ In.	45.00
Jar, Storage, Green Aqua, Wide Mouth, Rolled Lip, c.1780, 9½ x 5 In. ....*illus*	308.00
Jar, Storage, Light To Medium Yellow Topaz, Applied Ring On Lip, Open Pontil, c.1800, 12½ In. .	300.00
Jar, Storage, Yellow Olive Green, Wide Mouth, Flared Rim, c.1780, 10 x 4½ In. ....*illus*	168.00
Jar, Tobacco, Globe Tobacco Co., Yellow, 6-Sided, Ground Lip	69.00
Jar, Utility, Bright Moss Green, Applied Lip, Pontil, New England, 13 In.	440.00
Jar, Utility, Cobalt Blue, 4-Sided, Flared Lip, Pontil, c.1810, 11 In.	440.00
Jug, Ackers High Grade Groceries, Pottery, Brown, Cream, Qt.	125.00
Jug, Aqua, Globular, Applied Handle, Lip, Crimped Foot, Open Pontil, c.1850, 3 In.	245.00
Medicine, Apothecary, Baluster Shape, Paneled, Fluted Neck, Footed, Bullet-Shaped Stopper, 18 In. .	390.00
Medicine, Apothecary, Cased Cranberry, Gilt, Hand-Painted Label, Enameled, Polished Pontil, 7 In. .	143.00
Medicine, Apothecary, Cover, Pulv. Lapis. P., Pottery, Cobalt Blue, 6⅝ In.	448.00
Medicine, Apothecary, Foley Cathartic Tables, Square, Clear, Stopper, 1880, 9 In.	259.00
Medicine, Apothecary, Leech, Bisque, White, Lid, Germany, 1820-35	3360.00
Medicine, Apothecary, McDonald's Improved Liver Pills, Free-Blown, Clear, Stopper, 1906, 9 In. ..	79.00
Medicine, Apothecary, P & S Cough Drops, Free-Blown, Clear Stopper, c.1890, 11½ In.	139.00
Medicine, Apothecary, Pear Shape, Blown Glass, Steeple-Shaped Faceted Stopper, 20 In.	720.00
Medicine, Apothecary, Pear Shape, Spiral Ribbed Collar & Finial, Spread Foot, 29½ In.	660.00
Medicine, Apothecary, Porcelain, White, Hand-Painted Label, Ungt. Zinci, 10 x 6 In.	115.00
Medicine, Apothecary, Pyrex, Tongue Depressors, 7½ x 2⅞ In.	20.00
Medicine, Beekman's Pulmonic Syrup, Olive Green, 8-Sided, Double Collar, 7¼ In.	7280.00
Medicine, Billings Clapp & Co., Boston, Yellow Olive, Cylindrical, 1865, 7 In.	139.00
Medicine, C. Brinckerhoff's Health Restorative, Olive Green, Sloping Mouth, 7 In.	770.00
Medicine, C. Brinckerhoff's Health Restorative, Olive Yellow, Collared Mouth, 7 In.	2128.00
Medicine, C. Brinckerhoff's Health Restorative, Yellow Olive Green, Pontil, 7⅜ In. .....*illus*	1904.00
Medicine, C. Ellis & Co., Philada, Blue Aqua, Embossed, Open Pontil, c.1840, 7 In.	79.00
Medicine, C. Heimstreet & Co., Cobalt Blue, 8-Sided, Open Pontil, Double Collar, c.1850, 7 In.	246.00
Medicine, C.W. Merchant, Chemist, Lockport, N.Y., Emerald Green, Applied Top, 7⅜ In. *illus*	336.00
Medicine, Cook's Balm Of Life, Golden Amber, Applied Top, 9¾ In.	139.00
Medicine, Diehl's Condition Powders For Horse, Cattle & Swine, Teal Blue, Green, 7 In.	39.00
Medicine, Dr. Baker's Pain Panacea, Aqua, Rectangular, Open Pontil, 5 In.	60.00
Medicine, Dr. C. Grattan's Diphtheria Remedy, Aqua, Tooled Lip, 6¾ In.	66.00
Medicine, Dr. D. Fahrney & Son, Teething Syrup For Babes, Clear, 5½ In.	22.00
Medicine, Dr. D.C. Kellinger, N.Y., Aqua, Cylindrical, Open Pontil, 6⅛ In.	69.00
Medicine, Dr. E.G. Gould's Pin Worm Syrup, Embossed	39.00
Medicine, Dr. H. Van Vleck's Family, Aqua, Cylindrical, Open Pontil, 6¾ In.	300.00
Medicine, Dr. Humphrey's Medicated Holland Gin, Aqua, Square, Qt.	48.00
Medicine, Dr. Josephus, Great Shoshonees Remedy, Aqua, Rectangular, 8½ In.	85.00
Medicine, Dr. Keeler's Vermifuge Syrup, Aqua, Rectanglular, Open Pontil, 5 In.	160.00
Medicine, Dr. Kellinger's Magic Fluid, Aqua, Rectangular, Open Pontil, 3¾ In.	145.00
Medicine, Dr. Kelling's Pure Herb, Aqua, Cylindrical, Pontil, Applied Mouth, 1850, 6⅜ In. 100.00 to 200.00	
Medicine, Dr. M. Bowman's Genuine Healing Balsam, 8-Sided, Open Pontil, 5½ In.	90.00

Bottle, Flask, Scroll, Yellow Green,
Applied Ring Mouth, Iron Pontil, Pt.
$280.00

Bottle, Flask, Success To The Railroad,
Moss Green, Tooled Lip, Open Pontil, Pt.
$448.00

Bottle, Flask, Sunburst, Yellow Amber,
Tooled Lip, Pontil, ½ Pt.
$784.00

Bottle, Flask, Union,
Clasped Hands & Eagle, Medium Amber,
Applied Ring, ½ Pt.
$280.00

Bottle, Flask, Washington, Father Of His Country, Cobalt Blue, Sheared Lip, Open Pontil, Pt.
$5600.00

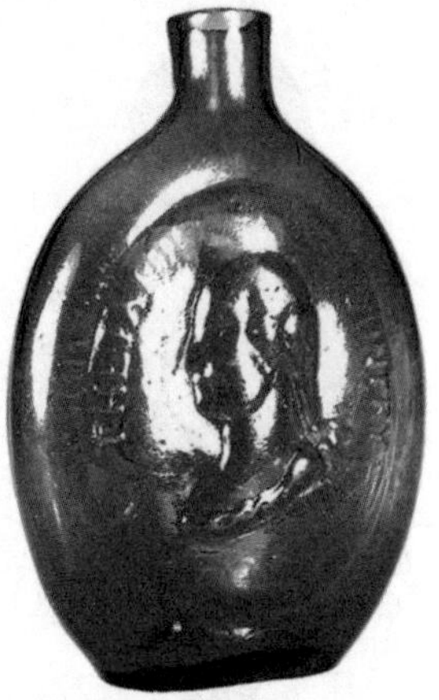

Bottle, Flask, Washington & Eagle, Emerald Green, Sheared Lip, Open Pontil, Pt.
$12320.00

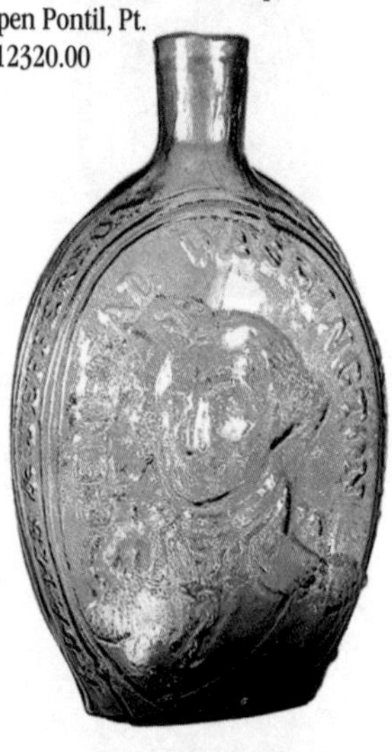

Bottle, Fruit Jar, A. Stone & Co., Philada, Blue Aqua, Internal Screw Threads, Glass Lid, Pt.
$1120

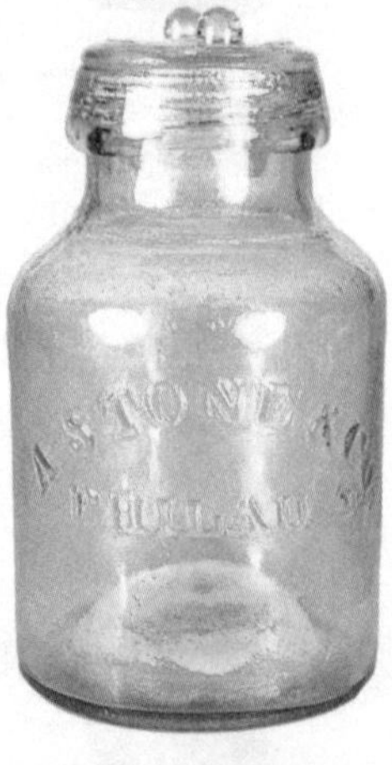

Medicine, Dr. Pettit's Canker Balsam, Aqua, Oval, Open Pontil, 3½ In. 175.00

Medicine, Dr. S. Feller's Eclectic Liniment, 8-Sided, Aqua, Open Pontil, 4½ In. 175.00

Medicine, Dr. S.A. Weaver's Canker & Salt Rheum Syrup, Aqua, Applied Top, 9½ In. 55.00

Medicine, Dr. Steph. Jewett's Celebrated Pulmonary Elixir, Aqua, Open Pontil, 5½ In. 325.00

Medicine, Dr. Thatcher's Liver & Blood Syrup, Tenn, Amber Panel 40.00

Medicine, English Remedy, W.H. Hooker & Co. Sole Agents North & South America, 6 In. 50.00

Medicine, F. Stearns & Co., Pure Fruit Tablets, Aqua, 18 In. 50.00

Medicine, Furst-McNess Co., Freeport, Ill., Aqua, 6¼ In. 5.00

Medicine, Gargling Oil, Lockport, N.Y., Blue Green, 5½ In. 35.00

Medicine, Gottschall's Liniment, Clear, Cylindrical, Mother & Girl Label, 5 In. 39.00

Medicine, H. Lake's Indian, Aquamarine, Open Pontil, Applied Ring Mouth, 1850, 8 In. 1680.00

Medicine, Hall's American Cough Syrup For Diseases Of Throat, Lungs, Aqua, 1906, 10 In. .. 39.00

Medicine, Healy & Bigelow Indian Sagwa, Aqua Blue, Indians, 6 In. 45.00

Medicine, Herrick's German Horse Liniment, L.W. Warner, Aqua Panel 30.00

Medicine, J.B. Wilde & Co., Blue, Aqua, Open Pontil, Applied Mouth, c.1850, 6¾ In. 78.00

Medicine, L.Q.C. Wishart's Pine Tree, Blue, Green, Applied Mouth, c.1865, 7⅞ In. 280.00

Medicine, L.Q.C. Wishart's Pine Tree Tar, Embossed Tree, Tooled Top, 10 In. 275.00

Medicine, Laboratory Of G.W. Merchant, Chemist, Lockport, N.Y., Blue Green, 5⅝ In. 179.00

Medicine, Life Plant Trademark, Embossed Eagle, Amber, Oval, 8½ In. 69.00

Medicine, Lynch's Celebrated Dyspectic Cordial, Forest Green, Iron Pontil, 7½ In. 9520.00

Medicine, M.B. Roberts Vegetable Embrocation, Green, Cylindrical, Open Pontil, 5½ In. 439.00

Medicine, Mrs. M.N. Gardner's Indian Balsam Of Liverwort, Aqua, Cylindrical, 1840-60, 5⅛ In. . 101.00

Medicine, Owl Drug Co., San Francisco, Embossed Owl, Aqua Green, Tooled Top 80.00

Medicine, Paine's Celery Compound, Amber, Front & Back Label Pictures Celery Stalk 59.00

Medicine, Rev. I.R. Gates Magamoose Co., Blue Aqua, Cathedral, 8½ In. 39.00

Medicine, Rodericks Wild Cherry Cough Balsam, Aqua, Label, 6 In. 25.00

Medicine, Scovill's Blood & Liver Syrup, Blue, Green, Curved Panels, 10 In. 85.00

Medicine, Scovill's Blood & Liver Syrup, Square Panel, 10 In. 25.00

Medicine, Shaker Cherry Pectoral Syrup, Aqua, Pontil, Canterbury, N.H., 5¼ In. 160.00

Medicine, Smelling Salts, Seahorse, Cobalt Blue, Applied Rigaree, 2¼ In. 199.00

Medicine, Swift's Syphilitic Specific, Cobalt Blue, Strap-Sided, c.1875, 9⅛ In. 1232.00

Medicine, T.A. Slocum Psychine For Consumption & Lung Problems, Clear 25.00

Medicine, U.S.A. Hosp. Dept., Amber, Green, Applied Top, 9 In. 605.00

Medicine, U.S.A. Hosp. Dept., Clear, Flared Lip, Smooth Base, 5 In. 110.00

Medicine, U.S.A. Hosp. Dept., Olive Yellow, Double Collar, 4-Piece Mold, c.1865, 9 In. 560.00

Medicine, U.S.A. Hosp. Dept., Topaz, Copper, Double Collar, 4-Piece Mold, c.1865, 9⅜ In. 672.00

Medicine, U.S.A. Hosp. Dept., Yellow, Amber, Double Collar, 4-Piece Mold, c.1865, 9⅜ In. 280.00

Medicine, U.S.A. Hosp. Dept., Yellow, Amber, Double Collar, 4-Piece Mold, c.1865, 9 In. 784.00

Medicine, Vaughn's Vegetable Lithontriptic Mixture, Buffalo, Blue Aqua, Iron Pontil, 8 In. . *illus* 2688.00

Medicine, W.W. Clarks Infallible Worm Syrup, Phila, Aqua, Rolled Lip, c.1855, 4 In. 19.00

Medicine, Warner's Safe Nervine, Slug Plate, 7 In. 120.00

Milk, Big Elm Dairy Company, 7Up Green, 1925, Qt., 9 In. 168.00

Milk, Del Rico Dairy, La Fiesta De Santa Fe, Enjoy Delicious Ice Cream, 3-Color Pyro, Qt. 647.00

Milk, Milk's Emulsion, Amber, 8 In. 15.00

Milk, Norwood Bros. Dairy, Bartlett, Tenn., Pt. 4.00

Milk, Nowlin's Dairy, Wickenburg, Embossed, Slug Plate 75.00

Milk, University Of Wisconsin, Embossed, Round, 1914, Pt. 50.00

Mineral Water, C.A. Cole, Cobalt Blue, Ten Pin, Applied Tapered Collar, 8⅜ In. 1344.00

Mineral Water, C.A. Cole, Green, Ten Pin, Applied Tapered Collar, c.1850, 8¾ In. 2016.00

Mineral Water, Carbutt & Hamilton, Blue, Aqua, Ten Pin, Applied Mouth, c.1860, 7⅞ In. 616.00

Mineral Water, Clarke & Co., Blue, Green, Iron Pontil, Applied Mouth, c.1850, Pt., 7⅞ In. .. 420.00

Mineral Water, Clarke & Co., Emerald Green, Iron Pontil, Applied Mouth, c.1850, Pt., 7⅞ In. 258.00

Mineral Water, Clarke & Co., Olive Green, Applied Mouth, 3-Piece Mold, 9½ In. 190.00

Mineral Water, Clarke & White, Deep Olive Green, High Shoulder, Applied Mouth, c.1860, Qt. 78.00

Mineral Water, Clarke & White, Olive Green, Applied Mouth, 3-Piece Mold, Qt., 9 In. 146.00

Mineral Water, Congress & Empire Spring Co., Emerald Green, Sloping Mouth, 7¾ In. 66.00

Mineral Water, Congress & Empire Spring Co., Hotchkiss' Sons, New York, Blue Green, Qt. .. 157.00

Mineral Water, Consolidated Ice Co., Blue, Aqua, Applied Mouth, Wooden Carrying Case, 2 Gal. . 90.00

Mineral Water, Eureka Spring Co., Aqua, Round, Applied Mouth, c.1870, 8⅞ In. 280.00

Mineral Water, G.W. Weston & Co., Saratoga, N.Y., Yellow Olive, Cylindrical, Pontil, Pt. 364.00

Mineral Water, Geyser Spring, Saratoga Springs, Aquamarine, Sloping Mouth, Collar, 7 In. . 33.00

Mineral Water, Haskins Spring Co., Emerald Green, Cylindrical, Applied Collar, Qt. 1008.00

Mineral Water, Hawthorn Spring, Saratoga, N.Y., Orange Amber, 1865-75, Qt. .... *illus* 90.00

Mineral Water, Lewis & Lappeus, 10-Sided, Blue, Applied Collared Mouth, Pontil, 1850, ½ Pt. 1010.00

Mineral Water, Marlboro Red Spring, Emerald Green, Cylindrical, Collared Mouth, Pt. 3920.00

Mineral Water, P. Conway, Philada, Cobalt Blue, Blob Top, Iron Pontil, 1840-60, 7½ In. 224.00

Bottle, Fruit Jar, Trademark Lightning, Putnam On Base, Citron, Qt.
$448.00

Bottle, Ink, Harrison's Columbian, Cylindrical, Cobalt Blue, Inward Rolled Lip, Open Pontil, 2 In.
$784.00

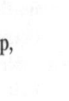

Bottle, Ink, Teakettle, 11-Sided, Cobalt Blue, Ground Lip, Brass Collar & Cap, 2⅜ In.
$224.00

Bottle, Ink, Butler's, Cincinnati, 12-Sided, Blue Aqua, Rolled Lip, Open Pontil, 2¼ In.
$202.00

Bottle, Ink, Pitkin Type, 36 Ribs, Swirled To Left, Dark Olive Green, Tooled Disc Mouth, OP, 1⅝ In.
$1008.00

Bottle, Ink, Umbrella, 8-Sided, Aqua, Rolled Lip, Label, Jet Black, For School Use, 2½ In.
$101.00

Bottle, Ink, Geometric, Yellow Olive Green, 3-Piece Mold, Tooled Disc Mouth, 1½ In.
$179.00

Bottle, Ink, Teakettle, 6-Sided, Milk Glass, Raised Flowers, Brass Collar & Cap, 2⅜ In.
$560.00

Bottle, Ink, Umbrella, 8-Sided, Blue Green, Inward-Rolled Lip, OP, 2⅝ In.
$112.00

Bottle, Jar, Storage, Green Aqua, Wide Mouth, Rolled Lip, c.1780, 9½ x 5 In. $308.00

Bottle, Medicine, C.W. Merchant, Chemist, Lockport, N.Y., Emerald Green, Applied Top, 7⅜ In. $336.00

Bottle, Pickle, Cathedral, Emerald Green, Iron Pontil, Willington Glass Works, 8½ In. $4760.00

Bottle, Jar, Storage, Yellow Olive Green, Wide Mouth, Flared Rim, c.1780, 10 x 4½ In. $168.00

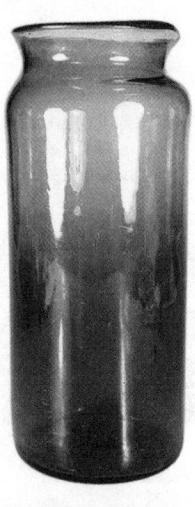

Bottle, Medicine, Vaughn's Vegetable Lithontriptic Mixture, Buffalo, Blue Aqua, Iron Pontil, 8 In. $2688.00

Bottle, Poison, Hobnail, Olive Green, Tooled Mouth, Pontil, 5⅝ In. $476.00

Bottle, Medicine, C. Brinckerhoff's Health Restorative, Yellow Olive Green, Pontil, 7⅜ In. $1904.00

Bottle, Mineral Water, Hawthorn Spring, Saratoga, N.Y., Orange Amber, 1865-75, Qt. $90.00

Mineral Water, Polk & Co., Cobalt Blue, Ten Pin, Applied Tapered Collar Mouth, 8 In.	. . . . .	952.00
Mineral Water, Richfield Sulphur, B&R, Richfield Springs, N.Y., Blue Green, 1850, Pt.	. . . . .	3080.00
Mineral Water, Ritter, Cinn., Aqua, 10-Sided, Teardrop, Iron Pontil	. . . .	135.00
Mineral Water, Saint Leon, Cylindrical, Emerald Green, Applied Sloping Collar, Pt.	. . . .	784.00
Mineral Water, Saratoga High Rock Spring, 1767, Rock, Blue Emerald Green, 1870, Qt.	. . . .	4480.00
Mineral Water, Saratoga Spring Co., Emerald Green, Applied Mouth, 1870, 7⅜ In.	. . . .	78.00
Mineral Water, Saratoga Spring Co., Emerald Green, Applied Mouth, 1870, Qt., 9¾ In.	. . . .	157.00
Mineral Water, Saratoga Spring Co., Red Amber, Reversed S, Sloping Mouth, Collar, Dimples, 9 In.	. .	121.00
Mineral Water, Saratoga Spring Co., Yellow Amber, Applied Mouth, 1870, Qt., 10 In.	. . . .	100.00
Mineral Water, Superior, Iron Pontil, Blue, Squat, 10-Sided, Union Glassworks	. . . .	595.00
Mineral Water, Susquehanna Springs, Emerald, Applied Sloping Collar Mouth, 1870, Qt.	. .	5650.00
Mineral Water, Syracuse Springs, Yellow, Olive Tone, Cylindrical, Sloping Collar, Qt.	. . . .	3080.00
Mineral Water, Washington Spring, Emerald Green, ½ Pt.	. . . .	345.00
Mineral Water, Washington Spring Co, Bust Of Washington, Emerald Green, 1860-80, Pt.	. . .	1568.00
Mineral Water, White Sulphur, Blue Green, Applied Sloping Collar Mouth, 1870, 8¾ In.	. . . .	1045.00
Mineral Water, Witter Springs, Wm. S. Co., San Francisco, Amber, Cylindrical, 9½ In.	. . . . . .	29.00
Pepper Sauce, 8-Sided, Aqua, Scalloped, 3 Neck Rings, Open Pontil, c.1840, 9¾ In.	. . . .	89.00
Pepper Sauce, 8-Sided, Aqua, Scalloped, Open Pontil, 9 In.	. . . .	259.00
Pepper Sauce, 12-Sided, Green Aqua, Open Pontil, Inward-Rolled Lip, 1850, 11 In.	. . . .	132.00
Pepper Sauce, Blue, Spiral, Embossed, S & P Pat.	. . . .	295.00
Pepper Sauce, Cathedral, 4-Sided, Aqua, 8¾ In.	. . . .	55.00
Pepper Sauce, Cathedral, 6-Sided, Green, Aqua, 18 Windows, Acorn Designs, 8¾ In.	. . . . . .	119.00
Pepper Sauce, Cathedral, Aqua, Applied Top, Pontil, 8¾ In.	. . . . 100.00 to 209.00
Pepper Sauce, Heinz, 1906, 8 Oz., 6¼ In.	. . . .	149.00
Pepper Sauce, W.K. Lewis & Co., 8-Sided, Green, Applied Lip, Graphite Pontil, 10½ In.	. . . . .	495.00
Pepper Sauce, W.M. & P., N.Y., Blue Green, Sheared, Tooled Mouth, Pontil, 1850, 9 In.	. . . . .	308.00
Perfume bottles are listed in their own category.		
Pickle, 7Up Green, 3-Piece Mold, Cylindrical, 10 In.	. . . .	69.00
Pickle, C.P. Sanborn & Son, Union, Boston, Yellow Olive, Sheared Lip, c.1885, 5 In.	. . . .	120.00
Pickle, Cathedral, 4-Sided, Green, Applied Top, Square Graphite Pontil, 11¾ In.	. . . .	1210.00
Pickle, Cathedral, 6-Sided, Applied Top, Light Aqua, 1880s, 11½ In.	. . . .	100.00
Pickle, Cathedral, 6-Sided, Blue, Aqua, Rolled Lip, 1860, 13 In.	. . . . 123.00 to 190.00
Pickle, Cathedral, 6-Sided, Blue Green, Rolled Mouth, 1870, 13 In.	. . . .	3080.00
Pickle, Cathedral, 6-Sided, Golden Amber, Tooled Mouth, 1870, 13 In.	. . . .	1680.00
Pickle, Cathedral, Aqua, 11½ In.	. . . .	265.00
Pickle, Cathedral, Aquamarine, Tooled Mouth, 7½ In.	. . . .	1680.00
Pickle, Cathedral, Blue, Aqua, Double Windows	. . . .	48.00
Pickle, Cathedral, Blue Aqua, Leafy Branches, Applied Mouth, 1865, 11⅜ In.	. . . .	280.00
Pickle, Cathedral, Blue Green, Diamonds, Crown, Rolled Lip, 1865, 11 In.	. . . .	728.00
Pickle, Cathedral, Blue Green, Fluted Shoulders & Neck, Iron Pontil, Applied Mouth, c.1860, 11 In.	. .	1100.00
Pickle, Cathedral, Emerald Green, Iron Pontil, Willington Glass Works, 8½ In.	. . . . *illus*	4760.00
Pickle, Cathedral, Green Aqua, 11½ In.	. . . .	230.00
Pickle, Cathedral, Light Green, Beveled Corners, Rolled Mouth, Iron Pontil, 1850, 11 In.	. . . .	1232.00
Pickle, Cathedral, Light Green, Rolled Lip, 11¾ In.	. . . .	299.00
Pickle, Cylindrical, Pale Green, Fluted Shoulder, Iron Pontil, 11½ x 4 In.	. . . .	1792.00
Pickle, Goofus, Vase Form, Cornflower Blue, Flowers, Ground Mouth, 15½ In.	. . . .	784.00
Pickle, Goofus, Vase Form, Topaz, Flowers, Roses, Ground Mouth, 1890, 15½ In.	. . . .	1064.00
Pickle, Shaker Brand, Aqua, Applied Lip, Paper Label, c.1900, 7 x 2 x 2 In.	. . . .	770.00
Pickle, Wm. Underwood & Co., Boston, Cylindrical, 7 Panels, Green, Pontil, 11 In.	. . . .	2128.00
Poison, Amber, Tooled Lip, Slug Plate, 1900, 3 In.	. . . .	3640.00
Poison, DP, Embossed Skull & Crossbones, Cobalt Blue, Hobnails, Casket, Label, 1885, 7½ In.	. .	995.00
Poison, Flask, Ice Blue, Square Hobnails, Pontil, Inward-Rolled Lip, c.1850, 5½ In.	. . . .	420.00
Poison, Flask, Olive Green, Hobnails, Pontil, Sheared, Tooled Mouth, c.1830, 5⅝ In.	. . . .	476.00
Poison, Friedgen, Yellow Green, Tooled Lip, Ribs, 1900, 6⅞ In.	. . . .	4480.00
Poison, Hobnail, Olive Green, Tooled Mouth, Pontil, 5⅝ In.	. . . . *illus*	476.00
Poison, It Kills Bed Bugs, Cream, Blue Letters, Cylindrical, Handle, 1885, 6¾ x 4½ In.	. . . . . .	1792.00
Poison, S & D, Amber, Tooled Mouth, 1900, 4⅞ In.	. . . .	179.00
Poison, Triangular, Cobalt Blue, 3½ In.	. . . .	25.00
Sarsaparilla, Adamur, Green Plant, Amber, Rectangular, Paneled Sides, Tooled Mouth, 8¾ In.	*illus*	202.00
Sarsaparilla, B. Whitcomb's Beer, Stoneware, Gray, Cobalt Slip Letters, 10 In.	. . . . *illus*	392.00
Sarsaparilla, B.F. Williams Syrup, Iodid Of Potass, Aqua, Pontil, c.1855, 9 In.	. . . .	1045.00
Sarsaparilla, Botanic, Blue Aqua, Applied Square Collar, 8¼ In.	. . . . *illus*	67.00
Sarsaparilla, Catlins, For The Blood, St. Louis, Amber, Tooled Mouth, c.1890, 8¼ In.	. . . .	232.00
Sarsaparilla, Chas. Cable & Son, Po'keepsie Premium, Blue Green, Blob Mouth, c.1850, 7 In.	. .	525.00
Sarsaparilla, Custer's Extract, Pale Aqua, Tooled Mouth, c.1900, 9 In.	. . . .	209.00
Sarsaparilla, Dana's, Belfast, Maine, Aqua	. . . .	412.00

Bottle, Sarsaparilla, Adamur, Green Plant, Amber, Rectangular, Paneled Sides, Tooled Mouth, 8¾ In.
$202.00

Bottle, Sarsaparilla, B. Whitcomb's Beer, Stoneware, Gray, Cobalt Slip Letters, 10 In.
$392.00

Bottle, Sarsaparilla, Botanic, Blue Aqua, Applied Square Collar, 8¼ In.
$67.00

Bottle, Sarsaparilla, Dr. Townsend's, Albany, N.Y., Blue Aqua, Applied Top, Iron Pontil, 9½ In.
$672.00

Bottle, Seal, Old Mill Whiskey, Whitlock & Co., Yellow Amber, Cone Shape, Pontil, 8¼ In.
$1680.00

B

Bottle, Snuff, Agate, Applied Flowers, Double Gourd Shape, Jade Stopper
$561.00

Snuff Bottles

At the same time the Chinese were developing small bottles to hold snuff, Europeans were creating snuff boxes, which have also become collectibles. The Chinese needed bottles rather than boxes, according to historians, because Chinese apparel had no pockets. The bottles, with their sealed stoppers, could be hidden up a sleeve.

Bottle, Snuff, Amber, Carved, Men Under Pine Tree, Round, Jade Stopper
$1298.00

Bottle, Snuff, Cloisonne, Phoenix Bird In Cartouche, Oval, Gilt Foo Dog Handles, 18th Century
$708

Sarsaparilla, Dr. Buchan's, Olive Amber, Applied Sloping Collar Mouth, 1885, 9¼ In.	280.00
Sarsaparilla, Dr. Clarke's, Olive Green, Tooled Mouth, c.1890, 8½ In.	405.00
Sarsaparilla, Dr. Cronk's Compound, Deep Blue, Aqua, Pontil, Applied Sloping Collar, 8⅝ In.	616.00
Sarsaparilla, Dr. Denison's, Aqua, Oval, Open Pontil, Applied Tapered Mouth, 1850, 7⅝ In.	532.00
Sarsaparilla, Dr. Guysott, Compound Extract Of Yellow Dock, Aqua, Double Collar, c.1860, 9 In.	405.00
Sarsaparilla, Dr. Guysott, Yellow Dock, John D. Park, Cincinnati, Aqua, Oval, IP, c.1850, 9⅝ In.	440.00
Sarsaparilla, Dr. Ira Baker's Honduras, Apple Green, Tooled Lip, 1890, 10⅛ In.	200.00
Sarsaparilla, Dr. J. Townsend's, N.Y., Chocolate Amber, Applied Mouth, Pontil, 9¾ In.	1568.00
Sarsaparilla, Dr. J. Townsend's, New York, Blue, Green, Iron Pontil, Tapered Mouth, 10 In.	190.00
Sarsaparilla, Dr. Reinhausers, Hydriodated, Aqua, Collar, Open Pontil, c.1850, 8⅝ In.	4400.00
Sarsaparilla, Dr. Townsend's, Albany, N.Y., Blue Aqua, Applied Top, Iron Pontil, 9½ In. *illus*	672.00
Sarsaparilla, Dr. Townsend's, Albany, N.Y., Olive Green, Applied Top, Open Pontil, 9½ In.	303.00
Sarsaparilla, Dr. Townsend's, Albany, N.Y., Amber, Applied Mouth, Square, Pontil, 1860, 9 In.	3375.00
Sarsaparilla, Dr. Townsend's, Green, Applied Tapered Lip, Iron Pontil, 9¾ In.	110.00
Sarsaparilla, E. Carroll's, Aquamarine, Applied Blob Mouth, c.1860, 7⅜ In.	336.00
Sarsaparilla, E.A. Olendorf, Orange Amber, Applied Top, Lightning 1890-95, 8¾ In.	235.00
Sarsaparilla, H. Boese's Root Beer, Tan Pottery, 12-Sided, Salt Glaze, 1855, 9⅝ In.	200.00
Sarsaparilla, John Bull, Blue, Aqua, Iron Pontil, Applied Mouth, 1850, 9⅛ In.	336.00
Sarsaparilla, Kennedy's, Celery Compound, Amber, Tooled Mouth, c.1890, 9¾ In.	187.00
Sarsaparilla, Log Cabin, Rochester, N.Y., Yellow Olive Amber, Applied Mouth, c.1890, 9 In.	198.00
Sarsaparilla, Masury's Cathartic, Blue Aqua, Double Collar, 1860, 9 In.	224.00
Sarsaparilla, Old Townsend's, N.Y., Blue Green, Applied Sloping Collar, Iron Pontil, c.1850, 9 In.	357.00
Sarsaparilla, Old Townsend's, N.Y., Yellow Green, Tooled Mouth, c.1885, 10¼ In.	154.00
Sarsaparilla, Post's, Aqua, Double Collar, 1860, 8⅜ In.	715.00
Sarsaparilla, Stoneware, Salt Glaze, Light Gray, c.1860, 10½ In.	90.00
Sarsaparilla, Thos. A. Hurley's, Compound Syrup, Aqua, Collar, Iron Pontil, 1850, 9½ In.	880.00
Scent, 8-Sided, Corseted, Cobalt Blue, Rolled Collar Mouth, 6⅛ In.	840.00
Scent, 8-Sided, Corseted, Teal Green, Round Tooled, Smooth Base, 4⅝ In.	1792.00
Scent, Amber, Cylinder, Embossed, 2 Stars, 8¾ In.	59.00
Scent, Amber, Double Headed Eagle, Emperor's Crown, Flower, Leaves, 3½ In.	440.00
Scent, Bloodstone, Carved, Disc Shape, Chatelaine Hook, Cabochon, Scotland, 3 In.	805.00
Scent, Blue, Flowers, Cameo, Silver Neck Mount, Screw Cap, Laydown, 1884, 11 In.	4800.00
Scent, Cloisonne, Silver, Oval, Turquoise Ground, Medallion, Flowers, Russia, 2¾ In.	518.00
Scent, Cobalt Blue, Applied Gilt Flowers, Flared Lip, Polished Pontil, Stopper, 1825, 3¼ In.	112.00
Scent, Cobalt Blue, Coat Of Arms, French Crown, City Of Orleans, 3 In.	220.00
Scent, Cylindrical, Enameled Silver, Pastoral Scene, Woman Gathering Flowers, 2½ In.	288.00
Scent, Dancing Indian, Apple Green, Open Pontil, Rolled Lip, 1850, 4¾ In.	213.00
Scent, Double Gourd, Millefiori, Punties, Twists, 6¾ In.	275.00
Scent, Duck Head, Cameo, Silver Screw Cap, Laydown, 1884, 9 In.	8400.00
Scent, Egg Shape, Vertical Ribs, Teal Green, Pigeon Blood Striations, Pontil, 1840, 3 In.	560.00
Scent, Fish Shape, Silver Articulated, Engraved, Red Cabochon Eyes, 6 In.	690.00
Scent, Green, Leaves, Flowers, Cameo, Silver Neck Mount, Screw Cap, 1901, 5 In.	1800.00
Scent, Lion, Blue, Aqua, Open Pontil, Tooled Lip, 1850, 4⅜ In.	364.00
Scent, Mandolin Shape, Nickel Silver, Repousse Scenes, Children, Lakeside, 6¾ In.	288.00
Scent, Persian Style, Champleve Cap, Band, Gilt Accents, Vermeil Silver Finish, 3⅛ In.	518.00
Scent, Porcelain, Inverted Pear Shape, Matte Gray, Gilding, Green Ground, Flowers, 8½ In.	705.00
Scent, Quiver Shape, Paneled Interior, Nickel Silver Plate, Filigree Mount, Stopper, 4 In.	862.00
Scent, Silver Case, Cut Panels, Engraved Design, Birmingham, c.1792, 1⅞ In.	200.00
Scent, Sultan & Consort, Hookah, Bird, Porcelain, Jacob Petit, Paris, 6 x 4 In., Pair	613.00
Scent, Tortoiseshell, Round, Cut Panels, Silver Cap, Stopper, Bimingham, c.1902, 3 In.	230.00
Scent, Triple Overlay, Blue Cut To White, Bulbous, Waisted, Silver Plated Cap, 3⅜ In.	200.00
Scent, Urn Shape, Enameled Silver, Scroll, Leaf Design, Glass Jewels, 2½ In.	400.00
Scent, Urn Shape, Silver, Tooled, Courting Couples, Leaf Scrolls, 3¾ In.	345.00
Scent, Violin Shape, Cobalt Blue, Shaded, Open Pontil, Rolled Lip, 1850, 5⅝ In.	1792.00
Seal, All Souls, Deep Olive Amber, Cylinder, Clover Leaf Pontil, Sheared Mouth, c.1780, 10⅝ In.	840.00
Seal, Black Glass, Deep Olive Green, Pontil, Sheared Mouth, Applied String Lip, c.1785, 10 In.	560.00
Seal, Chestnut Grove, Whiskey, Puce, Applied Handle, Embossed, 1860, 8¾ In.	418.00
Seal, HHC, Black Glass, Applied String Lip, Pontil, 1800, 10¾ In.	420.00
Seal, Old Mill Whiskey, Whitlock & Co., Yellow Amber, Cone Shape, Pontil, 8¼ In. *illus*	1680.00
Seal, Sidney Breese Wine, Magnum, Yellow Olive, Sheared Mouth, String Rim, Pontil, 1765, 11 In.	18800.00
Seal, Whiskey, Star, Amber, Cone Shape, Ribs, Pontil, Applied Double Collar, Handle, 1870, 8 In.	1456.00
Seal, Whitlock & Co., Cognac, Amber, Globular, Applied Ringed Mouth, Handle, 6 In.	448.00
Seal, Wm. Wilson Wine, Dark Olive Amber, Pontil, Sheared Mouth, String Lip, 1761, 8¾ In.	1344.00
Snuff, Agate, Applied Flowers, Double Gourd Shape, Jade Stopper *illus*	561.00
Snuff, Agate, Flattened Oval, Carved, Depicts Shi Shi, Cub, Chinese	413.00
Snuff, Agate, Lion Mask Handles, Rose Quartz Stopper, Chinese, 2 In.	294.00

Snuff, Agate, Yellow, Carved, Man Under Tree, Flattened Oval, Chinese	236.00
Snuff, Agate Moss, Gilt Wirework, Coral & Turquoise Cabochons, 3½ In.	72.00
Snuff, Amber, Carved, Men Under Pine Tree, Round, Jade Stopper .... *illus*	1298.00
Snuff, Amethyst, Phoenix, Flowers, Chinese, 2¾ In.	353.00
Snuff, Bone, Cylindrical, 2 Cranes, Leaves, Chinese	118.00
Snuff, Chalcedony, Broad Flattened Flask, Shou Medallions, Amethyst Stopper, 2¾ In.	261.00
Snuff, Chalcedony, Oval Flask, Gray Stone, Black Banding, Rose Quartz Stopper, 2½ In.	98.00
Snuff, Cinnabar, Lacquer, Flask Shape, Chinese, 19th Century, 2¼ In.	86.00
Snuff, Cloisonne, Phoenix Bird In Cartouche, Oval, Gilt Foo Dog Handles, 18th Century *illus*	7080.00
Snuff, Glass, Aesthetic, Caramel, Black, Silver Cap, London Hallmark, c.1897, 3 In.	230.00
Snuff, Glass, Aubergine Overlay, Ducks, Flowers, Chinese	165.00
Snuff, Glass, Dark Olive Amber, Rectangular, Semi-Flared Lip, Pontil, 1815, 4¾ In.	137.00
Snuff, Glass, Dragon, Phoenix, Flowers, Cameo, Pear Shape, 2½ In.	176.00
Snuff, Glass, Enameled, Flattened Oval, Scrolling Leaves, Birds, Chinese	266.00
Snuff, Glass, Forest Green, 4-Sided, Sheared Mouth, Pontil, Dip Mold, 1815, 4¼ In.	489.00
Snuff, Glass, Gray, Green, Double Gourd, Jade Stopper, Chinese, 2 In.	558.00
Snuff, Glass, Milk, Overlaid, Flattened Circle, Dragons, Mask Handles, Chinese, 2¾ In.	94.00
Snuff, Glass, Olive Amber, Chamfered Corners, Pontil, 1815, 6¾ In.	285.00
Snuff, Glass, Olive Amber, Sheared Mouth, Open Pontil, New England, 1820, 4¼ In.	100.00
Snuff, Glass, Olive Green, Chamfered Panels, Pontil, 1815, 4¼ In.	88.00
Snuff, Glass, Olive Green, Sloped Neck, Sheared & Fire Polished Lip, Pontil, 1810, 4½ In. ...	265.00
Snuff, Glass, Painted Birds, Flowers, Leaves, Flattened Oval, Jade Stopper, Signed, Ku Ye Shien ..*illus*	266.00
Snuff, Glass, Painted Interior, Portrait, Emperor Qianlong, Flattened Rectangle ......*illus*	325.00
Snuff, Glass, Painted Interior, Riverscape, Flattened Oval, Chinese	767.00
Snuff, Glass, Splash, Black Gold, Flattened Octagon, Chinese	443.00
Snuff, Glass, White, Cafe-Au-Lait, Flattened Oval, Chinese	295.00
Snuff, Glass, White, Double Gourd, Chinese	266.00
Snuff, Glass, White & Pink, Flattened Oval, Carved, Double Carp, Chinese	472.00
Snuff, Glass, Yellow Amber, Chamfered Corners, Flared, Sheared Mouth, Open Pontil, 1815, 5½ In. ..	358.00
Snuff, Glass Green, Imitating Jade, Flattened Oval, Chinese, 19th Century	118.00
Snuff, Horn, Banded, 19th Century, 1¾ x ¾ In.	78.00
Snuff, Ivory, Chicken Shape, Chinese, 2¾ In.	234.00
Snuff, Ivory, Confronting Dragons, Flattened Egg Shape, Carved, Chinese	443.00
Snuff, Ivory, Elephant Shape, Howdah, Multicolored, Chinese, 3¾ In.	527.00
Snuff, Ivory, Figures In Landscape, Flattened Oval, Chinese	5015.00
Snuff, Ivory, Man, Woman, Multicolored, Hand Carved, Chinese, Early 1900s, 4¼ In.	82.00
Snuff, Jade, Carved, Chinese, c.1900, 2½ In.	322.00
Snuff, Jade, Frog, Leaf, Coral Stopper, 2¼ In.	499.00
Snuff, Jade, Green, White, Brown Inclusions, Flattened Circle, Coral Stopper, 2½ In.	184.00
Snuff, Jade, Tan, Striations, Chinese, 2 In.	588.00
Snuff, Jade, White, Carved, Butterfly, Flattened Oval, Chinese	885.00
Snuff, Jade, White, Ladyfinger Shape, Chinese	472.00
Snuff, Lapis, Blue, Bird Shape, Oriental, 1½ x 2½ In.	88.00
Snuff, Lapis, Blue, Fruit & Monkeys Shape, Oriental, 3 In.	117.00
Snuff, Lapis Lazuli, Blue, Black Base, Chinese, 2 In.	293.00
Snuff, Mother-Of-Pearl, Boatman, Farmer, Chinese, 2¼ In.	588.00
Snuff, Peking Glass, Red Overlay On White, Precious Objects, Flattened, Oval ....*illus*	354.00
Snuff, Peking Glass, Striated, Tapered, Bulbous, 2½ In.	82.00
Snuff, Porcelain, Blanc-De-Chine, Flattened Oval, Carved, Depicts Lohan, Chinese	1652.00
Snuff, Porcelain, Bottle Shape, Mountains, Figures, Bridge In Riverscape, Chinese	201.00
Snuff, Porcelain, Copper Red, Painted, Cylindrical, Chinese, 2⅝ In.	413.00
Snuff, Porcelain, Dragon, Turquoise Glaze, Chinese, 20th Century, 3 In.	1645.00
Snuff, Porcelain, Famille Rose, Figures, Bridge, Mountains, Painted, Bottle Shape......*illus*	201.00
Snuff, Porcelain, Famille Rose, Flattened Oval, Carved, Musicians, Chinese	1770.00
Snuff, Porcelain, White, Glazed, Fu Dog, Chinese	649.00
Snuff, Rock Crystal, Reverse Painted, Water Lilies, Fish, Signed, Chinese	2832.00
Snuff, Rock Crystal, Round Shoulders, Lion, Mask Handles, Chinese, 2 In.	529.00
Snuff, Rose Quartz, Squirrel & Nuts Shape, Oriental, 2 In.	88.00
Snuff, Smoky Quartz, 3 Friends, Bamboo, Pine, Prunus, Poems, Flattened Circle, Chinese, 2 In. ..	235.00
Snuff, Smoky Quartz, Tourmaline Stopper, Chinese, 2¼ In.	176.00
Snuff, Zoizite Stone, Fruit Shape, Plum, Ruby, Oriental, 2 In.	94.00
Soda, Allens Red Tame Cherry, Reverse Painted Label, Aluminum Cup Cap, 11½ In.	2200.00
Soda, Beam & Yount, Teal, Blue, Green, Squat, Philadelphia	89.00
Soda, Cole & Co., C.A. Cole, C.F. Brown, Baltimore, Green, 10-Pin, Sloping Collar, 8¾ In. *illus*	2016.00
Soda, Coon & Spencer's Nectarian, Sapphire Blue, Collared Mouth, Iron Pontil, 8⅛ In.	1792.00
Soda, Crystal, Deep Cobalt Blue, Footed, Applied Blob Mouth, 1872, 7½ In.	364.00

Bottle, Snuff, Glass, Painted Birds, Flowers, Leaves, Flattened Oval, Jade Stopper, Signed, Ku Ye Shien
$266.00

Bottle, Snuff, Glass, Painted Interior, Portrait, Emperor Qianlong, Flattened Rectangle
$325.00

Bottle, Snuff, Peking Glass, Red Overlay On White, Precious Objects, Flattened, Oval
$354.00

Bottle, Snuff, Porcelain, Famille Rose, Figures, Bridge, Mountains, Painted, Bottle Shape
$201.00

Bottle, Soda, Cole & Co., C.A. Cole, C.F. Brown, Baltimore, Green, 10-Pin, Sloping Collar, 8¾ In. $2016.00

Bottle, Soda, Crystal Soda Water Co., Patented Nov 12 1872, Cobalt Blue, Blob Top, Pt., 7½ In. $364.00

Bottle, Soda, E.G. Ware, Philad A-D, Blue Green, Applied Sloping Collar, Iron Pontil, 7½ In. $1064.00

Bottle, Soda, F.J. Brennen, Shenandoah, Pa., Cobalt Blue, Blob Top, Pony, 7 In. $1232.00

Soda, Crystal Soda Water Co., Patented Nov 12 1872, Cobalt Blue, Blob Top, Pt., 7½ In. *illus*	364.00
Soda, Crystal Soda Water Co., Patented November 12, 1872, Applied Top, Blue, Pt.	160.00
Soda, D. Bacon, Aqua, Blob Top, Squat, Harrisburg, Pa.	99.00
Soda, D. O'Kane, Green, Applied Sloping Mouth, Collar, Iron Pontil, 7 In.	55.00
Soda, Dr Pepper, Commemorative, Texas Vs. Oklahoma Football Game, 1973, 16 Oz.	25.00
Soda, E.G. Ware, Philad A-D, Blue Green, Applied Sloping Collar, Iron Pontil, 7½ In. *illus*	1064.00
Soda, E.L. Billings Sac City Geyser, Light Blue, Applied Top	30.00
Soda, F.A. Jennings, Cobalt Blue, Cylindrical, Tooled Mouth, Smooth Base, ½ Pt., 6½ In.	2128.00
Soda, F.J. Brennen, Shenandoah, Pa., Cobalt Blue, Blob Top, Pony, 7 In. *illus*	1232.00
Soda, G.W. Brandt, Carlisle, Emerald Green, Blob Toop, Squat, Iron Pontil	295.00
Soda, Glencoe Bottling Co., Applied Top, ACWL On Base, 8½ In.	70.00
Soda, Green, John Beck, Camden, N.J., Blob Top	129.00
Soda, H. Nash & Co., Root Beer, Cincinnati, Cobalt Blue, 12-Sided, Blob Top, Iron Pontil, 8½ In.	896.00
Soda, Henry H. Ellis, Smooth Base, Vertical Embossing, Blob Top	300.00
Soda, Hires Carbonated Beverages, Whittled, Embossed, Aqua	20.00
Soda, J & A Dearborn & Co., New York Water, Applied Top, Iron Pontil, Blue	200.00
Soda, J.L. Leavitt, Olive Green, Cylindrical, Collared Mouth, 1865, 8¼ In.	616.00
Soda, J.W. Harris, New Haven, Conn., Cobalt Blue, 8-Sided, Blob Top, Iron Pontil, 7¾ In. *illus*	1064.00
Soda, Knickerbocker, Applied Top, Iron Pontil, Light Green	450.00
Soda, Kramer Bros., Natural Set Up, Green, White, Red ACL, Dice, Contents, Cap	19.00
Soda, Lazy-B Beverage, Hi Partner, Red & White, Color Label, 1951, 10 Oz	12.00
Soda, Levi Bender, Aqua, Tapered Shoulder, Squat, Blob Top	100.00
Soda, Pearson Bros. Bodie, Tooled Top, Applied Top, 1882-91	2800.00
Soda, Polk & Co., Barnum's Building, Baltimore, Cobalt Blue, 10-Pin, 8 In. *illus*	952.00
Soda, S. Smith, 10-Sided, Sapphire Blue, Applied Collared Mouth, Iron Pontil, Pt., 7¼ In.	532.00
Soda, S.B. Winn, Ginger Ale, Salem, Mass., Light Aqua	18.00
Soda, Smile, Aqua, Embossed, c.1920, 19 x 5½ In.	187.00
Soda, Smile Brand Soda Pop, Aqua, 1920s, 18 x 5 In.	190.00
Soda, Walter & Brother, Teal Blue-Green, Double Collar, Squat	69.00
Soda, Ward's Lemon-Crush, Original Cap, 12 In.	280.00
Target Ball, Amber, 7 Bands, Sheared Lip, 1885, 2⅝ In.	504.00
Target Ball, Bogardus, Olive Green, Sheared Lip, Dots, Diamonds, c.1877, 2⅝ In.	1650.00
Target Ball, Bogardus, Pat'd Apr 10 1877, Diamond, Sapphire Blue, Sheared Lip, 2⅝ In. *illus*	672.00
Target Ball, Bogardus, Pat'd Apr 10 1877, Diamond, Yellow Amber, Sheared Lip, 2⅝ In. *illus*	4480.00
Target Ball, Bogardus, Pat'd Apr. 10 1877, Diamond, Orange Amber, Sheared Lip, 2⅝ In.	532.00
Target Ball, Clear With Mottled Cobalt Blue, Sheared Wide Mouth, England, c.1900, 2¾ In.	715.00
Target Ball, Clear With Mottled Turquoise Blue, Wide Mouth, Sand Grain Finish, England, 2¾ In.	605.00
Target Ball, Cobalt Blue, 2 5-Point Stars, Long Neck, Sheared Lip, 2⅛ In. *illus*	168.00
Target Ball, Cobalt Blue, 7 Bands, Sheared Lip, 1885, 2⅝ In.	532.00
Target Ball, Cobalt Blue, Sheared Lip, 1885, 2⅝ In.	50.00
Target Ball, Diamond, Amethyst Tint, Man Shooting, Feather Stuffing, England, c.1890, 2⅝ In.	358.00
Target Ball, Diamond, Clear, Man Shooting, Sheared Lip, England, c.1890, 2⅝ In.	230.00
Target Ball, Diamond, Cobalt Blue, Van Cutsem, St. Quentin, 2½ In.	195.00
Target Ball, Diamond, Man Shooting, Pink Amethyst, Sheared Lip, 2⅝ In.	616.00
Target Ball, Diamond, Yellow, Green, Czechoslovakia, 1890, 2⅝ In.	258.00
Target Ball, Glasshutten Dr. A Frank, Diamond, Olive, Charlottenburg, Germany, 1885, 2¾ In.	300.00
Target Ball, Ira Paine's, Yellow, Olive Tone, Sheared Lip, 3-Piece Mold, Pat. Oct. 23, 1877, 2⅝ In.	420.00
Target Ball, Man Shooting, Light To Medium Emerald Green, Sheared Lip, 2⅝ In. *illus*	532.00
Target Ball, Squares, Cobalt Blue, Sheared Lip, France, 1890, 2¾ In.	146.00
Target Ball, Squares, Yellow Green, Sheared Lip, France, 1890, 2¾ In.	308.00
Target Ball, W.W. Greener St., Diamond, Amethyst, Sheared Lip, 1890, 2⅝ In.	532.00
Tonic, Green, Aqua, 5-Sided, Open Pontil, Applied Mouth, c.1850, 6 In.	420.00
Tonic, Rohrer's, Expectoral Wild Cherry, Lancaster, Pa., Amber, Embossed, 10¼ In.	248.00
Tonic, Rohrer's Wild Cherry, Yellow Amber, Double Collar Mouth, 1860, 10 In.	392.00
Whiskey, Acorn & Old Continental, Stoneware, Mini-Jug, Cream, Black Stencil	59.00
Whiskey, Amber, Embossed Grapes & Vine, Applied Lip, Iron Pontil, 1875, 9½ In.	1760.00
Whiskey, Amber, Pinched Waist, Applied Double Collar, Handle, c.1870, 8½ In.	420.00
Whiskey, Amber, Pinched Waist, Double Collar Lip, Handle With Rigaree, Pontil, c.1860, 8 In.	330.00
Whiskey, Avan Hoboken & Co., Olive Green, Applied Seal, Rolled Lip, 9½ In.	33.00
Whiskey, Backbar, Amethyst, 8-Pillars, Polished Pontil, Swirled Neck, 1840-60, 11¾ In.	725.00
Whiskey, Backbar, Dark Cobalt Blue, Applied Collar, Pontil, Blown, 1840-60, 10½ In.	220.00
Whiskey, Backbar, Imperial Cabinet, Tooled Top, Amber Brown	700.00
Whiskey, BB Extra Superior, Amber, Applied Top, 10½ In.	143.00
Whiskey, Bourbon, Plum Puce, Applied Squared Lip, 9⅜ In.	358.00
Whiskey, Casper's, Cobalt Blue, Qt.	495.00
Whiskey, Chestnut Grove, Orange Amber, 10 Ribs, Applied Mouth, Handle, c.1870, 5⅛ In.	168.00

Whiskey, Chestnut Grove, Wharton's, Amber, Teardrop, 1850, 5¼ In. ....*illus*	420.00
Whiskey, Dr. Bauer's Wild Cherry Cordial, Schlesing & Benders, S.F., 1890	90.00
Whiskey, Dr. Girard's Ginger Brandy, Yellow Amber, Cone Shape, Double Collar, 9¼ In.	1232.00
Whiskey, E.G. Booz Old Cabin, 1840, 7½ In.	3738.00
Whiskey, Edward Oullahan Trademark, Pioneer Liquor House, Stockton Cala., Embossed Bear .	100.00
Whiskey, Greeley's Bourbon, Barrel, Copper Salmon, Applied Disk Lip, Embossed, c.1865, 9 In. ..	469.00
Whiskey, Griffith Hyatt & Co., Baltimore, Yellow Amber, Jug, Pontil, 7½ In. ....*illus*	728.00
Whiskey, I.W. Harper Gold Medal, Stoneware, Cream, Anchors & Rope, Qt.	69.00
Whiskey, J.F.T. & Co., Amber, Jug, Ribs, Pontil, Double Collar, Handle, 1870, 7⅛ In.	616.00
Whiskey, J.H. Cutter Old Bourbon, Orange Amber, Cylindrical, Crown, 11½ In.	39.00
Whiskey, John H. Hamm, Label Under Glass, Original Stopper, 10 In.	1320.00
Whiskey, McHenry 1812, Amber, Square, Wreath Logo, Swirled Neck, Qt.	59.00
Whiskey, Myers & Co. Pure Fulton Whiskey, Jug, Stoneware, Cream, Blue Letters, Gal.	89.00
Whiskey, O'Donnel's Old Irish, Pottery, Jug, Cream, Brown Glaze Neck, Handle, 1900, 7¾ In.	179.00
Whiskey, Old Crow 1880 Pure Sour Mash, Black, Gold Label, Qt.	39.00
Whiskey, Old Kentucky Bourbon, Amber, Barrel Shape, Ribbed Bands, Applied Lip, 9½ In. ..	382.00
Whiskey, P. Hoppe's Special Schiedam Schnapps, Olive Yellow, Applied Top, 7½ In.	69.00
Whiskey, Schenleys Golden Wedding, Amber, Paper Label, Screw Top, Mid 1900s, 8 In.	118.00
Whiskey, Song Bird On Blossom, Merry Christmas, Happy New Year, Label Under Glass, 5 x 4 In.	605.00
Whiskey, Star, Medium Orange Amber, Ribs, Pontil, Double Collar, Tooled Spout, 1870, 8 In.	672.00
Whiskey, Turner Brothers, Honey Amber, Olive Tint, Barrel, Applied Square Lip, 10 In.	385.00
Whiskey, Udolpho Wolfe's, Schiedam, Embossed, Olive Amber, Applied Lip, Collar, 1850, 9½ In. ..	450.00
Whiskey, Udolpho Wolfe's Aromatic Schnapps, Olive Green, Applied Top, 9¼ In.	165.00
Whiskey, Udolpho Wolfe's Aromatic Schnapps, Schiedam, Tobacco Amber, Applied Top, 9⅞ In. .*illus*	336.00
Whiskey, Watson's Dundee, Brown, Tan, Man In Kilt, Triangular Spout, Scotland, ¼ Gal.	350.00
Whiskey, Whitney Glass Works, Flora Temple, Copper, Ringed Mouth, Handle, 1859, 10 In. ..	448.00
Whiskey, Wicklow Distillery, Old Irish, Pottery, Jug, Cream, Brown Glaze Neck, Handle, 7¾ In.	202.00
Whiskey, Wicklow Distillery, Owl On Branch, Jug, Pottery, Black Transfer, 7¾ In. ......*illus*	190.00
Whiskey, Yellow, Green, Cylindrical, Applied Double Collar, 11 In.	69.00
Wine, Dutch Onion, Green, Mid 18th Century, 7¼ In.	295.00
Wine, Dutch Onion, Medium Olive Green, Applied Lip, Kick Up Base, Pontil, 8¼ In.	88.00
Wine, Dutch Onion, Medium Olive Yellow, Sheared Mouth, String Rim, 2 x 2³⁄₁₆ In.	840.00
Wine, Olive, Yellow, Bulbous, Multicolored Shop Scene, Sheared Mouth, 10½ In.	3360.00
Wine, Onion, Blue Green, Applied String Lip, Open Pontil, 7¼ In. ....*illus*	213.00
Wine, Onion, Dark Olive Green, Applied String Lip, Pontil, 5⅝ In. ....*illus*	1344.00
Wine, Onion, Deep Olive Green, Sheared Mouth, Applied String Lip, Open Pontil, 1730, 7¼ In. ..	112.00
Wine, Onion, Olive Green, Sheared Mouth, Applied String Lip, Pontil, c.1730, 6⅞ In.	123.00
Wine, Onion, Yellow, Green, Sheared Mouth, String Rim, 10¾ In.	3360.00
Wine, Onion, Yellow, Olive Amber, Sheared Mouth, Applied String Lip, c.1730, 8 In.	90.00
Wine, Onion, Yellow, Olive Green, Sheared Lip, Applied String Lip, c.1730, 8⅛ In.	100.00
Wine, Shaft & Globe, Olive Green, Bulbous, Sheared Mouth, c.1655, ½ Pt.	7280.00

BOTTLE CAPS for milk bottles are the printed cardboard caps used since the 1920s. Crown caps, used after 1892 on soda bottles, are also popular collectibles. Unusual mottoes, graphics, and caps from bottlers that are out of business bring the highest prices.

Clover Leaf Dairy, Green & White, 4 In.	1.00
Crown, Donald Duck Cream Soda, Cork Lined, Walt Disney Productions	23.00
Crown, Donald Duck Soda, Yellow, White, Blue, Cork, Commercial Beverage Co., 1953	5.00
Crown, Red Fox Ale, Red, White Lettering, Cork Lined, Largay Brewing Co., Connecticut	7.00
Crown, Stegmaier Porter, Yellow, Black Letters, Cork Lined, Standard Brewing Co.	22.00
University Of Maryland, Pasteurized Milk, College Park, Md.	96.00
Yoo-Hoo, Me For, New York Yankees, Early 1960s, 8-Piece	405.00

BOTTLE OPENERS are needed to open many bottles. As soon as the commercial bottle was invented, the opener to be used with the new types of closures became a necessity. Many types of bottle openers can be found, most dating from the twentieth century. Collectors prize advertising and comic openers.

Alligator, Cast Iron, Wilton Products, 1¼ x 6 In.	138.00
Alligator, Head Up, Cast Iron, John Wright Co., 3¾ x 2¾ In.	252.00
Alligator & Boy, Cast Iron, 1947, 2¾ In.	145.00
Amish Boy, Red Shirt, Black Pants, Hat, Cast Iron, 1935, 4 x 2 In.	193.00
Ballantine Ale & Beer, Metal, Handy Walden, 3½ In.	8.00
Bartender, Corkscrew, Signed, 8 x 3 In.	50.00
Bavaria, Bottle Shape, Brass, Brazil, 5¼ x 1⅜ In.	8.00
Beanie Bert, 1988 FBOC Convention, Cast Iron, 4 x 2 In. .... 275.00 to 336.00

Bottle, Soda, J.W. Harris, New Haven, Conn., Cobalt Blue, 8-Sided, Blob Top, Iron Pontil, 7¾ In.
$1064.00

Bottle, Soda, Polk & Co., Barnum's Building, Baltimore, Cobalt Blue, 10-Pin, 8 In.
$952.00

Bottle, Target Ball, Bogardus, Pat'd Apr 10 1877, Diamond, Sapphire Blue, Sheared Lip, 2⅝ In.
$672.00

Bottle, Target Ball, Bogardus, Pat'd Apr 10 1877, Diamond, Yellow Amber, Sheared Lip, 2⅝ In.
$4480.00

Bottle, Target Ball, Cobalt Blue, 2 5-Point Stars, Long Neck, Sheared Lip, 2⅛ In. $168.00

Bottle, Target Ball, Man Shooting, Light To Medium Emerald Green, Sheared Lip, 2⅝ In. $532.00

Bottle, Whiskey, Chestnut Grove, Wharton's, Amber, Teardrop, 1850, 5¼ In. $420.00

Bottle, Whiskey, Griffith Hyatt & Co., Baltimore, Yellow Amber, Jug, Pontil, 7½ In. $728.00

Bear Head, Black, Cast Iron, Wall Mount, John Wright Co., 3¾ x 3⅛ In.	196.00
Billy Goat, Cast Iron, John Wright Co., 1950, 2¾ x 2¾ In.	84.00
Black Caddy, Nickel Plated, Cast Iron, 1932, 6 x 2 In.	840.00
Black Face, Cast Iron, Wall Mount, Wilton Iron Works, 1940s, 4 x 3½ In.	125.00
Boomerang, Penguins, Fish, Boats, Fish, Aluminum	12.00
Boy Winking, Cast Iron, Wall Mount, Wilton Prod., 3¾ x 3⅝ In.	2016.00
Bulldog, White, Cast Iron, Wall Mount, Wilton, 1947, 4⅛ x 3¾ In.	308.00
Canada Goose, Cast Iron, Wilton Products, 1947, 1¾ x 3⅝ In.	140.00
Canvas Back, Cast Iron, 1947, 1¹³⁄₁₆ x 2⅞ In.	196.00
Cathy Coed, Girl With Books, Pledge Dance '57, Cast Iron, L & L Favors, 4½ In.	1008.00
Clown, Red & White Polka Dot Bowtie, Cast Iron, Wall Mount, Wilton, 4 x 4 In.	84.00
Cockatoo, Cast Iron, John Wright Co., 1950, 3¼ x 2⅞ In.	224.00
Corkscrew, Boot, Figural, Marked, Blackinton, c.1930, 3⅞ In.	275.00
Cowboy, Drunk, Cactus, Cast Iron, Woodstock, N.Y., John Wright Co., 3¾ x 2⅝ In.	504.00
Cowboy, Guitar, Cast Iron, John Wright Co., 4¾ x 3⅛ In.	168.00
Cowboy, In Chaps, Cast Iron, Wilton Products, 4½ x 2¾ In.	448.00
Dinky Dan, Initiatory Formal '53, Zme On Sweater, Cast Iron, 3⅞ x 2⅛ In.	504.00
Dodo Bird, Multicolored, Cast Iron, John Wright Co., 2¹³⁄₁₆ x 2¹¹⁄₁₆ In.	252.00
Dolphin, Chrome, 6½ In.	9.00
Elephant, Walking, Black, White, Pink, Cast Iron, Wilton Products, 1947, 2½ x 3¼ In.	28.00
Elephant, Walking, Red, Black, Cast Iron, 1947, 2½ In.	165.00
Elephant, White, Cast Iron, Flat, 1950, 3 x 2 In.	56.00
Falls City Beer, It's Pasteurized, Bitter Free, Vaughn, 3⅞ x ¾ In.	12.00
Fish, Green, Yellow, Orange, Flat, Cast Iron, 1947, 2 x 3¾ In.	140.00
Fish, Tail Up, Cast Iron, John Wright Co., 1940s, 2⁵⁄₁₆ x 4⅝ In.	168.00
Football Player, Ashtray, Colgate Weekend '54, Joe Alexander, Iron, L & L Favors, 4 x 2 In.	252.00
Foundry Man, Cast Iron, John Wright Co., 3⅛ x 2⅝ In.	140.00
Four Eyes Man, Cast Iron, Wall Mount, John Wright Co., 4 x 4 In.	28.00
Freddie Frosh, Pledge Party '63, Cast Iron, L & L Favors, 4 x 2 In.	392.00
Frenchman, Yellow Shirt, Red Ascot, Belt, Brown Boots, Beret, Cast Iron, 6¼ In.	45.00
Grass Skirt Greek, Cast Iron, Signed Boiler, Md., 4⅞ x 1½ In.	616.00
Handy Hans, Pledge Formal '65, Beta Sigma Rho, Cast Iron, L & L Favors, 3⅞ x 2⅜ In.	392.00
Hard-Hat Shape, Metal, Aldrich Engineering, Newark, N.J.	11.00
Horse Tail, Wilton Products, Inc., Box, Signed WO 36, 5¼ In.	303.00
Lady's Leg, Pocket Knife, Celluloid, Imperial, Providence, R.I., c.1920, 5 x 1 In.	190.00
Miss Four Eyes, Painted, Cast Iron, Box, 1954, 3¾ In.	84.00
Monkey, Brown, Cast Iron, John Wright Co., 1947, 2⅝ x 2¹¹⁄₁₆ In.	504.00
New York Central, Wood, Steel Ring, Stamped, Edlund Co., Pat. Nov 7-33, USA, 4½ In.	7.50
Paddy The Pledgemaster, Spring Formal '55, R Lambda Phi, Cast Iron, Gadzik Phila, 3⅞ x 2¼ In.	252.00
Palm Tree, Cast Iron, Wilton Products, 4⁹⁄₁₆ x 2⅝ In.	504.00
Parrot, Can Punch, Cast Iron, John Wright Co., 5 x 3 In.	84.00 to 165.00
Parrot, Cast Iron, Wilton Products, 3¼ x 3¼ In.	28.00 to 168.00
Parrot, On Black Perch, Timonium Fair, Md., Signed JW, 5½ In.	56.00
Parrot, On Perch, 1987 FBOC 10th Convention, Cast Iron, 5½ In.	55.00
Parrot, On Perch, Vine, Cast Iron, 4⅝ x 3¼ In.	616.00
Parrot, Virginia Beach, Cast Iron, John Wright Co., 4 x 2 In.	275.00
Patty Pep, Ashtray, N. Sigma, Cast Iron, L & L Favors, 4 In.	448.00
Pelican, Cast Iron, Wilton Products, 1947, 3⅜ x 3¾ In.	392.00
Penguin, Wood, Hand Carved, Corkscrew, France, c.1930, 5 In.	95.00
Pheasant, Cast Iron, John Wright Co., 2¼ x 3⅞ In.	336.00
Reynolds Toys, Bear, Black, Holding Sign, Painted, Aluminum, No. 40, 4⅝ In.	112.00
Rooster, Cast Iron, John Wright Co., 3¾ x 2¾ In.	193.00 to 224.00
Sammy Samoa, Cast Iron, Signed, L & L Favors, 4⁵⁄₁₆ x 2 In.	392.00
Sawfish, Cast Iron, Wilton Products, 2¹⁄₁₆ x 5¾ In.	672.00
Seagull, Atlantic City, N.J., Cast Iron, John Wright, 3¼ x 2¾ In.	28.00
Seagull, Cast Iron, John Wright Co., 1950s, 3¼ x 2¾ In.	196.00
Seahorse, Cast Iron, John Wright Inc., 1950s, 4¼ x 2¼ In.	196.00
Squirrel, Gray, Cast Iron, John Wright Co., 1950s, 2 x 2⅞ In.	224.00
Straw Hat, Ashtray Base, Sign Post, Baltimore, Md., Cast Iron, John Wright Co., 4 x 3 In.	28.00
Toucan, Cast Iron, John Wright Co., 3⅜ x 2⅞ In.	140.00
Trout, Cast Iron, Wilton Products, 1947, 1⅝ x 4⅞ In.	280.00
Wood, C.B. Wagner, Patent 1900	20.00

BOW is an English porcelain works started in 1744 in East London. Bow made decorated porcelains, often copies of Chinese blue and white patterns. The factory stopped working about 1776. Most items sold as Bow today were made after 1750.

Candlestick, Flowers, Scrolls, Shells, Yellow, Blue, Painted, Rococo, c.1760, 4½ In., Pair	2280.00
Figurine, Saltbox Player, Yellow Jacket, Puce Hat, Seated On Rock, c.1758, 5 In.	1920.00
Figurine, Sportswoman, Flower Dress, 3-Sided Hat, Fountain, Dog, Green Base, c.1752-53, 4¾ In.	1320.00
Figurine, Troubadour, Seated, On Tree Stump, Singing, Strumming Guitar, c.1755-60, 5⅞ In.	720.00
Figurine, Turkish Woman, Headdress, Puce Coat, Skirt, Applied Flowers, Leaves, c.1760, 7 In.	2280.00
Tureen, Cover, Partridge, In Nest, Applied Grass, Feathers, Marked, c.1758, 7½ In., Pair	14400.00

BOXES of all kinds are collected. They were made of thin strips of inlaid wood, metal, tortoiseshell, embroidery, or other material. Additional boxes may be listed in other sections, such as Advertising, Ivory, Shaker, Tinware, and various Porcelain categories. Tea Caddies are listed in their own category.

Agate Sides, Brown, Figured, Beveled, Gilt Brass Frame, Agate Ball Feet, 2 x 3½ x 2 In.	720.00
Art Nouveau, Jeweled, Inset Classical Room Scene, c.1900, 17 x 11 x 4¼ In.	295.00
Arts & Crafts, Silver Crest, Bronze, Patina, Zigzag Decoration, 1915, 3¾ In.	245.00
Bakelite, Black & Yellow, Round, Barrel Shape Finial, Lid, c.1935, 3½ In.	323.00
Band, Black, Polychrome Tulips & Flowers, Nailed Lap, 4¼ x 8¾ In.	176.00
Band, Cover, Green Paint, Stenciled, Interlocking Finger Bands, 6¾ x 14⅝ In. *illus*	495.00
Band, Cover, Old Blue Paint, Finger Jointed, 4¾ x 12¼ In. *illus*	143.00
Band, Finger Joint On Lid & Base, 1⅛ x 3½ In.	121.00
Band, Heart Shape, Wallpaper Covered, Cream, Blue Wavy Combed Design, 1 x 3 In.	1998.00
Band, Old Blue Paint, Finger Jointed, Stenciled, Pumice, 3 x 6⅝ In.	1045.00
Band, Oval, Blue, White Floral Pattern, Holds Doll's Woven Straw Hat, 2½ x 3⅝ In.	880.00
Band, Oval, Wallpaper, Country Estate Scene, c.1835, 11 x 13 In.	1058.00
Band, Oval, Wallpaper, Flowers, Multicolored, Boston Newspaper Lined, 1840, 4⅝ x 9 In.	588.00
Band, Oval, Wallpaper, Flowers, White Blossoms, Blue Ground, 11 x 13 In.	118.00
Band, Oval, Wallpaper, Fruit Compotes, Swan Handles, Newspaper Lined, Hannah Davis, 13 x 19 In.	1610.00
Band, Oval, Wallpaper, Mythological Scenes, Mid 1800s, 10 x 13 In.	1000.00
Band, Oval, Wallpaper, Neoclassical Garden Scene, c.1835, 12¾ x 14¾ In.	470.00
Band, Oval, Wallpaper, Squirrel, Giraffe Patterns, Blue Ground, Label, 13 x 16 In.	1410.00
Band, Painted, Black & White Flowers, Salmon Ground, Lancaster Co., 2⅜ x 6½ In.	1430.00
Band, Painted, Blue, Green Ground, Colorful Flower Basket, Festoon Border, 3¾ x 8 In.	275.00
Band, Wallpaper, Flowers, Blue Ground, Tin Latch, Dome Lid, 2½ x 3 x 4¼ In.	999.00
Band, Wallpaper, Heart Shape, Pink Cutwork Flowers, Green Leaves, 1⅝ x 3⅜ In.	1998.00
Band, Wallpaper, Poplar, Stenciled, Sliding Lid, 2½ x 6⅞ x 3⅞ In.	777.00
Band, Wooden, Wallpaper, Hannah Davis, Landscape, c.1834, 15½ x 15½ In.	2115.00
Beaded Leather, Wood, Tassels, Swags, Castle, Figures, Beveled Mirror, 1700s, 17 x 13 In.	7480.00
Bentwood, Oval, Opposing Fingers, Copper Tacks, Green Paint, Impressed, Levi Beal, 2 x 5 In.	517.00
Bentwood, Oval, Opposing Fingers, Copper Tacks, Green Paint, Notched, Initials, BFH, 2 x 5 In.	373.00
Bentwood, Oval, Opposing Fingers, Copper Tacks, Natural, Carved, D. Newton, 2¼ x 5½ In.	747.00
Bentwood, Oval, Opposing Fingers, Copper Tacks, Old Gray Paint, 1⅜ x 4¾ In.	747.00
Bentwood, Oval, Scalloped Edge Finger, Iron Rosehead Tacks, Patina, 3¼ x 9 In.	288.00
Bible, Oak, Fan & Floral Carving, Beehive Feet, Strap Hinges, Iron Lock, 1700s, 11 x 23 In.	489.00
Bible, Walnut, Pine, Poplar, Dovetailed, Rose Head Nails, Ball Feet, Base Molding, 17 x 15 In.	546.00
Book, Mahogany, Carved Panel, Kit, Biding Drawer, Gilt Edge, 10¼ x 8 In.	220.00
Book, Mahogany, Inlaid, Bird On Branch, Shaped Line, Herringbone, Drawer, 8 x 5½ In.	165.00
Book Shape, Pine, Painted, Hinged Lid, Faux Black Marble, Ladies Book 1839, 13 x 7 In.	764.00
Boulle, Tortoiseshell Veneer, Brass Foliage Inlay, Brass Lock, 6½ x 3¼ In.	460.00
Brass, Hinged Lid, Red, Gold Designs, Chinese, 8 x 20 x 10 In.	70.00
Brass & Copper, Art Nouveau Relief Decoration, Enameled Inset, Hinged Lid, 3 x 5 x 4 In.	705.00
Bride's, Bentwood, Laced Seams, Couple & Tulips On Lid, German Text, 1820, 12 x 19 In.	1840.00
Bride's, Bentwood, Laced Seams, Decoupage, Painted Flowers, 12¼ x 18¼ x 7¼ In.	518.00
Bride's, Bentwood, Tulips, Songbird, Blue Ground, Hand Painted, 10 x 17 x 8 In.	1092.00
Bride's, Painted, White, Orange Dress, Raised Arms, Flowers, Swirls, 6 x 16¼ In.	523.00
Bride's, Paper Lithograph, German Script, Flower Bands, Red Border, 7¼ x 19½ In.	220.00
Calamander Wood, Rectangular, Fitted Interior, Tray, 2 Lidded Bottles, Mid 1800s, 5 x 10 In.	398.00
Candle, Brass, Shaped Crest, 5½ In.	61.00
Candle, Hanging, Pine, Divided, Red Paint, Wrought Iron Straps, Lift Lid, Double Crest, 16 x 9 In.	1495.00
Candle, Hanging, Tin, Cylindrical, 15 In.	330.00
Candle, Pine, Slide Lid, 5½ x 10 x 4 In.	518.00
Candle, Pine, Square Nails, Slide Lid, Incised, 8 x 13½ x 5½ In.	805.00
Candle, Poplar, Red Paint, Yellow Striping, Tulips, ANW 1834, 6¾ x 10¼ In.	8912.00
Candle, Slide Lid, Painted, Heart Handle, Signed D.Y. Ellinger, 5 x 15 x 6½ In.	1586.00
Candle, Softwood, Dovetailed, Red Grain Paint, Finger Notch, Slide Lid, 5⅜ x 15⅜ In.	154.00
Candle, Softwood, Dovetailed, Red Paint, Green Oxidized, Black Moldings, 4 x 13 x 8 In.	2420.00
Candle, Softwood, Dovetailed, Red Paint, Slide Lid, 9½ x 13¾ In.	358.00

Bottle, Whiskey, Udolpho Wolfe's Aromatic Schnapps, Schiedam, Tobacco Amber, Applied Top, 9⅞ In.
$336.00

Bottle, Whiskey, Wicklow Distillery, Owl On Branch, Jug, Pottery, Black Transfer, 7¾ In.
$190.00

Bottle, Wine, Onion, Blue Green, Applied String Lip, Open Pontil, 7¼ In.
$213.00

Bottle, Wine, Onion, Dark Olive Green, Applied String Lip, Pontil, 5⅝ In.
$1344.00

Box, Band, Cover,
Green Paint, Stenciled,
Interlocking Finger Bands,
6¾ x 14⅝ In.
$495.00

Box, Band, Cover,
Old Blue Paint,
Finger Jointed, 4¾ x 12¼ In.
$143.00

Box, Cutlery, 2 Sections,
Wood, Shaped Cutout Handle,
6 x 15 x 9¾ In.
$201.00

Box, Knife, Mahogany,
Inlaid, Urn Shape,
Silver Shield Escutcheon,
Georgian, 26 In., Pair
$10925.00

Candle, Softwood, Dovetailed, Red Wash, Notched Finger Hold, Slide Lid, 4 x 10 x 5 In.	187.00
Candle, Softwood, Raised Panel, Chip Carved Edge, Slide Lid, 4¼ x 14⅝ In.	248.00
Candle, Walnut, Dovetailed, Finger Notch, Chamfered Lid, Slide Lid, 5⅜ x 13 x 7 In.	198.00
Candle, Walnut, Dovetailed, Finger Notch, Slide Lid, 3½ x 11¾ In.	105.00
Charity, Molded Lid, Stenciled, Nailed Construction, 5¾ x 9½ In.	138.00
Chest, Woman's Face, Flowers, Yellow & Red Pinstripes, Turned Feet, Dentil, Lehnware, 6 x 8½ In.	3575.00
Chip Carved, Slide Lid, Figural, Bird, Folk Art, 2½ x 4 In.	173.00
Cigarette, Ashtray, Bonzo Figure, Wood, 1930s, 5 x 9 x 6 In.	284.00
Conestoga Wagon, Blue Paint, Mounted To Partial Side Of Wagon, Scroll Hasp, 27 x 25 In. .	7700.00
Conestoga Wagon, Double Scroll Hasp Plate, Terminal, Blue Paint, Lid, 6¼ x 13½ In.	688.00
Cordials, Mahogany, Interior Slot, Fitted Compartments, Lift Top Lid, 8¼ x 6⅝ In.	978.00
Cover, Bentwood, Laced Joints, Rounded Corners, Painted Flowers, Folk Art, 3¼ x 8¼ In. ...	288.00
Cutlery, 2 Sections, Wood, Shaped Cutout Handle, 6 x 15 x 9¾ ....*illus*	201.00
Decanter, Lacquered Wood, Fox Hunting Print, Fitted Interior, Amber Glass Carafes, 9 x 11 In. .	53.00
Deed, Oak, Carved, Lock, 1920, 7 x 15 x 8 In.	230.00
Desk, Tooled Leather, French Gilt, Red Matte Interior, 8 x 10 x 7 In.	564.00
Desk, Traveling, Inlaid Woods, 19th Century, 15½ In.	7200.00
Ditty, Honey Birch, Washington On Horse, Hinged Gutta-Percha Lid, Civil War, 4½ x 3 In. ...	325.00
Document, Brass, Studded, Geometric Design, James Wyer, London, 19th Century, 22 In. ...	791.00
Document, Brass Tacks, Bail Handle, Hide Lid, Inscribed, Martha Hale, Bradford, Mass., 4 x 14 In. ..	110.00
Document, Burr, Inlaid, Ormolu Mounted, Mother-Of-Pearl, Hinged Lid, c.1820, 12 x 24 In. .	7800.00
Document, Copper Mounted, Brass Footed, Key, Bail Handle, Ball Feet, Hipped Lid, 9¾ x 19 x 9 In. .	1116.00
Document, Pine, Molded Sides, Escutcheon, Lock, Handle, Hinged Lid, 6½ x 15 x 11 In.	230.00
Document, Queen Anne, Walnut, Raised & Boxed Panels, Inlaid Star, Bracket Feet, 11 x 18 x 12 In. .	940.00
Document, Softwood, Old Dry Green Paint, Dovetailed, Brass Escutcheon, 6 x 15 In.	330.00
Document, Softwood, Paint Decorated, Brown Swirl Over Blue Paint, 4 x 15 In.	413.00
Document, Walnut, Shield Form Escutcheon, Iron Closure, Bull Ring Handle, Wire Hinges, 5 x 11 In.	825.00
Dovetailed, Painted Yellow, Red, Black, 12 x 24 x 12 In.	575.00
Dovetailed, Pine, Yellow Paint, Red Hearts, Black Horse, Red Barn, Trees, Dome Lid, 15 x 8 In. ..	144.00
Dovetailed, Poplar, Salmon & Black Vines, Geometrics, Lock, Dome Lid, Hinged, 12½ x 24 x 12 In. .	978.00
Dresser, Burl, Fruitwood, Inlaid Leafy Scrolls, Serpentine Lid, Ball Feet, 3¼ x 6⅝ In.	55.00
Dresser, Burl Walnut, Dome Lid, Drawer, Silver Plated Jars, 9 x 12 In.	529.00
Dresser, Porcelain, France, c.1930, 4 x 5 x 8 In.	117.00
Dresser, Walnut, Carved, Continental, c.1890, 7 x 6¼ x 10¼ In.	205.00
Embroidered, Fountain, Birds, Trees, Insects, Pink Lining, Silver Knob, Ball Feet, c.1640 ...	2950.00
Enamel, Painted, Mountain Scene, Continental, 3¾ In.	363.00
Enamel, Portrait In Interior, France, 18th Century, 1½ x 3¼ In.	234.00
English Oak, Walnut, 2 Books Shape, Opens, Storage, Square Legs, 19½ x 19 x 15½ In.	1175.00
Figural, Dove, Hardwood, Inside Compartment, Painted, Folk Art, 5 x 9½ In.	431.00
Figured Malachite, Polished Black Slate, Rectangular, Lid, Italy, 2 x 7½ x 4½ In.	900.00
Game, Wooden, 4 Compartments, Painted Scenic Lids, c.1820, 6¼ x 8 x 2¼ In.	900.00
Gilt Metal, Oval, Double Portrait, Ivory Reserve, Carved, 5¼ x 6⅝ In.	1287.00
Globe Shape, Olga Kosterneikova, Signed, Russia, c.1940, 3 x 3½ In.	176.00
Glove, Rosewood, Brass, Mother-Of-Pearl & Pewter Inlaid Decoration On Lid, 3 x 10 In.	360.00
Japanned, Louis XIV, Black, Gilt, Dome Lid, Chinoiserie Scene, 4 x 11½ x 8½ In.	3000.00
Jewelry, Brass Inlaid, Macassar Ebony, Tray, 19th Century, 7¾ x 5½ In.	660.00
Jewelry, Burl & Fruitwood Veneer, Inlaid Shell, Ivory Keyhole, Fitted Interior, Drawer, 9 x 6 x 4 In. ..	661.00
Jewelry, Gilt Bronze, Enamel, Roses, Scrolls, Sky Blue Ground, Taupe Satin Interior, 5 x 10 In.	2702.00
Jewelry, Mahogany, Satinwood String Inlay, Lion's Mask Handles, Brass Ball Feet, 5 x 9 In. ..	940.00
Jewelry, Turtle Shell, Incised Dragon, Chinese, 3½ x 5⅜ In.	351.00
Knife, Curly Maple, Pine, Canted Sides, Serpentine Edges, Cutout Handle, 12 x 13 In.	316.00
Knife, George III, Mahogany, Inlaid, Hinged Serpentine Lid, 9¾ x 15 x 11 In.	384.00
Knife, Georgian, Mahogany, Serpentine Front, Yew Inlay, Fitted Interior, Slant Lid, 15 x 8 In.	705.00
Knife, Georgian Spiral Rope, Slant Front, Banded Mahogany, Cutlery Grill, 14 x 8¾ x 10 In. ..	880.00
Knife, Georgian Style, Mahogany, Fruitwood Band, Slant Front, Hinged Lid, 9 x 15 x 9 In. ...	767.00
Knife, Mahogany, Dovetailed, Cutout Handle, 19th Century, 7 x 14 In.	1265.00
Knife, Mahogany, Dovetailed, Heart Cutout, Acorn Finials, Beveled Edge Lift Lids, 11 x 9 In. ..	546.00
Knife, Mahogany, Inlaid, Fitted Interior, England, c.1800, 14 x 10 x 11 In.	819.00
Knife, Mahogany, Inlaid, Urn Shape, Silver Shield Escutcheon, Georgian, 26 In., Pair ..*illus*	10925.00
Knife, Mahogany, Inlaid Band, Ivory Keyhole Escutcheon, Slant Lid, 15⅝ x 10 x 12½ In.	230.00
Knife, Pine, Grain Paint, Scalloped Edges, Double Heart Cutout Handle, 4 x 8 x 12 In.	259.00
Knife, Walnut, Scalloped Edge, Divider, Drawer, Geometric Inlays, Handle, 8 x 13 x 9 In.	2750.00
Knitting Needle Case, Cardboard, Wallpaper, Flattened Cylindrical Case, 9 In.	323.00
Lacquer, Diamond Shape, Gold, Brown Ground, Cranes, Landscapes, Japan, 7 x 12¼ In.	1080.00
Lacquer, Mother-Of-Pearl Inlay, 10¾ x 10 x 10½ In.	354.00
Lap Desk, Federal, Mahogany, Fold-Out Writing Surface, Tambour Lid, 16 x 10 In. ....*illus*	1016.00

Leather, Brassbound, Paper Lined, John Gilbert, 12 x 5½ x 7¼ In.	177.00
Leather, Spanish, Brass Nail Heads, Velvet Lining, Early 1800s, 10½ x 10½ In.	4600.00
Letter, Georgian Style, Mahogany, Inlaid, Sloped Lid, 15 In. *illus*	259.00
Letter, Papier-Mache, Mother-Of-Pearl, Flower Medallion, 13 x 4½ x 10 In.	354.00
Letter, Tortoise, Inlaid, Hinged, Checkerboard Banding, 19th Century, 3½ x 9¾ In.	748.00
Letter, Victorian, Leather Hinges, Silver Mounted, 1897, 12 x 8 x 5 In.	620.00
Logs, Twig Carry Handle, Black Forest, 8 x 13 x 8 In.	300.00
Mahogany, Brass Top Handle, Escutcheon, Hinged Lid, 5 x 8½ In.	117.00
Mahogany Veneer, Canted, 3 Compartments, Paneled, Dome Lid, Hinged, 7 x 6 In.	235.00
Malachite, Brass Inlay, Book Form, Leopard-Printed Fur Inside, Lid, 2 x 10 x 7 In.	960.00
Maple, Rosewood, Ebony, Inlaid Tunbridge Block Pattern, Silver & Pink Paper Lining, 5 x 12 In.	381.00
Oak, Dovetailed, Carved, Painted Relief Grapes, Vines, Brass Hinges, 19th Century, 12 x 23 In.	201.00
Oak, Grain Painted Geometric, Red, White, Black Striping, Lift Lid, 2¼ x 4⅞ x 3¼ In.	529.00
Painted, White & Blue Flowers, Finger Notch, Square Nails, Slide Lid, Lancaster Co., 4 x 10¾ x 7 In.	1100.00
Painted, White & Orange Flowers, Black Stems, Dark Blue Ground, Wire Nails, 2⅛ x 5½ x 3½ In.	660.00
Pantry, Bentwood, Swallowtail Fingers, Copper Tacks, Green Flowers, 3⅜ x 9½ In.	431.00
Pencil, Dixons Typhonite Eldorado, Master Drawing Pencil, Cardboard, 7¼ x 2 In.	10.00
Pencil, Felix The Cat, American Pencil Co., 1936, 1¼ x 4 x 8½ In.	112.00
Pine, Black Ground, Flowers, Buildings, Dome Lid, Hinged, 10½ x 7 x 5 In.	2990.00
Pine, Blue, Brass Swing Handle, Iron, Brass Hasp, Dome Lid, Hinged, 6⅜ x 13 x 9½ In.	940.00
Pine, Brass Swing Handle, Putty Whorls, Dome Lid, Hinged, 5⅜ x 10¼ x 5⅜ In.	588.00
Pine, Dovetailed, Mahogany Sides, Tiger Maple Posts, Federal, Lift Lid, 1800s, 23 x 19 In.	1265.00
Pine, Drawer, Iron Ring Pull, Tulip Blossoms, Hinged Lid, 7¼ x 13½ x 7½ In.	4406.00
Pine, Geometric Painted, Iron Latch, Turquoise, Yellow, Green, Hinged Lid, c.1845, 9 x 20 In.	1175.00
Pine, Iron Lock Plate, Black, White Putty, Hinged Lid, 10¼ x 29 x 13½ In.	1410.00
Pine, Iron Mounted, Painted Decoration, Metal Escutcheon, c.1883, 10 x 15¾ In.	345.00
Pine, Red & Blue Paint, Raised Panel, Finger Holds, Slide Lid, Marked, KOD, 8½ x 32½ x 10½ In.	460.00
Pine, Painted, Cast Iron Swing Handle, Lock, Wallpaper, Hinged Lid, 7¾ x 8¾ In.	500.00
Pine, Poplar, Painted, Polychrome, Flowers, Dome Lid, 3½ x 7½ In.	440.00
Pine, Red, Green Blossoms, Scalloped Borders, Dome Lid, Hinged, 3 x 5 x 3 In.	499.00
Pine, Red, Mustard Comb, Circles, Wavy Bands, Dome Lid, Hinged, 15¾ x 24¾ x 13½ In.	470.00
Pine, Red Over Mustard Vinegar, Dome Lid, 4½ x 8¾ In.	3335.00
Pine, Smoke Decorated, Iron Lock, Newspaper Lined Interior, Hinged Lid, c.1830, 7 x 18 In.	294.00
Pine, Walnut, Dovetailed, Chip Carved Geometrics, Original Paint, Slide Lid, 4½ x 9 x 7 In.	460.00
Pipe, Cherry, Brown Paint, Cutout, Pierced Backboard, Brass Knobs, 20½ x 4⅝ x 4 In.	8813.00
Pipe, Curly Maple, Dovetailed Drawer, 16½ x 4½ x 4½ In.	115.00
Pipe, Mahogany, Shell & Line Inlay, Tapered, Shaped Handing Plaque, 19 x 8 In.	144.00
Pipe, Pine, Red Stain, Dovetailed Drawer, 18 x 9½ In.	345.00
Pipe, Poplar, Red Stain, Stepped, Cutout Sides, Curved Crest, Dovetailed Drawer, 4½ x 17½ In.	1840.00
Pipe, Wall, Softwood, Dovetailed Drawer, Tall Compartment, Red Paint, 15 x 5 In.	495.00
Porcelain, Bronze Mounted, Multicolored, Courting Couples, Flowers, Lion Head Feet, 8 In.	646.00
Putty Fan, Paneled Borders, Dome Lid, c.1830, 12¾ x 26 x 12 In.	2468.00
Rectangular, Multicolored Outlined Panels, Dome Lid, Hinged, 11¼ x 34½ x 12 In.	2468.00
Rosewood, Bombe Shape, Brass Mount, Marbleized Paper Lining, Paw Feet, William IV, 7 x 5 In.	646.00
Rosewood, Carved, Victorian, Late 19th Century, 5 x 9 x 6½ In.	410.00
Rosewood, Citron Shape, Leaves, Branches, 2 Sections, Wood Stand, Chinese, 7 In.	470.00
Rosewood, Inlaid, Silver, Mother-Of-Pearl, Malachite, Soapstone, Chinese, 5½ x 4¼ In.	1003.00
Round, Wooden, Mustard Paint, Pineapple Stencil, Roses, Handles, Lid, 11½ x 6 In.	546.00
Saffron, Cover, Salmon, Strawberry & Vine, Mushroom Finial, Lehnware, 3½ In. *illus*	3850.00
Salt, Wall, Softwood, Dovetailed, Arched Backboard, Painted, Brown, 11½ x 11½ In.	165.00
Salt, Wall, Softwood, Dovetailed Construction, Peaked Backboard, 10 x 11 x 7 In.	303.00
Salt, Wall, Walnut, Scalloped Backboard, Slant Lift Lid, Drawer, 18 x 13¼ In.	523.00
Sarcophagus Shape, Figured Maple, Dovetailed, 3 Lidded Compartments, 6½ x 10 In.	575.00
Seed, Bentwood, Round, Laced Seams, Incised Cherry Branch, Anno 1899, 2 x 1½ In.	115.00
Silver Gilt, Stone, Floral Finial, Filigree, Applied Tree, Lobed Lid, Chinese, 7¼ In.	863.00
Snuff, Dog's Head, Painted, Wood, 19th Century, 2 In.	520.00
Softwood, Black Tulips, Gold Hearts, Red Ground, Pine Tree & Flower, Oval, 3 x 6⅝ In.	550.00
Softwood, Dovetailed, Dome Lid, 6½ x 12 x 8¾ In.	77.00
Softwood, Dovetailed, Green & Brown Rag Design, 7¼ x 17¾ x 9½ In.	143.00
Softwood, Dovetailed, Red Paint, 5-Sided, 5 Fabric Sewing Balls, 2¼ x 7¾ In.	880.00
Softwood, Red Rag Design, Yellow, Log House, Paper Lithograph On Hinged Lid, 2 x 6⅝ x 4½ In.	132.00
Softwood, Slide Lid, 4 Compartments, Finger Notch, 1¾ x 9 x 3⅝ In.	99.00
Stationary, Napoleon III, Mother-Of-Pearl, Brass, Silvered Inlaid, c.1870, 5 x 6½ In.	1040.00
Storage, Lid, Bentwood, Pine, 5-Finger, Iron Tacks, Oval, Lid, 5 x 12 In.	529.00
Storage, Softwood, Gesso Molding, Shell, Shield, Red & Yellow Marbleized Panels, 7⅝ x 20 x 12 In.	66.00
Strong, Iron, Steel Sides, Heavy Mounts, Handle, Lift-Out Tray, Lock, Key, Early 1900s, 11 x 15 In.	288.00

Box, Lap Desk, Federal, Mahogany, Fold-Out Writing Surface, Tambour Lid, 16 x 10 In. $1016.00

TIP

To clean a veneered box or one made of porcupine quills or matchsticks, use a vacuum cleaner hose covered with a nylon stocking.

Box, Letter, Georgian Style, Mahogany, Inlaid, Sloped Lid, 15 In. $259.00

Box, Saffron, Cover, Salmon, Strawberry & Vine, Mushroom Finial, Lehnware, 3½ In. $3850.00

Box, Travel Case,
Rosewood, Hinged Lid,
Lift-Out Tray, Compartment,
11 Glass Bottles, 7 x 12 x 9 In.
$460.00

Box, Wall, Walnut,
Dovetailed, Shaped Pierced
Crest, 8¼ x 14 x 7 In.
$990.00

Box, Wood, Beadwork,
Woman, Animals, Parrot,
Bible Scenes, Gold Feet,
c.1670, 8½ x 12 x 8½ In.
$10800.00

Strong, Poplar, Iron Handle Compartment, Lift Lid, 19th Century, 17 x 21 In.	353.00
Tantalus, Boulle Inlaid, Lacquered Cut Glass Bottles, France, Late 19th Century, 10½ In.	381.00
Tantalus, Gilt Brass, 3 Cut Glass Bottles, Continental, 20th Century, 15½ In.	304.00
Tantalus, Glass, Wood, Brass Holder, 3 Decanters, Sherry, Gin, Rye, 13 x 14 In.	351.00
Tantalus, Leather Bound Books Box, Gilt Enameled, Baccarat Decanters, 19th Century	550.00
Tantalus, Oak, 3 Decanters, England, 19th Century, 13 x 13 In.	468.00
Tantalus, Oak, Locked Case, Nickel, Rope Twist Detail, 3 Cut Glass Decanters, 16 x 7 In.	489.00
Tin, Taper, Storage, Candlesnuffer Attached, 4 In.	770.00
Tobacco, Bentwood, Leather Clad, Incised Decoration, 18th Century, 3¼ x 2¼ In.	234.00
Tobacco, Lacquer, Portrait, Russian Emperor, Black Ground, Red Interior, Russia, 4¼ In.	1528.00
Travel Case, Aucoc Aine A Paris, Toilette Set, Rosewood, Leather Interior, Mirror, 12 x 9 In.	374.00
Travel Case, Rosewood, Hinged Lid, Lift-Out Tray, Compartment, 11 Glass Bottles, 7 x 12 x 9 In. *illus*	460.00
Tulip & Star, Polychrome, Initials, WS, May 24, 1858, Slide Lid, 1¾ x 4¾ In.	440.00
Vanity, Prison, Mixed Woods, Parquetry, Ebonized, Satinwood, Late 1800s, 10 x 6 In.	531.00
Vanity, Restauration, Hand Colored, Engraved, Eglomise, Gilt Brass, Round, Troubadour, 6½ In.	570.00
Wall, Chip Carved, Green Paint, 13 x 7 x 6 In.	863.00
Wall, Drawer, Heart Cutout, Compartments, Dovetailed, Green Paint, Slant Lid, 12½ x 11½ x 8 In.	1725.00
Wall, Pine, Dovetailed Case, Drawer, Beaded Edge, Heart Cutout, Slant Lid, 12 x 15 In.	374.00
Wall, Softwood, Carved, Shield Shape, Diamond Hanger, Stylized Scrolls, 12½ x 8¼ In.	275.00
Wall, Walnut, Dovetailed, Shaped Pierced Crest, 8¼ x 14 x 7 In. *illus*	990.00
Wallpaper, Cylindrical, Yellow, Brown Flowers, 2⅞ x 2¼ In.	705.00
Wallpaper, Orange, Yellow Flowers, Blue, German Newspaper Lined, 1835, 3⅜ x 4 x 5 In.	646.00
Walnut, Dovetailed, 3 Gouged Finger Holds, Divided Interior, Chamfered Slide Lid, 3⅝ x 12 In.	165.00
Wood, Beadwork, Dutch Style, Leaves, Scrolls, Insects, Birds, Animals, Elizabethan, 12 x 8 x 9 In.	3819.00
Wood, Beadwork, Woman, Animals, Parrot, Bible Scenes, Gold Feet, c.1670, 8½ x 12 x 8½ In. *illus*	10800.00
Wood, Carved Jade, Medallion, Brass Fitted, 3 x 10 x 4 In.	47.00
Wood, Decorated, Flecked Paint, Primary Colors, Tulips, Flowers, 12½ x 8 In.	633.00
Wood, Orange Wallpaper, Oblong, 2 Bands, Blue Square, White Flowers, 2¼ x 3 x 4½ In.	353.00
Wood, Painted, Composition, Banding, Flower, Leaves, Dots, c.1940, 1½ x 3¾ In.	95.00
Wood, Painted, Swag, Stars, Flowers, Blue, Dome Lid, 5¾ x 8½ x 4¾ In. *illus*	460.00
Wood, Red Lacquered, Phoenix Bird, Chinese Export, 5½ x 12 In.	295.00
Wood Pin Construction, Painted, Tulip, Leaves, Slide Lid, 5 x 12¼ In.	248.00
Writing, Asian Hardwood, Bronze Trefoil Mounted, Chinese, 12 In.	1200.00
Writing, Mahogany, Rosewood Interior, Pen Compartments, England, 8 x 22 In.	176.00
Writing, Regency, Rosewood, Brassbound, Fitted Interior, 28 x 12 In.	411.00
Writing, Rosewood, Marquetry, Satin Birch, 4 Compartments, 19th Century, 16 x 9¾ In.	895.00
Writing, Stand, Inlaid Diamond Panels, Geometric Shapes, Fitted Interior, Slant Lid, 26 x 16 In. *illus*	575.00
Zodiaque, Line Vautrin, Gilt Bronze, Parcel Gilt, Mother-Of-Pearl, c.1950, 1¼ x 3½ In.	7200.00

BOY SCOUT collectibles include any material related to scouting, including patches, manuals, and uniforms. The Boy Scout movement in the United States started in 1910. The first Jamboree was held in 1937. Girl Scout items are listed under their own heading.

Armband, Explorer Emergency Service, 3 x 5 In.	13.00
Belt, Web, Boy Scout Buckle, Scout Logo, 26-28 In.	32.50
Bugle, Rexcraft Official, Unlacquered Brass, Gold Cord, Braid Attached, 17 In.	385.00
Buttons, Uniform, Emblem, Be Prepared, Wire Shank, 1911-33, ⅞ In.	10.00
Calendar, 1941, A Scout Is Helpful, Norman Rockwell, Full Pad, 8 x 14 In.	80.00
Camp Cookware Set, Emblem, Green Canvas Sack, Pan, Cove, Cup, Aluminum, Regal	28.50
Canteen, Royal Boy Scout, Royal, Green Canvas Sack, Emblem, Aluminum	24.00
Clock, Boy Scout Holding 2 Flags, Pendulum, 2 Weights, Keebler Of Philadelphia, 5 In.	495.00
Doll, Felt, Stamped Felt Face, Straw Torso, Original Hang Tag, c.1930	125.00
Drum, Pictures Of Scouts In Various Duties, Marked June 4, 1913, Anthony's Toy	115.00
Flashlight, 90 Degree Head, Belt Clip, Scout Logo, Bridgeport Metal Mfg., 7 x 2 In.	68.00
Happy Scout Birthday, Recruitment Card, Form, Envelope, c.1960, 4¼ x 5⅜ In.	5.00
Knife, Silver Side Plates, Scout Holding Flag, Camping Scene, 3½ In.	275.00
Marionette, Cub Scout Uniform, Wood, Box, Instruction Book, 1949, 13 In.	585.00
Paperweight, Brass Emblem, 4¼ x 3½ In.	29.00
Patch, Jamboree, Delhi, India, 1937, 2¾ x 2 In.	185.00
Patch, Jubilee Express, 1959, 2 x 2½ In.	5.50
Pin, Strengthen The Arm Of Liberty, Gold Tone, ¾ x ½ In.	28.50
Ring, American Eagle, Wings, Sterling Silver, Onyx, Scout Insignia, 1950s, Size 10	55.00
Ring, Cub Scout, Wolf Head, Sterling Silver, Size 6	28.50
Shirt, Baseball Style, Short Sleeves, Patches, Olive Green, Size 12, 1970s	180.00
Songbook, Paperback, 100 Songs, 1985 Edition	10.00
View-Master Reels, View-Master, Boy Scout Jamboree, 1955	75.00

TIP

When restoring antiques or houses, take color pictures before and after for records of colors used, exact placement of decorative details, and insurance claims.

BRADLEY & HUBBARD is a name found on many metal objects. Walter Hubbard and his brother-in-law, Nathaniel Lyman Bradley, started making cast iron clocks, tables, frames, andirons, lamps, chandeliers, sconces, and sewing birds in 1854 in Meriden, Connecticut. The company became Bradley & Hubbard Manufacturing Company in 1875. Charles Parker Company bought the firm in 1940. Their lamps are especially prized by collectors.

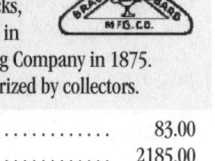

Frame, Mask Of Bacchus, Cast Iron, Mirrored, c.1900, 14 In.	83.00
Lamp, Hanging, Ox Blood, Opalescent Cranberry Hobnail Shade, 19 x 36 In.	2185.00
Lamp, Oil, Brass, Marked, The B & H, 1894, 16¼ In.	139.00
Lamp, Oil, Pear Shape, Copper Base, Scrolled Feet, Fleur-De-Lis, 25 In.	250.00
Lamp, Openwork Vine & Berries, Spelter, Caramel Slag Shade, Paneled, 22 In. ....*illus*	1980.00
Lamp, Student, Double, Electrified	2300.00
Letter Holder, Cherubs, Signed, 7 x 9½ In.	250.00
Mirror, Dresser, Beveled Mirror, Gilt Design, Cast Iron, Marked, 15 x 12 In.	145.00
Stationary Holder, Gilt Bronze, 2 Tiers, Footed, Figural Dragons, 11 x 8 In.	465.00

BRASS has been used for decorative pieces and useful tablewares since ancient times. It is an alloy of copper, zinc, and other metals. Additional brass items may be found under Bell, Candlestick, Tool, or Trivet.

Bed Warmer, Goat, Flowers, Turned Wood Handle, 43½ In.	460.00
Bed Warmer, Grain Painted Handle, Hinged Lid, Chase Decoration, 10 x 40 In.	345.00
Bed Warmer, Maple Handle, 19th Century, 41 x 10 In.	117.00
Bed Warmer, Pierced, Engraved Lid, Turned Wood Handle, 43½ In.	230.00
Bed Warmer, Tooled Decoration, Turned Walnut Handle, 45 In.	303.00
Bed Warmer, Tooled Design, Punched Holes, Wrought Iron Handle, 44 In.	460.00
Bottle Jack, Iron Hanger, Round, John Linwood, Warrantee, England, 19th Century, 17 In.	431.00
Bottle Pin, Precursor To The Corkscrew, Tapered, Open Handle Top, 1600s	650.00
Bowl, Cover, Cone Shape, Ball Finial, Albert Reimann, c.1920, 5½ In.	205.00
Bucket, Apple Butter, Wrought Iron Swing Handle, 10½ x 16 In.	1020.00
Bucket, Georgian Style, Mahogany, Spiral Rib, Swing Handle, Brass Collar, 17 In., Pair	4230.00
Candlesnuffer, Cone Shape, Ball Finial, 2½ In.	22.00
Candlesnuffer, Scissors, 4¾ In.	22.00
Castor, Pepper, c.1780s, 4 In.	345.00
Cigar Cutter, Bear, Climbing Rocks, Nickel Cutter, Striker Ribs, Lever, 5¼ In.	110.00
Cigar Cutter, Monkey On To Hat, Figural, 4½ In.	220.00
Cigar Cutter, Woman, Hands Up, Cigar Cutter In Center Of Body, Presses Legs Together, 2 In.	220.00
Cigar Cutter, Woman On Chamber Pot, Figural, 1¼ In.	330.00
Coffeepot, Wood Handle, France, c.1730	895.00
Dog Collar, Inscribed, England, 18th Century	595.00
Doorknocker, Hand Knocking, Scalloped Backplate, 6¼ x 2¾ In. ....*illus*	85.00
Easel, Desk Top, 20th Century, 19 x 8 In.	117.00
Ewer, Renaissance Style, Patinated, Bas-Relief Cupids, Ivy, Mounted As Lamp, 21 x 8 In.	147.00
Figure, Lion, Lying Down, On Base, Applied Dark Brown Patina, Hollow, 10 x 20 In., Pair	345.00
Gong, Held Between 2 Ivory Tusks, Oak Base, 18¾ x 17 In.	230.00
Hand Warmer, Cover, Objects, Chinese, 4¾ x 5½ In.	384.00
Humidor, Relief Decoration, Panels, Exotic Figures, Caldwell, 12 x 7¾ In.	3910.00
Magnifier, On Stand, George V, Swing, Georgian Style, Reversing Lens, Early 1900s, 13 In.	360.00
Mailbox, Steel, Black, Polished, Hinged Lid, U.S. Mail, Cutler Mail Chute Co., 37 x 22 In.	633.00
Medallion, 4 Clasped Hands, True To The End, Engraved, 1775	395.00
Model, Cannon, Field, Cast, Adjustable Carriage, .22 Caliber Cartridge, Disarmed, 11 In.	472.00
Model, Cannon, Touch Hole, Cast Iron Carriage, 12½ x 32 x 12 In.	690.00
Mug, England, c.1740-60	450.00
Paperweight, Man's Face, Switzerland, 3¼ x 2¼ In.	28.00
Pipe Tamper, Holland, 1670	325.00
Pitcher, Dovetailed, Added Rim At Base, Continental, 19th Century, 7 In.	69.00
Plaque, George Washington, Holding Rolled Map, Hand On Sword, Embossed, c.1820, 7 In.	738.00
Plate, Alms, Hammered, Repousse Tulip Center, Text, Tooled Border, Germany, 17 In. Diam.	546.00
Ruler, Engraved, 18th Century	350.00
Samovar, Square-Footed Base, Small Teapot, 19th Century, 2 x 13 x 16 In.	117.00
Sconce, Circular, Wall Mount, Scrolled Arms, Bobeche, Tulip Shaped Cups, 6 x 12 In.	717.00
Sconce, Wall, Tulip Tops, Jarvie, 13 x 6 In., Pair	3000.00
Serving Dish, Hors D'Oeuvres, Crab Shape, 13¼ x 11¾ In.	61.00
Spoon, Seal, c.1570	395.00
Spoon, Serving, Wrought Iron, Flattened, Pierced End, Shaped Brass Bowl, 11 In.	28.00
Tieback, Victorian, Flaming Torch Backplate, Bellflowers, Ribbons, 5 x 3½ In., 8 Piece	382.00
Tieback Set, Classical Style, High Relief Rosette, c.1825, 4 In., 4 Piece	720.00

Box, Wood, Painted, Swag, Stars, Flowers, Blue, Dome Lid, 5¾ x 8½ x 4¾ In. $460.00

Box, Writing, Stand, Inlaid Diamond Panels, Geometric Shapes, Fitted Interior, Slant Lid, 26 x 16 In. $575.00

Bradley & Hubbard, Lamp, Openwork Vine & Berries, Spelter, Caramel Slag Shade, Paneled, 22 In. $1980.00

TIP

To clean intricate brass hardware, try this: Remove the hardware from the furniture. Soak it in a solution of equal parts lemon juice and water for about a half hour. Brush with an old toothbrush. Rinse and wipe dry. Rub paste wax on the brass.

Brass, Doorknocker, Hand Knocking, Scalloped Backplate, 6¼ x 2¾ In. $85.00

TIP

If your piece of old brass is covered with a protective coat of lacquer, it should not be cleaned. Test a darkened area with a dab of brass polish. If it stays dark, it has been lacquered and cannot be cleaned until the lacquer is removed from the entire piece.

Tinder Lighter, Flintlock, Iron, Wood, Early 18th Century, 6½ x 3½ In. 2880.00
Urn, Mantel, Indian, Ornate Handles, c.1900, 14 x 7 In., Pair 176.00
Vase, Bulbous, Tapered, Wide Mouth, Geometric Design, WMF, Germany, c.1930, 6 In. 206.00

BRASTOFF, *see Sascha Brastoff category.*

BREAD PLATE, *see Pressed Glass patterns.*

BRIDE'S BASKETS OR BRIDE'S BOWLS were usually one-of-a-kind novelties made in American and European glass factories. They were especially popular about 1880 when the decorated basket was often given as a wedding gift. Cut glass baskets were popular after 1890. All bride's baskets lost favor about 1905. Bride's baskets and bride's bowls may also be found in other glass sections. Check the index at the back of the book.

BRIDE'S BASKET
Blue, Mother-Of-Pearl, Diamond-Quilted, 13 In. 1250.00
Blue, Multicolored Enamel, Cherub Silver Plated Frame, 15 In. 588.00
Blue Satin, Ruffled Rim, Raised Dots, Brown Enamel, 14 In. 411.00
Blue Satin, Yellow Coralene, Silver Plated Frame, Middletown, 12 In. ....*illus* 470.00
Chartreuse, Gold Vines, Allover Silver Mica, Pinched Sides, Ruffled Edge, 9½ In. 575.00
Cranberry Glass, Cherub, Birds, Gilt Stand, 6½ x 2 In. 99.00
Cranberry Glass, Opalescent Swirl, Silver Plated Frame, c.1870, 11½ In. 695.00
Cranberry Glass, Thumbprint, Enameled, Berries, Leaves, 9 In. 1500.00
Cranberry Glass, White, Amber Rigaree Edge, 2½ x 8¼ In. 225.00
Cranberry To White Bowl, Silver Plated Figural Meriden Frame, Ruffled Edge 980.00
Custard Glass, Enameled, Filigree Handle, Cherub Shooting Bow, 7 In. 850.00
Cut Glass, Stepped Bands, Tiffany & Co. Frame, c.1907, 11 In. 3120.00
Green, Flared, Ruffled Edge, Molded Handle, 9 x 6 In. 65.00
Opaque Pink, White, Flared, Crimped Edge, 1880s 65.00
Pink, Enameled, Flowers, Leaves, 8½ x 4¼ In. 895.00
Pink, Mother-Of-Pearl, Diamond-Quilted, Leaves, Silver Plated Frame, 12 In. 588.00
Pink, Ruffled Edge, Silver Plated, Cherub Support Frame, 8½ In. 650.00
Pink Opalescent, Enameled Flowers, Tufts Frame, 4 Paw Feet, c.1900, 10½ In. ....*illus* 206.00
Silver, Pierced Trumpet Foot, Pierced, Engraved, c.1910, 23 In. 4560.00
Silver, Vase Form, Acanthus Leaves, Bellflower Swags, Gorham, 1917, 19 In. 4200.00
Striped Pink Satin, Cased, Ruffled Edge, Silver Plated Frame, 4-Footed Branches, Wilcox, 10¾ In. 220.00

BRIDE'S BOWL
Apricot Cased, Cream Exterior, Shell Shape, Applied Clear Edge, 10½ In. 230.00
Blue, Satin, Birds On Gold Stems, 9¼ In. 235.00
Opal, Satin, Shell Shape, Red Flowers, White Scrolling, 10½ In. 201.00
Rose, Cased White, Ruffled Edge, Crimped, Kanawa, 1970s, 10 x 4 In. 95.00

BRISTOL glass was made in Bristol, England, after the 1700s. The Bristol glass most often seen today is a Victorian, lightweight opaque glass that is often blue. Some of the glass was decorated with enamels.

Barber Bottle, Opal, Enameled, Gold Trim, c.1900, 7 In. 58.00
Bottle, Scent, Opal, Enameled, Flowers, 8 In., Pair 195.00
Bottle, Scent, Stopper, Black, Enameled Flowers, Gold Leaves, c.1800, 8½ x 3 In. 40.00
Cup, Opal, Flower & Leaf Decoration, Flared Rim, Base, Applied Handle, 3 In. 33.00
Decanter, Stopper, Opal, Frosted, Flowers, Pontil, 11½ In. 30.00
Decanter, Stopper, Opal, Pedestal Base, Gold Trim, 9⅞ In. 89.00
Mug, Remember Me, Applied Handle, Gold Grape, Leaf Surround, Pontil, c.1880, 3¼ In. 75.00
Tray, Calling Card, Opal, Enameled, Victorian, c.1890, 5 x 6 In. 95.00
Tureen, Sauce, Cover, Opal, Floral Border, c.1775, 7¾ In. 1767.00
Vase, Blue, Enameled, White Flowers, c.1900, 7 In. 35.00
Vase, Cream, Orange Enameled, Ruffled Rim, Leaves, Flowers, Victorian, 5¾ In. 25.00
Vase, Green & Red Flowers, White, England, 12½ In. 29.00
Vase, Opal, Bird, Nest With Eggs, Vines, Leaves, Flowers, 12 x 7½ In. 175.00
Vase, Opal, Cased Pink Interior, Ruffled Edge, Flowers, Butterfly, 5¼ In. 35.00
Vase, Opal, Enameled Flowers, Leaves, Butterflies, Lavender, 10 x 5 In. 45.00
Vase, Opal, Twisted Stem, Victorian, 10 x 3 In. 40.00
Vase, Pink, Blue & White Flowers, Urn Shape, Stylized Tulip Neck, Footed, 15 In., Pair 201.00
Vase, Serpents, Fluted Top, Pedestal Base, 12 In., Pair 210.00

BRITANNIA, *see Pewter category.*

BRONZE is an alloy of copper, tin, and other metals. It is used to make figurines, lamps, and other decorative objects. Bronze lamps are listed in the Lamp category. Pieces listed here date from the eighteenth, nineteenth, and twentieth centuries.

Ashtray, Bach, Oscar, Blue Iridescent Glass, Seahorse Holders, Dolphin, c.1922, 41 x 7 In.	558.00
Ashtray, Bonzo, 3¾ In.	29.00
Ashtray, Gilt, Main Dans Les Flots, Line Vautrin, Enameled, c.1950, 4¾ In.	9600.00
Bill Clip, Frog, On Lily Pad, Figural, 5½ x 2½ x 1½ In.	90.00
Bottle, Enameled, Coconut, Fleur-De-Lis Filigree, France, 18th Century, 8½ In.	588.00
Bowl, Footed, Shell Shape, Sea Serpent Handle, 13½ In.	191.00
Bowl, Hurley, E.T., Web & Spider, Sculpted, Original Patina, Signed, 5½ In. Diam.	1250.00
Box, Glove, Blue Satin Tufted Lining, Country Town Scene, 1800s, 10 x 3½ In.	450.00
Box, Rectangular, Hinged Cover, Phoenix, 4 Wheeled Feet, India, 19th Century, 7½ In.	118.00
Box, Seahorse Design, Sculpted, Lid, Original Patina, Signed, Hurley, E.T., 4¾ In.	990.00
Bust, Asian Woman, 5 x 3½ In.	146.00
Bust, Bauer, Theodore, Crazy Horse, New York, Patina, 14 x 8 In.	5280.00
Bust, Carpeaux, J.B., Le Rieur Napolitain, 4 x 2½ x 2½ In.	405.00
Bust, Carrier-Belleuse, Albert Ernest, Young Virgil, Marble Socle, Mid 1800s, 20 In.	2478.00
Bust, Lussman, Anton, Pierrot, Black Patina, Germany, c.1920, 10¼ In.	420.00
Bust, Mich, Jean, Girl With Hair Bow, Brown Patina, Signed, 14¼ In.	1528.00
Bust, Weisse, Henry, Woman In Turkish Costume, Signed, Germany, 1800s, 27 In.	4130.00
Cannon, Oak Carriage, 19th Century, 31 In.	5378.00
Cannon, Oak Carriage, 19th Century, 34 In.	5975.00
Cannon, Signal, Pearce, J., Carved Oak Carriage, Stamped, 1800s, 6 x 8⅛ x 16½ In.	1410.00
Cauldron, Hoofed Feet, Iron Bail Handle	495.00
Censer, Foo Dog Final, Handles, Chinese, 15½ In.	826.00
Censer, Ribbed, Loose Loop Form Handles, Japan, 7½ In.	944.00
Censer, Riverscape, Dragon Form Handles, Japan, 11 In.	325.00
Censer, Silver Inlaid, Handles, Japan, 9½ x 11½ In.	472.00
Censer, Tripod, Foo Dog Finial, Chinese, 13 x 8 In.	3521.00
Censer, Tripod, Shaped Cartouches, Arabic Calligraphy, Chinese, 1700s, 3 x 5 In.	2950.00
Censer, Tripod, Xuande Mark, Chinese, 5½ x 6 In.	472.00
Censer, Warrior, Dragon Form Finial, Chinese, 7 In.	767.00
Charger, Nude Center, Mythological Battle Of Amazons, Nudes, Mask & Serpent Rim, Patina, 27 In.	1380.00
Compote, Charles X Style, Cut Crystal Bowl, Beaded Rim, Stepped Base, 8½ x 13 In.	1725.00
Dish, Beach, Chester, Figural, Wood Elf, Seated By Rock Dish, 5 x 4 In.	1610.00
Dish, Reclining Nude, Full Moon, Owl, Art Deco, Handles, c.1930, 7 x 10 In.	495.00
Doorknocker, Figural, Male & Female Nudes Clinging To Slings, 1900, 19 x 12 In.	940.00
Ewer, Dragon Spout, Finial, Japan, 1868-1911, 23 In.	1116.00
Ewer, Ho Shape, Animal Form Spout, Handle, Finial, Japan, 19th Century, 12 In.	764.00
Frame, Eraud, Malachite, Easel Back, Hand Painted Picture, Lady, Signed, 7⅜ x 5⅝ In.	761.00
Garniture, Gilt, Ormolu, Opaline Glass, Lily Sprays, Victorian, 1800s, 34½ x 14 In., Pair	705.00
Garniture, Mantel, Green Onyx, Black Slate, Portico Shape, Clock, 18¾ In., 3 Piece	2540.00
Garniture Set, Louis XV, Clock, Porcelain, Turtle Doves, Scrolls, Swags, c.1860, 11½ In.	443.00
Garniture Set, Patinated, Gilt, Clock, 3-Light Candelabrum, France, Late 1800s, 19½ In.	1143.00
Girandole, 4 Arms, Bronze, Crystal, Spire Finials, France, 26½ x 11 In., Pair	1997.00
Gong, Bell Shape, Teakwood, Chinese, c.1930, 17 x 11 In.	59.00
Hand Mirror, Erte, Indo-China, Signed R.K. Parker, 1988, 7 x 11½ In.	854.00
Hibachi, Figural, Elephant Head Handles, Japan, 8 x 8½ In.	649.00
Humidor, Lift Cover, Chest Form, Stylized Flower, Strapwork, 3½ x 11 x 6½ In.	191.00
Incense Burner, 4 Characters, Cast Square, Chinese, 18th Century, 5¼ In.	3819.00
Incense Burner, Wood Base, Chinese, 4½ x 5½ In.	68.00
Jar, Wine, Geometric, Mask Handles, Chinese, 7¾ In.	1410.00
Jardiniere, Birds, Lotus Branches, Oriental, Early 1900s, 11 In.	200.00
Jardiniere, Gilt, Pierced, Scrolling Body, Lion's Head Masque, Paw Feet, Tin Line, 14 x 6 In.	177.00
Jardiniere, High Relief, Horned Dragons, Chasing Each Other, Engraved, 12 x 17 In.	1140.00
Jardiniere, Urn Shape, Incised Rim Pattern, Flying Dragon, High Relief, 37 x 25 In.	1058.00
Jewelry Box, Hinged Lid, 2 Girls Carrying Casket, Multicolored Stones, 7¼ x 7½ x 4 In.	1116.00
Mask, Lion's Head, Gilt, Appliques, Sand Cast, Hollow, Continental, 16 x 9 In., Pair	2703.00
Match Holder, Ashtray, Embossed Cherubs, 4¼ x 5½ In.	11.00
Mirror, Characters, Central Boss, Chinese, 5½ In.	264.00
Mirror, Stand, Animal Rest, Chinese, 5½ In.	1528.00
Pen Wiper, Figural, Hissing Cat, Arched Back, Badger Bristles, Vienna, 4½ In.	1440.00
Penholder, Camel, Chinese, 4 x 5 In.	1652.00
Planter, 2 Sections, Round Top, Handles, 3 Figural Legs, 1-Legged Fauns, Claw Feet, 35 x 16 In. *illus*	2185.00
Planter, Patinated, Basket Weave Neck, Floral Swags, Lion's Head Handles, 25 In., Pair	1058.00

Bride's Basket, Blue Satin, Yellow Coralene, Silver Plated Frame, Middletown, 12 In.
$470.00

Bride's Basket, Pink Opalescent, Enameled Flowers, Tufts Frame, 4 Paw Feet, c.1900, 10½ In.
$206.00

Bronze, Planter, 2 Sections, Round Top, Handles, 3 Figural Legs, 1-Legged Fauns, Claw Feet, 35 x 16 In.
$2185.00

Bronze, Sculpture, Bonheur, Rosa, Un Mouton Broutant, 6½ x 9¼ In. $1912.00

Bronze, Sculpture, Gallo, I., Woman With Greyhound, Patina, Signed, 25 x 17 x 8½ In. $1058.00

Bronze, Sculpture, Hagenauer, Christ, Austria, 6¾ In. $470.00

Planter, W.H. Jackson Co. Founders, New York, c.1920, 4¾ x 5 In.	936.00
Plaque, Cupid, Raised Relief, France, 9 In.	94.00
Plaque, Proctor, Pony Express Rider, Horse Galloping, Round, 16⅝ In.	6463.00
Plaque, Wyon, Edward William, Children At Play, Mounted On Marble, Mid 1800s, 7 In.	460.00
Sculpture, 2 Mountain Goats, 11½ x 8¾ x 5 In.	764.00
Sculpture, 2 Neoclassical Style Female Figures, 20th Century, 22 In.	244.00
Sculpture, 2 Tigers Attack Elephant, Japan, 1868-1911, 16 In.	1175.00
Sculpture, 3 Dogs Huddled Over Outcrop, 8⅝ x 15 x 7 In.	1528.00
Sculpture, African Antelope, Standing Alert, Grazing, 1½ & 2⅜ In., Pair	235.00
Sculpture, Amazon Warrior Holding Spear, Wearing Beads, 9 In.	443.00
Sculpture, Anfrie, Charles, Pastorale, Young Girl, Classical Attire, Late 1800s, 19 In.	1282.00
Sculpture, Angel, Upholding Cylinders, Olive Brown Patina, Red Marble Socle, Italy, 9⅝ In.	600.00
Sculpture, Animal, Benin, Nigeria, 24 In.	468.00
Sculpture, Antelope, Verdigris Patinated, Reclining, 41½ x 57 In.	2040.00
Sculpture, Apollo, Seated In Toga, Laurel Wreath, Holding Scroll, 17½ In.	2938.00
Sculpture, Arts Decoratif, Ivory, Spanish Dancers, Brown & Black Marble Base, 15 x 19 In.	1645.00
Sculpture, Atalanta, After Pierre Le Faguays, Early 20th Century, 11 In.	665.00
Sculpture, Aube, Jean Paul, Reclining Man, Cherub, Brown Patina, Signed, 19⅝ In.	3900.00
Sculpture, Bach, Bruno, Woman Of The Night, Marble Base, Signed, 12 In.	4465.00
Sculpture, Barye, A.L., Lion, Brown, Black, Green Patina, Signed, 7½ In.	3055.00
Sculpture, Barye, A.L., Stag, Standing, Patina, Marble Plinth, Signed, 6 x 6½ In.	1763.00
Sculpture, Barye, Antoine Louis, Lioness, Standing, Dark Patina, 8 x 11 In.	6613.00
Sculpture, Batiste, Paul Jean, The Kiss, 21½ In.	6463.00
Sculpture, Bear Climbing Tree, Verdigris Patina, Continental, 20th Century, 49 In.	920.00
Sculpture, Bearded Man On Toboggan, Boy, Black Slate Base, Russia, 20th Century, 5⅝ x 4 In.	588.00
Sculpture, Belskie, Abraham, Mercury, Kneeling, Holding Globe, Signed, 3¼ In.	4700.00
Sculpture, Benin, Leopard, African Tribal, 22 x 15 In.	214.00
Sculpture, Bergman, Arab, Cold Painted, Signed, Austria, 5½ x 5 In.	1705.00
Sculpture, Bergman, Nymph, Gilt, c.1910, 5 In.	614.00
Sculpture, Bermann, Frog Band, Cold Painted, Stamped, Vienna, 1950s, 7 In., 4 Piece	3500.00
Sculpture, Blondat, Max, Gilt, First Kiss, Boy, Girl Preparing To Kiss, Signed, 24¼ In.	5640.00
Sculpture, Bodhisattva, Gilt, Tibet, Wood Base, 4 In.	590.00
Sculpture, Boisseau, E., Troubadour, Playing Lute, Societe Des Bronzes De Paris, Cast, Patina, 31 In.	1093.00
Sculpture, Bonheur, Horse, Jockey, Green Marble Base, 8 x 7 In.	472.00
Sculpture, Bonheur, Rosa, Un Mouton Broutant, 6½ x 9¼ In. ....*illus*	1912.00
Sculpture, Boy, Reading Book, Carrying Bundle Of Sticks, Early 20th Century, 11½ In.	403.00
Sculpture, Buddha, Arakan Style, Burmese, 18th Century, 27½ In.	7670.00
Sculpture, Buddha, Burmese, Gilt, Standing, Stepped Lotus Base, 19th Century, 18¼ In.	1003.00
Sculpture, Buddha, Crowned, Pala Mandrola, Inscription, India, 12th Century, 5 In.	767.00
Sculpture, Buddha, Gilt, Thai, Bangkok Period, 19th Century, 24 In.	649.00
Sculpture, Buddha, On Lotus Throne, Embracing Consort, Bowl, Nepal, Early 1900s, 6 x 4 In.	58.00
Sculpture, Buddha, Seated, Cross-Legged, Blue Paint, Cast, 8½ In.	4312.00
Sculpture, Buddha, Seated, Signed, Japan, 19th Century, 12 x 9 In.	410.00
Sculpture, Buddha, Seated On Lotus Throne, Korea, 18th Century, 4¾ In.	3173.00
Sculpture, Buddha, Standing, Early 20th Century, 41 In.	1521.00
Sculpture, Burro, Alert, Bridled, Patinated Bronze, Cano, 19th Century, 5½ In.	720.00
Sculpture, Bust, Aeneas, Gilt, Patinated, 19¼ In.	5700.00
Sculpture, Bust, Woman With Headscarf, Flower Bodice, Green Marble Socle, 21½ In.	3290.00
Sculpture, Calandrelli, Woman Surprised At The Bath, Rosso Antico Marble Base, 15 In.	673.00
Sculpture, Campajola, Tom, Enrico Caruso, Angel Playing Harp, Dark Brown, Signed, 1921, 10½ x 13½ In.	1135.00
Sculpture, Canova, A., Venus, Holding Fruit, Cast, Brown Patina, 20th Century, 45½ In.	977.00
Sculpture, Car, Benz, 2-Wheel Daimler, 2 Men, 1885, 27 x 19 In.	8210.00
Sculpture, Carrier, Anna, Woman, Children, Signed, 22 In.	3300.00
Sculpture, Cat, Hissing Tabby, Vienna Bronze, Cold Enameled, Wire Whiskers, 5 In.	840.00
Sculpture, Cat, Tabby, Little Red Riding Hood, Cold Enameled, Vienna, 1800s, 2½ In.	780.00
Sculpture, Cat & Mouse In Old Shoe, Austria, 1¼ x 3¼ In.	633.00
Sculpture, Chinese, Gilt, Court Officials, Holding Ruyi, Sword, Early 1900s, 6 In., Pair	460.00
Sculpture, Chipaurs, D.H., Dancer, Pebbled Studded Body Suit, Leg Up, Head Turned, 21¾ In.	920.00
Sculpture, Clesinger, Jean Baptiste, Bust, Christ, Thorn Crown, Patinated, France, 1867, 25 In.	1175.00
Sculpture, Cockatiel, White & Gray, On Perch, Vienna, Cold Enameled, Late 1800s, 4 x 3 In.	540.00
Sculpture, Coming Through The Rye, Green Marble Base, After Remington, 32 x 20 x 27 In.	878.00
Sculpture, Dancing Faun Of Pompeii, Patinated, Oval Marble Base, Italy, 15 In.	600.00
Sculpture, Deer, Patinated, Italy, Early 20th Century, 8½ In., Pair	328.00
Sculpture, Deity, Lord Of The Dance, India, 19th Century, 16 In.	499.00
Sculpture, Deity, Natarat, Hindu, Multiarmed, 20th Century, 41 x 28 In.	1170.00
Sculpture, Dog, Afghan Hound Standing, Rectangular Base, 9¾ x 3¾ In.	940.00

Sculpture, Dog, Mastiff, Male, Chocolate Patinated, Early 20th Century, 6 In.	150.00
Sculpture, Dog Watching Rabbit Under Leaf, Oval Base, 7¾ x 12⅝ x 5¼ In.	1528.00
Sculpture, Dogs, 2 Hunting Dogs Watching Quail In Brush, 8¾ x 16⅜ x 7⅝ In.	2350.00
Sculpture, Dolphins, Leaping Through Wave, Alabastrite, 12½ x 5¾ x 11 In.	29.00
Sculpture, Dragon Holding Pearl, Stamped, 12 In.	266.00
Sculpture, Drouot, Edouard, Woman, Joueuse De Pipeaux, Mounted As Lamp, 22 In.	585.00
Sculpture, Dubois, P., Troubadour, Boy, Standing, Playing Lute, Brown Patina, 1865, 45 In.	1150.00
Sculpture, Eagle, Marble Base, 3¼ x 5½ In.	660.00
Sculpture, Eagle Head, Patinated, Polished Beak, Eyes, Black Marble Base, 13 x 7 In., Pair	116.00
Sculpture, Elephant, Black Marble Base, 3 Elephant Heads, Tusks, Trunks, Patina, 12½ In.	230.00
Sculpture, Elephant, Kneeling, Trunk Curled Around Vessel, Thai, Early 1800s, 9 x 15 In.	920.00
Sculpture, Elephant, Standing On One Leg, Trunk Pointed Up, Mahogany Base, 19 In.	9600.00
Sculpture, Equestrienne, Patinated, Prancing Horse, 48 x 47 In.	2160.00
Sculpture, Erte, Evening In 1922, Standing Woman, Stylized, c.1980, 17 In.	2183.00
Sculpture, Falconet, Nude, Bather, Cast, Brown Patina, Marked, 1757, 22¾ In.	690.00
Sculpture, Fayral, Nude, Flowers, Bird In Hands, Marble Base, Signed, 12 In.	310.00
Sculpture, Female Figure, Neoclassical, Continental, 20th Century, 27 In.	1220.00
Sculpture, Figure Holding Deer, Court Costume, Gilt, 1368-1644, 6 In.	588.00
Sculpture, Foo Dogs, Seated, Rectangular Plinth, Chinese, 8 x 5½ In., Pair	236.00
Sculpture, Fox, On Prowl, Cast, Marble Base, 7½ In.	115.00
Sculpture, French, Daniel Chester, John Harvard, 7½ x 3¾ x 6 In.	1076.00
Sculpture, Frishmuth, Harriet Whitney, The Leaf, Nude Woman, Standing, 27 In.	5750.00
Sculpture, Frishmuth, Harriet Whitney, Vine, Gorham Co. Founders, c.1921, 12½ In.	16500.00
Sculpture, Gallo, I., Woman With Greyhound, Patina, Signed, 25 x 17 x 8½ In. *illus*	1058.00
Sculpture, Gardet, George, Lions, c.1900, 19 x 14½ In.	2938.00
Sculpture, Girl On Chair, 12 In.	176.00
Sculpture, Greek Dancer, Brown Patina, 13 In.	236.00
Sculpture, Group, Winged Man Holding Female, Black Marble Base, 12¾ In.	236.00
Sculpture, Guanyin Seated Holding Septum, Wearing Crown, Chinese, 15 In.	8850.00
Sculpture, Guy, E., Crouching Lion, Gilt, Slate Base, Early 20th Century, 7½ x 29½ In.	1265.00
Sculpture, Hagenauer, Christ, Austria, 6¾ In. *illus*	470.00
Sculpture, Hagenauer, Greyhound, Austria, 8½ x 10¼ In.	1998.00
Sculpture, Haines, Peter, Abstract, Animal, Patina, 5¾ In.	1035.00
Sculpture, Haines, Peter, Abstract, Patina, Black Marble Base, 8½ In.	863.00
Sculpture, Haines, Peter, Neolithic Animal, Patina, 5⅝ In.	518.00
Sculpture, Hand, Gilt, Sino-Tibet, 17th Century, 7½ In.	1416.00
Sculpture, Hoffman, Malvina, Egyptian Dancer, Nyota Inokaa, Parcel Gilt, 11 x 12½ In. *illus*	10158.00
Sculpture, Horse, Running, Wood Base, Oriental, 4½ x 6 In.	81.00
Sculpture, Horse, Standing On Back Legs, Alabaster Base, 21½ In., Pair	373.00
Sculpture, Horses, Rearing, Veined Marble Plinth, Pair, 12½ In.	6000.00
Sculpture, Iffland, Franz, Cupid, Marble Base, 12¼ In.	510.00
Sculpture, Innocence, Chryselephantine, Ivory, Gold Yellow Patinated, c.1920, 14¾ In.	11800.00
Sculpture, Jennewein, Carl Paul, Greek Dance, Cold Painted, Early 1900s, 20½ In.	13307.00
Sculpture, Joan Of Arc, Marble Base, France, 21 In.	646.00
Sculpture, Jules, Pierre, 2 Whippets With Ball, 6 x 8½ x 4¾ In. *illus*	3585.00
Sculpture, Kauba, Carl, Lariat Chase, Indian Chief, Lariat Overhead, Horse, 11 x 10 In.	2588.00
Sculpture, Kauba, Carl, Mounted Indian Chief, Early 1900s, 26 x 17 In.	1495.00
Sculpture, Kauba, Carl, Warrior On Horseback, Signed, 27 In.	16500.00
Sculpture, Laurent, Eugene, Psyche, 1800s, 9½ In.	614.00
Sculpture, Lion, 2-Part Tail, Bronze Base, 9 In.	288.00
Sculpture, Lion, Lying Down, Gilt, Chased, Oak-Footed Stand, 7 x 16 In.	587.00
Sculpture, Lion, Paw On Gilt Sphere, Patinated, Oval Mahogany Stand, 7 x 10½ In.	998.00
Sculpture, Lion, Roaring, Cast, Bronze Base, 9½ In.	115.00
Sculpture, Lion, Roaring, Dark Brown, Applied Patina, Red Marble Base, 8 In.	288.00
Sculpture, Lion, Standing, Platform Base, 19th Century, 9 x 16 x 4½ In.	489.00
Sculpture, Lorenzi, Josef, 2 Women Dancing, Patina, Signed, 14¾ In.	4935.00
Sculpture, Ludwig, W., Bust, Lady Of The Wind, Gilt, Patinated, 29 In.	1645.00
Sculpture, Male, Bearded, With Staff, Female Fertility Figure, Africa, 19th Century, 14 In.	895.00
Sculpture, Male, Marble Base, 20th Century, 7½ x 12 In., Pair	840.00
Sculpture, Male Figure, Neoclassical, Sword, Plough, After A. Caudez, 28 In.	585.00
Sculpture, Man, Palms Facing Out, Benin Style, 14½ In.	236.00
Sculpture, Marly Horse, Rearing, Groom, Brown Patination, Pair, 15¾ In.	244.00
Sculpture, Masseau, P., Gilt, Le Secret, c.1894, 11 In.	6000.00
Sculpture, Mercie, Marius-Jean-Antonin, Waterloo, c.1907, 34 x 17½ x 13 In.	8963.00
Sculpture, Mercury, Standing, Black Marble Base, 19 In.	585.00
Sculpture, Meunier, Constantine, Dock Worker, Belgium, 1831-1905, 15½ In.	1250.00

Bronze, Sculpture, Hoffman, Malvina, Egyptian Dancer, Nyota Inokaa, Parcel Gilt, 11 x 12½ In. $10158.00

Bronze, Sculpture, Jules, Pierre, 2 Whippets With Ball, 6 x 8½ x 4¾ In. $3585.00

Bronze, Sculpture, Picault, E., Le Penseur, Man, Draped, Holding Scroll, Eagle, 27 x 14 In. $2032.00

Bronze, Teapot, Embossed Dragon In Waves, Mt. Fuji, Dragon Handle, Meiji Period, Japan, 8 In. $118.00

TIP

Outdoor bronze sculptures need special care. Wash with soap, water, and a little ammonia to remove oil and dirt. Then rinse, dry, and rub with a cloth dipped in olive oil or boiled linseed oil. Rub with a dry cloth to remove extra oil. Outdoor bronzes should be oiled several times a year.

Brownies, Figurine, Brownie Sitting, Knees Up, Palmer Cox, Porcelain, Painted Features, 4 In. $460.00

Sculpture, Middle Eastern Man, On Horseback, With Rifle, 7 x 6 In.	345.00
Sculpture, Middle Eastern Merchant Holding Drapery, Nude Woman, 4½ x 5⅜ In.	2468.00
Sculpture, Moigniez, Jules, Eagle, Perched On Branch, 31½ In.	1163.00
Sculpture, Monk, Gilt, Sino-Tibet, 14 In.	561.00
Sculpture, Monk Holding Mouse, Gilt, Chinese, 6¾ In.	649.00
Sculpture, Nannin, R., Victorian Woman Wearing Gown, Gilt, Marble Plinth, France, 13¼ In.	4025.00
Sculpture, Napoleon III, Maternity, Mother & Child, Patinated, 1800s, 10 x 10¼ In.	1997.00
Sculpture, Neandross, Sigurd, Cougar, Standing, Brown Patina, 1894, 5 x 11 In.	575.00
Sculpture, Neptune, After Giovanni Bologna, Dark Patina, Marble Socle, 22 x 7½ In.	1528.00
Sculpture, Nude Woman, Hand Rests On Natural Stump, Square Base, 19¼ In.	1035.00
Sculpture, Nude Woman, Seated, Folded Legs, France, 10 In.	395.00
Sculpture, Omerth, Georges, Harlequin, Carved Ivory, 8¾ In.	1413.00
Sculpture, Omerth, Georges, Moissonneuse, Carved Ivory, 7¾ In.	1522.00
Sculpture, Pecheuse Bretonne, Signed Base, After Gustabe Obiols, 26½ In.	732.00
Sculpture, Picault, E., Le Penseur, Man, Draped, Holding Scroll, Eagle, 27 x 14 In. ....*illus*	2032.00
Sculpture, Picault, E.L., Woman, Spread Winged Eagle, 1833-1915, 37½ In.	8050.00
Sculpture, Poertzel, Otto, Aristocrats, Woman, 2 Dogs, Ivory Face, Hands, 19 In.	21600.00
Sculpture, Poncin, Albert, Panther, Brown Black Finish, Signed, c.1925, 8 x 18 In.	1880.00
Sculpture, Powell, Ace, Moccasin Maker, 1970s, 5½ x 5½ In.	345.00
Sculpture, Rabbit, Sitting, 16 In., Pair	410.00
Sculpture, Roberdetti, Cat, Seated, Cold Enameled, Vienna Bronze, Signed, 2 In.	330.00
Sculpture, Rooster, Peter France, 1 Of 8, c.1995, 18 x 19 In.	3627.00
Sculpture, Running Back, Marble Plinth, Green, Brown Patina, 9½ In.	1195.00
Sculpture, Russell, C.M., Lone Buffalo, Early 1900s, 5 x 8½ In.	805.00
Sculpture, Russell, C.M., Oh Mother What Is It?, Wolf, 4¼ x 7 In.	374.00
Sculpture, Satyr & Bacchus, Grapevines, Tree Trunk, Fauno E Bacco, Marble Base, Italy, 18 In.	546.00
Sculpture, Seated Nude, After Etienne Maurice Falconet, France, 7½ In.	935.00
Sculpture, Seikoku, Ivory, Trunk Down, Japan, c.1900, 6 In.	301.00
Sculpture, Smith, Maria Kirby, Mule, 20th Century, 13¾ x 14¼ In.	748.00
Sculpture, Swaying Dancer, Brown Patina, After Claire Colinet, 20th Century, 18½ In.	325.00
Sculpture, Sykes, Charles, Woman, Body, Running, Attached Wings, Signed, 15 x 7½ In.	995.00
Sculpture, Syrian Archers, Cast, Stepped Base, 10 x 4½ In., Pair	115.00
Sculpture, Szczevlewski, Whistler, Boy, Hands In Pockets, Barefoot, Base, Tiffany & Co., 1889, 16½ In.	1610.00
Sculpture, Tiger, Prowling Stance, Fierce Growling Expression, Base, 1868-1912, 21½ In.	575.00
Sculpture, Vajrabhairava In Yab-Yum, Gilt, Turquoise Jewels, Sino-Tibetan, 8¾ x 3¼ In.	1793.00
Sculpture, Vanderlei, Phil, Otter, Cold Cast, 3½ x 14 In.	263.00
Sculpture, Vase, Chinese Designs, Horned Mask, Verdigris Patina, 8¾ In.	115.00
Sculpture, Wheeler, Hughlette, Horse, Man Scent, Patina, 5½ x 8½ In.	2530.00
Sculpture, Woman & Child, Gilt, Green Velvet Lined Base, 12½ x 11 In.	236.00
Sculpture, Woman Bust On Marble Base, 10½ In.	224.00
Sculpture, Woman Carrying Bucket, Patina, Wood Base, 17½ In.	978.00
Sculpture, Woman Dancer, Holding Up Skirt, Brown, Green Patina, Art Deco, 13½ In.	558.00
Sculpture, Woman Standing Next To Sail, Windblown, Art Deco, Signed G. Mikles, 9¾ x 4 In.	2346.00
Sculpture, Zurini, Emanuel, Car, Cadillac Roadster, 16¼ x 3½ In.	3376.00
Tazza, Center Bust Of Woman, Ring Of Ivy & Berries, Rolled Edge, 5¾ x 9 In.	52.00
Tazza, Portrait, Court Lady, Enamel, Dore, Jeweled, Raised Gilt, Dragon Handles, 1800s	750.00
Teapot, Embossed Dragon In Waves, Mt. Fuji, Dragon Handle, Meiji Period, Japan, 8 In. *illus*	118.00
Tieback, Empire Style, Flower Design, Swags, Stamped J.C., 6⅜ In., 4 Piece	793.00
Tieback, Winged Cherubs Riding Cornucopia, 1890, 13 In., Pair	650.00
Tobacco Jar, Indian, Buffalo, Brown Patina, Abastenia St. Leger, 6⅞ In.	8963.00
Tray, Art Nouveau, After Daniel Camragne, 8 x 12¾ In.	585.00
Tray, Card, Gilt, Legend, British Can Be Shot Here, Woman Exposing Buttocks, 6 In.	240.00
Triptych, Gilt, Hinged Doors, Applied Filigree, 6¾ x 5½ In.	558.00
Urn, Cut Crystal, Gilt, Baccarat Style, France, 21 x 10 In., Pair	2115.00
Urn, Mantel, Marble, Patinated, France, Late 19th Century, 13 In., Pair	2079.00
Vase, Animals, Relief, Japan, 12 In.	354.00
Vase, Beaker, Flared Mouth, Scalloped Rim, Relief Casting, Dragon, Chinese, 4½ In.	413.00
Vase, Bird Perched On Flowering Branch, Japan, 5½ In., Pair	118.00
Vase, Bottle, Champleve, Dragon Handles, Fan Patterned, Geometric, Chinese, 26 x 8 In.	94.00
Vase, Depicts Dragon, Wave, Taotie Mask, 2 Qilin Head, S-Shape Tung Handles, 7¼ In.	325.00
Vase, Dragon, Flowers, Japan, 16 In.	295.00
Vase, Dressler, 2 Fauns, Grapevines, 1916, 13½ In.	1058.00
Vase, Figure, Many Arms, Gilt, Chinese, 7½ In.	7050.00
Vase, Fish-Form Handles, Squat Baluster, Japan, 10½ In.	561.00
Vase, Gilt, Panel Cut Glass, Trumpet Shape, Sparrows Mount, 14 In.	1800.00
Vase, Gold, Silver, Geometric, Mask Handles, Chinese, 18th Century, 7¼ In.	3819.00

Vase, Keiten, Squat Oval, Patina, Marked, Japan, 20th Century, 6¾ In.	261.00
Vase, Molded Dragon, Turned Wood Base, Japan, 19th Century, 30 In.	764.00
Vase, Showa, Bears Attacking Tiger, Relief Animals, Gold, Verdigris Ground, 19 x 11 In.	1320.00
Vase, Wine, Ching Dynasty, 19th Century, 23½ x 13½ In.	330.00

BROWNIES were first drawn in 1883 by Palmer Cox. They are characterized by large round eyes, downturned mouths, and skinny legs. Toys, books, dinnerware, and other objects were made with the Brownies as part of the design.

Book, Brownie Primer, Banta-Benson, 1920, 7⅞ x 6 In., 94 Pages	15.00
Book, Brownies & The Farmer, Palmer Cox, 1902	24.00
Book Cover, Mother Mouse, 2 Baby Mice, Palmer Cox, 10 x 7 In.	30.00
Cup, Soccer, 19th Century, 3 x 3 In.	90.00
Cup & Saucer, Transfer, Brownies Singing, Child's, c.1890, 6⅜ x 2½ In.	135.00
Doll, Cloth, Lithographed, Cotton Stuffing, c.1892, 7 In.	195.00
Figurine, Brownie Sitting, Knees Up, Palmer Cox, Porcelain, Painted Features, 4 In. . . . *illus*	460.00
Knife, Fork, Standing On Daisy Handles, Malabar, Early 1900s, 7¼ & 6¼ In.	24.00
Mold, Ice Cream, Pewter, 4½ In.	81.00
Planter, Man's Face, Big Eyes, Ears, Palmer Cox, c.1895, 4¾ In.	125.00
Plate, Brownies Around Edge, Fluted Edge, Gold Trim, Marked, Child's, 8½ In.	90.00
Plate, Sage, Gray, Blue, Mustard, Gold Rims, Marked TST Latona	85.00
Postcard, Halloween, Brownies Chased By Jack-O'-Lantern, c.1920	30.00
Stickpin, Brass, Enamel, Red Pants, Jacket, 2¼ In.	20.00
Store Figure, Kinyons Brownies Cure All, Early 1900s, 11½ In.	813.00
Toothpick, Resting On Stump, Late 1800s, 7¼ & 2⅜ In.	250.00
Trivet, 4 Relief Scenes, 6¼ In.	100.00

BRUSH Pottery was started in 1925. George Brush first worked in 1901 in Zanesville, Ohio. He started his own pottery in 1907, but it burned to the ground soon after. In 1909 he became manager of the J.W. McCoy Pottery. In 1911, Brush and J.W. McCoy formed the Brush-McCoy Pottery Co. After a series of name changes, the company became The Brush Pottery in 1925. It closed in 1982. Old Brush was marked with impressed letters or a palette-shaped mark. Some new pieces are being marked in raised letters or with a raised mark. Collectors favor the figural cookie jars made by this company. Because there was a company named Brush-McCoy, there is great confusion between Brush and Nelson McCoy pieces. See McCoy category for more information.

Bank, Pig, Spotted, 6 In.	15.00
Bowl, Scenic, Green, Signed Cusick, Marked 93, 5¼ x 2½ In.	20.00
Cookie Jar, Bear, Brown, Marked 014 USA, 11 In.	15.00
Cookie Jar, Cow, Brown & Tan Glaze, No. W 10, 8¼ x 10 In. . . . . *illus*	25.00
Figurine, Swan, Yellow, Marked Brush USA Pottery, 1925-80, 5¼ x 6 In.	17.00
Figurine, Turtle, 4⅞ x 2 In.	22.00
Flowerpot, Saucer, Olive Green, Wood Grain Design, Marked Brush USA, 5½ x 5¾ In.	20.00
Garden Frog, Green, Brown, Brush-McCoy, 8 x 14½ In. . . . . *illus*	575.00
Jar, Strawberry, Onyx, Brush-McCoy, 6½ x 6½ In. . . . . *illus*	10.00
Jardiniere, McCoy, Green Overglaze, Cream Ground, Woman Figure, c.1912, 8 x 10 In.	118.00
Jardiniere, Pedestal, Greek Key Design, Lion Handles, Ivory Glaze, Gray Marbling, 30¼ In.	165.00
Jug, Clock, Green Onyx, German Clock, 6¾ In.	88.00
Music Box, Decanter, Onyx, Stopper, 9½ In.	25.00
Planter, Windowsill, Dark Green, 12 x 4½ x 4 In.	17.00
Vase, Green Onyx, 8 x 5 In.	15.00

BRUSH-MCCOY, *see Brush category and related pieces in McCoy category.*

BUCK ROGERS was the first American science fiction comic strip. It started in 1929 and continued until 1967. Buck has also appeared in comic books, movies, and, in the 1980s, a television series. Any memorabilia connected with the character Buck Rogers is collectible.

Card, Membership, Buck Rogers Rocket Rangers, Used, 1944, 2¼ x 3⅞ In.	112.00
Costume, Halloween, Buck Rogers, Ben Cooper, Medium, Box, 1978	20.00
Game, Buck Rogers Battle For The 25th Century, Board, TSR, 1988	61.00
Game, Pinball Machine, Buck Rogers In The 25th Century, Gottlieb, 1979	495.00
Game, Siege Of Gigantica, 3 Boards, Box, 8 x 16 In.	440.00
Lunch Box, Buck Rogers In The 25th Century, Thermos, Metal	30.00
Lunch Box, Thermos, Aladdin, 1979	150.00
Pencil Box, Cardboard, Snap Closure, American Pencil Co., c.1935, 12 x 14½ In.	168.00
Pin, I Saw Buck Rogers 25th Century Show, Did You?, Lithograph, 1934, 1¼ In. . . . . . . *illus*	311.00

Brush, Cookie Jar,
Cow, Brown & Tan Glaze,
No. W 10, 8¼ x 10 In.
$25.00

Brush, Garden Frog,
Green, Brown, Brush-McCoy,
8 x 14½ In.
$575.00

Brush, Jar,
Strawberry, Onyx, Brush-McCoy,
6½ x 6½ In.
$10.00

TIP
Need a quick measurement at an antiques show? A penny is ¾ inch in diameter; a dollar bill is almost 6 inches long.

Buck Rogers, Pin, I Saw Buck Rogers
25th Century Show, Did You?, Lithograph,
1934, 1¼ In.
$311.00

Buck Rogers, Toy, 25th Century
Destroyer Ship, Metal, Painted, Box,
Tootsietoy, 5 In.
$634.00

Buffalo Pottery Deldare, Plaque, An
Evening At Ye Lion Inn, Signed Delany,
1908, 13½ In.
$230.00

Buffalo Pottery Deldare, Plate,
Ye Village Gossips, Men Talking, Lang,
c.1908, 10 In.
$206.00

Pin, Strange World Adventures Club, Blue, Silver, 1939, 1¼ In.	3717.00
Pin, World's Fair, Century Of Progress, Lithograph, 1934, 1⅛ In.	140.00
Pocket Watch, Insert, Ingraham, Box, 1935, 2¾ x 7 In.	5014.00
Ring, Personalized, H, Birthstone, Brass, Adjustable, Cocomalt, 1934	235.00
Toy, 25th Century Destroyer Ship, Metal, Painted, Box, Tootsietoy, 5 In. ......*illus*	634.00
Toy, Atomic Pistol, Steel, Gold, Trigger Pops, Daisy, Box, 10 In.	300.00
Toy, Atomic Pistol, U-235, Holster, Metal, Daisy Mfg. Co., 1946, 10 In.	1735.00
Toy, Cardboard Helmet, Rocket Pop Pistol, Einson Freeman Co., Inc., 1934, 10½ x 11 In.	560.00
Toy, Draconian Marauder, No. 85012, Mego, Box, 1979	58.00
Toy, Model Kit, Starfighter Space, No. 6030, Sealed, Box, 1979	56.00
Toy, Robot, Walking Twiki, Buck Rogers In The 25th Century, Mego, Box, 1979	61.00
Toy, Rocket Police Patrol, Tin Lithograph, Windup, 1939, 4 x 12 x 4½ In.	948.00
Toy, Rocket Ship, 25th Century, Tin, Windup, Marx, Box, 12 In.	2200.00
Watch, Combination, Pocket, Wrist, Leather Band, Photorific Products, Box, c.1972	493.00

BUFFALO POTTERY was made in Buffalo, New York, after 1902. The company was established by the Larkin Company, famous manufacturers of soap. The wares are marked with a picture of a buffalo and the date of manufacture. Deldare ware is the most famous pottery made at the factory. It has either a khaki-colored or green background with hand-painted transfer designs.

BUFFALO POTTERY

Cup & Saucer, Willow	25.00
Gravy Boat, Cream, Pink Flowers, Gold Trim, 3¼ x 8 In.	13.00
Mug, Maroon Edge, Green, Mark, Restaurant Ware, 1940, 3¾ In.	10.00
Pitcher, Demi, Gazebo, Landscape, Blue, White, 1909, 5½ In.	70.00
Pitcher, Gloriana, Female Nymphs, Flowers In Garden, Foxes On Rim, Marked, 1908, 9 In.	295.00
Pitcher, Marine, Sailors, Ships, c.1907, 9 In.	205.00
Pitcher, Robin Hood, Sounding Horn, Marked, 1906-07, 8¼ x 6¼ In.	295.00
Pitcher, Roosevelt Bears, Sepia Transfers, 7⅞ In.	1490.00
Plate, Dinner, Scalloped, Pink & White Floral Decals, Gold Trim, c.1920, 9½ In.	12.00
Platter, Forest Scene, Buck Guarding Doe, R.K. Beck, c.1918, 11¼ x 15¼ In.	230.00
Platter, Horse Chariot, Oval, Restaurant Ware, 1940, 7 x 4⅞ In.	8.00
Saucer, Niagara Green Line, Restaurant Ware, 5½ In.	3.00
Tankard, Maritime Theme, Ships, Sailors, Lighthouse, Flow Blue, Marked, 9 In.	175.00

BUFFALO POTTERY DELDARE

Card Tray, Fallowfield Hunt, Signed E. Wayson, 1908, 8 In.	350.00
Charger, An Evening At Ye Lion Inn, Marked, 1908, 13¾ In.	1800.00
Humidor, Dome Lid, Ye Lion Inn, 8-Sided, Marked, 1909, 6¾ In.	190.00
Mug, Dr. Syntax Again Filled Up His Glass, Emerald, 1911, 5½ In.	600.00
Mug, Fallowfield Hunt, 4¼ In.	285.00
Pitcher, Their Manner Of Telling Stories, Signed, Gewlman, 1908, 6 In.	175.00
Pitcher, This Amazed Me, Van Horn, Marked, 1908, 9 In.	325.00
Pitcher, To Demand My Annual Rent, Signed, Stiner, Marked, 1908, 8 In.	225.00
Plaque, An Evening At Ye Lion Inn, Signed Delany, 1908, 13½ In. ......*illus*	230.00
Plate, Dr. Syntax Observing Man Wooing Susan, Emerald, 10 In.	345.00
Plate, Fallowfield Hunt, The Start, 1908-09, 14 In.	350.00
Plate, Ye Village Gossips, Men Talking, Lang, c.1908, 10 In. ......*illus*	206.00
Plate, Ye Village Street, Signed G. Eaton, 7¼ In.	250.00
Relish, Ye Olden Times, Oval, Signed, Dowlman, Marked, 1908, 12 In.	175.00
Tankard, The Great Controversy, Stiner, 1908, 12¼ In. ......*illus*	115.00

BUNNYKINS, *see Royal Doulton category.*

BURMESE GLASS was developed by Frederick Shirley at the Mt. Washington Glass Works in New Bedford, Massachusetts, in 1885. It is a two-toned glass, shading from peach to yellow. Some pieces have a pattern mold design. A few Burmese pieces were decorated with pictures or applied glass flowers of colored Burmese glass. Other factories made similar glass also called Burmese. Related items may be listed in the Fenton category, the Gundersen category, and under Webb Burmese.

Berry Bowl, Ruffled Edge, 4½ x 1⅛ In.	150.00
Biscuit Jar, Cover, Charles Dickens Verse, Handles, 7 x 5½ In.	8912.00
Bowl, Folded Sides, Applied Yellow Drip Rim, Salmon Pink, Round Base, 2½ x 6 In.	1050.00
Bowl, Rectangular, Folded, 5¼ In.	25.00
Bowl, White Daisies, Green Leafy Stems, Squat, Folded-Over Rim, Footed, 7 In.	431.00

Candy Dish, Salmon Shading To Yellow Interior, Diamond Pattern, Tooled Rim, 2¾ x 6 In. .	345.00
Condiment Set, Cruet, Salt, Pepper, Ribbed, Derby Silver Plated Holder, 7¾ In., 3 Piece *illus*	1840.00
Condiment Set, Melon Ribbed, Shakers, Mustard, c.1890, 4 In., 3 Piece	176.00
Condiment Set, Pillar Shape, Ribbed, Pairpoint Holder, Open Handle, 7¼ In. . . . .*illus*	411.00
Creamer, Cone Shape, Crimped Rim, 5¼ In.	173.00
Cruet, Melon Ribbed, Teardrop Stopper, c.1890, 6¾ In.	206.00
Lamp, Fairy, Candle, 3-Piece Dome, Cup & Base, Quadrafold Base, 6 In. . . . .*illus*	1495.00
Lamp, Fairy, Candle, Clarke Base, 3¾ In.	150.00
Pitcher, Water, Painted Flowers & Verse, Gold Tracery, 6¾ In.	6613.00
Punch Cup, 2⅝ In.	175.00
Rose Jar, Cover, Enameled English Ivy, Dickens Verse, Handles, 7 x 5½ In. . . . .*illus*	8913.00
Sugar & Creamer, Crimped Edge	150.00
Sugar & Creamer, Disk-Footed Creamer, 3-Footed Sugar, Glossy, 4 In.	345.00
Tankard, Pitcher, Glossy, 9 In.	650.00 to 748.00
Toothpick, Diamond-Quilted, 1¾ In.	450.00
Toothpick, Diamond-Quilted, Bulbous, Square Mouth, 2¾ In.	173.00
Toothpick, Hat Shape, Blue Threading At Collar, 2 In.	288.00
Toothpick, Urn Shape, 2¾ x 2¼ In.	725.00 to 850.00
Tumbler, Acid Finish, Paper Label, 3⅝ In.	197.00
Tumbler, Enameled Rose Design, 3¾ In.	201.00
Vase, Berry & Leaf, 2½ x 3¼ In.	225.00
Vase, Coralene Decoration, 7 In.	2500.00
Vase, Enameled Flowers & Leaves, Flared & Ruffled Rim, 4¼ In. . . . .*illus*	230.00
Vase, Grecian Shape, Pedestal Base, Flowers, 7 In.	1175.00
Vase, Jack-In-The-Pulpit, 12½ In., Pair	800.00
Vase, Jack-In-The-Pulpit, Crimped, Refired Yellow Rim, 6⅞ In.	475.00
Vase, Ostrich Egg, Trifold Rim, 3 Reeded Feet, 6¼ In. . . . .*illus*	115.00
Vase, Queen's Pattern, Enameled Daisies, Matte Glaze, Egg Shape, 9¾ x 4¾ In. . . . .*illus*	7188.00
Vase, Raised White Seeds, Fall-Colored Leafy Branches, Oval, Trifold Rim, 3½ In.	575.00
Vase, Stick, Bulbous, Art Nouveau Flowers, Gold Tracery, 2 Small Scrolled Handles, 12 In. . . .	9200.00
Vase, Stick, Squat, 7 In. . . . .*illus*	118.00
Vase, Storks, Egyptian Landscape, Raised Gold, No. 260, 11 x 5½ In.	10925.00
Vase, Striped Wild Flowers Decoration, Squat Stick Shape, 9¾ In.	2415.00
Whiskey Taster, Diamond-Quilted, Gold Rim, Daisies, Leaves, 2⅞ x 2¼ In.	750.00

BUSTER BROWN, the comic strip, first appeared in color in 1902. Buster and his dog, Tige, remained a popular comic and soon became even more famous as the emblem for a shoe company, a textile firm, and other companies. The strip was discontinued in 1920. Buster Brown sponsored a radio show from 1943 to 1955 and a TV show from 1950 to 1956. The Buster Brown characters are still used by Brown Shoe Company, Buster Brown Apparel, Inc., and Gateway Hosiery.

Balloon Blowerhead, Fiber Glass, Original Paint, 1960s, 21 x 24 In.	308.00
Bank, Buster & Tige, Cast Iron, A.C. Williams, 5¼ In. . . . .*illus*	460.00
Bank, Horseshoe, Horse, Buster Brown, Tige, Gold, Black, Cast Iron, Arcade, 5 x 4 In.	336.00
Book, Bread Book Of Rhymes, Wells Boettler Bakery, 1904, 4 x 6 In., 12 Pages	140.00
Box For Camera, My Camera, Cardboard, Ansco Co., 3¾ x 6 x 4½ In.	210.00
Button, Metal, 2-Piece, Metal Shank, ½ In.	12.50
Clicker, Buster Brown Shoes, Buster & Tige, Tin, 2⅛ In.	81.00
Clicker, Buster Brown Shoes, Buster & Tige In Color, Celluloid, 1900s, 1¼ In.	170.00
Clicker, Buster Brown Shoes, Celluloid, Round, Early 1900s, 1¼ In.	197.00
Clicker, For Happy, Healthy Feet, Tread Straight, Yellow, 1930s, 3¾ In.	45.00
Clock, Buster Brown, Tige, America's Favorite Children's Shoes, Electric, 15 x 15 In.	950.00
Display, Buster Brown Feeding Cracker To Tige, Die Cut, Tin, Painted, 2 Piece, 39 & 32 In. . .	12650.00
Doorknocker, Sitting On Fence, Tige, Cast Iron, Hubley, No. 200, 4¾ x 2 In.	825.00
Figure, Tige, Metal, Bead Eyes, 1 x 1 In.	29.00
Finger Puppet, Die Cut Mask, Buster Brown Image, Multicolored, 8½ In.	13.00
Fob, Buster Brown Shoes, 2-Sided, Celluloid, 1920s, 1¾ In.	168.00
Match Holder, Visit Our Modern Bakery, Bread, Tige, Tin Lithograph, 6¾ x 2 x ¾ In.	925.00
Mirror, Buster Brown Shoes, Buster & Tige, Celluloid, Pocket, 1¾ In.	121.00
Mirror, Buster Brown Shoes, Buster Brown & Tige, St. Louis, 2⅛ In.	132.00
Pan Scraper, Buster Brown Bread, Schmidt's, 3½ x 2¾ In.	425.00
Pin, Buster Brown Bread, Resolved That The Best Bread People Eat, Celluloid, 1½ In.	61.00
Pocket Mirror, Buster Brown & Tige, Vacation Days Carnival, c.1946	39.00
Postcard, Circus Theme, Leather, c.1910	12.00
Rattle, Sterling Silver, Buster & Tige, Mother-Of-Pearl Teething Bar . . . .*illus*	215.00
Ring, Buster Brown, Tige, Froggy, Midnight The Cat, Brass, Adjustable, Late 1940s	115.00

Buffalo Pottery Deldare, Tankard, The Great Controversy, Stiner, 1908, 12¼ In. $115.00

Burmese Glass, Condiment Set, Cruet, Salt, Pepper, Ribbed, Derby Silver Plated Holder, 7¾ In., 3 Piece $1840.00

Burmese Glass, Condiment Set, Pillar Shape, Ribbed, Pairpoint Holder, Open Handle, 7¼ In. $411.00

Burmese Glass, Lamp, Fairy, Candle, 3 Piece Dome, Cup & Base, Quadrafold Base, 6 In. $1495.00

Burmese Glass, Rose Jar, Cover, Enameled English Ivy, Dickens Verse, Handles, 7 x 5½ In. $8913.00

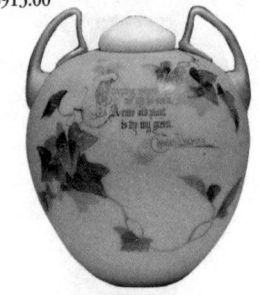

Burmese Glass, Vase, Enameled Flowers & Leaves, Flared & Ruffled Rim, 4¼ In. $230.00

Burmese Glass, Vase, Ostrich Egg, Trifold Rim, 3 Reeded Feet, 6¼ In. $115.00

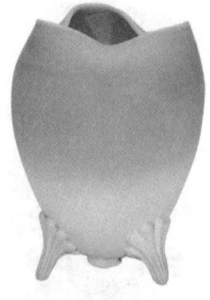

Burmese Glass, Vase, Queen's Pattern, Enameled Daisies, Matte Glaze, Egg Shape, 9¾ x 4¾ In. $7188.00

Rocking Horse, Buster, Tige, Painted, Red, Wood, Metal Springs, 34 x 28 x 20 In.	550.00 to 605.00
Sign, Buster Brown Bread, By Golden Sheaf, Buster & Tige, 19 x 27 In.	1650.00
Sign, Buster Brown Shoes, For Boys & Girls, Buster Brown & Tige, Cast Iron, 17½ In. Diam.	11200.00
Stringholder, Buster & Tige, Plaster, Painted, 1938, 7½ x 8 In. ....*illus*	345.00
Tin, Buster Brown Cigars, 2 For 5 Cents, Man In Chair, Buster, Tige, 50 Count, 5 x 5 In. ..	1540.00 to 2050.00
Tin, Mustard, Buster Brown & Tige, Steinwender-Stoffregen Coffee Co., Paper Label, 2½ In.	220.00
Toothpick, Figural, Bisque, Pink, c.1910, 6 In.	407.00
Toy, Buster Brown Stands In Cart, Pulled By Tige, Cast Iron, Kenton, c.1910	385.00
Toy, Wagon, Metal, Spoke Wheels, Undercarriage, Wood Floor, Handle, 15 x 26 In.	1680.00
Valentine, Mechanical, Eyes Move, Made In USA, 6½ In.	25.00

BUTTER CHIPS, or butter pats, were small individual dishes for butter. They were the height of fashion from 1880 to 1910. Earlier as well as later examples are known.

Black Transfer, Scalloped Rim, Mellor & Taylor, c.1900, 3 In.	12.00
Blue Forget-Me-Not Flowers, c.1908, 3 In.	35.00
Ironstone, Blue Flowers, Gold, Scalloped Rim, c.1880, 2¼ In.	24.00
Ironstone, Multicolored Flowers, Gold Trim, Alfred Meakin, c.1890, 2½ In.	28.00
Royal Blue, Gold Lines, Royal Doulton, British Airways, 4 In.	28.00
Scalloped Rim, Gold Leaf Border, c.1910, 3¼ In.	14.00
Stoneware, Art Deco, Green Bands, Gold Band, c.1925, 3½ In.	12.00
Stoneware, Floral Border, Dogwood, c.1930, 3 In.	16.00

BUTTER MOLDS *are listed in the Kitchen category under Mold, Butter.*

BUTTON collecting has been popular since the nineteenth century. Buttons have been known throughout the centuries, and there are millions of styles. Gold, silver, or precious stones were used for the best buttons, but most were made of natural materials, like bone or shell, or from inexpensive metals. Only a few types are listed for comparison.

2 Stars, 4 Holes, Phila., Penn., ⅝ In.	22.00
A.N. Rosenbloom, 4 Holes, Phila., Penn., 2 Stars, ⅝ In.	22.00
Bakelite, Heart Center, Butterscotch Color, 2 Holes, ⅞ In.	10.00
Bakelite, Navy Anchor, Black, 1940s, 1¼ In.	20.00
Bakelite, Red Star, Cream, Round Clear Plastic Applied Shank, 1 In.	12.50
Brass, Floral Cornucopia, Painted Back, Round Wire Shank, Stamped, 2 Piece, 1³⁄₁₆ In.	20.00
Brass, Floral Cornucopia, Painted Metal Back, Round Wire Shank, Stamped, 1³⁄₁₆ In.	20.00
Brass, Flower Bouquet, Cut Steel, Tin Back, 19th Century, 1¼ In.	30.00
Brass, Military, Coat, King Charles I, c.1640	150.00
Brass, Stamped, Silver Collet, U-Shape Wire Shank, 2 Piece, 1¼ In.	15.00
Burl Wood, Patina, 3¾ In.	200.00
Celluloid, Pearl Center, Metal Back, Self Shank, 2 Piece, 1½ In.	2.50
Cupids, Climbing Brick Wall, Victorian, 1½ In.	65.00
Cut Steel, Lion, Standing, Shield, Brass Shank, Victorian, Pierced, Stamped, c.1870, ¾ In.	14.50
Cut Steel, Reticulated, Stamped, Pierced, Rolled Edge, Victorian, c.1870, 1¼ In.	18.00
Cut Steel, Victorian, 1 In.	22.00
Enamel, Pink & Blue Flowers, France, ⅞ In.	85.00
Gold Plate, Vest, Edwardian, Abalone Inset, Brass Loop, Fitted Box, c.1900, ½ In.	85.00
Goofus Glass, Painted Flowers, Red Ground, ⅜ In.	9.00
Luster, Black, Glass, Gold, Silver, ½ In.	9.00
Luster, Black, Gold, Glass, 1 In.	8.00
Luster, Black, Silver, Glass, ¾ In.	8.00
Luster, Silver, Black Glass, c.1880, ⅝ In.	5.00
Metal, Bugler, 1½ In.	12.50
Metal, Flower Shape, Amber Gold Rhinestones, Round Wire Loop, 1 In.	15.00
Metal, Neptune With Trident, Black Painted Back, Victorian, 1⅜ In.	35.00
Metal, Raised Grapes, Leaves, 3 Sections, Cut Steel, Foldover Shank, Gold Wash, Victorian	23.00
Milk Glass Cameo Center, Banded Copper, Brass Border, Victorian, 1½ In.	20.00
Mother-Of-Pearl, Fish, Self-Carved Shank, ¾ In.	10.00
Mounted Collection, 100+ Buttons, Oval Frame, Victorian, c.1940, 19 x 13 In.	234.00
Over The Wall, 2 Cupids Climbing Brick Wall, Victorian, 1½ In.	65.00
Plastic, Moonglow, Raised Shank, 1¾ In.	8.00
Pot Metal, Silver, 2 Center Sapphire Rhinestones, 1 x ¾ In.	12.50
Purple Elm, Brown Patina, Northern China, Early 20th Century, 2¾ In.	50.00
Scottie Dog Head, Black, 1¼ In.	12.50
Uniform, US Navy, 13 Stars, Rope, Eagle, Anchor, Post 1941, ¹⁵⁄₁₆ In.	25.00
Wood, Hat Shape, Green, Red Trim	2.50

BUTTONHOOKS have been a popular collectible in England for many years but are now gaining the attention of American collectors. The buttonhooks were made to help fasten the many buttons of the old-fashioned high-button shoes and other items of apparel.

Bakelite Handle, V Shape, Flat Back, Step Cut Sides, 3¾ In.	29.00
Mother-Of-Pearl, 1890, 2¼ In.	66.00
Steel, 1900, 4½ In.	5.75
Steel, Folding, Late 19th Century, 2¾ In.	17.00
Sterling, Repousse, Anchors, Marked, Sterling 225, 4½ In.	125.00
Sterling Silver, c.1900, 5½ In.	65.00
Sterling Silver, Repousse, Anchor Hallmark, Gorham, 4½ In.	125.00
Sterling Silver, Repousse, Marked, Sterling, 3 In.	50.00

BYBEE POTTERY was started in 1845 and is still working. The Lexington, Kentucky, firm makes pottery that is sold at the factory. Pieces are marked with the name or with the name enclosed by the outline of the state of Kentucky.

Bank, Pig, Standing, Brown, 5½ In.	9.00
Bank, Pig, Standing On 2 Legs, 5⅝ In.	16.00
Batter Bowl, Brown, Handle, Marked, Bybee Ky 18, 7½ In.	18.00
Pitcher, Blue, Wheel Thrown, 8 In.	65.00
Strawberry Jar, Gloss Black, Cornelison Bybee Pottery, Incised Stamp, 4 x 5 In.	36.00

CALENDARS made to hang on the wall or to be displayed on a desk top have been popular since the last quarter of the nineteenth century. Many were printed with advertising as part of the artwork and were given away as premiums. Calendars with guns, gunpowder, or Coca-Cola advertising are most prized.

1883, Brown's Iron Bitters, Revolving, Jester, 6¼ x 5½ In.	80.00
1890, Hood's Sarsaparilla, Girl, Red Hat, Full Pad, 9¾ x 5½ In.	190.00
1895, Hinckel Brewing Co., Lager Beers, Woman, Pink Hat, Die Cut, 13 x 7½ In.	200.00
1896, Bartholomay Brew Co., Woman Holding Glass, Full Pad, Frame, 46 x 36 In.	2750.00
1896, California Powder Works, San Francisco, Blond Woman, 15 x 19 In.	7200.00
1898, Norton Bros., Tin Lithograph, Folding, Pocket, 3⅜ x 3¾ In.	413.00
1899, Winchester Ammunition, 2 Hunting Scenes, A.B. Frost, Full Pad, Frame, 29 x 17 In.	805.00
1903, Eagle Ore Sampling Co., Full Pad, Oak Frame, 22 x 14 In.	6600.00
1903, Hill's Cascara Quinine Bromide Pills, 35 Tablets For 25 Cent, Full Pad, 9½ x 5½ In.	145.00
1905, Wells County Bank, 4 Dogs, January Only, Bluffton, In., 16 x 21 In.	180.00
1906, O.H. Allison, Plumbing, Heating & Roofing, 15 x 10 In.	146.00
1907, Scherling Bros., Dealers In General Merchandise, 17 x 10½ In.	146.00
1908, California Wine House, 3 Girls In Boat, Flowers, Die Cut, Embossed, Cardboard, 12 x 16 In.	150.00
1909, Deering Harvesting Machines, Woman, Gold Border, 26 x 17 In.	1800.00
1909, DuPont Explosives, Dog With Puppies, 29 x 21 In.	325.00
1909, E. & W. Chandler, General Merchandise, Wedding Journey, Full Pad, 14 x 11 In.	100.00
1910, DeLaval, Lady, Hat, Red Shawl, 25½ x 17½ In.	1430.00
1910, Notebook, Walter E. Koenig, Jobber In Auto Tires & Supplies, Celluloid	41.00
1910, Pratts Veterinarian Supplies, Woman With Horse, Emp Bros., 12½ x 8 In.	310.00
1911, Parman & Heinze, Dry Goods & Notions, 18 x 12 In.	157.00
1911, Swifts Lowell Fertilizer Co., Girl Feeding Chickens, Full Pad, 24¼ x 15 In.	660.00
1912, DuPont, Powder Wagon, Lake Erie Commodore, September Page, 30 x 19 In.	275.00
1915, Eureka Fly Killer, Hiawatha's Wedding Journey, Ferris, Full Pad, 14½ x 24½ In.	374.00
1916, Bargain Store, Girl, Blue Dress, Bow, Flowers, Die Cut, Cardboard, Frame, 24 x 18 In.	210.00
1916, Weed Chains, 4 Ladies Dressed In Different Seasons, 10 x 30 In.	1550.00
1918, Horton Bristol Goodwin, Bristol Rods, Woman Fishing From Canoe, 22 x 37 In.	1650.00
1924, Round Oak Stoves, Doe-Wah-Jack, Brings Message Of Good Cheer, Indian, Girl, 20⅝ x 10⅝ In.	687.00
1924, Winchester, Hunter Shooting Ducks, October To December Pages, 14 x 28 In.	2655.00
1925, Rooster Snuff, Rooster On Fence, Farmer, Horses, 16½ x 8½ In.	1808.00
1926, Triner's Bitter Wine, Ailments & Remedies For All Kinds Of Sickness, 26 x 13½ In.	40.00
1927, J.S. Thomas Dry Goods Clothing Store, Little Red Riding Hood, 14½ x 22 In.	154.00
1927, United States Cartridge Co., Shot-Shells Cartridges, Ducks, January Only, 35 x 16 In.	700.00
1928, Hercules Powder Co., This Trip We All Go, October Page, 29½ x 13 In.	425.00
1928, Stevens Firearms, Pioneers, 11 Months On Pad, 28½ x 16 In.	2250.00
1928, Western Ammunition, Snow Geese, Lynn Bogue Hunt, 28½ x 15 In.	575.00
1929, Clothesline, Novelty, Original Box	75.00
1929, US Shot Shells Cartridges, Come On, What Ails Yer, December Only, 35 x 16 In.	1850.00
1930, Hercules Powder Co., Let's Go, Man, Dogs, 30 x 13 In.	725.00

C

Burmese Glass, Vase, Stick, Squat, 7 In.
$118.00

Buster Brown, Bank, Buster & Tige, Cast Iron, A.C. Williams, 5¼ In.
$460.00

Buster Brown, Rattle, Sterling Silver, Buster & Tige, Mother-Of-Pearl Teething Bar
$215.00

Buster Brown, Stringholder, Buster & Tige, Plaster, Painted, 1938, 7½ x 8 In.
$345.00

Calendar, 1939,
Drink Nehi, Royal Crown Cola,
Woman In Rowboat, 24 x 12 In.
$1170.00

Calendar, 1950,
Royal Crown Cola, Ann Blyth,
24 x 11¼ In.
$58.00

TIP

If you have a book or other small item that smells peculiar, put it in a large plastic bag with kitty litter. Seal it and let it stand for about a week.

1930, John Morrell Co., Morrell's Pride Liver Cheese, 30 x 14 In. 40.00
1930, US Shot Shells Cartridges, Hunter Behind Scarecrow, January Only, 31½ x 16 In. 1850.00
1931, US Shot Shells Cartridges, Opportunity, Hunter, Dog, Full Pad, 31½ x 16 In. 1900.00
1937, Quinlans Garage, Hunter Sleeping, Dogs, Full Pad, 14 x 8 In. 110.00
1939, Drink Nehi, Royal Crown Cola, Woman In Rowboat, 24 x 12 In. .... *illus* 1170.00
1940, 7Up, I Like 7Up, It Likes Me, Image Of Blond, Full Pad, 15 x 24 In. 85.00
1941, Newells Cowboy Store, Cowboy On Horse, Full Pad, 27 x 18 In. 70.00
1947, Bachelders Service Station, Goodyear Tires, Take Me Too, Boy, Dog, Full Pad, 16 x 9½ In. 40.00
1947, Mutual Benefit Life Insurance Co., Evening Landscape, 33¼ x 16 In. 264.00
1948, Hercules Powder Co., Veterans, Full Pad, 30 x 13 In. 275.00
1949, Hercules Powder Co., 100th Anniversary Of Western Mining Industry, No Pad, 30 x 13 In. 275.00
1950, Royal Crown Cola, Ann Blyth, 24 x 11¼ In. .... *illus* 58.00
1950-51, DeLaval, Indians, 35 x 16 In. 27.00
1957, Kelly Tires, Paper Lithograph, Metal Bands, 16 x 33 In. 330.00
Desktop, DeLaval Cream Separators, Tin Lithograph, Rolling Calendar, 5½ x 6⅝ In. 1430.00

CALENDAR PLATES were very popular in the United States from 1906 to 1929. Since then, plates have been made every year. A calendar and the name of a store, a picture of flowers, a girl, or a scene were featured on the plate.

1776-1976 Bicentennial, Gold Trim, 9¼ In. 12.00
1909, J. Cornelius, General Merchandise, Bird, Ribbon, Calendar Pages, 8¼ In. 21.00
1909, Santa Claus, Car, Toys, Compliments Of H.C. Kase, Elysburg, Pa., American China Co., 7⅜ In. 55.00
1910, C.F. Company, 8¾ In. 30.00
1915, Panama Canal, Compliments Of D. Trozzo Co., Pittsburgh, Dresden, 7½ In. 28.00
1953, Debutante, Homer Laughlin 25.00
1953, Jubilee Line, Homer Laughlin, 10¼ In. 11.00
1957, Windmill, Gold On White, Taylor Smith Taylor, 10¼ In. 20.00
1961, Zodiac, God Bless Our House, Brown, Alfred Meakin 18.00
1962, Windmill, Sailboats, Gold Decoration, Flower Rim, Taylor Smith Taylor, 10 In. 20.00
1970, Zodiac, God Bless Our House, Blue, Alfred Meakin, 9 In. 12.00
1972, Season Poem, William Browne, Mount Clemens 7.50
1975, Zodiac, Metallic Gold, Green Rim, 10¼ In. 7.50

CAMARK POTTERY started in 1924 in Camden, Arkansas. Jack Carnes founded the firm and made many types of glazes and wares. The company was bought by Mary Daniel. Production was halted in 1983.

Ashtray, Delphite Blue, Flower, Scalloped Edge, 3½ x 1¼ In. 35.00
Basket, White, 4¾ In. 36.00
Bowl, Center, Pink Semimatte, Vertical Ribs, Scalloped, 10 x 3¾ In. 30.00
Candleholder, 3-Light, Green, Frosted, 7⅜ x 6 In., Pair 145.00
Figurine, Frog, 2¾ x 4 In. 49.00
Figurine, Hound Dog, Squatting, 2 x 4 In. 40.00
Figurine, Satin Ivory, Cat Peering In Fishbowl, 9 x 9½ In. 85.00
Flower Frog, Olive Green, 1970s, 2¾ x 4 In. 10.00
Lamp, Electric, Honey Brown Onyx Glaze, Urn Shape, Shade, 3⅝ In. 175.00
Mug, Royal Blue, Handles, 5¾ In. 200.00
Mustard, Green Drip, 3 In. 45.00
Pitcher, Mustard Yellow Matte, 6⅛ In. 50.00
Pitcher, White, Rose Decals, 11 In. 45.00
Planter, Double Swans, 7½ x 7½ In. 50.00
Planter, Green, Double Basket, 4¾ x 5¾ In. 35.00
Planter, Light Blue, Urn Shape, 5½ In. 45.00
Vase, Blue, Stipple, Triangle, 2½ x 3⅜ In. 50.00
Vase, Blue Drip, Triangle, 2½ x 3½ In. 50.00
Vase, Blue Matte, Bulbous, Arts & Crafts, 1930, 6⅜ In. 45.00
Vase, Bud, Brown, 4 In. 25.00
Vase, Flowers, 2 Handles, 9¼ In. 125.00
Vase, Green Matte, Blue Drip, 2 Handles, 5⅛ In. 85.00
Vase, Light Blue, Cornucopia, c.1950, 6 x 10 In. 45.00
Vase, Ring, Black, 5 In. 75.00
Vase, Rose, Footed, 8 In. 95.00
Vase, Satin White, Ruffled Edge, 4¾ In. 50.00
Vase, Water Lily, 7½ In. 195.00

CAMBRIDGE GLASS Company was founded in 1901 in Cambridge, Ohio. The company closed in 1954, reopened briefly, and closed again in 1958. The firm made all types of glass. Their early wares included heavy pressed glass with the mark *Near Cut*. Later wares included Crown Tuscan, etched stemware, and clear and colored glass. The firm used a *C* in a triangle mark after 1920.

Apple Blossom, Bowl, Gold Krystol, Flared, 4-Footed, 11½ In.	70.00
Apple Blossom, Dish, Mayonnaise, Gold Krystol, 4-Footed	33.00
Apple Blossom, Plate, Tea, Gold Krystol, 7½ In.	10.00
Apple Blossom, Sandwich Server, Gold Krystol, Center Handle, 10½ In.	50.00
Ball, Decanter Set, Amber, Clear Stopper, 4 Mushroom Tumblers, 2-Qt. Jug, 5 Piece ....*illus*	50.00
Bashful Charlotte, Flower Frog, Jade, 11 In.	129.00
Bashful Charlotte, Flower Frog, Light Emerald Green, 11 In.	114.00
Bashful Charlotte, Lamp Base, Vaseline, 8 In., Pair	100.00
Bluebell, Cocktail, Narrow Optic, 2½ Oz., 4 Piece	165.00
Bunny Box, Cover, Crystal, 7 In.	500.00
Calla Lily, Candlestick, Emerald Green, 6½ In., Pair	75.00
Candlelight, Bowl, Flared Rim, 4-Footed, 10 In.	75.00
Candlelight, Plate, 8½ In.	35.00
Candlelight, Sherbet, 6¼ In.	22.50
Caprice, Bowl, 5 In.	10.00
Caprice, Bowl, Moonlight Blue, 4-Footed, 13½ In. .....*illus*	32.00
Caprice, Bowl, Moonlight Blue, Alpine, Oval, Handles, 4-Footed, 11 In.	104.00
Caprice, Bowl, Moonlight Blue, Alpine, Ruffled Edge, 4-Footed, 12 In.	65.00
Caprice, Bowl, Moonlight Blue, Crimped Edge, 3-Footed, 10½ In.	70.00 to 75.00
Caprice, Bowl, Moonlight Blue, Oval, Handles, 4-Footed, 9 In.	80.00
Caprice, Cake Salver, 2 Piece	145.00
Caprice, Candelabrum, 3-Light, Bobeches, Prisms, 7½ In.	100.00
Caprice, Candelabrum, 5-Light, Bobeches, Prisms, 11 In.	300.00
Caprice, Candelabrum, 5-Light, Center Bobeche, Prisms, 8½ In.	157.00
Caprice, Candlestick, 3-Light, Mandarin Gold, 6 In., Pair	100.00
Caprice, Candlestick, Alpine, Bobeche, Prisms, 7 In., Pair	45.00
Caprice, Candlestick, Moonlight Blue, 2½ In., Pair	50.00
Caprice, Celery Dish, Oval, 9 In.	15.00
Caprice, Claret, Moonlight Blue, 4½ Oz.	150.00
Caprice, Compote, Moonlight Blue, 6 In.	85.00
Caprice, Cruet, Moonlight Blue, Clear Stopper, 3 Oz.	45.00
Caprice, Cruet, Stopper, 3 Oz.	25.00
Caprice, Cup & Saucer, Moonlight Blue, Alpine	45.00
Caprice, Dish, Jelly, Handles, 5 In.	8.00
Caprice, Dish, Mayonnaise, Larosa, 6 In.	50.00
Caprice, Dish, Mayonnaise, Moonlight Blue, Underplate, Ladle, 8 In.	75.00
Caprice, Goblet, Blown Bowl, 9 Oz.	15.00
Caprice, Nut Dish, Moonlight Blue, 2½ In.	15.00 to 35.00
Caprice, Parfait, Blown, 5 Oz.	45.00
Caprice, Pitcher, Ball, 80 Oz.	75.00
Caprice, Relish, 4 Sections, 12 In.	50.00
Caprice, Rose Bowl, 4-Footed, 6 In.	55.00
Caprice, Rose Bowl, Moonlight Blue, 4-Footed, 6 In.	110.00
Caprice, Sherbet, Blown Bowl, Moonlight Blue, Tall, 6 Oz.	25.00 to 30.00
Caprice, Sugar & Creamer, Medium	40.00
Caprice, Sugar & Creamer, Mocha, Medium	35.00
Caprice, Tumbler, Iced Tea, 12 Oz.	25.00
Caprice, Tumbler, Juice, Moonlight Blue, Footed, 5 Oz.	30.00
Caprice, Tumbler, Moonlight Blue, Footed, 10 Oz.	30.00
Caprice, Vase, Ball, Moonlight Blue, 5 In.	150.00
Carmen, Bowl, Everglades, 10 In.	1136.00
Carmen, Candy Box, Cover, Georgian	105.00
Carmen, Cigarette Holder, Footed	75.00
Carmen, Decanter, Straight Sides, Long Neck, Striped Silver Overlay, 28 Oz.	202.00
Carmen, Nut Cup, 4-Toed, 3 In.	45.00
Cascade, Sugar & Creamer, Emerald Green	45.00
Chantilly, Creamer	21.00
Chantilly, Goblet, 10 Oz.	150.00
Chantilly, Saltshaker, Metal Lid	20.00
Cleo, Bowl, Light Emerald Green, 9¼ In.	25.00

C

Cambridge Glass, Ball, Decanter Set, Amber, Clear Stopper, 4 Mushroom Tumblers, 2-Qt. Jug, 5 Piece
$50.00

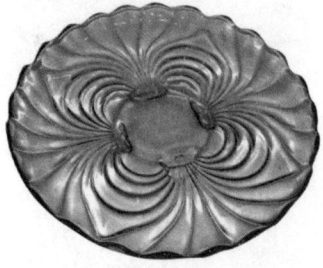

Cambridge Glass, Caprice, Bowl, Moonlight Blue, 4-Footed, 13½ In.
$32.00

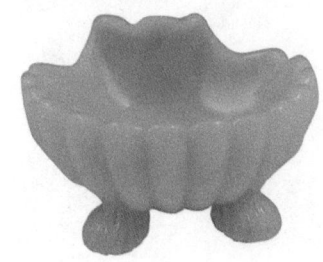

Cambridge Glass, Crown Tuscan, Salt, Seashell, Footed, 2½ x 1½ In.
$7.50

Cambridge Glass Colors

The most popular Cambridge Glass Company colors made during the 1920s and '30s were given special names in the advertising. Look for Amberina (shaded red amber), Carmen (ruby), Crown Tuscan (pink opaque), Ebony, Moonlight Blue, Peach-Blo (pink) Royal Blue, and several shades of Emerald Green.

Cambridge Glass, Decagon, Bowl, Vegetable, Oval, Peach-Blo, 10½ In. $6.00

Cleo, Cheese & Cracker Set, Light Emerald Green, Decagon		25.00
Cleo, Dish, Mayonnaise, Peach-Blo, Handles		10.00
Cleo, Underplate Only, For Gravy Boat, Pink		13.00
Corinth, Tray, Footed, 14 In.		22.00
Crown Tuscan, Ashtray, Shell, 3-Toed, Gold, 4 In.		8.00
Crown Tuscan, Bowl, Fruit, Flying Lady, Footed, 10 In.		350.00
Crown Tuscan, Bowl, Salad, Seashell, 13 In.		55.00
Crown Tuscan, Candlestick, 2-Light, Keyhole, 6 In., Pair		45.00
Crown Tuscan, Candy Box, Cover, 3 Sections, Charleton Gardenia, 8 In.		45.00
Crown Tuscan, Cigarette Box, Cover, Shell, 4½ x 3½ In.		20.00
Crown Tuscan, Ivy Ball, Keyhole, 8 In.		40.00 to 50.00
Crown Tuscan, Jar, Cover, Yardley		35.00
Crown Tuscan, Salt, Seashell, Footed, 2½ x 1½ In.	*illus*	7.50
Crown Tuscan, Torte Plate, Seashell, Charleton Rose, 14 In.		65.00
Crown Tuscan, Vase, Bud, Footed, 10 In.		45.00
Crown Tuscan, Vase, Bud, Footed, Charleton Rose, 10 In.		115.00
Daffodil, Candy Box, Cover, Cut 6-Sided Knob, 6 In.		85.00
Daffodil, Compote, Tall Stem, 6 In.		60.00
Daffodil, Tumbler, Iced Tea, Footed, 12 Oz.		25.00
Decagon, Bowl, Vegetable, Oval, Peach-Blo, 10½ In.	*illus*	6.00
Decagon, Plate, Pink, 8½ In.		8.95
Diane, Cocktail, 3 Oz., 6 Piece		45.00
Diane, Compote, Blown, 5⅜ In.		45.00
Diane, Compote, Tall, 7 In.		60.00
Diane, Dish, Pickle, 9 In.		40.00
Diane, Epergne		55.00
Diane, Goblet, 9 Oz.		22.00
Diane, Icer, Shrimp Cocktail, 2 Piece		45.00
Diane, Lamp, Hurricane, Etched, 17 In.		100.00
Diane, Plate, Salad, 8 In.		12.00
Diane, Relish, 2 Sections, Handle, 6 In.		35.00
Diane, Relish, 5 Sections, 12 In.		15.00
Dolphin, Candlestick, Emerald Green, Flat Round Base, 9½ In.		215.00
Doric Column, Candlestick, Amber, 9½ In., Pair		175.00
Draped Lady, Flower Frog, 13 In.		170.00
Draped Lady, Flower Frog, Amber, 8½ In.		175.00
Draped Lady, Flower Frog, Peach-Blo, 8½ In.		150.00
Draped Lady, Flower Frog, Peach-Blo Satin, 8½ In.		165.00
Ebony, Basket, 10½ In.		75.00
Ebony, Candlestick, 3-Light, Keyhole, 6½ In.		20.00
Elaine, Candlestick, 2-Light, 6 In., Pair		210.00
Elaine, Candlestick, 3-Light, 6 In., Pair		75.00
Elaine, Compote, Tall, Blown, 5⅜ In.		45.00
Elaine, Cordial, 1 Oz.		90.00
Elaine, Dish, Mayonnaise, Underplate		45.00
Elaine, Goblet, 6¼ In.		27.50
Elaine, Goblet, Water, 10 Oz.		25.00
Elaine, Sherry, 2 Oz.		45.00
Everglade, Bowl, Swan Handles, Light Emerald Green, Frosted Trim, 14 In.		400.00
Everglade, Bowl, Vaseline, 9½ In.		80.00
Everglade, Candlestick, Blue, Pair		70.00
Everglade, Platter, Swan Handles, Willow Blue, 16 In.		45.00
Everglade, Sherbet, Amber		55.00
Everglade, Sugar & Creamer, Willow Blue		60.00 to 135.00
Everglade, Tray, Tulip, Milk Glass, 16 In.		225.00
Everglade, Vase, Tulips, Purple & Gold Flash, 10½ In.		1100.00
Fernland, Plate, Near Cut, 10¾ In.		20.00
Figurine, Squirrel, Frosted		65.00
Firenze, Plate, Salad, 7½ In., 12 Piece		110.00
Firenze, Tumbler, Footed, 12 Oz.		40.00
Flower Frog, Gold Krystol, Round, No. 2899		102.00
Flower Frog, Mocha, 2 Children		184.00
Georgian, Basket, Smoke Handle		45.00
Georgian, Candy Box, Cover, Mandarin Gold		50.00
Georgian, Tumbler, Smoke, 12 Oz.		20.00
Georgian, Tumbler, Willow Blue, 9 Oz.		10.00

Gloria, Decanter, Royal Blue, Gold Encrusted, Pinched Sides	990.00
Granada, Cocktail, 3 Oz.	10.00
Gyro-Optic, Vase, Keyhole Stem, Midnight Blue, 12 In.	95.00
Harvest, Cocktail, Crystal, 3 Oz.	15.00
Heatherbloom, Goblet, Apple Blossom Etch	85.00
Heatherbloom, Vase, Clear Stem & Foot, 10 In.	375.00
Helio, Vase, Bud, Ruffled Edge, Footed, 10 In.	165.00
Imperial Hunt Scene, Goblet, Green, 9 Oz.	40.00
Imperial Hunt Scene, Salt, Green, 2½ In.	90.00
Imperial Hunt Scene, Sandwich Server, Pink, Center Handle	166.50
Imperial Hunt Scene, Tumbler, Pink, Gold Encrusted	90.00
Jenny Lind, Punch Cup	10.00
Keyhole, Ivy Ball, Emerald Green, Clear Stem & Foot, 8½ In. *illus*	30.00
Krystolshell, Sugar & Creamer	30.00
Laurel Wreath, Claret, 4½ Oz.	22.50
Laurel Wreath, Sherbet, 4½ Oz.	12.50
Lily Of The Valley, Sugar & Creamer	175.00
Lorna, Celery Dish, Red Enamel Trim, Handles, 11 In.	45.00
Martha Washington, Basket, Ebony, Handles, 10½ In.	50.00
Martha Washington, Compote, Gold Encrusted, Blossom Time Etch, 6 In.	90.00
Martha Washington, Finger Bowl, Amber, 3½ In.	14.78
Minerva, Cordial, 1 Oz.	85.00
Minerva, Ice Bucket, Chrome Handle	55.00
Mt. Vernon, Compote, Heatherbloom, Twisted Stem, 4½ In.	225.00
Mt. Vernon, Creamer, Royal Blue	50.00
Mt. Vernon, Mug, Royal Blue, 14 Oz.	50.00
Mt. Vernon, Tumbler, Milk Glass, 10 Oz.	25.00
No. 402, Vase, Amber, Ball Bottom, Etched, 12 In.	100.00
Nude, Brandy, Amethyst, Frosted Stem, Clear Foot, 1 Oz., 6½ In. *illus*	178.00
Nude, Brandy, Royal Blue, Frosted Stem, Clear Foot, 1 Oz., 6½ In.	255.00
Nude, Candlestick, Crown Tuscan, 9 In., Pair	250.00
Nude, Claret, Vichy Etch, 4½ Oz.	911.00
Nude, Cocktail, Amethyst, 3 Oz.	90.00
Nude, Cocktail, Carmen, Clear Stem & Foot, 3 Oz.	180.00
Nude, Cocktail, Pistachio, 3 Oz.	150.00
Nude, Cocktail, Royal Blue, Crown Tuscan Stem, 3 Oz.	329.00
Nude, Compote, Carmen, 7 In.	250.00
Nude, Compote, Seashell, Crown Tuscan, 5 In.	75.00
Nude, Compote, Seashell, Crown Tuscan, Charleton Rose, 7 In.	150.00
Nude, Compote, Smoke, Clear Stem & Foot, 7 In.	425.00
Nude, Ivy Ball, Carmen, Clear Stem & Foot	275.00
Peach-Blo, Plate, Apple Shape, 8 In.	150.00
Peach-Blo, Tray, Center Handle	10.00
Peacock, Pitcher, Water, Tankard, Rayed Base, 11¾ In.	231.00
Plainware, Candy Jar, Cover, Azurite, 1 Lb.	75.00
Portia, Cordial, 1 Oz.	50.00
Portia, Cruet, Ball Stopper, 2 Oz.	40.00
Portia, Relish, 5 Sections, Amber, 12 In.	40.00
Portia, Sugar & Creamer	25.00
Portia, Vase, Pillow, Crown Tuscan, 9 In.	558.00
Ram's Head, Bowl, Peach-Blo, 8½ In.	175.00
Rolling Pin, Milk Glass, Wood Handles	95.00
Rose Lady, Flower Frog, Pink	149.00
Rose Point, Bowl, Rcrimped Edge, 13 In.	80.00
Rose Point, Candlestick, 3-Light, 6 In., Pair	125.00
Rose Point, Candy Box, Cover, Ram's Head, 6 In.	195.00
Rose Point, Compote, Tall, Gold Encrusted, 5⅜ In.	105.00
Rose Point, Cup & Saucer	30.00
Rose Point, Decanter, Footed, 28 Oz.	350.00
Rose Point, Decanter, Steeple & Wafer Stopper, No. 1388	1775.00
Rose Point, Epergne, 4 Piece	100.00
Rose Point, Goblet, Water, 10 Oz.	35.00
Rose Point, Plate, Dinner, 10½ In.	140.00
Rose Point, Relish, 4 Sections, Handle, 15 In.	125.00
Rose Point, Sherbet, Tall, 6 Oz.	60.00
Rose Point, Sugar & Creamer, Gold Encrusted	76.00

C

Cambridge Glass, Keyhole, Ivy Ball, Emerald Green, Clear Stem & Foot, 8½ In. $30.00

Cambridge Glass, Nude, Brandy, Amethyst, Frosted Stem, Clear Foot, 1 Oz., 6½ In. $178.00

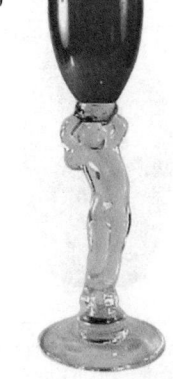

Cambridge Glass, Seashell, Vase, Footed, 6 x 7 In. $47.00

Cameo Glass, Perfume Bottle, Frosted, Leafy Branches, Round, Flared Silver Collar & Lid, 4¼ In. $264.00

Cameo Glass, Vase, Amethyst Stemmed Lilies, Frosted, Martele, Richardson, 2½ In. $353.00

Cameo Glass, Vase, Burgundy Medallions, Lake Scenes, Art Deco Flowers, Oval, D'Argyl, 13 In. $940.00

Cameo Glass, Vase, Cascading Flowers, Leaves, Butterfly, Red On White On Blue, Shouldered, 9 In. $5175.00

Rose Point, Sugar	10.00
Rose Point, Sugar & Creamer	40.00 to 45.00
Rose Point, Tumbler, Iced Tea, 12 Oz., 5½ In.	35.00 to 60.00
Rose Point, Wine, 3½ Oz.	50.00
Rose Point, Wine, Amethyst, Clear Stem & Foot	275.00
Roselyn, Cordial, 1 Oz.	30.00
Sea Gull, Flower Frog, 8½ In.	45.00
Seashell, Cocktail, Dolphin Stem, 4½ Oz.	25.00
Seashell, Dish, Emerald Green, Oval, 4-Footed, 8 In.	10.00
Seashell, Vase, Footed, 6 x 7 In. ....*illus*	47.00
Stackaway, Ashtray Set, Moonlight Blue, Wood Base, 5 Piece	55.00
Sunburst & Wheat, Pitcher, 8½ x 6½ In.	35.00
Swan, Dish, Crown Tuscan, 8½ In.	125.00
Swan, Dish, Crown Tuscan, Charleton Gardenia, 8 In.	152.00
Swan, Dish, Ebony, 10½ In.	275.00
Swan, Dish, Emerald Green, 3 In.	35.00
Swan, Dish, Emerald Green, 6½ In.	100.00
Swan, Dish, Emerald Green, 8½ In.	125.00
Swan, Dish, Gold Krystol, 3 In.	40.00
Swan, Dish, Light Emerald Green, Style II, 3 In.	35.00
Swan, Dish, Mandarin Gold, 3 In.	35.00
Swan, Dish, Mandarin Gold, 8½ In.	125.00
Swan, Dish, Mandarin Gold, Style III, 3 In.	30.00
Swan, Dish, Mocha, 3 In.	85.00
Swan, Dish, Peach-Blo, 6½ In.	100.00
Swan, Dish, Peach-Blo, 8½ In.	140.00
Swan, Dish, Peach-Blo, Style I, 8½ In.	50.00
Swan, Dish, Royal Blue, 3 In.	125.00
Swan, Dish, Style II, 3 In.	15.00
Swan, Punch Cup	100.00
Sweet Pea, Vase, Azurite, 7 In.	30.00
Sweet Pea, Vase, Blue, Gold Encrusted, Etched, 7 x 8¼ In.	315.00
Tahoe, Cordial, Moonlight Blue, 1 Oz.	50.00
Tally-Ho, Cordial, Amber, 1 Oz.	35.00
Tally-Ho, Salt & Pepper, Royal Blue	75.00
Tally-Ho, Sherbet, Low, Elaine Etch	40.00
Tally-Ho, Stein, 12 Oz.	30.00
Tally-Ho, Tumbler, Elaine Etch, Footed, 12 Oz.	50.00
Tally-Ho, Tumbler, Forest Green, 2½ Oz.	18.00
Tally-Ho, Tumbler, Handle, Amber, 2½ Oz.	5.00
Twist, Muddler, Forest Green, 4½ In.	45.00
Wild Rose, Punch Cup, Carmen, 5 Oz., 8 Piece	120.00
Wild Rose, Vase, Squared Cylinder, 9 In.	95.00
Wildflower, Cake Plate, Gold Encrusted, Handles, 12½ In.	115.00
Wildflower, Candy Box, Cover, Gold Encrusted, Footed	159.00
Wildflower, Cocktail Shaker, Chrome Cover	75.00
Wildflower, Compote, 6 In.	40.00
Wildflower, Cordial, 1 Oz.	50.00
Wildflower, Pitcher, Ball, 80 Oz.	200.00
Wildflower, Plate, 7½ In.	12.00
Wildflower, Plate, Salad, 8 In.	10.00
Wildflower, Relish, 5 Sections, 12 In.	45.00
Wildflower, Sherbet, Tall, 6 Oz.	45.00
Wildflower, Soup, Dish, Gold Encrusted	105.00
Wildflower, Tumbler, Barrel, 13 Oz.	38.00
Willow, Cup & Saucer, Blue Encrusted, Gold Band	65.00
Willow, Plate, Blue Encrusted, Gold Band, 6¾ In.	35.00
Willow, Plate, Blue Encrusted, Gold Band, 8 In.	45.00

CAMEO GLASS was made in much the same manner as a cameo in jewelry. Parts of the top layer of glass were cut away to reveal a different colored glass beneath. The most famous cameo glass was made during the nineteenth century. Signed cameo glass pieces are listed under the glasswork's name, such as Daum or Galle.

Biscuit Jar, Gray, Grecian Warriors, Metal Collar, Lid, G. De Feure, c.1910, 7½ In.	764.00
Biscuit Jar, Prussian Blue, Ginkgo, Band Borders, Metal Lid, 7 In.	1035.00

Bowl, Brass Mount, Brown, Green, Art Nouveau, 10 x 7 In.	508.00
Bowl, Green, Gray, Silver Flowers, France, 6 In.	353.00
Flask, Textured, Green Stemmed, Red Flowers, Hammered Flip Cover, France, c.1900, 5 In. . .	500.00
Perfume Bottle, Frosted, Leafy Branches, Round, Flared Silver Collar & Lid, 4¼ In. . . . . . .*illus*	264.00
Vase, Amethyst Dragonfly, Iris, Frosted, Flat Sides, Verriere Nancy, 8 In.	230.00
Vase, Amethyst Stemmed Lilies, Frosted, Martele, Richardson, 2½ In. . . . .*illus*	353.00
Vase, Blue, Lake Scene, Red Sailing Ship, Tapered, Signed, J. Michel, 3¾ In.	345.00
Vase, Buds, Flowers, Leaves, Rose, Frosted Ground, Shouldered, Pantin, 14 In.	940.00
Vase, Burgundy Medallions, Lake Scenes, Art Deco Flowers, Oval, D'Argyl, 13 In. . . . . . .*illus*	940.00
Vase, Cascading Flowers, Leaves, Butterfly, Red On White On Blue, Shouldered, 9 In. . . .*illus*	5175.00
Vase, Cobalt Blue Flowers, Martele, Signed, Richardson, 12 In.	1208.00
Vase, Green & Red, Art Nouveau, Squatwide Mouth, Frosted, Signed, Honesdale, 6¼ In.	460.00
Vase, Green Translucent, Amethyst Flowers, Martele Rim, Cylindrical, 8 In.	374.00
Vase, Leaves, Light Green Ground, c.1890, 7¼ In.	1320.00
Vase, Pink Flowers, Leaves, Orange Ground, c.1890, 4 In.	1320.00
Vase, Red Vines & Grape Leaves, Frosted Interior, Elongated Neck, Flared Rim, 17½ In.	2233.00
Vase, Rose Du Barry, Stemmed Leafy Fuchsia, Shouldered, 4¾ In.	805.00
Vase, Rose Fuchsia, Leaves, Frosted Ground, Shouldered, Tapered Neck, Pantin, 6½ In.	588.00
Vase, Stick, Enameled Purple Flowers, Textured Ground, Tapered, 5¾ In.	460.00
Vase, Sweet Peas & Leaves, Chartreuse, Frosted Ground, Tapered, Arsall, 16¾ In. . . . . . .*illus*	360.00
Vase, Textured Green, Gold Enameled, Silver Acorns, Leaves, Cylindrical, 11¾ In.	1410.00
Vase, Translucent Green, Gold Highlights, Crimson Leaves, Oval, Signed, St. Louis, 7 In. . . .	575.00
Vase, Trumpet, Amethyst Flowers, Frosted Ground, Tapered, 9 In.	403.00
Vase, Trumpet, Pink Butterflies, Stemmed Flowers, Frosted, Metal, c.1900, 16¼ In.	1645.00
Vase, Wheel Carved, Apple Blossoms, Blue, Gold Trim, Burgun & Schverer, 10 In. . . . . . .*illus*	33350.00
Vase, White Flowers, Leaves, Cranberry Ground, Urn Shape, c.1890, 5 In.	1320.00
Vase, Yellow, Brown Lake Scene, Trees, Castle, Bulbous, Footed, J.M. Paris, 8 In.	805.00

CAMPAIGN *memorabilia is listed in the Political category.*

CAMPBELL KIDS were first used as part of an advertisement for the Campbell Soup Company in 1906. The kids were created by Grace Drayton, a popular illustrator of the day. The kids were used in magazine and newspaper ads until about 1951. They were presented again in 1966; and in 1983, they were redesigned with a slimmer, more contemporary appearance.

Bank, Boy & Girl, Cast Iron, Gold Paint, Embossed, A.C. Williams, 3⁵⁄₁₆ In. . . . .*illus*	138.00
Bowl, 1984 Sarajevo Olympic Games, Corelle, Marked, 1 x 8 In.	12.50
Bowl, Covered, Marked, 1998, 4½ x 5 In.	7.50
Dish, Girl Holding Doll, Marked, Buffalo Pottery, c.1904, 7½ In.	96.00
Doll, Bicentennial Boy, Red, White, Blue, Revolutionary War Era, 10 In.	115.00
Doll, Boy, Blue Shorts, White Shirt, Posable Arms, Eugene Doll & Novelty Co., Box, 1984, 7½ In. .	45.00
Doll, Boy, Vinyl, Red & White Checkered Shirt, Blue Overalls, White Socks, Shoes, 9½ In.	45.00
Doll, Girl, Chef, Porcelain, Red Hair, Red Shirt, Green Shorts, Striped Socks, Apron, Tag, 10 In.	125.00
Doll, Girl, Cloth, Blue Eyes, Blond Hair, Carrying Doll, Marked, 16 In.	55.00
Doll, Girl, Composition Head, Cloth Body, Pink Flowered Dress, 11 In.	95.00
Doll, Girl, Vinyl, Red & White Gingham Dress, Bow, Bloomers, Socks, Shoes, 9½ In.	45.00
Doll, Girl, White Dress, Flowers, Posable Arms, Eugene Doll & Novelty Co., Box, 1984, 7½ In.	45.00
Figure, Boy, Blue Overalls, Carrying Case Of Soup, Original Box	15.00
Spoon, Boy, 6 In.	25.00
Spoon, Girl, 6 In.	25.00
Spoon, M'm! M'm! Good! Slogan, Kids Image, Back Stamped, Oneida Ltd, 4½ In.	35.00
Stringholder, Incised On Bottom, 1950s, 6¾ In.	395.00

CAMPHOR GLASS is a cloudy white glass that has been blown or pressed. It was made by many factories in the Midwest during the mid-nineteenth century.

Decanter, Light Blue Forget-Me-Nots, Stopper, 7 x 5½ In.	135.00
Powder Jar, Art Deco, Green, Footed, 4¾ In.	35.00
Vase, Top Hat, Daisy & Button, Light Blue, 2½ x 3½ In.	135.00

CANDELABRUM refers to a candleholder with more than one arm to hold many candles; a candlestick is designed to hold one candle. The eccentricity of the English language makes the plural of candelabrum into candelabra.

2-Light, Sconce, Silver, Baskets, Acanthus & Ribbon, Charles S. Harris, England, 7 x 11 In., Pair .	1997.00

Cameo Glass, Vase, Sweet Peas & Leaves, Chartreuse, Frosted Ground, Tapered, Arsall, 16¾ In.
$360.00

Cameo Glass, Vase, Wheel Carved, Apple Blossoms, Blue, Gold Trim, Burgun & Schverer, 10 In.
$33350.00

SECURITY TIP

Be sure you have photographs and descriptions of your collections in case of a robbery. Keep them in a safe place away from your house.

Campbell Kids, Bank, Boy & Girl, Cast Iron, Gold Paint, Embossed, A.C. Williams, 3⁵⁄₁₆ In.
$138.00

TIP
Check the supports on wall-hung shelves once a year. Eventually a heavy load will cause "creep," the metal brackets will bend, and the shelf will fall.

Candelabrum, 2-Light, Woman's Bust, Bronzed Cast Iron, Flowing Hair Supports, Art Nouveau, 12½ In. $275.00

Candlesticks
The seventeenth-century brass candlestick had a square base and fluted column. In the 1700s, a smaller candlestick base was made because it took up less space on the gaming table. In the eighteenth century, candlesticks had hexagonal or ornamented bases, and candelabra were used to give more light. In the nineteenth century, candlesticks became larger and more ornate. By the 1850s, oil lamps replaced the candle as a main source of illumination.

2-Light, Silver, Domed Base, Scroll Arms, Mexico, 5 x 8½ In., Pair 323.00
2-Light, Silver, Fluted, Inverted Bell Nozzles, Domed Foot, John Scofield, England, 17 In., Pair 4320.00
2-Light, Tin, Painted, Vertically Adjustable, Ring Finial, 18¾ In. 440.00
2-Light, Woman's Bust, Bronzed Cast Iron, Flowing Hair Supports, Art Nouveau, 12½ In. *illus* 275.00
2-Light, Wrought Iron, 3-Footed, Penny Feet, Crimped Tin Candle Cups, 56½ In. 1925.00
3-Light, 2nd Empire, Bronze, Figural, France, 20 x 9¾ In. 350.00
3-Light, Convertible, D.S. Spaulding, c.1940, 10¼ x 9 In., Pair 88.00
3-Light, Sheffield Plate, c.1810, 20 In. 1247.00
3-Light, Silver, D.S. Spaulding, Convertible, c.1940, 10¼ x 9 In. 234.00
3-Light, Silver, P.G. Lopez, Mexico, 20th Century, 12 In., Pair 671.00
3-Light, Silver, Scrolled Arms, Amsterdam, c.1960, 12½ In., 4 Piece 1662.00
3-Light, Silver, Ivory, Round Base, Scrolling Acanthus Feet, Fluted Shaft, 12 In., Pair 944.00
3-Light, Silver Plate, 2 Scrolling Arms, International, 16¾ x 15½ In., Pair 1265.00
3-Light, Silver Plate, 20th Century, 18¾ x 16 In. .... 59.00 to 70.00
3-Light, Silver Plate, Victorian, Elkington & Co., 21¼ In., Pair 1033.00
3-Light, Sterling Silver, Convertible, Gorham, 12 x 12 In. 350.00
3-Light, Sterling Silver, Crown, Convertible, 15 x 12 In., Pair 585.00
3-Light, William IV, Gilt Bronze, Cut Glass, Canopied, c.1835, 22¼ x 12 In., Pair 2115.00
4-Light, Bronze, Malachite, France, 19th Century, 15 x 6 In., Pair 819.00
4-Light, Empire, Gilt, Ebonized Brass, Tapered Shaft, Scroll Feet, 20½ In., Pair 588.00
4-Light, Figural, Drop Decoration, Early 20th Century, 17¾ In., Pair 120.00
4-Light, Louis XV Style, Bronze, Acanthus Arms, S-Scroll Base, 19⅜ In., Pair 470.00
4-Light, Porcelain, Schierholz, Denmark, 18 In. 70.00
5-Branch, Brass, Flowing Scrolled Leaves, 17½ In., Pair 805.00
5-Light, Art Nouveau, Gilt Parcel, 19 x 14 In. 2880.00
5-Light, Bronze, Black Marble Base, c.1880, 22¼ x 11 In., Pair 1287.00
5-Light, French Style, Brass, 20½ x 11 In., Pair 206.00
5-Light, Glass Cups, Wire Rods, Cast Glass Disk, Skrufs Glassworks, c.1964, 14 In. 470.00
5-Light, Louis XV Style, Bronze, Porcelain, Flower Heads, Pair, 16½ In. 176.00
5-Light, Louis XVI Style, Gilt Bronze, Serpentine Arms, Cherub, Onyx Base, Pair, 25 In. 1880.00
5-Light, Renaissance Revival, Blue Enamel, Gilt Brass, 23 In., Pair 440.00
5-Light, Silver, Square Base, Column, Czechoslovakia, c.1929, 24¾ In. 1628.00
5-Light, Tin Candlecup, Embossed Scalloped Borders, 6½ x 12 In., Pair 118.00
5-Light, Turkish Style, Cloisonne, Black Onyx, Bobeches, Finials, 18½ In., Pair 235.00
5-Light, White Marble Urn, Bronze, Gilt Metal Branches, France, 1800s, 23 In., Pair 3042.00
6-Light, Brass, Cut Glass Swags, Prisms, Octagonal, 18th Century, 26 In., Pair 345.00
6-Light, French Empire Style, Bronze Dore, Columnar Shafts, 19th Century, 34 In. 5900.00
6-Light, Napoleon III, Gilt Bronze, Footed Supports, Scroll Base, 28 x 15 In., Pair 2530.00
7-Light, Belle Epoque, Gilt Bronze, Brass, Multicolored, Flowers, Leaves, 40 In., Pair 352.00
7-Light, Figural, Rococo Style, Gilt Metal, Cherub Base, 31 x 14 In., Pair 644.00
7-Light, Sevres Style, Porcelain, Gilt Bronze, Scroll Arms, 36 x 16 In., Pair 2468.00
9-Light, Neoclassical Style, Giltwood, Gilt, Iron, Cut Glass, Italy, c.1850, 30 x 16 In., Pair 2585.00
12-Light, Tin, Star Base, Weighted, 10½ x 27½ In. 1485.00
50-Light, Louis XVI Style, White Marble, Ormolu, Urn Shape, Lily Stem Arm, 24¾ In. 529.00
Brass, 2 Riveted Coils, Tapered Holders, Jarvie, 10½ x 7¾ In. 4800.00
Brass, Girandole, Cornstarch Blue, Trumpet Shape Shade, White Marble, 17 In., Pair 1320.00
Brass, Girandole, Leatherstocking, Gilt, White Marble, Cut Glass, Prisms, c.1848, 3 Piece 1080.00
Girandole, 6-Light, Directoire, Gilt Brass, Crystal Hung, Marble, 34 x 17 In., Pair 1528.00
Girandole, Daniel Boone & Indians, Brass, Marble, Cornelius & Co., 3 Piece 632.00
Silver, Repousse Pattern, Scrolled Arms, S. Kirk & Son, 14¾ In. 1980.00
Wrought Iron, Double Adjustable, Trefoil Base, 21¾ x 12 In. 360.00

CANDLESTICKS were made of brass, pewter, glass, sterling silver, plated silver, and all types of pottery and porcelain. The earliest candlesticks, dating from the sixteenth century, held the candle on a pricket (sharp pointed spike). These lost favor because in times of strife the large church candlesticks with prickets became formidable weapons, so the socket was mandated. Candlesticks changed in style through the centuries, and designs range from classic to rococo to Art Nouveau to Art Deco.

Art Deco, Orange, 3-Sided Base, Round Holder, 8¾ In., Pair 58.00
Baluster Shaft, Round Base, Concave Drip Plate, Dutch, 17th Century, 7 In., Pair 1380.00
Beechwood, Louis XV Style, Pricket, Shell, Leaves, Lobed, France, c.1865, 10 In., Pair 940.00
Beechwood, Wrought Iron, Italian Provincial, Round Turned Base, Caged Column, 11 In. 36.00
Bell Metal, Baluster Shaft, Octagonal Base, 17th Century, 5 In., 2 Piece 345.00
Bell Metal, Baluster Shaft, Square Base, 17th Century, 3½ x 4¼ In., Pair 546.00
Bell Metal, Copper Hue, Queen Anne, 8⅞ In., Pair 575.00

Blown Glass, Amber, Quilted, Holder, 2½ In., Pair	72.00
Blown Glass, Drip Pans, Base, Twist Spiral Stems, Holder, 9¾ In., Pair	935.00
Brass, Baluster, c.1900, 8 In., Pair	29.00
Brass, Baluster Shaft, Round Stepped Base, Late 18th Century, 10 In., Pair .... *illus*	201.00
Brass, Baluster Stem, Bobeche, Cylindrical Cup, Notched Base, 18th Century, 9 In., Pair	359.00
Brass, Baluster Stem, Square Base, Seam, 7 In., Pair	489.00
Brass, Baluster Turned Stem, Cylindrical Bobeche, Notched Base, Joseph Wood, 7 In., Pair ..	896.00
Brass, Beehive, 3⅜ In.	44.00
Brass, Beehive, Push-Up, Marked England, 10¾ In., Pair	172.00
Brass, Beehive, Stepped Base, Push-Up, 11 In., Pair	121.00
Brass, Beehive, Turned Shaft, Round Base, 9½ In., Pair	55.00
Brass, Beehive, Turned Shaft, Shaped Base, 10¾ In., Pair	28.00
Brass, Capstan, 17th Century	195.00
Brass, Capstan, Bell Shape Base, 2 Extraction Holes, 17th Century, 3¾ x 4¾ In.	206.00
Brass, Cast, Baluster Turned Post, Square Base, Dutch, 17th Century, 5½ In., Pair	633.00
Brass, Cast, Chippendale, 18th Century, 7⅜ x 4½ In., Pair	1560.00
Brass, Cast, Square Base, Stylized Hoof Feet, Baluster Turned Post, 6¾ In.	431.00
Brass, Cast, Square Base, Stylized Hoof Feet, Continental, 1700s, 8¼ In.	115.00
Brass, Cast Iron, Spring Loaded, Bulbous Chimney, Holder, 14½ In.	451.00
Brass, Chippendale, 18th Century, 7¼ x 4¼ In., Pair	420.00
Brass, Cone Base, Incised Lines, Turned Shaft, Continental, 10½ x 6 In.	230.00
Brass, Dish Shape Base, Central Column, Ring Handle, Ejector, 4 x 6 In.	144.00
Brass, Dome Base, Baluster Stem, 2 Ejector Holes, 7½ In.	230.00
Brass, Dome Base, Rings, Socket, Mid-Drip Pan, 9 In.	316.00
Brass, Drip Pan, Joining Handles, Saucer Bases, 6¾ In., Pair	55.00
Brass, Eagle Shape, Claw Foot, Late 20th Century, 35 In.	527.00
Brass, Enameled, Louis XV, Baluster Stem, Shaped Base, Late 1800s, 5 In., Pair	144.00
Brass, Faceted Base, 6 In.	86.00
Brass, Fan Reflector, 12¾ In.	28.00
Brass, Flared Base, Push-Up, 6 In., Pair	121.00
Brass, Griffin Shape, c.1910, 6 In., Pair	47.00
Brass, Hogscraper, 18th Century, 8 In., Pair	695.00
Brass, Leaves, Threaded Post, Removable Bobeche, 9¾ In., Pair	230.00
Brass, Oval Shaft, Stepped Oval Base, Push-Up, Embossed H, 9 In., Pair	88.00
Brass, Pricket, 8 In.	55.00
Brass, Pricket, Archaic, Ball Centered On Standard, 3-Footed, 6¾ In., Pair	291.00
Brass, Push-Up, 4¼ In.	33.00
Brass, Push-Up, 10 In., Pair	23.00
Brass, Queen Anne, Beehive Shape Ring Stem, Rounded Corner Base, 7½ In., Pair	230.00
Brass, Sand Cast, Wide Drip Pan, Dutch, 12 In., Pair	950.00
Brass, Scalloped Base, Push-Up, England, 1700s, 8¼ In., Pair	978.00
Brass, Scalloped Lip & Base, Push-Up, Marked EK, c.1800, 7¾ In., Pair	1955.00
Brass, Seamed, Panel & Ring Stems, Octagonal Base, Knopped Push-Up, 7 In., Pair	776.00
Brass, Spiral Twist Stem, Scalloped Edge Base, 5 In.	345.00
Brass, Spring Loaded, Pierced Gallery Collar, 7¼ In.	11.00
Brass, Spring Loaded, Weighted Base, 8¾ To 13¾ In.	33.00
Brass, Spun, Flared, Zeta Model, Original Patina, Signed, Jarvie, 6 x 6 In.	360.00
Brass, Square Base, Filled Bottom, Central Column, Turned Rings, 5½ In., Pair	200.00
Brass, Tiered, Baluster Turned Shafts, Shaped Base, Curved Drip Pans, 8 In., Pair	5875.00
Brass, Twisted Shaft, Square Base, Continental, Early 1700s, 6 In.	345.00
Brass, Wax Jack, Tankard Shape, Openwork Acanthus Leaves & Tassels, Wax Taper, 4 x 3 In. *illus*	920.00
Brass-Over-Metal, Ecclesiastical Style, c.1900, 19 In., Pair	59.00
Bronze, Champleve, Flowers, Japan, 9¼ In., Pair	142.00
Bronze, Figural, Seahorse, E.T. Hurley, c.1916, 13 In., Pair	3360.00
Bronze, Gilt, Altar, 19th Century, 13½ In., Pair	147.00
Bronze, Gilt, Patinated, Porcelain Flowers, Tripod, 12½ In., Pair	880.00
Bronze, Marble, Porcelain Flowers, c.1900, 15¾ In., Pair	3159.00
Bronze, Marble Base, Patina, 12 In., Pair	100.00
Bronze, Sea Dragon, 25 In.	146.00
Bronze, Silvered, c.1903, 12 In., Pair	9000.00
Cast Iron, Baluster Post, Scalloped, Relief Scroll, Shell, 1900s, 10 In.	1035.00
Cast Iron, Holder, 11¼ In.	66.00
Chamber, Brass, Rectangular Saucer Base, Scissor, Cone Snuffer, 5 x 6½ In. ....*illus*	205.00
Chamber, Brass, Red Boulle, Napoleon II, Fretwork, Tortoiseshell, c.1825, 3¾ x 2¼ In.	695.00
Chamber, Silver, Leaf Base, Flower Form Ring Handle, Flower Nozzle, Russia, 3½ In.	1062.00
Chamber, Silver, Lobed, Paris, c.1768, 1½ x 8½ In.	1170.00

C

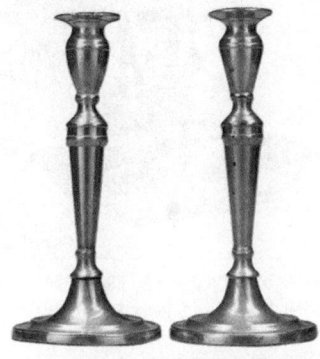

Candlestick, Brass, Baluster Shaft, Round Stepped Base, Late 18th Century, 10 In., Pair
$201.00

TIP

Candle wax on your antique metal candlesticks? Put the candlesticks in the freezer. After a few hours, the wax will easily flake off. If there is a large lump of wax in the candle cup, run hot water on the stick until the wax melts. Do not let water get into the hollow base.

Candlestick, Brass, Wax Jack, Tankard Shape, Openwork Acanthus Leaves & Tassels, Wax Taper, 4 x 3 In.
$920.00

Candlestick, Chamber, Brass, Rectangular Saucer Base, Scissor, Cone Snuffer, 5 x 6½ In. $205.00

Candlestick, Chamber, Snuffer, Silver, George III, Elizabeth Jones, England, 1791, 3⅝ In. $1170.00

Candlestick, Chamber, Snuffer, Silver, Solomon Hougham, London, 1802, 4½ x 6½ In. $920.00

Candlestick, Silver, Federal Style, Tapered Stem, Oval Base, Black, Starr & Frost, 12 In., Pair $920.00

Chamber, Snuffer, Silver, George III, Elizabeth Jones, England, 1791, 3⅝ In. . . . . *illus*	1170.00
Chamber, Snuffer, Silver, Solomon Hougham, London, 1802, 4½ x 6½ In. . . . . *illus*	920.00
Clambroth, Paneled, 9 In.	115.00
Cloisonne, Pricket, Crane Shape, Lotus Leaf In Mouth, Rockwork Base, Chinese, 6 In., Pair .	3055.00
Cranberry Glass, Brass Base, Top, Swirl, 10 In., Pair	86.00
Cut Crystal, Crystal Drops, Regency, c.1830, 10 In.	146.00
Cut Glass, Anglo-Bohemian, Panel Cut, Van Dyke Knop, 1800s, 12 In., Pair	210.00
Giltwood, Pricket, Carved, Neoclassical Style, Armorial Shield, Tripod, 24 In., Pair	2040.00
Glass, Honey Amber, Drawn Out Socket, Baluster, Open Pontil, 1840-65, 6¾ In.	1230.00
Glass, Littala, Festivo, Molded, Rough Surface, Initialed TS, 1967, 12 In., Pair	353.00
Glass, Opaque Blue, Pressed, Pewter Insert, Cross, Embossed, Ripley & Co., 1868, 10½ In. . . .	515.00
Hog Scraper, Brass, 18th Century, 8 In., Pair	895.00
Hog Scraper, Brass, Push-Up, Wedding Band, Signed, Shaw's Birm, 7⅛ In.	431.00
Hog Scraper, Steel, Push-Up, Round Base, Column Shaft, 5½ x 3¾ In., Pair	345.00
Hog Scraper, Tin, Push-Up, Flared Rim, Looped Hook, Dome Base, 8¼ In.	248.00
Iron, Birdcage, Wood Base, 7½ In.	660.00
Iron, Spiral, Wood Base, Carry Handle, Push-Up, 8¾ In.	72.00
Ivory, Carved, Low Relief, Domestic Scenes, Flowers, Wood Base, Chinese, 8 In., Pair	240.00
Onyx, Green, Gilt Metal, Mounted As Lamp, Early 20th Century, 11 In., Pair	561.00
Onyx, Taupe, Bronze Mounted, Columnar Shaft, Corinthian Capital, 6½ In., Pair	660.00
Pewter, Peg Lamp Holder, Smith & Co., ¾ In.	209.00
Pewter, Push-Up, Melon Shape Glass Peg Inserts, Spouts, 13 In., Pair	523.00
Pewter, Queen Anne, Octagonal Base, 7 x 4¼ In., Pair	316.00
Rock Crystal, Tapered, In 3 Sections Stepped Base, Turned Socket, 8½ In., 4 Piece	1680.00
Rosewood, Table Mount, Adjustable Arm, 14½ x 20½ In.	275.00
Satin Glass, Reverse Painted Shade	32.00
Silver, Cartier, No. 055, 6½ x 2 In.	322.00
Silver, Chamber Stick, Coin, Round, Applied Border, Ring Handle, c.1850, 2¾ x 6 In.	748.00
Silver, Chinese, c.1900, 5½ In.	450.00
Silver, Clark's Pyramid, Monogram, Match Safe, Holder, 2¾ In.	88.00
Silver, Dutch, c.1900, 11 x 5 In., Pair	585.00
Silver, Federal Style, Tapered Stem, Oval Base, Black, Starr & Frost, 12 In., Pair . . . . . . *illus*	920.00
Silver, Fluted Sconce, Removal Nozzle, Tapered Cylindrical, England, 12 In.	7050.00
Silver, Gadroon Border, Urn Shape Socket, Detachable Nozzle, c.1765, 3 In., Pair	3360.00
Silver, Garland Decorations, Birmingham, England, c.1907, 4½ In., Pair	299.00
Silver, Georgian, Fluted Columns, Corinthian Capitals, Square Base, Sheffield, 13 In., 4 Piece .	1880.00
Silver, Germany, Early 20th Century, 9½ In., Pair	707.00
Silver, Hand Wrought, Original Finish, Kalo, Impressed Mark, No. 9557, 7½ x 4 In.	1700.00
Silver, Openwork Bobeches, Base, Bellflowers, Shield, c.1916, 11 In., Pair	748.00
Silver, Oval, Baluster, Conforming Base, Gorham, c.1926, 10½ In., 4 Piece	690.00
Silver, Petticoat Style, Square Base, Knopped Baluster Stems, Russia, 12¼ In.	1652.00
Silver, Pinched Waist, Flowers, Shells, Scrolls, England, c.1827, 10 In., Pair	1619.00
Silver, Rococo Style, Shaped Base, Baluster Stem, Acanthus, 13 In., Pair	2280.00
Silver, Round, Stop Fluted Tapered Column, Gadrooned, Beaded, Sheffield, 12 In., Pair	546.00
Silver, Virginia Pattern, Dominick & Haff, c.1900, 8 In.	176.00
Silver Plate, Brass, Round Base, Tubular Stem, c.1969, 16 & 12½ In., 3 Piece	840.00
Silver Plate, Classical Style, Columnar Shape, England, c.1950, 8 In., Pair	47.00
Silver Plate, Gadrooning, Bobeches, Sheffield, Boulton, c.1800, 11¼ In., 4 Piece	4900.00
Silver Plate, Oval, Fluted Columns, Reeded Borders, Mid 1800s, 10 In., Pair	345.00
Silver Plate, Oval, Reeded & Gadrooned Border, Old Sheffield, 5½ In., Pair . . . . *illus*	431.00
Silver Plate, Oval, Squat, Gadrooned Band, Flared Nozzle, Oval Base, 5¾ In., Pair	146.00
Silver Plate, Oval Scalloped Form, Reeded Design, Late 1800s, 11½ In., 4 Piece	259.00
Silver Plate, Scrolling Feet, Acanthus Leaf, Baluster Shape, Polish, 1800s, 11½ In.	295.00
Silver Plate, Sheffield, 19th Century, 11½ In., Pair	206.00
Silver Plate, Taper Stick, Fused, Tapered Stem, Round Reeded Base, 18th Century, 6½ In., Pair .	288.00
Silver Plate, Tapered, Round Base, Hexagonal Dome, Monogram, Meriden, 9 In., Pair	146.00
Silver Plate, Tapered Stem, Vase Shaped Nozzle, Navette Base, Elkington, 12 In., Pair	705.00
Silver Plate, Victorian, Martin Hall & Co., Late 19th Century, 11 In., Pair	312.00
Spring Loaded, Painted Tin Shade, 2 Sockets, Holder, 15 In.	83.00
Sterling Silver, Baluster Stem, Repousse, Round, Flowers, Birds, 12 In., Pair	2415.00
Sterling Silver, Cobalt Blue Enamel, Meka Of Denmark, c.1930, 2 x 3 In., Pair	234.00
Sterling Silver, Ebonized Wood, 1877, 8½ In., Pair	3600.00
Sterling Silver, Preisner, 6 In., Pair	117.00
Sterling Silver, Stepped Spread Foot, Kalo, 7½ x 4 In. . . . . *illus*	1680.00
Tin, Deep Dish, Holder, 4¾ x 9½ In.	105.00
Tin, Embossed, Holder, 2 In.	94.00

C

Tin, Glass Globe, Folding Doors, Traveling, Holder, 6 In.	187.00
Tin, Glass Hurricane Shade, Smoke Bell Top, Holder, 13¼ In.	165.00
Tin, Mechanical, Adjustable Reflector, Holder, 14¼ In.	2420.00
Tin, Push-Up, Mid Drip, 6½ In.	275.00
Tin, Push-Up, Saucer Base, 4½ In.	28.00
Tin, Push-Up, Weighted, Mid Drip, 8½ In.	279.00
Wood, Adjustable, Floor Stand, Holder, 23 To 30½ In.	2860.00
Wood, Adjustable Column, Turned Base, Drip Pan, Socket, 39 In.	518.00
Wood, Demi-Silvered, Pricket, Carved, Neoclassical, Vase Shape, 13½ In., Pair	3360.00
Wood, Pressed Glass Sockets, Turned, Painted Flower Base, 11½ In.	61.00
Wood, Yellow, Green, White, Brown Hurricane Shade, Birch Trees, 21¼ In.	275.00
Wood Base, Spiral, Side Ejector, Hanging Hook, 18th Century, 8 In.	345.00
Wrought Iron, 3-Footed, Wood Base, 12 In.	275.00
Wrought Iron, Adjustable, Slide, Round Drip Pan, 23 In.	385.00
Wrought Iron, Adjustable Table, Drip Pan, 3-Footed, Stand, Push-Up, 20 In.	440.00
Wrought Iron, Alpine, Holder, 7½ In.	220.00
Wrought Iron, Articulated Arm, Dovetailed Wood Base, 4 Parts, 34 In.	550.00
Wrought Iron, Hanging Splint, Twist Stem, Holder, 20½ In.	495.00
Wrought Iron, Open Twist Shaft, 11 In., Pair	165.00
Wrought Iron, Spiral, Wood Base, Holder, 7½ In.	358.00
Wrought Iron, Spiral Column, Triangular Pan, 3-Footed, Hook, 13½ In., Pair	201.00
Wrought Iron, Spiral Twist, Triangular Drip Pans, 6⅜ In., Pair	473.00
Wrought Iron, Splint Holder, 3-Footed, Trim Scissors, 49¾ In.	1485.00
Wrought Iron, Taper, Double Drip Pan, Arrowhead Form, Holder, 10¼ In.	688.00
Wrought Iron, Wood, Cantilever Arm, Holder, 18th Century, 6½ In.	77.00

CANDLEWICK *items may be listed in the Imperial Glass and Pressed Glass categories.*

CANDY CONTAINERS have been popular since the late Victorian era. Collectors have long favored the glass containers, but now all types, including tin and papier-mache, are collected. Probably the earliest glass container sold commercially was the Liberty Bell made in 1876 for sale at the Centennial Exposition. Thousands of designs were made until the cost became too high in the 1960s. By the late 1970s, reproductions were being made and sold without the candy. Containers listed here are glass unless otherwise described. A Belsnickle is a nineteenth-century figure of Father Christmas. Some candy containers may be listed in Toy or in other categories.

Angel, Bisque Head, Blue Glass Eyes, Rabbit Fur Robe, Germany, 16 In. *illus*	4125.00
Baby Chick, Glass	75.00
Barney Google, Glass	250.00
Baseball Player, Blue & White Uniform, Papier-Mache, Composition, c.1910-15, 11 In.	2241.00
Baseball Player, Mustache, Holding Ball, Original Clothes, Cloth, 9½ In.	2128.00
Belsnickle, Lichen Moss Robe, Brown Hood, Holding Sprigs, 8 In. *illus*	1495.00
Bicycle Horn, Glass, Rubber, 5¾ In.	22.00
Billiken, Closure, Glass	200.00
Black Boy, On Jack-O'-Lantern, Blue Cap, Germany, 2¾ In.	550.00
Black Cat, Arched Back, Nodder, Spring Tail, Marked, Germany, 6½ In.	550.00
Black Cat, On Jack-O'-Lantern, Composition, 3½ In. *illus*	1100.00
Black Cat, Painted, Glass, 3½ In.	1430.00
Boy, Rabbit Suit, Holding Easter Egg, Gold, Blue, Pink, Composition, 7¼ In.	88.00
Car, Jeep Scout, Embossed On Sides, Willys Jeep, Closure On Side, Glass	30.00
Car, Oldsmobile, Red, Black, Glass, 1941, 7¾ In.	385.00
Car, West Bros. Co. Limousine, Red Tin Wheels, Closure, Glass	200.00
Carrot Man, Black Face, White Top Hat, Germany, 4 In.	110.00
Cat, Lying On Floor, Playing With Ball, Separates At Head, Composition, 10 In. *illus*	1610.00
Chick In Eggshell Car, Glass	250.00
Clock, Mantel, Red Paint, Paper Dial, Glass	150.00
Clock, Painted, Glass	80.00
Dog, Bulldog, Round Base, Victory Glass, c.1930, 4¹⁄₁₆ x 2 In.	50.00
Dog, Bulldog, Seated, Painted, Glass	138.00
Dog, Mutt, No. 11, Glass Hat	100.00
Dog, Pug, 3 In. *illus*	440.00
Dog, Sitting, Black Eyes, Glass, 3 x 2½ In.	25.00
Doll, Sleep Eyes, Open Mouth, Teeth, Wig, Wax, Rattan Cover, Leon Lamothe, France, 9¾ In.	220.00
Donkey & Cart, Glass, 2 x 4½ In.	18.00 to 25.00
Drug Store, Village, Tin, 3 In.	40.00

Candlestick, Silver Plate, Oval, Reeded & Gadrooned Border, Old Sheffield, 5½ In., Pair
$431.00

Candlestick, Sterling Silver, Stepped Spread Foot Kalo, 7½ x 4 In.
$1680.00

TIP

Always use a metal polish on the metal it was made for. Don't clean silver with pewter or chrome polish. The wrong formulation may scratch the metal.

C

Candy Container, Angel,
Bisque Head, Blue Glass Eyes,
Rabbit Fur Robe, Germany, 16 In.
$4125.00

TIP

*Most glass candy
container reproductions
do not have original-
looking closures or
paint or old candy.*

Candy Container, Belsnickle,
Lichen Moss Robe, Brown Hood,
Holding Sprigs, 8 In.
$1495.00

Egg, Red, Black Cats, Arched Backs, Dresden Paper Trim, Germany, 4 In.	550.00
Elephant, Pink, Styrene Plastic, 3¼ x 3 x 2 In.	12.00
Elephant With Howdah, Closure, Glass	200.00
Engine House, Village, Tin, 3 In.	130.00
Farmer, In Overalls, Jack-O'-Lantern Face, Composition, Germany, 5 In.	550.00
Fire Engine, Blue Glass, Closure	75.00
Fox, Learned, Closure, Glass	150.00
Foxy Grandpa On Rabbit, Nodding Head, Fur Covered Rabbit, Germany, 7 In.	335.00
Girl & Cat, By Pumpkin, 3 In.	385.00
Girl Nodder, Pulling Pumpkin, 4 In.	385.00
Gun, Mercury Glass, 3¾ x 7½ In.	40.00
Gun, Pistol, Glass, 8 x 4½ In.	60.00
Gun, Pistol, Green Glass, 6 In.	18.00
Happifats On Drum, Closure, Glass	400.00
Hat, Military, 2 Eagles, Ribbed, Glass, Play-Toy Co., 1920-30, 3 x 3¾ In.	65.00
Hat Box, World Travel Labels, Pressed Paper, Dresden *illus*	248.00
Hen On Nest, Glass, 4½ x 5 x 2½ In.	32.00
Iron, Clear Glass, Plug	40.00
Jack-O'-Lantern, Plastic, Union Products Inc., 1950s, 3½ In.	25.00
Jack-O'-Lantern, Slanted Eyes, Closure, Glass	350.00
Jack-O'-Lantern, White Dress, Yellow Boots, Marked, Germany, 4½ In.	248.00
Jack-O'-Lantern Face, Black Top Hat, Squeaker Toy, 6½ In.	715.00
Jack-O'-Lantern Head, On Owl's Body, Lantern, Composition, 6 In.	1870.00
Jack-O'-Lantern Woman, Cardboard Face, Hat, Crepe Paper Clothes, Germany, 8 In.	248.00
Jetson, Sprockets, Candy Cigarettes, 2 x 3¼ x 5 In.	143.00
Jitney Bus, Glass, Tin Top, Metal Wheels, 4 In. *illus*	660.00
Kitten, Walking, Gray Stripes, Cloth Collar, Composition, 3½ x 4¾ In.	187.00
Koala Bear, Stippled Glass, Bakelite, Marked, San Diego Zoo, 6½ In.	40.00
Lantern, Glass, Paper Label, Marked, Gallery Originals, 6½ In.	12.00
Lantern, Red Tin Top & Bottom, Glass, U.S.A. Avor, 3½ In.	33.00
Lantern, Victory Glass, 4 In.	40.00
Lantern, Wire Bail, Tin Screw Lid, Glass, 7½ In.	65.00
Liberty Bell, Green, Pressed Glass, Westmoreland, c.1920	55.00
Man-In-The-Moon, Smiling, Ball Form, Cardboard, 3½ In.	605.00
Orange, Whimsical Man, Vest, Green Hat, 6 In.	193.00
PEZ, Boy With Cap, Hard Plastic, Vinyl Hair, Cap, 4½ In.	45.00
PEZ, Donald Duck, 1960s, 4¼ In.	143.00
PEZ, Easter Bunny, With Palette & Paintbrush, Plastic, 1950s, 4½ In. *illus*	288.00
PEZ, Mickey Mouse, Plastic, 1960s, 4 In.	143.00
PEZ, Peter Pan, Hard Plastic, Vinyl Hair, Cap, 1960s, 4¼ In.	112.00
PEZ, Pluto, Movable Ears, 1960s	12.00
PEZ, Santa Claus, Plastic, 1950s, 3¾ In.	75.00
PEZ, Space Trooper, Blue, Plastic, 1950s, 4 In. *illus*	173.00
PEZ, Spaceman, Plastic, 1950s, 4½ In.	100.00
PEZ, Spaceman, Raised Letters, Cocoa-Marsh, Cereal Premium, 1950s, 4 In. *illus*	127.00
Piano, Wood, 3-Footed, Grandette Mfg., Chicago, 6 x 8¾ In.	176.00
Policeman, Bobby, Blue Eyes, Mustache, Wire Handle, Paper	4400.00
Pouch The Dog, Glass, 1940s	20.00
Princess Theatre, Village, Tin, 3 In.	40.00
Pumpkin Man, On Duck, Spring Arms, Marked, Germany	880.00
Rabbit, Basket On Arm, Closure, Glass	150.00
Rabbit, Blue & White Shirt, Blue Shorts, Purple Hat, Composition, Cloth, Germany, 9 In.	330.00
Rabbit, Bowtie, Egg Crate, Painted, 10 In.	121.00
Rabbit, Brown Flocked, Carrot In Backpack, Glass Eyes, Germany, 1920, 6 In.	110.00
Rabbit, Carrot In Mouth, Standing, Brown, Beige, Composition, 12⅝ In.	660.00
Rabbit, Clown Suit, Polka Dots, Composition, 7¾ In.	99.00
Rabbit, Crouching, Closure, Glass	150.00
Rabbit, Lying Down, Brown, Black, White, Grass, Cardboard, Composition, 5⅝ x 7 In.	55.00
Rabbit, Pulling Cart, Composition, Stamped, Germany, 7¼ In.	99.00
Rabbit, Pulling Cart, Duck, Wood, Composition, c.1920, 8 In.	650.00
Rabbit, Pulling Moss Covered Cart, Composition, 4⅜ x 8⅞ In.	275.00
Rabbit, Seated, Glass	140.00
Rabbit, Standing, Carrot In Front Paws, Brown, Orange, Composition, 9⅛ In.	248.00
Rabbit, Ukulele, Red & White Shirt, Yellow Bow, Spring Ears, Stamped, Germany, 7½ In.	33.00
Rabbit, Walking, Brown, Composition, 9¼ x 9⅝ In.	440.00
Rabbit, Walking, Painted, Glass Eyes, Separates At Neck, Germany, 9½ In. *illus*	546.00

Candy Container, Black Cat,
On Jack-O-Lantern,
Composition, 3½ In.
$1100.00

Candy Container, Hat Box,
World Travel Labels,
Pressed Paper, Dresden
$248.00

Candy Container, PEZ,
Space Trooper, Blue, Plastic,
1950s, 4 In.
$173.00

Candy Container, Cat,
Lying On Floor, Playing With Ball,
Separates At Head,
Composition, 10 In.
$1610.00

Candy Container, Jitney Bus,
Glass, Tin Top,
Metal Wheels, 4 In.
$660.00

Candy Container, Dog,
Pug, 3 In.
$440.00

Candy Container, PEZ,
Easter Bunny, With Palette & Paintbrush,
Plastic, 1950s, 4½ In.
$288.00

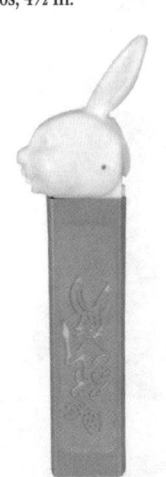

Candy Container, PEZ,
Spaceman, Raised Letters,
Cocoa-Marsh, Cereal Premium,
1950s, 4 In.
$127.00

Candy Container, Rabbit,
Walking, Painted,
Glass Eyes, Separates At Neck,
Germany, 9½ In.
$546.00

Candy Container, Santa Claus,
In Chimney, Cardboard, Paper,
Cotton Santa, Lithographed Face, 6 In.
$385.00

Candy Container, Skier, Child,
Bisque Head & Hands, Glass Eyes,
White Snowsuit, Wood Skis, 9 In.
$1265.00

Candy Container, Santa Claus,
Bisque Head, Crepe Paper Suit,
Composition Hands,
On Box, Germany
$138.00

Candy Container, Santa Claus,
On Elephant, Elephant Nodder Head,
Container Under Blanket, 6 In.
$880.00

Candy Container, Spark Plug,
Horse, Orange Blanket, Glass,
King Features, Copyright 1923, 3 In.
$115.00

Candy Container, Santa Claus,
Composition, Red Cotton Robe,
Separates At Legs, Box, 24 In.
$4125.00

Candy Container, Santa Claus,
On Zeppelin, Container In Rocket,
Germany, 6 x 5 In.
$770.00

Candy Container, Turkey,
Thanksgiving, Papier-Mache,
Painted, Metal Feet, 7 In.
$275.00

Rocking Horse, Clown Rider, Clear Glass	225.00
Rolling Pin, Closure, Glass	275.00
Roosevelt Bears, Bugle Form, Milk Glass, c.1910, 5½ In.	295.00
Rooster, Composition, Multicolored, Metal Legs, 3 In.	83.00
Rooster, Composition, Multicolored, Metal Legs, Germany, 10½ In.	880.00
Rooster, Composition, Multicolored, Wood Legs, Mounted On Board, 5¼ In.	83.00
Sack, String Attached To Top, 7 Bisque Babies, Composition, 2¾ In.	33.00
Santa Claus, At Chimney, Glass	110.00
Santa Claus, Banded Coat, Closure, Glass	300.00
Santa Claus, Belsnickle, Holding Feather Tree, White Coat, Composition, 10½ In.	660.00
Santa Claus, Bisque Head, Crepe Paper Suit, Composition Hands, On Box, Germany ...*illus*	138.00
Santa Claus, Composition, Painted, Molded, Mica Snow, 1890, 16 In.	2860.00
Santa Claus, Composition, Red Cotton Robe, Separates At Legs, Box, 24 In. ....*illus*	4125.00
Santa Claus, Holds Sucker, Bottle Brush Tree, Plastic, 1950s, 3¼ x 4 In.	34.00
Santa Claus, In Chimney, Cardboard, Paper, Cotton Santa, Lithographed Face, 6 In. ...*illus*	385.00
Santa Claus, On Elephant, Elephant Nodder Head, Container Under Blanket, 6 In. .....*illus*	880.00
Santa Claus, On Green Skis, Holds 10 Lollipops, Sears, 1940s, 4½ In.	21.00
Santa Claus, On Zeppelin, Container In Rocket, Germany, 6 x 5 In. ....*illus*	770.00
Santa Claus, Plastic Head, 2 Piece, Closure	100.00
Santa Claus, Square Chimney, Closure, Glass	450.00
Santa Claus, With Double Cuff, Closure, Glass	200.00
Santa's Boot, Candy Closure, Sticker, Cardboard	35.00
School House, Village, Tin, 3 In.	40.00
Skeleton Ghost, Cardboard, Composition, Muslin Robe, Germany, 6 In.	825.00
Skier, Child, Bisque Head & Hands, Glass Eyes, White Snowsuit, Wood Skis, 9 In. ......*illus*	1265.00
Skookum, Closure, Glass	200.00 to 350.00
Snowman, Mittens Around Neck, Tin, Darlington, Box, 8 In.	7.00
Spark Plug, Horse, Orange Blanket, Glass, King Features, Copyright 1923, 3 In. ......*illus*	115.00
Spark Plug, Horse, Painted, Cast Iron	250.00
Spinning Top, Metal, Victory Glass Co., 1920s, 3¾ In.	14.00
Tank, Marked, Victory Glass, 2⅛ x 4⅛ x 1⅝ In.	40.00
Telephone, Glass, Plastic Mouthpiece, Contents, Stough Co., Pa., 3½ In.	85.00
Telephone, Kiddie, With Candy, Glass	45.00
Telephone, Large Glass Receiver	200.00
Toonerville Trolley, Depot Line, Glass, Fontaine Fox, 1922, 3½ In.	560.00
Toys & Confectionary Store, Village, Tin, 3 In.	40.00
Turkey, Black, Red, Composition, Metal Legs, 4½ x 8½ In.	358.00
Turkey, Composition, Metal Legs, Multicolored, Germany, 14¼ In.	1650.00
Turkey, Fan Of Feathers, Multicolored, Composition, Metal Legs, Stamped, Germany, 5¼ In.	99.00
Turkey, Small Fan Of Feathers, Multicolored, Composition, Metal Legs, 4 In.	209.00
Turkey, Thanksgiving, Papier-Mache, Painted, Metal Feet, 7 In. ....*illus*	275.00
Uncle Sam Hat, Closure, Glass	75.00
Uncle Sam On Rabbit, Composition, 5 x 6 In.	990.00
Veggie Man, On Chicken, Springs For Arms, Marked, Germany, 4 In.	495.00
Veggie Man, On Gourd, Spring On Nose, 3½ In.	303.00
Veggie Man, Seated, Yellow Shirt, Black Shoes & Hat, 4 In.	165.00
Witch, On Black Cat, Mohair, Glass Eyes, Composition Head, 9 x 13 In.	8250.00
Witch, Smiling, Composition, 6 In.	4950.00

CANES and walking sticks were used by every well-dressed man in the nineteenth century, but by World War I the style had changed. Today canes are used by few but the infirm. Collectors prize old canes made with special features, like hidden swords, whiskey flasks, or risqué pictures seen through peepholes. Examples with solid gold heads or made from exotic materials are among the higher-priced canes. See also Scrimshaw.

Animal Handle, Wood, Carved, 8 In.	117.00
Eagle Handle, Tapered Ebony Shaft, Carved, Inset Black Eyes, c.1850, 34¼ In.	1675.00
Face, Tree, Stylized Heart, Cross, Bird, c.1877, 35¾ In.	110.00
Glass, Blown, Light Green, Spiral Twist Handle, 36 In.	11.00
Head, Black Man, Carved, Painted, Smiling, Applied Stone Eyes, Teeth, Folk Art, 35 In.	500.00
Horn, English Silver Ferule, Hallmark, Monogram, 1899, 34 In.	345.00
Ivory, 2 Dog Heads, Glass Eyes, Horn Ferrule, T-Shape Handle, Hardwood Shaft, 35 In.	230.00
Ivory, 5 Cat Faces, Jet Bead Eyes, Silver Collar, Brass Ferrule, Hardwood Shaft, 35½ In.	575.00
Ivory, Alligator, Mouth Open, Embossed Gold Collar, Ebonized Wood Shaft, 35¾ In. ...*illus*	345.00
Ivory, Buffalo Head, Carved, Silver Collar, Rosewood Shaft, 34½ In.	920.00
Ivory, Child, Sleeping In Bed, Rosewood Shaft, L-Shape Handle, Horn Ferrule, 34 In.	403.00

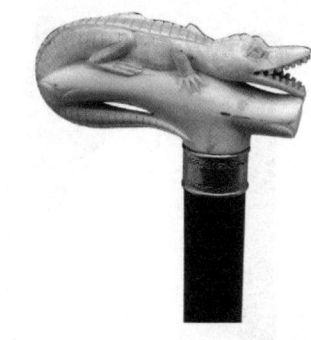

Cane, Ivory, Alligator, Mouth Open, Embossed Gold Collar, Ebonized Wood Shaft, 35¾ In. $345.00

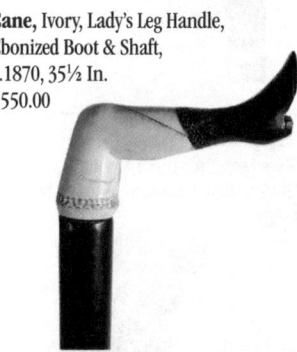

Cane, Ivory, Lady's Leg Handle, Ebonized Boot & Shaft, c.1870, 35½ In. $550.00

Cane, Novelty, Opera-Glass Handle, Mother-Of-Pearl, Gilt Metal, Enamel, France, 36 In. $550.00

Cane, Novelty, Stiletto Hatchet,
Pierced Steel, Metal Ferrule,
Bamboo Shaft, 35 In.
$250.00

Cane, Wood, Dog Head,
Glass Eyes, Pull-Down Mouth,
Silver Collar, Tapered Shaft, 36¾ In.
$460.00

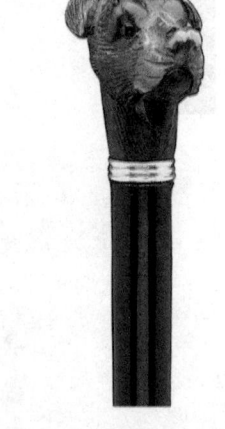

Cane, Wood, Parrot Head,
Painted, Horn Ferrule,
Malacca Shaft, 37 In.
$288.00

Ivory, Dog, Retriever, Open Mouth, Glass Eyes, Horn Ferrule, Walnut Wood Shaft, 34 In.	575.00
Ivory, Dog, St. Bernard, Basket In Mouth, L-Shape Handle, Inscribed, 35 In.	450.00
Ivory, Dove, Oriental, Glass Eyes, Textured Feathers, Bamboo Shape, 34 In.	1150.00
Ivory, Eagle, Branch, Leaf Cluster, Brass Collar, Ebonized Shaft, 36 In.	460.00
Ivory, Elephant, Dark Collar, Ivory Ferrule, Rosewood Shaft, 36 In.	720.00
Ivory, Finial, Captain's, Renaissance, Carved, Engraved, Brass, Globe Shape, 3¼ In.	270.00
Ivory, Fox Den, Stag Horn Shape, L-Shape Handle, Stick Wood Shaft, 34½ In.	805.00
Ivory, Lady's Leg Handle, Ebonized Boot & Shaft, c.1870, 35½ In. ....*illus*	550.00
Ivory, Lion, Female, Ebony Shaft, Anglo-Indian, Early 20th Century, 39¼ In.	288.00
Ivory, Lion Head, Fur, Open Mouth, Glass Eyes, Gold Collar, Ebonized Shaft, 37 In.	690.00
Ivory, Mice Eating Corn On The Cob, Oriental Flowers, Birds, Brass Ferrule, 36 In.	575.00
Ivory, Narwhal, Knot Top, Baleen Bands, Silver Tip, 36 In.	4600.00
Ivory, Narwhal, Unicorn Of The Sea, Repousse Brass Cap On Handle, Ebony Tip, 48 In.	2875.00
Ivory, Silver Collar, Tapered, Ebony Shaft, L-Shape Handle, Engraved, 35½ In.	115.00
Ivory, Tiger, Crouching, Pierced Tail, Glass Eyes, L-Shape Handle, Exotic Wood Shaft, 36 In.	660.00
Novelty, Doctor's, Silver Knob, Black Paint, Masonic Calipers, Surgical Instruments, 35 In.	172.00
Novelty, Opera-Glass Handle, Mother-Of-Pearl, Gilt Metal, Enamel, France, 36 In. .....*illus*	550.00
Novelty, Peep Hole, Monkey Head With Cap, Glass Eyes, 33 In.	77.00
Novelty, Phrenology, Ivory Handle, Marked Head, Decoder, Snakewood Shaft, c.1850	6160.00
Novelty, Stiletto Hatchet, Pierced Steel, Metal Ferrule, Bamboo Shaft, 35 In. ....*illus*	250.00
Presentation, Doctor's, Silver Plated Handle, Syringe & Scalpel Inside, 1892, 35 In.	230.00
Silver Overlay, Rooster Head, Double, Metal Ferrule, Hardwood Crook Shaft, 35½ In.	575.00
Sterling Silver, Sheep Head, Modeled Fur, Horn Ferrule, Ebonized Shaft, 34 In.	575.00
Sterling Silver, Swan, Glass Eyes, Feathers, L-Shape, Beak, Exotic Wood Shaft, 34½ In.	1035.00
Sword, Bamboo Shaft, Brass Collar, Push Button Release, 34 In.	144.00
Walking Stick, Abraham Lincoln, Lincoln Inaugural, His Fence Rail, Silver Grip	4183.00
Walking Stick, Alligators, Spiral Decoration, Early 20th Century, 38 In.	345.00
Walking Stick, Bear, Dancing, Holding Grapevine, Inserted Tin Pan, 40 x 20 In.	5875.00
Walking Stick, Bear, Standing, Outstretched Paws, Footed Base, Copper Pan, 40 In.	2350.00
Walking Stick, Carved, Ebony, Chinese Style Decoration, Silver Knob, Copper Tip, 36 In.	92.00
Walking Stick, Carved Face, Tall Hat, Relief, 39½ In.	39.00
Walking Stick, Ivory, Boar Head, Carved, France, 19th Century	1404.00
Walking Stick, Ivory, Horse Head, Edwardian, 4¼ In.	527.00
Walking Stick, Ivory Knob, Mother-Of-Pearl, Baleen Star, Silver Discs, c.1840	795.00
Walking Stick, Snake, Coiling, Red, Black, Early 20th Century, 37 In.	71.00
Walking Stick, Spiral, Human Figure Handle, c.1890, 10-In. Figure	9500.00
Walking Stick, Telescope Handle, 3 Draw, Scrimshaw, Stanley, London, 36½ In.	336.00
Walking Stick, Wood, Bird Of Prey, Rabbit, Vine Shaft, Ivory Tip, Richard R. Haines, 34 In.	2151.00
Walking Stick, Wood, Carved, Folk Art, 37 In.	717.00
Wood, Bird, Carved Feathers, Sawtooth Cuff, White & Gray Paint, 35 In.	2310.00
Wood, Burl Knot, Man's Head, Beard, Mustache, Glass Eyes, Bone Ferrule, 39½ In.	200.00
Wood, Dog, Great Dane, Detailed Fur, Glass Eyes, Closed Mouth, Birch Shaft, 36 In.	1840.00
Wood, Dog, Running, Relief Carved Horse On Shaft, Old Brown Paint, 35½ In.	248.00
Wood, Dog Head, Brown, Glass Eyes, Pull-Down Articulating Mouth, Silver Collar, 37 In.	460.00
Wood, Dog Head, Foxhound, Painted, Glass Eyes, Mottled Shaft, 37¾ In.	1150.00
Wood, Dog Head, Glass Eyes, Pull-Down Mouth, Silver Collar, Tapered Shaft, 36¾ In. ..*illus*	460.00
Wood, Ebonized, Gold Filled Heads, Repousse Flowers, Scrolled, Victorian, 2 Piece	205.00
Wood, Gold Filled Top, Samuel Daniels, R.F.S. & Co., 19th Century, 33 In.	316.00
Wood, Monk Handle, Shoulder Bust, Dark Finish, 43 In.	403.00
Wood, Parrot Head, Painted, Horn Ferrule, Malacca Shaft, 37 In. ....*illus*	288.00
Wood, Snake Head, Swallowing Shaft, Spread Wing Eagle, Indian In Headdress, 35 In.	138.00
Wood, Yew, Wild Boar, Oak Leaves, Fierce Face, Garnet Eyes, Silver, c.1870, 36½ In.	863.00

CANTON CHINA is blue-and-white ware made near the city of Canton, in China, from about 1785 to 1895. It is hand decorated with Chinese scenes. Canton is part of the group of porcelains known today as Chinese Export Porcelain.

Basket, Undertray, Landscape, Reticulated Sides, 3¼ x 8 x 6¾ In.	632.00
Basket, Undertray, Reticulated Sides, Strap Handles, 3¾ x 6¼ x 5¼ In.	1380.00
Bidet, House, Landscape, Figure-8 Form, Mahogany Base, Turned Legs, Early 19th Century	1912.00
Bowl, Riverscape, Cut Corner, Late 19th Century, 10 In.	633.00
Bowl, Riverscape, Scalloped, 10 In.	388.00
Bowl, Round, Notched & Shaped Rim, 10 In. ....*illus*	633.00
Bowl, Scalloped, Orange Peel Bottom, 19th Century, 2¼ x 10 In.	460.00
Bowl, Undertray, Fruit Basket, Cut Corner, Pierced Design, 3¾ x 4¾ In.	558.00
Bowl, Vegetable, Footed, Orange Peel Glaze, Boar Head Handles, Stem-Shaped Finial, 12½ In.	748.00

C

Butter, Cover, 12-Sided Base, Pointed Finial, 7 x 5 In. . . . .*illus*	115.00
Charger, Back Painted, Asian Leaf Spray, 19th Century, 16¼ In.	470.00
Coffeepot, Riverscape, Dome Lid, Ball Finial, 9½ In.	359.00
Cup & Saucer, Demitasse, Late 1800s, 2⅝ In., 14 Piece	264.00
Cup & Saucer, Rose, 19th Century, 2⅛ & 6¼ In., 6 Piece	264.00
Dish, Hot Water, Riverscape, 19th Century, 9½ In.	325.00
Ginger Jar, Hawthorne, Cover, 10 x 8 In.	275.00
Jug, Beer, Leaves, Rain & Cloud Border, Bulbous, Long Neck, 19th Century, 12½ In.	1076.00
Jug, Cider Cover, Foo Dog Finial, Strap Handles, Leaf Terminal, 8 In.	2938.00
Jug, Cider, Cover, Riverscape, Foo Dog Finial, 19th Century, 6¾ In.	478.00
Pitcher, Applied Handle, Fishtail End, 6½ In.	173.00
Pitcher, Riverscape, 19th Century, 5¾ In.	179.00
Planter, Landscape, 7½ x 8½ In.	20.00
Plate, Bread & Butter, Bridge & Pagoda In Landscape, 5¾ In., 8 Piece	115.00
Plate, Soup, 19th Century, 9 In., 8 Piece	880.00
Platter, 8-Sided, 11¾ x 14½ In.	288.00
Platter, City Scene, 8-Sided, Cut Corner, 17 x 13¾ In.	920.00
Platter, Cut Corner, 16½ x 20 In.	748.00
Platter, Late 19th Century, 12 x 9 In.	173.00
Platter, Oblong Hexagonal, Chinese Export, Early 19th Century, 20 x 16 In.	1150.00
Platter, Pagodas On Island, Oval, 12½ x 9¼ In.	20.00
Platter, Riverscape, 19th Century, 15 x 11¾ In.	568.00
Sauce, Loop Handle, Scalloped, Spout, 3 x 7½ In.	230.00
Soup, Dish, Bridge & Pagoda, 10 In., Pair	115.00
Teapot, Flowers, Panels, Interior Scenes, Bamboo Handle, c.1900, 4½ In.	104.00
Teapot, Landscape, High Dome Lid, 9 In.	460.00
Tureen, Bridge & Pagodas, Boar's Head Handles, Cut Corner, 5 x 12 In.	288.00
Tureen, Cover, Boar's Head Handle, 19th Century, 9 x 12 x 9 In.	1265.00
Tureen, Cover, Stem Knop, Boar's Head Handles, Chamfered, Footed, 8½ x 8¾ In.	323.00
Vase, Famille Rose, Tapering Body, Lion's Head Handles, 19th Century, 23½ In.	540.00
Vase, Panels, Dignitaries, Warriors, Foo Dog & Puppy Handles, Baluster Shape, 34½ In. *illus*	6000.00
Vase, Scroll, Flowers, Butterfly, Bird, Turquoise Ground, c.1920	210.00

CAPO-DI-MONTE porcelain was first made in Naples, Italy, from 1743 to 1759. The factory moved near Madrid, Spain, reopened in 1771, and worked to 1834. Since that time, the Doccia factory of Italy acquired the molds and is using the crown and N mark. Societe Richard Ceramica is a modern-day firm often referred to as Ginori or Capo-di-Monte. This company also uses the crown and N mark.

Candlestick, Leaves, Pink & Green, Gold Trim, 2 x 2½ In., Pair	20.00
Candy Dish, Swan, Applied Flowers, Leaves, Marked	20.00
Casket, Temple Shape, Shaped Reserves, Classical Scenes, 4 Squat Feet, 7½ x 14 In. . . .*illus*	2271.00
Compote, Cupids, Flowers, 13¾ x 12 In.	1450.00
Figurine, Classical Youth, Man With Shield, Sword, Fleur-De-Lis In Circle, c.1755, 15 In. . . .	3900.00
Figurine, Courtier, c.1900, 13 In.	105.00
Figurine, Dancer, Orange Shawl, 9 In.	82.00
Figurine, Geppetto, Making Pinocchio, 8 x 9 In.	94.00
Figurine, Man, Seated On Park Bench, 7 x 8 In.	88.00
Figurine, Peasant Woman, Marked, Signed, Lartori, 12 x 6½ In.	300.00
Pitcher, Peaches & Vines, Ivory Wood Grain Textured Ground, Marked, 9 x 7 In.	30.00
Pitcher, Underplate, Gilt Scrolls, Paneled Figural Scenes, Portraits, 14 In. . . . .*illus*	300.00
Plaque, Pan At Censer, Attendants, Canted Corners, Cupids, Openwork, Frame, 20 x 17 In. . .	633.00
Teapot, Cover, Ball Shape, 3 Paw Feet, Scroll Handle, Fruit Finial, 6 x 10 In.	374.00
Urn, Cover, 3-Footed Pedestal, Tricornered Base, Reticulated Band, 12 In., Pair	489.00
Urn, Tripod Base, Gilt, Putti Scenes, Lamp Mounted, 36 In.	142.00
Vase, Hand Painted, Scenic, 21 x 11 In., Pair	146.00

CAPTAIN MARVEL was introduced in February 1940 in Whiz comic books. An orphan named Billy Batson met the wizard, Shazam, and whenever he said the magic word he was transformed into a superhero. A movie serial was released in 1940. The comic was discontinued in 1954. A second Captain Marvel appeared in 1966, a third in 1967. Only the original was transformed by shouting "Shazam."

Bank, Magic Dime Saver, Captain Marvel Flying, Holding Money, Square 2½ In.	140.00
Beanie, Skull Cap, Felt, 3 Images, Label, Fawcett Publications, 1945, 10 In.	280.00
Blotter, Captain Marvel, Scorpion, Fawcett Publications, 1941, 3¼ x 6⅞ In.	336.00
Book, Punch-Outs, Comic Heroes, Unused, 11¾ x 8½ In., 6 Pages	551.00

Canton China, Bowl, Round, Notched & Shaped Rim, 10 In. $633.00

Canton China, Butter, Cover, 12-Sided Base, Pointed Finial, 7 x 5 In. $115.00

Canton China, Vase, Panels, Dignitaries, Warriors, Foo Dog & Puppy Handles, Baluster Shape, 34½ In. $6000.00

TIP

Mayonnaise can be used to remove old masking tape, stickers, or labels from glass or china.

Capo-Di-Monte, Casket,
Temple Shape, Shaped Reserves,
Classical Scenes,
4 Squat Feet, 7½ x 14 In.
$2271.00

Capo-Di-Monte, Pitcher,
Underplate, Gilt Scrolls,
Paneled Figural Scenes,
Portraits, 14 In.
$300.00

Card, Greeting, Valentine,
Girl In Yellow Rain Suit,
To My Valentine, Cardboard, Germany
$2.00

Figure, Captain Marvel Jr., Plastic, Kerr Company, 1946, 5 In.	739.00
Figure, Mary Marvel, Kerr Company, 1946, 5½ In.	1293.00
Figure, Mary Marvel, Plastic, Painted, R.W. Kerr, Box, 1946, 7 x 4 x 2¼ In.	1848.00
Patch, Felt, Captain Marvel Jr., Shield Shape, Fawcett Publications, 1946, 3 x 4 In.	168.00
Patch, Felt, Mary Marvel, Shield Shape, Fawcett Publications, 1946, 3 x 4 In.	185.00
Pennant, Felt, Clouds, Fawcett Publications, 1948, 8 x 14½ In.	246.00
Pin, Captain Marvel Club, Shazam, Lithograph, 1946, ⅞ In.	164.00
Pin, Captain Marvel Club, Shazam, Tin Lithograph, 1948, 1⅛ In.	56.00
Ring, Compass, Rocket Raider, Brass, Adjustable Band, c.1946	672.00
Wristwatch, Chromed Metal Case, Green Strap, Fawcett, Box, 1948, 6¼ x 3¾ In.	840.00

CAPTAIN MIDNIGHT began as a network radio show in September 1940. The first comic book appeared in July 1941. Captain Midnight was really the aviator Captain Albright, who was to defeat the Nazis. A movie serial was made in 1942 and a comic strip was published for a short time. The comic book version of Captain Midnight ended his career in 1948. Radio premiums are the prized collector memorabilia today.

Badge, Book, Secret Squadron, Instructions, Radio Premium, Envelope, 1945	275.00
Badge, Secret Squadron, Decoder, 1945, 2½ In.	73.00
Badge, Secret Squadron, Decoder, Photograph, 1942, 2⅛ In.	164.00
Cup, Secret Squadron, Plastic, Decal, 3 x 4 In.	18.00
Decoder, Brass, Plastic, Ovaltine, 1948, 2 In.	125.00 to 164.00
Folder, Official Commission Secret Instructions, 1942, 6½ x 3¼ In.	224.00
Handbook, Official Secret, Mailing Envelope, Ovaltine, 1941, 3¼ x 6½ In.	271.00
Mug, Ovaltine, Heart Of A Hearty Breakfast, Shake-Up, Blue Lid	75.00
Ring, Mystic Sun, Gold Color, Brass Base, Pamphlet, Ovaltine, 1946	616.00

CARAMEL SLAG, *see Imperial Glass category.*

CARDS listed here include advertising cards (often called trade cards), baseball cards, playing cards, and others. Color photographs were rare in the nineteenth century, so companies gave away colorful cards with pictures of children, flowers, products, or related scenes that promoted the company name. These were often collected and stored in albums. Baseball cards also date from the nineteenth century when they were used by tobacco companies as giveaways. Gum cards were started in 1933, but it was not until after World War II that the bubble gum cards favored today were produced. Today over 1,000 cards are issued each year by the gum companies. Related items may be found in the Christmas, Halloween, Paper, Postcard, and Movie categories.

Advertising, Adam's Yellow Kid Chewing Gum, No. 4, Yacht Theme, 1896, 2¾ x 4⅜ In.	60.00
Advertising, Adam's Yellow Kid Chewing Gum, No. 24, Scotsman, 1896, 2¾ x 4⅜ In.	47.00
Advertising, American Eagle Toy Savings Bank, Eagle, Eaglets, Frame, c.1883	110.00
Advertising, Continental Insurance Co., 4 Pug Dogs, 5¼ x 8¼ In.	60.00
Advertising, Dam-I-Ana Benedictine Invigorator, If You Appreciate Me Drink, 5 x 3¼ In.	325.00
Advertising, Geo. H. Clark & Co., Speaking Dog Bank, Frame	220.00
Advertising, Great Atlantic & Pacific Tea Co., 5 People, Baby, Cardboard, 1886, 6 x 8 In.	50.00
Advertising, Harlequin, Transformation Deck, Kenney Tobacco Co., c.1889, 52 Piece	960.00
Advertising, Humpty Dumpty Toy Savings Bank, Clown, Selchow & Righter, 5½ x 3½ In.	375.00
Advertising, J.H. Weigman & Sons, Uncle Sam Bank, Frame	220.00
Advertising, Jolly Nigger, Toy Bank, Cary, Fulton & Co., Self-Framed, Type 1, 1882 Patent	308.00
Advertising, Kennedy, Spaulding & Co., Stump Speaker Bank, Frame	220.00
Advertising, Lautz Bros. Soap, Pure Healthy, Woman In White Dress, Hat, Flowers, c.1900	12.00
Advertising, Lily Leaf Brand, Pigs, Playing Baseball, c.1900	114.00
Advertising, Lorillard's Climax Plug Tobacco, Hold-To-Light, 10 Cents, 5 x 3½ In.	150.00
Advertising, N. Klinger, Whitewater Brewery, Whitewater, Wis., 3⅝ x 6 In.	306.00
Advertising, Picture Gallery Toy Savings Bank, Excelsior Series, Self-Framed, c.1885	8960.00
Advertising, Purity Cut Plug, 10¼ x 6¼ In.	120.00
Advertising, Quaker Oats, Packing Room, 1893, 5 x 7½ In.	40.00
Advertising, Rough On Rats, 15 Cents A Box, They Must Go., Forbes, Boston, 7 x 5 In.	525.00
Advertising, S.O. Barnum & Sons, Co., Trick Pony Bank, Frame	193.00
Advertising, Samson, Largest Elephant Ever, People, W.W. Coles Colossal Shows, 8 x 5 In.	40.00
Advertising, Soapine, Dirt Killer, Whale, Kendall Mfg. Co., 6 x 3¼ In.	40.00
Advertising, Supreme Flints, Highest Quality, 24 Packs Of Flint, Japan, 10 x 6½ In.	55.00
Advertising, Trick Dog Toy Savings Bank, Self-Framed, 6 Piece, 1885 Patent	9520.00
Advertising, Trick Pony Bank, Self-Framed, Kipp Bros., 1885 Patent	392.00
Advertising, Trick Pony Bank, Self-Framed, Shepard Hardware Co., 1885 Patent	392.00
Advertising, Wahl, Ansteth & Smith, Punch & Judy Back	66.00
Advertising, Warren Powder Mills, Gunpowder, Hunting Scene, 5½ x 7 In.	198.00

Baseball, Pee Wee Reese, Bowman, No. 21, 1950	814.00
Baseball, Whitey Ford, Topps, No. 35, 1960	611.00
Basketball, Michael Jordan, Rookie, Fleer, No. 57	6065.00
Calling, Babies Head In Rose, Victorian, Hidden Name, Salesman's Sample, 2 Piece	5.00
Football, Ollie Matson, Topps, No. 50, 1959.	814.00
Football, Tom Fears, Bowman, No. 43, 1955.	987.00
Football, Sonny Jurgenson, No. 110, 1963.	1086.00
Greeting, Fortune-Teller, Young Woman By The Sea, Sipping Tea, c.1886, 5½ x 8 In.	12.00
Greeting, New Year's, Jan 1 On Scroll, Ribbons, Roses, Blue Matte, c.1930, 7¼ x 5¼ In.	12.00
Greeting, Valentine, Cutout, Watercolor Accents, Verses, Gilt Frame, Penn., 18 x 18 In.	431.00
Greeting, Valentine, Girl In Yellow Rain Suit, To My Valentine, Cardboard, Germany ...*illus*	2.00
Greeting, Valentine, Heavy Paper, 6 Hearts, Tulips, Starflower, Verse, 1820, 10 x 12 In.	710.00
Greeting, Valentine, Puppy With String Tied To Tail, 1950s, 4 x 8 In.	15.00
Greeting, Valentine, Sawtooth Crescent & Heart Cutouts, Verse, Frame, 1830, 12½ In.	121.00
Greeting, Valentine, Wizard Of Oz, Die Cut Glossy, 4 x 6 In.	84.00
Playing, As Nas, Tempera, On Papier-Mache, Persia, c.1860, 20 Cards	1560.00
Playing, Berlin Theatrer, Photograph, Germany, c.1900, 53 Cards	2040.00
Playing, Black & Red Plaid, P. Grimard, Paris, Late 1800s, 52 Cards	132.00
Playing, Border Index, Paper Fabrique Company, Middletown, Ohio, c.1878, 52 Cards	1200.00
Playing, Deck, Ecstasy, Maxfield Parrish, Glassine Wrap, Slipcase Box, 1930s	233.00
Playing, Deck, The Waterfall, Maxfield Parrish, Slipcase Box, 1930s	256.00
Playing, Edison Mazda Lamps, Linen, Parrish, Waterfall Cover Box, c.1930	121.00
Playing, Gallant Highlanders Deck, Plaid Back, John J. Leby, N.Y., c.1845, 52 Cards	1680.00
Playing, Humphrey's Deck, Blue Geometric Back, James Y. Humphrey, Phila., c.1816, 52 Cards .	4200.00
Playing, Le Plaisier, Is My Delight, Das Vergnugen, Illustrated, Box, 24 Cards	1800.00
Playing, Metamorphosen Fur Kinder, Figures In 3 Sections, Box, 1800s, 28 Cards	240.00
Playing, Mughal Ganjifa, Ivory, Hand Painted, Lacquered, Deccan, India, Box, c.1850, 95 Cards .	7200.00
Playing, Pep Boys, Pinochle, Red Box, 1940s	126.00
Playing, Press, Brass, Palm Tree Central Screw, Elephant Heads, 4 x 5¼ x 7½ In.	1200.00
Playing, Splendid Plug Tobacco, American Playing Card. Co., c.1786, 52 Cards	180.00
Playing, Tout Est Bin Qui Finit Bien, Illustrated, 4 Series, France, Box, c.1900, 39 Of 40 Cards	180.00
Tarock, Military, Emperor Franz Josef, Deck 4, Josef Glanz, Vienna, c.1885, 2 x 4 In., 54 Piece .	600.00
Tarock, Opera, Stencil, Engraved, Carl Titze & Schinkay, Vienna, c.1870, 4 x 2½ In., 54 Piece .	1440.00
Tarot, Besancon, Woodblock, Louis Carey, Strasbourg, c.1795, 4¹³/₁₆ x 2½ In., 78 Piece	9600.00
Tarot, Dellarocca, Stencil, Ferdinando Gumppenberg, Milan, c.1830, 78 Piece	2880.00
Tarot, La Gravure Originale, Copper Engraving, Yves Jobert, France, c.1973, 12 x 7 In., 16 Piece .	1560.00
Tarot, Lombardy, Woodblock, Stencil, Ietro Milesi, c.1870, 4 x 2¼ In., 78 Piece	1440.00
Tarot, Major Arcana, Silk Screen, Taylor McCall, Bocaccio Press, Santa Fe, c.1975, 22 Piece .	960.00
Tarot, Muchery, B.P. Grimaud, Paris, c.1927, 5 x 3 In., 48 Piece	240.00
Tarot, Piedmont, Letter Press, Stencil, Torino, Alessandro Viassone, c.1926, 4 x 2 In., 78 Piece .	180.00
Tarot, Princesse, Stencil, Line Engraving, Watilliaux, Paris, c.1880, 4 x 2⅝ In., 78 Piece	180.00
Tarot, Recchi, Copper Engraving, Giacomo Recchi, Oneglia, c.1820, 4⅜ x 2½ In., 78 Piece ..	5040.00
Tarot, Stencil, Copper Engraving, Gumppenberg, Milan, c.1812, 4³/₁₆ x 2⅛ In., 78 Piece	6600.00

CARLSBAD is a mark found on china made by several factories in Germany, Austria, and Bavaria. Many pieces were exported to the United States. Most of the pieces available today were made after 1891.

Biscuit Jar, Lid, Blue Iris, Green Leaves, Marked, 6½ x 5 In.	70.00
Bowl, Purple Iridescent, Applied Gilt Handles, 3¾ In., 3 Piece ....*illus*	324.00
Dish, Mint, Pink Flowers, White Ground, Gold Rim, 4 In.	18.00
Rose Bowl, Yellow Flowers, Brown Leaves, Gold Accent, Crown Mark, 4¾ x 5 In.	85.00
Shaving Mug, Magenta Flowers, Blue Collar, Gold Squiggles, Marx & Gutherz, c.1895	59.00
Soup, Dish, Blue Flowers, Brown Vines, Marx & Gutherz, Late 1800s, 9½ In.	45.00
Tureen, Cover, Blue Flower Sprays, Handles, Marked, LS & S, c.1895-1917	55.00

CARLTON WARE was made at the Carlton Works of Stoke-on-Trent, England, beginning about 1890. The firm traded as Wiltshaw & Robinson until 1957. It was renamed Carlton Ware Ltd. in 1958. The company went bankrupt in 1995, but the name is still in use.

Bowl, Kingfisher, Rouge Royale, Enamel, Gilt, 1½ x 7½ In.	170.00
Bowl, Persian, Blue Ground, Footed, 9½ In.	221.00
Card Holder, Rouge Royale, Gold Trim, Stamped, 3¼ x 5¼ In.	85.00
Cup & Saucer, Blue On White Marbleized, Gold Trim, Art Deco, 1930s	28.00
Cup & Saucer, Blue Royale, Gold Interior, c.1920	65.00
Cup & Saucer, Cobalt Blue, Gold Interior, Angular Handle	60.00
Cup & Saucer, Dark Red Luster, Quatrefoil, Gilt Interior, Handle, 1920s	60.00

TIP

To remove old trade cards you find glued in albums, practice on the scrapbook page that's least desirable. Put the page in cool water for an hour. If the cards don't float loose, switch to hot water. But the hotter the water, the greater the risk of fading colors. Once the card is off the page, rinse the back and rub spots until you feel no more glue. Let the card air-dry until damp, then press it between blotting papers weighted down by books for a few days. (Blotting paper can be found at office supply stores.)

Carlsbad, Bowl, Purple Iridescent, Applied Gilt Handles, 3¾ In., 3 Piece
$324.00

Carlton Ware, Teapot, Cameo, Black Matte Glaze, Medallion, Dancers, Flame Luster Band, 7 In.
$300.00

Carnival Glass, Apple Tree, Pitcher, Blue, 9½ In. $300.00

Carnival Glass, April Showers, Vase, Cobalt Blue, 7 In. $65.00

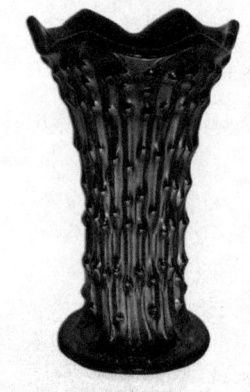

Carnival Glass, Basket, Blue $65.00

Carnival Glass, Beaded Cable, Rose Bowl, 3-Footed, Ribbed Interior, Green $90.00

Cup & Saucer, Pagoda, Black Ground, Red Rim, Gilt, Gold Interior, c.1927		95.00
Cup & Saucer, Wisteria Tree, Birds, Enamel, Green Luster, Gold Interior		135.00
Cup & Saucer, Yellow Luster, Gold Interior, c.1920		48.00
Dish, 2 Female Wrestlers, Luster, 7¼ In.		232.00
Dish, Art Deco, Rouge Royale, Dark Red, Mottled Black, Gilt, 1¾ x 12⅜ x 7¼ In.		106.00
Dish, Blue Royale, 1930s, 9 In.		103.00
Dish, Dogwood, Oval, No. 2564, 1930-40		78.00
Dish, Fish Shape, Green Purple, Marked, 4½ x 4¼ In.		50.00
Dish, Leaf Shape, Green, Red Flowers & Leaves, Incised, No. 976		50.00
Dish, New Stork, Rouge Royale, 4 x 7 In.		125.00
Eggcup, Navy Blue Shoes, Walking Ware, 1960s		28.00
Plaque, Australian Purple Lily, 10½ In.		105.00
Plate, Donkey Race, Transferware, Marked, 7½ In.		185.00
Plate, Escargot, White, Snail Shape, Raised Chain Leaf Design, 6 Wells, 7⅜ In.		20.00
Teapot, Cameo, Black Matte Glaze, Medallion, Dancers, Flame Luster Band, 7 In. *illus*		300.00
Teapot, Red Baron, Lucy May		50.00
Vase, Armand Luster, Chicks In Tree, Orange Ground, 8 In.		137.00
Vase, Cover, Pagoda, Blue Ground, 13 In.		148.00
Vase, Kang He, Pheasant, Rocks, Blue Ground, 9½ In.		179.00
Vase, Pagoda, Blue Ground, 10½ In.		127.00
Vase, Spider Web, Rouge Royale, Enamel, Gilt, Bulbous, 5 x 5 In.		240.00
Vase, Stylized Butterflies & Plants, Black & White, Orange Ground, 18 In.		499.00

CARNIVAL GLASS as an inexpensive, iridescent, pressed glass made from about 1907 to about 1925. More than 1,000 different patterns are known. Carnival glass is currently being reproduced.

Abbottmaid Ice Cream, Plate, 6th Anniversary, Ice Cream Slice, Original Mailer, 6½ In.		55.00
Acanthus, Bowl, Aqua, Deep		75.00
Acanthus, Bowl, Smoke, Deep		55.00
Acanthus, Chop Plate, Marigold		115.00 to 225.00
Acanthus, Chop Plate, Smoke		325.00
Acanthus, Compote, Dark Aqua, 5 In.		20.00
Acorn, Bowl, Ruffled Edge, Red		250.00
Acorn Burrs, Butter, Amethyst		190.00
Acorn Burrs, Pitcher, Amethyst, Signed, 1½ Qt., 9 In.		575.00
Acorn Burrs, Punch Set, Green, 8 Piece		1800.00
Acorn Burrs, Spooner, Amethyst		55.00
Acorn Burrs, Water Set, Amethyst, 7 Piece		450.00
Acorn Burrs & Bark pattern is listed here as Acorn Burrs.		
Amaryllis pattern is listed here as Tiger Lily.		
American Beauty Roses pattern is listed here as Wreath Of Roses.		
Apple Blossom Twigs, Bowl, Ruffled Edge, Peach Opalescent		85.00 to 105.00
Apple Blossom Twigs, Plate, Blue, 9 In.		205.00
Apple Blossom Twigs, Plate, White, 9 In.		125.00
Apple Tree, Pitcher, Blue, 9½ In. *illus*		300.00
April Showers, Vase, Amethyst, 11½ In.		50.00
April Showers, Vase, Cobalt Blue, 7 In. *illus*		65.00
April Showers, Vase, Lime Green, Marigold Iridescence, 13 In.		115.00
April Showers, Vase, Peacock Tail Interior, Amethyst, 12 In.		40.00
April Showers, Vase, White, 11 In.		250.00
Argonaut Shell pattern is listed here as Nautilus.		
Asters, Chop Plate, Marigold, 10 In.		200.00
Aurora pattern is listed here as Flowers.		
Australian Butterfly & Bells, Compote, Marigold		90.00
Australian Butterfly & Bush, Compote, Amethyst		120.00
Australian Emu, Compote, Marigold, 5¾ x 9¾ In.		500.00
Australian Kangaroo, Bowl, Ruffled Edge, Amethyst		250.00
Australian Kangaroo, Sauce, Ruffled Edge, Amethyst		275.00
Australian Kiwi, Sauce, Ruffled Edge, Marigold		255.00
Australian Magpie, Bowl, 8-Sided, Serrated Edge, Amethyst		65.00
Australian Magpie, Bowl, Pie Crust Edge, Amethyst		185.00
Australian Swan, Bowl, Ruffled Edge, Marigold, Large		55.00
Autumn Acorn, Bowl, Green		60.00
Autumn Acorn, Bowl, Marigold, Crimped Ruffled Edge, 8½ In.		55.00
Banded Medallion & Teardrop pattern is listed here as Beaded Bull's-Eye.		

Basket, Amethyst	60.00
Basket, Aqua Opalescent	195.00 to 325.00
Basket, Blue ....*illus*	65.00
Basket, Blue Opalescent	275.00
Basket, Ice Green	85.00
Basket, Lavender	105.00
Basket, Marigold	40.00 to 55.00
Basketweave, Basket, Open Edge, Amethyst, Small	85.00
Basketweave, Basket, Open Edge, Aqua, Small	55.00 to 95.00
Basketweave, Basket, Open Edge, Black Amethyst, Small	30.00 to 75.00
Basketweave, Basket, Open Edge, Blue, Small	40.00 to 55.00
Basketweave, Basket, Open Edge, Celeste Blue, Large	195.00
Basketweave, Basket, Open Edge, Green, Small	65.00 to 120.00
Basketweave, Basket, Open Edge, Ice Green, Large	85.00
Basketweave, Basket, Open Edge, Lime Green, Small	25.00 to 40.00
Basketweave, Basket, Open Edge, Pink, Small	80.00
Basketweave, Basket, Open Edge, Red, Small	115.00 to 175.00
Basketweave, Basket, Open Edge, Ruffled Edge, Aqua	30.00
Basketweave, Basket, Open Edge, Ruffled Edge, Celeste Blue, Small	300.00
Basketweave, Basket, Open Edge, Sides Folded Up, Aqua, Small	65.00
Basketweave, Basket, Open Edge, Sides Folded Up, Red, Small	145.00
Basketweave, Bowl, Open Edge, White, Small	150.00
Basketweave, Hat, Open Edge, Jack-In-The-Pulpit, Light Green, Red Iridescence	250.00
Battenburg Lace No. 1 pattern is listed here as Hearts & Flowers.	
Battenburg Lace No. 2 pattern is listed here as Captive Rose.	
Battenburg Lace No. 3 pattern is listed here as Fanciful.	
Beaded Bull's-Eye, Vase, Marigold, 7 In.	30.00
Beaded Cable, Rose Bowl, 3-Footed, Amethyst, 4½ In.	50.00
Beaded Cable, Rose Bowl, 3-Footed, Aqua Opalescent, Butterscotch Iridescence	165.00 to 195.00
Beaded Cable, Rose Bowl, 3-Footed, Blue	70.00
Beaded Cable, Rose Bowl, 3-Footed, Marigold	65.00
Beaded Cable, Rose Bowl, 3-Footed, Ribbed Interior, Green ....*illus*	90.00
Beaded Medallion & Teardrop pattern is listed here as Beaded Bull's-Eye.	
Beaded Shell, Mug, Marigold	25.00
Beads & Flowers, Plate, Amethyst, 6 In.	25.00
Big Basketweave, Basket, Marigold	30.00
Big Basketweave, Vase, Amethyst, 9½ In.	155.00
Big Basketweave, Vase, Amethyst, 11 In.	215.00
Big Basketweave, Vase, Blue, 11 In.	105.00
Big Basketweave, Vase, Celeste Blue, 10 In.	750.00
Big Basketweave, Vase, Marigold, 9½ In.	25.00
Big Basketweave, Vase, White, 10 In.	75.00
Blackberry, Basket, Open Edge, Amethyst	25.00
Blackberry, Basket, Open Edge, Powder Blue	35.00
Blackberry, Compote, Green	180.00
Blackberry A pattern is listed here as Blackberry.	
Blackberry B pattern is listed here as Blackberry Spray	
Blackberry Bramble, Compote, Ruffled Edge, Green	35.00 to 45.00
Blackberry Spray, Hat, Jack-In-The-Pulpit, Crimped & Ruffled Edge, Aqua Opalescent	675.00
Blackberry Spray, Hat, Ruffled Edge, Red	15.00
Blackberry Spray, Hat, Ruffled Edge, Reverse Amberina Opalescent	800.00
Blackberry Wreath, Bowl, Crimped & Ruffled Edge, Green, 10¼ In. ....*illus*	40.00
Blackberry Wreath, Bowl, Ruffled Edge, Satin, Amethyst, 7 In.	85.00
Blossomtime, Compote, Ruffled Edge, Amethyst	85.00
Blossomtime, Compote, Ruffled Edge, Marigold	85.00
Blueberry, Tumbler, Blue	40.00
Bo Peep, Mug, Marigold	35.00
Broken Arches, Punch Set, Amethyst, 13 Piece	800.00
Brooklyn Bridge, Bowl, Ruffled Edge, Marigold	135.00 to 205.00
Bull's-Eye & Beads, Vase, Amethyst, 11 In.	115.00
Bushel Basket pattern is listed here as Basket.	
Butterfly, Bonbon, Ribbed Exterior, Green	700.00
Butterfly & Berry, Berry Bowl, Marigold, Master	55.00
Butterfly & Berry, Berry Set, Blue, 7 Piece	300.00
Butterfly & Berry, Butter, Marigold	45.00
Butterfly & Berry, Fernery, Blue, Whimsy	1500.00

Carnival Glass, Blackberry Wreath, Bowl, Crimped & Ruffled Edge, Green, 10¼ In.
$40.00

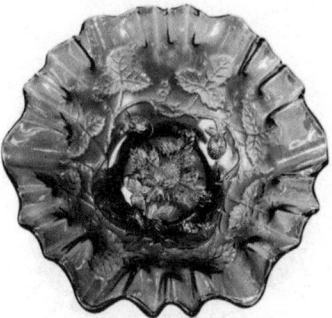

Carnival Glass
Fenton Art Glass Company tried to imitate the handmade iridescent glass of Tiffany and Loetz. In 1907 Fenton made a line called Venetian Art. It is part of what collectors now call carnival glass, mainly because the glass was often given away as prizes at carnivals.

TIP

*To clean carnival glass,
use a soft brush,
room-temperature
water, a sponge, and
a gentle detergent.
Window cleaner
is also OK.*

Carnival Glass, Butterfly & Berry,
Tumbler, Green, 6 Piece
$450.00

Carnival Glass, Butterfly & Tulip, Bowl,
Footed, Amethyst, 5¼ x 10 In.
$400.00

Carnival Glass, Daisy & Plume,
Rose Bowl, Amethyst
$165.00

Butterfly & Berry, Spooner, Blue		125.00
Butterfly & Berry, Tumbler, Green, 6 Piece	*illus*	450.00
Butterfly & Berry, Vase, Amber, 9 In.		40.00
Butterfly & Berry, Vase, Blue, 6½ In.		85.00
Butterfly & Fern, Pitcher, Blue		300.00
Butterfly & Grape pattern is listed here as Butterfly & Berry.		
Butterfly & Plume pattern is listed here as Butterfly & Fern.		
Butterfly & Stippled Rays pattern is listed here as Butterfly.		
Butterfly & Tulip, Bowl, Footed, Amethyst, 5¼ x 10 In.	*illus*	400.00
Butterfly & Tulip, Bowl, Ruffled Edge, Lavender		325.00
Buzz Saw, Cruet, Green, 4 In.		150.00 to 245.00
Buzz Saw, Cruet, Green, 6 In.		325.00
Buzz Saw, Cruet, Marigold, 6 In.		85.00
Cactus Leaf Rays pattern is listed here as Leaf Rays.		
Captive Rose, Plate, Amethyst, 9 In.		550.00
Captive Rose, Plate, Blue, 9 In.		425.00
Carolina Dogwood, Bowl, Peach Opalescent		35.00
Carolina Dogwood, Bowl, Ruffled Edge, Blue Opalescent		275.00
Cattails & Fish pattern is listed here as Fisherman's Mug.		
Cattails & Water Lily pattern is listed here as Water Lily & Cattails.		
Cherries & Mums pattern is listed here as Mikado.		
Cherry, Bowl, 3-Footed, Folded Edge, Amethyst, 8½ In.		80.00
Cherry, Bowl, Ruffled Edge, Peach Opalescent, 10 In.		85.00
Cherry, Plate, Crimped Edge, Amethyst, 6 In.		115.00
Cherry, Sauce, Ruffled Edge, Amethyst, 6 In.		55.00
Cherry & Cable, Berry Set, Marigold, 7 Piece		150.00
Cherry Chain, Bowl, Amethyst, Ruffled Edge, 10 In.		105.00 to 210.00
Cherry Chain, Plate, Blue, 6 In.		45.00 to 50.00
Cherry Wreathed pattern is listed here as Wreathed Cherry.		
Christmas Cactus pattern is listed here as Thistle.		
Christmas Plate pattern is listed here as Poinsettia.		
Christmas Rose & Poppy pattern is listed here as Six Petals.		
Chrysanthemum Wreath pattern is listed here as Ten Mums.		
Circle Scroll, Vase, Amethyst, 6 In.		115.00
Cobblestone, Bowl, Ruffled Edge, Amethyst		350.00
Cobblestone, Bowl, Ruffled Edge, Green, Silver Iridescence		110.00
Cobblestone, Bowl, Ruffled Edge, Marigold		250.00
Coin Spot, Compote, Ruffled Edge, Peach Opalescent		20.00
Colonial, Candlestick, Wisteria		250.00
Colonial Lady, Vase, Amethyst		700.00
Colonial Lady, Vase, Marigold		700.00
Columbia, Compote, Ruffled Edge, Smoke		165.00
Columbia, Plate, Dome-Footed, Whimsy, Marigold		30.00
Concave Diamonds, Tumbler, Celeste Blue		10.00
Coral, Plate, Marigold, 9 In.		2500.00
Corinth, Vase, Aqua, 8 In.		50.00
Corn, Bottle, Marigold		165.00
Corn, Bottle, Smoke		450.00
Corn, Vase, Stalk Base, Amethyst		275.00
Corn, Vase, Stalk Base, Green		900.00
Corn, Vase, Stalk Base, Ice Green		175.00 to 225.00
Corn, Vase, Stalk Base, Sapphire		2750.00
Cosmos, Bowl, Green, 6 In.		25.00
Cosmos & Cane, Banana Boat, Honey Amber		115.00
Cosmos & Cane, Compote, Cuspidor Shape, Whimsy, Amber		825.00
Cosmos & Cane, Tumbler, Honey Amber		35.00
Courthouse, Bowl, Ruffled Edge, Amethyst		275.00
Crackle, Vase, Auto, Marble Holder, Marigold		75.00
Dahlia, Tumbler, Green, 4 In.		20.00
Daisy, Basket, Clambroth		55.00
Daisy, Basket, Smoke		70.00
Daisy & Drape, Vase, Cupped, Amethyst		85.00 to 105.00
Daisy & Drape, Vase, Cupped, Marigold		200.00
Daisy & Drape, Vase, Cupped, White		85.00 to 105.00
Daisy & Drape, Vase, Flared, Aqua Opalescent		350.00
Daisy & Drape, Vase, Flared, Blue		500.00

Daisy & Drape, Vase, Straight, Aqua Opalescent 450.00
Daisy & Lattice Band pattern is listed here as Lattice & Daisy.
Daisy & Plume, Banana Boat, Footed, Peach Opalescent 55.00
Daisy & Plume, Candy Dish, Footed, c.1905, 8 x 3½ In. 55.00
Daisy & Plume, Rose Bowl, Amethyst ....*illus* 165.00
Daisy Band & Drape pattern is listed here as Daisy & Drape.
Daisy Cut, Bell, Marigold 150.00
Daisy Squares, Rose Bowl, Crimped Edge, Green 210.00
Daisy Wreath, Bowl, Blue Opalescent, Ruffled Edge 145.00
Dandelion, Mug, Aqua Opalescent 75.00
Dandelion, Mug, Blue 185.00
Dandelion, Mug, Marigold 100.00
Dandelion, Pin Tray, Amethyst 250.00
Dandelion, Pin Tray, Green 175.00
Dandelion, Water Set, Tankard, Green, 6 Piece 1050.00
Dandelion Variant pattern is listed here as Paneled Dandelion.
Davidson's Society Of Chocolates, Plate, Amethyst, Handgrip .... 450.00 to 775.00
Diamond & Sunburst, Wine Set, Marigold, 6 Piece 145.00
Diamond Band pattern is listed here as Diamonds.
Diamond Cut Shields, Water Set, Marigold, 5 Piece 175.00
Diamond Lace, Pitcher, Amethyst ....*illus* 165.00
Diamond Lace, Tumbler, Amethyst .... 30.00 to 40.00
Diamond Lace, Water Set, Amethyst, 7 Piece .... 300.00 to 350.00
Diamond Point, Vase, Amethyst, 9 In. 65.00
Diamond Point, Vase, Amethyst, 10 In. 40.00
Diamond Point, Vase, Green, 11 In. 40.00
Diamond Point, Vase, Marigold, 11 In. .... 45.00 to 65.00
Diamond Point, Vase, Sapphire, 10½ In. 1900.00
Diamond Point & Daisy pattern is listed here as Cosmos & Cane.
Diamond & Rib, Vase, Amethyst, 7 In. 500.00
Diamond & Rib, Vase, Amethyst, 10 In. 30.00
Diamonds, Pitcher, Marigold 105.00
Diving Dolphins, Bowl, Ruffled Edge, Footed, Marigold, 7 In. 175.00
Dogwood & Marsh Lily pattern is listed here as Two Flowers.
Dogwood Sprays, Bowl, Pedestal, Amethyst, 5 x 8 In. ....*illus* 100.00
Double Scroll, Candlestick, Red, Pair 250.00
Double Scroll, Console Set, Smoke, 3 Piece 75.00
Double Star, Water Set, Green, 7 Piece .... 200.00 to 350.00
Double Stem Rose, Bowl, Ruffled Edge, Dome Foot, Lavender 450.00
Dragon & Lotus, Bowl, Ice Cream, Amber, 9 In. 165.00
Dragon & Lotus, Bowl, Ice Cream, Cherry Red, 9 In. 175.00
Dragon & Lotus, Bowl, Ice Cream, Marigold, 9 In. ....*illus* 90.00
Dragon & Lotus, Bowl, Ruffled Edge, Amber, 9 In. 25.00
Dragon & Lotus, Bowl, Ruffled Edge, Amethyst, 9 In. .... 80.00 to 95.00
Dragon & Lotus, Bowl, Ruffled Edge, Blue, 9 In. .... 65.00 to 120.00
Dragon & Lotus, Bowl, Ruffled Edge, Cherry Red, 9 In. 275.00
Dragon & Lotus, Bowl, Ruffled Edge, Green, 9 In. 105.00
Dragon & Lotus, Bowl, Ruffled Edge, Marigold, 9 In. .... 105.00 to 275.00
Dragon & Lotus, Bowl, Ruffled Edge, Red, 9 In. 350.00
Dragon & Strawberry, Bowl, Ice Cream, Blue, 9 In. 250.00
Drape & Tie pattern is listed here as Rosalind.
Drapery, Candy Dish, Blue 275.00
Drapery, Candy Dish, Ice Blue 110.00
Drapery, Candy Dish, Marigold 135.00
Drapery, Candy Dish, White .... 95.00 to 125.00
Drapery, Rose Bowl, Aqua Opalescent, Butterscotch Iridescence 135.00
Drapery, Rose Bowl, Aqua Opalescent .... 185.00 to 240.00
Drapery, Rose Bowl, Cobalt Blue ....*illus* 135.00
Drapery, Rose Bowl, Ice Blue 275.00
Drapery, Rose Bowl, Marigold 250.00
Drapery, Vase, Blue, 8½ In. .... 195.00 to 375.00
Drapery, Vase, Ice Green, 7½ In. 95.00
Drapery, Vase, Lime Green, 7 In. 155.00
Drapery, Vase, Marigold, 7½ In. 55.00
Drapery, Vase, White, 9 In. 55.00
Dreibus Parfait Sweets, Plate, Lavender, 6 In. 1200.00

Carnival Glass, Diamond Lace,
Pitcher, Amethyst
$165.00

Carnival Glass, Dogwood Sprays,
Bowl, Pedestal, Amethyst, 5 x 8 In.
$100.00

Carnival Glass, Dragon & Lotus, Bowl,
Ice Cream, Marigold, 9 In.
$90.00

Carnival Glass, Drapery, Rose Bowl,
Cobalt Blue
$135.00

C

How Was Carnival Glass Made?

An iridescent finish is added to molded glass to make carnival glass. The glass, usually colored, is pressed in the mold, then removed. Additional shaping may be done by hand. Then the piece is sprayed with a coating of liquid metallic salts to create the iridescent finish.

Carnival Glass, Fine Cut & Roses, Rose Bowl, Amethyst
$145.00

Carnival Glass, Floral & Grape, Pitcher, Blue
$150.0

Eagle Furniture, Plate, Card Tray Shape, Amethyst	950.00
Eat Paradise Sodas, Plate, Amethyst, 6 In.	475.00
Egyptian Band pattern is listed here as Round-Up.	
Emaline pattern is listed here as Zipper Loop.	
Embroidered Mums, Bowl, Electric Blue, 8½ In.	750.00
Embroidered Mums, Plate, Ribbed Back, Ice Green, 9 In.	800.00
Enameled Cherries, Pitcher, Blue	65.00
Enameled Cherries, Tumbler, Blue	35.00
Estate, Pin Dish, Footed, Smoke	90.00
Estate, Sugar, Marigold	10.00
Estate, Sugar & Creamer, Blue Opalescent	35.00
Fan & Arch pattern is listed here as Persian Garden.	
Fanciful, Bowl, Ruffled Edge, Amethyst, 8½ In.	250.00
Fanciful, Bowl, Ruffled Edge, Marigold Exterior Only	20.00
Fanciful, Bowl, Ruffled Edge, Peach Opalescent, 8½ In.	95.00
Fanciful, Bowl, Ruffled Edge, White, 8½ In.	80.00
Fanciful, Plate, Blue, 9 In.	135.00
Fantail, Berry Bowl, Footed, Amethyst, Master	25.00
Fantasy pattern is listed here as Question Marks.	
Farmyard, Bowl, Ruffled Edge, Square, Amethyst, 8 In.	675.00
Fashion, Creamer, Smoke	35.00
Fashion, Sugar, Green	40.00
Fashion, Sugar & Creamer, Marigold	110.00
Fashion, Tumbler, Marigold	20.00
Feathers, Vase, Green, 10½ In.	50.00
Feathers, Vase, White, 7 In.	300.00 to 325.00
Fenton's Butterfly pattern is listed here as Butterfly.	
Fern Panels, Hat, Ruffled Edge, Red	95.00
Field Rose pattern is listed here as Rambler Rose.	
Field Thistle, Creamer, Marigold	80.00
Fine Cut & Roses, Rose Bowl, Amethyst *illus*	145.00
Fine Cut & Roses, Rose Bowl, Green	50.00
Fine Cut & Roses, Rose Bowl, White	200.00
Fine Rib, Vase, Aqua, 9½ In.	45.00
Fine Rib, Vase, Ice Green, 11 In.	165.00
Fine Rib, Vase, Red, 10 In.	105.00 to 225.00
Fine Rib, Vase, Red, Silver Iridescence, 10 In.	125.00
Fine Rib, Vase, Ruffled Edge, Blue, 10 In.	55.00
Fine Rib, Vase, Ruffled Edge, Red, 9 In.	325.00
Fish & Flowers pattern is listed here as Trout & Fly.	
Fisherman's Mug, Amethyst	20.00 to 35.00
Fisherman's Mug, Marigold	35.00 to 85.00
Fishnet, Epergne, Peach Opalescent	150.00 to 155.00
Fishscales & Beads, Plate, Marigold, 7 In.	25.00
Fishscales & Beads, Plate, White, 7 In.	65.00
Fleur-De-Lis, Bowl, Green, 9½ In.	175.00
Floral & Diamond Point pattern is listed here as Fine Cut & Roses.	
Floral & Grape, Pitcher, Blue *illus*	150.00
Floral & Grape, Water Set, Blue, 5 Piece	275.00
Floral & Grape, Water Set, Blue, 7 Piece	175.00
Floral & Grapevine pattern is listed here as Floral & Grape.	
Floral & Optic, Bowl, Footed, Red	195.00
Florentine, Candlestick, Celeste Blue, 8½ In., Pair	60.00
Flower Pot pattern is listed here as Butterfly & Tulip.	
Flowering Almonds pattern is listed here as Peacock Tail.	
Flowers, Rose Bowl, Marigold	25.00
Flowers & Frames, Bowl, Ruffled Edge, Dome Foot, Amethyst	105.00
Fluffy Bird pattern is listed here as Peacock.	
Fluffy Peacock, Tumbler, Green	65.00
Fluffy Peacock, Water Set, Amethyst, 5 Piece	450.00
Fluffy Peacock, Water Set, Amethyst, 7 Piece	800.00
Flute, Toothpick, Amethyst	30.00 to 50.00
Four Flowers Variant, Plate, Amethyst, 6½ In.	300.00
Four Pillars, Vase, Amethyst, 12 In.	50.00
Four Pillars, Vase, Aqua Opalescent, 10 In.	105.00
Four Pillars, Vase, Blue, 6¾ In.	85.00

Four Pillars, Vase, Green, 12 In.	75.00
Four Pillars, Vase, Olive Green, 11 In.	20.00
Four Pillars, Vase, Ribbed Interior, Blue, 7 In.	55.00
Four-Seventy-Four, Punch Bowl & Base, Emerald Green	4000.00
French Knot, Hat, Square, White	195.00
Frolicking Bears, Cuspidor, 1982 ICGA, Red	75.00
Frollicking Bears, Cuspidor, 1983 ICGA, Vaseline Opalescent	85.00
Fruits & Flowers, Bonbon, Aqua Opalescent	475.00
Fruits & Flowers, Bonbon, Blue	55.00
Fruits & Flowers, Bonbon, Electric Blue ....*illus*	105.00
Fruits & Flowers, Bonbon, Green	40.00
Fruits & Flowers, Bonbon, Ice Blue	325.00 to 475.00
Fruits & Flowers, Bonbon, Ice Green	400.00
Fruits & Flowers, Bonbon, Marigold	50.00 to 55.00
Fruits & Flowers, Bonbon, Sapphire	400.00
Fruits & Flowers, Bowl, Ruffled Edge, Blue, 7 In.	100.00
Garden Mums, Bowl, Central Shoe Store, Crimped & Ruffled Edge, 6 In. ....*illus*	646.00
Garden Path, Bowl, Ice Cream, Peach Opalescent, 11 In.	275.00
Garden Path, Rose Bowl, Marigold	85.00
Garland, Rose Bowl, Blue	30.00
Garland, Rose Bowl, Marigold	15.00 to 40.00
Gervutz Brothers Furniture, Plate, Amethyst, Handgrip	1200.00
Golden Grapes, Rose Bowl, Marigold	15.00
Good Luck, Bowl, Pie Crust Edge, Ribbed Back, Amethyst, 8½ In.	275.00 to 550.00
Good Luck, Bowl, Pie Crust Edge, Ribbed Back, Blue, 8½ In.	125.00 to 200.00
Good Luck, Bowl, Pie Crust Edge, Ribbed Back, Green, 8½ In. ....*illus*	300.00
Good Luck, Bowl, Pie Crust Edge, Ribbed Back, Marigold, 8½ In.	105.00 to 125.00
Good Luck, Bowl, Ruffled Edge, Basketweave Back, Amethyst, 8½ In.	175.00
Good Luck, Bowl, Ruffled Edge, Basketweave Back, Green, 8½ In.	305.00
Good Luck, Bowl, Ruffled Edge, Ribbed Back, Amethyst, 8½ In.	165.00 to 200.00
Good Luck, Plate, Basketweave Back, Amethyst, 9 In.	225.00 to 350.00
Good Luck, Plate, Basketweave Back, Marigold, 9 In.	425.00
Good Luck, Plate, Ruffled Edge, Basketweave Back, Amethyst, 9 In.	250.00
Good Luck, Plate, Ruffled Edge, Basketweave Back, Marigold, 9 In.	300.00
Good Luck, Plate, Stippled, Ribbed Back, Blue, 9 In.	775.00
Good Luck, Plate, Stippled, Ribbed Back, Marigold, 9 In.	500.00
Gothic Arches, Vase, Flared, Marigold, 11 In.	195.00
Gothic Arches, Vase, Smoke, 10 In.	850.00
Grape & Cable, Banana Boat, Amethyst	200.00
Grape & Cable, Berry Bowl, Amethyst, Master	95.00
Grape & Cable, Berry Bowl, Blue, Master	550.00
Grape & Cable, Bonbon, Stippled, Green	185.00
Grape & Cable, Bowl, 3-Footed, Stippled, Blue, 6½ x 10¾ In.	400.00
Grape & Cable, Bowl, Amethyst, 12 In.	100.00
Grape & Cable, Bowl, Basketweave Back, Amethyst, 11 In.	80.00
Grape & Cable, Bowl, Centerpiece, Turned-Up Sides, White	200.00
Grape & Cable, Bowl, Ruffled Edge, Ribbed Back, Stippled, Ice Green	700.00
Grape & Cable, Bowl, Stippled, Pie Crust Edge, Ribbed Back, Ice Blue	825.00
Grape & Cable, Bowl, Stippled, Ruffled Edge, Amethyst, 10 In.	275.00
Grape & Cable, Breakfast Set, Amethyst	205.00
Grape & Cable, Butter, Cover, Amethyst	65.00 to 110.00
Grape & Cable, Butter, Cover, Green	200.00
Grape & Cable, Butter, Cover, Marigold, 6 x 8 In.	225.00
Grape & Cable, Candlestick, Amethyst	95.00
Grape & Cable, Candlestick, Green, Pair	300.00
Grape & Cable, Candlestick, Marigold, Pair	225.00
Grape & Cable, Cologne Bottle, Marigold	105.00
Grape & Cable, Compote, Ruffled Edge, Amethyst	250.00
Grape & Cable, Creamer, Amethyst	65.00
Grape & Cable, Decanter, Stopper, Marigold, 13 In.	175.00 to 495.00
Grape & Cable, Dish, Sweetmeat, Amethyst	130.00 to 195.00
Grape & Cable, Fernery, Amethyst	650.00
Grape & Cable, Fernery, Marigold	600.00
Grape & Cable, Hatpin Holder, Amethyst	125.00 to 200.00
Grape & Cable, Hatpin Holder, Footed, White	225.00
Grape & Cable, Hatpin Holder, Green	220.00 to 450.00

Carnival Glass, Fruits & Flowers, Bonbon, Electric Blue
$105.00

Carnival Glass, Garden Mums, Bowl, Central Shoe Store, Crimped & Ruffled Edge, 6 In.
$646.00

Carnival Glass, Good Luck, Bowl, Pie Crust Edge, Ribbed Back, Green, 8½ In.
$300.00

Carnival Glass, Hanging Cherries, Pitcher, Marigold
$625.00

Carnival Glass, Heart & Vine, Bowl, Green, 8½ In.
$85.00

Grape & Cable, Hatpin Holder, Marigold	125.00
Grape & Cable, Humidor, Marigold	95.00
Grape & Cable, Humidor, Stippled, Blue	425.00
Grape & Cable, Pin Tray, Green, Epoxy Base	185.00
Grape & Cable, Pin Tray, White	500.00
Grape & Cable, Pitcher, Ice Green	350.00
Grape & Cable, Pitcher, Smoke	900.00
Grape & Cable, Plate, Amethyst, 9 In.	75.00
Grape & Cable, Plate, Card Tray Shape, Amethyst, 6 In.	30.00 to 55.00
Grape & Cable, Plate, Footed, Blue, Silver Iridescence, 9 In.	10.00
Grape & Cable, Plate, Footed, Marigold, 9 In.	45.00
Grape & Cable, Plate, Green, 9 In.	45.00
Grape & Cable, Plate, Handgrip, Amethyst, 7 In.	60.00
Grape & Cable, Plate, Handgrip, Green, 7 In.	105.00
Grape & Cable, Plate, Marigold, 9 In.	135.00
Grape & Cable, Plate, Ribbed Back, Stippled, Amethyst, 9 In.	425.00
Grape & Cable, Powder Jar, Amethyst	120.00
Grape & Cable, Powder Jar, Green	200.00 to 250.00
Grape & Cable, Powder Jar, Marigold	45.00
Grape & Cable, Punch Bowl, Base, Marigold	800.00
Grape & Cable, Punch Bowl, Base, White	10000.00
Grape & Cable, Punch Bowl, Stippled, Cobalt Blue, 8 Piece	1700.00
Grape & Cable, Punch Set, Amethyst, 14 Piece	1550.00 to 2000.00
Grape & Cable, Spooner, Amethyst	60.00 to 100.00
Grape & Cable, Spooner, Marigold	25.00
Grape & Cable, Sugar, Cover, Amethyst	45.00 to 75.00
Grape & Cable, Tray, Dresser, Amethyst, 11¼ In.	155.00
Grape & Cable, Tray, Dresser, Marigold, 11¼ In.	115.00
Grape & Cable, Tray, Dresser, White, 11¼ In.	450.00
Grape & Cable, Water Set, Amethyst, 7 Piece	225.00
Grape & Cable, Water Set, Marigold, 5 Piece	155.00
Grape & Cable Variant, Bowl, Ruffled Edge, Ribbed Back, Sapphire	850.00
Grape & Gothic, Tumbler, Blue	40.00
Grape Arbor, Berry Bowl, Footed, Marigold	75.00
Grape Arbor, Tumbler, Amethyst	80.00
Grape Arbor, Tumbler, Ice Blue	125.00
Grape Arbor, Water Set, Tankard, Marigold, 7 Piece	350.00
Grape Delight, Rose Bowl, Footed, White	55.00
Grape Delight pattern is listed here as Vintage.	
Grape Leaves, Bowl, Marigold, 9 In.	10.00
Grape Wreath Variant, Bowl, Ruffled Edge, Amethyst, 8 In.	85.00
Grapevine Diamonds pattern is listed here as Grapevine Lattice.	
Grapevine Lattice, Bowl, Ruffled Edge, Amethyst, 7 In.	35.00
Grapevine Lattice, Bowl, Ruffled Edge, White, 7 In.	10.00 to 30.00
Grapevine Lattice, Plate, Amethyst, 7 In.	147.00
Grapevine Lattice, Water Set, Tankard, Marigold, 7 Piece	55.00
Greek Key, Bowl, Ruffled Edge, Basketweave Back, Amethyst	225.00
Greek Key, Tumbler, Green	65.00
Hanging Cherries, Creamer, Marigold	25.00
Hanging Cherries, Pitcher, Marigold	*illus* 625.00
Hattie, Chop Plate, Amethyst	900.00 to 1800.00
Heart & Vine, Bowl, Green, 8½ In.	*illus* 85.00
Heart & Vine, Plate, Blue, 9 In.	175.00 to 400.00
Hearts & Flowers, Bowl, Ruffled Edge, Ice Blue	175.00
Hearts & Flowers, Bowl, Ruffled Edge, Ribbed Back, Frosted, White	110.00
Hearts & Flowers, Compote, Ruffled Edge, Aqua Opalescent	325.00
Hearts & Flowers, Compote, Ruffled Edge, Blue	375.00
Hearts & Flowers, Compote, Ruffled Edge, Ice Blue	700.00
Hearts & Flowers, Compote, Ruffled Edge, Ice Green	90.00
Hearts & Flowers, Compote, Ruffled Edge, Marigold	80.00 to 115.00
Hearts & Flowers, Compote, Ruffled Edge, White	105.00
Hearts & Flowers, Plate, Ribbed Back, Marigold, 9 In.	400.00 to 710.00
Hearts & Flowers, Plate, Ribbed Back, Pastel Marigold 9 In.	900.00
Heavy Grape, Chop Plate, Amber	255.00 to 265.00
Heavy Grape, Chop Plate, Amethyst	400.00
Heavy Grape, Chop Plate, Marigold	145.00

Heavy Grape, Chop Plate, White	875.00
Heavy Grape, Plate, Amethyst, 8 In.	95.00
Heavy Grape, Plate, Clambroth, 8 In.	55.00
Heron, Mug, Black Amethyst, Silver Iridescence	10.00
Hex, Candlestick, Marigold, Pair	375.00
Hobnail pattern is listed in this book as its own category.	
Hobstar & Feather, Punch Set, Tulip Shape, Amethyst, Gold Iridescence, 8 Piece ......*illus*	2700.00
Hobstar & Tassels, Bowl, Amethyst, Metal Frame, 7 In.	135.00
Hobstar & Torch pattern is listed here as Double Star.	
Hobstar & Waffleblock, Basket, Marigold	100.00
Hobstar Band, Pitcher, Tankard, Marigold	55.00
Hobstar Flowers, Compote, Ruffled Edge, Marigold	55.00
Holly, Bonbon, Handles, Marigold ......*illus*	40.00
Holly, Bowl, Crimped & Ruffled Edge, Blue	60.00
Holly, Bowl, Ruffled Edge, Marigold Opalescent	375.00
Holly, Compote, Ruffled Edge, Green	25.00
Holly, Hat, Blue	15.00
Holly, Nut Dish, Blue	35.00
Holly, Plate, Blue, 9 In.	165.00 to 225.00
Holly, Plate, Marigold, 9 In.	80.00 to 165.00
Holly & Berry, Bowl, Ruffled Edge, Peach Opalescent	45.00
Holly Wreath, Bowl, Marigold, 8¼ In.	30.00
Homestead, Chop Plate, Amber	2200.00
Homestead, Chop Plate, Marigold	325.00
Homestead, Chop Plate, White	600.00
Honeycomb, Rose Bowl, Peach Opalescent	85.00
Honeycomb Collar pattern is listed here as Fishscales & Beads.	
Horse Medallions pattern is listed here as Horses' Heads.	
Horses' Heads, Bowl, Footed, Pink	200.00
Horses' Heads, Bowl, Ice Cream, Marigold	15.00
Horses' Heads, Bowl, Jack-In-The-Pulpit Edge, Footed, Blue	95.00
Horses' Heads, Bowl, Marigold	125.00
Horses' Heads, Plate, Marigold, 7 In.	65.00 to 125.00
Horses' Heads, Rose Bowl, Footed, Blue	85.00
Horses' Heads, Rose Bowl, Powder Blue, Gold Iridescence	300.00
Imperial Flute, Celery Vase, Amethyst	1500.00
Imperial Flute, Punch Set, Green, 10 Piece	300.00
Imperial Flute, Toothpick, Amethyst	45.00
Imperial Grape, Basket, Marigold	30.00
Imperial Grape, Basket, Smoke	65.00
Imperial Grape, Bowl, Ruffled Edge, Amethyst	145.00
Imperial Grape, Bowl, Ruffled Edge, Marigold	10.00
Imperial Grape, Bowl, Ruffled Edge, Smoke	350.00
Imperial Grape, Carafe, Amber	2700.00
Imperial Grape, Carafe, Amethyst ......*illus*	125.00
Imperial Grape, Carafe, Emerald Green, Blue Iridescence	4000.00
Imperial Grape, Carafe, Green	35.00
Imperial Grape, Carafe, Pinched Neck, Flared, Amethyst	255.00
Imperial Grape, Cup & Saucer, Green	20.00 to 45.00
Imperial Grape, Cup & Saucer, Marigold	20.00
Imperial Grape, Nut Dish, Amethyst	300.00
Imperial Grape, Pitcher, Amethyst	105.00
Imperial Grape, Plate, Amethyst, 6 In.	65.00 to 95.00
Imperial Grape, Plate, Green, Silver Iridescence, 6 In.	25.00
Imperial Grape, Plate, Marigold, 6 In.	45.00
Imperial Grape, Plate, Marigold, 9 In.	75.00
Imperial Grape, Punch Set, Amethyst, 9 Piece	1200.00
Imperial Grape, Tumbler, Amethyst	10.00
Imperial Grape, Wine Bottle, Stopper, Marigold	195.00
Imperial Grape, Wine Bottle, Stopper, Smoke	250.00
Imperial Grape, Wine Set, Amethyst, 6 Piece	300.00
Imperial Grape, Wine Set, Marigold, 7 Piece	60.00
Imperial Square, Pitcher, Square, Marigold	25.00
Intaglio pattern is listed here as Hobstar & Feather.	
Interior Of Cherries & Mums pattern is listed here as Mikado.	
Inverted Strawberry, Candlestick, Green	145.00

Carnival Glass, Hobstar & Feather, Punch Set, Tulip Shape, Amethyst, Gold Iridescence, 8 Piece
$2700.00

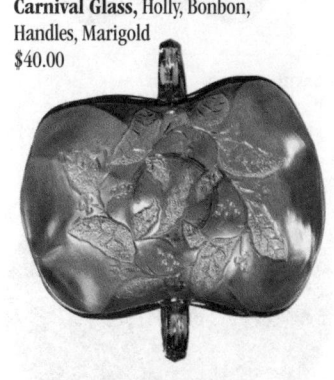

Carnival Glass, Holly, Bonbon, Handles, Marigold
$40.00

Carnival Glass, Imperial Grape, Carafe, Amethyst
$125.00

Carnival Glass, Leaf Chain, Plate, Marigold, 7 In.
$40.00

C

Carnival Glass, Little Flowers,
Bowl, Green, 10¼ In.
$70.00

Carnival Glass, Louisa,
Rose Bowl, Teal
$30.00

Carnival Glass, Luster Rose,
Water Set, Marigold,
8½-In. Pitcher, 7 Piece
$106.00

Carnival Glass Sets

Some carnival glass patterns were made in full sets that include bowls, plates, and accessories in numerous sizes. Other patterns were for novelties made in only one shape.

Irish Lace pattern is listed here as Louisa.	
Kimberly pattern is listed here as Concave Diamonds.	
Kittens, Bowl, 2 Sides Turned Up, Amethyst	250.00
Kittens, Bowl, 2 Sides Turned Up, Blue	300.00
Kittens, Bowl, 2 Sides Turned Up, Marigold	65.00
Kittens, Bowl, 4 Sides Turned Up, Amethyst	215.00
Kittens, Bowl, 4 Sides Turned Up, Marigold	45.00
Kittens, Bowl, Cereal, Blue	250.00
Kittens, Bowl, Cereal, Marigold	50.00 to 85.00
Kittens, Cup & Saucer, Marigold	155.00 to 165.00
Kittens, Plate, Marigold	55.00
Kittens, Toothpick, Blue	115.00 to 195.00
Kittens, Toothpick, Marigold	80.00
Knotted Beads, Vase, Blue, 9 In.	45.00
Knotted Beads, Vase, Green, 10 In.	175.00
Labelle Elaine pattern is listed here as Primrose.	
Labelle Poppy pattern is listed here as Poppy Show.	
Labelle Rose pattern is listed here as Rose Show.	
Lattice & Daisy, Tumbler, Powder Blue Slag	100.00
Lattice & Grape, Water Set, Tankard, Blue, 7 Piece	275.00
Lattice & Grapevine pattern is listed here as Lattice & Grape.	
Lattice & Points, Vase, Blue, 8 In.	30.00
Lattice & Points, Vase, Marigold, 8½ In.	30.00
Leaf & Beads, Rose Bowl, Amethyst	115.00 to 155.00
Leaf & Beads, Rose Bowl, Aqua Opalescent, Butterscotch Iridescence	165.00 to 300.00
Leaf & Beads, Rose Bowl, Aqua Opalescent	75.00
Leaf & Beads, Rose Bowl, Blue	95.00
Leaf & Beads, Rose Bowl, Ice Green	275.00
Leaf & Beads, Rose Bowl, Rayed Interior, Emerald Green, Blue Iridescence	750.00
Leaf & Beads, Rose Bowl, Rayed Interior, Green	60.00
Leaf & Beads, Rose Bowl, Rayed Interior, Marigold	30.00 to 55.00
Leaf & Beads, Rose Bowl, Sunflower Interior, Amethyst	85.00
Leaf & Beads, Rose Bowl, White	175.00
Leaf Chain, Bowl, Ruffled Edge, Blue, Silver Iridescence, 7 In.	8.00
Leaf Chain, Plate, Blue, 9 In.	800.00
Leaf Chain, Plate, Blue, Silver Iridescence, 7 In.	25.00
Leaf Chain, Plate, Marigold, 7 In. ....*illus*	40.00
Leaf Chain, Plate, Pastel Marigold, 9 In.	125.00
Leaf Columns, Vase, Green, 10 In.	60.00
Leaf Medallion pattern is listed here as Leaf Chain.	
Leaf Pinwheel & Star Flower pattern is listed here as Whirling Leaves.	
Leaf Rays, Nappy, Trocornered, Amethyst	45.00
Leaf Swirl, Compote, Amethyst	75.00
Lincoln Land, Rose Bowl, Aqua Opalescent	25.00
Lined Lattice, Vase, Amethyst, 6 In.	350.00
Lined Lattice, Vase, Amethyst, 9 In.	40.00
Lion, Bowl, Blue, 7 In.	225.00
Lion, Bowl, Ruffled Edge, Blue, 7 In.	315.00
Lions, Bowl, Marigold, 7 In.	100.00
Little Barrel, Green	75.00
Little Barrel, Marigold	45.00
Little Fishes, Berry Bowl, Ruffled Edge, Footed, Blue, Master	155.00
Little Fishes, Sauce, Ruffled Edge, Footed, Amethyst	50.00
Little Fishes, Sauce, Ruffled Edge, Footed, Aqua	195.00
Little Fishes, Sauce, Ruffled Edge, Footed, Marigold	80.00
Little Flowers, Berry Set, Green, 7 Piece	105.00
Little Flowers, Bowl, Crimped & Ruffled Edge, Amethyst, 10 In.	40.00
Little Flowers, Bowl, Green, 10¼ In. ....*illus*	70.00
Little Stars, Bowl, Ruffled Edge, Amethyst, Silver Iridescence, 9 In.	195.00
Loganberry, Vase, Amber	350.00 to 800.00
Loganberry, Vase, Amethyst	1150.00
Loop & Column pattern is listed here as Pulled Loop.	
Looped Petals pattern is listed here as Scales.	
Lotus & Grape, Bonbon, Marigold	18.00
Lotus & Grape, Bowl, Ruffled Edge, Marigold	10.00
Louisa, Rose Bowl, Amethyst	40.00 to 80.00

Louisa, Rose Bowl, Green	115.00
Louisa, Rose Bowl, Teal ....*illus*	30.00
Lucille, Water Set, Blue, 7 Piece	700.00
Luster Rose, Butter, Cover, Amethyst	450.00
Luster Rose, Water Set, Marigold, 8½-In. Pitcher, 7 Piece ....*illus*	106.00
Magnolia & Poinsettia pattern is listed here as Water Lily.	
Many Fruits, Punch Set, Amethyst, 8 Piece	650.00
Maple Leaf, Butter, Cover, Amethyst	165.00
Maryland pattern is listed here as Rustic.	
Melinda pattern is listed here as Wishbone.	
Melon & Fan pattern is listed here as Diamond & Rib.	
Memphis, Berry Bowl, Lavender	90.00
Mikado, Compote, Blue	275.00
Mitered Ovals, Vase, Crimped & Ruffled Edge, Green	20000.00
Mitered Ovals, Vase, Green, 10 In.	7500.00
Moonprint, Candlestick, Marigold	165.00
Morning Glory, Vase, Amethyst, 7 In.	65.00
Morning Glory, Vase, Funeral, Marigold, 15 In.	230.00
Morning Glory, Vase, Marigold, 4½ In.	20.00
Morning Glory, Vase, Marigold, 5 In.	150.00
Morning Glory, Vase, Marigold, 7 In.	150.00
Morning Glory, Vase, Smoke, 5 In.	80.00
Multi Fruit & Flowers pattern is listed here as Many Fruits.	
Mums & Greek Key pattern is listed here as Embroidered Mums.	
Nautilus, Sugar, Whimsy, Amethyst	55.00
Nautilus, Sugar, Whimsy, Peach Opalescent	45.00
Nesting Swan, Bowl, Ruffled Edge, Frosted Marigold	105.00
Nugget, Creamer, Blue	55.00
Oak Leaf & Acorn pattern is listed here as Acorn.	
Oak Leaf pattern is listed here as Leaf Swirl.	
Octagon, Compote, Aqua Teal	75.00
Octagon, Decanter, Green	90.00
Octagon, Pitcher, Amethyst	500.00
Octagon, Pitcher, Marigold	35.00
Omnibus, Water Set, Marigold, 9 Piece	275.00
Open Rose, Bowl, Ruffled Edge, Footed, Amethyst, 8 In. ....*illus*	60.00
Open Rose, Plate, Amber, 9 In.	300.00
Orange Tree, Bowl, Fruit, Blue	180.00
Orange Tree, Bowl, Fruit, Ruffled Edge, Footed, Marigold	45.00
Orange Tree, Bowl, Ice Cream, Green	400.00
Orange Tree, Bowl, Ruffled Edge, Red	1850.00
Orange Tree, Hatpin Holder, Blue, 6¾ In. ....*illus*	130.00
Orange Tree, Loving Cup, Blue	115.00 to 265.00
Orange Tree, Mug, Amethyst	85.00
Orange Tree, Mug, Aqua	85.00
Orange Tree, Mug, Blue	15.00
Orange Tree, Mug, Marigold	10.00
Orange Tree, Mug, Red	115.00
Orange Tree, Plate, Blue, 9 In.	125.00 to 200.00
Orange Tree, Plate, Clambroth, 9 In.	45.00
Orange Tree, Plate, Marigold, 9 In.	200.00
Orange Tree, Plate, Serrated Edge, Marigold, 9 In.	165.00
Orange Tree, Plate, Stippled, Serrated Edge, Blue, 9 In.	400.00
Orange Tree, Shaving Mug, Amethyst	15.00
Orange Tree, Shaving Mug, Black Amethyst	50.00
Orange Tree, Shaving Mug, Blue	10.00 to 18.00
Orange Tree, Shaving Mug, Marigold	15.00
Orange Tree, Shaving Mug, Red	250.00
Oriental Poppy, Tumbler, Amethyst	130.00
Palm Beach, Banana Boat, Marigold	135.00
Palm Beach, Rose Bowl, Gooseberry Interior, White	155.00
Palm Beach, Vase, Pinched, Amethyst, 4 In.	195.00
Paneled Dandelion, Pitcher, Tankard, Amethyst	350.00
Paneled Dandelion, Tumbler, Amethyst	65.00
Paneled Dandelion, Water Set, Tankard, Amethyst, 6 Piece	55.00
Paneled Dandelion, Water Set, Tankard, Blue, 7 Piece	400.00

Carnival Glass, Open Rose, Bowl, Ruffled Edge, Footed, Amethyst, 8 In.
$60.00

Carnival Glass, Orange Tree, Hatpin Holder, Blue, 6¾ In.
$130.00

Carnival Glass, Peacock & Grape, Bowl, Ruffled Edge, Footed, Green $205.00

Carnival Glass, Peacock & Urn, Bowl, Ice Cream, Ruffled Edge, Blue, 6 In. $100.00

Carnival Glass, Peacock At The Fountain, Water Set, Blue, 5 Piece $450.00

Carnival Glass, Peacocks, Plate, Serrated Edge, Ribbed Back, Green, 9 In. $500.00

Paneled Dandelion, Water Set, Tankard, Green, 7 Piece	550.00
Pansy, Bowl, Amethyst, 9 In.	65.00 to 85.00
Pansy, Dish, Pickle, Oval, Marigold	115.00
Pansy, Dish, Pickle, Oval, Ruffled Edge, Amethyst	75.00 to 85.00
Pansy, Dish, Pickle, Oval, Smoke	215.00
Pansy, Nappy, Amethyst, Handle	45.00
Pansy, Plate, Ruffled Edge, Green	45.00
Pansy, Plate, Ruffled Edge, Lavender	75.00
Pansy, Plate, Ruffled Edge, Marigold	65.00
Pansy, Plate, Ruffled Edge, Smoke	170.00
Panther, Berry Bowl, Footed, Blue, 10 In.	300.00
Panther, Berry Bowl, Footed, Olive Green, 10 In.	300.00
Panther, Berry Bowl, Ruffled Edge, Footed, Marigold, 10 In.	65.00
Panther, Berry Bowl, Ruffled Edge, Footed, Blue, 5 In.	75.00
Panther, Berry Set, Ruffled Edge, Footed, Marigold, 6 Piece	135.00
Parlor Panels, Vase, Marigold, 6 In.	135.00
Pastel Swan, Salt, Ice Green	5.00
Pastel Swan, Salt, Marigold	55.00
Peach, Tumbler, White	55.00
Peacock, Berry Bowl, Amethyst	85.00 to 90.00
Peacock, Plate, Ruffled Edge, Amethyst, 6 In.	350.00
Peacock & Dahlia, Bowl, Aqua, 7 In.	30.00
Peacock & Grape, Bowl, Green, 8¾ In.	40.00
Peacock & Grape, Bowl, Ruffled Edge, Amethyst	60.00
Peacock & Grape, Bowl, Ruffled Edge, Footed, Green ....*illus*	205.00
Peacock & Grape, Bowl, Ruffled Edge, Footed, Marigold	80.00
Peacock & Grape, Bowl, Ruffled Edge, Footed, Red	85.00
Peacock & Grape, Bowl, Ruffled Edge, Footed, Smokey Blue	175.00
Peacock & Grape, Bowl, Ruffled Edge, Marigold	30.00
Peacock & Grape, Bowl, Spatula Foot, Green, 7¾ In.	40.00
Peacock & Grape, Plate, Marigold, 9 In.	700.00
Peacock & Urn, Bowl, Ice Cream, Amethyst, 6 In.	45.00 to 95.00
Peacock & Urn, Bowl, Ice Cream, Blue, 6 In.	75.00
Peacock & Urn, Bowl, Ice Cream, Ice Blue, 10 In.	650.00
Peacock & Urn, Bowl, Ice Cream, Marigold, 10 In.	250.00 to 400.00
Peacock & Urn, Bowl, Ice Cream, Marigold, 6 In.	70.00
Peacock & Urn, Bowl, Ice Cream, Ruffled Edge, Blue, 6 In. ....*illus*	100.00
Peacock & Urn, Bowl, Ice Cream, Slightly Ruffled Edge, Blue, 10 In.	2100.00
Peacock & Urn, Bowl, Ice Cream, White, 6 In.	45.00 to 95.00
Peacock & Urn, Bowl, Marigold, 8½ In.	60.00
Peacock & Urn, Bowl, Ruffled Edge, Frosted Amethyst	145.00
Peacock & Urn, Compote, Ruffled Edge, Amethyst	1000.00
Peacock & Urn, Compote, Ruffled Edge, Aqua	85.00
Peacock & Urn, Compote, Ruffled Edge, Blue	55.00
Peacock & Urn, Plate, Blue, 9 In.	275.00 to 450.00
Peacock & Urn, Plate, Marigold, 9 In.	135.00 to 250.00
Peacock & Urn, Plate, White, 9 In.	200.00
Peacock At The Fountain, Berry Set, Amethyst, 7 Piece	275.00
Peacock At The Fountain, Bowl, Fruit, Aqua Opalescent	6500.00
Peacock At The Fountain, Bowl, Fruit, Marigold	300.00
Peacock At The Fountain, Compote, Ice Blue	530.00
Peacock At The Fountain, Punch Set, Marigold, 8 Piece	450.00
Peacock At The Fountain, Spooner, Marigold	40.00
Peacock At The Fountain, Tumbler, Amethyst	80.00
Peacock At The Fountain, Tumbler, Blue	110.00
Peacock At The Fountain, Water Set, Blue, 5 Piece ....*illus*	450.00
Peacock Eye & Grape pattern is listed here as Vineyard.	
Peacock On Fence pattern is listed here as Peacocks.	
Peacock Tail, Bowl, Crimped Edge, 4-Sided, Green	255.00
Peacock Tail, Bowl, Green, 8½ In.	130.00
Peacock Tail & Daisy, Bowl, Ruffled Edge, Blue Milk Glass	1100.00
Peacocks, Bowl, Pie Crust Edge, Ribbed Back, Amethyst	350.00
Peacocks, Bowl, Pie Crust Edge, Ribbed Back, Green	400.00
Peacocks, Bowl, Ruffled Edge, Ribbed Back, Amethyst	250.00
Peacocks, Bowl, Ruffled Edge, Ribbed Back, Aqua Opalescent	400.00 to 900.00
Peacocks, Bowl, Ruffled Edge, Ribbed Back, Blue	500.00

C

Peacocks, Bowl, Ruffled Edge, Ribbed Back, Marigold	315.00
Peacocks, Plate, Amethyst, 9 In.	350.00
Peacocks, Plate, Green, Gold Iridescence, 9 In.	550.00
Peacocks, Plate, Ice Green, 9 In.	250.00
Peacocks, Plate, Serrated Edge, Ribbed Back, Amethyst, 9 In.	325.00
Peacocks, Plate, Serrated Edge, Ribbed Back, Blue, 9 In.	550.00
Peacocks, Plate, Serrated Edge, Ribbed Back, Green, 9 In. ....*illus*	500.00
Peacocks, Plate, Serrated Edge, Ribbed Back, Horehound, 9 In.	725.00
Peacocks, Plate, Serrated Edge, Ribbed Back, Ice Blue, 9 In.	600.00
Peacocks, Plate, Serrated Edge, Ribbed Back, Lime Green, 9 In.	105.00
Peacocks, Plate, Serrated Edge, Ribbed Back, Marigold, 9 In.	85.00 to 185.00
Peacocks, Plate, Serrated Edge, Ribbed Back, Smokey Lavender, 9 In.	800.00
Peacocks, Plate, Serrated Edge, Ribbed Back, White, 9 In.	225.00
Peacocks, Plate, White, 9 In.	175.00
Persian Garden, Bowl, Fruit, Base, Peach Opalescent	375.00
Persian Garden, Chop Plate, Serrated Edge, Peach Opalescent ....*illus*	2000.00
Persian Garden, Plate, Marigold, 6 In.	40.00 to 100.00
Persian Garden, Plate, Peach Opalescent, 6 In.	250.00
Persian Garden, Plate, White, 6 In.	125.00
Persian Medallion, Bonbon, Celeste Blue	350.00
Persian Medallion, Bonbon, Lime Green	95.00
Persian Medallion, Bowl, Fruit, Grape & Cable Exterior, Amethyst ....*illus*	250.00
Persian Medallion, Compote, Crimped Edge, Marigold	35.00
Persian Medallion, Hair Receiver, Blue	65.00 to 135.00
Persian Medallion, Hair Receiver, Marigold	25.00 to 85.00
Persian Medallion, Plate, Blue, 6 In.	65.00 to 105.00
Persian Medallion, Plate, Blue, 7 In.	30.00
Persian Medallion, Plate, Blue, Silver Iridescence, 9 In.	40.00
Persian Medallion, Plate, Marigold, 6 In.	15.00 to 35.00
Persian Medallion, Rose Bowl, Marigold	75.00
Petal & Fan, Plate, Crimped Edge, Amethyst, 6 In.	105.00
Petal & Fan, Sauce, Ruffled Edge, Amethyst	215.00
Petals, Compote, Ruffled Edge, Green	50.00
Peter Rabbit, Bowl, Ice Cream, Blue	1560.00
Pine Cone, Bowl, Ice Cream, Blue, 7 In.	25.00 to 105.00
Pine Cone, Plate, Marigold, 6 In.	50.00
Pine Cone, Plate, Marigold, 7 In.	145.00 to 155.00
Pine Cone Wreath pattern is listed here as Pine Cone.	
Pinwheel, Vase, Marigold, 6 In.	90.00
Plaid, Bowl, Ruffled Edge, Blue	300.00
Plaid, Bowl, Ruffled Edge, Celeste Blue	10000.00
Plaid, Bowl, Ruffled Edge, Marigold	75.00
Plain Jane, Basket, Marigold	10.00
Plain Jane, Basket, Smoke	55.00 and 70.00
Plain Jane, Basket, White	10.00
Plume Panels, Vase, Amber, 13 In.	105.00
Plume Panels, Vase, Marigold, 11 In.	25.00
Poinsettia, Pitcher, Milk, Amethyst	1000.00
Poinsettia, Pitcher, Milk, Marigold	65.00 to 85.00
Poinsettia & Lattice, Bowl, 3-Footed, Electric Blue, 8¾ In. ....*illus*	440.00
Pond Lily, Bonbon, Card Tray Shape, Amethyst	50.00
Pony, Bowl, Ruffled Edge, Marigold	60.00
Pony Rosette pattern is listed here as Pony.	
Poppy, Compote, Marigold	650.00
Poppy, Dish, Pickle, Blue	150.00
Poppy, Dish, Pickle, Marigold	65.00
Poppy Scroll pattern is listed here as Poppy.	
Poppy Show, Bowl, Ruffled Edge, Pastel Marigold	350.00
Poppy Show, Bowl, Ruffled Edge, White	145.00
Poppy Show, Plate, Blue, 9 In.	875.00
Poppy Show, Plate, Ice Blue, 9 In.	475.00
Poppy Show, Plate, Marigold, 9 In.	600.00
Poppy Show, Plate, Marigold, Pink & Yellow Iridescence, 9 In.	1250.00
Poppy Show, Plate, White, 9 In.	235.00 to 275.00
Primrose, Bowl, Ice Cream, Amethyst, 9¾ In. ....*illus*	100.00
Primrose, Bowl, Ruffled Edge, Marigold, 8½ In.	75.00

C

Carnival Glass, Persian Garden, Chop Plate, Serrated Edge, Peach Opalescent
$2000.00

Carnival Glass, Persian Medallion, Bowl, Fruit, Grape & Cable Exterior, Amethyst
$250.00

Carnival Glass, Poinsettia & Lattice, Bowl, 3-Footed, Electric Blue, 8¾ In.
$440.00

Carnival Glass, Primrose, Bowl, Ice Cream, Amethyst, 9¾ In.
$100.00

Carnival Glass, Raspberry,
Pitcher, Milk, Amethyst
$90.00

Carnival Glass, Scroll Embossed,
Plate, Aqua, 9 In.
$115.00

Carnival Glass, Singing Birds,
Mug, Amethyst
$145.00

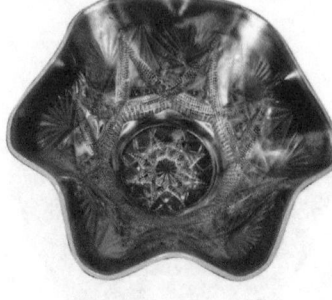

Carnival Glass, Ski Star, Bowl,
Peach Opalescent, 10½ In.
$10.00

Princess Lace pattern is listed here as Octagon.

Pulled Loop, Vase, Aqua, 10½ In.	225.00
Pulled Loop, Vase, Blue, 11 In.	45.00
Pulled Loop, Vase, Peach Opalescent, 10 In.	20.00
Puzzle, Bonbon, Amethyst	90.00
Puzzle, Bonbon, White	125.00
Question Marks, Cake Plate, Ruffled Edge, Footed, Peach Opalescent	225.00
Question Marks, Candy Dish, Pedestal, Marigold Opalescent, Handles, 4 x 7 In.	55.00
Question Marks, Compote, Crimped Edge, Marigold	20.00
Question Marks, Compote, Crimped Edge, Peach Opalescent	15.00
Question Marks, Compote, Marigold, 2 x 7 In.	25.00
Question Marks, Dish, Handles, Pedestal Base, Marigold, 4 x 7 In.	55.00
Question Marks, Plate, Footed, Marigold, 7 In.	85.00
Rabbit, Bank, Marigold, Large	40.00
Rambler Rose, Tumbler, Marigold	30.00
Raspberry, Gravy Boat, Amethyst	65.00
Raspberry, Pitcher, Milk, Amethyst	*illus* 90.00
Raspberry, Pitcher, Water, Amethyst	50.00
Raspberry, Pitcher, Water, Green	300.00
Raspberry, Pitcher, Water, Marigold	85.00
Raspberry, Tumbler, Amethyst	25.00
Raspberry, Tumbler, Marigold	55.00
Raspberry, Water Set, Amethyst, 7 Piece	200.00 to 550.00
Raspberry, Water Set, Green, 7 Piece	350.00
Rays & Ribbons, Bowl, Amethyst, 9 In.	220.00
Rays & Ribbons, Bowl, Crimped Edge, Amethyst, 9 In.	400.00
Rib & Drape, Vase, Marigold, 5 In.	65.00
Ribbon Tie, Bowl, Crimped Ruffled Edge, Blue	60.00
Ribbon Tie, Plate, Crimped Ruffled Edge, Marigold, 9¼ In.	150.00
Ring Optic, Vase, Swung, Pink, 13 In.	165.00
Ripple, Vase, Amethyst, 9 In.	45.00
Ripple, Vase, Aqua, 9 In.	135.00
Ripple, Vase, Aqua Teal, 10½ In.	160.00
Ripple, Vase, Funeral, Amethyst, 18 In.	1000.00
Ripple, Vase, Funeral, Green, 18 In.	95.00
Ripple, Vase, Green, 11 In.	40.00
Ripple, Vase, Green, 14 In.	200.00
Ripple, Vase, Lavender, 10 In.	400.00
Ripple, Vase, Marigold, 7 In.	30.00
Ripple, Vase, Marigold, 11½ In.	40.00
Ripple, Vase, Marigold, 12 In.	18.00
Ripple, Vase, Smoke, 11½ In.	125.00
Rising Sun, Butter, Cover, Marigold	95.00
Rising Sun, Tumbler, Juice, Marigold	65.00
Rococo, Vase, Marigold	35.00 to 45.00
Rococo, Vase, Smoke	205.00
Rosalind, Bowl, Amethyst, 10 In.	60.00
Rose & Ruffles pattern is listed here as Open Rose.	
Rose Garden, Rose Bowl, Blue	45.00
Rose Pinwheel, Bowl, Ruffled Edge, Marigold	425.00
Rose Show, Bowl, Ruffled Edge, Aqua Opalescent, 8½ In.	800.00 to 900.00
Rose Show, Bowl, Ruffled Edge, Marigold, 8½ In.	700.00
Rose Show, Plate, Marigold, 9 In.	750.00
Rose Show, Plate, White, 9 In.	275.00
Roses & Loops pattern is listed here as Double Stem Rose.	
Rosette, Bowl, Ruffled Edge, Footed, Amethyst	75.00
Rosette & Prisms pattern is listed here as Rosette.	
Round-Up, Bowl, Ruffled Edge, Peach Opalescent	500.00
Round-Up, Bowl, Ruffled Edge, White	115.00
Round-Up, Plate, White, 9 In.	145.00
Rustic, Vase, Amethyst, 17 In.	255.00
Rustic, Vase, Blue, 18½ In.	950.00
Rustic, Vase, White, 17 In.	135.00
Sailboat & Windmill pattern is listed here as Sailboats.	
Sailboats, Sauce, Ruffled Edge, Aqua	65.00
Sailboats, Sauce, Ruffled Edge, Marigold	25.00

C

Scales, Compote, Amethyst, 7¼ In.	20.00
Scroll & Flower, Vase, Marigold	500.00
Scroll Embossed, Bowl, Ruffled Edge, File Back, Amethyst, 8 In.	85.00
Scroll Embossed, Bowl, Ruffled Edge, Smoke, 10 In.	115.00
Scroll Embossed, Compote, Ruffled Edge, Amethyst, Small	175.00
Scroll Embossed, Compote, Ruffled Edge, Green, Small	35.00
Scroll Embossed, Plate, Amethyst, 9 In.	200.00 to 325.00
Scroll Embossed, Plate, Aqua, 9 In. *illus*	115.00
Scroll Embossed, Plate, Marigold, 9 In.	100.00
Scroll Embossed, Sauce, Ruffled Edge, File Back, Amethyst, Electric Blue Iridescence	165.00
Scroll Embossed, Sauce, Ruffled Edge, File Back, Clambroth	185.00
Scroll-Cable pattern is listed here as Estate.	
Sea Lanes pattern is listed here as Little Fishes.	
Seacoast, Pin Tray, Amethyst	700.00
Seacoast, Pin Tray, Green	600.00
Seaweed, Bowl, Crimped & Ruffled Edge, Marigold, 10¼ In.	275.00
Shell & Sand, Bowl, Ruffled Edge, Amethyst	300.00 to 305.00
Shell & Sand, Bowl, Ruffled Edge, Green, Metal Frame	170.00
Shell & Sand, Bowl, Ruffled Edge, Lavender	215.00
Shell & Sand, Bowl, Ruffled Edge, Marigold	75.00
Shell & Sand, Plate, Aqua, 9 In.	75.00
Singing Birds, Mug, Amethyst *illus*	145.00
Singing Birds, Mug, Blue	55.00 to 90.00
Singing Birds, Mug, Green	80.00 to 85.00
Singing Birds, Mug, Lavender	75.00
Singing Birds, Mug, Stippled, Marigold	45.00
Singing Birds, Tumbler, Amethyst, 4 In.	65.00
Singing Birds, Water Set, Green, 7 Piece	550.00 to 800.00
Single Flower, Bowl, Crimped Edge, Peach	35.00
Six Petals, Bowl, Ruffled Edge, Marigold	25.00
Six Petals, Bowl, Ruffled Edge, White	65.00
Six Petals, Bowl, Tricornered, Amethyst	85.00
Six Sided, Candlestick, Marigold	85.00
Six Sided, Candlestick, Smoke, Marigold Iridescence	75.00
Ski Star, Berry Set, Ruffled Edge, Peach Opalescent, 5 Piece	105.00
Ski Star, Bowl, Peach Opalescent, 10½ In. *illus*	10.00
Ski Star, Bowl, Ruffled Edge, Amethyst, 5 In.	45.00
Ski Star, Bowl, Ruffled Edge, Peach Opalescent, 5 In.	60.00
Ski Star, Plate, Handgrip, Footed, Peach Opalescent	110.00
Soda Gold, Water Set, Smoke, 5 Piece	325.00
Soutache, Plate, Crimped Edge, Dome Foot, Peach Opalescent	80.00
Spider Web pattern is listed here as Soda Gold.	
Stag & Holly, Bowl, Crimped Ruffled Edge, Marigold, 10½ In.	60.00
Stag & Holly, Bowl, Footed, Marigold	65.00
Stag & Holly, Bowl, Ice Cream, Footed, Amber	175.00
Stag & Holly, Bowl, Ice Cream, Footed, Amethyst	650.00
Stag & Holly, Bowl, Ice Cream, Footed, Aqua	550.00
Stag & Holly, Bowl, Ice Cream, Footed, Blue	130.00
Stag & Holly, Bowl, Ice Cream, Footed, Green	425.00
Stag & Holly, Bowl, Ice Cream, Footed, Lime Green, Marigold Iridescence	100.00
Stag & Holly, Bowl, Ruffled Edge, Blue, 10½ In.	325.00
Stag & Holly, Bowl, Ruffled Edge, Footed, Amethyst	55.00
Stag & Holly, Chop Plate, Footed, Marigold	750.00
Stag & Holly, Rose Bowl, Marigold	85.00 to 125.00
Star Of David, Bowl, Ruffled Edge, Amethyst	65.00
Star Of David, Bowl, Ruffled Edge, Marigold	55.00
Star Of David & Bows, Bowl, Ruffled Edge, Dome Foot, Amethyst	65.00
Star Of David & Bows, Bowl, Ruffled Edge, Dome Foot, Marigold, 8½ In.	120.00
Star Of David Medallion pattern is listed here as Star Of David & Bows.	
Stippled Clematis pattern is listed here as Little Stars.	
Stippled Diamond & Flower pattern is listed here as Little Flowers.	
Stippled Leaf & Beads pattern is listed here as Leaf & Beads.	
Stippled Peacocks, Plate, Ribbed Back, Blue, 9 In.	850.00
Stippled Peacocks, Plate, Ribbed Back, Marigold, 9 In.	850.00
Stippled Ribbons & Rays pattern is listed here as Rays & Ribbons.	
Stippled Three Fruits, Bowl, Ruffled Edge, Footed, Blue	500.00

C

Carnival Glass, Thistle, Bowl, Pie Crust Edge, Amethyst, 7¾ In. $275.00

Carnival Glass, Three Fruits, Plate, 12-Sided, Marigold, 9 In. $220.00

Carnival Glass, Wishbone, Epergne, Amethyst $500.00

CARNIVAL GLASS

Carousel, Frog,
Leaping, Pine, Saddle Blanket,
Glass Eyes, Herschell-Spillman,
c.1911, 29 x 48 In.
$72000.00

Carousel, Goat, Pine, Painted,
Glass Eyes, Bridle, Saddle,
Gustav Dentzel, c.1905, 59 x 56 In.
$15600.00

Carousel, Horse,
Baby, Wood, Gray Paint,
Red & Green Saddle, Stand,
Parker, 31 x 23 In.
$330.00

Stippled Three Fruits, Bowl, Ruffled Edge, Footed, Green	185.00
Strawberry, Bonbon, Lime Green Opalescent	150.00
Strawberry, Bowl, Pie Crust Edge, Amethyst	105.00
Strawberry, Bowl, Ruffled Edge, Basketweave Back, Green	55.00
Strawberry, Bowl, Ruffled Edge, Ribbed Back, Amethyst	300.00
Strawberry, Bowl, Stippled, Ruffled Edge, Ribbed Back, Lime Green	1100.00
Strawberry, Compote, Ruffled Edge, Marigold	150.00
Strawberry, Plate, Basketweave Back, Amethyst, 9 In.	85.00 to 105.00
Strawberry Wreath, Bowl, Square, Amethyst, 9 In.	410.00
Stream Of Hearts, Compote, Marigold, 6½ In.	30.00 to 65.00
Sunflower pattern is listed here as Dandelion.	
Swirl Hobnail, Cuspidor, Amethyst	575.00
Swirl Hobnail, Cuspidor, Marigold	750.00
Ten Mums, Bowl, Ruffled Edge, Green, 9 In.	90.00
Thin Rib, Vase, Amethyst, 10 In.	40.00
Thin Rib, Vase, Ice Green, 10½ In.	250.00
Thin Rib, Vase, Sapphire, 11½ In.	600.00
Thin Rib, Vase, White, 10 In.	90.00
Thistle, Banana Boat, Footed, Amethyst, 10½ In.	160.00
Thistle, Bowl, Blue, 8½ In.	94.00
Thistle, Bowl, Ice Cream, Blue, 7¾ In.	70.00
Thistle, Bowl, Pie Crust Edge, Amethyst, 7¾ In. *illus*	275.00
Three Fruits, Bowl, Amethyst, 8¾ In.	59.00
Three Fruits, Bowl, Horehound, 8½ In.	200.00
Three Fruits, Bowl, Ruffled Edge, Ribbed Back, Collar Base, Stippled, White	325.00
Three Fruits, Bowl, Stippled, Blue Opalescent, 8½ In.	100.00
Three Fruits, Bowl, Stippled, Ruffled Edge, Footed, Aqua Opalescent	450.00 to 525.00
Three Fruits, Plate, 12-Sided, Amethyst, 9 In.	60.00
Three Fruits, Plate, 12-Sided, Blue, 9 In.	165.00
Three Fruits, Plate, 12-Sided, Green, 9 In.	105.00
Three Fruits, Plate, 12-Sided, Marigold, 9 In. *illus*	220.00
Three Fruits, Plate, Amethyst, 9 In.	40.00
Three Fruits, Plate, Stippled, Ribbed Back, Amethyst 9 In.	145.00
Three Fruits, Plate, Stippled, Ribbed Back, Blue, 9 In.	225.00 to 650.00
Three Fruits, Plate, Stippled, Ribbed Back, Marigold, 9 In.	300.00
Tiger Lily, Pitcher, Green, 8½ In.	200.00
Tornado, Vase, Amethyst, Small	275.00
Tornado, Vase, Green, Small	750.00
Tornado, Vase, Marigold, Small	300.00
Town Pump, Amethyst, Silver & Gold Iridescence	275.00
Tree Trunk, Vase, Amethyst, 10½ In.	80.00 to 115.00
Tree Trunk, Vase, Amethyst, 9 In.	60.00
Tree Trunk, Vase, Blue, 10½ In.	105.00
Tree Trunk, Vase, Elephant's Foot, Amethyst, 13 In.	1600.00
Tree Trunk, Vase, Green, 12 In.	300.00
Tree Trunk, Vase, Green, 13 In.	350.00
Tree Trunk, Vase, Green, Blue Iridescence, 10 In.	175.00
Tree Trunk, Vase, Ice Blue, 10½ In.	195.00
Tree Trunk, Vase, Ice Green, 10½ In.	250.00
Tree Trunk, Vase, Irregularly Ruffled Edge, Elephant's Foot, Amethyst, 13½ In.	7750.00
Tree Trunk, Vase, Marigold, 10 In.	40.00
Tree Trunk, Vase, Marigold, 11 In.	95.00
Tree Trunk, Vase, Sapphire, 9 In.	750.00
Tree Trunk, Vase, Squat, Amethyst, 6½ In.	95.00
Tree Trunk, Vase, Squat, Green, 7½ In.	55.00
Tree Trunk, Vase, White, 11 In.	190.00
Trout & Fly, Bowl, Ice Cream, Green	350.00
Trout & Fly, Bowl, Ruffled Edge, Frosted Green	400.00
Two Flowers, Bowl, Ruffled Edge, Footed, Blue, Large	275.00
Two Flowers, Chop Plate, Footed, Marigold	550.00
Two Fruits, Bonbon, Sections, Handles, Marigold	8.00
Venetian, Vase, Serrated Foot, Green	350.00
Victorian, Bowl, Amethyst, 11¼ In.	225.00
Vineyard, Pitcher, Amethyst, Silver Iridescence, 9¼ In.	150.00
Vineyard, Tumbler, Marigold	10.00
Vineyard, Water Set, Amethyst, 6 Piece	175.00

Vineyard, Water Set, Serrated Edges, Amethyst, 6 Piece	400.00
Vintage, Bowl, Crimped & Ruffled Edge, Amethyst	40.00
Vintage, Bowl, Ice Cream, Hobnail Back, Marigold	325.00
Vintage, Bowl, Ruffled Edge, Persian Blue, 9 In.	500.00
Vintage, Epergne, Amethyst	135.00
Vintage, Epergne, Blue, Small	85.00
Vintage, Epergne, Blue	120.00
Vintage, Epergne, Green	130.00
Vintage, Epergne, Marigold	170.00
Vintage, Plate, Amethyst, 7 In.	25.00
Vintage, Plate, Green, 7 In.	20.00
Waffleblock, Basket, Aqua	100.00
Waffleblock, Basket, Clambroth	15.00
Waffleblock, Punch Bowl, Aqua Teal, Marigold Base	35.00
Water Lily, Berry Bowl, Ruffled Edge, Marigold, Master	45.00
Water Lily, Sauce Bowl, Ruffled Edge, Lime Green Opalescent	350.00
Water Lily & Cattails, Saucer, Marigold	5.00
Water Lily & Cattails, Toothpick, Whimsy, Marigold	45.00
Western Thistle, Tumbler, Marigold	40.00
Whirling Leaves, Bowl, Green, 10 In.	70.00
Wide Panel, Basket, Amethyst	65.00
Wild Blackberry, Bowl, Ruffled Edge, Amethyst	65.00
Wild Grapes pattern is listed here as Grape Leaves.	
Wild Strawberry, Plate, Handgrip, Green, 8 In.	165.00
Wild Strawberry, Plate, Handgrip, Marigold, 8 In.	120.00
Wildflower, Plate, Blue, 9 In.	200.00
Windflower, Plate, Blue, 9 In.	105.00
Windmill, Bowl, Ruffled Edge, Amethyst	140.00
Windmill, Bowl, Ruffled Edge, Aqua	35.00
Windmill, Bowl, Ruffled Edge, Smoke	65.00
Windmill, Dish, Pickle, Ruffled Edge, Marigold	105.00
Windmill Medallion pattern is listed here as Windmill.	
Wishbone, Bowl, 3-Footed, Amethyst, 8½ In.	85.00 to 150.00
Wishbone, Bowl, Ruffled Edge, Marigold, 8½ In.	55.00
Wishbone, Epergne, Amethyst	illus 500.00
Wishbone, Plate, Footed, Amethyst, 9 In.	400.00 to 410.00
Wishbone & Spades, Plate, Amethyst, 6 In.	170.00 to 275.00
Wreath Of Roses, Punch Bowl, Base, Flared Rim, Marigold	425.00
Wreathed Cherry, Banana Boat, Peach Opalescent	50.00
Wreathed Cherry, Pitcher, Amethyst	215.00
Zipper Loop, Lamp, Kerosene, Marigold, 9 In.	275.00 to 325.00
Zipper Loop, Lamp, Kerosene, Smoke, 9 In.	350.00
Zipper Loop, Lamp, Kerosene, Smoke, 11 In.	185.00 to 225.00
Zippered Heart, Rose Bowl, Green	550.00

CAROUSEL or merry-go-round figures were first carved in the United States in 1867 by Gustav Dentzel. Collectors discovered the charm of the hand-carved figures in the 1970s, and they were soon classed as folk art. Most desirable are the figures other than horses, such as pigs, camels, lions, or dogs. A jumper is a figure that was made to move up and down on a pole; a stander was placed in a stationary position.

Frog, Leaping, Pine, Saddle Blanket, Glass Eyes, Herschell-Spillman, c.1911, 29 x 48 In. *illus*	72000.00
Giraffe, Raised Head, Glass Eyes, Carved, Painted, Gastav Dentzel, c.1908, 69 x 60 In.	33000.00
Goat, Pine, Painted, Glass Eyes, Bridle, Saddle, Gustav Dentzel, c.1905, 59 x 56 In. *illus*	15600.00
Horse, Baby, Wood, Gray Paint, Red & Green Saddle, Stand, Parker, 31 x 23 In. *illus*	330.00
Horse, Galloping, Head Up, Open Mouth, Carved, Painted, Herschel-Spellman, 54 x 40 In.	1320.00
Horse, Jewels On Bridle, Chest Strap, Setters Head On Cantle, C.W. Parker, c.1917, 59 In.	2530.00
Horse, Jumper, Glass Eyes, Orange & Green Saddle, C.W. Parker, c.1912, 48 x 60 In.	5400.00
Horse, Jumper, Glass Jewels, Fish Scale Armor, C.W. Parker, Leavenworth, Kan., 38 x 78 In. *illus*	19550.00
Horse, Outside Row Stander, Jewels, Gustav Dentzel, c.1885, 64 x 62 In.	11000.00
Horse, Painted, Legs Down, Molded Mane, Hyen, 78 In.	4675.00
Horse, Standing, Raised Front Leg, Eagle Saddle, Pine, Gustav Dentzel, c.1880, 60 x 61 In.	12000.00
Horse, Wood, Carved, Painted, Black, Green, Orange, Glass Eyes, 53 In.	1035.00
Horse, Wood, Blanket, Diamonds, Brass Pole, Alan Hershell, N. Tonawanda, N.Y., c.1926 *illus*	1100.00
Mask, Depicts 4 Winds, Painted, Mounted To Board, Cast Iron, 11½ In., 4 Piece	935.00
Mirror, Carved, Multicolored, Coney Island, c.1920, 35 x 19 In.	2640.00

Carousel, Horse,
Jumper, Glass Jewels,
Fish Scale Armor, C.W. Parker,
Leavenworth, Kan., 38 x 78 In.
$19550.00

Carousel, Horse,
Wood, Blanket, Diamonds,
Brass Pole, Alan Hershell,
N. Tonawanda, N.Y., c.1926
$1100.00

Carousel, Tiger,
Pine, Painted, Stripes,
Saddle, Philadelphia Toboggan Co.,
c.1904, 50 x 60 In.
$78000.00

Carriage, Baby Buggy, Wicker, 2 Sleigh Runners, Wakefield, 36 x 48 In. $205.00

Carriage, Baby Buggy, Wicker, Umbrella, 53 In. $175.00

Cash Register, National, Model 92 $891.00

Cash Register, National, Model 313, Nickel Plated Brass, 17 In. $690.00

Mirror, Seated Clown, Wood, Carved, Legs Shaped Around Oval Glass, 24 x 13 In. 10925.00
Panel, Chariot, Griffin Wagon, Wood, Carved, Multicolored, Early 20th Century, 33 x 71 In. . . 777.00
Seal, Carved, Head Turned To The Side, Black Paint, 19th Century, 22 x 45 In. 15000.00
Tiger, Pine, Painted, Stripes, Saddle, Philadelphia Toboggan Co., c.1904, 50 x 60 In. . . .*illus* 78000.00
Woman, Victorian, Scroll Work, Cast Iron, 2-Piece Cast, 12 x 8¼ In., Pair 1064.00

CARRIAGE means several things, so this category lists baby carriages, buggies for adults, horse-drawn sleighs, and even strollers. Doll-sized carriages are listed in the Toy category.

Baby Buggy, Double, Metal Wheels, Wood Basket, Leather Hood, Brass, 50 x 49 . . . . 1100.00
Baby Buggy, Painted, Wood Wheels, Mid 19th Century, 52 In. 408.00
Baby Buggy, Upholstered Rim, Stick & Ball Detail, Porcelain Handles, 1800s, 37 x 20 In. . . . 950.00
Baby Buggy, Victorian, Wicker, Curlicues, Beadwork, Birdcage Design, 1890s, 38 x 25 In. . . . 1650.00
Baby Buggy, Victorian, Wicker, Curlicues, Beadwork, Twist Wrapped Foot Rest, 1890s, 42 x 26 In. 2450.00
Baby Buggy, Wicker, 2 Sleigh Runners, Wakefield, 36 x 48 In. . . . . *illus* 205.00
Baby Buggy, Wicker, Umbrella, 53 In. . . . . *illus* 175.00
Baby Buggy, Wicker, Upholstered Rim, Stick & Ball Sides, Porcelain Handles, 1800s, 37 x 43 In. . 950.00
Baby Buggy, Wicker Shell, Scroll Design, Cast Iron, c.1900, 33 x 44 x 21 In. 575.00
Horse Form, Wood, 4 Wheels, Metal Mounts, India, 17 In. 201.00
Sleigh, Wood, Push, Paris Mfg., 42 In. 345.00
Wagon, Farm, John Deere, Wood, Steel, Spoked Wooden Wheels, Blue, 1930s, 54 x 144 In. . . . 3450.00

CASH REGISTERS were invented in 1884 because an eye on the cash was a necessity in stores of the nineteenth century, too. John and James Ritty invented a large model that resembled a clock and kept a record of the dollars and cents exchanged in the store. John Patterson improved the cash register with a paper roll to record the money. By the early 1900s, elaborate brass registers were made. About World War I, the fancy case was exchanged for the more modern types.

National, Brass, Filigree, Receipt Attachment, Marble Shelf, 17 x 16 In. 633.00
National, Brass, Marble Inset, 17 In. 198.00
National, Model 1½, 16 x 17½ x 15 In. 826.00
National, Model 6, Base, Personalized Cover Plate, Restored, 17½ x 22 In. 5225.00
National, Model 6, No. S38760, 2 Key Rows, Leaf Cast Case, 15 x 22 In. 3290.00
National, Model 50, Brass, 17 x 10 In. 2420.00
National, Model 67, Bohemian Design Cabinet, Restored, 17½ x 21 In. 2007.00
National, Model 92 . . . . *illus* 891.00
National, Model 313, Brass, c.1910, 21 x 16 x 10 In. 1497.00
National, Model 313, Brass, Early 20th Century, 17 In. 705.00
National, Model 313, Keyboard Lock, 1897 . . . . 1495.00
National, Model 313, Nickel Plated Brass, 17 In. . . . . *illus* 690.00
National, Model R-313, Serial No. 11-3652, Refurbished, 1908-20 . . . . 324.00
National, Nickel Plated, Saloon, Filigree, Key, Counter, 17¼ x 17 x 16½ In. 575.00

CASTOR JARS for pickles are glass jars about six inches in height, held in special metal holders. They became a popular dinner table accessory about 1890. Each jar had a top that was usually silver or silver plate. The frame, also of a silver metal, had a handle that arched above the jar and a hook that held a pair of tongs. By 1900, the pickle castor was out of fashion. Many examples found today have reproduced glass jars in old holders. Additional pickle castors may be found in the various Glass categories.

Pickle, Clarissa, Square Base & Handle, 9 In. 173.00
Pickle, Coin Spot, Amberina, Ribbed, Leaf-Embossed Frame, Tongs, Meriden, 9¼ In. 1150.00
Pickle, Coin Spot, Blue, Multicolored Enameled Flowers, Squat, Frame, Roger Bros., 9 In. . . . 705.00
Pickle, Coin Spot, Cranberry, Cylindrical, Embossed Metal Frame, Tongs, 12½ In. 470.00
Pickle, Coin Spot, Cranberry, Squat, Silver Plated Frame, 4-Footed, c.1900, 12 In. 353.00
Pickle, Cranberry, Enameled Flowers, 4 Griffins, Rose Garden, Embossed Frame, Tufts, 12½ In. . 1265.00
Pickle, Cranberry, Optic Ribbed, Flowers, Silver Plated Frame, Tongs, Knickerbocker, 11 In. . . 489.00
Pickle, Daisy & Button, Amber, Pierced Scrolls, Middletown Frame, 11 In. . . . . *illus* 323.00
Pickle, Daisy & Button, Amberina, Silver Plated Frame, Tongs, 11 In. 145.00
Pickle, Daisy & Button, Black Amethyst, Silver Plated Frame, Tongs, 11 In. 145.00
Pickle, Daisy & Button, Cranberry Ice, Silver Plated Frame, Tongs, 11 In. 145.00
Pickle, Etched Birds, Clear, Reed & Barton Holder, Heart Handles, Embossed Flowers, 10 In. . . 460.00
Pickle, Fern, French Opalescent, Tongs, Silver Plated Frame, 11 In. 110.00
Pickle, Fern, Light Lavender Opalescent, Silver Plated Frame, Tongs, 11 In. 110.00
Pickle, Fern & Daisy, Blue Opalescent, Silver Plated Frame, Tongs, 11 In. 96.00

Pickle, Frosted Glass, Melon Ribbed, Oval, Cucumber Finial, Silver Plated Frame, Wilcox, 10 In.		230.00
Pickle, Honeycomb, Cranberry Opalescent, Pierced Frame, 4-Footed, 12 In.		460.00
Pickle, Honeycomb, Cranberry Opalescent, Silver Plated Frame, Tongs, 11 In.		145.00
Pickle, Honeycomb, Green Opalescent, Silver Plated Frame, Tongs, 11 In.		110.00
Pickle, King's Crown, Ruby Stained, Silver Plated Frame, 8¾ In.		660.00
Pickle, Pink Satin, Gold, Blue Flowers, Enameled, Oval, Metal Frame, c.1900, 10 In.		353.00
Pickle, Rainbow Swirl, Diamond Optic, Blue & White Flowers, Silver Plated Frame, 10 In.	*illus*	353.00
Pickle, Scalloped Swirl, Ruby Stained, Silver Plated Frame, Tongs, 9¾ In.		220.00
Pickle, Treebark, Ribbed, Pink Vines & Flowers, Reticulated Frame, Toronto, 12 In.		1093.00

CASTOR SETS holding just salt and pepper castors were used in the seventeenth century. The sugar castor, mustard pot, spice dredger, bottles for vinegar and oil, and other spice holders became popular by the eighteenth century. These sets were usually made of sterling silver. The American Victorian castor set, the type most collected today, was made of silver plated Britannia metal. Colored glass bottles were introduced after the Civil War. The sets were out of fashion by World War I. Be careful when buying sets with colored bottles; many are reproductions. Other castor sets may be listed in various porcelain and glass categories in this book.

3 Bottles, Jumbo Pattern, Metal Lid & Frame, 9¼ In.		440.00 to 935.00
3 Bottles, Silver Plate, Revolving, Cut Glass Bottles, 18 x 12½ In.		70.00
3 Bottles, Tree Stump, Stand, Metal Cover & Loop Handle Frame, 5½ In.		55.00
4 Bottles, Clear, Square, Silver Plated Frame, 7½ In.		49.00
4 Bottles, King's Crown, Ruby Stained, Silver Plated Frame, 9½ In.	*illus*	330.00
5 Bottles, Early Thumbprint, Pewter Stand, 8½ In.		935.00
5 Bottles, Gothic Pattern, Britannia Stand, 3-Footed, 9¾ In.		77.00
5 Bottles, Jacob's Ladder, Domed Foot, Silver Plated Frame, 17½ In.		99.00
5 Bottles, Silvered, Flower Repousse Frame, 18 In.		94.00
6 Bottles, Silver Plated Frame, No. 35, Meriden, c.1880		115.00
7 Bottles, Cut Glass, Silver On Copper Frame, Oval Handle, 4 Paw Feet, 9 In.	*illus*	118.00
7 Bottles, Square, Silver Plated Frame, Victorian, c.1860, 11½ In.		950.00

CATALOGS *are listed in the Paper category.*

CAUGHLEY porcelain was made in England from 1772 to 1814. Caughley porcelains are very similar in appearance to those made at the Worcester factory. See the Salopian category for related items.

Jug, Cover, Chinese Figures, Chinoiserie, Gilt, Pinecone Knop, Crossed Swords Mark, 6¼ In.		3900.00
Serving Dish, Asparagus, Fisherman & The Cormorant, Blue Detail, Diaper Border, 3 x 3 In.		335.00
Tea Caddy, Chinoiserie, Blue Printed, Knopped Lid, Porcelain, c.1790, 4½ In.		312.00
Tea Caddy, Fluted, Gilt Highlights, Scattered Flowers, c.1790, 4¾ In.		214.00

CAULDON Limited worked in Staffordshire, Great Britain, and went through many name changes. John Ridgway made porcelain at Cauldon Place, Hanley, until 1855. The firm of John Ridgway, Bates and Co. of Cauldon Place worked from 1856 to 1859. It became Bates, Brown-Westhead, Moore and Co. from 1859 to 1862. Brown-Westhead, Moore and Co. worked from 1862 to 1904. About 1890, this firm started using the words *Cauldon* or *Cauldon Ware* as part of the mark. Cauldon Ltd. worked from 1905 to 1920, Cauldon Potteries from 1920 to 1962.

Cuspidor, Green, Castle, Clouds, Flowers, 1800s, 6 x 8 In.		59.00
Pitcher, Abraham Lincoln, With Malice Toward None, Charity For All, 7 x 6½ In.		1016.00
Plate, Service, Blue & Gilt Banded, White Center, 20th Century, 10¼ In., 12 Piece		413.00

CELADON is the name of a velvet-textured green-gray glaze used by Chinese, Japanese, Korean, and other factories. The name refers both to the glaze and to pieces covered with the glaze. It is still being made.

Bowl, Blue, Crackle, 9 In.		235.00
Bowl, Ching Dynasty, Chinese, 2 x 7 In.		66.00
Bowl, Flower Shape, Porcelain, Chinese, 5 In.		2478.00
Bowl, Glazed, Korea, 6½ In.		295.00
Bowl, Inlaid Porcelain, White & Black Slip, Fruit & Leaf Decoration, Korea, 8 In.		266.00
Bowl, Interior With Lotus Flower Medallion, Thailand, 15th Century, 11 In.		295.00
Bowl, Korea, 7 In.		177.00
Bowl, Lotus, Petal Shape, Chinese, 13 In.		590.00
Box, Cover, Jade, Bird Shape, 2 x 3½ In., Pair		2832.00
Brush Washer, Crackled Glaze, Lotus Shape, Chinese, 4¾ In.		1888.00

Castor Jar, Pickle, Daisy & Button, Amber, Pierced Scrolls, Middletown Frame, 11 In.
$323.00

Castor Jar, Pickle, Rainbow Swirl, Diamond Optic, Blue & White Flowers, Silver Plated Frame, 10 In.
$353.00

Castor Set, 4 Bottles, King's Crown, Ruby Stained, Silver Plated Frame, 9½ In.
$330.0

Castor Set, 7 Bottles, Cut Glass, Silver On Copper Frame, Oval Handle, 4 Paw Feet, 9 In.
$118.00

Celadon, Vase, Maebyong Form, Circles, Cranes, Clouds, Choson Dynasty, Korea, 13½ x 6 In.
$805.00

Censer, Longquan, Tripod, Trigram Design, Chinese, 14th Century	1038.00
Cuspidor, Porcelain, Flowers, Chinese, 19th Century, 8 In.	236.00
Figurine, Jizo, Standing On Lotus Base, Hands In Prayer, Marked, Early 20th Century, 9½ In.	69.00
Jar, Dragons, 5-Clawed, Clouds, Embossed, Bulbous, Pinched Neck, Qianlong Mark, 14 In.	1200.00
Jar, Porcelain, Ribbed, Globular Body, Late 19th Century, Japan, 9 In.	236.00
Plate, Brick Red, Brown Foot, Leaf Edge, 1735-96, 9½ In.	3055.00
Vase, Blue & White, Baluster, Flared Lip Rims, Applied Foo Dog Handles, 17 In., Pair	300.00
Vase, Copper Red, Pear Shape, Garlic Mouth, Ilin In High Relief, 9½ In.	1121.00
Vase, Cover, Jade, Flattened Oval Shape, Flowering Branch, High Relief, 5 In., Pair	354.00
Vase, Cover, Tripod, Crosshatch, Jade Finial, 1800s, 9¾ x 8½ In.	303.00
Vase, Incised, Scrolling Leaf Decoration To Shoulder & Ribbed Body, Chinese, 11 In.	177.00
Vase, Maebyong Form, Circles, Cranes, Clouds, Choson Dynasty, Korea, 13½ x 6 In. ....*illus*	805.00
Vase, Mallet, Porcelain, Handles, Song Dynasty, Chinese, 9 In.	1888.00
Vase, Ming, Elongated Baluster Shape, Flared Lip Rim, Low Relief, Rockwork, 11½ In.	1320.00
Vase, Porcelain, Bulbous, Elongated Neck, Ming Dynasty, Chinese, 6 In.	708.00
Vase, Porcelain, Flowerhead, Scrolling Foliage, Mounted As Lamp Base, 12½ In.	224.00
Vase, Thailand, 18 x 9 In.	264.00
Vase, Viking Ships Panels, Matte Glaze, Steiger, 3½ x 4 In.	1920.00

Betty Harrington
Betty Harrington was a designer at the Ceramic Arts Studio soon after it opened. Collectors often call the Ceramic Arts Studio figures "Harrington" figures because she designed so many of them. These figurines are the most popular Ceramic Arts Studio pieces collected today. Betty Harrington died in March 1997.

CELLULOID is a trademark for a plastic developed in 1868 by John W. Hyatt. Celluloid Manufacturing Company, the Celluloid Novelty Company, Celluloid Fancy Goods Company, and American Xylonite Company all used celluloid to make jewelry, games, sewing equipment, false teeth, and piano keys. The name *celluloid* was often used to identify any similar plastic. Celluloid toys are listed under Toy.

Baby Carriage Clips, Duck Shape, Squeeze Heads To Open, 4 In.	80.00
Box, Accessory, Manicure, Woman In Rowboat, Blue Silk Lining, 3 x 9¼ In.	365.00
Box, Glove, Purple Poppies, Cottage, Tree Filled Landscape, Brass Clasp, 13 x 3¼ In.	245.00
Case, Calling Card, Carved, Figure Cartouches, Landscapes, Chinese, 3¼ x 1¾ In.	59.00
Comb, Clear, Blue Sets, 1869-1910, 5¾ x 3¾ In.	185.00
Dresser Set, Bevel Edge, Oval Mirror, Silver Top Brush, Monogram, 3 Piece	50.00
Hand Mirror, Ivory Pyralin, Marked, Dubarry	60.00
Luggage Tag, Transatlantique French Line, Havre & New York, Leather Strap, c.1930	29.00
Manicure Tools, Nail File, Cuticle Tool, Nail Buffer, America, 1900-20	18.00
Mirror, Packard Car, Handheld, 13½ x 7½ In.	342.00
Mirror & Lipstick Holder, RMS Queen Mary, c.1940, 2½ In.	94.00
Notebook, Plant Line, Steamship, Twin Screw, 2¾ x 4 In.	29.00
Stamp Holder, Miller Triple X Side Seat, Haverford Cycle, Philadelphia, 1¼ x 2¼ In.	368.00
Stamp Holder, Ride A Monarch & Keep In Front, 1¼ x 2¼ In.	62.00

CELS *are listed in this book in the Animation Art category.*

CERAMIC ART COMPANY of Trenton, New Jersey, was established in 1889 by J. Coxon and W. Lenox and was an early producer of American belleek porcelain. It became Lenox, Inc. in 1906. Do not confuse this ware with the pottery made by the Ceramic Arts Studio of Madison, Wisconsin.

Pitcher, Cider, Flowers, American Belleek, c.1900, 5¾ In.	176.00

CERAMIC ARTS STUDIO was founded about 1940 in Madison, Wisconsin, by Lawrence Rabbett and Ruben Sand. Their most popular products were expensive molded figurines. The pottery closed in 1955. Do not confuse these products with those of the Ceramic Art Co. of Trenton, New Jersey.

Figurine, Boy & Girl, Shelf Sitter, Leaning In For Kiss, Marked, 5 In.	165.00
Figurine, Covered Wagon, 2¼ x 2⅞ In.	24.00
Figurine, Dance Moderne Man, 1952, 9½ In.	95.00
Figurine, Dog, Dachshund, Standing, 2½ x 3½ In.	125.00
Figurine, Dutch Boy & Girl, Hanz Hides Bouquet Of Tulips, 6½ In., Pair	195.00
Figurine, Elsie The Elephant, 1949, 5 In.	81.00
Figurine, Katrinka, Chubby Dutch Girl, 1955, 6¼ In.	55.00
Figurine, Lamb, 1948, 3¾ In.	41.00
Figurine, Russian Man & Woman, 1950s, 5¼ In., Pair	90.00
Figurine, Sultan On Pillow, Marked, 1951, 4½ In.	99.00
Figurine, Winter Belle, 1950s, 5¼ In.	75.00
Plaque, Greg The Dancer, 1950s, 9½ In.	55.00
Salt & Pepper, Calico Cat, Gingham Dog, 3 In.	135.00

Salt & Pepper, Fighting Cocks, 1949 .... 80.00
Salt & Pepper, Polar Bear Mom, Baby Nesting, Marked, 4½ In. 95.00
Salt & Pepper, Siamese Cats, Thai & Thai-Thai, 1952 .... 80.00
Shaker, Mother Rabbit, 4½ In. 24.00
Shelf Sitter, Dog, Collie, 5⅛ In. 70.00
Shelf Sitter, Harmonica Boy, 1948, 4 In. 105.00
Shelf Sitter, Oriental Boy & Girl Sitting, Sun-Lu, Su-Lin, Red, Yellow, 5½ In. 85.00
Shelf Sitter, Persian Cat, 5½ In. 70.00
Shelf Sitter, Persian Cat, White, c.1950, 5½ In. 49.00
Vase, Bud, Bamboo, Wing-Sang, Marked, 1947, 7 In. 39.00

CHALKWARE is really plaster of Paris decorated with watercolors. One type was molded from Staffordshire and other porcelain models and painted and sold as inexpensive decorations in the nineteenth century. This type is very valuable today. Figures of plaster, made from about 1910 to 1940 for use as prizes at carnivals, are also known as chalkware.

Ashtray, Bonzo, Playful Pose, Butt In Air, Black, White, 1935, 5 x 5 In. 88.00
Ashtray, Bonzo, Seated, Green Figure, Orange Ashtray, 1930s, 5 x 6 In. 147.00
Bank, Dog, Pug, Standing, Brown Spots, Red Facial Features, 7½ x 8½ In. 248.00
Compote, Fruit, Multicolored, Kissing Live Birds, Hollow, 11½ In. 770.00
Figurine, Baby Snooks, Crying, 4 In. 29.00
Figurine, Bird, On Platform, Brown, Multicolored, 3½ In. 242.00
Figurine, Birds, Leaves, Berries, Green, Brown, Cylindrical Base, c.1840, 10 In. 3000.00
Figurine, Cat, Seated, Bow Around Neck, Multicolored, Hollow, 6¾ In. 100.00
Figurine, Cat, Seated, White, Gray, Pink Ears, Collar, Hollow, 6¼ In. 688.00
Figurine, Cat, Seated, Yellow Trim, 6⅝ In. 518.00
Figurine, Dog, Poodle, Dimpled Chest, White, Black, Green, 7⅛ x 6 In. 132.00
Figurine, Dog, Poodle, Seated, Gold Paint, Dimpled Body, Square Base, Hollow, 6¼ In. 138.00
Figurine, Dog, Poodle, Standing, 7⅛ In. 230.00
Figurine, Dog, Poodle, Standing, Dimpled Chest, Multicolored, Hollow, 8 x 6¼ In. 248.00
Figurine, Dove, On Stump, Multicolored, 11 In. 99.00
Figurine, Horse, Yellow & Black Mane, Hollow, Rock Form Oval Base, 10 x 8 In. 176.00
Figurine, Lovebirds, 2 Birds Facing Each Other, Oval Base, 9½ In. 402.00
Figurine, Mae West, Painted, Sparkle Accents, 1930s, 14¼ In. .... *illus* 345.00
Figurine, Parrot, 1870s, 10½ In. 3500.00
Figurine, Parrot, Perched On Mound, Red & Black Highlights, Hollow, 7⅛ In. 28.00
Figurine, Pelican, Painted, 6 In. 1793.00
Figurine, Rabbit, Seated, Painted, 6 In. 132.00
Figurine, Ram, Standing, 7¾ In. 1725.00
Figurine, Ram, Standing, Red, Yellow, Black, Hollow, Stepped Rectangular Base, 8¾ x 6 In. . 495.00
Figurine, Sheep, Lying Down, Dimpled Body, Hollow, Oval Gold Base, 3¾ x 4¾ In. 154.00
Figurine, Sheep, Lying Down, With Lamb, 9 x 6½ In. 402.00
Figurine, Squirrel, Seated, Holding Nut In Mouth, Multicolored, Oval Base, 5¾ In. 303.00
Figurine, Stag, Lying Down, Multicolored, Green Vine Surrounds Base, 10 In. 231.00
Figurine, Stag, Lying Down, Multicolored, Oval Base, 6¼ x 4 In. .... *illus* 1540.00
Figurine, Stag, Lying Down, Multicolored, Rectangular Base, Hollow, 10½ x 8 In., Pair 1650.00
Figurine, Stag, Lying Down, Smoke Decorated, Rectangular Base, Hollow, 9⅜ x 8 In. 138.00
Garniture, Basket Of Fruit, Original Paint, 11 In. 288.00
Garniture, Mantel, Fruit, Multicolored, White Plinth, 13¾ In. 2938.00
Model, Capitol Building, Stained Glass Panels, Front Openings, Lighted, 18 In. 440.00
Vase, Art Nouveau, White, Standing Woman, Holding Vine, 22¼ x 10 In. 144.00

CHARLIE CHAPLIN, the famous comic and actor, lived from 1889 to 1977. He made his first movie in 1913. He did the movie *The Tramp* in 1915. The character of the Tramp has remained famous, and in the 1980s appeared in a series of television commercials for computers. Dolls, candy containers, and all sorts of memorabilia with the image of Charlie's Tramp are collected. Pieces are being made even today.

Candy Container, Glass, Painted, Coin Slot, Borgfeldt Dist., 3½ In. .... *illus* 83.00
Doll, Papier-Mache Face & Arms, Soft Cloth Legs, Gee Tumbling Toys, Windup, 12 In. 85.00
Figure, Original Paint, Cast Iron, 3 x 1⅛ In. 252.00
Match Holder, Bisque, Schafer & Vader, c.1920 .... 228.00
Pencil Box, Tin Lithograph, Signed, Henry Cline, 7¾ x 2¼ x ¾ In. 75.00
Thimble, Chaplin, Movable Black Hat, Navy Jacket, Cane, Pewter, Painted 20.00
Toy, Hat Tipper, Pull String, Mechanical, Tin Lithograph, Germany, 1930s, 4 In. 166.00
Toy, Walker, Cane Spins, Felt Clothes, Windup, Schuco, Box, 6½ In. .... *illus* 936.00

Chalkware, Figurine, Mae West, Painted, Sparkle Accents, 1930s, 14¼ In. $345.00

Chalkware, Figurine, Stag, Lying Down, Multicolored, Oval Base, 6¼ x 4 In. $1540.00

Charlie Chaplin, Candy Container, Glass, Painted, Coin Slot, Borgfeldt Dist., 3½ In. $83.00

C

Charlie Chaplin, Toy,
Walker, Cane Spins, Felt Clothes,
Windup, Schuco, Box, 6½ In.
$936.00

CHARLIE McCARTHY was the ventriloquist's dummy used by Edgar Bergen from the 1930s. He was famous for his work in radio, movies, and television. The act was retired in the 1970s.

Bank, Charlie McCarthy, Seated On Trunk, Movable Jaw, 5½ In.	175.00
Bank, Charlie McCarthy, Standing, Hand In Pockets, Right Glancing Eyes, Composition, 9⅜ In.	85.00
Book, Big Little, Story Of Charlie McCarthy, By Edgar Bergan, No. 1456, 1938	45.00
Charm, Charlie McCarthy Head, Movable Mouth, 2 x 1 In.	29.00
Dummy, Cloth Stuffed, Plastic Head, Movable Jaw, 28 In.	44.00
Dummy, Composition, Cloth Body, Effanbee, Late 1930s, 19½ In.	246.00
Game, Radio Party, Chase & Sanborn Premium, Envelope, 1938	100.00
Pencil Sharpener, Bakelite	65.00
Pin, Edgar Bergen's Charlie McCarthy, An Effanbee Play Product, c.1938, 1 In.	73.00
Pin, Letter Of Introduction At Loew's, Red Border, 1938, 1¼ In.	123.00
Puppet, Charlie McCarthy, Composition Head, 1938	45.00
Puppet, Juro Novelty Co., 1970s	130.00
Radio, Charlie Sits On Edge Of Case, Plastic, Majestic, c.1938, 6 x 7 In. ....*illus*	575.00
Salt & Pepper, Charlie McCarthy, Bust, Pottery, 1940s, 3 In.	79.00
Spoon, Charlie McCarthy, Silver Plated, 6 In. .... 15.00 to 29.00	
Toy, Benzine Buggy, Tin, Windup, Marx, Box, 1930s, 8 In. .... 784.00 to 950.00	
Toy, Car, Whoopee, Mortimer Snerd, Tin, Windup, Marx, 8 In.	575.00
Toy, Charlie McCarthy, Holding Cane, Walker, Celluloid, Windup, 7¼ In.	295.00
Toy, Charlie McCarthy, Standing, Movable Jaw, Marx, 12¼ In.	100.00
Toy, Charlie McCarthy, Walker, Tin, Windup, Marx, 8 In.	247.00
Toy, Crazy Car, Benzine Buggy, Tin, Windup, Action, Marx, 7 In.	220.00
Toy, Drummer, Strike Up The Band, Tin, Windup, Marx, Box, 8 In. .... 1650.00 to 1792.00	
Toy, Gentleman Ventriloquist, Celluloid, Windup, C & K, Japan, Box, 1930s, 7 In.	575.00
Toy, Mortimer Snerd, Drummer, Drum, Tin Lithograph, Windup, Marx, 8½ In. ......*illus*	633.00
Toy, Mortimer Snerd, Hometown Band, Tin Lithograph, Marx, Box, c.1936, 8½ In.	1456.00
Toy, Mortimer Snerd, Tin, Windup, Hat Flips, Vibrates, Marx, Box, 8¼ In.	634.00
Toy, Private Car, Charlie & Mortimer, Black, Red, Yellow, Tin, Windup, Marx, 16 In.	1650.00

Charlie McCarthy, Radio,
Charlie Sits On Edge Of Case, Plastic,
Majestic, c.1938, 6 x 7 In.
$575.00

CHELSEA porcelain was made in the Chelsea area of London from about 1745 to 1769. Some pieces made from 1770 to 1784 are called Chelsea Derby and may include the letter *D* for *Derby* in the mark. Ceramic designs were borrowed from the Meissen models of the day. Pieces were made of soft paste. The gold anchor was used as the mark but it has been copied by many other factories. Recent copies of Chelsea have been made from the original molds. Do not confuse Chelsea porcelain with Chelsea Grape, a white pottery with luster grape decoration.

Bowl, Exotic Birds, Landscape, Soft Paste, Scalloped Border, Blue, Gilt, 2¼ x 9½ In.	316.00
Box, Bonbonniere, Cover, Lady's Head, Mob Cap, Puce Ribbon, Gold Mount, c.1755, 2 In.	8400.00
Box, Bonbonniere, Lady, Seated, Spaniel On Lap, Flowered Dress, c.1760, 1⅞ In.	1320.00
Box, Cover, Basket Form, White, Flowers, Bird On Branch, Gold & Enamel Mount, c.1760, 1⅛ In.	1680.00
Candlestick, Flowers, Leaves, Scrolls, Applied Flower Garland, Gilt, Gold Anchor Mark, c.1755, 7 In.	1920.00
Cooler, Wine, Cupid, Claret Ground, Gilt, Scroll Handles, Chelsea Derby, c.1770, 6¼ In., Pair	6000.00
Cup & Saucer, Exotic Birds, Alternating Blue Panels, Scrolls, Gilt, Gold Anchor Mark, c.1760	5400.00
Figurine, Flower Seller, Basket Strapped To Back, Applied Flowers, Red Anchor Mark, c.1755, 9 In.	1560.00
Figurine, Maiden, Skirt Filled With Flowers, Square Base, Gilt, Chelsea Derby, c.1770, 8¾ In.	990.00
Figurine, Peacock, Head Turned, Tree Stump, Applied Leaves, Red Anchor Mark, c.1750, 8 In.	1080.00
Inkstand, 2 Pen Trays, Pounce Pot, Pots, Cherubs, Puce, Gilt, 4-Footed, Pierced, c.1765, 10⅝ In.	5100.00
Pitcher, Lavender, Embossed Garland, 5¾ In.	105.00
Plate, Botanical, Puce Flowers, Cactus Stem, Leaf Sprays, Fruit, Insects, Red Anchor Mark, 9¼ In.	2700.00
Plate, Flowers, Bouquets, Gilt, Blue Enamel Border, Scroll Rim, Gold Anchor Mark, c.1765, 9 In.	600.00
Scent Bottle, Yellow Rope Design, Flower Sprays On Neck, Eau De Senteur, Stopper, 3⅛ In.	720.00
Vase, Potpourri, Birds, Butterflies, Gilt Scrolls, Reticulated Panel, 7½ In., Pair ....*illus*	9600.00

Charlie McCarthy, Toy,
Mortimer Snerd, Drummer,
Drum, Tin Lithograph, Windup,
Marx, 8½ In.
$633.00

CHELSEA GRAPE pattern was made before 1840. A small bunch of grapes in a raised design, colored with purple or blue luster, is on the border of the white plate. Most of the pieces are unmarked. The pattern is sometimes called Aynsley or Grandmother. Chelsea Sprig is similar but has a sprig of flowers instead of the bunch of grapes. Chelsea Thistle has a raised thistle pattern. Do not confuse these Chelsea patterns with Chelsea Keramic Art Works, which can be found in the Dedham category, or with Chelsea porcelain, the preceding category.

Sugar & Creamer, Lavender Blue Grape Leaves, Relief, 3-In. Sugar	45.00

CHELSEA KERAMIC ART WORKS *items are listed in the Dedham category.*

CHINESE EXPORT porcelain comprises all the many kinds of porcelain made in China for export to America and Europe in the eighteenth, nineteenth, and twentieth centuries. Other pieces may be listed in this book under Canton, Celadon, Nanking, and Rose Medallion.

Basin, Blue & White, Fitzhugh, 16 In.	767.00
Basin, Cranes, Peonies, 8-Sided, Multicolored Overglaze, 14½ In.	570.00
Basin, Famille Verte, Figures, Garden, Blue Underglaze, Turned Out Rim, 19th Century, 11 In. Diam.	108.00
Basin, Storage, Cover, Famille Rose, Flowers, Shell Handles, Iron Red, 8 x 9 In.	780.00
Bottle, Pilgrim, Fish, Cherry Blossoms, Salamander Handles, Blue, 8 In., Pair	403.00
Bough Pot, Pierced Cover, Figures, Landscape, Flared, Leaf Handles, 11 In., Pair	1410.00
Bowl, Blue & White, 2 Scholars, Landscape, 19th Century, 11 In.	118.00
Bowl, Blue & White, Fish, Foo Dog, 16½ x 15¾ In., Pair	826.00
Bowl, Center Bouquet, Fleur-De-Lis Border, Gilt Flower Ground, 11¼ In.	1020.00
Bowl, Center Medallion, Landscape, Hunter, Dog, Shell Border, 1700s, 16 In.	4560.00
Bowl, Cover, Famille Rose, Flowers, Characters, 7¾ In.	443.00
Bowl, Cover, Fitzhugh, Green, Rectangular, Gilded Pinecone Knop, 5½ x 8 In.	558.00
Bowl, Famille Rose, Bird, Flowers, 3 In.	266.00
Bowl, Famille Rose, Center Bouquet, Draped Border, Ships, 1700s, 10¼ In.	1020.00
Bowl, Famille Rose, Figures, 10½ In.	295.00
Bowl, Famille Rose, Figures, Scalloped, 9½ In.	212.00
Bowl, Famille Rose, Flower Filled Vases, Turquoise Interior, Octagonal, 9¼ In.	590.00
Bowl, Famille Rose, Flowering Branches, Green Ground, 3½ In., Pair	3658.00
Bowl, Famille Rose, Flowers, 4½ x 10¾ In.	826.00
Bowl, Famille Rose, Flowers, 14½ In.	3304.00
Bowl, Famille Rose, Flowers, Faux Basket Weave, Blue, 10 In.	510.00
Bowl, Famille Rose, Lotus Heads, Scrolling Leaves, 6 In.	3894.00
Bowl, Famille Rose, Peony, Ruby Ground, 5⅞ In.	2478.00
Bowl, Famille Rose, Phoenix Bird, Flowers, 18th Century, 11 In., Pair	708.00
Bowl, Famille Rose, Woman Under Flowering Tree, Holding Scepter, 7½ In.	3540.00
Bowl, Famille Verte, Landscape, Seated Figure, Blue Ground, Gilt, Trellis Border, c.1720, 7 In.	890.00
Bowl, Famille Verte, Rice, Dragon Rondels, Cafe Au Lait Glaze, 8½ In.	764.00
Bowl, Figures, Hexagonal, 19th Century, 7 In.	499.00
Bowl, Iron Red & White, 6 Characters, 2¾ x 6 In., Pair	1416.00
Bowl, Peony, Arms, Of New York State, Colored Enamels, Gilt, c.1795, 11½ In.	3840.00
Bowl, United States Eagle, Carnation, Initials, Gilt, c.1800, 11½ In.	2640.00
Bowl, Urn Reserves, Flower Bouquets, Gilt Edges, 18th Century, 10¼ In.	2530.00
Box, Cover, Flowering Prunus Tree, Birds, Blue Lotus, 4½ In. Diam.	295.00
Box, Famille Rose, Figures, 19th Century, 3¾ In.	295.00
Brush Washer, Famille Rose, Dragon, 19th Century, 4½ In.	1298.00
Brushpot, Bamboo, Dragons, Pearls, 5 In.	206.00
Brushpot, Blue & White, 7 x 7½ In.	2360.00
Brushpot, Famille Rose, Figures, 5½ In.	590.00
Brushpot, Figures In Landscape, 2 Circles, Cylindrical, 18th Century, 7¼ x 8 In.	2350.00
Brushpot, Immortals, Landscape, Carved Bamboo, 6 In.	5288.00
Cachepot, Famille Rose, Flowers, Calligraphy, Footed, 3¾ x 7 In.	207.00
Cake Stand, 4 Panels, Scalloped Rim, Tapered, Pedestal, Band, Late 19th Century, 4½ x 10½ In.	575.00
Candlestick, Sepia, Blue Underglaze, Enamel, Gilt Starred Border, c.1900, 5 In.	2400.00
Censer, Blue & White, Dragons Chasing Pearl Of Wisdom, 7¾ In.	502.00
Censer, Duck Form, 3¾ x 5 In.	561.00
Charger, Blue & White, Butterflies, Peonies, Fretwork Border, 1800s, 15¼ In.	329.00
Charger, Blue & White, Central Reserve, Roosters, Flower Band, 11 In.	174.00
Charger, Blue & White, Cranes, Tree, 3 Friends, Flower Border, Octagonal, 17 In.	1140.00
Charger, Blue & White, Flowers, Diamond Border, 1700s, 12½ In.	293.00
Charger, Blue & White, Kraak Style, Bird, Flowers, 12½ In.	177.00
Charger, Boys Dancing In Celebration With Dragon, 13½ In.	248.00
Charger, Carp, Jumping, Waves, Cliffs, Trees, Storks, Blue, Red Symbol, Signed, 16¾ In.	747.00
Charger, Famille Rose, Flowers, 22 In.	2360.00
Charger, Famille Rose, Flowers, c.1760, 15¼ In.	1180.00
Charger, Famille Rose, Mandarin, Figures, Flowers, Panels, 13½ In.	633.00
Charger, Flowers, Iron Red, Blue, c.1700, 15½ In.	332.00
Charger, Orange Fitzhugh, American Eagle, Mahogany Stand, 22 x 18 In.	2350.00
Cup, Cover, Armorial, Silver Base, 18th Century, 6½ x 6½ In.	468.00
Cup, Famille Rose, Overlapping Lotus Petal Rows, c.1820, 2 x 3⅜ In., Pair	805.00
Cup, Wine, Famille Rose, Hall For Cultivation Of Virtue, 2½ In., Pair	649.00
Cup & Saucer, Famille Rose, Mythology Scene, Judgment Of Paris, 4¾ In., 4 Piece	826.00
Dish, Armorial, Leaf Shape, Sepia Sailing Ship, Blue & Red Geometric Border, 8½ In.	470.00
Dish, Blue & White, Birds, Flowers, Square, 5½ In.	206.00

Chelsea, Vase, Potpourri, Birds, Butterflies, Gilt Scrolls, Reticulated Panel, 7½ In., Pair
$9600.00

Chinese Export, Mug, 3-Masted Ship, Rattan Covered Pewter Handle, 4½ In.
$288.00

TIP

When packing teapots to move, do not tape the lid to the pot. The tape may leave a stain and the lid may chip if it is handled roughly or just bumps around while being moved in a car.

C

Chinese Export Porcelain

Chinese potters made restrained, simple pottery or porcelain for use in their own country. When the first few pieces were brought back to Europe by Marco Polo in the late thirteenth century, Chinese porcelain was considered a rarity worth more than gold. Europeans were not able to make porcelain until the eighteenth century, when the secret was discovered at Meissen, Germany. During the eighteenth century, when trading with the Orient became more common, the ships of England and Holland brought back dishes to please European tastes. We call them Chinese Export porcelain or China trade porcelain.

Chinese Export, Plate,
Armorial, Shield, Banner,
Touch Not The Cat Gloveless, 9 In.
$288.00

Chinese Export, Platter,
Famille Rose, Roses & Leaves,
Scalloped Edge, 13¾ x 10¾ In.
$633.00

Dish, Condiment, Blue & White, Center Decoration, Fitzhugh, 10 In.	540.00
Dish, Famille Rose, Lotus, 18th Century, 8⅜ In.	354.00
Dish, Famille Rose, Pink Flower Clusters, Turquoise Band, c.1730, 8¾ In., Pair	5980.00
Dish, Lotus Scrolls, Blue Underglaze, 1862-73, 6¼ In.	235.00
Dresser Set, Silver, Repousse Chrysanthemum, Wang Hing & Co., c.1900, 9 Piece	1610.00
Ewer, Cover, Flowers, Baluster, 8 In.	885.00
Ewer, Famille Rose, Flowers, Tibetan Style, 8 In.	826.00
Figurine, Doves, Turquoise, 19th Century, 8 In.	3000.00
Figurine, Famille Rose, Dignitary & Child, 24 In.	944.00
Figurine, Famille Rose, Lion & Boy, c.1800, 8 x 6½ In.	1770.00
Figurine, Famille Rose, Phoenix, 23½ In.	2242.00
Figurine, Famille Rose, Taoist Dignitary, 9 In.	354.00
Figurine, Famille Verte, Dignitary Wearing Robes, Cranes, Clouds, 12½ In.	590.00
Figurine, Foo Dog, Green, 6 In., Pair	295.00
Figurine, Foo Dog, White Marble, Carved, Ming Dynasty Style, 28 x 10 x 15 In., Pair	960.00
Figurine, God Of Wealth, Holding Child, 20th Century, 11 In.	176.00
Figurine, Goddess Of Mercy, Seated, Wearing Long Robes, Veil, Holding Vase, 16 In.	1770.00
Figurine, Hawk, Crouching, Pierced Rockwork Base, Multicolored, 8¾ x 11 In.	360.00
Figurine, Horse, Standing, Turquoise Glaze, 19th Century, 6⅛ In., Pair	4800.00
Figurine, Official, Blue & White, 17th Century, 13¼ x 7¼ In.	6490.00
Figurine, Parrot, Standing, Blanc De Chine, Rockwork Base, c.1900, 8¼ In., Pair	200.00
Figurine, Phoenix, Turquoise Glaze, Pierced Base, 19th Century, 15½ In.	4200.00
Figurine, Rooster, Turquoise, Aubergine, 10 In., Pair	118.00
Flask, Famille Rose, Pilgrim, Peacock, Warriors On Horseback, 10 In., Pair	944.00
Flask, Pilgrim, Leaves, Loop Form Handle, 7¼ In.	531.00
Ginger Jar, Blue & White, Lid, Foo Dog Handles, 23 x 14 In., Pair	1998.00
Group, 3 Roosters, Turquoise Glaze, c.1900, 11 In.	2700.00
Group, 5 Dogs, Standing, Seated, Turquoise Glaze, Aubergine Base, 4⅜ In.	2400.00
Group, 5 Roosters, Turquoise Glaze, 9⅞ In.	4500.00
Incense Burner, Famille Jeune, Dragons, Shou Character, Clouds, 10½ In.	999.00
Jar, Black Fish, Scrolling, Flowers, Cream Glaze, 11 x 14 In.	3525.00
Jar, Blue & White, Foo Dog, 13 In.	354.00
Jar, Cover, Animals, Grisaille, White, Electrified, 14½ In., Pair	708.00
Jar, Cover, Armorial, 18th Century, 6 x 4¾ In.	293.00
Jar, Cover, Blue & White, 11 In.	2950.00
Jar, Cover, Blue & White, Butterfly, Flower Cartouche, 9½ In.	236.00
Jar, Cover, Blue & White, Calligraphy, Butterfly, Leaves, 17 In.	472.00
Jar, Cover, Blue & White, Dragons, Baluster, 25 In.	1100.00
Jar, Cover, Enameled Crest & Armorials, Garden Seat Shape, Cash Shaped Lid, 5 In., Pair	352.00
Jar, Cover, Famille Jeune, Warriors, Enamels, Hexagonal, 19th Century, 20 In.	1880.00
Jar, Cover, Famille Rose, Dragons, Flowering Branches, 16 In.	561.00
Jar, Cover, Famille Rose, Flower Heads, 2 In., Pair	472.00
Jar, Cover, Famille Verte, Qilin, Mythical Creature, 9½ In.	153.00
Jar, Cover, Figures In Garden, Wucai-Style Baluster, 19th Century, 14¼ In., Pair	8400.00
Jar, Famille Rose, Bird Perched, Flowering Prunus Tree, Peony, Painted, 9 In.	649.00
Jar, Famille Rose, Flowers, Exotic Birds, Rectangular Panels, 25½ In.	259.00
Jar, Landscape, Flowering Trees, Blue Underglaze, 1662-1722, 8 In.	353.00
Jardiniere, Blue & White, Flowers, 4-Sided, 15 x 8½ In.	295.00
Jardiniere, Undertray, Blue & White, Bird, Flowering Branches, 12 x 14½ In.	502.00
Mug, 3-Masted Ship, Rattan Covered Pewter Handle, 4½ In. ....*illus*	288.00
Mug, Famille Rose, Flower Handle, 1700s, 4¼ In.	720.00
Mug, Famille Rose, Landscape, Cylindrical, Dragon Frame, 1700s, 6 In.	420.00
Mug, Tobacco Leaf, c.1785, 6 In.	4800.00
Painting, Figurines, Reverse Glass, c.1840, 15½ x 23 In.	274.00
Pitcher, Famille Rose, Mandarin, Paneled, Octagon, 6½ In.	862.00
Planter, Blue & White, Dragon, 9¼ x 14 In.	561.00
Planter, Famille Rose, Flowers, 11¾ In.	443.00
Plate, Famille Rose, Flowers, 18th Century, 9½ In., 10 Piece	1770.00
Plate, Armorial, Shield, Banner, Touch Not The Cat Gloveless, 9 In. ....*illus*	288.00
Plate, Chrysanthemums, Blue, Iron Red, Gilding, 9 In., Pair	450.00
Plate, Dinner, Armorial Crest, Flower Border, Gilt Fleur-De-Lis Edges, 9 In., 6 Piece	587.00
Plate, Famille Rose, Arbor, Figures Seated, Trellis Border, c.1740, 9¼ In.	6600.00
Plate, Famille Rose, Armorial, Gilt, 18th Century, 9 In., Pair	510.00
Plate, Famille Rose, Figures In Garden, Flower Border, Turquoise Ground, 11 In.	441.00
Plate, Famille Rose, Flowers, Open Hand Scroll, Flower Scroll Border, 9 In., Pair	960.00
Plate, Famille Verte, Figures In Garden, Blue Underglaze, 14¾ In.	2115.00

C

Plate, Famille Verte, Flowers, Doucai, 8 In., Pair	266.00
Plate, Farm Animals, Mountains, Multicolored, Enameled, 9¾ In.	823.00
Plate, Fitzhugh, Orange, c.1820, 9¾ In., Pair	413.00
Plate, Judgment Of Paris, Multicolored Enamel, Iron Red Rim, Gilt Shells, 9 In.	529.00
Plate, Millefiori, Gold Ground, 6¼ In., Pair	257.00
Plate, Pomegranates, Blue & Red, Crosshatch & Floral Border, White Ground, 12 In.	300.00
Plate Set, Octagonal, Blue Underglaze Borders, Genre Scenes, 9 In., Pair	240.00
Platter, Blue & White, Landscape, Octagonal, 14½ In.	390.00
Platter, Famille Rose, Landscape, Oval, Gilt Monogram, c.1790, 14 In.	6600.00
Platter, Famille Rose, Roses & Leaves, Scalloped Edge, 13¾ x 10¾ In. ....*illus*	633.00
Platter, Famille Rose, Tobacco Leaf, Blossom, Flowers, Sprigs, 11 x 8 In.	4366.00
Platter, Pink Trellis, Scroll Border, Flower Sprays, Late 18th Century, 17½ In.	1195.00
Platter, Sauceboat, Blue & White, Fitzhugh, Oval, 12½ x 10 In.	130.00
Platter, Tobacco Leaf, 12⅛ In.	8400.00
Platter, Tobacco Leaf, 18¼ In.	15600.00
Platter, Well, Tree, Fitzhugh, Crest, 18th Century, 16 In.	944.00
Platter Set, Graduated Sizes, Blue & White, Early 1800s, 14 In., 4 Piece	337.00
Punch Bowl, Famille Rose, Armorial, Hearts, Gilt Flowers, Late 1700s, 5 x 12 In.	1955.00
Punch Bowl, Birds, Butterflies, Flowers, Panels, 19th Century, 6½ x 16¼ In.	2243.00
Punch Bowl, Famille Rose, Figures, Landscape, Flower Border Interior, 4¾ x 11 In.	1410.00
Punch Bowl, Famille Rose, Floral Medallion, Gilt, 1700s, 12 In.	720.00
Punch Bowl, Famille Rose, Flower Border, c.1800, 4¾ x 11½ In.	1610.00
Punch Bowl, Famille Rose, Flowers, Fleur-De-Lis Border, 15 In.	1800.00
Punch Bowl, Famille Verte, Butterflies, Leaves, c.1900, 14½ In.	1280.00
Punch Bowl, Farm, King Charles II Hiding In Tree, c.1760, 10¼ In.	8400.00
Punch Bowl, Hunting Scene, Horseman, Spearhead Border, c.1770, 15¾ In.	9000.00
Punch Pot, Cover, Figures, Bamboo, Fruit, Vine Border, c.1760, 7½ In.	1440.00
Punch Pot, Fitzhugh, Armorial, Oval, Double Strap Handles, Spout, 11 In.	840.00
Saucer, Famille Rose, Butterfly, Flowers, 6¼ In.	531.00
Screen, Table, Famille Verte, Scholar, Page, Enamels, 9½ In.	1058.00
Teapot, Cover, Famille Rose, Bird, Flowers, Pink Ground, 4 In.	295.00
Teapot, Cover, Famille Rose, Reserve Panels, Canal Scene, 6½ In.	360.00
Teapot, Cover, Tobacco Leaf, 5½ In.	2400.00
Teapot, Famille Rose, Figures, Pavilion, 5½ In.	1003.00
Teapot, Figures In Garden, Reserve Panels, Mons, Gilt Trim, 10½ In.	1175.00
Teapot, Flowers, Bird, Iron Red, Chocolate Brown, Gilt, 5 In.	1416.00
Teapot, White Ground, Encrusted With Flowers, 18th Century, 5½ In.	1018.00
Tray, Famille Rose, Rectangular, Floral, Round Footed, 11½ x 7½ In.	295.00
Tureen, Soup, Cover, Armorial, Valentine, Demi-Wolf Crest, Pheasants, Peonies, Blue, 11 In.	1140.00
Tureen, Soup, Cover, Stand, Rabbit Handles, Flower Knop, 15⅛ In.	2868.00
Tureen, Undertray, Cover, Famille Rose, Flowers, Footed, Gilt Mushroom Finial, 9 x 12 In., 3 Piece	1438.00
Vase, Baluster, Blue & White, c.1900, 24 In.	270.00
Vase, Baluster, Blue & White, Foo Dog, Flower Head, Scrolling Leaves, 11¼ In.	944.00
Vase, Baluster, Blue & White, Hawks On Rock, Peony Branches, 11¾ In.	3600.00
Vase, Baluster, Famille Verte, Flowers, Facets, 12 In.	3422.00
Vase, Baluster, Pheasant On Rockwork, Peonies, Imari Style, 1700s, 26 In.	570.00
Vase, Blue & White, Butterfly, Cong, 4-Sided, Round Rim, 13 In.	3304.00
Vase, Blue & White, Dragon, Garlic Mouth, 13¼ In.	531.00
Vase, Blue & White, Dragons Chasing Pearl Of Wisdom, 3½ In.	767.00
Vase, Blue & White, Flowers, Garlic Mouth, 10½ In.	1003.00
Vase, Blue & White, Mountainscape, 19th Century, 15 In., Pair	472.00
Vase, Blue & White, Riverscape, 14 In.	236.00
Vase, Bottle, Famille Rose, Dragon Chasing Pearl Of Wisdom, Turquoise, 24 In.	530.00
Vase, Bottle, Flowers, Turquoise, 14 In.	764.00
Vase, Bottle, Peach Bloom, 10 In.	502.00
Vase, Cover, Baluster, Dragon Handles, Mandarin Style, 1800s, 13 In.	1320.00
Vase, Double Gourd, Blanc-De-Chine, 5¾ In.	1652.00
Vase, Double Gourd, Blue & White, Foo Dogs, Clouds, 19 In., Pair	1762.00
Vase, Double Gourd, Tea Dust Glaze, 8¼ In.	3186.00
Vase, Dragon, Iron Red & White, 8¾ In.	236.00
Vase, Famille Rose, Birds, Plants, Yellow Ground, Flared Neck & Rim, 13½ In., Pair	705.00
Vase, Famille Rose, Butterflies, Birds, Roses, Foo Dog & Ring Handles, 14 x 7 In., Pair ..*illus*	805.00
Vase, Famille Rose, Dragons, Phoenix Birds, Yellow Ground, 16½ In.	325.00
Vase, Famille Rose, Enamel, Gilt, Applied Chilong, Neck Shishi, 1800s, 18 In.	881.00
Vase, Famille Rose, Flowers, 1912-49, 13 In.	142.00
Vase, Famille Rose, Flowers, Imperial Yellow Ground, 6½ In.	1062.00

Chinese Export, Vase, Famille Rose, Butterflies, Birds, Roses, Foo Dog & Ring Handles, 14 x 7 In., Pair
$805.00

Chinese Export Porcelain for the European and American Markets

The porcelains wanted in Europe and the United States were different from those made for Asians. The porcelain was not as thin and the designs were usually distinctly European. Dishes with family coats of arms, figures in European clothes, American flags, ships, biblical and mythological scenes were made for the European and American markets.

C

Chocolate Glass, Dolphin, Dish, Cover, 4⅜ x 7¼ In. $143.00

Christmas, Belsnickle, Composition, Cloth, Horsehair, Wood Teeth, 1870s, 25 In. $25300.00

Christmas, Belsnickle, White Robe, Blue & Green Trim, Composition, Feather Tree, Germany, $935.00

Christmas, Figure, Santa Claus, Bisque, Red Robe, Holding Feather Tree, Germany, 7½ In. $385.00

Vase, Famille Rose, Garniture, Cylindrical, Flared Rim, Blue Underglaze, 26 In., Pair	480.00
Vase, Famille Rose, Immortals, Clouds, 12¼ In.	531.00
Vase, Famille Rose, Millefleur, Iron Red Seal Mark, 10 In., Pair	531.00
Vase, Famille Rose, Peaches, Flowering Tree, 19th Century, 18 In.	649.00
Vase, Famille Rose, Ponds, Harvesting Women, 10 x 5 In., Pair	374.00
Vase, Famille Rose, Yen Yen, Bird In Flowering Tree, 1800s, 15½ In.	1180.00
Vase, Famille Verte, 6 Characters, 19⅞ In.	2714.00
Vase, Famille Verte, Figurines & Riverscape, 20th Century, 17 In.	354.00
Vase, Famille Verte, Mythical Animals, 10½ In.	1770.00
Vase, Famille Verte, Woman, Phoenix, Man, Dragon, 18 In.	1763.00
Vase, Fish, Doucai, 7½ In.	189.00
Vase, Fish, Turquoise Overlay, 9½ In., Pair	649.00
Vase, Flambe, Baluster, Purple, Blue Glaze, 19th Century, 9¾ In.	940.00
Vase, Flambe, Silver Mounts, 5½ In.	413.00
Vase, Flower Scrolling, Acanthus Leaves, Diaper, Pear Shape, 18th Century, 10½ In.	1645.00
Vase, Flowers, Calligraphy, Iron Red & White, 23 In., Pair	649.00
Vase, Foo Dog, Iron Red & White, 15½ In., Pair	826.00
Vase, Foo Dog, Iron Red & White, 22½ In.	189.00
Vase, Garlic Mouth, Tea Dust, Globular, 2 Handles, 8¼ In.	384.00
Vase, Globular, Tea Dust, Olive Green Glaze, 14 In.	1416.00
Vase, Immortals, Red, Blue Underglaze, Enamel, 5¾ In.	588.00
Vase, Immortals, Reticulated Turquoise Ground, Panels, 9 x 5 In.	551.00
Vase, Iron Red, 18th Century, 9 In.	1416.00
Vase, Prunus Tree, Imperial Yellow, Bird, Square, 11 In.	260.00
Vase, Tobacco Leaf, Cylindrical, Flared Neck & Base, 7¾ In., Pair	646.00
Vase, Water Plants, Acanthus Leaves, Thunder, Yellow Ground, 13¾ In.	1998.00
Warming Dish, Blue & White, Oval, Hot Water Reservoir, c.1835, 2 x 12 In.	375.00
Warming Dish, Fitzhugh, Green, Early 19th Century, 10¾ In., Pair	294.00
Washbowl, Woman Carrying Fruit, Raised Rim, Border Writing, 4 x 11 In.	173.00
Water Drum, Peach Bloom, 4 In., 6 In. Diam	644.00
Wine Pot, Camellia Leaf Green, 4 Characters, Late 19th Century, 6 In.	470.00

CHINTZ is the name of a group of china patterns featuring an overall design of flowers and leaves. The design became popular with English makers about 1928. A few pieces are still being made. The best known are designs by Royal Winton, James Kent Ltd., Crown Ducal, and Shelley. Crown Ducal and Shelley are listed in their own sections.

Anemone, Cup & Saucer, Lord Nelson, 4⅛ In. Cup	125.00
Balmoral, Sugar & Creamer, Royal Winton, Ascot Style, Gold Trim Edge	140.00
Evesham, Cup & Saucer, Demitasse, Royal Wonton	360.00
Hazel, Plate, 4-Sided, Gold Trim, Royal Winton, 7 In.	140.00
Marina, Cup & Saucer, Lord Nelson	98.00
Marina, Vase, Bud, Gold Rim, Footed, Flared, Lord Nelson, 5¼ In.	195.00
Mayfair, Wall Pocket, Crocus Flower Shape, Royal Winton, 8½ In.	850.00
Melody, Plate, Royal Crown, 9 In.	215.00
Midwinter Coral, Saltshaker, Plated Top, 6 x 2½ In.	150.00
Old Cottage, Bowl, Royal Winton, 1¼ x 7¼ x 10 In.	108.00
Rose, Cup & Saucer, Yellow, Gold Trim, Scalloped Edge	30.00
Rose Time, Cup & Saucer, Lord Nelson	80.00
Summertime, Ashtray, Royal Winton, 4½ In.	65.00
Summertime, Nut Dish, Royal Winton, 2 x 3¼ In.	45.00

CHOCOLATE GLASS, sometimes mistakenly called caramel slag, was made by the Indiana Tumbler and Goblet Company of Greentown, Indiana, from 1900 to 1903. It was also made at other National Glass Company factories. Fenton Art Glass Co. made chocolate glass from about 1907 to 1915. More recent pieces have been made by Imperial and others.

Argonaut, Butter, Cover	125.00
Cactus, Berry Bowl, Greentown, c.1900, 3½ x 8¼ In.	110.00
Cactus, Biscuit Jar, Cover, Greentown, 8 In.	145.00
Cactus, Biscuit Jar, Greentown, c.1903, 6 x 5⅜ In.	88.00
Cactus, Biscuit Jar, Greentown, c.1903, 8 x 5½ In.	145.00
Dolphin, Dish, Cover, 4⅜ x 7¼ In. .... *illus*	143.00
Feather Pattern, Pitcher, Greentown, 8 In.	1410.00
Leaf Bracket, Berry Bowl, Greentown, 2 x 4¾ In.	60.00
Leaf Bracket, Butter, Cover, Greentown, c.1900, 5⅛ x 7¼ In.	145.00
Leaf Bracket, Celery Tray, 11 x 5⅝ In.	90.00

Leaf Bracket, Nappy, Handle, Greentown	110.00
Squirrel, Pitcher, 9 In.	358.00
Wild Rose With Festoon, Lamp, Kerosene, Embossed Flowers, 10 In.	950.00

CHRISTMAS collectibles include not only Christmas trees and ornaments listed below, but also Santa Claus figures, special dishes, and even games and wrapping paper. A Belsnickle is a nineteenth-century figure of Father Christmas. A kugel is an early, heavy ornament made of thick blown glass, lined with zinc or lead, and often covered with colored wax. Christmas cards are listed in this section under Greeting Card. Christmas collectibles may also be listed in the Candy Container category. Christmas trees are listed in the section that follows.

Christmas, Figure,
Santa Claus, Robe,
Wood Carrier On Back, Feather Tree,
Germany, 8 In.
$825.00

Badge, Santa Wants To See You At Kaufmann's, 1¼ In.	74.00
Bank, Santa Claus, On Base, Tree Holder, Bronze Wash, Cast Iron, M 56, 7¼ In.	220.00
Banner, Headquarters For Christmas Toys, Santa Claus In Chimney, Linen, 1900s, 36 x 60 In.	2200.00
Belsnickle, Composition, Cloth, Horsehair, Wood Teeth, Box, 1870s, 25 In. .... *illus*	25300.00
Belsnickle, Papier-Mache, Felt, Pipe Cleaners, Painted Face, Japan, 6 In.	30.00
Belsnickle, Papier-Mache, Gold Coat, Feather Tree, 11¼ In.	825.00
Belsnickle, Papier-Mache, Mica-Covered Lavender Coat, Feather Tree, Berry, 7½ In.	715.00
Belsnickle, Papier-Mache, Mica-Covered Seafoam Green Coat, Feather Tree	10.00
Belsnickle, White Robe, Blue & Green Trim, Composition, Feather Tree, Germany, 12 In. *illus*	935.00
Boot, Santa Claus, Rippin Good Cookie, 10 In.	135.00
Candlestick, Tin, Glass, Multicolored, 8-Sided, Holder, 3¼ In.	72.00
Candy Containers are listed in the Candy Container category.	
Chop Plate, Holly, Burleigh Ware, Round, 13 In.	48.00
Figure, Father Christmas, Paper Crackers, Wood, Carved Head & Hands, 16 x 6 In.	350.00
Figure, Father Frost, Holding Staff, Bag Of Flowers, Papier-Mache, Cloth, Russia, 28 In.	288.00
Figure, Santa Claus, Belsnickle-Style, Holding Feather Tree, 1900s, 10 In.	530.00
Figure, Santa Claus, Bisque, Red Robe, Holding Feather Tree, Germany, 7½ In. ......*illus*	385.00
Figure, Santa Claus, Composition, Rabbit Fur Beard, Windup, Prewar Germany, 6 In.	250.00
Figure, Santa Claus, Red & White Outfit, Black Boots, Straw Filled, Germany, c.1920, 18 In. .	495.00
Figure, Santa Claus, Robe, Wood Carrier On Back, Feather Tree, Germany, 8 In. ......*illus*	825.00
Figure Set, Angel Musicians, Composition, West Germany, U.S. Zone, 3¾ In., 6 Piece ..*illus*	58.00
Figurine, Christmas Island, Christmas Cabin, Pendelfin	84.00
Game, Marble, Santa Claus In Car, Wood, Lithograph, 6 In. ....*illus*	1760.00
Greeting Card, King Features Popular Comics, Box, c.1945	522.00
Greeting Card, To Sweet Little Daughter, Little Girl On Santa Claus' Lap, 4¼ x 7 In.	6.00
Humidor, Santa Claus, Germany, 8 In. ....*illus*	1210.00
Mold, Santa Claus, Chocolate, Metal, 8½ In.	110.00
Nativity Set, Papier-Mache, Manger, Figures, Germany, 1920s, 15 Piece	495.00
Nodder, Reindeer, Fur, Antlers, Windup	1980.00
Nodder, Reindeer, Keywind, Germany, 14 x 12 In. ....*illus*	4675.00
Nodder, Santa Claus, Tin, Celluloid, Windup, Box, Masudaya	150.00
Noisemaker, Clicker Chirper, Santa, Flying Plane, Meet Me At American Dry Goods, 1¼ In. .	139.00
Pin, Brooklyn Eagle, Santa Claus Aid Society, Santa Holding American Flags, Celluloid, 1¾ In. ..	495.00
Pin, Burke, Fitzsimons, Hone Store, Santa Claus, Rochester, N.Y., 1½ In.	69.00
Pin, Hazelton Shopping, Santa Claus, Celluloid, 1¼ In.	13.00
Pin, Key, Schrafft's, Key To A Merry Christmas, White, Red, Green, Celluloid, 1¼ In.	19.00
Pin, L. Wertheimer, Santa Claus, Gives Presents To Doughboy, World War I, 1¼ In.	303.00
Pin, Mr. Bingle, Holding Candy Cane, Red, Green, White, Black, Celluloid, 1 In.	14.00
Pin, Santa Claus, Bi-Plane, Wanamaker's, Merry Christmas, Celluloid, 1½ In.	632.00
Pin, Santa Claus, Boston Store's Toy Contest, I'm A Candidate, Celluloid, 1¼ In.	75.00
Pin, Santa Claus, Climbing In Chimney, Toys, Metal Covered Back, c.1930, 1½ In.	140.00
Pin, Santa Claus, Give Something Electrical, Celluloid, 1910s, 1¼ In.	240.00
Pin, Santa Claus, Goerke's Toyland, Celluloid, 1910s, 1¼ In.	85.00
Pin, Santa Claus, I Am At Joyce Green Co., Toys, Teddy Bear, c.1908, 1½ In.	280.00
Pin, Santa Claus, I Am At The Bon Marche Seattle, 1900-12, 1¼ In.	192.00
Pin, Santa Claus, I Am At The May Co., 1900-12, 1½ In.	265.00
Pin, Santa Claus, I Am At The May Co., Holly & Berries Around Hat, Celluloid, 1 In.	15.00
Pin, Santa Claus, Merry Christmas, Celluloid, 1¼ In. .... 13.00 to 22.00
Pin, Santa Claus, Merry Christmas, Happy New Year, Head Only, Holly, Celluloid	24.00
Pin, Santa Claus, People's Outfitting Co., Celluloid, 1910s, 1¼ In.	98.00
Pin, Santa Claus, Polar Bear, Otter, North Pole, 1¼ In.	117.00
Pin, Santa Claus, Roth's Variety Store, Celluloid, 1930s, 1½ In.	171.00
Pin, Santa's Good Behavior Award, Late 1940s, 1¼ In.	45.00
Pin, Santa's Guest, North Pole, New York, 1¼ In.	17.00

Christmas, Figure Set,
Angel Musicians, Composition,
West Germany, U.S. Zone,
3¾ In., 6 Piece
$58.00

Christmas, Game,
Marble, Santa Claus In Car, Wood,
Lithograph, 6 In.
$1760.00

C

Christmas, Humidor,
Santa Claus, Germany, 8 In.
$1210.00

Christmas, Nodder,
Reindeer, Keywind,
Germany, 14 x 12 In.
$4675.00

Christmas, Puppet,
Santa Claus, Wood, Paper,
Jointed, Pull String,
Arms & Legs Move, 12 In.
$220.00

Pin, Smiling Christmas Store Santa, 1924-39, 1 In.	407.00
Pin, Spiegel, Santa Claus, Your Spiegel J & R Store, Lithograph, 1¼ In.	25.00
Pin, Stowell Co., Santa Claus, 2 Children, 1919, 1¼ In.	141.00
Plates that are limited edition are listed in the Collector Plate category or in the correct factory listing.	
Postcard, Santa Calus, Looking In Window, Scenic, Hold-To-Light, Die Cut	1058.00
Postcard, Santa Claus, Attached Beard, Hat	705.00
Postcard, Santa Claus, In Car, Hold-To-Light, Die Cut	764.00
Postcard, Santa Claus, Walking By Sleigh, Reindeer	1058.00
Puppet, Santa Claus, Wood, Paper, Jointed, Pull String, Arms & Legs Move, 12 In. .....*illus*	220.00
Puzzle, Santa Claus Travels, Cardboard Blocks, McLoughlin Bros., 1897, 13½ x 11 In.	798.00
Puzzle, The Night Before Christmas, Cube, Wood Box, McLoughlin Bros., 14 x 11 In. ...*illus*	1650.00
Sheet Music, Santa Claus Is Coming To Town, John Frederick Coots, Eddie Canter, 1934	14.00
Spinner, 2 Santa Clauses, Merry Christmas, Celluloid, Victor & Co., 1910s, 1¼ In.	120.00
Stocking, E.T., Felt, Tree & Star, 1982, 15 In.	11.00
Toy, Jack-In-The-Box, Santa Claus, Wood, Paper, Cloth Santa, Germany, 5 In. ....*illus*	1045.00
Toy, Santa, On Scooter, Tin, Plastic, Battery Operated, Masudaya, Box, 8 In.	121.00
Toy, Santa & Reindeer, Painted, Cast Iron, Hubley, 16 In.	1760.00
Toy, Santa Claus, Composition, Rabbit Fur Beard, Windup, Prewar Germany, 6 In.	285.00
Toy, Santa Claus, On Blue Sleigh, 2 Brown Reindeer, Red, Gold Highlights, Cast Iron, Hubley, 15 In.	605.00
Toy, Santa Claus, On Blue Sleigh, White Reindeer, Red, Gold Highlights, Cast Iron, Hubley, 14 In.	467.00
Toy, Santa Claus, On Skis, Tin Lithograph, Windup, KSK, Japan, Box, 1950s, 5½ In.	216.00
Toy, Santa Claus, On Sleigh, 2 Reindeer, Arms Move, Bells, Tin, Windup, Strauss, 11 In.	3300.00
Toy, Santa Claus, Rings Bell, Windup, Alps Of Japan, Box	110.00
Toy, Santa Claus, Roly Poly, 1910, 4¼ In.	275.00
Toy, Santa Claus, Roly Poly, Composition, 1910, 8 In.	495.00
Toy, Santa Claus, Roly Poly, Composition, Papier-Mache, Germany, 6 In. ....*illus*	83.00
Toy, Santa Claus, Roly Poly, Felt, Fur Beard, Hand Painted, Composition, 11½ In.	672.00
Toy, Santa Claus, Roly Poly, Smiling, Red, White, Black, Painted, Composition, Schoenhut, 9 In.	616.00
Toy, Santa Claus, Roy Poly, Pointed Cap, Red, White, Blue, Hand Painted, Pressed Cardboard, 8¾ In.	224.00
Toy, Santa Claus, Walker, Yellow Sack, Marx, Box, 1960s, 3 In.	30.00
Toy, Santa Claus, Walker, Tin, Windup, Waddles, Holds Present, Chein, 5½ In.	440.00
Toy, Santa Claus, With Reindeer, Bells, Guide Wheels, Windup, Strauss, 11 In.	3300.00
Toy, Santee Sleigh, 2 Reindeer, Santa Claus, Windup, Tin Lithograph, Strauss, 10½ In.	1175.00 to 550.00
Wall Decoration, Santa Claus, Fur Robe, Girls, Mica Highlights, 3 Sections, 34 In. ....*illus*	1045.00
Wristwatch, Rudolph, Red-Nosed Reindeer, Rudolph On Dial, Box Top Only, 1939, 7 In. *illus*	310.00

CHRISTMAS TREES made of feathers and Christmas tree decorations of all types are popular with collectors. The first decorated Christmas tree in America is claimed by many states, including Pennsylvania (1747), Massachusetts (1832), Illinois (1833), Ohio (1838), and Iowa (1845). The first glass ornaments were imported from Germany about 1860. Dresden ornaments were made about 100 years ago of paper and tinsel. Manufacturers in the United States were making ornaments in the early 1870s. Electric lights were first used on a Christmas tree in 1882. Character light bulbs became popular in the 1920s, bubble lights in the 1940s, twinkle bulbs in the 1950s, plastic bulbs by 1955. In this book a Christmas light is a holder for a candle used on the tree. Other forms of lighting include light bulbs. Other Christmas memorabilia is listed in the preceding section.

Aluminum, 200 Branches, 4-Color Wheel, Spartus, Original Box, 7 Ft.	240.00
Bottle Brush, Green, White Paint Depicting Snow, Red Balls, 3¾ In.	7.00
Bottle Brush, Rotates, Plays Silent Night, Mercury Glass Bulbs, 1940s, 17 x 6 In.	165.00
Feather, 6 Branches, Berries, Tin Candle Cups, White Pot, 9¼ In.	72.00
Feather, Goose, Cast Iron Stand, 53 In. ....*illus*	58.00
Feather, Ornaments, Candles, Musical Stand, Revolves, Silent Night, W. Germany, 12 In. *illus*	248.00
Feather, Red Tipped Branches, Wood Base, Germany, Early 20th Century, 45 In.	294.00
Garland, Glow In The Dark, Plastic Bells, Clambroth White, 1960s, 96 In.	29.00
Holder, Green Glaze, Stoneware	500.00
Kugel, Glass, Gold, Embossed Cap, 4½ In.	77.00
Kugel, Glass, Grape Cluster, Cobalt Blue, Embossed Cap, 4¾ In.	715.00
Kugel, Glass, Grape Cluster, Green, Embossed Cap, 3¾ In.	660.00
Kugel, Glass, Green, Embossed Cap, 7½ In.	303.00
Kugel, Glass, Light Green, Embossed Cap, 4 In.	99.00
Kugel, Glass, Red, Embossed Cap, 7½ In.	770.00
Kugel, Glass, Silver, Embossed Cap, 6 In.	55.00
Kugel, Grape Cluster, Gold, Mercury Glass, Germany, 9 In. ....*illus*	920.00
Light, 15-Diamond Pattern, Olive Yellow, Flared & Rolled Lip, England, c.1880, 3 In. ...*illus*	101.00
Light, Acme Fairy Lamp Co., Hobnails, Yellow Amber, Screw Cap, c.1895, 4⅝ In.	123.00
Light, Bohemian Glass, Brock's Illumination Lamp, Red, Tooled Lip, France, 4⅛ In. ...*illus*	56.00

Christmas, Puzzle, The Night Before Christmas, Cube, Wood Box,
McLoughlin Bros., 14 x 11 In.
$1650.00

Christmas Tree, Kugel,
Grape Cluster, Gold, Mercury Glass,
Germany, 9 In.
$920.00

Christmas, Toy, Jack-In-The-Box,
Santa Claus, Wood, Paper, Cloth Santa,
Germany, 5 In.
$1045.00

Christmas, Wristwatch, Rudolph,
Red-Nosed Reindeer, Rudolph On Dial,
Box Top Only, 1939, 7 In.
$310.00

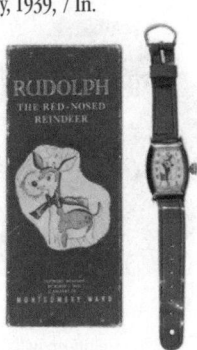

Christmas Tree, Light, 15-Diamond Pattern,
Olive Yellow, Flared & Rolled Lip, England,
c.1880, 3 In.
$101.00

Christmas, Toy, Santa Claus, Roly Poly,
Composition, Papier-Mache, Germany, 6 In.
$83.00

Christmas Tree, Feather, Goose,
Cast Iron Stand, 53 In.
$58.00

Christmas Tree, Light, Bohemian Glass,
Brock's Illumination Lamp, Red, Tooled Lip,
France, 4⅛ In.
$56.00

Christmas, Wall Decoration,
Santa Claus, Fur Robe, Girls,
Mica Highlights, 3 Sections, 34 In.
$1045.00

Christmas Tree, Feather,
Ornaments, Candles, Musical Stand,
Revolves, Silent Night,
W. Germany, 12 In.
$248.00

Christmas Tree, Light, Glass,
Allover Diamond, Teal Green, Sheared Lip,
England, c.1880, 3½ In.
$100.00

Christmas Tree, Light Set,
Cinderella, Disneylights, 12 Plastic Ball Lights,
Decals, Mazda, Box
$230.00

Christmas Tree, Ornament,
Elf On Reindeer, Pack, Holding Feather Tree,
Pressed Paper, Dresden
$935.00

Christmas Tree, Ornament, Fox,
Spun Cotton, Paper Jacket, Hat & Boots,
Holding Dead Fowl, Germany, 5¼ In.
$690.00

Christmas Tree, Ornament, Golfer,
Cotton, Paper Clothes & Club, Painted Face,
Germany, 5½ In.
$431.00

Christmas Tree, Ornament, Kugel,
Grapes, Blue, Embossed Cap, 7 In.
$1210.00

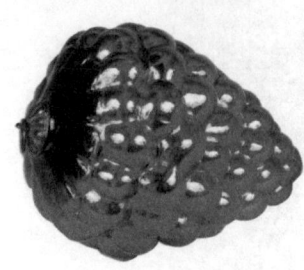

Christmas Tree, Ornament, Kugel,
Green, Embossed Cap, France, 6 In.
$154.00

Christmas Tree, Ornament, Kugel,
Turnip Shape, Silver, Embossed Cap, 5¾ In.
$110.00

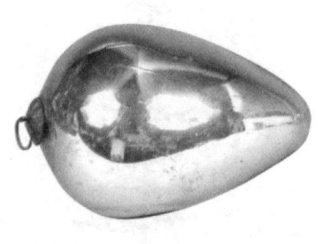

Christmas Tree, Ornament,
Lock & Key, Silver, Lock Holds Candy Box,
Pressed Paper, Dresden
$275.00

Christmas Tree, Ornament, Santa Claus,
Toy Sack, With Boy & Girl, Pressed Paper,
Dresden, 3 In.
$660.00

Christmas Tree, Stand,
3 Santas On Legs, Metal, Painted, 12 In.
$2200.00

Christmas Tree, Stand, Father Christmas,
Basket, Cast Iron, Twig Screws,
Evergreen Base, 7½ In.
$1760.00

Light, Brocks Illumination Lamp, Diamonds, Ruby Red, Bohemia, c.1895, 4 In.	206.00
Light, Glass, Allover Diamond, Teal Green, Sheared Lip, England, c.1880, 3½ In. *illus*	100.00
Light, Internal Broken Ribs, Ruby Red, Polished Rim, England, 1870-1900, 3⅝ In.	235.00
Light, Queen Victoria, Diamonds, Yellow Topaz, England, c.1895, 3½ In.	420.00
Light, Registered D.R.G.M., Diamonds, Yellow Green, Screw Cap, Germany, c.1895, 3⅝ In.	112.00
Light Set, Cinderella, Disneylights, 12 Plastic Ball Lights, Decals, Mazda, Box *illus*	230.00
Ornament, Baby's 1st Christmas, Bear On Sled, Hallmark Keepsake, Box, 1984, 3 In.	27.00
Ornament, Bear, Raised, Lavender Ball, Glitter, Glass, Russia, 2¼ In.	15.00
Ornament, Bird, Blue, Gold Glitter, Glass, Clip, c.1950, 6 In.	19.00
Ornament, Bird, Red, Gold Glitter, Glass, Clip, c.1950, 6 In.	19.00
Ornament, Brownie, String Jointed, Composition, Painted, 3¼ In.	110.00
Ornament, Chick, Rust Orange, Clip On, Mercury Glass, 3 In.	19.00
Ornament, Concave Rainbow, Red Center, Orange, Mercury Glass, E. Germany, 1950s, 3¼ In.	16.00
Ornament, Elf On Reindeer, Pack, Holding Feather Tree, Pressed Paper, Dresden *illus*	935.00
Ornament, Flower Basket, Blown Glass, Pink, Diamond Dust Trim, 2½ In.	9.00
Ornament, Flower Basket, Green Basket, White, Red, Blue Flowers, Glass, 2 In.	15.00
Ornament, Fox, Spun Cotton, Paper Jacket, Hat & Boots, Holding Dead Fowl, Germany, 5¼ In. *illus*	690.00
Ornament, Golfer, Cotton, Paper Clothes & Club, Painted Face, Germany, 5½ In. *illus*	431.00
Ornament, Grape Cluster, Blue, Glossy Finish, Mercury Glass, Japan, 3½ In.	11.00
Ornament, Grape Cluster, Blue, Mercury Glass, Japan, 3½ In.	11.00
Ornament, Grape Cluster, Fuchsia, Blown Glass, USA, 3¾ In.	8.00
Ornament, Grape Cluster, Green, Mercury Glass, Japan, 3½ In.	11.00
Ornament, Grape Cluster, Red, Mercury Glass, Japan, 3½ In.	11.00
Ornament, Grape Cluster, Silver, Blown Glass, No. HA47, Marked, GDR, 2¼ In.	9.00
Ornament, Indian Woman, Blown Glass, Red Dress, Matching Headpiece, Gold Glitter, 6 In.	60.00
Ornament, Kugel, Grapes, Blue, Embossed Cap, 7 In. *illus*	1210.00
Ornament, Kugel, Green, Embossed Cap, France, 6 In. *illus*	154.00
Ornament, Kugel, Turnip Shape, Silver, Embossed Cap, 5¾ In. *illus*	110.00
Ornament, Lock & Key, Silver, Lock Holds Candy Box, Pressed Paper, Dresden *illus*	275.00
Ornament, Mandolin, Glass, Russia, 2¾ In.	17.00
Ornament, Mr. Christmas, Faceted, Plastic, Silver, Box, 1960s, 2⅜ In.	10.00
Ornament, Mrs. Claus, Fuchsia, Glass, Russia, 3¼ In.	16.00
Ornament, Nutshell, Fireside Scene, Hallmark Keepsake, Box, 1½ In.	15.00
Ornament, Owl, Copper, White & Pink Accents, Glass, Russia, 2½ In.	17.00
Ornament, Papier-Mache, Wreath, Bells, Glass Bead, Chenille, Early 1900s, 12 In.	17.00
Ornament, Pinecone, Blown Glass, Gold, 2¾ In.	9.00
Ornament, Pinecone, Blown Glass, Red, 1¾ In.	9.00
Ornament, Pinecone, Silver, White Frost Glitter, 3¾ In.	15.00
Ornament, Pocketwatch, Glass, Gold Paint, Russia, 2½ In.	19.00
Ornament, Santa Claus, Toy Sack, With Boy & Girl, Pressed Paper, Dresden, 3 In. *illus*	660.00
Ornament, Snowman, White Chenille, Orange Scarf, Black Pipe, Plastic Hat, 1950s, 2 In.	17.50
Ornament, Train, Hallmark, Yesteryears Collection, Box, 1976, 2¾ x 4 In.	150.00
Ornament, Umbrella, Closed, Red, Green, Gold Handle, Mercury Glass, 5 In.	18.00
Ornament, Wreath Of Memories, Red Ribbon, Hallmark Keepsake, 1987	27.00
Ornament Set, Jewelbright Durable, Box, Decor Novelties Inc., 3 Piece	15.00
Stand, 3 Santas On Legs, Metal, Painted, 12 In. *illus*	2200.00
Stand, Cast Iron, Green Paint, Embossed, Crosshatch, c.1900, 5½ x 17 In.	75.00
Stand, Father Christmas, Basket, Cast Iron, Twig Screws, Evergreen Base, 7½ In. *illus*	1760.00
Stand, Nativity, Papier-Mache Manger, Composition Figures, Musical, Rotates *illus*	3300.00
Stand, Rotating, Musical, 1878, 14 x 9 In.	650.00
Stand, Santa Claus & Holly Design, White, Brown, Northwest Terra-Cotta, 9 x 16 In.	1080.00
Stand, Silver Glitter, Rotating, White, 10 In.	16.00
Stand, Wooden Picket, 5 Tiers, Stepped Square Pedestal, White, 7 x 9¾ x 9¾ In.	323.00
Topper, Angel, Composition, Paper Banner, Gloria In Excelsis, Germany, 8 In. *illus*	1265.00
Topper, Angel, Silvered Glass, Spun Glass Wings & Cloud, Globe Cover, Dresden, 9 In. *illus*	230.00
Topper, Expandable Cardboard, Stars Cutouts, Colored Foil, Glitter, 8 In.	16.00
Topper, Royalites Starlite, Illuminated, Molded Styrene Plastic, Box, 1950s, 8 x 6 In.	16.00
Topper, Star, Green & Silver Tinsel, Germany, 11½ x 9 In.	45.00

CHROME items in the Art Deco style became popular in the 1930s. Collectors are most interested in high-style pieces made by the Connecticut firms of Chase Brass & Copper Co. and Manning-Bowman & Co.

Ashtray, Bonzo, 2¾ In.	59.00
Ashtray, Cigar, Art Deco, Racehorse, Jockey, Marked, Park Sherman, 1950s, 1 x 7½ In.	25.00
Ashtray, DC-3 Plane, TWA Logo, 1940s	354.00

Christmas Tree, Stand, Nativity, Papier-Mache Manger, Composition Figures, Musical, Rotates
$3300.00

Christmas Tree, Topper, Angel, Composition, Paper Banner, Gloria In Excelsis, Germany, 8 In.
$1265.00

Christmas Tree, Topper, Angel, Silvered Glass, Spun Glass Wings & Cloud, Globe Cover, Dresden, 9 In.
$230.00

Chrome, Siphon, Black Enamel Top, Norman Bel Geddes, Soda King, 11 x 4½ In. $94.00

Cigar Store Figure, Indian Chief, Arm Raised, Feathered Headdress, Painted, Wood, Square Base, 46½ In. $4200.00

TIP

Some repairs make the sale of an antique very difficult, if not impossible. Don't buff pewter. Don't wash ivory. Don't repaint old toys. Don't tape old paper. Don't wash oil paintings.

Candlestick, Hexagonal Socket, Cylindrical & Hexagonal Stem, Round Base, 8¼ In.	118.00
Candy Box, Polished, Harry Layon, Chase Brass & Copper Co., 4¾ x 3 In.	25.00
Cocktail Shaker, Art Deco, Walnut Trim, Jay Ackerman, Manning Bowman Esquire, 1941	100.00
Dish, Cover, Round, Car & Piano Finials, 10½ In., Pair	235.00
Siphon, Black Enamel Top, Norman Bel Geddes, Soda King, 11 x 4½ In. . . . .*illus*	94.00
Sugar & Creamer, Cordiality Tray, Art Deco, Revere Copper & Brass, 1930s, 12 & 2¾ In.	32.00

CIGAR STORE FIGURES of carved wood or cast iron were used as advertisements in front of the Victorian cigar store. The carved figures are now collected as folk art. They range in size from counter type, about three feet, to over eight feet high.

Indian, 2-Sided, Multicolored, Wood Plank, Traditional Dress, Head Dress, 61 In.	1155.00
Indian, Carved, Painted, Arm Raised, Feather Headdress, 20th Century, 46½ In.	4200.00
Indian, Chief, Arm Raised, Feathered Headdress, Painted, Wood, Square Base, 46½ In. .*illus*	4200.00
Indian, Feather Headdress, Cigars On Base, Holding Leaves, Attributed To Samuel Robb, 66 In.	23100.00
Indian, Feather Headdress, Fringed Cloak, Holding Tobacco, 74 x 18 In.	23500.00
Indian, Feather Headdress, Fur On Shoulders, Attributed To Thomas Brooks, Wheels, 86 In.	36750.00
Indian, Feather Headdress, Holding Mallet, On Blue Tin Box, Drawer, J. Jiminez, 17 x 4 x 5 In.	24000.00
Indian, Feather Headdress, Outstretched Arm, Early 1900s, 67½ x 21 In.	4700.00
Indian, Full Headdress, Scouting, Carved Wood, Early 1900s, Life Size	605.00
Indian, Maiden, Cast Zinc, William Demuth & Co., Original Paint, 69 In.	26680.00
Indian, Papier-Mache, Wood Base, Tobacco, Cigars, Life Size	4950.00
Indian, Pine, Carved, Painted, Feathered Headdress, Holding Tobacco Leaf, c.1880, 74 In.	47500.00
Indian, Princess, Holding Tobacco Leaves, Cast Iron, Shaped Base, 25 In.	4481.00
Man, Colonial, Lighting Pipe, Cast Metal, Painted, 27 In.	690.00
Sir Walter Raleigh, Pine, Painted, Zinc Sword Guard, Charles Demuth, N.Y., c.1880, 73 In. . . .*illus*	30000.00
Turk, Reclining, Bearded, Turban, Smoking Long Stemmed Pipe, 19 x 48 In.	8813.00

CINNABAR is a vermilion or red lacquer. Pieces are made with tens to hundreds of thicknesses of the lacquer that is later carved. Most cinnabar was made in the Orient.

Bowl, Cover, Carved Design, Basket Weave Bottom, Chinese, 1800s, 6 In.	216.00
Box, Cover, Carved, Round, Chinese, 19th Century, 5½ In.	139.00
Box, Figures, Landscape, c.1900, 6¼ In.	81.00
Box, Hand Carved, Chinese, 3¾ x 5½ In.	47.00
Box, Rectangular, Carved, Dragon, Flowers, Chinese, 6⅛ In.	1062.00
Ginger Jar, Figures, Landscape, Carved, Oval, Marked, Chinese, Early 20th Century, 6 In.	184.00
Table, Altar, Diaper Pattern, Pierced Apron, Carved, Chinese, 32 x 48 In.	3218.00
Tray, Phoenix Bird Decoration, Clouds, Chinese, 7½ x 6 In.	767.00
Urn, Converted To Lamp, Chinese, 19 In.	146.00
Vase, Baluster, Chinese, c.1900, 9 In., Pair	279.00
Vase, Figures, 7½ In.	1180.00
Vase, Figures, Landscape, Baluster, Late 19th Century, 10¼ In.	204.00
Vase, Sages, Amid Mountain Motifs, Chinese, 7½ In.	350.00

CIVIL WAR mementos are important collectors' items. Most of the pieces are military items used from 1861 to 1865. Be sure to avoid any explosive munitions.

Battle Report, Assault On Fort Fisher, Handwritten, Kidder R. Breese, Jan. 16 1865	3803.00
Bayonet, 18 In.	53.00
Bayonet, 20½ In.	42.00
Bayonet, 21 In.	53.00
Bayonet, Scabbard, Hanger, Marked US, 19 In.	85.00
Binoculars, Mother-Of-Pearl, Brass, Leather Case, Silk Lined, Labeled, Marchand Paris	95.00
Binoculars, Signal Glasses, Brass Tubes, Black Enamel Finish, Etched, Extend To 7 In.	150.00
Buckle, Brass, Confederate, Snake	61.00
Button, Brass Front, Stars, Round Metal Shank, Embossed, Wanamaker & Brown, 1860s	22.00
Cane, Oak, Carved, Confederate Pow, Entwined Snake, Camp Chase, 1862, 34½ In.	2106.00
Canteen, Bull's-Eye	224.00
Canteen, Wood, Iron Strapping, c.1860, 7¾ x 4½ In.	543.00
Creamer, Bull Run Battlefield, Light Blue, Beige, Black Writing, Squares, 1907, 3½ In.	47.00
Dice, Bone, Handmade, ⅜ In.	55.00
Dog Tag, General McClellan, Brass, No Holes, c.1861, 1¼ In.	266.00
Flag, Battle, Confederate, Veteran's Camp 3, Bunting Cloth, 38 x 38 In.	484.00
Flask, Wrapped, Pewter Cap	67.00
Game, Jolly Exempts, Triangular Pieces, ¼ Face, Lee & Shepard, Box, c.1863, 39 Piece	1320.00
Hat, Campaign Cord, Union, Gold Thread Acorns, Cord, 6th Vermont, Silas O. Dwinell	135.00

Hat Wreath, GAR, Stamped, Brass, Soldered Back Loop	50.00
Kettle, Coffee, Camp, Copper, Brass Spout, Pitted Handle, c.1860	245.00
Knife, Mess, 2-Piece Bone Grips, Steel Blade, Lamson & Goodnow Mfg., 9 In.	25.00
Knife, Mess, Bone Grip, Lamson Goodnow & Co., S. Falls Works, Mass., 5 In.	95.00
Map, Ohio, Color, Railroads, Towns, Rivers, Johnson's Atlas, 26 x 17 In., 1863	85.00
Ribbon, Carte De Visite, General Lee, Memoriam, Oct. 12, 1870	115.00
Ribbon, Gettysburg Reunion, Red, Marked Gettysburg 1863, 1911, 6 In.	95.00
Saber, Cavalry, Scabbard	665.00
Scarf, Silk, Cannon, Patriotic Theme	385.00
Shaving Kit, Gutta-Percha, Friction Fitted Lid, Decorated, c.1851, 3¼ In.	395.00
Shot Glass, Union Forever, Bumper To The Flag, 3 In.	203.00
Surgeon's Amputation Saw, Knife	96.00
Surgeon's Kit, Field, Instruments, Leather Case, 10 Piece	777.00
Surgeon's Scalpel Blade, Leather Case	121.00
Sword, Brass Guard, Knight's Head, Leather Hanger, 26 In.	121.00
Sword, Officer's, 38 In.	303.00
Sword, Staff & Field Officers, Scabbard, 1860	157.00
Trumpet, Field, Presentation, Emeil Castagnino, Co. B 1st Cal., Silver Plate, 16 In.	1404.00
Trumpet, Navy, Hand Hammered, Engraved, C.F. Schmitz, 10th Indiana, 1861	2925.00

CKAW, *see Dedham category.*

CLAMBROTH glass, popular in the Victorian era, is a grayish color and is somewhat opaque, like clam broth. It was made by several factories in the United States and England.

Barber Bottle, 8-Sided, Ringed Neck, c.1910, 6¾ In.	48.00
Canister, Hoosier Style, White	55.00
Canister, Red Lid	48.00
Vase, Enameled, Ruffled Edge, Gold Luster Stripe, Bristol	75.00
Vase, Flowers, Leaves, Stemmed, Gold Trim, 9⅞ In.	48.00
Vase, Gold Trim, 9⅞ In.	48.00

CLARICE CLIFF was a designer who worked in several English factories, including A.J. Wilkinson Ltd., Wilkinson's Royal Staffordshire Pottery, Newport Pottery, and Foley Pottery after the 1920s. She is best known for her brightly colored Art Deco designs, including the Bizarre line. She died in 1972. Reproductions have been made by Wedgwood.

Biarritz, Dinner Service, c.1935, 20 Piece	470.00
Bizarre, Ginger Jar, Geometric, Red, Purple, Blue, Green, 9½ In.	823.00
Bizarre, Vase, Abstract Flowers, Turquoise Ground, Flared, 8 In.	546.00
Budgies, Vase, Newport Pottery, 12½ In.	179.00
Chrysanthemum, Vase, Panels, Wide Mouth, Flared Foot, Marked, 8 In.	940.00
Clematis, Tureen, Cover, 10½ x 5½ In.	82.00
Crocus, Jug, Handle, Yellow Spout, White Ground, 8 In.	1530.00
Fantasque, Sandwich Server, Octagonal Plate, 11¾ x 5⅝ In.	646.00
Fantasque, Sandwich Set, Dish, 6 Octagonal Plates, Orange Flowers, Fruit, 7 Piece	764.00
Harvest, Platter, Peach & Brown Flowers, White Ground	65.00
Inspiration, Vase, Trees, Bridge, Teal Ground, Marked, 10 In.	940.00
Killarney, Charger, Geometric, Green, Cream, Brown, Marked, 17¾ In.	1116.00
Latona, Charger, Ribbed Body, Orange, Rust, Green, Blue, Stylized Trees, 18¼ In.	764.00
Patina, Vase, Stylized Tree, Textured, Scalloped Rim, Tapered, Cylindrical, 6 In.	588.00
Plaque, Budgies, Newport Pottery, 9 In.	148.00
Plaque, Flying Goose, Newport Pottery, 15¼ In.	116.00
Plaque, Lady In Bonnet In Trees, Newport Pottery, 8¼ In., Pair	295.00
Plaque, Swallows, Newport Pottery, 8¾ In., Pair	274.00

CLEWELL ware was made in limited quantities by Charles Walter Clewell of Canton, Ohio, from 1902 to 1955. Pottery was covered with a thin coating of bronze, then treated to make the bronze turn different colors. Pieces covered with copper, brass, or silver were also made. Mr. Clewell's secret formula for blue patinated bronze was burned when he died in 1965.

Bowl, Copper Clad, 3-Footed, Original Patina, Marked, 421, 2½ x 5 In.	390.00
Bowl, Copper Clad, Eclipse Electrotype & Engraving Co., Cleveland, 3⅝ In.	173.00
Bowl, Copper Clad, Verdigris Patina, Folded-In Sides, 2 x 7½ In.	92.00
Vase, Copper Clad, Bronze, Verdigris Patina, Baluster, 17¼ x 8½ In.	2280.00
Vase, Copper Clad, Etched, Fish, Swimming, Sea Plants, Bulbous, 8 x 5¼ In.	1080.00
Vase, Copper Clad, Green Patina, Bulbous, Shouldered, Flared Rim, 5⅜ In.	1495.00

Cigar Store Figure, Sir Walter Raleigh, Pine, Painted, Zinc Sword Guard, Charles Demuth, N.Y., c.1880, 73 In. $30000.

C

TIP

Civil War re-enactors have been warned that some old medical instruments could still carry germs or viruses that are infectious. Be very careful when handling any old medical items. They should be carefully cleaned and disinfected.

Clewell, Vase, Copper Clad, Swollen Shape, 9 x 4½ In. $3600.

Clock, Advertising, Red Goose Shoes, Electric, Red Goose, 14 In. $660.00

Clock, Ansonia, Shelf, Austria Model, Oak Case, Etched Vase Of Flowers, c.1900, 20 In. $206.00

Clock, Ansonia, Shelf, China, Shaped, Scrolls, Pink, Gold Trim, Pendulum, Key, 11 x 12 In. $878.00

Vase, Copper Clad, Original Patina, Flared, Marked, No. 361-2-6, 10¼ x 4½ In.	1150.00
Vase, Copper Clad, Swollen Shape, 9 x 4½ In. ....*illus*	3600.00

CLEWS *may be listed in the Staffordshire category.*

CLIFTON POTTERY was founded by William Long in Newark, New Jersey, in 1905. He worked there until 1909 making lines including Crystal Patina and Clifton Indian Ware. Clifton Pottery made art pottery until 1911 and then concentrated on wall and floor tile. By 1914 the name had been changed to Clifton Porcelain and Tile Company. Another firm, Chesapeake Pottery, sold majolica marked *Clifton Ware.*

Bottle, Olde Coach House, Bristol, Stratford, Woolhampton, Transfer, Wood Stopper	30.00
Candlestick, Indian Ware, Red Clay, Geometrics, No. 194, Pueblo Viejo, Az., 9½ x 5 In., Pair .	290.00
Jar, Indian Ware, Redware, Stamped, Homolobi, Arizona, c.1910, 5 x 7 In.	81.00
Vase, Green Matte Glaze, Caramel Drip, Crystal Glaze, Bottle Shape, c.1905, 10½ In.	785.00
Vase, Indian Ware, Terra-Cotta, Dark Brown Paint, Bulbous, Stamped, 1906, 2¾ In.	200.00

CLOCKS of all types have always been popular with collectors. The eighteenth-century tall case, or grandfather's, clock, was designed to house a works with a long pendulum. In 1816, Eli Terry patented a new, smaller works for a clock, and the case became smaller. The clock could be kept on a shelf instead of on the floor. By 1840, coiled springs were used and even smaller clocks were made. Battery-powered electric clocks were made in the 1870s. A garniture set can include a clock and other objects displayed on a mantel.

Advertising, Alka-Seltzer, Speedy, Television Form, c.1961, 5¼ In.	58.00
Advertising, Animated, Zonweiss Tooth Powder, Girl Brushing Teeth, 4½ x 4 x 2½ In.	1430.00
Advertising, Bull Durham Smoking Tobacco, Pouch Shape, 1910-20, 12 x 9 x 5½ In.	474.00
Advertising, Cat's Paw, Advertising Products, Pre-Double Bubble, 15 In.	550.00
Advertising, Champion Spark Plugs, Art Deco, Neon, 26 x 4 x 14 In.	440.00
Advertising, Chocolat Revillon, 8-Day, Japy Freres Pendulette Movement, c.1920, 23 In.	908.00
Advertising, Col. Sanders, Minutes & Hours, 4-Sided, Light-Up, 20 x 20 In.	275.00
Advertising, Dowagiac Drills & Seeders, Pocket-Watch Shape, Electric, 10½ x 7 In.	1700.00
Advertising, Dr Pepper, Drink Dr Pepper, Good For Life, Call Again, No Cord, 16 x 22½ In. ..	1344.00
Advertising, Dr Pepper, Drink Dr Pepper, Composition, Green, Red, Black, 14½ In. Diam. ...	300.00
Advertising, Drink Brownie Chocolate Soda, Square, Pam Clock Co., 1950s, 4 In.	140.00
Advertising, Expert TV & Radio Service, Work Guaranteed, Tubes, Box, Metal, Light-Up, 15 In.	295.00
Advertising, Galat's Corndale Meats, Double Bubble, 15 In.	77.00
Advertising, Gem Damaskeene Razor, Man Holding Baby, Wood, 33 x 22 x 3½ In.	900.00
Advertising, Greyhound Lines, Telechron, 15 In.	110.00
Advertising, Hubbard's Sunshine Feed, Double Bubble, 15 In.	110.00
Advertising, Iroquois Beer, Indian Head, Full Headdress, International Breweries Inc.	575.00
Advertising, Iroquois Beer Ale, Double Bubble, 15 In.	385.00
Advertising, It's Cleaning Time, Neon, Pressed Steel, Red, White, Blue, 32 In.	523.00
Advertising, Jolly Tar Pastime, Old Honesty, Composition, Pendulum, Baird & Co., 30 x 18 In.	1700.00
Advertising, KCKN Radio, 1340 On Every Dial, 3-Sided, Black, Red, White, Light-Up, 23 x 18 In. .	110.00
Advertising, Marathon City Brewing Co., Drink Marathon Beer, Union Made, 15 x 8 x 3½ In. .	500.00
Advertising, Nebo Cigarette, Wood, Man, Key, Pendulum, Gilbert Clock Co., 7½ x 40 In.	8050.00
Advertising, Old Mr. Boston, Fine Liquors, Flask Form, Yellow, Black, 22 In.	300.00
Advertising, Pittsburg, Glass, Mirror, Pre-Double Bubble, 15 In.	121.00
Advertising, RCA Victor, Nipper, Stainless Case, Square, 1940s	204.00
Advertising, Reddy Kilowatt Cook Electrically, Telechron, 15 In. Diam.	743.00
Advertising, Red Goose Shoes, Electric, Red Goose, 14 In. ....*illus*	660.00
Advertising, Rexall, Bisma-Rex, Double Bubble, 15 In.	110.00
Advertising, Sidney Clock Co., Owego, N.Y., c.1885, 28 x 72 x 10 In.	9900.00
Advertising, St. Charles Evaporated Milk, 12 In.	565.00
Advertising, Sundial Shoes, Time Will Tell Wear, Bronze Pot Metal, Alarm, c.1920, 5 In.	17.00
Advertising, Three Feathers, Metal, Glass, Chrome, Hammer Bros., 12 In.	385.00
Advertising, Ward's Orange Crush, Orange Crush Time, Black, Western Union, 32 x 15 In. ..	224.00
Advertising, Zonweiss Tooth Powder, Girl Brushing Teeth, Round, Footed, 4¼ In.	1430.00
Amphitrite, Pursued By Dolphin For Neptune, Ormolu, c.1825, 16½ x 21 In.	2310.00
Ansonia, Cadet Style, Cast Metal Case, Bee Movement, c.1880, 4¼ In.	275.00
Ansonia, Correct Time, 30-Hour Lever Movement, Glass Dial, c.1901, 10 In.	94.00
Ansonia, Crystal Regulator, No. 2, Porcelain, Pink, Flowers, c.1905, 17½ In.	5775.00
Ansonia, Improved Bee Alarm, 30-Hour Lever Movement, c.1914, 3¾ In.	44.00
Ansonia, Regulator, Brass Frame, Beveled Edge, Onyx, Ormolu Acanthus Leaves, 15½ In. ...	2070.00
Ansonia, Shelf, Architectural, Gilt Metal, Painted, Time & Strike, 12½ x 5¾ In.	153.00
Ansonia, Shelf, Austria Model, Oak Case, Etched Vase Of Flowers, c.1900, 20 In. ....*illus*	206.00

Ansonia, Shelf, Black Onyx, Keywind, c.1875, 10½ x 14 In.		293.00
Ansonia, Shelf, Blue, Flowers, Open Escapement, Time, Strike, Marked, Recruit, c.1905		715.00
Ansonia, Shelf, Brass Sailor, Fisherman, Brass Dial, 17 In.		690.00
Ansonia, Shelf, China, Shaped, Scrolls, Pink, Gold Trim, Pendulum, Key, 11 x 12 In.	*illus*	878.00
Ansonia, Shelf, Crest, Cast Metal Rococo Case, 8-Day, Time & Strike, c.1904, 12½ In.		165.00
Ansonia, Shelf, Parisian, Walnut Case, 8-Day, Time & Strike, c.1890, 23½ In.		330.00
Ansonia, Shelf, Flowers, Cathedral Bell Strike, American Wringer Co., Extra 8-Day, Dresden		440.00
Ansonia, Shelf, Pink, Flowers, Key, Pendulum, 11 x 12 In.		825.00
Ansonia, Shelf, Porcelain, Painted, White, Blue, c.1890, 11 x 9 In.		293.00
Ansonia, Shelf, Recluse, Blue Porcelain Case, Time & Strike, c.1901, 11 In.		413.00
Ansonia, Steeple, Mahogany, Reverse Painted Glass, Rose & Vine Border, 20 x 10 In.		345.00
Ansonia, Swing No. 2, Child On Swing, 1-Day, c.1895, 8 In.		1155.00
Ansonia, Swinging Arm, Fisher, Original Paper Dial, c.1885, 3-In. Canister, 22½ In.		3410.00
Ansonia, Tacoma Pattern, Hand Painted Flowers, c.1900, 10½ In.		235.00
Art Deco, Onyx, White Metal, Angel, Harp, Male Scribe, Caramel, c.1930, 22 x 24 In.		353.00
Art Deco, Wood, Carved, Nude Female, Rectangular Base, Round Dial, c.1930, 10½ In.		206.00
Arts & Crafts, Copper, Riveted Strap, Enameled Dial, Key Wind, Swiss, 7 x 10 In.		294.00
Bakers, Walnut Case, Carved Corners, 8-Day, Time & Strike, France, c.1900, 16 In.		193.00
Banjo, Howard, E., No. 1, Weight Driven		5463.00
Banjo, Howard, E., No. 4, Fruitwood Case, Rosewood, 8-Day, Weight Driven, c.1870, 32 In.		2530.00
Banjo, Federal, Mahogany, Eglomise, Parcel Gilt, Eagle On Ball Finial, 1800s, 40 x 11 In.		5310.00
Banjo, Federal, Mahogany, Gilt Gesso, Eglomise, 8-Day Movement, c.1820, 34¼ In.		1645.00
Banjo, Federal, Parcel Gilt, Eglomise Panel, c.1810, 42 x 10½ x 4 In.		3000.00
Banjo, Gilbert, c.1900, 30½ x 10½ In.		146.00
Banjo, Mahogany, Eagle Finial, Reverse Painted Throat & Tablet, Mass., 19th Century, 29 In.		1434.00
Banjo, Mahogany, Painted Face, Opaque Panel, Door, c.1850, 29 x 11 x 3¾ In.		796.00
Banjo, Mahogany, Thermometer, Satinwood Inlay, Eglomise, 36 x 10 In.		9360.00
Banjo, Sessions, White House, Reverse Decorated, Early 20th Century, 34 In.		106.00
Banjo, Waterbury, Willard, No. 1, Mahogany, c.1900, 42 x 10 In.		1300.00
Banjo, Willard, Simon, Mahogany, Eglomise Panel, Flame Finial, Boston, c.1810, 34 In. *illus*		3000.00
Banjo, Willard, Simon, Mahogany, Reverse Glass Panel, 2 Fighting Ships, 42 In. *illus*		3450.00
Becker, Gustav, Shelf, Mahogany, Dome Case, c.1900, 23 In.		118.00
Becker, Gustav, Wall, Walnut, Carved & Turned Columns & Finials, Key, 30 x 17 x 8 In. *illus*		826.00
Birge & Fuller, Gothic, Candle Finials, Time & Strike, Wagon Spring, c.1845, 25½ In.		990.00
Black Forest, Carved Birds Crest, Scrolled Acanthus, 19th Century, 26 In.		764.00
Black Forest, Cuckoo, Eagle, Hare, Pheasant, Rifles, Oak Leaves, Branches, 48 x 30 In. *illus*		11750.00
Black Forest, Cuckoo, Shelf, Forest Motif, Carved, Germany, c.1915, 16 In.		495.00
Black Forest, Figural, Chamois Standing, Rockery Base, Preying Eagle, 24 In.		3760.00
Black Forest, Oak, Carved, Fish, Birds, Stag's Head, Antlers, 37 In.		1180.00
Black Forest, Wall, Oak, Roman Numerals, 22 x 17 In.		382.00
Boye, Charles, Pedestal, Black Marble, Time & Strike, Gilt Bronze Numerals, c.1880, 9 In.		143.00
Bracket, Ebonized Case, Brass Swing Handle, Glass Door, Early 18th Century, 11 x 9 In.		3450.00
Bracket, Edwardian, Brass, Inlaid Mahogany Case, c.1900, 18¼ In.		370.00
Bracket, Smith-Patterson, Brass, Beveled Glass, Key, 4½ x 3 x 2½ In.		70.00
Bradley & Hubbard, Blinking Eye, Cast Iron, 19th Century, 16 In.		915.00
Bradley & Hubbard, Lion, Lying Down, Blinking Eye, Cast Iron, 8½ x 10⅝ In.		2520.00
Bradley & Hubbard, Parade, 30-Hour, Stamped Brass Case, Glass Inserts, c.1885, 13 In.		1100.00
Brewster & Ingrahams, Beehive, New Haven Strike, Mahogany Panel Door, c.1850, 20 In.		99.00
Brown, J.C., Shelf, Acorn, 8-Day, Fusee Movement, Forestville, Conn., c.1848, 24 In.		18700.00
Carriage, Chinoiserie, Lacquered Case, France, c.1900, 6½ In.		435.00
Carriage, Engraved Brass Case, Beveled Glass Panels, Grand Sonnerie, 5¾ In.		3335.00
Carriage, Gilt Brass, Striking Movement, France, c.1900, 7 In.		270.00
Carriage, Grand Sonnerie, France, 19th Century, 7 In.		1522.00
Carriage, Nickel Plated, Tole Scenes, Musical Box, Keywind, 19th Century, 8 In.		840.00
Carriage, Porcelain Dial, Brass Anglaise Riche Case, Beveled Glass, 8-Day, 7½ In.		294.00
Cartier, Desk, 2½ x 5½ In.		702.00
Cartier, Lion, Growling, On Rock, Spelter, Bronze Patina, Key, 21 x 26 x 8 In.		518.00
Chinoiserie Case, Lamb's Tongue, Musicians, 7 Jewel, Tiffany & Co., 9½ In. *illus*		1840.00
Cuckoo, Carved, Glass Eyed Stag Pediment, Rabbit, Bird, Double Cuckoos, 28 In.		460.00
Cuckoo, Flower-Turbaned Lady, Blinking Eye, Time & Strike, Germany, c.1900, 14½ In.		550.00
Cuckoo, Frankfield, Bird & 5 Leaf, 30-Hour, Cast Plate Movement, Germany, c.1920, 24 In.		138.00
Davies, H.J., Young American, Milk Glass Front, Gold Paint, 30-Hour, c.1857, 7 In.		263.00
Demosthenes Bust, Bronze & Sienna Marble, 8-Day, Time & Bell Strike, c.1850, 21 In.		770.00
Desk, Rouge Marble Case, Bronze Mounts, Stamped, Austria, c.1900, 9¾ In.		705.00
Drocourt, Carriage, Grand Sonnerie, Brass Architectural Case, Columns, c.1890, 7 In.		3300.00
Drury, Mahogany, Victorian, Round, Late 19th Century, 14¾ In.		900.00

Clock, Banjo, Willard, Simon,
Mahogany, Eglomise Panel, Flame Finial,
Boston, c.1810, 34 In.
$3000.00

Clock, Banjo, Willard, Simon,
Mahogany, Reverse Glass Panel,
2 Fighting Ships, 42 In.
$3450.00

Clock, Becker, Gustav, Wall, Walnut,
Carved & Turned Columns & Finials, Key,
30 x 17 x 8 In.
$826.00

Clock, Black Forest, Cuckoo, Eagle, Hare, Pheasant, Rifles, Oak Leaves, Branches, 48 x 30 In.
$11750.00

Clock, Chinoiserie Case, Lamb's Tongue, Musicians, 7 Jewel, Tiffany & Co., 9½ In.
$1840.00

Clock, Figural, Pedro Friedberg, Mahogany, Red Legs, Gold Hour Hands, 13½ x 10½ In.
$14400.00

Eli Terry & Sons, Shelf, Pillar & Scroll, Mahogany, Eglomise, Mt. Vernon	956.00
Elliot Of London, Carriage, Chinoiserie, Lacquer, Red, c.1960, 8 x 4½ In.	146.00
Farcot, Balance, Brass, Ebonized Panel, 8-Day, Exposed Platform, Paris, c.1890, 10¾ In.	220.00
Farcot, Shelf, Swinging Doll, White Marble Case, Ormolu, France, c.1880, 9¼ In.	908.00
Farmer & Co., Desk, Jade, Chinoiserie, Silver Gilt Mounted, 1900s, 7 x 9 In.	5520.00
Federal, Mahogany, Pillar & Scroll, Flower Spandrels, Gilt, Brass Urn Finials, 32 x 18 In.	3680.00
Federal, Pillar & Scroll, Painted Wood Face, Brass Urn Finials, 31 x 18 In.	230.00
Figural, Pedro Friedberg, Mahogany, Red Legs, Gold Hour Hands, 13½ x 10½ In. ...*illus*	14400.00
Forestville Mfg., Column & Cornice, 2-Weight, 30-Hour, Bristol, Conn., c.1845, 28¼ In.	1045.00
French, Art Deco, Westminster Chime, Oak Case, 8-Day Time, Odo, c.1910, 27¾ In.	193.00
French, Cartel, George III, Giltwood, Eagle Finial, Single Movement, Pendulum, 31 In.	4230.00
French, Cartel, Glass Dial, Brass Trim, 8-Day, Keywind, c.1900, 13½ In.	165.00
French, Lyre Shape, Dore Bronze, Veined Pink Marble, c.1900, 12¾ x 5¾ In.	1521.00
French, Putto, Seated, Marble Veneer, Bronze Bezel, 19th Century, 20 In.	500.00
French, Romulus & Remus, Bronze, Marble Base, c.1900, 5¾ In.	330.00
German, Louis XVI Style, Gilt Bronze, Round Dial, Engine Turned Brass, 6 In.	210.00
German, Porcelain Case, White, Yellow Flowers, Applied Gold, 30-Hour, c.1910, 10 In.	17.00
German, Souvenir, Rothenburg Ob Der Tauber, Painted Image, 30-Hour, c.1935, 3¼ In.	110.00
German, Spring Driven, Reeded Pillars, Corinthian Capitals, 8-Day, c.1890, 32½ In.	248.00
Gilbert, Regulator, Stripped Oak Case, Pressed Molding, 8-Day, c.1913, 36 In.	303.00
Gilbert, Shelf, Mission Oak Case, c.1910, 19½ In.	184.00
Gilbert B. Owen Co., Shelf, Oak, Eastlake Style, Keywind, c.1880, 20 x 12 x 5 In.	293.00
Gravity, Ratchet Upright, Cast Brass Case, Reverse Painted Dial, c.1921, 10½ In.	330.00
Hamburg American Clock Co., Blue & White, Inverted Dish Shape, Germany, c.1920, 11 In.	44.00
Hot Air Balloon, Bronze, Round Dial, Porcelain Numbers, Zodiac Signs, 27 x 10 In. ...*illus*	7475.00
Howard, E. & Co., Wall, Dial, Marble, Painted Wood Case, Signed	1904.00
Howard Miller, Starburst, No. 2202, Salmon Spikes, Electric, G. Nelson, 18¾ In. ......*illus*	330.00
Ingraham, E., Shelf, Oriental, 8-Day, Time & Strike, c.1880, 17½ In.	880.00
Ingraham, E., Violet Model, Gingerbread, Oak Case, 8-Day, Time & Strike, c.1915, 22 In.	99.00
Ingraham, Shelf, Vaseline Glass, Cuttings, Half Moon Shape, Victorian, 14 In. ....*illus*	411.00
International Time Recording Co., Wall, Oak Case, Timecard Punch, 48 x 17 In. ...*illus*	780.00
Ithaca Calendar, Walnut, 2 Dials, 1865, 21 x 10½ In. ....*illus*	644.00
Ives, Chauncey, Pillar & Scroll, Mahogany, Columns, Brass Finials, Reverse Glass Painting, 30 In.	2415.00
Ives, Joseph, Shelf, Wagon Spring, Mahogany Case, Ebonized, Paw Feet, 29 x 16 In.	11550.00
Japy Freres, Knight's Helmet, Nickel Plated Brass, France, c.1890, 13 In.	165.00
Japy Freres, Portal, Rosewood, Flowers, Scroll Inlay, Cast Iron, Spiral Columns, 19 x 9⅝ In.	440.00
Japy Freres, Square, Metal, Pendulum, Painted, 8-Day, France, c.1925, 12½ In.	66.00
Jerome & Co., Steeple, Rosewood, 30-Hour, New Haven Movement, c.1875, 15¼ In.	121.00
Jerome & Darrow, Shelf, 8-Day, 40 In.	430.00
Jessner, Joseph, Shelf, Gilt Bronze Case, Austria, c.1815, 9 In.	598.00
Junghans, Cottage, Faux Bamboo Frame, Time & Strike, Hamburg, U.S. Trademark ...*illus*	117.00
Junghans, Porcelain China Dial, Blue & White Checkerboard, 8-Day, c.1910, 18¾ In.	121.00
Karl Griesbaum & Co., Whistler, Man, Brown Coat, Bowler Hat, Germany, c.1935, 14 In.	743.00
Kienzle, Regulator, R-A Style, Gong Strike, 8-Day, Germany, c.1900, 35 In.	193.00
Kroeber, F., Mahogany, Victorian, N.Y., c.1887, 20½ x 4½ In.	263.00
Kroeber, Florence, Porcelain, Urn, Pressed Brass Base, 8-Day, Time & Strike, c.1880, 18½ In.	539.00
Lawson Time, Desk, Zephyr, K.E.M. Weber, c.1934, 3½ x 3¾ x 8½ In. ....*illus*	540.00
LeCoultre, Atmos, Jean-Leon Reutter, Mid 20th Century, 9½ In.	470.00
LeCoultre, Atmos, Square Case, Round Dial, Jean-Leon Reutter, c.1970, 9¼ In.	481.00
LeCoultre, Shelf, Atmos, Brass Frame, Glass Panels, 15 Jewels, 9¼ In.	1888.00
LeCoultre, Zodiac, Lucite, Gilt Brass, Blue Ground, Square Face, c.1960, 6 In.	855.00
Leroy & Fils, Carriage, Brass, Beveled Glass, Case, Grand Sonniere, 6½ In.	6095.00
Linden, Humpback, 8-Day, Germany, c.1950, 9 x 16 x 4 In.	41.00
Litchfield Mfg. Co., 30-Hour Time & Alarm Lever, Litchfield, Conn., c.1850, 12 In.	138.00
Lux, Cat, Blinking Eye, Arms Attached To Nose, Tail Pendulum, Keywind, 5 In. ....*illus*	440.00
Lux, Clown, Blinking Eye, Arms Attached To Nose, Red Hat & Collar, Keywind, 6 In. ....*illus*	385.00
Marionnet, A., Bacchus, Art Nouveau, Bronze, Vining, Bell Strike, c.1895, 18 In.	330.00
Marti, Samuel, Regulator, Cloisonne, Corniche Case, 8-Day, Gong Strike, c.1895, 10½ In.	1155.00
Mayer, Dog, Panting Tongue, Wagging Tail, Metal, Embossed, c.1885, 5 In.	550.00
Munroe, Matthew, Shelf, Federal, Mahogany, Inlaid, Concord, Mass., c.1800, 33 x 14 x 6 In. *illus*	8400.00
Mystery, Annular Dial, Mini Urn, Blue Cobalt Enamel, Silver Case, 6 Cameos, c.1900, 4½ In.	3850.00
Nelson, G., Wall, Brushed Silver Metal, Transparent Dial Face, Brass Works, Pendulum, 12 In.	411.00
New Haven, Bingham, Cast White Metal Case, Gold Plate, 30-Hour, c.1917, 7¼ In.	55.00
New Haven, Eastlake, c.1890, 22½ x 16 In.	88.00
New Haven, Guilford, 1-Day Alarm, Original Box, c.1930, 3½ In.	3.00
New Haven, Shelf, Mahogany, Ogee, c.1840, 26 x 15 In.	70.00
New Haven, Steeple, 19th Century, 20 In. ....*illus*	69.00

C

Clock, Hot Air Balloon, Bronze, Round Dial, Porcelain Numbers, Zodiac Signs, 27 x 10 In. $7475.0

Clock, Howard Miller, Starburst, No. 2202, Salmon Spikes, Electric, G. Nelson, 18¾ In. $330.00

Clock, Ingraham, Shelf, Vaseline Glass, Cuttings, Half Moon Shape, Victorian, 14 In. $411.00

Clock, International Time Recording Co., Wall, Oak Case, Timecard Punch, 48 x 17 In. $780.00

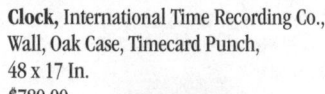

Clock, Ithaca Calendar, Walnut, 2 Dials, 1865, 21 x 10½ In. $644.00

Grandmother Clock

A *grandmother clock* is is a smaller version of a grandfather clock. It should be less than six feet six inches in height. Grandmother clocks were first popular from about 1750 to 1850. Modern versions are made today.

Clock, Junghans, Cottage, Faux Bamboo Frame, Time & Strike, Hamburg, U.S. Trademark $117.00

Clock, Lawson Time, Desk, Zephyr, K.E.M. Weber, c.1934, 3½ x 3¾ x 8½ In. $540.00

Clock, Lux, Cat, Blinking Eye, Arms Attached To Nose, Tail Pendulum, Keywind, 5 In. $440.00

Clock, Lux, Clown, Blinking Eye,
Arms Attached To Nose, Red Hat & Collar,
Keywind, 6 In.
$385.00

Clock, Munroe, Matthew, Shelf,
Federal, Mahogany, Inlaid, Concord, Mass.,
c.1800, 33 x 14½ x 6½ In.
$8400.00

Clock, New Haven, Steeple,
19th Century, 20 In.
$69.00

Clock, New Haven, Wall, Oak, Carved Lions'
Heads & Flowers, Shaped Sides, Glass Door,
25 x 15 In.
$385.00

Clock, Seth Thomas, Regulator, Brass Case,
Lion, Standing, Flower Swags On Dial,
15 x 8 In.
$748.00

Clock, Seth Thomas, Regulator, No. 2, Oak,
8-Day, 34 In.
$1112.00

Clock, Seth Thomas, Shelf, Walnut, Gilt Trim,
Brass Works, 30-Hour, 15½ x 12 x 5 In.
$69.00

Clock, Shelf, Faux Tortoiseshell, Gilt Bronze
Scroll Mount, Medaille, 1886,
16 x 9 In.
$978.00

Clock, Shelf, Gilt Bronze, Diana, Cherubs,
Gravet Movement, France,
19th Century, 19 x 14 In.
$2151.00

Timepiece or Clock?

In clock collector's lingo, a timepiece
is an instrument that measures time
but does not strike. A clock keeps
time and has a striking mechanism
that sounds on the hour and
sometimes the quarter hour.

New Haven, Wall, Oak, Carved Lions' Heads & Flowers, Shaped Sides, Glass Door, 25 x 15 In. ..*illus*	385.00
New Haven, Walnut Case, 8-Day, Time & Strike, c.1890, 26½ In.	198.00
Parker, Drum Alarm, Bell Shape Base, 30-Hour Lever, Meriden, Conn., c.1910, 7 In.	55.00
Porcelain Shield, Embossed Pendulum, 30-Hour, Fluted Iron Weight, c.1879, 5¾ In.	550.00
Regulator, Mahogany, Burl Veneer Case, Turned Quarter Columns, 16¾ x 7½ In.	748.00
Regulator, Music Box, Oak, Corinthian Columns, Jos. Coch, 17 x 7½ In.	2070.00
Regulator, Victorian, Fruitwood, Burl Veneer, Turned Finials, Weights, Pendulum, 17 x 8 In.	4255.00
Regulator, Vienna, Ebonized Case, Racetrack Door, 8-Day, Austria, c.1880, 45 In.	495.00
Regulator, Walnut, 2-Train, Spindles, Half-Hour Strike, Germany, 20th Century, 31 In.	2350.00
Round Drop, Inlaid Case, 8-Day, Time & Bell Strike, c.1890, 27 In.	550.00
Royal Bonn, Ansonia, Shelf, Blue, Pendulum, Key, Royal Vonn, 13 x 14 In.	825.00
Royal Bonn, Ansonia, Shelf, White, Flowers, Porcelain, Open Escapement, Time, Strike, c.1881	825.00
Sessions, Shelf, Decorated Wood, Flowers, Shaped, Early 1900s, 12½ x 11 In.	47.00
Seth Thomas, Cherry Case, 1-Day Movement, c.1870, 10½ In.	55.00
Seth Thomas, Cottage, Octagon Top, Alarm c.1870, 9 In.	220.00
Seth Thomas, Cottage D, Mahogany, Time & Alarm, Thomaston, c.1870, 9 In.	110.00
Seth Thomas, Lodge, Alarm, Nickel Plate, 30-Hour Lever Movement, c.1904, 7½ In.	110.00
Seth Thomas, Long Case, Oak, Gothic Style Apron, 2 Finials, Roman Numerals, 8-Day, 67 x 23 In.	2038.00
Seth Thomas, Mahogany, 2 Weights, Bone Kite Escutcheons, 2 Columns, Paw Feet, 8-Day, 36 In.	265.00
Seth Thomas, Mahogany, Ogee, Thomaston, Conn., c.1850, 25 x 15½ In.	94.00
Seth Thomas, Mahogany, Town Scene, Pillar & Scroll, Eglomise, 30-Hour Movement, 31 x 17¾ In.	3190.00
Seth Thomas, Regulator, Beveled Glass, Brass, Standing Lion, Flowers, Swags, 15 x 8 In.	748.00
Seth Thomas, Regulator, Brass Case, Lion, Standing, Flower Swags On Dial, 15 x 8 In. .*illus*	748.00
Seth Thomas, Regulator, No. 2, Oak, 8-Day, 34 In. ....*illus*	1112.00
Seth Thomas, Regulator, No. 3, Pendulum, Oak Case, 8-Day, 42 x 40 In.	4816.00
Seth Thomas, School, 8-Day Oak Case, c.1924, 21½ In.	220.00
Seth Thomas, Shelf, Adamantin, Faux Marble, 8-Day, Time & Strike, c.1896, 11½ In.	171.00
Seth Thomas, Shelf, Burled Finish, Sonora Chimes, c.1900, 14 In.	323.00
Seth Thomas, Shelf, Double Dial, Time & Strike, Calendar, Dome Top, 15½ x 5¼ In.	890.00
Seth Thomas, Shelf, Eastlake Style, 20 In.	88.00
Seth Thomas, Shelf, Eastlake Style, 22 x 12 In.	82.00
Seth Thomas, Shelf, Mahogany, Keywind, 8 x 15¼ In.	65.00
Seth Thomas, Shelf, Mahogany, Westminster Chime, 8-Day, c.1921, 14 In.	209.00
Seth Thomas, Shelf, No. 99, Marble, Black Marble, 8-Day, Time & Strike, c.1882, 10¾ In.	176.00
Seth Thomas, Shelf, Rosewood, c.1880, 15 x 11 In.	82.00
Seth Thomas, Shelf, Walnut, Gilt Trim, Brass Works, 30-Hour, 15½ x 12 x 5 In. ......*illus*	69.00
Seth Thomas, Wall, Rosewood, 8-Day, 25 x 14¾ In.	351.00
Shelf, Alabaster Case, Carved, France, 19th Century, 19½ In.	716.00
Shelf, Art Deco, Brass, Alabaster, Octagonal, Mermaids, 9¾ x 16 In.	120.00
Shelf, Art Deco, Zodiac, Bronze, 8-Day, Round, 11½ x 9¾ In.	1554.00
Shelf, Black Marble, Year Duration, France, c.1900, 15½ In.	495.00
Shelf, Black Slate, Patinated Metal, Enamel Numbers, Tiffany & Co., 19⅛ In.	588.00
Shelf, Brass, Enameled Gilt, France, Late 19th Century, 13½ In.	563.00
Shelf, Bronze, Marble, Figural, Neoclassical Male Sculptor, Seated, 1800s, 17 x 12 In.	1404.00
Shelf, Chamois Trophy Head, Scrolled Branch, Leaf, Carved, Black Forest, c.1900, 15 In.	880.00
Shelf, Charles X, Bronze Dore, Beloved Memory, Allegorical Figure, 1800s, 17 x 13 In.	2938.00
Shelf, Eagle, Holding Globe Between Wings, Patinated Spelter, Gilt, France, c.1880, 10 In.	1045.00
Shelf, Edwardian Baroque, Rosewood, Arch, Westminster Chime, Brass Pomegranate Finials, 29 In.	3525.00
Shelf, Elephant, Bronze, Ormolu, Clock & Cupid Surmount Elephant, c.1860, 23 In.	3575.00
Shelf, Faux Tortoiseshell, Gilt Bronze Scroll Mount, Medaille, 1886, 16 x 9 In. ....*illus*	978.00
Shelf, Federal, Mahogany, Eglomise, Brass Mounted, Pillar & Scroll, c.1825, 31 x 17 x 35 In.	1320.00
Shelf, Federal, Mahogany, Pillar & Scroll, Painted, Gilt Dial, c.1825, 31¾ In.	1410.00
Shelf, Gilt Bronze, Diana, Cherubs, Gravet Movement, France, 19th Century, 19 x 14 In. *illus*	2151.00
Shelf, Gilt Bronze, Silk Thread, Fruit, Woman In Asian Dress, France	7475.00
Shelf, Greco-Roman Style, Onyx, Brass, France, 20th Century, 12 x 13 x 6 In.	468.00
Shelf, Ingraham, E., Steeple, Mahogany, Frosted Glass, Vase Of Flowers, c.1938, 11¼ In. *illus*	295.00
Shelf, Japy Freres, Bronze, Marble Base & Mount, c.1880, 18 x 11 In.	2340.00
Shelf, Japy Freres, Louis XVI Style, Gilt Bronze, Angel, Cherubs, 16¼ In.	4406.00
Shelf, Louis XV, Faux Tortoiseshell, Ormolu Mounted, France, 29 x 15½ In.	1783.00
Shelf, Louis XVI Style, Bronze, Beveled Glass, Enamel Dial, 20½ In.	2350.00
Shelf, Louis XVI Style, Figural, Gilt Bronze, Marble, Calendar, 2-Train Movement, 14 In.	2468.00
Shelf, Lyre Shape, Gilt Bronze Mounted, Composition, Marble, Enameled, 17½ In.	960.00
Shelf, Mahogany, Barometer, Calendar, Time, Pendulum Window, France, 19 x 19 In. ..*illus*	2559.00
Shelf, Malachite, Arched Portico Shape, Gilt Bronze Sunburst Pendulum & Trim, 15 In.	3840.00
Shelf, Marble, Bronze, Scrolling, Figures, France, c.1880, 21 x 16 In.	263.00
Shelf, Marble, Onyx Case, Gazelles, c.1930, 24 In.	205.00

Clock, Shelf, Ingraham, E., Steeple, Mahogany, Frosted Glass, Vase Of Flowers, c.1938, 11¼ In.
$295.00

Clock, Shelf, Mahogany, Barometer, Calendar, Time, Pendulum Window, France, 19 x 19 In.
$2559.00

Windup Clocks

Windup clocks were made in art deco and later styles. Marble, onyx, chrome, brass, copper, Bakelite, Formica, celluloid, and glass were used for clock cases for living room and bedroom clocks. Eight-day windups were sometimes made in unusual modern shapes. Clever clocks were shaped like airplanes or statues with an added clock face. A series of clocks with neon trim was fashionable. A windup alarm clock with a cartoon character like Mickey Mouse or Popeye moving its arms to point to the time was made for children's bedrooms.

C

Clock, Tall Case, Thomas Nauman, Cherry, Arched Glazed Door, Iron Dial, Black Paint, 89 In.
$3910.00

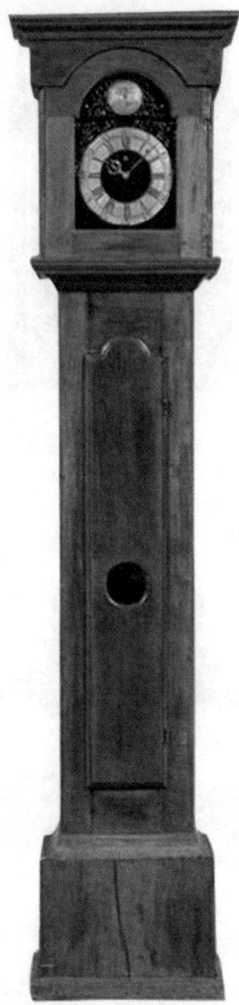

The Clock Face Game
Bet your friends they can't draw a picture of the numbers on an old grandfather clock face. Try it. The Roman numeral VI on a clock face was placed upside down on clocks made before 1900. The bottom of the numeral always faces the center on early clocks or on authentic reproductions. Most clocks made before 1850 use the Roman numeral IIII instead of IV for four.

Shelf, Nelson, G., Mahogany, Brass Fittings, 13½ x 12 x 6¼ In.	176.00
Shelf, Neoclassical, Parcel Gilt, Walnut, Temple Shape, Putti, Wreath, 20½ In.	180.00
Shelf, Onyx Base, Reclining Female Figure, France, Early 20th Century, 14 x 17 In.	468.00
Shelf, Ormolu, Enameled Dial, Roman Numerals, Rectangular Case, c.1825, 14 x 9 x 4¾ In.	4800.00
Shelf, Porcelain, 4 Seasons, Meissen, 19 In.	4348.00
Shelf, Porcelain, Ormolu, Blue Case, Gilt Highlights, Painted Landscape, 21 x 14½ In.	2530.00
Shelf, Tortoiseshell, Gilt Mounted, Robert A. Paris, France, 19th Century, 15½ In.	437.00
Shelf, Werner & Sons, Porcelain, Dresden, 15 x 10 In.	263.00
Shelf, Windmill, 11 In.	45.00
Simplex Time Recorder, Oak Case, Flat Cornice Top, Pendulum, Key, 15½ x 18 In.	920.00
Skyscraper, Paul Frankl, Bakelite, Circular Glass Dial, Mirror, c.1932, 7½ In.	588.00
Snider, Ball, White Face, Dark Red, Red & White Balls, After Nelson, 1950s, 1½ In.	160.00
Stuhl, Wood, Carved, 30-Hour, Time & Strike, c.1810, 27 In.	660.00
Swinging Arm, Art Nouveau Statue, 8-Day, Bell Strike, c.1890, 29 In.	5280.00
Tall Case, A. Willard, Federal, Mahogany Inlaid, Pierced Fretwork, c.1800, 92 In.	47000.00
Tall Case, Boignard, Mahogany, Channel Island, 8-Day, Strike Movement, 85 In.	3563.00
Tall Case, Brevetto Turati, Molded Fiberglass, c.1970, 66½ In.	307.00
Tall Case, Caleb Wheaton, Federal, Inlaid, Figured Mahogany, c.1785, 96 x 21 In.	33000.00
Tall Case, Cherry, Carved, Molded Arched Cornice, Brass Ball Finials, Late 1700s, 94 In.	6463.00
Tall Case, Cherry, Tombstone Door, Turned Columns, 30-Hour, Wood Movement, 94 In.	3220.00
Tall Case, Chippendale, Mahogany, Block & Shell, Carved, Newport, c.1775, 96 x 23 In.	13200.00
Tall Case, Classical, Mahogany Panels, Curved Door, Broken-Arch Pediment, 84 x 19 In.	2760.00
Tall Case, Colonial Clock Co., Moon Dial, Westminster Chimes, Early 1900s, 82 In.	1058.00
Tall Case, David Gobrecht, Chippendale, Cherry, Broken-Arch Top, Dentil Molding, 103 In.	11000.00
Tall Case, F. Willard, Federal, Figured Mahogany, Massachusetts, c.1790, 101 x 20 In.	7200.00
Tall Case, Federal, Cherry, Pierced Fretwork, Tombstone Door, 8-Day Movement, 90 In.	5288.00
Tall Case, Federal, Inlaid Mahogany, Andrews Family, Roxbury, Mass., c.1816, 99 x 21 In.	20400.00
Tall Case, Federal, Mahogany, Eagle Crest, Glazed Panel Door, 63 x 14 In.	1770.00
Tall Case, Federal, Mahogany, Veneer, Swan's-Neck Crest, Finials, 8-Day Movement, 95 In.	5580.00
Tall Case, French Provincial, Walnut, Oval Glazed Door, Burl Panels, 92 x 18 In.	2115.00
Tall Case, George Eby, Chippendale, Walnut, Poplar, Arch, Columns, 8-Day, Manheim, Pa., 94½ In.	2530.00
Tall Case, George III, Mahogany, Arched Bonnet, Open Fretwork, 2-Train Movement, 87½ In.	4406.00
Tall Case, George III, Mahogany, Painted Face, Swan's-Neck Crest, 2-Train Movement, 90 In.	2703.00
Tall Case, Georgian, Black Lacquer, Japanned, Chinoiserie, 85 x 19 In.	10620.00
Tall Case, Hoadley, Painted, Fretwork, Ball Finials, Arched Cornice, c.1825, 80 In.	3055.00
Tall Case, Hopkins & Lewis, Cherry, Curly Maple, Broken-Arch Pediment, Rosettes, 30-Hour, 89 In.	1840.00
Tall Case, John Felsher, Chippendale, Cherry, Carved, c.1805, 91½ x 19 x 11½ In.	8400.00
Tall Case, John Wainwright, Brass Works, Squared Hood Top, 79 x 14½ x 10 In.	288.00
Tall Case, L. Watson, Federal, Pine Case, Wood Dial, Cincinnati, c.1834, 93 x 18 In.	5290.00
Tall Case, Mahogany, Brass, Germany, Late 19th Century, 87 In.	703.00
Tall Case, Mahogany, Scrolled Pediment, Arching Glazed Door, 91½ x 26 x 11¾ In.	2714.00
Tall Case, Oak, Boxwood, Swan's-Neck, Lunar Arch, 2-Train Movement, England, 88 In.	2585.00
Tall Case, Oak, Fluted Columns, Inlaid Plinths, Bracket Feet, Second Hand, Calendar, 81 In.	2070.00
Tall Case, Osborn, Chippendale, Cherry, Painted Iron Dial, 97 In.	5175.00
Tall Case, Parlange Fils & Freres, Cherry, Stepped Cornice, Arched, France, 17 x 11 In.	2643.00
Tall Case, Peter Stretch, Queen Anne, Walnut, Philadelphia, c.1740, 96 x 20½ In.	18000.00
Tall Case, Pine, White Enamel Face, Brass Spandrels, Tombstone Door, 102 In.	1000.00
Tall Case, Renaissance Revival, Mahogany, Carved Bonnet, 5 Chimes, Early 1900s, 93 In.	6573.00
Tall Case, Riley Whiting, Pine, Arched Door, Scroll Cut, Skirt, Red & Black Grain, 86 In.	1725.00
Tall Case, Seth Thomas, Poplar, Pine, Carved Hood, Flower-Painted Dial, Feet, 30-Hour, 86½ In.	805.00
Tall Case, Sheraton, Cherry, Broken-Arch Top, Bull's-Eye Rosettes, 8-Day Movement, 99 In.	3740.00
Tall Case, Sheraton, Mahogany, Scrolling Broken-Arch Crown, c.1830, 88 x 19 In.	4600.00
Tall Case, Thomas Bennett, Cherry & Walnut, Early 19th Century, 84 In.	2165.00
Tall Case, Thomas Nauman, Cherry, Arched Glazed Door, Iron Dial, Black Paint, 89 In. *illus*	3910.00
Tall Case, Transitional, Mahogany, Broken-Arch Top, Scrolled Rosettes, 90 In.	2540.00
Tall Case, W. Lewis Warren, Walnut, Poplar, Broken-Arch, Arched Door, Flower-Painted Dial, 93 In.	2415.00
Tall Case, Walnut, Broken-Arch Top, Chip-Carved Rosettes, Astragal Door, 96 In.	2640.00
Tambour, Seth Thomas, Flemish Oak, 8-Day Round Movement, c.1915, 9¾ In.	418.00
Terry, Eli & Samuel, Shelf, Pillar & Scroll, Scroll Top, Reverse Painted Panel, 31 x 18 In.	1035.00
Tiffany clocks that are part of desk sets made by Louis Comfort Tiffany are listed in the Tiffany category. Clocks sold by the store, Tiffany & Co., are listed here.	
Tiffany, Bronze, Violet Marble, Medici Tomb, Night & Day, Figures, 8-Day, Bell, c.1890, 19 In.	6375.00
Travel, Jaeger-LeCoultre, Lapis Lazuli, Brass, Roman Numerals, Fitted Case, 3 x 1¾ In.	585.00
Wag-On-Wall, Flowers, Blue Columns, Brass Works, Weights, Pendulum, 9¾ x 13¾ In.	230.00
Wall, Delft, 13 In.	369.00
Wall, German, Oak, Leaded Glass Panel, 30 x 13 x 6 In.	189.00

Wall, Mother-Of-Pearl Inlay, Bull Hoofprint Form, France, 1800s, 24 x 19 In.		675.00
Wall, Walnut, Hand Carved, Germany, Late 19th Century, 37 x 14 x 7 In.		527.00
Wall, Walnut, Handmade, 35 x 16 In.		176.00
Wall, Wood, Carved, Spool Turned, Rosettes, Stepped Finials, Pendulum, Germany, 48 In.		558.00
Wall, Wood, Half Column Pillar		250.00
Walnut, Carved, Turned Posts, Finials, Shaped Lower Section, c.1910, 30 x 16 In.		117.00
Waltham, Art Nouveau, Inlaid, Easel, Back Wind, 8-Day, c.1925, 10½ In.		121.00
Warren Telechron Co., Bakelite, Ivory & Brown, Brass Framed Face, Alarm, c.1930, 4½ In.		88.00
Waterbury, 2 Pilgrims, Blunderbuss, Carved, Oak, 2-Weight, 28½ x 26 In.	*illus*	920.00
Waterbury, Regulator, Crystal, Gilt Brass, 8-Day, c.1908, 15½ x 7½ In.	*illus*	633.00
Waterbury, Shelf, Cherry Case, c.1900, 12 In.		82.00
Waterbury, Shelf, Parlor, Green, Daisies, Gold Trim, Porcelain, c.1891, 11 In.	*illus*	288.00
Waterbury, Shelf, Parlor No. 94, Porcelain, 8-Day, Time & Strike, c.1900, 12 In.		248.00
Waterbury, Shelf, Rosewood, Eglomise, Steeple, 8-Day, c.1850, 20 In.		176.00
Waterbury, Walnut, Calendar, 2 Dials, Victorian, 23½ In.		499.00
Welch, E.N., Steeple, Rosewood, Alarm, 30-Hour, Time & Strike, c.1860, 20 In.		132.00
Welch Spring, Rosewood, Arched, Turned Columns, Perpetual Calendar, 2 Dials, 18 In. *illus*		550.00
Werner, Walnut Case, 8-Day, Time & Strike, Germany, c.1890, 47 In.		440.00
Whistler, Baseball Player, Take Me Out To The Ball Park, c.1970, 15 In.		2145.00

CLOISONNE enamel was developed during the tenth century. A glass enamel was applied between small ribbons of metal on a metal base. Most cloisonne is Chinese or Japanese. Pieces marked *China* are twentieth-century examples.

Belt Buckle, Dragon Clasp, Blue Passion Flower Design, Early 18th Century, 5¾ In., 2 Piece	1150.00
Bowl, Cover, Dragons, Phoenixes, 5¾ In.	500.00
Bowl, Flowers, Butterflies, Birds, Turquoise Ground, Chinese, 11 x 14 In.	2938.00
Bowl, Low, Chinese, 3¼ x 12 In.	281.00
Box, Peacock, Peonies, Flowers & Butterflies Inside, Dome Lid, Bracket Feet, 4 x 6 In.	259.00
Box, Silver, Cylindrical, Fahua Palette, Hardstone Lion On Lid, 5½ In.	230.00
Cachepot, Hardstone Trees, Chinese, 12 In., Pair	295.00
Charger, Birds, Basket Of Flowers, 1868-1912, 12 In.	192.00
Charger, Blue Ground, Decorated Border, Quail, Cranes, Flowers, Japan, 1800s, 18 In., Pair	3528.00
Charger, Center Inset, Carved Panels Of Bone, Chinese, 23 x 2 In.	823.00
Dish, Pigeon Blood Ginbari, 5 In.	85.00
Figure, Flying Horse Of Gansu, Blue, Gold Mane, Hooves, Chinese, 1900s, 17 In.	176.00
Ginger Jar, Dover, Pointed Brass Finial, Brass Fittings, Blue, Dome Lid, 8 x 5 In., Pair	460.00
Ginger Jar, Green Ground, Flowers, Scroll Design, Dome Lid, 7 x 6 In., Pair	518.00
Jar, Bronze, Flowers, Green Ground, Double Handles, 18 In.	345.00
Jar, Ginger Jar Shape, Lid, Chinese, 13¼ In.	354.00
Jardiniere, Chrysanthemums, Birds, Blue On Black, Lion's Head Handles, 17 x 14 In.	287.00
Jardiniere, Flower Lappets, 1868-1912, 5 In. Diam.	69.00
Panel, Wireless, Heart Shape, Crane In Landscape, Japan, 9¾ In.	502.00
Plate, Cranes, Flowers, Blue Ground, Japan, 1868-1911, 12 In.	529.00
Plate, Peonies, Birds, Shell Form Medallions, Brocade Ground, 1868-1912, 10 In.	230.00
Screen, Table, 4 Panels, Birds, Flowers, 20th Century, 7¼ x 13 In.	431.00
Teapot, Bird & Butterfly Medallions, White Ground, Oval, 1868-1912, 6½ In.	92.00
Teapot, White Ground, Green, Red, Blue & Lavender Design, Gold Trim, 2 In.	30.00
Temple Jar, Tapered, Dome Lid, Black Ground, Yellow Flowers Leaves, 14½ In.	690.00
Vase, Blue To White Ground, Berries On Branch, Birds, 7½ x 7½ In., Pair	1840.00
Vase, Butterflies, Inverted Pear Shape, 1868-1912, 7½ In.	57.00
Vase, Celadon Silver, Green Blue Ground, Roses On Stems, 12 In.	1200.00
Vase, Chrysanthemums, Basse Taille Ground, Pear Shape, Chinese, 9 In.	470.00
Vase, Chrysanthemums, Leaves, Moth, Red Metallic Ground, Elongated Baluster, Japan, 10 In.	300.00
Vase, Cobalt Blue Ground, 19th Century, 6 In., Pair	605.00
Vase, Dignitaries, Canopy Chariot, 3 Panels, Electrified, Chinese, 14 In.	148.00
Vase, Dragon, Brown Ground, Seed Form, 1868-1912, 5¾ In.	259.00
Vase, Dragon, Peach Shaped Medallions, Phoenixes, Chinese, 17th Century, 12½ In.	4406.00
Vase, Egrets In Lotus Pond, Flower Border, Japan, 19th Century, 12 In.	323.00
Vase, Flowers, Vases, Bowls, Plants, Double Bulbous, 13 In., Pair	275.00
Vase, Flowes, Blue Ground, Chinese, 10½ In.	2360.00
Vase, Flying Bluebirds, Flowers, Gray Green, Blue, White Flared Rim, Tapered, Footed, 12 In., Pair	1150.00
Vase, Java Finches, Pink Blossoms, Green Ground, Japan, 12 In., Pair	345.00
Vase, Morning Glories, Purple Flowered Ground, Pear Shape, Chinese, 13 In.	24.00
Vase, Openwork, Lotus Scrolls, Blue, Green, Border On Vase & Neck, 15¾ In.	660.00
Vase, Patterned Body, 4 Bronze Buttresses, Agate Roundels, c.1900, 13½ x 8½ In.	528.00

Clock, Waterbury, 2 Pilgrims, Blunderbuss, Carved, Oak, 2-Weight, 28½ x 26 In. $920.00

Clock, Waterbury, Regulator, Crystal, Gilt Brass, 8-Day, c.1908, 15½ x 7½ In. $633.00

Clock, Waterbury, Shelf, Parlor, Green, Daisies, Gold Trim, Porcelain, c.1891, 11 In. **$288.00**

Clock, Welch Spring, Rosewood, Arched, Turned Columns, Perpetual Calendar, 2 Dials, 18 In. **$550.00**

Wedding Dresses

The average woman was married in her best dress until the late nineteenth century. The dress was not white because it was to be worn to church or for visiting. White wedding dresses became the fashion after Queen Victoria's wedding in 1840. By the 1870s, women wanted white wedding gowns made in Paris, or at least a copy of a French dress. Dresses were handed down to others, so look out for restyled bodices or sleeves and added trim. The most collectible dresses have the original lace, beading, and embroidery.

Vase, Peacock On Rockery, Japan, 8¾ In.	153.00
Vase, Swirling Flowers, Mulberry Ground, Japan, 20th Century, 5 In.	235.00
Vase, Temple, Mums, Geometric Flower Bands, Vining, Teakwood Base, 25½ In.	345.00
Vase, Treebark, Brown Tones, 5 In.	375.00
Vase, Urn Shape, Dragon Motif, Mounted As Lamp, c.1900, 12 In.	173.00
Vase, Wireless, Silver Wire, Ando Mark, Japan, Early 20th Century, 10¾ In.	1180.00

CLOTHING of all types is listed in this category. Dresses, hats, shoes, underwear, and more are found here. Other textiles are to be found in the Coverlet, Movie, Quilt, Textile, and World War I and II categories.

Bathing Suit, Right Side Drape, Catalina, 1950s, Large	140.00
Belt, Official Tom Corbett Space Cadet, Yale, On Card, 1950s, 6½ x 13 In.	187.00
Cap, Railroad, Blue & White Stripes, Lee Brand, 1940-50, Size 6¾ In.	55.00
Cap, Space Patrol Rocket, Bailey, Hollywood, 1950s, 7 x 11¾ In.	336.00
Chaps, Batwing, Metal Conchas, Child's, c.1920, 24 In.	1300.00
Coat, Blue Silk, Kesi Panels On Front & Back, Chinese, 45 In.	826.00
Coat, Brown Bear, Quilted Lining, 1900s, Size 48	750.00
Coat, Mink, Full-Length, Caramel Color, Hook Closure, Silk Interior, Size 8	575.00
Corset, Dancing, Flapper, Wraparound, Tea Rose Pink Brocade, 1925	50.00
Dress, Evening, Blue & Silver, Brocade, 1950s, Size 10	75.00
Dress, Evening, Flapper, Beaded, Loop Of Beads Hang From Hem, Off-White, 1920s	75.00
Dress, Silk Taffeta, Maroon Lined In White Cotton, 1865, 33-In. Bust, 23-In. Waist	195.00
Earmuffs, Shmoo, Box, c.1949	240.00
Gloves, Lace, Fingers Out, Ruffle At Wrist, White, 1940s	60.00
Hat, Leather, Round, 18th Century	1800.00
Jacket, Motorcycle, Leather, Tan With Black Sleeves, Bate Of California, 1960s, Large	500.00
Jacket, Silk, Black, Embroidered, Flowers, Satin Stitch, Woman's, Chinese	708.00
Jockey Silks, Cap, Horse Racing, Brown & Green Strips, New Orleans, 1930s	375.00
Kimono, Silk, Crane, Brocade Decoration, Black Ground, Japan	224.00
Mittens, Amish, Wool, Pink, Dog Applique, Flannel Lining, 1930s, 6 x 4 In.	300.00
Mukluks, Hide Sole, Fur Bodies, Beaded Borders, 8¾ x 9 In.	115.00
Nightgown, Victorian, White Cotton, Pintucking On Bust, Button Front, c.1890	50.00
Obi, Silk, Gold Thread, Japanese, 120 In.	18.00
Playsuit, Vest, Calling Cards, Paladin, Have Gun Will Travel, In Package	249.00
Robe, Burgundy Silk, Embroidered Dragon, Gold Buttons, Chinese, 19th Century	3540.00
Robe, Silk, Embroidered, Dragons, Figures, Multicolored, Frame, 69 x 38 x 4 In.	881.00
Sash, Metis, From I Assumption, Quebec, 1885, 153 x 8 In.	14850.00
Scarf, Silk, Yellow On Cream Ground, Emilo Pucci, 1960s, 28 In.	300.00
Scarf, Vive Le Vent, Clipper Ships, Rigging, Flags, Blue, Brown, White Ground, Hermes	382.00
Shawl, Embroidered, Silk, Floral Motifs, Turquoise, Asia, 64 x 67 In.	354.00
Shoes, Black Leather Penny Loafer, G.H. Bass, 1960s, Size 7½ In.	50.00
Shoes, Wedding, White, Leather, Pearl Buttons, Scalloped High Tops, c.1900	110.00
Skirt, Embroidered, Red Silk, Depicts Dragons, Phoenix, Chinese, 19th Century, 53 In.	177.00
Skirt, Poodle, Gray Felt, Pink & Black Poodle, Sequin Collar With Chain, 1950s, Size 12	70.00
Skirt, White Silk, Embroidered, Gold Threads, Dragon, Phoenix, Flowers, Chinese	502.00
Sweater, Beaded, Black Wool, Sequins, Zado Of California, 1960s, Size 38	55.00
Sweater Jacket, Red Polyester Knit, Foldover Collar, 1970s	35.00
Sweater Suit, Ivory, Virgin Wool, Jantzen, 1960s	30.00
Tie, Clip-On, Bret & Bart Maverick Look-A-Likes, Warner Brother, 1959, 7 x 4 In.	200.00
Top Hat, Black Wool, Grosgrain Band, 6½ x 2 In.	89.00
Top Hat, Black Wool Felt, Ribbon Band, Feather, Size 7⅝, 5 x 2¼ In.	59.00
Tunic, Coachman's, 1830s	650.00
Vest, Black Silk, Velvet, Chinese	325.00
Vest, Brocade, Gold Embroidery, Cream Felt, Red Jewels, Turkey, c.1900, 14 In., Child's	264.00

CLUTHRA glass is a two-layered glass with small bubbles and powdered glass trapped between the layers. The Steuben Glass Works of Corning, New York, first made it in 1920. Victor Durand of Kimball Glass Company in Vineland, New Jersey, made a similar glass from about 1925. Durand's pieces are listed in the Durand category. Related items are listed in the Steuben category.

Vase, Amethyst, Steuben, 8 In.	1900.00
Vase, Green, Bulbous, Flared Rim, Steuben, 10½ In. ....*illus*	1495.00
Vase, Lime Green, Flared Rim, Steuben, 7½ In.	460.00
Vase, Multicolored, Confetti Ribbon Design, 8 In.	425.00
Vase, Pink Shading To White, Steuben, c.1920, 5½ In.	995.00

Vase, Pink, Shouldered, Steuben, 6½ In.	275.00
Vase, Pink, Steuben, 6½ In.	316.00
Vase, Rose, Steuben, 8 In.	2200.00
Vase, Trumpet, White, Blue Border, Steuben, 6¾ In.	920.00
Vase, Trumpet, White, Pink Cintra Rim, Steuben, 17 In.	633.00
Vase, Urn Shape, Lime Green, Ground Pontil, 10 In. .... *illus*	1140.00
Vase, White, Green, Pink & Yellow, 5 In.	295.00

COALPORT ware has been made by the Coalport Porcelain Works of England from 1795 to the present time. Early pieces were unmarked. About 1810–25 the pieces were marked with the name *Coalport* in various forms. Later pieces also had the name *John Rose* in the mark. The crown mark has been used with variations since 1881. The date 1750 is printed in some marks, but it is not the date the factory started. Some pieces are listed in Indian Tree.

COALPORT
BONE CHINA
MADE IN ENGLAND
EST. 1750

Bowl, Vegetable, Arcadia, Scalloped Rim, Oval, 1¾ x 8¾ x 6¾ In.	45.00
Bowl, Vegetable, Shrewsbury, Gold Trim, Oval, 3 x 9 x 6 In.	65.00
Cachepot, Stand, Gilt, Painted, Reserves, c.1820, 8½ In.	1767.00
Creamer, Samarkand, 4¾ In.	28.00
Cup & Saucer, Geneva, Athens Shape, Gold Trim	38.00
Cup & Saucer Set, Scalloped, Gold Trellis Work, Scrolled, Footed Cup, c.1940, 16 Piece	795.00
Dinner Service, Spearpoint, White, Navy Blue Rim, Gold Edge, 1900s, 180 Piece	1496.00
Figurine, Age Of Elegance, Royal Gala, 1992-96, 7 In.	56.00
Plate, Bread & Butter, Arcadia, Scalloped Rim, 5¾ In.	25.00
Plate, Bread & Butter, Flowers, Scalloped Rim, Gold Trim, 6 In.	12.00
Plate, Cobalt Blue, Gold, Flower Sprays, Gilt Grids, 9 In., 12 Piece	420.00
Plate, Dinner, Anniversary Pattern, Louis XVI, Gilt, Cobalt Blue Ground, 11 In., 12 Piece	3360.00
Plate, Salad, Arcadia, Scalloped Rim, 7¾ In.	30.00
Plate Set, Flow Blue, Gilded Design, White Ground, 8 In.	290.00
Platter, Arcadia, Scalloped Rim, 15 x 11¾ In.	70.00
Platter, Flowers, Scalloped Border, 14 In.	200.00
Soup, Cream, Underplate, Harebell, Handles	45.00
Soup, Cream, Underplate, Pembroke	30.00
Soup, Dish, Harebell, Rim, 1½ x 7½ In.	35.00
Sugar Basin, Cover, Finger, Japan Pattern, c.1810, 5½ In.	988.00
Tray, Mint, Ming Rose, Scalloped Rim, 8½ In.	35.00
Vase, Cover, Hong Kong, 20th Century, 8¼ In., Pair	208.00
Vase, Ming Rose, Flowers, White Ground, Bulbous, Flared, 1960s, 6½ In.	10.00

COBALT BLUE glass was made using oxide of cobalt. The characteristic bright dark blue identifies it for the collector. Most cobalt glass found today was made after the Civil War. There was renewed interest in the dark blue glass in the late 1930s and dinnerwares were made.

Banana Boat, Moon & Stars, Handle	48.00
Biscuit Jar, Cover, Grape, Oak Leaf, Handles, 5 x 6 In.	80.00
Bowl, 3½ x 8 x 14 In.	35.00
Bowl, Chrome Stand, 5½ x 2½ In.	40.00
Butter, Dome Cover, Pressed Grape, 4 x 3 In.	28.00
Candleholders, 7 In., Pair	48.00
Candy Dish, Iron Shape, Extra Base	20.00
Candy Dish, Shell Cover, Nautical, Dolphin Feet, 6½ In.	44.00
Candy Jar, 8 x 6½ In.	56.00
Compote, Tooled Ruffled Rim, Applied White Rim Band, 8 Ribs, 5½ In., Pair	529.00
Creamer, Aurora, 1930, 4½ In.	30.00
Decanter, 6 Glasses, Egg Shape Case, Footed, Painted, Flowers, Victorian, c.1870	205.00
Dish, Holder, Silver Plated, 3 x 3¾ & 1½ In.	16.00
Eggcup, Chicken, 2¾ x 2⅝ In.	22.00
Figurine, Shoe, Woman's, Cuban Heel, Beaded Band, c.1930, 4¾ x 3 In.	10.00
Figurine, Sleigh, Westmoreland, 9 x 5 In.	175.00
Ginger Jar, Bird, Flower, Tree, White, Gold, Green, 5¾ x 4½ In.	42.00
Goblet, King's Crown, 4¼ In.	10.00
Nut Dish, Scalloped Rim, 5½ In.	24.00
Pitcher, Ice Lip, 1934-41, 68 Oz., 8 In.	550.00
Pitcher, Mt. Vernon Scene, Curved Handle, 5½ x 5¾ In.	30.00
Plate, Moderntone, 1934-42, 6¾ In.	11.00
Punch Set, Fan & File, Child's, 13 Piece	31.00
Sherbet, King's Crown, 3¼ x 3¾ In.	12.00

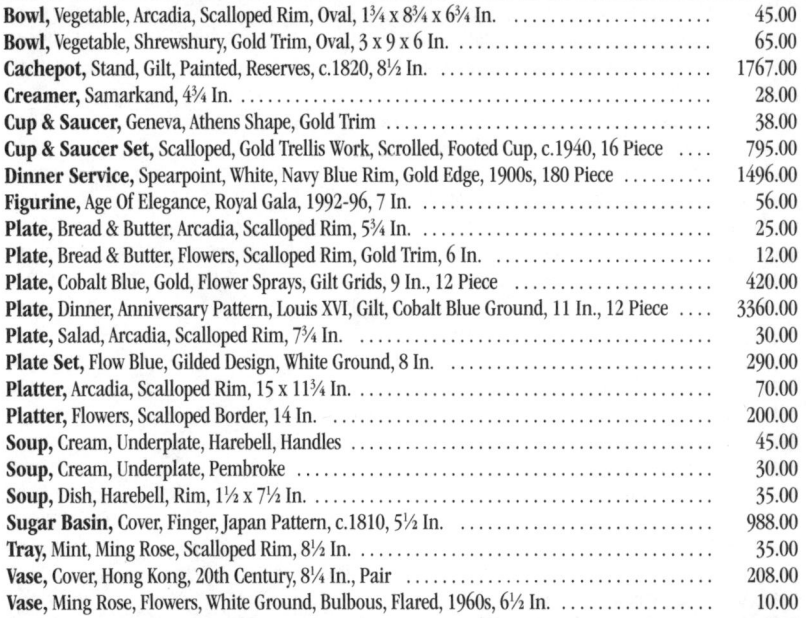

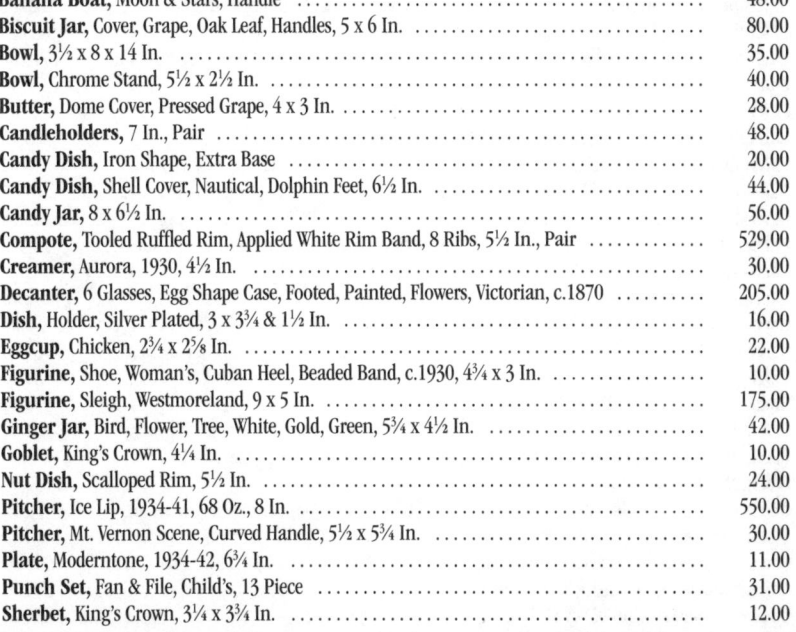

Christening Gowns
The first time a child was seen in public was for the christening ceremony. The baby was dressed up and introduced to the neighbors. By the eighteenth century, christening gowns were white. Many were embroidered, and most had matching bonnets. The expensive gowns were often used for more than one child and then handed down. Many have names and dates embroidered on the inside.

Cluthra, Vase, Green, Bulbous, Flared Rim, Steuben, 10½ In.
$1495.00

Cluthra, Vase, Urn Shape, Lime Green, Ground Pontil, 10 In.
$1140.00

C

Coca-Cola Slogans

Date original Coca-Cola items from slogans used in the advertising campaigns: *Drink Coca-Cola* (1886), *Deliciously Refreshing* (1904), *The Pause That Refreshes* (1929), *It's the Real Thing* (1942), *Things Go Better with Coke* (1954), *Coke Is It* (1982), and *Coca-Cola. Enjoy* (2000).

Coca-Cola, Bottle, Seltzer, Amber Glass, Wagner Spigot, 1920s, 12 In. $585.00

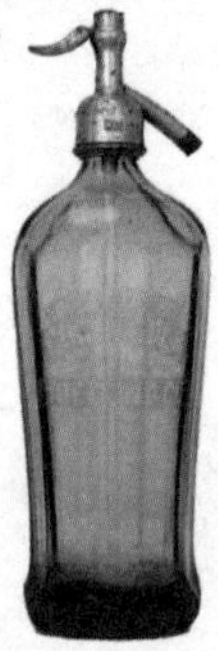

Coca-Cola, Bottle Topper, Bottle Cap, Drink Coca-Cola, We Let You See The Bottle, Tin, 1950s $495.00

DRINK
Coca-Cola
"Coke"
ASK FOR IT   EITHER WAY
WE LET YOU SEE THE BOTTLE

Coca-Cola, Dispenser Head, Counter, Cornelius, Metal, Plastic, 3 Taps, 15 In. $316.00

Toothpick, Top Hat	38.00
Vase, Clear, Applied Base, Hand Blown, 11½ In.	48.00
Vase, Clear Handles, White Lining, 8 x 4 In.	65.00
Vase, Enameled Flowers, Bottle Shape, Gilt, Mounted As Lamp, Victorian, 28 In., Pair	165.00
Vase, Ring Bottom, Fluted Mouth, 13¾ In.	45.00
Vase, Triangular, 9½ In.	10.00
Vase, Trumpet, Gilt Metal, Glass Inserts, 9½ In., Pair	47.00
Wall Pocket, Blue, 8¼ x 2 In.	30.00

COCA-COLA was first served in 1886 in Atlanta, Georgia. It was advertised through signs, newspaper ads, coupons, bottles, trays, calendars, and even lamps and clocks. Collectors want anything with the word *Coca-Cola*, including a few rare products, like gum wrappers and cigar bands. The famous trademark was patented in 1893, the *Coke* mark in 1945. Many modern items and reproductions are being made.

Ashtray, 50th Anniversary, Red, Black, Gold, Porcelain, 1936, 5½ In. Diam.	680.00
Badge, 6th Annual Bottlers Convention, Ribbon, Atlanta, Ga., 1914, 4½ x 2½ In.	994.00
Bank, Dispenser Shape, Drink Coca-Cola, Tin Lithograph, Linemar, Box, 1950s, 10 In.	1448.00
Bank, Vending Machine, Work Refreshed, Red, White, Plastic, 1950s, 6 In.	55.00
Blotter, Ink, Wholesome Refreshment, 2 Boy Scouts With Coke Cooler, 7½ In.	25.00
Bookmark, Drink Coca-Cola, 5 Cents, Girl, Red, Diecut, 1904, 6 x 2 In.	502.00
Bookmark, Drink Coca-Cola, 5 Cents, Girl, White Dress, Mug, Flowers, Red, 1904, 6¼ x 2 In.	330.00
Bookmark, Drink Coca-Cola, 5 Cents, Girl Holding Cup, Flowers, Purple, 1903, 6¼ x 2 In.	265.00
Bookmark, Drink Coca-Cola, Girl, Heart Shape, Celluloid, 1900, 2 x 2¼ In.	95.00
Bookmark, Drink Coca-Cola, Refreshing, 5 Cents, Girl, Heart Shape, Celluloid, 1896, 2⅜ x 2¾ In.	1760.00
Bookmark, Drink Coca-Cola, Refreshing, Delicious, Celluloid, c.1900, 2¼ x 1¾ In.	282.00 to 377.00
Bookmark, Girl Holding Glass, Drink Coca-Cola, 5 Cents, Purple, 1903, 6¼ x 2 In.	265.00 to 472.00
Bottle, Amber, Straight-Sided, Marked Lewisburg, Tenn.	770.00
Bottle, Amber, Straight-Sided, Marked McMinnville, Tenn.	2310.00
Bottle, Biedenharn, Straight-Sided, Vicksburg, Miss., 7½ In.	138.00
Bottle, Property Of Coca-Cola Bottling Co., Hutchinson, c.1900	2640.00
Bottle, Seltzer, Amber Glass, Wagner Spigot, 1920s, 12 In. *illus*	585.00
Bottle Opener, Baseball Player, Canton City Bottling Co., 3¼ In.	55.00
Bottle Opener, Counter, Red Lettering	36.00
Bottle Topper, Bottle Cap, Drink Coca-Cola, We Let You See The Bottle, Tin, 1950s *illus*	495.00
Calendar, 1903, Hilda Clark, Holding Glass Of Coke, Frame, 15½ x 7½ In.	4950.00
Calendar, 1911, Coca-Cola Girl, Hamilton King, December Only, Frame, 17 x 10 In.	3575.00
Calendar, 1912, Victorian Girl, Full Pad, 30¾ x 12¼ In.	5500.00
Calendar, 1914, Betty, Partial Pad, 32 x 13 In.	1298.00
Calendar, 1915, Elaine, Holding Bottle, 31 x 12¼ In.	2200.00
Calendar, 1915, Elaine, Holding Cup, 31 x 12¼ In.	1430.00
Calendar, 1919, Girl With Knitting Bag, Holding Bottle, December	4690.00
Calendar, 1919, Girl With Knitting Bag & Glass, August	2640.00
Calendar, 1922, Summer Girl At Baseball Game, Glass Of Coke & Bottle, 11 x 29 In.	440.00
Calendar, 1927, Girl With Bouquet Of Flowers, Glass Of Cola	620.00
Calendar, 1930, Girl In Bathing Suit, Holding Bottle, Sitting On Rock, Frame, 24½ x 12 In.	715.00
Calendar, 1931, Barefoot Boy, Dog, Norman Rockwell, 24 x 12 In.	1150.00 to 1250.00
Calendar, 1931, Tom Sawyer Drinking Coke, 22 x 14½ In.	121.00
Calendar, 1936, 50th Anniversary, Girl & Fisherman, Boat, Frame, 24 x 12 In.	385.00
Calendar, 1937, Fishin' Hole, Boy, Fishing Pole, Dog, January Page, Paper, 24 x 12 In.	410.00
Calendar, 1941, Skating Girl, Bimonthly, 20¼ x 14½ In.	165.00
Calendar, 1950, Sign Of Good Taste, Button Top, Tin, Pad, 8 x 19 In.	523.00
Carrier, 6-Pack, Pause, Go Refreshed, Red, Yellow, Metal Trim, Wood, c.1940, 9⅜ x 8 x 5⅜ In.	143.00
Carrier, Aluminum, 12-Pack, 7¼ x 16¼ x 5½ In.	92.00
Carrier, Drink Coca-Cola, Pause, Go Refreshed, Wings, 6 Bottles, Wood, 1940s	291.00
Carrier, Hinged Lid, Metal, 72 Bottles, Embossed, 31½ x 9 x 16½ In.	60.00
Cigar Band, Embossed, Bottle, 3 In.	84.00
Clock, Art Deco, Electric, Aluminum Face On Masonite, 1948, 37 x 18 In.	330.00
Clock, Dome, Princess, Drink Coca-Cola, 1950s, 8½ x 6 In.	990.00
Clock, Drink Coca-Cola, Black Chapter Ring, Red Center, Mid 20th Century, 18 In. Diam.	82.00
Clock, Drink Coca-Cola, Bottle, Yellow, White, Red, Light-Up, Electric, Metal, 15½ In.	275.00
Clock, Drink Coca-Cola, Green, Red, White Lines, Electric, 15½ In.	137.00
Clock, Drink Coca-Cola, Silver Chapter Ring, Red Center, Mid 20th Century, 18 In. Diam.	35.00
Clock, Silhouette Girl, 8-Sided, Red, Green, White, Neon, 1939, 18 In.	1100.00
Clock, Spinner, Silhouette Girl, Diamond, Red, Black, White, Neon, 1939, 18 In. Diam.	990.00
Clock, Square, Neon, Lackner, 16 x 5 x 16 In.	248.00
Cooler, Model No. A39B5K, 59 In.	605.00

Cooler, Music Box, Rotating Doll, 1950s, 13 x 8 x 20 In.	825.00
Cooler, Soda Fountain, Horizontal, 8 Ft.	165.00
Counter Light, Clock, Square, Price Bros., 20 x 5 x 9 In.	110.00
Dispenser, Cut Glass, Gold Writing, Footed, Regd No. 179154, Etched, 1891, 24½ In.	15340.00
Dispenser, Syrup, Countertop, c.1950, 24 x 12 In.	900.00
Dispenser, Syrup, Cover, Urn, c.1890, 22 In.	2475.00
Dispenser Head, Counter, Cornelius, Metal, Plastic, 3 Taps, 15 In. .... *illus*	316.00
Display, Bottle, Stop For A Pause, Go Refreshed, Policeman, Frame, Canada, 1938, 16 x 10¾ In.	7150.00
Display, Bottle, Styrofoam, Brown, Green, White, 1950s, 42 In.	515.00
Display, Daily Double Key Chain & Pocket Knife, Cardboard, 12 Knives, 1959	247.00
Display, Santa Claus, For Food, For Fun, For Friends, Cardboard, Easel Back, 20 x 13 In.	63.00
Display, Take Home This Handy 6 Carton Box, Blue, Red, White, Die Cut, Carton, 1936, 10 x 13 In.	398.00
Display Sign, Masonite Kay, Airplane, 1940s, 6 x 27 In.	935.00
Doll, Delivery Boy, Composition, Striped Cloth Uniform, Coca-Cola Patch, Buddy Lee, 13 In. *illus*	605.00
Doll, Santa Claus, Holding Bottle, Rubber Face, Hands, Plastic Boots, 17 In.	83.00
Door Knob, Brass, Coca-Cola, Raised Letters, 2⅜ In.	590.00
Door Pull, Bottle, Plastic & Metal, Have A Coke, 1950s	200.00
Door Pull, Bottle Shape, 1950s, 2 x 8 In.	110.00
Door Pull, Refresh Yourself, Tin, 3 x 6 In.	220.00
Door Push, Come In & Have A Coca-Cola, Red, Yellow, White, Porcelain, Canada, 1940s .. 415.00 to 460.00	
Door Push, Drink Coca Cola, Ice Cold In Bottles, Red, White, Porcelain, 1950s, 4 x 35 In.	247.00
Door Push, Drink Coca-Cola, Bottle, Embossed, Tin Lithograph, 1930, 12½ x 4½ In.	448.00
Door Push, Girl, In Bonnet, Glass, 9 x 3 In.	106.00
Door Push, Porcelain, c.1940, 8 x 4 In.	495.00
Door Push, Thanks, Call Again For A Coca-Cola, Red, Yellow, White, Porcelain, Canada, 1940s ..	415.00
Fan, Coca-Cola, 5 Cents, Flared Glass, 2-Sided, Rattan & Rice Paper, 1900-10	98.00
Hair Receiver, Drink Coca-Cola, Yellow, Red, Celluloid, 2½ x 4½ In.	165.00
Hat, Drink Coca-Cola, Warning, Canvas, 1905-10	247.00
Holder, 6-Pack, Cardboard, c.1927, 7 x 5 x 12 In.	39.00
Holder, Note Pad, Candlestick Telephone, 8½ In.	385.00
Ink Blotter, Wholesome Refreshment, 2 Boy Scouts With Coke, 7 x 3 In.	25.00
Jug, Syrup, Drink Coca-Cola, Red, Black, Tin Lithograph, 1939, Gal.	400.00
Knife, Pocket, Corkscrew, Opener, Embossed Brass Case, c.1905-15, 1 x 3½ x ¼ In.	66.00
Lamp, Bottle Shape, Red Paint, Metal Cap, Bronze Colored Base, 1920s, 20 In. ....*illus*	12100.00
Light, Counter, Pause & Refresh, Waterfall, Price Bros., 20 x 5 x 9 In.	550.00
Machine, V-29, On Stand, 28 x 24 x 58 In.	715.00
Menu Board, Special To-Day, Makes Good Food Taste Better, Embossed, Tin, Canada, 25 x 17 In.	198.00
Meter, Mileage, Travel Refreshed, Mileage, Route Information, Side Knob, Greenwood, Miss., 1950s .	825.00
Meter, Mileage, Travel Refreshed, Mileage, Route Information, Wheels, Crescent Beach, S.C., 1950s .	1540.00
Mirror, Girl, Drinking From Glass, Drink Coca-Cola, Oval, 1906, 3½ In.	672.00
Mirror, Girl, Green Flower Dress, Holding Cup, Drink Coca-Cola, Celluloid, Oval, 1907, 2¾ x 1¾ In.	440.00
Mirror, Girl, Holding Bottle, Drink Coca-Cola, Celluloid, Oval, 1916, 2¾ x 1¾ In.	354.00
Mirror, Girl, Holding Bottle, Drink Coca-Cola, Oval, 1916, 3½ In.	504.00
Mirror, Girl, Holding Bottle, Golf Course, Drink Coca-Cola, Oval, 1920, 3½ In.	672.00
Mirror, Girl, Holding Bottle Of Cola, Celluloid, Lithograph, Whitehead & Hoag, 1916, 2¾ x 1¾ In.	230.00
Mirror, Girl, Holding Cup, Drink Coca-Cola, 5 Cents, Celluloid, Oval, 1914, 2¾ x 1¾ In.	413.00
Mirror, Girl, Holding Glass, Drink Coca-Cola, Oval, 1907, 3½ In.	504.00
Mirror, Girl, Large Brim Hat, Drink Delicious Coca-Cola, Oval, 1911, 3½ In.	555.00
Mirror, Girl, Red Hat, Dress, Drink Coca-Cola, Bastian Bros. Co., Celluloid, Oval, 1908, 2¾ x 1¾ In. .	1045.00
Mirror, Girl, Sitting At Table, Drink Coca-Cola, Celluloid, Oval, 1909, 2¾ x 1¾ In.	440.00
Mirror, Girl, White Dress, C On Necklace, Drink Coca-Cola, Celluloid, Oval, 1906, 2¾ x 1¾ In.	303.00
Mirror, Girl, Wide Brim Hat, Rose, Drink Coca-Cola, Celluloid, Oval, 1910, 2¾ x 1¾ In. 330.00 to 611.00	
Mirror, Woman, Yellow Dress, Holding Bottle, Drink Coca-Cola, Celluloid, Oval, 1920, 2¾ x 1¾ In. .	330.00
Park Bench, Oak, Cast Iron, 6 Ft.	154.00
Pencil, Red, Logo, 6 Packs Of 12 Pencils, Box, 8 x 5¾ In. ....*illus*	29.00
Pencil Sharpener, Bottle Form, Red Paint, Metal, c.1950, 1¾ In.	25.00
Penholder, Counter, Store, Celluloid Over Cast Iron, Yellow, Pen Hangs From Chain	540.00
Pin, Brendan Bowyer Endorses Coke, ¼ In.	20.00
Plate, Beautiful Girl, Tin Lithograph, Square, Vienna Art, Frame, 10 In. ....*illus*	410.00
Plate, Girl, Long Brown Hair, Tin Lithograph, Vienna Art, Frame, 1908, 10 In.	385.00
Plate, Girl With Gold Tam, Vienna Art, Gold Gesso Frame, Shadowbox, 1910	660.00
Plate, Girl With Low Cut Top, Vienna Art, Gold Gesso Frame, Shadowbox, 1910	770.00
Plate, Girl With Red Tam, Vienna Art, Gold Gesso Frame, Shadowbox, 1910	515.00
Plate, Half-Full Bottle & Cup, Drink Coca-Cola, Knowles, 1930s, 7¼ In.	198.00
Plate, Topless Woman, Vienna Art, Gold Gesso Frame, Shadowbox, 1910	715.00
Plate, Vienna Art, 1908-12, 10 In.	28.00

Coke Fantasies
Coca-Cola collectibles that are not issued by the Coke company are called "fantasies." Some have been around so long they fool collectors. They probably will never have much value. Items Coca-Cola never made or licensed: Brass belt buckles marked "Tiffany Studios," pocketknives, paper Chinese lantern shades, cash register plates, and trays titled "The Romance of Coca-Cola."

Coca-Cola, Doll, Delivery Boy, Composition, Striped Cloth Uniform, Coca-Cola Patch, Buddy Lee, 13 In. $605.00

Coca-Cola, Lamp, Bottle Shape, Red Paint, Metal Cap, Bronze Colored Base, 1920s, 20 In. $12100.00

Coca-Cola, Pencil, Red, Logo, 6 Packs Of 12 Pencils, Box, 8 x 5¾ In. $29.00

Coca-Cola, Plate, Beautiful Girl, Tin Lithograph, Square, Vienna Art, Frame, 10 In.
$410.00

C

Coca-Cola, Sign, Fountain Service, Green, Red, White, Flange, Hanging Bracket, 1936, 26 x 22 In.
$1525.00

Coca-Cola, Sign, Girl Carrying Basket Of Bottles, Home Refreshment On The Way, Cardboard, 50 x 30 In.
$55.00

Coca-Cola, Sign, Santa Claus With Bottle, Cardboard, Cutout, 1950s, 48 x 34 In.
$85.00

Playing Cards, Drink Coca-Cola In Bottles, Blue Border, Hund & Eger Bottling Co., 1938 . . .	575.00
Playing Cards, Playing, Poker, Girl Holding Coke Bottle, Full Deck, 1961	45.00
Postcard, Delightfully Carbonated, Woman In Drivers Seat, 3¼ x 3½ In.	354.00
Radio, Bottle, Red, 1930s	2090.00
Radio, Cooler, Red, Box, 1950s, 9½ In.	385.00
Ring, Bottle, 50 Year Service, Signet, 14K Gold, 10 Diamond Chips, Man's	1650.00
Sign, 4 Seasons, Delicious & Refreshing All Season Long, Cardboard, Frame, 1923, 10 x 20 In.	6600.00
Sign, 6-Pack, 6 Bottles, There's Nothing Like A Coke, Tin, Die Cut, 13 x 11 In.	1210.00
Sign, 6-Pack, 6 For 25 Cents, Tin, Cutout, 1950, 13 x 11 In.	1320.00
Sign, 6-Pack, Delicious & Refreshing, Tin, Cutout, 1954, 13 x 11 In.	715.00
Sign, 6-Pack, King Size, Beige, Red, White, Embossed, Tin, Cutout, 1963, 36 x 31 In.	1320.00
Sign, 6-Pack, King Size, Red, White, Green, Tin, Cutout, 1960s, 36 x 31 In.	1320.00
Sign, 6-Pack, Regular Size, Tin, Cutout, 19844, 13 x 11 In.	1980.00
Sign, 6-Pack, Take Home A Carton, Drink Coca-Cola, Red, Yellow, Tin, 1938, 18 x 54 In.	370.00
Sign, 6-Pack, Take Home A Carton, Green, White, Red, Brown, Tin, 1951, 28 x 20 In.	1320.00
Sign, 12-Pack, Tin, Die Cut, 1954, 13 x 19 In.	2750.00
Sign, 50th Anniversary, 2 Bathing Beauties, Cardboard, 1936, 29 x 50 In.	605.00
Sign, 1903, Girl, Cup & Letter Opener, Drink, Delicious & Refreshing, Tin, Self-Framed, 6 In. Diam.	2100.00
Sign, 1923 Bottle, Die Cut, c.1933, 12 x 38 In.	220.00
Sign, Aviator Girl, Your Thirst Takes Wings, Cardboard, Frame, 1940, 35½ x 19½ In.	6600.00
Sign, Betty, Tin Lithograph, Self-Framed, 1914, 41 x 31 In.	2750.00
Sign, Bottle, Sprite Kid, Red, Yellow, White, Brown, Tin Lithograph, c.1947, 12¾ In. Diam. . .	825.00
Sign, Bottle, White Ground, Porcelain, 1950s, 24 In.	275.00
Sign, Cameo, Lillian Nordica, Celluloid, Shadowbox Frame, Chain, 1904, 11 x 8¼ In.	17600.00
Sign, Cap, Bottle, Coca-Cola, Tin, 1954, 24 In.	715.00
Sign, Coca-Cola, Bottle, Red, White, Green, Yellow, Brown, Tin, Marked, A.A.W., Round, 45 In.	305.00
Sign, Coca-Cola Pepsin Gum, Reversed Glass, Beveled, Copper Frame, c.1900, 17 x 9 In. . . .	1695.00
Sign, Coke, Pause, Fishtail, Tin, 18 x 40 In. . . . . 55.00 to 110.00
Sign, Diner With Eggs, Bacon, Bottle, Tin, 24 x 48 In.	220.00
Sign, Drink, With Girl, Tin, 1941, 12 x 34 In.	248.00
Sign, Drink Coca-Cola, 3 Bottles, Tin, Self-Framed, 1930s, 18 x 54 In.	440.00
Sign, Drink Coca-Cola, Brass, 10½ x 22 In.	250.00
Sign, Drink Coca-Cola, Girl Holding Bottle, Tin, Self-Framed, 32 x 56 In.	247.00
Sign, Drink Coca-Cola, Ice Cold, Bottle, Red, White, Green Lines, Tin, 1960s, 18 x 54 In. . . .	215.00
Sign, Drink Coca-Cola, Ice Cold, Bottle, Tin Lithograph, Embossed, c.1937, 19 x 27 In.	577.00
Sign, Drink Coca-Cola, Ice Cold, Tin, Horizontal, 27½ x 19 In.	275.00
Sign, Drink Coca-Cola, Porcelain, 30 x 10 In.	440.00
Sign, Drink Coca-Cola, Refreshing, Girl Leaning On Ship Wheel, Cardboard, 1936, 26 x 53 In.	3080.00
Sign, Drink Coca-Cola, Refreshing, Red, White, Plastic, Metal, Light-Up, 1960s, 11 x 8 In. . . .	345.00
Sign, Drink Coca-Cola, Reversed Letter, Silver Foil, Mother-Of-Pearl, 23 x 16 In.	12.00
Sign, Drink Coca-Cola, Script, Porcelain, Die Cut, 1930s, 5½ x 18 In. . . . . 385.00 to 605.00
Sign, Drink Coca-Cola Fountain Service, Porcelain, Horizontal, 28 x 12 In.	468.00
Sign, Drink Coca-Cola In Bottles, Aluminum, Embossed, 17½ x 7½ In.	230.00
Sign, Drink Ice Cold, 1923 Bottle, Tin, c.1937, 19 x 27 In.	220.00
Sign, Drink Ice Cold, Bottle, Flange, Tin, 17 x 22 In.	220.00
Sign, Drink In Bottle, Button, Porcelain, 36 In.	110.00
Sign, Drink In Bottles, 5 Cents, Horizontal, Tin, 6 x 24 In.	83.00
Sign, Drink In Bottles, Please Pay Cashier, Light-Up, Price Bros., 20 x 39 In.	220.00
Sign, Drink Refresh, Round, 2-Sided, Porcelain, 1939, 30 In.	55.00
Sign, Drink They All Expect, Girl, Man, Cardboard, 1942, 27 x 16 In.	770.00
Sign, Fishtail, Sign Of Good Taste, Bottle, Red, White, Green, Brown, 1960, 12 x 31½ In. . . .	192.00
Sign, Fountain Service, Drink Coca-Cola, Green, Gold, Red, 2-Sided, Porcelain, 1936, 22 x 26 In.	1430.00
Sign, Fountain Service, Drink Coca-Cola, Green, Red, White, Porcelain, 1930s, 42 x 63 In. . . .	1320.00
Sign, Fountain Service, Green, Red, White, Flange, Hanging Bracket, 1936, 26 x 22 In. *illus*	1525.00
Sign, Fountain Service, Horizontal, Porcelain, 29½ x 12 In.	358.00
Sign, Fountain Stationary, Porcelain, 1940s, 55 x 46 In.	1870.00
Sign, Girl Carrying Basket Of Bottles, Home Refreshment On The Way, Cardboard, 50 x 30 In. *illus*	55.00
Sign, Girl Holding Glass, Red, Green, White, Tin, Embossed, Oval, 1926, 13 x 19 In.	2200.00
Sign, Girl Putting Coke In Refrigerator, Cardboard, 1940, 16 x 27 In.	358.00
Sign, Grocery, Coca-Cola Refreshes You Best, Flange, 15 x 18 x 2 In.	308.00
Sign, Have A Coke, Refresh Yourself, Arrow, Fluorescent Light, Glass, 1950s, 11 x 18 x 3 In. . .	2090.00
Sign, He's Coming Home Tomorrow, Girl Pulling Wagon, Frame, Canada, 1944, 27 x 16 In. .	519.00
Sign, Hilda Clark, Gold Leaf Border, Diecut, Paper, Embossed, 1898, 8 x 6 In.	3850.00
Sign, Hilda Clark, Holding Pen, Tin, Embossed, 1899, 19 x 27 In.	6095.00
Sign, Ice Cold, Sold Here, 1923 Bottle On Left, Tin, 20 x 28 In.	220.00
Sign, Ice Cold, Sold Here, Round, Tin, c.1932, 20 In.	220.00
Sign, Ice Cold Coca-Cola Sold Here, Tin, Lithograph, Embossed, c.1931, 19½ x 38 In.	165.00

Sign, Jackie Cooper, It's So Good & Good For You, Cardboard, 1930s, 26 x 53 In. 2640.00
Sign, Lillian Nordica, Delicious, Refreshing, Celluloid, Frame, 1904, 25¼ x 18½ In. 13200.00
Sign, Maureen O'Sullivan, Weissmuller, Come Up Smiling, Cardboard, Frame, 29¾ x 13¾ In. 2750.00
Sign, Pause, Drink Coca-Cola, Bottle, Tin, Embossed, 1940, 54 x 18 In. 405.00
Sign, Pause, Please Pay When Served, Electric, 10 x 19 In. 330.00
Sign, Pause, Refresh, Hanover, Light-Up, 23 x 24 In. 300.00
Sign, Policeman, Fishtail, Cast Iron Base, 30 x 64 In. 550.00
Sign, Policeman, Slow School Zone, Tin, April, 1950, 60 In. 3080.00
Sign, Reclining Girl, With Fountain Glass, Die Cut, 24 x 50 In. 688.00
Sign, Refreshing, Drink Coca-Cola, Wood, Metal Hanger, 8 x 24 In. 168.00
Sign, Santa Claus With Bottle, Cardboard, Cutout, 1950s, 48 x 34 In. ....*illus* 85.00
Sign, Shop Refreshed, Girl With Hat Box, Dispenser, 23½ x 41 In. 2640.00
Sign, Soda Fountain, Fiberglass, 24 In. 165.00
Sign, Speedway Diner, Die Cut, 2-Sided, Porcelain, 46 x 54 In. 650.00
Sign, Take A Case Home Today, Quality Refreshment, Case Of 24 Bottles, Tin, 1957, 28 x 20 In. 1430.00
Sign, They All Want, Waitress, Cardboard, 1940s, 20 x 36 In. 385.00
Sign, Trolley, Tired?, Coca-Cola Relieves Fatigue, Sold Everywhere, 5 Cents, Frame, 10¼ x 20½ In. .. 825.00
Sign, Work Safely, Light-Up, Hanover, 16 x 3 x 16 In. 225.00
Sign, Yes!, Girl With World, Cardboard, 1944, 20 x 36 In. 413.00
Sign, You Work Better Refreshed, Girl Mechanic, Cardboard, 36 x 20 In. 4950.00
Stadium Vendor's Caddy, 1930s 504.00
Stamp Carrier, Compliments Of Coca-Cola Co., Girl, Red Dress, 1902, 2½ x 1½ In. 550.00
Stringholder, Take Home In Cartons, Tin, 1940s, 16 x 12 In. 2300.00
Table & Chairs, Diner Style, 1950s, 30 In., 3 Piece 154.00
Thermometer, 2 Bottles, Drink Coca-Cola, Tin, 1942, 16 x 7 In. 300.00
Thermometer, 1923 Bottle, Die Cut, Tin, 5 x 16 In. 176.00
Thermometer, Bottle, Embossed, 1950-60, Spain, 18 x 6¼ In. 30.00
Thermometer, Bottle, Embossed, Tin, 1935, 17 In. 275.00
Thermometer, Bottle, Gold, Red, Tin, Cardboard Box Sleeve, 1937, 15 In. 650.00
Thermometer, Bottle, Thirst Knows No Season, Red, White, Green, Masonite, 1940s, 17 x 6¾ In. 275.00
Thermometer, Bottle, Tin, Die Cut, 1956, 17 In. 55.00
Thermometer, Coke Bottle Shape, Pressed Tin, Donasco, 17 In. 110.00
Thermometer, Drink Coca-Cola, Be Really Refreshed, Red, White, 1959, 12 In. Diam. 650.00
Thermometer, Drink Coca-Cola, Red, Green, 1948, 12 In. 650.00
Thermometer, Drink Coca-Cola, Red, White, c.1950, 12 In. Diam. 192.00
Thermometer, Drink Coca-Cola, Thirst Knows No Season, Girl, Porcelain, Canada, 1939, 16½ In. . 650.00
Thermometer, Embossed Tin, c.1950, 10 In. 123.00
Thermometer, Enjoy Coca-Cola, Red Cap Shape, Metal, Glass, 1960s, 12 In. ....*illus* 161.00
Thermometer, Sign Of Good Taste, Refresh Yourself, Red, White, Tin, 1950s, 30 In. 800.00
Thermometer, Testing, Tin, 4½ In. 440.00
Thermometer, Twin Bottles, 1941, 7 x 15½ In. 495.00
Tip Tray, 1903, Hilda Clark, Delicious, Refreshing, Round, 4 In. .... 1210.00 to 1440.00
Tip Tray, 1903, Hilda Clark, Gold Border, 6 In. ....*illus* 6600.00
Tip Tray, 1909, Exhibition Girl, St. Louis World's Fair, Oval, 6¼ x 4¼ In. 350.00
Tip Tray, 1910, Coca-Cola Girl, Drink Delicious Coca-Cola, 6⅛ x 4⅜ In. .... 252.00 to 1100.00
Tip Tray, 1916, Elaine, Girl With Basket Of Flowers, 6⅛ x 4⅜ In. .... 237.00 to 390.00
Tip Tray, 1920, Golfer Girl Holding Glass, Oval, 6⅜ x 4½ In. 550.00
Tip Tray, Drink Coca-Cola, 5 Cents, Reverse Paint On Glass, 7 In. Diam. 715.00
Toy, Dispenser, Drink Coca-Cola, Andy Guard, No. 1500, Box, 1960s, 10 x 6 In. 110.00
Toy, Dispenser, Glasses, Plastic, Bottle, Box, 9 In. 123.00
Toy, Playtown Luncheonette, Drink Coca-Cola, Breakfast Menu, Masonite, c.1940, 7 x 10 x 4 In. . 550.00
Toy, Truck, 10 Original Bottles, Rubber Tires, Metalcraft 950.00
Toy, Truck, Coke Bottles, Delicious, Refreshing, Yellow, Red, Tin Lithograph, 1950s, 17 In. ... 550.00
Toy, Truck, Electric Lights, Metalcraft, 11½ In. 750.00
Toy, Truck, Steel, 9 Cases Of Coke, Hand Truck, Marx, Box, 12½ In. 349.00
Toy, Truck, Tin Lithograph, Battery Operated, Sanyo, Japan, Box, 1960s, 12½ In. ... 370.00 to 541.00
Tray, 1903, Hilda Clark Holding Cup, Delicious, Refreshing, Flower Border, 9½ Diam. 15400.00
Tray, 1905, Lillian Nordica, Drink Carbonated Coca-Cola In Bottles, 12⅞ x 10⅝ In. 6600.00
Tray, 1909, Exhibition Girl, St. Louis World's Fair, Oval, 13¼ x 10½ In. 880.00
Tray, 1909, Exhibition Girl, St. Louis World's Fair, Oval, 16½ x 13½ In. 1870.00
Tray, 1910, Coca-Cola Girl, Hamilton King, 13¼ x 10½ In. 311.00
Tray, 1913, Hamilton King, Girl, Large Hat, Oval, 15 x 12½ In. 323.00
Tray, 1914, Betty, Passaic Metalware Co., 15½ x 12⅜ In. 418.00
Tray, 1916, Elaine, Girl With Basket Of Flowers, 19 x 8½ In. .... 190.00 to 956.00
Tray, 1921, Autumn Girl Holding Glass, 13 x 10 In. .... 450.00 to 784.00
Tray, 1922, Summer Girl, 13¼ x 10½ In. ....*illus* 359.00

Coca-Cola, Thermometer, Enjoy Coca-Cola, Red Cap Shape, Metal, Glass, 1960s, 12 In.
$161

Coca-Cola, Tip Tray, 1903, Hilda Clark, Gold Border, 6 In.
$6600.00

Coca-Cola, Tray, 1922, Summer Girl, 13¼ x 10½ In.
$359.00

Coca-Cola, Tray, 1926, Golfing Couple, 13¼ x 10½ In.
$591.00

Coca-Cola, Tray, 1927, Fountain Sales, Soda Jerk, 13¼ x 10½ In. $1290.00

Coca-Cola, Tray, 1931, Barefoot Boy, Dog, Norman Rockwell, 13¼ x 10½ In. $936.00

Coca-Cola, Tray, 1939, Springboard Girl, White Swimsuit, 13¼ x 10½ In. $465.00

Coca-Cola, Tray, 1942, 2 Girls At Car, 13¼ x 10½ In. $215.00

Tray, 1923, Flapper Girl, Fox Fur Stole, 13¼ x 10½ In.	200.00 to 777.00
Tray, 1925, Party Girl, Fur Stole, 13¼ x 10½ In.	395.00
Tray, 1926, Golfing Couple, 13¼ x 10½ In.	*illus* 591.00
Tray, 1927, Fountain Sales, Soda Jerk, 13¼ x 10½ In.	*illus* 1290.00
Tray, 1928, Bobbed Hair Girl, 13¼ x 10½ In.	529.00 to 717.00
Tray, 1930, Swimsuit Girl, 13¼ x 10½ In.	450.00
Tray, 1930, Telephone Girl, 13½ x 10 In.	210.00
Tray, 1931, Barefoot Boy, Dog, Norman Rockwell, 13¼ x 10½ In.	*illus* 936.00
Tray, 1933, Francis Dee, 13¼ x 10½ In.	717.00
Tray, 1934, O'Sullivan & Weissmuller, 10½ x 13¼ In.	717.00 to 1450.00
Tray, 1935, Madge Evans, American Art Works, 13½ x 10 In.	310.00
Tray, 1936, Hostess, Evening Gown, American Art Works, 13¼ x 10½ In.	190.00 to 400.00
Tray, 1937, Running Girl, Swimsuit	388.00
Tray, 1938, Girl At Shade, Yellow Dress, Hat, 13¼ x 10½ In.	130.00 to 215.00
Tray, 1939, Springboard Girl, White Swimsuit, 13¼ x 10½ In.	*illus* 465.00
Tray, 1940, Sailor Girl, Fishing, American Art Works, 10½ x 13¼ In.	160.00 to 260.00
Tray, 1941, Skater Girl, Seated On Log, 13¼ x 10½ In.	198.00 to 538.00
Tray, 1942, 2 Girls At Car, 13¼ x 10½ In.	*illus* 215.00
Tray, 1953, Menu Girl, 13¼ x 10½ In.	205.00
Tray, 1950s, Girl With Umbrella, French Words, 13¼ x 10½ In.	199.00
Vending Machine, Cavalier, Model No. CS-72, 81 Bottles, 9 Shelves, 1950, 57 x 26 In.	3618.00
Watch Fob, Drink Coca-Cola, Bottle, Celluloid, Leather Strap, 2-Sided, 1¾ In.	925.00
Whistle, Thimble Form, Red Paint, Aluminum, 1 In.	165.00

COFFEE MILLS are also called coffee grinders, although there is a difference in the way each grinds the coffee. Large floor-standing or counter-model coffee mills were used in the nineteenth-century country store. Small home mills were first made about 1894. They lost favor by the 1930s. The renewed interest in fresh-ground coffee has produced many modern electric mills and hand mills and grinders. Reproductions of the old styles are being made.

Acme, No. 60, Yellow, Red, Board Mount, Crank Handle	413.00
Arcade, Crystal, No. 3, Wall Mount, 24 In.	360.00
Arcade, Crystal, No. 3, Wall Mount, c.1900, 18¾ In.	176.00
Arcade, Crystal, No. 25, Wall Canister, In Cover, Black Metal Frame, 11½ In.	150.00
Arcade, Imperial, Drawer, Wood, Crank Handle, Late 19th Century, 7 In.	145.00
Armin Trosser, Wood, Chrome, Stamped, Germany, Mid 1900s, 9 x 4½ In.	75.00
Brighton, Wall Hung, Black Japanned Finish, Glass Catch, Logo, 1905 Patent	275.00
Coles, No. 7, Painted, Metal Receiver, Embossed, Eagle, Pat. Dec. 27, 1887, 27 x 16 In.	1575.00
Dienes, Bird's-Eye Maple, Drawer, Crank Handle, W. Germany, 7 x 4½ In.	77.00
Elgin National, 2 Wheels, Lid, Red Paint, Pinstriping, Woodruff & Edwards Co., 23 In.	468.00
Enterprise, 2 Wheels, Lid, Eagle Finial, Drawer, Painted, Stenciled, Pat. Oct. 21, 1873, 24 In.	550.00
Enterprise, Drawer, Porcelain Knob, 1873, 28 x 17 In.	*illus* 440.00
Enterprise, No. 2, Red, Drawer, 12½ In.	605.00
Enterprise, No. 3, Iron Hopper, Patent July 12, 1898, 10½-In. Wheels, 15 In.	*illus* 935.00
Enterprise, No. 7, Cast Iron, Old Red Paint, Eagle Finial, Wood Drawer, 24 In.	770.00
Enterprise, No. 9, Cast Iron, 22-In. Wheels	3000.00
Enterprise, No. 12, 2 Wheels, 29 In.	770.00
Enterprise, No. 218, Floor Model, Eagle Finial, 35-In. Wheels, 70 In.	3393.00 to 4800.00
Ever-Ready, No. 2, Red, Gold, Board Mounted, Crank Handle, Bronson-Walton Co., Cleveland	248.00
Freidag, Wardway, Glass, Green Paint, Fineness Adjusting Mechanism, 16½ In.	150.00
Grand Union, Cast Iron, Red Paint, Grand Union Tea Co.	300.00
Griswold Mfg., Cast Iron, Red, Lift Front Door, Wood Base, 6½ x 10½ In.	580.00
J. Fischer, Cherry, Drawer, Iron Bowl, Crank Handle, 8¾ x 6¾ In.	72.00
King Coffee Mill, No. 22, Cup, Board Mount, Crank Handle, Belmont Hardware Co.	440.00
Kissling & Mollman, Hopper, Wood, Brass, Drawer, Germany, c.1890, 9¾ x 6¾ In.	400.00
Landers, Frary & Clark, No. 11, Paint, Wood Base, Drawer, Turned Handle, 12½ In.	*illus* 649.00
Landers, Frary & Clark, Universal, No. 01, Cast Iron, Original Paint, Wall Mount, 13¼ In.	175.00
None Such, Tin Lithograph, Wood Base, 10 x 5¾ x 6¼ In.	523.00
Pritz, Cherry, Tiger Maple, Drawer, Pewter Bowl, Iron Handle, Hanover, Pa., 1839, 10 x 7 In.	2255.00
Regal, No. 44, Cast Iron, Tin Hopper, Black Enamel, Wall Mount, 14 In.	125.00
Spong & Co., No. 3, Cast Iron, Black, Gold, White Enamel, Wall Mount, Crank Handle	50.00

COIN SPOT is a glass pattern that was named by the collectors for the spots resembling coins, which are part of the glass. Colored, clear, and opalescent glass was made with the spots. Many companies used the design in the 1870–90 period. It is so popular that reproductions are still being made.

Compote, Ruby, 7 x 8 In.	68.00
Perfume Bottle, Ruffled Edge, Opalescent Round Stopper, 4½ In.	45.00
Pitcher, French Blue, Amber Reeded Handle, 6 In.	144.00
Pitcher, Lime Green, Opalescent Ruffled Edge, 9 In.	350.00
Sugar Shaker, Sapphire Blue, Northwood, 5 In.	260.00
Syrup, Dew Drop, Sapphire Blue, Hobbs Brockunier, 5 In.	375.00
Water Set, Cranberry, Clear Rope Twist Handle, 8¼-In. Pitcher, 8 Piece ... *illus*	147.00

COIN-OPERATED MACHINES of all types are collected. The vending machine is an ancient invention dating back to 200 B.C., when holy water was dispensed in a coin-operated vase. Smokers in seventeenth-century England could buy tobacco from a coin-operated box. It was not until after the Civil War that the technology made modern coin-operated games and vending machines plentiful. Slot machines, arcade games, and dispensers are all collected.

Arcade, Bally, Magic Ball, Chicago, c.1937, 24 x 74 In.	1650.00
Arcade, Electric Treatment Shocker, Stamped 3880, Mills Novelty Co., 23 In.	28600.00
Arcade, Electricity Is Life Shocker, Oak Stand, Cast Iron Base, 15 x 54 In.	3190.00
Arcade, Marksman Sharp-Shooter, Blue, Red, Yellow, Cylindrical, 5 Cent, 72 In.	440.00
Arcade, Personality Indicator, Exhibit Supply Co., Oak, Nickel Feet, 83 In.	1870.00
Arcade, Pot Of Gold, 5 Cent, Metal, 16½ x 13 In.	220.00
Arcade, Shocker, 1 Cent, Oak, 13½ In.	825.00
Arcade, Shocker, 1 Cent, Wood Case, Cast Aluminum Facade, Marquee, 19½ In.	1210.00
Arcade, Target, Indians Shooting At Target, 1 Cent, Wood, Metal, 19 x 21 In.	550.00
Baseball, Play Ball, Baseball Diamond, Exhibit Supply Co., Chicago, 19 x 12 In. ...*illus*	1870.00
Coin Changer, Victorian, Walnut, Hopkins & Rowdsen Mfg., 18½ In.	1430.00
Crane, Claw, Oak Case, Marquee, Iron, 76 In.	2640.00
Fortune Teller, Exhibit Supply, Color Of Your Eyes, Oak, 72 In.	6050.00
Fortune Teller, Palm Reader, 1 Cent, Quartersawn Oak, Cast Legs, 60 In.	1430.00
Fortune Teller, Swami, Fortune & Napkin Dispenser, 1 Cent, Metal, 9 x 9 In.	220.00
Fortune Teller, Wizard, 1 Cent, Wood, Aluminum, c.1920, 19 x 14 In.	1700.00
Game, Best Hand, Metal, Mechanical, 2 Person, 1930s, 20 In.	300.00
Golf, Aristocrat, 5 Cent, Mahogany Case, Brass Putter	1100.00
Gum, Black Jack, Klix, Metal, 7 x 8 In.	247.00
Gum, Caille, One Cent, Oak, Cast Nickel Marquee, 17½ In.	935.00
Gum, Daval, Aluminum Casting, 9 x 11 In.	660.00
Gum, Kelly Chicago Gambling, Pepsin Stick Gum, Wood, 1920-30	1650.00
Gum, Lucky Boy, Kentucky c.1933, 8½ x 12 In.	848.00
Gum, Pepsin, Penny Drop, Quartersawn Oak Case, 20½ In.	330.00
Gum, Pulver, Delivers A Tasty Chew, Policeman, Porcelain, 20 In.	660.00
Gum, Pulver, Yellow Kid, One Cent Delivers A Tasty Chew, 20 x 8¾ In. ...*illus*	702.00
Gum, Roth's, Pansy Gum & Fortune, 1 Cent, Metal, Wood, 20 x 5 x 4 In.	6600.00
Gum, Zeno, 1 Cent, Wood, Key, 16½ x 7 In.	715.00
Gum, Zeno Chewing Gum, Drop 1 Cent, Yellow, Black, 16½ x 7 In.	660.00
Gumball, Baby Grand, 5 Cent, Wood, Metal, Glass, 13 x 7 In.	27.00
Gumball, Baseball Card, Premier, 2 Cent, Red Paint, 1950s ...*illus*	526.00
Gumball, Chicago, Nickel Plated Case, Marquee, c.1909, 18½ In.	4675.00
Gumball, Columbus, No. 21, Porcelain, Cast Iron, 13½ In.	550.00
Gumball, Consolidated, 1 Cent, Cast Aluminum, Art Deco Case, 19 In.	605.00
Gumball, Homerun Baseball Game, 1 Cent, Wood, Glass, Metal, c.1950	927.00
Gumball, Mills, Slot, Award Card, Bell Boy, Metal, Wood Base, c.1930	2475.00
Gumball, Premiere, Baseball Card, 2 Cent, Metal, 1950s	495.00
Lighter Fluid, Taxibriquet, 5 Cent, Original Packing, 9½ In.	176.00
Lung Test, Caille, Little Wonder, Quartersawn Oak, Glass Globe, 27 In.	4125.00
Music Box, C.H. Miles, Oak Case, Nickel Accents, 64½ In.	23100.00
Music Box, Edison, Phonograph, Stand, Quartersawn Case, c.1893, 57½ In.	17600.00
Music Box, Leonard, Player Piano, Quartersawn Oak Frame, Leaded Glass, 65 In.	4950.00
Music Box, Organ, Barrel, Atlantic, Oak, 85 In.	1760.00
Music Box, Polyphon, Mahogany, Discs, 92½ In.	6900.00
Music Box, Regina, Double Comb, Door, Dragon, Automatic Changer, 25-In. Discs ...*illus*	19890.00
Music Box, Renaissance Revival, Walnut, Discs, 84¾ x 42 In.	14950.00
Mutoscope, Caille, Auto, Quartersawn Oak, Nickel Face Plate, 54 In.	4675.00
Mutoscope, Card Reel, Original Box, 11 In.	358.00
Pinball, Bally-Round, Wood, c.1930	440.00
Pinball, Pete's Penny Ante, Poker, Wood, c.1934, 8½ x 19½ In.	780.00
Pinball, Playing Card Front, 1 Cent, Wood, Glass, 24 x 16 x 9 In.	440.00
Ride, Horse, Saddle, 25 Cent, c.1940, 55 x 67 In.	1050.00

Coffee Mills, Enterprise, Drawer, Porcelain Knob, 1873, 28 x 17 In.
$440.00

Coffee Mill, Enterprise, No. 3, Iron Hopper, Patent July 12, 1898, 10½-In. Wheels, 15 In.
$935.00

Coffee Mill, Landers, Frary & Clark, No. 11, Paint, Wood Base, Drawer, Turned Handle, 12½ In.
$649.00

Coin Spot, Water Set, Cranberry, Clear Rope Twist Handle, 8¼-In. Pitcher, 8 Piece
$147.00

Coin-Operated Machine, Baseball,
Play Ball, Baseball Diamond,
Exhibit Supply Co.,
Chicago, 19 x 12 In.
$1870.00

Coin-Operated Machine, Gum,
Pulver, Yellow Kid,
One Cent Delivers A Tasty Chew,
20 x 8¾ In.
$702.00

Coin-Operated Machine, Gumball,
Baseball Card, Premier, 2 Cent,
Red Paint, 1950s
$526.00

Shooting Gallery, Tratsch, Challenger, 1 Cent, Metallic Balls, 1925, 22 x 9 In. ....*illus*	634.00
Skill, 3 Jacks, Silver Metal Front, Lock On Top, 13 x 12 In. ....*illus*	660.00
Skill, Catch, Coin Drop, Countertop, Mahogany, Glass Inserts, 29 In.	1045.00
Skill, Gambling, Select-Em, Dice, Gum, 25 Cent, 14 x 10 x 5 In.	110.00
Skill, J.F. Frantz, Bicentennial Kicker & Catcher, 1 Cent, Red, White, Blue, 21 x 14 In.	275.00
Skill, Jennings, Rockaway, Penny Drop, c.1930	1870.00
Skill, Kicker & Catcher, 1 Cent, Red, Metal, 18 x 14 In.	440.00
Skill, Penny Drop, Oak, Glass, Reward Card, 13½ In.	523.00
Skill, Steeplechase, 1 Cent, 18 x 14 In.	1210.00
Skill, Tratsch, Challenger Shooting Gallery, 1 Cent, Wood, Metal, Glass, 1925, 22 x 9 In.	605.00
Skill, Tug Of War, Mickey Finn, Cast Iron, Oak Marque, Base, c.1904, 76 In.	49500.00
Slot, 5 Cent, Painted Metal, Oak Sides, Base, 26 x 16 In.	1645.00
Slot, Black Bart, Electrified, 25 Cent, 3 Reel Slot, 78 In.	1323.00
Slot, Caille, Ben Hur, Nickels, c.1920, 22½ In.	4510.00
Slot, Jennings, Wood, 25 Cent, 25 In.	1210.00
Slot, Mills, Automatic Salesman, Oak, Nickel, Cast Aluminum, 25 In.	1210.00
Slot, Mills, Gooseneck, 5 Cent, 3 Reel, Oak, Iron Pedestal, 16 x 25 In.	1495.00
Slot, Mills, Gumball Dispenser, Bell Boy, Key, 1930s ....*illus*	2633.00
Slot, Mills, Hi Top, 10 Cent, 3 Reel, 16 x 26 In.	575.00
Slot, Mills, Jumbo Parade, Wood, 5 Cent, 51 In.	137.00
Slot, Mills, Junior, No. 6, Floor Model, Cast Iron, 57 In.	6600.00
Slot, Mills, Poinsettia, 5 Cent, c.1930, 25 x 16 In.	1750.00
Slot, Mills, Upright, 50 Cent, Quartersawn Oak, Nickel, Chicago, 67 In.	23100.00
Slot, New Deal, 1 Cent, Metal, 14 x 11 In.	880.00
Slot, New Deal, Trade, 1 Cent, Painted Card Suits, 14 x 11 In. ....*illus*	936.00
Slot, Pace, Aluminum, Golf Symbol Reel, 50 Cent, Oak, Iron, 15¾ x 24 In.	920.00
Slot, Watling, Roll-A-Top, Bird Of Paradise, 25 Cent, Art Deco Case, 27 In.	6050.00
Sobriety Test, Booze Barometer, 5 Cent, 19 x 18 In.	330.00
Stamp, Postage, American Vending Machine Co., Countertop	3025.00
Strength Tester, Grip & Lung, Caille, 5 Cent, Quartersawn Oak, 25 In.	16500.00
Strength Tester, Mercury, Athletic Scale Grip, 1 Cent, Metal, Glass, 19 x 15 In.	220.00
Strength Tester, Puncher, Caille Olympia, Cast Iron, Oak, Nickel Plate, 83 In.	18700.00
Trade Stimulator, Ball Gum, Gumball, Metal, 12 x 8 In.	495.00
Trade Stimulator, Cardinal, Spell It, Gumball, 5 Cent, 12 x 11 In.	1450.00
Trade Stimulator, Cigar, Oak, 20th Century Novelty Co., 17 x 10 In.	2860.00
Trade Stimulator, Mills, Puritan Bell, Cash Register Form, c.1922	825.00
Trade Stimulator, Nevada, Pressed Aluminum Face, Pressed Steel, 11 In.	22.00
Trade Stimulator, Pok-O-Reel, Gumball, Key, 12 x 12 In.	1100.00
Trade Stimulator, Superior, Art Deco, Mahogany, Cast Aluminum, 12 In.	660.00
Vending, 3 Mounted On One Stand, 50 x 29 In.	41.00
Vending, Alka-Seltzer, Be Wise Alkasize, Pedestal, 15 In.	504.00
Vending, Apples, Key, Apple Vendor Co., New Way Mfg. Co., Seattle, 32 x 20 x 12 In. ....*illus*	2750.00
Vending, Autosales Gum & Chocolate Co., Chiclets Stollwerck Chocolate, Porcelain, Wood, 33 In. .	8250.00
Vending, Butter Kist Peanut, Nickel, Glass, Quartersawn Oak, 30 In.	1760.00
Vending, California Dispenser Co., Vend-A-Bar, Li'l Abner & Daisy Mae, 1950s	550.00
Vending, Exhibit Supply Co., Beauty Card, 5 Cent, 52 Different Photos Of Risque Girls, Oak .	2475.00
Vending, Fresh Hot Nuts, Art Deco Style, Metal, Stand	495.00
Vending, Happy Home, Wood, Cast Iron Base, 70 In.	3850.00
Vending, Hen Lays Egg, Seated On Basket, Zinc, Crank, Paris, 21 In.	2820.00
Vending, Hershey Bars, 1 Cent, Metal, 25 x 4 In.	385.00
Vending, Hershey's, 1 Cent, Green, White, Brown, Metal, Glass, 20 x 10 In.	92.00
Vending, Hershey's Candy Bar, 5 Cent, Brown, White, 18 x 9 In.	448.00
Vending, Hershey's Milk Chocolate, 1 Cent, Glass Front, Doesn't Work, 20 x 11 In. .....*illus*	85.00
Vending, Horoscope, Exhibit Supply, Oak Case, Cast Legs, 72 In.	2750.00
Vending, Kodak Film, Eastman Autographic Film Cartridge, Metal, 9 x 27 x 9 In.	137.00
Vending, Match, Advance, Cast Iron, Base, Glass Globe, 17½ In.	1760.00
Vending, Matchbox, 1 Cent	800.00
Vending, Metal, Table Top, Key, 28½ x 12⅝ x 10 In.	209.00
Vending, Mills, Candy, Windmill, Wood, Cast Iron, Pressed Steel, 58 In.	3080.00
Vending, National, Mint & Gum, 5 Cent, Metal, Glass, 15½ x 6¾ In.	137.00
Vending, Peanut, Smiling Sam, Marquis Coin Receiver, 14 In.	4720.00
Vending, Pencil, Parker, Cast Aluminum, Art Deco Case, 9 In.	385.00
Vending, Postcard, Mutoscope, Goofy Giggles, 10 Cent, 1940s, 79 x 18 In.	176.00
Vending, Wilbur's Sweet Clover Chocolate & Pepsin Gum, 1 Cent, Porcelain, Wood, 33 x 9 In. .	8800.00
Viewing, Mills, Autostereoscope, No. 860, 73 In.	4700.00
Viewing, Mills, Quartoscope, Floor Model, Quartersawn Oak, 64 In.	6050.00

Viewing, Stereo Viewer, Glass, Mahogany Case, 3 Drawers, France, 11 x 10 x 11 In.	1725.00
Wishing Well, Exhibit Supply, Maple Case, Reverse Painted Glass, 84 In.	1320.00

COLLECTOR PLATES are modern plates produced in limited editions. Some may be found listed under the factory name, such as Bing & Grondahl, Royal Copenhagen, Royal Doulton, and Wedgwood.

Avon, Christmas, 1976, Bringing Home The Tree, Wedgwood, 3rd Edition, 8¾ In.	14.00
Fairmont, DeGrazia, DeGrazia & His Mountain, Angel, Candle, Larry Toschik, 10½ In.	50.00
Fairmont, DeGrazia, Flower Boy, 4th Issue, 1979, 10¼ In.	133.00
Fairmont, DeGrazia, Flower Girl, 3rd Issue, 1978, 10¼ In.	133.00
Fairmont, DeGrazia, Little Cocopah, Indian Girl, 5th Issue, 1980, 10¼ In.	109.00
Fairmont, DeGrazia, Sunflower Boy, 10th Issue, 1985, 10¼ In.	106.00
Kaiser, Children's Prayers, Now I Lay Me Down To Sleep, Box, 7½ In.	17.00
Kaiser, Christmas, 1970, Waiting For Christmas, 7⅝ In.	18.00
Kaiser, Christmas, 1971, Silent Night, 2nd Issue, Box	22.00
Kaiser, Christmas, 1972, Coming Home For Christmas, 3rd Issue, Box	45.00
Kaiser, Christmas, 1973, Toui, Holy Night, 4th Issue, 7¾ In.	15.00
Kaiser, Christmas, 1978, T. Shoener, Shepherds In The Field, Box, 8½ In.	21.00
Kaiser, Christmas, 1985, Gerda Neubacher, Christmas Eve, Box, 7½ In.	27.00
Kaiser, Classic Fairy Tales, Dorothea King, Tom Thumb, 4th Issue, Box, 7⅝ In.	28.00
Kaiser, Classic Fairy Tales, Gerda Neubacher, Frog King, 7½ In.	30.00
Kaiser, Classic Fairy Tales, Gerda Neubacher, Hansel & Gretel, 7½ In.	21.00
Kaiser, Classic Fairy Tales, Gerda Neubacher, Hansel & Gretel, Box, 7½ In.	27.00
Kaiser, Classic Fairy Tales, Gerda Neubacher, Little Red Riding Hood, 7½ In.	28.00
Kaiser, Classic Fairy Tales, Gerda Neubacher, Sleeping Beauty, 6th Issue, Box	48.00
Kaiser, Classic Lullabies, G. Neubacher, Rockabye Baby On The Treetop, 1985, 7½ In.	28.00
Kaiser, Classic Lullabies, G. Neubacher, Sleep Baby Sleep, 1st Issue, Box, 1985	27.00
Kaiser, Dance Ballerina Dance, R. Clarke, At The Barre, 1982, 7½ In.	23.00
Kaiser, Dance Ballerina Dance, R. Clarke, First Slippers, 1982, 7½ In.	23.00
Kaiser, Dance Ballerina Dance, R. Clarke, Opening Night, Box, 1982, 7½ In.	31.00
Kaiser, Dance Ballerina Dance, R. Clarke, Pirouette, Box, 1982, 7½ In.	27.00
Kaiser, Dance Ballerina Dance, R. Clarke, Recital, Box, 1982, 7½ In.	28.00
Kaiser, Dance Ballerina Dance, R. Clarke, Swan Lake, Box, 1982, 7½ In.	27.00
Kaiser, First Fish To Market, Dorothea King, 4th Issue, 7⅝ In.	28.00
Kaiser, Holiday Week Of The Family Kappelmann, Friday, Box, 1986, 7⅝ In.	36.00
Kaiser, Holiday Week Of The Family Kappelmann, Monday, 1st Issue, Box, 1984, 7¾ In.	36.00
Kaiser, Holiday Week Of The Family Kappelmann, Saturday, Box, 1986, 7⅝ In.	36.00
Kaiser, Holiday Week Of The Family Kappelmann, Sunday, Box, 1986, 7⅝ In.	36.00
Kaiser, Holiday Week Of The Family Kappelmann, Thursday, Box, 1985, 7⅝ In.	36.00
Kaiser, Holiday Week Of The Family Kappelmann, Tuesday, Box, 1984, 7⅝ In.	36.00
Kaiser, Holiday Week Of The Family Kappelmann, Wednesday, Box, 1985, 7⅝ In.	36.00
Kaiser, Little Clowns, L. Trester, Red Mask, 7½ In.	21.00
Kaiser, Memories Of Christmas, Gerda Neubacher, Wonder Of Christmas, 1983, 7½ In.	28.00
Kaiser, Mother's Day, 1971, Mare & Foal, 1st Issue, 7⅝ In.	75.00
Kaiser, Through A Woodland Window, R. Hersey, Mr. Badger's Fireside, Box, 7½ In.	30.00
Kaiser, Tribute To Children, Hibel, Giselle, 1st Issue, 1984	55.00
Kaiser, Tribute To Children, Hibel, Wendy, 3rd Issue, 1984	55.00
Kaiser, Yesterday's World, L. Trester, A Time Dreaming, Box, 1978, 10 In.	28.00
Knowles, Alaska, Dog Sled, Polar Bear, Mt. McKinley, Totem Pole, 18K Gold Trim, 8 In.	220.00
Knowles, American Holidays, Valentine's Day, 1981, 5539C, Certificate, Box	40.00
Knowles, Annie & Sandy, Bill Chambers, 1982, 8½ In.	18.00
Knowles, Annie & Sandy, Li'l Orphan Annie, Bill Chambers, Box, 1982, 8½ In.	35.00
Knowles, Christmas, 1988, Rockwell, Santa Claus, Box, 8¼ In.	22.00
Knowles, Colonial, Portrait For Bridegroom, Rockwell, 1987, 9 In. .... 18.00 to 20.00
Knowles, Colonial, Unexpected Proposal, Rockwell, 1986, Box, 9 In.	20.00
Knowles, Gone With The Wind, Scarlett, Box, 1978	65.00
Knowles, Rockwell, Rediscovered Women, Waiting On The Shore, Box	30.00
Knowles, Toy Shop Window, Rockwell, 1977, 8½ In.	22.00
Knowles, Wizard Of Oz, James Auckland, Wizard Bidding Farewell	38.00
Konigszelt, Christmas, 1979, Hedi Keller, Adoration, Box, 9½ In.	25.00
Konigszelt, Christmas, 1980, Hedi Keller, Flight Into Egypt, 9½ In.	22.00
Konigszelt, Christmas, 1981, Hedi Keller, Return Into Galilee, Box, 9½ In.	25.00
Konigszelt, Christmas, 1982, Hedi Keller, Following The Star, Box, 9½ In.	26.00
Konigszelt, Christmas, 1983, Hedi Keller, Rest On The Flight, Box, 9½ In.	25.00
Konigszelt, German Half-Timbered Houses, Frauhausen, Certificate, Box	27.00

C

Coin-Operated Machine, Music Box, Regina, Double Comb, Door, Dragon, Automatic Changer, 25-In. Discs
$19890.00

Coin-Operated Machine, Shooting Gallery, Tratsch, Challenger, 1 Cent, Metallic Balls, 1925, 22 x 9 In.
$634.00

Coin-Operated Machine, Skill, 3 Jacks, Silver Metal Front, Lock On Top, 13 x 12 In.
$660.00

Coin-Operated Machine, Slot, Mills, Gumball Dispenser, Bell Boy, Key, 1930s
$2633.00

Coin-Operated Machine, Slot,
New Deal, Trade, 1 Cent,
Painted Card Suits, 14 x 11 In.
$936.00

Coin-Operated Machine, Vending,
Hershey's Milk Chocolate, 1 Cent,
Glass Front, Doesn't Work,
20 x 11 In.
$85.00

Coin-Operated Machine, Vending,
Apples, Key, Apple Vendor Co.,
New Way Mfg. Co.,
Seattle, 32 x 20 x 12 In.
$2750.00

Konigszelt, German Half-Timbered Houses, Lake House In Immenstaad, Certificate, Box	27.00
Konigszelt, German Half-Timbered Houses, Middle Franconian In Ernhofen, Certificate	25.00
Konigszelt, German Half-Timbered Houses, Moselle River In Rissback, Certificate	25.00
Konigszelt, German Half-Timbered Houses, Westphalian House Near Delbruck, Certificate	25.00
Konigszelt, Grimm's Fairy Tales, Golden Goose, Certificate, Box	36.00
Konigszelt, Grimm's Fairy Tales, Hansel & Gretel, Certificate, Box, 1986	19.00
Konigszelt, Grimm's Fairy Tales, Rapunzel, Certificate, Box, 1982, 7¾ In.	24.00
Konigszelt, Grimm's Fairy Tales, Rumpelstiltskin, Certificate, Box, 1981	19.00 to 24.00
Konigszelt, Grimm's Fairy Tales, Snow White, Certificate, Box, 1981	38.00
Konigszelt, Grimm's Fairy Tales, Tale Of The Golden Goose, Certificate, Box, 1984, 8 In.	19.00
Konigszelt, Sulamith's Love Song, Die Musik, Box, 1982, 7¾ In.	24.00
Porsgrund, Christmas, 1968, Church, 7 In.	75.00
Porsgrund, Christmas, 1969, Three Wise Men, 7 In.	75.00
Porsgrund, Christmas, 1970, Flight From Egypt, 7 In.	25.00
Porsgrund, Christmas, 1971, Baby Jesus, Mary, Joseph, 7 In.	25.00
Porsgrund, Christmas, 1973, Angels, 7 In.	25.00
Porsgrund, Christmas, 1974, Shepherds, 7 In.	50.00
Porsgrund, Christmas, 1978, Farm, 7 In.	25.00
Porsgrund, Christmas, 1979, Boats On Water, 7 In.	25.00
Porsgrund, Christmas, 1982, Snow Village, 7 In.	25.00
Porsgrund, Father's Day, 1971, Fishing, Fars Dag, Box, 5 In.	20.00
Porsgrund, Mother's Day, 1971, Boy & Geese, 5 In.	20.00
Porsgrund, Mother's Day, 1972, Boy In Tree Watching Doe & Fawn, 5¼ In.	10.00 to 18.00
Porsgrund, Mother's Day, 1975, Mors Dag, 5 In.	32.00
Schmid, Bavarian Christmas, 1971, Christmas In The Tyrol, Box, 9½ In.	30.00
Schmid, Bicentennial, 1976, Peanuts, Snoopy On Liberty Bell, C. Schulz, 7½ In.	20.00
Schmid, Christmas, 1974, Hummel, Guardian Angel, 7¾ In.	12.00
Schmid, Christmas, 1975, Raggedy Ann, Gifts Of Love, Box, 7½ In.	30.00
Schmid, Christmas, 1976, Disney, Building A Snowman, Box, 7½ In.	14.00
Schmid, Christmas, 1977, Hummel, Herald Angel, 7¾ In.	18.00
Schmid, Mother's Day, 1973, Hummel, Der Kleine Fischer, 7½ In.	19.00
Villetta, American Family, Rockwell, Homerun Slugger, 1980, 8½ In.	25.00

COMIC ART, or cartoon art, is a relatively new field of collecting. Original comic strips, magazine covers, and even printed strips are collected. The first daily comic strip was printed in 1907. The paintings on celluloid used for movie cartoons are listed in this book under Animation Art.

Drawing, Country Cousin, Abner & Monty, Umbrella, No. 13, 1936, 12 x 9½ In.	280.00
Drawing, Klondike Kid, Mickey Mouse, Running, Whip, No. 69, 1932, 9½ x 12 In.	336.00
Drawing, Mad Doctor, Mickey Mouse, Pluto, No. 103, 1933, 9½ x 12 In.	431.00
Drawing, Mickey's Orphans, Pluto, Moose Head, No. 84, 1931, 9½ x 12 In.	112.00
Drawing, Snow White, Seq. 10a, Scene 22, 1937, 10 x 12 In.	957.00
Drawing, Wayward Canary, Mickey Mouse, Airplane, No. 45, 1932, 4 x 5½ In.	308.00
Strip, Dennis The Menace, Hank Ketcham, April 5, 1952, 8 x 6½ In.	1650.00
Strip, Freckles & His Friends, June 26, 1940, 5 x 16¾ In.	125.00
Strip, Funny Business, Roger Bollen, January 15, 1979, 9 x 7 In.	11.00
Strip, Garfield, Jim Davis, September 25, 1978, 4 x 14 In.	1100.00
Strip, Henry, Carl Anderson, February 14, 1967, 5½ x 20 In.	11.00
Strip, Jeanie, Gil Fox, August 28, 1952, 4½ x 16½ In.	44.00
Strip, Li'l Abner, Al Capp, December 18, 1941, 5½ x 22 In.	220.00
Strip, Little Lulu, Marge, July 26, 1967, 6 x 20 In.	44.00
Strip, Nancy, Ernie Bushmiller, November 3, 1941, 5 x 22 In.	264.00
Strip, Rex Morgan M.D., May 5, 1982, 5⅞ x 16⅞ In.	120.00
Strip, Sunday, Captain & The Kids, Rudolph Dirks, Oct. 13, 1968, 15½ x 22½ In.	165.00
Strip, Sunday, Flash Gordon, Mac Raboy, Dec. 25, 1955, 15 x 19½ In.	1086.00
Strip, Sunday, Prince Valiant, Hal Foster, Inscription, Autograph, 1943, 11 x 8 In.	2710.00
Strip, Sunday, Tarzan, Gray Morrow, No. 2771, Sept. 23, 1984, 13½ x 19½ In.	121.00
Strip, Toonerville Folks, Fontaine Fox, February 17, 1937, 10 x 9½ In.	220.00
Strip, Wizard Of Id, Johnny Hart, January 11, 1967, 5 x 17½ In.	440.00

COMMEMORATIVE items have been made to honor members of royalty and those of great national fame. World's fairs and important historical events are also remembered with commemorative pieces. Related collectibles are listed in the Coronation and World's Fair categories.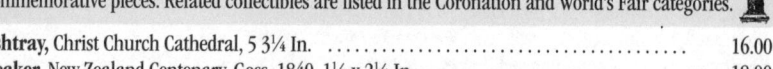

Ashtray, Christ Church Cathedral, 5 3¼ In.	16.00
Beaker, New Zealand Centenary, Goss, 1840, 1½ x 2¼ In.	18.00

C

Coach, Fisher Body Division, 75th Anniversary, Enamel, 1983, 8 x 13 In.	293.00
Cup, Prince Andrew & Sarah Ferguson Wedding, Royal Crown Derby, c.1960	150.00
Cup & Saucer, Duke Of York & Princess May Wedding, 1893	155.00
Glass, Kentucky Derby, 1985, 5⅜ x 2¾ In.	7.00
Honey Pot, Cover, British Union, Yellow Ground, Pottery, c.1825	3840.00
Humidor, King George V & Queen Mary, 1911	145.00
Jug, Wellington Provincial Centenary, Goss, 1840, 1940, 3 x 3⅜ In.	17.00
Pitcher, King George V & Queen Mary Silver Jubilee, 1935, 5 In.	60.00
Plaque, Charles & Diana Wedding, Maidstone, England, 1981	25.00
Plate, Franklin D. Roosevelt, Marked, Maastricht, Holland, 10 In.	95.00
Plate, Jasper Dip, Blue, Relief Portrait, Christian IX, Denmark, Wedgwood, 7 In.	118.00
Plate, King Edward VIII Abdicated, Year Of 3 Kings, 1936	125.00
Plate, King George IV Visit To Scotland, 1822	495.00
Plate, Princess Elizabeth Birth, Paragon, c.1926, 7 x 1¾ In.	195.00
Plate, Queen Elizabeth & St. Lawrence Seaway, Tuscan Bone China, 1959	48.00
Sauceboat, Queen Caroline, 1821	350.00
Trinket Box, Diana, People's Princess, 1961-97, Staffordshire	20.00
Trinket Dish, Queen Elizabeth, Silver Jubilee, Royal Grafton, c.1977, 4½ In.	5.00

COMPACTS hold face powder. A woman did not powder her face in public until after World War I. By 1920, the beauty parlor, permanent waves, and cosmetics had become acceptable. A few companies sold cake face powder in a box with a mirror and a pad or puff. Soon the compact was designed by jewelers and made of gold, silver, and precious materials. Cosmetic companies began to sell powder in attractive compacts of less valuable metal or plastic. Collectors today search for Art Deco designs, commemorative compacts from world's fairs or political events, and unusual examples. Many were made with companion lipsticks and other fittings.

Enamel, Aluminum, Elephant Shape, Black, Cream, France, c.1930	840.00
Enamel, Continental Silver, Carved Ivory Inset Plaque, Houbigant, France, c.1930, 3 In.	585.00
Enamel, Continental Silver, Inset Ivory Plaque, Italy, c.1968, 2½ x 3¼ In.	702.00
Enamel, Continental Silver, Lighter Case, c.1930, 2¼ x 1½ In.	644.00
Enamel, Continental Silver, Lobed, Oval, Austria, c.1960, 3⅜ x 3⅝ In.	1170.00
Enamel, Continental Silver, Vermeil, Fan Shape, Italy, c.1968, 3⅛ x 4 In.	1404.00
Enamel, Continental Silver, Vermeil, Round, Austria, c.1950, 2 ¹³⁄₁₆ In.	468.00
Enamel, Continental Silver, Vermeil Interior, Italy, c.1944, 2⅝ x 3¼ In.	936.00
Enamel, Continental Silver, Vermeil Interior, Italy, c.1968, 2⁷⁄₁₆ x 3⅛ In.	936.00
Enamel, Inset Oval Carved Ivory Plaque, Houbigant, France, c.1930, 2¼ x 1½ In.	468.00
Enamel, Italian Continental Silver, Hinged, Austria, c.1944, 3 x 4 In.	995.00
Gilt Brass, Enamel, Rotary Telephone Dial, Blue, White, France, c.1930	1365.00
Silver, Enamel, Pierced Filigree Lid, Beveled Mirror, Early 20th Century, 1¾ In.	59.00
Silver, Enamel, Vermeil, Amorous 18th Century Couple, c.1930, 1½ x 2¼ In.	761.00
Sterling Silver, Enamel, Vermeil, Austria, c.1930, 2¼ x 2⅜ In.	1404.00

CONSOLIDATED LAMP AND GLASS COMPANY of Coraopolis, Pennsylvania, was founded in 1894. The company made lamps, tablewares, and art glass. Collectors are particularly interested in the wares made after 1925, including black satin glass, Cosmos (listed in its own category in this book), Martele (which resembled Lalique), Ruba Rombic (1928–32 Art Deco line), and colored glasswares. Some Consolidated pieces are very similar to those made by the Phoenix Glass Company. The colors are sometimes different. Consolidated made Martele glass in blue, crystal, green, pink, white, or custard glass with added fired-on color or a satin finish. The company closed for the final time in 1967.

Berry Set, Coreopsis, 9 Piece	45.00
Biscuit Jar, Coreopsis, Cover, Large	55.00
Biscuit Jar, Coreopsis, Satin, Large	50.00
Butter, Cover, Florette, Pink On White Cased, Satin	385.00
Catalonian, Bowl, Emerald Green, 8½ In.	140.00
Catalonian, Candlestick, Emerald Green, Footed, Pair	135.00
Catalonian, Vase, Green, Flared, 5½ In.	145.00
Condiment Set, Coreopsis	85.00
Cruet, Coreopsis	95.00
Dish, Sweetmeat, Coreopsis, Satin, Metal Frame	95.00
Lamp, Coreopsis, Large	70.00
Pickle Castor, Coreopsis	190.00
Pitcher, Guttate, Pink Cased Satin, Draped, Camphor Handle, 9½ In.	288.00
Salt & Pepper, Coreopsis	25.00
Sugar Shaker, Cone Pattern, Opaque Pink, 5½ In. .... *illus*	106.00

Consolidated Lamp and Glass,
Sugar Shaker, Cone Pattern,
Opaque Pink, 5½ In.
$106.00

Consolidated Lamp and Glass,
Vase, Dancing Girls,
Cream Ground, Oval, 12 In.
$235.00

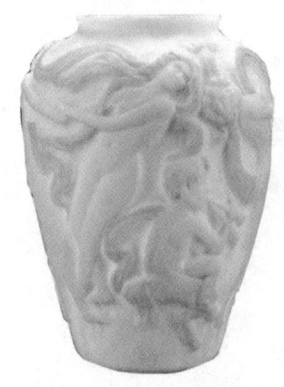

Consolidated Lamp and Glass,
Water Set, Opal Glass,
Lattice Bands, Pink Roses, 13 Piece
$118.00

TIP

If the metal top on your saltshaker won't unscrew, try this: Turn the saltshaker upside down in a small bowl of white vinegar. Let it soak for about 12 hours. The cap should then be loose.

Cookie Jar, Brooklyn Bum, Dodger Cap, Gap-Toothed, Cigar, Ceramic, Prototype, 1953, 12 x 11 In. $429.00

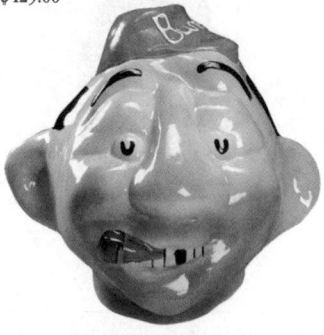

Cookie Jar, Derby Dan Muggsy, Black Mustache & Hat, Ceramic, Pfaltzgraff $30.00

Cookie Jar, Donkey & Milk Wagon, Yellow, Green, Black Cover, Cat Finial, Bisque, 9 x 12½ In. $30.00

TIP

Treat your antiques like your grandparents: Have proper respect for their age, but don't exaggerate their fragility.

Syrup, Coreopsis	80.00
Table Set, Coreopsis, 4 Piece	125.00
Vase, 2 Brown Birds, Blue Flowers, Green Leaves, Ivory Ground, Pillow Form, 6⅜ In.	115.00
Vase, Dancing Girls, Cream Ground, Oval, 12 In. ....*illus*	235.00
Vase, Lovebirds, Relief, Branches, Bulbous, c.1933, 10 In.	2468.00
Vase, Ruba Rhombic, Oval, Lavender, Oblique Faceted Design, 12 In.	1008.00
Water Set, Coreopsis, 7 Piece	35.00
Water Set, Opal Glass, Lattice Bands, Pink Roses, 13 Piece ....*illus*	118.00

CONTEMPORARY GLASS, *see Glass-Contemporary.*

COOKBOOKS are collected for various reasons. Some are wanted for the recipes, some for investment, and some as examples of advertising. Cookbooks and recipe pamphlets are included in this category.

American Country Inn, Hardback, 1987, 510 Pages	10.00
Betty Crocker, 101 Delicious Bisquick Creations, Movie Stars Photos, 1933, 32 Pages	12.00
Betty Crocker, Cookie Cookbook, Spiral Bound, Hard Cover, 1963, 156 Pages	12.00
Betty Crocker, Good & Easy Cookbook, Spiral Bound, 1962, 192 Pages	12.00
Betty Crocker, Picture Cook Book, 5-Ring Notebook, 1st Edition, 1950, 463 Pages	125.00
Betty Crocker, Picture Cooky Book, General Mills, 1948, 44 Pages	35.00
Carnation, Mary Blake, 1948, 6½ x 9½ In., 93 Pages	10.00
Celebrity Cookbook, James S. Black & Co., Post 1950, 112 Pages	8.00
Cooking The Scandinavian Way, Pre 1950, 260 Pages	10.00
Everyday Banana Recipes, 1927, 7 x 5 In., 20 Pages	23.00
General Foods, Learn To Bake You'll Love It, 1947, 8½ x 5½ In., 80 Pages	12.00
Good Housekeeping's Egg & Cheese, Pasta Cookbook, Post 1950, 68 Pages	7.50
Good Housekeeping's Hamburger & Hot Dog Book, Post 1950, 68 Pages	7.50
Good Housekeeping's Party Pie Book, 1958	7.50
Good Housekeeping's Salads Cookbook, Post 1950	7.50
How To Cook With Budweiser Beer, 1950s, 42 Pages	65.00
Knox Gelatin, Salads, Desserts, Pies, Candies, 1930-40, 9 x 6¾ In., 40 Pages	12.00
Pet Milk, Better Babies, 1938, 30 Pages	5.00
Pillsbury 2nd Grand National 100 Prize Winning Recipes, 1951, 100 Pages ... 30.00 to	45.00
Plantation Cookery Of Old Louisiana, 1st Edition, 1938	25.00
Recipe Book, Calumet, 1931, 7 x 5 In., 31 Pages	8.00
Royal Recipes, Time Tested, 1950s, 8½ x 5½ In., 31 Pages	8.00
Treasury Of Meat Recipes, Nation Livestock & Meat Board, 1940s, 40 Pages	15.00

COOKIE JARS with brightly painted designs or amusing figural shapes became popular in the mid-1930s. Many companies made them and collectors search for cookie jars either by design or by maker's name. Listed here are examples by the less common makers. Major factories are listed under their own names in other categories of the book, such as Abingdon, Brush, Hull, McCoy, Metlox, Red Wing, and Shawnee. See also the Disneyana category.

Apple Shape, 7 In.	24.00
Aunt Jemima, Red Dress, White Apron, Plastic, Quaker Oats, 1950s, 10 In.	237.00
Barn, Red Roof, Overflowing Hayloft, Treasure Craft, 8½ x 9 In.	70.00
Bear, Kraft-T Marshmallows, Regal China, 15 In.	395.00
Bear, With Eyes Open, American Bisque, 11¾ In.	124.00
Bear Police Chief, Brown, Black, Yellow, Twin Winton, 11 In.	39.00
Betsy Ross, Blue Dress, White Apron, American Flag, Original Sticker, Enesco	590.00
Brooklyn Bum, Dodger Cap, Gap-Toothed, Cigar, Ceramic, Prototype, 1953, 12 x 11 In. *illus*	429.00
Chili Pepper Cow, Marked, Omnibus, 1980	145.00
Chuck E Cheese's 20th Anniversary, K & L Enterprises, 1997, 15 In.	150.00
Cow, Bessie, Twin Winton, 8 x 12 In.	100.00
Daisy Cow, Marked, Omnibus, 1990	135.00
Dalmatian, Bone Handle, Carol Eldridge, 8½ x 8¾ In.	35.00
Dancing Rabbits, Omnibus, 9¾ In.	75.00
Derby Dan Muggsy, Black Mustache & Hat, Ceramic, Pfaltzgraff ....*illus*	30.00
Derby Dan Muggsy, Pfaltzgraff Stamp	33.00
Donkey & Milk Wagon, Yellow, Green, Black Cover, Cat Finial, Bisque, 9 x 12½ In. ...*illus*	30.00
Edible Express, Airplane, Omnibus, c.1980	125.00
Elsie The Cow, Pottery Guild, 1940s, 11½ In.	436.00
Feed Sack, American Bisque, 1958, 9½ In.	85.00
Fujiya, Yum-Ee-Yum, Girl's Head, Blue Bow, 1960s, 7½ In.	320.00
Gingerbread House, Painted Details, Roof Cover, Cleminson's, 5⅞ In. ....*illus*	25.00

Happy Hooligan, Majolica, 1920s, 9¾ In.	712.00
Hey Diddle Diddle, Yellow, RRP. Co., 9½ In.	35.00
Jim Beam Bottle Club, United States Image, Regal China, 9½ In.	65.00
Kitten With Yarn Ball, Fitz & Floyd	95.00
Lamb, Hands In Pockets, Yellow & Green, American Bisque, 10½ In.	255.00
Little Old Lady Holding Broom, Blue Apron, Abingdon, 8 In. ....*illus*	20.00
Mailbox, U.S. Cookie Mail, Doranne Of California, 10 In.	75.00
Mama Bear, Fitz & Floyd, 11 In.	245.00
Mammy, Green Trim, Incised, Brayton Laguna, 1940s, 12 In.	495.00
Milk Wagon, American Bisque, Marked, U.S.A. 740, 9 In.	185.00
Night Before Christmas, Santa On Roof Top, Fitz & Floyd, 1990	83.00
Old Barn, Bird In Nest On Roof, Stamped, Twin Winton, 11½ x 8½ x 7½ In.	65.00
Pin In Baby Diaper, Regal China, 1950s, 11 In.	290.00
Poodle At Cookie Counter, Marked, Twin Winton, 13½ In.	250.00
Potbellied Stove, Marked, Twin Winton, 12½ x 7 In.	65.00
Quaker Oats, Regal China, Box, 1978, 9¾ x 5¼ In.	150.00
Queen Of Hearts, Incised, Fitz & Floyd, 1992, 10½ In.	275.00
Rio Rita, Fitz & Floyd, 10¾ In.	295.00
Rooster, American Bisque, 10¾ x 8¼ In.	110.00
Rooster, Orange, Turquoise, Brown, Yellow, Beige, Stamped, Twin Winton, 11½ In.	85.00
Santa Driving Rolls-Royce, Fitz & Floyd, 1987	450.00
Santa Going Down Chimney, Fitz & Floyd, 1993, 14 In.	130.00
Santa On Motorcycle, Fitz & Floyd	1000.00
Santa's Sleigh, Fitz & Floyd, Box	75.00
Shoe House, Dark Tan, Marked, Twin Winton, 10¼ In.	30.00
Sinclair Oil Dinosaur, Green Glazed, Name On Front, 1943, 9 x 10 In.	560.00
Smokey The Bear, Bottom Inscription, Made In USA Cookie Jarrin', 1997, 11½ In.	140.00
Squirrel On Top Of Nut, Cookie Nut, Marked, Twin Winton, 11 x 9 x 8 In.	25.00
Squirrel With Cookie Jar, Twin Winton, 10¾ x 9½ x 6½ In.	45.00

COORS ware was made by the Coors Porcelain Company of Golden, Colorado, a company founded with the help of the Coors Brewing Company. Its founder, John Herold, started the Herold China and Pottery Company in 1910. The company name was changed in 1920, when Herold left. Dishes were made from the turn of the century. Coors stopped making nonessential wares at the start of World War II. After the war, the pottery made ovenware, teapots, vases, and a general line of pottery, but no dinnerware—except for special orders. The company is still in business making industrial porcelain. For more information, see *Kovels' Depression Glass & Dinnerware Price List.*

COORS
U.S.A.

Baker, Rosebud, Blue, 10⅞ x 7¼ In.	135.00
Batter Bowl, Rosebud, Green, Handle, 5 x 8 In.	115.00 to 125.00
Batter Bowl, Rosebud, Orange, Handle, 12¼ In.	150.00
Batter Bowl, Rosebud, Yellow, Handle, 8¼ In.	100.00
Bean Pot, Rosebud, Blue, Cover, 4¼ In.	70.00
Bean Pot, Rosebud, Green, Cover, 4¼ In.	55.00
Bowl, Pudding, Coorado, Ivory, 5¾ In.	75.00 to 125.00
Bowl, Pudding, Rosebud, Red, 5¾ In.	45.00
Cake Plate, Rosebud, Orange, 11 In.	70.00
Casserole, Rosebud, Blue, Triple Service, Cover, 5¾ In.	95.00
Casserole, Rosebud, Yellow, Triple Service, Cover, 5¾ In.	65.00
Cookie Jar, Dusty Rose, Flowers, Cover, 10 In.	125.00
Cookie Jar, Rosebud, Red, Handles, Cover, Marked	75.00
Cup & Saucer, Rosebud	25.00
Dish, Rosebud, Handle, 1½ x 6 In.	30.00
Dutch Casserole, Rosebud, Orange, Green Cover, 5½ In.	100.00
Egg Bowl, Rosebud, Green, Shirred, Handles, 6¾ In.	50.00
Loaf Pan, Rosebud, Red, 5 x 9 In.	50.00
Pie Plate, Coorado, Ivory, 10¾ In.	140.00
Pie Plate, Rosebud, Blue, 10 In.	90.00
Pie Plate, Rosebud, Orange, 10 In.	75.00
Pitcher, Rosebud, Green, Large, Cover	55.00
Pitcher, Tilt Ball, Teal, Ice Lip, No. 190, 8 x 7 In.	95.00
Ramekin, Rosebud, Red, Handle, Cover	50.00
Refrigerator Set, Lid, Coorado, Ivory	150.00
Refrigerator Set, Rosebud, Red, Pair	95.00
Salt & Pepper, Barley Hops, Thermo Porcelain, 4¾ In.	30.00

Cookie Jar, Gingerbread House, Painted Details, Roof Cover, Cleminson's, 5⅞ In. $25.00

C

Andy Warhol's Cookie Jars
Pop artist Andy Warhol was a collector of just about everything, including cookie jars. The 1987 auction of more than 125 of his ceramic cookie jars brought $250,000! Cookie jar prices went up immediately after his sale, but collectors were disappointed that prices for most jars soon went down to more reasonable levels, $50 to $300 each.

Cookie Jar,
Little Old Lady Holding Broom,
Blue Apron,
Abingdon, 8 In.
$20.00

C

Copeland, Platter, Turkey, Blue & White, Oval, Staffordshire, England, 17¼ x 13½ In. $86.00

TIP

To hang copper molds in your kitchen, try this: Mount a solid brass or wooden curtain rod across the top of the hanging area. Molds can then be hung by hooks and easily moved when new ones are added.

Copper, Bed Warmer, Hinged Cover, Pierced & Tooled Cover, Turned Handle, 45½ In. $385.00

Salt & Pepper, Wheat Stalks, Tapered, 4½ In.	31.00
Teapot, Turquoise, 2 Cup	22.00
Tumbler, Rosebud, Blue, 4½ In.	20.00
Vase, Art Deco, Aqua Green Matte Glaze, White Interior, Handles, Stamped, 5¼ In.	50.00
Vase, Art Deco, White Matte Glaze, Aqua Green Interior, Handles, Stamped, 5¼ In.	50.00
Vase, Berthoud, Blue, White, Satin, Handles, Marked, 8 In.	95.00

COPELAND pieces listed here are those that have a mark including the word Copeland used between 1847 and 1976. Marks include *Copeland Spode* and *Copeland & Garrett.*

COPELAND
SPODE
ENGLAND

Charger, Portrait, Dutch Painter, 1872-79, 12 In.	495.00
Cheese Dish, Cover, Brown, Rust, Blue, Cream, Fluted, c.1840, 11¾ In.	1880.00
Compote, 3 Graces, 21 In.	1295.00
Figurine, Dog, Russian Wolf Hound, Bisque, c.1950, 10 x 13 In.	205.00
Figurine, Ruth, Standing, Wheat Sheaves, 19th Century, 29½ In.	147.00
Font, Basalt, Black, Paneled Square Sides, 4 Columns, c.1870, 5⅜ In.	1175.00
Plate, Aesop's Fables, Copeland & Garrett, 10 In.	225.00
Plate, Dessert, Imari Flower & Fence Pattern, Entwined C's Mark, 8½ In., Pair	323.00
Platter, Turkey, Blue & White, Oval, Staffordshire, England, 17¼ x 13½ In. ....*illus*	86.00
Platter Drain, Earthenware, Oval, Hand Painted, 6, 8, &13 In., 3 Piece	263.00

COPELAND SPODE appears on some pieces of nineteenth-century English porcelain. Josiah Spode established a pottery at Stoke-on-Trent, England, in 1770. In 1833, the firm was purchased by William Copeland and Thomas Garrett and the mark was changed. In 1847, Copeland became the sole owner and the mark changed again. W.T. Copeland & Sons continued until a 1976 merger when it became Royal Worcester Spode. Pieces are listed in this book under the name that appears in the mark. Copeland Spode, Copeland, and Royal Worcester have separate listings.

Bowl, Blue, White, 5½ In.	18.00
Bowl, Chelsea Bird, Square, 9 In.	125.00
Bowl, Fruit, Peacock, 8¾ In.	125.00
Bust, Princess Alexandra, Parian, Signed, Mary Thornycroft, c.1863, 15 x 9 In.	1880.00
Cup, Coronation, King Edward VIII, 1937	30.00
Cup & Saucer, India Tree, Rust	18.00
Dish, Entree, Platters, Ermine Pattern, 3 Piece	53.00
Gravy Boat, Nancy, 9 x 5 In.	28.00
Ice Cream Set, Blue, Gold Flowers, Fishscale Design, c.1900, 13 Piece	805.00
Pitcher, George Washington, Centennial, 1876, 11 In.	436.00
Plate, Dessert, Chintz, 9 In.	20.00
Plate, Dinner, Buttercup, 10⅜ In.	28.00
Plate, Dinner, Morning Glory, Mansard, 10¾ In.	30.00
Plate, Dinner, Peplow, 1920s, 10 In.	22.00
Plate, Red Transferware, 10 In.	68.00
Platter, Nancy, 9½ x 12¾ In.	55.00
Platter, Nancy, 11 x 14¾ In.	95.00
Sugar, Mansard, 5 In.	20.00

COPPER has been used to make utilitarian items, such as teakettles and cooking pans, since the days of the early American colonists. Copper became a popular metal with the Arts & Crafts makers of the early 1900s, and decorative pieces, like desk sets, were made. Other pieces of copper may be found in the Arts & Crafts, Bradley & Hubbard, Kitchen, Roycroft, and other categories.

Bed Warmer, Birds Design, Pierced & Tooled, Turned Handle, 46½ In.	110.00
Bed Warmer, Engraved Bird, Turned Handle, England, 47 In.	144.00
Bed Warmer, Hinged Cover, Pierced & Tooled Cover, Turned Handle, 45½ In. ....*illus*	385.00
Bed Warmer, Oval, Loop Handle, 45 In.	90.00
Belt Buckle, Round, Hand Forged, Circular Pattern, Center Tong, c.1680, 4 x 3½ In.	177.00
Bowl, Enameled, Signed Schwarcz, 1964, 2¼ x 9¼ x 8½ In.	2700.00
Bowl, Fruits, Flowers, Aubergine Ground, Turquoise Interior, Bats, Chinese, 7 In.	441.00
Box, Engraved Gilt, Pastorale, After F. Boucher, 19th Century, 4 In.	184.00
Box, Hammered, Riveted, Circular Finial, Impressed Mark, Gustav Stickley, 2½ x 7½ In.	2400.00
Box, Wood, Depicting Siege De La Bastille, Round, Repousse Detail, Late 1700s, 3½ In.	155.00
Candle Wax Pourer, Turned Wood Handle, W.B. Berry & Co., Boston, Mass., 22 In. ....*illus*	978.00
Candy Dish, Hammered, Flared Top, Foot, Glass Ball, R. Cauman, 4½ x 6¾ In.	1080.00
Chamber Pot, Dovetailed, Flat Lip, Handle, Ireland, c.1800	250.00

Coffeepot, Wood Handle, Dovetailed, England, c.1750	395.00
Flagon, Ale, Bail Handle, Dutch, 18th Century, Gal.	210.00
Jar, Cover, Silver, Hardstone Inset, Tibetan, 9¾ In.	224.00
Jardiniere, Arts & Crafts, 6½ x 7½ In.	234.00
Jardiniere, Hand Wrought, Stickley Bros., 10½ x 18 In.	2640.00
Kettle, Apple Butter, Dovetailed, Forged Iron Swing Handle, 16 x 23 In.	220.00
Kettle, Apple Butter, Iron Swing Handle, Stamped, J.P. Schaum, 18¾ x 28 In.	523.00
Kettle, Apple Butter, Molded Rim, Iron Swing Handle, 1800s, 27 In.	155.00
Kettle, Dovetailed, Iron Bail Handle, Lid, 17 x 26 In.	230.00
Kettle, Hot Water, Dovetailed, Acorn Lid Finial, England, 1800s, 13 In.	180.00
Kettle, Water, Dome Lid, Brass Acorn Finial, Swing Handle, 10½ x 10½ In.	58.00
Kettle, Wrought Iron Handle, Drum Shape, Rolled Edge, France, 14 x 22 In.	420.00
Log Bucket, Edwardian, Arts & Crafts Style, Hammed, Riveted, 12 x 15 In.	780.00
Molds are listed in the Kitchen category.	
Mug, Ale, Heavy Hammered, 1700s	210.00
Pail, G. Stickley, Hammered, Embossed, Spade Shape Motif, Riveted Handles, 13 x 12 In.	2640.00
Penholder, Horse, Metal Base, 7½ x 5 In.	65.00
Photo Album, Hammered, Wood, 8¾ x 11 In.	205.00
Planter, Oval, Scrolled Iron Stand, 17 In., Pair ....*illus*	805.00
Plaque, Relief, African Antelope, 14 x 10 In.	18.00
Plate Warmer, Hinged Plate & Handle, Urn Pedestal, Tripod Base, 17½ In. ....*illus*	2415.00
Pot, Dovetailed, Scrolled Handles, Tripod Ball Feet, 11 x 12¾ In.	66.00
Pot, Wrought Iron, Long Handle, Scrolled Hook, Copper Bowl, Stamped, J. Moyer, 19 In.	33.00
Tag, Slave, Oblong, Octagonal, Hole Punch, Charleston, S.C., 1805	2450.00
Teakettle, Dovetailed, Gooseneck Spout, Dome Lid, Brass Bulbous Finial, 12 In.	198.00
Teakettle, Dovetailed, Gooseneck Spout, Dome Lid, Brass Mushroom Finial, J. Miller, 11 In.	633.00
Teakettle, Dovetailed, Gooseneck Spout, Dome Lid, Brass Mushroom Finial, W. Heyser, 12 In.	880.00
Teakettle, Dovetailed Seams, Raised Design, Swivel Handle, 7 In.	58.00
Teakettle, Gooseneck Spout, Swing Carry Handle, E. Miller, 7 In.	303.00
Teakettle, Gooseneck Spout, Swing Carry Handle, F. Steinman, 8 In.	1650.00
Teakettle, Gooseneck Spout, Swing Handle, Dovetailed, John W. Schlosser, York, Pa., 7 In.	523.00
Teakettle, Gooseneck Spout, Swing Handle, Dovetailed, Stamped, G & H Nessenthler, 1876, 6 In.	330.00
Teakettle, Gooseneck Spout, Swing Handle, Dovetailed, Stamped, Harbeson, Philadelphia, 6¾ In.	3190.00
Teakettle, Gooseneck Spout, Swing Handle, Dovetailed, Stamped, John Kidd, Reading, Pa., 7⅜ In.	440.00
Tray, G. Stickley, Oval, Riveted Handles, Original Patina, 24 x 11½ In.	3240.00
Tray, Hammered, Original Patina, Impressed, Als Ik Kan, Gustav Stickley, 12 x 18 In.	750.00
Vase, Arts & Crafts, Brass Washed, Hammered, Blossoms, Blue, White, 12 x 6 In., Pair	840.00
Vase, Cylindrical, Pierced Strapwork Handles, Silver, Rim, Athenic, Gorham, 16¼ In.	881.00
Vase, Hammered, Applied Malachite Foot, Original Patina, 4 In.	180.00
Vase, Hand Wrought, 2 Handles, Stickley Bros., c.1910, 9½ In.	7200.00
Wall Pocket, Hand Hammered, Curving Design, 15 x 11 In., Pair	294.00

COPPER LUSTER *items are listed in the Luster category.*

CORALENE glass was made by firing many small colored beads on the outside of glassware. It was made in many patterns in the United States and Europe in the 1880s. Reproductions are made today. Coralene-decorated Japanese pottery is listed in the Japanese Coralene category.

Vase, Cream Ground, 2 Flower Branches, Yellow & Green, Brown Stem, 5 In.	150.00
Vase, Diamond-Quilted, Mother-Of-Pearl, Gilt Foot, Bohemia, Late 1800s, 10½ In.	558.00
Vase, Lemon Gold Design, Fleur-De-Lis, Diamond Pattern, 6¼ In.	475.00
Vase, Pumpkin Chrysanthemum, Nippon, Japan, 9 In. x 6½ In.	1500.00
Vase, Roses, Nippon, Japan, c.1910, 4¼ x 5¾ In.	250.00
Vase, Yellow To White, Satin, Bulbous, 7 In.	177.00

CORDEY China Company was founded by Boleslaw Cybis in 1942 in Trenton, New Jersey. The firm produced gift shop items. In 1969 it was acquired by the Lightron Corp. and operated as the Schiller Cordey Co., manufacturers of lamps. About 1950 Boleslaw Cybis began making Cybis porcelains, which are listed in their own category in this book.

Figurine, Gentleman, 11 In.	57.00
Figurine, Mallard Ducks, 14 In., Pair	495.00
Figurine, Man, Plumed Hat, Red Beard, 7½ In.	30.00
Figurine, Woman, 16 In.	119.00
Figurine, Woman, Gold Tiara, 6½ In.	48.00
Lamp, Woman, 1950s, 25½ In.	96.00
Vase, Rose, Bud, Leaves, 12¼ x 6½ In.	85.00

Copper, Candle Wax Pourer, Turned Wood Handle, W.B. Berry & Co., Boston, Mass., 22 In. $978.00

Copper, Planter, Oval, Scrolled Iron Stand, 17 In., Pair $805.00

Copper, Plate Warmer, Hinged Plate & Handle, Urn Pedestal, Tripod Base, 17½ In. $2415.00

C

Coverlet, Jacquard,
Charles Young,
Mechanicksburg, Penn., 1836,
Elizabeth Barnard, 83 x 79 In
$920.00

Coverlet, Jacquard,
Flower Medallions, Eagles, Foxes,
Doves & Churches Border, E.S.,
1830, 86 x 68 In.
$201.00

TIP

Machine sewing started about 1850. After that date many quilts were still hand-sewn, but at least this tip will help if you spot a machine-made quilt with characteristics of the pre-1850 period.

CORKSCREWS have been needed since the first bottle was sealed with a cork, probably in the seventeenth century. Today collectors search for the early, unusual patented examples or the figural corkscrews of recent years.

Advertising, Cognac Barnett, 7 In.	46.00
Advertising, Old Crow Bourbon, Crow, Plastic Cap, Cigar, Gold Metal Cane, Wood, 6¼ In.	12.50
Advertising, Schlitz Beer, Wood, Nickel-Plated Steel, c.1900, 3⅝ In.	45.00
Anheuser-Busch, Beer Bottle Shape, Nickel Over Silver, 2¾ x 2½ In.	154.00
Antler, Mounted, Woman, Swept-Up Hair, Repousse Roses, Sterling Silver, c.1900	1150.00
Bakelite, Marbled Orange & Brown, Chromed Metal, 5 x 3⅝ In.	10.00
Bakelite, Mottled Brown, Caramel-Colored Handle, 3¾ x 5 In.	18.00
Barrel, Painted, Marked, Richaud, c.1950, 4½ In.	55.00
Boar's Tusk, Silver Ends, Buffalo Head On 1 End, Bottle Brush On Other End, 7½ In.	1582.00
Butterfly, Red, Valezina, 6½ In.	95.00
Clown, Mouth Open, Dotted Shirt, Painted, Late 1920s	326.00
Dog, English Setter, Figural, Brass, 4¾ x 3 In.	78.00
Dog, Terrier, Standing, Brass, Marked, England, 1933, 4½ In.	85.00
Golf Ball, Plastic, 4¼ In.	7.50
Golf Clubs & Bag, Figural, Silver Plated, International Silver, Box, 3½ In.	35.00
Horn Handle, 5 In.	35.00
Kingscrew Patent, England, Mid 19th Century, 7½ In.	353.00
Lady's Leg, Black & White Stripes, Celluloid, Marked, SRD, 5¼ In.	330.00
Lady's Leg, Folding, Metal, Celluloid, 2¾ In.	413.00
Lady's Leg, Green & White Stripes, Celluloid, Germany, 2⅜ x 1¼ In.	550.00 to 660.00
Lady's Leg, Pink & White Stripes, Celluloid, Germany, 2¾ x 1¼ In.	523.00 to 660.00
Penguin, Wood, Hand Carved, France, 1930s, 5 In.	95.00
Pig, Brass, Silver, Corkscrew Tail, 1900s	112.00
Riding Boot, Sterling Silver, Gorham, Stamp On Heel, 6 In.	125.00
Silver Plated, Cork Puller, Italy, 7½ In.	19.00
Soldier, Mahogany, Carved, Removable Head, Marked, Brevete S.G.D.G., c.1930	65.00
Wood & Steel, Adjustable Compression Spring, 6½ In.	88.00
Wood Handle, Red, Sliding Cap, Painted, 3¾-In. Handle	14.00

CORONATION souvenirs have been made since the 1800s. Pottery, glass, tin, silver, and paper objects with a picture of the monarchs and date have been sold at many coronations. The pieces that mention King Edward VIII, the king who was never crowned, are not rare; collectors should be sure to check values before buying. Related pieces are found in the Commemorative category.

Bank, Queen Elizabeth II, Crown Shape, Cast Iron, England, Box, 1953, 3¼ In.	84.00
Cup & Saucer, King Edward VII, Coronation & Throne Chair, Aynsley, 1902	95.00
Cup & Saucer, King Edward VII, Sepia Portraits, Hand Enameling, R.H. & S.L. Plant, 1902	95.00
Cup & Saucer, Plate, Queen Elizabeth II, Trio Myott, Ironstone, 2¾ x 6 & 7 In.	88.00
Cup & Saucer, Queen Elizabeth II, Sepia Portrait, Duchess China, 1953	68.00
Handkerchief, King Edward VIII, 11 x 11 In.	65.00
Knife, Pocket, King George VI, 1937	64.00
Mug, King Edward VII, Coat Of Arms Of Empire Countries, Flowers, Gilt, 1902	75.00
Mug, King George V, Lithophane, 1911	145.00
Mug, Queen Elizabeth II, Flags, 1953, 3 In.	28.00
Open Salt, Queen Elizabeth II & Prince Philip, Blue Jasper, Wedgwood, 1953	68.00
Pin, King Edward VII & Queen Alexandra, Corporation Of Liverpool, 1902, 1¾ In.	56.00
Pin Tray, Queen Elizabeth II, Royal Crown Derby, c.1953	25.00
Plate, King George V & Queen Mary, 1911	175.00
Plate, King George VI, Beaded Dates & Names, Pressed Glass, 1937, 9¾ In.	158.00
Plate, King George VI, Ox Roasting In Middlesboro, Blue, White, 1911	75.00
Plate, King George VI & Queen Elizabeth, Pressed Glass, 1937, 9¾ In.	158.00
Plate, Queen Elizabeth II, Burgundy Border	45.00
Program, Queen Elizabeth II, June 2, 1953, 9¾ x 7 In.	58.00
Salt & Pepper, Queen Elizabeth II, Milk Glass, Metal Screw Top, 3-Sided, June 2, 1953, 3 In.	45.00
Teapot, Queen Elizabeth II & Prince Philip, Blue Jasper, Wedgwood, 1953	145.00
Teaspoon, King George VI & Queen Elizabeth, Silver Plate, Art Deco, 1937, 4½ In.	20.00
Tin, Toffee, Queen Elizabeth, Philip, Blue Boy Toffees, George W. Horner & Co., 1953, 5 x 4⅜ In.	45.00
Toby Jug, George VI, Royal Winton, Grimwades	228.00
Tray, George V & Queen Mary, Coat Of Arms, 1911, 9½ x 6¼ In.	165.00

COSMOS is a pressed milk glass pattern with colored flowers made from 1894 to 1915 by the Consolidated Lamp and Glass Company. Tablewares and lamps were made in this pattern. A few pieces were also made of clear glass with painted decorations. Other glass patterns are listed under Consolidated Lamp and also in various glass categories. In later years, Cosmos was also made by the Westmoreland Glass Company.

Butter, No Cover	12.50
Condiment Set	100.00
Lamp, Miniature	75.00
Pitcher, Pink Band, Flowers, Seamless Daisy, c.1898, 9 In.	255.00
Salt & Pepper	40.00
Syrup	45.00
Table Set, 4 Piece	275.00
Water Set, 7 Piece	275.00

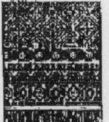

COVERLETS were made of linen or wool during the nineteenth century. Most of the coverlets date from 1800 to the 1880s. There was a revival of hand weaving in the 1920s and new coverlets, especially geometric patterns, were made. The earliest coverlets were made on narrow looms, so two woven strips were joined together and a seam can be found. The weave structures of coverlets can include summer and winter, double weave, overshot, and others. Jacquard coverlets have elaborate pictorial patterns that are made on a special loom or with the use of a special attachment. Quilts are listed in this book in their own category.

Double Weave, 3 Colors, Flowers, Peacock Corner Blocks, 92 x 86 In.	358.00
Double Weave, Birds, Medallions, Flower Corner Blocks, Navy, White, 19th Century, 90 x 75 In.	239.00
Double Weave, Blue, White, Somerset Ohio, L. Hesse Weaver, 1849	468.00
Double Weave, Geometric Blocks, Pine Tree Border, 2 Panel, 71 x 84 In.	173.00
Double Weave, Snowflakes, Pine Trees, Green & White, 2 Panel, 1930s, 74 x 86 In.	200.00
Jacquard, 8-Point Stars, 3 Colors, 2 Piece, 102 x 84 In.	558.00
Jacquard, Blue, White, Flower, Leaf & Flower Border, Fishkill, D. County, 1842, 78 x 91 In.	320.00
Jacquard, Birds Feeding Young, Urns, Fruit, Flowers, Blue, Double Town Border, 98 x 78 In.	288.00
Jacquard, Black, White, Sunburst, Birds, Trees, Wm. Lowmiller, Muncy, 1842, 74 x 98 In.	248.00
Jacquard, Blue, Red, Cream, Flowers, Birds, Wm. Lowmiller, Muncy, Ly Co., 1840, 73 x 96 In.	660.00
Jacquard, Blue, Red, Green, Cream, Sunburst, Trees, Wm. Lowmiller, 1836, 76 x 100 In.	990.00
Jacquard, Blue, Red, Green, Tan, Flower, Strawberry Medallion, Ohio, 70 x 82 In.	684.00
Jacquard, Blue, Red, Mustard, Bird & Rose Border, Peter Goodman, 1852, 96 x 76 In.	260.00
Jacquard, Blue, Red, Roses, Vines, Emanuel Meily, Lebanon, 1836, 76 x 91 In.	546.00
Jacquard, Blue, White, Eagle, Agriculture & Manufacturers Foundation, 1829, 78 x 92 In.	468.00
Jacquard, Blue & Red, Double Rose Border, Signed, G. Renner & P. Leidig, 1842, 81½ x 78 In.	388.00
Jacquard, Blue & White, Medallions, 8-Point Stars, c.1851, 97 x 78 In.	1410.00
Jacquard, Capitol In Washington, Olive Leaves, Stars, Blue, Red, White, 1846, 78 x 85 In.	805.00
Jacquard, Centennial, Geometric, Memorial Hall, 80 x 74 In.	944.00
Jacquard, Central Flower Medallion, Flower Vine Border, 5 Colors, 77 x 80½ In.	132.00
Jacquard, Charles Young, Mechanicksburg, Penn., 1836, Elizabeth Barnard, 83 x 79 In. *illus*	920.00
Jacquard, Blue, Muir Family, Medallions, Cotton, 78 x 84 In.	173.00
Jacquard, Double Rose, Grapevine Border, 4 Colors, C. Yordy, Willow St., 1848, 74 x 80 In.	568.00
Jacquard, Double Rose, Grapevine Border, Red, Blue, White, Isaac Kepner, 1848, 74 x 80 In.	299.00
Jacquard, Double Rose, Grapevine Border, Red, Navy, White, Davis Steiner Brecknock, 75¾ x 83 In.	327.00
Jacquard, Exotic Birds Feeding Their Young, Christian & Heathen, 19th Century, 86½ x 78 In.	388.00
Jacquard, Flower, Bird & Snowflake Border, Red, Blue, Green, White, Mathias Mann, 91½ x 80 In.	440.00
Jacquard, Flower, Leaves, 4 Colors, Berry Corner Blocks, Elisabeth Medary, c.1840, 84 x 102 In.	523.00
Jacquard, Flower, Snowflake, Birds, Trees, Red, White, Blue, Wm. Lowmiller, Muncy, 1840, 72 x 91 In.	154.00
Jacquard, Flower & Snowflake, Eagle & Tree Border, Blue, White, Red, M. Frailey, 1835, 72 x 94 In.	302.00
Jacquard, Flower Medallions, Birds, Trees, Red, Blue, Green, White, J. Unger, 1845, 82 x 91 In.	440.00
Jacquard, Flower Medallions, Bird, Tree Border, Red, Blue, Green, H. Hersh, 1848, 82 x 91 In.	550.00
Jacquard, Flower Medallions, Blue, White, Signed, Jay A. Van Vleck Gallipolis, O., 80 x 92 In.	402.00
Jacquard, Flower Medallions, Eagles, Foxes, Doves & Churches Border, E.S., 1830, 86 x 68 In. *illus*	201.00
Jacquard, Flower Medallions, Rooster, Tree Border, Red, Blue, White, Benja Kiehl, 1836, 90 x 77 In.	777.00
Jacquard, Flowers, 2 Colors, C. Fehr, Emmaus, Pa., c.1838, 76 x 102 In.	193.00
Jacquard, Flowers, 3 Birds & Berry Border, Red, Blue, Black, Green, F. Gish, 1852, 92 x 76 In.	303.00
Jacquard, Flowers, 4 Colors, Joseph Smith, Millerstown, c.1839, 78 x 88 In.	121.00
Jacquard, Flowers, Bird Border, Black, Red, Andrew Hoover, Hanover, Pa., c.1840, 92 x 76 In.	275.00
Jacquard, Flowers, Leaves, 3 Colors, Isaac Kepner, Pottstown, Pa., c.1842, 100 x 80 In.	275.00
Jacquard, Flowers, Leaves, 4 Colors, Joseph Deavler, c.1860, 80 x 88 In.	248.00
Jacquard, Flowers, Red, Blue, Green, White, F. Hershey, W. Brosey, Manheim, Pa., 1847, 91 x 77 In.	2970.00
Jacquard, Flowers, Snowflakes, Isaac Kepner, Pottstown, Pa., c.1843, 90 x 80 In.	138.00

Coverlet, Jacquard, Medallion, Flower, Bird & Tree Border, J. Unger, Willow St. 1845, 82 x 91 In. $440.00

Coverlet, Jacquard, Medallion, Flower, Floral Vine Border, 5 Colors, 77 x 80½ In. $132.00

Coverlet Markings

Woven coverlets often have a woven corner block with the name of the weaver or the name of the owner, the county or city, or the date. Sometimes weavers used logos or special designs—a sailboat, a flower, an eagle, or a star—or wove slogans, like "United We Stand, Divided We Fall," in the corner or border.

C

Coverlet, Jacquard, Red, White, Center Medallion, Temple Design, Eagles, Stags, Birds, 1855, 77 x 87 In. $1265.00

Cowan, Figurine, Man With Sword, Woman, Multicolored Glaze, 9 x 6¼ In., Pair $1800.00

Coverlet Colors

The wool of black sheep was used for black. For other colors, white wool was dyed. Indigo was used for blue, cochineal (a Mexican insect) for scarlet. Red came from madder root, and goldenrod and sumac made yellow. Alder bark made tan; hickory or walnut hulls were used to make dark brown.

Jacquard, Flowers, Sunburst, Vine, Snowflake, Red, White, Blue, Barbara Kready, 1839, 91 x 82 In.	523.00
Jacquard, In God We Trust, Red, Yellow, White, Grape & Cornucopia Border, 94 x 83 In.	431.00
Jacquard, Medallion, Flower, Bird & Tree Border, J. Unger, Willow St., 1845, 82 x 91 In. *illus*	440.00
Jacquard, Medallion, Flower, Floral Vine Border, 5 Colors, 77 x 80½ In. *illus*	132.00
Jacquard, Memorial Hall, Red, Brown, Green Wool, Cotton, 82 x 78 In.	588.00
Jacquard, Navy Blue, Red, Cotton, Sarah Lamb, Basil Ohio 1839, 82 x 88 In.	575.00
Jacquard, Period Patriotic, United We Stand, Flowers, Eagles, 42 Stars, 1857, 89 x 79 In.	1265.00
Jacquard, Red, Blue, Mustard, Cabbage Rose Border, John Kachel, 1839, 100 x 83 In.	690.00
Jacquard, Red, Medallion, Triangles, Eagle, Plume Border, 74 x 79 In.	288.00
Jacquard, Red, White, Center Medallion, Temple Design, Eagles, Stags, Birds, 1855, 77 x 87 In. *illus*	1265.00
Jacquard, Red, White, Sunburst, Eagle, Diamond Border, Lowmiller, Muncy, 1845, 78 x 98 In.	220.00
Jacquard, Red & Blue, Flower Medallion, Washington Bust, c.1869, 78 x 78 In.	144.00
Jacquard, Star & Medallion Center, Peace & Plenty 1855, 72 x 90 In.	489.00
Jacquard, Star Medallion, Flower Border, H. Stager, Mount Joy, Pa., 81 x 81 In.	275.00
Jacquard, Stars, Eagles, Doves, Mary Nunemacher John Kaufman, 1842	1093.00
Jacquard, Stars & Flowers, Blue Field, Fence, Trees Border, Harry Tyler, 1839, 87 x 77 In.	1840.00
Jacquard, Sunburst, 4 Colors, Grapevine Border, P. Rasweiler, Millersburg, 1847, 72 x 102½ In.	299.00
Jacquard, Sunbursts, Flowers, Red, Blue, Green, White, M. By John Kachel, 1841, 84 x 94½ In.	448.00
Jacquard, Tree & Flower Border, 2 Panel, Mary Adams, 1840, 76 x 92 In.	400.00
Jacquard, White Ground, Flowers, Snowflake, Pennsylvania, 1842, 90 x 79 In.	708.00
Overshot, Blue On Blue, 19th Century, 66½ x 80 In.	480.00
Overshot, Checkerboard Variation, Blue & Red, 3 Panel, 87 x 70 In.	374.00
Overshot, Geometric, Red, Blue, White, 2 Panel, 71 x 88 In.	230.00
Single Weave, Center Medallion, Black & Natural Wool, Geometric Border, 65 x 88 In.	92.00

COWAN POTTERY made art pottery and wares for florists. Guy Cowan made pottery in Rocky River, Ohio, a suburb of Cleveland, from 1913 to 1931. A stylized mark with the word *Cowan* was used on most pieces. A commercial, mass-produced line was marked *Lakeware*. Collectors today search for the Art Deco pieces by Guy Cowan, Viktor Schreckengost, Waylande Gregory, or Thelma Frazier Winter.

Bookends, Camels, Brown Crackled Glaze, Alexander Blazys, 8¾ x 9½ In.	3900.00
Bookends, Sunbonnet Girl, Green Matte Crystalline Glaze, Impressed, 7¼ In.	230.00
Candleholder, Larkspur Blue, 3¼ In.	40.00
Candleholder, Pink, Swirled, 1¾ x 4 In., Pair	25.00
Candlestick, Yellow Glaze, Seahorse Shape, 4¼ In., Pair	65.00
Candlestick, Yellow Matte, 3⅜ In., Pair	75.00
Charger, Leaping Maidens, Leaves, Beige Semimatte Glaze, Stamped, 12¾ In.	1140.00
Figurine, Man With Sword, Woman, Multicolored Glaze, 9 x 6¼ In., Pair *illus*	1800.00
Flower Frog, Blue Luster, 8½ & 3 x 1¼ In.	145.00
Flower Frog, Scarf Dancer, Ivory Glaze, Art Deco	375.00
Flower Frog, Toadstool, 1924-25, 4¾ x 5½ In.	500.00
Plaque, Jazz Theme, Victor Schreckengost	4888.00
Snack Set, Light Blue, 6-Sided, 2 Piece	105.00
Vase, Blue Luster, 3⅜ x 2⅞ In.	75.00

CRACKER JACK, the molasses-flavored popcorn mixture, was first made in 1896 in Chicago, Illinois. A prize was added to each box in 1912. Collectors search for the old boxes, toys, and advertising materials. Many of the toys are unmarked.

Ad, Sailor Doll Recalls Long-Time Snack, 9¾ In.	20.00
Ad, Woman Handing Out Cracker Jack For Halloween, c.1954, 9½ x 12½ In.	12.50
Booklet, Riddles, c.1920, 3 x 5 In., 40 Pages	125.00
Bookmark, Metal, Spaniel, 2⅝ In.	20.00
Card, Christy Mathewson, c.1915	1911.00
Charm, Ship, Metal, 1910-20	8.50
Cookie Jar, Borden, Happy Memories Collectibles, Box, 1997, 13 In.	448.00
Lantern, Metal, Celluloid, Red Insert, c.1910, 1⅛ In.	35.00
Puzzle, Donkey, Cardboard, 1½ In.	10.00
Puzzle, Maze	10.00
Puzzle, Pinball, High Flyer, Mother Goose, On Flying Goose	10.00
Puzzle, Pinball, Money Tree, Mix'n & Match'm Picture Dominoes, Set No. 1	10.00
Spinner, Red, Blue	95.00
Tape Measure, Angelus Marshmallows, Celluloid, Round, 1½ In.	103.00
Thimble, For A Good Girl, Metal, 1910-20, Pair	12.00
Toy, Cop On Motorcycle, Metal	90.00
Toy, Dominos, Picture, Instructions, 1971, 28 Piece	8.00

Toy, Goat, Marbleized Pink, Plastic, Stand-Up, 1940s, 1⅜ In.	7.00
Toy, Golf Club, Plastic, 1950s, 3³⁄₁₆ In.	2.00
Toy, Horse Drawn Carriage, Angelus Marshmallows, Red, White, Blue, Tin Litho, ⅞ x 2⅛ In.	22.00
Toy, Sedan Automobile, Metal, 1920s	60.00
Toy, Shovel, Metal, 1920s, 1 In.	3.00
Toy, Spoon & Fork, Tin, 1930s, 2 In.	10.00
Toy, Toonerville Trolley, Tin, Nifty, Germany, 2 In.	495.00
Whistle, Flat, 1 x 2⅝ In.	110.00

CRACKLE GLASS was originally made by the Venetians, but most of the ware found today dates from the 1800s. The glass was heated, cooled, and refired so that many small lines appeared inside the glass. It was made in many factories in the United States and Europe.

Bowl, Clear, Turquoise Stem & Foot, 8 In.	75.00
Bowl, Turquoise, Scalloped Rim, 12 In.	105.00
Creamer, Amber, 3½ In.	20.00
Creamer, Blue, 3½ In.	22.00
Cruet, Tricornored Spout, Clear Pulled Handle, Bright Red, 7 In.	30.00
Decanter, Rainbow, 15 In.	225.00
Lemonade Set, Topaz, Cone Shaped Tumblers, Footed, 8-In. Pitcher, 7 Piece	325.00
Pitcher, Amber, 7½ In.	95.00
Pitcher, Deep Amethyst, Clear Handle, 4¾ In.	75.00
Pitcher, Green, Long Neck, Clear Handle	30.00
Pitcher, Handle, Ruffled Edge, 4¾ x 9 In.	30.00
Pitcher, Rainbow, 8½ In.	95.00
Pitcher, Rainbow, Cupped Top, Bulbous Bottom, 9 In.	85.00
Pitcher, Ruby, Hand Blown, Applied Crystal Handle, 5 x 3 In.	45.00
Pitcher, Teal Blue, 5¼ In.	30.00
Pitcher, Yellow, 3¾ In.	30.00
Rose Bowl, Green, 3 In.	10.00 to 30.00
Vase, Applied Yellow Rosettes, 7½ In.	110.00
Vase, Clear, Royal Blue Pedestal, 8¾ x 6⅝ In.	46.00
Vase, Ruby, Fan, Pulled Rim, 7 In.	85.00
Vase, Turquoise, Applied Snake Rigaree, Flared Rim, Pontil, 5¼ In.	20.00

CRANBERRY GLASS is an almost transparent yellow-red glass. It resembles the color of cranberry juice. The glass has been made in Europe and America since the Civil War. It is still being made, and reproductions can fool the unwary. Related glass items may be listed in other categories, such as Northwood, Rubina Verde, etc.

Compote, Clear Base, c.1880, 4 x 8½ In.	67.00
Cruet, Inverted Coin Dot	45.00
Dish, Cover, Thumbprint, Applied Paneled Finial, 7¾ In.	115.00
Dresser Box, Cover, Gold & White Paneled Decoration, Metal Holder, 4-Footed, c.1890, 4 In. *illus*	235.00
Epergne, 2-Lily, Baskets, Ruffled Edge, 1900, 19 In.	1100.00
Epergne, 3-Lily, Ruffled Edge Base, c.1880, 22 In.	282.00
Epergne, 4-Lily, Applied Decoration	650.00
Lamp Shade, Fluted, c.1880, 9½ In., Pair	92.00
Pitcher, Opalescent Swirl, Ruffled Rim, Egg Shape, c.1950, 10 In.	176.00
Pitcher, Round Indents, Hand Blown, Ruffled Edge, 9 In.	146.00
Sugar Shaker, Faceted, Silver Plated Cover, c.1900, 6 In.	75.00
Tray, Enameled, Blue Flowers, c.1870, 2 x 13½ In.	117.00
Vase, Art Nouveau, Sterling Silver Overlay, Trumpet Shape, Scalloped, 15 In.	2703.00
Vase, Enameled, Stork, Tree, Beaded Edge, Gold Trim, Milk Glass Interior, Footed, 12 In., Pair	1035.00
Vase, Satin Glass, Silver Overlay, Footed, 9 In.	65.00

CREAMWARE, or queensware, was developed by Josiah Wedgwood about 1765. It is a cream-colored earthenware that has been copied by many factories. Similar wares may be listed under Pearlware and Wedgwood.

Basket, Chestnut, Basket Weave, Leaves & Nuts Inside, Footed, 5 x 10 x 7 In. *illus*	403.00
Bowl, Tavern Scene, Man With Pipe, Barrel Shape Table, Hound Dog, Staffordshire, 6 In.	1560.00
Bowl, Whaling Scene, Transfer, c.1810, 10 In.	283.00
Cheese Dish, Lid, Transfer, Flower Sprigs, c.1920, 10¼ x 8½ In.	106.00
Coffeepot, Dome Lid, Baluster, William Greatbatch, 1765-70, 9⅜ In.	5400.00
Creamer, Cow, Brown, White, Calf Feeding, Bird Finial, Rectangular Plinth, 18th Century	1016.00
Creamer, Cow, Lead Glazed, Enamel, Staffordshire, Late 18th Century, 5 In.	823.00

Cranberry Glass, Dresser Box, Cover, Gold & White Paneled Decoration, Metal Holder, 4-Footed, c.1890, 4 In.
$235.00

Creamware, Basket, Chestnut, Basket Weave, Leaves & Nuts Inside, Footed, 5 x 10 x 7 In.
$403.00

Creamware, Platter, Lead Glaze, Gadrooned, Scallop Rim, Brown Ground, Staffordshire, 15¼ In.
$1058.00

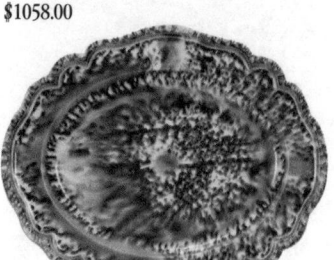

Creamware, Wall Pocket, Lead Glaze, Flowers, Scroll Framed Cartouche, 9½ In.
$294.00

Crown Ducal, Plate, Asiatic Pheasants, Mulberry Transfer, 9¼ In.
$38.00

Figurine, Cat, Sitting, Wrapped Tail, Brown & Green Drip Glaze, Staffordshire, 6¼ In.	12000.00
Figurine, Charity, Standing, Child In Arms, Lead Glaze, Staffordshire, c.1800, 8½ In.	176.00
Figurine, Farmer, Tree, Staffordshire, Victorian, c.1820, 5 In.	195.00
Figurine, Lion, Lead Glaze, Multicolored, Staffordshire, 18th Century, 5½ In.	8225.00
Figurine, Water Buffalo, Brown Tortoiseshell Lead Glaze, Applied Leaves, Staffordshire, 5¼ In.	881.00
Jug, Fluted Mask, Beaded Rim, Baluster Shape, Footed, Inscribed, c.1771, 8 In.	1800.00
Loving Cup, Chinese Figures, Gardens, Multicolored, Enamel, Handles, 7¾ In.	940.00
Pitcher, Milk, Lid, Embossed Fruit	42.00
Platter, Lead Glaze, Gadrooned, Scallop Rim, Brown Ground, Staffordshire, 15¼ In. ....*illus*	1058.00
Punch Pot, Cover, Lead Glaze, Globular, Crabstock Handle, Spout, Staffordshire, 7 In. 999.00 to	1175.00
Punch Pot, Cover, Lead Glaze, Globular, Crabstock Handle, Spout, Staffordshire, 9 In.	1763.00
Tankard, Blue, Emblem, Vine, England, c.1760, Qt.	1200.00
Teapot, Cover, Prodigal Son Receives Patrimony, William Greatbatch, c.1782, 5 In.	4200.00
Teapot, Cover, Shell, 4-Lobe Melon Form, Crooked Handle, Claw Feet, 18th Century, 5 In.	2030.00
Teapot, Harlequin & Columbine, Discovered By Pierrot, Beaded, Shaped Handle, 5 In.	6600.00
Teapot, House Form, Hand, Holding Bird's Head Spout, Serpent Handle, 18th Century, 4⅝ In.	568.00
Wall Pocket, Lead Glaze, Female Mask Head, Leaves, 1700s, 9 In.	382.00
Wall Pocket, Lead Glaze, Flowers, Scroll Framed Cartouche, 9½ In. ....*illus*	294.00

CREDIT CARDS, credit tokens, metal charge plates, phone cards, and other similar collectibles that replace money are now part of the numismatic collecting hobby.

Esso Gas & Oil, Humble Oil & Refining Co., Plastic, 1962	30.00

CREIL, France, had a faience factory as early as 1794. The company merged with a factory in Montereau in 1819. They made stoneware, mocha ware, and soft paste porcelain. The name *Creil* appears as part of the mark on many pieces. The Creil factory closed in 1895.

Inkwell, Insert, Cover, Imari Pattern, c.1920, 3¾ In.	146.00
Lazy Susan, Center Bowl, Imari Style, Impressed Mark, 1893, 4¾ In.	350.00
Platter, Imari Style, 15¾ x 13 & 17 x 14½ In., 2 Piece	1840.00
Platter, Roasted Meats, Oval, Imari Style, Brass Frame, 1800s, 19 x 16 In.	180.00

CROWN DUCAL is the name used on some pieces of porcelain made by A. G. Richardson and Co., Ltd., of Tunstall and Cobridge, England. The name has been used since 1916.

Biscuit Jar, Cameo	350.00
Cake Plate, Roma, Flowers, Grapes, Vines, Leaves, Gold Trim	195.00
Charger, Orange & Yellow Flowers, Charlotte Rhead, 13½ In.	263.00
Creamer, Florentine, Off-White, 3½ In.	18.00
Cup, Berkshire, Florentine Shape, Flowers, Blue, Green, Yellow Border, 2⅜ In., Pair	7.00
Cup & Saucer, Blink Bonnie Thistle	28.00
Cup & Saucer, Bristol, 1930s, 3¾ In.	25.00
Cup & Saucer, Florentine, 2⅜ x 5⅞ In.	10.00
Cup & Saucer, Florentine, Cobalt Blue Band, Gold Trim	35.00
Cup & Saucer, Tulips & Freesias, Yellow Ground, 12 Piece	250.00
Gravy Boat, Underplate, Blink Bonnie Thistle, 7¾ & 8½ In.	45.00
Mug, Princess Margaret, 1930s	165.00
Mug, Pub Scene, Man Drinking, Man Shaking Dice, 5½ x 4¼ In.	40.00
Plate, Asiatic Pheasants, Mulberry Transfer, 9¼ In. ....*illus*	38.00
Plate, Bread & Butter, 1930s, 6¼ In.	9.00
Plate, Bread & Butter, Bristol, Embossed, Scalloped, 1931	20.00
Plate, Bread & Butter, Colonial Times, 1900-20, 6 In.	16.00
Plate, Bread & Butter, Tulip & Freesia, 12 Piece	150.00
Plate, Coach House, 11 In.	40.00
Plate, Dessert, Rosalie, Florentine Shape, 6⅞ In.	5.00
Plate, Fruit, Cobalt Blue, Gold Ring, 8 In.	40.00
Plate, Fruit, Wheat, Cobalt Blue, Gold Ring, 9 In.	40.00
Plate, Game Bird, Laurel, Mallard, Quails, Maroon Band, 8 Piece	320.00
Plate, George Washington, Surrender Of Cornwallis, 1932, 10½ In.	98.00
Plate, Majolica, Florentine Shape, Royal, Cobalt Blue, 10½ In.	125.00
Plate, Memorial, George Washington & Mother, 9 In.	45.00
Plate, Mulberry, 10½ In.	105.00
Plate, Salad, Blue, Colonial Times, Speak For Yourself, John, 8 In.	30.00
Plate, Salad, Colonial Times, Blue, Scalloped, 8 In.	25.00
Plate, Tulip & Freesia, Yellow Ground, Enamel, 12 Piece	250.00

Platter, Blink Bonnie Thistle, 16½ x 13½ In.		65.00
Platter, Rosalie, Florentine Shape, 12¼ x 9¾ In.		10.00
Saucer, Colonial Times, 1900-20, 5¾ In.		11.00
Soup, Dish, Underplate, Tulip, Freesia, Yellow Ground, 4¾ & 1⅝ In., 8 Piece		200.00
Tray, Eggcup, Pansy Chintz, 4 Egg Rests, 6½ In.		95.00
Vase, Apple Green, Cream, Orange, Pewter, Signed Charlotte Rhead, 1930, 5¾ In.		275.00
Vase, Art Deco, Color Splotches, Cream Matte, Overglaze, 1940s, 5½ x 7¼ In.		245.00
Vase, Art Deco, Cream, Mottled Ocher, Blue, Beige Matte Glaze, c.1940, 10 x 6 In.		325.00
Vase, Art Deco, Star Shape, Charlotte Rhead, 7 x 4¾ In.		225.00

CROWN MILANO glass was made by Frederick Shirley at the Mt. Washington Glass Works about 1890. It had a plain biscuit color with a satin finish. It was decorated with flowers and often had large gold scrolls.

Basket, Spatter Glass, Satin Finish, Thorny Applied Handle, Signed, 8 In.		500.00
Biscuit Jar, Cover, Beige, Raised Gold Mums & Leaves, Oval, 10 In.		805.00
Biscuit Jar, Cover, Light Blue Shaded To White, Dotted Art Nouveau Flowers, 7 In.		920.00
Biscuit Jar, Cover, Opal, Tan, Enameled Water Lilies, Metal Lid, 6½ In.	350.00 to	403.00
Biscuit Jar, Cover, Oval, Opal, Blue Flowers, Gold Scrolling, 7 In.		259.00
Biscuit Jar, Cover, White, Flower Sprays, Gold Scrolling Medallions, Turtle Finial, 7 In.		460.00
Biscuit Jar, Green, Molded Hobnail, Raised Jeweled Starfish, Seaweed, Butterfly Finial, 9 In.		1265.00
Dish, Sweetmeat, Cream, Raised Enameled Starfish, Applied Jewels, Metal Lid, Handle, 6 In. *illus*		470.00
Dish, Sweetmeat, Molded Stars, Raised Jeweled Starfish, Squat, Embossed Metal Lid, 6 In.		518.00
Ewer, Opal, Mauve & Amber Scrolls, Raised Gold Branches, Pink Rope Twist Handle, 13 In.		978.00
Jar, Jeweled, Spirals, Silver Plated Lid, Turtle Finial, Twig Handle, c.1900, 4 x 5 In.		1850.00
Jar, Stopper, Flower Clusters, Snail Handles, Enamel Gold Band, Signed, 6 x 4¼ In. *illus*		1035.00
Lamp, Red & Yellow Mums, Gray Ground, Domed Shade, Gilt Metal Fittings, 12 In.		11500.00
Puff Box, Crosshatch Cutting, Embossed Roses, Swirl On Lid, 4½ In.		195.00
Sugar & Creamer, Cream Shaded To Yellow, Pansies, Gold Trim		288.00
Sugar & Creamer, Opal, Flowers, Gold Scrolls, Reed Handles, 4 In.		690.00
Syrup, Wild Roses, Silver Spout, Bulging Ovals, 3⅞ In. *illus*		690.00
Vase, Coralene Gold Branch Design, White, Mt. Washington, 4½ In.		250.00
Vase, Daffodils, Cream Ground, Cylindrical, Ring Collar, 13 In.		633.00
Vase, Flowers, Gold, Mauve & Blue, Flared Rim, Applied Handles, c.1900, 12 In.		294.00
Vase, Swirl Design, Raised Gold, Wild Rose Design, 8 In.		1750.00
Vase, Swirled Neck, Raised Gold Beads, Colorful Panels, 8½ In.		230.00

CROWN TUSCAN *pattern is included in the Cambridge Glass category.*

CRUETS of glass or porcelain were made to hold vinegar, oil, and other condiments. They were especially popular during Victorian times and have been made in a variety of styles since the eighteenth century. Additional cruets may be found in the Castor Set category and also in various glass categories.

Citron, Gold Hummingbird, Red Black Flowers, Blue Stopper, Rope Twist Handle, 7 In.	374.00
Clear, Green & White Peppermint Swirl, Round, Clear Ball Stopper & Reeded Handle, 6 In.	155.00
Cut Glass, Cranberry Cut To Clear, Notched Neck, Hobstars, Cut Handle, Faceted Stopper, 7 In.	104.00
Pressed Glass, Daisy Stopper, Anchor Hocking, c.1960	5.00
Pyrex, Stopper, Anchor Hocking, 4½ In.	3.00
Vaseline Opalescent, Alaska Pattern, Faceted Clear Stopper, 5 In.	144.00

CT GERMANY was first part of a mark used by a company in Altwasser, Germany, in 1845. The initials stand for C. Tielsch, a partner in the firm. The Hutschenreuther firm took over the company in 1918 and continued to use the *CT*.

C.T.

Bowl, Flowers, Mint Green, Flowers, Handles, 13½ In.	210.00
Bowl, Lady, Portrait, Black Hair, Blue Dress, Gold Trim, 6 In.	58.00
Chocolate Pot, Lavender Violets, Gold	1295.00
Coffeepot, Flowers, Fancy Handle, Gold	1295.00
Dish, Flowers, Fluted, Reticulated, 8 In.	82.00
Dish, Pink & Gold Design, Divided, Gilt Twig Handle, Pre 1900	95.00
Plate, Dinner, Poppies, Pink, Scalloped Border, 8½ In.	75.00
Plate, Quail Scene, Landscape, Brown Scalloped Edge, Gilt, Pre 1920, 11½ In.	75.00
Platter, Pink Flowers, Emerald Green Trim, Gold Fleur-De-Lis, Round, Signed, 12 In.	25.00
Teapot, Pink Roses, Green Leaves, Gold Striping, Crown Mark	20.00
Tray, Fruits, Scalloped Edge, Gold Design, 12½ In.	32.00
Vase, Blue & Pink Flowers, Gold Rim, Cylindrical, Handle, Footed, 10½ x 5¾ In.	100.00

Crown Milano, Dish, Sweetmeat, Cream, Raised Enameled Starfish, Applied Jewels, Metal Lid, Handle, 6 In.
$470.00

Crown Milano, Jar, Stopper, Flower Clusters, Snail Handles, Enamel Gold Band, Signed, 6 x 4¼ In.
$1035.00

Crown Milano, Syrup, Wild Roses, Silver Spout, Bulging Ovals, 3⅞ In.
$690.00

C

Cup Plate, Dot, Rings, 20-Petal Border, Plain Shoulder, 62 Scallops, Olive Green, 3 In. $143.00

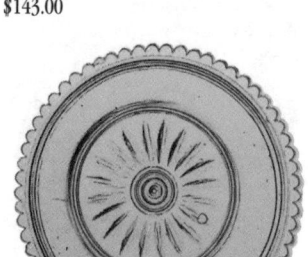

Cup Plate, Dot Center, Posy Border, Plain Rim, Opaque Swirled Light Blue, 3⅝ In. $3300.00

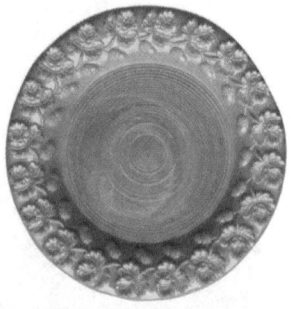

Cup Plates from Dr. Ruff
The dark areas on some of the pictured cup plates are labels showing they came from the collection of Dr. Augustine Ruff, an early cup plate collector. This provenance adds value to the plates.

Cup Plate, Flower, 15 Even Diamond Scallops, Lavender, 3½ In. $413.00

CUP PLATES are small glass or china plates that held the cup while a diner of the mid-nineteenth century drank coffee or tea from the saucer. The most famous cup plates were made of glass at the Boston and Sandwich factory located in Sandwich, Massachusetts. There have been many new glass cup plates made in recent years for sale to gift shops or limited edition collectors. These are similar to the old plates but can be recognized as new.

4 Hearts, Bull's-Eyes, Posies, 19 Scallops & Double Points, Lavender, 3¹⁄₁₆ In.	176.00
6-Point Center, Comet-Tail Band, 36 Bull's-Eye Scallops, Blue, 3⅜ In.	44.00
6-Point Diamond Starflower, 17 Wheat Sheaf Scallops, Clear, 3¼ In.	33.00
6-Point Star, Rounded Hexagon Border, Stippled, 24 Beads & Reels, Clear, 3¼ In.	55.00
8-Point Starflower, Scroll Border, 65 Scallops, Gray, Blue, Brown, European, 3¾ In.	154.00
8-Point Starflower, Scroll Border, 65 Scallops, Honey Amber, European, 3¾ In.	55.00
16-Petal Flower, Scroll Border, 16 Even Scallops, Clear, 3⁷⁄₁₆ In.	44.00
Anthemion, Scrolling Vines, Stippled Ground, 24 Scallops & Points, Clear, 3⁷⁄₁₆ In.	66.00
Anthemion, Wheat Sheaf Border, 8-Sides, 7 Scallops Between Corners, Clear, 3½ In.	77.00
Beaded Ring Fleurette, In Triangle, Acanthus, 58 Scallops, Peacock Blue, 3⅜ In.	468.00
Beaded Ring Fleurette, In Triangle, Acanthus, 58 Scallops, Peacock Green, 3⅜ In.	495.00
Bull's-Eye, Diamond-Point Bull's-Eyes, 8 Serrated Scallops & Point, Teal, 3⁹⁄₁₆ In.	88.00
Bull's-Eye, Rings, 20-Petal Border, 34 Bull's-Eye Scallops, Yellow Green, 3⅝ In.	44.00
Bull's-Eye, Scrolled Anthemion, Fleur-De-Lis, Trefoils, 66 Scallops, Blue, 3⁵⁄₁₆ In.	22.00
Cavetto, Circled Stars, Oakleaf & Sheaf Border, 19 Scallops & Points, Clear, 3½ In.	330.00
Concentric Rings, Plain Border, 22 Scallops & Points, Amber, 3¼ In.	187.00
Dahlia, Stippled Ground, Palmette Border, 16 Scallops & Points, Clear, 2¹⁵⁄₁₆ In.	55.00
Dahlia, Stippled Ground, Palmette Border, 28 Scallops & Points, Blue, 2¾ In.	330.00
Diamond-Point Bull's-Eye, C-Scroll Border, 34 Bull's-Eye Scallops, Clear, 3⁹⁄₁₆ In.	44.00
Dot, Rings, 20-Petal Border, Plain Shoulder, 62 Scallops, Olive Green, 3 In. ....*illus*	143.00
Dot Center, Posy Border, Plain Rim, Opaque Swirled Light Blue, 3⅝ In. ....*illus*	3300.00
Flower, 7-Posy Border, Graduated Stiple Band, Rope Rim, Clear, 3⁷⁄₁₆ In.	33.00
Flower, 15 Even Diamond Scallops, Lavender, 3½ In. ....*illus*	413.00
Flower, Shield Border, Opaque White, 10-Sided Rope Rim, Fiery Opalescent, 3⅝ In.	33.00
Flower, Wheat Sheaf Border, 55 Even Scallops, Light Blue, 3⅜ In. ....*illus*	605.00
Overlapping Hearts, Arrows, Stippled Lyre Border, 24 Scallops, Opalescent, 3½ In.	88.00
Plain Center, Flower Baskets Border, Clear Rope Rim, Fiery Opalescent, 3¾ In.	1760.00
Plain Center & Borders, Rim Folded Outward, Clear, Pontil, 3⅞ In.	99.00
Posy, Beaded Swag, Leaves, Sheafs & Leaves, 42 Scallops, Fiery Opalescent, 3½ In.	66.00
Posy, Oak Leaves, Roses, Scrolled Anthemion, 53 Stippled Scallops, Clear, 3⁹⁄₁₆ In.	44.00
Rose & Pansy, Stippled Ground, 30 Bull's-Eye Scallops, Soft Blue, 3 In.	154.00
Star, 5-Point Stars, Stippled, Rope Border, 34 Scallops, Light Green, 3¼ In. ....*illus*	209.00
Star Center, Sheen, Posy Border, Plain Rim, Opaque Light Blue, Dark Swirl, 3⅜ In.	1760.00
Swirled Rosette, Flower Baskets Border, Rope Rim, Opalescent To Clear, 3¾ In.	55.00

CURRIER & IVES made the famous American lithographs marked with their name from 1857 to 1907. The mark used on the print included the street address in New York City, and it is possible to date the year of the original issue from this information. Earlier prints were made by N. Currier and use that name from 1835 to 1847. Many reprints of the Currier or Currier & Ives prints have been made. Some collectors buy the insurance calendars that were based on the old prints. The words *large, small,* or *medium folio* refer to size. The original print sizes were very small (up to about 7 x 9 In.), small (8.8 x 12.8 In.), medium (9 x 14 In. to 14 x 20 In.), large (larger than 14 x 20 In.). Other sizes are probably later copies. Other prints by Currier & Ives may be listed in the Card category under Advertising and in the Sheet Music category. Currier & Ives dinnerware patterns may be found in the Adams or Dinnerware categories.

American Express Train, Frances F. Palmer, 22 x 30 In.	15600.00
American Farm Scenes, Sleigh, Pond, N. Currier, Frances F. Palmer, 21 x 28 In.	2160.00
American Farm Scenes, Spring, Farmer, Plow, Oxen, N. Currier, Frame, 1853, 18 x 25 In.	1058.00
American Homestead Autumn, Trees, Apples, House, Frame, 16 x 20 In.	1093.00
American Homestead Summer, Mahogany Veneer Frame, 16 x 20 In.	288.00
American National Game Of Baseball, Frame, 17 x 21 In.	220.00
Assassination Of President Lincoln, Mat, Frame, 1865, 17 x 21 In.	274.00
Bound Down The River, Frame, 1870, 10 x 14 In.	1293.00
Brook Trout Fishing, Frame, c.1872, 11 x 14 In.	705.00
Camping Out, Some Of The Right Sort, N. Currier, Frame, c.1856, 22 x 30 In.	1763.00
Champion Pacer Johnston, Bashaw Golddust, c.1884, 25½ x 36 In.	1560.00
Check, Keep Your Distance, N. Currier, Frame, 1853, 20 x 24 In.	3525.00
City Of Peking: Pacific Mail Steamship Co., Frame, 13 x 14 In.	588.00
Clipper Ship, Dreadnought, Off Sandy Hook, N. Currier, 1854, 23 x 30 In.	1880.00

Course Of True Love, 2 Cats Sitting On Pillow, Mahogany Veneer Frame, 1875, 13 x 10 In.	121.00
Custer's Last Charge, Frame, 1876, 10 x 14 In.	940.00
Fording The River, Frame, 12¾ x 17⅛ In.	1116.00
Game Dog, 1879, 13⅜ x 17⅝ In.	235.00
General William H. Harrison, 12¼ x 10½ In.	263.00
Girard Avenue Bridge, Fairmount Park, Philadelphia, c.1860, 11 x 14⅞ In.	538.00
Gray's Elegy In A Country Church Yard, Color, 16 x 23 In.	1180.00
Great Fire At Boston, Frame, 13 x 16 In.	3055.00
Home In The Wilderness, Frame, 1870, 10 x 15 In.	1058.00
Iroquois, Black Wood Frame, c.1881, 13¼ x 9¾ In.	920.00
Last Hit In The Game: A Home Run, 1886, 13 x 17½ In.	1058.00
Main Of Cocks, The First Battle, Double Mat, Frame, 7½ x 13⅞ In.	420.00
New York Yacht Club Regatta, 17 x 27⅝ In. *illus*	8400.00
Pioneer's Home, Hand Colored, Frame, 24 x 31⅝ In.	777.00
Quail Shooting, S. Palmer's Setters, Molded Frame, 24 x 32 In.	4485.00
Scenery Of The Wissahickon Near Philadelphia, c.1860, 14 x 11 In.	418.00
Snipe Shooting, N. Currier, Frame, 16½ x 23 In.	1645.00
Sperm Whale, In A Flurry, N. Currier, Frame, c.1852, 10 x 14 In.	1645.00
Trolling For Bluefish, Hand Colored, Frame, 23¾ x 31¼ In.	11950.00
Whale Fishery, Laying On, N. Currier, Frame, c.1852, 10 x 14 In.	1998.00
Won By A Neck, 23¾ x 30⅞ In. *illus*	2160.00
Woodlands In Winter, Frame, 10 x 14 In.	1058.00
Zachary Taylor, 11 Presidents, 10 x 14 In.	176.00

CUSTARD GLASS is a slightly yellow opaque glass. It was made in England in the 1880s and was first made in the United States in the 1890s. It has been reproduced. Additional pieces may be found in the Cambridge, Fenton, Heisey, and Northwood categories. Custard glass is called Ivorina Verde by Heisey and other companies.

Argonaut Shell, Berry Bowl, Gold Trim, 5 In.	85.00
Argonaut Shell, Pitcher, Custard Glass, Gold Trim, 8¼ x 4¾ In.	470.00
Argonaut Shell, Sugar & Creamer, 7 In.	450.00
Bead Swag, Tumbler, Gold Trim	30.00
Bowl, Windmill, Scalloped Ruffled Rim, 2¾ x 8 In.	29.00
Chrysanthemum Sprig, Compote, Gold Trim, c.1900, 5 In.	50.00
Chrysanthemum Sprig, Spooner	129.00
Chrysanthemum Sprig, Toothpick	259.00
Diamond With Peg, Mug, Hand Painted, Rose, 2¾ x 2¾ In.	65.00
Diamond With Peg, Napkin Ring, Seneca, S.D., Roses, Souvenir	155.00
Geneva, Sugar & Creamer, Green, Gold Trim	185.00
Georgia Gem, Butter, Cover, 7 In.	325.00
Georgia Gem, Spooner, 4 x 12 In.	86.00
Harvest Flower, Glass, Raised Wheat & Floral, 4¼ In.	75.00
Little Gem, see Georgia Gem pattern in this category.	
Louis XV, Cruet, Gold Highlights	45.00
Maize is its own category in this book.	
Maple Leaf, Berry Set, Gold Trim, 7 Piece	450.00
Maple Leaf, Table Set, Gold Trim, 4 Piece	725.00
Maple Leaf, Toothpick	1195.00
Maple Leaf, Water Set, Gold Trim, 7 Piece	450.00
Ring & Band, Creamer, Souvenir, 2½ In.	59.00
Sawtooth Rim, Toothpick, Souvenir, Gold, Pink Roses	25.00
Scroll & Lattice, Dresser Bottle, Blue Pansies, Gold Trim, 9 In., Pair	125.00
Wild Bouquet, Toothpick	1159.00

CUT GLASS has been made since ancient times, but the large majority of the pieces now for sale date from the brilliant period of glass design, 1880 to 1905. These pieces have elaborate geometric designs with a deep miter cut. Modern cut glass with a similar appearance is being made in England, Ireland, and the Czech and Slovak republics. Chips and scratches are often difficult to notice but lower the value dramatically. A signature on the glass adds significantly to the value. Other cut glass pieces are listed under factory names.

Basket, Engraved Flowers, 12 In.	35.00
Berry Bowl, Hobstar & Lancet, 8 In.	120.00
Berry Bowl, Interlaced Hobstars, Scalloped & Notched Edge, 4 x 8 In.	150.00
Bottle, Double Ogee, Blue Flashed, Stopper, 3½ In.	33.00

Cup Plate, Flower, Wheat Sheaf Border, 55 Even Scallops, Light Blue, 3⅜ In.
$605.00

Cup Plate, Star, 5-Point Stars, Stippled, Rope Border, 34 Scallops, Light Green, 3¼ In.
$209.00

Currier & Ives, New York Yacht Club Regatta, 17 x 27⅝ In.
$8400.00

Currier & Ives, Won By A Neck, 23¾ x 30⅞ In.
$2160.00

Cut Glass, Charger, Hobstar, Lace, 5-Point Stars, Laurel Wreaths, Notched Edges, c.1900, 13½ In. $353.00

Cut Glass, Decanter, Diamond Point Bands, Silver Plated Label, English, 10 In., Pair $403.00

Cut Glass, Dresser Bottle, Clear To White To Blue, Enameled, Gold Trim, 7¼ In., Pair $1150.00

TIP

American brilliant period cut glass will fluoresce a pale lime green under a black light. Newly cut glass will look purple-pink under the same light.

Bowl, Centerpiece, Amethyst To Clear, Footed, 5½ x 15½ In.	79.00
Bowl, Centerpiece, Faceted Round Base, Ball Stem Supports, Scalloped Rim, 9 x 12 In.	130.00
Bowl, Fern, 3-Footed, 7½ x 4½ In.	359.00
Bowl, Ice Cream, Hobstar & Buzz, Russian Cut, Brilliant, 1900s, 16½ In.	150.00
Bowl, Intaglio, Flowers & Wreath, Footed, 4 x 14¾ In.	330.00
Bowl, Oval, Square Foot, Anglo-Irish, c.1800, 9 In.	217.00
Bowl, Pinwheels, Fans, 8 In.	59.00
Bowl, Swirls, Hobstars, Crosshatching, Scalloped Sawtooth Rim, 9 x 2½ In.	42.00
Bowl, Trifle, Engraved Tulips, Design Guild, 5½ x 10½ In., Pair	230.00
Carafe, Starbursts, Geometric Designs, Brilliant, c.1915, 8½ x 5½ In., Pair	529.00
Celery Vase, Strawberry Diamond & Fan, Urn Shape, Scalloped Rim, Footed, 8⅞ In.	330.00
Charger, Hobstar, Lace, 5-Point Stars, Laurel Wreaths, Notched Edges, c.1900, 13½ In. *illus*	353.00
Cigar Holder, Ruby To Clear, Intaglio Flowers, 6½ In.	66.00
Claret Jug, Diamond, Rose, Fan, Brilliant, Sterling Silver Collar, c.1897, 13 In.	382.00
Compote, Cover, Rolled Rim, Intaglio, 16¾ In., Pair	633.00
Compote, Engraved Cornflowers, 9 In.	25.00
Cordial Set, Waterford, Kylemore, 4 In., 6 Piece	59.00
Decanter, Cranberry To Clear, 20th Century, 15¾ In.	146.00
Decanter, Diamond Point Bands, Silver Plated Label, English, 10 In., Pair *illus*	403.00
Decanter, Engraved, Medial & Neck Band, Flutes, Plain Lip, Pontil, 11¼ In.	198.00
Decanter, Engraved Flower & Trellis, Oval Prism Stopper, 15½ In., Pair	720.00
Decanter, Peacock Green, 8 Flutes, Applied Rim, 12¼ In.	1045.00
Decanter, Sawtooth Band, Fluted Columns, Silver Rim, Stopper, 14½ In.	46.00
Decanter, Whiskey, Cranberry To Clear, Faceted, Ovals, X's, Stopper, 10½ In.	230.00
Dish, Sweetmeat, Cover, Scalloped Foot, Knopped Stem, Flared Bowl, 18 In., Pair	472.00
Dish, Sweetmeat, Underplate, Jewel Decoration, Clear, Frosted Bowl, Ruby Flashed Edge, 8½ In.	705.00
Dresser Bottle, Clear To White To Blue, Enameled, Gold Trim, 7¼ In., Pair *illus*	1150.00
Eggcup, Cobalt Blue To White To Clear, Flute, Star-Cut Base, 2¾ In.	77.00
Goblet, Green Cut To Clear, Flower Sprays, Scrolls, 5½ In., 8 Piece *illus*	1528.00
Goblet, Hobstar, Wine, 7½ In., 12 Piece	705.00
Ice Pail, Octagonal, c.1900, 4¼ x 4 In.	71.00
Ice Tub, Hobstar, Arched Hobnail, Engraved Rosettes, Tab Handles, 5½ In. *illus*	71.00
Lamp, Mushroom Shade, Pinwheel, Prisms, 11½ x 19 In.	1035.00
Pitcher, Bronze Spout, Rim, Dragon Handle, Italy, 8 In.	70.00
Pitcher, Engraved, Stemmed Flowers, 10½ In.	35.00
Pitcher, Hobstar, Engraved Sunflower & Wheat, 7½ In.	55.00
Pitcher, Pinwheel, 12½ In.	82.00
Pitcher, Stars, Brilliant, 8 In.	71.00
Powder Box, Cover, Silver Fittings, 4½ x 5¼ In.	94.00
Scent Bottle, Blue To Clear, Groove, Crosshatch, 3½ In.	143.00
Scent Bottle, Blue To White To Clear, Punty, Oval, Stopper, 2⅛ In.	154.00
Scent Bottle, Cobalt Blue, Punty, Hinged Brass Cap, Blue Jewel, 4½ In.	198.00
Scent Bottle, Double, Cased Ruby, Hinged, Screw, Silver Caps, Stopper, 4 In.	176.00
Scent Bottle, Double, Cased Teal Green, Center Hinge, Hinged Screw Caps, Chain, 5¼ In.	253.00
Scent Bottle, Ogee, Opaque Black, Hinged Gilt Repousse, Cap, 3⅛ In.	154.00
Scent Bottle, Panel, Emerald Green, Hinged Brass Cap, 2 In.	121.00
Scent Bottle, Pink To White To Clear, Punty, Elongated, Hinged Cap, 3 In.	303.00
Scent Bottle, Purple To Clear, Diamond, Groove, Hinged Silver Cap, 3⅝ In.	165.00
Scent Bottle, Ruby To Clear, Star, Punty, Groove, Paneled Neck, 3¼ In.	154.00
Scent Bottle, Sunburst, Violet Blue, Hinged Silver Cap, 3¼ In.	88.00
Scent Bottle, White To Clear To Green, Punty, Teardrop, Hinged Brass Cap, 3½ In.	165.00
Shade, Blue Cut To Clear, 5 Panels, Open Flowers, Greek Key, Oval, 4½ x 11 In.	588.00
Sugar, Cover, Cobalt Blue, Paneled Stem, Footed, Hexagonal Finial, 8¾ In.	1320.00
Sugar, Cover, Medium Amber, Octagonal Bowl, 8 Scallop Rim, Footed, 9 In.	66.00
Sugar, Cover, Yellow Amber, Applied Round Foot, Faceted Base, Knop, Ireland, c.1820, 6¾ In.	170.00
Syrup, Diamonds, Silver Mounted, c.1840, 6½ x 5 In.	353.00
Tumbler, Strawberry Diamonds, Fans, Roundels, Rays, 3½ In.	132.00
Tumbler Set, Ruby To Clear, 8 Panels, 4⅛ In., 6 Piece	55.00
Vanity Set, Flowers, Trailing Stems, Red Cut To Clear, Stylized Leaves, c.1930, 5 Piece	588.00
Vase, Alternating Bands Of Hobstars & Fans, 12 In.	120.00
Vase, Circle, Ellipse, Electric Blue, Gauffered Rim, Hexagonal Base, 7¼ In.	605.00
Vase, Cone Shape, Sunburst Hobstar, 12½ In.	59.00
Vase, Daisy & Button Bands, Engraved Flowers, Round, Pedestal Base, 9¼ In. *illus*	59.00
Vase, Engraved Allover Flowers, Star & Fan, 7½ x 14½ In.	117.00
Vase, Engraved Tom Turkey, Sweden, 6½ x 7 In.	165.00

Cut Glass, Goblet, Green Cut To Clear, Flower Sprays, Scrolls, 5½ In., 8 Piece
$1528.00

Czechoslovakia Glass, Perfume Bottle, Pink, Jeweled Metalwork, 1920s, 5⅛ In. $900.00

Cut Glass, Ice Tub, Hobstar, Arched Hobnail, Engraved Rosettes, Tab Handles, 5½ In. $71.00

Czechoslavakia Glass, Perfume Bottle, Blue, Jeweled Metalwork, Dauber, Hoffman, 1930s, 6½ In. $3000

Czechoslovakia Glass, Perfume Bottle, Shoe Shape, Black, Metalwork, Jade Stopper, Hoffman, 1920s, 4½ In. $18000.00

Cut Glass, Vase, Daisy & Button Bands, Engraved Flowers, Round, Pedestal Base, 9¼ In. $59.00

Czechoslavakia Glass, Perfume Bottle, Blue, Jeweled Metalwork, Putto Stopper, Morlee, 1920s, 3¾ ¯ $480.00

Czechoslovakia Glass, Vase, Angular Panels, Clear & Acid Etched, Flared, c.1930, 12 In. $263.00

Cybis, Figurine, Jester, 16 In. $940.00

Czechoslovakia Glass, Perfume Bottle, Jeweled Metalwork, Stopper, Seated Lovers, 1920s, 5¾ In. $2160.00

Czechoslovakia Pottery

Pottery and porcelain have been made in Bohemia since the late eighteenth century. At the end of World War I in 1918, Bohemia joined Moravia and Slovakia to form Czechoslovakia.

Czechoslavakia Pottery, Pitcher, Cat, Sitting, Yellow, Black, Red, Ditmar Urbach, 8⅜ In. $403.00

Czechoslavakia Pottery, Vase, Fruit, Yellow & Orange Ground, Flared Rim, Footed, 7⅛ In. $58.00

Vase, Hobstar, Fan, Combination Pattern, 10 In.	230.00
Vase, Hobstar & Harvard Alternating Panels, Sunburst Base, Pinched Waist, 12 In.	240.00
Vase, Hobstar & Notched Prism, Flared Neck, Loop Handles, Bulbous, 10½ In.	900.00
Vase, Silver Mounted, William Comyns, London, c.1912, 5½ In., Pair	227.00

CUT VELVET is a special type of art glass, made with two layers of blown glass, which shows a raised pattern. It usually had an acid finish or a texture like velvet. It was made by many glass factories during the late Victorian years.

Vase, Diamond-Quilted, Victorian, 8¼ In.	375.00

CYBIS porcelain is a twentieth-century product. Boleslaw Cybis came to the United States from Poland in 1939. He started making porcelains in Long Island, New York, in 1940. He moved to Trenton, New Jersey, in 1942 as one of the founders of Cordey China Co. and started his own Cybis Porcelains about 1950. The firm is still working. See also Cordey.

CYBIS

Bust, God Of Love, Eros, 9½ In.	590.00
Bust, Victoria, Pink Bow, Flowers, Blue Eyes, White Dress, Blue Dots, 10 In.	395.00
Bust, Victorian Lady, Big Lace Collar	65.00
Bust, Virgin Mary, Praying, 20th Century, 7½ In.	235.00
Figurine, Bunny, Mr. Snowball, 4½ In.	40.00 to 100.00
Figurine, Dandy Man, Cordey, 6½ In.	55.00
Figurine, Duckling, Flapping Little Wings, 1940s, 4¼ In.	83.00
Figurine, Eleanor Of Aquitaine, Katharine Hepburn, No. 461, 13½ In.	2000.00
Figurine, Elephant, Seated, 5 In.	351.00
Figurine, Jester, 16 In. ....*illus*	940.00
Figurine, Madonna With Bird, 1956, 11½ In.	560.00
Figurine, Owl, On Branch, 4½ In.	75.00
Figurine, Skylark, 6⅛ In.	420.00
Figurine, Squirrel, Mr. Fluffy Tail, No. 630, 8 In.	285.00

CZECHOSLOVAKIA is a popular term with collectors. The name, first used as a mark after the country was formed in 1918, appears on glass and porcelain and other decorative items. Although Czechoslovakia split into Slovakia and the Czech Republic on January 1, 1993, the name continues to be used in some trademarks.

CZECHOSLOVAKIA GLASS

Basket, Art Deco, Blown, Red, Green Waves, 10½ x 6¾ In.	275.00
Beverage Set, Pitcher, Tumblers, Hand Blown, c.1950, 6 & 14 In., 7 Piece	111.00
Cocktail Set, Amber, Gold Rings, Band, Engraved Roses, 7 Piece	153.00
Liqueur Set, Amethyst Cut To Clear, 13¾ In., 3 Piece	176.00
Liqueur Set, Ruby Flashed, Engraved Flowers, 1920s, 7 Piece	1925.00
Perfume Bottle, Blue, Jeweled Metalwork, Dauber, Hoffman, 1930s, 6½ In. ...*illus*	3000.00
Perfume Bottle, Blue, Jeweled Metalwork, Putto Stopper, Morlee, 1920s, 3¾ In. ...*illus*	480.00
Perfume Bottle, Cameo, Black Fuchsia, Red Ground, Atomizer, 9 In.	431.00
Perfume Bottle, Jeweled Metalwork, Stopper, Seated Lovers, 1920s, 5¾ In. ...*illus*	2160.00
Perfume Bottle, Lead Crystal, Elongated Diamond Stopper, Multifaceted, 5¾ In.	12.00
Perfume Bottle, Pink, Jeweled Metalwork, 1920s, 5⅛ In. ...*illus*	900.00
Perfume Bottle, Shoe Shape, Black, Metalwork, Jade Stopper, Hoffman, 1920s, 4½ In. .*illus*	18000.00
Vase, Angular Panels, Clear & Acid Etched, Flared, c.1930, 12 In. ...*illus*	263.00
Vase, Applied Snake, Cobalt Blue, Mottled Red, Green, 14 In., Pair	59.00
Vase, Black, Silver Overlay, c.1930, 12 In., Pair	88.00
Vase, Orange, 12 In.	195.00
Vase, Orange, Ruffled, Pontil Mark, 6⅛ x 3³⁄₁₆ In.	33.00
Vase, Red, Orange, Yellow, Brown, 6¼ In.	68.00
Vase, Yellow, 7⅛ In.	24.00

CZECHOSLOVAKIA POTTERY

Figurine, Nude, Seated, Black, Turquoise Hair, 1950s, 10½ In.	288.00
Fish Set, Fish & Water Plant Decoration, c.1885, 24-In. Platter, 11 Piece	316.00
Pitcher, Cat, Sitting, Yellow, Black, Red, Ditmar Urbach, 8⅜ In. ...*illus*	403.00
Pitcher, Toucan, Hand Painted, Ditmar Urbach, c.1920, 9 x 7 In.	205.00
Sculpture, Mother & Child, Miroslav Klinger, 1970, 21 In.	185.00
Vase, Fruit, Yellow & Orange Ground, Flared Rim, Footed, 7⅛ In. ...*illus*	58.00

D'ARGENTAL is a mark used in France by the Compagnie des Cristalleries de St. Louis. The firm made multilayered, acid-cut cameo glass in the late nineteenth and twentieth centuries. D'Argental is the French name for the city of Munzthal, home of the glassworks. Later they made enameled etched glass.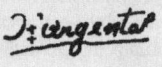

Vase, Blue, Red Stems Flowers, Leaves, Vines, Squat, Signed, 9 In.	350.00
Vase, Blue & Purple Overlay, Rose Ground, Leaves, Art Deco Style, c.1920, 4¼ In.	1315.00
Vase, Bottle, Dutch Landscape, Windmill, Village, Signed, 7 In.	600.00
Vase, Citron, Blue Fruit, Leafy Branches, Bulbous, Stick, Signed, c.1920, 12 In.	1116.00
Vase, Citron, Crimson Flowers, Thorny Branches, Leaves, Bulbous, Flared Rim, 10 In., Pair	3450.00
Vase, Grapes, Leaves, Yellow Shaded To Red Shaded To Brown Ground, 13½ In. ....*illus*	920.00
Vase, Landscape, Sailboats On Water, Orange, Etched Yellow Ground, Signed, 8 In.	940.00
Vase, Sailing Ships, Crimson, Blue Ground, Cylindrical, Signed, 11 In.	900.00
Vase, Stick, Citron, Ruby Thistle Branches & Leaves, Signed, 12 In.	700.00
Vase, Stylized Amber Fronds, Green Ground, c.1905, 4½ In.	780.00

DANIEL BOONE, a pre–Revolutionary War folk hero, was a surveyor, trapper, and frontiersman. A television series, which ran from 1964 to 1970, was based on his life and starred Fess Parker. All types of Daniel Boone memorabilia are collected.

Book, Adventures Of, Katherine W.E. Wilke, Soft Cover, 1962, 64 Pages	4.00
Book, Little Golden Book, 1st Edition, Irwin Shapiero, Miriam Story Hurford, c.1956	22.00
Knife, Barlow, Fess Parker, On Card, Camillus Cutlery Company, 6¾ x 3¼ In.	95.00
Lunch Box, Aladdin, 1955	250.00
Lunch Box, Kaboodle Kit, Vinyl, Standard Plastic Products, 1964	392.00
Lunch Box, Metal, Fess Parker, No Thermos, King-Seeley Thermos Co., c.1965	41.00
Playset Figure, Holding Rifle, Marx, 3¼ In.	15.00
Postcard, Birthplace, Reading, Penn., Linen, Stichler & Co., 1930-45	2.00
Ring, Plastic, Raised Head, Gold, Red Plastic, 1960s	15.00
View-Master Set, Guest Star George Gobel, 21 Views	10.00

DAUM, a glassworks in Nancy, France, was started by Jean Daum in 1875. The company, now called Cristalleries de Nancy, is still working. The *Daum Nancy* mark has been used in many variations. The name of the city and the artist are usually both included.

Bird, Toucan, Amber Pate-De-Verre Beak, 10 In. ....*illus*	777.00
Bowl, Amber Blown, Wrought Iron Mount, Foil Inclusions, Handles, 4-Footed, 11 In.	1058.00
Bowl, Aqua, Yellow, Enamelled Landscape, Round, Cameo, Signed, 1900s, 4 x 8½ In.	3000.00
Bowl, Blown Glass, Wrought Iron Mounts, Signed, 1910-25, 6 x 7 In.	1912.00
Bowl, Centerpiece, Blue, Foil Inclusion, Footed, Signed, 5 x 14 In.	1650.00
Bowl, Centerpiece, Mottled Russet & Brown, Gold Foil Inclusions, Flared, Footed, Signed, 12¼ In.	345.00
Bowl, Centerpiece, Sky Blue, Purple, Footed Base, Signed, 1895, 9 In. ...... 275.00 to 295.00
Bowl, Landscape, Lake, Mountains, Yellow, Boat Shape, Signed, 4¾ In.	1350.00
Box, Cover, Enameled Flowers, Gold Trim, Knob Finial, Signed, c.1910, 3¼ In.	5040.00
Box, Cover, Enameled Flowers, Leaves, Gold Trim, Signed, c.1910, 3 In.	4560.00
Box, Cover, Hydrangea, Dragonflies, Opalescent Ground, Enameled, Gold Trim, c.1900, 3¼ In.	5700.00
Box, Cover, Landscape, Village, Enameled, Gold Trim, c.1900, 2¼ In.	3840.00
Box, Dome Lid, Blackbirds, Enameled, Cameo, c.1910, 3¾ In.	8400.00
Box, Pink & Purple Fuchsia Blossoms On Vines, Round Cover, Cameo, 2⅝ x 4¼ In. ....*illus*	2760.00
Ceiling Light, Cameo Glass, Grapes, Leaves, Wrought Iron, 3 Chains, c.1905, 15½ In.	5040.00
Compote, Landscape, Trees, Lake, Green, Round Foot, Mottled Yellow, Red Ground, 4¾ In.	3500.00
Cordial, Green, Gold Mistletoe, Cameo, Signed, 2 In.	316.00
Cordial Set, Clear, Black Accents, Round Tray, Decanter, 6 Cordials, 8 Piece	234.00
Decanter, Fleur-De-Lis Shape Cut Stopper, 11½ x 5¼ In.	850.00
Ewer, Fall Leaves, Amethyst & Yellow Berries, Mottled Green, Branch Handle, 11 In.	8338.00
Ewer, Green Flowers, Pointed Spout, Cameo, c.1910, 9¼ In.	9000.00
Figurine, Elephant, Lucy, Seated	775.00
Figurine, Owl, Blue, Textured, Signed, c.1925, 9¼ In.	588.00
Figurine, Owl, Clear, Inverted Bead Eyes, Signed, 8¼ x 4½ In.	398.00
Figurine, Peacock, Blue Green, Textured, Signed, c.1925, 13¾ In.	1763.00
Goblet, Blue Spatter, Hollow Stem, Cobalt Blue, Internally Painted, 5¾ x 3 In.	170.00
Ice Bucket, Tsar Nicholas II Coronation, Silver Mounted, Enameled, Gold Trim, c.1896, 4 In.	7200.00
Inkwell, Cover, Mottled Glass, Applied Insect, c.1915, 4¾ In.	3120.00
Inkwell, Red Orchids, 2 Spider Webs, Amethyst To Yellow, Cameo, Signed, 4½ In.	2185.00
Jar, Cover, Crimson Stemmed Flowers, Frosted, Cameo, Signed, 8 In.	881.00
Jar, Dome Lid, Blackbirds, Enameled, Cameo, c.1910, 4½ In.	9600.00
Jar, Enameled Flowers, Gold Trim, Dark Rose, Rectangular Stopper, Signed, c.1905, 4 In., Pair	7800.00

D'Argental, Vase, Grapes, Leaves, Yellow Shaded To Red Shaded To Brown Ground, 13½ In. $920.00

Daum, Bird, Toucan, Amber Pate-De-Verre Beak, 10 In. $777.00

Daum, Box, Pink & Purple Fuchsia Blossoms On Vines, Round Cover, Cameo, 2⅝ x 4¼ In. $2760.00

Daum, Lamp, Sailboats, Brown Shaded To Yellow Green, Domed Shade, Bronze Foot, 18½ In.
$7170.00

Daum History

Cut and enameled glass, often with heraldic crests, was made by Daum at first. In 1885 Daum's sons Auguste (1853–1909) and Antonin (1864–1930) introduced art nouveau-style pâte-de-verre and cameo glass. Pieces were decorated with flowers, landscapes, and other natural forms. In 1900 Daum joined Emile Gallé and Louis Majorelle to found the École de Nancy. Daum started making free-form clear glass in the 1950s. It reintroduced pâte-de-verre glass in 1966, using contemporary designs. Daum glass is still being made.

Daum, Perfume Bottle, Pink, Gold Fleur-De-Lis, Etched Stopper, Gold Trim, 9½ In.
$2875.00

Jar, Enameled Flowers, Round Stopper, Signed, c.1905, 4¾ In., Pair 9600.00
Jar, Mushroom, Stopper, Enameled, Cameo, c.1910, 5¼ In. 3840.00
Lamp, Etched, Vertical Ribs, Zigzag Borders, Frosted, Iron Mount, Art Deco, c.1930, 19 In. 5100.00
Lamp, Sailboats, Brown Shaded To Yellow Green, Domed Shade, Bronze Foot, 18½ In. ..*illus* 7170.00
Lamp Shade, Mottled Orange, Egg Shape, 6½ In. 200.00
Open Salt, Spoon, Clear, France, 2½ In., 8 Sets 234.00
Paperweight, Frog, Green, 2½ In. 239.00
Perfume Bottle, Pink, Gold Fleur-De-Lis, Etched Stopper, Gold Trim, 9½ In. .....*illus* 2875.00
Plate, Relief Molded Portrait, Beethoven, Pate-De-Verre, Amethyst Glass, Signed, 9¾ In. 495.00
Salt, Blue, Summer Scene, Green Silhouetted Trees, Blue Horizon, Oval, Signed, 2 In. 920.00
Salt, Bridge, Tree & Mountains, Bucket Form, Signed, 1¼ In. 520.00
Salt, Clear, 2½ In., 8 Piece 88.00
Salt, Red Sweet Peas, Green Stems, Amethyst Shaded To Amber, Oval, Signed, 2 In. 975.00
Salt, Sailboats, Windmills, Opalescent, 2 Square Handles, 1¼ In. 719.00
Salt, Venetian Scene, Gondola, Sailboat, Oval, Cameo, 1¼ x 2 In. 1900.00
Salt, Winter Scene, Etched, Enameled, Cameo, c.1920, 2 x 1¼ In. 2250.00
Salt, Yellow, Winter Landscape, Snow Covered Trees, Gray Forest, Cameo, Signed, 2 In. 1090.00
Soup, Coupe, Green, Yellow, Pink, Mottled, Etched Vines, Cameo, 11 x 9¾ In. 4130.00
Tumbler, Sailboats Against Foggy Shoreline, Mottled Yellow, 5 In. 1955.00
Vase, Amber, Stylized Leaf & Lines, Etched, Cylindrical, Art Deco, c.1930, 13 In. 2233.00
Vase, Amethyst, Geometric, Circular Foot, Flared Rim, Signed, 7 In. 236.00
Vase, Amethyst, Leaves, Yellow, Green, Textured, Bulbous Stick Shape, Footed, 20 In. 4600.00
Vase, Black Silhouetted Trees, Green & Crimson Sky, Rectangular, Signed, 8½ In. 1725.00
Vase, Blackbird, Enameled, Cameo, 4⅝ In. 5760.00
Vase, Bleeding Heart, Etched, Enameled, Mottled Amber Ground, c.1900, 4½ In. 1800.00
Vase, Burgundy, Black, Enameled Martele, Cameo, c.1905, 15¾ In. 7800.00
Vase, Clear, Flared, Pointed Rim, 8⅛ In. 148.00
Vase, Cover, Landscape, Rainy, Enameled, Cameo, c.1910, 3 In. 5400.00
Vase, Cranberry, Cased Interior, Iron Mount, Geometric Panels, Footed, 12½ In. .....*illus* 2868.00
Vase, Crimson Flowers, Green, Orange, Mottled, Footed, Signed, 8 In. 1775.00
Vase, Crocus, Shaded Purple To Mottled Yellow Ground, Martele, 11¾ In. .....*illus* 28750.00
Vase, Dark Purple, White, Cameo, Signed, c.1905, 3½ In. 2400.00
Vase, Flower, Green, Light Green, Martele, Cameo, c.1910, 14½ In. 9000.00
Vase, Flowering Dogwood, Mottled Crimson Shaded To Yellow, Cameo, 10½ In. 8855.00
Vase, Flowers, Fire Polished, Square, Signed, 7½ In. 1100.00
Vase, Forest, Tall Trees, Mottled Green, Enameled, Cameo, Signed, c.1920, 14 In. 5875.00
Vase, Gold Enameled Flowers, Stems, Signed, c.1910, 10⅞ In. 6600.00
Vase, Green, Gold Speckled Enamel, Art Deco, Signed, 17 In. 1920.00
Vase, Green, Orange, Martele, Cameo, Signed, 5¼ In. 6600.00
Vase, Green, Purple, Light Blue, Enameled, Cameo, Signed, 4 In. 2880.00
Vase, Green Cameo Flowers, Frosted Amber Body, Footed, Gold Enamel, 16 In. 1016.00
Vase, Green Trees, Gray & Amethyst Ground, Elongated, Bottle Shape, Signed, 2¾ In. 1050.00
Vase, Ivy, Motto Frieze, I Die Where I Take Hold, Etched, Gold Enameled, 1890, 11 In. 2400.00
Vase, Lake Scene, Silhouetted Trees, Burnt Orange Sky, Bulbous, Cylindrical Rim, 8¼ In. 1485.00
Vase, Landscape, Autumn, Silhouetted Trees, Tapered, Rolled Foot & Rim, 14 In. 3360.00
Vase, Landscape, Mountain, Green, Orange, Frosted Ground, Cameo, Signed, 13 In. 3480.00
Vase, Landscape, Rain, Wind Blown Trees, Raised Raindrops, Bulbous, Stick, 1 In. 1600.00
Vase, Lily-Of-The-Valley, Blossoms, Leaves, Frosted, Opalescent, Square, 4¾ x 2 In. 750.00
Vase, Mottled Amber, Crimson, Engraved, Bulbous, Cameo, 8½ In. 1495.00
Vase, Mottled Blue, Crimson & Amethyst Orchids, Cameo Cobwebs, Signed, 3½ In. 1955.00
Vase, Mottled Clear, Wrought Iron Mounted, Gold Foil Inclusions, Louis Majorelle, c.1915 ..... 4800.00
Vase, Pillow, Iris, Amethyst Shaded To Powder Blue, 1½ In. 1380.00
Vase, Pillow, Irises, Mottled Amethyst Shaded To Gray, Signed, 4 In. 1438.00
Vase, Pillow, Opalescent Pink, Tall Green Trees, Red Forest, Signed, 1¾ In. 1100.00
Vase, Pillow, White Flowers, Amethyst Ground, 4 x 7 In. .....*illus* 2588.00
Vase, Pond, Egrets, Multicolored, Gold Trim, Mauve Ground, Cameo, c.1890, 8½ In. 7200.00
Vase, Poppies, Cranberry, Brown Leaves, Frosted & Mottled Orange Ground, Footed, 7½ In. ....*illus* 10638.00
Vase, Prairie, Field Of Flowers, Grass, Pink Sky, Flared, 5-Sided Mouth, 7¼ x 5¾ In. ...*illus* 3450.00
Vase, Purple, Acid Etched, Flared Mouth, c.1925, 12 In. 5040.00
Vase, Purple, Red Strawberries, Gold Stems, Signed, 1¾ In. ..... 500.00 to 575.00
Vase, Red Flowers, Green Leaves, Amethyst & Yellow Mottled, Rectangular, 5 In. 1778.00
Vase, Rose Red, Gold Mica Inclusions, Cased Black, 4¾ x 2 In. 1250.00
Vase, Rosehips, Leaves, Green, Red, Orange, Mottled Purple Ground, Cameo, 19¾ x 6 In. 4500.00
Vase, Scarlet Geranium Blossoms, White & Yellow Spangled Ground, 15 In. 2400.00
Vase, Snow-Covered Village, Windmills, Mottled Blue Ground, Rectangular, Cameo, 4¾ In. 3738.00
Vase, Stacked Arches, Oval, Round Foot, Cameo, Signed, 9 In. 353.00

Vase, Stick, Amethyst Mums, Gray, Amber, Enameled, Bulbous, Cameo, Signed, 15 In.	3055.00
Vase, Stick, Blue To Gray, 3 Blackbirds On Winter Tree, Bulbous, Signed, 3 In.	520.00
Vase, Stick, Blue To Gray, Summer Scene, Green Pasture, Bulbous, Signed, 3 In.	1265.00
Vase, Stick, Crimson Tobacco Flowers, Yellow Ground, Footed, Cameo, Signed, 12¼ In.	2585.00
Vase, Stick, Rain Scene, Windblown Trees, Bulbous, Signed, 1 In.	1840.00
Vase, Stick, Swan, Gray & Green Trees, Bulbous, Cameo, 3 In.	2760.00
Vase, Summer Trees, Green, Crimson Opalescent, Yellow, Broken Egg, Signed, 2 In.	1380.00
Vase, Sunflowers, Martele, Gold Leaves, Streaked Red Ground, c.1900, 15¾ In.	3480.00
Vase, Tall Pine Trees, Orange Lake, Mountains, Oval, Footed, Cameo, 15 In.	2990.00
Vase, Teal, Art Deco Fuchsias, Frosted Mottled, 9½ In.	1093.00
Vase, Thistle, Autumn Palette, Frosted Opalescent Ground, Baluster, Signed, 16¾ In.	7200.00
Vase, Windblown Trees In The Rain, Rectangular, Cameo, 4¾ In.	5750.00
Vase, Windmill Shoreline, Ships, Frosted, Textured, Gray, Oval, Folded Rim, Cameo, 2¾ In.	805.00
Vase, Winter Woods, Yellow Orange Sky, Bulbous, Wide Mouth, Cameo, 4 In.	3000.00
Vase, Yellow, Red, Brown Overlay, Trees, Boats, Internally Decorated, c.1900, 4½ x 7 In.	872.00

DAVENPORT pottery and porcelain were made at the Davenport factory in Longport, Staffordshire, England, from 1793 to 1887. Earthenwares, creamwares, porcelains, ironstone, and other ceramics were made. Most of the pieces are marked with a form of the word *Davenport*.

DAVENPORT
LONGPORT
STAFFORDSHIRE

Bowl, Vegetable, Base, Alpine Amusement, Blue Transfer, Staffordshire, 3 x 9½ x 12¾ In.	176.00
Platter, Blue Printed, Landscape, Leaf & Vine Border, Oval, 1810-15, 22 In.	385.00
Platter, Montreal Well & Tree, Blue & White, c.1835, 18 In.	516.00

DAVY CROCKETT, the American frontiersman, was born in 1786 and died in 1836. The historical character gained new fame in 1954 when the Walt Disney television show ran a series of episodes featuring Fess Parker as Davy Crockett. Coonskin caps and buckskins became popular and hundreds of different Davy Crockett items were made.

DAVY CROCKETT
CONGRESSMAN

Bandanna, Scenic, Black & Red, Printed, 16⅝ x 17⅛ In.	20.00
Cookie Jar, Gold Luster, Embossed Name At Collar, Regal China, 1955, 11½ In.	280.00
Cookie Jar, Marked, Brush, c.1956, 10¼ In.	425.00
Doll, Cloth, Coonskin Hat, Moccasins, Hallmark, Original Tag, 1979, 7 In.	16.00
Doll, Plastic, Accessories, Box, 1950s, 8 In.	140.00
Frontier Wagon, Covered, Tin, Friction, 5¼ x 2½ In.	250.00
Glass, When Davy Met An Indian Foe, Yellow, Brown & Orange, 5¼ In.	10.00
Label, Bread End, Ballad Of Davy Crockett, Waxed Paper, c.1955, 2 In., 16 Piece	280.00
Movie Poster, King Of The Wild Frontier, Buena Vista, 1955, 27 x 41 In.	489.00
Mug, Anchor Hocking Fire-King, Red, Signed	35.00
Mug, Hazel Atlas, 3 In.	15.00
Pencil Pouch, Frontierland, Starring Fess Parker, Pencil Sharpener, 8 x 4 In.	26.00
Pin, Davy Crockett, Indian Fighter, Big Yank, Lithograph, c.1955, 1⅜ In.	31.00
Pin, Davy Crockett, Indian Scout, Lafayette Theatre, Now Playing, 1950, 1¼ In.	61.00
Plate, Legends Of The West Perillo, Signed, Vague Shadows, 1981, 10¼ In.	54.00
Plate, Parian, 1984, 8½ In.	24.00
Powder Horn, Official, Plastic, Daisy, Box, c.1955, 7 In.	246.00 to 312.00
Record, Ballad, Little Golden Record, Disney, Sandpipers, Mitch Miller, 7½ x 6¾ In.	20.00
Ring, Brass, Crossed Rifles, Powder Horn, Adjustable Bands, c.1955	31.00
Sheet Music, Ballad Of Davy Crockett, Fess Parker, c.1954	15.00
Tie Bar, Original Box, c.1957	23.00
Toy, Horse, Play, Cardboard, Die Cut, 2-Sided, Pied Piper, Box, 1950s, 25 x 18 In.	168.00
Wristwatch, Bradley Time, Box, c.1956, 2½ x 4 x 5½ In.	1491.00

DE MORGAN art pottery was made in England by William De Morgan from the 1860s to 1907. He is best known for his luster-glazed Moorish-inspired pieces. The pottery used a variety of marks.

Bowl, Ruby Luster, Ibex, Tulip Border, Charles Passenger, Wedgwood Blank, 10 In.	4700.00
Bowl, Ruby Luster, Viking Ship At Sea, Charles Passenger, c.1885, 7½ In.	2938.00
Compote, Dragon Center, Leaf & Berry Design, Blue Luster Glaze, Marked, Fred Passenger, 3 x 9 In.	6450.00
Dish, Ruby Luster, Fish Border, Cherub, Charles Passenger, Wedgwood Blank, 9¼ In.	3819.00
Plaque, Stylized Flowers, Luster Glaze, Impressed, Charles Passenger, 9 In.	1910.00
Tile, Fish, Ruby Luster, Wood Frame, c.1885, 6 In.	1293.00

DE VEZ was a signature used on cameo glass after 1910. E. S. Monot founded the glass company near Paris in 1851. The company changed names many times. Mt. Joye, another glass by this factory, is listed in its own category.

de Vez

D

Daum, Vase, Cranberry, Cased Interior, Iron Mount, Geometric Panels, Footed, 12½ In.
$2868.00

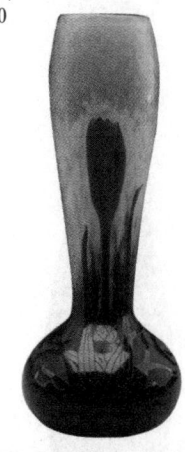

Daum, Vase, Crocus, Shaded Purple To Mottled Yellow Ground, Martele, 11¾ In.
$28750

Daum, Vase, Pillow, White Flowers, Amethyst Ground, 4 x 7 In.
$2588.00

Daum, Vase, Poppies, Cranberry, Brown Leaves, Frosted & Mottled Orange Ground, Footed, 7½ In.
$10638.00

Daum, Vase, Prairie, Field Of Flowers, Grass, Pink Sky, Flared, 5-Sided Mouth, 7¼ x 5¾ In.
$3450.00

De Vez, Vase, Egyptian Scene, Pyramids, Palm Trees, Lake, Sailboats, Camphor Ground, Tapered, 9½ In.
$420.00

Decorated Tumbler, Game Bird, Pheasant, Milk Glass, Federal, 5 In.
$8.00

Decorated Tumbler, Geese Cattails, Forest Green, Anchor Hocking, 5¼ In.
$10.00

Perfume Bottle, Cameo, Mountain Lake Scene, Yellow, Orange, Brown, Citrine, 6 In. 1350.00
Perfume Bottle, Mountain Lake Scene, Signed, 6 In. 1340.00
Vase, Amber, Vertical Ribs, Teal Green Overlay, Carved, Butterflies, Flowers, 7¾ In. 1200.00
Vase, Blue & Pink, Flying Ducks, Bottle Shape, Signed, 4½ In. 575.00
Vase, Blue Palm Trees, Mountains, Pink & Yellow Sky, Bulbous Stick Shape, 6 In. 431.00
Vase, Bud, Decorated, Raised & Cut Pink Flowers, White Satin Glass, Signed, c.1910 1400.00
Vase, Egyptian Scene, Pyramids, Palm Trees, Lake, Sailboats, Camphor Ground, Tapered, 9½ In. *illus* 420.00
Vase, Etching, Wheel Carved, Landscape, Seated Woman, 7 In. 764.00
Vase, Stick, Brown Flowering Vines Over Green & Blue Lake Scene, Footed, 7½ In. 431.00
Vase, Vertically Ribbed, Amber, Butterflies & Flowers, Signed, 8 In. 1200.00

DECORATED TUMBLERS have been made by Anchor Hocking, Federal, Hazel Atlas, Libbey, and other companies since the 1930s, when the pyroglaze process of printing was introduced. The barware and other glasses feature drinking jokes, characters, or decorative geometric patterns. Swankyswigs are listed in their own category. Decorated tumblers may also be listed in Advertising, Coca-Cola, Pepsi-Cola, and many other categories.

Carnation, Gold Trim, Hazel Atlas, 9 Oz., 5 In. 7.00
Chris. Schmidt, Lager Beer, Etched Glass, Belle Plaine, Minn. 1025.00
Coin, Frosted, Black, Gold, Deco, 5 In. 3.00
Deco Gold & Black Star, Federal, 5¾ In. 2.00
Deco Gold & Black Star, Federal, 6¾ In. 3.00
Flowers & Stripes, Orange, White, Blue, 9½ Oz. 12.50
Game Bird, Canada Goose, Milk Glass, Federal, 5 In. 8.00
Game Bird, Grouse, Milk Glass, Federal, 5 In. 8.00
Game Bird, Pheasant, Milk Glass, Federal, 5 In. *illus* 8.00
Game Bird, Quail, Milk Glass, Federal, 5 In. 8.00
Geese Cattails, Forest Green, Anchor Hocking, 5¼ In. *illus* 10.00
Green Hornet, Mike Axford, Golden Jersey Milk Co., c.1938, 4¾ In. 678.00
Green Hornet, WXYZ 7:30 PM, Golden Jersey Milk Co., c.1938, 4¾ In. 448.00
Hellenic, Blue, Ribbed, Jasperware Decal, Jeannette, 5 In. 6.50
Hellenic, Gold Trim, White Classic Greek Figures, Green Ground, Jeannette, 5 In. 9.00
Hoe Down, Forest Green, Anchor Hocking, 5¼ In. 16.00
Horse Car, Royal Ruby, 13½ Oz., 5 In. 14.00
Milano, Anchor Hocking, 6¾ In. 9.00
New Years, Federal, 4¾ In. 6.50
Open Sleigh, Forest Green, 6¾ In. 16.00
Partners All, Forest Green, Anchor Hocking, 5¼ In. 16.00
Scottie Dog, Red Bands, 4½ In. 8.00
Thistle, Federal, 4¾ In. 4.00

DECOYS are carved or turned wooden copies of birds, fish, or animals. The decoy was placed in the water or propped on the shore to lure flying birds to the pond for hunters. Some decoys are handmade; some are commercial products. Today there is a group of artists making modern decoys for display, not for use in a pond.

Black Duck, Carved, Painted, Wood, Glass Eyes, Ken Harris, N.Y., 5⅝ x 15 In. 353.00
Black Duck, Mason Premier Grade, Repaint, 17¼ In. 198.00
Bluebill Drake, Tack Eye, Old Repaint, 13¾ In. 110.00
Bluebill Hen, Hollow Body, Old Repaint, 11½ In. 341.00
Blue-Winged Teal Drake, Mason Detroit Grade, Painted, 11¾ In. 2090.00
Brant, Hollow Body, Old Repaint, Barneget Bay, N.J., 16¼ In. 154.00
Brant, Hollow Body, Painted, 17½ In. 28600.00
Bufflehead Hen, Mason Detroit Grade, Repaint, 11½ In. 330.00
Canada Goose, Black, White, Old Repaint, Signed, Ward Brothers, Crisfield, Md., 1936, 23½ In. 8800.00
Canada Goose, Carved, Head Features, Painted, Wood, Mid 20th Century, 11 x 24 In. 411.00
Canada Goose, Carved, Preening, Painted, Glass Eyes, Stand On Iron Legs, 32 x 18 In. 690.00
Canvasback Drake, Mason Detroit Grade, 16 In. 110.00
Canvasback Drake, Mason Premier Grade, 19¾ In. 132.00
Canvasback Drake, Old Repaint, Attributed To Wash Barnes, 15 In. 330.00
Canvasback Drake, Susquehanna River, Repaint, c.1930, 17½ In. 176.00
Canvasback Hen, Old Repaint, Attributed To Bill Heverin, L. Pannock, 15¼ In. 467.00
Canvasback Hen, Old Repaint, Attributed To Wash Barnes, 15 In. 577.00
Coot, Original Paint, Signed, R. Madison Mitchell, 1962, 12 In. 275.00
Curlew Shorebird, Balsa, Original Paint, Metal Beak & Legs, 14 In. 385.00
Duck, Carved, Painted, Applied Glass Bead Eyes, Early 1900s, 5½ x 11½ In. 118.00
Duck, Home Made, Milk Carton, Applied Painted Canvas, Wood, Reed Wrapped, 12 In. 69.00
Duck, Merganser, Painted, Canvas Stretched, Glass Eye, Frame, Wood Base, 23 In. 7200.00

Fish, Blue Gill, Spearing, Painted, Signed, Bud Stewart, 5½ In.	193.00
Fish, Brook Trout, Chuck Vogel, 12 In.	248.00
Fish, Brown, Painted, Wood, Leather Tail, Glass Eyes, Lake Chautauqua, c.1910, 8½ In.	522.00
Fish, Carp, A.J. Downey, 11 In. ....*illus*	403.00
Fish, Flowers, Green, Red, White Flowers, Hinkley, Minn., Leroy Howell, 6½ In.	963.00
Fish, Folk Art, Pale Blue, Green, White Pattern, Frank Mizra, 9¼ In.	1980.00
Fish, Glass Eyes, Open Mouth, Signed, Bud Stewart, 4½ In.	254.00
Fish, Golden Shiner, Painted Eyes, Oscar Peterson, 6½ In.	440.00
Fish, Green & Yellow Paint, Red Mouth & Gills, Tack Eyes, Lake Chautauqua, 7 In.	560.00
Fish, Lumberjack, Otto Bishop, Signed, 13½ In.	28.00
Fish, Orange & Black, Frank Mizra, 7½ In.	193.00
Fish, Paddletail, Daugherty, 12 In.	59.00
Fish, Painted, Wood, Copper & Yellow, Metal Fins & Tail, Kenneth Bruning, 6 In.	1180.00
Fish, Painted, Wood, Metal Fins & Tail, William Faue, 7 In.	742.00
Fish, Perch, Painted, Andy Trombley, 1950s, 9 In.	2596.00
Fish, Pike, Painted, Bud Stewart, 7 In.	206.00
Fish, Rainbow Trout, Painted Wood, Kenneth Bruning, 6¾ In.	2200.00
Fish, Shiner, Natural Finish, Burned-In Scales, Lac Du Flambeau, Wis., Ross Allen Sr., 6¾ In.	259.00
Fish, Smallmouth Bass, Flitter Finish, Signed, Bud Stewart, 1980s, 7½ In.	165.00
Fish, Snake, Jointed, Signed, Bud Stewart, 13 In.	207.00
Fish, Spearing, Bass, Painted, Glitter, Bud Stewart, 8½ In.	177.00
Fish, Spearing, Coldwater, Mich., O.A. Turner, 1920s	110.00
Fish, Sturgeon, Blue & Yellow Sucker, Boyne City, Mich., Cal Deming, 23¾ In.	1035.00
Fish, Sunfish, Glass Eyes, Painted, Lead Weights, Bud Stewart, 5½ In.	177.00
Fish, Sunfish, Metal Fins, Neenah, Wis., Lou Schifferl, 9 In.	230.00
Fish, Trout, Mark Bruning, 12 In.	144.00
Fish, Trout, Paw Paw, Tack Eyes, 7½ In.	460.00
Fish, Turtle, Painted, Signed, Bud Stewart, 6 In.	678.00
Fish, Walleye, Painted, Metal Fins, Lead Weights, Oscar Peterson, 7½ In.	1180.00
Fish, Walleye, Signed DW, Michigan, Dennis Wolf, 12 In.	248.00
Fish, White Eyes, Painted, Signed, Bud Stewart, 7 In.	193.00
Goldeneye Drake, Old Repaint, Lebouf Quebec, 13¼ In.	176.00
Goose, Old Repaint, Signed, Crisfield, Md., L.T. Ward, 1939, 24½ In.	19250.00
Goose, Original Paint, Signed, Havre-De-Grace, Md., R. Madison Mitchell, 1956, 24¼ In.	523.00
Goose, Tack Eye, Hollow Body, Old Repaint, Barneget Bay, N.J., 23 In.	578.00
Hooded Merganser, Painted, Glass Eye, Vermont, Brent Borden, 1979, 13½ In. ...*illus*	540.00
Mallard Drake, Original Paint, Attributed To Pratt, 15¾ In.	254.00
Merganser, Green Head, Orange Bill, Old Repaint, 19 In.	204.00
Merganser, Painted Eyes, Leather Crest, 5⅞ x 18 In.	881.00
Owl, Wood, Carved, Painted, Slats, Steel & Leather Mounts, Hanging, 27 In.	2070.00
Peep, Shorebird, Yellow Legs, Carved Wing Detail, Original Paint, 7 In.	660.00
Pintail Drake, Signed, 1948 Lem & Steve Ward, Repainted, 1972 By Lem, 16¾ In.	2530.00
Pintail Drake, Traces Of Old Paint, 16 In.	797.00
Quail, Tin, Multicolored, Voice Box, 10 In.	550.00
Red-Breasted Merganser, 16 In.	144.00
Red-Breasted Merganser, 17 In.	633.00
Redhead Drake, H.V. Shourds, New Jersey ...*illus*	720.00
Redhead Drake, Ward Brothers, 16 In.	5463.00
Redhead Hen, Madison Mitchell, 1972, 15 In.	403.00
Redhead Hen, W. Minto Jr., 16 In.	231.00
Robin Snipe Shorebird, Old Repaint, Mounted To Wood Block, 7¾ In.	880.00
Root Head Stick Up Duck, Old Repaint, Eastern Shore Of Virginia, c.1910, 11¾ In.	176.00
Shorebird, Brown, Black Dots, Original Paint, T. Rogers, 10½ In.	797.00
Shorebird, Old Paint, Mounted To Wood Block, c.1910, 10 In.	552.00
Spearing, Newt, Red Spots, Easton, Pa., Jon Sahl, 5 In.	92.00
Swan, White Paint, Tack Eyes, Horseshoe Weight, Early 1900s, 24 x 9 x 18 In.	450.00
Victor Dove, Papier-Mache, Clothespin Clip, Original Paint, 8½ In.	28.00
Widgeon Drake, Raised Carved Wing Feathers, Patrick R. Godin, 16 In. ...*illus*	345.00
Wood Duck, Painted, Woodville, N.Y., Ken Harris, 12½ In. ...*illus*	978.00
Yellow Leg Shorebird, Original Paint, H.V. Shourds, 8¾ In.	8800.00

DEDHAM Pottery was started in 1895. Chelsea Keramic Art Works was established in 1872 in Chelsea, Massachusetts, by members of the Robertson family. The factory closed in 1889 and was reorganized as the Chelsea Pottery U.S. in 1891. The firm used the marks *CKAW* and *CPUS*. It became the Dedham Pottery of Dedham, Massachusetts. The factory closed in 1943. It was famous for its crackleware dishes, which picture blue outlines of animals, flowers, and other natural motifs. Pottery by Chelsea Keramic Art Works and Dedham Pottery are listed here.

Decoy, Fish, Carp,
A.J. Downey, 11 In.
$403.00

Decoy, Hooded Merganser, Painted,
Glass Eye, Vermont, Brent Borden,
1979, 13½ In.
$540.00

Decoy, Redhead Drake, H.V. Shourds,
New Jersey
$720.00

Decoy, Widgeon Drake, Raised Carved
Wing Feathers, Patrick R. Godin, 16 In.
$345.00

Decoy, Wood Duck, Painted, Woodville,
N.Y., Ken Harris, 12½ In.
$978.00

Dedham, Elephant, Dish,
Child's, Stamped, 7½ In.
$960.00

Dedham, Polar Bear, Plate, Stamped, 10 In. $480.00

Chelsea and Dedham Marks

The Monogram for Chelsea Keramic Art Works or the name Chelsea Keramic Art Works, Robertson & Sons was used from about 1875 to 1889.

A cloverleaf with the initials CPUS was used from 1891 to 1895.

 Dedham Pottery mark (1895-1932)

 Dedham Pottery mark (1896-1943)

Dedham, Poppy, Plate, Stamped, 6¼ In. $480.00

Dedham, Rabbit, Coffeepot, Cobalt Stamp, 7 x 9 In. $720.00

Birds In Orange Tree, Plate, Impressed, 1895, 8½ In.	257.00
Clover, Plate, Embossed, 8½ In.	400.00
Crab, 2, Plate, Indigo, Impressed Stamps, 8¾ In.	1680.00
Crab, Plate, 3 Crabs, 8¾ In.	1400.00
Crab, Plate, Seaweed, 8½ In.	1000.00
Crab, Plate, Seaweed, Indigo Stamp, 8½ In.	1140.00 to 1200.00
Crab, Plate, Waves, Marked, 5⅞ In.	295.00
Day & Night, Pitcher, Handle, Rooster On Side, Rabbit Mark, 5 In.	440.00
Day & Night, Pitcher, Rooster, Chickens, Owl, Refief, 5¼ In.	353.00
Dolphin, Plate, 8½ In.	400.00 to 850.00
Dolphin, Plate, 8¾ In.	1500.00
Dolphin, Plate, Indigo, Impressed Stamps, 8¾ In.	1800.00
Duck, Cup & Saucer	264.00
Duck, Plate, Marked, 8½ In.	115.00
Elephant, Dish, Child's, Stamped, 7½ In. _illus_	960.00
Elephant, Plate, 6½ In.	600.00
Elephant, Plate, Child's, 7¾ In.	750.00 to 1100.00
Elephant, Plate, Cobalt Stamp, Rabbit Die Stamp, 6½ In.	720.00
Flower Border, Plate, Unglazed, CPUS, 8½ In.	118.00
Goat & Putti, Plate, Rabbit Mark, 1929, 9 In.	575.00 to 585.00
Grape, Bowl, Rabbit Mark, 1929, 9 In.	210.00
Horse Chestnut, Nappie, Pre 1929 Mark, 6 In.	72.00
Lion Tapestry, Plate, 8½ In.	850.00
Magnolia, Plate, Marked, 10 In.	190.00
Mushroom, Plate, 8½ In.	800.00
Mushroom, Plate, Deep, 8½ In.	500.00
Mushroom, Plate, Indigo, Impressed Stamp, 8½ In.	600.00
Mushroom, Plate, Pink Overglaze, Indigo, Impressed Stamp, 8½ In.	960.00
Pineapple, Plate, Alternating With Raised Flowers, 8½ In.	400.00
Pineapple, Plate, Rabbit Die Stamp, 8½ In.	480.00
Pineapple, Plate, Raised, Impressed Cloverleaf, 10 In.	1080.00
Polar Bear, Plate, 8½ In.	450.00
Polar Bear, Plate, 10 In.	400.00 to 1500.00
Polar Bear, Plate, Stamped, 10 In. _illus_	480.00
Polar Bear, Plate, Indigo, 10 In.	1800.00
Polar Bear, Plate, Marked, 8¼ In.	378.00
Pond Lily, Plate, Marked, 10 In.	115.00
Poppy, Plate, 8½ In.	600.00
Poppy, Plate, Center Poppy, Cobalt & Rabbit Die Stamp, 6¼ In.	480.00
Poppy, Plate, Central Poppy, Poppy Pod Border, 6¼ In.	400.00
Poppy, Plate, Stamped, 6¼ In. _illus_	480.00
Poppy, Plate, Marked, 8½ In.	400.00
Rabbit, Charger, Maud Davenport, 12 In.	400.00
Rabbit, Clockwise, Charger, Maud Davenport, 12¼ In.	480.00
Rabbit, Cockwise, Coffeepot, Cobalt Stamp, 7 x 9 In.	720.00
Rabbit, Coffeepot, Cover, 7 x 9 In.	600.00
Rabbit, Coffeepot, Cobalt Stamp, 7 x 9 In. _illus_	720.00
Rabbit, Mixing Bowl, Blue Ink Stamp, 4 x 9 In.	115.00
Rabbit, Mug, Blue Ink Stamp, 4¼ In.	219.00
Rabbit, Plate, 1 Ear, 8½ In. _illus_	104.00
Rabbit, Plate, Soup, Indigo, Impressed, 3, 9¼ In.	780.00
Rabbit, Salt & Pepper, Bulbous, Blue Ink Stamp, 2⅝ In.	142.00
Rabbit, Sugar & Creamer, Blue Ink Stamp, 3 In.	380.00
Rabbit, Teapot, Blue & White, Marked, c.1932, 4½ In.	470.00
Swan, Cup & Saucer	470.00
Tapestry Lion, Plate, Indigo, 1968, 8¼ In.	2040.00
Tapestry Lion, Plate, Raised Lion, Moon, Leaves, 8¼ In.	1700.00
Turkey, Plate, 9¾ In.	230.00
Turtle, Plate, 6¼ In.	550.00
Turtle, Plate, 8½ In.	1900.00 to 2280.00
Turtle, Plate, Cobalt Stamp, Rabbit Die Stamp, 6¼ In.	660.00
Vase, Amber & Cobalt Blue Flambe Glaze, 6 x 4 In.	780.00
Vase, Baluster, Brown Glossy Flambe Glaze, Hugh Robertson, 10 x 6 In.	960.00
Vase, Baluster, Experimental, White & Beige Drip Glaze, Green Ground, 8½ x 4½ In.	2880.00
Vase, Brown & Green Thick Glaze, Baluster, Experimental, Robertson, 8½ x 4½ In.	2000.00
Vase, Brown, Green Glaze, 8½ x 4½ In.	2400.00
Vase, Brown Flambe Glaze, Baluster, Experimental, Hugh Robertson, 10 x 6 In.	1200.00

Vase, Green & Blue Thick Mottled Glaze, Bulbous, Robertson, 7 x 4 In.	1920.00
Vase, Green, Amber, White Volcanic Glaze, Experimental, Robertson, c.1900, 11 x 5½ In.	3750.00
Vase, Green, Oxblood Drip Glaze, Early 1900s, 11 In.	5581.00
Vase, Green Drip Glaze, White & Blue Base, 7 x 4 In.	1080.00
Vase, Green Opaque Drip Glaze, White Orange Peel Ground, 6 x 4½ In.	2040.00
Vase, Khaki Green Over Blue & Green Glaze, H. Robertson, 7¾ x 5 In.	1440.00
Vase, Mahogany & Oxblood Flambe, Experimental, Hugh Robertson, 8 x 6 In.	2300.00
Vase, Mahogany & Oxblood Flambe Glaze, H. Robertson, 8 x 6 In.	2760.00
Vase, Mottled Brown, Green, Volcanic Glaze, 8 x 6 In.	2400.00
Vase, Mottled Forest Green & Blue, Bulbous, Experimental, Robertson, 7¼ x 4¼ In.	1600.00

DEGENHART is the name used by collectors for the products of the Crystal Art Glass Company of Cambridge, Ohio. John and Elizabeth Degenhart started the glassworks in 1947. Quality paperweights and other glass objects were made. John died in 1964 and his wife took over management and production ideas. Over 145 colors of glass were made. In 1978, after the death of Mrs. Degenhart, the molds were sold. The D in a heart trademark was removed, so collectors can easily recognize the true Degenhart piece.

Bell, Liberty, Bicentennial, Blue, Opalescent, 1776-1976	18.00
Bell, Liberty, Bicentennial, Chocolate, 1776-1976	15.00
Bell, Liberty, Bicentennial, Pale Blue Opalescent, 1776-1976	14.00
Bell, Liberty, Bicentennial, Pink Opalescent, 1776-1976	14.00 to 18.00
Figurine, Owl On Books, Amber, 3½ In.	46.00
Figurine, Owl On Books, Bernard Boyd's Ebony, 3½ In.	74.00
Figurine, Owl On Books, Dark Chocolate Slag	10.00
Figurine, Owl On Books, Old Ivory Slag, c.1981	21.00
Figurine, Owl On Books, Pink Champagne Satin, c.1979	18.00
Figurine, Pooch, Sapphire Blue, 3 x 2½ x 1¾ In.	20.00
Figurine, Shoe With Cat, Amber, Marked, D Inside Heart, 3 x 5¾ In. . . . . *illus*	5.00
Mug, Stork & Peacock, Milk Glass, c.1972, Child's	18.00
Mug, Stork & Peacock, Pink, c.1972, Child's	18.00
Salt, Bird, Holding Cherry, Blue Milk Glass, c.1890-1911, 3 x 1½ In.	15.00 to 20.00
Salt, Bird, Holding Cherry, Ivory	25.00
Shoe, Baby, Vaseline	25.00
Slipper, Daisy & Button Pattern, Carmel Slag, c.1968	30.00
Slipper, Vaseline, 1970s	39.00
Toothpick, Bird, Amber, 1970s	10.00
Toothpick, Bird, Pink, 1970s	8.00 to 10.00
Toothpick, Forget-Me-Not, Milk Blue, 1970s	38.00
Toothpick, Forget-Me-Not, Toffee	43.00
Toothpick, Gypsy Pot, Cobalt Blue	25.00
Toothpick, Gypsy Pot, Honey Amber	16.00 to 20.00
Toothpick, Sweetheart, Beaded Heart, Jade Green	8.00
Toothpick, Sweetheart, Toffee Slag	45.00
Toothpick, Sweetheart, White, c.1968	30.00

DEGUE is a signature acid-etched on pieces of French glass made in the early 1900s. Cameo, mold blown, and smooth glass with contrasting colored rims are the types most often found.

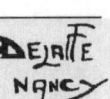

Vase, Bulbous, Red, Black, Wide Mouth, White Transparent Drape, Marked, c.1932, 16 In.	353.00
Vase, Fern Fronds, Brown, Urn Form, Signed, c.1932, 15¼ In.	1058.00
Vase, Mottled White, Purple Cased In Clear, Metal Mount, Wrought Iron, 14 x 16 In.	2000.00
Vase, Sunflowers, Orange Shaded To Brown, Mottled Pink Ground, Cameo, 18 In.	1058.00
Vase, White To Green, Blue Ground, Geometric, Tapered, Flared Rim, Cameo, 13½ In.	1116.00

DELATTE glass is a French cameo glass made by Andre Delatte. It was first made in Nancy, France, in 1921. Lighting fixtures and opaque glassware in imitation of Bohemian opaline were made. There were many French cameo glassmakers, so be sure to look in other appropriate categories.

Bowl, Centerpiece, Inside Decoration, Lilac Center, Amethyst-Footed Base, Signed, 3 x 14 In.	1250.00
Bowl, Centerpiece, Lilac Design, Amethyst-Footed, Signed, 3⅜ x 13¾ In.	1250.00
Bowl, Cinnamon Opalescent, Amethyst Band, Art Deco Flowers, Footed, Cameo, 12 In.	920.00
Vase, Pink, Fire-Polished Burgundy Flowers & Buds, Footed, 9¼ In. . . . . *illus*	1035.00
Vase, Pink & Mauve, Toadstool & Leaf Design, Signed	475.00

DELDARE, *see Buffalo Pottery Deldare.*

Dedham, Rabbit, Plate, 1 Ear, 8½ In. $104.00

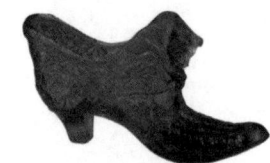

Degenhart, Figurine, Shoe With Cat, Amber, Marked, D Inside Heart, 3 x 5¾ In. $5.00

Delatte, Vase, Pink, Fire-Polished Burgundy Flowers & Buds, Footed, 9¼ In. $1035.00

Delft, Charger, Blue & White Floral Panels, 18th Century, 14 In. $288.00

Delft, Figurine, Horse, Standing, Right Leg Raised, Cold Paint, Canted Base, Mid 18th Century, 4¾ In. $1080.00

Delft, Plaque, Wall, Oval, Enamel, Figures Before Harbor, Blue, Green, Puce, 19th Century, 15½ In. $264.00

DELFT is a tin-glazed pottery that has been made since the seventeenth century. Delft was made in England in the eighteenth century. It is decorated with blue on white or with colored decorations. Most of the pieces sold today were made after 1891, and the name *Holland* usually appears with the Delft factory marks. The word *Delft* appears alone on some inexpensive twentieth- and twenty-first-century pottery from Asia and Germany that is also listed here.

Ashtray, Blue & White, Windmill, 3¾ In.	20.00
Ashtray, Shell Shape, Painted, Flowers, 5 In.	20.00
Ashtray, Wooden Shoe Shape, Blue & White, Flowers, 1950s, 5 x 2 In.	20.00
Ashtray, Wooden Shoe Shape, Windmill Scene, 2½ x 5 In.	13.00
Ashtray, Wooden Shoes, 3⅞ In.	10.00
Bell, Blue & White, Windmill Scene, Glass Bead Clapper, 3 In.	25.00
Bottle, Stopper, Blue & White, Windmill, House, Dike, Flowers, 11 In.	25.00
Bowl, Blue, White, Fluted, c.1740	495.00
Bowl, Blue & White, Landscape, 1682, 8⅝ In.	5850.00
Bowl, Multicolored, Landscapes, Mountains, Urn Mounted Pedestal, Yellow, Blue, Red, 6 x 12 In.	4830.00
Box, Lid, Windmill, Blue & White, 3-Sided, ⅞ x 1⅛ In.	29.00
Brick, Blue & White, Paneled Sides, Flowers, Birds, Mid 18th Century, 6½ In., Pair	2115.00
Candleholder, Aladdin Shape, Flowers, Windmill, 7 x 3¼ In.	40.00
Candleholder, Windmill, Blue & White, 4½ In., Pair	25.00
Candy Dish, Leaf Shape, Painted, Gold Rim, Holland	13.00
Charger, Blue, Central Urn, Flowers, Feathers, Fruit, Scrolled Edge, 13½ In.	1322.00
Charger, Blue, Flowers, 13⅝ In.	345.00
Charger, Blue & White, Kraak Style, 18th Century, 14 In.	186.00
Charger, Blue & White Floral Panels, 18th Century, 14 In. *illus*	288.00
Charger, Bristol, Blue, Pale Blue Ground, Sailing Ships, c.1700, 13¼ In.	8400.00
Charger, Royal Portrait, Equestrian King Charles II, Rearing Steed, c.1685, 17¼ In.	45000.00
Charger, Royal Portrait, King George I, Bristol, With Orb & Scepter, c.1715, 13¾ In.	19200.00
Charger, Stag, Stylized, Yellow, Flowers, Polychrome, Tin Glaze, 12 In., Pair	1495.00
Charger, Urn Of Flowers, Polychrome, Tin Glaze, 12¼ In., Pair	517.00
Chocolate Pot, Windmill, House, Water, Blue, White, 10 In.	199.00
Cup, Blue, Hand Painted, Windmill, Flower Spray, 3¼ In.	6.00
Decanter, Stopper, Blue & White, Embossed, 5 In.	45.00
Dutch House, Henkes Distilleries, Blue & White, Holland, 3 In.	20.00
Earrings, Clip, Round, Blue & White, Windmill, Silvertone Edge, ⅞ In.	30.00
Ewer, Windmill, House, Blue & White, Scroll Handle, 3 In.	27.00
Figurine, Horse, Standing, Right Leg Raised, Cold Paint, Canted Base, Mid 18th Century, 4¾ In. *illus*	1080.00
Jar, Cover, Bulbous Body, Cartouche, Playful Putto, 19th Century, 14¼ In.	472.00
Jar, Wooden Lid, Blue & White, Windmill, Sailboat, 4½ x 4 In.	65.00
Mug, Blue & White, Sailboat, Windmill, 7 x 3 In.	30.00
Mug, Heineken, Windmills	25.00
Pin, Earrings, Sterling Filigree, Windmills, Clip Earrings, 1¼ & ¾ x ⅞ In.	40.00
Pin, Flower, Blue & White, Silver Filigree, 1 x ⅝ In.	38.00
Pitcher, Blue & White, Ram, c.1935, 5 x 2½ In.	99.00
Pitcher, Genie, 5 x 3½ In.	11.00
Plaque, Blue & White, Dutch Landscape Scene, 11 x 17½ In.	708.00
Plaque, Depicting Ship, Inscribed Near E. Linnig, Holland, 20th Century, 5¾ x 5¾ In.	177.00
Plaque, Wall, Oval, Enamel, Figures Before Harbor, Blue, Green, Puce, 19th Century, 15½ In. *illus*	264.00
Plate, Applied Figure, Boy Holding Rabbit, Carrot, Windmill, 6 In.	20.00
Plate, Baby & Stork, 1954, 6¼ In.	50.00
Plate, Blue, White Decoration, Basket Of Fruit, Flowers, Blue Leaf Border, 1700s, 9 In.	230.00
Plate, Blue & White, Cabinetmaker Scene, 1769, 12½ In.	16380.00
Plate, Grapevines, Animals, Arbors, Blue, Tin Glaze, 8¾ In.	144.00
Plate Set, Wooden Shoe Maker, Blacksmith, Mother & Child, 9 In., 3 Piece	68.00
Platter, Hunting Scene, Blue & White, Boch, Holland, 15½ In.	79.00
Posset Pot, Cover, Bristol, Bulbous Body, Scrolled Handle, Curved Spout, c.1690, 6½ In.	12000.00
Pot, Flower, Bird On Branch, 6 x 6 x 5¼ In.	33.00
Punch Bowl, Blue, White, 3-Masted Ship, Success To The Devonshire, c.1761, 11 In.	14400.00
Punch Bowl, Man, Pastoral Setting, Inside Inscribed, One Bowl More & Then, 8½ In.	1200.00
Salt, Armorial, Footed, Cherub Head, Blue, Green, Ocher, Flowers, c.1640, 5 In.	28800.00
Salt & Pepper, Dutch Couple	20.00
Spoon Holder, Blue & White, Half Circle Shape, 6½ x 4 In.	28.00
Tankard, Blue, White, Inscribed, Ring Is Round & Haith No End, Strap Handle, c.1663, 5 In.	84000.00
Tea Caddy, Blue & White, Windmill, Square, Dome Lid, 6 x 3 In.	35.00
Tea Canister, Blue & White, Champered, Rectangular, Interior Scenes, c.1760, 3⅝ In.	15600.00
Teabag Holder, Square, Painted, Windmill Scene, Blue & White, Blue Trim, 3½ x 4 In., Pair	18.00

D

Teabag Holder, Teapot Shape, Painted, Blue & White	16.00
Tile, Canal Scene, 5⅞ x 5⅞ In.	15.00
Tile, Covered Bridge Scene, Blue & White	24.00
Tile, Painted, Blue & White, Windmills, Silver Holder, 4 x 4 In.	128.00
Tile, Religious, Mythological Scenes, 17th Century Dates, 5 x 5 In., 16 Piece	633.00
Tile, Religious Scenes, 19th Century, 5 x 5 In., 10 Piece	518.00
Tile, Tall Sailing Ship, Plymouth Rock, Blue & White, 1620	24.00
Tile, White Duck Flying, Blue Lake, Grasses, 4¾ x 12½ In.	345.00
Tile, Windmill, 4⅞ In.	15.00
Tile, Windmill, Canal, Canal Bank, Circle Border, Blue & White, Flowers	38.00
Tile, Windmills, Boat, Delfts Blauw, Holland, c.1910, 6 x 6 In.	38.00
Tile, Windmills, Sailing Ship, Circle Border, Blue & White	38.00
Trencher, Salt, Blue & White, Red Flower On Side, c.1710	550.00
Urn, Blue & White, Foo Dog Lid, Sailboat Scene In From, c.1790, 15 In.	750.00
Urn, Blue & White, Parrot Lid, Romantic Scene In Front, c.1785, 15 In.	750.00
Vase, 4 Sections, Cupids, Signed, 18th Century, 15½ x 10 In.	7500.00
Vase, Birds, Floral Chinoiserie, Bulbous, Ribbed, Dome Lid, Spread Foot, 13 x 7 In., Pair	1880.00
Vase, Brass Top, Green, Holland, 7½ In.	27.00
Vase, Bud, Windmill, Blue & White, Handle, 4½ x 1¾ In.	23.00
Vase, Bulbous, Painted, Flowers, Cook Pottery Co., N.J., c.1894, 3½ In.	42.00
Vase, Chinoiserie, Blue & White, Slender Neck, Late 18th Century, 10½ In., Pair	468.00
Vase, Cover, Temple Jar Shape, Flowers & Bird Cartouches, 18 x 9 In.	900.00
Vase, Pottery Covered, Oriental Style, Peacock Design, 11¼ In., Pair	527.00
Vase, Urn Shape, Floral Band, Cook Pottery Co., N.J., c.1894, 4½ In.	42.00

DENTAL cabinets, chairs, equipment, and other related items are listed here. Other objects may be found in the Medical category.

Cabinet, Eastlake, Walnut, Marble Top, Spindles, Paneled, Carved, c.1880, 71 x 28 In.	5950.00
Cabinet, Leaded Glass Doors, Pearl Inlay Knobs, Pat. 1899, 70 x 31 x 21 In.	5750.00
Cabinet, Oak, 12 Drawers, Raised Panel, Label Hardware, Tools, Teeth, c.1910, 14 x 15 In.	1450.00
Cabinet, Traveling, Walnut, Roll Top, 3 Shaped Shelves, Drawers, 30 x 20 In.	193.00
Cabinet, Walnut, 3 Tiers, Tambour Lid, 22 Drawers, 5 Lower Drawers, Doors, 59 x 45 In.	977.00
Cabinet, Walnut, Roll Top, Leather Top Pull-Out Shelf, Drawers, Marble Surface, 70 In.	5710.00
Chair, Red Velvet, Betz, Victorian	605.00
Chair, Wood, Civil War Era	633.00
Chart, Chart Of Dentistry, Dr. G.H. Michel & Co.	330.00
Dental Floss, Champion, 1¼ In.	18.00
Drill, Bone Handles, Civil War Era	1045.00
Drill, Cast Iron, Fly Wheel, Foot Pedal, Black Paint, Floor Model, 56½ In.	144.00
Kit, Leather Rollout Case, 19th Century	3575.00
Mirror, Celluloid, Drs. V.T. & R.S. Schlosser, Hagerstown, Md.	245.00
Mirror, Pocket, Celluloid, Round, Lollipop Handle, Boos Dental Labs, c.1902, 3½ In.	65.00
Sign, Tooth Shape, Wood, Bracket, 12 In.	2035.00
Tin, Co-Re-Ga, Trial Size, Brass Cap, Lithograph, Corega Chemical Co., Cleve., 2¼ In.	13.00
Training Aid, Molar, Ivory, Hand Carved, Mid 19th Century	85.00

DEPRESSION GLASS is an inexpensive glass that was manufactured in large quantities during the 1920s and early 1930s. It was made in many colors and patterns by dozens of factories in the United States. Most patterns were also made in clear glass, which the factories called *crystal*. If no color is listed here, it is clear. The name *Depression glass* is a modern one and also refers to machine-made glass of the 1940s through 1970s. For more descriptions, history, pictures, and prices of Depression glass, see the book *Kovels' Depression Glass & American Dinnerware Price List*.

1700 Line, Cup & Saucer, Royal Ruby ....*illus*	15.00
1700 Line, Cup & Saucer, Ivory	17.00
1700 Line, Plate, Dinner, Ivory, 9⅛ In.	12.50
1700 Line, Platter, Milk White, Oval, 9 x 12 In.	20.00
1700 Line, Sugar, Cover, Ruby, 5 In.	30.00
1700 Line, Sugar, Royal Ruby	9.00
Adam, Ashtray, Green, 4½ In.	34.00
Adam, Bowl, Cereal, Green, 5¾ In.	57.00
Adam, Bowl, Cover, Pink, 9 In. ....*illus*	90.00
Adam, Bowl, Dessert, Green, 4¾ In.	27.50
Adam, Bowl, Dessert, Pink, 4¾ In.	25.00
Adam, Bowl, Green, Oval, 10 In.	53.00 to 70.00

Depression Glass, 1700 Line, Cup & Saucer, Royal Ruby
$15.00

Depression Glass, Adam, Bowl, Cover, Pink, 9 In.
$90.00

Depression Glass, American Sweetheart, Bowl, Vegetable, Pink, 11 In.
$65.00

Depression Glass, American Sweetheart, Plate, Luncheon, Monax, 9 In.
$12.00

Depression Glass, Aurora, Creamer, Ritz Blue
$30.00

Depression Glass, Block Optic,
Candy Dish, Cover, Yellow, 2¼ In.
$72.00

Depression Glass, Bubble, Bowl,
Vegetable, Pink, 8½ In.
$6.00

Depression Glass, Bubble, Sherbet,
Forest Green
$14.00

Depression Glass, Cameo, Grill Plate,
Green, 10½ In.
$20.00

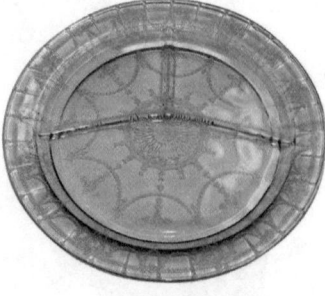

Adam, Bowl, Pink, 9 In.	30.00 to 40.00
Adam, Bowl, Pink, Square, 7¾ In.	35.00
Adam, Bowl Cover, Pink, 7⅝ In.	34.00
Adam, Bowl Cover, Pink, 9 In.	40.00
Adam, Butter, Cover, Pink	90.00
Adam, Butter, Cover Only, Pink	60.00
Adam, Butter, Pink	19.50
Adam, Cake Plate, Green, Footed, 10 In.	32.00 to 37.00
Adam, Cake Plate, Pink, Footed, 10 In.	30.00 to 38.00
Adam, Candy Dish, Lid, Pink, 2½ x 3⅛ x 4⅝ In.	110.00
Adam, Coaster, Green, 3¼ In.	25.00 to 32.00
Adam, Creamer, Green	32.00
Adam, Creamer, Pink	25.00 to 30.00
Adam, Cup, Green	29.00 to 30.00
Adam, Cup, Pink	22.50 to 35.00
Adam, Cup & Saucer, Pink	37.00 to 40.00
Adam, Grill Plate, Green, 9 In.	23.00 to 28.00
Adam, Grill Plate, Pink, 9 In.	25.00 to 28.00
Adam, Pitcher, Pink, 32 Oz.	25.00 to 49.00
Adam, Plate, Dinner, Green, 9 In.	32.00 to 40.00
Adam, Plate, Dinner, Pink, 9 In.	22.00 to 38.00
Adam, Plate, Salad, Green, 7¾ In.	18.00 to 20.00
Adam, Plate, Salad, Pink, 7¾ In.	18.00 to 22.00
Adam, Plate, Sherbet, Pink, 6 In.	7.00 to 12.00
Adam, Platter, Green, 11¾ In.	46.00
Adam, Platter, Pink, 11¾ In.	33.00 to 40.00
Adam, Relish, Pink, Sections, 8 In.	12.00
Adam, Salt & Pepper, Pink	95.00
Adam, Saucer, Green, 6 In.	7.00
Adam, Sherbet, Green	38.00
Adam, Sherbet, Pink	32.00
Adam, Sugar, Cover, Green	75.00
Adam, Sugar, Cover, Pink	50.00
Adam, Sugar, Cover Only, Pink	19.00
Adam, Tumbler, Footed, Green, 4½ In.	45.00
Adam, Tumbler, Footed, Pink, 4½ In.	33.00 to 40.00
Adam, Tumbler, Iced Tea, Footed, Pink, 5½ In.	85.00 to 95.00
Adam, Vase, Green, 7½ In.	150.00 to 155.00
Adam's Rib, Compote, Pink, Oval, 8 In.	18.00
Adam's Rib, Creamer, Marigold, 4 In.	18.75
Adam's Rib, Cup & Saucer, Green	9.00
American Pioneer, Plate, Luncheon, Pink, 8 In.	12.00
American Sweetheart, Berry Bowl, Pink, 9 In.	65.00
American Sweetheart, Bowl, Vegetable, Pink, 11 In. ....*illus*	65.00
American Sweetheart, Cup, Pink	18.00
American Sweetheart, Cup & Saucer, Monax	12.00
American Sweetheart, Plate, Dinner, Monax, 10¼ In.	28.00
American Sweetheart, Plate, Dinner, Pink, 9¾ In.	40.00
American Sweetheart, Plate, Luncheon, Monax, 9 In. ....*illus*	12.00
American Sweetheart, Plate, Salad, Pink, 8 In.	15.00
American Sweetheart, Sandwich Server, Monax, 12 In.	25.00
American Sweetheart, Sandwich Server, Pink, 12 In.	22.00
American Sweetheart, Saucer, Monax	3.00
American Sweetheart, Sherbet, Pink, 4¼ In.	22.00
American Sweetheart, Soup, Cream, Monax, 4½ In.	100.00
American Sweetheart, Sugar, Monax	8.00
American Sweetheart, Sugar, Pink	22.00
Anniversary, Relish, 4 Sections, Gold Trim, Metal Holder, 11 In.	75.00
Apple Blossom pattern is listed here as Dogwood.	
Aramis, Tumbler, Cobalt Blue, 12 Oz., 5 In.	20.00
Artura, Sandwich Server, Center Handle, Yellow	50.00
Aunt Polly, Bowl, Pickle, Blue, Handle, 7¼ In.	45.00
Aunt Polly, Bowl, Pickle, Green, Handles, 7¼ In.	20.00
Aurora, Bowl, Cereal, Pink, 5⅜ In.	14.00
Aurora, Bowl, Ritz Blue, 4½ In.	70.00
Aurora, Creamer, Ritz Blue ....*illus*	30.00

Aurora, Cup, Ritz Blue	16.00
Aurora, Cup & Saucer, Ritz Blue	20.00
Aurora, Tumbler, Ritz Blue, 10 Oz., 4¾ In.	28.00
Avocado, Bowl, Handles, Oval, 8 In.	11.00
Balda, Console, Pink, Rolled Edge, 12 In.	125.00
Ballerina pattern is listed here as Cameo.	
Bamboo Optic, Console, Pink, Rolled Edge, 13½ In.	95.00
Bamboo Optic, Creamer, Green	10.00
Bamboo Optic, Cup, Pink	6.00
Bamboo Optic, Plate, Luncheon, Pink, Round, 8 In.	8.00
Bamboo Optic, Plate, Salad, Pink, Octagonal, 7 In.	6.00
Bamboo Optic, Saucer, Pink, 5½ In.	4.00
Banded Rib pattern is listed here as Coronation.	
Banded Rings pattern is listed here as Ring.	
Block pattern is listed here as Block Optic.	
Block Optic, Berry Bowl, Green, 8½ In.	36.00
Block Optic, Berry Bowl, Pink, 4½ In.	12.00
Block Optic, Bowl, Cereal, Green, 5¼ In.	13.00
Block Optic, Butter, Cover Only	80.00
Block Optic, Candy Dish, Cover, Yellow, 2¼ In. .... *illus*	72.00
Block Optic, Cup, Pink	9.00
Block Optic, Cup & Saucer, Flared Rim, Green	15.00
Block Optic, Goblet, 9 Oz., 5¾ In.	15.00
Block Optic, Plate, Luncheon, Green, 8 In.	7.00
Block Optic, Plate, Luncheon, Pink, 8 In.	8.00
Block Optic, Plate, Sherbet, Green, 6 In.	4.00
Block Optic, Plate, Sherbet, Pink, 6 In.	3.00
Block Optic, Sandwich Server, 10¼ In.	15.00
Block Optic, Saucer, Green, Cup Ring	9.00
Block Optic, Sherbet, 5½ Oz., 3¼ In.	8.00
Block Optic, Sherbet, 6 Oz., 4¾ In.	10.00
Block Optic, Sherbet, Yellow, 5½ Oz., 3½ In.	25.00
Block Optic, Sugar, Pink	13.00
Block Optic, Sugar & Creamer, Green, Footed	28.00
Blue Mosaic, Bowl, Dessert, 5 In.	20.00
Blue Mosaic, Cup, 2½ x 3 In.	15.00
Blue Mosaic, Plate, Dinner, 10 In.	20.00
Blue Mosaic, Plate, Salad, 7¾ In.	22.00
Blue Mosaic, Platter, Oval, 12 x 9 In.	25.00
Bowknot, Cup, Green	10.00
Bubble, Berry Bowl, Milk White, 8⅜ In.	8.00
Bubble, Berry Bowl, Royal Ruby, 4½ In.	12.00
Bubble, Bowl, Cereal, 5¼ In.	9.00
Bubble, Bowl, Vegetable, Pink, 8½ In. .... *illus*	6.00
Bubble, Cocktail, Royal Ruby Bowl, Clear Stem & Foot, 3¼ In.	16.00
Bubble, Cup	4.00
Bubble, Plate, Dinner, Sapphire Blue, 9½ In.	9.00
Bubble, Sherbet, Forest Green .... *illus*	14.00
Bubble, Soup, Dish, 7¾ In.	10.00 to 15.00
Bubble, Tumbler, Iced Tea, Forest Green Bowl, Clear Stem & Foot, 5⅞ In.	13.50
Bubble, Tumbler, Lemonade, Royal Ruby, 12 Oz., 5⅞ In.	18.00
Bullseye pattern is listed here as Bubble.	
Butterflies & Roses pattern is listed here as Flower Garden With Butterflies.	
Buttons & Bows pattern is listed here as Holiday.	
Cabbage Rose pattern is listed here as Sharon.	
Cameo, Bottle, Water, Dark Green, White House Vinegar Premium	25.00
Cameo, Bowl, Vegetable, Green, Oval, 10 In.	30.00
Cameo, Cake Plate, Green, 3-Footed, 10 In.	40.00
Cameo, Candlestick, Green	70.00
Cameo, Compote, Mayonnaise, Green, 5⅜ In.	45.00
Cameo, Console, Pink, 3 Legs, 11 In.	75.00
Cameo, Cup	7.00
Cameo, Grill Plate, Green, 10½ In. .... *illus*	20.00
Cameo, Plate, Dinner, Green, 9½ In.	25.00
Cameo, Plate, Dinner, Yellow, 9½ In.	15.00
Cameo, Plate, Luncheon, Green, 8 In.	14.00

Depression Glass, Cherry Blossom, Creamer, Pink
$22.00

Depression Glass, Christmas Candy, Cup, Teal
$25.00

Depression Glass, Cloverleaf, Sherbet, Black
$20.00

Depression Glass, Colonial Fluted, Plate, Luncheon, Green, 8 In.
$9.00

Depression Glass, Doric,
Cup & Saucer, Pink
$12.00

Depression Glass, Doric & Pansy,
Child's Tea Set, Ultramarine, Box
$425.00

Depression Glass, Fire-King, Jar,
Grease, Lid, Ivory, Red Dots, 6 In.
$100.00

Depression Glass, Floral, Tumbler,
Juice, Green, Footed, 5 Oz., 4 In.
$25.00

Cameo, Plate, Salad, 7 In.	5.00
Cameo, Plate, Sherbet, Green, 6 In.	6.00
Cameo, Platter, Green, Oval, Tab Handles, 12 In.	30.00
Cameo, Relish, Green, 3 Sections, 3-Footed, 7½ In.	30.00
Cameo, Saltshaker, Green, Footed	40.00
Cameo, Sauce, 4¼ In.	7.00
Cameo, Sherbet, Green, Molded, 3⅛ In.	15.00
Cameo, Sugar, Green, 3¼ In.	22.00
Cameo, Vase, Green, 8 In.	65.00
Cape Cod pattern is listed in the Imperial category.	
Caprice Pattern is included in the Cambridge Glass category.	
Cherry Blossom, Berry Bowl, Green, 8½ In.	50.00
Cherry Blossom, Bowl, Delphite, Handles, 9 In.	25.00
Cherry Blossom, Cake Plate, Pink, 3 Legs, 10¼ In.	30.00
Cherry Blossom, Creamer, Pink *illus*	22.00
Cherry Blossom, Cup, Delphite	18.00
Cherry Blossom, Cup, Green	21.00
Cherry Blossom, Cup & Saucer, Pink	22.00
Cherry Blossom, Pitcher, Green, Scalloped Base, 36 Oz., 6¾ In.	65.00 to 75.00
Cherry Blossom, Plate, Salad, Green, 7 In.	25.00
Cherry Blossom, Sandwich Server, Pink, Handles, 10½ In.	32.00
Cherry Blossom, Sherbet, Green	20.00
Cherry Blossom, Sugar, Pink	18.00
Cherry Blossom, Sugar & Creamer, Cover, Pink	60.00
Cherry Blossom, Tea Set, Pink, Jeanette Jr., Box, 14 Piece	300.00
Cherry Blossom, Tumbler, Delphite, Footed, 4 Oz., 3¾ In.	24.00
Cherry Blossom, Tumbler, Pink, Footed, 9 Oz., 4½ In.	25.00
Cherry-Berry, Berry Bowl, 7½ In.	22.00
Cherry-Berry, Plate, Sherbet, Green, 6 In.	10.00
Cherry-Berry, Plate, Sherbet, Pink, 6 In.	12.00
Cherry-Berry, Sherbet, Green, Footed	10.00
Cherry-Berry, Sherbet, Pink	12.00
Chevron, Creamer, 4 x 2½ x 4 In.	19.00
Chevron, Pitcher, Milk, Ritz Blue, 4¼ In.	16.00 to 24.00
Chevron, Sugar, Pink	18.00
Chevron, Sugar & Creamer, Pink	33.00
Chevron, Sugar & Creamer, Ritz Blue, 3 In.	19.00
Chinex Classic, Plate, Castle Decoration, 9¾ In.	25.00
Christmas Candy, Creamer	8.50
Christmas Candy, Cup, Teal *illus*	25.00
Christmas Candy, Plate, Luncheon, 8¼ In.	1.95
Christmas Candy, Saucer, Teal	10.00
Christmas Candy, Sugar, 3¼ In.	8.50
Cloverleaf, Bowl, Salad, Green, 7 In.	115.00
Cloverleaf, Plate, Luncheon, Pink, 8 In.	10.00
Cloverleaf, Sherbet, Black *illus*	20.00
Cloverleaf, Sherbet, Green	10.00
Colonial, Berry Bowl, Green, 4½ In.	20.00
Colonial, Butter, Cover Only, Green	20.00
Colonial, Butter, Cover Only	12.00
Colonial, Creamer	16.00
Colonial, Cup, Green	14.00
Colonial, Cup	4.00
Colonial, Pitcher, 68 Oz., 7¾ In.	35.00
Colonial, Plate, Dinner, Pink, 10 In.	65.00
Colonial, Sherbet, Pink, 3⅞ In.	12.00
Colonial, Sugar, Cover Only	10.00
Colonial, Sugar, Green	18.00
Colonial, Tumbler, Whiskey, Pink, 1½ Oz., 2½ In.	18.00
Colonial Block, Creamer, Pink	15.00
Colonial Block, Sugar, Cover, Milk White	15.00
Colonial Block, Sugar, Cover, Pink	25.00
Colonial Block, Sugar, Green	15.00
Colonial Fluted, Bowl, Cereal, Green, 6 In.	18.00
Colonial Fluted, Cup & Saucer, Green	10.00
Colonial Fluted, Plate, Luncheon, Green, 8 In. *illus*	9.00

Colony Swirl, Cup, Capri Blue, 4 Oz., 2½ In. 4.00
Columbia, Bowl, Cereal, 5 In. 18.00
Columbia, Plate, Bread & Butter, 6 In. 3.00
Coronation, Berry Bowl, Royal Ruby, 4½ In. 8.00
Coronation, Berry Bowl, Royal Ruby, 8 In. 20.00
Coronation, Nappy, Handles, Royal Ruby, 6½ In. 20.00
Cracked Ice, Sugar & Creamer, Pink 95.00
Craquel, Sherbet, Green 9.00
Cremax, Cup & Saucer, Delphite 12.00
Cremax, Sugar, Delphite 10.00
Criss-Cross, Butter, Cover, 7¼ x 4¼ In. 25.00
Criss-Cross, Pitcher, 9 In. 19.00
Cube pattern is listed here as Cubist.
Cubist, Bowl, Dessert, Pink, 4½ In. 10.00
Cubist, Bowl, Dessert, Underplate, Gold Trim, 4½ & 6 In. 8.00
Cubist, Bowl, Salad, Green, 7¼ In. 24.00
Cubist, Butter, Cover, Pink 85.00
Cubist, Candy Jar, Cover, Pink 38.00
Cubist, Candy Jar, Green 15.00
Cubist, Creamer, Green, 3½ In. 15.00
Cubist, Creamer, Pink, 2⅝ In. 8.00
Cubist, Cup, Green 12.00
Cubist, Cup, Pink 10.00
Cubist, Plate, Sherbet, Pink, 6 In. 3.00
Cubist, Powder Jar, Cover, Pink, 3-Footed 32.00
Cubist, Powder Jar, 3-Footed 5.00
Cubist, Powder Jar, Cover Only, Green 20.00
Cubist, Salt & Pepper, Green 45.00
Cubist, Saucer, Green 3.00
Cubist, Saucer, Pink 3.00
Cubist, Sugar, Green, 3 In. 12.00
Cubist, Sugar, Pink, 2⅝ In. 6.00
Cubist, Sugar & Creamer 10.00
Daisy pattern is listed here as No. 620.
Dancing Girl pattern is listed here as Cameo.
Dewdrop, Creamer, 4 x 2⅞ In. 9.00
Diamond pattern is listed here as Miss America.
Diamond Line, Pitcher, Pink, 60 Oz. 48.00
Diamond Line, Relish, Green, Handle, Enameled 85.00
Diamond Line, Relish, Pink, Handle 70.00
Diamond Line, Tumbler, Pink, 9 Oz., 4 In. 12.00
Diana, Console, Flared, Scalloped, 12 In. 16.00
Diana, Cup, After Dinner 7.00
Diana, Cup, Pink 20.00
Diana, Cup & Saucer, After Dinner 12.00
Diana, Sherbet, Amber 12.00
Dogwood, Berry Bowl, Pink, 8½ In. 62.00
Dogwood, Cup, Pink, Thin 17.00
Dogwood, Cup & Saucer, Pink, Thin 18.00
Dogwood, Grill Plate, Pink, Border Design, 10½ In. 33.00
Dogwood, Saucer, Pink .... 5.00 to 7.00
Dogwood, Sugar, Pink, Footed, 3¼ In. 18.00
Dogwood, Tumbler, Pink, Molded Band, 10 Oz., 4¾ In. 25.00
Doric, Berry Bowl, Pink, 4½ In. 12.00
Doric, Cup & Saucer, Pink .... *illus* 12.00
Doric, Plate, Sherbet, Green, 6 In. 8.00
Doric, Relish, Pink, 8 x 8 In. 40.00
Doric, Saltshaker, Pink 22.00
Doric, Saucer, Pink 4.00
Doric, Sugar, Cover Only, Green 30.00
Doric, Tumbler, Pink, 9 Oz., 4½ In. 75.00
Doric & Pansy, Child's Tea Set, Ultramarine, Box .... *illus* 425.00
Doric & Pansy, Plate, Sherbet, Pink, 6 In. 8.00
Fascination, Sherbet, Lilac, 4½ In. 18.50
Fine Rib pattern is listed here as Homespun.
Fire-King, Batter Bowl, Jade-Ite 50.00

TIP
Glassware, old or new, requires careful handling. Stand each piece upright, not touching another. Never nest pieces. Wash in moderately hot water and mild detergent. Avoid wiping gold- or platinum-banded pieces while glasses are hot. Never use scouring pads or silver polish on glass. When using an automatic dishwasher, be sure the water temperature is under 180 degrees.

Depression Glass, Florentine No. 2, Sherbet, Yellow
$9.50

Depression Glass, Holiday, Pitcher, Milk, Pink, 16 Oz., 4¾ In.
$22.00

D

Depression Glass, Iris, Creamer, Iridescent
$12.50

Depression Glass, Madrid, Sugar, Cover, Yellow
$55.00

Depression Glass, Manhattan, Sandwich Server, Handles, 14 In.
$10.00

Fire-King, Bowl, Breakfast, Ivory, 5 In.	20.00
Fire-King, Bowl, Cereal, Stacking, 2¼ x 5 In.	7.00
Fire-King, Bowl, Milk White, 2¾ x 5 In.	9.00
Fire-King, Bowl, Ribbed, Jade-Ite, 1930s, 7 In.	40.00
Fire-King, Bowl, Sectons, Tab Handles, 2 x 8½ In.	9.50
Fire-King, Bowl, Vegetable, Ivory, Round, 8¼ In.	25.00
Fire-King, Cake Pan, Tab Handle, Ivory, 9 In.	15.00
Fire-King, Canister, Spice, Jade-Ite, 3 In.	59.00
Fire-King, Casserole, Milk White, 2¼ x 5⅛ In.	5.50
Fire-King, Casserole, White, Rectangular, 1½ Qt.	5.75
Fire-King, Creamer, White Laurel, 3½ x 4½ In.	25.00
Fire-King, Cup, Coffee, Ivory, 3 In.	9.50
Fire-King, Cup & Saucer, Ivory	10.00
Fire-King, Egg Plate, Ivory, Gold Trim, 9¾ In.	25.00
Fire-King, Eggcup, Footed, Jade-Ite	42.00
Fire-King, Flowerpot, Ivory, 3¾ In.	25.00
Fire-King, Jar, Grease, Lid, Ivory, Red Dots, 6 In. ......*illus*	100.00
Fire-King, Jar, Grease, Tulip Lid, Ivory, 4½ In.	40.00
Fire-King, Loaf Pan, Ivory, 9⅝ In.	15.00
Fire-King, Loaf Pan, Peach Luster, Qt.	5.00
Fire-King, Loaf Pan, Peach Lustre, Handles, 8 x 2½ In.	10.00
Fire-King, Mixing Bowl, Ivory, 8 In.	20.00
Fire-King, Mixing Bowl, Ivory, 9 In.	40.00
Fire-King, Mixing Bowl, Milk White, 2 Spouts, 2 Qt., 4¼ x 10¼ In.	17.50
Fire-King, Mixing Bowl, Swirl, Milk White, 7 In.	12.00
Fire-King, Mixing Bowl, Swirl, Milk White, 9 In.	12.00
Fire-King, Mug, Ivory	25.00
Fire-King, Mug, Milk White, 3½ In.	6.50 to 10.00
Fire-King, Mug, Peach Lustre	36.00
Fire-King, Plate, Dinner, Ivory, 9⅛ In.	12.50
Fire-King, Plate, Salad, Ivory, 7¾ In.	15.00
Fire-King, Range Set, Shakers, Ivory, 4½ In., 2 Piece	50.00
Fire-King, Saltshaker, Horizontal Ribs, Jade-Ite	58.00
Fire-King, Shaker, Spice, Jade-Ite, 6 Oz.	35.00
Fire-King, Trivet, Ivory, Handles, 8½ In.	25.00
Fire-King, Trivet, Tab Handle, Ivory	35.00
Fire-King, Vase, Bud, Jade-Ite, No. 519, 6¼ In.	25.00 to 29.00
Fleurette, Creamer	7.00 to 13.50
Fleurette, Platter, 9 x 12 In.	14.00 to 19.00
Fleurette, Soup, Dish, 6¼ In.	12.00
Fleurette, Sugar, Cover, 4 In.	15.00
Fleurette, Sugar & Creamer, 4⅛ x 3⅜ In.	30.00
Floral, Bowl, Vegetable, Pink, 9 In.	24.00
Floral, Cup, Green	12.50
Floral, Plate, Dinner, Green, 9 In.	22.00
Floral, Relish, Sections, Green, 8 In.	22.50
Floral, Salt & Pepper, Green, Footed	49.00
Floral, Tumbler, Footed, Pink, 5¼ In.	55.00
Floral, Tumbler, Juice, Green, Footed, 5 Oz., 4 In. ......*illus*	25.00
Floral & Diamond Band, Berry Bowl, Green, 8 In.	35.00
Floral & Diamond Band, Sherbet, Green	10.00
Florentine No. 1, Plate, Salad, Gold Rim, 8½ In.	8.50
Florentine No. 1, Salt & Pepper, Green, Footed, 4 In., Pair	40.00
Florentine No. 2, Sherbet, Yellow ......*illus*	9.50
Flower & Leaf Band pattern is listed here as Indiana Custard.	
Flower Garden With Butterflies, Plate, Blue Green, 8¼ In.	45.00
Flower Garden With Butterflies, Tray, Pink, Oval, 10 In.	85.00
Flower Rim pattern is listed here as Vitrock.	
Fruits, Berry Bowl, Green, 8 In.	115.00
Fruits, Cup, Green	9.50
Fruits, Plate, Luncheon, Green, 8 In.	14.00 to 16.50
Fruits, Sherbet, Footed, Pink, 3 x 3½ In.	17.50
Fruits, Tumbler, Pink, Combination Fruits, 4 In.	39.00
Golden Anniversary, Creamer, Ivory	6.50
Gray Laurel, Bowl, Dessert, 5 In.	9.50
Gray Laurel, Creamer	15.00

D

Gray Laurel, Plate, Dinner, 9⅛ In.	12.50 to 14.00
Gray Laurel, Plate, Salad, 7¾ In.	12.50 to 15.00
Gray Laurel, Platter, 11 In.	25.00
Gray Laurel, Soup, Dish, 7½ In.	20.00 to 25.00
Gray Laurel, Sugar, 5 In.	15.00
Hairpin pattern is listed here as Newport.	
Heritage, Bowl, Fruit, 3⅛ x 10½ In.	15.00
Heritage, Plate, Dinner, 9¼ In.	8.00 to 12.50
Hex Optic pattern is listed here as Hexagon Optic.	
Hexagon Optic, Pitcher, Marigold, 9½ x 6 In.	50.00
Hexagon Optic, Tumbler, Marigold, 5 In.	5.00 to 9.00
Hexagon Optic, Tumbler, Marigold, 6½ In.	15.00
Holiday, Berry Bowl, Pink, 5¼ In.	15.00
Holiday, Cup & Saucer, Pink, Buttons & Bows, Jeanette Glass Co.	18.00
Holiday, Pitcher, Pink, 52 Oz., 6¾ In.	35.00
Holiday, Pitcher, Milk, Pink, 16 Oz., 4¾ In. ....*illus*	22.00
Holiday, Plate, Dinner, 9 In.	20.00
Holiday, Plate, Sherbet, Pink, 6 In.	10.00
Holiday, Sherbet, Pink	10.00
Holiday, Soup, Dish, Pink, 7¾ In.	60.00
Holiday, Sugar, Cover Only, Pink, 3½ In.	15.00
Homespun, Butter, Cover, Pink	90.00
Homespun, Coaster	1.75 to 4.00
Homespun, Creamer, Pink	6.50
Homespun, Cup, Pink	8.50 to 14.00
Homespun, Plate, Dinner, Pink, 9¼ In.	25.00
Homespun, Plate, Pink, Child's, 4½ In.	14.00
Homespun, Plate, Sherbet, Pink, 6 In.	8.00
Homespun, Platter, Pink, 12 In.	18.00
Homespun, Saucer, Pink, Child's	12.00
Homespun, Sherbet, Pink	24.00
Homespun, Sherbet	35.00
Homespun, Sugar, Cover, Pink	15.00 to 27.00
Homespun, Tumbler, Iced Tea, Pink, Footed, 15 Oz., 6½ In.	48.00
Homespun, Tumbler, Pink, 9 Oz., 4¼ In.	15.00 to 33.00
Homespun, Tumbler, Pink, Flared Rim, 8 Oz., 4¼ In.	15.00
Homespun, Tumbler, Pink, Footed, 5 Oz., 3⅜ In.	15.00
Homespun, Tumbler, Pink, Footed, 7 Oz., 3⅞ In.	8.50 to 10.00
Honeycomb pattern is listed here as Hexagon Optic.	
Horizontal Ribbed pattern is listed here as Manhattan.	
Indiana Custard, Berry Bowl, 5½ In.	23.00
Indiana Custard, Plate, Dinner, 9¾ In.	45.00
Indiana Custard, Sugar, Cover, Ivory	52.00
Iris, Berry Bowl, Iridescent, 8 In.	16.00
Iris, Berry Bowl, Iridescent, Ruffled Edge, 9 In.	12.00
Iris, Bowl, Fruit, Iridescent, Ruffled Edge, 11½ In.	14.00
Iris, Candy Jar, Cover, 6½ x 6 In.	245.00
Iris, Creamer, Iridescent ....*illus*	12.50
Iris, Cup, 3 x 3½ In.	14.00
Iris, Sandwich Server, Iridescent, 11¾ In.	30.00
Iris, Sauce, Ruffled Edge, 5¼ In.	9.00
Iris, Sherbet, Iridescent	14.00
Iris, Sherbet	22.00
Iris, Sugar	10.00
Iris, Tumbler, Iridescent, Footed, 6 In.	20.00
Iris, Vase, 9 In.	26.00
Iris, Vase, Iridescent, 9 In.	20.00
Iris & Herringbone pattern is listed here as Iris.	
Jane Ray, Plate, Dinner, Jade-Ite, 9 In.	24.50
Jane Ray, Platter, Jade-Ite, 12 x 9 In.	40.00
Jane Ray, Sugar & Creamer, Jade-Ite	39.00
Jubilee, Plate, Salad, Yellow, 8¼ In.	30.00
Jubilee, Saucer, Yellow, 6 In.	8.00
Knife & Fork pattern is listed here as Colonial.	
Lace Edge pattern is listed here as Old Colony.	
Laced Edge Is Listed In The Imperial Glass category.	

D

Depression Glass, Mayfair Open Rose, Pitcher, Pink, 37 Oz., 6 In.
$62.00

Depression Glass, Miss America, Relish, 4 Sections, Pink, 8¾ In.
$40.00

Depression Glass, Moderntone, Tumbler, Cobalt Blue, 9 Oz., 4 In.
$36.00

Depression Glass, Moonstone, Candy Dish, Cover
$38.00

Depression Glass, Newport, Sugar, Amethyst
$14.00

Depression Glass, No. 620, Cup & Saucer, Amber
$4.50

Depression Glass, Oyster & Pearl, Relish, Pink, Sections, Handles, 10½ In.
$25.00

Depression Glass, Patrician, Sherbet, Green
$12.00

Depression Glass, Petalware, Platter, Pink, 13 In.
$25.00

Lake Como, Plate, Dinner, Blue Scene, 9⅛ In.	45.00
Laurel, Cup & Saucer, Jade Green, Child's	75.00
Laurel, Plate, Jade Green, Child's, 5¾ In.	24.00
Laurel, Sugar & Creamer, Jade Green, Child's	230.00
Lido, Pitcher, Golden Glow, 65 Oz.	45.00
Lido, Tumbler, Golden Glow, 4 In.	8.00
Lido, Tumbler, Juice, Golden Glow, 3½ In.	6.00
Line 300 pattern is listed in the Paden City category as Peacock & Wild Rose.	
Lorna pattern is included in the Cambridge Glass category.	
Madrid, Ashtray, Amber, 6 In., Pair	1035.00
Madrid, Butter, Cover, 7 In.	52.00
Madrid, Candleholder, Iridescent, 2½ In.	40.00
Madrid, Cookie Jar, Cover, Amber, 5¼ In.	60.00
Madrid, Cookie Jar, Cover, Pink, 5¼ In.	40.00
Madrid, Pitcher, Blue, Square, 60 Oz.	225.00
Madrid, Pitcher, Juice, Amber, 36 Oz., 5½ In.	45.00
Madrid, Sugar, Cover, Yellow *illus*	55.00
Madrid, Sugar & Creamer, Amber	50.00
Madrid, Tumbler, Blue, 12 Oz., 5½ In.	50.00
Manhattan, Barware, Tumbler, Amber, Footed, 9 Oz.	6.00
Manhattan, Barware, Tumbler, Whiskey, 8 Piece	35.00
Manhattan, Bowl, Fruit, Handles, 9¼ In.	35.00
Manhattan, Bowl, Fruit, Pink, 9¼ In.	44.00
Manhattan, Candlestick, Square, 4½ In.	11.00
Manhattan, Candy Dish, 3-Footed, Pink, 6¼ In.	12.50 to 15.00
Manhattan, Candy Dish, Cover, 3-Footed, 6¼ In.	24.00
Manhattan, Cocktail, Avocado Green, 4 Oz., 5¾ In.	5.00
Manhattan, Goblet, Water, Avocado Green, Bartlett Collins, 5⅞ In.	5.00
Manhattan, Pitcher, Tilted, 80 Oz.	50.00
Manhattan, Salt & Pepper, Pink, Square, 2 In.	45.00
Manhattan, Sandwich Server, Handles, 14 In. *illus*	10.00
Manhattan, Sauce, Handles, 4½ In.	11.00
Manhattan, Tumbler, Iced Tea, Avocado Green, Footed, 6¼ In.	6.00
Manhattan, Vase, 8 In.	30.00
Martha Washington Pattern is included in the Cambridge Glass category.	
Mayfair, Federal, Tumbler, Amber, 9 Oz., 4½ In.	35.00
Mayfair Open Rose, Bowl, Green, 11¾ In.	110.00
Mayfair Open Rose, Cookie Jar, Blue	95.00
Mayfair Open Rose, Cookie Jar, Cover, Pink, Satin	60.00
Mayfair Open Rose, Creamer, Pink	25.00
Mayfair Open Rose, Pitcher, Pink, 37 Oz., 6 In. *illus*	62.00
Mayfair Open Rose, Plate, Luncheon, Pink, 8½ In.	35.00
Mayfair Open Rose, Tumbler, Iced Tea, Footed, Pink, 5¾ In.	50.00
Meadow Green, Casserole, 1½ Qt.	7.50
Meadow Green, Casserole, 2 Qt.	8.50
Meadow Green, Loaf Pan	6.25
Miss America, Bowl, Pink, Oval, 10 x 8 In.	50.00
Miss America, Compote, Pink, 5 x 6½ In.	100.00
Miss America, Plate, Dinner, Pink, 10¼ In.	50.00
Miss America, Relish, 4 Sections, Pink, 8¾ In. *illus*	40.00
Moderntone, Cup, Amethyst	11.00
Moderntone, Cup, Cobalt Blue	10.00
Moderntone, Cup, Platonite, Pink	4.00
Moderntone, Cup & Saucer, Cobalt Blue	13.00 to 13.50
Moderntone, Custard Cup, Cobalt Blue	13.00
Moderntone, Plate, Dinner, Cobalt Blue, 9 In.	14.50
Moderntone, Plate, Dinner, Platonite, Fired-On Gray, 9 In.	16.00
Moderntone, Plate, Sherbet, Cobalt Blue, 6 In.	6.00
Moderntone, Sandwich Server, Amethyst, 10½ In.	40.00
Moderntone, Sherbet, Platonite, Fired-On Yellow	7.00
Moderntone, Sherbet, Platonite, Pastel Pink, 3 x 3¼ In.	15.00
Moderntone, Soup, Cream, Amethyst, 4½ In.	30.00
Moderntone, Soup, Cream, Cobalt Blue	25.00
Moderntone, Sugar, Cobalt Blue	15.00
Moderntone, Sugar & Creamer, Pink	20.00
Moderntone, Tumbler, Cobalt Blue, 9 Oz., 4 In. *illus*	36.00

D

Moderntone, Tumbler, Whiskey, Pink	24.00
Moderntone Little Hostess Party, Tea Set, Autumn Colors, 16 Piece	245.00
Moderntone Little Hostess Party, Tea Set, Turquoise, Rust, Gold, Gray, 16 Piece	325.00
Moderntone Platonite, Sugar & Creamer	12.00
Moon & Star, Ashtray, Green, 8½ In.	22.00
Moondrops Pattern is listed in the New Martinsville category.	
Moonstone, Berry Bowl, Ruffled Edge, 5½ In.	18.00
Moonstone, Bonbon, Heart, 6½ In.	18.00
Moonstone, Candleholder, Pair	20.00
Moonstone, Candy Dish, Cover . . . . *illus*	38.00
Moonstone, Cigarette Box, Cover, 5½ x 3½ In.	36.00
Moonstone, Cup & Saucer	12.00
Moonstone, Plate, Luncheon, 8¾ In.	15.00
Moonstone, Relish, Opalescent, 3 Sections, Clover	18.00
Moonstone, Sherbet, 3⅜ In.	9.00
Moonstone, Sugar & Creamer	20.00
Moroccan Amethyst, Bowl, Colony, 5¾ In.	12.00
Moroccan Amethyst, Cocktail Mixer, 16 Oz.	35.00
Moroccan Amethyst, Cup & Saucer, Hexagonal	15.00
Moroccan Amethyst, Goblet, 9 Oz., 5¾ In.	12.00
Mt. Vernon Pattern is included in the Cambridge Glass category.	
Newport, Sugar, Amethyst . . . . *illus*	14.00
No. 601 pattern is listed here as Avocado.	
No. 620, Bowl, 7¼ x 2½ In.	10.00
No. 620, Creamer, Amber	9.00
No. 620, Cup & Saucer, Amber . . . . *illus*	4.50
Old Colony, Bowl, Cereal, 6½ In.	20.00
Old Colony, Creamer, Pink	60.00
Old Colony, Cup & Saucer, Pink	55.00
Old Colony, Plate, Dinner, Pink, 10½ In.	30.00
Old Colony, Relish, 5 Sections, Pink, 12¾ In.	48.00
Old Colony, Tumbler, Footed, Pink . . . . 95.00 to 125.00	
Old Florentine pattern is listed here as Florentine No. 1.	
Open Lace pattern is listed here as Old Colony.	
Open Rose pattern is listed here as Mayfair Open Rose.	
Optic Design pattern is listed here as Raindrops.	
Orange Blossom, Bowl, Dessert, 1⅝ x 5¼ In.	5.00
Orange Blossom, Creamer, 4⅛ In.	7.00
Orange Blossom, Cup, 2¼ In.	4.00
Orange Blossom, Plate, Dinner, 9¾ In.	10.00
Orange Blossom, Saucer	1.00
Orange Blossom, Sugar, 3⅝ In.	5.00
Oyster & Pearl, Bowl, Fruit, Platonite, Fired-On Green, 10½ In.	24.00
Oyster & Pearl, Bowl, Pink, Handles, Deep, 6½ In.	18.00
Oyster & Pearl, Relish, Pink, Sections, Handles, 10½ In. . . . . *illus*	25.00
Parrot pattern is listed here as Sylvan.	
Patrician, Sherbet, Green . . . . *illus*	12.00
Peach Lustre, Cup & Saucer	10.00
Peacock & Wild Rose pattern is listed in the Paden City category.	
Petal Swirl pattern is listed here as Swirl.	
Petalware, Platter, Pink, 13 In. . . . . *illus*	25.00
Poinsettia pattern is listed here as Floral.	
Poppy No. 1 pattern is listed here as Florentine No. 1.	
Poppy No. 2 pattern is listed here as Florentine No. 2.	
Pretty Polly Party Dishes, see the related pattern Doric & Pansy.	
Princes, Vase, Green, Frosted, 8 x 5¼ In.	35.00
Prismatic Line pattern is listed here as Queen Mary.	
Provincial pattern is listed here as Bubble.	
Queen Mary, Candlestick, 2-Light, 4½ In., Pair . . . . *illus*	26.00
Queen Mary, Cup	12.00
Queen Mary, Plate, Bread & Butter, 6⅝ In.	5.00
Radiance pattern is listed in the New Martinsville category.	
Raindrops, Plate, Luncheon, Green, 8 In. . . . . *illus*	6.00
Raised Grapevine, Pitcher, Ice Lip, Gold Band, 9 In.	45.00
Ring, Tumbler, Whiskey, Multicolored Rings, 1½ Oz., 2½ In.	20.00
Rope pattern is listed here as Colonial Fluted.	

Depression Glass, Queen Mary, Candlestick, 2-Light, 4½ In., Pair
$26.00

D

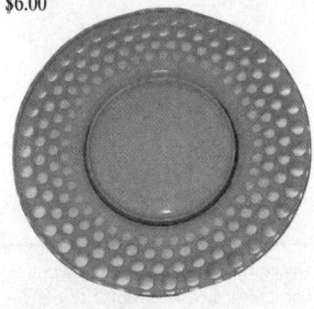

Depression Glass, Raindrops, Plate, Luncheon, Green, 8 In.
$6.00

Depression Glass, Royal Lace, Cup & Saucer, Cobalt Blue
$32.00

Depression Glass, Royal Lace, Sherbet, Cobalt Blue, Etched, Chrome Holder, 3½ In., 6 Piece
$118.00

Depression Glass, Royal Ruby, Tumbler, 6 Piece
$58.00

D

Depression Glass, Sharon,
Cup & Saucer, Green
$28.00

Depression Glass, Shell Pink,
Box, Cover, Butterfly
$213.00

Depression Glass, Sportsman Series,
Cocktail Shaker, Angelfish
$75.00

Depression Glass, Swirl, Bowl,
Vegetable, Ultramarine, Footed,
Tab Handles, 10 In.
$10.00

Depression Glass, Sylvan,
Parrot, Sherbet, Cone Shape,
Amber, 2¾ In.
$30.00

Royal Lace, Sherbet, Cobalt Blue, Etched, Chrome Holder, 3½ In., 6 Piece	*illus*	118.00
Royal Lace, Cup & Saucer, Cobalt Blue	*illus*	32.00
Royal Ruby, Tumbler, 6 Piece	*illus*	58.00
Sailboat pattern is listed here as Sportsman Series.		
Sandwich Anchor Hocking, Punch Set, Ivory, 13 Piece		110.00
Saxon pattern is listed here as Coronation.		
Scroll Band, Pitcher, Blue, Green, Bartlett Collins, 80 Oz.		15.00
Sharon, Cup & Saucer, Green	*illus*	28.00
Shell Pink, Box, Cover, Butterfly	*illus*	213.00
Spiral Flutes pattern is listed in the Duncan & Miller category as Swirl.		
Spoke pattern is listed here as Patrician.		
Sportsman Series, Cocktail Shaker, Angelfish	*illus*	75.00
Sportsman Series, Tumbler, Roly Poly, Sailboat, Cobalt Blue, 2½ In.		12.00
Star Of David, Relish, Sections, 10 In.		7.00
Stars & Bars, Vase, White, 6 In.		6.50
Sunburst, Bowl, 11 In.		25.00
Swirl, Bowl, Vegetable, Ultramarine, Footed, Tab Handles, 10 In.	*illus*	10.00
Swirl, Candy Dish, Cover, Pink, Footed, 6½ In.		180.00
Sylvan, Parrot, Sherbet, Cone Shape, Amber, 2¾ In.	*illus*	30.00
Vertical Ribbed pattern is listed here as Queen Mary.		
Vitrock, Kitchen Set, Grease Jar, Salt, Pepper, Sugar & Flour Shakers, 5 Piece		60.00
Wheat, Baking Pan, Handles, 2⅛ x 10½ x 6½ In.		12.00
Wheat, Cake Pan, Round, Handles, 2 x 8 In.		11.00
Wheat, Casserole, Handles, Qt., 4¼ x 7¼ In.		10.00
Wheat Barware, Pitcher, Ice Lip, 80 Oz.		15.00
White Ship pattern is listed here as Sportsman Series.		
Wild Rose pattern is listed here as Dogwood.		
Windmill pattern is listed here as Sportsman Series.		
Windsor, Compote, 5½ x 6 In.		20.00
Windsor, Soup, Cream, Pink, 5 In.	*illus*	28.00
Windsor Diamond pattern is listed here as Windsor.		
Yorktown, Sugar & Creamer, Cover		15.00

DERBY has been marked on porcelain made in the city of Derby, England, since about 1748. The original Derby factory closed in 1848, but others opened there and continued to produce quality porcelain. The Crown Derby mark began appearing on Derby wares in the 1770s.

Basket, Chelsea, Oval, Oval, 2 Handles, Painted, Flowers, Scalloped Edge, c.1780, 9 In.	437.00
Figurine, Africa, Blackamoor Boy, Elephant Headdress, Cornucopia, Fruit, Lion, c.1780, 5½ In.	3900.00
Figurine, Boar, Puce & Red Spots, Flowers, Leaves, Grass, Oval Base, c.1750-55, 4½ In.	2880.00
Figurine, Diana, Holding Bow, Reaching For Arrow, Dog, Applied Flowers, c.1760-65, 11 In.	1680.00
Figurine, Dog, Pug, Gilt Collar, Gray, Puce, Scroll Molded Oval Base, 2⅝ & 2⅞ In., Pair	1320.00
Fruit Basket, Reticulated, Multicolored, Gilt Flowers, 19th Century, 10½ x 7 In.	29.00
Group, Couple, Seated, Star-Shape Flowers, Harlequin, Gilt, Scroll Molded Base, c.1765, 12⅜ In.	5760.00
Plate, Dessert, Imari Palette, Scalloped Gadroon Border, Early 1900s, 9 In., 12 Piece	1265.00
Tureen Stand, Topographical, Landscape, c.1800, 14½ In.	478.00
Vase, Gilt Decorated, Scrolled Handles, Red Ground, Gilt Flowers, c.1880, 15½ In.	1015.00
Vase, Japonesque, c.1880, 4½ In.	268.00

DICK TRACY, the comic strip, started in 1931. Tracy was also the hero of movies from 1937 to 1947 and again in 1990, and starred in a radio series in the 1940s and a television series in the 1950s. Memorabilia from all these activities are collected.

Badge, Dick Tracy Detective, Cleveland News, Brass, Early 1930s, 1⅜ In.		50.00
Badge, Secret Service Patrol, Second Year Member, Brass, Quaker, 1939, 1⅝ In.		112.00
Book, Dick Tracy Meets The Night Crawler, 1945		9.00
Book, Mystery Of The Purple Cross, Whitman No. 4071, 1938, 7¼ x 9½ In., 316 Pages		460.00
Comic Art, Daily Cartoon, Chester Gould, August 25, 1948, 6 x 20 In.		792.00
Dinner Set, Homer Laughlin, 1940s		200.00
Figure, Composition, Painted, Movable Head, 1930s, 13 In.	*illus*	575.00
Fingerprint & Microscope Outfit, J. Pressman, Box, 1930s, 2½ x 11½ x 13½ In.		246.00
Flashlight, Flip Switch, Original Package, 1962, 8½ x 4 In.		149.00
Lamp, Figural, Image Of Tracy & Sparkle Plenty Shade, Plastoc Mfg., 1951, 9 In.		2040.00
Pin, Member, Secret Service Patrol, Celluloid, Canada, 1938, 1¼ In.		84.00
Pocket Knife, Cream Colored Grips, Image Of Tracy Holding Gun, 1930s, 3 In.		185.00
Standee, Cardboard, Die Cut, Junio Ties, 10¼ x 15¼ In.		1120.00
Toy, Bonnie Braids, Crawls, Windup, Marx, Box, 11 In.	*illus*	140.00

Toy, Camera, Insignia On Front, c.1950	50.00
Toy, Ringer Washing Machine, Sparkle Plenty, Instructions, Kalon Redro, Box, 14 In.	115.00
Toy, Riot Car, Tin Lithograph, Friction, Marx, 1950s, 7½ In.	136.00
Toy, Squad Car, Friction, Green, Marx, 6¾ In.	250.00
Toy, Squad Car, No. 1, Tin Lithograph, Windup, Marx, 1950s, 6¾ In.	161.00
Toy, Squad Car, Tin, Dick Tracy, Sam Catchum, Battery Operated, Siren, 8½ x 20 x 5 In.	407.00
Toy, Submachine Gun, Tops Plastic, Water Gun, Box, c.1951, 12 In.	264.00
Toy, Tommy Gun, Die Cast, Orange Plug, Strap, Box, 20 In. *illus*	518.00
Washing Machine, Sparkle Plenty, Ringer, Instructions, Comic Strip, Kalon, 14 In.	115.00

DICKENS WARE *pieces are listed in the Royal Doulton and Weller categories.*

DINNERWARE used in the United States from the 1930s through the 1950s is listed here. Most was made in potteries in southern Ohio, West Virginia, and California. A few patterns were made in Japan, England, and other countries. Dishes were sold in gift shops and department stores, or were given away as premiums. Many of these patterns are listed in this book in their own categories, such as Autumn Leaf, Azalea, Coors, Fiesta, Franciscan, Hall, Harker, Harlequin, Red Wing, Riviera, Russel Wright, Vernon Kilns, Watt, and Willow. For more information, see *Kovels' Depression Glass & Dinnerware Price List*.

Adam Antique, Platter, Steubenville, 10½ In.	22.00
Alyce, Creamer, Harmony House	24.00
Aristocrat, Cup & Saucer, Demitasse, 23k Gold Trim, Salem China	8.00
Aristocrat, Cup & Saucer, Salem China	8.00
Athena, Cup & Saucer, Johnson Brothers	13.00
Autumn Gold, Cup, Homer Laughlin	5.00
Autumn Harvest, Plate, Dinner, Taylor, Smith & Taylor . . . . *illus*	8.00
Autumn Harvest, Sugar & Creamer, Taylor, Smith & Taylor	11.00
Autumn Spiral, Serving Bowl, Taylor, Smith & Taylor	12.00
Aztec, Cup & Saucer, Iroquois	15.00
Aztec, Plate, Dinner, Iroquois, 10 In.	9.00
Ballerina, Chop Plate, Iris Decal, Tab Handles, Universal, 11⅝ In.	22.00
Ballerina, Creamer, Gray, Universal	12.00
Ballerina, Cup & Saucer, Burgundy, Universal	10.00
Ballerina, Plate, Bread & Butter, Burgundy, Universal, 6¼ In.	10.00
Ballerina, Platter, Chrysanthemum, Tab Handles, Universal, 12 In.	35.00
Bells Of Ireland, Bowl, Vegetable, Harmony House, 9½ In.	15.00
Biscayne, Plate, Dinner, Salem China, 9⅜ In.	14.00
Blossom Top, Salt & Pepper, Blue Ridge	45.00
Blue Bonnet, Cup & Saucer, Harmony House	20.00
Blue Bonnet, Sugar & Creamer, Harmony House	20.00
Blue Vineyard, Platter, Oval, Iroquois, 12 In.	20.00
Blue Wheat, Platter, Oval, Taylor, Smith & Taylor, 13⅜ x 9½ In.	28.00
Bluebell Bouquet, Bowl, Blue Ridge, 9¼ In.	45.00
Bluebird, Bowl, Blue Trim, Taylor, Smith & Taylor, 2½ x 5¼ In.	24.00
Bluebird, Gravy Boat, Attached Underplate, Edwin M. Knowles, 3½ x 7 In.	53.00
Bluebird, Plate, Dinner, Steubenville, 9 In.	35.00
Bluebird, Platter, 12-Sided, Salem China, c.1920, 10⅞ In.	175.00
Boutonniere, Salt & Pepper, Taylor, Smith & Taylor	18.00
Boutonniere, Sugar & Creamer, Taylor, Smith & Taylor	48.00
Buchanan, Plate, Dinner, Blue Ridge, 9⅜ In.	24.00
Bunny, Bowl, 23K Gold Trim, Salem China, Child's, 6 In.	20.00
Buttercup, Sugar & Creamer, Edwin M. Knowles	10.00
Cameo Rose, Chop Plate, Blue, White, Harmony House, 12 In.	15.00
Castle On The Lake, Cup & Saucer, Johnson Brothers	68.00
Cattail, Soup, Dish, Harmony House	15.00
Center Bowl, Yellow, Footed, Homer Laughlin, 12 In.	176.00
Century, Creamer, Homer Laughlin, 1930s	10.00
Century, Platter, Homer Laughlin, 1930s, 15¼ In.	20.00
Century, Platter, Tab Handles, Salem China, 11½ In.	15.00
Clairmont, Serving Bowl, Gold Lines, Taylor, Smith & Taylor	12.00
Classic, Plate, Dinner, Edwin M. Knowles, 9¼ In.	9.00
Colonial Couple, Bowl, Berry, 23K Gold Trim, Salem China, 5½ In.	7.00
Colonial Couple, Bowl, Cereal, 23K Gold Trim, Salem China, 6¼ In.	8.00
Colonial Couple, Soup, Dish, 23K Gold Trim, Salem China, 8½ In.	9.00
Colonial Village, Cup & Saucer, Salem China	15.00

Depression Glass, Windsor, Soup, Cream, Pink, 5 In. $28.00

Dick Tracy, Figure, Composition, Painted, Movable Head, 1930s, 13 In. $575.00

Dick Tracy, Toy, Bonnie Braids, Crawls, Windup, Marx, Box, 11 In. $140.00

Dick Tracy, Toy, Tommy Gun, Die Cast, Orange Plug, Strap, Box, 20 In. $518.00

Dinnerware, Autumn Harvest, Plate, Dinner, Taylor, Smith & Taylor $8.00

Dinnerware, Eva Zeisel, Casserole, Duck Head Cover, Blue, Brown, Western Stoneware, 1953, 7½ x 9 In. $2760.00

Dating Dinnerware by Decorations

Colonial scenes and figures dressed in period costume were popular dinnerware designs in the 1930s because of the interest in the restoration of Colonial Williamsburg. Mexican and Hawaiian themes were trendy in the late 1930s and 1940s, and hand-painted and decal designs of cactus or hula dancers were common. Disney-inspired designs also appeared on dinnerware in the 1940s. Rustic-looking, California-inspired, mix-and-match pottery was "in" on dinnerware for young marrieds in the 1950s. In the 1950s, western designs seemed to follow the popularity of movie cowboys like Tom Mix and Hopalong Cassidy. Stars, planets, and other space-related patterns came in by the late 1950s.

Crabapple, Plate, Dinner, Blue Ridge, 9½ In.	15.00
Dauphine, Platter, Harmony House, 12⅝ x 9¼ In.	25.00
Day Lily, Plate, Dinner, Taylor, Smith & Taylor, 10 In.	11.00
Debutante, Casserole, Cover, Homer Laughlin, 4¼ x 10 In.	34.00
Devonshire, Bowl, Cereal, Johnson Brothers	5.00
Devonshire, Bowl, Vegetable, Johnson Brothers, 8 In.	16.00
Dinner Rose, Creamer, Crooksville	26.00
Dinner Rose, Cup & Saucer, Gold Trim, Crooksville	12.00
Dinner Rose, Plate, Bread & Butter, Crooksville, 6 In.	8.00
Dinner Rose, Saucer, Crooksville	4.00
Dinner Rose, Sugar, Cover, Crooksville	35.00
Dogwood, Pitcher, Pink, Ice Lip, Universal, 2 Qt., 6 In.	45.00
Duchess, Chamber Pot, Homer Laughlin, 1920s, 9 x 5 In.	45.00
English Chippendale, Bowl, Vegetable, Cover, Red, Johnson Brothers, 8¾ In.	192.00
English Chippendale, Cup & Saucer, Red, Johnson Brothers	28.00
English Chippendale, Sugar, No Cover, Red, 4-Footed, Handles, Johnson Brothers, 2½ In.	28.00
English Village, Cup & Saucer, Salem China	18.00
Eva Zeisel, Casserole, Duck Head Cover, Blue, Brown, Western Stoneware, 1953, 7½ x 9 In. *illus*	2760.00
Fairlane, Plate, Dinner, Steubenville, 10½ In. *illus*	7.00
Ferndale, Gravy Boat, Harmony House	15.00
Forsythia, Sugar, Cover, Edwin M. Knowles	9.00
French Peasant, Relish, Blue Rim, Leaf Shape, Blue Ridge, 11 In. *illus*	20.00
Fruit Basket, Relish, Blue Ridge, 6¼ x 10½ In.	25.00
Garden Bouquet, Gravy Boat, Attached Underplate, Johnson Brothers, 9 In.	55.00
Garden Bouquet, Platter, Oval, Johnson Brothers, 10 x 8¼ In.	24.00
Garden Bouquet, Platter, Oval, Johnson Brothers, 12 x 9½ In.	28.00
Georgetown, Cup & Saucer, Salem China	15.00
Georgetown, Plate, Dinner, Salem China, 10¼ In.	28.00
Georgetown, Saucer, Salem China, 6⅛ In.	8.00
Grape, Plate, Luncheon, Blue Ridge, 8⅜ In.	15.00
Grapes, Butter, Cover, Iroquois	26.00
Grapes, Coffee Carafe, Iroquois	56.00
Harvest, Pie Baker, Universal, 10 In.	20.00
Harvest Time, Mug, Johnson Brothers, 3½ In.	20.00
Harvest Time, Plate, Bread & Butter, Johnson Brothers, 6¼ In.	6.00
Heritage, Bowl, Vegetable, White, 8-Sided, Oval, Johnson Brothers, 9 In.	15.00
Heritage, Cup & Saucer, White, Johnson Brothers	15.00
Highlander, Coffeepot, Harmony House, 5 Cup	15.00
Hollyhocks, Platter, Platinum Rim, Fluted, Oval, Universal, 11 x 8¾ In.	28.00
Honey Hen, Plate, Bread, Harmony House, 6¼ In.	10.00
Hostess, Soup, Dish, Edwin M. Knowles	10.00
Indian Tree, Platter, Oval, Johnson Brothers, 11½ x 9 In.	40.00
Iris, Plate, Bread & Butter, Homer Laughlin, 6 In.	14.00
Iva-Lure, Berry Bowl, Crooksville, 5½ In.	8.00
Iva-Lure, Bowl, Vegetable, Crooksville, 8½ In.	26.00
Iva-Lure, Cup & Saucer, Crooksville	15.00
Iva-Lure, Gravy Boat, Stand, Crooksville, 9½ x 5¼ In.	48.00
Iva-Lure, Plate, Bread & Butter, Crooksville, 6 In.	8.00
Iva-Lure, Plate, Dinner, Crooksville, 10 In.	15.00
Iva-Lure, Plate, Salad, Crooksville, 8 In.	12.00
Iva-Lure, Saucer, Crooksville	5.00
Ivy Twine, Plate, Bread & Butter, Taylor, Smith & Taylor, 6¾ In.	3.00
Ivy Twine, Saucer, Taylor, Smith & Taylor	3.00
Jamestown, Plate, Bread & Butter, Johnson Brothers, 6 In.	5.00
Jamestown, Saucer, Johnson Brothers	3.50
Jean, Plate, Dinner, Homer Laughlin, 10 In.	15.00
Kraft, Salt & Pepper, Blue, Homer Laughlin	22.00
Largo, Pitcher, Ice Lip, Universal, 2 Qt., 6 In.	40.00
Lazy Daisy, Plate, Dinner, Iroquois, 10 In.	8.00
Lazy Daisy, Platter, Avocado Green, Taylor Smith & Taylor, 13½ In.	19.00
Lazy Daisy, Platter, Blue & Yellow Daisies, Ben Siebel Design, Iroquois	16.00
Lazy Daisy, Platter, Oval, Iroquois, 12 In.	12.00
Liberty, Teapot, Homer Laughlin, 1954, 8 In.	17.50
Maple Leaf, Bowl, Dessert, Salem China, 6⅛ In.	6.00
Maple Leaf, Plate, Dinner, Salem China, 10 In.	8.00
Marigold, Platter, Homer Laughlin, 1935, 11½ In.	12.50

Mary, Creamer, Harmony House	14.00
Mary Bello, Sugar & Creamer, Royal China	14.00
Mayflower, Plate, Dinner, Edwin M. Knowles, 10 In.	8.00
Melody, Plate, Salad, Edwin M. Knowles, 7½ In.	12.00
Memory Lane, Bowl, Red, Royal China, 5¾ In.	6.00
Memory Lane, Plate, Dinner, Pink, Royal China, 10 In. ......*illus*	12.00
Moderne, Creamer, Harmony House	14.00
Moderne, Sugar, Cover, Handles, Harmony House	15.00
Monticello, Creamer, Harmony House	15.00
Monticello, Sugar, Cover, Handles, Harmony House	25.00
Monticello, Sugar, Cover, Handles, Salem China	20.00
Moselle, Soup, Dish, Triumph Shape, Homer Laughlin, 1950s, 8 In.	8.00
Moss Rose, Plate, Bread & Butter, Universal, 6 In.	5.00
Mount Vernon, Creamer, Harmony House	15.00
Mount Vernon, Cup, Harmony House	15.00
Nora, Sugar, Cover, Handles, Harmony House	18.00
Northstar, Berry Bowl, Salem China, 5¼ In.	9.00
Old Britain Castles, Platter, Green, Johnson Brothers	68.00
Old Britain Castles, Saucer, Pink, Johnson Brothers	8.00
Old Britain Castles, Sugar & Creamer, Green, Johnson Brothers	48.00
Old English Clover, Gravy Boat, Johnson Brothers, 7¾ x 4 In.	18.00
Old English Clover, Plate, Salad, Johnson Brothers, 8 In.	6.00
Old English Clover, Soup, Dish, Flat, Johnson Brothers, 8 In.	8.00
Old English Clover, Sugar, Cover, Handles, Johnson Brothers, 4 In.	15.00
Olde English Countryside, Mug, Johnson Brothers	13.00
Olde English Countryside, Teapot, Brown, 4-Footed, Johnson Brothers, 4 Cup	148.00
Pastoral, Bowl, Fruit, Green, Taylor, Smith & Taylor	10.00
Pebbleford, Saucer, Honey Gold, Taylor, Smith & Taylor	3.00
Pennsylvania, Bowl, Salad, Homer Laughlin, 1960, 9 In.	15.00
Petal Lane, Saucer, Taylor, Smith & Taylor	3.00
Petal Lane, Serving Bowl, Platinum Trim, Taylor, Smith & Taylor	12.00
Piccadilly, Bowl, Vegetable, Homer Laughlin, 1940, 9 In.	16.00
Platinum Garland, Bowl, Fruit, Harmony House, 5½ In.	18.00
Poinsettia, Plate, Salad, Blue Ridge, 7¼ In.	15.00
Poppy, Pie Baker, Silver Trim, Universal, 8½ In.	22.00
Poppy, Platter, Red Trim, Oval, Universal, 13½ x 10⅜ In.	18.00 to 20.00
Puritan, Sugar, Cover, Handles, Footed, Edwin M. Knowles	8.00
Quadra Granite, Plate, Dessert, Square, 7¼ In.	6.00
Reveille, Plate, Dinner, Yellow, Red Trim, Taylor, Smith & Taylor	12.00
Ridge Daisy, Plate, Dinner, Blue Ridge, 9½ In.	12.00
Ring-O-Roses, Creamer, Blue Ridge	14.00
Ring-O-Roses, Cup & Saucer, Blue Ridge	16.00
Rooster, Cup, Taylor, Smith & Taylor	12.00
Rosalinde, Plate, Dinner, Blue Ridge, 9¼ In.	25.00
Rose Chintz, Cup & Saucer, Johnson Brothers	18.00
Rose Mist, Baker, Oval, Platinum Trim, Taylor, Smith & Taylor	12.00
Rosebud, Cup & Saucer, Harmony House	12.00
Rosebud, Plate, Dinner, Harmony House, 10¼ In. ......*illus*	15.00
Rosebud, Saucer, Harmony House	5.00
Rosedale, Soup, Dish, Rim, Harmony House, 8½ In.	18.00
Shadow Fruit, Creamer, Ice Lip, Blue Ridge, 3½ In.	20.00
Shasta Daisy, Platter, Coupe Shape, Taylor Smith & Taylor, 11⅜ In.	15.00
Sheraton, Plate, Bread & Butter, Johnson Brothers, 6¼ In.	5.00
Simplicity, Cup & Saucer, Turquoise, Salem China	5.00
Simplicity, Plate, Dinner, Turquoise, Salem China, 10 In.	7.00
Simplicity, Plate, Salad, Turquoise, Salem China, 7¼ In.	4.00
Simplicity, Soup, Dish, Turquoise, Salem China, 8 In.	5.00
Simplicity, Sugar, Cover, Turquoise, Handles, Salem China, 3½ In.	8.00
Sophisticated Lady, Plate, Dinner, Harmony House, 10¼ In.	15.00
Southern Belle, Saucer, Harmony House, 5⅞ In.	6.00
Staffordshire Bouquet, Plate, Dinner, Johnson Brothers, 10 In.	10.00
Staffordshire Bouquet, Saucer, Johnson Brothers, 5¾ In.	7.00
Starlite, Bowl, Vegetable, Oval, Regal China, 10¾ In.	22.00
Starlite, Creamer, Regal China, 5½ In.	15.00
Starlite, Cup & Saucer, Regal China	17.00
Starlite, Plate, Dinner, Regal China, 10½ In.	17.00

Dinnerware, Fairlane, Plate, Dinner, Steubenville, 10½ In. $7.00

Dinnerware, French Peasant, Relish, Blue Rim, Leaf Shape, Blue Ridge, 11 In. $20.00

Dinnerware, Memory Lane, Plate, Dinner, Pink, Royal China, 10 In. $12.00

> **TIP**
> *Don't use a repaired plate for food. It could be a health hazard.*

Dinnerware, Rosebud, Plate, Dinner, Harmony House, 10¼ In. $15.00

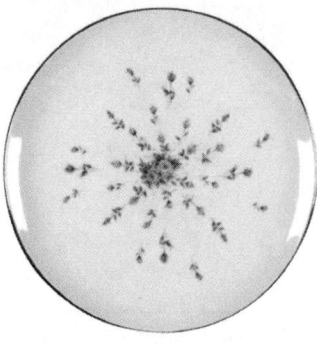

Dinnerware, Teapot, Round, Shaped Handle, Paul Schreckengost, c.1938, 7 x 11 In. $4800.00

Dionne Quintuplets, Doll, Madame Alexander, Composition, Baby, Basket, Tag, Clippings, 7-In. Dolls $345.00

Dionne Quintuplets, Madame Alexander, Composition, Merry-Go-Round, Animal Gondolas, 7½ In. $4125.00

Starlite, Soup, Dish, Regal China, 7¾ In.	14.00
Starlite, Sugar, Cover, Handles, Regal China, 2¾ x 6½ In.	18.00
Symphony, Plate, Luncheon, Chartreuse, Harmony House, 9¼ In.	18.00
Symphony, Plate, Luncheon, Gray, Harmony House, 9¼ In.	8.00
Symphony, Plate, Luncheon, Pink, Harmony House, 9¼ In.	8.00
Teapot, Round, Shaped Handle, Paul Schreckengost, c.1938, 7 x 11 In. ....*illus*	4800.00
Tiajuana, Platter, Oval, Edwin M. Knowles, 13½ x 10 In.	26.00
Tierra, Gravy Boat, Underplate, Harmony House	15.00
Triumph, Plate, Luncheon, Platinum Rim, Taylor, Smith & Taylor	10.00
Trotter, Plate, Dinner, Crooksville, 10 In.	22.00
Triumph, Soup, Coupe, Homer Laughlin, 1950s, 8 In.	7.50
Vellum, Bowl, Vegetable, Oval, Regal China	14.00
Vellum, Gravy Boat, Attached Underplate, Regal China	16.00
Vellum, Soup, Dish, Regal China	8.00
Victory, Platter, Oval, Salem China, 11¼ In.	40.00
Virginia Rose, Bowl, Scalloped Rim, Homer Laughlin, 3 x 6 In.	25.00
Watteau Pareek, Plate, Bread & Butter, Johnson Brothers, 7½ In.	5.00
Watteau Pareek, Plate, Dinner, Johnson Brothers, 9 In.	9.00
Wild Cherry, Cup & Saucer, Blue Ridge	10.00
Windemere, Plate, Dessert, Taylor, Smith & Taylor, 7⅛ In.	3.00
Winnie, Plate, Dinner, Blue Ridge, 9⅜ In.	15.00
Wood Hyacinth, Platter, Universal, 12 x 11 In.	23.00
Woodfield, Cup & Saucer, Golden Fawn, Steubenville	13.00
Woodfield, Cup & Saucer, Salmon Pink, Steubenville	15.00
Woodfield, Plate, Dinner, Gray, Steubenville, 9 In.	7.00
Woodhue, Bowl, Fruit, Harmony House, 5½ In.	18.00

DIONNE QUINTUPLETS were born in Canada on May 28, 1934. The publicity about their birth and their special status as wards of the Canadian government made them famous throughout the world. Visitors could watch the girls play; reporters interviewed the girls and the staff. Thousands of special dolls and souvenirs were made picturing the quints at different ages. Emilie died in 1954, Marie in 1970, Yvonne in 2001. Annette and Cecile still live in Canada.

Ad, Karo Syrup, 1937, 8¼ x 12 In.	10.00
Doll, Baby, Madame Alexander, Pillow Bed, Molded Hair, 1930s, 16 x 22 In., 5 Piece	588.00
Doll, Composition, Socket Head, Painted Hair, Sleep Eyes, 2 Outfits, c.1935	425.00
Doll, Madame Alexander, Composition, Baby, Basket, Tag, Clippings, 7-In. Dolls ....*illus*	345.00
Doll, Toddler, Madame Alexander, Composition, Sunsuits, 1930s, 7¼ In., 5 Piece	588.00
Fan, Playing At Beach, Paper, Home Science Bakery, Pittsburgh, Penn., 1936	15.00
Madame Alexander, Composition, Merry-Go-Round, Animal Gondolas, 7½ In. ......*illus*	4125.00
Magazine, Click, Cover Story, 13301, 52 Pages	14.00
Paper Dolls, Here We Are Three Years Old, Whitman, 1937	40.00
Spoon Set, Full Body, Carlton, Silver Plate, 1930s	129.00

DIRK VAN ERP was born in 1860 and died in 1933. He opened his own studio in 1908 in Oakland, California. He moved his studio to San Francisco in 1909 and the studio remained under the direction of his son until 1977. Van Erp made hammered copper accessories, including vases, desk sets, bookends, candlesticks, jardinieres, and trays, but he is best known for his lamps. The hammered copper lamps often had shades with mica panels.

Bookends, Copper, Hammered, Pierced Lunette, Oak Tree, 4¼ x 5½ In.	1800.00
Bowl, Copper, Hammered, Flared, Footed, Patina, Impressed Mark, 2½ x 11 In.	440.00
Box, Copper, Hammered, Cover, 4 Cutout Designs, Patina, Impressed Mark, 2 x 4 In.	550.00
Box, Copper, Hammered, Round Handle, Cover, Original Patina, Signed, 4½ x 3½ In. Diam.	700.00
Lamp, Copper, Hammered, 3-Light, Mica, 3-Paneled, 20 x 18 In.	6000.00
Lamp, Electric, Hand Wrought Copper, Mica, Stenciled, Shade, c.1920, 11 In.	8400.00
Vase, Copper, Hammered, Flaring Rim, Open Box Mark, 3 x 6 In.	540.00
Vase, Copper, Hammered, Shouldered, Wide Mouth, Windmill Mark, 6¼ x 5 In. ....*illus*	3335.00
Vase, Copper, Hammered, Wrinkled Neck, Bulbous, 8½ x 7½ In.	10200.00

DISNEYANA is a collector's term. Walt Disney and his company introduced many comic characters to the world. Collectors search for examples of the work of the Disney Studios and the many commercial products modeled after his characters, including Mickey Mouse and Donald Duck, and recent films, like *Beauty and the Beast* and *The Little Mermaid*.

Ashtray, 3 Little Pigs, Luster, 3½ In.	29.00
Ashtray, Bambi, Lying Down, Goebel, Hummel, Full Bee, 4 In.	72.00
Ashtray, Bambi, Standing, Goebel, Hummel, 3 In.	72.00
Ashtray, Donald Duck, Twins, Long Bills, Luster, 4 In.	342.00
Ashtray, Donald Duck & Pluto, Cart, Luster, 5 In.	522.00
Ashtray, Little Hiawatha, Ceramic, 4 In.	29.00
Ashtray, Louie Duck, Green Hat, Hockey Stick, Skates, Goebel, Hummel, 4 In.	65.00
Ashtray, Mickey & Minnie Mouse, Pluto, Luster	291.00
Ashtray, Mickey & Minnie Mouse, Seated, Luster, Japan, 3¼ In.	80.00
Ashtray, Mickey Mouse, Black, White, Ceramic, Belgium, 7½ In.	920.00
Ashtray, Mickey Mouse, Full Body, Flat, Black, White, Belgium, 5⅛ In.	555.00
Ashtray, Mickey Mouse, Hard Rubber, Early 1930s, 4¼ In.	179.00
Ashtray, Mickey Mouse, Large Ears, Seated, 3½ x 4¼ In.	59.00
Ashtray, Mickey Mouse, Playing Mandolin, Luster, Japan, 4 In.	59.00
Ashtray, Mickey Mouse, Playing Violin, Spring Legs, Japan, 4½ In.	240.00
Ashtray, Thumper, Goebel, Hummel, 4½ In.	56.00
Bank, 3 Little Pigs, Keylock Trap, Tin Lithograph, 3⅛ In.	160.00
Bank, Alice In Wonderland, Mad Hatter, Register, Tin Lithograph, Girard, Pa., c.1951, 4 In.	605.00
Bank, Dopey, Crown Toy & Novelty, 7 In.	125.00
Bank, Mickey Mouse, Hands On Hips, Cast Metal, 1970-80, 20 In.	252.00
Bank, Mickey Mouse, Hands On Hips, Red Shorts, Aluminum, France, 9 In.	715.00
Bicycle, Donald Duck, Shelby, Yellow, Donald Headlight, 1949	2629.00
Book, Big Little Book, Donald Duck & His Misadventures, 1937	45.00
Book, Big Little Book, Mickey Mouse & The Bat Bandit, 1935	25.00
Book, Farmyard Symphony, Whitman, 1939	45.00
Book, Golden Touch, Whitman, 1937	95.00
Book, Professor Ludwig Von Drake Dog Expert, Whitman, 1962	22.50 to 25.00
Book, Ugly Ducking, Whitman, 1939	45.00
Book Bag, Snow White & Seven Dwarfs, Pencil Case, Plaid, 1940-50	95.00
Booklet, Mickey Mouse, Spanish Advertising, Scott's Emulsions	85.00
Bowl, 3 Little Pigs, Dancing, Tin Lithograph, 3 In.	248.00
Bowl, Mickey Mouse, ABCs, Bavarian China, 8 In. ....*illus*	138.00
Bowl, Mickey Mouse, Large Alphabet, Beetleware, 1930s	65.00
Box, Pencil, Mickey Mouse Figure, Composition, Dixon, 1930s, 5½ x 8½ In.	1232.00
Brush Set, Mickey Mouse, Wooden Handle, Mm Decal, Henry Hughes, Box, 4¼ In.	72.00
Candlestick, Goofy, Cast Iron, John Wright, No. 222, 4 x 5 In.	252.00
Card, Lobby, Dumbo, RKO, 1941	1380.00
Card, Lobby, Snow White & Seven Dwarfs, Show Sensation Of Generation, RKO, 11 x 14 In.	598.00
Card, Snow White & Seven Dwarfs, Valentine, Walt Disney Ent., 5½ x 3 In., 8 Piece	100.00
Catalog, Mickey Mouse, Walt Disney Mickey Mouse Merchandise, Kay Kaman Ltd., 1936-37	2475.00
Cel, see Animation Art category.	
Clock, Alarm, Mickey Mouse, Windup, Bayard, France, 1977, 5 In.	84.00
Clock, Alarm, Pluto, Metal Case, Bayard, 1964, 5 In.	168.00
Clock, Donald Duck, Metal Case, Bayard, France, 1960s, 5 In.	271.00
Condiment Set, Mickey Mouse, China, 4-In. Mustard, 2-In. Salt & Pepper ......*illus*	117.00
Cookie Jar, Alice In Wonderland, Regal China, c.1951, 13½ x 8 x 9 In.	1176.00
Cookie Jar, Mickey Mouse, Standing Behind Film Canister, 13½ x 9½ x 8½ In.	45.00
Cookie Jar, Mickey Mouse & Friends, Skiing, Earthenware, 11 x 10 In.	34.00
Cookie Jar, Snow White & Seven Dwarfs, Enesco, Japan, 10 In.	1456.00
Cookie Jar, Winnie The Pooh, Piglet, Flower Bed, Box, 11 x 8 In.	49.00
Cutouts, Mickey Mouse, Snow White & Seven Dwarfs, Post Toasties Box, c.1938	110.00
Display, Mickey Mouse, Old King Cole, Red Pants, Papier-Mache, c.1930, 42 In.	840.00
Display, Minnie Mouse, Old King Cole, Polka Dot Skirt, Fiber Glass, c.1930, 42 In.	448.00
Doll, Donald Duck, Band Leader, Knickerbocker, c.1938, 16½ In.	4312.00
Doll, Figaro, Composition, Jointed, Tag, Knickerbocker, 1940, 7 In.	276.00
Doll, Mickey Mouse, Composition Feet, Cloth, Pie Eyes, Knickerbocker, 1930s, 12 In.	480.00
Doll, Mickey Mouse, Cowboy, Composition, Chaps, Holster, Guns, Knickerbocker, 10 In.	1035.00
Doll, Mickey Mouse, Easter Parade, Rubber Tail, Tag, Knickerbocker, 1930s, 12½ In.	11180.00
Doll, Mickey Mouse, Felt Cover, Ear Button, Steiff, Germany, 7 In. ......*illus*	702.00
Doll, Mickey Mouse, Pie Eyes, Lenci, 14 In.	224.00
Doll, Mickey Mouse, Stuffed, Cloth, Rubber Tail, Tag, Knickerbocker, 1930s, 16 In.	19096.00
Doll, Mickey Mouse, Stuffed, Felt, Cowboy, Composition Feet, c.1933, 12 In.	504.00
Doll, Mickey Mouse, Stuffed, Felt, Green Pants, Charlotte Clark, c.1934, 20½ In.	1008.00
Doll, Mickey Mouse, Stuffed, Felt, Red Pants, Charlotte Clark, c.1934, 20½ In.	5320.00
Doll, Minnie Mouse, Nifty, Borgfeldt, 14 In.	385.00
Doll, Pinocchio, Wood, Composition, Ideal, 10 In.	412.00

D

> **TIP**
> *Hard plastic dolls will mildew if kept in a damp environment.*

Dirk Van Erp, Vase, Copper, Hammered, Shouldered, Wide Mouth, Windmill Mark, 6¼ x 5 In.
$3335.00

Disneyana, Bowl, Mickey Mouse, ABCs, Bavarian China, 8 In.
$138.00

Cartoon Toys

Modern comic toys include characters from newspapers, movies, and television, like Peanuts, SpongeBob, and the many Disney characters. All sorts of toys have been made to resemble famous comic characters such as Mickey and Minnie Mouse, the Yellow Kid, Maggie and Jiggs, or Snoopy. Each toy usually dates from the time of the strip or cartoon, but many revivals occur.

Disneyana, Condiment Set, Mickey Mouse, China, 4-In. Mustard, 2-In. Salt & Pepper
$117.00

Disneyana, Doll, Mickey Mouse, Felt Cover, Ear Button, Steiff, Germany, 7 In.
$702.00

Disneyana, Pitcher, 3 Little Pigs, Big Bad Wolf Handle, Wade, Heath, England, 10 In.
$165.00

Disneyana, Toy, 3 Little Pigs Band, Tin, Windup, Schuco, 5 In., 3 Piece
$527.00

Doll, Pinocchio, Wood, Composition, Jointed, Ideal, Box, 1940, 7½ In.	280.00
Doll, Pinocchio, Wood, Jointed, Kreuger, Original Tag Dated 1939, 16 In.	285.00
Doll, Pluto, Straw Filled, White, Fur, Felt, c.1930, 12 In.	112.00
Doll, Shaggy Dog, Stuffed, Felt Outfit, Gund, Tag, c.1959, 14 In.	274.00
Doorstop, Donald Duck, Stop & Enter Sign, Cast Iron, 1971, 8 x 5 In.	140.00
Egg Holder, Mickey Mouse, Porcelain, 1930s	165.00
Fan, Silly Symphony, Cardboard, Wood Handle, 14 x 8¼ In.	84.00
Figurine, Donald Duck, Facing Right, Painted, Bisque, Japan, Marked, 6 In.	137.00
Figurine, Donald Duck, Playing Violin, Bisque, 1930s, 4½ In.	295.00
Figurine, Dumbo, Goebel, 1950s, 4 In.	168.00
Figurine, Horace Horsecollar & Clarabelle Cow, Bisque, Japan, 1930s, 5 In., Pair	1670.00
Figurine, Mary Poppins, 2 Medicine Spoons, Musical, Enesco, 1964, 7 In.	524.00
Figurine, Mickey & Minnie Mouse, Big Head, String Tails, Movable, Celluloid, c.1930, 4¾ In.	308.00
Figurine, Mickey Mouse, Black & White, Porcelain, 3¼ In.	150.00
Figurine, Mickey Mouse, Fun-E-Flex, Red Shorts, Yellow Shoes, Original Tail & Ears, 7 In.	385.00
Figurine, Mickey Mouse, Lollipop Hands, Composition Head, Wire Tail, Wood, Jointed, 9½ In.	1064.00
Figurine, Mickey Mouse, Lollipop Hands, Wood, Chest Decal, Borgfeldt, c.1930, 7 In.	672.00
Figurine, Mickey Mouse, Playing Violin, Bisque, Japan, 1930s, 4 In.	325.00
Figurine, Mickey Mouse, Rubber, 3 In.	125.00
Figurine, Mickey Mouse, Sword, Bisque, Prewar Japan, 4 In.	210.00
Figurine, Minnie Mouse, Playing Violin, Bisque, Japan, 1930s, 5¾ In.	560.00
Figurine, Minnie Mouse, Rocking Chair, Tin, Windup, Linemar, Box, 7 In.	750.00
Figurine, Minnie Mouse, Umbrella, Bisque, Prewar Japan, 4 In.	210.00
Figurine, Pegasus, Fantasia, No. 19, Black, Vernon Kilns, 1940	217.00
Figurine, Pegasus, Fantasia, No. 19, Gray, Vernon Kilns, 1940	240.00
Figurine, Pinocchio, Plaster, Composition, France, c.1950, 8 In.	675.00
Figurine, Satyr, Fantasia, Hands On Hips, Ceramic, No. 2, Vernon Kilns, 1940, 4½ In.	196.00
Figurine, Snow White, Bring Back The Heart, Box, Certificate	149.00
Figurine, Snow White, Chalk, c.1933, 9½ In.	121.00
Figurine, Snow White, Humph, Box, Certificate	149.00
Figurine, Snow White & Seven Dwarfs, Britain, 1938-39	336.00
Figurine, Sprite, Fantasia, Crossed Arms, Ceramic, No. 11, Vernon Kilns, 1940, 4¾ In.	196.00
Figurine, Tinkerbell, Bone China, Enesco, 1960s, 1½ In.	224.00
Figurine, Unicorn, Fantasia, No. 15, White, Vernon Kilns, 1940	240.00
Figurine, Unicorn, Fantasia, No. 18, Gray, Vernon Kilns, 1940	240.00
Figurine Set, 3 Little Pigs, Bisque, Borgfeldt, Box, Prewar, 3½ In., 3 Piece	625.00 to 850.00
Figurine Set, 3 Little Pigs, Bisque, Japan, 1930s, 3½ In., 3 Piece	165.00
Figurine Set, Snow White & Seven Dwarfs, Painted, Bisque, Box, Japan, 8 Piece	247.00
Figurine Set, Snow White & Seven Dwarfs, Wade, England, c.1938, 6½-In. Snow White	1453.00
Game, Mickey Mouse, Bagatelle, Wolverine, Box, 1970s, 10 x 15½ In.	62.00
Game, Mickey Mouse, Bagatelle, Wood, Chad Valley, Box, c.1935, 24 In.	392.00
Game, Mickey Mouse, Circus, Marks Bros., Box, c.1934, 9½ x 20 In.	504.00 to 992.00
Game, Snow White & Seven Dwarfs, Board, Parker Brothers, 1938	350.00
Hanky Set, Mickey Mouse, Herrmann Handkerchief, Box, 1930s, 7¼ In., 3 Piece	196.00
Lantern, Mickey Mouse, 50 Glass Slides, Labels, Leather Case, 14 x 18 x 12 In.	330.00
Lantern, Pluto, Tin Lithograph, Linemar, 1950s, 8 In.	153.00
Lighter, Mickey Mouse, Stainless Steel, Zippo, c.1970, 2¼ In.	265.00
Lunch Box, Disney Characters, Metal, Uruguay, c.1950, 6½ x 8¾ x 3½ In.	616.00
Lunch Box, Disney Firefighters, Metal, Dome Top, Aladdin Industries Inc., 1969	154.00
Lunch Box, Disney's New Mickey Mouse Club, Flying Sailboat, Mouseketeers, Aladdin, 1977	45.00
Lunch Box, Mickey Mouse Club, Metal, Aladdin Industries, 1963	205.00
Map, Mickey Mouse, Globetrotters, Cutouts, NBC, Bread Premium, 20 x 26 In.	110.00
Marionette, Mickey Mouse, Composition Head, Cardboard Ears, Fur, Germany, 8 In.	280.00
Marionette, Mickey Mouse, Hestwood, Box, 1933, 12 In.	1478.00 to 1680.00
Marionette, Pluto, Hestwood, Box, 1933, 9½ In.	2464.00
Mold, Mickey Mouse, Chocolate, 1931, 7 In.	395.00
Movie Poster, Alice In Wonderland, Style A, RKO, 1951, 22 x 28 In.	489.00
Movie Poster, Bambi, RKO, Re-Release, 1948, 27 x 41 In.	633.00
Movie Poster, Donald Duck, Sea Scouts, RKO, 1939, 27 x 41 In.	9200.00
Movie Poster, Dumbo, RKO, 1941, 27 x 41 In.	8050.00
Movie Poster, Fantasia, Denmark, RKO, 1940s, 24 x 33½ In.	1837.00
Movie Poster, Peter Pan, RKO, 1953, 27 x 41 In.	805.00
Movie Poster, Pinocchio, RKO, 1940, 22 x 28 In.	4888.00
Movie Poster, Pluto's Christmas Tree, RKO, 1952, 27 x 41 In.	2760.00
Movie Poster, Sleeping Beauty, Buena Vista, 1959, 27 x 41 In.	956.00
Movie Projector, Mickey Mouse, 4 Films, 11 In.	99.00

Napkin Ring, Mickey Mouse, Celluloid, Hand Painted, England, 1930s	275.00
Newsreel, Mickey Mouse Club, Film, Record, Sleeve, Screen	115.00
Night-Light, Dopey, Tin & Paper Lithograph, Kiddy Lite, Box, 1938	475.00
Nodder, Donald Duck, Celluloid, Pendulum, Metal Base, Windup, 1930s, 6 In.	985.00 to 1050.00
Nursery Set, Mickey Mouse, Wardrobe, Bed, Rocker, Table, High Chair, Tri-Ang	450.00
Pail, Mickey & Minnie Mouse, Atlantic City, Tin, Ohio Art, 8 In.	2200.00
Pail, Mickey Mouse, Donald Duck, Stars, Yellow, Red, Blue, Tin Litho, Happynak, 5 In.	248.00
Pail, Mickey Mouse, Pinocchio, Jiminy Cricket, Square, Willow Prod., Australia, c.1945, 6 x 5 In.	224.00
Pail, Mickey Mouse, Pluto, Goofy, Donald Duck, Amusement Park, J. Chein & Co., 7 In.	84.00
Pail & Shovel, 3 Little Pigs, In Spanish, Tin Lithograph, Handle, 5 In.	385.00
Pail & Shovel, 3 Little Pigs, Who's Afraid Of The Big Bad Wolf, Tin Lithograph, 4½ In.	220.00
Pail & Shovel, 3 Little Pigs, Yellow, Footed, Tin Lithograph, Marked, 7 In.	1540.00
Pail & Shovel, Donald Duck, Beach, Tug-O-War, Nephews, Tin Litho, Ohio Art, 1939, 4¼ In.	275.00
Pail & Shovel, Donald Duck, On Boat, Tin Lithograph, Ohio Art, 4½ In.	385.00
Pail & Shovel, Snow White & Seven Dwarfs, Shovel, Handle, Tin, 6 In.	140.00
Pencil Holder, Fifer, Pig Race, Car, Wood, 11 Pencils, Spain, 1930s, 6 In.	224.00
Pencil Sharpener, Donald Duck, Plastic, Scalloped Edge, Catalin, 1930s, 1⅛ In.	117.00
Pencil Sharpener, Pluto, Sitting, Doghouse, Green, Red, Yellow Swirl, Bakelite, 1⅛ In. Diam.	90.00
Pin, Donald Duck, Jackets, Norwich Knitting Co., c.1935, 1¼ In.	411.00
Pin, Donald Duck, With Toothbrush, 1 In.	136.00
Pin, Mickey Mouse, Hands Behind Back, Red, Black, White Ground, Celluloid, 1 In.	85.00
Pin, Mickey Mouse, Running, Evening Ledger Comics, Red, Celluloid, c.1938, 1¼ In.	416.00
Pin, Mickey Mouse Club, Mickey Mouse, Black, White, Red Ground, Celluloid, 1928, 1 In.	154.00
Pin, Mickey Mouse Club, Ritz Theatre, c.1947, ⅞ In.	325.00
Pin, Mickey Mouse In Underwear, Celluloid, Paper Back, 1928-30, ¾ In.	160.00
Pin, Mickey Mouse On Skis, 1⅛ In.	112.00
Pin, Minnie Mouse, Oooh Mickey, Evening Ledger Comics, Celluloid, c.1938, 1¼ In.	672.00
Pitcher, 3 Little Pigs, Big Bad Wolf Handle, Painted, Ceramic, 8¼ In.	248.00
Pitcher, 3 Little Pigs, Big Bad Wolf Handle, Wade, Heath, England, 10 In. .... *illus*	165.00
Pitcher, Mickey Mouse, Porcelain, 4 In.	125.00
Pitcher, Snow White & Seven Dwarfs, Squirrel, Birds, Wade Heath, England, 8¾ In.	220.00
Plate, Donald Duck, 3 Sections, Patriot China Co., 1930, 8 In.	65.00
Plate, Mickey & Minnie Mouse, Dancing, Happy Days, Royal Paragon China, 8 In.	1525.00
Puppet, Jiminy Cricket, Pelham, Original Box, 9½ In.	196.00
Puzzle, Jigsaw, The Love Bug, Whitman, 8 x 11 In.	45.00
Radiator Badge, Mickey Mouse, Pie Eyes, Brass, 6 In.	108.00
Radio, Mickey Mouse, Disney Characters, Emerson, Black, Silver, 1930s	1100.00
Radio, Mickey Mouse, Emerson, 1933, 7½ x 7 In.	920.00
Rattle, Mickey Mouse, Life Preserver, Celluloid, Japan, 1930s, 4¼ In.	3349.00
Rattle, Mickey Mouse, Music Notes, Celluloid, Japan, 1930s, 8 x 2 In.	336.00
Rattle, Snow White & Seven Dwarfs, Playing Instruments, Celluloid, 1938, 6 x 2¼ In.	168.00
Ring, Donald Duck, Instruction Sheet, Kellogg's Pep, Living Toy, Box, 1949	448.00
Sculpture, Mickey Mouse, Puttin' On The Ritz, Bronze, No. 43/50, c.1994, 10¾ In.	1045.00
Sheet Music, Mickey Mouse, Mickey's Son & Daughter, 1935	237.00
Sheet Music, Pinocchio, When You Wish Upon A Star, 1930s	55.00
Shovel, Snow, Mickey Mouse, Snowball Fight Scene, Tin, Wood, Ohio Art, 27 In.	385.00
Sign, Donald Duck Cola, Tops For Flavor, Die Cut, 8 In.	162.00
Sign, Mickey Mouse, White Eyes, Yellow, Green, Red, Neon, 14¼ x 16½ In.	478.00
Tea Set, Mickey & Minnie Mouse, Ceramic, France, 1930s, Service For 12	1650.00
Tea Set, Mickey Mouse, China, Japan, Box, 1930s, 12 Piece	448.00
Tea Set, Mickey Mouse, Minnie Decals, France, Adult Size, 1930s, 12 Piece	1650.00
Tea Set, Mickey Mouse, Tin Lithograph, Ohio Art, 11 Piece	271.00
Toothbrush Holder, Donald Duck, Bisque, Japan, 1930s, 5 In.	315.00
Toothbrush Holder, Mickey & Minnie Mouse, Bisque	225.00
Toothbrush Holder, Mickey Mouse, Bisque, 6 In.	275.00
Toothbrush Holder, Mickey Mouse Wiping Pluto's Nose, Bisque	325.00
Toothbrush Holder, Toby Tortoise, China, Maw & Sons, c.1936, 4 In.	308.00
Toy, 3 Little Pigs, Bisque, Borgfeldt, Prewar, Japan, Box, 3 Piece	765.00
Toy, 3 Little Pigs, Tin, Windup, Linemar, Postwar, 3 Piece	743.00
Toy, 3 Little Pigs Band, Tin, Windup, Schuco, 5 In., 3 Piece .... *illus*	527.00
Toy, 20,000 Leagues Under The Sea, Nautilus, Sutcliffe, Tin, Windup, Box, 9¾ In.	248.00
Toy, Cinderella, Prince Charming, Waltzing, Plastic, Windup, Irwin Corp., Box, 5½ In. *illus*	108.00
Toy, Disney, Bus, Bell Rings, Push Toy, Tin, Pressed Wood, Gong Bell Co., Box, 20 In.	672.00
Toy, Disney Ferris Wheel, Tin, Windup, Chein, 16 In.	205.00
Toy, Disney Ferris Wheel, Tin, Windup, Chein, 1950s, 17 In.	550.00
Toy, Disney Roller Coaster, Tin, Windup, Chein, 19 In.	330.00

Disneyana, Toy, Cinderella, Prince Charming, Waltzing, Plastic, Windup, Irwin Corp., Box, 5½ In. $108.00

Disneyana, Toy, Donald Duck, Roly Poly, Celluloid, Japan, 5 In. $715.00

Disneyana, Toy, Mickey & Minnie Mouse, Pluto, Washing Machine, Tin, Ohio Art, 7 In. $350.00

Disneyana, Toy, Sand Pail, 3 Little Pigs, Tin Lithograph, 3½ In. $358.00

Disneyana, Watch, Mickey Mouse, Original Strap & Fob, Ingersoll
$440.00

Disneyana, Watch, Pocket, Mickey Mouse, Silver, White Dial, Arms As Hands, Ingersoll, 2 In.
$335.00

Disneyana, Wristwatch, Little Pig, Red Band, Box, U.S. Time, 1947, 7 In.
$660.00

Toy, Donald Duck, Driver, Tin, Plastic, Battery Operated, Marx, 1953, 7 In.	357.00
Toy, Donald Duck, Driver, Tin, Windup, Linemar, Box, 1950s	750.00
Toy, Donald Duck, Drummer, Tin Lithograph, Windup, Linemar, Japan, 6 In.	248.00
Toy, Donald Duck, Fireman, Climbing, Windup, Linemar, 7 In.	300.00
Toy, Donald Duck, Goofy, Duet, Tin, Windup, Marx, 1946, 10 In.	330.00
Toy, Donald Duck, Goofy, Duet, Tin, Windup, Marx, Box, 1940s, 10 In.	825.00 to 985.00
Toy, Donald Duck, On Box, Bends Over, Eats Out Of Bowl, Windup, 1930s, 6½ In.	650.00
Toy, Donald Duck, Pluto Cart, Celluloid, Tin, Windup, Prewar Japan, Borgfeldt, Box, 9 In.	3300.00
Toy, Donald Duck, Pulling Huey, Walks, Quacks, Tin, Linemar, Japan, Box, 5½ In.	448.00
Toy, Donald Duck, Race Car, Tin, Celluloid, Occupied Japan, Box, 3 In.	336.00
Toy, Donald Duck, Roly Poly, Celluloid, Japan, 1930s, 7 In.	542.00
Toy, Donald Duck, Roly Poly, Celluloid, Japan, 5 In. *illus*	715.00
Toy, Donald Duck, Talking, Pull Toy, No. 765, Fisher-Price, Box, c.1955, 8 In.	138.00
Toy, Donald Duck, Tricycle, Celluloid, Tin, Red Cap, Linemar, 1950s, 4 In.	252.00
Toy, Donald Duck, Tricycle, Windup, Japan, MT, Box	120.00
Toy, Donald Duck, Twirling Tail, Plastic, Donald Vibrates Around Holding Umbrella, Marx, 6 In.	247.00
Toy, Donald Duck, Waddler, Bobble Head, Battery Operated, Tin, Linemar, Box, 6 In.	495.00
Toy, Donald Duck, Waddler, Long Billed, Celluloid, Windup, 5¼ In.	523.00
Toy, Donald Duck, Walker, Long Bill, Waddles, Celluloid, Windup, 5½ In.	1150.00
Toy, Donald Duck & Nephews, Pull Toy, Fisher-Price, 1941, 13 In.	135.00
Toy, Dumbo, Acrobatic Elephant, Tin, Windup, Marx, Box, 4 In.	715.00
Toy, Dumbo, O Elefante Voador, Flies, Box, 10 In.	336.00
Toy, Figaro, Rolls Over, Rubber Ears, Tin, Windup, Marx, Box, 5 In.	385.00
Toy, Goofy, Car, El Coche Que Anda, Tin, Windup, Box	224.00
Toy, Goofy, Unicycle, Rubber Ears, Tin, Windup, Paper Label, Linemar, 1950s	485.00
Toy, Goofy, Unicycle, Tin, Windup, Linemar, 1950s	575.00
Toy, Johnny Tremain, Horse, Accessories, Box, c.1957, 9¾ x 12½ In.	193.00
Toy, Mickey & Minnie Mouse, Handcar, Composition, Steel, Lionel, Box, 10 In.	605.00
Toy, Mickey & Minnie Mouse, Handcar, Wells, Box, England, 8 In.	990.00
Toy, Mickey & Minnie Mouse, Pluto, Washing Machine, Tin, Ohio Art, 7 In. *illus*	350.00
Toy, Mickey Mouse, Air Mail Airplane, Blue, Propeller, Rubber Wheels, Sun Rubber, 1950s, 6 In.	88.00
Toy, Mickey Mouse, Balloon Vendor, Eyes Move, Monkeys, Tin, Windup, Germany, 7 In.	385.00
Toy, Mickey Mouse, Climbing, Cardboard, String, Dolly Toy Co., Box, c.1935, 9 In.	280.00 to 440.00
Toy, Mickey Mouse, Dipsy Car, On Tractor, Tin, Windup, Linemar, Box, 5½ In.	750.00
Toy, Mickey Mouse, Dipsy Car, Tin, Windup, Linemar, Box	750.00
Toy, Mickey Mouse, Driver, Tin, Plastic, Windup, Marx, Box, 7 In.	616.00
Toy, Mickey Mouse, Driver, Windup, Marx, Box, 1950s, 6½ In.	474.00
Toy, Mickey Mouse, Handcar, Tin Lithograph, Wells Of England, Box	1195.00
Toy, Mickey Mouse, Laundry Set, Pail, Board, Hanger, Ohio Art, Box	495.00
Toy, Mickey Mouse, Laundry Set, Pail, Board, Hanger, Tin Lithograph, Box, 9 In.	275.00
Toy, Mickey Mouse, Magician, Tin, Battery Operated, Linemar, 10 In.	770.00
Toy, Mickey Mouse, On Unicycle, Tin, Cloth, Windup, Japan, Linemar, 5 In.	192.00
Toy, Mickey Mouse, Playing Saxophone, Cymbals, Tin, Squeeze, Germany, 6 In.	385.00
Toy, Mickey Mouse, Pluto Pulling, Celluloid, Tin, Windup, Prewar Japan, Borgfeldt, Box, 9 In.	3575.00
Toy, Mickey Mouse, Race Car, Orange, Tin, No. 5, Windup, 1930s, 4 In.	225.00
Toy, Mickey Mouse, Ramblin' Mickey, Waddles, Celluloid, Windup, 1930s, 7¼ In.	1650.00
Toy, Mickey Mouse, Ricycle, Tin, Windup, Japan, 5 In.	330.00
Toy, Mickey Mouse, Riding Horse, Celluloid, Tin Base, Windup, Marked, Occupied Japan, 6 In.	2090.00
Toy, Mickey Mouse, Scooter Jockey, Head Bobs, Plastic, Windup, Mavco, Box, 6 In.	165.00 to 175.00
Toy, Mickey Mouse, Sparkler, Black, White, Tin, Chein, 5½ In.	385.00
Toy, Mickey Mouse, Sparkler, Tin Lithograph, Nifty, Box, 1931, 5½ In.	616.00
Toy, Mickey Mouse, Waddler, Windup, Celluloid, 1930s	1450.00
Toy, Mickey Mouse, Walker, Wire Tail, Red Pants, Celluloid, Windup, c.1934, 7 In.	668.00
Toy, Mickey Mouse, Washing Machine, Tin Lithograph, Ohio Art, c.1930	235.00
Toy, Mickey Mouse, Whirligig, Celluloid, 10 In.	605.00
Toy, Mickey Mouse, Whirligig, Mickey Balanced On 1 Leg, Borgfeldt, 1930s, 9½ In.	2700.00
Toy, Mickey Mouse, Whirligig, On Ball, Celluloid, Windup, Japan, Box, 8 In.	2200.00
Toy, Mickey Mouse, Whirligig, On Cart, Celluloid, Windup, Japan, Box, 7 In.	440.00
Toy, Mickey Mouse, Xylophone, Pull Toy, No. 798, Fisher-Price, Box, 11 In.	1430.00
Toy, Mickey Mouse, Xylotone Player, Linemar, 7 In.	201.00
Toy, Mickey Mouse & Donald Duck, Rowboat, Celluloid, Japan, 6 In.	550.00
Toy, Mickey Mouse Print Shop, No. 35, Fulton Specialty, Box, c.1935, 6¼ x 6½ In.	136.00
Toy, Minnie Mouse, On Horse, Bobbin', Celluloid, Wood, Japan, 1930s, 4¾ x 5½ In.	801.00
Toy, Minnie Mouse, Rocking Chair, Knitting, Tin, Windup, Linemar, Box, 7 In.	205.00 to 743.00
Toy, Pinocchio, Carousel, Windup, Tin, Composition, Wood Base, France, 14 In.	280.00
Toy, Pinocchio, Tricycle, Tin, Vinyl, Windup, Korea, Box, 4½ In.	110.00

Toy, Pluto, Drum Major, Whistle, Cane, Bell, Tin Lithograph, Windup, Linemar, 6½ In.	275.00
Toy, Pluto, Roll Over, Long Wire Tail, Walt Disney, Marx, 1939, 8 In.	145.00 to 225.00
Toy, Pluto, Roll Over, Tin, Windup, Marx, 1939, 9 In.	225.00
Toy, Pluto, Roll Over, Tin, Windup, Rubber Ears, Marx, Box, 1930s	425.00 to 450.00
Toy, Pluto, Slinky, Tin, Windup, Linemar, 8 In.	220.00
Toy, Pluto, Tin, Rubber Ears, Depress Tail, Spring Wind, Walt Disney, 1939, 8 In.	60.00
Toy, Pluto, Tricycle, Tin, Celluloid, Windup, Linemar, Box, 3¾ In.	650.00
Toy, Pluto, Walker, Moving Head, Rubber Ears & Tail, Plush, Battery Operated, Linemar, 5 In.	387.00
Toy, Pluto, Wise, Crouched, Nose To Ground, Tin Lithograph, Windup, Marx, Box, 1939, 8 In.	550.00
Toy, Professor Ludwig Von Drake, Squeak, Rubber, 7½ In.	135.00
Toy, Ramp Walker, Donald Duck, Composition, Wilson, 1939	495.00
Toy, Ramp Walker, Mickey Mouse, Pushing Lawn Roller, Marx, 1950s	75.00
Toy, Ramp Walker, Pluto, Marx, 1950s	75.00
Toy, Sand Pail, 3 Little Pigs, Tin Lithograph, 3½ In. ....*illus*	358.00
Toy, Tea Set, Donald Duck, Porcelain, Occupied Japan, Box, 11 Piece	193.00
Toy, Train, Disney Land Express, 4 Cars, Tin, Windup, Marx, Box, 12 In.	138.00
Toy, Train, Mickey Mouse Meteor, Engine, 4 Cars, Disney Characters, Windup, Marx	850.00
Toy, Zorro, On Horse, Plastic, Unopened Package, Lido, c.1958, 7½ x 9 In.	246.00
Trolley, Tin, Red Roof, Yellow, Green, Dayton, 16 In.	165.00
Wall Pocket, Mickey & Minnie Mouse, Luster, Orange Rim, 1930s	217.00
Watch, Mickey Mouse, Original Strap & Fob, Ingersoll ....*illus*	440.00
Watch, Pocket, Donald Duck, Ingersoll, Box, 1939, 2 x 2 In.	1232.00
Watch, Pocket, Mickey Mouse, Celluloid Dial, Ingersoll	1663.00
Watch, Pocket, Mickey Mouse, Silver, White Dial, Arms As Hands, Ingersoll, 2 In. ......*illus*	335.00
Watering Can, 3 Little Pigs, Who's Afraid Of The Big Bad Wolf, Tin Lithograph, 4½ In.	330.00
Wristwatch, Alice In Wonderland, Tea Cup, U.S. Time, Box, 1950, 3 x 5 In.	862.00
Wristwatch, Cinderella, Slipper, U.S. Time, Box, 1950, 5 x 5 x 5 In.	448.00
Wristwatch, Goofy, Runs Backwards, 17 Jewels, Helbros, Plastic Case, 1972	896.00
Wristwatch, Jiminy Cricket, Chrome Case, Ingersoll, 20th Birthday Box, 1948	355.00
Wristwatch, Little Pig, Red Band, Box, U.S. Time, 1947, 7 In. ....*illus*	660.00

DOCTOR, *see Dental and Medical categories.*

DOLL entries are listed by marks printed or incised on the doll, if possible. If there are no marks, the doll is listed by the name of the subject or country or maker. Notice that Barbie is listed under Mattel. G.I. Joe figures are listed in the Toy section. Eskimo dolls are listed in the Eskimo section and Indian dolls are listed in the Indian section. Doll clothes and accessories are listed at the end of this section. The twentieth-century clothes listed here are in mint condition.

A.M., 302, Bisque Socket Head, Black Glass Sleep Eyes, Open Mouth, Teddy, Cape, 1920s, 13 In.	264.00
A.M., 323, Bisque Socket Head, Googly Eyes, Smiling, Mohair, 5-Piece Composition Body, 11 In.	805.00
A.M., 323, Bisque Socket Head, Googly Eyes, 5-Piece Body, Toddler, c.1920, 8 In.	952.00
A.M., 341, Dream Baby, Solid Dome, Bisque Flange Head, Cloth Body, Celluloid Hands, 9½ In.	75.00
A.M., 351, Bisque Socket Head, Solid Dome, Sleep Eyes, 5-Piece Composition, Body, 23 In.	288.00
A.M., 370, Bisque, Kid Leather Body, Box, c.1900, 20½ In.	147.00
A.M., 370, Bisque Shoulder Head, Sleep Eyes, Mohair, Kid Body, Rivet-Jointed, Box, 28 In.	431.00
A.M., 390, Bisque Socket Head, Human Hair, Cardboard, Composition, Jointed, Wood, 23 In.	200.00
A.M., 390, Bisque Socket Head, Sleep Eyes, Human Hair, Composition, Jointed, Wood, 30 In.	374.00
A.M., 390, Bisque Socket Head, Stationary Eyes, Synthetic Wig, Composition, Jointed, 23 In.	115.00
A.M., 550, Bisque Socket Head, Sleep Eyes, Mohair, Wood, Composition, Jointed, Boy, 15 In.	604.00
A.M., 590, Bisque Socket Head, Sleep Eyes, Teeth, 5-Piece Composition, Jointed, Baby, 13 In.	230.00
A.M., 990, Bisque Socket Head, Sleep Eyes, Teeth, Mohair, Composition, Baby, 20 In.	288.00
A.M., Bisque Socket Head, Set Eyes, Human Hair, Composition, Jointed, 1894, 17 In.	201.00
A.M., Flora Dora, Bisque Shoulder Head, Blue Glass Eyes, Leather Body, 22 In. ......*illus*	115.00
A.M., Just Me, Bisque Socket Head, Googly Eyes, Mohair, 5-Piece Composition, 7½ In.	1208.00
A.M., Just Me, Bisque Socket Head, Googly Sleep Eyes, 5-Piece Composition, 9 In.	1725.00
A.M., Queen Louise, Bisque Head, Green Eyes, Open Mouth, 22 In.	185.00
A.M., Queen Louise, Bisque Socket Head, Synthetic Wig, Composition, Jointed, Wood, 25 In.	316.00
Advertising, Buddy Lee, Phillips 66, Composition, Green Outfit, 13 In.	392.00
Advertising, General Electric Radio, Drum Major, Wood, Jointed, 20 In. ....*illus*	935.00
Advertising, Marky Maypo, Vinyl, Squeak Toy, 1960s, 9 In.	140.00
Advertising, Miss Sunbeam Bread, Vinyl, Navy Dress, Blond Hair, Houseman Inc., 1970, 14 In.	115.00
Advertising, Radiotron, General Electric Radio, Wood, String Jointed, Parrish, 18 In. ..*illus*	634.00
Advertising, Sunshine Biscuit, Elephant, Cloth, Stuffed, For Sunshine Animal Crackers, 5 In.	358.00
Advertising, Taco Bell, Chihuahua Dog, Talking, 1990s, 6 In.	10.00
Alexander Dolls are listed in this category under Madame Alexander.	

View-Master

View-Master was invented in 1939 in Portland, Oregon, by William Gruber. His hobby was stereo photography. Since then more than a billion of the viewers have been sold. The U.S. military used the viewers for training during World War II. After the war, adults bought them to view reels of national parks and other tourist sites. View-Master got a license to picture Disney characters in 1951 and it became a popular children's toy.

Doll, A.M., Flora Dora, Bisque Shoulder Head, Blue Glass Eyes, Leather Body, 22 In.
$115.00

Doll, Advertising, General Electric Radio, Drum Major, Wood, Jointed, 20 In.
$935.00

Doll, Advertising, Radiotron, General Electric Radio, Wood, String Jointed, Parrish, 18 In.
$634.00

Doll, American Character, Tiny Tears, Plastic Head, Sleep Eyes, Vinyl, Suitcase, 12 In.
$69.00

Doll, Arranbee, Nancy Lee, Composition, Clear Sleep Eyes, Lashes, Blond Mohair Wig, 20 In.
$58.00

Alt Beck & Gottschalck, 1353, Bisque Head, Blue Sleep Eyes, Mohair, Early 1900s, 14½ In.	176.00
Alt Beck & Gottschalck, Bisque Shoulder Head, Turned Right, Cloth Stitched Body, Jointed, 27 In.	575.00
American Character, Betsy McCall, Hard Plastic, Jointed, Schoolgirl Dress, c.1960-63, 8 In.	178.00
American Character, Betsy McCall, Hard Plastic, Mussed Hair, Jointed, 8 In.	58.00
American Character, Betsy McCall, Hard Plastic, Mussed Hair, Jointed, Pony Pals, c.1958, 8 In.	144.00
American Character, Betsy McCall, School Days, Vinyl, Sleep Eyes, Brown Hair, 1959, 14 In.	700.00
American Character, Betsy McCall, Vinyl, Jointed, Trunk, Clothing, c.1958-59, 14 In.	230.00
American Character, Cloth, Felt Swivel Head, Mohair, Jointed Arms, Legs, 17 In.	1792.00
American Character, Lillian, Felt Swivel Head, Painted Features, 5 Piece, 17 In.	2576.00
American Character, Muslin, Flat Face, Painted, Shaped Body, Stitch-Jointed Limbs, 18 In.	952.00
American Character, Patrick, Felt Swivel Head, Painted Features, Mohair, Felt, Jointed, 18 In.	2352.00
American Character, Tiny Tears, Plastic Head, Sleep Eyes, Vinyl, Suitcase, 12 In. *illus*	69.00
American Character, Toni, Vinyl, Jointed, Tagged Dress, 10½ In.	144.00
Armand Marseille Dolls are listed in this category under A.M.	
Arranbee, Nancy, Composition, Open Mouth, Sleep Eyes, Mohair, Jointed, Box, 14 In.	460.00
Arranbee, Nancy Lee, Cinderella, White Coiffure Dress, Leaves & Flowers, 1949, 14 In.	850.00
Arranbee, Nancy Lee, Composition, Clear Sleep Eyes, Lashes, Blond Mohair Wig, 20 In. *illus*	58.00
Arranbee, Nursing Bottle Baby, Bisque Head, Solid Dome, Sleep Eyes, Stuffed Cloth Body, 12 In.	201.00
Automaton, Bebe Rose, Bisque Head, Papier-Mache, Open Spring, Roullet Et Decamps, 9 In.	572.00
Automaton, Bebe Rose, Jumeau Bisque, Head, Papier-Mache, Roullet Et Decamps, 10½ In.	5875.00
Automaton, Carousel, Riders On Gondolas & Horses, Silk Canopy, France, 12 x 12 In. *illus*	2300.00
Automaton, Cat Jumping, Fur, Hoop With Bells, Windup, Roullet Et Decamps, 6½ In.	588.00
Automaton, Cats' Tea Party, Fur Covered, Grain Painted, Multicolored, c.1890, 12 x 8½ In.	2585.00
Automaton, Cobbler, Nodding, Storefront, Papier-Mache, Hammer In Hand, Windup, 21 In.	1293.00
Automaton, Dancer, Man, Bisque Socket Head, Mohair, Castanets, Tambourine, Lambert, 26 In.	3163.00
Automaton, Goat, Nodding, Fur, Articulated Head, Glass Eyes, Papier-Mache, 17 x 11 In.	353.00
Automaton, Rabbit In Cabbage, Open Spring Movement, Papier-Mache, 4 Movements, 11 In.	3525.00
Automaton, Rabbit Violinist, Fur Covered, Glass Eyes, Roullet Et Decamps, 18½ In.	4406.00
Automaton, Shepherdess, Papier-Mache Landscape, Gustave Vichy, c.1880, 16 x 20 In.	12925.00
Automaton, Smoking Man, Bisque Head & Hands, Leopold Lambert, c.1895, 24 In. *illus*	5750.00
Bahr & Proschild, 204, Bisque Socket Head, Paperweight Eyes, Wood, Composition, 15 In.	978.00
Bahr & Proschild, 641, Bisque Socket Head, Blue Glass Sleep Eyes, Boy, 12 In. *illus*	173.00
Bahr & Proschild, 678, Bisque Socket Head, Sleep Eyes, Human Hair, Composition, Baby, 16 In.	374.00
Barbie Dolls are listed in this category under Mattel.	
Bergner, Bisque Socket Head, 3 Faces, Mohair, Papier-Mache, Cloth, Cardboard Body, 12 In.	978.00
Bisque, Black, Jointed Arms, Legs, Original Clothes, Japan, 6 In.	75.00
Bisque, Boy & Girl, Flower & Bee, Painted Eyes, Watermelon Mouth, 5 & 5½ In.	294.00
Bisque, Stiff Neck, Painted Features, Human Hair, Pin-Jointed, Painted Shoes, 5 In.	29.00
Bisque, Stiff Neck, Sleep Eyes, String-Jointed, Painted Shoes, Stockings, 4 In.	109.00
Bisque Flange Head, Solid Dome, Sleep Eyes, Cloth Body, Jointed, Composition Limbs, 20 In.	374.00
Bisque Shoulder Head, Dome, Googly Eyes, Mohair Wig, Jointed Hips, c.1915, 5 In.	368.00
Bisque Shoulder Head, Molded Hair, Painted Eyes, Muslin Body, Bisque Limbs, 7 In.	52.00
Bisque Shoulder Head, Molded Hair, Cloth Legs, Oilcloth Arms, Kid Body, Boy, 17 In.	259.00
Black, Heubach, Bisque Socket Head, Sleep Eyes, Painted, Composition, Toddler, 7½ In.	633.00
Black dolls are also included in the Black category.	
Bru Jne, 9, Bisque Socket Head, Paperweight Eyes, Throwing Kiss, Composition, Wood, 22 In.	3960.00
Bru Jne, Bisque, Paperweight Eyes, Mohair, Mona Lisa Smile, Gusseted Kid Body, 18 In.	4140.00
Bru Jne, Bisque Socket Head, Shoulder Plate, Glass Eyes, Human Hair, c.1870, 17 In. *illus*	11000.00
Bru Jne, Bisque Swivel Head, Enamel Eyes, Mohair Wig, Kid Body, Jointed, 13 In.	3300.00
Bru Jne, Bisque Swivel Head, Glass Enamel Eyes, Gusset-Jointed, c.1873, 23 In.	5775.00
Bruno Schmidt, 2042, Bisque Socket Head, Painted Eyes, Ball-Jointed, c.1912, 16 In.	1540.00
Bucherer, Jiggs, Felt Body, Oilcloth Clothes, 1930s, 19½ In.	448.00
Bye-Lo, Bisque Flange Head, Brown Sleep Eyes, Celluloid Hands, Twins, Basket, c.1925, 10 In. *illus*	605.00
Bye-Lo, Bisque Flange Head, Solid Dome, Sleep Eyes, Celluloid Hands, 15 In.	161.00
Bye-Lo, Bisque Head, Blue Sleep Eyes, Painted Hair, Cloth Frog Body, 18 In. *illus*	144.00
Chad Valley, Bonzo, Cloth, Plush, Cream-Color Velvet, Adjustable Arms & Legs, 1925, 12 In.	1005.00
Chase, Boy, Molded & Painted, Stitch-Jointed, Blue Clothes, 27 In. *illus*	546.00
China Head, Flat Top, Cloth Body, Organdy Lace-Trimmed Dress, Painted Boots, 7½ In. *illus*	201.00
China Shoulder Head, Blond Spillcurl, Blue Eyes, Closed Mouth, Cloth Body, c.1870, 13 In.	235.00
China Shoulder Head, Blue Eyes, Molded Hair, 3-Mold, Print Dress, With Dolly, 25 In.	1116.00
China Shoulder Head, Blue Painted Eyes, Pink Tinted Mouth, Cloth Body, Germany, 1870s, 15 In.	147.00
China Shoulder Head, Dolley Madison, Molded Hair & Bow, Painted Eyes, Cloth Body, 25 In. *illus*	345.00
China Shoulder Head, Molded Painted Curls, Blue Eyes, Cloth Body, c.1865, 19 In. *illus*	575.00
China Shoulder Head, Windblown Hair, Pink Tint, Molded Wavy Hair, 1840s, 16½ In.	2585.00
Cloth, Brown Muslin, Flat Face, Embroidered, Yarn Hair, Boy, Girl, American, 17 In., Pair	224.00
Cloth, Cotton, Silk, Stuffed Cotton Head, Bodice, Painted Facial Features, c.1820, 9½ In.	382.00

Doll, Automaton, Carousel, Riders On Gondolas & Horses, Silk Canopy, France, 12 x 12 In.
$2300.00

Doll, Automaton, Smoking Man, Bisque Head & Hands, Leopold Lambert, c.1895, 24 In.
$5750.00

Doll, Bahr & Proschild, 641, Bisque Socket Head, Blue Glass Sleep Eyes, Boy, 12 In.
$173.00

Doll, Bru Jne, Bisque Socket Head, Shoulder Plate, Glass Eyes, Human Hair, c.1870, 17 In.
$11000.0

Doll, Bye-Lo, Bisque Flange Head, Brown Sleep Eyes, Celluloid Hands, Twins, Basket, c.1925, 10 In.
$605.00

Doll, Bye-Lo, Bisque Head, Blue Sleep Eyes, Painted Hair, Cloth Frog Body, 18 In.
$144.0

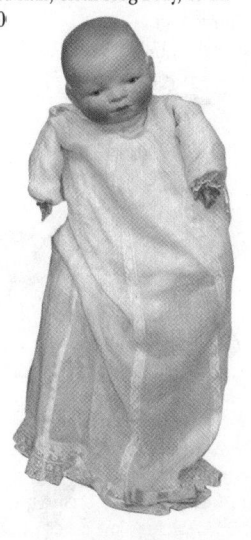

Doll, Chase, Boy, Molded & Painted, Stitch-Jointed, Blue Clothes, 27 In.
$546.00

Doll, China Head, Flat Top, Cloth Body, Organdy Lace-Trimmed Dress, Painted Boots, 7½ In.
$201.00

Doll, China Shoulder Head, Dolley Madison, Molded Hair & Bow, Painted Eyes, Cloth Body, 25 In.
$345.00

Doll, China Shoulder Head,
Molded Painted Curls, Blue Eyes, Cloth Body,
c.1865, 19 In.
$575.00

Doll, Door Of Hope, Manchu Woman,
Pear Wood Head, Carved Headdress,
Cloth Body, 11 In.
$9200.00

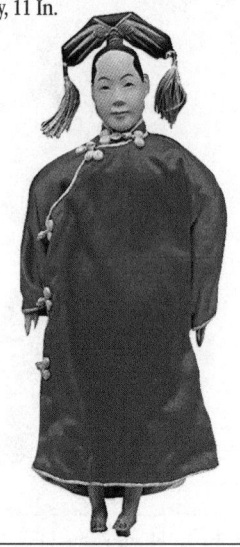

Doll, Freundlich, Gen. MacArthur,
Composition, Painted Features,
Molded Hat, 19 In.
$403.00

Doll, Composition, WAC, Painted Features,
Green Women's Army Uniform, 16 In.
$316.00

Doll, Effanbee, Colonial Historical Replica,
Plastic, White Upswept Wig,
Dress & Coat, 14 In.
$460.00

Doll, Frozen Charlie, China, Pink Luster,
Molded & Painted Hair & Features, Clenched
Fists, 16½ In.
$1320.00

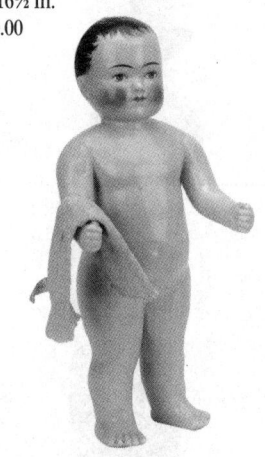

Doll, Composition, Yellow Kid, Big Ears,
Open Mouth, 2 Teeth, Cloth Body,
Straw Stuffing, 13 In.
$1610.00

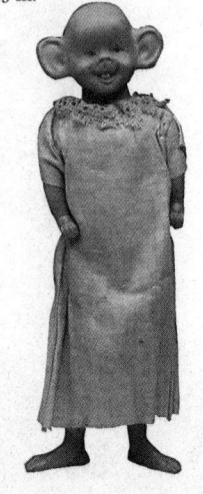

Doll, Fannie Brice, Composition,
Molded Brown Hair,
Original Clothes, 13 In.
$115.00

Frozen Charlottes

Frozen Charlottes, one-piece china
dolls with immovable arms and legs,
were made from the 1850s until
the 1920s. The boy doll was called
"Frozen Charlie." The dolls usually
had their arms at their sides or
pointing straight forward. They were
made from one-inch high, dollhouse
size, up to about 15 inches. Most are
about three inches high.

Cloth, Maggie Bessie, Stitch-Jointed, Oil-Painted Features, Late 1800s, 15 In.	16500.00
Cloth, Notre Dame Fighting Irish, Stuffed, 1950s, 11 In.	45.00
Cloth, Painted Features, Gusseted, Attached Limbs, Cotton Body, Wood-Chip Stuffing, 34 In.	2990.00
Composition, WAC, Painted Features, Green Women's Army Uniform, 16 In. ....*illus*	316.00
Composition, Yellow Kid, Big Ears, Open Mouth, 2 Teeth, Cloth Body, Straw Stuffing, 13 In. *illus*	1610.00
Composition Head, Shoulder Plate, Sleep Eyes, Teeth, Human Hair, Cloth Body, 29 In.	144.00
Damerval & Laffranchy, Bisque Socket Head, Composition Body, Gentleman, 1909-16, 13 In.	1210.00
Demalcol, Bisque Socket Head, Cardboard Pate, Googly Sleep Eyes, Mohair, 10 In.	776.00
Denamur, Bisque Socket Head, Paperweight Eyes, Composition, Jointed, Wood, Bebe, 17 In.	891.00
Door Of Hope, Kindergarten Child, Carved Wood Head, Hands, Early 1900s, 6 In.	999.00
Door Of Hope, Manchu Woman, Pear Wood Head, Carved Headdress, Cloth Body, 11 In. *illus*	9200.00
Dorothy Heizer, Ben Franklin, Cloth, Long White Wig, Gray Suit, 10 In.	2115.00
Dorothy Heizer, Blue Boy, Cloth, Blue Silk Costume, Holding Hat, 9½ In.	2468.00
Dorothy Heizer, Isabella Of Castille, Queen Of Spain, Red Velvet Dress, Jewel Casket, 10 In.	3055.00
Dressel, Flapper, Bisque Socket Head, Sleep Eyes, Mohair, Composition, Wood, Jointed, 14 In.	3024.00
Effanbee, Anne Shirley, Composition, Blue Sleep Eyes, Closed Mouth, Hair, 1930, 15 In.	95.00
Effanbee, Candy Kid, Composition, Closed Mouth, Sleep Eyes, Jointed, 12½ In.	374.00
Effanbee, Colonial Historical Replica, Plastic, White Upswept Wig, Dress & Coat, 14 In. *illus*	460.00
Effanbee, Fairy Princess, Composition, Painted Features, Blue Eyes, Trousseau, 1935, 6 In.	890.00
Effanbee, Patsy Ann, Composition, Jointed, 19 In.	104.00
Effanbee, Patsy Lou, Composition Socket Head, Bobbed Hair, Button Nose, 1935, 21 In.	735.00
Effanbee, Rosemary, Composition Shoulder Head, Limbs, Tin Sleep Eyes, Cloth Body, 22 In.	115.00
Fannie Brice, Composition, Molded Brown Hair, Original Clothes, 13 In. ....*illus*	115.00
Fashion, Bisque Head, Cobalt Blue Eyes, Mohair, Papier-Mache Clog Shoes, 13 In.	4480.00
Fashion, Bisque Swivel Head, Glass Eyes, Blond Mohair, Kid, Gusset-Jointed, France, 16 In.	5280.00
Fashion, Bisque Swivel Head, Glass Eyes, Mohair, Kid, Gusset-Jointed, France, 16 In.	3190.00
Fashion, Bisque Swivel Head, Glass Eyes, Mohair, Kid Body, France, c.1885, 12 In.	2090.00
Fashion, Bisque Swivel Head, Kid-Edge, Glass Eyes, Blond Mohair, Gusset-Jointed, France, 13 In.	2860.00
Fashion, Bisque Swivel Head, Kid-Edged Shoulder Plate, Paperweight Eyes, Kid Body, France, 16 In.	3300.00
Fashion, Papier-Mache Shoulder Head, Painted Features, Human Hair, France, c.1850, 13 In.	1320.00
Fashion, Porcelain, Glass Eyes, Blond Mohair, Kid, Gusset-Jointed, Porcelain Arms, France, 13 In.	2970.00
Fireman, Composition Head, Painted Features, Tribute, Philadelphia, c.1852, 25 In.	4113.00
French, Bisque Head, Glass Sleep Eyes, Mohair Lashes, Painted Features, 24 In.	3410.00
French, Bisque Socket Head, Paperweight Eyes, Mohair, Composition, Wood, Jointed, Bebe, 27 In.	7975.00
French, Bisque Swivel Head, Glass Eyes, Mohair, Kid Over Wood, Dowel-Jointed, 15 In.	4290.00
French, Bisque Swivel Head, Painted, Mohair Moustache, Goatee, Jointed, Metal Hands, 18 In.	4620.00
French, Bisque Swivel Head, Shoulder Plate, Enamel Eyes, Mohair, Kid, Gusset-Jointed, 20 In.	4510.00
French, Bridegroom, Bisque Swivel Head, Glass Eyes, Mohair, Muslin, Jointed, 15 In.	5940.00
French, Cloth, Swivel Head, Painted, Googly Eyes, Mohair, 5-Piece Body, Jointed, 16 In.	715.00
French, Fortune Teller, Porcelain Shoulder Head, Muslin Body, Pedestal, 9½ In.	1485.00
French, Leather Swivel Head, Oil-Painted Features, Twill Body, Stitch-Jointed, c.1920, 8 In.	1870.00
French, Papier-Mache Swivel Head, Dowel-Jointed, Muslin, Wood Limbs, Baby, 20 In.	1210.00
French, Polichinelle, Papier-Mache, White Mohair, Wood Body, 30 In.	2530.00
French, Soldier, Papier-Mache, Composition Socket Head, 5-Piece Body, Costume, 14 In.	1120.00
Freundlich, Gen. MacArthur, Composition, Painted Features, Molded Hat, 19 In. ......*illus*	403.00
Frozen Charlie, China, Painted Features, Molded Brush Hair, c.1880, 12½ In.	403.00
Frozen Charlie, China, Pink Luster, Molded & Painted Hair & Features, Clenched Fists, 16½ In. *illus*	1320.00
Frozen Charlotte, China, Pink Luster Head, Painted Features, Molded Body, Germany, 16 In. *illus*	375.00
G.I. Joe Figures are listed in the Toy category.	
Gaultier, Bisque Swivel Head, Kid Edge, Glass Eyes, Mohair, Gusset-Jointed, 16 In.	3360.00
Gebruder Heubach, 6969, Bisque Socket Head, Sleep Eyes, Girl, Pouty, 18 In.	5940.00
Gebruder Heubach, 7246, Bisque Socket Head, Sleep Eyes, Boy, Pouty, c.1912, 18 In.	2530.00
Gebruder Heubach, 7602, Molded & Painted Features, Boy, Navy Suit & Hat, 11 In. ...*illus*	230.00
Gebruder Heubach, Baby Stuart, Molded Bonnet, Composition Body, Early 1900s, 12 In.	1175.00
Gebruder Heubach, Bisque, Baby In Shoe, Sculpted Hair, c.1910, 12 In.	3850.00
Gebruder Heubach, Bisque, Baby In Tub, Googly Eyes, Sculpted Hair, 5 In.	798.00
Gebruder Heubach, Bisque, Baby Lying On Stomach, Sculpted Hair, Googly Eyes, 11 In.	495.00
Gebruder Heubach, Bisque, Black, Baby, Smiling, Flannel Slip, 14 In.	1410.00
Gebruder Heubach, Bisque, Dutch Boy & Girl Seated, Sculpted, Googly Eyes, 8 In., Pair	578.00
Gebruder Heubach, Bisque, Girl Dressing, Googly Eyes, Chair, 13 In.	1650.00
Gebruder Heubach, Bisque, Girl Waking From Nap, Down-Glancing Eyes, Chair, 13 In.	825.00
Gebruder Heubach, Bisque, Painted Features, Sculpted Curls, Head Tilted, Girl, 6½ In.	550.00
Gebruder Heubach, Boy & Girl Blowing Bubbles, Bisque, Sculpted, Seated, 14 In., Pair	2200.00
Gebruder Heubach Dolls may also be listed in this category under Heubach.	
Gebruder Kuhnlenz, Bisque Socket Head, Brown, Sleep Eyes, Ball-Jointed, c.1895, 20 In.	3740.00
German, Bisque, Painted Features, Hip-Jointed, Crocheted Romper, Baby, 6 In.	138.00

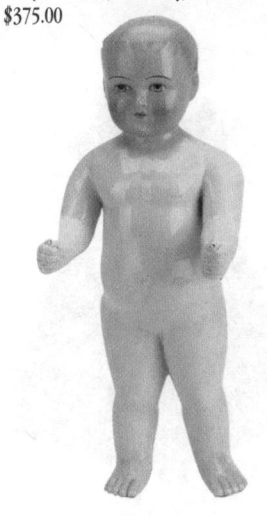

Doll, Frozen Charlotte, China, Pink Luster Head, Painted Features, Molded Body & Limbs, Germany, 16 In.
$375.00

Doll, Gebruder Heubach, 7602, Molded & Painted Features, Boy, Navy Suit & Hat, 11 In.
$230.00

Doll, German, Papier-Mache Shoulder Head, Cloth Body, Leather Arms, 1880s, 19 In.
$115.00

Doll, German, Parian, Braided Coronet, Painted Features, Bisque Limbs, c.1880, 18 In. $660.00

Doll, German, Wood, Tuck Comb, Painted Tendrils, Peg, Limbs, Cloth Dress, 2¾ In. $431.00

Doll, Handwerck, 283, Bisque Head, Brown Glass Sleep Eyes, Ringlet Wig, White Dress & Hat, 20 In. $173.00

German, Bisque, Sculpted Hair, Painted, Googly Eyes, Woman, 11 In.	336.00
German, Bisque Head, Painted, Open Mouth, Sleep Eyes, Composition, Baby, 19½ In.	63.00
German, Bisque Head, Solid Dome, Flanged Neck, Muslin, Composition Hands, Baby, 13 In.	770.00
German, Bisque Shoulder Head, Sculpted Hair, Painted, Muslin Body, Papier-Mache, 21 In.	880.00
German, Bisque Shoulder Head, Solid Dome, Paperweight Eyes, Kid Body, Gusseted, 17 In.	633.00
German, Bisque Shoulder Head, Turned Right, Sleep Eyes, Human Hair, Gusset-Jointed Kid, 20 In.	259.00
German, Bisque Socket Head, Brown Complexion, Sleep Eyes, Mohair, Wood, Composition, 30 In.	3360.00
German, Bisque Socket Head, Dark Tint, Mohair, 5-Piece Jointed Composition, Indian, 17 In.	863.00
German, Bisque Socket Head, Glass Eyes, Blond Mohair, Wood, Composition, 25 In.	4400.00
German, Bisque Socket Head, Glass Eyes, Mohair, Teeth, Wood, Ball-Jointed, 21 In.	2860.00
German, Bisque Socket Head, Sleep Eyes, Mohair, Composition, Wood, Ball-Jointed, 18 In.	6820.00
German, Bisque Socket Head, Sleep Eyes, Synthetic Wig, Painted Composition, Jointed, 23 In.	115.00
German, Composition, Glass Eyes, Blond Mohair, Muslin, Composition Limbs, c.1910, 15 In.	523.00
German, Lubina, Black Bisque Shoulder Head, Painted Features, Molded Curly Hair, 1880s, 10 In.	264.00
German, Papier-Mache Shoulder Head, Cloth Body, Leather Arms, 1880s, 19 In. ......*illus*	115.00
German, Papier-Mache Shoulder Head, Sculpted Hair, Curls, Chignon, Kid Body, Wood Limbs, 7 In.	468.00
German, Parian, Braided Coronet, Painted Features, Bisque Limbs, c.1880, 18 In. .....*illus*	660.00
German, Pilot, Composition Head, Cloth, Parachute, Box, c.1930, 10½ In.	1275.00
German, Porcelain, Pink Tint, Sculpted Hair, Muslin, Jointed, 17 In.	1100.00
German, Porcelain, Sculpted Hair, Muslin, Stitch-Jointed, Porcelain Limbs, 22 In.	440.00
German, Porcelain Shoulder Head, Muslin, Stitch-Jointed, Porcelain Limbs, 10 In.	672.00
German, Porcelain Shoulder Head, Painted Features, Muslin, Porcelain Limbs, 20 In.	440.00
German, Wood, Painted Features, Tuck Comb, Articulated Body, Grodner Tal, c.1850, 7 In.	2240.00
German, Wood, Tuck Comb, Painted Tendrils, Peg, Limbs, Cloth Dress, 2¾ In. ....*illus*	431.00
Greiner, Papier-Mache, Enamel Eyes, Muslin, Stitch-Jointed, Leather Arms, 24 In.	764.00
Greiner, Papier-Mache, Enamel Eyes, Muslin, Stitch-Jointed, Leather Arms, 31 In.	728.00
Half Dolls are listed in the Pincushion Doll category.	
Handwerck, 99, Bisque Socket Head, Sleep Eyes, Synthetic Wig, Composition, Wood, 23 In.	374.00
Handwerck, 109, Bisque Head, Blue Sleep Eyes, Open Mouth, Nurse's Outfit, 22 In.	382.00
Handwerck, 109, Bisque Head, Brown Sleep Eyes, Open Mouth, Blond Mohair Wig, 18 In.	470.00
Handwerck, 109, Bisque Socket Head, Sleep Eyes, Composition, Wood, Jointed, 15 In.	230.00
Handwerck, 109, Bisque Socket Head, Sleep Eyes, Pierced Ears, Mohair, Composition, 22 In.	173.00
Handwerck, 283, Bisque Head, Brown Glass Sleep Eyes, Ringlet Wig, White Dress & Hat, 20 In. *illus*	173.00
Handwerck, Bisque Socket Head, Glass Sleep Eyes, Composition, Wood, Jointed, 42 In.	3190.00
Handwerck, Simon & Halbig Bisque Head, Brown Glass Sleep Eyes, Brunette, 28 In. ...*illus*	546.00
Harold Lloyd, Oilcloth, Hands In Pockets, Yours For Happiness, 1930s, 11¾ In.	203.00
Hertel Schwab, 149, Bisque Socket Head, Sleep Eyes, Ball-Jointed, c.1912, 13 In.	5060.00
Hertel Schwab, 152, Bisque Socket Head, Sleep Eyes, Mohair, Composition, Baby, 13 In.	288.00
Hertwig, Glazed Porcelain Shoulder Head, Painted Features, Cloth Body, China Limbs, 14 In. ..*illus*	275.00
Heubach, see also Gebruder Heubach in this category.	
Heubach, 300, Bisque Head, Blue Sleep Eyes, Teeth, 5-Piece Bent-Limb Body, 14 In. ....*illus*	144.00
Heubach, 342, Bisque Socket Head, Sleep Eyes, Mohair, 5-Piece Composition, Baby, 18½ In.	200.00
Heubach, 417, Bisque Head, Mohair Wig, Composition, Toddler Boy, Girl, 12 In. ....*illus*	1380.00
Heubach, Bisque Shoulder Head, Laughing, Velvet Sailor Suit, Boy, 13½ In. ...,.....*illus*	235.00
Heubach, Bisque Socket Head, Googly Eyes, Composition, Mohair Wig, 21 In. ....*illus*	9900.00
Heubach, Bisque Socket Head, Mohair, Composition, Jointed, Wood, Stick Legs, 11 In.	200.00
Horsman, Babyland Rag, Cloth, Painted Features, Human Hair, Dress & Hat, 31 In. ...*illus*	316.00
Horsman, Composition, Painted Features, Jointed Shoulders, Hips, 10 In.	518.00
Horsman, Hug-Me Kiddies, Mask Face, Glass Googly Eyes, Striped Dress, 9½ In. ......*illus*	748.00
Horsman, Patty Duke, Red Sweater, Blue Jeans, Telephone, Star Pin, 1965, 7 In.	150.00
Huret, Bisque, Socket Head, Painted Eyes, Sad Jester, c.1905, 18 In.	10450.00
Ideal, Baby Snooks, Composition Head, Painted Features, Wood Body, Cable Limbs, 13 In.	132.00
Ideal, Bud Abbott & Lou Costello, Who's On First, Baseball Uniforms, 1983, 10 In., Pair	515.00
Ideal, Deanna Durbin, Composition, Original Clothes & Feathered Hat, 21 In. ....*illus*	546.00
Ideal, Little Miss Revlon, Vinyl, Mussed Hair, Jointed, Tagged Clothes, c.1955-59, 10½ In.	144.00
Ideal, Mama, Composition Head, Arms & Legs, Cloth Body, 1920s, 16 In.	300.00
Ideal, Mary Hartline, Plastic, Blue Sleep Eyes, Blond, 5-Piece Body, 1959, 8 In.	300.00
Ideal, Patti Playpal, Vinyl, Blue Eyes, Brown Wig, Jointed, 35 In.	98.00
Ideal, Saucy Walker, Plastic Head, Brunette, Blue Sleep Eyes, Open Mouth, 1952, 14 In.	510.00
Ideal, Shirley Temple, Stowaway, Blue Silk Chinese Blouse, 1982, 12 In.	33.00
Ideal, Toni, Hard Plastic, Blue Eyes, Brown Wig, Jointed, c.1950, 21 In.	75.00
Indian Dolls are listed in the Indian category.	
Izannah Walker, Stockinet Head, Oil-Painted Features, Muslin Body, c.1860, 20 In. ...*illus*	4950.00
J.D.K., 260, Bisque, Composition Body, Starfish Hands, Incised, 9 In.	935.00
J.D.K. Dolls are also listed in this category under Kestner.	
Jumeau, Bisque Head, Paperweight Eyes, Composition, Jointed, Wood, 1907, 19½ In.	1380.00

Doll, Handwerck, Simon & Halbig Bisque Head, Brown Glass Sleep Eyes, Brunette, 28 In.
$546.00

Doll, Heubach, 417, Bisque Head, Mohair Wig, Composition, Toddler Boy, Girl, 12 In.
$1380.00

Doll, Horsman, Hug-Me Kiddies, Mask Face, Glass Googly Eyes, Striped Dress, 9½ In.
$748.00

Doll, Hertwig, Glazed Porcelain Shoulder Head, Painted Features, Cloth Body, China Limbs, 14 In.
$275.00

Doll, Heubach, Bisque Socket Head, Googly Eyes, Composition, Mohair Wig, 21 In.
$9900.00

Doll, Ideal, Deanna Durbin, Composition, Original Clothes & Feathered Hat, 21 In.
$546.00

Doll, Heubach, 300, Bisque Head, Blue Sleep Eyes, Teeth, 5-Piece Bent-Limb Body, 14 In.
$144.00

Doll, Horsman, Babyland Rag, Cloth, Painted Features, Human Hair, Dress & Hat, 31 In.
$316.00

Doll, Izannah Walker, Stockinet Head, Oil-Painted Features, Muslin Body, c.1860, 20 In.
$4950.00

Doll, Jumeau, Bisque Head, Brown Paperweight Eyes, Blond Wig, Pink Dress, 15 In.
$3163.00

Doll, K * R, 68, Simon & Halbig, Bisque Head, Glass Sleep Eyes, Jointed Body, 26 In.
$460.00

Doll, Kestner, China Shoulder Head, Molded Black Hair, Painted Features, Cloth Body, 26 In.
$748.00

Doll, Jumeau, Bisque Socket Head, Paperweight Eyes, Human Hair, Kid Body, Ermine Stole, 23 In.
$4675.00

Doll, K * R, 100, Kaiser Baby, Painted Eyes, Bent-Limb Body, Asian Features, 19½ In.
$259.00

Doll, Lenci, Dutch Girl, Wooden Clogs, Holding Tulip, Mascotte, 9 In.
$173.00

Doll, K * R, 43, Bisque Head, Glass Eyes, Burgundy Plaid Dress & Hat, 18 In.
$115.00

Doll, Kathe Kruse, Hannerle, IX, Blond Hair, Blue & White Dotted Dress & Headband, Box, 14½ In.
$288.00

Doll, Lenci, Spanish Toreador, Pressed Felt, Black Mohair Wig, 17 In.
$3738.00

Jumeau, Bisque, Paperweight Eyes, Human Hair Wig, Composition, 19 In.	2300.00
Jumeau, Bisque Head, Brown Paperweight Eyes, Blond Wig, Pink Dress, 15 In. . . . .*illus*	3163.00
Jumeau, Bisque Head, Closed Mouth, Brown Paperweight Eyes, Bebe, 20½ In.	1645.00
Jumeau, Bisque Socket Head, Glass Sleep Eyes, Composition, Wood, Jointed, Bebe, 38 In. . . .	5775.00
Jumeau, Bisque Socket Head, Open Mouth, Jointed Body, c.1900, 21 In.	403.00
Jumeau, Bisque Socket Head, Paperweight Eyes, Composition, Jointed, Wood, Bebe, 11 In. . .	4760.00
Jumeau, Bisque Socket Head, Paperweight Eyes, Composition, Wood, Jointed, Bebe, 26 In. . .	6720.00
Jumeau, Bisque Socket Head, Paperweight Eyes, Human Hair, Composition, Jointed, Wood, 22 In. . .	2818.00
Jumeau, Bisque Socket Head, Paperweight Eyes, Human Hair, Composition, Wood, 20 In. . . .	3410.00
Jumeau, Bisque Socket Head, Paperweight Eyes, Human Hair, Kid Body, Ermine Stole, 23 In. *illus*	4675.00
Jumeau, Bisque Socket Head, Paperweight Eyes, Mohair, Composition, Bebe, 20 In.	8500.00
Jumeau, Bisque Socket Head, Paperweight Eyes, Mohair, Composition, Jointed, Wood, 11 In. .	4025.00
Jumeau, Bisque Socket Head, Paperweight Eyes, Mohair, Composition, Wood, Jointed, 22 In. .	10640.00
Jumeau, Bisque Socket Head, Paperweight Eyes, Mohair, Gusset Joints, Fashion, 16 In.	2070.00
Jumeau, Bisque Socket Head, Paperweight Eyes, Mohair, Kid Body, Stitched Fingers, 13 In. . .	1955.00
Jumeau, Bisque Socket Head, Sleep Eyes, Human Hair, Composition, Wood, Jointed, 17 In. . .	896.00
Jumeau, Bisque Swivel Head, Enamel Eyes, Blond Mohair, Kid Body, Jointed, Fashion, 15 In.	2530.00
K * R, 43, Bisque Head, Glass Eyes, Burgundy Plaid Dress & Hat, 18 In. . . . .*illus*	115.00
K * R, 68, Simon & Halbig, Bisque Head, Glass Sleep Eyes, Jointed Body, 26 In. . . . .*illus*	460.00
K * R, 100, Kaiser Baby, Painted Eyes, Bent-Limb Body, Asian Features, 19½ In. . . . .*illus*	259.00
K * R, 101, Bisque Socket Head, Painted, Mohair, Composition, Jointed, Wood, 11½ In.	1495.00
K * R, 121, Bisque Socket Head, Sleep Eyes, Teeth, Mohair, 5-Piece Jointed Composition, Baby, 20 In.	604.00
K * R, 122, Bisque Socket Head, Metal Eyelids, Wobble Tongue, Composition, Jointed, Wood, 22 In. .	1265.00
K * R, 126, Bisque Socket Head, Flirty Eyes, Teeth, Tongue, Mohair, Composition, Baby, 22 In. . . .	575.00
K * R, 126, Bisque Socket Head, Sleep Eyes, Open Mouth, 5-Piece Body, Mohair, Baby, 11 In. .	403.00
K * R, 132, Bisque Socket Head, Glass Flirty Eyes, Painted Features, Jointed, Toddler, 15 In. . .	1870.00
K * R, 192, Bisque Socket Head, Lever-Operated Eyes, Mohair, Composition, Jointed, Wood, 14 In. . . .	1668.00
K * R, 115/A, Bisque Head, Blue Eyes, Blond Wig, Royal Stuart Tartan, Boy, c.1927, 16 In. . . .	3525.00
K * R, 115/A, Bisque Head, Pouty, Sleep Eyes, Embroidered Shirt, Velvet Pants, Toddler, 15 In. . . .	2115.00
K * R, 116/A, Bisque Head, Blue Sleep Eyes, Smiling Mouth, Upper Teeth, c.1920, 11 x 16 In.	1175.00
K * R, Bisque Socket Head, Brunette Mohair Braids, Composition, Wood, Jointed, 10 In.	3410.00
K * R, Bisque Socket Head, Human Hair, Composition Body, Washed Finish, 32 In.	403.00
K * R, Bisque Socket Head, Painted, Human Hair, Composition, Jointed, Wood, Toddler, 16 In. . .	4760.00
K * R, Bisque Socket Head, Sleep Eyes, Mohair, Composition, Jointed, Wood, 11 In. . . 374.00 to 460.00
K * R, Marie, Bisque Head, Painted Eyes, Closed Mouth, Composition Body, c.1910, 18½ In. . .	2703.00
K * R, Mein Liebling, Bisque Socket Head, Sleep Eyes, Mohair Wig, c.1912, 18 In.	5060.00
K * R, Mein Liebling, Simon & Halbig, Blue Sleep Eyes, Jointed, White Cotton Dress, 24 In. . .	1785.00
Kathe Kruse, Cloth, Oil-Painted Features, Hair, Stitch-Jointed Shoulders, Jointed Legs, 17 In. . .	4400.00
Kathe Kruse, Cloth, Painted Features, Hair, Tab-Jointed Limbs, Stitched Fingers, 16 In.	2645.00
Kathe Kruse, Hannerle, IX, Blond Hair, Blue & White Dotted Dress & Headband, Box, 14½ In. .*illus*	288.00
Kathe Kruse, Socket Head, Painted Features, Muslin Body, Jointed Shoulders, Hips, 18 In. . .	1792.00
Kenner, Baby Wet & Care, Accessories, General Mills Fun Group, Box, 1978, 13 In.	56.00
Kestner, 129, Bisque Socket Head, Sleep Eyes, Mohair, Composition, Wood, Jointed, 18 In. . . .	1456.00
Kestner, 143, Bisque Head, Blue Sleep Eyes, Composition Body, Original Clothing, 16 In. . . .	764.00
Kestner, 143, Bisque Socket Head, Sleep Eyes, Mohair, Composition, Wood, Jointed, 12 In. . . .	604.00
Kestner, 147, Bisque Shoulder, Sleep Eyes, Mohair, Kid Body, Bisque Arms, 23 In.	144.00
Kestner, 147, Bisque Shoulder Head, Blue Sleep Eyes, Open Mouth, Inset Teeth, 26½ In.	235.00
Kestner, 164, Bisque Socket Head, Human Hair, Cardboard, Composition, Wood, Jointed, 27 In. .	546.00
Kestner, 172, Gibson Girl, Bisque Shoulder Head, c.1900, 20 In.	3850.00
Kestner, 172, Gibson Girl, Bisque Shoulder Head, Sleep Eyes, Upturned Chin, Satin Dress, 17 In. . .	1351.00
Kestner, 191, Bisque Socket Head, Composition Body, Ball-Jointed, Boy, c.1910, 18 In.	4400.00
Kestner, 221, Bisque Socket Head, Googly Eyes, Mohair, Composition, Wood, Jointed, Toddler, 17 In.	9520.00
Kestner, 226, Bisque Socket Head, Sleep Eyes, Painted, 5-Piece Composition, Baby, 22 In. . . .	896.00
Kestner, 243, Bisque Socket Head, Amber Complexion, Sleep Eyes, Chinese Baby, 19 In.	5824.00
Kestner, 243, Bisque Socket Head, Sleep Eyes, Human Hair, Composition, Chinese Boy, 16 In. .	4140.00
Kestner, 249, Bisque Socket Head, Sleep Eyes, Composition, Jointed, Wood, Child, 20 In.	575.00
Kestner, 257, Bisque Socket Head, Sleep Eyes, Mohair, 5-Piece Composition Body, Baby, 16 In. .	374.00
Kestner, Baby Jean, Bisque Socket Head, Glass Eyes, Painted, Mohair, Composition, 17 In. . .	935.00
Kestner, Bisque Head, Brown Sleep Eyes, Upper Inset Teeth, Chinese Baby, 13½ x 18 In.	3819.00
Kestner, Bisque Shoulder Head, Sleep Eyes, Human Hair, Kid Body, Rivet-Jointed, 17 In. . . .	1265.00
Kestner, Bisque Socket Head, Glass Sleep Eyes, 4 Teeth, Braids, Composition, Wood, 40 In. . .	3190.00
Kestner, Bisque Socket Head, Gray Sleep Eyes, Pouty Mouth, Blond Human Hair, 16 In.	3105.00
Kestner, Bisque Socket Head, Sleep Eyes, Human Hair, Composition, Jointed, 10 In.	1150.00
Kestner, Bisque Socket Head, Sleep Eyes, Human Hair, Composition, Wood, Jointed, 23 In. . .	1725.00
Kestner, Bisque Socket Head, Sleep Eyes, Mohair, Jointed, Composition, Wood, 21 In.	5600.00
Kestner, Bisque Socket Head, Sleep Eyes, Mohair Wig, Composition, Wood, Jointed, 34 In. . . .	1120.00

Doll, Madame Alexander, Cissy, Hard Plastic, Sleep Eyes, Red Polka-Dot Dress, Hat, 20 In. $201.00

Doll, Madame Alexander, Sonja Henie, Plastic, Sleep Eyes, Mohair, Skating Clothes, 14 In. $144.00

Doll, Mattel, Barbie, Ash Blond, Black & White Swimsuit, Flowered Sun Dress, Box, 12 In. $188.00

Doll, Mattel, Barbie, Bubble Cut, Blond, Cheerleader Outfit, Stand, Box, 12 In. $176.00

Doll, Mattel, Barbie, No. 4, Brunette, Ponytail, Black & White Swimsuit, Accessories, Box $441.00

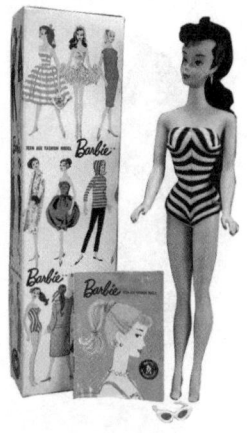

Doll, Morimura Bros., Bisque Head, Brown Glass Sleep Eyes, Jointed Body, 30 In. $58.00

Kestner, Bisque Socket Head, Solid Dome, Sleep Eyes, Jointed Composition, Baby, 25 In.	748.00
Kestner, China Shoulder Head, Molded Black Hair, Painted Features, Cloth Body, 26 In. *illus*	748.00
Kestner, Hilda, Bisque Socket Head, Glass Eyes, Mohair, Composition, Jointed, Toddler, 23 In.	5060.00
Kestner, Hilda, Bisque Socket Head, Glass Sleep Eyes, Composition, Bent Limbs, Baby, 22 In.	2310.00
Kestner, Hilda, Bisque Socket Head, Sleep Eyes, Teeth, Mohair, Composition, Jointed, Baby, 17 In.	1725.00
Kestner, Socket Head, Glass Eyes, Painted Hair, Composition Body, Toddler, 14 In.	294.00
Kestner dolls are also in this category under J.D.K.	
Kewpie dolls are listed in the Kewpie category.	
Kley & Hahn, 525, Bisque Socket Head, Painted Eyes, Composition, Ball-Jointed, c.1912, 18 In.	1320.00
Knickerbocker, Dagwood, Composition Head, Large Ears, Black Suit, 1935, 14 In.	3100.00
Lenci, Boy, Felt, Painted, Mohair, Cloth Body, Jointed Shoulders, Hips, 13 In.	288.00
Lenci, Boy, Felt Head, Painted Features, Mohair, Cloth Body, Stitched Fingers, Mascotte, 9 In.	316.00
Lenci, Boy, Felt Swivel Head, Chubby Face, Up-Glancing Eyes, Mohair, 11 In.	458.00
Lenci, Boy, Felt Swivel Head, Googly Eyes, Mohair, Muslin, Jointed, 19 In.	825.00
Lenci, Boy, Felt Swivel Head, Googly Eyes, Mohair, Muslin, Pajamas, Robe, 15 In.	1320.00
Lenci, Cowboy, Felt Swivel Head, Painted, Googly Eyes, 5-Piece Body, 14 In.	1155.00
Lenci, Dutch Girl, Wooden Clogs, Holding Tulip, Mascotte, 9 In. *illus*	173.00
Lenci, Elf, Felt, Brown Complexion, Pointed Ears, Googly Eyes, 7 In.	3300.00
Lenci, Girl, Felt Head, Painted Features, Mohair Braids, Cloth Body, Tab-Jointed, Mascotte, 8 In.	288.00
Lenci, Girl, Felt Swivel Head, Googly Eyes, Mohair, Muslin Body, Felt Limbs, 18 In.	1870.00
Lenci, Girl, Felt Swivel Head, Googly Eyes, Mohair Braids, Muslin Body, 27 In.	1870.00
Lenci, Girl, Felt Swivel Head, Painted, Blond Mohair Wig, Felt Body, Jointed, 14 In.	1760.00
Lenci, Girl, Felt Swivel Head, Painted Features, Googly Eyes, Felt Body, Jointed, 12 In.	880.00
Lenci, Girl, Felt Swivel Head, Painted Features, Googly Eyes, Muslin Body, 20 In.	1870.00
Lenci, Golfer, Felt Swivel Head, Painted, Googly Eyes, Felt Body, Jointed, 16 In.	3300.00
Lenci, Golfer, Sports Series, Brown Golf Bag, 2 Clubs, 18 In.	3300.00
Lenci, Italian Girl, Felt Swivel Head, Painted Features, 5-Piece Cloth Body, Jointed, 16 In.	1792.00
Lenci, Italian Girl, Felt, Swivel Head, Painted Features, Mohair, Jointed Shoulders, Hips, 14 In.	896.00
Lenci, Madame Pompadour, Pressed Felt, Blond Wig, Painted Eyes, Jointed, 27 In.	2575.00
Lenci, Spanish Toreador, Pressed Felt, Black Mohair Wig, 17 In. *illus*	3738.00
Limbach, Parian Shoulder Head, Painted Eyes, Open-Close Mouth, 20 In.	259.00
Madame Alexander, Agatha Portrette, Plastic, Sleep Eyes, Brunette, Female Body, 1968, 10 In.	150.00
Madame Alexander, Alice In Wonderland, Cloth, Painted Features, Googly Eyes, Yarn Hair, 16 In.	288.00
Madame Alexander, Alice In Wonderland, Hard Plastic, Sleep Eyes, Jointed, 15 In.	178.00
Madame Alexander, Amish Girl & Boy, Hard Plastic, Bent Knee, Black Outfit, 8 In., Pair	140.00
Madame Alexander, Amy, Little Women, Hard Plastic, Sleep Eyes, Synthetic Wig, Walker, 8 In.	201.00
Madame Alexander, Annabelle, Hard Plastic, Sleep Eyes, Blond, Pink Linen Dress, 1952, 15 In.	475.00
Madame Alexander, Annabelle, Hard Plastic, Sleep Eyes, Synthetic Wig, Jointed, 1952, 18 In.	316.00
Madame Alexander, Annabelle, Hard Plastic, Sleep Eyes, Synthetic Wig, Jointed, 1952, 18 In.	550.00
Madame Alexander, Baby Clown, Hard Plastic, Sleep Eyes, Caracul Wig, Jointed, Walker, 8 In.	430.00
Madame Alexander, Ballerina, Hard Plastic, Synthetic Wig, Quizkin Body, Jointed, 8 In.	489.00
Madame Alexander, Binnie Walker, Hard Plastic, Sleep Eyes, Synthetic Wig, Jointed, 18 In.	374.00
Madame Alexander, Binnie Walker, Plastic, Auburn, Dress For Matinee, 1955, 18 In.	850.00
Madame Alexander, Bobby Q, Cloth, Painted Features, Googly Eyes, Yarn Wig, 15 In.	430.00
Madame Alexander, Brenda, Vinyl, Sleep Eyes, Auburn Hair, Black Lace Chemise, 1964, 20 In.	150.00
Madame Alexander, Bunny, Muslin, Embroidered Face, Shoebutton Eyes, Whiskers, 16 In.	153.00
Madame Alexander, Cecile, Composition, Googly Eyes, Mohair, Jointed, Toddler, Box, 8 In.	345.00
Madame Alexander, Chatterbox, Vinyl, Jointed, Tagged Clothes, c.1961, 24 In.	35.00
Madame Alexander, Cissette, Ballerina, Hard Plastic, Sleep Eyes, Synthetic Wig, Jointed, 10 In.	200.00
Madame Alexander, Cissette, Bride, Hard Plastic, Sleep Eyes, Synthetic Wig, Walker, 10 In.	345.00
Madame Alexander, Cissette, Hard Plastic, Bubble Cut, Sleep Eyes, Jointed, 10 In.	178.00
Madame Alexander, Cissette, Hard Plastic, Sleep Eyes, Synthetic Hair, Jointed, Walker, 10 In.	254.00
Madame Alexander, Cissette, Plastic, Brown Hair, Afternoon Dress, High Heels, 1960, 10 In.	600.00
Madame Alexander, Cissette, Plastic, Brunette, High Heels, Chemise, Lace Teddy, 10 In.	550.00
Madame Alexander, Cissette, Plastic, Sleep Eyes, Blond, Sun Bathing, 1962, 10 In.	225.00
Madame Alexander, Cissy, Brunette, Plastic, Red & White Evening Grown, Jewelry, 1958, 21 In.	3200.00
Madame Alexander, Cissy, Hard Plastic, Mussed Wig, Vinyl Arms, 20 In.	345.00
Madame Alexander, Cissy, Hard Plastic, Sleep Eyes, Red Polka-Dot Dress, Hat, 20 In. *illus*	201.00
Madame Alexander, Cousin Mary, Hard Plastic, Synthetic Wig, Jointed, Walker, 8 In.	374.00
Madame Alexander, Cowboy On Horse, Hard Plastic, Jointed, Western Clothes, 1987, 8 In.	121.00
Madame Alexander, David Copperfield, Cloth, Molded Felt Face, Blond Wig, Red Hat, 1930s, 16 In.	445.00
Madame Alexander, Davy Crockett, Hard Plastic, Caracul Wig, Jointed, Walker, Box, 8 In.	138.00
Madame Alexander, Elsie, Lavender Ball Grown, Sleep Eyes, Blond, 1964, 17 In.	550.00
Madame Alexander, Fairy Princess, Composition, Mohair Wig, Sleep Eyes, Box, 18 In.	295.00
Madame Alexander, Fairy Princess, Composition, Sleep Eyes, Red Gown, 1938, 15 In.	710.00
Madame Alexander, Flora McFlimsey, Composition, Sleep Eyes, Freckles, Jointed, 15 In.	403.00

Madame Alexander, Flora McFlimsey, Composition, Synthetic Wig, Freckles, Jointed, 13 In.	414.00
Madame Alexander, Godey Portrette, Plastic, Sleep Eyes, Auburn Hair, 1968, 10 In.	225.00
Madame Alexander, Gold Rush, Hard Plastic, Sleep Eyes, Synthetic Wig, Jointed, Walker, 10 In. .	259.00
Madame Alexander, Jenny Lind, Hard Plastic, Jointed, Tagged Outfit, c.1969, 10 In.	81.00
Madame Alexander, Leslie, Vinyl, Sleep Eyes, Synthetic Wig, Jointed, 17 In.	288.00
Madame Alexander, Lissy, Ballerina, Hard Plastic, Sleep Eyes, Jointed, 12 In.	431.00
Madame Alexander, Lissy, Hard Plastic, Sleep Eyes, Synthetic Wig, Jointed, 12 In. . . 178.00 to 374.00	
Madame Alexander, Little Minister, Hard Plastic, Synthetic Hair, Jointed, 8 In.	1380.00
Madame Alexander, Maggie, Hard Plastic, Sleep Eyes, Synthetic Wig, Jointed, Walker, 20 In.	518.00
Madame Alexander, Maggie Mixup, Hard Plastic, Bent Knee, Tagged Outfit, Walker, 8 In. . .	230.00
Madame Alexander, Margaret O'Brien, Composition, Mohair Wig, Jointed, Tagged Outfit, 21 In.	345.00
Madame Alexander, Margaret O'Brien, Composition, Sleep Eyes, 5-Piece Body, 18 In.	1344.00
Madame Alexander, Margaret O'Brien, Plastic, Sleep Eyes, Brown Wig, 1946, 14 In.	2355.00
Madame Alexander, Margot, Plastic, Blond, Blue Sheath Dress, 1961, 10 In.	475.00
Madame Alexander, Marlo Thomas, Vinyl, Sleep Eyes, Synthetic Hair, Jointed, 17 In.	431.00
Madame Alexander, Mary Rose Bride, Hard Plastic, Sleep Eyes, Floss Wig, Jointed, 17 In. ...	604.00
Madame Alexander, Marybell, The Doll That Gets Well, Vinyl, Medical Supplies, 1960, 16 In.	175.00
Madame Alexander, McGuffey Ana, Composition, Googly Eyes, Mohair, Jointed, Case, 9 In. .	748.00
Madame Alexander, McGuffey Ana, Composition, Sleep Eyes, Mohair, Jointed, 15 In. 375.00 to 1008.00	
Madame Alexander, McGuffey Ana, Hard Plastic, Sleep Eyes, Synthetic Hair, Jointed, 8 In. . .	144.00
Madame Alexander, Melinda Portrette, Plastic, Blond, High Heels, 1968, 10 In.	125.00
Madame Alexander, Nina Ballerina, Plastic, Sleep Eyes, Brown Hair, Tutu, 1949, 17 In.	1100.00
Madame Alexander, Oliver Twist, Cloth, Felt Face, Painted Features, Googly Eyes, Mohair, 16 In.	316.00
Madame Alexander, Polly Pigtails, Hard Plastic, Plaid Dress, Brunette, c.1949, 17 In.	625.00
Madame Alexander, Prince Charles, Hard Plastic, Sleep Eyes, Synthetic Wig, Jointed, 8 In. .	178.00
Madame Alexander, Princess, Composition, Tin Sleep Eyes, Human Hair, 13 In.	178.00
Madame Alexander, Princess Elizabeth, Composition, Jointed, Tagged Clothing, Box, 14 In.	489.00
Madame Alexander, Queen Portrette, Plastic, Brunette, Ivory Brocade Gown, 1972, 10 In. . .	150.00
Madame Alexander, Renoir Portrette, Plastic, Sleep Eyes, Brunette, 1968, 10 In.	200.00
Madame Alexander, Romeo, Hard Plastic, Sleep Eyes, Caracul Wig, Jointed, Walker, 8 In. . .	460.00
Madame Alexander, Scarlett, Composition, Sleep Eyes, Synthetic Wig, Jointed, 11 In.	345.00
Madame Alexander, Snow White, Hard Plastic, Jointed, Tagged Clothes, 1972-77, 8 In.	58.00
Madame Alexander, Snow White, Plastic, Sleepy Eyes, Black Wig, Gold Gown, 1952, 15 In. .	550.00
Madame Alexander, Sonja Henie, Plastic, Sleep Eyes, Mohair, Skating Clothes, 14 In. *illus*	144.00
Madame Alexander, Southern Belle, Hard Plastic, Sleep Eyes, Synthetic Wig, Walker, 8 In. .	178.00
Madame Alexander, Southern Belle Portrette, Plastic, Blond, Sleep Eyes, 1968, 10 In.	200.00
Madame Alexander, Susie-Q, Cloth, Painted Features, Googly Eyes, Yarn Wig, Box, 15 In. . .	662.00
Madame Alexander, Sweet Violet, Hard Plastic, Jointed, 18 In.	144.00
Madame Alexander, Tiny Tim, Cloth, Felt Face, Painted, Closed Mouth, Googly Eyes, Mohair, 16 In.	345.00
Madame Alexander, Tippi Ballerina, Hard Plastic, Jointed, Tagged Clothes, 8 In.	115.00
Madame Alexander, Wendy Bride, Hard Plastic, Sleep Eyes, Blond Wig, Jointed, 14 In.	431.00
Madame Alexander, Wendy-Kins, African, Brown Body, Black Hair, 1966, 8 In.	100.00
Madame Alexander, Wendy-Kins, Billy Walker, Plastic, Sleep Eyes, Reddish Blond, 1963, 8 In.	200.00
Madame Alexander, Wendy-Kins, Eskimo, Brown Body, Harpoon, 1966, 8 In.	200.00
Madame Alexander, Wendy-Kins, Hawaiian, Brown Body, Grass Skirt, 1966, 8 In.	150.00
Madame Alexander, Wendy-Kins, Plastic, Red Dress & Rainwear, 8 In.	700.00
Madame Alexander, Wendy-Kins, Southern Belle, Plastic, Blond, Blue Taffeta Dress, 8 In. . .	475.00
Madame Alexander, Wendy-Kins, Vietnamese, Light Brown Body, 1966, 8 In.	50.00
Madame Alexander, Winnie Walker, Plastic, Sleep Eyes, Synthetic Wig, Clothes, Box, 15 In. .	575.00
Marion Kaulitz, Composition, Socket Head, Painted Eyes, Ball-Jointed, c.1910, 18 In.	10450.00
Marotte, Bisque Head, Closed Mouth, Blue Eyes, Wood Torso, Flange Neck, Late 1800s, 15 In. .	382.00
Mary Hoyer, Hard Plastic, Sleep Eyes, Mohair Wig, Jointed, Vintage Clothes, c.1950, 14 In. . .	546.00
Mason & Taylor, Gesso Over Wood, Swivel Head, Sculpted, Pewter Hands, Feet, c.1880, 11 In. .	1540.00
Mattel, Barbie, Ash Blond, Black & White Swimsuit, Flowered Sun Dress, Box, 12 In. ...*illus*	188.00
Mattel, Barbie, Bride, Bubble Cut, White Lips, Blond Hair, Red Nails, 1967, 11 In.	200.00
Mattel, Barbie, Bubble Cut, Blond, Cheerleader Outfit, Stand, Box, 12 In. ....*illus*	176.00
Mattel, Barbie, Bubble Cut, Brunette, Career Girl Outfit, Stand, 1961, 11½ In.	385.00
Mattel, Barbie, Color Magic, Midnight & Ruby Red, Red Hair, Swim Suit, 1966, 11 In.	1900.00
Mattel, Barbie, No. 2, Blond, Ponytail, Black & White Swimsuit, Sunglasses, Stand, 11 In. ...	5500.00
Mattel, Barbie, No. 4, Brunette, Ponytail, Black & White Swimsuit, Accessories, Box ....*illus*	441.00
Mattel, Barbie, Ponytail, Brunette, Blue Eyes, Black & White Striped Suit, Accessories, Box, c.1960 . .	1348.00
Mattel, Barbie, Stewardess, American Airlines, Flight Bag, Box, 1961-64	474.00
Mattel, Barbie, Sweater Girl, Blond, Ponytail, Orange Knit Sweater, Gray Skirt, 1959, 11 In. .	9000.00
Mattel, Barbie & Ken, Guinevere & King Arthur, Purple Gown, Sword, Helmet, 1964, 12 In. . .	150.00
Mattel, Beany, Propeller On Hat, 11 Phrases, 1962, 17 In.	400.00
Mattel, Cecil, Plush, Green Felt, Plastic Eyes, Pull String, Talker, 1960s, 14 In.	135.00

Doll, Puppet, Punch & Judy, Stage, Wood, Cardboard, Cloth Curtains, 8 Puppets, 24 In.
$800.00

Doll, Raggedy Ann & Andy, Cloth, Button Eyes, Yarn Hair, Mitten Hands, Georgene, 19 In.
$316.00

Doll, S.F.B.J., 60, Bisque Head, Glass Sleep Eyes, Composition, Jointed, Lace Dress, 16 In.
$173.00

TIP

Check your dolls regularly to be sure no insects have moved into the sawdust filling or tasty wool fabrics.

D

Doll, Schoenhut, 405, Twins,
Boy & Girl, Intaglio Painted Eyes,
Blond Wigs, Clothes, 15 In.
$1093.00

Doll, Schoenhut, Wood,
Painted Features, Spring-Jointed,
Cotton Romper, Boy, 17 In.
$880.00

Doll, Simon & Halbig, 151,
Bisque Socket Head, Mohair Braids,
Teal Dress, Pinafore, 14 In.
$4313.00

Mattel, Charmin' Chatty, Blond, Traveling Around The World Series, Accessories, 1962, 25 In. ...	1125.00
Mattel, Donny Osmond, Costume, Microphone, Osbro Productions, 1976, 12 In.	85.00
Mattel, Ken, Prince, Green Cape, Diamond-Like Buttons, Tights, Box, 1964	415.00
Mattel, Mindy, From Mork & Mindy, Posable, Paramount Pictures, 1979, 9 In.	55.00
Mattel, Shrinkin Violette, Black Shiny Shoes, Blond, Purple Dress, Talker, 1963	430.00
Mattel, Skipper, School Girl, Jacket, Shirt, Pleated Skirt, Carrying Books, 1965	240.00
Mattel, Tutti, Melody In Pink, Blond, Vinyl, Posable, Piano, Box, 1965, 6½ In.	375.00
Morimura Bros., Bisque Head, Brown Glass Sleep Eyes, Jointed Body, 30 In. ....*illus*	58.00
Norah Wellings, Mistress Mary, Felt, Swivel Head, Orange Organdy Gown, 1935, 17 In.	620.00
Paper Dolls are listed in their own category.	
Papier-Mache, Shoulder Head, Turned Right, Paperweight Eyes, Mohair, Cloth Body, 20 In. .	403.00
Parian, Shoulder Head, Painted Features, Hair, Cloth, Stuffed, Kid, Stitched Fingers, 15½ In.	345.00
Pincushion Dolls are listed in their own category.	
Porcelain Shoulder Head, Mustache, Goatee, Stitch-Jointed, Jester's Cap, Germany, 14 In. .	1018.00
Puppet, Groucho Marx, Love Happy, Felt, Vinyl Head, c.1949, 11 In.	224.00
Puppet, Hand, Cat, Felix, Cloth, Pliable Vinyl Head, Ribbon, Header Card, Gund, c.1950s, 9¾ In.	84.00
Puppet, Hand, Composition, Character Figures, Painted, Cloth Outfits, Carved, 19 In., 4 Piece ...	743.00
Puppet, Hand, Francis The Talking Mule, Cloth, Rubber Head, c.1950, 11½ In.	246.00
Puppet, Hand, Martin & Lewis Trio, Cloth, Pliable Vinyl Heads, 2 Sided Heads Combo, c.1950s	407.00
Puppet, Hand, Wonder Woman, Vinyl, Pliable Head, Ideal, 1966, 10½ In.	246.00
Puppet, Mighty Mouse, Corduroy Body, Vinyl Head, c.1950	92.00
Puppet, Punch & Judy, Stage, Wood, Cardboard, Cloth Curtains, 8 Puppets, 24 In. .....*illus*	800.00
R. John Wright, Maria, Felt, Painted Features, Brown Mohair Wig, Jointed, 20 In.	403.00
Rabery & Delphieu, Bisque Socket Head, Paperweight Eyes, Bebe, c.1885, 15 In.	4510.00
Raggedy Ann & Andy, Cloth, Button Eyes, Yarn Hair, Mitten Hands, Georgene, 19 In. . .*illus*	316.00
Raggedy Ann & Andy, Muslin, Red Mop Hair, Original Clothing, Averill, 1950s, 20 In.	2455.00
Raynal, Cloth, Swivel Head, Painted, Googly Eyes, Mohair, Jointed, c.1930, 16 In.	1155.00
Renwal, Nurse, With Hat, 1951-52, 4 In.	100.00
Rosko, Call Me Baby, Crawls, Battery Operated, Box	71.00
S & H dolls are also listed here as Simon & Halbig.	
S.F.B.J., 60, Bisque Head, Glass Sleep Eyes, Composition, Jointed, Lace Dress, 16 In. ....*illus*	173.00
S.F.B.J., 230, Bisque Socket Head, Paperweight Eyes, Composition, Wood, Jointed, 14 In.	3024.00
S.F.B.J., 236, Bisque Socket Head, Sleep Eyes, Teeth, Tongue, Human Hair, Jointed, Toddler, 15 In.	460.00
S.F.B.J., Bisque Head, Brown Paperweight Eyes, Rosy Cheeks, Human Hair, c.1900, 23 In. ...	588.00
S.F.B.J., Bisque Socket Head, Flirty Eyes, Human Hair, Wood, Composition, Walker, Kisser, 22 In. .	489.00
S.F.B.J., Bisque Socket Head, Sleep Eyes, Mohair, 5-Piece Jointed Composition, 8 In.	288.00
Sad Sack, Vinyl, Fabric Clothing, Sterling Doll Tag, 1950s, 20 In.	570.00
Sasha, Harlequin, Vinyl, Clothes, c.1984, 16 In.	178.00
Sasha, Prince Gregor, Vinyl, Jointed, Clothes, c.1983, 16 In.	149.00
Sasha, Socket Head, Tan Complexion, Scout Uniform, Gotz, c.1960, 16 In.	952.00
Schmitt & Fils, Bisque Socket Head, Pressed, Paperweight Eyes, Composition, Wood, 11⅛ In. .	5750.00
Schmitt & Fils, Bisque Socket Head, Sleep Eyes, Composition, Jointed, Wood, 18 In.	10640.00
Schoenau & Hoffmeister, 4900, Bisque Socket Head, Glass Slant Eyes, Mohair, Jointed, 8½ In. .	431.00
Schoenhut, 301, Wood Socket Head, Intaglio Eyes, Mohair, Jointed, Girl, 16 In.	460.00
Schoenhut, 316, Wood, Painted Teeth, Mohair, Jointed, Metal Springs, 19 In.	405.00
Schoenhut, 405, Twins, Boy & Girl, Intaglio Painted Eyes, Blond Wigs, Clothes, 15 In. .*illus*	1093.00
Schoenhut, Boxer, Jack Dempsey, Sculpted Black Curly Hair, Gloves, Trunks, 14 In.	11163.00
Schoenhut, Miss Dolly, Open-Close Mouth, Brown Decal Eyes, Blond Mohair Wig, 20 In. ...	265.00
Schoenhut, Wood, Painted Features, Spring-Jointed, Cotton Romper, Boy, 17 In. ......*illus*	880.00
Schoenhut, Wood, Sober Face, Brown Eyes, Blond, Pink Shoes, Girl, 1911, 14 In.	355.00
Schoenhut, Wood Socket Head, Intaglio Eyes, Teeth, Mohair, Spring-Jointed, Boy, 16 In.	7040.00
Schoenhut, Wood Socket Head, Mohair, Spring-Jointed, Sailor Suit, 21 In.	1540.00
Shaker, Bisque Head, Satin Dress, Pearl Buttons, Palm Leaf Bonnet, Kid Trim, Germany, 17 In. .	702.00
Shaker, Porcelain Head, Blue Eyes, Open Mouth, Wool Dress, Kid Body, Bonnet, 13 In.	1287.00
Shirley Temple Dolls are included in the Shirley Temple category.	
Simon & Halbig, 151, Bisque Socket Head, Mohair Braids, Teal Dress, Pinafore, 14 In. .*illus*	4313.00
Simon & Halbig, 164, Bisque Socket Head, Amber Tint, Glass Sleep Eyes, Asian Woman, 23 In.	3740.00
Simon & Halbig, 739, Bisque Socket Head, Brown Complexion, Composition, Jointed, 18 In. .	3472.00
Simon & Halbig, 749, Bisque Socket Head, Glass Sleep Eyes, Teeth, Blond Mohair, 11 In. ...	1155.00
Simon & Halbig, 1039, Bisque Socket Head, Mohair, Composition, Wood, Jointed, 16 In. ...	575.00
Simon & Halbig, 1078, Bisque Socket Head, Sleep Eyes, Composition, Wood, Jointed, 27 In. .	1064.00
Simon & Halbig, 1079, Bisque Socket Head, Human Hair, Composition, Wood, Jointed, 21 In. .	896.00
Simon & Halbig, 1079, Bisque Socket Head, Sleep Eyes, Composition, Jointed, 8½ In.	575.00
Simon & Halbig, 1079, Bisque Socket Head, Sleep Eyes, Human Hair, Jointed, 28 In.	431.00
Simon & Halbig, 1079, Bisque Socket Head, Sleep Eyes, Mohair, Composition, Wood, Jointed, 21 In.	460.00
Simon & Halbig, 1079, Bisque Swivel Head, Glass Sleep Eyes, Mohair, Teeth, Pierced Ears, 18 In. ...	935.00

Simon & Halbig, 1079, Porcelain Head, Mohair, Composition, Jointed, 28 In.	443.00
Simon & Halbig, 1358, Bisque Socket Head, Cafe-Au-Lait Complexion, c.1910, 18 In.	5225.00
Simon & Halbig, Bisque Head, Blue Eyes, Open Mouth, Upper Teeth, Cotton Dress, 26 In. . . .	353.00
Simon & Halbig, Bisque Socket Head, Glass Sleep Eyes, Human Hair, Composition, Child, 35 In.	3850.00
Simon & Halbig, Bisque Socket Head, Sleep Eyes, Mohair, Composition, Wood, Jointed, 16 In. . .	374.00
Simon & Halbig, Wood & Composition, Mohair Wig, Walker, 16 In.	400.00
Steiff, Celluloid Socket Head, Flocked, Glass Eyes, 5-Piece Body, c.1935, 17 In.	605.00
Steiner, Bisque Socket Head, Cardboard Pate, Mohair Wig, Paperweight Eyes, 10½ In.	2875.00
Steiner, Bisque Socket Head, Googly Eyes, Cardboard, Mohair, Composition, 7¾ In.	374.00
Steiner, Bisque Socket Head, Human Hair, Paperweight Eyes, Composition, Jointed, Wood, 16 In.	6325.00
Steiner, Bisque Socket Head, Human Hair, Paperweight Eyes, Kid Body, Wheels, Key Wind, 15 In.	1265.00
Steiner, Bisque Socket Head, Mohair, Lever-Activated Sleep Eyes, Composition, Jointed, 11 In. . .	4802.00
Swaine & Co., Bisque Head, Solid Dome, Sleep Eyes, Composition Body, Marked D.V., Baby, 14 In.	776.00
Terri Lee, Plastic, Socket Head, Brown Eyes, Cowgirl Outfit, 1950s, 16 In.	1075.00
Uncle Sam, Bisque Head, No Goatee, c.1928, 17½ In.	999.00
Van Rozen, Bisque Socket Head, Sleep Eyes, Composition & Wood Body, c.1915, 17 In.	7425.00
Vogue, Cowboy & Cowgirl, Brother & Sister Series, Composition, Blond Wig, 1943, 8 In., Pair	600.00
Vogue, Ginny, Anchor's Aweigh, Dark Brown Hair, Blue & White Sailor Outfit, Hat, Posable, 8 In.	35.00
Vogue, Ginny, Away We Go, Plastic, Sleepy Eyes, Blond, Sundress, Bonnet, Walker, 1955, 8 In.	300.00
Vogue, Ginny, Ballerina, Frolicking Fables, Plastic, Brown Sleep Eyes, Blue Tutu, 1951, 8 In. .	750.00
Vogue, Ginny, Bo Peep, Frolicking Fables, Plastic, Blue Eyes, Auburn Wig, 1951, 8 In.	1300.00
Vogue, Ginny, Holiday Girl, Blond Hair, Blue Velour Dress, 1984	35.00
Vogue, Ginny, Hope, Plastic, Sleepy Eyes, Blond Wig, Pink Dress, Snap Shoes, 1952, 8 In.	1200.00
Vogue, Ginny, Israel, Far-Away Lands Series, Hard Plastic, Jointed, 8 In.	58.00
Vogue, Ginny, Skier, Gadabout Series, Plastic, Blue Eyes, Brown Pigtails, Ski Outfit, 1953, 8 In. . .	800.00
Vogue, Ginny, Steve & Eve, Brother & Sister Series, Plastic, Plaid Outfit, 1951, 8 In., Pair	1100.00
Vogue, Ginny, Wee Willie Winkie, Frolicking Fables, Plastic, Blue Eyes, Auburn, 1952, 8 In. . .	600.00
Vogue, Jill, Plastic, Blond, Sleep Eyes, Sailor Dress, No. 3166, 1959, 8 In.	60.00
Vogue, Toddler, Mary Had A Little Lamb, Composition, Painted Features, Googly Eyes, Mohair, 8 In. .	604.00
Vogue, Valerie, Composition, Googly Eyes, Jointed, 1942, 7 In.	190.00
Wax Over Papier-Mache, Shoulder Head, Glass Eyes, Box, c.1890, 16 In. . . . .*illus*	115.00
Wax Over Papier-Mache, Shoulder Head, Glass Eyes, Human Hair, Germany, c.1880, 28 In. *illus*	173.00
Wax Shoulder Head, Blue Glass Sleep Eyes, Closed Mouth, Blond Wig, Cloth Body, 20 In. . .	176.00
Wax Shoulder Head, Enamel Eyes, Mohair Wig, Muslin Body, Wax Limbs, England, 17 In. . .	1705.00
Wood, Carved, Brown Hair, Enamel Eyes, Turban, Dowel-Jointed, Italy, 14 In.	660.00
Wood, Enamel Eyes, Human Hair, Dowel-Jointed Legs, 26 In.	5600.00
Wood, Hand Carved, Painted Hair, Shaded Coloring, Dowel-Jointed, Costume, Accessories, 18 In. . . .	825.00
Wood, Round Face, Elongated Throat, Painted Hair, Blush Spots, Dowel-Jointed, c.1850, 6 In. . . .	550.00
Wood, Socket Head, Carved, Painted Curls, Eyes, Tenon-Jointed Body, Boy, 29 In.	2703.00

DOLL CLOTHES

Cissette, Afternoon Dress, Pink Silk Gauze, Satin, Rhinestones, Box, c.1958	475.00
Cissette, Ball Gown, Ruffled Tiered Tulle, Satin Bodice, Appliques, No. 0745, c.1962	350.00
Cissette, Ballerina, Aqua Satin, Tulle, Rhinestones, Coronet, Slippers, Box, c.1960	250.00
Cissette, Ballerina, Pink Satin, Tulle, Rhinestones, Tulle Neck Ruffle, Box, c.1960	100.00
Cissette, Ballerina, Pink Satin, Tulle, Sleeve Ruffles, Ballet Slippers, Box, c.1960	375.00
Cissette, Bridesmaid Dress, Tulle, Swiss Dots, Appliques, Woven Bonnet, c.1960	475.00
Cissette, Lingerie, Teddy, Nightgown, Bathrobe, Panties, Slip, Lace, Alexander, c.1960	200.00
Cissette, Party Dress, Ivory Taffeta Faille, Rose Pattern, Pouf Sleeves, c.1958	350.00
Cissette, Party Dress, Pink Nylon, Rose Print Design, Lace Collar, No. 0721, c.1960	175.00
Cissette, Wedding Gown, White Tulle, Long Sleeves, No. 0755, Box, c.1963	325.00
Cissy, Rose Satin Evening Gown, Tulle Wrap, Petticoat, Box, c.1958	975.00
Dress, Aqua French Silk Faille, Lined, Flowers, Lace Edge, Pleats, Princess Style, 38 In.	275.00
Elise, Afternoon At Home, No. 16-46, Box, c.1958	250.00
Elise, Ball Gown, Pink Tulle, Organdy, Taffeta Bodice, No. 19-45, Box, c.1960	400.00
Elise, Ballerina, Pink Tutu, Satin Bodice, Pink Nylon Tights, No. 17-40, Box, c.1958	100.00
Elise, Ballerina, White Tutu, Satin Bodice, Pink Nylon Tights, Box, c.1958	75.00
Elise, Blue Coat, Flared, Woven Hat, Pink Bow, No. 158, c.1957	250.00
Elise, Party Dress, Pink Nylon, Velvet Lace, Ruffled Collar, Box, c.1960	400.00
Elise, Peignoir Set, Pink Nylon, Lace Trim, Box, c.1960	150.00
Elise, Sporty Set, White Pique, Blouse, Skirt, Bermuda Shorts, Box, c.1958	175.00
Housecoat, Rose Satin, White Cotton Collar, Cuffs, Madame Alexander, c.1955	25.00
Lissy, Bridesmaid Dress, Dotted Swiss Tulle, Pink Bodice, Lace Coronet, c.1958	350.00
Lissy, Party Dress, Navy Blue Taffeta, White Straw Hat, No. 1151, c.1957	300.00
Lissy, Pinafore Dress, Pink Sateen, Blue, White Pinafore, White Bonnet, c.1956	700.00
Margot, Capri Set, Blue & White Nylon Satin Jacket, Orange Pants, No. 0960, Box	225.00

Doll, Wax Over Papier-Mache, Shoulder Head, Glass Eyes, Box, c.1890, 16 In. $115.00

Doll, Wax Over Papier-Mache, Shoulder Head, Glass Eyes, Human Hair, Germany, c.1880, 28 In. $173.00

> **TIP**
> *If you have a vinyl doll with dirt or pencil marks on the head or body, try this: Wrap the doll so that only the marked part shows. Rub the mark with solid vegetable shortening and put the doll in the sun for the day. Try this for several days and the mark should disappear.*

Doorstop, 3 Puppies In Basket, Bulldogs, Cast Iron, M. Rosenstein, 1932, 7 x 7⅜ In. $230.00

Doorstop, Church, Stained Glass Windows, Cast Iron, No. 12502, 7½ x 5½ In. $1980.00

Doorstop, Cockatoo, On Branch, Multicolored, Cast Iron, Signed, L.A.C.S. 711, 8¼ x 6 In. $303.00

Doorstop, Dog, Fox Terrier, Cast Iron, Creations Co., 6¾ x 7¼ In. $248.00

Doorstop, Dog, Setter, White, Black, Cast Iron, Hubley, 8⅞ x 15½ In. $440.00

Quintuplets, Baby Gown, Pink Cotton, No. 0315, Box, c.1964, 4 Piece	50.00
Skipper, Learning To Ride, No. 1935	175.00
Terri Lee, Bathrobe, Blue Nylon, No. 5607, Envelope, c.1957	25.00
Wendy, Beth, Charteuse Cotton Dress, Lilac Pinafore, Alexander-Kins, c.1956	50.00
Wendy, Marme, Brown, Yellow Gown, White Pique Collar, Taffeta Apron, c.1956	50.00
Wendy, Riding Outfit, White Knit Top, Brown Checked Pants, Hat, Boots, Box, c.1964	100.00
Wendy-Kins, Angel, Turquoise Taffeta, Silver, Bodice, Wings, No. 0618, Box, c.1961	50.00
Wendy-Kins, Bride, Lace Ruffle Tiered Bodice, Taffeta Petticoat, No. 0670, Box	175.00
Wendy-Kins, Bridegroom, Black Jacket, Striped Trousers, No. 0331, Box, c.1957	150.00
Wendy-Kins, Pink Organdy Dress, Ruffled Lace Bodice, No. 621, c.1965	75.00

DONALD DUCK *items are included in the Disneyana category.*

DOORSTOPS have been made in all types of designs. The vast majority of the doorstops sold today are cast iron and were made from about 1890 to 1930. Most of them are shaped like people, animals, flowers, or ships. Reproductions and newly designed examples are sold in gift shops.

2 Kittens, Cast Iron, Hubley, 7¼ x 5½ In.	94.00
3 Kittens In Basket, Cast Iron, Signed, M. Rosenstein, Wilton Products, 1932, 7 x 10 In.	672.00
3 Puppies In Basket, Bulldogs, Cast Iron, M. Rosenstein, 1932, 7 x 7⅜ In. *illus*	230.00
Amish Man, Hand In Pocket, Red Shirt, Black Vest, Hat, Painted, Cast Iron, 8½ x 3½ In.	88.00
Amish Woman, Holding Basket, Red Shirt, Black Skirt, Painted, Cast Iron, 8¼ x 4 In.	88.00
Asian Couple, Kneeling, Kissing, Cast Iron, 4⅝ x 4⅝ In.	165.00
Bathing Beauties, Art Deco, 2 Bathers, Parasol, Painted, Iron, Hubley, 11 x 5 In.	1792.00 to 2750.00
Bellhop, Black, Luggage, Gold Overall Paint, Cast Iron, 7½ x 5 In.	1210.00
Blowfish, White, Painted, Cast Iron, 8¼ x 7 In.	2090.00
Blue Boy, Cast Iron, Bradley & Hubbard, 8½ x 5 In.	880.00
Bobby Blake, Teddy Bear, Green Base, Painted, Cast Iron, Hubley, 9½ x 5¼ In.	413.00
Bridesmaid, Silhouette, Flowers, Cast Iron, No. 5, Albany Foundry, 11¼ x 10¼ In.	7840.00
Butler, Checkered Base, 2 Sections, Cast Iron, Bradley & Hubbard, 11½ x 5¾ In.	495.00
Cabin, In Woods, Cast Iron, National Fdry., No. 78, 4⅝ x 10 In.	275.00
Camel, 2 Humps, Cast Iron, 7 x 9 In.	448.00
Camel, Running, 1 Hump, Painted, Cast Iron, No. S118, 6⅞ x 7⅞ In.	336.00
Cat, Black, Seated, Flat Back, 12½ In.	425.00
Cat, Black, Seated, Yellow Eyes, Cast Iron, Hubley, 12½ In.	460.00
Cat, Black, White Outline, Raised Back, Carlisle Fdry. Co., 9¼ x 5¾ In.	138.00
Cat, Fireside, White, Gray, Blue Eyes, Cast Iron, No. 335, Hubley, 10¾ In.	3080.00
Cat, On Rug, Full Figure, Cast Iron, National Foundry, 2⅞ x 6⅞ In.	784.00
Cat, Persian, Green, Eyes, Original Bow, Cast Iron, No. 302, Hubley, 8½ x 6½ In.	1792.00
Cat, Siamese, Blue Eyes, Cast Iron, 10½ x 6 In.	5320.00
Cat, Striped, Scratching Girl, Blue Dress, Painted, CJO, 9 x 4 In.	1870.00
Cat, White, Seated, Green Eyes, Painted, Hollow, Cast Iron, Hubley, 10 x 4 In.	99.00
Church, Stained Glass Windows, Cast Iron, No. 12502, 7½ x 5½ In. *illus*	1980.00
Clown, Hunched Over, Blue Hat, Red Outfit, White Face, Painted, Cast Iron, 10 x 4 In.	1320.00
Clown, Red, White, Black, Ruffled Collar & Cuffs, Cast Iron, 11½ x 5¾ In.	2240.00
Cock, Duck, Fighting, Cast Iron, Signed, Stadig, 8¾ x 9⅝ In.	3920.00
Cockatoo, On Branch, Multicolored, Cast Iron, Signed, L.A.C.S. 711, 8¼ x 6 In. *illus*	303.00
Cockatoo, On Stump, Cast Iron, Albany Fdry. Co., 7¼ x 8½ In.	385.00
Colonial Woman, Bustled Dress, Yellow Shawl, Flowers, Painted, Cast Iron, 8 x 4 In.	88.00
Cottage, Cape Cod, Light & Dark Green Roof, Cast Iron, Eastern Specialty, 5¾ x 8¾ In.	220.00
Cottage, Flowers, Green Grass Base, Hubley, 5¾ x 7½ In.	110.00
Cottage, Hollyhocks, Cast Iron, Albany Foundry, 5¾ x 8¾ In.	220.00
Crow, Eating Berries, Glass Eye, Woodland Base, Painted, Cast Iron, 5¼ x 4¾ In.	220.00
Daisy Bowl, No. 452, Hubley, 7½ x 6 In.	193.00 to 224.00
Dancer, Nude, Art Deco Style, Cast Iron, 5 x 4½ In.	165.00
Dapper Dan, Walking With Cane, Cast Iron, No. 1224, Judd Co., 8⅜ x 5¼ In.	1760.00
Dog, Bloodhound, Full Figure, Cast Iron, 6¾ x 5¾ In.	3640.00
Dog, Cocker Spaniel, Sitting, Cast Iron, Wilton Products, Inc., 6⅞ x 7 In.	330.00
Dog, Dachshund, Red Collar, Multicolored, Cast Iron, 9½ In.	588.00
Dog, Doberman Pinscher, Full Figure, Cast Iron, Hubley, 7⅞ x 7⅞ In.	1008.00
Dog, English Bulldog, Standing, Cast Iron, No. 460, Hubley, 4⅝ x 5½ In.	660.00
Dog, Fox Terrier, Cast Iron, Creations Co., 6¾ x 7¼ In. *illus*	248.00
Dog, Scottie, Cast Iron, 6¼ x 8 In.	146.00
Dog, Setter, Bird In Mouth, Cast Iron, No. 105, National Fdry., 7 x 12 In.	495.00
Dog, Setter, White, Black, Cast Iron, Hubley, 8⅞ x 15½ In. *illus*	440.00

Dog, St. Bernard, Barrel Around Neck, Cast Iron, 8 x 11 In.	385.00
Dog, Terrier, Cast Iron, Repainted, c.1900, 10 In.	24.00 to 94.00
Dresser, Welsh, Slate, Inscribed, A Present To Jane Thomas, 10⅜ x 9 In.	209.00
Drum Major, Marching, Baton, Painted, Cast Iron, 13½ x 5 In.	275.00
Duck, Top Hat, Blue Pants, Walking, Profile, Painted, Cast Iron, 7½ x 4¼ In.	303.00
Dutch Couple, Kissing, Cast Iron, No. 332, Hubley, 4¾ In.	225.00
Eagle, Cast Iron, c.1890, 6½ x 5½ In.	263.00
Edgar Allen Poe House, Cast Iron, Hand Painted, Bradley & Hubbard, 6 x 7½ In.	495.00
El Capitan, Marching, Gun On Shoulder, Cast Iron, 7¾ x 5 In.	1904.00
Elephant, Picking Coconuts, Tree, Cast Iron, No. 13, National Foundry, 14 x 10 In.	896.00
End Of Trail, Man, Slumped Over Horse, Cast Iron, 9¾ x 9¼ In.	92.00
Fisherman, Hands In Pockets, 15½ In.	895.00
Flapper Girl, Holding Parasol, Cast Iron, Toledo Stove Co., 9½ In.	1870.00
Flapper Girl, Holding Parasol, Pink Dress, Cast Iron, Toledo Stove Co., No. 8, 9½ x 4¾ In.	1232.00
Flapper Girl, Profile, Layered Dress, Parasol, Painted, Cast Iron, H Caine, 1922, 9 In.	1210.00
Flower Basket, Cast Iron, No. 357, Hubley, 8¼ x 5½ In.	248.00
Flower Basket, Dogwood, Berries, Cast Iron, 8¾ x 6⅜ In.	83.00
Flower Basket, Lilies Of The Valley, Blue Bow, Cast Iron, No. 189, Hubley, 10½ x 7½ In.	275.00
Flower Basket, Mixed Flowers, Cast Iron, No. 69, Hubley, 10¾ x 6½ In.	252.00
Flower Basket, Yellow Poppies, Handle, Iron, Signed, C.H.F. Co., 10½ x 8⅝ In. ..... *illus*	660.00
Flower Vase, Gladiolas, Cast Iron, No. 489, Hubley, 10 x 8 In.	193.00
Flower Vase, Tulips, Pink, Yellow, Fluted, Cast Iron, No. 148, Albany, 8½ x 7 In.	330.00
Flowerpot, Poppies, Cast Iron, No. 330, Hubley, 7 x 6 In.	248.00
Fox, Sleeping, Cast Iron, 6½ x 12¼ In.	112.00
Fox Head, Old Black Paint, Cast Iron, 5¾ x 5¼ In.	460.00
French Basket, Cast Iron, No. 69, Hubley, 11 x 6¾ In.	138.00
French Girl, Cast Iron, No. 23, Hubley, 9¼ x 5½ In.	728.00
Frog, Original Green Paint, Cast Iron, 3 x 5 In.	55.00
Fruit Basket, Natural Colors, 11½ x 11½ In.	440.00
Fruit Basket, Original Paint, Cast Iron, 9⅞ In.	385.00
Fruit Bowl, Cast Iron, No. 456, Hubley, 7 x 7 In.	275.00
Fruit Bowl, Marked CN, Hubley, 7 In.	160.00
Fruit Bowl, Oranges, Plums, Grapes, Ribbed Bowl, Cast Iron, No. 456, Hubley, 7 In. ...*illus*	230.00
Gazelle, Cast Iron, No. 410, Hubley, 6½ x 5 In.	224.00
Geese, Cast Iron, No. 291, 8¼ x 6¼ In.	2520.00
Gen. George Washington, Woodland Ground, Painted, Cast Iron, Albany Foundry, 9 x 5 In.	100.00
Girl, Dancing, Arms Above Head Holding Dress, Painted, National Foundry, 9 x 6¾ In.	2475.00
Girl, Feeding Geese, Red Dress, Cast Iron, 9¾ x 11⅝ In.	2240.00
Girl, Holding Dress, Art Deco Base, Painted, Cast Iron, Bradley & Hubbard, 13 x 6½ In.	3300.00
Girl, Holding Flower Basket, Yellow Dress & Hat, Cast Iron, 9 x 3¾ In.	550.00
Girl, Holding Sunbonnet, Braided Rug, Painted, Cast Iron, Waverly Studios, 8¼ x 5 In.	550.00
Gladiolas, Cast Iron, No. 484, Hubley, 10 x 7¾ In.	165.00
Gnome, Cast Iron, Painted, 11 In. ..... *illus*	201.00
Gnome, Green Hoodie, White Beard, Cast Iron, 13¼ In.	88.00
Gnome, Standing, Full Figure, Cast Iron, Hubley, 11 In.	146.00
Golfer, Putting, Original Paint, Cast Iron, Hubley, 8½ x 7 In.	3300.00
Golfer, Putting, Red Jacket, Brown Nickers, Hat, Painted, Cast Iron, Hubley, 8⅜ x 7 In.	248.00
Grapes, On Vine, 2 Bunches, Shaped Vine, Cast Iron, Albany Fdry. Co., 11 x 7 In. ......*illus*	165.00
Grapes, On Vine, Cast Iron, Albany Fdry. Co., 8 x 6⅝ In.	193.00
Halloween Girl, Holding Jack-O'-Lantern, Ghost Costume, Littco Label, 13⅞ x 8¾ In.	72800.00
Harlow House, Oversized Shingle Roof, Cast Iron, Signed, No. 1677, 5 x 5 In.	3360.00
Heron, Red, Yellow, Blue, Painted, Cast Iron, Marked, BB Noes Co., 7½ x 5⅛ In.	220.00
Horse Sloped Base, Brass, 20th Century, 9⅜ x 12¼ In.	206.00
House, Edgar Allen Poe, Brass, Japanned, Bradley & Hubbard, 6 x 7½ In.	100.00
House, Old Mill, Bridge, Brass, AM Greenblatt Studios, 9¾ x 7¼ In.	110.00
Irises, White, Purple, Cast Iron, No. 469, Hubley, 10⅜ x 6¾ In.	275.00
Iron, Frog, Cast, Multicolored, Black, Red Highlights, 19th Century, 6 x 4½ In.	118.00
Jonquil Daffodils, Cast Iron, No. 453, Hubley, 7⅜ x 6 In.	448.00
Lafayette, On Horse, Cast Iron, 15⅜ x 8⅜ In., Pair	224.00
Lighthouse, Caretakers Cottage, Painted, Cast Iron, National Foundry, 6¼ x 8 In.	248.00
Lighthouse, Highland Cape Cod, Houses, Figural, Painted, Cast Iron, 9 x 7¾ In.	880.00
Lincoln Cabin, Cast Iron, No. 8687, Signed, Judd Co., 3⅞ x 4⅞ In.	56.00
Lion, Full Figure, Cast Iron, 7 x 8 In.	196.00
Lion, Full Figure, Cast Iron, England, 19th Century, 14½ In.	263.00
Lobster, Red, Partially Emerged In Green Base, Painted, Cast Iron, 12 x 6½ In.	303.00
Lovebirds, Nestling, Tropical Foliage, Sloped Base, Painted, Cast Iron, 7 x 3¾ In.	220.00

Doorstop, Flower Basket, Yellow Poppies, Handle, Iron, Signed, C.H.F. Co., 10½ x 8⅝ In. $660.00

Doorstop, Fruit Bowl, Oranges, Plums, Grapes, Ribbed Bowl, Cast Iron, No. 456, Hubley, 7 In. $230.00

Doorstop, Gnome, Cast Iron, Painted, 11 In. $201.00

Doorstop, Grapes, On Vine, 2 Bunches, Shaped Vine, Cast Iron, Albany Fdry. Co., 11 x 7 In. $165.00

Doorstop, Orange Tree, In Pot, Round Ribbed Base, Cast Iron, 12⅛ x 6⅝ In. $5500.00

Doorstop, Parlor Maid, Serving Cocktails, Cast Iron, Signed Fish, No. 268, Hubley, 9¼ x 3½ In. $1760.00

Doulton, Pitcher, Stylized Flowers, Mottled Gray & Pink, Snake Handle, 7¾ In. $349.00

Doulton, Pitcher, Tan, Salt Glaze, Black Flowers, Cylindrical, Stoneware, 1880, 9 In. $263.00

Doulton, Umbrella Stand, Flow Blue, Floral Band, Gold Trim, Stepped Cylinder, 24 x 11 In. $403.00

Maid, Black Dress, White Apron, Cast Iron, No. 1242, Judd Co., 9 x 4¾ In.	220.00
Mammy, Blue Dress, Red Scarf, White Apron, Cast Iron, Hubley, 13¼ In.	239.00
Mammy, Painted, Cast Iron, Early 20th Century, 13¼ In.	239.00
Marigolds, Cast Iron, No. 315, Hubley, 7½ x 8 In.	110.00 to 336.00
Mary Quite Contrary, Painted, Cast Iron, Littco, 12½ x 9½ In.	784.00
Mexican Guitar Player, Painted, Cast Iron, No. 951, 12 In.	3080.00
Minuet Girl, Dancing, Painted, Cast Iron, CJO, 8½ x 5 In.	193.00
Monkey, Full Figure, 3-Piece Casting, Cast Iron, 8¾ x 7 In.	308.00
Monroe Tavern, Tree In Front, Lexington, Mass., 5⅜ x 8⅝ In.	2750.00
Mouse, On Wedge Of Cheese, Cast Iron, Painted, 2¼ x 1½ x 5⅞ In.	1998.00
Narcissus, Cast Iron, No. 266, Hubley, 7½ x 7 In.	220.00
Orange Tree, In Pot, Round Ribbed Base, Cast Iron, 12⅛ x 6⅝ In. ......*illus*	5500.00
Organ Grinder, Monkey At Feet, Painted, Cast Iron, 2-Sided, 10 x 5¾ In.	193.00
Ostrich, Cast Iron, Signed, S120, 8½ x 9 In.	224.00
Owl, Glass Eyes, Cast Iron, Pat. Pend. For, 7¼ x 3¾ In.	336.00
Owl, On Books, Cast Iron, Signed, Eastern Specialty Mfg., 9½ x 6⅛ In.	952.00 to 2200.00
Owl, On Pedestal, Cast Iron, No. 7797, Bradley & Hubbard, 15½ x 5 In.	896.00
Owl, On Pedestal, White, Cast Iron, No. 7797, Bradley & Hubbard, 15½ x 6 In.	3025.00
Owl, On Stump, Gray, White, Cast Iron, Bradley & Hubbard, 8 x 4¼ In.	715.00
Owl, On Stump, Holly Berries, Cast Iron, No. 254, Hubley, 10 x 4½ In.	248.00 to 392.00
Parlor Maid, Serving Cocktails, Cast Iron, Signed Fish, No. 268, Hubley, 9¼ x 3½ In. ..*illus*	1760.00
Parrot, Albany Foundry, 12½ In.	195.00
Parrot, On Stump, Cast Iron, No. 1010, Blodgett Studio, Lake Geneva, Wis., 12 x 6 In.	140.00
Parrot, On Tree Stump, Painted, Cast Iron, National Foundry, 7½ x 6 In.	66.00
Peacock, Multicolored, Painted, Cast Iron, 6¼ x 6¼ In.	358.00
Penguin, Cast Iron, Creations Company, 1930, 3 x 3¾ In.	560.00
Penguin, Tuxedo, Top Hat, 2-Piece Casting, Painted, Cast Iron, Hubley, 10½ x 4 In.	660.00
Penguin, Yellow, Red, Black, Cast Iron, No. 1, Taylor Cook, 1930, 9½ x 5⅜ In.	2240.00
Petunias & Asters, Cast Iron, No. 470, Hubley, 9½ x 6½ In.	193.00
Phlox Flowers, Cast Iron, No. 473, Hubley, 5¾ x 4½ In., Pair	112.00
Pilgrim, Boy, Cast Iron, Boye, 2-Sided, Full Figure, Marked CJO, 9 In.	500.00
Police Boy, In Diaper, Dog, Cast Iron, 10⅝ x 7¼ In.	1120.00
Poppies & Cornflowers, Cast Iron, No. 265, Hubley, 7¼ x 6½ In.	165.00 to 308.00
Poppies & Daisies, Cast Iron, No. 491, Hubley, 7¼ In.	138.00
Rabbit, Dressed In Tails, Top Hat, Cast Iron, No. 89, National Foundry, 8¼ x 4⅞ In.	728.00
Rabbit, Pushing Wheelbarrow, Easter Eggs, Wedge, Cast Iron, Littco, 11⅝ x 9 In.	4200.00
Red Riding Hood & Wolf, Painted, Cast Iron, Albany Foundry, 7¼ In.	1100.00
Rooster, 2-Sided, Painted, Cast Iron, Spencer, 13¼ x 10¾ In.	440.00
Roses, Cast Iron, No. 445, Hubley, 8¾ x 7⅞ In.	275.00
Rumba Dancer, Green Tiered Skirt, Red Bandanna, 11 x 6⅜ In.	9900.00
Sailor, Multicolored, Cast Iron, 12 In.	201.00
Screech Owl, On Stump, Painted, Cast Iron, Marked, CJO-1287, 10¼ x 6 In.	5225.00
Senorita, Yellow Dress, Basket Of Flowers, Profile, Painted, Cast Iron, Marked No. 40, 10 x 7 In.	495.00
Ship, On High Seas, Painted, Cast Iron, AM Greenblatt Studios, 10 x 12 In.	248.00
Ship, On Rough Sea, Painted, Cast Iron, Albany Fdry. Co., 187, 8⅛ x 9½ In.	784.00
Sign, Trade, Cow, Scroll Work, 19th Century	1912.00
Snooper, Detective, Black Trench Coat, Yellow Pants, Top Hat, Cast Iron, 13 x 4 In.	770.00
Snow Owl, On Stump, Cast Iron, No. 1287, Judd Co., 10 x 6 In.	952.00
Southern Belle, Blue Dress, Holding Hat & Flowers, National Foundry, 11¾ x 6 In.	385.00
Southern Belle, Green Dress, Holding Hat, Cast Iron, National Foundry, 11¼ x 6 In.	112.00
Squirrel, Seated, Eating Nut, Cast Iron, Gray, 9 In.	489.00
Squirrel, Sitting Up, With Nut, Cast Iron, Hubley, 9¼ x 5¾ In.	616.00
Tiger Lily, Cast Iron, No. 472, Hubley, 10¾ In.	248.00
Tropical Woman, Bowl Of Fruit On Head, Cast Iron, Signed, 1000, 11⅝ x 6⅛ In.	672.00
Turtle, Light Yellow Citron Glass, Drawn Out Head & Feet, 1880-1920, 6 In.	110.00
Uncle Sam, Red, White, Blue, Cast Iron, 12⅛ x 5¼ In.	12320.00
Whistling Jim, Boy, Bare Feet, Rolled Up Pants, Cap, Bradley & Hubbard, 16¼ In.	1430.00
Windmill, 2 Cottages, Cast Iron, Signed, A.M. Greenblatt Studios, 1926, 11⅞ x 9 In.	1904.00
Windmill, Cottages, Cast Iron, No. 8, Roland, 11 x 8⅝ In.	165.00
Witch, Riding Broomstick, Bat, Ring, Painted, Cast Iron, 6⅝ x 6½ In.	5600.00
Woman, Arched Back, Art Deco, Copper Electroplated Iron, No. 154, 5 x 4 In.	308.00
Woman, Entering House, Cast Iron, No. 50, Eastern Specialty Co., 8¼ In.	440.00
Woman, Hat Box, Carpet Bag, Mary Newton, Cast Iron, Sarah Symonds, 12 x 6⅝ In.	672.00
Woman, In Red Canoe, Forest Ground, Cast Iron, 4½ x 10 In.	1120.00
Woman, Multi-Layered Shawl, Bustled Blue Dress, Painted, Cast Iron, 8¼ x 3½ In.	110.00
Woman, Old Fashioned, Blue Dress, Cast Iron, No. 296, Hubley, 7¾ x 4 In.	168.00

Woman, Skiing, Full Figure, Red Scarf, Cast Iron, 12½ x 5 In.	1344.00
Woman, Victorian, Walking, Flower Basket, Parasol, Cast Iron, Bradley & Hubbard, 11 x 7 In.	715.00
Zinnias, Cast Iron, No. 267, Hubley, 9¾ x 8½ In.	616.00

DORCHESTER POTTERY was founded by George Henderson in 1895 in Dorchester, Massachusetts. At first, the firm made utilitarian stoneware, but collectors are most interested in the line of decorated blue and white pottery that Dorchester made from 1940 until it went out of business in 1979.

DORCHESTER POTTERY WORKS BOSTON, MASS.

Bed Warmer, No. 8088, Stamped, 11 x 5 In.	95.00
Bottle, Hot Water, Salt Glaze, Marked, 10½ x 6¼ In.	250.00
Foot Warmer, Marked, 12 In.	325.00
Plate, Pussy Willow, Blue Swirl Ground, 1950s, 12¾ In.	275.00
Pot, Lid, Lily Of The Valley, Blue Ground, Handles, Marked, 4½ x 7 In.	195.00

DOULTON pottery and porcelain were made by Doulton and Co. of Burslem, England, after 1882. The name *Royal Doulton* appeared on their wares after 1902. Other pottery by Doulton is listed under Royal Doulton.

Bust, George V & Queen Mary, Brown Stoneware, Leslie Harridine, c.1910, 7½ In., Pair	470.00
Candlestick, Gilt Brass, Stoneware, Frank A. Butler, Lambeth, 1880s, 8 In., Pair	520.00
Group, Steeplechase, Stoneware, George Tinworth, c.1885, 6 In.	7638.00
Jug, Carrara, Female Mask Head, Blue Flowers, Gold Trim, Leaves, c.1880, 7⅛ In.	499.00
Jug, Water, For Sir Edward Lee & Co., Stoneware, Lambeth, c.1900, 7½ In.	123.00
Match Holder, A Match For You, Tan Glaze, Sterling Silver Rim, 2⅞ In.	92.00
Menu Holder, Group, Potters, George Tinworth, c.1885, 3¾ In.	2820.00
Menu Holder, Trumpet Blowers, Porcelain, George Tinworth, c.1890, 3½ In.	3408.00
Pitcher, Stylized Flowers, Mottled Gray & Pink, Snake Handle, 7¾ In. .....*illus*	349.00
Pitcher, Tan, Salt Glaze, Black Flowers, Cylindrical, Stoneware, 1880, 9 In. .....*illus*	263.00
Salt Cellar, Stoneware, Round, Incised Leaf Design, Raised Square Base, c.1885, 3½ In.	235.00
Tile, Picture, 2 Panels, Earthenware, H.A. Miles, Enameled, Andromache, c.1900, 16 In.	764.00
Umbrella Stand, Flow Blue, Floral Band, Gold Trim, Stepped Cylinder, 24 x 11 In. ....*illus*	403.00
Vase, Birds In Marsh Grass, Mottled Blue Green Glaze, Flared Rim, 1884, 11 In. ....*illus*	978.00
Vase, Mottled Gray Ground, Stylized Flowers, c.1939, 9 In.	508.00
Vase, Stick, Brown Flowers, Green Blue & Brown Panels, Beaded, Bulbous, 5¼ In.	115.00
Vase, Stoneware, Cartouches, Dogs, Birds, Hannah Barlow, c.1880, 11½ In., Pair	3819.00
Vase, Stoneware, Edith Lupton, Lambeth, c.1883, 10 In.	144.00
Vase, Stoneware, Eliza Simmance, Lambeth , c.1905, 13 In.	349.00
Vase, Stoneware, Trumpet Shape, Incised Flowers, Scrolled Panels, c.1880, 7 In., Pair	441.00
Vase, Stylized Flowers & Leaves, Green, Blue & Black, Flared Rim, 1927, 10½ In. ......*illus*	1075.00

DRAGONWARE is a form of moriage pottery made since the late 19th century. Moriage is a type of decoration on Japanese pottery. Raised white designs are applied to the ware. White dragons are the major raised decorations on the moriage called dragonware. The background can be one of many different colors. It is still being made.

Biscuit Jar, No Lid, Gray & White Body, Blue Eyes, Pink & Blue Ground, Handle, 3 In.	9.00
Bowl, Rice, Marked, 4½ In.	13.00
Bucket, Dragon, Dark Gray, White, Blue, Pink Ground, 3 In.	9.00
Candlestick, Cylindrical, Flared Holder, Square Foot, Nippon, 10 In. ....*illus*	176.00
Creamer, Kutani, 3¾ x 4½ In.	25.00
Cup, Moriage, 1½ In.	5.00
Cup, Tea, 4 x 2½ In.	60.00
Cup, Yellow, Occupied Japan, 1½ In.	5.00
Cup & Saucer, Demitasse, 1930, 2¼ & 4½ In.	20.00
Cup & Saucer, Demitasse, Blue, Pink	45.00
Cup & Saucer, Dragon Lithophane	55.00
Cup & Saucer, Geisha, Gray, Pink, Blue	10.00
Cup & Saucer, Niagara Falls, 1¼ In.	14.00
Cup Set, Demitasse, Sugar & Creamer, White Opalescent, Lithophane, 15 Piece	85.00
Incense Burner, Animals, Handles, 3½ x 3 In.	12.00
Incense Burner, Footed, Handles, High Top, 3¾ In.	20.00
Olive Dish, Black, White, Brown Edge, Blue, Pink Ground, Handle	22.00
Plate, Salad, Blue, Black, Pink, Gold, 7¼ In.	5.00 to 8.00
Plate, Salad, Blue, Pink, Gold, 7¼ In.	7.50
Salt & Pepper, Brown, 2½ In.	15.00
Salt & Pepper, Prospect Point, Niagara Falls, Domed Top, 2¾ In.	20.00

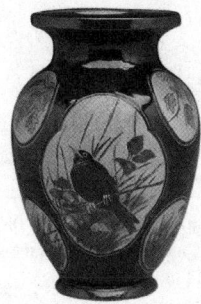

Doulton, Vase, Birds In Marsh Grass, Mottled Blue Green Glaze, Flared Rim, 1884, 11 In.
$978.00

Doulton, Vase, Stylized Flowers & Leaves, Green, Blue & Black, Flared Rim, 1927, 10½ In.
$1075.00

Dragonware, Candlestick, Cylindrical, Flared Holder, Square Foot, Nippon, 10 In.
$176.00

Dragonware, Vase, Oval, Buttressed Tab Handles, 4-Footed, Green Wreath Mark, c.1920, 8 In.
$323.00

Dresden, Desk Set, Cherubs & Flowers, Gold Trim, Inkwell, Letter Holder, 7-In. Tray, 3 Piece
$71.00

Duncan & Miller, Pall Mall, Dish, Swan, Emerald Green, Crystal Neck, 8½ x 12 In.
$25.00

Duncan & Miller, Sandwich, Relish, 3 Sections, 12 In.
$17.00

Durand, Ginger Jar, Cover, Blue Iridescent, White Pulled Hearts & Vines, Fluted Finial, 9¼ In.
$8050.00

Durand, Vase, Gold Iridescent, 5 Combed White Feathers, Green Bands, Shouldered, 6¾ In.
$1093.00

Saltshaker, Brown, 6-Sided, 3¾ In.	15.00
Saucer, Demitasse, 4¾ In.	4.00
Saucer, Geisha Lithophane, Blue Luster Ground, Moriage Dragon, 5½ In.	13.00
Sugar & Creamer, Charcoal Gray, Black, 3¼ & 4¼ In.	20.00
Teapot, Pearlized, Luster Ware, 7¼ x 2⅝ In.	25.00
Vase, Oval, Buttressed Tab Handles, 4-Footed, Green Wreath Mark, c.1920, 8 In. *illus*	323.00
Wall Pocket, Carmel Luster, Metallic Brass Rim Glaze, 7 In.	100.00

DRESDEN china is any china made in the town of Dresden, Germany. The most famous factory in Dresden is the Meissen factory. Figurines of eighteenth-century ladies and gentlemen, animal groups, or cherubs and other mythological subjects were popular. One special type of figurine was made with skirts of porcelain-dipped lace. Do not make the mistake of thinking that all pieces marked *Dresden* are from the Meissen factory. The Meissen pieces usually have crossed swords marks, and are listed under Meissen. Some recent porcelain from Ireland, called *Irish Dresden,* is not included in this book.

Box, Cover, Oval, Schumann, c.1940, 4 x 8 In.	47.00
Candelabrum, 5-Light, c.1900, 20 x 15 In., Pair	585.00
Centerpiece, Gilt Bronze Mounted, Serpentine Rim, Floral Spray, 1800s, 6 x 17 x 13 In.	235.00
Charger, Flowers, Hand Painted, c.1930, 13 In.	100.00
Cup & Saucer, Baker's Cocoa Woman, Gilt Handle, Figural Silver Spoon	495.00
Cup & Saucer Set, Creme Brule, 8 Sets	105.00
Desk Set, Cherubs & Flowers, Gold Trim, Inkwell, Letter Holder, 7-In. Tray, 3 Piece *illus*	71.00
Dish, Duck Shape, Schumann, 20th Century, 6½ x 9½ In., Pair	82.00
Figurine, 2 Women, Playing Mandolin, Piano, 8 x 12 In.	70.00
Figurine, Cherubs, White 5½ In., 4 Piece	205.00
Figurine, Napoleonic Style, Soldiers, 12 In., 3 Piece	295.00
Figurine, Woman Reading Book To Boy & Girl, c.1970, 8 x 10 In.	70.00
Group, 18th Century Couple Having Tea, Lamp Mount, 25 x 11 In.	29.00
Plate, Flower Rimmed, 9½ x 11 Piece	585.00
Plate Set, Cabinet, Leaf Shape, Flowers, Scalloped Edge, 8 In., 11 Piece	644.00
Plate Set, Dessert, Floral Spray Center, Reticulated Border, Gilt, 7⅛ In., 12 Piece	189.00
Urn, Cover, Schumann, Early 1900s, 24¾ In.	936.00

DUNCAN & MILLER is a term used by collectors when referring to glass made by the George A. Duncan and Sons Company or the Duncan and Miller Glass Company. These companies worked from 1893 to 1955, when the use of the name *Duncan* was discontinued and the firm became part of the United States Glass Company. Early patterns may be listed under Pressed Glass.

Basset Town, Sugar, Silver Colored Rim, c.1891-94, 2⅞ x 2¾ In.	15.00
Button Panel, Celery Tray, Cupped Rim	28.00
Canterbury, Basket, 10 x 7½ In.	185.00
Canterbury, Cruet, 5½ In.	30.00
Canterbury, Plate, Dessert, 7¾ In.	10.00
Canterbury, Relish, 3 Sections, 10½ In.	35.00
Canterbury, Rose Bowl, 5¼ x 3¼ In.	25.00
Canterbury, Tumbler, 5⅜ In.	15.00
Canterbury, Vase, Sapphire Blue, Cloverleaf Shape, Flared, 2⅝ x 4½ In.	28.00
Caribbean, Bowl, Gold Encrusted, Handles, 6 In.	15.00
Caribbean, Bowl, Handles, 6 x 2¼ In.	15.00
Caribbean, Plate, Serving, 4-Footed, 12 In.	30.00
Caribbean, Punch Set, Clear Bowls, Red Handles, 18-In. Underplate, 11-In. Bowl, 15 Piece	400.00
Cornucopia, Vase, 12¼ In.	35.00
First Love, Champagne, 6 Oz., 4¾ In.	20.00
First Love, Cigarette Box, Cover, 3 x 5 In.	140.00 to 285.00
First Love, Plate, Scalloped Rim, 8 In.	29.00
First Love, Sugar, 4 In.	24.00
Gable, Toothpick, 8-Sided, 16-Point Cut Star, Base, 1905, 2¼ In.	42.00
Georgian, Tumbler, Whiskey, Green, 3¾ In., 4 Piece	30.00
Herringbone, Ladle, Mayonnaise, 4¾ In.	25.00
Hobnail, Champagne, 4½ In.	16.00
Hobnail, Relish, 3 Sections, Handles, Clear, 10 In.	35.00
Lily Of The Valley, Wine, 5 In.	25.00
Pall Mall, Dish, Swan, Emerald Green, Crystal Neck, 8½ x 12 In. *illus*	25.00
Pall Mall, Swan, Ruby, Clear Head & Neck, 6¼ x 8 x 4¾ In.	41.00

Sandwich, Candlestick, Milk Glass, 4 In.	25.00
Sandwich, Dish, Grapefruit, Flat Rim, 6 In.	30.00
Sandwich, Relish, 3 Sections, 12 In. ....*illus*	17.00
Sandwich, Sundae, Amber, Flared, 3½ In.	25.00
Sandwich, Torte Plate, 12 In.	35.00
Sandwich, Tray, Scalloped, Handles, 1924-55, 8 In.	30.00
Sylvan, Swan, Pink Opalescent, 13 x 9¾ In.	195.00
Tear Drop, Goblet, 5¾ In.	14.00
Tear Drop, Relish, Heart Shape, Sections, Handle, 7½ In.	30.00
Tear Drop, Tumbler, Whiskey, Footed, 3 Oz., 3 In.	14.00
Terrace, Relish, Sections, Silver Overlay, Grapes, Leaves, 6 In.	32.00

DURAND art glass was made from 1924 to 1931. The Vineland Flint Glass Works was established by Victor Durand and Victor Durand Jr. in 1897. In 1924 Martin Bach Jr. and other artisans from the Quezal glassworks joined them at the Vineland, New Jersey, plant to make Durand art glass. They called their gold iridescent glass Gold Lustre.

Ginger Jar, Cover, Blue Iridescent, White Pulled Hearts & Vines, Fluted Finial, 9¼ In. . .*illus*	8050.00
Lamp, Gourd Shape, Pulled Iridescent Design, 28 In.	360.00
Lamp Base, Green Heart & Vine, Orange Ground, 16 In.	400.00
Perfume Bottle, Blue Iridescent, Allover Gold Threading, Gold Foot, 7½ In.	1035.00
Shade, Torchere, Marigold Iridescent, Blue Iridescent Coils, 8½ In.	633.00
Sherbet, Ambergris Shaded To Blue, White Pulled Feathers, Amber Iridescent Foot, 4 In.	201.00
Vase, Blue Hearts & Vines, Shape No. 1717, 10 In.	1035.00
Vase, Blue Iridescent, 7¾ x 4¾ In.	1053.00
Vase, Blue Iridescent, Allover Gold Threading, Shouldered, Flared Rim, 8½ In.	575.00
Vase, Blue Iridescent, Gold Around Neck, White Heart & Vines, Baluster, Signed, 6 In.	2223.00
Vase, Blue Iridescent, Gold Iridescent Foot, Signed, 11¾ In.	850.00
Vase, Blue Iridescent, Threaded, No. 1722-8, Signed, 8 In.	450.00
Vase, Blue Iridescent, White Hearts & Vines, Shouldered, 10½ In.	1898.00
Vase, Gold, Blue Pulled Feathers, White Trim, Flower Sprays, 7 In.	1035.00
Vase, Gold Iridescent, 5 Combed White Feathers, Green Bands, Shouldered, 6¾ In. . . . .*illus*	1093.00
Vase, Gold Iridescent, Baluster, Flared Rim, Signed, 6 In.	345.00
Vase, Gold Iridescent, Flared, Pontil, Signed, 7¾ In.	518.00
Vase, Gold Iridescent, Green Lappets, Pontil, 12 In.	960.00
Vase, Gold Iridescent, Signed, Footed, 12 In.	1494.00
Vase, Iridescent, Purple & Gold, Urn Shape, White Swirls, c.1925, 7 In.	910.00
Vase, King Tut, Blue Iridescent Shaded To Green, White Design, Bulbous, Flared, 6¾ In.	978.00
Vase, King Tut, Gold Iridescent, White Swirls, Stick, Bulbous Base, 14½ In.	2776.00
Vase, King Tut, Green Luster, Gold Iridescent Coils, Bulbous, Footed, Flared, 6¾ In.	2013.00
Vase, King Tut, Opal On Blue, Ruffled Rim, Tapered Body, Cylindrical Foot, 6½ In.	1763.00
Vase, Lady Gay Rose, Pink, Gold Iridescent Pulled Feather, Shoulder, 10½ In.	9200.00
Vase, Moorish Crackle, Blue On Clear, Cobalt Blue Lip, Baluster, 6 In.	633.00
Vase, Moorish Crackle, Green, Vertical Gold Crackled Bands, Shouldered, Flared Rim, 6¾ In.	1265.00
Vase, Moorish Crackle, Gold Iridescent, White & Blue, Bulbous, Flared Rim, 7 In. . . . . . .*illus*	1495.00
Vase, Opal Luster, Gold Iridescent Coils, Shoulder, Flared Rim & Foot, 10½ In.	1265.00
Vase, Orange Iridescent, Blue Green Highlights, Gold Foot, Flared, 13¾ In.	518.00
Vase, Purple & Gold, White Swirls, Urn Shape, 1925, 6¾ In.	910.00
Vase, Stick, Cranberry Cut To Clear, Crisscross Oval, Punties, Bulbous Base, 16½ In.	2300.00

ELFINWARE is a mark found on Dresden-like porcelain that was sold in dime stores and gift shops. Many pieces were decorated with raised flowers. The mark was registered by Breslauer-Underberg, Inc., of New York City in 1947. Pieces marked *Elfinware Made in Germany* had been sold since 1945 by this importer.

Elfinware

Figurine, Boot, White, Painted Flowers, Gold Accents, Scalloped Top, Marked, 5 In.	9.00
Figurine, Shoe, Flower, Green Trim, 5 In.	145.00
Watering Can, Applied Flowers & Spinach, Marked, 2¼ In.	65.00

ELVIS PRESLEY, the well-known singer, lived from 1935 to 1977. He became famous by 1956. Elvis appeared on television, starred in twenty-seven movies, and performed in Las Vegas. Memorabilia from any of the Presley shows, his records, and even memorials made after his death are collected.

Hanky, Elvis, Playing Guitars, Singing, Scalloped Edges, Cotton, c.1956, 13 x 13½ In.	224.00
Movie Poster, Jailhouse Rock, MGM, 1957, ½ Sheet	978.00
Movie Poster, Jailhouse Rock, MGM, Australia, 1957, 1 Sheet	920.00

E

Durand, Vase, Moorish Crackle, Gold Iridescent, White & Blue, Bulbous, Flared Rim, 7 In.
$1495.00

Elvis Presley, Skirt, Sock Hop, Felt Applique, Elvis Playing Guitar, Music Notes, Metallic Beads, 28 In.
$863.00

TIP

Sunlight and heat can harm most antiques. Wood, paper, textiles, glass, ivory, leather, and many other organic materials will discolor, fade, or crack. Cover sunny windows with blinds or curtains or apply a sun-filtering plastic coating to the windows. These coatings can be found at hardware and window stores, or be installed by special companies listed in the Yellow Pages. Information is available from museums or art conservators and online.

Enamel, Frame, Champleve Flowers, Leaves, Scrolls, Easel Back, France, 11 x 7 In.
$1135.00

Twentieth-Century Enamels

Enameling is not a new art. The basic techniques used today were discovered by the sixteenth century. Arts and Crafts artists used enamel, but sparingly, in the early 1900s. Copper trays had a few enamel leaves and copper-covered bowls were made with metal tops with an enameled circle set in a bezel. In the 1920s and '30s, Boston artists, like Elizabeth Copeland, Katharine Pratt, and Gertrude Twichell, made enameled clockfaces and jewelry. By the 1950s, the new midcentury style of enamels was nationwide.

Movie Poster, King Creole, Re-Release, Paramount, 1959, 1 Sheet	489.00
Movie Poster, Le Rock Du Bagne, MGM, France, 1957, 63 x 47 In.	2070.00
Movie Poster, Love Me Tender, 20th Century Fox, 1956, ½ Sheet	276.00
Movie Poster, Viva Las Vegas, MGM, 1964, 1 Sheet	1150.00
Pin, Love Me Tender, Lithograph, 1956, ⅞ In.	185.00
Poster, It Happened At The World's Fair, Reveille Amplifier, MGM, 1963, 60 x 40 In.	2990.00
Skirt, Sock Hop, Felt Applique, Elvis Playing Guitar, Music Notes, Metallic Beads, 28 In. *illus*	863.00

ENAMELS listed here are made of glass particles and other materials heated and fused to metal. In the eighteenth and nineteenth centuries, workmen from Russia, France, England, and other countries made small boxes and table pieces of enamel on metal. One form of English enamel is called Battersea and is listed under that name. There was a revival of interest in enameling in the 1930s and a new style evolved. There is now renewed interest in the artistic enameled plaques, vases, ashtrays, and jewelry. Enamels made since the 1930s are usually on copper or steel, although silver was often used for jewelry. Graniteware is a separate category and enameled metal kitchen pieces may be included in the Kitchen category.

Ashtray, Copper, Roof Tops Pattern, Sascha Brastoff, 7 In.	150.00
Ashtray, Red, Gold Metal Leaf Trim, Evans, 6 In.	15.00
Ashtray, Scraffito Squiggles, Multicolored, 1950s, 6 In.	19.00
Bowl, Blue, Gold Lines, Small Jewels, Gerte Hacker, 7½ In.	60.00
Bowl, Peking, Flowers, Chinese, 7 In.	472.00
Box, Copper, Round, Green, Lid Flower Design, White Inside, Brass, 2½ x 1½ In.	20.00
Box, Cover, Turquoise & White French Moire, Gold Plated Interior, Round, ⅞ x 2 In.	518.00
Box, Patch, Red, 18K Yellow Gold, 1⅛ x 1½ In.	3510.00
Box, Wood Crescent, Jewels, Enamel Insert, Bovano, Conn., 1953, 7½ x 4 In.	75.00
Buckle, Red Guilloche, Silver Fleur-De-Lis, France, 19th Century, 3 x 3 In.	150.00
Button, Floral, Wire Shank, 1⅛ In.	65.00
Candlestick, Champleve, Bronze, Painted, Leaves, Scrollwork, 1800s, 8 x 4¼ In.	274.00
Cigarette Case, Brass, Red, Blue, White, Depicting Animals, People, White Back, 5 x 3 In.	110.00
Cigarette Case, Leaves, Brass, Blue Leaves, Green Overlay, 4 x 3 In.	90.00
Dish, Blue, Red, Jewels, Edwards Star, 8¾ In.	55.00
Dish, Sunburst, Brown Tones, 4-Sided, Bovano, 8½ In.	50.00
Frame, Champleve Flowers, Leaves, Scrolls, Easel Back, France, 11 x 7 In. *illus*	1135.00
Holy Water Font, Champleve, Green Onyx Plaque, Arabesques, Gold, 1800s, 11½ In.	895.00
Incense Jar, Molded Cover, Foil, Multicolored, Rosewood Base, Japan, c.1890, 4½ In.	1170.00
Lighter, Starfish, Brown, White, c.1962, 4½ x 2½ In.	36.00
Matchbox, White, Strike Plate On Top Of Lid, France	58.00
Plaque, Cherub, Among Flowers, Green Guilloche Enamel Ground, 2⅞ & 1¼ In.	588.00
Plaque, Copper Plate, Abstract Pattern, Green Ground, Yellow & White Swirls, 1950s, 4 In.	15.00
Plaque, Courting Couple, Brass Rococo Frame, Signed CSK, Austria, c.1840, 7 x 5 In.	995.00
Plaque, Jovial Musician, Playing Mandolin, On Copper, Frame, Late 1800s, 10 x 6 In.	805.00
Plaque, Stylized Water & Skyscape, Blue, White, Orange Sun, Boat, Frame, 1950s, 8 x 12 In.	147.00
Plate, Blue, Yellow, Jewels, Annemarie Davidson, 1960s, 7½ In.	150.00
Plate, Gold Center, Green Border, Jeweled, Yellow Initials, 7½ In.	20.00
Sculpture, Cavallo, Horse, Copper, 956, Signed, Gio Ponti, 7½ x 15½ In.	6900.00
Sculpture, Diavolo, Devil Face, Copper, Gio Ponti, 1956, 5½ x 8½ In.	3600.00
Vanity Kit, Blue Enameled Handles, 7 Tools, Leather Case, Early 20th Century	206.00
Vase, Champleve, Bronze Vase, Chinese, c.1900, 9¾ In.	117.00

ERICKSON glass was made in Bremen, Ohio, from 1943 to 1961. Carl and Steven Erickson designed and made free-blown and mold-blown glass. Best known are pieces with heavy ball bases filled with controlled bubbles.

Ashtray, Amethyst, Bubble, 6 In.	65.00
Ashtray, Teal Green, Bubble, 5 In.	50.00
Bowl, Green, Free-Form, 7½ In.	60.00
Bowl, Ruby Red, Bubble, 7½ In.	28.00
Console, Bubble Ball, 12 & 4 In.	475.00
Console, Green, Bubble, 9¾ x 4¼ In.	375.00
Console Set, Smoke Gray, 6½ x 12¼-In. Bowl, 5½-In. Candlestick, 3 Piece *illus*	130.00
Nut Dish, Amethyst	145.00
Vase, Amber, 7 In.	65.00
Vase, Bud, Amber, 8 In.	45.00
Vase, Bud, Amber, Controlled Bubble Base, 10 In.	30.00
Vase, Bud, Clear, Bubble Base, 8 In.	45.00

Vase, Bud, Clear, Teal Blue Controlled Bubble Base, 8 In. 45.00
Vase, Console, Smoky Green, 10½ In. 275.00

ERPHILA is a mark found on Czechoslovakian and other pottery and porcelain made after 1920. This mark was used on items imported by Ebeling & Reuss, Philadelphia, a giftware firm that is still operating in Pennsylvania. The mark is a combination of the letters *E* and *R* (Ebeling & Reuss) and the first letters of the city, Phila(delphia). Many whimsical figural pitchers and creamers, figurines, platters, and other giftwares carry this mark.

Bowl, Cheery Chintz, Open Weave, Oval, 10 x 6⅝ x 2¾ In. 55.00
Bowl, Flowers, Luster, Rim Trim, 9 9/16 In. 18.00
Bowl, Poppies, 1920-30s, 10⅛ x 2⅝ In. 30.00
Cake Plate, Flower Garlands, Bouquet, Gold Trim, 11¼ In. 36.00
Candy Dish, Woman, Nude, 6 In. 275.00
Dresser Box, Madame Pompadour, c.1920-30s, 5¼ In. 185.00
Figurine, Cat, Tabby, Gray Pastel, 1933, 4 In. 80.00
Figurine, Dog, Basset Hound, Puppy, Sitting, 4 x 3½ In. 18.00
Figurine, Dog, Beagle, Puppy, Sitting, 4 x 3½ In. 18.00
Figurine, Dog, Great Dane, Harlequin, 2 x 3 In. 32.00
Figurine, Dog, Spaniel, 4 x 4½ In. 65.00
Figurine, Elephant, 1¾ In. 15.00
Nut Dish, Windsor Chintz, Multicolored, Flowers, 2½ x 2¾ In. 26.00
Oyster Plate, Wells, Flowers, Gold Trim, 8⅞ x 1½ In. 115.00
Pitcher, Cream Ground, Orange Poppies, Green Leaves, 6 In. 50.00
Pitcher, Goat, Orange, Red, Black, 7 In. 200.00
Pitcher, Granny, 6 In. 8.00
Plate, Cheery Chintz, 10½ In. 75.00
Plate, Lemon, Pearl Luster, 1920s-30s, 6⅛ x 1¾ In. 18.00
Sugar, Cheery Chintz, Flowers, Multicolored, 2¾ 26.00
Sugar & Creamer, Cheery Chintz, Gilt Painted Scroll 40.00
Teapot, Cairn Terrier With Newspaper, 9 x 7 In. 85.00
Teapot, Cat, 7½ In. 170.00
Teapot, Cow, 1920s-30s, 7¼ In. 245.00
Teapot, Dachshund, 7½ In. 170.00
Teapot, Georgian Leaf, 8 In. 170.00
Teapot, Pig, 1920s-30s, 7¼ In. 265.00
Teapot, Poodle, Majolica, 1920-30, 8½ In. 265.00
Teapot, Terrier, 8 x 6 In. 135.00

ES GERMANY porcelain was made at the factory of Erdmann Schlegelmilch from 1861 to 1937 in Suhl, Germany. The porcelain, marked *ES Germany* or *ES Suhl*, was sold decorated or undecorated. Other pieces were made at a factory in Saxony, Prussia, and are marked *ES Prussia*. Reinhold Schlegelmilch made the famous wares marked *RS Germany*.

Candy Dish, Shell Shape, 5½ In., 2 Piece 10.00
Jardinere, Woman, Gold Frame Medallion, Holly Wreath, 1900-10, 11¾ In. 170.00

ESKIMO artifacts of all types are collected. Carvings of whale or walrus teeth are listed under Scrimshaw. Baskets are in the Basket category. All other types of Eskimo art are listed here. In Canada and some other areas, the term *Inuit* is used instead of Eskimo.

Doll, Cloth & Seal Fur, Hand Carved Wood Face, 1930s, 21 In. 468.00
Figure, Eskimo On Whale, Inuit, Wolf Original, 7 In. 117.00
Figure, Man, Bone, Carved, Inset Eyes, 5 x 2½ In. 145.00
Figure, Man, Seal, Soapstone, Signed, Inuit, 9 x 4½ In. 293.00
Figure, Penguin, Soapstone, Carved, Inuit, 8 In. 540.00
Figure, Seal, Soapstone, Carved, Signed, Inuit, 8 x 3 In. 153.00
Moccasin Boots, Deer Hide, Rabbit Fur Trim, Cloth Design, Inuit, 1900s, 8 x 5 In. 250.00
Sculpture, Inuit Hunter, Stone, Hand Carved, Signed B.J., 1980s, 4 x 3 x 1½ In. 295.00

ETLING glass pieces are very similar in design to those made by Lalique and Phoenix. It was made in France for Etling, a retail shop. It dates from the 1920s and 1930s.

ETLING
FRANCE

Vase, Frosted Glass, Molded Design, Stylized Lily Pond Fronds, Blue Wash, 10 In. 323.00

Ebeling & Reuss

Importer Ebeling & Reuss, established in 1886, imported antique-looking mustache cups and smoking sets by about 1935. Soon it was selling dinnerware and humorous pottery and porcelain, including animal-shaped pitchers from Czechoslovakia. Ebeling & Reuss imported giftware from many countries. During World War II, it found new supplies in South America, Mexico, and China. Recent imports are from Asia.

Erickson, Console Set, Smoke Gray, 6½ x 12¼-In. Bowl, 5½-In. Candlestick, 3 Piece
$130.00

E

TIP

If you are remodeling or redecorating, think about antiques and collectibles displayed near the work area. A workman will hammer on a wall without worrying about the shelves on the other side.

Faience, Bowl, Tulips & Birds, Swirl Border, Redware, 18¾ In. $518.00

Faience, Candlestick, Rampant Lion, Holding Helmet Shape Socket, Blue, White, 11 In., Pair 460.00

Fairing, Box, Child With Cross, Lying On Ground, Pink Blanket, Bisque, 2¼ x 3 In. 66.00

Fairing, Trinket Box, Wallpaper, Leather Hinges, Dome Lid, 2 x 3½ x 2¼ In. 550.00

FABERGE was a firm of jewelers and goldsmiths founded in St. Petersburg, Russia, in 1842, by Gustav Faberge. Peter Carl Faberge, his son, was jeweler to the Russian Imperial Court from about 1870 to 1914. The rare Imperial Easter eggs, jewelry, and decorative items are very expensive today.   **ФАБЕРЖЕ КФ**

Bookmark, Silver, Sword Shape, Sapphire, 6 Rose Cut Diamonds, c.1890	14500.00
Cigarette Case, Karelian Birch Wood, Victorian	275.00
Cigarette Case, Red Enamel, Portrait, Empress Catherine II, Cyrillic Signature, 4⅜ In.	11700.00
Compact, Triangle, Silver One Side, Gold Other, Original Box	85.00
Egg, Red, Jeweled Crown Inside, Jade Base, Russian Eagle	400.00
Goblet Set, Honors Anna Pavlova, 1980, 12 Piece	1000.00
Kovsh, Drinking Vessel, Boat Shaped Body, Handle, Russian Silver, Jewels, c.1895, 14 In.	58300.00

FAIENCE refers to tin-glazed earthenware, especially the wares made in France, Germany, and Scandinavia. It is also correct to say that faience is the same as majolica or Delft, although usually the term refers only to the tin-glazed pottery of the three regions mentioned.

Bowl, Tulips & Birds, Swirl Border, Redware, 18¾ In. ....*illus*	518.00
Candlestick, Rampant Lion, Holding Helmet Shape Socket, Blue, White, 11 In., Pair ...*illus*	460.00
Jardiniere, Sunflowers, Verse, Slip Decorated, Carved, Handles, Avon 1903, 11 x 18 In.	1840.00
Jug, Figural, Seated Woman, Cook Pot, White Cat, Handle, Hat Spout, Galle, c.1890, 11 In.	2779.00
Pitcher & Basin, Foley, c.1915, 11 x 17 In.	41.00
Plate Set, Birds, Scrolls, Cornucopia, Butterflies, Blue Banner, Gien, 9¾ In., 7 Piece	460.00
Temple Jar, Turquoise High Glaze Over Red Clay, California Faience, 10 In.	299.00
Tureen, Cover, Goose, On Grassy Mound, Painted, Continental, Late 18th Century, 15¼ In.	9000.00
Urn, Continental, White Body, Multicolored Swags, Floral Spray, 9¼ In., Pair	212.00
Urn, Multicolored, Landscape, Boat, Serpent Handles, Pear Finials, 22½ In., Pair	1200.00
Vase, Flowers, Green Glaze, Bulbous, Cylindrical Neck, Reticulated Rim, Handles, FMC, 16 In.	3360.00
Vase, Quintel, Blue & White, Pendant Floral Spray Decoration, Anglo-Dutch, 6 In.	150.00

FAIRINGS are small souvenir boxes and figurines that were sold at country fairs during the nineteenth century. Most were made in Germany. Reproductions of fairings are being made, especially of the famous *Twelve Months After Marriage* series.

Box, Child With Cross, Lying On Ground, Pink Blanket, Bisque, 2¼ x 3 In. ....*illus*	66.00
Figurine, 2 Cats, On Side Of Pot, Pink Flower, Green Leaves, Heart Shaped Base, 2 x 2½ In.	8.00
Figurine, Girl In Cape, Standing, 4¾ In.	130.00
Figurine, Oysters Sir, Woman Selling Variety Of Shellfish, c.1880, 3¼ x 2¼ x 4 In.	185.00
Figurine, Welsh Tea Party, 3 Women At Table, Stamped, Germany, 4 x 3½ In.	75.00
Group, 3 O'Clock In The Morning, Man, Woman, 3 x 3 x 2 In.	315.00
Match Safe, Couple, Standing, 3½ x 2½ In.	115.00
Notion Box, Boy In Rowboat, Germany, 3½ x 4¼ In.	82.00
Striker, Boors, 2½ x 2¼ In.	110.00
Striker, Shoes, Flower Buckles, 2¼ x 2 In.	90.00
Trinket Box, Blue & Orange Flower Wallpaper, Tin Hasp & Closure, Dome Lid, 3 x 5 x 3⅞ In.	1320.00
Trinket Box, Center Flowers, Openwork, Chip Carved Sawtooth Rim, Lili Bohn, 1858, 1 x 2½ In.	220.00
Trinket Box, Child Holding Doll & Trumpet, 2½ x 1½ In.	345.00
Trinket Box, Dovetailed, Painted, Blue Ground, Flowers, Tulips, Dome Lid, 6¼ x 7¼ In.	5500.00
Trinket Box, Dresser Shape, Mirror, Trinket On Top, White, 4 x 3 x 2½ In.	45.00
Trinket Box, Dresser Shape, Watch In Center, Mirror, 5 x 3½ In.	165.00
Trinket Box, Enamel, Gilt, Brass, Jeweled, Blue Ground, France, Late 19th Century, 5½ In.	326.00
Trinket Box, Softwood, Old Green Paint, Dovetailed, Coffin Lid, 4 x 6¾ In.	275.00
Trinket Box, Victoria's Crown, Gold On Beads, 4 x 5 x 3 In.	135.00
Trinket Box, Wallpaper, Leather Hinges, Dome Lid, 2 x 3½ x 2¼ In. ....*illus*	550.00
Trinket Box, Walnut, Alligatored Varnish, Dovetail, Hinged Mirror, c.1905, 8½ x 5½ In.	115.00
Trinket Box, Walnut, Dovetailed, Incised Design, Dome Lid, 3½ x 7 In.	193.00
Trinket Box, Walnut, Relief Carved, Shaped Panels, Maltese Cross Decoration, 5¼ x 8¾ In.	209.00

FAIRYLAND LUSTER *pieces are included in the Wedgwood category.*

FAMILLE ROSE, *see Chinese Export category.*

FANS have been used for cooling since the days of the ancients. By the eighteenth century, the fan was an accessory for the lady of fashion and very elaborate and expensive fans were made. Sticks were made of ivory or wood, set with jewels or carved. The fans were made of painted silk or paper. Inexpensive paper fans printed with advertising were giveaways in the late nineteenth and early twentieth centuries. Electric fans were introduced in 1882.

F

2 Ladies, Gentleman, Mother-Of-Pearl, Lace, Painted, Folding, Edwardian, c.1910, 13 x 22 In.	176.00
Advertising, American Dairy, Cardboard, Wooden Handle	3.00
Advertising, Burke Drug Co., The Real Drug Store, 14¾ In.	16.00
Advertising, Celebrated Shelburne Grill, Atlantic City, Wood, Paper Lithograph, 1890s	36.00
Advertising, Dominican Republic Steamship, Wood Handle, 8¼ x 7¾ In.	44.00
Advertising, Ford, Women In Car By Water, 1920s, 10½ x 8 In.	133.00
Advertising, Garrett Scotch Snuff, Man, Woman, Flowers, Warehouse, 1932-33 Calendars	45.00
Advertising, Poe Vineyard, Kenton, Ohio, Cardboard Paddles, Oak Case, Clockwork, c.1875, 28 In.	440.00
Advertising, Putnam Dyes, Paper, Picture Of Founder With Grandchild, 1920s, 7⅜ In.	10.00
Advertising, Putnam Fadeless Dye, Sherman Bros.	12.00
Advertising, Spanish Language, Girl, Plastic Handle	8.00
Advertising, U.S. Tires, Motorists, Cardboard, Wood Handle, 9⅝ x 8 In.	132.00
Cardboard, Star Spangled Banner, Generals, Wood Handle, c.1914, 14 x 9 In.	112.00
Electric, Airplane Form, 28 x 22 In. Propellers	3025.00 to 4125.00
Electric, Chrome, Hunter Century, 1940s, 16 In.	175.00
Electric, Desk, Lectrohome, On-Off Switch, 115 Volts, 6 Amps, Model 65100-6	35.00
Electric, Diehl, 110-120 Volts, Finderne, N.J., 1950s, 21 x 20 In.	125.00
Electric, Emerson, Oscillating, 4 Brass Blades	75.00
Electric, Emerson, Type 29648, Black, Glossy, 4 Brass Blades, 16 In.	150.00
Electric, Eskimo, Bersted, Bullet Back, Model No. 081002, Turquoise, 1940s, 10½ x 9 In.	80.00
Electric, Eskimo, Black Base, Tin Blades, Bersted Mfg. Co., Fostoria, 60 Cycle, 10 x 9 In.	49.00
Electric, General Electric, Ice Cream Parlor, 9 x 7 In.	275.00
Electric, General Electric, Pancake Motor, No. 215638	565.00
Electric, Handybreeze, Teal, Cast Iron Base, Enameled, Chicago Electric Mfg. Co, 12 x 9 In.	58.00
Electric, Original Breeze-Spreader, Victor, 1940s, 16 In.	125.00
Electric, Robbins & Myers, Brass, 3-Speed, Oscillating, 4 Brass Blades, c.1910, 13 x 17 In.	225.00
Electric, Trico, Vacuum, Metal, Air Hose Attachment, Adjustable Arm, 6½ In.	100.00
Electric, Westinghouse, Oscillating, 2 Vanes, Brass, 16 x 13 In. *illus*	575.00
Electric, Westinghouse, Partners, 2-Sided, No. 162635, 1915, 16 x 13 In.	1760.00
Electric, Westinghouse, Wind Vane, Oscillating, No. 115675, 1910	961.00
Fabric, Hand Painted, Flower, Blue, White, Ivory Guards, 27 In.	260.00
Fabric, Metallic, Ivory Spins, Flower Design, Folding, 17 In.	16.00
Fabric, Painted, Cranes, Tao Lengyue, Ink & Color, 20½ In.	78.00
Fabric, Painted, Sequined, Flowers, Black, 1890s, 26 In.	350.00
Hand Painted, Black Lacquer Casket, Courting Scene, Bamboo Blades, 1800s, 10 x 2 x 2 In.	245.00
Ivory, Carved, 22 Sticks, Dancing Figures, Relief, Painted Vellum, Feast, 22 x 11 In. *illus*	150.00
Ivory, Linen, Lace Trim, Embroidered Flowers	40.00
Ivory, Paper, Lithographed Scene, Elegant Ladies, Gilt Shadowbox Frame, 21 x 20 In. *illus*	230.00
Ivory, Pierced, Mother-Of-Pearl Guards, Court Scenes, France, c.1800, 10½ In. *illus*	431.00
Lace, 18 Mother-Of-Pearl & Bone Sticks, Fabric Lined Box, Tiffany & Co., 14 x 26 In. *illus*	230.00
Lace, Ivory Spokes, 2 Women, Man, 17 In.	13.00
Metal, Fabric, Folding, Ivory, Bone Spines, Flowers, 17 In.	16.00
Mirror, Pique, Shadowbox Shaped Frame, Romantic Scene, 22¼ x 14¼ In.	2495.00
Painting, Immortal & Demons, Chen Zaofent, Ink & Color, On Fabric, 1800s, 20¼ In.	52.00
Paper, Birds, Flowers, Folding, 10⅜ In.	5.00
Paper, Painted, Sequined, Silver, Thistle, Flowers, 18½ In.	95.00
Paper, Red, Couple In Garden, Bouquet Of Flowers, 24½ In.	250.00
Paper, Woman In Canoe, Feeding Swans, 25 Ribs, 8½ x ⅜ In.	17.00
Satin, Feather, Ivory Guards, Sticks, 12 x 23 In.	335.00
Satin, Ivory, Open Dot, Carved Pattern	250.00
Satin, Mourning, Black, 25½ x 13½ In.	250.00
Silk, Bone Frame, Hand Painted, c.1900	41.00
Silk, Flowers, Brass Members, 9¾ x 5 x ⅞ In.	84.00
Silk, Ivory, Embroidered, Painted Gold Fish, Flowers, Birds, Butterfly, Tassel, 8½ x 15½ In.	50.00
Silk, Ivory, Pearl Buttons, Woman With Upswept Hairdo, Staircase, Roses, c.1800s, 11½ In.	895.00
Silk, Ivory Ribs, Mother-Of-Pearl Buttons, Goldtone Metal Loop	60.00
Silk, Painted, Gold Foil, Paper, Wood Sticks, Black Guards, 26½ In.	150.00
White Swan Feathers, Turned Bone Handle, Cockade Style, Mother-Of-Pearl, 1860s, 12½ In.	295.00
Wicker, Pleated, Braided Handle, Tan Border, 13½ x 11 In.	9.00
Wood, Pierced, Oriental Hand, Tassels, 8 x 14 In.	13.00

FAST FOOD COLLECTIBLES *may be included in several categories, such as Advertising, Coca-Cola, Toy, etc.*

FEDERZEICHNUNG, *see Loetz category.*

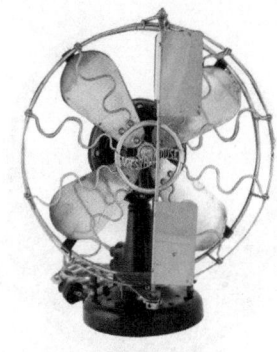

Fan, Electric, Westinghouse, Oscillating, 2 Vanes, Brass, 16 x 13 In. $575.00

Fan, Ivory, Carved, 22 Sticks, Dancing Figures, Relief, Painted Vellum, Feast, 22 x 11 In. $150.00

Fan, Ivory, Paper, Lithographed Scene, Elegant Ladies, Gilt Shadowbox Frame, 21 x 20 In. $230.00

Fan, Ivory, Pierced, Mother-Of-Pearl Guards, Court Scenes, France, c.1800, 10½ In. $431.00

Fan, Lace, 18 Mother-Of-Pearl & Bone Sticks, Fabric Lined Box, Tiffany & Co., 14 x 26 In. $230.00

Fenton, Curtain, Basket, Amethyst Opalescent, Carnival, Ruffled Edge, 8 In. $65.00

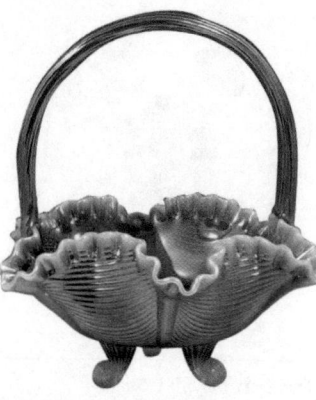

Fenton, Daisy & Fern, Lamp, Oil, Cranberry Opalescent, Ruffled Edge, 17 In. $206.00

Fenton, Drapery, Vase, Blue Satin, Ruffled Edge, 8 In. $41.00

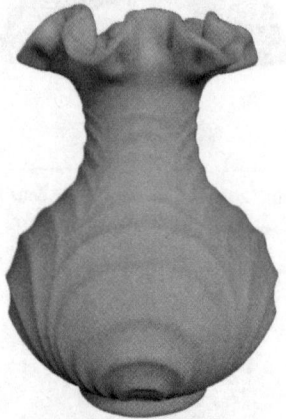

FENTON Art Glass Company, founded in Martins Ferry, Ohio, by Frank L. Fenton, is now located in Williamstown, West Virginia. It is noted for early carnival glass produced between 1907 and 1920. Some of these pieces are listed in the Carnival Glass category. Many other types of glass were also made. Spanish Lace in this section refers to the pattern made by Fenton.

Adam's Rib, Pitcher, Blue, 7½ In.	139.00
Aqua Crest, Saucer	20.00
Basket Weave, Bowl, Custard, Lace Edge, 5 x 3 In.	24.00
Basket Weave, Bowl, Green, Satin, 5 x 5 In.	30.00
Basket Weave, Candle Light, Cameo Satin	75.00
Basket Weave, Candlelamp, Custard Satin	75.00
Beaded Melon, Pitcher, Squat, Rosalene, 3½ x 5 In.	40.00
Beaded Melon, Rose Bowl, Burmese	95.00
Beaded Melon, Vase, Blue Satin, Ruffled Edge, 5¾ x 3¾ In.	22.00
Bicentennial, Compote, Cover, Independence Blue, Large	11.00
Bicentennial, Jar, Old Abe Eagle, Independence Blue, 1776-1976	63.00
Blackberry Spray, Bowl, Custard	48.00
Blackberry Spray, Bowl, Hat Shape, Custard	48.00
Burmese, Bowl, Enameled, Butterflies & Berries, 3-Footed	140.00
Burmese, Fairy Light, 1960s	65.00
Burmese, Ginger Jar, Cover, Diamond Optic	220.00
Burmese, Vase, Enameled, Raspberries, 7½ In.	60.00
Cameo, Vase, Satin, Wave Crest	25.00
Cameo Satin, Bell, Enameled, Painted, Sunset, 6 In.	44.00
Christmas Classics, Bell, Snowy Scene, Church In Woods, c.1978, 5¾ In.	95.00
Coin Dot, Bowl, Topaz, Opalescent, 3¼ x 6¾ In.	76.00
Coin Dot, Cruet, Cranberry Opalescent, Clear Handle & Stopper, 6½ In.	195.00
Coin Dot, Jug, Blue Opalescent, Squat	65.00
Coin Dot, Pickle Castor, Cranberry, Embossed, Grape & Leaf, Metal Frame, 10½ In.	135.00
Coin Dot, Shade, Globular, Honeysuckle Opalescent, 7 In.	20.00
Coin Dot, Water Set, Cranberry Opalescent, 6 Barrel Tumblers, Ice Lip Jug, 1940s, 7 Piece	425.00
Cranberry Hearts, Basket, 10½ In.	145.00
Curtain, Basket, Amethyst Opalescent, Carnival, Ruffled Edge, 8 In. *illus*	65.00
Custard Satin, Bell, Christmas Faith	45.00
Custard Satin, Egg, Hand Painted, Green Roses, Louise Piper, 3½ In.	65.00
Custard Satin, Fairy Lamp, Blue Roses, Signed, Laura Long, 2 Sections	35.00
Custard Satin, Fairy Lamp, Coralene Daisy, J. Chapman	50.00
Custard Satin, Fairy Light, Blue Roses, 4½ x 3¼ In.	40.00
Custard Satin, Vase, Ruffled Edge, 8 In.	35.00
Daisy & Button, Boot, Colonial Amber, c.1970, 4 x 4¼ In.	14.00
Daisy & Fern, Lamp, Oil, Cranberry Opalescent, Ruffled Edge, 17 In. *illus*	206.00
Daisy & Fern, Pitcher, Opalescent Vaseline, 9½ In.	310.00
Daisy & Fern, Pitcher, Tumblers, Blue Opalescence, c.1910-20, 7 Piece	650.00
Diamond Optic, Compote, Dolphin Handles, Tangerine	125.00
Diamond Optic, Tumbler, Red Ruby, c.1933, 8 Piece	250.00
Dolphin, Vase, Fan, Jade Green, Handles, Footed, Early 1900s, 3 x 5 In.	165.00
Dot Optic, Apothecary Jar, Ruby Overlay	275.00
Dot Optic, Bowl, Ruby Overlay, Snowcrest, 10 In.	85.00
Drapery, Vase, Blue Satin, Ruffled Edge, 8 In. *illus*	41.00
Emerald Crest, Epergne, 3-Lily, Spanish Lace, 11 In. *illus*	94.00
Figurine, Bear, Blue Satin	75.00
Figurine, Bird Of Happiness, Blue Satin, 7 In.	22.00
Figurine, Elephant, Blue Satin	75.00
Figurine, Fawn, Blue Satin	75.00
Figurine, Mouse, Blue Satin	75.00
Figurine, Praying Boy, Blue, 4 In.	20.00
Figurine, Praying Girl, Blue, 4 In.	20.00
Figurine, Whale, Blue Satin	75.00
Garden Of Eden, Plate, Cobalt Blue, Marigold, 1985	82.00
Georgian, Ice Bucket, Rose Pink, 6 x 5¼	65.00
Georgian, Pitcher, Rose Pink, 7¾ In.	65.00
Hobnail, Basket, Amber, Ruffled Edge, 13 In. *illus*	4.00
Hobnail, Basket, Blue Opalescent, 6⅜ x 4¼ In. *illus*	16.00
Hobnail, Basket, French Opalescent, Footed	48.00
Hobnail, Bowl, Milk Glass, 3-Toed, 8 x 4 In.	12.00

Hobnail, Candleholder, 2-Light, Milk Glass, 8 In.	55.00
Hobnail, Candleholder, Milk Glass, Gold Tone Wire Feet, Low, c.1967	20.00
Hobnail, Candleholder, Milk Glass, Ruffled Edge, 5 x 2 In., Pair	15.00
Hobnail, Candleholder, Ruby, 3½ In., Pair	125.00
Hobnail, Candlestick, Milk Glass, Bowl Base, Footed, 4 In.	35.00
Hobnail, Candy Jar, Cover, Milk Glass, Footed, c.1967	30.00
Hobnail, Compote, Custard Satin, 6 In.	35.00
Hobnail, Compote, Milk Glass	35.00
Hobnail, Condiment Set, Milk Glass, 6 Piece	125.00
Hobnail, Epergne, 1-Lily, Milk Glass, 3½ x 7 In.	65.00 to 95.00
Hobnail, Epergne, 1-Lily, Rose, Pastel, 3½ x 7 In.	150.00
Hobnail, Epergne, 1-Lily, Turquoise, 3½ x 7 In.	150.00
Hobnail, Jam Set, French Opalescent, 3 Piece	25.00
Hobnail, Jar, Apothecary, Cover, Milk Glass	180.00
Hobnail, Lavabo, Milk Glass, Brass Spigot, 3 Piece	175.00
Hobnail, Marmalade, Blue Opalescent, Underplate, Ruffled Edge	90.00
Hobnail, Marmalade, Milk Glass	80.00
Hobnail, Planter, Custard Satin, Oval	45.00
Hobnail, Shade, Globular, Honey Amber Overlay, 7 In.	20.00
Hobnail, Syrup, French Opalescent, 6 In.	125.00
Hobnail, Tumbler, Barrel, French Opalescent	20.00
Hobnail, Vase, Cranberry Opalescent, 1940s, 4 In.	75.00
Hobnail, Vase, Custard Satin, 6 In.	35.00
Hobnail, Vase, Fan, Milk Glass, 4 In.	53.00
Hobnail, Vase, Milk Glass, 11 In.	60.00
Hobnail, Vase, Milk Glass, Ruffled Edge, 7¼ In.	45.00
Hobnail, Vase, Springtime Green, Flared & Ruffled Edge, 1977, 5 In. ....*illus*	10.00
Hobnail, Vase, Turquoise, Footed, 4½ In.	40.00
Hobnail, Water Set, Topaz Opalescent, 9 Piece	265.00
Ivory Crest, Basket, 10 In.	125.00
Ivory Crest, Epergne, 3-Lily, Candleholders, 6½ In., 6 Piece	25.00
Jamestown Blue, Bowl, c.1957, 8½ In.	25.00
Lavender Petals, Pitcher	110.00
Lavender Petals, Vase, 10 In.	110.00
Lily-Of-The-Valley, Basket, 8 In.	55.00
Lincoln Inn, Goblet, Water, Wisteria, 9 Oz.	65.00
Lincoln Inn, Plate, Luncheon, Pink, 8 In.	15.00
Lincoln Inn, Plate, Salad, Wisteria, 7½ In.	45.00
Lincoln Inn, Sherbet, Wisteria, Tall	55.00
Lovebirds, Vase, Lime Sherbet	50.00
Magnolia & Berry, Candy Dish, French Opalescent, 1990s, 10½ In.	115.00
Magnolia & Berry, Rose Bowl, French Opalescent, Ruffled Edge, 1990s, 9½ In.	39.00
Melon Rib, Vase, Custard, 5½ In.	50.00
Moon & Star, Water Set, Topaz Opalescent, 8 Piece	395.00
Mother's Day, Plate, Madonna Of The Rose Hedge, White, 1979, 9 In.	25.00
Paneled Daisy, Candy Box, Lime Sherbet, 8 In.	55.00
Paneled Daisy, Candy Dish, Cover, Blue Satin, 1970s	34.00
Peach Crest, Basket, 10 In.	50.00 to 65.00
Peach Crest, Basket, Melon Ribbed, c.1950	195.00
Peach Crest, Bowl, Shell Shape	55.00
Peach Crest, Pitcher, Asian Garden	105.00
Peach Crest, Rose Bowl	5.00
Peach Crest, Vase, 6½ In.	20.00 to 60.00
Peach Crest, Vase, Violets In The Snow, 6½ In.	56.00
Persian Medallion, Compote, Custard, 6¾ x 4¼ In.	37.00
Plymouth, Goblet, Ruby Red, 8 Piece	325.00
Plymouth, Sherbet, Ruby Red, 1933, 8 Piece	275.00
Polka Dot, Rose Bowl, Cranberry Opalescent, c.1955, 5 In.	180.00
Poppy, Lamp, Student, Blue Satin, 20 In.	175.00
Prayer Rug, Bowl, Custard, Scalloped Sawtooth Edge, c.1915	40.00
Rib Optic, Lemonade Set, Green Opalescent, Cobalt Blue Handles, 1924, 6 Piece	500.00
Ribbon Tie, Bowl, 2¾ x 8¼ In.	46.00
Rosalene Springtime, Basket	120.00
Rose, Bowl, Vaseline Opalescent, 9½ x 3¼ In.	120.00
Rose, Candlestick, Sky Blue, Slag, Pair	35.00
Rose Crest, Epergne Set, Lily Center, 6½ In., 6 Piece	25.00

Fenton, Emerald Crest, Epergne,
3-Lily, Spanish Lace, 11 In.
$94.00

Fenton, Hobnail, Basket, Amber,
Ruffled Edge, 13 In.
$4.00

Fenton, Hobnail, Basket,
Blue Opalescent, 6⅜ x 4¼ In.
$16.00

Fenton, Hobnail, Vase, Springtime
Green, Flared & Ruffled Edge, 1977, 5 In.
$10.00

Fenton, Wide Optic, Vase, Green, Grape & Leaf Etch, Spread Foot, Pewter Overlay, 9½ In.
$206.00

Fiesta, Cobalt Blue, Syrup, Green Top With Handle, 5¾ In.
$411.00

Fiesta, Cobalt Blue, Teapot, 6 Cup
$110.00

Fiesta, Light Green, Carafe
$170.00

Fiesta, Light Green, Mixing Bowl, No. 5
$175.00

Rose Pastel, Basket, Handle	30.00
Rose Pastel, Compote, Crystal Crest, Large	33.00
Silver Crest, Basket, Hobnail, Ruffled Edge, 6 x 5 In.	38.00
Silver Crest, Bell, Spanish Lace, 6 x 4¼ In.	32.00
Silver Crest, Bell, Spanish Lace, Violets In The Snow, 1974	28.00
Silver Crest, Bowl, Chip, Heart Shape, Large	250.00
Silver Crest, Bowl, Spanish Lace, 9½ In.	50.00
Silver Crest, Candleholder, Enameled, Violets In The Snow, Pair	40.00
Silver Crest, Candlestick, Spanish Lace, c.1970, Pair	40.00
Silver Crest, Candy Box, Cover, Spanish Lace	33.00
Silver Crest, Candy Dish, Spanish Lace, Footed, 6¾ x 6½ In.	40.00
Silver Crest, Saucer	20.00
Silver Crest, Shade, Globular, 6 In.	20.00
Snow Crest, Vase, Amber, 7½ In.	15.00
Spanish Lace, Vase, Violets In The Snow, Signed, K. Haught, 8 In.	52.00
Spiral, Decanter, Cranberry Opalescent, Crimped Edge, Spout, 10½ In.	297.00
Spiral, Lamp, Hurricane, French Opalescent, c.1938	45.00
Stars & Stripes, Basket, Amethyst Opalescent, 7 In.	89.00
Stretch Glass, Vase, Handkerchief, Ruby Red	95.00
Stretch Glass, Vase, Plume, Ruby Red	80.00
Trumpet, Vase, Mandarin Red, c.1932, 8¼ In.	472.00
Vasa Murrhina, Vase, Rose Adventurine, White Ground, c.1968, 5 In.	80.00
Velva Rose, Vase, Square Top, 2 In.	25.00
Water Lily, Bowl, Yellow Satin, 1970s, 8¾ x 3 In.	40.00
Wave Crest, Vase, 5¾ In.	35.00
Wide Optic, Vase, Green, Grape & Leaf Etch, Spread Foot, Pewter Overlay, 9½ In. ......*illus*	206.00
Wild Strawberry, Compote, 5¼ In.	26.00
Wisteria, Butterfly, Vase, Turquoise, 8½ In.	100.00

FIESTA, the colorful dinnerware, was introduced in 1936 by the Homer Laughlin China Co., redesigned in 1969, and withdrawn in 1973. It was reissued again in 1986 in different colors and is still being made. New colors are being introduced. The simple design was characterized by a band of concentric circles, beginning at the rim. Cups had full-circle handles until 1969, when partial-circle handles were made. Harlequin and Riviera were related wares. For more information about Fiesta, its colors and prices, and prices of American dinnerware, see the book *Kovels' Depression Glass & Dinnerware Price List.*

Chartreuse, Bowl, Fruit, 4¾ In.	35.00
Chartreuse, Cup & Saucer	45.00
Chartreuse, Grill Plate, 11¾ In.	30.00
Chartreuse, Saucer	6.00
Cobalt Blue, Bowl, Fruit, 5½ In.	20.00
Cobalt Blue, Plate, Deep, 8½ In.	50.00
Cobalt Blue, Saucer	4.50
Cobalt Blue, Syrup, Green Drip Cup, 6 In.	411.00
Cobalt Blue, Syrup, Green Top With Handle, 5¾ In. ......*illus*	411.00
Cobalt Blue, Teapot, 6 Cup ......*illus*	110.00
Cobalt Blue, Tidbit, 3 Tiers	12.50
Forest Green, Bowl, Fruit, 5½ In.	40.00
Gray, Bowl, Fruit, 5½ In.	40.00
Gray, Cup, Tea	38.00
Gray, Cup & Saucer	11.00
Gray, Grill Plate, 11¾ In.	30.00
Gray, Nappy, 8½ In.	65.00
Gray, Plate, 6 In.	9.00
Ivory, Bowl, Dessert, 6 In.	75.00
Ivory, Bowl, Fruit, 4¾ In.	35.00 to 40.00
Ivory, Bowl, Fruit, 5½ In.	50.00
Ivory, Cup, After Dinner	25.00
Ivory, Plate, 6 In.	7.00 to 10.00
Ivory, Plate, 7 In.	20.00
Ivory, Plate, 9 In.	25.00
Ivory, Plate, 10 In.	35.00 to 60.00
Ivory, Plate, Compartment, 10½ In.	50.00
Ivory, Plate, Deep, 8 In.	50.00 to 60.00
Ivory, Platter, Oval, 12 In.	75.00

Ivory, Saucer, Tea		5.00
Ivory, Shaker, Pair		25.00
Ivory, Soup, Cream		50.00
Ivory, Tumbler, Juice		50.00
Ivory, Tumbler, Water		90.00
Light Green, Carafe	*illus*	170.00
Light Green, Chop Plate, 13 In.		40.00
Light Green, Mixing Bowl, No. 5	*illus*	175.00
Light Green, Plate, Deep, 8½ In.		38.00
Light Green, Saucer		2.50
Mauve Blue, Platter, 11 In.		17.50
Medium Green, Bowl, Fruit, 4¾ In.		36.00
Medium Green, Bowl, Fruit, 5½ In.		95.00
Medium Green, Bowl, Salad, Individual, 7½ In.		150.00
Medium Green, Casserole		1600.00
Medium Green, Chop Plate, 13 In.		500.00
Medium Green, Creamer, Ring Handle		40.00
Medium Green, Cup, Tea		60.00
Medium Green, Mug		135.00
Medium Green, Plate, 6 In.		35.00
Medium Green, Plate, 9 In.		75.00
Medium Green, Plate, 10 In.		135.00
Medium Green, Plate, 7 In.		13.00
Medium Green, Plate, Deep, 8½ In.		150.00
Medium Green, Saucer, Tea		15.00
Medium Green, Teapot, 6 Cup		2000.00
Red, Cup, Tea		32.50 to 35.00
Red, Nappy, 8½ In.	*illus*	35.00
Red, Pitcher, Water, Disk		150.00
Rose, Candleholder, Tripod		32.00
Rose, Cup & Saucer		15.00
Rose, Plate, 10½ In.		15.00
Rose, Sauceboat, Footed	*illus*	10.00
Rose, Saucer		6.00
Turquoise, Ashtray		60.00
Turquoise, Bowl, Fruit, 4¾ In.		25.00 to 30.00
Turquoise, Bowl, Fruit, 5½ In.		40.00
Turquoise, Bowl, Plate, Deep, 8½ In.		50.00
Turquoise, Casserole, Cover, 7½ In.		80.00 to 195.00
Turquoise, Chop Plate, 13 In.		60.00
Turquoise, Coffeepot, Cover		195.00
Turquoise, Creamer, Ring Handle		22.00
Turquoise, Cup, Tea		17.50 to 35.00
Turquoise, Marmalade, Cover	*illus*	130.00
Turquoise, Mug, Tom & Jerry		35.00
Turquoise, Mug		75.00
Turquoise, Nappy, 8½ In.		55.00
Turquoise, Pitcher, Water, Disk		160.00
Turquoise, Plate, 6 In.		8.00 to 10.00
Turquoise, Plate, 7 In.		15.00
Turquoise, Plate, 9 In.		8.00 to 20.00
Turquoise, Plate, 10 In.		28.00 to 40.00
Turquoise, Plate, Compartment, 10½ In.		30.00 to 45.00
Turquoise, Platter, Oval, 12 In.		75.00
Turquoise, Saucer, After Dinner		20.00
Turquoise, Saucer, Tea		3.00 to 5.00
Turquoise, Saucer		25.00
Turquoise, Shaker, Pair		20.00
Turquoise, Soup, Cream		60.00
Yellow, Bowl, Dessert, 6 In.		35.00 to 50.00
Yellow, Bowl, Fruit, 4¾ In.		16.00 to 30.00
Yellow, Bowl, Fruit, 5½ In.		40.00
Yellow, Bowl, Plate, Deep, 8 In.		50.00
Yellow, Carafe		400.00
Yellow, Casserole		195.00
Yellow, Coffee Set, Sugar, Cover, Creamer, 10½-In. Pot, 3 Piece	*illus*	118.00

Fiesta, Red, Nappy, 8½ In.
$35.00

Fiesta, Rose, Sauceboat, Footed
$10.00

Fiesta, Turquoise, Marmalade, Cover
$130.00

Fiesta, Yellow, Coffee Set, Sugar, Cover, Creamer, 10½-In. Pot, 3 Piece
$118.00

Fiesta, Yellow, Pitcher, Water, Disk
$60.00

Fiesta, Yellow, Relish, 5 Inserts, 11 In.
$147.00

Firefighting, Grenade,
H Inside Shield, Cobalt Blue, Hobnails,
Ground Lip, 6¼ In.
$3080.00

Firefighting, Grenade, Imperial Fire
Extinguisher, Crown, Lime Green,
Bulbous, Ground Lip, 6⅝ In.
$336.00

Firefighting, Grenade, LB, Turquoise
Blue, Vertical Ribs, Ground Lip,
France, 5⅛ In.
$336.00

Fireglow, Vase, Enameled Bird On
Branch & Flowers, Cylindrical Neck,
5 x 4 In.
$30.00

Yellow, Creamer, Stick	75.00
Yellow, Creamer	30.00
Yellow, Cup, After Dinner	60.00
Yellow, Cup, Tea	7.00
Yellow, Cup & Saucer	15.00
Yellow, Grill Plate, 11¾ In.	30.00
Yellow, Mixing Bowl, No.5	250.00
Yellow, Mug, Tom & Jerry	30.00
Yellow, Mug	75.00
Yellow, Nappy, 8½ In.	60.00 to 75.00
Yellow, Pitcher, Water, Disk	*illus* 60.00
Yellow, Plate, 6 In.	5.00 to 8.00
Yellow, Plate, 7 In.	15.00 to 20.00
Yellow, Plate, 9 In.	8.00
Yellow, Plate, 10½ In.	15.00 to 40.00
Yellow, Relish, 5 Inserts, 11 In.	*illus* 147.00
Yellow, Sauceboat	45.00
Yellow, Saucer, Tea	5.00
Yellow, Saucer	3.00
Yellow, Soup, Cream	60.00
Yellow, Sugar, Individual	150.00
Yellow, Tray, Utility	75.00

FINCH, *see Kay Finch category.*

FINDLAY ONYX AND FLORADINE are two similar types of glass made by Dalzell, Gilmore and Leighton Co. of Findlay, Ohio, about 1889. Onyx is a patented yellowish white opaque glass with raised silver daisy decorations. A few rare pieces were made of rose, amber, orange, or purple glass. Floradine is made of cranberry-colored glass with an opalescent white raised floral pattern and a satin finish. The same molds were used for both types of glass.

Celery Vase, Opal, Silver Molded Branching Flowers, 6½ In.	230.00
Muffineer, 5½ In.	1495.00
Spooner, Flowers, Leaves, 1889, 4½ In.	1200.00
Sugar, Platinum Luster, 5½ x 3½ In.	650.00
Syrup, Opal, Silver Flowers & Vines, Applied Opalescent Handle, Metal Flip Lid, 7 In.	575.00
Vase, Flowers, Leaves, 1889, 5 In.	1995.00

FIREFIGHTING equipment of all types is wanted, from fire marks to uniforms to toy fire trucks. It is said that every little boy wanted to be a fireman or a train engineer 75 years ago and the collectors today reflect this interest.

Alarm Box, Gamewell, Cast Iron, Lock, Key, Lantern, 32 In.	176.00
Bucket, Leather, Copper Rim, Nobes & Hunt, c.1916, 21 In.	546.00
Bucket, Leather, Copper Rivets, Bentwood Rim, 9 x 11 In.	633.00
Bucket, Leather, G. Critzon, Union, Gold Stencil, Leather Swing Handle, 12 In.	825.00
Bucket, Leather, Painted, Denver Fire Society, John Dunn, 1825, 13 In.	1070.00
Bucket, Leather, Painted, Gilt Crest, Red Painted Canvas, 1800s, 18 In.	173.00
Bucket, Leather, Painted, Maine No. 54, Green, Handle, 12 In.	863.00
Bucket, Leather, Painted, S. Sawyer	1035.00
Bucket, Leather, Riveted, Red, Gold, Black, Metal Band, Leather Handle, 10 x 12 In.	230.00
Bucket, Leather, Wood, Leather Rim Handle, Red, Black, Gold, Green, 8¾ x 12 In.	633.00
Bucket, W. Brosey Globe, Black Ground, Yellow Letters, Tin, Bail Handle, 1852, 14 In.	633.00
Cabinet Card, 2 Firemen, Connecting Hose, Palais Studio, Butte, Montana	450.00
Chromolithograph, Last Alarm, Horse Drawn Steamer, Racing To Blaze, 18 x 27 In.	264.00
Fire Gong, Gamewell, Clockwork Motor, Beveled Glass Door, 37 In.	4113.00
Fire Hydrant, Model 82, Chapoman Valve Mfg. Co., Boston, Cast Iron, 1890, 33 In.	170.00
Fire Mark, Man, Running With Torch, Holding Trumpet, Banner, Cast Iron, 11¾ In.	220.00
Fire Mark, Snake, Cast Iron, Philadelphia, Painted, c.1830, 11½ In.	575.00
Grenade, Babcock, Non-Freezing, Chicago, Cobalt Blue, 1880-95, 7⅝ In.	2128.00
Grenade, Babcock, Non-Freezing, Elmira, N.Y., Gold Amber, 1880-95, 7½ In.	2128.00
Grenade, Deutsche Loschgranate Eberhardt, Fire Hydrant, Copper Amber, Germany, 8 In.	469.00
Grenade, Du Progres, Extinctives, Yellow Amber, Pontil, Tooled Lip, Germany, c.1880, 5 In.	232.00
Grenade, Extincteur, Waffle, Systeme Labbe, Anchor, L'Incombustibilte, Paris, Yellow, 6¾ In.	220.00
Grenade, Extincteur, Waffle, Systeme Labbe, L'Incombustibilte, Paris, Amber, France, 6¾ In.	198.00
Grenade, H Inside Shield, Cobalt Blue, Hobnails, Ground Lip, 6¼ In.	*illus* 3080.00
Grenade, Hayward's Hand, Cobalt Blue, Tooled Lip, Vertical Pleats, 1880-1900, 6 In.	392.00

Grenade, Hayward's, Yellow Amber, Olive Tone, 1880-90, 6¼ In.	308.00
Grenade, Hazelton's High Pressure Chemical, Keg, Yellow Amber, c.1890, 11¼ In.	420.00
Grenade, Imperial Fire Extinguisher, Crown, Lime Green, Bulbous, Ground Lip, 6⅝ In. *illus*	336.00
Grenade, Kalamazoo, Automatic, Cobalt Blue, 1880-95, 11⅛ In.	560.00
Grenade, Labbe, Anchor, L'Incombustibilte 139, Paris, Yellow Amber, France, 6¾ In.	220.00
Grenade, LB, Turquoise Blue, Vertical Ribs, Ground Lip, France, 5⅛ In. *illus*	336.00
Grenade, Lime Green, Ribs, Sheared, Ground Lip, France, 1889-1900, 6⅝ In.	1456.00
Grenade, System Labbe, Yellow Amber, Contents, France, 1880-1900, 5¾ In.	308.00
Grenade, Turquoise Blue, Vertical Ribs, Sheared, Ground Lip, Contents, c.1890, 5 In.	784.00
Grenade, Vertical Ribs, Round Panels, Sheared Lip, France, c.1880-1900, 5 In.	264.00
Hose Rack, Cast Iron, Red Paint, Wall Mount, Lattice Frame, Pierced Lettering, 19 In.	176.00
Stickpin, Celluloid, Fireman At Fire, c.1890, 1½ In.	114.00
Stickpin, Northwestern Volunteer Firemen's Ass'n., Ashland, O., 1929, 1¼ In.	22.00

FIREGLOW glass is attributed to the Boston and Sandwich Glass Company. The light-tan-colored glass appears reddish brown when held to the light. Most fireglow has an acid finish and enamel decoration, although it was also made with a satin finish.

Vase, Enameled Bird On Branch & Flowers, Cylindrical Neck, 5 x 4 In. *illus*	30.00

FIREPLACES were used to cook food and to heat the American home in past centuries. Many types of tools and equipment were used. Andirons held the logs in place, firebacks reflected the heat into the room, and tongs were used to move either fuel or food. Many types of spits and roasting jacks were made and may be listed in the Kitchen category.

Andirons, Brass, Acorn Finial, Baluster, Iron Shaft, Penny Feet, Late 18th Century, 23 In.	657.00
Andirons, Brass, Arts & Crafts, Ball Top, Tiered Disc, Columned Base, 22 x 8 x 32 In.	1200.00
Andirons, Brass, Belted Ball, Reel Turned Support, Spurred Legs, Ball Feet, 1800s, 19 In.	920.00
Andirons, Brass, Cabriole Legs, Urn Columns, Lobed Base, Scrolled Capitals, 1900s, 26 In.	201.00
Andirons, Brass, Chippendale, Urn Finials, Tapered, Cylindrical, Ball & Claw Feet	588.00
Andirons, Brass, Contemporary, 5 Stacking Forms, Asian Style, 13 x 11 In.	5015.00
Andirons, Brass, Double Lemon Top, Spurred Legs, Ball Feet, Early 1800s, 21 In.	510.00
Andirons, Brass, Faceted & Ball Spire Top, Spur & Ball Legs, 18½ In.	403.00
Andirons, Brass, Faceted Ball, Urn Finial, Baluster Shaft, Plinth Base	657.00
Andirons, Brass, Federal, Double Lemon Finials, Beaded Borders, Octagonal Shaft, 21 In.	1840.00
Andirons, Brass, Federal, Iron, Lemon Top, Cabriole Legs, Ball Feet, 16 x 8 In.	353.00
Andirons, Brass, Federal, Iron Ball, Steeple Topped, Pedestal Plinth, 18 x 22 In.	1058.00
Andirons, Brass, Federal, Octagonal Plinth, Urn Finials, Penny Feet, 13½ In.	978.00
Andirons, Brass, Federal, Steeple & Ball Top, Arched Spurred Legs, Slipper Feet, 18 In.	259.00
Andirons, Brass, Federal, Steeple Top, c.1800, 21 x 11 x 8¼ In.	1680.00
Andirons, Brass, Federal, Urn Shape Finial, Square Plinth, Cabriole Legs, 15½ In.	1093.00
Andirons, Brass, Figure Holding Urn With Flame, Curved Paw Feet, 25 In.	230.00
Andirons, Brass, Fleur-De-Lis, Scroll Feet, c.1910, 15 x 9 In.	468.00
Andirons, Brass, Iron, Ball Top, Baluster Shaft, Spurred Cabriole Legs, 15 x 10 In.	353.00
Andirons, Brass, Iron Belted, Double Lemon Top, Cabriole Legs, 18 x 8½ In.	353.00
Andirons, Brass, Ivy Leaf Decoration, 12½ In.	150.00
Andirons, Brass, Regency Style, Reeded Baluster, Support, Arched Leg, 29 In.	1998.00
Andirons, Brass, Spool Form Shafts, Scrolled Legs With Spurs, Ball Feet, 12½ In.	253.00
Andirons, Brass, Spur Arches, Ball Feet, Finials, Hand Wrought Rod, 1800s, 16 In.	460.00
Andirons, Brass, Steel, Peened Rods, Tapered Columns, Slipper Feet, 5½ In.	690.00
Andirons, Brass, Torch Form, Flame Finials, Iron Rods, Marked, Patent Dec. 8, 1908, 22 In.	316.00
Andirons, Brass, Wrought Iron, Incised, Bellflowers, c.1770, 31 In.	9000.00
Andirons, Brass Plate, Iron Shafts, Knife Blade, Acorn Finials, Arched Legs, 19 x 8 x 15 In.	264.00
Andirons, Bronze, Cast Iron, Dolphin Pedestal, Encircling Trident, Early 1900s, 21 In.	705.00
Andirons, Bronze, Regency, Figural, Whippet, Reclining, Profile, Swag Pier, 9 x 9 In.	4347.00
Andirons, Cast Iron, Figural, George Washington, Early 20th Century, 14½ In.	120.00
Andirons, Fender, Brass, Paw Feet, Tin Back, 36 x 11 x 9 In.	431.00
Andirons, Gilt Brass, Georgian Style, Paneled, Cannonballs, Ball & Claw Feet, 23 x 12 In.	1175.00
Andirons, Gilt Brass, Lighthouse Form, Cabriole Legs, Ball Feet, 20 x 10 In.	235.00
Andirons, Iron, Anchor, Joined By Chain, 18 x 13 x 16 In.	625.00
Andirons, Iron, Arts & Crafts, Architectural Shape, Black, c.1903, 19¾ In.	353.00
Andirons, Iron, Arts & Crafts, Sunflower Finial, Tripod Foot, Early 20th Century, 26 In.	572.00
Andirons, Iron, Black Man & Woman, Drop-In Billet Bars, 16½ In.	345.00
Andirons, Iron, Block Form, Arts & Crafts, 22½ x 14 x 29 In.	191.00
Andirons, Iron, Brass, Faceted Flame Finials, Penny Feet, Late 1700s, 25 In.	1315.00
Andirons, Iron, Dachshund, Black Paint, 20th Century, 8 x 21 In.	173.00
Andirons, Iron, Dressed Women, Firedog Shanks, c.1850-70, 16 In.	1485.00

Fireplace, Andirons, Iron, Figural, George Washington, Standing, Drapery, Star, 20 In.
$460.00

Fireplace, Andirons, Iron, Hessian Soldiers, Fire Dogs, 19⅝ x 20½ In.
$275.00

Fireplace, Andirons, Iron, Wrought, Tole, Bird Form, Pierced Headdress, 21 x 29 x 6 In.
$826.00

Fireplace, Bellows, Turtle Back, Painted Fruit, Flowers, Mustard, Brass Nozzle, 18 In., Pair
$288.00

Fireplace, Chenet, Andirons, Brass, Louis XVI Style, Urn, Flame Finial, Openwork Bellflower, 15½ In., $518.00

Fireplace, Fender, Iron, Wrought, Openwork Spirals, Green Leather Pleated Seat, 24 x 83 In. $1673.00

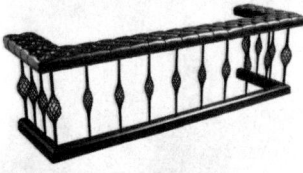

Fireplace, Hook, Steel, Sawtooth Trammel, Engraved Wheat, Heart, Cross, Iron Knobs, 35 x 16 In. $1035.00

Fireplace, Screen, Pole, Mahogany, Baluster, Urn Finial, Oval Panel, Embroidered Flowers, 54 In. $418.00

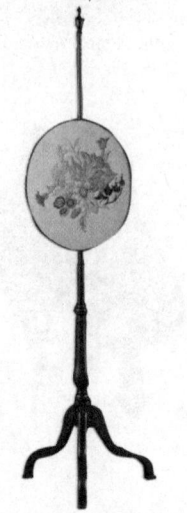

Andirons, Iron, Figural, George Washington, Standing, Drapery, Star, 20 In. *illus*	460.00
Andirons, Iron, Figural, Posed, Early 20th Century, 16 x 13 In.	410.00
Andirons, Iron, Figural, Woman Holding Vessel, 17 In.	201.00
Andirons, Iron, Flat Curved Posts, Cast Brass Rosette Finial, Tulips, Gold Paint, 22½ In.	143.00
Andirons, Iron, George Washington, Drapery, Star, Gilt, Log Rests, Mid 19th Century, 20 In.	460.00
Andirons, Iron, George Washington, Standing, Holding Book, 20¾ In.	632.00
Andirons, Iron, Gothic, Arched Form, Black, c.1850, 17 In.	1998.00
Andirons, Iron, Hammered, Arts & Crafts, 21 x 11½ x 22 In.	144.00
Andirons, Iron, Hessian Soldiers, Fire Dogs, 19⅝ x 20½ In. *illus*	275.00
Andirons, Iron, Labrador Dog, Verdigris Patina, Richard Clancy, Mass., 13½ In.	1998.00
Andirons, Iron, Owl, 21½ In.	1695.00
Andirons, Iron, Punch & Judy, Black Base, Painted, England, 17 In.	550.00
Andirons, Iron, Scrolled Figural Design, 19th Century, 14½ In.	546.00
Andirons, Iron, Wrought, Arts & Crafts, Scrolls, Spirals, Hammered, c.1925, 27¾ In.	353.00
Andirons, Iron, Wrought, Brass Dome Finials, Curved Feet, 28½ In.	115.00
Andirons, Iron, Wrought, Flattened Shafts, Faceted Finials, Penny Feet, 13 In.	193.00
Andirons, Iron, Wrought, Nailhead Tops, Scrollwork Base, 30½ x 25 In.	293.00
Andirons, Iron, Wrought, Penny Feet, Twisted Posts, Faceted Finials, 16½ In.	115.00
Andirons, Iron, Wrought, Spanish Colonial Style, Glazed Terra-Cotta, 22 x 18 In.	177.00
Andirons, Iron, Wrought, Tole, Bird Form, Pierced Headdress, 21 x 29 x 6 In. *illus*	826.00
Andirons, Round, Leaf Decoration, Paw Feet, Early 20th Century, 12½ x 25 In.	293.00
Bellows, Brass, Leather, Carved Bone, Middle Eastern, 19th Century, 16 In.	47.00
Bellows, Cornucopia Of Fruit, Stenciled, Painted, Rosewood, Grained Ground, 17½ In.	880.00
Bellows, Faux Tortoiseshell, Painted, Stenciled, 19th Century, 17 In.	359.00
Bellows, Oak, Carved, English Coat Of Arms, Long Handle, Brass Nozzle, 8½ x 45 In.	200.00
Bellows, Painted, Yellow, Decorated	403.00
Bellows, Turtle Back, Painted Fruit, Flowers, Mustard, Brass Nozzle, 18 In., Pair *illus*	288.00
Broom, Hearth, Splintered Shavings, 53½ In.	523.00
Chenet, Andirons, Brass, Louis XVI Style, Urn, Flame Finial, Openwork Bellflower, 15½ In. *illus*	518.00
Chenet, Andirons, Bronze, Pan, Leaf Scrolls, Flute, Figural, France, 16 x 18 x 13 In.	4025.00
Chenet, Andirons, Gilt Brass, Garlands, Flame Finial, France, Late 1800s, 13¾ In.	1143.00
Chenet, Andirons, Gilt Brass, Louis XVI Style, Garland Draped Urns, 1800s, 18 x 12½ In.	235.00
Coal Grate, Brass, Steel, Arching Back Plate, 26 x 26 x 13 In.	1416.00
Coal Grate, Engraved, Serpentine Brass Front, Pierced Grill, Figures, 32 x 30 In.	805.00
Coal Scuttle, Brass, Oval, Sloped Lid, Acanthus Side, Rear Lifting Handles, 20 In.	176.00
Coal Scuttle, Brass, Swivel Handle, Dutch, 19 In.	29.00
Coal Scuttle, Copper, Swing Handle, 4½ In.	44.00
Coal Scuttle, Gilt Brass, Helmet Form, Shell-Ribbed, Guilloche Border, Handle, 19 In.	646.00
Fender, Brass, Curved, Pierced Flowers, Stylized Paw Feet, Leaves, 41 x 8 In.	121.00
Fender, Brass, Iron, Serpentine, Lemon Finials, Vertical Wirework, 1800s, 13 x 57 In.	1116.00
Fender, Brass, Serpentine, Pierced, Flowers, Drapes, England, 39 x 9½ In.	115.00
Fender, Brass, Wire, Scroll, Lemon Top Finials, Early 19th Century, 13 x 53 x 15 In.	1380.00
Fender, Bronze, Empire, Polished, Embossed Rosettes, Griffin Torcheres, 7 x 51 In.	1763.00
Fender, Gilt Brass, Bowed Front, Reticulated, 4 Paw Feet, 8 x 53 x 12 In.	205.00
Fender, Gilt Brass, Club, Colonnade Style, Black Leather Tufted Seat Top, 20 x 66 x 24 In.	1410.00
Fender, Gilt Brass, Twisted Upper Rail, Spindled Lower Rail, D-Shape, 6½ x 48 In.	176.00
Fender, Iron, Wrought, Openwork Spirals, Green Leather Pleated Seat, 24 x 83 In. *illus*	1673.00
Fender, Tool Holder, Brass, Pierced Screen, Embossed Center Rib, Scalloped Feet, 47 x 15 In.	827.00
Fender, Wirework, Brass Rails & Finials, Ball Feet, England, Early 1800s, 17½ x 34 In.	999.00
Fender, Wirework, Brass Rim, Scrolled Ends, 40½ x 6½ In.	316.00
Fender, Wirework, D-Shape, 19th Century, 12 x 44½ x 14 In.	345.00
Fender, Wirework, D-Shape, Brass Rim, Sloped Iron Floor, 13 x 28 In.	115.00
Fender, Wirework, Scroll, Brass Top Rail, Ball Finials, Early 19th Century, 12½ x 45 x 15 In.	920.00
Fender, Wirework, Serpentine, Scrolled, Brass Rim, Finials, 15 x 53 In.	1265.00
Fender, Wirework, Steeple Finials, Brass Rim, c.1800, 15½ x 47½ In.	920.00
Fender, Wirework, Swags, Brass Rim, Ball Finials, c.1800, 16 x 69 In.	690.00
Fire Dogs, Arched Back Legs, Penny Feet, Angled Front Legs, 15 x 7 In.	460.00
Fire Dogs, Brass, Tongs, England, 18th Century, 7 x 6 In.	234.00
Fire Grate, Cast Iron, Lion Mounts, 19th Century, 37 In.	835.00
Fire Screen, Federal, Walnut, Mahogany, Oval, Paint On Silk, Bird, Flowers, 54 In.	385.00
Fire Screen, Federal Style, Mahogany, Turned Pole, Sliding Folding Panel, 50 x 16 In.	374.00
Fire Screen, Louis XV Style, Giltwood, Carved, Serpentine Crest, 41 x 31 In.	353.00
Fire Screen, Stained Glass, Leaded, Woman Holding Flowers, Brass, Claw Feet, 33 x 20 In.	748.00
Fire Screen, Victorian, Brass, Scrolling Supports, Round Frame, Wood Handle, 29 x 19 In.	176.00
Fire Screen, Victorian, Rosewood, Twist Carved Frame, Needlepoint, 1800s, 56 x 34 In.	624.00
Fireback, Cast Iron, Indian Princess, Dogs, Tree, Scroll, Drapery Beadwork, 35 x 35 In.	1265.00

Firedog, Utensil Rest, Wrought Iron, Dog Shape, Elongated Neck, 6⅜ x 12 In.	165.00
Footman, 4 Curved Feet, Stretchers, Cutout Pinwheels, Diamonds, Copper, 13 x 14 x 19 In. . .	104.00
Hearth Broom, Paint Decorated, 26 In.	86.00
Hearth Grill, Wrought Iron, Toray, Tripod Base, Pierced Wrought Handle, 27 In.	294.00
Hearth Set, Brass Stand, Dragon Finial, Griffin Loops, 4-Footed, Claw Tongs, 34 In., 5 Piece	840.00
Hook, Steel, Sawtooth Trammel, Engraved Wheat, Heart, Cross, Iron Knobs, 35 x 16 In. *illus*	1035.00
Insert, Federal Style, Brass, Cast Iron, Arched Fireback, Slatted Log Holder, 29 x 36 In.	235.00
Mantel Is Listed In The Architectural category.	
Reflector, Brass, Wrought Metal, Helmet Shape, Repousse Design, 24 x 21 In.	345.00
Screen, Art Nouveau, Oil Painted, Flowers, Birds, Painted Gold, c.1900, 57 x 39 In.	1250.00
Screen, Biedermeier, Mahogany, Shield-Form Needlework Screen, 1835, 29 In.	645.00
Screen, D-Shape, Brass Rim, Scrolled Wirework, England, Early 1900s, 13 x 53 In.	230.00
Screen, Faux Bamboo, Nature Morte, Taxidermied Bird, Victorian, 39 x 26 In., Pair	4112.00
Screen, Ironwork, Paneled Iron, Scrolled Feet, Polished Steel, Brass Hinges, 39 x 40 In.	115.00
Screen, Louis XV Style, Giltwood, Multicolored, Oval, Tapestry, Young Boy, 39½ x 17 In.	528.00
Screen, Louis XV Style, Giltwood, Multicolored, Oval, Aubusson Tapestry, c.1810, 40 x 17 In. .	528.00
Screen, Mahogany, Shield-Form Needlework, Earred Crest, 4 Legs, Biedermeier, 1835	645.00
Screen, Mahogany, Urn Finial, Turned Vase Column, Floral Needlepoint Screen, 59 In.	402.00
Screen, Marquetry, Colored Wood Inlay, Bamboo Turned, c.1900, 41 x 48 In.	94.00
Screen, Pole, Georgian, Mahogany, Carved, Tripod Base, Needlepoint Panel, 60 x 25 In.	1495.00
Screen, Pole, Hickory, Oval Maple Screen, Rose Head Nails, 51 In.	460.00
Screen, Pole, Late Georgian, Rosewood, Shield Shape Screen, Floral, Early 1800s, 55 In.	187.00
Screen, Pole, Mahogany, Baluster, Urn Finial, Oval Panel, Embroidered Flowers, 54 In. *illus*	418.00
Screen, Pole, Mahogany, Needlework, Inlay, Tapered, 8-Sided, 3 Legs, 25 x 14 In.	360.00
Screen, Pole, Queen Anne Style, Needlepoint Panel, Tripod Base, 44 In.	110.00
Screen, Victorian, Rosewood, Applied Scrolling, Painted Beach Scene, 46 In.	780.00
Screen, Walnut, Needlepoint, France, 40 x 30 x 16 In.	3776.00
Screen, William IV, Mahogany, Shield Shape, Needlework Flower, 68 In.	600.00
Screen, Wirework, Scrolls & Swags, Brass Rim, 24 x 42 x 14 In. . . . .*illus*	403.00
Stand, Kettle, Triangular, Wrought Iron, Tripod, Penny Feet, Heart, Rope Twist, 13½ In.	104.00
Tinderbox, Brass, Handle, 9 In.	55.00
Tinderbox, Copper, Contents, 3 In.	308.00
Tinderbox, Flintlock, Iron, Tin, 4¼ In.	743.00
Tinderbox, Tin, Flint Striker, Damper, Japanned, 4 x 4¼ In.	358.00
Tinderbox, Tin, Round, Finger Loop, Candle Socket, Interior Damper, 4¼ x 3 In.	144.00
Tongs, Iron, Ember, 12¾ In.	143.00
Tool Set, Iron, Forged, Turned, Skimmer, Spit Holder, Roast Holder, 19th Century	259.00
Trammel, Iron, Hand Forged, Sawtooth Bar, 34½ In.	33.00
Trammel, Iron, Hand Forged, Tooled Design, Rope Twist Shaft, Square Links, 54 In.	88.00
Trammel, Maltese Cross, Acorn Finials, Cast Iron, Winch Operation, 48½ In.	288.00
Trammel, Wrought Iron, Fish Design, Adjustable, Loop Handle, 41 To 70 In.	805.00

FISCHER porcelain was made in Herend, Hungary, by Moritz Fischer. The factory was founded in 1839 and continued working into the twentieth century. The wares are sometimes referred to as Herend porcelain.

MF

Box, Cover, Flowers, Strawberry Finial, Round, 4½ In.	125.00
Figurine, Madonna & Child, Seated, No. 5420, 16 In. . . . .*illus*	470.00
Figurine, Owl, Perched On Books, 12 In. . . . .*illus*	316.00
Figurine, Parrot, Painted, 8¼ In., Pair	527.00
Plate, Dinner, Fortuna, 10¾ In., 6 Piece	266.00
Platter, Rothschild Bird, Oval, Pink Ribbon Trim, 15¾ In.	384.00
Tureen, Cover, Rothschild Bird, Lemon Finial, 10 x 8 In.	826.00
Tureen, Cover, Underplate, Flowers, Fish, Gold Trim, Fish Handles, 4½ In. . . . .*illus*	800.00
Tureen, Soup, Under Tray, Poisson, Blue Ground, 11 In.	649.00
Vase, Persian Decoration, Overall Flowers, Tall Neck, Flared Rim, 28 In.	587.00
Vase, Rothschild Bird, 4½ In., Pair	413.00

FISHING reels of brass or nickel were made in the United States by 1810. Bamboo fly rods were sold by 1860, often marked with the maker's name. Lures made of metal, or metal and wood, were made in the nineteenth century. Plastic lures were made by the 1930s. All fishing material is collected today and even equipment of the past thirty years is of interest if in good condition with original box.

Catalog, Dame Stoddard Co., Tackle, c.1910, 161 Pages, 7 x 9¾ In. . . . .*illus*	360.00
Creel, Basket, Hinged Birchbark Top, Center Square Hole, 10 x 12 x 7 In. . . . .*illus*	1093.00
Creel, Basket, Rattan, French Weave Leather Bound, 14½ x 6½ x 10 In. . . . .*illus*	120.00

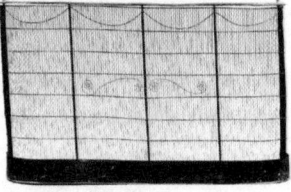

Fireplace, Screen, Wirework, Scrolls & Swags, Brass Rim, 24 x 42 x 14 In.
$403.00

Fischer, Figurine, Madonna & Child, Seated, No. 5420, 16 In.
$470.00

Fischer, Figurine, Owl, Perched On Books, 12 In.
$316.00

Fischer, Tureen, Cover, Underplate, Flowers, Fish, Gold Trim, Fish Handles, 14½ In.
$800.00

FISHING

Fishing, Catalog, Dame Stoddard Co., Tackle, c.1910, 161 Pages, 7 x 9¾ In.
$360.00

Fishing, Display, Paul Bunyan Flyrod Lures, 12 Dinky Lures In 4 Colors, 8 x 11 In.
$210.00

Fishing, Lure, Moonlight Bait, Bass Seeker, Red Head, Gold Metallic Flitter, Glass Eye, Box
$60.00

Fishing, Creel, Basket, Hinged Birchbark Top, Center Square Hole, 10 x 12 x 7 In.
$1093.00

Fishing, Display, Shurkatch Fishing Tackle Co. Bobbers, Beats All, Stand-Up, 11 Bobbers
$240.00

Fishing, Lure, R.L. Clewell, Snakerbait, Green, Yellow, Treble Hooks, Roller Bearing Swivel, Box
$450.00

Fishing, Creel, Basket, Rattan, French Weave Leather Bound, 14½ x 6½ x 10 In.
$120.00

Fishing, Lure, Action Frog Corp., Frog, Plastic, Propeller-Driven Legs, Box, 3 x 7 In.
$480.00

Fishing, Lure, Rhodes, Mechanical Swimming Frog, Oblong Weight, Kalamazoo Tackle Co., Box
$240.00

Fishing, Creel, E. Robicheau, Wood, Slat Sides, Painted Trout, Maine, 1977, 8 x 15 In.
$805.00

Fishing, Lure, Heddon, Darting Zara, Jointed, Wood, Glass Eyes, Bullfrog Pattern, Hooks, Box
$570.00

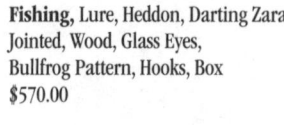

Fishing, Lure, Shakespeare, Bass Trolling Bug, Reed Head, Hair Body, Box
$342.00

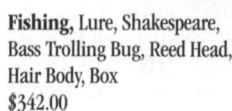

Creel, E. Robicheau, Wood, Slat Sides, Painted Trout, Maine, 1977, 8 x 15 In. ....*illus*	805.00
Creel, Ed Cummings, Wicker, Twisted Reed Hinges, Peg Latch, 7 x 14 x 7 In.	59.00
Creel, Turtle, Leather Trimmed, Rattan Weave, Hemp Cord, 7 x 14 x 8 In.	688.00
Creel, Woodhouse, Leather Trimmed, Hand Tooled, Cheyenne, Wyo., 16 x 10 x 8 In.	413.00
Display, Paul Bunyan Flyrod Lures, 12 Dinky Lures In 4 Colors, 8 x 11 In. ....*illus*	210.00
Display, Shurkatch Fishing Tackle Co. Bobbers, Beats All, Stand-Up, 11 Bobbers ....*illus*	240.00
Display, South Bend, Bass Oreno, Fish & Feel Fit, Die Cut, c.1927, 30 x 48 In.	2750.00
Eel Drag, Iron, 12 Teeth, 25 In.	431.00
Eel Gig, Iron, J.D. Fordham, Hooked Tines On Each Side Of Blade, Sag Harbor, N.Y., 16 In. ..	374.00
Harpoon, Whale, Carved, Crosshatching, Metal Banding, Detachable Point, Incised, 59 In. ...	600.00
License, 1917, California, Paper, 1 Dollar	13.00
License, 1936, New York Nonresident Button, Orange, White & Black, 1¼ In.	75.00
License, 1937, Maryland, Resident Angler's Button, Cellomet Prod., 1¾ In.	63.00
Lure, Action Frog Corp., Frog, Plastic, Propeller-Driven Legs, Box, 3 x 7 In. ....*illus*	480.00
Lure, Blackbird, Twin Treble Feet, Red Bead Eyes, Brown Feathers, 3½ In.	275.00
Lure, Bud Stewart, Crippled Duck, Folk Art, Signed, 4 In.	325.00
Lure, Chapman, Mermaid Spinner, Swivel, Feathered Treble Hook, Box, 2½ In.	330.00
Lure, Chapman, Water Nymph, Brass Wings, Painted, 4 In.	266.00
Lure, Creek Chub, Baby Wiggler, No. 200, Painted Gills, Belly Fins, Box	605.00
Lure, Creek Chub, Gar Minnow, Green Gar Pattern	443.00
Lure, Creek Chub, Kingfish Pikie, Yellow & Black Stripe, Screw Eye, Nickel Plate	236.00
Lure, Creek Chub, Weed Bug, Yellow Body, Gold Wing, Red Bead Eyes, Wire Leader	266.00
Lure, Creek Chub, Wigglefish In Frog	2805.00
Lure, Cummings, Bass Getter, Jersey Rigged, Gray Finish, Box	275.00
Lure, Heddon, Bubbling Bud, Full Wings, Gold, Green Stripes	523.00
Lure, Heddon, Bug-A-Bee, Red, Tail, Mustache, Pair	303.00
Lure, Heddon, Crazy Crawler, Cone Tail, Green Glow Worm, Luminous Belly Ribs	495.00
Lure, Heddon, Darting Zara, Jointed, Wood, Glass Eyes, Bullfrog Pattern, Hooks, Box ...*illus*	570.00
Lure, Heddon, Little Luny, c.1927, 3¾ In.	147.00
Lure, Heddon, Minnow, Underwater, No. 159K, Goldfish Scale	1121.00
Lure, Heddon, Musky Minnow, Black Sucker, Box	3186.00
Lure, Heddon, Punkinseed, c.1940, 2 In.	141.00
Lure, Heddon, Shiner Scale, Runtie, Wood	495.00
Lure, Heddon, Spindiver, L Rigging, Glass Eyes	649.00
Lure, Heddon, Stanley, Musky SOS Minnow, No. 372, White, Red Head, Bowtie Prop	678.00
Lure, Heddon, Surface Minnow, Stenciling On Belly, Red Painted Collar	89.00
Lure, Heddon, Tiny Tease, Painted, Pair	220.00
Lure, Heddon, Underwater Minnow, No. 101, Wooden Box	1760.00
Lure, Heddon, Underwater Minnow, No. 150, High Forehead	9735.00
Lure, Heddon, Underwater Minnow, Wooden Box, Papers, 1904	8360.00
Lure, Heddon, Vamp, Round Nose, Glass Eyes, L Rigging, Diving Lip, Rainbow Finish	561.00
Lure, Heddon, Westchester, Tail Feathers	550.00
Lure, Joe Pepper, Minnow, Jersey, Yellow, Gold Spots, Glass Eyes, Feather Hook, 1⅝ In.	798.00
Lure, Lake George, Floater, Water Witch, Green, White, Red Painted Cork Ball, Multi-Hook ..	1650.00
Lure, Minnow, Wood Body, Red Bead Eyes, Painted Metal Diving Lip, 3¼ In.	28.00
Lure, Moonlight Bait, Bass Seeker, Red Head, Gold Metallic Flitter, Glass Eye, Box ......*illus*	60.00
Lure, Moonlight Bait, Pikaroon, Yellow, Painted Eye, Black Eye Shadow, Red Nose, 5¼ In. ...	170.00
Lure, Musky Dead Sure Bait, Nickel Plate Rig, Box, Rochester, N.Y., Box, 6 In.	83.00
Lure, Musky Gee Wiz Frog, Wood Head, Rubber Body, Box, 5¾ In.	743.00
Lure, Pardee Shape, Minnow, Brass, 3 Treble Hooks, Glass Eyes, 6⅜ In.	853.00
Lure, Pepper, Baby Roamer, Front Spinner, Glass Eyes, Green Back, Painted Gills, 1¾ In. ...	220.00
Lure, Pepper, Frog, Composite, Belly Hook, Painted Eyes, Arrowhead Spinner, 1¾ In.	275.00
Lure, Pepper, Frog, Green, Black & Yellow Spots, Double Hook, 3 In.	385.00
Lure, Pepper, Revolving Minnow, Wooden Box	1416.00
Lure, Pepper, Roman, Spider, Notched Head, White, Red Face, Double Hooks, String Legs ...	266.00
Lure, Pflueger, Surprise Minnow, Maroon Box	1770.00
Lure, Plunk Oreno, South Bend, Tack Eyes, Black, Original Box	193.00
Lure, R.L. Clewell, Snakerbait, Green, Yellow, Treble Hooks, Roller Bearing Swivel, Box .*illus*	450.00
Lure, Rhodes, Mechanical Swimming Frog, Oblong Weight, Kalamazoo Tackle Co., Box *illus*	240.00
Lure, Sea Devil Bug, Tuttle, Saltwater Hook, Red, White, Black, Wire Wrapped, 5 In.	83.00
Lure, Seagull Pollywog, Yellow, Black Glass Eyes, 2 Hooks, 4¼ In.	148.00
Lure, Shakespeare, Barnacle Bill, White Iris Glass Eyes, Red Head, White Body, Glitter	440.00
Lure, Shakespeare, Bass Trolling Bug, Reed Head, Hair Body, Box ....*illus*	342.00
Lure, Shakespeare, Jim Dandy, Crippled Minnow, Glass Eyes, Blue Back Rainbow, 4 In.	207.00
Lure, Shakespeare, Red Wonder Bug, No. 6331-R1, Full Wings & Tail, Card, 3 In. ......*illus*	120.00
Lure, Shakespeare, Revolution, Acorn Shape, Mickey Mouse Style Spinner	236.00

Fishing, Lure, Shakespeare,
Red Wonder Bug, No. 6331-R1,
Full Wings & Tail, Card, 3 In.
$120.00

Fishing, Minnow Trap, Green Glass,
Galvanized Bands & Feet,
Perforated Lid, 11 In.
$60.00

Fishing, Net, Trout,
Carved Handle With Trout, Hand
$96.00

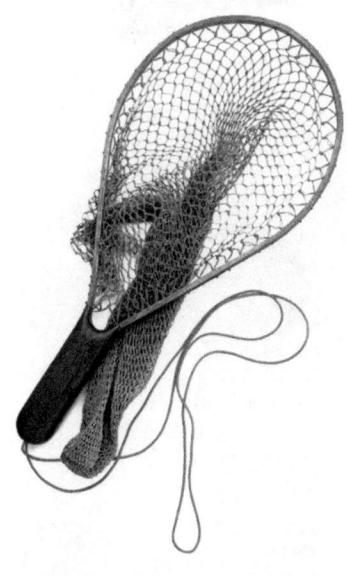

F

Fishing, Reel, Abu Garcia, Casting,
Model 4601CA, Left-Handed
$60.00

Fishing, Reel, B.F. Meek & Sons,
Bait Casting, No. 7, German Silver,
Box, 1⅝ In.
$1200.00

Fishing, Reel, Hardy, Trout, The Perfect,
Brass Foot, Box, 3⅜ x ¾ In.
$300.00

Fishing, Reel, Heddon,
Bait Casting, No. 3-35, German Silver,
Celluloid Handles, Case, Box
$570.00

Fishing, Rod, Abercrombie & Fitch,
Passport, Glass, Cork Handle,
Box, 4 Ft. 8 In.
$1200.00

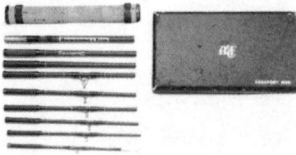

Lure, Shakespeare, Tarpalunge, Carved Eye, Green Mullet, Box		605.00
Lure, South Bend, Big Pike Oreno, Pearl Finish, Blue & Pink Spots, Glass Eyes, 5¼ In.		1320.00
Lure, South Bend, Minnow, Maroon Box		7480.00
Lure, South Bend, Minnow, Underwater, No. 903, White Hex Screw Eyes, Painted, 3 Hooks		325.00
Lure, South Bend, Mouse Oreno, Gray Flock, Black Bead Eyes, Tail, Original Box		148.00
Lure, South Bend, Pantella Minnow, 5 Hooks, Pointed Props, Painted Tack Eyes, Rainbow		177.00
Lure, South Bend, Truck Oreno, Box		7080.00
Lure, South Bend, Woodpecker, Luminous, Red Head, Original Box		148.00
Lure, South Bend, Zane Grey Teaser		207.00
Lure, Springfield Novelty Co., Half Charmer, White, Green Stripes, Nose, 1⅞ In.		89.00
Lure, Welch & Graves, Minnow, Glass, 3 Treble Hooks, Cork Stopper, Wire Leader, 3¾ In.		649.00
Mackerel Splitter, Wood, Steel, Carved, Incised Leaf Shape Handle, 1800s, 9 In.		118.00
Minnow Bucket, Falls City, Expert, Oval, Lift-Out Interior, Bail Handle, 10 Qt., 13 x 8 In.		330.00
Minnow Bucket, Falls City, Winner, Green, Gold, Silver Stenciling, 9½ x 9 In.		440.00
Minnow Trap, Green Glass, Galvanized Bands & Feet, Perforated Lid, 11 In.	*illus*	60.00
Minnow Trap, Shakespeare, Glass, Harness, Perforated Lid, 13 In.		303.00
Net, Trout, Carved Handle With Trout, Hand	*illus*	96.00
Reel, Abu Garcia, Casting, Model 4601CA, Left-Handed	*illus*	60.00
Reel, Ames, True Temper, Trolling, Model 923C, Glass Rod, Lever Free Spool, Level Wind		28.00
Reel, B.F. Meek & Sons, Bait Casting, No. 3, Blue Grass, Serial No. 5746		303.00
Reel, B.F. Meek & Sons, Bait Casting, No. 7, German Silver, Box, 1⅝ In.	*illus*	1200.00
Reel, Bill Ballan, Trout, Model 50, Leather Reel Bag		193.00
Reel, E. Holzmann, Casting, German Silver, Hard Rubber, Mother-Of-Pearl, 3 x 1³⁄₁₆ In.		6490.00
Reel, Edward Vom Hofe, Saltwater, Model 621, Silver, Hard Rubber, 4¼ x 2¼ In.		193.00
Reel, Edward Vom Hofe, Surf Casting, Silver, Hard Rubber, Click & Drag Level, Size 3/0		220.00
Reel, Edward Vom Hofe, Trout, Click, Size 2 Handle Plate, 2⅝ In.		550.00
Reel, Edward Vom Hofe, Trout, German Silver, Rubber, Size 2, 2¼ In.		742.00
Reel, Edward Vom Hofe, Trout, Size 3½ Handle Plate, 2¼ In.		110.00
Reel, H.L. Leonard, Trout, Bronze, Nickel Silver, Aluminum, Pat. No. 191813, 2¼ In.		4070.00
Reel, Hardy, Salmon, Saint John, Smooth Foot, Rim Check, 4 In.		220.00
Reel, Hardy, Salmon, Silex, Alloy, Smooth Brass Foot, Ivorine Handles, c.1911		177.00
Reel, Hardy, Tournament Casting, Alloy, Carrete Reflejo No. 1, c.1938, 3⅝ x 1 In.		55.00
Reel, Hardy, Trout, Bougle, Mark II Version, Brass Foot, Marked, c.1930, 3¼ In.		2090.00
Reel, Hardy, Trout, Mark II, Wide Drum, Ribbed Foot, Silver Line Guide, c.1945, 3½ In.		550.00
Reel, Hardy, Trout, The Perfect, Brass Foot, Box, 3⅜ x ¾ In.	*illus*	300.00
Reel, Hardy, Trout, The Perfect, Mark II, Wide Drum, Right Hand Wind, c.1935, 3½ In.		385.00
Reel, Hardy, Trout, The Princess, Left Hand Wind, 3⅜ In.		176.00
Reel, Heddon, Bait Casting, No. 3-35, German Silver, Celluloid Handles, Case, Box	*illus*	570.00
Reel, Orvis, SSS, Salmon, Fly, Dual Handle, Left Hand Wind, 9/10 Weight Line	138.00 to	165.00
Reel, Otto Zwarg, Salmon, Fly, Model 400, Click Switch, Drag Regulator, 3⅝ x 1½ In.		770.00
Reel, Pflueger, Hawkeye, Trout, German Silver, Rubber, Marked, 2½ In.		110.00
Reel, Philbrook & Paine, Trout, Fly, Raised Pillar, Orange & Black Rubber, 2¼ x 1 In.		9020.00
Reel, Seamaster, Fly, Mark III, Left Hand, Zippered Case, 3¼ In.		1402.00
Reel, Virginia Reel, Trout, Nickel Plate, Automatic, Hendryx, c.1903, 2¾ x 1½ In.		1045.00
Reel, Wm. Mills & Son, Trout, Telephone-Style Spool Latch, Marked, 3 In.		295.00
Rod, Abercrombie & Fitch, Passport, Glass, Cork Handle, Box, 4 Ft. 8 In.	*illus*	1200.00
Rod, Abercrombie & Fitch, Trout, 3 Piece, 1 Tip, Glass Insert Guide, Sack, Leather Case, 8 Ft.		148.00
Rod, B.F. Nichols, Trout, 3/2, Flip Ring Guides, Rattan Handle, Wood Case, Sack, 10 Ft.		495.00
Rod, Charles Daley, Bass, 2/2, Para Taper, 8 Ft. 6 In.		110.00
Rod, Dickerson, Trout, 8015 Guide Special, 2/2, 6/7 Weight Line, Bag, Tube, Cap, 8 Ft.		3186.00
Rod, Goodwin, Trout, Granger Victory, Bag, Tube, 9 Ft.		330.00
Rod, Hardy, Salmon, 3/2, Bag, Label, 12 Ft. 9 In.		83.00
Rod, Hardy, Trout, Fairy, 3/2, White Agate Stripper, Bag, Tube, 9 Ft.		83.00
Rod, Hardy, Trout, The Phantom, Cork Reel Seat, Agate Stripper, Bag, Tub, 6 Ft. 10 In.		413.00
Rod, Heddon, Salmon, Model 36, Double Handed, Bag, Tube, 10 Ft.		110.00
Rod, Heddon, Trout, Black Beauty, 3 Piece, 2 Tip, Bag With Label, 8 Ft. 6 In.		220.00
Rod, Heddon, Trout, Model 17, Cork Handle, Tube, 1930s, 6 Ft. 6 In.		531.00
Rod, Leonard & Mills, Fly, 2 Tips, 9 Ft. 9 In., 4 Piece		165.00
Rod, Leonard Duracane, Trout, Model 756, Impregnated, Bag, Tube, No. 6 Line, 7 Ft. 6 In.		908.00
Rod, Orvis, Madison, Trout, 2/1 Impregnated, No. 4 Line, Bag, Tube, 6 Ft. 6 In.		358.00
Rod, Orvis, Trout, Model 99 Impregnated, 1 Tip, Bag, Tube, 7 Ft. 6 In.		358.00
Rod, Stoddard, Trout, Special, 3/2, Bag, Tube, 8 Ft. 6 In.		165.00
Rod, Winston, Trout, 2 Tips, Copper & Gold Wraps, Maroon, 8 Ft., 2 Piece		1760.00
Rod Case, Don Woodhouse, Cheyenne, Wyo., Tooled Saddle Leather, 42 x 5 In.		325.00
Spear, Eel, E. & M. Co., No. 11, Iron, Black & Gold Paint, 11 Barbed Tines, 14½ In.		288.00
Spear, Eel, Early Winter, Iron, 6 Hooked Tines, Shaped Handle, New Jersey, 32½ In.		288.00
Spear, Eel, Susquehanna Type, Iron, Wood Handle, Child's, 34 In.		345.00

Spear, Fish, Iron, Tapered Handle, 7 8-In. Tines, 18 In.	288.00
Tackle Box, B.F. Meek & Sons, No. 99, Black, Gold, 3 Lift-Out Trays, 9 x 9 x 4 In.	743.00
Tackle Box, John Wheelock, Wood, Canvas, Worcester, Mass., 1858, 10 x 28 x 9 In.	288.00
Tackle Box, Metal, Tole Painting, Charles A. Blakslee, 15½ x 9½ x 7½ In.	115.00
Tackle Box, Storage, 3 Drawers, Cherry-Stained Pine, 18 x 8 x 10½ In.	138.00
Trophy, Walleye, Mounted, Glass & Wood Display Case, 26-In. Fish, 23 x 41 x 21-In. Case	374.00
Winding Board, Bone, U-Shape End Cutouts, 1800s, 1 x 2¼ In.	110.00

FLAGS *are included in the Textile category.*

FLASH GORDON appeared in the Sunday comics in 1934. The daily strip started in 1940. The hero was also in comic books from 1930 to 1970, in books from 1936, in movies from 1938, on the radio in the 1930s and 1940s, and on television from 1953 to 1954. All sorts of memorabilia are collected, but the ray guns and rocket ships are the most popular.

Advertisement, Newspaper, Atlanta Georgian, April 1934, 16¼ x 21¼ In.	112.00
Book, Tournament Of Death, Pop-Up, c.1935, 8 x 9¼ In., 16 Pages	280.00
Comic Art, Carlos Garzon, Comic Book No. 26, Page 23, 1979, 18 x 12 In.	55.00
Lobby Card, Walking Bombs, 1940, 11 x 14 In.	360.00
Lunch Box, Plastic, Aladdin Industries Inc., 1979	84.00
Movie Poster, New Worlds To Conquer, Universal, 1938, 27 x 41 In.	1955.00
Puppet, Hand, Cloth, Silk Screened, Pliable Vinyl Head, c.1950s, 10 In.	168.00
Toy, Clicker Gun, Tin Lithograph, Futuristic, Rings, Exhaust Ports, Marx, c.1950, 10 In.	309.00
Toy, Rocket Fighter, No. 5, Sparks, Tin Lithograph, Windup, Marx, Box, c.1930, 12 In.	3360.00
Toy, Squirt Gun Set, Plastic, Chest Plate, Belt, Compass, Esquire, On Card, 1952, 12 x 8 In.	560.00

FLORENCE CERAMICS were made in Pasadena, California, from World War II to 1977. Florence Ward created many colorful figurines, boxes, candleholders, and other items for the gift shop trade. Each piece was marked with an ink stamp that included the name *Florence Ceramics Co.* The company was sold in 1964 and although the name remained the same the products were very different. Mugs, cups, and trays were made.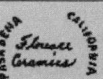

Candy Dish, Pink, Oval, Fluted, Curled Rim, 7 x 5 In.	50.00
Figurine, Ballerina, Ruffles, 7 In.	140.00
Figurine, Betsy, White, Gold Trim, 7½ In.	110.00
Figurine, Blue Boy, 12 In.	350.00
Figurine, Children, Oriental, Boy, Girl, 2 Piece	95.00 to 125.00
Figurine, Claudia, Holding Flowers, Light Blue Dress	300.00
Figurine, David, 7½ In.	75.00 to 95.00
Figurine, Deborah, Holding Flowers, Moss Green Dress, Bow, 9½ In.	450.00
Figurine, Delia, Holding Gold Trim Muff, 7¾ In.	95.00 to 120.00
Figurine, Dolores, Bonnet, Shawl, Gloves, 8¼ In.	595.00
Figurine, Girl, Holding Blue Bird, 5 In.	95.00
Figurine, Girl, Holding Hat, 7¼ In.	150.00
Figurine, Girl, In Nightgown, 5½ In.	98.00
Figurine, Jenevieve, Holding Muff, Pink Dress, Green Trim, Purse, Hat, 8 In.	155.00
Figurine, Marie Antoinette, French Style Dress, 10 In.	695.00
Figurine, Musette, Royal Red Dress, White Trim, Hat, Flower, Ringlets, 8¾ In. ....*illus*	350.00
Figurine, Sarah, Gray Dress, Red Hat, Purse, 7½ In.	95.00
Figurine, Twins, Red Hair, Hand Painted Features	70.00
Figurine, Woman, Holding Parasol, Amber, Blue Dress, 9½ In.	695.00
Figurine, Woman, Pink Dress, 6½ In.	70.00
Figurine, Woman, Velvet Gown, Pearls, 15 In.	2495.00
Flower Holder, Girl, Bee Nice	50.00
Flower Holder, June, 7 In.	40.00
Flower Holder, Patsy, 6 In.	40.00
Flower Holder, Polly, 6 In.	50.00
Group, Choir Boys, Black Bases, 5 Piece	250.00
Group, Story Hour, Mother, Son, Daughter, 8 x 7 In.	1000.00
Planter, Girl, Blond Hair, White Coat	45.00
Plaque, Woman, Blond Hair, 9 x 6½ In.	75.00
Vase, Daisy, White Dress, Flowers	40.00
Wall Pocket, Violet, 7 In.	95.00 to 145.00

FLOW BLUE was made in England and other countries about 1830 to 1900. The dishes were printed with designs using a cobalt blue coloring. The color flowed from the design to the white body so that the finished piece has a smeared blue design. The dishes were usually made of ironstone china. More Flow Blue may be found under the name of the manufacturer.

Florence, Figurine, Musette, Royal Red Dress, White Trim, Hat, Flower, Ringlets, 8¾ In.
$350.00

F

Flow Blue, Pitcher, Oriental Scene, 8-Sided, Shaped Handle, Ironstone, 5 In.
$132.00

Flow Blue, Platter, Turkeys In Field, Leaf & Game Bird Border, Gold Trim, 19 x 16 In.
$288.00

TIP

Plastic bubble wrap can ruin the glaze on old ceramics. If the wrap touches the piece for a long time in a hot storage area, it may discolor the glaze or adhere to the surface in an almost permanent glob.

Folk Art, Bird Tree, Polychrome, Tiered Tree, 7 Birds, Wood Carving, Don Noyes, 19½ In. $1035.00

Folk Art, Rooster, Yellow, Black, Red, Signed, Lonnie & Twyla Money, 30 In. $1265.00

Folk Art, Whirligig, Man Milking Cow, Wood, Painted, 16 x 14 In. $85.00

Bowl, Vegetable, Osborne, Blue, 8½ x 2¼ In.	145.00
Bowl, Vegetable, Osborne, Blue, Oval, 9 x 6⅞ In.	155.00
Centerpiece, La Belle China, c.1900, 6 x 10 x 13 In.	117.00
Charger, Meat, Oval Cartouches, Oriental Scene, 14½ In.	545.00 to 600.00
Fish Platter, Oval, Melbourne, Grindley, 24 x 11½ In.	575.00
Jam Jar, Footed, Melbourne, Grindley, 5½ In.	345.00
Open Salt, Dip Cellar, Double, Cherub, Footed, Applied Roses, 4½ x 3½ In.	32.00
Pitcher, Oriental Scene, 8-Sided, Shaped Handle, Ironstone, 5 In. *illus*	132.00
Plate, Chain Of States, State Names Around Edge, Decus Et Tutamen Ab Illo, 9 In.	50.00
Plate, Cobalt Blue, Oriental Scene, 10 In.	275.00
Plate, Cottage Scene, People By Lake's Edge, 3⅝ In.	149.00
Platter, Temple, 13¾ x 10½ In.	560.00
Platter, Turkeys In Field, Leaf & Game Bird Border, Gold Trim, 19 x 16 In. *illus*	288.00
Soup, Dish, Navy Blue, 1905, 7¾ In.	45.00
Teapot, Melbourne, Grindley, 10 In.	575.00

FLYING PHOENIX, *see Phoenix Bird category.*

FOLK ART is also listed in many categories of this book under the actual name of the object. See categories such as Box, Cigar Store Figure, Paper, Weather Vane, Wooden, etc.

Bear, Wood, Chainsaw Carved, Painted, Homer Green, 17 x 39 In.	230.00
Bird, On Branch, Acorn Shape, Plaque, Multicolored, 5¾ In.	187.00
Bird, Perched On Driftwood, Polychrome, Signed, Robert Hogg, 7⅜ x 6½ In.	121.00
Bird, Perched On Log, Multicolored, 4½ x 6½ In.	138.00
Bird Tree, Polychrome, Tiered Tree, 7 Birds, Wood Carving, Don Noyes, 19½ In. *illus*	1035.00
Birdhouse, Carved, Painted, Indian Figures, James Harold Jennings, 12 x 8 In.	748.00
Birdhouse, Oriole On Perch, Painted, Green, Orange, Blue, 4 x 4⅜ In.	250.00
Boat, 2 Masts, Man In Crow's Nest, Sailors, Feb. 2, 1878, 7½ x 7½ In.	2530.00
Bowling Pin, Man, Carved Facial Features, White Paint, 12 In.	468.00
Bowling Pin, Penguin Shape, Turned Wood, Applied Beak, Black & White Paint, 12¼ In.	431.00
Bust, Statue Of Liberty, Brown Stain, Wood Carving, Signed, E. Reed, 11 In.	1495.00
Cat, Folk Art, Linvel Barker, Crockett, Kentucky, Folk Art, 11¼ x 4½ In.	1610.00
Crocodile, Orange, Blue Paint, Bulbous Plastic Eyes, Carved, J.R. Lewis, 7 x 19 In.	288.00
Cup, Coconut, Hoof Shape, Carved, Flowers, Eagle, Coat Of Arms, Silver Hook, 2 x 4 In.	978.00
Diorama, Castle, Wood, Plaster, Wire, Mirrored Windows, Moat, Drawbridge, Figures, 18 x 12 In.	230.00
Diorama, Log Cabin, Outhouse, Split Log Fence, Root Trees, Birds, Tinfoil Fire, 27 x 20 In.	73.00
Dragon, Wood, Rattlesnake Tail, Wings, Ulysses Davis, Savannah, 28 x 3½ In.	7820.00
Eagle, Spread Wing, Crosshatch Breast, Arched Wings, Black, 13 x 21¼ In.	605.00
Eagle, Spread Wing, Talons, Downward Neck, Open Beak, Gold Wash, 9½ x 25 In.	209.00
Figure, Black Man, Walking Dog, Carved, Wood, Fabric, Popcorn, 49 x 18 In.	920.00
Figure, Man, Gears, Stars, Carved, James Harold Jennings, 23½ x 17½ In.	1035.00
Figure, Penguins, Carved, Painted, Black & White, Wood Carving, 8, 10, 12 & 20 In.	1880.00
Figurehead, Lady, Holding Torch, Hand On Waist, Carved, Wood, Painted, 52 In.	8050.00
Figurehead, Vine, Dove, Sea Serpents, Wood, Signed, E. Reed, 12 x 10 In.	1380.00
Gourd, American Flag, U.S.A., Painted, B.F. Perkins, Marked, 1995, 11 In.	115.00
Hand, Pointing, Pine, Carved Herringbone Sleeve, Cufflink, Mounting Chains, 13 x 52 In.	2990.00
Hearth Brush, Walnut, Carved, Golliwog Face, Horsehair Bristle, 22½ In.	518.00
Howling Wolf, Wood, Carved, Charles Keeton, 31 x 11 In.	863.00
Jug, Encrusted, Shells, Screws, Glass, 20th Century, 10 x 6¼ In.	176.00
Maenad, Sandstone, Signed, Snakes, Grapes, E. Reed, 1980, 17½ In.	3450.00
Marriage Dome, Coronet, Mirror, Flowers, Velvet Cushion, France, c.1915, 20 x 15 In.	605.00
Marriage Dome, Gold Plated, Blossom Earrings, Gloves, Photograph, France, c.1928, 21 x 13 In.	605.00
Marriage Dome, Gold Plated, Flowers, Velvet Cushion, France, c.1890, 20 x 14 In.	1430.00
Marriage Dome, Gold Plated, Mirror, Flowers, Wheat, Doves, France, c.1915, 20 x 13 In.	715.00
Marriage Dome, Gold Plated, Mirrors, Crown, Silk Lined Book, c.1900, 22 x 14 In.	715.00
Marriage Dome, Gold Plated, Mirrors, Doves, Photograph, Lace, France, c.1900, 21 x 13 In.	770.00
Mask, Welcome, Northwest Coast Haida, Cedar, Canada, 1930s, 19 x 15 In.	950.00
Monkey Holding Hat, Seated On Horse, Carved, Painted, 1860, 15 x 34 In.	4800.00
Owl, Balsa, Multicolored, Crosshatched Breast, 6¾ In.	350.00
Owl, Old Paint, Glass Eyes, Ohio, Folk Art, 10½ In.	431.00
Oxen & Cart, Carved, Glass Case, 36 x 14 In.	173.00
Parrot, Multicolored, Speckled Body, Incised Feathers, Green Mound, W. Schimmel, 5 In.	13750.00
Rattle, Layered Panels, Rounded Ends, Long Pointed Handle, Wood, Red & Black Paint, 8¾ In.	209.00
Rattlesnake, Painted, Brass Screw Eyes, Composition, 17¼ In.	825.00

Rooster, Antler Spurs, Glass Eyes, Wood Carving, Stand, 8-Sided, Horn Feet, Signed, 18 In. . .	1495.00
Rooster, Carved, White Wash, Tapered Column Mount, Stepped Base, Gold Paint, 41½ In. . .	440.00
Rooster, Multicolored, Black, White, Red, Yellow, Green Mound, W. Schimmel, 4⅜ In.	13200.00
Rooster, Yellow, Black, Red, Signed, Lonnie & Twyla Money, 30 In. . . . .*illus*	1265.00
Sailor's Toothpick, Nude Woman, Carved Ebony, Ivory Blade, Shotgun Shell Case, 3 In. . . .	460.00
Scarecrow, Wood, Jointed Arms & Hips, Carved Toes, Fingers, Features, Cloth, Stand, 41 In. .	4600.00
Seal, Curled Flippers, Glass Inset Eyes, Wood, Carved, Lid On Back, Green, Black, 25 In.	13800.00
Snake, Gourd, Minnie Black, Painted, Applied, 5½ x 18 In.	288.00
Snake, Root, Painted, Red, White, Black, 76 In.	316.00
Stag, Stripes, Multicolored, Iron, 4¾ x 6¾ In.	248.00
Swan, Wood, Carved, Painted, Shaped Body, Neck, Flat Bottom, 18 x 39 In.	1150.00
Tiger, Wood, Carved, Painted, JR Lewis, Kentucky, c.1990, 8¾ x 24 In.	288.00
Totem, Beavers, Applied Eyes, Painted, Homer Green, 52 In.	200.00
Totem, Indian Head, Stars, Suns, Moons, James Harold Jennings, 109 x 13 In.	690.00
Tree, 9 Birds On Drooping Branches, Nest, Multicolored, Conical Wood Block, 21⅜ In.	209.00
Tree, 9 Carved Doves, Iron, Wood, Painted, 55¼ x 33 x 30 In.	6600.00
Tree, Wood Block, 8 Birds On Branches, 6-In. Birds, 26 In.	187.00
Tugboat, Black, Red, Green, Tin Stack, Lake St. Clair, 1892, 15 x 34 In.	4125.00
Uncle Sam, Hinged Shoulders, Carved, Painted, Winford Gibson, 24½ In.	374.00
Uncle Sam, Painted, Red, White, Blue, Jointed Arms, Wood, Carved, 61 In.	518.00
Whimsy, Hearts, Pine, Carved, Telescopes, 5 Extensions, Dark Stain, 33 x 4 In.	1035.00
Whimsy, Wooden Circle, 11½ In.	144.00
Whirligig, Canoe, Man, Paddle Arms, Man, Top Hat, S.E. Snyder, Montour Co., Pa., 32¼ In. .	1265.00
Whirligig, Cyclist, Red, White, Blue, Yellow, Aluminum, Wood, c.1920, 24 x 34 In.	252.00
Whirligig, Duck, Flying, Cutout Wings, Flat Tail, Tin Feet, Original Paint, 23¾ In.	330.00
Whirligig, Indian, Feather Headdress, Wood, Carved, Painted, 19th Century, 23 x 6 In.	15600.00
Whirligig, Indian, Wooden, Carved, Painted, Flattened Full Figure, 1800s, 10¼ In.	470.00
Whirligig, Indian In Canoe, Paddle, Pine, Sheet Metal Feathers, Loin Cloth, 20½ In.	3000.00
Whirligig, Man, Inset Glass Bead Eyes, Arrow, Propeller, Multicolored, 16⅜ x 12½ In.	176.00
Whirligig, Man, On Stool, Milking Cow, Multicolored, Green Base, Tin Pail, 10 x 18¾ In. . . .	50.00
Whirligig, Man, Pine, Tin, Bottle Cap Hat, Ears, Stylized Face, Paddles, 23 In.	6000.00
Whirligig, Man Hoeing Shrubbery, Wood, Carved, Painted, Propeller, 21 x 19¼ In.	588.00
Whirligig, Man Milking Cow, Wood, Painted, 16 x 14 In. . . . .*illus*	85.00
Whirligig, Military Officer, Wooden, Carved, Painted, Black Helmet, Red Jacket, 22 In.	1523.00
Whirligig, Policeman, Revolving Arms, Blue Uniform, Hat, Red, White & Blue, 24 In.	805.00
Whirligig, Sailor, Wooden, Carved, Painted, Tin, Rotating Arms, c.1865, 19 In.	2468.00
Whirligig, Seated Man, Chased By Woman With Rolling Pin, Tin, Wood, Painted, 38 In.	374.00
Whirligig, Windmill, Black Man Turning Shaft, Red Paint, Stand, 37 x 31¼ In.	248.00
Whirligig, Woman Working Churn, Dasher Moves Up & Down, Wire, Nails, 23 In.	201.00

FOOTBALL *collectibles may be found in the Card and the Sports categories.*

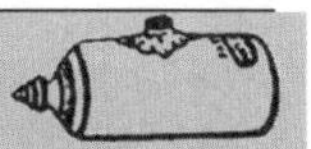

FOOT WARMERS solved the problem of cold feet in past generations. Some  warmers held charcoal, others held hot water. Pottery, tin, and soapstone were the favored materials to conduct the heat. The warmer was kept under the feet, then the legs and feet were tucked into a blanket, providing welcome warmth in a cold carriage or church.

Copper, Brass Cap, Handle, 11½ In.	75.00
Copper, Brass Top, Anchor, 11 x 8½ In.	169.00
Copper, Dome Cover, Acorn Finial, Handles, 13¼ x 12 In.	500.00
Copper, Mesh Handle, 9 x 4 In.	250.00
Granite, Wire Handle, 8 x 6 In.	20.00
Metal, Galvanized, 9 x 12 In.	25.00
Pottery, Doulton Lambeth, Transfer Decoration, c.1900, 9 In. . . . .*illus*	71.00
Stool, Oak, Carved, Hinged Front, Brass Handle, 8 x 9 In.	700.00
Wooden, Ceramic Tile Top, 10 x 8½ In.	150.00

FOSTORIA glass was made in Fostoria, Ohio, from 1887 to 1891. The factory was moved to Moundsville, West Virginia, and most of the glass seen in shops today is a twentieth-century product. The company was sold in 1983; new items will be easily identifiable, according to the new owner, Lancaster Colony Corporation. Additional Fostoria items may be listed in the Milk Glass category.

American, Appetizer Set, 10½-In. Tray, 7 Piece	400.00
American, Bowl, 3 x 6½ In.	48.00
American, Bowl, Centerpiece, Tricornered, 3-Toed	8.00

Foot Warmer, Pottery,
Doulton Lambeth, Transfer Decoration,
c.1900, 9 In.
$71.00

F

TIP

Be sure the dishes you put in a microwave oven are microwave-safe. New dishes are usually marked. Older dishes are not. To test a dish, put it in the microwave next to a glass of cold water. Heat it on high for one minute. If the dish is cool but the water is hot, it is okay to put the dish in the microwave. If the dish is hot, don't use it in a microwave.

Fostoria, American,
Compote, 6 In.
$24.00

Fostoria, American,
Pitcher, 48 Oz., 7 In.
$95.00

Fostoria, Baroque,
Sandwich Server, Topaz,
Center Handle, 4½ x 11½ In.
$80.00

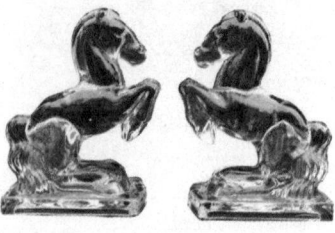

Fostoria, Bookends,
Rearing Horse, 7⅜ In.
$125.00

Fostoria, Coin, Compote,
Ruby, 6½ x 8½ In.
$65.00

American, Candleholder, Octagonal Foot, 6 In.	35.00
American, Candlestick, 2-Light, Round Foot, 4 x 8 In., Pair	58.00
American, Candy Dish, Cover, 7½ In.	45.00
American, Celery Dish, 3-Part, Oval, 10½ x 7 In.	45.00
American, Compote, 6 In. ....*illus*	24.00
American, Dish, Jelly	15.00
American, Goblet, Water, 9 Oz.	15.00
American, Ice Bucket, 3½ x 5½ In.	45.00
American, Jug, Ice, ½ gal.	120.00
American, Pitcher, 48 Oz., 7 In. ....*illus*	95.00
American, Plate, Salad, 7¾ In.	15.00
American, Puff Box, Cover, Gold Colored Metal Frame, 2½ x 3 In.	250.00
American, Relish, 4 Sections, 9 x 6½ In.	48.00
American, Sherbet, 5 Oz., 3½ In.	15.00
American, Sherbet, Underplate	14.00
American, Vase, Bud, Flared, Hexagonal Foot, 8½ In.	28.00
American Lady, Claret, 3 Oz., 4 In.	16.50
American Lady, Sherbet, Amethyst	45.00
Arcady, Tumbler, Juice, Crystal, 6 Oz., 4½ x 3¾ In.	8.00
Argus, Goblet, Olive Green, 10 Oz.	20.00
Argus, Sherbet, Olive Greem, 5 In., Pair	12.00
Argus, Sugar, Open, Olive Green	59.00
Baroque, Bowl, Topaz, 11 In.	65.00
Baroque, Goblet, 10 Oz., 6¾ In.	16.00
Baroque, Sandwich Server, Topaz, Center Handle, 4½ x 11½ In. ....*illus*	80.00
Baroque, Sugar & Creamer, Footed	35.00
Beacon, Sherbet, 6 Oz., 5½ In.	10.00
Beverly, Platter, Amber, 12 In.	45.00
Bookends, Rearing Horse, 7⅜ In. ....*illus*	125.00
Brocaded Palms, Plate, Handle, Green	55.00
Brocaded Palms, Sandwich Server, Center Handle, Ice Green	80.00
Buttercup, Sandwich Server, 14 In.	65.00
Century, Cake Plate, Handles, Original Label, 12 In.	30.00
Century, Candy Dish, Flared Rim, 3-Footed, 7½ In.	18.00
Century, Cruet, Oil, 5 Oz.	45.00
Century, Mustard Jar, Cover, Spoon, 4 In.	65.00
Century, Pitcher, 48 Oz.	110.00
Century, Sandwich Server, Center Handle, 11½ In.	28.00
Chintz, Centerpiece Set, Oval Bowl, Double Candlesticks, 3 Piece	145.00
Chintz, Champagne, 6 Oz., 5½ In., 6 Piece	53.00
Chintz, Plate, Salad, 7½ In.	15.00
Coin, Candlestick, 4⅝ In.	20.00
Coin, Cigarette Urn, Green	51.00
Coin, Compote, Ruby, 6½ x 8½ In. ....*illus*	65.00
Coin, Creamer, 3½ In.	12.00
Coin, Decanter, Stopper, 10 In.	225.00
Coin, Nappy, Handle, 1⅞ x 5³⁄₁₆ In.	15.00
Coin, Tumbler, Juice, 9 Oz.	15.00
Coin, Vase, Footed, 8 In.	29.00
Coin, Wedding Bowl, Cover, 8 In.	35.00
Colonial Prism, Toothpick	45.00
Colony, Candlestick, 16 In.	120.00
Colony, Goblet, 9 Oz.	15.00
Contour, Candlestick, Black, 4½ In., Pair	75.00
Contour, Goblet, Pink, 10 Oz., 5¾ In.	24.50
Corsage, Plate, Salad, 7¾ In.	15.00
Dolly Madison, Goblet, Claret, 4 Oz., 4¾ x 2½ In., 4 Piece	50.00
Dolly Madison, Goblet, Cordial, Oz., 3¼ In.	20.00
Fairfax, Candlestick, Emerald Green, Footed, 4½ In., Pair ....*illus*	18.00
Fairfax, Plate, Salad, Amber, 8¾ In.	14.00
Fairfax, Plate, Salad, Green, 7½ In.	15.00
Heather, Compote, 4¾ In.	35.00
Heirloom, Bonbon, White Opalescent, 5 In.	31.50
Heirloom, Bowl, Blue Opalescent, 6 x 9 In.	275.00
Heirloom, Bowl, Green Opalescent, 21 Points, c.1970, 6 x 8 In.	85.00
Heirloom, Plate, Green Opalescent, c.1970, 16 In.	95.00

F

Heirloom, Vase, Canary Opalescent, 10 In. 145.00
Hermitage, Ice Bowl, Blue 20.00
Hermitage, Sherbet, Topaz, 5½ Oz. 18.00
Horizon, Berry Bowl, Cinnamon, 5 In. 22.00
Horizon, Bowl, Cinnamon, 6 In. 26.00
Horizon, Candy Dish, Cover, Spruce Green, 5 In.. .... 48.00
Horizon, Coaster, Cinnamon 12.00
Horizon, Console, Spruce Green, 12 In. 48.00
Horizon, Console, Spruce Green, Handles, 12 In. 48.00
Horizon, Cup & Saucer, Cinnamon 24.00
Horizon, Plate, Dinner, Cinnamon, 10 In. 32.00
Horizon, Plate, Salad, Cinnamon, 7 In. .... 8.00 to 15.00
Horizon, Plate, Salad, Spruce Green, 7 In. 15.00
Jamestown, Cake Plate, Handles, Silver Flowers, 9½ In. 45.00
Jamestown, Goblet, Blue, 10 Oz., 5⅞ In. 15.00
Jamestown, Goblet, Light Blue, 10 Oz., 5⅞ In. 24.00
Jamestown, Pitcher, Amber, Qt., 6 In. 48.00
Jamestown, Sherbet, 7 Oz., 4⅛ In. 14.00
Jamestown, Sherbet, Light Blue, 7 Oz., 4¼ In. 20.00
Jamestown, Tray, Handles, 9¼ In. 27.50
Jamestown, Tumbler, Iced Tea, Amber, 11 Oz., 6 In. 10.00
Jamestown, Tumbler, Iced Tea, Light Blue, Footed, 11 Oz., 6 In. 24.00
Jamestown, Tumbler, Iced Tea, Pink, 12 Oz., 5⅛ In. 26.00
Jamestown, Tumbler, Iced Tea, Pink, Footed, 11 Oz., 6 In. 24.00
Jamestown, Tumbler, Juice, Ruby, Footed, 5 Oz., 4¾ In. 26.00
Jamestown, Wine, Light Blue, 3 Oz., 4½ In. 24.00
June, Compote, Topaz, 5 In. .... 50.00 to 55.00
June, Plate, Pink, 6¼ In. 8.25
June, Sandwich Server, Center Handle, Topaz, 12 In. 35.00
June, Tumbler, Juice, Footed, Pink, 4½ In. 48.00
June, Wine, 3 Oz. 32.00
Karnak, Tumbler, Marine Blue, 14 Oz. 20.00
Lafayette, Plate, Luncheon, Topaz, 8½ In. 16.00
Lafayette, Plate, Wisteria, 10¼ In. 60.00
Lido, Bowl, Flared Rim, 11 In. 80.00
Lido, Bowl, Floral, Handles, 3½ x 13 In. 85.00
Lido, Bowl, Handles, 4-Footed, 3½ x 10½ In. 40.00
Lido, Plate, Salad, 7½ In. 7.50
Lido, Plate, Salad, Azure, 7½ In. 12.50
Manor, Wine, 4 Oz. 34.00
Mayfair, Plate, Lemon, Wisteria, Handles, 6½ In. .... *illus* 10.00
Mesa, Bowl, Trifle, Amber, 7¼ In. 33.00
Midnight Rose, Celery Dish, 11¾ In. 45.00
Midnight Rose, Dish, Mayonnaise, Sections, Handles, 2⅜ x 8¾ In. 45.00
Midnight Rose, Goblet, 7⅝ In. 42.00
Midnight Rose, Relish, Sections, 1⅝ x 6⅛ x 8⅛ In. 25.00
Midnight Rose, Serving Dish, Oval, Handles, 2⅜ x 9 x 5⅛ In. 26.00
No. 2329, Console Set, Amber, Etched, Gold Trim, 10¾-In. Bowl, 3 Piece .... *illus* 20.00
Pioneer, Plate, Burgundy, 8¾ In. 30.00
Regal, Toothpick 35.00
Romance, Cup & Saucer 33.00
Romance, Goblet, Footed, 9 Oz. 32.50
Scepter, Goblet, Yellow, 9 Oz. 32.00
Seascape, Bowl, Pink Opalescent, 2½ x 6 In. 45.00
Virginia, Candleholder, Pair 30.00
Virginia, Goblet, Blue, 7 In. 15.00
Wavecrest, Cocktail, Azure, Clear Stem, Foot, 4¾ In. 28.00
Wavecrest, Cordial, Topaz, Clear Stem, Foot, 3⅞ In. 65.00
Wavecrest, Goblet, Blue, Clear Stem, Foot, 7½ In. 35.00
Wisteria, Tumbler, Iced Tea, 12 Oz. 45.00
Woodlands, Compote, Jelly, Green, Footed, 5½ x 4½ In. 15.00

FOVAL, *see Fry category.*

FRAMES *are included in the Furniture category under Frame.*

TIP

A glass vase or bowl can be cleaned with a damp cloth. Try not to put the glass in a sink filled with water. Hitting the glass on a faucet or the sink is a common cause of breakage.

Fostoria, Fairfax, Candlestick, Emerald Green, Footed, 4½ In., Pair
$18.00

Fostoria, Mayfair, Plate, Lemon, Wisteria, Handles, 6½ In.
$10.00

Fostoria, No. 2329, Console Set, Amber, Etched, Gold Trim, 10¾-In. Bowl, 3 Piece
$20.00

Franciscan, Autumn,
Plate, Salad, 8 In.
$10.00

Franciscan, Carmel,
Plate, Luncheon, 8¼ In.
$12.00

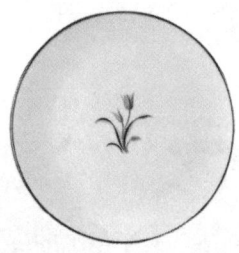

Franciscan, Desert Rose, Bowl,
Vegetable, Round, 9 In.
$20.00

Franciscan, Jamoca,
Plate, Dinner, Brown,
Gold, 10¾ In.
$10.00

Franciscan, Maypole, Plate,
Dinner, 10¾ In.
$15.00

FRANCISCAN is a trademark that appears on pottery. Gladding, McBean and Company started in 1875. The company grew and acquired other potteries. They made sewer pipes, floor tiles, dinnerwares, and art pottery with a variety of trademarks. In 1934, dinnerware and art pottery were sold under the name Franciscan Ware. They made china and cream-colored, decorated earthenware. Desert Rose, Apple, El Patio, and Coronado were best-sellers. The company became Interpace Corporation and in 1979 was purchased by Josiah Wedgwood & Sons. The plant was closed in 1984 but a few of the patterns are still being made. For more information, see *Kovels' Depression Glass & Dinnerware Price List*.

Apple, Bowl, Fruit, 5¼ In.	10.00
Apple, Creamer, 2¾ In.	12.00 to 15.00
Apple, Pitcher, Milk, 6¼ In.	75.00
Apple, Plate, Bread & Butter, 6½ In.	6.00
Apple, Plate, Dinner, 10½ In.	9.00 to 25.00
Apple, Plate, Luncheon, 9½ In.	12.00
Apple, Platter, 17 In.	55.00
Apple, Relish, 3 Sections, 11¾ In.	50.00
Aurora, Bowl, 10¼ In.	60.00
Autumn, Bowl, Vegetable, 13½ x 6½ In.	15.00
Autumn, Pitcher, Milk, 8½ In.	25.00
Autumn, Plate, Salad, 8 In. *illus*	10.00
Birchbark, Plate, Bread & Butter, 6⅜ In.	7.00
Birchbark, Plate, Dinner, 10½ In.	34.00
Birchbark, Plate, Salad, 8¼ In.	11.00
Bouquet, Napkin Ring, 4 Piece	75.00
Capistrano, Bowl, Maroon, Satin Yellow, 10 x 15 In.	65.00
Capistrano, Candlestick, Satin Ivory, 3⅜ In.	60.00
Capistrano, Planter, Goose, 7½ In.	50.00 to 75.00
Carmel, Cup & Saucer, 1¾ In.	12.00
Carmel, Plate, Bread & Butter, Dessert, 6⅜ In.	10.00
Carmel, Plate, Luncheon, 8¼ In. *illus*	12.00
Catalina, Coaster, Green, 4 In.	50.00
Coronado, Bowl, Cereal, Satin Ivory, 6¼ In.	65.00
Coronado, Bowl, Fruit, Satin Coral, 6 In.	70.00
Coronado, Bowl, Salad, Satin Ivory, 10½ In.	70.00
Coronado, Bowl, Vegetable, Satin Turquoise, 10½ In.	70.00
Coronado, Chop Plate, Satin, Coral, 14 In.	55.00
Coronado, Coffeepot, Satin Turquoise, 7½ In.	35.00
Coronado, Cup & Saucer, Satin, Coral	12.00
Coronado, Cup & Saucer, Satin, Turquoise	12.00
Coronado, Gravy Boat, Satin Yellow	56.00
Coronado, Lid, Casserole, Satin, Turquoise, 7¾ In.	6.00
Coronado, Plate, Dinner, Satin, Coral Gloss, 10⅜ In.	14.00
Coronado, Plate, Dinner, Satin, Turquoise Gloss, 10⅜ In.	14.00
Coronado, Plate, Salad, Satin, Coral, 7¼ In.	10.00
Coronado, Plate, Salad, Satin, Coral Crescent, 9⅜ In.	60.00
Coronado, Platter, Satin, Coral, 15¼ x 11½ In.	45.00
Coronado, Salt & Pepper, Off-White	30.00
Coronado, Soup, Dish, Satin, Coral Gloss, 6⅛ In.	4.00
Coronado, Soup, Dish, Satin Ivory, 6¼ In.	30.00
Coronado, Sugar, Satin, Turquoise	20.00
Coronado, Teapot, Cover, Satin Coral	65.00
Coronado, Teapot, Satin Ivory, Cover	65.00
Coronado, Tumbler, Satin Ivory, 5¼ In.	50.00
Country Craft, Platter, Russet Brown, 13¾ In.	9.00
Del Rio, Plate, Dinner, 10½ In.	15.00
Denmark, Gravy Boat, Underplate, 8½ In.	55.00
Denmark, Plate, Dinner, 9½ In.	25.00
Desert Rose, Bowl, Salad, 10 In.	40.00
Desert Rose, Bowl, Vegetable, Cover, 1½ Qt.	25.00
Desert Rose, Bowl, Vegetable, Divided, Oval, 10¾ In.	45.00
Desert Rose, Bowl, Vegetable, Round, 9 In. *illus*	20.00
Desert Rose, Chop Plate, 14 In.	50.00
Desert Rose, Creamer, 4½ In.	16.00
Desert Rose, Cup & Saucer, 6 Piece	55.00
Desert Rose, Plate, Dessert, 7 In.	4.00
Desert Rose, Plate, Dinner, 9½ In.	10.00

Desert Rose, Plate, Dinner, 10⅝ In.	8.00 to 25.00
Desert Rose, Plate, Salad, 8 In.	6.00
Desert Rose, Platter, 14 In.	52.00
Desert Rose, Platter, Oval, 12½ In.	45.00
Desert Rose, Salt & Pepper, 6½ In.	70.00
Desert Rose, Saltshaker, 6¼ In.	50.00
Dogwood, Cup & Saucer, 4 In.	12.00
Dogwood, Plate, Dinner, 10½ In.	14.00
Dogwood, Plate, Salad, 8 In.	10.00
El Patio, Bowl, Relish Apple, Green, 8¾ In.	50.00
El Patio, Bowl, Salad, Maroon, 11 In.	65.00
El Patio, Carafe, Cobalt Blue, 7½ In.	75.00
El Patio, Carafe, Flame Orange, 7½ In.	50.00
El Patio, Carafe, Golden Glow, Cover	60.00
El Patio, Carafe, Redwood, 7½ In.	50.00
El Patio, Chop Plate, Gray, 14 In.	45.00
El Patio, Cup, Coral, 4⅜ In.	25.00
El Patio, Cup, Eggplant, 4⅜ In.	50.00
El Patio, Gravy Boat, Bright Yellow	50.00
El Patio, Gravy Boat, Cobalt Blue	45.00
El Patio, Gravy Boat, Liner, Redwood	50.00
El Patio, Gravy Boat, Maroon	50.00
El Patio, Gravy Boat, Satin Gray	50.00
El Patio, Jug, Golden Glow, 7¼ In.	50.00
El Patio, Sugar, Coral, 3¾ In.	25.00
El Patio, Tumbler, Apple Green, Banded, 3½ In.	25.00
El Patio, Tumbler, Eggplant, 3½ In.	65.00
El Patio, Tumbler, Redwood, 3½ In.	25.00
El Patio, Tumbler, White, 3¼ In.	30.00
Fern Dell, Bread Tray, 18 In.	25.00
Floral, Candlestick, Satin Gray, Pair	25.00 to 55.00
Forget Me Not, Cup & Saucer	27.00
Hacienda, Coffeepot, 8 Cups, 8¾ In.	28.00
Hacienda Gold, Bowl, Vegetable, 9¼ In.	25.00
Hacienda Gold, Pitcher, Milk, 6¼ In.	20.00
Hacienda Gold, Pitcher, Water, 7 In.	25.00
Hacienda Gold, Platter, 14 In.	9.00
Indian Summer, Cup & Saucer	17.00
Ivy, Bowl, Vegetable, 7¼ In.	55.00
Ivy, Bowl, Vegetable, 8 ¼ In.	65.00
Ivy, Plate, 6½ In., 4 Piece	30.00
Jamoca, Plate, Dinner, Brown, Gold, 10¾ In. *illus*	10.00
Kaolena, Vase, Swirl, 7¾ In.	65.00
Kaolena, Wall Skillet, 7⅜ In.	25.00
Madeira, Goblet, Dark Green, Pair	15.00
Maypole, Plate, Dinner, 10¾ In. *illus*	15.00
Maytime, Gravy Boat, Underplate	28.00
Montecito, Cup, Coral	25.00
Montecito, Plate, Luncheon, Ruby, 9⅜ In.	50.00
Montecito, Soup, Dish, Coral	50.00
Mountain Laurel, Bowl, Fruit, 6¼ In.	15.00
Mountain Laurel, Soup, Dish, 8¼ In.	15.00
Oasis, Pepper Mill, 6 In.	30.00
Padua, Tile, Tea	65.00
Pebble Beach, Plate, Dinner, 10½ In., 4 Piece	28.00
Poppy, Salt & Pepper	50.00
Radiance, Bowl, Vegetable, 8¼ In.	25.00
Radiance, Gravy Boat, Underplate, 6¼ In.	45.00
Renaissance Gold, Cup & Saucer	50.00
Renaissance Gold, Plate, Dinner, 10⅝ In. *illus*	74.00
Spice, Platter, 16½ In.	30.00
Strawberry Fair, Salt & Pepper	50.00
Tara, Bowl, Vegetable, 9 In.	28.00
Tara, Platter, 12½ x 9½ In.	28.00
Tiempo, Coffeepot, 7½ In.	75.00
Tiempo, Plate, Dinner, Apricot, 8⅞ In. *illus*	17.00
Tiempo, Plate, Dinner, Yellow, 9¾ In.	17.00

F

Franciscan, Renaissance Gold, Plate, Dinner, 10⅝ In. $74.00

Franciscan, Tiempo, Plate, Dinner, Apricot, 8⅞ In. $17.00

Potter's Vocabulary

Coiling: A method that uses long ropelike rolls of clay, coiled to form the shape, then smoothed on the inside and outside.

Sgraffito: A design scratched or cut through slip or glaze before the pottery is fired. The color underneath shows.

Slip: Clay mixed with water to the consistency of heavy cream. It can be cast in a plaster mold. Slip also is spread on pottery as decoration.

Wheel turned: Pottery made by putting a lump of clay on a wheel, then shaping it with your hands as the wheel spins.

Frankoma Pottery, Bowl,
Lazybones, Prairie Green,
Free-Form Shape, Footed, 7½ In.
$5.00

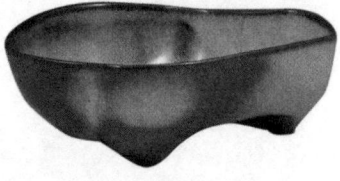

Frankoma Pottery, Casserole,
Cover, Mayan Aztec,
Prairie Green, 4½ x 10 In.
$20.00

Frankoma Pottery, Figurine,
Ponytail Girl, Prairie Green,
No. 106, 9¾ In.
$45.00

Frankoma Pottery, Figurine,
Puma, Reclining, Desert Gold,
No. 116, 9½ In.
$20.00

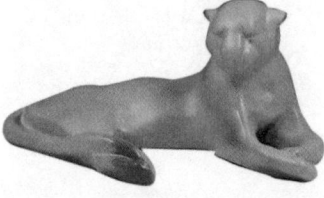

Tiempo, Plate, Salad, 8 In. Square	16.00
Tiempo, Soup, Dish, Dark Brown, 6½ In.	17.00
Topaz, Cup & Saucer	10.00
Tropico, Bowl, Ivory, 3-Footed, 9⅝ In.	65.00
Tropico, Bowl, Yellow, 3-Footed, 9⅝ In.	65.00

FRANKART, Inc., New York, New York, mass-produced nude dancing lady lamps, ashtrays, and other decorative Art Deco items in the 1920s and 1930s. They were made of white lead composition and spray-painted. *Frankart Inc.* and the patent number and year were stamped on the base.

Lamp, 2 Female Nudes, Stretched Legs, Holding White Stepped Globe, 1928, 19½ In.	2350.00
Lamp, Double Lady, Nude, Holding Green Glass Globe, Art Deco, 7½ x 5 In.	1800.00
Lamp, Sarsaparilla, Art Deco, Nude, Aluminum, Crackle Glass Globes, 7 x 9 x 5 In.	250.00

FRANKOMA POTTERY was originally known as The Frank Potteries when John F. Frank opened shop in 1933. The factory is now working in Sapulpa, Oklahoma. Early wares were made from a light cream-colored clay from Ada, Oklahoma, but in 1956 the company switched to a red burning clay from Sapulpa. The firm made dinnerwares, utilitarian and decorative kitchenwares, figurines, flowerpots, and limited edition and commemorative pieces. John Frank died in 1973 and his daughter, Joniece, inherited the business. Frankoma went bankrupt in 1990. It was bought by Richard Bernstein in 1991 and closed in 2004. The pottery was bought by H.B. "Det" and Crystal Merryman in 2005 and is in business as Frankoma, Inc.

Ashtray, Arrowhead, Prairie Green, 7 In.	15.00
Ashtray, Arrowhead, Woodland Moss, 7 In.	15.00
Bank, Pig, White	25.00
Bowl, Lazybones, Prairie Green, Free-Form Shape, Footed, 7½ In. ....*illus*	5.00
Butter, Plainsman, Prairie Green	15.00
Candleholder, Flame, Pedestal Base	20.00
Casserole, Cover, Mayan Aztec, Prairie Green, 4½ x 10 In. ....*illus*	20.00
Cornucopia, Prairie Green, 9½ In.	30.00
Cup, Plainsman, Prairie Green	7.00
Figurine, Bird, Prairie Green, 3 In.	7.00
Figurine, Coyote Pup, Prairie Green, 7¾ In.	15.00
Figurine, Indian Chief, Prairie Green, 8 In.	20.00
Figurine, Indian Maiden, Prairie Green, 13 In.	15.00
Figurine, Madonna, Prairie Green, 8 In.	20.00
Figurine, Mare & Colt, Prairie Green, 12 In.	15.00
Figurine, Mother Bird, Prairie Green	7.00
Figurine, Ponytail Girl, Desert Gold, 9¾ In.	28.00
Figurine, Ponytail Girl, Prairie Green, No. 106, 9¾ In. ....*illus*	45.00
Figurine, Puma, Reclining, Desert Gold, No. 116, 9½ In. ....*illus*	20.00
Gravy Boat, Handle, Prairie Green, Plainsman	20.00 to 25.00
Gravy Boat, West Wind, Prairie Green	20.00
Mug, Prairie Green, Plainsman	5.00
Mug, Cowboy, Desert Gold	13.00
Pitcher, Lazybones, Prairie Green, Ada Clay, 7 In.	20.00
Pitcher, Wagon Wheel, Prairie Green, 2 Qt.	15.00
Planter, Prairie Green, Footed, Gracetone, 4½ In.	15.00
Planter, Praying Hands, Prairie Green, 7½ In.	20.00
Plate, 1st Presbyterian, 75th Anniversary, 1970	15.00
Plate, Conestoga Wagon, Prairie Green, 1971	100.00
Plate, Statue Of Liberty, Prairie Green, 1986	20.00
Plate, Texas, 28th State, Prairie Green, Plainsman, 8½ In.	25.00
Platter, Prairie Green, Plainsman, 9 In.	10.00
Platter, Prairie Green, Plainsman, 13 In.	15.00
Salt & Pepper, Wagon Wheel, Prairie Green	15.00 to 20.00
Sugar & Creamer, Wagon Wheel, Prairie Green	13.00
Toothbrush Holder, Owl, Brown Satin, Sapulpa Clay, 5 In.	10.00
Trivet, Iowa, Prairie Green	10.00
Trivet, Stars & Stripes, Prairie Green	13.00
Trivet, Unicorn, Prairie Green	15.00
Vase, Bud, Crocus, Prairie Green, 8 In.	10.00
Vase, Bud, Crocus, Sunflower Yellow, 8 In.	10.00
Vase, Prairie Green, 8-Sided, 9½ In.	30.00
Wind Chime, Bell, Prairie Green	15.00

FRATERNAL objects that are related to the many different fraternal organizations in the United States are listed in this category. The Elks, Masons, Odd Fellows, and others are included. Also included are service organizations, like the American Legion, Kiwanis, and Lions Club. Furniture is listed in the Furniture category. Shaving mugs decorated with fraternal crests are included in the Shaving Mug category.

American Order Of United Workmen, Paperweight, John Upchurch, c.1868, 3 In.	59.00
Eagles, Tumbler, Red Enamel Decoration, Waynesboro, Lodge 1758, Libbey	4.00
Eastern Star, Bowl, Painted, 22K Gold, 10 In.	15.00
Eastern Star, Change Plate, Porcelain, Royal Winton Of England, 4½ x 3½ In.	15.00
Eastern Star, Cup & Saucer, Marked	12.00
Eastern Star, Paperweight, Star, Red, North Dakota School Of Mines, 5-Sided, 1 x 5 In.	115.00
Eastern Star, Pin, Shriner Chain, Multicolored Enamel, 14K Gold	55.00
Eastern Star, Punch Bowl, Salt Glazed, Cobalt Blue, Leaves, c.1870, 11 x 19 In. *illus*	4200.00
Elks, Pin, Chillicothe Ohio Fair, Celluloid	85.00
Knights Of Pythias, Badge, Ribbon, 29th Annual Convention, Dayton, 1898, 6½ x 2 In.	25.00
Knights Of Pythias, Fob, Gold Link Chain, Enamel, American Flag, Other Symbols	130.00
Knights Of Pythias, Pendant, 14K Gold, Black Onyx, Letters F-C-B, Coat Of Arms	149.00
Knights Templar, Mug, Carnival Glass, Dandelion, Ice Blue	325.00
Knights Templar, Mug, Carnival Glass, Dandelion, Marigold	220.00
Masonic, Apron, Ornamental Silver, Gold Metallic Fringe, Trim	350.00
Masonic, Apron, Painted, Lambskin, Silk, Symbols, 19th Century, 13½ x 13½ In. *illus*	978.00
Masonic, Belt Buckle, 33rd Degree, Scottish Rite, Berbamot Brass Works, 1978	35.00
Masonic, Champagne Glass, Syria Temple, Westmoreland, Shriners On Camels, 1911, 5 In.	88.00
Masonic, Dish, Pottery, White, Blue Lodge, Golden Gate Lodge, Chagrin Falls, Ohio	10.00
Masonic, Face Jug, Redware, Applied Hair Coil, Incised G, Early 1800s, 12 In. *illus*	18000.00
Masonic, Headdress, Silk, Brass, c.1890	68.00
Masonic, Knife, Pocket, Pine Knot, 3 Blades, 4 In.	130.00
Masonic, Pin, Annual Guest Night, 12 Symbols, 1920s, 1¾ In.	94.00
Masonic, Pitcher, Silver Luster, Scrolls, Transfer, William Hamilton, Lodge No. 500, 9 In.	33.00
Masonic, Rainbow Girls, Bracelet, Charm, 13 Symbol Charms, Silver, 1950s	33.00
Masonic, Ring, 32nd Degree, Full Cut Diamond, 14K Gold, Enamel & Gold Symbols	950.00
Masonic, Sword, Bowtie Guard, Wrapped Grip, Scabbard, c.1870, 28-In. Blade	288.00
Masonic, Toothpick, Barrel Shape, Hand Painted, Westmoreland Glass, 1905, 2 In.	40.00
Odd Fellows, Box, Arc Of Covenant, Carrying Rods, Link Gallery, Blue, Red, 12 x 36 In.	748.00
Odd Fellows, Code Of Laws, State Of Nebraska, 82 Pages, c.1907, 3¾ x 6¾ In.	15.00
Odd Fellows, Pin, 10K Gold, Enamel, 3-Link Chain, Red, White Blue, ⅜ x ⁷⁄₁₆ In.	17.00
Odd Fellows, Pin, Sash, Metal Insignia, Fisher, Minnesota, 7¾ x 2¼ In.	43.00
Odd Fellows, Pin, Service, Marcasite	8.00
Odd Fellows, Sign, Porcelain, Round, Metal Band, Red, White, Blue, 29½ In. *illus*	475.00
Odd Fellows, Sign, Red Heart In Hand, Ioof, Metal, Raised Black Letters, 25 x 49 In.	2300.00
Odd Fellows, Watch Fob, Gold Filled, Enameled, Letters F-L-T, 5¼ x ¾ In.	130.00
Odd Fellows, Wood Carving, Staff, Heart In Hand, Walnut, Regalia, Indiana, 59 In.	2760.00
Rebekah Assembly, Brooch, Mourning, Braided Hair, 3-Link Chain	300.00
Shriner, Ashtray, Frying Pan Shape, Harwal China, 6⅛ In.	15.00
Shriner, Band Hat, Sahara, Pine Bluff, Arkansas, 1890	35.00
Shriner, Bell, Zuhrah, Fez Shape, Ceramic, High Gloss, Minneapolis	65.00
Shriner, Fez, Khiva, Maroon, Tassel Pin, Rhinestones, Gold Tone Crescent, 7¼ In.	75.00
Shriner, Money Clip, Enamel	28.00
Shriner, Mug, Hat Shape, Relpo Mark, Japan	5.00
Shriner, Pin, Enamel, 14K Gold Wreath Border, Shriner's Cap, Round, Victorian, ¾ In.	65.00
Shriner, Pin, Fez, Masonic Past Masters, Ora Jewelers, Pave Rhinestone, 2½ x 2 In.	13.00
Shriner, Pin, Old Lodge Hat, C Closure, Brass, ¾ x 3 In.	35.00
Shriner, Plate, Restaurant War, Akdar Temple Scammell, Blue, Gold, 1920s, 7 In.	30.00
Shriner, Tie Bar Clasp, Hickok, Goldtone, Enamel, 1½ x ½ In.	8.50
Shriner, Tile, Tube Lined, Wheeling, Symbols, Yellow Glaze, 1940s, 4¼ x 4¼ In.	85.00
Shriner, Toothpick, Amethyst Glass, Barrel Shape, Westmoreland Glass, 1905, 2 In.	38.00
Shriner, Toothpick, Syrian Temple	40.00

FRY GLASS was made by the H.C. Fry Glass Company of Rochester, Pennsylvania. The company, founded in 1901, first made cut glass and other types of fine glasswares. In 1922 it patented a heat-resistant glass called Pearl Ovenglass. For two years, 1926–1927, the company made Fry Foval, an opal ware decorated with colored trim. Reproductions of this glass have been made. Depression glass patterns made by Fry may be listed in the Depression Glass category. Some pieces of cut glass may also be included in the Cut Glass category.

Fraternal, Eastern Star, Punch Bowl, Salt Glazed, Cobalt Blue, Leaves, c.1870, 11 x 19 In.
$4200.00

Fraternal, Masonic, Apron, Painted, Lambskin, Silk, Symbols, 19th Century, 13½ x 13½ In.
$978.00

Fraternal, Masonic, Face Jug, Redware, Applied Hair Coil, Incised G, Early 1800s, 12 In.
$18000.00

Fraternal, Odd Fellows, Sign, Porcelain, Round, Metal Band, Red, White, Blue, 29½ In.
$475.00

Fulper, Bookends, Books, 1 Flat,
1 Open On Top,
Mottled Green & Tan Glaze, 5 In.
$374.00

Fulper, Bowl, Blue Onyx Glaze,
2 Open Loop Handles, 3 x 7¼ In.
$100.00

Fulper, Candleholder,
Glossy Blue Glaze, Angular Handle,
Arts & Crafts, 2¼ x 5¾ In.
$75.00

Fulper, Vase, Chinese Blue Flambe
Glaze, Bulbous, Handles, 5⅞ In.
$259.00

Vasekraft

The Fulper Pottery began
making its *Vasekraft* art
ware line in 1909. This
pottery had classical shapes
and new glazes. Best-known
Mirror Glaze, a high-gloss,
crystalline glaze; *Mission
Matte*, a brown-black glaze
with shaded greens, and the
expensive rose shades.

FRY GLASS

Bean Pot, Qt.	45.00
Bowl, Fan, Pinwheel, Inset Hobstars, Elongated Mitres, 3½ x 8 In.	65.00
Bowl, Scallope d Rim, Hobstar, Starburst, c.1934	450.00
Bowl, Whirling Star, c.1950	97.00
Candlestick, Pearl, Jade Green Treading & Trim, 12 In.	250.00
Casserole, Cover, Marked Fry Oven Glass, 3 x 8¼ In.	55.00
Casserole, Cover, Opalescent, 3 x 8½ In.	55.00
Casserole, Cover, Pearl, Opalescent, 8 In.	35.00
Cup & Saucer, Pearl, Delft Blue Handle	875.50
Custard Cup, 4 Oz.	10.00
Custard Cup, 6 Oz., 2¼ x 3¼ In.	10.00 to 12.00
Custard Cup, Crystal, Flower, Embossed, 1919	6.00 to 10.00
Goblet, Cocktail, 14K Gold Rim, 1920s, 5 Piece	143.00
Goblet, Emerald Green, Needle Etched, Footed	45.00
Goblet, Wine, Grape Pattern, 5 x 4 In.	20.00
Loaf Pan, Satin Finish, 3 x 9 x 4½ In.	20.00
Pie Plate, 9 In.	18.00
Plate, Flashed Star & Fan, 10 In.	625.00
Plate, Fruit, Hand Painted, 8½ In., 4 Piece	75.00
Plate, Salad, Clear, Gold Trim, 7½ In.	6.00
Platter, Opalescent	35.00
Platter, Pearl, Wheel Cut Leaf Patten	27.00
Platter, Silver Plate Server, Pearl, Aluminum Oxide, 16 In.	75.00
Reamer, Green	45.00
Reamer, Juicer, Scalloped Rim, 6½ x 8 In.	40.00
Sherbet, Pink, Bubble Girl, Lotus Nudes, c.1920	65.00
Sherbet, Pink, Daisy, 12 Petals, Footed, Paneled, 5¼ In.	19.00
Trivet, Pearl, 8 In.	29.00
Tumbler, 1917, 3¾ In.	19.00
Tumbler, Black Glass, Scalloped Feet, 13 Oz., 5½ In.	39.00
Tumbler, Crystal, Handle, Yellow, Gold Trim, 12 Oz., 4¾ In.	45.00
Tumbler, Iced Tea, 5¼ In.	19.00
Tumbler, Lemonade, Pearl, Delft Blue Handle, 5¼ In.	135.00
Tumbler, Pink, Footed, Paneled, Cone Shape, 4½ In.	19.00
Wine, Bubble Blower, Lotus Nudes, c.1920	65.00

FRY FOVAL

Bowl, Fruit, Delft Blue Foot, 7¼ x 12 In.	695.00
Candlestick, Opalescent, Pearl, Jade Green, 1921-32, 12 In.	250.00
Casserole, Cover, Vine, Flower, 8 In.	35.00
Cup & Saucer, Clambroth Opalescent, Applied Delft Blue Handle	65.00
Cup & Saucer, Pearl, Delft Handle	95.00
Cup & Saucer, White Opalescent, Applied Delft Blue Handle	65.00
Custard Cup, Pearl, 4 Oz., 1920-30	10.00
Custard Cup, Pearl, 6 Oz., 1920-30	12.00
Goblet, Swags, Flowers, Scrolls, Bulbous, Bell Shape Bowl, Lady's Leg Stem, 6½ In.	28.00
Tumbler, Lemonade, Delft Handle, 5¼ In.	150.00
Vase, Jack-In-The-Pulpit, Opalescent, Green Rim, Footed, 10½ In.	230.00

FULPER Pottery Company was incorporated in 1899 in Flemington, New Jersey. They made art pottery from 1909 to 1929. The firm had been making bottles, jugs, and housewares from 1805. Doll heads were made about 1928. The firm became Stangl Pottery in 1929. Stangl Pottery is listed in its own category in this book.

Bean Pot, Cover, Vented, 2-Tone, Handle, 5 In.	75.00
Bookends, Books, 1 Flat, 1 Open On Top, Mottled Green & Tan Glaze, 5 In. ....*illus*	374.00
Bookends, Ramses II, Marked, Oriental Letters, c.1920, 8½ In.	575.00
Bowl, Blue, White, Green, 9 In.	540.00
Bowl, Blue Onyx Glaze, 2 Open Loop Handles, 3 x 7¼ In. ....*illus*	100.00
Bowl, Chinese Blue Flambe Dripped Over Famille Rose Glaze, 2½ x 9 In.	92.00
Bowl, Double Handles, Green Crystalline Exterior, Brown Flambe Interior, 3⅜ x 7 In.	147.00
Bowl, Effigy, Cat's-Eye Flambe Glaze Interior, Mustard Matte Exterior, 7¼ x 11 In.	720.00
Candleholder, Blue, Arts & Crafts, Marked, 5¾ x 2¼ In.	88.00
Candleholder, Glossy Blue Glaze, Angular Handle, Arts & Crafts, 2¼ x 5¾ In. ......*illus*	75.00
Candleholder, Green Crystalline Glaze, Ink Stamp, 1¼ In.	28.00
Candleholder, Mottled Blue Matte Glaze, Low Form, Impressed, Vertical Ink Mark, 2 x 7 In.	58.00

F

Candleholder, Mottled Purple Matte Glaze, Broad Form, Stamped, Prang Mark, 7 In.	87.00
Candlestick, Barley Sugar Twist, Mirror Glaze, Stoneware, 1920, 11⅛ In., Pair	705.00
Candlestick, Ivory To Brown To Pastel Blue, Faceted Sides, Flared, Marked, 10 In., Pair	300.00
Cruet, Rose Matte, Marked, 4⅝ In.	154.00
Lamp, Chinese Blue Flambe Glaze, Hemispherical Shade, Inset Slag Glass, 17 x 9¼ In.	4800.00
Lamp, Leopard Skin Crystalline Glaze, Leaded Glass Shade, Mushroom Shape, 17 x 17 In. ..	36000.00
Lamp, Stained Glass Border, Mottled Amber, Gray, Green Glaze, Round Top, 22½ In.	2300.00
Lemonade Set, Cream With Rose Matte Glaze, 1915, 11-In. Pitcher, 6 Piece	710.00
Mug, 2nd Reunion, Vertical Ink Stamp, 1913, 4 In.	11.00
Trivet, Blue Crystalline, Glaze, 6½ In.	265.00
Vase, Baluster, Cucumber Frothy Matte Glaze, 12 x 4¾ In.	1020.00
Vase, Blue, Double Handle, Marked, 10¼ In.	385.00
Vase, Blue Crystalline Glaze, Round, 3 Handles, Footed, Impressed, 7 In.	175.00
Vase, Blue Over Green, Flambe Glaze, 6½ In.	259.00
Vase, Brown Matte Glaze, Double Handles, Vertical Ink Stamp, c.1915, 4½ In.	382.00
Vase, Bullet, Rose Matte Over Brown, Marked, 6¾ In.	220.00
Vase, Cat's-Eye, Gunmetal Glaze, Squat, Buttressed Handles, Stamped, c.1910, 7 x 8½ In. ...	495.00
Vase, Chinese Blue Crystalline Flambe Glaze, Handles, 9½ x 7 In.	480.00
Vase, Chinese Blue Flambe Glaze, Bulbous, Handles, 5⅞ In. ....*illus*	259.00
Vase, Chinese Blue Frothy Flambe Glaze, 17½ x 7 In.	1440.00
Vase, Crescent Shape, Multitoned Green Crystalline Glaze, Footed, Label, Stamped, 9 x 8 In. ..	375.00
Vase, Cucumber Crystalline Glaze, Flared, 2 Elongated Handles, 8 In.	173.00
Vase, Cucumber Crystalline Glaze, Oval, Raised Mark, 9¼ In.	370.00
Vase, Frothy Moss To Rose Flambe, Squat, Buttressed Handles, Marked, c.1914-20, 6 x 8 In. .	595.00
Vase, Gray Over Dark Blue Matte Glaze, Squat, 4 Buttressed Handles, 4-Footed, 2½ x 5 In. ...	173.00
Vase, Green Glaze, Bottle Neck, Marked, 7⅞ In.	143.00
Vase, Green Onyx Glaze, Squat, 2 Angular Handles, 4½ x 6 In. ....*illus*	130.00
Vase, Green Semigloss & Matte Rose Glaze, Squat, Buttressed Handles, 6 x 8½ In. .....*illus*	70.00
Vase, Ikebana, Mushroom, Elephant's Breath Flambe Glaze, 10 x 4½ In.	1020.00
Vase, Light Blue & Mottled Tan Glaze, Striations, Round, 2 Handles, 6½ x 8½ In. ......*illus*	420.00
Vase, Moss To Rose Flambe Glaze, Squat, Buttressed Handles, c.1914-20, 7½ In.	595.00
Vase, Mottled Blue Glaze, Flared Rim, 10 In. ....*illus*	80.00
Vase, Multitoned Green Glaze, 3 Handles, Marked, 6½ x 4½ In.	200.00
Vase, Pinched Waist, Handles, Marked, 7⅞ In.	292.00
Vase, Robin's-Egg Blue, Gray, Blue Striations, Gold Speckles, 1909-35, 7 In.	550.00
Vase, Runny Brown, Green, Blue Glaze, Metallic Crystals, Handles, 9¼ In.	201.00
Vase, Tear Shape, Mirror Black Over Copper Dust Crystalline Glaze, 12½ x 7 In.	2280.00

FURNITURE of all types is listed in this category. Examples dating from the seventeenth century to the 1970s are included. Prices for furniture vary in different parts of the country. Oak furniture is most expensive in the West; large pieces over eight feet high are sold for the most money in the South, where high ceilings are found in the old homes. Condition is very important when determining prices. These are NOT average prices but rather reports of unique sales. If the description includes the word *style*, the piece resembles the old furniture style but was made at a later time. It is not a period piece. Garden furniture is listed in the Garden Furnishings category. Related items may be found in the Architectural, Brass, and Store categories.

Armchairs Are Listed Under Chair In This category.

Armoire, Aesthetic Revival, Walnut, Roof Frieze, Trefoil Finials, Mirrored Door, 82 In.	2400.00
Armoire, Belle Epoque, Blondwood, Figured, Arched Crest, Beveled Mirror, 100 x 48 In.	1058.00
Armoire, Chippendale, Walnut, 2 Doors, 2 Drawers, Panels, Interior Cross Beam, 87 x 49 x 25 In. ..	46200.00
Armoire, Dutch Provincial, Walnut, Twist Columns, Door, Geometric Panels, 81 x 48 In. ...	4320.00
Armoire, Empire, Mahogany, Gilt Bronze Mount, Paw Feet, Mirror Door, 89 x 44 In.	4602.00
Armoire, French Provincial, Ebony Accented Walnut, Domed Cornice, 98 x 58 In.	1440.00
Armoire, French Provincial, Fruitwood, Elm, 2 Shaped-Panel Doors, Apron, 86 x 56 In.	3290.00
Armoire, French Provincial, Fruitwood, Oak, Ogee Cornice, 2 Doors, Geometric Panels, 83 In.	1880.00
Armoire, French Provincial, Fruitwood, Rounded Cornice, Inlaid Frieze, 85 x 56 In.	3840.00
Armoire, French Provincial, Oak, Fruitwood, 2 Paneled Doors, Drawer In Center, 78 x 41 In.	3840.00
Armoire, French Provincial, Oak, Molded Cornice, 2 Paneled Doors, 87 x 56 In.	4320.00
Armoire, French Provincial, Painted, 19th Century, 92 x 51 In.	1196.00
Armoire, French Provincial, Walnut, 2 Full Length Shaped-Panel Doors, 93 x 56 In.	6300.00
Armoire, Louis Philippe, Rosewood, Mirrored Door, Shelves, Drawer, 26 x 11½ In.	529.00
Armoire, Louis XV, Fruitwood, Molded Cornice, Shaped Panel Doors, 82 x 54 In.	2040.00
Armoire, Louis XV, Provincial, Cherry, Paneled Doors, 93½ x 72 x 24 In.	2938.00
Armoire, Louis XV Style, Fruitwood, Star Frieze, Canted Corners, Paneled Door, 75 x 43 In. ..	3995.00
Armoire, Louis XVI Style, 3 Elliptical Mirrored Doors, Drawers, 71 x 58 x 18 In.	4700.00

Fulper, Vase, Green Onyx Glaze, Squat, 2 Angular Handles, 4½ x 6 In. $130.00

Fulper, Vase, Green Semigloss & Matte Rose Glaze, Squat, Buttressed Handles, 6 x 8½ In. $70.00

Fulper, Vase, Light Blue & Mottled Tan Glaze, Striations, Round, 2 Handles, 6½ x 8½ In. $420.00

Fulper, Vase, Mottled Blue Glaze, Flared Rim, 10 In. $80.00

Furniture, Barstool, Philip Johnson, Chrome, Cushions, Knoll, 30 x 17 In., 4 Piece
$5700.00

Furniture, Bed, Camp, Regency, Mahogany, Canopy, E. Argles, London, 73 x 76 x 42 In.
$4200.00

Furniture, Bed, Four-Poster, Federal, Maple, Leaf-Carved Posts, 85 x 59 x 82 In.
$1035.00

Armoire, Neoclassical, Figured Mahogany, New York, c.1825, 89½ x 66½ In.	4800.00
Armoire, Neoclassical, Mahogany, c.1825, 89½ x 66½ x 24 In.	5700.00
Armoire, Neoclassical, Walnut, Parquetry, Flowers, Geometric Panels, 100 x 58 In.	14688.00
Armoire, Pine, Painted, 2 Doors, Continental, Mid 19th Century, 76 x 56 In.	563.00
Armoire, Pine, Painted, Door, Continental, Early 19th Century, 72 x 48 In.	409.00
Armoire, Pine, Paneled Doors, Quebec, 19th Century, 59¾ In.	3044.00
Armoire, Provincial Empire, Walnut, Arched Top, 2-Paneled Doors, 100 x 58 In.	1920.00
Armoire, Provincial Louis XV Style, Cherry, Domed Crest, 2-Paneled Doors, 96 x 63 In.	3760.00
Armoire, Renaissance Revival, Walnut, Mid 19th Century, 104½ x 59 In.	3055.00
Armoire, Rococo Revival, Rosewood, 2 Mirrored Doors, Finial, Drawer, 85 x 41 x 21 In.	1880.00
Bakers Rack, Wrought, Scrolled Pediment, Slattered Shelves, 87 x 59 In.	235.00
Banquette, Foot Rest, Walnut, Carved, Open Back, Scrolled Arms, Upholstered, 41 x 79 In.	826.00
Barstool, Philip Johnson, Chrome, Cushions, Knoll, 30 x 17 In., 4 Piece ....*illus*	5700.00
Bed, Aesthetic Revival, Bird's-Eye Maple, Faux Bamboo, Spindles, 69 x 56 In.	8225.00
Bed, Burr Maple, Walnut, Carved, Drapery, Beaded Tassel, Continental, 52 x 92 In.	6600.00
Bed, Camp, Regency, Mahogany, Canopy, E. Argles, London, 73 x 76 x 42 In. ....*illus*	4200.00
Bed, Chippendale Style, Mahogany, Four-Poster, Carved, 79½ x 57½ In.	4800.00
Bed, Curly Maple, Double, Posts, Shaped Headboard, 60 x 78 In.	288.00
Bed, Federal, Bird's-Eye Maple, Tall Post, Ebonized, Early 1800s, 92 x 53 In.	2938.00
Bed, Four-Poster, Curly Maple, Turned, Queen Size, 82 x 67 In.	2530.00
Bed, Four-Poster, Federal, Maple, Leaf-Carved Posts, 85 x 59 x 82 In. ....*illus*	1035.00
Bed, Four-Poster, Federal, Tiger Maple, Ash Rails, Turned Urn & Baluster Posts, 77 x 50 In.	2530.00
Bed, Four-Poster, Mahogany, Walnut, Ring & Baluster Posts, 99 x 65 x 81 In. ....*illus*	1610.00
Bed, Four-Poster, Pencil, Rails, Finials, Slats, Queen Size, 86 x 66 x 82 In.	403.00
Bed, Four-Poster, Regency, Mahogany, Veneered, Molded, 80 x 82 x 81 In.	6168.00
Bed, Four-Poster, Rococo, Mahogany, Carved, Cluster Posts, Lotus Capital, 110 x 60 In.	7638.00
Bed, Four-Poster, Sheraton, Maple, Reeded Posts, Shaped Headboard, 69 x 53 x 78 In.	646.00
Bed, Four-Poster, Sheraton, Maple & Pine, Acorn Finials, 1800s, 92 x 60 In.	2380.00
Bed, Four-Poster, Victorian, Walnut, Paneled Headboard, Turned Finials, 90 x 57 In.	323.00
Bed, French Provincial, Fruitwood, Carved, Linen Upholstery, 45 x 32 In.	6900.00
Bed, Half-Tester, Victorian, Walnut, Faux Grained Rosewood, Carved, 104 x 63 In.	4406.00
Bed, Hardwood, Turned Posts, Cannonball Finials, Shaped Headboard, Rope, 56 x 70 In.	403.00
Bed, Infirmary, Shaker, Pine, Maple, Turned Legs, Rope, Hancock, c.1850, 33 x 65 In.	702.00
Bed, Italian, Painted Decorated, Arched Headboard, Trompe L'Oeil, 66 x 83 In.	1495.00
Bed, Limbert, No. 51170, Oak, 5 Vertical Slats, c.1920, 47 x 42 In.	470.00
Bed, Louis XVI Style, Giltwood, Polychrome, Padded, 47 x 53½ x 88 In.	4700.00
Bed, Paint Decorated, Center Round Vignette, Flowers, Leaves, Swag Panels, 61 x 53 In.	1100.00
Bed, Painted, Old Red, Urn Finials, Rope, 46 x 50 In.	259.00
Bed, Painted, Turned Posts, Acorn Finials, Scrolled Headboard, Rope, 55 x 52½ In.	661.00
Bed, Pineapple Post, Mahogany, Acanthus Leaves, Footboard, 49 x 75 In., Pair	1007.00
Bed, Polychrome Marriage Scene, Continental Style, 60 In.	708.00
Bed, Post, Mahogany, Shaped Headboard, Pencil Posts, Canopy, c.1820, 87 x 73 In.	2185.00
Bed, Rococo Revival, Mahogany, Posts, Paneled Headboard, Carved Crest, 73 x 90 In.	4800.00
Bed, Rosewood, Fan Cartouche, Turned Posts, Footboard, Mid 1800s, 75 x 64 In.	4113.00
Bed, Roycroft, Arts & Crafts, Oak, Youth, Signed	6900.00
Bed, Shaker, Pine, Maple, Turned & Square Posts, Mortised, Pegged, Hancock, c.1850, 34 x 68 In.	468.00
Bed, Sleigh, Empire, Mahogany, Paneled, Curved Side Rails, Block Feet, 40½ x 79 In.	1765.00
Bed, Sleigh, Empire, Mahogany, Scrolled, Upholstered, Gilt Swan Supports, 45 x 52 In.	6325.00
Bed, Sleigh, Empire Style, Painted Flowers, Birds, Gilt Scrolls, 42 x 91 x 58 In. ......*illus*	2415.00
Bed, Sleigh, Mahogany, Scrolled Head & Footboard Veneer, Block Feet, 1890	755.00
Bed, Sleigh, Neoclassical, Mahogany, Scrolled Head & Footboard, Block Feet, 36 x 42 In.	705.00
Bed, Spool, Walnut, Turned Headboard, Spindles, Rails, Scalloped Ends, 1800s, 49 x 78 In.	259.00
Bed, Tiger Maple, Poplar, Pitched Pediment Head & Footboards, 51 x 50 In.	345.00
Bed, Trundle, Cherry, Poplar, Cannonball Posts, Scalloped Headboard, 18 x 64 x 45 In.	374.00
Bed, Trundle, Walnut, Arched Head & Footboards, Baluster Posts, 26 x 73 In.	978.00
Bed, Turned Posts, Blue Paint, Knob Finials, Swelled Feet, Early 1800s, 33 x 43 In.	940.00
Bed, Victorian, Walnut, Carved, Pierced Scroll Crest, c.1870, 80 x 62 In.	470.00
Bed, Walnut, Dark Refinish, Urn Finials, Scalloped Headboard, 52 x 62 In.	374.00
Bed, William & Mary, Turned Walnut, England, c.1740, 37 x 51½ In.	5100.00
Bed Frame, Brass, Black Paint, 19th Century, 28½ In.	246.00
Bed Steps, George IV, Mahogany, 3 Leather Treads, Hinged Well, 28 x 31 x 19 In. ......*illus*	8400.00
Bed Steps, Victorian, Mahogany, Potty Seat, White Ceramic Commode, 18 x 19 In.	460.00
Bed Steps, William IV, Mahogany, Lift Top Treads, Pullout Commode, Leather, 26 x 19 In.	1410.00
Bedroom Set, Bird's-Eye Maple, Dresser, Double Bed, 56 x 75 x 24 & 70 x 63 In.	382.00
Bedroom Set, Enameled Metal, 2 Single Beds, Norman Bel Geddes, c.1935, 7 Piece	1645.00
Bedroom Set, Mahogany, Armoire, Bed, Armchair, Ottoman, Table, 2 Tables, 8 Piece	3450.00

Bedroom Set, Oak, Carved Scroll, Flowers, Gilt Metal Mounts, Early 1900s, 2 Piece	1560.00
Bench, 2 Seats, Carved Legs, Gilt Skirt, Padded Armrest, Upholstered, 45 x 27 x 16 In.	403.00
Bench, Beech, Chinese, 18½ x 44 x 13 In.	354.00
Bench, Biedermeier, Ash, U-Shaped Seat, Turned Armrests, Splayed Legs, 26 x 30 In.	780.00
Bench, Black Forest, 2 Bears, Plank Shape Seat, Glass Eyes, 38 x 25 In. . . . . *illus*	11162.00
Bench, Bucket, Bootjack, 53 In.	86.00
Bench, Bucket, Softwood, 2 Tiers, Apple Green Paint, Mortised Supports, 21 x 31 In.	413.00
Bench, Bucket, Softwood, Red Paint, 5 Shelves, Stepped Back Top, 65 x 42 In. . . . . *illus*	2420.00
Bench, Bucket, Softwood, Red Paint, Well, Half-Moon Cutout Legs, 31 x 85 x 20 In.	4950.00
Bench, Bucket, Softwood, Scrolled, Cutout Ends, 2 Scrub Top Shelves, Red Paint, 38 x 44 In.	907.00
Bench, Ebonized Wood, Steel Rod, H. Bertoia, Knoll International, c.1952, 72 In.	563.00
Bench, Elm, Carved Leaves, Shanxi Province, Chinese, 18th Century, 20 x 51 In., Pair	354.00
Bench, English Country, Pine Wash, Drawer, Scalloped Backsplash, 1800s, 38 x 39 x 20 In. .	176.00
Bench, G. Nakashima, Walnut, 18 Hickory Spindles, Arms, Plank Seat, Tapered Legs, 31 x 64 In.	16730.00
Bench, G. Nakashima, Walnut, Butterfly Joint, Free Edge, 21 Hickory Spindles, 30 x 81 x 34 In. . .	40630.00
Bench, G. Nelson, Platform, No. 4692, Herman Miller, c.1948, 14 x 18 x 72 In. . . . . *illus*	840.00
Bench, George I, Walnut, Upholstered, 6 Legs, 19 x 49¾ x 21 In.	2124.00
Bench, Georgian Style, Mahogany, Carved, Needlepoint Seat, Cabriole Legs, 19 x 22 In. . . .	1225.00
Bench, Georgian Style, Needlepoint, Upholstered, Winged Figural Legs, 36 x 17 In.	322.00
Bench, H. Bertoia, Slats, Knoll, 1952, 15½ x 18¼ In. . . . . *illus*	960.00
Bench, H. Bertoia, Wood, Slats, Metal Supports, Cushions, 1952, 15 x 72 x 19 In.	1800.00
Bench, Hall, G. Stickley, Board Back, Seat, Butterfly Joints, 76 x 78 In. . . . . *illus*	5400.00
Bench, Library, Georgian, Mahogany, 8 Legs, Leather, 1900s, 17 x 38 In.	770.00
Bench, Louis XIV Style, Fruitwood, Carved, Scrolled Arms, Scalloped Seat Rail, 22 x 31 In. . .	411.00
Bench, Louis XV, Beech, Padded, Serpentine Seat, Cabriole Legs, 53 In.	6600.00
Bench, Louis XV, Polychrome, Parcel Gilt, Padded Arms, c.1900, 24 x 27 In.	2400.00
Bench, Louis XVI Style, Giltwood, Carved, Outscrolled Side Panels, 28 x 20 In.	3680.00
Bench, Mahogany, Carved, Scroll Arms, Upholstered Seat, 20th Century, 26 In.	499.00
Bench, Mortised, Red Wash, Arched Cutouts, Shaped Legs, 18 x 40 In.	605.00
Bench, Neoclassical, Crotch Walnut, Scalloped Crest Raid, S-Scrolls, Palmettes, 30 x 47 In. . .	780.00
Bench, Neoclassical, Mahogany, Ebonized Frieze, Curule Legs, Stretcher, 16 x 20 In.	880.00
Bench, Neoclassical, Mahogany, Serpentine Back, Carved Crest, Bracket Feet, 32 x 45 In. . . .	1080.00
Bench, Oak, Carved Leaf Scrolls, Flowers, Panels, Lift Top Center, 44 x 17½ x 36½ In.	690.00
Bench, Oak, Carved Skirt, Turned Legs, H-Stretchers, Floral Upholstery, 1800s, 19 x 89 In. . .	1840.00
Bench, Oak, Splayed, Barley Twist Legs, Mortised Cross Stretcher, 1600s, 35 x 9 In.	960.00
Bench, Pier, Regency Style, Gilt Brass, Carved, Parcel Gilt, Ebonized, 1800s, 27 x 44 In.	840.00
Bench, Pine, Convex Shape, Gray, Cutout Base, Medial Stretcher, 21 x 73 x 23 In.	2468.00
Bench, Pine, Trestle, Painted, Red, Yellow, Blue Hearts, Scrolls, Red Ground, 22 x 36 In. . . .	144.00
Bench, Pine, Turned Dowel Crest, 8 Splats, Scrolled Arms, Continental, 36 x 88 x 15 In.	472.00
Bench, Renaissance Style, Faux Painted, Pilasters, 19th Century, 66 x 76 x 16½ In.	2990.00
Bench, Rococo Style, Walnut, Carved, Scrolling Arms, Legs, Stretcher, 1800s, 24 x 22 In. . . .	88.00
Bench, Shaker, Pine, Bucket, 2 Shelves, Painted, 23½ x 50 x 9½ In.	881.00
Bench, Shaker, Pine, Original Red Paint, Bootjack Ends, Inset Braces, 16 x 43 x 9¾ In.	1872.00
Bench, Softwood, Heart, Polychrome Vine, Black Stripes, Canted Legs, 16¾ x 36 In.	330.00
Bench, Softwood, Mortised, Old White Paint, Shaped Peak Cutout Legs, 65½ In.	358.00
Bench, Spanish Style, Walnut, Scalloped Carved Splat, Arms, Plank Seat, 37 x 53 In.	1347.00
Bench, Window, English Oak, Molded Edge, 6 Turned Legs, Box Stretcher, 18 x 84 x 14 In. . .	352.00
Bench, Windsor, Spindle Back, Black Paint, Eagle & Designs On Tablet, 1800s, 32 x 84 In. . .	518.00
Bench, Windsor, Turned Half Spindles, Scroll Arms, Plank Seat, 8 Legs, Pa., 35 x 71 In. . *illus*	480.00
Bench, Wrought Iron, Oak Split Seat, Back, Scrolled Ears, Arms, 37 x 51 In.	316.00
Bookcase, 3 Doors, Gallery Top, 12 Panes, Cast Hardware, 44¼ x 55 x 12 In.	4200.00
Bookcase, 4 Lacquer Elm Shelves, Chinese, 1900s, 75 x 35 In., Pair	1534.00
Bookcase, 12 Pane Doors, Copper Pulls, Gallery Top, Through Tenons, 57 x 52 In.	4200.00
Bookcase, Arts & Crafts, Oak, 3 Tiers, Glass Doors, Macey Furniture Co., c.1920, 48 In.	764.00
Bookcase, Arts & Crafts, Oak, 4 Posts, 2 Glass Doors, c.1916, 58 x 32 In.	764.00
Bookcase, Arts & Crafts, Oak, 4 Shelves, Glass Panel Door, c.1905, 57 x 14 x 48 In.	1024.00
Bookcase, Arts & Crafts, Oak, Flared Cornice, Glazed Doors, Copper, Scotland, 85 x 53 In. . . .	3290.00
Bookcase, Arts & Crafts, Oak, Roycroft, 4 Pane Door, 55 x 40 In.	7150.00
Bookcase, Barrister, Oak, 4 Sections, Sliding Glass Panels, Early 1900s, 34 x 12 In.	646.00
Bookcase, Biedermeier, Walnut, 2 Astragal Panel Doors, Block Feet, 71 x 46 In.	1645.00
Bookcase, Carlton, Sottsass, Laminate, 2 Drawers, Memphis, c.1981, 76 x 75 In. . . . . . . *illus*	9000.00
Bookcase, Chest, Edwardian, Satinwood, Painted, Shelves, Drawers, Door, 73 x 40 x 15 In. . .	3819.00
Bookcase, Chest Base, Neoclassical Style, Mahogany, 2 Doors, 4 Drawers, 84 x 49 In. . . *illus*	374.00
Bookcase, Desk, Shaker, 2 Doors, 3 Drawers Over 4, New Lebanon, N.Y., c.1860, 79 x 41 In. .	2633.00
Bookcase, Door, 3 Shelves, Corbels, Shaped Top, Arched Apron, 57¼ x 29½ x 14 In.	5400.00
Bookcase, Federal Style, Inlaid Mahogany, Astragal Glazed Door, c.1900, 52 x 26 In.	518.00

Furniture, Bed, Four-Poster, Mahogany, Walnut, Ring & Baluster Posts, 99 x 65 x 81 In.
$1610.00

Furniture, Bed, Sleigh, Empire Style, Painted Flowers, Birds, Gilt Scrolls, 42 x 91 x 58 In.
$2415.00

Furniture, Bed Steps, George IV, Mahogany, 3 Leather Treads, Hinged Well, 28 x 31 x 19 In.
$8400.00

Furniture, Bench, Black Forest, 2 Bears, Plank Shape Seat, Glass Eyes, 38 x 25 In.
$11162.00

Furniture, Bench, Bucket, Softwood, Red Paint, 5 Shelves, Stepped Back Top, 65 x 42 In.
$2420.00

Furniture, Bench, G. Nelson, Platform, No. 4692, Herman Miller, c.1948, 14 x 18 x 72 In.
$840.00

Furniture, Bench, H. Bertoia, Slats, Knoll, 1952, 15½ x 18¼ In.
$960.00

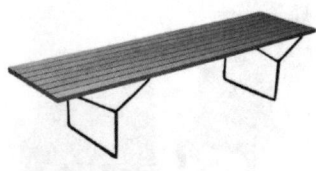

Furniture, Bench, Hall, G. Stickley, Board Back, Seat, Butterfly Joints, 76 x 78 In.
$5400.00

Bookcase, French Provincial, Painted, Molded Crown, Paneled Doors, 70 x 49 In.	2360.00
Bookcase, G. Stickley, 2 Doors, 8 Panels, Iron V-Pulls, 56 x 48 x 13 In.	6600.00
Bookcase, G. Stickley, 3 Doors, Mitered Mullion, 12 Panes Per Door, 56 x 73 In.	13200.00
Bookcase, G. Stickley, Open, 4 Fixed Shelves, Mortised Tenons, Red Decal, 45 x 39 In.	10200.00
Bookcase, George II Style, Mahogany, Revolving, 4 Sides, Pierced Gallery, 35 x 33 In.	940.00
Bookcase, George III, Inlaid Mahogany, Broken Arch Crown, Glazed Doors, 99 x 48 In.	8625.00
Bookcase, George III, Mahogany, Dentil Cornice, Glazed Door, 25 x 14 In., Pair	3525.00
Bookcase, George III, Mahogany, Doors, Shelves, Writing Surface, 89 x 50 x 20 In.	7050.00
Bookcase, George III Style, Mahogany, 2 Glazed Doors, 4 Shelves, Plinth, 79 x 48 x 15 In.	2350.00
Bookcase, George III Style, Mahogany, 2 Glazed Doors, Bracket Feet, 70 x 48 x 13 In.	1880.00
Bookcase, George III Style, Mahogany, Doors, Ball, Claw Feet, 86 x 55 x 14½ In.	6768.00
Bookcase, Golden Oak, Mirrored Backsplash, Glazed Cabinets, c.1900, 62 x 70 In.	588.00
Bookcase, Gothic, Mahogany, Carved, Dentil Molding, Fretwork, c.1840, 71 x 55 In.	4406.00
Bookcase, Hepplewhite, Mahogany, 2 Doors, 72 x 46 x 14 In.	2530.00
Bookcase, Hepplewhite Style, Mahogany, Glazed Doors, French Back, 87 x 50 In.	2937.00
Bookcase, Heywood-Wakefield, M321, Wheat Finish, 3 Shelves, 33 x 36 x 11 In.	323.00
Bookcase, Heywood-Wakefield, M326, Wheat Finish, 2 Doors, 33 x 36 x 11 In.	176.00
Bookcase, L. & J.G. Stickley, 1 Door, 16 Panes, Gallery Top, Copper Pull, 55 x 33 x 12 In.	4500.00
Bookcase, L. & J.G. Stickley, 2 Doors, Gallery, 12 Panes, Copper Pulls, 55 x 49 x 12 In.	7200.00
Bookcase, Late Neoclassical, Mahogany, Molded Cornice, Doors, Grill Work, 113 x 75 In.	370.00
Bookcase, Louis XVI Style, Kingwood, Sevres Style, 2 Parts, Gilt Metal, 69 x 46 x 16 In.	5875.00
Bookcase, Napoleon III, Burr Walnut, Ebonized, Gilt Metal Mounted, 44 x 36 x 18 In.	2233.00
Bookcase, Neoclassical, Mahogany, Marble Top, Glazed Doors, X-Braces, 90 x 48 In., Pair	3680.00
Bookcase, Oak, Fixed Shelves, 2 Doors, Wood Strap Hinges, 62 x 34 In. *illus*	230.00
Bookcase, Oak, Paneled Doors, Slant Lid, Drawers, Pigeonholes, Dutch, 98 x 39 x 21 In.	1645.00
Bookcase, Oak, Revolving, 4 Tiers Of Shelves, X-Shape Base, Casters, 61 x 24 In.	2415.00
Bookcase, Queen Anne Style, Black Lacquer, Mother-Of-Pearl, 38½ x 20 x 88 In.	805.00
Bookcase, Regency, Mahogany, 3 Sections, Open Shelves, 88 x 82 x 22½ In.	2350.00
Bookcase, Regency Style, Satinwood, Fruitwood, Shelves, Rotating Base, 36½ x 21 In.	1645.00
Bookcase, Renaissance Revival, Mahogany, Carved, 68 x 54 In., Pair	1003.00
Bookcase, Revolving, Slat Sides, Book Holder Shelf, Tripod Base, 38 x 18 In. *illus*	330.00
Bookcase, Secretary, George III, Mahogany, Glazed Doors, Tracery, c.1800, 94 x 49 In.	6756.00
Bookcase, Stickley Bros., 2 Doors, 16 Panes, Copper Hardware, 52¼ x 48 x 12½ In.	2520.00
Bookcase, Walnut, Hickory, Tiger Maple, 2 Piece, 85 x 41 In.	4125.00
Bookrack, G. Stickley, Mahogany, Revolving, 9½ x 13 x 13 In.	2520.00
Bookrack, Regency, Brass Inlaid Mahogany, Revolving, Tabletop, 13¾ x 10 In.	510.00
Bookstand, French Provincial, Mixed Wood, 2-Sided, Pedestal Base, 74 x 26½ In.	1180.00
Bookstand, G. Stickley, Tapered Legs, 2 Shelves, Spindled Ends, Paper Label, 30 x 24 In.	5100.00
Bookstand, William IV, Mahogany, Inlay, Brass Mounted, 46½ In.	998.00
Box, Shirtwaist, Cherry, Birch, Hinged, American, 19th Century, 17 x 31 x 19 In.	88.00
Box, Writing, Stand, Mahogany, Brass Bound, Stretcher, Mid 1800s, 14 In.	603.00
Box-On-Stand, Hinges, Mahogany, Metal Mounted Cover, 18 x 13 x 12 In.	354.00
Bracket, Rococo Style, Walnut, Carved, Scroll Motif, Continental, 12½ x 10 In., Pair	470.00
Breakfront, Black Lacquer, Chinoiserie, 3 Glazed Doors Over 4 Doors, 79 x 55 In. *illus*	590.00
Breakfront, Queen Anne Style, Mahogany, 4 Doors, Mullions, Shelves, 76 x 21 x 86 In.	1150.00
Buffet, Charles X, Elm, Plank Top, Drawer, 2 Shaped Panel Doors, Bracket Feet, 40 x 70 In.	3600.00
Buffet, Classic, Walnut, Carved, Heart & Shell Motif, Drawers, Shelf, Doors, 57 x 61 In.	7000.00
Buffet, French Provincial, 2 Sections, Late 18th Century, 104 x 48 In.	2342.00
Buffet, French Provincial, Fruitwood, 2 Drawers Over Cupboard Doors, 37 x 51 In.	2280.00
Buffet, French Provincial, Oak, 2 Drawers, Inlaid Sunburst, 2-Paneled Doors, 44 x 53 In.	1997.00
Buffet, Louis Philippe, Painted Fruit, Drawer, 2 Doors, c.1830, 40 x 45 In.	4900.00
Buffet, Louis XV, Fruitwood, 3 Drawers Over Cupboard Doors, 40 x 51 In.	1680.00
Buffet, Louis XV, Walnut, Carved, Scalloped Front, Leaf Carved Frieze, 38 x 49 In.	4800.00
Buffet, Louis XV Style, Provincial, Pine, Marble Top, Drawers, 2 Doors, 40½ x 94 x 22 In.	1997.00
Buffet, Louis XVI Style, Marble Top, Painted, Ribbon, Leaf, Flowers, 1800s, 40 x 51 In.	8000.00
Buffet, Mahogany, Louis XVI Style, Marble Top, Paneled Doors, 44 x 59 x 19 In.	1888.00
Buffet, Oak, Lozenge Carved Doors, Shelved Alcove, 65⅜ x 75½ x 19 In.	224.00
Buffet, Queen Anne Style, Walnut, 4 Drawers, c.1925, 42 x 50 x 22 In.	118.00
Bureau, Baroque, Oak, Carved, Paneled Slant Front, Interlacing Designs, 40 x 51 In.	5280.00
Bureau, Dressing, Rococo Revival, Faux Rosewood, Marble Top, 86 x 43 In.	1440.00
Bureau, Dressing, Rococo Revival, Rosewood, Marble Top, Carving, Flowers, 100 x 45 In.	1020.00
Bureau, Federal, Mahogany, Inlay, Bowfront, 4 Drawers, c.1810, 37½ x 40 In.	1998.00
Bureau, Federal, Mahogany, Overhanging Top, Elliptic Front, 4 Drawers, 36 x 40 In.	3408.00
Bureau, George III, Mahogany, Slant Top, Bombe, 3 Drawers, Paw Feet, 45 x 55 In.	3055.00
Bureau, Georgian Style, Drop Front, Japanned, Chinoiserie, Fitted, 24 x 18 x 10 In. *illus*	1200.00
Bureau, Louis XVI Style, Inlaid Kingwood, Cylinder, Lady's, 20th Century, 29½ In.	768.00

Bureau, Louis XVI Style, Mahogany, Brass Inlay, Drawers, Writing Surface, 16 x 14 x 7 In. . .	2700.00
Bureau, Napoleon III, Kingwood, Ormolu Mounted, Drawers, c.1850, 45 x 54 x 23 In.	1527.00
Bureau, Regency, Mahogany, Kneehole, Leather Top, Inlaid Drawers, 1800s, 28 x 46 In.	1495.00
Bureau, Rococo Revival, Rosewood, Mirror Plate, 2 Parts, Scrolls, 93 x 48 x 21½ In.	5640.00
Bureau, Tambour, George III, Mahogany, Fitted Interior, Tooled Top, c.1790, 45 x 46 In.	5875.00
Bureau, Walnut, Herringbone Banded, Slant Lid, 5 Over 2 Drawers, 38 x 36 In.	1880.00
Bureau-Bookcase, Georgian, Walnut, Serpentine Crest, Mirrored Doors, Slots, 96 x 22 In. . .	15275.00
Bureau-Bookcase, Queen Anne, Walnut, Inlay, Mirrored Doors, 80 x 37 x 21 In.	7050.00
Cabinet, 2 Over 3 Drawers, Grain Painted, Gray, White, 19 x 19 In.	288.00
Cabinet, Aesthetic Revival, Inlay, Parcel Gilt, Rosewood, Mahogany, 49 x 61 In.	54000.00
Cabinet, Architect's Blueprint, Stacked, Storage, 1950-60, 67 x 45½ x 34½ In.	6346.00
Cabinet, Art Deco, Mahogany, Burl, Tiger Maple, 2 Sections, Germany, 58 x 79 In. . . . . . *illus*	345.00
Cabinet, Art Nouveau, Oak, Carved, Stained Glass Upper Doors, c.1900, Pair	3650.00
Cabinet, Barber, Shaving Mug, Cherry, Poplar, 72 Mugs, 1880s, 97 x 44 In.	4900.00
Cabinet, Biedermeier, Mahogany, Drawer, 2 Doors, Shaped Top, Mid 1800s, 30 In.	905.00
Cabinet, Black & Gold Lacquer, Jewel, Bone Pull, Mandarins In Garden, 15 x 13 In.	300.00
Cabinet, Bread, French Provincial, Walnut, 16 Turned Spindles, Door, 34 x 39 x 20 In.	863.00
Cabinet, Chimney, Paneled Door, Molded Cornice, Mixed Wood, 1800s, 72 x 25 In.	1265.00
Cabinet, China, G. Stickley, 2 Doors, 16 Panes, Arched Apron, 64 x 40 x 15 In.	5100.00
Cabinet, China, Heywood-Wakefield, M175, Wheat Finish, Glass Doors, 65 x 34 x 18 In. . . .	323.00
Cabinet, China, Limbert, 2 Doors, 2 Panes Over Pane, Plate Rail, Shelves, 62 x 46 In.	3120.00
Cabinet, China, Limbert, Door, 3 Fixed Shelves, 56½ x 46¾ In.	3000.00
Cabinet, China, Limbert, Door, 3 Shelves, 2 Exterior Shelves, Corbels, 57 x 44 In.	6000.00
Cabinet, Chinoiserie, Faux Bamboo, Painted, Red Ground, Gilt, 35½ x 43 In., Pair	2185.00
Cabinet, Continental, 2 Doors, Sponge Painted, Brass Fittings, 86 x 54 x 17¼ In.	5993.00
Cabinet, Corner, Cherry, Molded Cornice, 3 Doors, 3 Drawers, Scrolled Feet, c.1825	3107.00
Cabinet, Corner, Chippendale, Mahogany, Greek Key Carved Frieze, 2 Doors, 95 x 36 In. . . .	2596.00
Cabinet, Corner, Elm, Red Lacquered, Ducks, Doors, Shelf, Chinese, 71 x 35 x 26 In., Pair . . .	1652.00
Cabinet, Corner, George III, Mahogany, 12-Pane Doors, 70 x 34 x 20 In.	881.00
Cabinet, Corner, George III, Mahogany, Molded Cornice, Glazed Doors, 85 x 40 In.	3120.00
Cabinet, Corner, Hanging, George III Style, Mahogany, Glazed Door, 36 x 26 In.	499.00
Cabinet, Corner, Pine, Asymmetrical Shape, 3 Open Shelves, Drawers, 80 x 62 In.	1035.00
Cabinet, Corner, Pine, Leaf-Pierced Frieze, 3 Shelves, Paneled Door, Plinth Base, 74 x 29 In. .	499.00
Cabinet, Corner, Walnut, Flat Top, Glass Door, 3 Shelves, Paneled Door, 38 x 19½ In.	585.00
Cabinet, Corner, White Pine, Hanging, Iron Butterfly Hinges, c.1840, 28 In.	1200.00
Cabinet, Countertop, 8 Graduated Drawers, Walnut Front, Pine, 1800s, 27 x 12 In.	575.00
Cabinet, Demilune, Mahogany, Marquetry, Marble Top, Door, 35 x 23 In., Pair	5405.00
Cabinet, Directoire, Burled Ash, Mahogany, 2 Doors, Gilt Diamonds, Paw Feet, 54 x 44 In. . .	6900.00
Cabinet, Display, Art Deco, Walnut, Burl Walnut, Corner, 3 Glass Panels, 82 x 46 In.	411.00
Cabinet, Display, Edwardian, Mahogany, Inlay, Early 20th Century, 61 x 48 In.	1040.00
Cabinet, Display, Georgian, Gadrooned Bowfront, Glazed Doors, Shelves, 46 x 13 In.	510.00
Cabinet, Display, Glass Sides, Shelves, Gilt, Gold Leaf, 15 x 26½ In.	2530.00
Cabinet, Display, Neoclassical Style, Gilt Metal Mounts, Line Inlay, 51 x 22 In.	1920.00
Cabinet, Display, Victorian, Mahogany, Late 19th Century, 44 x 39 In.	594.00
Cabinet, Display, Walnut, Dark Stain, Curved Glass Sides, Door, Shelves, 23½ x 6½ In.	58.00
Cabinet, Elizabethan Revival, Oak, 3-Paneled Drawers, Barley Twist Legs, 38 x 23 In.	900.00
Cabinet, Elm, 2 Doors, 2 Shelves, Rectangular, Chinese, 69½ x 34 x 18 In.	531.00
Cabinet, Elm, Black Lacquered, Doors, Chinese, 71 x 44 x 19¾ In.	1888.00
Cabinet, Elm, Black Lacquered, Doors, Shelf, Chinese, 35 x 50½ x 17½ In.	620.00
Cabinet, Elm, Lacquered, 2 Doors, 2 Drawers, Shelf, Chinese, 68 x 43 In.	1298.00
Cabinet, Elm, Rectangular Top, 2 Drawers, Chinese, 32 x 43 In.	236.00
Cabinet, Elm, Red Lacquer, Doors, Painted Flowers, Chinese, 48 x 37 x 20 In.	413.00
Cabinet, Emile Galle, Walnut, Marquetry, c.1900, 39 x 55 x 15 In.	14400.00
Cabinet, File, 4 Stacked Sections, Paneled Sides, 51 x 14 x 24 In. . . . . *illus*	147.00
Cabinet, Finn Juhl, Walnut, Sycamore, Doors, Drawers, Shelves, 30 x 36 x 18 In.	1076.00
Cabinet, French Provincial, Oak, Marble Top, 19th Century, 39 x 57 In.	1033.00
Cabinet, G. Nelson, 4 Drawers, Cabinet Door, Shelves, Herman Miller, c.1962, 30 x 56 In. . . .	823.00
Cabinet, G. Nelson, Laminate, Doors, Herman Miller, 29½ x 33½ x 17 In.	508.00
Cabinet, G. Nelson, Laminate, Glass, Drawers, Herman Miller, 29½ x 33½ x 17 In.	478.00
Cabinet, G. Stickley, 8-Pane Glass Doors, 3 Shelves, Copper V-Pulls, Paper Label, 64 x 42 In. .	7800.00
Cabinet, G. Stickley, Safecraft, Drawer, Cabinet Door, Strap Hinges, Red Decal, 34 x 21 In. . . .	4800.00
Cabinet, George I, Walnut, Oyster, 2 Short, 2 Long Drawers, 1700s, 83½ x 60 In.	9400.00
Cabinet, George III, Mahogany, Reticulated Broken Arch Crest, 100 x 40 In.	1293.00
Cabinet, Georgian, Mahogany, Gadrooned Bowfront, Backsplash, 2 Doors, 48 x 15 In.	510.00
Cabinet, Georgian Style, Marble Top, Drawer, Beveled Glass Doors, 1900s, 52 x 15 In.	293.00
Cabinet, Glove, 18 Drawers, The Practical Glove Holder, 1897, 13 x 16 In.	800.00

Furniture, Bench, Windsor,
Turned Half Spindles, Scroll Arms,
Plank Seat, 8 Legs, Pa., 35 x 71 In.
$480.00

Furniture, Bookcase, Carlton, Sottsass,
Laminate, 2 Drawers, Memphis, c.1981,
76 x 75 In.
$9000.00

Furniture, Bookcase, Chest Base,
Neoclassical Style, Mahogany, 2 Doors,
4 Drawers, 84 x 49 In.
$374.00

F

Furniture, Bookcase, Oak, Fixed
Shelves, 2 Doors, Wood Strap Hinges,
62 x 34 In.
$230.00

Furniture, Bookcase, Revolving, Slat
Sides, Book Holder Shelf, Tripod Base,
38 x 18 In.
$330.00

Furniture, Breakfront, Black Lacquer,
Chinoiserie, 3 Glazed Doors Over
4 Doors, 79 x 55 In.
$590.00

Cabinet, H. Glass, Swingline, Lacquered Masonite, Birch, c.1952, 42 x 32 In. .... *illus*	3838.00
Cabinet, Hanging, Finn Juhl, Walnut, Sycamore, Doors, Drawers, Shelves, 20 x 32 x 15 In. ..	299.00
Cabinet, Japanese, Rosewood, 3 Shelves, 2 Doors, Carved, Dragon, Prunus, 81 x 43 In.	1534.00
Cabinet, Library, Cherry, Bird's-Eye Maple, Inlay, 3 Glass Doors, Shelves, 87 x 14 In.	2468.00
Cabinet, Library, Regency, Gilt Rosewood, Black Faux Marble, 2 Glazed Doors, 34 x 58 In. ..	4113.00
Cabinet, Library, Regency, Mahogany, 2 Sections, Grill Inset Doors, Shelves, 94 x 46 x 18 In.	3290.00
Cabinet, Louis XV, Satinwood, Serpentine Front, France, 52 In.	956.00
Cabinet, Louis XVI, Mahogany, Bronze Mounted, Fluted Stiles, 7 Drawers, 65 x 44 In.	9400.00
Cabinet, Louis XVI Style, Oak, Carved, France, Late 19th Century, 63 In.	1433.00
Cabinet, Mahogany, Cherry, c.1820, 46½ x 44½ In.	1058.00
Cabinet, Mahogany, Marble Top, France, Early 19th Century, 44½ In.	2559.00
Cabinet, Mahogany, Polychrome, Fitted Case, Round Panel, Marble, 40 x 79 In.	6900.00
Cabinet, Music, Aesthetic Revival, Backsplash Shelf, Mirrored Doors, 59 x 25 In.	460.00
Cabinet, Music, Burled Walnut, Gallery Top, Glazed Door, Shelves, 1800s, 24 x 17 In.	936.00
Cabinet, Music, Renaissance Revival, Walnut, Burled, Ebonized, Gilt, c.1870, 42 x 46 In.	4700.00
Cabinet, Napoleon III, Brass Inlay, Ormolu, Ebonized, Marble Top, 51 x 47 x 19 In., Pair ...	8812.00
Cabinet, Napoleon III, Ebonized, Bronze Mounted, Cherry, c.1860, 48 x 66 In.	2280.00
Cabinet, Napoleon III Style, Kingwood, Marble Top, Bowed Front, 36 x 61 x 18 In.	2679.00
Cabinet, Neoclassical, Cabinet, Mahogany, Pediment Top, Columns, 66 x 39 In.	1440.00
Cabinet, Neoclassical, Mahogany, Front Frame & Panel Door, Columns, 1900s, 16 x 12 In. ..	690.00
Cabinet, Neoclassical, Mahogany, Marble Top, Ormolu, Boston, c.1830, 48 x 44 x 19 In. *illus*	2400.00
Cabinet, Neoclassical, Painted, Panel Door, Scandinavian, 36 x 18 x 17 In., Pair	3422.00
Cabinet, Oak, Curved Glass Panels, Beveled Glass Mirror Back, c.1900, 62 x 41 In. .....*illus*	206.00
Cabinet, Oak, Molded Cornice, Paneled Doors, Shelves, England, 71 x 51 x 22½ In.	1293.00
Cabinet, Oak, Rectangular Top, Glazed Door, Shelves, Plinth Base, 25 x 10 x 49 In.	117.00
Cabinet, Oak Bowfront, Mirrored Back, Shelves, Cabriole Legs, Paw Feet, 40 x 17 In.	360.00
Cabinet, Painted, Paneled Door, Molded Edge, Interior Shelf, Late 1900s, 36 x 22 In.	502.00
Cabinet, Peachwood, 2 Doors, Shelves, Zhe Jiang Province, Chinese, 1600s, 69 x 35 In.	767.00
Cabinet, Peachwood, Brown Lacquered, 4 Doors, 2 Drawers, Chinese, 65 x 27 x 17 In.	1416.00
Cabinet, Pine, 5 Graduated Drawers, Wooden Knobs, Red Paint, 21 x 13¼ x 9½ In.	1645.00
Cabinet, Pine, 7 Drawers, Brass Pulls, Footed, 20th Century, 50½ x 18 x 12 In.	170.00
Cabinet, Pine, Black Paint, 2 2-Pane Doors, 3 Drawers, Turned Feet, 39 x 42 x 15 In.	288.00
Cabinet, Polychrome, Painted, Leaf Sprays, Blue Ground, Continental, 71 x 45 x 21 In.	1410.00
Cabinet, Press, Dutch Rococo, Walnut, Figured, Double Doors, 1700s, 95 x 69 In.	5875.00
Cabinet, Red Lacquer, Paneled Doors, Gilt Figural, Shelf, Drawers, Chinese, 69 x 55 In.	1000.00
Cabinet, Regency, Rosewood, Walnut, Marble Top, 37¼ x 64 x 20½ In.	5400.00
Cabinet, Regency Style, Library Bookcase, Triangular Pediment, 85 x 80 In.	708.00
Cabinet, Regency Style, Mahogany, Pedestal, Paneled Frieze, Geometric, 34 x 17 In.	2174.00
Cabinet, Regency Style, Parcel Gilt, Ebonized, 2 Doors, Late 1800s, 64 x 47 x 21 In.	1645.00
Cabinet, Renaissance Revival, Ebonized & Burled Walnut, Porcelain Plaque, 49 x 50 In.	9987.00
Cabinet, Renaissance Revival, Inlaid Walnut, Burl Walnut, Glazed Doors, 111 x 70 In.	8816.00
Cabinet, Renaissance Style, Hardwood, Dentil Molded Edge, Drawers, 41 x 64 In.	1645.00
Cabinet, Restauration, Fruitwood, Ebonized Inlay, 2-Paneled Doors, Marble Top, 37 x 51 In.	3055.00
Cabinet, Robes, Elm, Carved Doors, Mandarin Panels, Railed Sides, Chinese, 45 x 42 In.	1020.00
Cabinet, Serving, L. Majorelle, Mahogany, Marquetry, c.1900, 57 x 52 x 20 In.	26400.00
Cabinet, Smoking, G. Stickley, Drawer, Cabinet Door, Shelves, Copper, 29 x 20 In.	2520.00
Cabinet, Spice, 8 Dovetailed Drawers, Wood, 19th Century, 17 In.	206.00
Cabinet, Spice, 10 Drawers In 2 Columns, White Porcelain Knobs, 15 x 14 x 7 In.	748.00
Cabinet, Steel, Veined Marble Top, 2 Doors, Interior Shelves, 37½ x 29 x 16 In.	3600.00
Cabinet, Utility, Formica, Metal, Walnut, Tubular Chrome, 31½ x 20½ x 17½ In.	60.00
Cabinet, Vitrine, Louis Philippe, Mahogany, Shelves, Glazed Doors, 1835, 55 x 42 In.	1763.00
Cabinet, Wall, 3 Drawers, Recessed Pulls, Denmark, 13¾ x 31½ x 15¾ In., Pair	239.00
Cabinet, Wall, Georgian Style, Hanging, Mahogany, 3 Tiers, Inlaid Doors, 35 x 15 x 7 In. ...	502.00
Cabinet, Walnut, 2 Doors, Shelf, Chinese, 46½ x 40 x 18½ In.	502.00
Cabinet, Walnut, Carved, Italy, 19th Century, 58 In.	471.00
Cabinet, Walnut, Doors, Shelf, Drawers, Ming Dynasty, Chinese, 73½ x 26 x 25 In.	1298.00
Cabinet, Walnut, Hanging, Canted Top, Dentil Molding, Raised Panel Door, 26 x 15 In.	413.00
Cabinet, Walnut, Red, 28 Drawers, 2 Doors, Chinese, 18th Century, 45 x 33 x 19 In.	1003.00
Cabinet, Wood, Black, Polychrome Lacquered, Painted Decoration, Chinese, 72 x 47 In.	826.00
Cabinet, Zelkova, Double Door, Brass Hardware, 7 Interior Drawers, 21 x 26½ In.	381.00
Cabinet-On-Stand, George III, Yellow Lacquer, Oriental Landscapes, 2 Doors, 58 x 32 In. ..	2585.00
Cabinet-On-Stand, Georgian Style, Mahogany, 2 Door, 28½ x 15 x 10½ In.	354.00
Cabinet-On-Stand, Green Japanned, 2 Sections, Doors, Chinoiserie Lacquer, 72 x 38 In. ...	2950.00
Caddy, Pie, Victorian, Wicker, Latticework Woven Shelves, Braiding, 1900s, 39 x 14 In.	495.00
Cake Stand, 3 Tiers, Mahogany, Inlay, 20th Century, 36 In.	229.00
Candlestand, Carved, Gilt, Winged Cherubs, Italy, 31 x 7 In., Pair	1100.00

F

Furniture, Bureau, Georgian Style, Drop Front, Japanned, Chinoiserie, Fitted, 24 x 18 x 10 In. $1200.00

Furniture, Cabinet, H. Glass, Swingline, Lacquered Masonite, Birch, c.1952, 42 x 32 In. $3838.00

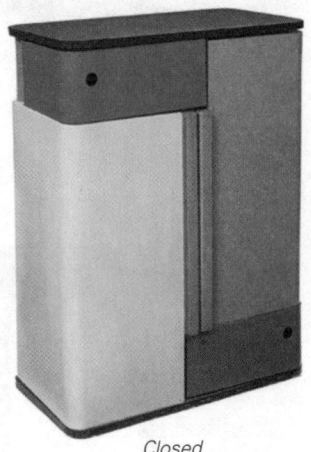

Closed

Open

Furniture, Cabinet, Art Deco, Mahogany, Burl, Tiger Maple, 2 Sections, Germany, 58 x 79 In. $345.00

Furniture, Cabinet, Oak, Curved Glass Panels, Beveled Glass Mirror Back, c.1900, 62 x 41 In. $206.00

Furniture, Cabinet, File, 4 Stacked Sections, Paneled Sides, 51 x 14 x 24 In. $147.00

Furniture, Cabinet, Neoclassical, Mahogany, Marble Top, Ormolu, Boston, c.1830, 48 x 44 x 19 In. $2400.00

Furniture, Candlestand, Federal, Mahogany, Satinwood, Inlay, Tilt Top, Spider Legs, 29 x 24 x 16 In. $166750.00

Furniture, Candlestand, Mahogany, Tilt Top, Shaped Edge, Urn Shaft, Snake Legs, Pad Feet, 28 In. $2185.00

Furniture, Cellarette, George III, Mahogany, 8 Sides, Brass Lion's Head Handles, 22 x 18 In. $1438.00

Furniture, Cellarette, Neoclassical, Figured Mahogany, Sarcophagus, 4 Paw Feet, N.Y., c.1825, 37 x 27 In. $15600.00

Furniture, Chair, Art Nouveau, Charles Rennie Macintosh, Spindles, Scotland, c.1906, 45 In. $2390.00

Furniture, Chair, Belter, Laminated Rosewood, Pierced, Flowers, C-Scrolls, Serpentine Front, 35 x 16 In. $1610.00

Furniture, Chair, Black Forest, Grotesque Mask, Pierced Scroll Back, Caryatids, 48 In., Pair $3290.00

Furniture, Chair, Black Forest, Scroll Back, Marquetry, Music Box In Seat, Child's, 30 In. $823.00

Furniture, Chair, Butterfly, Ferrari-Hardoy, Black Iron Frame, Brown Leather Seat, 30 x 36 In. $720.00

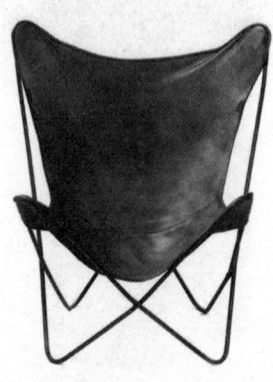

Candlestand, Cherry, Octagonal Beaded Top, Vase & Ring Turned Post, 25½ x 18 In.	382.00
Candlestand, Cherry, Round Top, Tapered Turned Support, Tripod Base, 24 x 14 In.	294.00
Candlestand, Cherry, Shaped Corners, Tripod Base, Tenn., c.1840, 28 x 22 In.	3105.00
Candlestand, Cherry, Tilt Top, Turned Shaft, Birdcage, Cabriole Legs, 31 x 24 In.	138.00
Candlestand, Cherry, Tripod Base, Slipper Feet, 14½ x 14 x 29½ In.	863.00
Candlestand, Chippendale, Curly Maple, Cherry, Round Top, Snake Feet, 25 x 15 In.	173.00
Candlestand, Chippendale, Mahogany, c.1780, 29½ x 19 In.	4800.00
Candlestand, Federal, Black, Oval Corners, Ring Turned Base, c.1800, 28 x 17 In.	881.00
Candlestand, Federal, Cherry, Square Top, Vase & Ring Turned Support, Tripod, 28 x 13 In. .	1058.00
Candlestand, Federal, Curly Maple, Ring & Vase, Tripod Base, Curved Legs, 28 x 17 In.	863.00
Candlestand, Federal, Mahogany, Inlay, Baluster Turned Shaft, Snake Feet, 29 x 17 In.	633.00
Candlestand, Federal, Mahogany, Satinwood, Inlay, Tilt Top, Spider Legs, 29 x 24 x 16 In. *illus*	166750.00
Candlestand, Federal, Mahogany, Square Top, Urn Shaft, Arched Legs, 1800s, 28 x 18 In. ...	598.00
Candlestand, Federal, Mahogany, Tilt Top, Ring Turned Support, c.1800, 29 x 18 In.	2115.00
Candlestand, Federal, Maple, Oval Corners, Turned Column, 17¾ x 28 In.	1668.00
Candlestand, Federal, Maple, Ring Turned Shaft, Arched Legs, Duck's Head Feet, c.1825, 29 In. .	896.00
Candlestand, Federal, Walnut, Molded Dish Top, Bulbous, Cabriole Legs, Pad Feet, 25 x 16 In. ..	275.00
Candlestand, Federal, Walnut, Red Paint, Shaped Top, Vase Column, Pad Feet, 26 x 14 In. ..	440.00
Candlestand, Federal, Walnut, Square Top, Ring Turned Shaft, 3-Footed, Spider Legs, 28 x 14 In. ..	660.00
Candlestand, Federal Style, Mahogany, Shaped Top, 3-Footed, Concave Legs, 30 In.	202.00
Candlestand, Folk Art, Tiger Maple, Lift Top, Yellow Pine, Paneled Front, 25 x 45 In.	1955.00
Candlestand, Hepplewhite, Birch, 8-Sided, Cock-Beaded, Turned Shaft, Tripod, 27 x 21 In. ..	2185.00
Candlestand, Hepplewhite, Bird's-Eye Maple, Birch, 8-Sided, Tripod Base, Red Paint, 30 In.	431.00
Candlestand, Iron, Adjustable, Tripod Base, 18th Century	1495.00
Candlestand, Mahogany, Carved, Inlay, 8-Sided, Urn Form Support, Paw Feet, 28 x 27 In. ..	5378.00
Candlestand, Mahogany, Tilt Top, Rectangular Top, Urn Turned Pedestal, 29 x 21 In.	316.00
Candlestand, Mahogany, Tilt Top, Shaped Edge, Urn Shaft, Snake Legs, Pad Feet, 28 In. *illus*	2185.00
Candlestand, Mixed Wood, Vasiform Turned Standard, Cabriole Legs, 27½ In.	72.00
Candlestand, Pine, Gameboard Top, Drawer, Turned Pedestal, Red & Yellow Paint, 29 In. ..	1035.00
Candlestand, Queen Anne, Cherry, Walnut, Oval, Vase Shaft, 3-Footed, 26 x 21 In.	275.00
Candlestand, Queen Anne, Mahogany, c.1770, 27¾ x 18½ In.	3000.00
Candlestand, Queen Anne, Mahogany, Dish Top, Birdcage, 18th Century, 28 x 11 In.	2478.00
Candlestand, Queen Anne, Mahogany, Tilt Top, Dish Top, c.1770, 27½ x 21 In.	4200.00
Candlestand, Queen Anne, Tilt Top, c.1760, 26 x 20 In.	6600.00
Candlestand, Queen Anne, Tilt Top, Walnut, Philadelphia, 1760-90, 29 x 21 In.	12000.00
Candlestand, Queen Anne, Walnut, Oval, Turned, Tapered Shaft, Spider Legs, 30 x 23 In. ...	303.00
Candlestand, Queen Anne, Walnut, Square, Bulbous Shaft, 3-Footed, Cabriole Legs, Pa., 28 In.	198.00
Candlestand, Red Paint, Round Top, Turned Stem, Raised Plinth, Splayed Legs, 29½ In. ...	1175.00
Candlestand, Shaker, Cherry, Square, Turned, 4 Peg Legs, Watervliet, N.Y., c.1870, 30 In. ...	1053.00
Candlestand, Shaker, Maple, Red Paint, Adjustable Arm, 2 Cups, Turned Shaft, Label, c.1800, 34 In.	4680.00
Candlestand, Shaker, Poplar, Turned Cherry Shaft, 4 Arched Spider Legs, 27 x 21 In.	7839.00
Candlestand, Softwood, Ratchet, Square Shaft, Iron Hardware, Mortised Legs, 43 In.	94.00
Candlestand, Softwood, Shaped Corner, Vasiform Shaft, Spider Legs, 31 x 19 In.	770.00
Candlestand, Tilt Top, Mahogany, Circular Top, Tripod Base, Cabriole Legs, 21½ x 28 In. ...	230.00
Candlestand, Tilt Top, Mahogany, Turned Post, Tripod Base, Octagonal Top, 29 In.	345.00
Candlestand, Tilt Top, Mahogany, Urn Shaft, 3 Footed Snake Legs, 27 x 18 In.	2185.00
Candlestand, Tilt Top, Maple, Brown & Yellow Graining, Turned Column, 27½ In.	1782.00
Candlestand, Tilt Top, Queen Anne, Mahogany, Dish Top, Baluster, Snake Feet, 19 x 21 In. ..	748.00
Candlestand, Tilt Top, Queen Anne, Walnut, Circular Top, Cabriole Legs, 26 x 20¾ In.	4406.00
Candlestand, Tilt Top, Walnut, Round, Turned Pedestal, Slipper Feet, 26 x 25 x 27 In.	603.00
Candlestand, Tilt Top, Federal Style, Poplar, Column Shaft, Snake Feet, 30 x 20½ In.	230.00
Candlestand, Walnut, 1-Board Top, Vase Turned Pedestal, Tripod Cabriole Base, 26½ In. ...	460.00
Candlestand, Walnut, Dish Top, c.1830, 27 x 20 In.	1080.00
Candlestand, Walnut, Swivel Top, Baluster Turned Support, Tripod Base, 27 x 20 In.	460.00
Candlestand, William & Mary, Maple, Pine, Turned, Rhode Island, c.1720, 22 x 13 In.	9600.00
Candlestand, Wrought Iron, American, 38½ In.	351.00
Candlestand, Wrought Iron, Tripod Base, Tapered Shaft, Rush Holder, 1700s, 29 In.	384.00
Canterbury, Federal, Mahogany, Rails On Shaped Spindles, Drawer, c.1820, 22 x 18 In.	5581.00
Canterbury, Federal, Mahogany, Spindles, Tapered Legs, Medial Shelf, c.1800, 20 x 13 In. ..	1763.00
Canterbury, George III, Mahogany, Drawer, Twist Carved Spindles, Brass Caster Feet, 23 In. .	881.00
Canterbury, Neoclassical, Mahogany, Lyre Shape Supports, Dividers, Drawer, 19 x 19 In. ...	1528.00
Canterbury, Regency, Spindle Turned Top, Dovetailed Drawer, Casters, 21 x 21 In.	546.00
Canterbury, Sheraton, Mahogany, Carrying Handle, Slat Top, Spindles, 19 x 19 In.	518.00
Canterbury, Walnut, Lyre Shape, Shaped Dividers, Shaped Apron, Bracket Feet, 22 x 22 In. .	470.00
Canterbury, William IV, Rosewood, Carved, Pierced Gallery, Turned Finials, 41 x 24 In.	1880.00
Canterbury, William IV, Rosewood, Divided Section, c.1830, 20½ x 20 In.	1410.00

F

Furniture, Chair, Chippendale, Ribbon Crest, Upholstered, Boston, Mass., c.1780, 37 In., Pair
$4200.00

Furniture, Chair, Corner, Chippendale, Mahogany, Pierced Urn Splats, Padded, N.Y., c.1770, 33 In.
$6600.00

Furniture, Chair, Corner, Chippendale, Walnut, Oak, Pierced Splat, England, 32 x 18 x 18 In.
$978.00

Furniture, Chair, Cornucopia, Belter, Rosewood Laminate, Vine & Floral Carving, 38 In. $5060.00

Furniture, Chair, Dan Johnson, Iron Frame, Wood Armrests, Upholstered, 26 x 30 In., Pair $1680.00

Furniture, Chair, Eero Saarinen, Grasshopper, Bentwood, Leather Upholstery, Knoll, 36 x 27 In. $1150.00

Furniture, Chair, Erik Magnussen, Z, Metal Frame, Sling Seat & Back, c.1968, 29 x 28 x 27 In. $840.00

Case, Bottle, Dovetailed, Dividers, Bracket Feet, Holds 36 Bottles, 1800s, 13 x 34 In.	230.00
Case, Cane, Oak, Hinged Lift Top, Glass On 4 Sides, Top, Removable Grate, 45 x 30 In.	1265.00
Cellarette, Burl Veneer, Inlay, Mother-Of-Pearl, Ebony, Lift-Out Tray, Brass, 13 x 11 In.	2415.00
Cellarette, Chinese Style, Brass Mounted, Black, Gold, Pontypool, Oval, 20 x 22 x 14½ In. ..	4512.00
Cellarette, Empire, Mahogany, Fitted Interior, Octagonal Pedestal, 29 x 22½ In.	767.00
Cellarette, Federal, Inlaid Walnut, Hepplewhite, Lift Top, Door, String Inlay, 30 x 23 In.	5206.00
Cellarette, George III, Mahogany, 8 Sides, Brass Lion's Head Handles, 22 x 18 In. .....*illus*	1438.00
Cellarette, George III, Mahogany, Brass Bound, 25 x 18 In.	2530.00
Cellarette, Neoclassical, Figured Mahogany, Sarcophagus, 4 Paw Feet, N.Y., c.1825, 37 x 27 In. .*illus*	15600.00
Cellarette, Satinwood Veneer, Rosewood Inlay, Tassels, 6 Bottles, Brass Handles, 10 x 6 x 8 In.	1265.00
Chair, 3 Black Tubular Legs, Round Wood Back, Stefan Siwinski, c.1958, Pair	1945.00
Chair, 3-Legged Skastool, Bent Plywood, Red, Varnished, Tan, Wegner, c.1963	958.00
Chair, Aalto, Lounge, Closed Loop Birch Frame, Upholstered, c.1950, 28 In.	2468.00
Chair, Aesthetic Revival, Faux Bamboo, Overupholstered Seat, 33½ In., Pair	316.00
Chair, Aesthetic Revival, Mahogany, Burl Maple, Gilt Incised, Padded Back, Seat, 4 Piece ..	705.00
Chair, Anglo-Indian, Openwork, Vine & Leaf Carving, Upholstered Seat, 36 In., Pair	460.00
Chair, Arne Jacobsen, Swan, Upholstered, Aluminum Pedestal, Swivel Base, 1958, 32 In.	1410.00
Chair, Art Deco, Leather, Embossed Faux Alligator Finish	644.00
Chair, Art Deco, Mahogany, Gilt Bronze, Arms, Normandie Dining Room, 34½ x 22 In.	14340.00
Chair, Art Nouveau, Charles Rennie Macintosh, Spindles, Scotland, c.1906, 45 In. .....*illus*	2390.00
Chair, Art Nouveau, Walnut, Padded, Upholstered, Wings, Austria, 48 x 25 x 20¼ In.	472.00
Chair, Arts & Crafts, Morris, Oak, Adjustable Back, Cushions, c.1925, 39½ In.	2938.00
Chair, Arts & Crafts, Oak, Arms, Leather Seat Pad, c.1910	307.00
Chair, Bamboo, Lacquered, Openwork Splat, Plain Seat, Chinese, 40 x 24 In., Pair	1680.00
Chair, Banister Back, Shaped Crest Rails, Reeded Slats, Rush Seats, 40 x 20 In., Pair	489.00
Chair, Bar Harbor, Latticework, Braid Framing, Woven Seat, Arms, 1920s, 37 In.	875.00
Chair, Bar Harbor, Wicker, Wide Banding, Braid Framing, Latticework, 1920s, 37 x 28 In. ...	675.00
Chair, Baronial, Walnut, Carved, Painted, Continental, Fleur-De-Lis, Scroll Arms, 68 In., Pair .	3525.00
Chair, Baroque, Beech, Carved, Pierced Cresting, Stretcher, 52 In.	1645.00
Chair, Baroque, Fruitwood, Upholstered, Scroll Carved Terminals, 1600s, 41 x 24 In.	944.00
Chair, Baroque Style, Walnut, Carved, Overupholstered, Pair, Open Arm, Pair	1116.00
Chair, Baroque Style, Walnut, Overupholstered, Carved Arms, Pair, 17½ In.	1998.00
Chair, Baroque Style, Walnut, Padded Backrest, Scrolled Arms, Supports, England, 18 In., Pair ..	823.00
Chair, Baroque Style, Walnut, Reclining Children Armrests, Blackamoor Legs, 47½ In.	7200.00
Chair, Baroque Style, Walnut, Upholstered Backrest, Scrolled Arms, Pair, 19½ In.	2233.00
Chair, Bear, Vines, Glass Eyes, Lion Head On Legs, Carved Wood, Swiss, 1900s, 38 x 17 In., Pair ..	4370.00
Chair, Beech Frame, Upholstered Seat, 20th Century, Pair	348.00
Chair, Belter, Laminated Rosewood, Pierced, Flowers, C-Scrolls, Serpentine Front, 35 x 16 In. ..*illus*	1610.00
Chair, Bentwood, Scrolled Crest, Shaped Armrests, Hoof Feet, 35¼ x 19½ x 23 In.	2271.00
Chair, Bergere, Art Deco, Cream Paint, Scalloped Crest Rails, Velvet Upholstery, 39 In., Pair .	470.00
Chair, Bergere, Biedermeier, Cherry, Curved Crest, Downswept Arms, Square Legs, 34 In.	480.00
Chair, Bergere, Continental Louis XVI Style, Painted, Cane, Closed Arms, 31 In., Pair	1180.00
Chair, Bergere, Edwardian, Adam Style, Satinwood, Painted, Cane, c.1910, 37 x 26 In.	1410.00
Chair, Bergere, French Provincial, Fruitwood, Padded, Outscrolled Arms, 39½ In.	1057.00
Chair, Bergere, Louis XV Style, Fruitwood, Gilt, Green Polychrome, Upholstery, 1950s	1200.00
Chair, Bergere, Louis XV Style, Polychrome, Closed Arms, Late 1800s, 34 In., Pair	2232.00
Chair, Bergere, Louis XVI, Domed, Padded Back, Closed Padded Arms, 38 In., Pair	3840.00
Chair, Bergere, Louis XVI, Polychrome, Padded Back, Cushion Seat, Closed Arms, 36 In., Pair .	2880.00
Chair, Bergere, Louis XVI, Walnut, Carved, France, c.1870, 34 In., Pair	2250.00
Chair, Bergere, Louis XVI Style, Giltwood, Domed Padded Back, Seat, 42 In., Pair	4560.00
Chair, Bergere, Louis XVI Style, Green Painted, Spoon Backrest, Cane Seat, 17½ In.	235.00
Chair, Bergere, Pickle Finish, Upholstered, Closed Arms, France, c.1850, 39 x 31 In., Pair ...	16000.00
Chair, Bergere, Provincial Fruitwood, Domed, Padded Back, Seat, 47 In.	1320.00
Chair, Bergere, Regence Style, Fruitwood, Carved, Serpentine Crest, Padded, 40 x 29 In., Pair	590.00
Chair, Biedermeier, Fruitwood, Curved Crest, Ebonized, Splayed Splat, 33 In.	1175.00
Chair, Biedermeier, Fruitwood, Shaped Back, Scroll Inlaid Crest, Padded, 35½ In.	646.00
Chair, Biedermeier, Mahogany, Back Scrolled Crest, Fruitwood Panel, 37 In., Pair	1320.00
Chair, Biedermeier, Satinwood, Arched Crest, Openwork, Shell Inlay, Arms, 18½ In., Pair ...	550.00
Chair, Black Forest, Grotesque Mask, Pierced Scroll Back, Caryatids, 48 In., Pair ......*illus*	3290.00
Chair, Black Forest, Scroll Back, Marquetry, Music Box In Seat, Child's, 30 In. ....*illus*	823.00
Chair, Black Paint, Rush Seat, Turned, Early 18th Century	470.00
Chair, Butterfly, Ferrari-Hardoy, Black Iron Frame, Brown Leather Seat, 30 x 36 In. ....*illus*	720.00
Chair, Campaign, Mahogany, Anglo-Indian, Brass	490.00
Chair, Charles X Style, Fruitwood, Medallion Back, Swan Head Masks, Padded Seat	130.00
Chair, Chevallier, Louis Sognot, Cane, Bamboo, Arms, c.1953, 32 In., Pair	1560.00
Chair, Chinese Style, Black Lacquered, Horseshoe Back, Scroll Arms, 29 x 27 In., Pair	323.00

Chair, Chippendale, Cherry, Serpentine Crest Rail, Center Fan, Pair	1912.00
Chair, Chippendale, Cherry, Yoke Crest, Pierced Splat, Upholstered Seat, 38 In.	259.00
Chair, Chippendale, Mahogany, Carved, Arms, Stevenson, Philadelphia, c.1770, 41 In.	36000.00
Chair, Chippendale, Mahogany, Carved, Upholstered Seat, Child's, 30 In., Pair	527.00
Chair, Chippendale, Mahogany, Claw & Ball Feet, Cutout Splat, 38 x 23 x 18 In.	323.00
Chair, Chippendale, Mahogany, Crested, Padded Seat, Newport, c.1800, 38 In., Pair	7800.00
Chair, Chippendale, Mahogany, Pierced Slat, Cabriole Legs, Claw & Ball Feet, c.1780, 37 In.	3585.00
Chair, Chippendale, Mahogany, Scroll Carved Splat, Raked Stiles, 37 In.	2468.00
Chair, Chippendale, Mahogany, Serpentine Crest, Pierced Splat, 36½ In.	748.00
Chair, Chippendale, Mahogany, Shaped Crest Rail, Trellis Pierced Splat, Arms, 38 In.	450.00
Chair, Chippendale, Mahogany, Slip Seat, Philadelphia, 1780-1800, 38¼ In.	7200.00
Chair, Chippendale, Mahogany, Upholstered, Scrolling Arms, Box Stretcher, 35 In.	3525.00
Chair, Chippendale, Ribbon Crest, Upholstered, Boston, Mass., c.1780, 37 In., Pair .....*illus*	4200.00
Chair, Chippendale, Walnut, Serpentine Crest, Scrolled Ears, Cabriole Legs, 39 In., Pair	5378.00
Chair, Chippendale Style, Mahogany, Frame, Open Arms, Late 19th Century, Pair	768.00
Chair, Chippendale Style, Mahogany, Open Arms, 19th Century	553.00
Chair, Chippendale Style, Mahogany, Upholstered, Loose Cushions, 45 x 33 x 30 In.	590.00
Chair, Chippendale Style, Mahogany, Wing, Cabriole Legs, Claw & Ball Feet	1645.00
Chair, Club, Art Deco, Leather, Padded Arms, Tilt Back, Squab Cushion, 1900s, 33 In., Pair	4900.00
Chair, Club, Neoclassical, Mahogany, Ram's Head Terminals, Hoof Feet, 1800s, 28 x 25 In.	575.00
Chair, Club, Paul Laszio, Beige Upholstered, 1947, 31 x 39 x 35 In.	3300.00
Chair, Club, Tobia Scarpa, Bastiano, Rosewood, Black Leather, 30 x 35½ x 30 In., Pair	660.00
Chair, Colonial Revival, Cherry, Oak, Slat Back, Rush Seat, Box Stretchers, Arms, 42 In.	480.00
Chair, Commode, Chippendale, Serpentine Crest Rail, Pierced Splat, Needlepoint, Arms	777.00
Chair, Commode, George III, Mahogany, Carved, Drop In Cushion, Early 1800s	470.00
Chair, Concave Crests, Freehand Painted, Shells, Leaves, Gold, Red, c.1825, 35 In., Pair	1763.00
Chair, Continental, Walnut, Padded, Domed Back, Saddle Seat, Scrolling Arms, 34 In.	2640.00
Chair, Continental Style, Mahogany, Carved, Arms, Upholstered, Early 1900s, 46½ In.	472.00
Chair, Corner, Chippendale, Mahogany, Carved, Figured, c.1770, 31½ In.	5700.00
Chair, Corner, Chippendale, Mahogany, Pierced Urn Splats, Padded, N.Y., c.1770, 33 In. *illus*	6600.00
Chair, Corner, Chippendale, Walnut, Oak, Pierced Splat, England, 32 x 18 x 18 In. .....*illus*	978.00
Chair, Corner, Chippendale Style, Mahogany, Pierced Splats, Slip Seat, 30 x 17½ In.	212.00
Chair, Corner, French Provincial, Walnut, Woven Rush Seat, 25 x 22 In.	354.00
Chair, Corner, George III, Mahogany, Mid 18th Century, 34 In.	532.00
Chair, Corner, George III Style, Black Lacquer, Vase Splats, Gilt Oriental Accents, 33 In.	1500.00
Chair, Corner, Oriental, Padouk Wood, Carved, 20th Century	304.00
Chair, Corner, Victorian, Carved, Slip Seat, Red Velvet Upholstery, 32 x 17 In.	200.00
Chair, Cornucopia, Belter, Rosewood Laminate, Vine & Floral Carving, 38 In. ....*illus*	5060.00
Chair, Curvilinear Back, Openwork, Black Finish, White Silk Upholstery, Arms, 30 In.	353.00
Chair, Dagobert Style, Walnut, Gothic Style, Pierced Carving, c.1890, 36 x 24 In., Pair	3250.00
Chair, Dan Johnson, Iron Frame, Wood Armrests, Upholstered, 26 x 30 In., Pair ....*illus*	1680.00
Chair, Deck, Queen Elizabeth, Mixed Wood, Folding, Brass Tag, 68 x 22 x 32 In., Pair	431.00
Chair, Dutch, Marquetry, Upholstered Slip Seat, Flowers, Birds, 36 In.	180.00
Chair, Eames, LCW, Molded Plywood, P. Evans, Label, Herman Miller, c.1945	999.00
Chair, Eames, Lounge, Ottoman, Brown Leather, Casters, 1956	3300.00
Chair, Eames, Lounge, Ottoman, Molded Plywood, Leather, Herman Miller, c.1956	2559.00
Chair, Eames, Molded Fiberglass, Tubular Steel, Green, Herman Miller, c.1965, 3 Piece	256.00
Chair, Ebena-Lasalle, Pedestal, Upholstered, Laminated Wood, c.1967	614.00
Chair, Ebonized, Mother-Of-Pearl Inlay, Papier-Mache, Child's, 28 x 14 x 14 In.	443.00
Chair, Ebonized, Scrolled Leaf Back, Plank Seats, Anthemion Carved, Portugal, Pair	266.00
Chair, Edwardian, Mahogany, Leather Upholstered, Pillow Back, 40 x 44 In.	1175.00
Chair, Edwardian, Mahogany, Leather Upholstered, Tufted, 30 x 42 x 36 In., Pair	822.00
Chair, Eero Saarinen, Grasshopper, Angular Wood Frame, 1946, 35 x 26 x 37 In.	1920.00
Chair, Eero Saarinen, Grasshopper, Bentwood, Leather Upholstery, Knoll, 36 x 27 In. . .*illus*	1150.00
Chair, Eero Saarinen, Womb, Upholstered, 1947, 36 x 39 x 35 In.	900.00
Chair, Egyptian Revival, Ebonized, Gilt, Carved, Animal Figures, Symbols, 24 x 16 In.	2232.00
Chair, Elm, Carved Vertical Splat, Chinese, 18th Century, 20 x 18 x 15 In., Pair	708.00
Chair, Elm, Lacquered, Yoke Back, Foo Lion, Arm, Chinese, 46 x 24 x 18 In., Pair	531.00
Chair, Elm, Tall Back, Carved, Arched Crest, Volutes, Paneled Seats, Chinese, 46 In., Pair	805.00
Chair, Empire, Ebonized, Gilt, Upholstered, Scrolled Back, Sphinx Arm Supports, 40 In., Pair	2468.00
Chair, Empire, Mahogany, Grecian Style, Gilt Carved, Reed Crest, Papyrus, Early 1800s, 38 In.	1997.00
Chair, Empire, Mahogany, Open Arms, Carved, Silk Upholstery, 19th Century, Pair	2768.00
Chair, Empire Style, Mahogany, Padded Back, Seat, Arms, Caryatid Uprights, 38 In., Pair	1560.00
Chair, English Style, Green Leather, Tufted, Padded Back, c.1940, 43 In., Pair	4200.00
Chair, Erik Magnussen, Z, Metal Frame, Sling Seat & Back, c.1968, 29 x 28 x 27 In. ....*illus*	840.00
Chair, Fantasy, Carved, Winged Bird, Oval Seat, 3 Scrolled Feet, Italy, 29 x 26 In.	5581.00

Furniture, Chair, G. Nelson, Rounded Back, Birch Legs, Herman Miller, 1950s, 32 In., Pair
$2520.00

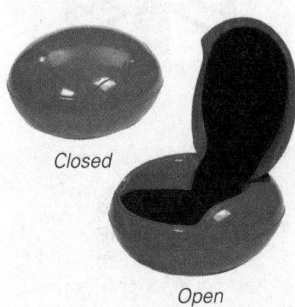

Furniture, Chair, Garden Egg, Fiberglass & Plastic Shell, Upholstery, Peter Ghyczy, 18 x 30 In.
$748.00

Closed

Open

Furniture, Chair, Gehrey, Easy Edges, Corrugated Cardboard, c.1971, 36 x 16 x 20 In.
$840.00

Furniture, Chair, George III, Mahogany, Shaped Back, Octagonal Fretwork, Padded Seat, Pair
$12000.00

Furniture, Chair, Hall, Art Nouveau, Mahogany, Marquetry, Shaped Seat & Back, 40 x 17 x 17 In. $316.00

Furniture, Chair, Maple, Hickory, Writing Surface, Rush Seat, Tennessee, c.1815, 47 x 29 In. $4140.00

Chair, Federal, Inlaid Mahogany, Shell Inlay Crest, Padded Back, Seat, Arms, 37 In.	1528.00
Chair, Federal, Mahogany, Needlepoint Seat, Saber Legs, Shaped Splat, 1800s, 33 In., Pair	450.00
Chair, Federal, Mahogany, Pierced & Carved Urn Splat, Scroll Arms, Connecticut, 40 In., Pair	575.00
Chair, Federal, Mahogany, Scrolled Back, Padded Arms, Seat, 40 x 24 In.	1528.00
Chair, Federal, Mahogany, Shieldback, S. Badlam Attribution, 1800-10, 37¾ In.	12000.00
Chair, Federal, Mahogany, Upholstered Arms, c.1790, 44 In.	2100.00
Chair, Federal, Mahogany, Vertical Slats, Lamb's Tongue Carving, Santo Domingo, 1790, Pair	767.00
Chair, Fiddle Back, Cherry, Plank Seat, c.1850, 35 x 17 x 17 In., Pair	118.00
Chair, Finn Juhl, Teak, Black Leather Back, Seat, France & Sons, 32 In.	1175.00
Chair, Flemish Style, Walnut, Carved, Open Arms, Scroll Feet, Stretchers, 44 x 25 In.	518.00
Chair, French Provincial, Needlework Upholstery, Open Arms, France, 20th Century	261.00
Chair, Fruitwood, 3 Salamander Back Slats, Arm, 37½ x 21½ x 17½ In.	5605.00
Chair, Fruitwood, High Back, Arms, Pigskin Upholstery, Loose Cushion, 46 x 31 In.	1180.00
Chair, Fruitwood, Parcel Gilt, Lyre Back, Flower Head Carved Crest, 35 In., Pair	1770.00
Chair, G. Nakashima, Walnut, Conoid, 8-Hickory Back Spindles, Saddle Seat, 35½ In., Pair	19120.00
Chair, G. Nelson, Rounded Back, Birch Legs, Herman Miller, 1950s, 32 In., Pair ......*illus*	2520.00
Chair, G. Stickley, Horizontal Back Slats, Flaring Legs, Leather Seat, 1901, 34 x 17 In.	12000.00
Chair, G. Stickley, Morris, 5 Side Slats, Cushions, Brown Leather, Drop Arm, 37 x 33 x 37 In.	5400.00
Chair, G. Stickley, Spindles, Drop In Cushions, Brown Suede Arms, 49 x 27½ x 22 In.	3360.00
Chair, G. Stickley, Spindles, Tacked On Leather Seat, 38½ x 18 In.	1020.00
Chair, G. Stickley, Willow, Square Openings, Cushions, Velvet, Arms, 32 x 33 x 26 In.	3120.00
Chair, Garden Egg, Fiberglass & Plastic Shell, Upholstery, Peter Ghyczy, 18 x 30 In. ....*illus*	748.00
Chair, Gehrey, Easy Edges, Corrugated Cardboard, c.1971, 36 x 16 x 20 In. ....*illus*	840.00
Chair, Gentleman's, Walnut Frame, Leather Upholstery, Mid 19th Century	307.00
Chair, George II Style, Mahogany, Carved, Eagle Heads, Baluster Splat, Upholstered, 19 In.	1880.00
Chair, George II Style, Mahogany, Yellow Upholstered, 20th Century, 42 x 31 In.	502.00
Chair, George III, Chippendale Style, Carved, 39 x 26 In., Pair	764.00
Chair, George III, Mahogany, Domed, Carved Crest, Pierced Baluster Splat, 37½ In.	540.00
Chair, George III, Mahogany, Fret Carved, Upholstered Back, Seat, 40 x 27 In.	3910.00
Chair, George III, Mahogany, Needlework Upholstered, Cabriole Legs, Claw, Ball Feet, 19 In.	1336.00
Chair, George III, Mahogany, Overupholstered, Marlboro Legs, c.1775, 18 In.	705.00
Chair, George III, Mahogany, Shaped Back, Octagonal Fretwork, Padded Seat, Pair ....*illus*	12000.00
Chair, George III, Padded Rectangular Back, Seat, Carved Arms, Cabriole Legs, 37 In.	1140.00
Chair, George III Style, Mahogany, Carved, Open Arm, Upholstered Seat, 1800s, 41 x 26 In.	1062.00
Chair, George III Style, Mahogany, Serpentine Crest, Pierced Splat, 38 In., Pair	353.00
Chair, George III Style, Mahogany, Shield Shape Back, Pierced Splat, 38 x 20 x 18 In., Pair	224.00
Chair, Georgian, Mahogany, Box Stretcher, Leather Upholstery, Open Arm, Early 1900s	884.00
Chair, Georgian, Needlepoint Upholstery, Padded Arms, c.1800	4250.00
Chair, Georgian Style, Mahogany, Carved, Needlepoint Upholstery, 38 In., Pair	3173.00
Chair, Georgian Style, Mahogany, Carved, Shaped Crest, Strapwork Splat, 38 In., Pair	575.00
Chair, Georgian Style, Mahogany, Serpentine Crest, Upholstered, Arms, 44 x 30 In.	472.00
Chair, Georgian Style, Open Arms, Upholstered Seat, 19th Century	348.00
Chair, Gilt, Stenciled, Spoon Shape Splats, Rush Seat, Turned Legs, c.1820, 35 In.	200.00
Chair, Giltwood, Round Back, Padded Serpentine Seat, Continental, 36 In., Pair	288.00
Chair, Gothic, Mahogany, Open Carved Crest, Open Arms, 50½ In.	3600.00
Chair, Gothic, Mahogany, Upholstered Panel, Trefoil Arch, Arms, 1800s, 56 In.	3600.00
Chair, Gothic, Oak, Arch Arm Supports, Front Skirt, 19th Century, 34½ x 24 In.	690.00
Chair, Great, Oak, Turned, Mass., c.1710, 43 In.	15600.00
Chair, H. Bertoia, Lounge, Ottoman, Wire Mesh, Black, 1951, 27 x 44 x 31 In.	660.00
Chair, Hall, Art Nouveau, Mahogany, Marquetry, Shaped Seat & Back, 40 x 17 x 17 In. *illus*	316.00
Chair, Hall, Peter Hunt, Painted Scene, Hearts, Trees, Arms, 1943	2645.00
Chair, Harp, Jorgen Hovelskov, Ebonized Ash, Flag Line, c.1968	972.00
Chair, Heart, V. Panton, Blue Wool Upholstery, 4 Pronged Base, 35 In.	1175.00
Chair, Heart Cone, Red, V. Panton, c.1959	1065.00
Chair, Hepplewhite, Mahogany, Carved, Serpentine, Vase Shape Splat, Arms, 17 In.	441.00
Chair, Hepplewhite Style, Mahogany, Shieldback, Early 1800s, 36 x 22 In., Pair	443.00
Chair, Heywood, Serpentine Rolled Crest, Curlicues, Beadwork, Ladies, 1890s, 39 In.	1450.00
Chair, High Back, Walnut, Open Arms, Upholstered, c.1880, 52 x 28 In., Pair	460.00
Chair, His & Hers, Walnut, Carved, Shield & Swag Crest, Leather, Late 1800s, Pair	460.00
Chair, Hitchcock, Pillow Back, Gold Fruit Stenciling, Black Ground, 18 x 34 In., 8 Piece	1120.00
Chair, Hoffmann, Tubular Steel, Chromed, Upholstered, Arms, 1931, 32 In.	4800.00
Chair, Hood, Louis XV, Painted, Carved, Blue Silk Upholstery, c.1900, 57 x 29 In.	12250.00
Chair, Hood, Louis XVI, Gold Silk Blend Upholstery, c.1870	7000.00
Chair, Horn, Arms & Legs, Brown, Black, White, Hide Covered, Late 1900s, 41½ In.	575.00
Chair, Horn, Back & Arms, Round Upholstered Seat, Gray Suede, Casters, 36 In.	546.00
Chair, Horn Buffalo Legs & Arm Sections, Reupholstered, c.1875, 42 x 28 In.	16650.00

Chair, Huang Huali, Horseshoe Back, Arms, 38½ x 24¼ x 22 In., Pair	5605.00
Chair, Iberian Baroque, Walnut, Carved, Scrolled Arms, Acanthus Back, 49 x 24 In.	881.00
Chair, Iberian Baroque, Walnut, Scroll Carved Splat, Acanthus Cartouche, 1700s	368.00
Chair, Italian Baroque, Walnut, Carved, Upholstered, Barley Twist Arms, 26 In., Pair	1998.00
Chair, Italian Fruitwood, Arched Back, Plaid Upholstery, Open Arms, 37 In., Pair	978.00
Chair, Italian Rococo, Painted, Parcel Gilt, Carved, Upholstered, Padded Arms, 45 In., Pair ..	5310.00
Chair, Jacobean Style, Mahogany, Padded, H-Stretcher, Arms, 36½ In., Pair	1292.00
Chair, Jean Prouve, Lacquered Metal, Oak Plywood, c.1950, 32 x 81 In. .... 4200.00 to 5400.00	
Chair, Kem Weber, Laminated Wood, Glazed Cloth, Chromium, Arms	120.00
Chair, Kem Weber, Lounge, Chrome, Black Upholstered, c.1935, 29 x 40 In.	3819.00
Chair, Kneeler, Prie-Dieu, Louis XV Style, Bead, Needlework, Padded Seat, France, 36 In.	708.00
Chair, Ladder Back, 4 Slats, Arms, Turned Stiles, Acorn Finials, Rush Seat, 46 In.	173.00
Chair, Ladder Back, 5 Graduated Arched Slats, Rush Seat, Turned, Arms	770.00
Chair, Ladder Back, 5 Slats, Rush Seat, Delaware Valley, Shaped Arms, Turned Legs, 16 In. ..	770.00
Chair, Ladder Back, Cypress, Pine, Turned Finials, Molded Splats, Deer Hide Seat	995.00
Chair, Ladder Back, Rush Seat, 4 Arched Slats, Turned Posts, Box Stretcher, 17 In.	413.00
Chair, Ladder Back, Sausage & Ring Turned Posts, Front Legs, Rush Seat, 41 In.	230.00
Chair, Lambing, English Oak, Shaped Wings, Padded Seat, 18th Century, 45½ In.	1247.00
Chair, Leather, Chrome, Tubular Steel, Arms, After Marcel Breuer, c.1940	205.00
Chair, Leather, Nail Heads, Serpentine Shape, Wings, Arms, 1900s, 41 In., Pair	6200.00
Chair, Lolling, Federal, Inlaid Mahogany, Upholstered, Mass., c.1800, 45½ In.	9000.00
Chair, Lolling, George III, Mahogany, Padded Arms, Upholstered Seat, 1700s, 42 In.	2350.00
Chair, Lolling, Mahogany, Inlay, Upholstered, Serpentine Backrest, 17½ In.	646.00
Chair, Louis Majorelle, Fruitwood, Marquetry, High Back, Arms, c.1900, 43¼ In.	960.00
Chair, Louis Majorelle, Walnut, Arms, c.1900, 37⅜ In., Pair	13200.00
Chair, Louis Philippe, Upholstered, Outscrolled Arms, 34 x 31½ x 22½ In.	354.00
Chair, Louis Philippe, Walnut, Carved, Arched Crest Rail, Padded Back, Seat, 40 In., Pair ...	266.00
Chair, Louis Philippe, Walnut, Carved, Padded Back, Seat, Arms, 39 x 24 x 21 In., Pair	590.00
Chair, Louis XIII, Fruitwood, Padded Back, Seat, Scroll Arms, 42½ In.	720.00
Chair, Louis XIII, Walnut, Carved, Gothic Motif, Arms, c.1900, 46 x 26 In., Pair	6000.00
Chair, Louis XIV, Oak, Carved Vase Shaped Splat, Arching Crest, France, 41 x 25 x 20 In.	767.00
Chair, Louis XIV Style, Arched Back, Scroll Arms, Needlepoint, Acorn Feet, 45 In., Pair	1762.00
Chair, Louis XV, Beech, Arched Backrest, Winged Cartouche, Cane Back, Seat, 35 In.	6000.00
Chair, Louis XV, Carved, Curved Back, Gilt, Arms, Brocade Upholstery, 1900s, 34 In.	785.00
Chair, Louis XV, Fruitwood, Carved, Linen Upholstery, 19th Century, 34 x 30 In., Pair	2600.00
Chair, Louis XV, Parcel Gilt, Painted, Upholstered, Padded Armrests, Cushion, 35 In.	2400.00
Chair, Louis XV, Walnut, Caved, Cartouche Backrest Crest, Padded Arms, 39 x 26 In.	1763.00
Chair, Louis XV Style, Bead & Channel Frame, Floral Cresting, Child's, 31 In.	374.00
Chair, Louis XV Style, Flower Carved Crest, Cushioned Seat, Padded Arms, 34 In.	1175.00
Chair, Louis XV Style, Fruitwood, Ribbon Carved Crest, Open Arms, Early 1800s, 42 In.	1116.00
Chair, Louis XV Style, Fruitwood, Upholstered, Arms, 32 x 23 In., Pair	472.00
Chair, Louis XV Style, Mahogany, Carved, 39½ x 28 In.	1410.00
Chair, Louis XV Style, Multicolored, Padded, Cabriole Legs, Peg Feet, 32¼ In., Pair	528.00
Chair, Louis XV Style, Polychrome, Padded & Scrolled Back, 32¼ In., Pair	528.00
Chair, Louis XVI, Carved, Water Gilt, Aubusson Tapestry Upholstery, 37½ In.	4700.00
Chair, Louis XVI, Rosewood, Carved, Open Arms, Upholstered Back, Seat, Arms, Pair	2183.00
Chair, Louis XVI Style, Beech Frame, Upholstered, Padded Arms, Early 1900s, Pair	2174.00
Chair, Louis XVI Style, Fluted Legs, Acanthus, Ribbon, Upholstered, Early 1900s, Pair	2530.00
Chair, Louis XVI Style, Fruitwood, Carved, Needlework Upholstered, 1900s, 41 x 26 In.	224.00
Chair, Louis XVI Style, Giltwood, Carved, Ribbon & Flower, Upholstered, 1900s, 38 In., Pair ..	1770.00
Chair, Louis XVI Style, Giltwood Frame, Open Arms, Velvet Upholstery, Early 1900s	328.000
Chair, Lounge, Caramel Leather Upholstery, Gray Metal Base, Knoll, 29 x 32 In.	1763.00
Chair, Lounge, Eames, Walnut Shell, Black Leather Upholstery, Herman Miller, 33 In., Pair .	1528.00
Chair, Lounge, Ottoman, Rosewood, Black Leather, 1956, 31 x 36 x 33½ In.	1800.00
Chair, Mahogany, Leather Upholstered, Tufted, Brass Tacks, Victorian, 19½ x 48 x 22 In.	2820.00
Chair, Mahogany, Lion Head Carvings, Claw Feet, Arm, 40 x 25 x 20 In.	206.00
Chair, Mahogany, Shieldback, Early 19th Century, Pair	369.00
Chair, Maple, Cane Seat, Vase Shaped Splat, 19th Century, 32 In., Pair	92.00
Chair, Maple, Hickory, Writing Surface, Rush Seat, Tennessee, c.1815, 47 x 29 In. .....*illus*	4140.00
Chair, Maple, Rush Seat, Pierced Backrest, Turned Tapered Legs, c.1825, Pair	131.00
Chair, Maple, Shaped Crest Rail, Open Vase Shaped Splat, New England, 38 In., Pair	920.00
Chair, Maralunga, Lounge, Magistretti, Steel Frame, Brown Leather, Atelier, 38 x 33 In., 4 Piece .	3055.00
Chair, Mario Villa, Wrought Metal, Empire Style, Gold, Sponged Violet Paint, 36 In., Pair ...	646.00
Chair, Mid Victorian, Open Back, Carved Horizontal Splat, Upholstered Seat, 4 Piece	416.00
Chair, Mies Van Der Rohe, Barcelona, Bar Frame, Black Leather Cushions, Knoll, 29 x 29 In. .	1645.00
Chair, Mies Van Der Rohe, Barcelona, No. MR 90, c.1929, 29 x 29 x 30 In., Pair ....*illus*	2640.00

Furniture, Chair, Mies Van Der Rohe, Barcelona, No. MR 90, c.1929, 29 x 29 x 30 In., Pair $2640.00

F

Furniture, Chair, N. Cherner, Walnut, Birch, Plycraft, Bernardo, 1950s, 31 x 25 In., Pair $2415.00

Furniture, Chair, Oak, Spindle & Cane Back, Cane Seat, Swivel, Pat'd April 1895, 43 x 20 In. $230.00

Furniture, Chair, Ottoman, Eames, Rosewood, Leather, Herman Miller, c.1956, 31 x 36 In. $3240.00

F

Furniture, Chair, Philippe Starck, Ed Archer, Leather Seat, Aluminum Leg, Driade, Italy, 39 x 18 In. $1035.00

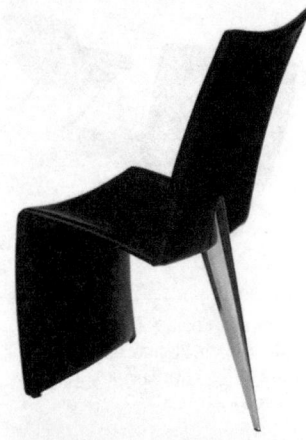

Furniture, Chair, Renaissance Revival, Hunzinger, Walnut, Upholstered, 39½ In., Pair $11950.00

Furniture, Chair, Robert Venturi, Queen Anne, Black, Green Padded Seat, Knoll, c.1984, 38 In. $3840.00

TIP

If the shine has worn off a spot on an old formica tabletop, try using auto-body rubbing compound on the spot.

Chair, Mies Van Der Rohe, Chromed Steel, Leather Cushions	508.00
Chair, Mies Van Der Rohe, No. MR533, Chromed Steel, Cantilevered, Canvas, Thonet, Pair	1116.00
Chair, Morris, G. Stickley, Open Arms, Drop In Seat, Morris Upholstery, 41 x 30 In.	1680.00
Chair, Morris, L. & J.G. Stickley, Spring Cushion, 39 x 32 x 35 In.	2640.00
Chair, Morris, L. & J.G. Stickley, Oak, Adjustable Back, 6 Vertical Slats, 42 x 32 In.	1410.00
Chair, Morris, Lifetime, 3 Vertical Arm Slats, Drop In Seat, Loose Back, Leather, 40 x 32 In.	3480.00
Chair, Morris, Oak, Reclining Back, Victorian, 43 x 30 x 32 In.	88.00
Chair, Morris, Wicker, Curlicues, Beadwork Panels, Rolled, Cabriole Legs, 1890s, 41 In.	1450.00
Chair, Mother-Of-Pearl Inlay, Lacquered, Shaped Crest, Victorian, 31 In., Pair	240.00
Chair, N. Cherner, Walnut, Birch, Plycraft, Bernardo, 1950s, 31 x 25 In., Pair *illus*	2415.00
Chair, Napoleon II, Louis XV Style, Padded, Scrolled Arms, Domed, Floral Crest, Arms, 39 In.	528.00
Chair, Napoleon III, Ebonized, Louis XV Style, Damask Upholstery, Arms, 1800s, Pair	1292.00
Chair, Napoleon III, Rococo Revival, Mahogany, Flower Crest, Cabriole Legs, Arms, Pair	880.00
Chair, Neoclassical, Mahogany, Adjustable Back, Padded Scrolling Arms, 42 In.	550.00
Chair, Neoclassical, Mahogany, Carved, Concave Crest, Ebony Stringing, c.1825, 33 In., Pair	5875.00
Chair, Neoclassical, Mahogany, Gondola Form, Vase Shaped, Slip Seat, 35⅝ In., Pair	201.00
Chair, Neoclassical, Mahogany, Serpentine Back, Padded Arms, Scroll Arms, 42 x 28 In.	2820.00
Chair, Neoclassical, Mahogany, Veneer, Scrolled Stiles, Splat, Upholstered, c.1830, 32 In.	323.00
Chair, Neoclassical, Painted, Pierced Cresting, Spindles, Shaped Splat, c.1815, 32 In.	558.00
Chair, Neoclassical Revival, Mahogany, Scrolled Back, Eagle Arms, 34 x 22 In., Pair	3525.00
Chair, Neogrec, Walnut, Medallion, Burl Inlay, Incised Decoration, c.1870, Pair	118.00
Chair, Nutting, Windsor, No. 432, Writing Arm, Black Paint, 2 Drawers, Paper Label	2750.00
Chair, Oak, Carved, Carved Supports, Flower Crest Back, Arms, Pair, 48 In.	646.00
Chair, Oak, Carved, Padded Back, Leather Upholstery, Acanthus Crest, 46 In.	4800.00
Chair, Oak, Maple, Banister Back, Serpentine Shape Arms, Woven Bark Seat, 43 x 22 In.	431.00
Chair, Oak, Spindle & Cane Back, Cane Seat, Swivel, Pat'd April 1895, 43 x 20 In. *illus*	230.00
Chair, Oak, Upholstered Seat, Back, Open Arms, Stretcher At Base, 17th Century	594.00
Chair, Oak, Wainscot, Paneled Back, Seat, Turned Legs, Stretchers, 45 x 18½ In., Pair	1093.00
Chair, Occasional, Beech Frame, Shaped Crest, Cane Back, Seat, France, Early1900s	217.00
Chair, Old Hickory, Cane Seat, Back, Footstool, Cane Deck, Arms, 44 x 29 & 15 x 20 In.	1200.00
Chair, Ottoman, Eames, Rosewood, Leather, Herman Miller, c.1956, 31 x 36 In. *illus*	3240.00
Chair, Painted, Slat Back, Reverse Graduated, Ring Turned Stiles, Arms, Late 1700s, 42 In.	705.00
Chair, Painted, Yellow, Brown, Turned Spindles, Arms, Rush Seat, Stretcher, 20 x 14 In.	220.00
Chair, Paul Laszlo, Pink Leather Upholstered, Arms, 28 x 35½ x 32 In.	3300.00
Chair, Philippe Starck, Ed Archer, Leather Seat, Aluminum Leg, Driade, Italy, 39 x 18 In. *illus*	1035.00
Chair, Pine, Yellow Painted, Stenciled, Fruit, 32 x 17½ In., Pair	323.00
Chair, Plank Bottom High Leg, Paint Decorated, Floral Crest, H-Stretcher, 22 In.	303.00
Chair, Plank Seat, Raked Crest, Arrow Spindles, Stretcher, Arms, 17½ In.	55.00
Chair, Provincial, Blue Paint, Flowers, Shaped Seat & Back, Splayed Legs, 36 In., Pair	822.00
Chair, Provincial, Fruitwood, Pierced Double Splat, Padded Seat, 32 x 16 x 14 In., Pair	59.00
Chair, Provincial Restauration, Fruitwood, 2 Splats, Rush Seat, Arms, 33 x 23 x 23 In.	352.00
Chair, Queen Anne, Cherry, Grain Painted, Vase Shape Splat, Rush Seat, 40½ In.	529.00
Chair, Queen Anne, Mahogany, Cabriole Legs, Pad Feet, Velvet Cover Seat, 39½ In.	920.00
Chair, Queen Anne, Mahogany, Cabriole Legs, Stretchers, Quilted Upholstery, 19½ In.	633.00
Chair, Queen Anne, Mahogany, Curved Crest, Shepherds' Crook Arms, Slip Seat, 38 In.	633.00
Chair, Queen Anne, Mahogany, Upholstered Back, Cabriole Legs, 1700s, 50 x 28 In.	6490.00
Chair, Queen Anne, Maple, Cherry, Vase Splat, Turned Posts, Stretchers, 15½ x 36 In.	144.00
Chair, Queen Anne, Maple, Yoke Crest, Vase Splat, Rush Seat, 40 In.	230.00
Chair, Queen Anne, Vase Splat, Turned Arms & Legs, Rush Seat, New England, 44½ In.	316.00
Chair, Queen Anne, Walnut, Balloon Seat, 1740-60, 40¼ In.	8400.00
Chair, Queen Anne, Walnut, c.1760, 39½ In.	2280.00
Chair, Queen Anne, Walnut, Flat Stretchers, c.1745, 40 In., Pair	16800.00
Chair, Queen Anne, Walnut, Needlepoint, Upholstered, 18 In.	1410.00
Chair, Queen Anne, Walnut, Shaped Crest, Urn Splat, Trapezoidal Seat, Cabriole Legs, c.1770	2151.00
Chair, Queen Anne, Walnut, Shaped Crest, Vase Splat, Leather Balloon Slip Seat, 37 In., Pair	978.00
Chair, Queen Anne, Walnut, Shaped Splat, Yoke Crest, Curved Arms, Cabriole Legs, 38 In.	489.00
Chair, Queen Anne, Walnut, Upholstered, Compass Seat, c.1750	8400.00
Chair, Queen Anne Style, Black Lacquer, Vase-Shaped Splat, Gilt Oriental Scene, 43 In., Pair	900.00
Chair, Queen Anne Style, Fruitwood, Crest Rail, Arms, Continental, 1900, 45 In., Pair	985.00
Chair, Queen Anne Style, Padded, Cabriole Legs, Spoon Feet, 37 x 22½ x 24 In., Pair	177.00
Chair, Queen Anne Style, Walnut, Marquetry, Needlework, Crook Arms, Dutch, Pair	1416.00
Chair, Queen Anne Transitional, Rush Seat, Vase Shape Splat, Stretcher, 39 In.	58.00
Chair, Regency, Mahogany, Reeded Panel Crest, Stiles, X Splat, Early 1800s, Pair	851.00
Chair, Regency, Painted, Ebonized, Openwork Backrest, Arm Supports, Cane Seat, 17 In.	353.00
Chair, Regency Style, Cane Seat, Reeded Crest, Splayed Legs, Arms, 35¾ In.	470.00
Chair, Regency Style, Mahogany, Cane Seat, Back, 36 x 17 x 14½ In.	2150.00

Chair, Regency Style, Mahogany, Hinged Seat, 4-Step Library Ladder, 35 x 22 x 26 In.	705.00
Chair, Regency Style, Mahogany, Upholstered, Padded, 33 x 22 x 19½ In.	590.00
Chair, Regency Style, Rosewood, Cane Seat, Brass Inlaid	120.00
Chair, Renaissance Revival, Burl Walnut, Carved, Medallion, Oval Back Padded Arms, 43 In.	118.00
Chair, Renaissance Revival, Hunzinger, Walnut, Upholstered, 39½ In., Pair ....*illus*	11950.00
Chair, Renaissance Revival, Walnut, Gilt, Flemish Tapestry Upholstery, 41 In., Pair	956.00
Chair, Renaissance Style, Walnut, Carved Arms, Backrest, X Form Base, Savonarola, Italy ...	2350.00
Chair, Rhode, Tubular Chrome, Charcoal Upholstery, Open Arm, 30½ In., Pair	418.00
Chair, Robert Venturi, Queen Anne, Black, Green Padded Seat, Knoll, c.1984, 38 In. ....*illus*	3840.00
Chair, Rocker, is listed under Rocker in this category.	
Chair, Rococo, Cane, Japanned, Cabriole Legs, Claw & Ball Feet, Pair, Continental, 16 In. ...	3290.00
Chair, Rococo, Laminated Rosewood, Serpentine Backs, Floral Crest, Mid 1800s, Pair	2350.00
Chair, Rococo, Rosewood, Laminate, Serpentine Crest Rail, Cabriole Legs, 39 In., Pair	4700.00
Chair, Rococo Revival, Rosewood, Belter Style, Laminated, Roses, Cabriole Legs, 1855	1645.00
Chair, Rococo Revival, Rosewood, Flower & Leaf Carved Crest, Brocade, 38 In., Pair	360.00
Chair, Rococo Revival, Rosewood, Laminated, Rosalie Without Grapes, 43 In.	3120.00
Chair, Rococo Style, Giltwood, Gesso, Scalloped Crest, Scroll Arms, 38 x 21 In., Pair	570.00
Chair, Rococo Style, Walnut, Slip Seat, Cabriole Legs, Continental, 18 In.	235.00
Chair, Rohde, Walnut, Leather Upholstered, Round, Arms, c.1935, 30 In.	8400.00
Chair, Rosewood, Inlay, Mother-Of-Pearl, Openwork Splats, Arms, 39½ In., Pair	348.00
Chair, Rosewood, Marble Inset, Chinese, 37½ x 25 In., Pair	590.00
Chair, Rosewood, Pierced Fret Back, Shaped Arms, Saddle Seat, Saber Legs, 33 In., Pair	3600.00
Chair, Rosewood, White Marble Inset, Chinese, 40 x 20½ x 16 In., Pair	295.00
Chair, Rush Seat, 3-Part Back, Baluster Turned Spindles, Urn Support, 1700s, 16 In.	110.00
Chair, Rush Seat, Yellow Paint, Gold Accents, Bamboo Turnings, 17½ In., Pair	94.00
Chair, Rustic, Log Construction, Woven Cane Seat, Back, Arms, 36½ x 24½ In., Pair	1800.00
Chair, Savonarola, Renaissance Style, Inlaid Mahogany, Ivory, Mother-Of-Pearl, 36 x 23 In. .	2400.00
Chair, Second Empire, Mahogany, Scrolled Backrest, Swan Form Arm Supports, France	705.00
Chair, Sergio Rodrigues, Lounge, Rosewood, White Leather, c.1968, 29 x 28½ x 32 In.	4800.00
Chair, Shaker, Birch, Pine, Canted Crest, 6 Spokes, Canterbury, N.H., c.1850, 25 In., Pair	2925.00
Chair, Shaker, Cherry, Original Varnish, Cane Seat, Tilters, Harvard, Mass., c.1850, 42½ In. .	702.00
Chair, Shaker, Enfield Tilter, Old Finish, Wool Tape Seat, Red & Olive, 41 In.	920.00
Chair, Shaker, Maple, 3 Slats, Tape Seat, Tilters, Mt. Lebanon, N.Y., c.1860, 24 In.	468.00
Chair, Shaker, Maple, Black Paint, Tape Seat, 4 Slats, Arms, Mt. Lebanon, N.Y., c.1925, 46 In.	1521.00
Chair, Shaker, Maple, Ocher Stained Varnish, 2 Slats, Tape Seat, Alfred, Me., c.1835, 30 In. ..	761.00
Chair, Shaker, Maple, Varnish, 4 Slats, Mushroom Arms, Rush Seat, Mt. Lebanon, c.1925, 45 In. .	2223.00
Chair, Shaker, No. 6, Rocker, Black Paint, Arm, Mt. Lebanon, 35 x 13¼ In.	940.00
Chair, Shaker, School, Birch, Maple, Pine, 4 Spindles, Revolving, New Lebanon, 1860, 30 In., Pair ..	1053.00
Chair, Shaw Walker, Aluminum, Wood, Arms, Pair	717.00
Chair, Slat Back, Black Painted, 47 x 16½ In.	176.00
Chair, Slat Back, Woven Cane Seat, Painted, Blue, Red, Yellow, Green, Child's, 16 x 6 In.	176.00
Chair, Slipper, Gold Upholstery, Fringed Edge, Kroehler, 1950s, 30 In., Pair	1440.00
Chair, Slipper, Rococo Revival, Barrel Back, Skirt, Arms, Upholstered, 30 x 26 In., Pair	1298.00
Chair, Slipper, Rococo Revival, Rosewood, Laminated, 44¾ In.	3760.00
Chair, Slipper, Victorian, Horn Back, Arms, Legs, Silver Plate Finials, Velvet, 45 In.	1725.00
Chair, Spanish, Curved Back, Carved Crest, Scroll Arms, Early 1700s, 43 x 24 In.	2300.00
Chair, Spindle, Maple, Black & Gold, Green & White Design, 8-Point Stars, Arms, 35 In.	230.00
Chair, Stickley & Brandt Co., Drop Arms, 3 Back Slats, Spring Leather Cushion, 38 x 35 In. ..	3900.00
Chair, Stickley & Brandt Co., Underarm Slat, Mortised Posts, Leather Cushions, 38 x 34 In. ..	3120.00
Chair, Stickley Bros., Inlaid Flowers, 42 x 18 x 16 In. ....*illus*	1140.00
Chair, Stool, Mies Van Der Rohe, Tan Leather, Stainless Steel Base, Knoll, 30 x 14 In.	2115.00
Chair, Tiger Maple, Lyre Back, Cane Seats, Painted Pillow Crests, c.1870, Pair	2350.00
Chair, Tub, George III, Hepplewhite, Mahogany, England, c.1790	2200.00
Chair, Tub, Georgian Style, Mahogany, Leather Upholstered, Padded, Cabriole Legs, 31 In. ..	646.00
Chair, Tub, Post Modern, Lucite, Upholstered Seat, Casters, c.1990, Pair	358.00
Chair, V. Panton, Plywood, Laminated, Ebonized, S-Shaped, c.1956, 31¼ In.	4800.00
Chair, Walnut, Balloon Back, Floral Tapestry, Round Footstool, Victorian, 38 In. ......*illus*	82.00
Chair, Walnut, Baroque, Padded, Back, Seat, Turned, Blocked Legs, Italy, 50½ In.	2820.00
Chair, Walnut, Carved, Arched Crest, Scroll, Serpentine Seat, Victorian, 38½ In., Pair	200.00
Chair, Walnut, Carved, Gothic Arch, Tufted Upholstery, c.1860, 63 x 27 In., Pair	375.00
Chair, Walnut, Carved, Hoop Back, Flowers, Serpentine Seat, Victorian, 37½ In., Pair	288.00
Chair, Walnut, Carved Frame, Open Arms, Upholstered, Victorian	246.00
Chair, Walnut, Lacquered, Yoke Back, Arms, Chinese, 17th Century, 40 x 23 In., Pair	5900.00
Chair, Wegner, Papa, No. AP 19, 1951, 29 x 33 In. ....*illus*	4800.00
Chair, Wegner, Walnut, Beech, c.1950s, Pair, 27¼ In.	6600.00
Chair, Wicker, Diamond Designs, Fancywork, Scallops, Victorian, 1890s, 37 x 30 In.	975.00

F

Furniture, Chair, Stickley Bros., Inlaid Flowers, 42 x 18 x 16 In.
$1140.00

Furniture, Chair, Walnut, Balloon Back, Floral Tapestry, Round Footstool, Victorian, 38 In.
$82.00

Furniture, Chair, Wegner, Papa, No. AP 19, 1951, 29 x 33 In.
$4800.00

Furniture, Chair, William IV, Oak, Curved Back, Carved Scroll Supports, Turned Legs, Leather
$3600.00

Furniture, Chair, Windsor, Bow Back, Carved Arms & Seat, White & Co., England, 27 In., Child's
$345.00

Furniture, Chair, Windsor, Comb Back, 7 Spindles, Shaped Crest, Saddle Seat, Yellow Paint, 47 In.
$575.00

Furniture, Chair, Windsor, Comb Back, Writing, 7 Spindles, Shaped Desk Arm, 41 x 29 In.
$518.00

Chair, Wicker, Hand Cane Back, Latticework, Curlicues, 1890s, 43 x 26 In.	1250.00
Chair, Wicker, Hand Cane Back, Seat, Cabriole Legs, Brass Caps, 1890s, 36 In.	875.00
Chair, Wicker, Natural, Beadwork, Loops, Curlicues, Cane Seat, 1890s, 41 In.	1450.00
Chair, Wicker, Photographer's, Victorian, Scalloped Edge, Wrapped Legs, c.1890s, 43 In.	2250.00
Chair, Wicker, Reception, Victorian, Curlicued Crest, Reed Wrapper Spools, c.1890s, 37 In.	757.00
Chair, Wicker, Serpentine Roll Frame, Hand Cane, 1890s, 36 In.	875.00
Chair, Wicker, Serpentine Rolled Crest, Beadwork, Cane, Arms, 1880s, 37 In.	975.00
Chair, Wicker, Serpentine Rolled Crest, Twist Wrapped Rosettes, Arms, Victorian, 34 In.	975.00
Chair, Wicker, Twist Wrapped Finials, Fancywork, Curlicue Arms, Victorian, 42 In.	1450.00
Chair, Wicker, Victorian, Cabriole Legs, Cane Seat, c.1890s, 40 In.	795.00
Chair, William & Mary, Maple, Shaped Crests, c.1790, 42 In.	1320.00
Chair, William & Mary, Oak, Carved, Leaf, Cane Backrest, Seat, Barley Twist Legs, Pair	353.00
Chair, William & Mary, Walnut, Arched Back, Upholstered, 42 x 28 In., Pair	805.00
Chair, William IV, Mahogany, Balloon Shape Backrest, Shield, C-Scrolls, c.1835, 17 In.	118.00
Chair, William IV, Oak, Curved Back, Carved Scroll Supports, Turned Legs, Leather ....*illus*	3600.00
Chair, Windsor, 4 Turned Spindles, Painted, Flowering Vines, c.1830, 34 In.	4113.00
Chair, Windsor, 6 Spindles, Black Paint, Splayed Legs, Stretcher, 34 In.	633.00
Chair, Windsor, 7 Spindles, Bamboo Turned, Saddle Seat, H-Stretcher	413.00
Chair, Windsor, 7 Spindles, Black, Stepped Crest, Shaped Seat, Turned Legs, Box Stretcher, 18 In.	154.00
Chair, Windsor, 7 Spindles, Red Over Green Paint, Turned Legs, H-Stretcher, Arms, Pa., 17 In.	6600.00
Chair, Windsor, 7 Spindles, Shaped Arms, Baluster Supports, H-Stretcher, 15¾ In.	1155.00
Chair, Windsor, 7 Spindles, Shaped Saddle Seat, Bamboo Turnings, 22 In.	990.00
Chair, Windsor, 7 Spindles, Side, Birdcage, Bamboo Turned, Box Stretcher, 17½ In. Seat	72.00
Chair, Windsor, Arrow Back, Painted, Multicolored, c.1815, Arms, 8 In.	418.00
Chair, Windsor, Bamboo Turnings, Tall Arms, Black Paint, 30 In.	374.00
Chair, Windsor, Bow Back, 7 Spindles, Hickory, Pine, Turned Legs, H-Stretcher, 37 In.	115.00
Chair, Windsor, Bow Back, Carved Arms & Seat, White & Co., England, 27 In., Child's ..*illus*	345.00
Chair, Windsor, Bow Back, Continuous Arm, c.1770	1750.00
Chair, Windsor, Brace Back, 7 Spindles, Bowed Crest Rail, c.1800, 39 In., Pair	3525.00
Chair, Windsor, Brace Back, 9 Spindles, Back Bow, Saddle Seat, c.1800, 36½ In.	1440.00
Chair, Windsor, Comb Back, 7 Spindles, Painted, Serpentine Crest Rail, c.1810, 44 In.	823.00
Chair, Windsor, Comb Back, 7 Spindles, Shaped Crest, Saddle Seat, Yellow Paint, 47 In. .*illus*	575.00
Chair, Windsor, Comb Back, 9 Spindles, Shaped Crest, Carved Ears, Phila., 17 In.	1320.00
Chair, Windsor, Comb Back, Ash, Maple, Chestnut, Turned Spindles, c.1790, 48½ In.	1410.00
Chair, Windsor, Comb Back, Bamboo Turnings, Shaped Pine Seat, 17 x 40 In.	143.00
Chair, Windsor, Comb Back, Knuckle Arm, Nutting, Label, 45 In.	1275.00
Chair, Windsor, Comb Back, Painted, Arms, Philadelphia, c.1790, 44¼ In.	14400.00
Chair, Windsor, Comb Back, Serpentine Crest, Carved Terminals, Turned Legs, Arms	2032.00
Chair, Windsor, Comb Back, Shaped Crest, Scrolled Arm Supports, Plank Seat, 39 x 25 In.	431.00
Chair, Windsor, Comb Back, Writing, 7 Spindles, Shaped Desk Arm, 41 x 29 In. ....*illus*	518.00
Chair, Windsor, Continuous Arm, 10 Spindles, Chestnut, S. Tracy, Conn., 35 x 22 In. ...*illus*	1725.00
Chair, Windsor, Continuous Arm, 36 In.	1150.00
Chair, Windsor, Fanback, 7 Spindles, Black Paint, Serpentine Crest, Bamboo Turnings, 36 In., Pair	978.00
Chair, Windsor, Fanback, 7 Spindles, Painted, Serpentine Crest Rail, c.1780, 34 In.	1000.00
Chair, Windsor, Fanback, 8 Spindles, Black Paint, Serpentine Crest, Reed Legs, 37 In.	387.00
Chair, Windsor, Fanback, Red Stain, Serpentine Concave Crest Rail, c.1780, 36 In.	441.00
Chair, Windsor, Late Georgian, Elm, Wheel Carved Splat, Spindles, Early 1800s, 6 Piece	2391.00
Chair, Windsor, Low Back, 14 Spindles, Saddle Seat, Black Paint, Continuous Arm	4600.00
Chair, Windsor, Painted, Stenciled Fruit, Green, Gold, Copper, Black, Pinstriping, c.1830, 27 In.	388.00
Chair, Windsor, Rod Back, 7 Spindles, Step-Down Crest, Bamboo Turnings, Black Paint, 34 In.	200.00
Chair, Windsor, Rod Back, Writing Arm, Graining, Yellow Striping, Lathrop Family, N.Y., 29 In.	230.00
Chair, Windsor, Sack Back, 7 Spindles, Continuous Arm, Black Paint, 37½ In.	2760.00
Chair, Windsor, Sack Back, Painted, D-Shape Seat, Bamboo Turned Legs, Arms, 44 In.	478.00
Chair, Windsor, Sack Back, Patina, New England, 38 x 25 In.	825.00
Chair, Windsor, Sack Back, Writing Desk, Tapered Legs, Arms, 34 In.	657.00
Chair, Windsor, Sack Back, Yellow Painted, Arms, c.1790	3000.00
Chair, Windsor, Thumb Back, Tablet Top, Painted, c.1815, 34¼ In., Pair	6000.00
Chair, Windsor, Thumb Back, Tablet Top, Painted, Flowers, c.1815, 35 In., Pair	9000.00
Chair, Windsor, Writing, Writing Arm & Footrest, Oversized, Drawer Under Seat, 44 In.	575.00
Chair, Wing, Bar Harbor, Magazine Pocket, Latticework, Braiding, 1920s, 42 x 29 In.	1150.00
Chair, Wing, Bar Harbor, Wicker, Mountain Top Style, Wide Arms, c.1910, 43 x 31 In.	975.00
Chair, Wing, Birch, Ebonized, Medallion, Padded Back, Continental, 17½ In., Pair	708.00
Chair, Wing, Chippendale, Leather Upholstery, Scalloped Crest, Scrolled Arms, 44 x 32 In.	858.00
Chair, Wing, Chippendale, Mahogany, 44 x 19 In.	1320.00
Chair, Wing, Federal, Mahogany, Rolled Arms, Square Legs, 48 x 35 In. ....*illus*	8625.00
Chair, Wing, Mahogany, Leather Tufted Upholstery, Cabriole Legs, Pad Feet, 40 In., Pair	352.00

F

Chair, Wing, Potty, Hole In Seat, Red Paint, 23½ x 11¾ x 7½ In. ....*illus*	173.00
Chair, Wing, Yellow & Gray Leather, Brass Tack Decoration, 46 x 31 In., Pair	1380.00
Chair, Wolfgang Hoffmann, Lounge, Chromium, Leather, Red	329.00
Chair, Yellow Paint, Stencil, Cane Seat & Back, 32½ In., Pair	603.00
Chair & Ottoman, Eames, No. 670 & 671, Rosewood, Leather, Herman Miller, 33 In. ...*illus*	3000.00
Chair & Ottoman, Edwardian, Mahogany, Leather Upholstered, 36 In., Pair	2585.00
Chair & Ottoman, Edwardian, Mahogany, Leather Upholstered, 41 x 20 x 36 In.	1997.00
Chair Set, 3 Slat Back, Turned Finials, Oak Split Seat, Tennessee, 1800s, 36½ In., 6	546.00
Chair Set, Balloon Back, Plank Bottom, Flower Crest, 17 In., 8	440.00
Chair Set, Bar, Iron, Steel, Post Modern, Curved Back, Scroll Arms, Woven Seat, 40 In., 4 ...	646.00
Chair Set, Bar, Steel, Deep Curved Back, Woven Seat, 1980s, 40 In., 4	650.00
Chair Set, Biedermeier, Birch, Curved Crest, Ebonized Wreath Splat, 39 In., 12	1320.00
Chair Set, Biedermeier, Fruitwood, Parcel Gilt, Padded, Saber Legs, 2 Armchairs, 12	14000.00
Chair Set, Biedermeier, Walnut, Crest, Narrow Splat, Tapered Legs, 35 In., 10	10800.00
Chair Set, Charles X, Fruitwood, Fan-Shape Splat, 2 Armchairs, c.1815, 37½ In., 6	3525.00
Chair Set, Charles X, Fruitwood, Portrait Medallion, Saber Legs, 2 Armchairs, 6	3525.00
Chair Set, Chippendale, Arched Crest, Rush Seat, Square Legs, 41 x 18 In., 5 ....*illus*	863.00
Chair Set, Chippendale, Mahogany, Cabriole Legs, Claw & Ball Feet, 12	6000.00
Chair Set, Chippendale, Mahogany, Carved, Pierced Splat, Fluted, Upholstered Seat, 39 In., 12 ..	4230.00
Chair Set, Chippendale, Mahogany, Domed Back, Gothic Arches, Square Legs, 43 In., 12 ...	4080.00
Chair Set, Chippendale, Rococo Style, Mahogany, Cabriole Legs, 2 Armchairs, 36 In., 12	8225.00
Chair Set, Chippendale, Serpentine Crest Rail, Square Legs, Upholstered, 6	7170.00
Chair Set, Chippendale, Walnut, Rococo Ribbonbacks, Shell Crest, 19 In., 5	880.00
Chair Set, Chippendale Style, Mahogany, Carved, 2 Armchairs, Pierced Splat, 12	7344.00
Chair Set, Chippendale Style, Rush Seat, Pierced Splat, 38 In., 6	1035.00
Chair Set, Eames, DCM, Herman Miller, 1958, 29¼ In., 4 ....*illus*	960.00
Chair Set, Elm, Turned, Rush Seat, Provincial, 18	5700.00
Chair Set, Empire Style, Giltwood, Painted, Cream, Carved Back, Saber Legs, 37 In., 6	999.00
Chair Set, English Queen Anne Style, Walnut, 2 Armchairs, Early 1900s, 40 In., 6	2242.00
Chair Set, Federal, Mahogany, Carved, Shieldback, c.1790, 37½ In., 6	4200.00
Chair Set, Federal, Mahogany, Reeded Spindles, Upholstered, 36 In., 12	14100.00
Chair Set, Federal, Mahogany, Square Back, N.Y., c.1800, 37 In., 12	54000.00
Chair Set, Finn Juhl, Walnut, Fabric Covered, Back, Seat, Cylindrical Legs, c.1952, 5	1912.00
Chair Set, Flemish Style, Beech, Leaf Carved Backrest, Scrolls, Overupholstered, 6	411.00
Chair Set, French Provincial, Oak, Domed Top, Oval Pierced Splat, Cane Seat, 34 In., 8	1560.00
Chair Set, G. Stickley, 3 Slats, Green Leather Seat, 37¼ x 17¾ x 16 In., 8	5400.00
Chair Set, G. Stickley, 5 Slats, Tacked Leather Seat, 36 x 25½ x 21½ In., 4	2880.00
Chair Set, G. Stickley, 5 Slats, Tacked Leather Seat, 37¾ x 25½ x 21½ In., 4	3600.00
Chair Set, G. Stickley, No. 370, Oak, 3 Slats, Woven Seat, c.1912, 36¼ In., 5	1293.00
Chair Set, George II Style, Walnut, Carved, Needlepoint Back, 4	5400.00
Chair Set, George III, Mahogany, Crossed Palm Frond Crest, 2 Armchairs, 14	6195.00
Chair Set, George III, Yew, Padded Seat, Late 18th Century, 4	1228.00
Chair Set, George III Style, Domed Crest, Stylized Sheaf Splat, Square Legs, Slip Seat, 38 In., 5 ..	1175.00
Chair Set, George III Style, Mahogany, Leaf-Carved Crest, 2 Armchairs, 39 In., 12	4230.00
Chair Set, Georgian, Mahogany, Carved, Pierced Splat, Slip Seats, 40 In., 8	590.00
Chair Set, Georgian Style, Mahogany, Openwork Splat, 39 In., 12	5750.00
Chair Set, Gothic Style, Oak, Pierced Crockets & Stretchers, Padded Seat & Back, 41 In., 4 ..	705.00
Chair Set, Grain Painted, Tablet Back, c.1825, 6	960.00
Chair Set, Half Arrow Back, Red, Black, Flowers, Leaves, Apple Green, 6	303.00
Chair Set, Half Spindle Plank Bottom, Black Ground, Stencil, 18 In., 4	1100.00
Chair Set, Knoll, Gray Metal Frame, Cream & Gray Heather Upholstered Seat, 32½ In., 6 ...	705.00
Chair Set, L. & J.G. Stickley, Ladder Back, Drop In Seats, 34½ x 17 x 16 In., 4	1440.00
Chair Set, L. & J.G. Stickley, Oak, Early 20th Century, 34½ x 16½ In., 4	460.00
Chair Set, Ladder Back, 3 Curved Slats, Splint Seat, Old Red Finish, 36 In., 6	518.00
Chair Set, Ladder Back, Mahogany, Acorn Finials, 2 Armchairs, 45 In., 6	384.00
Chair Set, Louis XV, Beech, Molded Cartouche, Upholstered, Cabriole Legs, 4	8400.00
Chair Set, Louis XV Style, Fruitwood, Leather Upholstered, Cabriole Legs, 38 In., 6	1645.00
Chair Set, Louis XV Style, Provincial, Polychrome, Curved Crest, Rush Seat, 38 In., 12	2585.00
Chair Set, Louis XV Style, Shell Cartouche, Carved, Cane, 1900s, 38 x 21 In., 4	472.00
Chair Set, Louis XVI, Beech, Lyre Back, Horseshoe Shaped Seat, Fluted Legs, 35 In., 4	3055.00
Chair Set, Louis XVI, Cane Back, Dore, Upholstered Seat, c.1940, 40 x 19 In., 6	4000.00
Chair Set, Louis XVI Style, Carved, Upholstered, Oval Backs, Fluted Legs, Arm, 38 In., 5	1000.00
Chair Set, Louis XVI Style, Floral Tapestry Upholstery, Mid 19th Century, 4	4094.00
Chair Set, Louis XVI Style, Painted, Turned Fluted Legs, Bulb Feet, 35 x 19 In., 6	1298.00
Chair Set, Lounge, Mesh Seats, Aluminum, Enameled, Richard Schultz, Knoll, 1967, 4	1293.00
Chair Set, Mahogany, Balloon Back, Wide Crest, Front Legs, Mohair, Arm, 9	1725.00

Furniture, Chair, Windsor, Continuous Arm, 10 Spindles, Chestnut Seat, S. Tracy, Conn., 35 x 22 In.
$1725.00

F

Furniture, Chair, Wing, Federal, Mahogany, Rolled Arms, Square Legs, 48 x 35 In.
$8625.00

Furniture, Chair, Wing, Potty, Hole In Seat, Red Paint, 23½ x 11¾ x 7½ In.
$173.00

FURNITURE

Furniture, Chair & Ottoman, Eames, No. 670 & 671, Rosewood, Leather, Herman Miller, 33 In.
$3000.00

Furniture, Chair Set, Chippendale, Arched Crest, Rush Seat, Square Legs, 41 x 18 In., 5
$863.00

Furniture, Chair Set, Eames, DCM, Herman Miller, 1958, 29¼ In., 4
$960.00

Furniture, Chest, Blanket, Federal, Poplar, 2 Drawers, New England, c.1830, 38 x 39 x 18 In.
$3300.00

Chair Set, Mahogany, Tree Of Life-Carved Back, Padded Seat, Fluted Legs, Italy, 36 In., 4	1440.00
Chair Set, Maple, Bowed Crest Rail, Splat, Upholstered, Saber Legs, Deco Style, 4	956.00
Chair Set, Neoclassical, Mahogany, Carved, Molded Crest, Leafy Shell Splat, 8	2160.00
Chair Set, Neoclassical, Rosewood, Upholstered, 2 Armchairs, 36¾ & 35½ In., 8	9600.00
Chair Set, Neoclassical, Scroll Back, Mahogany, Rosette Carved Splat, c.1820, 32 In., 6	3408.00
Chair Set, Neoclassical, Vasiform Splat, Saber Legs, Slip Covered Seat, 1800s, 6	183.00
Chair Set, Nutting, Windsor, Brace Back, No. 301, New England Turnings, 4	3580.00
Chair Set, Oak, Red Leather Upholstery, Carved, Late 19th Century, 6	409.00
Chair Set, Oval Padded Back, Seat, Fluted Legs, Cream Painted, 18th Century, Demark, 6	7800.00
Chair Set, Painted, Fruit, Flowers, Rectangular Splats, Spindles, c.1825, 34 In., 4	2585.00
Chair Set, Palmwood, Veneer, c.1950, 32 In., 8	5040.00
Chair Set, Parlor, Rococo, Rosewood, Carved, Oval Backs, Chintz Upholstery, 6	1645.00
Chair Set, Provincial, Fruitwood, Shaped Crest, 2 Horizontal Splats, Rush Seat, 45 In., 8	2800.00
Chair Set, Queen Anne, Maple, Carved, Spooned Crest Rail, Rush Seat, 42 In., 6	19975.00
Chair Set, Queen Anne, Rush Seat, Carved Yoked Crest Rail, Spanish Front Feet, 4	1315.00
Chair Set, Queen Anne Style, Olive Wood, Scrolled Splats, 2 Armchairs, 8	2645.00
Chair Set, Queen Anne Style, Solid Splat, Yoke Crest Rail, Red Paint, Splint Seat, 4	575.00
Chair Set, Queen Anne Style, Walnut, Padded, Upholstered, Cabriole Legs, 40 In., 6	354.00
Chair Set, Red Paint, Flowers, Shaped Crest, Splat & Angel Wing Corners, 32 In., 6	633.00
Chair Set, Regency, Mahogany, Carved, Paneled Crest Rail, 32 x 20 In., 8	4700.00
Chair Set, Regency, Mahogany, Curved Crest, 2 With Scroll Arms, 7	1292.00
Chair Set, Regency, Mahogany, Inlay, Tablet Back, 2 Armchairs, 33½ In., 8	2645.00
Chair Set, Renaissance Revival, Oak, Carved, Paw Feet, 2 Armchairs, 10	43475.00
Chair Set, Ribbonback, Mahogany, England, Late 1800s, 6	1008.00
Chair Set, Robsjohn-Gibbings, Mahogany, Upholstered, Widdicomb, 34 In., 6	1410.00
Chair Set, Rococo Revival, Dutch Oak, Carved, Padded Seat, Cabriole Legs, 46 In., 12	7403.00
Chair Set, Rococo Revival, Rosewood, Carved Crest, Upholstered, 45 In., 6	4320.00
Chair Set, Rosewood Legs, Frame, Blue Upholstery, Denmark, 1960, 30 In., 8	550.00
Chair Set, Shaker, Red & White Tape Seat, 38 In., 6	449.00
Chair Set, Teak, Curved Back, Seat, Denmark, c.1970, 4 Piece	384.00
Chair Set, Teak, Curved Back Rail, Rope Seat, Borge Mortenson, 31 In., 6	1645.00
Chair Set, Teak, Green Upholstery, Adjustable, Kai Christensen, 31 In., 8	2350.00
Chair Set, Thonet Style, Bentwood, Cane Seat, Early 20th Century, 36 In., 8	115.00
Chair Set, Victorian, Iron, Round Back & Seat, Scrolled Splat, Tubular Legs, Pad Feet, 36 In., 4	660.00
Chair Set, Victorian, Walnut, 38¾ x 22 x 18½ In., 6	252.00
Chair Set, Walnut, Carved, Dolphin Flanked Cartouche, Mid 1800s, 8	9988.00
Chair Set, Walnut, Gadrooned Crest, Curbed Splat, Cabriole Legs, Flemish, 4	1298.00
Chair Set, Walnut, Mother-Of-Pearl, Bone Inlay, Cabriole Legs, 39 In., 4	9600.00
Chair Set, Walnut, Plank Seat, Molded Edge, Shaped Crest, 1800s, 35 x 17 In., 6	115.00
Chair Set, Wegner, Stacking, Manufactured By Fritz Hansen, 1958, 29 In., 4	1955.00
Chair Set, Wegner, Wishbone, Twine Seat, Labels, Carl Hansen & Son, c.1955, 29 In., 4	1293.00
Chair Set, Windsor, Arrow Back, Painted, Bamboo Turnings, c.1830, 33 In., 6	470.00
Chair Set, Windsor, Maple, Curved Crest, Spindled Back, Saddle Seat, 35 In., 8	575.00
Chair Set, Windsor, Tablet Back, Bamboo Turnings, Paper Label, Rev. P.H. Dalton, 34 In., 5	2645.00
Chair Set, Windsor, Thumb Back, Step-Down Crest Rail, Arrow Splats, 34 In., 4	690.00
Chair Set, Wirework, Painted, Green, Arm, 3	478.00
Chair Set, Wood Laminate, Curvilinear Form, Philippe Starck, 1 Armchair, 34 In., 7	1410.00
Chair-Table, Maple, Pine, Seat With Arms, Box Stretcher Base, 29 x 50½ In.	1495.00
Chair-Table, Oak, Rounded Corner Top, Hinged Lid Compartment, Cushion, 30 x 54 In.	403.00
Chair-Table, Pine, 2-Board Top, Drawer, Turned Uprights, Dry Brown Finish, 35 In.	460.00
Chair-Table, Pine, Maple, Round, Medial Shelf, 28 x 41½ In.	2233.00
Chair-Table, Pine, Maple, Round Top, Battens, Dovetailed Drawer, 1800s, 29 x 45 In.	1150.00
Chair-Table, Pine, Poplar, Tilt Lift Top, Hinged Seat, Pa., 19th Century, 30 x 48 In.	863.00
Chair-Table, Scrubbed Top, Red Paint, 30 x 40 In.	1955.00
Chair-Table, Wicker, Rolled, Arched Spiral Twist Supports, Heywood, Victorian	2850.00
Chaise Longue, Barcelona, Chromium, Wool Upholstered, 70 x 29 x 27 In.	4481.00
Chaise Longue, Chippendale, Mahogany, Flame Stitch Upholstery, 1900s, 71 In.	780.00
Chaise Longue, Edwardian, Mahogany, Leather Upholstered, 25 x 68 In.	1292.00
Chaise Longue, Le Corbusier, Tubular Steel, Enameled Base, c.1980, 72 In.	333.00
Chaise Longue, Louis XV Style, Painted, Serpentine Crest, Upholstered Back, 34 x 60 In.	384.00
Chaise Longue, Magazine Pocket, Bar Harbor, Wicker, Cup Holder, Arched Foot Rest, c.1920s	1950.00
Chaise Longue, Marcel Breuer, Angular Frame, Upholstered, c.1936, 32 x 51 In.	2700.00
Chaise Longue, Wicker, Cushion, Rolled Back, Arms, Early 1900s, 37 x 61 x 33 In.	147.00
Chaise Longue, Wicker, Weave Pattern, Rosettes Arms, Full Skirt, Twist Feet, 1920, 58 In.	1850.00
Chest, 5 Drawers, Georgian, Mahogany, Early 19th Century, 36 In.	728.00
Chest, 6-Board, Decorated, Painted, Hinged, Interior Till, Lattice Surface, 27 x 45 In.	1175.00

Chest, 6-Board, Painted, Hinged Top, Applied Edge, Lidded Till, c.1825, 22 x 49 In. 3525.00
Chest, 6-Board, Pine, Painted, Molded Top, Cutout Ends, Abstract Earthworm, 24 x 50 In. ... 4113.00
Chest, Art Deco, Mahogany Veneer, Round Corners, Brass Hardware, Red Lion, 49 x 35 In. .. 1175.00
Chest, Blanket, 3 Tombstone Reserves, Vinegar Grain, Bracket Base, 1800s, 22 x 51 In. 3107.00
Chest, Blanket, 6-Board, Red Paint, Molded Edges, Bracket Base, c.1800, 17 x 17 x 47 In. ... 575.00
Chest, Blanket, Arches, Flowers, Hearts, Applied Edge, Molded Bracket Base, 1700s, 22 x 48 In. 2988.00
Chest, Blanket, Arts & Crafts Style, Figured Cypress, Copper Mounts, Iron, 16 x 47 In. 940.00
Chest, Blanket, Brown Grain Paint, Yellow Ground, Dovetailed, Pa., 23 x 44 In. 220.00
Chest, Blanket, Cherry, 6-Board, Turned Feet, 16 x 11¾ x 24 In. 863.00
Chest, Blanket, Chestnut, Dovetailed Case, Scalloped Apron, Inlay, 11½ x 5⅝ In. 546.00
Chest, Blanket, Chippendale, 3 Drawers, Red Paint, 38 x 18 x 42 In. 1265.00
Chest, Blanket, Chippendale, Paint Decorated, Softwood, Drawers, 27 x 51 In. 440.00
Chest, Blanket, Chippendale, Pine, Pa., c.1800, 20½ x 50½ In. 9600.00
Chest, Blanket, Chippendale, Pine, Painted, Blue, c.1795, 41 x 39 x 19 In. 9600.00
Chest, Blanket, Chippendale, Walnut, Heart Shaped Escutcheons, c.1780, 30 x 51 In. 1650.00
Chest, Blanket, Curly Maple, Dovetailed, Line Inlay, Keyhole, Miniature, 10 x 6 x 6 In. 2875.00
Chest, Blanket, Decorated, 3 Drawers, Concentric Circles, Glass Knobs, 28 x 50 In. 1320.00
Chest, Blanket, Dovetailed, Red Paint, 15 x 38 x 13 In. 125.00
Chest, Blanket, Drawer, Rag Design, Scrolled Apron, Bracket Feet, New Eng., 36 x 43 In. 2860.00
Chest, Blanket, English Oak, Lid, 8 Sunken Panels, Geometric Inlay, 28 x 60 In. 220.00
Chest, Blanket, Federal, Poplar, 2 Drawers, New England, c.1830, 38 x 39 x 18 In. ......*illus* 3300.00
Chest, Blanket, Federal, Softwood, Feather Grain Paint, Strap Hinges, Bracket Feet, 26 x 50 In. 715.00
Chest, Blanket, Figured Cherry, Poplar, Fitted Interior, 1800s, 25 x 50 In. 1955.00
Chest, Blanket, Garlands, Bouquets, Strap Hinges, Interior Drawers, 1900s, 28 x 45 In. 206.00
Chest, Blanket, Grain Paint, Green Base & Trim, 19th Century, 16½ x 41⅞ x 17 In. 360.00
Chest, Blanket, Hinged Lid, Columns, Hearts, Vines, Multicolored, 23 x 50 x 22 In. 3107.00
Chest, Blanket, Hinged Lid, Painted, Vases, Flowers, Bracket Feet, 25 x 52 x 23 In. 717.00
Chest, Blanket, Inlaid Figured Walnut, Applied Beaded Molding, 1800s, 23 x 49 In. 1093.00
Chest, Blanket, Lift Top, Pine, Flowers, Urns, Johannes Rank, 1799, 23 x 52 In. ....*illus* 3450.00
Chest, Blanket, Lift Top, Poplar, Painted, Turned Feet, c.1830, 26 x 43½ x 20 In. 7800.00
Chest, Blanket, Maple, Dovetailed, Ogee Bracket Feet, 17 x 8 In. 373.00
Chest, Blanket, Oak, Pine, Carved, Snipe Hinges, c.1790, 36 x 14 In. 1595.00
Chest, Blanket, Paint Decorated, Astragal Painted Panels, Adam Folier, 1782, 24 x 49 In. 3850.00
Chest, Blanket, Paint Decorated, Red Flame Graining, Molded Lid, Bracket Feet, 28 x 48 In. . 1980.00
Chest, Blanket, Painted, 2 Drawers, Bracket Base, Cadarina Weisen, 1769, 24 x 51 x 23 In. .. 1793.00
Chest, Blanket, Painted, 6-Board, Turned Feet, Blue, Red Panels, Grained, 21 x 35 In. 1955.00
Chest, Blanket, Painted, Multicolored, Tulip Design, 3 Drawers, c.1825, 52 x 22 In. 4183.00
Chest, Blanket, Painted, Robin's Egg Blue, 21 x 49 x 19 In. 173.00
Chest, Blanket, Painted, Signed, Stahly, 1868, 24 x 45 In. 2750.00
Chest, Blanket, Painted, Softwood, Christian Selzer, Miniature, 5½ x 12⅝ In. 468.00
Chest, Blanket, Painted, Stenciled, 2 Drawers, Maria Catrina Bushen, 1788, 28 x 48 In. 9560.00
Chest, Blanket, Pine, 6-Board, Strap Hinges, Oak Till, Bootjack Ends, 25 x 52 In. 7475.00
Chest, Blanket, Pine, 6-Board, Till, Scalloped Apron, Nail Construction, 43 x 17 x 25 In. 632.00
Chest, Blanket, Pine, Blue, Tapered Feet, Hand Planed, Iron Butt Hinges, 20 x 72 x 17 In. ... 505.00
Chest, Blanket, Pine, Dovetailed, Carved, Inlaid Design, Iron Lock, 37 x 19 In. 3105.00
Chest, Blanket, Pine, Dovetailed, Till, 3 Beaded Drawers, Bracket Feet, 48 x 31 In. 374.00
Chest, Blanket, Pine, Drawer, Lift Top, Red Paint, Brass Escutcheon Plate, 33 x 37 In. 2128.00
Chest, Blanket, Pine, Drawer, Offset Wrought Iron Hinges, Fitted Interior, 33 x 46 In. 248.00
Chest, Blanket, Pine, Grain Painted, Flowers, Hinged Lid, 1835, 22 x 50 x 26 In. ......*illus* 518.00
Chest, Blanket, Pine, Lift Top, Chrome Blue, Applied Molded Edge, 28 x 35½ In. 690.00
Chest, Blanket, Pine, Ocher Painted, 19th Century, 19½ x 43 x 20½ In. 1800.00
Chest, Blanket, Pine, Painted, Mitered Corners, Dovetailed Lift Top, Bracket Feet, 24 x 45 In. 374.00
Chest, Blanket, Pine, Painted Flowers, Turned Feet, 1840, 24½ x 36¼ x 18 In. 7800.00
Chest, Blanket, Pine, Red, Molded Edge, Open Till, Cutout Ends, Molded Base, 22 x 41 In. ... 230.00
Chest, Blanket, Pine, Red Smoke, Child's, 15 x 22½ x 11½ In. 3300.00
Chest, Blanket, Pine, Thumb Molded Drawer, Shaped Skirt, 1800s, 34 x 39 In. 568.00
Chest, Blanket, Pine, Yellow, Red Grain Painted, England, c.1830, 21 x 36 x 16 In. 3900.00
Chest, Blanket, Poplar, Lift Top, Dovetailed, Applied Molding, Painted, 1800s, 18 x 16 In. 460.00
Chest, Blanket, Red & White Paint, Dovetailed, 20 x 38 x 19 In. 863.00
Chest, Blanket, Red Paint, Miniature, 9 x 3 x 4 In. 144.00
Chest, Blanket, Salmon, Yellow Stamping, 2 Drawers, Black Molding, 29 x 44 In. 4950.00
Chest, Blanket, Salmon & Yellow Feathering, 2 Drawers, Red Molding, Turned Feet, 27 x 43 In. .. 3850.00
Chest, Blanket, Salmon & Yellow Feathering, Red Molding, Turned Feet, 16½ x 26 In. 5225.00
Chest, Blanket, Secret Panel, Red, Salmon, Black, Wayne, Ohio, c.1835, 26 x 43 In. 4180.00
Chest, Blanket, Shaker, Pine, Poplar, Drawer, Dovetailed, Arched Base, c.1825, 34 x 36 In. ... 8775.00
Chest, Blanket, Softwood, 2 Drawers, Dovetailed, Blue, Bail Handles, Bracket Feet, 27 x 45 In. . 4675.00

Furniture, Chest, Blanket, Lift Top, Pine, Flowers, Urns, Johannes Rank, 1799, 23 x 52 In. $3450.00

Furniture, Chest, Blanket, Pine, Grain Painted, Flowers, Hinged Lid, 1835, 22 x 50 x 26 In. $518.00

Furniture, Chest, Blanket, Softwood, Painted Urns, Flowers, Panels, J. & P. Rank, 21 x 51 In. $3850.00

Furniture, Chest, Burl Walnut, 6 Drawers, Butler's Desk Drawer, Pigeonholes, 60 x 37 In. $1035.00

F

Furniture, Chest, Campaign, Mahogany, 4 Drawers, Brass Corners, Handles, Legs, 43 x 39 x 19 In.
$2300.00

Furniture, Chest, Chippendale, Bowfront, Figured Mahogany, Inlay, Mass., 1785, 33 x 41 In.
$8400.00

Furniture, Chest, Federal, Cherry, Poplar, Pine, 4 Drawers, Turned Feet, Tenn., 44 x 46 x 21 In.
$805.00

Furniture, Chest, Hepplewhite, Mahogany Veneer, 4 Drawers, Shaped Skirt, 38 x 38 In.
$863.00

Chest, Blanket, Softwood, 2 Drawers, Lift Top, Graining, Cutout Legs, 43 x 37 In.	1546.00
Chest, Blanket, Softwood, 3 Drawers, Red Wash, Bracket Feet, 30 x 52½ x 22 In.	440.00
Chest, Blanket, Softwood, Blue Paint, Polychrome Flowers, 3-Panels, Dovetailed, 21 x 51 In.	3850.00
Chest, Blanket, Softwood, Brown Grain On Yellow, Turned Feet, Dovetailed, Till, Pa., 22 x 37 In. .	660.00
Chest, Blanket, Softwood, Dovetailed, Grain Paint, Molded Lid, Bracket Feet, 25 x 45 x 21 In.	1100.00
Chest, Blanket, Softwood, Dovetailed, Tulips, Red, Yellow, Bracket Feet, 23 x 50½ In.	852.00
Chest, Blanket, Softwood, Elongated Heart, Blue, Till, Bracket Feet, Dovetailed, 21 x 48 In. . .	1540.00
Chest, Blanket, Softwood, Flowers, Leaves, Ribbons, Bracket Feet, Cutout Ends, 13 x 18 x 10 In. . .	440.00
Chest, Blanket, Softwood, Green Ground, Black Squiggles, Molded Base, 18 x 34⅝ In.	385.00
Chest, Blanket, Softwood, Old Red Paint, Dovetailed, Turned Feet, 22½ x 31 In.	330.00
Chest, Blanket, Softwood, Original Blue Paint, Dovetailed, Bracket Feet, 20 x 37 x 15 In.	1650.00
Chest, Blanket, Softwood, Paint Decorated, Yellow Graining, Molded Lid, 23 x 44 In.	385.00
Chest, Blanket, Softwood, Painted, Tombstone Panels, Unicorns, Tulip Urns, 14 x 37 In.	1155.00
Chest, Blanket, Softwood, Painted Urns, Flowers, Panels, J. & P. Rank, 21 x 51 In. . . . . . . *illus*	3850.00
Chest, Blanket, Softwood, Sponging, Drawer, Dovetailed, New Eng., 20 x 39 In.	154.00
Chest, Blanket, Softwood, Yellow Graining, Dovetailed, Turned Feet, 24½ x 45½ x 22 In.	770.00
Chest, Blanket, Softwood, Yellow Graining, Fingerprint Dots, Sunken Panel, 26 x 50 In.	468.00
Chest, Blanket, Softwood, Yellow Graining, Lift Top, Panels, Doors, Dovetailed, 40 x 44 In. . .	385.00
Chest, Blanket, Walnut, 2 Cock-Beaded Drawers, Arched Feet, Molded Top, c.1800, 27 x 45 In. . .	1793.00
Chest, Blanket, Walnut, Chestnut, Inlaid Eagle, Dovetailed, 3 Drawers, 28 x 49 In.	805.00
Chest, Blanket, Walnut, Paint, Molded Lid, Dovetailed, Turned Feet, Strap Hinges, 24 x 51 In.	550.00
Chest, Blanket, White Pine, Dovetailed, Interior Till, Secret Drawer, 19½ x 43½ In.	633.00
Chest, Blanket, White Pine, N.Y., c.1830, 30 x 22½ In.	4200.00
Chest, Blanket, Wood, Green Paint, 18 x 44 x 17½ In.	360.00
Chest, Blanket, Yellow, Green Paint, Fan Decoration, Corners, 19 x 28 In.	1210.00
Chest, Bonnet, Cherry, Tiger Maple, 4 Drawers, Cork Banded, Turned Feet, c.1825, 42 x 47 In. .	1315.00
Chest, Bowfront, Mahogany, 3 Dovetailed Drawers, Applied Bead, England, 40 x 45 In.	1095.00
Chest, Burl Walnut, 6 Drawers, Butler's Desk Drawer, Pigeonholes, 60 x 37 In. . . . . *illus*	1035.00
Chest, Burl Walnut, Side Lock, 31 x 43 In.	800.00
Chest, Campaign, Camphorwood, Brass Mounted, 9 Drawers, 44 x 42 x 19½ In.	4406.00
Chest, Campaign, Camphorwood, Southeast Asian, 3 Over 2 Drawers, 43 x 20 In.	780.00
Chest, Campaign, Mahogany, 4 Drawers, Brass Corners, Handles, Legs, 43 x 39 x 19 In. . *illus*	2300.00
Chest, Campaign, Rosewood, Drawers, Bulb Feet, 40¼ x 36 x 15½ In.	11800.00
Chest, Cherry, 4 Drawers, 36½ x 38 In.	6900.00
Chest, Cherry, 4 Drawers, Red, Oval Brasses, c.1820, 45 x 53 In.	1430.00
Chest, Cherry, 4 Graduated Drawers, Federal Brasses, Unusual Feet, 42 x 38 In.	5060.00
Chest, Cherry, 6 Drawers, 46 In.	765.00
Chest, Cherry, Maple, Overhanging Edge, 4 Graduated Drawers, 40 x 38 In.	1840.00
Chest, Cherry, Raised Back, 2 Over 3 Graduated Drawers, 19th Century, 46 In.	544.00
Chest, Cherry, String Inlay, 5 Drawer, 42 x 18 x 46 In.	575.00
Chest, Chippendale, Birch, Red Painted, 4 Graduated Drawers, 35½ x 38 x 20½ In.	2350.00
Chest, Chippendale, Birch, Reverse Serpentine Front, Mass., c.1775, 34 x 39½ In.	7200.00
Chest, Chippendale, Bowfront, Figured Mahogany, Inlay, Mass., 1785, 33 x 41 In. . . . . *illus*	8400.00
Chest, Chippendale, Carved Maple, Reverse Serpentine, 4 Drawers, c.1780, 33 x 40 x 20 In. . .	9600.00
Chest, Chippendale, Cherry, 4 Drawers, 32 x 37½ x 29 In.	2400.00
Chest, Chippendale, Cherry, 4 Drawers, Brass Bails, Bracket Feet, 34 x 40 x 27 In.	3346.00
Chest, Chippendale, Cherry, 4 Graduated Dovetail Drawers, Fluted Column, 40 x 22 In.	4888.00
Chest, Chippendale, Cherry, Birch, Pine, Overhanging Top, Bracket Feet, 34 x 32 In.	1610.00
Chest, Chippendale, Cherry, Bowfront, 4 Dovetailed Drawers, Columns, 37 x 42 In.	2530.00
Chest, Chippendale, Cherry, Tiger Maple, 3 Over 6 Drawers, Apron, 68 x 46 In.	4070.00
Chest, Chippendale, Curly Maple, Pine, Poplar, Molding, 4 Drawers, 41 x 21½ In.	23000.00
Chest, Chippendale, Mahogany, 4 Drawers, 18th Century, 37 x 38½ x 20½ In.	600.00
Chest, Chippendale, Mahogany, Carved, 4 Drawers, 32½ x 37 x 22¾ In.	9600.00
Chest, Chippendale, Mahogany, Carved, Figures, 4 Drawers, c.1775, 32 x 35 x 20 In.	7800.00
Chest, Chippendale, Mahogany, Carved, Serpentine Front, Phila., 1800s, 42 x 48 In.	3300.00
Chest, Chippendale, Mahogany, Serpentine Front, 4 Drawers, c.1780, 34 x 40 x 22 In.	8400.00
Chest, Chippendale, Mahogany, Serpentine Front, c.1780, 35 x 40½ x 20½ In.	3300.00
Chest, Chippendale, Mahogany, Serpentine Front, Salem, c.1770, 33 x 40½ In.	42000.00
Chest, Chippendale, Maple, 2 Over 5 Drawers, Molded Edge, Cornice Molding, 55 x 38 In. . . .	2585.00
Chest, Chippendale, Maple, Cornice, 6 Graduated Drawers, 56½ x 36 x 19 In.	7638.00
Chest, Chippendale, Tiger Maple, Molded Cornice, 6 Thumb Molded Drawers, 51 x 36 In. . . .	5405.00
Chest, Chippendale, Walnut, 2 Over 4 Drawers, Cutout Bracket Feet, Black Paint, 41 x 40 x 22 In.	2090.00
Chest, Chippendale, Walnut, 4 Drawers, Chamfered Corners, Ogee Bracket Feet, 39 x 35 x 18 In. .	1540.00
Chest, Chippendale, Walnut, 5 Drawers Over 4, Cornice, Bracket Feet, c.1750, 62 x 38 In.	4487.00
Chest, Chippendale, Walnut, 10 Drawers, Molded Columns, Ogee Feet, Cornice, 1700s	8963.00
Chest, Chippendale, Walnut, Molded Lip, 4 Drawers, Ogee Feet, York County, 41 x 37¾ In. . . .	825.00

Chest, Chippendale, Walnut, Yellow Pine, Lift Top, 2 Drawers, Bracket Feet, N.C., 30 x 47 In.	3220.00
Chest, Chippendale Style, Elm, Cock-Beaded Drawers, 1800s, 57 x 43 In.	1534.00
Chest, Dower, Clover, Painted, Bracket Base, Strap Hinges, Pa., Late 1700s, 22 x 49 In.	1980.00
Chest, Dower, Painted, 31¾ In.	8625.00
Chest, Dower, Pine, Painted, Hinged Molded Top, Lidded Till, c.1798, 22 x 48 In.	1058.00
Chest, Dower, Softwood, Painted, Flowers, Panels, Birds, Strap Hinges, 1787, 22 x 50 In.	2530.00
Chest, Dressing, Gentleman's, Neoclassical, Mahogany, Carved, Mirror, 41 x 21 In.	1998.00
Chest, Empire, Mahogany, 3 Graduated Drawers, Shaped Feet, 17¾ x 17½ x 10 In.	359.00
Chest, Empire, Mahogany, Carved, Stepped Back, 3 Drawers, Columns, 41 x 37 In.	413.00
Chest, Empire, Mahogany, Flame Veneer, 3 Drawers, Reverse Painted Insets, Columns, 44 x 21 In.	460.00
Chest, Empire, Mahogany Veneer, Pine, Poplar, 2 Over 3 Drawers, 40 x 18½ In.	288.00
Chest, Empire, Painted, Brown Yellow Graining, Sunken Panel, 48 x 43 In.	110.00
Chest, Empire, Pine, Red & Black, 4 Drawers, Signed, John Blinn, 1800, 19 x 16 In.	5405.00
Chest, Federal, Bird's-Eye Maple Inlay, Bowfront, 4 Drawers, c.1810, 36 x 41 In.	5760.00
Chest, Federal, Cherry, 4 Cock-Beaded Drawers, Reeded Stiles, Turned Feet, 19th Century, 41 x 40 In.	837.00
Chest, Federal, Cherry, Ebony Inlay, Drawers, Bracket Feet, String Inlay, 44 x 46 x 22 In.	705.00
Chest, Federal, Cherry, Graduated Drawers, Molded Base, c.1800, 36 x 41 In.	1880.00
Chest, Federal, Cherry, Inlay, 4 Thumb Molded Graduated Drawers, 37 x 41 In.	1645.00
Chest, Federal, Cherry, Poplar, Pine, 4 Drawers, Turned Feet, Tenn., 44 x 46 x 21 In. *illus*	805.00
Chest, Federal, Cherry, Veneer, Walnut, Poplar, Drawers, Oval Brass, 42 x 25 x 46 In.	6325.00
Chest, Federal, Inlaid Walnut, Yellow Pine, 2 Short Over 3 Long Drawers, 39 x 40 In.	2530.00
Chest, Federal, Ivory Inlaid Mahogany, Serpentine Front, 4 Drawers, c.1810, 41 x 46 In.	9600.00
Chest, Federal, Mahogany, 4 Cock-Beaded Drawers, Inlaid Apron, Bracket Feet, 1800s, 37 x 41 In.	1912.00
Chest, Federal, Mahogany, 4 Cock-Beaded Drawers, Ring Turned Columns, Turned Legs, 38 x 40 In.	2151.00
Chest, Federal, Mahogany, Beaded Drawers, Fluted Stiles, Paneled Sides, 40 x 42 x 22 In.	1016.00
Chest, Federal, Mahogany, Inlay, 4 Drawers, 15½ In.	4481.00
Chest, Federal, Mahogany, Pine, Bowfront, 4 Drawers, Bone Escutcheons, 31 x 43 In.	805.00
Chest, Federal, Mahogany, Swell Front, 4 Drawers, 38⅝ x 42¾ x 23¾ In., Pair	5378.00
Chest, Federal, Mahogany Inlay, Bowfront, 14½ x 11 x 18½ In.	4780.00
Chest, Federal, Mahogany Inlay, Graduated Drawers, French Feet, 38 x 38 x 20¾ In.	3884.00
Chest, Federal, Maple, Cherry, 5 Cock-Beaded Drawers, Bracket Feet, c.1800, 39 x 43 x 20 In.	2271.00
Chest, Federal, Tiger Maple, 4 Graduated Drawers, Bracket Feet, c.1800, 38 x 38 x 18¼ In.	5378.00
Chest, Federal, Walnut, 2 Over 3 Drawers, Reeded Pilasters, 1800s, 39½ x 36 In.	633.00
Chest, Federal, Yellow Birch, Yellow Pine, Bellflower Inlay, 19th Century, 48 x 39 In.	10925.00
Chest, Federal Style, Mahogany, 3 Over 4 Drawers, Ernest Hagan, c.1902, 49 x 49 In.	633.00
Chest, Finn Juhl, Walnut, Sycamore, 4 Drawers, Bar Pulls, c.1952, 30¼ x 36 x 18 In.	1315.00
Chest, Folk Art, Blue Paint, Cornucopias, Lift Top, Pegged, Through Mortise, 24 x 83 In.	748.00
Chest, Folk Art, Oak, Painted, Lift Top, Compass Work, Orange, Blue, Green, 1800s, 43 x 45 In.	1150.00
Chest, G. Nakashima, Walnut, 3 Drawers, c.1960, 31¾ x 36 x 20 In.	7200.00
Chest, G. Nelson, Laminate, 3 Drawers, 29½ x 33½ x 17 In.	478.00
Chest, G. Nelson, Thin Edge, Oak, 5 Drawers, White Wire Pulls, c.1961, 41 x 40 In.	2350.00
Chest, G. Stickley, 9 Drawers, Overhang Top, Arched Toe Kick, Wood Pulls, 51 x 36 In.	4800.00
Chest, George II, Mahogany, 3 Short Over 3 Long Drawers, Bracket Feet, 36 x 42 In.	1410.00
Chest, George III, Inlaid Mahogany, 2 Over 3 Drawers, Early 1800s, 49 x 51 In.	652.00
Chest, George III, Mahogany, 4 Drawers, 18th Century, 36 x 36 x 19 In.	1528.00
Chest, George III, Mahogany, 5 Drawers, Banded Top, c.1785, 41 x 41 x 18 In.	2115.00
Chest, George III, Mahogany, Banded, Molded Edge, 3 Drawers, 34 x 47 x 22 In.	998.00
Chest, George III, Mahogany, Banded, Molded Edge, 3 Drawers, Bracket Feet, 35x 39 x 20 In.	1057.00
Chest, George III, Mahogany, Bowfront, 2 Drawers Over 3, 43 x 45½ x 22¼ In.	1645.00
Chest, George III, Mahogany, Bowfront, 2 Short Over 3 Drawers, c.1780, 41 x 41 In.	3525.00
Chest, George III, Mahogany, Bowfront, 5 Drawers, Early 19th Century, 41 In.	1638.00
Chest, George III, Mahogany, Crossbanded, 2 Over 3 Drawers, 36 x 44 x 21 In.	1998.00
Chest, George III, Mahogany, Dentil Molded Cornice, Drawers, Dressing Slide, 78 x 46 In.	8225.00
Chest, George III, Mahogany, Molded Edge, 3 Drawers, c.1785, 35 x 48 x 23 In.	998.00
Chest, George III, Mahogany, Rectangular Top, 2 Short Over 3 Long Drawers, 43 x 47 In.	1920.00
Chest, George III, Mahogany, Rounded Rectangular Top, Fitted Case, 4 Drawers, 36 x 36 In.	1680.00
Chest, George III Style, Mahogany, 2 Drawers Over 3, Bracket Feet, 43 x 40½ In.	1527.00
Chest, George III Style, Mahogany, 5 Drawers, Bracket Feet, 40 x 38½ x 17¾ In.	1128.00
Chest, George III Style, Mahogany, Bowfront, 2 Over 3 Drawers, 1800s, 41 x 40 In.	1534.00
Chest, George III Style, Mahogany, Drawers, 18th Century, 44 In.	2150.00
Chest, George III Style, Painted Oriental Landscapes, 2 Over 3 Drawers, 39 x 42 In.	4465.00
Chest, Georgian, Mahogany, Bowfront, 4 Drawers, Curved Apron, Early 1800s, 37 In.	2080.00
Chest, Georgian, Stepped Top, 3 Drawers, England, 35 x 18 In.	819.00
Chest, Georgian Provincial, Oak, Lift Top, Flat Bracket Feet, Pendant Scallop, 19 x 26 In.	146.00
Chest, Georgian Style, Inlaid Bowfront, 7 Drawers, Bracket Feet, 48 x 28 In.	413.00
Chest, Georgian Style, Walnut, Burled Panel, 2 Short Over 2 Long Drawers, 33 x 41 In.	2360.00

Furniture, Chest, Neoclassical, Cherry, Mahogany, Spiral-Turned Columns, 5 Drawers, 55 x 43 In. $805.00

Furniture, Chest, Oak, Plank Top, 2 Short & 2 Long Drawers, Carved, Bun Feet, 35 x 37 In. $4500.00

Furniture, Chest, Queen Anne, Walnut, Veneer, Inlay, Feather-Banding, c.1710, 37 x 37 In. $3900.00

Furniture, Chest, Sugar, Federal, Cherry, Hinged Top, Drawer, Square Legs, Tenn., 35 x 23 x 16 In. $6200.00

Furniture, Chest, William & Mary, Birch, 2 Over 4 Drawers, Ball Feet, R.I., c.1720, 39 x 37 x 20 In. $18000.00

Furniture, Chest, Wood, Multicolored Stylized Flowers, Blue Ground, Hinged Lid, 18 x 34 In. $201.00

Chest, Georgian Style, Walnut Inlay, Tall Boy, 2 Over 3 Drawers, Cabriole Legs, 62 x 39 In.	3173.00
Chest, Hepplewhite, Bowfront, Curly Maple, 4 Flame Grain Veneer Drawers, 41 x 21 In.	1380.00
Chest, Hepplewhite, Cherry, Poplar, 3 Graduated Dovetail Drawers, Vine On Stile, 38 x 37 In.	862.00
Chest, Hepplewhite, Figured Mahogany, Bowfront, 2 Over 3 Drawers, 41 x 42 In.	1265.00
Chest, Hepplewhite, Mahogany, 4 Graduated Cock-Beaded Drawers, 39 x 42 In.	1760.00
Chest, Hepplewhite, Mahogany, Line Inlay, Center Medallion, 4 Drawers, 47 x 46 In.	1540.00
Chest, Hepplewhite, Mahogany, Oak, Pine, 3 Drawers, Wooden Pulls, 13 x 5⅝ x 12¼ In.	604.00
Chest, Hepplewhite, Mahogany Veneer, 4 Drawers, Shaped Skirt, 38 x 38 In. ....*illus*	863.00
Chest, Hepplewhite, Walnut, 4 Drawers, Line Inlay, Scalloped Apron, Flared Feet, 37 x 39 In.	770.00
Chest, Hepplewhite, Walnut, Poplar, 2 Over 5 Drawers, Shaped Skirt, French Feet, 43 x 44 In.	920.00
Chest, Hepplewhite, Walnut With Poplar, 4 Drawer, French Feet, 38 In.	1725.00
Chest, Japanese, Lacquer, 19th Century, 11 x 11 In.	146.00
Chest, Jewelry, Chinese, Lacquered, Wood, 4 Drawers, 16 x 16 In.	82.00
Chest, Josef Frank, 3 Drawers, Mahogany, Printed Paper, c.1949, 30 x 52 x 17 In.	10800.00
Chest, Lift Top, Continental, Carved Floral Relief, 45½ x 17½ In.	450.00
Chest, Limbert, Arts & Crafts, Through Tenon Construction, 2 Over 2 Drawers, 35 x 35 In.	978.00
Chest, Liquor, Blue Paint, Fitted Interior, 10 x 11 x 16 In.	115.00
Chest, Louis Philippe, Mahogany, 3 Drawers, 19th Century, 39 x 45 In.	1957.00
Chest, Mahogany, 3 Drawers, Inlaid Shaped Apron, French Bracket Feet, 19th Century, 12 In.	837.00
Chest, Mahogany, 3 Long Drawers, Shaped Bracket Feet, 36½ x 36½ In.	295.00
Chest, Mahogany, 4 Drawers, 10 x 13 x 7¼ In.	4500.00
Chest, Mahogany, 5 Drawers, Ogee Mahogany Mirror, 41½ x 81 In.	403.00
Chest, Mahogany, 5 Drawers, Sabot Feet, Bronze Ring Pulls, Accents, 39 x 15 x 12½ In.	470.00
Chest, Mahogany, Block Front, 4 Drawer, Claw & Ball Feet, 32 x 32 In.	1150.00
Chest, Mahogany, Bowfront, 3 Drawers, Mid 19th Century, 36 In.	409.00
Chest, Mahogany, Bowfront, 4 Cock-Beaded Drawers, Stiles, Panels, 4 Feet, c.1815, 44 In.	956.00
Chest, Mahogany, Bowfront, 4 Cock-Beaded Drawers, Turned Pulls, Early 1800s, 37 x 42 In.	1434.00
Chest, Mahogany, Bowfront, 4 Drawers, 19th Century, 38 x 42½ x 23 In.	2714.00
Chest, Mahogany, Bowfront, 4 Drawers, Ivory Escutcheons, Brass Pulls, c.1800, 43 x 42 In.	881.00
Chest, Mahogany, Bowfront, Banded Top, Fluted, Beaded Edges, 42 x 43 x 23½ In.	440.00
Chest, Mahogany, Frieze, Applied Bead Molding, Drawers, 46 x 49 In.	1265.00
Chest, Mahogany, Sheraton, Rope Pilasters, Carved Fans, Scrolls, c.1835, 46 x 39½ In.	5170.00
Chest, Mahogany, Straight Front, Molded Edge, 4 Drawers, Bracket Feet, 36½ x 37 In.	1380.00
Chest, Medicine, Elm, 32 Drawers, 2 Doors, Chinese, 44 x 12½ In.	354.00
Chest, Mirror, Continental, Marble Top, Arched, 4-Panel Drawers, 1800s, 50 x 64 In.	224.00
Chest, Mixed Wood, Shaped Backboard, 2 Short & 3 Long Drawers, c.1860, 48 x 44 In.	863.00
Chest, Mule, White Pine, Dovetailed Drawer, Tang Hinges, Cut Nails, 1800s, 35 x 38 In.	1093.00
Chest, Mule, White Pine, Hinged, Cut Nails, Blue Paint, 1802, 35 x 38 x 18 In.	1095.00
Chest, Neoclassical, Birch, Lift Top, Hinged Lid, Painted, Flowers, Greek Figures, 17 x 45 In.	115.00
Chest, Neoclassical, Cherry, Mahogany, Spiral-Turned Columns, 5 Drawers, 55 x 43 In. .*illus*	805.00
Chest, Neoclassical, Cherry, Maple, Inlay, 7 Drawers, Shaped Skirt, Feet, c.1830, 50 x 43 x 20 In.	2390.00
Chest, Neoclassical, Figured Mahogany, Carved, 3 Drawers, New York, c.1830, 41 x 42 In.	1560.00
Chest, Neoclassical, Mahogany, Cherry, Shallow Drawers, Reeded Columns, 46 x 44 In.	600.00
Chest, Neoclassical, Mahogany, Drawers, Glass Pulls, Carved Pilasters, 52 x 47 In.	900.00
Chest, Neoclassical, Mahogany, Early 19th Century, Drawers, Tuned Feet, 47 x 44 In.	1320.00
Chest, Neoclassical, Walnut, Marble Top, 4 Drawers, Continental, 35½ x 29½ x 18½ In.	764.00
Chest, New England, Softwood, Lift Top, 4 Drawers, Top 2 False, Ogee Feet, 42 x 40 In.	358.00
Chest, Oak, Carved, 3-Panel Front, Flowers, Geometrics, Strap Hinges, England, 28 x 51 In.	920.00
Chest, Oak, Frame & Panel, 3-Panel Front, Lift Top, Iron Strap Hinges, 1700s, 22 x 42 In.	403.00
Chest, Oak, Lift Top, Dovetailed, Iron Hinges, Candle Box, Bracket Feet, England, 26 x 15 In.	403.00
Chest, Oak, Limbert, 5 Drawers, C-Shape Patinated Brass Pulls, 48 x 36 In.	999.00
Chest, Oak, Plank Top, 2 Short & 2 Long Drawers, Carved, Bun Feet, 35 x 37 In. ......*illus*	4500.00
Chest, Oak, Polychrome Painted Panels, 2 Birds, Bun Feet, 27 x 43 x 25 In.	998.00
Chest, Over 2 Drawers, Federal, Tiger Maple, Maple, Lift Top, c.1810, 37 x 38 In.	2820.00
Chest, Over Drawer, Painted, Pine, Poplar, Beaded Hinged Top, Drawer, 33 x 42 In.	3055.00
Chest, Over Drawers, Pine, Red Painted, Lift Top, Conn., Late 1700s, 43 x 39 In.	3055.00
Chest, Pine, 3 Dovetailed Drawers, Brass Pulls, Shaped Crest, Apron, 15 x 8 x 13 In.	2530.00
Chest, Pine, 4 Drawers, Brown Over Tan Graining, Backsplash, 16½ x 38 In.	489.00
Chest, Pine, 4 Drawers, Painted, Carved Backsplash, Elihu Nye, 1843, 41 x 30 In.	1872.00
Chest, Pine, 6-Board, Lift Top, Hinges, Yellow, Burnt Sienna Paint, 24¾ x 47 In.	1880.00
Chest, Pine, Blue Painted, 6-Board, Lift Top, Hinges, Child's, 15¾ x 31 x 13 In.	3290.00
Chest, Pine, Cherry Stained, Marquetry, 3 Drawers, Porcelain Pulls, 13 x 14¼ In.	4800.00
Chest, Pine, Hinged Top, 6-Board, 16½ x 29½ x 15 In.	264.00
Chest, Pine, Lift Top, Red Paint, 2 Drawers, Applied Molding, 44½ x 40½ x 17¾ In.	2468.00
Chest, Pine, Molded Lid, Cotter Pin Hinges, 2 Drawers, 41½ x 18 x 44 In.	748.00
Chest, Pine, Multicolored, Bavarian, Flowers, Green Ground, Bun Feet, 26 x 56 x 24 In.	999.00

Chest, Poplar, Grain Painted, Storage Well, Drawer, Bracket Feet, Early 1800s, 36 x 43 In. ...	767.00
Chest, Queen Anne, Maple, 6 Drawers, c.1770, 60¼ x 39 x 19½ In.	5700.00
Chest, Queen Anne, Maple, Carved, Figured, Salem, c.1770, 71½ x 39½ In.	16800.00
Chest, Queen Anne, Pine, 3 Graduated Drawers, Bracket Base, Late 1700s, 23 x 17 In.	1410.00
Chest, Queen Anne, Walnut, Veneer, Inlay, Feather-Banding, c.1710, 37 x 37 In. .... *illus*	3900.00
Chest, Queen Anne, Walnut, Veneer Inlay, 10 Drawers, Mass., c.1750, 72 x 39 In.	27025.00
Chest, Regency, Mahogany, 2 Short Over 3 Long Drawers, Splayed Bracket Feet, 42 x 42 In. ..	2232.00
Chest, Regency, Mahogany, Bowfront, Banded Top, 2 Over 3 Drawers, 45 x 40 In.	1920.00
Chest, Regency, Mahogany, Bowfront, Reeded Edge, Inlaid Stringing, 43 x 37 In.	2880.00
Chest, Regency, Mahogany, Molded Edge Top, 2 Over 3 Drawers, French Feet, 37½ x 43 In. ..	385.00
Chest, Regency, Mahogany, Rectangular Top, 4 Graduated Drawers, c.1825, 29 x 21 In.	1234.00
Chest, Rococo, Pine, Painted, Gray, Serpentine Top, Drawers, 37 x 40 x 25 In.	6463.00
Chest, Rococo Revival, Rosewood, 4 Double Serpentine Drawers, Cartouches, 36 x 46 In. ...	1092.00
Chest, Rococo Revival, Walnut, Marble Top, Bowfront, 3 Drawers, Fruit-Carved Pulls, 32 x 43 In.	587.00
Chest, Sea, Blue Paint, 37 x 16 x 14 In.	748.00
Chest, Secretary, Campaign, Teak, 5 Drawers, Shaped Apron, 19th Century, 37½ In.	2391.00
Chest, Seed, Cherry, Slant Top, 3 Compartments, 22 Drawers, 1800s, 23 x 18 In.	1434.00
Chest, Shaker, Cherry, Pine, 6 Drawers, Varnish, Dovetailed, Walnut Knobs, c.1850, 32 x 47 In.	8190.00
Chest, Shaker, Pine, 4 Drawers, Varnish, Walnut Knobs, Mass., 36 x 36 x 14 In.	3510.00
Chest, Shaker, Pine, 6 Over 3 Drawers, Backsplash, Harvard, Mass., c.1850, 27 x 17 x 9 In. ..	1989.00
Chest, Shaker, Pine, 7 Drawers, Dovetailed, Canted Feet, Mt. Lebanon, N.Y., c.1840, 66 x 45 In.	12285.00
Chest, Shaker, Walnut, Butternut, Poplar, 4 Drawers, Union Village, Ohio, c.1860, 47 x 19 x 42 In. .	3510.00
Chest, Shaker, Walnut, Poplar, Lift Top, Door, Drawers, Union Village, Ohio, c.1840, 30 x 36 In.	10530.00
Chest, Sheraton, Cherry, Inlay, Reeded Pilasters, Drawers, 46 x 45 In.	1528.00
Chest, Sheraton, Cherry, Veneer, Pine, Hickory, 4 Drawers, 41½ x 23 x 42½ In.	1725.00
Chest, Sheraton, Curly Maple, Pine, Chestnut, 4 Drawers, Beaded, Turned Legs, 42 x 39 In. ..	2990.00
Chest, Sheraton, Mahogany, 4 Drawers, Bowfront, Oval Corners, Turned Legs, 41 x 42 In. ...	550.00
Chest, Sheraton, Mahogany, 4 Drawers, Bowfront, Turned Feet, Reeded Columns, 39 x 42 x 20 In. ..	440.00
Chest, Sheraton, Mahogany, 4 Drawers, Reeded Stiles, Turned Feet, 39 x 37 x 21 In.	743.00
Chest, Sheraton, Mahogany, Bowfront, 4 Drawers, Crossbanded, 38 x 42 In.	1320.00
Chest, Sheraton, Mahogany, Veneer, Poplar, Writing Surface, 3 Drawers, 46 x 57 In.	2070.00
Chest, Sheraton, Mixed Wood, Shaped Backboard, Drawers, 49 x 42 In.	3450.00
Chest, Sheraton, Tiger Maple, Cherry, 4 Drawers, Reeded Half Columns, Turned Feet, 44 x 39 In.	1540.00
Chest, Sheraton, Walnut, Bird's-Eye Maple, Reeded Edge, Stiles, 4 Drawers, Turned Feet, 39 x 41 In. .	188.00
Chest, Softwood, Hinged Drop Door, Buddhist Symbols, Loop Handles, 32 x 34 In.	2880.00
Chest, Spice, Pine, 3 Drawers, Turned Wood Knobs, Black Paint, 8 x 18 x 9 In.	588.00
Chest, Storage, Shaker, Poplar, Painted, Lid, Bootjacks, Harvard, Mass., c.1830, 21 x 45 In. ..	2574.00
Chest, Storage, Walnut, Lift Top, Breadboard Ends, Door, Drawer, 17½ x 16¼ In.	358.00
Chest, Studded Copper Band, Cedar, Standard Red Cedar Chest Co., 48 x 20 x 20 In.	127.00
Chest, Sugar, Cherry, Dovetailed, Interior Drawers, Southern, 26 x 18 In.	2875.00
Chest, Sugar, Cherry, Dovetailed Case, 2 Drawers, Bone Kite Escutcheon, 16 x 15 In.	1035.00
Chest, Sugar, Federal, Cherry, Hinged Top, Drawer, Square Legs, Tenn., 35 x 23 x 16 In. *illus*	6200.00
Chest, Sugar, Federal, Cherry, Lift Top, Molded Edge Opening, 1800s, 36 x 32 In.	3910.00
Chest, Sugar, Federal, Spanish, Cedar, Faceted Top, Dovetailed, Top Shape Feet, 31 x 32 In. ..	3525.00
Chest, Sugar, Federal, Walnut, Hinged Top, Divided Interior, Early 1800s, 31 x 41 In.	3335.00
Chest, Sugar, Late Federal, Walnut, Sheraton Style, Divided Interior, c.1820, 32 x 38 In.	3819.00
Chest, Sugar, Mahogany, Chamfered Top, Drawer, 19th Century, 38 x 34 In.	1430.00
Chest, Sugar, Poplar, Lift Top, Fitted Interior, Dividers, 19th Century, 32 x 35 In.	2185.00
Chest, Sunflower, Joined, Oak, Pine, Carved, Wethersfield, Conn., c.1720, 40 x 48 In.	78000.00
Chest, Tiger Maple, 5 Drawers, Dividers, Dovetailed, Brass Escutcheons, 40 x 42 In.	4200.00
Chest, Tiger Maple, Grain Painted, 3 Drawers, Wood Knobs, Miniature, 11 x 8 x 13 In.	460.00
Chest, Tiger Maple, Molded Cornice, 8 Drawers, Shaped Shirt, Bracket Feet, 58 x 41 x 20 In. .	5378.00
Chest, Vanity, Boulle, Baccarat Jars, Sterling Silver Tops, c.1841, 13¾ x 10½ In.	10995.00
Chest, Walnut, 6 Drawers, Bracket Base, 23½ x 25¼ In.	3107.00
Chest, Walnut, Carved, Figural, Lift Top, Patina, 18th Century, 30 x 50 In.	2970.00
Chest, Walnut, Hinged Lid, Interior Till, Drawers, Early 19th Century, 25 x 36 In.	2640.00
Chest, Walnut, Lift Top, Hinged Top, Double Paneled Front, Sides, 1800s, 29 x 40 In.	748.00
Chest, Walnut, Lift Top, Poplar, Yellow Pine, Wrought Iron Hasp, 1800s, 21 x 37 In.	1093.00
Chest, Walnut Veneer, Brass Hardware, 6 Center Drawers, Mid 1900s, 31 x 72 In.	294.00
Chest, William & Mary, Birch, 2 Over 4 Drawers, Ball Feet, R.I., c.1720, 39 x 37 x 20 In. *illus*	18000.00
Chest, William & Mary, Yellow Pine, Flower Painted, 4 Drawers, 42¾ x 38 x 18 In.	4560.00
Chest, William IV, Mahogany, Bowed Top, 2 Over 3 Drawers, Plinth Base, 43 x 42 In.	1410.00
Chest, Wood, Multicolored Stylized Flowers, Blue Ground, Hinged Lid, 18 x 34 In. .....*illus*	201.00
Chest, Wood, Wrought Iron, Domed Top, Scrolled, Continental, 23 x 43 x 22 In.	411.00
Chest, Wooden, Korea, 53 x 37 x 19 In.	326.00
Chest, Work, Shaker, Butternut, Pine, 6 Drawers, Step-Down, Enfield, N.H., c.1850, 13 x 19 In. ..	3861.00

F

Furniture, Chest-On-Chest, Chippendale, Figured Mahogany, Pediment, Boston, Mass., 87 x 44 In.
$57000.00

Furniture, Chest-On-Frame, Sewing, Walnut, Hinged Lid, Scissor & Needle Inlay, Victorian, 28 In.
$353.00

Furniture, Chiffonier, Walnut, Teardrop Pulls, Queen Anne Legs, c.1925, 55 x 33 In.
$176.00

F

Furniture, Commode, Louis XV Style, Demilune, Metal Gallery, Marquetry, 29 x 18 In., Pair
$502.00

Furniture, Commode, Oak, Mirror & Towel Bar, 1 Long Over 2 Short Drawers & Door, 60 x 31 In.
$147.00

Furniture, Confidante, Mahogany, Fan Carved Back, Upholstered Seats, c.1880, 31 x 48 In.
$200.00

Furniture, Cradle, Softwood, Hooded, Brown Paint, Shaped Rockers, 28 x 39 x 13 In.
$99.00

Chest, Work, Shaker, Pine, Red Stain, Breadboard Top, 5 Drawers, Mt. Lebanon, N.Y., 30 x 40 In.	7020.00
Chest, Writing, Federal, 4 Drawers, 40 x 40 In.	2250.00
Chest, Yellow Grain Paint, 3 Drawers, Cutout Ends, 14½ x 13¾ In.	495.00
Chest, Yellow Pine, Lift Top, Slant Lid, H Hinges, South Carolina, 1800s, 40 x 38 In.	575.00
Chest-On-Chest, Chippendale, Figured Mahogany, Pediment, Boston, Mass., 87 x 44 In. *illus*	57000.00
Chest-On-Chest, George III, Mahogany, 9 Drawers, Bracket Feet, 73 x 43 In.	3290.00
Chest-On-Chest, George III, Mahogany, Bone Inlaid Escutcheons, 67 x 47 x 21 In.	1180.00
Chest-On-Chest, George III Style, Walnut, Veneered, Parcel Painted, 57 x 38 x 18 In.	354.00
Chest-On-Chest, Georgian, Mahogany, 2 Case, Dentil Cornice, 1700s, 70 x 46½ In.	1840.00
Chest-On-Chest, Georgian, Scottish, 3 Short Drawers, Shaped Bracket Feet	2938.00
Chest-On-Chest, Georgian, Walnut, 3 Short, 3 Long Drawers, 73½ x 40 x 22½ In.	3819.00
Chest-On-Chest, Mahogany, Early 19th Century, 71 x 42 In.	717.00
Chest-On-Frame, Blanket, Softwood, 2 Tiers, Mortised Top, Cutout Feet, 18 In., Pair	28.00
Chest-On-Frame, Queen Anne Style, Black Lacquer, Polychrome Chinoiserie, 62 x 44 In.	8400.00
Chest-On-Frame, Sewing, Walnut, Hinged Lid, Scissor & Needle Inlay, Victorian, 28 In. *illus*	353.00
Chest-On-Frame, William & Mary Style, Mixed Wood, 66¼ x 43¼ x 15½ In.	590.00
Chest-On-Frame, William & Mary Style, Oak, 5 Drawers, Turned Legs, 58 x 32 In.	635.00
Chiffonier, Walnut, Teardrop Pulls, Queen Anne Legs, c.1925, 55 x 33 In. *illus*	176.00
Chopping Block, Oak, Slab Cut From Fork In Tree, Legs, American, 1880, 32 x 16 In.	345.00
Clothespress, Southern Pine, Slanted Crown, Paneled Doors, Drawer, 81 x 64 In.	1610.00
Coat Rack, Arts & Crafts, Mahogany, Square, 4 Curved Supports, Brass Hooks, 70 In.	206.00
Coat Rack, Black Forest, Walnut, Bust Of Fox, Oak Leaf Plaque, 9 In.	382.00
Coat Rack, Costumer, G. Stickley, Shoe Feet, Iron Hooks, 72 x 22 x 13 In.	2280.00
Coat Rack, Iron, Column Center, Hooks, 66 In.	82.00
Coat Rack, Pine, Brown Stained, Brass Horn Hooks, Carved Backboard, 12 x 42 x 9 In.	235.00
Coat Tree, 4-Arm, Round, Octagonal Base, 72 In.	117.00
Cocktail Table, Widdicomb, Mahogany, Brass, Grand Rapids, 51 x 39 In.	82.00
Coffer, Far Eastern, Hardwood, Iron Clad, Iron Strapwork, 1800s, 34 x 47 In.	207.00
Coffer, Polychrome, Metal & Brass Tack Banding, Floral Band, Handles, 20 x 41 In.	1320.00
Commode, Baroque Style, Leather Covered, Serpentine, Drawers, Paw Feet, 33 x 38 x 21 In.	944.00
Commode, Biedermeier, Birch, 4 Drawers, Molded Edge Block, 40¼ x 51¼ x 24 In.	2832.00
Commode, Biedermeier, Cherry, Ebonized Trim, 2 Drawers, Splayed Feet, 33 x 42 In.	2280.00
Commode, Biedermeier, Walnut, Highly Figured, 3 Drawers, Turret Feet, 35 x 47 x 23 In.	6168.00
Commode, Bombe, Louis XV, Kingwood, Marquetry, Rouge Marble Top, Drawers	1293.00
Commode, Bombe, Louis XV Style, Ormolu Mounted, Lacquered, Marble, 34 x 30 In.	3120.00
Commode, Bombe, Venetian Style, Painted Decor, Rouge Griotte Marble, 35 x 58 In.	2818.00
Commode, Cherry, Marble Top, 4 Drawers, Continental, 33 x 27½ x 14½ In.	2596.00
Commode, Chinoiserie, 3 Fitted Drawers, Bracket Feet, England, 31 x 25 In.	6169.00
Commode, Continental Style, Fruitwood Veneers, Marble Top, 33 x 48 x 22 In.	2415.00
Commode, Directoire, Mahogany, Bronze Mount, Drawers, Gilt Brasses, 32 x 33 In.	3407.00
Commode, Empire, Mahogany, Ormolu Mounted, Marble Top, 3 Drawers, 37 x 51 In.	7920.00
Commode, Empire Style, Fruitwood, Marble Top, 25¼ x 23⅝ x 15½ In.	1880.00
Commode, Faux Marble Top, Painted, Floral Sprays, 4 Drawers, Tapered Legs, 41 x 44 In.	5280.00
Commode, Kingwood, Marble Top, 3 Drawers, Italy, Late 1800s, 34 x 51 x 21 In.	3995.00
Commode, Louis Philippe, Bird's-Eye Maple, 4 Drawers, c.1850, 18¼ x 21 x 11¼ In.	1762.00
Commode, Louis Philippe, Elm Burl, Brass Mounted, Marble Top, 39 x 52 In.	2880.00
Commode, Louis Philippe, Fruitwood, Marble Top, 36½ x 46½ In.	1020.00
Commode, Louis Philippe, Walnut, Black Marble Top, 4 Drawers, c.1900, 37 x 49 In.	2640.00
Commode, Louis Philippe, Walnut, Canted Corners, 4 Drawers, Bun Feet, 38 x 50 In.	2040.00
Commode, Louis Philippe, Walnut, Gray Marble Top, 4 Drawers, 35 x 51 x 21¾ In.	1292.00
Commode, Louis XV, Kingwood, Tulipwood, Marble Top, Cabriole Legs, 33 x 45 In.	5700.00
Commode, Louis XV, Rosewood, Kingwood, Marble, Cabriole Legs, 34 x 43 In.	8400.00
Commode, Louis XV Style, Bombe, Kingwood, Tulipwood, France, c.1885, 35 x 51 x 24 In.	2820.00
Commode, Louis XV Style, Demilune, Metal Gallery, Marquetry, 29 x 18 In., Pair *illus*	502.00
Commode, Louis XV Style, Kingwood, Marble Top, 4 Drawers, 28 x 15 In., Pair	900.00
Commode, Louis XV Style, Marquetry, Parquetry, Marble, Pair, 34 x 30 x 16 In.	14100.00
Commode, Louis XV Style, Tulipwood, Marquetry, Ormolu Mounted, 32 x 46 x 22 In.	1000.00
Commode, Louis XVI, Inlaid Marble Top, 3 Drawers Over 2, 33 x 51 x 21¾ In.	5900.00
Commode, Louis XVI, Kingwood, Rosewood, Marble Top, 3 Drawers, 36 x 33 In.	600.00
Commode, Louis XVI, Mahogany, Marble Top, 5 Drawers, Fluted Corners, 35 x 44 x 21 In.	4200.00
Commode, Louis XVI Style, Tulipwood, Marquetry, Ormolu Mounted, 30 x 22 x 13 In.	206.00
Commode, Neoclassical, Mahogany, Geometric, Medallion, 2 Drawers, 30 x 22 x 14¾ In.	1880.00
Commode, Neoclassical, Walnut, Parquetry, Lozenge, 3 Drawers, Italy, 34 x 51 In.	9000.00
Commode, Neoclassical, Walnut, Tulipwood, Marquetry, 37½ x 48½ x 23 In.	7200.00
Commode, Oak, 3 Drawers, Victorian, 34 x 32 x 18 In.	147.00
Commode, Oak, Mirror & Towel Bar, 1 Long Over 2 Short Drawers & Door, 60 x 31 In. *illus*	147.00

Commode, Petite, Louis XVI Style, Inlaid Kingwood, Ormolu Mounted, 36 x 31 In.	1645.00
Commode, Pine, Painted, Marble Top, 4 Drawers, Continental, 41 x 48 In.	1998.00
Commode, Provincial, Louis XVI, Oak, Carved, 4 Drawers, Scrolling, 43 x 51 In.	2640.00
Commode, Restauration, Walnut, Charcoal Marble Top, Frieze Drawer, 38 x 52 In.	2160.00
Commode, Rococo Style, Marquetry, Flowers, Geometrics, Sabot Feet, 34 x 55 In.	2115.00
Commode, Swedish Pine, Painted, Faux Lattice Panel Drawers, 39½ x 49 In.	2124.00
Commode, Walnut, 3 Drawers, Teardrop Pulls, Victorian, 35 x 30 x 16 In.	206.00
Commode, Walnut, Banded, Intricate Scrolling Inlay, Fitted Case, Drawers, 32 x 37 In.	2400.00
Commode, Walnut, Dentillated Frieze, Drawer, Classical Pilasters, 45 x 17 In.	3231.00
Commode, Walnut, Marquetry, Parquetry, 3 Drawers, Bracket Feet, Germany, 31 x 46 In. . . .	8400.00
Commode A Vantaux, Louis XV, Kingwood, Vernis Martin, c.1875, 46 x 34 In.	2940.00
Commode Chair, Provincial English, Mahogany, Tambour Seat, Pot Cupboard, 32 In.	411.00
Confidante, Mahogany, Fan Carved Back, Upholstered Seats, c.1880, 31 x 48 In. . . . . . .*illus*	200.00
Cradle, Acadian Cypress, Shaped Sides, Old Green, Black Paint, Early 1800s, 15 x 16 In.	1645.00
Cradle, Curly Maple, Turned Walnut Posts, Scalloped Rockers, 41 x 29 In.	259.00
Cradle, Softwood, Hooded, Brown Paint, Shaped Rockers, 28 x 39 x 13 In. . . . .*illus*	99.00
Credenza, Adam Style, Mahogany, Canted Corners, Painted Flowers, 2 Cane Doors, 32 x 48 In. . .	998.00
Credenza, Florence Knoll, Sliding Doors, c.1950, 28 x 72 x 18 In. . . . .*illus*	1440.00
Credenza, G. Nakashima, Walnut, 3 Sliding Doors, 4 Shelves, 4 Drawers, Signed, 32 x 84 In. .	45410.00
Credenza, G. Nakashima, Walnut, 4 Slat Sliding Doors, Shelf, Drawer, 32 x 84 x 20 In.	23900.00
Credenza, Neoclassical, Painted, Canted Top, 4 Drawers, Cupboards, Italy, 42½ x 84 In.	5100.00
Credenza, Regency, Rosewood, Brass Mounted, Grill Inset Doors, 34 x 43 x 16 In.	2468.00
Credenza, Renaissance Revival, Oak, Carved, Glass Doors, 38 x 56 x 20½ In.	823.00
Credenza, Rosewood, 2 Sliding Doors, 4 Center Drawers, Denmark, 31 x 19 In.	4994.00
Credenza, Walnut, 2 Sliding Doors, 4 Drawers, Harry Rubin, c.1960, 32 x 72 In.	470.00
Credenza, Wormley, Parkwood Top, Oak Door Fronts, Ash Case, Label, Dunbar, 38 x 66 In. . .	1763.00
Crib, G. Stickley, Spindles All Around, Cane Mattress Support, 34 x 55 In.	2280.00
Crib, Victorian, Reed Work Designs, Cane Wrapped Legs, c.1890, 49 x 46½ In.	1250.00
Cupboard, Bleached Pine, Paneled, Drawers, 2 Doors, Bracket Feet, c.1900, 68 x 46 In. .*illus*	115.00
Cupboard, Bonnetiere, Louis XV, Fruitwood, Cornice, Panel Door, Drawers, 84 x 41 In.	3840.00
Cupboard, Canning, Softwood, Green Paint, Drawer Over Paneled Door, 50 x 45 In. . . .*illus*	15950.00
Cupboard, Canning, Softwood, Painted, Paneled, Cutout Feet, 45 x 38 x 14 In. . . . .*illus*	3190.00
Cupboard, Canning, Softwood, Red Wash, Shaped Gallery, Square Feet, 61⅓ x 37⅜ In.	825.00
Cupboard, Cherry, 3 Shelves, 3 Doors, Molded, Rosettes, Bracket Feet, 82½ x 43 In.	2032.00
Cupboard, Corner, American Empire, 12 Glazed Panels, Drawer, 2 Doors, c.1845, 80 x 35 In. .	411.00
Cupboard, Corner, Butternut, Inlay, Crescents, Flowers, Panel Doors, c.1825, 48 x 21 In. . . .	2530.00
Cupboard, Corner, Central Fan, Glazed Doors, Serpentine Skirt, 91 x 46 x 25½ In.	9020.00
Cupboard, Corner, Cherry, 2 Doors, 8 Panes, Paneled Lower Doors, c.1820, 76 x 43 In.	3520.00
Cupboard, Corner, Cherry, 2 Sections, Molded Cornice, Recessed Doors, 83 In.	1195.00
Cupboard, Corner, Cherry, 12-Pane Upper Door, Step Back Molding, c.1820, 93 x 45 In.	6270.00
Cupboard, Corner, Cherry, Molded Cornice, Cupboard Doors, Recessed Panels, 88 x 43 In. . . .	3525.00
Cupboard, Corner, Cherry, Scalloped Apron, 2 Over 2 Flat Panel Doors, 85½ In.	1437.00
Cupboard, Corner, Edwardian, Mahogany, Inlay, 2 Sections, 3 Doors, 81 x 23 x 12 In. . .*illus*	1150.00
Cupboard, Corner, Figure On Horse, c.1935, 27 x 25 x 15 In.	1830.00
Cupboard, Corner, Grain Painted, 12-Pane Door, 2 Drawers, Paneled Doors, 87 x 45 In. *illus*	2013.00
Cupboard, Corner, Hanging, Pine, Door, 2 Drawers, Molded Cornice, Late 1700s, 49 x 30 In.	1500.00
Cupboard, Corner, Hanging, Shaker, Pine, Old Red Paint, 3 Shelves, Door, 23½ x 20 x 12 In.	585.00
Cupboard, Corner, Oak, 2 Doors, Carved Rosettes, Brass Pulls, Arches, 84 x 63 In.	588.00
Cupboard, Corner, Painted, Hinged Doors, Recessed Panels, 84 x 46 In.	6463.00
Cupboard, Corner, Painted, Turkey Breast Form, 2 Doors, 16 Panes, 2 Panel Doors, 81 x 47 In. . .	5750.00
Cupboard, Corner, Pine, 2 Doors Over Single Door, Brass H-Hinges, 76 x 40 x 19 In.	2185.00
Cupboard, Corner, Pine, 2 Sections, 9-Pane Door Over Drawer & Panel Door, Pa., 78 In.	4312.00
Cupboard, Corner, Pine, Brown, Mustard Graining, 12-Pane Door, 38 x 18½ x 84½ In.	7415.00
Cupboard, Corner, Pine, Painted, Glazed Door, Ontario, 19th Century, 87½ x 47 In.	1305.00
Cupboard, Corner, Poplar, 2 Doors, 20 Panes, Bull's-Eyes, Faux Grain, 84 x 58 In.	12650.00
Cupboard, Corner, Poplar, Molded Cornice, Double Pane Doors, 1800s, 79 x 42 In.	1265.00
Cupboard, Corner, Softwood, 2 Parts, 12-Pane Door, 2 Doors, Cutout Feet, 84 x 40 In.	1320.00
Cupboard, Corner, Softwood, 2 Sections, 2 Doors, 2 Drawers, Broken Arch Top, 82 x 38 In. . .	1073.00
Cupboard, Corner, Softwood, Hanging, Old Yellow Paint, Door, Raised Panels, 53 x 29 In. . . .	275.00
Cupboard, Corner, Victorian, Pine, Waxed, Mullioned, 2 Paneled Doors, 80 x 40 x 20 In.	1880.00
Cupboard, Corner, Walnut, 2 Sections, Scroll Neck Pediment, Glazed Doors, 95 x 52 In.	4140.00
Cupboard, Corner, Walnut, 4-Paneled Doors, Scalloped Base, c.1850, 80 x 48 In.	763.00
Cupboard, Corner, Walnut, 6 Pane Doors, Dentil Molded Cornice, 84 x 51 In.	1150.00
Cupboard, Corner, Walnut, Glazed Door, 12 Panes, Early 1800s, 79 x 47 In.	485.00
Cupboard, Corner, Walnut, Poplar, Panel Doors, Interior Shelves, Bracket Feet, 85 x 45 In. . .	10925.00
Cupboard, Corner, Walnut, Stepped Cornice, 2 Raised Panel Doors Over 2 Lower, 86 x 43 In. .	2990.00

Furniture, Credenza, Florence Knoll, Sliding Doors, c.1950, 28 x 72 x 18 In.
$1440.00

Furniture, Cupboard, Bleached Pine, Paneled, Drawers, 2 Doors, Bracket Feet, c.1900, 68 x 46 In.
$115.00

F

Furniture, Cupboard, Canning, Softwood, Green Paint, Drawer Over Paneled Door, 50 x 45 In.
$15950.00

Furniture, Cupboard, Canning, Softwood, Painted, Paneled, Cutout Feet, 45 x 38 x 14 In.
$3190.00

Furniture, Cupboard, Corner, Edwardian, Mahogany, Inlay, 2 Sections, 3 Doors, 81 x 23 x 12 In. $1150.00

Furniture, Cupboard, Corner, Grain Painted, 12-Pane Door, 2 Drawers, Paneled Doors, 87 x 45 In. $2013.00

Furniture, Cupboard, Hired Man's, Softwood, Red Wash, Slide Out Front, 30 x 39 x 20 In. $1980.00

Cupboard, Corner, Yellow Pine, Glazed, Flat Molded Cornice, Shelves, Door, 87 x 49 In.	3173.00
Cupboard, Decorative, Clock Front, Folk Art, Hand Painted, Germany, c.1920, 88 In.	117.00
Cupboard, Desk, Pine, Painted, 78½ x 49 x 12½ In.	4800.00
Cupboard, Dutch, 2 Sections, 24 Panes, Spoon Notches, c.1820, 86½ x 61 In.	4675.00
Cupboard, Dutch, Walnut, 2 Sections, 12 Panes, Spoon Notches, c.1830, 84 x 50 In.	9075.00
Cupboard, Federal, Pine, Grain Painted, 76¾ x 41¼ x 22¼ In.	4800.00
Cupboard, George III Style, Mahogany, Gadroon Edges, 2 Doors Over 2 Drawers, 44 x 44 In.	1292.00
Cupboard, Hanging, Cherry, Pine, Crown Molding, Raised Panel Door, Shelf, 30 x 25 In.	1380.00
Cupboard, Hanging, Door, 4 Panes, c.1820, 29 x 26½ In.	2200.00
Cupboard, Hanging, Dutch Provincial, 3 Doors, Carved Arch, Hearts & Scrolls, 16 x 13 x 10 In.	450.00
Cupboard, Hanging, Pine, 3 Doors, Brass Knobs, 3 Shelves, 13¾ x 11 In.	823.00
Cupboard, Hanging, Softwood, Dentil Molding Tiers, Panel Door, 30 x 23 In.	385.00
Cupboard, Hanging, Softwood, Dry Scraped, Sunken Panel, Cove Molded, Shelf, 27 x 26 In.	715.00
Cupboard, Hanging, Walnut, Rattail Hinges, Sunken Panel Door, 35 x 20 In.	4070.00
Cupboard, Hanging, Wood, Red & Blue Paint, Panel Door, Molded Cornice, 26 x 23 In.	505.00
Cupboard, Hired Man's, Softwood, Red Wash, Slide Out Front, 30 x 39 x 20 In. .... *illus*	1980.00
Cupboard, Jelly, Grained, 2 Door, 58 x 44 x 16 In.	575.00
Cupboard, Jelly, Grained, 4-Paneled Door, 15 x 32 x 87 In.	1150.00
Cupboard, Jelly, Poplar, Pegged & Cut Nail Construction, Shelves, 40 x 41 x 21 In. .... *illus*	805.00
Cupboard, Jelly, Raised Panel Door, Green Paint, 20 x 34 x 56 In.	345.00
Cupboard, Jelly, Softwood, 2 Drawers, 2 Doors, Half Moon Ends, Grain Paint, 49 x 41 In.	1870.00
Cupboard, Jelly, Yellow Paint, Arched Gallery, 2 Drawers, 2 Doors, 49 x 42 x 17 In. .... *illus*	2640.00
Cupboard, Mixed Woods, Step Back, Carved, Faith, Hope, Charity, 94 x 57 In.	2750.00
Cupboard, Napoleon III, Kingwood, Drawer, 2 Doors, c.1865, 29 x 15 x 12 In.	499.00
Cupboard, Napoleon III, Kingwood, Veneered Top, Drawer, 2 Doors, Cabriole Legs, 29 x 15 In.	449.00
Cupboard, Oak, Open Top, Shelves, Drawers, Doors, 50 x 19½ x 60 In.	115.00
Cupboard, Oak, Paneled & Tambour Doors, 3 Drawers, Enameled, c.1900, 68 x 43 In. . *illus*	449.00
Cupboard, Painted, Hanging, Arched Pediment, 2 Doors, Scrolls, Molded, Continental, 25 x 21 In.	2749.00
Cupboard, Pine, 2 Doors, 3 Shelves, Painted, 83½ x 56 x 21¾ In.	4406.00
Cupboard, Pine, Corner, 2 Parts, Cornice, 2 Doors, Shelves, Skirt, Bracket Feet, c.1800, 80 x 45 In.	1793.00
Cupboard, Pine, Open Top, Scalloped Edges, 4 Shelves, 2 Drawers, Scalloped Base, 75 x 46 In.	920.00
Cupboard, Pine, Painted, Step Back, Shelves, Open Storage Cove, Mid 1800s, 66 x 69 In.	2360.00
Cupboard, Pine, Scalloped Back, Door Panels, Splash Shelf Support, 74 x 48 x 26 In.	323.00
Cupboard, Poplar, Green Paint, Paneled Doors, Shelves, Cut Nails, 1800s, 61 x 37 In.	374.00
Cupboard, Poplar, Red Stain, Frame & Panel, Shelves, Tennessee, 1800s, 71 x 41 In.	460.00
Cupboard, Regency, Mahogany, 2 Doors, 4 Interior Drawers, Bracket Feet, 44 x 23 In., Pair	2820.00
Cupboard, Regency, Mahogany, Square Top, Paneled Door, Tapered Legs, Pad Feet, 37 In.	440.00
Cupboard, Shaker, Cherry, Thumbnail Molded Top, Hanging, N.Y., c.1840-50, 31 x 12 In.	3217.00
Cupboard, Shaker, Chest, Pine, Painted Yellow, Paneled Doors, New Lebanon, c.1850, 81 x 50 In.	42000.00
Cupboard, Shaker, Hanging, Pine, Painted, 4 Shelves, Bottle Holder, Harvard, Mass., 43 x 29 In.	3042.00
Cupboard, Shaker, Pine, 4 Shelves, Door, Peg, Painted, Mt. Lebanon, N.Y., 1850, 45 x 20 In.	2340.00
Cupboard, Shaker, Pine, 7 Shelves, 4-Panel Door, Signed, Arthur J., Harvard, 1850, 60 x 35 In.	1404.00
Cupboard, Shaker, Pine, Poplar, Red Stain, 4 Drawers, Door, New Lebanon, c.1850, 72 x 38 In.	33000.00
Cupboard, Shaker, Pine, Red Paint, Door, 5 Shelves, Gray Paint, Brass Pull, 68 x 29 x 16 In.	2574.00
Cupboard, Shaker, Walnut, Pine, Drawers, 2 Doors, Mortised, Union Village, c.1850, 57 x 53 In.	4212.00
Cupboard, Softwood, 2 Sections, 2 Panel Doors, Red Paint, Scalloped Apron, 88 x 45 In.	6050.00
Cupboard, Softwood, Green Over Red Paint, Drawer Over Door, Turned Feet, 50 x 44 In.	15950.00
Cupboard, Softwood, Old Yellow Paint, 2 Drawers, 2 Doors, Cutout Feet, 48½ x 42 In.	2640.00
Cupboard, Softwood, Yellow Paint, Door, Sunken Panels, Cutout Feet, 45 x 38 In.	3190.00
Cupboard, Spice, Walnut, 12 Drawers, Door, Bracket Feet, Molded Cornice, Late 1700s, 28 x 21 In.	3585.00
Cupboard, Spice, Walnut, Double Panel Door, 3 Drawers, c.1825, 19 x 14 x 12 In.	4400.00
Cupboard, Step Back, Pine, Pierced Pediment, Heart Decorations, Drawers, 85 x 64 In.	1495.00
Cupboard, Step Back, Walnut, 4 Doors, 3 Drawers, Chamfered, Early 1800s, 79 x 54 In.	4183.00
Cupboard, Step Back, Wood, 2 Doors Over 8 Drawers & Door, 64 x 71 x 24 In. .... *illus*	4830.00
Cupboard, Victorian, Pine, Kitchen, Waxed, 2 Sections, 2 Glazed Doors, 76 x 65 In.	1880.00
Cupboard, Wall, 2 Sections, Walnut, Dovetailed Drawers, Panel Doors, Turned Feet, 85 In.	1840.00
Cupboard, Walnut, Press, Glazed Doors, 4 Shelves, Panel Doors, Tenn., 89 x 59 In.	4830.00
Cupboard, Welsh, Oak, Step Back, 2 Sections, Cornice, Shelves, Early 1900s	1265.00
Cupboard, William IV, Mahogany, Door, Arched Panel, 37 x 25½ x 19½ In.	1562.00
Cupboard, William IV, Mahogany, Raised Edge, Tambour Door, Drawer, 31 x 20 In.	645.00
Cupboard, Windowsill, Bull's-Eye, 19th Century, Pa., 27 x 9½ x 15 In.	1100.00
Curio Stand, Burl, Teakwood, Chinese, 3½ x 12 In., Pair	176.00
Daybed, Arts & Crafts, Oak, Upholstered Pad, 78 In.	409.00
Daybed, Chinese, Elm, Shanxi Province, Ming Dynasty, 18½ x 85 In.	1888.00
Daybed, English Arts & Crafts, Stained Beech, Sloped Back, Upholstered, 28 x 80 In.	885.00
Daybed, Figured Maple, Turned Posts, Side Rails, Chamfered Rails, 25 x 25½ In.	115.00

Daybed, G. Nakashima, Walnut, Free-Edge Backboard, Exposed Joinery, Tapered Legs, 36 x 84 In.	19120.00
Daybed, Limbert, Cutouts, Leather Spring Cushions, 23 x 25 x 75 In.	3120.00
Daybed, Limbert, Raised Headrest, Broad Oak Sides, Square Legs, 25 x 79 In.	1200.00
Daybed, Louis Philippe, Rosewood, Arched Head & Footboard, 48 x 49 In.	1440.00
Daybed, Louis XVI, Upholstered, Padded Head & Footboard, Painted, 24 x 31 x 68 In.	2585.00
Daybed, Mahogany, Turned & Swelled Posts, Paneled Ends, Onion Turned Feet, c.1835	1434.00
Daybed, Napoleon III, Iron, Upholstered, Outscrolled Arms, Leaves, Casters, 31½ x 83 In.	2585.00
Daybed, Robsjohn-Gibbings, Widdicomb, c.1950, 14½ x 34 x 83 In. *illus*	7500.00
Daybed, Stickley Bros., Oak, Through Tenon Construction, Leather Upholstery, 25 x 29 In.	2415.00
Daybed, Stickley Bros., Raised Headrest, Loose Linen Cushions, 24½ x 77 In.	1080.00
Daybed, Tiger Maple, Turned Posts, New Mattress, c.1860, 72 In.	2900.00
Daybed, Walnut, Hoof Feet, Padded Seat, France, c.1870, 76 x 29 In.	5200.00
Daybed, Wicker, Latticework Panels, Woven Seat, Heywood-Wakefield, 1900	1650.00
Desk, 2 Drawer, 2-Board Flat Top, Wrought Iron Ring Pull, Continental, 29 x 68 In.	1150.00
Desk, Biedermeier, Walnut, 4 Drawers, 38¼ x 51¼ x 25 In.	4130.00
Desk, Bookcase, Chippendale, Inlaid Cherry, Connecticut, c.1780, 84 x 41 In.	21600.00
Desk, Bookcase, Chippendale, Mahogany, Elbert Anderson, N.Y., c.1796, 89 x 50 In.	21600.00
Desk, Bookcase Sides, Wicker, Canter Drawer, Brass Knob, c.1920s, 34 In.	1050.00
Desk, Butler's, Chippendale, Mahogany, Goddard-Townsend, c.1780, 40 x 46 In.	11400.00
Desk, Butler's, Empire, Mahogany, Projecting Frieze Panel, Glass Pulls, 52 x 48 In.	708.00
Desk, Butler's, Federal, Hepplewhite, Inlaid Mahogany, Secretary Drawer, 44 x 47 In.	3760.00
Desk, Butler's, Hepplewhite, 4 Faux Drawers, 4 Beaded Drawers, Bone Escutcheon, 43 x 43 In.	1210.00
Desk, Butler's, Neoclassical, Mahogany, Carved, Drawers, Drop Front, c.1835, 43 x 47 In.	863.00
Desk, Campaign, Mahogany, Lift Top, Easel-Back Writing Surface, Square Legs, 34 x 36 In.	2040.00
Desk, Campaign, Slant Front, Mahogany, Brass Inlay, Fitted Interior, Turned Legs, 41 x 41 In.	1800.00
Desk, Camphorwood, Rosewood, Mahogany, Book Rack, Inkwells, Lift Top, 10 x 25 x 15 In.	2200.00
Desk, Cherry, Lift Top, Yellow Pine, Poplar, Interior Compartments, 40 x 49 In.	1495.00
Desk, Chippendale, Cherry, Block Front, Compartmented, Fan Carved, 43½ x 40 In.	2468.00
Desk, Chippendale, Figured Maple, White Pine, Fitted Interior, Drawers, 44 x 41 In.	345.00
Desk, Chippendale, Mahogany, Block Front, Glazed Prospect Door, 1780, 43 x 40 In.	11163.00
Desk, Chippendale, Slant Front, Carved Walnut, c.1775, 42 x 39½ x 19½ In.	4200.00
Desk, Chippendale, Slant Front, Cherry, c.1780, 42½ x 39½ x 20½ In.	5100.00
Desk, Chippendale, Slant Front, Cherry, Glazed Tombstone Prospect Door, 48 x 36 In.	3819.00
Desk, Chippendale, Slant Front, Cherry, Inlay, Pa., c.1795, 43¼ x 40 x 20¾ In.	4200.00
Desk, Chippendale, Slant Front, Cherry, Oxbow Serpentine, 43½ x 42¾ In.	3525.00
Desk, Chippendale, Slant Front, Mahogany, 15¼ x 12 x 7½ In.	5700.00
Desk, Chippendale, Slant Front, Mahogany, 4 Drawers, 41½ x 41¾ x 23 In.	2271.00
Desk, Chippendale, Slant Front, Mahogany, 4 Drawers, Ogee Feet, Late 1700s, 43 x 39 In.	5676.00
Desk, Chippendale, Slant Front, Mahogany, 5 Drawers, 42 x 36½ x 24 In.	550.00
Desk, Chippendale, Slant Front, Mahogany, Pine, Poplar, 4 Drawers, High Bracket Feet, 43 x 41 In.	5750.00
Desk, Chippendale, Slant Front, Maple, 6 Drawers, Pigeonholes, 42 x 36 In.	3450.00
Desk, Chippendale, Slant Front, Maple, Birch, Pine Drawers, Prospect Door, 43 x 39 In.	1035.00
Desk, Chippendale, Slant Front, Pine, Bracket Feet, 4 Drawers, 36 x 41 In.	1208.00
Desk, Chippendale, Slant Front, Walnut, 4 Drawers, Door, Cubby Holes, 40½ x 39 In.	440.00
Desk, Chippendale, Slant Front, Walnut, 4 Graduated Drawers, Ogee Feet, 44 x 38 In.	1320.00
Desk, Chippendale, Walnut, 4 Drawers, Door, Scrolled Shell, Claw & Ball Feet, 32 x 40 In.	9350.00
Desk, Chippendale Style, Slant Front, Tiger Maple, 4 Drawers, Bracket Feet, Albert R. Winroth, 1929	4481.00
Desk, Circasian, Slant Front, Walnut, Veneered, 2 Drawers, Shelf, 48 x 39 In.	495.00
Desk, Credenza, Office, Streamline, Industrial Steel, Cantilevered, Leather Top, 30 x 66 In.	354.00
Desk, Cylinder, Victorian, Walnut, Burl, Pierced, Mirrored Gallery, 60 x 31 In.	403.00
Desk, Davenport, Burl Walnut, Writing Surface, Gallery Top, Drawers, c.1880, 37 x 24 In. *illus*	950.00
Desk, Davenport, Victorian, Walnut, 4 Side Drawers, Front Drawer, 38½ x 32 x 24 In.	558.00
Desk, Drop Front, Eastlake Style, Ladies, Oak, Drawers, Victorian, 1880s, 72 In.	1675.00
Desk, Emile Galle, Drop Front, Burled Walnut, Marquetry, c.1900, 43 x 30 x 19 In.	24000.00
Desk, Federal, Cherry, Inlay, 4 Drawers, Ebony Stinging, Bracket Feet, 43 x 45½ In.	1528.00
Desk, Federal, Cherry, Tambour, Hinged, Graduated Drawers, 46 x 38 x 20 In.	2980.00
Desk, Federal, Mahogany, Drop Front, Fitted Interior, 4 Drawers, 1900s, 41 x 38 In.	590.00
Desk, Federal, Mahogany, Figured Maple, Bowfront, New Eng., c.1810, 53 x 39 In. *illus*	8400.00
Desk, Federal, Mahogany, Inlay, Figured, c.1810, 48½ x 34½ x 20 In.	4200.00
Desk, Federal, Mahogany Veneer, String Inlay, Cylinder, c.1810, 48¾ x 46 In.	1998.00
Desk, Federal, Slant Front, Cherry, Tiger Maple, 4 Drawers, 19th Century, 42 x 41 x 22 In.	1195.00
Desk, Federal, Slant Front, Mahogany Ox Bow, White Pine, Boston, 1700s, 44 x 42 In.	5750.00
Desk, French Provincial Style, Drop Front, Painted, Late 19th Century, 29½ In.	246.00
Desk, G. Nakashima, Black Walnut, 3 Drawers, 1961, 29 x 60 x 27 In. *illus*	12000.00
Desk, G. Stickley, Chalet, Paneled Drop Front, Lower Shelf, Shoe Feet, 46 x 24¼ In.	3120.00
Desk, G. Stickley, Drawer, Wooden Knobs, Letter Holder, 33 x 32 x 20 In.	840.00

Furniture, Cupboard, Jelly, Poplar, Pegged & Cut Nail Construction, Shelves, 40 x 41 x 21 In.
$805.00

Furniture, Cupboard, Jelly, Yellow Paint, Arched Gallery, 2 Drawers, 2 Doors, 49 x 42 x 17 In.
$2640.00

Furniture, Cupboard, Oak, Paneled & Tambour Doors, 3 Drawers, Enameled, c.1900, 68 x 43 In.
$449.00

Furniture, Cupboard, Step Back, Wood, 2 Doors Over 8 Drawers & Door, 64 x 71 x 24 In.
$4830.00

Furniture, Daybed, Robsjohn-Gibbings, Widdicomb, c.1950, 14½ x 34 x 83 In.
$7500.00

Furniture, Desk, Davenport, Burl Walnut, Writing Surface, Gallery Top, Drawers, c.1880, 37 x 24 In.
$950.00

Furniture, Desk, Federal, Mahogany, Figured Maple, Bowfront, New Eng., c.1810, 53 x 39 In.
$8400.00

Desk, G. Stickley, Kneehole, 5 Drawers, Paneled Sides, Iron Hardware, 30 x 50 In.	1920.00
Desk, G. Stickley, Paneled Drop Front, Chalet, Shoe Feet, 45½ x 24 x 7 In.	2520.00
Desk, George III, Mahogany, Leather Top, Pedestal, Drawers, Doors, 31 x 48 x 35 In.	4406.00
Desk, George III Style, Mahogany, Leather Inset, Drawers, Cabriole Legs, 29 x 54 x 32 In.	4292.00
Desk, George III Style, Mahogany, Leather Surface, 5 Drawers, c.1900, 29 x 54 x 32 In.	1292.00
Desk, George III Style, Slant Front, Mahogany, 52 In.	3600.00
Desk, Georgian, Slant Front, Burled Walnut, Veneered, Drawers, 38 x 34¼ x 18 In.	2823.00
Desk, Hepplewhite, Slant Front, Cherry, 4 Graduated Cock-Beaded Drawers, 45 x 42 In.	990.00
Desk, Hepplewhite, Slant Front, Cherry, Oval Brasses, Drawers, Letter Slots, c.1810, 30 x 40 In.	2000.00
Desk, Hepplewhite, Slant Front, Maple, Cherry, Pine, Poplar, Drawers, 40 x 19 x 42 In.	3738.00
Desk, Hepplewhite, Slant Front, Walnut, 4 Cock-Beaded Drawers, Line Inlay, 47 x 39 In.	2200.00
Desk, Hunt, Oak, Black Forest, Receding Top, Carved Legs, Lion Heads, 52 x 50 x 29 In.	3760.00
Desk, I. Noguchi, Rudder, Label, Herman Miller, 1949, 27 x 36 x 50 In. *illus*	21600.00
Desk, Limbert, Slant Front, 2 Drawers, Fitted Interior, 41 x 36 x 18 In. *illus*	1265.00
Desk, Louis XV Style, Rosewood, Mahogany, Gilt Tooled Leather, 30¼ x 65 x 36 In.	6345.00
Desk, Louis XVI, Kidney Shape, Carved Front, Cabriole Legs, 30 x 43 x 22 In. *illus*	1175.00
Desk, Louis XVI, Mahogany, Gilt Bronze Mounted, Adjustable, 51 x 22 In.	617.00
Desk, Louis XVI Style, Roll Top, C Roll, Lady's, 2 Section, Scenes, Brass Gallery, 60 x 32 In. *illus*	4371.00
Desk, Louis XVI Style, Tulipwood, Kingwood, Marquetry, Parquetry, Lady's, 39 x 32 x 19 In.	1645.00
Desk, Louis XVI Style, Upper Cupboards, Mirror, France, Mid 1800s, 53 In.	5129.00
Desk, Napoleon III Style, Walnut, Ormolu, Pedestals, Drawer, Blind Door, 31 x 54 x 34 In.	1293.00
Desk, On Frame, Drop Front, 2 Drawers, 40 x 20 x 43 In.	1150.00
Desk, On Stand, Lift Top, Pine, Painted, Box Stretcher, 19th Century, 24¾ In.	261.00
Desk, On Stand, Lift Top, Pine, Painted, Tapered Legs, 19th Century, 24¾ In.	283.00
Desk, Osvaldo Borsani, Techno, Metal, Chrome, Rosewood, c.1958, 29 x 71 x 33 In.	8400.00
Desk, Oxbow, Chippendale, Mahogany Oxbow, Carved Shell Interior, Boston, 1700s, 45 x 41 In.	7150.00
Desk, Partners, L. & J.G. Stickley, Double Slant Top, 30 x 36 x 39 In. *illus*	1080.00
Desk, Partners, Quartersawn Oak, Griffin Legs, Drawer, False Front, Hoener Mfg., 55 x 37 In.	5854.00
Desk, Pedestal, Contemporary, Black Paint, 9 Drawers, Turned Corner Poles, 35 x 64 In.	205.00
Desk, Plantation, Hidden Compartment, Drop Down Writing Surface, 37 x 23 In.	527.00
Desk, Plantation, Sheraton, Painted, Paneled Doors, Latticework, 91 x 42 In.	3000.00
Desk, Queen Anne, Slant Front, Japanned, Fitted, Mass., c.1740, 41 x 39 In. *illus*	3600.00
Desk, Queen Anne, Slant Front, Walnut, Inlay, Fitted, Mass., c.1740, 41 x 36 In. *illus*	3600.00
Desk, Queen Anne Style, Maple, Figured, 19th Century, 40½ x 30 x 15½ In.	3900.00
Desk, Renaissance Revival, Bird's-Eye Maple, Burled Walnut, 71 x 44 In.	14950.00
Desk, Renaissance Revival, Walnut, Mahogany, Patent, 57¼ x 42½ x 31½ In.	8400.00
Desk, Rohde, Palladio, Kidney Shaped, 6 Drawers, Leather Trim, Brass Tacks, 29 x 56 In.	1410.00
Desk, Roll Top, C Roll, Maple, 2 Short Over 2 Long Drawers, Fitted Interior, 31 x 48 In. *illus*	1265.00
Desk, Roll Top, C Roll, Oak, 2 Pedestals, Pigeon Drawers, Swivel Chair, 45 x 60 In. *illus*	382.00
Desk, Roll Top, S Roll, Oak, 2 Pedestals, Pigeonholes, Late 1800s, 44 x 52 x 32 In.	705.00
Desk, Roll Top, S Roll, Victorian, Walnut, Card, Letter Files, Carved Pulls, 50 x 50 x 34 In.	705.00
Desk, Roll Top, Victorian, Walnut, Scalloped, Carved Crest, Burl Accents, 52 x 25 In.	3105.00
Desk, Rosewood, 7 Drawers, Brass Mounts, Chinese, 31 x 60 x 29¾ In.	325.00
Desk, Rosewood, Slant Top, Ivory, Ebony, Mahogany, Mother-Of-Pearl, 21 x 19 In.	19750.00
Desk, School, Old Green Paint, Canted Top, Double Lift Top, 30 x 47½ In.	165.00
Desk, School, Pine, Double, Cut Nail, Hinged Writing Board, 1800s, 30 x 40 In.	144.00
Desk, Schoolmaster's, Slant Front, Oak, Pine, Drawers, Pigeonhole, 28½ x 22 x 35 In.	288.00
Desk, Schoolmaster's, Slant Front, Walnut, Carved, 3 Cubbyholes, 36½ x 38 x 25 In.	690.00
Desk, Shaker, Cherry, Maple, 2 Doors, Drawer, 2-Piece, Slanted, c.1850, 64 x 31 In.	5850.00
Desk, Slant Front, Cherry, 4 Drawers, Bracket Base, Child's, 31 x 19¼ x 10⅞ In.	1912.00
Desk, Slant Front, Cherry, 6 Drawers, Molded Skirt, 42¾ x 37½ x 21 In.	1315.00
Desk, Slant Front, Chippendale, Walnut, 3 Cock-Beaded Drawers, Ogee Feet, 43 x 37 In.	1100.00
Desk, Slant Front, Curly Maple, Pine, 4 Drawers, Dovetailed, 40½ x 36¾ x 18½ In.	3335.00
Desk, Slant Front, Grain Painted, Dovetailed Top, Late 18th Century, 46 x 38 In.	590.00
Desk, Slant Front, Inlaid Walnut, Fitted Interior, Long Drawers, 1700s, 42 x 42½ In.	2950.00
Desk, Slant Front, Mahogany, Pigeonholes, Drawers, Paw Feet, 42 x 40 x 20 In.	529.00
Desk, Slant Front, Softwood, Gallery Top, 3 Drawers, Yellow, Bracket Feet, Apron, 49 x 35 x 23 In.	5500.00
Desk, Slant Front, Tramp Art, Chip Carved, Drawer, Carved Legs, Early 1900s, 38 x 24 In.	4500.00
Desk, Slant Front, Walnut Inlay, 41 x 43¾ In.	2271.00
Desk, Softwood, Countertop, Old Blue Paint, Canted Lid, Cubbyhole Interior, 17 x 21 In.	605.00
Desk, Southern Walnut, Pine, Writing Board Opens, Fitted Interior, 1800s, 33 x 28 In.	431.00
Desk, Stand Up, Kittinger, Mahogany, Leather, Pigeonholes, Drawer, 1900s, 51 x 36 In.	1495.00
Desk, Stand Up, Slant Front, Walnut, Dovetailed, 2 Doors, Pigeonholes, 50 x 36 In.	805.00
Desk, Stand Up, Walnut, Yellow Pine, Lift Top, Open Compartment, 35 x 19 In.	489.00
Desk, Table Top, Cherry, Dovetailed, Fitted Interior, Lift Top, Leather, 20 x 10¼ In.	173.00
Desk, Table Top, Slant Front, Oak, Carved, Applied Molding, 27¾ x 11 In.	546.00

Desk, Tambour, Mahogany, Brass Mounts, Fold Down, Portable, 7½ x 15 In.	489.00
Desk, Walnut, Blueberry Painted, Shaped, Scalloped Legs, Child's, c.1840, 54 x 30½ In.	1155.00
Desk, Wicker, Gallery, Kidney Shape, Wood Top, Cane Wrapped Legs, Drawer, 1920, 33 In. . . .	875.00
Desk, William & Mary, Slant Front, Oak, 4 Drawers, Ball Feet, Stepped Interior, 38 x 32 In. . .	770.00
Desk Stand, Rococo Style, Silvered Metal, Reticulated Scroll, 2 Inkwells, 12 x 9½ In.	294.00
Desk Top, Shaker, Trustees, Pine, Backsplash, Hinged Lid, Enfield, Conn., c.1860, 12 x 17 x 15 In. . .	410.00
Desk-Bookcase, Slant Front, Cherry, Pine, Poplar, 4 Doors, Square Legs, Tenn., 95 x 40 In. . . . . *illus*	6900.00
Dessert Trolley, Christofle, Mahogany, 6 Silver Trays, 2 Shelves, 1930s, 39 x 37 x 20 In.	2084.00
Dining Set, Art Deco Style, Walnut, Padded Seat, c.1940, 39 In., 8 Piece	614.00
Dining Set, Art Nouveau, Walnut, Carved Fruit, France, 29 x 54 x 46-In. Table, 7 Piece . *illus*	1300.00
Divan, Victorian, Wicker, Serpentine, Twist-Wrapped Rosettes, Heywood Bros. & Wakefield . .	1850.00
Dresser, Aesthetic Revival, Bird's-Eye Maple, Bamboo, Mirror, Horner, 75 x 48 In.	4406.00
Dresser, Carved, Mirror Drawer, Paneled Cabinet, Victorian, 66½ x 41 In.	460.00
Dresser, Desk, Pine, 1930s, 44½ x 30½ x 17 In.	110.00
Dresser, Early 18th Century Style, Oak, Carved, Early 20th Century, 76 x 84 In.	614.00
Dresser, Eastlake, Oak, 3 Drawers, Brass Pulls, Victorian, 71 x 40 x 20 In.	235.00
Dresser, Empire, Stepp Back, 3 Drawers, Diamond Paneled Frieze Drawer, 51 x 44 In.	413.00
Dresser, Fruitwood, Bone Inlay, 2 Parts, Shelves, Door, Drawers, 93¾ x 54½ x 23 In.	5581.00
Dresser, Limbert, 2 Over 2 Drawer, Pivoting Mirror, Bronze Hardware	1920.00
Dresser, Marble Top, Mirror, Walnut, Burl Veneer, Victorian, 47 x 20¾ In.	288.00
Dresser, Oak, 4 Drawers, Victorian, 72 x 42 x 21 In.	294.00
Dresser, Renaissance Revival, Walnut, Center Well, Marble Top, 86 x 49 x 20 In.	529.00
Dresser, Restauration, Mahogany, Marble Top, Oval Mirror, Scroll Supports, 67 x 41 In. . . .	1116.00
Dresser, Walnut, Carved, Burl Veneer, Marble Top, Victorian, 94 x 56 In.	489.00
Dresser, Welsh, English Oak, Molded Cornice, Shaped Frieze, Shelves, 76 x 45 In.	720.00
Dresser, Welsh, Pine, Pierced Frieze, 3 Open Shelves, 3 Short Drawers, Block Legs, 80 x 57 In. . .	940.00
Dressing Table, Rosewood, Walnut, Carved, Drawer, Cabriolet Legs, 1800s, 26 x 45 In.	15000.00
Dry Sink, Bucket Bench, Softwood, Old Gray Paint, Scalloped Edge, 24 x 25 In.	990.00
Dry Sink, Corner, Old Gray Paint, Shelf, Zinc Lined Well, 47½ x 36½ x 24 In.	1840.00
Dry Sink, Paint Decorated, 42 x 19 x 32 In.	978.00
Dry Sink, Pine, Blue, Gray, Red, Backsplash, Drain Board, Drawer, Doors, 24 x 13 x 18 In. . .	1093.00
Dry Sink, Shaker, Walnut, Pine, Child's, 26 x 24 x 15 In.	4406.00
Dry Sink, Softwood, Dovetailed, 2 Panel Doors, Old Red Paint, 34½ x 50 x 21 In.	880.00
Dry Sink, Softwood, Hooded, 2 Doors, Mustard Over Blue Paint, 19th Century, 34 x 42 x 18 In. . .	2310.00
Dry Sink, Softwood, Old Blue Paint, 2 Doors, Sunken Well, 36 x 42 In.	1210.00
Dry Sink, Softwood, Red Paint, Dovetailed Well, 2 Doors, Bracket Feet, 35 x 45 In. . . . . . *illus*	2090.00
Dry Sink, Walnut, Poplar, Shaped Gallery, Shelf Over Till, Drawers, 43½ x 43½ In.	1783.00
Dumbwaiter, Georgian, Mahogany, 3 Tiers, Urn Supports, Tripod Base, 47 x 24 In. . . . . *illus*	978.00
Dumbwaiter, Mahogany, 2 Tiers, Carved, Pineapple, c.1810, 21 In.	8050.00
Dumbwaiter, Regency, Mahogany, Round Top, Inlaid Sunburst, Splayed Legs, 42 x 24 In. . .	940.00
Dumbwaiter, William IV, Mahogany, Baluster & Block Supports, 1800s, 50 x 54 In.	1121.00
Easel, Empire Style, Mahogany, Gilt Tucked Swan Ends, Scepter Shaft, Tripod, 82 x 29 In. . . .	1410.00
Easel, Louis XV Style, Scrolled Leaf Pierced Crest, 3 Part, 71 x 25 x 27½ In.	561.00
Easel, Wicker, Butterfly Shaped Crest, Metal Frame Holder, 1890s, 62 In.	395.00
Etagere, Aesthetic Revival, Black Lacquered, Stepped Case, Shelves, c.1900, 73 x 48 In.	575.00
Etagere, Anglo-Indian, Bamboo, Black Lacquered, 4 Shelves, Gilt, 43 x 16 In., Pair	1800.00
Etagere, Chinese Chippendale, Pagoda Shape, Mahogany, 4 Tiers, Fretwork, 71 x 21 In.	3408.00
Etagere, Contemporary Style, Wooden, 6 Shelves, Casters, 13¼ x 19½ In.	205.00
Etagere, Corner, Anglo-Indian, Bamboo, Black Lacquered, Mirror Panels, 58 x 23 In.	300.00
Etagere, Corner, Mahogany, Graduated Shelves, Victorian, 64 x 24 In.	293.00
Etagere, Ebonized, Brass Hinges, Drawer Pull, Victorian, 55¼ x 35½ x 10 In.	1175.00
Etagere, Ebonized Wood, Gallery Top, Door, Painted, Incised, 55 x 35 In. . . . . *illus*	1175.00
Etagere, Mahogany, 6 Shelves, Victorian, c.1850, 61 In.	4320.00
Etagere, Neoclassical, Painted, 5 Shelves, Ring Turned Supports, c.1820, 56 x 19 In.	4700.00
Etagere, Rococo Revival, Rosewood, Carved Crest, Urn, Carved Scrolls, 100 x 67 In.	8100.00
Etagere, Rosewood, Rococo Revival, 88¾ In.	4025.00
Etagere, Walnut, 3 Shelves, Turned Supports, Brass Cuffs, Casters, c.1880, 40 x 36 In.	1000.00
Etagere, Wicker, Oak, Arched Curlicue Skirt, Heywood, 1890s, 47 x 18 In.	1950.00
Etagere, Wicker, Wakefield, Arched Wrapped Columns, 1880s, 58 x 19 In.	2650.00
Fernery, Wicker, Contoured Edge, Shapely Skirting, 30 In.	475.00
Fernery, Wicker, Natural, Wood Turned Frame, Loop Work, 1915, 31 In.	575.00
Footstool, Arts & Crafts, Oak, Brown Leather Cushion, Early 1900s, 13 x 16½ In.	489.00
Footstool, Charles X, Rosewood, Inlay, Red Damask, Oval, Ball Feet, 6 x 14 x 10 In., Pair . . .	2115.00
Footstool, Chippendale, Mahogany, Carved, 15 x 20 In.	385.00
Footstool, Chippendale, Walnut, Frame, Brocade Upholstery Seat, Late 1800s, 23 In.	780.00
Footstool, Chippendale, Walnut, Marlboro Legs, Slip Seat, 10 x 15½ In.	220.00

Furniture, Desk, G. Nakashima, Black Walnut, 3 Drawers, 1961, 29 x 60 x 27 In. $12000.00

F

Furniture, Desk, I. Noguchi, Rudder, Label, Herman Miller, 1949, 27 x 36 x 50 In. $21600.00

Furniture, Desk, Limbert, Slant Front, 2 Drawers, Fitted Interior, 41 x 36 x 18 In. $1265.00

Furniture, Desk, Louis XVI, Kidney Shape, Carved Front, Cabriole Legs, 30 x 43 x 22 In. $1175.00

Furniture, Desk, Louis XVI Style, Roll Top, C Roll, Lady's, 2-Section, Scenes, Brass Gallery, 60 x 32 In. $4371.00

Furniture, Desk, Partners, L. & J.G. Stickley, Double Slant Top, 30 x 36 x 39 In. $1080.00

Furniture, Desk, Queen Anne, Slant Front, Japanned, Fitted, Mass., c.1740, 41 x 39 In. $3600.00

Footstool, Chippendale, Walnut, Scrolled Apron, Square Legs, Leather Seat, 18 x 20 x 15 In.	523.00
Footstool, Chippendale Style, Walnut, Claw & Ball Feet, 17 x 19¼ x 14 In., Pair	144.00
Footstool, Continental, Mahogany, Carved, 20th Century, 22½ In., Pair	988.00
Footstool, Crewel Upholstered, Red Wool Fringe, Ring Turned Legs, 13 x 15 In.	3525.00
Footstool, G. Stickley, Tacked On Brown Naugahyde Deck, Finish Tacks, 9 x 16 In.	960.00
Footstool, Georgian Style, Mahogany, Carved, Slip Set, Scrolling Skirt, 20 x 24 In.	345.00
Footstool, Hickory, Maple, Rush Seat, Painted, Gray, 27¾ x 32 x 21½ In.	5700.00
Footstool, Louis XV, Fruitwood, Carved, Upholstered Top, Early 1900s, 9 x 16 In.	58.00
Footstool, Louis XVI, Giltwood, Carved, Floral Gros Point Upholstery, 12½ x 10 In.	210.00
Footstool, Mixed Wood, Pierced Shaped Top, Half Moon Cutouts, 5 x 13 In.	110.00
Footstool, Neoclassical, Mahogany, Ogee Base Molding, Bracket Feet, 15 x 21 In., Pair	518.00
Footstool, Neoclassical, Mahogany, Slip Seat, Ogee Frame, Scrolled Legs, c.1830, 18 x 24 In.	2160.00
Footstool, Neoclassical, Mahogany, Slip Seat, Ogee Molded Frieze, Turnip Legs, 8 x 15 In.	117.00
Footstool, Prairie School, Drop In Tacked On Deck, Red Leather, Stretchers, 17x 16 In.	300.00
Footstool, Roycroft, Tacked On Burgundy Leather Deck, Finish Tacks, 11 x 16 In.	1080.00
Footstool, Softwood, ½ Moon Cutout Legs, Brown Sponge Paint, White Pinstripes, 8 x 14 In.	110.00
Footstool, Walnut, Carved, Cabriole Legs, Damask Upholstery, Victorian, 17 x 24 In.	259.00
Footstool, Walnut, Scrolled Apron, Cutout, Mortised Legs, Drop Finials, 1928, 7 x 13 In.	88.00
Footstool, Walnut, Scrolled Apron, Shaped Legs, Peaked Cutout, 8 x 14¼ In.	88.00
Footstool, Wicker, Circular Woven Top, Wrapped Ball Feet, 1890, 13 x 15 In.	695.00
Footstool, Wicker, Contour Top, Diamond Designs, c.1900, 17 x 23 In.	675.00
Footstool, William & Mary, Walnut, Turned Legs, Needlepoint, Fringe, 21 x 18 In., Pair	3000.00
Footstool, Windsor, Pine, Splayed Leg, Oval Top, Early 18th Century, 20 x 12 In.	633.00
Frame, Branch Sides, Entwined Berries, Leaves, Acorns, Eagle & Crest, Black Forest, 56 x 44 In.	646.00
Frame, Brass Over Metal, Oval, Black & White Family Portrait, c.1890, 22 x 14 In.	35.00
Frame, Figural, Winged Archer, Torchbearer, Lilies Of The Valley, Heart, Banner, 34 x 26 In.	5225.00
Frame, Gilt Ormolu, Jeweled, Faux Turquoise, Reticulated Flowers, c.1940, 3½ x 3 In.	150.00
Frame, Giltwood, Flowers, Latticework, Floral Vine, 32 x 24 In.	472.00
Frame, Iron, U.S. Army, Eagle Top, Flags, Drum, Judd Company, c.1917, 6 x 8 In.	175.00
Frame, Napoleon III, Giltwood, Gilt Gesso, Oval Center, Leaf Scrolls, Swags, Shells	750.00
Frame, Neoclassical, Gilt, Red Velvet, Acanthus Leaves, 19th Century, 18 x 20 In.	200.00
Frame, Painted, Mitered, Yellow Rag, Ebony Ground, 14⅞ x 10⅞ In.	44.00
Frame, Rococo Style, Bronze, Patinated, Standing, Early 1900s, 16 x 13 In.	82.00
Frame, Rohlfs, Eagle Shape, Rustic, 1904, 11 x 9¾ In.	1080.00
Frame, Softwood, Molded, Painted, Red Striping, Yellow Ground, 9 x 11¼ In.	495.00
Frame, Softwood, Painted, Black Striping Over Red Flamed Ground, 13½ x 9½ In.	275.00
Frame, Softwood, Painted, Brown Striping Over Yellow Ground, 13¼ x 9½ In.	165.00
Frame, Softwood, Painted, Red Striping On Black Ground, 10¾ x 9½ In.	303.00
Frame, Softwood, Painted, White, Green Polka Dot, Rosette, Medallion, 9½ x 7⅜ In.	880.00
Girandole, Louis XVI Style, Giltwood, Composition, Flaming Urn, Swag, 42 x 22 In.	805.00
Hall Stand, Black Forest, Bear, Cub, Branch Hooks, Mirror, Leaf Frame, 89 In. *illus*	19975.00
Hall Stand, Ebonized Beech, 4 Hooks, Beveled Mirror, Umbrella Holder, 77 In.	9000.00
Hall Stand, Wrought Metal, Mirrored Panel, Early 20th Century, 32 x 6 x 79 In.	450.00
Hall Tree, Carved Bear, Holding Hoop, Copper Pan, Black Forest, 34 In.	5405.00
Hall Tree, Victorian Style, Cast Iron, Porcelain Drip Pan, 78 x 28 x 15 In.	990.00
Hall Tree, Walnut, Marble Top, Cast Iron Pans, Victorian, 86 x 36 x 13 In.	500.00
Hamper, Clothes, Wicker, Flat Weaving, Woven Diamond Designs, 1920s, 23 x 20 In.	165.00
Hat Rack, Black Forest, Fox Head, Holding Branch, Double Hook In Jaws, 12½ In. *illus*	1175.00
Hat Rack, Black Forest Type, Carved Animal Heads, Horn Hooks, 67 In.	4872.00
Hat Rack, Carved, Bird, Brance Perch, Oak Leaves, 3 Iron Hooks, Black Forest, 9 x 17 In.	132.00
Hat Rack, Walrus Tusk, Wood Mount, Nickel Pegs, 21 In.	176.00
Hat Rack, Wooden, Painted, Black, Green, Gilt, Scrolled Wire Hooks, 3⅜ x 25 In.	2350.00
Headboard, Italian Rococo Style, Carved, Painted, Upholstered, 65 x 60½ In.	165.00
Headboard, Walnut, Carved, Fruit, Nut, Turned Finials, Victorian, 62 x 58½ x 4½ In.	325.00
Highboy, Chippendale, Mahogany, Broken Arch Top, Swag Carved Molding, 95 x 42 In.	11000.00
Highboy, Chippendale, Walnut, Maple, Birch, Cabriole Legs, Claw & Ball Feet, 67 x 37 x 22 In.	6486.00
Highboy, Chippendale Style, Mahogany, 13 Drawers, Columns, Claw & Ball Feet, 93 x 43 In.	6900.00
Highboy, Federal Style, Bonnet Top, Broken Pediment, 1900s, 24½ x 12 In.	767.00
Highboy, George III, Mahogany, Dentil Molded Crown, 5 Drawers, 1800s, 69½ x 48 In.	3680.00
Highboy, Jacobean Style, Oak, Early 20th Century, 54 x 25 In.	389.00
Highboy, Mahogany, Modified Bonnet Top, 10 Drawers, 19th Century, 40 x 32 In.	1580.00
Highboy, Queen Anne, Cherry, 2 Sections, Carved Sunbursts, 10 Drawers, 71 x 34 In. *illus*	4600.00
Highboy, Queen Anne, Cherry, Pine, 10 Drawers, Shaped Skirt, Cabriole Legs, New Eng., 72 x 38 In.	8625.00
Highboy, Queen Anne, Cherry, Pine, Poplar, 9 Drawers, Cabriole Legs, Pad Feet, 71 x 39 x 20 In.	6325.00
Highboy, Queen Anne, Mahogany, 8 Drawers, Pendants, Pad Feet, Mid 1700s, 69 x 42 In.	20315.00
Highboy, Queen Anne, Mahogany, Oak, 8 Drawers, Cabriole Legs, England, 64 x 40 x 24 In.	1610.00

Furniture, Desk, Queen Anne, Slant Front, Walnut, Inlay, Fitted, Mass., c.1740, 41 x 36 In.
$3600.00

Furniture, Desk, Roll Top, C Roll, Maple, 2 Short Over 2 Long Drawers, Fitted Interior, 31 x 48 In.
$1265.00

Furniture, Desk, Roll Top, C Roll, Oak, 2 Pedestals, Pigeon Drawers, Swivel Chair, 45 x 60 In.
$382.00

Furniture, Desk-Book[...] Cherry, Pine, Poplar, 4 [...] Square Legs, Tenn., 95 [...]
$6900.00

Furniture, Dining Set, Art Nouveau, Walnut, Carved Fruit, France, 29 x 54 x 46-In. Table, 7 Piece
$1300.00

Furniture, Dry Sink, Softwood, Red Paint, Dovetailed Well, 2 Doors, Bracket Feet, 35 x 45 In.
$2090.00

FURNITURE

Furniture, Dumbwaiter, Georgian, Mahogany, 3 Tiers, Urn Supports, Tripod Base, 47 x 24 In.
$978.00

Furniture, Hat Rack, Black Forest, Fox Head, Holding Branch, Double Hook In Jaws, 12½ In.
$1175.00

Furniture, Highchair, Oak, Applied Carvings, Cane Seat, Wheels, 37 In.
$206.00

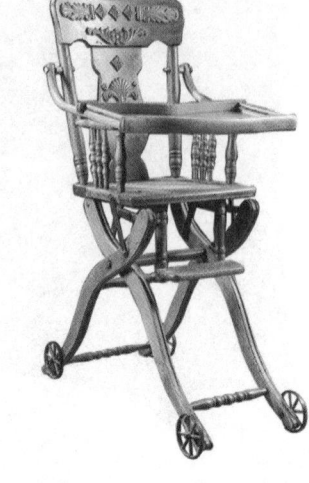

Furniture, Etagere, Ebonized Wood, Gallery Top, Door, Painted, Incised, 55 x 35 In.
$1175.00

Furniture, Highboy, Queen Anne, Cherry, 2 Sections, Carved Sunbursts, 10 Drawers, 71 x 34 In.
$4600.00

Furniture, Highchair, Windsor, Bentwood Back, Turned Spindles, Blue Paint, 30½ In.
$518.00

Furniture, Hall Stand, Black Forest, Bear, Cub, Branch Hooks, Mirror, Leaf Frame, 89 In.
$19975.00

Furniture, Lounge Set, Ebonized Wood, Silk Upholstery, 2 Sofas, Table, 1950s, 75 x 16 x 38 In.
$978.00

F

Highboy, Queen Anne, Maple, 18th Century, 72½ x 38 In.	12075.00
Highboy, Queen Anne, Maple, Drawers, Cabriole Legs, New Hampshire, 39 x 72 In.	5060.00
Highboy, Queen Anne, Tiger Maple, Cherry, 8 Drawers, Cabriole Legs, 74½ In.	2300.00
Highboy, Queen Anne, Walnut, 10 Drawers, Shaped Skirt, Cabriole Legs, Drake Feet, 18th Century	4780.00
Highboy, Queen Anne, Walnut, 12 Drawers, Shells, Drake Feet, Mid 1700s, 77 x 44 In.	20315.00
Highboy, Queen Anne Style, Walnut, 11 Drawers, Cabriole Legs, 61 x 40½ x 22½ In.	9518.00
Highboy, William & Mary, Oak, Carved, Fluted & Floral Scroll Drawers, 58 x 38 In.	2143.00
Highchair, Arts & Crafts Style, Oak, Pierced Back, 39 x 18 x 18 In.	353.00
Highchair, Bentwood, Turned Spindle Supports, Black Paint, Late 1800s, 32 In.	300.00
Highchair, Bentwood Windsor, Spindle Back, Plank Seat, Early 1900s, 27 x 15 In.	115.00
Highchair, Hickory, Maple, Ladder Back, Arched Splat, Splayed Legs, 20 x 33½ In.	748.00
Highchair, Image Of Yellow Kid, Wood, c.1890, 42 In.	1345.00
Highchair, Maple, Ash, Slat Back, New England, Late 1700s, 35½ In.	294.00
Highchair, Oak, Applied Carvings, Cane Seat, Wheels, 37 In. ....*illus*	206.00
Highchair, Oak, Spindle Back, Victorian, 40 x 17 x 19 In.	118.00
Highchair, Pine Plank Bottom, Spindle Back, Arm Supports, Turned Legs, 31 x 17 In.	69.00
Highchair, Thumb Posts, 3 Arrow Back Spindles, Bamboo Turnings, 37 In.	144.00
Highchair, Tray, Windsor, Spindle Back, Footrest, 19th Century, 33 In.	131.00
Highchair, William & Mary, Flat Back, New England, c.1740, 37½ In.	3840.00
Highchair, Windsor, Bentwood Back, Turned Spindles, Blue Paint, 30½ In. ....*illus*	518.00
Highchair, Windsor, Black & Red Graining, Yellow Striping, Walnut Arms, 34 In.	546.00
Highchair, Windsor, Bow Back, Maple, Turned Spindles, 36 x 16½ x 18 In.	71.00
Highchair, Windsor, Plank Seat, Faux Bamboo Spindles, 19th Century, 36 x 20 In.	374.00
Highchair, Wood, Red Paint, Yellow Pinstripes, J.T. Quigley, Chardon, Oh., 31 x 23 In.	288.00
Hoosier Cabinet, Frosted Glass Doors, 44 x 70 In.	1695.00
Huntboard, Federal, Inlaid Walnut, Pine, Dovetailed, Fred Fraser, c.1949, 41 x 57 In.	978.00
Huntboard, Federal, Mahogany, 3 Drawers, Arched Center, 40 x 61 x 20 In.	1495.00
Huntboard, Federal Style, Cherry, Inlaid Tiger Maple, 38¾ x 21½ x 44 In.	1840.00
Huntboard, Georgian Style, Mahogany, Serpentine Top, 3 Drawers, 33½ x 54 In.	3172.00
Huntboard, Yellow Pine, Hepplewhite, 2-Board Top, Drop Front, 44 x 51 In.	10200.00
Hutch, Pine, Scalloped Sides, Bracket Feet, c.1850, 81 x 48 x 19 In.	441.00
Jardiniere, Carved, Grape Motif, Pedestal, 34 x 18 x 24 In.	2800.00
Jardiniere, Regency Style, Mahogany, Slatted Body, Metal Liner, 47 x 13¾ In., Pair	705.00
Jardiniere, Regency Style, Tole, Pierced Brass Gallery, 29 x 18 x 13 In., Pair	1410.00
Kas, 2 Doors, Drawer, Panels, 3 Shelves, Removable Feet, Finish, N.J., 18th Century, 77 x 55 In.	4025.00
Kas, Softwood, Blue Paint, 2 Doors, Molded Cornice, Panels, Ogee Feet, 64 x 45 x 22 In.	4125.00
Kneeler, Prie-Dieu, Provincial, Fruitwood, Armrest, Slatted Back, Rush Seat, 34 In.	117.00
Kneeler, Prie-Dieu, Napoleon III, Oak, Padded Crest, Seat, Carved Thorny Cross, 36 In.	450.00
Knife Box, Federal Style, Urn Finials, Line & Astragal Inlay, Berkey & Gay, 26 In., Pair	2415.00
Knife Box, Urn, Figured Mahogany, Line & Barber Pole Inlay, 1800s, 26 x 10 In., Pair	10925.00
Lap Desk, English Walnut, Slant Top, 2 Side Drawers, 4½ x 13 x 12 In.	322.00
Lap Desk, Mahogany, 3 Inkwells, Brass Handles, Victorian, 24 x 8 x 11¾ In.	354.00
Lap Desk, Mahogany, Brass Inlay, Tooled Leather Writing Surface, 1800s, 7 x 18 In.	431.00
Lap Desk, Mahogany, Brass Mounted, Victorian, 17¾ x 8 x 11¼ In.	413.00
Lap Desk, Mahogany, Rosewood, Inlaid Flowers, Ebonized, Leather Surface, 6 x 17 In.	1560.00
Lap Desk, Oak, Marquetry, Brass Nameplate, England, Victorian, 6 x 13½ x 9 In.	275.00
Lap Desk, Papier-Mache, Mother-Of-Pearl Inlay, Figures, Sloped Top, Victorian, 13½ In.	264.00
Lectern, Oak, Carved, Pedestal, c.1880, 41½ x 30½ x 19 In.	71.00
Library Ladder, French Provincial, Oak, Fold-Out Ladder, Square Legs, 34 x 18 x 14 In.	1800.00
Library Ladder, George III Style, Mahogany, Scrolled Sides, 3 Steps, Brass Edges, 40 x 16 In.	499.00
Library Ladder, Regency, Mahogany, Hinged, 8 Rungs, 38 In.	528.00
Library Ladder, Regency Style, Mahogany, Folding, 4 Graduated Rungs, Brass Tread, 34 In.	325.00
Library Ladder, Regency Style, Mahogany, Folding, 5 Rungs, Brass Tread, 44 In.	470.00
Library Ladder, Regency Style, Mahogany, Folding, Hinged, 3 Rungs, 25¼ In.	264.00
Library Steps, Fruitwood, Brass Inset Mounts, Hinged Frame, 4 Steps, 34 x 30 In.	1293.00
Linen Press, Cherry, Yellow Pine, Poplar, Panel Doors, Rattail Hinges, 76 x 38 In.	4370.00
Linen Press, George III, Mahogany, 2-Paneled Doors, 4 Drawers, Fluted Frieze, 78 x 52 In.	4465.00
Linen Press, George III, Mahogany, Geometric Pediment, Cornice, 1700s, 82 x 51 In.	4320.00
Linen Press, George III Style, Mahogany, Molded Cornice, Fitted Cast, 75 x 53 In.	2640.00
Linen Press, Oak, Carved Tavern Scene Panels, Cherubs, 30 x 24 x 20 In.	764.00
Linen Press, Oak, Paneled Doors, 3 Drawers Over 2, Bracket Feet, 78 x 54 x 20 In.	2950.00
Linen Press, Regency, Mahogany, Cornice, Banded Doors, Geometric, c.1820, 84 x 53 In.	4406.00
Liqueur Set, Regency, Mahogany, 6 Blown Glass Bottles, c.1830, 10 x 7 In.	764.00
Liquor Cabinet, Napoleon III, Tortoiseshell, Mahogany, Brass, Lacquer, 1800s, 75 x 13 In.	4875.00
Liquor Set, Black Forest, Etched Crystal Decanters, Glasses, c.1860, 15½ x 12 In.	4900.00
Lounge Set, Art Deco, Woven, Latticework Frame, Braiding, 1920s, Daybed, 2 Chairs	3450.00

Furniture, Mirror, Chippendale, Mahogany, Inlay, Reverse Painted, Colonial House, 57 x 23 In.
$748.00

Furniture, Mirror, Dressing, Figured Mahogany, Inlay, Serpentine Front, Ivory Finials, 25 x 17 In.
$288.00

Furniture, Mirror, Dressing, Sheraton, Mahogany, Inlay, 5-Drawer Stand, 28 x 28 x 9 In.
$403.00

Furniture, Mirror, Federal, Mahogany Frame, Acorn Drops, Reverse Painted, Water Scene, 35 x 20 In. $374.00

Furniture, Mirror, George III, Giltwood, Scrolled Panels, Birds, Arched Center, 51 x 43 In. $7200.00

Lounge Set, Ebonized Wood, Silk Upholstery, 2 Sofas, Table, 1950s, 75 x 16 x 38 In. ...*illus*	978.00
Lounge Set, Stick Wicker, Sofa, Chair, Armchair, 1920s	5500.00
Love Seat, Contemporary, Upholstered, Love's Barrier Textile, Loose Cushions, 30 x 63 In. ..	472.00
Love Seat, Georgian Style, Mahogany, Carved, Padded Back, Loose Cushion, 37 x 29 In.	431.00
Love Seat, Walnut, Carved, Upholstered, Wood Arms, Padded Sides, 35 x 49 x 28 In.	826.00
Lowboy, Chippendale, Carved Swag, Cabriole Legs, Claw & Ball Feet, 35 x 20 In.	244.00
Lowboy, Chippendale Style, Mahogany, 4 Drawers, Cabriole Legs, Claw & Ball Feet, 31 x 33 In.	2868.00
Lowboy, Chippendale Style, Mahogany, Fan Motif, Drawers, 20th Century, 31 x 34 In.	224.00
Lowboy, English Oak, Drawer, Overhang Top, Cabriole Legs, Mid 1700s, 29 In.	2495.00
Lowboy, English Oak, Frieze, Fitted Drawers, Trumpet & Vase Shape Legs, 27 x 30 In.	1560.00
Lowboy, Queen Anne, Walnut, Banded, 2 Short Over Long Drawer, 1700s, 26 x 29 In.	3120.00
Lowboy, Queen Anne Style, Curly Maple, Eldred Wheeler, Mass., Label, 30 x 34 In.	2530.00
Lowboy, Queen Anne Style, Oak, Rectangular Overhang Top, Early 1800s, 27 x 30 In.	1200.00
Lowboy, Walnut Veneer, Herringbone Inlay, Williamsburg, Baker Furniture, 32 x 34 In.	2415.00
Mammy Bench, Windsor, Rocker, Poplar, Shaped Plank Seat, Scroll Arms, 31 x 52 In.	748.00
Map Case, Renaissance Revival, Walnut, 7 Long Drawers Over 6, 2 Panel Doors	550.00
Mirror, Architectural, Federal, Reverse Painted Panel, Naval Battle, 1800s, 30 x 19 In.	575.00
Mirror, Architectural, Reverse Painted, Walnut, Reeded Cornice, Acorn Drops, 20 x 36 In. ...	403.00
Mirror, Art Deco, Rectangular, Beveled Edges, Chrome Corner Moldings, 36 x 48 In.	353.00
Mirror, Baroque, Giltwood, Carved, Leafy Scrolls, Flowers, 65 x 42 In.	5760.00
Mirror, Baroque, Giltwood, Shell Carved Scrolling Pediment, 18th Century, 55 x 44 In.	4130.00
Mirror, Baroque Style, Giltwood, Bombe Crest, Wirework, Portugal, Pair, 20 In.	2468.00
Mirror, Biedermeier, Walnut Veneer, Inlay, Arched Crest, 37½ In.	147.00
Mirror, Black Boule, Gilt Banded, Cenotaph Form, 37 x 28 In.	1116.00
Mirror, Brass, Line Vautrin, Talosel Resin, Glass, Fabric Netting, c.1950, 12¾ In.	36000.00
Mirror, Bull's-Eye, Giltwood, Carved, Eagle On Rockwork, Early 1800s, 48 x 25 In.	3819.00
Mirror, Chardon, Line Vautrin, Talosel Resin, Glass, Convex, c.1953, 9 In.	14400.00
Mirror, Charles X, Giltwood, Plaster, Molded Frame, 53¾ x 23½ In.	1116.00
Mirror, Cheval, Gothic Style, Mahogany, Spire Crest, Tracery, 78 x 32 In.	4560.00
Mirror, Cheval, Mahogany, Carved, Turned Posts, Paw Feet, 77 x 52 In.	2868.00
Mirror, Cheval, Mahogany, Oval, Swivel Mechanism, 27½ x 48 In.	60.00
Mirror, Cheval, Ormolu Mounted, Neoclassical, Figured Mahogany, c.1820, 76 x 40 In.	1200.00
Mirror, Cheval, Rococo Revival, Mahogany, Beveled, Carved Crest, 76 x 35 In.	1920.00
Mirror, Chippendale, Ebony, Stenciled Gold Highlights, Scrolled Crest & Ears, 20 x 13 In. ...	495.00
Mirror, Chippendale, Gilt Eagle Pediment, 23½ x 48 In.	488.00
Mirror, Chippendale, Giltwood, Carved, Pagoda Crest, Phoenixes, 64 x 38 In.	5520.00
Mirror, Chippendale, Mahogany, Carved, Eagle, Giltwood, Fretwork, c.1800, 29 x 16 In.	330.00
Mirror, Chippendale, Mahogany, Giltwood, Phoenix Finial, England, c.1770, 52 x 23 In.	6000.00
Mirror, Chippendale, Mahogany, Giltwood, Swans Neck Center, Phoenix, Late 1700s, 66 In. .	7170.00
Mirror, Chippendale, Mahogany, Inlay, Reverse Painted, Colonial House, 57 x 23 In. ...*illus*	748.00
Mirror, Chippendale, Mahogany, Parcel Gilt, Figured, England, c.1770, 50 x 22¾ In.	5700.00
Mirror, Chippendale, Mahogany, Pine, Bird On Crest, Gesso, 21¼ In.	575.00
Mirror, Chippendale, Mahogany, Scrolled Crest, Feathered Ears, 26 x 14 In.	193.00
Mirror, Chippendale, Mahogany, Scrolled Frame, Molded Liner, c.1804, 32 x 18 In.	646.00
Mirror, Chippendale, Mahogany, Scrolled Frame, String Inlay, c.1790, 36½ x 19 In.	470.00
Mirror, Chippendale, Mahogany, Shaped Crests, 22½ x 22 In.	201.00
Mirror, Chippendale, Mahogany Veneer, Molded Corners, Burl Frame, 32 In.	173.00
Mirror, Chippendale, Mahogany Veneer, Phoenix Crest, Openwork, 33 x 18 In.	489.00
Mirror, Chippendale, Mahogany Veneer, Scalloped Crest, Gilt Plume, 29 In.	201.00
Mirror, Chippendale, Pine, 2 Brass Candlelights, Giltwood, Phoenix, Swags, 54 x 26 In.	5462.00
Mirror, Chippendale, Walnut, Parcel Gilt, c.1760, 46½ In.	8400.00
Mirror, Chippendale Style, Mahogany, Parcel Gilt, Phoenix Crest, 45 x 20 In.	4602.00
Mirror, Chippendale Style, Mahogany Flame Grain Veneer, Phoenix Crest, 1900s, 40 In.	230.00
Mirror, Chippendale Style, Walnut, Shaped, Scrolled, Pendant, 19th Century	359.00
Mirror, Courting, Border, Floral Reverse Painted Glass, Continental, 1800s, 17 x 12 In.	345.00
Mirror, Courting, Mahogany Veneer, Line Inlay, Crest, Reverse Painted Glass, 18 x 8 In.	86.00
Mirror, Courting, Multicolored, Carved, Pierced Scrolled Leaves, 91 x 9½ In.	558.00
Mirror, Courting, Reverse Painted, Marbleized, Jesse Haines, Muncy, Pa., 1856, 8 x 6 In. ..	1320.00
Mirror, Directoire Style, Giltwood, Sunburst, 12 Rays, Round Glass, Italy, 26 In.	440.00
Mirror, Directoire Style, Sunburst, Convex, Circular, Giltwood, Italy, 20 In.	998.00
Mirror, Dressing, Aesthetic Revival, Polished Steel, Round, Beveled, Pierced, 1800s, 18 x 16 In. ..	293.00
Mirror, Dressing, Figured Mahogany, Inlay, Serpentine Front, Ivory Finials, 25 x 17 In. .*illus*	288.00
Mirror, Dressing, Georgian Style, Walnut, Flanking Finials, Drawers, 1800s, 28 x 27 In.	295.00
Mirror, Dressing, Jenny Lind, Multicolored, Painted, Cast Iron, Cherub Finial, 24 x 14 In. ...	1528.00
Mirror, Dressing, Mahogany, Tilting, Fitted Case, Drawer, Ogee Bracket Feet, 23 x 17 In.	201.00
Mirror, Dressing, Mahogany Veneer, Mahogany, On Stand, Ball Finials, 14 x 8½ In.	86.00

Mirror, Dressing, Regency, Mahogany, Urn Finials, Trestle Base, Paw Feet, 24 x 19 In.	147.00
Mirror, Dressing, Rococo Style, Painted, Italy, 28½ In.	382.00
Mirror, Dressing, Sheraton, Mahogany, Inlay, 5-Drawer Stand, 28 x 28 x 9 In. *illus*	403.00
Mirror, Elm, Chinese, 52⅛ x 2 x 45 In.	325.00
Mirror, Empire, Split Column, Giltwood, 42 x 25 In.	690.00
Mirror, Empire Style, Giltwood, Painted Triangular Pediment, Fluted Sides, 38 x 26 In.	1920.00
Mirror, Faux Bamboo, Carved, Giltwood, Beveled, 48¼ x 40¼ In.	1200.00
Mirror, Federal, Carriage, House, Giltwood, Cove Cornice, Reverse Painted Panels, 40 x 22 In.	863.00
Mirror, Federal, Flower Garland, Eagle Finial, Applied Gesso, Shell, Gold Paint, 44¼ x 23 In.	230.00
Mirror, Federal, Gilt Gesso, Carved, Carved Scroll Crest, Rosettes, Flower Urn, 55 x 21 In.	5288.00
Mirror, Federal, Giltwood, 2 Sections, Acorn Frieze, Applied Ornament, 40 x 25 In.	920.00
Mirror, Federal, Giltwood, Applied Rope Twist, Half-Columns, Cornice Drops, Shells, 24½ In.	288.00
Mirror, Federal, Giltwood, Reverse Painted Panel, Naval Battle Scene, 43½ x 19¼ In.	2233.00
Mirror, Federal, Mahogany, Carved, Cornice, Frieze, Columns, Ring Turned, Flowers, 30 x 17 In.	201.00
Mirror, Federal, Mahogany, Giltwood, Fret Carved, c.1800, 52¼ x 21¼ In.	9000.00
Mirror, Federal, Mahogany Frame, Acorn Drops, Reverse Painted, Water Scene, 35 x 20 In. *illus*	374.00
Mirror, Federal, Panel, Reverse Painted, Woman With Cornucopia, 2 Sections, 27 x 18 In.	1610.00
Mirror, Federal, Reverse Painted, 19th Century, 36½ x 21 In.	2880.00
Mirror, Federal, Reverse Painted, ¾ Rope Twist Columns, Sailing Ships, 26 x 33 In.	978.00
Mirror, Federal, Reverse Painted, Fluted Columns, Acanthus Leaf Capitals, 33 x 20 In.	920.00
Mirror, Federal Style, Giltwood, 3 Sections, Cornice, Ball Drops, Bellflowers, 27 x 69 In.	690.00
Mirror, Folk Art, Applied Chip Carved Decorations, Fan Corners, Rosettes, 20 x 20 In.	316.00
Mirror, Frame, Giltwood, Carved Acanthus, Ogee Inner Molding	1527.00
Mirror, G. Nakashima, Black Walnut, Free Edge, 78 x 23½ In.	5875.00
Mirror, George I, Giltwood, Bird Mask Carved Pediment, Bell Flowers, 47 x 26 In.	472.00
Mirror, George III, Giltwood, Scrolled Panels, Birds, Arched Center, 51 x 43 In. *illus*	7200.00
Mirror, George III, Mahogany, Parcel Gilt, Leaf Carving, c.1765, 44½ x 26 In.	1292.00
Mirror, George III Style, Giltwood, Faux Tortoiseshell, Oval, 36 x 27 In., Pair	3120.00
Mirror, George III Style, Mahogany, Toilet, 20th Century, 26 x 20 In.	205.00
Mirror, George III Style, Walnut, Giltwood, Beveled, Winged Eagle, Frame, 62 x 32 In.	5875.00
Mirror, George V, Giltwood, Parcel Ebonized, Bull's Eye, Carved, 37 x 21 In.	1440.00
Mirror, Georgian, Fret Carved Frame, Early 20th Century, 28½ x 16 In.	374.00
Mirror, Georgian, Gilt Gesso, Over Wood, Enclosed Urn, Pierced Scrolling, 45 x 26 In.	1416.00
Mirror, Georgian, Mahogany, Carved, Scrolling Frame, Gilt Fillet, 28 x 18 In.	431.00
Mirror, Georgian Style, Giltwood, Carved, Shell Cartouche, Corn Stalks, 44 x 30 In.	1150.00
Mirror, Gilt Gesso, Rectangular, Rolled Over, Ruled Linenfold Frame, 53 x 40 In.	236.00
Mirror, Giltwood, Carved, Octagonal, 18th Century, 13¾ x 12¼ In.	1320.00
Mirror, Giltwood, Convex, Round, Eagle, Bellflower Garland, Ebonized Trim, 44 In.	2040.00
Mirror, Giltwood, Oval, 40 x 34 x 2¼ In.	413.00
Mirror, Giltwood, Polychrome, Parcel Gilt, Carved, Italy, c.1780, 29 x 39 In.	9750.00
Mirror, Giltwood, Rectangular, C-Scrolls, Leaf Trails, Plume Finial, Continental, 49 In.	4800.00
Mirror, Giltwood, Reverse Painted, Knight, On Horseback, Split Spindle, 29 x 14 In.	266.00
Mirror, Giltwood, Ribbon Accents, Urn & Flame Crest, Drape & Leaf Garlands, 60 In.	431.00
Mirror, Giltwood, Turned Frame, Leaves, Flowers, c.1830, 35 x 17½ In.	388.00
Mirror, Giltwood, Turned Pilasters, Wreaths, Brass Rosettes, c.1835, 23 x 56 In.	418.00
Mirror, Girandole, Classical Gilt, Gesso, 1810-20, 53 x 38 In.	7200.00
Mirror, Girandole, Giltwood, Eagle, Ball Decoration, Frame, Scrolls, 38 x 27 In.	2070.00
Mirror, Gothic Style, Giltwood, Carved, Lancet Arch, Spire, Crockets, 71½ x 30 In.	3600.00
Mirror, Hanging, 4 Hammered Double Hooks, 3 Single Hooks, Limbert, 25 x 37½ In.	2160.00
Mirror, Hat Rack, 4 Sets Of Cattle Horns, Carved Wood Skulls, Framed Mirror, 50 x 45 In.	460.00
Mirror, Italian Provincial, Iron, Gilt, Open Acanthus Leaves, Oval, 25½ x 22½ In.	381.00
Mirror, Italian Rococo, Reticulated, Wide Frame, Leaf Scrolling, Acanthus, 49 x 74 In.	7050.00
Mirror, Late Neoclassical, Giltwood, Round, Molded Frame, c.1840, 24 In.	840.00
Mirror, Louis Philippe, Giltwood, Molded Beaded Frame, 67½ x 55½ In.	1762.00
Mirror, Louis Philippe, Mahogany Veneer, Psyche Shape, c.1840, 61 x 34 In.	2800.00
Mirror, Louis XIV, Giltwood, Shell Shape, Scroll Decoration, 35 x 28 In.	900.00
Mirror, Louis XV, Carved, Beveled Arch, Scallops, Floral Pendant, 1920, 63 x 38 In., Pair	1997.00
Mirror, Louis XV, Giltwood, Rocaille Craved Crest, Molded Framework, 62 x 32 In.	499.00
Mirror, Louis XV Style, Giltwood, Carved, Cartouche Shape, Scrolling, 45 x 28 In.	94.00
Mirror, Louis XVI, Carved, Silver Gilt, Pegged Mortise & Tenon, 1700s, 33 x 20 In.	316.00
Mirror, Louis XVI, Gilt Gesso, Carved Wood, Leaf Carved Crest, 1800s, 102 x 55 In.	5310.00
Mirror, Louis XVI Style, Giltwood, Gesso Over Wood, Late 19th Century, 36 x 42 In.	354.00
Mirror, Louis XVI Style, Giltwood, Pierced Ribbon Crest, Domed & Beveled, 69 x 36 In.	2040.00
Mirror, Louis XVI Style, Mahogany, Giltwood, Bow Crest, 56½ x 42 In.	235.00
Mirror, Louis XVI Style, Walnut, Stained, Inverted Scallop, 35¼ x 16 In.	940.00
Mirror, Mahogany, Carved, Scrolling Frame, Gilt Bird, Mid 1800s, 30 x 17 In.	633.00

Furniture, Mirror, Neoclassical Style, Ebonized, Gilt Trim, Reverse Painted Castle, 34 x 18 In.
$460.00

Furniture, Mirror, Rococo Revival, Cartouche Shape, Beaded, Beveled Glass, France, 55 x 41 In.
$633.00

Furniture, Patio Set, Heywood-Wakefield, Rattan, Upholstered Cushions, Sofa, Chair, 2 Piece
$588.00

Furniture, Pedestal, Napoleon III, Pietra Dura, Gilt Bronze, Leaves, Fruit, Bird, France, c.1860, 45 x 17 In.
$1743.00

Furniture, Pie Safe, Poplar,
Mustard Yellow Paint, 2 Doors,
Punched Tin Panels, 65 x 45 x 24 In.
$1093.00

Furniture, Pie Safe, Walnut, Softwood,
2 Drawers, 2 Doors, Pierced Tin Panels,
Wheels, Rays, 51 x 44 In.
$1760.00

Furniture, Press, Jackson, Walnut,
Pine, 2 8-Pane Doors, Shelves,
2 Drawers, N.C., 97 x 42 In.
$6900.00

Mirror, Mahogany, Reverse Painted, Paddlewheel Steamship, c.1830, 21½ x 12¼ In.	717.00
Mirror, Mahogany, Shield Form, 17¼ x 12 In.	470.00
Mirror, Mahogany, Stepped, Molded Cornice, Carved Balusters, 41¾ x 23 In.	568.00
Mirror, Micro Mosaic Band, Spiral Twist, Octagonal, Venetian, 1800s, 31 x 26 In.	2124.00
Mirror, Molded Frame, Mahogany Veneer, 18th Century, 25½ x 22½ In.	863.00
Mirror, Molded Resin Frame, Gilt Finish, Leafy Scrolls, Shells, 47½ x 25 In.	115.00
Mirror, Mother-Of-Pearl, Bone, North African, 85 x 39¼ In.	3600.00
Mirror, Napoleon III, Giltwood, Carved, Arched Top, Oval, 70 x 51 In.	3120.00
Mirror, Neoclassical, Carved, Giltwood, Convex, c.1815, 39¾ x 26 x 10 In.	6000.00
Mirror, Neoclassical, Ebonized, Giltwood, Split Baluster, Rosettes, c.1830, 41 x 20 In.	16450.00
Mirror, Neoclassical, Giltwood, Portugal, c.1810, 37 x 18 In.	3600.00
Mirror, Neoclassical, Giltwood, Split Column Frame, Corner Rosettes, 38 x 20 In.	470.00
Mirror, Neoclassical, Mahogany, Molded Cornice, Brass Rosettes, 47 x 25 In.	633.00
Mirror, Neoclassical, Mahogany, Veneer, Reeded Cornice, Drop Pendants, c.1825, 36 x 19 In.	235.00
Mirror, Neoclassical, Painted, Trumeau, Black Ground, Bellflower Swags, 43 x 22 In.	390.00
Mirror, Neoclassical Style, Ebonized, Gilt Trim, Reverse Painted Castle, 34 x 18 In. ....*illus*	460.00
Mirror, Neoclassical Style, Giltwood, Carved, Scrolling Leaves, Eagle, 45 x 37 In.	1680.00
Mirror, Oval, Giltwood, Leaf & Berry Design, Victorian, 50 x 30 In.	403.00
Mirror, Pier, Eastlake, Burled Walnut, Sunflower, Scrolls, Columns, Marble Shelf, 107 In.	2040.00
Mirror, Pier, Federal, Reverse Painted, Giltwood, England, c.1815, 36 x 63¼ In.	4800.00
Mirror, Pier, Georgian Style, Giltwood Frame, Mid 20th Century, 49 x 22 In.	761.00
Mirror, Pier, Neoclassical, Giltwood, Split Columns, Reverse Painted, c.1830, 47 x 25 In.	1293.00
Mirror, Pier, Neoclassical, Mahogany, Giltwood, Ogee Molded Frame, 51 x 27 In.	881.00
Mirror, Pier, Neoclassical Style, Arched Mullioned Fanlight Panel, Arrows, 71 x 30 In.	3840.00
Mirror, Pier, Original Gilt, Label, Isaac L. Platt, N.Y., c.1820, 61 x 30½ In.	2250.00
Mirror, Pier, Renaissance Revival, Giltwood, Medallion, Cornucopia, Swags, 76 x 40 In.	720.00
Mirror, Pier, Victorian, Beveled Edge, Pink Marble Top, Gilt Decoration, 91 x 30 In.	489.00
Mirror, Pier, Walnut, Carved Crest, Turned Pillars, Marble Shelf, Victorian, 95 x 26 x 10 In.	646.00
Mirror, Queen Anne, Mahogany, Arched, Scrolled Crest, Molded, 18th Century, 15 In.	1195.00
Mirror, Queen Anne, Mahogany, Veneered, c.1740, 46½ x 14½ In.	6600.00
Mirror, Queen Anne, Walnut, Parcel Gilt, 42 x 23 In.	2880.00
Mirror, Queen Anne Style, Walnut Frame, Late 19th Century, 37 x 17 In.	972.00
Mirror, Regence, Giltwood, Rectangular, Arched Pediment, Shell Finial, 48 x 25½ In.	5100.00
Mirror, Regency, Bull's Eye, Giltwood, Convex, Carved, Ebonized, 39 In.	1680.00
Mirror, Regency Style, Giltwood, Convex, Fan-Carved Crest, Leopard, 54 x 37 In.	1527.00
Mirror, Restauration, Beech, Carved, Parcel Gilt, Ivory Paint, 30½ x 25 In.	763.00
Mirror, Restauration, Giltwood, Plaster, Carved, Neoclassical, 27 x 23 In.	420.00
Mirror, Restauration Style, Beech, Carved, Painted, Parcel Gilt, 65 x 31 In.	2880.00
Mirror, Reverse Painted, House, Half Turnings, Corner Blocks, Giltwood, 22½ x 13 In.	316.00
Mirror, Rococo, Bronze Dore, Rocaille Pattern, C-Scrolls, Leaves, 32 x 20 In., Pair	3120.00
Mirror, Rococo, Gesso, Rectangular, Molded Edge Frame, 19th Century, 42 x 36 In.	708.00
Mirror, Rococo Revival, Cartouche Shape, Beaded, Beveled Glass, France, 55 x 41 In. ..*illus*	633.00
Mirror, Rococo Style, Walnut, Leaf Carved Giltwood, 41 x 21 In.	165.00
Mirror, Round, Wood Frame, Silenzio On Frame, 21¼ In.	390.00
Mirror, Sailing Ship, Reverse Painted, Gilt & Black Paint, Brass Rosettes, 29 x 15 In.	489.00
Mirror, Scroll, Cutout Crest, Mahogany, 22½ x 12⅛ In.	198.00
Mirror, Shaker, Tiger Maple, Original Finish, Beveled Glass, 14½ In.	1170.00
Mirror, Shaving, G. Stickley, Shoe Feet, V Top, 21½ x 23½ In.	1920.00
Mirror, Shaving, George IV, Brass, Ebony Inlaid Mahogany, Swing, Drawers, 32 x 20 In.	840.00
Mirror, Shaving, Pine, Inlay, Bracket Feet, 2 Dovetailed Drawers, Glass Pulls, 18 x 16 In.	172.00
Mirror, Shaving, Teak, Triptych, Tooled Leather, 9 x 22 In.	41.00
Mirror, Sheraton, Applied Baluster Columns, Stencil, Reverse Painted Tablet, 24 x 13½ In.	110.00
Mirror, Sheraton, Applied Half Columns, Painted, Gilt Capitals, 32 x 16 In.	193.00
Mirror, Sheraton, Painted, Applied Reeded Columns, Reverse Painted Panel, 21 x 12½ In.	165.00
Mirror, Sunburst, Gilt Brass, Directoire Style, Rope Twist Frame, Italy, 39 In.	660.00
Mirror, Table, Brass, Gilt, Mounted, Mahogany, France, c.1900, 13¾ In.	353.00
Mirror, Toilet, Victorian, Chinoiserie Decoration, Mid 19th Century, 34 In.	348.00
Mirror, Tortoise-Patterned Bone, Ogee Molded, Ebonized, Octagonal, Dutch, 34 x 27 In.	2232.00
Mirror, Trumeau, Empire, Beech, White Paint, Napoleon Profile, 57 x 44 In.	2280.00
Mirror, Trumeau, Louis XVI Style, Giltwood, Cartouche Form, 1900s, 44 x 30 In.	354.00
Mirror, Trumeau, Louis XVI Style, Giltwood, Crest, Scrolling Bracket, c.1900, 80 x 24 In.	826.00
Mirror, Trumeau, Painted, Arched Panel, Still Life, Flowers, Giltwood, 1800s, 63 x 28 In.	575.00
Mirror, Trumeau, Painted, Parcel Gilt, Oval Reserve, Putto, 1900s, 71 x 43 In.	354.00
Mirror, Venetian, Rococo Style, Rocaille Crest, Candle Arms, 28 x 14 In., Pair	3720.00
Mirror, Venetian Style, Octagonal, Pierced Scrolling, Leaf Mounted Crest, 50¾ x 45½ In.	472.00
Mirror, William & Mary, Shaped Ogee Frame, Fruitwood Oyster Veneers, 31 x 25 In.	1093.00

Mirror, Wood, Painted, Decoration, Carved, 49 x 32 In.	263.00
Mirror Frame, Chippendale, Walnut, Scrolled Crest & Ears, 18 x 11½ In.	176.00
Mirror Frame, Porcelain, Gallub & Hofman, Germany, c.1900, 14 x 9¾ In.	351.00
Ottoman, Club Style, Mahogany, Leather, Brass Nailhead Trim, Octagonal Legs, 17 x 38 In.	1116.00
Ottoman, Mahogany, Leather Upholstered, Opens, 22¼ x 39 x 23½ In.	2115.00
Ottoman, Neoclassical, Mahogany, Scrolled Legs, Bulbous Medial Stretcher, 20 x 21 In.	720.00
Ottoman, Split Reed, Wicker, Scalloped Edge, Upholstered Cushion, c.1920s, 16 x 19 In.	475.00
Ottoman, William IV Style, Mahogany, 2 Frieze Drawers, Upholstered, Pineapple Feet, 44 In.	1140.00
Overmantel Mirror, see Architectural category.	
Parlor Set, Art Deco, Diamond Designs, Woven Seats, Shaped Skirting, 1920s, 4 Piece	4250.00
Parlor Set, Art Deco, Latticework, Diamond Designs, Kaltex Co., 1920s, 3 Piece	3850.00
Parlor Set, Art Deco, Wicker, Diamond Designs, Braiding, 1920s, 4 Piece	6500.00
Parlor Set, Art Deco, Wicker, Woven, Diamond Designs, Scooped Arms, 1920s, 4 Piece	4650.00
Parlor Set, Art Nouveau, Wicker, Leaf Designs, Full Skirting, 1920s, 3 Piece	3950.00
Parlor Set, Egyptian Revival, Pottier & Stymus, New York, c.1870, 4 Piece	8400.00
Parlor Set, Karpen, Art Nouveau, Carved Rail, Vine, Leaves, Woman, Flowing Hair, 3 Piece	1800.00
Parlor Set, Louis XV, Giltwood, Upholstered, Padded Cartouche Back, 7 Piece	1534.00
Parlor Set, Louis XVI Style, Giltwood, Carved, Padded, Settee, 2 Chairs	3995.00
Parlor Set, Red Leather, Brass Studded Arm Fronts, 2 Cushion Sofa, Armchair	1265.00
Parlor Set, Renaissance Revival, Walnut, Carved, Velvet Upholstery, c.1870, 3 Piece	14400.00
Parlor Set, Rococo Revival, Laminated Rosewood, Carved Grape Cluster, 4 Piece	15525.00
Parlor Set, Rococo Revival, Rosewood, Brocade Upholstery, Sofa, 2 Armchairs	4560.00
Parlor Set, Rococo Revival, Rosewood, Cabochon Cartouche, 50 x 72-In. Sofa, 3 Piece	8812.00
Parlor Set, Wicker, Bar Harbor, Contoured Backs, Latticework, Sofa, Chair, Rocker	3950.00
Parlor Set, Wicker, Serpentine Rolled Back, Arms, Beadwork, Heywood, Victorian, 3 Piece	3950.00
Patio Set, Heywood-Wakefield, Rattan, Upholstered Cushions, Sofa, Chair, 2 Piece *illus*	588.00
Pedestal, 1 Stacked & Tiered Columns, Rose Mottled Marble, Tile, 43 In.	1175.00
Pedestal, Anglo-Indian, Brass, Ebonized, Round Base, 42 In., Pair	206.00
Pedestal, Art Deco, Onyx, Carved, Red, Brown, Green, Cream, Reeded Column, 38 x 13 In.	382.00
Pedestal, Bronze Mounted, Onyx, Square Top, Baluster Support, 40½ x 11 In.	259.00
Pedestal, Buff Marble, Square Top, Ormolu Mounted, Italy, Early 20th Century, 45½ In.	293.00
Pedestal, Empire Style, Alabaster, Gilt Bronze Mount, Swivel Top, 32 x 15 In.	529.00
Pedestal, George III Style, Painted, 20th Century, 36 In., 3	1171.00
Pedestal, Georgian, Mahogany, Carved, Urn Shape Standard, 20th Century, 38 In.	572.00
Pedestal, Gilt, Cobalt Blue Ceramic, 4 Columns, Multicolored, Vignettes, 8 In.	176.00
Pedestal, Gilt Metal Mounted, Turned Marble, 20th Century, 45½ In., Pair	692.00
Pedestal, Giltwood, Fluted Column, Swag, Tasseled Rosette, Step Base, 40 x 11 In.	1410.00
Pedestal, Louis XVI Style, Marble, Carved Capitals, Fluted Columns, 39 x 12 In., Pair	1880.00
Pedestal, Marble, Brass, Champleve Frieze, Mask Mounts, 1800s, 44 x 12 In.	4140.00
Pedestal, Marble, Veined White, Banded Columnar Shaft, Octagonal Base, 40 x 13 In.	717.00
Pedestal, Napoleon III, Pietra Dura, Gilt Bronze, Leaves, Fruit, Bird, France, c.1860, 45 x 17 In. *illus*	1743.00
Pedestal, Oak, Carved, Column Shape, Square Top, Capitol, 37 x 12 In.	805.00
Pedestal, Onyx, Beige Veined, Columnar Shaft, Square Plinth, 1800s, 39¾ x 10 In.	777.00
Pedestal, Poplar, Red Stained, 5-Sided Top, 25 x 20 x 18 In.	764.00
Pedestal, Renaissance Revival, Patinated Bronze, Female Masks, 41 x 13 In., Pair	1763.00
Pedestal, Wood, Fluted Column, Capital, Marble Inset, Stepped Base, 1900s, 36 x 15 In., Pair	345.00
Pediment, Giltwood, Carved, Arched, C-Scrolls, Shell Carved, Early 1900s, 30 x 97 In.	460.00
Pie Safe, Pine, 10 Tins, 67 x 50 In.	3950.00
Pie Safe, Pine, Pierced Tin Stars & Diamonds, 2 Drawers, 2 Doors, Bracket Base, 19th Century	227.00
Pie Safe, Pine, Punched Tin Panels, Brown Painted, 53½ x 42 x 18 In.	9988.00
Pie Safe, Poplar, 12 Punched Tin Panels, Sunflowers, Geometrics, Turned Legs, 62 x 40 x 18 In.	1380.00
Pie Safe, Poplar, Blue Paint, 2 Doors, 3 Tulips, Hearts, Punched Tin Panels, 39 x 49 In.	4600.00
Pie Safe, Poplar, Mustard Paint, 2 Doors, Punched Tin Panels, 65 x 45 In.	1093.00
Pie Safe, Poplar, Mustard Yellow Paint, 2 Doors, Punched Tin Panels, 65 x 45 x 24 In. *illus*	1093.00
Pie Safe, Shaker, Pine, Purple Over Blue, Hinged Door, Screen, Harvard, Mass., 34 x 27 x 19 In.	117.00
Pie Safe, Tiger Maple, Mahogany, Drawer, 2 Doors, Punched Tin Panels, 43 x 43 In.	5290.00
Pie Safe, Tin Door, Punched Hearts & Stars, American, c.1875, 48 x 43 x 22 In.	1235.00
Pie Safe, Walnut, 2 Drawers, 2 Doors, Punched Tin Panels, Wheel, Stars, Cutout Feet, 51 x 43 In.	1760.00
Pie Safe, Walnut, Inset Tins, Stylized Urn, Grape, Leaves, 34½ x 50 x 17 In.	10560.00
Pie Safe, Walnut, Pine, 4-Panels, 6 Tins, Punched Pinwheel, 2 Doors, Shelves, 57 x 49 In.	1955.00
Pie Safe, Walnut, Softwood, 2 Drawers, 2 Doors, Pierced Tin Panels, Wheels, Rays, 51 x 44 In. *illus*	1760.00
Planter, Wire, Green Paint, 29 In.	316.00
Planter, Wrought Iron, Copper Bowl, Scrolls, 3-Footed, c.1930, 50 In.	250.00
Press, Jackson, Walnut, Pine, 2 8-Pane Doors, Shelves, 2 Drawers, N.C., 97 x 42 In. *illus*	6900.00
Print Stand, Neoclassical, Folding, Mahogany, Ratcheted Adjustable Sides, 43 x 30 In.	2185.00
Rack, Baking, Brass, Iron, Painted, Glass Shelves, France, Early 20th Century, 69 x 44 In.	748.00

Furniture, Rocker, Adirondack, Twig, 6 Back Slats, X-Stretcher Base, Sweet Water, Tex., Pair
$825.00

F

Furniture, Rocker, Ladder Back, 4 Slats, Turned Arms & Stiles, Oak Split Seat, 42 x 19 x 16 In.
$259.00

Furniture, Rocker, Platform, Aesthetic Revival, Oak, Turned Decoration, Victorian, 35 x 24 In.
$106.00

Furniture, Rocker, Shaker, Ladder Back, Shawl Bar, Pommels, Tape Seat, Mt. Lebanon, N.Y., 41 x 24 In.
$1035.00

Furniture, Rocker, Stickley, Quaint, Bentwood Back, Arms, Spindles, Stenciled, 35 x 23 In. $210.00

Furniture, Rocker, Stickley & Brandt Co., High Back, 3 Vertical Slats, 42 x 30 x 30 In. $1320.00

Furniture, Rocker, Victorian, Bentwood, Arched Back, Painted Decoration, 40 In. $176.00

Rack, Baking, Brass, Wrought Iron, 3 D-Shape Tiers, Scrolling Supports, 89 x 37 In.	920.00
Rack, Baking, French Provincial Style, Scrolling Iron, Wine Storage, 1900s, 87 x 49 In.	443.00
Rack, Drying, Pine, 3 Mortised Bars & Shoe Feet, High Arches, 34 x 37 In.	144.00
Rack, Hanging, Fruitwood, Ebonized, 3 Shelves, Spindled Galleries, Molded Base, 45 x 53 In.	352.00
Rack, Magazine, Mahogany, Gilt Metal, Folding, Turned Standard, Tripod, 32 x 18 In.	325.00
Rack, Magazine, Walnut, Shelves, France, c.1900, 43 x 23 In.	4000.00
Rack, Magazine, Wormley, No. 4765, Walnut & Birch, Dunbar, 1952, 28 x 25 In.	4825.00
Rack, Plate, G. Stickley, No. 903, Arched Top, Chamfered Board Back, Signed, 23 x 46 In.	7200.00
Rack, Quilt, Regency, Mahogany, 3 Tiers, Block Accents, Cabriole Supports, 35 x 24 x 13 In.	323.00
Recamier, William IV, Leather, Dome Back, Anglo-Colonial, c.1850, 45 x 85 x 26 In.	1057.00
Rocker, Adirondack, Twig, 6 Back Slats, X-Stretcher Base, Sweet Water, Tex., Pair ......*illus*	825.00
Rocker, Aesthetic Revival, Oak, Turned Decoration, Victorian, 35 x 24 x 30 In.	106.00
Rocker, Art Deco, With Arm, Wicker, Full Skirting, c.1920s, 33½ In.	675.00
Rocker, Bar Harbor, Braid Framed Banding, Shaped Skirt, Spring Seat, 1920s, Child's	395.00
Rocker, Bar Harbor, Latticework, Braid Framing, Full Skirt, 1920s, 23 x 16 In.	350.00
Rocker, Barrel Back, Green Paint, Comb Over U-Shape Arm Rail, 8 Spindles, Child's, 18 In.	86.00
Rocker, Chair, Victorian, Wicker, Serpentine Roll, Twist Wrapped, Skirting, Heywood	2650.00
Rocker, Footstool, L. & J.G. Stickley, 6 Arm Slats, Drop In Vinyl Seat, 36 x 33 In.	3360.00
Rocker, G. Stickley, 3 Horizontal Back Slats, Tacked On Seat, Black Naugahyde, 32 x 25 In.	480.00
Rocker, G. Stickley, 3 Horizontal Slats, Squared Arms, Child's, 24¾ x 18 x 19 In.	316.00
Rocker, G. Stickley, 3 Slats, Tacked On Seats, Arm, Child's, 25¾ x 18¼ x 14 In.	1020.00
Rocker, G. Stickley, Ladder Back, Leather Tacked Seat, Child's, 25 x 18 In., Pair	1020.00
Rocker, Gentleman's, Victorian, Wicker, Rolled Crest, Curlicued Skirting, c.1890s, 43 In.	1250.00
Rocker, L. & J.G. Stickley, 6 Slats, Spring Seat, Leather Cushion, 36 x 31 x 35 In.	3360.00
Rocker, Ladder Back, 4 Slats, Turned Arms & Stiles, Oak Split Seat, 42 x 19 x 16 In. ...*illus*	259.00
Rocker, Ladder Back, Knobby Finials, Graduated Splats, Shaped Arms, 43 In.	1150.00
Rocker, Ladder Back, Walnut, Hickory, River Cane Seat, 42 x 18½ In.	23.00
Rocker, Limbert, Ebonized, Oak, Curved Arm, Back Slats, Corbels, 33½ x 30 x 28 In.	2400.00
Rocker, Maple, Ladder Back, Woven Seat, Knobby Finials, 19th Century, 32 In.	199.00
Rocker, Oak, Slat Back, Carved Plank Seat, Arms, 1920s, 41 x 27 x 24 In.	147.00
Rocker, Old Hickory, Curved Back, Bentwood, Split Ash Seat, Back, Arms, 39 x 26 In.	600.00
Rocker, Phoenix, Vertical Slats, Drop In Cushions, Arms, 32 x 30 & 36 x 30 In., Pair	1320.00
Rocker, Platform, Aesthetic Revival, Oak, Turned Decoration, Victorian, 35 x 24 In. ...*illus*	106.00
Rocker, Sawn Oak, Carved Lion Head Arms, Velvet Upholstery, 42 x 26½ In.	550.00
Rocker, Shaker, 3 Curved Slats, Taped Seat, Mt. Lebanon, 33½ In.	173.00
Rocker, Shaker, Bird's-Eye Maple, Red Brown, 3 Slats, Rush Seat, Canterbury, N.H., c.1840, 41 In.	702.00
Rocker, Shaker, Ladder Back, Shawl Bar, Pommels, Tape Seat, Mt. Lebanon, N.Y., 41 x 24 In. *illus*	1035.00
Rocker, Shaker, Maple, 4 Slats, Beige & Tan Stripe Seat, Mt. Lebanon, N.Y., c.1860-70, 44 In.	702.00
Rocker, Shaker, Maple, Old Red Paint, Tape Seat, 3 Slats, Child's, Alfred, Maine, c.1840, 30 In.	819.00
Rocker, Shaker, No. 0, Maple, 3 Slats, Mushroom Caps, Tape Seat, Mt. Lebanon, N.Y., 23½ In.	4212.00
Rocker, Shaker, No. 4, Ladder Back, Acorn Finials, Tape Seat, Mt. Lebanon, 35 x 22 In.	518.00
Rocker, Shaker, No. 6, Ladder Back, Shawl Rod, Mushroom Pommels, Tape Seat, 41 x 24 In.	1035.00
Rocker, Shaker, No. 6, Maple, 4 Slats, Mushroom Caps, Tape Seat, Mt. Lebanon, 42 In.	1521.00
Rocker, Shaker, No. 6, Maple, Dark Stain, Tape Seat & Back, Arms, Mt. Lebanon, N.Y., c.1870, 41 In.	468.00
Rocker, Shaker, No. 6, Maple, Shawl Bar, 4 Ladder Slats, Tape Seat, 20th Century, 40 x 24 In.	460.00
Rocker, Shaker, No. 7, Maple, 4 Slats, Shawl Bar, Mushroom Caps, Tape Seat, Mt. Lebanon, 42 In.	3042.00
Rocker, Shaker, No. 7, Maple, 4 Slats, Shawl Bar, Tape Seat, Plush Covers, Stool, Mt. Lebanon, 41 In.	1170.00
Rocker, Shaker, No. 7, Maple, Stained, Shawl Bar, 4 Slats, Rush Seat, Mt. Lebanon, N.Y., 41 In.	2574.00
Rocker, Shaker, Tiger Maple, Ladder Back, Oval Finials, Rush Seat	13145.00
Rocker, Stickley, Quaint, Bentwood Back, Arms, Spindles, Stenciled, 35 x 23 In. ......*illus*	210.00
Rocker, Stickley & Brandt Co., High Back, 3 Vertical Slats, 42 x 30 x 30 In. ....*illus*	1320.00
Rocker, Thumb Back, Paint Decorated, 38 In.	58.00
Rocker, Victorian, Bentwood, Arched Back, Painted Decoration, 40 In. ....*illus*	176.00
Rocker, Victorian, Oak, Triple Pressed Back Panels, 40 In. ....*illus*	47.00
Rocker, Victorian, Rolled Crest, Arms, Beadwork, Heywood Bros., 1890s, 28 x 19 In.	625.00
Rocker, Victorian, Wicker, Cane Back, Rolled Back & Arms, c.1890s, 43 In.	975.00
Rocker, Victorian, Wicker, Rolled Back, Wave Patterns & Beadwork, Whitney Reed, 1890s	975.00
Rocker, Wicker, Brown, Spring Seat, Handcraft, 36 x 26 x 30 In. ....*illus*	94.00
Rocker, Wicker, White Paint, Flat Arms, 3 Cushions, Spring Seat, 32 x 27½ In. ....*illus*	161.00
Rocker, Windsor, Bow Back, Bamboo Turnings, 7 Spindle Back, 30 In.	144.00
Rocker, Windsor, Comb Back, Birdcage, 6 Bamboo Turned Spindles, Front Stretcher	110.00
Rocker, Windsor, Comb Back, Nantucket, c.1800, 41½ In.	4800.00
Rocker, Windsor, Writing Arm, Blue Gray Paint, Bamboo Turnings, Stenciled, 3 Slats, 16½ In.	220.00
Rocker & Ottoman, V. Kagan, Walnut Frame, Tweed Upholstery, Knoll, 32 x 42 In. .....*illus*	10800.00
Screen, 3-Panel, Bentwood Frame, Looped Finials, Lace Panels, Victorian, 63 x 55 In. ...*illus*	94.00
Screen, 3-Panel, Brass Over Wood, Hammered, Armorial, Shield, Lion, 36 x 39½ In.	200.00

Screen, 3-Panel, Dressing, Oak, Stick & Ball, Red Cloth, 60 x 64 In. 705.00
Screen, 3-Panel, Etched Glass, Reeds, Cattails, Azure Tint, 72 x 24 In. 1150.00
Screen, 3-Panel, Glazed, Louis XVI Style, Carved Giltwood, Flower Fabric, 22 x 69 In. 705.00
Screen, 3-Panel, Instruments, Postcards, Flowers, Fornasetti, 59 x 20 In. . . . . *illus* 4200.00
Screen, 3-Panel, Leaves, Carved, Pierced, Folding, Indo-Persian, 20th Century, 62 x 61 In. . . 206.00
Screen, 3-Panel, Louis XVI Style, Giltwood, Carved, Flowers, 22 x 69 In. 705.00
Screen, 3-Panel, Oak, Silvered Metal Figures, Scrolls, Leaves, Arts & Crafts, 67 x 62 In. 646.00
Screen, 3-Panel, Oak Frame, Canvas, Flower Paintings, c.1900, 72 x 62 In. 206.00
Screen, 3-Panel, Tapestry, c.1900, 69½ x 75 x 4 In. 3000.00
Screen, 3-Panel, Wood, Carved Frame, Painted Aquatic Scene, 64 x 76 In. . . . . *illus* 11500.00
Screen, 4-Panel, Continental Style, Folding, Paint, Oil On Gilt Canvas, 1900s, 70 x 80 In. . . . 1003.00
Screen, 4-Panel, Coromandel, Black Ground, Gilt, Pagoda, Landscape, 72 x 64 In. 644.00
Screen, 4-Panel, Floor, Tooled Leather, Painted, Arched Top, Gilt, Flowers, 69 x 58 In. 489.00
Screen, 4-Panel, Lithographed Die-Cuts, People & Animals, Victorian, 74 x 88 In. . . . . *illus* 353.00
Screen, 4-Panel, Needlework, Labeled Childhood, Youth, Manhood, Old Age, 1800s 1485.00
Screen, 4-Panel, Porcelain, Lacquered Frame, Famille Rose, Bone Appliques, 72 x 74 In. 2538.00
Screen, 4-Panel, Russet Vellum, Fleur-De-Lis Stencils, Burlap Back, France, 84 x 48 In. 720.00
Screen, 4-Panel, Stickley, Arts & Crafts, Oak, Early 1900s, 60 x 95 In. 8280.00
Screen, 5-Panel, George III, Pine, Painted, Folding, Inset Panels, 85 x 85 In. 2360.00
Screen, 6-Panel, Folding, Grisalle Papier Peinte, Block Print, Faux Marble, 79 x 120 In. 1058.00
Screen, 6-Panel, Louis XVI Style, Giltwood, Oval Frames, Portraits, Mirrors, Fabric . . . . *illus* 2390.00
Screen, 6-Panel, Painted Oriental Landscape, Gold, Applied Figures, 72 x 102 In. 518.00
Screen, 8-Panel, Coromandel, Court Scene, Pavilions, Trees, Chinese, 84 x 136 In. 4800.00
Screen, 12-Panel, Coromandel, Landscape, Palace, Gardens, Courtiers, Animals, 108 x 20 In. . . . 2640.00
Screen, Biedermeier, Needlework, Mahogany Frame, Shield Shape, Scrolled Legs, 28 x 24 In. . 646.00
Screen, Chinese, Lacquer, Black Crackle, Gilt, Soapstone Designs, c.1900, 30 x 19 In. 259.00
Screen, Dressing, Heywood Bros., Bar Harbor, Wicker, Oak, c.1900, 68 x 69 In. 1950.00
Screen, Leather, Black & Crimson, Embossed Mandarin's Garden Decoration, 72 x 74 In. . . . 2880.00
Screen, Leather, Cartouche Shape, Flower Basket, Shaped Wood Handle, 36 x 37 In. . . . *illus* 177.00
Screen, Table, Chinese Scholar's, Rosewood Frame, Pierced, Gray Marble Slab, 14 x 11 In. . . 763.00
Screen, Table, Rosewood, White Jade Inset, Plaques With Leaves, Dragon, 14 x 15 In. 826.00
Secretary, Baroque Style, Mixed Woods, Marquetry, Germany, 77 x 47 x 21 In. 8850.00
Secretary, Biedermeier, Drop Front, Birch, Ebonized, Drawers, Drop Front, 46 x 44 In. 1652.00
Secretary, Biedermeier, Drop Front, Fruitwood Veneer, Ebonized Columns, 61 x 43 In. 1150.00
Secretary, Breakfront, George III, Chinoiserie, Mid 1900s, 71 x 42 In. 489.00
Secretary, Breakfront, Regency, Mahogany, Molded Cornice, 4 Doors, 94 x 104 In. 16500.00
Secretary, Commode, Louis Philippe, Drop Front, Walnut, Leather Inset, 38 x 41 In. 5040.00
Secretary, Eastlake, Lock Side, Gallery Top, 52 x 33 x 19 In. . . . . *illus* 805.00
Secretary, Eastlake Style, Walnut, Cylinder, Paneled Doors, Glass Door, 95 x 33 x 20 In. . . . 1528.00
Secretary, Empire, Drop Front, Mahogany, Drawers, France, 54¾ x 32¼ x 18½ In. 7200.00
Secretary, Empire, Mahogany, Pediment, Frieze, Panel Doors, Early 1800s, 80 x 43 In. 1770.00
Secretary, Federal, 2 Sections, Foldover Surface, Fitted Top, 44 x 40 In. . . . . *illus* 4888.00
Secretary, Federal, 2 Upper Doors, Fold-Out Writing S urface, 3 Drawers, 36 x 21 In. 1200.00
Secretary, Federal, Drop Front, Mahogany, Tambour Door, 46¾ x 34½ x 18 In. 2360.00
Secretary, Federal, Mahogany, Figured Maple, 4 Drawers, Urn Finials, Lady's, 86 x 40 In. . . . 9600.00
Secretary, French Empire, Mahogany, Doors, Drawer, 57 x 38 x 17 In. 2360.00
Secretary, George III, Mahogany, Dentil Molded Cornice, 95 x 96 In. 27500.00
Secretary, George III, Mahogany, Inlay, Reeded Edge, Drop Front, c.1785, 46 x 48 In. 5100.00
Secretary, George III, Mahogany, Swan's Neck Pediment, Glazed Doors, 92 x 41 In. 5520.00
Secretary, George III, Multicolored, Glazed Door, Drawers, 83 x 26 x 18 In. 9106.00
Secretary, George III, Slant Front, Mahogany, 2 Glazed Doors, 87 x 43 x 23 In. 6462.00
Secretary, George III, Slant Front, Mahogany, 2 Glazed Doors, Leather Inset, 87 x 43 x 22 In. . . 4230.00
Secretary, Georgian, Mahogany, Inlay, Glazed Doors, 5 Drawers, 99 x 38 x 22 In. . . . . . *illus* 6325.00
Secretary, Georgian Style, Slant Front, Yew, Double Arched, 1900s, 85 x 43 In. 1770.00
Secretary, Hepplewhite, Cherry, Poplar, Fitted Interior, Drawers, 40 x 88 In. 2070.00
Secretary, Louis XVI Style, Mahogany, Marble Top, Brass Mounted, 55 x 29 x 15 In. 1880.00
Secretary, Mahogany, 2 Doors, Shelves, Drawers, Foldover Desk, 70 x 42 In. 805.00
Secretary, Neoclassical, Drop Front, Mahogany, Paneled Drop Front, 58 x 34 In. 1762.00
Secretary, Pine, Glazed Doors, Fold Down Surface, 75½ x 43½ In. 920.00
Secretary, Sheraton, 2 Glazed Doors Up, Foldover Writing Surface, 2 Drawers, 70 x 39 In. . . 1610.00
Secretary, Victorian, Walnut, Mahogany, Drop Front, Cubbyholes, Drawers, 83 x 34 In. 690.00
Server, American Arts & Crafts Style, Oak, 37½ x 40 x 20 In. 443.00
Server, Bird's-Eye Maple, 2 Tiers, 5 Drawers, Turned Legs, 40½ x 38 x 19 In. 863.00
Server, Cherry, Poplar, Drawer, Lower Scalloped Shelf, Turned Legs, 37 x 33 In. 489.00
Server, Cypress, 2-Board Top, Plain Skirt, Mid 19th Century, 30 x 60 In. 940.00
Server, Edwardian, Mahogany, Scrolled Back Rail, Frieze Drawers, c.1890, 60 x 53 In. 1175.00

Furniture, Rocker, Victorian, Oak, Triple Pressed Back Panels, 40 In.
$47.00

Furniture, Rocker, Wicker, Brown, Spring Seat, Handcraft, 36 x 26 x 30 In.
$94.00

Furniture, Rocker, Wicker, White Paint, Flat Arms, 3 Cushions, Spring Seat, 32 x 27½ In.
$161.00

Furniture, Rocker & Ottoman, V. Kagan, Walnut Frame, Tweed Upholstery, Knoll, 32 x 42 In.
$10800.00

Furniture, Screen, 3-Panel, Bentwood Frame, Looped Finials, Lace Panels, Victorian, 63 x 55 In. $94.00

Furniture, Screen, 3-Panel, Instruments, Postcards, Flowers, Fornasetti, 59 x 20 In. $4200.00

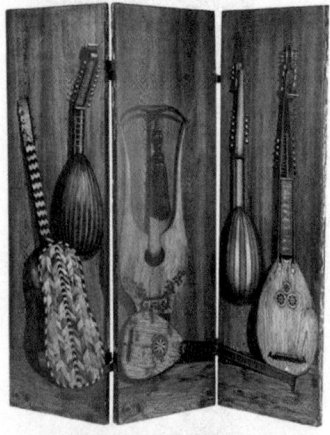

Server, Empire Style, Plank Top, Paneled Frieze Drawer, 20th Century, 33 x 35 In.	266.00
Server, Federal, Mahogany, 2 Beaded Drawers, Double Doors, Turned Legs, c.1825, 41 x 46 In.	4183.00
Server, Federal, Mahogany, Veneer, Carved, Elliptical Front, c.1820, 36 x 37 In.	11163.00
Server, G. Stickley, 3 Drawers, Open Shelf, Hammered Copper Pulls, 39 x 48 In.	3360.00
Server, G. Stickley, 3 Drawers Over Linen Drawer, Oval, Copper Pulls, 39 x 48 x 20 In.	3900.00
Server, George II Style, Mahogany, Carved, Bowed, Marlboro Legs, 29 x 48 In.	2006.00
Server, George III, Mahogany, Shaped, Bow Top, Drawers, 36 x 62 x 26 In.	3055.00
Server, George III, Mahogany Inlay, Serpentine Top, 2 Drawers, 33 x 45 In.	1410.00
Server, Grain Painted, Drawer, Doors, Turned Columns & Feet, 52 x 20 In. ....*illus*	2185.00
Server, Inlaid Gilt Metal, Porcelain Mounted, Drawer, Lower Shelf, France, 37 x 23 In.	1652.00
Server, Mahogany, Recessed Tilt Tooled Leather Insert, Arched Apron, 1800s, 32 x 42 In.	1888.00
Server, Neoclassical, Cherry, Tiger Maple, 2 Short Over Long Drawer, c.1830, 41 x 38 In.	2468.00
Server, Regency, Drop Leaf, Mahogany, 2 Drawers, 4 Brass Claw Feet, c.1800, 28 x 59 x 28 In. .	881.00
Server, Renaissance Revival, Oak, Carved, 2 Tiers, Drawers, Turned Supports, 43 x 42 In. ...	502.00
Server, Sheraton, Pine, ¾ Backsplash, Drawers, Cupboard Doors, 51 x 42 In.	546.00
Server, Sheraton, Pine, Grain Paint, 2 Drawers, Dovetailed, Overhang, 32 x 51 x 24 In.	1380.00
Server, Victorian, Mahogany, Band Inlay, Leaf Corbels, Late 1800s, 30 x 65 In.	460.00
Server, Victorian, Mahogany, Bowed Front, Fitted Case, Paneled, 41 x 46 In.	1920.00
Server, William IV, Mahogany, Pierced Gallery, Molded Top, Paneled, c.1840, 50 x 50 In. ...	2232.00
Server, William IV, Mahogany, Shaped Gallery, Drawer, Shaped Plinth, 38 x 44 In.	411.00
Serving Cart, Heywood-Wakefield, Maple, Oak, Bamboo, Rattan, 28 x 31 In. ....*illus*	60.00
Serving Cart, Mahogany, Galleried Top, Low Shelf, Legs Fitted With Wheels, 29 x 24 In.	118.00
Settee, Black Paint, Spindle Back, Ball Finials, Upholstered, 17 x 71 In.	1155.00
Settee, Charles II Style, Walnut, Cane, 3 Chairback, 54 x 62 x 20 In.	2327.00
Settee, Double 3-Slat Chairback, Figured Maple Posts, Oak Split Seat, 35 x 35 In. .....*illus*	144.00
Settee, Edwardian, Inlaid Mahogany, Padded Seat, Open Arms, Early 20th Century, 53 In. ..	553.00
Settee, Elm, Rectangular, Open Work, Leaves, 2 Drawers, 21 x 74 x 23 In.	767.00
Settee, Empire, Mahogany, Scrolled Arm, Claw Feet, Eagles Head, Child's, 36 x 54 In.	940.00
Settee, Federal, Mahogany, Carved Ribbon, Tassels, Wheat, Cane Seat, Back, 36 x 60 In. *illus*	1880.00
Settee, Federal Style, Inlaid Mahogany, Oval Patera Inlay, Scrolled Arms, 39 x 48 In.	1175.00
Settee, Federal Style, Mahogany, Cane Seat, Back, 36 x 60 x 21½ In.	1880.00
Settee, Federal Style, Mahogany, Reeded Supports, Reeded Legs, 1875, 38 x 48 In.	1175.00
Settee, Finn Juhl, Nils Vodder, No. NV-53, Walnut Frame, Green Upholstery, 21 x 51 In. .*illus*	2400.00
Settee, French Art Deco, Curved Back, Channeled Upholstery, 27 x 58 In. ....*illus*	1440.00
Settee, G. Nakashima, Walnut, Spindle Back, Cushion, 28 x 48 In.	5378.00
Settee, G. Stickley, Even Arm, Tapered Posts, Slats, Leather Cushions, 39 x 60 x 27 In.	3360.00
Settee, George II, Mahogany, Shaped Backrest & Arms, Upholstered, Ireland, 42 x 59 In. *illus*	4200.00
Settee, George II Style, Mahogany, Camelback, Padded Crest, Arms, 37 x 65 x 31 In.	1180.00
Settee, George III Style, Mahogany, Upholstered, 20th Century, 79 In.	819.00
Settee, Georgian, Mahogany, Leather, Carved, Arched Acanthus Back, 35 x 55 x 23 In.	2232.00
Settee, Giltwood, Raised Finials, Tufted Upholstery, Italy, 1800s, 34 x 55 x 29 In.	4300.00
Settee, L. & J.G. Stickley, Drop Arm, 7 Slats, Underarm Slats, Cushion, 37 x 77 x 28½ In.	3250.00
Settee, L. & J.G. Stickley, Drop Arm, 16 Slats, Open Arms, Cushion, 38½ x 76 x 26 In.	2160.00
Settee, L. & J.G. Stickley, Drop Arm, Slats, Spring Cushion, 34½ x 79 x 31½ In.	3240.00
Settee, L. & J.G. Stickley, Cherry, Wide Arms, Paneled Sides, Upholstered, 84 In.	2233.00
Settee, Mahogany, 4 Chairback, Leaf Carved, Serpentine Crest, Portugal, 40 x 70 In.	2714.00
Settee, Mahogany, Double Back, Pierced Splats, Cabriole Legs, Claw & Ball Feet, 38 x 54 In. .	1840.00
Settee, Mahogany, Shaped Crest Rail, Leaf Inlay, Padded Back, Ormolu Paws, 36 x 76 In. ...	1200.00
Settee, Majorelle, Art Nouveau, Carved Walnut Frame, Velvet, 43 x 62 In. ....*illus*	5463.00
Settee, Plank Bottom, Paint Decorated, Brown, Floral Splat, Scrolled Arms, 74 x 21 In.	660.00
Settee, Queen Anne Style, Mahogany, Crested 3 Chairback, Slip Seat, 44½ x 56 In.	212.00
Settee, Regency, Mahogany, Cane, Outswept Legs, Brass Cuffs, 1820, 35 x 89 In.	5875.00
Settee, Rocker, Rustic, 2-Panel Back, Seat, Applied Bark, 36 x 39½ In.	345.00
Settee, Rococo Revival, Walnut, Serpentine Rail, Carved, Upholstered, 39 x 64 In., Pair	1057.00
Settee, Rush Seat, Bamboo Turnings, 3-Part Back, Yellow Paint, 33½ x 67 In.	4950.00
Settee, Shaker, Maple, Curved Arms, 24 Spindles, 8 Legs, Mid 19th Century, 31 x 110 In. ...	16800.00
Settee, Softwood, Half-Spindle, Green Paint, Scrolled Arms, Turned Legs, Box Stretcher, 17 x 75 In. .	5225.00
Settee, Spindle Back, Plank Bottom, H-Stretcher, Bulbous Turnings, 78½ In.	550.00
Settee, Twig & Root, Adirondack, 49 x 18 In., Pair	3850.00
Settee, Victorian, Mahogany Veneer, Serpentine Back, Scroll Arms, Upholstered, 60 x 23 In. .	345.00
Settee, Victorian, Wicker, Rolled Crest & Arms, Diamond Design, Full Skirting, 1915	2850.00
Settee, William & Mary Style, Mahogany, Carved, Canted Winged Back, 49 x 47 In.	980.00
Settee, Windsor, Arrow Back, Stenciled, Painted, Turned Legs, Stretchers, c.1825, 72 In. ...	1195.00
Settee, Windsor, Bamboo Turnings, Shaped Crest, Plank Seat, Cut Corners, Incised, 17 x 84 In. ..	2875.00
Settee, Windsor, Maple, Spindle Back, 19th Century, 33 x 72 In.	94.00
Settee, Windsor, Yellow Paint, Double Back, 6 Spindles, 34 x 17½ In.	235.00

Settee, Windsor Style, Bamboo Turnings, Walter Seeley, 35½ x 46 x 18 In.	1430.00
Settee, Wing, Bar Harbor, Wicker, Full Skirting, Latticework, Ball Feet, 1900, 41 In.	1750.00
Settle, Ash, Woven Hickory Bark Seat, Back, 1900s, 36 x 37 In.	230.00
Settle, G. Stickley, No. 225, Even Arm Form, 5 Vertical Slats, Leather Cushion, 78 In.	9000.00
Settle, G. Stickley, Arts & Crafts, Leather Upholstery, Arms, 37½ x 71½ In.	2300.00
Settle, L. & J.G. Stickley, Even Arm, Vertical Slats All Around, 39 x 84 In.	6000.00
Settle, L. & J.G. Stickley, Oak, Straight Rails, Leather Seat, 34 x 76 x 31 In. .... *illus*	3105.00
Settle, L. & J.G. Stickley, Prairie, Oak, c.1915, 29 x 84 x 37 In.	19200.00
Settle, L. & J.G. Stickley, Prairie, Paneled Sides, Leather Upholstery, 29 x 85 In.	16800.00
Settle, Limbert, Drop Arm, Vertical Slats, Leather Cushions, 30 x 76 x 31 In.	6600.00
Settle, Limbert, Even Arm, Broad Vertical Back Slats, Drop In Leather Cushion, 36 x 73 In.	4200.00
Settle, Spindle Back, Scrolled Arms, Shaped Crest, Brown & Green Paint, Alligatored, 10 x 18 In.	633.00
Shadowbox, Mahogany, Stepped Shelves, Oriental, c.1950, 34 x 20 In.	88.00
Shelf, Acrylic, Pewter & Brass, Italy, 9 x 7 In., Pair	59.00
Shelf, Black Forest, Chamois Bust, Horns, Plaque, Brackets, 12½ In.	940.00
Shelf, Black Forest, Walnut, Figural, Eagle, Spread Wings, Scalloped, Pair, 14 x 20 In.	1175.00
Shelf, Carved, Compass Etched, Pa., 19th Century, 19 x 69½ In.	3840.00
Shelf, Fernery, 2 Shelves, Braiding, Wicker, c.1920s, 29 In.	575.00
Shelf, Giltwood, Cherub, Gilding, 8 x 6½ In.	440.00
Shelf, Hanging, Brown Stained, 3 Graduated Shelves, Cutout Ends, 27 x 32½ x 6¾ In.	1293.00
Shelf, Hanging, Pine, Scrolled Ends, 4 Tiers, 37¾ x 30 x 8½ In.	1645.00
Shelf, Hanging, Red Paint, 5 Tiers, Wooden Spindles, 32 x 28 x 8½ In.	470.00
Shelf, Louis XVI Style, Giltwood, Carved, Mirrored, Mid 1800s, 30 x 9½ In., Pair	600.00
Shelf, Mahogany, Whale End, 3 Shelves, 19th Century, 20½ x 19 In.	1763.00
Shelf, Napoleon III, Giltwood, Carved, Louis XV Style, Bracket, Serpentine, 14 x 13 In.	780.00
Shelf, Rococo Style, Painted, Parcel Gilt, Serpentine Top, Continental, 8 x 30 In.	142.00
Shelf, Victorian, Walnut, Tiered, Canted, Scrolling Leaf Inlay, 42 x 21½ In.	1020.00
Sideboard, Adams, Mahogany, Demilune, Crossbanded D Top, Inlay, 38 x 72 In.	4400.00
Sideboard, Arts & Crafts, Oak, Mirror Back, Wood Pulls, Early 1900s, 52 x 48 In.	316.00
Sideboard, Empire, Mahogany, Gadroon Border, 3 Over 4 Drawers, 74 x 26 In.	488.00
Sideboard, Federal, Inlay, Figured Mahogany, Newport, R.I., c.1800, 38¾ x 66 In.	15600.00
Sideboard, Federal, Mahogany, Doors, Tapered Legs, Cuffed Feet, 19th Century, 41 x 70 In.	2703.00
Sideboard, Federal, Mahogany, Figured, Inlay, 5 Drawers, S.C., c.1800, 36 x 65 In. ....*illus*	10200.00
Sideboard, Federal, Mahogany, Inlay, 2 Doors, 2 Drawers, N.C., 36 x 65 In. ....*illus*	6325.00
Sideboard, Federal, Mahogany, Inlay, D-Shape Center, Reeded Legs, S.C., 40 x 68 In. ...*illus*	6900.00
Sideboard, Federal, Mahogany, Inlay, Elliptical Front, c.1815, 41½ x 71½ In.	11163.00
Sideboard, Federal, Mahogany, Outset Center, 7 Drawers, Acanthus Carved, 42 x 82 x 28 In.	4183.00
Sideboard, Federal, Mahogany, Scrolled Gallery, Elliptical Center, c.1815, 47 x 65 In.	2115.00
Sideboard, Federal, Mahogany, Serpentine, Drawer Over Doors, 1800s, 41 x 66 In.	2714.00
Sideboard, Federal, Mahogany, Veneer, Inlay, Arched Back, Drawers, c.1820, 51 x 75 In.	2350.00
Sideboard, Federal, Mahogany Inlay, 1790-1810, 40¾ x 59 x 22¾ In.	3840.00
Sideboard, Federal, Serpentine Front, 1 Long, 2 Short Drawers, Early 1900s, 72 x 26 In.	585.00
Sideboard, G. Stickley, 3 Center Drawers, 2 Cupboard Doors, Copper Pulls, 48 x 65 In.	6600.00
Sideboard, G. Stickley, Center Drawers, 2-Paneled Doors, 8 Legs, 50 x 70 In.	192000.00
Sideboard, G. Stickley, Plate Rack, 1drawer Over 2 Drawers, Doors, 46 x 49 x 18 In.	4200.00
Sideboard, G. Stickley, Strap Hinge, 3 Drawers, Doors, Iron Hardware, 48 x 56 x 21 In.	7200.00
Sideboard, George III, Mahogany, Bowed Top, Banded, Tambour Cupboard, 37 x 64 In.	4800.00
Sideboard, George III, Mahogany, Bowfront, Drawers, 2 Cellarettes, 35 x 60 In.	826.00
Sideboard, George III, Mahogany, Frieze Drawer, Cupboard Doors, c.1800, 39 x 70 In. *illus*	3000.00
Sideboard, George III, Mahogany, Satinwood Banded, Demilune Top, Drawers	9106.00
Sideboard, George III, Mahogany, Satinwood Inlay, 4 Drawers, 37½ x 78 x 30½ In.	9988.00
Sideboard, George III Style, Mahogany, Bow Top, Drawer Flanked, 36 x 60 x 23 In.	998.00
Sideboard, George III Style, Mahogany, Shaped Front, 3 Drawers, Spade Feet, 36 x 48 In.	2585.00
Sideboard, Georgian, Mahogany, Bowfront, Storage Door, Early 1800s, 35 x 78 In.	2596.00
Sideboard, Georgian, Walnut, Breakfront, Early 20th Century, 66½ In.	707.00
Sideboard, Hepplewhite, Line & Banded Inlay, Mahogany, 35 x 73 In.	2990.00
Sideboard, Hepplewhite, Mahogany, Poplar, Drawer, 4 Doors, Spindles, Tapered Legs, 47 x 71 In.	3737.00
Sideboard, Hepplewhite Style, Mahogany, Inlay, 5 Drawers, Door, Spade Feet, 36 x 64 In.	2300.00
Sideboard, Limbert, Mirrored Backboard, 2 Half Drawers Over 2 Cabinets, 52 x 21 In.	1880.00
Sideboard, Mahogany, Bowed, Shaped Top, Drawer, Cupboard Doors, 1900s, 40 x 74 In.	5760.00
Sideboard, Mahogany, Bowfront, Line Inlay, 3 Drawers, 6 Doors, Greek Key Cuffs, 43 x 72 In.	1320.00
Sideboard, Mahogany, Serpentine, Molded Edge Top, Frieze Drawer, 1800s, 33 x 68 In.	502.00
Sideboard, Neoclassical, Mahogany, 3 Band Inlaid Dovetailed Drawers, Doors, 45 x 72 In.	1265.00
Sideboard, Neoclassical, Mahogany, Carved, Crossbanded Splash Rail, c.1835, 52 x 61 In.	3525.00
Sideboard, Neoclassical, Mahogany, Carved Arched Backsplash, Drawers, 67 x 74 In.	3525.00
Sideboard, Paul Evans, Bronze, Sculpted Sides, Slate Top, 33 x 48 x 21 In. ....*illus*	6600.00

F

Furniture, Screen, 3-Panel, Wood, Carved Frame, Painted Aquatic Scene, 64 x 76 In.
$11500.00

Furniture, Screen, 4-Panel, Lithographed Die-Cuts, People & Animals, Victorian, 74 x 88 In.
$353.00

Furniture, Screen, 6-Panel, Louis XVI Style, Giltwood, Oval Frames, Portraits, Mirrors, Fabric
$2390.00

Furniture, Screen, Leather, Cartouche Shape, Flower Basket, Shaped Wood Handle, 36 x 37 In. $177.00

Furniture, Secretary, Eastlake, Lock Side, Gallery Top, 52 x 33 x 19 In. $805.00

Furniture, Secretary, Federal, 2 Sections, Foldover Surface, Fitted Top, 44 x 40 In. $4888.00

Furniture, Secretary, Georgian, Mahogany, Inlay, Glazed Doors, 5 Drawers, 99 x 38 x 22 In. $6325.00

Sideboard, Pesce, Painted, 2 Carved Doors, 31 x 96 x 18 In. ....*illus*	4200.00
Sideboard, Quartersawn Oak, Oval Mirror, Lion Heads, Man Of The North Heads, 87 In.	770.00
Sideboard, Regency, Mahogany, Line Strung, Double Pedestal, Paw Feet, 48 x 86 x 25 In. ...	2115.00
Sideboard, Regency, Mahogany Inlay, 3 Drawers Over 4 Doors, 39 x 79 x 22 In.	1293.00
Sideboard, Regency Style, Mahogany, Reeded Edge, Drawers, 19th Century, 32 x 48 In.	2242.00
Sideboard, Renaissance Revival, Walnut, Mirror, Marble Top, Doors, Drawers, 95 x 74 x 24 In. ..	1175.00
Sideboard, Sheraton, Walnut, Poplar, Bowfront, Drawer, 2 Doors, 6 Legs, 39 x 63 In.	1955.00
Sideboard, Victorian, Mahogany, Figured, Paneled Back, Backsplash, Drawers, 57 x 96 In. ..	2990.00
Sideboard, Victorian, Oak, Beveled & Scalloped Mirror, Turned Posts, 61 x 50 x 23 In.	264.00
Sideboard, Victorian, Oak, Beveled Glass Mirror, Claw Feet, 66 x 50 x 24 In.	529.00
Sideboard, William IV, Mahogany, 3 Drawers, Paneled Doors, 39 x 74 x 22 In.	4406.00
Silver Chest, Federal, Mahogany, Hinged Lid, Dovetailed, Brass Pulls, 1800s, 34 x 33 In.	1265.00
Sofa, Art Deco, Wicker, Diamond Design, Spring In Frame, Full Skirting, c.1920s, 35 x 72 In.	1850.00
Sofa, Art Moderne, Russet Leather, 3-Part Back, Roll Arms, Bun Feet, 39 x 86 In.	1290.00
Sofa, Auto, Chevrolet Model, Backseat, Corbin, Retro, 1957, 68 x 38 x 30 In.	2420.00
Sofa, Bastiano, Tobia Scarpa, Rosewood, Black Leather, 1960, 21½ x 83 x 29½ In.	1440.00
Sofa, Biedermeier, Maple, Serpentine Backrest, Cresting, Carved Roundels, 82 In.	1785.00
Sofa, Biedermeier, Serpentine Backrest, S-Scrolled Arms, Upholstered, 82 In.	1765.00
Sofa, Chippendale, Arched Back, Rolled Arms, Square Legs, Upholstered, 38 x 89 In.	1610.00
Sofa, Chippendale, Camelback, Mahogany, Rolled Arms, Upholstered, 70 In.	1725.00
Sofa, Chippendale, Camelback, Upholstered, Padded Back, Scrolled Arms, 36 x 78 In.	767.00
Sofa, Chippendale, Mahogany, Camelback, Outscrolled Arms, Upholstered, 39 x 81 In.	1840.00
Sofa, Chippendale, Mahogany, Moire Upholstery, Mass., c.1780, 43 x 78 In.	3840.00
Sofa, Chippendale Style, Miller & Ripper, Mahogany, Camelback, Phila., 1980s, 40 x 77 In. ..	5040.00
Sofa, Chippendale Style, Sofa, Cherry, Yellow Damask Upholstery, Marlboro Legs, 72 In.	975.00
Sofa, Duncan Phyfe School, Family Crest, Painted, New York, c.1810, 77 x 22 In.	13750.00
Sofa, Dutch Empire, Marquetry, Serpentine Crest, Scroll Arms, 37 x 78 In.	4720.00
Sofa, Empire, Mahogany, Scrolled Back, Hairy Paw Feet, Upholstered, 31 x 82 In.	1150.00
Sofa, Empire, Mahogany, Scrolled Back Crest, Carving, Padded, Upholstered, 35 x 88 In.	3304.00
Sofa, Empire, Mahogany, Serpentine, Carved Crest, Padded Triple Hump, 39 x 83 In.	354.00
Sofa, Federal, Mahogany, Maple, Inlay, Figured, c.1790, 36 x 75¾ x 24 In.	9600.00
Sofa, Federal, Mahogany, Maple, Upholstered, Rolled Pillows, 8 Legs, 36 x 85 x 24 In.	4560.00
Sofa, Federal, Mahogany, Tiger Maple, Carved, Reeded Baluster, Portsmouth, 34 x 79 In. ...	1495.00
Sofa, Florence Knoll, Oatmeal Upholstery, 6 Upholstered Legs, c.1954, 84½ In.	1645.00
Sofa, George III, Mahogany, Overupholstered Backrest, Arms, 64 In.	4700.00
Sofa, George III, Mahogany, Serpentine Back, Coiled Arms, Tapestry Upholstery, 38 x 97 In. .	8812.00
Sofa, George III Style, Inlaid Mahogany, Downswept Crest Rail, 1900s, 32 x 53 In.	1357.00
Sofa, Knoll, Velvet Upholstery, Fringe, 20th Century, 73 In.	1087.00
Sofa, Leather, Tufted Back, 3 Loose Seat Cushions, Cabriole Legs, 72 In.	632.00
Sofa, Lodge, Antler Legs, Arms & Crest, Imitation Leather Upholstery, 71 x 25 x 45 In.	345.00
Sofa, Louis XV Style, Carved Beech, Serpentine Frame, Upholstered, 81 In.	3055.00
Sofa, Louis XV Style, Fruitwood, Arch Arms, Upholstered, 1900s, 36 x 84 In.	826.00
Sofa, Louis XV Style, Fruitwood, Double Arched Crest Rail, Upholstered, 38 x 60 In.	1012.00
Sofa, Louis XVI, Giltwood, Leaf Carved Crest, Late 1800s, 35 x 51 In.	885.00
Sofa, Louis XVI, Walnut, Carved, France, c.1880, 34 x 45 In.	3000.00
Sofa, Mahogany, Carved, Rolled Crest, Upholstered Back, Paw Feet, Casters, 36 x 82 In.	1195.00
Sofa, Mahogany, Carved, Scrolled, Gadroon Crest, Upholstered, 1825, 34 x 75 In.	1315.00
Sofa, Mahogany, Inlaid Crest Rail, Upholstered, Padded Back, Bolsters, c.1840, 38 x 75 In. ..	3658.00
Sofa, Mahogany, Rolled Arched Crest, Upholstered Back, Paw Feet, Casters, 34 x 84 In.	1554.00
Sofa, Mahogany, Wing, Serpentine Top, Claw & Ball Feet, 46 x 64 x 32 In.	2040.00
Sofa, Marshmallow, G. Nelson, Enameled, Polished Steel Base, 18 Cushions, 31 x 52 In. *illus*	20400.00
Sofa, Meeks, Box, Neoclassical, Mahogany, Scroll Crest, Ogee Rails, 38 x 84 In.	1528.00
Sofa, Neoclassical, Mahogany, Carved, Arms, Tufted Upholstery, 30 x 54 In., Pair	1645.00
Sofa, Neoclassical, Mahogany, Carved, Upholstered, Duncan Phyfe, c.1820, 33 x 88 In.	13200.00
Sofa, Neoclassical, Mahogany, Dolphin, Rolled Crest, Acanthus Leaf Terminals, 18 x 86 In. ..	8800.00
Sofa, Neoclassical, Mahogany, Upholstered, Carved, Paneled, Arms, Early 1800s	4780.00
Sofa, Neoclassical, Mahogany, Veneer, Carved, Scrolled, Paneled Crest, c.1825, 33 x 89 In. ...	3173.00
Sofa, Painted, Scroll Decorated Back, Padded Seat, Arms, 80 In.	3738.00
Sofa, Paul Laszlo, Beige Upholstered, 1947, 30 x 98 x 36 In.	6600.00
Sofa, R.J. Horner, Mahogany, Winged Griffin Sides, Gadrooned Apron, 29 x 56 In. .....*illus*	2875.00
Sofa, Regency, Faux Rosewood, Padded Back, Rounded Crest, Stenciled, 33 x 83 In.	4080.00
Sofa, Regency Style, Camelback, Outscrolled Arms, 20th Century, 35 x 88 In.	561.00
Sofa, Rococo, Rosewood, Carved, Triple Back, Curved Arms, Mid 1800s, 48 x 71 In.	3173.00
Sofa, Rococo Revival, Rosewood, Double Chairback, Panel, 46 x 80¼ x 27 In.	5170.00
Sofa, Sectional, Richard Schultz, Teal Leather Like Upholstery, Wooden Legs, 29 x 40 In. ...	59.00
Sofa, Sheraton, Inlaid Mahogany, Arched Crest, Padded Side Panels, 35 x 68 In.	2070.00

Furniture, Server, Grain Painted, Drawer, Doors, Turned Columns & Feet, 52 x 20 In. $2185.00

Furniture, Serving Cart, Heywood-Wakefield, Maple, Oak, Bamboo, Rattan, 28 x 31 In. $60.00

Furniture, Settee, Double 3-Slat Chairback, Figured Maple Posts, Oak Split Seat, 35 x 35 In. $144.00

Furniture, Settee, Federal, Mahogany, Carved Ribbon, Tassels, Wheat, Cane Seat, Back, 36 x 60 In. $1880.00

Furniture, Settee, Finn Juhl, Nils Vodder, No. NV-53, Walnut Frame, Green Upholstery, 21 x 51 In. $2400.00

Furniture, Settee, French Art Deco, Curved Back, Channeled Upholstery, 27 x 58 In. $1440.00

Furniture, Settee, George II, Mahogany, Shaped Backrest & Arms, Upholstered, Ireland, 42 x 59 In. $4200.00

Furniture, Settee, Majorelle, Art Nouveau,
Carved Walnut Frame, Velvet, 43 x 62 In.
$5463.00

Furniture, Settle, L. & J.G. Stickley, Oak, Straight Rails,
Leather Seat, 34 x 76 x 31 In.
$3105.00

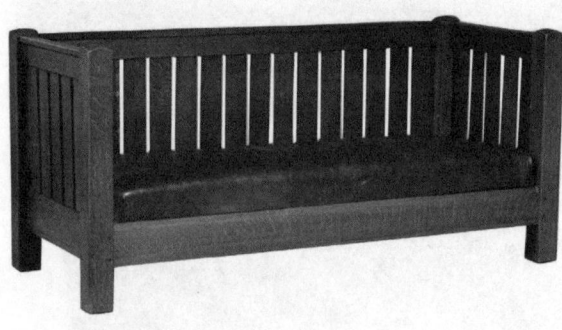

Furniture, Sideboard, Paul Evans, Bronze, Sculpted Sides,
Slate Top, 33 x 48 x 21 In.
$6600.00

Furniture, Sideboard, Federal, Mahogany, Figured, Inlay,
5 Drawers, S.C., c.1800, 36 x 65 In.
$10200.00

Furniture, Sideboard, Federal, Mahogany, Inlay, 2 Doors,
2 Drawers, N.C., 36 x 65 In.
$6325.00

Furniture, Sideboard, Federal, Mahogany, Inlay, D-Shape Center,
Reeded Legs, S.C., 40 x 68 In.
$6900.00

Furniture, Sideboard, George III, Mahogany, Frieze Drawer,
Cupboard Doors, c.1800, 39 x 70 In.
$3000.00

Sofa, Tubular Chrome, Black Circular Seats, Howell Furniture Co., c.1940, 42 In.	1175.00
Sofa, Turned Spindle Back, Upholstered Seat, Loose Pillows, 1800s, 72 In.	326.00
Sofa, Victorian, Carved Grapes, Serpentine Front Rail, Tufted Upholstery, 39 x 80 In.	230.00
Sofa, Victorian, Louis XV Style, Finger Molded Medallion, 36 x 59 In.	264.00
Sofa, Vinyl Upholstered, Red, 3 Cushions, Chromium, Wood, 66 In.	418.00
Sofa, Wicker, Rounded Upholstered Back, 3 Cushions, Open Arms, 36 x 68 In. ....*illus*	390.00
Sofa, Wool Upholstery, Tubular Chromed Steel Frame, Fritz Hansen, 29 x 50 In.	1410.00
Sofa, Wormley, Mahogany, Curved Legs, Striped Upholstery, Dunbar, 27 x 84 In. ......*illus*	1800.00
Sofa, Wormley, Upholstery, Dunbar, c.1958, 29 x 34 x 56 In. ....*illus*	2040.00
Spice Chest, Arts & Crafts, Oak, Inlay, c.1910, 13½ x 11 In.	146.00
Stand, 2 Tiers, Mahogany, Faux Painted Rosewood, Cartouche Shape Top, 28 x 22 In.	115.00
Stand, Aesthetic Revival, Mahogany, 4 Shelves, Inset Tooled Leather Side Panels, 48 x 23 In.	1680.00
Stand, Black Forest, Animal, Glass Eyes, Rocky Outcrop, Copper Pan, 55 x 23 In. ......*illus*	8695.00
Stand, Black Forest, Walking Stick, Bear, Standing, Holding Cane, Copper Pan, 40 In. ..*illus*	2350.00
Stand, Blackwood, Square Top, C-Scrolls, Circular Legs, Chinese, 45 x 17¼ In.	826.00
Stand, Brass, 3 Tiers, Leaves, Mythical Creatures, Austro-Hungarian, c.1900, 30 x 15 In.	230.00
Stand, Cherry, 3 Drawers, Wooden Knobs, 29 x 25 x 20 In.	5750.00
Stand, Cherry, Curly Maple Legs, 2 Dovetailed Drawers, 28 x 17 In.	374.00
Stand, Cherry, Drawer, Tapered Molded Legs, 27 x 21 x 18½ In.	330.00
Stand, Cherry, Mahogany, 2 Crossbanded Drawers, Molded, Turned Legs, 29 x 21¾ In.	495.00
Stand, Cherry, Painted, Splayed Chamfered Legs, 15½ x 15 x 12 In.	235.00
Stand, Cherry, Poplar Top, 2 Short Over 1 Long Drawer, 28 x 21 In.	2300.00
Stand, Cherry, Tapered Leg, Tulip Foot, 30 x 18 In.	550.00
Stand, Chippendale, Walnut, 2-Board Top, Square Turned Legs, 27½ x 22 In.	187.00
Stand, Directoire, Mahogany, Marble Top, Drawer, Fluted Supports, 27 x 17 In.	1080.00
Stand, Drawer, Red Paint, 18 x 19 x 29 In.	144.00
Stand, Dressing, Mahogany, Swing Mirror, 3 Drawers, Animal Legs, 64¾ x 34¾ In.	2510.00
Stand, Drop Leaf, Sheraton, Cherry, Poplar, Rounded Corners, Drawer, 28 x 16 x 21 In.	403.00
Stand, Drop Leaf, Walnut, 2 Drawers, Bird's-Eye Maple, Red Paint, Turned Legs, 29 x 32 x 20 In. .	550.00
Stand, Elm, Square, Beaded Apron, Rectangular Legs, Chinese, 1800s, 30 x 17 In.	708.00
Stand, Empire, Flame Maple, 2 Drawers, Pedestal, c.1820, 30 x 21 x 15 In.	850.00
Stand, Federal, Cherry, Drawer, 3-Board Top, Chamfered Edges, 19th Century, 28 x 23 In. ...	518.00
Stand, Federal, Cherry, Figured Top, Ring & Baluster Support, Tripod Base, 27 x 18 In. .*illus*	431.00
Stand, Federal, Cherry, Grain Painted, Drawer, 1866, 30 x 21½ x 22 In.	5700.00
Stand, Federal, Cherry, Poplar, Dovetailed Drawer, 19th Century, 28½ x 18 In.	575.00
Stand, Federal, Cherry, Poplar, Drawer, 1-Board Top, Compass Work, 27 x 23 In.	3680.00
Stand, Federal, Maple, Red Painted, Drawer, c.1805, 27½ x 21 x 20½ In.	3600.00
Stand, Federal, Pine, Yellow, Drawer, 26 x 18 x 18 In.	2350.00
Stand, Federal, Tiger Maple, 2 Drawers, Turned Legs, Peg Feet, 1800s, 28 x 20 In.	1793.00
Stand, Federal, Tiger Maple, Maple, Overhang Top, Turned Legs, c.1825, 29 x 20 In.	3055.00
Stand, Federal, Walnut, Overhanging Top, Drawer, Tapered Legs, Tenn., 27 x 26 In. ....*illus*	374.00
Stand, Federal, Walnut, White Cedar, Walnut, Splayed Legs, Box Stretcher, 28 x 17 In.	575.00
Stand, Fern, American Aesthetic, Square, Brass, 4 Bracket Supports, Pad Feet, 1880, 32 In. ..	1410.00
Stand, Fern, Gilt Metal, Curving Rod Posts, Rope Drapery, Tassels, 45 x 13 In.	120.00
Stand, Fern, Wicker, Pedestal, Urn Design, Handles, Latticework Panel, c.1900, 36 In.	575.00
Stand, Floor, Metal, Tiered, Scalloped, c.1930, 37 x 13 In.	117.00
Stand, Folio, William IV, Mahogany, Bun Feet, c.1835, 49 x 34 In.	2225.00
Stand, G. Stickley, Drawer, Rectangular Top, Square Legs, 1912, 30 x 24 In.	1865.00
Stand, Hepplewhite, Hardwood, Inlay, Tapered Legs, 2 Drawers, 28 x 23 In.	575.00
Stand, Hepplewhite, Hardwood, Square Legs, Drawer, Dovetailed, 26 x 19 In.	58.00
Stand, Hepplewhite, Inlay, Drawer, Porcelain Knob, Corner Fans, Lined Top, 29 x 20 In.	1150.00
Stand, Hepplewhite, Pine, 2-Board Top, Canted Skirt, Drawer, Tapered Legs, 17 x 20 In.	402.00
Stand, Hepplewhite, Walnut, Pegged Construction, Drawer, 28 In.	258.00
Stand, Louis XV Style, Black Lacquered, Drawers, 32 x 16½ x 13 In.	1974.00
Stand, Louis XV Style, Marquetry Scrolls, Marble Top, c.1950, 30 x 16 x 12 In., Pair	235.00
Stand, Magazine, Barber Bros., 4 Shelves, Single Slat Sides, 38 x 22 x 13 In. ....*illus*	510.00
Stand, Magazine, Emile Galle, Fruitwood, Marquetry, c.1900, 26 x 24 x 12 In.	7200.00
Stand, Magazine, G. Stickley, 3 Shelves, Arched Panels, Harvey Ellis, 41½ x 22 x 13 In.	2160.00
Stand, Magazine, L. & J.G. Stickley, 3 Slats, Arched Side Rail, 4 Shelves, 42 x 21 x 21 In.	2520.00
Stand, Magazine, L. & J.G. Stickley, Trapezoidal, 4 Shelves, Mortised, 42 x 20 In.	4800.00
Stand, Magazine, Limbert, Trapezoidal, Cut Out, Shelves, 40 x 24 x 13¾ In.	2400.00
Stand, Magazine, Stickley Bros., No. 4600, 3 Shelves, Slat Back, 16 x 13 x 31 In.	1100.00
Stand, Mahogany, Cherry, Cock-Beaded Drawer, Open Well, Scalloped Edge, 29 x 19 In.	2860.00
Stand, Mahogany, Corner, Ebony Columns, Brass, Mirror Back, Marble Top, 32 x 27 In.	863.00
Stand, Mahogany, Marble Top, Octagonal, Brescia Marble Inset, Chinese, 34 x 16 In.	540.00
Stand, Maple, Red Paint, Drawer, 27 x 19 x 17½ In.	1645.00

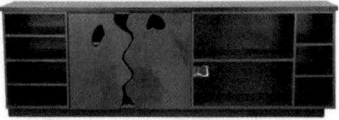

Furniture, Sideboard, Pesce, Painted, 2 Carved Doors, 31 x 96 x 18 In. $4200.00

Furniture, Sofa, Marshmallow, G. Nelson, Enameled, Polished Steel Base, 18 Cushions, 31 x 52 In. $20400.00

F

Furniture, Sofa, R.J. Horner, Mahogany, Winged Griffin Sides, Gadrooned Apron, 29 x 56 In. $2875.00

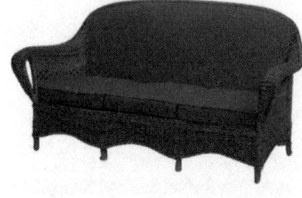

Furniture, Sofa, Wicker, Rounded Upholstered Back, 3 Cushions, Open Arms, 36 x 68 In. $390.00

Furniture, Sofa, Wormley, Mahogany, Curved Legs, Striped Upholstery, Dunbar, 27 x 84 In. $1800.00

Furniture, Sofa, Wormley, Upholstery, Dunbar, c.1958, 29 x 34 x 56 In. $2040.00

Furniture, Stand, Black Forest, Animal, Glass Eyes, Rocky Outcrop, Copper Pan, 55 x 23 In. $8695.00

Furniture, Stand, Black Forest, Walking Stick, Bear, Standing, Holding Cane, Copper Pan, 40 In. $2350.00

Furniture, Stand, Federal, Cherry, Figured Top, Ring & Baluster Support, Tripod Base, 27 x 18 In. $431.00

Stand, Marble Top, Octagonal, Chinese, Early 20th Century, 12 x 24 In.	92.00
Stand, Music, Bar Harbor, Latticework, Braid Framing, Oriole Co., c.1910, 37 x 18 In.	975.00
Stand, Music, Double, Regency, Mahogany, Giltwood Lyre, 55 In.	720.00
Stand, Music, George III, Tilt Top, Tripod Base, Slipper Feet, 20 x 14½ In.	633.00
Stand, Music, Heywood, Wicker, Braiding, Latticework, Lyre Design, 1890s, 53 In.	1450.00
Stand, Music, Mahogany, Sheet, Brass Railings, Griffins, 50 x 20¾ x 16½ In.	294.00
Stand, Music, Regency, Lacquered, Lyre Support, c.1810, 28½ x 20 x 14½ In.	15000.00
Stand, Music, Restauration, Mahogany, Gilt, Patinated Bronze, Marble, 17½ x 13½ In.	6168.00
Stand, Music, Victorian, Wicker, Curlicues, Spools, Heywood, 1890s, 37 x 17 In.	1650.00
Stand, Music, Victorian, Wicker, Fancywork, Turned Finials, Beadwork, 1890s, 37 x 19 In.	875.00
Stand, Music, Victorian, Wicker, Ornate Shaped Crest, Beadwork, 1890s, 59 x 20 In.	1950.00
Stand, Music, Wicker, Stick Style, Tall Gallery, Curlicues, Finials, 1890s, 32 x 16 In.	1050.00
Stand, Music, Wicker, Wood Shelves, Casters, 1880s, 21 x 16½ In.	875.00
Stand, Notched Corners, Apron, Pencil Turned Legs, Yellow, Red Striping, 19th Century, 30 x 21 In.	1434.00
Stand, Plant, Arts & Crafts, Hammered, Applied Details, Iron, Painted Copper Finish, 10 x 38 In.	600.00
Stand, Plant, Arts & Crafts, Oak, 4 Posts, 2 Rails, 6 Hourglass Slats, c.1912, 35⅝ In.	470.00
Stand, Plant, Arts & Crafts, Oak, Square Top, Slat Sides, 4 Square Posts, 15 x 35 In.	176.00
Stand, Plant, Cast Iron, Lion Mask, Bas Relief, Square, 20th Century, 16½ x 22¼ In., Pair	531.00
Stand, Plant, G. Stickley, Cloud-Lift Aprons, Mortised Stretcher, 28 x 15 In.	1560.00
Stand, Plant, Limbert, Oak, Apron Panels, Shaped Corbels, 34¼ x 14 x 14 In.	1800.00
Stand, Plant, Pine, 3 Tiers, Painted, 44½ In.	283.00
Stand, Plant, Poplar, Raised Scalloped Edge, Turned Legs, Red Paint, 19 x 20 x 60 In.	863.00
Stand, Plant, Relief Figures, Birds, Lead, 16 x 16 In., Pair	1404.00
Stand, Plant, Stickley Bros., No. 135, Square, Notched Apron, Flared Legs, Cross Stretcher, 34 In.	820.00
Stand, Plant, Wrought Iron, Copper, Leaf & Flowers, Tripod Base, Early 1900s, 45 In.	460.00
Stand, Plant, Wrought Iron, Pierced, Painted Black, Tripod, Scroll Top, 30 x 15 In.	173.00
Stand, Poplar, Drawer, Removable Overhanging Top, Early 19th Century, 30 x 36 In.	1175.00
Stand, Reading, Mahogany, Pedestal, Drawer, Adjustable, England, c.1850, 40½ In.	7850.00
Stand, Renaissance Revival, Walnut, Ebonized, Painted Details, Dish Top, Turned Legs, 33 In.	2640.00
Stand, Renaissance Revival, Walnut, Marble Top, 4-Paneled Drawers, Carved Pulls, 30 In., Pair	2640.00
Stand, Rococo Revival, Rosewood, Marble Top, 19th Century, 29 x 24 In.	2400.00
Stand, Rosewood, Carved, Round, Marble Insert, Pierced Skirt, Chinese, 35 x 15 In.	345.00
Stand, Rosewood, Marble Top, Round Top, Pierce Carved, Chinese, c.1890, 16 x 18 In.	259.00
Stand, Rosewood, Mottled Marble, Shaped Apron, Scrolling Legs, Chinese, 30 x 14 In.	189.00
Stand, Rosewood, Square Top, Beaded Legs, Chinese, 32 x 13⅞ x 13⅞ In.	590.00
Stand, Round Top, Marble, Early 20th Century, 18 x 18 In.	183.00
Stand, Roycroft, Little Journeys, Overhanging Tops, Shoe Feet, 26 x 26 In., Pair	1315.00
Stand, Shaker, Maple, Poplar, Drawer, Dovetailed, Turned Legs, 25¾ x 16½ In.	1287.00
Stand, Shaker, Pine, Red Paint, Square, Turned Legs, Canterbury, N.H., c.1840, 27 x 17 In.	1989.00
Stand, Shaker, Walnut, 3 Drawers, Brass Pulls, Union Village, Oh., c.1850, 33 x 26 In.	4680.00
Stand, Shaving, Green, Stylized Flowers, Gold Trim, Baltimore, 62 x 14 x 14 In. ......*illus*	575.00
Stand, Shaving, Renaissance Revival, Walnut, X-Form Base, Oval Mirror, 65 In.	1320.00
Stand, Sheraton, Cherry, Pine, 2 Drawers, Rope Turned Legs, Peg Feet, 29 x 18 In.	633.00
Stand, Sheraton, Mahogany, 2 Drawers, Oval Corners, Spiral Legs, 28 x 18 In.	770.00
Stand, Sheraton, Mahogany, Bowfront, Reeded Top, Drawers, 30 x 37 In.	176.00
Stand, Sheraton, Maple, Cut Corners, Drawers, Wooden Knob, Splayed Legs, 19 x 27 In.	345.00
Stand, Sheraton, Tulipwood, Quatrefoil Top, Wreath, Ribbon, Swags, 27 x 20 In. ......*illus*	705.00
Stand, Sheraton, Walnut, Cherry, Tapered Legs, Ball Feet, Drawer, Brass Pull, 27 x 18 In.	489.00
Stand, Smoking, Arts & Crafts, Door, Pipe Cutouts, Overhang Shelf, 30 x 14 In.	300.00
Stand, Smoking, Black Forest, Wood, Carved, Bear At Base, 3 On Tray, 34½ In.	1126.00
Stand, Smoking, Eero Saarinen, 1956, 22 x 13 In.	300.00
Stand, Smoking, Various Metals, Drop Lid, Side Compartments, Ring Handles, 38 x 21 In.	480.00
Stand, Softwood, 2-Board Top, Tapered Legs, 30½ x 22¾ In.	110.00
Stand, Softwood, Drawer, Old Red Paint, Turned Legs, Tulip Feet, 28¾ x 19 x 17 In.	220.00
Stand, Softwood, Drawer, Red & Black Rosewood Grain, Tapered Legs, New Eng., 28 x 22 x 17 In.	220.00
Stand, Softwood, Drop Leaf, 2 Drawers, Old Red Paint, Turned Legs, 29¼ x 21¾ In.	275.00
Stand, Softwood, Painted, Red Wash, Drawer, Overhang Top, 30 x 21 In.	303.00
Stand, Softwood, Red Paint, Dovetailed, Tapered Legs, 28¾ x 17¾ x 20 In.	467.00
Stand, Softwood, Red Paint, Drawer, Dish Rim Top, Flower Knob, Tapered Legs, 28 x 19 x 19 In.	1870.00
Stand, Softwood, Red Paint, Smoke Design, Shaped Corners, Turned Legs, Pa., 29 x 19 In.	330.00
Stand, Softwood, Splay, Drawer, Old Red Paint, Tapered Legs, 29½ x 17½ In.	1100.00
Stand, Stickley Bros., Drawer, Tapered Posts, Label, 28 x 21 x 17 In. ......*illus*	2600.00
Stand, Table, Black Forest, Carved Bear & Cub, Hinged Head For Storage, 32 x 24 In.	5500.00
Stand, Tiger Maple, Softwood, Drawer, Turned Legs, 29⅜ x 20½ In.	209.00
Stand, Urn, George III Style, Gallery, Fretwork, Fitted Cup Slide, 27 x 13 In. ......*illus*	3000.00
Stand, Victorian, Rosewood, Walnut Top, 3 Carved Women's Bust, Goat Feet, 28 x 17 In.	1430.00

Stand, Walnut, 2 Drawers, Carved, Chamfered Edges, Flower Swag, Turned Legs, 29 x 21 In. . . 1980.00
Stand, Walnut, 2-Board Top, Molded Apron, Square Tapered Legs, 28½ x 24 x 17½ In. 303.00
Stand, Walnut, Chinese, 20¼ x 17½ x 13 In. 295.00
Stand, Walnut, Drawer, 2 Oversized Wood Knobs, Turned Legs, Tall Feet, 29 x 21 In. 550.00
Stand, Walnut, Drawer, Overhanging Top, Shaped Corners, Early 19th Century 1000.00
Stand, Walnut, Poplar, Splayed, Tapered Legs, Cutouts, Drawer, 18 x 17 x 27 In. 748.00
Stand, Wig, Queen Anne Style, Mahogany, Round Top, 3 Supports, Triangular Drawer, 31 In. 960.00
Stool, Barcelona, Knoll, Leather Strapping, Brown Leather Cushion, Steel, 15 x 24 In. 521.00
Stool, Chinese Provincial, Elm, Rectangular Seat, Square Legs, Early 1900s, 21 x 19 In., Pair 470.00
Stool, Chippendale, Walnut, Leather Top, Scrolled Apron, Square Legs, 18 x 20 x 15 In. . *illus* 523.00
Stool, Dagobert, Eclectic, Tufted Silk & Needlepoint Upholstery, 1800s, 20 x 18 In. 2400.00
Stool, Duet, Louis XV, Giltwood, Carved, Kidney Shape, Pierce Carved Back, 24 x 39 In. 431.00
Stool, Egyptian, Oak, Ebonized, Leather Upholstered, c.1901, 16 x 24 x 24 In. 9600.00
Stool, Elm, Marble Top, Chinese, 18½ x 15¼ In., Pair 670.00
Stool, English Oak, Padded Needlework, Turned, Tapered Legs, Bulb Feet, 17 x 18 x 12 In. .. 70.00
Stool, G. Nakashima, 1 Piece Figural Walnut Seat, Mira, 1984, 35 In. 1645.00
Stool, G. Nakashima, Walnut, Grass Cord, Rectangular, Cylindrical Legs, 12 x 16 x 17 In. ... 2988.00
Stool, George II Style, Mahogany, Padded, Shaped Frieze, Cabriole Legs, 22 x 21 x 18 In. 822.00
Stool, George III, Book Form Top, Leather Bound, Carpet Lined, 20 x 22 x 16 In. ......*illus* 6000.00
Stool, George III, Mahogany, Needlepoint Upholstered, Flower Scrolls, 18 x 18 x 20 In. 3819.00
Stool, George III, Mahogany, Padded Top, Cabriole Legs, Shell Carving, 19 x 24 In. 450.00
Stool, Giltwood, Padded, Needlework Top, Scrolled Toes, Mid 1800s, 6 x 17½ In., Pair 1200.00
Stool, Gout, Baltimore, Painted, Frederick City Novelty, Scrolled Shape, 7 x 15 In. 2520.00
Stool, Hemba, Round Seat, Crouching Figure Supports, Ceremonial, Congo, 15½ In. 502.00
Stool, Jacobean, Tapestry, Upholstered, H-Stretcher, Ring Turned Legs, 16 x 19 x 15 In. 1528.00
Stool, Joint, Jacobean, Rectangular, Ring Turned Legs, Stretchers, 21 x 23 In. 1058.00
Stool, Louis Philippe, Fruitwood, X-Shaped Ends, Stretcher, Needlework Seat, 16 x 15 In. ... 480.00
Stool, Louis XIII, Walnut Base, Carved, Needlepoint Top, 1800s, 23 x 18 In., Pair 1975.00
Stool, Louis XV, Beech, Serpentine Rails, Flower Heads, c.1745, 16 x 25 In., Pair 8400.00
Stool, Louis XV, Walnut, Padded Top, Cabriole Feet, Acanthine Carving, 9½ x 17 In. 180.00
Stool, Mahogany, Acanthus Carved & Scrolled Stretcher & Legs, Padded Top, 17 x 20 In. 822.00
Stool, Milking, Mahogany, Pine, Rectangular, Center Carrying Hole, Peg Legs, 12 x 16 In. ... 120.00
Stool, Milking, Old Paint, Cupped Plank Seat, Canted Legs, T-Stretcher, 11 In. 440.00
Stool, Napoleon III, Giltwood, Padded, Tufted, Faux Bamboo Frieze, 21 In. 2610.00
Stool, Napoleon III, Giltwood, Padded, Upholstered, Velvet, Faux Bamboo, 17¾ x 20 In. 2256.00
Stool, Neoclassical Style, Burl, Upholstered, Padded, 12¾ x 31½ x 17¾ In. 1116.00
Stool, Oak, Joint, Molded Edge Top, Turned Legs, Stretcher, 1800s, 21 x 16 In., Pair 561.00
Stool, Oak, Rectangular, Box Stretcher, Block & Column Legs, 14 x 17 x 10 In. 600.00
Stool, Philippe Starck, WW, Burnished Aluminum, Green 1384.00
Stool, Piano, Louis XV Style, Beech, Cabriole Legs, Revolving Seat, 19 x 16¾ In. 917.00
Stool, Pine, Scooped Round Seat, Bamboo Turnings, Brown Paint, Yellow Striping, 24 In. ... 259.00
Stool, Regency, Mahogany, Padded, Pineapple Feet, c.1850, 16 x 50 x 34 In., Pair 3290.00
Stool, Regency Style, Rosewood, Tufted Top, Palmetto-Carved Feet, 14 x 49 x 30 In. 1997.00
Stool, Rococo Revival, Mahogany, Upholstered, Scalloped Apron, 18 x 19 In., Pair 1440.00
Stool, Shaker, Maple, Walnut Stain, Wool Plush Cover, Mt. Lebanon, N.Y., c.1880, 7 In. 351.00
Stool, Shaker, Pine, 2-Step, Red Stain, X Cross Brace, Hand Held Cut In Top, N.Y., 20 x 17 In. 1989.00
Stool, Shaker, Pine, Gray Paint, 3 Steps, Arched Sides, Mt. Lebanon, N.Y., c.1850, 24 x 18 In. . 702.00
Stool, Shaker, Pine, Red Paint, 2 Steps, Bootjack Sides, Harvard, Mass., c.1860, 21 x 15 In. .. 819.00
Stool, Shaker, Wood, Paint, Shaped Legs, Incised Rings, Webbing, 9 x 13 In. ....*illus* 173.00
Stool, Vanity, Egyptian Revival, Peach Upholstered Seat, Cast Figural Legs, 20 x 21 In. 387.00
Stool, Windsor, Stylized Leaves & Flowers, Original Green Paint, 8 x 12 In. 1035.00
Stool, Wood, Splay Legs, Hand Riveted Legs & Stretchers, Early 20th Century, 22 In. 400.00
Stool, Wood, Turned, 3 Legs, England, Early 19th Century, 12½ In. 229.00
Table, 17th Century Style, Oak, Early 20th Century, 60 x 28 In. 430.00
Table, 18th Century Style, Drop Leaf, Oval Top, 2 Swing Legs, 1900s, 21 x 21 x 12 In. 201.00
Table, 2 Drawers, Yellow Pine, Old White Paint, Southern, 1800s, 29 x 27 In. 489.00
Table, 2 Tiers, Round, Marquetry, Floral Motif, c.1900 .... 6500.00
Table, 2-Board, Plain Apron, Tapered Square Legs, 25½ x 36 x 16 In. 2400.00
Table, 3-Board, Red Paint, 54 x 35 In. 1980.00
Table, Adirondack, 12 Supports, 30 x 24 x 24 In. 6050.00
Table, Altar, Asian Hardwood, Carved, Scalloped Apron, 34 x 42½ x 21¼ In. 5700.00
Table, Altar, Elm, Rectangular Legs, Chinese, 36 x 81½ x 20 In. 1180.00
Table, Altar, Mahogany, Carved, Rectangular, Block Legs, Chinese, 35¾ x 69 x 17¾ In. 1292.00
Table, Anglo-Indian, Inlaid Decoration, Early 20th Century, 26 x 24 In. 457.00
Table, Anglo-Indian Regency, Rosewood, Carved, Drawer, Trestle Base, 29 x 30 In. 649.00
Table, Art Deco, Mirrored Glass, Rosettes, Continental, 25 x 26¾ x 16¼ In. 998.00

Furniture, Stand, Federal, Walnut, Overhanging Top, Drawer, Tapered Legs, Tenn., 27 x 26 In.
$374.00

Furniture, Stand, Magazine, Barber Bros., 4 Shelves, Single Slat Sides, 38 x 22 x 13 In.
$510.00

Furniture, Stand, Shaving, Green, Stylized Flowers, Gold Trim, Baltimore, 62 x 14 x 14 In.
$575.00

Furniture, Stand, Sheraton, Tulipwood, Quatrefoil Top, Wreath, Ribbon, Swags, 27 x 20 In.
$705.00

Furniture, Stand, Stickley Bros., Drawer, Tapered Posts, Label, 28 x 21 x 17 In. $2600.00

Furniture, Stand, Urn, George III Style, Gallery, Fretwork, Fitted Cup Slide, 27 x 13 In. $3000.00

Furniture, Stool, Chippendale, Walnut, Leather Top, Scrolled Apron, Square Legs, 18 x 20 x 15 In. $523.00

Table, Art Deco, Pedestal, Wicker, Wood Top, Woven Skirting, c.1915, 29 x 48 In.	975.00
Table, Art Deco, Wicker, Cane Wrapped Edge, Bottom Shelf, Splayed Legs, 1920s, 30 In.	1850.00
Table, Art Moderne, Directoire Style, Giltmetal, Glass Top, Tubular Legs, 17 x 16 In., Pair	1800.00
Table, Art Nouveau, Satinwood, Rosewood, Marquetry, 2 Tiers, 30 x 26½ In.	4500.00
Table, Arts & Crafts, Oak, Round Leather Top, 4 Post Legs, Shelf, c.1912, 29 x 36 In.	646.00
Table, Asian Hardwood, Block Legs, Bracket Spandrels, 34 x 47 x 13½ In.	3900.00
Table, Bamboo, Lacquered, Square Top, Decoupage Border, Anglo-Indian, 28 x 20 x 20 In.	264.00
Table, Bamboo, Lacquered, Square Top, Decoupage Border, Birds, Anglo-Indian, 28 x 19 In.	411.00
Table, Bar Harbor, Oval, Wicker, Latticework Skirting, c.1920s, 31 In.	795.00
Table, Bar Harbor, Round, Wicker, Woven Top & Shelf, Wrapped Legs, c.1920s, 28 In.	425.00
Table, Biedermeier, Curly Birch, Round, Disc Stretcher, Shaped Tapered Legs, 31 x 20 In.	2400.00
Table, Biedermeier, Mahogany, Ebonized, Round Top, Bulbous Standard, 27 x 18 In.	1200.00
Table, Biedermeier, Mahogany, Raised Edge, Inlaid Star, Turned Supports, 39 x 21 In.	2160.00
Table, Biedermeier, Walnut, Projecting Oval Top, Drawer, Continental, 32 x 31 In.	531.00
Table, Birch, 2-Board Top, Plain Apron, Drawer, Tapered Legs, 25½ x 17½ x 18 In.	900.00
Table, Black Forest, Tilt Top, Walnut, Marquetry, Eagle, Tripod Base, 30 x 31 In. *illus*	1410.00
Table, Blue Paint, 3-Board Top, Plain Apron, Drawer, 27½ x 38 x 23 In.	3000.00
Table, Bookcase, Oak, 26 x 14 In.	695.00
Table, Bookshelf, Paul Laszlo, 1947, 22½ x 23½ x 30 In.	660.00
Table, Bookshelf With Removable Tray, Floral Fabric Under Glass, 1920s, 27 In.	975.00
Table, Burl, Plank Top, Stump Pedestal, Hexagonal, Rustic, 31 x 48 In.	489.00
Table, Capital, Wood, Carved, Painted, Cast Iron Mounts, Round Glass Top, Continental, 30 In.	639.00
Table, Card, 2 Gatelegs, Kittinger, Walnut, 2 Pullout Candle Shelves, Label, 29 x 36 In.	575.00
Table, Card, Chippendale, Mahogany, Folding Overhang Top, c.1795, 28 x 34 In.	11750.00
Table, Card, Chippendale, Mahogany, Serpentine Front, New York, c.1790, 28 x 34 In.	42000.00
Table, Card, Empire, Mahogany, D-Shape Top, Carved Post, 4 Paw Feet, 30 x 36 In. *illus*	1840.00
Table, Card, Empire, Mahogany, Swivel, Flip Top, Carved, Pedestal, Paw Feet, 36 x 35 In.	1380.00
Table, Card, Federal, Mahogany, Demilune, 1800-20, 29¼ x 36 x 17½ In.	960.00
Table, Card, Federal, Mahogany, Figured, Inlay, c.1790, 29 x 36 x 17 In.	3900.00
Table, Card, Federal, Mahogany, Foldover Top, Reeded Legs, Casters, 30 x 36 In., Pair	3910.00
Table, Card, Federal, Mahogany, Inlay, Serpentine Front, Mass., c.1800, 30 x 36 x 18 In.	9600.00
Table, Card, Federal, Mahogany, Maple, Reeded Legs, Peg Feet, New Eng., 1800s, 29 x 36 In., Pair	10755.00
Table, Card, Federal, Mahogany, Maple, Serpentine Flip Top, Frieze Drawer, 28 x 34 In.	1062.00
Table, Card, Federal, Mahogany, Oval Corners, Apron, Square Tapered Legs, c.1810, 29 x 36 In.	1195.00
Table, Card, Federal, Mahogany, Pine, Biscuit Corners, Tapered Reeded Legs, 37 x 30½ In.	1092.00
Table, Card, Federal, Mahogany, Shaped Top, Inlaid Edge, c.1810, 26 x 35½ In.	5580.00
Table, Card, Federal, Mahogany, Urn Pedestal, 4 Saber Legs, Brass Paw Feet, 32 x 16 In.	200.00
Table, Card, Federal, Mahogany, Veneer, Carved Legs, Eagle Heads, Brass Caps, 36 x 18 x 29 In.	8913.00
Table, Card, Gothic, Mahogany, Foldover Top, Bird's-Eye Knots, 29 x 31½ In.	230.00
Table, Card, Hepplewhite, Mahogany, Oval Corners, Tapered Legs, Leaf, 29 x 36 In.	575.00
Table, Card, Hepplewhite, Mahogany, Pine, Birch, Elliptical Front, Serpentine Ends, 29 x 36 In.	2300.00
Table, Card, Hepplewhite, Mahogany Veneer, Pine, Shell Inlay, 36 x 16 x 30 In.	2645.00
Table, Card, Neoclassical, Mahogany, Foldover Top, Molded Apron, 30 x 36 In.	4800.00
Table, Card, Sheraton, Cherry, Shaped Top, Tapered Legs, Ball Feet, 29 x 37 In. *illus*	1035.00
Table, Card, Sheraton, Mahogany, Flip Top, Serpentine Front, Reeded Legs, Peg Feet, 28 x 36 In.	546.00
Table, Card, Sheraton, Mahogany, Serpentine Front, Oval Inlay, Swing Leg, 30 x 35 In.	360.00
Table, Card, Sheraton, Mahogany, Shaped Top, Reeded Edge, Reeded Leg, 30 x 36 In.	1870.00
Table, Card, Walnut, Square, Leather Top, Upholstered Chairs, Art Deco, c.1930, 5 Piece *illus*	264.00
Table, Cast Iron, Marble Top, Trestle Base, Stretcher, 25½ x 29½ x 16 In.	354.00
Table, Center, Biedermeier, Maple, Ebonized, Oval Top, 19th Century, 30 x 40 In.	3173.00
Table, Center, Black Forest, Carved, Marquetry, Tripod Pedestal, 30 x 29 In.	1410.00
Table, Center, Black Forest, Inlay, Carved, 19th Century, 29 x 22 In.	2400.00
Table, Center, Charles X, Walnut, Round, Drop Leaves, c.1825, 29 x 39 In.	780.00
Table, Center, Empire, Mahogany, Decorated, Round Stretcher, Curved Legs, 48 In.	4158.00
Table, Center, Empire Style, Elm, String Inlay, Ebonized Edge & Bun Feet, 30 x 46 In.	4080.00
Table, Center, Greek Revival, Marquetry Floral, Round Top, Mid 1800s, 31 x 23 In.	3068.00
Table, Center, Mahogany, Carved, Round, Acanthus Leaf Support, Paw Feet, 29½ x 35 In.	4481.00
Table, Center, Mahogany, Iron Mount, Bulbous Legs, Stretchers, 30 x 47 In.	1800.00
Table, Center, Mahogany, Marquetry, Round Top, Platform Base, Continental, 30 x 41 In.	920.00
Table, Center, Neoclassical, Mahogany, Carved, Tilt Top, Rosewood Disc, Paw Feet, 29 x 42 In.	9900.00
Table, Center, Neoclassical Style, Mahogany Gilt, Painted, Parcel, Russia, 30 x 48 In.	9600.00
Table, Center, Oak, Black Forest, Tripod Pedestal, Hoof Feet Legs, 27 x 26½ In.	823.00
Table, Center, Oak, Shelf, Spindle Gallery, Victorian, 31 x 38 x 24 In.	206.00
Table, Center, Regency, Burl Oak, Tilt Top, Ebony Band, Paw Feet, 29½ x 55½ In.	3055.00
Table, Center, Regency Style, Rosewood, Inlaid Marble, Circular Top, 29 x 33½ In.	3525.00
Table, Center, Renaissance Revival, Burled Walnut, Ebonized, Marquetry, c.1870, 29 x 37 In.	4700.00

Table, Center, Rococo Revival, Crotch Walnut, Marble Top, Carved Stretcher, 29 x 45 In.	1800.00
Table, Center, Rococo Revival, Rosewood, Marble Turtle Top, 30 x 40 In.	7200.00
Table, Center, Rococo Style, Carved, Giltwood, Pink, Gray Marble Top, 50½ x 32 In.	4183.00
Table, Center, Victorian, Ash, Turned Design, 31 In.	59.00
Table, Center, Victorian, Burl Walnut, Marble Top, Squared Oval, 31 x 31 In. ....*illus*	1020.00
Table, Center, Victorian, Circassian Walnut, Mid 19th Century, 55 x 41 In.	819.00
Table, Center, Victorian, Marble Turtle Top, Carving, Drop Pendants, 28 x 38 In.	920.00
Table, Center, Walnut, Cabriole Style Legs, Victorian, 29 x 31 x 20 In.	94.00
Table, Center, Walnut, Relief Carved, 4 Kneeling Mermaid Supports, 30 x 39 In. ....*illus*	10925.00
Table, Center, Wicker, Cane Wrapped Posts, Top Lifts Off, c.1910, 27½ In.	1050.00
Table, Center, William IV, Chinoiserie, Tilt Top, Decorated, 39 In.	958.00
Table, Center, William IV, Mahogany, Round, 5 Turned & Bulbous Legs, Casters, 28 x 46 In. ..	1320.00
Table, Cherry, Walnut, 2-Board Top, Splayed Legs, Chamfered Edges, Brackets, 32 x 32 In. ..	345.00
Table, Chinese Chippendale, Mahogany, 2 Tiers, 20th Century, 16 In., Pair	389.00
Table, Chippendale, Mahogany, Extension, Oval Top, Crank Mechanism, 1900s, 29 x 41 In. .	259.00
Table, Chippendale, Walnut, Drop Leaf, Marlboro Swing Leg, 29 x 54 In.	385.00
Table, Chippendale, Walnut, Tilt Top, Bulbous Vase Post, Late 1700s, 27 x 30 In.	764.00
Table, Chippendale Style, Mahogany, Molded Top, 4 Drawers, Carved, 1800s, 35 x 41 In.	896.00
Table, Coffee, Contemporary, Iron, Slate, Bow Shape Base, Casters, 22 x 46 In.	1080.00
Table, Coffee, Edwardian, Chinoiserie, Black Lacquer, Landscape, c.1900, 17 x 30 In.	429.00
Table, Coffee, Edwardian Style, Satinwood, Recessed Top, Painted Decoration, 18 x 48 In. ...	460.00
Table, Coffee, G. Nakashima, Black Walnut, Free Edge, Butterfly Joint, 45 x 43 In.	34655.00
Table, Coffee, G. Nakashima, Walnut, Cone Shape, Free Edge, Tapered Leg, 37 x 36 In.	21510.00
Table, Coffee, G. Nakashima, Walnut, Rectangular, Free Edge, Cylindrical Leg, 13 x 73 In.	20315.00
Table, Coffee, G. Nakashima, Walnut, Round Top, 3 Butterfly Joints, 1955, 12 x 39 In.	8810.00
Table, Coffee, Hickory, 14 x 30 In.	3300.00
Table, Coffee, I. Noguchi, Walnut Base, Folds, 3-Sided Plate Glass Top, 16 x 50 x 36 In.	598.00
Table, Coffee, Louis XV, Oak, Mirrored Glass, Polychromed Leaf Band, 19 x 36 In.	570.00
Table, Coffee, Mahogany, Brass, Bisected, 4-Step Library Ladder, 21 x 35 x 36 In.	998.00
Table, Coffee, Molded Plastic, Off White, Italy, c.1970, 12 x 27 x 27 In.	77.00
Table, Coffee, Paul Laszio, Wood, 2 Solid Pedestals, 1947, 14 x 48 x 23 In.	2160.00
Table, Coffee, Pietra Dura, Painted, Round, Slab Base, 44 In.	588.00
Table, Coffee, Regency Style, Mahogany, Lyre Form Supports, Casters, 22 x 36 In.	587.00
Table, Coffee, Regency Style, Yew, Leather Panel, Drawer, 22 x 42 x 20 In.	224.00
Table, Coffee, Rosewood, Floating Top, 4 Triangular Legs, Denmark, c.1962, 20 x 59 In.	764.00
Table, Coffee, V. Kagan, Walnut, Glass, c.1950, 15¼ x 52 x 30⅛ In.	6600.00
Table, Coffee, W. Platner, Oak Laminate Top, Wire Rod Base, Round, c.1960s, 15 x 36 In.	940.00
Table, Coffee, Wegner, Teak Top, Birch Frame, Gettema Workshops, 18 x 34 In.	235.00
Table, Coffee, Wormley, Walnut, 6 Inset Tiffany Tiles, Dunbar, 17 x 77 In.	13255.00
Table, Collector's, Louis XVI, Gilt Bronze Mounted, Variegated Marble Top, 33 x 35 In.	764.00
Table, Conservatory, Napoleon III, Iron, Marble Top, Molded Edge, 32 x 51 In.	1560.00
Table, Console, 18th Century Style, Marble Top, Early 20th Century, 29 In.	634.00
Table, Console, Adam Style, Rosewood, Burl, Giltwood, Demilune Top, Pair, 32 x 54 In.	3290.00
Table, Console, Charles X, Satinwood, Inlaid Scrolls, Curved Sides, Stretcher, 33 x 50 In.	5280.00
Table, Console, Contemporary, Demilune, Black Paint, Inset Marble Top, Drawer, 45 x 15 In.	2340.00
Table, Console, Demilune, Banded, Painted Bellflowers, Spade Feet, 32 x 36 x 18 In.	1020.00
Table, Console, Demilune Top, Gilt, Polychrome, Grapevines, Italy, Late 1800s, 34½ In.	763.00
Table, Console, Directoire Style, Ebonized, Brass, x Form Stretchers, 39¾ x 36 x 11 In.	1292.00
Table, Console, Federal, Mahogany, Banded Front, 33 x 51 In.	2588.00
Table, Console, Federal, Pine, Black Painted, 29 x 39 x 19½ In.	2820.00
Table, Console, Florentine, Painted, Gilt, Hand Carved, Hoof Feet, Italy, 1600, 77 x 39 In. ...	100000.00
Table, Console, French Empire, Mahogany, Marble Top, 32 x 53 x 19 In.	1416.00
Table, Console, Fruitwood, Marble Top, Mottled Serpentine Top, Gilt Bronze, 27 x 31 In.	224.00
Table, Console, George III Style, Mahogany, Pierced Frieze, 31 x 48 x 18 In., Pair	1116.00
Table, Console, George III Style, Painted, Adam Style, Floral Spray, Drawers, 31 x 45 In.	294.00
Table, Console, Italian Rococo Style, Giltwood, Carved, Mottled Rouge Marble Top, 33 x 40 In.	224.00
Table, Console, Italian Style, Giltwood, Marble Top, Scrolled Pendant Apron, 37 x 45 In., Pair .	7080.00
Table, Console, Lacquered, Continental, Early 19th Century, 20 In.	819.00
Table, Console, Lifetime, 6 Legs, Corbels, Drawer, Bell Shaped Pulls, 31 x 67 x 22 In.	9600.00
Table, Console, Louis XIII, Chestnut, Carved, c.1820, 64 x 19 In.	11500.00
Table, Console, Louis XVI, Marble Top, Polychrome, Parcel Gilt, Fluted Legs, 31 x 36 In.	3000.00
Table, Console, Mahogany, Demilune, Square Legs, Painted Vines, Spade Feet, 33 x 38 In., Pair ..	940.00
Table, Console, Mirror, Rococo, Silver Gilt, Marble Top, Swagged Drapery Shape, 32 x 52 In. .	3600.00
Table, Console, P. Evans, Slate Top, Patinated Metal, 20th Century, 60 x 13 In.	2938.00
Table, Console, Pine, Cabriole Front Legs, 19th Century, 48 In.	500.00
Table, Console, Regency, Gilt Bronze Mount, Galleried Shelf, Mirror Back, 50 x 42 In.	1293.00

F

Furniture, Stool, George III, Book Form Top, Leather Bound, Carpet Lined, 20 x 22 x 16 In.
$6000.00

Furniture, Stool, Shaker, Wood, Paint, Shaped Legs, Incised Rings, Webbing, 9 x 13 In.
$173.00

Furniture, Table, Black Forest, Tilt Top, Walnut, Marquetry, Eagle, Tripod Base, 30 x 31 In.
$1410.00

Furniture, Table, Card, Empire, Mahogany, D-Shape Top, Carved Post, 4 Paw Feet, 30 x 36 In.
$1840.00

Furniture, Table, Card, Sheraton, Cherry, Shaped Top, Tapered Legs, Ball Feet, 29 x 37 In. $1035.00

Furniture, Table, Card, Walnut, Square, Leather Top, Upholstered Chairs, Art Deco, c.1930, 5 Piece $264.00

Furniture, Table, Center, Victorian, Burl Walnut, Marble Top, Squared Oval, 31 x 31 In. $1020.00

Furniture, Table, Center, Walnut, Relief Carved, 4 Kneeling Mermaid Supports, 30 x 39 In. $10925.00

Table, Console, Regency, Rosewood, D-Shape Marble Top, 34½ x 31 x 25½ In.	940.00
Table, Console, Regency Style, Ebonized Mahogany, Ormolu Mounts, Plinth Base, 32 x 54 In.	1527.00
Table, Console, Restauration, Mahogany, Marble Top, Drawer, Scroll Supports, 33 x 31 In.	1320.00
Table, Console, Restauration, Mahogany, Marble Top, Scroll Legs, Mirrored Back, 36 x 42 In.	3360.00
Table, Console, Rococo Revival, Carved, Bleached, Pickled, Mahogany, 32 x 53 In.	2160.00
Table, Console, Walnut, Carved, Marble Top, 20th Century, 27 In.	164.00
Table, Console, Walnut, Highly Figured, Scrolled Supports, Shaped Plinth Base, 31 x 33 In.	1920.00
Table, Console, William IV, Mahogany, Marble Top, Metal Gallery, Ireland, 47 x 37 In. ..*illus*	4800.00
Table, Contemporary, Red Lacquer, Curving Scroll Under Sides, 1900s, 17 x 60 In.	236.00
Table, Contemporary, Tripod, Drawer, Marble Top, 15 x 13½ In., Pair	176.00
Table, Corner, Rococo Style, Giltwood, Marble Top, 1 Cabriole Leg, 1800s, 37 x 24 In.	850.00
Table, D. Deskey, Walnut, Lacquered, Chromed, c.1929, 20¼ In.	9000.00
Table, Danish Modern, Convertible, c.1956, 21 x 47 x 24 In. ....*illus*	1200.00
Table, Danish Modern, Mahogany, c.1958, 20 x 18½ x 18½ In.	84.00
Table, Demilune, Split Reed, Wood Top, Split Reed Skirting, Cane Wrapped Legs, c.1920s	425.00
Table, Demilune, Wicker, Oak Top, Cane Wrapped Legs, 1920s, 25¾ In.	425.00
Table, Dining, Biedermeier, Burled Top, Apron, Tapered Legs, 2 Sections, 29 x 47 In.	1100.00
Table, Dining, Danish Modern, Teak, Oval, 4 Leaves, Mid 1900s, 29 x 133 In.	201.00
Table, Dining, Directoire, Light Oak, Extension, Round Top, Drop Leaves, 31 x 49 In.	960.00
Table, Dining, Drop Leaf, Cherry, 2 Sections, Spiral Turned Legs, 29 x 44 x 86 In. ...*illus*	863.00
Table, Dining, Drop Leaf, Chippendale, Maple, Skirt, Marlboro Legs, 28 x 42 In.	2233.00
Table, Dining, Drop Leaf, Federal, Mahogany, 2 Sections, Swing Leg, 29 x 45 In.	940.00
Table, Dining, Drop Leaf, Gateleg, Cherry, Turned Legs, 19th Century, 47¾ In.	367.00
Table, Dining, Drop Leaf, Neoclassical, Mahogany, Carved, Reeded Edge, c.1820, 29 x 42 In.	2350.00
Table, Dining, Drop Leaf, Queen Anne, Walnut, c.1760, 28½ x 54½ In.	9600.00
Table, Dining, Drop Leaf, Queen Anne, Walnut, Cabriole Legs, 28 x 41½ x 18½ In.	1554.00
Table, Dining, Drop Leaf, Queen Anne, Walnut, Philadelphia, c.1760, 29 x 42 In.	2400.00
Table, Dining, Dunbar, 2 Leaves, Oriental Style, 29 x 52 x 39 In.	478.00
Table, Dining, Edwardian, Mahogany, Carved, Round Top, Leaf Carving, 1800s, 29 x 48 In.	1175.00
Table, Dining, Eliel Saarinen, Birch, Black Laminate, 2 Leaves, c.1941, 29 x 72 x 34 In.	5400.00
Table, Dining, Empire Style, Mahogany, Urn Pedestal, Beaded, Scrolled Feet, Leaves, 30 x 60 In.	920.00
Table, Dining, English Regency, Inlaid Mixed Wood, Parcel Gilt, 1900s, 30 x 66 In.	1062.00
Table, Dining, Federal, 2 Sections, Cherry, Shaped Ends, Skirt, Reeded Legs, 29 x 50 In.	431.00
Table, Dining, Federal, 2 Sections, Figured Veneer Top, Diamond & Bellflower, 32 x 47 In.	1035.00
Table, Dining, Federal Style, Mahogany, 2 Pedestal, Molded Top, 2 Leaves, 29 x 90 In.	2160.00
Table, Dining, Finn Juhl, Teak, c.1952, 29 x 63 x 43 In.	657.00
Table, Dining, Florence Knoll, Wood Veneer, Chromed Metal, Drawer, 30 x 95 In.	1293.00
Table, Dining, Folding, B. Mathsson, Karl Mathsson, 1936, 29 x 36 x 110 In. ....*illus*	5100.00
Table, Dining, French Provincial, Draw Top, 20th Century, 30 x 38 In.	2124.00
Table, Dining, French Provincial, Neoclassical, Fruitwood, Pewter Mounted, 31 x 39 In.	1560.00
Table, Dining, G. Nakashima, Walnut, Round, Rectangular Tapered Legs, 28 x 57 In.	7120.00
Table, Dining, G. Stickley, 5 Legs, Leaves, Cross Stretchers, 30 x 54 In.	7200.00
Table, Dining, G. Stickley, Circular, Plank Legs, Octagonal Apron, 29 x 59 In.	3600.00
Table, Dining, G. Stickley, Circular Top, Pedestal, Shaped Feet, 6 Leaves, 28 x 54 In.	3900.00
Table, Dining, G. Stickley, Split Pedestal, Trumpet Shape Stretchers, 6 Leaves, 29 x 54 In.	7200.00
Table, Dining, George III, Inlaid Mahogany, Demilune Ends, 29 x 54 In.	4320.00
Table, Dining, George III, Inlaid Mahogany, Round Top, Reeded Edge, Brass Paws, 37 x 77 In.	7200.00
Table, Dining, George III Style, Mahogany, Crossbanded Frieze, Leaves, 30 x 48 In.	999.00
Table, Dining, George III Style, Mahogany, Extension, Early 20th Century, 30 x 42 In.	708.00
Table, Dining, George III Style, Mahogany, Twin Pedestal, 30-In. Leaf, 1900s, 53 x 92 In.	1945.00
Table, Dining, Georgian, Mahogany, 20th Century, 30 x 46 x 102 In.	1196.00
Table, Dining, Mahogany, 2 Parts, D-Shape, Cylindrical Support, 30 x 54 x 94 In.	8365.00
Table, Dining, Milo Baughman, Rectangular, Stainless Steel Panel Supports, 28 x 78 In.	1880.00
Table, Dining, Neoclassical, Mahogany, Round Extension Top, Cluster Column, 30 x 52 In.	2645.00
Table, Dining, P. Evans, Bronze, Glass, 1972, 29 x 96 x 48 In.	8400.00
Table, Dining, Poplar, Oak, Lazy Susan Center, Turned Legs, 33 x 49 In. ....*illus*	1035.00
Table, Dining, Queen Anne Style, Mahogany, 3 Pedestals, Oval Top, 2 Leaves, 17 x 30 In.	6169.00
Table, Dining, Regency Style, Mahogany, Circular, Banded, Medallion, Leaves, 31 x 60 In.	10281.00
Table, Dining, Regency Style, Mahogany, Inlaid Greek Key Border, 4 Splayed Legs, 30 x 78 In.	2640.00
Table, Dining, Renaissance Revival, Oak, Pedestal, Winged Female Legs, Paw Feet, 30 x 58 In.	19975.00
Table, Dining, Renaissance Revival, Walnut, Leaf Carved Baluster Legs, 28 x 65 x 45 In.	325.00
Table, Dining, William & Mary, 3 10-In. Leaves, Shaped Legs, Early 1900s, 49 x 54 In.	176.00
Table, Directoire Style, Gilt Brass, Glass Top, H-Stretcher, Reeded Legs, 18 In., Pair	1680.00
Table, Dough, French Provincial, Fruitwood, Plank Top, Storage Bin, Splayed Legs, 29 x 54 In.	2040.00
Table, Drafting, Sheraton, Mahogany, Lift Top, Shelves, Frieze Drawer, 29 x 31 In. ...*illus*	13800.00
Table, Drawer, Red & Black Grained, 18 x 18 x 29 In.	403.00

Furniture, Table, Console, William IV, Mahogany, Marble Top, Metal Gallery, Ireland, 47 x 37 In.
$4800.00

Furniture, Table, Danish Modern, Convertible, c.1956, 21 x 47 x 24 In.
$1200.00

Furniture, Table, Dining, Drop Leaf, Cherry, 2 Sections, Spiral Turned Legs, 29 x 44 x 86 In.
$863.00

Furniture, Table, Dining, Folding, B. Mathsson, Karl Mathsson, 1936, 29 x 36 x 110 In.
$5100.00

Furniture, Table, Dining, Poplar, Oak, Lazy Susan Center, Turned Legs, 33 x 49 In.
$1035.00

Furniture, Table, Drafting, Sheraton, Mahogany, Lift Top, Shelves, Frieze Drawer, 29 x 31 In.
$13800.00

Furniture, Table, Dressing, Mustard Paint, Grapes & Leaves, Drawer, 34 x 34 In.
$1265.00

Furniture, Table, Drop Leaf, Gateleg, Oval, Rustic Hickory Co., For John Wanamaker, 30 x 36 In.
$2415.00

Gateleg Table

The gateleg table was first made during the seventeenth century. Usually the more legs on the gateleg table, the more expensive the table.

Furniture, Table, Empire, Figured Mahogany, Hinged Top, Mirror, 26 x 20 In. $518.00

Furniture, Table, Game, George I Style, Serpentine Top, Needlework, 29 x 35 In. $1416.00

Furniture, Table, Drop Leaf, Spindle Gatelegs, Old Hickory, 29 x 36 x 15 In. $1800.00

Furniture, Table, Federal, Mahogany, 2 Drop Leaves, 2 Drawers, Lower Bag Drawer, 28 x 18 In. $1495.00

Furniture, Table, Game, Regency, Tulipwood Veneer, Brass Inlay, Arched Feet, 29 x 36 x 18 In. $6600.00

Furniture, Table, Drop Leaf, Walnut, Burl, Oval Top, Scrolled Trestle Legs, 29 x 39 In. $441.00

Furniture, Table, Folding, Rosewood, Black Laminate Top, Dunbar, 22 x 26 x 23 In. $840.00

Furniture, Table, George III, Mahogany, Gallery, Turned Pedestal, Cabriole Legs, 29 x 20 In. $4800.00

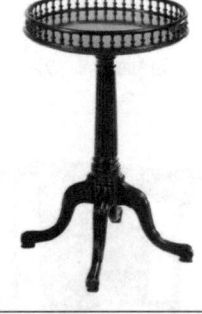

Furniture, Table, Drop Leaf, William & Mary Style, Gateleg, Shaped Skirt, Drawer, 29 x 46 In. $1093.00

Furniture, Table, Frederic Weinberg, Horse Shape, Wrought Iron, Glass Top, 41 x 33 In. $2160.00

Furniture, Table, Heywood-Wakefield, Wheat Finish, Stepped, Arched Legs, 23 x 16 x 30 In., Pair $294.00

Table, Dressing, Aesthetic Revival, Faux Bamboo, Mirror, 2 Drawers, c.1885, 63 x 40 In.	1293.00
Table, Dressing, Beau Brummel, Edwardian, Mahogany, Doors, Drawer, 34 x 21 In.	540.00
Table, Dressing, Chippendale Style, Mahogany, 4 Drawers, Shell, Columns, 35 x 38 In.	2415.00
Table, Dressing, Duncan Phyfe, Classical, Swivel Mirror, Lyre Shape Supports, 56 x 36 In. ...	3680.00
Table, Dressing, Edwardian, Chinoiserie, 3-Part Mirror, c.1900, 69 x 49 In.	1164.00
Table, Dressing, Figured Maple, 34 x 16 x 33 In.	288.00
Table, Dressing, Louis XVI, Giltwood, Kidney Shape, 3-Part Mirror, 72 x 51 In.	531.00
Table, Dressing, Louis XVI, Satinwood, Mahogany, Pull-Up Mirror, 3 Drawers, 28 x 18 In. ...	940.00
Table, Dressing, Mustard Paint, Grapes & Leaves, Drawer, 34 x 34 In. ....*illus*	1265.00
Table, Dressing, Neoclassical, Mahogany, Carved, Mirror, Drawers, Marble Top, 81 x 38 In. ..	1763.00
Table, Dressing, Painted, Scrolled Backboard, Stenciled Fruit, c.1830, 29 x 31 In.	1528.00
Table, Dressing, Poplar, Painted, Stenciled, c.1820, 43 x 34 x 19½ In.	1200.00
Table, Dressing, Queen Anne, Walnut, c.1750, 28 x 34 x 20 In.	15000.00
Table, Dressing, Queen Anne, Walnut, Carved, Boston, c.1760, 28¾ x 22 In.	3600.00
Table, Dressing, Queen Anne, Walnut, Figured, Trifid Feet, Mid 1700s, 29 x 36 In.	7480.00
Table, Dressing, Queen Anne, Walnut, Pine, 1 Over 3 Drawers, Pad Feet, 28 x 31 x 20 In. ...	2300.00
Table, Dressing, Rococo Revival, Rosewood, Marble Top, Arched Mirror, 71 x 48 In.	2880.00
Table, Dressing, Rosewood, Mirror, 3 Drawers, Chinese, 33 x 27½ x 15¾ In.	413.00
Table, Dressing, Sheraton, Mustard Ground, Flowers, Hourglass Shelf, Turned Leg, 35½ In. .	400.00
Table, Dressing, Sheraton, Paint Decorated, Mustard Ground, Flowers, Gallery, 35 x 36 In. ..	330.00
Table, Dressing, Tiger Maple, 3 Drawers, Apron, Cabriole Legs, Pad Feet, 26 x 24 In.	1045.00
Table, Drop Leaf, Birch, Mortise & Tenon, Tapered Legs, 28½ x 48 In.	288.00
Table, Drop Leaf, Cherry, Turned Legs, 28 x 39 In.	382.00
Table, Drop Leaf, Chippendale, Mahogany, 3-Board Top, Swing Legs, 28 x 51 x 47 In.	460.00
Table, Drop Leaf, Chippendale, Maple, 28 x 41¼ x 40½ In.	1410.00
Table, Drop Leaf, Chippendale, Pine, Maple, Rounded Leaves, Swing Legs, 16 x 48 In.	862.00
Table, Drop Leaf, Chippendale, Walnut, Marlboro Legs, X-Stretcher, 28 x 36½ In.	825.00
Table, Drop Leaf, Clover Leaf, Inlay, Sprays, Vine, Cabriole Legs, c.1920, 28 x 20 In.	403.00
Table, Drop Leaf, Corner, Georgian Style, Burled Walnut, Folding, 27 x 30 x 29¾ In.	1416.00
Table, Drop Leaf, Drawer, Turned Legs, Stretcher, 19 x 12 In.	117.00
Table, Drop Leaf, Empire, Mahogany, Grained Board, Ogee Style, 29 x 39 In.	230.00
Table, Drop Leaf, English Oak, 20 x 21 In.	275.00
Table, Drop Leaf, Federal, Cherry, Splayed Legs, 29 x 16 x 36 In.	705.00
Table, Drop Leaf, Federal, Mahogany, Pedestal, 29 x 42 x 49 In.	708.00
Table, Drop Leaf, Federal, Walnut, Drawer, Tapered Legs, Early 19th Century, 29 In.	1195.00
Table, Drop Leaf, Figured Maple, 2 Drawers, 19th Century, 27 In.	1305.00
Table, Drop Leaf, G. Stickley, Oak, Gateleg, Drawer, Signed, Red Decal, c.1910, 24 In.	2115.00
Table, Drop Leaf, Gateleg, Oval, Rustic Hickory Co., For John Wanamaker, 30 x 36 In. ..*illus*	2415.00
Table, Drop Leaf, Gateleg, Stained Oak, Oval Top, England, 20th Century, 29 x 41 In.	295.00
Table, Drop Leaf, Gateleg, William & Mary, Walnut, 2 Drawers, Apron, 28 x 57 x 48 In.	26400.00
Table, Drop Leaf, George III, Mahogany, Frieze Drawer, X-Stretcher, 26 x 26 x 35 In.	529.00
Table, Drop Leaf, George III, Mahogany, Round Top, 2 Leaves, Pad Feet, 27½ x 39 In.	1880.00
Table, Drop Leaf, Georgian, Mahogany, Cabriole Legs, Claw & Ball Feet, 27 x 42 x 56 In.	2585.00
Table, Drop Leaf, Green Paint, Flowers On Corner, Signed, Dated Aug. 11, 1948	175.00
Table, Drop Leaf, Mahogany, 38½ x 24½ x 28 In.	300.00
Table, Drop Leaf, Mahogany, Carved, Flowerhead, Leaf Carved Legs, 28 x 22 x 32 In.	1315.00
Table, Drop Leaf, Mahogany, D-Shape, Drawer, Reeded Legs, c.1820	900.00
Table, Drop Leaf, Mahogany, Tapered Legs, Claw & Ball Feet, 27 x 30¾ x 30¾ In.	590.00
Table, Drop Leaf, Queen Anne, Cherry, Chestnut, Turned Legs, 40 In., 15 In. Leaves	805.00
Table, Drop Leaf, Queen Anne, Cherry, Rounded Top & Leaves, Pad Feet, 42 x 41 In. Open ...	3737.00
Table, Drop Leaf, Queen Anne, Demilune, Shaped Skirt, Cabriole Legs, 1700s, 27 x 42 In. ...	2629.00
Table, Drop Leaf, Queen Anne, Mahogany, D-Shape Leaves, Tapered Legs, c.1770, 29 In.	2749.00
Table, Drop Leaf, Queen Anne, Mahogany, Oak, D-Shape Leaves, Cabriole Legs, 27 x 60 x 61 In. .	1955.00
Table, Drop Leaf, Queen Anne, Mahogany, Turned Legs, Pad Feet, 30 x 32 In.	805.00
Table, Drop Leaf, Queen Anne, Walnut, Pa., 28 x 40 In.	1100.00
Table, Drop Leaf, Queen Anne, Walnut, Veneer, Oak, 44 x 14 x 27¾ In.	863.00
Table, Drop Leaf, Regency, Mahogany, Drawers, Splayed Legs, 27½ x 18¾ x 37 In.	2585.00
Table, Drop Leaf, Regency, Rosewood Inlay, Frieze Drawer, Pedestal, 28¾ x 43 x 41 In.	529.00
Table, Drop Leaf, Regency Style, Yew, Drawers, Lyre Form Base, 28 x 60 x 24 In.	590.00
Table, Drop Leaf, Shaker, Cherry, Drawer, Butterfly Supports, Mt. Lebanon, c.1830, 26 x 34 In.	12550.00
Table, Drop Leaf, Shaker, Cherry, Maple, Tapered Legs, Canterbury, N.H., c.1825, 26 x 36 In. .	4212.00
Table, Drop Leaf, Shaker, Cherry, Pine, Drawer, Turned & Tapered Legs, c.1840, 28 x 45 In. ..	1404.00
Table, Drop Leaf, Sheraton, Cherry, Pine, Swing Leg, Beaded Apron, 30 x 45 x 59 In. Open ..	374.00
Table, Drop Leaf, Sheraton, Cherry, Swing Legs, Alligatored, Ohio, 29 x 47 x 22 In.	431.00
Table, Drop Leaf, Sheraton, Gateleg, Cherry, Pine, Turned Legs, 29 x 42½ In.	402.00
Table, Drop Leaf, Sheraton, Mahogany, Twist Carved Legs, Brass Feet, c.1800, 30 x 29 In. ...	998.00

F

Furniture, Table, Huang Huali, Cloud Brackets, Horse Hoof Legs, Chinese, 34 x 37 x 18 In.
$690.00

Furniture, Table, Majorelle, Inlaid Lake Scene, Flowers, c.1900, 31 x 23 In.
$3000.00

Furniture, Table, Oak, Free-form Scalloped Top, Lower Shelf, 30 x 24 x 24 In.
$708.00

Furniture, Table, Pembroke, 2 Shaped Leaves, Drawer, Square Legs, 26 x 33 In.
$863.00

Furniture, Table, Pembroke, Federal, Figured Mahogany, Inlay, R.I., c.1800, 27 x 32 x 32 In.
$3000.00

Furniture, Table, Pembroke, George III, Satinwood, Crossbanded, Marquetry, 28 x 30 In.
$3600.00

Furniture, Table, Pembroke, Sheraton, Mahogany, String Inlay, England, 27 x 32 x 19 In.
$725.00

Furniture, Table, Picnic, Pine, Painted, Dovetailed, Table & 2 Chairs, 25 x 55 x 18 In.
$690.00

Table, Drop Leaf, Spindle Gatelegs, Old Hickory, 29 x 36 x 15 In. ....*illus*	1800.00
Table, Drop Leaf, Tavern, Queen Anne Style, Pine, D-Shape Leaves, Apron, 29 x 81 x 52 In. ..	940.00
Table, Drop Leaf, Walnut, 2 Drawers, Ceramic Knobs, c.1850, 29 x 16½ x 23 In.	147.00
Table, Drop Leaf, Walnut, Burl, Oval Top, Scrolled Trestle Legs, 29 x 39 In. ....*illus*	441.00
Table, Drop Leaf, Walnut, Maple Front Drawers, Barley Twist Legs, 28 x 24 x 38 In.	382.00
Table, Drop Leaf, Walnut, Red Wash, Drawer, Turned Legs, Tulip Feet, 29 x 42 x 36 In.	660.00
Table, Drop Leaf, Walnut, Square Tapered Legs, 28 x 37 x 36 In.	660.00
Table, Drop Leaf, Wegner, Teak, Brass, 1950s, 27½ x 93½ x 34 In.	3900.00
Table, Drop Leaf, William & Mary, Oak, D-Shape Leaves, Stretchers, 29 x 28 x 36 In.	1645.00
Table, Drop Leaf, William & Mary Style, Gateleg, Shaped Skirt, Drawer, 29 x 46 In. ....*illus*	1093.00
Table, Duncan Phyfe Style, Mahogany, D-Shape, Tilt Top, Brass Caps, 38 x 47 x 22 In.	575.00
Table, Ebonized, Gilt, Painted Flower Bouquet, 21½ x 21¾ In.	165.00
Table, Edwardian, Adam Style, Satinwood, Painted, Ribbons, Vines, Medallion, 29 x 24 In. ..	2040.00
Table, Edwardian, Mahogany, Painted, Early 20th Century, 22 In.	1305.00
Table, Edwardian, Walnut, Banded, Square, Lower Shelf, Turned Supports, 23 x 18 In., Pair .	1880.00
Table, Edwardian Style, Mahogany, Painted, Shaped Top, Piecrust Edge, 27½ x 33 In.	374.00
Table, Eero Saarinen, Knoll, Wood Laminate Top, Cast Metal Base, c.1957, 20½ x 16 In.	353.00
Table, Elm, Black Lacquered, Chinese, 18¼ x 44 x 19 In.	354.00
Table, Elm, Carved, Italian Style, Rectangular Top, Scrolled Supports, 30 x 49 In.	1880.00
Table, Elm, Chinese, 19½ x 22 x 22½ In.	153.00
Table, Elm, Chinese, Ming Dynasty, 33¼ x 37 x 16½ In.	708.00
Table, Elm, Green Stone, Chinese, 31½ x 37½ x 16½ In.	649.00
Table, Elm, Rectangular Top, Drawer, Cabriole Scroll Legs, Chinese, 17 x 35 In.	283.00
Table, Elm, Red Lacquered, Chinese, 31 x 51 x 13 In.	885.00
Table, Emile Galle, 2 Shelves, Marquetry, Flowers, c.1900	1995.00
Table, Empire, Figured Mahogany, Hinged Top, Mirror, 26 x 20 In. ....*illus*	518.00
Table, Empire, Mahogany, Circular, Accordion Action Extension, Carved Ends, 29 x 46 In. ...	1793.00
Table, Empire, Round, Mahogany, Lyre Supports, Brass Mounts, c.1840, 29 x 33 In.	3700.00
Table, Empire Style, Bird's-Eye Maple, Bronze Capped Feet, 26 x 30 x 22 In.	940.00
Table, Empire Style, Fruitwood, Octagonal, 3-Sided, Ball Feet, 23 x 28 In.	176.00
Table, Empire Style, Polychrome, Marble Top, Crossover Legs, 17½ x 39 In.	822.00
Table, English Provincial Queen Anne, Fruitwood, Pierced Gallery, Shelf, 30 x 20 In., Pair ..	1880.00
Table, Farm, Painted, Apple Green, 2 Drawers, 64 x 27 x 31 In.	1898.00
Table, Farm, Provincial, Oak, Planked Top, Frieze Drawer, Tapered Legs, 30 x 63 In.	1320.00
Table, Farm, Walnut, Pine Top, 3-Board Top, 2 Drawers, Turned Legs, 30 x 50 In.	1760.00
Table, Federal, Cherry, Overhanging Top, Beaded Edge, Drawer, c.1800, 28 x 20 In.	4113.00
Table, Federal, Mahogany, 2 Drop Leaves, 2 Drawers, Lower Bag Drawer, 28 x 18 In. ...*illus*	1495.00
Table, Federal, Mahogany, Birdcage, Tilt Top, Turned Support, Claw & Ball Feet, 29 In.	54970.00
Table, Federal, Mahogany, Ebony Inlay, Drop Leaves, c.1815, 28 x 25 In.	3910.00
Table, Federal, Mahogany, Graduated Drawers, Turreted Spiral Carved Legs, 29 x 19 In.	1998.00
Table, Federal, Mahogany Inlay, Hinged, Serpentine Top, Bird's-Eye Maple, 30 x 35 In.	5175.00
Table, Federal, Pembroke, Cherry, Drawer, Cross Stretcher, 18 x 34½ x 27 In.	1207.00
Table, Federal, Pembroke, Cherry, Pine, Serpentine Top, Drawer, Inlay, 36 x 28 In.	920.00
Table, Federal, Pembroke, Figured Maple, New England, c.1810, 29 x 20 In.	2160.00
Table, Federal, Tiger Maple, Rounded Drop Leaves, Drawer, Tapered Legs, 28 x 18 In.	1645.00
Table, Federal Revival, Inlaid Mahogany, Galleried Oval Top, 1900s, 27 x 26 In., Pair	360.00
Table, Finn Juhl, Rosewood, Oval Top, Tapered Legs, 2 Leaves, 118 x 28½ x 55 In.	9560.00
Table, Finn Juhl, Teak, 3 Corner, Cylindrical Tapered Legs, 20 x 21 x 19¾ In.	120.00
Table, Finn Juhl, Teak, Tray Top, Molded Legs, Apron Stretcher, 15 x 23½ x 16½ In.	448.00
Table, Flemish, Oak, Carved, Trestle Base, Lion Masks, Dolphin Base, 1800s, 31 x 40 In.	590.00
Table, Folding, Rosewood, Black Laminate Top, Dunbar, 22 x 26 x 23 In. ....*illus*	840.00
Table, Frederic Weinberg, Horse Shape, Wrought Iron, Glass Top, 41 x 33 In. ....*illus*	2160.00
Table, French Provincial, Canted Triangular Top, Leather Inset Surface, 26 x 24 In.	1140.00
Table, French Provincial, Farm, Elm, Plank Top, H-Stretcher, 30 x 88 x 31 In.	2400.00
Table, French Provincial, Farm, Elm, Plank Top, Trestle Base, 29 x 66 x 34 In.	1020.00
Table, French Provincial, Fruitwood, Farm, End Drawers, Square Legs, 30 x 50 In.	117.00
Table, French Provincial, Fruitwood, Raised Edge, Frieze Drawer, Square Legs, 26 x 20 x 14 In. ..	660.00
Table, French Provincial, Fruitwood, Turreted Corners, Cabriole Legs, 25 x 23 In.	1440.00
Table, French Transitional, Gilt Metal Mount, Mahogany, Round, Early 1900s, 29 x 24 In. ..	1180.00
Table, Fruitwood, Tile Top, Stretchers, Continental, 20th Century, 17 x 18½ In.	708.00
Table, G. Nakashima, Walnut, Cone Shape, 2-Board, Butterfly, Drawing, Signed, 35 x 60 In. .	31070.00
Table, G. Nakashima, Walnut, Cone Shape, Cross-Legged, 4-Sided Top, 21 x 26 x 26 In.	15530.00
Table, G. Nakashima, Walnut, Terminal Support, Flared Legs, 19 x 29 x 26 In., Pair	13145.00
Table, G. Stickley, Tea, Shaped Legs, Flower-Form Top, Lower Shelf, 23¼ x 19 In.	8400.00
Table, G. Stickley, Trestle, Bungalow, Mortised Lower Shelf, c.1902, 38 x 36 In.	4500.00
Table, Game, Anglo-Indian, Bamboo, Lacquered, Leather Inset, Stretcher, 31 x 25 In.	360.00

Table, Game, Art Deco Style, Mahogany, Inlay, Reeded Legs, Brass Cuffs, 29 x 23 x 32 In. 748.00
Table, Game, Bagatelle, Mahogany, Felt Lined, Ivory Counters, Balls, Cues, 39 x 48 x 24 In. . . 823.00
Table, Game, Black Lacquer, Gold Flowers, Scrolls, Turned Pedestal, Tripod Base, 31 x 25 In. 1175.00
Table, Game, Charles X, Mahogany, Writing Surface, Drawer, 28½ x 21 x 15 In. 1175.00
Table, Game, Chippendale, George III, Mahogany, Flip Top, c.1780, 29 x 30 In. 9488.00
Table, Game, Chippendale, Mahogany, Cock-Beaded Drawer, Label, C.L. Prickett, 29 x 35 In. . 890.00
Table, Game, Chippendale, Mahogany, Inlaid Fans, Banding, Cabriole Legs, 29 x 31 In. 1840.00
Table, Game, Empire, Mahogany, Flip Top, Columnar Pedestal, Plinth Base, 28 x 36 In. 708.00
Table, Game, Federal, Flame Birch, Mahogany, Inlay, New England, c.1800, 30 x 35 In. 3600.00
Table, Game, Federal, Inlaid Mahogany, Flip Top, Eagle & Serpent, c.1810, 30 x 36 In. 2070.00
Table, Game, Federal, Mahogany, c.1795, 35 In. 3600.00
Table, Game, Federal, Mahogany, Flip Top, Deep Apron, Peg Feet, Early 1800s, 27 x 36 In. . . . 826.00
Table, Game, Federal, Mahogany, Inlay, Figured, Mass., c.1800, 29¼ x 36 In. 1440.00
Table, Game, Federal, Mahogany, Inlay, Flip Top, String Inlay, 30 x 36 In. 1058.00
Table, Game, Flip Top, Maple, Pine, Breadboard Ends, Drawer, 19 x 37 x 29½ In. 3450.00
Table, Game, George I Style, Serpentine Top, Needlework, 29 x 35 In. . . . . *illus* 1416.00
Table, Game, George II, Mahogany, Demilune, 28¾ x 29¾ x 14 In. 4200.00
Table, Game, George II, Mahogany, Veneered, Demilune, c.1760, 29 x 28½ x 15 In. 4800.00
Table, Game, Georgian, Figured Mahogany, Inlay, Serpentine Flip Top, 30 x 36 In. 529.00
Table, Game, Heywood-Wakefield, Flip Top, Wheat Finish, 30 x 32 x 16 In. 294.00
Table, Game, Inlaid Designs, Italy, c.1880, 31½ x 35 In. 7250.00
Table, Game, Lacquer, Wood, Carved, Round Top, Checkerboard, Birdcage, 33 x 25 In. 940.00
Table, Game, Mahogany, Carved, Felt, Reeded Columns, Brass, c.1815, 30 x 36 In., Pair 27485.00
Table, Game, Mahogany, Fruitwood Marquetry, Flip Top, Felt, Dutch, 31 x 40 In. 499.00
Table, Game, Neoclassical, Carved, Figured, N.Y., c.1815, 29½ x 36 In., Pair 4800.00
Table, Game, Queen Anne, Burl Walnut, Scalloped Top, Cabriole Legs, Pad Feet, 29 x 33 In. . 489.00
Table, Game, Queen Anne, Oak, Circular Legs, Pad Feet, 28 x 13¼ In. 881.00
Table, Game, Rectangular, Rounded Corners, Faux Bamboo Legs, 29 x 36 x 18 In. 660.00
Table, Game, Regency, Mahogany, Demilune Top, Turned Tapered Legs, Peg Feet, 29 x 36 In. 998.00
Table, Game, Regency, Satinwood, Mahogany, Ebonized Edge, c.1810, 29 x 36 x 18 In. 2115.00
Table, Game, Regency, Tulipwood Veneer, Brass Inlay, Arched Feet, 29 x 36 x 18 In. . . . .*illus* 6600.00
Table, Game, Rococo Revival, Walnut, Flip Top, Swivel, Storage Well, 1800s, 34 x 18 In. 9000.00
Table, Game, Roulette, Felt Top, Claw Foot Legs, 1900s, Full Size 1770.00
Table, Game, Spanish Style, Oak, 3 Marble Panels, Iron Stretchers, 29 x 99 x 39 In. 1410.00
Table, Game, William IV, Mahogany, Shaped Top, Rose-Carved Frieze, Pedestal, 29 x 34 In. . . 2232.00
Table, Gateleg, Drop Leaf, Incised Floral Decoration, Triangular Top, 27 x 14 In. 153.00
Table, Gateleg, Walnut, Foldover, Folding Leaf, Ring & Baluster Legs, 1700s, 28 x 44 In. 518.00
Table, Gateleg, William & Mary, Maple, Oval, Turned Ring Legs, 1785, 27 x 15 x 43 In. 2500.00
Table, George III, Mahogany, 2 Drawers, Spade Feet, Late 18th Century, 36 x 66 In. 2685.00
Table, George III, Mahogany, Bowed Top & Frieze, Drawer, Tapered Legs, 30 x 38 In. 1410.00
Table, George III, Mahogany, Bowfront, Frieze Drawer, 28½ x 34 x 20½ In. 558.00
Table, George III, Mahogany, Carved, Octagonal Top, Tooled Leather, c.1780, 31 x 51 In. 7050.00
Table, George III, Mahogany, Carved Blind Fret, 18th Century, 32½ x 51 x 24 In. 7638.00
Table, George III, Mahogany, Demilune, Frieze, Spade Feet, 1800s, 31 x 40 In., Pair 1320.00
Table, George III, Mahogany, Gallery, Turned Pedestal, Cabriole Legs, 29 x 20 In. . . . . . .*illus* 4800.00
Table, George III, Mahogany, Inlay, Drop Leaves, Drawers, c.1790, 28 x 66 In. 3120.00
Table, George III, Mahogany, Tripod, Tilt Top, Birdcage Supports, Baluster, 29 x 32 x 26 In. . 1175.00
Table, George III, Oak, Tripod, Round Top, Piecrust Edge, Birdcage Support, 31 x 32 In. 720.00
Table, George III Manner, Inlaid Mahogany, 47 In. 860.00
Table, George III Style, Mahogany, Metal Gallery, Marble Slab, Tripod Base, 26 x 24 In. 201.00
Table, George III Style, Mahogany, Pink & Green Marble Top, Scrolled Drawer, 32 x 36 In. . . 587.00
Table, Georgian, Rosewood, Turned Legs, Stretcher, 2 Drawers, Early 1900s, 41 In. 693.00
Table, Georgian, Walnut, Triangular, Drop Leaf, Pad Feet, Mid 18th Century, 40½ In. 520.00
Table, Georgian, Yew, Drop Leaf Top, Banded Edge, 1800s, 28 x 36 In. 1057.00
Table, Georgian Style, Mahogany, Carved, Oval, Thumbnail Edge, c.1890, 29 x 49 In. 1380.00
Table, Georgian Style, Mahogany, Tilt Top, Piecrust, Spiral Pedestal, 1700s, 28 x 28 In. 1416.00
Table, Georgian Style, Walnut, Carved, Burl Veneer, Shaped Top, Cabriole Legs, 31 x 42 x 19 In. . 1880.00
Table, Giltwood, Carved, Round, White & Gray Marble Insert, Continental, 33 x 44 In. 1955.00
Table, Glass Top, Wrought Iron Base, Branches, Lemons In Relief, Italy, 24 x 20 In. 558.00
Table, Gueridon, Directoire Style, Gilt Brass, Mahogany, Marble Top, 30 x 15 In., Pair 2468.00
Table, Gueridon, Neoclassical, Gilt Brass, Verde Antico, 3-Part Base, 27 x 21 In., Pair 2938.00
Table, Hand Pedestal, Surrealist, Wood, Glass Top, Costa Achillopoulo, 1934 . . . . 43964.00
Table, Harden, 5 Slats, Shelf, Mortised Legs, Square, 26 x 18½ In. 2280.00
Table, Hardwood, Pierce Screen Center, Black Lacquer Frame, Chinese, 18 x 45 In. 978.00
Table, Harvest, Drop Leaf, 2-Board Top, Rounded Corners, Red Paint, 28 x 72 x 28 In. 805.00
Table, Harvest, Drop Leaf, Pine, c.1850, 30 x 85 x 45 In. 588.00

Furniture, Table, Pine, Tilt Top, Oval, Painted, Hudson River Valley, 18th Century, 27 x 52 In. $1955.00

Furniture, Table, Poplar, Painted, 2-Board Top, Drawer, Tapered Square Legs, 28 x 36 x 28 In. $345.00

Furniture, Table, Regency, Mahogany, Drop Leaf Ends, 2 Drawers, 28 x 36 x 28 In. $1093.00

Furniture, Table, Renaissance Revival, Marquetry, Washington, 1876 Centennial, 28 x 27 In. $4183.00

F

Furniture, Table, Sewing, Regency, Satinwood, Inlay, Painted Children, Lift Top, 1800s, 30 x 22 In. $2588.00

Furniture, Table, Tavern, Mixed Woods, Box Stretchers, Ring & Baluster Legs, 25 x 33 In. $633.00

Furniture, Table, Tea, Tilt Top, Queen Anne, Mahogany, Dish Top, Birdcage, Pad Feet, 28 x 32 In. $3450.00

Furniture, Table, Thulin, Oak, Carved Arts & Crafts Designs, Drawer, Square Legs, 26 x 40 In. $1955.00

Table, Harvest, Pine, Sawbuck, 30 x 95½ x 35 In.	3819.00
Table, Harvest, Pine & Poplar, 4 Vase & Ring Turned Legs, 1830, 29 x 67 x 26 In.	1655.00
Table, Harvest, Softwood, Shaped Trestle Base, Mid Stretcher, Marked, HES, 91 x 34 In.	1870.00
Table, Harvest, Yellow Pine, 3-Board Top, Tapered Square Legs, 1800s, 29 x 41½ In.	345.00
Table, Hepplewhite, Mahogany, Semicircular, 53½ x 26 x 19½ In., Pair	863.00
Table, Heywood-Wakefield, Wheat Finish, Stepped, Arched Legs, 23 x 16 x 30 In., Pair . . *illus*	294.00
Table, Huang Huali, Cloud Brackets, Horse Hoof Legs, Chinese, 34 x 37 x 18 In. . . . . . . *illus*	690.00
Table, Hunt, Mahogany, Folding, Shaped Top, X-Shaped Stretcher, Chamfered Legs, 27 x 29 In. . .	470.00
Table, Hunt, Oak, Carved Skirt, Animal Form Legs, Black Forest, c.1900, 30 x 50 x 68 In.	8225.00
Table, I. Noguchi, Black Laminate Top, Round, Metal Wirework Base, Knoll, 38⅝ In.	1528.00
Table, Ironstone Platter Top, Garden Scene, Stretcher, 18 x 15 In.	819.00
Table, Italian Baroque, Walnut, Drawer, Incised Carving, Stretcher, 1700s, 24 x 33 In.	1955.00
Table, Kitchen, Cypress Wood, Louisiana, 3-Board Top, Blue Paint, 1885, 27 x 59 x 34 In. . . .	1465.00
Table, Kittinger, Contemporary Regency, Oval, Mahogany, Tray Top, Stretcher, 18 x 39 In. . . .	266.00
Table, L. & J.G. Stickley, 25 Tile Top, Sea Green, 4 Square Legs, 18 x 38 In.	825.00
Table, L. & J.G. Stickley, Flared Cross Stretchers, Square Shelf, 29 x 24 x 24 In.	1080.00
Table, L. & J.G. Stickley, Oak, Cut Corners, Square Legs, Angled Lower Shelf, 29 x 36 In.	441.00
Table, L. & J.G. Stickley, Oak, Drop Leaf, No. 553, 30 x 41¾ In.	4560.00
Table, L. & J.G. Stickley, Trestle, Lower Shelf, Mortised Tenons, 29½ x 72 In.	3600.00
Table, Lacquered, Matted Hardwood, Stainless Top, Folding Top, 16 x 50 In.	2468.00
Table, Late Federal, Mahogany, Drop Leaf, Drawer, Peg Feet, 1900s, 30 x 40 In.	354.00
Table, Lazy Susan, Yellow Pine, Swiveling Top, Tapered Square Legs, 1900s, 34 x 54 In.	1495.00
Table, Leather Tray Top, Patinated Metal Stand, 19 x 36¾ x 21 In.	130.00
Table, Library, American Classical, Figured Mahogany, Drop Leaf, Paw Feet, 29 x 24 In.	1955.00
Table, Library, Chinese Chippendale, Mahogany, Leather Top, Fret Carving, 31 x 48 x 24 In. .	1265.00
Table, Library, English Oak, Carved, Gadrooned Frieze, Lion Heads, 32 x 46 x 30 In.	6000.00
Table, Library, G. Stickley, 2 Drawers, Interior Corbels, Lower Shelf, 30 x 42 In.	1320.00
Table, Library, G. Stickley, 2 Drawers, Oval Iron Pulls, 30 x 48 x 30 In.	1920.00
Table, Library, G. Stickley, 2 Drawers, Wooden Knobs, V Shape Apron, 30 x 36 x 24 In.	10200.00
Table, Library, G. Stickley, Cross Stretchers, Mortised, Hexagonal, 29½ x 48 In.	5100.00
Table, Library, Henri IV Style, Mahogany, Carved Scrolls, Reeded Column Ends, 31 x 49 In. . .	1880.00
Table, Library, Jacobean, 2 Drawers, Faux Painted Marble Top, Spiral Legs, 30 x 48 In.	748.00
Table, Library, Late Georgian, Mahogany, Raised Stretcher, Leather Inset Top, 47 x 33 In. . . .	2807.00
Table, Library, Limbert, Chalet Style, Wood Knobs, Lower Shelf, 29 x 48 In.	510.00
Table, Library, Limbert, Ebon-Oak, Square Copper Knobs, 29½ x 42 x 26 In.	2760.00
Table, Library, Limbert, Oak, 2 Drawers, Corbel Supports, c.1912, 29 x 47 x 32 In.	940.00
Table, Library, Limbert, Oak, Model No. 164, 2 Drawer, Lower Shelf, c.1912, 29 x 43 In.	940.00
Table, Library, Regency, Rosewood, Leather Writing, Paneled, 28¾ x 48 x 26 In.	1880.00
Table, Library, Renaissance Revival, Burled Walnut, Canted Corners, Leather Top, 30 x 47 In. .	4320.00
Table, Library, Renaissance Revival, Mahogany, Acanthus Leaf Carved, 31 x 66 x 30 In.	118.00
Table, Library, Renaissance Revival, Marquetry, Carved, Late 1800s, 30 x 40 In.	7200.00
Table, Library, Renaissance Revival, Walnut, Carved, Fluted Frieze, Drawers, 32 x 59 In.	2820.00
Table, Library, Rosewood, Leather, Round, Scrolled Feet, 1830, 28 x 47 In.	2350.00
Table, Library, Stickley Bros., Drawer, Oak Pulls, Mortised Stretchers, 30 x 44 In.	720.00
Table, Library, Wicker, Oak Top, Twin Arched Supports, c.1920s, 30 x 52 In.	1250.00
Table, Library, William IV, Rosewood, Faux Mahogany, Brass Inlay, 30 x 58 x 26 In.	3900.00
Table, Lifetime, Puritan Line, Gateleg, Extension, Arched Lower Stretcher, 31 x 48 In.	1680.00
Table, Limbert, Ebon-Oak, Canted Legs, Cross Stretchers, Leaves, 29½ x 54 In.	2640.00
Table, Limbert, Oval, Canted Cutout Sides, 29½ x 45 x 29½ In.	3240.00
Table, Lodge, Antler, Oak Top, Crossed Legs, Entwined Antlers, 30 x 45 x 31 In.	1265.00
Table, Louis XIII, Oak, Hand Carved Bird, Glass Top, c.1900, 28 x 41 In.	2400.00
Table, Louis XIII, Walnut, Turned Supports, Stretcher, c.1870, 30½ x 41 In.	3500.00
Table, Louis XIII, Walnut, Twist Supports, Stretcher, France, c.1850, 29 x 59 In.	6000.00
Table, Louis XV, Giltwood, Shaped Rose Marble Top, Carved Apron, 1700s, 28 In.	520.00
Table, Louis XV, Mahogany, Ormolu Mounted, Raised Edge, Drawer, Slide, 26 x 18 In.	4320.00
Table, Louis XV Style, Fruitwood, Gilt Metal, Mottled Slab, France, 34 x 26 x 19 In.	413.00
Table, Louis XV Style, Fruitwood, Inset Leather Top, Shaped Frieze, Drawer, 28 x 37 In.	1320.00
Table, Louis XV Style, Inlaid Satinwood, Late 19th Century, 12½ x 27 In.	1740.00
Table, Louis XV Style, Inlaid Veneer, Gilt Metal Mounted, 20th Century, 29 x 24 In.	224.00
Table, Louis XV Style, Inlay, Mixed Wood, 28 x 16¾ In.	708.00
Table, Louis XV Style, Marquetry, Gilt Metal Mounted, 2 Tiers, 1900s, 28 x 24 In.	472.00
Table, Louis XV Style, Marquetry, Marble Top, 29 x 16 x 11 In., Pair	4406.00
Table, Louis XV Style, Tulipwood, Kingwood, Drawers, Inlaid Flowers, 29 x 18 In.	8400.00
Table, Louis XVI, Mahogany, Marble Shelves, Brass Handles, Casters, 32 x 22 x 14 In.	4200.00
Table, Louis XVI, Mahogany, Marquetry, Cornucopia, Tambour Door, Drawer, 27 x 142 In. . .	2880.00
Table, Louis XVI Style, Giltwood, Carved, Ribbon Frieze, Reed Legs, Late 1800s, 29 x 27 In. . .	1351.00

Table, Louis XVI Style, Kingwood, Satinwood, Brass Gallery, 29½ x 27½ x 15 In.	4113.00
Table, Louis XVI Style, Mahogany, Late 19th Century, 25½ In.	768.00
Table, Louis XVI Style, Mahogany, Round, Piecrust Inlay, Pierced X-Form Stretcher, 28 In.	1800.00
Table, Louis XVIII, Figured Kingwood, Chestnut, Drop Leaves, Leather Top, 29 x 50 In.	1997.00
Table, Mahogany, 2 Drawer, Inlaid Top, Tapered Legs, Early 19th Century, 29 x 20 In.	418.00
Table, Mahogany, Bronze Mounted, Inset Tooled Leather, Carved, Drawers, 31 x 41 In.	3643.00
Table, Mahogany, Claw & Ball Feet, c.1930, 27 x 18 x 18 In.	176.00
Table, Mahogany, Drop Leaf, Painted Gilt Apron, Octagonal Tapered Shaft, 28 x 53 In.	880.00
Table, Mahogany, Mother-Of-Pearl & Brass Inlay, Birds, Butterflies, Flowers, Octagonal, 23 In.	470.00
Table, Majorelle, Inlaid Lake Scene, Flowers, c.1900, 31 x 23 In. ....*illus*	3000.00
Table, Marble Top, Rectangular Top, Quadruped Base, 19th Century, 19 x 14 In.	92.00
Table, Mariani, Figural, Nude Woman, Arms Holding Glass Top, Art Deco, 23 x 56 In.	1530.00
Table, Mies Van Der Rohe, Smoked Glass Top, Round, Tubular Steel Frame 19½ x 27 In.	235.00
Table, Mixed Wood, Inlay, Starburst, Tripod Base, Octagonal, Continental, 30 x 28 x 28 In.	826.00
Table, Mixed Wood, Oval Scrub Top, Apron, Splay Legs, Red Paint Base, 25 x 33 x 25 In.	1155.00
Table, Mixed Wood, Shaped & Cutout Corners, Tapered Legs, 27 x 36 x 25 In.	2750.00
Table, Mixing, Poplar, Gray Marble Over 2-Board Top, 1800s, 32 x 24 In.	431.00
Table, Molded Edge, Brass Inset Trivet, Baker Furniture, 18 x 18½ x 10½ In.	115.00
Table, Mongolian, Wood, Polychrome, 2 Drawers, 2 Doors, 18th Century, 19 x 56 In.	590.00
Table, Moorish, Hardwood, Octagonal, Arched Legs, Mother-Of-Pearl, 25 x 18 In., Pair	1320.00
Table, Napoleon III, Brass Inlay, Ormolu, Mounted, Ebonized, Marble Top, 23 x 23 In.	2820.00
Table, Napoleon III, Mahogany, Ormolu Mounted, Marble Top, Paw Feet, 30 x 14 In.	587.00
Table, Neoclassical, Giltwood, Figured Mahogany, Ebony, Phila., c.1820, 29 x 42 In.	19200.00
Table, Neoclassical, Inlaid Marble, Gilt, Round Top, Black Roundel, 32½ x 44 In.	6756.00
Table, Neoclassical, Mahogany, 2 Pedestal, Acanthus Carved, Paw Feet, 29 x 54 In.	2115.00
Table, Neoclassical, Mahogany, Carved, c.1835, 98 x 52 In.	4994.00
Table, Neoclassical, Mahogany, Drop Leaf, Drawer, 28 x 39 In.	230.00
Table, Neoclassical, Mahogany, Figured, Drop Leaves, Acanthus Carved Base, 29 x 41 In.	1035.00
Table, Neoclassical, Mahogany, Molded Drawer, Paw Feet, c.1830, 34 x 23 In.	1880.00
Table, Neoclassical, Mahogany, Veneer, Carved, Shaped Leaves, Drawers, c.1820, 28 x 39 In.	1175.00
Table, Neoclassical, Mahogany Inlay, Round Top, Radiating Panels, c.1825, 30 x 36 In.	2700.00
Table, Neoclassical, Rosewood, Round, Paneled Standard, Concave Tripod Base, 29 x 21 In.	1080.00
Table, Neoclassical, Stick Lamp, Reeded Column, Trefoil Onyx, Scrolling, 63 In.	360.00
Table, Neoclassical Giltwood, Mahogany, Drop Leaf, Frieze, Fluted Column, 30 x 43 In.	575.00
Table, Neoclassical Revival, Mahogany, 8 Leaves, Column Pedestal, 30 x 48 In.	1800.00
Table, Nesting, Edwardian, Mahogany, Oval Inset Panel, Splayed Feet, c.1900, 27 In., 4 Piece	1057.00
Table, Nutting, Colonial Style, Medial Stretcher, Trestle Base, 19 x 13 In.	518.00
Table, Oak, Free-Form Scalloped Top, Lower Shelf, 30 x 24 x 24 In. ....*illus*	708.00
Table, Oak, Limbert, No. 146, Oval Top, Corbel Supports, Median Shelf, 30 x 30 In.	1528.00
Table, Oak, Split Pedestal, Claw Feet, Round, Victorian, 30 x 45 In.	147.00
Table, Paul Laszio, Black, Crisscross Stretcher, 1947, 15 x 26 x 24 In.	840.00
Table, Pedestal, 2 Tiers, Inlaid Mahogany, Raised Edge, 20th Century, 30 x 24 In., Pair	326.00
Table, Pedestal, Eero Saarinen, White Top, c.1956, 20½ x 20 In.	660.00
Table, Pedestal, Georgian, Mahogany, Crossbanded, Drop Leaf, Drawer, Early 1800s, 33 x 19 In.	572.00
Table, Pembroke, 2 Shaped Leaves, Drawer, Square Legs, 26 x 33 In. ....*illus*	863.00
Table, Pembroke, Chippendale, Mahogany, Poplar, Oak, Drawer, Dovetailed, 29 x 32 In.	3450.00
Table, Pembroke, Federal, Cherry, Rectangular, Drawer, Tapered Legs, 28 x 18 x 36 In.	299.00
Table, Pembroke, Federal, Figured Mahogany, Inlay, R.I., c.1800, 27 x 32 x 32 In. .....*illus*	3000.00
Table, Pembroke, Federal, Mahogany, Beaded Drawers, Reeded, Tapered, Legs, c.1800, 28 In.	837.00
Table, Pembroke, Federal, Mahogany, Oval Top, Cuff Inlay, 29 x 36 In.	8050.00
Table, Pembroke, George III, Satinwood, Crossbanded, Marquetry, 28 x 30 In. ....*illus*	3600.00
Table, Pembroke, George III Style, Satinwood, Mahogany, 28 x 32 x 20 In.	767.00
Table, Pembroke, Hepplewhite, Cherry, Straight Apron, Tapered Legs, Stretcher, 34 x 53 In.	863.00
Table, Pembroke, Hepplewhite, Walnut, Drawer, Tapered Legs, 29¾ x 32¾ In.	303.00
Table, Pembroke, Mahogany, Butterfly, Bowed Top, Shaped Leaves, 29 x 24 In.	430.00
Table, Pembroke, Mahogany, Pine, Dovetail Drawer & 1 False, String Inlay, 30 x 36 x 20 In.	460.00
Table, Pembroke, Sheraton, Mahogany, Scalloped, Drawer, 30 x 20 In.	5206.00
Table, Pembroke, Sheraton, Mahogany, String Inlay, England, 27 x 32 x 19 In. ....*illus*	725.00
Table, Pembroke, Sheraton, Oak, Hinged, Turned Legs, Tapered Feet, 28 In.	460.00
Table, Pembroke, Sheraton, Walnut, Poplar, Drawer, Rope Turned Legs, 28 x 36 x 18 In.	345.00
Table, Picnic, Pine, Painted, Dovetailed, Table & 2 Chairs, 25 x 55 x 18 In. ....*illus*	690.00
Table, Pier, Grain Painted, Gilt Stenciled, Marble Top, 30¾ x 36¾ x 18½ In.	2880.00
Table, Pier, Mahogany, Carved, Gadroon Edge, Ogee Apron, Flower, Acanthus, 34 In.	2629.00
Table, Pier, Mahogany, Gilt Stenciled, Bronze Mount, Marble Top, 37 x 41 x 18 In.	5400.00
Table, Pier, Neoclassical, Mahogany, Carrara Marble Top, Turned Columns, 31 x 42 In.	2233.00
Table, Pier, Neoclassical, Mahogany, Gilt Stenciled, Marble Top, Phila., c.1820, 39 x 42 In.	54000.00

Furniture, Table, Tray, Papier-Mache, Painted Flowers, Faux Bamboo Stand, 20 x 32 In.
$944.00

Furniture, Table, Wicker, Paint, Glass Top, 2 Tiers, 29 x 36 x 24 In.
$173.00

Furniture, Table, William & Mary, Gateleg, Drawer, Philadelphia, c.1720, 29 x 15 x 36 In.
$4500.00

Furniture, Table, Yellow Pine, Paint, 2-Board Top, 2 Drawers, Southern, 29 x 26 x 32 In.
$489.00

F

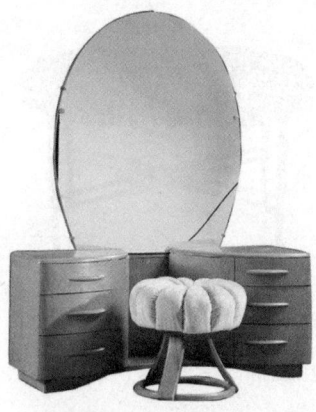

Furniture, Vanity, Heywood-Wakefield, Coronet, Wheat Finish, Pouffe Stool, c.1941, 65 x 53 In.
$353.00

Hollywood Deco

Hollywood Deco is a modern term describing the extreme art deco designs used for the decorating in movies like *The Thin Man* (1934). The furnishings look glamorous and theatrical. The Hollywood-inspired furniture, with round mirrors, chrome, blue glass, plastic, and blond wood, ranged from poor quality to expensive custom-made.

Furniture, Vitrine, Vernis Martin, Painted Courting Scene, Ormolu Mount, 59 x 26 In.
$940.00

Table, Pier, Neoclassical, Mahogany, King Of Prussia Marble Top, Frieze, Phila., 40 x 43 In.	5170.00
Table, Pier, Neoclassical Style, Rosewood Inlay, Swan Carved Monopods, 40 x 52 x 26 In.	2585.00
Table, Pier, Rococo Revival, Mahogany, Serpentine Marble Top, Frieze, 36 x 37 In.	1200.00
Table, Pine, Black Paint, Center Brace Under Top, New England, Early 1800s, 28 x 36 In.	863.00
Table, Pine, Green Sponge Paint, 2-Board Top, Tripod Panel Legs, Circular, 31 x 30 In.	9600.00
Table, Pine, Lacquered, Panel Inset Apron, Horse Hoof Feet, Chinese, Pair, 32 x 18 x 13 In.	411.00
Table, Pine, Poplar, Red Paint, Drawer, Overhang Top, Pa., 1800s, 28 x 22½ In.	431.00
Table, Pine, Tilt Top, Oval, Painted, Hudson River Valley, 18th Century, 27 x 52 In. *illus*	1955.00
Table, Pine, Yellow Paint, Plain Apron, Drawer, Tapered Legs, 27 x 17 x 22 In.	6600.00
Table, Poplar, Painted, 2-Board Top, Drawer, Tapered Square Legs, 28 x 36 x 28 In. *illus*	345.00
Table, Provincial, Mahogany, Scalloped Frieze, Dish Top, Cabriole Legs, 29 x 33 In.	2280.00
Table, Provincial, Oak, Farm, Planked Top, H-Stretcher, Bun Feet, 65 x 28 In.	1292.00
Table, Provincial, Polychrome, Marble Top, 2 Frieze Drawers, Lower Shelf, 30 x 55 x 24 In.	1880.00
Table, Quartersawn Oak, Carved, Sawn Top, Reeded Square Legs, 29½ x 89 In.	575.00
Table, Queen Anne, Poplar, Maple Legs, Porringer Top, 18th Century, 26 x 34 In.	1265.00
Table, Queen Anne, Walnut, Leaves, Arched Skirt, Cabriole Legs, Late 1700s, 29 x 48 In.	2749.00
Table, Queen Anne, Walnut, Poplar, Pine, Drawer, Turned Legs, Pad Feet, Pa., 30 x 46 In.	1150.00
Table, Queen Anne Style, Mahogany, Gateleg, Drop Leaves, Drawers, 1800s, 29 x 36 In.	470.00
Table, Queen Anne Style, Walnut, Back Lip, Tooled Red Leather Insert, Drawer, 26 x 22 In.	173.00
Table, Reading, George III, Oak, Easel Back, Barley Twist Stand, 3 Splayed Feet, 31 x 16 In.	1920.00
Table, Red Lacquer, D-Form, Incised Flowers, Chinese, 31½ x 34 x 17 In., Pair	472.00
Table, Red Lacquer, Rectangular Top, Plain Skirt, Chinese, c.1950, 18 x 53 In.	2242.00
Table, Refectory, Baroque Style, Olive Wood, Figured Burl, Carved Pedestals, 32 x 155 In.	4994.00
Table, Refectory, Carved Oak, Elizabethan Style, 28½ x 90 x 33 In.	3600.00
Table, Refectory, English Oak, Early 20th Century, 102 x 44 In.	1767.00
Table, Refectory, English Oak, Straight Stretchers, Turned Legs, Late 1800s, 58 x 31 In.	780.00
Table, Refectory, Jacobean, Oak, Carved, Turned, Carved Legs, Mannerist Skirt, 29 x 83 In.	10925.00
Table, Refectory, Jacobean, Oak, Plank Form, Box Stretcher, Urn Form Legs, 31 x 102 x 30 In.	4700.00
Table, Refectory, Oak, Round, Turned Legs, Stretcher, 32 x 99 x 30 In.	660.00
Table, Refectory, Renaissance Revival, Walnut, 3 Drawers, Carved, Lions, 31¼ x 31½ In.	5875.00
Table, Regency, Burl Oak, Tilt Top, Circular, Ebony Banding, 3-Footed, c.1815, 30 x 56 In.	3055.00
Table, Regency, Mahogany, Drop Leaf Ends, 2 Drawers, 28 x 36 x 28 In. *illus*	1093.00
Table, Regency, Mahogany, Line Inlay, Baluster Turned Base, Elm Pedestal, 28 x 49 In.	1840.00
Table, Regency, Mahogany, Marble Top, 3 Scrolling Supports, 15½ In.	1340.00
Table, Regency, Mahogany, Round, Green Leather Top, 6 Wells, 4 Splayed Legs, 30 x 53 In.	3525.00
Table, Regency, Mahogany, Tilt Top, Banded, Splayed, Reeded Legs, 29 x 68 x 47 In.	5640.00
Table, Regency, Polychrome Wood, Marble Top, D-Shape, Dolphin Support, 32 x 29 In.	720.00
Table, Regency, Round Top, Figured Mahogany, Ring & Baluster Pedestal, 30 x 41 In.	2300.00
Table, Regency Style, Mixed Wood, Octagonal, Revolving, 28 x 18½ x 18½ In.	826.00
Table, Regency Style, Walnut, Inlay, Medial Shelf, Drawer, 20th Century, 23 x 18 In.	201.00
Table, Renaissance Revival, Marquetry, Washington, 1876 Centennial, 28 x 27 In. *illus*	4183.00
Table, Rococo Revival, Transitional, Walnut, Marble Top, Carved Scrolls, 29 x 45 In.	2640.00
Table, Rococo Style, Cast Iron, Marble Top, Pierced Leaf Pedestal, 29 x 19 x 19 In.	236.00
Table, Rosewood, 2 Drawers, Arne Vodder, c.1958, 21 x 12½ x 16 In.	1920.00
Table, Rosewood, Mother-Of-Pearl, Butterflies, Flowers, Chinese, c.1880, 23 x 18 In.	633.00
Table, Rosewood, Rectangular Top, Beaded Skirt, Chinese, 34 x 44 x 12½ In.	413.00
Table, Sawbuck, 2-Board Top, Cross Leg Base, 29 x 66 In.	345.00
Table, Sawbuck, Softwood, Scrub Top, Breadboard Ends, X-Base, Stretcher, 28 x 38 x 21 In.	935.00
Table, Scroll Top, Projecting Top, Rosette Carved Ends, 29½ x 45 In.	354.00
Table, Sewing, Cherry, 2 Drawers, Turned Legs, c.1840, 29 x 22 In.	1035.00
Table, Sewing, Ebonized, Gilt, Papier-Mache, Flowers, England, 27 x 21 x 16 In.	212.00
Table, Sewing, Federal, Cherry, Poplar, Lift Top, Veneer Front, 1800s, 26 x 24 In.	1725.00
Table, Sewing, Federal, Mahogany, Inlay, Figured, c.1800, 29 x 19½ x 15½ In.	5700.00
Table, Sewing, Federal, Mahogany, Inlay, Figured, c.1805, 30 x 20½ x 16¾ In.	4200.00
Table, Sewing, Federal, Mahogany, Veneer, Carved, Drawers, Salem, c.1825, 28 x 22 In.	2820.00
Table, Sewing, Federal, Mahogany, Veneer, Oval Corners, Drawer, c.1820, 28 x 22 In.	1958.00
Table, Sewing, Federal, Tiger Maple, 2 Drawers, 19th Century, 27 x 18 In.	649.00
Table, Sewing, Federal Style, Mahogany, 2 Drawers, Lyre Trestle Base, 31¾ x 19 In.	472.00
Table, Sewing, Leatherwood, Maple, Poplar, Dovetailed, Early 19th Century, 30 x 23 In.	1495.00
Table, Sewing, Lift Top, Walnut, Open Compartment, Turned Legs, Inscription, c.1860, 30 x 24 In.	690.00
Table, Sewing, Louis XV Style, Black Lacquered, Hinged, Avian Scene, 29 x 17 In.	1080.00
Table, Sewing, Louisana Cypress, Overhang Top, Drawer, c.1830, 30 x 28 In.	764.00
Table, Sewing, Neoclassical, Mahogany, Carved, Gadrooned Top, Drop Leaves, 27 x 16 In.	588.00
Table, Sewing, Neoclassical, Mahogany, Veneer, 2 Drawers, c.1825, 31 x 24 In.	1645.00
Table, Sewing, Oak, 3 Drawers, Side Bins, c.1920, 29 x 31 x 20 In.	94.00
Table, Sewing, Pine, 2-Board Top, Dovetailed Drawer, Pullout Bag, 20 x 19 x 30 In.	374.00

F

Table, Sewing, Pine, Painted, 2 Drawers, Tapered Legs, Alfred, Maine, c.1850, 27 x 36 In.	1404.00
Table, Sewing, Regency, Satinwood, Inlay, Painted Children, Lift Top, 1800s, 30 x 22 In. *illus*	2588.00
Table, Sewing, Rococo Revival, Rosewood, Lift Top, Cupboard, Drawers, 32 x 21 x 16 In.	1762.00
Table, Sewing, Rococo Revival, Walnut, Rosewood, Drawer, X-Stretchers, 34 x 23 In.	1140.00
Table, Sewing, Shaker, Birch, Pine, 3 Drawers, Enfield, N.H., c.1840, 28 x 35 In.	30420.00
Table, Sewing, Shaker, Butternut, Cherry, Pine, Varnish, Drawer, 27 x 32 x 22 In.	16380.00
Table, Sewing, Shaker, Pine, Carved Cherry Legs, Chamfered, c.1890, 26 x 36 x 19 In.	2106.00
Table, Sewing, Softwood, White Paint, Scrub Top, Feathered Accents, 29 x 27 In.	990.00
Table, Sewing, Victorian, Burl, Cartouche Shape Top, Veneers, Drawers, 29 x 20 In.	230.00
Table, Sewing, Walnut, Pine Top, 2-Board Top, Drawer, Turned Legs, Tulip Feet, 30 x 42 In. ..	440.00
Table, Sewing, Walnut, Pine Top, Molded Lip Drawer, Turned Legs, Stretcher, 31 x 46 In.	495.00
Table, Sewing, Wicker, Victorian	250.00
Table, Sewing, Wicker, Wrapped Handle, Birdcage Design, Heywood Bros., 1890s	795.00
Table, Shaker, Cherry, Pine, Round, Drawer, Snake Legs, Mt. Lebanon, c.1880, 27 x 36 In. ...	1755.00
Table, Shaker, Maple, Cherry, Yellow Base, Scrubbed Top, Turned Legs, c.1840, 28 x 24 In. ...	936.00
Table, Shelf, Wicker, Woven Skirting, Wood Turned Legs, c.1920s, 24 In.	475.00
Table, Side, Adam Style, Mahogany, Carved Garland, Early 1900s, 30 x 42 x 20 In.	1057.00
Table, Side, G. Nakashima, Wepman, Walnut, Free Edge, Tripod Legs, 17 x 26 x 20 In.	5378.00
Table, Side, George III, Mahogany, 18th Century, 27½ x 32 x 19 In.	3960.00
Table, Side, L. & J.G. Stickley, Bookcase, 12 Panes, 2 Doors, Copper Pulls, 24 x 26 x 17 In. ...	2060.00
Table, Side, Pine, Lacquered, Chinese, 19th Century, 31½ x 17¾ x 12¾ In., Pair	411.00
Table, Side, Regency, Mahogany, Drawer, Reeded Legs, c.1915, 33 x 43 In.	2232.00
Table, Side, Regency Style, Mahogany, Dovetailed Drawer, Kittinger Label, 27 In., Pair	475.00
Table, Side, Renaissance Style, Walnut, Carved, Griffin, 2 Tiers, 30 x 24 x 24 In.	1534.00
Table, Side, Sheraton Style, Cherry, Square, Drawer, Turned Legs, 1855, 29½ In.	205.00
Table, Side, Sheraton Style, Cherry, Square, Single Drawer, 1855, 29½ In.	205.00
Table, Slab, End-Grain Tree Slice, Rustic Tripod Base, 29½ x 38 In.	1035.00
Table, Softwood, Salmon & Red Paint, 3-Board Top, Square Tapered Legs, 28½ x 48 x 30 In.	825.00
Table, Softwood, Sawbuck, 2-Board Scrub Top, X-Stretcher, Salmon Paint, 28 x 56 In.	440.00
Table, Softwood, Yellow Grain Paint, Drawer, Shelf, Turned Legs, Ball Feet, Pa., 29 x 37 In. ..	1870.00
Table, Sorting, Shaker, Pine, Blue Paint Over Red, Raised Sides, c.1880, 34 x 84 In.	2106.00
Table, Spanish, Oak, Iron Trestle, Carved, Lyre Supports, c.1920, 78½ x 35 In.	5400.00
Table, Spanish, Pine, Drop Leaf, Carved Lyre Supports, c.1850, 48 x 29 In.	3400.00
Table, Spider, Mahogany, Collinson & Lock, Octagonal, Marquetry, c.1880, 29 x 32 In.	1225.00
Table, Spider, Mahogany, Octagonal Top, Concave Shelf, Curved Legs, 1880, 29 In.	1225.00
Table, Square Base, Urn Pedestal, Round Top, Painted, 20th Century, 20 In., Pair	692.00
Table, Stacking, Chinese, Black Lacquered, 5 Triangle Shape Stands, 9¾ x 28 In.	489.00
Table, Steel, Chrome Plated, Glass Top, Triangular Base, 16 x 46 In.	299.00
Table, Stickley Bros., No. 2832, 8-Sided Top, V-Shape Apron, Label, Signed, 27 x 20 In.	1320.00
Table, Sunderland, Rosewood, Gadroon Edge, Baluster Supports, 30 x 36 In.	2644.00
Table, Tavern, 1-Board Pine Top, Maple Base, Drawer, Turned Legs, Button Feet, 34 x 21 In. .	920.00
Table, Tavern, 2-Board Pine Top, Red Paint, Dovetailed Drawer, New England, 44 x 27 In. ...	2990.00
Table, Tavern, Breadboard Ends, Block & Ring Turned Legs, Late 1700s, 25 x 31 In.	430.00
Table, Tavern, Chestnut, 3 Splayed Legs, Round, 25½ In.	2310.00
Table, Tavern, Chippendale, Poplar, 3 Drawers, Baluster Legs, H-Stretcher, 30 x 59 In.	546.00
Table, Tavern, Colonial Style, Conant & Ball, Oval Top, Turned Legs, 29 x 21 In.	49.00
Table, Tavern, Drawer, Chrome Yellow Paint, 39 x 21 x 28 In.	1150.00
Table, Tavern, Federal, Pine, Maple, 2 Drawers, c.1850, 30 x 60 x 33 In.	3600.00
Table, Tavern, Mixed Woods, Box Stretchers, Ring & Baluster Legs, 25 x 33 In. ....*illus*	633.00
Table, Tavern, Moravian, Walnut, Poplar, Stretcher Base, 18th Century, 30 x 54 In.	8050.00
Table, Tavern, Oval Top, Scrubbed Surface, Red Paint, New England, 25 x 30 In.	1380.00
Table, Tavern, Oval Top, Turned Legs, Stretcher, 26 x 23 x 25½ In.	1521.00
Table, Tavern, Pine, Maple, Painted, Breadboard Ends, Stretcher Base, Drawer, 27 x 33 In. ..	1495.00
Table, Tavern, Queen Anne, Maple, Figured, c.1760, 25¾ x 32 x 25 In.	2400.00
Table, Tavern, Rectangular Top, Breadboard Ends, Frieze, Turned Legs, 36 x 21 In.	244.00
Table, Tavern, Red Paint, Drawer, 37 x 22 x 30 In.	863.00
Table, Tavern, Walnut, Drawer, Turned Legs, Peg Feet, 19th Century, 30 x 36 x 25 In.	4481.00
Table, Tavern, Walnut, Molded Edge, 2 Drawers, Turned Legs, 27 x 31 x 27 In.	657.00
Table, Tavern, Walnut, Pine, 1-Board Top, Dovetailed Drawer, 27 x 29 x 19 In.	575.00
Table, Tea, Chippendale, Mahogany, Birdcage, Urn Turned Shaft, Cabriole Legs, 28 x 29 In. .	748.00
Table, Tea, Chippendale, Mahogany, Dish Top, Cabriole Legs, Claw & Ball Feet, 28½ In.	8365.00
Table, Tea, Chippendale, Mahogany, Round, Molded Rim, Birdcage, Slipper Feet, c.1775	3346.00
Table, Tea, Chippendale, Mahogany, Tilt Top, Piecrust Top, Claw & Ball Feet, 28 x 30 In.	3630.00
Table, Tea, Chippendale, Walnut, Dish Top, Birdcage Support, Slipper Feet, 1760, 28 In.	2200.00
Table, Tea, Chippendale Style, Mahogany, Pierced Gallery, Chinese, 27 x 24 x 17 In., Pair ...	1057.00
Table, Tea, George II, Mahogany, Tilt Top, Birdcage Support, Pedestal, 30 x 36 In.	2760.00

F

Furniture, Wall Unit, G. Nelson,
5 Walnut Shelves, Dividers, Herman
Miller, 1950s, 96 x 49 In.
$3000.00

Furniture, Wall Unit, Gio Ponti
$6000.00

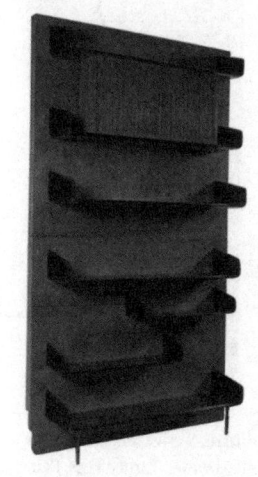

Furniture, Wall Unit, McCobb,
Enameled Metal Frame, 49 x 47 x 13 In.
$960.00

Furniture, Washstand, Corner, Federal, Mahogany, Line Inlay, Drawer, 43 x 28 x 18 In.
$805.00

Furniture, Washstand, Federal, Painted, Lower Shelf, 38 x 18½ x 16 In.
$384.00

Furniture, Washstand, Scroll Back, Cutouts, Drawer, Turned Legs, Painted, Maine, 36 x 17 In.
$115.00

Table, Tea, Georgian, Mahogany, Inlay, D-Shape Foldover Top, 1900s, 36 In.	1195.00
Table, Tea, Irish Georgian, Tray Top, Mahogany, Carved Shell Knees, 30 x 30 In.	5750.00
Table, Tea, Mahogany, Round, Baluster Turned Support, Cabriole Legs, Snake Feet, 9 x 9 In.	269.00
Table, Tea, Mahogany, Tray Top, Cabriole Legs, Slipper Feet, Ireland, 26 x 27 In.	6670.00
Table, Tea, Queen Anne, Mahogany, Maple, c.1755, 25 x 31 In.	4800.00
Table, Tea, Queen Anne, Mahogany, Tilt Top, c.1780, 11¾ x 10½ In.	6600.00
Table, Tea, Queen Anne, Maple, Oval, Scalloped Skirt, Conn., c.1750, 24¾ x 34 In.	2700.00
Table, Tea, Queen Anne, Oval, Red Paint, 3-Board Top, 28 x 32 x 27 In.	920.00
Table, Tea, Queen Anne, Walnut, Tilt Top, Birdcage Construction, 27 x 31 In.	550.00
Table, Tea, Queen Anne Style, Kittinger, C-Scroll Cabriole Legs, 2 Shelves, Label, 29 In.	1093.00
Table, Tea, Queen Anne Style, Mahogany, Cabriole Legs, Paw Feet, 29 x 37 x 25¾ In.	4230.00
Table, Tea, Regency, Mahogany, Rectangular, Canted Corners, 4 Splayed Legs, 25 x 20 x 12 In.	3525.00
Table, Tea, Tilt Top, Chippendale, Mahogany, Philadelphia, c.1770, 29 x 34 In.	4800.00
Table, Tea, Tilt Top, Chippendale, Mahogany, Pineapple, Cabriole Legs, 28 x 32 In.	660.00
Table, Tea, Tilt Top, George III, Mahogany, Piecrust, 27½ In.	3840.00
Table, Tea, Tilt Top, Mahogany, Birdcage Support, Tripod Base, Paw Feet, 26 x 32 x 32 In.	2185.00
Table, Tea, Tilt Top, Queen Anne, Mahogany, Dish Top, Birdcage, Pad Feet, 28 x 32 In. . .*illus*	3450.00
Table, Thonet, Fruitwood, Round, Bentwood Legs, Cross Stretchers, 31 x 33 In.	411.00
Table, Thulin, Oak, Carved Arts & Crafts Designs, Drawer, Square Legs, 26 x 40 In. . . . .*illus*	1955.00
Table, Tilt Top, Black Forest, Walnut, Satinwood, Marquetry, 30 x 31 x 23 In.	2232.00
Table, Tilt Top, Federal, Mahogany, Oval, Ring-Turned Support, Curved Legs, 24 x 30 x 21 In. .	144.00
Table, Tilt Top, Figured Walnut, Star Inlay, Raised Edge, Oval, 3 Shaped Legs, 29 x 35 In. . . .	3290.00
Table, Tilt Top, George III, Mahogany, Birdcage, Spiral Twist Turned Standard, 28 x 35 In. . .	2938.00
Table, Tilt Top, George III, Mahogany, Dish Top, Vase Form Pedestal, 29 x 24 In.	1680.00
Table, Tilt Top, George III, Mahogany, Inlay, Round, Tripod, Inlaid Patera, 38 x 23 In.	240.00
Table, Tilt Top, George III, Mahogany, Tripod, 3 Splayed Cabriole Legs, 28 x 32 In.	500.00
Table, Tilt Top, George III, Oak, Cabriole Legs, Snake Feet, 27¾ x 26 x 28 In.	316.00
Table, Tilt Top, Mahogany, Carved, Circular, Pedestal, 29½ x 52 In.	2115.00
Table, Tilt Top, Painted, Round Top, Faux Marble Panel, Top, Early 1800s, 30 x 20 In.	880.00
Table, Tilt Top, Papier-Mache, Mother-Of-Pearl, c.1840	4500.00
Table, Tilt Top, Queen Anne Style, Walnut, Ring, 28 x 32 x 31½ In.	708.00
Table, Tilt Top, Square, Burl, Figured, Lotus-Carved, Splayed Tripod Base, 30 x 34 In.	2115.00
Table, Tilt Top, Victorian, Mahogany, Burl, Polychrome, 28 x 23 x 15 In.	352.00
Table, Tilt Top, Victorian, Mahogany, Molded Edge, 3 Splayed Legs, 28 x 41 In.	411.00
Table, Tilt Top, Victorian, Papier-Mache, Mid 19th Century, 25 In.	409.00
Table, Tray, Brass, Benares, Folding Carved Base, Early 20th Century, 31 In.	154.00
Table, Tray, Butler's, Oak, Mahogany Stand, Hinged Sides, Cutout Handles, 19 x 18 In.	411.00
Table, Tray, Butler's, Stand, Georgian, Mahogany, Mid 19th Century, 30 In.	1171.00
Table, Tray, Mahogany, Mortise & Tenon Construction, Lamb's Tongue Chamfers, 37 In.	230.00
Table, Tray, On Stand, Georgian, Oval, Satinwood, Bamboo-Form Stand, 1810, 27 x 21 In. . .	3850.00
Table, Tray, On Stand, Tole, Yellow, Cross Stretcher, Turned Legs, Italy, 1900s, 28 In.	208.00
Table, Tray, Papier-Mache, Painted Flowers, Faux Bamboo Stand, 20 x 32 In. . . . .*illus*	944.00
Table, Tray, Regency Style, Mahogany, Hand Grips, 37 x 36 x 19 In.	1092.00
Table, Tray, Victorian, Black Lacquer, Papier-Mache, Oval, Upswept Rim, 23 x 29 In.	1035.00
Table, Trestle, Arts & Crafts, Oak, Rectangular, Median Shelf, Tenons, c.1916, 48 x 30 In.	499.00
Table, Trestle, L. & J.G. Stickley, Overhang Top, Lower Shelf, Through Tenons, 29 x 48 In.	1320.00
Table, Trestle, Shaker, Pine, Maple, Birch, Chamfered Leg, Arched Base, c.1840, 28 x 38 In. . .	15210.00
Table, Trestle, Shaker, Pine, Scrubbed, Red Paint, Pegged, Mortised, Brackets, 91 In.	8775.00
Table, Trestle, Spanish, Walnut, Carved, Scrolling Legs, Stretchers, 32 x 70 In.	6490.00
Table, Venetian, Polychrome, Raised Edge, Polychrome Floral Spray, 25 x 20 In.	240.00
Table, Venetian Rococo Style, Applied Shells, Branch-Stretcher, Painted Octopus, 28 x 25 In.	2185.00
Table, Victorian, Marble Top, Stretcher, Casters, 19th Century, 32 x 22 In.	936.00
Table, Victorian, Marble Top, Walnut, Turtle Top, Reclining Spaniel On Base, 37 x 23 In.	1495.00
Table, Victorian, Rosewood, Marble Top, Turned Legs, Scrolled Feet, 28 x 32 x 22 In.	441.00
Table, Victorian, Rosewood, Serpentine Top, Leaf Carved Base, Cabriole Legs, 29 x 43 x 17 In. .	470.00
Table, Victorian, Woven Cane Top, Shelves, Birdcage, Heywood Bros., 1890s, 26 x 37 In.	795.00
Table, Victorian Style, Mahogany, Penshell, Carved, Round Top, 31 x 40 In.	1610.00
Table, Wake, English Oak, Rounded Rectangular Top, Oval Drop Leaves, 30 x 84 In.	3900.00
Table, Walnut, 2 Drawer, Line Inlay, Square Tapered Legs, 29¾ x 48¼ In.	2860.00
Table, Walnut, Drop Leaf, Oval, Floral Decoration, Tapered Legs, c.1790, 28½ x 46½ In.	978.00
Table, Walnut, Drop Leaves, c.1960, 30 x 41 In.	351.00
Table, Wicker, Paint, Glass Top, 2 Tiers, 29 x 36 x 24 In. . . . .*illus*	173.00
Table, Widdicomb, Walnut, Octagonal, 2 Tiers, Cork Base, c.1960, 24 x 27 In., Pair	764.00
Table, William & Mary, Gateleg, Drawer, Philadelphia, c.1720, 29 x 15 x 36 In. . . . . . .*illus*	4500.00
Table, William & Mary, Gateleg, Flower & Leaf Swags, Ball Feet, 27 x 28 In.	770.00

F

Table, William & Mary, Marquetry, Walnut, Drawers, Twisted Legs, Stretcher, 37 x 24 In. 2390.00
Table, William & Mary, Walnut, Painted, Drawer, England, c.1720, 28 x 32 x 22 In. 5700.00
Table, Wine, Elm, Rectangular Top, Green Stone Inset, Chinese, 1600s, 36 x 39 In. 590.00
Table, Wine, Pedestal, Wood, Lacquered, Figural Landscapes, Butterflies, Japan, 27 In. 103.00
Table, Wine Tasting, French Provincial, Tilt Top, Fruitwood, 1890s, 29½ In. 1340.00
Table, Wood, Front Legs Formed As Legs & Feet, Glass Top, Sulton Rogers, 20 x 19 In. 633.00
Table, Wormley, Walnut, 2 Blue Inset Tiffany Tiles, Dunbar, 24 x 25 x 21 In. 7475.00
Table, Writing, Art Nouveau, Painted, Incised, Decorated, c.1890, 28 x 20 x 30 In. 246.00
Table, Writing, Burl Walnut, Leather Top, England, 29¾ x 35½ x 23½ In. 890.00
Table, Writing, Campaign Style, Mahogany, Folding, 31½ x 24 x 24 In. 1416.00
Table, Writing, Edwardian, Mahogany, Robert Adam Style, Leather Top, Lady's, 31 x 39 In. .. 1800.00
Table, Writing, Federal, Mahogany Inlay, Drawer, 1790-1810, 30 x 42 x 20½ In. 3600.00
Table, Writing, George II Style, Walnut, Carved, Frieze Drawer, Early 1800s, 30 x 34 In. 920.00
Table, Writing, Inlaid Mahogany, Late 19th Century, 51 In. 457.00
Table, Writing, Louis Philippe, Mahogany, Leather Inset Surface, Easel Back, 29 x 32 In. 1680.00
Table, Writing, Louis XV, Provincial, Walnut, Scalloped Apron, Raised Edge, 28 x 30 In. 1416.00
Table, Writing, Louis XV Style, Kingwood, Gilt Bronze, Bookmatch Top, 30 x 34 In. 8519.00
Table, Writing, Louis XVI, Tulipwood, Marble Top, Slide, Inkwell, Sand Pot, 28 x 20 In. 9600.00
Table, Writing, Mahogany, Oak, Pine, Drawers, Ebonized Heads, England, 32 x 48 x 29 In. .. 1150.00
Table, Writing, Walnut, Drawer, Tapered Legs, North Carolina, Early 1800s, 30 x 31 In. 1150.00
Table, Writing, William IV, Kidney Shape, Dish Edge, Pierced Supports, 29 x 38 In. 940.00
Table, Writing, William IV, Rosewood, 2 Hinged Sections, Easel Back, Fluted Legs, 31 x 71 In. 8225.00
Table, Wrought Iron, Slate Top, Painted, Neoclassical Figures, Black Ground, 17 x 46 In. ... 4700.00
Table, Yellow Pine, Paint, 2-Board Top, 2 Drawers, Southern, 29 x 26 x 32 In. ....*illus* 489.00
Table, Yellow Pine, White Paint, 1-Board Top, Tapered Square Legs, 31 x 26 In. 546.00
Tabouret, L. & J.G. Stickley, Octagonal, Mortised Legs Through Top, 17 x 15 In. 780.00
Tabouret, L. & J.G. Stickley, Octagonal Top, Mortised Legs, Stretchers, 20 x 18 In. 1200.00
Tabouret, Louis XVI, Giltwood, Oval Padded Seat, Fluted Legs, Late 1800s, 15 x 20 In. 295.00
Tabouret, Wood Top, Wicker, Woven Skirting, c.1900, 18½ In. 495.00
Tea Cart, Bar Harbor, Oak Top, Shelf, Wicker, 4 Wood & Rubber Wheels, Heywood Bros. 975.00
Tea Table, Tilt Top, Chippendale, Mahogany, Lobed Top, Carved Legs & Feet, 27 x 28 In. 863.00
Tea Table, Tilt Top, Chippendale, Mahogany, Urn Shaft, Carved Slipper Feet, 28 x 27 In. 805.00
Tea Table, Tilt Top, Queen Anne, Mahogany, Oak, Baluster Shaft, Snake Feet, 28 x 29 In. ... 403.00
Torchere, Louis XVI Style, Polychrome, 3-Paneled Supports, Urn Shelf, Bun Feet, 48 x 11 In. 705.00
Trolley, Drinks, Alvo Altair, Bentwood, Black Tile Top, Wicker Basket, 23 x 25 x 36 In. 359.00
Umbrella Stand, Bear Above Mirror, Adult Bear On Base, Hooks, Black Forest, 78½ In. 4140.00
Umbrella Stand, Oak, Cutout Scrolls On Sides, Tapered, Arts & Crafts, 29 x 17 x 9 In. 230.00
Umbrella Stand, Victorian, Wicker, Turned Wood Framework, Panels, Spools, 1890s 525.00
Umbrella Stand, Wrought Iron, Rectangular, Scrolled Panel, Early 1900s, 30 x 22 In. 270.00
Vanity, Bench, Mirror, Artisans Shop, Maple, Dovetailed, Floral Carving, 1941 .... 288.00
Vanity, Heywood-Wakefield, Coronet, Wheat Finish, Pouffe Stool, c.1941, 65 x 53 In. ...*illus* 353.00
Vanity, Louis XV, Walnut, Gilt Oval Mirror, Cane Inset, France, c.1900, 54 x 35 In. 4250.00
Vitrine, Baroque Style, Walnut, Scrolled Leaf Crest, Glazed Panel, 81 x 44 x 18 In. 1770.00
Vitrine, Edwardian, Mahogany, Hinged, Glazed, Blind Fret Carved, c.1900s, 28 x 20 In. 660.00
Vitrine, Edwardian, Mahogany, Marquetry, Oval, Early 1900s, 30 x 25 In. 3068.00
Vitrine, Emile Galle, Burled Walnut, Marquetry, c.1900, 57 x 25 x 13½ In. 20400.00
Vitrine, Empire Style, Brass Inlay, Gilt Bronze, Mahogany, Galleried Top 1645.00
Vitrine, Empire Style, Mahogany, Brass Inlay, Beveled Glass Top, 30 x 25 In. 1000.00
Vitrine, Louis XV Style, Glass Sides, Mirrored, Pair, 72 x 25 x 13½ In. 1175.00
Vitrine, Louis XV Style, Mahogany, Gilt Brass Mounted, Brass Gallery, c.1900, 61 x 30 In. ... 1680.00
Vitrine, Louis XV Style, Tulipwood, 20th Century, 73 x 28 In. 973.00
Vitrine, Mahogany, Carved, Marble Top, Beveled Glass, Cabriole Legs, 40 x 39 In. 3300.00
Vitrine, Pine, Fluted Columns, Paneled Half Blind Door, Bunt Feet, 70 x 38 x 16 In. 382.00
Vitrine, Vernis Martin, Painted Courting Scene, Ormolu Mount, 59 x 26 In. ....*illus* 940.00
Wagon Seat, Mixed Woods, Slat Back, Turned Arms, Legs, Rush Seat, 29 In. 144.00
Wall Hook, Double, Figural, Elephant Masque, Gilt Lacquered Brass Plate, 7 In., Pair 2640.00
Wall Unit, G. Nelson, 5 Walnut Shelves, Dividers, Herman Miller, 1950s, 96 x 49 In. ....*illus* 3000.00
Wall Unit, Gio Ponti ....*illus* 6000.00
Wall Unit, McCobb, Enameled Metal Frame, 49 x 47 x 13 In. ....*illus* 960.00
Wardrobe, Art Nouveau, English Oak, Inlay, Early 20th Century, 80 x 62 In. 413.00
Wardrobe, Arts & Crafts, Canted Sides, Top Overhang, Open Shelf, Copper, 76 x 46 In. 1800.00
Wardrobe, Chippendale, George III, Mahogany, Double Doors, 83 x 50 In. 1035.00
Wardrobe, Empire Style, Mahogany, Ormolu Mounted, Mirrored Door, 94 x 69 x 21 In. 2115.00
Wardrobe, Figured Maple, Mirror Front, Carved Crest, Early 1900s, 78 x 46 In. 652.00
Wardrobe, George III, Mahogany, 2-Paneled Doors, 2 Drawers, Bracket Feet, 78 x 47 x 23 In. ... 387.00

Furniture, Washstand, Walnut, 2 Tiers, Drawer, Turned Legs, Green Paint, Tenn., 28 x 20 x 19 In.
$115.00

F

Furniture, Wastebasket, P.S. Heggen, Teak, Molded, 2 Handles, Norway, 17 x 15 x 8 In.
$570.00

Furniture, Whatnot Shelf, Corner, Victorian, Walnut, Openwork, 3 Shelves, 29 In.
$264.00

G. Argy-Rousseau, Lamp, Dune Flowers, Purple, Amber, Roses, Leaves, Pate-De-Verre, 13 In. $690.00

G. Argy-Rousseau, Pendant, Green Parrot, Round, Silk Cord, Pate-De-Verre, Signed, 2⅜ In. $2185.00

G. Argy-Rousseau, Vase, Earth Tone Leaves, Mottled Yellow, Pate-De-Verre, 6½ In. $6900.00

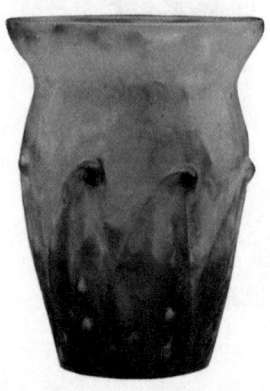

Wardrobe, Mahogany, Scroll Finial, Mirror, Draw, Claw Feet, 82 x 38 x 22 In.	646.00
Wardrobe, Mahogany, Walnut, Molded Cornice, Panel Doors, Shelves, c.1840, 84 x 50 In.	1793.00
Wardrobe, Maple, Mirrored Door, Drawer, Flattened Ball Feet, 36 x 18 In., Pair	3585.00
Wardrobe, Poplar, 4-Panel Door, Shaker Village, 84 x 42 In.	1050.00
Wardrobe, Provincial, Pine, Oblong, 3 Drawers, Paneled Door, 43 x 37 x 18 In.	1645.00
Wardrobe, Victorian, Mahogany, Canted Cornice, Fitted Cabinets, c.1840, 84 x 58 In.	2115.00
Wardrobe, Walnut, Inlay, Dentil Molding, Panel Doors, Fruitwood Inlay, 78 x 47 In.	880.00
Wardrobe, William IV, Satinwood, Doors, 2 Over 4 Drawers, c.1850, 82 x 92 In.	2233.00
Wash Tub, Red Paint, Trencher Style, Drain Hole, Turned Legs, 34 x 51 x 16 In.	990.00
Washstand, Cherry, ¾ Backsplash, 2 Drawers, Doors, c.1870, 33 x 44½ In.	1955.00
Washstand, Cherry, Dovetailed, Scalloped Gallery, Turned Legs, 28 x 19 x 37 In.	373.00
Washstand, Corner, Federal, Mahogany, Line Inlay, Drawer, 43 x 28 x 18 In. ....*illus*	805.00
Washstand, Decorated, Cantilevered Top, Chrome Yellow Paint, Decorated	518.00
Washstand, Federal, Corner, Inlaid Flower & Line Decoration, 24 x 17 x 44 In.	183.00
Washstand, Federal, Mahogany, Inlay, N.Y., 19th Century, 40 x 24 x 17 In.	600.00
Washstand, Federal, Maple, Mahogany, 2 Tiers, Trapezoidal, Drawer, 37½ x 27 In.	590.00
Washstand, Federal, Painted, Backsplash, Medial Shelf, Drawer, Early 1800s, 38 x 19 In.	384.00
Washstand, Federal, Painted, Lower Shelf, 38 x 18½ x 16 In. ....*illus*	384.00
Washstand, George III, Corner, Mahogany, Shaped Backsplash, Shelf, 3 Legs, 37 x 26 In.	528.00
Washstand, George III, Mahogany, Corner, Backsplash, Medial Shelf, Drawer, 34 x 23 In.	1416.00
Washstand, Iron, Brass, Victorian, 36 x 20 In.	118.00
Washstand, Mahogany, Burled On Pine, Empire, Door, Drawer, 28 x 20½ x 16 In.	147.00
Washstand, Marble Top, Rectangular Top, Drawer, Flat Panel Door, 1800s, 27 x 15 In.	88.00
Washstand, New England, Mixed Woods, Scrolled Sides, Medial Shelf, 31 x 27 x 18 In.	944.00
Washstand, Painted, Scrolled Backsplash, Pierced Top, Shelf, c.1830, 27 x 14 In.	235.00
Washstand, Painted, Shaped Backsplash, Shelf, Pierced Top, c.1835, 37 x 18 In.	1000.00
Washstand, Pine, Old Paint, Turned Legs, Shelf Across Stretcher, 35¼ x 17½ x 28 In.	288.00
Washstand, Pine, Poplar, Red & Orange Paint Design, Drawer, Turned Front Legs, 36 x 21 In.	690.00
Washstand, Rococo Revival, Rosewood, Marble Top, Serpentine Top, Backsplash, 40 x 36 In.	2160.00
Washstand, Scroll Back, Cutouts, Drawer, Turned Legs, Painted, Maine, 36 x 17 In. ...*illus*	115.00
Washstand, Scrolled Back Splash, Stenciled, Pierced Top, c.1830, 36 x 16½ In.	470.00
Washstand, Sheraton, Mahogany Veneer, Dovetailed, Drawer In Lower Base, 39 x 20 In.	230.00
Washstand, Victorian, Walnut, Burl Walnut, Marble Top, Backsplash, 38 x 30 In.	235.00
Washstand, Walnut, 2 Tiers, Drawer, Turned Legs, Green Paint, Tenn., 28 x 20 x 19 In. .*illus*	115.00
Washstand, Walnut, Towel Bars, Drawers, Panels, England, 34½ x 38 x 17 In.	230.00
Wastebasket, P.S. Heggen, Teak, Molded, 2 Handles, Norway, 17 x 15 x 8 In. ....*illus*	570.00
Wastebasket, Stickley Bros., Wooden Slats, Hammered Iron Hoops, 14 x 12 In.	1355.00
Whatnot Shelf, Corner, Victorian, Walnut, Openwork, 3 Shelves, 29 In. ....*illus*	264.00
Whatnot Shelf, Grain Painted, 2 Shelves, Faux Marble, Mustard, Amber Paint, 23 x 21 In.	201.00
Whatnot Shelf, Wood, 3 Tiers, Heart Pediment, Pillar & Arrow Decoration, 21 x 6½ In.	230.00
Whatnot Stand, Victorian, Wicker, Spiral Turned Posts, Splayed Legs, 1890s, 42 x 23 In.	1150.00
Window Seat, George III, Mahogany, Adam Style, Padded Seat, Scrolled Arms, 30 x 50 In.	3120.00
Window Seat, George III, Mahogany, Padded Seat, Outscrolled Arms, Spade Feet, 49 In.	3210.00
Wine Cooler, Georgian, Mahogany, Brass Mounts, Oval, Metal Liner, 1800s, 20 x 25 In.	748.00
Wine Cooler Table, Directoire Style, Mahogany Inlay, Figured, Oval, 26 x 23 In.	823.00
Workbench, Engraver's, Pine, Maple, Mahogany, Lidded Compartment, 40 x 43 In.	546.00
Workbench, Maple, Through Mortise Construction, Vises, Paint Trace, 33 x 43 In.	546.00

G. ARGY-ROUSSEAU is the impressed mark used on a variety of objects in the Art Deco style. Gabriel Argy-Rousseau, born in 1885, was a French glass artist. In 1921, he formed a partnership that made pate-de-verre and other glass. He worked until 1952 and died in 1953.

G-ARGY-ROUSSEAU

Box, Cover, Leaves, Brown, Biege, Pate-De-Verre, c.1920, 3¾ In.	4200.00
Box, Cover, Papyrus, Amethyst & Red Flowers, Pate-De-Verre, Round, 3⅛ In.	4600.00
Figurine, Elephant, Pate-De-Verre, Mottled, Green, Signed, 4½ x 5½ In.	4500.00
Lamp, Dune Flowers, Purple, Amber, Roses, Leaves, Pate-De-Verre, 13 In. ....*illus*	690.00
Paperweight, 2 Moths, Mottled Green, Pate-De-Verre, Signed, 2¾ In.	2520.00
Pendant, Green Parrot, Round, Silk Cord, Pate-De-Verre, Signed, 2⅜ In. ....*illus*	2185.00
Vase, 4 Thistles, Purple Ground, Pate-De-Verre, Signed, c.1920, 6 In.	5700.00
Vase, Earth Tone Leaves, Mottled Yellow, Pate-De-Verre, 6½ In. ....*illus*	6900.00
Vase, Mottled Amber & Red, Cascading Design, Pate-De-Verre, Signed, 7 In.	5175.00

GALLE was a designer who made glass, pottery, furniture, and other Art Nouveau items. Emile Galle founded his factory in France in 1874. After Galle's death in 1904, the firm continued to make glass and furniture until 1931. The name *Galle* was used as a mark, but it was often hidden in the design of the object. Galle glass is listed here. Pottery is in the next section. His furniture is listed in the Furniture category.

Cachepot, Barrel Shape, Blue Grapes & Vines, Etched, 3 Branch, Cameo, 7¼ In.	235.00
Chalice, Islamic Style, Enameled, Gilt, c.1880, 8 x 4½ In.	21000.00
Charger, White Peace Lily, Black Ground, Signed, 1904, 14 In.	475.00
Cup & Saucer, Wildflowers, Blue, Pink, Green, Zigzag Border, Rope Twist Handle, Signed ...	382.00
Night-Light, Frosted Dome Shade, Green Butterflies, Bronze Baluster Base, Cameo, 6¾ In. ..	748.00
Perfume Bottle, Etched Flowers, Amber Ground, Gilt Flower Stopper, 4½ In. ...._illus_	5175.00
Pitcher, Vaseline, Pink Flowering Branch, Butterfly In Flight, Cone Shape, c.1890, 8½ In.	1058.00
Powder Box, Dome Cover, Poppies, Amber & Rose, Cushion Shape, Signed, 1885, 9 In.	1100.00
Scent Bottle, Purple, Sterling Mounted, Cameo, c.1910, 4 x 3 In.	950.00
Tray, Coat Of Arms, Cobalt Blue Slip, White Ground, Signed, 9⅝ In.	431.00
Tumbler, Monogram, Cameo, c.1910, 4 In.	995.00
Vase, Amber, Brown, Fuchsia Flowers, Early 1900s, 5 In.	809.00
Vase, Amethyst & White Flowering Branches, Frosted Pink Ground, Cylindrical, 6½ In.	575.00
Vase, Amethyst Flowers, Citron Ground, Cylindrical, Flared, Footed, 6¼ In.	575.00
Vase, Apricot Dragonflies, Water Lilies, Blue Frosted Ground, Signed, 19 In. ...._illus_	12075.00
Vase, Banjo, Frosted Pink, Green Leaves, 6½ In.	575.00
Vase, Banjo, Green & White Maple Leaves, Seed Pods, Amethyst Frosted Ground, 6½ In.	460.00
Vase, Banjo, Madder Brown, Yellow Ground, Cameo, c.1900, 6½ In.	1121.00
Vase, Blue & Purple Bellflowers, Amber To Frosted Ground, Square, 11¾ In. ...._illus_	8050.00
Vase, Brown Flowers & Leaves, Peach Ground, Cameo, Signed, 6¾ In.	940.00
Vase, Brown Stemmed Garden, Yellow, Bulbous, Signed, 3¾ In.	400.000
Vase, Burnt Orange, Frosted Ground, Bulbous, Trefoil Rim, Cameo, Signed, 5 In.	646.00
Vase, Carved Leaves & Berries, Brown On Frosted Green, Cameo, 7½ In.	660.00
Vase, Chrysanthemum, Amber, Fire Orange Ground, Cameo, Signed, 4½ x 3½ In.	720.00
Vase, Citron, Red Stemmed Leaves & Flowers, Boat Shaped, Cameo, Signed, 7 In.	345.00
Vase, Columbines, Brown, Frosted Gold Ground, Cameo, Signed, 5⅛ In.	588.00
Vase, Flowers, Brown, Enameled, Flat Rim, Beveled Edge, 12¼ In.	4700.00
Vase, Flowers, Green, Purple, Brown, Mottled Ground, Cameo, 12½ In.	18800.00
Vase, Fruit, Leaves, Brown, Orange Shaded To Green, Pinched Neck, 10 In. ...._illus_	3107.00
Vase, Green Thistles, Frosted Ground, Cameo, Signed, c.1904, 12½ In.	1058.00
Vase, Honeysuckle, Mauve, Yellow Ground, Cameo, Signed, 9½ In.	1800.00
Vase, Islamic Style, Gilt, Enameled, Applied Circular Bosses, c.1890, 8 x 9 In.	33600.00
Vase, Landscape, Hills, Trees, Enameled, Urn Shape, 5⅞ In.	9600.00
Vase, Landscape, Mountain, Mauve, Blue, Green, Yellow Ground, c.1900, 12½ In.	9000.00
Vase, Landscape, Village, Brown To Teal To Clear, Pedestal Foot, Cameo, 10¼ In.	3525.00
Vase, Landscape, Wooded Lake, Amber, Frosted Yellow Ground, Cameo, Signed, 7¾ In.	2640.00
Vase, Lavender Over Cream, Fuchsias, Tapered, Flared Rim, Cameo, Signed, 10 In.	1175.00
Vase, Mold-Blown Water Lilies, Green & Brown, Frosted Ground, Cameo, 8¼ In.	2530.00
Vase, Moorish Design, Multicolored Enamel, Cylindrical, 12 Cabochons, c.1890, 6 In.	2115.00
Vase, Morning Glory, Purple, Green, White, Martele Ground, Cameo, c.1900, 11 In.	9600.00
Vase, Nymphs, Enameled, 4 Prunts, c.1890, 6½ x 9 In.	11400.00
Vase, Polar Bears, Iceberg, Aqua Ground, Flared Rim, Cameo, 11 x 10¾ In. ...._illus_	34500.00
Vase, Poppies, Crimson, Frosted White, Egg Shape, Footed, Cameo, 4¾ In.	900.00
Vase, Purple, Flowers, Leaves, Gold Ground, Cameo, c.1900, 11½ In.	2151.00
Vase, Red Leaves & Fruit, Frosted Handles, Orange Neck, Pillow, 5 In.	1175.00
Vase, Shepherd, Tree Covered Hillside, Peach, Cameo, 5¼ In.	34500.00
Vase, Spider Chrysanthemum, Rose, Amber, Russet, Bulbous, Cupped Rim, Cameo, 5¼ In. ..	960.00
Vase, Stick, Citron, Crimson Leafy Stem Flowers, Trifold Rim, 10 In.	2233.00
Vase, Stick, Flowers, Leaves, Green, Pink Over Yellow, Applied Handles, Cameo, 14½ In.	1645.00
Vase, Stick, Green Leaves, Seed Pods, Frosted Ground, Signed, 12 In.	1435.00
Vase, Stick, Olive Green Shaded To Pink, Flowers, Seed Pods, c.1904, 10½ In.	920.00
Vase, Stick, Peach Frosted, Green Leaves, Seed Pods, Cameo, Signed, 12 In.	1438.00
Vase, Stick, Trailing Flower, Ocher, Celery, Pink, Bulbous Base, Flared Rim, Cameo, 8 In.	1080.00
Vase, Stick, Trumpet Flowers, Purple, Sea Green, Bulbous Base, Pinched Rim, 10⅜ In.	4113.00
Vase, Stylized Poppies, Purple, Shaded Frosted Ground, 8 In.	1058.00
Vase, Swamp Flowers, Yellow, Turquoise Ground, Cameo, 8 In.	6500.00
Vase, Trumpet, Purple Wisteria Pod, Hanging From Vine, Frosty Yellow, Cameo, 12 In.	970.00
Vase, Violet, Clematis, Cupped Oval, Signed, c.1900, 4¾ In.	1950.00
Vase, Wisteria, Matte Pink, Green, White, Frosted Olive Ground, Cameo, c.1900, 23 In.	2760.00
Vase, Wisteria Blossoms, Twining Vine, Frost, Saffron, Amethyst Ground, 17¼ In.	1955.00

GALLE POTTERY was made by Emile Galle, the famous French designer, after 1874. The pieces were marked with the initials *E. G.* impressed *Em. Galle Faiencerie de Nancy,* or a version of his signature. Galle is best known for his glass, listed above.

Candlestick, Rampant Lion, Castellated Candle Sockets, 16½ In., Pair	1150.00
Clock, Blue Oval Top, Molded Art Nouveau Flowers, Japy Frere Works, Scroll Feet, 16 In.	2468.00

Galle, Perfume Bottle, Etched Flowers, Amber Ground, Gilt Flower Stopper, 4½ In.
$5175.00

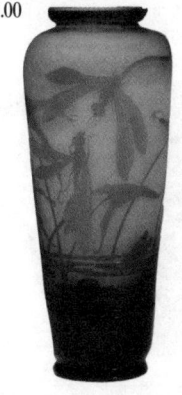

Galle, Vase, Apricot Dragonflies, Water Lilies, Blue Frosted Ground, Signed, 19 In.
$12075.00

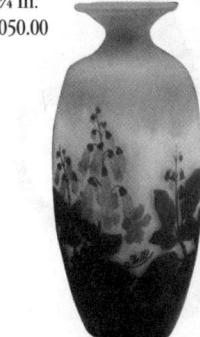

Galle, Vase, Blue & Purple Bellflowers, Amber To Frosted Ground, Square, 11¾ In.
$8050.00

Galle, Vase, Fruit, Leaves, Brown, Orange Shaded To Green, Pinched Neck, 10 In.
$3107.00

G

Galle, Vase, Polar Bears, Iceberg, Aqua Ground, Flared Rim, Cameo, 11 x 10¾ In. **$34500.00**

Galle Pottery, Ewer, Dragonfly, Crackled Ground, Embedded Gold Leaves, Faience, 7¼ In. **$2703.00**

G

Galle Pottery, Pitcher, French Peasant Smoking Pipe, Faience, 12 x 7 In. **$863.00**

Galle Pottery, Pot-De-Creme, Cover, Painted Ships In Ovals, Delft Blue, Footed, 3 In. **$288.00**

Cup & Saucer, Botanical Sprays, Landscape, Pink, Gold, Pinched Waist, 3½ x 6 In.	....	725.00
Cup & Saucer, Faience	....	725.00
Ewer, Dragonfly, Crackled Ground, Embedded Gold Leaves, Faience, 7¼ In.	.........*illus*	2703.00
Ewer, Pale Blue, Chrysanthemum Sprays, Enameled, Optic Rib, Signed, 1890s, 7 In.	....	780.00
Pitcher, French Peasant Smoking Pipe, Faience, 12 x 7 In.	.......................*illus*	863.00
Pot-De-Creme, Cover, Painted Ships In Ovals, Delft Blue, Footed, 3 In.	..............*illus*	288.00
Vase, Berries, Butterfly, Crescent Moon, Cream, Gray Ground, Crimped, Handles, 9 In.	......	1998.00
Vase, Sunflower Shape, Thistles, Blue, Faience, 6½ In.	...........................*illus*	978.00

GAME collectors like all types of games. Of special interest are any board games or card games. Transogram and other company names are included in the description when known. Other games may be found listed under Card, Toy, or the name of the character or celebrity featured in the game.

Airplane Dominoes, Parker Brothers, Box, Early 1900s	....	46.00
All Aboard For Chicago, Railroad Tracks, Cities, Parker Brother, Board, 7 x 11 In.	....	1210.00
All In The Family, Milton Bradley, Card, 1972	....	35.00
Alvin & Chipmunks, Board, Hasbro, 1960	......	175.00
American Boys, Boy Scouts At Work In Mountains, McLoughlin Bros., 1913, 19 x 10 In.	....	300.00
Balcony Bound, Pinball, Marble, Tin, Hoge	....	56.00
Baseball, Pinch Hitter, Marble, Key Wind, Joseph Schneider Games, c.1938, 24 x 12 In.	.....	295.00
Beany & Cecil Ring Toss, Wood Characters, Box, Pressman Toys, 1962, 14 x 20 In.	...*illus*	202.00
Board, Backgammon, Painted Red, Black, 19th Century, 16½ x 16½ In.	....	4200.00
Board, Checkers, 2-Sided, Painted, Mitered Molding, Yellow On Red, 19 x 28 In.	....	500.00
Board, Checkers, 2-Sided, Painted, Red & Blue, 26½ x 16½ In.	....	518.00
Board, Checkers, 2-Sided, Wood, Inlaid, Diamonds, c.1876, 14½ x 15 In.	....	470.00
Board, Checkers, 2-Sided, Wood, Painted, Yellow, Black, Red Ground, 15 x 24 In.	....	705.00
Board, Checkers, Applied Molding, Mustard Yellow, Dark Red, Black Ground, 30 x 22 In.	....	382.00
Board, Checkers, Black & White Painted Squares, Red Border, Folding, 14 x 14 In.	....	575.00
Board, Checkers, Black & Yellow, Rectangular, Applied Mitered Molding, 17 x 25 In.	....	1293.00
Board, Checkers, Box, Square, Slide Lid, Leaves, Brass Ring Handle, 14 x 14 In.	....	5100.00
Board, Checkers, Burgundy Paint, Black & Red Squares, 13 x 13 In.	....	1150.00
Board, Checkers, Decoration, Pinstripes, Red, Black & Gold Detail, 35 x 17½ In.	....	345.00
Board, Checkers, Green, Yellow Blocks, Red Pinstripe Border, Wood, Paint, Folding, 9 In.	...	1210.00
Board, Checkers, Painted, Black, Brown, Early 19th Century, 16¼ x 14¾ In.	....	5760.00
Board, Checkers, Painted, Leather, Wood, 19th Century, 16½ x 16½ In.	....	4800.00
Board, Checkers, Parcheesi, Black, Red, Green, Gilding, Beveled Edges, 19¾ x 20 In.	....	5750.00
Board, Checkers, Pine, Brown & Black, Gold Paint, Applied Edge, 19½ x 24 In.	....	748.00
Board, Checkers, Poplar, Red & Black Paint, 13 x 13 In.	....	690.00
Board, Checkers, Rose Stenciled, Grain Painted, Early 20th Century, 22 x 35 In.	....	235.00
Board, Checkers, Salmon, Black Blocks, White & Black Border, Wood, Painted, 16 In.	......	385.00
Board, Checkers, Slate, Marbleized, Jas. Foote Gen'l, Staltington, Pa., 1800s, 22 x 22 In.	....	956.00
Board, Checkers, Wood, 2-Sided, Mitered Molding, Yellow, Green, 9½ x 19½ In.	....	2468.00
Board, Checkers, Wood, Painted, Applied Molding, Dividers, Dark Brown, White, 18 x 31 In.	.	588.00
Board, Checkers, Wood, Painted, Green, Salmon, White, 17 x 17½ In.	....	3173.00
Board, Checkers, Wood, Painted, Square, Applied Molding, Salmon, Black, 16⅜ x 16 In.	....	1998.00
Board, Checkers, Yellow & Black, Pine, Rectangular Panel, 19th Century, 19 x 31 In.	....	1000.00
Board, Checkers & Parcheesi, Painted, Multicolored, 18 x 17¾ In.	....	600.00
Board, Checkers & Parcheesi, Painted, White, Black, Green, 1800s, 16½ x 14½ In.	....	720.00
Board, Chinese Checkers, Painted Orange, Blue, White, Yellow, Black, 1800s, 15 x 15 In.	...	960.00
Board, Coin Toss, Tabletop, Numbered Squares, Bull's-Eye Center, Frame, 47½ In.	....	2750.00
Board, Cribbage, Banded Inlay, Starburst, Diamonds, Drawers, 1800s, 17½ x 7½ In.	....	403.00
Board, Cribbage, Bone, Carved, No Pegs, 10 x 7 x 3¼ In.	....	92.00
Board, Cribbage, Ivory Inlaid, Ball Feet, Inscribed, England, 18th Century	....	550.00
Board, Parcheesi, 2-Sided, Black Ground, Blue, Orange, Green, 27 x 27 In.	....	1495.00
Board, Parcheesi, 2-Sided, Cloud Pattern Decoration, Maine, 21 x 33 In.	....	1150.00
Board, Parcheesi, 12 x 12 Draughts, Marquetry, Quebec, c.1900, 19 x 32 In.	....	283.00
Board, Parcheesi, Checkers, 2-Sided, Painted Pine, 18½ x 20 In.	....	3000.00
Board, Parcheesi, Checkers, Painted, Multicolored, Early 20th Century, 21 x 21 In.	....	2700.00
Board, Parcheesi, Green Ground, Red, Black, Home In Center, Wood, 20 x 19¾ In.	....	825.00
Board, Parcheesi, Multicolored, Artist Board, Wood Frame, 20½ In.	....	468.00
Board, Parcheesi, Multicolored, Painted, Wooden, Square, Rounded Corners, 18 x 19 In.	...	6463.00
Board, Parcheesi, Painted, Black, Brown, Hinged, 19th Century, 17½ x 17¼ In.	....	1920.00
Board, Parcheesi, Painted, Black, White, Red, Green, Yellow, 20th Century, 18 x 18 In.	......	13200.00
Board, Parcheesi, Painted, White, Brown, Incised, 19th Century, 18½ x 18½ In.	....	11400.00
Board, Parcheesi, Pine, Painted, Incised Lines, Red, Yellow, Green, Blue, 18 x 18 In.	....	588.00
Board, Parcheesi, Wood Frame, Multicolored Paint, Square, 20½ In.	...............*illus*	468.00

Board, Pine, Multicolored, Original Paint, Geometric, 20¼ In.	209.00
Board, Pine, Painted, Square, Recessed Corner Pockets, 30¾ x 31 In.	5875.00
Box, Belgian Great Mogul Cards, Burl Wood, Papier-Mache, Mother-Of-Pearl, 1880, 6 x 9 In.	1080.00
Box, Compendium, Coromandel, Wood, Hinged, England, Mid 19th Century, 8¼ x 13 In.	2400.00
Box, Compendium, Victorian, Mahogany, England, c.1889, 13 x 17½ In.	7200.00
Box, Dominoes, Mahogany, Brass, Hinged Lid, Lift-Out Tray, Bone & Ebony Dominoes, 5½ x 16 In.	705.00
Box, Ivory, Silver, Carved, Side Panels, Latticework, Chinese, c.1800, 5 x 9½ In.	9600.00
Box, Lacquer, Dragon Head Legs, Hinged, Chinese, Early 19th Century, 6 x 12¼ In.	1320.00
Box, Playing Card, Needlework, Ribbed Pattern Paper, Wood Frame, Tray, c.1850, 6 x 8½ In.	420.00
Box, Poker Chip, Divided Interior, 411 Chips, Abercrombie & Fitch Co., Hinged Lid, 6 x 11 In.	115.00
Chess Set, Board, Ivory, Chinese	561.00
Chess Set, Red, Gold Anodized Aluminum Chess Pieces, Man Ray, 1945-47	11400.00
Chess Set, Wood, Carved, Encased, Chinese, c.1960, 4½ x 18 In.	117.00
Chit Chat, Hugh Downs Game Of Conversation, Milton Bradley, Board, 1963	20.00
Clown Ring Toss, Transogram, 1950	75.00
Combat Bagatelle, Louis Marx, Box, c.1965, 10 x 16 x 1 In.	84.00
Croquet, Thors Croquet, England, Box, c.1900	1275.00
Dexterity Puzzle, Cats & Mice, Round, Prewar Germany	45.00
Dice, Painted, White, Black, 7½ In.	748.00
Domino, Box, Bone, Book Shape, Tortoiseshell Pattern, Hinged Lid, c.1815, 1¾ x 2¾ In.	1800.00
Domino, Box, Bone, Cards, Cribbage Side Rails, Watercolor, Peaked Slide Lid, c.1815, 4 x 10 In.	3840.00
Donkey Shooting, Donkey, Black Man, Clown, Ringmaster, Tin, Strauss, 1920s, 18 In.	750.00
Family Affair, Where's Mrs. Beasley, Whitman, Board, 1971	165.00
Fish Pond, McLoughlin Bros., 1890	12.00
Footitt Et Chocolat, Tossing Hat, Wood Box, France, c.1900, 8½ x 8½ In.	175.00
Funnies, World's Funniest Card Game, 1924, 6 x 6½ x 1 In.	224.00
Funny Bones, Parker Brothers, Card, 1968	8.00
Geewiz Horse Race, Wolverine Of Pittsburgh, 1930s	155.00
Grand Loterie, Roulette Wheel, Playing Sticks, Prizes, Wood Box, France, 15 x 12 In.	990.00
Great Blockade, Linen On Paper Board, W. Childs, England, 21 x 14 In. _illus_	1900.00
Green Ghost, Glows In The Dark, Transogram, Board, Original Box, 1965	200.00
High Speed Race World Champion, Track, Gates, Lithograph, Japan, Box, 8½ In.	468.00
Jigsaw Puzzle, Aunt Jemima Pancake Flour, Pickaninny Doll, Die Cut, Cardboard, 4 x 3 In.	143.00
Jigsaw Puzzle, Circus, Lithographed, 3 Puzzles, Box, McLoughlin, 12 x 10 In. _illus_	750.00
Jigsaw Puzzle, Effanbee Doll, 6 Puzzles, Box, 1940s	150.00
Jigsaw Puzzle, Fire Engine, Cardboard, McLoughlin Toys & Games, Wooden Box, 1887	625.00
Jigsaw Puzzle, Fire Engine, Fire Fighting Scene, McLoughlin, 17½ x 25 In.	687.00
Jigsaw Puzzle, Flintstones, Sliding Squares, On Card, Late 1960s, 5 x 6 In.	164.00
Jigsaw Puzzle, Huckleberry Hound & Yogi Bear, Sliding Squares, On Card, c.1969, 5 x 6 In.	99.00
Jigsaw Puzzle, Regular Fellers Marble Puzzle, Box, Japan	308.00
Jigsaw Puzzle, Santa's Workshop, Inlaid Heavy Cardboard, Lowe, 1940s	10.00
Jigsaw Puzzle, Sting Ray, Wood, 20 Pieces, Ponda, John Waddington, 1960s, 6 x 8 In.	84.00
Jolly Marble, Circus Performers, Hinged Tier, Cups, Paper On Wood, 1892, 21 x 19 In.	990.00
Jump Jockey, Electric, Steeplechasing, Trang, England, 1960, 18 x 22 In.	55.00
Justice League Of America, Flash, Cardboard, Hasbro, Board, Box, 1967, 8½ x 16½ In.	228.00
Kentucky Derby, Dice, 1930s, 10 x 12 In.	555.00
King Pin Bowling, No. 300, Tin, Baldwin Company, 1930s	110.00
Land Of The Giants, Ideal, Board, 1968	260.00
Little Orphan Annie's Treasure Hunt, Board, 1933	112.00
Lost In Space, Milton Bradley, Board, Box, 1965	47.00
Louisa, Built-In Board, Playing Pieces, McLoughlin, 16½ x 18 In. _illus_	150.00
Mechanical Teacher, ABCs, Numbers, Wood, Cycloo Toy, Marble, 1818	168.00
Merry Go Round, Built-In Board, Wood Tokens, Parker Bros., 21 x 14 In. _illus_	325.00
Merry Milkman, All Pieces, Instructions, Hasbro, Board, 1950, 12 x 18 In.	200.00
Mighty Comics Superheroes, Transogram, Board, Box, 1966, 7¾ x 15 In.	209.00
Mutt & Jeff's Jokes, Gilbert, Box, 1920s, 8½ x 12½ x 1 In.	328.00
Mystery Gun, Tin Lithograph, No. 55, McDowell Mfg., Box, 1920s	225.00
Name That Tune, Milton Bradley, Board, 1959	34.00
Nancy Drew Mystery, Parker Brothers, Board, 1957	68.00
Outer Limits, Milton Bradley, Board, Box, 1964, 9½ x 19 In.	287.00
Parcel Post Toy Town, Antique Truck, Bradley, 1910	195.00
Parlor Keeps, Lithograph, Wood, Marble, c.1880	392.00
Peter Max Chesset, Kontrell, Box, 1971, 12 x 24¼ In.	154.00
Pinball, Painted Pine, Arched, Green, Gray, White, Pin Nails, Slots, Board, 20 x 10 In.	2100.00
Pinhead, Hide & Seek, Remco, Board, 1959	10.00
Planet Of The Apes, Milton Bradley, Board, 1974	42.00
Press, Playing Card, Nickel Plated, Cast Iron, Flowers, Fleur-De-Lis, c.1880, 9 x 5 In.	1300.00

Galle Pottery, Vase, Sunflower Shape, Thistles, Blue, Faience, 6½ In.
$978.00

Game, Beany & Cecil Ring Toss, Wood Characters, Box, Pressman Toys, 1962, 14 x 20 In.
$202.00

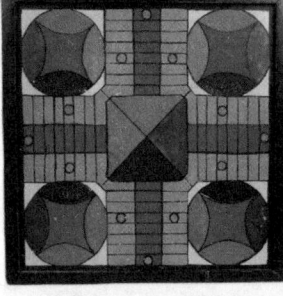

Game, Board, Parcheesi, Wood Frame, Multicolored Paint, Square, 20½ In.
$468.00

Game, Great Blockade, Linen On Paper Board, W. Childs, England, 21 x 14 In.
$1900.00

Game, Jigsaw Puzzle, Circus, Lithographed, 3 Puzzles, Box, McLoughlin, 12 x 10 In. $750.00

Game, Louisa, Built-In Board, Playing Pieces, McLoughlin, 16½ x 18 In. $150.00

Game, Merry Go Round, Built-In Board, Wood Tokens, Parker Bros., 21 x 14 In. $325.00

Game, Show Horse, Board, Spinner, Award Cards, Playing Pieces, Box, 19 x 9½ In. $518.00

Rawhide Cattle Drive, No Dice, Berwick, England, Box, c.1960, 11 x 17 In.	296.00
Shoot A Loop, Tin Lithograph, Wolverine, Marble	39.00
Show Horse, Board, Spinner, Award Cards, Playing Pieces, Box, 19 x 9½ In. ......*illus*	518.00
Snake Eyes, No. 27, Selchow & Righter, Board, 1957, 7½ x 11½ In.	250.00
Snuffy Smith's Barney Google, Complete, Box	50.00
Space:1999, Omnia, Board, 1974	20.00
Target, Buster Brown, Paper Lithograph On Wood, Manufactured By Bliss, 24 x 10 In.	259.00
Target, Carnival, Oriental Man, Green Fan, Red Pants, Iron, Wood Base, 13⅝ x 5¾ In.	15680.00
Target, Man From U.N.C.L.E., Plastic, Cardboard, Ideal, Box, c.1965, 15 In.	220.00
Target, Removable Marble Shooters, Iron Score Wheels, Kyser & Rex, 10 x 10 In. ......*illus*	1495.00
Target, Shooting Gallery, Horned Ram, Cast Iron, Bullet Holes, 31 x 26 In.	1380.00
Target, Teddy Roosevelt, Elephant, Schoenhut, c.1910, 11 In.	150.00
Targeteer BB, Original Box, Daisy	220.00
Touring, Parker Brothers, Card, 1958	13.00 to 15.00
Trip Round The World, Map Board, Spinners, Tokens, McLoughlin, 22 x 16 In. ......*illus*	250.00
Trump Indicator, Card Holder, Lady, Stylized, Celluloid, Marbleized Mustard, 4¼ In.	720.00
Trump Indicator, Leprechaun, Lead, Painted, Flip Style, 5¼ In.	660.00
Trump Indicator, Pig, Brass, Brass Scroll, Flip Style, 4 In.	360.00
Underwater Maze, Transogram, Board, 1966	165.00
Wheel, Gambling, Bird Decals, Center Hub, White Ground, Blue Number Outer Ring, 23 In.	39.00
Wheel, Gambling, Multicolored, Green Shaft, Painted Red X Base, Early 1900s, 25 x 18 In.	294.00
Wheel, Gambling, Painted Concentric Circles, Ship Wheel Spokes, Number Border, 27 In.	743.00
Wheel, Gambling, Pierced Center Holes, Painted, Outer Ring Numbers, 42 In.	94.00
Wheel, Gambling, Red & White, Christmas Inscription, 77-In. Hanging Chain, 1904-05	350.00
Wheel, Gambling, Red Star Center, White Ground, 35½ In.	110.00
Wheel, Gambling, Turned Multicolored Stand, Iron Legs, Star, Finials, H.C. Evans, 89 x 61 In.	550.00
Wheel Gambling, Painted, 2-Sided, Wrought Iron Hub, Geometric Fretwork, 30 In.	470.00
Wheel Gambling, Wood, Iron, Painted, 6-Point Spoke, Black, White, Tripod, 26½ x 20 In.	441.00
Wheel Of Fortune, Painted Wheel, Electrified, Light Bulbs, Wood Cased Box, 30 x 30 In.	385.00
Willie Mays Say Hey, Board, 1950s, 9 x 14 In.	575.00
Wizard Of Oz, Blue & White, 5 Main Characters, England, Card, Box, 1939, 44 Cards	170.00
Wolf Man Mystery Game, Hasbro, 1963, 15½ x 18½ In.	206.00
Wonderful Wizard Of Oz, Fairchild, Board, 1957	140.00
Wonderful Wizard Of Oz, Parker, Board, 19½ x 10 In.	220.00
Yacht Race, Spinner, McLoughlin Bros., Board, Pat. Dec. 27, 1887, 8 x 16 In.	138.00
Yard Balls, Carrying Tray, Burlwood, 4½ In Ball, 6¾ x 22 x 5¾ In. Tray, 5 Piece	160.00

GAME PLATES are plates of any make decorated with pictures of birds, animals, or fish. The game plates usually came in sets consisting of twelve dishes and a serving platter. These sets were most popular during the 1880s.

2 Pheasants Flying, Marked Germany, Leuchtenburg, 8¼ In.	25.00
Fish, Sand & Sea, Scalloped Edge, Gold Trim, Flambeau China, c.1900, 9⅞ In.	135.00
Fish, Seaweed, Transfer Printed, Gold Rim, Signed Lea, Bawo & Dotter, c.1910, 8½ In.	85.00
Mallard Pair, Transfer, Hand Painted, Gold Detail, Haviland, 9 In.	175.00

GARDEN FURNISHINGS have been popular for centuries. The stone or metal statues, wire, iron, or rustic furniture, urns and fountains, sundials, and small figurines are included in this category. Many of the metal pieces have been made continuously for years.

Bench, Flower Urn Pattern, Rococo Revival, Cast Iron, Mid 1800s, 41 x 46 In.	3525.00
Bench, Scroll & Horseshoe Back, Openwork, Cabriole Legs, Iron, 35 x 43 In. ......*illus*	2070.00
Bench, Scroll Back & Apron, Grape Pattern, White Paint, Cast Iron, 1900s, 30¾ x 40 In.	288.00
Bench, Scrolls, Flower Crest, Arch Back, Arms, Cabriole Legs, Iron, 1800s, 32 x 62 In.	1315.00
Bench, Scrolls, Renaissance Style, Iron, Kramer Bros., Dayton, c.1900, 38 x 46 In., Pair	920.00
Bench, Shield & Leaf, Curved Back, Pierced Seat, Cast Iron, 1900s, 30½ x 37½ In.	115.00
Bootscraper, 2 Arched Fish, Scrolled Tails, On Canted Plate, Iron, 8 In.	105.00
Bootscraper, Columns, Incised, Outward Turned Ends, Faceted Terminals, Iron, 7¾ In.	385.00
Bootscraper, Lyre Shape, Oval Pan, Fluted & Scalloped Edge, Iron, Black Paint, 11 x 9 In.	300.00
Bootscraper, Lyre Shape In Tray, Scalloped Border, Iron, 10 x 12 x 9½ In.	65.00
Bootscraper, Men Sawing, Cast Iron, 6 x 16½ In.	460.00
Bootscraper, Satyr & Lioness Masks, Oval, Iron, Old Black Paint, 5 x 18 x 11 In.	900.00
Bootscraper, Twisted Supports, Iron, Blacksmith Made, New England	350.00
Chair, Green Pads, Metal, Salesman Sample, 1950s, 22 x 9 In.	27.00
Chair, Pierced Design, Round Seat, Curved Legs, White Paint, Cast Iron, 20th Century, 31 In.	58.00
Chair Set, Fern Pattern, White Paint, Cast Iron, E.T. Barnum, 3 Piece	1444.00
Figure, Alpine Boy, After Haubner, Metal, 25 In.	293.00

Figure, Black Man & Woman, Sitting, Arms On Lap, Limestone, c.1900, 22 In., Pair	90.00
Figure, Deer, Reclining, Lead, 23 x 22 In., Pair	2574.00
Figure, Deity, Ganesha, Standing Elephant, Bronze, 72 x 31 In.	3510.00
Figure, Duck, Head Raised, Marble, White, 23 In.	585.00
Figure, Geese, Cast Iron, 20 In., Pair	381.00
Figure, Putto, Holding Flowers, Square Cloud Base, Carrara Marble, Carved, 28 In.	1560.00
Figure, Rabbit, White Paint, Seated, Ears Up, Cast Iron, Late 1900s, 11 x 9½ In., Pair	805.00
Figure, Satyr, With Tambourine, Pedestal, Flower Petal Border, Bronze, 32 In. ....*illus*	1035.00
Figure, Woman, Allegorical, Summer, Robed, Holding Sheaf Of Wheat, Cast Stone, 27 In.	824.00
Figure, Young Fruit Gatherer, Wearing Straw Hat, Cast Stone, 27½ In.	528.00
Fountain, Boy, With Calla Lily, Cast Iron, J.L. Mott, 52 In.	5462.00
Fountain, Boy With Goose, Fish Heads, Bronze, 26 x 13 In.	748.00
Fountain, Children In Fountain, White Marble, Continental, 20th Century, 68 x 31 In.	3450.00
Fountain, Mermaid, Lotus, Bronze, 62 x 36 In.	2500.00
Fountain, Scalloped Shell Basin, Cherubs, Cast Iron, 3 Tiers, 81 x 40 In.	6169.00
Fountain, Wall, Armorial, Cast Stone, 20th Century, 28 In.	957.00
Fountain, Wall, Classical Style, Cherub, Shells, Scallop Basin, Black Masonry, 34 x 19 In.	88.00
Fountain, Wall, Lion's Mask, Demilune Basin, Shaped Border, Cast Lead, 32 x 18 In.	2880.00
Fountain, Wall, Roaring Lion Mask, Colonial Metalcrafters, Tyler, Texas, 20 x 16 In.	205.00
Hitching Post, Horse Head, Cast Iron, 44 In.	440.00
Hitching Post, Jockey, Arm Extended With Ring, Square Base, Iron, 47 In.	748.00
Horse Tether, Hand Cut Granite, Iron Ring, Mid To Late 1800s	125.00
Lawn Sprinkler, Alligator, Red Paint, Cast Iron, 10 In.	165.00
Lawn Sprinkler, Frog, Alligator Style Back, Green, Cast Iron, 11 x 8¾ In.	1120.00
Lawn Sprinkler, Frog, On Ball, Green, Red, Yellow, Cast Iron, Signed, Nuyda, 10 x 7 In.	1904.00
Lawn Sprinkler, Frog, On Rock, Copper Over Plaster, 9½ x 8⅝ In.	1344.00
Lawn Sprinkler, Frog, Seated On Ball, Red & Brown Paint, Cast Iron, 9 In.	165.00
Lawn Sprinkler, Frog, Spread Legs, Green, Yellow, Cast Iron, 8⅝ x 14 In.	2520.00
Lawn Sprinkler, Frog, Seated On Ball, Pedestal Base, 4 Footed, 12½ x 7½ In.	550.00
Lawn Sprinkler, Mallard Duck, Brown, Green, White, Orange, Cast Iron, Signed, B & H	2240.00
Lawn Sprinkler, Mermaid, Fluted Base, Staff Is Sprinkler, Iron, 14 x 7 In. ....*illus*	3300.00
Lawn Sprinkler, Sambo, Original Label, 35 In.	360.00
Lawn Sprinkler, Wood Duck, Painted, Signed, Nuyda, Cast Iron, 13½ x 8 In.	3640.00
Lawn Sprinkler, Wood Duck, Shell Shape Base, Cast Iron, Nuydea, 13½ x 8 In. ......*illus*	825.00
Ornament, Boy & Girl, On Seesaw, Bronze, 24 x 54 In.	880.00
Ornament, Cherub, Cement, France, c.1900, 31 In.	175.00
Plant Stand, see Furniture, Stand, Plant	
Seat, Bat, Bird, Flowers, Celadon, White, Chinese Export, 18 x 12 In.	472.00
Seat, Flowers, Reticulated, Chinese Export, Early 1900s, 19 x 14 In.	430.00
Seat, Riverscape, Chinese, 18 In.	708.00
Spigot, Brass, Magic Incised On Turnkey, Patented Oct. 28 1870, 5 In.	45.00
Statue, Iron, 4 Seasons, 4 Women, Holding Seasonal Items, Brown Patina, 44 In., 4 Piece ...*illus*	1560.00
Table, Inlaid Marble Top, Black Paint, Lion Mask, Round, Claw Feet, Cast Iron, 29 x 26 In.	460.00
Urn, Dome Lid, Terra-Cotta, White Paint, Relief Acanthus, Stepped Square Base, 32 In., Pair	780.00
Urn, Elephant Mask Handles, Applied Tree, Birds, Foo Dog Lid, Openwork, Brass, 39 In.	2640.00
Urn, Gray Paint, Ribbed, 2 Handles, Footed, Cast Iron, 16½ x 35 In., Pair	381.00
Urn, Pedestal, Cast Iron, 42 x 25¼ In., Pair	2650.00
Urn, Pedestal, Concrete, 26 & 24 In.	454.00
Water Pump, Red Paint, Pinstriping, Bay State Pump, Jos. Breck & Sons, Boston, 76 In.	288.00
Watering Can, Brass, 20th Century, 17 x 21 x 8 In.	70.00
Watering Can, Brass Rose, England, 2 Gal.	65.00
Watering Can, Copper & Brass, England, c.1790	695.00

GARDNER Porcelain Works was founded in Verbiki, outside Moscow, by the English-born Francis Gardner in 1766. The Gardner family retained ownership of the factory until 1891 and produced porcelain tablewares, figurines, and faience.   ΓΑΡΔΗΕΡΖ

Bowl, Round, Roses, Red, Orange, Flowers, Foliage, Victorian Woman, Moscow, 1800s	275.00
Cup & Saucer, White, Painted, Flowers, Gold Swirls, Moscow, 1890s, 3 x 4¾ In.	450.00
Figurine, Bisque, Man Playing Accordion, Early 20th Century, 7 x 4½ In.	4800.00
Figurine, Dancing Peasant, Rust Dress, Leaf Sprigged White Apron, Bisque, 8 In.	1175.00
Figurine, Man, Carrying Tray Of Buns, Basket, Sampling Wares, 8⅜ In.	823.00
Figurine, Mother & Child Ironing, Seated Outdoors, Bisque, 4 In.	764.00
Figurine, Peasant Girl, Holding Pitcher, Beaker, Basket On Back, Bisque, 8 In.	2233.00
Figurine, Peasant Girl, Regional Dress, Holding Wheat Sheaf, Bisque, 9 In.	1175.00
Figurine, Peasant Woman, 2 Children, On Bench, Feeding Baby, Bisque, 5¾ In.	1528.00
Group, 2 Boys, Cracking Colored Eggs, Seated On Bench, 6 In.	881.00

Game, Target, Removable Marble Shooters, Iron Score Wheels, Kyser & Rex, 10 x 10 In. $1495.00

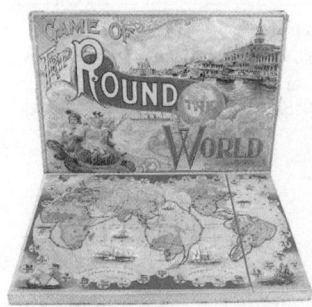

Game, Trip Round The World, Map Board, Spinners, Tokens, McLoughlin, 22 x 16 In. $250.00

Garden, Bench, Scroll & Horseshoe Back, Openwork, Cabriole Legs, Iron, 35 x 43 In. $2070.00

Garden, Figure, Satyr, With Tambourine, Pedestal, Flower Petal Border, Bronze, 32 In. $1035.00

Garden, Lawn Sprinkler, Mermaid, Fluted Base, Staff Is Sprinkler, Iron, 14 x 7 In. $3300.00

Garden, Lawn Sprinkler, Wood Duck, Shell Shape Base, Cast Iron, Nuydea, 13½ x 8 In. $825.00

Garden, Statue, Iron, 4 Seasons, 4 Women, Holding Seasonal Items, Brown Patina, 44 In., 4 Piece $1560.00

GAUDY DUTCH pottery was made in England for the American market from about 1810 to 1820. It is a white earthenware with Imari-style decorations of red, blue, green, yellow, and black. Only sixteen patterns of Gaudy Dutch were made: Butterfly, Carnation, Dahlia, Double Rose, Dove, Grape, Leaf, Oyster, Primrose, Single Rose, Strawflower, Sunflower, Urn, War Bonnet, Zinnia, and No Name. Other similar wares are called Gaudy Ironstone and Gaudy Welsh.

Bowl, Adams, 2 x 9 In.	15.00
Bowl, Adams, Scalloped Rim, 4 x 2½ In.	85.00
Coffeepot, Dome Lid, Flowers, Scrolled Handle, Acanthus Leaf Molded Spout, 12 In.	2300.00
Coffeepot, Single Rose, Blue Band, 10¾ In.	2875.00
Creamer, Oyster, Helmet Shape, 4½ In. *illus*	143.00
Cup & Saucer, Adams, Handleless	65.00
Cup & Saucer, Butterfly, Handleless	834.00
Cup & Saucer, Grape, c.1860	195.00
Cup & Saucer, Oyster, Handleless, Red Rim	176.00
Cup & Saucer, Single Rose, Handleless *illus*	187.00
Cup & Saucer, Single Rose, Handleless, Blue Rim	187.00
Cup & Saucer, Urn, 2½ x 5⅝ In.	220.00
Cup & Saucer, War Bonnet, Handleless, 2½ x 5½ In.	193.00
Cup & Saucer Set, Single Rose, 2⅜ x 5½ In., 8 Piece	715.00
Pitcher, Carnation, 6¼ In.	550.00
Pitcher, Cream, Single Rose, 4¾ In.	110.00
Pitcher, Cream, Sunflower, Snake Handle, c.1831, 5½ In.	116.00
Pitcher, Oyster, 7½ x 4 In.	75.00
Plate, Adams, 9 In.	65.00
Plate, Butterfly, 7⅜ In.	144.00
Plate, Butterfly, 9⅞ In.	4485.00
Plate, Butterfly, Blue Border, 9⅞ In.	1840.00
Plate, Single Rose, Blue Rim, 9⅞ In.	1207.00
Plate, Toddy, Grape, 4½ In.	385.00
Plate, Urn, 6¼ In.	288.00
Plate, Urn, Paneled Border, 9¾ In.	747.00
Saucer, Single Rose, 5⅝ In.	138.00
Soup, Dish, Grape, 9⅞ In.	403.00 to 550.00
Sugar, Cover, Dove, Molded Shell Handles, Quatrefoil Rim, 6¼ In.	575.00
Sugar, Cover, Sunflower, Molded Handles, Scalloped Gallery Rim, 5½ In.	1610.00
Sugar, Single Rose, Shell Shape Handles, 4¾ In.	330.00
Teapot, Butterfly, 5½ In.	718.00
Teapot, Oyster, Paneled Borders, 6⅛ In.	2530.00
Teapot, Single Rose, 7 In.	805.00
Waste Bowl, Carnation, 3 x 5⅜ In.	385.00

GAUDY IRONSTONE is the collector's name for the ironstone wares with the bright patterns similar to Gaudy Dutch. It was made in England for the American market after 1850. There may be other examples found in the listing for Ironstone or under the name of the ceramic factory.

Bowl, Vegetable, Octagonal, Fern, Flowers, 9 x 7 In.	116.00
Cake Plate, Tulip, 8¼ In.	175.00
Cup & Saucer, Morning Glory & Strawberry	300.00
Cup & Saucer, Paneled, Strawberry, 3 x 5⅞ In.	165.00
Plate, Blackberry, 8½ In.	94.00
Plate, Copper Luster, Pink Luster Border, 8¼ In.	150.00
Plate, Morning Glory & Strawberry, 8¾ In.	350.00
Plate, Paneled, Half Ripe Strawberry, 8½ In.	149.00
Plate, Paneled, Strawberry, 8 In.	193.00
Plate, Primrose, 8¼ In.	350.00
Plate, Seeing Eye, 8¼ In.	350.00
Teapot, Morning Glory, Gothic Shape, 10 x 8½ In.	155.00
Waste Bowl, Seeing Eye, 3½ x 5 In.	280.00

GAUDY WELSH is an Imari-decorated earthenware with red, blue, green, and gold decorations. Most Gaudy Welsh was made in England for the American market. It was made from 1820 to about 1860.

Cake Plate, Sunflower, c.1860, 7¾ In.	195.00
Cake Plate, Tulip, 8¼ In.	175.00

Cake Plate, Tulip, 10 In.	145.00
Cup & Saucer, Angels Trumpet	195.00
Cup & Saucer, Venus	195.00
Jug, Dutch, 8-Sided, c.1830, 6¼ In.	295.00
Jug, Grape, Octagonal, Impressed Mark, c.1930, 6¼ In.	295.00
Jug, Llanelly Poppy, c.1840, 7¼ In.	350.00
Jug, Poppies, Orange, Blue, Green Leaves, 4 In.	350.00
Mug, Forget-Me-Not, 1830-40, 3 In.	450.00
Pitcher, Baluster, Inscribed, Mary Brayshaw Died Febry 3 1837, 8 In.	1016.00
Plate, Flower Basket II, 9 In.	175.00
Plate, Flowers, Gold Edged Leaves, Vines, 1903, 6 In.	30.00
Plate, Grapevine, Square, 8½ In.	175.00
Plate, Lotus, 9 In.	195.00
Plate, Strawberry, 8¾ In.	350.00
Plate, Tulip, Square, 8½ In.	175.00
Sugar, Cover, 4¾ In.	135.00
Tea Set, Tulip, Teapot, Sugar, Lid, Creamer, Cups, Saucers, Plates, Waste Bowl, 26 Piece	374.00
Teapot, Flow Blue, 7 In.	40.00

GEISHA GIRL porcelain was made for export in the late nineteenth century in Japan. It was an inexpensive porcelain often sold in dime stores or used as free premiums. Pieces are sometimes marked with the name of a store. Japanese ladies in kimonos are pictured on the dishes. There are over 125 recorded patterns. Borders of red, blue, green, gold, brown, or several of these colors were used. Modern reproductions are being made.

Cup & Saucer, Demitasse, Lithophane, 2¼ In.	10.00 to 35.00
Cup & Saucer, Lithophane, Cover	48.00
Sugar & Creamer, Cover	48.00
Tea Set, Dragon Spout, Lithophane, 21 Piece	149.00 to 200.00
Teapot, Lithophane, Charcoal Gray, Blue, Pink, 6 In.	12.00

GENE AUTRY was born in 1907. He began his career as the "Singing Cowboy" in 1928. His first movie appearance was in 1934, his last in 1958. His likeness and that of the Wonder Horse, Champion, were used on toys, books, lunch boxes, and advertisements.

Award Ribbon, Snake River Stampede, Medallion, Frame, July 11, 1950, 12½ In.	168.00
Belt, Vinyl, Buckle, Keeper, 1950s, 31 In.	140.00
Boots, Rubber, Brown, 4 Buckles, Servus, Box, 1950s, 9½ In.	112.00
Cap, Military Style, Cloth, Red, 1940s, 9 x 4 In.	102.00
Cap Gun, Cast Iron, Nickel Finish, Red Grips, Kenton, 1950s, 6½ In.	474.00
Cap Gun, Die Cast Nickel, Horsehead Grips, 1950s, 7½ In.	185.00
Cap Gun, Die Cast Nickel, Plastic Grips, Buzz Henry, Box, 1950s, 7½ In.	310.00
Cap Gun, Repeating, Cast Iron, Orange Grips, Kenton, Box, 1950, 8½ In.	1879.00
Cowboy Hat, Wool, Hat Band, Images, Chin Strap, 12½ x 14 x 4 In.	246.00
Display, Friendship Ring, Cardboard, Easel Back, 1940s, 7½ In.	671.00
Display, Gene Autry & Champion, Cardboard, Stand-Up, 59 x 31 In. ....*illus*	440.00
Figure, Composition, Plaster, Painted, c.1940, 12½ In.	560.00
Knife, Rubber, Suede Sheath, 1950s, 11-In. Sheath, 8½-In. Knife	112.00
Lunch Box, Melody Ranch, Rearing Up On Horse, Lasso, Thermos, Universal, 1954	325.00
Movie Poster, Colorado Sunset, Republic, 1939, 27 x 41 In.	1035.00
Movie Poster, Yodelin' Kid From Pine Ridge, Republic, 1937, 27 x 41 In.	575.00
Outfit, Chaps, Vest, 1940s, 28-In. Chaps, 12-In. Vest	224.00
Paper Dolls, Gene Autry At Melody Ranch, Unpunched, Whitman, 1951, 14 x 11 In.	84.00
Pin, Guitar Club, Gene, On Horse, Holding Guitar, c.1950, 1 In.	84.00
Ring, Horseshoe Nail Ring, On Card, 1950s	140.00
Tie Slide, Gene Autry & Champ, Silvered Brass, President Product, On Card, 2¾ In.	154.00
Toy, Guitar, Gene Autry Emenee, Case, 31 In.	338.00
Toy, Gun, Cap, Cast Iron, Pearl Grip, Kenton, 1939, 8¾ In.	125.00
Window Card, Gene Autry & Company In Person, Die Cut, 14 x 11 In.	133.00
Wristwatch, 6-Shooter, New Haven, 1951, 2¼ x 5¾ In.	949.00
Wristwatch, New Haven, Box, 1-In. Dial, 5 x 5 In.	392.00

GIBSON GIRL black-and-blue decorated plates were made in the early 1900s. Twenty-four different 10½-inch plates were made by the Royal Doulton pottery at Lambeth, England. These pictured scenes from the book *A Widow and Her Friends* by Charles Dana Gibson. Another set of twelve 9-inch plates featuring pictures of the heads of Gibson Girls had all-blue decoration. Many other items also pictured the famous Gibson Girl.

Gaudy Dutch, Creamer, Oyster, Helmet Shape, 4½ In.
$143.00

Gaudy Dutch, Cup & Saucer, Single Rose, Handleless
$187.00

G

Gene Autry, Display, Gene Autry & Champion, Cardboard, Stand-Up, 59 x 31 In.
$440.00

Gillinder, Bust, Lincoln, Frosted, Embossed A. Lincoln, Centennial Exhibition, 6 In.
$110.00

Gillinder, Salt & Pepper, Melon, White Opalescent, Late 1800s, 3 In.
$110.00

"Elegant" Glass

Glass collectors use the term *elegant* to refer to American hand-pressed items made from about 1925 to 1955. Even though the glassware was produced in large quantities, the "elegant" factories used higher-quality raw materials and employed skilled glassmakers. Several companies, like Heisey and Fostoria, called their glassware *American crystal.*

Doll, Plastic, Storybook, Gray Sleep Eyes, Jointed, Clothing, Box, 7½ In.	28.00
Fashion Print, Frame, 19th Century, 50 x 39 In., 3 Piece	3750.00
Plate, Mr. Waddles Arrives Late & Finds Her Card Filled, c.1900, 10½ In.	250.00
Plate, Quiet Dinner With Dr. Bottles, Reads Miss Babbles Book, c.1900, 10½ In.	250.00
Plate, Some Think She Has Remained In Retirement Too Long, c.1900, 10½ In.	250.00
Postcard, You Are The Apple Of My Eye, Leather, Postmark, Stamp, 1906	9.00
Print, Frame, Oval, A. Fox, c.1907, 8 x 10 In.	24.00

GILLINDER pressed glass was first made by William T. Gillinder of Philadelphia in 1863. The company had a working factory on the grounds at the Centennial and made small, marked pieces of glass for sale as souvenirs. They made a variety of decorative glass pieces and tablewares. **GILLINDER**

Bread Tray, Luck & Puck	195.00
Bust, Lincoln, Frosted, Embossed A. Lincoln, Centennial Exhibition, 6 In. ....*illus*	110.00
Celery Vase, Frosted Lion, Footed, c.1877, 8¾ In.	48.00
Cologne, Ruffles, Stopper, 8 x 4 In.	75.00
Compote, Cover, Early American Pattern, Footed, c.1876, 9 In.	295.00
Cup, Lion, 2 In.	110.00
Mug, Liberty Bell, Snake Handle, Centennial Exhibition, 3⅝ In.	176.00
Paperweight, Lion, Frosted, 1876 Philadelphia Centennial Exhibition, 5½ x 3 In.	175.00
Salt & Pepper, Melon, White Opalescent, Late 1800s, 3 In. ....*illus*	110.00
Salt & Pepper, White, Blue Forget-Me Not Flowers, 3 In.	110.00

GIRL SCOUT collectors search for anything pertaining to the Girl Scouts, including uniforms, publications, and old cookie boxes. The Girl Scout movement started in 1912, two years after the Boy Scouts. It began under Juliette Gordon Low of Savannah, Georgia. The first Girl Scout cookies were sold in 1928.

Bank, Coin, Yellow, Orange, Plastic, Girl Scout Insignia, 3¾ x 2¼ In.	4.00
Bookends, GS, Eagle, Spread Wings, Wood, Metal, 5¾ In.	19.00
Bookmark, GS, Green, Metal, Early 1970, 1¾ In.	5.00
Camera, 620, Official Girl Scout, Black Case, Herbert George Co., 1940s	56.00
Coin, Honor The Past, Serve The Future, Oath, 50th Anniversary, 1 In.	8.00
Compass, Rotating Aluminum Dial, Silva, Laporte, Ind.	14.00
Figurine, Girl Scout, Spelter, Copper Coated, 6 In.	125.00
Handbook, Aqua, Yellow, Copyright 1940	10.00
Handbook, Brownie Scout, Hardback, 1960, 95 Pages	10.00
Handbook, Intermediate Program, Girl, Green, Yellow, Dust Jacket, 6th Imprint, 1944	50.00
Hat, Green, GS, Bow, Wide Brim, Cotton, Box, Cat. No. 2-150, Size 23, Cardboard	51.00
Pocketknife, Green, Insignia, Bottle Opener, Screwdriver, Ring, Kutmaster, 5¾ In.	15.00
Pocketknife, Single Blade, Brownie, Be Wise, Beware, Use Me With Care, Kutmaster, 3 In.	15.50
Record, Our Songs, 78, 1950s	15.00
Songbook, Pocket, Cultural Group Songs, Lute On Cover, 1956	5.00

GLASS-ART. Art glass means any of the many forms of glassware made during the late nineteenth or early twentieth century. These wares were expensive and production was limited. Art glass is not the typical commercial glass that was made in large quantities, and most of the art glass was produced by hand methods. Later twentieth-century glass is listed under Glass-Contemporary, Glass-Midcentury, or Glass-Venetian. Even more art glass may be found in categories such as Burmese, Cameo Glass, Tiffany, Venini, and other factory names.

Bowl, Centerpiece, Spider Webbing, Burgundy To Clear Ground, Wurttenberg, 5 x 10 In. *illus*	300.00
Bowl, Etched Brown Leaf, Berries, Frosted, Paynaud, 8¼ x 9 In.	1170.00
Bowl, Fish, Marquetry, 1970s, 18 In.	128.00
Bowl, Green Opaque, Optic Ribbed Body, Lacy Band At Rim, New England, 3 In.	489.00
Bowl, Iridescent, Golden Pink, Fluted Rim, White Interior, c.1910, 3½ In.	176.00
Bowl, Iridescent, Silvered Brass Mounted, Austria, c.1900, 10 In.	308.00
Bowl, Kew Blas, Iridescent, Undulating, Stretched Rim, 7¾ In.	411.00
Compote, Nautilus Shell, Pink Custard, Free-Blown, Early 1900s, 7 x 6½ In.	175.00
Console, Figural, Flower Frog, Seated Woman, Embossed Roses, 10 x 5¾ In.	280.00
Dish, Oyster Shape, Blue, Turquoise, Green, 6½ x 4½ In.	20.00
Figurine, Man In Hat, Sea Of Sweden, 9½ In.	29.00
Liquer Set, Peach, Opaque Red Rim, White Handle, Nude Female, 7¾ x 3½ In., 7 Piece	294.00
Pitcher, Vaseline, Bulbous, Overall Threading, Amethyst Loop Handle, 9 In. ....*illus*	118.00
Shade, Globe, Clear, Molded, Art Deco Style, 15 x 12 In.	146.00
Sugar, Green Opaque, 2 Applied Handle, Lacy Band At Rim, New England, 3½ In.	489.00

G

Vase, 6 Paneled Sides, Green, Fluted, Radiant-Cut Base, c.1915, 6¼ In. 382.00
Vase, Amber, Internal Swirls, Gray, Green, Blue Flowers, M. Peisner, 8½ In. 411.00
Vase, Amber, Iridescent Red, Flared Top, Flattened, Polished Rim, 13 In. 230.00
Vase, Amethyst, Acid Etched, Leaping Gazelle, Charles Catteau, 11 In. .... *illus* 6325.00
Vase, Amethyst, Enameled, Stylized Flowers, Art Nouveau, c.1900, 10 x 4½ In. 293.00
Vase, Blue Iridescent, Blossoming Hawthorne Tree, Shouldered, Flared Rim, 10¼ In. 891.00
Vase, Bubbled Blue, Spiral Wrapping, c.1890, 8 In. 600.00
Vase, Cobalt Blue, Red, Cranberry, Spiral Stripes, Flared Rim, Bulbous Body, 11 In. 705.00
Vase, Gold Aventurine, Hooked Internal Decoration, Cone Shape, Monart, 8¾ In. 86.00
Vase, Green, Gold, Ribbed, Bubbles, Italy, c.1940, 8½ x 7½ In. 360.00
Vase, Intaglio Cut, Peaches, Etched Leaves, Inverted Rim, Wide Shoulder, Neusom, 9 In. 881.00
Vase, Iridescent, Copper Mounted, Austria, c.1900, 8 In. 287.00
Vase, Moire Fern, Lundberg Studios, c.1999, 7 x 6 In. 321.00
Vase, Moorish Style, Satin Finish, Blue Enamel, Gilt Metal Rim Ornament, 25½ In. 1175.00
Vase, Opalescent, Enameled, Berries, Leaves, Gold, Green Ruffles, Hollow Stem, c.1890, 7 x 10 In. 295.00
Vase, Oval Mouth, Flared Silver Rim, Neck, Oval, Faceted Amethyst Cut To Clear, 9¼ In. 470.00
Vase, Paperweight, Iris Garden, Pink, Purple Iris & Other Flowers, C. Heilman, 7 In. 323.00
Vase, Paperweight, Willow & Iris, Orange, Internal Decoration, C. Heilman, 7 In. 353.00
Vase, Pink, Gilt Metal Overlay, Art Nouveau, 4¼ x 3¼ In. 94.00
Vase, Pulled Design, Blue & Gold Iridescent, Pear Shape, Footed, 7 x 3 In. 120.00
Vase, Ruby, Flashed, Enameled, 8¾ In., Pair 94.00
Vase, Tangerine, Purple, Wrought Iron Cage Frame, Leaves, Berries, 6¾ In. .... *illus* 1320.00

GLASS-BLOWN. Blown glass was formed by forcing air through a rod into molten glass. Early glass and some forms of art glass were hand blown. Other types of glass were molded or pressed.

Apothecary Jar, Cover, Twisted Body, 16 x 4 In., Pair 459.00
Apothecary Jar, Metal Lid, Latin Gilt Label, Black, Red, 10½ x 4¾ In., Pair 411.00
Bank, Clear, Chicken Finial, Raised Supports, Rigaree, Leaf, Coin Slot, 10¼ x 4 In. 2860.00
Bell, Cranberry, Ribs, Opal Rim, Swirled Rib Handle, Whimsy, 13 x 6 In. 77.00
Birdcage, Font, Clear, Hollow Finial, Crimped Wafer Stem, Applied Trough, 7¼ In. 88.00
Birdcage, Font, Cobalt Blue, Finial, Ringed Wafer Stem, Applied Trough, 6⅛ In. 66.00
Bowl, Aqua, Flared Folded Rim, Thumb Hold, 1820-40, 3¼ x 10 In. 469.00
Bowl, Aqua, Wide Tapered Body, Pontil, 1840-60, 3½ x 10 In. 110.00
Bowl, Clear, Footed, Continental, 19th Century, 10 In. 268.00
Bowl, Cobalt Blue, 8 Ribs, Folded Rim, Footed, 4 x 3½ In. .... *illus* 978.00
Bowl, Medium Amber, Flared Rim, Domed Base, Pontil, 5½ x 9⅛ In. 1100.00
Bowl, Opaque White, Flared Rim, Pontil, 5¼ x 12¾ In. 132.00
Bowl, Peacock Blue, Drawn Out Foot, Flared Rim, Pontil, 2¼ x 5 In. 105.00
Canister, Flanged Lid, Wafer Finial, Applied Cobalt Blue Rings, 5 x 10⅝ In. 431.00
Chalice, Clear, Engraved, Neoclassical Cartouche, Monogram, Flower Spray, 8 In. 523.00
Chalice, Cover, Clambroth, Bucket Bowl, 3-Part Stem, Knop, Pontil, 16½ In. 220.00
Compote, Amethyst, Folded Rim, Knop Baluster, Footed, Flint Pontil, c.1855, 1½ In. 143.00
Compote, Blue Opalescent, Enameled, Applied Baluster, Footed, 2½ x 3¾ In. 80.00
Compote, Clear, Leaf, Applied Solid Stem, Footed, Engraved, 6⅜ In. 121.00
Creamer, 3-Piece Mold, Tooled Rim, Pinched Spout, Pontil, c.1825, 4 In. .... *illus* 672.00
Creamer, Clear, Folded, Tooled Rim, Ribbed, Hollow Handle, Rayed Base, 4¾ x 3 In. 1870.00
Creamer, Cobalt Blue, Pattern Molded, Applied Handle, England, 1820-50, 3 In. 220.00
Creamer, Cobalt Blue, Rigaree, Crimped Rim & Spout, Pontil, 4½ In. .... *illus* 672.00
Creamer, Cobalt Blue, Tooled Rim, Applied Handle, Footed, Pontil, 4⅜ x 3¼ In. 6325.00
Creamer, Lily Pad, Red Amber, Squat, Pulled Peaks, Handle, 4½ x 2¾ In. 7700.00
Creamer, Opaque White, Bulbous, Tapered Neck, Solid Handle, Disc Foot, 5¼ In. 132.00
Cruet, Clear, Cartouche, Flower Engraved, Silver Mounted, 7½ x 2¾ In. 209.00
Cruet, Cobalt Blue, Folded Rim, Rayed Base, Tam-O-Shanter Stopper, 7¼ In. 330.00
Cruet, Cobalt Blue, Rayed Base, Tam-O-Shanter Stopper, Pontil, 6⅝ In. 99.00
Cruet, Cobalt Blue, Rayed Base, Tam-O-Shanter Stopper, Pontil, 7 In. .... 121.00 to 143.00
Cup, Dark Cobalt Blue, Applied Handle, Knopped Baluster & Foot, 1840-60, 4 In. 160.00
Decanter, Amethyst, 10 Neck Flutes, 11 Basal Flutes, Bar Lip, Metal Pourer, 11 In. 1210.00
Decanter, Clear, Frosted Band, Swags, Tassels, Teardrop Stopper, Pontil, 12 In. 198.00
Decanter, Clear, Rayed Base, Stopper, Pontil, Qt., 7¾ In. 110.00
Decanter, Clear, Rigaree, Gadrooning, Neckrings, Footed, Pontil, Norway, 1750-70, 8 In. 170.00
Decanter, Clear, Ringed Base, Pontil, ¼ Pt., 4¼ In. 66.00
Decanter, Cobalt Blue, Pontil, Qt., 9 In. 1980.00
Decanter, Cut Grape & Leaves, Ribs, Applied Neckrings, Stopper, Pontil, 1860-80, 9 In. 35.00
Decanter, Electric Blue, 10 Flutes, Applied Ring, 6-Panel Stopper, 13 In. 143.00

Glass-Art, Bowl, Centerpiece, Spider Webbing, Burgundy To Clear Ground, Wurttenberg, 5 x 10 In.
$300.00

Glass-Art, Pitcher, Vaseline, Bulbous, Overall Threading, Amethyst Loop Handle, 9 In.
$118.00

Glass-Art, Vase, Amethyst, Acid Etched, Leaping Gazelle, Charles Catteau, 11 In.
$6325.00

Glass-Art, Vase, Tangerine, Purple, Wrought Iron Cage Frame, Leaves, Berries, 6¾ In.
$1320.00

Glass-Blown, Bowl, Cobalt Blue, 8 Ribs, Folded Rim, Footed, 4 x 3½ In. $978.00

Glass-Blown, Creamer, 3-Piece Mold, Tooled Rim, Pinched Spout, Pontil, c.1825, 4 In. $672.00

Glass-Blown, Creamer, Cobalt Blue, Rigaree, Crimped Rim & Spout, Pontil, 4½ In. $672.00

Glass-Blown, Jug, Claret, Green Tint, Melon Ribbed Base, Cut Neck, Stopper, 10½ In., Pair $15600.00

Decanter, Medium Olive Green, Flared Lip, Rayed Base, Pontil, 7¼ x 3 In.	770.00
Decanter, Purple Blue, Folded Lip, Ringed Base, Pontil, 5⅜ In.	88.00
Decanter, Teal Green, Opaque White Plume, Rolled Lip, Ring, Pontil, 10½ In.	770.00
Doorstop, Turtle, Whimsy, Aquamarine, Pulled Head, Tail, Feet, 2½ x 3½ x 6½ In.	11.00
Ewer, Hallmark, Sterling Silver Collar, London, England, c.1847, 9 In.	585.00
Figurine, Dog, Applied Feet, Head, Tail, Rigaree, Millville, N.J., 1860-1920, 5½ In.	230.00
Figurine, Frozen Charlotte Doll, Clear, Multicolor Filigree Rings, Whimsy, 6 x 2 In.	1045.00
Figurine, Turtle, Aqua, Teal Tones, Molded Head, Drawn Feet, 1860-1900, 6 In.	58.00
Fly Trap, Clear, Applied Feet, 7½ x 5 In.	210.00
Fly Trap, Clear, Applied Neck Ring, 3 Tab Feet, Ground Rim, 7 x 5½ In.	154.00
Fly Trap, Clear, Applied Neck Ring, 3 Tab Feet, Tam-O-Shanter Stopper, 8¼ In.	187.00
Fly Trap, Clear, Bottle Shape, Ball Stopper, 3-Footed, 8½ In.	720.00
Fly Trap, Hanging, Cloche Shape, Wire Suspension, Gutta Percha Stopper, 6½ In.	210.00
Goblet, Clear, Oval Bowl, Ball Knop, Domed Disc Base, Seeds, 12½ In.	499.00
Goblet, Clear, Oval Bowl, British Coins In Hollow Ball Knop, Disc Foot, 8⅞ In.	470.00
Goblet, Dark Amethyst, Bulbous, 3 Rings, Double Step Base, Pontil, 1820-35, 7 In.	515.00
Goblet, Olive Green, Cone Shape, Bulbous Stem, Disc Foot, 6¾ In., 6 Piece	180.00
Goblet, Opal Applied Baluster Stem, Pontil, 1840-60, 6 x 5¾ In.	1045.00
Hat, Amber, Flared Rim, Pontil, 1860-80, 2¼ In.	55.00
Hat, Aqua, Flared Rim, Pontil, 1860-80, 3 In.	55.00
Hat, Aqua, Folded Rim, Pontil, 1830-50, 5½ In.	112.00
Hat, Dark Blue Green, Flared Rim, Pontil, 1820-40, 2¼ In.	405.00
Hat, Dark Cobalt Blue, Flared Rim, Pontil, 1860-1900, 2 In.	55.00
Hat, Light Sapphire Blue, Folded Rim, Pontil, 1860-90, 5¾ In.	112.00
Hat, Purple Amethyst, Flared, Inward Folded Rim, Pontil, 1810-30, 1½ In.	305.00
Hat, Red Amber, Folded Rim, Open Pontil, 1830-60, 2¾ In.	220.00
Hat, Whimsy, Cobalt Blue, Open Pontil, 1860-1900, 1½ x 3½ In.	70.00
Honey Pot, Cover, Cobalt Blue, Pinched Waist, Funnel Foot, Folded Rim, 1820-50, 6½ In.	225.00
Hurricane Shade, Baluster, Etched Bands, Greek Key, Shells, Leaves, 21 x 8 In.	2232.00
Jar, Cover, Aqua, Painted Rooster & Star, Rolled Lip, Pontil, 1850-70, 9¾ In.	153.00
Jar, Cover, Clear, Cobalt Blue Rims, Ribbed Applied Ring Handle, 8½ In.	165.00
Jar, Cover, Olive Amber, Squat, Angled Shoulder, Flared Rim, Pontil, 7¾ x 4½ In.	2090.00
Jar, Utility, Dark Amethyst, Folded Lip, Pontil, 1850-75, 7 In.	94.00
Jug, Amber, Cylindrical, Bulbous, Handle, Pontil, 1840-60, 8 x 4 In.	1008.00
Jug, Blue Aqua, Bulbous, Flared Rim, Threading, Footed, Pt., 5½ x 3⅜ In.	4070.00
Jug, Claret, Green Tint, Melon Ribbed Base, Cut Neck, Stopper, 10½ In., Pair _illus_	15600.00
Jug, Lily Pad, Blue Aqua, Squat Bulbous, Swirled Peaks, Flared Rim, Qt., 7 In.	7700.00
Jug, Red Amber, Squat, Tooled Band, 6¼ x 3½ x 3½ In.	3630.00
Jug, Tumble-Up, Beaker Cap, Engraved Flowers, Flat Sides, Spain, 9½ In.	480.00
Loving Cup, Cover, Cobalt Blue, Medial Groove, Folded Rim, 2 Handles, Footed, 7 In.	44.00
Mug, Clear, Enameled, Multicolored Flowers, Pulled Handle, Pontil, 4 x 2½ In.	187.00
Mug, Cover, Tulips, Flared Base, Applied Handle, 6⅛ In.	297.00
Mug, Engraved, Flowers, Scrolls, Flared Base, Applied Handle, 6¾ In.	231.00
Mug, Engraved, Scrolled Tulip, Vines, Bulbous, Flared Base, Applied Handle, 5½ In.	176.00
Mug, Engraved, Tulip, 2-Handled Urn, Flared Foot, Applied Handle, 6⅝ In.	275.00
Nappy, Clear, Folded Rim, Rayed, Ringed Base, Pontil, 1½ x 5 In.	66.00
Nappy, Clear, Inward Folded Rim, Rayed Base, Pontil, 1½ x 6 In.	77.00
Nappy, Ribs Swirled To Right, Clear, Rim Folded, 11 Dots, 1⅜ x 5¾ In.	66.00
Pan, Clear, Folded Rim, 12-Diamond Base, Pontil, 1⅝ x 7 In.	66.00
Pitcher, Aqua, Bulbous, Gadrooning, Crimped Foot, Applied Ribbed Handle, 7 In.	2576.00
Pitcher, Bird, Green, Aqua Iridescent, Crimped Foot, Handle, Spout, Pontil, 5 x 8¾ In.	170.00
Pitcher, Bulbous, 3-Piece Mold, Wide Neck, Tooled Rim, Sheared Mouth 6 x 4¾ In.	1992.00
Pitcher, Clear, Bulbous, Tooled Rim, Tooled Rim, Spout, Applied Handle, 6⅜ In.	1344.00
Pitcher, Cobalt Blue Threaded Rim, 16 Ribs, Applied Handle, c.1860, 7 In.	115.00
Pitcher, Cover, Amber, Applied Handle, Footed, Ball, South Jersey, c.1850, 7½ In.	2035.00
Pitcher, Flared Rim, Horizontal Ribbing, Pinched Lip, Ear Shape Handle, 8 In.	440.00
Pitcher, Lily Pad, Aqua, Threaded At Neck & Handle, Crimped Foot, 7 In. _illus_	202.00
Pitcher, Orange Amber, Crimped Spout, Rigaree & Disc Foot, 8⅞ In. _illus_	6160.00
Plate, Clear, Folded Rim, Rayed, Ringed Base, Pontil, 1 x 6½ In.	66.00
Pomade Jar, Figural, Bear, Light Amethyst, Deep Amethyst, Clambroth, 3¾ In.	728.00
Punch Bowl, Baluster Shape, Flared & Rolled Rim, Early 1800s, 11¼ In.	374.00
Punch Bowl, Cover, Underplate, Blue, Pear Shape, 20th Century, 17½ x 10 In.	176.00
Rolling Pin, Black Olive Amber, Splotches, Knob Handles, 15½ In.	88.00
Rolling Pin, Clear, Red, Blue Marbrie Loops, Plaster Filled, Knob Handles, 12½ In.	209.00
Rolling Pin, Clear, Spatter, Red, Blue Spots, Plaster Filled, Knob Handles, 16 In.	220.00
Rolling Pin, Fiery Opalescent, Knob Handles, 15 In.	143.00

Imitation—The Sincerest

Form of Flattery

Almost every known type of glassware—pressed, blown, colored, clear—has been reproduced or reissued since the nineteenth century. Some reissues are from original molds, which makes identification difficult but not impossible. Some repros have fake marks.

Glass-Blown, Pitcher, Lily Pad, Aqua, Threaded At Neck & Handle, Crimped Foot, 7 In.
$202.00

Glass-Blown, Pitcher, Orange Amber, Crimped Spout, Rigaree & Disc Foot, 8⅛ In.
$6160.00

Glass-Blown, Tumbler, Flip, Cobalt Blue, 3-Piece Mold, Tooled Rim, Pontil, 5⅞ In.
$6720.00

Glass-Blown, Vase, Witch's Ball Cover, Olive Green, Pontil, Mid 19th Century, 6 x 4 In.
$748.00

Glass-Blown, Witch's Ball, Internal Die-Cut Flowers, Cherubs, Silver Plated Frame, 17 In.
$235.00

Glass-Bohemian, Bowl, Clear, Applied Frog, Oval, Folded Rigaree Rim, Harrach, c.1890, 4 In.
$764.00

Glass-Bohemian, Mantel Set, Pink, Enameled Birds In Trees, c.1880, 19-In. Jar, 3 Piece
$206.00

Glass-Bohemian, Pokal, Cover, Finial, Blue Cut To Clear, Flowers, Faceted, Footed, 14 In.
$441.00

Glass-Bohemian, Vase, Blue Iridescent, Platinum Iridescent Overlay, Metal Surround, 23 In. $2400.00

Glass-Bohemian, Vase, Cobalt Blue, Applied White Streamers, Scalloped Rim, 10½ In. $345.00

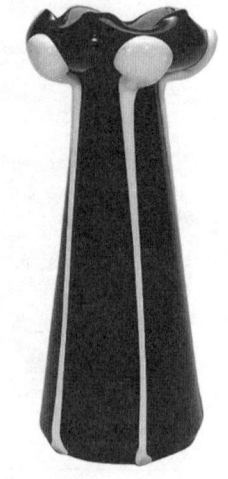

Glass-Bohemian, Vase, Mottled Red & Green, Applied Cobalt Blue Snake, 14 In., Pair $59.00

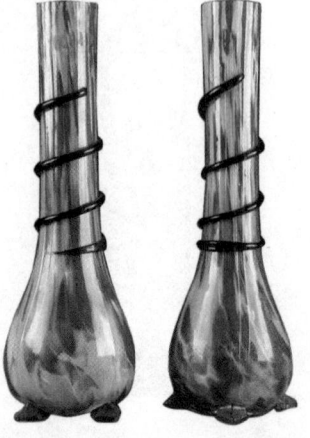

Rolling Pin, Light Green, 4 Pence Coin, Inside Handles, Knobs, 13 In.	303.00
Rolling Pin, Red Amber, Knobs Handles, 15 In.	154.00
Salt, 16 Broken Swirled Ribs, Applied Cobalt Blue Rim, Footed, Pontil, 1800-30, 3 In.	418.00
Salt, Blue, Orange, Teal Inclusions, Footed, Pontil, Millville, 1860-1900, 3¾ In.	112.00
Salt, Yellow Olive, 16 Diamonds, Applied Foot, 1850-70, 2 x 3¾ In.	112.00
Scent Bottle, Latticinio, Clear, Red, Opaque White Threads, Flattened Oval, Hinged Cap, 4 In.	198.00
Sugar, 8-Pillar, Folded Rim, Applied Baluster, Footed, 1840-60, 4½ x 5¾ In.	112.00
Sugar, Clear, Cupped Bowl, Folded Rim, Funnel Foot, Pontil, 4½ x 3⅝ In.	440.00
Sugar, Clear, Flower Sprays, Swags, Folded Funnel Foot, Engraved, 3 x 4⅜ In.	330.00
Sugar, Cobalt Blue, 16 Ribs, Inward Folded Rim, Drawn Foot, Pontil, 1840-70, 5 In.	143.00
Sugar, Cover, Sawtooth Bands, Engraved, Applied Double Handle, Footed, 6¾ In.	94.00
Sugar & Creamer, Opalescent, Amethyst Spatter, Pontil Scar, c.1900, 3 In.	39.00
Tumbler, Clear, 6-Point Star, Ring Pontil, 3⅜ x 2½ In.	88.00
Tumbler, Clear, 16-Diamond Base, Tapered, Pontil, 2¾ x 2¼ x 1½ In.	165.00
Tumbler, Clear, Multicolored Flowers, Bird, Enamel, Pontil, 3 x 2½ x 1⅝ In.	110.00
Tumbler, Enameled, Bird Perched On Stump, Floral Band, 3 In.	297.00
Tumbler, Flip, Clear, 18 Diamonds, Ring Base, Pontil, 4¾ x 3¾ In.	121.00
Tumbler, Flip, Clear, Engraved, Swag Around Rim, Molded Fluted, 6 In.	83.00
Tumbler, Flip, Clear, Inward Rolled Rim, Tulips, Pontil, 3½ In.	66.00
Tumbler, Flip, Clear, Ribs, Rayed Base, Pontil, 4⅜ x 3½ In.	132.00
Tumbler, Flip, Cobalt Blue, 3-Piece Mold, Tooled Rim, Pontil, 5⅞ In. ....*illus*	6720.00
Tumbler, Flip, Engraved, Bird On Branch, 3 In.	99.00
Tumbler, Flip, Engraved, Clear, Bird On Branch, Pontil, 4 In.	66.00
Tumbler, Flip, Engraved, Flower, Stylized Leaves, 6¼ In.	138.00
Tumbler, Flip, Engraved, Molded Flutes, Engraved Lines, Flowers, 5½ In.	72.00
Tumbler, Flip, Engraved, Sunburst, Bird On Tulip, 7 In.	138.00
Tumbler, Flip, Engraved, Tulip, 2 Handled Urn, Scrolled Accents, 8¼ In.	220.00
Tumbler, Flip, Tulip, Lattice & Scroll, 6½ In.	193.00
Tumbler, Gray Green, Birds, Hears, Flower Spray, Engraved, Pinched Waist, 3½ In.	33.00
Tumbler, Rummer, Amethyst, Oval, Applied Knop Stem, Footed x 4¼ In.	22.00
Tumbler, Tavern, Clear, Rayed, Ring Base, Pontil, 3½ x 3 In.	242.00
Vase, Green Aqua, Engraved, Applied Baluster, Footed, Rough Pontil, c.1830, 9 In.	1780.00
Vase, Hyacinth, Amethyst, Cone Shape, Pontil, 6⅝ x 2½ x 3⅛ In.	55.00
Vase, Hyacinth, Green, Cone Shape, Removable Bowl, 2 Parts, 7⅞ x 2⅝ In.	165.00
Vase, Hyacinth, Opal, Pink Pulled Looping, Flared Mouth, Pontil, 1840-60	660.00
Vase, Witch's Ball, Cover, Clear, White Drag Looping, Flared Rim, Footed, c.1865, 6 In.	274.00
Vase, Witch's Ball Cover, Marbrie Loop, Baluster Form, Knop Stem, Footed, 13 In.	990.00
Vase, Witch's Ball Cover, Olive Green, Pontil, Mid 19th Century, 6 x 4 In. ....*illus*	748.00
Wine, Button Knop Stem, Flint, 4⅛ In., 4 Piece	39.00
Wine, Clear, Conical Bowl, Button Stem, Pontil, 4 In.	253.00
Wine, Clear, Funnel Bowl, Engraved, Flowers, Leaves, Opaque Twist Stem, 5¾ In.	275.00
Witch's Ball, Cover, Vase, Cobalt Blue, Applied Baluster, Footed, c.1840, 10¾ In.	950.00
Witch's Ball, Cranberry, White Drag Looping, Open Pontil, 1840-60, 2¾ In.	306.00
Witch's Ball, Internal Die-Cut Flowers, Cherubs, Silver Plated Frame, 17 In. ....*illus*	235.00
Witch's Ball, On Stand, Boston, c.1850, 14 In., Pair	4800.00
Witch's Ball, Red & Blue Splotches, White Interior, Open End Pontil, 1840-60, 3 In.	284.00
Witch's Ball, Teal, Chalk Interior, Paper Insert, Girls, Flowers, Open Pontil, c.1875, 5 In.	112.00

GLASS-BOHEMIAN. Bohemian glass is an ornate overlay or flashed glass made during the Victorian era. It has been reproduced in Bohemia, which is now a part of the Czech Republic. Glass made from 1875 to 1900 is preferred by collectors.

Beaker, Gold, Opaline, Blue, Enameled, c.1870, 5 In.	326.00
Bottle, Faceted Cut To Clear, Amber, Blue Vertical Bands, Flowers, Stopper, 18 In.	115.00
Bowl, Clear, Applied Frog, Oval, Folded Rigaree Rim, Harrach, c.1890, 4 In. ....*illus*	764.00
Bowl, Iridescent Green, Ruffled Edge, c.1900, 14¼ In.	205.00
Compote, Diamond, Quilted, Ribbed Bowl, Iridescent, Bronze Stem, c.1900, 12 In.	235.00
Decanter, Ruby Cut To Clear, 14 In.	88.00
Dresser Box, Cranberry, Optic Ribbed, Enameled Flowers, 4-Footed Holder, 5 In.	288.00
Goblet, Ruby, Gilt, Gold Enameled, Figurines, Twisted Stems, 9 In., 9 Piece	690.00
Lamp, Ruby Flashed Font, Wheel Cut Design, Brass Column, Marble Base, 15 In.	144.00
Lustres, Ruby Cut To Clear, Enameled, Late 19th Century, 13 In., Pair	826.00
Mantel Set, Pink, Enameled Birds In Trees, c.1880, 19-In. Jar, 3 Piece ....*illus*	206.00
Pokal, Cover, Finial, Blue Cut To Clear, Flowers, Faceted, Footed, 14 In. ....*illus*	441.00
Tumbler, Cobalt Blue To Cranberry, Engraved Deer, Star Cut Base, 5 x 3¾ In.	518.00
Vase, Amberina, Bulbous Urn, Diagonal Swirl, Amber Rigaree, Harrach, 10 In.	288.00

Glass-Bohemian, Vase, Opalescent, Melon Ribbed, Enameled Flowers, Dotted, Flared Neck, 7 In.
$184.00

Glass-Bohemian, Vase, Opaline, Reeded Green Opalescent Teardrops, Silver Mica, Kralik, 8 In.
$118.00

Glass-Bohemian, Vase, Pepita, Red To Green, Scalloped Rim, Rindskopf, 13½ In., Pair
$353.00

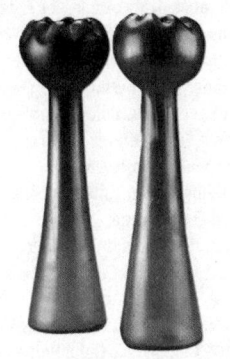

Glass-Bohemian, Vase, Translucent Feather Enamels, Gold Tracery, c.1920, 5¾ In.
$264.00

Glass-Contemporary, Bowl, Black, Purple, Mauve, Orange, Toots Zynsky, 11 x 11 In.
$7475.00

It's Pretty, But Is It Old?

Most people know art glass when they see it. Most is colorful, often shaded from one color to another, and embellished with fancy details like ruffles and three-dimensional fruit and flowers. But is it the original old glass? In the 1930s, there was renewed interest in nineteenth-century glass styles. Several factories, including Fenton Art Glass Company, Gunderson Glass Works, and Pairpoint Manufacturing Company, introduced glassware that imitated the styles of the 1880s.

Dale Chihuly

Dale Chihuly (1941–present) is the best-known of the late twentieth-century studio glassmakers. Chihuly blew early pieces himself. After several injuries, he had others do the glassblowing. He continued designing the pieces.

Glass-Contemporary, Group, Persian, Waves, Rims, Free-Form, Dale Chihuly, 4 Piece
$4888.00

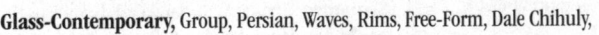

Glass-Contemporary, Vase,
Beige Iridescent, Blue, Caramel King Tut,
Orient & Flume, 6 In.
$230.00

G

Glass-Contemporary, Vase,
Cobalt Blue Cypriot,
Gold Iridescent Lava, C. Lotton, 4 In.
$633.00

Glass-Contemporary, Vase, Coral,
Spring Green Overlay, Scallops, Labino,
1981, 6¼
$259.00

Glass-Midcentury, Mobile,
Fused Discs, Michael & Frances Higgins,
c.1965, 34 In.
$4080.00

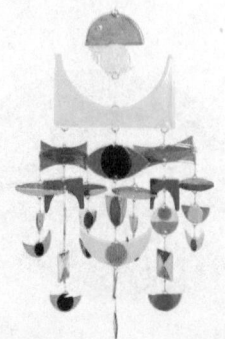

Vase, Blue Iridescent, Platinum Iridescent Overlay, Metal Surround, 23 In. . . . . *illus*	2400.00
Vase, Blue Iridescent On Green, Cameo Ribbons, Metal Foot, Karl Goldberg, 15 In.	690.00
Vase, Blue Oil Spot Iridescence, Yellow, Polished Foot, Art Deco, 8¾ In.	480.00
Vase, Clear, Enameled, Max Rade, For Fritz Heckert, c.1890, 5¼ In.	239.00
Vase, Clear, Intaglio Cut, Applied Amber Handles, 4½ x 5½ In.	475.00
Vase, Cobalt Blue, Applied White Streamers, Scalloped Rim, 10½ In. . . . . *illus*	345.00
Vase, Cobalt Blue, Art Nouveau, Silver Overlay, Flowers, 9½ In.	184.00
Vase, Cobalt Blue Flowers, Yellow Enameled Scrolls, Cameo, 5¾ In.	104.00
Vase, Coral, Free-Form, Allover Iridescent Finish, Kralik, 7¼ In.	173.00
Vase, Dancing Nudes, Frosted, Molded, c.1925, 14¼ In.	147.00
Vase, Ebony, Yellow, Green, Amethyst, Blue, 12⅛ In.	345.00
Vase, Engraved Forest Scene, Cylindrical, 10 In., Pair	201.00
Vase, Fan, Opal, Red Threading, Art Deco, c.1915, 9 In.	82.00
Vase, Garniture, Cranberry Cut To Clear, Brilliant, Engraved, 16½ In., Pair	1440.00
Vase, Iridescent, Amethyst, Applied Coil, Silver Rim, Bottle, Kralik, 7½ In.	144.00
Vase, Iridescent, Amethyst & Gold Waves, Cylindrical, Trifold Rim, c.1900, 13 In.	470.00
Vase, Iridescent, Chipped Ice Chip, Honesdale, Early 1900s, 4½ In.	179.00
Vase, Iridescent, Threaded, Red, Pallme-Koenig, 6 In.	735.00
Vase, Iridescent Purple, Green, Rose Highlights, Threading, Pallme-Koenig, 4 In.	645.00
Vase, Iridescent Purple, Red, Rolled Rim, Pallme-Koenig, 8½ x 9 In.	750.00
Vase, Iridescent White, Threading, Urn Shape, 3-Footed Metal Holder, 10½ In.	118.00
Vase, Mottled Burnt Sienna, Iridescent Purple, Early 1900s, 8½ In.	335.00
Vase, Mottled Red & Green, Applied Cobalt Blue Snake, 14 In., Pair . . . . *illus*	59.00
Vase, Opalescent, Melon Ribbed, Enameled Flowers, Dotted, Flared Neck, 7 In. . . . . *illus*	184.00
Vase, Opaline, Reeded Green Opalescent Teardrops, Silver Mica, Kralik, 8 In. . . . . *illus*	118.00
Vase, Pepita, Red To Green, Scalloped Rim, Rindskopf, 13½ In., Pair . . . . *illus*	353.00
Vase, Phoenix Bird, Exotic Flowers, Platinum, Gold Luster, Custard Glass	748.00
Vase, Red, Exterior Threading, Polished Pontil, Pallme-Koenig, 6 In.	735.00
Vase, Stick, Peachblow, Gold Enameled Flowers, Harrach, c.1880, 8⅞ In.	425.00
Vase, Translucent Feather Enamels, Gold Tracery, c.1920, 5¾ In. . . . . *illus*	264.00
Vase, Trumpet, Amber Cut To Clear, Hunting Dog, Footed, 9½ In.	294.00
Vase, Trumpet, Green, Silver Overlay, Flowers, Urns, Victorian Lady, Cherubs, 34 In.	1495.00
Wedding Cup, Figural, Woman, Bronze, Enameled Bowl, Skirt, Fritz Heckert, 8 In.	920.00
Wedding Cup, Figural, Woman, Bronze, Green Ribbed Skirt, Red Top, 10½ In.	698.00
Wine, Balloon, Art Nouveau Panel, Peacocks, Ladies, Signed Vedar XIV, 7½ In.	58.00

GLASS-CONTEMPORARY includes pieces by glass artists working after 1975. Many of these pieces are free-form, one-of-a-kind sculptures. Paperweights by contemporary artists are listed in the Paperweight category. Earlier studio glass may be found listed under Glass-Midcentury or Glass-Venetian.

Berry Bowl Set, Opalescent, Drapery, Blue, 7 Piece	195.00
Bowl, Black, Purple, Mauve, Orange, Toots Zynsky, 11 x 11 In. . . . . *illus*	7475.00
Bowl, Hand Blown, Purple, Signed, Curt Brock, 1983, 5 x 9 In.	351.00
Bowl, Peachblow, Ruffled Edge, Kanawha, c.1970, 7 x 3¾ In.	26.00
Bowl, Transparent Blue, Pinched Sides, Signed, Labino, 3¾ In.	235.00
Decanter, Clear, Double Handle, Italy, c.1920, 11 x 6½ In.	117.00
Goblet, Toasting, Pulled Leaves, Amber Bowl, Flower Form, 7⅝ In.	115.00
Group, Persian, Waves, Rims, Free-Form, Dale Chihuly, 4 Piece . . . . *illus*	4888.00
Perfume Bottle, Yellow Opalescent, Pulled Feathers, Lundberg, 7¾ In.	259.00
Pitcher, White, Amber Spatter, Pilgrim Glass, 4½ In.	36.00
Sculpture, Finding Man, Sand Cast, B. Vallien, 1994, 21¾ x 8 In.	7800.00
Sculpture, Janus, Sand Cast, Painted Metal Base, B. Vallien, 19¾ x 9½ In.	7880.00
Sculpture, Organic Basket Shape, Translucent Blue, Red, Green, D. Lotton, 13 In.	460.00
Sculpture, Tension Released, 2 Arcs, 1 Sliced, Red, White, Blue, Littleton, 1979, 14 In.	15200.00
Vase, Amberina, Red, Orange, Cream, Satin, Pilgrim, 4½ In.	25.00
Vase, Amethyst, Blue Iridescent Swirls, Oval, Signed, Charles Lotton, 11 In.	1298.00
Vase, Antique Ivory, Double Loops, Silvery Blue, Caramel, C. Lotton, 6 In.	518.00
Vase, Beige Iridescent, Blue, Caramel King Tut, Orient & Flume, 6 In. . . . . *illus*	230.00
Vase, Blue, Gold Iridescent, Oil Spots, Ribbed, Lundberg, 5⅜ In.	81.00
Vase, Black, White, Foldover Flap, T. Zuccheri, 1989, 12½ In.	4200.00
Vase, Blue Iridescent, Raised Vertical Ribs, Tapered, Labino, 1971, 9 In.	403.00
Vase, Bud, Gold Iridescent, Orient & Flume, c.1975, 3¾ In.	88.00
Vase, Clear Cased, Yellow & Black Fish Swimming, Sea Grass, Orient & Flume, 7 In.	345.00
Vase, Clearl, Cased Black-Eyed Susans, Oval, Orient & Flume, 6 In.	403.00
Vase, Cobalt Black, Silvery Blue, Pulled Loops, Flower Form, C. Lotton, 12 In.	1265.00
Vase, Cobalt Blue, Gold, Crowded Shoots Rising, C. Lotton, 5¼ In.	489.00

Vase, Cobalt Blue Cased, Dogwood Branch Band, Shouldered, Foot, Orient & Flume, 7¼ In.	259.00
Vase, Cobalt Blue Cypriot, Gold Iridescent Lava, C. Lotton, 4 In. ....*illus*	633.00
Vase, Coral, Spring Green Overlay, Scallops, Labino, 1981, 6¼ In. ....*illus*	259.00
Vase, Cypriot, Blue Iridescent, Gold Iridescent Lava, C. Lotton, 1977, 5½ In.	690.00
Vase, Encased Iris, Shallow Bowl, Signed, David Lotton, c.1991, 6½ In.	384.00
Vase, Flower Form, Iridescent Gold, Red Heart, Vines, Footed, Lundberg, 13½ In.	288.00
Vase, Gold, Globe, Iridescent Blue Feathers, C. Lotton, 3¼ In.	230.00
Vase, Gold Iridescent, Acorn, Branches, Egg Shape, Footed, Orient & Flume, 10 In.	633.00
Vase, Gold Iridescent, Moire Fern, Green Pulled Feathers, Flared, Lundberg, 11 In.	382.00
Vase, Golden Honey, Sprouting Shoots, Leaves, Silvery Blue, C. Lotton, 8½ In.	920.00
Vase, Green, Silvery Blue Flowers, Gourd Shape, Orient & Flume, 9 In.	288.00
Vase, Green Iridescent, Blue Threaded Decoration, Scalloped Rim, 9 In.	460.00
Vase, Iridescent, Stylized Flowers, Carl Radke, 13¼ x 7 In.	293.00
Vase, Iridescent Gold, Lundberg Studios14¼ x 3 In.	263.00
Vase, Jack-In-The-Pulpit, Blue Iridescent, Ribbed Neck, Base, Lundberg, 13 In.	176.00
Vase, Jack-In-The-Pulpit, Iridescent, Charles Lotton, 1977, 12½ In.	287.00
Vase, King Tut, Bulbous, Pinched, Red Iridescent, Blue Iridescent, 7 In.	1150.00
Vase, King Tut, Dark Blue, Caramel, Iridescent Beige, Orient & Flume, 5⅞ In.	230.00
Vase, Lava, Cypriot Body, Golden Flow, Magenta, Gold, Blue, Lotton, 1986, 4¾ In.	863.00
Vase, Mottled Green Leaves, Blue, Green Spattered Ground, D. Lotton, 4⅛ In.	575.00
Vase, Multicolored Patches, Purple Ground, Steve Nelson, 5⅛ In.	92.00
Vase, Opalescent, Green Lily Pads, Flared Disc Rim, 8½ In.	144.00
Vase, Paperweight, Cranberry, Mica, Cased Flowers, D. Merritt, 11 In.	230.00
Vase, Peachblow, Hobnail, Red Interior, Kanawha, Ruffled Edge, 6 In.	48.00
Vase, Pink, Purple Striations, Tim Maycock, c.1988, 15¾ In.	192.00
Vase, Pink Flowers, Blue Stems, Mottled Pink Ground, Flared Rim, C. Lotton, 8 In.	920.00
Vase, Purple Iridescent, Relief Swirls, Globular, Polished Pontil, Labino, 5 In.	646.00
Vase, Ruby, Organic Shape, Pinched, Flared & Flattened Rim, Labino, 7 In.	633.00
Vase, Ruby Red, Orange, Red Flowers, Silvery Blue Leaves, Vines, Lotton, 5⅞ In.	978.00
Vase, Stick, Cranberry, Green, Blue Cascading Feathers, Bulbous Base, 9 In.	805.00
Vase, Tall Stem, Footed, Wavy Edge, Iridescent, Lundberg Studios, 14 x 5 In.	234.00
Vase, Translucent Ruby, Pink Clematis, Cylindrical, Tapered, D. Lotton, 1993, 10 In.	633.00
Vase, Turquoise Blue, Satin Sheen, Silver Split Leaf, Magenta, C. Lotton, 6¾ In.	633.00
Vase, Whirled Stems, Pink, White Flowers, Multicolored Leaves, Lotton, 10 In.	1725.00

GLASS-CUT, *see Cut Glass category.*

GLASS-DEPRESSION, *see Depression Glass category.*

GLASS-MIDCENTURY refers to art glass made from the 1940s to the early 1970s. Some glass factories, such as Baccarat or Orrefors, are listed under their own categories. Earlier glass may be listed in the Glass-Art and Glass-Contemporary categories. Italian glass may be found in Glass-Venetian.

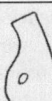

Bowl, Blue, Holmegaard, 5½ x 4¾ In.	28.00
Bowl, Clear, Littala Kanttarelli, Tapio Wirkkala, c.1955, 5 In.	164.00
Candlestick, Green Leaf, Green Ground, White Points, Higgins, 3 x 5¼ In., Pair	360.00
Charger, Opaque Circles, Green, Red, Blue, Striated Ground, Anne Warff, 24 In.	353.00
Decanter, Kluk-Kluk, Clear, Holmegaard, 1950s	125.00
Decanter, Smokey Gray, Per Lutken, Holmegaard, 1950s	49.00
Dish, Abstract, Gold, Black, Higgins, 10½ x 8½ In.	235.00
Dish, Acid Etched, Radiating Lines, 3-Sided, Michael Higgins, 1960s, 10 x 8 In.	345.00
Dish, Flower, Green, White, Blue, Yellow, Rectangular, Higgins, 4 x 7¼ In.	135.00
Mobile, Fused Discs, Michael & Frances Higgins, c.1965, 34 In. ....*illus*	4080.00
Plaque, Mary, Relief, Original Frame, Edris Eckhardt, 1973, 14 x 12 In. ....*illus*	1560.00
Plate, 3 Diamond Shape Sections, Peacock, White Ground, Green, 12½ In.	275.00
Platter, Emancipation Of Woman, Rectangular, Maurice Heaton, 14 In. ....*illus*	275.00
Platter, Fused, Blue Ground, Higgins, Early 1960s, 12⅜ In.	150.00
Vase, Amber, Gunnel Nyman, c.1948, 14 In.	718.00
Vase, Blown, Fused, Flared, Multicolored, c.1955, 12⅞ In.	6000.00
Vase, Blue, Amethyst To Green, Free-Form, Sweden, 9½ In.	147.00
Vase, Blue, Green, c.1955, 10½ x 5 x 3½ In.	360.00
Vase, Bud, Goberal Ware, Copper, 2½ x 4 In.	41.00
Vase, Clear, Round Foot, Gerda Stromberg, Strombergshyttan, 1950s, 8¾ In.	171.00
Vase, Coquille, Clear, Black Cased, Stylized Penguin Shape, Flygsfors, 15 In.	58.00
Vase, Engraved, Underwater Scene, Oval, Signed, Strombergs, Sweden, 6 In. ....*illus*	71.00
Vase, Frosted, Spout, Ground Cover, Urn Shape, Holmegaard, 8½ x 3½ In.	79.00

Glass-Midcentury, Plaque, Mary, Relief, Original Frame, Edris Eckhardt, 1973, 14 x 12 In. $1560.00

G

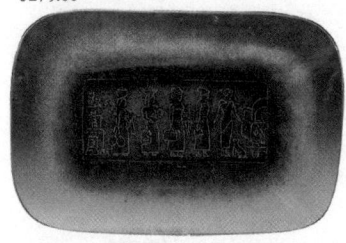

Glass-Midcentury, Platter, Emancipation Of Woman, Rectangular, Maurice Heaton, 14 In. $275.00

Glass-Midcentury, Vase, Engraved, Underwater Scene, Oval, Signed, Strombergs, Sweden, 6 In. $71.00

Glass-Midcentury, Vase, Paperweight, Blue, Scalloped Folded Rim, Whitefriars, 7 In. $71.00

Glass-Venetian, Chandelier, 6-Light, Applied Flowers & Leaves, Murano, 21 x 19 In. $1600.00

Glass-Venetian, Figurine, Bird, Alessandro Pianon, Vistosi, 1962, 7 In. $6900.00

Glass-Venetian, Sculpture, Internal Decoration, Green Lattice Over Ruby, Murano, 13 In. $147.00

Vase, Gold Iridescent, Shouldered, Squat, 2¾ In.	58.00
Vase, Irregular Shape, Blue, Per Lutken, Holmegaard, 1950s	58.00
Vase, Molar, Emerald Green, Cased In Clear, Ground Pontil, Whitefriars	150.00
Vase, Nude Women, Etched, Enameled, V. Lindstrand, 1930, 4¾ In.	9600.00
Vase, Paperweight, Blue, Scalloped Folded Rim, Whitefriars, 7 In. ....*illus*	71.00
Vase, Savoy, White, Alvar Aalto, Iittala Finland, Label	50.00
Vase, Smoky Glass, Trapped Bubbles, Narrow Mouth, Oval, Pukeberg, 17 In.	118.00
Vase, Sommerso, Amethyst, Whitefriars, 9¾ In.	35.00
Vase, Spiral Cut, Clear, Whitefriars	59.00

GLASS-VENETIAN. Venetian glass has been made near Venice, Italy, since the thirteenth century. Thin, colored glass with applied decoration is favored, although many other types have been made. Collectors have recently become interested in the Art Deco and fifties designs. Glass was made on the Venetian island of Murano from 1291. The output dwindled in the late seventeenth century but began to flourish again in the 1850s. Some of the old techniques of glassmaking were revived, and firms today make traditional designs and original modern glass. Since 1981, the name *Murano* may only be used on glass made on Murano Island. Other pieces of Italian glass may be found in the Glass-Contemporary and Glass-Midcentury categories of this book.

Bonbon, 2 Black Dancers Holding Cup, Black, Gold Aventurine, Murano, 12 x 8 In.	470.00
Bottle, Black & Gold Spiraling Lines, Flattened Rim, Dino Martin, 8½ In.	115.00
Bowl, Black, Brown & Clear Lines, Folded Flower Form, Tyra Lundgren, Venini, 7 x 12 In.	748.00
Bowl, Flower, Ruby Red, Gold Highlights, Raised Flowers, Leaves, 3¼ x 7½ In.	195.00
Bowl, Glass, Black, Footed, Wide Rim, Venini Sommerso, Venini Italia, 1960s, 10 In.	214.00
Bowl, Multicolored, Archimede Seguso, c.1975, 8 x 13½ x 7¾ In.	1140.00
Bowl, Rose, Venini Battuto, Frosted, Engraved, Venini Italia, c.1960, 9 In.	1069.00
Bowl, Sommerso, Clear, Bubbled, Footed, Folded Rim, Carlo Scarpa, Venini, 4 x 15 x 11 In.	633.00
Candlestick, Clear Serpent Stem, Gold Aventurine, Ribs, Bobeche, Footed, 12¾ In.	173.00
Candlestick, Gold, Silver Speckled, Dolphin Stem, Fluted Top, Woven Gold, 6 In.	475.00
Candlestick, Gold Metallic Waffle Optic, Green Stem, Applied Leaves, 5½ In.	425.00
Carafe, Filigrana, Vertical Stripes, Narrow Neck, Murano, 1950s, 10¼ In.	150.00
Chandelier, 6-Light, Applied Flowers & Leaves, Murano, 21 x 19 In. ....*illus*	1600.00
Compote, Swan, Gold, Emerald, White, Swan Stem, Ruffled Edge, Swirled, 7 x 6 In.	525.00
Egg, Red, Gray, Black & Yellow Interior Decoration, Taglie Pietra, 1982, 10 x 9 In.	920.00
Figurine, Aqua, Vistosi, Alessandro Pianon, c.1962, 7 In.	6900.00
Figurine, Bird, Alessandro Pianon, Vistosi, 1962, 7 In. ....*illus*	6900.00
Figurine, Cockatiel, Murano, Oggetti, 1980s, 9 In.	164.00
Figurine, Eyeball, Globular, Cased Clear On White, Brown Iris, Italy, 8½ In.	999.00
Figurine, Fish, Tosialberto Murano, 1968, 5 x 11½ In.	510.00
Garniture, Murano, Fish, 3 Vases, Amber, 7¼ To 10¾ In., 3 Piece	413.00
Group, Figurine, Madonna & Child, Dark Shaded To Dark Gray, Lichio, 19½ In.	263.00
Jardiniere, Rococo Style, Hand Painted, Scalloped Bases, 24 x 32 In., Pair	1528.00
Scent, Bottle, Silver Foil, Portrait Cane, St. Mark's Lion, Brass Hinged Cap, 2⅜ In.	143.00
Sculpture, Fish, 1968, Signed, Tosi Alberto, 5 x 11½ In.	510.00
Sculpture, Gazelle, Cendese, c.1965, 13½ In.	600.00
Sculpture, Internal Decoration, Green Lattice Over Ruby, Murano, 13 In. ....*illus*	147.00
Vase, Blue & Green Sommerso, c.1955, 10½ In.	360.00
Vase, Bottle, Irregular Shape, Amber, Scandinavian, 1950s, 10 In.	125.00
Vase, Bud, Murano, 1970s, 7¾ x 2¾ In.	155.00
Vase, Bullicante, Gold Inclusions, Lavender, Ribbed Body, Alfredo Barbini, 16 In.	177.00
Vase, Bullicante, Peach Colored Body, Red Trailing Trim, Murano, 9 In.	413.00
Vase, Cased Rainbow Colors, Red Interior, Cylindrical, Murano, 12 In. ....*illus*	118.00
Vase, Fazzoletto, Smokey, White Zanfirico, Venini, 11½ x 10½ In. ....*illus*	1800.00
Vase, Filigrana, Diagonal Swirl Stripes, Corseted, Murano, 1950s, 9¾ In.	278.00
Vase, Frosted, Ribs, Pear Shape, Elongated Neck, Flared Rim, Footed, Murano, 12 In.	510.00
Vase, Green Bullicante, Gold Foil Inclusions, Flavio Poli, Seguso Vetri D'Arte, 8½ In.	480.00
Vase, Latticinio, Diagonal Swirls, 1950s, 11¾ In.	321.00
Vase, Occhi, T. Scarpa, c.1960, 7½ In.	9600.00
Vase, Olive Green, Blue Iridescent, Cane Flowers, Swirled Brown Base, 12 In.	403.00
Vase, Red Agate, Barovier & Toso, 1980s, 11½ In.	128.00
Vase, Ritiglia, Green, Signed, Fulvio Bianconi, Venini, 1992	2938.00
Vase, Ruby, Multicolored Murrines, Canes, Gold & Silver Inclusions, V.E.M., 20 x 9 In.	3000.00
Vase, Silver Leaf Inclusions, Murrine, Italy, c.1955, 10½ In.	4800.00
Vase, Sommerso, Green, 1950s, 13½ In.	92.00

GLASSES for the eyes, or spectacles, were mentioned in a manuscript in 1289 and have been used ever since. The first eyeglasses with rigid side pieces were made in London in 1727. Bifocals were invented by Benjamin Franklin in 1785. Lorgnettes were popular in late Victorian times. Opera Glasses are listed in their own category.

Black, Celluloid, Folding, Hand-Painted Leather Case, Woman Reading At Desk	....	139.00
Brass, Folding Arms, Impressed, W. Ball, Late 18th Century	....	191.00
Brass, Sliding Bow, Half-Round Nose Piece, Patina, c.1780, 4½ x 6 In.	....	502.00
Lorgnette, Gold, Diamonds, Enameled Flowers, Embossed Rococo Handle, 4½ In.	....*illus*	411.00
Spectacles, Celluloid, Tortoiseshell	....	95.00
Spectacles, Gold, Mahogany Trap Case, Suede Lined, France	....	210.00
Spectacles, Marbled Frames, Bifocals, 1950s	....	25.00
Spectacles, Metal Frames, Civil War Era	....	75.00
Sun, Silver-Gray, Cat's Eye, 1960s	....	15.00
Sun, Tortoise Frame, Cool Ray, Polaroid	....	22.00
Sun, Tortoiseshell Color, Pink Rhinestones	....	25.00
Sun, Woman's, Animal Print, Red Highlights, Liz Claiborne	....	25.00

GLIDDEN Pottery worked in Alfred, New York, from 1940 to 1957. The pottery made stoneware, dinnerware, and art objects.

Bowl, Turquoise Matrix Glaze, No. 22, Signed, 11 x 9 In.		25.00
Vase, Turquoise, Ball, No. 49, Incised, 6½ In.	....	85.00
Vase, Rolled Rim, Mottled, Turquoise Matrix, No. 86, 7½ In.	....	45.00
Vase, Turquoise Rose, No. 87, 8 In.	....	45.00
Planter, Turquoise Matrix, No. 104, 2 x 4¼ x 2⅜ In.	....	21.00
Vase, Blue Green, No. 124, Marked, 8 In.	....	48.00
Casserole, Lid, Mottled, Green Teal, Specks, No. 165	....	20.00

GOEBEL is the mark used by W. Goebel Porzellanfabrik of Oeslau, Germany, now Rodental, Germany. Many types of figurines and dishes have been made. The firm is still working. The pieces marked *Goebel Hummel* are listed under Hummel in this book.

Cruet Set, Ducks	....	32.00
Cruet Set, Squirrels	....	32.00
Figurine, Blumenkinder, Accompanist, Girl Strumming Banjo, 7½ In.	....	95.00
Figurine, Blumenkinder, First Date, Stamped, Impressed, 1970, 9 x 4 In.	....	175.00
Figurine, Blumenkinder, Patient, Girl Taking Care Of Sick Puppy, 1972, 8 In.	....	175.00
Figurine, Co-Boy, Rick, Firefighter, 1982, 7 In.	....	142.00
Figurine, La L'Aitiere Flamande, Woman Pouring Milk, Dog Cart, c.1914, 7½ In.	.....*illus*	203.00
Figurine, Meditation, No. 80, 73/V, No. 2, 14 In.	....	702.00
Figurine, Whoosit, Orange Hair, No. 11707 11, Marked, 4½ In.	....	23.00

GOLDSCHEIDER has made porcelains in three places. The family left Vienna in 1938 and started factories in England and in Trenton, New Jersey. The New Jersey factory started in 1940 as Goldscheider-U.S.A. In 1941 it became Goldscheider-Everlast Corporation. From 1947 to 1953 it was Goldcrest Ceramics Corporation. In 1950 the Vienna plant was returned to Mr. Goldscheider and the company continues in business. The Trenton, New Jersey, business, called Goldscheider of Vienna, imports all of the pieces.

Figurine, Ballerina, Signed, Dakon, 10½ x 18 x 11 In.	....	1750.00
Figurine, Bust Of Woman, In Spring, Hand Holds Ribbon, Marked, c.1945, 5½ In.	....	85.00
Figurine, Bust Of Woman, In Winter, Hand Holds Hat, Marked, c.1945, 5¼ In.	....	115.00
Figurine, Butterfly Lady, Signed, Lorenzl, 11 x 10 In.	...........................*illus*	1998.00
Figurine, Country Girl, Picking Up Basket, Stamped, 14 x 11½ x 8 In.	....	900.00
Figurine, Diana With Borzoi, Signed, Latour, c.1912, 24 x 8 In.	....	3500.00
Figurine, Dog, Springer Spaniel Puppy, 4½ In.	....	65.00
Figurine, Female, Head, Form Curly Hair, Orange, 6¾ In.	....	440.00
Figurine, Female Head, White, Green Accents, Terra-Cotta, c.1925, 12½ In.	....	999.00
Figurine, Flamenco Dancer, Art Nouveau, M. Linder, Pre 1940, 19 x 13 x 8 In.	....	2500.00
Figurine, Lady, No. 257, 6¾ In.	....	85.00
Figurine, Lady With Hat, Marked, 11 In.	....	185.00
Figurine, Latina, Girl Posing, Marked, 13 x 5½ x 5 In.	....	1500.00
Figurine, Madonna, Marked, 5 x 4 In.	....	295.00
Figurine, Nude Woman Next To Cow, Signed, 14 x 18 x 6½ In.	....	4500.00
Figurine, Pierroette, Woman Sitting In Chair, Early 1920s, 14 x 12 x 6 In.	....	1500.00

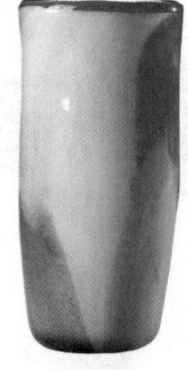

Glass-Venetian, Vase, Cased Rainbow Colors, Red Interior, Cylindrical, Murano, 12 In.
$118.00

G

Glass-Venetian, Vase, Fazzoletto, Smokey, White Zanfirico, Venini, 11½ x 10½ In.
$1800.00

Glasses, Lorgnette, Gold, Diamonds, Enameled Flowers, Embossed Rococo Handle, 4½ In.
$411.00

Goebel, Figurine, La L'Aitiere Flamande, Woman Pouring Milk, Dog Cart, c.1914, 7½ In.
$203.00

Goldscheider, Figurine, Butterfly Lady, Signed, Lorenzl, 11 x 10 In. $1998.00

Goofus Glass, Roses, Bowl, Green Stems, 10¾ x 1¾ In. $60.00

China Souvenirs

Collecting souvenirs made by Goss and other companies was a fad in England about 1900. Tourists bought inexpensive souvenirs of the resorts, historic spots, people, places, and buildings they visited. Goss made many white porcelain souvenir items decorated with coats of arms or local scenes. It is said that ninety percent of the homes in England had at least one Goss china piece.

Figurine, Prince Of Wales, No. 255, 7⅛ In.	125.00
Figurine, Quadrille, Signed, P. Porcher, c.1950, 6¼ In.	60.00
Figurine, Shakesperian Actress, Signed, Lorenzl, 15 x 8 x 5 In.	900.00
Lamp, Nude Woman Under Tree, Signed, Fago, 12 x 9 In.	2500.00
Statue, Virgin Mary, Marked, Fumo, 9 In.	40.00

GOLF, see Sports category.

GOOFUS GLASS was made from about 1900 to 1920 by many American factories. It was originally painted gold, red, green, bronze, pink, purple, or other bright colors. Many pieces are found today with flaking paint, and this lowers the value.

Apple, Plate, 8½ In.	50.00
Bird & Grape, Vase, 9 In.	90.00
Blossoms & Palms, Bowl, 1906	75.00
Blue Grapes, Vase, 1905, 8 In.	95.00
Butterflies, Plate, Red & Gold, Branches Between 12 Panels, 12 In.	45.00
Carnation, Bowl, 9 In.	95.00
Carnation, Bowl, Gold, Red	22.00
Dahlia & Fan, Berry Bowl, Ruffled, 9 In.	35.00
Dancing Lady, Vase, 9 In.	175.00
Embossed Peach, Bowl, Opalescent Edge, 11¾ In.	145.00
Flowers & Lattice, Tray, 10¾ In.	18.00
Fruit, Dish, Black, Gold, 8-Sided, 5½ In.	23.00
Galleon At Sea, Vase, 1925, 10 In.	42.00
Intaglio Fruit, Bowl, Ruby Cranberry, Gold Luster, Ruffled Edge	30.00
Iris, Bowl, 9 In.	34.00
Iris, Plate, Red, Gold, 1897-1912	12.00
La Belle Rose, Plate, 9 x 2½ In.	65.00
La Belle Rose, Plate, 11 In.	35.00 to 60.00
Last Supper, Bread Tray, Red, Black, Gold, 11 x 7 In.	20.00
Nasturtium, Plate, 7⅝ In.	65.00
Peacock, Vase, 10½ In.	50.00
Petals, Plate, Red, 10 In.	26.00
Pine Cones & Panels, Bowl, Green Ground, Sawtooth Edge, 8¾ In.	60.00 to 65.00
Pine Cones & Panels, Plate, 6½ In.	70.00
Poppy, Vase, 8-Sided, 8 In.	100.00
Puffy Grape, Vase, 7½ In.	4.00
Puffy Poppy, Vase, 8 In.	40.00
Puffy Rose, Vase, 5½ In.	53.00
Red Flowers, Bowl, 6 Petals, 8½ x 3 In.	28.00
Red Iris, Berry Set, Gold Ground, 7 Piece	200.00
Red Iris, Bowl, 1¾ x 10⅝ In.	15.00
Red Roses, Plate, 8½ In.	50.00
Red Roses, Platter, 10¾ In.	29.00
Rose On Fishnet, Vase, c.1910, 6 In.	50.00
Rosebuds, Candy Dish, Cover	15.00
Rosebuds, Dish, Ribbed Rim, Round	25.00
Rosebuds, Vase, Gold, Green, Red, 1800s	15.00
Rosebuds, Vase, Puffy, 5⅛ In.	15.00
Roses, Bowl, Green Stems, 10¾ x 1¾ In. ....*illus*	60.00
Roses, Dish, Sauce	20.00
Roses, Jar, Vanity, Cover	105.00
Roses, Tray, 11 In.	45.00
Roses In Snow, Bowl, Ruffled & Scalloped Edge, 9¼ In.	43.00
Roses In Snow, Plate, 10½ In.	100.00
Roses In Snow, Vase, 10 In., Pair	110.00
Sawtooth Edge, Bowl, Multicolored, 9⅛ In.	60.00
Single Rose, Bowl, 9¼ In.	34.00
Single Rose, Vase, 4-Sided, 10½ In.	55.00
Tree Rose, Vase, 9¾ In.	105.00
Tree Rose, Vase, 12½ In.	95.00
Two Apples, Plate, Thistles, Scrolls, 8⅜ In.	20.00
Wild Rose, Bowl, 2½ In.	65.00

G

GOSS china has been made since 1858. English potter William Henry Goss first made it at the Falcon Pottery in Stoke-on-Trent. The factory name was changed to Goss China Company in 1934 when it was taken over by Cauldon Potteries. Production ceased in 1940. Goss China resembles Irish Belleek in both body and glaze. The company also made popular souvenir china, usually marked with local crests and names.

Bowl, Dessert, Apple, Pear, Grapes, Beige Ground, Staffordshire, 5⅛ x 1¼ In., 6 Piece	20.00
Casserole, Cover, Fruit, Tab Handles, Staffordshire, 8½ In.	20.00
Cup & Saucer, Tintagel Crest, Saucer, 4¾ In., Cup, 4 x 1½ In.	28.00
Jug, Load Of Mischief, 6¾ In.	527.00
Loving Cup, Swanage Coat Of Arms, Swan Wearing Crown, 2 Handles, 1870-90s	36.00
Mug, Wellington, Lightning Shaped Handle, 1940, 2¾ x 4 In.	23.00
Pot, Arms At Abbotsford Crest, Eagle, 1¾ x 2 In.	17.00
Pot, Souvenir, Swan, Treherbert Crest, Coal Mine, Woman In Welsh Dress, 2 x 1¾ In.	25.00
Urn, Pembroke Dock Crest, 4 x 2⅛ In.	55.00
Vase, New Zealand Centenary, 1840-1940, 3½ In.	17.00
Vase, New Zealand Centenary, Auckland, 1840-1940, 3¼ In.	16.00
Vase, New Zealand Centenary, Dunedin Scene, 1840-1940, 2¼ x 1 In.	16.00

GOUDA, Holland, has been a pottery center since the seventeenth century. Two firms, the Zenith pottery, established in the eighteenth century, and the Zuid-Hollandsche pottery made the brightly colored art pottery marked *Gouda* from 1898 to about 1964. Other factories followed. Many pieces featured Art Nouveau or Art Deco designs. Pattern names in Dutch, listed here, seem strange to English speaking collectors.

Ashtray, Black & White, Gold Trim, 4 In.	22.00
Ashtray, Bols Genever Liqueurs, Green	20.00
Ashtray, Round, Flowers, Leaves, Yellow, Green, Brown, 7 x 1¼ In.	65.00
Bell, Delft, Dutch Girl, 2¾ In.	35.00
Bowl, Berdino, 5-Sided, Painted, 1940s, 9 In.	125.00
Bowl, Black, Yellow, Orange, Green, 6 x 8¾ In.	525.00
Cake Plate, Prize, Art Deco, Floral Center, Footed, c.1915, 8 x 2 In.	170.00
Chamberstick, Imans, Loop Handle, c.1928, 7 In., Pair	226.00
Humidor, Tobacco, Goedewaagen, c.1977	55.00
Jardiniere, Royal Zwaro, Dark Brown, Rose, Turquoise Droplets	42.00
Jug, Painted Flowers, Multicolored, Goedewaagen, 5⅜ x 4½ In.	30.00
Pitcher, Flowers, High Glaze, c.1930, 5 x 4 In.	230.00
Pitcher, Painted, Royal Goedewaagen, 8 In.	35.00
Pitcher, Petunias, Art Nouveau, Red, Purple, Blue, Green, Yellow, Marked, 6 In.	345.00
Plate, Unique Metalique, Scalloped Edge, Iridescent Copper Luster, c.1950, 8¼ In.	350.00
Vase, Art Nouveau Flower, Amphora Shape, 2 Handles, 10½ In. ....*illus*	259.00
Vase, Double Handles, c.1920, 9½ x 6½ In.	280.00
Vase, Floral & Leaf, High Glaze, 10½ In.	450.00
Vase, Flowers, Blue, Yellow, Red, Gray Matte Ground, Squat, Lady's Leg Bottle Neck, 5 In.	259.00
Vase, Flowers, Leaves, Black Ground Moss Green Inside, Egg Shape, Wide Mouth, 3½ In.	173.00
Vase, Geometric Flower, Early 20th Century, 6½ x 4½ In.	185.00
Vase, Gourd Shape, Geometric, Hand Painted, Signed, 5¼ In.	94.00
Vase, Juliana, Painted, Cream Ground, Ivora, c.1920, 10¼ In., Pair	1200.00
Vase, Painted, Signed Roos, Goedewaagen, c.1935, 10 In.	175.00
Vase, Pastel Blossoms, Basket Shape, Signed, 14 x 13 In.	2400.00
Vase, Regina, Stylized Flowers, Bulbous Center, Blue High Glaze, Spattered, 6¼ In.	55.00
Vase, Regina 204 WB, Holland, 6⅝ x 3¾ In.	275.00
Vase, White Abstract Shapes, Blue Spiraled Lines, Gray Ground, Long Neck, Blanca, 5 In. ...	173.00

GRANITEWARE is an enameled tinware that has been used in the kitchen from the late nineteenth century to the present. Earlier graniteware was green or turquoise blue, with white spatters. The later ware was gray with white spatters. Reproductions are being made in all colors.

Berry Bucket, Blue & White, Granite Lid, 5¼ In.	18.00
Berry Bucket, Blue & White Swirl, Tin Lid, 4 x 5 In.	105.00
Berry Bucket, Blue & White Swirl, Tin Lid, 6 x 8 In.	125.00
Berry Bucket, Gray, Tin Lid, 4 x 5 In.	25.00
Berry Bucket, Gray, Tin Lid, 5 x 6 In.	22.00
Biscuit Cutter, White & Cobalt	40.00
Bread Box, Blue, Round	27.00
Buttermelt, Peacock, 4 x 4 In.	39.00

Gouda Marks

Plateelbakkerij Zuid-Holland (PZH)
Mark used 1926

Zenith Plateelbakkerij en Pijpenfabrieken
Mark used c.1920

Plateelfabriek Ivora
Mark used c.1925

Plateelfabriek Regina
Mark used after c.1938

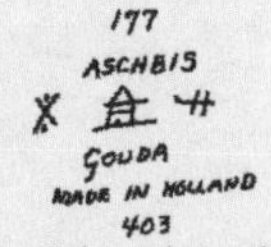

Firma Eduard Antheunis
Mark used c.1920

Gouda, Vase, Art Nouveau Flower, Amphora Shape, 2 Handles, 10½ In. $259.00

Graniteware, Coffeepot, Gray, Straight Spout, Tin Lid, 12⅝ In. $22.00

Graniteware, Ladle, Green & White Swirl, Ebonized Turned Wood Handle, 14½ In. $715.00

Graniteware, Lavabo, Marbled Pink, Green & White, 2 Sections, 24 In. $173.00

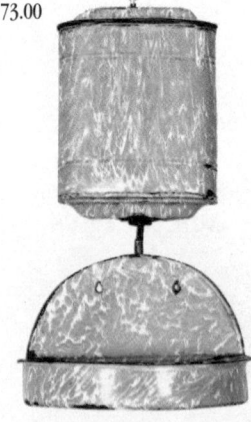

Graniteware, Tea Set, Orange, 3½-In. Teapot, 15 Piece $173.00

Cake Pan, Blue & White, 8 x 10 In.	15.00
Can, Cream, Blue & White Swirl, Tin Lid	70.00
Can, Cream, Gray, Tin Lid	23.00
Can, Cream, Gray, Tin Lid, Boston, 7 In.	55.00
Can, Cream, Lid, 9 In.	85.00
Candleholder, Blue & White, Columbia Terra Haute	35.00
Candleholder, White, Adjustable	65.00
Churn, Light Blue, White, Handles, Wood Lid, 18 In.	675.00
Coaster, Blue & White, 4 Piece	10.00
Cocoa Dipper	40.00
Coffee Boiler, 10 In.	45.00
Coffee Boiler, Blue & White Mottled, Granite Lid	50.00
Coffee Boiler, Blue & White Swirl, 6 x 8 In.	55.00
Coffee Urn, White, Handles, 18 In., 4 Piece	400.00
Coffeepot, Blue & White Swirl, Granite Lid, 9 In.	65.00
Coffeepot, Granite Lid	30.00
Coffeepot, Gray, Straight Spout, Tin Lid, 12⅝ In. *illus*	22.00
Coffeepot, Wood Handle, 10 x 10 x 6½ In.	95.00
Coffeepot, Wood Handle	20.00
Comb Case, Embossed Star, Gray	205.00
Dish, Blue Swirl, Blue & White, White Enamel Inside, 8 x 2½ In.	15.00
Dishpan, Blue Swirl, Blue & White, White Enamel Inside, 12 x 3 In.	25.00
Double Boiler, Gray, Tin Lid	4.00
Foot Tub, Oval	15.00
Frypan, 9 In.	50.00
Funnel, Gray, Large	13.00
Grater, Solid Blue	20.00
Kettle, Preserve, Lip Strainer, Gray	65.00
Kettle, Straight-Sided, Large	50.00
Kitchen Set, Rack, Sieve, Ladle, White, 17 In., 3 Piece	215.00
Ladle, Green & White Swirl, Ebonized Turned Wood Handle, 14½ In. *illus*	715.00
Ladle, Windsor, Columbian Swirl	50.00
Lavabo, Marbled Pink, Green & White, 2 Sections, 24 In. *illus*	173.00
Loaf Pan, Rectangular	40.00
Measure, Riveted, Gray, ½ Pt.	105.00
Mold, Melon, Gray, Stamped L&G	27.00
Mold, Strawberry, Onyxware, Kemp's Pearl Enameled Ware, Paper Label	45.00
Mold, Turk's Head, Turban, Tube Style, Blue	20.00
Muffin Pan, 6 Cup	155.00
Muffin Pan, 12 Cup, Gray Underspray	65.00
Muffin Pan, Gray, Turk's Head, 8-Hole	45.00
Pail, Chamber, Blue, Granite Lid	25.00
Pan, Blue, White, 7 In.	12.00
Pan, Blue, White, 16 x 5 In.	36.00
Pan, Oval, Small, Marked, Elite	55.00
Pie Plate, Blueberry, Gray	5.00
Pitcher, Gray, Strap Handle, Riveted Sides, 13 In.	625.00
Pitcher, Water, 8½ In.	65.00
Pitcher, Water, Bulbous, 6½ In.	75.00
Pitcher, White, Dark Blue Trim, 4½ In.	15.00
Potty, Lid, Gray, Small	8.00
Pudding Dish, Oblong, 8 x 5¾ x 1⅛ In.	15.00
Roaster, Flat Top, Oval, Blue & White Swirl, Side Holds On Lid, 15 In.	115.00
Roaster, Insert, Relish, Salesman Sample, Lisk	600.00
Roaster, Large	30.00
Salt Box, Wood Lid, Hanging, Solid Blue	40.00
Saltshaker, White	22.00
Sign, Restroom, Men & Ladies, White Enamel	35.00
Slop Jar, Gray	8.00
Soap Dish, Hanging, Solid Blue	45.00
Soup, Dish, Gray	10.00
Strainer, Sink, White & Cobalt Blue	35.00
Tea Set, Child's, 15 Piece	250.00
Tea Set, Orange, 3½-In. Teapot, 15 Piece *illus*	173.00
Tea Strainer, Solid Blue	15.00
Teakettle, Gray	20.00

Teapot, Bell Shape, Pewter Rim, Gray	950.00
Teapot, Blue, Snow On Mountain	12.50
Teapot, Blue & White Speckled, Wood Handle, 8 In.	20.00
Teapot, Blue & White Swirl, Granite Lid, 9 In.	55.00
Teapot, Navy Blue, White Speckled	10.00
Trivet, Gray Speckled	15.00
Vase, Dark Blue Swirl, 6 x 3⅛ In.	17.00

GREENTOWN glass was made by the Indiana Tumbler and Goblet Company of Greentown, Indiana, from 1894 to 1903. In 1899, the factory became part of National Glass Company. A variety of pressed glass was made. Additional pieces may be found in other categories, such as Chocolate Glass, Holly Amber, Milk Glass, and Pressed Glass.

Austrian, Creamer, 4½ In.	25.00
Austrian, Saltshaker, Pewter Lid, c.1907, 4 In.	60.00
Austrian, Tumbler, 3⅝ In.	45.00
Austrian, Vase, Footed, 10 In.	85.00
Austrian, Wine	30.00
Bird & Strawberry, Creamer, c.1914, 4¼ x 3 In.	55.00
Cord Drapery, Spooner, 4 x 4½ In.	45.00
Dewey, Tray, Condiment, Green, 8½ x 4¾ In.	17.00
Heron, Celery Vase, 8⅞ x 3⅝ In.	59.00
Holly, Dish, Pickle, Handles, 8⅞ x 4 In.	75.00
Laverne, Tumbler, Footed, c.1880, 5⅛ In.	30.00
Pleat Bands, Cake Stand, Child's, 4 x 6½ In.	75.00
Teardrop & Tassel, Butter, No Lid, 1¾ x 6⅜ In.	48.00

GRUEBY Faience Company of Boston, Massachusetts, was incorporated in 1897 by William H. Grueby. Garden statuary, art pottery, and architectural tiles were made until 1920. The company developed a green matte glaze that was so popular it was copied by many other factories making a less expensive type of pottery. This eventually led to the financial problems of the pottery.

Bowl, Applied Leaves, Green Matte Glaze, Squash Shape, 4½ x 5½ In.	1920.00
Jar, Oil, Pumpkin Matte Glaze, Handle, Round Spout, Rolled Rim, 3½ In. ....*illus*	978.00
Paperweight, Scarab Beetle, Mottled Green Matte Glaze, 1 x 2¾ In.	288.00
Paperweight, Scarab Beetle, Oatmeal Matte Glaze, 1 x 3 In.	345.00
Tile, Cellist, Busy At Work, Blue Slip, Dark Caramel Matte Ground, Red Clay, 6 In.	432.00
Tile, Green Tree, Blue Sky, Clouds, Matte Glaze, Square, 6 In.	1955.00
Tile, Horses, Ivory, Cuenca, Blue Sky, Signed, K.C., Square, 6 In.	2640.00
Tile, Mermaid, Looking In Mirror, Brown, Yellow Matte Ground, Red Clay, 6 In.	735.00
Tile, Ship, Ivory, Brown, Blue, Gray Ground, Cuenca, Signed, S.R., Square 6 In.	1200.00
Tile, St. George & Dragon, Blue, Green, Ocher, 9 In.	7638.00
Tile, Stork, 2 x 4 In.	59.00
Tile, The Pines, Cuenca, Signed RD, Square, 6 In.	3480.00
Tile, Tulip, Red, Green, 6 In.	2200.00
Tile, Yellow Tulip, Green Ribbed Leaf Blades, White Ground, c.1905, 6 In.	2585.00
Trivet, Bear & Tree, Bronze Base, Initials M.C., 4¼ x 1½ In.	936.00
Trivet, Lion & Tree, Bronze, 4¼ x 1½ In.	936.00
Vase, Gourd Shape, Green Matte Glaze, Tooled, Applied Leaves, Kendrick, 12 x 8 In. ....*illus*	24000.00
Vase, Green Matte, Applied Vertical Leaves & Buds, Long Stems, Signed, 9 In.	2400.00
Vase, Green Matte Glaze, Applied Flowers, Leaves, Shouldered, Ruth Erickson, 5 x 5 In.	2200.00
Vase, Green Matte Glaze, Overlapping Leaves, Feathered, Spherical, 3¼ x 4¾ In.	1080.00
Vase, Green Matte Glaze, Tooled, Applied Full-Height Leaves, Yellow Buds, 12 x 5 In.	10800.00
Vase, Green Matte Glaze, Tooled Leaves, 4-Sided Pinched Rim, Marked, 4½ x 5½ In.	1265.00
Vase, Leathery Green Matte Glaze, Tooled Panels, Cylindrical Neck, 7 In.	1380.00
Vase, Leathery Green Matte Glaze, Vertical Panels, Cylindrical Rim, 5⅝ In. ....*illus*	1035.00
Vase, Oval, Indigo Matte Glaze, Tooled, Applied Full-Height Leaves, 8 x 4 In.	1140.00

GUNDERSEN glass was made at the Gundersen-Pairpoint Glass Works of New Bedford, Massachusetts, from 1952 to 1957. Gundersen Peachblow is especially famous.

Bowl, Peachblow, Flared Rim, 1940s, 9 x 3½ In.	50.00
Nappy, Camellia Heart Shape, Applied Loop Handle, 7¼ x 2¾ In. ....*illus*	86.00
Vase, Cornucopia, Ruby Red, Paperweight Base, Controlled Bubbles, 8½ In.	125.00
Vase, Fan, Marina Blue, 6½ x 10 In.	150.00

Grueby, Jar, Oil,
Pumpkin Matte Glaze, Handle,
Round Spout, Rolled Rim,
3½ In.
$978.00

G

Grueby, Vase, Gourd Shape,
Green Matte Glaze, Tooled,
Applied Leaves, Kendrick, 12 x 8 In.
$24000.00

Grueby, Vase,
Leathery Green Matte Glaze,
Vertical Panels, Cylindrical Rim, 5⅝ In.
$1035.00

Gundersen, Nappy,
Camellia Heart Shape,
Applied Loop Handle, 7¼ x 2¾ In.
$86.00

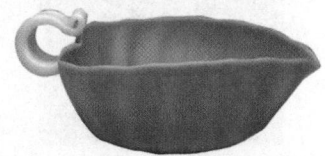

Gundersen, Vase, Cornucopia, Ruby, Ruffled Rim, Paperweight Base, Bubbles, 11½ In. $60.00

Gustavsberg, Vase, Green Flowers, Green Ground, Round, Ekberg, 1904, 6¾ x 6 In. $265.00

Gutta-Percha, Case, Union, Fireman Rescuing Child, Tintypes, Littlefield, Parsons, 3 In. $303.00

Vase, Ruby Red, Urn Shape, Swirl Connector, Polished Pontil, 11¾ x 6¼ In.	125.00
Vase, Cornucopia, Ruby, Ruffled Rim, Paperweight Base, Bubbles, 11½ In. *illus*	60.00

GUSTAVSBERG ceramics factory was founded in 1827 near Stockholm, Sweden. **Gustafsberg** It is best known to collectors for its twentieth-century artwares, especially Argenta, a green stoneware with silver inlay.

Bowl, Leaf Shape, Yellow, Stig Lindberg, 1950s, 7 x 6 x 3½ In.	175.00
Bowl, Mermaid Medallion, Silver, Turquoise Ground, Shaped Banded Rim, Argenta, 11 In.	176.00
Bowl, Reptile, Leaf Shape, Blue, Signed, Stig Lindberg, 1950s, 10½ x 5 In.	95.00 to 125.00
Bowl, Silver Fish, Bubbles, Footed, Argenta, Signed, Anchor Mark, 6 In.	295.00
Box, Cover, Green, Silver Woman's Figure On Cover, Argenta, 1930s, 5¾ In.	299.00
Dish, Sgreffitto, Signed, Josef Ekberg, 1925, 5½ In.	75.00
Figurine, Cat, Murre, Signed, Lisa Larsson, 1982-87, 3¾ In.	75.00
Figurine, Cat, Stripes, Marked, 4¼ x 11 In.	250.00
Vase, Black Glaze, Iridescent Silver Spots, Signed, Stig Lindberg, 3⅞ x 2¾ In.	185.00
Vase, Fish On Chain, Argenta, Wilhelm Kage, 3¼ x 3½ In.	125.00
Vase, Flowers, Green, Argenta, Squat, c.1930, 3 x 4½ In.	295.00
Vase, Geometrics, Pale Green & Blue, Footed, Signed, Joseph Exberg, 1920	975.00
Vase, Gray Glaze, Swen Wejsfelt, 6 x 4¾ In.	175.00
Vase, Grazia, Stig Lindberg, 5⅜ In.	75.00
Vase, Green Flowers, Green Ground, Round, Ekberg, 1904, 6¾ x 6 In. *illus*	265.00
Vase, Lily Of The Valley, Mottled Green, Argenta, Stamped, Anchor, 5 In.	475.00

GUTTA-PERCHA was one of the first plastic materials. It was made from a mixture of resins from Malaysian trees. It was molded and used for daguerreotype cases, toilet articles, and picture frames in the nineteenth century.

Button, Cameo, Brass Base, Victorian, ¾ In.	24.00
Button, Pirate Boot, Raised, Lid To Late 1800s, 1 In.	20.00
Cape Clasp, Fern, Carved, Brass, 1¼ x 2 In.	135.00
Case, Oval, Daguerreotype, Young Lady, Floral, Maroon Velvet, Metallic Trim, 3 x 2 In.	165.00
Case, Union, Ambrotype, Hinged, Velvet Interior, Holmes Booth Hayden, 3 x 2½ In.	245.00
Case, Union, Ambrotype, Man, Grape Cluster, Oval, ⅙ Plate	225.00
Case, Union, Ambrotype, Young Man, 1/16 Plate	135.00
Case, Union, Ambrotype, Young Woman, 1/16 Plate	145.00
Case, Union, Angel Holding Flowers, Littlefield, Parsons & Co., 2½ x 2 In.	110.00
Case, Union, Cherub Grabbing Stag Antlers, Littlefield, Parsons & Co., 3 x 2¾ In.	55.00
Case, Union, Daguerreotype, Baby Boy, Gold Foil Frame, c.1857, 3 x 2½ In.	100.00
Case, Union, Fireman Rescuing Child, Tintypes, Littlefield, Parsons, 3 In. *illus*	303.00
Case, Union, Man, Horse, Greeting, Man, Woman, Dog, A.P. Critchlow & Co., 4¼ x 3¼ In.	99.00
Case, Union, Tintype, Gilt & Burnished Hinge, Scovill Mfg. Co., 3 x 2½ In.	245.00
Case, Union Seashells, Twisted Rope, S. Peck & Co., 3¼ x 2¾ In.	99.00
Case, Union Woman, Seated, Child, Dog, Cat, Littlefield, Parsons & Co., 5 x 4 In.	55.00
Case, Washington Memorial, Virginia, Photograph, 4 x 5 x 1 In.	423.00
Locket, Chain, Angel, Chunky, c.1860, 19½ x 1¼ In.	295.00
Mirror, Beveled Glass, Wood Back, Silvered, c.1880, 19 x 14 In.	650.00
Mirror, Flowers, Nodding Violet, Black, Marked, Diatite, March 19, 1872, 10 x 4 In.	155.00
Mirror, Hand, Black, Oval, Marked Florence, 1880s, 9 x 3½ In.	85.00
Mirror, Sailboat, Flowers, 9 x 3¼ In.	125.00
Mirror, Victorian Style, Beveled Glass, Wood Back, c.1880, 19 x 14 In.	650.00
Pendant, Cameo, Ivory, 14K Rose Gold Frame, c.1900, 3½ x 2 In.	1295.00
Pin, Victorian, Carved, Floral Relief, Twisted Rope, 1860s	50.00
Shoe Buckle, Rose, Cameo, Tortoiseshell, Brass Clasps, Beveled, 2⅜ x 1¾ In.	52.00
Shuttle, Tatting	45.00
Thermometer, Fancy Design, Easel Back, 1850s	145.00

HAEGER Potteries, Inc., Dundee, Illinois, started making commercial artwares in 1914. Early pieces were marked with the name *Haeger* written over an *H*. About 1938, the mark *Royal Haeger* was used in honor of Royal Hickman, a designer at the factory. The firm is still making florist wares and lamp bases. See also the Royal Hickman category.

Bookends, Calla Lily, Blue, Incised Mark	24.00
Candleholder, Coral Pink, Art Deco	15.00
Cigarette Box, Cube, Checkered, Persian Gray, Stylized Fish Finial, 7 x 4 In.	60.00
Console, Yellow, 11 x 7½ In.	30.00
Figurine, Dog, Poodle, Black & White, 8 In. *illus*	10.00

Figurine, Nude Woman, 17½ In.	150.00
Figurine, Swan, Greenbrier, 15 In.	165.00
Figurine, Swan, Mauve Glaze, Loop Neck, 8½ In.	30.00
Pitcher & Bowl, 9½ & 7 In.	40.00
Planter, Console, Brown Drip Glaze, 12 x 4½ In.	27.00
Planter, Ruffled, Petal Shape, 5 x 8 In.	11.00
Planter, Top Hat, Apple Green	16.00
Vase, Bird Of Paradise, Variegated Turquoise, c.1937, 13½ In.	49.00
Vase, Bottle Neck, Etruscan Red, 5 In.	120.00
Vase, Console, White Matte, 16 x 7 In.	38.00
Vase, Leaf, Petal Shape, Embossed, 12½ x 5 In.	65.00
Vase, Swan, Mauve Agate, Closed Loop Neck, 8½ x 5½ In.	30.00
Vase, Urn Shape, Gold, Cream Interior, 9 x 7 In.	85.00

HALF-DOLL, *see Pincushion Doll category.*

HALL CHINA Company started in East Liverpool, Ohio, in 1903. The firm made many types of wares. Collectors search for the Hall teapots made from the 1920s to the 1950s. The dinnerwares of the same period, especially Autumn Leaf pattern, are also popular. The Hall China Company is still working. For more information, see *Kovels' Depression Glass & Dinnerware Price List.* Autumn Leaf pattern dishes are listed in their own category in this book.

Blue Garden, Casserole, Gold Trim, Handles, Lid, 8¼ x 5¼ In.	89.00
Bow Knot, Teapot, Oval, Ribbed Body, Pink & Puce Decoration, Cup	176.00
House 'N Garden, Creamer, Brown Glaze, 4½ In.	3.00
McCormick, Teapot, Gray, 2 Cup, 4⅝ In. ....*illus*	10.00
Pretzel, Cookie Jar, Pretzel Handles, 7 x 7½ In.	22.00
Red Poppy, Bread Box, Metal, 31 x 11 In.	150.00
Red Poppy, Hurricane Lamp, Globe	85.00
Red Poppy, Waste Can, Pedal, Metal, 13 x 11 In.	225.00
Rose White, Dip Jar, Cover, No. 658, 3½ x 5⅞ In. ....*illus*	4.00

HALLOWEEN is an ancient holiday that has changed in the last 200 years. The jack-o'-lantern, witches on broomsticks, and orange decorations seem to be twentieth-century creations. Collectors started to become serious about collecting Halloween-related items in the late 1970s. The papier-mache decorations, now replaced by plastic, and old costumes are in demand.

Bank, Pirate With Drum, Orange Plastic, Green, Black Trim, Yellow Wheels, 8 In. .....*illus*	180.00
Costume, Alvin Chipmunk, Cloth, Plastic Mask, Ben Cooper, c.1962, Child's Size 8-10	58.00
Costume, Fireman, Helmet, Eagle Finial, Lithograph, Shield, Horn, Ax, Schoenhut, Child's, 4 Piece .	1725.00
Cutout, Cat, Hissing, Legs Move, 1940s, 13 x 12 In.	35.00
Cutout, Pumpkin, Owl, 1960s, 4 Piece	35.00
Cutout, Witch, Howling Cat With Pumpkin, 1960s, 2 Piece	35.00
Decorations, Tablecloth, Cake, Witches, Doll Witch Centerpiece, Nut Cups, 1930s	35.00
Figure, Boy Holding Pumpkin, Red Shirt, Brown Pants, Chalk, 16 In.	616.00
Jack-O'-Lantern, Cat, Pressed Papier-Mache, Paint, Tissue, Wire Bail Handle, 5 x 7 In.	50.00
Jack-O'-Lantern, Orange, Blue & White Eyes, Paper, Wire Handle, 1920s, 8 In.	165.00
Jack-O'-Lantern, Plastic, Orange, Union Products Inc., 1950s, 3½ In.	25.00
Jack-O'-Lantern, Pressed Papier-Mache, Paint, Tissue Face, Wire Bail Handle, 6 x 7 In.	70.00
Jack-O'-Lantern, Unglazed, Cutout Eyes, Mouth, Stoneware, B.B. Craig, Vale, N.C., 9¼ In. ..	374.00
Lantern, Black Cat, Bowtie, Pressed Cardboard, Paper Eyes, 6 In.	330.00
Lantern, Devil, c.1920, 5½ In. ....*illus*	3575.00
Lantern, Devil, Paper Eyes & Mouth, 4 In.	825.00
Lantern, Jack-O'-Lantern, Blue, Glass, Embossed, Tin Screw Top, Bail Handle, 4 x 4 In.	248.00
Lantern, Jack-O'-Lantern, Yellow, Metal Handle, c.1920, 5 In.	935.00
Lantern, Jack-O'-Lantern Ghost, Cardboard, Metal Handle, c.1920, 4 In.	440.00
Lantern, Witch, Paper Eyes & Mouth, Red Scarf, Handle, 8 In.	7150.00
Nodder, Black Cat, Composition, Wood Neck, Germany, 5 In.	220.00
Nodder, Veggie Man, Multicolored, 6 In.	248.00
Noisemaker, Cat, Painted, Wood, Composition, 8 x 4 In.	176.00
Noisemaker, Jack-O'-Lantern, Cat, Witch, Devil, Bat, Wood Handle, Tin Litho, c.1950, 4 In. .	110.00
Owl, Pulp, 10 In.	110.00
Paper, Article, Fads & Frills For Halloween, Witch, Photo, 1905, 11 x 16 In.	35.00
Pin, Jack-O'-Lantern, Lion's Club, 1930s, 1¼ In.	75.00
Postcard, Child Carving Pumpkin, Embossed, 1917	30.00
Postcard, Mechanical, Girl Holding Jack-O'-Lantern, Ellen Clapsaddle	264.00
Postcard, Mechanical, Pumpkin Moves Over Child's Head, Clapsaddle	275.00

Haeger, Figurine, Dog, Poodle, Black & White, 8 In.
$10.00

Hall China, McCormick, Teapot, Gray, 2 Cup, 4⅝ In.
$10.00

Hall China, Rose White, Dip Jar, Cover, No. 658, 3½ x 5⅞ In.
$4.00

TIP

Be careful where you put a fresh pumpkin or gourd. Put a plastic liner underneath them. A rotting pumpkin will permanently stain wood or marble.

Halloween, Bank, Pirate With Drum, Orange Plastic, Green, Black Trim, Yellow Wheels, 8 In. $180.00

Halloween, Lantern, Devil, c.1920, 5½ In. $3575.00

Halloween, Postcard, Woman On Pumpkin, Black Cat, Bat, Halloween Greetings, Verse, S.S., Winsch $441.00

Halloween, Standup, Jack-O'-Lantern Playing Saxophone, Die Cut, Germany, 27 In. $248.00

Postcard, Scared Boy, Don't Be Scared On Halloween, Postmark 1916		25.00
Postcard, Witch On Broom, Jack-O'-Lantern, Boy, Winsch		588.00
Postcard, Woman In Front Of Jack-O'-Lantern, Winsch		588.00
Postcard, Woman On Jack-O-Lantern, Kicking Up Leg, Samuel Schmucker		441.00
Postcard, Woman On Pumpkin, Black Cat, Bat, Halloween Greetings, Verse, S.S., Winsch *illus*		441.00
Pumpkin, 2-Sided Faces, Cutout, Bottom Open, Papier-Mache, 10 x 8¼ In.		320.00
Pumpkin Head Man, Orange, Pulp, 9½ In.		220.00
Standup, Jack-O'-Lantern Playing Saxophone, Die Cut, Germany, 27 In. *illus*		248.00
Witch On Motorcycle, White Face & Hands, Orange Dress & Hat, 4 x 6 In.		1236.00

HAMPSHIRE pottery was made in Keene, New Hampshire, between 1871 and 1923. Hampshire developed a line of colored glazed wares as early as 1883, including a Royal Worcester-type pink, olive green, blue, and mahogany. Pieces are marked with the printed mark or the impressed name *Hampshire Pottery* or *J.S.T. & Co., Keene, N.H.* Many pieces were marked with city names and sold as souvenirs.

Bowl, Artichoke, Green Matte Glaze, Impressed Mark, c.1905, 3 x 4¾ In.		382.00
Bowl, Good Luck Symbols On Shoulder, Green Matte Glaze, Folded Sides, 2¼ x 7 In.		127.00
Ewer, Green, 9½ x 8½ In.		395.00
Ewer, Green Matte Glaze, c.1803-1903, 9½ x 9½ x 6¼ In.		795.00
Vase, Blue, Carved Design To Shoulder, 4¼ x 5½ In.		365.00
Vase, Blue Jean Blue Crackled Glaze, Black Graphite, Marked, 7⅛ In.		515.00
Vase, Brown, 4¼ x 5¼ In.		355.00
Vase, Curdled Blue Matte Glaze, Shouldered, Wide Mouth, 5 In.		173.00
Vase, Dark & Light Blue Matte Glaze, Squat, Marked, 3 x 6 In.		250.00
Vase, Flowing Blue Glaze, 8¼ In.		615.00
Vase, Green Matte Glaze, 2½ x 6 In.		365.00
Vase, Green Matte Glaze, Squat, Marked, 6½ In.		729.00
Vase, Melon Shape, Runny Green Matte Glaze, Stamped, 5 In.		748.00
Vase, Mocha Brown, 7½ In.		425.00
Vase, Molded Leaves, Curdled Blue Matte Glaze, Swollen Neck, 6½ In.		374.00
Vase, Organic Green, Lightning Bolt Handles, Impressed, 7⅝ In.		400.00

HANDEL glass was made by Philip Handel working in Meriden, Connecticut, from 1885 and in New York City from 1893 to 1933. The firm made art glass and other types of lamps. Handel shades were made not only of leaded glass in a style reminiscent of Tiffany but also of reverse painted glass. Handel also made vases and other glass objects.

Humidor, Masonic, Red, Green, Marked, No. 2379-194, 6 In.		605.00
Humidor, Milk Glass, Dog, Landscape, Silver Plated Cover, Pipe Handle, 7 x 5½ In. *illus*		1093.00
Lamp, 4 Panels, Metal Overlay, Leaf, Border, Bronzed Metal Base, Patina, 20 x 11 In.		1500.00
Lamp, 6 Panels, Chipped Ice, Aquatic Scene, Bronze Base, Mermaid, 23 In. *illus*		54625.00
Lamp, 9 Panels, Metal Overlay, Geometrics, Landscape, Bronze Base, Patina, 24 x 20 In.		3500.00
Lamp, 9 Panels, Metal Overlay, Hawaiian Tropic, Palm Trees, 24 x 20 In. *illus*		9775.00
Lamp, Chipped Ice, Asian Scene, 3 Sockets, Bronze Base, 24 x 18 In.		18000.00
Lamp, Copper Overlay, Floral, Green Slag Glass, Arts & Crafts, 28 x 20 In.		18000.00
Lamp, Desk, Leaded Glass Shade, Socket Bronze Base, 5 x 5¼ In.		2200.00
Lamp, Desk, Tropical Moon, c.1910, 14 In.		1842.00
Lamp, Domed Shade, Bird, Macaws, Chipped Ice, Pierced Metal Base, 24 x 18 In. *illus*		16675.00
Lamp, Domed Shade, Birds Of Paradise, c.1910, 23½ In.		10236.00
Lamp, Domed Shade, Japanese Garden, Tapered Melon-Ribbed Base, 23 x 18 In.		6463.00
Lamp, Domed Shade, Landscape, Double Sockets, 17 x 22 In.		1763.00
Lamp, Domed Shade, Mountain, Lakes, Trees, Teroma, Tree Base, 18 In.		6900.00
Lamp, Domed Shade, Nocturnal Landscape, Moon, Bronze Base, Patina, 23 x 18 In.		5500.00
Lamp, Domed Shade, Winter Scene, Sunset, Tree Form Base, 13½ In. *illus*		3450.00
Lamp, Electric, Faceted Slag Glass Shade, Brown, Green Cattails, Bronze Base, 28 x 32 In.		5100.00
Lamp, Gothic, Leaded Glass Shade, Green Amber, Ruby, Bronze Base, 5 Sockets, 31 x 26 In.		3900.00
Lamp, Green Steuben Glass Shade, Bronzed Base, Verdigris, 55½ x 6 In.		7200.00
Lamp, Hanging, Leaded, Luster Glass Shade, Parrots, Branches, Socket, Bronze Mount, 22 In.		5100.00
Lamp, Landscape, Earth Tones, Cased Interior, 3 Sockets, Acorn Pulls, 24 x 18 In.		4406.00
Lamp, Leaded Glass Shade, White, 3 Sockets, Bronze Base, 3 Curved Legs, 16 x 23 In.		3700.00
Lamp, Metal Overlay, Grapevine, Carmel & Green Slag Glass, Tree Trunk Base, 25 In.		3525.00
Lamp, Mosserine Shade, Arts & Crafts Flowers, Peach Ground, Harp Base, 18½ In. *illus*		1725.00
Lamp, Orange Iridescent, Allover Aqua & Quartz Lava Decoration, Art Deco, 4 In. *illus*		1035.00
Lamp, Reverse Painted Landscape, Etched Glass, Hemispherical, 3 Socket Base, 24 x 18 In.		7800.00
Lantern, Copper Over Carmel & White Slag Glass, Original Patina, Chain, 22½ x 16 In.		2900.00
Vase, Cameo, Yellow Peonies, Ferns, Leaves, Frosty Textured Ground, Mosher, 9¾ In.		1050.00

H

Handel, Humidor, Milk Glass, Dog, Landscape,
Silver Plated Cover, Pipe Handle, 7 x 5½ In.
$1093.00

Handel, Lamp, 6 Panels, Chipped Ice,
Aquatic Scene, Bronze Base,
Mermaid, 23 In.
$54625.00

Handel, Lamp, 9 Panels, Metal Overlay,
Hawaiian Tropic, Palm Trees, 24 x 20 In.
$9775.00

Handel, Lamp, Domed Shade,
Bird, Macaws, Chipped Ice,
Pierced Metal Base, 24 x 18 In.
$16675.00

Handel, Lamp, Domed Shade,
Winter Scene, Sunset,
Tree Form Base, 13½ In.
$3450.00

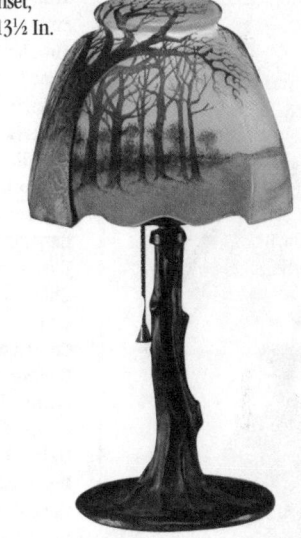

Big Three Lampmakers

Collectors' most wanted names in early 20th-century American electric lamps are Tiffany, Handel, and Pairpoint. The three companies made glass lampshades in art nouveau and art deco styles. Lamp bases were usually bronze. Table lamps by the "big three" sell for the highest prices, but there are similar, signed lamps by less famous makers.

Handel, Lamp, Mosserine Shade,
Arts & Crafts Flowers,
Peach Ground,
Harp Base, 18½ In.
$1725.00

Handel, Lamp,
Orange Iridescent,
Allover Aqua & Quartz Lava
Decoration, Art Deco, 14 In.
$1035.00

Handel, Vase, Trees,
Lake, Mountains, Chipped Ice,
Teroma, Shouldered,
Flared Rim, 7½ In.
$1840.00

Vase, Trees, Lake, Mountains, Chipped Ice, Teroma, Shouldered, Flared Rim, 7½ In. . . . *illus*	1840.00
Vase, Yellow Flowers & Green Leaves, Egg Shape, Ruffled Edge, 1910, 10 In.	630.00

HARDWARE, *see Architectural category.*

HARKER Pottery Company of East Liverpool, Ohio, was incorporated in 1890 in East Liverpool, Ohio. The Harker family had been making pottery in the area since 1840. The company made many types of pottery but by the Civil War was making quantities of yellowware from native clays. They also made Rockingham-type brown-glazed pottery and whiteware. The plant was moved to Chester, West Virginia, in 1931. Dinnerwares were made and sold nationally. In 1971 the company was sold to Jeannette Glass Company and all operations ceased in 1972. For more information, see *Kovels' Depression Glass & Dinnerware Price List.*

Advertising, Ashtray, Compliments Of Werres Variety Store, 6-Sided, 5½ In.	9.00
Advertising, Ashtray, Honey Bear Farm, Powers Lake, Wis., Turquoise	12.00
Advertising, Plate, Souvenir Of Luck, Wis., Woodland Scene, 6 In.	8.00
Alpine, Bowl, Vegetable, Divided, Intaglio, Cameoware, 10½ x 7⅜ In.	13.00
Alpine, Cup & Saucer, Intaglio, Cameoware	10.00
Alpine, Plate, Salad, Intaglio, Cameoware, 8¼ In.	8.00
Alpine, Platter, Intaglio, Cameoware, 13½ x 10½ In.	25.00
Alpine, Salt & Pepper, Intaglio	19.00
Alpine, Soup, Dish, Intaglio, Cameoware	8.00
Alpine, Sugar & Creamer, Intaglio, Cameoware	13.00
Amy, Custard Cup, 2¼ In.	9.00
Amy, Plate, Luncheon, 7¼ In.	5.50
Amy, Rolling Pin, 13 In.	89.00
Amy, Teapot, Cover Only	9.00
Bakerite, Bowl, Gold Trim, 9 In.	33.00
Bakerite, Pie Baker, c.1930	8.00
Blue Basket, Creamer, 3 In.	8.00
Calico Tulip, Platter, 12 In.	11.00
Cameoware, Bowl, Blue, Scalloped Rim, 9 In.	10.00
Cameoware, Pie Baker, Blue, Rose, 10 In.	22.00
Chesterton, Plate, Dinner, 9 In.	8.00
Chesterton, Platter, 13 In.	14.00
Colonial Lady, Pie Baker, 9 In.	22.00
Compass Rose, Creamer, 4⅝ In.	9.00
Currier & Ives, Pie Lifter, 9 In.	18.00
Dainty Flowers, Creamer, Blue, Cameoware	11.00
Dainty Flowers, Plate, Luncheon, Blue, Cameoware, 7 In.	7.00
Dainty Flowers, Platter, Blue, Cameoware, 11 In. . . . . *illus*	25.00
Deco Dahlia, Casserole, Cover Only, c.1930, 6⅞ In.	9.00
Deco Dahlia, Pie Lifter, 9¼ In.	20.00
Dogwood, Bowl, Fruit, 5¾ In.	7.00
Dogwood, Cup & Saucer	13.00
Dogwood, Plate, Dinner, 10 In.	15.00
Dogwood, Soup, Dish, 7½ In.	9.00
Emmy, Rolling Pin, 14½ In.	89.00
Emmy, Syrup, Cover, 5½ x 4¼ In.	22.00
English Ivy, Batter Bowl, Cover, 7 In.	33.00
Godey, Bowl, Gadroon, Gold Trim, 6⅛ In.	4.50
Intaglio, Creamer, Green, Cameoware, 4 In.	3.00
Intaglio, Cup, Green, Cameoware, 3¾ In.	3.00
Intaglio, Plate, Bread & Butter, Green, Cameoware, 6 In.	2.50
Intaglio, Saucer, Green, Cameoware, 6 In.	2.00
Jewel Weed, Casserole, Cover Only, 7 In.	9.00
Jewel Weed, Custard Cup, 3⅜ In.	9.00
Laurelton, Plate, Dinner, Turquoise, White, 10 In.	5.00
Lovelace, Bowl, 6 In.	3.00
Lovelace, Plate, Bread & Butter, 6⅛ In.	3.00
Lovelace, Plate, Bread & Butter, Gold Trim, 6¼ In.	15.00
Mallow, Casserole, Cover, Qt., 4¼ x 6½ In.	35.00
Mallow, Rolling Pin	90.00
Melrose, Bowl, Vegetable, 6 x 4 In.	24.00
Modern Tulip, Cake Plate, Metal Holder	18.00
Modern Tulip, Rolling Pin, 13 In.	77.00

H

Pate-Sur-Pate, Creamer, Teal ....*illus*	25.00
Pate-Sur-Pate, Platter, Teal, 13¾ x 10 In.	12.00
Petit Point, Fork, 8⅝ In.	23.00
Petit Point, Pie Baker, 10¼ In.	20.00
Petit Point, Pie Baker, Silver Trim, 9 In.	16.00
Petit Point, Pie Lifter, 9 In.	20.00
Petit Point, Spoon, 9 In.	15.00
Pink Poppy, Casserole, Cover, 8½ In. ....*illus*	35.00
Red Apple, Cup & Saucer	13.00
Red Apple, Plate, Bread & Butter, 6 In.	6.00
Red Apple, Spoon, 8⅞ In.	20.00
Shellridge, Plate, Bread & Butter, 6 In.	8.00
Silhouette, Plate, Man & Woman Riding Horses, 9 In.	25.00
Tulip Bouquet, Rolling Pin, 15 In.	89.00
Vintage, Bowl, Vegetable, Gadroon, 9 In.	20.00
Vintage, Plate, Bread & Butter, 6 In.	4.00
Vintage, Tidbit Tray, Rose, 10 In. ....*illus*	14.00
Wild Rose, Pie Lifter, 9¼ In.	28.00

HARLEQUIN dinnerware was produced by the Homer Laughlin Company from 1938 to 1964, and sold without trademark by the F. W. Woolworth Co. It has a concentric ring design like Fiesta, but the rings are separated from the rim by a plain margin. Cup handles are triangular in shape. Seven different novelty animal figurines were introduced in 1939. For more information on Harlequin dinnerware, see *Kovels' Depression Glass & Dinnerware Price List.*

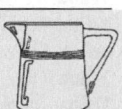

Chartreuse, Salt & Pepper	18.00
Coral, Plate, Deep, 8 In.	8.95
Gray, Cup & Saucer	11.00
Gray, Pitcher, Water	85.00
Gray, Plate, Dinner, 10 In.	10.00
Green, Cup	8.00
Green, Plate, 7 In.	15.00
Green, Plate, Bread & Butter, 6¼ In.	6.95
Green, Plate, Salad, 7¼ In.	15.00
Green, Saucer	4.95
Mauve Blue, Bowl, Fruit, 5½ In.	20.00
Mauve Blue, Bowl, Oatmeal, 36s, 6½ In.	35.00
Mauve Blue, Bowl, Salad, Individual, 7½ In.	50.00
Mauve Blue, Creamer, Individual	40.00
Mauve Blue, Cup, Tea	15.00
Mauve Blue, Eggcup	50.00
Mauve Blue, Plate, Bread & Butter, 6¼ In.	4.95
Mauve Blue, Plate, Bread & Butter, 7 In.	20.00
Mauve Blue, Plate, Deep, 8 In.	35.00
Mauve Blue, Plate, Dessert, 6 In.	8.00
Mauve Blue, Plate, Dinner, 10 In.	45.00
Mauve Blue, Plate, Luncheon, 9 In.	25.00
Mauve Blue, Saltshaker	12.50
Mauve Blue, Saucer, Tea	5.00
Mauve Blue, Soup, Cream	40.00
Medium Green, Cup .... 6.00 to 15.00
Medium Green, Plate, 7 In.	15.00
Medium Green, Plate, Deep, 8 In. .... 8.95 to 9.95
Rose, Cup	15.00
Rose, Cup & Saucer	15.00
Rose, Eggcup, Double	22.50
Rose, Pitcher, Water, Ice Lip	8.00
Rose, Plate, 7 In.	10.00
Rose, Saucer	12.00
Rose, Soup, Dish	18.00
Rose, Sugar, Cover	25.00
Spruce Green, Cup & Saucer, After Dinner	125.00
Turquoise, Bowl, Cereal, 7½ In.	7.00
Turquoise, Bowl, Fruit, 5½ In.	12.00
Turquoise, Bowl, Oatmeal, 36s, 6½ In.	25.00

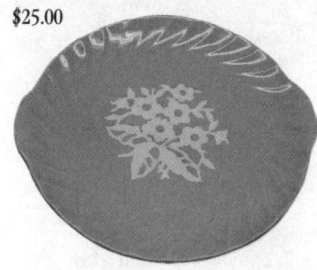

Harker, Dainty Flowers, Platter, Blue, Cameoware, 11 In. $25.00

Harker, Pate-Sur-Pate, Creamer, Teal $25.00

Harker, Pink Poppy, Casserole, Cover, 8½ In. $35.00

Harker, Vintage, Tidbit Tray, Rose, 10 In. $14.00

H

TIP
If your stainless steel knife blades stain in a dishwasher, rinse them, then dry or clean them with silver polish.

Plate Sizes and Shapes

Dessert	6 inch
Bread & Butter	7 inch
Salad	7½ inch
Luncheon	8–9 inch
Breakfast	9 inch
Dinner	10 inch
Grill	10½ inch, divided into three sections
Sandwich	11–13 inch serving plate, usually with 2 handles
Chop	13-inch serving plate

Harlequin, Turquoise, Plate, Dinner, 10 In. $30.00

Harlequin, Yellow, Cup & Saucer $24.00

Harlequin, Yellow, Pitcher, Water $150.00

Turquoise, Bowl, Salad, Individual, 7½ In.	20.00 to 30.00
Turquoise, Creamer, Individual	30.00
Turquoise, Creamer	10.00
Turquoise, Cup	7.00 to 15.00
Turquoise, Cup, Tea	12.00
Turquoise, Eggcup	40.00
Turquoise, Eggcup, Double	30.00
Turquoise, Nut Dish	25.00
Turquoise, Plate, Bread & Butter, 7 In.	10.00
Turquoise, Plate, Deep, 8 In.	25.00
Turquoise, Plate, Dessert, 6 In.	6.00
Turquoise, Plate, Dinner, 10 In. *illus*	30.00
Turquoise, Plate, Luncheon, 9 In.	15.00
Turquoise, Saucer, Tea	3.00
Turquoise, Soup, Cream	35.00
Yellow, Bowl, Fruit, 5½ In.	12.00
Yellow, Bowl, Oatmeal, 36s, 6½ In.	25.00 to 32.00
Yellow, Bowl, Salad, Individual, 7¼ In.	24.00 to 30.00
Yellow, Breakfast Set, 3 Piece	15.00
Yellow, Cup, Tea	12.00
Yellow, Cup & Saucer *illus*	24.00
Yellow, Cup	7.50 to 12.00
Yellow, Eggcup	40.00
Yellow, Gravy Boat	16.00
Yellow, Nut Cup	25.00
Yellow, Pitcher, Water *illus*	150.00
Yellow, Plate, Bread & Butter, 7 In.	10.00
Yellow, Plate, Deep, 8 In.	25.00
Yellow, Plate, Dessert, 6 In.	6.00
Yellow, Plate, Dinner, 10 In.	30.00
Yellow, Plate, Luncheon, 9 In.	15.00
Yellow, Saucer, Tea	3.00
Yellow, Soup, Cream	35.00
Yellow, Soup, Dish	18.00

HATPIN collectors search for pins popular from 1860 to 1920. The long pin, often over four inches, was used to hold the hat in place on the hair. The tops of the pins were made of all materials, from solid gold and real gemstones to ceramics and glass. Be careful to buy original hatpins and not recent pieces made by altering old buttons.

Black, Egg Shape, 9 In.	49.00
Black Carved Lucite Bead, Pink Enamel Bead, Sapphire, Filigree Prong Setting, 6 In.	6.00
Black Enamel, Caged, Scrolls, Gold Flowers, Seed Pearl Center, Faceted, Gilt, 7½ In.	495.00
Carnival Glass, Butterfly, Amethyst *illus*	55.00
Carnival Glass, Dimples & Brilliance, Purple	65.00
Carnival Glass, Flying Bat, Purple	160.00
Carnival Glass, Horned Owl, Purple, 6 In.	850.00
Carnival Glass, King Spider, Amethyst	800.00
Carnival Glass, Turban, Purple	35.00
Coin Cluster, 8 Coins, 1¾ x 1¾ x 6½ In.	55.00
Crystal, Green Faceted, Bead Bottom, ½ x 1¼ x 8⅛ In.	75.00
Crystals, Sapphire Blue & Aurora Faceted Goldtone Filigree, 5 In.	18.00
Glass, Bead, Amethyst, Barrel Shape, Goldstone, Brass Ball, Finial, 6 In.	15.00
Glass, Iridescent & Baby Blue Faceted Crystals, Silvertone Filigree, 5⅓ In.	18.00
Glass, Pink & Clear Faceted Crystals, Satin Gold Ball, Goldtone Filigree, 5½ In.	418.00
Glass, Pink Frosted Tube Crystal, Faceted Accents, Goldtone Filigree, 9 In.	15.00
Glass Beads, Catherine Lippert, Purple, Pink, 7¼ In.	26.00
Green Crackle Glass, Geometric, Brass Filigree Caps, 8 In.	15.00
Iridescent Cone Shaped Crystal, Crystals, Goldtone Filigree Caps, Silvertone Stem, 8 In.	10.00
Micro Mosaic, Goldtone, ¾ x 1⅜ x 8¼ In.	65.00
Paperweight Glass, Venetian, Murano, Round, ¾ x 7⅞ In.	60.00
Plastic, Pink, Flowers, Rhinestone, Lucite Beads, Crystals, 9 In.	8.00
Silver, Art Nouveau, Charles Horner, England, 11½ In. *illus*	145.00
Silver, Metal, Dog, Terrier, Green Glass Eyes, England, 8¾ In. *illus*	425.00
Silver, Repousse Leaf, Horner, Hallmarks, Chester, England, 1911, 1¼ x 11 In.	195.00
Twin Gators, Carnival Glass, Amethyst	600.00

HATPIN HOLDERS were needed when hatpins were fashionable from 1860 to 1920. The large, heavy hat required special long-shanked pins to hold it in place. The hatpin holder resembles a large saltshaker, but it often has no opening at the bottom as a shaker does. Hatpin holders were made of all types of ceramics and metal. Look for other pieces under the names of specific manufacturers.

Porcelain, Bird, Figural, On Branch, 4 Holes, Marked, Germany, 6 In.	49.00
Porcelain, Boot, Woman's, Flowers, Green, Pink, Gold Trim, 9 Holes, 6 In.	18.00
Porcelain, Butterfly, Flower Blossoms, Pink, Noritake, 5 In.	65.00
Porcelain, Green, Pink, Gold Trim, 10 Holes, 6 In.	25.00
Porcelain, Hand Painted, Nippon, 5 In.	95.00
Porcelain, Pierrot Boy, Dog, Germany, 7⅛ In. .... *illus*	400.00
Porcelain, Roses, Bavaria, 5 In.	125.00

HAVILAND china has been made in Limoges, France, since 1842. The factory was started by the Haviland Brothers of New York City. Pieces are marked *H & Co.*, *Haviland & Co.*, or *Theodore Haviland*. It is possible to match existing sets of dishes through dealers who specialize in Haviland china. Other factories worked in the town of Limoges making a similar chinaware. These porcelains are listed in this book under Limoges.

HAVILAND & CO.

Bowl, Cereal, Trailing Oak Leaf & Rose Vine, 7¾ In.	28.00
Bowl, Flowers, Scalloped Rim, Footed, 5 In.	75.00
Bowl, Fruit, Greek Key, Yellow, Black Outlined, Gold Trim, 4⅞ x 1 In.	18.00
Bowl, Pink, Yellow Roses, Scalloped, Fluted, Embossed, Oval, 1888-96	65.00
Bowl, Vegetable, Greek Key, Yellow, Black Outlined, 10 x 8¼ x 2¼ In.	50.00
Bowl, Vegetable, Pink, Roses, Green Leaves, White Ground, Oval, Embossed Scrolls, 10 In.	94.00
Butter, Cover, Gold, White, 15 In.	125.00
Butter Chip, 3¾ In., 8 Piece	20.00
Chocolate Pot, Painted Pink Roses, 10½ x 5¾ In.	395.00
Creamer, 4 x 3⅞ In.	40.00
Creamer, Hanging Basket, Orange, Yellow Flowers, 5¾ x 2⅜ In.	52.00
Cup, Embossed, Pink Roses, Green Leaves, White Ground, 2¼ In.	35.00
Cup & Saucer, Blue Garland, Scalloped, Platinum Trim, 3⅛ In.	12.00
Cup & Saucer, Moss Rose, c.1880, 2⅝ In.	6.00
Cup & Saucer, Yellow Poppies, Blue Ground, Gold Trim, 2 x 3¼ & 5½ In.	35.00
Custard Cup, Underplate, Scalloped Edge, Limoges, 15 Piece	59.00
Dessert Set, Berry Bowl, Plate, Serving Bowl, Scalloped Rim, Flowers, c.1900	325.00
Dish, Lobster, Shell Shape, 2 Sections, Birds, Duck, Iris, Label, 12 In.	415.00
Gravy Boat, Attached Underplate, Greek Key, Yellow, Black Outlined, 7 x 2½ In.	50.00
Jardiniere, Raised Flowers, Leaves, Brown Mottled Ground, Rectangular, 30 x 11 In.	588.00
Plate, Blue, Yellow Flower Garlands, 9½ In.	20.00
Plate, Bread & Butter, Greek Key, Yellow, Black Outlined, Gold Trim, 6⅛ In.	18.00
Plate, Bread & Butter, Limoges Chanson, 6⅝ In.	16.00
Plate, Bread & Butter, Twilight Rose, Flowers, Leaves, Roses, 6 In.	12.00
Plate, Dinner, Blue Garland, 10 In.	12.00
Plate, Greek Key, Yellow, Black Outlined, 9¾ In.	30.00
Plate, Luncheon, Hanging Basket, Orange, Yellow Flowers, Chanson, 10 In.	33.00
Plate, Salad, Antonette, Pink, Green Flowers, White Ground, Scalloped, 7½ In.	12.00
Plate, Salad, Hanging Basket, Orange, Yellow Flowers, 7⅝ In.	22.00
Platter, Blue Garland, 15 x 11 In.	40.00
Platter, Bowknots, Blue, Pink Flowers, Green Leaves, 16½ In.	65.00
Platter, Elizabeth, Green Leaf Border, Roses, 16 x 12 In.	145.00
Platter, Greek Key, Yellow, Black Outlined, 13¾ x 10 In.	50.00
Platter, Greek Key, Yellow, Black Outline, Gold Trim, 11¼ x 8½ In.	40.00
Platter, Rose Sprays, c.1800, 15¾ x 11 In.	155.00
Platter, Trailing Flower Sprays, Green Vine, Victorian, 15¼ x 10¼ In.	165.00
Salt, Oporto Master, Pink Flowers, 7 Piece	80.00
Saucer, Blue Flowers, Green Leaves, 5½ In.	15.00
Saucer, Pink, Yellow Roses, Queen Anne's Lace, 5⅜ In.	18.00
Soup, Dish, Pink Flower Vine, Green Leaf Border, Gold Trim, White Ground, 7½ In.	25.00
Soup, Dish, Pink Rose Spray, Blue Flowers, 7½ In.	17.00
Tray, Oval, Hanging Basket, Orange, Yellow Flowers, Chanson, 8 x 5 In.	42.00
Tureen, Cover, Porcelain, 2 Handles, 7¼ x 11½ In.	205.00
Vase, Women & Flowers, Shouldered, Signed, De Feure, Marked, 5½ x 4 In.	650.00

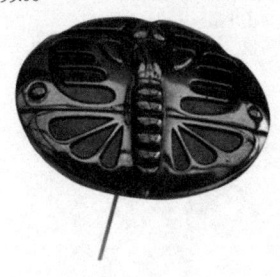

Hatpin, Carnival Glass,
Butterfly, Amethyst
$55.00

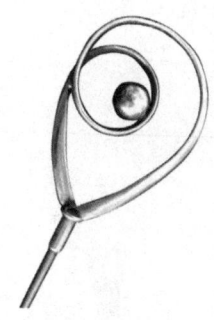

Hatpin, Silver,
Art Nouveau, Charles Horner,
England, 11½ In.
$145.00

H

Hatpin, Silver, Metal,
Dog, Terrier, Green Glass Eyes,
England, 8¾ In.
$425.00

Hatpin Holder, Porcelain,
Pierrot Boy, Dog,
Germany, 7⅛ In.
$400.00

Hawkes, Pitcher, Hobstar,
Blazes, Fan Cut Top,
Hobstar Applied Handle,
Signed, 9 In.
$715.00

Hawkes, Vase, Queen Pattern,
Flared, Scalloped & Notched Rim,
Signed, 11 In.
$881.00

Head Vase, Woman, Blond,
Red & White Hat, National Potteries,
No. C3307, 5¼ In.
$45.00

Head Vase, Woman, Blond,
Striped Hat, Floral Pin,
Pastel Colors, 6⅛ In.
$26.00

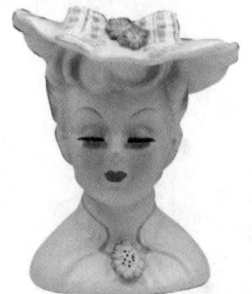

HAWKES cut glass was made by T. G. Hawkes & Company of Corning, New York, founded in 1880. The firm cut glass blanks made at other glassworks until 1962. Many pieces are marked with the trademark, a trefoil ring enclosing a fleur-de-lis and two hawks. Cut glass by other manufacturers is listed under either the factory name or in the general Cut Glass category.

Bowl, Astor, Strawberry Diamonds, Crosshatch Triangles, Fan Edge, 8 In.	290.00
Bowl, Floral Sprays, Beaded Swags, Hanging Tassels, Signed, 10¼ x 4½ In.	350.00
Bowl, Fruit, Scalloped & Notched Edge, 4 x 12 In.	1200.00
Butter Tub, 48-Points, Sunburst Star, 4 x 2 In.	125.00
Candlestick, Ribbons, Floral Spray, Signed, 14 In.	650.00
Cocktail Mixer, Intaglio, Gamecock, Silver Rim, c.1925, 10 In.	675.00
Cocktail Shaker, Art Deco, Sterling Silver Cap, Strainer, Signed, 12¼ x 3⅝ In.	875.00
Compote, Intaglio Flower Spray, Sterling Foot, 6½ In.	295.00
Console, Floral Spray, Pearls, Footed, 10½ x 2½ In.	55.00
Ice Bucket, Art Deco, 5 Panels, Metal Frame, Tongs, c.1920-30, 10½ In.	175.00
Knife Rest, Faceted, Dumbbell Shape, Signed, 4¾ In.	95.00
Lid, Sterling Silver, Signed, 4½ In.	165.00
Pitcher, Hobstar, Blazes, Fan Cut Top, Hobstar Applied Handle, Signed, 9 In. ....*illus*	715.00
Pitcher, Star-Petaled Flowers, Pinched Neck, Cut Notched, 11¼ In.	210.00
Punch Bowl, Hobstars, Fans, Crosshatching, Signed, 15 x 13¾ In.	1093.00
Salt, 2 Birds, Triangular, 6 Piece	300.00
Salt, Intaglio Floral Garland, Tub Shape, Handles, 1⅛ x 1¾ In.	50.00
Vase, Queen Pattern, Flared, Scalloped & Notched Rim, Signed, 11 In. ....*illus*	881.00

HEAD VASES, generally showing a woman from the shoulders up, were used by florists primarily in the 1950s and 1960s. Made in a variety of sizes and often decorated with imitation jewelry and other lifelike accessories, the vases were manufactured in Japan and the U.S.A. Less elaborate examples were made as early as the 1930s. Religious themes, babies, and animals are also common subjects. Other head vases are listed under manufacturers' names and can be located through the index and the back of this book.

Candy, Brunette, Green Striped Dress, Straw Hat, Necklace, Betty Lou Nichols, 6 In.	655.00
Clown, Relpo, 7¼ In.	55.00
Graduate, Blond Hair, Cap & Gown, Swinging Tassel, Box, 5 In.	70.00
Lotus & Manchu, Oriental Man & Woman, Stamped, Ceramic Arts Studio, 8 In., Pair	229.00
Madonna, Marked, Napcoware, 5 x 3½ In.	32.00
Teen, Ash Blond, Red Bow & Dress, White Collar, Earrings, Relpo, 7 In.	300.00
Woman, Blond, Black Bristle Eyelashes, Green Cape, White Flowers, Ucagco, 5 In.	85.00
Woman, Blond, Black Matte Dress, Applied Eyelashes, Earrings, Inarco, 5½ In.	168.00
Woman, Blond, Pearl Earrings, Necklace, Hand On Face, Ardco Foil Label, 1950-60, 6 In.	225.00
Woman, Blond, Red & White Hat, National Potteries, No. C3307, 5¼ In. ....*illus*	45.00
Woman, Blond, Striped Hat, Floral Pin, Pastel Colors, 6⅛ In. ....*illus*	26.00
Woman, Blond, Turquoise, Gold Trim, Hand, Eyelashes, Earrings, Necklace, Rubens, Box, 6 In.	168.00

HEDI SCHOOP Art Creations, North Hollywood, California, started about 1945 and was working until 1954. Schoop made ceramic figurines, lamps, planters, and tablewares.

Hedi Schoop S

Ashtray, Duck, Gold Embossed, Inscribed, 5½ x 8 In.	40.00
Box, Butterfly, Yellow, White, Marked, 3½ x 6 In.	55.00
Figurine, Dancing Lady, Black & Gold Billowing Dress, Marked, 9 In.	110.00
Figurine, Dancing Lady, Pink Dress, Gold Trim, Marked, 9½ In.	110.00
Figurine, Dutch Boy & Girl, My Sister & I, 11½ In., Pair	165.00
Figurine, Exotic Lady, Green & Black Dress, Pink, Gold Accents, Marked, 12½ In.	55.00
Figurine, Exotic Lady, Green Dress, Gold Accents, Marked, 12½ In.	125.00
Figurine, Hungarian Man & Woman, Marked, 10 & 10½ In., Pair	150.00
Figurine, Marguerita, Marked, 12½ In.	125.00
Figurine, Oriental Man, Marked, 12½ In.	58.00
Figurine, Rooster, Green, Brown, Marked, 13 In.	125.00
Figurine, Spanish Dancer, Aqua & Cream Dress, Gold Trim, 9 & 10 In., Pair	250.00
Figurine, Woman, With Buckets, White Dress, Marked, 13½ In.	125.00
Planter, Figurine, Girl Holding Flowers, Pink Skirt, Green Shirt, Marked, 9¼ x 6⅞ In.	75.00
Planter, Horse, Pink & White, Green Saddle, Signed, 9¾ x 10½ In.	75.00
Planter, Tyrolean Girl, Marked, 11 In.	75.00
Tray, Butterfly, Gold & White Wings, Gold Rim, Marked, 8 In.	42.00
Tray, Butterfly, Multicolored, Gold Rim, Marked, c.1950, 8 In. ....*illus*	35.00
Vase, Fan, Pink, Beige, Gold Trim, Signed, 7 x 12 In.	100.00

HEINTZ ART

HEINTZ ART Metal Shop used the letters *HAMS* in a diamond as a mark. Otto Heintz took over the Arts & Crafts Company in Buffalo, New York, in 1903. By 1906 it had become the Heintz Art Metal Shop. It remained in business until 1930. The company made ashtrays, bookends, boxes, bowls, desk sets, vases, trophies, and smoking sets. The best-known pieces are made of copper, brass, and bronze with silver overlay. Similar pieces were made by Smith Metal Arts and were marked *Silver Crest*. Some pieces by both companies are unmarked.

Candlestick, Organic Design, Silver On Bronze, Original Patina, Impressed Mark, 8 x 4½ In..	150.00
Candlestick, Silver On Bronze, Applied Leaf & Berry, Original Patina, 14½ x 6 In.	900.00
Candlestick, Silver On Bronze, Triangular, Stylized Landscape, 4 x 3¾ In.	1140.00
Desk Set, Lamp, Inkwells, Letter Holder, Calendar, Pen Tray, Mark, 9 In., 7 Piece ......*illus*	880.00
Humidor, Art Nouveau, Silver On Bronze, Cylindrical, Signed, 6 In.	120.00
Inkwell, Hinged Cover, Mission Style, Compartments, Cup, Silver On Bronze, 8 x 6 In.	115.00
Inkwell, Silver On Bronze, Leaf & Berry Design, Insert, 6¾ In.	275.00
Inkwell, Wooden, Sterling On Bronze, Leaf & Berry, Original Insert, 7 In.	275.00
Lamp, Flowers, Silver On Bronze, Original Patina, Impressed Mark, 15½ x 6 In., Pair	725.00
Pin, Bar, Copper Base, Silver On Bronze, 2 x ⅜ In.	83.00
Pin, Bar, Leaf & Berry, Silver On Bronze, Original Patina, 3 In.	175.00
Pin, Bar, Organic, Silver On Bronze, Original Patina, 1½ In.	140.00
Pin, Bar, Organic, Silver On Bronze, Original Patina, 2 In.	175.00
Pin, Bird, Silver On Bronze, Original Patina, Marked, 2 In.	360.00
Pin, Lily, Silver On Bronze, Original Patina, 2 In.	760.00
Pin, Moth, Silver On Bronze, Original Patina, 1½ In.	760.00
Pin, Windmill, Silver On Bronze, Original Patina, Marked, 1¼ In.	360.00
Vase, Bamboo, Silver On Bronze, Cylindrical, Flared Base, Patina, Marked, 9 x 3 In.	600.00
Vase, Bamboo, Silver On Bronze, Flared, Original Patina, Marked, 8 x 4 In.	320.00
Vase, Bamboo, Silver On Bronze, Original Silver Patina, Marked, 6 x 3 In.	210.00
Vase, Birds, Silver On Bronze, Original Silver Patina, Impressed Marked, 10 x 3 In.	415.00
Vase, Bronze, Iris, Silver On Bronze, 11½ x 5 In. ......*illus*	200.00
Vase, Bronze, Sterling Silver Columns, Bulbous Base, Flared Rim, Handles, 9 In. ......*illus*	147.00
Vase, Flowers, Applied, Sterling Silver On Bronze, Flared, Silver Patina, Marked, 6½ In.	240.00
Vase, Flowers, Applied, Sterling Silver On Bronze, Patina, Marked, 7½ In.	495.00
Vase, Organic Design, Applied, Sterling Silver On Bronze, Patina, Marked, 8 In. ...... 240.00 to	360.00
Vase, Sterling Silver On Bronze, Handles, Pat. 1912, 9 In.	147.00
Vase, Stick, Bronze, c.1910, 11 In.	495.00

HEISEY

HEISEY glass was made from 1896 to 1957 in Newark, Ohio, by A. H. Heisey and Co., Inc. The Imperial Glass Company of Bellaire, Ohio, bought some of the molds and the rights to the trademark. Some Heisey patterns have been made by Imperial since 1960. After 1968, they stopped using the *H* trademark. Heisey used romantic names for colors, such as Sahara. Do not confuse color and pattern names. The Custard Glass and Ruby Glass categories may also include some Heisey pieces.

Animal, Asiatic Pheasant	250.00
Animal, Colt, Standing	35.00
Animal, Goose, Stopper Only	60.00
Animal, Goose, Wings Down	55.00
Animal, Pheasant, Ring Neck ......*illus*	60.00
Animal, Rabbit, Paperweight	95.00
Animal, Rooster, Vase	55.00
Animal, Scottie, Frosted	75.00
Aqua Caliente, Cocktail, Tally Ho Etch, 4 Oz.	10.00
Aristocrat, Candlestick, 15 In., Pair	625.00
Aristocrat, Candy Jar, Cover, Cobalt Blue	150.00
Athena, Candlestick, 2-Light, Pair	100.00
Athena, Sugar & Creamer, Tray ...... 10.00 to	15.00
Athena, Wine, 2½ Oz.	55.00
Banded Flute, Cruet, Stopper, 4 Oz. ...... 8.00 to	15.00
Beaded Panel & Sunburst, Creamer	10.00
Beaded Panel & Sunburst, Cruet, Stopper, 6 Oz.	40.00
Beaded Panel & Sunburst, Nappy, 8 In.	10.00
Beaded Swag, Punch Cup, Ruby Flashed, Engraved, Joe, 1907	20.00
Beaded Swag, Toothpick	10.00
Beaded Swag, Water Set, Ruby Stain, Gold Trim, 9½-In. Pitcher, 5 Piece	198.00
Beehive, Plate, 14 In.	25.00
Cabochon, Candlette, Pair	15.00
Cabochon, Dawn, Goblet, 9 Oz.	5.00

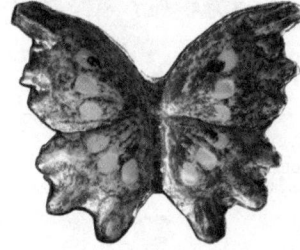

Hedi Schoop, Tray, Butterfly, Multicolored, Gold Rim, Marked, c.1950, 8 In.
$35.00

Heintz Art, Desk Set, Lamp, Inkwells, Letter Holder, Calendar, Pen Tray, Mark, 9 In., 7 Piece
$880.00

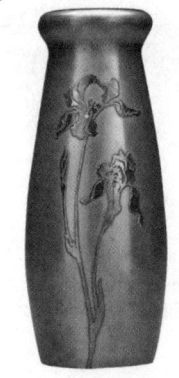

Heintz Art, Vase, Bronze, Iris, Silver On Bronze, 11½ x 5 In.
$200.00

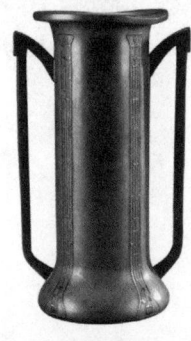

Heintz Art, Vase, Bronze, Sterling Silver Columns, Bulbous Base, Flared Rim, Handles, 9 In.
$147.00

Heisey, Animal, Pheasant,
Ring Neck
$60.00

Heisey., Coarse Rib,
Sugar, Cover, Moongleam
$50.00

Heisey, Double Rib & Panel, Basket,
Flamingo, 8¼ In.
$235.00

Heisey, Empress, Sugar,
Sahara, Dolphin-Footed,
3 Handles
$30.00

Cascade, Candlestick, 3-Light, Pair	40.00
Cecelia, Vase, Saturn Optic, 10½ In.	90.00
Charter Oak, Goblet, Flamingo, 8 Oz., 7 In.	70.00
Charter Oak, Goblet, Moongleam, 8 Oz., 7 In.	20.00
Christos, Decanter, Silver Overlay, Stopper	75.00
Clarence, Bottle, Sherry, Oval, Stopper	60.00
Coarse Rib, Jar, Cover, Amber Stain	20.00
Coarse Rib, Dish, Jelly, Footed, Moongleam	25.00
Coarse Rib, Jug, 3 Pt.	50.00
Coarse Rib, Sugar, Cover, Moongleam .... *illus*	50.00
Cobel, Cocktail Shaker, Mallard Duck, Stopper, Painted, Signed, Lilli Henderson, 2 Qt.	105.00
Cobel, Cocktail Shaker, Rooster Stopper, 1 Qt.	65.00
Cockade, Bowl, Gardenia, 11 In.	50.00
Colonial, Jar, Cover, Potpourri, Lavender, Footed, 2½ Oz.	60.00
Colonial, Vase, 3 Handles, 12 In.	525.00
Colonial Panel, Cruet, Stopper	10.00
Colonial Star, Plate, 5 In., 4	15.00
Comet, Champagne, 5 Oz., 4⅝ In.	25.00
Comet, Goblet, Oyster Cocktail, 4 Oz., 3¼ In.	15.00
Comet, Goblet, Water, 10 Oz., 5¾ In.	35.00
Comet, Plate, Luncheon, Square, 8 In.	35.00
Comet, Sherbet, 4 Oz., 3¼ In.	15.00
Comet, Tumbler, Footed, 8 Oz., 5⅞ In.	25.00
Comet, Tumbler, Footed, 10 Oz., 5¾ In.	40.00
Comet, Tumbler, Juice, Footed, 5 Oz., 4½ In.	30.00
Continental, Bottle, Water	35.00
Continental, Eggcup, 4 Piece	20.00
Convex Circle, Nappy, 9½ In.	45.00
Cornucopia, Vase, 10 In., Pair	55.00
Country Club, Cocktail, Winchester '73 Etch, 4 Oz.	220.00
Country Club, Tumbler, Winchester '73 Etch, 10 Oz.	120.00 to 230.00
Cristos, Decanter, Flamingo, 1 Qt.	70.00
Crystolite, Ashtray, Matchbook Holder	25.00
Crystolite, Bowl, 5 In.	15.00
Crystolite, Bowl, Gardenia, Square, 10 In.	55.00
Crystolite, Candleblock, Banded, 3 In., Pair	30.00
Crystolite, Candleblock, Round, 2½ In., Pair	55.00
Crystolite, Candlestick, 1-Light, Pair	25.00
Crystolite, Candlestick, 2-Light, Pair	45.00
Crystolite, Candy Box, Cover, 7 In.	20.00
Crystolite, Candy Dish, Shell, 7 In.	15.00
Crystolite, Cheese Dish	15.00
Crystolite, Cigarette Box, Cover, 4 In.	20.00
Crystolite, Claret, Blown Bowl, 3½ Oz.	8.00
Crystolite, Coaster, 4 In.	15.00
Crystolite, Compote, 5 In.	15.00
Crystolite, Cruet, Stopper	40.00
Crystolite, Dish, Conserve, 2 Sections, Handle	20.00 to 30.00
Crystolite, Dish, Pickle, Leaf, 9 In.	25.00
Crystolite, Dish, Pickle, Oval, 6 In.	15.00
Crystolite, Hurricane Lamp Base, Pair	20.00
Crystolite, Jug, ½ Gal.	65.00
Crystolite, Nappy, 4 In.	15.00
Crystolite, Nappy, 5 In.	30.00 to 35.00
Crystolite, Nut Dish, Swan, Master	30.00
Crystolite, Plate, 10½ In., 8 Piece	120.00
Crystolite, Plate, Coupe, 7½ In.	25.00
Crystolite, Relish, Oval, 3 Sections, 13 In.	25.00
Crystolite, Tumbler, 10 Oz.	25.00
Crystolite, Tumbler, Soda, Footed, 5 Oz.	50.00
Crystolite, Vase, Footed, Flared, 6 In.	25.00
Cupid & Psyche, Ashtray, Moongleam	50.00
Cut Block, Creamer, Souvenir, Scalloped Edge, c.1910	68.00
Delaware, Champagne, 6½ Oz., 4 Piece	30.00
Diana, Plate, Wabash, 6 In., 5 Piece	15.00
Double Rib & Panel, Basket, Flamingo, 8¼ In. .... *illus*	235.00

H

Double Rib & Panel, Tumbler	5.00
Duck, Ashtray, Flamingo	145.00
Duplex, Tray, Candy Dish, Flamingo	60.00
Duquesne, Wine, Titania Etch, 3 Oz.	65.00
Eagle, Plate, Moongleam	50.00
Elephant, Mug, Amber	475.00
Elephant, Mug	250.00
Elizabeth, Candlestick, 10 In.	210.00
Empress, Bowl, Floral, Lion's Head, Handles, 4-Footed, 10 In.	260.00
Empress, Compote, Sahara, Oval, 7 In.	65.00
Empress, Cover, Flamingo	60.00
Empress, Dish, Mayonnaise, Moongleam	70.00
Empress, Plate, Chateau Etch, 7 In., 12	10.00
Empress, Plate, Salad, Sahara, 8⅛ In.	42.00
Empress, Plate, Sahara, Square 7 In.	40.00
Empress, Sherbet, Sahara, 4 Oz., 3½ In.	20.00
Empress, Sugar, Sahara, Dolphin-Footed, 3 Handles ......*illus*	30.00
Empress, Sugar & Creamer, Sahara	45.00
Empress, Tray, Condiment, 8 In.	25.00
Empress, Vase, Antarctic Etch, 8 In.	25.00
Fancy Loop, Creamer, Hotel	8.00
Fancy Loop, Cruet, Stopper	25.00
Fancy Loop, Toothpick	25.00
Fandango, Bowl, Footed	35.00
Fandango, Cruet, Stopper, 4 Oz.	35.00
Fandango, Cruet, Stopper, 6 Oz.	15.00
Federal, Candlestick, 9 In., Pair	75.00
Fern, Relish, 3 Sections, Handles, Footed	10.00
Flat Panel, Bowl, Floral, Octagonal, Flamingo	15.00
Flat Panel, Candy Jar, 1 Lb.	40.00
Flat Panel, Cruet, Stopper, 4 Oz.	8.00
Flat Panel, Cruet, Stopper, 6 Oz.	15.00
Flat Panel, Relish, Oval, Keystone Silver Plated Holder, 14 In.	25.00
Flat Panel, Spooner	15.00
Flat Panel, Syrup, 5 Oz.	25.00
Flat Panel, Tobacco Jar, Cover	100.00
Fleur-De-Lis, Plate, Moongleam, 8 In.	30.00
Four Leaf, Candlestick, Pair	40.00
Gascony, Tumbler, Footed, Ambassador Etch	20.00
Gibson Girl, Bowl, Floral, Gold, Black	20.00
Grape Cluster, Candlestick, Pair	100.00
Greek Key, Banana Boat, Octagonal, Pedestal Base, 3 x 7½ In.	20.00
Greek Key, Bowl, 7½ In.	65.00
Greek Key, Bowl, 8½ In.	135.00
Greek Key, Celery Dish, Oval, 12 In.	30.00
Greek Key, Cheese & Cracker Set, 2 Piece	170.00
Greek Key, Cocktail, 3½ Oz.	25.00
Greek Key, Cruet, Stopper	25.00
Greek Key, Dish, Banana Split, Footed, 7½ In.	35.00
Greek Key, Dish, Jelly, Handle	10.00 to 25.00
Greek Key, Dish, Lemon, Individual, 4½ In.	100.00
Greek Key, Ice Tub, Small	110.00
Greek Key, Jar, Crushed Fruit, Cover, 2 Qt.	650.00
Greek Key, Nappy, Handles	45.00
Greek Key, Nut Dish	20.00
Greek Key, Punch Cup	15.00
Greek Key, Sherbet, 4½ Oz., 3½ In.	15.00 to 22.50
Groove & Slash, Cruet, Stopper, 6 Oz.	60.00
Hartman, Punch Cup	15.00
Hartman, Tumbler	30.00
Hazelwood, Oyster Cocktail, Renaissance Etch	10.00
Horsehead, Bookend	90.00
Horseshoe, Sugar & Creamer, Sahara	425.00
Hydrangea, Goblet	270.00
Impromptu, Plate, 8 In., 9 Piece	50.00
Ipswich, Candlestick	55.00

Heisey, Lariat, Vase,
Fan, 8 In.
$15.00

Heisey, Mercury, Candlestick,
Moongleam, 3½ In.
$30.00

H

Colored Pressed Glass
American pressed glass factories suffered hard times during the 1890s. Few new patterns were introduced. Imported glass from Europe influenced tastes. Buyers wanted handmade decorative accessories and novelties, not glass tableware. Manufacturers tried to compete by producing colored pattern glass. Pieces were made using old molds, but they were made of colored glass and embellished with gold trim or enameled flowers.

Heisey, Miss Muffet, Candlestick, Moongleam, Footed, 3 x 4¼ In., Pair
$38.00

Heisey, Petticoat Dolphin, Compote, Moongleam Bowl, Clear Stem, 7⅜ In.
$235.00

Heisey, Pinwheel & Fan, Nappy, 8 In.
$55.00

Ipswich, Sugar, Sahara	35.00
Ipswich, Sugar	28.00
Jack-Be-Nimble, Candleholder, Pair	25.00
Jamestown, Cocktail, 3 Oz., 3 Piece	25.00
Jamestown, Goblet, Palmetto Cutting, 9 Oz.	12.00
Jamestown, Sherry, 2 Oz.	50.00
Kalonyal, Compote, Jelly	45.00
Kalonyal, Creamer, Ruby Stained, 4¾ In.	55.00
Kalonyal, Dish, Pickle	10.00
Kalonyal, Plate, 8½ In.	50.00
Kalonyal, Punch Set, Flared Bowl, Underplate, Cups, 10 Piece	200.00
Kingfisher, Flower Frog, Hawthorne	300.00
Lariat, Ashtray, 4 In.	15.00
Lariat, Basket, 8½ In.	70.00
Lariat, Bowl, Crimped Flower, 12 In.	10.00
Lariat, Candlestick, 2-Light, Pair	20.00
Lariat, Candlestick, 3-Light, Pair	35.00
Lariat, Candy Dish, Cover, 5 In.	20.00
Lariat, Candy Dish, Cover, Etched	75.00
Lariat, Cruet, Stopper, Handle	10.00
Lariat, Punch Set, Bowl, Underplate, Cups, 12 Piece	395.00
Lariat, Relish, 3 Sections, 12 In.	105.00
Lariat, Relish, Etched, Round, 10 In.	35.00
Lariat, Vase, Fan, 8 In. ....*illus*	15.00
Legionnaire, Cordial, Arcadia Etch	35.00
Legionnaire, Goblet, Yorktown, 10 Oz.	25.00
Legionnaire, Wine, Yorktown, 3 Oz.	45.00
Liberty, Candlestick, Marigold, 3 In.	210.00
Lobe, Dish, Pickle & Olive, Sections, Moongleam	40.00
Lodestar, Bowl, Dawn, 12 In.	200.00
Lotus, Sandwich Server, Center Handle, Sahara, 12 In.	110.00
Mars, Candlestick, Moongleam, Pair	15.00
Marshall, Cocktail Shaker, Rooster Stopper	70.00
Marshall, Decanter, Barcelona Cut, 1 Pt.	50.00
Mercury, Candlestick, Moongleam, 3½ In. ....*illus*	30.00
Minuet, Goblet, 9 Oz., 8¼ In.	35.00
Minuet, Jam Jar, Cover, Apple, Toujours	25.00
Minuet, Plate, Salad, 7 In. .... 15.00 to 20.00	
Minuet, Sugar & Creamer, Queen Ann	25.00
Miss Muffet, Candlestick, Moongleam, Footed, 3 x 4¼ In., Pair .....*illus*	38.00
Narrow Flute, Celery Tray, 12 In.	40.00
Narrow Flute, Compote, Jelly, 5 In.	25.00
Narrow Flute, Creamer, Moongleam	45.00
Narrow Flute, Cruet, Stopper, 4 Oz.	25.00
Narrow Flute, Cruet, Stopper, Gold Trim, Flower Enamel, 6 Oz.	20.00
Narrow Flute, Dish, Grapefruit	40.00
Narrow Flute, Dish, Jelly, Handles	8.00
Narrow Flute, Dish, Pickle, Flamingo, 6 In.	35.00
Narrow Flute, Goblet	25.00
Narrow Flute, Jam Jar, Cover	65.00
Narrow Flute, Mustard, Cover, Gold Trim, Flower Enamel	15.00
Narrow Flute, Nappy, Jelly, Handle	15.00
Narrow Flute, Nut Dish	10.00
Narrow Flute, Sugar & Creamer, Hotel	30.00
Narrow Flute, Sugar & Creamer	15.00
Navy, Plate, Cobalt Center, 7 In.	110.00
New Era, Tumbler, Pilsner, 16 Oz.	90.00
Oak Leaf, Coaster, Flamingo, 4 Piece	110.00
Oak Leaf, Coaster, Hawthorne	95.00
Octagon, Bonbon, Marigold, Empress Etch	15.00
Octagon, Celery Dish, Cutting	25.00
Octagon, Cheese Plate, Handles, 6 In.	8.00
Old Colony, Plate, Empress, 10½ In.	90.00
Old Dominion, Goblet, Sahara, 10 Oz.	20.00
Old Gold, Ashtray	95.00
Old Sandwich, Ashtray, Cobalt Blue	35.00

Old Sandwich, Cruet, Stopper, 2½ Oz.	20.00
Old Sandwich, Jug, Sahara, ½ Gal.	150.00
Old Sandwich, Mug, 12 Oz.	35.00
Old Sandwich, Mug, Moongleam, 12 Oz.	250.00
Old Sandwich, Soda, Moongleam, 12 Oz.	25.00
Old Sandwich, Soda, Sahara, 8 Oz.	15.00
Old Sandwich, Toddy, Moongleam, Footed	55.00
Old Williamsburg, Candelabrum, 2-Light, Bobeches, Short Base	60.00
Old Williamsburg, Cup & Saucer	10.00
Orchid Etch, Bowl, Floral, Waverly, 12 In.	25.00
Orchid Etch, Candlestick, 3-Light, Cascade	80.00
Orchid Etch, Cruet, Stopper, Waverly	130.00
Orchid Etch, Sauce Bowl, Queen Ann	40.00
Orchid Etch, Sherbet, Tyrolean	8.00
Orchid Etch, Torte Plate, Waverly	40.00
Paneled Cane, Cruet, Stopper, 8 Oz.	50.00
Patrician, Candlestick, 9 In., Pair	35.00
Patrician, Candlestick, Toy, Pair	30.00
Peerless, Compote, 5 In.	8.00
Peerless, Cruet, Stopper, 6 Oz.	20.00
Peerless, Dish, Sundae	8.00
Peerless, Sherbet	8.00
Peerless, Toothpick	10.00
Peerless, Tumbler, Footed, 7 Oz.	10.00
Penguin, Decanter, 1 Pt.	400.00
Pentagon, Nut Dish, Flamingo	100.00
Pentagon, Nut Dish, Moongleam	150.00
Petal, Sugar & Creamer, Flamingo	8.00
Petal, Sugar & Creamer, Moongleam	45.00
Petticoat Dolphin, Compote, Moongleam Bowl, Clear Stem, 7⅜ In. ....*illus*	235.00
Phyllis, Sugar & Creamer, Canary	750.00
Pillows, Cruet, Stopper, 6 Oz.	80.00
Pillows, Rose Bowl, Footed	105.00
Pineapple & Fan, Berry Bowl, Oval, 10 In.	25.00 to 35.00
Pineapple & Fan, Compote, Fluted, Square	55.00
Pineapple & Fan, Creamer, Hotel	25.00
Pineapple & Fan, Molasses Jug, Metal Lid	25.00
Pineapple & Fan, Vase, 6½ In.	65.00
Pinwheel & Fan, Bowl, 4¾ In.	17.00
Pinwheel & Fan, Nappy, 8 In. ....*illus*	55.00
Plain & Fancy, Tumbler, Pied Piper Etch	10.00
Plain Band, Tankard, 1 Pt.	20.00
Plantation, Butter, Cover, ¼ Lb.	75.00
Plantation, Cake Stand, 12 In.	200.00
Plantation, Candlestick, 3-Light	85.00
Plantation, Cocktail, 3 Oz.	22.00
Plantation, Compote, Ivy Etch, 5 In.	35.00
Plantation, Cruet, Stopper, 4 Oz.	25.00
Plantation, Cruet, Stopper, 6 Oz.	80.00
Plantation, Dish, Jelly, Handles, Silver Overlay	15.00
Plantation, Goblet, 10 Oz., 6 Piece	60.00
Plantation, Goblet, Ivy Etch, 10 Oz., 2 Piece	30.00
Plantation, Jam Jar, Cover, Pineapple Shape	130.00
Plantation, Relish, 3 Sections	40.00
Plantation, Sherbet, Ivy Etch, 6 Oz.	35.00
Plantation, Tumbler, Iced Tea, Footed, 12 Oz.	25.00
Plantation, Tumbler, Ivy Etch, 5 Oz.	35.00
Plantation, Vase, Flared, 5 In.	50.00
Plateau, Goblet, Flamingo, 10 Oz.	10.00
Plateau, Rose Bowl, Moongleam	140.00
Pleat & Panel, Bowl, Vegetable, Oval, 9 In.	35.00
Pleat & Panel, Cruet, Stopper, 3 Oz.	15.00
Pleat & Panel, Cruet, Stopper, Flamingo, 3 Oz.	50.00
Pleat & Panel, Cruet, Stopper, Moongleam, 3 Oz.	45.00
Pleat & Panel, Cup & Saucer, Flamingo, 8 Piece	75.00
Pleat & Panel, Jam Jar, Cover, Flamingo	40.00

Heisey, Pleat & Panel, Vase, Flamingo, 8 In. $60.00

Heisey, Rose Etch, Goblet, 9 Oz., 6½ In. $36.00

Heisey, Sunburst, Bowl,
5 Sides, 10 In.
$100.00

Heisey, Twist, Bonbon,
Moongleam, Folded Sides,
Handles, 6¾ In.
$17.00

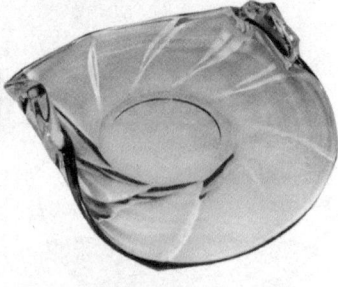

Heisey, Twist, Cruet,
Flamingo, 4½ In.
$125.00

Pleat & Panel, Nappy, 8½ In.	20.00
Pleat & Panel, Plate, Flamingo, 10½ In.	110.00
Pleat & Panel, Vase, Flamingo, 8 In. .... *illus*	60.00
Pointed Oval & Diamond Point, Pitcher	55.00
Pony Stem, Cocktail, 3 Oz.	425.00
Prince Of Wales Plume, Tumbler	30.00
Priscilla, Bowl, 9 In.	15.00
Priscilla, Dish, Jelly, Handles, 6 In.	20.00
Priscilla, Jug, ½ Gal.	40.00
Priscilla, Mustard Jar, Cover	20.00
Priscilla, Tumbler, Pilsner, Cobalt Blue, 16 Oz., 10 In.	2300.00
Prism Band, Decanter, Flamingo, 1 Pt.	50.00
Prison Stripe, Bowl, 8 In.	10.00
Provincial, Plate, Buffet, Limelight, 17 In.	170.00
Provincial, Sugar & Creamer	20.00
Provincial, Tumbler, Iced Tea, Zircon, Footed, 12 Oz.	100.00
Provincial, Tumbler, Soda, Zircon, Footed, 12 Oz.	80.00
Punty & Diamond Point, Cologne, Sterling Cap	40.00
Punty & Diamond Point, Molasses Jug	80.00
Punty Band, Cake Salver	75.00
Punty Band, Champagne, Ruby Stained, 5 In.	77.00
Punty Band, Cruet, Stopper, 6 Oz.	20.00
Punty Band, Salt & Pepper	10.00
Puritan, Compote, 5 In.	8.00
Puritan, Cruet, 4 Oz.	10.00
Puritan, Cruet, 6 Oz.	15.00
Puritan, Jar, Pickle, Knob Cover	60.00
Puritan, Jug, 1 Pt.	65.00
Puritan, Jug, 3 Pt.	25.00
Puritan, Nappy, Ice Cream, Flared, 4 Piece	25.00
Puritan, Salt, Master	30.00
Puritan, Tankard, 1 Pt.	15.00
Puritan, Tankard, Lid, 1 Pt.	100.00
Quator, Bonbon, 6 In.	45.00
Queen Ann, Dish, Jelly, Round	35.00
Queen Ann, Dish, Lemon, Cover	30.00
Queen Ann, Sugar & Creamer, Everglades Etch, Pair	70.00
Recessed Panel, Candy Jar, Cover, Gray Cutting, 1 Lb.	45.00
Recessed Panel, Vase, Pinched Neck, 7 In.	155.00
Regency, Puffbox, Cover	75.00
Revere, Jam Jar, Cover, Gold Design	15.00
Revere, Legionnaire, Plate, 8 In., 4 Piece	25.00
Ridge & Star, Plate, Moongleam, 6 In., 4 Piece	35.00
Ridgeleigh, Candle Vase, Insert, Zircon	140.00
Ridgeleigh, Candlestick, Square Footed, 4 In., Pair	15.00
Ridgeleigh, Cocktail Shaker, 1 Pt.	250.00
Ridgeleigh, Cruet, Stopper	10.00
Ridgeleigh, Cup & Saucer	45.00
Ridgeleigh, Decanter, 1 Pt.	115.00
Ridgeleigh, Dish, Jelly, Sections	8.00
Ridgeleigh, Jam Jar, Cover	55.00
Ridgeleigh, Salt & Pepper	10.00
Ridgeleigh, Sugar & Creamer	15.00
Ridgeleigh, Tumbler, Roly Poly, Coaster Base	35.00
Ridgeleigh, Tumbler, Soda, Flared, 12 Oz.	30.00
Ridgeleigh, Vase, Straight, 8 In.	70.00
Ridgeleigh, Vase, Straight, 10 In.	280.00
Ring Band, Dish, Ivorina Verde	38.00
Rococo, Creamer, Sahara	150.00
Rooster, Vase	45.00
Rooster Head, Cocktail, 3 Oz.	50.00
Rose Etch, Champagne, 6 Oz.	15.00
Rose Etch, Goblet, 9 Oz., 6½ In. .... *illus*	36.00
Rose Etch, Vase, Violet, Waverly, 4 In.	65.00 to 70.00
Saturn, Toothpick, 3 In.	50.00
Skirted Panel, Candlestick, Toy, Pair	40.00

Solitaire, Ashtray, Sahara	20.00
Spanish, Goblet, Springtime Etch, 10 Oz.	45.00
Spencer, Decanter, Stopper, Moongleam	300.00
Stanhope, Dish, Jelly, Handles	40.00
Sunburst, Bowl, 5 Sides, 10 In. *illus*	100.00
Sunburst, Tray, Ice Cream, 16 In.	65.00
Sweet Ad-O-Line, Goblet, 14 Oz.	10.00
Thumbprint & Panel, Vase	65.00
Toujours, Jam Jar, Apple, Cover, Minuet	95.00
Touraine, Tumbler, Amber	20.00
Trefoil, Ashtray, Moongleam	25.00 to 50.00
Trident, Candlestick, 2-Light, Moongleam	70.00
Trident, Candlestick, 2-Light, Sahara, Pair	95.00
Tudor, Dish, Mayonnaise, Underplate	50.00
Tudor, Jam Jar, Cover, Flamingo	55.00
Tulip, Vase, Cobalt Blue	725.00
Twist, Bonbon, Moongleam, Folded Sides, Handles, 6¾ In. *illus*	17.00
Twist, Cocktail, Flamingo, 3 Oz., Pair	60.00
Twist, Cruet, Flamingo, 4½ In. *illus*	125.00
Twist, Plate, Moongleam, 6 In.	10.00
Twist, Sugar & Creamer, Flamingo	105.00
Twist, Tumbler, Soda, Footed, Marigold, 12 Oz.	15.00
Victorian, Bottle, Rye, Stopper	65.00
Victorian, Compote, 5 In.	40.00
Victorian, Tumbler, Footed, 10 Oz.	15.00
Victorian Girl, Bell	25.00
Warwick, Bowl, Floral, 11 In.	45.00
Warwick, Bowl, Floral, Cobalt, 11 In.	325.00
Warwick, Candleholder, 3 In. *illus*	32.00
Warwick, Candlestick, 2-Light, Pair	40.00
Warwick, Vase, Cobalt, 9 In.	460.00
Warwick, Vase, Sahara, 9 In.	250.00
Waverly, Butter, Cover, Square	15.00
Waverly, Candy Box, Cover	40.00
Whirlpool, Bowl, Floral, 11½ In.	20.00
Whirlpool, Cruet, Ipswich Stopper, 4 Oz.	20.00
Whirlpool, Dish, Mayonnaise, Footed	15.00
Whirlpool, Plate, Buffet, 13 In.	20.00
Whirlpool, Sugar & Creamer, Tray	30.00
Wide Flat Panel, Sugar & Creamer, Butter Chip Cover, Stacking *illus*	90.00
Windsor, Candlestick, 9½ In.	20.00
Winged Scroll, Creamer, Ivorina Verde	25.00
Winged Scroll, Cruet, Stopper, Gold Trim	80.00
Winged Scroll, Sugar, Cover, Canary	625.00
Winged Scroll, Toothpick	115.00
Yeoman, Ashtray, Monogram	10.00
Yeoman, Ashtray, Moongleam, Bowtie	170.00
Yeoman, Ashtray, Moongleam	40.00
Yeoman, Candy Box, Bottom Only	10.00
Yeoman, Cologne, Stopper, Engraved	80.00
Yeoman, Cologne, Stopper, Etched	75.00
Yeoman, Cruet, Stopper, 2 Oz.	10.00
Yeoman, Cruet, Stopper, Moongleam, 4 Oz.	80.00
Yeoman, Plate, 10½ In.	90.00
Yeoman, Sandwich Server, Handle, Wheel Etch, 10 In.	25.00

HEREND, *see Fischer category.*

HEUBACH is the collector's name for Gebruder Heubach, a firm working in Lichten, Germany, from 1840 to 1925. It is best known for bisque dolls and doll heads, their principal products. They also manufactured bisque figurines, including piano babies, beginning in the 1880s, and glazed figurines in the 1900s. Piano Babies are listed in their own category. Dolls are included in the Doll category under Gebruder Heubach and Heubach. Another factory, Ernst Heubach, working in Koppelsdorf, Germany, also made porcelain and dolls. These will also be found in the Doll category under Heubach Koppelsdorf.

Heisey, Warwick, Candleholder, 3 In.
$32.00

Heisey, Wide Flat Panel, Sugar & Creamer, Butter Chip Cover, Stacking
$90.00

Higbee, Celery Vase, Spirea Band, Blue, 8 In.
$125.00

H

Higbee, Pitcher, Owl, Blue,
Molded Eyes, 9 x 5 In.
$187.00

Higbee, Sugar, Bear,
Glass Menagerie, 4⅜ In.
$70.00

Holt-Howard, Cheese Dish,
Cover, Stinky Cheese,
Mouse & Cheese Finial,
1958, 4½ In.
$15.00

Candy Container, Girl On Snowball, 1920s	365.00
Figurine, Bubble Blower, No Pipe, 11½ In.	750.00
Figurine, Chinese Twins, Gold Trim, 1900s, 5 & 5½ In., Pair	400.00
Figurine, Dancing Girl, 1900s, 12 In.	400.00
Piano Baby, Bonnet Girls, Blue Intaglio Eyes, Red Lips, Blond, 1900s, 3½ x 4½ In.	400.00
Piano Baby, Lying On Back, Smiling, Foot Up In Air, Signed, 5½ x 8½ In.	595.00
Piano Baby, White Gown, Ribbons, Blue Eyes, Open Mouth, Blond, 1900s, 11 x 7½ In.	600.00

HIGBEE glass was made by the J. B. Higbee Company of Bridgeville, Pennsylvania, about 1900. Tablewares were made and it is possible to assemble a full set of dishes and goblets in some Higbee patterns. Most of the glass was clear, not colored. Additional pieces may be found in the Pressed Glass category by pattern name.

Banana Boat, Floral Oval, c.1910, 8 In.	50.00
Banana Stand, 10-Pointed Star, c.1907, 7 x 9⅜ In.	36.00
Berry Bowl, Twin Teardrops, Flared, Scalloped, Sawtooth Rim, c.1915, 4 In.	35.00
Bowl, Floral Oval, c.1910, 7 x 2 In.	45.00
Bowl, Hickman, Oval, c.1904, 8 x 4 In.	20.00
Bowl, Madora, Footed, c.1910, 2⅜ x 3¼ In.	18.00
Butter, Cover, Homestead, Engraved Fern & Leaf, Footed, c.1885, 8 x 7¾ In.	42.00
Cake Stand, Feathered Medallion, 9⅜ x 4⅝ In.	38.00
Cake Stand, Rosette & Palms, c.1905, 9¾ x 5¼ In.	45.00
Candy Dish, Thistle, Pink, 5 x 5¼ In.	55.00
Celery Vase, Cut Log, Scalloped Rim, c.1896, 7½ x 4½ In.	65.00
Celery Vase, Spirea Band, Blue, 8 In..*illus*	125.00
Compote, Floral Oval, c.1910, 6¾ In.	20.00
Compote, Fortuna, Gothic Arch, c.1918, 6¾ x 8¼ In.	40.00
Compote, Gala, c.1913	65.00
Compote, Paneled Thistle, c.1910, 9 In.	40.00
Cordial, Georgian, 1 Oz., 3¼ In.	20.00
Creamer, Cut Log, c.1891	18.00
Creamer, Drum, Child's, c.1890, 2¾ In.	75.00
Dish, Banana Split, Twin Teardrops, c.1905, 3¾ In.	20.00
Dish, Sweetmeat, Sheaf & Diamond, Footed, c.1907, 5 x 5¼ In.	15.00
Goblet, Spirea Band, Blue	30.00
Mug, Advertising, Higbee Sanitary Bottle, Vacuum, 2 x 2 In.	80.00
Mug, Butterfly & Spray, Child's, c.1883, 3½ x 3¼ In.	42.00
Mug, Drum & Eagle, Child's, c.1885	35.00
Mug, Willow Oak, Blue, 1800s	18.00
Pitcher, Cut Log, c.1896, 12 In.	77.00
Pitcher, Owl, Blue, Molded Eyes, 9 x 5 In. *illus*	187.00
Pitcher, Water, Oaken Bucket, 8¼ In.	77.00
Relish, Hickman, Cupped Edge, Marquise Shape, c.1900, 1¼ x 5½ In.	45.00
Spoon Rest, Willow Oak, Blue, Pressed Daisies, 1800s	12.00
Spooner, Drum, Child's, c.1890, 2⅝ x 1¾ In.	75.00
Sugar, Bear, Glass Menagerie, 4⅜ In. *illus*	70.00
Sugar Shaker, 6-Sided, Star Burst Bottom, 4⅝ x 2½ In.	25.00
Tumbler, Oaken Bucket, c.1880, 3¼ In.	10.00
Vase, 10-Point Star, 17 In.	40.00
Vase, Cut Log, Swung, c.1889, 15¾ & 16¼ In., Pair	65.00
Wine, Georgian, 3 Oz., 4½ In.	17.00

HISTORIC BLUE, *see factory names, such as Adams, Ridgway, and Staffordshire.*

HOBNAIL glass is a style of glass with bumps all over. Dozens of hobnail patterns and variants have been made. Clear, colored, and opalescent hobnail have been made and are being reproduced. Other pieces of hobnail may also be listed in the Duncan & Miller and Fenton categories.

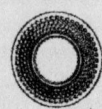

Bell, Amber & Topaz, Opalescent	30.00
Bottle, Dresser, Opalescent, Cork Stopper, 6 In.	30.00
Bowl, Centerpiece, Pink Exterior, Coral Interior, Victorian, c.1870, 5 x 6 In.	146.00
Cuspidor, Green	700.00
Ice Bucket, Bucket Shape, 2 Handles, 5½ x 7 In.	65.00
Relish, Clear, Gold Rim, 10 x 7½ In.	10.00
Tumbler Set, Anchor Hocking, Chrome Holder, 16 Oz., 8 Piece	45.00
Vase, Opalescent, Daisy Petal, Footed, Early 1900s, 3 x 5½ In.	80.00

HOCHST, or Hoechst, porcelain was made in Germany from 1746 to 1796. It was marked with a six-spoke wheel. Be careful when buying Hochst; many other firms have used a very similar wheel-shaped mark.

Figurine, Diana, Leaning, Rocky Plinth, Gold Quiver, Crown Wheel Mark, c.1770, 11¾ In. . .	3900.00
Group, Girl, Placing Flower On Sleeping Boy, Pedestal, Urn, Dog, Crown Wheel Mark, 7 In. . .	3840.00
Group, Man, Flute, Lady, Seated, Flowers, Sheep, Dog, Crown Wheel Mark, c.1770, 7¾ In. . . .	3840.00

HOLLY AMBER, or golden agate, glass was made by the Indiana Tumbler and Goblet Company of Greentown, Indiana, from January 1, 1903, to June 13, 1903. It is a pressed glass pattern featuring holly leaves in the amber-shaded glass. The glass was made with shadings that range from creamy opalescent to brown-amber.

Cake Stand, Pedestal Base, 5 x 9 In.	4800.00
Compote, Cover, 12 x 8½ In.	4100.00
Cruet, Original Stopper, 6½ In.	2100.00
Pitcher, Syrup, 6 In.	3400.00
Water Set, 9-In. Pitcher, 4 Piece	4500.00

HOLT-HOWARD was an importer that started working in 1949 in Stamford, Connecticut. The company sold many types of table accessories, such as condiment jars, decanters, spoon holders, and saltshakers. The figures shown on some of its pieces had a cartoon-like quality. The company was bought out by General Housewares Corporation in 1969. Holt-Howard pieces are often marked with the name and the year or *HH* and the year stamped in black. The *HH* mark was used until 1974. There was also a black and silver label. Production of Holt-Howard ceased in 1990. Similar pieces by the same Holt-Howard designer are being made today and are marked *GHA*.

Apple Jar, Cover, Marked, 1962, 6⅜ In.	28.00
Ashtray, Cat, Says Meow, 5 x 4½ In.	85.00
Bottle, Italian Dressing, Pixie, c.1959, 7½ In.	195.00
Bowl, Melon, Yellow & Green, 2¼ In.	35.00
Butter, Rooster, 6¼ In.	14.00
Candle Cup, Original Label, Holes	35.00
Candleholder, Angel, 1960	14.00
Candleholder, Santa In Car, 1959, 3½ In.	28.00
Candleholder, Santa	25.00
Candy Holder, Santa Boots, Red & White, Holly Leaves & Berries, 2¾ In.	15.00
Cheese Dish, Cover, Stinky Cheese, Mouse & Cheese Finial, 1958, 4½ In. . . . . *illus*	15.00
Coffeepot, Server, Rooster, 1960, 4 x 8 In.	125.00
Cookie Jar, Lemon Face, Yellow, Green & Pink, 6½ In.	115.00
Cookie Jar, Rooster, 1961, 5¾ In.	185.00
Cruet, Russian Dressing, Pixie, 7½ In.	175.00
Egg Nog Set, Santa, 7½-In. Pitcher, 7 Piece . . . . *illus*	65.00
Jar, Ketchup, Rooster Design, Red & Yellow, 4½ In.	70.00
Jar, Mustard, Pixie, 1958	125.00
Jar, Onion, Pixie, Spoon, 1958	335.00
Mug, Bottom Imprint, 1967, 2½ In., 4 Piece	60.00
Ornament, Bell, Holly Berries, 1960, 3½ In.	12.00
Pitcher, Rooster, 1964, 4½ In.	125.00
Salt & Pepper, Angel, 3⅞ In.	10.00
Salt & Pepper, Kozy Kitten, Meow Noisemaker Base, 1958, 4½ In. . . . . *illus*	45.00
Salt & Pepper, Pony Tail, 3½ In.	32.00
Shaker, Rooster, 4½ In.	40.00
Stringholder, Cozy Kitten, 4¾ In.	85.00

HOPALONG CASSIDY was a character in a series of twenty-eight books written by Clarence E. Milford, first published in 1907. Movies and television shows were made based on the character. The best-known actor playing Hopalong Cassidy was William Lawrence Boyd. His first movie appearance was in 1919, but the first Hopalong Cassidy film was not until 1934. Sixty-six films were made. In 1948, William Boyd purchased the television rights to the movies, then later made fifty-two new programs. In the 1950s, Hopalong Cassidy and his horse, named Topper, were seen in comics, records, toys, and other products. Boyd died in 1972.

Barette, Painted, Grass, c.1950, 2 In.	75.00
Birthday Card, You're 12, Buzza Cardoza, 1950s, 6 x 5 In.	49.00
Box Only, Genuine Handkerchiefs, 1950s, 9 x 9 In.	112.00
Bracelet, By Coro, Silver Brass, 1950s	246.00

Holt-Howard, Egg Nog Set, Santa, 7½-In. Pitcher, 7 Piece
$65.00

Holt-Howard, Salt & Pepper, Kozy Kitten, Meow Noisemaker Base, 1958, 4½ In.
$45.00

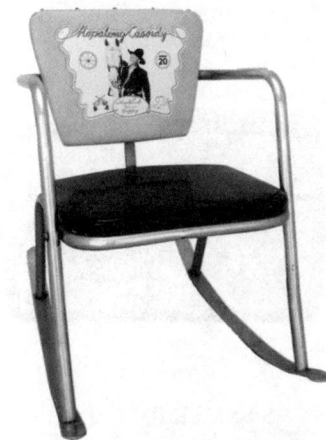

Hopalong Cassidy, Chair, Rocker, Hopalong & Topper, Metal & Vinyl, 24 x 15 In.
$260.00

H

TIP
Do not pour detergent directly on stainless steel. It will stain.

TIP

When repairing a table or toy take digital pictures at each step. Even photograph the screws and nails so you can put everything back in the same place. The photos in reverse order are a step by step guide to what to do.

Hopalong Cassidy, Lunch Box, Metal, Blue, Thermos, Aladdin, 1950, 7½ x 8½ x 3½ In. $248.00

Hopalong Cassidy, Radio, Hoppy Riding Topper, Steel, Embossed, Arvin, No. 441T, 9 x 5 x 4 In. $895.00

SECURITY TIP

Re-key all locks when you move to a new house or apartment or if you lose a key.

Chair, Rocker, Hopalong & Topper, Metal & Vinyl, 24 x 15 In. .... *illus*	260.00
Clock, Alarm, Hopalong On Topper, Black, Metal, Round, US Time Corp., 5 In.	287.00
Comic Book, No. 95, Night Raiders Of Twin River, DC Comics, No. 1954	25.00
Crayon, Black, 3⅜ x ⅜ In.	20.00
Crayon, Blue, 3¼ x ⅜ In.	20.00
Display, Cardboard, 2 Ballpoint Pens, 5 x 8½ x 13½ In.	752.00
Drinking Straws, Contents, Box, c.1950, 9 In.	100.00
Game, Cardboard, Stroehmann's Sunbeam Bread, 1950s, 10¾ x 13¾ In.	168.00
Game, Lasso, Board, Plastic Figure, Rules, Transogram, c.1950	149.00
Game, Target, Tin Lithograph, Wire Stand, Marx, 1950s, 27 x 16 In.	172.00
Headdress, Cloth, Vinyl Inset, Feathers, Big Chief Hoppy, Child's	165.00
Knife, Hopalong Cassidy, Novelty Cutlery, Ireland, 1940s, 3½ In.	135.00
Lamp, Horsehead, Glass, Glass Finial, c.1950s, 27 In.	280.00
Lobby Card, Hopalong Rides Again, Paramount, 1935	1610.00
Lunch Box, Metal, Blue, Thermos, Aladdin, 1950, 7½ x 8½ x 3½ In. .... *illus*	248.00
Lunch Box, Metal, Red, Thermos, Aladdin, 1950, 7½ x 8½ x 3½ In.	303.00
Movie Poster, Hopalong Cassidy Returns, Paramount, 1936, 27 x 41 In.	13225.00
Movie Poster, Range War, Paramount, 1939, 27 x 41 In.	863.00
Mug, Hopalong Cassidy, Holding 6-Gun, Lassoing, Steer, Blue, Milk Glass, 3 x 3 In.	38.00
Mug, Hopalong On 1 Knee, 3 In.	38.00
Neckerchief, Hopalong, Topper, Bar 20 Ranch, Cotton, 1950s, 36 x 24 In. .	55.00
Outfit, Western, 1950s, 18-In. Shirt, 26-In. Pants	112.00
Pen, Ballpoint, Refill, Plastic Head, Box, c.1950	168.00
Pin, Detroit News, Red Ground, Lithograph, 1⅛ In.	62.00
Pin, For Democracy, 1, Bill Boyd, 1¼ In.	226.00
Pin, Hopalong & Topper, Red, Photo, 1¾ In.	18.00
Pin, Hopalong Cassidy's Saving Rodeo, Bronco Buster, Red, Black, White, 2 In. ...	20.00
Pin, I Follow Hoppy In The Albany Times-Union, Lithograph, 1⅜ In.	56.00
Pin, Old Hopalong Cassidy, Photo, Celluloid, 2¼ In.	55.00
Radio, Hoppy Riding Topper, Steel, Embossed, Arvin, No. 441T, 9 x 5 x 4 In. .... *illus*	895.00
Range Rifle, Tin, Vinyl Strap, Marx, 1950s, 30½ In.	392.00
Rocker, Hopalong & Horse, Black Seat, Vinyl, Metal, 24 x 15 In.	247.00
Rug, Topper, Fence, Hopalong Cassidy In Writing, Chenille, 24 x 37 In. ..	165.00
Sheet Music, If I Had My Way, 1929, 12 x 9 In.	33.00
Shirt, Little Champ, Size 8 In.	123.00
Shooting Gallery, Tin, Windup, Automatic Toy Co., Original Box, 18 In. ..	385.00
Thermos Bottle, Yellow, Red Cap, Aladdin, Box, 1950s, 6½ In.	146.00
Toothbrush, Hopalong Cassidy, Dr. West's Miracle Tuft, Black, c.1950, 5¼ In. ...	75.00
Toy, Hopalong, Holding Hat, Topper, Plastic, Painted, Ideal, 6 x 5 In., 3 Piece ...	195.00
Toy, Hopalong & Topper, Die Cast Metal, Painted, Tiempo Toys, 2¼ In., 2 Piece ..	75.00
Trash Can, Hopalong Cassidy On Horse, Ropes, Cactus, Metal, 12½ x 10 In.	165.00
Tumbler, Hopalong, Topper, What Does Milk At Lunchtime Do?, Milk Glass, 5 x 3 In.	45.00
View-Master Reel, No. 955, Hopalong & Topper, Cattle Rustler, 1950s	9.00
Wristwatch, Metal Case, Leather Bands, US Time Corp., Box, 1950s	336.00
Writing Folder, Hopalong On Topper, Paper, Envelopes, 1950, 11 x 8½ In. .	231.00

HORN was used to make many types of boxes, furniture inlays, jewelry, and whimsies.

Box, Tobacco, Portrait, Queen Anne, England, c.1702	795.00
Cup, Dark Patina, Cow Horn, 3½ In.	50.00
Cup, Gray, Ivory, Brown, Cow Horn, 3¼ In.	33.00
Figurine, Carved, Sage, Chinese, 7½ In.	590.00
Figurine, Immortal, Holding Flower Filled Basket, Chinese, 12¼ In.	1298.00
Figurine, Immortal, Rhinoceros Horn, Chinese, 8 In.	472.00
Hide Scraper, Elk Horn, Wrought Iron Blade, Early 1900s, 9 In.	127.00
Jewelry Box, Bone, Carved, Hinged Handles, Napoleonic Pow, c.1814, 8½ x 4½ In.	1180.00
Ladle, Sheep's Horn, Raven's Head Handle, Red & Black Decoration, 15½ x 12 x 5½ In.	575.00
Ladle, Steer Horn, c.1900, 9½ x 2½ In.	81.00
Pie Bird, Carved, Detailed Wing, Glass Eyes, Base, Leafy Carving, 3⅞ In.	72.00
Spice Set, Lid, Patina, Round, 3 Sizes, 18th Century, 3 Piece	850.00

HOWARD PIERCE began working in Southern California in 1936. In 1945, he opened a pottery in Claremont. He moved to Joshua Tree in 1968 and continued making pottery until 1991. His contemporary-looking figurines are popular with collectors. Though most pieces are marked with his name, smaller items from his sets often were not marked.

Howard Pierce

Figurine, Bird, Cream, Brown, Textured Wings, Signed, Pair	80.00
Figurine, Bird, Light Brown, Head Pointing Down, 2¾ In.	25.00
Figurine, Bird, Robin, Orange Breast, Marked, 3 In.	60.00
Figurine, Deer, Resting, Brown, Marked, 5½ In.	70.00
Figurine, Dog, Droopy Ears, Stamped, 8 & 6 In., Pair	100.00
Figurine, Dove, Blue, Marked, 9 In.	60.00
Figurine, Girl With Container, Stamped, 9 In.	70.00
Figurine, Goose, Gray, Black, White, 11 In., 8½ In., Pair	165.00
Figurine, Madonna & Child, Gold Leaf Finish, 13½ In.	85.00
Figurine, Natives, Black & White Matte Glaze, 7¾ & 7¼ In., 2 Piece	75.00
Figurine, Quail Family, Mother, 2 Chicks, Light Gray, 6 In., 3¼ In., 2 In., 3 Piece	65.00 to 75.00
Figurine, Quails On Branch, Stamped, 6½ In.	35.00
Figurine, Raccoon, Brown Matte, Marked, 8½ In.	115.00
Figurine, Seal, Stamped, 5¼ x 6 In.	80.00
Sign, Pottery Show Calif., 1985, Marked, 3 x 6 In.	100.00
Vase, Arcature, White Tree & Deer, Green, Center Opening, Incised, 9 x 6 In.	95.00

HOWDY DOODY and Buffalo Bob were the main characters in a children's series televised from 1947 to 1960. Howdy was a redheaded puppet. The series became popular with college students in the late 1970s when Buffalo Bob began to lecture on campuses.

Bag, Ice Cream, Premium, Chocolate Covered Ice Milk, Wax Paper, c.1950	10.00
Band, Howdy Doody, Buffalo Bob, Windup, Doin' The Howdy Doody, Unique Art, 8 In. ...*illus*	1755.00
Behavior Chart, Jolly Jumbo, Box, c.1949, 18½ x 13 In.	196.00
Book, Fishing Trip, Whitman Cozy Corner, Child's, Kagran Corp., 1955	18.00
Box, Royal Pudding, Vanilla, Howdy Doody Trading Card, No. 1, Unopened, c.1955	108.00
Bubble Pipe, Carabell, Plastic, Original Card, Lido Toy, 4½ In.	88.00
Camera Outfit, Sun-Ray, Plastic, Battery, Silver Rich Corp.	75.00
Card Set, Howdy Doody Cookies, Envelope, Kagran, 1951, 3 x 2 In., 42 Piece	560.00
Christmas Cards, Mailing Envelope, Mars Candy, 1950-54, Set Of 8	95.00
Clarabell Horn Ring, Brass, With Howdy & Clarabell	165.00
Cookie Jar, Purinton Pottery, 1950s, 9¾ In.	900.00
Costume, Official Pl'a-Time, Collegeville, Original Box, Copyright Kagram	120.00
Costume, Patterned Shirt, Canvas Mask, Box, Collegeville, Child's Size 8	121.00
Doll, Jointed, Wood, Composition, Original Box, Noma-Cameo, 12¾ In.	633.00
Doll, Princess Summerfall-Winterspring, Plastic, Beehler Arts, Box, 1950s, 8 In.	110.00
Doll, Princess Summerfall-Winterspring, Plastic, Virga, Box, Early 1950s, 8 In.	734.00
Glass, Welch's Jelly, Train, Blue, White, Clarabell & Princess, 1953	25.00
Head Vase, 1988, 7 In.	45.00
Jacket, Buffalo Bob Says Howdy Doody For President, Yellow, Corduroy, 1948	1195.00
Lamp, Circus, Wood Triangular Base, Howdy Figure, Illustrated Shade, 13½ In.	550.00
Night-Light, Figural, Leco Electric Manufacturing Co., 1950s, 6 x 17 x 2 In.	203.00 to 345.00
Ornament, Christmas, 50th Anniversary, Hallmark Keepsake, Box, 1997	13.00
Pencil Set, Character, Original Package, Different Colors, 1988, 6 Piece	20.00
Pin, It's Howdy Doody Time, 1970s, 6 In.	334.00
Puppet, Finger, Foam Rubber, 1950s	35.00
Puppet, Hand, Cloth, Rubber Head, c.1950s, 9 In.	92.00
Puppette, Controllable Eyes & Mouth, Plastic, Pride Products, 13 In.	138.00
Puzzle, Circus Star, Highwire, Tray Frame, Whitman Publishing, 1950s, 9 x 11 In.	27.00
Ring, Flashlight, Premium, Battery	195.00
Ring, Plastic, Jack-In-The-Box, Red Top, Premium, 1950s	588.00
Shoe Bag, Vinyl, Insert Card, Box, c.1950, 8 x 15 In.	196.00
Sign, Store, For Welch's Grape Jelly & Grapelade, 1951, 10 x 13 In.	247.00
Sign, Store, Royal's Pudding, Paper Over Cardboard, 19½ In.	1320.00
Spoon, Cereal, Character Handle, Premium, Crown Silver Plate, 7 In.	42.00
Squeak Toy, Clarabell, Peter Puppet Playthings, Original Box, Rubber, 7 In.	88.00
Strawholder, Plastic, Clip On Glass, 48 Straws, Old Colony Paper Prod., 2½ In.	94.00
Toy, Clarabell, Stands On Hands, Wobbles, Battery, Tin, Linemar, 5 In.	550.00
Toy, Doodler, Magic Drawing Toy, Box, c.1949, 13 x 18½ In.	739.00
Toy, Howdy Doody Drives Go-Cart, Windup, Ny-Lint Co.	275.00
Toy, One Man Band, Rocket Whistle, Clarabell Horn, Slide Whistle, Trophy Products	137.00
Toy, Phineas T. Bluster, Squeak, Kagran, 1950s, 7 In.	115.00
Toy, Put On You Own Puppet Show, 5 Figures, Kagran, On Card, 1950s, 7 x 11 In.	84.00
Toy, Swings, Plastic, Cloth, Tin, Lever, Arnold, Germany, 14 In.	92.00
Toy, Television Set, Color, Plastic, 5 Films, All American Plastic Toy Co., Box	165.00
Toy, Television Set, Premium, Plastic, Palmolive	71.00

Howdy Doody, Band, Howdy Doody, Buffalo Bob, Windup, Doin' The Howdy Doody, Unique Art, 8 In. $1755.00

Howdy Doody, Wristwatch, Red Band, Die Cut Howdy Doody Display Box, Kagran, 7 In. $880.00

H

Hull, Imperial, Planter,
Sea Serpent, Green, 5¾ In.
$38.00

Hull, Planter, Pig, White,
Pink Flowers, 5 x 8¼ In.
$15.00

Hull, Red Riding Hood,
Cookie Jar, Red Cape,
Floral Border On Dress, 13 In.
$118.00

Hull, Tray, Gingerbread Man,
Brown Glaze, 10 In.
$3.00

Ukulele, Green Plastic, Nylon Strings, Emenee, Kagran, Box, 1950s	. . . .	316.00
Wristwatch, Red Band, Die Cut Howdy Doody Display Box, Kagran, 7 In.	. . . . *illus*	880.00

HULL pottery was made in Crooksville, Ohio, from 1905. Addis E. Hull bought the Acme Pottery Company and started making ceramic wares. In 1917, A. E. Hull Pottery began making art pottery as well as the commercial wares. For a short time, 1921 to 1929, the firm also sold pottery imported from Europe. The dinnerwares of the 1940s, including the Little Red Riding Hood line, the high gloss artwares of the 1950s, and the matte wares of the 1940s, are all popular with collectors. The firm officially closed in March 1986.

Blossom Flite, Console, Pink, 1955, 16½ x 6½ In.	33.00
Blossom Flite, Pitcher, c.1955, 5½ In.	59.00
Bow Knot, Vase, Pink & Green, 12½ In.	374.00
Camellia, Vase, Pillow, Pink & Green, 6½ x 5¼ In.	55.00
Camellia, Vase, Swan, 6¾ In.	66.00
Cookie Jar, Apple, 6 x 9 In.	117.00
Cookie Jar, Duck, 12 In.	149.00
Ebb Tide, Basket, Green & Pink Glaze, 16½ In.	127.00
Fiesta, Planter, 4 x 7¾ x 3¾ In.	33.00
Imperial, Planter, Sea Serpent, Green, 5¾ In. . . . . *illus*	38.00
Imperial, Vase & Bowl, Pitcher, Brown, Embossed Rose, Olive Green, Sponge Trim, 7 In.	50.00
Magnolia, Vase, Pink Gloss, 12½ In.	121.00
Magnolia, Vase, Cornucopia, Double, Pink Matte, Shaded To Blue, 12¾ x 7⅞ In.	132.00
Magnolia, Vase, Cornucopia, Matte Shaded To Blue, 8½ x 9 In.	44.00
Magnolia, Vase, Dusty Rose, Yellow Matte, Marked, c.1946, 10½ In.	210.00
Parchment & Pine, Basket, 6 In.	28.00
Parchment & Pine, Basket, 16½ In.	44.00
Planter, Pig, White, Pink Flowers, 5 x 8¼ In. . . . . *illus*	15.00
Red Riding Hood, Cookie Jar, Red Cape, Floral Border On Dress, 13 In. . . . . *illus*	118.00
Red Riding Hood, Wall Pocket, Gold Collar, 8⅝ x 5¼ In.	350.00
Regal, Vase, Cornucopia, c.1950, 4½ x 10 In.	15.00
Sun Glow, Wall Pocket, Iron Shape, Pansy, Butterfly, Gloss Yellow, 1950s	125.00
Sun Glow, Wall Pocket, Whiskbroom Shape, 8¼ In.	125.00
Tray, Gingerbread Man, Brown Glaze, 10 In. . . . . *illus*	3.00
Tulips, Ewer, Pink Shaded To Blue, Scroll Handle, Footed, c.1930, 13 In. . . . . *illus*	62.00
Water Lily, Console Shape, Marked, c.1948, 13½ In.	180.00
Wildflower, Candleholder, 4¼ In.	70.00
Wildflower, Vase, Cornucopia, Gold Trim, 8½ x 7½ In.	61.00
Wildflower, Vase, Cornucopia, Pink & Cream, 11 In.	44.00
Wildflower, Vase, Cream, Tan Foot, 5½ x 4½ In.	44.00
Wildflower, Vase, Pink & Blue, 6¼ x 6¼ In.	61.00
Woodland, Ewer, Dawn Rose, Gray, Base, 13½ In.	39.00
Woodland, Teapot, Blue, Pink, 1940s, 6 In.	83.00
Woodland, Wall Pocket, Pink, Yellow, Green, 7½ In.	150.00

HUMMEL figurines, based on the drawings of the nun M.I. Hummel (Berta Hummel) are made by the W. Goebel Porzellanfabrik of Oeslau, Germany, now Rodenthal, Germany. They were first made in 1935. The *Crown* mark was used from 1935 to 1949. The company added the *bee* marks in 1950. The *full bee* with variations, was used from 1950 to 1959; *stylized bee,* 1957 to 1972; *three line mark,* 1964 to 1972; *last bee,* sometimes called *vee over gee,* 1972 to 1979. In 1979 the V bee symbol was removed from the mark. *U.S. Zone* was part of the mark from 1946 to 1948; *W. Germany* was part of the mark from 1960 to 1990. The *Goebel, W. Germany* mark, called the *missing bee* mark, was used from 1979 to 1990; *Goebel, Germany* with the crown and *WG,* originally called the *new mark,* was used from 1991 through part of 1999. The newest version of the bee mark with the word *Goebel,* the *current mark* or *Goebel with full bee,* was adopted in 2000. A special *Year 2000* backstamp was also introduced. Porcelain figures inspired by Berta Hummel's drawings were introduced in 1997. These are marked *BH* followed by a number. They are made in the Far East, not Germany. Other decorative items and plates that feature Hummel drawings have been made by Schmid Brothers, Inc., since 1971.

Candleholder, No. 37, Herald Angles, Stylized Bee	46.00
Figurine, No. 6/1, Sensitive Hunter, 1979 . . . . 215.00 to 410.00
Figurine, No. 10/1, Flower Madonna, Vee Over Gee	71.00
Figurine, No. 23/1, Adoration, Millennium Bee	94.00
Figurine, No. 68/0, Lost Sheep, Vee Over Gee	93.00
Figurine, No. 71, Stormy Weather, Stylized Bee	147.00
Figurine, No. 84/0, Worship, Crown Mark	527.00
Figurine, No. 152/0/A, Umbrella Boy, Millennium Bee	176.00

H

Figurine, No. 226, The Mail Is Here, Millennium Bee	263.00
Figurine, No. 256, Knitting Lesson, New Mark	205.00
Figurine, No. 331, Crossroads, Missing Bee	205.00
Figurine, No. 333, Blessed Event, Vee Over Gee	176.00
Figurine, No. 340, Letter To Santa Claus, Vee Over Gee	147.00
Figurine, No. 364, Supreme Protection	234.00
Figurine, No. 405, Sing With Me, New Mark	205.00
Figurine, No. 487, Let's Tell The World, Missing Bee	2199.00
Figurine, No. 600, We Wish You The Best, New Mark	575.00
Figurine, No. 635, Welcome Spring, New Mark	1979.00
Figurine, No. 668, Strike Up The Band, New Mark	575.00
Figurine, No. 766, Here's My Heart, New Mark	660.00
Font, Holy Water, No. 207, Heavenly Angel, Stylized Bee	199.00
Lamp Base, No. 44/B, Out Of Danger, Full Bee	147.00
Plate, Annual, 1971, Heavenly Angel	35.00
Plate, Annual, 1972, Hear Ye, Hear Ye, 7½ In.	100.00
Plate, Annual, 1973, Globe Trotter, 32 Stars, 7½ In.	225.00
Plate, Christmas, 1974, Guardian Angel, 7¾ In.	13.00
Plate, Christmas, 1975, Christmas Child, 7¾ In.	20.00
Plate, Christmas, 1977, Herald Angel, 7¾ In.	20.00
Plate, Mother's Day, 1972, Boy With Toys, 7¾ In.	75.00
Plate, Mother's Day, 1982, Flower Basket, 7¾ In.	23.00
Plate Set, Annual, Bisque, 1976-1979, 5 Piece	176.00

HUTSCHENREUTHER Porcelain Company of Selb, Germany, was established in 1814 and is still working. The company makes fine quality porcelain dinnerwares and figurines. The mark has changed through the years, but the name and the lion insignia appear in most versions.

Breakfast Set, Dresden Pattern, 18 Piece	94.00
Figurine, Mephistopheles, Karl Tutter, Mid 20th Century, 7½ In.	185.00
Figurine, Nude Nymphet, Feeding Fawn, 1930s, 4½ In.	950.00
Group, Eagles Diving For A Catch, 25½ In.	250.00
Group, Swans In Flight, 13 x 10 In.	275.00
Plaque, Ruth Harvesting Grain, Gilt Scroll Frame, 8¾ x 5⅞-In. Plaque	2013.00
Plate, Pink Roses, Aqua Blue Border, Gold Trim, Marked, c.1956, 8 In.	35.00
Tray, Pansies, Hand Painted, Gold Handles, Marked, 12 x 10½ In.	135.00

ICONS, special, revered pictures of Jesus, Mary, or a saint, are usually Russian or Byzantine. The small icons collected today are made of wood and tin or precious metals. Many modern copies have been made in the old style and are being sold to tourists in Russia and Europe and at shops in the United States. Rare, old icons have sold for over $50,000.

Elijah, Saints Peter & Paul, Wood, Silvered, Brass Riza, 11½ x 10 In.	420.00
Holy Napkin, Face Of Christ, Moscow, 1878, 3½ x 3 In. ....*illus*	529.00
Madonna, Seated, Holding Book Out To Baby Jesus, Walnut, Carved, Dark Patina, 22 In.	977.00
Madonna & Child, Portable, Green Fabric Box, Bronze Crucifix, 5 x 6¼ In.	384.00
Major Feasts, Wooden, Painted, c.1850, Russia	1100.00
Resurrection, Life Of Christ Scenes, Oil, Tempera, Panel, Russia, Late 1800s, 12½ x 14 In.	708.00
St. Alexei, Sergei & Basil In Arch, Wood, Brass Argente Riza, Russia, 13 x 11 In.	440.00
St. Barbara, Catherine & Alexandra In View Of Christ, Wood, Polychrome, Russia, 13 x 11 In.	705.00
St. George, Slaying Dragon, Overlaid, Silver Plate, Cyrillic Script, Russia, 12 x 10 In.	390.00
St. George, Slaying Dragon, Russia, 1780-1810, 12¾ x 10 In. ....*illus*	2703.00
St. Ivan Bogoslovski, Color On Wood, 18th Century, Russia, 11¾ x 9¼ In.	1714.00
St. John The Evangelist, Wooden, Painted, Russia, 1850s	1050.00
St. Nicholas, Metal Oklad, Color On Panel, Eastern, 7½ x 5¼ In.	637.00
St. Nicholas, Miracle Worker, Silver Oklad, Russia, Late 19th Century, 3 x 2 In.	536.00
St. Nicholas, Tempera, On Wood, Russia, Early 20th Century, 11¼ x 13½ In.	590.00
Traveling, Crucifixion, Saints, Gilded Cloisonne Enamel, Brass, 1875, 6½ x 3¾ In.	500.00
Virgin & Child, Saints Sergius & Nicholas, Sterling Silver Repousse, Moscow, 1886, 10 x 10 In.	470.00

IMARI porcelain was made in Japan and China beginning in the seventeenth century. In the eighteenth century and later, it was copied by porcelain factories in Germany, France, England, and the United States. It was especially popular in the nineteenth century and is still being made. Imari is characteristically decorated with stylized bamboo, floral, and geometric designs in orange, red, green, and blue. The name comes from the Japanese port of Imari, which exported the ware made nearby in a factory at Arita. Imari is now a general term for any pattern of this type.

Hull, Tulips, Ewer, Pink Shaded To Blue, Scroll Handle, Footed, c.1930, 13 In.
$62.00

Icon, Holy Napkin, Face Of Christ, Moscow, 1878, 3½ x 3 In.
$529.00

Icon, St. George, Slaying Dragon, Russia, 1780-1810, 12¾ x 10 In.
$2703.00

IMARI

Imari, Charger, Ladies In Kimonos,
Dancing With Fans,
Red Ground, 15¾ In.
$374.00

Imari, Dish, Bird Shape,
Molded Feathers,
Flower Basket In Cartouche,
14 x 12 In.
$978.00

Imari, Vase, Phoenix In Garden,
Flowers, Cartouches, Shouldered,
Flared Rim, 13¾ In.
$230.00

Basin, Bottle, Flowering Peonies, Chinese, 18th Century, 10¾ & 9½ In.		3540.00
Bowl, 2 Ducks Among Flowering Branch, Japan, 14¾ In.		384.00
Bowl, Barber's, Flowers, Blue Lotus, Scrolling Vine, Early 1800s, 1¾ x 11 In.		403.00
Bowl, Beige Ground, Red Leaves, White Flowers, Brown Vine, 1955-70, 4⅛ x 2½ In.		40.00
Bowl, Center Decorated, Flower Vase, Paneled Sides, Footed, 4 x 10 In.		144.00
Bowl, Cover, Birds, Trees, Flowers, Cobalt Blue Border, Rooster Finial, 21 x 15 In.		294.00
Bowl, Cover, Flower & Brocade, Japan, 6 x 8½ In.		472.00
Bowl, Fish, Reserve Panels, Flowers, Blue, Gilt, Boat Shape, Early 1900s, 12 x 8 In., Pair		960.00
Bowl, Flower Filled Vase, Cavetto, Flowers Panels, Japan, 8½ In.		224.00
Bowl, Flower Filled Vase, Panels, Japan, 9¼ In.		189.00
Bowl, Flowers, Scalloped Edge, Japan, 12¼ x 6½ In.		590.00
Bowl, Flying Crane, Flower, Brocade, Japan, 18 In.		2124.00
Bowl, Foo Dog Center, Flower Garden Border, 8 Lobes, 6-Character Mark, Late 1800s, 7 In.		84.00
Bowl, Lobed Edge, Double Ringed Foot, Japan, c.1900, 3¼ x 7½ In.		234.00
Bowl, Lobed Edge, Double Ringed Foot, Japan, c.1900, 4 x 8¾ In.		263.00
Bowl, Lobed Edge, Double Ringed Foot, Japan, c.1900, 4 x 9¾ In.		322.00
Bowl, Scalloped Edge, 19th Century, 10 x 3¾ In.		475.00
Bowl, Scalloped Rim, Brocade & Flowers, Gilt Highlights, Japan, 8¾ In.		266.00
Brushpot, Cylinder Shape, Flowers, Bands, Rust, Cobalt Blue, 6 x 4 In.		201.00
Charger, 3 Seasons, Japan, 18½ In.		325.00
Charger, Bird & Flowers, Japan, 14½ In., 3 Piece		236.00
Charger, Flower Filled Vase, Scalloped Rim, Japan, 18½ In.		561.00
Charger, Flowering Vase, 2 Birds, c.1900, 2¾ x 18 In.		690.00
Charger, Flowers, Foo Dogs, Fish, Peonies, Blossoms, Propeller Roundel, c.1912, 12 In.		850.00
Charger, Flowers, Japan, Edo Period, 13¼ In.		1770.00
Charger, Flowers, Scalloped Rim, Japan, 15 In., Pair		384.00
Charger, Ladies In Kimonos, Dancing With Fans, Red Ground, 15¾ In.	*illus*	374.00
Charger, Octagonal, Scalloped Rim, 12 In., Pair		575.00
Charger, Scalloped Edges, Flower Cartouches, Fish, Cobalt Blue Ground, 15 In., Pair		1093.00
Charger, Women, Children, Brocade Borders, 19th Century, 22 In.		500.00
Dish, Bird Shape, Molded Feathers, Flower Basket In Cartouche, 14 x 12 In.	*illus*	978.00
Dish, Flowering Tree, Cart, 19th Century, 9¼ In.		132.00
Dish, Samurai, Men, Entertaining Ladies, Fish Shape, Japan, 3 x 14½ In., Pair		3680.00
Dresser Jar, Crane, Rectangular, 1868-1912, 5 In.		120.00
Jar, Cover, Landscape, Cockerels, Iris, Bamboo, Hexagonal, 36 In.		1997.00
Jardiniere, Flowers, Japan, 8¾ x 12¼ In.		472.00
Plate, Ship, Fired Gold Accents, Japan, c.1930, 9½ In.		439.00
Plate, Soup, Mandarin Orange, Flowers, Scalloped Rims, Gilt, Cobalt Blue, 9½ In., 10 Piece		1645.00
Platter, Man, Woman, Rectangular, Japan, c.1920, 11¼ x 14¼ In.		936.00
Punch Bowl, Chinese, c.1710, 15¾ In.		1770.00
Serving Plate, Courtyard Scene, Repeating Panel Border, Lobed, Late 1800s, 2 x 12 In.		176.00
Vase, Baluster, Iron Red, Green, Underglaze Blue, 8½ & 9 In., 2 Piece		374.00
Vase, Cover, Flower Panels, Japan, 19 In.		472.00
Vase, Flower Filled Vase Design, Children At Play, Japan, 12 In., Pair		236.00
Vase, Flowers, Brocade, Japan, 17½ In.		413.00
Vase, Flowers & Bird, Japan, 11 In.		354.00
Vase, Phoenix In Garden, Flowers, Cartouches, Shouldered, Flared Rim, 13¾ In.	*illus*	230.00

IMPERIAL GLASS Corporation was founded in Bellaire, Ohio, in 1901. It became
a subsidiary of Lenox, Inc., in 1973 and was sold to Arthur R. Lorch in 1981. It was sold
again in 1982, and went bankrupt in 1984. In 1985, the molds and some assets were sold.
The Imperial glass preferred by the collector is freehand art glass, carnival glass, slag glass,
stretch glass, and other top-quality tablewares. Tablewares and animals are listed here.
The others may be found in the appropriate sections.

IMPE
RIAL

Animal, Donkey, Caramel Slag	*illus*	32.00
Animal, Elephant, Carmel Slag, 4 x 6¾ In.		40.00
Animal, Mallard, Ruby Red, 3 Piece	*illus*	105.00
Animal, Mallard, Wings Down, Blue, Frosted, 4¾ In.		50.00
Animal, Mallard, Wings Up, Carmel Slag, Marked, 6½ In.		30.00
Animal, Scottie, Carmel Slag, 3½ In.		45.00
Art Glass, Vase, Blue & Bronze Iridescent, Egg Shape, 3 Looped Handles, c.1920, 7 In.	*illus*	175.00
Art Glass, Vase, Citron, Green Loopings, Gold Flecks, Shouldered, Flared Rim, 5½ In.		403.00
Art Glass, Vase, Orange Iridescent, Blue Draped Loops, Ruffled, 3 Pull-Down Handles, 6 In.		1150.00
Art Glass, Vase, Orange Iridescent, Blue Hearts & Vines, 3 Pull-Down Handles, 6¾ In.		1333.00
Art Glass, Vase, Peachblow, Frosted, 7¾ In.		145.00

Imperial, Animal, Donkey,
Caramel Slag
$32.00

Imperial, Candlewick, Punch Set,
Bowl, Underplate, Cups, 14 Piece
$300.00

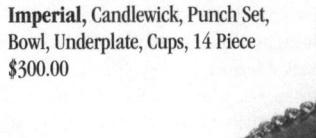

Imperial, Animal, Mallard,
Ruby Red, 3 Piece
$105.00

Imperial, Cape Cod,
Cruet, Azalea
$45.00

Imperial, Daisy & Button,
Cruet, Purple Slag,
Original Stopper, 7 In.
$30.00

Imperial, Art Glass, Vase,
Blue & Bronze Iridescent, Egg Shape,
3 Looped Handles, c.1920, 7 In.
$175.00

Imperial, Cathay, Bowl,
Dragon, Antique Blue,
Satin, 7¾ x 5 In.
$336.00

Imperial, Diamond Quilted,
Creamer, Pink
$12.00

Imperial, Candlewick, Bowl,
Ruby, Crimped, Square, Footed, 9¼ In.
$175.00

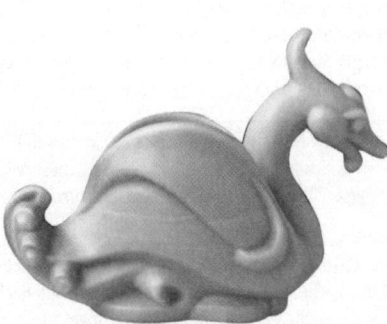

Imperial, Laced Edge, Vase,
Seafoam Green Opalescent,
Footed, 5 In.
$46.00

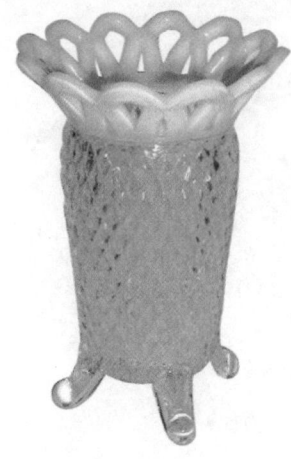

Imperial, Purple Slag,
Dish, Lion Cover,
Lace Edge Base, 7½ In.
$145.00

Indian, Basket, Apache, Utility,
Twine Construction, Horizontal Bands,
Hide Trim, 14 In.
$891.00

Beaded Block, Bowl, Round, 7 In.	20.00
Beaded Block, Bud Vase, Cobalt Blue, 5⅛ In.	25.00
Beaded Block, Creamer	12.00
Beaded Block, Dish, Jelly, Pink, Footed, 5 In.	20.00 to 30.00
Candlewick, Bowl, Ruby, Crimped, Square, Footed, 9¼ In. ....*illus*	175.00
Candlewick, Punch Set, Bowl, Underplate, Cups, 14 Piece ....*illus*	300.00
Cape Cod, Cruet, Azalea ....*illus*	45.00
Cape Cod, Sherbet, 3⅝ In.	6.00
Cape Cod, Tumbler, Footed, 5½ In.	6.00 to 9.00
Caramel Slag, Basket, Marked, 10 In.	150.00
Caramel Slag, Bowl, Rose Pattern, 3-Footed, 8 In.	33.00
Caramel Slag, Cruet, Stopper, Raised Flowers, c.1880, 5¾ In.	70.00
Caramel Slag, Pitcher, Windmill, 36 Oz.	85.00
Cathay, Bowl, Dragon, Antique Blue, Satin, 7¾ x 5 In. ....*illus*	336.00
Daisy & Button, Cruet, Purple Slag, Original Stopper, 7 In. ....*illus*	30.00
Dewdrop, Bowl, 10½ In.	17.50
Diamond Block, Bowl, Lily, Pink, 5 In.	18.00
Diamond Block, Creamer, Green	15.00
Diamond Block, Dish, Jelly, Green, Handle, 4½ In.	16.00
Diamond Block, Dish, Pickle, Green, Handles, Oval, 6½ In.	20.00
Diamond Block, Dish, Pickle, Pink, Handles, Oval, 6½ In.	20.00
Diamond Block, Sugar & Creamer, Green	30.00
Diamond Quilted, Black, Crimped Edge, 7 In.	20.00
Diamond Quilted, Bowl, Pink, Straight Edge, 7 In.	20.00
Diamond Quilted, Candlestick, Black, Enameled, Pair	35.00
Diamond Quilted, Candlestick, Black, Flat Base	18.00
Diamond Quilted, Candlestick, Blue, Flat Base	18.00
Diamond Quilted, Candlestick, Green, Domed Base	25.00
Diamond Quilted, Candlestick, Green, Flat Base	15.00
Diamond Quilted, Candlestick, Pink, Flat Base, Pair	30.00
Diamond Quilted, Compote, Cover, Green, 11½ In.	140.00
Diamond Quilted, Creamer, Black	15.00
Diamond Quilted, Creamer, Pink ....*illus*	12.00
Diamond Quilted, Cup, Black	17.00
Diamond Quilted, Nappy, Black, Handle, 5½ In.	18.00
Diamond Quilted, Nappy, Pink, Handle, 5½ In.	15.00
Diamond Quilted, Plate, Luncheon, Green, 8 In.	12.00
Diamond Quilted, Plate, Luncheon, Pink, 8 In.	12.00
Diamond Quilted, Plate, Sherbet, Blue, 6 In.	8.00
Diamond Quilted, Punch Bowl Base, Green	250.00
Diamond Quilted, Saucer, Black	6.00
Diamond Quilted, Sugar, Black	15.00
Diamond Quilted, Sugar, Green	10.00
Diamond Quilted, Sugar, Pink	10.00
Diamond Quilted, Sugar & Creamer, Green	22.00
Laced Edge, Bowl, Fruit, Diamond, 3½ x 10 In.	40.00
Laced Edge, Candleholder, 4¼ In., Pair	50.00
Laced Edge, Vase, Katy Blue, 7 In.	40.00
Laced Edge, Vase, Seafoam Green Opalescent, Footed, 5 In. ....*illus*	46.00
Purple Slag, Ashtray, Nautical, 4-Sided, 4 x 4 In.	75.00
Purple Slag, Box, Cover, Bee Finial, 5 In.	125.00
Purple Slag, Box, Cover, Butterfly Finial, 5½ In.	125.00
Purple Slag, Compote, Grapes, Scalloped Rim, Footed, Marked, 4 x 5½ In.	105.00
Purple Slag, Dish, Lion Cover, Lace Edge Base, 7½ In. ....*illus*	145.00

INDIAN art from North America has attracted the collector for many years. Each tribe has its own distinctive designs and techniques. Baskets, jewelry, pottery, and leatherwork are of greatest collector interest. Eskimo art is listed in another category in this book.

Amulet, Southern Plains, Ute, Sun, Moon, Face, Multicolored Elk, Fringe, Beads, 3¾ In.	4700.00
Awl Case, Sioux, Rawhide, Fully Beaded, Tapered, Fringe, Early 1900s, 20 In.	374.00
Bag, Apache, Beaded, Fringe, Cross Design, Silk Backing, Mirror, 19th Century, 11½ In.	748.00
Bag, Bandolier, Cree, Leather, Beaded Strap	133.00
Bag, Beaded, Gold, Green Tassels, Thread Sewn, Hide Handles, 22 In.	201.00
Bag, Doctor, Sioux, Czech Bead, Red, Yellow, Blue, White, American Flags, 5 x 13 In.	2990.00
Bag, Iroquois, Triangular, Cloth, Hide, Beaded, Strap, c.1900, 6 x 5 In.	150.00

Bag, Nez Perce, Cornhusk, Triangles, Stripes, c.1890, 19½ x 13 In.	1380.00
Bag, Ojibwa, Bandolier, Cloth, Multicolored Flowers, Beaded Tabs, Yarn Danglers, 42 In.	2820.00
Bag, Ojibwa, Bandolier, Multicolored Flowers, Bugle Bead, Yarn Danglers, 39 In.	1645.00
Bag, Ojibwa, Bandolier, Trade Cloth, Beaded, Flower, Loomed Panel, Strap, Geometric, 35 In.	2468.00
Bag, Plateau, Cornhusk, Multicolored, Calico Lining, Geometric, 19th Century, 18 In.	411.00
Bag, Plateau, Cornhusk, Multicolored, Geometric, 19th Century, 19 In.	823.00
Bag, Plateau, Cornhusk, Multicolored, Geometric, c.1900, 11 In.	441.00
Bag, Plateau, Cornhusk, Multicolored, Geometric, c.1900, 20 In.	646.00
Bag, Sioux, Moccasin Style Bead	121.00
Bag, Tobacco, Sioux, Sinew-Sewn, Red, Green, Yellow, Purple, Buffalo, Fringe, 24 In.	11500.00
Bag, Yakima, Leaves, Eagle, Flag, Beaded, Thread Sewn, c.1900, 8¾ x 7¾ In.	633.00
Ball, Northern Plains, Beaded, Stripes, Pink, Yellow, Light Blue, Wrist Strap, c.1890, 2 In.	657.00
Bandolier, Ojibway, Loom Beaded, c.1880, 37½ x 11 In.	4025.00
Bandolier Bag, Chippewa, Beaded, Flowers, Military Braid, Early 1900s, 42 x 12 In.	633.00
Basket, Algonquin, Ash, Splint, Multicolored Paint, Decorated Bands, Handles, 6 x 13 In.	275.00
Basket, Algonquin, Ash, Splint, Multicolored Paint, Lid, Paper Liner, 12 x 12 In.	385.00
Basket, Apache, Checkered, Modified Crosses, Early 1900s, 2½ x 14 In.	1725.00
Basket, Apache, Coiled Olla, Split Willow, Devil's Claw Bark, Bulbous, Flared Rim, 9¼ In.	1815.00
Basket, Apache, Flared, Stepped Lattice, Center Circle, Early 1900s, 4½ x 14½ In.	920.00
Basket, Apache, Olla, Oval, Flared Rim, Multiple Stepped Diagonals, 22½ In.	5875.00
Basket, Apache, Utility, Twine Construction, Horizontal Bands, Hide Trim, 14 In. ......*illus*	891.00
Basket, Apache, Willow, Devil's Claw, Geometric Bands, 4¾ x 10½ x 9 In.	575.00
Basket, Ash, Loop Handles, Upper & Lower Blue Band, 4½ x 10¼ In.	44.00
Basket, Attu, Northwest, Multicolored, Yarn Hourglasses, c.1900, 8 x 5½ In.	1410.00
Basket, Cherokee, Multicolored, Geometric Design, Wood Handle, 1920s, 8 x 11 In.	550.00
Basket, Cherokee, River Cane, Square To Round, Concentric Bands, Geometric, 12 In.	863.00
Basket, Chitimacha, River Canes, Fishbone Pattern, Natural Dyes, c.1930, 5 In.	823.00
Basket, Choctaw, Low, Open, Herringbone Pattern, Twill Weave, Natural Dyes, c.1900, 11 In.	646.00
Basket, Cowlitz, Coil, Red & Brown Stepped Pattern, Openwork Rim, c.1900, 4 x 8 In.	546.00
Basket, Klickitat, Imbricated, Rim Loops, Woven Handle, Early 1900s, 6½ x 12½ In.	575.00
Basket, Northeast, Wood, Splint, Painted, 9½ x 13½ In.	353.00
Basket, Northeast, Wood, Splint, Painted, 9 x 12½ In.	470.00
Basket, Papago, Cover, Handle, Stepped Design, c.1950, 9 x 9 In.	184.00
Basket, Papago, Triangles, Flared, 7 x 13 In. ....*illus*	59.00
Basket, Pima, Bowl, Greek Key Bands, Braided Rim, Flared, 6¼ x 19¼ In.	1380.00
Basket, Pima, Coiled, Pictorial, Flared Sides, 7 Lizards, 6¼ x 10¼ In.	470.00
Basket, Pima, Flared, Banded, c.1925, 6¾ x 12 In.	690.00
Basket, Pima, Swirled Stepped Diagonals, Braided Rim, Late 1800s, 3¾ x 12½ In.	518.00
Basket, Pima, Swirls, Multicolored, Braided Rim, 4 x 12½ In.	374.00
Basket, Pima, Whirlwind Design, Braided Devil's Claw Rim, Early 1900s, 2 x 6 In.	40.00
Basket, Pomo, Beaded Points, Coiled, Diagonals, Feathers, 2½ x 4¾ In.	633.00
Basket, Pomo, Bowl, Coiled, Globe, Multicolored Feathers, c.1900, 1¾ x 4¼ In.	1116.00
Basket, River Cane, Bloodroot, Butternut Dye, Eva Wolfe, Late 1970s, 18 x 13½ In.	4370.00
Basket, Seed, Hopi, Cover, Wide Coils, Paper Label, 7 x 8 In.	115.00
Basket, Seneca, Cylindrical, Lidded, Plaited Ash Splints, Red Bands, Handles, 14½ x 11 In.	144.00
Basket, Southeastern, Coiled, Pine Needles, Raffia, Round, Tall Handles, 1900s	59.00
Basket, Southwest, Stepped Diagonals, Braided Rim, 5½ x 20½ In.	1380.00
Basket, Washo, Coil, Moths, Red & Black, Braided Rim, 4¼ x 8½ In.	1380.00
Belt, Navajo, Black, Inlaid Coral & Silver, 9 Conchas, Mother-Of-Pearl Flowers, 50½ In.	805.00
Belt, Navajo, Black Leather, 9 Silver Panels & Beads, Coral Cabochons, Sterling, 41 In.	1955.00
Belt, Navajo, Black Leather, Turquoise Cabochons, Silver Panels & Buckle, 46 In.	1840.00
Belt, Navajo, Silver Oval & Bow-Shaped Medallions, Turquoise, 38 In. ....*illus*	382.00
Belt, Turquoise, Silver, Linked Medallions, Centered Oval Turquoise, 42 In.	410.00
Blanket, Saddle, Navajo, Multicolored Serrated, Banded, Fringe, 30½ x 24 In.	1880.00
Bolo, Zuni, Sun, Inlaid, Silver Tips, Turquoise, Delger Cellicion, 3½-In. Sun ....*illus*	264.00
Bow & Arrow, Plains, Painted, Child's, 37½ In.	33.00
Bowl, Northwest Coast, Bentwood, Carved, Bear, Abalone Eyes, 5½ x 4¾ In.	102000.00
Bowl, Pueblo, Santa Fe, Pottery, c.1861, 2 x 5½ In.	527.00
Bowl, Santa Clara, Black On Black, Carved Avanyu, Triangular Tonus, Signed, 5 x 9 In.	8050.00
Bowl, Santa Clara, Pottery, Black On Black, Bulbous, Tapered Top, 5 x 3½ In. ....*illus*	147.00
Bowl, Santa Clara, Pottery, Blackware, Oval, Carved Avanyu, 8 x 7½ In.	5288.00
Box, Storage, Cover, Algonquin, Birch Bark, Leaves, 10 x 13½ In.	764.00
Box, Storage, Cover, Algonquin, Bird, Leaves, 9½ x 10 x 13½ In.	353.00
Bracelet, Navajo, Central Spinner, Inlaid, Silver, Turquoise, Coral, Bird, Abstract Design, 3 In.	430.00
Breastplate, Plains, Cowry Shells, Bead Fringe, Hairpipes, Early 1900s, 42 x 10 In.	1093.00
Canoe, Birch Bark, Alberta, Canada, Algonquin, Early 20th Century	3248.00

Indian, Basket, Papago, Triangles, Flared, 7 x 13 In. $59.00

Indian, Belt, Navajo, Silver Oval & Bow-Shaped Medallions, Turquoise, 38 In. $382.00

Indian, Bolo, Zuni, Sun, Inlaid, Silver Tips, Turquoise, Delger Cellicion, 3½-In. Sun $264.00

Indian, Bowl, Santa Clara, Pottery, Black On Black, Bulbous, Tapered Top, 5 x 3½ In.
$147.00

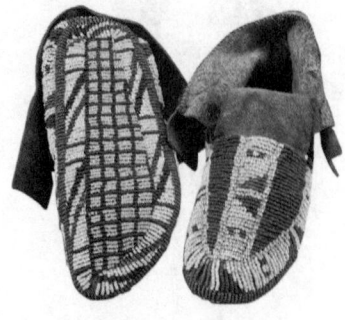

Indian, Moccasins, Sioux, Beaded Tops & Soles, Crimped Cuffs, Women's, 7¾ In.
$1410.00

Canoe, Painted, Pressed Cardboard, Ribbed Interior, Paddle, 17¼ In.	440.00
Case, Bow, Crow, Otter Skin, Beaded In Pink, Blue, White Green, White Heart, 55 In.	21850.00
Choker, Crow, Beaded Orange & Whit Shells, c.1900, 12 In.	135.00
Clapper, Tshimsian, Paddle Shape, Stylized Creature, Bound Handle, c.1900, 23 In.	546.00
Cradle, Crow, Doll, Blue, Green, White, White Heart, Hood Cover, 14½ In.	10350.00
Cradle, Doll, Sioux, Beaded Hide, Red Heart, Yellow & White Beads, 1880, 18 x 5 In.	10925.00
Cradle, Karok, Twine, Sunshade, 19 In.	940.00
Cradle, Sioux, Buffalo Hide, Quillwork, Beadwork, Feathers, Bells, 1870s, 36 x 13 In.	4313.00
Cradle, Sioux, Hide, Beaded, Crosses, Squares, Stepped Diamonds, c.1880, 23 In.	4481.00
Cradle, Sioux, Hide, Beaded Geometrics, White Ground, Brass Hawk Bells, c.1890, 28 In.	5019.00
Cradle, Sioux, Tanned Hide, Calico Cloth, Beaded Flap, Tree Dweller, Crosses, c.1890, 28 In.	5676.00
Cradle, Ute, Wood, Hide, Cloth, Beaded, Stained Hide Attachments, Cloth Sack, Fringe, 29 In.	4400.00
Cradleboard, Ute, Hide-Covered Wood, Beaded Geometrics, Muslin Doll, c.1880, 22 In.	3384.00
Cuffs, Ute, Blue Ground, Lazy Stitch Beading, Valero Stars, c.1910, Boy's, 4¼ x 4½ In.	633.00
Dagger, Tlingit, Steel & Yew Wood, Carved, Bear Or Wolf Form Hilt	28800.00
Dance Club, Pawnee, Ball End, c.1950, 18 x 3 In.	230.00
Dance Roach, Plains, Porcupine Hair Headdress, Horsehair Trim, Early 1900s, 12 In.	259.00
Dance Yoke, Sioux, Fully Beaded, Flowers, Sisseton Reservation, 1930s, Girl's, 15 x 17 In.	316.00
Doll, Cheyenne, Woman Holding Child, Red Wool Dress, Beaded, 12¾ x 4½ In.	316.00
Doll, Crow, Beaded Hide, Sinew-Sewn, Coated With Red Pigment, Facial Features, 11 In.	3450.00
Doll, Crow, Cotton, Hide, Horsehair, Wool Dress, White Seed Beads, c.1890, 6¼ In.	1370.00
Doll, Seminole, Palmetto Fiber Head, Cotton Hide Clothes, Man, Woman, c.1930, 22 In., Pair	747.00
Doll, Skookum, Male, 36 In.	1265.00
Doll Dress, Sioux, Deerskin, Green & Red Triangles, Beadwork, Hide Fringe, c.1880, 11 In.	1912.00
Dress, Cheyenne, Lazy Stitched, Sinew Sewn, Fringe, Early 1900s, 46 x 25 In.	1610.00
Dress Yoke, North Plains, Sioux, Girl's, Buffalo Hide, Fringed, Beaded, c.1870, 17 In.	9400.00
Drum, Kwakiutl, Crescent & Full Moon Sides, Painted Face, Leather, Sinew, Fabric, 13 x 3 In.	431.00
Drum, N.W. Coast, Totemic Images, Trade Wool, Hiada Indian, Wolf Clan, Canada, 1930s, 4 x 13 In.	374.00
Envelope, Sioux, Parfleche, Mineral Painted, Early 1900s, 14 x 7 In.	863.00
Fetish, Sioux, Seed Beaded, Tin Cones, Horsehair, c.1950, 12 x 6 In.	518.00
Gauntlets, Nez Perce, Beaded, Flowers, Early 1900s, 16 In.	1265.00
Goggles, Northwest Coast, Wood, Carved, Tied & Knotted At Nose, 7¾ x 1¾ x 1½ In.	978.00
Headdress, Prairie, Roach, Dyed Red Deer & Porcupine Hair, c.1890, 7¼ x 6 In.	2032.00
Headdress, Prairie, Roach, Dyed Red Deer & Porcupine Hair, Chin Strap, c.1920, 7 x 9 In.	2510.00
Headdress, Sioux, Trail Feather, Beaded, Tradecloth Trailer, Rabbit Fur, c.1910, 21 x 46 In.	1265.00
Horns, Sioux, Buffalo, Center Beaded Panel, Red, Green, White, c.1895, 8 x 12 In.	657.00
Jacket, Plains, Scout, Beaded, Pictures Indians On Horseback, c.1900	3410.00
Jar, Hopi, Pottery, Multicolored, Signed, Al Adams, 3 x 6 In.	147.00
Jar, Pottery, Pueblo, Multicolored, 7 In.	1320.00
Jar, Santa Clara, Blackware, Matte, Carved, 2⅝ x 3 In.	58.00
Jar, Seed, Pottery, Hopi, 3 Color Geometric, Corn Woman, Multicolored, 5 x 11 In.	5875.00
Kachina, Hopi, Wood, Shalako Mana, Red & Black Paint, 3 Stepped Panels, 10¾ In.	21600.00
Knife, Crooked, Carved, Cat Head, 9 In.	115.00
Knife, Crooked, Carved, Signed Joe Founier, 11 In.	173.00
Knife Sheath, Beaded, Blue, White Heart, Red, Yellow, Blue Ground, 9¾ In.	2530.00
Lacrosse Stick, Plains, Hickory, Heat Branded Circles	19200.00
Ladle, Northwest Coast, Horn, Carved, Tapered & Curved Handle, Carved Heads, Frog, 10 In.	345.00
Lamp, Basket, Pima, Coiled, Tray, Base, Shade, 10 In.	3290.00
Leggings, Central Plains, Lakota, Beaded Panels, Multicolored Geometric, Woman's, 14 In.	411.00
Leggings, Central Plains, Lakota, Fringed, Multicolored, Geometric, Man's, 37 In.	1880.00
Leggings, Southern Cheyenne, Green Ocher, Horseshoes, Beaded, Fringe, c.1910, 35 x 14 In.	1495.00
Leggings, Southern Plains, Apache, Beaded Hide, Tabs, Fringe, Boy's, 19½ In., Pair	2350.00
Log Caddy, Penobscot, Birch Bark, Wood, Leaf, Animals, 20 x 14½ x 22 In.	7638.00
Mask, Carved Wood, Multicolored, Hollow Oval, Pierced Mouth, Eyes, 8½ In.	1763.00
Moccasins, Algonquin, Flower Beading, Multicolored, Velvet Cuffs, Silk Binding, 10 In.	144.00
Moccasins, Beadwork, Buckskin, Sinew Sewn, Lazy Stitch, Early 1900s, 10½ In.	1150.00
Moccasins, Blackfoot, Ceremonial Black, Beaded Vamp, Lazy Stitch, 1890, 10½ In.	1335.00
Moccasins, Central Plains, Cheyenne, Hard Sole, Multicolored, Geometric, 10½ In.	880.00
Moccasins, Central Plains, Lakota, Beaded, Divided Tongue, Multicolored, 9½ In.	2958.00
Moccasins, Central Plains, Lakota, Hard Sole, Multicolored, Geometric, 11 In.	1000.00
Moccasins, Central Plains, Lakota, Hard Sole, Multicolored, Geometric, Child's, 6 In.	323.00
Moccasins, Cheyenne, High Top, Woman's, 1800s, 17 x 9½ In.	4510.00
Moccasins, Cheyenne, U-Shaped Beaded Panel, c.1890, 9½ In.	837.00
Moccasins, Chippewa, Puckered Toe, Beaded Velvet Panels, Early 1900s, 9½ In.	316.00
Moccasins, Cree, Embroidered Hide, Floral, Blue Silk Bow, Child's	4200.00
Moccasins, Deerskin, Red, Green, Yellow Beads On White Ground, 10¾ In.	220.00

Moccasins, Huron, Hide, Quillwork Panels, Rows Of Metal Cones, 10½ In.		51000.00
Moccasins, Northern Arapaho, Rawhide Sole, Beaded, Lazy Stitch, Late 1800s, 9½ In.		1610.00
Moccasins, Northern Plains, Center Row Of Cones, 19th Century, 11 In.		880.00
Moccasins, Northern Plains, Tanned & Rawhide, Ocher Rub, Beaded Flowers, c.1890, 11 In.		14434.00
Moccasins, Plains, Beaded, Yellow Ocher, c.1900, 10 In.		1116.00
Moccasins, Plains Cree, Fully Beaded, Elk Hide, c.1925, 10½ In.		920.00
Moccasins, Sioux, Beaded Tops & Soles, Crimped Cuffs, Women's, 7¾ In.	*illus*	1410.00
Moccasins, Sioux, Deerskin, Ocher Rub, Sinew Sewn, Beaded Crosses, c.1880, 7¾ In.		777.00
Moccasins, Sioux, Parfleche Soles, Beaded Vamp, c.1890, 10½ In.		1058.00
Moccasins, Southern Plains, Arapaho, Beaded, Hard Sole, Multicolored, Geometric, 9½ In.		1528.00
Mug, Anasazi, Black & White, 4⅜ x 4 In.		1155.00
Necklace, Apache, Shawl Shape, Beaded Steps, Beadwork Bottom, c.1890, 10 x 21 In.		837.00
Necklace, Naja Pendant, 10 Squash Blossom, Silver Beads, Turquoise, 15 In.		266.00
Necklace, Navajo, Squash, 10 Blossoms, 15 Turquoise Cabochons, Stamped FG, 27 In.		2185.00
Necklace, Navajo, Squash Blossom, 12 Silver Blossoms, Turquoise Cabochons, 28½ In.		633.00
Necklace, Navajo, Squash Blossom, 14 Blossoms, 5 Turquoise Cabochons, 1940s, 22 In.		288.00
Necklace, Navajo, Squash Blossom, Flutes, Beads, Silver, Turquoise, 1935, 3 x 3-In. Naja *illus*		287.00
Necklace, Navajo, Squash Blossom, Silver, Turquoise, Red Coral, 26 In.		936.00
Necklace, Shadowbox, Squash Blossom, 14 Silver Blossoms, Turquoise Cabochons, 25 In.		863.00
Necklace, Southwestern, Squash Blossom, Sterling, Fluted Beads, Jade Naja, 23 In.		374.00
Necklace, Zuni, Squash Blossom, Silver, Petit Point Turquoise, 1940s, 21 In.		920.00
Olla, Apache, Cross-Banded Diamonds, Crosses, 10½ x 9 In.		2415.00
Olla, Southwest, Pottery, Black, Cream, Abstract, Painted, Globe, 12 x 14½ In.		1763.00
Olla, Yavapai, Figural, Coiled, 9 Humans, 4 Dogs, 13 Wolves, 9 Deer, 19 x 18 In.		24150.00
Pad, Saddle, Cree, Floral Beadwork, Pink & Red, Blue, Orange, Green, 25 x 27 In.		7475.00
Parfleche, Cheyenne, Rawhide, Painted, 1930s, 6 x 3½ In.		489.00
Parfleche, Sioux, Buckskin, Full Beaded Front, Lazy Stitch, Early 1900s, 8 x 12½ In.		2588.00
Pipe, Assiniboin, Wood, Stone Bowl, Scalloped Design		45000.00
Pipe, Haida, Effigy, Copper Bowl, Raven, Bear, Inlaid Abalone Trim, 1910, 10 x 1 x 2 In.		2300.00
Pipe, Plains, Classic T Bowl, Quill Work, Horse Hair Drop, Ash Stem, 1800s, 27½ In.		2750.00
Pipe Bag, Beaded, Flower & Leaf Panels, Fringe, Inscribed, Sioux Dakota, Early 1900s		1195.00
Pipe Bag, Sioux, Antelope Hide, Beadwork, Buffalo Rawhide Slats, c.1880, 36 x 6 In.		2875.00
Pouch, Apache, Beaded Hide, Multicolored, Geometric, Cone Danglers, Fringe, 10½ In.		1293.00
Pouch, Blackfoot, Beaded Hide, 4¾ In.		5400.00
Pouch, Cheyenne, Hide, Beaded, 12¼ In.		764.00
Pouch, Southern Plains, Beaded Hide, Flap, Multicolored, Geometric, Danglers, 7 In.		2115.00
Rattle, Kwakiutl, Owl, Wood, Carved & Painted, 12½ x 5 x 4½ In.		5060.00
Rattle, Peyote, Gourd, Engraved, Painted, Sun, Lightning, Wood, Hide Handle, Beaded, 12 In.		1619.00
Rattle, Salish, Northwest Coast, Wood, Carved, Painted, Sunburst Shape, Wool Fringe, 11 x 6 In.		1265.00
Ring, Hopi, Silver, Coral, Turquoise & Lapis Bands, Signed, Loloma, 20th Century		7800.00
Ring, Navajo, Silver, Coral, c.1950		59.00
Rug, Navajo, 2 Diamonds, Central, Brown, Tan, White Carded Ground, 55 x 34 In.		374.00
Rug, Navajo, 2 Gray Hills, Diamond, Fret Edged Corners, Stepped Borders, 87 x 68 In.		2468.00
Rug, Navajo, 2 Gray Hills, Geometric, Brown, White Fret Border, 20th Century, 122 x 63 In.		5288.00
Rug, Navajo, 3 Serrated Diamonds, Red Field, Stepped & Barpole Borders, 86 x 60 In.		2070.00
Rug, Navajo, Banded Geometrics, Multicolored, Gray Ground, 62 x 41 In.		1800.00
Rug, Navajo, Black, Red, Gray Ground, 20th Century, 81 x 43 In.		470.00
Rug, Navajo, Brown & White Geometric, Beige Field, 1920s, 49 x 75 In.		518.00
Rug, Navajo, Diamonds, Red, Cream, Black On Brown Ground, Red Border, c.1920, 69 x 51 In.		500.00
Rug, Navajo, Diamonds, Zigzag, Red, Gray, Brown, Transitional, c.1910, 98 x 72 In.		700.00
Rug, Navajo, Diamonds & Stripes, Red, Brown, Black, Tan Ground, c.1940, 76 x 56 In.		475.00
Rug, Navajo, Eye Dazzler, Serrated Designs, c.1930, 77¾ x 52¼ In.		978.00
Rug, Navajo, Ganado, Double Dye, Red, Gray, Black, White, 57 x 30 In.		173.00
Rug, Navajo, Geometric, Red, Black, Cream, On Gray Ground, c.1920, 84 x 54 In.		700.00
Rug, Navajo, Geometric, Stepped Squared, Brown, Cream, c.1930, 66 x 34 In.		750.00
Rug, Navajo, Multicolored Banded, Central Lightning, 19th Century, 76 x 50 In.		940.00
Rug, Navajo, Multicolored Diamond Rows, 82¼ x 50½ In.		1265.00
Rug, Navajo, Pictorial, Red, Brown, Beige, 58 x 37 In.		1020.00
Rug, Navajo, Reservation, Serrated Diamond, Multicolored, 60 x 43 In.		2415.00
Rug, Navajo, Storm Pattern, Zigzags, Geometrics, Crabs, Arrows, 46 x 72 In.		1495.00
Rug, Navajo, Stripes, Red, Green, Brown, Ivory, Orange, 51 x 36 In.		960.00
Rug, Navajo, Stripes, Stylized Diamonds, Gray, Black, Brown, Chinle Revival, c.1930, 70 x 49 In.		475.00
Rug, Navajo, Stylized Diamonds, Black & Purple Stripes, Red, Hubbell, Moki, c.1900, 71 x 48 In.		3600.00
Rug, Navajo, Stylized Diamonds, Red, Brown, Gray On Cream Ground, c.1940, 77 x 38 In.		425.00
Rug, Navajo, Wool, Serrated Diamond, Crosses, Whirling Log, 75½ x 44½ In.		1293.00
Rug, Navajo, Yei, Cornstalks, Feathers, c.1930, 56½ x 80 In.	*illus*	3465.00

Indian, Necklace, Navajo, Squash Blossom, Flutes, Beads, Silver, Turquoise, c.1935, 3 x 3-In. Naja
$287.00

American Indian Jewelry
Early jewelry worn by American Indians was made for their use in ceremonies and as portable wealth. Later jewelry was made to sell to tourists. In 1935 Congress tried to promote development in Indian communities. New silversmiths were trained, and guilds and cooperatives were formed. Indian jewelry became more artistic and more expensive. After World War II, new Indian artists made jewelry pieces with a modern look using traditional materials. Indian trade jewelry is lighter in weight and more highly polished than older jewelry. It is often decorated with arrows, suns, thunderbirds, and other traditional designs.

Indian, Rug, Navajo, Yei, Cornstalks, Feathers, c.1930, 56½ x 80 In. $3465.00

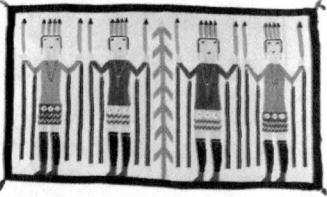

Inkstand, Ormolu, Harlequin, Bowing, Art Nouveau, 2 Pots, 3-Footed, 10 In. $588.00

Saddle, Crow, Wood, Buffalo Hide, Beaded Pommel & Cantle, Fringe, Hawk Bells, c.1875, 17 In.	8365.00
Saddlebag, Sioux, Bead, Cobalt, Rose, 3 Triangles & Tin Cones, Fringe, 49 x 15 In.	7475.00
Sash, Huron, Finger Woven, Long Fringe, Early 1800s, 150 In.	440.00
Serape, Navajo, Serrated Diamonds, Checkerboard, Moki Striped, c.1870, Man's, 73½ x 53 In.	131450.00
Sewing Bag, Omaha, Buffalo Hide, Hair Attached, Beaded Edges, Scalloped Flap, c.1865, 8 x 12 In.	1016.00
Shirt, Cree, Buckskin, Flowers, Crosses, 1890s, 32 x 19 In.	633.00
Shirt, Crow, Red, 1940s	605.00
Shirt, Plains, Scout, Hide, Pullover Form, Collar, Fringed Seams, 33 In.	880.00
Shirt, Prairie, Beaded, Black Ground, c.1900, 36 In.	2350.00
Shirt, Seminole, Patchwork, Appliqued Cotton, Rayon, c.1930, Man's, 35 In.	470.00
Shirt, Southern Plains, Comanche, Pony Beaded Cloth, Hide Strips, Fringe, 30 In.	7050.00
Shirt, Wild West Show, Hide, Multicolored, Embroidered, Flowers, Clamshell Buttons, 35 In.	940.00
Snowshoes, Cree, Bear Paw Style	92.00
Spoon, Northwest Coast, Totemic, Goat Horn, 9 In.	468.00
Spoon, Potlatch, Northwest Coast, Carved Totemic Figures, 10½ In.	110.00
Tile, Zia, Multicolored, Bird, Plants, c.1950, 6 x 6 In.	1725.00
Tobacco Bag, Crow, Deerskin, Yellow Ocher Rub, Beaded Flowers, Fringe, c.1885, 26 x 5 In.	3884.00
Tobacco Bag, Southern Cheyenne, 19th Century, 16 x 3¼ In.	413.00
Totem Pole, Northwest Coast, 7 Figures, 25½ In.	863.00
Tray, Basket, Hopi, 3rd Mesa, Multicolored, Butterfly Maiden, 1920s, 8½ In.	460.00
Tray, Basket, Hopi, Coiled, Radiating Design, Yellow, Brown, Black, 11¾ In.	230.00
Tray, Basket, Pima, 10 Human Figures With Star Design, 14½ In.	853.00
Vase, Olla, Pueblo, Center Handle, Black, Santa Clara, 9¼ In.	83.00
Vest, Central Plains, Lakota, Beaded Hide, Multicolored Geometric, 20 In.	4113.00
Vest, Nez Perce, Fully Beaded, Flowers, Early 1900s, Man's, 2½ x 21 In.	3163.00
Vest, Yakima, Flowers, Full Beaded, Late 1800s, Man's, 22 x 19 In.	2875.00
Wall Hanging, Seal Of Cherokee Nation, Star, Oak Leaves, Acorns, Appliqued, Frame, 1869, 32 In.	633.00
Wall Pocket, Northwest, Tlingit, Beaded, Cloth, 3 Panels, Eagle, Frog, Bear, Flower, 10 x 27½ In.	5580.00
Wall Pocket, Plains, Beaded, Wood Frame, 15 In.	165.00
War Club, Plains, Granite, Double Cone Head, Rawhide, 21 In.	242.00
War Club, Sioux, Buffalo Horn, Wood Haft, Hide Bound, Fully Beaded, c.1900, 27 x 8½ In.	489.00
Weaving, Chimayo, Central Lozenge, Multicolored Stripes, Fringe, c.1910, 67 x 38 In.	460.00
Weaving, Navajo, 4 Yei Figures, c.1950, 18 x 36 In.	127.00
Weaving, Navajo, Elongated Chevrons, Sawtooth Edge, c.1940, 66¼ x 43 In.	546.00
Weaving, Navajo, Eye Dazzler, Serrated Diamonds, c.1940, 84¼ x 49 In.	1495.00
Weaving, Navajo, Serrated Diamond, c.1930, 66 x 37 In.	1150.00
Wedding Jar, Olla, Southwest, Redware, Handle, Pedestal, 12 x 10 In.	1058.00

INDIAN TREE is a china pattern that was popular during the last half of the nineteenth century. It was copied from earlier Indian textile patterns that were very similar. The pattern includes the crooked branch of a tree and a partial landscape with exotic flowers and leaves. Green, blue, pink, and orange were the favored colors used in the design.

Creamer, Pink Flowers, Black Hearts, Gold Trim, Bowtie Border, No. 2, Stamped, 3¾ In.	15.00
Ramekin, Pink Flowers, Blue & Green Leaves, Gold Trim, Greek Key Border, Stamped, 1¼ x 4 In.	22.00
Serving Bowl, Oval, Warwick, 1940, 1¾ x 7 x 5¼ In.	12.00
Serving Bowl, Scammell's Trenton China, Oval, 2 x 9 x 7 In.	12.00
Soup, Dish, Pink Flowers, Black Hearts, Gold Trim, Bowtie Border, No. 2, Stamped, 7⅜ In.	15.00

INKSTANDS were made to be placed on a desk. They held some type of container for ink, and possibly a sander, a pen tray, a pen, a holder for pounce, and even a candle to melt the sealing wax. Inkstands date to the eighteenth century and have been made of silver, copper, and glass. Additional inkstands may be found in these and other related categories.

Bronze, Blotter, Dore, France, 19th Century, 10 x 5½ In.	1250.00
Bronze, Cherub, Holding Grapes, Ewer, Ram Heads, 19th Century	495.00
Bronze, Vines, Pierced, France, 6 x 9 x 19 In.	293.00
Burl Walnut, Painted Black, Pedestal Footed, Cathedral, c.1880, 14 x 6¼ In.	475.00
Cut Glass, Double, Obelisk, Thermometer, Black Glass Tray, Pen Rest, 3⅜ x 1⅝ In.	175.00
Gilt Bronze, American Bison, Cut Panel Crystal, c.1900, 7 In.	940.00
Gilt Bronze, Tortoiseshell Glass, 2 Wells, Covers, Storage Chest, 16 In.	499.00
Gilt Bronze, Victorian, Rococo Scrolled Base, Threaded Glass Well, 8½ In.	499.00
Glass, Art Deco, Rectangular Base, Pen Rests, 2 Davis Automatic Wells, 12 x 6½ In.	143.00
Glass, Clear, Pewter Cap, Gold Plated, Rosette Shape, 1¾ In.	125.00
Inkwell, Sander, Box, Boat Shape, Silver Plate, England, 19th Century, 3 x 9½ x 3½ In.	288.00
Marble, Bronze, Master, France, 19th Century, 14 x 7 In.	293.00
Marble, Green, Arched Clock Center, Gold Eagle, Swags, Gilt Pots, Top Shape Feet, 11 x 13 In.	1020.00

I

Milk Glass, Igloo, Kettle Shape Metal Carrier, 1875-95, 3½ In. 532.00

Ormolu, Harlequin, Bowing, Art Nouveau, 2 Pots, 3-Footed, 10 In. *illus* 588.00

Pewter, Double, Rectangular, 2 Compartments, Lids, 6 Pen Holes, 2 Drawers, c.1790, 4¾ In. 1838.00

Porcelain, Bisque, 2 Dogs Attacking Boar, Inkwell, Sander, Continental, 7 In. 118.00

Pressed Glass, Blue, Thermometer, Hinged Top, 3½ In., 4 Piece 253.00

Pressed Glass, Daisy & Button, Thermometer, Hinged Top, 3¼ In. 121.00

Pressed Glass, Electric Blue, Ribs, Hinged Brass Tops, Pen Ledge, Rayed Base, 2⅛ In. 231.00

Rectangular, Paw Feet, Bolted Strapwork, Silver, c.1830, 14 In. 7200.00

Silver Plate, Cover, Bun Supports, Hinged Dome, 2 Wells, c.1930, 3½ x 5¾ In. 58.00

Silver Plate, Cranberry, Pen Rest, 2 Bottles, Elkington & Co., c.1871, 7½ x 6 In. 450.00

Slate, Clock, Figural Brass, Roman Gladiator, Trumpet, 13½ x 8½ In. 750.00

Walnut, Tags, Patent Model, Gutta-Percha, Beveled Ink Reservoir Base, 1860s 425.00

Wood, Painted Black, Blue Pressed Glass, Sander, Nib, Wafer Bowl, Pen Rest, 8 x 4½ In. 275.00

INKWELLS, of course, held ink. Ready-made ink was first made about 1836 and was sold in bottles. The desk inkwell had a narrow hole so the pen would not slip inside. Inkwells were made of many materials, such as pottery, glass, pewter, and silver. Look in these categories for more listings of inkwells.

Bakelite, Green, 2 Pens, 9 x 4 In. 225.00

Boulle, Crystal, Deep Cut Pattern, Brass, Bronze Inlay, 19th Century 1400.00

Brass, Ceramic, Domed Cover, Allover Flowers, Victorian, c.1870, 5 x 2½ In. 47.00

Brass, Ceramic Liner, Engraved, Finial, c.1860, 4¼ In. 155.00

Brass, Hinged Lid, Ceramic Insert, 2⅝ x 3 In. 150.00

Brass, Mahogany, 2-Tone, Decorative Center, Glass Insert, 19th Century 295.00

Brass, Metal Liner, Covered Bottom, c.1850, 3⅞ x 2¾ In. 145.00

Brass, Pivot Cover, Spool Shape, c.1690-1730 350.00

Bronze, Boar's Head Shape, 4 x 7 In. 117.00

Bronze, Embossed, Pen Tray, Hinged Lid, Seminude Woman, 5 Putti, 2 Wells, 7 x 16 In. *illus* 3450.00

Bronze, Pen Rest, Arts & Crafts, Patina, O & K Co., 2¼ x 11 In. 176.00

Bronze, Renaissance Style, Patinated, Masks, Lidded Wells, Avian Handles, 3 x 9 In. 123.00

Bronze, Roses, Butterflies, Ormolu, Landscape, Paris, c.1870 325.00

Cameo Glass, Engraved Glass Base, Multicolored, Acid Etched, 2¾ x 3¾ In. 642.00

Cast Iron, Blown Glass Well, Elk Head, Large Antlers, Painted, 3 x 6½ In. 138.00

Cast Metal, Bear, Painted, Jennings Brothers, 19th Century 225.00

Cast Metal, Bronze Finish, Art Nouveau, Hinged Cover, Glass Insert, Jennings, 3 x 3½ In. 125.00

Cast Metal, Hinged Lid, Woman In Water, Flowing Hair, Ceramic Insert, 8½ x 7 x 3 In. 125.00

Champleve, Enamel, Metal Line Design, Urn Shape, 4-Footed, Tray, c.1900, 2½ x 7 In. 165.00

Champleve, Enamel, Bronze, Green Onyx, Pen Rest, 19th Century, 3 x 5 In. 295.00

Copper, Hammered, Arts & Crafts, Applied Decoration, Glass Insert, 4 x 4¼ In. 495.00

Copper, Hammered, Double, Brass Hinges, Arts & Crafts, Gustav Stickley, 11 x 7 In. *illus* 4313.00

Cut Glass, Cover, Flaubert, Baccarat, 6 In. *illus* 200.00

Cut Glass, Frosted, On Brass Tray, Hinged Brass Top, Greek Theme, 9½ x 4½ In. 450.00

Cut Glass, Silver Top, Tray, Swag, Ball Feet, c.1900, 4¾ x 3½ In. 400.00

Glass, Black Amethyst, 3½ In. 185.00

Glass, Blown, Aqua Green, Uncontrolled Bubble, Sheared Pontil, Stopper, 4 x 4¾ In. 275.00

Glass, Blown, Barrel Cobalt Blue, Spout, Brass Collar, 2⅛ x 2 In. 143.00

Glass, Blown, Olive Green, 14-Diamond Base, Pontil, 2 x 2⅝ In. 209.00

Glass, Blown, Yellow Olive Green, Plain Base, Pontil, 1¾ x 2¼ In. 220.00

Glass, Blown Molded, Olive Amber, 16-Diamond Base, Pontil, 1¾ x 2 In. 209.00

Glass, Blown Molded, Olive Amber, Plain Base, Pontil, ½ x 2¼ In. 143.00

Glass, Bottle, Aqua Green, Applied Top, Pontil, 3⅓ x 3½ In. 230.00

Glass, Brass Lid, Gold Wash, Star, c.1860, 2 x 3½ In. 235.00

Glass, Bristol, Cobalt Blue, Cut Flutes, Polished Pontil, Hinged Bronze Top, c.1790, 5 x 2½ In. 650.00

Glass, Cobalt Blue Funnel Well, Red, Yellow, Green, Blue Devils Fire, 1865-75, 4¼ In. 335.00

Glass, Cow Horn, 9 x 4 x 3 In. 175.00

Glass, Dark Aqua, Applied Baluster, Round Foot, Open Pontil, 1840-60, 5 In. 280.00

Glass, Gold Plated Pewter Cap, Rosette Shape, 1¾ In. 125.00

Glass, Leather Pen Rest, 4¾ x 3¾ In. 48.00

Glass, Paperweight, Clear, Abstract, Blue, White, Texas Glass Co., 4½ In. 60.00

Glass, Pitkin Type, 36 Ribs, Swirled To Left, Inverted Conical, Yellow Olive, 1¾ x 2 In. 672.00

Lucite, Red, Clear, Penholder, Pen, 3 x 3 x 3 In. 145.00

Majolica, Tin, Glazed, Leaf Decorated Underplate, Apple Shape, c.1900, 5¾ x 3 In. 225.00

Metal, Camel, Reclining, Saddle, Painted, Glass Insert, Hinged Lid, 5½ x 8 In. 345.00

Metal, Terrier, With Pups, Victorian, c.1890, 4 x 5¾ In. 205.00

Millefiori, Concentric Rings Of Canes, Clear Ground, Domed Stopper, 5¾ In. *illus* 1265.00

TIP

Watch out for exploding antiques! Guns, shells, powder cans, nitrate movie film, and some chemicals left in old bottles or cans are dangerous. If you don't know about these items, contact your local police or fire department for help.

Inkwell, Bronze, Embossed, Pen Tray, Hinged Lid, Seminude Woman, 5 Putti, 2 Wells, 7 x 16 In. $3450.00

Inkwell, Copper, Hammered, Double, Brass Hinges, Arts & Crafts, Gustav Stickley, 11 x 7 In. $4313.00

Inkwell, Cut Glass, Cover, Flaubert, Baccarat, 6 In. $200.00

Inkwell, Millefiori,
Concentric Rings Of Canes,
Clear Ground, Domed Stopper, 5¾ In.
$1265.00

Inkwell, Ram's Horns,
Silver Mount, Stag's Head, Hoof,
2 Wells, Walker & Hall,
Sheffield, 9 x 22 In.
$2880.00

Inkwell, Wood, Skull,
Snake Interlaced Through Ear,
Eye, Head, Hinged Lid,
Glass Well, 2⅝ In.
$101.00

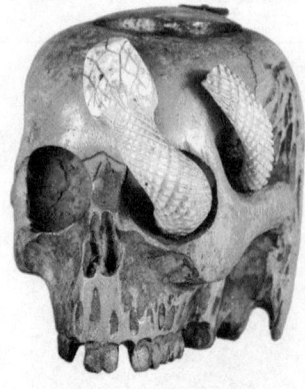

Onyx, Bronze Moose, 10¾ x 5 In.	117.00
Opaline Insert, Napoleon III, Gilt Ormolu, Enameled, Medallion, William The Conqueror	395.00
Porcelain, Cover, Pink Flowers, Cream Ground, RS Prussia	175.00
Porcelain, Gilt Bronze Mounted, Hand Painted, 19th Century, 5¼ In.	646.00
Porcelain, Painted, Round, Mushroom Shape Cover, Star Cutouts, Tray, 5 x 3½ In.	125.00
Porcelain, Pounce Pot, Pomegranate, Flower, Ocher, Yellow, Puce, c.1760, 3¼ In., 2 Piece	1440.00
Pot Metal, Bulldog, Wearing Derby Hat, 3½ In.	275.00
Pressed Glass, Early Thumbprint, Rayed Base, Hinged Brass Mount, Stopper, 3 x 3½ In.	253.00
Ram's Horns, Silver Mount, Stag's Head, Hoof, 2 Wells, Walker & Hall, Sheffield, 9 x 22 In. ....*illus*	2880.00
Scalloped Edges, Blue, Opalescent, Swirls, 19th Century	55.00
Silver, Crystal, Scallops, Flowers, Cut Starburst, c.1898, 2½ x 3½ In.	750.00
Silver, Hawkesworth Eyre Ltd., Sheffield, Edwardian, c.1904, 4 x 4½ In.	293.00
Silver, Repousse, Cut Crystal, c.1890, 3 x 2⅜ In.	290.00
Silver Plate, 2 Owls, Twig Base, Glass Eyes, Meriden Silver Plate Co., 6 x 7½ In.	345.00
Silver Plate, Alpaca Cover, Hand Hammered, c.1905, 4¼ In.	8400.00
Silver Plate, White Metal, Flowers, Art Nouveau, Jennings Brothers, 3 x 3 In.	125.00
Soapstone, Carved, Square, Swirled Domed Filler Hold, 4 Dipping Holes, 1799, 3 In.	705.00
Stoneware, Cobalt Blue Leaves, Center Well, 5 Quill Holes, P.J. Houghtaling, 8 x 2 In.	3335.00
Stoneware, Round, Filler Hole, 2 Dipping Holes, Incised Letters, 1770, 1½ x 3½ In.	4113.00
Toleware, Traveling, Double Lid, Stainless Lid, Small Ink Bottle, 2¼ x 1½ In.	68.00
Traveling, Mary Troby, London, George III, Silver Plate, c.1810, 1¼ In.	26.00
Traveling, Pocket Watch Form, Brass, England, c.1700	475.00
White, Gold Decoration, Limoges, France, c.1960, 1¾ x 8 In.	351.00
Wood, Bear On Log, Hinged Lid, Glass Well, Pen Trough, Black Forest, 7 x 6¼ In.	495.00
Wood, Skull, Snake Interlaced Through Ear, Eye, Head, Hinged Lid, Glass Well, 2⅝ In. .*illus*	101.00
Wooden, Treen, Turned, Soft Finish, Pottery Insert, Brown Salt Glaze, 3 x 4⅞ In.	403.00

INSULATORS of glass or pottery have been made for use on telegraph or telephone poles since 1844. Thousands of different styles of insulators have been made. Most common are those of clear or aqua glass; most desirable are the threadless types made from 1850 to 1870.

Brookfield, Dark Green, Teeth Along Bottom, 3½ In.	18.00
Brookfield, No. 010, Aqua, Amber Swirls	25.00
Brookfield, No. 010, Green Aqua	220.00
Brookfield, No. 450, Side Wire Groove, Single Petticoat, Embossed, Yellow Green	255.00
C.E.W., No. 020, Frothy Aqua	1000.00
C.E.W., No. 030, Dark Purple	700.00
C.E.W., No. 030, Straw	550.00
California, No. 010, Yellow	1075.00
Columbia, No. 040, Dark Aqua	150.00
Diamond, No. 040, Milky Aqua, Wire Groove, Dome	20.00
Diamond, No. 135, Midnight Blue	370.00
Duquesne, No. 020, Light Cornflower Blue, Embossed	110.00
E.C. & M. Co. S.F., Tobacco Amber, 4 In.	3960.00
Good, No. 010, Side Wire Groove, Single Petticoat, Annealing Lines In Dome, Purple	125.00
Good, No. 010, Side Wire Groove, Single Petticoat, Green, Solid Dome, Amber Swirls	100.00
H.G. Co., Aqua Glass, Embossed H, 4¼ x 3¼ In.	5.00
H.G. Co., No. 070, Side Wire Groove, Double Petticoat, Dark Cornflower Blue	360.00
Hemingray, Green, Threaded, Wood Pin, Straw Marks, Bubbles, Pat. Oct. 8, 1907, 4¼ In.	8.00
Hemingray, No. 56, Clear, Corrugated Base, Embossed 22-57	12.00
Hemingray, No. 040, Side Wire Groove, Double Petticoat, Annealing Line In Dome, Carnival	170.00
Hemingray, No. 040, Side Wire Groove, Double Petticoat, Mustard Yellow, Clouds Of Milk	425.00
Hemingray, No. 070, Side Wire Groove, Double Petticoat, Dark Cobalt Blue	420.00
Hemingray, No. 070, Side Wire Groove, Double Petticoat, Red Amber	275.00
Hemingray, No. 090, Yellow Amber	485.00
Hemingray, No. 240, Side Wire Groove, Double Petticoat, Sapphire Blue	960.00
Hoop Skirt, Mahogany Glaze	15.00
Knowles, No. 030, Blue	220.00
Locke, No. 010, Glowing Peacock Blue	1900.00
McLaughlin, No. 030, Citrine Green	250.00
Pyrex, No. 453, 1 Piece, Light Yellow	40.00
Santa Ana, No. 020, Yellow Green	175.00
Side Wire Groove, Single Petticoat, Annealing Lines On Dome, Bubbles, Teal Green, Pat. 1871	670.00
Star, No. 010, Grooves, Open Bubble On Umbrella, Front Base, Blue Aqua	95.00
Telegraphos, No. 030, Yellow Golden	200.00
W.E. Mfg., No. 010, Side Wire Groove, Single Petticoat, 4, Lime Green, Milky Swirls	85.00

Whitall Tatum, Peach, 4 x 3¾ In.	18.00
Zicme, Glass Spool, Nail Nobs, Columbia, Cranberry Violet	95.00

IRISH BELLEEK, *see Belleek category.*

IRON is a metal that has been used by man since prehistoric times. It is a popular metal for tools and decorative items like doorstops that need as much weight as possible. Items are listed here or under other appropriate headings, such as Bookends, Doorstop, Kitchen, Match Holder, or Tool. The tool that is used for ironing clothes, an iron, is listed in the Kitchen category under Iron and Sadiron.

Ashtray, Frying Pan, Wagner Ware	14.00
Ax Head, Curved Blade, Talicot, Hand Forged, 19th Century, 6½ x 9¾ In.	259.00
Ball & Chain, Yale Lock, 6½-In. Ball, 36-In. Chain	316.00
Bell, Plantation, Cast, Signed On Yoke, Brackets, Clapper, Wheel, G.S. Bell Co., 31 x 24 In.	2115.00
Book Press, Dolphin Design On Molded Base, Marked 3, 22 x 11½ x 14 In.	374.00
Box, Arts & Crafts, Raised Dome, Relief Decorated, Flowers, Early 1900s, 2½ x 9 In.	176.00
Box, Chiseled, Naturalistic, Scrolling Vines, Hand Forged, Mid 1800s	450.00
Box, Document, Casket Shape, Decorative Swags, Rope Twist, Black Painted, 12 x 8 In.	189.00
Bullet Mold, Small Caliber, Scissor Shape, Flintlock Rifle Mold, Hand Forged, c.1776, 5 In.	257.00
Candle Mold, Cast, Double France, 11 In.	115.00
Candle Snuffer, Scissor Shape, 6½ In.	61.00 to 88.00
Candle Snuffer, Signed, 18th Century	110.00
Candleholder, 3-Footed, 11 In.	247.00
Card Holder, Frog, Green, Yellow, Cast Iron, Hubley, ⅜ x 2⅛ In.	685.00
Carousel Head, Viking, Cast Iron, Signed, 46, No. 1, 1919, 11¾ x 7⅞ In., Pair	1456.00
Cigar Cutter, Dunce, Boy, Seated With Slate, Painted, Blade Inside Mouth, Pat. 1885, 6¼ In.	330.00
Coin Tray, Cast, Nickel Slots, Pat., 1890, 11¼ x 6½ In.	105.00
Compote, Oval, Pierced Scroll, Leaf Design, Domed, Fluted, 7⅞ x 22½ In.	3290.00
Cork Sizer, Alligator, 3 Diameters, 4½ x 11 In.	170.00
Cuspidor, Dragon, Turtle, Hinged Lid, Removable Pan, 5 x 12 x 9 In.	425.00
Cuspidor, Turtle, Bronze Finish, Pat.1891, 13 x 10 In.	530.00
Cuspidor, Turtle, Copper Flashed, Removable Pan, Golden Jacobs, Chicago, 4 x 11 x 13 In.	240.00
Cuspidor, Turtle, Green Paint, Hinged Back, Early 20th Century, 14 In.	146.00
Cuspidor, Turtle, Metal Shell, Removable Pan, 5 x 14 x 11 In.	250.00
Directional, Heart, S-Shape Hangers, 19th Century, 35 In.	385.00
Doorknocker, Skier, Holding Skis, Cast, 12½ In. *illus*	410.00
Figure, Black Man, In Chair, Top Hat, Cast, Painted, 8¼ In.	443.00
Figure, Bonzo, Tin Umbrella, Painted, Early 1930s, 5 In.	80.00
Figure, Bust, Horses Head, Cast, Wood Plinth, 13½ In.	21.00
Figure, Deer, Brown, White, Black Eyes & Nose, Cast, Rectangular Base, Buck, Doe, Fawn	5750.00
Figure, Dog, Standing, Cast Iron, Poultney, Vermont Foundry, 1800s, Life Size	8050.00
Figure, Felix The Cat, Painted, Signed Felix On Chest, 2⅞ x 2½ In.	336.00
Figure, Great Dane, Cast, Rectangular Plinth, 20th Century, 43 x 22 In., Pair	880.00
Figure, Guanyin, Seated On Lotus Throne, Holding Vase, Chinese, 15 In.	1357.00
Figure, Kuan Ti, Goddess Of War, Standing, Chinese, 12 In.	881.00
Figure, Mermaid, Silhouette, Hand Forged, Incised Scales, Mass., c.1850, 9¼ In.	575.00
Figure, Rhinoceros, Charging Pose, Cast, 11 x 8¼ x 17½ In., Pair	235.00
Figure, Statue Of Liberty, White, Cast, 18 x 5⅜ In.	392.00
Game Hanger, Hand Forged, Round Frame, Triple Drop Hooks, 15 x 9½ In.	110.00
Game Hook, Wrought, 4 Crown Hooks, Suspended From Chains, Ring Hanger, 10½ x 12 In.	201.00
Handcuffs, No Key, From Calabases, California, Jail, 1880s	440.00
Ladles, Wrought, Brass Bowl, Ring Terminal, 9¾ & 12 In., 2 Piece	209.00
Lamp Hanger, Wrought, Center Heart, Repeated Scroll On Crest, 7½ In.	187.00
Lamp Hanger, Wrought, Notched Round Crest, Semi Circular Hook, 5½ In.	28.00
Letter Holder, Automobile, Roadster, Cast Iron, Judd Co., 4¼ x 5⅝ In.	308.00
Mailbox, Owl, Arts & Crafts, 11½ x 9½ In.	205.00
Ornament, Tree, Birds, Fruits, Flowers, In Basket, Painted, 20th Century, 13¼ In., Pair	748.00
Padlock, Figural, Hunchback Clown, Pointy Cap, Hinged Arm, Cast, 3 In. *illus*	1150.00
Paperweight, Boy Fishing, Kissing Girl, Pink Dress, Blue Coat & Pants, 3 x 2½ In.	168.00
Paperweight, Bunny, White, Brown, Black, 3 x 2½ In.	280.00
Paperweight, Colt, Brown, Black, White, Hubley, 4 In.	140.00
Paperweight, Dog, Boston Bull Dog, Red Collar, Hubley, 3 x 3½ In.	252.00
Paperweight, Dog, Cocker Spaniel, Hubley, Box, 2½ x 3½ In.	336.00
Paperweight, Dog, Fido, Hubley, 1½ In.	112.00
Paperweight, Dog, Scottie, Hubley, 3 x 3½ In.	140.00

Iron, Doorknocker, Skier, Holding Skis, Cast, 12½ In. $410.00

Iron, Padlock, Figural, Hunchback Clown, Pointy Cap, Hinged Arm, Cast, 3 In. $1150.00

TIP

Andirons get tarnished and covered with resin from the smoke so should be cleaned with liquid metal polish and 0000-grade steel wool.

TIP
To clean small pieces of iron, try soaking them in white vinegar for 24 to 48 hours.

Iron, Plant Hanger, Girl Holding Doll, Cast, Painted, 2-Sided, CJO, Judd Co., 7 x 10 In.
$259.00

Iron, Plant Hanger, Parrot On Branch, Cast, Painted, 2-Sided, 7 x $10\frac{1}{2}$ In.
$173.00

Iron, Tieback, Flowers, Woven Basket, Cast, Painted, $2\frac{1}{8}$ x $1\frac{3}{8}$ In., Pair
$146.00

TIP
Old iron heating grates have a new use. Put them on the outdoor mat to be used as mud scrapers.

Paperweight, Dog, Sealyham, White, Brown, Red Collar, Hubley, $2\frac{1}{4}$ x $3\frac{1}{2}$ In. 392.00
Paperweight, Duck, Top Hat, Yellow, Black, Blue, Red, $2\frac{1}{4}$ x $1\frac{3}{4}$ In. 392.00
Paperweight, Dutch Girl, Blue Dress, White Checkered Apron, Hubley, $2\frac{3}{4}$ x 2 In. 56.00
Paperweight, Dutchess, Yellow Dress, Black Hat, Hubley, 3 x $1\frac{3}{4}$ In. 252.00
Paperweight, Elephant, Trunk Up, Gray, Green Base, 2-Piece Casting, 5 x 4 In. 56.00
Paperweight, Flapper Duck, Hubley, 4 In. 798.00
Paperweight, Hat, G.A.R., Washington D.C., 1915, $2\frac{3}{4}$ x $1\frac{3}{4}$ In. 56.00
Paperweight, Kitten, Pink Bow, White, Hubley, 3 In. 224.00
Paperweight, Lion, Yellow, Brown, 3 x $3\frac{1}{4}$ In. 392.00
Paperweight, Lobster, Red Paint, $2\frac{3}{4}$ x 6 In. 308.00
Paperweight, Mannequin De Pis, Boy Peeing In Bowl, 4 x $3\frac{1}{4}$ In. 392.00
Paperweight, Peter Rabbit, Pink Pants, Hubley, 3 x $1\frac{1}{4}$ In. 504.00
Paperweight, Pheasant, Hubley, $3\frac{1}{2}$ x $2\frac{3}{4}$ In. 252.00
Paperweight, Quail, Hubley, $2\frac{3}{4}$ x 3 In. 336.00
Paperweight, Sailboat, Provincetown, Mass., Hubley, $2\frac{3}{4}$ x $3\frac{3}{4}$ In. 280.00
Paperweight, Skater, Girl, Blue Coat, Green Pants, Hubley, 3 x $1\frac{1}{2}$ In. 224.00
Paperweight, Wire Haired Terrier, Box, Hubley, 3 x $3\frac{1}{2}$ In. 224.00
Pencil Holder, 3 Bears, Yellow, Brown, Green, Cast, Wilton, $1\frac{1}{2}$ x $2\frac{3}{8}$ In. 140.00
Pencil Holder, Ducks, Mama & Baby, Painted, White, Yellow, Green, Cast, Wilton, 2 x $1\frac{3}{4}$ In. 224.00
Pencil Holder, Dutch Girl, Pail, Blue Dress, Yellow Shoes, Cast, Wilton, $2\frac{3}{4}$ x $1\frac{1}{2}$ In. 140.00
Pencil Holder, Indian Head, Painted, White, Brown, Black, Red, Cast, Wilton, $2\frac{1}{8}$ x $1\frac{5}{8}$ In. .. 56.00
Pencil Holder, Penguin, Painted, Cast, Wilton, $2\frac{1}{8}$ x $1\frac{7}{8}$ In. 168.00
Pencil Holder, Peter Rabbit, Holding Carrots, Blue Pants, Bowtie, Cast, Wilton, $2\frac{5}{8}$ x $1\frac{5}{8}$ In. 280.00
Pencil Holder, Puss 'n Boots, Painted, Black Hat, Boots, White, Red, Wilton, $2\frac{3}{4}$ x $1\frac{1}{2}$ In. ... 196.00
Place Card Holder, Dog, Pomeranian, Painted, Brown, Black, Cast, Hubley 392.00
Place Card Holder, Elephant, Trunk Raised, Painted, Gray, White, Pink, Cast, Hubley 392.00
Place Card Holder, Frog, Painted, Green, Yellow, Black, Cast, Hubley 504.00
Place Card Holder, Pig, Painted, Red, White, Blue, Green, Brown, Cast, Hubley 728.00
Place Card Holder, Swan, Painted, White, Yellow, Pink, Cast, Hubley 196.00
Place Card Holder Set, Cast, 6 Flowerpots, 6 Baskets, Hubley, Box 1568.00
Plant Hanger, Girl Holding Doll, Cast, Judd Co., 7 x 10 In. 280.00
Plant Hanger, Girl Holding Doll, Cast, Painted, 2-Sided, CJO, Judd Co., 7 x 10 In. .....*illus* 259.00
Plant Hanger, Parrot On Branch, Cast, Painted, 2-Sided, 7 x $10\frac{1}{2}$ In. ....*illus* 173.00
Plaque, Bird On Leafy Branch, Oval, Cast Iron, 5 x $3\frac{1}{4}$ In. 132.00
Pomade Jar, Bear, Separate Body & Head, Original Paint, 1850-87, $3\frac{3}{4}$ In. 2560.00
Radiator Cover, Cast, Gilded, Floral & Bird Decoration, Late 19th Century, 56 In. 3638.00
Safe, Alpine Safe Co., Cincinnati, Oh., Pinstripes, Graphics, Combination, 15 x 22 x 17 In. .. 1760.00
Scroll Weights, Duck Shape, Chinese, 3 x 5 In. 94.00
Shield, Woman's Mask, Lion Masks, Relief, Cast, Battle Scene, Bracket Handle, 25 x $17\frac{1}{2}$ In. . 805.00
Spurs, Round, Tilting, Fire Gilded Wheels, France, 10 x 5 In., Pair 2645.00
Stand, Plant, Art Deco, 38 In. 448.00
Striker, Kneeling Man, Shape, c.1785, $5\frac{1}{2}$ In. 1955.00
Taper Jack, Shaped Handle, Crab Claw Holder, Curved Legs, Ball Feet, $4\frac{3}{4}$ In. 743.00
Tieback, Flowers, Woven Basket, Cast, Painted, $2\frac{1}{8}$ x $1\frac{3}{8}$ In., Pair ....*illus* 146.00
Toast Rack, Forged, Twisted Concentric Arches, Scrolled Finials, Rotating Pan, 18 x 13 In. .. 330.00
Toast Rack, Rectangular, Round Terminal, Revolving, Handle 99.00
Tongs, Pipe, Blacksmith Made, New England 250.00
Tongs, Pipe, Spring Activated Handle, Bowl Scrape, Tobacco Tamp, Wrought, 17 In., Pair ... 1410.00
Windmill Weight, Bull, Cast, Molded, 19th Century, 13 x $15\frac{1}{2}$ In. 3840.00
Windmill Weight, Bull, Silhouette, Cast Iron, Fairbury Windmill Co., $24\frac{1}{2}$ In. 1495.00
Windmill Weight, Bull Silhouette, Flat, Fairbury Windmill Co., 25 x $18\frac{1}{2}$ In. 632.00
Windmill Weight, Horse, Bobtail, Wooden Base, Dempster Mill Mfg., 17 x 18 In. ... 374.00 to 603.00
Windmill Weight, Horse, Long Tail, Wooden Base, Dempster Mill Mfg., $19\frac{1}{2}$ In. 862.00
Windmill Weight, Rooster, Elgin Wind Power & Pump Co., Elgin, 1900s, 9 In. 825.00
Windmill Weight, Rooster, Marked, Elgin, No. 2, Early 1900s .... 450.00 to 748.00
Wishing Well, Bucket & Pulley, Fleur-De-Lis, Hearts, Shields, Circles, $84\frac{1}{2}$ x 36 In. 1840.00

IRONSTONE china was first made in 1813. It gained its greatest popularity during the mid-nineteenth century. The heavy, durable, off-white pottery was made in white or was decorated with any of hundreds of patterns. Much flow blue pottery was made of ironstone. Some of the decorations were raised. Many pieces of ironstone are unmarked, but some English and American factories included the word *Ironstone* in their marks. Additional pieces may be listed in other categories, such as Chelsea Grape, Chelsea Sprig, Flow Blue, Gaudy Ironstone, Mason's Ironstone, Moss Rose, Staffordshire, and Tea Leaf Ironstone.

Bowl, Beavers, Maple Leaves, White, Molded, 19th Century, $7\frac{1}{2}$ In. 109.00

Bowl, Ladyfinger Ribs, White, W.H. Grindley & Co., England, c.1890, 3 x 4¾ In.	20.00
Bowl, Vegetable, Cover, White, Niagra Fan Shape, Anthony Shaw, c.1856	245.00
Coffeepot, White, Wheat & Clover, Turner & Tomkinson, c.1860-72, 10 In.	295.00
Cup & Saucer, Handleless, Brown Transfer, Rose, Blue, Mustard, Green Enamel, Challinor	104.00
Cuspidor, Flowers, Multicolored, Scalloped Edge, 5½ x 7 In.	679.00
Gravy Boat, Forget Me Not, E & C Challinor, England, Late 1800s, 4½ x 8½ In.	75.00
Jar, Cover, Flowers, Grecian Border, Blue Ground, c.1890, 16 In.	146.00
Jar, Cover, Oriental Pattern, 5 x 4½ In.	18.00
Pitcher, Black Minstrel Band, I Wish I Was In Dixxy Land, Hand Painted, 8½ In.	777.00
Pitcher, Ceres Shape, White, Elsmore & Forster, c.1859, 9 In.	395.00
Pitcher, T & R Boote, Waterloo Potteries, England, 1895, 7 x 7½ In..	100.00
Pitcher, Water, White, Molded Tulip Design, 9 In.	150.00
Pitcher & Bowl, Black Transfer, Lions & Emblem Mark, Victoria Ware, Pitcher 9½ In.	95.00
Plate, Imari, England, c.1800, 9 In., 2 Piece	41.00
Plate Set, Flowers, Argyll, England, c.1850, 10½ In., 6 Piece	146.00
Platter, Davenport Of New York, c.1850, 13 x 17½ In.	205.00
Platter, Oxford Pattern, F. Sons, Burslem, 19th Century, 14 To 17½ In., 3 Piece	88.00
Platter, Painted Imari Border, Booths, c.1916, 17¼ x 33¾ In.	35.00
Saucer, Forget Me Not	8.00
Saucer, Loop & Dot, Challinor	4.00
Soap Dish, Lid, Insert, White, Wheat & Hops, c.1850s	225.00
Soap Dish, Oval, Royal Ironstone China, Alfred Meakin, Eng., 5½ x 4 x 1½ In.	10.00
Sugar, Panelled Grape, White, Jacob Furnival, c.1845-70, 8 In.	145.00
Tea Set, Creamer, Sugar, Teapot, Raised Relief Leaf, Red Cliff, 12 In., 3 Piece	47.00
Teapot, White, Panelled Grape Shape, Jacob Furnival, Mid 1800s, 10½ In.	300.00
Teapot Lid, Wheat & Clover, 3⅜ In.	35.00
Tureen, Sauce, Underplate, Ladle, White, President, John Edwards, c.1855	475.00
Vase, Mandalay Red, 6½ x 4½ In., Pair	59.00

ISPANKY figurines were designed by Laszlo Ispanky, who began his American career as a designer for Cybis Porcelains. In 1966, he established his own studio in Pennington, New Jersey; since 1976, he has worked for Goebel of North America. He works in stone, wood, or metal, as well as porcelain. The first limited edition figurines were issued in 1966.

Bust, Woman, Ribbon On Shoulder Strap & In Her Hair, 10¼ x 7 x 3 In.	250.00
Figurine, Elizabeth, Blond Hair, Pink Gown, Holding Flowers, 8 In.	275.00
Figurine, Maiden, On Recliner Cupped In Flowers, Goebel, 8 x 8 In.	95.00
Figurine, Owl, American Wildlife Series, Attached Wood Stand, c.1982, 7 In.	145.00
Figurine, Swan, Light Blue Color On Wings, Goebel, 5¼ x 7 In.	125.00
Plate, Twelve Tribes Of Israel, Old Testament Series, Goebel, 1978, 12 In.	78.00

IVORY from the tusk of an elephant is thought by many to be the only true ivory. To most collectors, the term *ivory* also includes such natural materials as walrus, hippopotamus, or whale teeth or tusks, and some of the vegetable materials that are of similar texture and density. Other ivory items may be found in the Scrimshaw and Netsuke categories. Collectors should be aware of the recent laws limiting the buying and selling of elephant ivory and scrimshaw.

Bowl, Narcissus, Signed, Japan, 1926-89, 5½ In., Pair	295.00
Box, Brass, Swan Shape Finial, Footed, Empire, Lid, Continental, Early 1800s, 4½ x 4 In.	439.00
Box, Carved, Warriors, Flowers, Hexagonal, Chinese, 19th Century, 9 x 8 x 4 In.	4700.00
Box, Reticulated, Chinese, 1½ x 7½ x 2½ In.	207.00
Box, Scholars, Calligraphy, Flowers, Inlaid Lacquer, Hexagonal, Chinese, 1800s, 3½ In.	470.00
Bracelet, Carved, Domino Shapes, High Relief, Attendants, Chinese, 7½ x 1⅝ In.	118.00
Brush Holder, Carved Figures, Japan, 8½ In.	2243.00
Brush Pot, Figures, Landscape, Carved, 19th Century, 6¾ In.	660.00
Brush Pot, Landscape, Figures, Chinese, 3¼ In.	1298.00
Bust, Goddess Of Mercy, Smile, Downcast Eyes, Earrings, Chinese	1112.00
Card Case, Figures In Landscapes, Carved, Undercut, Oval Cartouche, Chinese, 4¼ In.	761.00
Card Case, Hinged Lid, Oval Inset, Carved Lilies, Blue Silk & Paper Interior, 4¼ In. ....*illus*	388.00
Casket, Scrolling Vines & Vines All Over, 4 Elephant Feet, India, 4 x 10 x 5 In.	720.00
Cigar Cutter, Curved, Polished Ivory Handle, Metal Cutter, Press Down, 5¼ In.	110.00
Cigarette Holder, Dragon, Hand Carved, 4 In.	47.00
Cricket Cage, Flowers, Scale, Mounted Gourd, Baluster Shape, Carved, Chinese, 6 In.	2006.00
Doctor's Doll, Carved, Rosewood Stand, Chinese, 2 x 6 In.	351.00
Doctor's Doll, Wearing Bracelet, Earrings, Holding Fan, Chinese, 10½ In.	590.00
Figurine, 2 Geisha Girls, Japan, 7 In.	205.00

Ivory, Card Case, Hinged Lid, Oval Inset, Carved Lilies, Blue Silk & Paper Interior, 4¼ In. $388.00

Ivory, Figurine, Man Walking,
With Violin & Cane,
Ebonized Wood Plinth Base, 8¼ In.
$956.00

Ivory, Patch Box,
Boy Playing Horn In Garden,
Copper Foil Backing, Gilt Metal Bezel,
Round, 2½ In.
$199.00

TIP

*Clean ivory beads and
jewelry with denatured
alcohol, not water.*

Figurine, 2 People Embracing, India, 5½ In.	117.00
Figurine, Beautiful Woman, Wearing Long Robes, Holding Flowering Branch, Chinese, 6 In.	177.00
Figurine, Boy, On Knee, Holding Vase, Japan, 3¼ In.	82.00
Figurine, Buddha, Seated, Bearded, Wearing Beaded Necklace, Japan, 6 In.	413.00
Figurine, Camel, Africa, 6½ x 5¼ In.	176.00
Figurine, Chinese Father & Child, Polychrome, Early 20th Century, 3¾ In.	878.00
Figurine, Christ, Crucified, 18th Century, 9 In.	1293.00
Figurine, Christ, Crucified, Goa, 18th Century, 8 In.	823.00
Figurine, Christ, The Good Shepherd, Goa, 6¾ In.	1763.00
Figurine, Cloisonne Enamel, Beautiful Woman, Holding Fan, Chinese, 13 In.	177.00
Figurine, Corpus Christie, Hair, Pierced Crown Of Thorns, Tongue, Toe, Fingernails, 9 In.	1880.00
Figurine, Court Lady, Chinese, 10¼ In.	1652.00
Figurine, Deity Seated On Lotus Throne, Buddha, Attendants, Chinese, 11 x 13 x 7 In.	944.00
Figurine, Eagle, Raised Wing, Perched On Ball, Oval Base, 4 In.	495.00
Figurine, Elder, Teak Base, Chinese, 7 x 3¼ In.	205.00
Figurine, Emperor Seated On Dragon Armchair, Chinese, 5 In.	1770.00
Figurine, Farmer, Basket Of Eggs, Holding Hatchling, 19th Century, 4¾ In.	1116.00
Figurine, Farmer Holding Basket Of Ducks, Japan, 19th Century, 8 In.	940.00
Figurine, Female Musician, Long Robes, High Chignon, Holding Flute, Chinese, 5 In.	142.00
Figurine, Fisherman, Holding Basket & Crane, Chromed, Chinese, 8½ In.	380.00
Figurine, Fisherman, Holding Catch, Seated, Wooden Base, 6¼ In.	316.00
Figurine, Fisherman, Holding Fish, Standing On Rocks, Japan, 6¼ In.	210.00
Figurine, Fisherman, Japan, 19th Century, 6¼ In.	235.00
Figurine, Fishmonger, Basket On Back, Japan, 9¼ In.	400.00
Figurine, Fist, Clenched, Carved, Red, White, Blue Spiral Shaft, Stepped Molded Base, 3 In.	66.00
Figurine, Foo Dog, Mounted On Wood Base, Chinese, Early 20th Century, 5 In.	266.00
Figurine, Gentleman, Period Costume, Continental, c.1900, 7 In.	307.00
Figurine, Giraffe Mother, Feeding Baby, Wood Base, c.1940	664.00
Figurine, Girl, Playing Flute, Wood Plinth, India, 7½ x 9½ In.	350.00
Figurine, Goddess Of Mercy, Girl, c.1940, 10 In., Pair	305.00
Figurine, Goddess Of Mercy, Holding Lotus Blossom, Chinese, 11 In.	380.00
Figurine, Immortal, Holding Peach, Staff, Beard, Long Robes, Chinese, 9¾ In.	472.00
Figurine, Immortal, Wearing Long Robes, Beard, Holding Branch, Chinese, 8½ In.	354.00
Figurine, Immortal, Wearing Robes, Holding Lotus Branches, Beard, Chinese, 12 In.	702.00
Figurine, Japanese Vendor, 2½ In.	70.00
Figurine, Lion, Wood Base, 2½ x 5 In., Pair	234.00
Figurine, Man, Goat, Carrying Boy, Flowers, Japan, 5 In.	380.00
Figurine, Man, Manchu Costume, Chinese, 15 In.	646.00
Figurine, Man, Seated 2 Fruit Baskets, Engraved, Wood Base, Japan, 7 x 6¾ In.	598.00
Figurine, Man & Monkey, Japan, 8 In.	351.00
Figurine, Man & Woman, Rosewood Stand, Chinese, c.1900, 8¼ x 8½ In., Pair	527.00
Figurine, Man Walking, With Violin & Cane, Ebonized Wood Plinth Base, 8¼ In. ......*illus*	956.00
Figurine, Man Wearing Long Robes, Beard, Holding Fish, Pipe, Chinese, 9 In.	354.00
Figurine, Mary Magdalene, Goa, 18th Century, 5 In.	1410.00
Figurine, Mother & Child, Tree Trunk, Parrot, Multicolored, 16 x 5 In.	900.00
Figurine, Old Man, Holding Fan, Scroll, Chinese, 9¾ In.	443.00
Figurine, Old Man, Japan, c.1900, 5 In.	41.00
Figurine, Putto, Holding Vessel, Grapes, Vines, 20th Century, 20 x 20 In.	999.00
Figurine, Reclining Oriental Woman, Wooden Base, 6½ In.	431.00
Figurine, Sage, With Staff, Japan, 3 In.	234.00
Figurine, Ship, Lanterns, Flag, Passengers, Chinese, 10 In.	413.00
Figurine, Tannhauser, Pilgrim's Shell, Harp, Venusberg, 19th Century, 5⅝ In.	863.00
Figurine, Vishnu, Multiarmed, Seated, On Lily Pad, Hindu, Teakwood Stand, 9¼ x 5 In.	936.00
Figurine, Warrior, Armored, Chinese, 14 In.	1116.00
Figurine, Warrior, Standing, Chinese, 27½ In.	2633.00
Figurine, Woman, Holding Child, Chinese, 10 In., Pair	1763.00
Figurine, Woman, Mourning, Cast Cement, Multicolored, Folds, 19th Century, 22 In., Pair	118.00
Figurine, Woman, Standing, Chinese, 15 In.	646.00
Figurine, Woman Holding Fan, Branch Of Flowers, Chinese, 11 In.	646.00
Group, Beautiful Woman, Holding Lotus Branch, Child On Dog, Crane, Chinese, 5¾ In.	413.00
Group, Virgin & Child, France, 19th Century, 14 In.	1410.00
Okimono, Boy With Dog, 19th Century, Japan, 1 In.	382.00
Okimono, Crab, Wood Plinth, Japan, 10½ In.	382.00
Okimono, Immortal, Elaborate Dress, Japan, 20th Century, 12 In.	499.00
Okimono, Lion, Wood Plinth, Japan, 9 In.	71.00
Okimono, Man, Beard, Long Robes, Holding Cup & Fan, 6½ In.	413.00

I

Okimono, Man, Selling Baskets, Signed, Japan, 4¼ In.	189.00
Okimono, Man Holding Child, Branch, Japan, 7 In.	561.00
Okimono, Man In Hood, Long Robes, Beard, Holding Bowl, Japan, 6 In.	295.00
Okimono, Man In Robes, Holding Fan, Signed, Japan, 5¼ In.	502.00
Okimono, Man On Horseback, Japan, 8 In.	649.00
Okimono, Monkey Trainer, 2 Monkeys, Boy, Flute, Japan, c.1900, 2½ In.	131.00
Okimono, Narcissus, Japan, 9½ In.	1000.00
Okimono, Peddler, Carrying Pole With Baskets, Fan, Signed, Japan, 10¼ In.	826.00
Okimono, Prophet, Wood Pedestal, Japan, 20th Century, 11½ In.	353.00
Okimono, Samurai, Swords In Belt, Japan, 6¾ In.	177.00
Okimono, Woman, Cherry Blossom, Lotus Branches, Chinese, 11½ In., Pair	646.00
Okimono, Woman, Lotus Blossom, Wood Plinth, Japan, 20th Century, 10 In.	323.00
Paginator, Silver Mounted, Late 19th Century, 17½ In.	143.00
Paginator, Silver Mounted, London, c.1898, 15½ In.	291.00
Panel, Angel Holding Crown, 19th Century, 4¾ x 2 In.	235.00
Panels, Mother-Of-Pearl Inlay, 19th Century, 3¾ x 2½ In.	935.00
Patch Box, Boy Playing Horn In Garden, Copper Foil Backing, Gilt Metal Bezel, Round, 2½ In. *illus*	199.00
Pen, Letter Opener, Glass Inset, Ste. Anne De Beaupre Image, c.1900	85.00
Puzzle Ball, Carved, Pierced, 18th Century, 11 In.	881.00
Puzzle Ball, Carved, Pierced, Chinese, 5½ In.	176.00
Puzzle Ball, Flowers, Vines, Stand, Buddhist Saint & Bat, 19th Century, 15 In.	510.00
Puzzle Ball, Pierced, Elephant Stand, Chinese, 7½ In.	561.00
Scene, Architectural, Carved, Japan, 4½ x 5 In.	380.00
Shoehorn, Shell, Eagle & Shield, Carved, Inscribed, Lt. McBride, God Speed, Aug. 1, 1789	1850.00
Sphere, Deities, Animals, Children, Carved, Japan, 19th Century, 2½ In.	1175.00
Stamp, Dragon, Block, Carved, 3 x 2½ In.	275.00 to 670.00
Tankard, Carved, Continental Europe, Late 19th Century, 9½ In.	4299.00
Triptych, Figural, Woman, Holding Bouquet, Skirt Opens, Full Round, 19th Century, 9¼ In.	2350.00
Tusk, 23 In.	385.00
Tusk, Carved, Dragons, Chinese, 8 x 25 In.	2106.00
Tusk, Carved, Figures, Buddha, 19th Century, Burmese, 18 In., Pair	1888.00
Tusk, Carved, Teakwood Stand, Chinese, 25 In.	1053.00
Tusk, Engraved, Elephant, Figural Scene, Chinese, 26½ In.	1170.00
Tusk, Walrus, Figures, Mythical Animals, Indonesia, 23½ In.	354.00
Urn, Cover, Carved, Chinese, c.1900, 7 x 6 In.	819.00
Vase, Birds, Flowers, Mother-Of-Pearl, Coral, Horn, Japan, 1868-1911, 13½ In.	3055.00
Vase, Dragon, Carved, Cylindrical, Pinched Waist Neck, Reticulated Feet, Chinese, Pair	325.00
Wrist Rest, Flowering Gourd, Landscape, Chinese, 19th Century, 7½ In.	3290.00

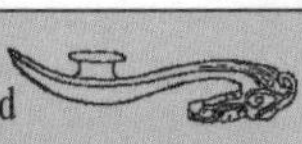

JADE is the name for two different minerals, nephrite and jadeite. Nephrite is the mineral used for most early Oriental carvings. Jade is a very tough stone that is found in many colors from dark green to pale lavender. Jade carvings are still being made in the old styles, so collectors must be careful not to be fooled by recent pieces. Jade jewelry is found in this book under Jewelry.

Bowl, Carved, Chinese, 3¼ x 7½ In.	468.00
Bowl, Carved, Dragon Mask, Ring Handles, Chinese, 7⅞ x 4 x 2¾ In.	650.00
Bowl, Carved, Green, Chinese, 2¼ x 5 In., Pair	293.00
Bowl, Carved, Open, Flared Rim, Chinese, 20th Century, 1¾ x 4 In.	88.00
Bowl, Cover, Celadon, Apple Green, Chinese, 4 In.	236.00
Bowl, Spinach Green, Carved, Phoenix, Dragon, Chinese, 8 In.	944.00
Bowl, Spinach Green, Shallow, Chinese, 11½ In.	1416.00
Box, Cover, Spinach Green, Carved, Rectangular, Leaves, Low Relief, Chinese, 5¼ x 3¼ In.	354.00
Box, Tortoiseshell, Carved, Bird, Leaf Decoration, Chinese, 1⅜ x 3½ In.	1770.00
Bracelet, Carved, 3¼ In.	205.00
Brush Washer, Celadon, Round, 3 Handles, Chinese, 1¼ x 3½ In.	2360.00
Brush Washer, Chinese, 3½ x 8 In.	4720.00
Brush Washer, Green, Snails, Incurved Rim, Chinese, 19th Century, 6½ In.	1645.00
Brushpot, Chinese, 4½ In.	2360.00
Carving, Celadon, Dragons, Chasing Flaming Pearl Of Wisdom, Russet Inclusions, 5 In.	325.00
Censer, Celadon, Flowers, Lion Mask Jump Rings, Chinese, 6 x 8 In. *illus*	5581.00
Censer, Cover, Foo Dogs, Brocade Balls, Mask, Ring Handles, Paw Feet, 1800s, 13¾ In.	3900.00
Censer, Cover, Frieze Masks, Swastikas, Dragon Mask, Spinach Green, 3 Paw Feet, 1800s, 8 In.	2280.00
Censer, Dome Cover, Bowl Shape Body, Hydra Finial, Tripod, Dragon Handles, 5½ In.	267.00
Cup, Lavender, Gray, Apple Green, Fitted Stand, Chinese, 19th Century, 2 In., Pair	353.00
Cup, White, Russet Rivering, Carved, Leaves, Footed Rim, 2 In.	780.00

Jade, Censer, Celadon, Flowers, Lion Mask Jump Rings, Chinese, 6 x 8 In. $5581.00

Jade
Real jade is actually one of two minerals, nephrite or jadeite. The most valuable jade is known as "Imperial Jade," which is a clear, dark green color. Both are usually a pale to dark green color, but they also occur in nature in a variety of other colors, including black, red, pink, violet, and white. Because jade is a hard, compact stone, it can only be carved by abrasives, not cutting tools. Antique Chinese carved jade can be very valuable.

TIP

You can tell a piece of jade by the feel. It will be cold, even in warm weather.

Jasperware, Dish, Cover, Blue, White Winged Angels, Columns, Oak Leaf Border, c.1900, 10½ In. $94.00

Costume Jewelry Colors

Jewelry was made to go with the fashions of the day.

1910s: Pale purple glass, amethyst, and opals.

1920s: Black, crystal, black, silver or bright colors like red, yellow, blue, and green.

1930s: Bright-colored stones and rhinestones.

1940s: Red, white, and blue were popular.

1950s and '60s: Turquoise, chartreuse, coral, red, royal blue, and other strong colors.

1960s: Yellow.

1970s: Gray-green and rust.

1980s: Mauve and teal.

1990s: Sage green, pumpkin, and wheat.

2000: Red violet, magenta, and plum.

Figurine, Bird, On Branch, Wood Base, 7 In.	234.00
Figurine, Birds, Perched On Rockery, Chinese, 20th Century, 5½ x 1½ In., Pair	239.00
Figurine, Birds, Serpents, Egg Shape, Gray, Chinese, 8 x 6 In.	234.00
Figurine, Boy, Chinese, 2½ In.	1298.00
Figurine, Buddha, Chinese, 3¾ In.	47.00
Figurine, Children, White, Chinese, 4¼ In.	708.00
Figurine, Dog, White, Chinese, 3 In.	561.00
Figurine, Dragon, Celadon, Chinese, 4 In.	823.00
Figurine, Elephant, Brown, Chinese, 1½ x 2 In.	531.00
Figurine, Foo Dog, Snail Curl Manes, Draped Plinths, Chinese, 18½ x 8 In., Pair	1195.00
Figurine, Foo Dog, White, Chinese, 5¼ In.	944.00
Figurine, Goat, Rodents, Carved, Ching Dynasty, Chinese, 3 In.	770.00
Figurine, Horse, Reclining, Cafe-Au-Lait, Chinese, 1½ x 3¼ In.	2242.00
Figurine, Horse, Reclining, Chinese, 1¾ In.	1052.00
Figurine, Horse, Saddle, Tang Style, Standing 4 Square, Chinese, 1900s, 9½ x 8½ In.	329.00
Figurine, Lion, Hardstone, Teakwood Base, 4 x 7 In.	82.00
Figurine, Mythical Beast, Reclining, Chinese, 1¾ x 1¾ In.	944.00
Figurine, Mythical Beast, Reclining, White, Chinese, 2¼ In.	2596.00
Figurine, Sage, Standing, Wood Base, 12 In.	351.00
Figurine, Water Buffalo, Serpentine, Carved, 4 x 5 In.	82.00
Group, Deer, Dragon, Birds, Pale Green, Chinese, 7½ In.	177.00
Group, Running Horses, Carved, Chinese, 20th Century, 13 x 13½ In.	176.00
Jar, Cover, Cranes, Rams, Celadon Gray Stone, Chinese, 5¾ In.	7638.00
Koro, Mottled, Lavender Ground, Carved & Pierced Cover, Dragon Finial, Handles, 8 x 9 In.	3525.00
Mystery Ball, Stand, Carved, Chinese, 5 In.	70.00
Pendant, Figural, Brown, Hongshan Culture, Chinese, 3¼ In.	708.00
Pendant, Figural, Mythical Animal Shape, Chinese, 2½ In.	177.00
Pendant, Monkey, Holding Peach Branch, Gray, Brown Inclusions, Chinese, c.1900, 1½ In.	120.00
Pendant, White, Apple Green, Carved Fish, Chinese, 3¾ x 2½ In.	885.00
Pendant, White, Quilin, Cafe-Au-Lait Inclusions, Chinese, 18th Century, 3 In.	1298.00
Picture, Ox, Reclining, Carved, Chinese, 1 x 3 In.	18.00
Plaque, Chicken Bone, Archaic Style Phoenixes, Chinese, 18th Century, 4 In., Pair	529.00
Sculpture, Lettuce Bunch, Carved, Wood Base, Chinese, 3 x 6 In.	136.00
Seal, Dragon, Spinach Green, Fitted Rosewood Box, Chinese	2478.00
Stamp, Block, Dragon, Carved, Wood Base, Chinese, 5½ x 3½ In.	235.00
Table Screen, Spinach Green, Chinese, 8 x 5 In.	502.00
Teapot, Celadon, Rectangular, Flowering Prunus, Taotie Masks, C-Shape Handle, 4½ In.	1062.00
Tree, Carnelian, Cloisonne Pot, c.1950, 13 In.	275.00
Urn, Carved, Chinese, 8 x 4¼ In.	410.00
Vase, Cover, Celadon, Fattened Oval Pear Shape, Qilin Shape Handles, Chinese, 5½ In.	266.00
Vase, Lotus Flowers, Buddha's Hand Citrons, Chinese, 19th Century, 6¼ x 5½ In.	2585.00
Vase, Spinach Green, Pine & Lotus Tree, Crane, Chinese, 6½ In.	767.00
Wedding Bowl, Carved, White, Round Border, Calligraphy, Foo Dog, 5½ x 7 In.	3304.00

JAPANESE CORALENE is a ceramic decorated with small raised beads and dots. It was first made in the nineteenth century. Later wares made to imitate coralene had dots of enamel. There is also another type of coralene that is made with small glass beads on glass containers.

Nappy, Leaf Shape, Nippon, 1940-50, 6 x 4⅞ x 2½ In.	45.00
Plate, Country Scene, Cobalt Blue, Gold, Nippon, 7½ In.	120.00
Serving Dish, Pink Roses, Scalloped Edge, Gold Trim, Side Handle, Nippon, 9 x 2 In.	165.00
Vase, 3 Painted Panels, Flowers, White, Green Ground, 3 Handles, Nippon, 5 In.	144.00
Vase, Flower, Nippon, 5 x 4 In.	575.00
Vase, Flowers, Leaves, Gold Trim, Nippon, 12½ In.	175.00
Vase, Flowers, Purple, Pink, Brown Satin Ground, Nippon, 5¾ x 4¾ In.	350.00
Vase, Roses, Nippon, 4¼ In.	250.00

JAPANESE WOODBLOCK PRINTS *are listed in this book in the Print category under Japanese.*

JASPERWARE can be made in different ways. Some pieces are made from a solid-colored clay with applied raised designs of a contrasting colored clay. Other pieces are made entirely of one color clay with raised decorations that are glazed with a contrasting color. Additional pieces of jasperware may also be listed in the Wedgwood category or under various art potteries.

Dish, Cover, Blue, White Winged Angels, Columns, Oak Leaf Border, c.1900, 10½ In. ....*illus*	94.00
Plaque, Green, White Allegorical Figures, c.1900, 5⅜ x 9⅜ In.	82.00

JEWELRY, whether made from gold and precious gems or plastic and colored glass, is popular with collectors. Values are determined by the intrinsic value of the stones and metal and by the skill of the craftsmen and designers. Victorian and older jewelry have been collected since the 1950s. More recent interests are Art Deco and Edwardian styles, Mexican and Danish silver jewelry, and beads of all kinds. Copies of almost all styles are being made. American Indian jewelry is listed in the Indian category. Tiffany jewelry is listed here.

Bangle, Sterling Silver, Engraved Rope Twists, Spratling, Mexico, 1940s, 5½ In.	1410.00
Belt, Calfskin, Carnelian, Amethyst, Quartz, Garnet, Lapis-Lazuli, Serpentine, Judith Leiber	317.00
Belt, Snakeskin, Amethyst, Rose Quartz, Lapis-Lazuli, Onyx, Gilt Brass Buckle, Judith Leiber	212.00
Bracelet, 5 Translucent Green Cabochons, 14K Gold Mount, Mid 1800s, 3 In. ....*illus*	325.00
Bracelet, 6 Rows Of Clear Rhinestones, Joseph Wiesner	54.00
Bracelet, Amazonite Pyramids, Onyx, 18K Gold, Art Deco, 7⅝ In.	2350.00
Bracelet, Amethysts, Leaf-Shaped Links, 14K Gold, Tiffany & Co., 7¾ In.	1293.00
Bracelet, Bakelite, Bangle, Apple Juice, Reverse Carved, Flowers, 3¼ x 1 In. ....*illus*	235.00
Bracelet, Bakelite, Bangle, Butterscotch, Wood Laminate, Marbled Black & Green, 8 In., Pair	235.00
Bracelet, Bakelite, Bangle, Creamed Corn, Carved, 7¾ In.	235.00
Bracelet, Bakelite, Bangle, Lime Green, Cream Dots, 8 In.	500.00
Bracelet, Bakelite, Bangle, Overlay Cutback, Black & Green, 7¾ In.	323.00
Bracelet, Bakelite, Bangle, Polka Dots, Red, Yellow, 7¾ In.	500.00
Bracelet, Bakelite, Bangle, Red, Carved, 7¾ In.	206.00
Bracelet, Bakelite, Bangle, Yellow, Cream Dots	595.00
Bracelet, Bakelite, Bangles, Butterscotch, Marbled Dots, 1940s, 8 In., Pair	500.00
Bracelet, Bakelite, Cuff, Laminate, Mustard, Dark Green, 7 In.	264.00
Bracelet, Bangle, 18K Bicolor Gold, Flexible Links, Marina B., 5¾ In.	1175.00
Bracelet, Bangle, Diamond, Citrine, Pearls, 14K Gold, Victorian, c.1880	6768.00
Bracelet, Bangle, Diamond, Enamel, 18K Gold, Le Nouvelle Bague, 6½ In., Pair	2938.00
Bracelet, Bangle, Hinged, 18K Yellow Gold, Polished, Tapered Oval, 1⅛ In.	767.00
Bracelet, Bangle, Hinged, Diamond, Enamel, 18K Gold, Marked, La Nouvelle Bague, 7 In.	823.00
Bracelet, Bangle, Hinged, Diamonds, 18K Gold, Tiffany & Co., 6¾ In.	2938.00
Bracelet, Bangle, Hinged, Sterling Silver, Antonio Pineda, Mexico ....*illus*	1680.00
Bracelet, Bangle, Love, 18K Gold, Cartier, 6 In.	1645.00
Bracelet, Bangle, Snake, Tortoiseshell Plastic, 2¼ x 1⅛ In.	65.00
Bracelet, Bangle, Sterling Silver, Georg Jensen, 7¾ In.	441.00
Bracelet, Bangle, Sterling Silver, Marked, Gucci, 7¾ In.	646.00
Bracelet, Bangle, Sterling Silver, Wrapped Geometric, Ed Weiner, ½ x 2¾ In. ....*illus*	1800.00
Bracelet, Bangle, Stingray Shape, 752 Tsavorites, 45 Diamonds, 2 Sapphires	4349.00
Bracelet, Blue, Green, Molded Nautilus Shell, Edlee	125.00
Bracelet, Blue Enamel Rings, Rhinestone Links, Ciner	130.00
Bracelet, Cameo, Coral, Art Nouveau Lady, Etruscan Disc, 14K Gold, 13 Slides, 7 In.	500.00
Bracelet, Catalin, Philadelphia, Yellow, Red, Green, Black, 1940s	5250.00
Bracelet, Cerisier, Cherry Tree, Blue, c.1928, 1⅛-In. Links	7200.00
Bracelet, Charm, 10K & 14K Gold, 16 Charms, Ship, Horse, Train, Car, Shoes, 7¼ In.	880.00
Bracelet, Charm, 14K Gold, 11 Airplanes, Moving Propellers, 7 In.	2468.00
Bracelet, Charm, 3 Strands, 11 Charms, Diamonds, Stones, 14K Gold, 5¼ In. ....*illus*	400.00
Bracelet, Charm, Judaic, 10K & 14K Gold, 12 Charms For 12 Tribes, 7½ In.	823.00
Bracelet, Charm, Napier	86.00
Bracelet, Charm, Padlock Clasp, 6 Charms, Onyx, Bloodstones, 9K Gold, 7 In. ....*illus*	690.00
Bracelet, Charm, Typewriter, Moving Platen, 1950s, 7 In.	19.00
Bracelet, Concentric Wirework Rings, Beadwork, Silver, Hector Aguilar, Mexico, 7 In.	1058.00
Bracelet, Crystal, Reverse Painted Fox, Hunter, Rider, 14K Gold, 6¾ In.	1880.00
Bracelet, Cuff, Sterling Silver, Renior	34.00
Bracelet, Dahlias, Frosted, c.1927, ¾-In. Links	2280.00
Bracelet, Dark Blue & Green Stones, Schiaparelli, 2 In.	1090.00
Bracelet, Diamond Florets, Ruby, Emerald, Moonstone, Garnet, Sapphires, India, 6½ In.	1175.00
Bracelet, Diamonds, 7 Cultured Pearls, 14K Yellow Gold, Victorian	2006.00
Bracelet, Diamonds, Gemstones, Leaf-Shaped Rubies, 18K White Gold Links, Art Deco	7403.00
Bracelet, Flexible, Peacock Feather, Blue, Green Enamel, 18K Yellow Gold, 7 In.	1170.00
Bracelet, Georgia O'Keeffe, Silver, Engraved, Black Suede, Hector Aguilar, 6¾ In. .....*illus*	3525.00
Bracelet, Gilt Bronze, Enameled, Diamond Shapes, Line Vautrin, c.1950, 6¾ In.	7800.00
Bracelet, Gold Metal, Alternating Medallions & Purple Stones, Leo Glass	41.00
Bracelet, Hinged, Amethyst, Round, Pear & Oval Cuts, 14K Gold, 6¼ In.	1175.00
Bracelet, Hinged, Black Enamel, Bird, Leaves, 14K Gold, Victorian, 5⅝ In.	529.00
Bracelet, Link, 14K Yellow & Pink Gold, Hungary	1029.00
Bracelet, Link, Abstract Shape, Engraved, Sterling Silver, Los Castillo, Mexico, 7 In. ...*illus*	529.00
Bracelet, Link, Bakelite & Wood	133.00

Jewelry, Bracelet,
5 Translucent Green Cabochons,
14K Gold Mount,
Mid 1800s, 3 In.
$325.00

Jewelry, Bracelet, Bakelite,
Bangle, Apple Juice, Reverse Carved,
Flowers, 3¼ x 1 In.
$235.00

Jewelry, Bracelet, Bangle,
Hinged, Sterling Silver,
Antonio Pineda, Mexico
$1680.00

Jewelry, Bracelet, Bangle,
Sterling Silver, Wrapped Geometric,
Ed Weiner, ½ x 2¾ In.
$1800.00

Jewelry, Bracelet, Charm,
3 Strands, 11 Charms,
Diamonds, Stones, 14K Gold, 5¼ In.
$400.00

TIP
Diamonds clean well in club soda.

Jewelry, Bracelet, Charm,
Padlock Clasp, 6 Charms, Onyx,
Bloodstones, 9K Gold, 7 In.
$690.00

Jewelry, Bracelet, Georgia O'Keeffe,
Silver, Engraved, Black Suede,
Hector Aguilar, 6¾ In.
$3525.00

Jewelry, Bracelet, Link,
Abstract Shape, Engraved,
Sterling Silver,
Los Castillo, Mexico, 7 In.
$529.00

Jewelry, Bracelet, Link,
Round & Ball Shaped, Sterling Silver,
Hector Aguilar, Mexico, 8 In.
$999.00

Bracelet, Link, Round & Ball Shaped, Sterling Silver, Hector Aguilar, Mexico, 8 In. . . . .*illus*	999.00
Bracelet, Lucite, Lustered, Blue, Domed, Interior Bubbles, 3 In.	7.00
Bracelet, Mesh, Buckle, Turquoise Cabochons, 14K Gold, Victorian, 1 x 9½ In. . . . . .*illus*	215.00
Bracelet, Mesh, Strap, 14K Yellow Gold, Austro-Hungary	877.00
Bracelet, Mesh, Strap, Black Enamel, 14K Yellow Gold, Buckle Clasp	722.00
Bracelet, Moonstone, Cabochons, Scrolls, Buds, Sterling Silver, Marked, Georg Jensen	1880.00
Bracelet, Pearls, Rubies, Diamonds, Center Plaque, Spacers, c.1900, 7 In., Pair	4700.00
Bracelet, Platinum, Emerald, Diamonds, Beaded Edge, Art Deco, 6¾ In.	15275.00
Bracelet, Raisins, Grapes & Vines, Yellow Amber Glass, R. Lalique, c.1919, 3¼ In. . . . . .*illus*	2040.00
Bracelet, Rondelles Plates, 36 Discs, Frosted, Black Enamel, 1927	6463.00
Bracelet, Sapphire, Diamond, 14K Bicolor Gold, Tiffany & Co., c.1950	2468.00
Bracelet, Sapphires, Diamonds, Channel Set, Baguette, 14K Gold, Retro, Cartier	11163.00
Bracelet, Scarab, Gem Set, Sapphire, Ruby, Diamond Melee, Egyptian Revival, 7¼ In.	1175.00
Bracelet, Scarab, Hardstone, Carved, Tiger's Eye, Onyx, Carnelian, Moonstone, 7 In.	236.00
Bracelet, Silver, 8 Hinged Panels, Carved Scenes, Tibet, 7 In.	384.00
Bracelet, Sterling Silver, 18K Gold, H-Shape Links, Integral Clasp, Hermes, 7⅜ In.	1116.00
Bracelet, Sterling Silver, 18K Gold, Sven Boltenstern, c.1972, 6¾ In.	3055.00
Bracelet, Sterling Silver, Abstract Geometric Links, Marked, Los Castillo, 6½ In.	441.00
Bracelet, Sterling Silver, Chain Links, Abstract Designs, Hector Aguilar, Mexico, 7 In.	764.00
Bracelet, Sterling Silver, Crisscross Links, Silver Balls, Hector Aguilar, Mexico, 7¼ In.	1763.00
Bracelet, Sterling Silver, Danish Modern Style, Abstract Links, No. 88A, Henning Koppel	2115.00
Bracelet, Sterling Silver, Hinged Links, Amethyst Cabochons, William Spratling, 8 In.	1995.00
Bracelet, Sterling Silver, Interlocking Abstract Links, Henning Koppel, Georg Jensen	2115.00
Bracelet, Sterling Silver, No. 294, Georg Jensen	495.00
Bracelet, Sterling Silver, Obsidian, 7 Segments, Crescent Shaped, Los Ballesteros, 1900s	470.00
Bracelet, Sterling Silver, Obsidian, Antonio Pineda, Mexico	1440.00
Bracelet, Sterling Silver, Rectangular Panels, Banded Wire Links, Hector Aguilar, 7 In.	2350.00
Bracelet, Sterling Silver, Wide Concave Links, Antonio Pineda, Mexico, 6 In.	1116.00
Bracelet, Tank Track, 14K Gold, Retro, 7⅜ In.	1880.00
Bracelet, Yellow Jade, Carved, Dragon Heads, Chinese, 3¾ In.	177.00
Bracelet & Earrings, Bakelite, Creamed Corn, Blue Green, Carved, Geometric, 8-In. Bangle	294.00
Bracelet & Earrings, Dragon, Har	585.00
Bracelet & Necklace, Sterling Silver, Mesh, Beveled Links, Mexico, 15-In. Necklace	558.00
Bracelet & Pin, Bakelite, Butterscotch, Carved, Daisy, Cuff Bracelet, 5¾ In.	588.00
Bracelet & Pin, Celluloid, Red Rhinestone Accents, Leg Shape Pin, 2¼-In. Pin	176.00
Bracelet & Ring, Cuff, 18K Gold, Michael Good, 4⅞ In., Size 8½ Ring	1410.00
Buckle, Mask, Sterling Silver, Black Stone Cabochon Eyes, Hubert Harmon, 5½ In.	2468.00
Buttonhook, 14K Gold, Enameled Flowers In Hat-Shaped Basket, Chain, c.1880 . . . . .*illus*	212.00
Cigarette Case, 18K Bicolor Gold, Rod Sided, Woven Decoration, 4⅜ x 3¾ In.	2340.00
Cigarette Case, Brass, Engraved, Applied Flowers, Birds, Japan, 4¼ x 2¾ In.	60.00
Cigarette Case, Silver, Gilt, Art Deco Style, European, 1920s, 3 In.	390.00
Cigarette Case, Textured Grid Surface, Gold, Czechoslovakia, 1930s, 4¼ In.	1282.00
Clip, Diamonds, Platinum, Art Deco, Cartier, Box	30550.00
Clip, Monkeys, Sterling Silver, Faceted, Painted, Marked, Coro Duet, 1¼ x 2 In.	235.00
Clip, Rooster, Sterling Silver, Engraved Accents, Los Castillo, Taxco, Mexico, 1¾ In.	294.00
Cuff Links, Dragons, Coral, Carved, ⅝ In.	353.00
Cuff Links, Dumbbell, Trace Link Chain, 18K Gold, ¾ In.	764.00
Cuff Links, Foot, Brass, Applied Bead Accents, Hubert Harmon, Mexico, c.1940, 1¼ In.	411.00
Cuff Links, Jade Disc, Gold, Carved, Rectangular Panels, 1⅛ x ⁷⁄₁₆ In.	201.00
Cuff Links, Knot Shape, 18K Gold, Marked, Van Cleef & Arpels, ⅞ In.	1410.00
Cuff Links, Leaves, Sterling Silver, Marked, M. Buccellati, Pouch	588.00
Cuff Links, Monkey, 14K Gold, Labradorite, Cabochon Red Stone Eyes, 1¼ In.	2468.00
Cuff Links, Rectangular Quartz, 14K Gold Mount, Button Back, Victorian, ¾ In. . . . . .*illus*	150.00
Cuff Links, Sterling Silver, Foot Shape, Marked, Hubert Harmon, 1½ In.	529.00
Cuff Links, Tiger's Head, 18K Yellow Gold, Enamel, Gemstone, Wing Back, Italy	1003.00
Cuff Links & Tie Tack, Frog Shape, 18K Gold, Enamel, Garnet Cabochon Eyes, David Webb .	1645.00
Earrings, 14K Gold, Gem Set, Coral, Cabochon, Turquoise, Clip-On, Seaman Schepps, 1 In. .	1410.00
Earrings, 18K Gold, Clip-On, Schlumberger, Tiffany & Co., Box, 1¼ In.	1528.00
Earrings, 18K Gold, Marked, Zolotas, Pouch, 2¼ In.	823.00
Earrings, 18K Gold, Rosewood, Wirework Bound, Seaman Schepps, 1 x ⅞ In.	1645.00
Earrings, Adam & Eve & Tree Of Life, Gilt Bronze, Clip-On, Line Vautrin, c.1950, ⅞ In.	1920.00
Earrings, Amber, Orange Cabochon, Sterling Silver, Marked, Georg Jensen, 1995, 1 In.	470.00
Earrings, Amethyst, Carved Leaves, 14K Gold, 2½ In.	646.00
Earrings, Aquamarine, Diamond, Square Cut, 18K White Gold Mount, 1⅛ x ½ In.	1380.00
Earrings, Basket Weave, Bombe Shape, 18K Gold, Garrard & Co., Box	588.00
Earrings, Bird On Leaf, Sterling Silver, Marked, Georg Jensen, ⅞ In.	235.00

Earrings, Blue & Green Stones, Schiaparelli	213.00
Earrings, Buckle Shape, Clip-On, 14K Gold, Retro, 1¼ In.	529.00
Earrings, Button, Sterling Silver, Oval Hematite Cabochon, Paloma Picasso, Tiffany & Co.	124.00
Earrings, Carnelian Cabochon, Suspended Flower, 18K Gold, 2 In.	1293.00
Earrings, Diamond, Cultured Pearl, Bead & Bezel Set, Platinum, Art Deco, 1½ In.	2585.00
Earrings, Double C Shape, Clip-On, 18K White Gold, Marked, Cartier, ¾ In.	881.00
Earrings, Double Hoop, 14K Gold, Clip-On, Cartier, 1 In.	588.00
Earrings, Emeralds, Diamonds, Trapezoid Cut, Platinum, Art Deco, 7¼ In.	470.00
Earrings, Enamel, Bicolor Gold, Victorian, 2 In.	2233.00
Earrings, Honeycomb, 18K Gold, Marked, DM, 1⅛ In.	529.00
Earrings, Hoop, Crimped, Full Cut Diamond Melee, 14K Gold, Clip-On, 1¼ In.	940.00
Earrings, Hoop, Patinated Steel, 14K Gold, Cultured Pearl, Diamond, Marsh's, Box	2115.00
Earrings, Hoop, Sterling Silver, Wide, Tapered, Marked, Georg Jensen	264.00
Earrings, Jadeite Cabochon, 2 Beads, 14K Bicolor Gold, Art Deco, Bippart, Griscom & Osborn	705.00
Earrings, Lapis, Diamonds, 3 Strands, 18K Gold, Van Cleef & Arpels, ⅜ In.	1528.00
Earrings, Large Pearl Cabochons, Rows Of Clear Rhinestones, L. Vrba	90.00
Earrings, Moon & Stars, South Sea Pearl, Diamond, White Gold, ¾ In.	1175.00
Earrings, Pearl, Grape Cluster, 14K Gold	425.00
Earrings, Rooster, Sterling Silver, Engraved, Clip-On, Los Castillo, 1¾ In. ....*illus*	294.00
Earrings, Shrimp, Blue Chalcedony, 18K White Gold, 1¼ x ¾ In.	1645.00
Earrings, Tanzanite, Prong Set, Oval Cut, 14K Gold, ½ In.	382.00
Earrings, Turbo Shell, Ruby Cabochon, 14K Gold, 1 In.	1880.00
Earrings, Turquoise Cabochon, 18K Gold, Rope Work Frame, Tiffany & Co., ½ In.	1880.00
Earrings, Wing & Star, Brass, Hubert Harmon, Taxco, Mexico	353.00
Earrings & Pin, Sterling Silver, Janiye, 1½-In. Pin, 1⅛-In. Earrings	264.00
Earrings & Ring, Sterling Silver, Turquoise, Bezel Set, Marked, Georg Jensen	881.00
Fibula, Silver, Diamond, Pearl, Flower Shape, Collet Set, 2⅛ In.	264.00
Hair Comb, Brass, Hand Wrought, Alexander Calder, c.1960, 6¼ x 5 In. ....*illus*	36000.00
Hatpins are listed in this book in the Hatpin category.	
Lavaliere, 14 Yellow Diamonds, 144 Brilliant Cut Diamonds, 18K Bicolor Gold	3805.00
Locket, 14 Cut Rubies, 18 Halved Pearls, 18K Yellow Gold, Victorian	962.00
Locket, Bar & Link Chain, Sterling Silver, Arts & Crafts, Marked, Alo, 23½ In.	880.00
Locket, Cameo, Hardstone, Classical Warriors, 14K Gold, 2¼ In.	235.00
Locket, Lion Mask, Gemstones, Yellow Gold, Renaissance Revival, 1⅜ In.	472.00
Locket, Pearls, Gold Vermeil, Black Enamel Overlay, Engraved Cross, 1800s, 2 x 1½ In.	345.00
Necklace, 3 Heshi Birds, Mother-Of-Pearl, Tortoiseshell Spacers, 28 In.	125.00
Necklace, 30 Metal Ojime Beads, Mythical Creatures, Flowers, Gourds, Gold Clasp, 24 In.	3055.00
Necklace, 31 Ceramic Scarabs, Lotus Flower, Ankh, Wing, 14K Gold, Egypt, 42 In.	823.00
Necklace, 103 Full Cut Diamonds, Prong Set, 14K White Gold, Riviere, 15½ In.	4113.00
Necklace, 180 Rose Cut Garnets, Gilt Metal, Bohemia, Victorian, c.1880, 15½ In.	935.00
Necklace, 14K Yellow Gold, Flexible, Flared Drop Pendant, Denmark, c.1960	224.00
Necklace, 18K Yellow Gold, 135 Pink Pearls, 3 Strands, Lobster Claw Clasp, 21 In.	3304.00
Necklace, Akoya Pearls, 3 Graduated Strands, 14K White Gold & Sapphire Bar Clasp	826.00
Necklace, Amethyst, Silver, Glasgow Rose Design, Paper Clip Chain, Kalo, 18 In.	2700.00
Necklace, Angel Skin Coral, 10 Strands, Gold, Coral Flower Clasp, Italy, 1960s, 20 In.	325.00
Necklace, Bakelite, Licorice, Faceted Beads, Fringe, 14¾ In.	264.00
Necklace, Beads, Gadrooned, 3 Strands, 14K Gold, Tiffany & Co., 18 In.	2115.00
Necklace, Branch Coral, Spanish Silver Coins, Charms, Peru	177.00
Necklace, Chain, Gem Set, Champleve Enamel, Renaissance Revival, 26¾ In.	18800.00
Necklace, Charm, Typewriter, 2 Cutout Hearts, Gold Tone Metal, Monet	35.00
Necklace, Coral Beads, 3 Cabochons, 4 Strands, Teardrop Pendants, c.1850, 28 In. ....*illus*	767.00
Necklace, Cultured Pearls, 2 Strands, 14K Yellow Gold Diamond Clasp, 18 In.	620.00
Necklace, Cultured Pearls, Graduated Sizes, Art Deco, 16 In.	470.00
Necklace, Diamond Melee, Bezel Set, Platinum, Marked, Tiffany & Co., 15¼ In.	3819.00
Necklace, Festoon, Blue & Gold Beads, Tassel Pendant, Frerich	59.00
Necklace, Foxtail Fringe, Enamel Accents, 15K Gold, Floral Mount, Victorian, 17¼ In.	764.00
Necklace, Link, Flexible, Enameled Pendant, Lapis Ball Drop, Egyptian Revival, 15½ In.	1003.00
Necklace, Moonstone, Glass, Quartz, Ceramic, Amethyst, 24K Gold Plated, Box, 1994, 16½ In.	4200.00
Necklace, Nephrite, 2 Dragons, Butterflies, Silver	2115.00
Necklace, Opals, Pearls, Pink Quartz, 4 Strands, Thread Tieart Decosylvia Gottwald, Peru	649.00
Necklace, Pendant, 2 Hands, Brown & White Stone, Chain, Silver, William Spratling, 11 In.	2468.00
Necklace, Pendant, Bird, Wood, Silver, Leather Cord, 2¼ x 1⅞ In.	411.00
Necklace, Pendant, Black Opal, Diamonds, Arts & Crafts, William Bramley, 15 In.	17625.00
Necklace, Pendant, Black Opal Composite, 14K Bicolor Gold, Retro, 17 In.	764.00
Necklace, Pendant, Blue, Round, Silver Neck Wire, Royal Copenhagen, Mid 1900s, 16 x 5½ In.	823.00
Necklace, Pendant, Cross, Carved Black Onyx, 173 Diamonds, Chain, 18K White Gold	1631.00

Jewelry, Bracelet, Mesh, Buckle, Turquoise Cabochons, 14K Gold, Victorian, 1 x 9½ In. $215.00

Jewelry, Bracelet, Raisins, Grapes & Vines, Yellow Amber Glass, R. Lalique, c.1919, 3¼ In. $2040.00

Jewelry, Buttonhook, 14K Gold, Enameled Flowers In Hat-Shaped Basket, Chain, c.1880 $212.00

TIP
A signature on a piece of jewelry adds 30% to the value. Look at the pin shank, pin back, and catch for the signature.

Jewelry, Cuff Links,
Rectangular Quartz, 14K Gold Mount,
Button Back, Victorian, ¾ In.
$150.00

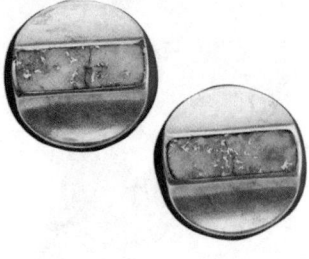

Jewelry, Earrings, Rooster,
Sterling Silver, Engraved, Clip-On,
Los Castillo, 1¾ In.
$294.00

Jewelry, Hair Comb, Brass,
Hand Wrought, Alexander Calder,
c.1960, 6¼ x 5 In.
$36000.00

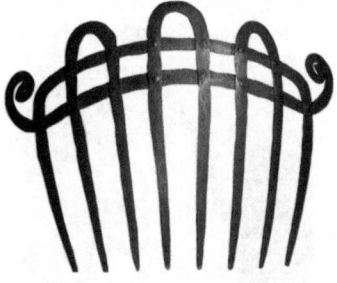

Jewelry, Necklace, Coral Beads,
3 Cabochons, 4 Strands,
Teardrop Pendants, c.1850, 28 In.
$767.00

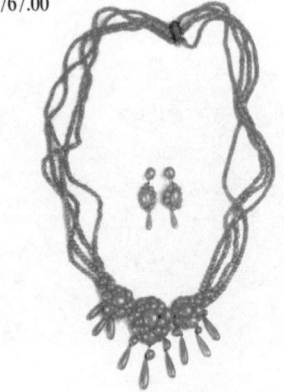

Necklace, Pendant, Diamonds, European Cut, Seed Pearls, 18K Gold, c.1920, 16 In. ...*illus*	717.00
Necklace, Pendant, Emerald, 85 Diamonds, Chain, 14K Yellow Gold, 17 In.	2580.00
Necklace, Pendant, Flowers, Oval Blue Stone, Chain, Arts & Crafts, c.1927, 17½ x 15 In.	264.00
Necklace, Pendant, Glass, Intaglio, Classical Scene, Freshwater Pearl, 18K Gold, 1½ In.	470.00
Necklace, Pendant, Glass, Woman Reclining In Flowers, Baton Link Chain, R. Lalique, 20 In.	3819.00
Necklace, Pendant, Pin, Starburst, 14K Gold, Diamond Melee, 18K Gold Link Chain, 1 In. ..	440.00
Necklace, Pendant, Sterling Silver, Silver & Rubber Chain, Georg Jensen, Denmark, 15 In. ..	227.00
Necklace, Pendant, Tourmaline Wings, Ball Chain, 18K Gold, Art Nouveau, 1⅝ x 18 In.	1645.00
Necklace, Pendant, Trace Link Chain, Multiple Strands, 18K Gold, Tiffany & Co., 16½ In. ...	940.00
Necklace, Peruvian Opal, Seed Pearls, Faceted Garnet Rondels, Gold Chain, Riviera, 16 In. .	105.00
Necklace, Serpent, Coiled, Sterling Silver, Enamel, Mexico, 30 In.	1754.00
Necklace, Slide, Diamond, Moon, Star, Sunburst, 18K Gold, Morelli	793.00
Necklace, Starburst, Seed Pearls, 9K Gold, Fancy Link Chain, Victorian, 16¾ In.	1410.00
Necklace, Sterling Silver, 17 Links, Domed Pyramids, Strap Links, H. Aguilar, 16 In.	2115.00
Necklace, Sterling Silver, Alternating Spade & Tear Shaped Links, Mexico, 16 In.	176.00
Necklace, Sterling Silver, Obsidian, Antonio Pineda, Taxco, Mexico	3000.00
Necklace, Stylized Snake Head, Wraps Around To Tail, Hinged, Spratling, 5 In.	1998.00
Necklace, Textured Fringe, Foxtail Chain, 18K Gold, Bulgari, 14 In.	4113.00
Necklace, Torsade, 8 Strands Nematite Beads, Swan, 18K Gold, Natan, Brazil, 16 In.	2006.00
Necklace, Watch Pendant, Tassels, 18K Gold, Louis Favre Sandor ....*illus*	388.00
Necklace, White Glass Beads, Hand Knotted, Beige, Ivory, Japan, 27 In.	35.00
Necklace & Earrings, 18K Gold, Black Cord, Marked, Elsa Peretti, Tiffany & Co., 33 In.	1058.00
Necklace & Earrings, Coral, Ribbed Leaves, 132 Beads, 18K Gold, 17½-In. Necklace	940.00
Necklace & Earrings, Coral Beads, 3 Flowers, Box Clasp, Victorian, c.1850	767.00
Necklace & Earrings, Mesh, Blue Art Glass Stone & Baguettes, Hobe	104.00
Necklace & Earrings, Pearls, Diamond Melee, 18K Gold Mounts, Art Deco	3525.00
Necklace Set, Bracelet, Drop Earrings, Sterling Silver, Art Deco Style, Birks	103.00
Necklace Set, Bracelet, Earrings, Clip-On, Sterling Silver, Marcasite, Theodore Fahrner, c.1940 ..	264.00
Necklace Set, Bracelet, Earrings, Turquoise, Sterling Silver, TNC, Mexico, c.1940	808.00
Necklace Set, Cameo, Lava, Multicolor, Bracelet, Pin, Earrings, Flower Wreaths, Victorian, Box .	2115.00
Necklace Set, Diamond Melee, Blue & Teal Enamel, Bicolor Gold, La Nouvelle Bague, 4 Piece	2350.00
Parure, 14K Rose Gold, Onyx, Seed Pearls, Necklace, Earrings, Bracelet, Victorian	823.00
Parure, Demi, Cameo, Hardstone, 14K Gold, Maiden, Flowing Hair, 2 Pins, 1⅞-In. Pin	1175.00
Parure, Demi, Coral, Fringe, 18K Gold, Ram's Head, Suspended Urns	3173.00
Parure, Demi, Grape, Engraved, Gilt Metal, Pin, Earrings, Fitted Leather Box	323.00
Parure, Demi, Seed Pearls, Enamel, 14K Gold, Victorian, Leather Box, 1¾ x 1¼ In.	646.00
Pendant, Boulder Opal, Diamond, Bezel Set, Garland Frame, Art Nouveau, 1½ In.	2468.00
Pendant, Citrine, Faceted, Oval, Bezel Set, 18K Gold	325.00
Pendant, Colombes, Woman Holding Dove, Red, c.1920, 1⅝ In.	1200.00
Pendant, Emerald, Bow Shape, 10K Gold, Silver, Edwardian, 2½ In.	353.00
Pendant, Flowers, Paste, Mother-Of-Pearl, Applied Beads, Rope Twist, 18K Gold, Box	880.00
Pendant, Foo Dog, Crouching, Ball, Moving Tongue, Eyes, 24K Gold, 1½ In.	1763.00
Pendant, Gilt Bronze, c.1950, 2⅝ x 2½ In.	1440.00
Pendant, Graines, Seeded Stems, Triangular, Amethyst, 1¾ In.	1020.00
Pendant, Green Jade Figure, Seated, Lapis, Diamond, Pearl, Gold Frame, Chain, 14K Gold ..	2090.00
Pendant, Heart, Diamonds, Blue Enamel, 18K Bicolor Gold, La Nouvelle Bague, ¾ In.	1000.00
Pendant, Ivory, Carved, Orange Coral Mosaic, Sterling Silver, Oval, Cilia Sebiri, 2⅝ In.	177.00
Pendant, Jade, Yellow, Carved, Chinese, 1¼ x 2 In.	118.00
Pendant, Jadeite, Carved, Carp, Lotus, Birds, 3½ In.	826.00
Pendant, Libellules, Dragonflies, Green, c.1920, 2⅛ In.	1920.00
Pendant, Lion's Head, Flowers, Beads, Wire Twist, 18K Gold, Ernesto Pierret, 1¾ In.	4818.00
Pendant, Masks, Comedy & Tragedy, Inscription, 14K Gold, Art Nouveau, 1½ In.	705.00
Pendant, Micro Mosaic, St. Peter's Basilica, Onyx Field, Silver Mount, 1¼ x 1¾ In.	299.00
Pendant, Nantucket Basket, Cover, 14K Gold, 1 In.	294.00
Pendant, Opal Cabochons, 7 Oval, 14K Yellow Gold, Birks	588.00
Pendant, Panier De Fruits, Fruit Basket, Frosted, Gray Patina, c.1922, 1½ In.	720.00
Pendant, Pate-De-Verre, Green Glass, Pinecone, Silk Ribbon, G. Argy-Rousseau, c.1915 *illus*	2151.00
Pendant, Pate-De-Verre, White & Purple Flowers, Silk Cord, Tassel, 2½ In. ....*illus*	1840.00
Pendant, Pin, Fish, Diamond Eyes, 14K Gold, 2¼ x 1 In.	472.00
Pendant, Pin, Pearls, Diamonds, 14K Gold, Edwardian, Howard & Co., 1¼ x 1⅜ In.	14100.00
Pendant, Pin, Platinum, Diamonds, Millegrain Accents, Trace Link Chain, Art Deco, 2½ In. ..	6463.00
Pendant, Pin, Swallow, Bead Set, Rose Cut Diamond Melee, Pink Stone Eye, 2 In.	353.00
Pendant, Pin, Waterfall, Diamond Melee, 18K Gold, 2¾ In.	382.00
Pendant, Scarab, Mosaic, Red, White, Blue Border, Roma, Victorian, 2¼ In. ....*illus*	1058.00
Pendant, Serpents, Snakes, Blue, c.1920, 1¾ In.	2160.00
Pendant, Silver, 18K Gold, Sven Boltenstern, 3 In.	2703.00

Jewelry, Necklace, Pendant, Diamonds, European Cut, Seed Pearls, 18K Gold, c.1920, 16 In.
$717.00

Shoplifters Liked Rhinestones

Jonas Eisenberg added rhinestone clips made with imported Swarovski crystals to his dark dresses. His jewelry, crystal clips, buttons, and pins, was so popular with shoplifters, he started a separate company, Eisenberg Ice, to sell just the jewelry in 1935. Early pieces were marked *Eisenberg Original* or with the letter *E* in script. The name *Eisenberg Ice* was the mark in 1950. From the 1950s to the 1970s there were no marks, but in the 1970s the *Eisenberg Ice* label returned. It is still used on Eisenberg Ice jewelry, which still features clear and colored crystal from Swarovski.

Jewelry, Necklace, Watch Pendant, Tassels, 18K Gold, Louis Favre Sandor
$388.00

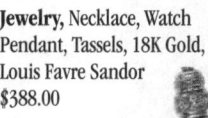

Jewelry, Pendant, Pate-De-Verre, White & Purple Flowers, Silk Cord, Tassel, 2½ In.
$1840.00

Jewelry, Pin, 2 Dolphins, Sterling Silver, Georg Jensen, 1¾ In.
$102.00

Jewelry, Pin, Abstract Shape, Sterling Silver, Ed Weiner, 2¼ In.
$480.00

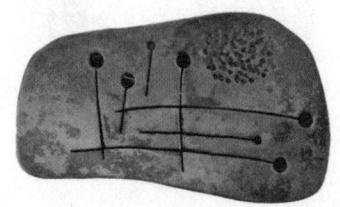

Jewelry, Pendant, Pate-De-Verre, Green Glass, Pinecone, Silk Ribbon, G. Argy-Rousseau, c.1915
$2151.00

Jewelry, Pendant, Scarab, Mosaic, Red, White, Blue Border, Roma, Victorian, 2¼ In.
$1058.00

Jewelry, Pin, Bakelite, Horse's Head, Red Brown, Leather Collar, Brass Chain, 3¾ x 3 In.
$176.00

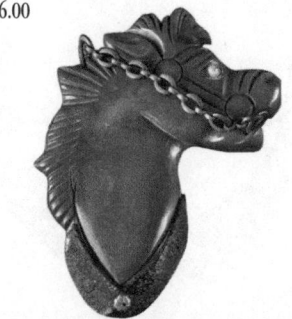

Jewelry, Pin, Bow, Amethyst Cabochon, Gold, Swag Chain, Slip Case Locket, Victorian, 2¾ In.
$206.00

Jewelry, Pin, Diamonds, Black Onyx Cabochons, Emeralds, Platinum, c.1930, 2 In.
$5975.00

Jewelry, Pin, Mourning, Onyx Panel, Diamonds, Seed Pearls, Gold Flowers, Scrolls, 1¾ In.
$235.00

Jewelry, Pin, Butterfly, Diamonds, Rubies, Sapphires, Opal, Gold Mount, c.1880, 1¾ x 1 In.
$598.00

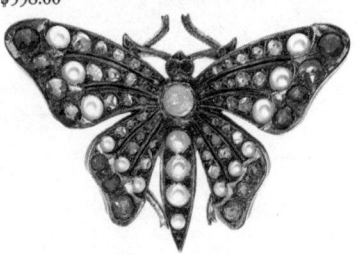

Jewelry, Pin, Diamonds, Pierced Platinum-Topped 18K Gold Mount, Edwardian, c.1910, 2 In.
$2629.00

Jewelry, Pin, Poodle, Seated, Sapphire Eyes, Diamond Bowtie, 14K Gold, 4½ In.
$130.00

Jewelry, Pin, Cameo, Shell, Woman's Profile, Gold Frame, Victorian, 2⅝ x 2¼ In.
$717.00

Jewelry, Pin, Horseshoe, 3-Leaf Clovers, Translucent Enamel, Victorian, 2¾ In.
$118.00

Jewelry, Pin, Sea Horse, Jadeite, Carved, Silver Scroll Mount & Chain, Mid 20th Century, 3 In.
$24.00

Jewelry, Pin, Cultured Pearls, 26 Graduated Old Mine Diamonds, Crescent Shape, 14K Gold
$1000.00

Jewelry, Pin, Mourning, Flowers, Seed Pearls, Lock Of Hair, Gold Frame, Victorian, 2 In.
$598.00

Jewelry, Pin, Spider, Oval Enamel Body, Diamonds, Rubies, Early 20th Century, 2⅝ In.
$1800.00

Pendant, Silver, Green Stone, Aztec Style, Mid 20th Century, 2¼ In. 176.00
Pendant, Sorbier, Rowan Tree, Electric Blue, Silk Cord, Lalique, c.1920, 2 In. . . . . . . 840.00 to 1140.00
Pendant, Watch, Diamonds, Onyx Highlights, 18 Jewel Movement, Art Deco, Cartier 21150.00
Pin, 2 Dolphins, Sterling Silver, Georg Jensen, 1¾ In. . . . . *illus* 102.00
Pin, 2 Ducks, Marked, Georg Jensen, 2 In. 411.00
Pin, 2 Hounds, Reverse Painted Glass, 14K Gold, 1⅜ x ⅝ In. 1880.00
Pin, 13 White Cultured Pearls, Branch Design, 14K Gold, Mikimoto, 1¼ In. 470.00
Pin, 14K Gold Coil Mount, Garnet, Pearl Border, Victorian, c.1880, 1½ In. 561.00
Pin, Abstract Shape, Sterling Silver, Ed Weiner, 2¼ In. . . . . *illus* 480.00
Pin, Abstract Shape, Sterling Silver, Marked, Georg Jensen, 1¾ In. 411.00
Pin, Abstract Shape, Sterling Silver, Tone Vigeland, Norway, 1960s, 2 In. 353.00
Pin, Bakelite, Boot, Licorice, Butterscotch, 3 x 2 In. 176.00
Pin, Bakelite, Fish, Butterscotch, Brass Stud, 3 In. 411.00
Pin, Bakelite, Horse's Head, Butterscotch, Glass Eyes, Brass Bridle, c.1925, 3½ x 2 In. 94.00
Pin, Bakelite, Horse's Head, Caramel, Leather Collar, Brass Chain, c.1925, 3¾ x 3 In. 176.00
Pin, Bakelite, Horse's Head, Red, Glass Eyes, Brass Bridle, c.1925, 3½ x 2 In. 206.00
Pin, Bakelite, Horse's Head, Red Brown, Leather Collar, Brass Chain, 3¾ x 3 In. . . . . *illus* 176.00
Pin, Bakelite, Horse's Head, Yellow, Resin Washed, Brass Bridle, c.1925, 3¼ In. 147.00
Pin, Basket, Pansies, Pearls, Enamel, 14K Gold, A.J. Hedges & Co., 2½ x 2¾ In. 443.00
Pin, Bee, Diamonds, 10K Gold, Retro, 1⅝ In. 341.00
Pin, Bird, Diamonds, Demantoid Garnet, 18K Bicolor Gold, Retro, 2¾ In. 1763.00
Pin, Bird, Goofus Glass, C-Clasp, Victorian 100.00
Pin, Bird, Pearl, Jade Insects, Pearl Head, Ruby Eyes, 18K Gold, Italy 325.00
Pin, Black Opal, Plique-A-Jour Enamel, 18K Gold, Art Nouveau, Whiteside & Blank 5580.00
Pin, Bow, Amethyst Cabochon, Gold, Swag Chain, Slip Case Locket, Victorian, 2¾ In. . . .*illus* 206.00
Pin, Bow, Platinum, Sapphire, Diamond, Millegrain Accents, Art Deco, 2 In. 4406.00
Pin, Butterfly, Diamonds, Rubies, Sapphires, Opal, Gold Mount, c.1880, 1¾ x 1 In. . . . .*illus* 598.00
Pin, Butterfly, Jadeite, Carved, Pierced Wings, Flexible Antennae, 14K Gold, 2 In. 382.00
Pin, Butterfly, Ruby, Sapphires, Diamonds, Marquise & Full Cut, 18K Patinated Gold, 1¼ In. 4583.00
Pin, Calla Lily, Sterling Silver, Los Castillo, Mexico, Mid 20th Century, 4½ In. 235.00
Pin, Cameo, Bacchante, Carved, Ivory, 18K Yellow Gold Mount 1039.00
Pin, Cameo, Classical Maiden, Agate, Rose Garland, 18K Gold, Engraved, ¾ In. 1410.00
Pin, Cameo, Classical Woman, 2 Children, Carved Shell, Silver Filigree, 2¼ x 1¾ In. 750.00
Pin, Cameo, Grecian Goddess, Gutta-Percha, Black Ground, 1860s 125.00
Pin, Cameo, Man, Silhouette, Scrolled Frame, 14K Gold, 1⅜ x 1⅝ In. 588.00
Pin, Cameo, Shell, Woman's Profile, Gold Frame, Victorian, 2⅝ x 2¼ In. . . . . *illus* 717.00
Pin, Cameo, Woman, Bird, Carved Shell, Gold Filled Frame, c.1900, 2½ In. 106.00
Pin, Cameo, Woman, Dove, Carved Shell, Gold Filled Frame, c.1900, 2 In. 118.00
Pin, Cameo, Woman With Bandeau, Curls, Hardstone, Seed Pearls, 14K Gold, 2¼ x 1⅞ In. . . 881.00
Pin, Cameo, Zeus, Coral, Leaf Frame, 18K Gold, 1¾ x 1¼ In. 1763.00
Pin, Circle, 36 Brilliant Cut Round Diamonds, Platinum, Mid 20th Century, 1³⁄₁₆ In. 1003.00
Pin, Circle, Diamonds, Platinum, Art Deco, Marked, Tiffany & Co., c.1930, 1 In. 2006.00
Pin, Copper & Silver, Abstract Triangular Shape, Marked, Jauquet, c.1985, 2½ In. 247.00
Pin, Crab, 35 Single Cut Diamonds, Bicolor Gold, Pave, 18K Gold, 1¼ In. 940.00
Pin, Crown, Pearls, Moriage Style, Victorian 225.00
Pin, Cultured Pearls, 26 Graduated Old Mine Diamonds, Crescent Shape, 14K Gold . . . .*illus* 1000.00
Pin, Dachshund, Enamel, Rose Cut Diamond Ears, Ruby Eyes, Emerald Collar, 1½ In. 705.00
Pin, Demantoid Garnet, Ruby, Pearl, Art Nouveau, Marcus & Co., 1⅜ x 1½ In. 7050.00
Pin, Deux, Clear, Frosted, Gray Patina, Pink Foil, Gilt Metal, Stamped, c.1913, 2¼ In. 3900.00
Pin, Diamonds, 208 Brilliant Cut, Platinum, Double Geometric Clips, c.1940, 3¼ In. 7080.00
Pin, Diamonds, Bead Set, Openwork, Platinum, Art Deco, Dreicer, 1¾ In. 3290.00
Pin, Diamonds, Black Onyx Cabochons, Emeralds, Platinum, c.1930, 2 In. . . . . *illus* 5975.00
Pin, Diamonds, European & Single Cut, Emerald, Platinum, Art Deco, 2 x ¾ In. 7638.00
Pin, Diamonds, Pierced Platinum-Topped 18K Gold Mount, Edwardian, c.1910, 2 In. . .*illus* 2629.00
Pin, Diana, Moonstone Intaglio, Old Mine Cut Diamonds, 14K Gold, ⅞ x ¾ In. 1410.00
Pin, Dog, Sapphire Eyes, Diamond Set Collar, 18K Gold, Tiffany & Co., 1¾ x 1¼ In. 826.00
Pin, Dolphin, Ruby Eye, 14K Gold, 1¾ In. 353.00
Pin, Dragon, Jadeite, Single Cut Diamond, Platinum, Art Deco 3643.00
Pin, Dragonfly, Tortoiseshell, Silver, Wm. Spratling, Wire Back Clips, 2 x 2½ In., Pair 1410.00
Pin, Elephant Head, Diamonds, Emerald Eyes, 14K Bicolor Gold, 1½ In. 472.00
Pin, Enamel, Topaz, Pearl, 14K Gold, c.1900 . . . . 635.00
Pin, Fan, Rhinestone, Multicolor, Gold Plated, Trifari, 1950s, 2½ In. 58.00
Pin, Fire Opal, Onyx, Sterling Silver, Sam Kramer, c.1950, 4 x 1¾ In. 6463.00
Pin, Fish, 14K Gold, Bailey Banks & Biddle, 2¼ In. 353.00
Pin, Fish, Enamel, Ruby Eye, 18K Gold, Cartier, 1¼ In. 1293.00
Pin, Fish, Unicorn, Abstract Scene, 14K Gold, Marked, Eric DeKolb, 1½ x 1¾ In. 353.00

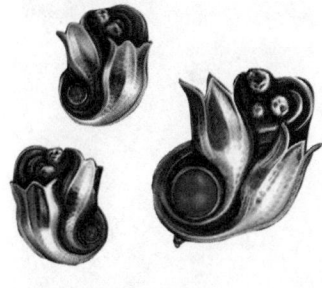

Jewelry, Pin & Earrings,
Flower, Red Coral Bead,
Sterling Silver, Georg Jensen
$600.00

Jewelry, Pin & Earrings,
Seed Pearls, 18K Gold,
Victorian, 2½-In. Pin, 1½-In. Earrings
$598.00

Jewelry, Ring, 2 Heart-Shaped Rubies,
Rose Cut Diamonds, Gold Mount,
Early 1900s, Size 7¾
$510.00

J

TIP

*Put your pearls on after
you finish using hair
spray or perfume. Both
will discolor the pearls
and amber beads.*

TIP
One antique earring can still be used. Have the jeweler make it into a stickpin, a tie tack, a charm for a bracelet or a ring. If it is a clip-on, use it like a lapel pin; if it is for a pierced ear, attach it through the knit of a sweater. Some earrings can be hung in the center of a strand of pearls, an old-fashioned adaptation of the new "pearl enhancers."

Jewelry, Ring, 3 Turquoise Cabochons, 2 Old European Cut Diamonds, Victorian
$431.00

Jewelry, Ring, 5 Opals, Graduated Sizes, Diamonds, 14K Gold, Edwardian
$745.00

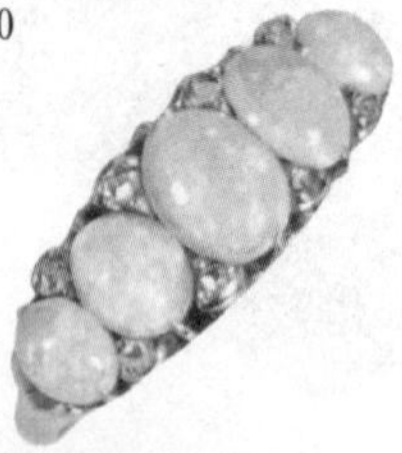

Newark, Home of Gold Jewelry
Most of the gold jewelry made in the United States before the 1930s was made in Newark, New Jersey. The name of the retailer, not the maker, was often used as the mark.

Pin, Flower, Black Enamel, Old Mine Cut Diamond, 14K Gold, Art Nouveau, Tiffany, 1½ In. . 1058.00
Pin, Flower, Freshwater Pearl, Engraved Leafy Stem, 18K Gold, Art Nouveau, 1⅜ In. 382.00
Pin, Flower, Jadeite, Enamel Highlights, 14K Gold, Art Deco, 1½ In. 441.00
Pin, Flower, Pearl, Old Mine Cut Diamond Melee, 14K Gold, Art Nouveau, 1¼ In. 470.00
Pin, Flower, Topaz, Citrine, Diamond, Cartier, London, c.1930 .... 17625.00
Pin, Flower Shape, Rose Cut Diamond, Garnet, Victorian Silver, c.1870 .... 1692.00
Pin, Flowers, Goofus Glass, Reverse Painted, Domed Shape, Gold Frame, Victorian, 1⅜ x 1 In. 56.00
Pin, Flowers, Leaves, Gutta-Percha, Wood, Carved, Victorian, c.1880, 2¼ x 1¾ In. 275.00
Pin, Gazelle, Red Lucite Head, Turquoise Horns, Hattie Carnegie 305.00
Pin, Gem Set Flower, Diamond, Lapis, Turquoise, 18K Gold, Hammerman Bros., 2 In. 646.00
Pin, Golfer, Sterling Silver, Painted Crystal, 2¾ x ⅞ In. 118.00
Pin, Hardstone Cabochon, Sterling Silver, Hammered, Matl, Taxco, Mexico, 1¾ In. 323.00
Pin, Heart, Sterling Silver, Pearl, Fronds, Georg Jensen, 1¼ In. 206.00
Pin, Horse, Riding Whip, Cabochon Ruby, 14K Bicolor Gold, Sloan & Co., 3½ In. 470.00
Pin, Horseshoe, 3-Leaf Clovers, Translucent Enamel, Victorian, 2¾ In. ....*illus* 118.00
Pin, Insect, Wings, Baroque Pearl Abdomen, Diamond, 18K White Gold 330.00
Pin, Jade, Ducks On Pond, Flowers, Green & Orange Enamel, 14K Gold, 2 In. 940.00
Pin, Landscape, Agate, Diamonds, Oval, 18K Gold, 1½ x ¾ In. 558.00
Pin, Leaf, Berry, Amber, Cabochon, Marked, Georg Jensen, 1¾ x 1⅜ In., 2 Piece 764.00
Pin, Leaf, Sapphire, Ruby, 18K Gold, Tiffany & Co., 2 In., Pair 1293.00
Pin, Leaves, Blue Stone Cabochon, Sterling Silver, Georg Jensen, 1⅜ In. 294.00
Pin, Love Birds, Goofus Glass, Amethyst Rhinestones, Bird Cages, C-Clasp, Victorian 125.00
Pin, Lover's Eye, Portrait, Blue Eye, Gold, Double Row Seed Pearls, Oval, 1 In. 3819.00
Pin, Lover's Eye, Portrait, Blue Eye, Gold, Seed Pearls, Teardrop Shape, ⅞ In. 2702.00
Pin, Lyre, Old Mine Cut Diamonds, Silver Mount, 1¼ In. 3525.00
Pin, Mabe Pearl, Sapphire, Diamond, Marked, Yard 1239.00
Pin, Maple Leaf, Diamond, 18K Gold, Tiffany & Co., 2½ In. 1116.00
Pin, Marcasite, Hematite, Sterling Silver, Marked, Theodor Fahrner, c.1926, 5⅜ In. 470.00
Pin, Meduse, Profile, Clear, Frosted, Gray Patina, Foil, Gilt, Stamped, c.1912, 1 In. 2280.00
Pin, Micro Mosaic, Architectural Scene, Onyx, 18K Yellow Gold, ¾ x 1 In. 356.00
Pin, Micro Mosaic, Butterfly, Twisted Wire, 18K Yellow Gold, Oval 658.00
Pin, Moonstone, Bezel Set, Leaf, Tendril, 14K Gold, Arts & Crafts, Edward Oakes, 1½ In. 5875.00
Pin, Moonstone, Cabochon, Oval Cut Garnet, 14K Bicolor Gold, 2¾ In. 1116.00
Pin, Mother-Of-Pearl, Gold Mount, 1752 .... 250.00
Pin, Mourning, Flowers, Seed Pearls, Lock Of Hair, Gold Frame, Victorian, 2 In. ....*illus* 598.00
Pin, Mourning, Grapes, Victorian, 2¼ x 1¾ In. 59.00
Pin, Mourning, Onyx Panel, Diamonds, Seed Pearls, Gold Flowers, Scrolls, 1¾ In. .....*illus* 235.00
Pin, Mourning, Winged Angel Holding Child, Vulcanite, Victorian 400.00
Pin, Onyx, Carved, 9 Rose Cut Diamonds, 14K Yellow Gold, Dutch 520.00
Pin, Opal Cabochons, Diamond Melee, Bezel Set, Platinum, Art Deco, 2 In. 1528.00
Pin, Oval, Gold, Black Enamel Border, Mourning Scene On Ivory, 1785, 1½ In. 7200.00
Pin, Pansy, Purple & Cream Enamel, Diamond Accents, 14K Gold, Marked 1116.00
Pin, Penguin, Turquoise Cabochon, 18K Gold, 1⅜ In. 588.00
Pin, Piggy Bank, Sterling Silver, 3 Graduated Coins, Flowers On Pig, Mexico, 4 In. 705.00
Pin, Pink Sapphire, Diamond Scroll, Prong Set, Platinum, 14K Gold, c.1915, 1⅛ In. 940.00
Pin, Pink Stones, Paisley Shape, Sherman 105.00
Pin, Poinsettia, Alfred Philippe, Trifari 1325.00
Pin, Poodle, Seated, Sapphire Eyes, Diamond Bowtie, 14K Gold, 4½ In. ....*illus* 130.00
Pin, Regimental, Sphinx, Plinth, Platinum, Diamonds, Pave Set, Egyptian Revival, 1¼ In. .. 2115.00
Pin, Rhinestone, Green Aurora Borealis, Clover Shape, 2½ In. 50.00
Pin, Ribbon, 14K Gold, Retro, 1¾ In. 235.00
Pin, Ribbon, Ruby, Diamonds, Bead & Bezel Set, 14K Rose Gold, Retro, 2¼ In. 940.00
Pin, Roses On The Vine, Goofus Glass, Giltwood Backing 72.00
Pin, Sailfish, Tackle, Rod, Reel, Enamel, Seed Pearls, 14K Gold, c.1940, 4 In. 3055.00
Pin, Sailfish, Diamond, Enamel, 18K Gold, Platinum, 3 In. 4348.00
Pin, Salamander, Opal Cabochons, Peridot, Pave Set, 14K Gold, 2 In. 529.00
Pin, Sapphires, Diamonds, Circle, Platinum, Art Deco, 1¼ In. 1175.00
Pin, Scotties, Celluloid, Japan, c.1950, 1¾ In. 15.00
Pin, Scrolls, Flexible Drops, Gems, 18K Gold, Arts & Crafts, F.G. Hale, 2½ x 2 In. 10575.00
Pin, Sea Horse, Jadeite, Carved, Silver Scroll Mount & Chain, Mid 20th Century, 3 In. ..*illus* 24.00
Pin, Seahorse, Sterling Silver, Coral Cabochon Eye, Matl, Taxco, Mexico, 2½ In. 264.00
Pin, Shamrocks, Enamel, Horseshoe Shape, Victorian, 2¾ In. 118.00
Pin, Ship, Full Sail, Silver, May 2, 1932 .... 20.00
Pin, Snowflake, Sapphire, Diamonds, Palladium Mount, Tiffany & Co., Box, c.1940, 1⅜ In. . 7638.00
Pin, Spider, Oval Enamel Body, Diamonds, Rubies, Early 20th Century, 2⅝ In. ....*illus* 1800.00

Pin, Starfish, Rhinestones, Brass Openwork, Gold Plate, Coro, 2¾ In. 85.00
Pin, Sterling Silver, Bow, 6 Amethyst Drops, Movable Mount, Antonio Pineda, c.1950, 4 In. 1763.00
Pin, Sterling Silver, Clasped Hands, North & South America, William Spratling, 1½ In. 353.00
Pin, Sterling Silver, Interlocking V Shapes, Scroll Ends, Line & Ball, Hector Aguilar, 2⅝ In. 353.00
Pin, Sterling Silver, Leaf Bud, Scrolled Tendril, Georg Jensen, 2 In. 118.00
Pin, Sterling Silver, No. 77, Georg Jensen 268.00
Pin, Sterling Silver, Ruskin Porcelain Panel, Oval, 1½ In. 31.00
Pin, Stylized Leaves, Sterling Silver, Round, Georg Jensen, 2½ In. 147.00
Pin, Swirl, 14K Gold, Cartier, 1⅞ In. 705.00
Pin, Tadpole, Diamond, Sapphire, Emeralds, Onyx, 18K White Gold, 2 In. 657.00
Pin, Textured 18K Yellow Gold Free Form Loops, Diamond, Sapphire, 2½ In. 649.00
Pin, Topaz Stone, Surrounded By 8 Chieftains, Aztec, Castlecliff, 1960s 125.00
Pin, Wasp, Garnet, Diamonds, European, Single Cut, 1⅝ x 1 In. 7638.00
Pin, Woman With Basket Of Fruit, Man With Guitar, Sterling Silver, Fred Davis, 2⅜ In., Pair 881.00
Pin, Zodiac, Virgo Woman, 18K Gold, 2¼ x 1¾ In. 470.00
Pin & Bracelet, Bakelite, Bangle, Carved, Applied Daisy, 8-In. Bracelet, 3-In. Pin 206.00
Pin & Earrings, Diamond Melee, 14K Gold, Cartier, Fitted Box, 1¾ x ¾ In. 1645.00
Pin & Earrings, Flower, Red Coral Bead, Sterling Silver, Georg Jensen *illus* 600.00
Pin & Earrings, Ribbed Squares, 18K Gold, Marked, Tiffany & Co. 940.00
Pin & Earrings, Ruby, Diamonds, 18K Gold, Tiffany & Co., 1½-In. Pin, ⅞-In. Earrings 2468.00
Pin & Earrings, Seed Pearls, 18K Gold, Victorian, 2½-In. Pin, 1½-In. Earrings *illus* 598.00
Pin & Earrings, Seed Pearls, Gold, Drops, Renaissance Revival, 2¼ & 2⅛ In. 1530.00
Pin & Earrings, Sun & Moon, Sterling Silver, Copper, Spratling, c.1942, 3⅜ & 1¼ In. 1293.00
Ring, 2 Heart-Shaped Rubies, Rose Cut Diamonds, Gold Mount, Early 1900s, Size 7¾ *illus* 510.00
Ring, 3 Diamonds, 2 Pear Shape, 1 Full Cut, Platinum, Tiffany & Co., Size 4¾ 5875.00
Ring, 3 Turquoise Cabochons, 2 Old European Cut Diamonds, Victorian *illus* 431.00
Ring, 5 Opals, Graduated Sizes, Diamonds, 14K Gold, Edwardian *illus* 745.00
Ring, 11 Diamonds, White Gold Filigree Mount, Art Deco, Size 7 413.00
Ring, Abstract Shape, 30 Yellow Sapphires, 30 Rubies, 14K White Gold 181.00
Ring, Alligator, Sapphire, 14K Gold, Size 7¼ 470.00
Ring, Amethyst, Step Cut, Cushion Shape, 18K Gold, Man's, Size 8¾ 470.00
Ring, Angel Skin Coral Cabochon, Diamond, Navette Shape, 14K Gold, Size 8 201.00
Ring, Ballerina, Orange Brown Marquise Cut Diamond, 16 Diamonds, Platinum, Size 6½ 5580.00
Ring, Black Opal, Single Cut Diamonds, Platinum, 18K White Gold, Art Deco 1998.00
Ring, Bombe Shape, 18K Gold, Tiffany & Co., Size 6½ 353.00
Ring, Bypass, Snake, Rose Cut Diamonds, Ruby Melee Accents, 14K Gold, Size 6½ 1410.00
Ring, Chrysoberyl, Cat's Eye, Diamond, Platinum, Ladies, Size 6½ 403.00
Ring, Diamond, 14K White Gold, Reeded, Box, Cartier, ¾ x 3⅞ In. 1150.00
Ring, Diamond, Citrine, Ruby, 18K Gold, Retro, Size 6 2820.00
Ring, Diamond, Cushion Cut Sapphire, Platinum, 18K Gold, Edwardian, Size 5½ 2585.00
Ring, Diamond, Old European Single Cut, Platinum, Art Deco, Size 5 *illus* 2760.00
Ring, Diamond, Star Sapphire, Platinum, Art Deco 2820.00
Ring, Diamond Melee, Bead Set, 18K White Gold, Marked, Cartier, Size 6½ 3819.00
Ring, Diamonds, Oval 18K White Gold, Filigree Mount, Ciner 1195.00
Ring, Diamonds, Rubies, Platinum, 14K Pink Gold Mount, c.1940, 1 In. *illus* 508.00
Ring, Emeralds, Diamond, Bezel Set, Lion's Head, Foil Back, Leaf Motifs, Size 5 9400.00
Ring, European Cut Diamond, Bead Set, Platinum, Art Deco, Size 5 2350.00
Ring, Hardstone, Cabochon, Oval, Green, Grapevine, 14K Gold, Arts & Crafts, Size 5¾ 470.00
Ring, Hematite, Cabochon, Bezel Set, Sterling Silver, Georg Jensen, 1¼ In., Size 7 In. 353.00
Ring, Iolite, 34 Diamonds, Prong Set, 18K White Gold, Size 6½ In. 1175.00
Ring, Lapis, 18K Gold, Marked, Tiffany & Co., Size 4½ 646.00
Ring, Lapis, Bezel Set, 18K Gold, Georg Jensen, Size 6¾ 1000.00
Ring, Lapis, Intaglio, Classical Figure, Leafy Shoulders, 18K Gold, Size 6½ 1293.00
Ring, Lion Of Judah, Hebrew Letters, Sapphire, Intaglio, 18K Gold, Size 9½ 3525.00
Ring, Navette Shape, 23 Old Mine Diamonds, 14K Gold, Victorian, Size 7 1058.00
Ring, Opal, Diamond Melee, Scrolls, Art Deco, Inscribed, Dec. 1933, Size 5¾ 2233.00
Ring, Panther's Head, Black Lacquer Spots, Peridot Eyes, Onyx Nose, 18K Gold, Cartier 6490.00
Ring, Paste Stone, Faceted, Black Enamel, Gold Scrolls, Inscribed, 1764, Size 7 9600.00
Ring, Puzzle, Diamond Melee, 18K White Gold, Chaumet, Paris, Size 5¾ 1293.00
Ring, Ruby, Diamond Melee, Bead Set, 18K Gold, Craig Drake, Size 7¾ 1293.00
Ring, Sapphire, 20 Small Diamonds, 18K White Gold, Canada 774.00
Ring, Sapphire, Diamonds, Gypsy Mount, 14K White Gold, Size 9½ 575.00
Ring, Sapphire, Star Set, 14K Gold, Marked, Tiffany & Co., Size 6 382.00
Ring, Seal, Winged Figure, Helmet, Suit Of Armor, Amethyst, Intaglio, Size 8¼ 705.00
Ring, Serpent, Relief Cast, Rubies, Sapphires, Textured, 18K Gold 384.00

Jewelry, Ring, Diamond, Old European Single Cut, Platinum, Art Deco, Size 5
$2760.00

Jewelry, Ring, Diamonds, Rubies, Platinum, 14K Pink Gold Mount, c.1940, 1 In.
$508.00

Jewelry, Stickpin, Dog's Head, Western Terrier, Painted, Porcelain, Round Gold Mount
$294.00

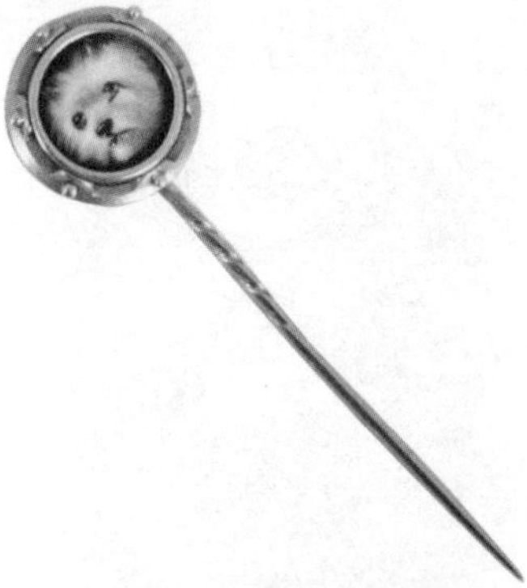

TIP
Gemstones are colder to the touch than glass. Colored gems like emeralds, rubies, and sapphires should not appear scratched. If there are scratches, the "stone" is probably colored glass.

Ring, Smoky Topaz, Pearl, 14K Yellow Gold, Coiled Border, Size 6	212.00
Ring, Spiral Bands, 18K Gold, William Spratling, Size 7	2938.00
Ring, U.S. Military Academy, West Point, Gold, Green Stone, 1918	1497.00
Ring, Wide Band, 4 Applied Relief Elephants, 56 Diamonds, 14K Bicolor Gold	1087.00
Stickpin, Dog's Head, Western Terrier, Painted, Porcelain, Round Gold Mount ....*illus*	294.00
Stickpin, Egyptian Style, Enamel, Pearls, 14K Gold	52.00
Stickpin, Flowers, Hummingbird, Bow, Ribbons, Goldtone, Flat, Oval, 2⅜ x 1¼ In.	20.00
Tiara, Sterling Silver, Gold Washed, Pear Cut Diamonds	5053.00
Watch Chain, 14K Gold, Interlocking Oval Links, 44 In.	823.00
Watch Chain, Round Links, Bean Shape Slide, 10K Yellow Gold, Lady's, Victorian, 48 In. ...	148.00
Watches are listed in their own category.	
Wristwatches are listed in their own category.	

JOHN ROGERS

JOHN ROGERS statues were made from 1859 to 1892. The originals were bronze, but the thousands of copies made by the Rogers factory were of painted plaster. Eighty different figures were created. Similar painted plaster figures were produced by some other factories. Rights to the figures were sold in 1893 and they were manufactured for several more years by the Rogers Statuette Co. Never repaint a Rogers figure because this lowers the value to collectors.

Group, Council Of War, Lincoln, Grant, Stanton, 1868, 24 x 15 x 12 In. ....*illus*	2645.00
Group, Is It So Nominated In The Bond?, Scene From Merchant Of Venice, 23 x 19 In.	288.00
Group, Parting Promise, Man Parting From Lady Love, Putting Ring On Finger, 22 In.	633.00
Group, Phrenology At The Fancy Ball, Painted, 1886, 20 x 9 x 8 In. ....*illus*	920.00
Group, Rip Van Winkle On The Mountain, 21 x 9½ In.	460.00
Group, Rip Van Winkle Returned, 21 x 9 In.	518.00
Group, School Days, Children & Hand-Organ Player With Monkey, 22 x 12 In.	805.00
Group, Shaughraun & Tatters, Vagabond Teaching Dog Tricks, Fiddle, 20 In.	575.00
Group, Traveling Magician, Sleeping Tambourine Girl, Man & Boy, 1877, 23 x 15 In.	3565.00
Group, Uncle Ned's School, Black Family, Father Shining Shoes, Girl Reading, 1868, 20 In.	1035.00
Group, Weighing The Baby, 1876, 21 x 15 x 11 In.	293.00
Group, Wounded Scout, 1864, 23 x 11 In.	690.00
Group, Wounded To The Rear Or One More Shot, Civil War Soldiers, 23½ In. ....*illus*	690.00

JOSEF ORIGINALS

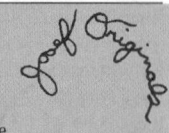

JOSEF ORIGINALS ceramics were designed by Muriel Joseph George. The first pieces were made in California from 1945 to 1962. They were then manufactured in Japan. The company was sold to George Good in 1982 and he continued to make Josef Originals until 1985. The company was then sold to Southland Corporation. The name is now owned by Applause, and the Birthday Girl series is still being made.

Figurine, Angel, June, Pearl, Gold Lines On Wings, 5½ In.	13.00
Figurine, Birthday Girl, No. 4, Marked, 3½ In.	35.00
Figurine, Birthday Girl, No. 5, Marked, 4½ In.	35.00
Figurine, Birthday Girl, No. 11, Marked	18.00 to 35.00
Figurine, Doll Of The Month, January, Girl With Muff	50.00
Figurine, Doll Of The Month, May, Pink, Bouquet Of Roses, c.1960, 3½ In.	45.00
Figurine, Ecology Girl, Blue Flowers, c.1974-75, 4¼ In.	43.00
Figurine, Ecology Girl, Ladybug, c.1974-75, 4¼ In.	43.00
Figurine, Mouse Bride, Flower On Head, 2¾ In.	24.00
Figurine, Ostrich Family, 2 Adults, 3 Babies, 1960, 5 Piece	177.00
Figurine, Sugar & Creamer, Santa	20.00

JUDAICA

JUDAICA is any memorabilia that refers to the Jews or the Jewish religion. Interests range from newspaper clippings that mention eighteenth- and nineteenth-century Jewish Americans to religious objects, such as menorahs or spice boxes. Age, condition, and the intrinsic value of the material, as well as the historic and artistic importance, determine the value.

Bracelet, Charm, Sterling Silver, Mother-Of-Pearl, Blue Enamel, Star Of David, 8 In.	150.00
Candlestick, Sabbath, Corinthian Column, Sterling Silver, c.1800, 11⅝ In., Pair	3000.00
Candlestick, Sabbath, Silver, Baluster Stems, Rococo Scrolls, Flowers, Russia, 1870, 15 In., Pair	5100.00
Candlestick, Sabbath, Silver, Square Bases, Germany, 1793, 10½ In., Pair	1680.00
Case, Esther Scroll, Parcel Gilt Silver, 20th Century, 17 In.	5700.00
Case, Esther Scroll, Parcel Gilt Silver, Ottoman, Mid 19th Century, 8½ In.	3600.00
Case, Esther Scroll, Silver, Austria, Mid 19th Century, 5⅝ In.	5100.00
Charity Box, Pewter, Copenhagen, c.1901, 4⅝ In.	3600.00 to 6000.00
Charm, Tribal, Sterling Silver, 10K Gold, Flag Of Ephraim, Grapes, 1 x 1½ In.	85.00

J

John Rogers, Group, Council Of War, Lincoln, Grant, Stanton, 1868, 24 x 15 x 12 In. $2645.00

Charms, Tribal, Issachar Emblem, 10K Gold, Sterling, Donkey, Rope Loop, ¾ x 1⅛ In.	90.00
Cover, Light Switch, Shabbat, Sterling Silver, Red Wood Frame, 5 x 3½ In.	150.00
Cup, Brass, Silver Inlay, 19th Century, 4⅛ In.	1287.00
Cup, Kiddush, Silver, Engraved Blessing, Hallmarks, France, 18th Century, 3 x 3 In.	300.00
Cup, Kiddush, Sterling Silver, Beaker Shape, Repousse Vines, Grapes, 3½ In.	100.00
Cup, Kiddush, Sterling Silver, Engraved, Scrolling, Zigzag, 1970s, 5½ In.	160.00
Curtain, Torah Ark, Jeweled, Red Velvet, Gold Fringe, Northern Africa, Mid 1900s, 55 In. . . .	150.00
Decanter Set, Shabbat, Sterling Silver, Hollowware, Star Of David, c.1920, 7 Piece	600.00
Dish, Latke, Ceramic, Man & Wife Figures, Apple Dish, Box, Lotus International, 5 & 12 In. .	85.00
Dresser Box, Porcelain, Star Of David, Flowers, Ruffled Rim, Gilded, Footed	50.00
Egg Holder, Passover, Silver Gilt, Germany, 1787-90, 2⅞ In.	4800.00
Figurine, Jewish Peddler, Porcelain, c.1830, 5⅜ In.	2700.00
Inkwell, Silver, Domed, Chased, Fruiting Leaves, Hebrew Inscription, c.1920, 3¾ In.	3600.00
Jar, Lid, Jewish Theme, Ceramic, 4 x 9 In.	65.00
Lamp, Hanukkah, Plated Copper, 8 Oil Fonts, Pear Shape Servant Light, 6 x 5 In.	123.00
Lamp, Hanukkah, Silver, Flowers, Scrolls, 8 Wick Holders, Hinged Cover, 5½ x 5 In.	1440.00
Mantel, Torah, Embroidered, Bazalel Era, Velvet, Green, Palestine, c.1940, 30½ In.	500.00
Mantel, Torah, Embroidered, Brown, Cotton, Palestine, Early 20th Century, 26 In.	175.00
Marriage Casket, Domed, Embossed, Gilt Leather, Germany, 4⅝ In.	3300.00
Megillah, Esther Scroll, Parcel Gilt Silver, Gem Set Case, 20th Century	7800.00
Menorah, Art Glass, Paperweight, Crystal Block Laser Sculpture, Beveled, 2 In.	215.00
Menorah, Hanukkah, Brass, Wall Mounted, 15 x 9 In.	176.00
Menorah, Silver, Pogorzelsk, Minsk, Russia, 1892, 26½ In.	4275.00
Mezuzah, Gilt Silver, Window Shape, Hebrew Script, Israel, 6¾ In.	295.00
Mezuzah, Kosher Klaf, Olive Wood, Engraved Stripes, Mid 20th Century, 6 In.	75.00
Mezuzah, Silver, Gold, Cylindrical, Engraved, Man On Horseback, Gemstone, Scroll, 5 In. . . .	1416.00
Paperweight, Caithness, Star Of David, 3-Dimensional, Blue Ground, Bubbles, 3¼ In.	110.00
Paperweight, Chai, Caithness, Spaced Bubbles, Blue Ground, Signed, 3¼ In.	210.00
Paperweight, Star Of David, Art Glass, Crystal Block, Laser Sculpture, Shalom, 3 In.	195.00
Paperweight, Star Of David, Millefiori, 30th Anniversary Of Israel, Whitefriars, 1978, 3 In. .	500.00
Paperweight, Star Of David, Perthshire, White Stardust Canes, Millefiori Garland, 2½ In. . .	170.00
Pin, Sterling Silver, Yemenite Style, Filigree, Amethyst, Canted Corners, 1900s, 1¼ In.	175.00
Plaque, Sidur, Copper, Leather Cover, Bezalel, Palestine, Early 1900s	150.00
Plate, Mizrach, Gilded, Painted, 10 In.	200.00
Postcard, Synagogue, 10 Fold-Out Pictures, Black & White, Leporello, Romania, c.1909	75.00
Prayer Scroll, Gold, Silver, 7 Inset Jewels, Encased, 19th Century, 5 In.	1112.00
Spice Box, Bsamim, Brass, Polish, Arched, Filigree Work, Early 1800s, 8 In.	300.00
Spice Box, Silver, Fruit Form, Palmettes, 4¾ In.	3300.00
Spice Box, Sliding Cover, Pewter, Rectangular, Ball Feet, Cherub Handle, 1793, 3⅜ In.	3000.00
Spice Tower, Parcel Gilt Silver, Filigree, c.1830, 10⅝ In.	8400.00
Spice Tower, Silver, Cubic Filigree Body, Spire, Flag, Rope Twist Supports, 9 In.	329.00
Tallis, Bag, Ateret Latalit Silver, Repousse Silver Rectangles, Germany, 19th Century, 25 In. .	150.00
Tallis Bag, Ateret, Silver Thread, Sewn Patterns, Rounded Ends, 28 x 3¼ In.	100.00
Tallis Bag, Silk, Embroidered, Flowers, Foliage, Star Of David, c.1923, 10¾ x 8½ In.	75.00
Tfillin Bag, Embroidered, Bezalel Period, Blue Velvet, Cotton, Palestine, Star Of David	75.00
Tfillin Bag, Silk, Cotton Lining, Drawstring Top, Palestine, c.1948, 7 x 9½ In.	45.00
Tfillin Bag, Yemenite, Embroidered, Black Velvet, Palestine, c.1940, 6 x 7 In.	45.00
Torah Cover, Silver Plate, Plaque Shape, Rococo, Oval Reserves, Hebrew Script, 14 x 10 In. .	705.00

JUGTOWN Pottery refers to pottery made in North Carolina as far back as the 1750s. In 1915, Juliana and Jacques Busbee set up a training and sales organization for what they named Jugtown Pottery. In 1921, they built a shop at Jugtown, North Carolina, and hired Ben Owen as a potter in 1923. The Busbees moved the village store where the pottery was sold to New York City. Juliana Busbee sold the New York store in 1926 and moved into a log cabin near the Jugtown Pottery. The pottery closed in 1959. It reopened in 1960 and is still working near Seagrove, North Carolina.

Bowl, Chinese Blue Glaze, Oval, Round Stamp Mark, c.1920-30, 4½ x 10½ x 14 In.	440.00
Figurine, Catfish, Speckled Brown Glaze, Charles Moore, 5½ In.	85.00
Fountain, Water Sound, Rocks, Burgundy Glass, 9½ In., 2 Piece	85.00
Jar, Green Frogskin Glaze, 4 Handles	475.00
Pitcher, Floating Blue, Red Glaze, Pulled Handle, H.T. Robbins	75.00
Vase, Blue, Green Glaze, 4⅛ In.	475.00
Vase, Chinese Blue Glaze, Shouldered, Flattened, 5½ x 7 In. . . . . *illus*	390.00
Vase, Chinese White Glaze, Band Of Incised Lines, Round, 8½ In.	470.00
Vase, Chinese White Glaze, Bulbous, Incised Band Decoration, Flared Rim, 9½ In.	264.00
Vase, Green & Red Sponged Glaze, 20th Century, 15¾ In.	6463.00

John Rogers, Group,
Phrenology At The Fancy Ball,
Painted, 1886, 20 x 9 x 8 In.
$920.00

John Rogers, Group,
Wounded To The Rear
Or One More Shot,
Civil War Soldiers, 23½ In.
$690.00

Jugtown, Vase,
Chinese Blue Glaze, Shouldered,
Flattened, 5½ x 7 In.
$390.00

Jukebox, Seeburg, Model 147,
Trashcan, Red Plastic Trim,
78 RPM, 1947, 58 In.
$1017.00

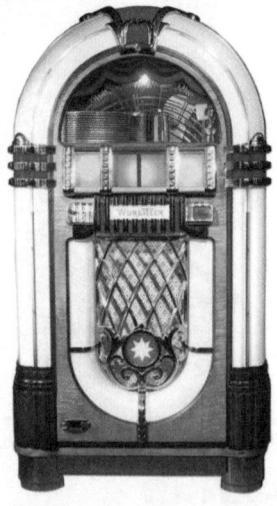

Jukebox, Wurlitzer, Model 1015,
Bubbler, 78 RPM, c.1947, 60 In.
$5265.00

Kay Finch
Kay Finch was a dog-show
judge, and her ceramic
canine figurines show her
understanding of dogs'
anatomy. Many of her
animals—cats, elephants,
monkeys, and pigs —have
very human expressions.

JUKEBOXES play records. The first coin-operated phonograph was demonstrated in 1889. In 1906 the Automatic Entertainer appeared, the first coin-operated phonograph to offer several different selections of music. The first electrically powered jukebox was introduced in 1927. Collectors search for jukeboxes of all ages, especially those with flashing lights and unusual design and graphics.

Seeburg, Model 147, Trashcan, Red Plastic Trim, 78 RPM, 1947, 58 In. ....*illus*	1017.00
Seeburg, Vogue, Red, c.1939, 56 x 34 In.	1171.00
Wurlitzer, Model 1015, Bubbler, 78 RPM, c.1947, 60 In. ....*illus*	5265.00
Wurlitzer, Model 1100, Arched Case, 24 Selections, 78 RPM, c.1948, 57½ In.	3819.00
Wurlitzer, Model 750, Tube Type, 24 Selections, 78 RPM, c.1941, 56 x 32 x 29 In.	3105.00
Wurlitzer, Model 780, 24 Selections, 78 RPM, c.1941, 38 x 60 In.	1430.00
Wurlitzer, Model 81, Countertop, Tortoiseshell, 24 Selections, c.1941	14690.00
Wurlitzer, Model 850A, Tulip, 24 Selections, 78 RPM, c.1941	38500.00
Wurlitzer, Victory, Replacement Cabinet, Girl, Jester, 1943-45, 67 In.	4950.00

KATE GREENAWAY, who was a famous illustrator of children's books, drew pictures of children in high-waisted Empire dresses. She lived from 1846 to 1901. Her designs appear on china, glass, and other pieces.

Button, 2 Children Sitting On Fence, Umbrella, Purple, Loop Shank, 1 In.	49.00
Calling Card Holder, Victorian, Silver Plate, 2 Sisters, Dog, 7¼ In.	550.00
Fairing Girl, Porcelain, Shaker Bonnet, Painted, c.1890, 4⅛ In.	51.00
Match Safe, Bronze, Boy & Girl, On Fence, Umbrella, 1981, 3 x 2 In.	325.00
Napkin Ring, Boy, Lying On Back On Rectangular Base, Openwork	995.00
Napkin Ring, Child Feeds Dog, Silver Plate, Meriden-Britannia	505.00
Napkin Ring, Figural, Girl With Rifle, Silver Plate, Miller, 3¼ In. ....*illus*	441.00
Napkin Ring, Girl, Sitting On Branches	1250.00
Napkin Ring, Girl On Swing, Silver Plate, Reed & Barton, Late 1800s, 5½ In.	765.00
Napkin Ring, Silver Plate, Boy, Leaning On Ring, Open Latticework, Tufts, Napkin	995.00
Napkin Ring, Silver Plate, Figural, Girl, Puppy, Simpson Hall Miller, Late 1800s, 3¾ In.	823.00
Paper Dolls Book, Kathy Allert, Kate Greenaway & Family, 4 Dolls, Outfits, Uncut	10.00
Pitcher, Children, Leaves, Flowers, Blown Glass, 9 In., Pair	1300.00
Saltshaker, Girl, In Bonnet, Fairings, c.1890, 4⅛ In.	51.00

KAY FINCH Ceramics were made in Corona Del Mar, California, from 1935 to 1963. The hand-decorated pieces often depicted whimsical animals and people. Pastel colors were used.

Kay Finch
CALIFORNIA

Figurine, Cat, Persian, 10¾ In.	595.00
Figurine, Choir Boy, Blond, 5½ In.	25.00 to 65.00
Figurine, Duck, Peep, 1950s, 4 In.	65.00
Figurine, Elephant, Mumbo, 4½ In.	46.00
Figurine, Lamb, Kneeling, 2¼ In.	84.00
Figurine, Lamb, Rearing, 5¾ In.	96.00
Figurine, Mama Duck, 4½ In.	199.00
Figurine, Mr. & Mrs. Bird, 1949, 4½-In. Male, 3-In. Female	170.00
Figurine, Peasant Girl, 7 In.	44.00
Figurine, Scandie Girl, 5 In.	52.00
Figurine, Squirrels, Mama & Papa, 3½ In.	100.00

KAYSERZINN, *see Pewter category.*

KELVA glassware was made by the C. F. Monroe Company of Meriden, Connecticut, about 1904. It is a pale, pastel-painted glass decorated with flowers, designs, or scenes. Kelva resembles Nakara and Wave Crest, two other glasswares made by the same company.

KELVA

Box, Collars & Cuffs, Pink Flowers, Blue Watermark Ground, Marked, 5½ x 8 In.	1320.00
Box, Hinged Cover, Black, 4½ x 4½ In.	875.00
Box, Hinged Cover, Oak Leaf Mold, Blue Mottled Ground, Square, Signed, 4½ In.	600.00
Box, Pink Rose, Gray Ground, 6-Sided, 3¼ x 3½ In.	175.00
Cigarette Holder, Blue Flowers, Brown Mottled Ground, Footed, 3½ In.	300.00
Jewelry Box, Blue Flowers, Red Mottled Ground, Round, Hinged Cover, Signed, 3¾ In.	150.00
Jewelry Box, Pink Flowers, Blue Mottled Ground, Square, Hinged Cover, Signed, 4 In.	400.00
Lamp Base, Pink Flowers, Green Mottled Ground, 13½ In.	150.00
Pin Tray, Pink Flowers, Gray Ground, Handles, 5 In.	125.00
Vase, Pink Flowers, Cobalt Blue Mottled Ground, Pink Border, Enameled Beads, 8¾ In.	500.00

J

KEMPLE glass was made by John Kemple of East Palestine, Ohio, and Kenova, West Virginia, from 1945 to 1970. The glass was made from old molds. Many designs and colors were made. Kemple pieces are usually marked with a *K* on the bottom. Many milk glass pieces were made with or without the mark.

Ashtray, Coal Bucket, Milk Glass, 2¼ x 3 In.	5.00
Bonbon, Sunburst Pattern, Milk Glass, Footed, Handles, No. 46, Marked	25.00
Bowl, Quintec Pattern, Amber Marigold, 3¼ x 7½ In.	25.00
Compote, Martec Pattern, Honey Amber, Footed, Marked, 1970s	15.00
Dish, Hen On Nest Cover, Milk Glass, Marked, 7¼ x 6 In.	65.00
Goblet, Lace & Dewdrop, Amber, 5⅞ x 3⅛ In.	15.00
Pitcher, Lace & Dewdrop, Milk Glass, 4½ In.	20.00
Plate, Milk Glass, Cabin In Woods, Snow, Icy Pond, Hand Painted, Lacey Edge, 7¼ In.	20.00
Plate, Milk Glass, Paneled Edge, Signed, John E. Kemple, 7 In.	12.00
Plate, Milk Glass, Sheaf Of Wheat Border, 7½ In.	25.00
Plate, Milk Glass, Shell & Club, Marked, 7 In.	12.00
Plate, Milk Glass, Water Wheel Scene, Hand Painted, Heart-Pierced Rim, 7¼ In.	20.00
Plate, Milk Glass, Windmill, Hand Painted, Heart-Pierced Rim, 7¼ In.	20.00
Plate, Milk Glass, Winter Scene, Hand Painted, Heart-Pierced Rim, 7¼ In.	20.00
Plate, Shell & Club, Pink Rose, Green Leaves, Hand Painted, 7 In.	12.00
Relish, Yutec, Yellow, 4-Part Mold, Scalloped Rim	35.00
Sugar, No Lid, Lace & Dewdrop, Milk Glass, 4⅛ x 4⅜ In.	9.00
Toothpick, Amber, Indian Chief Front & Back, 1960s, 3¼ In.	16.00

KENTON HILLS Pottery in Erlanger, Kentucky, made artwares, including vases and figurines that resembled Rookwood, probably because so many of the original artists and workmen had worked at the Rookwood plant. Kenton Hills opened in 1939 and closed during World War II.

Bowl, Spanish Red, 5 Lobes, 2¼ x 5¼ In.	*illus*	138.00
Figurine, Evening Star, Oriental Woman, Sitting, White, Marked, 9⅛ In.		180.00
Vase, Pink, Beaded & Striped Bands, Oval, William Hentschel, 3⅞ In.	*illus*	92.00
Vase, Raised Decoration, Brazilian Cat's-Eye Glaze, W.E. Hentschel, 11½ x 6 In.	*illus*	600.00
Vase, Stylized Orchard Decoration, Footed, W.E. Hentschel, 5 x 6 In.	*illus*	510.00

KEW BLAS is the name used by the Union Glass Company of Somerville, Massachusetts. The name refers to an iridescent golden glass made from the 1890s to 1924. The iridescent glass was reminiscent of the Tiffany glass of the period.

Vase, Bud, Gold Iridescent, White Ground, Drag Loop, Flat To Elongated Neck, 5¾ In.		540.00
Vase, Gold Iridescent Pulled Feathers, Opal Ground, Cone Shape, Flared Rim, 4 In.		316.00
Vase, Green, Gold Curled Tips, Opal Shoulder, Combed Feathers, Gold Iridescent, 8¾ In.		1150.00
Vase, Green & Gold Zipper, Yellow, Gold Iridescent Rolled Rim, 6¼ In.	*illus*	1150.00

KEWPIES, designed by Rose O'Neill, were first pictured in the *Ladies' Home Journal*. The figures, which are similar to pixies, were a success, and Kewpie dolls and figurines started appearing in 1911. Kewpie pictures and other items soon followed. Collectors search for all items that picture the little winged people.

Ashtray, Marble, Brass Figure, Art Brass Co., N.Y., 3 x 4¾ In.		129.00
Bank, Chalk, Coy, 11 In.		85.00
Bisque, Arms & Ankles Crossed, Wicker Chair, c.1912		375.00
Bisque, Buttonhole, Raised Arms, Germany		200.00
Bisque, Glass Eyes, Socket Head, Composition Body, 11 In.		6050.00
Bisque, Holding Luggage & Umbrella, 3½ In.		150.00
Bisque, Jointed Arms, Molded & Painted Features, Tied To Pink Lace Pillow, 5 In., Pair		275.00
Bisque, Seated, 3¾ In.		25.00
Bisque, Side-Glancing Eyes, Jointed Arms, 5-Piece Composition, Bunny Suit, 6 In.		840.00
Bisque, Side-Glancing Eyes, Jointed Arms, Red, Blue Crepe Paper Costume, 4½ In.		784.00
Bisque, Side-Glancing Eyes, Socket Head, 5-Piece Composition, Germany, 10 In.		6440.00
Bisque, Trailing Flowers, Pomander, Open Bottom, Impressed KW, 3¾ In.		95.00
Celluloid, Jointed Arms, Japan, 1945-52, 5 In.		18.00
Celluloid, Jointed Arms, Ribbon & Lace Dress, Original Wig, Japan, 3 In.		65.00
Chalk, Grass Skirt, 12 In.		175.00
Clock, Jasperware, 30-Hour Lever Movement, Porcelain, Germany, c.1910, 4 In.		358.00
Composition, Left-Glancing Eyes, Jointed, Starfish Hands		3249.00
Composition, Noma Toys Ltd., Box, 11 In.	*illus*	374.00

Kate Greenaway, Napkin Ring, Figural, Girl With Rifle, Silver Plate, Miller, 3¼ In.
$441.00

Kenton Hills, Bowl, Spanish Red, 5 Lobes, No. 184, 2¼ x 5¼ In.
$138.00

Kenton Hills, Vase, Pink, Beaded & Striped Bands, Oval, William Hentschel, 3⅞ In.
$92.00

K

Kenton Hills, Vase, Raised Decoration, Brazilian Cat's-Eye Glaze, W.E. Hentschel, 11½ x 6 In.
$600.00

Kenton Hills, Vase, Stylized Orchard Decoration, Footed, W.E. Hentschel, 5 x 6 In.
$510.00

KEWPIE

Kew Blas, Vase,
Green & Gold Zipper, Yellow,
Gold Iridescent Rolled Rim, 6¼ In.
$1150.00

Kewpie, Composition,
Noma Toys Ltd., Box, 11 In.
$374.00

Kewpie, Composition,
Right-Glancing Eyes, Standing,
Jointed, 10 In.
$175.00

Kewpie, Cup & Saucer,
Green Tree Pattern, Porcelain,
Royal Rudolstadt, c.1914
$258.00

Composition, Right-Glancing Eyes, Standing, Jointed, 10 In. ....*illus*	175.00
Cup & Saucer, Green Tree Pattern, Porcelain, Royal Rudolstadt, c.1914 ....*illus*	258.00
Planter, Pink, USA Pottery, 5¾ In.	38.00
Porcelain, Red Cross Outfit, 1983, 3½ In.	29.00
Porcelain, Right-Glancing Eyes, Playing Harp, Camille Naudot, c.1930	75.00
Postcard, Hazelwood Ice Cream, Valentine Heart, 2 Kewpies, Rose O'Neill ....*illus*	323.00
Ragsy, Rubber, Left-Glancing Eyes, Blue, Cameo, 1960s, 8 In.	89.00
Red Vinyl, Cameo, 10 In.	75.00
Rubber, Cameo, 10 In.	75.00

KING'S ROSE, *see Soft Paste category.*

KITCHEN utensils of all types, from eggbeaters to bowls, are collected today. Handmade wooden and metal items, like ladles and apple peelers, were made in the early nineteenth century. Mass-produced pieces, like iron apple peelers and graniteware, were made in the nineteenth century. Also included in this category are utensils used for other household chores, such as laundry and cleaning. Other kitchen wares are listed under manufacturers' names or under Advertising, Iron, Tool, or Wooden.

Board, Slaw, Lollipop Handle, 22⅝ x 7⅝ In.	55.00
Board, Slaw, Walnut, Crest, Double Heart Cutout, 16¾ x 7 In.	220.00
Bowl, Chopping, Burl, Carved Rim, Patina, 5¾ x 15½ In.	1265.00
Bowl, Dough, Butter, Wooden, 19th Century, 19 x 6 In.	245.00
Bowl, Dough, Maple, Oval Form, 13¾ x 22¾ x 4⅝ In.	144.00
Bowl, Ladle, Burl, Hand Carved, 14 & 16 In.	225.00
Box, Pantry, 3-Sided, Red Paint, Stripes, Birds, Flowers On Lid, Laced Seams, 7 In.	1495.00
Box, Pantry, Bentwood, Original Brown Paint, Copper Tacks, Abstract Design On Lid, 5 x 9¾ In. .	201.00
Box, Pantry, Bentwood, Pine, Ash, Painted Green, J. Burr, Round, Fitted Lid, 3½ x 6¾ In.	240.00
Box, Pantry, Lapped Seams, Tacks, Green Paint, Rust Color Hearts, Yellow Dots, 6 x 2½ In. ..	460.00
Box, Pantry, Old Green Paint, Finger Joint, 7¼ x 17¾ x 9½ In.	715.00
Box, Pantry, Pine, Bent Ash, Lapped Side, Fingers, Iron Tacks, Blue Paint, Lid, 3¾ x 7¼ In. ..	4348.00
Box, Pantry, Pine, Bent Ash, Rosehead Nails, Red Paint, Lapped Finger, Lid, 7¾ x 11 In.	646.00
Box, Pantry, Small Finger Lapped, Oval, Chrome Yellow Paint, 3 x 3½ x 1¼ In.	1725.00
Bread Bin, White With Brown, Enamel, Germany, 12 x 6 In.	85.00
Broiler, Round, Rotating, Tripod Base, Iron, 25 x 3 In.	115.00
Butter Mold, Look Under Mold, Butter In This category.	
Butter Paddle, Burl, 9¼ In.	154.00
Butter Paddle, Dog Head Handle, Tiger Maple, Carved, Tack Eyes, 10⅜ x 5¼ In.	8250.00
Butter Paddle, Tiger Maple, Scrolled Terminal On Handle, 10⅛ In.	55.00
Butter Paddle, Tiger Maple Wood, Dog Head Form Handle, 10 x 5¼ In.	8250.00
Butter Stamp, 5 Fish, Facing Right, Notched Border, c.1840, 3 In.	1100.00
Butter Stamp, Acorns, Branch, Carved Oak Leaves, 3¾ In.	94.00
Butter Stamp, Anchor, Rope Border, 3½ In.	92.00
Butter Stamp, Cow, Tree, Leafy Branches, Serrated Edge, 3½ In.	165.00
Butter Stamp, Cow, Tree, Leafy Branches, Serrated Edge, 4¼ In.	165.00
Butter Stamp, Cow, Tree, Leafy Branches, Serrated Edge, 4⅝ In.	149.00
Butter Stamp, Eagle, Leafy Branch, Star, Serrated Edge, 3⅜ In.	248.00
Butter Stamp, Eagle, On Leafy Branch, Star Serrated Edge, 4⅜ In.	303.00
Butter Stamp, Eagle, Spread Wings, Snowflake, Coggled Rim, Round, 4⅛ In.	330.00
Butter Stamp, Eagle, Star, Laurel Branch, Handle, 4½ In.	345.00
Butter Stamp, Fish, 3 Large & 2 Small, Notched Border, c.1840, 3 In. ....*illus*	1170.00
Butter Stamp, Flower, Leafy Stems, Serrated Edge, 4⅛ In.	44.00
Butter Stamp, Flower Urn, Handles, Small Flowers, Leaves, Serrated Edge, 4½ In.	550.00
Butter Stamp, Flowers, Crescent Leaf, Leaf Decoration, Serrated Edge, 2⅛ In.	248.00
Butter Stamp, Goat, Lying Down, Fence, Scalloped Border, c.1880, 2⅛ In.	110.00
Butter Stamp, Horse, Standing Under Tree, Double Line Border, c.1880, 2⅛ In. ......*illus*	260.00
Butter Stamp, Maple Leaf, Notched Border, Patina, c.1880, 3½ In.	110.00
Butter Stamp, Peafowl, Standing In Grass Under Tree, Notched Border, c.1880, 2 In.	92.00
Butter Stamp, Rooster, Crowing, Standing On 2 Branches, Notched Border, 4⅝ In.	165.00
Butter Stamp, Rooster, Leaf & Fern Stems, Serrated Edge, 4½ In.	825.00
Butter Stamp, Rooster, Leaves, Carved, Notched Rim, 4½ In.	1210.00
Butter Stamp, Sheaf Of Wheat, Concentric Lines Border, Bell Shape Case, 4⅛ In.	66.00
Butter Stamp, Sheaf Of Wheat, Stars, Leafy Vine Rim, 2 In.	110.00
Butter Stamp, Sheep, Branch Over Sheep's Back, Notched Border, Patina, 3⅛ In.	247.00
Butter Stamp, Sheep, In Grass Under Tree, Double Lined Border, c.1880, 2⅛ In.	247.00
Butter Stamp, Sheep, Tree, 4 In. ....*illus*	880.00

Butter Stamp, Sheep, Tree, Grass, Leaves, Round, 4 In. ... 880.00

Butter Stamp, Snowflake, Primitive, Lollipop, 4⅜ x 10¾ In. ... 248.00

Butter Stamp, Strawberry, Hatch Carved, Incised Leafy Stem, Elongated, 3 In. ... 44.00

Butter Stamp, Sunflower, Patina, c.1860, 4⅜ In. ... 220.00

Butter Stamp, Tulip, Shaped Leaves, Serrated Edge, 4⅛ In. ... 77.00

Cake Board, Wood, Carved, Man Wearing Plumed Headdress, Frock Coat, 16 x 7 In. ... 441.00

Canister, Warming, Arched Door, Punched, 2 Pan Inserts, Lift Handles, Scroll Handle, 9 In. ... 61.00

Canister Set, Windmill Scene, Blue & White, Coffee Mill, Saltbox, Germany, 16 Piece ... *illus* 82.00

Cauldron, Copper, Hammered, Brass & Wrought Iron Mounted, 18 x 25 In. ... 410.00

Cauldron, Gilt Brass, Wrought Iron Handles, England, 9 x 17¾ In. ... 146.00

Churn, Cast Iron, Hand Pump, Gear & Belt Mechanism, Camp Bro., 1884, 35 x 12 In. ... 259.00

Churn, Dasher, Slat Sides, Tapered, 4 Steel Bands, Lid, 22 In. ... *illus* 141.00

Churn, Dasher, Slatted, Metal Bands, Tapered, 24 x 10½ In. ... *illus* 115.00

Churn, Dasher, Wood, Old Blue Paint, Turned Lid, Tin Bands, 24¼ In. ... 660.00

Churn, Dasher, Wood, Old Red Paint, Concave Lid, Tin Bands, 26 In. ... 358.00

Churn, Dasher, Yellow Pine, Blue Gray Paint, Metal Bands, 41 In. ... 360.00

Churn, Ladle, Red Paint, Sliding Wood Collar, c.1850, 9½ x 19 In. ... 895.00

Churn, Tin, Elgin, c.1920, 18 x 12 In. ... 35.00

Churn, Windsor Style, Green Paint, Rocker Base, 33¼ x 36 x 13 In. ... *illus* 144.00

Churn, Wood, Cradle Type, Iron Wheel & Crank Handle, Stenciled, 33 x 14 In. ... *illus* 147.00

Coffee Bin, Countertop, Roll-Up Lid, Stencil, 9 x 7 x 6 In. ... 825.00

Coffee Grinders are listed in the Coffee Mill category.

Coffee Maker, Expobar, 15 x 10 In. ... 760.00

Coffee Mills are listed in their own category.

Cooker, Trout, Cast, 2-Sided, Fish Shape, Lid, Iron, Stamped, Arbra, 1800s, 3 x 12 x 6 In. ... 1440.00

Cookie Cutter, Acorn, Tin, 4¾ x 4⅛ In. ... *illus* 115.00

Cookie Cutter, Bat, Flying, Tin, Stamped H, 4⅝ In. ... 61.00

Cookie Cutter, Bear, Standing, Tin, 8 In. ... 105.00

Cookie Cutter, Belsnickle, Long Beard, Tin, 1900, 6 In. ... 210.00

Cookie Cutter, Butterfly, Tin, 3½ x 4⅜ In. ... *illus* 29.00

Cookie Cutter, Chimney Sweep, Tin Plated, Mid 1800s, 8 x 6 In. ... 670.00

Cookie Cutter, Christmas Animals, Plastic, Wilton, c.1989, 4 To 4½ In., 9 Piece ... 25.00

Cookie Cutter, Church Shape, Tin, 1940s, 4 x 3¾ In. ... 13.00

Cookie Cutter, Dog, Running, Strap Handle, Tin, 8¾ In. ... 44.00

Cookie Cutter, Dog, Strap Handle, Tin, Stamped, E.P. Barrett, Williamsport, Pa., 3 In. ... 248.00

Cookie Cutter, Eagle, Spread Wings, Strap Handle, Tin, 8 In. ... 319.00

Cookie Cutter, Elephant, Strap Handle, Tin, Stamped 42, 4 In. ... 44.00

Cookie Cutter, Fish, Leaping, Tin, 3¾ In. ... 11.00

Cookie Cutter, Fish, Strap Handle, Tin, 5 In. ... 11.00

Cookie Cutter, Giraffe, Tin, 6½ In. ... 28.00

Cookie Cutter, Horse, Running, Strap Handle, Tin, 4¾ In. ... 28.00

Cookie Cutter, Horse, Running, Strap Handle, Tin, 5½ In. ... 55.00

Cookie Cutter, Horse, Running, Strap Handles, Tin, 11½ x 9⅛ In. ... 100.00

Cookie Cutter, Horse, Short Legs, Tin, 7 In. ... 50.00

Cookie Cutter, Horse, Stylized Tail, Tin, 5 In. ... 50.00

Cookie Cutter, Jack-O'-Lantern, Frowning, Strap Handle, Tin, Stamped HF, 3¼ In. ... 72.00

Cookie Cutter, Man, In Hat, Hands In Pockets, Strap Handle, Tin, Stamped 464, 8 In. ... 121.00

Cookie Cutter, Man, In Hat, Saluting, Strap Handle, Tin, 8½ In. ... 44.00

Cookie Cutter, Man, On Horseback, Loop Handle, Flat Plate, 8 x 8 In. ... 110.00

Cookie Cutter, Rabbit, Running, Strap Handle, Tin, Stamped, E.P. Barrett, Williamsport, Pa., 3 In. ... 193.00

Cookie Cutter, Rooster, Loop Handle, Flat Plate, 6⅜ x 7½ In. ... 231.00

Cookie Cutter, Squirrel, Seated, Double Crossed Strap Handle, Tin, 9¼ x 8 In. ... 440.00

Cookie Cutter, Stag, Running, Strap Handle, Tin, 3½ In. ... 20.00

Cookie Cutter, Stag, Short Legs, Strap Handle, Tin, 5⅛ In. ... 39.00

Cookie Cutter, Woman, In Long Dress, Puffy Sleeves, Bonnet, Tin, Strap Handle, 9 x 5 In. ... 523.00

Corn Holder, Bakelite, Kob-Knobs, Original Box, 8 Piece ... 35.00

Cream, Separator, Oak, Metal Hoops, Round, 2 Handles, England, 1800s, 8 x 24¾ In. ... 940.00

Crimper, Brass Rollers, England, Late 19th Century, 9 In. ... 147.00

Crimper, Brass Rollers, Fine Tooth, England, Late 19th Century, 10½ In. ... 147.00

Crimper, Brass Rollers, Knox, Late 19th Century, 8-In. Rollers ... 118.00

Cutlery Tray, Dovetailed, Center Divider, Heart Cutout, Scalloped Edges, 7 x 17 In. ... 220.00

Cutlery Tray, Mahogany, Dovetailed, Scalloped Edges, Center Handle, 19th Century ... 495.00

Cutlery Tray, Mustard Paint, Center Cutout Handle, 19th Century ... 395.00

Cutlery Tray, Softwood, Center Divider, Cutout Handle, Drawer, Brass Knob, 9 x 15 In. ... 330.00

Cutlery Tray, Walnut, Dovetail Construction, Lid, Pennsylvania, 18th Century ... 450.00

Dough Box, Cover, Softwood, Yellow, Dovetailed, 8⅝ x 24⅝ x 10 In. ... *illus* 275.00

Kewpie, Postcard,
Hazelwood Ice Cream, Valentine Heart,
2 Kewpies, Rose O'Neill
$323.00

Kitchen, Butter Stamp, Fish,
3 Large & 2 Small, Notched Border,
c.1840, 3 In.
$1170.00

Kitchen, Butter Stamp, Horse,
Standing Under Tree,
Double Line Border, c.1880, 2⅛ In.
$260.00

Kitchen, Butter Stamp,
Sheep, Tree, 4 In.
$880.00

K

Kitchen, Canister Set, Windmill Scene, Blue & White, Coffee Mill, Saltbox, Germany, 16 Piece
$82.00

Kitchen, Churn, Dasher, Slat Sides, Tapered, 4 Steel Bands, Lid, 22 In.
$141.00

Kitchen, Churn, Dasher, Slatted, Metal Bands, Tapered, 24 x 10½ In.
$115.00

Dough Box, On Stand, Pine, Hinged Top, Tapered Splayed Legs, 27 x 23 x 16 In.	*illus*	460.00
Dough Box, On Stand, Red Paint, Dovetailed, Turned Legs, 27¾ x 39 x 21 In.	*illus*	1045.00
Dough Box, Painted, Red Wash, Black Stripes, Splay Lets, 1800s, 40 x 18 x 28 In.		975.00
Dough Box, Pine, Brown & Mustard Grain Paint, Canted, Splayed, Turned Legs, 25 x 34 x 18 In.		575.00
Dough Box, Pine, Dovetailed, Arched Ends, Cutout Handles, 14 x 16 x 33½ In.		431.00
Dough Box, Pine, Dovetailed, Stenciling On Lid, c.1880, 17 x 29 x 11 In.		27.00
Dough Box, Stand, Old Red Paint, Dovetailed, Turned Tapered Legs, 28 x 39 x 21 In.		1045.00
Dough Box, Walnut, Dovetailed, Old Red Paint, Scrubbed Top, Tulip Feet, Stand, 26 x 36 In.		330.00
Dough Box, Wood, Grain Painted, Yellow, Bread Painted On Lid, 11 x 37 x 17 In.		825.00
Dough Box, Wood, Old Green Paint, 9½ x 33 x 15½ In.		165.00
Dough Box, Wood, Painted, Red Feather Graining, Pierced Handles, 13¼ x 29½ In.		880.00
Dough Box, Wood, Turned Legs, Fitted With Table Top, 41 In.		209.00
Dough Cutter, Wood T-Handle, Stamped, Griffin Didle, 5 In.		61.00
Dough Scraper, Brass, Tin Handle, Brass End Cap, Stamped, J.B., 4 In.		990.00
Dough Scraper, Iron, Brass, Stamped Peter Derr, c.1858, Incised Lines, 4 In.		1760.00
Dough Scraper, Iron, Brass Ferrule, Wood Handle, Peter Derr, c.1840, 8 In.		1430.00
Dough Scraper, Pierced Heart, Snowflakes, Circle, Lowers, Forged Iron, 1835, 3 x 4 In.		4180.00
Dough Scraper, Scrolled Rattail Terminal, Forged Iron, 5 In.		72.00
Dough Scraper, Tin, Brass, J.B., 4 In.		495.00
Dough Tray, Softwood, Red Paint, Scrubbed Top, Flared Apron, 28 x 42½ In.		935.00
Dough Trimmer, Wrought Iron, Thistle Shape, Rattail, Twisted Horns Ring, 9¾ In.		105.00
Dry Measure, Old Blue Painted, Tin Bands, 5½ x 7¼ In., Pair		605.00
Egg Timer, Humpty Dumpty, On Brick Wall, Painted, Cast Iron, 3½ x 3 In.		77.00
Egg Timer, Little Red Riding Hood, 3½ In.		110.00
Flat Iron, Cleaner, Ideal, Original Label, Pat. April 13, 1897		20.00
Flat Iron, Gas Hose, Colt Carbide, J.B. Colt Co., N.Y., c.1903		30.00
Flour Bin, Brown Lettering & Date, Enamel, 1930, 13 x 10½ In.		85.00
Food Chopper, Ax Head Blade, Turned Wood Handle, Whitesmithed, 7 x 8¾ In.	*illus*	33.00
Food Chopper, Cast Iron Frame, Flywheel, Hand Crank, Rotating Tin Basin, 17 x 24 In.		173.00
Food Chopper, Crescent Blade, Turned Wood Handle, Podmore, 7 x 7¼ In.	*illus*	11.00
Food Chopper, Glass, Measuring Lines, Tin Cover, Hazel-Atlas, 7½ In.		15.00
Fork, Toasting, Iron, Brass Inlaid Handle, Pennsylvania, 1868, 17 In.		590.00
Fork, Wrought Iron, Brass Inlay, Rattail, Handle, Pierced Hole, Tulip, Initials, c.1819, 19 In.		495.00
Fork, Wrought Iron, Brass Inlay, Rattail, Leafy Stem, Stamped Koch, 9¾ In.		352.00
Fork, Wrought Iron, Ring Terminal, Stamped, J.W. Snyder, 21 In.		44.00
Fork, Wrought Iron, Round Loop Hanger, Stamped, J. Schmidt, c.1845, 18 In.		413.00
Funnel, Wood, Turned, 7 In.		55.00
Grater, Nutmeg, Silver, Touchmark SM, Inscribed, c.1778		6435.00
Gridiron, Hand Wrought Iron, Folding, 19th Century, 9 x 22 x 10½ In.		460.00
Grill, Iron, 5 Grates, Diamond & Donut Handle, 4-Footed, 18th Century, Miniature		450.00
Ice Cream Cone Holder, Glass, Metal Lid, Light Bulb, 18 x 9 In.		850.00
Ice Cream Freezer, Knibb Home Ice Cream Freezer, Chrome, 1960s		27.00
Iron, Buttonhole Press		25.00
Iron, Charcoal, Dragonhead, Brass Heat Shield, Berlinger, Late1800s, 6⅝ In.		950.00
Iron, Charcoal, Embossed Max Elb, Dresden, Germany, Early 1900s		1000.00
Iron, Charcoal, Rochford's Canadian, Patent May 6, 1868		225.00
Iron, Combination, Fluter, Riverside Fox, 7 In.	*illus*	176.00
Iron, Daisy No. 2, Central Oil & Gas Stove Co., Pat. May 16, 1893		45.00
Iron, Electric, Coleman, Model 41, Automatic, Bakelite Handle, Pat. 1935		35.00
Iron, Electric, Dead Man's Handle, Release Turns Off Iron, Simplex, c.1893		3000.00
Iron, Electric, Glass, Detroit Appliance Co., Low Wattage, For Lingerie, Fine Fabrics, c.1945		700.00
Iron, Electric, Never-Lift, Control Dial, Proctor, 1940s		70.00
Iron, Electric, Never-Lift, Headlight, Bakelite Handle, Proctor, 1940s		40.00
Iron, Electric, Petit Point, Model 410, Waverly Tool Co., Sandusky, Ohio, Pat. 1942		15.00
Iron, Electric, Silver Streak, Chromium Plated, Corning Glass Works, c.1942, 9 In.		6600.00
Iron, Electric, Steam-O-Matic, Rival, Rear Control, 1940s		10.00
Iron, Flounce, Ox Tongue, England, Late 19th Century		15.00
Iron, Fluter, Adjustable Serrated Rollers, Susan B. Knox, Pat. Nov. 20, 1866		110.00
Iron, Fluter, Clark, Buffalo, N.Y., Pat. Feb. 11, 1879		50.00
Iron, Fluter, Dudley, Pat. Mar. 8, 1870		350.00
Iron, Fluter, Erie, Detachable Cold Handle, 1890s, 6 In.		82.00
Iron, Fluter, Erie, Detachable Handle, Griswold Mfg. Co., Erie, Penn., 1890		115.00
Iron, Fluter, Sauerbier & Son, Pat. Nov. 20, 1866		105.00
Iron, Gas, Humphrey, Pat. Feb. 10, 1914		10.00
Iron, Gas, Ideal, Brass Tank, Wood Handle, 1915, 7½ In.	*illus*	1175.00
Iron, Gas, Jubilee, Tin Warming Burner, Omaha, Neb., Pat. By Wm. Pitt, Oct. 31, 1899		80.00

Kitchen, Churn, Windsor Style, Green Paint, Rocker Base, 33¼ x 36 x 13 In. $144.00

Kitchen, Churn, Wood, Cradle Type, Iron Wheel & Crank Handle, Stenciled, 33 x 14 In. $147.00

Kitchen, Cookie Cutter, Acorn, Tin, 4¾ x 4⅛ In. $115.00

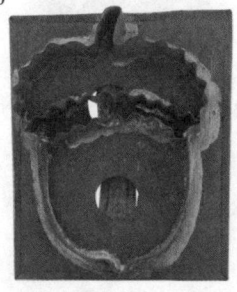

Kitchen, Cookie Cutter, Butterfly, Tin, 3½ x 4⅜ In. $29.00

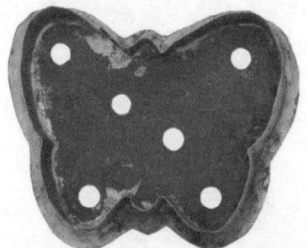

Kitchen, Dough Box, Cover, Softwood, Yellow, Dovetailed, 8⅝ x 24⅝ x 10 In. $275.00

Kitchen, Dough Box, On Stand, Pine, Hinged Top, Tapered Splayed Legs, 27 x 23 x 16 In. $460.00

Kitchen, Dough Box, On Stand, Red Paint, Dovetailed, Turned Legs, 27¾ x 39 x 21 In. $1045.00

K

Kitchen, Food Chopper, Ax Head Blade,
Turned Wood Handle,
Whitesmithed, 7 x 8¾ In.
$33.00

Kitchen, Food Chopper, Crescent Blade,
Turned Wood Handle,
Podmore, 7 x 7¼ In.
$11.00

Kitchen, Iron, Combination, Fluter,
Riverside Fox, 7 In.
$176.00

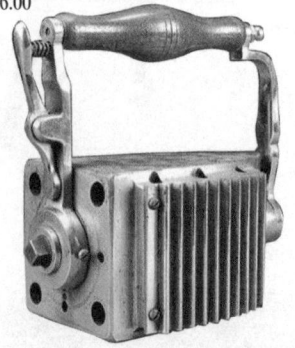

Kitchen, Iron, Gas, Ideal, Brass Tank,
Wood Handle, 1915, 7½ In.
$1175.00

Kitchen, Mold, Chocolate,
Turkey, Removable Tail,
Eppelsheimer's Spinning Top, No. 4922
$115.00

Kitchen, Mold, Jelly, Redware,
Tan, Manganese Splotches, Circles,
Flower On Reverse, 4 In.
$176.00

Kitchen, Mold, Pig Head In Relief,
Cast Iron, Round, Scalloped Border,
2 Handles, 8¾ In.
$230.00

Refinishing Kitchenware

Kitchenware—metal or wooden—
should never, never be repainted,
refinished, or restored if you want
it because of its value as an antique.
If you plan to use the piece,
refinishing or restoring might add
to the usefulness, but will detract
from its value to the serious collector.
Rusty iron can be cleaned, but don't
repaint the piece.

Kitchen, Mortar & Pestle, Lignum Vitae,
Early 19th Century, 10-In. Pestle
$173.00

Kitchen, Mortar & Pestle,
Wood, Turned, 7¼ In.
$110.00

Iron, Gas, Red Enamel, Red Handle, Model 4A, Coleman, 1930	800.00
Iron, Gas, Rhythm, No. 375, Green & Black Enamel, Trivet, Radiation, England	10.00
Iron, Gas, Uneedit, Louis Rosenbaum, New York, Pat. 1913	20.00
Iron, Goffering, Brass, Double Barrel, Tripod Base, Late 19th Century, 15 In.	588.00
Iron, Goffering, Monkey Tail, With Poker, Cast, England, 18th Century	650.00
Iron, Goffering, Stack, Welsh, Early 19th Century	400.00
Iron, Goffering, With Rod, W. Bullock Co., England	80.00
Iron, Lace, Cold Handle, No. 1, Trivet, Kenrick, c.1900	445.00
Iron, Lace, Hot Water, Glazed Pottery, Chinese, Late 1800s	550.00
Iron, Laundress, Arthur Y. Hubbell, Elmira, N.Y., Pat. Oct. 1, 1867	10.00
Iron, Pyrex Electric Silver Streak, Green, Saunders, 1940s	1800.00
Iron, Pyrex Electric Silver Streak, Red, Saunders, 1940s	700.00 to 2100.00
Iron, Silver Streak, Clear Pyrex	1100.00
Iron, Sleeve, Mary Sweeney, No. 6, Baird & Co., July 18, 1899	100.00
Iron, Slug, Laundry, Reversible, Economist, 2 Slugs	550.00
Iron, Slug, Magic No. 1, Sensible Trivet, Nelson W. Streeter, Groton, N.Y., c.1876	110.00
Iron, Slug, Polishing, O.K. Family Laundry, Iron, Slug, H.P. Carver, Racine, Wis., Jan. 3, 1899	450.00
Iron, Tailor's Goose, Blacksmith Made, American, Mid 1800s	35.00
Iron, Universal Gas Iron Co., Rock Island, Ill., Jewel Type, Pat. April 14, 1914	15.00
Iron Heater, Eagle No. 2, Gas, 2 Laundry Irons, 20th Century, 16 In.	176.00
Iron Heater, Fletcher Russell T2, 2 Laundry Irons, Early 20th Century, 18 In.	176.00
Iron Heater, J.M.B. Davidson, Stove Top, 3 Sadirons, 19th Century, 25 In.	294.00
Iron Heater, Monitor, Stove Top, 2 Geneva Flat Irons, 20th Century, 8 In.	71.00
Ironing Board, Shirt Bosom Stretcher, King, Dunkirk, N.Y., c.1876	10.00
Kettle, Brass, Spun, Forged Iron Swing Handle, 12⅞ x 19¼ In.	99.00
Kettle, Cast Iron, 3-Footed, Bail Handle, 19th Century, 24 In.	147.00
Kettle, Cast Iron, Flared Rim, 2 Mounted Holes, Louisiana, 60 x 23 In.	2115.00
Kettle, Copper, Wrought Iron Handle, 19th Century, 17½ In.	147.00
Kettle, Iron, J. Savery & Son, New York, 1866	45.00
Kettle, Iron, Tilter, Initials, J.K., 9⅝ In.	660.00
Kettle, Sugar, Cast Iron, Flared Rim, Goden's F & M Co., Columbus, Ga., 18 In.	3360.00
Kettle, Sugar, Cast Iron, Marked, Goldens, Columbus, Georgia, 57 In. Diam.	2820.00
Kettle, Sugar, Iron, Wide Lip, Pitted Surface, 1800s, 28 In.	1175.00
Kettle Stand, Brass, Cabriole Legs, Penny Feet, Pierced Sides, 1800s, 16 x 12 x 13 In.	795.00
Kraut Cutter, Maple, Chip Carved Border, Flowers, Heart, Marked, BF, 12 x 3½ In.	144.00
Kraut Cutter, Walnut, Scroll Cutout, Heart, 18¾ x 6 In.	314.00
Ladle, Iron, Brass Bowl, Diamond & Teardrop, Rattail Terminal, Whitesmithed, 1858, 15 In.	605.00
Ladle, Iron, Copper Bowl, Scrolled Terminal, 18½ In.	44.00
Ladle, Iron, Revolving, Wrought, Double Rope Twist Arches, Notched Handle, 17¼ In.	154.00
Ladle, Maple, Carved, One Piece Construction, Dark Patina, c.1825	185.00
Ladle, Mixed Metal, Hammered, Bronze Cherries On Handle, Gorham, c.1885, 6 In.	650.00
Ladle, Women, Birds, Flowers, Scrolled Handle, Wood, Sri Lanka, 17 In.	206.00
Ladle, Wood, Hollowed Out Bowl, 18¼ In.	33.00
Ladle, Wrought Iron, Brass, Hook Terminal, Stamped, J. Schmidt, 19¼ In.	358.00
Ladle, Wrought Iron, Brass Bowl, Rattail End, 9¼ In., Pair	248.00
Ladle, Wrought Iron, Copper Bowl, Diamond Shape Handle, Stamped, Peter Derr, 8 In.	1650.00
Ladle, Wrought Iron, Hook Terminal, Stamped, J. Schmidt, c.1847, 15 In.	363.00
Ladle, Wrought Iron, Rattail End, J. Schmidt, 10½ In.	248.00
Lard Container, Smoke On White Ground, Loop Side Handles, Ring Finial, Tin, 8¾ x 6½ In.	110.00
Lemon Squeezer, Maple, Lignum Vitae Wood Center, c.1890	58.00
Loaf Pan, Redware, Coggled Rim, 5 Sets Wavy Lines, Yellow Slip, 10 x 15½ In.	1265.00
Loaf Pan, Redware, Coggled Rim, Yellow Slip, Crisscross Lines, 10½ x 13 In.	144.00
Loaf Pan, Redware, Slip Decorated, Coggled Rim, Yellow Strip, Bacon Strip, 10¾ x 15½ In.	3819.00
Loaf Pan, Redware, Slip Decorated, Oval, Yellow Slip Squiggle, Coggled Rim, 3 x 10 In.	1528.00
Loaf Pan, Redware, Yellow Slip, Coggled Rim, 11¾ x 16 x 3 In.	1092.00
Loaf Pan, Redware, Yellow Slip Bands, Coggled Rim, 15½ x 17⅝ x 4¼ In.	977.00
Loaf Pan, Redware, Yellow Slip Design, Incised Running Deer, Signed, 13 x 16 In.	230.00
Match Holders can be found in their own category.	
Match Safes can be found in their own category.	
Meat Tenderizer, Crosshatched Ends, Stoneware, 3¾ x 2⅝ In.	121.00
Meat Tenderizer, Hammer, Blue, Crosshatch, Sawtooth, Stars, Diamonds, Stoneware, 5 x 4 In.	7700.00
Mixing Bowl, Mix With Roelofs & Vanderbok, Rock Valley, Ia., Blue, Basketweave, Stoneware	55.00
Mixing Bowl, Redware, Manganese Splotches, Interior Glaze, Applied Handles, 8½ x 16¼ In.	1320.00
Mixing Bowl, Redware, Manganese Splotches, Interior Glaze, Handle, 7¾ x 16 In.	550.00
Mold, Butter, Lollipop, Swirling Rosettes, 2-Sided, Blue Paint, Long Handle, 2 x 12 In.	1783.00
Mold, Butter, Maltese Cross, 4 Panels, Birds, Deer, Flowers, Star, Hinged, 12½ x 12½ In.	108.00

Kitchen, Pan, Cornstick,
7 Ears, Griswold, 8½ In.
$29.00

Kitchen, Sadiron, Scroll Handles,
3 Sadirons, J.F. Rathbone & Co.,
Nov. 25, 1862, 20½ In.
$323.00

Kitchen, Sprinkler Bottle,
Dutchman, Ceramic, 8 In.
$194.00

K

Kitchen, Stringholder, Globe Shape, Cutout Holes, 4 Arched Feet, Cast Iron, 6 x 4 In. $236.00

Kitchen, Sugar Cutter, Crescent Shape, Tooled Decoration, Whitesmithed, 10 In., Pair $220.00

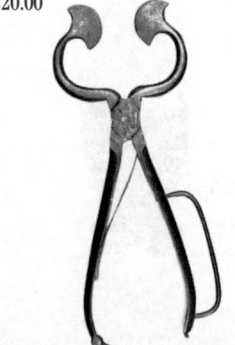

Kitchen, Teakettle, Copper, Swing Handle, Mushroom Finial, W. Heyser, Chambersburg, Pa., 12 In. $880.00

Mold, Candle, see also Tinware category.	
Mold, Candle Mold, 6 Candles, Shaped Handle, Copper	395.00
Mold, Chocolate, Rabbit, Split, Pressed Metal, Repousse Zinc, 18 In.	600.00
Mold, Chocolate, Turkey, Removable Tail, Eppelsheimer's Spinning Top, No. 4922 ..... *illus*	115.00
Mold, Food, Fish, Redware, Manganese Splotches, Incised Scales, Arched, 12¼ In.	495.00
Mold, Food, Fish, Redware, Mottled Glaze, 4 Scrolled Feet, 2¾ x 5 x 12¼ In.	385.00
Mold, Food, Jumping Fish, Redware, Brown Daubed Glaze, 10 In.	173.00
Mold, Food, Rabbit, Redware, Running, Impressed, 2, 5⅞ In.	550.00
Mold, Food, Santa, Embossed, Hello Kiddies, Griswold, 1930s, 12 In.	160.00
Mold, Ice Cream, see Pewter category.	
Mold, Jelly, Redware, Tan, Manganese Splotches, Circles, Flower On Reverse, 4 In. ..... *illus*	176.00
Mold, Lion's Head, Wood, Carved, 19th Century	131.00
Mold, Pig Head In Relief, Cast Iron, Round, Scalloped Border, 2 Handles, 8¾ In. ..... *illus*	230.00
Mold, Snowman Carrying Firewood, Wood, 15½ x 9 x 8 In.	450.00
Mold, Turk's Head, Redware, Green Glazed Exterior, Orange To Green Interior, 5½ x 13 In. ..	248.00
Molds may also be found in the Pewter and Tinware categories.	
Mortar, Fruitwood, Incised, Carved, Marble Pestle, Turkey, 5¾ x 12½ In.	763.00
Mortar & Pestle, Brass, 3 x 2½ & 4¾ In.	129.00
Mortar & Pestle, Bronze, 4¼ x 5½ & 7 In.	165.00
Mortar & Pestle, Iron, 4½ x 6 In.	265.00
Mortar & Pestle, Lignum Vitae, Early 19th Century, 10-In. Pestle ....*illus*	173.00
Mortar & Pestle, Porcelain, 2¾ x 4¾ & 8 In.	69.00
Mortar & Pestle, Walnut, 7 x 5¼ & 5¾ In.	125.00
Mortar & Pestle, Wood, Lignum Vitae	52.00
Mortar & Pestle, Wood, Treen, Old Green Paint, 7½ In.	77.00
Mortar & Pestle, Wood, Turned, 7¼ In. ....*illus*	110.00
Pan, Cornstick, 7 Ears, Griswold, 8½ In. ....*illus*	29.00
Pan, Meatloaf, Primrose Pattern, Fireking, Anchor Hocking Glass Co., c.1960, 5 x 9 In.	12.00
Pan, Poaching, Blue, Enamel, France, 20 x 6 x 5 In.	48.00
Pan, Spider, Iron, Tall Legs, Shaped Handle, Scrolled Terminal, Hand Forged, 32 In.	330.00
Pants Press, Nu-Pantz Creaser, Meta Fuel, c.1920, 7 In.	45.00
Pea Sheller, Wood, Metal, Orange & Blue Paint, Early 20th Century, 22 x 51 In.	144.00
Peel, Baker's, Maple, Tapered Tongue, 6 Ft.	95.00
Peel, Wrought Iron, Heart Decorated, Square Blade, Round Handle, 19 x 4½ In.	518.00
Peel, Wrought Iron, Tapered Blade, Faceted Terminal, 26½ In.	44.00
Peeler, Apple, Cast Iron, Hudson Parer Co., Leominster, Mass., Patd. Jan. 1882	35.00
Peeler, Apple, Turntable 98, Goodell Co., Antrim, N.H., c.1898, 11 In.	61.00
Pie Crimper, Bird, Lizard, Wood, Mid 19th Century, 3½ x 8 In.	211.00
Pie Crimper, Brass, Concentric Incised Lines, Turned Handle, Peter Derr, 6⅝ In.	3300.00
Pie Crimper, Brass, Wrought Iron, Brass Sawtooth Wheel, Hexagonal Handle, 7¾ In.	83.00
Pie Crimper, Ivory, Ebony Inlaid Band	1485.00
Pie Top Cutter, Crisscross Lattice, Clough Products, Kansas, 1952	10.00
Pie Wheel, Forged Iron, Heart Terminal, Incised Flowers, Snowflakes, Scroll Ends, 9 In.	2530.00
Pitcher, White, Enamel, Blue Trim, France, 16½ In.	85.00
Pot, Brass, Iron Handle, Copper Rivets, 18th Century	550.00
Pot, Brass, Wrought Iron, Long Handle, Turned, Iron Ferrule, Spun Brass Bowl, 22½ In.	39.00
Pot, Indigo, Cast Iron, Mounting Post, 31 x 64 In.	7638.00
Pot, Lid, Loop Handle, Iron, Bulbous, 3-Footed, Rope Twist Swing Handle, 13½ In.	413.00
Pot Rack, Iron, Half Orb, 6 Hooks, 24 x 17 In.	176.00
Press, Bacon, Pig, Wood, Iron, Impressed, The Chef's Tools, Late 1800s, 4 x 7 x 4⅜ In.	1440.00
Reamers are listed in their own category.	
Rice Cooker, Brass, Pierced Cover, c.1820, 9 x 13 In.	59.00
Roaster, Iron, Coffee, Hinged Door, Turned Wooden Handle, 52 In.	259.00
Roaster, Iron, Wrought, Drip Pan, Tilting Fork, Ram's Horn Support, Ring, 18½ In.	275.00
Rolling Pin, Pastry Board, Sheet Metal, c.1880	895.00
Rolling Pin, Tiger Maple, 1 Piece, 19th Century	195.00
Rolling Pin, Wood, Whalebone, Rectangular Diamond Pattern, Inlay, 19th Century	3450.00
Rolling Pin, Wood Handle, Turned, Stretcher, 13½ In.	275.00
Sadiron, Inclined Handle, Knauer & Warwick, Pittsburgh, Penn., Pat. July 31, 1866	50.00
Sadiron, Locking Handle, W.H.C. Sadiron, Wrightsville Hardware Co., 1900	170.00
Sadiron, Scroll Handles, 3 Sadirons, J.F. Rathbone & Co., Nov. 25, 1862, 20½ In. .....*illus*	323.00
Sadiron, Set, Howell, Harper No. 1 Handle, Pat. Aug. 27, 1907	330.00
Sadiron, Thermo-Cell, Landers Frary & Clark, New Britain, Conn., Pat. June 13, 1911	70.00
Sadiron Set, 2-Piece Wood Handle, 3 Irons, Chalfant, Box, c.1878	176.00
Salt & Pepper Shakers are listed in their own category.	
Scoop, Metal, Wood Handle, 1920s, 9 x 3½ In.	200.00

K

Skewer Set, 4¼ x 4¼ In. & 7½ To 9½ In., 6 Piece	330.00
Skillet, Griswold, Square, No. 129, 10 x 4½ In.	24.00
Skillet, Rattail Style, Brace Under Handle, Marked, Late 18th Century, 8 x 18 x 9 In.	460.00
Skimmer, Brass, Wrought Iron, Hook Terminal, Pierced Brass Bowl, J. Schmidt, 1848, 19¾ In.	413.00
Skimmer, Tin, Hooded, Copper Rivets, Bentwood Handle, 26¼ In.	297.00
Skimmer, Tin, Tallow, Hooded, Wood Handle, 23¼ In.	396.00
Skimmer, Wrought, Iron, Pierced Bowl, J. Schmidt, c.1847, 20 In.	193.00
Smoothing Board, Carved, Horse Handle, Scandinavian, c.1780	1800.00
Smoothing Board, Horse Handle, Norway, c.1770	900.00
Smoothing Board, Pinwheel Medallions, Inset Handles, Scratch Carved, 1840s	104.00
Spatula, Griddle Cake, Heart Form, Handle, Brass, Polished, Scotland, 18th Century	325.00
Spatula, Wrought Iron, Heart Cutout Tail Handle, Stamped Accents, 20 In.	248.00
Spatula & Meat Fork, Brass, Inlaid, 1903	61.00
Spice Box, Brass, Double Lids, 19th Century	450.00
Spice Box, Nutmeg Grater, Tin, Embossed Rosettes, Loop Handle, Divided Interior, 5 In.	165.00
Spice Box, Oak, 8 Drawers, Stencil Label, 19th Century, 18 In.	105.00
Spice Box, Oak, Late 19th Century, 16 x 9¼ x 5¼ In.	176.00
Spice Box, Shaped Gallery, 2 Rows Of 3 Drawers, Old Green Paint, 21½ x 14 In.	798.00
Spice Box, Softwood, Dovetailed, Red Wash, Divider, Finger Notch, Slide Lid, 3 x 9 x 5 In.	413.00
Spice Box, Tin, Asian Scenes, Figures, England, 19th Century, 13 Piece	4500.00
Spice Box, Walnut, Button Finials, Lift-Out Boxes, Dovetailed, 3½ x 11 In.	198.00
Spice Box, Walnut, Heart Shape Cutout On Crest, Divided Interior, Lift Lid, 6½ x 14 x 8 In.	460.00
Spice Grinder, Drawer, Wood, Dovetailed, Cast Iron, 5½ x 4¼ In.	85.00
Spit, Bird, Wrought Iron, 3 Arched Footed Base, Knob Top, 2 Prong Spikes, 26 In.	1150.00
Sprinkler Bottle, Asian Man, Rubber & Stainless Stopper, Original Top, 1950s, 7½ In.	125.00
Sprinkler Bottle, Dutch Boy, Ceramic, Green & White	95.00
Sprinkler Bottle, Dutchman, Ceramic, 8 In. .... illus	194.00
Sprinkler Bottle, Elephant, Ceramic, Sprinkles From Trunk	25.00
Sprinkler Bottle, Sprinkle Plenty, Oriental Man, Yellow, Green, Cardinal China, c.1951	32.00
Sprinkling Bottle, Clothespin Shape	70.00
Stringholder, Ball, Painted, Orange, Yellow, Green, 3-Footed, Cast Iron, 6¾ x 5 In., 3 Piece	840.00
Stringholder, Cat, Black, Green Eyes, Cast Iron, 7 x 3½ In.	336.00
Stringholder, Cat, Gray Tabby, Green Eyes, Bow, Cast Iron, Tin Bottom, 6 x 5 In.	1344.00
Stringholder, Girl At Mirror, Cast Iron, CJO, 7¾ x 5⅝ In.	896.00
Stringholder, Globe Shape, Cutout Holes, 4 Arched Feet, Cast Iron, 6 x 4 In. .... illus	236.00
Stringholder, Ice Skater, Cast Iron, Signed, CJO, 7 x 7¼ In.	504.00
Stringholder, Louis XVI, Brass, Round, Bronze Patination, Gilt, Scissors, 4 x 4 In.	330.00
Sugar Cutter, Crescent Shape, Tooled Decoration, Whitesmithed, 10 In., Pair .... illus	220.00
Sugar Cutter, Crescent Terminals, Tooled Shaft, Whitesmithed, 9½ In.	176.00
Teakettle, Brass, Tilting, Stand, Copper, England, c.1890	185.00
Teakettle, Copper, Handle, Mushroom Finial, W. Heyser, Chambersburg, Pa., 12 In. .... illus	880.00
Teapot, Brass, Ivory Handle, Openwork Footed Burner, 19th Century, 14 In.	92.00
Teapot, Bail Handle, Louis & Co., Lexington, Ky., Brass, 19th Century, 7½ In. .... illus	2415.00
Timer, Ceramic, Chrome Face, Bakelite Knob, 4¼ x 4¼ In. .... illus	10.00
Toasting Rack, Wrought Iron, Hinged Wood Handle, Horseshoe Feet, 6¾ x 19 x 13 In. ..illus	431.00
Tongs, Scissors, Iron, 4¼ In.	110.00
Trivet, see Trivet category.	
Utensil Holder, Blue, Enamel, France, c.1930, 13 x 20 In.	95.00
Waffle Iron, Blue Enamel, Round, Open Handle, Marked 8.9.10, 15 In. .... illus	69.00
Waffle Iron, Chrome Plated, Round, Model W36, Winchester, 5 x 9 In. .... 270.00 to 275.00	
Waffle Iron, Samson United, Chrome	65.00
Waffle Iron, Wagner, Cast Iron, Stand, Double Handles, Sidney, Ohio, 1910	295.00
Waffle Iron, Wrought Iron, Tooled Designs, Man On Horseback, 1804, 30½ In.	259.00
Wash Tub, Trencher Style, Pierced Drain Hole, Turned Legs, Red Paint, 34 x 51 x 16 In. illus	990.00
Washboard, Blue Ribbon, Blue Enamelware, 43 In.	173.00
Washboard, Redware, Brown Alkaline Glaze, c.1860, 13 In.	1375.00
Washing Machine, Paramount, Steam, Copper & Cast Metal, Crank, Pat. 1916, 20 In.	155.00
Washstick, Black Tin Base, Wood Handle, 23 In.	22.00
Waste Can, Red Poppy, Pedal, Metal, 13 x 11 In.	225.00

KNIFE collectors usually specialize in a single type. In the 1960s, the United States government passed a law that required knife manufacturers to mark their knives with the country of origin. This seemed to encourage the collectors, and knife collecting became an interest of a large group of people. All types of knives are collected, from top quality twentieth-century examples to old bone- or pearl-handled knives in excellent condition.

Kitchen, Teapot, Cylindrical, Bail Handle, Louis & Co., Lexington, Ky., Brass, 19th Century, 7½ In.
$2415.00

Kitchen, Timer, Ceramic, Chrome Face, Bakelite Knob, 4¼ x 4¼ In.
$10.00

TIP

Some people say you should shine the chrome on your 1940s toaster with club soda or lemon juice.

Kitchen, Toasting Rack, Wrought Iron, Hinged Wood Handle, Horseshoe Feet, 6¾ x 19 x 13 In.
$431.00

Kitchen, Waffle Iron, Blue Enamel, Round, Open Handle, Marked 8.9.10, 15 In.
$69.00

K

Kitchen, Wash Tub, Trencher Style, Pierced Drain Hole, Turned Legs, Red Paint, 34 x 51 x 16 In. $990.00

Kosta, Lamp, Green, Ghostly White Owls, Frosted Shade, Sandeberg, 10⅞ In. $633.00

Kosta, Vase, Internal White Festoons, Ruby Interior, Lindstrand, 1950-52, 6 In. $325.00

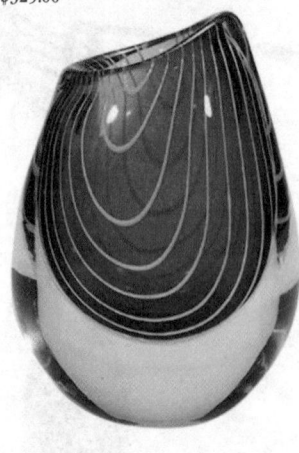

Bone Handle, Folding, Brass, England, 18th Century	....	285.00
Bowie, Golden Bear, Soligen Blade, Leather Holster, 9¾ In.	....	109.00
Bowie, Horn Handle, Etched Eagle, Justice For All, 15 In.	....	242.00
Bowie, Stag Handle, IXL, George Wostenholm & Sons, 14¼ In.	....	300.00
Bowie, Stag Handle, IXL, George Wostenholm & Sons, 15 In.	....	300.00 to 360.00
Bowie, Stag Handle, R. Cooper, Sheffield, 15¼ In.	....	360.00
Bullet, Remington, Folding, 2 Blades, 4½ In.	....	358.00
Crooked, Steel, Carved Wood Handle, Heart, Geometric, Frog Head, 8¼ In.	....	382.00
Horn Handle, Folding, Saw Blade, Late 1700s, 13¼ In.	....	425.00
Pocket, Lady's Leg, Converts To Bottle Opener, Imperial Providence, 1920s, 5 In.	....	190.00
Pocket, Mini Shoe, Black, Gutta-Percha, Star Mfg. Co., Germany, Early 1900s	....	75.00
Stag Handle, Hunting, c.1960, 10 In.	....	42.00
Trench, Model 1917, Triangular Blade, Leather Scabbard	....	538.00

KNOWLES, TAYLOR & KNOWLES *items may be found in the KTK category.*

KOREAN WARE, *see Sumida.*

KOSTA, the oldest Swedish glass factory, was founded in 1742. During the 1920s through the 1950s, many pieces of original design were made at the factory. Kosta and Boda merged with Afors in 1964 and created the Afors Group in 1971. In 1976, the name Kosta Boda was adopted. The company merged with Orrefors in 1990 and is still working. **KOSTA**

Bottle, Mottled Light Blue, Hexagonal, Amber Tapered Neck, Flattened Rim, B. Vallien, 6 In.	..	115.00
Bowl, Fluted, Geometric Designs, Kosta Boda No. 49949, 9¼ x 10 In.	....	468.00
Candleholder, Sweethearts, Kjell Engman, 4¼ x 4¼ In.	....	20.00
Candlestick, Red Stripe, Footed, c.1980, 7½ In.	....	85.00
Lamp, Green, Ghostly White Owls, Frosted Shade, Sandeberg, 10⅞ In.	*illus*	633.00
Paperweight, Etched Face, Engraved, Hair, 1970, 4½ x 2½ In.	....	75.00
Paperweight, Hippopotamus, Submerged, Signed, 1¾ x 5¼ In.	....	28.00
Paperweight, Lion, c.1970, 2¾ In.	....	30.00
Paperweight, Mushroom, Signed, Kosta 97332 & Hart, 2¾ In.	....	265.00
Vase, Autumn, Oval, Internal Black Tree, Falling Leaves, Marked, 6½ In.	....	2350.00
Vase, Clear, Artist Collection, Kosta Boda, 10 In.	....	234.00
Vase, Internal White Festoons, Ruby Interior, Lindstrand, 1950-52, 6 In.	*illus*	325.00
Vase, Internal Multicolored Stripes, White, 1950-60, 5¾ x 6½ In.	....	295.00

KPM refers to Berlin porcelain, but the same initials were used alone and in combination with other symbols by several German porcelain makers. They include the Konigliche Porzellan Manufaktur of Berlin, initials used in mark, 1823–1847; Meissen, 1723–1724 only; Krister Porzellan Manufaktur in Waldenburg, after 1831; Kranichfelder Porzellan Manufaktur in Kranichfeld, after 1903; and the Krister Porzellan Manufaktur in Scheibe, after 1838. *K.P.M*

Bowl, Blue & White Overlapping Leaves, Raised Gilt Grapes, Branch Rim, 11 In.	....	330.00
Bowl, Hunter & Hunted, Trees, Art Deco, 7½ In.	....	230.00
Bowl, Vegetable, Flowers, Cream Ground, 2¾ x 9½ In.	....	34.00
Bowl, Vegetable, Flowers, Cream Ground, Gold Trim, 2⅝ x 8¾ In.	....	24.00
Box, Lid, Flowers, Gilt, Bud Finial, 3½ x 3¾ In.	....	115.00
Coffeepot, Flowers, 20th Century, 8¾ In.	*illus*	59.00
Compote, Pansies, White Ground, Gold Enamel, Basket Weave, 8¾ x 2⅜ In.	....	465.00
Compote, Spider Mum, Scepter Mark, 8¾ x 2⅜ In.	....	465.00
Cup & Saucer, Demitasse, Branch Handle, Flower Extensions, Gilt, 2½ x 1½ In.	....	125.00
Figurine, Street Musicians, Playing Zither, Bagpipes, Gong, Flute, 2 Men, 2 Women, 6 In., 4 Piece		480.00
Figurine, Woman, With Peacock, White, Gold, Egyptian Style, 8½ In.	....	38.00
Figurine, Women Carrying Baskets Of Fruit, Butterfly, 9¾ x 9¼ In., Pair	....	800.00
Group, Putti, With Lyre, Book, Scroll, Quill, Birds, Shaped Base, 5¼ x 6½ In.	*illus*	717.00
Hat Pin Holder, Red Luster, Flowers, 6 x 4½ In.	....	30.00
Jewelry Box, Violets, White Ground, 7½ x 3½ In.	....	56.00
Lithophane, see also Lithophane category.		
Plaque, Bust, Young Woman In Hat, Ruffled Bodice, Scarf, Scepter Mark, Oval Frame, 7 x 5 In.	..	2013.00
Plaque, Christopher Columbus In Chains, Scepter Mark, Gilt Frame, 9 x 6½ In.	....	2588.00
Plaque, Classical Maidens, Entflohen, Gilt Border, Royal Vienna, Signed, Wagner, Frame, 13 In.	..	23000.00
Plaque, Girl, Harlequin Costume, Oval, Frame, 14½ x 17½ In.	....	1800.00
Plaque, Girl, Long Curly Hair, Blue Eyes, Oval, Frame, 11 x 8 In.	*illus*	2243.00
Plaque, Girl, With Dog & Puppies, Lithophane, 5 x 6 In.	....	295.00
Plaque, Gypsy, Tambourine, Red Dress, Gold Cartouche Frame, 17 x 11 In.	....	4250.00

Plaque, Harem Women, Dancing, Musicians, 9¼ x 7⅝ In.	1800.00
Plaque, Long Hike, Incised, Scepter Mark, Frame, 7 x 9½ In.	4680.00
Plaque, Nude Psyche, Embracing Eros, At Pond's Edge, Gilt Frame, 6 x 9 In.	6900.00
Plaque, Psyche, In Moonlight, Gilt Frame, 6 x 9¼ In.	6325.00
Plaque, Queen Louise, Star Head Band, Scarf, 2¾ x 3⅓ In.	395.00
Plaque, Sailor, 4 x 3¼ In.	68.00
Plaque, Sistine Madonna, Saints Sixtus & Barbara, Cherubs, Gilt Frame, 7½ x 10 In.	5175.00
Plaque, Soldier's Farewell, Initials, Frame, Late 19th Century, 12 x 9¾ In.	3308.00
Plaque, Woman, Holding Candle, 2⅔ x 3⅓ In.	450.00
Plaque, Woman, In Bonnet, Bronze Standup, Signed, Frame, c.1890s, 3 x 3¾ In.	475.00
Plaque, Woman, With Big Hat With Roses, 2 x 2½ In.	275.00
Plaque, Woman Dressing, Lithophane, 4⅝ x 6 In.	340.00
Plaque, Young Girl, Brown, Wavy Hair, Hand On Chest, Oval, Marked, 10¾ x 8¾ In.	2875.00
Plate, Apples, Blossoms, Raised Gold, Cobalt Blue Border, 8¼ In.	450.00
Plate, Blue Border, Pink, White Flowers, Handles, 10½ In.	60.00
Plate, Dinner, Flowers, Cream Ground, Gold Trim, 9½ In.	16.00
Plate, Flower Bouquet, Ivory, Scalloped Gold Edge, 10⅝ In.	12.00
Plate Set, Openwork Border, c.1890, 10 In., 12 Piece	5450.00
Platter, 4 Eggcups, Rooster Watching Hens & Eggs, Cream Ground, 13⅝ & 2⅜ In.	1295.00
Platter, Flowers, Cream Ground, Gold Trim, 11 x 7¾ In.	24.00
Platter, Flowers, Cream Ground, Gold Trim, 14¾ x 10¼ In.	32.00
Sugar & Creamer, Green, Yellow, Blue Pansies, Gold Trim, 3¼ x 5½ In.	15.00
Teapot, Cover, Blue, White, 5¾ In.	21.00
Teapot, Cover, Silesia, Waldenburg, 7 In.	75.00
Vase, Cabbage Roses, Multicolored, Gold Trim, 7⅝ In.	20.00
Vase, Gold Flowers, Leaves, Green, Gold, Rust, Beaded Rim, 7 In.	38.00
Vase, Mythical Figure, Reticulated Edge, Figural Handles, Flowers, Butterflies, 8 x 9 In., Pair	1850.00
Vase, Rose Flowers, 6 In.	70.00

KTK are the initials of the Knowles, Taylor & Knowles Company of East Liverpool, Ohio, founded by Isaac W. Knowles in 1853. The company made many types of utilitarian wares, hotel china, and dinnerwares. They made the fine bone china known as Lotus Ware from 1891 to 1896. The company merged with American Ceramic Corporation in 1928. It closed in 1934. Lotus Ware is listed in its own category in this book.

K.T.&K.
CHINA

Bowl, Fluted, Gold, Violets, 8 In.	750.00
Bowl, Vegetable, Flower Border, Oval, 9¾ x 7½ x 2 In.	60.00
Bowl, Vegetable, Poppy, Blue, Orange, 10¼ In.	18.00
Butter, Cover, Swags Of Leaves, Gold Trim	25.00
Casserole, Cover, Gold Swag, Footed, Handles, c.1922, 5 x 10 In.	25.00
Casserole, Cover, Poppy, Blue, Orange, 11¾ In.	25.00
Plate, Dinner, Gooseberries, Gold Trim, 10⅜ In.	6.00
Plate, Luncheon, Ramona, Green Flowers, Gold Trim, c.1919, 9 In.	8.00
Plate, Salad, Traymore, c.1902, 8¼ In.	6.00
Platter, Flowers, Multicolored, Ivory, Oval, 1872-1929, 12½ x 9¼ In.	26.00
Platter, Granite, Oval, 1880-90, 13½ x 9 In.	89.00
Platter, Plymouth, Scalloped Rim, c.1900, 13 In.	20.00
Sauce, Underplate, Rose, Pink, Black Band, Gold Trim, 1909, 6½ In.	25.00
Sauceboat, Bird, Orange, Black, Flowers, Orange Rim, 1930s, 7¾ In.	18.00
Teapot, Gold Trim, Marked, 4¾ In.	16.00

KUTANI porcelain was made in Japan after the mid-seventeenth century. Most of the pieces found today are nineteenth-century. Collectors often use the term *Kutani* to refer to just the later, colorful pieces decorated with red, gold, and black pictures of warriors, animals, and birds.

Bell, Cobalt Blue, Red Cord, Hanger, 2½ In.	45.00
Bowl, Animal, Riverscape, 12 In.	649.00
Bowl, Landscape, Geishas, Samurai, c.1880, 6 In.	2950.00
Bowl, Orange, Red, Black Matte, c.1843, 13½ x 5½ In.	3500.00
Bowl, Scalloped, Samurai, Fan, Landscape, Water, c.1890, 2½ x 11 In.	195.00
Charger, Bird & Flower, Earthenware, 13⅛ In. ....*illus*	153.00
Creamer, Pagodas, Mountains	12.00
Dish, Dessert, Bamboo, Green, White Ground, Platinum Trim, 6⅛ In.	3.00
Dish, Green, Raised Foot Rim, 8-Sided, c.1920-50	25.00
Figurine, Buddha, Dog, 6 x 8 x 4 In.	440.00
Figurine, Dove On Tree Stump, Early 20th Century, 11 In.	150.00

KPM, Coffeepot, Flowers, 20th Century, 8¾ In. $59.00

KPM, Group, Putti, With Lyre, Book, Scroll, Quill, Birds, Shaped Base, 5¼ x 6½ In. $717.00

KPM, Plaque, Girl, Long Curly Hair, Blue Eyes, Oval, Frame, 11 x 8 In. $2243.00

K

Kutani, Charger, Bird & Flower,
Earthenware, 13⅛ In.
$153.00

Kutani, Vase, Triple, Fish,
Riverscape, Brocade, Japan, 9½ In.
$502.00

Kutani, Wine Pot, 100 Poets,
Late 19th Century, 9 In.
$294.00

Figurine, God Of Happiness, 7½ x 5 In.	193.00
Figurine, God Of Happiness, 10 x 6¼ In.	250.00
Figurine, God Of Happiness & Boy, 6½ x 8½ In.	550.00
Figurine, Woman, Seated With Dog, 7 In.	500.00
Incense Box, Cover, Yellow Flowers, Gold Trim, 6¼ x 4¾ x 2 In.	50.00
Incense Burner, Boy With Flute Finial, c.1900, 7 x 4½ In.	295.00
Incense Burner, Foo Dog Finial, c.1900, 5½ x 4 In.	195.00
Jar, Cover, Baluster, Buddhist Saints, Dragons, Scroll, Flowers, Red, Green, Black, 14 In.	400.00
Jar, Cover, Flower, Raised Enamel, c.1900, 6¼ x 5½ In.	145.00
Lazy Susan, 7 Dishes, Black Lacquer Base, c.1920, 4½ x 12½ In.	146.00
Plate, Bread & Butter, 6⅛ In.	12.00
Plate, Green, Gold Mums, 8-Sided, 6¼ In.	25.00
Platter, Pagodas, Mountains, 12½ In.	13.00
Sake Bottle, Bird & Flower Reserves, Gold, Red Ground, 6-Sided, 6 In., Pair	206.00
Sake Set, Decanter, Cups, 6 In., 7 Piece	185.00
Sake Set, Mountain, Hanging Wisteria, Lithophane, 8-Sided, Decanter, Cups, 7 Piece	125.00
Saucer, Pagodas, Mountains	5.00
Serving Bowl, Pagodas, Mountains, 9 In.	14.00
Sugar, Cover, Pagodas, Mountains	14.00
Sugar, Cover, Spoon Opening, Blue Flowers, 3 In.	28.00
Tea Bowl, 2 Men, Landscapes, 3 Reserves, Red, 4½ x 3 In.	100.00
Tea Bowl, Sunflower, Orange, Green, 5 x 3 In.	100.00
Tray Set, Chrysanthemum, Good Luck Flower, 7 Piece	69.00
Urn, Cover, Foo Dog Finial & Handles, c.1900, 38 x 24 In.	819.00
Vase, Butterfly, Women, Children, Landscapes, Flowers, 3-Footed, 1880, 8 x 3 In.	495.00
Vase, Cobalt Blue, Red, Gold, Oval, 5 x 2½ In.	13.00
Vase, Copper Red Riverscape, Earthenware, 10 In.	295.00
Vase, Gilt, Enamel, 4 Lobes, Chrysanthemums, Lappet Band, 14 In.	29.00
Vase, Triple, Fish, Riverscape, Brocade, Japan, 9½ In. ....*illus*	502.00
Vase, Wall, Iris, Blue, White, c.1920, 12 x 4½ In.	185.00
Wine Pot, 100 Poets, Late 19th Century, 9 In. ....*illus*	294.00

L.G. WRIGHT Glass Company of New Martinsville, West Virginia, started selling glassware in 1937. Founder "Si" Wright contracted with Ohio and West Virginia glass factories to reproduce popular pressed glass patterns, like Rose & Snow, Baltimore Pear, and Three Face, and opalescent patterns, like Daisy & Fern and Swirl. Collectors can tell the difference between the original glasswares and L.G. Wright reproductions because of colors and differences in production techniques. Some L.G. Wright items are marked with an underlined W in a circle. Items that were made from old Northwood molds have an altered Northwood mark—an angled line was added to the N to make it look like a W. Collectors refer to this mark as "the wobbly W." The L.G. Wright factory was closed and the existing molds sold in 1999.

Animal Dish, Duck Cover, Purple Slag	20.00
Argonaut, Shell, Sugar & Creamer, Chocolate Glass, 7 & 4⅞ x 6¼ In. ....*illus*	150.00
Beaded Curtain, Creamer, Opalescent, 4 x 5 In.	95.00
Beaded Curtain, Sugar & Creamer, Ruby Cased	225.00
Bicentennial, Platter, Raised, Frosted Log House, Mountain, Trees, Star, 1976	180.00
Bird With Cherry, Salt, Amberina, 4 x 3 In.	20.00
Bubble Optic, Lamp, Wall, Wild Rose, Ruffled Shade, 1960s, 9½ In.	275.00
Bunny, Toothpick, Amberina, c.1961 ....*illus*	18.00
Bunny, Toothpick, Cobalt Blue, c.1961	18.00
Chick On Nest, Salt, Opaque Blue, 2 x 2½ In.	11.00
Colonial Carriage, Ashtray, Amethyst, 3⅝ x 2 In.	20.00
Cosmos, Custard, Hand Painted	85.00
Daisy, Basket, Green, Handle, Scalloped Edged Foot, 4¼ x 6 x 3 In.	20.00
Daisy & Button, Ashtray, 3¾ x 2⅛ In.	15.00
Daisy & Button, Bowl, Boat Shape, Vaseline, 4½ In.	38.00 to 80.00
Daisy & Button, Goblet, Amber, 1960s, 6 x 3 In.	20.00
Daisy & Button, Goblet, Amethyst, 6 In., 6 Piece	96.00
Daisy & Button, Goblet, Blue, 1940s, 6¾ x 2¾ In.	20.00
Daisy & Button, Hat, 1960s, 2½ x 3 In.	9.00
Daisy & Button, Hat, Milk Glass, Wide Rim, 3¼ x 4½ In.	5.00
Daisy & Button, Pickle Castor, Amberina Carnival, 11 In.	145.00
Daisy & Button, Pickle Castor, Black Amethyst, Silver Plated Tongs, 11 In.	145.00
Daisy & Button, Pickle Castor, Cranberry Ice, Silver Plated Tongs, 11 In.	145.00
Daisy & Button, Salt, Green, 2¼ In.	14.00

Daisy & Button, Shoe, Blue, 5½ In.	15.00
Daisy & Button, Skillet, Pink, 1960	15.00
Daisy & Button, Slipper, Green, 5½ In.	12.00
Daisy & Button, Tumbler, Vaseline, 4 In.	45.00
Diamond Panel, Goblet, Fruit & Leaves, Amber, 6 In.	19.00
Diamond Panel, Goblet, Fruits, Beaded Stem, 6 In.	19.00
Dot Optic, Bowl, Blue, Snow Crest Edge, 1951, 10 x 4¼ In.	174.00
Eyewinker, Compote, Amber, 4¾ x 5⅝ In.	40.00
Eyewinker, Toothpick, Amber, 2½ x 2¼ In.	15.00
Fern & Daisy, Pitcher, Vaseline, Opalescent, 9½ In.	310.00
Flute, Epergne, 4 Lily, Blue Opalescent, Ruffled Edges, 1940s, 17 x 12 In. ......*illus*	1150.00
Grasshopper, Goblet, Amethyst, 6 In.	23.00
Inverted Optic Thumbprint, Vase, Cranberry	95.00
Inverted Thumbprint Optic, Pitcher, Blue, Ruffled Edge, Reeded Handle, 6½ In.	70.00
Jersey Swirl, Compote, Cover, 5¼ x 5 In.	15.00
Lamp, Peachblow, Beaded Drapery Font, Enameled Moss Rose, 21 x 8 In.	350.00
Maple Leaf, Creamer, Royal Blue	35.00
Maple Leaf, Spooner, Cobalt Blue	25.00
Moon & Star, Candlestick, Amberina, 6 x 4 In.	28.00
Moon & Star, Candy Dish, Amber, Footed	22.00
Moon & Star, Candy Jar, Cover, Ruby, 1968	65.00
Moon & Star, Compote, Amber	25.00
Moon & Star, Compote, Amber, Footed, 8 x 5¾ In.	25.00
Moon & Star, Console, 8 In.	38.00
Moon & Star, Goblet, Amberina, 12 Oz., 6 In.	35.00
Moon & Star, Goblet, Green, 12 Oz., 6 In.	10.00
Moon & Star, Goblet, Smoke, c.1981, 12 Oz., 6 In.	15.00
Moon & Star, Oil Lamp, Amber, 1940s, 12 In.	80.00
Moon & Star, Toothpick, Amber, c.1930, 3 In.	9.00
Moon & Star, Toothpick, Amber, Scalloped Rim, Flat Base, 2½ In.	25.00
Moon & Star, Vase, Amber	24.00
Moss Rose, Creamer, Custard Glass, Applied Handle, 5½ In.	125.00
Moss Rose, Cruet, Peachblow	135.00
Moss Rose, Lamp, Electric, Crimped, Fluted Rim, 9½ In.	175.00
Moss Rose, Pitcher, Milk, Custard Glass, Applied Handle, 6½ In.	135.00
Moss Rose, Plate, Swirl, Milk Glass, 8⅜ In.	68.00
Paneled Grape, Goblet, Blue Opalescent, 5¾ In.	38.00
Paneled Grape, Plate, Ruby, 9½ In.	40.00
Paneled Grape, Punch Bowl Set, Underplate, Cups, Ruby, 12 Piece	650.00
Paneled Grape, Wine, Ruby, 4 In.	28.00
Paneled Thistle, Pitcher, 1970s	36.00
Paneled Thistle, Pitcher, Green, 1970s	36.00
Paneled Thistle, Pitcher, Ice Blue, 1970s	36.00
Paneled Thistle, Relish, 1970s	18.00 to 20.00
Priscilla, Candy Dish, Cover, Ruby, Pedestal, 7½ x 4 In.	40.00
Priscilla, Candy Jar, Cover, Ruby, 5 x 4 In.	40.00
Pump & Trough, Vase, Blue Satin	150.00
Stars & Stripes, Tumbler, Cranberry Opalescent, Pair	105.00
Stork & Rushes, Berry Bowl, Marigold, 8¼ In.	125.00
Swirl, Tri Spout, Cruet Aqua Opalescent, Melon Ribbed, Stopper, Handle, 7 In.	95.00
Thistle, Bowl, Footed, 2¾ x 5 In.	12.00
Vase, Top Hat, Daisy & Button, Vaseline, Bent Brim, 2 x 3½ In.	70.00
Wedding Ring, Sherbet, Amber, 4½ x 4 In.	17.00
Wild Rose, Compote, Green	25.00
Wild Rose, Goblet, Cobalt Blue, 6½ x 3½ In.	20.00
Wild Rose, Vase, Crimped Rim, 8 In.	40.00
Wreathed Cherry, Creamer, Ruby, 4¾ x 5 In.	15.00

LACQUER is a type of varnish. Collectors are most interested in the Chinese and Japanese lacquer wares made from the Japanese varnish tree. Lacquer wares are made from wood with many coats of lacquer. Sometimes the piece is carved or decorated with ivory or metal inlay.

Bowl, Bread, Chinoiserie, Multicolored, Gilt, Black, Geishas In Garden, 2 x 13½ In.	293.00
Box, Black, Mottled, Red Flowers, Early 20th Century, 3 x 7 In.	34.00
Box, Hirmaki-E, Takamaki-E, Bird, Flower Reserves, Red Ground, Japan, 1900s, 9 In.	18.00
Box, On Stand, Black, Gilt Chinoiserie, Scrolled Stand, Russia, 1894, 7 x 10 x 6 In.	1175.00

L.G. Wright, Argonaut, Shell, Sugar & Creamer, Chocolate Glass, 7 & 4⅞ x 6¼ In. $150.00

L.G. Wright, Bunny, Toothpick, Amberina, c.1961 $18.00

L.G. Wright, Flute, Epergne, 4 Lily, Blue Opalescent, Ruffled Edges, 1940s, 17 x 12 In. $1150.00

LACQUER

Lacquer, Picnic Set,
Maple Leaves, Pinecones,
Decanter, Food Container,
Tray, 14 x 11 In.
$805.00

Lalique, Ashtray, Feuilles,
Leaves, Electric Blue,
c.1924, 6⅞ In., Pair
$1440.00

Lalique, Bonbonniere, Cigales, Cicadas,
Opalescent, Engraved R. Lalique,
c.1921, 10 In.
$1560.00

Lalique, Bowl, Perruches, Parakeets,
Opalescent, Blue Patina, R. Lalique,
c.1931, 9¾ In.
$4500.00

Box, Painted, Troika Running In Snow, Red Inside, Signed, Russia, Early 1970s, 5 x 3 In. ...	235.00
Box, Polychrome, Rectangular Top, Maharaja, Attendants, Silk Panel, India, 14 x 11 In.	177.00
Box, Work, Black, Gilt Lakeside Pavilion Scene, Brass Handles, Rectangular, 6 x 17 In.	1645.00
Box, Writer's, Black, Wood, Cloud, Crest, Brown, Gold Flat, Japan, 1920s, 8 x 5½ In.	300.00
Case, Cosmetics, Wood, Black, Gold, 4 Drawers, Copper Alloy Pull, Round, Japan, 1800s	650.00
Cigar Container, Oriental Style, Black, 6 Door, England, c.1920, 12 x 8 In.	176.00
Dish Set, Flowers, Plants, Wood, Red Brown, Black, Japan, Mid 1900s, 5 In., 5 Piece	250.00
Jewelry Box, Black, Circles, Phoenix Bird, Flowers, Gold, Red, c.1900, 6¼ x 5 In.	195.00
Jewelry Chest, Black, Carved, Raised Agates, Brass Hinges, Handles, Drawers, 11 x 13 In. ...	725.00
Pen Case, Persian, 1½ x 1¾ x 9½ In.	1760.00
Pen Case, Qalamdan, Gilt Flowers, Red Ground, Figures Outside, Qajar, 8½ In.	720.00
Picnic Set, Maple Leaves, Pinecones, Decanter, Food Container, Tray, 14 x 11 In. ......*illus*	805.00
Tea Bowl, Red, Gold Lacquer Chrysanthemum & Fern Medallion, Flared, Flared Foot, 6 In. .	96.00
Tea Caddy, Tin, Brown Red, Flat & Raised Gold, Bird In Tree, Lion Finial, Japan, 1900s, 5 In.	150.00
Tray, Chinoiserie, Giltwood, Bird & Flower Decoration, Black Ground, 28 x 20 In.	2468.00
Tray, Crumb, Wood, Black, Red, Japan, Early 20th Century, 9 x 8 In.	25.00
Tray, Hand Painted, Flowers, 11½ x 7½ In.	19.00
Water Bucket, Metal, Red, Cricket, Silver, Gold, Maruni Co., Japan, c.1950, 9 x 3 In.	200.00

LADY HEAD VASE, *see Head Vase.*

LALIQUE glass was made by Rene Lalique in Paris, France, between the 1890s and his death in 1945. The glass was molded, pressed, and engraved in Art Nouveau and Art Deco styles. Pieces were marked with the signature *R. Lalique.* Lalique glass is still being made. Pieces made after 1945 bear the mark *Lalique.* Jewelry made by Rene Lalique is listed in the Jewelry category.

R.LALIQUE

Ashtray, Archers, Dark Amber, Engraved, R. Lalique, 1922, 4½ In.	823.00
Ashtray, Archers, Opalescent, Molded R. Lalique, c.1922, 4½ In.	1140.00
Ashtray, Fauvettes, Warblers, Amber, Molded R. Lalique, c.1924, 6¾ In.	960.00
Ashtray, Feuilles, Leaves, Electric Blue, c.1924, 6⅞ In., Pair ....*illus*	1440.00
Ashtray, Serpent, Scolled Snake, Electric Blue, Engraved R. Lalique, c.1920, 4⅜ In.	2880.00
Belt Buckle, Papillons, Butterflies, Frosted, c.1911, 1¾ In.	2640.00
Blotter, Cherries, Clear, Frosted, Sepia, Metal Rocker, Molded R. Lalique, c.1920, 6½ In.	1680.00
Blotter, Grosses Feuilles, Leaves, Frosted, Sepia, Metal Rocker, R. Lalique, c.1920, 6½ In. ...	1680.00
Bonbonniere, Cigales, Cicadas, Opalescent, Engraved R. Lalique, c.1921, 10 In. ......*illus*	1560.00
Bookends, Faucon, Falcon, Art Deco, R. Lalique, 6¼ In.	3878.00
Bookends, Hirondelle, Swallow, Paper Label, Signed Lalique In Script, c.1950s, 6 x 4 In.	550.00
Bookends, Tete D'Aigle, Eagle Head, Clear, Frosted, Chrome Collar, Black Glass, c.1928, 7 In.	3600.00
Bottle, Fleurette, Mushroom Stopper, Frosted, 5 In.	81.00
Bowl, Anges, Kneeling Angels, R. Lalique, 1930, 14½ In.	4692.00
Bowl, Bulbes No. 2, Flower Bulbs, Opalescent, 3¼ x 8 In.	529.00
Bowl, Cernuschi, Roses, Clear, Frosted, Wheel Cut R. Lalique, 10⅝ In.	780.00
Bowl, Chiens, Dogs, Opalescent, Molded R. Lalique, c.1921, 9⅜ In.	1680.00
Bowl, Chiens, Greyhounds, R. Lalique, 1921, 9½ In.	588.00
Bowl, Coquilles, Shells, Opalescent, 1930s, 9½ In.	770.00
Bowl, Deux Moineaux, 2 Sparrows, Clear, Frosted, 1980s, 15¾ In.	720.00
Bowl, Eglantine, Wild Rose, Blue, R. Lalique, 1931, 9¾ In.	1410.00
Bowl, Fleur, Flower, Clear, Frosted, Gray, Black Enamel, Molded R. Lalique, c.1912, 4½ In. ..	900.00
Bowl, Fontainebleau, Molded, Grapevine, Opalescent, Blue Patination, 7 x 7½ In.	2749.00
Bowl, Gazelles, Opalescent, Blue Patina, Molded R. Lalique, c.1925, 11⅝ In.	1800.00
Bowl, Gui, Mistletoe, Opalescent, Mint Green, R. Lalique, 1921, 8⅛ In.	1175.00
Bowl, Helianthe, Blue Enameled, 1930s, 14 In.	564.00
Bowl, Lys, Lilies, Opalescent, Footed, Wheel Cut, R. Lalique, 1924, 9¼ In.	1564.00
Bowl, Mesanges, Birds, 3¾ x 9 In.	380.00
Bowl, Mesanges, Birds, Molded, Clear, Frosted, Signed, 9½ In.	206.00
Bowl, Muguet, Lilies Of The Valley, Opalescent, 1930s, 12½ In.	923.00
Bowl, Muguet, Lilies Of The Valley, Opalescent, Stenciled R. Lalique, c.1931, 12⅜ In.	3360.00
Bowl, Nemours, Flower Heads, Molded, Frosted, Signed, 10 In.	441.00
Bowl, Ondines, Water Nymphs, Opalescent, Molded R. Lalique, c.1921, 8 In.	1440.00
Bowl, Perruches, Parakeets, Opalescent, Blue Patina, R. Lalique, c.1931, 9¾ In. ......*illus*	4500.00
Bowl, Plumes De Paon, Peacock Feathers, Alexandrite, Engraved R. Lalique, c.1932, 11 In. ..	1680.00
Bowl, Poissons, Fish, Opalescent, Stenciled R. Lalique, c.1931, 11½ In., Pair	1560.00
Bowl, Poissons, Fish Radiating Around Bowl, c.1931, 3½ x 9¼ In.	717.00
Bowl, Rosace, Radiating Triangles, Blue, Footed, Stenciled R. Lalique, 1930, 12½ In.	3097.00
Bowl, Saint-Denis, Smoky Green, Footed, Sepia Patina, R. Lalique, 1926, 8⅛ In.	1410.00

L

Lalique, Drinking Set, Jaffa,
Vertical Bands, Frosted,
Art Deco, c.1931, 9-In. Jug, 8 Piece
$2280.00

Lalique, Perfume Bottle,
D'Heraud, La Phalene,
Nymph, Butterfly Wings,
Frosted Amberina, 3½ In.
$7200.00

Lalique Glassware

Lalique made many types of
glassware, including vases, tableware,
perfume bottles, jewelry, figurines,
hood ornaments, clocks, and lamps.
The most famous are decorated with
classical figures.

Lalique, Hood Ornament,
Longchamp A, Horse Head, R. Lalique,
c.1929, 4⅞ In.
$7200.00

Lalique, Perfume Bottle,
Helene, Clear & Frosted,
c.1950, 5½ In.
$720.00

Lalique, Perfume Bottle, Saks,
Tresor De La Mer, Opalescent,
Shell Stopper, Box, 5¾ In.
$216000.00

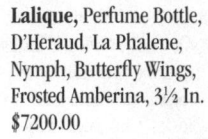

Lalique, Lamp, Graines, Seeds,
Clear & Frosted, Stenciled R. Lalique,
c.1930, 7¾ In.
$1440.00

Lalique, Perfume Bottle,
Roget & Gallet, Le Jade, Green,
Gray Patina, 3¼ In.
$1800.00

Lalique, Perfume Bottle, Worth,
Je Reviens, Blue & Opaque Aqua,
Silver Case, 5½ In.
$1800.00

L

Lalique, Perfume Bottle, Worth, Sans Adieu, Green, Wooden Box, c.1929, 4¼ In. $1080.00

Lalique, Vase, Courges, Squash, Electric Blue, c.1914, 7⅛ In. $8400.00

Lalique, Vase, Davos, Opalescent Bubble Clusters, In Diamonds, Brown, Bulbous, 1932, 11 In. $3346.00

Bowl, Sirene, Mermaid, Opalescent, c.1920, 14⅜ In.	7800.00
Bowl, Sirene, Mermaid, Opalescent, Molded R. Lalique, 1920, 14½ In.	7200.00
Bowl, Underplate, Vigne Striee, Bacchanalian Mask, Grapevine, Frosted, 6½-In. Plate	353.00
Bowl, Volubilis, Morning Glories, Opalescent, Frosted, Signed, 8½ In.	382.00
Bowl, Volubilis, Morning Glories, Opalescent Yellow, Molded R. Lalique, c.1921, 8½ In.	780.00
Box, Bombay, Birds On Cover, Frosted, Sepia Patina, c.1933, 4¾ In.	6240.00
Box, Cleones, Beetles, Opalescent, Molded Lalique, c.1921, 10 In.	3000.00
Box, Cover, Cheveux De Venus, Flower On Cover, Frosted, Gray Stain, 2 x 2⅔ In.	1150.00
Box, Pervenches, Periwinkles, Frosted, Sepia Patina, c.1929, 4½ In.	3600.00
Box, Primeveres, Wild Roses, Opalescent, Stenciled, R. Lalique, c.1930, 8 In.	3480.00
Box, Quatre Papillons, 4 Butterflies, Frosted, Blue Patina, c.1911, 3¼ In.	2280.00
Box, Roger, Birds & Cabochons, Opalescent, c.1926, 5⅜ In.	1920.00
Box, Tokio, Chrysanthemum, Blue, Molded Lalique, c.1921, 6¾ In.	8400.00
Box, Tokio, Chrysanthemum, Opalescent, Molded Lalique, c.1921, 6¾ In.	2880.00
Ceiling Light, Soleil, Stylized Sunbursts, 1926, 12 x 32½ In.	9600.00
Clock, Cinq Hirondelles, 5 Swallows, Enameled Glass, c.1920, 5¾ In.	5040.00
Clock, Dahlia, Frosted, Black Enamel Petal Edges, 5-Sided, Molded R. Lalique, 6¾ In.	2133.00
Clock, Deux Colombes, 2 Doves, Frosted, Sepia, Arched, Round Face, Signed R. Lalique, 9 In.	5033.00
Clock, Deux Figurines, Clear, Frosted, Metal Base, 1926, 15¼ In.	3480.00
Clock, Moineaux, Sparrows, Frosted, Sepia, Demilune, Round Face, R. Lalique, 1924, 8½ In.	1763.00
Clock, Roitelets, Wrens In Circle, Clear, Frosted, Black Enamel Numbers, c.1931, 7⅝ In.	3000.00
Cocktail, Edward, Rooster Stem, Clear, Blue Enamel, Engraved R. Lalique, c.1924, 5⅞ In.	510.00
Cocktail Shaker, Thomery, Grape Vines, c.1928, 9⅛ In.	5040.00
Decanter, Clos Sainte-Odile, Frosted, Low Relief Cameo, Berry Stopper, c.1927, 7½ In.	896.00
Decanter, Marienthal, Emerald Green, Engraved, R. Lalique, 1928, 5¼ In.	2938.00
Decanter, Parme, Clear & Frosted Circles, Post 1945, 10½ In.	308.00
Decanter, Satyre, Horned Satyr Handle, Engraved, R. Lalique, 1923, 9½ In.	1706.00 to 1920.00
Decanter, Sirenes Et Grenouilles, Mermaids & Frogs, Gray Patina, c.1911, 15¾ In.	9600.00
Decanter, Six Tetes, 6 Heads, Frosted, c.1914, 14¼ In.	7200.00
Dish, Pansy, Frosted To Clear, c.1920, 7 In.	234.00
Drinking Set, Jaffa, Vertical Bands, Frosted, Art Deco, c.1931, 9-In. Jug, 8 Piece *illus*	2280.00
Figurine, Bison, Clear, Frosted, Rectangular Plinth, Marked, c.1931, 3¾ x 4¾ In.	777.00
Figurine, Chat Assis, Cat, Seated, 8½ In.	761.00
Figurine, Chat Couche, Cat, Crouching, 3½ x 9 In.	702.00
Figurine, Cote D'Azur, Woman, R. Lalique, 1929, 6½ In.	4302.00 to 10200.00
Figurine, Elephant, Trunk Raised Over Head, 6¼ x 6½ In.	420.00
Figurine, Grande Ovale Tete Penchee, Woman, R. Lalique, 1919, 14½ In.	9384.00
Figurine, Lion, Frosted, Clear, 7½ In.	585.00
Figurine, Moyenne Voilee, Woman, Opalescent, Blue Patina, R. Lalique, c.1912, 5½ In.	3360.00 to 5100.00
Figurine, Perdrix Inquiete, Partridge, Molded, Frosted, Signed, 5½ In.	147.00
Figurine, Suzanne, Woman In Gown, Bronze Base, R. Lalique, 10¾ In.	12925.00
Figurine, Tete De Cheval, Horse Head, Clear, Polished Glass, Wheel Cut Lalique, c.1960, 16¼ In.	5400.00
Frame, Deux Figurines Et Fleurs, 2 Women, Flowers, Engraved Lalique, c.1912, 5⅛ In.	4800.00
Goblet, Bague Chiens, Hound Dogs, Ring Base, Sepia Stain, Engraved, 5⅜ In., 8 Piece	2300.00
Grape Bath, Muscat Grape Vines, Opalescent, Stenciled, R. Lalique, 1938, 6½ In., Pair	1763.00
Hood Ornament, Archer, R. Lalique, 1926, 4⅞ In.	2559.00
Hood Ornament, Cinq Chevaux, Frosted, 5 Horses, c.1925, 4 In.	11400.00
Hood Ornament, Coq Houdan, Rooster, Chrome Collar, R. Lalique, 1929, 8 In.	3360.00 to 6463.00
Hood Ornament, Coq Nain, Dwarf Cockerel, Large Plume, Clear, R. Lalique, 1928, 8 In.	1440.00 to 3696.00
Hood Ornament, Faucon, Falcon, Chrome Collar, Signed, R. Lalique, 1925, 7¼ In.	4159.00
Hood Ornament, Grande Libellule, Dragonfly, Frosted & Clear, Signed, R. Lalique, 9 In.	5206.00
Hood Ornament, Grande Libellule, Dragonfly, Silver Collar, Marble, R. Lalique, 1928, 8 In.	8602.00
Hood Ornament, Longchamp A, Horse Head, R. Lalique, c.1929, 4⅞ In. *illus*	7200.00
Hood Ornament, Perche, Fish, Clear, Frosted, Gray Patina, Molded R. Lalique, 6¼ In.	1560.00
Hood Ornament, Pintade, Guinea Fowl, Chrome Collar, Glass Base, R. Lalique, 1929, 5 In.	6463.00
Hood Ornament, Sanglier, Wild Boar, Gray Patina, R. Lalique, 1929, 3½ In.	776.00
Hood Ornament, Sirene, Crouching Mermaid, Frosted, Molded R. Lalique, 1920, 4⅛ In.	4066.00
Hood Ornament, Tete D'Aigle, Eagle's Head, Chrome Collar, R. Lalique, 1928, 4½ x 5 In.	2981.00
Hood Ornament, Tete De Belier, Ram's Head, Frosted, Polished, R. Lalique, 1928, 4½ In.	9227.00
Hood Ornament, Tete De Coq, Rooster Head, Clear, Frosted, Lucite, R. Lalique, c.1928, 7 In.	2400.00
Hood Ornament, Tete D'Epervier, Sparrowhawk, Clear, R. Lalique, 1928, 2⅛ In.	1410.00
Hood Ornament, Tete D'Epervier, Sparrowhawk, Opalescent, Lalique, c.1928, 2½ In.	3600.00
Inkwell, Biches, Doe, Black, c.1912, 6 In.	6000.00
Inkwell, Cover, Quatre Sirenes, 4 Mermaids, Blue Patina, Frosted, R. Lalique, 1920, 6 In.	2938.00
Inkwell, Cover, Quatre Sirenes, 4 Mermaids, Molded, Opalescent, R. Lalique, 6 In.	3760.00
Inkwell, Cover, Serpents Snakes, Amber, Engraved, R. Lalique, 6¼ In.	7050.00

L

Inkwell, Nenuphar, Water Lily, Clear, Frosted, Gray Patina, Engraved, c.1910, 2¾ In.	1440.00
Lamp, Graines, Seeds, Clear & Frosted, Stenciled R. Lalique, c.1930, 7¾ In. . . . .*illus*	1440.00
Lemonade Set, Hesperides, Jug, 8 Tumblers, Tray, Clear, Frosted, Stenciled, c.1931, 17 In. . . .	2160.00
Menu Holder, Pinsons, Finches, Clear, Frosted, Engraved R. Lalique, 1924, 1¾ In., Pair	360.00
Mirror, Anemones, Clear, Frosted, Metal Backing, Glass, Stamped Lalique, c.1913, 15 In. . . .	8400.00
Mirror, Hand, Deux Chevres, Mountain Goats, Grapevines, R. Lalique, 1919, 6½ In.	705.00
Paperweight, Chouette, Barn Owl, Art Deco Style, Stenciled, R. Lalique, 1931, 3½ In.	470.00
Paperweight, Daim, Deer, Clear, Frosted, Molded R. Lalique, c.1929, 3⅛ In.	960.00
Paperweight, Deux Aigles, 2 Eagles, Molded, R. Lalique, 1914, 4 In.	1058.00
Paperweight, Rhinoceros, Clear, Frosted, Stenciled R. Lalique, c.1931, 4⅜ In.	4200.00
Paperweight, Toby, Elephant, Clear, Frosted, Stenciled R. Lalique, c.1931, 3½ In. . . .	1440.00
Perfume Bottle, Amphitrite, Shell, Figurine Stopper, Frosted, Gray Patina, c.1920, 3¾ In. . .	2160.00
Perfume Bottle, Aster, Clear, Black Patina, Box, Engraved R. Lalique, c.1913, 3½ In.	5400.00
Perfume Bottle, Capricornes, Clear, Frosted, Blue Patina, R. Lalique, c.1912, 3 In.	2640.00
Perfume Bottle, Deux Anemones, Clear, Frosted, Sepia, Flower Top, c.1929, 3⅝ In.	3120.00
Perfume Bottle, D'Heraud, La Phalene, Nymph, Butterfly Wings, Frosted Amberina, 3½ In. *illus*	7200.00
Perfume Bottle, D'Orsay, Ambre D'Orsay, Black, White Patina, Lalique, c.1911, 5 In.	1800.00
Perfume Bottle, D'Orsay, Poesie D'Orsay, Frosted, Sepia Patina, c.1914, 5¾ In.	2880.00
Perfume Bottle, Forvil, La Perle Noire, Clear, Topaz, Molded R. Lalique, c.1922, 4⅜ In. . . .	2880.00
Perfume Bottle, Forvil, Tube Fleurs, Clear, Frosted, Sepia Patina, R. Lalique, c.1924, 4 In. . .	1140.00
Perfume Bottle, Gabilla, La Violette, Enameled, c.1925, 3⅜ In.	6600.00
Perfume Bottle, Guerlain, Bouquet De Faunes, Pierced Stopper, 4¼ In.	489.00
Perfume Bottle, Helene, Clear & Frosted, c.1950, 5½ In. . . . .*illus*	720.00
Perfume Bottle, Jay Thorpe, Jaytho, Clear, Frosted, Sepia Patina, c.1928, 5⅞ In.	840.00
Perfume Bottle, Nina Ricci, L'Air Du Temps, Dove Stopper, Cut Crystal, 4 x 3 In.	176.00
Perfume Bottle, Roger & Gallet, Flausa, Clear, Frosted, c.1912, 4½ In.	4800.00
Perfume Bottle, Roger & Gallet, Paquerettes, Clear, Frosted, 1919, 3¼ In.	2640.00
Perfume Bottle, Roget & Gallet, Le Jade, Green, Gray Patina, 3¼ In. . . . .*illus*	1800.00
Perfume Bottle, Rosace Figurines, Clear, Frosted, Sepia Patina, Figural Stopper, 4⅞ In.	3600.00
Perfume Bottle, Saks, Tresor De La Mer, Opalescent, Shell Stopper, Box, 5¾ In. . . . . . .*illus*	216000.00
Perfume Bottle, Silvered Metal Top, Atomizer, Round Frosted Glass, Dancing Putti, 5 In. . . .	235.00
Perfume Bottle, Worth, Blue Patination, Stars, c.1924, 9½ In.	2032.00
Perfume Bottle, Worth, Dans La Nuit, Clear, Blue Enamel, R. Lalique, c.1924, 9¾ In.	2400.00
Perfume Bottle, Worth, Je Reviens, Blue & Opaque Aqua, Silver Case, 5½ In. . . . .*illus*	1800.00
Perfume Bottle, Worth, Je Reviens, Skyscraper, Dark Blue, Blue Stopper, Chrome, 5 In. . . .	960.00
Perfume Bottle, Worth, Sans Adieu, Green, Wooden Box, c.1929, 4¼ In. . . . .*illus*	1080.00
Perfume Burner, Faune, Clear & Frosted, Figural Stopper, R. Lalique, c.1930, 8¼ In. . . .	10200.00
Perfume Burner, Marcus & Bardel, Danseuses Egyptiennes, Frosted, Black, c.1926, 5 In. . . .	1800.00
Pin, Deux Aigles, 2 Eagles, Frosted, Green Patina, c.1911, 3¾ In.	2640.00
Pitcher, Tumblers, Chene, Oak Leaves, Post 1945, 8½ In., 9 Piece	1230.00
Plate, Bague Chiens, Hunting Dogs, Trees, Birds, Engraved, 8⅜ In., 8 Piece	3470.00
Plate, Coquilles, Shells, Opalescent, R. Lalique, c.1924, 10¼ In.	717.00
Plate, Coquilles, Shells, Opalescent, Wheel Cut, R. Lalique, c.1924, 11¾ In.	1320.00
Plate, Oursins, Sea Urchin, Opalescent Frosted, R. Lalique, 10 In.	264.00
Plate, Plumes De Paon, Peacock Feathers, Alexandrite, R. Lalique, c.1932, 12 In.	1920.00
Plate Set, Fleur, Acid Stamp, c.1932, 7¼ In., 10 Piece	598.00
Powder Box, Panier De Roses, Rose Basket, Frosted, Blue, R. Lalique, c.1919, 3⅜ In.	2400.00
Powder Box, Pommier Du Japon, Apple Tree, White Patina, R. Lalique, c.1919, 3¼ In.	2520.00
Powder Box, Quatre Papillons, 4 Butterflies, Opalescent, R. Lalique, c.1911, 3 In.	3120.00
Powder Box, Quatre Scarabees, 4 Beetles, Blue, White, R. Lalique, c.1911, 3⅜ In.	3120.00
Sconce, Frosted, Dahlias, 1921, Pair, 8 In. . . . . 2640.00 to 3600.00
Seal, Trois Papillons, 3 Butterflies, Clear, Frosted, Engraved R. Lalique, c.1919, 2½ In. . . .	2400.00
Swizzle Stick Set, Barr, Champagne, Box, 4¾ In., 12 Piece	2640.00
Vase, Albert, Smoky Gray, Sparrow Hawk Head Handles, Wheel Cut, R. Lalique, 6⅛ In.	1410.00
Vase, Archers, Hunting Swooping Birds, Butterscotch, R. Lalique, c.1921, 10½ In.	11633.00
Vase, Archers, Hunting Swooping Birds, Smoky Green, Cased, No. 893, 1921, 10½ In.	6022.00
Vase, Archers, Swooping Birds, Clear, Frosted, Blue Patina, R Lalique, c.1921, 10½ In.	5100.00
Vase, Armorique, Overlapping Leaves, Opalescent, c.1927, 8¾ In.	7800.00
Vase, Avallon, Birds & Grapes, Yellow Amber, Wood, Wheel Cut R. Lalique, c.1927, 6 In.	6000.00
Vase, Bacchantes, Frieze Of Female Nudes, Frosted, Amber Patina, R. Lalique, 9½ In.	7188.00
Vase, Bacchantes, Frieze Of Female Nudes, Frosted, Gray Patina, R. Lalique, 9½ In.	5463.00
Vase, Bacchantes, Frieze Of Female Nudes, Frosted, R. Lalique, 9½ In. . . . . 1763.00 to 5760.00
Vase, Bagatelle, Molded, Clear, Frosted, Signed, 7 In.	235.00
Vase, Bandes De Roses, Vertical Bands, Clear, Frosted, Sepia Patina, Lalique, c.1919, 9 In. . . .	3900.00
Vase, Beautreillis, Opalescent, Trellis, Art Deco, Wheel Cut, R. Lalique, 1927, 5½ In.	1175.00
Vase, Beauvais, Graduated Cointed Fern Leaves, Stenciled, R. Lalique, 1931, 8 In.	3225.00

Lalique, Vase, Languedoc, Aloe Leaves, Emerald Green, Engraved R. Lalique, c.1929, 8⅞ In.
$19200.00

Lalique, Vase, Malesherbes, Loquat Leaves, Cased Jade Green, White Patina, c.1927, 8⅞ In.
$8400.00

Lalique, Vase, Meduse, Wavy Tentacles, Cased Red, Engraved R. Lalique, c.1921, 6½ In.
$7200.00

L

LALIQUE

Lalique, Vase, Ormeaux, Overlapping Elm Leaves, Deep Amber, R. Lalique, c.1926, 6½ In. $2160.00

Lalique, Vase, Pensees, Pansies, Clear, Frosted, Violet Enamel, Lavender Patina, c.1920, 5 In. $5700.00

Lalique, Vase, Poissons, Fish, Emerald Green, c.1921, 9⅛ In. $192000.00

Lalique, Vase, Ronces, Thorns, Green, Raised White Decoration, c.1921, 9¼ In. $2117.00

Vase, Beliers, Smoky Topaz, Ibex Handles, Wheel Cut Signed, R. Lalique, 8¼ In.	1763.00
Vase, Blown-Out Figures Of Man & Woman, & Pan, Marked, 8½ In.	615.00
Vase, Blown-Out Figures Of Man, Woman, Pan, Acid Etched Mark, 8½ In.	600.00
Vase, Blown-Out Figures Of Man, Woman, Pan, Acid Etched Mark, 9 In.	515.00
Vase, Boutons D'Or, Buttercups, 1930s, 5½ In.	975.00
Vase, Bresse, Swirling Feathers, Amber, White Patina, Stenciled, R. Lalique, c.1931, 4 In.	3000.00
Vase, Camaret, 4 Rows Of Fish, Opalescent, Engraved R. Lalique, c.1928, 5¼ In.	1920.00
Vase, Canards, Ducks, Amber, R. Lalique, c.1931, 5⅜ In.	3120.00
Vase, Canards, Ducks, Spiral Formation, Blue Patina, Art Deco, R. Lalique, 1931, 5¼ In.	995.00
Vase, Ceylan, 8 Parakeets, On Branches, Opalescent, Frosted, Signed, R. Lalique, 9½ In.	7188.00
Vase, Chamarande, Opalescent, Rose Handles, Patina, Wheel Cut, R. Lalique, 1926, 8 In.	3878.00
Vase, Champagne, Pointed Cabachons, Bright Green, R Lalique, c.1927, 6½ In.	3900.00
Vase, Champagne, Pointed Cabochons, Opalescent, c.1927, 6½ In.	3000.00
Vase, Chardons, Thistles, Green Patina, Signed, R. Lalique, 7½ In.	1265.00
Vase, Charmilles, Overlapping Leaves, Black Patina, 14 In.	3585.00
Vase, Claude, Molded, Clear, Frosted, Signed, 13½ In.	176.00
Vase, Courges, Squash, Electric Blue, c.1914, 7⅛ In. ....*illus*	8400.00
Vase, Courges, Molded Gourds, Opalescent, Blue Patina, R. Lalique, c.1914, 7¼ In.	3000.00
Vase, Courlis, Curlews, Deep Green, White Patina, Stenciled R. Lalique, c.1931, 6½ In.	6600.00
Vase, Courlis, Curlews, Yellow Amber, White Patina, Stenciled R. Lalique, c.1931, 6½ In.	8400.00
Vase, Cover, Cariatides, Frosted, c.1920, 7¾ In.	2880.00
Vase, Cover, Sylvia, Clear, Frosted, Blue Patina, Bird Handles, R. Lalique, c.1929, 8⅝ In.	9000.00
Vase, Cover, Sylvia, Frosted, Molded Bird Handles, c.1929, 9 In.	7800.00
Vase, Cover, Tourterelles, Turtle Doves, Gray, Egg Shape, Lovebird Finial, 1925, 11 In. . 5875.00 to 8225.00	
Vase, Danaides, Female Nudes, Pour Water From Urn, Blue Patina, Signed, R. Lalique, 7 In.	7475.00
Vase, Danaides, Female Nudes, Pour Water From Urns, Opalescent, c.1930, 7 In.	4309.00
Vase, Dauphins, Fish In Waves, Opalescent, Frosted, Signed, R. Lalique, 5½ In.	2070.00
Vase, Davos, Opalescent Bubble Clusters, In Diamonds, Brown, Bulbous, 1932, 11 In. ..*illus*	3346.00
Vase, Dentele, Frosted Glass, Notched Ribs, Articulated Bands, c.1912, 7½ In.	685.00
Vase, Domremy, Thistles, Blue Patina, Bulbous, Flared Rim, 8½ In.	1683.00
Vase, Domremy, Thistles, Dark Gray Patina, c.1926, 8¼ In.	1434.00
Vase, Epis, Leaves & Flared Ribs, Clear, Frosted, Signed, c.1931, 6¾ In.	470.00
Vase, Espalion, Allover Ferns, Blue, Engraved R. Lalique, c.1927, 7 In.	3600.00
Vase, Espalion, Allover Ferns, Jade Green, Engraved R. Lalique, c.1927, 7 In.	5700.00
Vase, Feuilles, 3 Rows Of Leaves, Clear, Frosted, Signed, 7½ In.	382.00
Vase, Florence, Band Of Cherubs, Clear, Frosted, Brown Enamel, Sepia, c.1937, 7⅞ In.	6000.00
Vase, Formose, Smoky Gray, R. Lalique, 1924, 8¾ In.	2115.00
Vase, Formose, Swirling Carp, Cased Opalescent, Blue Patina, R. Lalique, 6¼ In., Pair	3525.00
Vase, Formose, Swirling Carp, Clear, Frosted, Molded R. Lalique, c.1924, 5¾ In.	1920.00
Vase, Formose, Swirling Carp, Red, Tropical Fish, 1924, 6¼ In.	4524.00
Vase, Fougeres, 4 Rows Of Molded Leaves, Emerald Green, c.1912, 6 In.	4800.00
Vase, Fougeres, 4 Rows Of Molded Leaves, Gray, c.1912, 6¼ In.	3600.00
Vase, Fougeres, 4 Rows Of Molded Leaves, Mauve, c.1912, 6⅛ In.	6600.00
Vase, Gobelet 6 Figurines, Clear, Frosted, Blue Patina, Engraved R. Lalique, c.1912, 8 In.	3900.00
Vase, Grenade, Blue, White Enamel, Engraved R. Lalique, 4¾ In.	2520.00
Vase, Gui, Mistletoe & Berries, Pea Green, Molded R. Lalique, c.1920, 6½ In.	2400.00
Vase, Hirondelles, Swallows, Squat, Flared, Footed, Marc Lalique, 4¾ x 4½ In.	411.00
Vase, Honfleur, Flowing Leaf Handles, Brown Patina, Signed, R. Lalique, 5½ In.	1610.00
Vase, Honfleur, Flowing Leaf Handles, Leaf & Berry Motif, c.1927, 5 In.	837.00
Vase, Lagamar, Geometric Bands, Clear, Frosted, Black Enamel, R. Lalique, c.1926, 7 In.	9600.00
Vase, Laiterons, Overall Arched, Serrated Leaves, Amber, White Patina, c.1931, 3⅛ In.	1140.00
Vase, Languedoc, Aloe Leaves, Cased Opalescent, Stenciled, R. Lalique, 1929, 11½ In.	7109.00
Vase, Languedoc, Aloe Leaves, Clear, Frosted, Stenciled, R. Lalique, 1929, 11½ In.	4265.00
Vase, Languedoc, Aloe Leaves, Emerald Green, Engraved R. Lalique, c.1929, 8⅞ In. ....*illus*	19200.00
Vase, Languedoc, Gray, Aloe Leaves, c.1929, 8¾ In.	7800.00
Vase, Lilas, Lilac Leaves, Clear, Wheel Cut, R. Lalique, c.1930, 9¼ In.	1549.00
Vase, Lobelia, Flared Rim, Embossed Ferns, Molded, Clear, Frosted, Signed, 7¼ In.	147.00
Vase, Malesherbes, Loquat Leaves, Cased Jade Green, White Patina, c.1927, 8⅞ In. .....*illus*	8400.00
Vase, Malesherbes, Loquat Leaves, Clear, Frosted, Sepia Patina, R. Lalique, c.1927, 9 In.	3000.00
Vase, Malesherbes, Loquat Leaves, Frosted, Pear Shape, Engraved, R. Lalique, 1927, 10 In.	1549.00
Vase, Margaret, Clear, Frosted, Blue Patina, Rectangular Handles, c.1929, 9 In.	8400.00
Vase, Marguerites, Daisies, Sepia Patina, Bulbous, Rolled Rim, Stenciled R. Lalique, 8 In.	1148.00
Vase, Marisa, Vertical Fish, Gray, Frosted, c.1927, 9 In.	6600.00
Vase, Meduse, Spiraling Tentacles, Amber, c.1921, 6⅜ In.	4200.00
Vase, Meduse, Spiraling Tentacles, Green, c.1921, 6½ In.	6000.00
Vase, Meduse, Spiraling Tentacles, Opalescent, 1921, 6⅜ In.	4200.00

Vase, Meduse, Wavy Tentacles, Cased Red, Engraved R. Lalique, c.1921, 6½ In. . . . . *illus*	7200.00
Vase, Moissac, Overlapping Raised Leaves, Opalescent, Wheel Cut R. Lalique, c.1927, 5 In. . . .	2160.00
Vase, Moissac, Overlapping Raised Leaves, Topaz, Wheel Cut R. Lalique, c.1927, 5 In.	2040.00
Vase, Monnaie Du Pape, Money Plant, Opalescent, Blue Patina, R. Lalique, c.1914, 9 In.	3000.00
Vase, Nivernais, Olive Cabochons, Bright Green, Engraved R. Lalique, c.1927, 6⅝ In.	3360.00
Vase, Nivernais, Olive Cabochons, Cased Opalescent, c.1927, 6⅝ In.	3120.00
Vase, Ormeaux, Elm Leaves, Amber, Signed, R. Lalique, 1926, 6¼ In.	1410.00
Vase, Ormeaux, Elm Leaves, Jade Green, Engraved, R. Lalique, 6¼ In.	2115.00
Vase, Ormeaux, Elm Leaves, Red Amber, Engraved R. Lalique, c.1926, 6½ In.	2880.00
Vase, Ormeaux, Overlapping Elm Leaves, Deep Amber, R. Lalique, c.1926, 6½ In. . . . . . *illus*	2160.00
Vase, Ornis, Frosted, Bird Handles, Wheel Cut, R. Lalique, 1926, 7½ In.	1410.00
Vase, Ornis, Opalescent, Bird Handles, Wheel Cut, R. Lalique, c.1926, 7½ In. . . . . . . 3480.00 to 4850.00
Vase, Palissy, Snail Shells, Opalescent, Gray Patina, R. Lalique, c.1926, 6½ In.	3600.00
Vase, Pan, Pan Pipes, Portrait, Sepia Patina, R. Lalique, 1937, 12½ In.	5162.00
Vase, Pensees, Pansies, Clear, Frosted, Violet Enamel, Lavender Patina, c.1920, 5 In. . . . *illus*	5700.00
Vase, Perigord, Opalescent, c.1928, 5½ In.	2520.00
Vase, Perruches, Parakeets, Electric Blue, Signed, R. Lalique, 1920s, 10 In.	7755.00
Vase, Perruches, Parakeets, Opalescent Green, Blue, Green Patina, R. Lalique, c.1931, 10 In.	9600.00
Vase, Petrarque, Frosted, Bird Handles, c.1929, 8⅝ In.	7200.00
Vase, Pierrefonds, Frosted, Volute Handles, c.1926, 6 In.	6000.00
Vase, Poissons, Fish, Cased Red, Engraved, R. Lalique, c.1924, 9¼ In.	14624.00
Vase, Poissons, Fish, Emerald Green, c.1921, 9⅛ In. . . . . *illus*	192000.00
Vase, Poissons, Fish, Opalescent, Blue Patination, c.1921, 9¼ In.	3884.00
Vase, Poissons, Fish, Opalescent, Sea Green Patina, Engraved, R. Lalique, c.1921, 8¼ In. . .	3525.00
Vase, Poissons, Fish, Opalescent, Sepia Patina, R. Lalique, c.1921, 9¼ In.	3522.00
Vase, Poissons, Fish, Sepia, Frosted, Round, Raised Rim, R. Lalique, c.1921, 9¼ In.	3781.00
Vase, Rampillon, Cabochons & Flowers, Yellow Amber, R. Lalique, c.1927, 5 In. . . . . 1560.00 to 2280.00
Vase, Ronces, Thorns, Green, Raised White Decoration, c.1921, 9¼ In. . . . . *illus*	2117.00
Vase, Ronces, Thorns, Red Amber, Molded R. Lalique, c.1921, 9 In.	5100.00
Vase, Ronsard, Gray, Females In Rose Wreath Handles, R. Lalique, 1926, 8¼ In.	4524.00
Vase, Royat, Vertical Molded Ridges, Clear, Frosted, Signed, 1936, 6¼ In.	176.00
Vase, Saint-Emilion, Frosted, Green Applied Bird Handles, Leaves, c.1942, 9¾ In.	2151.00
Vase, Saint-Marc, Bands Of Birds, Opalescent, R. Lalique, c.1939, 6¾ x 6½ In.	1560.00
Vase, Sauterelles, Grasshoppers, Clear, Frosted, Engraved R. Lalique, c.1913, 10½ In.	5100.00
Vase, Sirenes Avec Bouchon, Mermaids, Figural Stopper, R. Lalique, 13¾ In.	11633.00
Vase, Sophora, Leaves, Amber, c.1926, 10 In.	12000.00
Vase, Soudan, 3 Bands Of Running Gazelles, Opalescent, Blue Patination, c.1928, 7 In.	3346.00
Vase, Soustons, Molded Leaves, Frosted, c.1935, 9 In.	1793.00
Vase, Tanega, Clear, Applied Green Leaf, Engraved, Lalique, 14¼ In.	1320.00
Vase, Tournesols, Sunflowers, Clear, Frosted, Yellow Patina, R. Lalique, c.1927, 4½ In.	720.00
Vase, Tristan, Flaring Leaf Handles, Clear, Green Patina, Stenciled R. Lalique, c.1928, 8 In. . .	4200.00
Vase, Tulipes, Molded, Frosted, Clear Tulips, c.1927, 8¼ In.	1912.00
Vase, Tulipes, Molded Tulips, Opalescent, c.1927, 8½ In.	3600.00
Vase, Violettes, Violet Leaves, Green Patina, Frosted, R. Lalique, 1921, 6¾ In.	1163.00

LAMPS of every type, from the early oil-burning Betty and Phoebe lamps to the recent electric lamps with glass or beaded shades, interest collectors. Fuels used in lamps changed through the years; whale oil (1800–1840), camphene (1828), Argand (1830), lard (1833–1863), turpentine and alcohol (1840s), gas (1850–1879), kerosene (1860), and electricity (1879) are the most common. Other lamps are listed by manufacturer or type of material.

Adjustable, Ripod Base, 2-Light Candlestand, Shepherd's Crook, Iron, N. Carolina, c.1820, 49 In.	2415.00
Advertising, AC Sparkplug, Porcelain, Black, White, c.1950, 19 x 5 In.	80.00
Advertising, Borden's, Figural, Elsie, Night-Light, Hard Plastic, 8 x 5 x 10 In.	83.00
Advertising, Champion Sparkplug, Porcelain, White, Metal, c.1950, 21 x 5½ In.	80.00
Advertising, Dutch Boy Paint, Composition, 15 In.	165.00
Advertising, Guinness Beer, Pelican, Ceramic, 17½ x 6½ In.	550.00
Advertising, Hamm's, Bear, Ceramic, c.1960s, 14 In.	166.00
Advertising, Ken-L-Ration, Little Friskies Dog, Plaster, 1940s, 13 In.	190.00
Advertising, Ken-L-Ration, Little Friskies Dog, Plastic Head, Bulb, c.1950s, 13 In.	140.00
Aladdin, A-1248, Venetian Art-Craft, Ebony	595.00
Aladdin, B-25, Victoria, Ceramic	495.00
Aladdin, B-25, Victoria, Ceramic, B Burner, New Wick, Flame Spreader	625.00
Aladdin, B-25, Victoria, Ceramic, Oil Fill, No Burner	325.00
Aladdin, B-28, Simplicity, Rose	170.00
Aladdin, B-39, Washington Drape, Clear Crystal, Burner	50.00

Lamp, Aladdin, Domed Shade, Reverse Painted, Cottage Scene, Trees, Flowers, 15 In.
$106.00

Aladdin Lamps

Today's collectors like the glass model Aladdin lamps made in the 1930s. They were made in amber, peach, white, moonstone, cobalt blue, red, and other colors. The glass finials for these lamps are often missing today and can sell for over $100 each.

Lamp, Betty, Brass, Peter Derr, Iron Arm & Hanger, Stamped, P.D., 1835, 5¾ In.
$3575.00

Lamp, Chandelier, 5-Light, Chrome, Opalescent Glass Shades, Icicles, Sabino, 31 x 26 In. $3600.00

Lamp, Chandelier, Duffner & Kimberly, Trumpet Vine, Cone Shape, Bronze Chain, 28 In. $22913.00

Lamp, Electric, 2 Nude Women Holding Shade, Amber Glass, Ice Chip Surface, 11 x 8 In. $345.00

Lamp, Electric, Cylindrical Shade, Leaf Applique, Rembrandt Art Pottery, 40 In. $59.00

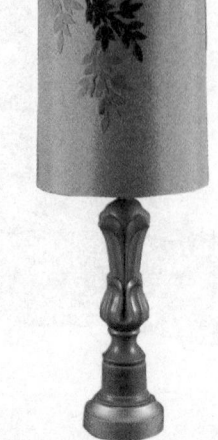

Aladdin, B-48, Washington Drape, Green, Bell Stem	275.00
Aladdin, B-52, Washington Drape, Amber Crystal, Filigree Stem	195.00
Aladdin, B-53, Washington Drape, Clear	50.00
Aladdin, B-55, Washington Drape, Crystal Amber, Plain Stem, Burner	125.00
Aladdin, B-60, Short Lincoln Drape, Alacite	475.00 to 495.00
Aladdin, B-60, Short Lincoln Drape, Alacite, No Burner	500.00
Aladdin, B-62, Short Lincoln Drape, Ruby Crystal, Burner	700.00
Aladdin, B-70, Solitaire, White Moonstone	1949.00
Aladdin, B-75, Alacite, Table Lamp, Scallop Foot	160.00
Aladdin, B-80, Beehive, Clear Crystal	98.00
Aladdin, B-87, Vertique, Rose Moonstone	395.00
Aladdin, B-88, Veritique, Yellow Moonstone, 3 Line Chimney, Model B Chicago Burner	650.00
Aladdin, B-92 Veritique, Green Moonstone, Burner	400.00
Aladdin, B-93, Vertique, White Moonstone	795.00
Aladdin, B-101, Corinthian, Amber Crystal	150.00
Aladdin, B-104, Corinthian, Clear Font, Black Foot	160.00
Aladdin, B-105, Corinthian, Clear Font, Green Foot	140.00
Aladdin, B-106, Corinthian, Clear Font, Amber Foot	120.00
Aladdin, B-110, Corinthian, White Moonstone, Burner	190.00
Aladdin, B-111, Cathedral, Green Moonstone, Burn, Chimney	300.00
Aladdin, B-112 Cathedral, Rose Moonstone, Burner, Chimney	255.00
Aladdin, B-122, Majestic, Green Moonstone	200.00
Aladdin, B-126, Corinthian, Moonstone Bowl, Rose Moonstone Foot	170.00
Aladdin, Domed Shade, Reverse Painted, Cottage Scene, Trees, Flowers, 15 In. *illus*	106.00
Aladdin, G-17, Opalique, Table Lamp	90.00
Aladdin, G-24, Light Blue, Cupid, Table Lamp	175.00
Aladdin, G-47C, Hoppy Bullet Lamp, No Shade, New Decal	65.00
Aladdin, G-62, Electric	30.00
Aladdin, G-64, Moonstone Table Lamp	65.00
Aladdin, G-95, Alacite, Millefleur Finial	100.00
Aladdin, G-141, Moonstone, Table Lamp	55.00
Aladdin, G-172, Alacite, Old Formula	55.00
Aladdin, G-189, Tree Trunk Opalique, No Feet	110.00
Aladdin, G-190, Opalique, 10-In. Fluted Shade, Bouquet Crystal Finial	225.00
Aladdin, G-201, Desk, Alacite, Old Formula	85.00
Aladdin, G-202, Alacite, Table Lamp, Angelia Finial	30.00
Aladdin, G-225, Alacite, Lyre	225.00
Aladdin, G-236, Alacite, Table Lamp, Scroll Finial	37.00
Aladdin, G-241, Alacite, Illuminated Base, Wheat Finial	70.00
Aladdin, G-256, Alacite, Table Lamp	48.00
Aladdin, G-265, Alacite, Table Lamp, Wheat Finial	32.00
Aladdin, G-282, Alacite, Table Lamp, Turn Key Finial	40.00
Aladdin, G-294D, Alacite, Colonial Scene	30.00
Aladdin, G-298D, Alacite, Floral, Illuminated Base, Bouquet Finial	65.00
Aladdin, G-333, Alacite, Bride & Groom, Illuminated Base, Forest Green Finial	130.00
Aladdin, G-333, Forest Green, Finial	130.00
Aladdin, G-355C, Gun, Holster Night-Light	205.00
Aladdin, G-375, Dancing Ladies Urn, Lid	775.00
Aladdin, M-146, Table, Lancet Finial, Shade, 16 In.	40.00
Aladdin, Model C, B-180 Aluminum	22.00
Aladdin, No. 1251, Floor, 641, Aladdinite, 20½ Shade	675.00
Aladdin, Short Lincoln Drape, Clear, Cobalt, 1995	85.00
Argand, Bronze, Patinated, Rhyton Shape, Bud Finial, Scrolled Arm, Lotus, c.1830, 12 In., Pair	2585.00
Argand, Cut Glass Shade, Mask Decorated Urns, Fluted, Ribbed Palm Trunk, 28 x 18 In.	5581.00
Betty, Brass, Peter Derr, Iron Arm & Hanger, Stamped, P.D., 1835, 5¾ In. *illus*	3575.00
Betty, Copper, Iron, 4¼ In.	154.00
Betty, Grease, Cast Iron, Colonial, Double, Hanger Hook, Black Patina, c.1750, 6 In.	177.00
Betty, Grease, Tin, Acorn Tipped Design, Hanger Cutouts, c.1780, 6 x 3 x 3½ In.	384.00
Betty, Grease, Tin, Acorn Tipped Design, Hanger Cutouts, c.1780, 9½ x 2½ x 3½ In.	207.00
Betty, Iron, Bokar Type, 3⅛ In.	715.00
Betty, Iron, Bokar Type, 5 In.	94.00
Betty, Iron, c.1800, 6 In.	94.00
Betty, Tin, Sand Weighted, 8 In.	149.00
Betty, Wood, Screw Type, Holder, 26 In.	5610.00
Betty, Wrought Iron, Chicken Finial, Flattened Reservoir, Swing Arm, Twist Hanger, 7 In.	165.00
Betty, Wrought Iron, Iron Arm, Twisted Handle, Chain Pick, Wick Channel, 4⅜ In.	330.00

L

Lamp, Electric, Dagwood & Daisy Base, Tree Trunk, Blondie Comics On Shade, 1949, 11 In.
$473.00

Lamp, Electric, Dome Shade, Tooled, Jewels, Arm Supports, Wiener Werkstatte, 22 In.
$3565.00

Lamp, Electric, Figural, Frog Holding Shade, Bronze, Opalescent Glass Cabochons, 14 In.
$2473.00

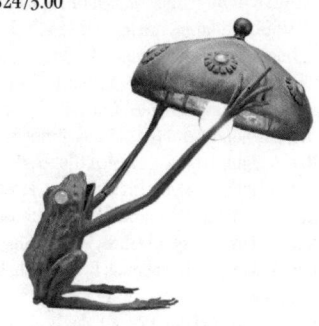

Lamp, Electric, Figural, Woman Playing Croquet, Brass Shade, Jewels, 16 x 8 In.
$2013.00

Lamp, Electric, G. Nelson, Bubble, Saucer Shape, Fiberglass Over Wire, H. Miller, 10 x 26 In.
$450.00

Lamp, Electric, Hanging, Domed Shade, Cranberry Hobnail, Brass Frame, Prisms, 27 In.
$316.00

Lamp, Electric, Hanging, Emerald Glass, Beehive, Honeycomb, Brass, Pull Chain, 14 In.
$82.00

Lamp, Electric, Hanging, Fun 13 Alu, Verner Panton, Discs, Chains, c.1976, 35 x 43 In.
$2280.00

Collectible Lamps

Any old lamp (even an early light bulb) is of interest to either a collector or a decorator. The very old oil-burning Betty and Phoebe lamps, china oil lamps, candle-burning fairy lamps, or leaded glass shades on art nouveau electric lamps can be found in homes that are modern in every other detail.

Lamp, Electric, Hanging, Pink Opalescent Shade, Ruffled Rim, Brass Mount, Chains, 9 In. $264.00

Lamp, Electric, Moe Bridges, Landscape, Trees, Mountains, Signed Shade & Base, 14 In. $176.00

Lamp, Electric, Palm Tree, 2-Light, Man With Turban, Holding Rifle, Riding Camel, 20 In. $3565.00

Bouillotte, 3-Light, Louis XVI, Gilt Bronze, Winged Female Cast Arms, Tole Shade, 24½ In.	708.00
Bouillotte, 3-Light, Louis XVI Style, Candle Arms, Laurel Swags, Ormolu, Pair, 11¾ In.	3600.00
Bouillotte, Double Arm, Green Tole Shade, Early 20th Century, 27 x 17 In., Pair	720.00
Bouillotte, Restauration Style, Gilded Brass, Black Tole Paint, Faux Candles, 26 x 16 In.	1680.00
Bradley & Hubbard lamps are included in the Bradley & Hubbard category.	
Burmese, Ducks, Enameled, Guba, 11½ In.	4200.00
Camphene, Brass, Petticoat, Wick Supports, 7 In.	44.00
Camphene, Clear Glass, 12-Sided Glass, Peg, 3 Brass Wick Burners, 6 In.	248.00
Camphene, Diamond Point Glass Fonts, Brass, Marble Base, 13 In., Pair	385.00
Chandelier, 3-Light, Art Deco, Frosted Globes, Bronze Tone, Early 1900s, 30 In.	360.00
Chandelier, 3-Light, Art Deco, Nickel Plated, Frosted Glass, France, 30 In.	351.00
Chandelier, 4-Light, Art Deco, Nickel Plated, Frosted Glass, France, 24 In.	300.00
Chandelier, 4-Light, Camphor Glass, Panels, Shades, Signed Muller Freres, 26 x 32 In.	7500.00
Chandelier, 4-Light, Prairie School, Brass Wash, Panels, Rosebuds, Amber Slag, 22 x 27 In. . .	1200.00
Chandelier, 5-Light, Art Deco, Nickel Plated, Frosted Glass, France, 29 In.	480.00
Chandelier, 5-Light, Crystal, Prism Bobeche, Candy Cane Ornaments, 24 x 24 In., Pair	1150.00
Chandelier, 5-Light, Chrome, Opalescent Glass Shades, Icicles, Sabino, 31 x 26 In. . . . .*illus*	3600.00
Chandelier, 5-Light, Gilt Metal, Crystal Pendants, Continental Style, 26 x 18½ In.	295.00
Chandelier, 5-Light, Louis XVI Style, Provincial Giltwood, Scrolled Candle Arms	823.00
Chandelier, 5-Light, Rococo, Gilt Brass, Porcelain, Leafy Arms, Glass Drops, 18 x 19 In. . . .	235.00
Chandelier, 5-Light, Wrought Iron, Steel, Electrified, Steel Ring, Scrolled Base, 32 x 25 In. . .	460.00
Chandelier, 6-Light, Art Deco, Nickel Plated, Frosted Glass, France, 34 In.	540.00
Chandelier, 6-Light, Art Deco, Nickel Plated, Frosted Globes, France, 36 In.	540.00
Chandelier, 6-Light, Art Deco, Opalescent Glass, France, 29 In.	900.00
Chandelier, 6-Light, Baronial Style, Wrought Iron, Pyramid Shape, 1800s, 44 x 24 In.	720.00
Chandelier, 6-Light, Cut Glass, Prisms, French Style, 20th Century, 21 In.	609.00
Chandelier, 6-Light, Gilt Metal, Flower Form, 20th Century, 36 x 30 In.	988.00
Chandelier, 6-Light, Louis XIV, Dragon, Parcel Bronzed, Gilded, Carved, 37 x 27 In.	5040.00
Chandelier, 6-Light, Louis XVI Style, Argente, Iron, Electrified, France, 52 x 30 In.	411.00
Chandelier, 6-Light, Louis XVI Style, Corbeille Shape, Brass, Cut Glass Prisms, 50 x 25 In. . .	2400.00
Chandelier, 6-Light, Regency Style, Gilt, Patinated Metal, Bell Shape, Scroll Arms, 28 x 27 In.	360.00
Chandelier, 6-Light, Rococo, Giltwood, Wrought Iron, Cut Glass, Early 1900s, 32 x 25 In. . . .	2880.00
Chandelier, 8-Light, Cut Glass, Spears, Triple Canopy, Electrified, England, 47 x 37 In.	4935.00
Chandelier, 8-Light, Gas, Electric, Longwy, 39 In.	9500.00
Chandelier, 8-Light, Georgian Style, Etched Bronze, Onion Standard, 22 x 25 In.	1416.00
Chandelier, 8-Light, Gilt, Iron, Faux Candles, Amethyst Glass, Electrified, Italy, 25 x 21 In. . .	822.00
Chandelier, 8-Light, Gilt Brass, Cobalt Blue Glass, Flower Heads, Chains, 38 x 31½ In.	2115.00
Chandelier, 8-Light, Louis XVI, Cut Brass, Wrought Iron, Cut Glass, c.1900, 37 x 32 In.	2160.00
Chandelier, 8-Light, Neoclassical, Crystal, Prism Drops, 26 x 32 In.	234.00
Chandelier, 8-Light, Regency Style, Bronze, 43 In.	3231.00
Chandelier, 8-Light, Sheet Iron, Lapped & Soldered Joints, Curved Arms, c.1800, 19 In.	14500.00
Chandelier, 8-Light, Wrought Iron, 20th Century, 35 In.	217.00
Chandelier, 10-Light, Georgian Style, Crystal, Cut Bowl Shaped, 33 x 20 In.	1298.00
Chandelier, 10-Light, Georgian Style, Crystal, Scalloped Bowl, 42 x 28 In.	413.00
Chandelier, 11-Light, Louis XV, Gilt Bronze, Circlet & Urn Bosy, 2 Tiers, 31 x 29 In.	1997.00
Chandelier, 12-Light, 2 Tiers, Brass, Ringed Center Post, Globe, 20th Century, 28 x 26 In. . . .	431.00
Chandelier, 12-Light, 2 Tiers, Wire Candle Arms, Wooden Hub, 15¼ x 24 In.	5288.00
Chandelier, 12-Light, Directoire, Italian Provincial, Wrought Iron, Turned Wood, 37 x 44 In. . .	1320.00
Chandelier, 12-Light, Electric, Brass, Fluted Arms, Acanthus, Laurel Leaf, 26 x 26 In.	863.00
Chandelier, 12-Light, Louis XVI Style, Cut Glass, Gilt Bronze, Urn Shape Corona, 60 x 31 In.	4583.00
Chandelier, 12-Light, Tin Candle Cups, Turned Center Post, 28½ x 23½ In.	201.00
Chandelier, 25-Light, Crystal, Gilt Metal, Scrolling Design, Teardrop Prisms, 42 x 36 In.	2070.00
Chandelier, 48-Light, Regency Style, Gilt Bronze, Cage Shape, 20th Century, 53 x 45 In.	2596.00
Chandelier, 4 Tiers, Triangular Glass Pendants, Venini, 1960s, 38 In.	2350.00
Chandelier, Art Nouveau, Cameo, Le Verre Francais, Striated Glass, 5¼ x 15½ In.	3290.00
Chandelier, Brass, 4 Hanging Lanterns, Caramel Slag Glass, Central Post, 33 x 21 In.	780.00
Chandelier, Brass, Milk Glass, Canopy, 4 Bell Shape Hanging Shades, c.1910, 25 x 21 In. . . .	805.00
Chandelier, Duffner & Kimberly, Trumpet Vine, Cone Shape, Bronze Chain, 28 In. . . .*illus*	22913.00
Chandelier, Faceted Cut Glass Prisms, Tiers Of Brass Rings, Ball Drop, Openwork, 36 In. . . .	403.00
Chandelier, Hand Blown, Tulip Shape, Art Deco, c.1920, 13 x 9 In.	410.00
Colonial Ware, Opal, Mallards, Gold Cattails, Ball Shade, Notched Rim, 36 In.	5175.00
Crusie, Double Well, Shaped Crest, Twisted Iron Hanger, Tin, 5¾ In.	55.00
Electric, 2 Nude Women Holding Shade, Amber Glass, Ice Chip Surface, 11 x 8 In. . . . .*illus*	345.00
Electric, 3-Light, Pull Chain, Bronze, Marble, Flame Finial, Edward F. Caldwell, 32 In.	3000.00
Electric, A. Noll, Mahogany, Ivory, Ebony, Mica Shade, c.1925, 64¼ In.	9600.00
Electric, Acrylic, Yellow, Black Base, Doug Ball, John Berezowsky, c.1969, 8 x 17½ In.	154.00

Lamp, Electric, Pheasant, Metal,
Amber Glass, Foil Inserts, Marble,
Chapelle, 17 x 20 In.
$6163.00

Lamp, Electric, Swing Arm,
Arteluce, 80 In.
$16800.00

Lamp, Fluid, Sinumbra, Baluster Stem,
Bronze Dore, Dome Shade,
Electrified, 26 In.
$805.00

Lamp, Electric, Pullman Car Company,
Norman Bel Geddes,
c.1933, 15 x 14 In.
$3900.00

Lamp, Electric, Turquoise,
Tripod Base, Ralph O. Smith,
Greta Grossman,
1949, 49 In.
$5400.00

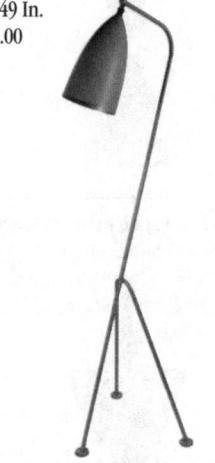

Lamp, Grease, Iron,
Fluted Pan, Long Spout,
Wrought Hanging Hook,
c.1770, 6½ x 5 In.
$306.00

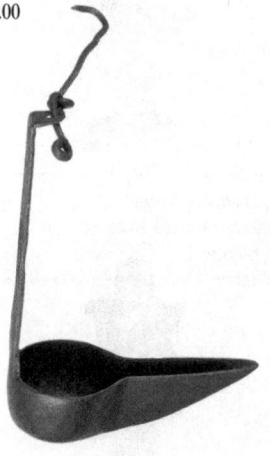

Lamp, Electric, Reverse Painted Shade,
Jefferson, Trees, Lake, Orange,
Brown, 22 x 16 In.
$1495.00

Lamp, Fairy, Candle, Figural,
Bisque, Bulldog, Glass Eyes,
Doghouse Frame, 4½ x 4 In.
$230.00

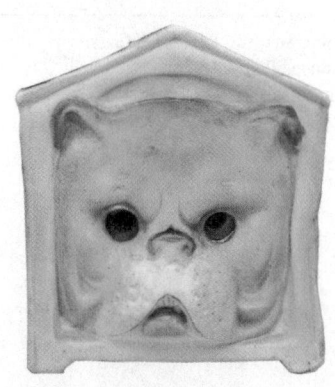

How Bright the Light?

The light from one regular
sixty-watt light bulb is equal to the
light from twenty-five double-wick
whale-oil lamps used in the
nineteenth-century.

Lamp, Kerosene, Brown Pottery Pig, Incised Words On Pig, Hornet Burner, 3⅜ In.
$14950.00

Lamp, Kerosene, Cranberry, Honeycomb Pattern, Applied Feet, Nutmeg Burner, 6¼ In.
$920.00

Lamp, Kerosene, Cranberry Opalescent, Seaweed, Nutmeg Burner, 7¾ In.
$2185.00

Lamp, Kerosene, Figural, Porcelain Lion Head, Hornet Burner, 3¾ In.
$173.00

Lamp, Kerosene, Gone With The Wind, Opal Glass Font, Painted, Ormolu Mounts, 27 In.
$353.00

Lamp, Kerosene, Milk Glass, Fired-On Flowers & Bird, Burner For Round Wick, 8 In.
$403.00

Lamp, Kerosene, Parlor, Ruby Glass, Roses, Ormolu Mount, Connecticut, Late 1800s, 21 In.
$235.00

Lamp, Kerosene, Pink Cased Glass, Diamond Puffed Pattern, Nutmeg Burner, 8 In.
$288.00

Lighting Fuel

Light came from flames before 1876, but the flames were fed by a variety of fuels. Each lamp style was determined by the needs of the fuel.

Candles: Colonial America

Whale Oil: 1800–1840

Argand: 1780s–1850s

Lard Oil: 1840s–1850s

Turpentine (Camphene): 1820s

Turpentine and Alcohol (Burning Fluid): 1840s–1850s

Gas (coal gas): early 1800s–early 20th century; popular 1850–1879

Kerosene: 1860–present

Electricity: 1879–present

Fluorescent: 1927

Halogen: 1980s

Lamp, Kerosene, Porcelain, Milk Glass Shade, Victorian Scene, P&A Victor Burner, 9 In.
$420.00

Electric, Alabaster, Ball & Baluster Shape, Art Deco, Italy, 41 In.	300.00
Electric, Art Deco, Pale Frosty Pink, Acid Cut, Urns, Gilt Metal Base, Shade, France, 16 In.	518.00
Electric, Art Deco Style, Desk, Nickel Silver, Cymbal Shaped Shades, 22½ In., Pair	2657.00
Electric, Art Deco Style, Stainless Steel, 71½ In.	2591.00
Electric, Art Glass, Metal, Leaf, Scrolling, Amber Textured Shade, France, 1910s, 9¾ In.	448.00
Electric, Art Moderne, Beveled Mirrored, Flared, Octagonal, Mirrored Base, 32½ In., Pair	1762.00
Electric, Art Nouveau, Bronze, Beaded, Lily Vine, Bowl Shape Shade, Emile Galle	886.00
Electric, Atomic, Chrome, Glass, c.1970, 26 In.	205.00
Electric, Bankers, Steuben, Double, Aurene Shades, Iridescent, Metal Foot, 6¾ x 22 In.	2415.00
Electric, Bar, Glass, Art Deco, c.1930, 10 In., Pair	176.00
Electric, Bergman, Bronze, Boudoir, Figural, Painted, Man, Woman Reclining, 13 In.	8400.00
Electric, Bergman, Bronze, Boudoir, Figural, Painted, Man Seated In Tent, 14½ In.	13200.00
Electric, Bisque, Nude Children, Standing, Pedestal Base, France, Early 1900s, 10¼ In., Pair	173.00
Electric, Brass, Canting Kettle, 10½ In.	66.00
Electric, Brass, Green Glass Globe, Bulbous, 6¼ In.	193.00
Electric, Bridge, Colonial Style, Iron, Brass Accents, Urn Top, 57 In.	58.00
Electric, Bronze, Figural, Parrot, Cold Painted, Multicolored, Lantern Style Fixture, 15 In.	518.00
Electric, Bronze, Figural, Woman, Hands Holding Socket, Beaded Shade, 4¼ In.	999.00
Electric, Bronze, Orange, Brown Flower-Form Shade, Held By Bird's Beak, 14 x 9½ In.	1020.00
Electric, Bulbous Metal Base, Mottled Green Leaded Glass Shade, Vine, Leaves, 18 x 16 In.	5288.00
Electric, Candlestick, Cut Glass, Hurricane, Faceted Lusters, c.1940s, 23¼ In., Pair	207.00
Electric, Candlestick, Enameled, White, Red, Black Wood Bases, 21 In., Pair	1800.00
Electric, Carriage, Wrought Iron, Painted White, c.1900, 12 x 26 In., Pair	35.00
Electric, Caterpillar, Silver, Black Shade & Base, Floor, 55 In.	294.00
Electric, Cattail, Gilt Brass, Gilbert Poillerat Style, Gilt Cord Bands, Mid 1900s, 24 In., Pair	2280.00
Electric, Ceiling, Artichoke, Aluminum, Poul Henningsen, Louis Poulsen, c.1958, 24 In.	3360.00
Electric, Ceiling, Brass, Custard Glass Shade, Pheasants, 30 x 4 In.	165.00
Electric, Ceiling, Faceted, Hammered Pierced Frame, Caramel Slag, 4 Sockets, 16 x 34 In.	900.00
Electric, Ceiling, Turtleback, Acorn, Amber, Orange, Geometric Green, White Ground, 16 In.	10350.00
Electric, Charles & Fils, Plant Shape, Cast Aluminum, Blade Shape Leaves, 21 x 20 In.	3173.00
Electric, Charlottenborg, 3 Shades, Flared Top Plate, Poul Henningsen, 20 x 26 In.	646.00
Electric, Chrome, Round Mount, Dome, Protruding Socket Rays, 10 Spheres, 8½ x 14 In.	82.00
Electric, Chromium Plated Metal, Lacquered Wood, Walter Von Nessen, c.1930, 15⅛ In.	6600.00
Electric, Cloisonne, Black Ground, Flowers, 2 Sockets, Blue Shade, 26 In.	200.00
Electric, Columnar, Cut Glass, Diamond Cut, Brass Base, Electrified, Victorian, 39½ In.	294.00
Electric, Copper, Hammered, 3 Sockets, Silk Lined Wicker Shade, G. Stickley, 22 x 18 In.	6600.00
Electric, Copper, Hammered, Walrus Tusk Base, 3 Sockets, Albert Berry, 25 x 7 x 5 In.	8400.00
Electric, Cut Glass, Harvard & Daisy, Cut Glass, 18½ In.	275.00
Electric, Cylindrical Shade, Leaf Applique, Rembrandt Art Pottery, 40 In. ....*illus*	59.00
Electric, Dagwood & Daisy Base, Tree Trunk, Blondie Comics On Shade, 1949, 11 In. ..*illus*	473.00
Electric, Desk, Art Deco, Swing Arm, Round Stem, Chrome & Copper Shade, c.1930, 19 In.	1116.00
Electric, Dome Shade, Tooled, Jewels, Arm Supports, Wiener Werkstatte, 22 In. ....*illus*	3565.00
Electric, Duffner & Kimberly, Arts & Crafts, Geometric Leaded Glass Shade	4888.00
Electric, Figural, Frog Holding Shade, Bronze, Opalescent Glass Cabochons, 14 In. ....*illus*	2473.00
Electric, Figural, Squirrels Around Tree Trunk, Blue Case Glass, 8¾ In.	85.00
Electric, Figural, Woman Playing Croquet, Brass Shade, Jewels, 16 x 8 In. ....*illus*	2013.00
Electric, Fixture, Hanging, Brass Washed, 2 Frosted Shades, Prairie School, 36 x 22½ In.	300.00
Electric, Frosted Glass, Brushed Steel, Murano, Late 20th Century, 73 In.	1330.00
Electric, G. Nelson, Bubble, Saucer Shape, Fiberglass Over Wire, H. Miller, 10 x 26 In. ..*illus*	450.00
Electric, G. Stickley, Copper, Hammered, Silk Shade, Crossed Base, Shoe Feet, 58 x 14 In.	11400.00
Electric, Gilt Metal, Slag Glass, Molded Base, Acanthus, Square Shade, Yellow, White, 21 In.	266.00
Electric, Giltwood, Rock Crystal, Pair, 21 In.	8400.00
Electric, Green Slag, Polished Brass Frame, Hexagonal Shade, Palm Fronds, 22 x 14 In.	764.00
Electric, Hammered Copper, 2 Sockets, Handles, Wicker Shade, G. Stickley, 26 x 20 In.	6600.00
Electric, Hammered Copper, 4 Panel Mica Shade, Bulbous Base, Kopper Kraft, 20 x 24 In.	7800.00
Electric, Hanging, 5-Light, Neoclassical, 12 x 28 In.	90.00
Electric, Hanging, Brass, Swirled Amberina Hobnail Shade, 14 In.	5280.00
Electric, Hanging, Cranberry Dome, Hobnail, Scrolled Brass Frame, Prisms, 16 In.	264.00
Electric, Hanging, Cut Glass, 6 Brass Wire Ribs, Glass Beads, Rosettes, Prisms, 20 x 13 In.	660.00
Electric, Hanging, Domed Shade, Cranberry Hobnail, Brass Frame, Prisms, 27 In. ....*illus*	316.00
Electric, Hanging, Emerald Glass, Beehive, Honeycomb, Brass, Pull Chain, 14 In. .....*illus*	82.00
Electric, Hanging, Flower Basket, Drop Tassel, 4 Socket Arms, Leaf Surround, Cast Iron, 15 In.	88.00
Electric, Hanging, Fun 13 Alu, Verner Panton, Discs, Chains, c.1976, 35 x 43 In. ....*illus*	2280.00
Electric, Hanging, Gilt Iron, 3-Part Armature, Gilt Roman Helmet, Fleur-De-Lis, 29 x 6 In.	1527.00
Electric, Hanging, Leaded Glass, Cherry & Leaf Border, Pink Slag, Geometric, 25 x 16 In.	403.00
Electric, Hanging, Modern, Chrome, Glass, c.1960, 18 In.	154.00

Lamp, Kerosene, Rainbow, Mother-Of-Pearl, Diamond Quilted, Ruffled Top, 9¼ In. $3163.00

Lamp, Kerosene, Student, Cased Emerald Green Shade, Manhattan Brass Co., 22½ In. $413.00

Lamp, Oil, 3 Tiers, Pedestal, Satin Glass, Gold Enamel Decoration, 9¾ In. $4025.00

L

TIP

If you find an old lamp with part of a light bulb still in the socket, try this. Push a fresh potato or a wine cork down into the old socket. Turn it and it will probably unscrew the old light bulb base.

Lamp, Oil, Blown Glass Font, Pewter Base, Hinged Reservoir, C-Scroll Handle, 14½ In. $288.00

Lamp, Oil, Bronze, Shell Font, Dolphin Finial, Masks, Horse, Fish, Etched Shade, 15 In. $3850.00

Lamp, Oil, Empire Revival, Japanned Metal, Black, Urn Shape, Tapered Shade, 27 In. $411.00

Electric, Hanging, Opaline Glass, Restauration, Gilt Bronze Mounted, Putto, 8 In.	1657.00
Electric, Hanging, Pink Opalescent Shade, Ruffled Rim, Brass Mount, Chains, 9 In. . . *illus*	264.00
Electric, Harlequin, Art Deco, Patinated Metal, Millefiori Shade, 8½ x 13 In.	499.00
Electric, Le Ministre, Wrought Iron, Glass, Edgar Brandt, Daum, c.1925, 20¾ In.	18000.00
Electric, Leaded Glass, Lotus Blossoms, Slag Glass, 3 Sockets, Bronze, Seuss, 24 x 18 In.	4200.00
Electric, Leaded Glass Shade, Lilies, Bronze Paw Base, Bent Glass Novelty, c.1890, Floor	4140.00
Electric, Lips, Plastic, Steel, Art Deco, c.1970, 51 In.	7200.00
Electric, Louis XV Style, Rock Crystal, Gilt Metal, Pair, 18½ In.	6600.00
Electric, Louis XVI Style, Leaf Arms, Pierced Base, Metal Shade, 2 Light, 22½ In.	649.00
Electric, Marble, Arabescato, Rib, Leaf Carved Baluster Shape, Octagonal Base, 1900s, 40 In.	540.00
Electric, Marble, Carved, Cockatiel Decoration, Early 20th Century, 14¾ In.	88.00
Electric, Metal, Steel, Painted, Adjustable, Karl Trabert, For G. Schanzenbach, c.1933, 18 In.	461.00
Electric, Moe Bridges, Landscape, Trees, Mountains, Signed Shade & Base, 14 In. . . *illus*	176.00
Electric, Monkey, Art Deco, M. Leverrier, Seated, Variegated Marble, c.1922, 6 x 6 In.	705.00
Electric, Moss Rose, Fluted Rim, L.G. Wright, 9½ In.	175.00
Electric, Mountains, Harbor, Boat, Birds, Tree, Pagoda, Wood Base, Moriage, 9½ In.	45.00
Electric, Mushroom, Murano, Cream Domed Shade, Maroon Trim, Cylindrical Base, 20 In.	353.00
Electric, Night-Light, Scrappy, Margie, Yippy, Oopy, 1930s, 6 x 3½ In.	140.00
Electric, Noguchi Style, Chrome, Cork, Cylinder Shade, 1950s, 58 x 11 In.	118.00
Electric, Onyx, Green, Ormolu, Enameled Details, Urn, Leaf Scrolled Arms, 1900s, 64 In.	633.00
Electric, Palm Tree, 2-Light, Man With Turban, Holding Rifle, Riding Camel, 20 In. . . *illus*	3565.00
Electric, Patinated Metal, Cased, Cut To Clear Red, Mushroom Shade, 19 x 13 In.	617.00
Electric, Patinated Metal, Temple Facade Shape, Glass Pediment, Mario Villa, 23 x 16 In.	529.00
Electric, Pheasant, Metal, Amber Glass, Foil Inserts, Marble, Chapelle, 17 x 20 In. . . *illus*	6163.00
Electric, Porcelain, Flowers, Urn Shape, Fred Cooper, 19¼ In.	177.00
Electric, Portrait, Translucent Green, Urn Shape, Medallions, Bohemian Glass, Pair, 24 In.	264.00
Electric, Pullman Car Company, Norman Bel Geddes, c.1933, 15 x 14 In. . . *illus*	3900.00
Electric, Reading, Gibigiana, Achille Castigliono, For Flos Lighting, c.1980, 16 In.	409.00
Electric, Reverse Painted, Gilt Metal, Conical Shade, Landscape, 2 Sockets, Jefferson, 23 In.	1763.00
Electric, Reverse Painted Shade, 2 Deer, Woodland Landscape, Coralene, 22 x 15 In.	633.00
Electric, Reverse Painted Shade, Island Sunset, Urn Shape Metal Base, 14 x 7½ In.	382.00
Electric, Reverse Painted Shade, Sunset Shore, Gothic Metal Base, Early 1900s, 22 x 14 In.	460.00
Electric, Reverse Painted Shade, Jefferson, Trees, Lake, Orange, Brown, 22 x 16 In. . . *illus*	1495.00
Electric, Reverse Painted Shade, Moe Bridges, Landscape, Incised Lines On Base, 21 In.	1528.00
Electric, Reverse Painted Shade, Moe Bridges, Trees, Shoreline, Cabochon Base, 21 In.	1093.00
Electric, Shade, Windmill, House, River, 8¾ x 17 In.	230.00
Electric, Sinumbra, Gilt Brass, Patinated Metal, Swirled Base, Leaves, 30 x 12 In.	2703.00
Electric, Slag Glass, Painted Metal, Panel Shade, Neoclassical Base, Early 1900s, 24 In.	380.00
Electric, Square Oak Base, Hammered Copper Knob, Rattan Shade, G. Stickley, 23 In.	2468.00
Electric, Stained Glass, Bronze, Nude Woman Base, Octagonal Shade, Painted Panels, 23 In.	460.00
Electric, Stainless Steel, Bowl Top, 4-Slat Stem, Stepped Base, Ball Feet, Art Deco, 72 In.	1390.00
Electric, Statuette, Bronze, Rose Arbor, Cast, Glass Shade, Gustav Schmidt, c.1867, 23 x 12 In.	1763.00
Electric, Stoneware, Churn, Stylized Dotted Flowers, c.1870, 18 In.	688.00
Electric, Street, Tin, Green Paint, Cast Iron, Spread Wing Eagle Finial, Phila., 44 x 17 In.	523.00
Electric, Street, Tin, Iron, Scrolled Support Arm, Angled Panes, Dome Top, 22 x 31 In.	110.00
Electric, Street Lamp, Cement & Brass, Westinghouse Plaque, 1920s, 29 In., Pair	1200.00
Electric, Student, Brass, Molded Glass Font, Milk Glass Hobnail Shade, Perfection Patent	595.00
Electric, Student, Nickel Plated, C.A. Kleeman	450.00
Electric, Stylized Swan Holding Lantern, Aldo Tura, Milano, 15½ In., Pair	1920.00
Electric, Swing Arm, Arteluce, 80 In. . . *illus*	16800.00
Electric, Table, Cranberry Flashing, Urn Shape, Diamond Pattern, 30 In., Pair	29.00
Electric, Tiffany Style, Patinated Metal, Columnar Base, Dragonfly Shade, 23 x 14 In.	360.00
Electric, Tin, Green Paint, Conical Base, 2 Candle Bulb Holders, Jerry Martin, 24 In.	358.00
Electric, Torino, Robot Shape, Chrome, Switch Nose, Socket Head & Hands, 28 x 16 In., Pair	5100.00
Electric, Tree Form, Squirrels, Leather Ears, Folk Art, 41 In.	2310.00
Electric, Tripod Base, Wrought Iron, Mica Shade, Painted Ships, Samuel Yellin, 60 x 19 In.	4800.00
Electric, Turban Shade, White, Blue, Red, Sliced Canes, 3 Prong Spider, Millefiori, 22 In.	588.00
Electric, Turquoise, Tripod Base, Ralph O. Smith, Greta Grossman, 1949, 49 In. . . *illus*	5400.00
Electric, Urn Base, Domed Shade, Weave Pattern Changes, Twin Bulb, 1920s, 23 x 17 In.	795.00
Electric, Urn Shape, Bronze Dore, Crystal, c.1930, 19 In.	70.00
Electric, Weave Pattern Designs, Latticework Panels, Scalloped Base, 1920s, 62 x 26 In.	1250.00
Electric, Wicker, Lattice Panels, Woven, Braiding, Domed Shade, c.1915, 68 x 28 In.	1650.00
Electric, Wicker, Latticework, Scalloped Edge, Urn Base, Cane Wrapped Handles, 23 In.	795.00
Electric, Wrought Metal, Mulitcolor, Reverse Painted Shade, Flower, 20½ In.	117.00
Fairy, Candle, Figural, Bisque, Bulldog, Glass Eyes, Doghouse Frame, 4½ x 4 In. . . *illus*	230.00
Fairy, Candle, White Satin Glass, 6½ x 4½ In.	16.00

Fat, Brass, Elongated Wick Channel, Lighthouse Top, Hook Hanger, Continental, 5¼ In.	66.00
Fat, Cast Iron, Hinged Lid, Saucer Base, Oval, 3¼ In.	165.00
Fat, Iron, Hunting Dogs Design On Sides, Continental, 17th Century	395.00
Fluid, Brass, Adjustable Shade, Early 19th Century, 16¾ In.	58.00
Fluid, Brass, Tin, Embossed Handles, 4¼ In.	66.00
Fluid, Clear Waterfall Base, Teal Green Font, Tooled Rim, Ponti, 7¼ In.	6720.00
Fluid, Old Sheffield, Plate, Removable Top, Wire Leaf Decoration, Beehive Base, 7 x 3 In. . . .	115.00
Fluid, Sinumbra, Baluster Stem, Bronze Dore, Dome Shade, Electrified, 26 In. . . . . *illus*	805.00
Fluid, Sinumbra, Gilt Lacquered, Bronze, Brass, Satin Glass, Cut, Prisms, Marble, 30½ In. . .	1920.00
Gas, 4-Light, Brass, Gilt Lacquered, Rococo Style, Troubadour Style, Gasolier, 35 x 29 In.	4560.00
Gas, Elizabethan Revival, Spelter, Patinated, Figural, Man In Period Clothing, c.1875, 45 In.	673.00
Grease, Hanger, 4 Spouts & Wicks, Square Base, Black, c.1750, 5½ In. . . . . 153.00 to 207.00
Grease, Hanging, Cast Bronze, 7 Flame Troughs, 18th Century, 19 In.	400.00
Grease, Iron, Double Hinged Reservoir, Caduceus, Turtle Base, Hand Forged, 29 x 14 In. . . .	2300.00
Grease, Iron, Fluted Pan, Long Spout, Wrought Hanging Hook, c.1770, 6½ x 5 In. . . . *illus*	306.00
Grease, Wrought Iron, Double, Shaped Back, Twist Hanger, 5⅜ In.	28.00
Handel lamps are included in the Handel category.	
Kerosene, Banquet, Cased Cranberry, White Overlay, Gold Detail, Marble Base, 25 In., Pair . .	500.00
Kerosene, Bigler, Applied 6-Sided Base, Brass Collar, 10½ In., Pair	170.00
Kerosene, Blown Glass, Blue, Clear Chimney, 9½ In.	39.00
Kerosene, Blue To Clear, Moorish Window Stem, Brass Mounts, Marble Base, 15¼ In.	3300.00
Kerosene, Brass, Nickel Plated, Circular Wick, Chimney, Shade, 20¼ In.	132.00
Kerosene, Brass, Spout, Removable Font, Weighted Base, 19¼ In.	83.00
Kerosene, Brown Pottery Pig, Incised Words On Pig, Hornet Burner, 3⅜ In. . . . . *illus*	14950.00
Kerosene, Carriage, Adjustable Socket, Match Holder, 9⅛ In.	83.00
Kerosene, Carriage, Beveled Glass Window, Burner, Brewster & Co., 15¼ In., Pair	138.00
Kerosene, Ceiling, Cast Iron, Double Bracket, Glass Fonts, 36 In.	116.00
Kerosene, Clear, Bull's-Eye & Leaf Mold, 11 In.	40.00
Kerosene, Clear Beehive Base, White Opalescent Coral, 12 In.	275.00
Kerosene, Cranberry, Applied Clear Handle, 5 In.	90.00
Kerosene, Cranberry, Honeycomb Pattern, Applied Feet, Nutmeg Burner, 6¼ In. . . . . . *illus*	920.00
Kerosene, Cranberry Opalescent, Seaweed, Nutmeg Burner, 7¾ In. . . . . *illus*	2185.00
Kerosene, Cranberry Swirl, 7½ In.	200.00
Kerosene, Domed Shade, Green, Gold Hearts, Vines, Gold Threads, Fostoria, 14 In.	6900.00
Kerosene, Embossed Cosmos, Emerald Green, Milk Glass Shade, 16 In.	45.00
Kerosene, Embossed Flowers, Lavender, 12½ In.	150.00
Kerosene, Enameled Flowers, Cranberry, Clear Base, 15½ In.	250.00
Kerosene, Figural, Porcelain Lion Head, Hornet Burner, 3¾ In. . . . . *illus*	173.00
Kerosene, Gilt Brass, Bronze, 3 Legs, Garland, Ram's Masque, Hoof Terminals, 70 In.	2400.00
Kerosene, Glass, Brass, Bulbous, Globe Shade, Iris Designs, c.1890, 25 x 10 In.	184.00
Kerosene, Glass, Cobalt Blue Font, Shade, 7¾ In.	143.00
Kerosene, Glass Font, Metal Stem, Base, Eagle Burner, 10 In.	39.00
Kerosene, Globe, Chimney, Silver, Copper, Japanese Style, Hammered, Gorham, 19 In.	7500.00
Kerosene, Globe, Murbelle, Carved, Molded, Relief, Pewter Base, Signed, c.1930, 7 x 6 In. . . .	293.00
Kerosene, Gone With The Wind, Arab Scene, Embossed Lion Head Mold, Brown, 22 In.	400.00
Kerosene, Gone With The Wind, Hand Painted, 30 x 9 In.	88.00
Kerosene, Gone With The Wind, Hyacinth, Carnival Glass, Pastel Marigold, 20½ In.	1500.00
Kerosene, Gone With The Wind, Opal Glass Font, Painted, Ormolu Mounts, 27 In. . . . *illus*	353.00
Kerosene, Gone With The Wind, Poppy Mold, Red Satin, 23 In.	600.00
Kerosene, Gone With The Wind, Rose & Mold Scroll, Red Satin, 22½ In.	700.00
Kerosene, Gone With The Wind, Roses & Ruffles, Green Opaque, 16½ In.	300.00
Kerosene, Gothic Style, Cast Iron, Hexagonal Font, Arched Window, 1900s, 15 x 5 In., Pair . .	1058.00
Kerosene, Greek Key, Goofus Glass, Matching Clear Shade, Painted Base, 18½ In.	50.00
Kerosene, Green Pressed Glass, Enamel Decoration, Square, 10½ In.	100.00
Kerosene, Hanging, Nickel Font, Leafy Scrolls, Opaque White Shade, Smoke Bell, 16 x 32 In.	92.00
Kerosene, Milk Glass, Fired-On Flowers & Bird, Burner For Round Wick, 8 In. . . . . . . *illus*	403.00
Kerosene, Parlor, Pink Diamond Quilted Mother-Of-Pearl Shade, Bronze, Flowers, 19 In. . . .	460.00
Kerosene, Parlor, Ruby Glass, Roses, Ormolu Mount, Connecticut, Late 1800s, 21 In. . . *illus*	235.00
Kerosene, Peg, Satin Glass, Yellow Font, Shade, Swirl, Brass Burner, Kosmos-Brenner, 24 In.	300.00
Kerosene, Persian, Longwy, 1875-80, 11 In.	995.00
Kerosene, Pink Cased Glass, Diamond Puffed Pattern, Nutmeg Burner, 8 In. . . . . *illus*	288.00
Kerosene, Pink Depression Glass, 12 In.	60.00
Kerosene, Pittsburgh Glass, Etched Shade, Painted, River Landscape, 21 x 16 In.	1140.00
Kerosene, Place Des Victoires, No. 3, Columnar, Blown Glass Chimney, Greek Key, 26 In. . . .	1140.00
Kerosene, Polychrome, White Opal Glass, Rococo Style, Brass Mounts, 28 In.	210.00
Kerosene, Porcelain, Milk Glass Shade, Victorian Scene, P&A Victor Burner, 9 In. . . . . *illus*	420.00

Lamp, Oil, Juno, Hanging, Embossed Brass, Tin Shade, Edward Miller & Co., 29¾ In. $88.00

Lamp, Oil, Pressed Glass, Amber Font, Blue Pedestal, 12 In., Pair $118.00

Lamp, Oil, Success P.L.B. & G. Co., Purple & Blue Flowers, Bronzed Iron Base, 25½ In. $495.00

L

Lamp, Oil, Tin Pan
$146.00

Lamps, Oil, Tin Pig, 5 x 7 In.
$146.00

Lamp, Oil, Wedding Stand,
Clambroth, Blue & Clear, Ripley & Co.,
1870, 12½ In.
$3850.00

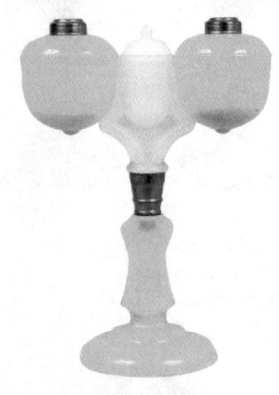

Lamp, Pink Planet Space,
Glass, 12 In.
$175.00

Kerosene, Pressed Glass, Bellflower Single Vine, Right Facing Vine, Round Foot, 7½ In.	55.00
Kerosene, Pressed Glass, Bellflower Single Vine, Scalloped Edge, Black Square Base, 10 In.	825.00
Kerosene, Pressed Glass, Bull's-Eye, Fleur-De-Lis & Heart, No. 1 Brass Collar, 8 In.	220.00
Kerosene, Pressed Glass, Cable, Reeded Brass Stem, Square Stepped Marble Base, 11 In.	77.00
Kerosene, Pressed Glass, Clear, 14¾ In., Pair	44.00
Kerosene, Pressed Glass, Giant Prism, Thumbprint Band, Wafer Stem, Brass, 12 In.	715.00
Kerosene, Pressed Glass, Three Face, No. 5, Brass No. 1 Atwood Collar, 8¾ In.	605.00
Kerosene, Pressed Glass, Three Face, No. 6, Brass No. 2 Atwood Collar, 10¼ In.	715.00
Kerosene, Pressed Glass, Three Face, No. 8, Brass No. 1 Atwood Collar, 9⅝ In.	715.00 to 2310.00
Kerosene, Pressed Glass, Washington, Engraved Flowers, Fiery Opalescent Base, 12 In.	187.00
Kerosene, Rainbow, Mother-Of-Pearl, Diamond Quilted, Ruffled Top, 9¼ In. ....*illus*	3163.00
Kerosene, Ruby Cut, Clear, Flowers, Brass Reeded Stem, Brass Marble, 11¼ In.	605.00
Kerosene, Santa, Carrying Sack Of Toys, Coralene, Snow Trim, 9½ In.	700.00
Kerosene, Sparking, Blown Glass, Round Base, Knob Stem, Reservoir, Burner, 4½ In.	300.00
Kerosene, Stand, White Cut To Green Alabaster, Opaque Opalescent Base, 9⅞ In.	990.00
Kerosene, Student, Cased Emerald Green Shade, Manhattan Brass Co., 22½ In. ......*illus*	413.00
Kerosene, Student, Nickel Plated, Log Cabin, 17 In.	303.00
Kerosene, Student, Nickel Plated, White Cased Glass Shade	375.00
Kerosene, Student, Tin, Painted, Adjustable Candle Holder, Conical Shade, Snuffer, 19 In.	1410.00
Kerosene, Swirl Type Glass Font, Chimney, 10½ In.	28.00
Kerosene, White Cut To Blue Alabaster, Brass Stem, Marble Base, 10⅛ In.	880.00
Kerosene, White To Blue, Alabaster Font, Gilded, Baroque Base, Brass Connector, 14⅛ In.	715.00
Kerosene Oil, Glass, Honeycomb Design, 21 x 6 In.	59.00
Kettle Roni, Brass Cylinder Reservoir, Incised Lines, Shaped Shaft, Peter Derr, 8½ In.	5500.00
Lard, Brass, Embossed, Removable Font, Dutch, 12¼ In.	72.00
Lard, Dutch, Removable Font, 12½ In.	72.00
Oil, 3 Tiers, Pedestal, Satin Glass, Gold Enamel Decoration, 9¾ In. ....*illus*	4025.00
Oil, Astral, Brass, Marble, Glass, Frosted, Cut, Flowers, Faceted Bands, Brass, 1800s, 30 x 12 In.	3525.00
Oil, Astral, Brass Font, Reeded Column, Marble Base, Cornelius & Co., 15 In.	115.00
Oil, Blown Glass, Pear Shaped Font, Copper Wheel, Etched Grapes, Snuffer Cap, 12 In.	230.00
Oil, Blown Glass, Twisted Stem, Pedestal Base, 3⅜ In.	88.00
Oil, Blown Glass Font, Pewter Base, Hinged Reservoir, C-Scroll Handle, 14½ In. ......*illus*	288.00
Oil, Brass, Neptune Head, 7¾ In., Pair	143.00
Oil, Brass, New Juno No. 2, Weighted Base, Hobnail Opalescent Shade, 15¾ In.	259.00
Oil, Brass, Opalescent Cranberry Swirl Ruffle Shade, Hinks Benetfink, London, 16½ In.	173.00
Oil, Bronze, Shell Font, Dolphin Finial, Masks, Horse, Fish, Etched Shade, 15 In. ......*illus*	3850.00
Oil, Clear, Free-Blown Glass, Font, 7¼ In.	72.00
Oil, Clear Glass, Blown In Mold, Free-Blown Font, 8 In.	72.00
Oil, Clear Glass, Free-Blown, Pedestal Base, 3½ In.	44.00
Oil, Clear Glass, Peg, Flat Wick Support, Barrel Form, 4¾ In.	550.00
Oil, Cranberry Opalescent Font, Coin Dot, Milk Glass Base, c.1885, 20¼ x 5½ In.	726.00
Oil, Custard Glass, Hand Painted, Enameled Rose, Garland, c.1890	375.00
Oil, Empire Revival, Japanned Metal, Black, Urn Shape, Tapered Shade, 27 In. ....*illus*	411.00
Oil, Finger, Blue Opalescent, Square Rib Front, Loop Finger Hold, Marked, P & A, 4½ In.	550.00
Oil, Finger, Cranberry Opalescent, Hobb's Snowflake, Footed	1430.00
Oil, Free-Blown Font, Blown In Mold, Pedestal Base, 3¼ In.	72.00
Oil, Free-Blown Glass, Blown In Mold Base, 7½ In., Pair	149.00
Oil, Green, Octagonal Panels, Graduated Bull's-Eye Column, Ball Stem, Flare Base, 9 In.	121.00
Oil, Honey Amber Snowstorm With A Twist, Hobbs & Brockunier & Co., c.1870	400.00
Oil, Hurricane, Cranberry, Opalescent, Daisy & Fern, Fenton, 20th Century, 17 In.	206.00
Oil, Juno, Hanging, Embossed Brass, Tin Shade, Edward Miller & Co., 29¾ In. ....*illus*	88.00
Oil, Microscope, Brass, Glass Font, V Shaped Base, Glass Stopper, Chimney, 15 In.	144.00
Oil, Non-Explosive, Embossed, Pink Opalescent Hobnail Shade, Nickel, 22 In.	259.00
Oil, Porcelain, Bronze, Signed, H. Kobert, Sevres, France, c.1850, 65 In.	2808.00
Oil, Pressed Glass, Amber Font, Blue Pedestal, 12 In., Pair ....*illus*	118.00
Oil, Pressed Glass, Beaded Heart, Frosted Hearts, 6½ x 4¾ In.	150.00
Oil, Pressed Glass, Columbian Coin, Clear Coins, No. 2 Taplin-Brown Collar, 10 In.	248.00
Oil, Pressed Glass, Columbian Coin, Clear Coins, No. 2 Taplin-Brown Collar, 12 In.	330.00
Oil, Pressed Glass, Columbian Coin, Frosted Coins, No. 2 Taplin-Brown Collar, 11 In.	440.00
Oil, Pressed Glass, Horn Of Plenty, Gilt Designs, Hexagonal Base, Baluster Stem, 9⅞ In.	316.00
Oil, Pressed Glass, U.S. Coin, Clear Quarter Coins, No. 1 Taplin-Brown Collar, 9½ In.	440.00
Oil, Pressed Glass, U.S. Coin, Frosted Dollar Coins, No. 2 Taplin-Brown Collar, 10 In.	990.00
Oil, Pressed Glass, U.S. Coin, Frosted Half-Dollar Coins, No. 2 Taplin-Brown Collar, 11½ In.	3740.00
Oil, Solar, Brass, Bronze, Satin & Cut Glass Shade, Cut Glass Prisms, Fluted Base, 24½ In.	960.00
Oil, Solar, Brass, Gilt Lacquered, Bronze, Glass Prisms, Satin Glass Shade, 23 In.	960.00
Oil, Solar, Gilt Lacquered, Brass Mounted, Ribbed Blue Opaline Glass, 32 In.	1320.00

L

Oil, Student, Melon Ribbed Shade, Brass Bridge, Drop Crystals, Plume & Atwood, 22 In.	....	690.00
Oil, Success P.L.B. & G. Co., Purple & Blue Flowers, Bronzed Iron Base, 25½ In.	*illus*	495.00
Oil, Tin, Box Form, Dish Base, 6½ In.		248.00
Oil, Tin, Corner, Red, 7¾ In.		94.00
Oil, Tin, Funnel Form, 4 In.		143.00
Oil, Tin, Pie Wedge Form Font, 5½ In.		39.00
Oil, Tin Pan	*illus*	146.00
Oil, Tin Pig, 5 x 7 In.	*illus*	146.00
Oil, Tin, Spout, Wire Hanger, Cape Cod Style, 8 In.		182.00
Oil, Urn Shape, Carcel, Napoleon III, Bronze, Neo-Grec Style, Mid 19th Century, 30 In., Pair		1880.00
Oil, Wedding Stand, Clambroth, Blue & Clear, Ripley & Co., 1870, 12½ In.	*illus*	3850.00
Oil, White Glazed Porcelain, Korea, 7¾ In.		295.00
Oil, Wrought Iron, 3-Legged, Double Pan, Adjustable Lamp, 19½ In.		220.00
Oil, Wrought Iron, Double Wick, 3-Footed, 9½ In.		1870.00
Pairpoint lamps are in the Pairpoint category.		
Pink Planet Space, Glass, 12 In.	*illus*	175.00
Rush, Iron, Wood, Tension Splint, Holder, 8¼ In.		468.00
Rush, Wrought Iron, Faceted Ball Counterweight, Cast Iron Base, 8½ In.		743.00
Rush, Wrought Iron, Twisted Stem, Flat Ring Base, Candleholder, 4¼ In.		275.00
Rush Holder, Wrought Iron, Adjustable, 3-Footed, 34 In.		385.00
Rush Holder, Wrought Iron, Sliding Trammel Type, 32½ In.		908.00
Sandwich Glass, Pink, White Loopings, Teardrop Font, Brass, Wafer, Marble, c.1870, 9½ In.		1430.00
Sconce, 1-Light, Wrought Iron, Patinated, Flambeau Shape, Pendant, Mexico, 1700s, 20 In.		270.00
Sconce, 2-Light, Art Deco, Metal, Lattice Overlay, 6½ x 8 In., Pair		235.00
Sconce, 2-Light, Branch Shape, 18th Century Manner, c.1920, 19 In., Pair		348.00
Sconce, 2-Light, Chinoserie, Gilt Brass, Parasol Backplate, France, 15¼ x 13½ In., Pair	....	2115.00
Sconce, 2-Light, Empire Style, Gilt Bronze, Torch Shape, Candle Cups, 21 x 15 In., Pair	....	360.00
Sconce, 2-Light, George I Style, Gilt Brass, Reverse-Cut Mirrored, Sunburst, 19 x 8 In., Pair	.	381.00
Sconce, 2-Light, Gilt Gesso, Leaves, Garland, Phoenix, Putti, Shelves, 1800s, 42 x 23 In., Pair	.	5175.00
Sconce, 2-Light, Giltwood, Carved, Italy, 20th Century, 27 In., Pair		447.00
Sconce, 2-Light, Louis XVI, Gilt Bronze, Shield Cartouche, Fluted Arms, Garlands, 21 In., Pair		1058.00
Sconce, 2-Light, Louis XVI, Wrought Iron, Cut Glass, Gilded, Pendants, 20 x 12 In., Pair	....	1560.00
Sconce, 2-Light, Louis XVI Style, Brass, Suspended Baskets, Bows, Roses, 19 x 11 In., Pair	...	390.00
Sconce, 2-Light, Naples, Scrolling Backplate, Rosettes, Scrolling Arms, 8½ x 6 In., Pair	....	177.00
Sconce, 3-Light, Louis XVI, Giltwood, Carved, Beaded Oval Shields, 39 x 14 In., Pair	....	2400.00
Sconce, 3-Light, Wrought & Cut Iron, Louis XV Style, Black, Parcel Gilt, 24 In., Pair	....	900.00
Sconce, Brass, Candle, Blown Glass Shade, 19th Century, 15½ In., Pair		2185.00
Sconce, Brass, Hood, Snuffer, 14 In.		121.00
Sconce, Candle, Amethyst Glass, Brass, Shield Shape, Brass Mount, 14 In., Pair	....	3408.00
Sconce, Candle, Polished Metal, Mirrored, Scalloped, 13 In., Pair		550.00
Sconce, Continental Rococo Style, Giltwood, Shell Shape Shelf, 15 x 19 In., Pair		499.00
Sconce, Gilt Brass, Blown Glass, Clipper Ship, Colonial Metalcrafters, 21 In., Pair		411.00
Sconce, Gilt Brass, Smoked Glass Pendant Shade, Colonial Metalcrafters, 23 In., Pair	......	1175.00
Sconce, Gilt Bronze, Acanthe, Jules & Andre Leleu, 1950s, 11¾ In., Pair		5760.00
Sconce, Gilt Bronze, Double Torsade, Jules & Andre Leleu, 1950s, 10¼ In., Pair	....	11400.00
Sconce, Gilt Metal, 8 Candle Cups, Leaf & Flower Decoration, 34 In.		489.00
Sconce, Gilt Wood, Carved, Metal, Birds, Bows, Italy, Early 20th Century, 45 x 13 In.	....	1135.00
Sconce, Glass, Gilt Metal, Molded, Fan Shape, c.1930, 13¼ In., Pair		588.00
Sconce, Lantern, 2 Arms, Louis XV Style, Wrought Iron, Backplate, Twist Standard, Pair	....	823.00
Sconce, Plastic, 5 Horizontal Movable Arcs, Over 5 Vertical Arcs, Brass Frame, 9 In.	....	118.00
Sconce, Renaissance, Brass, Mirrored, Beveled Glass, c.1865, 16½ x 14½ In.		381.00
Sconce, Tin, Candlecups, Pierced Drip Pans, 9⅞ x 10⅛ In., Pair		1175.00
Sconce, Tin, Double Wall, Crimped Edge, 10½ In.		231.00
Sconce, Wood, Amethyst Glass Candleholder, 12½ In.		72.00
Sinumbra, Brass, Cut, Frosted Shade, 31¼ In.		1073.00
Sinumbra, Bronze Dore Mounts, Round Font Supports, 19th Century, 26 x 11 In.	....	805.00
Tiffany lamps are listed in the Tiffany category.		
Torchere, Wrought Iron, Ebonized Wood, Tripartite 2 Tier Stand, 1600s, 62 x 22 In.	....	1180.00
Whale Oil, Acanthus Leaf Pattern, Clambroth Font, Blue Stepped Base, 11 In.	*illus*	840.00
Whale Oil, Applied Handle, Pontil, 1820-40, 2¼ x 3 In.		192.00
Whale Oil, Blown, Ball Font Stand, 5-Tier Quatrefoil Base, Cork Stopper, 9⅜ In., Pair	......	413.00
Whale Oil, Blown, Cobalt Blue Stem, Brass Base, 8½ In.		3335.00
Whale Oil, Blown Glass, Drop Burner, Applied Handle, 2 In.	253.00 to 264.00	
Whale Oil, Brass, Acorn Font, Baluster Stem, Round Base, 5⅞ In.		259.00
Whale Oil, Brass, Double Burner, Egg Shape Font, Round Stepped Base, 9 In., Pair	....	403.00
Whale Oil, Brass, Saucer, 4¼ In., Pair		303.00

Lamp, Whale Oil,
Acanthus Leaf Pattern,
Clambroth Font,
Blue Stepped Base, 11 In.
$840.00

L

Lighting Technologies

Incandescent light bulbs were first made by Thomas Edison in 1879.

Neon lamp were invented by George Claude in 1911. Neon was used primarily for signs.

Frosted light bulbs were made in 1925.

Fluorescent lighting was patented by Edmund Germer in 1927. It did not have widespread use until the 1970s.

Halogen lamps were used in the motion-picture industry in the early 1960s. Halogen lamps were used in many homes by the 1980s.

Track lighting was introduced in the 1960s.

Digital dimmers were first made in the 1980s.

LEDs are 21st century.

Lamp, Whale Oil, Pressed Glass, Arch, Canary, Cascade Base, Brass Collar, 10¼ In. $935.00

Lamp, Whale Oil, Pressed Glass, Three Printie, Sapphire Blue, Pewter Collar, 7⅝ In. $2970.00

Whale Oil, Brass, Seamed Construction, Signed, Webb, 7 In.	661.00
Whale Oil, Brass, Tuned Shaft, Round Base, 7 In.	77.00
Whale Oil, Flint Glass, Bulb Shape Font Over Stepped Square Base, Double Wick, 9¾ In.	165.00
Whale Oil, Flint Glass, Punty & Star, Flared, 6-Sided Base, 11 In.	77.00
Whale Oil, Free-Blown Clear Glass, Air Stem, Tin Drop Burner, 9¾ In.	495.00
Whale Oil, Free-Blown Clear Glass, Bulb Top Smoke Bell, 5¾ In.	66.00
Whale Oil, Free-Blown Glass, Pedestal, Drop Burner, 3½ In.	571.00
Whale Oil, Free-Blown, Globular, Clear, 2 Knop Stem, c.1800, 7½ x 4⅝ In.	1568.00
Whale Oil, Glass, 2-Part, Blown In, Burner, 5¼ In.	154.00
Whale Oil, Glass, Clear, Burners, Free-Blown Fonts, Blown-In Mold Bases, 10¾ In., Pair	220.00
Whale Oil, Glass, Sawtooth, c.1840, Pair, 10¼ In.	335.00
Whale Oil, Hanging, Glass Globe, Grapevine Embossed Brass Top, Bottom, 9¼ In.	115.00
Whale Oil, Horn Of Plenty, 9 Panels, Hexagonal Base, Brass Collar, 9¾ In.	110.00
Whale Oil, Peg, Clear Blown Glass, Ball Type	105.00
Whale Oil, Peg, Wrought Iron, Tin, Blown Glass, 20¼ In.	2200.00
Whale Oil, Pressed Glass, Arch, Canary, Cascade Base, Brass Collar, 10¼ In. .... *illus*	935.00
Whale Oil, Pressed Glass, Moon & Star, Finger, Rope Twist Base, Brass Collar, 4 In.	132.00
Whale Oil, Pressed Glass, Three Printie, Sapphire Blue, Pewter Collar, 7⅝ In. .... *illus*	2970.00
Whale Oil, Tin, 3-Part, 2-Part Base, Shade, Clear Faceted Glass, Weighted, 9½ In.	1018.00

LAMPSHADE

Caramel Slag Glass, Dome, Red Flowers, Yellow Centers, Green Leaves, 21½ In.	1175.00
Hanging, Art Glass, Leaded Glass, Stylized Peony Border, c.1910, 23 In.	1200.00
Leaded Glass, Painted, Multicolored, Flower & Fruit Decorated Rim, 22 In.	176.00
Mosaic, Domed, Brickwork, Blue Slag Glass, Tulips, 20th Century, 14½ In.	2585.00

LANTERNS are a special type of lighting device. They have a light source, usually a candle, totally hidden inside the walls of the lantern. Light is seen through holes or glass sections.

Barn, Swing Handle, Copper, Glass Globe, Marked, Union Ratchet, 10¾ In.	132.00
Brass, Curved Glass Window, Removable Burner, 9¾ In.	39.00
Brass, Skater's, Shaped Glass Shade, Swing Handle, 7 In.	143.00 to 176.00
Bronze, Leaded Glass, 13 x 11 In.	3000.00
Bronze, Patinated, Acanthus Hook, Urn Shape Finial, Pierced Gallery, 40 x 19 In., Pair	2468.00
Bronze, Patinated Brass, Pomegranate Finials, Louis XVI, Portico, Candles, 53 In.	7500.00
Candle, Glass, Keystone Form, Triangular Bracket Feet, 12½ In.	193.00
Candle, Tin, Mesh, Adjustable Candle Socket, 8¼ In.	88.00
Candle, Whale Oil, Tin, Glass, 11½ In.	275.00
Carriage, Brass, Copper, Scalloped, Beveled Glass, Etched Panels, Electrified, 1800s, 23 In., Pair	2468.00
Chinese, Metal Mesh Frame, Red Cloth Lining, Wood Base, 33 x 13½ In., Pair	345.00
Copper, Brass, Georgian Style, Pendant Faux Candle Lights, Portico, 27 x 13 In.	2640.00
Electric, Hanging, 3-Light, Blown Glass Hurricane, Brass Collar, Swags, 25 x 8 In.	470.00
Electric, Hanging, Trellis-Cut Glass Bowl, Gilt Brass, Colonial Metalcrafters, Texas, 20 In.	264.00
Firehouse, Tin, 6 Glass Panels, 11½ In.	182.00
Hanging, Cut Glass, Bell Shaped Globe, Brass Mounts, Smoke Cap, 24 In.	460.00
Hanging, Gilt, Brass Mounted, Frosted, Cut Glass, Bead Chains, Festoons, 17 x 18 In.	900.00
Hanging, Glass, Blown, Cut, Engraved, Inverted Bell Shape, c.1840, 18 x 12 In.	2760.00
Hanging, Hall, Globe, Bell Shape, Intaglio, Smoke Bell, Brass Mounts, 1800s, 27 In.	2990.00
Hanging, Hexagonal, 3 Brackets, Cast Iron, Tripod Lights, Electrified, 25 x 15 In.	411.00
Hanging, Melon Shaped, Green Glass Globe, Stenciled Mark, Early 1900s, 22½ x 10 In.	288.00
Iron, Openwork Sides, Arts & Crafts, Hinged Door, Painted Black, 8¾ In., Pair	805.00
Leaded Glass Panels, Stylized Glasgow Roses, Polychrome Slag Glass, 10 x 7½ In.	2040.00
Parcel Gilt, Tole Peinte, Black, Restauration, Electrified, France, 17 x 10 In., Pair	1200.00
Pillar, Mold Globe, Punched Tin Top, Font, Whale Oil Burner, Ring Handle, 12½ In.	1610.00
Punched, Sunburst & Ray, Tin, Loop Carry Handle, Cone Shape Top, 14⅝ In.	303.00
Silk Accordion, Pierced Tin Top, Bottom, 4¼ x 12 In.	66.00
Silver, Spring Loaded, Candle Socket, Mica Window, Match Holder, 8½ In.	66.00
Tin, 4 Panes, Rectangular, 12¼ In.	215.00
Tin, Candle, White, Glass Front Panel, Arched Back, Carry Handle, 12 In.	83.00
Tin, Conical Top, Pierced Star & Diamond, Ring Handle, 13¾ In.	61.00
Tin, Nonpareil, Square Body, Cylindrical Top, Pierced, Archer & Pancoast, 1864, 10 In.	143.00
Tin, Onion, Bulbous Glass Shade, Pierced Star & Diamonds, Ring Handle, 16 In.	154.00
Tin, Onion, Bulbous Shade, Wire Cage, Cone Top, Punched Holes, Ring Handle, 19½ In.	209.00
Tin, Onion, Oil Burner, Pierced Top, Base, Flared Base, Swing Handle, 11 In.	193.00
Tin, Paneled Glass Shade, Cone Top, Smoke Shield, Ring Handle, No Burner, 12½ In.	143.00
Tin, Triple Spout Wick Tubes, Lid, Loop Lift, Twisted Copper Swing Handle, 6 x 6¾ In.	143.00

Travel, Folding, Brass, 18th Century	895.00
Whale Oil, Tin, Brass Plate, Glass, Inverted Cone Shape, 6¾ In.	1073.00
Wooden, 4 Glass Panes, Bail Handle, 18th Century	359.00
Wrought Iron, Frosted Glass Liner, Renaissance, 12 x 6 In.	900.00
Wrought Iron, Hexagonal, Strawberry Hill Gothic, Glazed Panels, Portico, 33 x 14 In.	1800.00
Wrought Iron, Stained Glass, Hexagonal, Pebbled Glass, Scrolling, Portico, 40 x 14 In.	480.00

LE VERRE FRANÇAIS is one of the many types of cameo glass made by the Schneider Glassworks in France. The glass was made by the C. Schneider factory in Epinay-sur-Seine from 1918 to 1933. It is a mottled glass, usually decorated with floral designs, and bears the incised signature *Le Verre Français.*

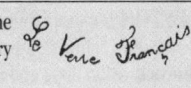

Bowl, Cameo Glass, Orange Ground, Blue Floral Enamel, 10½ x 4½ In.	732.00
Bowl, Orange, Red, Green, White Ground, Footed, Charder, 10 x 12 In. ....*illus*	4600.00
Jardiniere, Orange, Green Flowers, White Ground, 11 x 12 In. ....*illus*	5463.00
Vase, Amphora, Orange, Red Flowers, Yellow Ground, Metal, Art Deco, 7 In.	646.00
Vase, Bottle Form, Orange, Cascading Purple Leaf, Cameo, Signed, 6 In.	460.00
Vase, Fuchsia, Mottled Orange, Blue, Blue Bulbous Stem, Cameo, 16 In. ....*illus*	6325.00
Vase, Horseshoe Crab, Rose Shaded To Green, Orange, Cameo, Signed, 8 In.	529.00
Vase, Japanese Flower, Red, Mottled Orange Ground, Art Deco, 19 In.	3360.00
Vase, Mottled Orange, Brown Flowers, Mottled Pink, Cameo, Footed, 6½ In.	588.00
Vase, Pinched Waist, Amber & Orange, Art Deco Flowers, Chene Pattern, Signed, 22 In.	1840.00
Vase, Stylized Flowers, Yellow, Blue, Orange, 10 x 12 In.	837.00

LEATHER is tanned animal hide and it has been used to make decorative and useful objects for centuries. Leather objects must be carefully preserved with proper humidity and oiling or the leather will deteriorate and crack. This damage cannot be repaired.

Case, Accordion Fold, Portrait Of Young Woman, 19th Century, 5½ In.	35.00
Desk Folio, Gilt, Renaissance Style, Multicolor, Italy, Early 1900s, 15 x 12 In.	201.00
Harness, Brass, Draft Horse, Wood & Metal Pull Bar, 28 x 18 In. & 24½ In.	70.00
Rug, Cowhide, Russet, Natural Shape, 6 Ft. 2 In. x 7 Ft. 7 In.	210.00
Saddle, J.C. Higgins, Early 1900s, Child's	489.00
Shield, Round, Painted, Convex Surface, Flowers, Serrated Copper Bosses, India, 13 In.	267.00
Shot Bucket, Painted, Heraldic Shield, Canvas Lining, Swing Handle, 15½ x 8½ In.	470.00

LEEDS pottery was made at Leeds, Yorkshire, England, from 1774 to 1878. Most Leeds ware was not marked. Early Leeds pieces had distinctive twisted handles with a greenish glaze on part of the creamy ware. Later ware often had blue borders on the creamy pottery. A Chicago company named Leeds made many Disney-inspired figurines. They are listed in the Disneyana category.

LEEDS POTTERY.

Basket, Openwork, c.1800, 4½ x 10 x 12 In.	468.00
Bowl, Blue Feather Edge, Reticulated Body, Flared, Handles, Undertray, 11⅞ In.	358.00
Bowl, Flowers & Leaves, Multicolored, Flared, Broken Border, 4⅜ x 9¼ In.	193.00
Creamer, Blue & Yellow Flowers, Green & Brown Flower Design, Bulbous, 3⅝ In.	121.00
Creamer, Mustard Flowers, Green Leaves, Vine Around Rim, Bulbous, 3¾ In.	143.00
Cup, Blue & White Sprig, Running Vine, Handleless, Child's	83.00
Cup & Saucer, Blue Rim, Yellow & Brown Flowers, Blue Accents, 2¼ x 5 In.	55.00
Cuspidor, Lady's, Blue Flower Decoration, Funneled Top, C Handle, 2⅞ x 4 In.	440.00
Mustard, Blue, 2 Blue Rings, Feather Edge, Bulbous, Handle, 3 In.	58.00
Pitcher, Cream, Cobalt Blue Flowers, Leaves, Green, Yellow, Orange, Scalloped Rim, 5⅜ In.	83.00
Plaque, Roundel, Cream Glazed Portrait, Cleopatra, Green Ground, Late 1800s, 14⅜ In.	646.00
Plate, Blue Feather Edge, Green Sponge, Peafowl, 4⅜ In.	248.00
Plate, Blue Feather Edge, Oriental Scene, Scalloped Rim, 9⅝ In.	110.00
Plate, Eagle, Green Feather Edge, Spread Wings, Clutching Arrows, Olive Branch, 8 In.	1100.00
Plate, Eagle, Heraldic, Feather Edge Rim, c.1810, 3¾ In.	1888.00
Plate, Flower & Vine Decoration, Green Embossed Scalloped Rim, 8⅝ In. ....*illus*	358.00
Plate, Green Feather Edge, Flowers, Leaves, Swag, 7¾ In.	248.00
Plate, Green Feather Edge, Octagonal, Shield Decoration, 7⅞ In.	138.00
Plate, Green Feather Edge, Peafowl, Scalloped Rim, 7 In.	110.00
Platter, Blue, Feather Edge, Impressed Mark, 15½ x 12½ In.	98.00
Platter, Green Feather Edge, 15½ In.	132.00
Saucer, Blue, Feather Edge Border, Embossed, Stamped, Warranted Staffordshire, 3⅝ In.	88.00
Saucer, Eagle, Spread Wings, Clutching Arrows, Shield, Impressed E, 3¾ In.	33.00
Soup, Dish, Blue Feather Edge, Red Transfer Center, Eagle, Shield, Olive Branch, 8 In.	826.00
Sugar, Cover, Blue & White Pomegranate, Flowers, Beehive Finial, 5¼ In.	110.00

Le Verre Français, Bowl, Orange, Red, Green, White Ground, Footed, Charder, 10 x 12 In. $4600.00

Le Verre Français, Jardiniere, Orange, Green Flowers, White Ground, 11 x 12 In. $5463.00

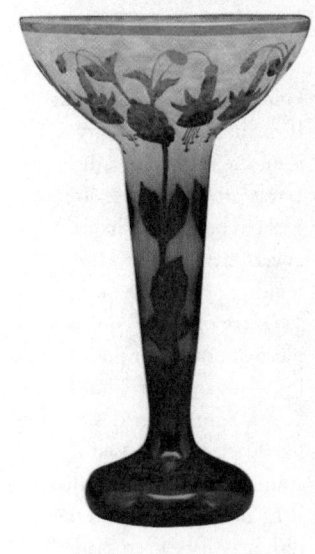

Le Verre Français, Vase, Fuchsia, Mottled Orange, Blue, Blue Bulbous Stem, Cameo, 16 In. $6325.00

L

Leeds, Plate,
Flower & Vine Decoration,
Green Embossed Scalloped Rim, 8⅝ In.
$358.00

Leeds, Waste Bowl, Flowers & Sunrays,
Blue Border, Lion Mask Handles,
3 x 4⅝ In.
$176.00

Country Names in Marks

If the name of a country is on the bottom of a dish, it was probably made after 1891. The United States government passed a law requiring the name of the "country of origin" on each piece of pottery or porcelain imported into the United States. Some countries, like England, had used the country's name years earlier. If England is the mark, the dish may have been made as early as 1850. The words "Made in..." were used after 1915.

Sugar, Cover, Blue Flowers, White Ground, Running Vine, Lion Mask Handles, 4⅛ In.		72.00
Sugar, Yellow Flower, Orange Accents, Green Leaves, Applied Handles, 3⅞ In.		72.00
Tureen, Sauce, Blue Feather Edge, Double Handles, Cover, Underliner, 7 x 5½ In.		288.00
Vase, Pearlware, Quintal, 5 Spouts, Feather Edge, Flowers, Early 19th Century, 7¾ In.		499.00
Waste Bowl, Flowers, Orange, Yellow, Leaves, Blue Rim, Lion Mask Handles, 3 x 4½ In.		176.00
Waste Bowl, Flowers & Sunrays, Blue Border, Lion Mask Handles, 3 x 4⅝ In.	*illus*	176.00

LEFTON is a mark found on pottery, porcelain, glass, and other wares imported by the Geo. Zoltan Lefton Company. The company began in 1941 and is still in business. It was restructured in 2002 and is now called The Lefton Company. The company mark has changed through the years, but because marks have been used for long periods of time, they are of little help in dating an object.

Ashtray, Fishing Hat Design, 6 x 5 x 3 In.		12.00
Basket, Holly, Green, 1971-72, 4¾ In.		14.00
Bell, Violets, White, Gold Trim, Marked, 1991		21.00
Bell, Yellow Rose, Gold Bow, 3 In.		18.00
Bonbon, Holly & Berry, Divided, Handle, Signed, 6¾ In.		40.00
Bookends, White, Poodle, Standing On Books, 1950s		65.00
Bowl, Forget-Me-Not, Scalloped Edge, 7¼ In.		14.00
Bowl, Handles, Carnation Pattern, Crown & L, 1940s, 8⅝ x 6¼ In.		22.50
Cake Stand, Happy Anniversary, White Flowers & Doves, Silver Bells		18.00
Candleholder, 25th Anniversary, Silver, Marked		18.00
Candleholder, Holly, Green, Label, 2 x 3¾ In., Pair		19.00
Candy Dish, 2 Cardinals, Holly, 5½ In.		10.00
Cookie Jar, Blue Flowers, Leaves, White & Blue, Wood Grain Effect, 1950s, 10 In.		66.00
Cookie Jar, Lion, Hubert, Harris Bank, 1992, 13½ In.		1120.00
Cup & Saucer, Demitasse, Violets, Hand Painted, Marked		48.00
Cup & Saucer, Fruit, Gold Trim, Signed G.Z., Lefton, Crown		80.00
Cup & Saucer, Fruit Intaglio		35.00
Cup & Saucer, Holly, Green, Red Berries, Sticker		12.00
Cup & Saucer, Victorian Scene, Courting Couples, Signed		38.00
Figurine, Angel, 3¾ In.		17.00
Figurine, Bird, Bunting, 5 In.		15.00
Figurine, Bird, Robin, Brown Body, Yellow To Red Breast, On Branch		14.00
Figurine, Birthday Girl, Brunette, 5 In.		15.00
Figurine, Bloomer Girl, Holding Candy Cane, Green Holly Halo, Gold Trim, 1950s		32.00
Figurine, Blue Birds, Perched On Dogwood Tree Branch, 6 In.		30.00
Figurine, Bunny, Standing On Hind Legs, Label, 4½ In.		8.00
Figurine, Butterfly, On Branch, Signed, 6 x 3½ In.		15.00
Figurine, Christmas Angel, Playing Drum, Pink, Gold		10.00
Figurine, Girl Holding Bunny, Pink Bow, Blue Coat, 3½ In.		15.00
Figurine, Graduation Girl, Holding Diploma, 4¾ In.		25.00
Figurine, Hummingbird, On Branch, 3¾ x 3½ In.		15.00
Figurine, Little Devil Playing Tennis, Red Outfit, Gold Horns	*illus*	28.00
Figurine, Old Man & Dog, 7 x 5 In.		22.00
Figurine, Poodle, Prissy, 7 In.		33.00
Hand, Applied Roses & Leaves, 7¼ In.		18.00
Pitcher, Applied Fruit, Flowers, Pink, Gold, Fancy Handle, Marked, 6 In.		58.00
Planter, Parakeet, Sprigs Of Leaves, Acorns, Crown Mark, 4¾ x 3¾ In.		110.00
Planter, Shoe, Lavender Flowers, 4½ In.		34.00
Planter, Stork & Baby Girl, White, Pink, Gold Trim, 1964, 7 x 6 In.		15.00
Plate, Dessert, Fruit, Brown, 7¼ In.		15.00
Relish, White Holly, 12 In.		30.00
Salt & Pepper, Coffee Grinder, Yellow, 1960s		13.00
Salt & Pepper, Noel, Christmas Tree, Star, Stockings, Candy Canes, 3⅜ & 3½ In.		18.00
Salt & Pepper, Owl Graduates, Rhinestone Eyes, Marked, 1956		17.00
Salt & Pepper, Rose Chintz, 2¾ In.		17.00
Salt & Pepper, Santa & Mrs. Claus, On Rocking Chairs, 4 In.		22.00
Salt & Pepper, Snowman & Snowlady, Red Hat, 4 In.		22.00
Toothbrush Holder, Flowers, 3¾ In.		15.00
Trinket Box, Hummingbird, Pink Flowers, Green Leaves, 3½ In.		35.00
Trinket Dish, Lefton 50th Anniversary, 4½ In.		15.00
Vase, Applied Fruit, Pink Ground, 6 In.		58.00
Vase, Baby Head, Foil Label, Japan, 1950s, 7 In.	76.00 to	95.00
Vase, Basket Weave, Flowers		15.00

L

Vase, Bud, 50th Anniversary, 6½ In.		15.00
Vase, Roses & Clematis, Gold Trim, Marked, 7½ In.		12.00
Votive Holder, Angel, Boy, Blue Robe, Golden Wings, 3¼ In.		15.00
Wall Pocket, Bowl & Pitcher Form, Yellow, Orange, Green, 5½ In., Pair		36.00
Wall Pocket, Lady Bluebird, 5½ x 6 In.		30.00

LEGRAS was founded in 1864 by Auguste Legras at St. Denis, France. It is best known for cameo glass and enamel-decorated glass with Art Nouveau designs. Legras merged with Pantin in 1920 and became the Verreries et Cristalleries de St. Denis et de Pantin Reunies.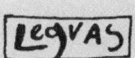

Bowl, Dogwood Blossoms, White Enameled, Green Ground, Gold Rim, Cameo, 4½ x 10 In. *illus*		2300.00
Bowl, Green & Crimson Leaves, Green Martele, Gold Trim, Cameo, 10 In.		316.00
Vase, Amethyst Branches, Textured Pink, Bulbous, Flared Rim, Cameo, 7 In.		403.00
Vase, Art Deco, Geometric, Cobalt Blue, Frosted Textured Body, Cameo, 8¾ In.		377.00
Vase, Art Deco Floral Medallions, Mottled End-Of-Day Ground, Signed, 18¼ In. *illus*		2013.00
Vase, Aubergine Vine Leaves, Grapes, Enamaled, Textured, Frosted, c.1910, 10½ In.		809.00
Vase, Branches With Leaves, Frosted, Red Enameled, Tapered, Footed, 18 In. *illus*		996.00
Vase, Deer & Bird By Tree, Mottled Brick Red, Cameo, Signed, 8½ In.		1035.00
Vase, Magenta Ivy, Pink Ground, Tricornered, Cameo, 16¾ In.		472.00
Vase, Medallion, Swans, Enameled, Mottled Orange, Yellow Graduate To Blue, Signed, 15 In.		264.00
Vase, Opaque Caramel, Underwater Scene, Seaweed, Bulbous, Cameo, Signed, 8 In.		460.00
Vase, Red Poppies, Mottled Orange, Enameled, Signed, 17¼ In.		646.00
Vase, Red Strawberries, Opaque Tan, Cameo, Signed, 3¼ In.		690.00
Vase, Scenic, Bridge Over Stream, Pink, Green Opalescent, Pillow Shape, Cameo, 4 In.		748.00
Vase, Scenic, Deer & Bird Trees, Mottled Brick Red, Swollen Shape, Cameo, 8½ In. *illus*		1035.00
Vase, Scenic, Lake, Trees, Sailboats, Enameled, c.1898, 10½ In.		275.00
Vase, Scenic, Summer Lake, Pink Shaded To Amethyst, Pinched Waist, Flat Sides, Cameo, 5 In.		604.00
Vase, Scenic, Winter, 2 Lugers Going Downhill, Enameled, 10½ x 5 In.		1500.00
Vase, Scenic, Winter Snow, Enameled, Elongated, 3-Lobed Top, 9 In.		500.00
Vase, Scenic, Winter Trees, Mottled Orange, Egg Shape, Footed, Cameo, Signed, 5½ In.		863.00
Vase, Scenic, Woodland, Enameled, 16 In.		900.00
Vase, Trees, Dark Green, Citron Ground, Shaped Sides, Cameo, 5 In.		230.00
Vase, Yellow Mottled, Orange Shading, Blue Upper Section, Peacocks, 5½ x 8½ In.		1750.00

LENOX is the name of a porcelain maker. Walter Scott Lenox and Jonathan Coxon Sr. founded the Ceramic Art Company in Trenton, New Jersey, in 1889. In 1906, Lenox left and started his own company called Lenox. The company makes a porcelain that is similar to Irish Belleek. Lenox was bought by Department 56 in 2005. The marks used by the firm have changed through the years and collectors prefer the earlier examples. Related pieces may also be listed in the Ceramic Art Co. category.

Bowl, Free-Form, Leaf Shape, Porcelain, 7 x 11½ In.		41.00
Cake Plate, Wallace Sterling Silver, c.1940, 12½ In.		23.00
Cup & Saucer, Golden Wreath, Gold Winding Leaves, Trimmed In Gold Band		30.00
Figurine, Rapunzel, 8 In.		23.00
Pitcher, Birds, Asian Style, Gourd Shape, Gilded Branch Handle, 10¼ x 5¼ In.		2760.00
Plate, Dinner, 2 Magenta Bands, Alternating Gilt Medallions, 10½ In., 12 Piece		1410.00
Plate, Dinner, Laurent, 10⅜ In.		52.00
Plate, Luncheon, Charmaine, 8¼ In.		22.50
Plate, Luncheon, Westwind, 7¾ In.		35.00
Urn, Irises, Pink, Gilded Handles, Painted, W. Morley, 13¼ In.		4500.00
Vase, Celadon Green, c.1940, 10 x 4 In., Pair		94.00
Vase, Primrose, Yellow, Oval, Painted, W. Morley, 14½ In.		3460.00

LETTER OPENERS have been used since the eighteenth century. Ivory and silver were favored by the well-to-do. In the late nineteenth century, the letter opener was popular as an advertising giveaway and many were made of metal or celluloid. Brass openers with figural handles were also popular.

Botanical, Flower Handle, Brass, India, 9½ x 1⅛ In.		15.00
Brass, Marble Handle		15.00
Eagle, Cast Iron, Brass Blade, 8 In.		168.00
India Deity, Brass, 8½ x 1½ In.		25.00
Jade Handle, 3 In.		29.00
Mother-Of-Pearl, Sterling Silver, Scrolling, Floral, Late 1800s, 5½ In.		125.00
Nude, Bronze, Original Patina, Signed, E.T. Hurley, 6¾ In.		600.00

Lefton, Figurine, Little Devil Playing Tennis, Red Outfit, Gold Horns
$28.00

Legras, Bowl, Dogwood Blossoms, White Enameled, Green Ground, Gold Rim, Cameo, 4½ x 10 In.
$2300.00

L

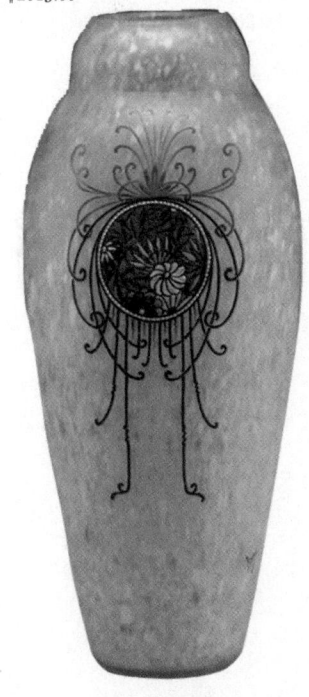

Legras, Vase, Art Deco Floral Medallions, Mottled End-Of-Day Ground, Signed, 18¼ In.
$2013.00

Legras, Vase, Branches With Leaves, Frosted, Red Enameled, Tapered, Footed, 18 In.
$996.00

Legras, Vase, Scenic, Deer & Bird Trees, Mottled Brick Red, Swollen Shape, Cameo, 8½ In.
$1035.00

Pewter Handle, Green, Red, Clear Stones, Prism Ball Finial	12.00
Silver, Entwined Handle With Ball On End, Magnifying Glass, 11 In., 2 Piece	220.00
Sterling Silver, Engraved, N. Hendricks, 3½ In.	15.00

LIBBEY Glass Company has made many types of glass since 1888, including the cut glass and tablewares that are collected today. The stemwares of the 1930s and 1940s are once again in style. The Toledo, Ohio, firm was purchased by Owens-Illinois in 1935 and is still working under the name Libbey Inc. Maize is listed in its own category.

Libbey

Beverage, Metallic Hostess Set, 5½ In.	36.00
Beverage, Pagoda, Original Box, 5¼ In., 8 Piece	35.00
Beverage Set, Ice Bucket, Tumblers, Silver Leaf, 7 Piece	10.00
Beverage Set, Pitcher, Tumblers, Fired-On, Turquoise, Orange, Yellow, 1960s, 7 Piece	40.00
Bowl, Talisman, Ribbed, Blue, Threading, Signed, 1⅜ x 4¼ In.	95.00
Candlestick, Morning Glory, Amethyst Cut To Opal, Ribbed, Flared, Footed, 3½ In., Pair	345.00
Celery Dish, Fan, Hobstars, Scalloped, Brilliant, Scalloped, 12 x 5 In.	225.00
Cocktail Set, Pitcher, Tumblers, Christmas, Original Box, 5 Piece	30.00
Compote, Amberina, Coin Spot Optic, Knopped Stem, Flared Amethyst Rim, Footed, 4 x 6 In.	978.00
Compote, Morning Glory, Amethyst Cut To Opalescent, 12 Ribbed, Clear Stem, Foot, 7 In.	1150.00
Cordial, Silver Leaf, 4¼ In., 6 Piece	18.00
Figurine, 3 Nude Women, 7 In.	35.00
Glass, Fish, 1950s	10.00
Goblet, Rock Sharpe, 1930s	8.00
Jug, Nash Green, Threading, Polished Pontil, Signed, 56 Oz., 9⅝ In.	425.00
Mug, Season's Greetings, Red, White Snowflakes, Footed, 6 In., 6 Piece	18.00
Plate, Rock Sharpe, 1940s	5.00
Sugar & Creamer, Golden Foliage, Original Box, 3¼ In.	20.00
Toothpick, Hat Shape, Peachblow, 2 In.	374.00
Toupee Holder, Cut Pattern, 3½ x 7½ In. .....*illus*	649.00
Tumbler, Butterfly, Brown, Orange, 3¾ In., 4 Piece	6.00
Tumbler, Daisy, White, Yellow, 10 Oz.	3.00
Tumbler, Daisy, White, Yellow, 14 Oz.	4.00
Tumbler, Gibraltar, Green, Ribbed Base, Stamped, 5⅛ x 3⅜ In.	6.00
Tumbler, Golden Foliage, 4½ In., 4 Piece	12.00
Tumbler, Go-With, Apple, Franciscan	9.00
Tumbler, Green, Banded Sections, Panel, 4¾ x 2½ In.	9.00
Tumbler, Highball, Golden Foliage, 5½ In., 7 Piece	20.00
Tumbler, Iced Tea, Rock Sharpe, 6⅜ In., 6 Piece	100.00
Tumbler, Juice, Silver Leaf, 1950s, 4 In., 6 Piece	13.00
Tumbler, Owl, On The Rocks, 4 Piece	10.00
Tumbler, Silver Leaf, 5¼ In., 4 Piece	17.00
Tumbler, Spiral, Iced Tea, Frosted, 7 In., 4 Piece	16.00
Vase, Flower Form, Amberina, Footed, Amber Stem, Fuchsia Top, Acid Stamp, 11½ In.	1093.00
Vase, Pink, Opalescent White, Tapered, Paneled, Rolled Rim, 10 In.	342.00
Vase, Pink Pulled Feather, Clear Foot, Signed, 7¾ In.	1150.00
Wine, Gold Leaf, 1950s, 10 Piece	40.00
Wine, Rock Sharpe, 5⅝ In., 14 Piece	8.00

LIGHTERS for cigarettes and cigars are collectible. Cigarettes became popular in the late nineteenth century, and with the cigarette came matches and cigarette lighters. All types of lighters are collected, from solid gold to the first of the recent disposable lighters. Most examples found were made after 1940. Some lighters may be found in the Jewelry category in this book.

Abraham Lincoln, Sitting On Bench, Copper, 4½ x 3½ x 2½ In.	90.00
Bell Shape, White, Pink Roses, Gold, Marked, Occupied Japan, 2¼ In.	22.00
Berra-Rizzuto Lanes, Celluloid, Brunswick, Bowler, 3 In.	766.00
Car Shape, Henry Miller Spring & Mfg. Co., Pittsburgh, Pa., 1940s	153.00
Cigar, Aleppo High Grade, C.H. Guppy Co., Cobalt Blue Globe, 15 In.	880.00
Cigar, Bulldog, Bronzed, White Lead, 4½ In.	138.00
Cigar, Butterfly Motif, Green Globe & Lighter Wicks, c.1890, 10 In.	385.00
Cigar, Cinco Cigars, Horse, Wicks, Globe, c.1900, 16½ In.	1320.00
Cigar, Drunk At Light Pole, Marble Base, Countertop, c.1890, 10 In.	413.00
Cigar, Man, Holding Globe On Pole, Cobalt Blue Globe, 18 In.	440.00
Cigar, Man, Holding Globe On Pole, Milk Glass Globe, Marble Base, 16 In.	531.00
Cigar, Man, Saluting, The Return, Cranberry Globe, 20 In.	472.00

L

Cigar, Poodle, Top Hat, Figural, Desk, Hinged Hat, 4 x 3 x 2½ In.	425.00
Dunhill, Silver, Gold Plated, 1970s	153.00
Electric, Wood Case, Chromed Torches, Universal Lighter Co., 1895 Patent, 8 x 8 In.	264.00
GE Automatic Dishwashers, Celluloid, Penguin, 1950s	29.00
Good Humor Ice Cream Company, Zippo, Gray Metal, Season 1956, 2¼ In.	125.00
Imco Gunlite, Gun Shape, Original Case, Instructions, Austria, 3 x 2¼ In.	72.00
Jay & Americans, Metal, Plastic, Scripto Inc., 1960s, 2¾ In.	78.00
Johnson's Wax Research Tower, F.L. Wright, 1940s, 5½ In. ....*illus*	345.00
Lava-Lite, Milford Concrete Products, Volcano, Celluloid	29.00
Limeliters, Tonight, In Person, RCA Victor, Nipper, Celluloid, Japan, 1960s	76.00
Maritime Company Of The Philippines, MCP, N.Y. Mets Home Schedule, 1969	240.00
New York Yankees, Best Wishes, Roger Maris, Nesor Rosen, 1961	264.00
Petty Girls, Celluloid, Table	103.00
Princess Phone, Lights, Telephone Planned Homes, Celluloid, Flat, Robin	29.00
Rathkamp Matchcover Society, Celluloid	41.00
Ronson, Matching Cigarette Case, Art Deco, Original Box, c.1940, 4¾ In.	47.00
Saltz Hotel & Country Club, Mount Freedom, N.J., Celluloid, Brother Lite	114.00
Willie Mays, 600 Home Runs, See Through, Scripto, 1970	1123.00
Yoo-Hoo, Drink Of Champions, Gil McDougald, N.Y. Yankees	766.00
Yoo-Hoo, Drink Of Champions, Yogi Berra, N.Y. Yankees	1123.00

LIGHTNING ROD BALLS are collected. The glass balls were at the center of the rod that was attached to the roof of a house or barn to avoid lightning damage.

Blue Glass, 5 In.	50.00
Blue Milk Glass, 1800s, 1⅛ In.	60.00
Blue Milk Glass, 5 In. Diam.	60.00
Ceramic, Brown Glaze, 3 x 2 In.	20.00
Milk Glass, 5 In. Diam	55.00
Milk Glass, Electra	50.00
Milk Glass, Salesman's Sample	55.00
Opaque Glass, Metal Caps	50.00

LIMOGES porcelain has been made in Limoges, France, since the mid-nineteenth century. Fine porcelains were made by many factories, including Haviland, Ahrenfeldt, Guerin, Pouyat, Elite, and others. Modern porcelains are being made at Limoges and the word *Limoges* as part of the mark is not an indication of age. Haviland, one of the Limoges factories, is listed as a separate category in this book.

Bowl, Centerpiece, Ceralene, 3½ x 9½ In.	234.00
Box, Enamel, Round, Hand Painted, Courting Scene, Signed, Gamet, 5¾ In.	1053.00
Cake Plate, Gold Stencil Inner Border, White Ground, Scrolled, J. Ouyat, c.1900, 9¾ In.	85.00
Compote, Raised Heavy Gold Edge, Pink Roses, White Ground, 8¾ In., 2 Piece	275.00
Cup & Saucer, Demitasse, Spode, Gold Band, 22 Piece	82.00
Cup & Saucer, Gold, White Enamel, Lacy, Le Tallec, 2½ x 2¼ & 5 In.	195.00
Dessert Set, Gold Gilt, Banded, Monogram, 14 Piece	293.00
Dessert Set, Rococo Style, Green, Gilt Edges, Hand Painted, 8 Piece	21.00
Game Set, Game Birds, Naturalistic Setting, Gold Border, 1920s, 15 Piece	2588.00
Humidor, Cover, Hand Painted Flowers, Initial P, Signed, GDA Manufacturer, 5 In.	195.00
Jar, Cover, Stylized Arrow & Bamboo Decoration, Blue, Silver Rim, C. Faure, 9 In.	5175.00
Jardiniere, Ferner, Painted Roses In Cartouche, Gold Trim, Scroll Feet, 7½ In. ......*illus*	294.00
Jardiniere, Painted Flowers, Gilt Rim, Footed, R. Delinieres, c.1900, 10 x 11½ In.	117.00
Jardiniere, Roses, Green Ground, c.1930, 9¼ x 11 In.	819.00
Jardiniere, Stand, Flowers, Red, Leaves, Green, 9 x 10 In.	527.00
Mug, Painted, Man Installing Wrought Iron Gate & Fence, O.R. Schellenberger	4680.00
Pitcher, Cider, Spider Web, Gold Highlights, Hand Painted, 6½ In.	175.00
Pitcher, Cider, Strawberry, Green Ground, Hand Painted, 5¾ In.	75.00
Place Setting, Haviland, Appetizer, Salad, Entree, c.1900, 7¼, 8½, 9½ In., 4 Sets	700.00
Plaque, Enamel, Man Drinking Wine, Gilt Wood Frame, Signed T. Leroy, 7 x 5 In.	2630.00
Plaque, Enameled, Painted, Cavalier, Gilt Bronze Frame, 7½ x 5½ In.	2925.00
Plaque, Enameled, Painted, Renaissance Troubadour, Gilt Bronze, Frame, 8 x 6 In.	2925.00
Plaque, Souls Awakening, Woman In Blue Velvet Robe, Holding Book, Frame, 7 x 9 In.	805.00
Plate, Cabinet, 10¾ In., 12 Piece	176.00
Plate, Dessert, Raised Gold, Pink Roses, White Ground, 8 In., 6 Piece	275.00
Plate, Dinner, Gilt Medallion, White Ground, Ivory, Gold Borders, 1800s, 8 Piece	480.00
Plate, Hand Painted, Children Playing, Tiffany & Co., 8 In., Pair	41.00

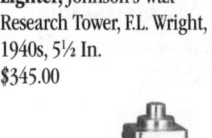

Libbey, Toupee Holder, Cut Pattern, 3½ x 7½ In. $649.00

Lighter, Johnson's Wax Research Tower, F.L. Wright, 1940s, 5½ In. $345.00

Limoges, Jardiniere, Ferner, Painted Roses In Cartouche, Gold Trim, Scroll Feet, 7½ In. $294.00

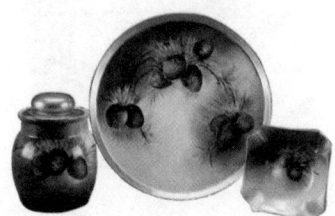

Limoges, Smoking Set, Pinecones, Tobacco Jar, Ashtray, 12-In. Platter, c.1900, 3 Piece $118.00

L

Limoges Factories

The best known of the Limoges, France, factories is Theodore Haviland, but porcelain was made by many Limoges firms, including Ahrenfeldt, Bernardaud, Charles Field Haviland; Delinieres & Company; William Guerin & Company; Lanternier; Jean Pouyat; and Martial Redon & Company. Collectors like the porcelain made in Limoges from 1850 to the 1930s.

Limoges, Vase, Green, White Art Deco Panels, Silvered Rim, Base, C. Faure, 12 x 8 In. $10350.00

Liverpool, Jug, Masonic Emblems, Black Transfer, 11 In. $1035.00

Punch Bowl, Painted Grapes, Gilt, Embossed, Blue & White Ground, 1900s, 8 In.	588.00
Punch Bowl Set, Painted, Berries, Leaves, Gold Trim, 4-Footed Stand, c.1919, 14 Piece	1725.00
Smoking Set, Pinecones, Tobacco Jar, Ashtray, 12-In. Platter, c.1900, 3 Piece *illus*	118.00
Tankard, Green, Gold Trim, Hand Painted, 15½ In.	350.00
Tray, Divided, Gilt Flowers, Hand Painted, c.1900, 12½ In.	59.00
Vase, Art Deco, Camille Faure, Zinnias, Enamel, Gold, Rose, Lavender, 5 In.	900.00
Vase, Fruiti Fiori, 9 In.	146.00
Vase, Green, Blue, Amethyst Swirls, Rust, White Accents, Egg Shape, C. Faure, 12 x 8 In.	7475.00
Vase, Green, White Art Deco Panels, Silvered Rim, Base, C. Faure, 12 x 8 In. *illus*	10350.00
Vase, Red & Yellow Flowers, Green Leaves, Gold & Green Ground, C. Faure, 4½ In.	575.00

LINDBERGH was a national hero. In 1927, Charles Lindbergh, the aviator, became the first man to make a nonstop solo flight across the Atlantic Ocean. In 1932, his son was kidnapped and murdered, and Lindbergh was again the center of public interest. He died in 1974. All types of Lindbergh memorabilia are collected.

Blotter Holder, Celluloid, Lindy & Spirit Of St. Louis Photograph, 3 x 7 In.	217.00
Button, 2 Great Flyers, Plucky Lindy & The Flexible Flyer, Red, White, Black, Celluloid	31.00
Button, Col. Charles A. Lindbergh, Photo, Black, White, Celluloid	52.00
Button, Conqueror, Capt. Charles Lindbergh, Portrait, Wings, Propeller, 1¼ In.	168.00
Button, Lucky Lindy, Welcome, Horseshoes, Celluloid, 1¼ In.	147.00
Button, Spirit Of St. Louis, Bakelite, Celluloid, Black Body, 3-D, On Card, 3 In.	204.00
Button, Spirit Of St. Louis, Bakelite, Celluloid, Cream Body, 3-D, 3 In.	59.00
Button, Spirit Of St. Louis, Rhinestones, 1 In.	186.00
Button, Welcome Lindbergh, Photo, White, Blue Ground, Celluloid	20.00 to 39.00
Button, Welcome Our Hero, Col. Chas. A. Lindbergh, 2¼ In.	767.00
Cigarette Case, Spirit Of St. Louis, Eiffel Tower, Statue Of Liberty, c.1927, 3 x 3¼ In.	311.00
Compact, Spirit Of St. Louis, New York-Paris, Silver, Germany, 1927, 2 In.	132.00
Figurine, Col. Charles A. Lindbergh, New York To Paris, Metal, Silver Paint, 8¼ In.	120.00
Figurine, Lindbergh, Standing, Flight Suit, Bronze, 13 In.	1673.00
Figurine, Spirit Of America, Pilot, Eagle, Globe, Plaster, Bronze Paint, Mazzolini Co.	657.00
Paperweight, Bust, Cast Iron, 3⅞ x 1⅝ In.	112.00

LITHOPHANES are porcelain pictures made by casting clay in layers of various thicknesses. When a piece is held to the light, a picture of light and shadow is seen through it. Most lithophanes date from the 1825–1875 period. A few are still being made. Many lithophanes sold today were originally panels for lampshades.

Angel At Night, Angel Carrying Child To Heaven, Town In Background, 4 x 6 In.	325.00
Cup & Saucer, Dragon, Geisha, Loop Handle, 3¾ x 2 & 5½ In.	50.00
Hunting, Signed, 5½ x 6½ In.	195.00
King Edward VII, Dated August 9th 1902	148.00
Lamp, 4 Castle, River Scenes, Kerosene, Signed, Germany, c.1900, 11 x 6 In.	2250.00
Shadowbox, Electric, Girls & Dog	475.00
Stein, Female With Harp, 8⅝ x 3³⁄₁₆ In.	225.00

LIVERPOOL, England, has been the site of many pottery and porcelain factories since the eighteenth century. Color-decorated porcelains, transfer-printed earthenware, stoneware, basalt, figurines, and other wares were made. Sadler and Green made print-decorated wares from 1756. Many of the pieces were made for the American market and feature patriotic emblems, such as eagles, flags, and other special-interest motifs. Liverpool pitchers are always called Liverpool jugs by collectors.

Figurine, Nun, Reading Bible, Flower Over Yellow Habit, Puce Veil, c.1760, 4½ In.	1440.00
Figurine, Nurse, Suckling Infant, Rectangular Base, c.1758-60, 5¾ In.	4570.00
Jug, 2 Scenes, Woman, Child, Spring, Love & Marriage Medallion, Black Transfer, c.1800, 6 In.	518.00
Jug, 3-Masted Ship, Peace, Plenty & Independence, Black Transfer, 10 In.	1725.00
Jug, American Ship, Criterion, Multicolored, Masonic Designs, 8 In.	3500.00
Jug, American Ship, Fanny's Farewell, James Bradburn, 10¾ In.	5800.00
Jug, Black Transfer, Governor Of Europe Stopped In His Career, Napoleon, 8⅜ In.	940.00
Jug, George Washington, Liberty & American Flag, 1805	3028.00
Jug, Masonic Emblems, Black Transfer, 11 In. *illus*	1035.00
Jug, Transfer, Hope, Woman With Anchor, Sailing Ship, 9 In.	5750.00
Jug, Washington, Gen'l Lafayette, Commemorative, Republican Quote Under Spout	316.00
Mug, Soft Paste, Black Transfer, 2 Young People, Butterfly, Short Verse, 6 In.	575.00
Tankard, George Washington, Sacred To Memory Of, Straight-Sided, 6 x 3¾ In.	1434.00
Teapot, Blue Printed, Flowers, Christian's, c.1770, 6 In.	458.00

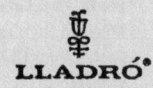

LLADRO is a Spanish porcelain. Juan, Jose, and Vicente Lladro opened a ceramics workshop in Almacera in 1951. They soon began making figurines in a distinctive, elongated style. In 1958 the factory moved to Tabernes Blanques, Spain. The company makes stoneware and porcelain figurines and vases in limited and unlimited editions. Dates given are first and last years of production.

Bust, Wanita, Young Girl, 1900s, 10 In.	441.00
Figurine, All Aboard, Boy Playing With Train, No. 7619, Box, 5 x 7 In.	90.00
Figurine, Doctor, No. 4602, c.1969, 14½ In. ....*illus*	82.00
Figurine, Dutch Girl, Basket, No. 1399, 10 In.	118.00
Figurine, Elephant, 9 x 8 In.	468.00
Figurine, Girl Kissing, No. 4873, c.1974, 7 In.	47.00
Figurine, Girl With Toy Wagon, Pulling Doll, No. 5044, c.1980, 11 In. ....*illus*	176.00
Figurine, Grand Dame, No. 1568, Box, 13½ In.	250.00
Figurine, I Love You Truly, Bride & Groom Dancing, No. 1528, 1987	465.00
Figurine, Little Pals, Clown, Puppies In Pocket, No. 7600, 8¾ In.	550.00
Figurine, Oriental Girl, Flower Decorating, No. 4840, 7½ In.	70.00
Figurine, The Kiss, After Klimt, No. 1871, 26 x 12 x 19½ In.	1708.00
Figurine, Wedding, No. 4808, 7½ In.	70.00
Figurine, Young Woman, Umbrella, 20th Century, 13 In.	223.00

Lladro, Figurine, Doctor, No. 4602, c.1969, 14½ In. $82.00

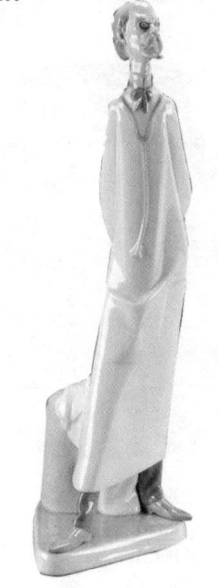

LOCKE ART is a trademark found on glass of the early twentieth century. Joseph Locke worked at many English and American firms. He designed and etched his own glass in Pittsburgh, Pennsylvania, starting in the 1880s. Some pieces were marked *Joe Locke,* but most were marked with the words *Locke Art*. The mark is hidden in the pattern on the glass.

Sherbet, Daisy, Optic Ribbed, Saucer Foot, Signed, 3¼ In.	90.00 to 95.00
Tumbler, Oysters, Seaweed, Coral, Polished Rim, 3⅝ In.	250.00
Vase, Amberina, Embossed, Storks, Rectangular, Arched Sides, 4½ In.	1380.00
Vase, Milk Glass, Embossed, Storks, Rectangular, Arched Sides, Pressed Storks, 4½ In.	575.00

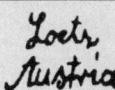

LOETZ glass was made in many varieties. Johann Loetz bought a glassworks in Austria in 1840. He died in 1848 and his widow ran the company; then in 1879, his grandson took over. Most collectors recognize the iridescent gold glass similar to Tiffany, but many other types were made. The firm closed during World War II.

Lladro, Figurine, Girl With Toy Wagon, Pulling Doll, No. 5044, c.1980, 11 In. $176.00

Basket, Silver-Plated, Frame, 6½ x 7 In.	117.00
Bowl, Gold, Green, Purple Iridescent, Folded Tricornered Rim, Signed, 8½ In.	472.00
Bowl, Marmorierte, Marbled Brown, Green, Scrolls, Oval, c.1890, 9 In.	441.00
Bowl, Marmorierte, Red, Gold Scroll Band, Amethyst Stalactites, Fan Form, 4¾ In. ....*illus*	382.00
Bowl, Mottled Green, Opalescent Ground, Dimpled On Sides, c.1900, 4½ x 7 In.	209.00
Bowl, Papillon, Gold Iridescent, Ruffled & Pinched Rim, 3¼ x 7¾ In.	294.00
Candlestick, Green, 9¼ In.	117.00
Compote, Iridescent Amber To Ruby, Scalloped Rim, Metal Base, 4 Footed, 11 x 9 In.	403.00
Inkwell, Green Iridescent Body, Brass Hinged Lid, Lion's Head In Relief, 2 x 4 In.	235.00
Jardiniere, Brown & Gold Swirls, Cylindrical, Ormolu Mount, Wreath, 6¼ In.	294.00
Shade, Gold & Blue Iridescent Glass, White & Green Pulled Feather, 5 In., 4 Piece	1200.00
Vase, 2 Green 4-Leaf Clovers, Iridescent, Ribbed, Ruffled Edge, 6¼ In.	148.00
Vase, Amber, Amethyst Bands, Oval, Tricornered Rim, Signed, c.1900, 5¼ In.	382.00
Vase, Argus, Phanomen, Platinum Over Tangerine, Bulbous, Pinched Shoulders, 4 In. .*illus*	1020.00
Vase, Art Glass, Iridescent, Orange Body, Rose, Green, Twisted Ribbing, Austria, 13 In.	236.00
Vase, Blue, Iridescent, Gold, 6¾ In.	717.00
Vase, Blue, Silver, 9 x 8¼ In.	215.00
Vase, Blue Iridescent, Pulled Feather, Gold & Blue Long Stem, Disc Foot, 12½ In.	764.00
Vase, Blue Iridescent, Silver Overlay Vine & Flowers, Flared Rim, Black, Starr & Frost, 5 In.	1116.00
Vase, Blue-Green Iridescent, Cylindrical, Fan-Shaped Rim, Footed, 24 In.	230.00
Vase, Brown Satin Glass, Applied Gold Design, Signed, Federzeichnung, 6 In. ......*illus*	1150.00
Vase, Cobalt Blue, Green & Blue Swirl, Sterling Silver Overlay, Scroll, 7 In.	1725.00
Vase, Craquelle, Blue & Green, Iridescent, Pierced Metal Frame, c.1900, 11 In.	176.00
Vase, Craquelle, Gold Iridescent, Squat, Tricornered Rim, 6½ In.	230.00
Vase, Diaspora, Blue Green Iridescent Lava, Pinched Waist, Flattened Rim, 7 In.	144.00
Vase, Diaspora, Gold Iridescent, Bulbous, Crimped & Folded Rim, 5¼ In. ....*illus*	660.00
Vase, Fan, Fluted Conical Shape, Iridescent Green, 7 Crimped Fingers, 12 In.	633.00
Vase, Federzeichnung, Cased, Glossy, Scrolls, Gold Tracery, Oval, Ruffled Edge, 7 In.	2013.00
Vase, Federzeichnung, Satin, Oval, Squared Rim, 8 In.	2070.00
Vase, Flower Frog, Iridescent White, 3 Green Feet, Melon Ribbed, Metal Lid, c.1900, 7½ In.	176.00
Vase, Gold Iridescent, Cylindrical, Raised Design, 14 In.	600.00

Loetz, Bowl, Marmorierte, Red, Gold Scroll Band, Amethyst Stalactites, Fan Form, 4¾ In. $382.00

L

Loetz, Vase, Argus, Phanomen,
Platinum Over Tangerine, Bulbous,
Pinched Shoulders, 4 In.
$1020.00

Loetz, Vase, Green Iridescent,
Magenta Highlights, Wrapped Snake,
Folded Rim, 13 In.
$896.00

Loetz, Vase, Opaque Purple To Amber,
Gold Enamel Scroll Medallions,
Ruffled Rim, 5½ In.
$411.00

Loetz, Vase, Brown Satin Glass,
Applied Gold Design, Signed,
Federzeichnung, 6 In.
$1150.00

Loetz, Vase, Oil Spot, Gold Iridescent,
Stretched Cutouts, Slightly Tapered,
12½ In.
$863.00

Loetz, Vase, Papillon Spots,
Blue Iridescent, Citron Top,
Ball Stem, Footed, Art Deco, 7 In.
$978.00

Loetz, Vase, Diaspora,
Gold Iridescent, Bulbous,
Crimped & Folded Rim, 5¼ In.
$660.00

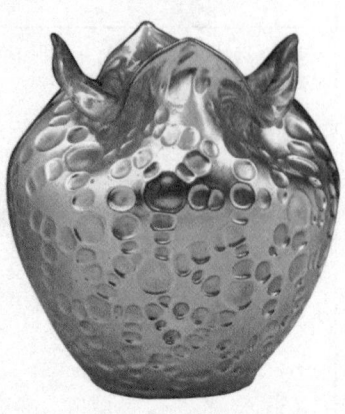

Loetz, Vase, Oil Spot, Red,
Silver Iridescent, Squared Shoulder,
Pinched, Bulbous Neck, 6 In.
$360.00

Loetz, Vase, Phanomen, Pink & Blue,
Flared Rim, 8¼ In.
$1020.00

L

Vase, Gold Iridescent, Double Gourd, Applied Ribs, Leaves, Vines, 6½ In.	288.00
Vase, Gold Iridescent Ribbons, Pinched Shoulder, Funnel Neck, Signed, 9¼ In.	705.00
Vase, Green Iridescent, Blue Leaves, Silver Overlay, Art Nouveau, Stylized Flowers, 7 In.	5288.00
Vase, Green Iridescent, Magenta Highlights, Wrapped Snake, Folded Rim, 13 In. *illus*	896.00
Vase, Green Iridescent, Threaded, Bulbous, Pinched Sides, Short Neck, 5½ In.	235.00
Vase, Green Iridescent, Trailing Tendril, Trefoil Lip, Engraved, 9½ In.	1920.00
Vase, Iridescent Gold, Bulbous, Art Nouveau Silver Overlay, Scrolling Flowers, 3¼ In.	633.00
Vase, Jack-In-The-Pulpit, Gold Iridescent, 14½ In.	2000.00
Vase, Jack-In-The-Pulpit, Gold Iridescent, Magenta Highlights, Austria, c.1900, 16¾ In.	1315.00
Vase, Lily, Iridescent Oil Spot, 17½ In.	2400.00
Vase, Medici, Amethyst, Blue Iridescent Oil Spot, Oval, Pinched Sides, 4 In.	748.00
Vase, Nautilus, Shell & Seaweed, Gold Iridescent, 10 In.	1600.00
Vase, Oil Spot, Gold Iridescent, Stretched Cutouts, Slightly Tapered, 12½ In. *illus*	863.00
Vase, Oil Spot, Red, Silver Iridescent, Squared Shoulder, Pinched, Bulbous Neck, 6 In. *illus*	360.00
Vase, Opaque Purple To Amber, Gold Enamel Scroll Medallions, Ruffled Rim, 5½ In. *illus*	411.00
Vase, Papillon, Blue, Green, Iridescent, 10 In.	633.00
Vase, Papillon, Gold Iridescent, Silver Overlay, Iris, Pinched Sides, Tricornered, 9½ In.	805.00
Vase, Papillon, Red, Metal Foot, 9 x 8 In.	960.00
Vase, Papillon Spots, Blue Iridescent, Citron Top, Ball Stem, Footed, Art Deco, 7 In. *illus*	978.00
Vase, Phanomen, Amber Iridescent, Blue Iridescent Pulled Feathers, Signed, 6¼ In.	1380.00
Vase, Phanomen, Amber Opalescent, Blue Iridescent Feather, Pinched Bottle Shape, 11 In.	1668.00
Vase, Phanomen, Blue Heart, Oval, Green Oil Spot, Graduating To Amethyst, 3½ In.	978.00
Vase, Phanomen, Pink & Blue, Flared Rim, 8¼ In. *illus*	1020.00
Vase, Phanomen Gre, Cobalt, 6¼ In.	1200.00
Vase, Purple, Blue, Greeniridescent, Diagonal Pulled Feathers, Blue Ground, 6½ In.	374.00
Vase, Rainbow Pattern, Twisting Body, Austria, c.1900, 10½ In.	502.00
Vase, Satin, Cased, Scrolls, Gold Tracery, Oval, Cylindrical Rim, Federzeichnung, 7 In.	1438.00
Vase, Seashell, Oil Spot, Gold Iridescent, Clear Vines Of Seaweed, 7 In. *illus*	900.00
Vase, Seashell, Yellow Iridescent, Green, Leaf Pod Base, Teal, Pink, 5½ x 11¾ In.	690.00
Vase, Silberiris, Iridescent Blue, Draped Loops, Egg Shape, c.1900, 3½ In. *illus*	225.00
Vase, Stick, Diaspora, Bulbous Base, Gold Iridescent, Tricornered Rim, Oil Spot, 10½ In.	690.00
Vase, Stick, Green Iridescent, Undulating Blue Bands, Bulbous Base, 12 In.	345.00
Vase, Stick, Green Iridescent Shaded To Purple, Optic Ribbed, Rolled Rim, K. Moser, 10 In.	575.00
Vase, Titania, Raspberry Pink Body, Apple Green Rim, Silver Overlay, Leafy Scroll, 8⅝ In.	3740.00
Vase, Translucent Green, Metal Overlay Rim, c.1900, 4 In.	870.00
Vase, Trumpet, Green, Iridescent, Tricornered Rim, Gold Bands, 9 In.	259.00
Vase, Water Lily, Iridescent Green, Dragonflies, Stems, Leaves, Gilt Metal Stand, 9½ In.	690.00

LONE RANGER, a fictional character, was introduced on the radio in 1932. Over three thousand shows were produced before the series ended in 1954. In 1938, the first Lone Ranger movie was made. Television shows were started in 1949 and are still seen on some stations. The Lone Ranger appears on many products and was even the name of a restaurant chain for several years.

Bank, Lone Ranger Strong Box, Zell, Box, 3⅜ x 3 In.	492.00
Bank, Mechanical, Lone Ranger, Lasso, Silver, Plastic, E.J. Kahn & Co., Box, 6¼ In.	3976.00
Bank, Money Bag, 100, 0, Cast Iron, No. 1262	295.00
Bedspread, Chenille, Hi-Yo Silver, 6 x 8 Ft.	223.00
Book, Secret Of Thunder Mountain, No. 14, Paperback, Bantam, 1930, 100 Pages	298.00
Calendar, 1953, Merita Bread, 14 x 8 In.	487.00
Comic Book, No. 5, Sept. 10, 1948, Edgar Church, Mile High Copy *illus*	630.00
Costume, Cloth Mask, Flannel Shirt, Reads Come On Silver, Collegeville, 1930s	403.00
Costume, Cowboy, Full-Like Chaps, Plaid Shirt, Vest, Hat, Mask, 1939	615.00
Costume, Tonto, Flannel Shirt, Leatherette Belt, Holster, Pla-Master, 1950s	149.00
Cowgirl Suit, Official, Shirt, Skirt, Fringe, Seneca, Box, 1930s, 14½ x 11½ In.	370.00
Cryptography Decoder, Premium Weber's Bread, 1943	145.00
Figurine, Lone Ranger, Chalkware, 15 In.	282.00
Flashlight, Signal Siren, Lone Ranger On Sides, United States Electric Mfg., 1950s	260.00
Flashlight, Signal Siren, Usalite, U.S. Electric Mfg. Co., Box, c.1948	153.00
Flashlight Pistol, Metal, Plastic, Lightbulb, Click Action, Box, c.1950s	739.00
Hat, Cloth, Sailor Type, Blue & Orange, 1939, 11 x 2 In.	58.00
Jugsaw Puzzles, 2 Puzzles In 1 Box, No. 3902, Whitman, Box, 1930s, 10 x 7½ In.	431.00
Makeup Kit, Miner's, Mailer, 2 Tins, Mask, Mustache, c.1939, 5 x 5¼ In.	224.00
Mask, Tonto, Unpunched, Merita Bread, Folder, c.1957, 11 x 7 In.	112.00
Pin, Lone Ranger, Hi-Yo Silver, Boston American, 1 In.	67.00
Pistol, Click, Smoking, Smoke Ammo & Muzzle Cap, 1950s, 9 In.	30.00

Loetz, Vase, Seashell, Oil Spot, Gold Iridescent, Clear Vines Of Seaweed, 7 In.
$900.00

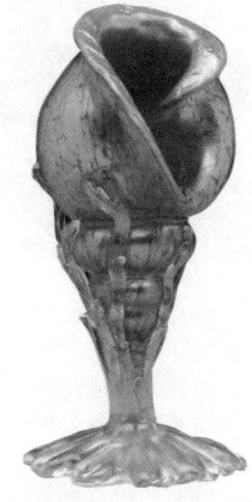

Loetz, Vase, Silberiris, Iridescent Blue, Draped Loops, Egg Shape, c.1900, 3½ In.
$225.00

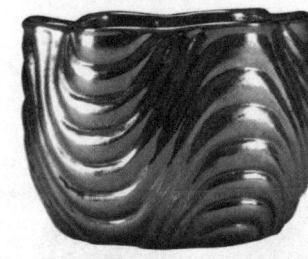

L

Lone Ranger, Comic Book, No. 5, Sept. 10, 1948, Edgar Church, Mile High Copy
$630.00

Lone Ranger, Record Player,
Lone Ranger, Silver, Lights Up,
Mercury, 1950s, 10 x 12 In.
$86.00

Longwy, Jardiniere, Stand,
Japonism, Lion's Mask Handles,
Metal Scroll, 12 x 26 In.
$800.00

Pistol, Flashlight, Plastic, White Grips, THR, 1950s, 9 In.	30.00
Poster, Boston's Logan Airport, Lone Ranger, Tonto, Black & White, 1970s, 21 x 22 In.	230.00
Puppet, Push, Blue Outfit, Plastic Head, By Kohner, 1940s, 5½ In.	145.00
Record Player, Lone Ranger, Silver, Lights Up, Mercury, 1950s, 10 x 12 In. ......*illus*	86.00
Ring, 6 Shooter, Kix, 1940s	204.00
Ring, Air Corps, Secret Compartment, Original Photographs, Kix, 1942	365.00
Sign, Merita Bread, Buy Merita Bread, It's Enriched, Embossed, Tin, 1954, 36 x 24 In.	6050.00
Socks, Sport-Wear Hosiery Mills Inc., Set Of 36 Pairs, Box, 1940s	85.00
Target Game, Gun, Darts, Box, Marx, 1946, 17 In. Diam.	450.00
Tonto Outfit, Holster, Gun, Knife, Headdress, Esquire Toy, Box, Late 1950s, 9½ x 13 In.	745.00
Toy, Lone Ranger, On Horse, Twirls Lasso, Windup, Marx, Box	585.00

LONGWY Workshop of Longwy, France, first made ceramic wares in 1798. The workshop is still in business. Most of the ceramic pieces found today are glazed with many colors to resemble cloisonne or other enameled metal. Many pieces were made with stylized figures and Art Deco designs. The factory used a variety of marks.

Bowl, Crown, Sailing Ship, Trefoils, Branches	200.00
Candleholder, Gargoyle, Brass, c.1890, 9 In., Pair	695.00
Charger, Birds, Flowers, 17 In.	2013.00
Charger, Renaissance, Triangular, Hanging Holes, 10½ In.	395.00
Dish, Bronze, Bamboo Frame, Flower, Leaf, 3½ x 5½ In.	55.00
Jardiniere, Stand, Japonism, Lion's Mask Handles, Metal Scroll, 12 x 26 In. ......*illus*	800.00
Plaque, City Scene, Faience, Rose Branch Border, Oval, 1880s, 10 x 11 In.	350.00
Tea Set, Blossoms, Branches, Pinks, Red, Turquoise Ground, 3 Piece	900.00
Tea Set, Butterflies, Insects, Turquoise Blue, 3 Piece	950.00
Tile, Spring Flowers	39.00
Trivet, Apple Blossom, c.1910, 11 In.	600.00
Trivet, Central Bird, Faience, Padded Feet, 8 In.	395.00
Trivet, Mosaic Style, Brass Mount, Serpent Handles, Paw Feet, 8½ x 11 In.	280.00
Trivet, Woman Dancing In Garden, Brown, Yellow, White, Stylized, Art Deco, Marked, 8 In.	180.00
Vase, Primavera, Grackle Glaze, White Ground, Gray Pattern, 1930s, 12 In.	588.00
Vase, Primavera, Orange & Maroon Circles & Wavy Bands, White Crackle Ground, 7½ In.	546.00

LONHUDA Pottery Company of Steubenville, Ohio, was organized in 1892 by William Long, W. H. Hunter, and Alfred Day. Brown underglaze slip-decorated pottery was made. The firm closed in 1896. The company used many marks; the earliest included the letters *LPCO.*

Vase, Aburamu & Iskan, Faience, Shape 350, Signed, ADF, 11¼ In.	1580.00

LOW art tiles were made by the J. and J. G. Low Art Tile Works of Chelsea, Massachusetts, from 1877 to 1902. A variety of art and other tiles were made. Some of the tiles were made by a process called "natural," some were hand-modeled, and some were made mechanically.

Tile, Bearded Gentleman, Blue Glaze, Frame, 6 x 4½ In.	184.00
Tray, Olive Green Glossy Glaze, Bronzed Metal Surround, 2 Shaped Handles, 1884, 18¾ In.	705.00

LOWESTOFT was a factory in Suffolk, England, which from 1757 to 1802 made many commemorative gift pieces and small, dated, inscribed pieces of soft paste porcelain. Related items may be found in the Chinese Export category.

Teacup & Saucer, Aqua, Oleander, Yellow Interior, Flower Center, 2½ & 5½ In.	118.00

LOY-NEL-ART, *see McCoy category.*

LUNCH BOXES and lunch pails have been used to carry lunches to school or work since the nineteenth century. Today, most collectors want either early tobacco advertising boxes or children's lunch boxes made since the 1930s. These boxes are made of metal or plastic. Boxes listed here include the original Thermos bottle inside the box unless otherwise indicated. Movie, television, and cartoon characters may be found in their own categories. Tobacco tin pails and lunch boxes are listed in the Advertising category.

LUNCH BOX

Adam-12, Aladdin, 1973	85.00
Alvin & Chipmunks, Green, White, Vinyl, No Thermos, King Seeley Thermos Co., 1963	165.00
Astronaut, Dome, Rockets & Moon Scene, King Seeley Thermos Co., 1960	140.00 to 154.00

Lunch Box, Bullwinkle,
Plastic, Universal Industries
$248.00

Lunch Box, Captain Kangaroo,
Vinyl, 1964
$290.00

Lunch Box, Gigi, French Poodle,
Eiffel Tower, Vinyl, Softie By Aladdin, 1962
$173.00

Lunch Box, Home Town Airport, Steel,
Dome, King Seeley Thermos Co., 1960
$819.00

Lunch Box, Jetsons, Steel, Dome, 1963
$878.00

Lunch Box, Space Explorer, Space Scenes, Metal, 1960
$82.00

Collectible Lunch Boxes

Children's vinyl lunch boxes, made from 1959 to 1982, don't sell for as much as metal ones, but they're attracting attention. Many collectors are driven by nostalgia—they want the boxes they carried to school decades ago.

LUNCH BOX

Lunch Box, Universal Movie Monsters, Frankenstein, Dracula, Metal, Aladdin, 1979
$230.00

Lunch Box, World Of Dr. Seuss, Vinyl, Aladdin, 1970
$58.00

A-Team, King Seeley Thermos Co., 1985	125.00
Ballerina, Aladdin, 1962	425.00
Banana Splits, Vinyl, King Seeley, 1960s	395.00
Barbie, By Ponytail, Vinyl, Flap, Snap Closure, King Seeley Thermos Co., 1962	395.00
Battle Kit, King Seeley Thermos Co., 1966	131.00
Battle Star Galactica, Aladdin, 1978	90.00
Black Hole, Aladdin, 1979	125.00
Boy On Rocket, Vinyl, Ardee Industries, 1960s	390.00
Bread Box, Campbell's Soup Can Shaped Thermos, Aladdin, 1968	400.00
Bugaloos, Metal, Embossed Panels, Aladdin, 1971	217.00
Bullwinkle, Plastic, Universal Industries *illus*	248.00
Cable Car, San Fransisco Nob Hill Trolley, Aladdin, 1962	495.00
Campus Queen, Metal, King Seeley Thermos Co., 1967	85.00
Captain Kangaroo, Vinyl, 1964 *illus*	290.00
Care Bears, Aladdin, 1984	50.00
Chan Clan, Metal, King Seeley Thermos Co., 1973	209.00
Circus Wagon, American Thermos, 1958	45.00
Clash Of The Titans, King Seeley Thermos Co., 1981	100.00
Close Encounters Of The Third Kind, Metal, King Seeley Thermos Co., 1977-78	112.00
Davy Crockett, Thermos, American Thermos Co., 1955, 8 In.	670.00
Denim Diner, Blue Patchwork Style Dog & Flowers, Red Vinyl Handle, Aladdin, 1975	125.00
Deputy Dawg, Vinyl, King Seeley Thermos Co., 1964	390.00
Disneyland, Metal, Castle, Congo Queen, Aladdin	339.00
Donny & Marie, Vinyl, Aladdin, 1976	122.00
Dream Boat, Vinyl, No Thermos, Feldco, 1960	476.00
Dukes Of Hazzard, Metal, Aladdin, 1980	110.00
Dynomutt, Metal, King Seeley Thermos Co., 1977	92.00
E.T. The Extra-Terrestrial, Aladdin, 1982	35.00
Fall Guy, Lee Majors, Walking Through Fire, Aladdin, 1981	85.00
Firehouse, Dome, American Thermos, 1959	75.00
G.I. Joe, Vinyl, King Seeley Thermos Co., 1960s	196.00
Gentle Ben, Metal, Aladdin, 1968	186.00
Get Smart, Metal, King Seeley Thermos Co., 1966	407.00
Gigi, French Poodle, Eiffel Tower, Vinyl, Softie By Aladdin, 1962 *illus*	173.00
Globe-Trotter, Metal, Dome, Aladdin, 1959	300.00
Gomer Pyle USMC, Metal, Aladdin, 1966	370.00
Goober & The Ghost Chasers, King Seeley Thermos Co., c.1974	236.00
Great Wild West, Western Theme, Indians, Cowboys, Thermos, Universal, 1959	600.00
Gremlins, Pink Corvette, Gremlins Driving, Aladdin, 1984	80.00
Gun Of Will Sonnett, Metal, King Seeley Thermos Co., 1968	339.00
Gunsmoke, Matt Dillon, U.S. Marshal, Metal, Aladdin, 1959	335.00
Hector Heathcoat, CBS Terrytoons Cartoons Image, Aladdin, 1964	295.00
Home Town Airport, Steel, Dome, King Seeley Thermos Co., 1960 *illus*	819.00
Hot Wheels, Mattel Hot Wheel Cars, King Seeley Thermos Co., 1969	100.00
Jetsons, Steel, Dome, 1963 *illus*	878.00
Kellogg's Cereal, Tony The Tiger, Rice Krispies, Aladdin, 1969	170.00
Krofft Super Show, Metal, Aladdin, 1976	90.00 to 203.00
Lance Link Secret Chimp, Metal, King Seeley Thermos Co., 1971	205.00
Land Of The Giants, Sci-Fi TV Show, Aladdin, 1968	87.00 to 185.00
Land Of The Lost, Metal, Aladdin, 1975	169.00
Laugh-In, Sock-It-To-Me, Brunch Bag, Yellow, Aladdin, 1968	225.00
Little Dutch Miss, Metal, Universal Industries, 1959	195.00
Little Friends, Metal, No Thermos, Aladdin, 1982	448.00
Little House On The Prairie, Metal, King Seeley Thermos Co., 1978	55.00
Loonie Tunes TV, Cartoon Characters In Scene, American Thermos	295.00
Lost In Space, Dome, Metal, King Seeley Thermos Co., 1967	305.00 to 410.00
Ludwig Von Drake In Disneyland, Metal, Aladdin, 1961	352.00
Lunch N Munch, Red, Vinyl, American Thermos, 1959	390.00
Lunch N Munch, Tan Pirate, Vinyl, American Thermos, 1959	335.00
Magic Of Lassie, Metal, King Seeley Thermos Co., 1978	92.00
Marvel Comics' Super Heroes, Metal, Aladdin, 1976	265.00
Mr. Merlin, King Seeley Thermos Co., 1982	125.00
Orbit, Astronaut Inside Space Capsule, King Seeley Thermos Co., 1963	295.00
Osmonds, Metal, Aladdin, 1973	102.00
Pac-Man, Vinyl, Aladdin, 1980	80.00

Partridge Family, Metal, King Seeley Thermos Co., 1971	168.00
Pebbles & Bamm-Bamm, Vinyl, Aladdin, 1978	240.00
Porky's Lunch Wagon, American Thermos, 1959	395.00
Psychedelic, Black & Yellow, Aladdin, 1969	450.00
Rat Patrol, Blowing Up German Vehicle, Jeep, Aladdin, 1967	100.00
Red Barn, Domed, American Thermos, 1957	175.00
Sabrina, Vinyl, Aladdin, 1972	388.00
Satellite, Space Scene, American Thermos, 1958	225.00
Secret Agent, Metal, King Seeley Thermos Co., 1968	136.00
Soupy Sales, Vinyl, Image Of Soupy, Blue Ground, King Seeley Thermos Co., 1966	300.00
Space Explorer, Space Scenes, Metal, 1960 ....*illus*	82.00
Space Travel, 2 Swing Handles, Decoware, 1940s	112.00
Space:1999, Landau, Bain, Metal, King Seeley Thermos Co., 1975	19.00
Speed Buggy, Metal, King Seeley Thermos Co., 1973	105.00
Star Trek, Mr. Spock, Capt. Kirk, McCoy, King Seeley Thermos Co., 1980	90.00
Teenager, School, Dancing, Baseball, American Thermos, 1957	195.00
Tom Corbett, Space Cadet, Metal, Aladdin, 1954	370.00
U.S. Mail, Aladdin, 1969	250.00 to 493.00
U.S. Submarines, Metal, American Thermos, c.1960	224.00
Universal Movie Monsters, Frankenstein, Dracula, Metal, Aladdin, 1979 ....*illus*	230.00
Voyage To The Bottom Of The Sea, Aladdin, 1967	350.00
Waltons, Aladdin, 1973	70.00
Washington Redskins, Metal, Okay Industries, 1970	280.00
Welcome Back Kotter, Barbarino, Brunch Bag, Vinyl, 1977	224.00
Wild Wild West, Metal, Aladdin, c.1969	451.00
Wonder Woman, Vinyl, Aladdin, 1977	168.00
World Of Dr. Seuss, Vinyl, Aladdin, 1970 ....*illus*	58.00
Yosemite Sam & Bugs Bunny, Vinyl, King Seeley Thermos Co., 1971	300.00

LUNCH BOX THERMOS

Alvin & The Chipmunks, King Seeley Thermos Co., 1963	35.00
Jr. Nurse, 3 Nurses In Blue Uniform, Aladdin, 1960s	50.00
Pete's Dragon, Pete Sitting On Dragon's Tail, Aladdin, 1978	75.00
The Osmonds, Portraits Of 5 Brothers & Donny Singing, Aladdin, 1973	100.00

LUNEVILLE, a French faience factory, was established about 1730 by Jacques Chambrette. It is best known for its fine biscuit figures and groups and for large faience dogs and lions. The early pieces were unmarked. The firm was acquired by Keller and Guerin and is still working.

Cup, Red, Yellow Flowers	20.00
Cup & Saucer, Green, White, Gold, Scrolls	15.00
Cup & Saucer, Raised Gold Flowers, Leaves, Victorian, 5⅞ & 3⅛ x 4¼ In.	65.00
Oyster Plate, 6 Wells, Flowers, 9¾ In., 6 Piece	700.00
Pitcher, Cornucopia, 8½ x 5 In.	90.00
Planter, Bird, Blue Wings, Red Plume, Flowers, Leaves, Gold Trim, Round, 15 x 21 In.	587.00
Plate, Asparagus, Artichoke, Blue, Green, Majolica, Barbotine, c.1890, 9 In.	225.00
Plate, Fruit, Painted, 8½ In., 6 Piece	205.00
Plate, Plum & Branch, Double Shaded Ground, Scalloped, Embossed, c.1900, 8½ In.	75.00
Potpourri Urn, Lid, Neoclassical, Blanc De Chine, Ram's Head Handles, 14 x 9 In., Pair	294.00

LUSTER glaze was meant to resemble copper, silver, or gold. The term *luster* includes any piece with some luster trim. It has been used since the sixteenth century. Some of the luster found today was made during the nineteenth century. The metallic glazes are applied on pottery. The finished color depends on the combination of the clay color and the glaze. Blue, orange, gold, and pearlized luster decorations were used by Japanese and German firms in the early 1900s. Tea Leaf pieces have their own category.

Blue, Sugar, Art Deco Style, Black & White Geometric Circle, Bavaria, 1930s, 3½ x 4 In.	17.00
Copper, Button, Plastic, Bow, 1⅛ In.	8.00
Copper, Cup & Saucer, Blue Decoration, Vines, 3 x 6¼ In., 8 Piece	374.00
Copper, Jug, 7 x 4 In.	35.00
Copper, Jug, Painted, Flowers, Victorian	175.00
Copper, Pepper Pot, Green Ground, 4½ In.	13.00
Copper, Pepper Pot, Sanded Band Decoration, c.1880	110.00
Copper, Pitcher, Badminton Scene, Mother & Child On Chaise, Yellow Band, 5½ In. ...*illus*	55.00
Copper, Pitcher, Canary Band, 3 Panels, Lafayette, Cornwallis, Fruit, Black Transfer, 6 In.	316.00

Luster, Copper, Pitcher, Badminton Scene, Mother & Child On Chaise, Yellow Band, 5½ In. $55.00

Luster, Orange, Jug, Ship, Amemnon In Storm, Verse, Sailor's Toast In Stormy Sea, 5 In. $345.00

Lustres, Opal & Clear,
Gold Trim, 10 Cut Prisms,
Bohemian, 13 In., Pair
$1880.00

Lustres, Pink Cut To Clear,
Gilt Cathedral Top, Moorish Windows,
Drops, Bohemian, 10 In.
$382.00

Lustres, Pink Opaline,
Chalice Form, Gold Scrolls,
Scalloped Rim, 8 Prisms
$235.00

Copper, Pitcher, Lafayette & Cornwallis, c.1825, Pair	1062.00
Copper, Sugar & Creamer, Fuchsia, Yellow Roses, Leaves, Gold Trim, Late 1800s, 4 In.	125.00
Fairyland Luster is included in the Wedgwood category.	
Gold, Decanter, 1960s, 10¼ In.	15.00
Gold, Pitcher, 8½ In.	18.00
Gold, Vase, Floral, Green Handles, Leaves, Blue, Yellow, 6¾ x 4¾ In.	35.00
Green Mottled, Vase, Oriental Style, Flowers, Royal Bradwell, Arthur Wood, 7⅝ In.	55.00
Orange, Jug, Ship, Amemnon In Storm, Verse, Sailor's Toast In Stormy Sea, 5 In. *....illus*	345.00
Peach, Cup & Saucer Set, Demitasse, Women, Child In Garden, Japan, 10 Piece	35.00
Peach, Rice Bowl, Black Trim, Footed, Japan	9.00
Peach, Shaker, Blue Top, Black Outline, 2¼ In., Pair	19.00
Pearl, Berry Set, Pink, Yellow Roses, Daisies, Blue Shading, Bavaria, 9 x 5½ In., 6 Piece	99.00
Pearl, Cup & Saucer, Painted, Flower Garlands, D&B Germany	15.00
Pearl, Eggcup, Blue Luster Foot, 2⅝ x 2 In., Pair	10.00
Pearl, Salt & Pepper, Conch Shell, Corks, Japan Stamp, 1950s	12.00
Pearl, Saucer, Black Band, Bavaria, 1900s, 5¾ In., Pair	22.00
Pearl, Vase, Milk Glass, White Pines, Cones	35.00
Pink, Cup & Saucer, Flowers, Leaves, Early 19th Century	75.00
Pink, Cup & Saucer, Handleless	85.00
Pink, Dish, Cover, Iridescent, c.1923, 5 In.	50.00
Pink, Goblet, Milk Glass, 5½ x 3 In.	20.00
Pink, Teapot, c.1820, 6 x 10 In.	234.00
Pink, Teapot, Deco, c.1925	100.00
Purple, Cup & Saucer, Art Nouveau, 2 & 2½ In.	38.00
Sunderland Luster pieces are in the Sunderland category.	
Tea Leaf luster pieces are listed in the Tea Leaf Ironstone category.	
White, Sugar & Creamer, 2⅜ In.	8.00
Yellow, Cup & Saucer, Pink Interior Flowers, 5½ x 3 In.	20.00

LUSTRE ART GLASS Company was founded in Long Island, New York, in 1920 by Conrad Vahlsing and Paul Frank. The company made lampshades and globes that are almost indistinguishable from those made by Quezal. Most of the shades made by the company were unmarked.

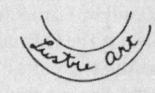

Vase, Gourd Shape, Amethyst Glass, Flowers, Carl Radke, Contemporary, 7 In.	106.00

LUSTRES are mantel decorations or pedestal vases with many hanging glass prisms. The name really refers to the prisms, and it is proper to refer to a single glass prism as a lustre. Either spelling, luster or lustre, is correct.

Blue, Ruffled Top, Prisms, Pair	425.00
Blue, Venetian, c.1880, 12 In., Pair	995.00
Clear, Engraved, Leaves, Deer, Castles, Floral Column, 10 Prisms, Bohemian, 12 In., Pair	1550.00
Cornflower Blue, Strawberry Motif, Pair	795.00
Cranberry, Baluster Base, Enameled, Flower Garlands, Prisms, 14 In., Pair	499.00
Cranberry, Enameled, 14½ x 7½ In., Pair	1995.00
Cranberry, Enameled, Gold Highlights, Late 19th Century, 14 x 7⅜ In., Pair	1275.00
Cranberry, Enameled, White Flowers, Gold, Blue, Scalloped Rim, Prisms, 14 In., Pair	540.00
Crystal, 22 Cut & Drop Prisms, Victorian, 18 In., Pair	118.00
Cut Glass, Drop Prisms, Continental, Late 19th Century, 13½ In., Pair	598.00
Green, Gold Trim, Victorian, Pair	1500.00
Opal & Clear, Gold Trim, 10 Cut Prisms, Bohemian, 13 In., Pair *................illus*	1880.00
Opaline, Triple Row Prisms, Ormolu Base, c.1890, 14 x 6¾ In.	315.00
Opaline Cased Glass, Cut To Amber, Painted Flowers, Bohemian, 14½ In., Pair	1200.00
Pink Cased Glass, Painted Flowers, Beads, Drumstick Prisms, Cut Finials, 14½ In., Pair	450.00
Pink Cut To Clear, Gilt Cathedral Top, Moorish Windows, Drops, Bohemian, 10 In. *...illus*	382.00
Pink Opaline, Chalice Form, Gold Scrolls, Scalloped Rim, 8 Prisms *..............illus*	235.00
Pink Overlay, Painted Gilt Flowers, Butterflies, Prisms, 7 In., Pair	1800.00
Ruby, Hand Painted, Floral Enamels, Cameo Medallions, 19th Century, Pair	700.00
Ruby Cut To Clear, Engraved Rose, Leaf Sprays, Back-Cut Albert Spear Pendants, 12¾ In.	660.00
Ruby Red Cut To Clear, Etched, Reindeer In Forest, Bohemian, Pair	245.00

LUTZ glass was made by Nicolas Lutz working at the Boston and Sandwich Glass Company from 1870 to 1888. He made delicate and intricate threaded glass of several colors. Other similar wares made by other makers are now known by the generic name Lutz.

Finger Bowl, Amber, Diamond Quilted, Threading, Crimped Rim, 5½ In.	58.00

MAASTRICHT, Holland, was the city where Petrus Regout established the De Sphinx pottery in 1836. The firm was noted for its transfer-printed earthenware. Many factories in Maastricht are still making ceramics.

Bowl, Oriental Scene, People, Blue & White, Marked, 3½ x 6 In.	95.00
Bowl, Vegetable, Blue Willow, c.1929, 8⅝ x 2 In.	25.00
Charger, Meat, Hindostan, Pagoda, Flow Blue, c.1860, 14½ In.	545.00
Plate, Couple At Table, Servant, Dog, Flowers, Leaves Border, Brown Transfer, 1800s, 7 In.	155.00
Plate, Dinner, Willow, Flow Blue, 9 In.	25.00
Plate, Grill, Gaudy Dutch, Rust, Cobalt Blue Flower Heads, Green, Magenta Leaves	45.00
Plate, Hindostan, Oriental Scene, Oval Cartouches, Flowers, Flow Blue, c.1860, 10 In.	275.00
Plate, Strawberries & Basket, 9½ In.	25.00
Plate, Timor Oriental Design, 8¼ In.	28.00

MACINTYRE, *see Moorcroft category.*

MAIZE glass was made by W. L. Libbey & Son Company of Toledo, Ohio, after 1889. The glass resembled an ear of corn. The leaves were usually green, but some pieces were made with blue or red leaves. The kernels of corn were light yellow, white, or light green.

Bowl, Green Leaves, Opalescent, 3¾ x 8 In.	150.00 to 295.00

MAJOLICA is a general term for any pottery glazed with an opaque tin enamel that conceals the color of the clay body. It has been made since the fourteenth century. Today's collector is most likely to find Victorian majolica. The heavy, colorful ware is rarely marked. Some famous makers include Minton; Griffen, Smith and Hill (marked *Etruscan*); and Chesapeake Pottery (marked *Avalon* or *Clifton*). Majolica made by Wedgwood is listed in the Wedgwood category.

Bank, Crying Baby, 4½ In.	150.00
Bowl, 2 Handles, Applied Rose, Petals, 4½ x 5 x 3½ In.	75.00
Bowl, Gnome, Lying On Back Holding Bowl, Painted, Late 19th Century, 6¾ In.	1957.00
Bowl, Leaves, Flowers, Green, Pink, Brown, 7½ In.	60.00
Bowl, Roses, Leaves, 10 x 8½ x 2 In.	145.00
Butter Pat, Leaves, Basket Weave, c.1920s, 3½ x 2¾ In.	135.00
Cachepot, Fern Fronds, Mottled Russet Ground, Lion's Head Handles, Palissy Ware, 8 x 8 In.	300.00
Cake Stand, Ivy Leaves, Brown Stem, Rustic Style, Etruscan, 19th Century, 9½ In.	205.00
Cake Stand, Picket Fence Pattern, Etruscan, 19th Century, 10 In.	235.00
Charger, Renaissance Style, c.1900, 20 In.	264.00
Clock, Elephant, 19th Century, 10 x 10⅝ x 4¼ In.	1250.00
Compote, Daisies, Pink Interior, Etruscan, 9 In. ....*illus*	382.00
Compote, Salad, Daisy, Gray Interior, Etruscan, 19th Century, 9 In.	147.00
Compote, Salad, Daisy, Pink Interior, Etruscan, 19th Century, 9 In.	382.00
Creamer, Flower, Blue Band, Square, c.1870, 4¼ In.	35.00
Dish, Cabbage Leaf, Crescent, 7½ x 4¾ x 1 In.	50.00
Dish, Leaf Shape, Green, Gold, Brown, 6½ x 6¼ In.	45.00
Dish Set, Leaf Shape, 7¾ To 8½ In., 6 Piece	575.00
Drainer, Asparagus, Cover, Cylinder Shape, c.1880	2150.00
Ewer, Wm. Schiller & Son., Germany, c.1870, 18¼ In.	350.00
Figurine, 18th Century Man & Woman, Painted, Raised Design, Italy, 16 x 6 In., Pair	351.00
Figurine, Alligator, Late 19th Century, 7 x 16 In.	351.00
Figurine, Blackamoor, Standing, France, c.1850, 58 x 12 In.	4388.00
Figurine, Child Standing Behind Sleigh, 6 x 6 In.	175.00
Figurine, Courtship, Man, Woman, 18th Century Dress, Italy, 10 x 5½ In., Pair	59.00
Figurine, Skater, c.1850, 7 In.	146.00
Humidor, Figural, Cigar Smoker, 6 In.	175.00
Humidor, Figural, Indian Chief, 8 In.	120.00
Humidor, Figural, Jockey, 5 In.	200.00
Humidor, Figural, Pipe Smoker, 5¾ In.	175.00
Humidor, Figural, Woman's Head, Art Nouveau, 7¼ In.	250.00
Humidor, Happy Hooligan Top, Lying Down, Foxy Grandpa, Front, c.1910, 8 x 7 x 5 In.	626.00
Jar, Druggist's, Flat-Sided, A. Di Luppoli, Hunter, Dog, Fox, Ribbon Handles, c.1705, 14 In.	480.00
Jardiniere, Pedestal, Blue Ground, White Flowers, Austria, 19½ x 6½ In.	176.00
Jardiniere, Red, Flower, Blue Interior, Continental, c.1880, 14½ In.	572.00
Jardiniere, Stand, Landscape, Mermaid, Scroll Leaf, Blue, Brown, Green, 40 x 17 In.	2520.00
Jug, Figural, Pig, 7¾ In.	74.00
Pedestal, Blue, Green, Black & Gold Glaze, Square, Tapered, Stepped Base, 45 In. .....*illus*	1265.00

Majolica, Compote, Daisies, Pink Interior, Etruscan, 9 In. $382.00

Majolica, Pedestal, Blue, Green, Black & Gold Glaze, Square, Tapered, Stepped Base, 45 In. $1265.00

Majolica, Pedestal, Ostrich, Brown, White Plumage, Naturalistic Ground, 26 In., Pair $2400.00

Majolica, Planter, Putti At Ends As Handles, Footed, 15½ x 20½ x 13 In. $518.00

Map, Africa, Woodcut, Animals, Sebastian, Frame, Munster, Germany, c.1550, 18½ x 22 In.
$896.00

Map, Globe, Kittinger, Bronzed Iron Frame, Mahogany Federal Style Stand, 36 In.
$805.00

Map, Republic Of Texas, Thomas G. Bradford, Weeks, Jordan & Co., 1838, 13 x 16¼ In.
$956.00

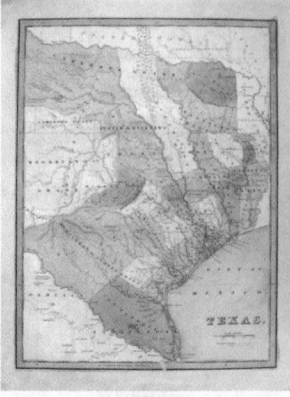

Pedestal, Blue, Green, Black Gold, 4-Sided Top, Stepped Base, Tapered Post, 46 x 11 In.	1265.00
Pedestal, Ostrich, Brown, White Plumage, Naturalistic Ground, 26 In., Pair ....*illus*	2400.00
Pitcher, Berries, Vines, Petal Base, 8 In.	173.00
Pitcher, Bird In Hand, c.1850, 7 In.	117.00
Pitcher, Corn, Figural, 9½ In.	455.00
Pitcher, Milk, Tree Trunk Spout, Leaves, Fruit, Branch Handle, 7 x 5¾ In.	40.00
Pitcher, Parrot, Figural, Incised, Stamped, 13 In.	425.00
Pitcher, Pig, Seated, Dressed As Waiter, Figural, 19th Century, 10 In.	176.00
Pitcher, Raised Leaves, Flowers, France, c.1900, 7½ In.	176.00
Pitcher, Rooster, Figural, Signed, USSR, 11¼ In.	495.00
Pitcher, Rooster, Inscribed Chante Clair Pour La France, Onnaing, 1900s, 9 In.	235.00
Planter, Figural, Wild Mallard Duck, 7½ x 12½ In.	150.00
Planter, Putti At Ends As Handles, Footed, 15½ x 20½ x 13 In. ....*illus*	518.00
Plate, Asparagus, Artichoke, c.1930, 9 In.	252.00
Plate, Crawfish, Palissy, 10 In.	375.00
Plate, Fruit, Basket Weave, 9 In.	125.00
Platter, Brown Cattails, White Lotus Blossoms, Lily Pads, 15 x 24 In.	6000.00
Server, Asparagus, Artichoke, Blue, Green, 14 x 11 In.	924.00
Teapot, Paneled, Chinese Man, Birds, 6 In.	3330.00
Tile, Dwarfs Working In Blacksmith Shop, Frame, Germany, c.1890, 10 x 16 In.	222.00
Tray, Water Lilies, Butterfly Handle, c.1874, 11 In.	4700.00
Urn, Handles, England, c.1900, 12 In., Pair	234.00
Vase, Moor Child Holding Plate, Tulip Shape, 11½ In.	250.00
Vase, Relief, Alligators, Frogs, Seashells, Palissy, 19th Century, 10 In., Pair	2160.00
Wall Pocket, Bird, Brown, Multicolored Glazes, 6¾ In.	38.00

MALACHITE is a green stone with unusual layers or rings of darker green shades. It is often polished and used for decorative objects. Most malachite comes from Siberia or Australia.

Figurine, Horse, Chinese, 20th Century, 7 In.	325.00
Figurine, Lion, Russia, c.1900, 4¼ x 9½ In.	354.00
Figurine, Quan Yin Holding Basket & Bird, Carved, 6 In.	92.00
Vase, 3 Couples In Various Poses, Grape Vines, Greek Mythology, Desna, 8¾ In.	300.00

MAPS of all types have been collected for centuries. The earliest known printed maps were made in 1478. The first printed street map showed London in 1559. The first road maps for use by drivers of automobiles were made in 1901. Collectors buy maps that were pages of old books, as well as the multifolded road maps popular in this century.

Africa, Woodcut, Animals, Sebastian, Frame, Munster, Germany, c.1550, 18½ x 22 In. ..*illus*	896.00
Battle Of Guilford, British, American Positions, Stedman, Engraved, Jan., 1794, 8 x 7½ In. . .	1495.00
Boston, Pocket, 35 Landmarks & Lighthouses, Ferry & Ship Routes, Color, 1910	364.00
California, Nevada, Fold-Out, Crowell & Kirkpatrick Co, Springfield, 1901, 13½ x 22 In.	35.00
Canada, Lower Province, Samuel Holland, London, James Wyld, c.1842, 22½ x 34½ In.	435.00
Canada, Ou De La Nouvelle France, Guillaume Delisle, 1730, 19¼ x 22¾ In.	905.00
Carolinas & Georgia, Copper Engraving, Emanuel Bown, c.1747, 16 x 19 In.	3450.00
Globe, Iron Legs, Label, Atlas School Supply Co., Chicago, c.1875, 22 In.	995.00
Globe, Kittinger, Bronzed Iron Frame, Mahogany Federal Style Stand, 36 In. ....*illus*	805.00
Globe, Terrestrial, 12 Colored Gores, Plaster Sphere, Stand, Rand McNally, 12 In., 35 In.	206.00
Globe, Terrestrial, Schedler's, Brass Polar, Meridian Ring, Iron Base, 14½ In.	588.00
Harrisburg, Land Survey, Tract Draft, East Hannover Township, Penn., c.1829, 7 x 7½ In.	264.00
Louisiana, Red River, Nicholas King, 1806	34720.00
New Orleans, Le Vieux Carre, Lucile Gillican, Louis Andrews, c.1929, 15 x 21½ In.	264.00
New York, Survey, Lithograph, Charles Magnus, c.1850, 18½ x 23 In.	885.00
North America, Mid Atlantic, Hand Colored, c.1780, 9¾ x 14 In.	944.00
North Hampshire, Hand Colored, Engraved, Willem Blaue, 1600s, 19¾ x 16¼ In.	708.00
Nova Scotia, Louisbourg, Jacques Nicolas Bellin, Paris, 1744, 8 x 11 In.	261.00
Ohio, Ohio River Bridge, Waterfront, Industrial, Business, T.R. Davis, 1872, 20 x 13 In.	200.00
Philippine Islands, Fold Out, Peerless 20th Century Pictorial Gazette, 1906, 22 x 14 In.	43.00
Republic Of Texas, Thomas G. Bradford, Weeks, Jordan & Co., 1838, 13 x 16¼ In. ....*illus*	956.00
Rhode Island, Engraved, Hand Colored, Daniel Friedrich Sotzmann, 29½ x 21¼ In.	2938.00
Rhode Island, Harding Harris, Cary's American Atlas 1796, 14 x 10 In.	705.00
United States, According To Treaty Of Peace 1783, A. Anderson, Frame, c.1796, 16 x 19 In.	1553.00
United States, Western, Indian Tribes, Mission, Forts, T. Kelly, 1925, 9 x 7 In.	200.00
United States Of America, British Possessions, Laurie & Whittle, 1794, 21 x 19 In.	146.00
Western Hemisphere, 16th Century New World, Sebastian Munster, 1552	7280.00

M

MARBLE collectors pay highest prices for glass and sulphide marbles. The game of marbles has been popular since the days of the ancient Romans. American children were able to buy marbles by the mid-eighteenth century. Dutch glazed clay marbles were least expensive. Glazed pottery marbles, attributed to the Bennington potteries in Vermont, were of a better quality. Marbles made of pink marble were also available by the 1830s. Glass marbles seem to have been made later. By 1880, Samuel C. Dyke of South Akron, Ohio, was making clay marbles and The National Onyx Marble Company was making marbles of onyx. The Navarre Glass Marble Company of Navarre, Ohio, and M. B. Mishler of Ravenna, Ohio, made the glass marbles. Ohio remained the center of the marble industry, and the Akron-made Akro Agate brand became nationally known. Other pieces made by Akro Agate are listed in this book in the Akro Agate category. Sulphides are glass marbles with frosted white figures in the center.

Advertising, Peltier Cotes Master Loaf, White, Green, $^{11}/_{16}$ In.		616.00
Agate, Flame, Green Base, Red, Yellow, $^{11}/_{16}$ In.		112.00
Agate, Pink, $2^5/_{16}$ In.		157.00
Agate, Sand Layer, Green, Yellow, Orange, Christensen, $^{21}/_{32}$ In.		140.00
Cloud, Multicolored Spots, Pontil, $1^{13}/_{16}$ In.		448.00
Clover Pattern, Banded, Opaque, Green Base, Orange, Red, White, $^{21}/_{32}$ In.		252.00
Latticinio, Core Swirl, 4 Stage, Red, Blue, Green, Yellow, $1^3/_4$ In. *illus*		106.00
Latticinio, Outer Swirl, Red, White & Blue, $2^5/_{16}$ In.		411.00
Latticinio, White Core, Multicolored Outer Bands, $1^{11}/_{16}$ In.		134.00
Latticinio, Yellow Core, Multicolored Outer Bands, $1^{11}/_{16}$ In.		123.00
Lutz, Black Opaque, Green Bands, 2 Pontils, $^3/_4$ In.		252.00
Lutz, Lavender, Green, $^3/_4$ In.		382.00
Lutz, Milk Opaque, Blue Bands, $^3/_4$ In.		392.00
Onionskin, 4 Panel, Blue & White, Yellow & Red, $1^5/_8$ In.		308.00
Onionskin, Cloud, Red, White, Blue, Pontil, $1^{15}/_{16}$ In.		840.00
Onionskin, Green, Pink, Blue, Yellow, $1^3/_4$ In.		258.00
Onionskin, Lutz, Black, $^3/_4$ In.		336.00
Onionskin, Lutz, Green, $^7/_8$ In.		448.00
Onionskin, Lutz, Multicolored, $^{11}/_{16}$ In.		195.00
Onionskin, Mica, 4 Lobes & Panels, Multicolored, $1^7/_8$ In.		560.00
Onionskin, Mica, 4 Panels, Multicolored, $1^{11}/_{16}$ In.		672.00
Onionskin, Mica, Red, White, Blue, $1^{11}/_{16}$ In.		728.00
Onionskin, Mottled Orange & Black, Yellow Base, 2 Pontils, $^{13}/_{16}$ In.		140.00
Onionskin, Multicolored, Straw Marks, $1^{37}/_{64}$ In.		140.00
Onionskin, Orange Swirl, Mica Flecks *illus*		294.00
Onionskin, Red, White, Blue, $1^{23}/_{64}$ In.		224.00
Onionskin, Red, White, Blue, Pink, $1^5/_8$ In.		448.00
Onionskin, Red, White, Blue, Pink, 2 Pontils, $1^3/_4$ In.		224.00
Onionskin, Red, White, Pink, Green, $1^3/_4$ In.		280.00
Onionskin, Red, Yellow, Green, $1^9/_{16}$ In.		235.00
Opaque, Clambroth, Pink & Green, $1^9/_{32}$ In.		308.00
Razor, Naked, Ribbon Swirl, Red, White, Blue, Green, $1^1/_{16}$ In.		840.00
Sailboat Scene, Hand Painted, China, $1^3/_{16}$ In.		784.00
Slag, Amber, Double Pontil, $^{15}/_{16}$ In. *illus*		168.00
Solid Core, Black & Yellow Core, Blue & White Outer Bands, $1^{11}/_{16}$ In.		134.00
Sulphide, 1 Cent Coin, Flying Eagle, Air Bubble At Top, 1958, $1^{19}/_{64}$ In.		448.00
Sulphide, Bear, Sitting, Straw Marks, $1^3/_4$ In.		28.00
Sulphide, Bird On Stump, $2^3/_{32}$ In.		56.00
Sulphide, Boy Playing With Sailboat, $1^3/_4$ In.		84.00
Sulphide, Cat, Sitting, $1^{31}/_{32}$ In.		56.00
Sulphide, Clear, Girl Sitting, Reading Book, 1 In.		260.00
Sulphide, Clear, White Love Birds Center, $1^7/_8$ In.		355.00
Sulphide, Dog, Setter, Air Bubbles, $2^{29}/_{64}$ In.		252.00
Sulphide, Eagle, Sitting, $2^3/_{32}$ In.		168.00
Sulphide, Falcon, On Stump, $1^5/_8$ In.		235.00
Sulphide, Girl, Sitting, With Doll, $1^5/_8$ In.		112.00
Sulphide, Girl, Standing, In Dress, Straw Marks, $1^1/_2$ In.		84.00
Sulphide, Horse, Pink Amethystine, $1^{11}/_{16}$ In.		235.00
Sulphide, Man Playing Guitar, $1^{15}/_{32}$ In.		112.00
Sulphide, Owl, On Pedestal, $2^3/_8$ In.		476.00
Sulphide, Razorback Boar, 1860-80, $2^1/_4$ In.		112.00
Sulphide, Shilling Coin, $1^{25}/_{64}$ In.		616.00
Sulphide, Squirrel, Holding Nut, $2^{29}/_{64}$		224.00

Glass Marbles
Venetian swirl glass marbles, clear glass with ribbons of colored glass, and End-of-Day glass marbles, with flecks of colored glass, are popular with collectors. An Indian swirl marble sold for $7,700 in 1995. Sulphides, marbles with frosted white figures of animals, flowers, or faces inside, are expensive. A double sulphide marble picturing both a lion and a dog sold in 1987 for $4,200.

M

Marble, Latticinio, Core Swirl, 4 Stage, Red, Blue, Green, Yellow, $1^3/_4$ In. $106.00

Marble, Onionskin, Orange Swirl, Mica Flecks $294.00

Marble, Slag, Amber, Double Pontil, $^{15}/_{16}$ In. $168.00

Marble Carving, Pedestal,
Nude Man, Woman, Astride Dolphin,
Wave, Holding Shell,
Tan, 40 In., Pair
$7768.00

Marblehead, Tile,
Ship, Blue Matte, Cream,
Early 20th Century, 4½ In.
$353.00

Marblehead, Vase,
Dark Blue Matte Glaze,
Flared, 5½ In.
$374.00

Swirl, White Core, Red, Green & Blue Middle Band, Yellow Outer Band, Pontils, 2 In.	252.00
Swirl, White Core, Red, Pink, Green Bands, Yellow Outside Layer, 1³⁷⁄₆₄ In.	196.00
Swirl, Yellow & White Core, Red & Green Middle Bands, White Outer Bands, 1⅞ In.	252.00
White Outer Bands, Divided Core, Multicolor Core, 1¹¹⁄₁₆ In.	235.00

MARBLE CARVINGS, such as large or small figurines, groups of people or animals, and architectural decorations, have been a special art form since the time of the ancient Greeks. Reproductions, especially of large Victorian groups, are being made of a mixture using marble dust. These are very difficult to detect and collectors should be careful. Other carvings are listed under Alabaster.

Bust, Benjamin Franklin, Black Stand, American School, Early 1800s, 14 x 8 In.	4560.00
Bust, Directoire Lady Of Fashion, White, Ribboned Hat, Lace Mantle, 17½ In.	1140.00
Bust, Girl, Lace Bonnet, Bead Necklace, Signed, F.G. Villa Milano, 1886, 18 In.	529.00
Bust, Girl Wearing Hat, Necklace, 15 In.	207.00
Bust, Girl Weeping, Dead Bird In One Hand, c.1880, 14 In.	2900.00
Bust, Man, 19th Century, 14 In.	588.00
Bust, Nefertiti, Inlaid, Multicolored, Mid 20th Century, 26½ x 13 In.	1528.00
Bust, Statesman Portrait, White, Signed, Pietro Costa, Florence, c.1861, 18½ In.	1062.00
Bust, Woman, Empire Dress, After J.P. Chinard, Signed, France, 1800s, 25 x 13 In.	1645.00
Medallion, Micro Mosaic, Inlaid, Roman Ruins, Scagliola Decoration, 1800s, 18 In.	3700.00
Obelisk, Decorative, 20th Century, 11 In., Pair	177.00
Obelisk, Noir Cihique, Polished, White Figuring, Louis XVI Style, 28 In., Pair	210.00
Pedestal, Blue, Column Shape, Square Top & Base, Louis XVI Style, 39 x 12 In.	660.00
Pedestal, Cove Molded Pediment, Inset Panels, Trailing Ivy, 1800s, 54 x 12 In.	1763.00
Pedestal, Green, 4-Sided Top, Column, Brass Inlay, Stepped Base, 40 x 11 In., Pair	2300.00
Pedestal, Nude Man, Woman, Astride Dolphin, Wave, Holding Shell, Tan, 40 In., Pair *illus*	7768.00
Pedestal, Ring Turned, Stepped Round Base, 9 x 32 In.	1035.00
Pedestal, Square Top, 20th Century, 39 In.	353.00
Pedestal, White, Brown, Carved Twist, 35½ x 14 In.	382.00
Plaque, Carrara, Allegorical, Night, Angel, Infant, Cased, Iron Roundel, 34 x 30 In.	2937.00
Ruin, Temple Of Castor & Pollux, Grand Tour, Corinthian Columns, Italy, 14 In.	1680.00
Statue, Cherub Hunter, Holding Rabbit, Winged, Pedestal, 19th Century, 40¼ In.	3290.00
Statue, Child, With Fruit Basket, European School, 20th Century, 30 In.	585.00
Statue, Cupid & Psyche, Antonio Canova, 19th Century, 23 x 25 In.	4465.00
Statue, Cupid & Psyche, Carrara, After Antonio Canova, Mid 1800s, 10 x 17 In.	235.00
Statue, Female, Standing At Well, Neoclassical, Early 20th Century, 20 x 13 In.	240.00
Statue, Foo Dog, White, Lambrequin Draped, Ribbed Pedestal, 28 x 10 In., Pair	960.00
Statue, Girl, Flowing Hair, White, Continental School, 20th Century, 15 In.	201.00
Statue, La Muse D'Andre Chenier, Denys Puech, 21 x 15 x 15 In.	5603.00
Statue, Panther, Crouching Concrete Base, Continental School, 1900s, 22 x 45 In.	920.00
Statue, Roman Male Athlete, Nude, Italian Carrara, 21¼ In.	176.00
Statue, Terpsichore, Carved, Seated Nude, Lyre, Klismos Chair, Florentine, 14 In.	1440.00
Statue, Venus At Her Bath, Carrara, Bois Peinte Pedestal, Italy, 71 x 13 In.	5288.00
Statue, Venus With Cupid At Her Toilette, Signed, P. Barranti, Italy, 1800s, 30 In.	1652.00
Urn, Classical Style, Variegated, Bronze Mounted, Gilt Bronze Finials, 21 x 11 In.	940.00
Urn, Empire, Black, Cassolette Shape, Bronze Dore, France, c.1870, 18 x 10 In.	600.00
Well Head, Octagonal, Stepped Base, Iron Arch Frame, Pulley, 1800s, 104 x 35 In.	8050.00

MARBLEHEAD Pottery was founded in 1905 by Dr. J. Hall as a rehabilitative program for the patients of a Marblehead, Massachusetts, sanitarium. Two years later it was separated from the sanitarium and it continued operations until 1936. Many of the pieces were decorated with marine motifs.

Bowl, Flower Holder, Blue Matte Glaze, 3½ In.	219.00
Bowl, Green Stippled Glaze, Brown Sea Leaf Border, 3 x 8½ In.	1998.00
Bowl, Lotus, Raised Leaves, Blue Glaze, Maroon Underglaze, c.1909, 4 In.	205.00
Chamberstick, Green Glaze, 3 Loop Handles, c.1907, 5 In.	265.00
Tile, Flower Bouquet, Wax Resist, Blue & Green Matte Glaze, 6 x 6 In.	600.00
Tile, Ship, Tan, On Yellow Ground, Frame, 10 In.	1400.00
Tile, Ship, Blue Matte, Cream, Early 20th Century, 4½ In. *illus*	353.00
Tile, Ship On Calm Water, Gray Matte Glaze, Blue Ground, 5 x 5 In.	1290.00
Vase, Black Crouching Panthers, Green Stylized Trees, Hannah Tutt, 7 x 5 In.	33600.00
Vase, Blue, Gray, Ocher, Grapevines, Bulbous, Marked, 1912, 3½ In.	3055.00
Vase, Blue Gray Glaze, Swollen Cylindrical Form, Impressed Cipher, 5 In.	264.00
Vase, Blue Matte Glaze, Swollen Shape, 3 In.	219.00
Vase, Blue Matte Glaze, Tapered, Impressed Ship Logo, c.1910, 5¹¹⁄₁₆ In.	550.00

Vase, Blue Stippled Body, Trees, Green Leaves, Red Berries, Blue Stem, 7 In. 3525.00
Vase, Blueberries, Green Leaves, Brown Stalks, Light Brown Ground, Marked, 5 In. 3390.00
Vase, Branches, Yellow Fruit, Green Leaves, Gray Ground, Hannah Tutt, 6¾ x 5 In. 7800.00
Vase, Bulbous, Incised, Painted, Indigo Decoration, Green Ground, 4 x 4¼ In. 2640.00
Vase, Butterflies, Blooms, Multicolored, Mustard Matte Ground, Barrel, 4½ x 4 In. 5100.00
Vase, Caramel, 7 Tree Trunks, Blue Green Leaves, c.1904, 4¼ In. 4113.00
Vase, Carnation Stylized, Tear Shape, Black, Dark Green Ground, 4½ x 3½ In. 3900.00
Vase, Dark Blue Matte Glaze, Flared, 5½ In. ....*illus* 374.00
Vase, Flowers Stylized, Brown, Indigo, Green Ground, Hannah Tutt, 5¼ x 6½ In. 3900.00
Vase, Melon Shape, Incised, Vines, Blue, Brown, Gray Ground, 9½ x 6½ In. 6000.00
Vase, Oatmeal Colored, Swollen Shape, Marked, 1908, 3¾ In. 330.00
Vase, Oval, Incised, Painted, Stylized Leaves, Brown, Green Ground, 5¼ x 3½ In. 1560.00
Vase, Pinched Waist, Geometric, Brown Squares, Indigo Stems, Green Ground, 8 x 4 In. 7200.00
Vase, Salmon Matte Glaze, Impressed, 7 In. 345.00
Vase, Stylized Geometric Tree, Dark Green, Indigo Ground, Cylindrical, 6 x 3¼ In. 4200.00
Vase, Tree, Stylized, Semi-Transparent Blue Glaze, Red Fruit, Hannah Tutt, c.1912, 7 In. 1645.00
Vase, Wide Mouth, Tapered Shape, Gray Stippled Glaze, 4⅜ In. 264.00

MARTIN BROTHERS of Middlesex, England, made Martinware, a salt-glazed stoneware, between 1873 and 1915. Many figural jugs and vases were made by the three brothers. Of special interest are the fanciful birds, usually made with removable heads. Most pieces have the incised name of the artists plus other information on the bottom.

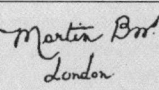

Figurine, Prehistoric Creature, Brown Mottled Glaze, Blue, Cream Glaze, Signed, 4½ In. *illus* 3738.00
Jar, Cover, Bird, Enamel, Ebonized Wood Base, Signed, 1888, 10¼ In. 11163.00
Jar, Cover, Bird, White Breast, Enamel, Mahogany Base, Signed, c.1900, 10 In. 7050.00
Jar, Cover, Enamel Decorated, Ebonized Wood Base, 1888, 10¼ In. 11163.00
Jardiniere, Scenic, Storks, Signed, c.1892, 9½ In. 5581.00
Jardiniere, Stork Scene, Vegetation, Signed, c.1892, 9½ In. Diam. 5581.00
Jug, Face, Signed, c.1898, 7¾ In. 10575.00
Jug, Fish, Globular Shape, 1886, 8¼ In. 5581.00
Jug, Fish, Vegetation, Globular, 1886, 8¼ In. 5581.00
Jug, Fish, Vegetation, Welcome Friends, Drinke With Noble Hearte, Signed, 1887, 15 In. 12925.00
Jug, Incised Fish, Welcome My Friends, Signed, 1887, 15¼ In. 12925.00
Jug, Smiling Face, Signed, c.1898, 7¾ In. 10575.00
Tobacco Jar, Bird Grotesque, Brown & Beige, Wooden Base, Signed, 11 In. ....*illus* 34500.00
Vase, Birds, Leaves, Blue, Brown, Tan Ground, London & Southall, Signed, 10 In. 1480.00
Vase, Orchids, Hummingbirds, Dragonflies, London & Southall, Signed, 1898, 10 In......... 3800.00
Vase, Sea Creatures, Brown, Tan Ground, London & Southall, Signed, 1907, 3 In. 1280.00

MARY GREGORY is the name used for a type of glass that is easily identified. White figures were painted on clear or colored glass as the decoration. The figures chosen were usually children at play. The first glass known as Mary Gregory was made about 1870. Similar glass is made even today. The traditional story has been that the glass was made at the Sandwich Glass works in Boston by a woman named Mary Gregory. Recent research suggests that it is possible that none was made at Sandwich. In general, all-white figures were used in the United States, tinted faces were probably used in Bohemia, France, Italy, Germany, Switzerland, and England. Children standing, not playing, were pictured after the 1950s.

Basket, Boy, Offering Girl Flowers, Dark Blue, Satin, 6½ x 4½ In. 65.00
Basket, Girl, Bird Watching, Cranberry, 8½ In. 155.00
Basket, Girl, Walking With Umbrella, Clear, 9½ In. 140.00
Bell, Boy, Chasing Bird, Trees, Mountains, Cobalt Blue, Clear Clacker, 5½ In. 85.00
Bell, Girl, Fishing, Ruby 52.00
Bell, Girl, On Fence, Ruby, 5 In. 36.00
Beverage Set, Girl, Holding Bird, Cobalt Blue, Gold Rim, Pitcher, 6 Tumblers 495.00
Bottle, Barber, Children, Playing Tennis, Cobalt Blue, 8¼ In., Pair 660.00
Bottle, Barber, Girl, Holding Twig, Teal, Pontil, Rolled Lip, 8 In. 385.00
Bottle, Barber, Girl, Holding Twig, Yellow Green, Pontil, Rolled Lip, 8 In. 132.00
Bottle, Barber, Girl, Playing Tennis, Cobalt Blue, Rolled Lip, Pontil, 1885-1925, 8 In. ....*illus* 213.00
Bottle, Barber, Girl, Sitting, Purple Amethyst, Pontil, Rolled Lip, 8 In. 121.00
Bottle, Barber, Girl, Sitting, Yellow Green, Pontil, Rolled Lip, 7¾ In. 220.00
Bottle, Barber, Palm Tree, Green, Tooled Mouth, 8 In. 2200.00
Bottle, Cologne, Stopper, Marquis Shape, 8¾ In. 195.00
Candle Set, Girl, Trees, Cranberry, Scallops, 5 x 6½ In., 3 Piece 495.00

Martin Brothers, Figurine, Prehistoric Creature, Brown Mottled Glaze, Blue, Cream Glaze, Signed, 4½ In. $3738.00

Martin Brothers, Tobacco Jar, Bird Grotesque, Brown & Beige, Wooden Base, Signed, 11 In. $34500.00

Mary Gregory, Bottle, Barber, Girl, Playing Tennis, Cobalt Blue, Rolled Lip, Pontil, 1885-1925, 8 In. $213.00

Mary Gregory, Vase, Maiden, Cobalt Blue, Bulbous, Cylindrical Rim, Beaded, Footed, 10¾ In. $264.00

M

Mason's Ironstone, Tureen, Cover, Canton Style Blue Transfer Decoration, Handles, Footed, 8 x 12½ In. **$460.00**

M

Massier, Vase, Flowers, Scrolls, Blue, Green, Red, Globular, 10 In. **$388.00**

Massier, Vase, Morning Glories, Gold & Blue Iridescent Glaze, Tapered, 1900, 3¾ In. **$1380.00**

Cream Pitcher, Girl, Tree, Cranberry, c.1870, 3 In.	205.00
Cup, Girl, Boy, In Silhouette, Catching Butterflies, Blue, 5½ In., Pair	115.00
Dresser Box, Woman & Dog, Dark Amethyst, Silver Plated Holder, Meridan, 5½ In.	600.00
Hair Receiver, Boy, Holding Hat, Cranberry Glass, 4 In. Diam.	275.00
Jug, Boy, In Blossom Bower, Green, 8¼ In.	365.00
Lamp, Hurricane, Little Drummer Boy, Clear, 11 In.	225.00
Lamp, Peg, Amethyst, Baluster Stem, Etched Shade, c.1950, 20½ In., Pair	294.00
Lampshade, Boy, Offering Girl Flowers, Blue Mist, Satin Glass, Milk Glass Base, 7½ In.	55.00
Lustres, Cranberry, White, 10½ In., Pair	205.00
Pickle Castor, Clear, Silver Plate, 9¾ In.	1500.00
Pitcher, Child, Walking, Blown Glass, c.1870, 4¾ In.	105.00
Pitcher, Woman, Picking Flowers In Field, Green, 1800s, 11 In.	135.00
Pitcher Set, Elk, Ruffled Rim, Applied Handle, Clear, Tumblers, 9¼ In., 3 Piece	139.00
Plate, Boy, Skating With Puppy, Blue Mist, Wicket Border, 9¼ In.	65.00
Rose Bowl, Trees, Deer, Cranberry, 3½ x 4 In.	95.00
Teapot Warmer, Red	130.00
Trinket Box, Red, Victorian, 2¾ x 2¼ In.	65.00
Tumbler, Girl, Amber, Flesh Tone Features	76.00
Vase, Beachcomber, Cranberry, 8½ In.	169.00
Vase, Bird, Trees, Mountains, Cranberry, 9½ x 9 In.	625.00
Vase, Boy, Fishing, Blue Satin, 7 x 3⅛ x 4¾ In.	73.00
Vase, Boy, With Rake & Puppy, Black, 1981, 7 x 3⅛ In.	78.00
Vase, Bud, Castle Scene, Blue, Trumpet Shape, 5⅞ In.	50.00
Vase, Children, Emerald Green, Gold Bands, 8½ In., Pair	195.00
Vase, Courting Couple, Optic Ribbed, Cobalt Blue, Pair, 10 In.	71.00
Vase, Garden Time, Cranberry, 8½ In.	124.00
Vase, Girl, In Swing With Puppy, Dark Blue Mist, 1960s, 8 In.	48.00
Vase, Hurricane, Amethyst Glass, Wood Base, 11¼ In., Pair	853.00
Vase, Maiden, Cobalt Blue, Bulbous, Cylindrical Rim, Beaded, Footed, 10¾ In. *illus*	264.00
Vase, Ruffled Edge, Cobalt Blue, 6 x 4¼ In.	45.00
Vase, Tea Party, Cranberry, 10 In.	185.00
Vase, Woman, Wavy Rim, Blue Satin, 4½ x 6 In.	395.00
Water Set, Optic Ribbed, Amber, c.1900, 9-In. Pitcher, 6 Tumblers	294.00

MASONIC, *see Fraternal category.*

MASON'S IRONSTONE was made by the English pottery of Charles J. Mason after 1813. Mason, of Lane Delph, was given a patent for this improved earthenware. He usually called it Mason's Patent Ironstone China. It resisted chipping and breaking so it became popular for dinnerwares and other table service dishes. Vases and other decorative pieces were also made. The ironstone was decorated with orange, blue, gold, and other colors, often in Japanese inspired designs. The firm had financial difficulties but the molds and the name Mason were used by many owners through the years, including Francis Morley, Taylor Ashworth, George L. Ashworth, and John Shaw. Mason's joined the Wedgwood group in 1973 and the name is still found on dinnerwares.

Bowl, Vegetable, 3 Sections, Griffin Handle, Scalloped Edge	160.00
Dish, Shell Shape, c.1820, 10½ In., Pair	333.00
Jug, Flowers, Dark Blue, Orange, Green, Peach, Yellow, 19th Century, 7¾ In.	450.00
Nappy, Japanese Style, Scalloped Rim, Handle, Embossed Leaf, Swag, Footed, 1813, 8 x 9½ In.	275.00
Plate, Mandarin & Attendants In Garden, Multicolored, 9¼ In., Pair	54.00
Plate, Peacock, Cobalt Blue, Light Blue, Orange, Peach, Gold, 9½ In.	335.00
Plate, Table & Flowerpot, 1813, 8¾ In.	175.00
Platter, Bird, Orange, Yellow, Pink, Brown Enamel, 9 x 6¼ In.	495.00
Platter, Roasted Meats, Imari, Lotus Decoration, Oval Well & Tree, 22 x 16 In.	587.00
Platter, Transfer Flowers, Blue, Yellow, Orange, Green, 15 x 12 In.	160.00
Serving Bowl, Underplate, Colored Pheasants, Octagonal, 4½ x 8½ & 9¾ In.	245.00
Tureen, Cover, Canton Style Blue Transfer Decoration, Handles, Footed, 8 x 12½ In. *illus*	460.00
Tureen, Soup, Underplate, Handle, Flowers, Orange, Yellow, Blue, 12¼ x 9 x 9 In.	475.00

MASSIER, a French art pottery, was made by brothers Jerome, Delphin, and Clement Massier in Vallauris and Golfe-Juan, France, in the late nineteenth and early twentieth centuries. It has an iridescent metallic luster glaze that resembles the Weller Sicardo pottery glaze. Most pieces are marked *J. Massier*. Massier may also be listed in the Majolica category.

Vase, Flowers, Blue, Green, Yellow, Maroon Iridescent, Cone Shape, Cylindrical Neck, 7 In.	370.00
Vase, Flowers, Scrolls, Blue, Green, Red, Globular, 10 In. *illus*	388.00

Vase, Green, Blue & Brown High Drip Glaze, Bulbous Bottom, 2 Wing Handles, 6⅞ In.	403.00
Vase, Morning Glories, Gold & Blue Iridescent Glaze, Tapered, 1900, 3¾ In. . . . . *illus*	1380.00

MATCH HOLDERS were made to hold the large wooden matches that were used in the nineteenth and twentieth centuries for a variety of purposes. The kitchen stove and the fireplace or furnace had to be lit regularly. One type of match holder was made to hang on the wall, another was designed to be kept on a tabletop. Of special interest today are match holders that have advertisements as part of the design.

Alligator, Cast Iron, Marlay Craig & Co., 2 x 9 x 4 In.	85.00
Banner Buggies, Russell Gardner Image, Tin Lithograph, 4⅞ x 3⅜ x 1¼ In.	302.00
Bear Cub, Chained To Tree, Figural, Brass, Hinged Head, 3 x 2½ In.	150.00
Boot, Cast Metal, Match For You, None For Woonsocket, Woonsocket Rubber Co., 3 x 3 In. . .	160.00
Bull Dog Cut Plug, De Luxe, Straight Leaf Tobacco, Tin, 6¾ x 3¼ In. . . . . *illus*	385.00
Bull Dog Cut Plug, Straight Leaf, Won't Bite, T.J. Carroll Groceries, Tin, Die Cut, 7 x 3 In. . . .	475.00
Cannon, Desk Top, Cast Iron, 3½ x 3 In., 2 Piece	120.00
Cat Climbing Kettle, Handle Back Plate, Embossed Barn Side, Cast Iron, 7½ In.	248.00
Ceresota, Prize Bread Flour Of Minnesota, Boy, Chair, Tin Lithograph, 5 x 3 In. 400.00 to 468.00	
Ceresota Flour, Figural, Boy Sitting On Bench, Tin Lithograph, c.1900, 5½ In. . . . . *illus*	353.00
Cigar Holder, Fashion Lady, Composition, Metal Inserts, 9 x 6½ x 3 In.	80.00
Columbia Mill Co., Lady Columbia, Embossed, Die Cut, 5½ x 2¼ In.	500.00
Deco Lady, Figural, 2-Piece Casting, Cast Iron, 5¼ x 3 In.	66.00
DeLaval, Separator Shape, Die Cut, Tin Lithograph, Box, 6¼ x 4 In.	605.00
Devil's Head, Grape Leaf Back Plate, Cast Iron, Embossed, 6 In.	193.00
Dog, Begging Paw, In House, Cast Iron, A.M. Nachi, 7¼ In.	605.00
Double Urn, Fancy Back Plate, Cast Iron, Stevens, Pat. 1867, 6 In.	66.00
Dutch Boy Paints, Dutch Boy, Embossed, Die Cut, Tin Lithograph, 6 x 3½ In. . . . . 375.00 to 770.00	
Eagle, Embossed, Electroplated, Cast Iron, 2 Holders, Wall Hanger, 8¾ In.	523.00
Egyptian Design, Cast Iron, Brass Plated Metal, 5 x 4 x 3 In.	70.00
Elephant Shape, Brass, c.1900, 2¼ In.	120.00
Fehrs Malt Tonic, King Toasting Lady Liberty, Flag, Eagle, Bottle Shape, 6¼ x 2 In.	210.00
Flag Shape, Chew Banner Fine Cut, Leaf Holder, Cast Iron, 7¼ In.	385.00
Friscoline, Ring-Up, Hanging Telephone, Embossed, Cast Iron, 6½ In.	467.00
Girl In Blue Bonnet, Sitting On Log Knitting, Figural, Majolica, 7 x 6½ In.	125.00
Gloomy Gus, Ceramic, Striker On Back Of Hat, 4½ x 3½ In.	80.00
Gold Dust Washing Powder, Black Twins, Logo, Metal, 3 x 1⅝ In.	469.00
Holyoke Coal & Wood, Coal Bucket Holder, Embossed, Cast Iron, Back Plate, 5 In.	138.00
Hotel Bell, Brass, Lever Style, 6 x 4½ In.	220.00
House, Removable Roof, Painted, Cast Iron, Embossed, Match Safe, Pat. 1883, 4 In.	550.00
Indian Motorcycle, Brass	126.00
Juicy Fruit, The Man, Made Famous, Red, White, Blue, 5 x 3¼ x 1 In.	100.00
Kirkman's Borax Soap, For Laundry, Woman, Washboard, Tin Lithograph, 7 x 3½ In.	2350.00
Man, Black Nose & Eyes, Your Good Old Pal, Schafer & Vater, 3¼ In.	170.00
Man Hoisting Mug, Pipe, Metal, Desk Top, 6 x 5 x 4½ In.	220.00
Man In Top Hat, Suit, Tie, Big Mouth, Schafer & Vater, 4 In.	170.00
Milwaukee Harvesting Machines, Always Reliable, Light Draft, Farmer, Tin, 5 x 3 In.	235.00
Monk Face Bust, Throne Back Plate, Cast Iron, 7¼ In.	99.00
Mother's Worm Syrup, Good As Honey, Children Eat Bread, Tin Lithograph, 7 x 2 In.	425.00
Moxie, Learn To Drink Moxie, Tin, Die Cut, 7 x 2½ In.	450.00
Old Hickory Wagons, Wagon, Kentucky Wagon Mfg Co., 5 x 3¼ In.	800.00
Old Judson, J.C. Stevens, Man, Woman, Girl, 5 x 3¼ x 1 In.	105.00
Plant System Railroad, Striker, Union Porcelain Works, 2 In.	375.00
Poodle Holding Top Hat, Cast Metal, 4½ x 3 In.	80.00
Prim Rose Cigars, 5 Cents, Green, Black, Jacob Livingston & Co., 6 x 3 x 3 In.	77.00
Rex Flintkote Roofing, For All Roofs, Barn, Tin Lithograph, 5 x 3½ In.	230.00
Royal Gall Remedy, Surgical Treatment For Animals, Tin Lithograph, 6 x 3 x 3 In.	962.00
San Felice Cigars, For Gentlemen Of Good Taste, Hinged Lid, Metal, Insert, 3 x 2 In.	143.00
Sharples Cream Separator Co., Woman, Milk Pails, Cows, Tin, 2 x 6¾ In. . . . . *illus*	385.00
Shoe, Women's, Lace-Up, Metal, 3¾ x 5 In.	145.00
Shrine Shape, 2 Crotal Bells, 12 In.	35.00
Solarine Metal Polish, Wise Wives Work Wonders With Solarine, Tin, 4 x 5 In. . . . . . . *illus*	165.00
Star, Circle, Back Plate, Marked, Standard Clark Hardware, Detroit, Michigan, Cast Iron, 7 In.	66.00
Stoneware, Open Well, Blue Outline, Hinged Lid, Signed, W.A. Rodgers, 1877, 6 x 4 In.	2420.00
Strike, Funny Face, Open Mouth, Metal, 4 In.	295.00
Striker, Boy, Riding Frog, Majolica, 7¼ In.	60.00
Striker, Cowboy, Standing With Rifle, Figural, Majolica, 10 In.	400.00

Match Holder, Bull Dog Cut Plug, De Luxe, Straight Leaf Tobacco, Tin, 6¾ x 3¼ In.
$385.00

Match Holder, Ceresota Flour, Figural, Boy Sitting On Bench, Tin Lithograph, c.1900, 5½ In.
$353.00

M

Match Holder, Sharples Cream Separator Co., Woman, Milk Pails, Cows, Tin, 2 x 6¾ In.
$385.00

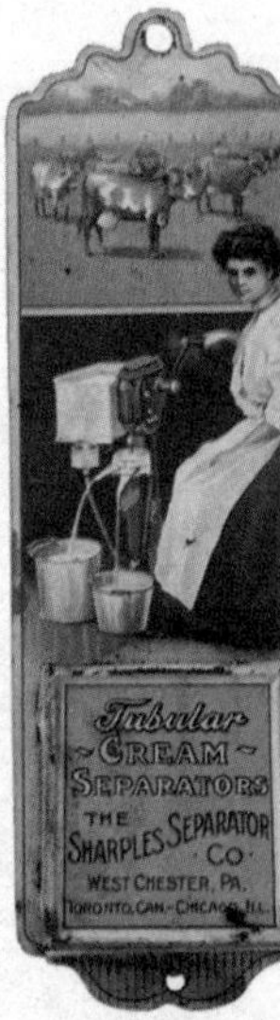

Match Holder, Solarine Metal Polish, Wise Wives Work Wonders With Solarine, Tin, 4 x 5 In.
$165.00

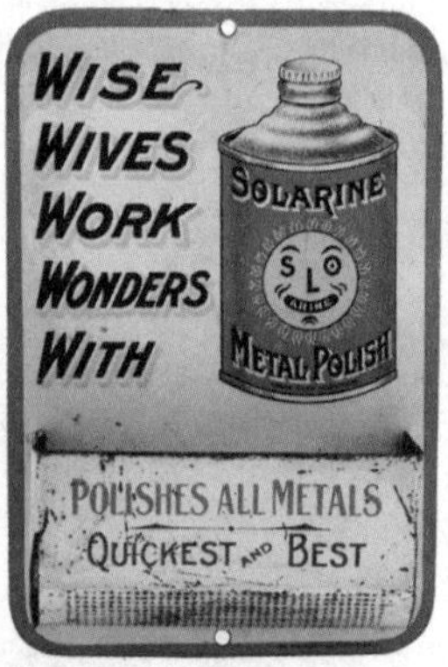

Match Safe, Mr. Punch, Cast Iron, Holding Feather Pen & Inkwell, Cast Iron, Zimmerman
$526.00

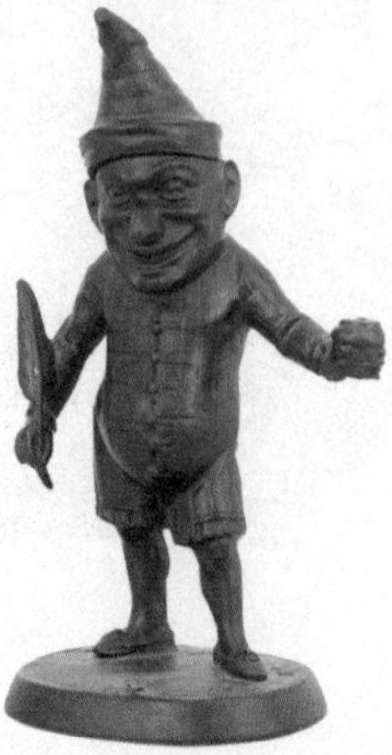

Striker, Gnome, Sitting Smoking Pipe, Figural, Majolica, 5½ x 6 In. 100.00
Striker, Monk, Holding Mug, Figural, Majolica, Full Body, 8 In. 200.00
Toad, Bronze, Brass Bucket Insert, 2 In. 110.00
Tubular Cream Separator, Cows, Woman Separating Cream, Girl, Tin Lithograph, 7 x 2 In. 350.00
Universal Stoves & Ranges, Best On Earth, Cribben & Sexton, 5 x 3¼ x 1¼ In. 120.00
Usher's O.V.G. Whisky, Edinburgh, Soldier, Spherical, Ceramic, 4 In. 120.00
Vulcan Plow Co., Die Cut, Tin Lithograph, 7⅞ x 2¾ In. 688.00
William Tell Flour, Makes Best Bread, Springfield, Ohio, 5 x 3¼ x 1¼ In. 300.00
Wilson & Co., Easton, Pennsylvania, Gold & Red Paint, Cast Iron, Wall Hanger, 6 In. 138.00
Wrigley Juicy Fruit, Man, Made Famous, Red, White, Black, Tin Lithograph, 4⅞ In. 138.00

MATCH SAFES were designed to be carried in the pocket. Early matches were made with phosphorus and could ignite unexpectedly. The matches were safely stored in the tightly closed container. Match safes were made in sterling silver, plated silver, or other metals. The English call these "vesta boxes."

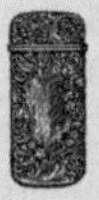

A.B.C. Tournament, Bowling Ball, Buffalo, N.Y., Celluloid, 1902, 2⅝ x 1½ In. 310.00
Agate, Banded, Bloodstone, Jasper, Gilt Mount, Diapered Motifs, 2 x ¾ x ⅝ In. 441.00
Anheuser-Busch, Silver, Purse Top, c.1900 .... 264.00
Arm & Hammer Soda, Church & Co., Gutta-Percha, 3 x 1¼ In. 350.00
Bicycle Riders, Man, Woman, Gutta-Percha, 1890s, 2 x 1½ In. 391.00
Bird, Hovering Over House, Nest Holder, Brass, 8 In. 110.00
Blatz Brewing Co., Silver, Milwaukee, Wisc. 133.00
Bowler Bros., Brewers, Fine Ales, Porter, Lager Beer, Worcester, Mass., Celluloid, c.1900 .... 240.00
Bowling, Art Nouveau, Silver, Late 1800s, 2½ x 1½ In. 310.00
Buffalo Brewing Co., Bohemian Beer, Celluloid, c.1900 .... 632.00
Buffalo Printing Ink Works, Buffalo Atop Ink Dauber, Celluloid 575.00
Cigar Box, Flowers, Scrolls, Enamel, Sterling Silver, Reeves & Sillcocks 1100.00
Conrad Eurich's Brewery, Sterling Silver, c.1900 .... 147.00
Dancing Lady, Purple Outfit, Green Legging, Enamel, Sterling Silver, 2⅝ x 1⅜ In. 590.00
Davenport Morris Chair, Langslow Fowler & Co., Celluloid 354.00
Fly Fishing, Silver, Early 1900s, 2¼ x 1¾ In. 504.00
Imperial Boilers, Utica Heater Co., Celluloid 522.00
Ironsides Company, Wire Rope, Celluloid 291.00
John Peterson, Bullfight, Celluloid 390.00
John Smith 5 Cent Cigar, Victorian Woman, Long Hair, Celluloid, c.1900 .... 632.00
King Albert High Grade Cigars, Celluloid, c.1900 .... 632.00
Look For The Union Label, Your Protection, Celluloid, c.1900 .... 632.00
Lotus Export, Adam Scheidt Brewing Co., Norristown, Pa., c.1900 .... 390.00
Miami Powder Co., Powder Keg, Red, White, Black, Celluloid, Metal, 2⅞ x 1⅕ In. 770.00
Mr. Punch, Cast Iron, Holding Feather Pen & Inkwell, Cast Iron, Zimmerman .... *illus* 526.00
National India Rubber Company, Nude Woman, Celluloid 474.00
Nude Woman, High Relief, Sterling Silver, 1⅜ x 2⅜ In. 138.00
O.C. Taylor, Golden Wedding, Smoke Our Hobby, Celluloid, c.1900 .... 632.00
Oak Bowling Alleys & Meeting Rooms, Silver, c.1895, 2¾ x 1½ In. 291.00
Owl Shape, Repousse, Hinged Lid, Japan, 2¾ In. 239.00
Potter's Shoes, J&M Shoe, Cincinnati, Celluloid 844.00
Relief Of Nude, Sterling Silver, 2⅜ x 1⅜ In. 137.00
Return Baltimore Rye, Thos. Carroll & Son, Celluloid 430.00
Round Oak Stoves, Ranges & Furnaces, Indian, Doe-Wah-Jack, Celluloid 430.00
Sauer's Flavoring Extract, Celluloid 696.00
Siesta, High Grade Nickel Cigar, Dietz & Mischler, Celluloid, c.1900 .... 928.00
Tadcaster Ale, Bowler Brothers, Worcester, Mass., Celluloid, c.1900 .... 240.00
Taylor Vs. Vardon, Sutton & Sons, Golf Course & Putting Greens, Celluloid, c.1900 .... 3450.00
United Brewery Workmen, Ask Your Support Against Prohibition, Celluloid, c.1917 .... 291.00
Vacuum Oil Co., Marine Engine Oil, Barrel, Celluloid Over Metal, 1⅜ x 2 x ⅜ In. 510.00
Voigt Brewery Co., Silver, Detroit, Mich. 217.00
Young Bros. Leaf Tobacco, Victorian Woman, Celluloid, c.1900 .... 474.00

McCOY pottery was made in Roseville, Ohio. Nelson McCoy and J.W. McCoy established the Nelson McCoy Sanitary and Stoneware Company in Roseville, Ohio, in 1910. The firm made art pottery after 1926. In 1933 it became the Nelson McCoy Pottery Company. Pieces marked *McCoy* were made by the Nelson McCoy Pottery Company. Cookie jars were made from about 1940 until December 1990, when the McCoy factory closed. Since 1991 pottery with the McCoy mark has been made by firms unrelated to the original company. Because there was a company named Brush-McCoy, there is great confusion between Brush and Nelson McCoy pieces. See Brush category for more information.

McCoy

Bank, Happy Face, 1970s, 4 In.	15.00
Bookends, Lily Bud, Aqua, 5¾ In.	115.00
Bookends, Lily Bud, White, 5¾ In.	65.00
Cookie Jar, Asparagus, 1977	30.00
Cookie Jar, Bananas, 1950-52	90.00
Cookie Jar, Barnums Animals, Nabisco Wagon, 1972, 11½ In.	168.00
Cookie Jar, Circus Horse, 1961	95.00
Cookie Jar, Clown, Bust, 10 In. *illus*	18.00
Cookie Jar, Coffee Grinder, 1961-68, 10 x 6½ In.	50.00
Cookie Jar, Cookie Bank, 1960s	75.00
Cookie Jar, Country Stove, Black, Marked, No. 236	65.00
Cookie Jar, Frontier Family, Late 1960s	15.00
Cookie Jar, Hamm's Bear, Brown, 1972, 12 In.	168.00
Cookie Jar, Keebler Elf Tree House, 1980s, 10 In.	15.00
Cookie Jar, World Globe, Airplane, 1960, 10 In.	400.00
Decanter, Apollo Astronaut, 12 In.	55.00
Decanter, Touring Car, 1932 Pierce-Arrow, 11 In.	30.00
Decanter, Train, McCormick, 1969, 4 Piece	100.00
Dish, Dog, Yellowgreen, Spaniel Feeder, 6 In.	70.00
Jar, Grease, Whale	75.00
Jardiniere, Butterfly, 7 In.	45.00
Jardiniere, Flowers, Green Matte Glaze, 8 x 6 In.	39.00
Mug, Nelson & Billie McCoy, 1981	35.00
Mug, Stoneware, Buccaneer, Raised Relief, 5 x 5 In.	35.00
Pitcher, Open Rose Design, Marked, Loy-Nel-Art, No.117, 8¼ In.	33.00
Planter, Apple, 1950, 6½ In.	85.00
Planter, Banana Boat, Calypso Line, 1950s, 11 In.	45.00
Planter, Bananas, 1950s, McCoy USA Mark, 6½ In.	115.00
Planter, Basketweave, Aqua, 1950s, 7½ In.	10.00
Planter, Basketweave, Yellow, 1950s, 7½ In.	20.00
Planter, Bird Dog, No Hunting, Marked, 1950s, 12½ x 8½ In.	116.00
Planter, Calypso Line, Barrel, Cold Paint, Late 1950s, 5 In.	55.00
Planter, Carriage With Umbrella, 1950, 9 In.	95.00
Planter, Cornucopia, Aqua, 1940s, 5 In.	40.00
Planter, Cornucopia, Yellow, 1940s, 5 In.	10.00
Planter, Flying Ducks, 10 In.	75.00
Planter, Frog With Umbrella, Mid 1950s, 7½ In.	60.00
Planter, Happy Snail, 1970, 10 In.	55.00
Planter, Lemon, 1950, 6½ In.	95.00
Planter, Liberty Bell, 10 In.	165.00
Planter, Old Mill, 7½ x 6½ In.	10.00
Planter, Orange, No Cold Paint, 1950s, 6½ In.	85.00
Planter, Pear, 1950s, 6½ In.	65.00
Planter, Pelican, Aqua, 1940, 7¾ In.	25.00
Planter, Pomegranate, 1950s, 6½ In.	195.00
Planter, Quail, Marked, 6⅞ x 8⅞ In.	28.00
Planter, Rabbit With Carrot, Cold Paint, 1950s, 7¼ In.	90.00
Planter, Scotties, 1950s, 9 In.	15.00
Planter, Zebra, 1950s, 8½ In.	625.00
Tankard, Pear Design, Loy-Nel-Art, 11½ In.	61.00
Tray, Art Deco Style, Light Blue High Glaze, Matte Orange, Gold Bottom, Footed, 3 x 9 In. *illus*	44.00
Vase, Aqua, Handles, 12 In.	85.00
Vase, Aqua, Ribbed, Handles, 9 In.	55.00
Vase, Aqua, Sand Dollar, 14 In.	85.00
Vase, Arrowhead, 1940s, 8 In.	65.00
Vase, Bird Of Paradise, Blue Green High Glaze, Handles, 8¼ x 6 In. *illus*	28.00
Vase, Blossomtime, Urn Form, 1940, 6½ In.	15.00
Vase, Blossomtime, Yellow, 1940s, 8 In.	20.00
Vase, Butterfly, Aqua, Handles, 10 In.	65.00
Vase, Chromeveil Design, Pink	35.00
Vase, Double Tulip, No. 74, 8 x 6¾ In. *illus*	45.00
Vase, Embossed Fish, Yellow, Handles, Large	50.00
Vase, Fan, Lime Green, Footed, 1940s, 6 In.	45.00
Vase, Fan, Oxblood Red, Footed, 1940s, 6 In. *illus*	16.00
Vase, Fawn, White & Maroon, 1954, 9 In.	45.00
Vase, Fish, Aqua, Dr. Seuss, Late 1930s-1940, 4¼ x 3¼ In.	55.00

McCoy, Cookie Jar, Clown, Bust, 10 In.
$18.00

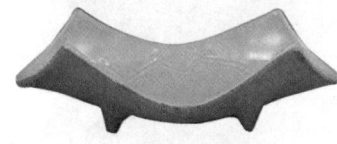

McCoy, Tray, Art Deco Style, Light Blue High Glaze, Matte Orange, Gold Bottom, Footed, 3 x 9 In.
$44.00

McCoy, Vase, Bird Of Paradise, Blue Green High Glaze, Handles, 8¼ x 6 In.
$28.00

M

TIP

Do not put water in a pottery container with an unglazed interior. The water will be absorbed and eventually stain the container.

McCoy, Vase, Double Tulip, No. 74, 8 x 6¾ In. $45.00

McCoy, Vase, Fan, Oxblood Red, Footed, 1940s, 6 In. $16.00

McCoy, Vase, Tulips, Green Ground, Wide Mouth, Rolled Rim, Marked, Loy-Nel-Art, 8 In. $75.00

McKee, Jar, Cover, Jade, 5⅝ x 6¼ In. $40.00

Vase, Grape, 1950s, 9 In.	35.00
Vase, Ivy, 1950s, 9 In.	85.00
Vase, Pigeon, Blue, Footed, 1940s, 4 In.	50.00
Vase, Rustic, 1940s, 9 In.	70.00
Vase, Sailboat, 1940s, 9 In.	95.00
Vase, Sunflower, Green, 1950s, 9 In.	30.00
Vase, Tulips, Green Ground, Wide Mouth, Rolled Rim, Marked, Loy-Nel-Art, 8 In. . . . . . *illus*	75.00
Vase, Wagon Wheel, Tan, Brown, 1954, 8 In.	36.00
Vase, Wild Rose, 1950s, 6½ In.	45.00
Wall Pocket, Baby Diaper, Teal Blue, 1950s, 7½ x 7½ In.	35.00
Wall Pocket, Country Time	15.00
Wall Pocket, Cuckoo, 1950s, 8 In.	65.00
Wall Pocket, Iron On Trivet, 1950s, 8 In.	20.00
Wall Pocket, Jester, Cold Paint, 8½ In.	20.00
Wall Pocket, Umbrella, 1950s, 8¼ In.	50.00

McKEE is a name associated with various glass enterprises in the United States since 1836, including J. & F. McKee (1850), Bryce, McKee & Co. (1850 to 1854), McKee and Brothers (1865), and National Glass Co. (1899). In 1903, the McKee Glass Company was formed in Jeannette, Pennsylvania. It became McKee Division of the Thatcher Glass Co. in 1951 and was bought out by the Jeannette Corporation in 1961. Pressed glass, kitchenwares, and tablewares were produced. Jeannette Corporation closed in the early 1980s. Additional pieces may be included in the Custard Glass and Depression Glass categories.

Bowl, Autumn, Seville Yellow, Oval, Footed, 5½ x 3¾ In.	30.00
Bowl, Cocotte, Custard, 1½ In.	19.00
Bowl, Sections, Opal, Marked	32.00
Bowl, Tom & Jerry, Opal, Red Design, Marked, 11½ In.	35.00
Canister, Cereal, Jade, 48 Oz., 5½ In.	130.00
Canister, Cereal, Script, Jade, 40 Oz., 5 In.	250.00
Canister, Coffee, Jade, 40 Oz., 5 In.	150.00
Canister, Sugar, Jade, 48 Oz., 5½ In.	150.00
Carafe, Cork Covered Glass Stopper, Marked, 6¾ In.	20.00
Compote, Jelly, Majestic, Chocolate Glass, c.1897, 5⅜ x 5¼ In.	650.00
Console, Autumn, Black, Handles, Oval, Footed, 9 In.	45.00
Console, Autumn, Jade Green, Handles, Oval, Footed, 9 In.	125.00
Custard Cup, Opal, Marked, Glasbake, 1¾ x 3¼ In.	3.00
Dish, Lid, Jade, Marked, 4 x 5 In.	66.00
Jar, Cover, Jade, 5⅝ x 6¼ In. . . . . . *illus*	40.00
Mixing Bowl, Bell, Jade, 7 In.	48.00
Mug, Green, Marked, Glasbake, 1940-50, 3½ In.	5.00
Plate, Sunbeam, c.1902, 7¼ In.	18.00
Punch Bowl, Daisy & Button, Opal, Ruffled Edge, 5½ x 4¼ In.	20.00
Punch Bowl, Underplate, Rotec, 12 Cups, Ladle, Early 1900s	165.00
Shaker, Pepper, Opal	28.00
Spice Set, Roman Arches, Jade, 4 In., 14 Piece	140.00
Spooner, Ribbed Palm, Scalloped, c.1863, 6 In.	50.00
Vase, Centipede, Green, Flared Base, 18 In.	45.00
Vase, Fan, Jade Green, Footed	165.00
Vase, Nortec, Green, Footed	45.00

MECHANICAL BANKS *are listed in the Bank category.*

MEDICAL office furniture, operating tools, microscopes, thermometers, and other paraphernalia used by doctors are included in this category. Veterinary collectibles are also included here. Medicine bottles are listed in the Bottle category. There are related collectibles listed under Dental.

Bleeder, Brass, Weigand & Snowden, Case, 4½ In.	81.00
Bloodletting Kit, 4 Glass Cups, Syringe, Tubing, Case, Brevete, 9 x 6 In.	1207.00
Bloodletting Kit, Physician's, Cups, Syringe, Lancet, Fitted Case, 4 x 8 In., 10 Piece	900.00
Cabinet, Apothecary, 10 Drawers, Green Paint, Red Panels, Shelves, 33 x 51 x 20 In.	575.00
Cabinet, Apothecary, 28 Drawer, Grain Painted, 45 x 10 x 28 In.	2013.00
Cabinet, Apothecary, 32 Drawers, Dovetailed, Walnut, Reverse Glass Labels, 76 x 34 In.	1035.00
Cabinet, Apothecary, Bracket Base, Center Foot, Green Over Red Paint, c.1825, 61 x 18 In.	2900.00
Cabinet, Apothecary, Cherry, 22 Drawers, Pewter Pulls, 1880	1695.00
Cabinet, Apothecary, Chinese, 2 Dovetailed Cases, 75 Drawers, 54 x 30 In.	1840.00

M

Cabinet, Apothecary, Oak, 18 Drawers, Overhanging Top, Metal Handles, 39 x 43 x 15 In. . . .	439.00
Cabinet, Apothecary, On Stand, 24 Drawers, Pine, Brass Pulls, 27 x 32 In.	518.00
Cabinet, Apothecary, Pine, Poplar, 20 Drawers, Wood Pulls, Decorated, 17 x 31 x 10 In.	1645.00
Cabinet, Apothecary, Shaker, Pine, 88 Drawers, Paint, Porcelain Pulls, c.1850, 44 x 40 In. . .	5557.00
Cabinet, Apothecary, Walnut, 12 Drawers, Chamfered Corners, Bracket Feet, 36 x 33 x 14 In.	550.00
Cabinet, First Aid, Tin, White Paint, Miller's Mutual Casualty Insurance Co., 17 x 12 In.	115.00
Cabinet, Oak, 6 Drawers, Lower Glass Case, Milk Glass Top & Gallery, 32 x 25 In.	316.00
Cabinet, Pharmacy, Mission Oak, 20 Vertical Drawers, Bronze, c.1940, 84 x 24 In.	1500.00
Case, Apothecary, Mahogany, 2 Doors, Drawer, Interior Drawers, Accessories, 13 x 15 In. . . .	632.00
Chart, Anatomy Of Human Ear, Zenith Radio Corporation, 21 x 15 In.	54.00
Chest, Apothecary, 16 Various Bottles, Compartments, Drawer, Mahogany Case, 9 x 8 In.	575.00
Container, Lid, Apothecary, Moss Green, White, 1880-1900, 6¼ In.	59.00
Electromagnet, Optometrist's, Remove Metal Particle From Eye, Pat. Feb. 12, 1907	500.00
Enema Kit, Ebony Handle, Accessories, Weiss Patent, Mahogany Case, 9 x 6 x 2 In.	403.00
Etui, 2 Lancets, Tortoiseshell Handles, Shagreen On Wooden Case, 2⅞ In.	316.00
Etui, 2 Lancets, Tortoiseshell Handles, Silver, London Hallmarks, 1891, 2⅜ In.	201.00
Etui, 6 Surgical Instruments, Tortoiseshell, Mother-Of-Pearl Handles, G. Turner, 2¾ In.	632.00
Etui, 8 Surgical Instruments, Shagreen, Thoms. McDonald, Tortoiseshell Handles, 6 In.	2185.00
Examining Table, Walnut, Reclines, Movable Footrest, Sink, W.D. Allison Co., 40 x 30 In. . . .	460.00
Eye Massage Machine, Neu-Vita Oculizer, Rubber, Foam, England, 6½ x 7½ In.	225.00
Eyecup, Teal Blue Green, W.T. & Co.	40.00
Hot Water Bottle, 10½ x 6 x 5¾ In.	250.00
Invalid Feeder, Red Cross On Top, Germany, Porcelain	75.00
Leech Jar, Cobalt Blue Glaze, Hand Painted, Banner, Royal Doulton, England, 9½ In.	8625.00
Leech Jar, Porcelain, Green, Crown & Banner Label, Dome Lid, Air Holes, 9½ In.	5980.00
Leech Jar, Staffordshire, Fluted Bands, Green, Labeled Leeches, Finial, Pierced Lid, 13 In. . . .	8625.00
Massager, Electric, Vibrator, Teal Green, Metal Housing, Wood Handle, Celluloid Head	32.00
Model, Human Heart, Teacher's, Removable Chambers & Valves, 17 In. . . . .*illus*	29.00
Mortician's Kit, Instruments, Interchangeable Handles, Mahogany, Savigny & Co., 10 x 5 In.	575.00
Otoscope, Cased Set, American Optical Company, 10¼ In.	69.00
Phrenology Head, Porcelain, Cranium Divided, Molded, L.N. Foster, 12 In.	294.00
Quack Device, Electric, Nervous Disease, W.H. Burnap, Brass, Mahogany, Crank, 5 x 10 In. .	748.00
Saddlebags, Leather, Fitted Wooden Interiors, 27 Glass Vials, Fold-Out Section, 7 x 8 In.	604.00
Saw, Surgeon's, Amputation, Checkered Ebony, Shepard & Dudley, N.Y., 15½ In.	105.00
Skull, Human, Opens For Teaching	440.00
Slide Case, Glass Door, 12 Trays, 175 Slides, Bone Knobs, 9 x 8 In.	518.00
Slide Case, Mahogany, Glass Panel Door, Ivory Knobs, 10 x 12 In.	374.00
Stethoscope, Blood Pressure Gauge, Leather Bag	45.00
Surgical Case, Rosewood, Fitted Interior, Lift-Out Trays, G. Teimann & Co., N.Y., 16 In.	230.00
Surgical Kit, 8 Instruments, Vial, Scalpel Blades, Wooden Case, Coexeter Univ., 7½ In.	230.00
Surgical Kit, Rosewood, Brass Corners & Plaque, Fitted Interior, Tools, 17 x 11 In. . . . .*illus*	6050.00
Surgical Kit, Skull Cutting Tools, 19th Century	3850.00
Surgical Kit, Traveling, Leather, Cloth, Folding, 7 Tools, Accessories, G. Tiemann, 1874, 5 In. .	402.00
Surgical Kit, Traveling, Leather, Folding, 14 Instruments, Horn Handles, 7 In.	460.00
Surgical Kit, Walnut, Fitted, Scalpels, Knives, Saws, G. Tiemann & Co., N.Y., 17 x 7 In.	6900.00
Surgical Needle Display, Surgicraft, Redditch, England, c.1935, 9½ x 28 In.	118.00
Syringe, Hard Rubber, Marked Goodyear, 1860s, 4⅞ In.	75.00
Tin, Royal Purple, Diarrhea Tables For Poultry, Calves, Pigs, 2¼ x 1⅞ x 1⅞ In.	55.00
Tin, Scotch Gall Remedy, For Man & Beast, Marshall Oil, Lithograph, 4 Oz., 3½ In.	275.00
Traveling Case, Physician's, Mahogany, Beaker, Bottles, Tins, Prescription, 1822, 8 x 7 In. . .	1320.00
Vampire Killing Kit, Ivory Cross, Pistol, Flask, Stake, Silver Bullets, Label, Box, 10 x 13 In. .	5463.00
Vibrator, Massager, Electric, Teal Green, Metal, Wood Handle, Celluloid Massage Head	32.00

MEISSEN is a town in Germany where porcelain has been made since 1710. Any china made in the town can be called Meissen, although the famous Meissen factory made the finest porcelains of the area. The crossed swords mark of the great Meissen factory has been copied by many other firms in Germany and other parts of the world. Pieces of Meissen dinnerware in the Onion pattern are listed in their own category in this book.

Bowl, Cobalt Ground, Crossed Swords Mark, 10½ In.	499.00
Bowl, Gilt, Multicolored, Gilt Molded Floral Bouquets, C-Scroll, 2¼ x 11 In., Pair	235.00
Bowl, Oval, Stipple Ground, Cobalt Blue, Gold Raised Shells, Scrolls, Scalloped, 11 In.	210.00
Bowl, Slop, Couple, Woods, Sprig, Scrollwork Border, Gilt, Crossed Swords Mark, 7 In.	1080.00
Box, Cover, Fan Shape, Pavilion, River, Kakiemon, Crossed Swords Mark, 1730-35, 4 In.	18000.00
Box, Pate-Sur-Pate, Cupid, Cover, 19th Century, 2 x 3½ In.	1053.00
Bread Bowl, Relief, Gilt, Painted Flowers, Crossed Swords Mark, 13 In.	294.00

Medical, Model, Human Heart, Teacher's, Removable Chambers & Valves, 17 In. $29.00

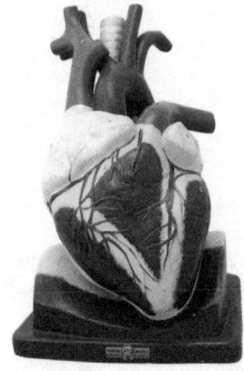

Medical, Surgical Kit, Rosewood, Brass Corners & Plaque, Fitted Interior, Tools, 17 x 11 In. $6050.00

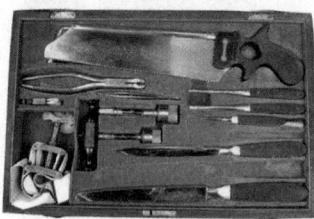

M

Dating Meissen

Old Meissen by the original factory can be identified. Many of the eighteenth-century figures continued in production during the nineteenth, twentieth, and twenty-first centuries. Old Meissen was skillfully decorated. It is heavier than new Meissen. The colors used can help to determine age. Maroon and yellowish chrome green were never used during the eighteenth century. Almost all the eighteenth-century figures had brown eyes. Blue or brown eyes were used in the nineteenth, twentieth, and twenty-first centuries. The porcelain used for early Meissen has a slightly green tinge, while later porcelain was dead white.

Meissen, Group, Cherub, Wind-Blown Hair, Putting Doves In Cage, Rocaille Base, 5 In. $3346.00

Meissen, Group, Drunken Silenus, On Donkey, With Bacchante, Faun & Cherub, 8½ In. $2032.00

Candelabra, 10-Light, Applied, Encrusted Flowers, Rocaille Cartouches, 29 In., Pair	6468.00
Clock, Diana, Huntsmen, Holding Rifle, Partridge, Deer, Rocaille Feet, 19th Century, 28 In.	6064.00
Coffee Service, Flower Sprigs, Painted Crossed Swords Mark, 20th Century, 20 Piece	520.00
Coffee Service, Yellow Tiger Pattern, 20th Century, 10½ In., 20 Piece	761.00
Compote, Cobalt Ground, Gilt Bordered Reserve, Flowers, 19th Century, 3¾ x 9 In.	443.00
Cup & Saucer, Floral, Late 19th Century, 5½ In.	227.00
Cup & Saucer, Flowering China Tree & Bird	230.00
Cup & Saucer, Flowers, Crossed Swords Mark, 3 In.	130.00
Dish, Leaf Shape, Curved Handle, Painted, White Ground, Flowers, c.1900, 8¾ In., Pair	192.00
Dish, Red Dragon, Crossed Swords Mark, c.1735-40, 11½ In.	1800.00
Figurine, African Woman, Holding Article, Crossed Swords, 6 In.	588.00
Figurine, Allegorical, Night, Late 19th Century, 6¾ In.	585.00
Figurine, Blackamoor, Turban, Puce Tunic, Flowers, Gilt, Crossed Swords Mark, 2⁷⁄₁₆ In.	600.00
Figurine, Boy, Crossed Swords Mark, 6¼ In.	764.00
Figurine, Boy, Playing Flute, Crossed Blue Swords Mark, 4¾ In.	323.00
Figurine, Cherub, Holding Blanket, Quiver, Crossed Swords Mark, 4⅞ In.	1058.00
Figurine, Cherub, Holding Flower Garland, 19th Century, 6½ In.	1410.00
Figurine, Cherub, Holding Flower Torchere, Crossed Swords Mark, 7½ In.	2115.00
Figurine, Cherub, Holding Garland, Crossed Swords Mark, 6 In.	1880.00
Figurine, Cherub, Holding Heart By Pedestal, Crossed Swords Mark, 5½ In.	999.00
Figurine, Cherub, Holding Torch To Plinth, Crossed Swords Mark, 5 In.	940.00
Figurine, Cherub, Seated, Hands, Wings Tied, Crossed Swords Mark, 4⅛ In.	441.00
Figurine, Child, Holding Letter, Captain Costume, Collar, Sword, Stump, c.1765-70, 4¾ In.	1080.00
Figurine, Classical Maiden Dancing With Garland, Blue Crossed Swords Mark, 9 In.	420.00
Figurine, Count Marcolini Period, Nobleman, Royal Vienna Pedestal, c.1814, 26 x 10 In.	10530.00
Figurine, Cupid, Bound Hands, Boy With Flowers, Pair, 4¼ x 5 In.	881.00
Figurine, Duck, Blue Crossed Swords Mark Under Glaze, 5½ In., Pair	1093.00
Figurine, Eros, Holding Marriage Contract Scroll, Holding Slipper Behind Back, 11 In.	1560.00
Figurine, Foo Dog, Seated Figure, Shaggy Hair, 19th Century, 8¼ In.	1880.00
Figurine, Hunter, Dog, Gun, Crossed Swords Mark, 5½ In.	940.00
Figurine, Lady, Green Dress, Bending Over, c.1900, 11 In.	890.00
Figurine, Lamb Feeder, 19th Century, 5¼ x 2⅛ In.	950.00
Figurine, Man, Holding Up Finger, Black Hat, Cloak, Dagger In Belt, c.1745-50, 6 In.	8758.00
Figurine, Man, Seated, Bowl In Hand, Eating Tool, Crossed Swords Mark, 4¾ In.	1410.00
Figurine, Man, Standing, Playing Goat Bagpipes, Dog Seated, c.1740-45, 5½ In.	6064.00
Figurine, Musician, Playing Mandolin, Crossed Swords Mark, 7¼ In.	1645.00
Figurine, Parrot, On Stump, Red, Blue, Yellow, Blue Crossed Swords Mark, 13 In., Pair	2115.00
Figurine, Parrot, Perched On Base, Leafy Branches, Green, Purple, 5¾ In.	323.00
Figurine, Partridge, Brown, Green Feathers, Ears Of Wheat, Impressed, No. 53, c.1741-45 In.	5100.00
Figurine, Peacock, Multicolored Plumage, Tree Stump Support, c.1730-35, 7 In.	3773.00
Figurine, Satyr, With Mandolin, Seated On Tree Trunk, 8½ In.	177.00
Figurine, Shepherd, With Bagpipes, Sheep, Dog At Feet, Crossed Swords Mark, 9¾ In.	646.00
Figurine, Shepherdess, Gathering Flowers, c.1900, 10 In.	534.00
Figurine, Woman, With Flower Basket, 20th Century, 4¼ In.	353.00
Group, 2 Bear Cubs, Frolicking, Brown Stoneware, 7½ In.	330.00
Group, 2 Cherubs, Playing Horn, Conducting, Crossed Swords Mark, 5 In.	2115.00
Group, Amphitrite & Attendant, Pulling Boy From Sea, Blue Crossed Swords Mark, 13 In.	1200.00
Group, Autumn, Shepherd, Shepherdess, Grapes, Goat, 20th Century, 7¾ In.	826.00
Group, Bacchus, Seated On Wine Barrel, Attendants, Putti, 12 x 10 x 6 In.	2185.00
Group, Cherub, Wind-Blown Hair, Putting Doves In Cage, Rocaille Base, 5 In. .....*illus*	3346.00
Group, Cherubs, Beside Barrel, Bale Of Cotton, Measuring Cloth, 19th Century, 5 In.	1880.00
Group, Cherubs, With Flowers, Seated, Making Garland, 6¾ In.	1645.00
Group, Children, Flower Headdress, Holding Bouquet, 4½ In.	940.00
Group, Drunken Silenus, On Donkey, With Bacchante, Faun & Cherub, 8½ In. .....*illus*	2032.00
Group, Europa & Bull, Putto, Rocaille Edged Base, Crossed Swords Mark, 9½ In. .....*illus*	3585.00
Group, Man & Woman, Cherub, 1880-1900, 9½ In.	1404.00
Group, Musicians, Violin, Bagpipe Players, c.1778, 9¼ In.	3773.00
Lamp, Electric, Ginger Jar, Indian Pattern, 18 In.	264.00
Mug, 2 Panels, Orange Ground, Flowers, Cherubs, Woods, 1800s, 3⅜ In.	330.00
Plate, Fish, 3 Insects On Basket Weave Border, Crossed Swords Mark, 10 In., 6 Piece	780.00
Platter, Phoenix & Dragon, Gilt & Brown Highlights, Marked, 1910, 14 In.	750.00
Salt, Double, Cover, Flowers Panels, Alternating Painted Sprigs, Gilt, 4-Footed, 6⅞ In.	1440.00
Salt, Girl Holding 2 Baskets, Late 19th Century, 6 x 5 In.	325.00
Scent Bottle, Double, Figural, Man, Brown Robe, Dead Goose, Basket, Child, 3 In.	1323.00
Scent Bottle, Pilgrim Flask, Female Bust Handles, Gadroon Lower Body, 3½ In.	1440.00
Tazza, Oval Bowl, Children Standing On Stumps Pedestal, Blue & White, 16 In., Pair	1610.00

Tea & Coffee Set, White Ground, Gold, Cobalt Overlay, Eagle Head Spout, 1900s, 5 Piece ...	790.00
Tea Bowl & Saucer, Acanthus Leaves, Gilt, Scrollwork, Incised, Saucer, c.1720, 6 In. Pair ...	7500.00
Tea Caddy, Cover, Couple, Landscape, Rectangular, Purple Border, Flowers, 7¼ In.	1080.00
Tete-A-Tete, Tea Set, Tray, Blue, Gilt, Fitted Box, c.1775, 12 Piece	16308.00
Urn, Cover, Courting Lovers, Flowers, Painted, 6 In.	206.00
Urn, Cover, Painted, Pastoral, Lovers, Crossed Swords Mark, 5¾ In.	881.00
Vase, Flowers, White Ground, Gold Trim, c.1900, 5½ x 2¾ In.	176.00
Vase, Masks, Classical Figures, Clouds, Gilt Edge, Female Busts, c.1790, 10 In., Pair	9433.00
Vase, Scenic, Gilt Scrollwork Cartouches, Dark Blue Ground, Flowers, 9¼ In., Pair	4043.00
Vase, Snake Handle, Egg Shape, Gilt Lappet Rim, Fluted Trumpet Foot, 15⅛ In.	2468.00
Wall Bracket, Giltwood, Scroll Support, Painted Crossed Swords Mark, c.1900, 6 In., Pair ..	468.00

MERCURY GLASS, or silvered glass, was first made in the 1850s. It lost favor for a while but became popular again about 1910. It looks like a piece of silver.

Atomizer, Blue, Hand Blown, 10 In.	125.00
Atomizer, Hand Blown, 7 In.	125.00
Candlestick, 12½ In.	95.00
Lamp, Electric, 11 In.	165.00
Saltcellar, 2 In.	20.00

METLOX POTTERIES was founded in 1927 in Manhattan Beach, California. Dinnerware was made beginning in 1931. Evan K. Shaw purchased the company in 1946 and expanded the number of patterns. Poppytrail (1946-1989) and Vernonware (1958-1980) were divisions of Metlox under E.K. Shaw's direction. The factory closed in 1989.

Antiqua, Bowl, Cereal, 7⅛ In.	9.00
Antique Grape, Bowl, Cereal, 7½ In.	39.00
Antique Grape, Mug	29.00
Autumn Berry, Plate, Salad, 7⅝ In. ....*illus*	12.00
Barkwood, Salt & Pepper, 3½ In.	14.95
Bluebird, Bowl, Vegetable, 10 In.	17.00
Bluebird, Cup & Saucer	9.00
Bluebird, Pitcher, Milk, 6 In.	20.00
Bluebird, Plate, Dinner, 10½ In.	15.00
Bluebird, Plate, Salad, 7¾ In.	9.00
California Ivy, Chop Plate, 13¼ In.	20.00
California Ivy, Cup	10.00
California Mobile, Bowl, 8¼ x 9¼ In.	59.00
California Peach Blossom, Coffeepot	125.00
California Provincial, Plate, Dinner, 10¼ In.	9.00
California Strawberry, Platter, 13 In.	48.00
California Strawberry, Salt & Pepper	20.00
Classic, Sugar & Creamer	28.00
Colonial Heritage, Plate, Luncheon, 7½ In.	7.00
Colonial Heritage, Sugar	12.00
Colorstax, Bowl, Cereal, Yellow, 6⅜ In.	15.00
Colorstax, Mug, Evergreen, 3¾ In.	15.00
Colorstax, Plate, Dinner, Fern, 10¾ In.	15.00
Colorstax, Plate, Dinner, Pink, 10¾ In.	15.00
Cookie Jar, Beulah Cow, 1960s, 11 In.	336.00
Della Robbia, Butter, 8¼ x 4⅞ In.	28.00
Della Robbia, Cup & Saucer	9.00
Della Robbia, Plate, Salad, 7⅝ In.	9.00
Della Robbia, Platter, 14½ In.	26.00
Gaiety, Creamer	19.95
Heavenly Days, Creamer	19.00
Nasturtium, Platter	30.00
Navajo, Bowl, Fruit, 6¾ In.	12.00
Navajo, Soup, Dish, 7 In.	15.00
Navajo, Teapot, Rattan Handle, 7 Cup	45.00
Pepper Tree, Teapot, 8½ In.	55.00
Provincial Fruit, Coffeepot, 11 In.	55.00
Red Rooster, Butter, Cover	26.00
Red Rooster, Platter, 13 In.	27.50
Red Rooster, Salt & Pepper, 3¾ In.	45.00
Sculptured Daisy, Bowl, Cereal, 7¼ In.	15.00

Meissen, Group, Europa & Bull, Putto, Rocaille Edged Base, Crossed Swords Mark, 9½ In. **$3585.00**

Meissen/Dresden China What's in a Name?
The word *Meissen* should mean any type of ceramic made at the original Meissen factory from 1710 to the present time. The English refer to Meissen as *Dresden*, the French use the word *Saxe*. People sometimes refer to Meissen porcelain as Dresden china. Dresden sold today is not made by the famous original Meissen factory. Until the mid-nineteenth century the term *Dresden china* was used to refer to porcelain made in the Meissen factory; then it was used for other porcelains that resembled the work of the famous factory. Most of it is from factories in or near the city of Dresden, which is 15 miles from Meissen. French, Italian, English, and other factories copied Meissen china. These pieces are Meissen-type or Dresden-type.

M

Metlox, Autumn Berry,
Plate, Salad, 7⅝ In.
$12.00

Mettlach, Stein, No. 1471,
½ Liter, Musicians, Inlaid Lid,
C. Warth.
$235.00

Mettlach, Stein, No. 2028,
½ Liter, Tavern Scene,
Inscribed Around Foot, Signed
$173.00

M

Sculptured Daisy, Sugar, Cover	20.00
Sculptured Zinnia, Butter, Cover	19.00
Susanna, Plate, Dinner, 10½ In.	12.00
Tickled Pink, Bowl, Vegetable, 7½ In.	30.00
Tickled Pink, Chop Plate, 13 In.	45.00
Vernon, Cup & Saucer	12.00
Vineyard, Platter, 12¼ In.	45.00
Wild Poppy, Plate, Dinner, 11 In.	12.00

METTLACH, Germany, is a city where the Villeroy and Boch factories worked. Steins from the firm are marked with the word *Mettlach* or the castle mark. They date from about 1842. *PUG* means painted under glaze. The steins can be dated from the marks on the bottom, which include a date-number code. Other pieces may be listed in the Villeroy & Boch category.

Ashtray, No. 2983, Art Nouveau, Etched, 2½ x 4½ In.	253.00
Beaker, No. 2327-1273, ¼ Liter, Drunken Man, PUG	163.00
Beaker, No. 2327-1287, ¼ Liter, Donkey Barmaid Feeding Fox Gentleman, PUG	163.00
Beaker, No. 2327-1290a, ¼ Liter, American Eagle, PUG	92.00
Beaker, No. 2781, ¼ Liter, Man & Woman, Cameo, Etched	58.00
Beer Tap, No. 2649, Knight In Castle Die, Kannenburg, Porcelain, Metal, 41 In.	2070.00
Bowl, No. 1659, Cover, Blue, Red & White Repeating Design, Ball Feet, Glazed, Relief, 4 In.	277.00
Bowl, No. 3420, Repeating Design, Glazed Relief, 3 x 7 In.	299.00
Butter, No. 3103, Cover, Art Nouveau, Etched, 4¾ x 5¼ In.	265.00
Inkwell, Pen Rest, Grape & Leaf, Hinged Lid, Compartments, 5¾ x 10½ x 7½ In.	303.00
Match Strike, No. 336, Cigar Holder, Boy, On Rocks, Leaning On Stump, Early Ware, 5¾ In.	230.00
Mug, No. 3095, ⅓ Liter, Drink Hires Root Beer, PUG	46.00
Pitcher, No. 7024, Phanolith, Flowers, Blue, White, 15 In.	546.00
Planter, No. 2415, Art Nouveau, Flowers, Etched, 7½ In.	785.00
Planter, No. 2423, Flowers, Art Nouveau, Etched, 5¼ x 12 In.	834.00
Plaque, No. 1044, Rustringen Im Kriegsjahr 1916, PUG, 9 In.	150.00
Plaque, No. 1044-5080, Castle, Ships, Delft, PUG, 17 In.	316.00
Plaque, No. 1044-5082, Windmill, People, Lake, Delft, PUG, 17 In.	316.00
Plaque, No. 2112, Gnome In Tree, Holding Bottles, Castle Mark, Etched, Schlitt, 16 In.	1380.00
Plaque, No. 2133, Gnome In Tree Drinking From Mug, Castle Mark, Etched, Schlitt, 16 In.	1380.00
Plaque, No. 2442, Trojan Warriors On Boat, Cameo Relief, 19 In.	690.00
Plaque, No. 2443, Trojan Lady & Servants, Cameo Relief, 19 In.	690.00
Plaque, No. 2508, Art Nouveau, Mermaid, Etched, 17 In.	1035.00
Plaque, No. 2874, Woman Holding Harp & Torch, Cameo Relief, 18 In.	690.00
Punch Bowl, No. 3037-1210, Students Drinking, Castle Heidelberg, PUG, No Lid, 5 Liter	287.00
Stein, No. 24, ½ Liter, Scenes Of People, 4 Panels, Relief, Inlaid Lid	133.00 to 253.00
Stein, No. 386, ½ Liter, Fraternal, Double Crest, Pewter Lid, Inscribed, G. Renz, 1905	418.00
Stein, No. 1403, ½ Liter, Men Bowling, Etched, Inlaid Lid, C. Warth	363.00
Stein, No. 1471, ½ Liter, Musicians, Inlaid Lid, C. Warth	*illus* 235.00
Stein, No. 1480, ½ Liter, Dwarfs, Etched, Inlaid Lid	230.00
Stein, No. 1526, 1 Liter, Munich Child, PUG, Pewter Lid	362.00
Stein, No. 1526-1143, 1 Liter, Cavaliers Drinking, PUG, Relief Pewter Lid, Child, H. Schlitt	403.00
Stein, No. 1526-1195, ½ Liter, Wheat & Hops, PUG, Pewter Lid	120.00
Stein, No. 1644, ½ Liter, Man Smoking, Tapestry, Etched, Silver Plated Lid	288.00
Stein, No. 1725, ½ Liter, Man & Woman, Etched, Inlaid Lid, C. Warth	282.00
Stein, No. 1740, ¼ Liter, Verse, Relief, Inlaid Lid	97.00
Stein, No. 1786, 1 Liter, St. Florian Extinguishing Fire, Dragon Handle, Etched, Pewter Lid	966.00
Stein, No. 1786, ½ Liter, St. Florian Extinguishing Fire, Dragon Handle, Etched, Pewter Lid	725.00
Stein, No. 1909-1109, ½ Liter, Musicians, PUG, Relief Pewter Lid With Lyre, H. Schlitt	332.00
Stein, No. 1909-1143, ½ Liter, Cavaliers Drinking, PUG, Pewter Lid, H. Schlitt	333.00
Stein, No. 1909-727, ⅓ Liter, Dwarfs Bowling, PUG, Pewter Lid, H. Schlitt	277.00
Stein, No. 1932, ½ Liter, Cavaliers Drinking, Etched, Pewter Lid, C. Warth	432.00
Stein, No. 1972, ½ Liter, 4 Ladies, Etched, Pewter Lid	303.00
Stein, No. 2001B, ½ Liter, Medicine, Etched, Relief, Inlaid Lid	604.00
Stein, No. 2001K, ½ Liter, Banking, Etched, Relief, Inlaid Lid	604.00
Stein, No. 2002, ½ Liter, Munchen, German Verse, Etched, Inlaid Lid	230.00 to 325.00
Stein, No. 2024, ½ Liter, Berlin, Shield, Etched, Inlaid Lid	604.00
Stein, No. 2025, ½ Liter, Cherubs, Etched, Inlaid Lid	366.00
Stein, No. 2028, ½ Liter, Tavern Scene, Inscribed Around Foot, Signed	*illus* 173.00
Stein, No. 2057, ⅓ Liter, Cherubs, Etched, Inlaid Lid	277.00
Stein, No. 2074, ½ Liter, Bird In Cage, Pewter Lid	1594.00

Stein, No. 2093, ½ Liter, Cards, Etched, Inlaid Lid	845.00
Stein, No. 2094, ½ Liter, Festive Scene, Etched, Inlaid Lid	664.00
Stein, No. 2123, ½ Liter, Knight Drinking, Etched, Inlaid Lid, H. Schlitt	1207.00
Stein, No. 2133, ½ Liter, Dwarf, Etched, Inlaid Lid, H. Schlitt	1864.00
Stein, No. 2140-869, ½ Liter, Field Artillerie Regt. Nr. 36, PUG, Pewter Lid, Weapons, Flags	575.00
Stein, No. 2177-960, ¼ Liter, Jester Playing Mandolin, PUG, Pewter Lid, H. Schlitt	159.00
Stein, No. 2230, ½ Liter, Man & Woman, Etched, Pewter Lid, H. Schlitt	368.00
Stein, No. 2231, ½ Liter, Cavaliers Drinking, Inlaid Lid, Music Box Base	380.00
Stein, No. 2382, ½ Liter, Der Durstige Ritter, Etched, Glazed, Inlaid Lid, H. Schlitt	316.00
Stein, No. 2382, 1 Liter, Der Durstige Ritter, Etched, Glazed, Inlaid Lid, H. Schlitt	778.00
Stein, No. 2388, ½ Liter, Pretzels, Inlaid Lid	313.00
Stein, No. 2391, 1 Liter, Lohengrin Wedding, Etched, Relief, Inlaid Lid	1450.00
Stein, No. 2479, ½ Liter, Hildebrand, 3 Scenes, Cameo, Relief, Inlaid Lid	654.00
Stein, No. 2580, ½ Liter, Dekannenburg, Etched, Inlaid Lid, H. Schlitt	725.00
Stein, No. 2580, 1 Liter, Dekannenburg, Etched, Inlaid Lid, H. Schlitt	948.00
Stein, No. 2690, 1¼ Liter, Drinking Scene, Etched, Inlaid Lid	1449.00
Stein, No. 2716, ½ Liter, Drinking Scene, Etched, Inlaid Lid, F. Quidenus	604.00
Stein, No. 2718, 1 Liter, David & Goliath, Etched, Glazed, Inlaid Lid	2186.00
Stein, No. 2722, ½ Liter, Shoemaker, Etched, Glazed, Inlaid Lid	788.00
Stein, No. 2765, 1 Liter, Knight Riding White Horse, Etched, Inlaid Lid, H. Schlitt	3019.00
Stein, No. 2778, ½ Liter, Carnival, Etched, Inlaid Lid	1362.00
Stein, No. 2823, ½ Liter, Woman With Schutzen Target, Etched, Relief Pewter Lid	363.00
Stein, No. 2828, ½ Liter, Wartburg, Houses, Tower, Etched, Relief, Inlaid Lid	2300.00
Stein, No. 2829, ½ Liter, Rodenstein, Etched, Relief, Inlaid Lid	1668.00
Stein, No. 2917, 1 Liter, Munchen Child, Scenes Of Munich, Lion & Shield, Inlaid Lid	923.00
Stein, No. 3000, ½ Liter, Women, 3 Panels, Etched, Pewter Lid, F. Ringer	425.00
Stein, Pewter Thumblift, Quidenus, Thirsty Knight, 8 To 9½ In., ½ Liter, 4 Piece	1410.00
Vase, No. 140, Leaf & Berry Design, Platinum, 10¼ In.	92.00
Vase, No. 1504, Repeating Design, Blue, Brown, Beige, Bulbous, Flared, Etched, 5¼ In.	265.00
Vase, No. 1700, Flowers, Brown, Blue, Beige, 3-Footed, Etched, 3¾ In.	173.00
Vase, No. 2472, Flowers, Art Nouveau, Etched, 4¾ In.	345.00
Vase, No. 2605, Flowers, Art Nouveau, Etched, 3 Handles, 4¾ In.	345.00
Vase, No. 3417, Repeating Design, Glazed Relief, 7¾ In.	277.00

MILK GLASS was named for its milky white color. It was first made in England during the 1700s. The height of its popularity in the United States was from 1870 to 1880. It is now correct to refer to some colored glass as blue milk glass, black milk glass, etc. Reproductions of milk glass are being made and sold in many stores. Related pieces may be listed in the Cosmos, Vallerysthal, and Westmoreland categories.

Bowl, Fruit, Open Lace Edge, Footed, 12⅛ In.	29.00
Box, Caramel, Cover, Dog Sitting On Lid, 6½ In.	100.00
Butter, Reclining Cow, Cover, Clear Base	70.00
Compote, Atlas, Scalloped Rim, Atterbury, 8 x 9¼ In. ....*illus*	30.00
Dish, Beaver Cover, Flaccus	500.00
Dish, Cannon On Drum Cover	40.00
Dish, Cat On Drum, Cover, Marked, Portieux	35.00
Dish, Cover, Dog, Split Rib Base, McKee	75.00
Dish, Dove Cover, Split Rib Base	12.00
Dish, Dove In Hand Cover, Atterbury	30.00
Dish, Duck Cover, Atterbury	25.00
Dish, Horse Cover, Split Rib Base, McKee	10.00
Dish, Lion Cover, Split Rib Base, Marked, McKee	255.00
Dish, Owl's Head Cover, Marked, McKee	175.00
Dish, Pickle, Fish, Atterbury	25.00
Dish, Pig Cover, Split Rib Base, McKee	775.00
Dish, Steerhead Cover, Marked, Challinor, c.1891	4500.00
Dish, Swan, Cover, Split Rib Base, McKee	105.00
Dish, Touring Car Cover, Painted	315.00
Figurine, Sphinx, On Platform, Black, Registration Mark, 6 x 10 In. ....*illus*	850.00
Jar, Grease, Bear, 1855-87, 3¾ In.	58.00
Lamp, Columbus, Nutmeg Burner, Shade, 10 In. ....*illus*	8625.00
Match Holder, Gnome	95.00
Pitcher, Ice Water, Silver Plated, Hinged Lid, Flower Handle, Dolphin Spout, 14 x 12 In.	920.00
Pitcher, Owl, Blue, Molded Eyes, 9 x 5 In.	187.00
Plate, Emerging Chick, 7¼ In.	30.00

Mettlach Was Famous
Mettlach steins were popular in America and won awards at the World's Fairs in the United States in 1876, 1893, and 1904.

Milk Glass, Compote, Atlas, Scalloped Rim, Atterbury, 8 x 9¼ In. $30.00

Milk Glass, Figurine, Sphinx, On Platform, Black, Registration Mark, 6 x 10 In. $850.00

M

Milk Glass, Lamp, Columbus, Nutmeg Burner, Shade, 10 In. $8625.00

Minton, Compote, Bisque & Turquoise, Reticulated Basket, Putti, Gold Trim, 12 In.
$764.00

Minton, Plaque, Urn, Flowers, Fruit, Stone Ledge, Giltwood Frame, Thomas Steel, 1850, 5 In.
$1800.00

Minton, Vase, Art Nouveau Flower, Slip Trail Outline, Shouldered, 7½ In.
$690.00

Plate, Flag, Eagle, Fleur-De-Lis, c.1903, 7 In.	40.00
Plate, Forget-Me-Nots In Snow, Cat, Tab Handles, 9 In.	154.00
Platter, Retriever	55.00
Sugar, Cover, Quince Shape, Green, Gold Leaves	40.00
Sugar Shaker, Grapes, Leaves, 4½ In.	20.00 to 35.00

MILLEFIORI means, literally, a thousand flowers. Many small pieces of glass resembling flowers are grouped together to form a design. It is a type of glasswork popular in paperweights and some are listed in that category.

Bowl, Leaf Shape, 12 x 9 In.	145.00
Figurine, Penguin, Satin Finish, 6⅛ In.	275.00
Flask, 4½ x 3½ In.	150.00
Vase, Bulb Shape, Simulated Vase Base, Flared Rim, 6⅝ x 4⅜ In.	475.00
Vase, Cased, Green, Orange Inside, Polished Pontil, 8¼ In.	375.00

MINTON china has been made in the Staffordshire region of England from 1793 to the present. The firm became part of the Royal Doulton Tableware Group in 1968, but the wares continued to be marked *Minton*. Many marks have been used. The word *England* was added in 1891. Minton majolica is listed in this book in the Majolica category.

Charger, Yellow Ground, Enamel Decorated, Perched Birds, c.1872, 13½ In.	823.00
Compote, Bisque & Turquoise, Reticulated Basket, Putti, Gold Trim, 12 In. ....*illus*	764.00
Ewer, Wing Jug Shape, Satyr Mask Handle, White Ground, Blossoms, 1900, 11 In.	320.00
Figurine, Dorothea, Parian, John Bell, 1851, 14¼ In.	390.00
Figurine, Miranda, Sitting On Rock, Sea Shell, 15½ In.	1395.00
Figurine, Queen Victoria, Carrying Bible, 19 In.	795.00
Jug, Cupid & Mermaid, Embossed Majolica, 12 In.	666.00
Plaque, Urn, Flowers, Fruit, Stone Ledge, Giltwood Frame, Thomas Steel, 1850, 5 In. . .*illus*	1800.00
Plate, Chinoiserie, Scenic, Pseudo Sevres Marks, c.1830, 8 In., 6 Piece	1663.00
Plate, Dinner, Raised Gold Borders, White Center Ground, Ivory Border, 9 In., 8 Piece	775.00
Plate, Gilded Border, Tiffany & Co., 10¾ In., 11 Piece	3220.00
Plate, Stylized Star Center, Royal Blue Border, Platinum Band, 10½ In., 12 Piece	360.00
Platter, Floral Sprigs, Blue & White, Minton, c.1830, 18½ x 15 In.	1450.00
Soup, Dish, Wide Band, Green, Gilded Scrollwork, c.1900, 1½ x 8¾ In., 12 Piece	1150.00
Tile, Shakespeare Series, John M. Smith, Victorian, England, 16 x 6 x 6 In.	2048.00
Vase, Art Nouveau Flower, Slip Trail Outline, Shouldered, 7½ In. ....*illus*	690.00
Vase, Cover, Gold Art Nouveau Flowers, Cream, Cobalt Blue, 6 In.	370.00
Vase, Earthenware, Painted, Elizabethan Style Figures, Landscapes, c.1856, 18 In., Pair	940.00
Vase, Pate-Sur-Pate, Venus, Minerva, Cupid Shooting Bow, Arrow, c.1910, 7¾ In., Pair.	5121.00
Vase, Stylized Flowers, Slip Trailing, Blue, Green Glaze, Bottle Form, Ribs, Secessionist, 8 In. .	431.00

MIRRORS *are listed in the Furniture category under Mirror.*

MOCHA pottery is an English-made product that was sold in America during the early 1800s. It is a heavy pottery with pale coffee-And-cream coloring. Designs of blue, brown, green, orange, black, or white were added to the pottery and given fanciful names, such as Tree, Snail Trail, or Moss. Mocha designs are sometimes found on pearlware. A few pieces of mocha ware were made in France, the United States, and other countries.

Bowl, Blue Band, Brown Pinstripe Rim, Brown, Black, White Leaves, Crow's Foot Bottom, 4 x 7 In. ..	440.00
Bowl, Blue Ground, Flared Edge, Brown, Rust, Zigzag Band, 4¼ x 10½ In.	11000.00
Bowl, Cover, Blue, Black, Green, Bands, Seaweed, Brown Ground, 7 x 10½ In.	11115.00
Bowl, Multicolored Bands, Cream Ground, Flared, 3½ x 7⅜ In.	605.00
Bowl, Seaweed, Black, Salmon Ground, Flared, 3¼ x 7⅛ In.	853.00
Bowl, Seaweed, Blue, Yellowware, 4 x 8 In.	220.00
Bowl, Seaweed, Blue, Yellowware, 6½ x 13 In.	137.00
Bowl, Seaweed, Green, 2 Bands, Yellowware, 6½ x 12 In.	247.00
Bowl, Seaweed Yellowware, 12 In.	403.00
Chamber Pot, Seaweed, Green, Blue, Double Bands, Handle, Yellowware	247.00
Compote, Marbleized, Footed, 3½ x 4⅞ In.	22.00
Creamer, Brown & Blue Bands, Bulbous, 5 In.	275.00
Mug, Brown, Black, White Slip Foil, Gray Band, Blue Stripes, Ear Handle, 3⅝ In. .....*illus*	165.00
Mug, Earthworm, Blue, Gray, Black	460.00
Mug, Earthworm, Double Banded	690.00
Mug, Earthworm, Ocher & Blue	805.00
Mug, Earthworm, White Ground, Brown Bands, Handle, 3⅞ In.	415.00

Mug, Marbleized, Straight-Sided, Applied Loop Handle, Brown, Ivory Blue Bands, 4 In.	275.00
Mug, Pearlware, Applied Strap Handle, Blue Bands, Marbled Lip, Late 1700s, 6 In.	1175.00
Mug, Pearlware, Applied Strap Handle, Taupe Band, Earthworm c.1830, 4½ In.	764.00
Mug, Seaweed, 6 Bands	288.00
Mug, Seaweed, Mocha Green, Brown Band, Tan, Yellowware, Ear Handle, Mark, 3¼ In.	413.00
Mug, Strap Handle, Leaf Terminal, Rest & Green Bands, c.1790, 3¾ In.	588.00
Pepper Pot, Blue & Brown Bands, 4⅛ In.	121.00
Pepper Pot, Cat's-Eye, Bulbous, Dome Top, Blue Ground, Rust, Brown Bands, 4¼ In.	2640.00
Pepper Pot, Cat's-Eye, Salmon Ground, Bulbous, Dome Top, 4⅞ In.	1760.00
Pepper Pot, Earthworm, Slate Band, Blue Button Finial, Footed Base, 4¾ In.	2640.00
Pepper Pot, Marbleized, Brass Screw Cap & Collar, Impressed 8 x 4¼ In.	94.00
Pitcher, Black, Brown & Blue Bands, Dendritic Design, 5½ In.	1725.00
Pitcher, Blue, Black Bands	805.00
Pitcher, Cat's-Eye, Blue Band, Salmon Ground, 7 In.	1870.00
Pitcher, Seaweed, Brown, Gray Ground, Brown Bands, Barrel Form, 4⅞ In.	275.00
Pitcher, Seaweed, Brown, Sandy Ground, Bulbous, Marked, Pt., 4⅞ In.	495.00
Pitcher, Seaweed, Green & Brown, Brown Rings, Yellowware, 6 In.	435.00
Salt, Footed, Seaweed, Brown, Gray Ground, 1⅞ In.	275.00
Salt, White Slip With Black Seaweed, Yellowware, Footed, Master, 2¼ x 3 In. ......*illus*	935.00

MONMOUTH Pottery Company started working in Monmouth, Illinois, in 1892. The pottery made a variety of utilitarian wares. It became part of Western Stoneware Company in 1906. The maple leaf mark was used until 1930. If *Co.* appears as part of the mark, the piece was made before 1906.

Bowl, Dark Brown Band, Marked, 3 x 5 In.	6.00
Casserole, Cover, Dark Tan, Burgundy Spatter, c.1967, 6 x 8½ In.	69.00
Cookie Jar, Brown Top, Cookies, Incised Maple Leaf, 7 x 5¾ In.	60.00
Cookie Jar, Green Glaze, Scroll Work Above Cookies, 7 x 6½ In.	32.00
Crock, Ice Water, Lid, Sponge, 4 Gal.	1750.00
Crock, Ice Water, Lid, Sponge, 8 Gal.	1100.00
Jug, Brown Top, Cookie Jug, Maple Leaf Mark	35.00

MONT JOYE, *see Mt. Joye category.*

MOORCROFT pottery was first made in Burslem, England, in 1913. William Moorcroft had managed the art pottery department for James Macintyre & Company of England from 1898 to 1913. The Moorcroft pottery continues today, although William Moorcroft died in 1945. The earlier wares are similar to the modern ones, but color and marking will help indicate the age.

Ashtray, Pomegranate, Blue Ground, Silver Rim	379.00
Bowl, Bulb, Pansies, Purple & Cream, 8 In.	999.00
Bowl, Columbine, Blue Ground, 4¼ In.	168.00
Bowl, Cover, Anemone, Blue Ground, c.1954, 5¾ In.	285.00
Box, Cover, Anemone, Yellow, Orange, Brown, Flambe Glaze, Impressed Mark, 5¼ In.	320.00
Box, Cover, Clematis, Purple, Green Ground, Impressed Mark, 1¾ In.	150.00
Box, Cover, Clematis, Red, Blue, Green, Round, Impressed Mark, 9¼ In.	345.00
Box, Cover, Hibiscus, Round, Brown Ground, 7 In.	253.00
Dish, African Lily, Blue Ground, 9¾ In.	357.00
Dish, Hibiscus, Flambe, 12¼ In.	800.00
Dish, Pomegranate, Blue Ground, Inverted Rim, c.1925, 4¼ In.	95.00
Dish, Wisteria, Blue Ground, c.1925, 4¼ In.	1054.00
Ginger Jar, Cover, Anemone, Blue Ground, 6½ In.	259.00
Ginger Jar, Cover, Anemone, Flambe, 6 In.	948.00
Ginger Jar, Rose Colored, Hibiscus On Green Ground, Impressed Maker's Mark, 8 In.	295.00
Ginger Jar, Rose Colored Hibiscus, Green Ground, Marked, 1968, 8½ In.	295.00
Jardinere, Coral, Hibiscus On Green Ground, Impressed Makers Mark, 1968, 7 In.	411.00
Lamp, Base, Hibiscus, Ivory, 12 In.	755.00
Lamp, Fruit, Birds, Blue, 11½ x 9½ In.	702.00
Mug, Coronation, King Edward & Queen Alexander, 3¾ In.	527.00
Pitcher, Anemones, Blue, Green Leaves, White Ground, Florian, Macintyre, 5¼ In.	550.00
Pitcher, Leaf & Berry, Blue, Green, Aqua, Impressed Mark, 4½ In.	295.00
Plaque, Hibiscus, Flambe, 8½ In.	432.00
Plaque, Lemons, Cream Ground, 10¼ In.	190.00
Plate, Cluny, Sally Tuffin, 6 In.	97.00
Powder Bowl, Domed Cover, Anemone, Green Ground, 4½ In.	337.00

Mocha, Mug, Brown, Black, White Slip Foil, Gray Band, Blue Stripes, Ear Handle, 3⅝ In.
$165.00

Mocha, Salt, White Slip With Black Seaweed, Yellowware, Footed, Master, 2¼ x 3 In.
$935.00

Moorcroft, Vase, Blackberries & Leaves, Flambe Glaze, 12¼ In.
$2070.00

Moorcroft, Vase, Imari Flowers, Cobalt Blue, Gold, Handles, Art Nouveau, Macintyre, 9 In., Pair
$475.00

Moorcroft, Vase, Leaves & Berries, Signed, William Moorcroft, c.1945, 13 In. $700.00

Morgantown, Barry, Pitcher, Venetian Green Handle & Foot, 9¾ In. $250.00

Morgantown, Crinkle, Sherbet, Pink $10.00

Morgantown, Golf Ball, Ivy Ball, Spanish Red, 6¾ In. $110.00

Moriage, Chocolate Pot, Allover Scrolls, Green Ground, Beaded Finial & Handle, 9½ In. $71.00

Tea Set, Buttercup Design, Teapot, Sugar, Creamer, 2 Cups, Saucers	759.00
Tea Set, Spring Flower, Impressed Mark, 4 Piece	550.00
Tea Set, Spring Flowers, Teapot, Coffeepot, 2 Creamers, Marked, 8½ In.	550.00 to 660.00
Vase, Alhambra, Tan Ground, Red & Blue Flowers, Swollen Shape, 9¼ In.	1725.00
Vase, Anemone, Blue Ground, 4 In.	816.00
Vase, Anemone, Blue Ground, Squat, 4¾ In.	370.00
Vase, Anemone, Green Ground, 1950s, 5 In.	337.00
Vase, Blackberries & Leaves, Flambe Glaze, 12¼ In. ....*illus*	2070.00
Vase, Blue Ground, Fruit Decoration At Shoulder, Mid 1900s, 5½ In.	467.00
Vase, Bulbous, Pomegranate, Stamped, 9½ x 5¼ In.	900.00
Vase, Clematis, Baluster Shape, Flambe Glaze, Marked, c.1940, 6¼ In.	1200.00
Vase, Clematis, Blue Ground, Footed, 4 In.	520.00
Vase, Clematis, Impressed Mark, Paper Label, Late 1940s, 12½ In.	1400.00
Vase, Cobalt Blue, Gold Art Nouveau Scrolls, Oval, Bulbous, Macintyre, 3½ In.	58.00
Vase, Columbine, Light Blue, Bulbous, c.1950, 3¾ In.	480.00
Vase, Columbine, Pedestal, Blue Green Ground, 3¾ In.	274.00
Vase, Coral, Hibiscus On Green Ground, Brown Signature, 1968, 10 In.	147.00
Vase, Flambe, Red, Gray, Courting Couple, E.H. Beardmore, Bernard Moore, c.1915, 4 In.	428.00
Vase, Florian Poppy, Blue Ground, Elongated Neck, 6¼ In.	1285.00
Vase, Imari Flowers, Cobalt Blue, Gold, Handles, Art Nouveau, Macintyre, 9 In., Pair ...*illus*	475.00
Vase, Leaf & Berry, Blue, Green, Aqua, Matte Overglaze, Impressed, 10 In.	550.00
Vase, Leaf & Berry, Green Ground, 3¾ In.	675.00
Vase, Leaves & Berries, Signed, William Moorcroft, c.1945, 13 In. ....*illus*	700.00
Vase, Orchid, Flambe Glaze, Impressed Mark, 9½ In.	735.00
Vase, Pansy, 14 In.	1793.00
Vase, Pansy, Blue Ground, Extended Neck, 4 In.	411.00
Vase, Pansy, Bulbous, Cobalt Blue Ground, c.1930, 4¼ In.	890.00
Vase, Pomegranate, Blue Ground, Low Set Handles, c.1925, 7 In.	800.00
Vase, Pomegranate, Blue Ground, Oval, c.1930, 6 In.	843.00
Vase, Pomegranate, Bottle Shape, Blue Ground, c.1925, 3½ In.	738.00
Vase, Pomegranate, Bulbous Bottom, Elongated Neck, Flared Rim, 12½ In.	3330.00
Vase, Pomegranate, Marked, c.1915, 8 In.	1500.00
Vase, Pomegranate, Red, Brown, Impressed, Cobridge, 6¼ In.	529.00
Vase, Pomegranate, Trumpet, Blue Ground, c.1925, 3½ In.	425.00
Vase, Spring Flowers, Purple, Pink, Yellow, Green Ground, Signed, 6 In.	475.00
Vase, Wisteria, Blue Ground, c.1920-30, 3½ In.	560.00
Wall Pocket, Blue Matte Glaze, Impressed Mark, c.1906, 5¼ In.	147.00

MORGANTOWN GLASS WORKS operated in Morgantown, West Virginia, from 1900 to 1974. Some of their wares are marked with an adhesive label that says *Old Morgantown Glass.*

Barry, Pitcher, Venetian Green Handle & Foot, 9¾ In. ....*illus*	250.00
Crinkle, Sherbet, Pink ....*illus*	10.00
Golf Ball, Candy Dish, Cover, Red, 6 x 5½ In.	750.00
Golf Ball, Cocktail Stem, Ruby, 3½ Oz., 4⅛ In.	40.00
Golf Ball, Ivy Ball, Spanish Red, 6¾ In. ....*illus*	110.00

MORIAGE is a special type of raised decoration used on some Japanese pottery. Sometimes pieces of clay were shaped by hand and applied to the item; sometimes the clay was squeezed from a tube in the way we apply cake frosting. One type of moriage is called Dragonware by collectors.

Bowl, Royal Dress, Dragon, Luster Gilt, 4¾ In.	100.00
Box, Turtle Back Shape, Mottled Green Ground, Flowers, 8 x 6 x 3½ In.	15.00
Chocolate Pot, Allover Scrolls, Green Ground, Beaded Finial & Handle, 9½ In. ....*illus*	71.00
Chocolate Pot, Green, White Coralene Decoration, 9 In., Pair	173.00
Chocolate Pot, Painted Roses, Lace Like, Nippon, 10 In.	995.00
Creamer, Dragonware, 3¼ In.	10.00
Cup & Saucer, Dragonware, After Dinner	45.00
Cup & Saucer, Mt. Fuji, Cherry Blossoms, Amber, Bamboo, Gold Enamel, Lusterware	45.00
Cup & Saucer, Pedestal, Fancy Handle, 2¾ x 5½ In.	38.00
Dish, Peach, Gold Ground, Embossed Beads, 10 In.	28.00
Dresser Tray, Landscape, Birch, Cherry Trees, Black Beading, Nippon, 8½ In.	65.00
Ewer, Flowers, Long Neck, 7 In.	175.00
Hair Receiver, Flowers, Cobalt Blue, Red, Yellow	75.00
Hair Receiver, Gold, Aqua, 3¼ In.	29.00

Incense, Cover, Gray, Dragonware, 3½ x 3 In.	12.00
Incense Burner, Cover, Figures, Satsuma Style, Brown, 4½ In.	28.00
Jam Jar, Cherries On Cover, Flowers, Brown Glaze, Spoon Slot, 4½ x 3½ In.	15.00
Knife, Spreader, Green, Gold Enamel Handle, 6¾ In.	10.00
Mustard, Rose Insert, Scallops, 3½ x 4½ In.	125.00
Plate, Landscape, Flowers, Nippon, 1910, 9 In.	175.00
Plate, Mountains, Water, Man In Boat, Wired Twirled Frame, 12 In.	35.00
Plate, Pink Roses, Green Leaves, Gold Band, Green Enamel	65.00
Salt & Pepper, Dragon, Washington D.C., 2½ In.	22.00
Serving Plate, 2 Tiers, Flower Band, White, Green, Gold, Nippon, 9 In.	40.00
Sugar, Flower, Gold Trim, Nippon, 3½ x 5 In.	10.00
Tea Set, Cover, Blue Luster, Plates, Cups, Saucers, Sugar, Creamer, 20 Piece	50.00
Tea Set, Dragonware, 1940s, 9 Piece	145.00
Tea Set, Teapot, Sugar & Creamer, Cover, Cups & Saucers, Green, Orange Luster, 15 Piece	175.00
Teapot, 8 Panels, Brown Glaze, 5 x 8 In.	19.00
Teapot, Child's, Dark Brown, Blue, Orange, Gold Trim	14.00
Tray, Vanity, Violets, Art Deco, Shallow Rim, Nippon, 10 In.	28.00
Urn, Cover, Raised Scroll, Early 20th Century, 9½ In.	47.00
Vase, Blue, Pink, Purple Poppies, White, Handles, 5 In.	325.00
Vase, Blue Ground, Pink, Purple Flower Sprays, Scrolling Handles, Nippon, 7½ In.	1000.00
Vase, Charcoal Gray Dragon, Pink, Luster Glaze, Gold Trim, 6½ In.	15.00
Vase, Cream, Black, Aqua, Rose, Burnt Orange, Green, Flat, 5¼ x 7 In.	175.00
Vase, Dogwood, 8½ x 3½ In., Pair	35.00
Vase, Flowers, Applied Turquoise Jewels, Cartouche, Nippon, 6¼ In.	500.00
Vase, Flowers, Cobalt Blue Handles, Gold, c.1900, 6½ x 5½ In., Pair	70.00
Vase, Owl, Tree Trunk, Gray, Blue, Brown, Handles, Nippon	1250.00
Vase, Pink, Luster Glaze, Gold Trim	225.00
Vase, Rooster, Flowers, Jewels, Bulbous, Ruffled Rim, Loop Handles, Nippon, 7 In. ....*illus*	411.00
Vase, Rose Flowers, Gold Gates, Swags, Pearl Beads, 1900-1920	225.00
Vase, Roses, Pink, White, Crimson, Gold Enamel, Green Leaves, Nippon, c.1891-1921, 11 In.	275.00
Wall Pocket, Bird, Luster, 8½ In.	40.00

MOSAIC TILE COMPANY of Zanesville, Ohio, was started by Karl Langerbeck and Herman Mueller in 1894. Many types of plain and ornamental tiles were made until 1959. The company closed in 1967. The company also made some ashtrays, bookends, and related giftwares. Most pieces are marked with the entwined *MTC* monogram.

Sculpture, Bear, Black Glaze Over Green, Impressed, 6⅛ x 10 In.	295.00
Tile, Cuerda Seca, Wooden Frame, Zanesville, c.1935, 4¼ x 4¼ In.	245.00
Tile, Paperweight, Abe Lincoln, Blue Ground, Relief, White Jasperware, 3 x 3½ In.	20.00

MOSER glass is made by Ludwig Moser und Sohne, a Bohemian (Czech) glasshouse founded in 1857. Art Nouveau-type glassware and iridescent glassware were made. The most famous Moser glass is decorated with heavy enameling in gold and bright colors. The firm, Moser Glassworks, is still working in Karlsbad, West Czech Republic. Few pieces of Moser glass are marked.

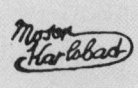

Basket, Cranberry, Enameled Leaves, Insects, Leaves, 3 Clear Rigaree Handles, 12 In.	2185.00
Basket, Smoke Green, Fern, Butterfly, Berry Enamel, Signed, 9 In.	900.00
Bowl, Cranberry, Medallion, Roman Warrior, Oval, 3 Scrolled Feet, Shaped Rim, 6 In. ..*illus*	705.00
Bowl, Green, Footed, Oval, Gold Enameled Floral Interior, 7¼ In.	180.00
Bowl, Green, Gold Enamel Flower Overlay, 3-Footed, 5 In.	175.00
Bowl, Optic Ribbed, Amber, Prussian Blue Rigaree Swags, Multicolored Enamel, 10 In.	690.00
Box, Cover, Green, 4 Medallions Of Pink & White Flowers, Rounded Square Shape, 5½ In.	144.00
Box, Hinged Cover, Raised Purple Rectangles, Gold, Cut Panels, Metal Rims & Clasp, 5 In.	625.00
Chalice, Amethyst To Clear Bowl, Etched Wreath, Gold, Long Stem, 12½ In.	345.00
Chalice, Marquetry Strawberries, Wheel Carved & Stained Leaves & Stems, 12¼ In.	1007.00
Charger, Cobalt Blue, 4 Shepherds In The Woods, Gold Scrolled Border, 15 In.	259.00
Cheese Dish, Cover, Green, Flowering Urns & Scrolls, Gold Dotted Peacock Eyes, 7 In.	633.00
Cordial, Green, Enamel, 3 In.	130.00
Cruet, Cranberry, Enamel Flowers, Clear Faceted Cut Steeple Stopper, 4¾ In.	250.00
Cruet, Green Translucent, Pinched Sides, Amber Handle & Stopper, Ferns, 9 In.	288.00
Cuspidor, Vaseline, Christmas Snowflake, Woman's	75.00
Decanter, Dragonfly, Flowers, Enameled, Yellow, Clear Pedestal, Handle, Stopper, 10½ In.	225.00
Dresser Box, Covered, Enameled Stork & Floral, Gilt Metal Mounts, 1920s, 6 x 4 In.	1380.00
Dresser Jar, Cobalt Blue, Gold Elephant & Palm Tree Frieze, 5½ In.	1265.00
Ewer, Emerald Green, Oak Leaves, Raised Acorn Jewels, Handle, Signed, 15 In.	1265.00

Moriage, Vase, Rooster, Flowers, Jewels, Bulbous, Ruffled Rim, Loop Handles, Nippon, 7 In. $411.00

SECURITY TIP
Have your chimney cleaned if you move into an old house or if you burn wood regularly. A creosote buildup can cause an explosion. Nesting animals can cause fire or smoke.

Moser, Bowl, Cranberry, Medallion, Roman Warrior, Oval, 3 Scrolled Feet, Shaped Rim, 6 In. $705.00

M

Moser, Punch Bowl, Cover, Etched, Green Tint, Pedestal Base, 14 In. $165.00

Moser, Vase, Enameled Oak Leaves, Gold Bee, Branches, Acorns, 4-Footed Base, 4¾ In. $1265.00

Mother-Of-Pearl Glass, Celery Vase, Herringbone, Melon Ribbed, Blue, 7 In. $235.00

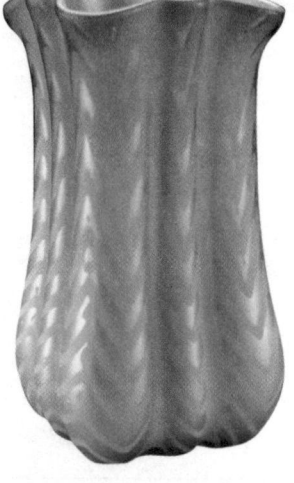

Mother-Of-Pearl Glass, Ewer, Rainbow, Herringbone, Tricornered Top, Frosted Handle, 6 In., Pair $690.00

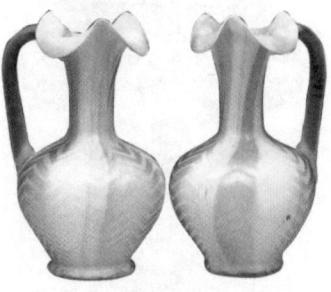

Ewer, Prussian Blue, Horn-Of-Plenty Shape, Applied Clear Reeded Feet & Handle, 11 In.	575.00
Finger Bowl, Enameled Feather, Applied Beads, 4¾ In.	90.00
Goblet, Green, Amber Twist Stem, Signed, 6½ In.	60.00
Perfume Bottle, Clear Green, Gold Embossed Band, c.1920, 4¼ In.	585.00
Perfume Bottle, Cranberry Glass, Enameled, Long Slender Neck, 19th Century, 8 In.	380.00
Perfume Bottle, Opaline, Enameled, 19th Century, 4 In.	160.00
Pitcher, Prussian Blue, Gold Scrolling, Flowers, Applied Crystal Handle, 6½ In.	1495.00
Pitcher, Tankard, Cranberry, White Branches, Gold Coralene Leaves, Blue Dots, Clear Handle, 10 In.	374.00
Plate, Cranberry, Gold Overlay, Enamel Flowers, 7 In.	1150.00
Punch Bowl, Cover, Etched, Green Tint, Pedestal Base, 14 In. *illus*	165.00
Ring Holder, Black Glass, Amethyst Bowl, Gold, Enameled, Scrolling Hearts, Vines	400.00
Rose Bowl, Amber, Multicolored Oak Leaves, Prunts, Acorn Jewels, Footed, Signed, 6 In.	1488.00
Scent Bottle, Stopper, Hexagonal, 5 In.	230.00
Spooner, Opalescent, 5½ In.	34.50
Tumbler, Juice, Amber, Enamel Flowers, Signed, 3¾ In.	140.00
Tumbler, Landscapes, Game Birds, Intaglio, Orange, Pink, Red, Green, 5 In., 6 Piece	550.00
Vase, Amber, Faceted, Mythological Warriors Frieze, Czechoslovakia, Signed, c.1920, 8 In. . . .	705.00
Vase, Amber, Sovereign Band, Gold, Classical Women Warriors, Faceted, Footed, Moser Karlsbad, 8 In.	290.00
Vase, Amber, Sovereign Band, Gold, Women Warriors, Faceted, Moser Karlsbad, 13 In.	465.00
Vase, Amethyst, Elephants, Palm Trees Frieze, Oval, Signed, c.1920	1116.00
Vase, Bud, 3 Prong, Cranberry, Leaves, Twisted Stem, Clear Shell Foot, 16 In.	1668.00
Vase, Bud, Green To Clear, Cylindrical, 6½ In.	225.00
Vase, Clear To Amber, Marquetry Eagle, Pond, Gold Reeds, Water Lilies, 14 In. . . . . . 2530.00 to 3450.00
Vase, Cranberry Cut To Green, Roman Figures, Cylindrical, c.1920, 10 In.	1058.00
Vase, Craquelle, Amber Crackle Glass, Enameled, Fish, Plants, Bulbous, 6½ In.	529.00
Vase, Craquelle, Pinched Sides, Amber Body, Enameled Seaweed, 5 In. . . . . 75.00 to 86.00
Vase, Deer & Tree, Green, Gold, Cylindrical, Signed, c.1900, 12 x 3 In.	345.00
Vase, Enameled Oak Leaves, Gold Bee, Branches, Acorns, 4-Footed Base, 4¾ In. . . . . . . *illus*	1265.00
Vase, Faceted, Cobalt Blue, Acid Etched Gold Band, Women Warriors, Signed, c.1920, 4½ In. .	300.00
Vase, Fan, Green, All Over Green Scrolling, Rigaree Waist, Gold Crimped Foot, 8 In.	259.00
Vase, Flower, Purple To Clear, Signed, c.1900, 5¾ x 2 In.	235.00
Vase, Flowers, Allover, Engraved, Green Shading To Clear, Scalloped Rim, 9 In.	808.00
Vase, Green, Gold Branch, 4 Pillars, Gilt Bronze Foot, c.1900, 11 In.	323.00
Vase, Green Flower, Leaves, Frosted, Flared, Carved, c.1900, 6 x 2 In.	365.00
Vase, Green Translucent, Underwater Scene, 2 Raised Fish, Shouldered, 9 In.	920.00
Vase, Marquetry, Purple Flower, Intaglio Leaves, Amethyst Rim & Foot, Bottle Shape, 9 In. . .	1438.00
Vase, Marquetry Flowers, Green, Pink, Yellow, Cameo, 8½ In.	2280.00
Vase, Purple, Gold, Painted Flowers, Flared, Footed, c.1950, 20 x 9 In.	165.00
Vase, Rubina, Ribbed, Pink & Yellow Mums, Gold Tracery Branches, 9½ In.	575.00
Vase, Translucent Green, Scrolling Gold Flowers, 2 Handles, Squat, 4 In.	115.00
Water Set, Cranberry, Gold Coralene Leaves, White Branches, Clear Twisted Handle, 5 Piece .	865.00
Wine, Clear Bowl, Cranberry Base, Enamel Flowers & Portrait, 5 In.	375.00

MOSS ROSE china was made by many firms from 1808 to 1900. It has a typical moss rose pictured as the design. The plant is not as popular now as it was in Victorian gardens, so the fuzz-covered bud is unfamiliar to most collectors. The dishes were usually decorated with pink and green flowers.

Plate, Dinner, Ironstone, KTK, 10 In.	25.00

MOTHER-OF-PEARL GLASS, or pearl satin glass, was first made in the 1850s in England and in Massachusetts. It was a special type of mold-blown satin glass with air bubbles in the glass, giving it a pearlized color. It has been reproduced. Mother-of-pearl shell objects are listed under Pearl.

Basket, Rainbow, Diamond Quilted, Ruffled Edge, Shaped Vaseline Handle, 8½ In.	1333.00
Biscuit Jar, Blue, Leaves & Stems, Gold Tracery, Round, Metal Lid, 7½ In.	575.00
Bride's Bowl, Egg Shape, Diamond Quilted, Tricornered Ruffled Rim, c.1890, 9½ In.	382.00
Celery Vase, Herringbone, Melon Ribbed, Blue, 7 In. . . . . *illus*	235.00
Cologne, Butterscotch, Diamond Quilted, Daisies, Clear Faceted Stopper, 6 In.	460.00
Dish, Sweetmeat, Blue Satin, Peacock-Eye Optic, Enameled Flowers, Flip Lid, 6 In.	345.00
Dish, Sweetmeat, White, Leaves, Acorns, Flowers, Gold Trim, 5½ In.	403.00
Ewer, Pink, Herringbone, Melon Ribbed, Late 1800s, 12 In.	176.00
Ewer, Rainbow, Herringbone, Crimped & Ruffled Edge, 9 In.	920.00
Ewer, Rainbow, Herringbone, Tricornered Top, Frosted Handle, 6 In., Pair . . . . *illus*	690.00
Pitcher, Diamond Quilted, Shouldered, Rectangular, c.1890, 8 In.	294.00
Pitcher, Tricornered Thumbprint, Blue & Pink Panels, Ruffled Edge, 9½ In.	460.00

Sugar & Creamer, Peach Shaded To Butterscotch, Coin Spot, Camphor Handles, 4½ In. ...	690.00
Sugar & Creamer, Pink, Diamond Quilted, Camphor Handle On Creamer, Ruffled Edges ...	1150.00
Toothpick, Blue	275.00
Vase, Apricot, Diamond Quilted, Camphor Branch Handles, 10⅜ In. ....*illus*	173.00
Vase, Bulbous Stick Form, Diamond Quilted, Shouldered, Late 1800s, 10¼ In.	71.00
Vase, Diamond Quilted, Peach, Shouldered, Flared Rim, 9¾ In. ....*illus*	71.00
Vase, Herringbone, Pink, Camphor Handles, Leaves, Ruffled Rim, 14 In. ....*illus*	470.00
Vase, Herringbone, Pink Shaded To White, Cased, Ruffled Edge, 1900, 9 In.	250.00
Vase, Orange, Herringbone, Camphor Handles, Urn Shape, 8 In.	115.00
Vase, Pink, Flat Sided, Air-Trapped Moire Design, 9¾ In.	1495.00
Vase, Rainbow, Diamond Quilted, Bulbous, Long Neck, Ruffled Rim, Camphor Handle, 7 In.	633.00
Vase, Ruby Cased, Vertical Stripes, Bulbous, Pinched Neck, 6 In.	518.00
Vase, Stick, Rainbow, Herringbone, Oval Body, Ruffled Edge, 8 In.	633.00
Vase, Yellow, Raindrop, Bulbous, Long Neck, Flared & Ruffled Edge, 6 In.	316.00

MOTORCYCLES and motorcycle accessories of all types are being collected today. Examples can be found that date back to the early twentieth century. Toy motorcycles are listed in the Toy category.

Francis-Barnett, Snipe, 1939	2310.00
Model, Pewter, Assembly Line, Harley-Davidson, Showcase, 26 In.	770.00
Pin, Harley-Davidson Distributors, Wagner Dolph Co., Rochester, N.Y., Oval	961.00
Pin, Yale Motorcycle, Celluloid Flag, 2 In.	226.00
Postcard, Photo, Harley-Davidson, Mailman, I Am With 235 Pounds Of Mail, 1914 ....*illus*	441.00
Poster, Harley-Davidson, Metal Frame, 31 x 6 In.	99.00
Sign, United States Chain Tread Motorcycle Tires, Stop Skidding, G. Hollrock, 38 x 20 In. ...	10100.00
Sign, Harley-Davidson, Motorcycle Sales & Service, Porcelain, Flange, 10 x 17 In.	550.00

MOUNT WASHINGTON, *see Mt. Washington category.*

MOVIE memorabilia of all types is collected. Animation Art, Games, Sheet Music, Toys, and some celebrity items are listed in their own section. A lobby card is 11 by 14 inches. A set of lobby cards includes seven scene cards and one title card. A one sheet, the standard movie poster, is 27 by 41 inches. A three sheet is 81 by 40 inches. A half sheet is 22 by 28 inches. A window card, made of cardboard, is 14 by 22 inches. An insert is 14 by 36 inches. A herald is a promotional item handed out to patrons. Press books, sent to exhibitors to promote a movie, contain ads & lists of what is available for advertising, i.e., posters, lobby cards. Press kits, sent to the media, contain photos and details about the movie, i.e., stars' biographies & interviews.

Banner, The Searchers, John Wayne, Warner Brothers, 1956, 24 x 83 In.	1920.00
Book, Spiral Bound, Exhibitors, Paramount Pictures, 1934-35 Season, 9¼ x 12¼ In.	336.00
Herald, Lost Horizon, Ronald Colman, 1937	15.00
Herald, The Fly, Vincent Price, 1958	9.50
Lobby Card, Baby Face, Barbara Stanwyck, Warner Brothers, 1933	978.00
Lobby Card, Big Store, Marx Brothers, 1941	339.00
Lobby Card, Bride Of Frankenstein, Karloff, Monster Thriller, Universal, 1935, 11 x 14 In. ..	10755.00
Lobby Card, Buck Privates, Abbott & Costello, 1941	149.00
Lobby Card, Day At The Races, Marx Brothers, MGM, 1937	4888.00
Lobby Card, Devil's Brother, Laurel & Hardy, MGM, 1933, 11 x 14 In.	403.00
Lobby Card, Dough Boys, Buster Keaton, MGM, 1926, 11 x 14 In.	517.00
Lobby Card, Harvey, Universal International, 1950	518.00
Lobby Card, High Sierra, Warner Brothers, 1941	633.00
Lobby Card, House Of Fear, Universal, 1945	374.00
Lobby Card, I Walked With A Zombie, RKO, 1943	1035.00
Lobby Card, I'm No Angel, Mae West, 1933	690.00
Lobby Card, It's A Wonderful Life, James Stewart, Donna Reed, 1946	460.00
Lobby Card, Notorious, Hitchcock, RKO, 1946	690.00
Lobby Card, Parachute Jumper, Douglas Fairbanks Jr., Bette Davis, 1932	374.00
Lobby Card, Rain, Joan Crawford, United Artists, 1932	1840.00
Lobby Card, Taxi, James Cagney, Warner Brothers, 1932	2530.00
Lobby Card, The Three Caballeros, RKO Radio Pictures, 1945	305.00
Pin, Give Crime A Break, Bring Back Inspector Clouseau, 3 In.	37.00
Pin, Sky Raiders Club, 12 Thrill Powered Chapters, Celluloid, 1941, 1¼ In.	303.00
Poster, 2001: A Space Odyssey, MGM, 1968, 1 Sheet	720.00
Poster, Arsenic & Old Lace, Cary Grant, 1944, 1 Sheet	783.00
Poster, Attack Of The 50 Foot Woman, Allied Artists, 1958, 1 Sheet	6613.00
Poster, Ben-Hur, Charlton Heston, 1959, 1 Sheet	310.00

Mother-Of-Pearl Glass, Vase, Apricot, Diamond Quilted, Camphor Branch Handles, 10⅜ In.
$173.00

Mother-Of-Pearl Glass, Vase, Diamond Quilted, Peach, Shouldered, Flared Rim, 9¾ In.
$71.00

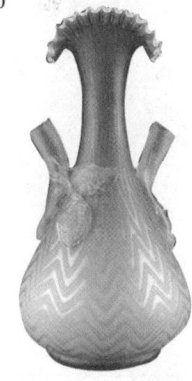

Mother-Of-Pearl Glass, Vase, Herringbone, Pink, Camphor Handles, Leaves, Ruffled Rim, 14 In.
$470.00

M

Motorcycle, Postcard, Photo, Harley-Davidson, Mailman, I Am With 235 Pounds Of Mail, 1914
$441.00

Mt. Joye, Vase, Art Nouveau,
Pink, Yellow Roses, Leafy Band,
Chipped Ice, Flared, 19 In.
$2280.00

Mt. Washington, Biscuit Jar,
Cover, Napoli, Palmer Cox Brownies,
Gold Enameled, Signed, 8 In.
$5463.00

Mt. Washington, Jug, Wine,
Colonial Ware, Lavender Flowers,
Gold Enameled Stems, 12 In.
$288.00

Mt. Washington, Muffineer,
Cranberry Glass, Fig Shape,
Gold Vines, Bark Texture, 3⅞ In.
$4600.00

Poster, Breakfast At Tiffany's, Audrey Hepburn, Paramount, 1961, Half Sheet	1840.00
Poster, Casey At The Bat, Cartoon Special, RKO, 1954, 41 x 27 In.	657.00
Poster, Duck Soup, Marx Brothers, Riding On Bullet, 1933, Half Sheet	28680.00
Poster, Enter The Dragon, Bruce Lee, Warner Brothers, 1973, 3 Sheet	633.00
Poster, For A Few Dollars More, Clint Eastwood, United Artists, 1967, 3 Sheet	863.00
Poster, Gaslight, Ingrid Bergman, Charles Boyer, MGM, 1944, 3 Sheet	960.00
Poster, Girl Crazy, Mickey Rooney, Judy Garland, 1943, Insert	285.00
Poster, Graduate, Anne Bancroft, Dustin Hoffman, 1968, 1 Sheet	956.00
Poster, Grand Hotel, Crawford, Garbo, John, Lionel Barrymore, 1932, Window Card	900.00
Poster, Guys & Dolls, Brando, Sinatra, Simmons, Blaine, MGM, 1955, 1 Sheet	508.00
Poster, Hell's Angels, Howard Hughes, Jean Marlow, 1930, Window Card	2613.00
Poster, How To Marry A Millionaire, Marilyn Monroe, 1953, 1 Sheet.	445.00
Poster, I Married A Monster From Outer Space, Paramount, 1958, 1 Sheet	336.00
Poster, Invaders From Mars, 20th Century Fox, 1953, 3 Sheet	1725.00
Poster, Invasion Of The Body Snatchers, Allied Artists, 1956, 3 Sheet	1150.00
Poster, Iron Butterfly, Fillmore West, Bill Graham, January, 1969, Window Card	616.00
Poster, Life & Adventures Of Buffalo Bill, 1915, 1 Sheet	2000.00
Poster, Merrie Melodies, Cartoon, Warner Brothers, 1940, 1 Sheet	2530.00
Poster, Mickey Mouse, Meller Drammer, United Artists, 1933, 41 x 27 In.	38837.00
Poster, Mickey Mouse, Mickeys Pal Pluto, United Artist, 1933, 41 x 27 In.	28680.00
Poster, Miracle On 34th Street, Maureen O'Hara, John Payne, 1947, 1 Sheet	2868.00
Poster, On The Waterfront, Marlon Brando, Columbia, 1954, Half Sheet	633.00
Poster, Pillow Talk, Rock Hudson, Doris Day, Universal, 1959, 1 Sheet	431.00
Poster, Planet Of The Apes, 20th Century Fox, 1968, Window Card	138.00
Poster, Rebecca, Hitchcock, United Artists, 1940, 1 Sheet	5750.00
Poster, Rebel Without A Cause, James Dean, Warner Brothers, 1955, Half Sheet	1265.00
Poster, Reform School Girl, American International, 1957, 1 Sheet	312.00
Poster, Roman Holiday, Paramount, Audrey Hepburn, 1962, 1 Sheet	173.00
Poster, Some Like It Hot, Marilyn Monroe, United Artists, 1959, 1 Sheet	1265.00
Poster, Spartacus, Kirk Douglas, Laurence Olivier, Universal, 1960, 1 Sheet	717.00
Poster, Tarzan & His Mate, Weissmuller, O'Sullivan, MGM, 1934, Half Sheet	1725.00
Poster, Taxi Driver, Robert Deniro, 1976, 1 Sheet	135.00
Poster, Ten Commandments, Charlton Heston, 1956, 1 Sheet	239.00
Poster, The Big Sleep, Humphrey Bogart, Lauren Bacall, 1946, 3 Sheet	11353.00
Poster, The Birds, Hitchcock, Universal, 1963, 1 Sheet	537.00
Poster, The Blue Dahlia, Alan Ladd, Veronica Lake, 1946, 1 Sheet	4481.00
Poster, The Dolly Sister, Grablehaver, Linen Back, 1945, 3 Sheet	410.00
Poster, The Great Escape, Steve McQueen, United Artists, 1963, 3 Sheet	633.00
Poster, The Outlaw, Jane Russell, United Artists, 1946, 1 Sheet	2070.00
Poster, The Sting, Newman, Redford, Universal, 1974, 1 Sheet	4313.00
Poster, They Died With Their Boots On, Flynn, Warner Brothers, 1945, 1 Sheet	1783.00
Poster, Thunderball, Sean Connery, United Artists, 1965, 3 Sheet	1610.00
Poster, To Kill A Mockingbird, Universal, 1963, 6 Sheet	1035.00
Poster, Tobor The Great, Republic, 1954, 1 Sheet	932.00
Poster, Vertigo, James Stewart, Kim Novak, Paramount, 1958, 1 Sheet	4481.00
Poster, West Side Story, United Artists, 1961, 1 Sheet	575.00
Poster, Wild Company, Fox, 1930, 3 Sheet	1150.00
Press Book, Boxcar Bertha, David Carradine, 1972	15.00
Press Book, The Brotherhood, Kirk Douglas, 1968	8.50
Press Kit, Gator, Burt Reynolds, 1976	10.50
Press Kit, Rain Man, Tom Cruise, Dustin Hoffman, 1988	9.99
Program, My Fair Lady, Audrey Hepburn, 1964	7.50
Program, Oliver, Mark Lester, 1963	5.00
Script, Something's Got To Give, Marilyn Monroe, 149 Pages, 1962	3479.00

MT. JOYE is an enameled cameo glass made in the late nineteenth and twentieth centuries by Saint-Hilaire Touvier de Varraux and Co. of Pantin, France. This same company made De Vez glass. Pieces were usually decorated with enameling. Most pieces are not marked.

Bowl, Amethyst Shaded To Clear, Stemmed Mums, Scalloped Gilt Rim, 8 In.	345.00
Cracker Jar, Vaseline, Optic Ribbed, Enameled Flowers, Embossed Metal Lid, 7½ In.	325.00 to 374.00
Jam Jar, Vaseline, Optic Ribbed, Enameled Flowers, Metal Lid, 5 In.	250.00 to 290.00
Rose Bowl, Cyclamen, Enameled, Gold Leaves, Stems, Scalloped Rim, Chipped Ice Ground, 4 In.	575.00
Vase, Acid Etched, Enameled Flowers, Rectangular, 6⅜ x 3 x 2½ In.	850.00
Vase, Art Nouveau, Pink, Yellow Roses, Leafy Band, Chipped Ice, Flared, 19 In. *illus*	2280.00
Vase, Clear Shaded To Amethyst, Enameled Flower, Ribbed, Ruffled Edge, 4¼ In.	230.00

Vase, Irises, Purple, White, Yellow, Enameled, Textured, Ruffled Edge, Bulbous, 6¾ In.	. . . . .	558.00
Vase, Ruby, Textured, Yellow Flowers, Gold Stems, Gold Rim, 6½ In.	. . . .	460.00
Vase, Stick, Green, Violets, Gold Leaves, Bulbous, Squat, 14 In.	. . . .	690.00
Vase, Trumpet, Silver, Gold Sunflowers, Gold Stalactite Border, Chipped Ice Ground, 10 In.	. .	920.00
Vase, Violets, Stemmed Leaves, Enameled, Hexagonal Rim, 3⅞ In.	. . . .	161.00

MT. WASHINGTON Glass Works started in 1837 in South Boston, Massachusetts. In 1870 the company moved to New Bedford, Massachusetts. Many types of art glass were made there until 1894, when the company merged with Pairpoint Manufacturing Co. Amberina, Burmese, Crown Milano, Cut Glass, Peachblow, and Royal Flemish are each listed in their own category.

Biscuit Jar, Cover, Blue Flowers, Gold Scrolling, Lid, Oval, 7 In.	. . . .	225.00
Biscuit Jar, Cover, Napoli, Palmer Cox Brownies, Gold Enameled, Signed, 8 In.	. . . .*illus*	5463.00
Biscuit Jar, Cream With Pink, Amethyst Flowers, Oval, 7 In.	. . . .	200.00
Biscuit Jar, Scrolling Medallion, Colonial Man & Woman, Silver Plated Lid, 10 In.	. . . .	489.00
Bowl, Cameo, Pink Cut To Opaque White, Ruffled Edge, Square, 4 x 8 In.	. . . .	646.00
Candlestick, Clambroth & Cornflower Blue, Frosted, 8½ In.	. . . .	316.00
Epergne, Vase, Trumpet, Amberina, Ruffled Base, c.1883, 9 In.	. . . .	2990.00
Jug, Wine, Colonial Ware, Lavender Flowers, Gold Enameled Stems, 12 In.	. . . .*illus*	288.00
Muffineer, Cranberry Glass, Fig Shape, Gold Vines, Bark Texture, 3⅞ In.	. . . .*illus*	4600.00
Muffineer, Fig Shape, Yellow Flowers, Leaves, Stems, Blue Textured, 4⅛ In.	. . . .	1390.00
Mustard, Cover, Fig Shape, Forget-Me-Not, Shaped Handle, 3 In.	. . . .	500.00
Pitcher, Verona, Blue, Purple Violets, Gold Trim, Optic Ribbed, Reeded Handle, 9 In.	. . . . . .	345.00
Saltshaker, Egg Shape, Flowers, Gold-Washed Metal Chick's Head, 3 In.	. . . .*illus*	460.00
Saltshaker, Fig Shape, Grape Leaves, Multicolored Berries, Texture, 3 In.	. . . .	377.00
Saltshaker, Melon Ribbed, Enameled Flowers, 2½ In.	. . . .	75.00
Sugar Shaker, Egg Shape, Blue To White, Dogwood Flowers, c.1890, 4¾ In.	. . . .	235.00
Sugar Shaker, Egg Shape, White Daisies, Green Leaves, 4½ In.	. . . .	230.00
Sugar Shaker, Fig Shape, Yellow, Pink Flowers, Green Leaves, 4 In.	. . . .	2300.00
Sugar Shaker, Melon Ribbed, Raised Daisy Cluster, Embossed Lid, 1890, 4 In.	. . . .	550.00
Toothpick, Square Mouth, Enameled Mums, 2¾ In.	. . . .	350.00
Toothpick, Yellow, White Chrysanthemums, Orange Bark, Lobed, 1¾ In.	. . . .*illus*	345.00
Tumbler, Lava, Black, Red, Purple, Blue, Green Glass Inclusions, c.1878, 3½ In.	. . . .	4830.00
Urn, Pink, Blue, White & Lavender, Shell Shape Handles	. . . .	1400.00
Vase, Blue, Mother-Of-Pearl, 6 In.	. . . .	81.00
Vase, Colonial Ware, Bedouins, Camels, Enameled, Bulbous, 3 Ring Handles, 12 In.	. . . .	5175.00
Vase, Egyptians, Camel, Cartouche, Stars, Medallions, Rust Ground, Handles, 13 In.	. . . .	28175.00
Vase, Enameled Guba Ducks, Prussian Blue Front & Back, 15 In.	. . . .	3750.00
Vase, Flared Rim, Gold Floral, Mauve, Applied Handles, 1900, 12 In.	. . . .	295.00
Vase, Mother-Of-Pearl, Shaded Blue, Herringbone, 4-Lobed Rim, 6 In.	. . . .*illus*	81.00
Vase, Urn Shaped, Fall Flowers, Footed, Applied Handles, 7 In.	. . . .	225.00

MUD FIGURES are small Chinese pottery figures made in the twentieth century. The figures usually represent workers, scholars, farmers, or merchants. Other pieces are trees, houses, and similar parts of the landscape. The figures have unglazed faces and hands but glazed clothing. They were originally made for fish tanks or planters. Mud figures were of little interest and brought low prices until the 1980s. When the prices rose, reproductions appeared.

Figurine, Old Lady, Cotton Bat Skirt, Umbrella, Basket, Late 1800s, 12 x 6½ In.	. . . .	575.00

MULBERRY ware was made in the Staffordshire district of England from about 1850 to 1860. The dishes were decorated with a reddish brown transfer design, now called mulberry. Many of the patterns are similar to those used for flow blue and other Staffordshire transfer wares.

Mulberry, Pitcher, English Scene, 4 In.	. . . .	65.00
Mulberry, Plate, Bochara, Pagoda, Bridge, Flowers, Ironstone, James Edwards, 9½ In.	. . . . . .	125.00
Mulberry, Plate, Haddon, Cows, Bridge, Castle, Scott Brothers, Southwick Pottery, 9½ In.	. . . . .	75.00
Mulberry, Plate, Man On Horse, Man Pushing Stubborn Mule, Earthenware, 9¼ x 1¼ In.	. . .	208.00
Mulberry, Platter, Gray Tones, Lake, Canadian Scene, Morely & Co., 17 x 14 In.	. . . .	400.00
Mulberry, Platter, Rose, Ironstone, Challinor, 13½ x 10½ x 1¼ In.	. . . .	200.00

MULLER FRERES, French for Muller Brothers, made cameo and other glass from about 1895 to 1933. Their factory was first located in Luneville, then in nearby Croismare, France. Pieces were usually marked with the company name.

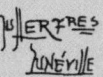

Mt. Washington, Saltshaker, Egg Shape, Flowers, Gold-Washed Metal Chick's Head, 3 In. $460.00

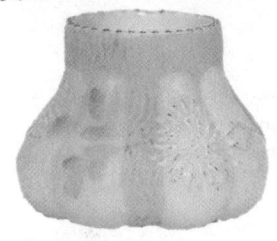

Mt. Washington, Toothpick, Yellow, White Chrysanthemums, Orange Bark, Lobed, 1¾ In. $345.00

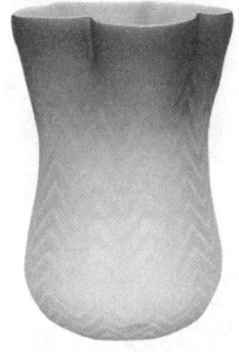

Mt. Washington, Vase, Mother-Of-Pearl, Shaded Blue, Herringbone, 4-Lobed Rim, 6 In. $81.00

M

TIP
Always wash antique china in a sink lined with a rubber mat or towels. This helps prevent chipping. Wash one piece at a time. Rinse and let it air dry. If you suspect a piece has been repaired, do not wash it. Clean with a soft brush dampened in a solution of ammonia and water.

Muncie, Vase, Blue Over Pink Matte Glaze, Tapered, 6½ In.
$58.00

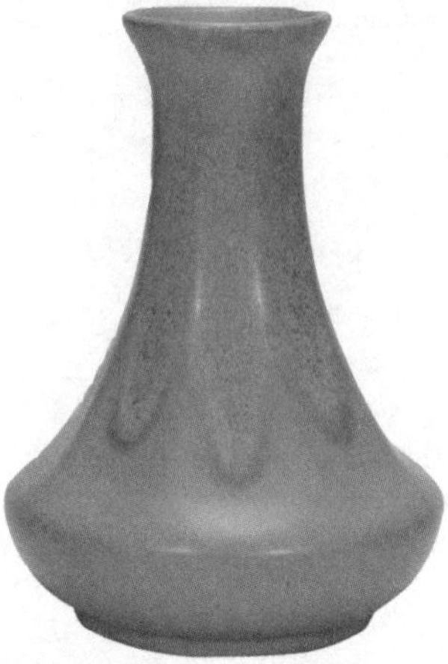

Muncie, Vase, Green Matte Over Pumpkin Glaze, Lobed, 2 Handles, No. 192-6, 7 x 7 In.
$65.00

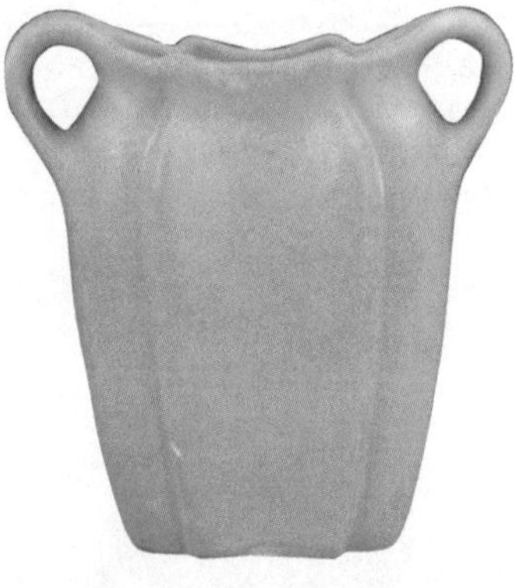

Muncie, Vase, Green Over Brown Matte Glaze, Shouldered, 2 Handles, 6 In.
$115.00

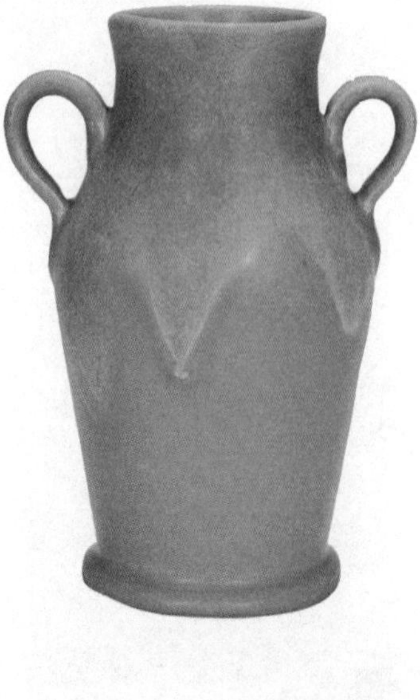

Chandelier, Dome Center Shade, 3 Gold Pendants, Purple, Ormolu Metalwork 1763.00
Chandelier, Wrought Iron, Glass, c.1900, 30 x 38 In. 7800.00
Vase, Birds, Background Trees, c.1920, 16 x 12 In. 1295.00
Vase, Birds In Flight, Trees, Mold Blown, Signed, c.1920, 16 x 12 In. 1295.00
Vase, Bulbous, Landscape, Waterscape, Brown Cut To Orange, Cameo, 11 In. 1410.00
Vase, Flitting Birds, Mold Blown, Trees, c.1920, 16 x 12 In. 1295.00
Vase, Flowers & Vines, Frosted, Wheel Carved, Cameo, 14 In. 1265.00
Vase, Landscape, Wooded Winter, Mauve, Amber Ground, Cameo, Signed, 4¼ In. 1200.00
Vase, Mottled Amber To Crimson, Allover Gold Mica, Oval, Cameo, Signed, 9 In. 690.00
Vase, Mottled Amethyst, Orange, Green, Silver Mica Patches, Cameo, Signed, 8 In. 403.00
Vase, Mottled Blue, Crimson, Sailing Ships, Urn Shaped, Footed, Cameo, Signed, 10 In. 1438.00
Vase, Mottled Yellow Shaded To Citron, Ruby Flowers, Bulbous, Cameo, 14 In. 4888.00
Vase, Orange, White Ground, Trees, Bushes, Brown, Green, Cameo, Signed, 9¾ In. 660.00
Vase, Orange To Purple, Signed, 1910-41, 6 In. 2500.00
Vase, Spherical, Mottled Orange & Purple, Flared Rim, Purple Feet, 12 In. 700.00
Vase, Trees, Mountains, Blue Lake, Sky, Flattened Bottle Shape, Loop Handles, 9 In. 7763.00
Vase, Yellow, Blue, Green, Butterflies, Pine Tree, Mottled, Signed, 9½ In. 3738.00
Vase, Yellow, Mottled Brown, Internally Decorated, Early 1900s, 13¾ In. 167.00
Vessel, Mottled Orange & Purple, Flared Rim, Footed, Signed, 12 In. 700.00

MUNCIE Clay Products Company was established by Charles Benham in Muncie, Indiana, in 1922. The company made pottery for the florist and giftshop trade. The company closed by 1939. Pieces are marked with the name *Muncie* or just with a system of numbers and letters, like *1A*.

MUNCIE

Bookends, Blue Over Rose Glaze, 6 x 6½ In. 270.00
Chamberstick, Blue Matte, Arts & Crafts, 4½ In. 50.00
Lamp, Dancing Nudes, Green Matte Glaze, Nude Finial, 27 In. 743.00
Lamp, Green Matte Over Rose Glazes, Art Deco, Marked, 6¼ In. 715.00
Pitcher, White Matte Over Blue, Marked, 4⅛ In. 50.00
Vase, Blue Glaze, 7 x 4½ In. 160.00
Vase, Blue Over Green, Handle, 11½ In. 253.00
Vase, Blue Over Green, Marked, Incised 3, 6¾ In. 55.00
Vase, Blue Over Pink Matte Glaze, Tapered, 6½ In. .... *illus* 58.00
Vase, Double Bud, Marked, 4¾ x 8½ In. 110.00
Vase, Fan, Blue Matte Over Rose, 7¾ In. 61.00
Vase, Flowing, Blue, Lavender & Rose Drip Glaze, 5¾ In. 120.00
Vase, Goldfish, Blue Over Green, Marked, 8⅛ In. 374.00
Vase, Green & Aqua Glaze, 6¼ In. 110.00
Vase, Green Matte Over Lilac, Handle, Marked, 10⅛ In. 187.00
Vase, Green Matte Over Pumpkin Glaze, Lobed, 2 Handles, No. 192-6, 7 x 7 In. .... *illus* 65.00
Vase, Green Matte Over Purple, 7¼ In. 160.00
Vase, Green Matte Over Rose, Double Handles, Marked, 5¼ In. 39.00
Vase, Green Matte Over Rose, Marked, 5½ x 6⅛ In. 28.00
Vase, Green Over Brown Matte Glaze, Shouldered, 2 Handles, 6 In. .... *illus* 115.00
Vase, Green Over Lavender Matte, 4¾ In. 110.00
Vase, Gunmetal Black, 2 Handles, No. 143, 6½ In. 99.00
Vase, Hand Thrown Form, Folded Rim, Dimpled Body, 9 In. 390.00
Vase, Peachskin, No. 102, Marked, 6½ In. 94.00
Vase, Pencil Holder, Rombic, No. 308, Green Matte, Pumpkin Glaze, R. Haley, 6 In. .... *illus* 500.00
Vase, Pinched Waist, Pastel Matte Glazes, Marked, 9¼ In. 105.00
Vase, Pillow, Green Gloss, No. 192, Marked, 9 In. 61.00
Vase, Shouldered, Green Matte Over Lilac, No. 115, Marked, 5¾ In. 121.00
Vase, White Matte Over Rose Glaze, 6¼ x 5 In. 120.00

MURANO, *see Glass-Venetian category.*

MUSIC boxes and musical instruments are listed here. Phonograph records, jukeboxes, phonographs, and sheet music are listed in other categories in this book.

Accordion, Hutschelli, Black Lacquer Case, Mother-Of-Pearl Accents, Case, Italy, 14 In. *.illus* 71.00
Accordion, Moreschi, Bakelite Case, Art Deco Chrome Accents, Travel Case, c.1935, 19 In. ... 71.00
Banjo Case, Wood, Applied Gold Stars & Scrolls, 38 x 13 In. 575.00
Bass, Church, J.G. Pickering, 2-Piece Back, Greenland, 1832, 31 1/16 In. 1763.00
Bow, Viola, Mirecourt, Ebony Frog, Parisian Eye, Nickel Adjuster, c.1920 .... 1410.00
Bow, Violin, F.N. Voirin, Octagonal, Ebony Frog, Pearl Eye, Silver, Ebony Adjuster, France 7838.00

M

Bow, Violin, Louis Morizot, Silver Mounted, Ebony Frog, Parisian Eye, France	3173.00
Box, Bremond, Organ, No. 8818, 10 Tunes, 21-Key Organ, Ebony, Enamel Inlay, 2 x 14 In. ..	1528.00
Box, Cylinder, 4 Mandolin Tunes, Rosewood Veneer, Marquetry, Swiss, 22 x 9 In.	4830.00
Box, Cylinder, 6 Bell Strikes, Dove Finials, Bee Hammers, Swiss, 11½ x 24½ In.	3740.00
Box, Cylinder, 6 Tunes, Burl Veneer Case, Ebonized, Brass Handles, Swiss, 34 x 13 In.	4140.00
Box, Cylinder, 8 Tunes, Grained Case, Rosewood Veneer Lid, Brass, Mother-Of-Pearl, 20 In. ..	940.00
Box, Cylinder, 8 Tunes, Marquetry, Rosewood Veneer Case, Swiss, 20¼ x 6⅞ In.	1265.00
Box, Cylinder, Capital Cuff, Model C, Spring Wind, 7 Tunes ....*illus*	6435.00
Box, Cylinder, Mermod Freres, No. 66535, 8 Tunes, Grained Case, c.1888, 17 In.	353.00
Box, Cylinder, Murgueter, Floral Marquetry, No. 3772, Swiss, 13-In. Cylinder, 5 x 23 x 9 In. ..	1265.00
Box, Cylinder, Nicole Freres, Marquetry, Rosewood, Musique De Geneve, 6 Tunes, 18 x 7 In. ..	125.00
Box, Cylinder, Orchestra, Wood Case, Flowers On Top, 12¾ In. ....*illus*	1755.00
Box, Cylinder, Paillard, No. 8112, 12 Airs, Rosewood Grain Case, 20 In.	588.00
Box, Cylinder, Reuge, Walnut Case, Ebonized Borders, Musical Motifs, 7½ In.	235.00
Box, Cylinder, Walnut Frame, Original Play List, 15 In.	468.00
Box, Donkey Organ, Frati & Co., Wood, Inlay, Gold Gilded Hand Point, 24 x 24 In.	3850.00
Box, Fruitwood, Mahogany, Cylinder, Brass Mounted, Ebonized, Parcel Gilt, 8½ x 18 In.	4800.00
Box, Lochmann's Walnut, Clock Top, Door, Cabinet, 160 Teeth, 7 Discs, c.1900, 84 In. ..*illus*	19576.00
Box, Nicoles Freres, Mahogany, Rosewood, Brass, Ivory, Mother-Of-Pearl, Boulle, 28 x 12 In. .	40250.00
Box, Polyphon, Model 49C, 4-Section Folding Lid, 118 Teeth, 16 Bells, Crank, c.1900 ...*illus*	39153.00
Box, Polyphon, Walnut, Germany, c.1894, 13 Discs	13, 900
Box, Regina, Beaded Cover, 73 Discs, Paper Lithographed Label, Copyright 1896	2645.00
Box, Regina, Corona, Mahogany Case, Model 33, Spindle Gallery, Urn Finials, 29 Discs, 28 x 39 In. ..	25300.00
Box, Regina, Double Comb, Mahogany Case, 20¾ In. ....*illus*	4973.00
Box, Regina, Mahogany, Case, Double Comb, 15½ In.	3300.00
Box, Regina, Mahogany Case, Double Comb, 20¾ In.	4025.00
Box, Regina, Mahogany Case, Double Comb, Folding Top, Stand, Celluloid Plaque, 29 In. ...	9988.00
Box, Regina, Mahogany Case, Double Comb, Regina On Inside Cover, 20¾ In.	4675.00
Box, Regina, Mahogany Case, Double Comb, Sliding Doors, 27 In.	10450.00
Box, Regina, Mahogany Case, Double Comb, Woman & Children Inside Cover, 20¾ In.	4025.00
Box, Regina, Mahogany Case, Double Comb, Woman & Children Inside Cover, No Crank, 16 In.	3525.00
Box, Regina, Mahogany Case, Double Combs, Serpentine Stand, 15½-In. Discs, 45 In.	6463.00
Box, Regina, Mahogany Case, Floor Cabinet, Double Comb, Disc, 19th Century, 37 In.	4230.00
Box, Regina, Mahogany Case, Sarcophagus Top, Rope Molding, 15½-In. Discs., 12 x 21 x 20 In. .	2750.00
Box, Regina, Oak Case, Double Comb, Door, Dragon Front, 27 In.	18700.00
Box, Regina, Oak Case, Double Comb, Woman & Children Inside Cover, 15½ In.	2750.00
Box, Regina, Oak Hexaphone, No. 103	8250.00
Box, Regina, Sublima, Upright, Mahogany	8625.00
Box, Regina Disc Changer, 27½ In., Quartersawn Oak Case, 67 In.	19800.00
Box, Reuge, Birth Of Christ Scene, Wood, Cover, Swiss, 3 x 5 x 8¾ In.	88.00
Box, Rosewood, Inlaid, Cylinder, Piccolo, No. 25034, Marque De Fabrique, 1800s, 22 In.	5000.00
Box, Singing Bird, Box, Tortoiseshell, Bontems, Barrel Mechanism, Gilt, 4 In.	3055.00
Box, Singing Bird, Cage, Bird Sings & Moves, Germany, 12 In.	715.00
Box, Singing Bird, Cage, Brass, Dome Top, Birds, Feathers, France, 19 x 9 In. ....*illus*	1495.00
Box, Singing Bird, Cage, Yellow, Red, Germany, 8½ In.	330.00
Box, Singing Bird, Enamel, Moving Beak, Landscape, Karl Griesbaum, 4 In.	3055.00
Box, Singing Bird, Feathers, Sterling Silver, Allover Rococo, 2½ x 4 x 2¾ In. ....*illus*	2875.00
Box, Singing Bird, Mechanical, Tin, Painted White, Red, Yellow, Blue, Flaps Wings, 6 In.	160.00
Box, Singing Bird, Metal Case, Egyptian Decor, Women, Eagle, Turler, Zurich, 4 x 3 In. .*illus*	288.00
Box, Singing Bird, Oval, Embossed, Cherubs, Leafy Vines, c.1970, 4½ x 2½ In.	2530.00
Box, Singing Bird, Pierced Brass Plate, Bombe Case, Acanthus, 4¼ x 2¼ In.	4600.00
Box, Singing Bird, Pops Up, Rococo, Mask, Dolphin, Sterling Silver, Marked, EB 925, 3 x 4 x 3 In.	2875.00
Box, Singing Bird, Yellow Plumage, Moving Head, Beak, Tail, Brass Cage, 10 In.	176.00
Box, Singing Bird In Cage, Real Feathers, Animated, Swiss, c.1920, 12 In.	385.00
Box, Singing Birds, Cage, Moving Heads, Beaks, Brass, Victorian, c.1890, 20 x 11 In.	5950.00
Box, Symphonion, Walnut Case, Diametric Combs, 10¾-In. Discs, 17 In.	1763.00
Box, Symphonion, Walnut Case, Double Diametric Combs, 9¼-In. Discs, 16 In.	646.00
Box, Tortoiseshell, Brass Pin Cylinder, Diamond Inlay, 3⅝ x 2¼ In.	345.00
Box, Troubadour, Circassian Walnut Case, 10 Discs, Picture In Lid, Germany, c.1895	1750.00
Box, Victrola, Victor, Model VV-IX, Oak, Hinged Lid, 20 Records, 15 x 20 x 17 In.	173.00
Clock, Picture, Oil, On Metal, Landscape, Mill, Castle, Key Wind, Vienna, 27 x 37 In.	3525.00
Concertina, Douglas & Co., Rosewood, Steel Reeds, Octagonal Case, 7 x 7¼ In.	1380.00
Contrabass, 2-Piece Back, Curl, Medium Curl Ribs, Brown Varnish, c.1900, 43 In.	7050.00
Drum, Gretsch, Mahogany, Maple, Twine, 12 x 14½ In.	230.00
Guitar, Acoustic, Yamaha, Model FG 230, Case, 43½ In.	147.00
Guitar, C.F. Martin, Model 00-18, Flat Top, Acoustic, Hard-Shell Case, 1970, 39½ In. ...*illus*	2070.00

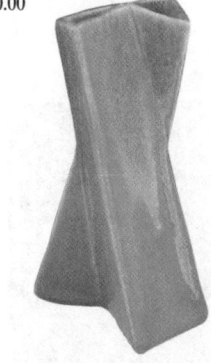

Muncie, Vase, Pencil Holder,
Rombic, No. 308, Green Matte,
Pumpkin Glaze,
R. Haley, 6 In.
$500.00

Music, Accordion, Hutschelli,
Black Lacquer Case,
Mother-Of-Pearl Accents, Case,
Italy, 14 In.
$71.00

M

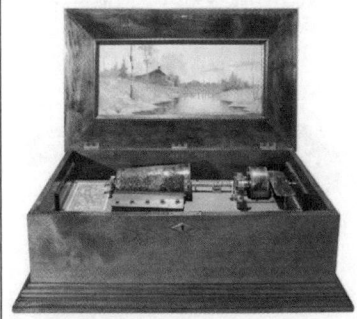

Music, Box, Cylinder, Capital Cuff,
Model C, Spring Wind, 7 Tunes
$6435.00

Music, Box, Cylinder, Orchestra,
Wood Case, Flowers On Top, 12¾ In.
$1755.00

Music, Box, Lochmann's Walnut, Clock Top, Door, Cabinet, 160 Teeth, 7 Discs, c.1900, 84 In. $19576.00

Music, Box, Polyphon, Model 49C, 4-Section Folding Lid, 118 Teeth, 16 Bells, Crank, c.1900 $39153.00

Music, Box, Regina, Double Comb, Mahogany Case, 20¾ In. $4973.00

Guitar, C.F. Martin, Model D-28, 242512, Acoustic, 1969	3173.00
Guitar, C.F. Martin, Model J-45, Rosewood, Maple, Mahogany Neck, 1942, 20¼ In.	2468.00
Harmonicon, Federal, Mahogany, Bird's-Eye Maple, 25 Glasses, 1800s, 39 x 39 x 28 In.	6844.00
Harp, Browne & Buckwell, N.Y., Giltwood, Plaster, Brass, Empire Style, 68 In.	6300.00
Harp, Erard Freres, Carved Giltwood, Gilt Brass Mounted, France, 1806, 62 x 30½ In.	3525.00
Harp, J. Erat Maker, Mahogany, Reeded Column, Burl Veneer, Case, 66 x 35 In.	5175.00
Harp, Lyon & Healy, Maple	7188.00
Harp, Painted, Parcel Gilt, Turned, Fluted, Downswept Crest Rail, Late 1800s, 68 x 31 In.	1770.00
Langlid, 10 Strings, 3 Pairs Unfretted Double Strings, Tuning Heads, 31 x 3½ In.	259.00
Mandolin, Gibson, F4, Maple Back, Truss Rod, Adjustable Bridge, 1922, 26 x 10 In.	8050.00
Mandolin, Gibson, Style A, No. 44936, Poplar, Cedar Neck, Case, 1906, 13¾ In.	705.00
Mandolin, Gibson, Style A-4, No. 21405, Poplar, Cedar Neck, Pearl Inlay, Case, 1914, 14 In.	1528.00
Melodeon, Mason & Hamlin, Boston, Rosewood, Music Stand, Scrolled Pedals, 32 x 46 In. *illus*	575.00
Nickelodeon, J.P. Seeburg, Arched Leaded Glass Panel, Eagle, Oak, 48 x 62 x 24 In.	8625.00
Nickelodeon, J.P. Seeburg, Oak, Stained Glass, c.1920	15400.00
Organ, Parlor, Walnut, Incised Decoration, Victorian, 48 x 53 x 23 In. *illus*	106.00
Organette, Celestina, Mechanical Orginette Co., 20-Note, Walnut Case, c.1881, 34 In.	764.00
Organette, Ehrlich, Patent 24-Note, Hand Crank, Grained Case, Incised, 20 Discs, 15½ In.	646.00
Phonograph, Victor E, Disc	1750.00
Piano, Baby Grand, Collard & Collard, Walnut, c.1900, 40¾ x 59¾ In.	5060.00
Piano, Baby Grand, Steinway & Sons, Model M, Mahogany, Bench, 55 x 66 x 38 In. *illus*	12650.00
Piano, Grand, Steinway, Harp Number 309229, Model S, Mahogany Case, Bench, 63 In.	10530.00
Piano, Grand, Steinway, Model L, Bench, 1929, 38¼ x 70¼ x 58 In.	8260.00
Piano, Grand, Steinway & Sons, Ebonized Finish, Brass Casters, Lift Top Bench, c.1913, 5 Ft. 6 In.	8050.00
Piano, Grand, Steinway & Sons, Model M, Mahogany, Patina, 1932, 68 x 56 In.	10350.00
Piano, Grand, Steinway & Sons, Rococo Revival, Scroll Sawn Music Stand, Gilt, 40 x 81 In.	3840.00
Piano, Upright, Schumann, Bench, Pyramidal, 55 x 62 x 27½ In.	4800.00
Pianoforte, William IV, William Stoddert & Son, Mahogany Case, Brass Casters	1175.00
Viola, 2-Piece Back, Narrow Curl Ribs, Orange, Case, Bow, Czechoslovakia, 1800, 15 In.	7050.00
Viola, A. Guadagnini, 2-Piece, Red, Orange Varnish, 1867, 15⁷⁄₁₆ In.	9400.00
Violin, 2-Piece Back, Medium, Narrow Curl Scroll, Golden Brown, France, c.1860, 14³⁄₁₆ In.	6463.00
Violin, Bow, J.W. Noble, Eldora, Iowa, c.1943, 18 In., Child's Half Size	118.00
Violin, Case, Students, c.1920	110.00
Violoncello, Giancinto Bertolazzi, 2-Piece Back, Orange, Brown Varnish, 1945, 29¾ In.	1763.00

MUSTACHE CUPS were popular from 1850 to 1900 when the large, flowing mustache was in style. A ledge of china or silver held the hair out of the liquid in the cup. This kept the mustache tidy and also kept the mustache wax from melting. Left-handed mustache cups are rare but are being reproduced.

Currier & Ives Landscape Scene, Gold Trim, 4 In.	19.00
Gay Nineties, Gold Trim, Enesco, 4 x 3¾ In.	68.00
Japonisme, Tan, Gold, England, 1880s *illus*	150.00
Man's Face, Eyebrows, Mustache, Raised, Eyes, Nose, Brown, Dark Brown, 3½ In.	12.00
Orange & Yellow Roses, Scalloped Shells, Gold Trim, Saucer	35.00
Pink Rose Bouquet, Luster, Marked, 248, Germany	25.00
Roses, Pink, Green Leaves, Gold Trim, Marked, Rm Bavaria, c.1920	60.00

MZ AUSTRIA is the wording on a mark used by Moritz Zdekauer on porcelains made at his works in Altrolau, Austria, from 1884 to 1909. The mark was changed to *MZ Altrolau* in 1909, when the firm was purchased by C.M. Hutschenreuther. The firm operated under the name Altrolau Porcelain Factories from 1909 to 1945. It was nationalized after World War II. The pieces were decorated with lavish floral patterns and overglaze gold decoration. Full sets of dishes were made as well as vases, toilet sets, and other wares.

MZ Austria

Creamer, Scalloped Pedestal, Flower Sprays, 1900s	15.00
Flowers, Blue, Purple, Red, Green Leaves, Blue Green Ground, Handle, 1900, 8½ In.	65.00
Gravy Boat, White, 9 x 4 In.	9.00
Plate, Poppies, Scalloped Edge, Gold Medallions, 7 In.	30.00
Plate, Roses, Scalloped, Gold Trim, c.1900	39.00
Plate, Salad, Abstract Rust Flowers, Maroon, Gold Border, 7¾ In.	12.00
Plate, Yellow Roses, 9½ In.	9.00
Salt Dip, 3-Footed, Pink, White Flowers, Gilt Rim, c.1900	20.00
Sugar & Creamer, Flowers	95.00
Sugar & Creamer, Purple, Pink Flowers, Green Leaves, 4¾ x 3¼ & 6 x 3¼ In.	150.00
Tray, Dresser, Aqua, Green, Coral, 8¼ In.	75.00
Tray, Dresser, Flowers, Green, Pink, White, 12¾ In.	85.00

M

Music, Box, Singing Bird, Cage, Brass,
Dome Top, Birds, Feathers,
France, 19 x 9 In.
$1495.00

Music, Box, Singing Bird, Feathers,
Sterling Silver, Allover Rococo,
2½ x 4 x 2¾ In.
$2875.00

Music, Box, Singing Bird, Metal Case,
Egyptian Decor, Women, Eagle,
Turler, Zurich, 4 x 3 In.
$288.00

Music, Guitar, C.F. Martin, Model 00-18,
Flat Top, Acoustic, Hard-Shell Case, 1970,
39½ In.
$2070.00

Music, Melodeon, Mason & Hamlin, Boston, Rosewood,
Music Stand, Scrolled Pedals, 32 x 46 In.
$575.00

Music, Organ, Parlor, Walnut,
Incised Decoration, Victorian, 48 x 53 x 23 In.
$106.00

Music, Piano, Baby Grand,
Steinway & Sons, Model M, Mahogany,
Bench, 55 x 66 x 38 In.
$12650.00

M

NAILSEA

Mustache Cup, Japonisme,
Tan, Gold, England, 1880s
$150.00

Nailsea, Epergne, Satin Glass Vases,
Crystal Stems, 3 Leaf Arms,
Mirror Base, 10 In.
$2243.00

Nailsea, Fairy Lamp, Cranberry,
Draped Loopings, Clear Holder,
Ruffled Base, c.1890, 5 In.
$411.00

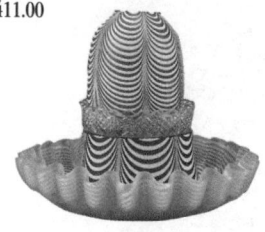

Nailsea, Lamp, Cranberry Loopings,
Crystal Wafer Foot, Burner, 7 In.
$3450.00

Nakara, Jewelry Box, Hinged Lid,
Pink Flowers, Light Blue, Round,
Signed, 4½ In.
$225.00

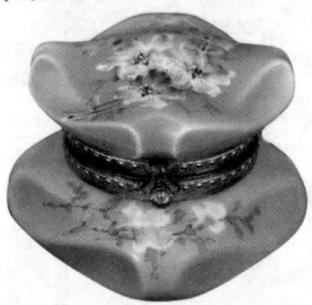

NAILSEA glass was made in the Bristol district in England from 1788 to 1873. It was made by many different factories, not just the Nailsea Glass House. Many pieces were made with loopings of either white or colored glass as decoration.

Epergne, Satin Glass Vases, Crystal Stems, 3 Leaf Arms, Mirror Base, 10 In. . . . . *illus*	2243.00
Fairy Lamp, Cranberry, Draped Loopings, Clear Holder, Ruffled Base, c.1890, 5 In. . . . . *illus*	411.00
Flask, Blue, Red, White Splotches, Flared Lip, Teardrop Shape, Pontil, 1800-30, 5½ In.	112.00
Flask, Milk Glass, Cranberry & Cobalt Blue Loopings, Tooled Lip, 8 In.	336.00
Flask, Milk Glass, Cranberry Herringbone, Red Band Lip, Pontil, 9⅜ In.	336.00
Flask, Stopper, White, Red, Pink, Swirls, 8¼ x 4½ In.	325.00
Jug, Green, White Splotches, Double Collar Lip, Handle With Curl, England, 1800-30, 7 In. . .	770.00
Jug, Green, White Splotches, Double Collar Lip, Handle With Curl, Pontil, 1800-30, 9 In. . . .	495.00
Lamp, Cranberry Loopings, Crystal Wafer Foot, Burner, 7 In. *illus*	3450.00
Paperweight, Foil Flowers, Green Bottle Glass, 5½ In.	230.00
Rolling Pin, Black Ground, Red, White, Gray Speckled, 13½ x 2 In.	200.00
Rolling Pin, Clear, Red, Blue, 14¼ x 2 In.	295.00
Sugar, Olive Green, White, Red, Footed, Pontil, 2½ x 4¼ In.	830.00
Sweetmeat, Cranberry & White Loopings, Rounded Square Handle, 5¼ In.	345.00
Sweetmeat, Lime Green & Opaque Spiral Bands, Satin, Swirled, Melon Ribbed, 5¾ In.	173.00
Vase, Blown, Red, White, Blue Loops, Applied Spiral, 15 In.	288.00
Vase, Cranberry, 5 In.	100.00
Wedding Bell, White Swirl, Clear Handle, 19th Century, 12¼ In.	206.00
Witch's Ball, Emerald Green, White Inclusions, Open End Pontil, 1840-60, 4¼ In.	95.00

NAKARA is a trade name for a white glassware made about 1900 by the C. F. Monroe **NAKARA** Company of Meriden, Connecticut. It was decorated in pastel colors. The glass was very similar to another glass, called Wave Crest, made by the company. The company closed in 1916. Boxes for use on a dressing table are the most commonly found Nakara pieces. The mark is not found on every piece.

Bonbon, Pink Flowers, Green Ground, 4½ In.	90.00
Box, Hinged Cover, Daisies, White Bead Enameling, Pink Ground, 6-Sided, 4 x 3½ In.	350.00
Box, Hinged Lid, Flowers, Lavender, 6-Sided, 4 x 3½ In.	325.00
Card Holder, Blue Flowers, Mauve, Signed, 2½ x 4 In.	30.00
Cigarette Holder, Flowers, White Enamel Beading, Brick Red & Pink Ground, 2¾ In.	400.00
Cigarette Holder, Pink Flowers, Pink & Green Ground, Signed, 2¾ In.	400.00
Dresser Box, Green, Portrait Medallion, Cherubs, Signed, C.F. Monroe, 3½ In.	288.00
Dresser Box, Green Bishops Hat Form, Pink Flowers, Signed, C.F. Monroe, 4 In.	345.00
Dresser Box, Playful Cherubs, Pink Flowers, Olive Green, 8 In.	1000.00
Humidor, Old Sport, Bulldog, Yellow, Brown, 6½ In.	300.00
Jewelry Box, Hinged Lid, Blue Applied Flowers, Light Blue Ground, 6-Sided, 3½ x 5 In.	150.00
Jewelry Box, Hinged Lid, Flowers, Green, Enamel Highlights, Oval, Signed, 5 In.	150.00
Jewelry Box, Hinged Lid, Iris, Orange, Signed, 3½ x 6 In.	100.00
Jewelry Box, Hinged Lid, Pink Flowers, Light Blue, Round, Signed, 4½ In. . . . . *illus*	225.00
Jewelry Box, Hinged Lid, Victorian Woman Portrait, Blue Ground, Round, Signed, 4½ In. . .	300.00
Jewelry Box, Hinged Lid, Violets, Green, Bishop's Hat Mold, Signed, 4½ x 5½ In.	350.00
Jewelry Tray, Beveled Mirror, Pink Flowers, Pink & Blue, Signed, 5 x 4 In.	700.00
Mustard Pot, Blue, White & Tan Beaded Circles, 8-Sided, Metal Handle & Flip Lid, 2¾ In. . .	489.00
Pin Tray, c.1900, 4½ In.	195.00
Salt, Open, Pink & Green, White Enamel Beading, Brick Red Ground, Handles, 1½ x 3 In. . .	600.00
Salt & Pepper, Puffy Mold, Pink Flowers, 4-Sided, Marked, 2 x 1¾ In.	220.00
Smoking Set, Lighter, Match Holder, Ash Tray, Basket Weave Form, Blue Flowers, 8 In.	300.00
Tobacco Humidor, Cover, Copper, 4⅜ In.	695.00
Vase, Pink Chrysanthemum, Blue Ground, Gold Ormolu Handles, Footed, Signed, 17½ In. . .	4200.00

NANKING is a type of blue-and-white porcelain made in Canton, China, since the late eighteenth century. It is very similar to Canton, which is listed under its own name in this book. Both Nanking and Canton are part of a larger group now called Chinese export porcelain. Nanking has a spear-and-post border and may have gold decoration.

Bowl, Blue & White, Gold Rim, 19th Century, 10 In.	345.00
Dish, Blue & White, Shallow, 19th Century, 16 In.	295.00
Plate, Dinner, Imperial, 19th Century, 9½ In., 12 Piece	823.00
Platter, Flowers, Butterfly Border, 8-Sided, Early 19th Century, 20 In.	2151.00
Platter, Pagoda Hut, Man On Bridge, Oval, Blue & White, Early 1800s, 12 x 9½ In.	525.00
Stand, Riverscape, Reticulated, Nanking, Blue & White, c.1800, 9¾ In.	472.00
Tureen, Cover, Riverscape, 10 x 9 In.	177.00
Tureen, Stand, Riverscape, Diamond Border, Rabbit Handles, Flower Knop, Oval, 8 x 11 x 15 In.	2868.00

N

NAPKIN RINGS were in fashion from 1869 to about 1900. They were made of silver, porcelain, wood, and other materials. They are still being made today. The most popular rings with collectors are the silver plated figural examples. Small, realistic figures were made to hold the ring. Good and poor reproductions of the more expensive rings are now being made and collectors must be very careful.

Bakelite, Figure, Rabbit, Butterscotch & Olive, Acrylic Eyes, 2¼ In., 6 Piece ....*illus*	264.00
Bone China, Forget-Me-Nots, Blue, Countess, England, 1960s, 2¼ x 1¾ In., Pair	28.00
Brass, Embossed, Putto, Black Case, Continental, 2½ x 8¾ In., 6 Piece	330.00
Ceramic, Figural, Toucan Bird, 12 Piece	30.00
Cloisonne, Fishscale, Japan, c.1900, Pair	220.00
Figural, Pan Prancing On Mound, Pairpoint, Silver Plated	950.00
Lucite, Lilac, Flower Shape, 1970s, 8 Piece	22.00
Milk Glass, Painted Roses, 6-Sided, Westmoreland, 2¼ In.	35.00
Pewter, Floral, Concave Center Band, Hand Hammered, 1½ In.	28.00
Pokerwork, Flowers, Leaves, Mid 1900s, 3⅜ In., Pair	17.00
Porcelain, Figural, Bonzo Dog, 1930s, 3 In.	39.00
Porcelain, Figural, Cherubs, Butterfly, Pink Luster, 2 x 3⅜ In.	225.00
Porcelain, Transferware, Flowers, Lord Nelson, 2 In., 4 Piece	10.00
Pottery, Bouquet Pattern, Franciscan, Original Box, 4 Piece	80.00
Pottery, Desert Rose, Hand Painted, Franciscan, 2 x 2½ In., 3 Piece	22.50
Silver Plate, Bud Vase, Figural, Cherub, Looking Into Mirror, Rockford	850.00
Silver Plate, Bud Vase, Figural, Flowers, Pods, Leaves, Webster	550.00
Silver Plate, Figural, 2 Butterflies On Fan, Meriden, Late 1800s, 4 In., 3 Piece	264.00
Silver Plate, Figural, 2 Winged Cherubs, Holding Ring, Meriden-Britannia, 3 In. .....*illus*	206.00
Silver Plate, Figural, Angel Blowing Horn, Flowers, Tiered Base, Simpson, Victorian	137.00
Silver Plate, Figural, Barrel, Leaf Branch Legs, Late 1800s, 2¼ In., 4 Piece	205.00
Silver Plate, Figural, Bird, On Leaf, 3½ In.	55.00
Silver Plate, Figural, Bird With Wishbone, Derby Silver Co.	55.00
Silver Plate, Figural, Boy & Puppy, Late 19th Century, 3 In.	559.00
Silver Plate, Figural, Boy Holding Foot, Derby Silver Co., 3¼ In.	118.00
Silver Plate, Figural, Boy Pulling Sled, Wilcox Silver Plate Co., 4 In.	226.00
Silver Plate, Figural, Bull, Late 1800s, 3¾ In., Pair	147.00
Silver Plate, Figural, Cherub, Butterfly, Flower, Marked, EDA, 4 In.	413.00
Silver Plate, Figural, Cherub, Ice Breaker, Bulldog, James Tufts, Late 1800s, 4½ In.	294.00
Silver Plate, Figural, Chicken & Rake, Round Base, Webster	650.00
Silver Plate, Figural, Child Feeding Dog, Meriden-Britannia Co.	505.00
Silver Plate, Figural, Conquistador, Toronto	1500.00
Silver Plate, Figural, Deer, Engraved Theodore, Meriden Co., 4 x 3¼ In.	59.00
Silver Plate, Figural, Dog, On Hind Legs, James W. Tufts, Boston, 4½ In.	118.00
Silver Plate, Figural, Dog Holding Rope In Mouth, Stamped, Victorian, 4 In.	715.00
Silver Plate, Figural, Eagle, Ring Balanced On Wings, Meriden-Britannia Co., 4 x 3½ In. ...	850.00
Silver Plate, Figural, Eskimo, Meriden, Late 1800s, 2½ In.	147.00
Silver Plate, Figural, Heron, Late 1800s, 4½ In.	646.00
Silver Plate, Figural, Infant & Frog, Barbour, 3¾ In. ....*illus*	294.00
Silver Plate, Figural, Jockey, Meriden, 3½ In. ....*illus*	764.00
Silver Plate, Figural, Lilies & Lily Pad, Rogers Smith, Late 1800s, 4 In., 3 Piece	147.00
Silver Plate, Figural, Pan, Pairpoint	950.00
Silver Plate, Figural, Parakeet On Branch, Leaf Base, Oval Ring, Toronto, Victorian	110.00
Silver Plate, Figural, Pewter, Floral, Branch, Leaves, c.1900, 2 x 3¼ In.	468.00
Silver Plate, Figural, Sailor Boy With Anchor, Reed & Barton, Late 1800s, 3½ In.	440.00
Silver Plate, Figural, Tennis Racquet, Meriden-Britannia Co.	550.00
Silver Plate, Figural, Turtle, Pulling Cherub, 3½ In.	236.00
Silver Plate, Figural, Woman, With Megaphone, Southington	950.00
Silver Plate, Figural, Woman, With Tennis Racket, Reed & Barton, Late 1800s, 3¼ In.	470.00
Sterling Silver, Enameled, Marked, Cyrillic Lettering, Russia, c.1890, 1½ In.	750.00
Sterling Silver, Figural, Arched Back Cat, Looks Down On Dog, Rogers, 1883, 4 In.	410.00
Sterling Silver, Trumpet Bud Vase Top, Birds, Vines, Footed, c.1873, 4¾ In. ....*illus*	896.00

NASH glass was made in Corona, New York, from about 1928 to 1931. A. Douglas Nash bought the Corona glassworks from Louis C. Tiffany in 1928 and founded the A. Douglas Nash Corporation with support from his father, Arthur J. Nash. Arthur had worked at the Webb factory in England and for the Tiffany Glassworks in Corona.

NASH

Bowl, Gold, Iridescent, Ribbed, Scalloped Rim, Footed, Polished Pontil, 6 In.	1900.00
Candlestick, Gold Iridescent, Wide & Ribbed Rims, Baluster Stem, Signed, 3¾ In., Pair	550.00
Compote, Chintz, Clear, Green Tint, Red Rim, Purple, 4 x 7½ In.	850.00

Napkin Ring, Bakelite, Figure, Rabbit, Butterscotch & Olive, Acrylic Eyes, 2¼ In., 6 Piece
$264.00

Napkin Ring, Silver Plate, Figural, 2 Winged Cherubs, Holding Ring, Meriden-Britannia, 3 In.
$206.00

Napkin Ring, Silver Plate, Figural, Infant & Frog, Barbour, 3¾ In.
$294.00

Napkin Ring, Silver Plate, Figural, Jockey, Meriden, 3½ In.
$764.00

Napkin Ring, Sterling Silver, Trumpet Bud Vase Top, Birds, Vines, Footed, c.1873, 4¾ In.
$896.00

N

Nash, Vase, Gold Iridescent, Magenta, Ribbed, Bulbous Neck, Flared Rim, Footed, 4 In.
$436.00

Nash, Vase, Red Orange, Pulled Olive Green & Blue Vertical Stripes, Flared Rim, 8 In.
$288.00

Nash, Vase, Yellow, Brown Chintz, Tapered Body, Flared Rim, 8¾ In.
$329.00

Nautical, Chest, Seaman's, Teak, 6-Board, Inlaid, Dovetailed, Iron Handles, 16 x 31 In.
$805.00

Tray, Gold Iridescent, Upturned Rim, Scalloped Edge, 16 Ribs, Polished Pontil, 4 In.	175.00
Vase, Gold Iridescent, Magenta, Ribbed, Bulbous Neck, Flared Rim, Footed, 4 In. *....illus*	436.00
Vase, Gold Iridescent, Magenta Highlights, Footed, 4 In.	436.00
Vase, Green With Glue Glass, Platinum, Enameled Flared Rim, 8 In.	330.00
Vase, Red Orange, Pulled Olive Green & Blue Vertical Stripes, Flared Rim, 8 In. *....illus*	288.00
Vase, Yellow, Brown Chintz, Tapered Body, Flared Rim, 8¾ In. *....illus*	329.00

NAUTICAL antiques are listed in this category. Any of the many objects that were made or used by the seafaring trade, including ship parts, models, and tools, are included. Other pieces may be found listed under Scrimshaw.

Bell Clock, Barometer, Thermometer, Chelsea, Claremont Model, 8-Day, 14½ In.	764.00
Binnacle, Wood, Brass Hood & Fittings, Kevin & Hughes Ltd., 54 In.	2990.00
Block, Double, Whale Ivory Sheaves, Bronze Thimble, 19th Century, 1¾ x 1¼ In.	1250.00
Block, Rigging, Whale Ivory Outer Shell, Bronze Hooks, c.1850, 3 x 1 In., Pair	1275.00
Boson's Whistle, Sterling Silver, Dragon Relief, China Trade, 2¾ In.	375.00
Bosun's Whistle, Silver, Engraved Leaves, Relief Crown Over Anchor, Y & W, 6 In.	875.00
Bridge Telegraph, Ship's, Brass, Double Faced, Chadburns Liverpool, Ltd., 43 In.	2473.00
Chart Case, Ship's, Green Paint, Dovetailed, Blanket Chest, Hinged, 13 x 12½ In.	805.00
Chest, Captain's, China Trade, Camphor Wood, Brass Bound, Ring Pull, 19 x 41 In.	1380.00
Chest, Seaman's, Black & Red Grain Painted, Dovetailed, Strap Hinged Lid, 18 x 43 x 17 In.	518.00
Chest, Seaman's, Hardwood, Compass Star Inlay, Interior Till, 19th Century, 19 x 37 In.	756.00
Chest, Seaman's, Leather Covered, Brass Tack & Corner Trim, 13 x 31 x 16 In.	374.00
Chest, Seaman's, Star & Pinwheel Inlay, Engraved Iron Lock Plate, Handles, 16 x 30 x 15 In.	863.00
Chest, Seaman's, Teak, 6-Board, Inlaid, Dovetailed, Iron Handles, 16 x 31 In. *....illus*	805.00
Chest, Seaman's, Till Interior, 40 x 17 x 16 In.	153.00
Chronometer, Joseph Sewill, Liverpool, No. 12239, Mahogany & Brass Box, c.1920	3475.00
Chronometer, Kelvin & Wilfrid, 2 Tiers, Brass Handles, Mahogany Case, No. 13975, 7 In.	441.00
Chronometer, Victor Kullberg, London, No. 3295, Ebony Fitted Case, 1875	5750.00
Chronometer, Whyte Thompson & Co., 2-Day, Fusee Movement, No. 5330, 7 In.	1528.00
Chronometer, Widenham, London, Silvered Face, Brass Gimbal, Mahogany Fitted Case	5275.00
Clock, Barometer, Port Hole Style, Brass, Late 20th Century, 10 x 23 In.	88.00
Clock, Chelsea, Brass, Chelsea Ships Bell, No. 878220, 10 In. Diam.	1150.00
Clock, Deck, U.S. Navy, Key Wind, Waterproof Case, 1943, 8½ In.	441.00
Clock, Seth Thomas, Brass Case, Bell, Silver Dial, 2 Keyholes, Vented, 6 In.	115.00
Clock, Ship's, Chelsea, Nickel Plated Brass, Silvered Face, No. 132071, 1919, 5½ In.	675.00
Clock, Ship's, Chelsea Clock Co., Brass, Abercrombie & Fitch, 7 In.	702.00
Clock, Ship's, Chelsea Clock Co., Constitution, Brass, 1912, 12 x 12 x 10 In.	4680.00
Clock, Ship's, Chelsea Lighthouse Establishment, Brass, Silver Dial, c.1900, 5⁵⁄₁₆ In.	1610.00
Compass, Binnacle, Brass, Glasgow, c.1900, 11 In.	264.00
Compass, Brass, Hanging Bracket, John Bliss & Co., c.1857, 5½ x 3¾ In.	1800.00
Compass, Brass, Removable Compass, Tapered Cone Housing, K. White, Boston, 12 x 9 In.	748.00
Compass, Gyro Compass, Repeater, Sperry Gyroscope Co., No.7382, 12 In.	235.00
Compass, John Bliss & Co., N.Y., Brass Housing & Gimbal, Bronze Hanging Bracket, 6 x 4 In.	1800.00
Compass, Navigation, F.L. West, London, Brass Case, Walnut & Brass Box, 4 x 1½ In. *....illus*	450.00
Compass, Ship's, U.S. Navy, Enclosed In Copper Hood, Lamp, 4-In. Compass, 8½ In.	184.00
Compass, T. Cook, London, Brass Case, Pedestal Base	58.00
Compass, Thomas Laughlin, Portland, Maine, Brass Case, Glass Top, c.1860, 3 In.	325.00
Compass, W.J. Johnson, Wing Divider	32.00
Diorama, Ship, 3-Masted, Glazed, Rigged, Wood Sails, Black Hull, 18 x 26 In.	1410.00
Diorama, Ship, 4-Masted, Cased, Rigged, Bark, White Hull, 8¾ x 6 In.	411.00
Diorama, Ship, Columbia, American Flag, Sailors, James Anderson, 1800s, 23¾ x 36 In.	863.00
Diorama, Ship, Glazed, Rigged, 3-Masted, Wood Sails, Lighthouse, 14 x 27 In.	1880.00
Diorama, Ship, Izac Webb, American Flag, Wood, Carved, Multicolor Paint, 16 x 36 In.	575.00
Diorama, Ship, Painted, Rigged, 3-Masted, Wood, Black Hull, 12 x 19 In.	441.00
Dirk, Naval, Georgian, Blue & Gold Decoration, Ivory Handle, Guard, c.1790, 10½ In.	2275.00
Diving Helmet, Deep Sea, Model 512, 4-Light, 12-Bolt Breast Plate, A.J. Morse, Stand	28200
Fid, Whalebone, Tapered Shaft, Incised & Turned End, c.1840, 5¼ In.	235.00
Footstool, Painted Blue, White Legs & Star	63.00
Gangplank, Rope, Mississippi Riverboat, Metal, Canvas Ring, Turk Head End, 20 Ft. x ¾ In.	920.00
Half-Model, Eva, 12 Wood Laminations, Female Figurehead, 12 x 48 In.	5875.00
Half-Model, Laminated Matchstick, Mid 20th Century, 7¼ x 18 In.	646.00
Half-Model, Laminated Wood, Early 20th Century, 6 x 30 In.	470.00
Half-Model, Painted, Red & White, Mounted On Board, 20 In.	288.00
Half-Model, Schooner, Laminated Wood, Carved, Maker's Inscription, 4 x 27 In.	1645.00
Half-Model, Stacked, Spruce, 1930s, 28 x 4¾ In.	1195.00
Half-Model, Wood, Blue Paint, 26¼ In.	105.00

Half-Model, Wood, Mounted Board In Frame, Painted, Smoke Stacks, 7 x 12 In.	61.00
Harpoon, Whaling, 2 Fluted Head, Iron, T. Humphrey, Valiant Whitby 1823, 32 In.	2750.00
Hull, Pond Boat, Double Paddle Oar, Hanging Weight, Keel, 79 In.	220.00
Kayak, Model, Skin, Bone Embellishment, c.1920, 17 In.	588.00
Kayak, Model, Skin, Sinew Sewn, Wood Frame, 11 In.	147.00
Knife, Rope, U.S. Navy, Square Tip, Stag Handles, Copper Bail, 8¼ In.	575.00
Knife, Whaling, Faroe Island, Inlaid Teak Handle, Sheath, Brass Bands, 12½ In.	2375.00
Lamp, Wing, Port & Starboard, F.H. Lovel & Co., New York, Pair	863.00
Lantern, Brass, Pierced, 360 Degree, 1 Red & 1 Blue Glass, 9 In., Pair	127.00
Lantern, Ship's, Copper, Brass, Japan, c.1957, 29 In.	326.00
Lantern, Ship's, Gimbal, Arm, Silver Plated, Brass, Ball Finial, 12 x 3 In., Pair	3450.00
Lantern, Ship's, Silver Plated Brass, Pierced Cylinder, Fall Finial, Gimbal Arm, 14 In., Pair	3450.00
Lantern, Ship's Masthead, Copper, Brass, 23 In. ....illus	390.00
Locket, Tortoiseshell, Hinged, Pierce Carving, Carved Chain, c.1889, 1½ & 17 In.	295.00
Model, Brigantine, Flying Cloud, Wood, Painted, Howard Moon, 1925, 24 x 37 In.	881.00
Model, Clipper Ship, Rainbow, Ivory, Whalebone, Baleen Veneer, Early 1900s, 16 x 25 In.	1998.00
Model, Fishing Dory, Accessories, 4 Oars, Bailing Scoop, 1940s, 43½ x 12 In.	485.00
Model, Fragata Espanola, Wood, Painted, c.1780, 31 In.	177.00
Model, Gun Ship, Belle-Poule, 3-Masted, Full Rigging, French Flags, Wood Stand, 36 In.	403.00
Model, Ship, 3-Masted, Whalebone, Ivory, 19th Century, 18 x 14 In.	4140.00
Model, Ship, Anna Hand, 3-Masted, Square Rigging, Cradle Stand, 48 In.	575.00
Model, Ship, Bone, Baleen, Straw Work, Carved, Napoleonic Prisoner-Of-War, 13½ In.	11755.00
Model, Ship, Cased, Rigged, 2-Masted Brig, Painted Details, Black Hull, 10 x 6½ In.	411.00
Model, Ship, Santa Maria, Germany, c.1920, 33 x 14 x 36 In.	468.00
Model, Ship, Sartari, Wood, 22 x 51 x 8 In.	650.00
Model, Ship, Schooner, The Bluenose, Full Rigging, 19 In.	144.00
Model, Ship, Technical, Wood, Freedom, 45 x 35 In.	585.00
Model, Ship, The Dolphin, Baltimore, Maryland, 2-Masted, Wood Cradle Stand, 22 In.	98.00
Model, Ship, Wood, 3-Masted, Carved, Painted, Black, Green Hull, Metal, 42 x 53 In.	940.00
Model, Whaling Ship, Charles Morgan, 3-Masted, Full Rigging, 29 In.	288.00
Model, Whaling Ship, Eagle, 3-Masted, Full Rigging, 25 In.	259.00
Model, Whaling Ship, Plank Seats, Barrels, Harpoons, 14 In.	201.00
Model, Whaling Ship, White Hull, Gray Sheerstrake, Equipment, Mahogany Base, 30 In.	2750.00
Napkin Ring, Naval Vessel Wood, Teak, Brass, H.M.S. Ganges, 2 x 1⅜ In.	75.00
Oars, Old Yellow Paint, Copper Sleeves On Ends, Copper Patch, 92 In., Pair	248.00
Octant, Brass Index Engraved Arm, Ivory, Bone Pencil Finial, c.1800, 18 In.	2250.00
Octant, Ebony, Ivory Scale & Vernier, Index Arm, Flags, Crown, Cannon, c.1780, 20 In.	2675.00
Octant, Engraved Arm, Flags, Cannon, Ivory Scale, Mahogany Frame, c.1790, 18¼ In.	2350.00
Octant, Ivory Inlay, Hinged Pine Case, Inscribed, Amos Latham, c.1783, 18 x 16 In.	3600.00
Oil Bailer, Whale Oil, Copper, Wood Pole, Rounded Rim, Iron Shank, 9 x 7 In.	1450.00
Plaque, Ship, 2-Masted, Black Hull, Green Ocean, Blue Sky, Wood, Carved, 11¾ x 15 In.	200.00
Pond Boat, Single Mast, 3 Sails, Dowel Mounted, Wood Stand, 30 In.	282.00
Propeller, Brass, Imprinted 502, 16 x 4½ In.	68.00
Rug, Ship, 3-Masted, Blue, White, Green, Brown, Green Border, Canvas, Late 1800s, 29 x 41 In.	1725.00
Sailor's Valentine, Shellwork, Heart, Anchor, Flowers, Shadowbox Frame, 10 x 12 In. .illus	1035.00
Sailor's Valentine, Shellwork, Heart, Flowers, Remember Me, 2-Sided, 9 x 9 In. ......illus	4600.00
Sailor's Valentine, Shellwork, Mahogany Veneer Case, Octagonal, 14½ In.	9500.00
Sailor's Valentine, Seashell Mosaic, 8-Point Star, Home Again, Octagonal, 14⅜ In.	5288.00
Sea Urchin Shell, Silvered Metal Mount, 16th Century German Style, 11 In., Pair	600.00
Sextant, Brass, Ivory Mounted, Imrocy & Son Minories, London, 11 In.	1035.00
Sextant, Lattice Pattern, Brass, 9-In. Radius, Ebony Handle, Telescopic Tubes, Case	558.00
Sextant, Leopold & Stevens, Box, U.S. Maritime Commission, 1944	213.00
Sextant, McMillan & Talbot, London, Mahogany Case, 2 Eyepieces, 10 x 11 In.	345.00
Sextant, Ross, London, Walnut & Brass Case, 4 x 5 In. ....illus	390.00
Sextant, Schick Inc., U.S. Navy Bureau Of Ships, Mahogany Case	146.00
Sextant, Troughton & Simms, London, Ebony Frame, Brass Scale, Mahogany Case, 10 In.	2950.00
Sextant, W. Cary, London, No. 2534, Brass Frame, Silver Scale, Ebony Handle, Fitted Case	3250.00
Sextant, Welag XXI 440, Brass, Steel Measuring Strip, Wood Handle, 9½ In. ....illus	575.00
Shell, Conch, Carved, Cameo, Classical Figure, Woman Riding Chariot, 2 Horses, 8¼ In.	288.00
Ship In Bottle, 3-Masted, Carved, Painted, Rigged, Ship, Wharf Scene, Early 1900s, 9¼ In.	382.00
Ship In Bottle, 3-Masted, Rigged, Flying American Flag, Carved, Wood Base, 12¼ In.	235.00
Ship In Bottle, 3-Masted, Wharf Scene, Brig, Rigged, Wooden Stand, Early 1900s, 13 In.	206.00
Ship In Bottle, 3-Masted, Wood, Carved, Rigged, Wharf Scene, Gal. Bottle, 12¼ In.	235.00
Ship In Bottle, 4-Masted, Sails, Rigged, Green Hull, Gallon Bottle, 11¼ In.	382.00
Ship In Bottle, Faux Painted Stand, Depicts Small Town Scene, c.1900, 14 x 7½ In.	1750.00

Nautical, Compass, Navigation, F.L. West, London, Brass Case, Walnut & Brass Box, 4 x 1½ In. $450.00

Nautical, Lantern, Ship's Masthead, Copper, Brass, 23 In. $390.00

N

Nautical, Sailor's Valentine, Shellwork, Heart, Anchor, Flowers, Shadowbox Frame, 10 x 12 In. $1035.00

TIP

Look through the wrong end of a telescope you plan to buy. If it can be focused, all the parts are there.

Nautical, Sailor's Valentine, Shellwork, Heart, Flowers, Remember Me, 2-Sided, 9 x 9 In. $4600.00

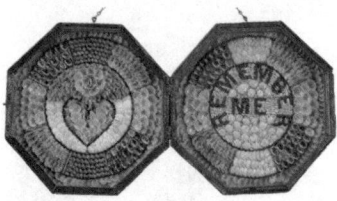

Nautical, Sextant, Ross, London, Walnut & Brass Case, 4 x 5 In. $390.00

Nautical, Sextant, Welag XXI 440, Brass, Steel Measuring Strip, Wood Handle, 9½ In. $575.00

Nautical, Ship's Wheel, Wood, Turned, Inlaid, Brass, 19 In. $180.00

Ship Model, see Nautical, Model.	
Ship's Wheel, Oak, Brass, Early 20th Century, 53½ In.	499.00
Ship's Wheel, Turned Spindle Spokes, Iron-Mounted Axle Plates, 47½ In.	633.00
Ship's Wheel, Wood, Brass Trim, Sailor's Rope Work Around Spoke, 43 In.	230.00
Ship's Wheel, Wood, Iron Bound, Old Red Paint, 43 In.	230.00
Ship's Wheel, Wood, Turned, Inlaid, Brass, 19 In. ....*illus*	180.00
Spotlight, Brass, Bail Handles, Model 3770, E & J Mfg. Co., Detroit, 9 x 11½ In.	230.00
Spyglass, Dollind, London, Single Draw Tube, Ivory, Leather, Shagreen, Fish Skin Case	2750.00
Steam Whistle, Brass, Cast Iron Base, Ballou Service & Instrument Co., N.Y., 50 In.	2200.00
Telescope, Brass, 4 Parts, Compass, Cap, Lawrance & Mayo, London, 33½ In.	288.00
Telescope, Brass, 5 Parts, Cap, Case, Brass Hardware, Ross London, 15 In.	431.00
Tiller, Boat, Carved, Eagle Head, Rope Rings, Twist, Oak, 38 In.	5750.00
Tiller, Boat, Carved, Oak, Arm Shape, Closed Hand, c.1849, 30 In.	1475.00
Tiller, Boat, Carved, Sea Serpent Head, Oak, Rope Twist, c.1850, 30 In.	4750.00
Tiller, Oak, Carved, Eagle Head, Spiral Rope, Rope Rings, 38 In.	5750.00
Tiller, Oak, Carved, Serpent Head, Scales, Twisted Rope, c.1850, 30 In.	4750.00
Tiller, Oak, Turk's Head Knot, Twisted Rope, Monkey Fist Knot, Hearts, Diamonds, 1843, 20 In.	3500.00
Watch, Chronometer, Hamilton, No. 22, 21 Jewel, U.S. Navy, Mahogany Fitted Case	1375.00
Watch, Chronometer, U.S. Navy, Hamilton, Mahogany Case, Hinged Lid, 2¾ In.	1375.00
Whale Gun, Brass, Iron Trigger, Hammer, Skeleton Stock, S. Eggers, New Bedford, 37 In.	8750.00
Whale Gun, Bronze, Iron Trigger, Hammer, Skeleton Stock, William Lewis, 34 In.	6850.00
Wing Divider, Hugh Warrington, 7 In.	60.00
Wing Divider, Pencil Holder, Pexto, 8 In.	45.00
Wing Divider, Pexto, 7 In.	50.00

NETSUKES are small ivory, wood, metal, or porcelain pieces used as toggles on the end of the cord that held a Japanese money pouch or inro. The earliest date from the sixteenth century. Many are miniature, carved works of art. This category also includes the ojime, the slide or string fastener that was used on the inro cord.

Agate Boy, With Fish, 1½ In.	176.00
Inro, New Years, Lobster, Pine Tree, Fruits, Gold, Silver, Brown & Red, Late 1800s	1000.00
Ivory, Buddha, Carved, Wood Stand, Japan, 4 Pipes, 3 In.	82.00
Ivory, Chick & Egg, Signed, Mitsuhiro, Cloth, Seal, Box, Mid 1800s	944.00
Ivory, Children & Dragon, 2 In.	117.00
Ivory, Clamshell Pile, 19th Century, 1¾ In.	52.00
Ivory, Demon On Umbrella, 2½ In.	443.00
Ivory, Demon Snatching Fan From Goddess Of Mirth's Hand, 19th Century, 2¼ In.	470.00
Ivory, Devil's Mask	472.00
Ivory, Dutchman Holding Rooster, Red, 18th/19th Century, 4 In.	1293.00
Ivory, Elder, Chinese, 2 In.	41.00
Ivory, Elephant Within Elephant, 2 In.	176.00
Ivory, Figures In Boat, 3 In.	944.00
Ivory, God Of Contentment & Demon, Signed, 1½ In.	236.00
Ivory, Gourds, 19th Century, 2 In.	118.00
Ivory, Haltered Ox, Wood Base, 18th Century, ¾ x 2¼ In.	5750.00
Ivory, Kabuki Actor, Rotating Face, 2½ In., Pair	146.00
Ivory, Male & Female, Erotic, Signed, 1¼ x 2¼ In.	657.00
Ivory, Man, Monkey On His Back, Carved, Early 20th Century, 1½ In.	146.00
Ivory, Man, Seated, Cutting Toenails, Late 19th Century, 1¼ In. ....*illus*	191.00
Ivory, Man & Child Riding Bird, 2 In.	176.00
Ivory, Man On Elephant, 2 In.	100.00
Ivory, Men Holding Boxes, Carved, Japan, 2 In., 2 Piece	117.00
Ivory, Miller, 2 Children, 19th Century, 1¾ In.	588.00
Ivory, Monk, Boy, Comical, 20th Century, 3 In.	161.00
Ivory, Monkey, Crouching On Turtle Back, 1¼ x 1¾ In.	146.00
Ivory, Mouse, Crouched In Rope Basket	561.00
Ivory, Mouse, Nibbling Candle, 19th Century, ½ In.	558.00
Ivory, Musicians, 3 Boys, 19th Century, 1½ In.	311.00
Ivory, Octopus & Erotic Lady, Japan, 2 In.	527.00
Ivory, Old Buddha, Child On Back, Carved, Japan, 1½ In.	59.00
Ivory, Rat, Wrapped In Leaf, 2¼ In.	293.00
Ivory, Seated Figure, Smoking Pipe, Demon, 1½ In.	264.00
Ivory, Sumo Wrestler, 1¾ In. ....*illus*	120.00
Wood, Demon, Signed, Morimitsu, 19th Century, 1½ In.	228.00
Wood, Dog Playing With Ball, 1½ In.	177.00

Wood, Mask, 2 In.	590.00
Wood, Mask, Signed, 19th Century, 1½ In.	176.00
Wood, Samurai, Signed, 19th Century, 1½ In.	208.00

NEW HALL Porcelain Manufactory was started at Newhall, Shelton, Staffordshire, England, in 1782. Simple decorated wares were made. Between 1810 and 1825, the *New Hall* factory made a glassy bone porcelain sometimes marked with the factory name. Do not confuse New Hall porcelain with the pieces made by the New Hall Pottery Company, Ltd., a twentieth-century firm.

Teapot, Mandarin Family, Shaped Sides, 6 x 9 In.	58.00
Teapot, Overglaze Multicolored Enamel, Early 1800, 4 x 7 In.	525.00

NEW MARTINSVILLE Glass Manufacturing Company was established in 1901 in New Martinsville, West Virginia. It was bought and renamed the Viking Glass Company in 1944. In 1987 Kenneth Dalzell, former president of Fostoria Glass Company, purchased the factory and renamed it Dalzell-Viking. Production ceased in 1998.

Addie, Cup, Amber	9.00
Addie, Plate, Bread & Butter, Green, 6⅛ In.	7.50
Addie, Plate, Luncheon, 8¼ In.	8.00
Addie, Plate, Luncheon, Green, 8¼ In.	8.00
Bookends, Elephant, Clear, 5½ x 6½ In., Pair	150.00
Crow's Foot, Bowl, Vegetable, Amber, Oval, 10 In.	45.00
Crow's Foot, Gravy Boat, Ruby, Footed, 7¼ In.	125.00
Janice, Relish, Divided, Handles, 1¹¹⁄₁₆ x 8½ In.	15.00
Moondrops, Candelabrum, 3-Light, Clear, 5½ x 7 In.	50.00
Moondrops, Creamer, Ruby, 3 In.	18.00
Moondrops, Cup, Dark Green	9.00
Prelude, Bonbon, Turned-Up Ends, Curlicue Handles, 5½ x 6½ In.	30.00
Radiance, Plate, 8½ In.	6.00
Radiance, Punch Cup, Crystal, 2½ In.	10.00
Shelf Support, Threaded Metal Spacer, Early 1900s, 10 In., Pair	30.00 to 40.00
Teardrop, Candelabrum, 2-Light	40.00

NEWCOMB Pottery was founded by Ellsworth and William Woodward at Sophie Newcomb College, New Orleans, Louisiana, in 1895. The work continued through the 1940s. Pieces of this art pottery are marked with the printed letters *NC* and often have the incised initials of the artist as well. Most pieces have a matte glaze and incised decoration.

Bowl, Blue, Green, Matte Glaze, White Flowers, Relief Molded, S. Irvine, 1926, 9½ In.	3100.00
Bowl, Caladiums, Seed Pods, Blue & Green Underglaze, Marked, 2⅞ x 7¼ In.	4994.00
Bowl, Flower, Trumpet, Blue, Yellow, 1915, 2½ x 5½ In.	780.00
Bowl, Irises, Blue, Pink Ground, Squat, A.F. Simpson, 1917, 4½ x 8 In.	2760.00
Bowl, Jonquil, Blue, Green, White, Anna Frances Simpson, 1918, 3 In.	1260.00
Bowl, Pink Freesia Blossoms, Blue Ground, Squat, A.F. Simpson, 1937, 5 x 8 In.	1920.00
Bowl, White Freesia, Green Leaves, Blue Ground, A.F. Simpson, 1919, 4 x 5 In.	2160.00
Breakfast Set, Spiderwort, Green, Orange, Indigo, Henrietta Bailey, 1907, 7 Piece	10800.00
Charger, Carved, 3 Fish, Blue, Blue Border, White Rim, Sabina Wells, c.1904, 9½ In.	6000.00
Charger, Oak Leaf Border, Delft Style, Painted, 8¾ In.	5600.00
Pitcher, Milk, Sailboats, Lake, Blue, Green, Pink Sky, A.F. Simpson, 4¼ x 4¾ In.	3480.00
Pitcher, Transitional, Carved, Pink Freesia, A.F. Simpson, 1917, 4 x 5 In.	3000.00
Tankard, Incised, High Glaze, Tree Of The Deepest Root, Pine Trees, c.1905, 5¾ In.	2266.00
Tile, Oaks, Oak Tree With Spanish Moss, Full Moon, Sadie Irvine, 10 x 7½ In.	16800.00
Vase, 3 Handles, Yellow Crocuses, Green Stems, Blue Ground, c.1909, 8½ x 9½ In.	21600.00
Vase, Bayou, Full Moon, Blue Glaze, Ground, Sadie Irvine, 1931, 9¾ x 6¾ In.	6600.00
Vase, Bayou Scene, Pink Sky, Sadie Irvine, 1919, 3½ x 4 In.	2880.00
Vase, Blue & Green, Matte Glaze, Relief Molded Flowers, Sadie Irvine, 1925, 7¼ In.	3100.00
Vase, Blue Blossoms, Blue Ground, Sadie Irvine, c.1925, 7½ x 4 In.	2040.00
Vase, Bulbous, Bayou, Full Moon, Blue Glaze, Ground, Sadie Irvine, 1932, 3½ x 4½ In.	2640.00
Vase, Bulbous, Gardenias, Cobalt Ground, Ada Lonnegan, 1904, 7 x 7 In.	12000.00
Vase, Carved, Cottage, Moonlit Bayou Scene, Sadie Irvine, 1918, 8 x 4 In.	4500.00
Vase, Cornflowers, Carved, Painted, Blue Ground, 10½ x 5 In.	2880.00
Vase, Daisies, Long Stems, Blue & Green Glaze, Flared, Irene Borden Keep, 13 x 6 In.	21850.00
Vase, Dogwood, White, Blue, Mushroom Slip Glaze, c.1916, 5⅝ In.	1410.00
Vase, Flowers, Carved, Pink, Blue, Green Matte Glaze, Bulbous Top, Sadie Irvine, 6 x 5 In.	2200.00
Vase, Fruit Trees, Squat, Marie Ross, 1904, 4¾ x 6 In.	4200.00
Vase, Gardenia Band, Blue, Green, Pink, Sadie Irvine, Marked, c.1929, 6⅜ In.	5288.00
Vase, Grapes, Blue, Purple, Pink, Green, Sadie Irvine, Marked, 1919, 8⅝ In.	2900.00

Netsuke, Ivory, Man, Seated, Cutting Toenails, Late 19th Century, 1¼ In.
$191.00

Netsuke, Ivory, Sumo Wrestler, 1¾ In.
$120.00

Newcomb, Vase, Incised Leaves, Red & Black Matte Glaze, Mazie Ryan, 1905, 8 In.
$3795.00

N

Newcomb Pottery Designs

Newcomb Pottery was usually blue-green with incised decorations emphasized with black from 1900 to 1910. Molded designs and dull matte glaze were used from about 1910 to 1930. Newcomb made vases, mugs, tea sets, candlesticks, and lamps. Designs were inspired by the landscape of the South with trees dripping moss and as full moon.

Niloak, Planter, Figural, Dog, Ozark Dawn Glaze, 4¼ In. $40.00

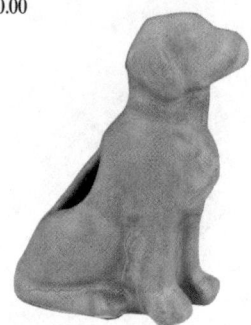

Niloak, Vase, Blue Matte, Wooded Scene, 10⅞ x 6 In. $28.00

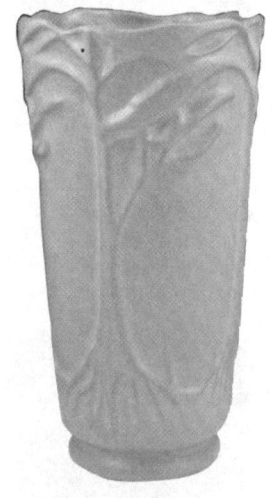

Niloak, Vase, Marbleized, Bulbous Top, 6½ In. $104.00

Vase, Incised Leaves, Red & Black Matte Glaze, Mazie Ryan, 1905, 8 In. . . . . *illus*	3795.00
Vase, Landscape, Bayou, Moonlit, 1923, 6¾ x 4¾ In.	1200.00
Vase, Landscape, Moss Laden Trees, Pink Sky, Carved, Shouldered, Sadie Irvine, 5 x 3 In.	2800.00
Vase, Leaves, Stacked, Green Semimatte Glaze, Oval, 9½ x 6 In.	2760.00
Vase, Match, Vellum Glaze, Lily Decoration, Blue Ground, 2 x 3 In.	3120.00
Vase, Moon & Moss, Matte Glaze, Blue, Green Underglaze, c.1933, 5½ In.	3525.00
Vase, Moon & Moss, Vellum Glaze, Bulbous, Sadie Irvine, 7 x 5 In.	7500.00
Vase, Mossy Oak Tree, Moon, Blue Glaze, Anna Frances Simpson, 1929, 4¾ In.	3105.00
Vase, Oak Tree, Spanish Moss, Full Moon, 1925, 6 x 3½ In.	3900.00
Vase, Oak Trees, Spanish Moss, Full Moon, A.F. Simpson, 1924, 6¼ x 5 In.	3600.00
Vase, Oak Trees, Spanish Moss, Vermillion Sky, 1928, 5¼ x 3 In.	3900.00
Vase, Pink Irises, Blue Ground, Sadie Irvine, c.1924, 10¾ x 6½ In.	5100.00
Vase, Pods, Leaves, Pink, Green, Spherical, 1925, 3¾ x 4½ In.	1320.00
Vase, Rain Mist Glaze, Ringed Beaker Shape, Flared, c.1945, 6 x 5 In.	780.00
Vase, Shaped Neck, Bulbous Body, Leaves, Stems, Turquoise, Blue, c.1920, 5 In.	3525.00
Vase, Spanish Moss, Trees, Louisiana Moon, 6½ In.	3100.00
Vase, Squat, Carved, Clusters Of Purple Grapes, Green Leaves, 1917, 4¼ x 7¼ In.	2400.00
Vase, Squat, Stylized Seed Pod Cross Section, Blue, Green, c.1901, 3¾ x 5¼ In.	16800.00
Vase, Stylized Leaves, Light, Dark Blue Ground, Bulbous, M.O. Delavigne, 6 x 4½ In.	3120.00
Vase, Stylized Trees, Blue, 8 x 5¾ In.	6630.00
Vase, Tall Pines, Moonlit Sky, A.F. Simpson, 1919, 8¼ x 3¾ In.	9000.00
Vase, Tapered, Carved, Ivory, Daffodils, Teal Ground, A.F. Simpson, 1908, 9 x 3½ In.	7800.00
Vase, Tear Shape, Espanol Pattern, Blue Glaze, Ground, Henrietta Bailey, 5¼ x 4 In.	3240.00
Vase, Vellum Glazed, Oleander, c.1922, 5½ In.	3120.00
Vase, White Morning Glories, Cylindrical, 1928, 8 x 3½ In.	2880.00
Vase, Windswept Landscape, Trees, Blue, Green, Ivory Sky, Oval, 5½ x 3¼ In.	3120.00
Vase, Wisteria Clusters, Blue Ground, Carved, Mazie Ryan, 8½ x 8½ In.	42000.00

NILOAK Pottery (Kaolin spelled backward) was made at the Hyten Brothers Pottery in Benton, Arkansas, between 1910 and 1947. Although the factory did make cast and molded wares, collectors are most interested in the marbleized art pottery line made of colored swirls of clay. It was called Mission Ware. By 1931 the company made castware, and many of these pieces were marked with the name Hywood.

Basket, Off-White, Marked, 3½ x 3 In.	7.50
Cornucopia, Flowers, Blue Matte, Marked, 7 In.	11.00
Cup, Bouquet, Pale Pink, Signed, 2½ x 3½ In.	24.00
Ewer, Eagle, Green Over White, Marked, 10 In.	75.00
Jar, Strawberry, White, Signed, 7 x 4 In.	35.00
Pitcher, Blue, Label, 3 In.	40.00
Pitcher, Flying Duck, 10 In.	65.00
Pitcher, Light Aqua Wash Over Ivory Body, Embossed, 6¾ In.	30.00
Pitcher, Yellow, 7 In.	40.00
Planter, Burma Camel, Recumbent, White & Tan Matte, Raised Mark, 3½ x 5 In.	34.00
Planter, Deer, 7 In.	55.00
Planter, Dog, Ozark Dawn Glaze, Marked, 4¼ In.	44.00
Planter, Dutch Shoe, Blue, Incised, 1932-47	20.00
Planter, Elephant, Glossy White, Sticker, 5¾ In.	55.00
Planter, Figural, Dog, Ozark Dawn Glaze, 4¼ In. . . . . *illus*	40.00
Planter, Satyr With Flute, Figural, Ribbed Bowl, Glossy Yellow, Marked, 7¼ In.	60.00
Planter, Squirrel, Brown Glaze, Stamped, 5¾ In.	40.00
Planter, Squirrel, Marked, 6 In.	65.00
Planter, Swan, Blue, Sticker, 7 In.	45.00
Planter, Swan, Light Blue, 7½ In.	40.00
Planter, Wishing Well, Closed Back, Pale Green, Brown Accents, Marked, 7¾ x 5 In.	48.00
Vase, Blue Matte, Wooded Scene, 10⅞ x 6 In. . . . . *illus*	28.00
Vase, Cornucopia, Rust Drip Glaze, Marked, 7⅛ In.	50.00
Vase, Cornucopia, Tan Matte Glaze, Green, Marked, c.1930-40, 7 x 7 In.	65.00
Vase, Fan, Wings, Light Blue, Footed, 5 x 6 In.	40.00
Vase, Marbleized, Brown, Green, Cream, 5½ In.	175.00
Vase, Marbleized, Brown, Tan, Blue, Satin Finish, 1900s, 6½ In.	125.00
Vase, Marbleized, Brown, Turquoise, Cream, Mission Ware, 10½ In.	525.00
Vase, Marbleized, Mauve, Blue, White, Green, 3¼ In.	195.00
Vase, Marbleized, Bulbous Top, 6½ In. . . . . *illus*	104.00
Vase, Marbleized, Pinched Waist, Marked, 5½ In.	175.00
Vase, Winged Victory, Blue, Marked, 6½ x 3¼ In.	24.00

NIPPON porcelain was made in Japan from 1891 to 1921. *Nippon* is the Japanese word for "Japan." A few firms continued to use the word *Nippon* on ceramics after 1921 as a part of the company name more than as an identification of the country of origin. More pieces marked Nippon will be found in the Dragonware, Moriage, and Noritake categories.

Bowl, Blossoms, Oasis Interior, Geometrics, Porcelain, Gilt, 3¼ x 7½ In.	35.00
Bowl, Lake Cottage, Swan, Blue Luster Rim, Peach Luster Interior, Red Mark, c.1920, 2 In.	50.00
Bowl, Mayonnaise, Ladle, Plate, Pink Roses, 3-Footed, 4½ x 2 & 5½ In.	55.00
Candlestick, Flower Panel, Green, White Coralene, Square Base, 9½ In., Pair . . . . *illus*	230.00
Chocolate Pot, Flowers, Blue M In Wreath Mark, c.1920, 9½ In.	47.00
Chocolate Pot, Iris Panel, Heavy Enamel Flowers, 8¼ In.	173.00
Chocolate Set, Pot, 9 In., Early 20th Century, 4 Cups & Saucers	118.00
Demitasse Set, Cranes, Palm Trees, Green Leaf Mark, c.1910, 10¼-In. Pot, 9 Piece . . . . *illus*	264.00
Dresser Set, Early 20th Century, Tray, 17 In., 8 Piece	323.00
Gravy Boat, Tray, Scalloped Edges, 8½ & 3½ In.	75.00
Gravy Boat, Violets, Rising Sun, 4 x 6 In.	65.00
Humidor, Man In Canoe Shooting Stag, Sunset, Cover, Disc Handle, 3 Buttressed Feet, 7 In.	86.00
Plaque, Water, Tree, 9 In.	125.00
Plate, Dessert, Azalea, 7½ In., 6 Piece	36.00
Plate, Lion & Lioness, Mountains, High Relief, 10¼ In.	575.00
Relish Set, Bluebird, Flowers, Enamel, Peach Luster, Blue Border, c.1912, 8 x 3 In., 5 Piece	70.00
Serving Dish, Flower Bouquet, Pink Garland, Trellis, Gold Band, Footed, 8½ x 3 In.	79.00
Sugar & Creamer, Nature Scene	64.00
Teapot, Geisha, 8½ x 5¼ In.	120.00
Toothpick, Circle With Cross, Oriental Scenes, Royal Satsuma	90.00
Tray, Farm On Lake, Beaded, 11½ x ¾ In.	250.00
Vase, Alpine Lake, Blue Flowers, Gold Enamel, Butterscotch Ground, c.1911, 8¾ In.	275.00
Vase, Blown Out, 4 Eagles On Rocks, Mountain Landscape, 10 x 6¼ In. . . . . *illus*	2760.00
Vase, Flowers, 2 Handles, c.1920, 6½ x 8 In.	53.00
Vase, Flowers, 9¼ In.	125.00
Vase, Flowers, Lake, Boat, c.1910, 10½ x 7¾ In.	176.00
Vase, Flowers, Satin, Jewels, Gold Trim, Maple Leaf Mark, c.1910, 10½ In. . . . . . . *illus*	470.00
Vase, Landscape, Flowers, Gold Trim, 2 Handles, 7¼ In., Pair	460.00
Vase, Rose, Pink, Red, Gold Moriage, c.1891-1921, 9 In.	200.00

NODDERS, also called nodding figures or pagods, are figures with heads and hands that are attached to wires. Any slight movement causes the parts to move up and down. They were made in many countries during the eighteenth, nineteenth, and twentieth centuries. A few Art Deco designs are also known. Copies are being made. A more recent type of nodder is made of papier-mache or plastic. These often represent sports figures or comic characters. Sports nodders are listed in the Sports category.

Andy Gump, Bisque, 4 In.	110.00
Bob's Big Boy, Checkered Pants, Decal On Chest, Composition, Japan, 1960s, 8 In. . . . . *illus*	330.00
Brylcreem Couple, Kissing, Magnet In Woman's Lips, Man's Cheek, 1950, 5½ In.	224.00
Charlie Weaver, Composition, Green Hat & Base, 1960s, 6½ In.	110.00 to 168.00
Cigar Boy, Bisque, Derby Hat, Porcelain, Germany, 6 In.	195.00
Leprechaun, Papier-Mache, Germany, c.1900	150.00
Man, Goatee, Green Hat, Coat, Blue Eyes, Brown Pants, Composition, Wood Base, 6¼ In.	132.00
Salt & Pepper Shakers are listed in the Salt & Pepper category.	
Skeezix, Bisque, 3 In.	110.00
Sweeping Lady, Wood, Painted, 7 In. . . . . *illus*	1400.00
Valentine, Man, Red & White Suit, Plastic, Spring Neck, 1950s, 6 In. . . . . *illus*	144.00

NORITAKE porcelain was made in Japan after 1904 by Nippon Toki Kaisha. The best-known Noritake pieces are marked with the M in a wreath for the Morimura Brothers, a New York City distributing company. This mark was used until the early 1950s. There may be some helpful price information in the Nippon category, since prices are comparable. Noritake Azalea is listed in the Azalea category in this book.

Basket Vase, Neil Roses, c.1910, 9 In.	750.00
Bowl, 3 Lobes, Moriage, c.1900, 7¼ In.	275.00
Bowl, Landscape, Moriage, c.1910, 7¼ In.	225.00
Bowl, Pink, Yellow & Purple Flowers, Shaped Shape, Gold Trim, 7 x 7 In.	15.00
Bowl, Seville, Cover, Oval, Handles, 12 x 8 In.	50.00
Chocolate Pot, Hand Painted, Fired Gold, c.1910, 9 In.	59.00

Nippon, Candlestick, Flower Panel, Green, White Coralene, Square Base, 9½ In., Pair
$230.00

Nippon, Demitasse Set, Cranes, Palm Trees, Green Maple Leaf Mark, c.1910, 10¼-In. Pot, 9 Piece
$264.00

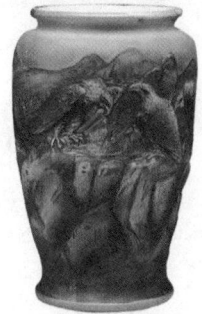

Nippon, Vase, Blown Out, 4 Eagles On Rocks, Mountain Landscape, 10 x 6¼ In.
$2760.00

Nippon, Vase, Flowers, Satin, Jewels, Gold Trim, Maple Leaf Mark, c.1910, 10½ In.
$470.00

Nodder, Bob's Big Boy, Checkered Pants, Decal On Chest, Composition, Japan, 1960s, 8 In. $330.00

Nodder, Sweeping Lady, Wood, Painted, 7 In. $1400.00

Nodder, Valentine, Man, Red & White Suit, Plastic, Spring Neck, 1950s, 6 In. $144.00

Chocolate Pot Set, Gold Floral Overlay Beading, 18 Piece 195.00
Creamer, Lorenzo, White, Blue, Gold Trim, Marked, 4¼ x 4½ In. 13.50
Creamer, Seville 23.00
Creamer, Sky Blue Luster, Floral Design Yellows, Pinks, Orange & Blue 25.00
Creamer, Up-Sa Daisy 17.00
Cup & Saucer, Griffin, Multicolored, Fleur-De-Lis, Red Wreath Mark 18.00
Cup & Saucer, Scenic, Ornate Gold Filigree 32.00
Cup & Saucer, Seville 23.00
Cup & Saucer, Susan Anne, Floral Design, 3¼ In. 16.00
Cup & Saucer, White Ground, Gold Flower Filled Urns, Bands Of Orange, 1940s 75.00
Demitasse Set, Butterflies, Blue, Gold Trim, Green M In Wreath, c.1920, 6-In. Pot, 4 Piece .. *illus* 294.00
Dish, Blue Luster, Yellow, White Flowers, Ivory Ground, 6½ In. 30.00
Dish, Butter, Spring Florals, Gold Enamel Medallions, 6½ In. 55.00
Dish, Flowers, Gold Trim, 6 In. 25.00
Dish, Vegetable, Croydon, Oval, 10½ x 7⅝ In. 35.00
Easter Egg, Spring Bonnet & Pink Flowers, Satin Lined Box, 1976 ..... 29.00
Gravy Boat, Tree In Meadow, Attached Underplate, 9 In. 45.00
Jar, Cover, Blue & Pink Flowers, 2 Handle, 8½ In. 38.00
Nappy, House By The Lake, Brown, Yellow & Blue, 5½ In. 28.00
Nappy, Lemon Dish, Orange & Teal Stylized Leaves, Marked 17.00
Nappy, Trees By The Lake, Brown, Purple, 5¾ In. 75.00
Plate, Baby Blue Ground, White Daisies, Trimmed In Gold, 8 Piece 32.00
Plate, Desert, Pink Flower Border, Marked, 6 In., 6 Piece 24.00
Plate, Dinner, Barrymore, 10⅝ In. 23.00
Plate, Dinner, Shenandoah, 10⅝ In. 24.00
Plate, Flowers, Black & Gold, Handles, Marked, Green M, Pre 1950s, 11 In. 35.00
Plate, The Oriental, 1920s, 10 In. 22.00
Plate, Zanzibar, White & Pink Flowers Design, 10½ In. 17.00
Platter, Daryl, Red Rose, Gold Trim, 16¼ In. 50.00
Platter, Doranne, 16⅜ In. 50.00
Platter, Pink Berries, Brown Leaves, Stems, Oval, 12⅛ In. 50.00
Salt & Pepper Set, Tray, Magenta Roses, c.1911 ..... 65.00
Shaker, Talcum, Blue Forget-Me-Nots, Gold Dots 250.00
Sugar, Cover, Goldcroft, Handles, 4 In. 24.00
Sugar, Cover, Goldmere, Gold Trim, Handles, 2¼ x 5 In. 35.00
Sugar, Cover, Oriental, Green, Nippon 65.00
Sugar, Cover, Polonaise, Handles 35.00
Sugar & Creamer, Dogwood Blossoms, Gold Accents, 4¾ In. 70.00
Syrup Set, Griffin, Multicolor, Fleur-De-Lis, Red Wreath 50.00
Tea Set, Oriental, Gold Finish, c.1925, 16 Piece 320.00
Trinket Dish, Art Deco Clown Sitting On Rim, Green M In Wreath, 5 In. ..... *illus* 147.00
Urn, Porcelain, Fired Gold Handles, c.1910, 6 x 6 x 5 In. 82.00
Vase, Flower & Woodland, Cobalt Blue Trim, Gold Highlights, Handles, 12¾ In. 275.00
Vase, Pagoda, Red, White Ground, S. Kimura, c.1930, 6¾ In. ..... *illus* 59.00
Vase, Purple, Gold, Green, Large Yellow Flowers, 5½ In. 235.00
Vase, Windmill, Landscape, Gilt, Handles, 7½ In. 72.00
Vase, Yellow, Cottage, Pond, Octagonal, Narrow Neck, Handles, Gold Trim, 6 x 4 In. 95.00

NORSE Pottery Company started in Edgerton, Wisconsin, in 1903. In 1904 the company moved to Rockford, Illinois. The company made a black pottery, which resembled early bronze relics of the Scandinavian countries. The firm went out of business in 1913.

Bowl, Band Of Owls, Verdigris On Black Ground, Footed, Marked, Impressed X, 3¾ In. 369.00
Bowl, Viking, Bronze Relics, Footed, Black, White, Bronze, Green, Impressed R, 4 x 8 In. 285.00

NORTH DAKOTA SCHOOL OF MINES was established in 1892 at the University of North Dakota. A ceramic course was included and pieces were made from the clays found in the region. Students at the university made pieces from 1909 to 1949. Although very early pieces were marked *U.N.D.*, most pieces were stamped with the full name of the university.

Bowl, Prairie Rose Encircled Shoulder, Pink, Margaret Cable, 2⅝ x 6 In. 432.00
Plate, Incised, Donkey, Rider In Sombrero, c.1951, 9½ In. 8400.00
Vase, Baluster, Irises, Indigo Ground, S. Mason, c.1935, 8 x 5 In. 4500.00
Vase, Bentonite, Allen, Yellow Birds, Terra-Cotta Ground, 5½ x 5½ In. 600.00
Vase, Bulbous, Prairie Rose, Flora Huckfield, 5¾ x 5¼ In. 840.00
Vase, Carved, Tepees, On River Front, M. Cable, 3½ x 7¼ In. 7800.00
Vase, Cowboy & Bronco, Riders, Horse, Mottled Tan Matte Glaze, Marked, 7¼ In. 2120.00

Vase, Gourd Shape, Bentonite, Firebirds, Suns, Red, Brown Ground, MLC, 4 In.	400.00
Vase, Incised, Yellow Blossoms, Celadon Matte Ground, 9 x 5 In.	10200.00
Vase, Indian On Horseback, Carved, Green, Incised, 151-N.D. Sioux, 6½ x 6 In.	600.00
Vase, Landscape, Incised, Green Matte Glaze, Tapered, Sorlie-Huck, 9 In.	13000.00
Vase, Light Blue High Glaze, Stepped Shoulder, M. Rognlie, 1947, 3½ In.	184.00
Vase, Maroon, 3 In.	115.00
Vase, Prairie Rose, Carved Stylized Flowers, Squat, 3 x 5 In. ....*illus*	540.00
Vase, Silhouetted Trees, Amber Ground, M.E.E. Collins, 8 x 5 In.	4500.00
Vase, Squat, Viking Ships, Bluegreen, Julia Mattson, 5 x 4 In.	1800.00
Vase, Wheat, Margaret Cable, Marked, 5½ In.	462.00

NORTHWOOD glass was made by the H. Northwood Co., founded in Wheeling, West Virginia, in 1901 by Harry Northwood. He worked for the Hobbs-Brockunier and LaBelle firms in the 1880s before operating his own glass plants in Martins Ferry, Ohio, and Ellwood City and Indiana, Pennsylvania. At the Wheeling factory, Harry Northwood and his brother Carl manufactured pressed and blown tableware and novelties in many colors that are collected today as custard, opalescent, goofus, carnival, and stretch glass. Pieces made between 1905 and about 1915 may have an underlined *N* trade mark. Harry Northwood died in 1919, and the plant closed in 1925.

Blown Twist, Celery Vase, 6 x 5½ In.	395.00
Chrysanthemum Sprig, Berry Bowl, Blue, Opaque, Gold Rim, 5 In.	185.00
Leaf Mold, Pickle Castor, Yellow Spatter, 10½ In.	950.00
Mother-Of-Pearl, Dish, Sweetmeat, Rose, Green & Blue Draped Loopings, 6½ In.	546.00
Rainbow & Cobweb, Compote, Blue, Footed, 1920s, 7 x 5 In.	56.00
Red Spatter, Water Set, Ribbed, Crimped Rim, 3¾-In. Tumblers, 9 Piece	374.00
Royal Ivy, Lamp, Gone With The Wind, Rubina, Ruby Chimney, 6½ In.	805.00
Royal Ivy, Pitcher, Rubina, c.1890, 8¼ x 6½ In.	85.00
Royal Oak, Salt, Rubina, 4-Sided, 3 In.	50.00

NU-ART, *see Imperial category.*

NUTCRACKERS of many types have been used through the centuries. At first the nutcracker was probably strong teeth or a hammer. But by the nineteenth century, many elaborate and ingenious types were made. Levers, screws, and hammer adaptations were the most popular. Because nutcrackers are still useful, they are still being made, some in the old styles.

Alligator, Cast Iron, Lift Tail, 13½ In.	125.00
Bird, Black Forest, Wood, Carved, Screw Type	350.00
Cast Iron, Ball Ends, Pliers Type, 1940s	18.00
Crossover Pliers, Nickel, Turned Handles, Convertible, Early 1900s, 5½ In.	18.00
Dog, Black, Cast Iron, Base, Harker Supply Co., 13 In.	285.00
Dog, Cast Iron, 2½ x 12 In.	95.00
Dog, On Base, Nickel Plated, 11 In.	132.00
Dog, Saint Bernard, Lift Tail To Open Mouth, 5½ x 14 In.	125.00
Gendarme, Wooden, Paris, 3 x 6 In.	36.00
Man, Iron, Old Sleepy Eyed, Hands In Pockets, Cast, Wood Base, 8½ x 5 In.	3640.00
Man, Standing, Hand In Pocket, Black Forest, Pliers Type	325.00
Squirrel, Cast Iron, Leaf Shape Platform, Tail Is Handle	55.00
Walnut Shape, Metal, Goldtone, Hinge Opening	20.00
William Shakespeare, Cottage, Brass, Pliers Type, Convertible, 1900, 5 In.	88.00
Wishing Well, Wood, Screw Top, Shells Fall In Well	16.00
Wolf's Head, Nickel Plated, Cast Iron, c.1920, 5 x 9½ x 4 In.	825.00
Woman, Seminude, Wooden, Left Leg Kicks Out, Engraved, 13 x 3¾ In.	68.00
Woman's Legs, Brass, 1½ x 5½ In.	55.00

NYMPHENBURG, *see Royal Nymphenburg.*

OCCUPIED JAPAN was printed on pottery, porcelain, toys, and other goods made during the American occupation of Japan after World War II, from 1945 to 1952. Collectors now search for these pieces. The items were made for export. Ceramic items are listed here. Toys are listed in the Toy category in this book.

Ashtray, Old Man's Head, Open Mouth, 2⅞ In.	29.00
Bank, Pig, Pink, Blue & Red Flower, 2¾ In.	40.00
Bowl, Black Glass, Gold Turtle & Rim, Marked, 2½ In.	20.00
Bowl, Leaves, Acorns, Flowers, Gilt, Mariuchi, 5 x 1¼ In.	22.00

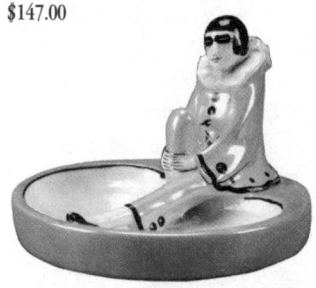

Noritake, Demitasse Set, Butterflies, Blue, Gold Trim, Green M In Wreath, c.1920, 6-In. Pot, 4 Piece
$294.00

Noritake, Trinket Dish, Art Deco Clown Sitting On Rim, Green M In Wreath, 5 In.
$147.00

Noritake, Vase, Pagoda, Red, White Ground, S. Kimura, c.1930, 6¾ In.
$59.00

North Dakota School of Mines, Vase, Prairie Rose, Carved Stylized Flowers, Squat, 3 x 5 In.
$540.00

Office, Arithmometer Tim, Ludwig Spitz, Berlin, No. 492, Wood Case, 1907
$1958.00

Ohr Pottery Victim of Katrina

A collection of 26 Ohr pots displayed on the Beau Rivage Casino's barge in Biloxi, Mississippi, was destroyed by Hurricane Katrina. Another barge landed on a gallery of the Ohr-O'Keefe Museum of Art under construction in Biloxi. All of the Ohr pottery being stored for the museum was safe.

Ohr, Vase, Cobalt Blue, Green Interior, Squat, Dimpled Shoulder, Lobed Neck, 3½ x 5¼ In.
$13200.00

Ohr, Vase, Mottled & Lustered Dark Teal Green, Dimpled Front, Folded Rim, 5 x 4½ In.
$5700.00

Creamer, Corn, Yellow, Green, Marked	28.00
Figurine, Accordion Player, Seated, Marked, 5 In.	30.00
Figurine, Basket, White, Marked, Red	20.00
Figurine, Black Native, Leaning On Stump, Marked, 5 In.	47.00
Figurine, Clown, Tuba, Blue Coat, Green Pants, Red Shoes, Stamped, 5¼ x 1½ In.	40.00
Figurine, Colonial Man, 4 In.	20.00
Figurine, Colonial Man, Woman, 4¾ x 3¼ In.	20.00
Figurine, Colonial Woman, Carrying Basket Of Flowers, 5 In.	22.00
Figurine, Cowboy, Drinking, 5½ In.	25.00
Figurine, Dutch Boy, Playing Accordion, 3 In.	15.00
Figurine, Dutch Girl, 4¼ In.	17.00
Figurine, Elephant, Green Glaze, 3 In.	19.00
Figurine, Lady, Blue & Yellow Dress, Gold Trim, Marked, 3 x 3 In.	23.00
Figurine, Puppies In A Basket, Marked, 3 x 3 In.	30.00
Mug, Old Salt Sailor, Eye Shut, Marked, 5½ In.	28.00
Pin Tray, Dog At Fire Hydrant, Marked, 2½ x 3 In.	21.00
Pitcher, Applied Leaves, Lemons, Brown, 3 In.	15.00
Planter, Donkey, 4 In.	15.00
Planter, Donkey & Cart, White, Brown, Black, Gray, 4 x 6¼ x 3 In.	40.00
Planter, Duck, Green, Blue, White, Beige, Brown	33.00
Plate, Bread, Leaves, Acorns, Flowers, Gilt, Mariuchi, 6¼ In.	22.00
Plate, Sailing Ship, Blue Sky, Water, White Clouds, Marked, 4 In.	22.00
Platter, Kingswood, Multicolored Flowers, Oval, Marked, 16 x 11¾ In.	35.00
Salt & Pepper, Birds, Blue, Orange, Yellow, Porcelain, 1945-52	15.00
Salt & Pepper, Ducks, Porcelain, 2 In.	20.00
Teapot, Old Salt Sailor, Marked, 4½ In.	35.00
Toothpick, Oriental Boy, Cachepot, Marked, H.K., 1945-52, 5 In.	40.00
Vase, Boy & Girl, Hats, Marked, Pair	50.00
Vase, Panda Bear, Climbing Tree, Porcelain, 1945-52, 3½ x 4 In.	22.00
Wall Pocket, Goose, Green, White, Brown, 9 x 10¾ In., 7 x 9½ In., 5 x 7¾ In., 3 Piece	50.00

OFFICE TECHNOLOGY includes office equipment and related products, such as adding machines, calculators, and check-writing machines. Typewriters are in their own category in this book.

Adding Machine, Gem Deluc, Model 307, Stand, 1915, 6½ x 6½ In.	105.00
Arithmometer, Pocket, Tasco, Vinyl Case, Instructions	22.00
Arithmometer Tim, Ludwig Spitz, Berlin, No. 492, Wood Case, 1907 ....*illus*	1958.00
Calculator, Texas Instrument, Advance Graphics, Manual, 7 x 3 In.	39.00
Calculator, Thatcher, No. 4012/4142, Keuffel & Esser Co., 1881, 22 In.	940.00
Check Writer, Paymaster, Mechanical, Ink, 19 Lbs.	150.00
Ticker Tape, Western Union, Self-Winding, Glass Dome, T.A. Edison, 1920s, 13 In.	1980.00

OHR pottery was made in Biloxi, Mississippi, from 1883 to 1906 by George E. Ohr, a true eccentric. The pottery was made of very thin clay that was twisted, folded, and dented into odd, graceful shapes. Some pieces were lifelike models of hats, animal heads, or even a potato. Others were decorated with folded clay "snakes." Reproductions and reworked pieces are appearing on the market. These have been reglazed, or snakes and other embellishments have been added.

Ashtray, Flower Form, Mottled Gunmetal, Green Glaze, Stamped, 1¾ x 4¾ x 4 In.	1920.00
Bank, Penny, Brown, Impressed, G.E. Ohr, Biloxi, Miss., 2⅝ x 2⅞ In.	575.00
Bowl, Bisque, Fired, Flat Shoulder, Dimpled Drum, 3 x 6 In.	1560.00
Bowl, Bisque Fired, Brown, Folded Rim, Dimpled, Stamped, 5¼ x 45¾ In.	4200.00
Bowl, Brown Glaze, Crumpled Edge, c.1897-1900, 2½ x 5¾ In.	7200.00
Bowl, Crumpled, Brown, Beige Glaze, c.1895-96, 5⅞ In.	3500.00
Bowl, Dark Green Glaze, Flower Form, Pinched, Squat, 2¼ x 4 In.	2280.00
Bowl, Dimpled, Folded, Green Glaze, 3½ x 4 In.	9600.00
Bowl, Scalloped Rim, Polychrome Sponge Glaze, Squat, 2¼ x 4¼ In.	5100.00
Hat, Torn, Folder, Floppy Rim, Green Speckled Glossy Glaze, 2½ x 6 In.	2520.00
Pitcher, Bisque, Fired, Clay, 3 x 6¼ In.	2160.00
Pitcher, Bisque, Fired, Marbleized Clay, 4 x 4½ In.	4500.00
Pitcher, Bisque Fired, Bulbous, Squeezed Heart Shape Handle, 1899, 9 x 6 In.	5700.00
Pitcher, Blue High Glaze Over Red Clay Body, Impressed, G.E. Ohr, 3 In.	1595.00
Pitcher, Bulbous, Bisque, Fired, Buff Clay, Twist, 6¼ x 5 In.	2520.00
Vase, Asymmetrical, Speckled Yellow & Green Matte Glaze, 4 x 3 In.	2400.00
Vase, Bottle Shape, Dimpled, Gray Brown Glaze, 4 x 2½ In.	1560.00

O

Vase, Brown Glaze, Black Spots, Pinched Waist, Crimped & Folded Rim, 3⅝ In.	3910.00
Vase, Burnt Baby, Lobed Rim, Dimpled, Red Glaze, 1893, 3 In.	4200.00
Vase, Burnt Baby, Pinched Rim, Dimpled, Olive Green Glaze, 1893, 3¼ In.	1200.00
Vase, Cabinet, Folded Rim, Notched Band, Gunmetal Brown Glaze, 4 x 3¼ In.	2040.00
Vase, Closed In Rim, Mottled Gray Brown Glaze, 3½ x 5 In.	1440.00
Vase, Cobalt Blue, Green Interior, Squat, Dimpled Shoulder, Lobed Neck, 3½ x 5¼ In. *...illus*	13200.00
Vase, Cut & Folded Top, Brown Glaze, Crystals, Impressed Mark, 3 x 5 In.	3900.00
Vase, Dark Brown Glaze, c.1897-1900, 3⅜ In.	5040.00
Vase, Dimpled, Spouted Rim, Green Mottled & Lustered Glaze, 5 x 4½ In.	5700.00
Vase, In Body Twist, Bisque, Fired, Inscribed, 2¾ x 3¾ In.	4200.00
Vase, Indigo, Amber Sponging, Amber Ground, Bulbous, Flower Form, 6 x 4½ In.	7200.00
Vase, Mottled & Lustered Dark Teal Green, Dimpled Front, Folded Rim, 5 x 4½ In. *.....illus*	5700.00
Vase, Multicolored, Glaze, Muted c.1897-1900, 5 In.	1920.00
Vase, Pinched Corners, Gunmetal Glaze, 3 x 5½ In.	2280.00
Vase, Pink Matte, Blue, Green, 2 Asymmetrical Handles, Signed, 4 x 5½ In.	10200.00
Vase, Red, Green & White Splatter Glaze, Bulbous, Rim, Indented, Impressed Mark, 3½ x 3½ In.	6600.00
Vase, Red, Green & Yellow Splatter Glaze, 2½ x 4 In.	4520.00
Vase, Squashed, Folded, Rounded Rim, Raspberry, Green, Blue Glaze, 2½ x 5 In.	13200.00
Vase, Squat, Dimpled Shoulder, Lobed Neck, Cobal Glaze, 3½ x 5 In.	13200.00
Vase, Squat, White Clay, Emerald Green Mirror Glaze, 2¼ x 4¼ In.	2520.00
Vase, Stove Pipe Neck, Black, Brown Sponged Glaze, 4½ x 3¾ In.	4500.00

OLD PARIS, *see Paris category.*

OLD SLEEPY EYE, *see Sleepy Eye category.*

ONION PATTERN, originally named bulb pattern, is a white ware decorated with cobalt blue or pink. Although it is commonly associated with Meissen, other companies made the pattern in the late nineteenth and the twentieth centuries. A rare type is called red bud because there are added red accents on the blue-And-white dishes.

Plate, Warming Dish, Blue, Hot Water Basin Below, Handles, 3 x 13 In.	144.00
Platter, Blue, Oval, Scalloped Edge, Meissen, 21 x 15 In., Pair	960.00
Tray, Blue, Plaque, Brass Frame, 2 Turned Handles, 20 x 13 In.	600.00
Tureen, Cover, Flow Blue, Oval, 6 x 11 In.	50.00
Vase, Blue, Fan Shape, 13 Openings, Lion's Head Ring Handles, 4 Scroll Feet, 12 In. *...illus*	978.00

OPALESCENT GLASS is translucent glass that has the tones of the opal gemstone. It originated in England in the 1870s and is often found in pressed glassware made in Victorian times. Opalescent glass was first made in America in 1897 at the Northwood glassworks in Indiana, Pennsylvania. Some dealers use the terms *opaline* and *opalescent* for any of these translucent wares. More opalescent pieces may be listed in Hobnail, Northwood, Pressed Glass, and other glass categories.

Alaska, Water Set, Vaseline Opalescent, Enameled Flowers, 6½ In., 7 Piece	700.00
Argonaut Shell, Tray, Vaseline, 8 x 6 In.	89.00
Beaded Fan, Dish, Green, Bull's-Eye, 8½ x 4½ In.	75.00
Blocked Thumbprint & Beads, Bowl, White, 7½ In.	50.00
Chrysanthemum Base Swirl, Syrup, Blue	350.00
Coin Dot, Syrup, Blue Opalescent, Metal Top, 7 In. *...illus*	118.00
Coin Dot, Tumbler, Blue	25.00
Coinspot, Compote, 1901, 7 x 4½ In.	45.00
Coinspot & Swirl, Syrup, Cranberry, 6¼ In.	195.00
Diamond, Candy Dish, Fan, 4-Footed, c.1907, 8¼ x 2½ In.	35.00
Diamond & Fan, Pitcher, Tumbler, Vaseline, 7¼ In.	500.00
Diamond & Star, Pitcher, Vaseline, 6¾ In.	270.00
Drapery, Butter, Cover Only, Blue, Gold Trim	60.00
Everglades, Bowl, Vaseline, Ruffled Edge, Footed, 9½ In.	80.00
Eyewinker, Candy Dish, Blue, 5½ In.	22.00
Eyewinker, Spooner, White, 5¾ In.	65.00
Feathers, Vase, White, 7 In.	5.00
Heirloom, Water Set, Footed Tumblers, Vaseline, 7 x 8 In., 5 Piece	225.00
Hobnail, Pitcher, Ruby, Applied Clear Reeded Handle, Hobbs, Brockunier, 8 In.	374.00
Hobnail, Sugar & Creamer, Blue, 3¼ In.	35.00
Intaglio, Creamer, White, 5⅛ In.	25.00
Inverted Fan & Feather, Owl, Vaseline, 7 x 2½ In.	195.00
Jackson, Green, Footed, Scalloped Rim, 3½ x 7½ In.	100.00

Onion Meissen
The blue-and-white "onion" Meissen has been made since the eighteenth century. The design, picturing peaches and pomegranates incorrectly called onions, is Chinese. The border fruit pointed only toward the center of the plate before 1800. Later the fruit alternately pointed in and out. Twentieth- and twenty-first-century pieces have the fruit pointing either way. Fewer of the "onions" or pomegranates are on newer plates. A pink version of the onion pattern and a Red Bud onion pattern date from the mid-nineteenth century. The Red Bud onion pattern had added gold and red overglaze decoration.

Onion Pattern, Vase, Blue, Fan Shape, 13 Openings, Lion's Head Ring Handles, 4 Scroll Feet, 12 In. $978.00

O

TIP
An unglazed rim on the bottom of a plate usually indicates it was made before 1850, or that it is Asian.

Opalescent Glass, Coin Dot, Syrup, Blue Opalescent, Metal Top, 7 In. $118.00

Opalescent Glass, Raindrop, Syrup, Cranberry, Crystal Reeded Handle, Hinged Lid, Oval, 7 In. $235.00

Opalescent Glass, Swirl, Pitcher, Cranberry, Bulbous, Ruffled Rim, Clear Handle, 10 In. $176.00

Jefferson Block, Celery Vase, 4 In.	95.00
Jewel & Fan, Bowl, Vaseline, 8 In.	60.00
Klondyke, Rose, Bowl, Vaseline	95.00
Leaf Chalice, Compote, White, 6 x 6¼ In.	50.00
Lined Heart, Vase, White, 11 In.	50.00
Many Loops, Bowl, Green	58.00
Meander, Bowl, Blue, Ruffled Edge	85.00
Meander, Bowl, Footed, Blue, c.1905, 9 In.	49.00
Opaline Brocade, Rose Bowl, Cranberry, 3⅝ x 4¼ In.	99.00
Opaline Brocade, Rose Bowl, Vaseline, Crimped Rim	140.00
Pearl Flower, Bowl, Blue, Ball Feet	65.00
Pearls & Scales, Compote, Vaseline, 3½ In.	250.00
Poinsettia, Bowl, White, 6¾ x 2¼ In.	42.00
Poinsettia, Tumbler, Blue, 4 In.	60.00
Raindrop, Syrup, Cranberry, Crystal Reeded Handle, Hinged Lid, Oval, 7 In. .... *illus*	235.00
Roulette, Dish, Green, 3¼ x 9 In.	25.00
Ruffles & Rings, Bowl, Green, Enameled, Daisy Band, 1906, 8 In.	69.00
Ruffles & Rings, Bowl, Ice Blue, 3 x 9½ In.	55.00
Ruffles & Rings, Bowl, White, Footed, 9½ In.	50.00
Shell & Dot, Bowl, White Ruffled Edge, c.1910	48.00
Star & Arch, Bowl, Vaseline, 6½ In.	60.00
Swirl, Pitcher, Cranberry, Bulbous, Ruffled Rim, Clear Handle, 10 In. .... *illus*	176.00
Thumbprint & Beads, Bowl, Green, 7¼ In.	50.00
Tokyo, Spooner, 4⅝ In.	19.00
Toothpicks are listed in the Toothpick category.	
Twiggs, Vase, Bud, Blue, 5 In.	35.00
Twist, Celery Vase, White, 6 x 5½ In.	395.00
Wheel, Bowl, Green, Footed, 9 In.	52.50
Wheel, Bowl, Green, 3 Loop Legs, 9 In.	55.00

OPALINE, or opal glass, was made in white, green, and other colors. The glass had a matte surface and a lack of transparency. It was often gilded or painted. It was a popular mid-Nineteenth-century European glassware.

Ashtray, Turquoise, Brass Mounts, 19th Century, 2⅜ In.	84.00
Bowl, Reticulated, Velvet Border, Wood Frame, 24 x 24 In.	290.00
Casket, Box Shape, White, Ormolu, Bohemian, 19th Century	895.00
Casket, Egg Shape, Blue, Ormolu, Twining Vine Basket Stand, 8 In.	795.00
Casket, Egg Shape, Bronze Nest, S-Shape Clasp, Triple Hinge	435.00
Casket, Egg Shape, Clambroth, Louis XVI Style Cutting, Gilt, 7 x 7¾ In.	650.00
Comport, Footed, Blue, 6¼ x 8½ In.	149.00
Cracker Jar, Storks, Embossed Metal Lid, Handle, Victorian, 10 In.	206.00
Dresser Set, Foil Label, Pierre Schneider, 3 Piece	212.00
Epergne, Layered, Gilt Ormolu, France, 19th Century	295.00
Goblet, Applied Blue Snake On Stem, c.1910, 2⅞ x 3 In.	67.00
Jar, Perfume, Cover, Gold Enameled, 6 In.	695.00
Lamp, Oil, c.1900, 6¼ In.	250.00
Mug, Gilt Silver Rim, 4¼ In.	75.00
Punch Set, Enameled Flowers, Vines, Tray, Tumblers, 15-In. Bowl, Cover, 10 Piece .... *illus*	411.00
Vase, Birds, Gold Rim, c.1910, 7¾ x 3⅜ In.	67.00
Vase, Enameled, Blue, Butterfly, France, 9½ In.	195.00
Vase, Mantel, Enameled, Birds In Flight, France, Pair	295.00

OPERA GLASSES are needed because the stage is a long way from some of the seats at a play or an opera. Mother-of-pearl was a popular decoration on many French glasses.

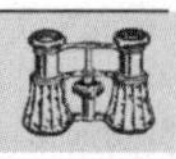

Brass, Black	40.00 to 99.00
Bronze Dore, Golden Luster, Mother-Of-Pearl, 4 x 2¾ In.	245.00
Butterfly, Coated Box	14.00
Chrome, Black, Etching, Raylite, 3 x 4½ In.	36.00
Chrome, Red, Flip-Up, 4¼ x 2½ In.	10.00
Enamel, Emerald Green, Cherubs, Lorgnette Handle	795.00
Lematire Paris, Pearl Eye Piece, Boy, Girl, Birds, Flowers, Enamel, L.M. Lederer, France, 3 x 4 In.	403.00
Lemoire, Mother-Of-Pearl, Gold Plated, Paris, Case, c.1900, 3 x 5 In.	41.00
Lorgnette, Mother-Of-Pearl, Lemoire Fabi Paris, 19th Century, 7½ x 3½ In.	295.00
Metal, Glass, Adjustable Focus, Case, Occupied Japan	32.00
Mother-Of-Pearl, Amber, Lorgnette, 6 In.	595.00

Mother-Of-Pearl, Auber Paris, c.1920	135.00
Mother-Of-Pearl, Blue, Silver Back, B.H. Stief Jewelry Co., 1900s, 6½ x 4 In.	173.00
Mother-Of-Pearl, Brass, Leather, Silk Lined Case	250.00
Mother-Of-Pearl, Brass, Lemoire, 4⅛ x 3 In.	95.00
Mother-Of-Pearl, Brass, Telescopic, Hardwood Partridge Stem, France, c.1900	850.00
Mother-Of-Pearl, Brass Engraved Monogram, c.1888, 4¼ x 2¾ In.	375.00
Mother-Of-Pearl, Colmunt Ft, Paris, Case ....*illus*	81.00
Mother-Of-Pearl, France, c.1890, 6¼ In.	144.00
Mother-Of-Pearl, Gilt Brass, Bronze, Bardou Paris, Swivel Handle, 4 x 1½ In.	118.00
Mother-Of-Pearl, Goldtone Metal, Leather Case, Satin Liner	55.00
Mother-Of-Pearl, Handle, A.J. Stark & Company, Denver, 6¼ x 4½ In.	201.00
Mother-Of-Pearl, Ivory Eye Lenses, Leather Case, Chevalier Paris	180.00
Mother-Of-Pearl, Jeweled, Brass Frame, Marked, Le Fils, Paris, 2 x 4½ x 2 In. ......*illus*	2020.00
Mother-Of-Pearl, Lemoire Paris, Inscribed, c.1900, 3⅞ x 2¼ In.	175.00
Mother-Of-Pearl, Mignon, c.1950	99.00
Mother-Of-Pearl, Tiffany & Co., France, c.1900, 3⅞ In.	140.00

Opaline, Punch Set, Enameled Flowers, Vines, Tray, Tumblers, 15-In. Bowl, Cover, 10 Piece
$411.00

ORPHAN ANNIE first appeared in the comics in 1924. The redheaded girl, her dog Sandy, and her friends have been on the radio and are still on the comic pages. A Broadway musical show and a movie in the 1980s made Annie popular again and many toys, dishes, and other memorabilia are being made.

Ashtray, Annie & Sandy, Lusterware, 4 In.	29.00
Bank, Annie Sitting By Sandy, Applause, 1982	30.00
Belt Buckle, 1981, 1¼ In.	35.00
Book, Big Little Book, Little Orphan Annie & The Haunted Mansion, 1941	42.50
Book, Big Little Book, Whitman Publishing, 1933	20.00
Book, Radio, Orphan Annie's Book About Dogs, Ovaltine Premium, 31 Pages, 1936	65.00
Bracelet, Identification, American Flag, Brass Links, Ovaltine, 1939, 6 In.	73.00
Button, Voter's, On Card, Ovaltine, 1931, 1¼ In.	448.00
Change Purse, Annie & Sandy, Snap Closure, Pink Vinyl, 3½ x 2½ In.	55.00
Comic Book, Little Orphan Annie In Circus, Cuppies & Leion Publishing, 1927	85.00
Comics, Radio Orphan Annie's 1939 Secret Society, 7 Golden Rules	60.00
Cook Stove, 7½ x 9½ x 5¼ In.	13.00
Doll, Arms Move, Celluloid, Japan, c.1930, 7½ In. ....*illus*	29.00
Doll, Composition, Red Dress, White Pantaloons, Sock, Leather Shoes, 10 In.	295.00
Doll, Knickerbocker, 15 In.	55.00
Doll, Knickerbocker, Cloth, 24 In.	75.00
Doll, Rcmco, Box, 1967, 16 In.	84.00
Doll Set, Annie & Sandy, Composition, Painted Eyes, Ralph Freundlich, Box, 12 In.	495.00
Foto Reel Viewer, Original Film, Premium, c.1938	95.00
Game, Little Orphan Annie Shipwrecked, Cuppies & Leon Publishing, 1931	65.00
Game, Little Orphan Annie Travel, Milton Bradley, Box	55.00
Glass, Drinking, Libbey, 1982, 6 In.	9.00
Lights, Christmas, Figural, Annie & Sandy, 3 In.	395.00
Lunch Box, Thermos, Aladdin, 1982	70.00
Marble, Orphan Annie, White & Black, Peltier, ¹¹⁄₁₆ In.	28.00
Mug, Ovaltine, 1930s	95.00
Mug, Ovaltine, Green Rim, Annie & Sandy Saying It's Good For Yuh, 3 In.	45.00
Mug, Shake-Up, Cream, Orange Top, Beetleware, Signed, Harold Gray	55.00
Mug, Shake-Up, Ovaltine, Caption, 7 In.	225.00
Mug, Shake-Up, Sandy, Ovaltine, 7 In.	55.00
Nodder, Annie & Sandy, Germany, Annie, 3½ In., Sandy, 1¼ In., Pair	225.00
Nodder, Bisque, c.1925, Germany, 3½ In.	75.00 to 110.00
Pillow, Square, 1940s, 10 In.	75.00
Pin, I'm An Inquirer, Rotocomic, c.1948, 1¼ In.	224.00
Pin, Picture Under Glass, Clasp On Back	35.00
Pin, Pittsburgh Post-Gazette, Serial Number, 1¼ In.	115.00
Pin, Sandy, Enamel, 1¼ In.	20.00
Plate, Annie & Sandy, Knowles, 8½ In.	35.00
Plate, Daddy Warbucks, Knowles, 1982, 8½ In.	39.00
Poster Order Form, Voters Button, Joe Corn Tassel, Ovaltine, 1931, 16¾ x 10¼ In.	743.00
Ring, February Birthstone, Brass Base, Ovaltine, 1936	496.00
Ring, Triple Mystery Silver Star, Secret Compartment, Ovaltine Premium, 1938	835.00
Salt & Pepper, Annie & Sandy, 1930s, 3 In.	47.00
Stove, Marx, 1930s, 8½ x 10 In.	40.00
Tin, Cocoa, Plastic, Cartoon With Annie	70.00

Opera Glasses, Mother-Of-Pearl, Colmunt Ft, Paris, Case
$81.00

Opera Glasses, Mother-Of-Pearl, Jeweled, Brass Frame, Marked, Le Fils, Paris, 2 x 4½ x 2 In.
$2020.00

Orphan Annie, Doll, Arms Move, Celluloid, Japan, c.1930, 7½ In.
$29.00

O

Orrefors, Vase, Fish Swimming, Teardrop Shape, Edward Hald, 7 In. $499.00

Overbeck, Bowl, Maroon, Green Interior, Flower Frog, 3 Flowers, 3 x 6½ In. $431.00

Overbeck, Vase, Pinecones, Matte Mustard & Green Glazes, E. & H. Overbeck, 8¾ x 4¾ In. $16800.00

O

Toothbrush Holder, Annie & Sandy, Bisque, Copyright F.A.S., Japan, 1950s, 4 In.	145.00
Tote Purse, Broadway Annie, The Musical, Red	45.00
Toy, Annie, Jumping Rope, Sandy, Suitcase In Mouth, Tin, Windup, Harold Gray, 5 In.	330.00
Toy, Sandy, Doghouse, Push Down Tail, Chases Ball, Tin Lithograph, Marx, Box, c.1939, 8 In.	336.00
Toy, Sandy, Tin, Windup, 1930s	153.00
Wall Pocket, Annie, Cutting Cake, Sandy, Lusterware, Orange Rim, 1930s	197.00
Wall Pocket, Annie & Sandy, Drinking Soda, Lusterware, Blue Rim, 1930s	108.00
Wristwatch, New Haven, Box, 1941, 4 x 7 x 1 In.	448.00
Wristwatch, New Haven, Box, 1948, 4 x 7 x 1 In.	336.00

ORREFORS Glassworks, located in the Swedish province of Smaaland, was established in 1898. The company is still making glass for use on the table or as decorations. There is renewed interest in the glass made in the modern styles of the 1940s and 1950s. In 1990, the company merged with Kosta Boda. Most vases and decorative pieces are signed with the etched name *Orrefors*.   *Orrefors*

Bottle, Stopper, 6 In.	28.00
Bowl, Art Deco Style, Ribbed, 4 x 6½ In.	95.00
Bowl, Flower Form, Mayflower, Jan Johanson, 3½ x 5 In.	43.00
Bowl, Fluted Columns, Signed, 5½ x 7½ In.	300.00
Bowl, Fluted Sides, Signed, 2 x 4¾ In.	135.00
Bowl, Pedestal, Aquamarine, Translucent, 3½ x 1¾ In., 2 Piece	125.00
Bowl, Raspberry Pattern, Anne Nilsson, Signed, 7¼ x 3 In.	50.00
Clock, Round, Carved Radiating Flutes, Original Label	75.00
Cordial, Coronation, Teardrop Base, Faceted Stems, 2⅝ In., 6 Piece	325.00
Decanter, Stopper, Engraved, Modernistic, 1950s, 11 In.	175.00
Ewer, Milk Glass, Loop Handle, 15 In.	125.00
Figurine, Punk, Erika Lagerbielke, Signed, c.1988, 13 x 8 In.	4500.00
Goblet, Coronation, 6 x 2¾ In.	20.00
Paperweight, Mushroom, Ruby Red, Yellow Spots, Curved Stem, 5 x 4 In.	85.00
Plate, Liberty Tree, c.1976, 10¼ In.	46.00
Plate, Notre Dame, Gold Embossed, Box, 9⅞ In.	60.00
Sculpture, Jonah & The Whale, No. 2407, 5 x 13 In.	410.00
Tumbler, Flip, Nude Woman, Holding Torch, Wheel Cut, Art Deco, Signed, c.1925	295.00
Vase, Ariel, The Girl & The Dove, Cobalt Blue, Amber Shaded Interior, 6 In.	2115.00
Vase, Bird On Branch, Etched, Hiles Landing, 1940s	60.00
Vase, Bottle, Blue Netting, Signed, Orrefors, Kraka 526, 8¾ In.	487.00
Vase, Cupid Holding Bow, Flowers, Engraved	125.00
Vase, Cut Crystal, Square, Paneled, 8½ x 4 In.	146.00
Vase, Dove, Flowers & Leaves, Amber & Blue Interior, Oval, 7½ In.	1495.00
Vase, Engraved, Vicke Lindstrand, c.1950, 8 In.	205.00
Vase, Fish, Graal, Swimming, Black, Oval, 4¾ In.	382.00
Vase, Fish Swimming, Teardrop Shape, Edward Hald, 7 In. *illus*	499.00
Vase, Gondolier, Amber, Blue Interior Design, Waves, Flowers, Oval, E. Ohrstrom, 5 In.	1610.00
Vase, Lily Of The Valley, Etched, 5 x 3¼ In.	89.00
Vase, Square, Signed, Nils Landberg, 1950s, 6 In.	45.00
Vase, Thunderstorm, People, Animals, Cobalt Blue, Label, E. Hald, 1920, 4⅜ In.	1528.00
Vase, Woman, Playing, Rectangular, Inscribed, 11 In.	147.00
Votive, Discus, Lars Hellsten, 5 In.	15.00

OTT & BREWER Company operated the Etruria Pottery at Trenton, New Jersey, from 1871 to 1892. They started making belleek in 1882. The firm used a variety of marks that incorporated the initials *O & B*.

Bust, Jesus Christ, Incised, Isaac Broome, 1876, 15¼ x 9 In.	3600.00
Bust, Virgin Mary, Incised, Isaac Broome, 1876, 15¼ x 8½ In.	3600.00
Cup & Saucer, Twig Handle, Bronze, Belleek, 3¼ & 2¼ x 5¾ In.	395.00
Dish, 2 Handles, Fluted, Oval, 2 x 6½ x 3¼ In.	195.00
Pitcher, Orchid, Delft Style, Reticulated Handle, 17¼ x 7½ In.	2280.00
Pitcher, Red Crown, Twig Handle, Bronze, Sword Mark, 5½ x 3½ In.	1295.00
Vase, Bird, Multicolored, Green Matte Ground, Bottle Shape, 10 x 5½ In.	7200.00

OVERBECK pottery was made by four sisters named Overbeck at a pottery in Cambridge City, Indiana. They started in 1911. They made all types of vases, each one-of-A-kind. Small, hand-modeled figurines are the most popular pieces with today's collectors. The factory continued until 1955, when the last of the four sisters died.

Bowl, Incised Morning Glories, Tan Matte Glaze, E & F Overbeck, 2½ x 6 In.	1610.00
Bowl, Maroon, Green Interior, Flower Frog, 3 Flowers, 3 x 6½ In. ....*illus*	431.00
Brooch, Southern Belle, Blond, Pink & Blue Striped Dress, 2 In.	175.00
Figurine, Bride & Groom, Multicolored Glaze, 5 In., Pair	16800.00
Figurine, Dog, Panting, White, Brown & Black Ears, Google Eyes, Incised, 3 In.	465.00
Figurine, Farmer, Holding Watermelon, Brown Floppy Hat, Blue Pants, 5⅛ In.	680.00
Figurine, Farmers Wife, Carrying Basket Of Apples, Blue Dress, Apron, Incised, 4¼ In.	515.00
Figurine, George & Martha Washington, Seated, Incised, 3⅞ & 3⅜ In., Pair	2130.00
Figurine, Man, Red Frock Coat, Blue Top Hat & Bow Tie, Incised, 4 In.	260.00
Figurine, Southern Belle, Blue Dress, Bonnet, Red & Blue Spots, Incised, 3⅜ In.	260.00
Figurine, Southern Belle, Striped Dress, Apron, Blue, Yellow Bonnet, Fan, Incised, 4⅛ In.	320.00
Figurine, Southern Belle, White Dress, Blue & Pink Spots, Marked, 4¼ In.	230.00
Figurine, Woman, Blue Dress, Pink Coat, Umbrella, Incised, 4¼ In.	230.00
Pitcher, Stylized Trees, Blossoms, Brown Matte Glaze Ground, Incised, 4¾ x 9½ In.	3120.00
Vase, Pinecones, Matte Mustard & Green Glazes, E. & H. Overbeck, 8¾ x 4¾ In. ....*illus*	16800.00
Vase, Stylized Flowers, Red & Green, Tan Ground, Marked, 11⅞ In.	13500.00
Vase, Stylized Flowers, Stems, Tan, Rust Glaze, Rolled Rim, E. & M.F. Overbeck, 11 In.	14900.00

OWENS Pottery was made in Zanesville, Ohio, from 1891 to 1928. The first art pottery was made after 1896. Utopian Ware, Cyrano, Navarre, Feroza, and Henri Deux were made. Pieces were usually marked with a form of the name *Owens*. About 1907, the firm began to make tile and discontinued the art pottery wares.

Ewer, Malachite Opalescent, Gold Inlay, Art Nouveau Flower, Green Beading, 10 In.	150.00
Pitcher, Daisies, Light Blue Ground, Straight Sides, Shaped Handle, No. 1015, 12⅜ In.	173.00
Tile, Deer, Leaping, Moonlit Forest, Cuenca, 11¾ x 17¾ In.	3120.00
Tile, Grapes, Purple, Green, Yellow, Carved, Frame, Marked, 5¼ In.	600.00
Tile, Hereford Cow, Cuenca, 12 x 12 In.	1560.00
Tile, Leaf, 3-Lobed, Molded, Green Matte Glaze, Square, 5¾ x 5¾ In.	173.00
Tile, Sailboat, Water, Cuenca, 11½ x 17¾ In.	2100.00
Tile, Swans On Water Lily Pond, Cuenca, 11¾ x 17¾ In.	5100.00
Vase, Aborigine, Geometrics, Brown & Black, Painted, Signed, JBO, No. 32, 7 x 4½ In.	175.00
Vase, Aborigine, Painted Geometric Design, Signed, JBO, 7 x 4½ In. ....*illus*	180.00
Vase, Aborigine, Triangles, Lines, Rust, Black, Tan Ground, Bulbous, Impressed No. 27, 6 In.	148.00
Vase, Arts & Crafts, Green Matte Glaze, Incised Lines, Cutouts In Neck, Impressed, 8 In.	1020.00
Vase, Dragonflies, Green Matte Glaze, Arts & Crafts, Maude Sibyl Pollock, 4 In.	1270.00
Vase, Humidor, Utopian, Portrait Of Young Girl, Green Ground, Footed, 7¾ In.	460.00
Vase, Lotus, Mushrooms, Shouldered, Charles Chilcote, 4¾ In.	460.00
Vase, Lotus, Trees, Stylized, Green On Blue Green Ground, Bulbous, Signed, Chilcote, 7 In.	690.00
Vase, Utopian, Bottle Neck, Flowers, Matte, Marked, 13¼ In.	110.00
Vase, Utopian, Carnations, Yellow & Orange, Bulbous, Tapered Neck, 8 In.	184.00
Vase, Utopian, Flowers, Brown Glaze, Bulbous, Signed, Impressed Mark, 8½ In.	230.00
Vase, Utopian, Ivy, Squat, Delores Harvey, 3½ x 8 In.	138.00
Vase, Utopian, Woodbine, Pinched Waist Shape, 5¾ In.	161.00
Vase, Utopian, Yellow, Orange Pansies, Brown Ground, Cylindrical, Impressed, 8⅛ In.	98.00
Vase, Utopian, Yellow, Orange Roses, Seal Brown Ground, Marked, 8 In.	115.00
Wall Pocket, Acorn Shape, Slip Decorated, Pansies, Brown Glaze, 7¾ In. ....*illus*	863.00

OYSTER PLATES were popular from the 1880s. Each course at dinner was served in a special dish. The oyster plate had indentations shaped like oysters. Usually six oysters were held on a plate. There is no greater value to a plate with more oysters, although that myth continues to haunt antiques dealers. There are other plates for shellfish, including cockle plates and whelk plates. The appropriately shaped indentations are part of the design of these dishes.

4 Wells, Parcel Gilt, Gilt Kelp, Limoges, 7⅜ In., 12 Piece	764.00
4 Wells, White Flowers, Green Leaves, Rectangular, 7 x 8½ In.	20.00
5 Wells, Blue Flowers, Gold Accents, Marked, RS, 10½ In.	60.00
5 Wells, Cream, Gold, Limoges, 9½ In.	35.00
5 Wells, Floral Spray, Gilt Rim, Limoges, Late 1800s, 8½ In., 12 Piece	295.00
5 Wells, Flowers, 1903-25	200.00
5 Wells, Gray, Blue, Purple, Green Flowers, Limoges	35.00
5 Wells, Pink, Beige, Black, Limoges	35.00
5 Wells, Pink, Blue Flower Transfer	165.00
5 Wells, Pink, Flowers, RS Prussia, 11 In.	60.00
5 Wells, Pink Roses, Pastel Ground, Gold Accents, Marked, RS, 10 In.	20.00
5 Wells, Purple & Green Flowers, Gray Green Edge, Limoges, 8½ In.	29.00
5 Wells, Purple Flowers, Green Leaves, Sea Foam Green Rim, Gold Accents, 8½ In.	27.00

Art Pottery

The term *art pottery* as it is used today by collectors includes handmade pottery and ceramics, including commercial florist lines, of companies that made art pottery from 1870 to about 1930. Sometimes it includes the work of studio potters from the 1920s through the 1940s.

Art pottery at first was hand thrown and hand decorated. Many of the art potteries started as one-man or one-woman operations and grew into large commercial factories.

Owens, Vase, Aborigine, Painted Geometric Design, Signed, JBO, 7 x 4½ In. $180.00

Owens, Wall Pocket, Acorn Shape, Slip Decorated, Pansies, Brown Glaze, 7¾ In. $863.00

Oyster Plate, 5 Wells, Turkey Style, Haviland, 1876-89, 8½ In. $550.00

Oyster Plate, 6 Wells, Faience, Quimper, 8¾ In. $250.00

Paden City, Gazebo, Sandwich Server, Center Handle, Blue, 11 In. $25.00

5 Wells, Raised Seaweed, Green Underglaze, Theo Haviland, 8¾ In.	600.00
5 Wells, Red Roses, Blue Forget-Me-Nots, Haviland, H & Co. Limoges, 1891	700.00
5 Wells, Shell Decoration	295.00
5 Wells, Southern Raccoon Oysters, Turkey Plate, Theodore R. Davis, Haviland & Co.	3500.00
5 Wells, Teal, Flowers, RS Prussia	60.00
5 Wells, Turkey Style, Haviland, 1876-89, 8½ In. ....*illus*	550.00
5 Wells, Underwater Decor, Coral Branches, Blue, Magenta, Pink, Square	375.00
5 Wells, White, Blue, Gold, Flowers, Gold Trim	35.00
5 Wells, White, Silver Accents, Limoges, 8½ In.	32.00
6 Wells, Basket Weave, Cream, Brown, Stoneware, Longchamp, Majolica	125.00
6 Wells, Black, White Fish Shape, Brown Leaves, Octagonal, 8¾ In.	29.00
6 Wells, Blue Diamond	170.00
6 Wells, Burgundy, White, Limoges, 9¼ In.	31.00
6 Wells, Burgundy Faded To Pink, Flowers, Gold Edging, Limoges, 8½ In.	31.00
6 Wells, Carl Tielsch, 9¼ In.	250.00
6 Wells, Cream, Coiffe Limoges Factory, Stamped, Limoges, France, 10 In.	40.00
6 Wells, Cream, Gold, Limoges, 9½ In.	35.00
6 Wells, Dark, Light Blue, Limoges, 9 In.	35.00
6 Wells, Faience, Quimper, 8¾ In. ....*illus*	250.00
6 Wells, Faience, Sarreguemines, c.1950, 9½ In.	154.00
6 Wells, Gold Accents, Carl Tielsch, 1880s, 9 In.	250.00
6 Wells, Heart Shape, Burgundy Faded To Pink, Flowers, Gold Rim, Limoges, 8½ In.	31.00
6 Wells, Longwy, 10 In.	95.00
6 Wells, Majolica, Blue, Green, Orange, Cream Ground, Starfish Center, 9½ In.	125.00
6 Wells, Majolica, Longwy, 10 In.	95.00
6 Wells, Majolica, Salmon, Teal, Sarreguemines, c.1890-1920	375.00
6 Wells, Multicolored, Metal Hanging Hooks	23.00
6 Wells, Salmon, Teal, c.1890-1920	375.00
6 Wells, Square, Carlsbad, 9 In.	175.00
6 Wells, White, Burgundy, White, Limoges, 9¼ In.	31.00
6 Wells, White, Gold, Pink Flowers, Limoges	31.00
6 Wells, White, Gold Accents, 8½ In.	31.00
6 Wells, White, Gold Accents, Limoges, 9 In.	35.00
7 Wells, Dark Blue, Flowers, Limoges	50.00
7 Wells, Platter, St. Clement, Majolica, 6 Piece	700.00
8 Wells, Roses, Pink & Yellow Flowers, White, Gold Accents, Marked, RS	20.00
Gilt Decorated, Marked CFH/GDM, Limoges, c.1890, 9 In., 10 Piece	1000.00
Shell Design, Gold Trim, Limoges, 1891-1900, 8½ In.	325.00

PADEN CITY Glass Manufacturing Company was established in 1916 at Paden City, West Virginia. The company made over twenty different colors of glass. The firm closed in 1951. Paden City Pottery is not listed here.

Black Forest, Candleholder, Green, Mushroom Style, 3 In., Pair	167.00
Black Forest, Console, Pink, 11 In.	119.00
Black Forest, Cracker Plate, Green, 10 In.	95.00
Black Forest, Dish, Mayonnaise, Pink	120.00 to 145.00
Black Forest, Ice Bucket, Green	119.00
Black Forest, Sugar, Pink	40.00
Bridal Bouquet, Candy Dish, Cover, Crystal, Footed	95.00
Chevalier, Cake Stand, Silver Plated Metal Base, 1935-50, 3 x 11¼ In.	38.00
Crocus, Tray, Center Handle, 5 x 11 In.	75.00
Crow's Foot, Bowl, Vegetable, Amber, Oval, 10 In.	45.00
Crow's Foot, Candlestick, Mushroom, Black, 2½ x 4½ In., Pair	79.00
Crow's Foot, Candy Dish, Cover, Black, 3¾ x 7 In.	75.00
Crow's Foot, Candy Dish, Cover Only, Green	16.00
Crow's Foot, Gravy Boat, Ruby, Footed, 4½ x 7⁷⁄₁₆ In.	110.00
Cupid, Cake Stand, Pink, Scalloped Edge, 2 x 11¼ In.	300.00
Figurine, Lion, Pony, Bubbles, 11½ In.	79.00
Figurine, Rooster, Chanticleer, Copenhagen Blue, c.1940, 9½ x 7 In.	325.00
Gadroon, Cup, Mulberry	39.00
Gadroon, Cup, Royal Blue	35.00
Gadroon, Plate, Bread & Butter, Mulberry, 6⅜ In.	17.00
Gadroon, Plate, Dinner, Mulberry, 9½ In.	47.00
Gadroon, Saucer, Royal Blue, 5½ In.	17.00
Gazebo, Bowl, Gold Trim, 9½ In.	45.00
Gazebo, Candlestick, Gold Trim, 6 In., Pair	90.00

O

Gazebo, Sandwich Server, Center Handle, Blue, 11 In. ....*illus*	25.00
Georgian, Goblet, Cobalt Blue, Footed, Low	20.00
Georgian, Tumbler, Iced Tea, Ruby, 12 Oz., 5 In.	6.00 to 13.00
Georgian, Tumbler, Juice, Ruby, 5 Oz., 3¼ In.	13.00
Largo, Bowl, 7 In.	28.00
Largo, Candelabrum, 2-Light, 5¼ x 7 In.	50.00
Lela Bird, Candy Dish, Cover, Footed, Green	281.00
Lela Bird, Dish, Mayonnaise, Underplate, Pink	210.00
Lela Bird, Plate, Green, 8 In.	43.00
Lido, Pitcher, Ball, Aquamarine, 96 Oz.	50.00
Maya, Bowl, Footed, 12 In.	25.00
Maya, Candelabrum, 2-Light, 5¾ In.	65.00
Party Line, Bowl, Pink, 9 In.	35.00
Party Line, Sherbet, Footed, 4½ Oz., 3⁵⁄₁₆ In.	10.00
Party Line, Tumbler, Pink, 5⅝ In.	15.00
Party Line, Tumbler, Pink, Footed, 3 In.	14.00
Party Line, Tumbler, Ruby, Footed, 5¾ In.	35.00
Peacock & Wild Rose, Bowl, Green, Rolled Edge, 2¾ x 11 In.	375.00
Penny, Cocktail, Ruby, Footed, 3 In.	14.00
Penny, Cup & Saucer	15.00
Penny, Sherbet, Cobalt Blue, 3¾ In.	16.00
Popeye & Olive, Bowl, Ruby, 5 In.	30.00
Popeye & Olive, Plate, Salad, Ruby, 8 In.	20.00
Popeye & Olive, Sherbet, Ruby, Footed, 3¼ In.	18.00
Rena, Shaker, Green, c.1930, 3⅛ In.	19.00
Utopia, Cheese Keeper, Cover, 5½ x 12 In.	90.00
Utopia, Compote, Cheriglo, 6½ In.	51.00
Vintager, Platter, 12 x 10 In.	22.00

PAINTINGS listed in this book are not works by major artists but rather decorative paintings on ivory, board, or glass that would be of interest to the average collector. Watercolors on paper are listed under Picture. To learn the value of an oil painting by a listed artist you must contact an expert in that area.

Miniature, Portrait, Girl, In Park, Holding Rosebud, Oval, Georgian, 3 x 2¼ In.	1645.00
Oil On Board, Amish Barn Raising, Arlene Fisher, Frame, 1976, 11 x 16½ In.	220.00
Oil On Board, Cemetery, Deserted, Thomas Allen Jr., 12¼ x 16 In.	646.00
Oil On Board, Harbor Scene, Sailboats, House, Landscape, Gilt Frame, 11¾ x 18 In.	5060.00
Oil On Canvas, Amish Farm, House, Barn, 2 Women Working, 30 x 40 In.	11550.00
Oil On Canvas, Day At The Beach, Dorothy Young Graham, c.1950, 20¼ x 16 In.	1410.00
Oil On Canvas, Landscape, Tree Lined Bank, Marsh Foreground, 9 x 7¼ In.	413.00
Oil On Canvas, Landscape, Trees By The Seashore, Sunset, 19¾ x 23½ In.	1020.00
Oil On Canvas, Mill, Fisherman, Waterfall, American School, Gilt Wood Frame, 30 x 45 In. .	460.00
Oil On Canvas, Mourning, Baby On Sofa, Angels In Background, Gilt Frame, 28 x 32 In. ...	12650.00
Oil On Canvas, Snapping The Whip, Girls Playing, Stetson, Frame, 1899, 12 x 20 In.	5175.00
Oil On Canvas, Still Life, Peaches, Joseph Henry Boston, Wood Frame, 20 x 24 In.	748.00
Oil On Canvas, Walking Along The Harbor, 18½ x 40 In.	147.00
Oil On Canvas, Winter Landscape, House, Barn, Snowy Road, 36 x 44 In.	10925.00
Oil On Copper, Portrait, Hispanic Woman, Pearl Necklace, Walnut Frame, 12 x 10 In.	230.00
Oil On Masonite, Farmyard Landscape, c.1955, 11 x 14 In.	382.00
Oil On Panel, Landscape, Pond, Percival Rosseau, Oak Frame, c.1879, 8½ x 10⅝ In.	1610.00
Oil On Panel, Skies Tell The Glory Of God, Symbolist School, Gilt Frame, 19 x 14 In.	246.00
On Ivory, Girl, Crossed Arms, Brown Hair, Brown Dress, White Collar, Oval, Signed, 3 x 2½ In. ..	173.00
On Ivory, Man, Black Coat, In Front Of Window, Drapes, Blue Sky, ½ Portrait, Frame, 3½ x 3 In.	270.00
On Ivory, Portrait, Double, Signed, Merey, Frame, 19th Century, Miniature	525.00
On Ivory, Portrait, Gentleman, Lock Of Braided Hair On Reverse, Oval Frame, 2¼ x 1¾ In. .*illus*	644.00
On Ivory, Portrait, Man, Black Jacket, Scarf, American School, Oval, Gilt Frame, 1800s, 2¾ x 2¼ In.	538.00
On Ivory, Portrait, Man, Black Jacket, Scarf, Red Chair, Bridport, Gilt Locket Frame, 3 x 2½ In. ..	1310.00
On Ivory, Portrait, Napoleon, Josephine, Oil, C. Duproche, Gilt Frame, 3¾ x 5 In., Pair	1652.00
On Ivory, Portrait, Pendant, Gilt Mount, Seed Pearls, Diamonds, Leather Box, 1845, 2 x 1½ In. .	598.00
On Ivory, Portrait, Woman, Engraved Locket, Lock Of Hair, 2 x 1¾ In. ....*illus*	468.00
On Ivory, Portrait, Woman, Short Hair, Dress, Gilt Locket Case, Oval, Engraved, 1800s, 2 x 1½ In.	478.00
On Ivory, Portrait, Young Man, American School, Oval, Frame, 19th Century, 2½ x 2 In. ...	359.00
Reverse On Glass, Boudoir Scene, Woman Combing Hair, Seated, Frame, 11¾ x 10 In.	489.00
Reverse On Glass, Katharina, Young Girl, Green Dress, Ebonized Frame, 8½ x 6½ In. .*illus*	165.00

Painting, On Ivory, Portrait, Gentleman, Lock Of Braided Hair On Reverse, 2¼ x 1¾ In. $644.00

Painting, On Ivory, Portrait, Woman, Engraved Locket, Lock Of Hair, 2 x 1¾ In. $468.00

Painting, Reverse On Glass, Katharina, Young Girl, Green Dress, Ebonized Frame, 8½ x 6½ In. $165.00

P

TIP

If possible, hang an oil painting on an inside wall away from direct sunlight.

Pairpoint, Compote, Peach Tree,
Red Ground, Silver Plated Floral Stand,
11 x 10 In.
$518.00

Pairpoint, Compote, Rosaria,
Diamond Quilted, Clear Stem,
4¾ x 9⅜ In.
$201.00

PAIRPOINT Manufacturing Company started in 1880 in New Bedford, Massachusetts. It soon joined with the glassworks nearby and made glass, silver-plated pieces, and lamps. Reverse-painted glass shades and molded shades known as "puffies" were part of the production until the 1930s. The company reorganized and changed its name several times but is still working today. Items listed here are glass or glass and metal. Silver-plated pieces are listed under Silver Plate.

Apothecary Jar, Cover, Dark Amethyst, Engraved, Pedestal Base, 14 In.	600.00
Apothecary Jar, Cover, Smokey Topaz, Engraved, Pedestal Base, 14¾ In.	500.00
Biscuit Jar, Brown, Blown-Out Mums, Enameled, Shaped Handle, 10 In.	604.00
Biscuit Jar, Mauve, Blueberries, Flowers, Melon Ribbed, Metal Lid, Shaped Handle, 9½ In.	633.00
Biscuit Jar, Opal, Green, Pink Flowers, Round, Metal Collar & Lid, Lion Cartouche Handles, 8 In.	345.00
Biscuit Jar, Pink, Shaded, Blown-Out Turtle, Silver Mount, Flowers, Branches, 4½ In.	470.00
Biscuit Jar, Sailboats, Shoreline, Faceted Sides, Molded Swags, Silver Plated Lid, 9 In.	518.00
Bowl, Amethyst, 12½ In.	495.00
Bowl, Amethyst, 4¼ x 9¾ In.	395.00
Bowl, Centerpiece, Satin, Birds, Flowers, Children Dancing, Enameled, c.1890, 9 x 8 x 8 In.	775.00
Bowl, Opal, Bird Nest, Enameled, Footed, 3¼ In.	75.00
Candlestick, Auroria, Bubble Ball Stem, 10 In., Pair	550.00
Candlestick, Green, 16 In.	525.00
Candlestick, Green, Controlled Bubble Ball Stem, Engraved Base, 11¾ In.	600.00
Candy Dish, Cover, Ruby, 9 x 6 In.	595.00
Candy Dish, Ruby, Footed, 9 x 6 In.	395.00
Casket, Silk Lining, Silver Highlights, Victorian, 7¼ x 6 In.	1500.00
Cocktail Mixer, Rooster, Engraved, Garlands, Star Cut Base, Sterling Silver Top, 7 x 4 In.	230.00
Compote, Barrington Cutting, 1920s, 7½ In.	165.00
Compote, Black, Bubble Ball Stem, 4⅛ x 6¼ In.	185.00
Compote, Black, Bubble Ball Stem, 7⅜ In.	450.00
Compote, Cover, Ruby, Polished Pontil, 9 x 6 In.	395.00
Compote, Cut Glass Bowl, Metal Base, Figural, Boy On Fish, 6½ x 7 In.	138.00
Compote, Green Translucent, Bubbles, Clear Faceted Knop, Spread Foot, 7 x 11 In.	92.00
Compote, Peach Tree, Red Ground, Silver Plated Floral Stand, 11 x 10 In. ....*illus*	518.00
Compote, Rosaria, Diamond Quilted, Clear Stem, 4¾ x 9⅜ In. ....*illus*	201.00
Compote, Ruby, 6⅝ x 8½ x 3⅛ In.	395.00
Compote, Ruby, Controled Bubble Ball Stem, 5¼ x 6⅞ In.	295.00
Console, Amethyst, Etched, 4¼ x 9¾ In.	395.00
Cornucopia, Ruby, Paperweight Base, Scalloped Top Edge, 11 In.	395.00
Cruet, Canaria, Yellow, Swirled, Faceted Clear Handle, 8 In.	58.00
Decanter, Amber, Engraved Grapes, Donut Shape, Stopper, 9 In.	350.00
Dish, Pink, Rolled Rim, Iridescent Edge, 7½ In.	85.00
Dresser Box, Round, Blue & Cream, Enameled Flowers, 5 In.	150.00 to 173.00
Holder, Razor Strop, Engraved, Silver Plate, Monogram	60.00
Lamp, Delft Scene, Paneled Milk Glass, Acorn Burner, Delft Mark, 8½ In. ....*illus*	345.00
Lamp, Puffy, Begonia, 4-Sided, Scalloped, Brass Base, Organic Form, 23 x 16 In. ......*illus*	51750.00
Lamp, Puffy, Owl, Bronze Colored Figural Base, 20 x 12½ In. ....*illus*	86250.00
Lamp, Puffy, Oxford Shade, Flowers, Burgundy Ground, Brass Base, c.1910, 18 x 14 In. ..*illus*	11950.00
Lamp, Puffy, Papillon, Butterflies, Roses, Bronze Base, Baluster Stem, 4-Footed, 15½ In.	1150.00
Lamp, Puffy, Papillon, Butterflies, Roses, Brass Base, Relief Flowers, 20 x 14 In.	4800.00
Lamp, Puffy, Papillon, Butterfly, Blue Flowers, Green Ground, Metal Base, 22 x 14 In. ..*illus*	4950.00
Lamp, Puffy, Papillon, Butterfly & Flowers, No. 3047½, Signed, 19 In.	3700.00
Lamp, Puffy, Papillon, c.1910, 14½ In.	2559.00
Lamp, Puffy, Red & Pink Roses, Buttressed Base, 21 x 12 In.	14300.00
Lamp, Puffy, Rose Bouquet, Variegated Green Ground, Silver Plated Art Nouveau Base, 20 x 12 In.	5175.00
Lamp, Puffy, Stratford Shade, Apple Blossoms, Roses, Brass Base, 15 x 8½ In. ....*illus*	3995.00
Lamp, Puffy, Torino Shade, Poppies, Herringbone, 4-Socket Base, 16 x 9½ In. ....*illus*	5175.00
Lamp, Radio, Flower & Butterfly Panel, Brass Holder, Stepped Rectangular, Base, 13½ In.	575.00
Lamp, Reverse Painted, Birds & Flowers, Wide Shoulder, 3-Stem Base, 22 In.	4113.00
Lamp, Reverse Painted, Butterflies, 8-Sided, 13 x 19 In.	823.00
Lamp, Reverse Painted, Cottage, Draped, Yellow, Orange, Green, Palm Base, 23 x 12 In. .*illus*	6613.00
Lamp, Reverse Painted, Domed Shade, Village Scene, Baluster-Shaped Base, 16 20 In.	1763.00
Lamp, Reverse Painted, Forest Scene, Brass Plated, Green Marble Base, 27 x 16 In.	1888.00
Lamp, Reverse Painted, Gazelle, 16 x 26 In.	4250.00
Lamp, Reverse Painted, Italian Garden Scene, 22 In.	8900.00
Lamp, Reverse Painted, Marine Scene, Ships, Beaded Fringe, 22 x 16 In.	4950.00
Lamp, Reverse Painted, Red Roses, White Scrolls, 5-Sided, Bronze Base, 12 In.	374.00
Lamp, Reverse Painted, Touraine Shade, Dutch Landscape, 2-Finish Base, Signed, 13 x 8 In.	550.00

Pairpoint, Lamp, Delft Scene,
Paneled Milk Glass, Acorn Burner,
Delft Mark, 8½ In.
$345.00

Pairpoint, Lamp, Puffy,
Oxford Shade, Flowers,
Burgundy Ground, Brass Base,
c.1910, 18½ x 14 In.
$11950.00

Pairpoint, Lamp, Puffy, Torino Shade,
Poppies, Herringbone, 4-Socket Base,
16 x 9½ In.
$5175.00

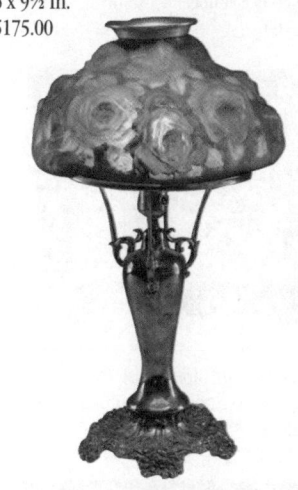

Pairpoint, Lamp, Puffy, Begonia,
4-Sided, Scalloped, Brass Base,
Organic Form, 23 x 16 In.
$51750.00

Pairpoint, Lamp, Puffy, Papillon,
Butterfly, Blue Flowers, Green Ground,
Metal Base, 22 x 14 In.
$4950.00

Pairpoint, Lamp, Reverse Painted, Cottage,
Draped, Yellow, Orange,
Green, Palm Base, 23 x 12 In.
$6613.00

Pairpoint, Lamp, Puffy, Owl,
Bronze Colored Figural Base,
20 x 12½ In.
$86250.00

Pairpoint, Lamp, Puffy,
Stratford Shade, Apple Blossoms,
Roses, Brass Base, 15 x 8½ In.
$3995.00

Pairpoint, Vase, Yellow,
Clear Crystal Ball Knop, Flared,
Footed, 11¾ In., Pair
$374.00

P

469

Paper, Cutwork, Scherenschnitte,
Urn, Flowers, Birds, Vines,
Ring Border, Frame, 7½ x 10 In.
$4113.00

Paper, Fraktur, Birth, 2 Sisters,
Verse, Frame, Early 19th Century,
8 x 9¾ In.
$1980.00

Paper, Fraktur, Birth & Baptism,
Freehand Circles, Leaves,
Bucks County, 1830, 10 x 13 In.
$413.00

Lampshade, Night-Light, Puffy, Yellow, Butterflies, Early 1900s, 3½ In., Pair	695.00
Perfume Bottle, Amethyst, Enameled Butterfly, 6¾ In.	375.00
Pickle Castor, Coin Spot, Cranberry, Blue Flowers, Fruit, Oval, Silver Plated Frame, 10 In.	518.00
Pickle Castor, Daisy & Button, Vaseline, Silverplated Embossed Holder, 10 In.	288.00
Pitcher, Celeste Blue, Clear Crackle Base, 10¼ x 7¾ In.	495.00
Pitcher, Pink, Lobes, c.1900-1920	275.00
Scent Bottle, Pillar Ribbed, Amethyst	45.00
Top Hat, Peachblow, 3 In.	125.00
Tumbler, Flambo, Black Foot, 3½ x 2⅜ In.	95.00
Vase, Amber, 11¾ x 5¼ In.	325.00
Vase, Amethyst, Polished Pontil, 11⅝ x 4 x 4¾ In.	350.00
Vase, Auroria, Grape Design, Bubble Ball Stem, Flared, 8 In.	425.00
Vase, Chalice Form, Amethyst, Pedestal Base, Engraved, 12½ In.	900.00
Vase, Chalice Form, Bubble Ball Stem, Applied Foot, 13 x 6¾ In.	230.00
Vase, Cobalt Blue, 1980s, 9 In.	175.00
Vase, Cobalt Blue, Bubble Ball Stem, 10 x 5 In.	395.00
Vase, Cranberry, Pontil, 11⅞ x 6¼ In.	395.00
Vase, Dark Amethyst, Grapes, Leaves, Vines, Engraved, 9 In.	300.00
Vase, Fan, Ruby, Flared Rim, Crimped, Footed, 6½ x 9¹⁵⁄₁₆ x 3¾ In.	650.00
Vase, Green, 8 In.	85.00
Vase, Magnum Diamond, Flared Rim, Bubble Ball Stem, Round Foot, 12 In., Pair	660.00
Vase, Opal, Guba Ducks, Yellow Sun, Crimson & Orange Sky, Enameled, Egg Shape, 12½ In.	460.00
Vase, Rosario, Pontil, 11⅞ x 6¼ In.	395.00
Vase, Ruby, 9⅞ In.	425.00
Vase, Ruby, 12 In.	495.00
Vase, Vaseline Cut, Silver Plate, c.1920, 15½ x 6 x 8 In.	1200.00
Vase, Viscania, Intaglio Cut, Pinched Waist, 9¾ In.	250.00
Vase, Yellow, Clear Crystal Ball Knop, Flared, Footed, 11¾ In., Pair ....*illus*	374.00

PALMER COX, BROWNIES, *see Brownies category.*

PAPER collectibles, including almanacs, catalogs, children's books, some greeting cards, stock certificates, and other paper ephemera, are listed here. Paper calendars are listed separately in the Calendar category. Paper items may be found in many other sections, such as Christmas and Movie.

Birth Record, Anna B. Cochran, Born July 6 1804, Watercolor, Ink, 2 Birds, 8½ x 6 In.	4700.00
Book, Bible, Fore-Edge, Painted, Windsor Castle, Marked Barritt, c.1856, 5 x 3¼ x 1½ In.	750.00
Book, Big Little Book, Scrappy, Whitman, Columbia Pictures, 1934	60.00
Book, Big Little Book, Tarzan-Lord Of The Jungle, Edgar Rice Burroughs, 1946	40.00
Book, Big Little Book, Wings Of The U.S.A., Illustrated By Thomas Hickey, 1940	35.00
Book, Lalique To Marbles Encyclopedia, 1978, 160 Pages	18.00
Booklet, General Cigar Co., Gracie Allen's Gift To Guy Lombardo, 1933, 20 Pages	47.00
Bookplate, Engraver's Proof, Jacqueline Kennedy, Frame, c.1958, 4½ x 3½ In.	1250.00
Bookplate, Elizabeth Biemersderfer, Ink & Watercolor, Maple Frame, 1817, 4 x 5 In.	431.00
Catalog, Marx, 1965, Toy Line, 11 x 8½ In., 72 Pages	218.00
Catalog, Sears & Roebuck, 1910, Motor Buggy	22.00
Catalog, Weeden Toys, 1889, Illustrated Pictures Of Steam Toys, Banks, 28 Pages	530.00
Cutwork, Scherenschnitte, Folk Art, Trees, Bird, Tulip, Heart, Penn. Dutch, 11 x 11 In.	230.00
Cutwork, Scherenschnitte, Heart Design, Flower Vase, Exotic Birds, Unicorns, Frame, 14 x 18½ In.	316.00
Cutwork, Scherenschnitte, Hearts, Tulips, Birds, Ledger Paper, Frame, 6¼ x 7 In.	110.00
Cutwork, Scherenschnitte, Multicolor Heart, Tulip, Diamond, Jan. 24, 1827, Frame, 7½ x 5¾ In.	55.00
Cutwork, Scherenschnitte, Urn, Flowers, Birds, Vines, Ring Border, Frame, 7½ x 10 In. ......*illus*	4113.00
Family Record, Painted, Multicolored, Watercolor, Pen, Ink, Mahogany Frame, 15 x 12 In.	235.00
Family Record, Watercolor, Thomas Sylvester, Polly Lane, 8 Children, Frame, 10 x 9½ In.	3173.00
Fraktur, 1812 Birth Of Salomon Gery, Berks County, Pennsylvania, 15 x 17 In.	690.00
Fraktur, 2 Birds, Red, Yellow Tulip, Watercolor, Pen, Ink, 6¾ x 4⅞ In.	3000.00
Fraktur, Baptism, Religious Text, Heart, Johann Jacob, Frame, c.1788, 13 x 8 In.	44.00
Fraktur, Barefoot Girl, Bird, Pen & Ink, Watercolor, c.1835, 7 x 3½ In.	2530.00
Fraktur, Birth, 2 Sisters, Verse, Frame, Early 19th Century, 8 x 9¾ In. ....*illus*	1980.00
Fraktur, Birth, Hand Lettered, Watercolor, Heinrich, Pa., 1797, 13 x 16 In.	235.00
Fraktur, Birth, Watercolor, Leah Tiefenbacken, March 1825, 12 x 15 In.	2400.00
Fraktur, Birth & Baptism, Angel Artist, Flowers, Swans, For Maria Berger, c.1816, 13 x 16 In.	4675.00
Fraktur, Birth & Baptism, Angels, Birds, Hand Drawn, c.1886, 15¼ x 12½ In.	770.00
Fraktur, Birth & Baptism, Christian Mertel, Winged Head, Stober, York Co., 1800, 12 x 16 In.	2200.00
Fraktur, Birth & Baptism, Emilie Grimm, Printed, Illuminated, Peter Otto, 1836, 16 x 13 In.	176.00

Fraktur, Birth & Baptism, Freehand Circles, Leaves, Bucks County, 1830, 10 x 13 In. . . . *illus*	413.00
Fraktur, Birth & Baptism, Johann Conrad Gilbert, Parrots, Vine, For Johannes Kolb, 1816, 8 x 13 In.	3575.00
Fraktur, Birth & Baptism, Man & Woman, Wine, Amelia Bucher, 1818, 10 x 8 In.	14850.00
Fraktur, Birth & Baptism, Printed, Illuminated, For Bertha Herbine, Pa., 1895, 17 x 14 In. . .	61.00
Fraktur, Birth & Baptism, Tulips, Birds, Burlwood Frame, 1845, 12½ x 16½ In.	1093.00
Fraktur, Birth Certificate, Christian Groh, Pen, Ink, Watercolor, 1823, 6½ x 7½ In.	3000.00
Fraktur, Birth Certificate, Wheels, Flowers, Mirror Image, Schollenberger, Feb. 2, 1839, Pa., 16 x 12 In.	770.00
Fraktur, Birth Record, Magdalene Beller, Watercolor, Ink, Berks County, Pa., 1798, 12 x 17 In.	2185.00
Fraktur, Bookmark, Watercolor, Ink, Frame, 3⅝ x 3 In.	155.00
Fraktur, Bookplate, 2 Hearts, Tulip, Watercolor, Pen, Ink, 1813, 1822, 7 x 4 In.	2700.00
Fraktur, Family Record, William Clark, Hannah Clark, 7 Children, 1817, 12 x 16 In.	3600.00
Fraktur, Heart, Bird, Tree, Vines, Albert Everett Logue, Mahogany Frame, 1909, 13 x 9 In.	413.00
Fraktur, Hearts, Text, Painted Suns, Flowers, Laid Paper, Friedrick Krebes, c.1802, 16 x 19 In. .	546.00
Fraktur, Lady On Horseback, Watercolor, Frederick Krebes, c.1784, 19 x 16 In.	6000.00
Fraktur, Marriage, Anthony Beffner & Maria Laurin Bockler, c.1795, 13 x 16 In.	600.00
Fraktur, Pennsylvania Births, Pen & Ink, Red Watercolor Accents, For Abraham King	17866.15
Fraktur, Potted Flowers, Scalloped Line Border, Frame, Early 19th Century, 5¾ x 2¼ In.	143.00
Fraktur, Presentation, Hennrich Klein, Basket Of Flowers, c.1825, 6½ x 8 In.	2200.00
Fraktur, Red & Green Vines, Rachel W. Fish, Nov. 11, 1831, Frame, 7½ x 6¾ In.	83.00
Fraktur, Scherenschnitte, Bird, Flowers, Sarah Shiner, Black Frame, 1813, 6 x 3½ In.	110.00
Fraktur, Scherenschnitte, Text, Eagle, Flowers, Contemporary Frame, c.1806, 12 x 11 In. . . .	440.00
Fraktur, Tulip Tree, 6 Birds, Snake, Daniel Stouffer, Frame, 1841, 10¼ x 7¾ In.	1265.00
Fraktur, Tulips, Birds, Flowers, Frame, Early 19th Century, 6¾ x 2¾ In.	110.00
Fraktur, Tulips, Flowers, Diamond Shapes, Leaves, Watercolor, Ink, 11¾ x 17 In.	1610.00
Fraktur, Vorschrift, Heart, Flowers, Scalloped Border, Frame, c.1876, 11½ x 8½ In.	633.00
Fraktur, Watercolor, Birds, Flowers, Pen & Ink Text, Frame, Pennsylvania, 10 x 9⅜ In.	1265.00
Fraktur, Watercolor, Exotic Birds On Flowering Branches, 1843, 9¼ x 7½ In.	999.00
Fraktur, Watercolor, Ink, Frame, c.1835, 9½ x 7¾ In.	388.00
House Blessing, Birds, Cherubs, Printed, Illuminated, Frame, 16 x 13½ In.	121.00
Magazine, Field & Stream, July, 1975	5.00
Magazine, Hit Parade, 17988, Lucille Ball On Cover	35.00
Magazine, Life, March 25, 1966	10.00
Magazine, Life, July 15, 1966	25.99
Magazine, Life, July 15, 1968	15.00
Magazine, Life, August 12, 1946, Loretta Young Cover	20.00
Magazine, Life, August 22, 1938, Fred Astaire & Ginger Rogers Dancing On Cover	1335.00
Magazine, Life, August 27, 1965	15.00
Magazine, Life, November 24, 1961, JFK Junior On Cover, Signed John Kennedy	369.00
Magazine, Life, December 21, 1936	35.00
Magazine, Life, The Best Of Life, 1973	89.00
Magazine, Memories, September 1990	8.00
Magazine, Modern Screen, May 1955, June Allyson On Cover	18.00
Magazine, Movie Life, January 1958, Judy Garland On Cover	25.00
Magazine, Newsweek, August 12, 1940, Duke & Duchess Of Windsor	20.00
Magazine, Photoplay, September 1952, Ann Blyth Cover	18.00
Magazine, Photoplay, April 1958, Pat Boone On Cover	18.00
Magazine, Photoplay, March 1959, Dick Clark On Cover	18.00
Magazine, Photoplay, May 1959, Tony Curtis & Janet Leigh & Baby Jamie Lee On Cover	25.00
Magazine, Playboy, December, 1953, Marilyn Monroe	2581.00
Magazine, Radio-TV Mirror, May 1952, Arthur Godfrey On Cover	15.00
Magazine, Record Time, April 1960, Volume 1, Number 1, Doris Day On Cover, 84 Pages	35.00
Magazine, Redbook, May 1955, Vol. 105, No. 1, Marlon Brando Cover	10.00
Magazine, Saturday Evening Post, April 2, 1938	8.00
Magazine, Saturday Evening Post, July 16, 1966	8.00
Magazine, Saturday Evening Post, November 6, 1965	8.00
Magazine, Screenland, September 1948, Humphrey Bogart & Lauren Bacall On Cover	45.00
Magazine, Song Hits, June 1937, Bing Crosby On Cover, Waikiki Wedding	50.00
Magazine, True, February 1961, 25th Anniversary Issue	15.00
Mask, Black Flame Of Amazon, Hi-Speed Gas, 1930s, 8¾ x 9¾ In.	84.00
Membership Kit, Captain Gallant Of Foreign Legion, Heinz, Mailer, 1955, 8 x 11 In.	85.00
Penmanship, Lord's Prayer, Flowers, Wreath, Lois Wentworth, 12 x 9 In.	248.00
Penmanship, Valentine, Folk Art, Scroll & Penwork, Heart Shape, Verse, 9½ x 9½ In.	230.00
Sack, Buffalo Woolen Mills, Brown, Lithograph Buffalo, 1800s, 40½ x 18 In.	48.00
Songbook, Bookplate, Tulip, Sawtooth Border, Hand Drawn, Samuel Saur, c.1791, 7 x 4 In. . .	220.00
Songbook, David Kulp, For Elisabeth Cassel, Tulips, Hand Drawn, 1812, 3¾ x 6½ In.	2750.00

Paper Doll, Lettie Lane, Family, Accessories, George W. Jacobs, c.1909, 11 x 16 In., 12 Sheets, Uncut $104.00

Paper Doll, Tabatha Of Bewitched, Magic Wand Corp., 1966, 9½ x 15 In., Uncut $173.00

P

Vorschrift, Alphabet, Number, Religious Text, For John Albrecht, Frame, c.1803, 8 x 13 In. . .	66.00
Vorschrift, Floral Letters, Religious Text, Alphabet, c.1820, 8 x 13 In.	1018.00
Wedding Certificate, Man, Woman, Verse, Symbols, Pen, Ink, Frame, 10¼ x 7¼ In.	1293.00
Whistle, Calliope, Band Playing, Cats Dancing, Man In Bed, Pat. 1889, Norwalk, Oh., 6 In. . .	33.00
Whistle, Green Paper, Clown Image Stand, Wood Block Base, Pink Feather, Japan, 4 In.	4.00

PAPER DOLLS were probably inspired by the pantins, or jumping jacks, made in eighteenth-century Europe. By the 1880s, sheets of printed paper dolls and clothes were being made. The first paper doll books were made in the 1920s. Collectors prefer uncut sheets or books or boxed sets of paper dolls. Prices are about half as much if the pages have been cut.

Airline Hostess & Pilot, Round The World Travel Clothes, Merrill, 1962	50.00
Baby Alive, General Mills Fun Group, Whitman, Box, 1973, Uncut	50.00
Bobbsey Twins Playbox, Treasure Books, 1958	40.00
Book, Eve Arden, Saalfield, 1956, 13¾ x 10½ In., 6 Pages, Uncut	67.00
Book, Sleeping Dolls, Queen Holden, No. 978, Whitman, 1940s, 14¾ x 9¾ In.	84.00
Debbie Darling, Wavy Hair, Front & Back Costumes, Yarn Hair, Saalfield, 1952	20.00
Dionne Quintuplets, Soon We'll Be Three Years Old, Whitman, 1936, 32 Pages	40.00
Drowsy, 29 Piece Wardrobe, Whitman, Box, 1975	45.00
Duffy, Heavy Cardboard, Whitman, 1969	95.00
Fanny Gray, House, Wooden Stand, 5 Outfits, Crosby Nichols & Co., Boxed, 6 x 8 In.	2703.00
Grace Kelly, Full Color, Tom Tierney, 1986, Uncut	20.00
Janet Leigh, Dresses By Janet, 2 Dolls, 1958, 6 Pages, Uncut	75.00
Jetsons, Cutouts, Whitman, 1963, 13 x 10 In., 8 Pages, Uncut	154.00
John Wayne, Tom Tierney, 1981, 16 Pages	14.00
Judy Garland, 3 Dolls, 30 Outfits, Tom Tierney, 1982, Uncut	15.00
Lettie Lane, Family, Accessories, George W. Jacobs, c.1909, 11 x 16 In., 12 Sheets, Uncut *illus*	104.00
Little Miss America, Saalfield, 13 Dolls, 8 Pages Of Clothes, 1947	50.00
Little Sweethearts, Susan & Karen, Stephens Publishing Co., Uncut	20.00
Mary Poppins, Activity Book, 4 Dolls, Golden Press, 1964, 16 Pages	40.00
Miss America, Whitman, 31 Piece Wardrobe, 1980	45.00
Nancy Reagan, Tom Tierney, 1983, Uncut	20.00
Pat Boone, Whitman, 1959	75.00
Raggedy Ann & Andy, Whitman Publishing, 1980, Uncut	15.00
Ronald Reagan, Tom Tierney, 1984	20.00
Singer World's Fair Dress Up Book, The Official 1964-65 New York World's Fair	75.00
Tabatha Of Bewitched, Magic Wand Corp., 1966, 9½ x 15 In., Uncut . . . . *illus*	173.00
Twiggy, 50 Cutout Accessories & Dresses, Mod Fashion, Whitman, 1967	95.00
White House Party Dresses, Famous Ladies At White House Parties, 1961	40.00

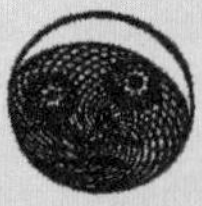

PAPERWEIGHTS must have first appeared along with paper in ancient Egypt. Today's collectors search for every type, from the very expensive French weights of the nineteenth century to the modern artist weights or advertising pieces. The glass tops of the paperweights sometimes have been nicked or scratched, and this type of damage can be removed by polishing. Some serious collectors think this type of repair is an alteration and will not buy a repolished weight; others think it is an acceptable technique of restoration that does not change the value. Baccarat paperweights are listed separately under Baccarat.

Advertising, B.D. Wood & Bros. Coal Merchants, Tugboat, New Orleans, White, Blue, Glass, 3 x 2 In. . . .	300.00
Advertising, Barr-Goodwin Lumber Co., House On Car, Orlando, Fla., 3½ In.	225.00
Advertising, Chalmers Motor Company, Brass, Rectangular, 2¼ x 3½ In.	80.00
Advertising, Famous Biscuit, Celluloid, Mirror, 4 In.	121.00
Advertising, Ford & Company, Mfgs. Of Vehicle Wheels, Round, Tippecanoe City, Ohio	98.00
Advertising, Goodyear, 15 Years Of Friendly Relations, Bronze, Medallion, 4 In.	115.00
Advertising, Mirror, Gilbert Brass Foundry Co., Palm, Celluloid, 4 In.	99.00
Advertising, National Cash Register Co., Bronze, 2¾ x 3 In.	275.00
Advertising, Star Headlight Co., Rochester, N.Y., Signal Light, 3 In. . . . . *illus*	154.00
Advertising, Thos. Evans & Co., Crescent Glass Works, Pittsburgh, Pa., June 5, 1882, 3 In. . .	385.00
Ayotte, Frog On Green Pond, Lily, Signed, 4 In.	1293.00
Ayotte, Poinsettia, Evergreen, 3¾ In.	1058.00
Ayotte, Salamander, Woodland Ground, Signed, 3¼ In.	1175.00
Borwski, Royal Blue Cartouche, Grotesque Mask, 5 In.	374.00
Boston & Sandwich, Poinsettia, Red Petals, Green Leaves, White Latticinio Ground, 3 In. . . .	420.00
Boston & Sandwich, Weedflower, Bud, Red & Striped Petals, Clear Ground, 3⅛ In. . . . *illus*	1093.00
Boston & Sandwich, Weedflower, Red, White, Blue, 3 In.	900.00
Butterfly, Multicolored, Wings Spread, Brown Body, Oval, 4 x 3¼ In.	3000.00
Caraluzzo, Orange & Red Rose Encased, Round Foot, Pontil, c.1950, 2¾ In.	94.00

Paperweight, Advertising, Star Headlight Co., Rochester, N.Y., Signal Light, 3 In. $154.00

Paperweight, Boston & Sandwich, Weedflower, Bud, Red & Striped Petals, Clear Ground, 3⅛ In. $1093.00

P

Paperweight, Clichy,
Green & Yellow Pastry Mold Cane Center, Pink
& White Swirls, 2¾ In.
$2070.00

Paperweight, Clichy, White & Green Rose
Cane Center, Turquoise & White Swirls, 3 In.
$6900.00

Paperweight, New England Glass Co.,
Millefiori, Eagles, Latticinio Swirls, Faceted,
8 Sides, 2¾ In.
$920.00

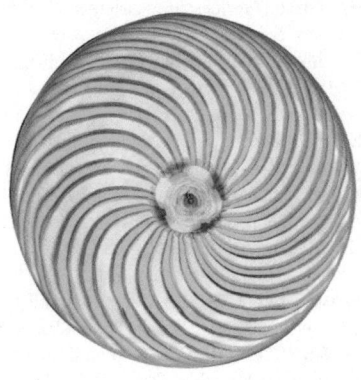

Paperweight, Clichy, Millefiori, Interlaced
Garlands, Pastry Mold Canes, White Muslin
Ground, 3 In.
$1380.00

Paperweight, Mushroom Shape Form,
Green Bottle Glass, England, 4 In.
$184.00

Paperweight, New England Glass Co.,
Millefiori, End-Of-Day, Canes, Twists,
White Latticinio, 2¾ In.
$575.00

Paperweight, Clichy, Sulphide,
Benjamin Franklin In Cameo,
Blue Ground, 2⅜ In.
$2185.00

Paperweight, New England Glass Co.,
Fruit Bouquet, White Double Swirl
Latticinio Basket, 2⅜ In.
$575.00

Paperweight, New England Glass Co.,
Millefiori, Nosegay, Garlands,
Clear Ground, 2⅝ In.
$748.00

P

Paperweight, Photo, Woman, Spray, Speckled Cushion Base, Domed, Faceted, Bohemia, 3½ In. $317.00

Paperweight, St. Louis, Clematis, Green Leaves, Flowers, Red & White Spiral Torsade, 3 In. $1725.00

Paperweight, St. Louis, Fruit Bouquet, Double Swirl White Latticinio Basket, 3 In. $920.00

Chinese, Jade, Mountain, Pine Trees, Celadon, 19th Century, 4 In.	147.00
Clichy, Cinquefoil, Millefiori Garland, Sodden Snow, 3½ In.	2500.00
Clichy, Green & Yellow Pastry Mold Cane Center, Pink & White Swirls, 2¾ In. . . . . *illus*	2070.00
Clichy, Millefiori, Interlaced Garlands, Pastry Mold Canes, White Muslin Ground, 3 In. *illus*	1380.00
Clichy, Millefiori Chequer, 2 Rose Canes, Faceted, 3 In.	3500.00
Clichy, Pansy & Clematis Bouquet, Red, White, Purple Yellow, Green, 3 In.	19500.00
Clichy, Pink & White Swirl, Blue Flower, 2¾ In.	2750.00
Clichy, Pink Millefiori Rose, Green Stem, Leaves, 2¾ In.	16500.00
Clichy, Sulphide, Benjamin Franklin In Cameo, Blue Ground, 2⅜ In. . . . . *illus*	2185.00
Clichy, White & Green Rose Cane Center, Turquoise & White Swirls, 3 In. . . . . *illus*	6900.00
D. Smallhouse, Red Octopus, On Blue Coral, Sea Forms, Box, 3½ In.	403.00
Desk Clock, Simmons Hardware's Motto, Pot Metal	825.00
G. Argy-Rousseau, Butterflies, Cube, Amber, Wings Spread, Signed, 1¾ x 2¼ In.	3000.00
Gentil, Millifiore, Yellow, c.1947	25.00
Gillinder Glass Co., Washington, Turned Sides, Beveled Edge, 1800s, 3 In.	295.00
Home Sweet Home, Tree, Log Cabin, Man, Milk Glass, Ground Base, c.1900, 3¾ In.	112.00
John Nickelson, Opalescent, Cylindrical, 4 Fountains, Gold Flecks, 1979, 5½ In.	489.00
Jon M. Wolfe, Conch Shell, Sea Creatures, Millefiori Patterns, 3⅜ In.	92.00
Latticinio, Pears, Vegetables, Leaves, Multicolored, 1½ x 2¼ In.	303.00
Latticinio, Petals, Blue, Central Cane, Green Stem, Leaves, 2 x 2¾ In.	385.00
Lewis, Silvery Moons, Blue & White Water, 1971, 4¼ In.	575.00
Lundberg, Amethyst Flower, Green Leaves, White Ground, Signed, 2¼ x 2¾ In.	480.00
Lundberg, Angels, Flowers, Doves, Blue Aurene, Lubomir Richter, 1989, 3 In.	900.00
Lundberg, Apple Blossoms, Blue, White, Green, Daniel Salazar, 1989, 2½ In.	267.00
Lundberg, Beta Fish, Purple, White, Blue, Red, Green, Daniel Salazar, 1989, 2½ In.	395.00
Lundberg, Daffodils, Green Leaves, Stem, Black Ground, Signed, 1984, 2 x 2¾ In.	518.00
Lundberg, Dragonfly, Flowers, Purple, Green, Brown, Daniel Salazar, 1989, 2¾ In.	570.00
Lundberg, Fire Spitting Dragon, Winged, Green, Gold Aurene, Lubomir Richter, 1989, 3 In.	735.00
Lundberg, Lady Slipper, Yellow, Amethyst, White Opalescent Ground, Signed, 1984, 2 x 2¾ In.	360.00
Lundberg, Mushrooms, Tan Ground, Green Leaves, 1989, 2½ In.	795.00
Lundberg, Pink Dahlia, 4 Tiers Of Petals, Green Leaves, Signed, 1983, 2¼ x 2¾ In.	480.00
Lundberg, Pulled Feathers, White, Blue, Brown, Yellow, Signed, 1977, 2¼ In.	60.00
Lundberg, Yellow Flowers, Green Leaves, Brown Branches, Daniel Salazar, 1989, 2½ In.	345.00
Magnum, Rock Of Ages, Cross, Vines, Milk Glass Ground, c.1900, 3¾ In.	170.00
Millefiori, Blue Iridescent, Applied Ribbed Serpent, 3½ In.	115.00
Mushroom Shape Form, Green Bottle Glass, England, 4 In. . . . . *illus*	184.00
New England Glass Co., Fruit Bouquet, White Double Swirl Latticinio Basket, 2⅜ In. *illus*	575.00
New England Glass Co., Millefiori, Eagles, Latticinio Swirls, Faceted, 8 Sides, 2¾ In. . *illus*	920.00
New England Glass Co., Millefiori, End-Of-Day, Canes, Twists, White Latticinio, 2¾ In. *illus*	575.00
New England Glass Co., Millefiori, Nosegay, Garlands, Clear Ground, 2⅝ In. . . . . . . *illus*	748.00
Orient & Flume, Blue Coral, Encrusted Sea Forms, Applied Red Octopus, Box, 3½ In.	403.00
Orient & Flume, Navy Blue, Iridescent Cameo Flowers, 1979, 3¾ In.	201.00
Peachblow, Pear Shape, Marble Base, 4½ x 2½ In.	260.00
Pear Shape, Rose To Yellow, 2½ x 3 In.	440.00
Photo, Woman, Spray, Speckled Cushion Base, Domed, Faceted, Bohemia, 3½ In. . . . . *illus*	317.00
Pressed Glass, Early Thumbprint Pattern, 2 Rows, Rayed Base, 3⅛ In.	242.00
Pressed Glass, Tumbler Shape, Gaines Pillar Pattern, 3½ In.	22.00
Provincetown, Mass., Sailboat, Cast Iron, 3¾ x 2¾ In.	280.00
Purple Pinwheel, Aqua, Red, White, Blue Inclusions, Pontil, c.1900, 3½ In.	58.00
Reddy Kilowatt, Your Electrical Servant, Cast Metal, Gold Paint, 1950s, 4½ In.	336.00
RMS Olympic, Ship, Rectangular, Rounded Ends, Early 1900s	197.00
Sambo, Smoking, Green Coat, Yellow Pants, Hat, Cast Iron, Hubley, 3 x 1⅜ In.	336.00
Sea Siren, Glass, Dome, Cardboard Base, 3⅛ x 1⅜ In.	55.00
Silvered Bronze, La Jalousie, Line Vautrin, c.1950, 3 x 2 In.	3360.00
Smith, Gordon, Dogwood Blossoms & Red Berries, Blue Ground, Signed, 2¾ In.	588.00
St. Louis, Blue Pelargonium, 1³⁄₁₆ In.	2500.00
St. Louis, Clematis, Green Leaves, Flowers, Red & White Spiral Torsade, 3 In. . . . . . . *illus*	1725.00
St. Louis, Cobalt Blue Double Clematis, Red & White Jasper Ground, 2⅝ In.	1500.00
St. Louis, Concentric Millefiori, Silhouettes, 3⅛ In.	7500.00
St. Louis, Fruit Bouquet, Double Swirl White Latticinio Basket, 3 In. . . . . *illus*	920.00
St. Louis, Millefiori, Butterfly & Garland, Red, Green & White Border, 3 In. . . . . *illus*	33350.00
St. Louis, Millefiori, Center Cane, Spaced Ring, Border Garland, 2½ In. . . . . *illus*	345.00
St. Louis, Millefiori, Mushroom, Concentric, 3 In.	4500.00
St. Louis, Millefiori, Nosegay & Garland, Faceted, 3⅛ In.	1500.00
Stankard, Blueberries, Pink & Yellow Flowers, Root Spirit, 4 Canes, Seeds, Signed, 2 x 3 In.	4372.00
Stankard, Yellow Floral, Red Ground, Signed, 3 In.	1410.00

Stankard, Yellow, White Flowers, Blueberries, Root Spirit, 3 Canes, Seeds, Signed, 2 x 3 In. . .	3565.00
Water Lily, Purple & Green, Applied Baluster, Footed, Polished Pontil, Early 1900s, 4¼ In. . .	170.00
Whitefriars, Floral Garlands, Interlocking, Cream, Blue, Lilac, Hexagonal	465.00
Whitefriars, Multicolored Garland, Intertwining Pattern, Hexagonal	440.00
Whitefriars, Star Of David, Millefiori, 5 Cane Rows, Blue, White	325.00

PAPIER-MACHE is made from paper mixed with glue, chalk, and other ingredients, then molded and baked. It becomes very hard and can be painted. Boxes, trays, and furniture were made of papier-mache. Some of the nineteenth-century pieces were decorated with mother-of-pearl. Papier-mache is still being used to make small toys, figures, candy containers, boxes, and other giftwares. Furniture made of papier-mache is listed in the Furniture category.

Box, Chinoiserie, Round, Lacquered Black, Gold Figural Scenes, 3 x 3¼ In.	37.00
Box, Man In Top Hat On Cover, Newspaper Lined, 12½ x 5½ In.	36.00
Caterpillar, Anatomical Model, Painted, Segmented Tiers, Case, 1800s, 30 In.	4700.00
Eyeglass Case, Abalone Design, Rectangular, Hinged, 6½ x 1½ In.	60.00
Figure, Tiger, Seated, String Stripes, Orange, Black, White, Red, Painted, 16 In.	1840.00
Head, Millinery, France, c.1900, 21 x 11 In.	585.00
Head, Millinery, Painted, France, c.1920, 21 x 12 x 7 In.	350.00
Letter Holder, Mother-Of-Pearl Inlay, England, c.1860, 9 In.	176.00
Mask, Noh, Tengu, Negoro Lacquer, Japan, Early 20th Century, 8 x 5½ In.	200.00
Pin Tray, 4¼ In.	45.00
Snuffbox, Black, Oval, Hinged Lid, Mid 19th Century, 2¼ x 3¼ In.	85.00
Snuffbox, Compass Star, Orange, White, Blue Ground, 2 In. Diam.	99.00
Snuffbox, Courtship Scene, Man In Top Hat, Lady, Long Dress, Bonnet, 2⅝ In. Diam.	121.00
Snuffbox, Cow, People, Locket Of Hair, Elizabeth Whitney, 1845, 3 In. Diam.	110.00
Snuffbox, Lid, Silver Inlay Design, 2½ In.	95.00
Snuffbox, Military Officer On Horseback, Oficer Der Krakuser, 3⅛ In. Diam.	165.00
Snuffbox, Woman Riding Horse, Man At Fence, 2⅞ In. Diam.	99.00
Tip Tray, Trio, Egyptian Hieroglyphic, Marked, Alfred E. Knobler, Japan, 3 Piece	39.00
Tray, Black Lacquer, Gilded, Graduated, 3 Piece	1500.00
Tray, Chinoiserie, Scalloped Edge, Gilt, Interior Scene, 31 x 24 In.	1298.00
Tray, Lacquered, Chinoiserie, Landscape, England, Mid 19th Century, 26¾ In.	641.00
Tray, Lacquered, Chinoiserie, Scalloped Edge, England, 19th Century, 25 In.	1496.00
Tray, Landscape, Flowers & Geometric Gilt Trim, England, c.1820, 30 x 23 In.	1762.00
Tray, On Stand, English Regency, Mother-Of-Pearl Inlay, c.1840, 3¾ x 10 In.	176.00
Tray, Parcel Gilt, Black Lacquered, Flowering Branch & Exotic Bird, 21 x 31 In.	4080.00
Tray, Regency, Oval, Floral, England, c.1840, 13½ x 17 In.	59.00
Tray, Shaped & Raised Edge, Multicolored Flower Basket, Victorian, 23 x 32 In.	1175.00

PARASOL, *see Umbrella category.*

PARIAN is a fine-grained, hard-paste porcelain named for the marble it resembles. It was first made in England in 1846 and gained in favor in the United States about 1860. Figures, tea sets, vases, and other items were made of Parian at many English and American factories.

Bowl, Cover, Underplate, Flower, Flower Finial, 8 In.	295.00
Bust, Abraham Lincoln, c.1862-63, 9 In.	717.00
Bust, Alfred Tennyson, 1867, 12½ x 9 x 6 In.	1695.00
Bust, Classical, Swag Mantle, Parian Socle, 19th Century, 10¾ In.	360.00
Bust, Diana, 6 x 3½ x 2¼ In.	350.00
Bust, King Edward VII, 1901-10, 8¼ In.	145.00
Bust, Lord Burton, c.1909, 8½ In.	65.00
Bust, President Garfield, c.1890, 9½ x 8½ In.	795.00
Bust, Queen Victoria, Jubilee, Robinson & Leadbeater, Waisted Round Socle, 1887, 21 In. . . .	2115.00
Bust, Sir Isaac Pitman, 1887, 10½ In.	195.00
Bust, William McKinley, Ionic Column Base, 11 x 5 In.	175.00
Creamer, Classical Figures, White Matte, Glossy, 3½ In.	75.00
Figurine, Bear, With Honey Pot, Circling Bees, Bisque, 19th Century, 4½ In.	350.00
Figurine, Bird, On Branch, Portugal, 5 In.	24.00
Figurine, Bird Seller, Bisque, 8 In.	115.00
Figurine, Boy, Hat, 3 Birds, Fruit, 14½ In.	795.00
Figurine, Courtly Man, Basket, Garlands, Rococo, 11½ In.	176.00
Figurine, Euterpe, Thalia, c.1870, 14 In., Pair	351.00
Figurine, Flutist, Seated, Bisque, 7 x 5 In.	105.00
Figurine, Girl With Dog, Bisque, c.1880, 8¾ In.	350.00
Group, Aphrodite & Eros, Kneeling Goddess, Embracing Eros, Round Base, 23 x 12 In.	1527.00

Paperweight, St. Louis, Millefiori, Butterfly & Garland, Red, Green & White Border, 3 In. $33350.00

Paperweight, St. Louis, Millefiori, Center Cane, Spaced Ring, Border Garland, 2½ In. $345.00

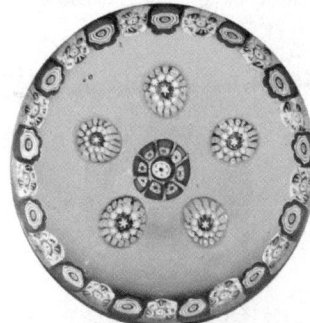

P

Paris, Vase, Garniture,
Flower Encrusted, Flared Rims,
Gold Trim, Jacob Petit,
8 In., Pair
$777.00

Pate-De-Verre, Paperweight,
Green Frog, Lily Pad, Blue Water,
Decorchemont, 5½ In.
$1725.00

Patent Model, Centrifugal Machine,
No. 215428, S. Baxendale,
May 20, 1879, 8 x 7¼ In.
$288.00

Pate-Sur-Pate, Vase, Brown,
Ivory Birds, Nest, Reeds, Oval,
Flattened, Flared Rim,
Ring Handles, 8¼ In.
$623.00

Group, Boy Kneeling Next To Girl, Bisque, Late 19th Century, 13 In.	425.00
Group, Children, Carrying Basket, Grapes, Leaves, Wheat, c.1865, 10 x 10 In.	850.00
Group, Three Graces, 6½ In.	40.00
Pitcher, Fern, Flowers, 8½ x 5½ In.	189.00
Pitcher, Napoleonic Battle, Blue & White, Relief, Labeled, Sam Alcock, 9¾ In.	260.00
Pitcher, Relief Molded, Classical, Maiden & Angel, Leaf Handle, Late 19th Century, 11 In.	117.00
Plaque, Morning & Night, Frame, 12 In.	1095.00
Plate, Buffalo Bill, 8½ In.	31.00
Plate, Buffalo Scout, With Horse, 10¼ In.	44.00
Plate, Jake, Children To Love, 1980, 10¼ In.	35.00
Plate, Johnny Appleseed, 1983, 8½ In.	29.00
Vase, Bacchus, Greek, c.1860, 5¼ x 4½ x 4 In.	250.00
Vase, Grape & Shell, 7½ In.	225.00
Wall Bracket, Shell Design, 8½ x 6½ x 5¾ In.	795.00

PARIS, Vieux Paris, or Old Paris, is porcelain ware that is known to have been made in Paris in the eighteenth or early nineteenth century. These porcelains have no identifying mark but can be recognized by the whiteness of the porcelain and the lines and decorations. Gold decoration is often used.

Basket, Oval, Reticulated, Multicolored Flowers, Gilt Details, 1800s, 7¾ x 8 In.	275.00
Basket, Pedestal, Pierced, Floral, Carved, Gold, White, 9 x 9¾ In.	695.00
Basket, Pierced, Gold, White, 4¾ x 8¾ In.	795.00
Bowl, Bleu Celeste, Gilt, Brass Mounted, Rococo Style, Floral Spray, Footed, 15½ In.	4080.00
Cachepot, Cornflower Decoration, Gilt Ram's Head Handles, 4½ In., Pair	1080.00
Centerpiece, Anneau D'Or, Navette Shape, Reticulated, Waisted Pedestal Base, 10 x 15 In.	470.00
Coffee Service, Tray, Vieux Paris, Parcel Gilt, Paint Decorated	1100.00
Coffee Set, White Ground, Grisaille & Landscapes, Service For 8	1800.00
Cup & Saucer, Baby Portrait, Baby In Clouds, c.1812	1200.00
Dresser Accessories, c.1950, 4 Piece	47.00
Figurine, Queen Mathilda, c.1900, 9 In.	234.00
Inkstand, White & Gold Glaze, Biscuit, Putto, Wine Barrel, On Barrow, Oval Base, 6 In.	2400.00
Pitcher, Milk, Louis XVI Pattern, White Ground, 10 In.	550.00
Plate, Cornflower Pattern, c.1780, 6 Piece	800.00
Plate, Dessert, Floral Center, Mulberry Border, 5 Gilt Old Ivory Scallop Shells, 8 Piece	720.00
Pots De Creme, Peach, Gilt Bands, White Ground, Handles, 2 Tiers, 11 Pots, 13 x 11 In.	676.00
Tureen, Anneau D'Or Pattern, Gilt Trim, Pomegranate Finial, Egyptian Mask Handles, 11 In.	480.00
Tureen, Tray, Round, Fruit Finial, Scrolled Handles, Gilt, Red Bands, Borders, 12 x 14 In.	470.00
Vase, Garniture, Flower Encrusted, Flared Rims, Gold Trim, Jacob Petit, 8 In., Pair .... *illus*	777.00
Vase, Gold, Swan Handles, Woman Holding Glass Of Red Wine, 10 In.	950.00
Vase, Hand Painted Floral Bouquets, Lavender Ground, Gilt, 10½ In., Pair	173.00
Vase, Rococo Style, Gilt Handles, Floral Detail, 10 x 5 In., Pair	1595.00

PATE-DE-VERRE is an ancient technique in which glass is made by blending and refining powdered glass of different colors into molds. The process was revived by French glassmakers, especially Galle, around the end of the nineteenth century.

Bowl, 2 Demon Masks, Laurel Wreaths, Ridges, Green, Impressed, Decorchemont, 2¼ x 3 In.	1300.00
Paperweight, Green Frog, Lily Pad, Blue Water, Decorchemont, 5½ In. .... *illus*	1725.00
Sculpture, Woman's Head, Hair Covered With Scarf, Golden Yellow, Signed, Despret, 3¼ In.	480.00

PATE-SUR-PATE means paste on paste. The design was made by painting layers of slip on the ceramic piece until a relief decoration was formed. The method was developed at the Sevres factory in France about 1850. It became even more famous at the English Minton factory about 1870. It has since been used by many potters to make both pottery and porcelain wares.

Plate, Art Nouveau, Woman, Eating Cherries From Basket, c.1900, 9 In.	495.00
Vase, Brown, Ivory Birds, Nest, Reeds, Oval, Flattened, Flared Rim, Ring Handles, 8¼ In. *illus*	623.00
Vase, Green Ground, Flat Sides, Gilt Rim, Maidens In Garden, 1880, 9 In.	1645.00

PATENT MODELS were required as part of a patent application for a United States patent until 1880. In 1926 the stored patent models were sold as a group by the U.S. patent office and individual models are now appearing in the marketplace.

Blind Slat Operator, Window Box, Wood, No. 119625, H.B. Lum, 1871	173.00
Carbureting Gases Apparatus, Tin, Painted, c.1859, 9 x 10 In.	353.00
Centrifugal Machine, No. 215428, S. Baxendale, May 20, 1879, 8 x 7¼ In. ....*illus*	288.00

Cotton Planter, E.T. Bostrom	460.00
Dental Chair Headrest, Wood, Steel Brackets, Rods, No. 171539, E.T. Starr, 1875	345.00
Egg Tester, No. 308791, E.W. Ptlaumer, 1884.	1093.00
Feed Water Heater & Filter, No. 226814, Wood, J.W. White, 1880	288.00
Horse Power Machine, Painted, Hunter & Co., 14¾ In.	330.00
Leg & Footrest, Wood, Cast Iron Locks, No. 183475, T. Weddle, 1876	259.00
Machinery For Cementing Shoe Uppers, No. 211567, J.B. Johnson, 1879, 11 In. *illus*	1150.00
Milking Stool, 3 Wheels, No. 196543, O. Scriven, Oct. 30, 1877, 11 x 7 x 5 In. *illus*	1725.00
Railway Station Indicator, No. 13824, C.A. McEvoy, 1855	575.00
Rudder Post Bearing, No. 163726, J.N. Bitting, Sr., 1875	518.00
Store Counter Seat, Wood, Spring Loaded, No. 244191, W.M. Corwin, 1881	891.00
Table, Extension, Walnut, Charles Utman, Hillsboro, Ohio, 1877, 7½ x 10 x 10 In. *illus*	825.00
Wagon Tire Bender, No. 25345, W. & I.H. Mosher, 1859	460.00
Washing Machine, No. 101592, C. Dean, 1870	403.00
Washing Machine, No. 95239, G.A. Leigh, 1869	460.00

PAUL REVERE POTTERY was made at several locations in and around Boston, Massachusetts, between 1906 and 1942. The pottery was operated as a settlement house program for teenage girls. Many pieces were signed *S.E.G.* for Saturday Evening Girls. The artists concentrated on children's dishes and tiles. Decorations were outlined in black and filled with color.

Bookends, Owls, On Tree Branch, Blue, S.E.G., Marked, Fannie Levine, 4 x 5 In.	1400.00
Bowl, Blue, Flared Rim, Narrow Round Foot, S.E.G., c.1919, 2¼ x 5½ In.	351.00
Bowl, Carved & Painted Stylized Pods, Sara Galner, S.E.G., c.1914, 5 x 11½ In. *illus*	3600.00
Bowl, Daffodils, Beige, White, Yellow Ground, 2½ x 8½ In.	1920.00
Bowl, Flared Rim, Ship Border, Blue, Green, Yellow, Brown, Black, 3½ x 9 In.	1410.00
Bowl, Flaring, Yellow Stylized Flowers, 1926, 2 x 10¼ In.	840.00
Bowl, Fruit, Blue, S.E.G., c.1923, 2½ x 8¼ In.	195.00
Bowl, Greek Key, S.E.G., Albina Mangini, 1914, 2½ x 8½ In.	2160.00
Bowl, Rosette Band, Her Bowl, Annie Barton, 1922, 1¾ x 5¾ In.	645.00
Bowl, White Geese, Yellow Ground, S.E.G., 4¼ x 10½ In.	5100.00
Candlestick, Pottery, High Glaze, Teal Blue, Speckling, 6½ In.	375.00
Children's Set, Rosettes, Inscribed, Dina Harris, S.E.G., 1922, 4½ In., 3 Piece	2985.00
Cup & Saucer, Lotus, Cuerda Seca, S.E.G., 1910, 2 x 4½ In.	1145.00
Mug, 3 Fishing Boats, Hilly Lakeside Landscape, 5 x 6 In.	2160.00
Plate, 3 Chicks, Mauve, Off-White, Janice, Her Plate, Initials PRP 5-4-40, 7½ In.	323.00
Tea Sct, 1917, 6 x 6 In.	985.00
Tea Set, Blue & White Semimatte Glaze, Teapot, Sugar, Creamer, Cup, Saucer	600.00
Tea Tile, Tulip, Green, Blue, White, Black Outline, Impressed, Initials EM 6-25, 4½ In.	353.00
Tile, Fox, Mustard Glaze, Celadon Ground, 5¼ x 5¼ In.	2880.00
Trivet, Trees, Landscape, Edith Brown, 1926, 5 In.	1485.00
Vase, Bud, Band Of Trees, Yellow Ground, Signed, 8 x 3 In.	3000.00
Vase, Cuerda Seca, Trees, Landscape, Yellow Ground, 7¾ x 3½ In.	3600.00

PEACHBLOW glass was made by several factories beginning in the 1880s. New England peachblow is a one-layer glass shading from red to white. Mt. Washington peachblow shades from pink to bluish-white. Hobbs, Brockunier and Company of Wheeling, West Virginia, made Coral glass that they marketed as Peach Blow. It shades from yellow to peach and is lined with white glass. Reproductions of all types of peachblow have been made. Related pieces may be listed under Gunderson and Webb Peachblow.

Basket, Diamond Quilted, Applied Twist Handle, Mt. Washington, 8½ In.	118.00
Bowl, Amber Rigaree Lip Wrap, Hobbs, Brockunier, 8½ In.	94.00
Bowl, Folded Rim, Satin Finish, c.1900	195.00
Creamer, Angular Shape, Square Mouth, Cream Handle, New England, 4½ In.	403.00
Cruet, Amber Reeded Handle & Faceted Stopper, Glossy, 7 In.	489.00
Cuspidor, Scalloped Top, Woman's, Mt. Washington, 5½ In.	875.00
Darner, Souvenir, Cambridge, Mass., Mt. Washington	250.00
Finger Bowl, Wheeling Drape, Hobbs, Brockunier, 2¾ x 5 In. *illus*	90.00
Paperweight, Pear Shape, New England, 4½ x 2⅞ In.	450.00
Pitcher, Bulbous, Square Mouth, Amber Frosted Handle, Hobbs, Brockunier, 7 In.	863.00
Pitcher, Square Mouth, Applied Amber Handle, Hobbs, Brockunier, 8½ In.	633.00
Punch Cup, Glossy, Amber Handle, Hobbs, Brockunier, 2¼ In., 4 Piece	489.00
Rose Bowl, Crimped Edge, Mt. Washington, 3⅞ x 4 In.	350.00
Rose Bowl, Ruffled Edge, Mt. Washington, 5¼ x 4½ In.	295.00
Sugar, Queen's Decoration, Gold & Red Trim, Square Mouth, Mt. Washington, 4½ In.	5750.00

Patent Model, Machinery For Cementing Shoe Uppers, No. 211567, J.B. Johnson, 1879, 11 In.
$1150.00

Patent Model, Milking Stool, 3 Wheels, No. 196543, O. Scriven, Oct. 30, 1877, 11 x 7 x 5 In.
$1725.00

Patent Model, Table, Extension, Walnut, Charles Utman, Hillsboro, Ohio, 1877, 7½ x 10 x 10 In.
$825.00

Paul Revere Pottery, Bowl, Carved & Painted Stylized Pods, Sara Galner, S.E.G., c.1914, 5 x 11½ In.
$3600.00

P

Peachblow Craze

In 1886 a seventeenth-century Chinese porcelain vase now known as the Morgan vase was sold. Several two-tone pink glasswares were being made, and to capitalize on the publicity of the sale of the Chinese vase and its peachblow glaze, some glass makers named their new vases "peachblow" or a similar name.

Peachblow, Finger Bowl, Wheeling Drape, Hobbs, Brockunier, 2¾ x 5 In. $90.00

Peachblow, Vase, Apple Form, Hobbs, Brockunier, 3½ In. $460.00

Names for Peachblow

Peachblow glass varies in color from one company to another. Even the names are confusing. Original trade ads used the term as one or two words. The companies themselves used different names in their ads: Coral, Peach Bloom, Peach Blow, Peach Skin, or Wild Rose.

Tumbler, Enameled Flowers, Leaves, Mt. Washington, c.1890	395.00
Tumbler, Glossy, New England, 3½ In.	144.00
Tumbler, Hobbs, Brockunier, 3¾ x 2¾ In.	250.00 to 450.00
Vase, Apple Form, Hobbs, Brockunier, 3½ In. ....*illus*	460.00
Vase, Bulbous, Square Mouth, Glossy, Hobbs, Brockunier, 7¼ In.	863.00
Vase, Egg Shape, Stand-Up Rim, Glossy, New England, 6½ In.	776.00
Vase, Glossy, Hobbs, Brockunier, 9 In.	295.00
Vase, Hawthorne, Egg Shape, Mt. Washington, 9½ x 4½ In. .....*illus*	5175.00
Vase, Jack-In-The-Pulpit, 8¼ x 4⅛ In.	195.00
Vase, Lily, Disc Foot, New England, 9¾ x 3¾ In.	520.00
Vase, Lily, Wild Rose, Tricorned Rim, Glossy, New England, 9½ In.	805.00
Vase, Morgan, Glossy, Glass Griffin Base, Hobbs, Brockunier, 10 In.	920.00
Vase, Morgan, Porcelain Griffin Base, Hobbs, Brockunier, 9¾ In.	635.00
Vase, Stick, Bulbous Base, Hobbs, Brockunier, 10 In.	978.00
Vase, Stick, Glossy, 1800s, 9 In.	850.00
Vase, Wild Rose, Bulbous Base, Lady's Leg Neck, Glossy, New England, 6¾ In.	633.00

PEANUTS is the tile of a comic strip created by cartoonist Charles M. Schulz (1922–2000). The strip, drawn by Schulz from 1950 to 2000, features a group of children, including Charlie Brown and his sister Sally, Lucy Van Pelt and her brother Linus, Peppermint Patty, and Pig Pen, and an imaginative and independent beagle named Snoopy. The Peanuts gang has also been featured in books, television shows, and a Broadway musical.

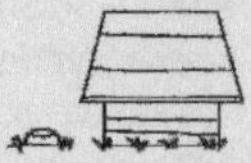

Book, All This & Snoopy Too, 1962	6.00
Bracelet, Enameled Figures, Snoopy, Charlie Brown, Lucy, 5¾ In.	32.00
Clock, Snoopy, Woodstock, Blue Plastic Case, Alarm, Battery Operated, Citizen, 5 x 4 x 2 In.	10.00
Comic Art, Daily Cartoon, Charles Schulz, April 26, 1958, 5½ x 27 In.	13200.00
Cookie Jar, Lucy, Benjamin & Medwin, Box, 2 x 7 In.	75.00
Cookie Jar, Snoopy, Woodstock, Snoopy Holding Glass Bowl With Wicker Lid, 13 x 18 In.	70.00
Cup, Woodstock Carrying Snoopy In Kerchief, 2⅛ In.	10.00
Doll Fabric Pattern, Peanuts Gang, Charlie Brown, Sally, Snoopy, Linus, Lucy, 23 x 16 In.	44.50
Doll, Lucy, Flat, Molded Pink Dress, Rubber, 5¼ In.	25.00
Figure, Charlie Brown, Bend-Em, 5½ In.	25.00
Figure, Lucy Van Pelt, It's The Great Pumpkin Charlie Brown, Memory Lane	17.00
Finger Puppet Set, Lucy, Snoopy, Violet, Peppermint Patty, Vinyl, 2½ In.	32.00
Keychain, Lucy & Linus, Classic, 2-Sided Plastic, Early 1970s, 3 x 3 In.	10.00
Mug, Lucy, Milk Glass, Avon, c.1969, 5 In.	13.00
Mug, Shampoo, Lucy With Balloon, Yellow, Metal Lid, Ball Finial, Avon, 1969, 5 Oz., 5 In.	27.00
Necktie, Charlie Brown & The Gang, Polyester, United Feature, Korea, c.1958	9.00 to 13.00
Night-Light, Snoopy, Woodstock, Heart, Bubble, Box, 1970s	10.00
Nodder, Charlie Brown, Resin, Box, 6¼ In.	14.00
Ornament, Ice Hockey Holiday, Panorama, Snoopy & Friends, Plastic, Hallmark, c.1979	85.00
Ornament, Snoopy Skiing, Sunglasses, Woodstock Perched On Skis, Hallmark, c.1984	45.00
Phone, Snoopy & Woodstock, Red & Yellow, Plastic, AT&T, 1976, 13 In.	160.00
Pin, Snoopy, Wearing Blue Snoopy Pin, c.1958, 2 In.	10.00
Puppet, Lucy, As Nurse, Push Button, Plastic, Ideal, c.1970, 4½ In.	30.00
Radio, Snoopy, Box, Carry Strap, Earphones, 6½ x 5 In.	115.00
Salt & Pepper, Charlie Brown, Lucy, On Sofa, Ceramic, Willets, c.1990, 4¼ x 3 In.	85.00
Snow Globe, Charlie Brown, Soccer, Resin, Box, 2½ In.	12.00
Stationary Holder, Snoopy, Paper, Envelopes, c.1958, 9¼ x 6 In.	22.00
Thermos Bottle, Charlie Brown At Bat, Yellow, Red Cap, Plastic, King Seeley, 1975, 8 Oz.	55.00
Top, Chein, Tin, Lithograph, Original Box, Late 1960s, 9 In.	83.00
Toy, Snoopy, Space Patrol, Bump & Go, Tin, Plastic, Battery Operated, Masudaya, Box, 11 In.	743.00
Toy, Snoopy's Dream Machine, DCS, Box, c.1970, 9 x 18 ½ x 3½ In.	103.00
Tumbler, 2 Charlie Brown, Snoopy, Lucy, 5½ In., 4 Piece	16.50
Tumbler, Camp Snoopy, There's No Excuse, McDonald's, c.1983	6.00
Tumbler, Camp Snoopy, Why Is Having Fun Always So Much Work, McDonald's, 1983, 6 In.	4.00

PEARL items listed here are made of the natural mother-of-pearl from shells. Such natural pearl has been used to decorate furniture and small utilitarian objects for centuries. The glassware known as mother-of-pearl is listed by that name. Opera glasses made with natural pearl shell are listed under Opera Glasses.

Knife Set, Blunt Blade, Floral Band, Landers Frary & Clark, 8 In., 6 Piece	165.00
Shadowbox, Carved, Last Supper, Elaborately Shaped Border, 10 In.	173.00
Spoon, Serving, Sterling Band, Paneled Bowl, 8½ In.	75.00

PEARLWARE is an earthenware made by Josiah Wedgwood in 1779. It was copied by other potters in England. Pearlware is only slightly different in color from creamware and for many years collectors have confused the terms. Wedgwood pieces are listed in the Wedgwood category in this book. Most pearlware with mocha designs is listed under Mocha.

Pearl

Bowl, Asian Decoration, Pagodas, Bouquets, Geometric Interior Border, 4 x 10½ In.	518.00
Bowl, Blue & White, Transfer, Scroll Border, Riley, Staffordshire, c.1825, 10 In.	350.00
Bowl, Bouquet In Center, Yellow, Ocher, Blue, Manganese, Pratt Style, c.1820	720.00
Bowl, Fruit & Flowers, Blue, c.1825, 9½ In.	250.00
Bowl, Spaniel & Bird, Blue & White, Transfer, Stevenson, c.1820, 9½ In.	425.00
Bowl, Vegetable, Open, Chinoiserie, Blue & White, Transfer, c.1830, 12 x 8½ In.	450.00
Bowl, Vegetable, Square, Dr. Syntax, 1st Tour, Blue & White, Transfer, c.1825, 11 In.	775.00
Bowl, White Gloss Glaze, Scalloped Edge, Johnson Bros., 7¾ x 2½ In.	10.00
Cheese Stand, Eastern Street Scene, Blue & White, Riley, c.1825, 12 In.	950.00
Coffeepot, English Country Scene, Blue & White, Transfer, c.1820, 11½ In.	450.00
Coffeepot, Milkmaid, Blue Transfer, Staffordshire, c.1825, 11 In.	1100.00
Coffeepot, Winged Mermen, Pegasus, Blue & White, Transfer, c.1825, 11½ In.	850.00
Creamer, Cow, Milkmaid, Green Sponged Base, c.1830	1750.00
Creamer, Orange Flowers, Green Leaves, Elongated Spout, Bulbous, Scroll Handle, 4¼ In.	138.00
Cup & Saucer, Birds Of Prey, Blue Transfer, Scalloped Edge, c.1825, 5½ In.	225.00
Cup & Saucer, Castle Scene, Transfer, Rust Color, 5½ In., Pair	28.00
Cup & Saucer, Handleless, Multicolored, Flower & Star, 2⅛ x 5¼ In.	193.00
Cup Plate, Girl Musician, Riley, Staffordshire, c.1825, 3½ In.	150.00
Cup Plate, Purple & White, Country Scene, Windmill, Children's, c.1835, 3¾ In.	95.00
Custard Cup, Flowers, Blue & White, Transfer, c.1825, 2½ x 3½ In.	250.00
Dish, Pickle, British View, Blue Transfer, Leaf Shape, c.1825, 5 x 4½ In.	200.00
Dish, Pickle, Floral, Blue & White, Transfer, c.1830, 3½ x 5 In.	350.00
Drainer, Forest Landscape, Chinoiserie, Spode, c.1820, 12¾ x 9 In.	295.00
Drainer, Vignette, Blue & White, Transfer, Staffordshire, c.1820, 13½ x 9½ In.	450.00
Figurine, Allegorical, Chaucer, Leaning On Pedestal, Wood, Polychrome, Late 1700s, 12 In.	881.00
Figurine, Britannia, Wood & Caldwell, Polychrome Enamel, Silver Luster, 1800s, 9½ In.	999.00
Figurine, Cradle With Baby, Sponged, 1820s, 3½ x 1¼ In.	475.00
Figurine, Hercules, Kneeling, Enamel, Pierced Globe, Staffordshire, c.1800, 11 In., Pair *illus*	1528.00
Figurine, St. George & Dragon, Lead Glaze, Gray Enamel, Staffordshire, 1700s, 11½ In.	1528.00
Figurine, Wicker Cradle, Green Glaze, Staffordshire, c.1790, 4 x 2 In.	250.00
Group, Drunken Parsons, Early 19th Century, 9 In.	764.00
Group, Remus & Romulus, Staffordshire, c.1820, 7½ In.	940.00
Group, Return From Egypt, Man & Woman Travelers, Staffordshire, 9½ In.	529.00
Infant Feeder, Swags, Floral, Blue Transfer, c.1830, 6¼ x 3¼ In.	650.00
Jug, Bacchus, Enameled, Dolphin Spout, Monkey Handle, Staffordshire, 12½ In.	1763.00
Jug, Classical Pattern, Milk, Blue & White, Transfer, 5½ In.	375.00
Jug, Neptune, Fountain, Brown & White, Transfer, c.1835, 8 In.	625.00
Jug, Rochester Castle, Blue Transfer, c.1825, 6 x 6½ In.	975.00
Knife Rest, Heart Ends, Blue, John Meir, c.1836, 3¾ In.	350.00
Mug, Satyr, Pointy Ears, Horns, Grapes, Leaf Crown, c.1800, 4½ In.	495.00
Pepper Pot, Blue & White, Transfer, Staffordshire, c.1830, 4 In.	155.00
Pepper Pot, Floral, Blue & White, Transfer, Staffordshire, c.1830, 4 In.	550.00
Pipe, Enamel, 4-Mask Bowl, Snake Stem, Hound Handle, Pratt Type, c.1800, 10 In.	1528.00
Pitcher, Squirrel & Rabbit, Blue Transfer, c.1830, 4 In.	425.00
Plate, Beemaster, Wedding Scene, Blue Transfer, c.1820, 8¼ In.	475.00
Plate, Boston State House, Rogers, c.1825, 10 In.	375.00
Plate, British Scenery, Man Fly Fishing, Children's, c.1825, 4½ In.	175.00
Plate, Cupid, Behind Bars, Blue & White, Transfer, Enoch Wood, c.1825, 9 In.	550.00
Plate, Eagle, With Shield, Blue, Sepia, Staffordshire, 6½ In.	777.00
Plate, Eel, Blue Transfer, Woodman, c.1825, 5¼ In.	350.00
Plate, Flower Rim, 4 In.	55.00
Plate, Flowers, Blue & White, Transfer, c.1820, 9½ In., Pair	350.00
Plate, Grapes, Grape Leaves, Blue & White, c.1820, 8¼ In.	350.00
Plate, Hunting Scene, Blue & White, Transfer, c.1825, 9 In.	375.00
Plate, Italian Scenery, St. Paul's, Rome, Blue & White, Transfer, c.1825, 10 In.	375.00
Plate, Leopard & Antelope, Blue & White, c.1820, 9¾ In.	495.00
Plate, Moulin Sur La Marne A Charenton, Blue & White, Transfer, Enoch Wood, 9 In.	525.00
Plate, Shell Pattern, Blue & White, Transfer, Stubbs & Kent, c.1820s, 10 In.	575.00
Plate, Shipping Series, Blue & White, c.1820, 10 In.	550.00
Plate, Soup, Blue & White, Transfer, Molded Border, Dixson Austin & Co., 10¼ In.	155.00

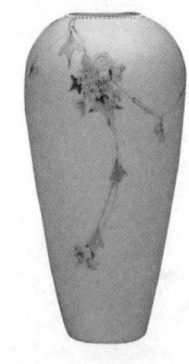

Peachblow, Vase, Hawthorne, Egg Shape, Mt. Washington, 9½ x 4½ In. $5175.00

Pearlware, Figurine, Hercules, Kneeling, Enamel, Pierced Globe, Staffordshire, c.1800, 11 In., Pair $1528.00

Pearlware, Tea Canister, Chinese Lady, Child, Old Man, Square, Low Relief, Staffordshire, c.1789, 4 In. $3000.00

Pearlware, Wall Pocket, Woman's Head & Bust, Pratt Type, c.1800, 9½ In. $646.00

P

Peking Glass, Vase, 4 Birds, F
lowering Prunus, Red Over, White,
Flared, Footed, 7½ In.
$1035.00

Peking Glass, Vase,
Flowering Trees & Bird In Flight,
Emerald Green, 6¼ In., Pair
$120.00

Peking Glass, Vase, Yellow,
Bottle Shape, Paneled Sides, 8¾ In.
$546.00

Plate, Soup, Gleaners, English Country Scene, Blue, c.1820, 9½ In.	475.00
Plate, Soup, Orange, Green, Clobbered, c.1820, 9½ In.	375.00
Plate, Trellis & Flowers, Children's, c.1830, 3¼ In.	145.00
Platter, Beehive & Vases, Blue Transfer, Stevenson & Williams, c.1825, 17 x 13 In.	1550.00
Platter, Birds, Butterflies, Flowers, Blue & White, Transfer, c.1825, 19 x 14½ In.	1250.00
Platter, British Views, Abington Abbey, Henshall, c.1820, 11 x 8½ In.	675.00
Platter, Chinoiserie, Blue & White, Transfer, c.1800, 20½ x 14¼ In.	450.00
Platter, Feather Edge, 1820s, 16¾ x 13½ In.	300.00
Platter, Flowers, Fruit, Blue Transfer, c.1825, 18½ x 14 In.	1650.00
Platter, Green Scalloped Edge, Molded Flowers, c.1830, 9¾ In.	150.00
Platter, India Vase, Blue Transfer, Staffordshire, c.1920, 17 x 13 In.	950.00
Platter, Mythical Beasts, Burnt Orange, Clobbered, c.1830, 19¼ In.	1200.00
Platter, Panoramic Scenery, Blue & White, Transfer, Staffordshire, c.1825, 21 In.	1550.00
Platter, Parkland Scenery, Blue & White, Transfer, c.1830, 18½ In.	1250.00
Platter, Tendril, Flow Blue & Mulberry, Floral, Vine, Staffordshire, 17 x 11½ In.	175.00
Platter, Vignette, Blue & White, Transfer, c.1820, 11½ x 8½ In.	375.00
Saucer, Elk, Blue & White, Transfer, c.1825, 5 In.	275.00
Saucer, Oriental Scene, Man Riding Zebra, Blue, White, Scalloped Rim, 4¾ In.	28.00
Sugar, Stately House, Grazing Cows, Blue & White, Transfer, Double Handles, c.1825	425.00
Tea Caddy, Pratt, Pottery Lid, Macaroni Figure, Staffordshire, c.1790, 6½ In., Pair	500.00
Tea Canister, Chinese Lady, Child, Old Man, Square, Low Relief, Staffordshire, c.1789, 4 In. *illus*	3000.00
Tea Set, Pink Luster Band, Grapevines, Flowers, Staffordshire, c.1825, 20 Piece	720.00
Teapot, Christmas Eve, Blue & White, Clews, c.1825	650.00
Teapot, Fruits & Flowers, Blue & White, Transfer, c.1830	550.00
Teapot, Tulips, Blue & White, Transfer, Children's, c.1800, 4 x 5½ In.	375.00
Toast Rack, Flowers, Leaves, Lace, Blue, Transfer, 8 x 4 In.	595.00
Toilet Box, Floral, Blue & White, Transfer, c.1825, 7½ x 3 In.	375.00
Tureen, Lid, Square, Don Quixote's Library, Staffordshire, c.1825	1150.00
Vase, Finger, Quintal Flower Horn, Green Glaze, c.1790, 8¾ In.	2500.00
Wall Pocket, Woman's Head & Bust, Pratt Type, c.1800, 9½ In. *illus*	646.00
Waste Bowl, Fluted, Blue & White Oriental, Transfer, 3½ x 6½ In.	160.00

PEKING GLASS is a Chinese cameo glass first made popular in the eighteenth century. The Chinese have continued to make this layered glass in the old manner, and many new pieces are now available that could confuse the average buyer.

Bowl, Butterflies, Mustard Yellow, 6¼ In., Pair	147.00
Bowl, Ducks, Lotus, Green Over White, 8¼ In.	118.00
Bowl, Yellow, Carved Teakwood Lotus Stand, 3 x 6 In., Pair	880.00
Brush Pot, Imperial Yellow, Cylindrical, 5½ x 4¾ In.	528.00
Charger, Jade Green, Shallow Cavetto, 11 In.	93.00
Vase, 4 Birds, Flowering Prunus, Red Over White, Flared, Footed, 7½ In. *illus*	1035.00
Vase, Buddhist Saints, Green, 5¼ In.	176.00
Vase, Flowering Trees & Bird In Flight, Emerald Green, 6¼ In., Pair *illus*	120.00
Vase, Lotus Plants, Blue To White, 20th Century, 8 In.	294.00
Vase, Pink, Round Bottom, Elongated Neck, Turned Foot, 6½ In., Pair	1320.00
Vase, Yellow, Bottle Shape, Paneled Sides, 8¾ In. *illus*	546.00

PELOTON glass is a European glass with small threads of colored glass rolled onto the surface of clear or colored glass. It is sometimes called spaghetti, or shredded coconut, glass. Most pieces found today were made in the nineteenth century.

Pitcher, Amber, Diagonal Swirls, Red, Blue, White Canes, Amber Reeded Handle, 7½ In.	288.00
Pitcher, Crackle, Multicolored Threads, Applied Clear Handle, 5½ In.	450.00
Pitcher, Water, Cranberry, Multicolored Threads, Reeded Handle, 9½ In. *illus*	288.00
Vase, Blue Threads, Enameled Leaf & Flowers, Gold Rim, 6¼ In. *illus*	259.00

PENS replaced hand-cut quills as writing instruments in 1780, when the first steel pen point was made in England. But it was 100 years before the commercial pen was a common item. The fountain pen was invented in the 1830s but was not made in quantity until the 1880s. All types of old pens are collected. Float pens that feature small objects floating in a liquid as part of the handle are popular with collectors. Advertising pens are listed in the Advertising section of this book.

PEN

Float, Frankfurt-Main, Blue, Airplane, Taxis On Runway, Offenbach Am Main	9.00

Fountain, Montblanc, Meisterstuck, No. 144, Original 14-C Nib, c.1958	235.00
Fountain, Mother-Of-Pearl, Engraved Gold Ferule, Red Velvet & Silk Box, Victorian, 5½ In.	85.00
Fountain, Parker, Blue Diamond, Vacumatic, Black, Gold Rim, Nib, 1940s	75.00
Fountain, Travel Size, Victorian, c.1870, 3 x 4¾ In.	250.00
Mother-Of-Pearl, Victorian, Engraved Gold Ferule, Velvet, Silk Box, 5½ In.	85.00
Perfumed, Arpege, Chanel No. 5, 14K Gold, Box	75.00
Provident Bank, Baseball Bat Shape, Blue Ink, 7¾ In.	6.00
Railroad, Sunshine Special Scenic Limited, Mother-Of-Pearl, Quikpoint Pen Co.	45.00
Risperdal Risperidone, Green Marble, Gold Accent, 5½ In.	5.00
Stripper, Woman Strips As Top Is Turned, 12 x 1¼ In.	55.00

PEN & PENCIL

Desk Set, Shaeffer, Art Deco, Black Marble, Speaker	250.00
Fountain, Montblanc, Meisterstuck, No. 92, 14K Yellow Gold, Box, c.1962, Pair	1598.00

PENCILS were invented, so it is said, in 1565. The eraser was not added to the pencil until 1858. The automatic pencil was invented in 1863. Collectors today want advertising pencils or automatic pencils of unusual design. Boxes and sharpeners for pencils are also collected. Pencil boxes are listed in the Box category.

PENCIL

Cross, Pendant, Gold Filled, Slides Up & Down, c.1850, 2¾ In.	255.00
Houston Oilers, Unsharpened, c.1986	8.00
Mechanical, 14K Gold Filled, N.Y., 5⅛ In.	55.00
Mechanical, Gold Filled, Victorian, 3¼ In.	155.00
Mechanical, Sterling Silver, Victorian, 3¼ In.	135.00
Mechanical, Wahl Eversharp, Gold Filled, 177C, With Tag	4.50
Silver, Scabbard Case, Man, Rifle, Federal Shooting Club Of Buenos Aires, c.1910, 4 In.	69.00
Telescoping, Gold Tone, Loop For Chain, Pat. Pend. Rubicon, 1950s, 4 In.	40.00

PENCIL SHARPENER

Alasco German Metal, Brass, 1 x ½ In.	18.00
Astronaut, Landing On Moon, Flag, Metal, 3 In.	5.00
Automobile, 1917 Model, 2 x 4 In.	49.00
Bakelite, Green, Child's, 1 In.	12.00
Baker's Cocoa, Cocoa Lady, Painted	125.00
Baseball Player, Metal, 4 In.	5.00
Black Face Caricature, Cast Metal, Germany, c.1930, 1¼ In.	36.00
Blackhawk Helicopter, Tin, 1½ x 4¼ In.	5.00
Boston Model, School, Metal, Crank Handle, 4 x 4½ In.	36.00
Camera, Metal, 2 x 2¼ In.	45.00
Car, Brass, Top Lifts To Reveal Sharpener, 1930s	126.00
Car, Metal, Hong Kong, 3 x 1¾ In.	10.00
Car Shape, 1917 Convertible, Red Bronze, Resin Top, 1¾ x 2¾ In.	19.00
Cash Register, Metal, 2¼ In.	5.00
Coffee Grinder, Red, Gold Eagle Decal, 5½ x 5¾ In.	45.00
Cowboy Boot, Metal, 2½ In.	5.00
Cupboard, Door & Drawers Open, Metal, Chinese, 2¾ x 1½ In.	6.00
Everglades Fan Boat, Metal, 2 x 2½ In.	5.00
Globe, Revolving, 3 Legs, 2 x 4 In.	49.00
Gramophone, Metal, 3 In.	5.00
Grandfather's Clock, Moving Pendulum, Metal, Brass Finish, 3¾ x 1¼ In.	8.00
Horse & Buggy, Metal, Die Cast, Black & Copper, 2¼ x 4 x 1¼ In.	5.00 to 12.00
Kitten In High Heel Shoe, Metal, 1960s, 2½ In.	15.00
Metal, Wood Base, U.S. Pencil Sharpening, Chicago, 1902, 6 x 4 x 3 In.	217.00
Owl, Metal, 2 In.	5.00
Phone, Candlestick, Removable Earpiece, Copper, 3½ In.	2.50
Pistol, 2 x 4 In.	25.00
Roneo, Mechanical, Cast Iron, Table Mount Clamp	325.00
Saddle, Metal, Copper Alloy, 3¼ In.	6.00
Sewing Machine, Metal, 2 In.	5.00
Stove, Drawer, Door Opens, Metal, Spain, 3 x 2⅝ x 1 In.	13.00
Toilet, Metal, 1¾ In.	5.00
Trolley Car, Metal, 3 In.	5.00
Violin, Metal, Bronze Patina, Germany	56.00
Volkswagen Bug, Yellow, 3 In.	8.00

Peloton, Pitcher, Water, Cranberry, Multicolored Threads, Reeded Handle, 9½ In. $288.00

Peloton, Vase, Blue Threads, Enameled Leaf & Flowers, Gold Rim, 6¼ In. $259.00

P

Types of Glass Decorations

Cameo cutting makes a design on multilayered glass by removing part of the top layer.

Chipped ice or *hammered glass* has a chipped appearance. Applying glue to the outside of the glass, then firing it, makes the glue crack. Pieces pop and a "hammered" look remains.

Frosted glass imitates the look of ancient glass. The dull, slightly iridescent look is made by acid treatment or sandblasting.

Pennsbury, Figurine, Bird, Nuthatch, No. 110, 3⅛ In. $45.00

Pennsbury, Figurine, Rooster, Blue, White, 12 In. $205.00

Pennsbury, Tray, Lovebirds, Heart, 7⅜ x 5¼ In. $15.00

PENNSBURY Pottery worked in Morrisville, Pennsylvania, from 1950 to 1971. Full sets of dinnerware as well as many decorative items were made. Pieces are marked with the name of the factory.

Pennsbury Pottery

Bookends, Bald Eagle, Marked, 8⅛ x 6½ In.	297.00
Creamer, Amish, Woman & Heart, 2½ In.	18.00
Creamer, Red Rooster, 4 Oz., 2½ In.	20.00
Creamer, Yellow Rooster, 4½ In.	45.00
Figurine, Birds On Gourds, 5⅛ In., Pair	61.00
Figurine, Chickadee, No. 111, Marked, 3 In.	66.00
Figurine, Large Wren, No. 106, Marked, 6½ In.	209.00
Figurine, Nuthatch, No. 110, 3⅛ In. ....*illus*	45.00
Figurine, Rooster, Blue, White, 10 In.	110.00
Figurine, Rooster, Blue, White, 12 In. ....*illus*	205.00
Figurine, Scarlet Tanager, Marked, 4 x 6¼ In.	253.00
Plaque, B & O Railroad Retired Workers, 1955, 5¾ x 7¾ In.	65.00
Plaque, Don't Stand Up While The Room Is In Motion, 6 In.	45.00
Plate, Baltimore & Ohio RR, Brown, Black, Yellow, Maroon, 5¾ In.	44.00
Plate, Christmas, Embossed, Holly, Berries, Children Stringing Popcorn, 1974, 8 In.	15.00
Sign, Display, Yellow Bird On Top	365.00
Tile, Amish, Hanging Hole, 4 In.	30.00
Tip Tray, Yellow Rooster, 6 x 8 In.	50.00
Tray, Fidelity Mutual 75th Anniversary, 1953, 7¼ In.	22.00
Tray, Lovebirds, Heart, 7⅜ x 5¼ In. ....*illus*	15.00
Vase, Slick Chick, Gourd, 5 In.	65.00

PEPSI-COLA, the drink and the name, was invented in 1898 but was not trademarked until 1903. The logo was changed from an elaborate script to the modern block letters in 1963. Several different logos have been used. Until 1951, the words *Pepsi* and *Cola* were separated by 2 dashes. These bottles are called "double dash." In 1951 the modern logo with a single hyphen was introduced. All types of advertising memorabilia are collected, and reproductions are being made.

Bank, Dispenser Shape, Be Sociable, Tin Lithograph, Linemar, Box, 1950s, 10 In.	2464.00
Bottle Crate, Wooden, 18 x 12 In.	48.00
Calendar, 1910, Woman Sipping Pepsi, American Lithographic Co., 19 x 10 In. .....*illus*	1298.00
Clock, Bottle Cap, Neon, 8-Sided, 18 In.	880.00
Clock, Bottle Cap, Pepsi, Light Refreshment, Light-Up, Metal, Plastic, Glass, c.1950, 16 In.	660.00
Clock, Neon, Pepsi-Cola Bottle Cap Center, Round, 18 In.	880.00
Clock, Say Pepsi Please, Double Bubble	775.00
Display, Store, Santa, Riding Reindeer, 54 In.	351.00
Figure, Woman & Bottle, Sparkling Quality, Plaster, Painted, Plasto Mfg., 10½ In.	2218.00
Glass, Big Baby Huey, Brockway Glass Company, 1970s, 5⅛ x 2¹³⁄₁₆ In.	15.00
Glass, Daffy Duck, Black Letters, Hardee's Giveaway, Warner Bros., 1973, 6¼ x 3⅛ In.	6.00
Glass, Stained Glass Design, Red, Blue Band, 5⅛ In., 5 Piece	27.00
Pen, Pepsi-Cola, Double Dash, Bottle-Shape Clip, 1930s, 5 In.	56.00
Sign, Bottle, Die Cut, Metal, c.1930, 29½ x 8⅛ In.	305.00
Sign, Bottle Cap, Drink Pepsi-Cola, Neon, 31 In. Diam.	672.00
Sign, Bottle Cap & Bottle, Vertical, Tin, 18 x 48 In.	330.00
Sign, Drink Pepsi-Cola, Refreshing & Healthful, 5 Cents, Double Dash, Tin, 1920s, 6 x 17 In.	385.00
Sign, More Bounce To Ounce, Vertical, Tin, 18 x 48 In.	330.00
Sign, Pepsi-Cola 5 Cent, Double Dash, Tin, Embossed, Yellow Ground, 1920s, 17 x 6 In.	385.00
Sign, Reverse Glass, Pepsi-Cola 5 Cents, Black Ground, 23½ x 12 In.	708.00
Sign, Take Home, 6-Pack, Light-Up, 9 x 4 x 12 In.	55.00
Sign, Woman Holding Bottle, Paper, 1940s, 20 x 14½ In.	728.00
Syrup Can, 1960s, Gal.	35.00
Thermometer, Bigger, Better, Bottle, Tin Lithograph, Box, c.1930s, 15½ x 6⅛ In.	770.00
Thermometer, Have A Pepsi, Bottle Cap, Embossed, Tin, Yellow, Red, White, Blue, 27 x 7 In.	135.00
Thermometer, Wall, Sheet Metal, Red, White & Blue Logo, 27 x 8 In. .....*illus*	40.00
Tip Tray, Woman In Green Dress & Hat, Green Border, Oval, 6 x 4½ In. .....*illus*	1100.00
Toy, Truck, Friction, Pepsi Caps, Japan, 1950s, 5 In.	245.00
Vending Machine, Vendo Model No. 50, Double Dash, Coffin Style, F.L. Jacobs, 60 x 27 In.	2230.00

PERFUME BOTTLES are made of cut glass, pressed glass, art glass, silver, metal, enamel, and even plastic or porcelain. Although the small bottle to hold perfume was first made before the time of ancient Egypt, it is the nineteenth- and twentieth-century examples that interest today's collector. DeVilbiss Company has made atomizers of all types since 1888 but no longer makes the perfume bottle tops so popular with collectors. These were made from 1920 to 1968. The glass bottle may be by any of many manufacturers even if the atomizer is marked *DeVilbiss*. The word *factice,* which often appears in ads, refers to store display bottles. Glass or porcelain examples may be found under the appropriate name such as Lalique, Czechoslovakia, Glass-Bohemian, etc.

Acid Etched Decoration, Flowers, Blue Ground, 7½ x 1¾ In.	189.00
Advertising, Nina Ricci, L'Air Du Temps, Eau De Toilette, 8 x 3 In.	50.00
Amber, Blown Glass, 5¾ x 4 In.	37.00
Art Deco, Blue, Ulric De Varens, Veronese UDV, Atomizer, 5⅜ x 3 In.	28.00
Art Glass, Bulbous, Turquoise Swirl, Satin Finish, Silver Cap, Birmingham, c.1887	633.00
Blown, Smoke Gray, Bubble Optic Design, Iridescent Round Stopper, 5 In.	15.00
Blue Glass, Frosted, Swirled, Brass Fittings, 2⅜ In. *illus*	48.00
Bourjois, Evening In Paris, Blue Glass, Blue & Silver Tassel *illus*	11.00
Brass Tone Sling Back High Heel Shoe, Rhinestones, Bow, 4½ x 2⅛ In.	20.00
Cachet Creme, Satin Glass, 4½ In.	7.00
Cameo Glass, Red, Flowering Branch, Teardrop Shape, Lay Down, Hinged Lid, 5¾ In.	1035.00
Carnations, Engraved, Sterling Silver Cap, Mount, Chased Repousse, 3½ In.	400.00
Cased Black Glass, Gold Flecks, Atomizer, 5¾ x 2½ In.	185.00
Celadon, Square, Oval Reserves, Birds, Gold Trim, Square Finial, Paris, 4 x 4 In.	270.00
Celluloid, Glass Ball Stopper, 5½ In.	18.00
Clear Cased Glass, Pink Orchid Blossoms, Greg Held, Orient & Flume, Box, 7¼ In.	259.00
Cologne, 8-Sided, Pinched Waist, Cobalt Blue, Tooled Mouth, 1850-70, 6⅞ In.	616.00
Cologne, 8-Sided, Pinched Waist, Teal Blue, Tooled Mouth, 1850-70, 4¾ In.	1120.00
Cologne, 8-Sided, Rolled Lip, Purple Amethyst, 1850-70, 4⅞ In.	246.00
Cologne, 8-Sided, Rolled Lip, Teal Blue, 1850-70, 4¾ In.	560.00
Cologne, 12-Sided, Cobalt Blue, Pontil, 1850-70, 7½ In.	179.00
Cologne, 12-Sided, Emerald Green, Tooled Mouth, 1850-70, 6½ In.	179.00
Cologne, 12-Sided, Sloped Shoulders, Apple Green, 1850-70, 4⅞ In.	213.00
Cologne, 12-Sided, Sloped Shoulders, Cobalt Blue, 1850-70, 4⅞ In.	134.00
Cologne, 12-Sided, Sloped Shoulders, Cobalt Blue, Pontil, 1850-70, 7½ In.	123.00
Cologne, 12-Sided, Sloped Shoulders, Purple Amethyst, 1850-70, 6⅛ In.	157.00
Cologne, 12-Sided, Sloped Shoulders, Teal Green, 1850-70, 6⅛ In.	179.00
Cologne, 21 Vertical Ribs, Flared Lip, Open Pontil, Midwestern, c.1830, 4¾ In.	89.00
Cologne, Baby Thumbprint, Canary Yellow, Pontil, Air Trap Stopper, 7¼ In.	468.00
Cologne, Blue To White To Clear, Punty Cuttings, Star Cut Base, Hollow Stopper, 5 In.	198.00
Cologne, Bunker Hill Monument, Cobalt Blue, Tooled Lip, c.1830, 11¾ In. *illus*	560.00
Cologne, Caithness Glass, Paperweight Base, Scotland, 5 In.	117.00
Cologne, Clear, Amber Staining, Hexagonal, Leaf, Star Cut Base, Tear Stopper, 7½ In.	22.00
Cologne, Clear, Pink Threads, Ribbed, Hollow Stopper, Pontil, 5⅞ In.	275.00
Cologne, Cobalt Blue, Pinched Waist, Tooled Lip, c.1865, 4¾ In.	138.00
Cologne, Cobalt Blue To Clear, Frosted Panel, Punty Panel Cuttings, Star Cut Base, 4 In., Pair	1760.00
Cologne, Cobalt Blue To Clear, Loop Cutting, Pontil, Rolled Rim, Hollow Stopper, 5¾ In.	275.00
Cologne, Cobalt Blue To Clear, Loop Cuttings, Pontil, Star Cut Base, Hollow Stopper, 6 In.	770.00
Cologne, Cobalt Blue To Clear, Oval, Groove Cuttings, Hollow Stopper, 9¾ x 3½ In.	1265.00
Cologne, Cobalt Blue To White To Clear, Pear Shape, Punty Cuttings, Stopper, 6 In.	385.00
Cologne, Cut Glass, Bell Shape, Footed, Flowers, Thumbprint Panels, Enamel Top, 6¼ In.	230.00
Cologne, Cylindrical, Milk Glass, Opalescent, Powder Blue, 1840-60, 13½ In.	336.00
Cologne, Cylindrical, Opalescent, Robin's-Egg Blue, Pontil, 1840-60, 9½ In.	146.00
Cologne, Dancing Indians, Milk Glass, Opalescent, 1840-60, 5 In.	3360.00
Cologne, Diamonds, Shell, Scrolls, Cobalt Blue, Violin Shape, Rolled Lip, OP, 5⅝ In. *illus*	1792.00
Cologne, Dina, Clear, Label Under Glass, Pontil, Tooled Lip, 1890, 9¾ In.	200.00
Cologne, Double Overlay, Grape, Rose To White, Star Cut Base, Hollow Stopper, 5 x 2 In.	880.00
Cologne, Figural, Flower Vendor & Wife, Bouquet Stopper, J. Petit, 9 In., Pair	1175.00
Cologne, Figural, Jeweled Crown On Cushion, Relief Flowers, Cross Stopper, J. Petit, 8 x 7 In.	3525.00
Cologne, H.E. Swan & Co., Sun Colored Amethyst, Herringbone Corners, 1850-80, 9 In.	392.00
Cologne, Horn Of Plenty, Embossed, Blown, 8½ x 2⅛ In.	100.00
Cologne, Milk Glass, 5 Stars, 3 Panels, Roped Corners, Tooled Lip, c.1865, 9¼ In.	121.00
Cologne, Milk Glass, Bead & Flute, 1850-80, 8⅛ In.	123.00
Cologne, Powder Blue Opalescent, Applied Lip, Pontil, c.1850, 10¾ In.	130.00
Cologne, Ruby, Oval, Panels, Polished Rim, Neck, Stopper, 6½ In.	132.00
Cologne, Silver Overlay, Scrolling Leaves, Stopper, c.1910, 5 In.	176.00
Cologne, Toilet Water, Cobalt Blue, 12-Sided, Neck Ring, Flared Lip, 1860, 6 In.	123.00
Cologne, White To Clear, Cranberry Case, Baluster, Groove Cuttings, Stopper, 9 x 4 In.	468.00
Cologne, White To Clear, Cranberry Case, Groove, Punty Cuttings, 6½ In.	715.00
Coty, Muguet Des Bois, Cologne Sprinkler, 1950s	5.00

Pepsi-Cola, Calendar, 1910, Woman Sipping Pepsi, American Lithographic Co., 19 x 10 In. $1298.00

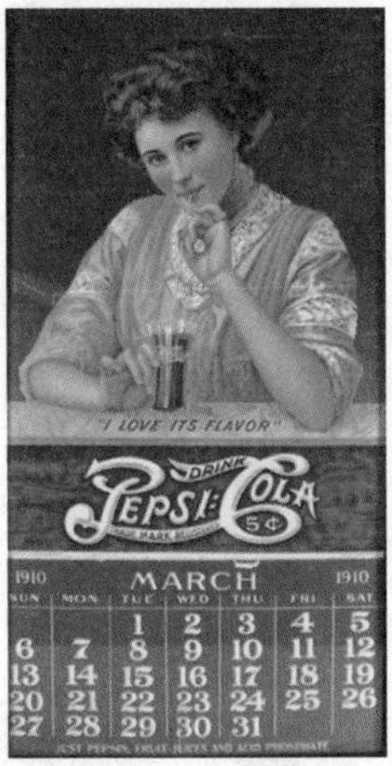

Pepsi-Cola, Thermometer, Wall, Sheet Metal, Red, White & Blue Logo, 27 x 8 In. $40.00

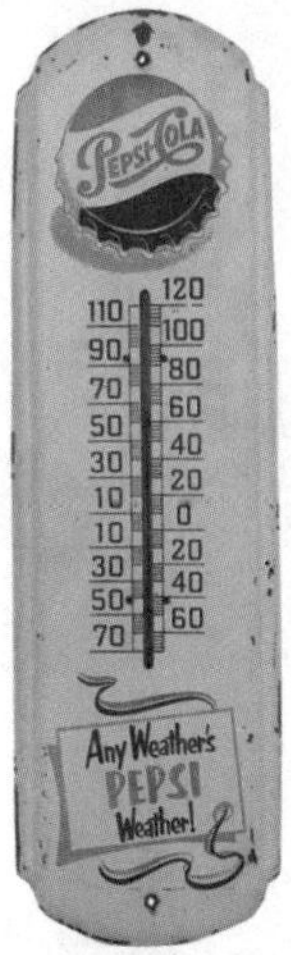

Pepsi-Cola, Tip Tray, Woman In Green Dress & Hat, Green Border, Oval, 6 x 4½ In. $1100.00

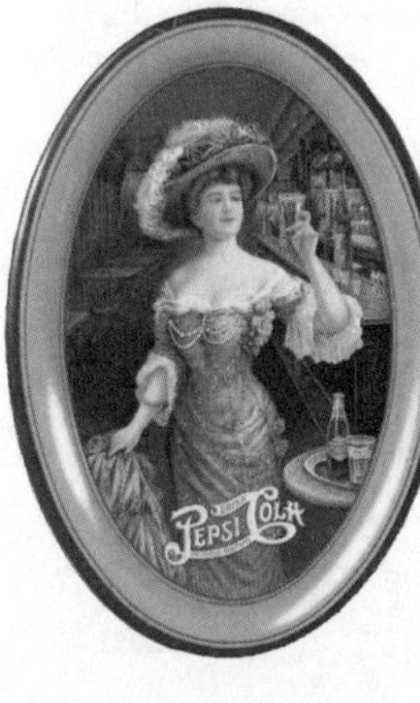

P

Perfume Bottle, Blue Glass, Frosted, Swirled, Brass Fittings, 2⅜ In. $48.00

Perfume Bottle, Bourjois, Evening In Paris, Blue Glass, Blue & Silver Tassel $11.00

Perfume Bottle, Cologne, Bunker Hill Monument, Cobalt Blue, Tooled Lip, c.1830, 11¾ In. $560.00

Perfume Bottle, Cologne, Diamonds, Shell, Scrolls, Cobalt Blue, Violin Shape, Rolled Lip, OP, 5⅝ In. $1792.00

Perfume Bottle, Dubarry, Blue Lagoon, Clear & Frosted Glass, Figural Stopper, J. Viard, c.1919, 4 In. $4440.00

Perfume Bottle, Glass, Green, Gold Top & Atomizer, 6 In. $230.00

Perfume Bottle, Harriet Hubbard Ayer, Muguet, Clear & Frosted Glass, Sepia, J. Viard, 1920s, 3¾ In. $570.00

Perfume Bottle, Langlois, Duska, Red & Black Glass, Art Deco, Box, 1920s, 4½ In. $780.00

Perfume Bottle, Lubin, Enigma, Crystal, Pyramid, Gold Sphinx, Box, Scarab Decoration, J. Viard, c.1921, 3½ In. $27600.00

Perfume Bottle, Lucien Lelong, Jabot, Clear & Frosted Glass, Box, c.1939, 3 In. $840.00

Perfume Bottle, Marquis, Niradjah, Black, Red Cased Stopper, Depinoix, Box, 1920s, 3¾ In. $7200.00

Crystal, Rectangular, Square Flat Stoppers, Quilted Pattern, 5¾ In., Pair	35.00
Cut Glass, Paneled, Uranium Yellow, Gilt Accents, Mushroom Stopper, 5 In.	374.00
Cut Glass, Pink, Bulb Spritzer, 3¼ x 2 In.	85.00
Cut Glass, Yellow Amber, Ringed & Paneled, Fan Scallops, Faceted Stopper, 9 In.	173.00
Dubarry, Blue Lagoon, Clear & Frosted Glass, Figural Stopper, J. Viard, c.1919, 4 In. . . *illus*	4440.00
Engraved Glass, Flat Sided, Silver Mounted, Continental, 1800s, 5¼ In.	120.00
Estee Lauder, Spellbound, Miniature, 1¼ In.	12.00
Faberge, 8-Sided, Alternating Concave, Flat Panels, Square Stopper	35.00
Faberge, Flambeau, 1960s, 3½ In.	58.00
Faberge, Satin Glass, Gold Arabesque Design, Satin Ball Stopper	55.00
Glass, Atlantis, 5½ x 2¾ In.	45.00
Glass, Green, Gold Top & Atomizer, 6 In. . . . *illus*	230.00
Globular, Raised Dots, Silk Hose, Atomizer Bulb, 1950s, 2½ In.	18.00
Gold, Gold Tone Cap, DeVilbiss Atomizer, 9 In.	460.00
Green, G.R. Bailey Perfumer, Purple Lilac, c.1900, 2¾ In.	25.00
Green, Green Crown Lid, Crown Perfume, London, c.1970, 1¾ In.	18.00
Harriet Hubbard Ayer, Muguet, Clear & Frosted Glass, Sepia, J. Viard, 1920s, 3¾ In. . . *illus*	570.00
Hattie Carnegie, Black Glass, Clear Stopper, Pyramid Shape, 4-Sided, 3 In.	510.00
Horse Cart, Blue Glass Keg, Enameled Flowers, Pincushion, 6½ x 3 In.	546.00
Hummingbird Stopper, Pink Glass, Wavy Design, Pearlescent, 5½ x 3¼ In.	25.00
Intoxication, Lime Cap, ½ Oz.	15.00
J.F. Fradley & Co., Art Deco, Crystal, Sterling Silver, c.1930, 6 In.	176.00
Lancome, Envol, Clear, Square, Molded, Dellhomme, 1958, 2 In.	575.00
Langlois, Duska, Red & Black Glass, Art Deco, Box, 1920s, 4½ In. . . . *illus*	780.00
Lubin, Enigma, Pyramid, Gold Sphinx, Box, Scarab, J. Viard, c.1921, 3½ In. . . . *illus*	27600.00
Lucien Lelong, Jabot, Clear & Frosted Glass, Box, c.1939, 3 In. . . . *illus*	840.00
Marquis, Niradjah, Black, Red Cased Stopper, Depinoix, Box, 1920s, 3¾ In. . . . *illus*	7200.00
Mikasa, Fan Shape Stopper, Label, Yugoslavia, 6 In.	65.00
Milk Glass, Embossed Latticework, Gold Stripe, Trim, Blue, 6½ In.	35.00
Milk Glass, Gold Trim, Atomizer, 3⅝ In.	36.00
Milk Glass, Violets Barrel, 2 In.	6.00
Monkey, Plush, Mohair, Head Comes Off, Label, Schuco, 5 In. . . . *illus*	330.00
Ofnah, Lead Glass Crystal, Foil Label, Germany, 1940s, 6½ x 3 In.	145.00
Opaque White, Teal Blue Decoration, Striped, Gilt, Painted Profile, 9⅜ In.	345.00
Overshot, Cranberry Flashing, Melon Ribbed Drapery Swag, Gilt, Atomizer, 5 In.	58.00
P. Brecher, Sous La Charmille, Enamel Flowers, J. Viard, Depinoix, c.1924, 2¾ In. . . . *illus*	2520.00
Palais Royal, Blue Opaline, Hinged, Ormolu Filigree, Eglomise, 1800s	525.00
Paneled Glass, Tortoiseshell Color, Tapered, Faceted Stopper, 7 In.	58.00
Paperweight, Green Heart, Glass Dabber, Imbedded Flowers, 3½ x 2¾ In.	9.00
Paperweight, Red Heart, Glass Dabber, Imbedded Flowers, 3½ x 2¾ In.	9.00
Porcelain, Glass, Cobalt Blue Enamel, c.1880, 2½ x 1 In.	410.00
Porcelain, Painted, Greek Figures, Pink, Lavender, Blue, Gold, 2½ x 2 In.	38.00
Prince Matchabelli, Wind Song, Cologne Spray Mist, Green Glitter, 1960s	5.00
Richard Hudnet, Gemey Perfume Cologne, 3 Fl. Oz.	22.00
Ritz Blue, Depression Glass, Mold Blown, Ground Glass Stopper, 5¾ In.	66.00
Set, Aphrodisia, Flambeau, Woodhue, Box, 1960s, 3 In., 3 Piece	49.00
Squat, Oval, Pressed Glass, Bakelite Shoulder, Gold Metal Band, 3 x 1¾ In.	22.00
Sterling Silver, Classical, Dolphin Shape, Melon-Ribbed Cap, 3 In.	400.00
Stopper, Overlay, Flowerhead Band, Heart Reserve, Sterling, 5 In.	176.00
Swirls, Bubbles, Shouldered, Embossed C In Square, Glass Co., 5⅝ In.	15.00
Teardrop Shape, Blue Glass, Red & Blue Banded Aventurine, Venetian, 1800s, 3 In.	71.00
Yellow, Flowers, Butterfly, Teardrop Shape, Twisted Silver Cap, Laydown, 4 In.	1150.00

PETERS & REED Pottery Company of Zanesville, Ohio, was founded by John D. Peters and Adam Reed in 1897. Chromal, Landsun, Montene, Pereco, and Persian are some of the art lines that were made. The company, which became Zane Pottery in 1920 and Gonder Pottery in 1941, closed in 1957. Peters & Reed pottery was unmarked.

Bowl, Dragonfly, Blue Glaze, 5⅛ In.	50.00
Bowl, Molded Vines, Green Matte Glaze, Folded Rim, 3 x 8 In.	196.00
Bowl, Moss Aztec, No. 403, Flowers, 3½ x 2¼ In.	28.00
Candleholder, Marbleized, 5½ x 1⅜ In.	28.00
Figurine, Frog, Green Matte, Open Mouth, Arts & Crafts, 3¾ x 2¾ In.	99.00
Flower Frog, Frog Shape, Green Crystalline Glaze, 2½ x 5 In. . . . *illus*	45.00
Vase, 3 Lion Heads, Connected By Floral Garlands, Brown Drip Glaze, 14 In. . . . *illus*	127.00
Vase, Landsun, Scenic, Yellow, Green, Brown, 9¾ In.	187.00

Perfume Bottle, Monkey, Plush, Mohair, Head Comes Off, Label, Schuco, 5 In. **$330.00**

Perfume Bottle, P. Brecher, Sous La Charmille, Enamel Flowers, J. Viard, Depinoix, c.1924, 2¾ In. **$2520.00**

TIP

To clean the residue out of an old perfume bottle, try this: Spray some window cleaner in the bottle, then rinse. If this fails, partially fill the bottle with nail polish remover and shake it. Wait about 15 minutes, empty, and rinse. It may help to poke at the residue with a shish kebab skewer. Do not get any liquids on the label. Avoid harsh glass stain removers.

Peters & Reed, Flower Frog, Frog Shape, Green Crystalline Glaze, 2½ x 5 In.
$45.00

Peters & Reed, Vase, 3 Lion Heads, Connected By Floral Garlands, Brown Drip Glaze, 14 In.
$127.00

Peters & Reed, Vase, Marbleized, Brown, Blue & Black High Glaze, Rolled Rim, 8 In.
$115.00

Vase, Marbleized, Brown, Blue & Black High Glaze, Rolled Rim, 8 In. . . . .*illus*	115.00
Vase, Standard Ware, Flowers, Slip Decorated, 9¾ x 6 In.	55.00
Vase, Zane Ware, Persian Blue Glaze, Baluster Shape, 10½ In.	173.00
Wall Pocket, Moss Aztec, Grapes, Vine, Coppery Matte Glaze, F. Ferrell, 7¾ In.	127.00

PETRUS REGOUT, *see Maastricht category.*

PEWABIC POTTERY was founded by Mary Chase Perry Stratton in 1903 in Detroit, Michigan. The company made many types of art pottery, including pieces with matte green glaze and an iridescent crystalline glaze. The company continued working until the death of Mary Stratton in 1961. It was reactivated by Michigan State University in 1968.

Bowl, Red & Turquoise Metallic Glaze, Flared, Impressed Mark, 2½ x 10 In.	575.00
Tile, Cat, Seated, Mottled Purple & Brown Matte Glaze, Raised, Frame, 7½ In.	675.00
Tile, Leaf, Acorns, Arts & Crafts, Black Glaze Base, Gold Iridescent, 5¾ x 5¾ In.	165.00
Tile, Sailboat On Water, Relief Molded, Wood Frame, c.1950, 6 x 6 In.	110.00
Vase, Black, Purple & Blue Volcanic Glaze, Flared, 15½ In.	4600.00
Vase, Blue Metallic Luster Glaze, Bulbous, Footed, 5 In. . . . .*illus*	374.00
Vase, Blue Over Gray Iridescent Glaze, Shouldered, 7⅝ In.	460.00
Vase, Bottle Shape, Leathery Green & Oxblood Matte Glaze, 7 x 4¾ In.	720.00
Vase, Iridescent Glaze, c.1920, 7½ x 5 In.	1053.00
Vase, Red, Green, Yellow, Iridescent Metallic Drip Glaze, Shouldered, Impressed Mark, 13 x 7½ In.	4750.00
Vase, Red, Blue, Gray Metallic Glaze, Shouldered, Marked, 6 x 5½ In.	230.00
Vase, Red & Green Metallic Drip Glaze Over Blue Ground, Flared, Impressed Mark, 3½ x 3½ In. . .	550.00

PEWTER is a metal alloy of tin and lead. Some of the pewter made after 1840 has a slightly different composition and is called Britannia metal. This later type of pewter was worked by machine; the earlier pieces were made by hand. In the 1920s pewter came back into fashion and pieces were often marked *Genuine Pewter*. Eighteenth-, nineteenth-, and twentieth-century examples are listed here.

Baptismal Bowl, Calder, Pedestal, Eagle Mark, Providence, R.I., 10⅛ In.	8250.00
Basin, J. Weekes, Marked, 5¾ In. Diam.	350.00
Basin, Thomas Melville II, Marked, c.1796-1824, 2 x 8 In.	575.00
Beaker, Tulip Form, Footed, Reeded Fillet, Touchmark, 1900s, 4 In.	89.00
Bedpan, Screw-Off Handle, Britain, 11 In.	179.00
Bowl, Harbeson, Hallmark, 11⅛ In.	1100.00
Bowl, Wassail, United States Shield On Side, Handles, Dutch, c.1785	950.00
Box, Tobacco, Cover, Ben Lord, Oval, Engraved, Late 18th Century	250.00
Candlestick, 17th Century Style, Bell Base, Circular Drip Tray, 1900s, 7¾ In.	90.00
Candlestick, Baluster Stem, Round, Stepped Base, Push-Ups, 9 In., Pair	201.00
Candlestick, Bulbous Base, Continental, 18th Century, 6 In., Pair	353.00
Candlestick, Inverted Cone, Ring Stems, Removable Bobeches, New York, 12 In., Pair	431.00
Candlestick, Square Base, Cut Corners, Acorn Knop, Continental, c.1700, 6 In., Pair	3585.00
Candlestick, Trumpet Base, Beaded Knop, Turned Design, Reeded Flange, 1800s, 2¼ In. . . .	269.00
Chalice, Leonard Reed & Barton, Marked, 6¾ In.	142.00
Chamber Pot, Handle, Smooth Patina, Dutch, c.1660, Child's	395.00
Charger, Lion, Flower, Bird, PY In A Beaded Tombstone Shape, Touchmarks, 16¼ In.	2950.00
Charger, Thomas Haward, Triple Reeded, Arms In Crossed Plume, c.1680, 26¾ In.	9415.00
Charger, Touchmarks, England, 16¾ In.	178.00
Clock, Liberty & Co., Tudric, Art Nouveau, c.1900, 4 In.	287.00
Coffee Urn, Baluster, 3 Scroll Legs, Ebonized Wood Feet, Finial, Handle, Dutch, 13 In. . .*illus*	212.00
Coffeepot, Ashbil Griswold, Bulbous, Polished, Repainted Handle, Finial, Marked, 10½ In. . .	373.00
Coffeepot, Baluster, Round Foot, Gooseneck Spout, Ebonized Handle, Finial, Dome Lid, 12 In.	400.00
Coffeepot, Baluster Shape, Wood Knob, Germany, 9 In.	59.00
Coffeepot, Boardman & Hart, Double Bulbous, Ivory Finial, Polished, Marked, N.Y., c.1830, 11½ In.	518.00
Coffeepot, F. Porter, Gooseneck Spout, Shaped Black Handle, Mushroom Finial, 10½ In. . . .	176.00
Coffeepot, G. Richardson, Polished, Repainted Handle & Finial, Cranston, R.I., c.1830, 11 In.	633.00
Coffeepot, George III Style, Shaped Spout, Scroll Handle, c.1900, 10 In. . . . .*illus*	47.00
Coffeepot, Israel Trask, Lighthouse, Bright-Cut Engraved Shield, Mass., 11¾ In.	2000.00
Coffeepot, Lighthouse, Polished, Wood Finial, Repainted Handle, 10¼ In.	431.00
Coffeepot, Roswell Gleason, 12½ In. . . . .*illus*	127.00
Coffeepot, Touchmark, A. Griswold, Conn., c.1842, 11¼ In.	403.00
Compote, Woodbury & Colton, Round, Dome Foot, 4 x 6¾ In.	550.00
Cup, Campbell & Co., U-Shape Bowl, 2 Double Curve Handles, Touchmarks, c.1840, Pt.	494.00
Cup, Communion, Calder, Tulip Shape, Marked, 6 In., Pair	1600.00
Cup, U-Shape, 2 S-Shape Handles, Dome Foot, Touchmarks, c.1775, Pt., 6½ In.	135.00

Cup, Wrigglework, 2 S-Shape Handles, Reeded Rim, Touchmark, c.1700, 7 In. 4484.00
Dish, Art Nouveau, Punched, Embossed Hearts, Swirls, Continental, c.1900, 14¼ In. 225.00
Dish, Deep, 9⅜ In. 215.00
Dish, Thomas King, Reeded Rim, Initials SW, Touchmark, c.1700, 16½ In. 1681.00
Ewer, Germany, c.1890, 21 In. 94.00
Flagon, Baluster Form, Hinged Flat Lid, Cast Thumbpiece, C-Scroll Handle, 10½ In. 4600.00
Flagon, Boardman & Co., Eagle Touchmark, 11 In. 960.00
Flagon, Communion, Sheldon & Feltman, c.1847, 10½ In. 374.00
Flagon, Heart Shape Lid, Acorn Thumbpiece, France, 1900s, 6½ In. 191.00
Flagon, Hunter With Dog, Pewter Lid, 1½ Liter, 13 In. 920.00
Flagon, Johann Christoph Heyne, Touchmark, Lancaster, c.1770, 11¾ x 6¼ In. 96000.00
Flagon, Reeded Drum, Knopped Dome Lid, Chairback Thumbpiece, c.1780, 12 In. 5381.00
Flagon, Shield, Weber Handwerks Zunft Zu Nurnberg, Animals On Base, c.1910, 23 In. 1265.00
Flagon, Shoemaker, Pewter Lid, 1½ Liter, 13 In. 1064.00
Flagon, Spire, Filleted Drum, S-Handle, Fishtail Terminal, Dome Lid, c.1725, 9 In. 5384.00
Flagon, T.D. Boardman, Scrolled Handle, 3-Wafer Spire Finial, 12 In. 460.00
Flagon, T.D. Boardman, Tapered, Dome Top, Scroll Thumbpiece, Handle, Touchmarks, 11 In. 2100.00
Flagon, Thomas Carpenter, Spire, Dome Lid, Chairback Thumbpiece, Touchmarks, c.1750, 9¾ In. . 7847.00
Food Carrier, Screw-On Top, Lift Top, 1900, 6½ In. 200.00
Jug, Ale, Naval, Bulbous, Overlapping Handle, Inscription, c.1828, 9½ In. 7622.00
Jug, Ale, Spout, Bulbous, Reeded Fillet, Curved Handle, Ball Terminal, c.1800, 9½ In. 1077.00
Jug, Spout, Ring Attached To Lid, 10¾ In. 59.00
Kettle, Hanging, Engraved, Switzerland, c.1826, 12 In. 369.00
Lamp, Camphene, 3¼ In. 55.00
Lamp, Camphene, Hand, 8¼ In. 187.00
Lamp, Fluid, Blown Glass Font, Hinged Reservoir, C-Scroll Handle, 14½ x 5½ In. 288.00
Lamp, Oil, No Globe, 11 In. 137.00
Lamp, Oil, Spout, 10¼ In. 105.00
Lamp, Oil, Spout, Flemish, 10¼ In. 66.00
Lamp, Open Pan, Saucer, Hinged Spout, Flemish, 5½ In. 83.00
Lamp, Whale Oil, Bell Form Font, Saucer, 7¼ In. 121.00
Lamp, Whale Oil, Double Bull's-Eye Lenses, 8¼ In. 605.00
Lamp, Whale Oil, Double Bull's-Eye Lenses, 8¾ In. 495.00
Lamp, Whale Oil, R. Gleason, Marked, 6½ In. 356.00
Lamp, Whale Oil, Roswell Gleason, Jacobs Mark 149, 6 In. 100.00
Lamp, Whale Oil, Whitlock, Saucer Base & Handle, Heavy Oxidation, Marked 225.00
Lamp Base, R. Gleason, Whale Oil Burner, Mass., Touchmark, c.1871, 5¾ In. 230.00
Measure, Baluster, Bud Thumbpiece, Marked, FRA, 5 x 3¼ In. 1304.00
Measure, Baluster, Flat Lid, Embryo Shell Thumbpiece, Touchmarks, Scotland, c.1826, Qt. . 3586.00
Measure, Bulbous, Domed Lid, Shell Thumbpiece, Glasgow, c.1840, Imperial ½ Gill 359.00
Measure, Bulbous, Domed Lid, Shell Thumbpiece, Glasgow, Imperial Pt., 6½ In. 515.00
Measure, Double Volute Thumbpiece, Flat Lid, S-Scroll Handle, Ball Terminal, c.1740, Qt. .. 1682.00
Measure, Fullerton, Paisley, Baluster, Flat Lid, Shell Thumbpiece, Stamped, Gal., 4¼ In. 852.00
Measure, Guernsey Channel Islands, Lid, Double Acorn Thumbpiece, Incised EN, 7½ In. ... 309.00
Measure, Harvester, Curved Handle, Ball Terminal, Touchmarks, c.1880, ½ Pt., 5 In. 515.00
Measure, Harvester, Squat, Curved Handle, Stamped, c.1880, ½ Gal. 1345.00
Measure, Loftus 321 Oxford St., Brass Rim, Mark, Pt., 4½ In. 104.00
Measure, M. Fothergill & Sons, Harvester Shape, S-Handle, Touchmark, c.1800, 7 In. 1971.00
Measure, Musten & Son, Haystack, Marked, Cork, Ireland, 19th Century, 3½ In. 717.00
Measure, W.R. Loftus Ltd., Brass Rim, Mark, Qt. 77.00
Measures, Graduated, Baluster, Quart To 1/12 Pint, 5 Piece 230.00
Mold, Cake, Fruit, Fluted, Continental, 1766, 13 In. 325.00
Mold, Candle, Tin Loop Handle, 15 In. 330.00
Mold, Ice Cream, E. & Co., Flying Witch Form, Marked, 5¼ In. 343.00
Mold, Ice Cream, Multi-Fruit Form, Cylindrical Sides, Fluted, 3 Parts, Marked, 3 Qt. 150.00
Mug, Abbott, Marked, 19, No. 3, Engraved, ½ Pt. 98.00
Mug, Ale, England, c.1780, ½ Pt. 265.00
Mug, Beaker Shape, Flared Rim, S-Shaped Handle, Flat Thumb Rest, 1700s, 3¼ In. 808.00
Mug, Bulbous, Scrolled Handle, Flared Footed Base, Monogram, 3⅝ In. 209.00
Mug, Carpenter & Hamberger, Tapered, S-Shaped Handle, c.1800, Imperial Qt. 1075.00
Mug, Ear Shape Handle, Touchmark, Crown Over, V.R., 4½ In. 275.00
Mug, Henry Joseph, Acanthus Leaf Handle, 18th Century, Qt. 695.00
Mug, J. Danforth, Touchmark, Crown X, Pt., 4½ In. 1892.00
Mug, John Townsend, Tulip Form, London, c.1760, Pt. 750.00
Mug, Squat, Tulip Shape, Single Curve Handle, c.1820, Pt. 202.00
Mug, T.D & S. Boardman, Cylindrical, Flared, C-Scroll Handle, Touchmark TD & SB, Qt., 6 In. 900.00

Pewabic, Vase, Blue Metallic Luster Glaze, Bulbous, Footed, 5 In.
$374.00

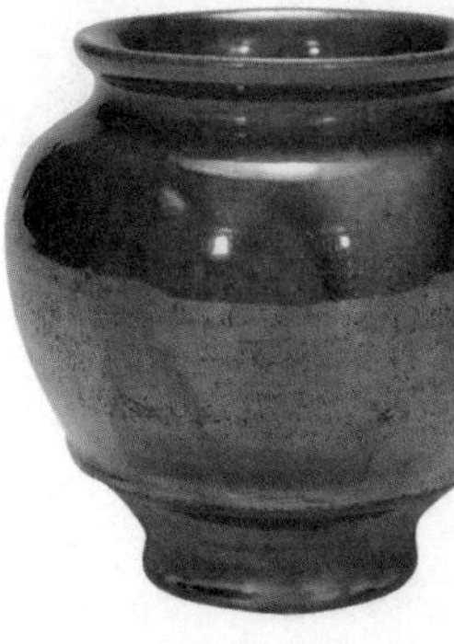

Pewter, Coffee Urn, Baluster, 3 Scroll Legs, Ebonized Wood Feet, Finial, Handle, Dutch, 13 In.
$212.00

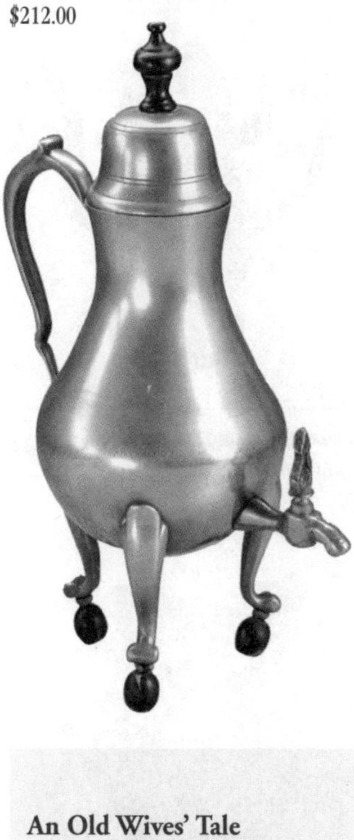

An Old Wives' Tale

Recently some have thought that eating from pewter plates can give you lead poisoning. If that were true, most of our ancestors would have died before their time. It is safe to serve any type of food on either shiny or dull pewter. The same tin that is in pewter has been used for years in the cans that store our food.

Pewter, Coffeepot, George III Style, Shaped Spout, Scroll Handle, c.1900, 10 In. $47.00

Pewter, Coffeepot, Roswell Gleason, 12½ In. $127.00

Pewter, Teapot, T.D. Boardman, Connecticut, 9¼ In. $397.00

Pewter, Vase, Hammered, 3 Handles, Impressed Mark, Tudric, 11½ x 6 In. $1020.00

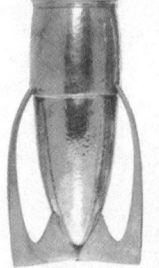

Mug, Tappit Hen, Crested, Erect Thumbpiece, Reeded Waist, Scotland, c.1800, 11¼ In.	1075.00
Mug, Tappit Hen, Crested, Erect Thumbpiece, Scotland, Chopin Capacity, c.1800, 9½ In.	2129.00
Mug, Tappit Hen, Domed Lid, Erect Thumbpiece, Initials, Scotland, c.1800, 11 In.	896.00
Mug, Tappit Hen, Lid, 5-Part Hinge, Crested, Scotland, Pt., 12 In.	501.00
Mug, Tappit Hen, Muirhead Moffat & Co., Scotland, Paper Label, c.1800, 4⅜ In.	2467.00
Mug, Tappit Hen, Reeded Waist, Mutchkin, Initials IR, Scotland, c.1800, 7¼ In.	1525.00
Mug, Truncated Cone Body, Single Curve Handle, Marked, c.1840, Gal., 11¼ In.	896.00
Pitcher, Bulbous, Long Spout, Bar Support, Touchmark, Switzerland, 12 In.	115.00
Pitcher, F. Porter, Bulbous Shape, Incised Lines, Shaped Handle, 6 In.	358.00
Pitcher, Syrup, 6¼ x 3½ In.	170.00
Pitcher, Water, Boardman & Hart, Hinged Lid, Spout Strainer, 7½ In.	205.00
Plate, Badger, 8½ In.	240.00
Plate, Broad Rim, Beaded, Shallow Bouge, 17th Century, 9 In.	583.00
Plate, E. Danforth, Touchmark, 12 In.	1225.00
Plate, J Martine, Single Reed Rim, Marked, 11 In.	375.00
Plate, John Underhill, Wrigglework, Reeded, Tulips, Leaves, Touchmarks, c.1720, 8⅝ In.	2802.00
Plate, Love Philadelphia, Touchmark, Lovebirds Under Tulip, London, 7¾ In.	176.00
Plate, Lovebird, London, Marked, 11 x 1½ In.	225.00
Plate, Nathaniel Austin, Reeded Brim, Initials SC, Cartouche, Hallmarks, 13½ In.	440.00
Plate, Thomas Danforth II, Hammered Bouge, Marked, 7¾ In.	143.00
Plate, W. Billings, Polished, Marked, c.1791-1806, 8¼ In.	862.00
Plate, Wm. Kirby, Single Reed, Eagle With Snake In Beak, Rising Sun, Marked, 9 In.	2550.00
Platter, Game, Kayserzinn, c.1900, 22 In.	246.00
Platter, Oval, Divided, Handles, 4 Ball Feet, England, 15½ x 21 In.	172.00
Platter, Thomas Alderson, GR IV, Oval, Touchmark, 17½ x 13¾ In.	1125.00
Platter, Warming, Hollow, Ball Feet, Cork Lined Plug, Townsend, Compton, Thomas, 20 In.	172.00
Porringer, Boardman, Round, Boss Bottom, Crown Handle, Touchmark, c.1830, 5 In.	382.00
Porringer, Commemorative, Queen Anne, England, c.1702, 6 In.	2800.00
Porringer, Crown Handle, Marked, IG, c.1800, 4⅝ In.	316.00
Porringer, Pierced Handle, 2 x 5¼ In.	55.00
Porringer, Pierced Twin Ears, Knurled Design In Bowl, Crowned Rose Touchmark, c.1700, 4½ In.	269.00
Porringer, Samuel Hamlin Jr., Pierced Handle, Engraved WW, 5¼ In.	450.00
Porringer, T.D. & S. Boardman, Old English Handle, 4 In. Diam.	204.00
Porringer, T.D. & S. Boardman, Polished, Crown Handle, Linen Mark, c.1830, 5 In. Diam.	518.00
Salt, Master, 17th Century Style, Octagonal Form, Touchmark BB, 1900s, 3¾ In.	358.00
Salt, Trencher, Cylindrical, Narrow Skirt Foot, Oval Molded Lip, c.1700, 1⅛ In., Pair	1232.00
Salt, Trencher, Round, Bulbous, Touchmark RB, c.1720, 1½ In.	538.00
Salt, Trencher, Round, Squat, Bulbous, Narrow Fillet, c.1720, 1⅜ In., Pair	1075.00
Snuffbox, Hancock & Jessop, Shoe Shape, Marked, 3¾ In.	219.00
Snuffbox, Hinged Lid, Engraved, WE, ¾ In. x 2¼ x 3 In.	327.00
Spoon, Child's, c.1660, 3½ In.	250.00
Spoon, Horse Hoof Knop, Shield Stem, Dutch, Mid 17th Century	295.00
Sugar, Sellew & Co., Acorn Final, Double Shaped Scroll Handles, Flared Base, 7½ In.	385.00
Sugar & Creamer, Wood Finial, 4¼-In. Sugar, 3¼-In. Creamer	182.00
Tankard, Allen Bright, S-Handle, Chairback Thumbpiece, Touchmark, Bristol, c.1750, 6½ In.	1682.00
Tankard, Allen Bright, Tulip Shape, Lid, Chairback Thumbpiece, Touchmark, c.1750, 6 In.	2018.00
Tankard, Anthony Saint Jacob, Cornwall, 8 In.	1463.00
Tankard, Barrel Terminal, IDS On Lip Of Lid, Ram's-Horn Thumbpiece, Qt.	7250.00
Tankard, Ingram & Hunt, Tulip Shape, Domed Lid, Palmette Thumbpiece, c.1780, 1½ Pt.	3025.00
Tankard, Reed & Barton, Admiral George Dewey, Glass Bottom, Hinged Lid, 9 x 4⅝ In.	529.00
Tankard, Samuel Cox, Domed Lid, Chairback Thumbpiece, Touchmark, c.1820, ½ Pt.	2915.00
Teapot, Bachelor's, Dixon & Son, Marked, 3½ In.	82.00
Teapot, Boardman & Hall, Philada., Black Painted Pewter Handle, Finial, 7½ In.	374.00
Teapot, Boardman & Hart, Polished, Repainted Handle & Finial, Touchmark, N.Y., c.1830, 7 In.	316.00
Teapot, Boardman & Hart, Polished, Marked, N.Y., 8 In.	374.00
Teapot, Boardman & Hart, Polished, New York, 8 In.	374.00
Teapot, Curtiss, Pear Shape, Footed, Interior Touchmark, Stamped 4 Times In Square, 8 In.	173.00
Teapot, Dunham, Marked, 12 In.	247.00
Teapot, Hiram Yale & Co., Polished, Wafer Finial, Painted, Marked, 7½ In.	345.00
Teapot, Jade, Agate Insets, Brass Beak, Strainer, Chinese, 9 In.	185.00
Teapot, Putnam, Gooseneck Spout, Shaped Black Handle, Floral Finial, 8½ In.	248.00
Teapot, R. Gleason, Painted Black Handle, Wooden Wafer Finial, Touchmark, 8¾ In.	402.00
Teapot, Scrolled Handle, Paneled Spout, Wafer Finial, 11½ In.	345.00
Teapot, Smith & Co. 2, Scrolled Handle, Petal Wafer Finial, Touchmark, 6½ In.	201.00
Teapot, Smith & Co., Urn Form, Flower-Form Knopped Dome Lid	250.00
Teapot, T.D. Boardman, Connecticut, 9¼ In. ....*illus*	397.00

Teapot, Thomas Danforth Boardman, Lion Touchmark, Connecticut, 1805-1850, 8½ In. ...	201.00
Tobacco Jar, Cover, Original Press, England, 18th Century	250.00
Tray, Osiris, c.1905, 27 In.	287.00
Tureen, Repousse Design, Pomegranate Finial, Early 19th Century, 10 x 14½ In.	395.00
Vase, Hammered, 3 Handles, Impressed Mark, Tudric, 11½ x 6 In. .... *illus*	1020.00
Vase, Hammered, Bulbous, Flared, Footed, 3 Upper Handles, Patina, Mark, Tudric, 11½ x 6 In. ..	350.00
Vase, Liberty & Co., Arts & Crafts, Tudric, Poplar Trees, For Old Time's Sake, 8 In.	429.00

PHOENIX BIRD, or Flying Phoenix, is the name given to a blue-and-white kitchenware popular between 1900 and World War II. A variant is known as Flying Turkey. Most of this dinnerware was made in Japan for sale in the dime stores in America. It is still being made.

Creamer, Flying Turkey, White Ground, 3¼ In.	25.00
Salt & Pepper, Flying Turkey, Marked Japan	36.00
Teapot, Flying Turkey, Blue & White, 4½ In.	95.00

PHOENIX GLASS Company was founded in 1880 in Pennsylvania. The firm made commercial products, such as lampshades, bottles, and glassware. Collectors today are interested in the "Sculptured Artware" made by the company from the 1930s until the mid-1950s. Some pieces of Phoenix glass are very similar to those made by the Consolidated Lamp and Glass Company. Phoenix made Reuben Blue, lavender, and yellow pieces. These colors were not used by Consolidated. In 1970 Phoenix became a division of Anchor Hocking, then was sold to the Newell Group in 1987. The company is still working.

Pitcher, Amberina, Lincoln Drape, Square Mouth, Reeded Amber Handle, 7¼ In.	201.00
Pitcher, Green Spatter, Bulbous, Flared Neck & Rim, Clear Reeded Handle, 8½ In.	144.00
Vase, Blue, White Birds Perched On Tree, Rectangular, Bulbous Sides, 6½ In., Pair	86.00
Vase, Figural, Seldon, Mold Blown, Dancing Muses, Pan, Blue, Cream, 12 In.	588.00
Vase, Pan With Nudes, Blown-Out, Gold, White Ground, 11½ In.	260.00
Vase, Phlox, Gray Ground, 11½ In.	50.00

PHONOGRAPHS, invented by Thomas Edison in 1877, have been made by many firms. This category also includes other items associated with the phonograph. Jukeboxes and Records are listed in their own categories.

Brunswick, Model 200, Disc, Floor Model, Oak, Oval, Grill, 12-In. Turntable, c.1923	250.00
Busy Bee, Grand, Disc, Red Morning Glory Horn, Oak, Silver, c.1905	200.00
Columbia, Model AJ, Disc, Oak Case, Black Horn, Brass Bell, 1903-05	1450.00
Columbia, Type BS, Eagle, Coin-Operated, Oak, Curved Glass Top, c.1898, 16 x 13 In.	4425.00
Edison, Diamond Disc, Chippendale, Floor Model, Edison Discs, 12-In. Turntable, c.1922, 51 In. .	382.00
Edison, Diamond Disc, Model C250, Floor Model, Oak, c.1915, 51½ In. .... *illus*	274.00
Edison, Fireside, Model A, Cylinder, Compact Table Model, Oak, Red Horn, c.1909 .....*illus*	385.00
Edison, Gem, Model B, Table Model, Black Horn, Wood Case, 1 Cylinder, 1905 ....*illus*	783.00
Edison, Gem, Model C, Cylinder, Table Model, Ribbed Horn, c.1907	499.00
Edison, Standard, Model E, Cygnet Horn, C Reproducer, Oak Case, c.1911	875.00
Edison, Triumph, Model E, Cygnet Horn, Cylinder, Oak, Speed Regulater, c.1910	3250.00
Fern-O-Grand Co., Disc, Baby Grand, Piano Shape, Mahogany, 78 RPM, 36 x 26 In.	470.00
Graphophone, Columbia, Type AP, No. 39608, Gilt Line, Transfer, 1887, 12 In.	323.00
Mandolina, Organette, Roller, Hand Crank, Walnut Case, Paper Roll, 20-Key	91.00
Needle Case, Cover, Talking Machine, Round, Tin	112.00
Sign, Victor Talking Machines, Dog, Machine, Sold Here, Tin Lithograph, 13½ x 20 In. .*illus*	1525.00
Sign, You Know It By This, His Master's Voice, Nipper, Enamel, 1910s, 28 x 20 In.	2355.00
Victor, Type E, Monach Junior, Oak Case, Black Horn, Belled, 7-In. Turntable, 9½ In.	999.00
Victor Victrola, VV-IXA, Tabletop, Oak, 2 Doors, 12-In. Turntable, 14 x 16 In.	165.00
Victrola, Figurine, Nipper, Plaster, 20 In.	70.00
Victrola, Model IX, Mahogany Case, Original Label, 2 Doors, 22 x 16 In. ....*illus*	440.00

PHOTOGRAPHY items are listed here. The first photograph was a view from a window in France taken in 1826. The commercially successful photograph started with the daguerreotype introduced in 1839. Today all sorts of photographs and photographic equipment are collected. Albums were popular in Victorian times. Cartes de visite, popular after 1854, were mounted on 2½-by-4-inch cardboard. Cabinet cards were introduced in 1866. These were mounted on 4¼ x 6½-inch cards. Stereo views are listed under Stereo Card. The cases for daguerreotypes are listed in the Gutta-Percha category. Stereoscopes are listed in their own section.

Phonograph, Edison, Diamond Disc, Model C250, Floor Model, Oak, c.1915, 51½ In. $274.00

Phonograph, Edison, Fireside, Model A, Cylinder, Compact Table Model, Oak, Red Horn, c.1909 $385.00

P

Phonograph, Edison, Gem, Model B, Table Model, Black Horn, Wood Case, 1 Cylinder, 1905
$783.00

Phonograph, Sign, Victor Talking Machines, Dog, Machine, Sold Here, Tin Lithograph, 13½ x 20 In.
$1525.00

Phonograph, Victrola, Model IX, Mahogany Case, Original Label, 2 Doors, 22 x 16 In.
$440.00

TIP

If you have an old, valuable tintype or photograph, have a copy made. Display the copy, and keep the original away from sunlight and dirt.

Album, Cabinet Card, Admiral Dewey Photo On Cover, Holds 28 Cards, 11 x 9 In. ..... *illus*	359.00
Album, Hard Cover, Gothic Design, Buckle Closures, 1860s, 6 x 5½ In.	185.00
Albumen Print, Bird's-Eye View Of Battlefield At Wounded Knee, 1891, 4¼ x 7¼ In.	837.00
Albumen Print, Market Square, Providence, 6 x 8 In.	88.00
Albumen Print, Wood Choppers' Huts In Virginia Forest, A.J. Russell, Mat, 10 x 12½ In.	405.00
Ambrotype, Abraham Lincoln, Velvet Lined Case, Cooper Union, ⅙ Plate	8365.00
Ambrotype, Black Baby, Leather Case, 1860s, ⅙ Plate	696.00
Ambrotype, Black Woman, Leather Case, 1860s, ⅙ Plate	321.00
Ambrotype, Civil War, New Hampshire Volunteer, Ruby Glass, Gilt Mat, Case, ⅙ Plate	176.00
Ambrotype, Civil War, Soldier, Rhode Island, ⅙ Plate	253.00
Ambrotype, Civil War, Union Officer, Black Attendant, Ruby Glass, ½ Plate	1150.00
Ambrotype, Civil War, Union Sergeant, Gilt Mat, Leather Case, ⅙ Plate	235.00
Ambrotype, Dairy Boy, Milk Can, Pail, Ruby Glass, ½ Case, ⅙ Plate	1280.00
Ambrotype, Dog On Chair, Leather Case, ⅑ Plate	125.00
Ambrotype, Elegant Lady, Gutta-Percha Frame, c.1858, 2¾ x 3¼ In.	75.00
Ambrotype, Gentleman, Hand Colored, Gold Watch Chain, Union Case, A. Schaefer, c.1860, ⅙ Plate	131.00
Ambrotype, Girl, Dark, Moody, Jewelry, Leather Case, ⅙ Plate	161.00
Ambrotype, Man, With Cane, Bent Arm, Leather Case, ¼ Plate	178.00
Ambrotype, Niagara Falls, Gilt Mat, Sept. 1856, ½ Plate	558.00
Ambrotype, Portrait, Girl, Tilted Position, J.H. Young, N.Y., ⅙ Plate	60.00
Ambrotype, Soldier, Civil War, Union, Gutta-Percha Case, ⅙ Plate, 3¼ x 2¾ In.	240.00
Ambrotype, Woman, Indian Head Case, ⅙ Plate	322.00
Cabinet Card, Charles Young, West Point Cadet, Pach Bros.	2151.00
Cabinet Card, Dog, Doll, Cello, 2 Sisters	345.00
Cabinet Card, Feminists, Belva Lockwood, Emily Faithfull	276.00
Cabinet Card, Fishing, 3 Men With Gear & Catch	150.00
Cabinet Card, Four Generals, 2 Grants, Sheridan, Sherman	178.00
Cabinet Card, Frame Maker, Holding Plane, A.L. Walline	395.00
Cabinet Card, Indian Girls With 2 Dogs, Open Parasol, Sewing Basket	104.00
Cabinet Card, Laura Bridgman Doing Craft Work, Unmounted	138.00
Cabinet Card, Locks At Pembroke, Ontario	69.00
Cabinet Card, Logging Trains, Humbolt County, Calif.	322.00
Cabinet Card, Machine & Its Inventor	178.00
Cabinet Card, Rocking Horse On Railroad Car	104.00
Cabinet Card, Russian Midget, Man In Military Service	138.00
Cabinet Card, Sailor Boys In Horrors, Shipboard Scene, Sailors In Drag	138.00
Cabinet Card, Sonora Hunters, 4 Men With Guns, 3 Smoking Pipes	748.00
Cabinet Card, Texas Banjo Player, In Woods, Pegs Stick Out From Banjo	104.00
Cabinet Card, Wild Men Of Borneo	92.00
Cabinet Card, Wolf Road, Cheyenne Indian	460.00
Camera, Brownie, No. 2, Eastman Kodak, Box, 6 In.	90.00
Camera, Brownie Hawkeye, Bakelite Plastic Box, Leather Carrying Case, Manual	45.00
Camera, Canon, ILF No. 102328, Chrome, Red Dot, 50 mm & 100 mm Lenses	235.00
Camera, Coronet Midget, Blue, Case ..... *illus*	595.00
Camera, Eastman, No. 2 View, Mahogany, Brass, Leather Bellows, Case, 8 x 10 In.	411.00
Camera, Field, ½ Plate, Mahogany, Nickel, Advertising Plaque, Bride's 1st Meal	235.00
Camera, Hasselblad, Model 500C, Carl Zeiss F/2.8 80 mm Lens, Neck Strap, 4½ In. ..... *illus*	460.00
Camera, Kodak, Six-20, 1938 ..... *illus*	2506.00
Camera, Nikon, F Photomic, Nikkor NC 2 Lens, 1962 ..... *illus*	235.00
Camera, Nikon, FE2, No. 2235382, Chrome, 24 mm Lens	176.00
Camera, Thornton-Pickard, Leather Bellows, Mahogany, Tripod, England, c.1900	385.00
Camera, Zeiss Ikon, Contax I, Black, Nickel, 2 Lenses, 1934 ..... *illus*	392.00
Carte De Visite, Adopted Slave Child, Posing With Drum	196.00
Carte De Visite, Arab On Horse	104.00
Carte De Visite, Arrival Of Dead Bodies At Fredericksburg, Matthew Brady, 1864	717.00
Carte De Visite, Black Boy, Dog, Hat	330.00
Carte De Visite, Captain John Loringer Worden	161.00
Carte De Visite, Charles Beach & Toys	222.00
Carte De Visite, Colonel Charles Denby	207.00
Carte De Visite, Fort Morgan, Alabama, Interior, Sandbagged Parapet	345.00
Carte De Visite, Locomotive & Crew, 9 Workers	161.00
Carte De Visite, Opera House, St. Cloud, Minn.	506.00
Carte De Visite, Sherman & Generals	150.00
Carte De Visite, Soldier Holding Sword	69.00
Carte De Visite, Vallejo Street Wharf	286.00
Carte De Visite, Water Batteries, Fort Morgan, Alabama	322.00

Photography, Album, Cabinet Card, Admiral Dewey Photo On Cover, Holds 28 Cards, 11 x 9 In.
$359.00

Photography, Camera, Coronet Midget, Blue, Case
$595.00

Photography, Camera, Hasselblad, Model 500C, Carl Zeiss F/2.8 80 mm Lens, Neck Strap, 4½ In.
$460.00

Photography, Camera, Kodak, Six-20, 1938
$2506.00

Photography, Camera, Nikon, F Photomic, Nikkor NC 2 Lens, 1962
$235.00

Photography, Camera, Zeiss Ikon, Contax I, Black, Nickel, 2 Lenses, 1934
$392.00

Photography, Magic Lantern, Jean Schoenner, Brass Lamphouse, Slides, Nuremberg, 12 In.
$230.00

Photography, Magic Lantern, Jean Schoenner, Tin, Wire Side Handles, Glass Shade, c.1880, 12 In.
$58.00

P

TIP

Photographs can be damaged by acidic paper, glue on envelope seams, ink from ballpoint pens, chemicals in glassine, moisture that can collect in plastic sleeves, etc. Acid-free boxes and envelopes are available at stores, online, and through catalogs.

Photography, Silver Print,
20 Mule Borax Team, Mat,
c.1890, 10 x 12 In.
$324.00

Photography, Tintype,
Civil War Union Soldier, Holding Saber,
Brass Shell, Mat, Union Case,
4 x 3 In.
$388.00

Carte De Visite, Windmill & Its Builder 178.00
Carte De Visite, Young Indians, From Choctaw Nation, Gannaway 400.00
Case, Daguerreotype, Gutta-Percha, Velvet Lining, Brass Insert, 3¾ x 3¼ In. 165.00
Daguerreotype, 2 Women, Holding Hands, ¼ Plate 100.00
Daguerreotype, 2 Women, One In Profile, Leather Case, ⅙ Plate 633.00
Daguerreotype, 3 Children, 1 Holding Toy Dog, ¼ Plate 60.00
Daguerreotype, Abraham Lincoln, Portrait, Brass Mat, Case, Stamped C.T. Rogers, ⅙ Plate . 1314.00
Daguerreotype, Advertising The California Fireman's Certificate, Frame, Full Plate 9380.00
Daguerreotype, Affectionate Women, Hold Hands, Arm Around Shoulder, ¼ Plate 219.00
Daguerreotype, Alice Mary Hawes, Age 4, ½ Plate 3480.00
Daguerreotype, Artist Reflecting, Sealed, ⅙ Plate 825.00
Daguerreotype, Bored Boy, ½ Plate 1508.00
Daguerreotype, Child & Black Nanny, Louisville, Ky., ⅙ Plate 1972.00
Daguerreotype, Couple, Woman Holding Book, Full Leather Case, ¼ Plate 45.00
Daguerreotype, Cutouts From Folk Art Painting, ⅙ Plate 1102.00
Daguerreotype, Dog, On Sofa, ⅙ Plate 1102.00
Daguerreotype, Dog, Seated On Stenciled Chair, ⅙ Plate 1275.00
Daguerreotype, Elderly Couple, Stamped, Cooley & Springfield, Case, ½ Plate 180.00
Daguerreotype, Elizabeth Moore Wardwell, Wife Of Edward Hooker, ⅙ Plate 196.00
Daguerreotype, Family Of 4, ½ Plate 130.00
Daguerreotype, Family Portrait, 2 Women, 2 Men, 1 Baby, Whole Plate 1972.00
Daguerreotype, Gentle Man, Folded Arms, Oval Mat, Case, ⅙ Plate 253.00
Daguerreotype, Girl, Ringlets, Spotted Dress, Mat, Full Case, ⅙ Plate 200.00
Daguerreotype, House, People Inside White Fence, ¼ Plate 1150.00
Daguerreotype, John Bull Blinking-Eye Clock, Bradley & Hubbard, ⅙ Plate 2900.00
Daguerreotype, Man, Scalloped Mat, Split Case, ⅙ Plate 30.00
Daguerreotype, Man & Woman, Farm Scene, Gutta-Percha Case, 3 x 2½ In. 325.00
Daguerreotype, Man & Woman, Woman With Arm In Sling, ½ Plate 348.00
Daguerreotype, Man Holding Scribing Tool, Half Case, ⅙ Plate 75.00
Daguerreotype, Man In Casket, ½ Plate 1392.00
Daguerreotype, Man With Beard & Man Without Beard, 3¼ In. 261.00
Daguerreotype, Mother & Daughter, Whitehurst, Mat, ½ Case, ⅙ Plate 240.00
Daguerreotype, New England Factory, Vermont, ⅙ Plate 1856.00
Daguerreotype, Portrait, Gentleman, Gilt Mat, Folding Leather Case, ½ Plate 147.00
Daguerreotype, Postmortem, Carrie Brewer Shillaber, Tinted, Case, ⅙ Plate 382.00
Daguerreotype, Postmortem, Mother Cradling Baby, Gilt Mat, Case, ⅙ Plate 353.00
Daguerreotype, Postmortem Of A Man, Full Leather Case, ⅙ Plate 250.00
Daguerreotype, Purser Thomas Breese, Uniform, c.1845, ¼ Plate 995.00
Daguerreotype, Rich Face, Benjamin Franklin Upton, ½ Case, ⅙ Plate 288.00
Daguerreotype, Side View Of Lady Holding Child, ⅙ Plate 754.00
Daguerreotype, Woman, Matching Dress & Cape, 1840s, ⅙ Plate 85.00
Daguerreotype, Woman Beside Pillar, Mat, Full Case, ⅙ Plate 135.00
Daguerreotype, Woman In Bonnet, Shows Patience, Wisdom, ⅙ Plate 178.00
Daguerreotype, Woman With Earring, Oval Mat, Leather Case, ⅙ Plate 161.00
Daguerreotype, Woman With Needlework, Leather Case, ⅙ Plate 150.00
Daguerreotype, Young Woman Wearing Cameo Brooch, ⅙ Plate 30.00
Head Holder, Photographer's, Cast Iron, Jenny Lind Model, Cupped Ears, 69 In. 1293.00
Magic Lantern, Jean Schoenner, Brass Lamphouse, Slides, Nuremberg, 12 In. .... *illus* 230.00
Magic Lantern, Jean Schoenner, Tin, Wire Side Handles, Glass Shade, c.1880, 12 In. . . *illus* 58.00
Magic Lantern, Pettibone, Spirit Illuminant, Hinged Reflector, Tin Lamphouse, 13 In. 294.00
Photograph, Beane's General Store, Moscow, Me., Bernice Abbott, 1960s, 15 x 19 In. 575.00
Photograph, Convicts In Swannanoa Cut, Chain Gang, T.H. Lindsey, 5 x 8 In. 956.00
Photograph, Grenada Spain, Panorama, No. 27, Louis De Clercq, 8 x 43½ In. 5750.00
Photograph, Harry Houdini, Signed, April 6 1922 My Birthday, 7 x 4½ In. 2860.00
Photograph, Maybeck's Palace Of Legion Of Honor, Brugiere, 1915, 14 x 11 In. 1200.00
Photograph, Military Bridge Across The Chickahominy, Va., D.B. Woodbury, 7 x 9 In. 690.00
Photograph, Our First Black Hero Of World's War, Black & White, Frame, 7 x 5 In. 51.00
Photograph, Pikes Peak, Colorado, From Palmer Park, 1925, 11 x 9 In. 30.00
Photograph, Platinum, Broken Arm, Ogallala Sioux, No. 1448, F.A. Rinehart 1035.00
Photograph, Platinum, Little Bird, Arapahoe Indian, Profile, F.A. Rinehart c.1898, 8⅞ x 6½ In. . 1093.00
Photograph, Platinum, Shot In The Eye, Sioux Indian, Heyn Bros., No. 343, c.1899, 8¾ x 6⅞ In. . . 1035.00
Photograph, Post Office, Caratunk, Maine, Bernice Abbott, 1960s, 15 x 18 In. 748.00
Photograph, Wilfrid Laurier, Montminy & Cie, Signed, Quebec, c.1910, 9¼ x 7 In. 544.00
Silver Print, 20 Mule Borax Team, Mat, c.1890, 10 x 12 In. .... *illus* 324.00
Silver Print, Bowery Scene, Weegee, 8 x 10 In. 1150.00
Silver Print, Crow Naming Ceremony, Baby, Mother, Grandmothers, c.1905, 4¾ x 6¾ In. . . . 2875.00

Silver Print, Marilyn Monroe, Reclining, Japanese Pattern, Cecil Beaton, 1960, 10 x 10⅝ In. .	2875.00
Silver Print, Projectile Humain, Ugo Zacchini Being Shot From Cannon, 7 x 5 In.	127.00
Silver Print, Woody Allen, Jazz Musician, Gilles Peress, 1980, 7¾ x 10 In.	276.00
Tintype, Abraham Lincoln, Portrait, Mounted On Card, Black Ribbon, ⅙ Plate	250.00
Tintype, Baby In Coffin, Decorated Mat, ½ Case, ¼ Plate	253.00
Tintype, Banjo & Fiddle Duo, Leather Case, ⅙ Plate	219.00
Tintype, Black Man, In Suit, Hat, Leather Case, 1870s, ⅙ Plate	72.00
Tintype, Blacksmith Works Forge, Lifts Horse's Leg, Tool Box, 5⅛ x 7 In.	178.00
Tintype, Child In Carriage, Oval, Thermoplastic Case, ⅑ Plate	90.00
Tintype, Civil War Enlisted Union Soldier, Bayonet, Gilt Mat, Case, ⅙ Plate	235.00
Tintype, Civil War Soldier, Holding Book, Thermoplastic Case, ⅑ Plate	260.00
Tintype, Civil War Soldier With Gun, Ohio Volunteer Militia, ⅙ Plate	368.00
Tintype, Civil War Union Soldier, Holding Saber, Brass Shell, Mat, Union Case, 4 x 3 In. illus	388.00
Tintype, Frame Maker, Man Holds Frame, Hammer, Points To Book On Knee	663.00
Tintype, John C. Fremont, Portrait, Embossed Leather Case, 2 x 1¾ In.	622.00
Tintype, John J. Crittenden, ID Card On Reverse, c.1862, 1⅓ x 1½ In.	72.00
Tintype, John Wilkes Booth, The Assassin, Verse, Carte De Visite Frame, ¾ x 1 In.	1314.00
Tintype, Kentucky Character, Leather Case, ⅙ Plate	178.00
Tintype, Lady, Leaning On Table, Lace Collar, Union Case, ¼ Plate	96.00
Tintype, North Carolina Confederates, Musical Instrument & Dog, 1860, ⅙ Plate	1105.00
Tintype, Officer Holding Sword, ¼ Plate	178.00
Tintype, Plasterer, Holds Brush, Pail, Paper Frame	150.00
Tintype, Spanish-American Soldier, Holding Rifle, Bayonet, Case, 1/16 Plate	167.00
Tintype, Wendell Phillips, Thermoplastic Case, 3¾ x 3¼ In.	239.00
Tintype, Woman, Dark Dress, Lace Collar, Union Case, ¼ Plate illus	96.00
Tintype, Young Soldier, Horn Emblem On Hat, Brass Mat, ⅑ Plate, 2 x 1½ In.	147.00

PIANO BABY is a collector's term. About 1880, the well-decorated home had a shawl on the piano. Bisque figures of babies were designed to help hold the shawl in place. They range in size from 6 to 18 inches. Most of the figures were made in Germany. Reproductions are being made. Other piano babies may be listed under manufacturers' names.

Baby In Papa's Shoe, Bisque, Gebruder Heubach, Germany, c.1910, 11 In.	6820.00
Black Baby, Eating Corn, Heubach, 1900s, 5¼ x 5¼ In.	800.00
Boy, Bisque, Signed Heubach Sunburst, 8½ x 5½ In.	595.00
Girl, With Pet, 4½ x 12 In.	499.00
Girl In Shoe, Hat, Bisque, Molded Hair, 1900s, 9 x 9 In.	400.00
Lying, Stretched Out, Looking Up, Sucking Thumb, Lefton, Pair	30.00
Lying On Back, Touching Foot, Bisque, No. 23/111, 7½ x 4 In.	250.00
Sitting, Blue Intaglio Eyes, Broad Smiling Mouth, Blond Hair, Pointy Curls, 15 In.	881.00
Sitting, Holding Cup, Yellow Dress, Pink Ruffles, Blue Bows, 12 In. illus	173.00
Twin Girls, Long Haired Wigs, Intaglio Blue Eyes, 1900s, 5 x 5 In.	400.00

PICKARD China Company was started in 1893 by Wilder Pickard. Hand-painted designs were used on china purchased from other sources. In the 1930s, the company began to make its own china wares in Chicago, Illinois. The company now makes many types of porcelains, including a successful line of limited edition collector plates.

Berry Bowl, Green Exterior, Cream Interior, Footed, Signed, Nessy, 4½ x 9½ In.	500.00
Bowl, Pink & Yellow Flowers, Cream Ground, Gold Highlights, Footed, Signed, P.G., 10 In.	325.00
Bowl, Raspberry Scene, Yellow & Green, Gold, Scalloped Rim, Signed, E. Challinor, 8¾ In.	450.00
Bowl, Strawberry Design, Rust Ground, Signed, Churn, 9¾ In.	225.00
Bowl, Violets, Cream Center, Gold, Footed, Signed, Fisher, 4 x 10 In.	450.00
Bowl, Walled Garden Scene, Pedestal, Vellum, Signed, E. Challinor, 2¾ x 9¼ In.	350.00
Cake Plate, Italian Garden Scene, Vellum, Handles, Signed, E. Challinor, 11 In.	175.00
Cake Plate, Pillars, Mountains & Lake Scene, Vellum, Handles, Signed, E. Challinor, 11 In.	350.00
Cake Plate, Walled Garden Scene, Vellum, Handles, Signed, 11 In.	150.00
Candleholder, Yellow Flowers, Pink, Gold Trim, Signed, Beukich, 5½ In.	90.00
Celery Dish, Italian Garden Scene, Vellum, Signed, F. Vobor, 13¼ In.	150.00
Celery Dish, Walled Garden Scene, Vellum, Signed, E. Challinor, 12½ In.	200.00
Charger, Gooseberry Scene, Gold Trim, Signed, 12 In.	200.00
Charger, Lotus, White Center, Gold, Signed, 12¼ In.	150.00
Cup & Saucer, Violet Flowers, Cream Ground, Gold Trim, Signed	60.00
Dish, Italian Garden Scene, Vellum, Handle, Signed, Marker, 6½ In.	70.00
Dish, Leaf Shape, Green, Violet, Gold Trim, Signed, H. Kevvy, 9 In.	150.00
Dresser Set, Blue Flowers, Gold Trim, White & Light Blue, Signed, Alex, 5 Piece	250.00
Humidor, Red Poppy, Rust Ground, Gold Trim, Signed, 7½ In.	700.00

Pickard, Vase, Purple Flowers, Trailing Stem, Gold Rim & Buttressed Handles, 9 In. $235.00

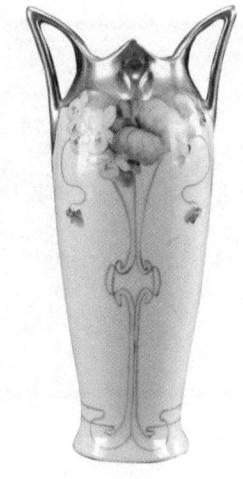

Picture, Engraving Set, Plants, Hand Colored, Giltwood Frame, P. Miller, 13 x 8¾ In., 12 Piece $9600.00

Silhouettes

The silhouette is a "cutout" paper picture, usually black, mounted on a white background. In America, the word "shade" was used until the French word came into use at the end of the eighteenth century. Early signed American silhouettes were made by Charles Willson Peale, William Bache, William Henry Brown, Augustus Day, William Doyle, Charles Peale Polk, and William King.

Jam Jar, Berries, Green Tones, Signed, Challinor, 5½ x 6¾ In., 3 Piece	450.00
Jam Jar, Fruit, Gold, Signed, Vokral, 5½ x 6 In., 3 Piece	475.00
Mayonnaise Set, Leaf & Violets, Cream, Gold Trim, Signed, Marker, 7 In., 2 Piece	200.00
Mug, Fruit, Dark Rose Ground, Signed, V. Meek, 3½ In.	150.00
Pin Tray, Violets, Cream & Gold, Rectangular, Signed, 6¼ In.	90.00
Pitcher, Cider, Blossom & Berry, Brown, Gold, Signed, Bitterly, 6¾ In.	350.00
Pitcher, Cider, Flower Field Scene, Vellum, 6-Sided, Signed, Marker, 8 In.	1100.00
Pitcher, Cider, Tropical Scene, Parrot, Iridescent Border, Gold Trim, Label, C. Marker, 6 In.	1700.00
Pitcher, Fruit, Heavy Gold, Pinched Waist, Signed, Marker, 8¾ In.	225.00
Pitcher, Water, Red Poppy, Light Green Ground, Gold, Signed, Fuchs, 10½ In.	1500.00
Plate, Autumn Lake Scene, Vellum, Signed, E. Challinor, 8¾ In.	200.00
Plate, Berry & Leaf, Cream Ground, Gold Border, Signed, E. Challinor, 6 In.	30.00
Plate, Blue & Pink Flowers, Cream Center, Gold Highlights, Signed, Richler, 8¾ In.	100.00
Plate, Fruit, Rose Ground, Signed, Hessler, 8¾ In.	70.00
Plate, Gold Serpentine & Flowers, Cream Center, Signed, E. Gibson, 8½ In.	75.00
Plate, Night Time Swan & Lake Scene, Vellum, Signed, Osborne, 9¼ In.	200.00
Plate, Nut, Brown Tones, Signed, Vokral, 8½ In.	60.00
Plate, Woodland Scene, Vellum, Signed, E. Challinor, 8½ In.	175.00
Salt & Pepper, White Daisy, Silver Bands, Gold, Signed, Passoni, 3 In.	25.00
Sugar & Creamer, Fruit, Gold, Square, Signed, Vokral	75.00
Sugar & Creamer, Night Time Ruins Scene, Vellum, Signed, E. Challinor	375.00
Tankard, Art Deco, Red, Pink, Blue, Green, Gold, Cream Ground, Signed, M. Rost. Derus, 14½ In.	5500.00
Tankard, Green, Mauve, Yellow, Signed, Seidel, 14¾ In.	2800.00
Tankard, Orange & Mauve Tones, Gold Trim, Signed, Seidel, 14¾ In.	1400.00
Tankard, Raspberry Scene, Orange & Mauve Tones, Gold Trim, Signed, Kiefus, 14½ In.	1500.00
Tray, Walled Garden Scene, Vellum, Signed, E. Challinor, 17½ x 6½ In.	500.00
Vase, Daisies, Gold & Silver Panels, Handles, Signed, Passoni, 13¾ In.	400.00
Vase, Night Time Palm Tree & Lake Scene, Vellum, Handles, Signed, F. James, 8¾ In.	1100.00
Vase, Night Time Woodland Scene, Vellum, Handles, Signed, Marker, 9¾ In.	1800.00
Vase, Pheasant, Vellum Flower Ground, Brocaded Gold, Handles, Signed, E. Challinor, 7¼ In.	100.00
Vase, Pink Rose, Gold, Green, Pinched Waist, Handles, Signed, Challinor, 16 In.	7000.00
Vase, Poinsettia, Cream, Orange, Gold Highlights, Signed, Gasper, 7½ In.	800.00
Vase, Purple Flowers, Trailing Stem, Gold Rim & Buttressed Handles, 9 In. ....*illus*	235.00
Vase, Violets, Green Tones, Signed, H. Kevry, 7¾ In.	275.00
Vase, Walled Garden Scene, Vellum, Signed, E. Challinor, 7¾ In.	400.00
Vase, Woodland & Flower Scene, Vellum, Pinched Waist, Signed, E. Challinor, 8¼ In.	550.00
Vase, Woodland & Flower Scene, Vellum, Handles, Signed, Marker, 7 In.	500.00

PICTURE FRAMES *are listed in this book in the Furniture category under Frame.*

PICTURES, silhouettes, and other small decorative objects framed to hang on the wall are listed here. Sandpaper pictures are black and white charcoal drawings done on a special sanded paper. Some other types of pictures are listed in the Print and Painting categories.

Album, Birds & Flowers, Zhang Dazhuang, Ink & Color, On Paper, 10¾ x 9¼ In.	623.00
Calligraphy, Birds, Raised Head, Diving Bird, Swan, Scrolls, G.B. Haines, 12 x 7½ In.	28.00
Calligraphy, Lord Will Provide, Leaves, Scroll, J. Appenzeller, c.1881, Frame, 22 x 24 In.	55.00
Calligraphy, Pen & Ink, Washington Portrait, Verses, Luther Tasker, Frame, 17 x 21 In.	1175.00
Diorama, Sailing Ship, American Flag, Wood, Toothpick, Cross Corner Frame, 13 x 14 In.	1380.00
Drawing, On Sandpaper, Winter Scene, Hunters, Bear, Fallen Tree, Frame, 19 x 26 In.	1955.00
Drawing, Pen & Ink, Landscape, New England, Barn, Distant Town, Eric Sloane, 14 x 18 In.	863.00
Drawing, Sandpaper, Landscape, Black & White, Boat, Stormy Sky, Gilt Liner, 19½ x 24 In.	230.00
Engraving, Fashion, French Fashion Designs, Hand Colored, 12⅞ x 10 In., 4 Piece	115.00
Engraving Set, Plants, Hand Colored, Giltwood Frame, P. Miller, 13 x 8¾ In., 12 Piece *illus*	9600.00
Etching, Hand Colored, Cancer Chelis Rubris, Titanokeratophyton, Mark Catesby	748.00
Etching, Hand Colored, Solea Lunata, Mark Catesby, Gilt Wood Frame, 14 x 20 In.	920.00
Etching, Hand Painted, Accipiter Pescatorius, Mark Catesby, 10 x 17¼ In.	431.00
Ink, Paint, Crayon, Men & Women Drinking, S.L. Jones, Frame, 17 x 20 In.	288.00
Ink & Color, On Paper, Buddhist Deities, Landscape, Thailand, 19th Century, 26 x 23 In.	443.00
Ink & Color, On Silk, Court Ladies Near Pavilion, Chinese, 19th Century, 18 x 27 In.	562.00
Ink & Color, Paper, Portfolio, Hindu Subjects, Hinged Cover, Anglo-Indian, 12 x 9 In.	2832.00
Memorial, In Memory Ezbon & John Taft Newell, 6 Mo., Watercolor, 1831, 14 x 18 In.	9200.00
Memorial, Sacred To The Memory Of, Monument, Clouds, Weeping Willow, 16 x 20 In.	1528.00
Memorial, To Washington, Watercolor, Pen & Ink, Grieving Woman, c.1834, 22 x 18 In.	3525.00
Mourning, Watercolor, Pen & Ink, On Silk, Classical, Tomb, England, c.1810, 11 x 9 In.	660.00
Mud, Sugar, Paint, On Plywood, Statue Of Liberty, Jim Sudduth, 37 x 20 In.	1035.00

Needlework, Embroidered, Manoah, Angel, Samson, Lion, Silk, Frame, c.1680, 22 x 25¾ In. 10800.00
Needlework, Embroidered, Silk, Girl Picking Flowers, Watercolor, Frame, 12 x 11 In. 633.00
Needlework, Embroidered, Wool, Silk, Watercolor, Woman, Cornucopia, Frame, 1803, 14 x 16 In. .. 719.00
Needlework, Gros & Petit Point, Calla Lily, Iris, Hydrangea, Panel, Frame, 20 x 24½ In. 300.00
Needlework, Maggie's Tea House, Carmel, Maine, Yarn, Punk Work Paper, 16 x 21 In. 345.00
Needlework, Panoramic Landscape, Lions, Asian, Early 20th Century, 46 x 70 In. 1800.00
Needlework, Sculpture, Flower Basket, Gilt Shadowbox Frame, c.1828, 24 x 26 In. 908.00
Needlework, Silk Thread, Ground, Man & Woman, Horse Cart, Country Lane, 8½ x 10 In. .. 411.00
Needlework, Woman, Girls Picking Berries, Matilda Werner, Frame, c.1862, 14 x 22 In. 1540.00
Needlework, Wool Work, Flower Bouquet, Shadowbox Frame, Porcelain Vase, 16 x 12 In. ... 115.00
Pastel, On Paper, Castle De Lemos Monforte De Lemos Spain, Pedro J. De Lemos, 13 x 10 In. 1320.00
Pen & Ink, King Fisher Bird, Flower, Written For Mam, 1800s, 9¾ x 6¼ In. 55.00
Pen & Ink, Old Snyder, Man In Wide Brimmed Hat, Lewis Miler, Walnut Frame, 5 x 3 In. ... 688.00
Pencil, Gouache, On Illustration Board, Bucolic Farm, Everett L. Bryant, 20 x 30 In. 1440.00
Pencil On Paper, Crowning Of Peace Following War, A.A. Von Werner, 1876, 14 x 10 In. 206.00
Pinprick, Ostrich, Paper, Feather Detail, Mat, Frame, 7 x 5½ In. 39.00
Scherenschnitte, Group, Animals, Feather, Bookmark, Gilt Frame, 10¾ x 8¼ In. 83.00
Scherenschnitte, Lovebirds, Branches, Painted Corner Block Frame, France, 8½ x 7 In. ... 83.00
Scherenschnitte, Park, Country House, Lake, Boat, Animals, c.1790, 15 x 25 In. 2596.00
Scherenschnitte, Tree In Urn, Birds, Walnut Frame, Label, Quaker Lady, 5½ x 3¾ In. *.illus* 303.00
Scherenschnitte, Valentine, Flower & Leaf, Swag, Ray Border, Frame, 11½ x 11½ In. 275.00
Scherenschnitte, Valentine, Hearts, Polychrome, Poem, 12 x 12 In. 28.00
Scherenschnitte, Valentine, Pinwheel, Tulips, Cutwork Stems, 12 x 12 In. 5500.00
Scherenschnitte, Valentine, Sawtooth Flower, Heart & Tulip Corners, 12½ x 12½ In. 28.00
Scherenschnitte, Valentine, Woman, Blue Dress, Cut Heart, Flowers, Frame, 8 x 8½ In. 39.00
Scroll, Chinese, Embroidery, Silk, Kingfishers, Flowering Lotus, Millet, Poem, 66 x 26 In. ... 840.00
Silhouette, Man, Full-Length Cutout, Signed, W. Seville, Burslem, Frame, 1836, 12 x 10 In. . 288.00
Silhouette, George Washington, Wax, Oval, Frame, 18th Century, 8 x 4 In. 400.00
Silhouette, Man, Woman, Ebonized Frame, Brass Leaf & Acorn Hanger, 3 x 2½ In., Pair 55.00
Silhouette, Man, Woman, Mahogany Veneered Frame, 4⅝ x 3⅝ In., Pair 110.00
Silhouette, Washington, Hollow Cut Bust, Peale Museum, Oval Frame, 4 x 3¾ In. 2415.00
Silhouette, Woman, Holding Flowers, Full Body, Gold Details, Ink Wash Ground, Frame, 15 x 13 In. 345.00
Silkscreen, Amish Auction, Barn, Man With Quilt, Crowd Of People, 22 x 27 In. 1128.00
Sketch, Pencil, Henry Hitchings, Post Mill's, Vt., 1870, 9 x 14 In. 173.00
Sketch, Watercolor, Omnibus Running From Phila., Xanthus Smith, 4 x 7 In. 518.00
Still Life, Flower, Blue Vase, Watercolor, On Paper, 19th Century, 19 x 22 In. 2070.00
Theorem, Amish Farm Scene, Goose, Dog, Pigs, 17½ x 23½ In. 1980.00
Theorem, Bantam Rooster, Yellow Ground, Painted Frame, 10 x 8 In. 413.00
Theorem, Bird, Berry In Beak, Flowering Stump, 7⅝ x 6¼ In. 1705.00
Theorem, Bird, Berry In Beak, Flowers, Geometric Border, Love D. Ellinger, Frame, 9 x 7¾ In. 3025.00
Theorem, Bird, Flower Tree, Frame, 11 x 7¾ In. 1375.00
Theorem, Bird, In Blue Urn, Flowers, Frame, 13 x 10 In. 2640.00
Theorem, Bird, On Arch, Heart, Flowers, Frame, 6 x 5¾ In. 1760.00
Theorem, Bird, On Flower Branch, Tulip, Heart, Frame, 9 x 7 In. 1045.00
Theorem, Bird, On Stump, Cherry In Beak, Frame, 9½ x 8 In. 2530.00
Theorem, Bird, On Stump, Flowers, Signed Happy Days, Frame, 8½ x 9¾ In. 1375.00
Theorem, Bird, On Stump, Grass, Flowers, Frame, 9¼ x 11½ In. 1650.00
Theorem, Bird, Orange, On Stump, Flowers, Berries, Frame, 9¾ x 8¼ In. 2420.00
Theorem, Bird, Polka Dot, Preening Bird, Floral Branch, 12 x 10 In. 413.00
Theorem, Blue & White Oriental Bowl, Fruit, Bird, Frame, 13 x 18 In. 2750.00
Theorem, Blue Compote Of Fruit, Yellow Bird With Cherry In Beak, Frame, 21 x 20 In. 935.00
Theorem, Blue Jug, Cowden & Wilcox, Bird, Painted Frame, 15 x 13 In. 825.00
Theorem, Bowl Of Fruit On Braided Mat, Frame, 12½ x 14½ In. 330.00
Theorem, Canton Bowl Of Fruit, Yellow Bird On Peach Branch, Frame, 18¾ x 22 In. 2475.00
Theorem, Cat, Calico, On Geometric Rug, Tassel Drapes, Frame, 15¾ x 19¾ In. 688.00
Theorem, Cat, Lying Down, Oval Blue Rug, Red Yarn Ball, 13 x 15 In. 275.00
Theorem, Cat, Lying In Basket, Holding Ball, Flowers, Frame, 13 x 14⅜ In. 303.00
Theorem, Cat, Spotted, Lying On Floor, Beaded Swag, Frame, 1988, 11¼ x 15¾ In. 413.00
Theorem, Cat, Striped, Ball Of Yarn, On Blue Rug, Frame, 12½ x 14½ In. 550.00
Theorem, Cat, With Ball, In Basket, Lawn, Flowers, Frame, 13¾ x 16¾ In. 3025.00
Theorem, Coiled Bee Skep Basket, Flowers, Bees, Grassy Mound, Frame, 17 In. 248.00
Theorem, Compote, Fruit, Flowers, Knife, Butterfly, Signed, Frame, 18½ x 23 In. 2750.00
Theorem, Compote, Fruit, Yellow Bird, Butterfly, Marble Slab, Knife, Frame, 22 x 25¾ In. ... 5500.00
Theorem, Dutch Country, Oil On Velvet, Signed, Frame, 22⅛ x 28¼ In. 6573.00
Theorem, Farm, Amish Boy, Ducks, Cocalico Country, Lebanon Co., Frame, 27½ x 33½ In. . 12100.00
Theorem, Flower Basket, Marble Slab, Hummingbird & Butterfly, Block Frame, 16½ In. 1540.00

Picture, Scherenschnitte, Tree In Urn, Birds, Walnut Frame, Label, Quaker Lady, 5½ x 3¾ In.
$303.00

18th-Century French Protest
In the 1760s, black paper picture cutouts were enjoyed by the French, including Finance Minister Etienne de Silhouette. M. Silhouette ignored the suffering of the rich and poor because of his heavy taxes. To protest, people dressed in black "*a la Silhouette*," claiming they were too poor to wear colors. The word silhouette was added to the French dictionary in 1835.

P

Picture, Theorem, Fruit Basket, Bird With Berry, Corner Block Frame, 17¾ x 19¾ In.
$2750.00

Picture, Watercolor, Mourning, Tomb, Girls, Memory Of My Sister, Gilt Frame, 10½ x 13 In. $3575.00

Pigeon Forge, Figurine, Chipmunk, 5½ In. $20.00

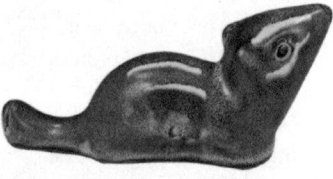

Pigeon Forge, Figurine, Owl, 4¼ In. $10.00

Theorem, Flower Basket, Reeded Urn, Grain Painted Frame, c.1830, 15 x 18 In.	1610.00
Theorem, Flower Basket, Watercolor, H.W. Hammond, Frame, 1840, 4¾ x 5¼ In.	489.00
Theorem, Flowers, Reverse Painted On Glass, 10 x 8 In.	575.00
Theorem, Fruit, On Oval Tray, Frame, 18⅞ x 23¼ In.	248.00
Theorem, Fruit, Watercolor, Velvet, Basket Of Fruit, Frame, Gilt Liner, 9 x 10 In.	632.00
Theorem, Fruit, Watercolor, Velvet, Gilt Frame, Attica, N.Y. Label, 16 x 18¾ In.	546.00
Theorem, Fruit, Watercolor, Velvet, Reverse Painted Black Liner, Gilt Frame, 9 x 11 In.	288.00
Theorem, Fruit & Watermelon Half, Molded Pine Frame, 21 x 27 In.	2185.00
Theorem, Fruit Basket, 2 Birds, Elaborate Tails, 13 x 15 In.	330.00
Theorem, Fruit Basket, Bird, Bees, Decorated Frame, 20 x 25 In.	1650.00
Theorem, Fruit Basket, Bird, Berry In Beak, Bee, Frame, 23⅜ x 29¼ In.	440.00
Theorem, Fruit Basket, Bird, Berry In Beak, Bees, Knife, Apple, Checkered Cloth, 15 x 19 In.	220.00
Theorem, Fruit Basket, Bird, Berry In Beak, Moth, Grasshopper, Signed, Frame, 14 x 17 In.	2530.00
Theorem, Fruit Basket, Bird, On Branch, Bees, 15½ x 19½ In.	1018.00
Theorem, Fruit Basket, Bird, On Branch, Bees, c.1972, 17½ x 21 In.	660.00
Theorem, Fruit Basket, Bird, On Branch, Leaves, Signed, Frame, 10¾ x 13¾ In.	2510.00
Theorem, Fruit Basket, Bird, With Berry, Corner Block Frame, 17¾ x 19¾ In. ....*illus*	2750.00
Theorem, Fruit Basket, Bird, With Berry, Molded Frame, 19¾ x 23¼ In.	770.00
Theorem, Fruit Basket, Pinecones On Cardboard Frame, Acorns, 10 x 10½ In.	374.00
Theorem, Fruit Basket, Reticulated, Blue Table, Grain Painted Frame, c.1830, 15 x 19 In.	1610.00
Theorem, Fruit Basket, Watercolor, Velvet, Dark, Grapes, Leaves, Frame, 21½ x 25¼ In.	1840.00
Theorem, Fruit Basket, Watermelon, Bird, Butterfly, Bees, Frame, 24 x 27¾ In.	4675.00
Theorem, Fruit Bowl, Blue & White Bowl, Bird, Signed, Wm. Rank, Frame, 13 x 15 In.	413.00
Theorem, Fruit Compote, Scalloped Edge, RSW, Frame, 9 x 11½ In.	253.00
Theorem, Grape Basket, Geometric Design, Bird, Frame, 14 x 19 In.	3410.00
Theorem, Hen On Nest, Emerging Eggs, Frame, 10 x 12 In.	303.00
Theorem, Painting, Watercolor, Paper, Still Life, Flowers, Basket, 1800s, 20 x 25½ In.	3120.00
Theorem, Parrot, On Jardiniere, Flowers, Frame, 9¾ x 8 In.	1600.00
Theorem, Parrot, On Tulip Pot, Sawtooth Border, Block Frame, Signed, 7¼ x 5½ In.	633.00
Theorem, Peacock, On Urn, Tulip, Flowers, Frame, 10 x 8½ In.	1760.00
Theorem, Pelican, Pecking Breast, Frame, 18½ x 14½ In.	1430.00
Theorem, Rebecca At The Well, Watercolor, On Silk, Burlwood Frame, 1800s, 16 x 21 In.	2530.00
Theorem, Rooster, Drooping Tulip Tree, Frame, 11 x 9 In.	143.00
Theorem, Rooster, On Grassy Mound, Tulips, Block Frame, 14 x 13¾ In.	1540.00
Theorem, Rooster, On Mound, Flowers, Corner Block Frame, Signed, 16⅜ In.	495.00
Theorem, Rooster, Standing On Mound, Tulip, Signed, Corner Block Frame, 6 x 7⅞ In.	990.00
Theorem, Rooster, Tulip Emerging, Painted Corner Block Frame, 9 x 10 In.	110.00
Theorem, Rooster, Tulips, Paint Decorated Frame, 18 x 16 In.	413.00
Theorem, Stenciled, Painted, Mary A. Gregg, New Hampshire, Dec. 30, 1826	920.00
Theorem, Still Life, Roses, Yellow Basket, Watercolor, Velvet, American School, 19 x 25 In.	246.00
Theorem, Strawberry, Small Pot, Paint Decorated Frame, 12 x 10 In.	220.00
Theorem, Strawberry Basket, Robin On Cherry Branch, Frame, 22 x 30 In.	3850.00
Theorem, Strawberry Basket, Yellow, Green & Red Bird, Vines, Frame, 13¾ x 15¾ In.	605.00
Theorem, Stylized Cherry Tree, 2 Yellow, Red Green Birds, Frame, 15 x 13 In.	1045.00
Theorem, Sulky, Dappled Horse, Rider In Yellow Vest, Frame, 10 x 12 In.	468.00
Theorem, Turkey, On Mound, Tulip, Berries, Frame, 9¼ x 7½ In.	2310.00
Theorem, Urn, 2 Birds, Flowers, Frame, 9¼ x 8¾ In.	1430.00
Theorem, Urn, Flowers, Butterflies, Bees, Signed, Frame, 9¾ x 8¼ In.	1480.00
Watercolor, Bermuda Street Scene, c.1907, 13⅝ x 20⅛ In.	748.00
Watercolor, Bird, Berry In Beak, Floral Stem, Decorated Frame, 3½ x 3 In.	578.00
Watercolor, Bird, Berry In Beak, Floral Vine, Decorated Frame, 5 x 3½ In.	275.00
Watercolor, Bird, Branch, Flowering Tree Stump, Painted Frame, 7 x 9 In.	770.00
Watercolor, Bird, Heart Center, Flowers, Painted Frame, 4 x 3¾ In.	743.00
Watercolor, Bird, On Branch, Painted Frame, Heart Corner Blocks, 7 x 7 In.	110.00
Watercolor, Bird, On Leafy Stem, Tulip, Frame, 11½ x 9 In.	633.00
Watercolor, Bird, Perched, Line & Dot Border, Burl Mahogany Frame, 4 x 3½ In.	3300.00
Watercolor, Bird, Serpentine Tulip Stem, Heart Base, 7 x 6 In.	1100.00
Watercolor, Bird, Tulips, Border, Painted Corner Block Frame, 5 x 4 In.	825.00
Watercolor, Building On Pond, Boat, Painted Wood Frame, 15½ x 15 In.	115.00
Watercolor, Country Landscape, Covered Bridge, V. Seagreaves, Frame, 10 x 16 In.	330.00
Watercolor, Cutout, Birds, Fern, Flowers, Signed, Mary Reyder, 5½ x 3¾ In.	220.00
Watercolor, Cutwork, Heart, Tulip, Bird, Drooping Stem, Frame, 8 x 10 In.	132.00
Watercolor, Cutwork, Valentine, Facing Birds, Branch, Hearts, 12 x 12 In.	143.00
Watercolor, Double Image, Polychrome Urn, Flowers, Frame, 18¾ x 14 In.	550.00
Watercolor, Easter Rabbit, Basket, Painted Corner Block Frame, 7 x 7 In.	220.00
Watercolor, Flower, Drooping Branches, Birds, Frame, 11 x 7 In.	1100.00

Watercolor, Flower Urn, Perched Bird, Flowers, Painted Frame, 12 x 14 In.	165.00
Watercolor, Gouache, Ink, Mountain Landscape, V. Toothaker, Mat, Frame, c.1909, 7 x 3 In.	1440.00
Watercolor, Grave Yard, Sheep, Stone Wall, 10 x 13½ In.	440.00
Watercolor, Group, Birds, Unicorn, Standing Lion, Painted Frame, 21½ In.	550.00
Watercolor, Indian Horse Dance, Paint Decorated Frame, 11⅜ x 11⅜ In.	28.00
Watercolor, Indian On Horseback, Feathered Head Dress, Frame, 11 x 13 In.	110.00
Watercolor, Indian On Horseback, Paint Decorated Frame, 11¼ x 14 In.	132.00
Watercolor, Indians On Horseback, Frame, 11¼ x 23¼ In.	132.00
Watercolor, Indians On Horseback, Frame, 13¼ x 15¼ In.	121.00
Watercolor, Love Birds, Elaborate Tails, Floral Stems, Frame, 14 x 11 In.	578.00
Watercolor, Marriage Certificate, Rev. Henry Young, Tulip & Heart Vines, 13 x 9½ In.	264.00
Watercolor, Mourning, Tomb, Girls, Memory Of My Sister, Gilt Frame, 10½ x 13 In. . . . *illus*	3575.00
Watercolor, Parrot, Tulip Branch, Paint Decorated Frame, 5¼ x 4¼ In.	798.00
Watercolor, Peafowl, Perched On Urn, Painted Corner Block Frame, 11 x 8 In.	550.00
Watercolor, Pen & Ink, Graphite, Portrait, Gentleman, Frame, 19th Century, 6 x 5 In.	646.00
Watercolor, Profile, Gentleman, Seated In Chippendale Chair, c.1840, 4 x 3 In.	345.00
Watercolor, Rooster, Drooping Tulip Tree, Painted Frame, 5¾ x 5 In.	138.00
Watercolor, Rooster, Tulip, Flowers, Painted Corner Block Frame, 8½ x 9 In.	303.00
Watercolor, Rooster, Tulip, Primitive, Painted Block Frame, 6¼ x 7½ In.	1210.00
Watercolor, Rooster, Tulips, Flowers, Paint Decorated Frame, 6 x 7 In.	275.00
Watercolor, Ruins Scene, Spectator, c.1876, 24 x 19⅝ In.	1955.00
Watercolor, Seated Woman, Black Dress, Windsor Chair, Jacob Maentel, Frame, 12 x 7 In. . .	8250.00
Watercolor, Tulip, Floral Stem, Heart Base, Geometric Design, 7 x 4 In.	825.00
Watercolor, Tulips, Urn, Birds, Sunray, Painted Frame, 8 x 7 In.	1375.00
Watercolor, Turkeys, Full Strut, Heart Corner Block Frame, 7 x 9 In.	176.00
Watercolor, Urn, Tulip, Opposing Birds, Berry Branch, 8 x 6½ In.	1540.00
Watercolor, Urn Of Flowers, Opposing Birds, Tulip, Flowers, 5½ x 6 In.	1375.00
Watercolor, Urn Of Flowers, Bird, Berry In Beak, Flowers, 13½ x 15½ In.	825.00
Watercolor, Winter Farm Landscape, Egbert Cadmus, 1934, 11½ x 15½ In.	235.00
Watercolor, Winter Snow Scene, Children Ice Skating, Frame, 9½ x 14 In.	468.00
Watercolor, Young Boy, Blue Dress & Kepi, Sword, Gilt Frame, 4½ x 3½ In.	440.00
Watercolor, Young Girl, Red Dress, With Flower, Handbag, Gilt Frame, 4½ x 3½ In.	523.00
Watercolor, Young Girl, Stone House, Holding Tulips, Walnut Frame, 9¾ x 7⅝ In.	440.00
Watercolor On Paper, Portrait, Man Standing, Full Cut Coat, Cap & Cane, Frame, 16 x 13 In. .	115.00

PIERCE, *see Howard Pierce category.*

PIGEON FORGE Pottery was started in Pigeon Forge, Tennessee, in 1946. Red clay found near the pottery was used to make the pieces. Molded or thrown pottery with matte glaze and slip decoration was made. The pottery closed in 2000.

Figurine, Chipmunk, 5½ In. . . . .*illus*	20.00
Figurine, Frog, Marked, 2¼ x 3½ In.	50.00
Figurine, Owl, 4¼ In. . . . .*illus*	10.00
Figurine, Owl, Marked, 7¼ In.	39.00
Pitcher, Plum High Glaze, White Interior, 3⅝ x 4¼ In. . . . .*illus*	20.00

PILKINGTON Tile and Pottery Company was established in 1892 in England. The company made small pottery wares, like buttons and hatpins, but soon started decorating vases purchased from other potteries. By 1903, the company had discovered an opalescent glaze that became popular on the Lancastrian pottery line. The manufacture of pottery ended in 1937. Pilkington's Tiles Ltd. has worked from 1938 to the present.

Charger, Royal Lancastrian, Luster, Redware Ground, Slip Galleon, Trees, 15⅝ In.	3819.00
Compote, Lapis Ware, Gray, Blue Repeating Triangles, Gladys Rogers, c.1935, 5 x 11 In.	431.00
Vase, Cobalt & Orange, Art Deco Geometric Band, Royal Lancastrian, 5¾ In., Pair . . . . .*illus*	360.00

PILLIN pottery was made by Polia (1909–1992) and William (1910–1985) Pillin, who set up a pottery in Los Angeles in 1948. William shaped, glazed, and fired the clay, and Polia painted the pieces, often with elongated figures of women, children, flowers, birds, fish, and other animals. Pieces are marked with a stylized *Pillin* signature.

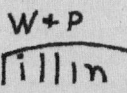

Tray, Young Woman Portrait, Multicolored, Incised, Pillin, 8¼ x 6 In.	1250.00
Vase, 4 Horses, Multicolored, Black Rim, Incised, Pillin, 5¼ In.	900.00
Vase, 4 Ladies, Birds, Mottled Blue & White, Bulbous, Signed, Polia Pillin, 9 x 7 In.	2400.00
Vase, Birds, Branches, Gray Ground, Flared, Footed, Signed, Polia Pillin, 4 x 5 In.	520.00
Vase, Blue Birds, White Ground, Bottle Form, Signed, Polia Pillin, 6 x 3½ In.	295.00

Pigeon Forge, Pitcher, Plum High Glaze, White Interior, 3⅝ x 4¼ In. $20.00

Pilkington, Vase, Cobalt & Orange, Art Deco Geometric Band, Royal Lancastrian, 5¾ In., Pair $360.00

P

Pillin, Vase, Woman With Birds,
Footed, Pillin, 4 x 4½ In.
$360.00

Pincushion Doll, Woman,
Porcelain Legs, Organdy Dress, 6 In.
$144.00

Pipe, Meerschaum,
Indians Attacking Bison,
Flower Form Bowl, Curved Amber Stem,
Case, 9½ In.
$1265.00

P

Pisgah Forest, Jar, Cover,
Green High Glaze, Rose Interior,
1951, 4 x 3¾ In.
$35.00

Vase, Bulbous, Red, Blue, Incised, W & P Pillin, 6⅜ In.		465.00
Vase, Figures, Birds, Patchwork Ground, Signed, Pillin, 4 x 4½ In.		495.00
Vase, Figures, Birds, Yellow Ground, Cylindrical, Signed, Polia Pillin, 2½ x 4 In.		920.00
Vase, Girl, Horse, Mottled Brown & White, Chalice, Signed, Pillin, 6½ x 3½ In.		450.00
Vase, Ladies, Mottled Red & White Ground, Signed, Polia Pillin, 2½ x 4 In.		430.00
Vase, Mother & Children, Green & Black Ground, Cylindrical, Signed, Pillin, 7 x 2½ In.		620.00
Vase, Woman, Horse, Mottled Brown & White, Chalice, Signed, Polia Pillin, 6½ x 3½ In.		450.00
Vase, Woman With Birds, Footed, Pillin, 4 x 4½ In.	*illus*	360.00
Vase, Yellow, Brown Speckles, Bulbous, Flattened, Elongated Neck, W & P Pillin, 9 In.		230.00

PINCUSHION DOLLS are not really dolls and often were not even pincushions. Some collectors use the term "half-doll." The top half of each doll was made of porcelain. The edge of the half-doll was made with several small holes for thread, and the doll was stitched to a fabric body with a voluminous skirt. The finished figure was used to cover a hot pot of tea, powder box, pincushion, whiskbroom, or lamp. They were made in sizes from less than an inch to over 9 inches high. Most date from the early 1900s to the 1950s. Collectors often find just the porcelain doll without the fabric skirt.

Woman, Porcelain, Holding Tray, Tea Cozy, Germany, c.1910, 19 In.		880.00
Woman, Porcelain, Nude, Arms Extended, Wire Armature Skirt, Germany, 12 In.		743.00
Woman, Porcelain Legs, Organdy Dress, 6 In.	*illus*	144.00
Woman's Head, Kidskin Top, Papier-Mache, France, 1830		2400.00

PIPES have been popular since tobacco was introduced to Europe by Sir Walter Raleigh. Carved wooden, porcelain, ivory, and glass pipes may be listed here.

Art Glass, Victorian, Blue & White Swirls, 31 In., 2 Piece		448.00
Art Glass, Victorian, White, Blue, 30 In., 3 Piece		448.00
Brass, Opium, Chinese, 13⅛ x 2¾ In.		59.00
Clay, Jonah, Whale, Holland, c.1620		250.00
Meerschaum, Indians Attacking Bison, Flower Form Bowl, Amber Stem, Case, 9½ In.	*illus*	1265.00
Meerschaum, Putti Design, 4¼ In.		234.00
Porcelain, Character, Skull, E. Bohne & Sohne, 11½ In.		303.00
Porcelain Bowl, Regimental, 28 Infantry Ehrenbreitstein 1911, Tet. Huls, Wood, 50 In.		345.00
Porcelain Bowl, Regimental, 67 Infantry Metz 1909-11, Res. Piehl, Wood, 43 In.		332.00
Tamper, King Charles II Head, Bronze, England, c.1665		395.00

PISGAH FOREST pottery was made in North Carolina beginning in 1926. The pottery was started by Walter B. Stephen, who had been making pottery in that location since 1914. The pottery continued in operation after his death in 1961. The most famous kinds of Pisgah Forest ware are the cameo type with designs made of raised glaze and the turquoise crackle glaze wares.

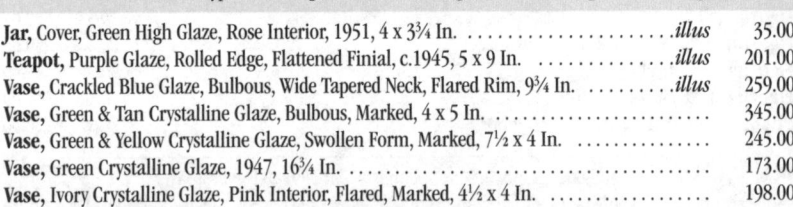

Jar, Cover, Green High Glaze, Rose Interior, 1951, 4 x 3¾ In.	*illus*	35.00
Teapot, Purple Glaze, Rolled Edge, Flattened Finial, c.1945, 5 x 9 In.	*illus*	201.00
Vase, Crackled Blue Glaze, Bulbous, Wide Tapered Neck, Flared Rim, 9¾ In.	*illus*	259.00
Vase, Green & Tan Crystalline Glaze, Bulbous, Marked, 4 x 5 In.		345.00
Vase, Green & Yellow Crystalline Glaze, Swollen Form, Marked, 7½ x 4 In.		245.00
Vase, Green Crystalline Glaze, 1947, 16¾ In.		173.00
Vase, Ivory Crystalline Glaze, Pink Interior, Flared, Marked, 4½ x 4 In.		198.00

PLANTERS PEANUTS memorabilia is collected. Planters Nut and Chocolate Company was started in Wilkes-Barre, Pennsylvania, in 1906. The Mr. Peanut figure was adopted as a trademark in 1916. National advertising for Planters Peanuts started in 1918. The company was acquired by Standard Brands, Inc., in 1961. Standard Brands merged with Nabisco in 1981. Some of the Mr. Peanut jars and other memorabilia have been reproduced and, of course, new items are being made.

Ashtray, Figural, Mr. Peanut, 3 Peanuts On Back, c.1930, 4 x 3 x 2½ In.		88.00
Bank, Lamp, Mr. Peanut, Light-Up, 10 In.		137.00
Bank, Mr. Peanut, Top Hat, Cane, Red, Plastic, 8½ In.		30.00
Box, Planters 5 Cents Peanuts, Mr. Peanut, Circus Parade, 8¾ x 7¾ x 2¾ In.		413.00
Box, Salted Peanuts, Cardboard, 16½ x 13½ x 11 In.		44.00
Canister, Glass, Paper Label, Large		205.00
Card, Mr. Peanut Holding Wreath Over Head, Seasons Greetings, 5½ x 2¾ In.		66.00
Container, Mr. Peanut, Detachable Hat, ½ Lb., 12 In.		385.00
Container, Mr. Peanut, Figural, Tan, Papier-Mache, Washington D.C., Label, ½ Lb., 12 In.		330.00
Container, Mr. Peanut, Figural, Papier-Mache, Golden State Exposition, ½ Lb., 12½ In.		600.00

Crate, Salted Peanuts, Mr. Peanut, Wood, 18½ x 30½ x 16 In. 99.00
Display, Chocolate, Jumbo Block, Peanuts, Tin, 1930-40, 7½ x 14 In. 825.00
Display, Mr. Peanut, Mouth & Eyes Light Up, Papier-Mache, Painted, c.1920, 50 In. 35750.00
Display, Woman, Die Cut, Cardboard, 10½ x 25 x 5 In. 288.00
Display, Woman Aviator, My These Planters Peanuts Are Delicious, Cardboard, c.1940, 2 Piece .. 825.00
Figure, Mr. Peanut, Wood, Jointed, Painted, Stick In Hand, 9 In. ....*illus* 193.00
Gate Post, Mr. Peanut, Cast Iron, Painted, 36 In. ....*illus* 4025.00
Jar, Barrel Shape, c.1935, 12½ In. 28.00
Jar, Clipper, Glass, Celluloid Label, Tin Lithograph Lid, Box, c.1939, 8 x 10 In. 2310.00
Jar, Planters Honey Roasted Peanuts, Glass, Enamel Label, 10½ x 7 In. 165.00
Jar, Planters Jumbo Block, Only Peanut Bar For Summer, Label, 9½ x 7½ x 4¾ In. 5700.00
Letter Opener, 2 Peanuts, Figural, Metal, Embossed, Wilkes-Barre, c.1920, 8½ In. 198.00
Letter Opener, Mr. Peanut, Inlaid Cloisonne Porcelain Enamel, 2-Sided, 9 x 1⅜ In. 520.00
Lighter, Mr. Peanut, Zippo, Box, 2¼ x 1½ x ⅜ In. 330.00
Mug, Mr. Peanut, Cobalt Blue, 3¾ In. 20.00
Party Pack, Salted Nuts, 3-4 Oz. Cans, Unopened, Box 170.00
Punch Board, Mr. Peanut, Planters Cocktail Peanuts, 2 Cents, Red, Yellow, Blue, 9¼ x 7½ In. 71.00
Puppet, Hand, Mr. Peanut, 1950s, 6½ In. 722.00
Salt & Pepper, Mr. Peanut, Ceramic, Glazed, Rhinestone Monocle, c.1960, 4½ In. ....*illus* 136.00
Sign, 1952 Times Square, 1997, 7½ x 19 In. 5079.00
Sign, Boston's WBZ Radio Station, Yellow, Red, Cardboard, 1921, 14 In. 575.00
Sign, Mr. Peanut, 14⅝ x 25⅛ In. 605.00
Sign, Mr. Peanut, Candy Apple, 10 Cents & 15 Cents, Red, White, Black, 44 x 28 In. 220.00
Sign, Planters Salted Peanuts, Mr. Peanut, Tin Lithograph, 9¾ x 23⅝ In. 578.00
Sign, Wbz Radio Station, Mac 'N' Moore, Cardboard, Boston, 14½ x 9 In. 632.00
Spoon, Serving, Mr. Peanut On End Of Handle, Slotted Well, Silver Plated 60.00
Tin, Planters Salt-In-Shell, Seaside Scene, Ocean, Net, White & Blue, 1920s, 10 Lb. 905.00
Toy, Mr. Peanut Pushing Cart, Red, Yellow, Green, Plastic, c.1950, 5¼ x 6¾ In. 330.00
Toy, Walker, Mr. Peanut, Plastic, Windup, 1950s, 9 In. ....*illus* 175.00
Wrapper, Old Fashioned Peanut Candy, Lady Smiling, 10 Oz., 5½ x 10½ In. 608.00

PLASTIC objects of all types are being collected. Some pieces are listed in other categories; gutta-percha cases are listed in photography, celluloid in its own category.

Bread Basket, Basket Weave, Pastel Pink, 1950s, 11½ x 7 In. 18.00
Clothesline Reel, Red, Retractable, Lusterware 25.00
Coaster Set, Holder, 4 Different Colors, Agate Plastics, 3½ x 3½ In. 18.00
Comb, Lady's Leg Form, Bakelite, White 28.00
Cup, Parfait Desert, 2 Pink, 2 Beige, Tan Specks, 3 x 3½ In., 6 Piece 19.00
Dinnerware Set, Brookpark Pattern, Pink, Rose Transfer, Melmac, 56 Piece 240.00
Hairbrush, Plastic Bristles, Handle Mirror, Snow White, Disney, 1980s, 11¼ In. 25.00
Key Chain, Golden Rose, Green Stem & Leaves, Lucite, 2¼ In. 25.00
Mug, Lucite, Glitter Leaf, Amber Gold, Insulated, 1950s 13.00
Platter, Thanksgiving Turkey, Melmac, Brookpark, Autumn Border, Corn & Leaves, 21¼ x 15¼ In. . 23.00
Pumps, Clear, Sling Back, Open Toe, Gold Flowers, Fabric Heels, Jack Rogers, Size 8½ In. ... 26.00
Recipe Box, Yellow, Painted Flowers, Metal Hinges, 1950s, 5¼ x 4 In. 24.00
Shoehorn, Stanley, Pink, 8¼ In. 8.00
Soap Dish, Pink Fish Soap, 3 Shell Shape Soap, Delagar, 5¾ In. 10.00
Spoon Holder, Mauve & White Pansy, Violas, Fronds, Lucite, 7 x 4¾ In. 24.00
Spoon Holder, Pear Shape, Red, Fuller Brush Co. 5.00
Tea Canister, Molded Green, Threaded Lid, Tri Foot Base, Bakelite, 1935, 5 x 3¾ In. 150.00
Thimble, Advertising, Sam W. Morris, Monroe, Mich., c.1950, ⅞ In. 4.00
Trinket Box, Lid, Tan, Silver Floral, Overlay, Knob Handle, 1950s, 4 x 3 In. 4.00
Tumbler, Basket Weave, Cottage 9.00
Tumbler Set, Pastel, Tupperware, 6½ In., 6 Piece 24.00
Weather Wizard, Old Lady & Kids, Green Marble Look, Nudell Plastic, 6¾ In. 23.00

PLATED AMBERINA was patented June 15, 1886, by Joseph Locke and made by the New England Glass Company. It is similar in color to amberina, but is characterized by a cream colored or chartreuse lining (never white) and small ridges or ribs on the outside.

Celery Vase, 6⅛ In. 8050.00
Pitcher, Tankard, Dark Amber Handle, 8½ In. 28000.00
Syrup, Tufts Silver Plated Fluted Flip Lid & Caddy, 6 In. 9200.00
Tumbler, Label, 3¾ In. 2070.00
Tumbler, Lemonade, Cylindrical, Amber Handle, 5 In. 4025.00
Vase, Lily, Tapered, Amber Disc Foot, 8 In. .... 3450.00 to 5750.00

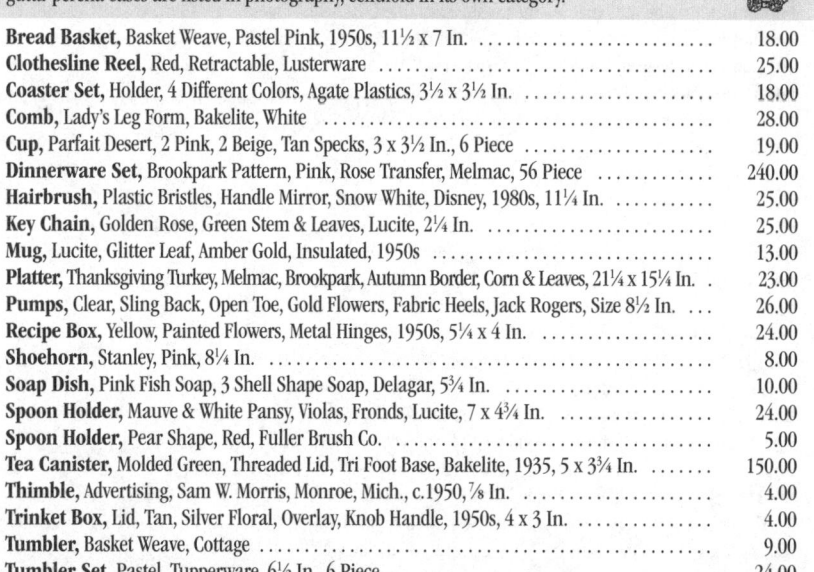

Pisgah Forest, Teapot, Purple Glaze, Rolled Edge, Flattened Finial, c.1945, 5 x 9 In. $201.00

Pisgah Forest, Vase, Crackled Blue Glaze, Bulbous, Wide Tapered Neck, Flared Rim, 9¾ In. $259.00

Planters Peanuts, Figure, Mr. Peanut, Wood, Jointed, Painted, Stick In Hand, 9 In. $193.00

Planters Peanuts, Gate Post, Mr. Peanut, Cast Iron, Painted, 36 In. $4025.00

P

Planters Peanuts, Salt & Pepper,
Mr. Peanut, Ceramic, Glazed,
Rhinestone Monocle, c.1960, 4½ In.
$136.00

Planters Peanuts, Toy, Walker,
Mr. Peanut, Plastic, Windup,
1950s, 9 In.
$175.00

Plique-A-Jour, Vase, Blue,
Russet & Amethyst Blossoms,
Metal Rim & Base, Japan, 5 In.
$863.00

PLIQUE-A-JOUR is an enameling process. The enamel is laid between thin raised metal lines and heated. The finished piece has transparent enamel held between the thin metal wires. It is different from cloisonne because it is translucent.

Vase, Blue, Russet & Amethyst Blossoms, Metal Rim & Base, Japan, 5 In. . . . .*illus*	863.00

POLITICAL memorabilia of all types, from buttons to banners, is collected. Items related to presidential candidates are the most popular, but collectors also search for material related to state and local offices. Memorabilia related to social causes, minor political parties, and protest movements are also included here. Many reproductions have been made. A jugate is a button with photographs of both the presidential and vice presidential candidates. In this list a button is round, usually with a straight pin or metal tab to secure it to a shirt. A pin is brass, often figural, sometimes attached to a ribbon.

Armband, For Hoover & The G.O.P., White Letters, Blue Ground, Red Border, Cloth, 16 In. . .	50.00
Armband, Herbert Hoover, Celluloid, Elastic Band, 4¾ x 3 In. . . . .*illus*	29.00
Ashtray, Uncle Sam & Matador Pulling On Cuba Cigar, Tobacco Leaf Shape Base, Porcelain	215.00
Autograph, George Washington, June, 1795	2400.00
Badge, Inaugural, Reagan, 1981, 3 In.	141.00
Badge, Lincoln, Union Campaign Club, 1864	4840.00
Badge, Police, Inaugural, Nixon, Agnew, Gold Finish, 1969, 3 In.	406.00
Badge, Samuel Tilden, Campaign, Tintype, Ribbon, 1876	1303.00
Badge, T. Roosevelt, Lion, Welcome Teddy, In Lion's Teeth, Aluminum, Lithograph, 2¼ x 2⅓ In. .	837.00
Ballot, Prohibition, James Black, Paper, 1872, 4¾ In.	128.00
Ballot, Z. Taylor, Virginia, Paper, 6½ In.	204.00
Bandanna, Benjamin, Morton, 38-Star Flag, 1888, 18½ x 19½ In.	256.00
Bandanna, Clay, Frelinghuysen Presidential Campaign, Frame, 29 x 31 In.	4927.00
Bandanna, Cleveland, Truman, Cotton, 1884, 19½ x 20¼ In.	282.00
Bandanna, Garfield, Arthur, Eagles, Red Ground, 1880, 19 x 19 In.	179.00
Bandanna, Harrison, Morton, Blue Ground, 1888, 22 x 20½ In.	478.00
Bandanna, Harrison, Morton, Protect Home Industry, Frame, 1888, 21 x 24 In.	246.00
Bandanna, Lincoln & His Generals In Command, 1864	4600.00
Bandanna, McKinley, Roosevelt On Horseback, Frame, 1900, 24½ x 25½ In.	4379.00
Bandanna, Presidential Victims Of Assassins, McKinley, Garfield, Lincoln, 15 x 15 In.	885.00
Bandanna, Protect Home Industry, Red, White, Blue, Frame, 24½ x 26 In.	325.00
Bandanna, Protection, Benjamin Harrison, Levi P. Morton, Cotton, c.1888, 23 x 24 In.	354.00
Bandanna, Taft, Sherman, U.S. Capitol, Women, Red, White, Blue, Black, 16½ x 17½ In. . . .	182.00
Bandanna, William Henry Harrison On Horseback, Tan, Frame, 1840, 28¼ x 26½ In.	1315.00
Bandanna, Winfield S. Hancock, William H. English, 1880	192.00
Bank, McKinley, Roosevelt, Elephant Shape, 2½ x 3½ In.	1434.00
Bank, Mechanical, The Great Political Feud, Ronald Reagan, Tip O'Neill, 1983, 5 x 9 In.	495.00
Bank, Taft-Sherman, Peaceful Bill, Smiling Jim, Bronze Finish, J.M. Harper, c.1908, 4 In. . . .	3025.00
Banner, Blaine, Logan, Plumed Knight, Black Jack, 24 x 38 In.	346.00
Banner, Buchanan, Breckinridge, Grand National, Currier, Frame, 1856, 16 x 12 In.	1016.00
Banner, FDR, Re-Elect Roosevelt, 1940, 54 In.	363.00
Banner, Fremont, Dayton, Grand National, Currier, 1856, 13¾ x 10 In.	598.00
Banner, Lewis Cass, William O. Butler, Grand National, 1848, 10 x 14 In.	555.00
Barrel, Harrison, Log Cabin Hard Cider, People's Choice, Tippecanoe, Barrel, Stand	1800.00
Baseball, Dukakis, Autographed	168.00
Bell, Votes For Women, Multi Porcelain, Old & Young Woman Faces, c.1915, 4 In.	590.00
Booklet, Clear Everything With Sidney, N.Y. Times, July 25, 1944, Pictures, 32 Pages	35.00
Booklet, Speech Of Madame Chiang Kai-Shek, Wellesley College, March 7, 1943, 16 Pages . .	20.00
Bottle, Policeman, Stop The Vote, Long Arm Raised, Figural, Bisque, Germany, 7¼ In.	2390.00
Box, William McKinley, Portrait, Flowers, Leaves, Multicolored, Gilt, 1896, 2¼ x 4 In.	405.00
Broadside, Grover Cleveland, Thomas Hendricks, Jugate, Nation's Choice, 21¾ x 16 In. *illus*	134.00
Broadside, Pro-Lincoln Campaign, Showing How The War Would End, 1864	180.00
Bumper Attachment, Al Smith, For President, Metal, 1928, 8 In. Diam.	79.00
Bumper Attachment, Herbert Hoover, For President, Metal, 1928, 8 In. Diam.	79.00
Bumper Sticker, For The Love Of Ike, 1956, 7½ In.	8.00
Bumper Sticker, McGovern, Shriver, 1972, 12 In.	3.00
Button, Adam Clayton Powell, Congressman, Late 1960s, 1¾ In., Pair	67.00
Button, Adlai Stevenson, Vote Democratic & Don't Let Them Take It Away, 2¼ In.	560.00
Button, Alaska Needs Johnson, Photo, Red, White, Blue, Celluloid, 1½ In.	1331.00
Button, America Needs Kennedy, John F. Kennedy, Celluloid, 4 In.	2541.00
Button, Andrew Jackson A.D. March 4, 1829, Inauguration, Plain Front, Brass, ¾ In.	263.00
Button, Anti Carter, Kennedy, You'll Get More Gas From Boston Bean, Celluloid, 1¾ In.	80.00

P

Button, Barry Goldwater, Don't Tarry, Nominate Barry, Celluloid, 1964, 3 12 In.	370.00
Button, Bryan, Beckham, For Governor Of Ky., Jugate, Celluloid, 1¾ In.	2300.00
Button, Bryan, Kern, Statue Of Liberty, Jugate, 1¾ In.	2500.00
Button, Bryan, Kitchen Club, Jugate, Celluloid, 1¼ In.	2000.00
Button, Bryan, United We Stand, Divided We Fall, No Trusts, Labor, 1896, 1¼ In.	7170.00
Button, Bryan & Sewall, Flag, Photo Of Both, Celluloid, 2 In.	590.00
Button, Bush, Quayle Rebus, Celluloid, 1988, 2⅜ In.	133.00
Button, Bush, Quayle Rebus, Celluloid, 1992, 2⅜ In.	133.00
Button, Calvin Coolidge, Trigate, 1¼ In.	777.00
Button, Carter, A Plain Peanut, Celluloid, 2¼ In.	110.00
Button, Carter, Metzenbaum, Ohio Senior Power, Celluloid, 1976, 1¾ In.	92.00
Button, Carter, Mondale, Celluloid, 2¼ In.	115.00
Button, Carter, Mondale, I Am For Alabama Cope, Photo, Green Letters, Celluloid, 2¼ In.	453.00
Button, Cassius Clay, Anti-Slavery Advocate, Celluloid, 1¼ In.	102.00
Button, Charles Hughes, My First Vote For President, 1916, 1¼ In.	1275.00
Button, Clinton, Gore, Alaska, Bald Eagle, 8 Gold Stars, Celluloid, 3½ In.	448.00
Button, Clinton, Gore, I'm With Magic, Earvin Johnson, Celluloid, 1992, 3½ In.	325.00
Button, Clinton, Gore, They Have Served Our Nation With Distinction, Celluloid, 9 In.	30.00
Button, Coolidge, 4th Of July Club, Liberty Bell, Red, White, Blue, Celluloid, ⅞ In.	258.00
Button, Coolidge, Dawes, 1924, ⅞ In.	131.00
Button, Cox, Red, White, Blue, 1920, 1¼ In.	508.00
Button, Democratic, In Your Guts You Know He's Nuts, Celluloid, 1964, 3½ In.	612.00
Button, Dewey, Warren, Vote Republican, Celluloid, 1¼ In.	2310.00
Button, Dukakis, Bentsen, '88, Black, White, Celluloid, 1½ In.	23.00
Button, Eisenhower, Broyhill, 6 In.	2114.00
Button, Eisenhower, I'm So Ikecited, Celluloid, 1950s, 2½ In.	182.00
Button, Eugene McCarthy, For President, Portrait, Celluloid, 1968, 1¾ In.	4.00
Button, FDR, Clean Sweep, Celluloid, 3½ In.	1870.00
Button, For President, Convict No. 9653, Red Border, 1920, 1 In.	1434.00
Button, Free Angela Davis, Union Bug, Lithograph, 3 In.	58.00
Button, Fremont, Lincoln, Harding Veteran Club, Ribbon, 2¼ In.	533.00
Button, George Wallace, For President, Portrait, Celluloid, 1968, 1¾ In.	4.00
Button, George Washington, G W, Long Live The President, Inaugural, Shank, 1789	1016.00
Button, George Washington, G W, Shank, 1789, ¾ In.	3287.00
Button, George Washington, Inaugural, Linked States, 1769	2384.00
Button, George Washington, Linked States, Long Live The President, Verdigris, Shank, 1789, 1¼ In.	1434.00
Button, Goldwater, Miller, 75, Red, White, Blue, Celluloid, 2¼ In.	413.00
Button, Governor Jim Cox, 1920, ½ In.	461.00
Button, Henry Clay, Clay, Frelinghuysen, Protection & Union, Brass, 1 In.	102.00
Button, Henry Clay, Oblique Portrait, Gilt Brass Shell, 1845, 1 In.	155.00
Button, Henry Wallace, Wallaces' Farmer, You Should Join This Army, 1900	261.00
Button, Hoover, My Country Tis Of Thee, The Crisis Is Here, Celluloid, 1928, 1¼ In.	1997.00
Button, Hubert H. Humphrey, For President, Portrait, Celluloid, 1968, 1¾ In.	4.00
Button, Hughes & Fairbanks, 1916, 1¾ In.	395.00
Button, Humphrey, Muskie Donkey Wobble, 1968, 3½ In.	242.00
Button, I Like Ike, Chimpanzee, Celluloid, 1950s, 1¼ In.	404.00
Button, I Like Ike, Red, White, Blue, 1952, ¾ In.	3.00
Button, Ike, Nixon, Don't Change The Team, 1956, 3½ In.	255.00
Button, Ike & Dick, They're For You, Jugate, 1952, 1½ In.	23.00
Button, Inaugural, Andrew Jackson, 1828	365.00
Button, Jackie Robinson Team For Rockefeller, Baseball Infield, 1968, 2 x 2 In.	282.00
Button, James M. Cox, Tyler Commercial College, Tyler, Texas, Photo, 1920, 1 In.	2400.00
Button, JFK Next President, Bug Eyes, Celluloid, 3½ In.	480.00
Button, JFK Vice President, Lithograph, 1956, 2¼ In.	467.00
Button, John F. Kennedy, New England Presents, 1956	515.00
Button, John W. Davis, For President, 1924, 1¼ In.	1195.00
Button, John W. Davis For Congress, 1 In.	478.00
Button, John William Davis For President, 1924, 1¼ In.	1302.00
Button, Keep Truman, Green Letters, White, Celluloid, 1948, 1 In.	773.00
Button, Keep U.S. Out Of War, United States, Red, White, Blue, ⅞ In.	9.00
Button, Marcus Garvey, Provisional President Of Africa, Portrait, 1921, 1¼ In.	125.00
Button, Martin Luther King, Peace Rally, Black, White Photo, April 27, 1968, 3 In.	48.00
Button, Martin Van Buren, Democracy, White Metal, 1840, 1½ In.	192.00
Button, Martin Van Buren Excelsior On Back, Ornate Front, Gilt Brass, c.1836, ¾ In.	209.00
Button, McGovern, Eagleton, Blue, White, 1972, 1⅛ In.	3.00
Button, McGovern, Shriver, Come Home America, Jugate, Celluloid, 1972, 3½ In.	7.00

Political, Armband, Herbert Hoover,
Celluloid, Elastic Band, 4¾ x 3 In.
$29.00

Political, Broadside, Grover Cleveland,
Thomas Hendricks, Jugate,
Nation's Choice, 21¾ x 16 In.
$134.00

Political, Button, McKinley,
Do You Smoke?, That's What McKinley
Promised, Factory, 1900, 2 In.
$1912.00

P

Reproduction Political Memorabilia

Beware of copies of political buttons, pins, and other political memorabilia. The 1972 Hobby Protection Act requires reproduction and fantasy political items to be marked with the word *reproduction* and the year of manufacture. Not all are.

Political, Button,
Trade In Your Ford In '76,
Gerald Ford As Hood Ornament
On An Edsel, 2½ In.
$137.00

Political, Figurine, Cartoonish Woman,
We Want The Vote!, Bisque, 3½ In.
$1554.00

Political, Flag,
Benjamin Harrison, 44 Stars,
Portrait, 1892, 7 x 10¼ In.
$1355.00

Political, Game, Votes For Women,
Suffragist Versus Anti-Suffragist,
Panko, Card, 52 Cards
$510.00

Button, McGovern Concert, C. King, J. Taylor, B. Streisand, Celluloid, 1972, 3½ In.	372.00
Button, McKinley, Do You Smoke?, That's What McKinley Promised, Factory, 1900, 2 In. *illus*	1912.00
Button, McKinley, Hobart, Bicycle Built For 2, Jugate, White, Blue, Brass Rim, Celluloid, 1⅛ In. . .	2031.00
Button, McKinley, Roosevelt, Eagle At Top, Celluloid, 1¼ In.	57.00
Button, McKinley, Teddy Roosevelt, Rough Rider, Celluloid, Jugate, 1¼ In.	446.00
Button, Mike Dukakis, Arizonans For Ducactus, Sand, Cactus, Votes, 1988, 2¼ In.	139.00
Button, Millard Fillmore, The Union, Portrait, White Metal, 1856, 1½ In.	156.00
Button, Mondale, Ferraro, We Are A Mirror Of America, Portrait, Celluloid, 1984, 1¼ In.	43.00
Button, Mondale, Ferraro, We Are A Mirror Of America, Portrait, Celluloid, 1984, 3½ In.	55.00
Button, Nelson Rockefeller, For President, Portrait, Celluloid, 1968, 1¾ In.	4.00
Button, Nixon, Pep, Peace, Economy, Prosperity, Celluloid, 1960, 3 In.	281.00
Button, Nixon Gone With The Wind, Donkey, Celluloid, 1972, 2⅛ In.	1045.00
Button, Parker, Davis, Sepia, Celluloid, Presidential Campaign, Jugate, 1904, 2¼ In.	363.00
Button, Peggy For First Lady, Yellow, Red Letters, Celluloid, 1¾ In.	346.00
Button, Profile In Courage, Elect John F. Kennedy Vice President, 1956, 2¼ In.	508.00
Button, Progressive Policies Become Law, Celluloid, ⅞ In.	32.00
Button, Reagan, Bush, Columbus Day Parade, Portraits, N.Y., 1984, Celluloid, 1¼ In.	35.00
Button, Reagan, Bush, Columbus Day Parade, Portraits, N.Y., 1984, Celluloid, 3½ In.	49.00
Button, Richard M. Nixon, For President, Portrait, Celluloid, 1968, 1¾ In.	5.00
Button, Robert F. Kennedy, For President, Portrait, Celluloid, 1968, 1¾ In.	6.00
Button, Ronald W. Reagan, For President, Portrait, Celluloid, 1968, 1¾ In.	13.00
Button, Roosevelt, Bull Moose Reception, Celluloid, Ribbon, 1912, ⅞ In.	797.00
Button, Roosevelt, Fairbanks, Flag, Celluloid, Jugate, 1904, 2⅛ In.	1150.00
Button, Roosevelt, Fairbanks, Sepia, Celluloid, Jugate, 1¼ In.	1507.00
Button, Roosevelt, For Humanity, Red, White, Blue, 1936, ¾ In.	9.00
Button, Roosevelt, Garner, Repeal & Prosperity, Jugate, Celluloid, 1932, 1¼ In.	1664.00
Button, Roosevelt, Member Georgia Roosevelt Club, Photo, 1¼ In.	2300.00
Button, Stop The War Now, Stop & Peace Sign, Red, White, c.1970, 3½ In.	9.00
Button, Taft, Sherman, Bloomington, Ill., Club No. 1, Ear Of Corn, Photo, 1¼ In.	2400.00
Button, Taft, Sherman, Jugate, 1908, 1¾ In.	388.00
Button, Taft, Sherman, Jugate, Celluloid, 1¾ In.	1331.00
Button, Teddy Roosevelt, Bull Moose, Caricature, Oval, 2⅜ x 1¹/₁₆ In.	7000.00
Button, Teddy Roosevelt, Michigan Volunteer Cavalry Reunion, Sept. 19, 1900, 1¾ In.	1200.00
Button, Teddy Roosevelt, Rough Rider, Mechanical, Hinged Mouth, 1¼ In.	825.00
Button, Theodore Roosevelt, Charles Fairbanks, Jugate, 1904, 1¼ In.	1292.00
Button, Theodore Roosevelt, Charles Fairbanks, Sagamore Hills, Jugate, 1¼ In.	605.00
Button, Theodore Roosevelt, For Vice President, 1¼ In.	808.00
Button, Theodore Roosevelt, Man Of The Hour, ⅞ In.	315.00
Button, Theodore Roosevelt, Square Deal & Straight Hand, 1⅜ In.	3850.00
Button, Theodore Roosevelt, Teddy's Terrors, Cartoon, 1¾ In.	812.00
Button, Together For McGovern, Rainbow, 3 In.	54.00
Button, Trade In Your Ford In '76, Gerald Ford As Hood Ornament On An Edsel, 2½ In. *illus*	137.00
Button, Truman, Barkley, White House, Red, Gold, Blue, 1948, ¾ In.	33.00
Button, Truman, Civil Rights Day, Celluloid, 1949, ⅞ In.	424.00
Button, Truman, Do It Again, Celluloid, 3½ In.	715.00
Button, Truman, Our President, Celluloid, 3 In.	891.00
Button, Truman, True-Man, Black, White, Celluloid, 1½ In.	303.00
Button, Uncle Sam Hanging Adolph Hitler, Let's Pull Together, c.1943, 1¾ In.	109.00
Button, Vote Democratic, Donkey, Flasher, Red, White, Blue, 1964, 2½ In.	6.00
Button, Vote Republican, Elephant, Flasher, Red, White, Blue, 1964, 2½ In.	6.00
Button, Warren G. Harding, For President, 1¾ In. 1016.00 to 1137.00	
Button, Warren Harding, Tyler Commercial College, Tyler, Texas, Photo, 1920, 1 In.	3250.00
Button, We Want Willkie, Blue Letters, White Ground, Red Rim, Celluloid, 1¾ In.	12.00
Button, William Henry Harrison, Major General, Brass, 1836, 1¼ In.	311.00
Button, William Howard Taft Riding GOP Elephant To Victory, 2⅛ In.	460.00
Button, William McKinley, Hot Stuff, McKinley, Mechanical, Celluloid, Brass, 1½ In.	956.00
Button, William McKinley, Ida McKinley, 3½ In.	168.00
Button, William McKinley, Memorium, Born Jan. 29, 1845, Shot Sept. 6, 1901, Portrait, 4 In. .	335.00
Button, William McKinley, National Steel Co., Ohio Works, 1900, Portrait, Flag, 2⅛ In.	478.00
Button, William McKinley, Portrait, American Flag, Gold Wreath, 3 In.	335.00
Button, William McKinley, Portrait, McKinley Sweeper Cigars, Black, White, ⅞ In.	204.00
Button, William McKinley, Riding Bicycle, To White House, Caricature, Celluloid, 1¼ In. . . .	1554.00
Button, Willkie, Ditch The Horse That Puts Us In The Middle Of The Stream, 1¾ In.	700.00
Button, Winfield Scott, Wreath, Lundys Lane, Vera Cruz, Cerro Gordo, White Metal, 1880, 1¼ In.	66.00
Button, Women's Suffrage, Let Ohio Women Vote, Whitehead & Hoag Back Paper, ¾ In.	898.00
Button, Woodrow Wilson, T.R. Marshall, J.E. Walscheid, Trigate	1625.00

Cane, Cleveland, Thurman Campaign, Rooster Top	1500.00
Cane, Harrison, Morton Heads, 1888, 34½ In.	2271.00
Cane, Jimmy Carter For President, 76, Embossed, 1976	42.00
Card, Christmas, White House, Image Of Red Room, John & Jacqueline Kennedy, 1962	500.00
Card, Committee, FDR, Political Action, 5¾ In.	28.00
Card, Dinner & Rally, For Adlai & Estes, November 13, 1956	12.00
Card, Ike & Mamie, Happy Birthday Celebration In Hershey, Pa., 10-13-53	12.50
Card, Our Teddy The Rough Rider, Aluminum, c.1904, 2 x 3½ In.	232.00
Carte De Visite, Lincoln & Cabinet, 1864	108.00
Carte De Visite, Stephen Douglas, Appleton	108.00
Carte De Visite, Victoria Woodhull, First Female Candidate For U.S. President	180.00
Chess Set, Watergate Personalities, Nixon King, 7 Republicans, 7 Democrats, 1972	350.00
Cigar, Taft, Blue Label, Light One Up For Bill, 9 In.	66.00
Cigar, Taft, Red Label, Victory, 9 In.	66.00
Cigar Box, Grover Cleveland, Stevenson, Paper American Flag, Wood, 6¾ x 8¾ x 4¾ In.	330.00
Cigar Box, Repeal Prohibition, Nation Needs A 5 Cent Cigar, Wood, 12½ In.	48.00
Cigar Box Opener, McKinley, Roosevelt, Hammer, Get Your Hammer Out, Now Knock, 4 x 2 In.	287.00
Cigarette Lighter, Goldwater, GOP Elephant With Glasses, 1¾ In.	59.00
Coaster, Barry Goldwater For President, Black, White, 1964, 3½ In.	4.00
Coloring Book, JFK, 1962, Unused, 10 x 13 In.	12.00
Compass, Coolidge, Dawes, Jugate, March 4, 1925, Celluloid, 1¼ In.	1706.00
Custard Cup, Abraham Lincoln, Presidential Pattern, Cover, 1800s, 2 x 2½ In.	32400.00
Daguerreotype, Daniel Webster, Brass Oval Frame	1080.00
Dish, Ice Cream, Rutherford B. Hayes, Presidential Pattern, Haviland, 7 x 7 In.	2880.00
Display, Woodrow Wilson, Flags, Pressed Cardboard, 1911	897.00
Dixie Bucks, Picturing Geo. Wallace, Confederate Flag & Soldier, 100 Bucks	7.50
Drawer Pull, George Washington, Portrait, Enamel, Brass, England, 1¼ x 3¼ In.	996.00
Envelope, Canceled, Bess Truman Day, Independence, Mo., Harry & Bess, Feb. 13, 1975	15.00
Envelope, Canceled, Hoover For President Slogan & Picture, Indianapolis 1932	18.00
Fan, Coolidge, Photos Of Presidents From Washington To Coolidge, Paddle Form, 10½ In.	44.00
Fan, FDR Portrait, Family Damp Wash Laundry, Waukesha, Wisc., 1936, 15 x 9 In.	105.00
Ferrotype, Abraham Lincoln, Portrait, 1860s, 1¼ In.	228.00
Ferrotype, Abraham Lincoln, Portrait, Beardless, Full Chest, Frame, 1 x ¾ In.	717.00
Ferrotype, Grant, Colfax, Brass Shell, Pinback	594.00
Ferrotype, James A. Garfield, E Pluribus Unum, Eagle, 1⅛ In.	287.00
Ferrotype, Stephen A. Douglas, 1860	212.00
Ferrotype, Ulysses Grant & Colfax, Portraits, 1868, 1 In.	131.00
Ferrotype, Ulysses S. Grant, Portrait, 1 In.	96.00
Figurine, Cartoonish Woman, We Want The Vote!, Bisque, 3½ In. *illus*	1554.00
Figurine, Cat, Gray Blue, Votes For Women, Porcelain, 3¼ In.	418.00
Figurine, Chalkware, Bust Of President John F. Kennedy, Linn Products, 1963, 8 In.	60.00
Figurine, Lincoln, On Horse, Staffordshire, 15¼ In.	2032.00
Figurine, Teddy Roosevelt, On Horse, Rough Rider Uniform, Painted, Composition, 5½ x 5 In.	311.00
Figurine, Warren Harding, Dog, Laddie Boy, Guarding Our President, 6½ x 6½ In.	528.00
Figurine, Woman, We Want The Vote, Spring Arms, Bisque, Germany, 3½ x 3 In.	1554.00
Flag, 12 Appliqued 5-Point Stars Around Larger Star, 13 Stripes, 6 Ft. 9 In. x 11 Ft. 6 In.	2530.00
Flag, Benjamin Harrison, 44 Stars, Portrait, 1892, 7 x 10¼ In. *illus*	1355.00
Flag, Campaign, Featuring 36 Stars, Uniformed General Grant, Grant & Colfax	6325.00
Flag, Garfield, Arthur, Campaign, 39 Stars, Frame, 1880, 31¾ x 24 In.	3892.00
Flag, Grover Cleveland, Portrait, Red, White, Blue, Black, 1884, 26½ x 17½ In.	1555.00
Flag, James G. Blaine, John A. Logan, President, Vice President, 23½ x 15½ In.	6346.00
Flag, McKinley & Hobart, 39 Stars, Stripes, Handmade, 68 x 44 In.	4600.00
Flag, Red, White, Blue, 21 Embroidered Stars, Metallic Fringe, Silk, 32½ x 40 In.	28680.00
Flag, Red, White, Blue, 26 Stars, 13 Stripes, Silk, Frame, c.1837, 31½ x 35 In.	5975.00
Flyer, Campaign, 1948, Progressive Party, Henry A. Wallace	40.00
Flyer, Operation Support, Pres. Kennedy's Program For Better Homes, 8½ x 14½ In.	6.00
Folder, Bill Clinton, Governor For Arkansas, 6 Pages	10.00
Folder, Bimetallism, 1896, 6 Pages	6.00
Folder, Goldwater In Air Force Uniform, Message To All Vests, 4 Pages	4.00
Folder, Ike, Michigan Gov. Fred Alger, Red, White, Blue, 6 Pages	5.00
Folder, People & Principles, Eisenhower, 10 Pages	5.00
Game, Coin Drop, Admiral Dewey Portrait, Wood, c.1900, 19½ x 10 x 6½ In.	567.00
Game, Theodore Roosevelt, 2½ In.	447.00
Game, Votes For Women, Suffragist Versus Anti-Suffragist, Panko, Card, 52 Cards *illus*	510.00
Gavel, Jim Wright, House Of Representatives, Wood, Signed, 14 In.	217.00
Handkerchief, Linen, Grover Cleveland, Adlai Stevenson, 1892, 17¼ x 18 In.	49.00

Political, Menu, Inaugural Ball, Benjamin Harrison, March 4, 1889, Flag, Cardboard, Ribbon, 5 x 6 In. $132.00

Political, Pin, Silver Bug, Bryan, Sewall, Jugate, Mechanical, 1896, 1¾ x 1½ In. $287.00

Political, Pitcher, Andrew Jackson Portrait, Hero Of New Orleans, Copper Luster, Shaped Handle, 6 In. $5975.00

TIP

All types of light— sunlight, fluorescent light, and electric lights—will eventually harm paper.

503

Political, Ribbon, Flag, Silk, Abraham Lincoln Photo, Brass Shell Frame, c.1864, 5 x ¾ In. $685.00

Political, Ribbon, Mrs. Benjamin Harrison, Celluloid Portrait, Red, White, Blue, 1892, 2 x 3¼ In. $114.00

Handkerchief, We Want Roosevelt, 1930s, 7 x 12 In.	70.00
Hat, College Youth For Nixon, Black, Yellow, 1960, 11 In.	22.00
Hatpin, Greeley, Tintype, 1872	5000.00
Invitation, Mrs. Truman At Home, Engraved Card, 1947, 3½ x 4½ In.	25.00
Invitation, Ulysses S. Grant, Inaugural Reception, 1869, 7 x 10 In.	448.00
JFK Football Player Bobbin' Head, 7 In.	840.00
Jug, Grotesque, Green Glaze, Cleter Meaders III, Jimmy Carter, President Of USA, 12½ In.	92.00
Label, Cigar Box, Woodrow Wilson, Square, 4½ In.	25.00
Label, Wine Bottle, Watergate With Anti Slogans, Budweiser, Unflattering Picture Of Nixon	16.00
Lamp, Oil, President Theodore Roosevelt, Milk Glass, White House, Eagle, 1900, 25 In.	3161.00
Lantern, Hayes, Wheeler, Paper, Red, White, Blue, 10 In.	392.00
License Plate, Attachment, Metal, We Need Roosevelt, 6½ In.	301.00
License Plate, Dwight Eisenhower, I Like Ike, Image Of Ike, 4 x 9 In.	115.00
License Plate, FDR, Democratic National Committee, 1936, 11½ In.	182.00
License Plate, FDR Inauguration, 1933	8100.00
License Plate, Forward With Roosevelt, 9½ In.	92.00
License Plate, Hoover For President, Blue Letters, White Ground, 12 In.	44.00
License Plate, John F. Kennedy For President, White Ground, Green Letters, 1960	310.00
License Plate, LaFollette For President, Progressive Party, 1924, 10 In.	242.00
License Plate, Prohibition, Repeal 18th Amendment, 12 In.	66.00
License Plate, Prohibition, Why Repeal 18th Amendment, Enforce It, 12 In.	105.00
License Plate, Repeal 18th Amendment, 14 In.	385.00
License Plate, Truman '48, 1948	713.00
License Plate Attachment, Wendell Willkie For President, Wood, 1940	145.00
Magazine, Jet, RFK, Luke Moore, May 30, 1963	7.00
Magazine, Time, Truman, FDR, Pony Edition, November 6, 1944, 6 x 8¼ In.	10.00
Match Holder, Woman, Votes For Women A Match For You, Weymouth, Wood, 1909	1554.00
Medallion, Blaine, Logan, Busts, Republicans Have Ruled Since 1860, 1884, 1 In.	29.00
Medallion, William Henry Harrison, Log Cabin, Hard Cider, Brass, 1840, 1 In.	43.00
Menu, Inaugural Ball, Benjamin Harrison, March 4, 1889, Flag, Cardboard, Ribbon, 5 x 6 In. *illus*	132.00
Mug, Abraham Lincoln, Portrait, President Abraham Lincoln, Ceramic, c.1862, 3¾ In.	837.00
Mug, Alfred E. Smith, March 23, 1911, 3⅝ In.	307.00
Mug, Portrait Of President Abraham Lincoln, 1860s	1477.00
Mug, Teddy Roosevelt, Elephant Handle, Ceramic, Toby Potteries, 7¾ In.	1315.00
Mustache Brush, Garfield & Wife, Milk Glass, Finger Hole, c.1880, 2½ x 5¼ In.	224.00
Newspaper, Dewey Defeats Truman, Chicago Tribune, Nov. 3, 1948, Frame, 31 x 24 In.	1175.00
Nodder, Democrat Donkey, Composition, 8 In.	64.50
Pail, William McKinley, A Full Dinner Pail, White, Gilt, American Flag Ribbon, 5 x 2½ In.	836.00
Painting On Ivory, General Lafayette, Wood Frame, Signed, G. Riviere, 4¼ In.	1494.00
Pamphlet, Hubert Humphrey For President Campaign, Autographed, 1968, 9 x 11 In.	40.00
Pamphlet, Rockefeller For President Campaign, Win With Rockefeller, 1960, 4 x 9 In.	40.00
Paper Hand-Out, Hand Shape, Give Me Your Hand, Jack Kennedy, 6 x 10 In.	69.00
Paperweight, Ulysses S. Grant, Portrait, Painted Brass Color, Steel, c.1880, 3 x 2½ In.	360.00
Parade Horn, McKinley As Napoleon, Painted Paper, 1896, 9 x 15 In.	10.00
Peace Pipe, Franklin Pierce, Ceramic, 1¾ x 2 In.	248.00
Pennant, Bobby Kennedy, Destined To Become President, Felt, 1968, 14 In.	45.00
Pennant, Bryan, Red, Blue, White Stars, 12 x 32½ In.	239.00
Pennant, Dewey For President, Purple, White, Felt, 1948, 26 In.	39.00
Pennant, Taft Inauguration, Felt, Red, Gold Glitter, 1909, 17 In.	186.00
Pennant, Truman For President, Felt, 1948, 25 In.	76.00
Pennant, Victory, Votes For Women, Black On Yellow, Felt, 35 In.	1135.00
Pennant, Vote For Hoover, Blue, White, Cloth, 3-Sided, 18 In.	44.00
Pennant, Votes For Women, 17 In.	363.00
Pennant, William Jennings Bryan, Felt, Blue & Red, 13 Stars, 1908, 32 x 12 In.	240.00
Photograph, GOP Presidential Candidate Wendell Willkie, Black & White, 1940, 8 x 11 In.	25.00
Photograph, Lincoln, Albumen, Springfield, Ill., Oval, Frame	4500.00
Photograph, Warren G. Harding, To George L. Kraatz, Fellow Mennonite, 1921, 13 x 10 In.	360.00
Picture, Lincoln & Hamlin, Frame	360.00
Pin, Alf Landon Notification, Double Felt Sunflower, Celluloid, 1936, 2¼ In.	502.00
Pin, Campaign, Grant, Colfax, 1868	450.00
Pin, Campaign, Seymour Blair, 1868	638.00
Pin, FDR, Photo, 3 Red, White, Blue Ribbons, 1920, 1¼ In.	7392.00
Pin, Flag, Hanging From Flagpole, Remember Pearl Harbor, Plastic, 1½ In.	65.00
Pin, Horace Greeley, Campaign, 1872	1077.00
Pin, Image Of William Henry Harrison, Hand Painted, 1840	847.00
Pin, John F. Kennedy, PT-109, Brass, 10 x 45 In.	33.00

P

Pin, Kennedy, Humphrey, Freeman, Matthews, 1960s, 2¼ In.	225.00
Pin, Lapel, American Flag, Cloth On Metal, 1888	9.00
Pin, McKinley, Teddy Roosevelt, Jugate, Brown, Full Dinner Bucket, 1¼ In.	46.00
Pin, Pansy, Harrison & Morton, Image Of Both, 1888	560.00
Pin, Pepsi-Cola, Relax, Donkey, Cowboy Hat, Democratic Convention, 1964, 3½ In.	62.00
Pin, Robert Taft Hopeful, Mad Magazine's Alfred E. Neuman, 1952, 4 In.	160.00
Pin, Rose, Velt, Theodore Roosevelt Rebus, Celluloid, 1¼ In.	878.00
Pin, Shield, McKinley For Protection	1549.00
Pin, Shield, Theodore Roosevelt, Charter Member, Celluloid, 1½ In.	318.00
Pin, Silver Bug, Bryan, Sewall, Jugate, Mechanical, 1896, 1¾ x 1½ In. ....*illus*	287.00
Pin, The Coming Of Carter, Caricature, 1976, 2⅜ In.	28.00
Pin, Theodore Roosevelt, Georgia Day, June 10, 1907, 2 In.	999.00
Pin, U.S. Grant, c.1868, 2 x 2½ In.	2750.00
Pin, Ulysses S. Grant, Portrait, White, Composite, 1 x 1⅓ In.	63.00
Pin, Whitehead & Hoag Co., What Makes An Ohio Delegate Happy, Celluloid	180.00
Pin, William Henry Harrison, Harrison & Reform, Log Cabin, Flag, White Metal, 1 In.	837.00
Pin, William Henry Harrison, Log Cabin, Sulphide, Gray Blue, White, Gold Border, ¾ In.	2032.00
Pipe Bowl, William Jennings Bryan, Embossed, 2¼ x 3 In.	83.00
Pitcher, Andrew Jackson Portrait, Hero Of New Orleans, Copper Luster, Shaped Handle, 6 In. .. *illus*	5975.00
Pitcher, James A. Garfield, Queensware, Wedgwood, 1881, 7¼ x 7½ In.	1554.00
Pitcher, William Henry Harrison, Copper Luster, c.1840, 5¼ In.	4183.00
Plaque, Hoover, Curtis, Photos, Eagle, Capitol Building, Shield Form, 2-Sided, Cardboard	297.00
Plaque, Theodore Roosevelt, Portrait, Bronze, Marked, 1900, 10 x 6¾ In.	538.00
Plate, Alphabet, Picturing James A. Garfield In Campaign Pose, 1880, 6 In.	80.00
Plate, Andrew Jackson, Pink Luster, Enoch Wood, c.1824, 8¾ In.	1416.00
Plate, Benjamin Harrison, Presidential Pattern, 1800s, 7¼ In.	1920.00
Plate, Dessert, Andrew Jackson, Presidential Pattern, 1800s, 8⅝ In.	22800.00
Plate, Howard, Taft, James Sherman, Past Republican Presidents, Tin Lithograph, 1908, 10 In.	330.00
Plate, James K. Polk, Presidential Pattern, Edouard Honore, 1800s, 9½ In.	22800.00
Plate, Mexican-American War, Texian Campaign, Purple Transfer, 1846, 8 In.	449.00
Plate, Scott & Pierce, Cast Iron, Oval, 12 x 10¼ In., Pair	1100.00
Plate, Temperance, Sobriety, Domestic Comfort, 5¾ In.	49.00
Plate, Ulysses S. Grant, Family, Chinese Export, Fish, 1800s, 9¾ In.	7800.00
Plate, Ulysses S. Grant, Presidential Pattern, Central Flower, 1800s, 8½ In.	1920.00
Plate, William McKinley, Protect & Plenty, c.1896, 9¼ In.	106.00
Pocket Knife, Taft & Sherman, 2 Blades, Names Stamped On Side, 1908, 3½ In.	156.00
Postcard, Bryan Post, Ear Of Corn Shape, Green Ribbon, Song Of The Corn Lyrics, 1908	360.00
Postcard, Inauguration Of President Roosevelt, Folded, Stiff Cardboard, 3½ x 16½ In.	129.00
Postcard, Teddy Roosevelt, Booker T. Washington, Visit Tuskegee Institute, 3½ x 5½ In.	190.00
Poster, FDR, Harry Truman, Missouri, 1940, 11 x 14 In.	159.00
Poster, FDR's Birthday Ball, Infantile Paralysis, Howard Chandler Christy, 1936, 24 x 13 In.	276.00
Poster, Fisk, Brooks, Prohibition, 1888, 11 x 17 In.	173.00
Poster, Franklin Roosevelt, Confidence, Ship, Portrait, c.1933, 25 x 19 In.	123.00
Poster, Gene McCarthy, Breath Of Fresh Air, 1968, 17 x 11 In.	33.00
Poster, Herbert Hoover, Charles Curtis, Iowa, State Candidates, 14 x 22 In.	193.00
Poster, Horace Greeley, Die Cut Cardboard, Hair, Mat, Frame, 1872, 20 x 26 In.	1461.00
Poster, Kennedy For President, Time For Greatness, 1960, 18½ x 28 In.	1150.00
Poster, McKinley, Hobart, Jugate, Flag, Blue Tinted, 1896 16½ x 21½ In.	118.00
Poster, Nixon's The One, Celebrities, Politicians, 1968, 28 x 20 In.	29.00
Poster, Pat Paulsen For President, 22¾ x 35 In.	60.00
Poster, Theodore Roosevelt, 1912, 20 x 16 In.	69.00
Poster, Women's Political Union, Suffrage Procession, May 23, 1910, 21 x 28 In.	5032.00
Poster, You Win When You Vote For Ike & Dick, 10 x 13 In.	135.00
Poster Stamp, Win With MacArthur, MacArthur Day, Slogans, June 13, 1942, 3½ x 5 In.	18.00
Presidential Ticket, Union, Lincoln, Johnson, Black Letters, Toned Newsprint, 7 x 3 In.	214.00
Program, Dinner, Inaugural, Mayflower Hotel, Seating Arrangements, 1949	10.00
Receipt, Donation For 1.00 For Senator Eugene McCarthy's 1968 Campaign	6.00
Record, Calvin Coolidge Campaign Speech, 1924, 4⅝ In.	84.00
Ribbon, Abraham Lincoln, Portrait, Beardless, Full Chest, Silk, 7½ x 2½ In.	3585.00
Ribbon, Abraham Lincoln, Silk, 3 x 7 In.	4619.00
Ribbon, Abraham Lincoln For President, Campaign, Paper, 1864, 3⅛ x 7⅝ In.	1321.00
Ribbon, Benjamin Harrison For President Campaign In Tipton, Black & White, 1888	80.00
Ribbon, Bookmark, Teddy Roosevelt, Bull Moose, Paper, 9 In.	144.00
Ribbon, Buchanan & Breckenridge, Democratic Candidate, 8 In.	3500.00
Ribbon, Cleveland & Hendricks, Sepia, Oak, Olive Spray, Jugate, 6 x 2½ In.	148.00
Ribbon, Fillmore, Know Nothing, 6½ In.	300.00

Political, Stickpin, Ulysses S. Grant, Portrait, Brass Frame, Stars & Stripes, 1868, 1 In. $191.00

Political, Textile, James A. Garfield, Chester A. Arthur, Portraits, Frame, 1880, 22 x 23 In. $110.00

Political, Tip Tray, Grand Old Party, President Taft, Vice President Sherman, Tin Lithograph, 1908, 4 In. $220.00

P

Political, Valentine, Girl, Boys,
No Votes, No Hearts, Votes For Women,
Cardboard, Die Cut
$84.00

If words could tell of all the love
within this heart of mine
I'd keep on speaking till I'd won your for my VALENTINE

Political Buttons

Pinback buttons were
first used during the 1896
presidential campaign of
William McKinley and
William Jennings Bryan.
Pictures and words were
printed on paper and
mounted under a layer of
transparent celluloid. In
1920, manufacturers used
lithographed tin. In the
1950s, some buttons were
coated with acetate, a clear
plastic (although some
collectors refer to these pins
as "celluloid" or "cello").

Look for buttons with
a picture of both the
presidential and vice
presidential candidates
(known as jugates), buttons
with just the printed names
of candidates, slogan buttons,
and "anti" buttons—those
against a candidate rather
than for one. Save old
buttons. Store them in a
dry place or display them
away from bright light.
Don't ignore other political
memorabilia, including
matchboxes, bumper stickers,
signs, and bandannas.

Ribbon, Flag, Silk, Abraham Lincoln Photo, Brass Shell Frame, c.1864, 5 x ¾ In. . . . . . *illus*	685.00
Ribbon, Fremont, Free Soil, 1856, 5 In.	100.00
Ribbon, George B. McClellan For President, 1864, 3⅜ x 7⅝ In.	2415.00
Ribbon, Harrison & Reform, We Will Take Him From The Plough, 1840, 6½ x 2½ In.	627.00
Ribbon, John Bell, Silk, 1860, 3 x 7 In.	1430.00
Ribbon, John Tyler, President Of The United States, Portrait, Eagle, Silk, 7⅓ x 3 In.	4183.00
Ribbon, Know Nothing Rare, 1854, 8 In.	128.00
Ribbon, La Guardia, Labor Party, McGoldrick, Morris, Levy, 7¼ In.	67.00
Ribbon, Lincoln & Hamlin, Romeo Wide Awakes For Abraham Lincoln, 1860	1663.00
Ribbon, McKinley, Sound Money, Chicago Jewelers, 1896, 6½ In.	41.00
Ribbon, McKinley, Welcome, Confederate Veterans, Macon, Ga., 1898	1100.00
Ribbon, Memorial, Andrew Jackson, Silk, W.L. Germon, Philadelphia, c.1845, 9 x 3 In.	354.00
Ribbon, Mourning, Lincoln, Issued By Albany Council	288.00
Ribbon, Mrs. Benjamin Harrison, Celluloid Portrait, Red, White, Blue, 1892, 2 x 3¼ In. *illus*	114.00
Ribbon, Native American Party, Know Nothing, 8 In.	206.00
Ribbon, People's Convention, Massachusetts, 1892, 6 In.	128.00
Ribbon, People's Convention Delegate, California, 1896, 8 In.	106.00
Ribbon, Sergeant Of Arms, Roosevelt, Johnson, Jugate, 1912 St. Louis State Convention	3827.00
Ribbon, Seymour, Blair, Silk, 1868	2324.00
Ribbon, Smith, Anti Prohibition, 6 In.	85.00
Ribbon, St. John, Prohibition, 1884, 6½ In.	230.00
Ribbon, Swallow, Prohibition, 1904, 6¼ In.	24.00
Ribbon, Taft, Sherman, Jugate, Celluloid, 2-Sided, I Bring Good Luck, 1⅝ In.	2263.00
Ribbon, Townsend, 1941, 5 In.	48.00
Ribbon, Ulysses S. Grant, People's Choice, Silk, Yellow, 7 x 2¼ In.	478.00
Ribbon, Ulysses S. Grant For President, Horandt & Sons, c.1868, 6½ x 1¾ In.	398.00
Ribbon, Washington, County Of Washington, Benevolent Society, Silk, 1808-15, 5¾ x 1¾ In.	239.00
Ribbon, William Henry Harrison, Log Cabin, Silk, 1840	482.00
Salt & Pepper, Peanut Shape, Cartoon Jimmy Carter, Marked Kimpie, 3 x 2 In.	30.00
Sand Picture, In Bottle, Patriotic, Eagle In Flight, American Flag, Late 1800s, 8¾ In.	10575.00
Sheet Music, Roosevelt's Rough Riders March, 2 Step, Roosevelt, Commanding Officers, 1898, 14 x 11 In.	287.00
Sheet Music, Set, Lincoln Quick Step, 1860	878.00
Sheet Music, Taylor Rough & Ready Polka, 1848, 6 Pages	168.00
Shield, McKinley, Enamel, Red, White, Blue, Stars, 1¼ In.	16.00
Sign, Cleveland Vs. Harrison, Butter, Sugar Price Comparison, Cream, Black, 22 x 74 In.	2875.00
Snuffbox, Martin Van Buren, Papier-Mache, ¾ x 2¾ In.	5975.00
Songbook, James K. Polk Campaign, 1844	810.00
Sponge Finger, Dukakis, Bentsen, No. 1, 22 In.	77.00
Spoon, Teddy Roosevelt, Lieut. Col. Theo. Roosevelt, American Flag, Portrait, Brass Plated, 4 In.	156.00
Statue, Suffragette, Look Out, Votes For Women Or Else, 5¾ In.	515.00
Sticker, Communist Party & Daily Workers Dr., 25 Cents, 1940, 2⅛ x 3¼ In.	2.00
Sticker, Nixon, Lodge, Cardboard, 1960, 3¾ In.	5.00
Stickpin, General Ulysses S. Grant, Ferrotype, 1860s	145.00
Stickpin, Harrison, Morton, Log Cabin, Shield Shape, 1888, ⅞ x 1¾ In.	179.00
Stickpin, Lincoln & Hamlin Ferrotype, 1860, ⅞ In.	1434.00
Stickpin, Scale, Woman Suffrage, Equal Legal Scales, 2 x ¾ In.	419.00
Stickpin, U.S. Grant, Ferrotype, c.1870, ¾ In.	199.00
Stickpin, Ulysses S. Grant, Portrait, Brass Frame, Stars & Stripes, 1868, 1 In. . . . . *illus*	191.00
Stud, Lapel, Cleveland, Thurman, Red, White, Blue, Silk On Metal, 1888, ¾ In.	25.00
Stud, William McKinley, Gold Bug, Portrait, Sound One Protection, Brass	311.00
Sugar, Cover, George Washington, Miss Liberty, Eagle, Brown, Blue, Castleford, c.1795, 5¼ In.	508.00
Textile, James A. Garfield, Chester A. Arthur, Portraits, Frame, 1880, 22 x 23 In. . . . . . . *illus*	110.00
Textile, William Henry Harrison, Log Cabin, Hard Cider, Mat, 9¾ x 6¾ In.	649.00
Ticket, McKinley Inaugural Dinner, Admit One, One Dollar, 1897, 4 x 2 In.	515.00
Ticket, National Democratic Convention, Cincinnati, 37793, 1880	478.00
Ticket, Ulysses S. Grant, Inauguration, Senate Floor, Green, Enameled Card, 3 x 5 In.	450.00
Ticket, Union Presidential, Lincoln, Andrews, Miami County, Ohio, 1864, 7 x 3½ In.	135.00
Tie, Harry Truman, Portrait, Rembrandt Hand Paints Work Of Art	99.00
Tie, Nixon For President, Elephant Lifting Hat, Blue, Red, White, 1960	22.00
Tintype, Garfield, Canal Barge, Oval Albumen Photo	1600.00
Tintype, Tilden, Hendricks, Brass Shield	1100.00
Tip Tray, Grand Old Party, President Taft, Vice President Sherman, Tin Lithograph, 1908, 4 In. *illus*	220.00
Tip Tray, Grand Old Party, President William Howard Taft, Photo, 1908, 4¼ In.	190.00
Toby Mug, Al Smith, Ceramic, 6¾ In.	87.00
Toy, JFK Musical Rocking Chair, Vinyl, Cloth Doll, Reading Paper, Windup, Karmar, 11 In.	460.00
Toy, Teddy Roosevelt, On Horse, Glass Eyes, Horsehair Mane, Metal Base, Steiff, 27 In.	7768.00

P

Tray, Cleveland, Hendricks, Pressed Glass, Frosted Center, 9½ x 11½ In.	770.00
Tray, FDR, Campaign, Keep Roosevelt In The White House, 10½ x 13 In.	85.00
Tray, McKinley, Roosevelt, Tin Lithograph, Oval, 1900, 13 x 16 In.	311.00 to 335.00
Valentine, Girl, Boys, No Votes, No Hearts, Votes For Women, Cardboard, Die Cut ......*illus*	84.00
Valentine, Votes For Women, Suffrage, Girl Standing On Box, 2 Boys, Verse, Cardboard, Die Cut	84.00
Vase, Abraham Lincoln, Bust Reads G. Grant, Opalescent, Scalloped Rim, Footed, c.1864, 5 In.	467.00
Vase, President Lincoln, High Relief Portrait, Porcelain, 1864, 3½ In.	384.00
Watch Fob, Coolidge & Dawes, Shield Shape, Strap, 1924, 5¼ x 1¾ In.	203.00
Watch Fob, Cox, President, Franklin Roosevelt, Vice Pres., Silvered Brass, 1920, 1½ In.	90.00
Watch Fob, Harding, President, Coolidge, Vice President, Silvered Brass, 1920, 1½ In.	70.00
Watch Fob, Teddy Roosevelt, Hunts Rhino, Brass, 1¼ In.	61.00
Window Sticker, Bob Taft For President, Red, White, Blue, 3 x 8 In.	9.00

POMONA glass is a clear glass with a soft amber border decorated with pale blue or rose-colored flowers and leaves. The colors are very, very pale. The background of the glass is covered with a network of fine lines. It was made from 1885 to 1888 by the New England Glass Company. First grind was made from April 1885 to June 1886. It was made by cutting a wax surface on the glass, then dipping it in acid. Second grind was a less expensive method of acid etching that was developed later.

Butter, Cover, Blue Cornflower, Reeded Finial, 1st Grind, 8 In.	1610.00
Celery Vase, Blue Cornflower, Ruffled Rim, Amber Ruffled Foot, 1st Grind, 4¾ In.	489.00
Finger Bowl, Berries, 2nd Grind, 5 In.	86.00
Pitcher, Band Of Blue Cornflowers On Amber Stems, Square Mouth, 1st Grind, 10 In.	546.00
Pitcher, Wheat Stocks, Blue Butterflies, New England, 2nd Grind, 11½ In.	3738.00
Tumbler, Cornflower, 1st Grind, 3½ In., Pair	144.00
Tumbler, Lemonade, Blue Cornflower Band, 2nd Grind, 6 In.	259.00
Tumbler, Lemonade, Blue Cornflowers, Loop Handle, 1st Grind, 5¾ In., 6 Piece	1725.00
Tumbler, Oak Leaves, 2nd Grind, 3⅝ In.	52.00

PONTYPOOL, *see Tole category.*

POOLE POTTERY was founded by Jesse Carter in 1873 in Poole, England, and has operated under various names since then. The pottery operated as Carter & Co. for several years and established Carter, Stabler & Adams as a subsidiary in 1921. The company specialized in tiles, architectural ceramics, and garden ornaments. Tableware, bookends, candelabra, figures, vases, and other items have also been made. The name Poole Pottery Ltd. was taken in 1963. The company went bankrupt in 2003, but is in business today with new owners.

Bowl, Delphis, Orange, Green, Black, Cut Sides, M. Anderson, 1965, 11 In.	185.00
Bowl, Scalloped Edge, 13½ x 13¾ In.	67.00
Eggcup, Stand, 4 In., Pair	70.00
Figurine, Fawn, Lying Down, 5¼ In.	100.00
Plate, Flowers In Center, Blue Edge, 7 In.	34.00
Plate, Girl In Red Dress	38.00
Vase, Alternating Stripes, Stylized Scrolls, Oval, Waisted, No. 700, 20th Century, 10½ In. *illus*	70.00
Vase, Atlantis, Brown, Strips, Bottle Shape, Earthenware, c.1975, 8½ In.	300.00

POPEYE was introduced to the Thimble Theatre comic strip in 1929. The character became a favorite of readers. In 1932, an animated cartoon featuring Popeye was made by Paramount Studios. The cartoon series continued and became even more popular when it was shown on television starting in the 1950s. The full-length movie with Robin Williams as Popeye was made in 1980. KFS stands for King Features Syndicate, the distributor of the comic strip.

Ad, It's A Circus, Die Cut, Cardboard, 1930, 6¼ x 9¾ In.	185.00
Ashtray, Popeye, Seated, Flexing Arms In Front, Chalkware, 1931, 10 In.	354.00
Ashtray, Popeye, Seated, Multicolored, Chalkware, 1930s, 10 x 7 In.	88.00
Ashtray, Popeye, Seated, Snufflers, Luster, 2¾ In.	29.00
Ashtray, Popeye, Standing, Multicolored, Chalkware, 1930s, 11 In.	88.00
Ashtray, Popeye, Standing, Multicolored, Chalkware, 1930s, 12 In.	120.00
Bank, Mechanical, Popeye Knockout, Straits Mfg. Co., 1930s	550.00
Bank, Popeye Knockout, Blue, Yellow, Straits Corp., c.1935, 2¼ x 3½ x 4¼ In.	986.00 to 1540.00
Bank, Treasure Chest, Characters, Tin, Lithograph, c.1960s, 4 x 6 x 3½ In.	246.00
Clock, Popeye & Swee'pea, Animated, Smiths, England, 1968, 5¼ In.	112.00
Comic Art, Daily Cartoon, E.C. Segar, July 18, 1936, 4½ x 20½ In.	4290.00
Cookie Jar, Popeye, Face, Pipe, American Bisque	392.00
Dish Set, Popeye, Plate, Bowl, Mug, Ceramic, TST Co., 1935, 3 Piece	252.00

Poole, Vase, Alternating Stripes, Stylized Scrolls, Oval, Waisted, No. 700, 20th Century, 10½ In. $70.00

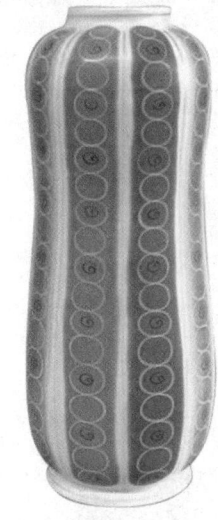

Popeye, Toy, Pail, Popeye The Sailor, Diving, Wimpy, Swee'pea, Tin, T. Cohn, c.1930, 3½ In. $1045.00

Popeye, Toy, Popeye, Bubble Blowing, Pipe, Tin, Battery Operated, Linemar, c.1960, 12 In. $260.00

Popeye is a Grocery Brand
Popeye has long been the logo on brands of fresh and canned spinach. There have also been Popeye iron-fortified white bread, Wimpy hamburger buns, Olive Oyl hot dog buns, and Swee' Pea wheat bread.

Popeye, Toy, Popeye, Heavy Hitter, Tin, Chein, Box, 1932, 11¾ In.
$8250.00

Popeye, Toy, Popeye & Olive Oyl, Dancing On Roof, Tin, Windup, Marx, 9 In.
$1540.00

Popeye, Toy, Popeye & Olive Oyl, Handcar, Stretchy, Pull Toy, Linemar, 7 In.
$990.00

Doll, Popeye, Cloth, Holding Spinach Can, No Pipe, Dean's, England, 1930s, 7 In.	165.00
Doll, Popeye, Cloth, Stuffed, Wood Pipe, Tag, Paramount, KFS, Japan, 1930s, 10 In.	696.00
Doll, Popeye, Wood, Jointed, Ideal, c.1935, 11½ In.	678.00
Doorstop, Popeye, Black Shirt, Blue Pants, No Pipe, Cast Iron, Hubley, 9 x 4½ In.	1232.00
Eggcup, Popeye, Smoking Pipe, Japan, 2½ In.	75.00
Figure, Alice The Goon, Plaster, Painted, 1930s, 9¼ In.	820.00
Figure, Eugene Jeep, Jointed, Wood, Composition, Wood Tail, 1935, 7 In.	610.00
Figure, Eugene Jeep, Jointed, Wood, Composition, Wood Tail, 1935, 13 In.	1528.00
Figure, Popeye, Jointed, Wood, Composition, Ideal, King Features, 15 In.	448.00
Figure, Sea Hag, Woman, Painted, Plaster, 1930s, 8½ In.	370.00
Figure, Wimpy, Painted, Plaster, c.1930s, 13 In.	336.00
Figurine, Popeye, Olive, Wimpy, Porcelain, Wade, Box, Set Of 3	105.00
Fly Swatter, Metal, Wood Handle, Paper Insert, Cutouts, Sales Sheet, c.1936, 24 In.	468.00
Game, Ask Popeye's Lucky Jeep, Box, 1936, 5¼ x 7½ In.	112.00
Game, Ring Toss, Pressboard Target, 3 Rings, Transogram, King Features, 1957, Box	138.00
Lunch Box, Popeye & Brutus Arm Wrestling, Aladdin, 1980	85.00
Lunch Box Thermos, Tying Boat To Dock, Olive Oyl, Wimpy, King Seeley Thermos Co., 1964	45.00
Mask, Popeye, Paper, Wrigley's Juicy Fruit, Einson-Freeman, Envelope, c.1930, 11 x 13 In.	318.00
Mug, Popeye, That's Nice, Eat Spinach, Ceramic, 1930s	85.00
Pail, Popeye At The Beach, Tin, Red Shovel, T. Cohn, c.1936, 3½ In.	745.00
Pail, Popeye The Sailor, Tin, Red Shovel, T. Cohn, c.1933, 3½ In.	616.00
Pencil Box, Popeye, Olive Oyl, Wimpy, No. 9107	55.00
Pin, Popeye Club, Avon Self Help, 1930s, ⅞ In.	165.00
Pin, Popeye The Sailor, Red, White Ground, Parisian Novelty, 1929, 1 In.	128.00
Pocket Watch, Popeye, Wimpy Chasing Burger, Dial Arms, Second Hand, c.1935	364.00
Popeye, Pirate Pistol, Clicks, Tin Lithograph, Marx, Box, c.1935, 10 In.	633.00
Poster, Popeye The Sailor, Fightin Pals, Paramount, 1940, 41 x 27 In.	3585.00
Poster, Popeye The Sailor, I Likes Babies & Infinks, Paramount, 1937, 41 x 27 In.	4183.00
Poster, Popeye The Sailor Nurse Mates, Popeye, Bluto, Swee'pea, Paramount, 1940, 41 x 27 In.	6573.00
Puzzle, Popeye, 4 Picture Puzzles, Saalfield, Box, c.1932, 8 x 10 In.	112.00
Toy, Pail, Popeye The Sailor, Diving, Wimpy, Swee'pea, Tin, T. Cohn, c.1930, 3½ In. ....*illus*	1045.00
Toy, Popeye, & Olive Oyl, Juggling, Tin Lithograph, Windup, Linemar, c.1960, 9 In.	1540.00
Toy, Popeye, Baggage, Wheelbarrow, Tin, Windup, Marx, Box, 1932, 8¼ In.	1650.00
Toy, Popeye, Barrel, Walker, Tin Lithograph, Tin, Windup, Chein, KFS 1932, 7 In. ... 523.00 to 650.00
Toy, Popeye, Barrel Walker, Tin Lithograph, Windup, Chein, Box, 1932, 7 In.	3300.00
Toy, Popeye, Basketball Player, Bounces Ball, Tin, Windup, Linemar, 1950s, 9 In.	715.00
Toy, Popeye, Boxer, Shadow, Tin Lithograph, Windup, Marx, Original Box, 7 In.	1210.00
Toy, Popeye, Bubble Blowing, Pipe, Tin, Battery Operated, Linemar, c.1960, 12 In. .....*illus*	260.00
Toy, Popeye, Champ, Boxing Ring, Big Fight, Tin, Celluloid, Windup, Marx, Box, c.1935, 7 In.	1430.00
Toy, Popeye, Dancing On Roof, Tin, Windup, Marx, Box, 1930s, 10 In.	825.00
Toy, Popeye, Drummer, Tin Lithograph, Chein, 1932, 7 In. .... 1584.00 to 5225.00
Toy, Popeye, Eccentric Airplane, Tin Lithograph, Windup, Marx, Box, 8 In.	2475.00
Toy, Popeye, Head Goes Up & Down, Celluloid, Windup, 1929, 8½ In. 390.00 to 575.00
Toy, Popeye, Heavy Hitter, Tin, Chein, Box, 1932, 11¾ In. ....*illus*	8250.00
Toy, Popeye, Heavy Hitter, Tin Lithograph, Windup, Chein, Original Box, 1930s, 12 In.	13200.00
Toy, Popeye, Horse Drawn Cart, Tin Lithograph, Celluloid, Windup, Marx, Box, 7½ In.	1100.00
Toy, Popeye, Lantern, Tin, Glass, Windup, Linemar, Box, 7½ In.	523.00
Toy, Popeye, Music Box, Tin Lithograph, Plastic Head, Cloth Outfit, KFS, Box, 11 In.	825.00
Toy, Popeye, Olive Oyl, Wimpy, Ramp Walker, Composition, Wood, Wilson, 1936, 5½ In., 3 Piece	224.00
Toy, Popeye, Parrot Cages, Carrying, Tin Lithograph, Marx, 8¼ In.	523.00
Toy, Popeye, Parrot Cages, Carrying, Tin Lithograph, Marx, Box, 8¼ In.	1320.00
Toy, Popeye, Roller Skater, Holding Platter, Tin, Windup, Linemar, 1950s, 6½ In.	460.00
Toy, Popeye, Roller Skater, Plate Of Spinach, Tin Lithograph, Windup, Linemar, 6½ In.	605.00
Toy, Popeye, Sparkler, Tin, Celluloid, Windup, Chein, Box, 5¼ In. 193.00 to 330.00
Toy, Popeye, Spinach Motorcycle, Movable Arms, Cast Iron, Hubley, c.1935, 5½ In.	750.00
Toy, Popeye, Spinach Wagon, Red, 3 Rubber Wheels, 1930s, 8 In.	611.00
Toy, Popeye, Tricycle, Goes In Circles, Bell, Tin, Celluloid, Windup, Linemar, Box, 1950s, 4 In.	1008.00
Toy, Popeye, Turnover Tank, Tin Lithograph, Windup, Linemar, 1950s, 4 In.	303.00
Toy, Popeye, Walker, Clenched Fists, Tin Lithograph, Windup, Chein, Box, c.1935, 6¼ In.	3300.00
Toy, Popeye, Walker, Name On Hat, Tin, Windup, King Features, Chein, 1932, 6 In.	385.00
Toy, Popeye & Mean Man, Fighters, Celluloid, Tin, Windup, Linemar, Box, 4 In.	3300.00
Toy, Popeye & Olive Oyl, Dancing On Roof, Tin, Windup, Marx, 9 In. ....*illus*	1540.00
Toy, Popeye & Olive Oyl, Dancing On Roof, Tin, Windup, Marx, 10 In. 550.00 to 1895.00
Toy, Popeye & Olive Oyl, Flyers, 2 Airplanes, Tin, Windup, Louis Marx, Box, 8 x 17 In.	4400.00
Toy, Popeye & Olive Oyl, Handcar, Stretchy, Pull Toy, Linemar, 1950s, 6½ In.	1804.00
Toy, Popeye & Olive Oyl, Handcar, Stretchy, Pull Toy, Linemar, 7 In. ....*illus*	990.00

Toy, Popeye Aeroplane, Pilot, Tin Lithograph, Windup, Marx, 8 In.	1540.00
Toy, Popeye Aeroplane, Pilot, Tin Lithograph, Windup, Marx, Box, 8 In.	3850.00
Toy, Popeye Express, Airplane, Train, Tunnels, Tin Litho, Windup, Marx, Box, 9 In.	1430.00 to 1971.00
Toy, Popeye Playing Xylophone, Wood, Pull Toy, KFS, 11 x 10 In.	250.00
Wallet, Popeye Hitting Brutus, Friends Clapping, Leather, Richard, Box, 1940s	226.00
Wrapper, Chewing Gum, Waxed Paper, Klene's, 1930s, 7 x 4¾ In.	185.00
Wristwatch, It's Popeye Time At Sheffield, Red Plastic Band, Popeye's Hand Moves, 1971	575.00

PORCELAIN factories that are well known are listed in this book under the factory name. This category and the two following list pieces made by the less well-known factories. Porcelain-Contemporary lists pieces made by artists working after 1975. Porcelain-Midcentury includes pieces made from the 1940s to the 1980s.

Ashtray, Frog On Lily Pad, Japan, 1950, 3½ In.	15.00
Biscuit Jar, Cover, Peaches, Tab Handles, Loop Finial, J & C Louise Mark, Koch, 7½ In. *illus*	118.00
Bottle, Cover, Blue & White, Rectangular, Chinese, 5½ x 4 In.	18.00
Bough Pot, Painted, Chinese, c.1908, 5 In., Pair	450.00
Bowl, Bamboo, Prunus Tree, 4 Reserves, Enclosing Figures, Famille Verte, 8½ In.	142.00
Bowl, Berlin, Topographical, Floral Reserves, Footed, 1800s, 14¼ In.	1039.00
Bowl, Bird & Flower, Swatow Blue, White, Chinese, 8 In.	354.00
Bowl, Butterflies, Peaches, Scalloped Rim, Painted, Chinese, Late 1800s, 6½ In., Pair	473.00
Bowl, Courting Scenes, Heart Shape Cutouts, Pedestal, Eisenberg, c.1920, 6⅞ x 10 In.	47.00
Bowl, Cover, Blossoms, Tendril Scroll, Clobbered Blue, White, Yellow Ground, 8½ In.	130.00
Bowl, Dragon, Blue & White, Chinese, 5 In., Pair	443.00
Bowl, Dragon, Blue & White, Chinese, 12¼ In.	325.00
Bowl, Dragon, Double Circle, Swatow, Blue & White, Chinese, 15¼ In.	2242.00
Bowl, Dragon Scrolls, Blue & White, Chinese, c.1627, 7¼ In.	270.00
Bowl, Dragons Chasing Flaming Pearl Of Wisdom, Yellow, Chinese, 4 In., Pair	1770.00
Bowl, Flower, Blue Ground, Gold Border, Green Interior, Chinese, c.1874, 8 In., Pair	291.00
Bowl, Flowers, Iron Red, Blue, Chinese, 4 In.	1770.00
Bowl, Flowers, Iron Red, White, Chinese, 18th Century, 8 In., Pair	1062.00
Bowl, Flowers, Leaves, Blue & White, Chinese, 3½ In.	295.00
Bowl, Flowers, Rose, Chinese, 18th Century, 7 In.	2950.00
Bowl, Flowers, Transferware, Upswept Rim, England, c.1820, 4¼ x 9½ In.	259.00
Bowl, Garden Scene, Sevres Style, Ormolu Mounted, 20 x 13½ In.	3995.00
Bowl, Hand Painted, England, 19th Century, 5½ x 10 In.	47.00
Bowl, Immortals, Landscape, Blue & White, Painted, Chinese, Late 1800s, 8 In.	195.00
Bowl, Mythical Beasts, Blue & White, Chinese, 19th Century, 7½ In.	726.00
Bowl, Peach, Flower, Calligraphy, Brocade Ground, Blue & White, Chinese, 8½ In.	4130.00
Bowl, Red, Chinese, 19th Century, 3½ x 6¾ In.	275.00
Bowl, Sages, Attendants, Lotus Shape, Aubergine, Yellow Ground, Chinese, 6 In.	411.00
Bowl, Warriors, Peonies, Alternating Reserves, Blue & White, Painted, 9 In.	1416.00
Box, Fish, Multicolored Painted Flowers, Oval Mahogany Base, Germany, 3 x 10 In.	411.00
Box, Flowers, Blue & White, Rectangular, Chinese, 2 x 4½ In.	59.00
Box, Hinged, Inset Plaque, Bronze, c.1900, 1½ x 3¾ In.	644.00
Box, Sewing, Gilt Brass Mounted, France, Late 19th Century, 8 In.	291.00
Brush Holder, Reticulated Duck & Lotus, Aubergine, Chinese, 19th Century, 5 x 4 In.	2124.00
Brush Washer, Brown, Leaf Shape, Chinese, 6 In.	413.00
Brush Washer, Flower Heads, Scrolling Foliage, Blue & White, Oval, Chinese, 3¼ In.	236.00
Brushpot, Blue & White, Chinese, 7 x 7½ In.	561.00
Cachepot, Famille Verte, Hexagonal, Panel Molded, Shaped Cartouche, Chinese	384.00
Cachepot, Flambe, Chinese, 10 In.	590.00
Cachepot, Flowers, Sevres Style, Bucket Form, Gilt Metal Rim, Handles, 11 x 10 In., Pair	978.00
Cachepot, Tree Branch, Blue, Celadon, Hexagonal, Japan, 9½ In.	189.00
Cake Plate, Apples, Handle, J & C Louise, Mark, Koch, Germany, c.1900, 11 In.	71.00
Cake Plate, Apples, Water, Handle, J & C Senta, Mark, Koch, Germany, c.1900, 10¼ In.	71.00
Cake Plate, Flowers, Blue Rim, Gilt, Hand Painted, Germany, c.1900, 10½ In.	41.00
Cake Plate, Peaches, Water, Handle, J & C Louise, Mark, Koch, Germany, c.1900, 11 In. *illus*	106.00
Candelabrum, 2-Light, Hutschenreuther, Germany, c.1930, 6½ x 9¾ In.	47.00
Candlestick, Cutout Base, Burnt Orange, Brown Matte Glaze, A. Robineau, 6 x 3½ In.	1440.00
Candlestick, Painted Scene, Sevres Style, Ormolu Mounted, France, 11 In.	646.00
Cassoulet, Ram's Heads, Ormolu Mount, Urn Shape, Pineapple Finial, 19½ In., Pair	259.00
Celery Vase, Grape, Water, J & C Louise, Mark, Koch, Germany, c.1900, 12 In.	147.00
Censer, Chinese Tripod, Flared Rim, White Glaze, Cafe Au Lait Edge, 3¾ x 8¾ In.	115.00
Charger, Apples, Water, J & C Louise, Mark, Koch, Germany, Early 20th Century, 12 In.	59.00
Charger, Blue & White, Chinese, 18th Century, 14 In.	293.00
Charger, Dragon, Scrolling Foliage, Blue & White, Painted, Chinese, 16 In.	1003.00

Porcelain, Biscuit Jar, Cover, Peaches, Tab Handles, Loop Finial, J & C Louise Mark, Koch, 7½ In. $118.00

Porcelain, Chocolate Set, Peaches, Scalloped Rim, J & C Louise Mark, Koch, 9½-In. Pot, 5 Piece $264.00

Porcelain, Figurine, Young Man Playing Soccer, Red Stripes, Hollohaza, Hungary, 10¼ In. $94.00

P

Nineteenth-Century American Porcelain

Porcelain was first made in America in about 1738. By the middle of the nineteenth century, Jersey Porcelain and Earthenware Company, Tucker and Hemphill, Smith Fife and Company, and Charles Cartlidge had all started, then closed. Late in the century, porcelain was being produced by Knowles, Taylor and Knowles of East Liverpool, Ohio (*Lotus ware* from about 1891 to 1896). Onondaga Pottery of Syracuse, New York, was making Imperial Geddo porcelain by 1891.

Trenton, New Jersey, had many porcelain manufacturers. Ceramic Art Company (1889) became Lenox, Inc., in 1906 and is still making porcelain. Ott and Brewer, Cook Pottery Company, Greenwood Pottery Company, and Willetts Manufacturing Company were other porcelain makers.

Porcelain, Group,
Courting Couple In Garden,
Pool, Lambs, Oval Base,
Sitzendorf, 9½ x 16½ In.
$1410.00

P

TIP
A good way to clean bisque is with a toothbrush and white toothpaste. Brush gently, then rinse completely in warm water.

Charger, Flowers, Blue & White, Japan, 18 In.	201.00
Charger, Peony, Ruyi & Bamboo Band, Blue & White, 11¼ In.	163.00
Charger, Pine Tree, Peony, Blue & White, Center Painted, Chinese, 14¾ In.	649.00
Charger, Portrait, Fashionable Woman, Hand Painted, E. Albert, France, c.1910, 19¾ In.	468.00
Charger, Rooster, Bird On Flowering Branch, Blue & White, Japan, 22 In.	767.00
Chocolate Set, Peaches, Scalloped Rim, J & C Louise Mark, Koch, 9½-In. Pot, 5 Piece *illus*	264.00
Coffee Set, Konigszelt Factory, Germany, c.1930, 15 Piece	82.00
Coffee Set, Shagreen, 6 Silver & Enamel Spoons, Case, 1930s, 12 Piece	416.00
Coffee Set, White & Turquoise Stripe, Augarten, Austria, c.1930, 19 Piece	308.00
Compote, Grapes, Footed, J & C Louise, Mark, Koch, Germany, c.1900, 9¼ In.	500.00
Creamer, Eagle's Head Handle	75.00
Cross, Oval Portrait, Christ, Brass, Velvet, Hand Painted, 10½ x 8¼ In.	234.00
Demitasse Set, Teapot, Creamer, Sugar, Cups, Saucers, Germany, 15 Piece	29.00
Dish, 4 Relief Fish, Beige Crackled Glaze, Interior Molded, Chinese, 1½ In.	354.00
Dish, Birds, Trees, Famille Verte, Chinese, 6¼ In., Pair	472.00
Dish, Blue & White, Footed, Chinese, Late 19th Century, 2 x 9⅜ In.	70.00
Dish, Copper Red, Blue, Iron Red Bat, Double Ring, Chinese, 6 In.	885.00
Dish, Doucai, Precious Objects, Flowers, Chinese, 8 In.	826.00
Dish, Dragon, Flower Heads, Scrolling Leaves, Blue & White, Ming Style, 12¾ In.	201.00
Dish, Lotus, Scrolling Leaves, Blue & White, Center Painted, Chinese, 6¼ In.	826.00
Dish, Wucai, Mythical Horse, Karst Landscape, Cloud Band, Chinese, Early 1900s, 8 In.	226.00
Dresser Box, Hinged Lid, Romantic Scene, Sevres Style, Gilt Bronze, Egg Form, 12 x 9¼ In.	3525.00
Egg, Jeweled, Cobalt Blue, Brass Mounted Box, Hinged Lid, France, 1900s, 13½ In.	1293.00
Ewer, Cream Glaze, Strap Handle, Lugs On 2 Sides, Short Spout, Chinese, 7⅝ In.	649.00
Ewer, Monk's Cap, Dragon & Phoenix, Blue & White, Chinese, 8¾ In.	325.00
Figurine, 2 Birds, White, One Standing, Other Squatting, Italy, 8½ In., Pair	115.00
Figurine, Allegorical, Astronomie, Germany, c.1840, 12 In.	205.00
Figurine, Bird, Multicolored Plumage, Rocky Base, Flowers, 8½ In., Pair	120.00
Figurine, Bird, Whip-Poor-Will, Tree Stump, Flowers, Mark, Red Anchor In Oval, England, 6¼ In.	1920.00
Figurine, Courting Couple, Furstenburg, Germany, 19th Century, 7 In.	105.00
Figurine, Dancing Peasant, Blue Coated, Raised Hand Holding Cap, 8⅞ In.	1175.00
Figurine, Eagles, Perched On Rockwork Base, 19th Century, 19½ In.	5100.00
Figurine, Floral Garlands, Blue & White, Schneeballen, 2 Handles, 1800s, 5 In.	1200.00
Figurine, Foo Dog, Blue & White, Chinese, 20 x 20 In.	176.00
Figurine, Foo Dog, Green Glaze, Square Base, Chinese, 7 In.	83.00
Figurine, Girl, Standing, Looking At Bird, Scavini, Lenci, c.1928, 12 In.	1645.00
Figurine, Girl Playing Bowls, Scheibe-Alsbach, Early 20th Century, 11 In.	207.00
Figurine, Goddess Of Mercy, Blanc De Chine, Early 20th Century, 17½ In.	550.00
Figurine, Goddess Of Mercy, Blanc De Chine, Chinese, 19th Century, 11½ In.	177.00
Figurine, Goddess Of Mercy, Seated On Elephant Back, Blanc De Chine, Chinese, 12½ In.	1180.00
Figurine, Griffin, Green & White, Wood Stand, 12 x 12 In., Pair	322.00
Figurine, Jane Seymour, Blue Underglaze, Germany, 8¼ x 3⅛ In.	225.00
Figurine, Lady, Seated On French Style Chair, 5 In.	117.00
Figurine, Lady, Sitzendorf, Germany, c.1900, 6¾ In.	41.00
Figurine, Man & Woman, Colonial Attire, Gathering Grapes, 1800s, 9½ In., Pair	201.00
Figurine, Maternita, Mother With Baby, Scavini, Lenci, c.1928, 12 In.	3055.00
Figurine, Minerva, Mars, White Glazed, Nymphenburg, Mid 1800s, 14 & 16 In., Pair	2006.00
Figurine, Napoleon, Standing, Royal Robe, Crown, Fired Gold Accents, 14 x 8½ In.	527.00
Figurine, Nude, Seated, Legs Crossed, Marked, 1764, 8 In.	303.00
Figurine, Owl, Stump, Glass Eyes, Gray, Ivory, Black, Marked, E. Bohne & Sohne, 20½ In.	719.00
Figurine, Parrot, White Glazed Column, Rudolstadt Volkstedt, 1900s, 15 In., Pair	561.00
Figurine, Poodle, Stylized, Bone China, Foley, 6½ In.	53.00
Figurine, Sheik, Continental, Late 19th Century, 15 In.	325.00
Figurine, Tiger, Sitting, Orange, Black, Yellow, 37 In.	1730.00
Figurine, Warrior, Hand Painted, Germany, 8 In.	88.00
Figurine, Young Man Playing Soccer, Red Stripes, Hollohaza, Hungary, 10¼ In. *illus*	94.00
Fishbowl, Flowers, Iron Red, Gilt, Chinese, 19th Century, 13½ In.	826.00
Garniture, Gu Form Vases, Candleholders, Censer, Blue & White, 5 Piece	1888.00
Ginger Jar, Blue & White, Chinese, c.1840, 7½ x 6 In.	146.00
Ginger Jar, Cover, Blue & White, Chinese, c.1900, 9½ In.	234.00
Ginger Jar, Famille Verte, Chinese, Ching Dynasty, 19th Century, 9½ In.	132.00
Ginger Jar, Jade Green, White, Black Wood Base, Chinese, c.1820, 8 x 7 In.	439.00
Group, Courting Couple In Garden, Pool, Lambs, Oval Base, Sitzendorf, 9½ x 16½ In. *illus*	1410.00
Group, Horses, Mythological, Base, Continental, 19 x 11 In.	878.00
Group, Musicians, Violin, Lute, Hurdy-Gurdy, Incised, D.V., Mennency, c.1760, 8 In.	1440.00
Group, Shoal Of Fish, Blue, White, Certificate, Box	459.00
Jar, Apothecary, Gilt, Painted Reserves, Busts, Galen, Hippocrates, France, 10½ In., Pair	1528.00

Jar, Apothecary, Lid, White, Transfer Printed, Green Scroll Form Labels, 11 x 5 In.	1140.00
Jar, Cover, Cabbage Leaf, Baluster, Gilt Foo Dog Handles, Chinese, 21 In., Pair	561.00
Jar, Cover, Flowers, Famille Verte, Chinese, 18¼ In.	531.00
Jar, Cover, Landscape & Figures, Blue & White, Chinese, 6½ In.	1416.00
Jar, Crane, Cloud, Blue & White, Korea, 8¼ In.	3422.00
Jar, Flowers, Blue & White, Octagonal, Korea, 6¼ In.	295.00
Jar, Gourd Shape, Chinese, 15 In., Pair	88.00
Jar, Lid, Buddhist Lions, Clouds, Blue & White, Chinese, Early 1800s, 8 x 8 In.	546.00
Jar, Lid, Double Happiness, Scrolling Lotus Field, Baluster, Blue & White, 17 x 10 In.	259.00
Jar, Lid, Ormolu Mounted, Lion Head Ring Mounts, Painted, Enamel, Gilt, 15 x 4 In.	230.00
Jar, Storage, Blue & White, Japan, 17½ In.	354.00
Jar, Wucai, Phoenix, Scrolls, Foliage, Flowers, Oval, 9 In.	885.00
Jardiniere, Birds, Flowers, Bronze Mounts, Blue & White, Continental, 21 x 14 In.	460.00
Jardiniere, Flowers, Blue & White, Japan, 10 x 11¾ In.	295.00
Jardiniere, Flowers, Pheasants, Famille Noire Enamel, Stand, Chinese, 12½ x 14 In.	70.00
Pitcher, Absinthe, Greyhound Shape, Mark On Collar, Cypp, France, 10 In. ....*illus*	115.00
Pitcher, Snowball, Footed, Germany, c.1900, 8½ In., Pair	118.00
Pitcher, Women Chattins, Burslem, 9½ x 5½ In.	59.00
Planter, Almond Shape, Brass Liners, Iron Frog, France, 1800s, 5½ x 13 In., Pair	1955.00
Planter, Blue On White, Chinese, 20th Century, 18 x 21 In.	176.00
Planter, Cherub, Flowers, Moore Bros., 1879, 8 In.	330.00
Planter, Frogs, Lotus Leaves, 13 In.	15.00
Planter, Frolicking Cherubs, France, Late 19th Century, 6¾ In., Pair	433.00
Plaque, Mountain Landscape, Oval Reserve, Blue & White, Chinese, 15½ x 10 In.	2478.00
Plaque, Young Woman, Hand Painted, Articulated Oval Frame, c.1900, 5 x 6 In.	761.00
Plate, Bucolic Scene, Hand Painted, Franz Arthur Bischoff, c.1900, 10½ In.	1872.00
Plate, Dinner, Flowers, Wide Gold & Thin Cobalt Blue Bands, Heinrich, 11 In., 12 Piece	360.00
Plate, Famille Jaune, Calligraphy Cartouches, Yellow Ground, Chinese, 9 In., Pair	767.00
Plate, Famille Verte, Chinese, 10½ In., Pair	1540.00
Plate, Flower, Vase, Blue & White, Chinese, 8¾ In., 5 Piece	1652.00
Plate, Flowers, T & V France, 8 In.	11.00
Plate, Phoenix Bird, Copper Red, Blue, Chinese, 8 In.	212.00
Plate, Scalloped, Flowering Vine, Iron Red, Cobalt Blue, Gilt, c.1840, 8⅜ In., 6 Piece	259.00
Plate, World, Governor General's Residence, Ottawa, Late 19th Century, 9¾ In.	54.00
Pot De Creme, Tucker, c.1820, 4 In., 9 Piece	472.00
Punch Bowl, Chinoiscrie, Man Fishing, Landscape, England, c.1780-1800, 4½ x 11 In.	708.00
Saucer, Flowers, Blue & White, Geometric, Chinese, 19th Century, 6½ In.	52.00
Stand, Turquoise, D Shape, 3-Footed, Chinese, 9¼ x 4¾ In., Pair	1180.00
Syrup, Cover, Peaches, J & C Louise, Koch, Germany, c.1900, 5 In.	177.00
Tazza, Flowers, Famille Verte, 18th Century, Chinese, 4 In.	590.00
Teacup Set, Flower Bouquet, Green Border, Cup, Saucer, Plate, Lowestoft, 1930s, 3 Piece	78.00
Teapot, High Relief Lid, Cardew, England, 8 x 10½ In.	59.00
Teapot, High Relief Lid, Tablecloth, Picnic Basket, Bottle, Fruit, England, 7½ x 9½ In.	88.00
Teapot, Puzzle, Famille Verte, Chinese, 19th Century, 8½ In.	826.00
Tray, Calling Card, Champleve, Classical Scene, Hand Painted, c.1900, 6½ x 11½ In.	936.00
Tray, Copper Trim, Binding, Geometric, Germany, 1920s, 12 In.	340.00
Tureen, Cover, Painted, Gold Bands, England, c.1850, 12¾ x 15½ In.	380.00
Umbrella Stand, Blue, White, Cylindrical, 24½ In.	225.00
Urn, Cover, Amorous Shepherds, Landscape, Painted, France, 1900s, 24 In., Pair	2360.00
Urn, Cover, Pastoral Scene, Sevres Style, Gilt Bronze, Baluster Shape, 27¼ In.	881.00
Urn, Cover, Woman, Cupid, Sevres Style, Ormolu Mounted, Signed, P. Roche, 12½ In.	646.00
Urn, Crackled Yellow Glaze, Manuel Jalanivich, 1930, 12½ x 4½ In., Pair	1920.00
Urn, Cupid & Venus, Cobalt Blue, Handles, Trumpet Foot, Plinth Base, Austria, 23½ In.	1763.00
Urn, Flowers, Parrot, Cover, 23 In., Pair	1287.00
Urn, Flowers, Yellow Ground, Black Border, 6-Sided, Wiltonware, 1935, 16 In.	265.00
Urn, Mantel, Domed Lid, Flower, Ribbons, Sevres Style, Trumpet Foot, Gilt Swags, 13½ In.	705.00
Urn, Oval Medallions, Portrait Of Woman, Flowers, Cranberry, Gold Scrolls, 12½ In. ...*illus*	3290.00
Vase, Acanthine Leaves, Rococo Style, Flowers, Jacob Petit, 7½ In.	780.00
Vase, Baluster, Aubergine, Turquoise, Flattened Ribbed, Chinese, 10½ In.	1121.00
Vase, Baluster, Flambe, Chinese, 19th Century, 15 In.	944.00
Vase, Baluster, Flowering Prunus Tree, Multicolored, Black Ground, Japan, 14¾ In.	212.00
Vase, Baluster, Powder Blue, 19th Century, 16 x 5½ In.	1416.00
Vase, Blue & White, 18th Century, Chinese, 12½ In.	3186.00
Vase, Bottle, Birds, Peonies, Rockwork, Flared Fluted Rim, Japan, 24 In.	440.00
Vase, Bottle, Copper Red, Chinese, 10 In.	1534.00
Vase, Bottle, Flowers, Blue & White, Chinese, 16 In.	2360.00
Vase, Bottle, Leaves, Blue & White, Korea, 5½ In.	236.00

Porcelain, Pitcher, Absinthe, Greyhound Shape, Mark On Collar, Cypp, France, 10 In.
$115.00

Porcelain, Urn, Oval Medallions, Portrait Of Woman, Flowers, Cranberry, Gold Scrolls, 12½ In.
$3290.00

Porcelain, Vase, Cobalt Blue Crystalline Glaze, Squat, Adelaide Robineau, 4¼ x 6 In.
$4200.00

P

Is It Pottery or Porcelain

- Porcelain is translucent. When a porcelain dish is held in front of a strong light, you can see the light through the dish. Pottery is opaque. You can't see through it.
- If a piece of pottery is held in one hand and porcelain in the other, the piece of porcelain will be colder to the touch.
- If a dish is broken, a porcelain dish will chip with small shell-like breaks; pottery cracks on a line.
- Pottery is softer and easier to break. Pottery will stain more easily. Porcelain is thinner, lighter, and more durable.

Porcelain, Watch Case, Woman, Seated, Rococo Style Scrolls, 8¾ x 7 In. $403.00

Vase, Bottle, Sang-De-Boeuf, Glazed, Chinese, 19th Century, 12½ In.	165.00
Vase, Bottle, Silver Mounted, Sang-De-Boeuf, Glaze, Early 1900s, 9¾ In.	944.00
Vase, Bouquets, Gilt, Urn Shape, Pink, Magenta Ground, Sevres Style, 18 In., Pair	940.00
Vase, Butterflies, Blue, Turquoise, Triangular, France, 7½ In., Pair	1095.00
Vase, Cartouches, Flowers, Blue & White, 1900s, 20 In., Pair	1560.00
Vase, Chrysanthemums, Blue & White, Baluster, Chinese, 22½ In.	1440.00
Vase, Civil War, John C. Fremont, Portrait, White, Gilt, Handles, Footed, 5¾ In.	418.00
Vase, Clair-De-Lune, Deer Shape Handles, Wood Stand, Chinese, 17½ In.	1062.00
Vase, Cobalt Blue Crystalline Glaze, Squat, Adelaide Robineau, 4¼ x 6 In. *illus*	4200.00
Vase, Copper Red, Pear Shape, Celadon At Mouth, 18th Century, 11 In., Pair	2596.00
Vase, Cover, 4-Footed, Chinese, 19th Century, 11 x 6 In.	330.00
Vase, Cover, Turquoise Glaze, Bronze Mounted Finial, Plinth, 19th Century, 9½ In.	353.00
Vase, Cymbidium, Franz, 13 In.	15.00
Vase, Dance Of The Daisies, Franz, 14 In.	20.00
Vase, Double Gourd, Multicolored, Iron Red, Leaves, Gilt Ground, Chinese, 11½ In.	6785.00
Vase, Double Gourd, Turquoise Glaze, Chinese, 19th Century, 3 In.	236.00
Vase, Double Handled, Yellow, Blue, Chinese, 14 In.	23.00
Vase, Doucai, Bat & Cloud, 4 In.	189.00
Vase, Dragon, Black Ground, Japan, 12¾ In.	189.00
Vase, Dragon, Chasing Flaming Pearl, Clouds, Blue & White, Korea, 11¾ In.	1888.00
Vase, Dragon, Iron Red Ground, Famille Verte, Chinese, 17½ In.	2006.00
Vase, Dragon & Bat Mounts, Monochrome Blue, Oval, Chinese, c.1850, 6½ In.	602.00
Vase, Figures, Gilt, Multicolored, Pink Ground, Floral Reserves, c.1860, 16 x 7½ In.	147.00
Vase, Figures Supporting Orb, Urn, Multicolored, England, 11½ In.	165.00
Vase, Flask, Moon, Dragons, Flaming Pearl Of Wisdom, Blue & White, Chinese, 18 In., Pair	1003.00
Vase, Flower Bouquet, 2 Handles, England, 10½ In.	212.00
Vase, Foo Dog Head, Monochrome, White, Molded, Ring Handles, Chinese, 11 In.	384.00
Vase, Foo Dogs, Flaming Pearls, Blue, Pear Shape, Gold Enamel, 15½ In.	206.00
Vase, Garniture, Courting Couple, Magenta, Satyr Mask Handles, Pomegranate Finial, 17 In., Pair	2040.00
Vase, Garniture, Gray Urn Supported By 2 Bisque Classical Maidens, Garlands, 15 In., Pair	3120.00
Vase, Gilt, Multicolored, Flare, Biscuit Applique, 16 x 8½ In.	330.00
Vase, Gilt, Rococo, Painted Flower Reserve, Franco Bohemian, 1800s, 16 In, Pair	660.00
Vase, Glazed, Enameled, 4 Handles, Paul Dachsel, c.1906, 10¾ In.	2880.00
Vase, Iris, Cream Body, Pink Petals, Green Leaves, Iris Shape, France, Early 1900s, 10 In.	212.00
Vase, Landscape, Eggshell, Painted, Orange, 1800s, 4½ In., Pair	385.00
Vase, Mantel, Green, Rose Reserves, Gilt, 2 Handles, England, c.1840, 12 In., Pair	413.00
Vase, Medallion, Phoenix, Branches, Medallion, Famille Rose, 17 In., Pair	3068.00
Vase, Peach Bloom, Chinese, 19th Century, 7 In.	354.00
Vase, Portland Style, Black Ground Glaze, Peach, White, Samuel Alcock, c.1840, 10 In.	646.00
Vase, Precious Objects, Immortal, Blue & White, Chinese, 4 In.	295.00
Vase, Reclining Figure, Pan, Ariadne, Cobalt Blue Ground, Gilt, c.1840, 13 In., Pair	201.00
Vase, Riverscape Cartouche, Blue & White, Chinese, 7 In.	413.00
Vase, Tea Dust Glaze, Chinese, 11 In., Pair	1180.00
Vase, Tree Stump, Figural Base, Woman, Man, Flare, Gilt, Multicolored, 13 x 11 In., Pair	529.00
Vase, Turquoise Glaze, Chinese, Early 20th Century, 9¾ In.	1650.00
Vase, Woman, Royal Vienna Style, Painted, Gilt Cartouche, Lavender Luster, 32½ In.	5875.00
Vase, Yellow Glaze, Chinese, Early 20th Century, 11½ In.	303.00
Watch Case, Woman, Seated, Rococo Style Scrolls, 8¾ x 7 In. *illus*	403.00

PORCELAIN-CONTEMPORARY lists pieces made by artists working after 1975.

Bust, Man With Pipe, Borsato, Milan, Italy, 8 In.	117.00
Charger, Lorna Bailey, 13 In.	5202.00
Figurine, Girl Holding Orange Flowers, Ispanky, 8 In.	275.00
Figurine, Man Eating Chicken, Borsato, Milano, Italy, 5½ In.	176.00
Figurine, Pots & Pans Maker, Borsato, Milano, Italy, 8 x 8½ In.	322.00
Plate Set, 12 Tribes Of Israel, Goebel, Laszlo Ispanky, 12 In., 12 Piece	78.00
Plate Set, Landmark, Interpace & Woodmere Studio, c.1980, 10⅝ In., 12 Piece	47.00
Sign, Dealer, Embossed Buffalo, 3½ x 3¾ In.	35.00

PORCELAIN-MIDCENTURY includes pieces made from the 1940s to the 1980s.

Bowl, Silver Plate Rim, Hanley, England	18.00
Clothes Brush, Woman, Tennis Player, Holding Racket, Marked, Made In Japan, 9 In.	113.00
Cup, Doucai, 6 Character Mark, Double Square, Chinese, 1¾ In., Pair	230.00
Cup & Saucer, Orange Flowers, Blue Border, Burgundy, Gold Enamel, Japan, c.1950	18.00

Cup & Saucer, Yellow Leaves, Rust, Green, White Ground, Japan, 1945-52	16.00
Dinner Service, Krister Manufactory, Landstuhl, Germany, c.1950, 84 Piece	293.00
Figurine, Elephant, Trumpeting, Tusks, Aynsley, 8¾ x 6 In.	205.00
Figurine, Foo Dog, Enameled, Chinese, 8¾ In., Pair	176.00
Figurine, Foo Dog, Meissen Style, 9¼ In.	266.00
Game Service, Wild Turkey, Johnson Bros., 13 Piece	351.00
Lemonade Set, Green Leaves, Yellow, Crown Devon, c.1950, 6 Tumblers, 8-In. Pitcher	82.00
Plate Set, Dinner, White, Gilt Rim, Rosenthal, 10¼ In., 11 Piece	295.00
Vase, Reduction Glaze, Signed, Joseph Panacci, 1989, 9½ In.	107.00
Vase, White Glaze, Lucie Rie, c.1965, 11½ In.	8400.00

POSTCARDS were first legally permitted in Austria on October 1, 1869. The United States passed postal regulations allowing the card in 1872. Most of the picture postcards collected today date after 1910. The amount of postage can help to date a card. The rates are: 1872 (1 cent), 1917 (2 cents), 1919 (1 cent), 1925 (2 cents), 1928 (1 cent), 1952 (2 cents), 1958 (3 cents), 1963 (4 cents), 1968 (5 cents), 1971 (6 cents), 1973 (8 cents), 1975 (7 cents), 1976 (9 cents), 1978 (10 cents), March 1981 (12 cents), November 1981 (13 cents), 1985 (14 cents), 1988 (15 cents), 1991 (19 cents), 1995 (20 cents), 2001 (21 cents), 2002 (23 cents), 2006 (24 cents), 2007 (26 cents). While most postcards sell for low prices, a small number bring high prices. Some of these are listed here.

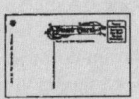

Atlantic City, Bathing Beauties, Postmarked 1923	10.00
Boston, Massachusetts, King's Chapel	6.00
Boston, Massachusetts, Old State House, Copyright 1905	5.99
Boston, Old State House, Wagons, People, Street Lights, Statues, 1905	6.00
Bouquet Brand Rock Lobster, Lobster, Tin, Linen ....*illus*	206.00
Bristol, New Hampshire, Central Square, 1906	6.00
Bristol Steel Fishing Rods, Man Fishing, Rod & Net, Philip R. Goodwin, 3½ x 5½ In.	145.00
Bristol Steel Fishing Rods, Man Scooping Fish Into Net, 1914, 5½ x 3 In.	115.00
Car, Door Opens & Small Postcards Drop Out, Grub Aus Wirzburg, Germany, 1953	12.00
Cocorico, Alphonse Mucha	294.00
Costumed Figures Dancing, Raphael Kirchner	235.00
Cowgirl, On Horse, Shading Face, Silk Embellishment, 1907 Postmark, Divided Back	25.00
DC Comics, Blackhawks, Best Wishes, 1960, 7 x 4 In.	280.00
Delivery Van, Palmer	176.00
Depot, Anamosa, Iowa, Bifold	33.00
French Quarter, New Orleans, Lacework, Linen, Color	8.00
Gator Diner, Linen	264.00
Governor Tyler Hotel, Restaurants, Virginia, Radford, c.1939	2.00
Grand Canyon National Park, Image Of Guest Arriving, 1912	13.00
Independence Hall Savings Bank, Still Bank, Linen	206.00
Katson's Drive-In, Albuquerque, N.M., Uniformed Server, Cars, Linen ....*illus*	118.00
L.H. Yeager Company, Allentown, Penn., Fruit Jar Quotes, Pictures, Jars, 1881	1881.00
Lobster, Gouache, Watercolor, Ink, Samuel L. Schmucker, 5 x 8 In.	3995.00
Mailman On Harley-Davidson, I Am With 235 Pounds Of Mail, 1914	441.00
Market Day, Williamsport, Pennsylvania, Divided Back, 1908	17.50
MGM Studios, The Story Of The Making Of Ben-Hur, 1969	20.00
Middletown, Conn., Main St. From Washington St., Looking South, Divided, 1916	17.50
Middletown High School, Middletown, N.Y.	7.00
Paris Expo, Alphonse Mucha, 1900	382.00
Penn Diner Inc., A Good Place To Eat, Linen	114.00
Rock Lobster, Bouquet Brand, Linen	206.00
Sarah Bernhardt From La Plume, Alphonse Mucha	323.00
Sea Horse, Gouache Watercolor, Ink, Samuel L. Schmucker, 1879-1921, 5 x 8 In.	3995.00
Shanghai, Busy Street Scene, c.1909	12.00
Simmons Hardware Co., Keen Kutter Tools, Cutlery, Hardware Items, 7 x 10½ In.	150.00
St. Mary's French Hospital, Lewiston, Maine, Postmarked, Auburn, Me.	7.00
Troop D, State Constabulary, Punxsutawney, Penn., Used, Divided, EC Kropp Co., 1912	25.00
Victorian Woman, Rooster, Cocorico, Alphonse Mucha ....*illus*	294.00
Warner Bros. Studio Promotional, Joan Crawford, Marked Oct. 8, 1947	10.00
Watkins Wagon, Horse Drawn	323.00
We Can't See You Papa, Children Looking Into Candlestick Telephone, Leather, c.1910	15.00
Woman, Gas Stove, Mechanical	118.00
Woman Looking In Mirror, Die Cut, Hold-To-Light, Raphael Kirchner	1175.00
Wonder Woman, Infantile Paralysis, Trimmed Edges, March Of Dimes, 1943, 6 x 8 In.	1758.00

Postcard, Bouquet Brand Rock Lobster, Lobster, Tin, Linen
$206.00

Postcard, Katson's Drive-In, Albuquerque, N.M., Uniformed Server, Cars, Linen
$118.00

Postcard, Victorian Woman, Rooster, Cocorico, Alphonse Mucha
$294.00

Early Postcards

The souvenir cards sold at the World's Columbian Exposition in Chicago in 1893 were probably the earliest picture postcards mailed in the United States. Before March 1907, the message had to be written on the picture side of the postcard (not the address side) to be mailed for a penny. By 1908 postcards had become very popular. Nearly 700 million were mailed annually in the United States. Historic views, special events, and cards by important postcard artists or publishers get the highest prices.

Poster, Chuck Berry, Grateful Dead, Fillmore Auditorium, March 19, 1967, Nude With Snake
$150.00

Poster, Cole & Walters 4 Ring Circus, Wild Animals, Silk Screen, Frame, c.1950, 31 x 25 In.
$132.00

Poster, Joan Baez, Concert, Berkeley, Tuesday, April 18, 1967, 13 x 22 In.
$215.00

Poster, The Clash, French Concert Tour, 18 Octobre, 1977, 43½ x 28½ In.
$299.00

POSTERS have informed the public about news and entertainment events since ancient times. Nineteenth-century advertising or theatrical posters and twentieth-century movie and war posters are of special interest today. The price is determined by the artist, the condition, and the rarity. Other posters may be listed under Movie, Political, and World War I and II.

Chuck Berry, Grateful Dead, Fillmore Auditorium, March 19, 1967, Nude With Snake *illus*	150.00
Circus, Christy Bros., Riverside Print Co., 1925, 3¼ x 8⅛ In., Set Of 4	165.00
Circus, Clyde Beatty, Cole Bros., 2 Sections, Folded, c.1950s, 92 x 128 In.	308.00
Circus, Ringling Bros. & Barnum & Bailey, 2 Sections, 9 Sheets, c.1945, 81 x 122 In.	590.00
Civil War, Confederate Veteran's Reunion, Jefferson Davis, 4 Flags, Richmond Va., 1896, 13 x 9¾ In.	717.00
Cole & Walters 4 Ring Circus, Wild Animals, Silk Screen, Frame, c.1950, 31 x 25 In. *illus*	132.00
Coppa Della Perugina, Color Lithograph, Frederico Seneca, Italy, 1900s, 39 x 56 In.	1121.00
Jardin De Paris, Lithograph, Jules Cheret, France, Early 1900s, 48 x 34 In.	1416.00
Jesse James, Missouri Law, Lige & Eliza Making Soldiers Toes Out, c.1890, 41½ x 27 In.	467.00
Jim Kweskin, Jug Band, Avalon Ballroom, Family Dog, 3rd Printing, 1966, 20 x 14 In.	74.00
Joan Baez, Concert, Berkeley, Tuesday, April 18, 1967, 13 x 22 In. *illus*	215.00
Keith Albee Theatre, Lum & Abner, Huntington, W.V., 1940s, 41½ x 28 In.	323.00
Little Eva's Temptation, Uncle Tom In Rocker, Eva Leaning, Frame, 28½ x 19⅞ In.	187.00
Maxfield Parrish, Poster Show, Penn. Academy Of Fine Arts, 1910s, 28½ x 41 In.	14340.00
McGovern Concert, Carole King, Barbara Streisand, James Taylor, 24¼ x 37 In.	1392.00
Night Circus, Shubert Theater, N.Y. Art Craft, Lithograph, On Canvas, 40 In., Pair	176.00
Overland Magazine, Maynard Dixon, Mat, Frame, 18½ x 13 In.	1080.00
Ringling Bros. & Barnum & Bailey, Lion, Tiger, Green, Purple, Red, Yellow, 37½ x 28 In.	55.00
Santana, Grass Roots, Fillmore West, Bill Graham, December, 1968, 21 x 14 In.	89.00
Super Session, Fillmore West, Bill Graham, September, 1968, 21 x 14 In.	565.00
The Clash, French Concert Tour, 18 Octobre, 1977, 43½ x 28½ In. *illus*	299.00
The Doors, Allmen Joy, Denver Dog, Family Dog, December, 1967, 22 x 13 In.	328.00
The Doors, Cow Palace, July 25, 1969, 22 x 13 In.	137.00
The Who, Grateful Dead, Fillmore West, Bill Graham, August, 1968, 22 x 28¼ In.	728.00
Uncle Tom's Cabin Co., Topsy, Stowes Mammoth, Red, White, Silk Screen, 27 x 41 In.	132.00
Woodstock, Concert, 3 Days Of Peace & Music, 1969, 36½ x 24 In. *illus*	2390.00

POTLIDS are just that, lids for pots. Transfer-printed potlids had their heyday from the 1840s to the early 1900s. The English Staffordshire potteries made ceramic containers with decorative lids for bear's grease, shrimp or meat paste, cold cream, and toothpaste. Printed advertising and pictures of historical events, portraits of famous people, or scenic views were designed in black and white or color. Reproductions have been made.

Atkinson's Celebrated Parisian Toothpaste, Printed In English & French, c.1890, 3 In.	200.00
Bears On Rock, Pratt, c.1860	350.00
Gentleman Reading Paper, Ceramic, Multicolored Transfer, c.1800s, 3⅝ In.	81.00
Pot, Burgess's Anchovy Paste, Hythe Road, London, c.1800s, 1½ x 3 In.	75.00
Pot, Creme De Savon, French Shaving Cream, Blue, Printed, c.1880, 4 In.	215.00
Pot, Royal Harbour, Ramsgate, Men & Women In Victorian Dress, Pratt, 2⅛ x 4 In.	89.00
Shakespeare's House, Stratford On Avon, Staffordshire, 3⅝ In.	55.00
Victorian Scene Of Children & Chicks, Basket Of Roses, Pratt, c.1870, 4¼ In.	275.00

POTTERY and porcelain are different. Pottery is opaque; you can't see through it. Porcelain is translucent. If you hold a porcelain dish in front of a strong light, you will see the light through the dish. Porcelain is colder to the touch. Pottery is softer and easier to break and will stain more easily because it is porous. Porcelain is thinner, lighter, and more durable. Majolica, faience, and stoneware are all pottery. Additional pieces of pottery are listed in this book in the categories Pottery-Art, Pottery-Contemporary, Pottery-Midcentury, and under the factory name. For information about pottery makers and marks, see *Kovels' Dictionary of Marks—Pottery & Porcelain: 1650–1850* and *Kovels' New Dictionary of Marks—Pottery & Porcelain: 1850 to the Present.*

3 Colors, Flambe Glaze, Grand Feu, Baluster, 7½ x 5 In.	9000.00
Bowl, Amphora, Pelican, c.1900, 9 In.	246.00
Bowl, Krater, Grand Tour, Red Figure, Man, Reclining, 2 Handles, Early 1900s, 14 x 11 In.	1320.00
Charger, Kingfishers, Maling Ware, Tubelined, 7 In.	190.00
Cheese Stand, Cover, Dudson, Late 19th Century, 9½ In.	330.00
Decanter, Musical, Daisy Daisy, Crown Devon Fieldings, 8½ In.	316.00
Dish, Indian In Canoe, Burleigh Ware	59.00
Dressing Table Set, Candlesticks, Tray, Bowl, Maling, Green Floral Luster, 4 Piece	116.00
Dressing Table Set, Candlesticks, Tray, Bowl, Maling, Red Floral Luster, 4 Piece	95.00

Egg Server, Demi, Aiden, 10¼ In.	35.00
Ewer, Bird Shape, Ocher, Chinese, 9 In.	354.00
Figurine, Cat, Black, Seated, Green Glass Eyes, Gilt Bows, Late 19th Century, 12 In., Pair	264.00
Figurine, Chicken, Red, Brown Glaze, Reggie Meaders, 13¾ In.	460.00
Figurine, Dog, Molded, Albany Glaze, Blue Green In Creases, 8½ x 9¾ In.	403.00
Figurine, Dog, Spaniel, Seated, Yellow Clay, Brown Glaze, Tooled Features, 10 In.	373.00
Figurine, Lion, Reclining On Platform, Dark Brown Glaze, 6¼ In.	588.00
Figurine, Lion, Lying Down, Log, Scalloped Base, Yellow Clay, Impressed, Neil A. Conner, 6 x 10 In.	489.00
Figurine, Owl, Standing On Book, Page Open To Owl Picture, Italy, 18¾ In.	546.00
Figurine, Panther, Orchies, Lejan, 1930s, 20½ In.	123.00
Figurine, Rooster, Blue Glaze, David Meaders, 14 In.	288.00
Figurine, Spaniel, Seated, Yellow Clay, Brown & Green Mottled Matte Glaze, 9½ In.	403.00
Figurine, Turkey, Detailed Feathers, White Clay, Earth Tone Glazes, 3¾ In.	345.00
Figurine, Woman Holding Vessel, Wearing Shawl, Long Dress, Hilton, 7¾ In.	1265.00
Ginger Jar, Cover, Rubens Ware, Hancock & Sons, c.1920, 7 In.	144.00
Inkwell, French Blue, Glazed, c.1930, 6½ In.	144.00
Jar, Egg Shape, Tooled Rim, Amber Glaze, John Bell, Impressed Mark, 5¼ In.	891.00
Jar, Lid, Buddhas, Floral Cartouches, 5 Colors, Brass Mount, Thai Bencharong, 9 In.	518.00
Jardiniere, Fish, Plant, 9 In.	3510.00
Jug, Borderware, Green Glaze, Bulbous, Ribbed Neck, Loop Handle, Mid 1700s, 4½ In.	1440.00
Jug, George III, Gray, Blue Flower Glaze, c.1760, 6 In.	1062.00
Jug, Heraldic Eagle, Clutching Arrows, 2 Flags, c.1876, 9 x 4 In.	2950.00
Jug, Parrots, Hand Painted, Burleigh Ware, 7½ In.	46.00
Jug, Rule Britannia, Kevin Francis, Limited Edition	63.00
Lamp Base, Tree Trunk, Squirrels, Birds, Hilton, 25½ In.	690.00
Mantel Urn, Painted Flower Bush, White Base, France, c.1940, 16½ x 9 In., Pair	146.00
Pen Tray, Fish, Green, Blue, Black, Crystalline Glaze, Pierrefonds, No. 578, 2¾ x 7¾ In.	1035.00
Pitcher, Agateware, Gilt Trim, Hinged Pewter Lid, Footed, 11 In. *illus*	230.00
Pitcher, Applied Grapevines, Blue Glaze, Green Highlights, Edwin Meaders, 10 In.	489.00
Pitcher, Cover, Penguin, Fish Handle, England, 19th Century, 8 In.	300.00
Pitcher, Game Hanging On Tree Trunk, Hound Handle, White Clay, Dark Brown Matte, 7 In.	144.00
Planter, Bisque, c.1951, 22 x 18½ In.	1020.00
Planter, Bisque, Double Cone, Inverted, c.1951, 16 x 20 In.	3000.00
Planter, Blue Glaze, c.1960, 15 x 12 In.	510.00
Planter, Crimson Glaze, c.1955, 11 x 13 In.	228.00
Planter, Crimson Glaze, c.1955, 11 x 17 In.	216.00
Planter, Double Cone, Red Glaze, c.1951, 20½ x 10 In.	780.00
Planter, Footed, Bisque Glaze, c.1955, 20 x 13 In.	1140.00
Planter, Footed, Black Glaze, c.1955, 24 x 17 In.	780.00
Planter, Gold, c.1955, 29½ In.	1680.00
Planter, Olive Green Glaze, c.1955, 14 x 17½ In.	600.00
Planter, White, Footed, c.1955, 20 x 13 In.	600.00
Plaque, Budgie Bird, Burleigh Ware, No. 12, 8½ In.	84.00
Plate Set, Flowers, Green, Gold, 19th Century, 6 Piece	125.00
Rooster, Speckled, Pitted Blue Glaze, David Meaders, 15 In.	230.00
Soup, Dish, Earthenware Rim, England, Mid 19th Century, 10½ In.	47.00
Tea Set, Nursery Rhymes, Original Box, Child's, Amersham Pottery, 15 Piece	105.00
Teapot, Flat Cover, Kyoyaki, Earthenware, Enameled, Sennin, Japan, c.1900, 6½ In.	206.00
Teapot, Flower Baskets, Bail Handles, Blue & White, 8¼ In.	86.00
Umbrella Stand, Roses, Brush Decoration, Ohio Pottery, c.1900, 18 In.	71.00
Vase, 2 Handles, Amphora, c.1900, 13½ In.	164.00
Vase, Baluster, Stylized Blossoms, Embossed, Alligatored Green Matte Glaze, 8 x 3½ In.	3600.00
Vase, Baluster, White Cinquefoils, Brown Ground, Underglaze, 5 x 4 In.	3600.00
Vase, Black Glaze, Egg Shape, 18 x 18 In.	180.00
Vase, Blossoms, Gilded, Cobalt Ground, Reticulated, Greenwood, 12½ x 6 In.	1250.00
Vase, Bulbous Base, Slender Neck, Amphora, c.1900, 6 In.	164.00
Vase, Cabinet, Blue, Green, Ipsen, 5 In.	179.00
Vase, Calligraphy, Islamic, Blue & Brown, 6½ In.	325.00
Vase, Campagna, Standing Cranes, Colored, Raised Gilt Enamels, Glazed Ground, 18½ In.	59.00
Vase, Egg Shape, Yellow Glaze, 14 x 14 In.	420.00
Vase, Face, White Ground, Blue Face, Bjorn Wiinblad, c.1979, 6½ In.	205.00
Vase, Figural, Young Girl, Near Fence, Beige, Acid Green, Gilt, Late 1800s, 20 x 9 In.	411.00
Vase, Pink & Green Glaze, Bulbous, Flared, 2 Handles, Burley & Winter, 12¼ In.	520.00
Vase, Pink & Green Glaze, Flared, Burley & Winter, Marked 201-K, 12¼ In.	210.00
Vase, Potpourri, French Provincial, Neoclassical, Tortoiseshell Glaze, Garland, 26 In.	1140.00
Vase, Red Glaze, Egg Shape, 23 x 22 In.	360.00

Poster, Woodstock, Concert,
3 Days Of Peace & Music,
1969, 36½ x 24 In.
$2390.00

Pottery, Pitcher, Agateware, Gilt Trim,
Hinged Pewter Lid, Footed, 11 In.
$230.00

Pottery-Art, Bowl, Free-Form,
Green Matte Shaded To Crimson,
North State Pottery, 8 In.
$35.00

Pottery-Art, Pitcher, Flowers, Gold Trim,
Branch Handle, Cincinnati Art Pottery,
Sara W., 1888, 10⅝ In.
$374.00

Pottery-Art, Vase, Green,
Brown & Blue Glaze, Organic Design,
4 Handles, Denbac, 9¼ In.
$390.00

Pottery-Art, Vase, Gres, Purple,
Teal & Gunmetal Frothy Glaze, Tapered
Neck, Adrien Dalpayrat, 9 x 6 In.
$3240.00

Pottery-Contemporary, Jar,
Cover, Fertility Figures,
Bronze Volcanic Glaze, Stoneware,
Scheier, 1983, 16 x 10 In.
$7200.00

Vase, Rooster, Sweeping Tail, Fan Shape Opening, Amphora, c.1900, 16 In.		308.00
Vase, Scalloped, 4-Sided Opening, Flame Painted, Gold Luster, Amber Glaze, 4¾ x 6 In.		1680.00
Vase, Sprinkler, Ding Ware, Song Dynasty, Chinese, 11 In.		212.00
Vase, Titian Ware, Multicolor, Fruit, Flowers, Footed, Hancock, England, 1920s, 14¼ In.		192.00
Vase, White Ground, Black Geometric, Humlebaek, 1930s, 14½ In.		616.00
Wig Stand, Swirl, Face, Broken China Teeth, B.B. Craig, Vale, N.C., 14 In.		1610.00
Wine Tureen, 10 Cups, Blue & White, Germany, c.1930, 12 x 10 In., 11 Piece		88.00

POTTERY-ART Art pottery was first made in America in Cincinnati, Ohio, during the 1870s. The pieces were hand thrown and hand decorated. The art pottery tradition continued until the 1930s when studio potters began making the more artistic wares. American, English, and Continental art pottery by less well-known makers is listed here. Most makers listed in *Kovels' American Art Pottery*, such as Arequipa, Ohr, Rookwood, Roseville, and Weller, are listed in their own categories in this book. More recent pottery is listed under the name of the maker or in another pottery category.

Bank, Bisque Fired, Pouch Shape, Signed, G.E. Ohr, 3 x 3 In.		1440.00
Bowl, Bisque Fired, Marbleized Clay, Pinched, Folded, Crenelated Rim, 4 x 7½ In.		2760.00
Bowl, Brown Speckled Glaze, Frederick Carlton Ball, Marked, 4 x 8¾ In.		35.00
Bowl, Free-Form, Green Matte Shaded To Crimson, North State Pottery, 8 In.	*illus*	35.00
Bowl, Turquoise Mottled Ground, Stylized Blossoms, Byrdcliffe, 5 x 10½ In.		570.00
Box, Cover, Raised Leaves & Berries, Blue Slip Glaze, Black Accents, Lachenal, 3½ x 6 In.		863.00
Charger, Glazed, Painted, Multicolor, c.1900, 16 In.		9600.00
Ewer, Bird Shape, Multicolored, Blue Tendril Handle, Beak Spout, C.H. Brannum Barum, 10 In.		152.00
Ewer, Nasturtiums, Standard Glaze, 1897, 10½ In.		460.00
Figurine, Woman, Green Top, Gray Skirt, Keramos, Wien, Austria, 8¼ In.		59.00
Jar, Flowers, Slip Decorated, Runny, Foamy Matte Celadon Glaze, Edgefield, 14 In.		4140.00
Jug, High Fired, Purple, Red, Cream Ground, Squared Handle, Rudkin, 1933, 8 In.		1443.00
Pitcher, Bisque Fired, Lobed Rim, Alberhill, c.1914, 11½ x 6 In.		1440.00
Pitcher, Flowers, Gold Trim, Branch Handle, Cincinnati Art Pottery, Sara W., 1888, 10⅝ In.	*illus*	374.00
Pitcher, Gres, Oxblood & Verdigris Mottled Glaze, Dalpayrat, 9 x 6 In.		1680.00
Urn, Oval, White Crackle Glaze, Jean Besnard, c.1930, 13 In.		5605.00
Vase, 2 Dragons, Flambe, Bulbous, Bernard Moore, 4¾ In.		333.00
Vase, 3 Orange Poppy Flowers, Standard Glaze, 14½ In.		2760.00
Vase, Art Nouveau, Crystalline Glaze, Blue, Gray, Yellow, Aultcliff, England, 1930s, 5½ x 3 In.		445.00
Vase, Blue, Green, Brown Crystalline Glaze, 4 Handles, Signed, Denbac, 10¼ In.		510.00
Vase, Blue & Green Crystals, Mustard Ground, Bulbous, Squat, Pierrefonds, 4¾ In.		460.00
Vase, Blue & Salmon Drip Glaze, Olive Ground, Tapered, Footed, Charles Greber, 10¾ In.		207.00
Vase, Blue & Yellow Crystalline Glazes, Egg Shape, Flared Rim, Footed, R. Guerin, Belgium, 30 In.		1265.00
Vase, Bottle Shape, Gres, 4-Sided, Blue Green & Gray Matte Glaze, Dalpayrat, 8½ x 5 In.		3000.00
Vase, Bottle Shape, Gres, 4-Sided, Purple & Gray Matte Glaze, Dalpayrat, 8½ x 5 In.		3240.00
Vase, Bottle Shape, Pinched, Red & Blue Drip Glaze Over Buff Clay, Dalpayrat, 5⅜ In.		978.00
Vase, Bud, Ducks, Fish, Bottle Shape, Persian Style, De Morgan, 5¾ x 3¼ In.		1680.00
Vase, Butterflies, Pierced Winglike Handles, Painted, Luster Glaze, c.1900, 12 x 7 In.		4500.00
Vase, Cabinet, Experimental, Lustered Brown Green & Oxblood Glaze, 3¼ x 3¼ In.		840.00
Vase, Carved Leaves, Crackle Glaze, Gray, White, Tapered, Art Deco, Rene Buthaud, 12 In.		1955.00
Vase, Carved Leaves, Green & Brown Semimatte Flambe Glaze, Walley, 5 x 4 In.		1320.00
Vase, Charcoal Gray, Herringbone, Germany, 10 In.		18.00
Vase, Cover, Bursley Ware, Charlotte Rhead, c.1950, 5½ In.		185.00
Vase, Cylindrical, Flared Rim, Stoneware, Red & Green Crystalline Glaze, Dalpayrat, 13¼ In.		4371.00
Vase, Daisies, Standard Glaze, Caroline Steinle, 1905, 5¼ In.		345.00
Vase, Double Gourd, Gray Metallic Crystalline Glaze, Green To Black Ground, St. Honore, 9 In.		403.00
Vase, Enameled Blue & Red Glaze, Stoneware, 2 Ear Handles, Dalpayrat, 4 In.		431.00
Vase, Flame Painted, Lustered Gold, Amber, Flat Shoulder, Flared, Brouwer, 6½ x 6 In.		2200.00
Vase, Flowers, Green, Brown Crystalline Glaze, Marked, M. Nancy, France, 12½ x 7½ In.		1900.00
Vase, Garniture, Barbotine Glazed, Rose & Poppy, Flared, Footed, France, 16 In., Pair		587.00
Vase, Glazed, Painted, Abstract, Blue, Cream, c.1928, 15¾ In.		8400.00
Vase, Gourd Form, Thick Blue & White Glaze, Signed, Mougin, 4 In.		345.00
Vase, Gray & Beige Stripe, Belgium, 5 x 7 In.		70.00
Vase, Green, Brown & Blue Glaze, Organic Design, 4 Handles, Denbac, 9¼ In.	*illus*	390.00
Vase, Green, Brown Matte Glaze, Lobes, Stamped, W.J. Walley, 7 x 4 In.		1200.00
Vase, Green, Oval, Sweden, 7½ In.		108.00
Vase, Green, Red, Purple Glaze, Swollen, Dalpayrat, Signed, A.P., No. 63, 5 In.		730.00
Vase, Gres, Purple, Teal & Gunmetal Frothy Glaze, Tapered Neck, Dalpayrat, 9 x 6 In.	*illus*	3240.00
Vase, Gres, Ribbed, Oxblood Glaze, Dalpayrat, 3¼ x 4 In.		1560.00
Vase, Handles, Lion's Head Medallions, Mottled Blue Glaze, Burley Winter, 21 x 17 In.		480.00

Vase, Indented, Mottled Brown, Red, Blue Matte Glaze, No. 63, Signed, Dalpayrat, 12 x 6 In.	3600.00
Vase, Iridescent, Pinched Sides, Cypriot Finish, Dugan, Early 1800s, 4½ In.	35.00
Vase, Leaves, Brown Matte Glaze, Oval, Tapered, Buttressed Handles, Denbac, No. 15, No Size	207.00
Vase, Marbleized Flambe Glaze, Red, Ivory, Squat, W.J. Walley, 4¼ x 4¾ In.	2520.00
Vase, Molded Trees, Green Matte Glaze, Bulbous Rim, Paul Dachsel, 7¾ In.	2530.00
Vase, Mottled Blue, Tan & Gray Glaze, Organic Shoulder, J. Wolfe, Mougin, 8 In.	920.00
Vase, Mottled Red, Blue, Green Glaze, Square, Dalpayrat, 9 x 5 In.	1700.00
Vase, Mushroom Form, Gray, Red, Green Glaze, Dalpayrat, 2 x 1½ In.	420.00
Vase, Ombroso, Rosettes, Blue, Green, Rose, Brown Glaze, 1915, 8⅛ In.	3105.00
Vase, Oval, Blue Crystals, Ivory & Gray Flambe Glaze, Robertson, 17 x 4 In.	1320.00
Vase, Oval, Green Crystalline Glaze, Signed, 8 In.	59.00
Vase, Owl Perched On Branch, Denmark, Stag Logo, 8½ In.	259.00
Vase, Painted, Sunflowers, Wardle, c.1900, 24 In.	293.00
Vase, Peacock Feathers, Crystalline Matte Glaze, Metal Mounts, Stones, Handles, Denbac, 7¾ x 3 In.	1020.00
Vase, Pear Shape, Specked Blue Matte Glaze, Arthur Baggs, 4½ x 3¾ In.	510.00
Vase, Pinched Waist, Pate-Sur-Pate, White Ivy On Green Matte Ground, Nonconnah, 11 x 4 In.	1680.00
Vase, Pinecone, Arts & Crafts, Green Shading, 5 x 8½ In.	1890.00
Vase, Piped, Painted Flowers, Gloss Glaze, 12½ In.	118.00
Vase, Roses & Crosses, Gray Stoneware, Blue Tapered, S. Frackleton, No. 101, 3¾ In.	4600.00
Vase, Speckled Red & Green Glaze, Pinewood, c.1948, 5½ In.	431.00
Vase, Squat, 2 Lizards Under Frothy Green & Brown Semimatte Glaze, 3¼ x 4¼ In.	4200.00
Vase, Squat, Cobalt Blue Crystalline Glaze, Adelaide Robineau, 4¼ x 6 In.	4200.00
Vase, Trees, Blue, Red, Black Glazes, Rectangular, R. Lachenal, 8¼ In.	633.00

POTTERY-CONTEMPORARY lists pieces made by artists working after 1975.

Bowl, Animals, Blue, Tan Interior, Red Clay, Signed, Scheier, 6⅛ x 11⅞ In.	2900.00
Bowl, Blue Band, Beige, Incised, Tapered, Marked, Gobble, 9 x 20 In.	345.00
Bowl, Dancing Figures, Green, Black Ground, Signed, Polia Pillin, 6 x 8 In.	1150.00
Bowl, Kayo O'Young, 1980s, 8 In.	103.00
Bowl, Red & Blue Glaze, Incised, Tapered, Marked, Gobble, 6¾ x 14 In.	173.00
Jar, Cover, Fertility Figures, Bronze Volcanic Glaze, Stoneware, Scheier, 1983, 16 x 10 In. *illus*	7200.00
Pitcher, Oval, Wavy Line, Kim Ellington, 10 In.	201.00
Pitcher, Runny Alkaline Glaze, Harold Hewell, 15½ In.	230.00
Sugar Sifter, Sunburst, Finned, Flame Jug, Lorna Bailey	84.00
Vase, Pedestal, Lid, 2 Bowl-Like Vessels, 3 Handles, Painted, Sylvia Hyman, 20 x 7½ In.	748.00

POTTERY-MIDCENTURY includes pieces made from the 1940s to about 1975.

Ashtray, No. 4, Fish Shape, Vermont, Ballard, 4½ x 3½ In.	23.00
Bottle, Ridged, Gunmetal Glaze, Stoneware, Peter Voulkos, 18¾ x 6 In. *illus*	5700.00
Bowl, Gold, Abstract Design, Brooklin, T. & S. Harlander, c.1960, 10¾ In.	214.00
Bowl, Pink & Bronze Matte Glaze, Sgraffito Lines, Flared, Lucie Rie, 4¾ x 9 In. *illus*	10200.00
Bowl, Red Glaze, Signed Beato, Beatrice Wood, c.1955, 4 x 7½ In. *illus*	2160.00
Charger, Glazed, Peter Voulkos, 1961, 12 In.	4200.00
Chess Set, Gladys Eleanor Montgomery, 1930s, 5½ In.	175.00
Dish, Divided, Figures, Parasol, Tree, Brock, California, 11 In. *illus*	1.00
Dish, No. 74, White Glaze, Twisted, Vermont, Ballard, 5½ In.	20.00
Feelie, Turquoise Glaze, Tan On Shoulders, Cabat, 3 x 3¾ In.	546.00
Feelie, Ultramarine Vellum Glaze, Cabat, 5½ x 4 In. *illus*	1680.00
Figurine, Siamese Cat, 1960s, 8 & 7¼ In., Pair *illus*	51.00
Figurine, Woman With Dove, Toucan, Baboon, Lemur, Edris Eckhardt, 11 In. *illus*	1840.00
Planter, Double Cone, White Glaze, La Tackett, c.1951, 20½ x 10 In.	1020.00
Planter, Figural, Landing Duck, Electrified, Van Nuys, 12 x 10 In.	41.00
Plate, Biscotti, Arranged On Doily, Trompe L'Oeil, P. Fornasetti, c.1950, 10 In. *illus*	359.00
Powder Jar, Nymolle, Jacob Bang, Denmark, c.1957	85.00
Vase, Blue & Purple Textured & Matte High Glazes, Cylindrical, Raymor, Italy, 14 In. *illus*	300.00
Vase, Egg, Foamy Blue Glaze, Red Highlights, Ben Owen, 6 x 4¾ In. *illus*	633.00
Vase, Floor, Runny Yellow, Green, Brown Glaze, Seagrove, N.C., 17 In.	259.00
Vase, Gourd Shape, Brown Clay, Turquoise & Tan Drip Glaze, Cabat, 5 x 3 In. *illus*	720.00
Vase, Luster Glaze, Signed, Laura Andreson, c.1970, 7 x 7½ In. *illus*	1920.00
Vase, No. 9, Seafoam Green, 8-Sided, Vermont, Ballard, 5 In.	40.00
Vase, No. 19, Green, Brown, Vermont, Ballard, 5¾ In.	50.00
Vase, Pottery, Blue & Green Glaze, Face, Brooklin, T. & S. Harlander, 1950s, 3¼ In.	342.00
Vase, Spool Shape, Blue, White, Black, Ettore Sottsass, Italy, 8¾ x 12 In. *illus*	1920.00

Pottery-Midcentury, Bottle, Ridged, Gunmetal Glaze, Stoneware, Peter Voulkos, 18¾ x 6 In.
$5700.00

Pottery-Midcentury, Bowl, Pink & Bronze Matte Glaze, Sgraffito Lines, Flared, Lucie Rie, 4¾ x 9 In.
$10200.00

Pottery-Midcentury, Bowl, Red Glaze, Signed Beato, Beatrice Wood, c.1955, 4 x 7½ In.
$2160.00

Pottery-Midcentury, Dish, Divided, Figures, Parasol, Tree, Brock, California, 11 In.
$1.00

Pottery-Midcentury, Feelie, Ultramarine Vellum Glaze, Cabat, 5½ x 4 In.
$1680.00

Pottery-Midcentury, Figurine, Siamese Cat, 1960s, 8 & 7¼ In., Pair
$51.00

Pottery-Midcentury, Figurine, Woman With Dove, Toucan, Baboon, Lemur, Edris Eckhardt, 11 In.
$1840.00

Pottery-Midcentury, Plate, Biscotti, Arranged On Doily, Trompe L'Oeil, P. Fornasetti, c.1950, 10 In.
$359.00

Pottery-Midcentury, Vase, Blue & Purple Textured & Matte High Glazes, Cylindrical, Raymor, Italy, 14 In.
$300.00

Pottery-Midcentury, Vase, Egg, Foamy Blue Glaze, Red Highlights, Ben Owen, 6 x 4¾ In.
$633.00

Pottery-Midcentury, Vase, Gourd Shape, Brown Clay, Turquoise & Tan Drip Glaze, Cabat, 5 x 3 In.
$720.00

Pottery-Midcentury, Vase, Luster Glaze, Signed, Laura Andreson, c.1970, 7 x 7½ In.
$1920.00

Pottery-Midcentury, Vase, Spool Shape, Blue, White, Black, Ettore Sottsass, Italy, 8¾ x 12 In.
$1920.00

P

Vase, Stylized Person, Signed, Lagardo Tackett, c.1955, 11 x 6½ In. . . . . *illus* 1800.00
Vase, Venini, Fazzoletto, Italy, 1950s, 7 In. 451.00

POWDER FLASKS AND POWDER HORNS were made to hold the gunpowder used in antique firearms. The early examples were made of horn or wood; later ones were of copper or brass.

POWDER FLASK

Brass, Eagle & Shield, Applied Motif, 6¾ x 1⅜ In. 235.00
Brass, Kangaroo, Nickel Plated, 7½ x 3½ x 1¼ In. 300.00
Copper, Bird, 2-Sided, G & JW Hawksley, Sheffield, 8 In. 425.00
Copper, Deer, Fox, Elk, 8 In. 350.00
Copper, Rabbit & Pheasants, James Dixon & Sons, 8½ In. 385.00
Engraved, Flowers, Flags, St. Augustine, Wood, Horn Screw Top, Signed, N.F., 1800s, 7 x 3¾ In. 574.00

POWDER HORN

Applied Silver & Medallion, Engraved W, Wood Plug, Beaded Fringe, 12 In. 55.00
Blown Glass, Amber, Applied Lower Ring, Knop, Pontil, 1850-70, 13 In. 285.00
Blown Glass, Marbrie White Looping, Clear, Stripe, Neck Ring, Rolled Lip, 11¾ In. 176.00
Blown Glass, Yellow To Red Amber, Flange Collar, Tooled Neck, Knop, 14½ In. 242.00
Brass, Crescent Shape, Openwork Arabesque, Inlay, Morocco, 1800s, 11½ In. 247.00
Carved, French & Indian Wars, New York Map, Hudson & Mohawk Rivers, 1740, 16 In. 6325.00
Concentric Rings, Turned, Wood Plug, Turned Rattlesnake Style Tip, 9½ In. 220.00
Engraved, British Coat Of Arms, Hunter, Dog, House, 19th Century, 10 In. 1265.00
Engraved, John Nalson, Hunter Shooting Stag, 1759, 13½ In. 2700.00
Engraved, Lion, Adam & Eve, Bird, Sun, Banner, Lizard, Carved Top, Signed, CSM, 1800s, 11 In. . 1265.00
Engraved, Moose, Woodsman & Rifle, Bennington, Vt., Aug. 15-16, 1777, 16 In. 120.00
Engraved, Overlapping Circles, Signed, Wm. M 1799, JM 1814, 14 In. 1035.00
Engraved, Port City, Ships, Houses, Benjamin Hills Horn, Early 19th Century, 19¼ In. 2703.00
Iron Collar Mount, Chain Hook, Wood End, Cork, 12 In., Pair 120.00
Leather Covered, Tooled Geometric Design, Early 1800s, 6½ x 2¾ In. 225.00
Painted, Indian, Canoe, Flag, Horse Head, Bowie Knife, Ship, Initials, Joseph Harrington, 14 In. . 3500.00
Silver End, Rolled Lip, Acorn, Leaves & Rosette Fasteners, Inscribed, Carl Geist, Berlin, 31 In. . . . 1020.00
Turned Tip, Wood Plug, 9½ In. 176.00

PRATT ware means two different things. It was an early Staffordshire pottery, cream-colored with colored decorations, made by Felix Pratt during the late eighteenth century. There was also Pratt ware made with transfer designs during the mid-nineteenth century in Fenton, England. Reproductions of the transfer-printed Pratt are being made. More Pratt may be listed in Potlid.

Cup Plate, Blue Glaze, Feather & Bar Edge, Pearlware, c.1820, 4 In. 250.00
Figurine, Man Standing At Column About To Sacrifice Lamb, 8 In. . . . . *illus* 288.00
Figurine, Ram, Lying Down, c.1800, 5½ In. 624.00
Group, Babes In The Wood, Multicolored, c.1800, 4 In. 229.00
Jug, Lord Wellington & General Hill, Staffordshire, c.1840, 6½ x 6½ In. 410.00
Jug, Red, Turned Decoration Below Rim, On Handle, Gold Bands, 19th Century 125.00

PRESSED GLASS was first made in the United States in the 1820s after the invention of glass pressing machines. Hundreds of patterns of pressed glass were made in complete table settings. Although the Boston and Sandwich Works was the most famous of the pressed glass factories, there were about sixteen other factories making pressed glass from 1830 to 1850, and still more from 1850 to 1900, when pressed glass reached its greatest popularity. It is now being widely reproduced. The pattern names used in this listing are based on the information in the book *Pressed Glass in America* by John and Elizabeth Welker. There may be pieces of pressed glass listed in this book in other categories, such as Lamp, Ruby, Sandwich, and Souvenir.

Acanthus pattern is listed here as Ribbed Palm.
Acorn & Oak Leaf, Spooner, Fiery Opalescent, 12-Scallop Rim, Flint, 5½ In. 110.00
Actress, Cake Stand, 6¾ x 10 In. 121.00
Actress, Cake Stand, Frosted Stem & Foot, 6¾ x 10 In. 99.00
Actress, Celery Vase, 8½ In. 110.00
Actress, Compote, Cover, 12½ In. 99.00
Actress, Compote, Cover, Frosted Accents, 12½ In. 110.00
Actress, Goblet, 6½ In. . . . . *illus* 66.00
Actress, Jam Jar, 6⅜ In. 44.00
Actress, Pitcher, 9 x 5 In. 220.00

Pottery-Midcentury, Vase, Stylized Person, Signed, Lagardo Tackett, c.1955, 11 x 6½ In. $1800.00

Pratt, Figurine, Man Standing At Column About To Sacrifice Lamb, 8 In. $288.00

P

TIP

A vase that has been drilled for a lamp, even if the hole for the wiring is original, is worth 30% to 50% of the value of the same vase without a hole.

Pressed Glass, Actress, Goblet, 6½ In.
$66.00

Pressed Glass, Beaded Circle, Tumbler, 3½ In.
$99.00

Is It Flint Glass?

Flint (lead glass) or *nonflint (lime glass)* are terms found in catalogs. Glassmakers used different amounts of lead in the glass for clarity. Most glass made before the 1860s has lead. Lime glass with clarity comparable to lead glass was developed in 1864 by William Leighton Sr., of Hobbs, Brockunier & Company. Nonflint lime glass of the 1800s should not be confused with *soda* or *bottle glass.* Bottle glass, green or brown, doesn't have lead and doesn't ring when struck.

Pressed glass factories made flint patterns in the 1870s and 1880s but found they couldn't compete with less expensive lime glass.

Actress, Saltshaker, 3⅛ In. 33.00

Actress, Table Set, Butter, Sugar, Creamer, 3 Piece 55.00

Almond Thumbprint, Tumbler, 2 Rows, 3¾ In. 99.00

Aquarium, Pitcher, 9¼ In. 275.00

Arched Cane & Fan, Sugar & Creamer, Green, Gold Bead 40.00

Argus, Table Set, Sugar, Cover, Creamer, Spooner, 3 Piece 154.00

Ashburton, Champagne, Cut, Gold Trim, 4¾ In. 44.00

Ashburton, Goblet, Cut, Flared Rim, 6 In. 22.00

Ashburton, Goblet, Double Knob Stem, 6⅝ In. 11.00

Ashburton, Goblet, Squared Stem, 6⅝ In. 22.00

Ashburton, Wine, Choked, Bowl, Gold Trim, 4¼ In. 55.00

Atlanta, Compote, 8¾ x 8 In. 53.00

Atlanta, Compote, Cover, Square, Lion Finial, 10 x 6 In. 66.00

Atlanta, Goblet, Square Lion, 6 In. 66.00

Atterbury Duck, Dish, Cover, Movable Glass Eyes, 11 In. 135.00

Aurora, Tray, Wine 25.00

Austrian, Saltshaker, Pewter Lid, 4 In. 60.00

Baby Face, Butter, Cover, Frosted Finial, Stem & Foot, 8½ In. 99.00

Baby Face, Celery Vase, Frosted Stem & Foot, 7¾ In. 187.00

Baby Face, Compote, Cover, Frosted Finial, Stem & Foot, 11½ x 8 In. 330.00

Baby Face, Creamer, Frosted Stem, 7¼ In. 242.00

Baby Face, Goblet, 6¼ In. .... 231.00 to 264.00

Baby Face, Goblet, Engraved Fern & Berry, 6⅜ In. 242.00

Baby Face, Sugar & Creamer, Cover, Frosted Finial, Stem & Foot 143.00

Baby Face, Table Set, Butter, Cover, Sugar, Spooner, Frosted Finial, Stem & Foot, 3 Piece 523.00

Baby Thumbprint pattern is listed here as Dakota.

Bakewell Block Knob, Tumbler, Ship's, 3⅞ In. 88.00

Balloon, Creamer, 1850s, 4 In. 450.00

Balloon, Sugar & Creamer, Cover, Molded Handle 605.00

Bar & Diamond pattern is listed here as Kokomo.

Barley & Oats pattern is listed here as Wheat & Barley.

Barley & Wheat pattern is listed here as Wheat & Barley.

Barred Ovals, Compote, 7¼ x 7 In. 50.00

Barrel Honeycomb, see the related pattern Honeycomb.

Barreled Block pattern is listed here as Red Block.

Basket Weave, Bowl, 3½ In. 18.00

Basket Weave, Cup & Saucer, Amber 30.00

Basket Weave, Goblet, 5½ In. 30.00

Beaded Bird, Salt & Pepper, Stand, Napkin Ring Handle, 4 In. 66.00

Beaded Circle, Tumbler, 3½ In. .... *illus* 99.00

Beaded Dart, Goblet, 5¾ In. 26.00

Beaded Shell, Tumbler, 3¾ In. 85.00

Beaded Swirl, Creamer, Amethyst, Jewel & Scallop Rim, 4½ In. 45.00

Bearded Head pattern is listed here as Viking.

Beaver Band, Goblet, 5½ In. 990.00

Bellflower, Bowl, Double Vine, 6 Clusters, Cut, Wafer Stem, Footed, 3¾ x 7½ In. 330.00

Bellflower, Celery Vase, Scallop & Point Rim, 8 In. 88.00

Bellflower, Compote, Double Vine, Cut, Hexagonal Stem, 16-Scallop Foot, 8½ x 10⅜ In. 4510.00

Bellflower, Compote, Flint, 7 In. 60.00

Bellflower, Compote, Left Facing On Bowl, Right Facing On Foot, 9 In. 165.00

Bellflower, Decanter, Double Vine, Left & Right Facing, Stopper, Qt., 9¾ In. 44.00

Bellflower, Decanter, Double Vine, Right Facing, Pewter Stopper, Pt., 9 In. 1800.00

Bellflower, Decanter, Double Vine, Right Facing, Pt., 8 In. 468.00

Bellflower, Decanter, Left Facing Vine, 3 Rows Cut Thumbprint, Pt., 12¼ In. 413.00

Bellflower, Decanter, Left Facing Vine, 3 Rows Cut Thumbprints, Bar Lip, Qt., 10 In. 220.00

Bellflower, Decanter, Left Facing Vine, Bar Lip, Qt., 9⅜ In. 77.00

Bellflower, Decanter, Left Facing Vine, Stopper, Qt., 12½ In. 303.00

Bellflower, Goblet, Looped Vines, Straight Sides, 5⅝ In. 66.00

Bellflower, Molasses Jug, Right Facing Vine, Handle, Hinged Tin Top, 7½ x 3¼ In. 275.00

Bellflower, Pitcher, Double Vine, Left & Right Facing, Applied Handle, 8½ In. 165.00

Bellflower, Pitcher, Double Vine, Left & Right Facing, Straight Sides, Applied Handle, 8¼ In. 715.00

Bellflower, Relish, Double Vine, Scoop Shape, 8½ x 4¾ In. 11.00

Bellflower, Tumbler, Coarse Ribs, 3½ In. 88.00

Bellflower, Tumbler, Cut, 4 Clusters, 3½ In. 88.00

Bicycle Girl, Pitcher, Scalloped Rim, 10¾ In. 1155.00

Bird & Strawberry, Goblet, 6½ In. 605.00

Birds & Flowers, Box, Ribbed, Lion Lying Down, Ribbed Band, Figural Lid, 6½ x 4 In.	220.00
Birds At Fountain, Goblet	55.00
Blackberry, Bowl, Fruit, 4 x 1 In.	19.00
Bleeding Heart, Cake Stand, 5½ x 9½ In.	110.00
Bleeding Heart, Cake Stand, 5¼ x 11 In.	132.00
Bleeding Heart, Compote, Cover, 9¼ x 7¼ In.	55.00
Bleeding Heart, Compote, Cover, 10¼ x 8¼ In.	66.00
Bleeding Heart, Egg Set, Tray, 4 Cups, 4 Domed Covers, 7¼ x 7 In. ....*illus*	1870.00
Bleeding Heart, Egg Set, Tray, 4 Cups, 7 In.	99.00
Bleeding Heart, Goblet, 6 In.	65.00
Bleeding Heart, Goblet, Metz Variation, 6¼ In., 6 Piece	132.00
Bleeding Heart, Nappy, Cover, 4¾ x 7¼ In.	55.00
Bleeding Heart, Nappy, Cover, Footed, 7¼ x 8¼ In.	44.00
Bleeding Heart, Pitcher, Applied Handle, Leaf Terminal, 8¾ In.	88.00
Bleeding Heart, Salt, Master	33.00
Bleeding Heart, Table Set, Nappy, Cover, Creamer, Spooner, 3 Piece	132.00
Bleeding Heart, Table Set, Sugar, Creamer, Spooner, 3 Piece	176.00
Bleeding Heart, Tumbler, 3¾ In.	110.00
Bleeding Heart, Tumbler, Footed, 5 In.	66.00
Bleeding Heart, Wine, 4 In.	77.00
Block & Fan, Biscuit Jar, Cover, 7½ In.	25.00
Block & Fan, Cruet, Stopper	15.00
Block & Star pattern is listed here as Valencia Waffle.	
Block & Thumbprint, Tumbler, 3⅞ In.	110.00
Bluebird pattern is listed here as Bird & Strawberry.	
Bow Tie, Cake Stand, Pedestal Foot, c.1889, 9 In.	225.00
Brilliant, Tumbler, 3¾ In.	77.00
Brilliant, Wine, Flint, 4⅝ In.	225.00
Broken Arches, Punch Bowl, With Stand, 12 x 5 In.	88.00
Broken Column, Bottle, Water, 8½ In.	225.00
Brooklyn, Goblet, 6 In.	99.00
Bullet Emblem, Sugar, Cover, 6 In.	88.00
Bull's Eye, Cordial, 3½ In.	88.00
Bull's Eye, Cruet, Panel-Cut Neck, Stopper, 7¾ In.	66.00
Bull's Eye, Eggcup, Cover, 5¼ In.	176.00
Bull's-Eye, Goblet, Cordial, 4 In.	25.00
Bull's-Eye & Bar, Champagne, 5¼ In.	550.00
Bull's-Eye & Bar, Eggcup, Clambroth, 3¾ In.	132.00
Bull's-Eye & Bar, Eggcup, Starch Blue, 3¾ In.	220.00
Bull's-Eye & Bar, Goblet, 6¼ In.	143.00
Bull's-Eye & Bar, Wine, 4⅛ In.	44.00
Bull's-Eye & Daisy, Water Set, Green Stained Bull's-Eyes, 7 Piece	174.00
Bull's-Eye & Fan, Berry Bowl, 3¾ x 8 In.	185.00
Bull's-Eye & Fan, Bowl, Star Base, 8½ In.	25.00
Bull's-Eye & Fan, Creamer	20.00
Bull's-Eye & Fan, Tumbler, Green, Gold Trim & Bull's-Eye, c.1900	40.00
Bull's-Eye & Fleur-De-Lis, Decanter, Flat Panel, Bar Lip, 10¾ In.	121.00
Bull's-Eye & Fleur-De-Lis, Goblet, 6⅜ In. ....*illus*	110.00
Bull's-Eye & Fleur-De-Lis, Pitcher, Applied Handle, 9¼ In.	880.00
Bull's-Eye & Rosette, Whiskey, 3⅛ In.	143.00
Bull's-Eye & Wishbone, Goblet, 6 In.	198.00
Bull's-Eye With Diamond Point, Celery Vase, Faceted Stem, Plain Foot, 9¼ In.	209.00
Bull's-Eye With Diamond Point, Compote, Hexagonal Stem, 7¼ In.	231.00
Bull's-Eye With Diamond Point, Compote, Octagonal Stem, Knop, 16-Scallop Foot, 7¼ In.	209.00
Bull's-Eye With Diamond Point, Creamer, Applied Handle, 6¼ In.	770.00
Bull's-Eye With Diamond Point, Goblet, 6¾ In.	99.00
Bull's-Eye With Diamond Point, Spooner, Gold Trim, Flared Rim, Round Foot, 5½ In.	66.00
Bull's-Eye With Diamond Point, Sugar, Cover, Hexagonal Stem, Round Foot, 9 In.	154.00
Bull's-Eye With Diamond Point, Tumbler, Whiskey, 3¼ In.	187.00
Bull's-Eye With Diamond Point, Wine, 4⅜ In.	303.00
Button Arches, Toothpick, Ruby Stained .... 45.00 to 65.00	
Button Stem, Wine, Flint, 4 x 2⅛ In.	60.00
Cabbage Leaf, Compote, Cover, Frosted, 10½ x 8¼ In.	330.00
Cabbage Leaf, Creamer, Frosted, 5¾ In.	88.00
Cabbage Leaf, Dish, Cover, Frosted, 5½ x 7½ In.	176.00
Cabbage Leaf, Pitcher, Amber, 10 In.	1980.00

Pressed Glass, Bleeding Heart, Egg Set, Tray, 4 Cups, 4 Domed Covers, 7¼ x 7 In. $1870.00

Pressed Glass, Bull's-Eye & Fleur-De-Lis, Goblet, 6⅜ In. $110.00

Pressed Glass, Classic, Pitcher, Milk, 4 Log Feet, 8¾ In. $550.00

P

Pressed Glass, Colonial Flute, Goblet, Fiery Opalescent, Polished Pontil, 6⅛ In. $468.00

Pressed Glass, Comet, Tumbler, 3½ In. $297.00

Pressed Glass, Cupid & Venus, Pitcher, Milk, Blue, 7¾ In. $550.00

Pressed Glass, Daisy & Button, Compote, Cover, Scalloped Edge, 13½ x 10 In. $231.00

Cabbage Leaf, Table Set, Butter, Cover, Sugar, Creamer, 3 Piece	275.00
Cabbage Rose, Tumbler	45.00
Cable, Goblet, 6⅜ In.	66.00
Cable, Spooner, 5¾ x 3½ In.	19.00
Cable, Tumbler, 3½ In.	154.00
Cable, Wine, 4 In.	77.00
Cable & Grape, Compote	26.00

Candlewick as a pressed glass pattern is properly named Banded Raindrop. There is also a pattern called Candlewick, which has been made by Imperial Glass Corporation since 1936. It is listed in this book in the Imperial Glass category.

Cane, Decanter, Stopper, Cranberry Stained, 9½ x 3¼ In.	20.00
Cane, Goblet	16.00
Canoe, Bowl, 15 In.	15.00
Cat & Dog, Pitcher, 9⅞ x 4 In.	358.00
Cathedral, Compote, Amethyst, 10½ In.	209.00

Centennial, see also the related patterns Liberty Bell and Viking.

Champion, Cake Stand	100.00
Cherry Lattice, Berry Bowl, 4½ In.	17.00
Cherry Tree, Dish, Pickle	20.00
Chilson, Goblet, 6⅝ In.	165.00
Chrysanthemum Sprig, Compote, Jelly	65.00
Classic, Goblet, 6 In.	176.00
Classic, Pitcher, 4 Log Feet, 9¾ In.	132.00
Classic, Pitcher, Milk, 4 Log Feet, 8¾ In. .... *illus*	550.00
Classic, Plate, Blaine, Frosted, 11½ In.	198.00
Classic, Plate, Grover Cleveland, Frosted, 11½ In.	165.00
Classic, Plate, Hendricks, Frosted, 11½ In.	495.00
Classic, Plate, Logan, Frosted, 11½ In.	99.00
Classic, Table Set, Butter, Sugar, Creamer, 3 Piece	187.00
Classic, Water Set, 7 Piece	1375.00
Classic Medallion, Compote, Footed	26.00
Cleat, Pitcher, Applied Solid Handle, 9 In.	220.00
Clipper Ship Etch, Goblet, 6 In.	275.00

Coin Spot pattern is listed in this book in its own category.

Colonial, Cruet	26.00
Colonial, Sugar, Double Handle	25.00
Colonial Flute, Goblet, Fiery Opalescent, Polished Pontil, 6⅛ In. .... *illus*	468.00
Colorado, Cup, Green	22.00
Columbian Coin, Cake Stand, Clear Coins, 6½ x 10 In.	99.00
Columbian Coin, Celery Vase, 6 In.	143.00
Columbian Coin, Compote, 7¾ x 8 In.	44.00
Columbian Coin, Compote, Cover, Frosted Coins, 11½ In.	176.00
Columbian Coin, Cruet, Frosted Coins, Stopper, 5½ In.	121.00
Columbian Coin, Finger Lamp, Frosted Coins, No. 1 Taplin-Brown Collar, 5¼ In.	1265.00
Columbian Coin, Goblet, Frosted Coins, Flared Rim, 6 In.	66.00
Columbian Coin, Mug, Beer, Gold Trim, 4¾ In.	143.00
Columbian Coin, Salt & Pepper	88.00
Columbian Coin, Wine, Frosted Coins, 4½ In.	121.00
Columned Thumbprints, Butter, Dome Lid, c.1905	40.00
Comet, Goblet, 6¼ In.	187.00
Comet, Tumbler, 3½ In. .... *illus*	297.00

Cosmos pattern is listed in this book as its own category.

Crane pattern is listed here as Stork.

Cupid & Venus, Creamer, Footed	90.00
Cupid & Venus, Pitcher, Milk, Blue, 7¾ In. .... *illus*	550.00
Cupid & Venus, Sherbet, 2¼ x 3⅔ In., Pair	49.00
Cupid & Venus, Spooner, Pedestal, 5¾ x 4¼ In.	45.00
Currant Pattern, Goblet, Buttermilk, 5 x 4 In.	40.00

Daisies In Oval Panels pattern is listed here as Bull's-Eye & Fan.

Daisy & Button, see also the related pattern Paneled Daisy & Button.

Daisy & Button, Ashtray, 3-Footed, 2½ x 4 In.	27.00
Daisy & Button, Bowl, Oblong, 9 x 6 In.	20.00
Daisy & Button, Butter, Helmet Cover, 6¼ In.	220.00
Daisy & Button, Compote, Cover, Scalloped Edge, 13½ x 10 In. .... *illus*	231.00
Daisy & Button, Condiment Set, Cobalt Blue, 3 Bottles, Holder, 7 In., 4 Piece .... *illus*	118.00
Daisy & Button, Plate, Square, 7 x 7 In.	25.00

Daisy & Button, Punch Cup, Blue, 3 Piece	65.00
Daisy & Button, Salt, Amber, 4½ x 1¾ In.	20.00
Daisy & Button, Shoe, 4⅛ x 1¾ In.	35.00
Daisy & Button, Tray, Ice Cream, Scalloped Rim, 9 x 5½ In.	95.00
Daisy & Button, Tumbler, Apple Green, 3 Piece	24.00
Dakota, Cake Stand, Cover, 13¾ x 9¼ In.	1100.00
Dakota, Finger Bowl, Engraved Flying Birds, 3 x 4¼ In.	209.00
Dakota, Salt, Blue	77.00
Dakota, Saltshaker, Engraved Fern & Berry, 3½ In.	99.00
Dakota, Table Set, Engraved Fern & Berry, 5 Piece	55.00
Dakota, Tray, Ruffled Edge, 13 In.	44.00
Dakota, Water Set, Engraved Fern & Berry, 10-In. Tankard Pitcher, 5 Piece	99.00
Deer & Doe With Lily-Of-The-Valley, Goblet, 5¾ In.	165.00
Deer & Dog, Butter, Cover, Frosted Finial	187.00
Deer & Dog, Celery Vase, 8½ In.	99.00
Deer & Dog, Claret, 4¾ In.	165.00
Deer & Dog, Compote, Cover, Frosted Finial, 13 In.	330.00
Deer & Dog, Cordial, Footed, 3½ x 1⅛ In.	275.00
Deer & Dog, Goblet, 6⅜ In.	66.00
Deer & Dog, Pitcher, Ribbed Handle, 10 In.	176.00
Deer & Dog, Sugar, Cover	220.00
Deer & Dog, Table Set, Butter, Cover, Sugar, Creamer, Spooner, 4 Piece	275.00
Deer & Oak Tree, Pitcher, 9 In.	132.00
Deer & Pine Tree, Cake Stand, 5¾ x 11 In.	187.00
Deer & Pine Tree, Compote, Cover, 12½ x 9 In.	66.00
Delaware, Berry Bowl, Emerald Green, Gold Trim, 8¼ In. . . . . . *illus*	75.00
Delaware, Spooner, Ruby Stained, Gold Trim, Early 1900s	50.00
Dew & Raindrop, Butter, Dome Lid, Round, 5½ x 7 In.	85.00
Dewdrop, Bread Plate, Sheaf Of Wheat, 11 In.	30.00
Dewdrop, Butter, Cover, 7½ x 5½ In.	85.00
Diamond, Berry Bowl, 4½ x 2 In.	8.99
Diamond, Pitcher, Tankard, Pewter Top, 14¼ In.	145.00
Diamond & Dot, Compote, Scalloped Rim, 6⅝ x 9 In.	40.00
Diamond Block, Vase, Footed, 8 x 4 In.	24.00
Diamond Cross, Relish, Ball Handles, 5½ x 7½ In.	40.00
Diamond Horseshoe pattern is listed here as Aurora.	
Diamond Peg, Creamer, Ruby Stained	36.00
Diamond Point, Cordial, 3⅜ In.	66.00
Diamond Point, Eggcup, Translucent Gray Blue, 3¾ In.	385.00
Diamond Point, Jug, Applied Handle, Octagonal Base, ½ Pt., 6¼ In. . .	154.00
Diamond Point, Spooner, Gold Trim, Round Foot, 5¾ In.	66.00
Diamond Point, Tumbler, 3¾ In.	99.00
Diamond Point, Tumbler, Lemonade, Handle, 3 In. . . . . 132.00 to 176.00	
Diamond Swirl, Pitcher, 8¼ In.	75.00
Diamond Thumbprint, Bowl, 24-Scallop Rim, Footed, 4¼ x 9½ In. . .	88.00
Diamond Thumbprint, Cake Stand, 24-Scallop Ruffled Edge, Footed, 5 x 9¼ In. . .	550.00 to 825.00
Diamond Thumbprint, Cake Stand, 26-Scallop Ruffled Edge, Footed, 6¼ x 12⅜ In.	990.00
Diamond Thumbprint, Celery Vase, 12-Scallop Rim, Short Ribbed Stem, 9¾ In.	132.00
Diamond Thumbprint, Champagne, 5¼ In.	220.00
Diamond Thumbprint, Compote, 24-Scallop Rim, Ribbed Stem, 6 x 8½ In.	88.00 to 99.00
Diamond Thumbprint, Compote, 26-Scallop Rim, Ribbed Stem, 7¾ x 10⅜ In.	121.00
Diamond Thumbprint, Compote, 26-Scallop Rim, Ribbed Stem, 9 x 11¼ In. . . . . . . *illus*	275.00
Diamond Thumbprint, Decanter, Applied Neck Ring, Flattened Lip, Stopper, 13 In.	176.00
Diamond Thumbprint, Decanter, Applied Neck Ring, Mushroom Stopper, Qt., 10¾ In. . . .	88.00
Diamond Thumbprint, Decanter, Bitters, Applied Square Lip, 6⅜ In. . .	66.00
Diamond Thumbprint, Goblet, 6½ In. . . . . 154.00 to 440.00	
Diamond Thumbprint, Jug, Bulbous, Applied Handle, Footed, ½ Pt., 6 In.	1595.00
Diamond Thumbprint, Pitcher, Baluster Shape, Applied Handle, Footed, 9½ In.	715.00
Diamond Thumbprint, Spooner, Straight Sides, 12-Scallop Rim, 6¼ In. .	33.00
Diamond Thumbprint, Sugar, Cover, 16-Scallop Rim, Lobed Finial, Footed, 8¾ In.	77.00
Diamond Thumbprint, Table Set, Butter & Sugar With Covers	220.00
Diamond Thumbprint, Tumbler, 3¾ In. . . . . 55.00 to 187.00	
Diamond Thumbprint, Tumbler, Lemonade, Pattern To Rim, Applied Handle, 3 In.	825.00
Diamond Thumbprint, Tumbler, Lemonade, Ring Over Pattern, Applied Handle, 2⅞ In. . . .	413.00
Diamond Thumbprint, Tumbler, Whiskey, No Ring, 3⅛ In.	187.00
Diamond Thumbprint, Tumbler, Whiskey, Ring Above Pattern, 3¼ In. . .	176.00

Pressed Glass, Daisy & Button, Condiment Set, Cobalt Blue, 3 Bottles, Holder, 7 In., 4 Piece
$118.00

Pressed Glass, Delaware, Berry Bowl, Emerald Green, Gold Trim, 8¼ In.
$75.00

Pressed Glass, Diamond Thumbprint, Compote, 26-Scallop Rim, Ribbed Stem, 9 x 11¼ In.
$275.00

Tumbler Sizes

A tumbler is a drinking glass, usually with a flat base. It never has a stem. Some tumblers are footed. Tumblers in several sizes have special names:

Whiskey or shot

1½–3 ounces, 2–2½ inches

Juice

4–7 ounces, 3¾–4½ inches, often footed

Old Fashioned

8 ounces, 2½ inches

Water

9–10 ounces, 4–5½ inches, often footed

Iced tea

12–16 ounces, 5½–6 inches, often footed

Pressed Glass, Draped Window, Goblet, 5⅝ In.
$715.00

Pressed Glass, Early Thumbprint, Compote, 7 Rows, Scalloped Rim, Fluted Stem, Flared, 11 x 12 In.
$358.00

Diamond Thumbprint, Wine, 4¼ In.	110.00 to 143.00
Dog & Cart, Salt, Amber, 3¼ x 1⅛ In.	55.00
Dog With Rabbit In Hole, Pitcher, 9¼ In.	198.00
Dolphin, Bowl, Oval, Cover, 4¼ x 5½ x 8⅜ In.	242.00
Dolphin, Compote, Blue, 9¾ In.	231.00
Dolphin, Compote, Vaseline, 9¾ In.	330.00
Dolphin, Punch Bowl, Base Only, 5⅛ x 8¼ In.	385.00
Doric pattern is listed here as Feather.	
Double Red Block, Wine, Ruby Stained, 4 x 2 In., 4 Piece	250.00
Double Sawtooth, Goblet	30.00
Double Wedding Ring pattern is listed here as Wedding Ring.	
Dragon, Compote, Cover, Seashell Finial, 9⅞ x 8¼ In.	1650.00
Dragon, Goblet, 5⅝ In.	1870.00
Drape, Mug, Gold Trim, 3⅛ In.	25.00
Draped Window, Goblet, 5⅝ In. .... *illus*	715.00
Drum & Eagle, Mug, 1885	35.00
E Pluribus Unum pattern is listed here as Emblem.	
Early Moon & Star, Table Set, Sugar, Cover, Creamer, Spooner, 3 Piece	605.00
Early Moon & Star, Tumbler, 3½ In.	132.00
Early Thumbprint, Berry Set, Opaque White, Fiery Opalescent, Scalloped Rim, 5 Piece	154.00
Early Thumbprint, Cake Stand, 4 Rows, Scalloped Rim, Hexagonal Foot, 4 x 11 In.	303.00
Early Thumbprint, Cake Stand, 4 Rows, Scalloped Rim, Hexagonal Stem, 13½ In.	440.00 to 660.00
Early Thumbprint, Compote, 7 Rows, Scalloped Rim & Foot, Fluted Stem, 10 x 10 In.	660.00
Early Thumbprint, Compote, 7 Rows, Scalloped Rim, Fluted Stem, Flared, 11 x 12 In... *illus*	358.00
Early Thumbprint, Compote, Cover, 7 Rows, Scalloped Rim, Ribbed Finial, 16 x 9 In.	5500.00
Early Thumbprint, Compote, Cover, 7 Rows, Scalloped Rim, Ribbed Finial, 18 x 10 In.	10450.00
Early Thumbprint, Compote, Cover, 7 Rows, Scalloped Rim, Ribbed Finial, 20 x 11 In.	24200.00
Early Thumbprint, Cordial, 3⅛ In.	231.00
Early Thumbprint, Decanter, 4 Rows, Applied Neck Ring, Qt., 11 In.	330.00
Early Thumbprint, Decanter, 4 Rows, Applied Neck Ring & Rolled Lip, Stepped Foot, 6¾ In.	825.00
Early Thumbprint, Decanter, 4 Rows Over 18 Ribs, Footed, Pewter Pour Spout, 10½ In.	143.00
Early Thumbprint, Goblet, 4 Rows, Ringed Stem, 6⅜ In.	187.00
Early Thumbprint, Nappy, Cover, 3 Rows, Scalloped Rim, Fluted Stem, 7½ In.	198.00
Early Thumbprint, Pitcher, 4 Rows, Applied Handle, 8½ In.	550.00
Early Thumbprint, Salt, 4 Rows, Flattened, Oval, 2 x 3¼ In.	121.00
Early Thumbprint, Syrup, 4 Rows, Applied Handle, Petal Base, Britannia Hinged Lid, 8½ In.	5225.00
Early Thumbprint, Tumbler, 3 Rows, 3¾ In.	22.00
Early Thumbprint, Tumbler, Flip, 4 Rows, 6⅞ In.	495.00
Early Thumbprint, Tumbler, Flip, 4 Rows, Plain Rim, 7¼ In.	1155.00
Early Thumbprint, Tumbler, Jelly, 4 Rows, Footed, 5 In.	77.00
Early Thumbprint, Tumbler, Whiskey, 3 Rows, 3¼ In.	77.00
Early Thumbprint, Tumbler, Whiskey, 4 Rows, Applied Handle, Footed, 3⅝ In.	220.00
Egyptian, Compote, Cover, Sphinx On Foot, 9¼ x 6¼ In.	330.00
Egyptian, Pitcher, 9⅜ In.	165.00
Elk & Doe, Goblet, 6 In.	187.00
Ellrose, Compote, Amber Stained, Scallop & Point Rim, 10 In.	468.00
Emblem, Table Set, Butter, Cover, Sugar, Creamer, 3 Piece	523.00
Empire, Salt, 2¼ x 1¾ In.	26.00
Etched Dakota pattern is listed here as Dakota.	
Excelsior With Maltese Cross, Tumbler, 3¼ In.	110.00 to 176.00
Excelsior With Maltese Cross, Tumbler, Lemonade, Handle, 3⅛ In.	220.00
Eyewinker, Tumbler, Jelly, Ruby Stained, 5 In.	55.00
Fan & Diamond, Pitcher, Footed, 8½ In.	50.00
Fan & Zig Zag, Bonbon, 6¾ In.	22.00
Feather, Toothpick, Scalloped Rim, 2¾ In.	77.00
Federal, Spooner, 3 Handles, 3¾ In.	125.00
Ferris Wheel, Pitcher, 8¼ In.	65.00
Fine Cut & Feather pattern is listed here as Feather.	
Fine Rib With Cut Ovals, Celery Vase, 4 Rows, Scalloped Rim, Plain Foot, 8½ In.	440.00
Fine Rib With Cut Ovals, Compote, 3 Rows, Hexagonal Stem, Scalloped Foot, 7½ In.	154.00
Fine Rib With Cut Ovals, Wine, 3 Rows, 4⅛ In.	33.00
Finecut & Block, Pitcher, Water, Amber Stained, 10 In.	88.00
Flamingo, Goblet, 6¼ In.	121.00
Flat Diamond & Panel, Lattice & Oval Panels, Goblet, 6 In.	132.00
Flat Diamond & Panel, Tumbler, 3⅝ In.	110.00
Fleur-De-Lis, Goblet, 5⅝ x 3⅛ In.	65.00

Floral & Raised Star, Pitcher, 8½ In.	49.00
Floral Medallion, Bowl, 9 x 8½ In.	89.00
Flower Band, Bowl, Cover, Oval, Frosted Love Birds Finial, 6⅝ x 9 In.	77.00
Flower Band, Butter, Cover, Frosted	77.00
Flower Band, Butter, Cover	88.00
Flower Band, Compote, Cover, Cherries On Band, Love Birds Finial, 12½ x 8 In.	187.00
Flower Band, Compote, Cover, Love Birds Finial, 9½ x 6 In.	55.00
Flower Band, Compote, Cover, Strawberry Band, Frosted Love Birds Finial, 11½ x 7 In.	143.00
Flower Band, Goblet, Frosted, 6⅜ In.	88.00 to 99.00
Flower Band, Jam Jar, Cover, 6¾ In.	33.00
Flower Band, Pitcher, Frosted, 9¼ In.	66.00
Flower Band, Pitcher, Milk, Frosted, 7½ In.	88.00
Flowered Tulip, Goblet, 6 In.	40.00
Fluted Scrolls, Pitcher, Scrolled Feet, 7¾ x 8½ In.	135.00
Flying Birds, Goblet, 5⅝ In.	77.00
Flying Robin pattern is listed here as Hummingbird.	
Four Petal, Sugar & Creamer, Pagoda Cover, Applied Handle, Short Stem, Footed	88.00
Fox & Crow, Pitcher, 8½ In.	231.00
Frog & Spider, Goblet, 6¼ In.	220.00
Frosted patterns may also be listed under the name of the main pattern.	
Frosted Chicken, Compote, Cover, Engraved Leaves, 12 In.	242.00
Frosted Chicken, Compote, Cover, Engraved Leaves, Oval, 13 x 8 In.	275.00
Frosted Chicken, Horseradish Jar, 6⅛ In.	176.00
Frosted Chicken, Jam Jar, Oval, 3 Panels, Ogee Corners, Flat Cover, 7 In.	550.00
Frosted Circle, Syrup, Tin Lid, 6 In.	33.00
Frosted Dog, Compote, Cover, 13¼ x 7⅞ In.	176.00
Frosted Dog, Compote, Cover, 14½ x 8¾ In.	242.00
Frosted Eagle, Butter, Cover, 7⅛ x 5⅞ In. ....*illus*	55.00
Frosted Eagle, Compote, Cover, 11½ x 7 In.	55.00
Frosted Eagle, Compote, Cover, Engraved Leaves, 12½ x 8 In.	99.00
Frosted Eagle, Jam Jar, 8½ x 3½ In.	193.00
Frosted Leaf, Goblet, 5¾ In.	55.00
Frosted Leaf, Tumbler, 3½ In.	132.00
Frosted Ribbon, Compote, Dolphin Stem, 9 x 10½ In.	66.00
Frosted Ribbon, Compote, Dolphin Stem, Rectangular, 6⅞ x 5¼ x 8 In.	88.00
Garden Of Eden, see also the related pattern Lotus & Serpent.	
Gargoyle, Goblet, 6¼ In.	242.00
Georgia Gem, Butter, Cover	80.00
Georgian, Compote, Jelly, 3½ x 5½ In.	24.00
Giant Baby Thumbprint, Champagne, 5 In.	66.00
Giant Bigler, Goblet, 6⅞ In. ....*illus*	77.00
Giant Prism With Thumbprint Band, Ale, Footed, 4⅜ In.	99.00
Giant Prism With Thumbprint Band, Celery Vase, 18-Scallop Rim, Wafer Stem, 9¼ In.	187.00
Giant Prism With Thumbprint Band, Champagne, 5¼ In.	253.00
Giant Prism With Thumbprint Band, Compote, 48-Scallop Rim, 8⅝ x 9¼ In.	330.00
Giant Prism With Thumbprint Band, Goblet, 6¼ In.	121.00
Giant Prism With Thumbprint Band, Punch Bowl, Stand, 48-Scallop Rim, 11½ x 12 In.	2200.00
Giant Sawtooth, Tumbler, Water, 3⅞ In. ....*illus*	110.00
Globe & Star, Pitcher, Air-Twist Handle, 9¼ In.	330.00
Goat's Head, Butter, Cover, Frosted Finial	99.00
Gonterman, Spooner, Frosted, Amber Stained Rim, 6 In. ....*illus*	275.00
Good Luck pattern is listed here as Horseshoe.	
Goose Boy, Compote, Frosted Stem & Foot, 8⅝ x 8 In.	165.00
Goose Girl, Compote, Frosted Stem & Foot, 8⅝ x 8 In.	154.00
Gooseberry, Table Set, Opaque White, Fiery Opalescent, 4 Piece	88.00
Gothic, Celery Vase, Hexagonal Baluster Stem, Wafer, Footed, 9¾ In.	176.00
Grand Army Of The Republic pattern is listed here as Historical.	
Grape, see also the related patterns Magnet & Grape and Magnet & Grape With Frosted Leaf.	
Grape With Vine, Syrup, Metal Lid	75.00
Grapevine, Mug, Cobalt Blue, 2¼ x 1⅞ In.	58.00
Grooved Bigler, Goblet, 6¾ In.	88.00
Guardian Angel, Sauce	23.00
Hairpin With Thumbprint, Goblet, 6 In.	44.00
Hamilton, Pitcher, Applied Handle, 8½ In.	248.00 to 550.00
Hamilton, Wine, 3¾ In.	55.00
Hamilton With Clear Leaf pattern is listed here as Hamilton With Leaf.	

Pressed Glass, Frosted Eagle, Butter, Cover, 7⅛ x 5⅞ In. $55.00

Pressed Glass, Giant Bigler, Goblet, 6⅞ In. $77.00

Pressed Glass, Giant Sawtooth, Tumbler, Water, 3⅞ In. $110.00

Reproductions and Look-alikes

Many patterns of pressed glass have been reproduced. Westward Ho, made about 1879, pictures a wounded deer, bison, log cabin, pine trees, and an Indian. It has been reproduced in the 1930s, 1980s, and 1990s. Learn the differences, like the size of the bison's legs or the details of the pine tree.

Companies including Fenton Glass Company and importer L.G. Wright sold other look-alikes in the 1960s and 1970s. Fenton still makes older patterns. Reproductions are imported into the United States every year.

Pressed Glass, Gonterman, Spooner, Frosted, Amber Stained Rim, 6 In.
$275.00

Pressed Glass, Harp, Goblet, 6¼ In.
$1760.00

Hamilton With Leaf, Tumbler, 3¼ In. 88.00
Hand With Torch, Cake Plate, Amber Stem & Foot, 8 x 11¼ In. 110.00
Harp, Goblet, 6¼ In. *illus* 1760.00
Harp, Spooner, Gold Trim, Round Foot, 4½ In. 77.00
Harvard Yard, Sauce, 6 Piece 55.00
Hawaiian Pineapple, Goblet, 6⅜ In. 99.00
Hawaiian Pineapple, Tumbler, 3⅝ In. 143.00
Heart & Bull's Eye, Tumbler, 3½ In. 132.00
Heart Plume, Pitcher 147.00
Heart With Thumbprint, Bowl, Straight Sides, Scalloped Rim, 8 x 4 In. 22.00
Heart With Thumbprint, Goblet, Ruby Stained, 5⅞ In. *illus* 2640.00
Heart With Thumbprint, Wine 65.00
Hero, Celery Vase, Enameled Daisies 54.00
Heron, Jam Jar, Cover, 6⅝ x 2¾ In. 176.00
Historical, Dish, Cover, Terrestrial Globe, Columbia Head Finial, 9½ x 8 In. 2750.00
Historical, Dish, Pullman Train Car, America, Daisy & Button Base, Roof Cover, 9½ In. 715.00
Historical, Goblet, 3 Presidents Etch, 6⅛ In. 77.00 to 99.00
Historical, Goblet, Greeley, Brown, 6¼ In. 2090.00
Historical, Goblet, New England Centennial, Barrel Shaped Bowl, 6¾ In. 198.00
Historical, Goblet, New England Centennial, Flared Rim, 6½ In. *illus* 198.00
Historical, Goblet, New England Centennial, Large Stem, 6½ In. 121.00 to 198.00
Historical, Mug, Ashburton, Union, Laurel Wreath, Flag, Muskets, Eagle In Ovals, 3½ In. 520.00 to 880.00
Historical, Mug, Beer, Centennial, Bell Shape, 4⅛ In. 110.00
Historical, Mug, Beer, Centennial, Flared Rim, 4 In. 220.00
Historical, Mug, Garfield & Lincoln, Loop Handle, 2½ In. 88.00
Historical, Mug, Independence Hall, 1876, 3¼ In. 77.00
Historical, Plate, President Garfield, Stippled Ground, 1800s, 10 In. 50.00
Historical, Plate, USS Texas, Spanish American War Ships, Gold Trim, Scalloped Edge, 6 In. 55.00
Historical, Plate, Volunteer, Soldier, American Flag, Crossed Muskets, Cannon, 9¾ In. 253.00
Historical, Platter, G.A.R., Medal On Ribbon In Center, 7⅝ x 11 In. 55.00
Historical, Platter, Teddy Roosevelt, Frosted Profile, Teddy Bears In Rim, 7½ x 10½ In. 242.00
Historical, Spooner, General Grant, Wreath-Framed Bust, Fiery Opalescent, 5 In. 330.00
Historical, Tray, Mormon Temple, Give Us This Day, Egyptian Pattern Rim, 8¾ x 13 In. 242.00
Historical, Tumbler, Remember The Maine, 3¾ In. 55.00
Historical, Tumbler, Union For Ever, Constitution, Flag, Flint, 3⅛ In. 110.00
Hobstar & Tassel, Bowl, Crimped, 7 In. 21.00
Hobnail pattern is in this book as its own category.
Holly, Compote, Cover, Hexagonal Faceted Stem, Stepped Foot, 8½ x 8 In. 303.00
Holly, Goblet, 5¾ In. 154.00
Holly, Sugar & Creamer 220.00
Holly Band, Pitcher, 8¼ In. 88.00
Honeycomb, Compote, Cover, Cable Rim, Hexagonal Stem, Acorn Finial, 10⅜ x 8½ In. 231.00
Honeycomb, Goblet, Fiery Opalescent, 6 In. 2310.00
Honeycomb, Pitcher, 8¼ x 5¾ In. 65.00
Horn Of Plenty, Butter, Cover, Washington's Head Finial 132.00
Horn Of Plenty, Celery Vase, 8¾ In. *illus* 88.00
Horn Of Plenty, Champagne, 5¼ In., 4 Piece 275.00
Horn Of Plenty, Compote, 6-Lobed Stem, Scalloped Rim, 7¼ x 8 In. 66.00
Horn Of Plenty, Compote, 6-Lobed Stem, Scalloped Rim, 8¾ x 9¼ In. 121.00
Horn Of Plenty, Dish, Sweetmeat, 6-Lobed Stem, Wafer Footed, 8¼ In. 209.00
Horn Of Plenty, Goblet, 6¼ In. 77.00
Horn Of Plenty, Pitcher, Applied Handle, Scalloped Foot, 8⅝ x 3⅝ In. 880.00
Horn Of Plenty, Plate, Canary, 6⅜ In. 358.00
Horn Of Plenty, Relish, Trefoil Shape, 7⅛ x 5 In. 55.00
Horn Of Plenty, Salt, Oval, 2¼ x 3¼ In. 88.00
Horn Of Plenty, Spooner, Amber Stained, 4¾ In. 358.00
Horn Of Plenty, Table Set, Butter, Cover, Sugar, Creamer, Spooner, 4 Piece 187.00
Horn Of Plenty, Tumbler, Whiskey, 3 In. 88.00 to 165.00
Horn Of Plenty, Waste Bowl, 8-Scallop Foot, 3½ x 5⅛ In. 303.00
Horse, Cat & Rabbit, Goblet, 6⅜ In. 385.00 to 935.00
Horsehead Medallion, Toothpick, c.1890s, 2 x 2 In. 55.00
Horseshoe, Bread Tray 46.00
Horseshoe, Pitcher, 9⅛ In. *illus* 115.00
Horseshoe, Relish, 7½ x 5 In. 12.99
Huber, Pitcher, Applied Handle, 8¼ In. 66.00
Hummingbird, Tumbler, 3¾ In. 90.00

Icicle With Chain Band, Goblet, 6¼ In.	66.00
Ida pattern is listed here as Sheraton.	
Idyll, Tumbler, 4 x 3 In.	35.00
Imperial, Dish, Pickle, 4¾ x 3¾ In.	20.00
Indiana Swirl pattern is listed here as Feather.	
Indiana Window, Nappy, 4½ In.	10.00
Inverted Fan & Feather, Toothpick, 3-Footed, 3½ In.	45.00
Inverted Fern, Tumbler, 3½ In.	110.00
Ivy In The Snow, Celery Vase, c.1898	45.00
Jewel & Block, Wine, 6 In.	15.00
Jeweled Diamond & Fan, Bowl, 4¾ In.	12.00
Jeweled Moon & Star pattern is listed here as Moon & Star.	
Jumbo, Butter, Cover	1650.00
Jumbo, Compote, Cover, Frosted Finial, Base & Ribbing, 12 x 7¼ In.	495.00
Jumbo, Goblet, 6¼ In.	715.00
Jumbo, Jam Jar, Frosted Finial & Base, 8 x 3 In.	1650.00
Jumbo, Pitcher, Blue, Footed, 9¾ In.	880.00
Jumbo, Spoon Rack, Frosted Finial, 11¼ x 5¾ In.	413.00
Jumbo, Sugar, Cover, Frosted Finial	413.00
Jumbo, Sugar, Cover, Man Under Handle	209.00
Jumbo, Table Set, Frosted, Man Under Handle, Butter, Sugar, Creamer, 3 Piece	385.00
Kansas, Jewel & Dewdrop, Pitcher, Milk, 7½ x 4¼ In.	132.00
King's Crown pattern is listed here as Ruby Thumbprint.	
Knights Of Labor, Platter, Oval, Blue, 8⅝ x 11¾ In.	143.00
Kokomo, Spooner, 4¾ In.	28.00
Lacy, Plate, Toddy, Strawberry Border, 14 Scallops & Point, Cobalt Blue, 4⅜ In.	154.00
Lacy, Plate, Toddy, Strawberry Border, 61 Scallops, Peacock Blue, 4⅜ In.	44.00
Lacy, Salt, Aqua, Scallop & Point Rim, 1¾ x 2⅛ x 2⅞ In.	220.00
Lacy, Salt, Beads, Ferns, Rayed Base, Paw Feet, Oblong, 2 x 2½ x 3 In.	44.00
Lacy, Salt, Claw Foot, Hexagonal, Scalloped Rim, 2¼ x 3⅛ In.	44.00
Lacy, Salt, Diamond Heart, Rectangular, Ribs, Scalloped Rim, 2 x 2⅛ x 3 In.	88.00
Lacy, Salt, Lafayet, Paddle Boat, Opalescent Blue, 1⅝ x 3½ In.	1344.00
Lacy, Salt, Light Green, Scalloped Rim, Star Base, 1¾ x 2⅛ x 3¼ In.	198.00
Lacy, Salt, Light Green, Star Under Base, Scallop & Point Rim, 2 x 3 x 2 In. .... *illus*	143.00
Lacy, Salt, Sapphire Blue, Shaped Rim, Oval, Pedestal, 2¼ x 2¼ x 3½ In.	330.00
Lacy, Salt, Stippling, V Shapes, Serrated Scalloped Rim, 1¼ x 2¼ x 3½ In.	602.00
Ladders With Diamond, Bonbon, Gold Trim, 6 x 4 In.	13.00
Lattice & Oval Panels pattern is listed here as Flat Diamond & Panel.	
Leaf & Star, Jar, Dresser, Metal Lid, 3 In.	18.00
Leaflets, Horseradish Jar, Cover, Frosted Dog Finial, 5¾ In.	77.00
Lee, Champagne, 5⅞ In.	110.00
Lee, Sugar, Cover, Scalloped Rim, Plain Foot, Pointed Finial, 8 In.	77.00
Lee, Wine, 4¾ In.	55.00
Liberty Bell, Mug, Child's, 2 x 1⅝ In.	225.00
Lily-Of-The-Valley, Salt, Cover, 4¼ In.	55.00
Lincoln Drape, Goblet, 6 In.	77.00
Lincoln Drape, Molasses Jug, Applied Handle, Silver Plated Hinged Lid, 6¾ In.	88.00
Lincoln Drape, Sugar, Cover, Rope Twist Trim, Rayed Foot, Tulip Finial, 8¼ In.	303.00
Lincoln Drape With Tassel, Goblet, 6 In.	242.00
Lion, Butter, Cover, Frosted, 4 x 2¾ In.	200.00
Lion, Cheese Dish, Frosted, Rampant Lion Finial, 5¾ In.	523.00
Lion, Compote, Cover, Frosted, Rampant Lion Finial, 12¾ In.	121.00
Lion, Pitcher, Frosted, 9 In.	330.00
Lion, Sherbet, Frosted, 4 In., Pair	45.00
Lion, Tray, Ice Cream, Tab Handles, 8 x 15 In.	44.00
Lion & Baboon, Butter, Cover, Clear Finial	303.00
Lion & Baboon, Butter, Cover, Frosted Finial	385.00
Little Samuel, Compote, 10¾ x 8 In.	143.00
Little Samuel, Compote, Flared, 10⅞ x 9⅛ In.	99.00
Little Samuel, Epergne, 18¼ In.	231.00
Log Cabin, Butter, Cover	176.00
Log Cabin, Compote, Cover, 9¼ x 4¼ x 6 In.	825.00
Log Cabin, Compote, Cover, 10½ x 7¼ In.	935.00
Log Cabin, Dish, Cover, 6⅞ x 5 x 8¾ In.	523.00
Log Cabin, Jam Jar, Vaseline, 6¾ In.	2200.00
Log Cabin, Pitcher, 8½ In.	495.00

Pressed Glass, Heart With Thumbprint, Goblet, Ruby Stained, 5⅞ In.
$2640.00

Pressed Glass, Historical, Goblet, New England Centennial, Flared Rim, 6½ In.
$198.00

Pressed Glass, Horn Of Plenty, Celery Vase, 8¾ In.
$88.00

P

SECURITY TIP
If you are moving, be sure to get special insurance coverage for damage to your antiques. You may want valuable pieces covered by your insurance, not by the mover's policy.

Pressed Glass

Pressed glass machines were invented in the 1820s. Molds were made of brass, iron, or other metal. A plunger forced the glass into the mold.

By the 1840s, American glasshouses were *firepolishing* their glass. It was reheated after shaping, "melting" the seams a little and smoothing the surface.

Pressed Glass, Horseshoe, Pitcher, 9⅛ In. $115.00

Pressed Glass, Lacy, Salt, Light Green, Star Under Base, Scallop & Point Rim, 2 x 3 x 2 In. $143.00

Pressed Glass, Moon & Star, Compote, 7¾ x 10⅝ In. $77.00

Log Cabin, Spooner, Blue, 4⅝ In.	468.00
Loop, Compote, 11 Loops, Octagonal Stem, 9-Loop Foot, 9¼ x 11¾ In.	253.00
Loop, Compote, Plain Base, Pittsburgh, c.1845, 9½ x 13 In.	1000.00
Loop, Goblet, 6 In.	14.00
Loop & Crystal, Goblet, 6 In.	22.00
Loop & Dart, Goblet, Buttermilk	60.00
Loop & Pillar, Syrup, 4 In.	65.00
Loops & Drops pattern is listed here as New Jersey.	
Lord's Prayer, Bread Tray	245.00
Lotus & Serpent, Goblet, 6 In.	99.00
Lotus & Serpent, Pitcher, 8½ In.	33.00
Magnet & Grape, Goblet, Engraved, Star Cut Foot, 6⅝ In.	11.00
Magnet & Grape, Wine, 4 In.	55.00
Magnet & Grape With Frosted Leaf, Tumbler, 3½ In.	44.00
Magnet & Grape With Frosted Leaf, Tumbler, Footed, 5⅞ In.	44.00 to 66.00
Magnet & Grape With Frosted Leaf & American Shield, Goblet, 6⅜ In.	176.00 to 209.00
Magnet & Grape With Frosted Leaf & American Shield, Sugar	22.00
Manting, Tumbler, 3¼ In.	99.00
Maple Leaf, Goblet, Vaseline, 6 In.	176.00
Mardi Gras, Spooner, Gold Trim, Children's, 2¾ In.	49.00
Minnesota, Mug, Gold Trim	15.00
Mirror & Fan, Goblet, Cordial, Gold Trim, 4¼ x 2¼ In.	13.00
Model Gem, Decanter, Ruby Stained, 12 In.	77.00
Monkey, Spooner, Fiery Opalescent, 5 In.	385.00
Monkey, Table Set, Butter, Cover, Sugar, Creamer, 3 Piece	523.00
Moon & Star, Compote, 7¾ x 10⅝ In. ....*illus*	77.00
Moon & Star, Compote, 8 In.	65.00
Moon & Star, Compote, Amber, 5¾ In.	25.00
Moon & Star, Compote, Cover, 16¼ x 10¼ In.	132.00
Moon & Star, Spooner, Gold Trim, Footed, 4¾ In.	22.00
Moon & Star, Syrup, 7 Sides, Applied Handle, 5¾ In.	99.00
Moon & Stork pattern is listed here as Ostrich Looking At The Moon.	
Morning Glory, Goblet, 5⅞ In.	1375.00
Nail, Pitcher, 9½ In.	65.00
Narcissus Spray, Plate, Handles, 6 In.	15.00
Naturalistic Lion, Goblet, 3 Panels, 5⅞ In.	3520.00
Netted Swan, Goblet, Blue, 6 In.	198.00
New England Pineapple, Goblet, 5½ In.	66.00
New England Pineapple, Salt ....*illus*	115.00
New England Pineapple, Tumbler, 3¾ In.	99.00
New Jersey, Butter, Gold Trim, Dome Lid, c.1900, 8 x 5½ In.	60.00
Old Abe pattern is listed here as Frosted Eagle.	
Orion pattern is listed here as Cathedral.	
Ostrich Looking At The Moon, Goblet, 5¾ In.	77.00
Ostrich Stork & Heron, Goblet, 5 In.	605.00
Oswego Waffle, Goblet, 5⅝ In.	22.00
Oval With Long Bars, Tumbler, Applied Handle, Footed, 4⅛ In.	303.00
Owl & Possum, Goblet, 6⅛ In.	132.00
Owl pattern is listed here as Bull's-Eye With Diamond Point.	
Owl In Fan pattern is listed here as Parrot.	
Palmette, Syrup	154.00
Paneled 44, Bowl, Footed, Double Handles, Pair	55.00
Paneled Cherries, Spooner, Gold Trim	65.00
Paneled Daisy, Bowl	40.00
Paneled Daisy & Button, Pitcher	26.00
Paneled Diamond Blocks, Salt, Ruby Stained	198.00
Paneled Dogwood, Berry Bowl, Emerald Green, 8 In.	35.00
Paneled Heather, Tumbler, 4¼ In.	15.00
Paneled Jewels, Goblet	55.00
Paneled Palm, Compote, Jelly, 4 x 7 In.	50.00
Paneled Scroll, Celery Vase, Stippled	42.00
Paneled Swan, Goblet, 5½ In.	385.00
Paneled Swan, Pitcher, Water, 9 In.	330.00
Paneled Thousand Eye, Goblet	25.00
Parrot, Goblet	95.00
Peacock Eye Gothic Arch & Palm, Creamer, Scalloped Foot, 4¼ In. ....*illus*	121.00

Pentagon, Decanter, Ruby Stained, Stopper, 10 In.	85.00
Philadelphia, Goblet, 6¼ In.	440.00
Pigs In Corn, Goblet, 6 In.	440.00
Pillow Encircled, Bowl, 8 x 4½ In.	14.00
Pillow In Oval, Creamer, 6¾ In.	50.00
Pinafore pattern is listed here as Actress.	
Pineapple, Bowl, 9 x 4 In.	50.00
Plain Smocking pattern is listed here as Smocking.	
Pointed Panel Daisy & Button pattern is listed here as Paneled Daisy & Button.	
Pointed Thumbprint pattern is listed here as Almond Thumbprint.	
Pointing Dog, Mug, Child's, 2¾ In.	36.00
Polar Bear, Goblet, Frosted, Flared Rim, 6 In.	165.00
Polar Bear, Pitcher, 9½ In.	605.00
Polar Bear, Water Set, 4 Piece	523.00
Prayer Rug pattern is listed here as Horseshoe.	
Prescut, Sugar & Creamer, Cover	9.00
Prism & Daisy Bar, Goblet	25.00
Prism & Diamond Point, Goblet, 6¼ In.	44.00
Quail Pie, Dish, Cover, Frosted	199.00
Queen, see also the related pattern Paneled Daisy & Button.	
Racing Deer & Doe, Pitcher, 8½ In.	88.00
Rainbow, Punch Bowl, Stand, 11 x 5½ In.	47.00
Red Block, Goblet, Ruby Stained, 5¾ In.	36.00
Red Block, Sugar & Creamer, Ruby Flashed	110.00
Reverse 44 pattern is listed here as Paneled 44.	
Reward, Goblet, Gold Stain	25.00
Rhode Island, Goblet, 6¼ In.	413.00
Ribbed Clover, Tumbler, 3½ In.	99.00
Ribbed Ivy, Decanter, Applied Lip, 7⅛ In.	231.00
Ribbed Ivy, Tumbler, Whiskey, 2¾ In.	176.00
Ribbed Ivy, Tumbler, Whiskey, Handle	350.00
Ribbed Palm, Champagne, Concave Leaves, 5½ In.	66.00
Ribbed Palm, Pitcher, Applied Handle, 9 In.	231.00
Rose & Ivy, Plate, Opaque Black, 8½ In.	44.00
Rose Sprig, Biscuit Jar, Dome Lid, Hexagonal Foot, 13¾ In.	99.00
Rose Sprig, Pitcher, Water, Vaseline, 9⅜ In.	165.00
Roses In The Snow, Compote	100.00
Rosette & Palms, Goblet	50.00
Royal Crystal, Butter, Covered, 5¾ In.	40.00
Royal Crystal, Toothpick, Ruby Stained	225.00
Ruby Rosette pattern is listed here as Hero.	
Ruby Thumbprint, Dish, Honey, Cover, Square, Wide Rim, 5½ x 7¾ In.	358.00
Ruby Thumbprint, Pitcher, Tankard	124.00
Ruby Thumbprint, Toothpick	35.00
Sandwich Star, Goblet, 6½ In.	825.00
Sandwich Star, Spooner, Hexagonal Body, 5 x 3¾ In.	210.00
Sandwich Star, Wine, 4⅝ In.	121.00
Sawtooth, Eggcup, Cover, Gold Trim, 5¼ In.	44.00
Sawtooth, Salt, Cover, Beaded Rim, Scalloped Foot, 3½ In.	77.00
Sawtoothed Honeycomb, Toothpick	52.00
Scarab, Wine, Rayed Foot, 4 In.	33.00
Sheraton, Berry Bowl, Amber, c.1889, 5 x 2¾ In.	21.00
Shrine, Goblet, 6 In.	75.00
Shrine, Pitcher, Gal.	77.00
Six Panel Fine Cut, Compote, Cover, Amber Stained, 12¾ In.	264.00
Smocking, Tumbler, 3½ In.	110.00
Spanish Coin pattern is listed here as Columbian Coin.	
Spearpoint Band, Toothpick, Ruby Stained	79.00
Square & Diamond Bands, Pitcher	40.00
Squirrel, Goblet, 6 In.	715.00
Squirrel, Pitcher, Plain Rim, 9 In.	209.00
Squirrel, Pitcher, Scalloped Rim, 8¾ In.	66.00
Squirrel, Sugar, Cover	253.00
Squirrel, Table Set, Butter, Cover, Sugar, Creamer, 3 Piece	468.00
S-Repeat, Condiment Set, Apple Green, 4 Piece	230.00
St. Bernard, Celery Tray, Dog Under Base, 4¾ x 11¼ In.	77.00

Pressed Glass,
New England Pineapple, Salt
$115.00

Pressed Glass, Peacock Eye
Gothic Arch & Palm, Creamer,
Scalloped Foot, 4¼ In.
$121.00

SECURITY TIP

If you have an entry door with a large window, put unbreakable glass in the window. The easiest way for a burglar to enter your house is by breaking the window in the door and reaching in to unlock the door. Even a small window in a door might be positioned so it is possible to break it and reach the door knob. Either put in unbreakable panes or install a slide bolt that will be out of reach.

P

Pressed Glass, Swan,
Goblet, 5¾ In.
$121.00

Dating Pressed Glass— 1820-1890s

Pressed glass patterns went in
cycles, just as skirt lengths do.

1820s-1830s: Simple, heavy
loops or ribbed effects.
Heavy glass.

1830s-1840s: Lacy patterns,
stippled backgrounds, allover
designs. Hearts, feathers,
lyres, sheaves of wheat,
eagles, and thistles were
popular motifs.

1850s: Simpler patterns, Argus
(thumbprint), Ashburton,
and Thousand Eye.

1860s: More elaborate
geometrics and stylized
flowers. Bellflower and Horn
of Plenty (Comet). Colored
glass after the Civil War.

1870s: Naturalistic patterns,
Grape, Rose in Snow, Daisy,
and Thistle. Figural details,
often frosted, Actress,
Classic, Lion, Three Face,
and Westward Ho.

1880s-1890s: Allover
geometric patterns, Daisy
and Button, imitated cut
glass. Delaware, Hidalgo,
Ruby Thumbprint, and
X-Ray were stained,
trimmed with gold, or
enameled with flowers.

St. Bernard, Compote, Cover, Frosted Finial, 9¼ In.	187.00
Star, Pitcher, Curved Spout, 8½ In.	52.99
Star, Platter, 12 In.	40.00
Star & Punty pattern is listed here as Moon & Star.	
Star & Zipper, Salt & Pepper, 2¾ In.	16.00
Star Band, Spooner, Double Handles, 4½ x 4 In.	15.00
Starburst, Celery Dish, 9¼ In.	8.00
Stork, Jam Jar, Cover, 6 In.	22.00
Stork, Pitcher, Water, 9 In.	176.00
Stork, Pitcher, Water, Frosted, 9½ In.	303.00
Stork, Sugar, Cover, Frosted	99.00
Stork, Sugar, Cover, Stork Finial	110.00
Stork, Table Set, Butter, Cover, Sugar, Creamer, Stork Finials, 3 Piece	143.00
Stork, Water Set, Frosted, 15½-In. Tray, 4 Piece	523.00
Stork Looking At The Moon pattern is listed here as Ostrich Looking At The Moon.	
Strawberry, Pitcher, 9¼ In.	77.00
Strawberry, Tumbler, Gold Trim, Maiden's Blush, 4⅛ In.	24.00
Sunk Honeycomb, Decanter, Ruby Stained, 13 In.	44.00
Superior, Tumbler, Ruby Stained, 3¾ In.	88.00
Swan, Goblet, 5¾ In. .... *illus*	121.00
Swan, Jam Jar, Cover	44.00
Swan, Pitcher, 9½ In.	110.00
Swan, Table Set, Butter, Sugar, Cover, Creamer, Spooner, 4 Piece	187.00
Swan Paneled, Tray, Water, Round, 11⅜ In.	154.00
Swinger, Toothpick, Ruby Stained, Gold Trim	49.00
Tackle Block, Goblet, 6 In.	264.00
Tacoma, Dish, Oblong	25.00
Tacoma, Salt, Sawtooth Edge	40.00
Teardrop & Tassel, Goblet, 5¾ In.	176.00
Texas, Goblet, Wine, Maiden's Blush, 4 In.	77.00
Thistleblow, Celery Dish, 5½ In.	18.00
Three Face, Cake Stand, 6¼ x 8¼ In.	66.00
Three Face, Cake Stand, 8⅛ x 10½ In.	99.00
Three Face, Celery Vase, Etched Birds & Nest, Scalloped Rim, 9 In.	605.00
Three Face, Champagne, Engraved Flowers & Leaves, 5½ In.	231.00
Three Face, Claret, 4¾ In.	165.00
Three Face, Claret, Engraved Bellflower, 4¾ In.	242.00
Three Face, Claret, Engraved Stylized Flowers, 4¾ In.	176.00
Three Face, Compote, 40 Beads, Piecrust Rim, 7⅞ x 7⅜ In.	550.00
Three Face, Compote, 44 Beads, Piecrust Rim, 8½ x 8½ In.	605.00
Three Face, Compote, 48 Beads, Piecrust Rim, 14⅛ x 9½ In.	2970.00
Three Face, Compote, Cover, 14½ x 9⅛ In.	198.00
Three Face, Compote, Cover, 44 Beads, Piecrust Rim, 13 x 8½ In.	2750.00
Three Face, Compote, Engraved Ivy, 9½ x 9¼ In.	220.00
Three Face, Compote, Geometric Engraving, 10½ x 10 In.	242.00
Three Face, Compote, Huber Bowl, Etched Daisies, 8½ x 8½ In.	357.00
Three Face, Creamer	187.00
Three Face, Jam Jar, Cover, Etched Stag & Doe, Quail Finial, 6½ In.	110.00
Three Face, Pitcher, Milk, Engraved Flowers, Qt.	2970.00
Three Face, Pitcher, Water, ½ Gal., 10 In.	413.00
Three Face, Table Set, Engraved Ivy, Butter, Cover, Sugar, Creamer, Spooner, 4 Piece	935.00
Three Face Medallion, Goblet, 6 In.	132.00
Three Graces, see also the related pattern Three Face.	
Three Sisters pattern is listed here as Three Face.	
Thumbprint, Candy Dish, Pedestal, 9½ x 5 In.	19.00
Thumbprint, Compote, Cover, 9 x 4½ In.	110.00
Thumbprint, Compote, Cover, 15 In.	4950.00
Thumbprint, Compote, Cover, 16¼ In.	5500.00
Thumbprint, Compote, Cover, 18¼ In.	10450.00
Thumbprint, Compote, Cover, 20 In.	24200.00
Thumbprint, Creamer	50.00
Thumbprint, Syrup, Britannia Hinged Lid, 8½ In.	5225.00
Thumbprint & Divided Diamond, Tumbler, 3¾ In.	99.00
Thumbprint & Hobnail, Goblet, 5⅞ In.	99.00
Tile, Goblet, 6 In.	17.50
Tobin pattern is listed here as Leaf & Star.	
Togo, Goblet	20.00

P

Tong, Creamer, Footed, Applied Handle	88.00
Toy, Castor Set, 2 Bottles, 2 Shakers, Britannia Stand, 7½ In.	99.00
Toy, Lemonade Set, Michigan, Gold Trim, 4-In. Pitcher, 7 Piece	88.00
Toy, Punch Set, Tulip & Honeycomb, 4¼-In. Footed Bowl, 7 Piece	55.00
Toy, Table Set, Nursery Rhyme, Butter, Spooner, Creamer, 4-In. Sugar, 4 Piece	99.00
Toy, Table Set, Rooster, Butter, Spooner, Creamer, 4½-In. Sugar, 4 Piece	242.00
Tree Of Life, Epergne, 6-Petal Lily, Scalloped Rim, 19 x 8 In.	735.00
Tree Of Life, Salt, Bird's Nest, 3 In.	66.00
Tree Of Life With Shell & Tassel, Mug, Blue, 2⅛ In.	77.00
Truncated Cube, Toothpick, Ruby Stained	25.00
Tulip, Tumbler, Lemonade, Handle, 2¾ In.	143.00
Tulip Band, Goblet, 6¾ In.	165.00
Tulip With Sawtooth, Cruet, Applied Handle, Rayed Foot, 7¾ In.	143.00
Tulip With Sawtooth, Decanter, 8-Scallop Rayed Base, Stopper, Qt., 14½ x 4½ In., Pair	303.00
Tulip With Sawtooth, Decanter, Bitters, Applied Neck Ring, Rayed Base, 6¾ In.	99.00
Tulip With Sawtooth, Eggcup, Cover, Paneled Acorn Finial, Rayed Foot, 5½ In.	121.00
Tulip With Sawtooth, Jar, Pickle, Rayed Base, Stopper, 5½ In.	88.00
Tulip With Sawtooth, Nappy, Cover, 14-Petal Rim, Hexagonal Finial, 5¾ In.	154.00
Tulip With Sawtooth, Pitcher, Scalloped Rayed Base, Applied Handle, 8⅞ In.	495.00
Tulip With Sawtooth, Table Set, Butter, Cover, Sugar, Cover, Creamer, 3 Piece	55.00
U.S. Coin, Ale, Frosted Half-Dollar Coins, Flared Rim, Footed, 6¾ In. .... *illus*	330.00
U.S. Coin, Berry Set, Frosted Coins, 5 Piece	440.00
U.S. Coin, Bowl, Frosted Dollar Coins, 3 x 9 In.	550.00
U.S. Coin, Bowl, Frosted Quarter Coins, 2 x 6⅝ In.	66.00
U.S. Coin, Cake Stand, Dollar Coins, 6½ x 10 In.	165.00
U.S. Coin, Cake Stand, Frosted Dollar Coins, 6½ x 10 In.	330.00
U.S. Coin, Compote, Cover, Dollar Finial, 11½ x 8 In.	468.00
U.S. Coin, Compote, Cover, Frosted Coins, Dollar Finial, 10¼ x 6⅞ In.	330.00
U.S. Coin, Compote, Cover, Frosted Coins, Dollar Finial, 11⅝ In.	715.00
U.S. Coin, Epergne, Frosted Coins, 5 x 8⅝ In.	1155.00
U.S. Coin, Finger Bowl, Frosted Quarters, 2⅜ x 4 In.	605.00
U.S. Coin, Goblet, Claret, Frosted Coins, Flared Rim, 4¾ In.	358.00
U.S. Coin, Goblet, Frosted Dime Coins, 6¼ In.	220.00
U.S. Coin, Goblet, Frosted Half-Dollar Coins, Straight Rim, 4¾ In.	275.00
U.S. Coin, Mug, Beer, 4¾ In.	385.00
U.S. Coin, Mug, Beer, Clear Coins, 4¾ In.	275.00
U.S. Coin, Pitcher, Dollar Coins, ½ Gal., 9½ In.	275.00
U.S. Coin, Pitcher, Frosted Dollar Coins, ½ Gal., 9½ In.	990.00
U.S. Coin, Saltshaker, Frosted Dime Coins, 3 In.	110.00
U.S. Coin, Spooner, Frosted Quarter Coins, 4⅝ In.	187.00
U.S. Coin, Sugar & Creamer, Cover, Dollar Finial, Frosted Coins	1375.00
U.S. Coin, Syrup, Frosted Quarter Coins, 6⅞ In.	440.00
U.S. Coin, Toothpick, Frosted Dollar Coins, 2⅞ In.	77.00
U.S. Coin, Toothpick, Ruby Stained, Dollar Coins, 2⅞ In.	660.00
U.S. Coin, Tray, Water, Frosted Coins, 10 In.	990.00
Union, Toothpick, Ruby Stained	85.00
Valencia Waffle, Compote, Cobalt Blue	57.00
Viking, Mustard, Cover, Applied Ring Handle, 4⅞ In.	154.00
Wading Heron, Pitcher, 9½ In.	198.00
Waffle, Champagne, 5¼ In.	66.00
Waffle, Compote, Dolphin Stem, Frosted Blocks, Domed Foot, 7½ x 8¼ In.	132.00
Waffle, Creamer, Applied Handle, Flint, 6¼ In.	325.00
Waffle, Goblet, 6½ In.	66.00
Waffle, Salt, Cover, Faceted Knop, Footed, 4¾ In.	358.00
Waffle, Tumbler, 3½ In. .... *illus*	77.00
Waffle & Thumbprint, Celery Vase, Faceted Knop Stem, Flared Rim, Footed, 9¼ In.	99.00
Waffle & Thumbprint, Spooner, Gold Trim, Flared, Footed, 4½ In.	44.00
Waffle & Thumbprint, Sugar, Cover	66.00
Waffle & Thumbprint, Syrup, Applied Handle, Hinged Britannia Lid, 5¼ In.	209.00
Waffle Block, Syrup, Pewter Lid, 6 In.	76.00
Washington, Celery Vase, Plain Rim & Foot, 8½ In.	66.00
Washington, Champagne, 4¾ In.	132.00
Washington, Cordial, 3¼ In.	358.00
Washington, Goblet, 5½ In.	33.00
Washington, Goblet, 6 In.	88.00
Washington, Goblet, Engraved, Alternating Flowers & Fruit, 6 In.	385.00

Decorations on Glass

Applied decoration: Glassmakers add blobs of hot glass to pieces. Lily-pad, looping, prunts, and threading are used.

Offhand or tooled decoration: Ruffled edges, air twisted or knopped stems, pinched waists, neck rings added to the hot glass with tools.

Molded decoration: Glass impressed with a design during the shaping process.

Special finishes: Colors created by adding chemicals to the glass or covering with oxides.

Exterior decoration: Acid etching, cutting, enameling, or engraving the surface of glassware. Camphor finish, satin, and casing created with vapors, acid, or another layer of glass.

Pressed Glass, U.S. Coin, Ale, Frosted Half-Dollar Coins, Flared Rim, Footed, 6¾ In. $330.00

Pressed Glass, Waffle, Tumbler, 3½ In. $77.00

Print, Audubon, Baltimore Oriole, Royal Octavo, Plate No. 217, 8½ x 10½ In.
$418.00

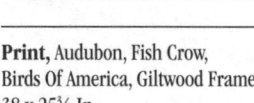

Print, Audubon, Fish Crow, Birds Of America, Giltwood Frame, 38 x 25⅝ In.
$1725.00

P

Print, Audubon, Little Screech Owl, Royal Octavo, Plate No. 40
$179.00

Washington, Wine, 4 In. 88.00
Wedding Ring, Jar, Pickle, Short Hexagonal Stem, Footed, Stopper, Rayed Finial, 6¾ In. 231.00
Westward Ho, Butter, Cover 143.00
Westward Ho, Compote, Cover, 12¾ x 7 In. 187.00
Westward Ho, Compote, Cover, 14½ x 8 In. 231.00
Westward Ho, Compote, Cover, Indian Finial, 6 In. 295.00
Westward Ho, Dish, Cover, 11⅜ x 5½ x 8¾ In. 231.00
Westward Ho, Dish, Cover, Oval, Footed, 10 x 5 x 7¾ In. 132.00
Westward Ho, Jam Jar, Cover, 7¼ x 3½ In. 413.00
Westward Ho, Pitcher, 9½ In. 176.00
Westward Ho, Sauce, Footed 25.00
Westward Ho, Table Set, Sugar, Creamer, Spooner, 3 Piece 187.00
Wexford, Candy Dish, Cover, 7 x 8 In. 25.00
Wheat & Barley, Compote, Jelly 45.00
Wheat & Barley, Mug, Paneled, Square Handle, 3¾ x 3¼ In. 30.00
Wild Bouquet, Biscuit Jar, Teal, Frosted, 8 x 5 In. 310.00
Wildflower, Celery Vase, Amber, 8 x 4 In. 24.00
Wildflower, Pitcher, Amber 45.00
Willow Oak, Bowl, 8 x 3 In. 35.00
Yoked Loop, Tumbler, 6 Panels, 18-Ray Base, 3⅝ In. 358.00
Zig Zag, Sauce, 5⅝ In. 8.00
Zig Zag Band, Butter, Cover, Squirrel Finial, 5½ x 6½ In. 303.00
Zig Zag Band, Sugar, Cover 413.00
Zipper Block, Dish, Ice Cream, 3¾ In. 15.00

PRINT, in this listing, means any of many printed images produced on paper by one of the more common methods, such as lithography. The prints listed here are of interest primarily to the antiques collector, not the fine arts collector. Many of these prints were originally part of books. Other prints will be found in the Advertising, Currier & Ives, Movie, and Poster categories.

J.W.Audubon

Audubon bird prints were originally issued as part of books printed from 1826 to 1854. They were issued in two sheet sizes, 26½ inches by 39½ inches and 11 inches by 7 inches. The quadrupeds were issued in 28-by-22-inch prints. Later editions of the Audubon books were done in many sizes, and reprints of the books in the original size were also made. The words *After John James Audubon* appear on all of the prints, including the originals, because the pictures were made as copies of Audubon's original oil paintings. The bird pictures have been so popular they have been copied in myriad sizes by both old and new printing methods. This list includes originals and later copies because Audubon prints of all ages are sold in antiques shops.

Audubon, American Flamingo, Bien Edition, Plate 375, Wood Frame, c.1860, 38 x 36 In. 9200.00
Audubon, Baltimore Oriole, Royal Octavo, Plate No. 217, 8½ x 10½ In. .... *illus* 418.00
Audubon, Belted Kingfisher, 1829, 39½ x 26⅜ In. 418.00
Audubon, Blue Jays, 11 x 7 In. 1673.00
Audubon, Cervus Leucurus, Long-Tailed Deer, Imperial Quadruped, 28 x 22 In. 2390.00
Audubon, Crested Titmouse, Tufted Titmouse, 38⅝ x 26 In. 2880.00
Audubon, Fish Crow, Birds Of America, Giltwood Frame, 38 x 25⅝ In. .... *illus* 1725.00
Audubon, Fremont's Squirrel & Sooty Squirrel, Imperial Quadruped, 28 x 22 In. 1135.00
Audubon, Great Footed Hawk, Peregrine Falcon, 27 x 39 In. 5760.00
Audubon, Large Tailed Skunk, Male, Natural Size, 27 x 21 In. 2880.00
Audubon, Lepus Sylvaticus, Gray Rabbit, Imperial Quadruped, 28 x 22 In. 1793.00
Audubon, Lepus Texianus, Texian Hare, Imperial Quadruped, 28 x 22 In. 3237.00
Audubon, Little Screech Owl, Royal Octavo, Plate No. 40 .... *illus* 179.00
Audubon, Loggerhead Shrike, 39½ x 26½ In. 3840.00
Audubon, Lutra Canadensis, Canada Otter, Imperial Quadruped, 28 x 22 In. 1076.00
Audubon, Prong-Horned Antelope, 21 x 27 In. 3360.00
Audubon, Red Headed Woodpecker, 39 x 26 In. 8400.00
Audubon, Vulpes Fulvus, Red Fox, Imperial Quadruped, 28 x 22 In. 1793.00
Audubon, Whooping Crane, Royal Octavo, Plate No. 313 .... *illus* 568.00
Audubon, Yellow Billed Magpie, Stellers Jay, Ultramarine Jay, Clark's Crow, 38 x 25 In. 6600.00
Catesby, Mark, Cuckow Of Carolina, Hand Colored, Frame, c.1754, 14 x 19 3/16 In. 2415.00
Catesby, Mark, Parrot Of Carolina, Gilt Wood Frame, 14 x 20½ In. 3680.00
Catesby, Mark, Pigeon Of Passage, Hand Colored, Frame, c.1754, 14¼ x 20½ In. 1840.00
Erte, Untitled, Silkscreen, Signed, Numbered, 236/300, 9 In. 205.00
Gould, Hummingbirds, Hylocharis Cyaneus, Frame, 34 x 27 In. 259.00

Icart prints were made by Louis Icart, who worked in Paris from 1907 as an employee of a postcard company. He then started printing magazines and fashion brochures. About 1910 he created a series of etchings of fashionably dressed women, and he continued to make similar etchings until he died in 1950. He is well known as a printmaker, painter, and illustrator. Original etchings are much more expensive than the later photographic copies.

Icart, Casanova, 1928, 13⅜ x 15 In.	*illus*	823.00
Icart, Dame Aux Camelias, 1938, 7¾ x 5¾ In.		153.00
Icart, Four Dears, 3 Women & 1 Doe, Pedestal, Urn, Drypoint, Signed, 1929, 29 x 22 In.		920.00
Icart, Japanese Garden, Hand Colored, Signed, 15 x 17¾ In.		900.00
Icart, Lady Of The Camelias, Drypoint, Hand Colored, c.1927, 17 x 21 In.		1126.00

Jacoulet prints were designed by Paul Jacoulet (1902–1960), a Frenchman who spent most of his life in Japan. He was a master of Japanese woodblock print technique. Subjects included life in Japan, the South Seas, Korea, and China. His prints were sold by subscription and issued in series. Each series had a distinctive seal, such as a sparrow or butterfly.

Jacoulet, Basket Weaver, 1948		840.00
Jacoulet, Joaquina & Her Mother At The Sermon Of Father Pons, 1947		780.00
Jacoulet, Karinjawa, Woodcut, Signed, Japan, c.1947, 15 x 11½ In.	*illus*	413.00
Jacoulet, Living God, 1952		780.00
Jacoulet, New Dress, 1938		600.00
Jacoulet, Oyster Stew, 1948		600.00
Jacoulet, Porcelain Garden Seat, 1936		720.00
Jacoulet, Water Pipe, Chinese, 1952		780.00

Japanese woodblock prints are listed as follows: Print, Japanese, name of artist, title or description, type, and size. Dealers use the following terms: Tate-e is a vertical composition. Yoko-e is a horizontal composition. The words Aiban (13 by 9 inches), Chuban (10 by 7½ inches), Hosoban (13 by 6 inches), Koban (7 by 4 inches), Nagaban (20 by 9 inches), Oban (15 by 10 inches), Shikishiban (8 x 9 inches), and Tanzaku (15 x 5 inches) denote approximate size. Modern versions of some of these prints have been made. Other woodblock prints that are not Japanese are listed under Print, Woodblock.

Japanese, Hiroshige, Boating In Harbor, Frame, Oban, Tate-e		132.00
Japanese, Hiroshige, Night Rain At Niehaka, Farming Village, c.1830, 17¼ x 23¼ In.		115.00
Japanese, Hiroshige, Otsuki Plain In Kai Province, Frame, Oban, Tate-e		270.00
Japanese, Hiroshige, Views Of The Tokaido Road, Frame, Oban, Tate-e		230.00
Japanese, Hokusai, 36 Views Of Fuji, c.1820, 10 x 15 In.		115.00
Japanese, Kiyohiro, Torii, Four Courtesans Near The Coast, Frame, 15 x 10 In.		440.00
Japanese, Kuniaki, Utagawa, Print Triptych, Takao-Zan Kaicho Senryu-Tenho No Zu, Signed		129.00
Japanese, Kunichika, Toyohara, Actor Nakamura Shikan, Others, Triptych, Oban		206.00
Japanese, Kunichika, Toyohara, Actor Sawamura Tossho As Kawamuraya Tokujiro		103.00
Japanese, Kunisada, Samurai, 14 x 10 In.	*illus*	354.00
Japanese, Kunisada, Theater, Color, Signed, Sealed, 1800s		201.00
Japanese, Kunisada, Utagawa, Lady In Kimono, Cockatoo, c.1820, 37 x 19 In.		920.00
Japanese, Masanobu, Kitao, The Fan Seller, Mat, Frame, c.1785, 16 x 10 In.		411.00
Japanese, Saito, Kiyoshi, Village In Winter, Signed, 1900s, 10¼ x 15 In.		1121.00
Japanese, Saito, Kiyoshi, Winter In Aizu, Signed, 16 x 21 In.		1121.00
Japanese, Saito, Kiyoshi, Young Girl, Color, Signed, 15¼ x 10 In.		295.00
Japanese, Yoshida, Hiroshi, Kyoto At Night, Color, 9½ x 14 In.		354.00
Japanese, Yoshida, Hiroshi, Mt. Rainier, c.1925, Oban		1337.00
Japanese, Yoshiku, Utagawa, Interior Restaurant Scene With Women, 1869, 14 x 9¾ In.		206.00
Nevelson, Untitled Abstract, Lithograph, Signed, 16⁄20, c.1967, 21½ x 41 In.		972.00

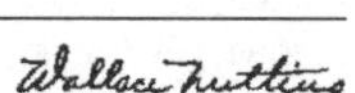

Nutting prints are now popular with collectors. Wallace Nutting is known for his pictures, furniture, and books. Nutting prints are actually hand-colored photographs issued from 1900 to 1941. There are over 10,000 different titles. Wallace Nutting furniture is listed in the Furniture category.

Nutting, A Peep Down The Street, Original Mat, Signed, Frame, 1915-25, 17 x 14 In.		1760.00
Nutting, Better Than Mowing, Original Mat, Signed, Frame, 1905-10, 20 x 16 In.		1210.00
Nutting, Mrs. Maloney, Original Mat, Signed, Frame, 1910-15, 14 x 11 In.		3300.00
Nutting, Pasture Dell, Original Mat, Signed, Frame, 1915-25, 12 x 15 In.		1980.00

Print, Audubon, Whooping Crane, Royal Octavo, Plate No. 313
$568.00

Print, Icart, Casanova, 1928, 13⅜ x 15 In.
$823.00

Print, Jacoulet, Karinjawa, Woodcut, Signed, Japan, c.1947, 15 x 11½ In.
$413.00

P

Print, Japanese, Kunisada, Samurai, 14 x 10 In. $354.00

Print, Woodblock, Miller, Lilian, Moonlit Scene, 5¼ x 3½ In. $360.00

Print, Woodblock, Sandzen, Birger, Pasture With Willows, c.1930, 6 x 8 In. $900.00

Purinton Pottery, Fruit, Grease Jar, Cobalt Blue Stripes, 5¼ x 6 In. $5.00

Purinton Pottery, Normandy Plaid, Sugar & Creamer $10.00

Parrish prints are wanted by collectors. Maxfield Frederick Parrish was an illustrator who lived from 1870 to 1966. He is best known as a designer of magazine covers, posters, calendars, and advertisements.

Parrish, Lute Players, Frame, c.1924, 21 x 33 In.	323.00
Parrish, Rubaiyat, Original Frame, 1917, 14 x 36 In.	437.00
Rockwell, Norman, Main Street Stockbridge At Christmas, Signed, Frame, 9 x 28½ In.	1150.00
Rockwell, Norman, Young Love, Offset, Signed, 15⅞ x 16 In.	345.00
Sullivan, Luke, Engraving Set, Woburn, Cliefden, Hampton Court, 14 x 19 In., 4 Piece	1062.00

Woodblock prints that are not in the Japanese tradition are listed here. Most were made in England and the United States during the Arts and Crafts period. Japanese woodblock prints are listed under Print, Japanese.

Woodblock, Baumann, Gustave, 3 Pines, Mat, Frame, 10½ x 9¼ In.	9000.00
Woodblock, Baumann, Gustave, Woodland Meadows, Mat, Frame, 9¼ x 11 In.	9600.00
Woodblock, Gearhart, Frances, Evening, Quartersawn Oak Frame, 1900s, 9½ x 5 In.	4200.00
Woodblock, Lum, Bertha, Mothers & Children, Frame, 1900s, 7 x 4½ In.	995.00
Woodblock, Miller, Lilian, Moonlit Scene, 5¼ x 3½ In. ....*illus*	360.00
Woodblock, Patterson, Margaret, Morning Glories, Mat, Frame, c.1930, 10 x 7¼ In.	4200.00
Woodblock, Sandzen, Birger, Pasture With Willows, c.1930, 6 x 8 In. ....*illus*	900.00
Woodblock, Watson, Ernest W., Cove, Seacoast, Frame, c.1940, 9½ x 12 In.	395.00
Woodcut, Esherick, Wharton Harris, February, Frame, 20th Century, 9½ x 8½ In.	575.00
Woodcut, Rist, Luigi, Still Life, Apples, Pear On Towel, Cutting Board, 11 x 8½ In.	1540.00
Woodcut, Van De Velde, Henri, Tropon, Eiweiss Nahrung, Mat, Frame, 1898, 20 x 16 In.	540.00

PURINTON POTTERY COMPANY was incorporated in Wellsville, Ohio, in 1936. The company moved to Shippenville, Pennsylvania, in 1941 and made a variety of hand-painted ceramic wares. By the 1950s Purinton was making dinnerware, souvenirs, cookie jars, and florist wares. The pottery closed in 1959.

Apple, Grease Jar, Fats, Pear, Lid	5.00
Fruit, Grease Jar, Cobalt Blue Stripes, 5¼ x 6 In. ....*illus*	5.00
Fruit, Pitcher, Apple & Pear, 5 In.	30.00
Fruit, Relish, 3 Sections, Hand Painted Fruit, Handle, 9¼ x 6¼ In.	6.00
Fruit, Sugar & Creamer, Apple & Pear	10.00
Normandy Plaid, Canister Set, Covers, 5¼ In. To 7½ In., 4 Piece	66.00
Normandy Plaid, Oil & Vinegar, 4¾ In.	6.00
Normandy Plaid, Sugar & Creamer ....*illus*	10.00
Pennsylvania Dutch, Beer Mug, 16 Oz., 4¾ In.	110.00
Small Grapes, Cookie Jar, Cover, 8 In.	17.00

PURSES have been recognizable since the eighteenth century, when leather and needlework purses were preferred. Beaded purses became popular in the nineteenth century, went out of style, but are again in use. Mesh purses date from the 1880s and are still being made. How to carry a handkerchief and lipstick is a problem today for every woman, including the Queen of England.

Alligator, Judith Leiber, Black, 3 Parts, Goldtone Hardware	2233.00
Beaded, Multicolored, Enameled Silver Frame, Chain Strap, Pink Lining, Tiffany, 1950s	310.00
Beaded, Persian Style, Engraved Vines, Sapphire Cabochon Clasp, Tiffany, 8½ x 6½ x 15 In. *illus*	1265.00
Crochet, Peacocks, Tortoiseshell Handle, 6¼ x 9½ In.	100.00
Crocodile, Brown, Goldtone Hardware, Shoulder Strap, Hermes	1763.00
Faux Tortoiseshell, Filigree Metal Feet	404.00
Leather, Birkin, Indigo Togo, Goldtone Hardware, Sleeper Bag, Hermes, Box	3878.00
Leather, Black Caviar, Open Oblong, Exterior Sleeve, Interior Pocket, Chanel, 14 x 10 In.	500.00
Leather, Constance, Black, Goldtone H & Hardware, Double Shoulder Strap, Pocket	1293.00
Leather, Clutch, Jige, Toile, H-Closure, Navy Blue, Box	353.00
Leather, Envelope, Arts & Crafts, Binding, Silk Lining, 4½ x 9 In.	165.00
Leather, Kelly, Birque, Goldtone Hardware, Shoulder Strap, Sleeper Bag, Hermes	2820.00
Leather, Kelly, Goldtone Hardware, Shoulder Strap, Noisette, Rain Protector, Box, Hermes	3290.00
Leather, Plastic Handle, Umbrella Shape	9.00
Linen, Crewel Work Flowers & Leaves, 8 x 10¼ In. ....*illus*	66.00
Linen, Envelope, Arts & Crafts, Stylized Design, Blue, Letter L, c.1920, ½ x 20 In.	110.00
Lizard, Box Shape, Taupe, Brass Handle, Satin Lining, Judith Leiber	1300.00
Lucite, Clutch, Gray, Silver & Black Sparkles, Gold Plated Clasp, 9 x 4½ In.	80.00
Mesh, Diamond, Sapphire, Ruby, Trace Link Chain, 14K Gold, Russia, c.1985, 4½ x 4 In.	5875.00

P

Purse, Beaded, Persian Style, Engraved Vines,
Sapphire Cabochon Clasp, Tiffany, 8½ x 6½ x 15 In.
$1265.00

Purse, Linen, Crewel Work Flowers & Leaves,
8 x 10¼ In.
$66.00

Purse, Mesh, Silver, Art Deco,
Brown, Tan, Pink, Chain Links,
Whiting & Davis, 5 x 7½ In.
$110.00

Purse, Mesh, Silver, Loop Handle,
Whiting & Davis, 8⅞ x 5¼ In.
$8.00

Purses, Mesh, Sterling Silver,
Engraved Frame, Flowers,
Ball-Shaped Tassels,
c.1900, 6 x 5 In.
$96.00

Purse, Sterling Silver, Dance Card Holder,
Engraved, Hinged Lid, Leather Box,
c.1890, 3½ x 2½ In.
$100.00

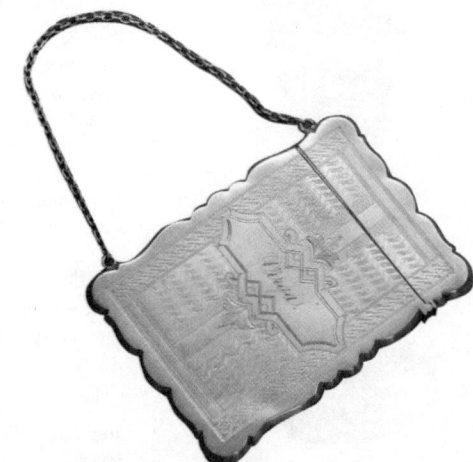

Q

Quezal, Basket, Ivorene, Green Pulled Feathers, Gold Iridescent Chain, Trim & Handle, 8 x 7½ In.
$7188.00

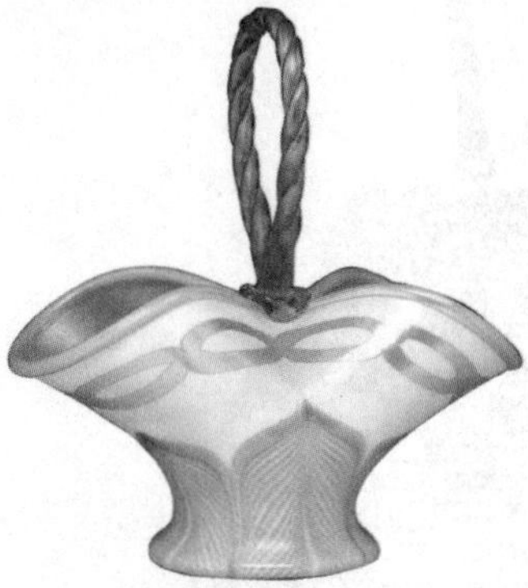

Quezal, Compote, Gold Aurene, Purple Highlights, Flared Rim, 5 x 8 In.
$300.00

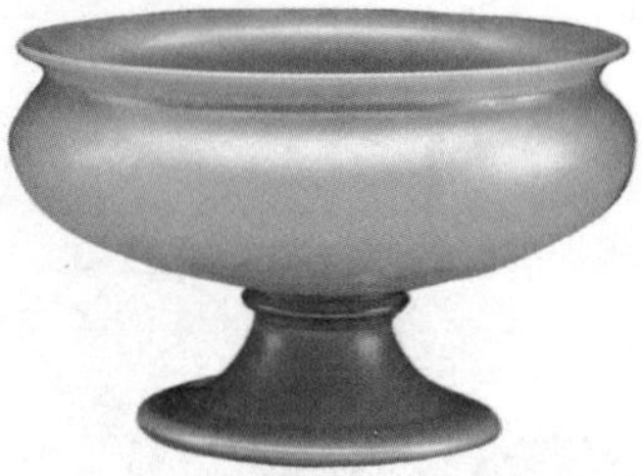

Quezal, Vase, Gold & Green Iridescent Pulled Feathers, Folded Rim, 8½ In.
$2739.00

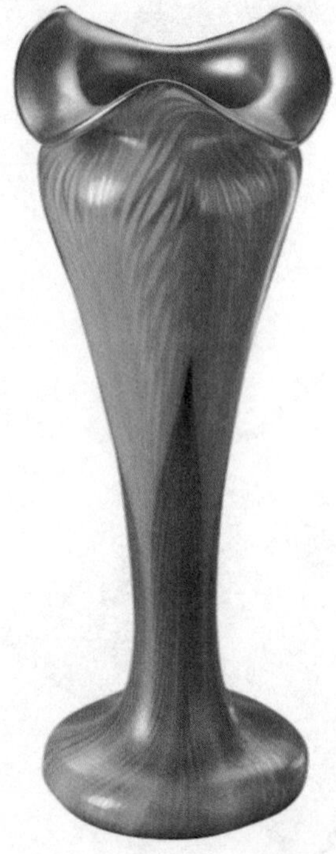

Mesh, Silver, Art Deco, Brown, Tan, Pink, Chain Links, Whiting & Davis, 5 x 7½ In. *illus* 110.00
Mesh, Silver, Loop Handle, Whiting & Davis, 8⅞ x 5¼ In. *illus* 8.00
Mesh, Silver Plate, Coin, Chain, Pear Shape, America, c.1920, 7 In. 85.00
Mesh, Sterling Silver, Engraved Frame, Flowers, Ball-Shaped Tassels, c.1900, 6 x 5 In. *illus* 96.00
Pigskin, Birkin, Porc Lisse, Haut Au Courroie, Goldtone Hardware 2820.00
Silk, Cabochon Rubies, Emeralds, Sapphires, Munshi Ganeshilal & Son, c.1945, 10 x 6 In. 2900.00
Sterling Silver, Coin, Engraved Nosegay, Russia, 1914, 5 x 1¾ x ½ In. 470.00
Sterling Silver, Dance Card Holder, Engraved, Hinged Lid, Leather Box, c.1890, 3½ x 2½ In. *illus* 100.00

Quezal

QUEZAL glass was made from 1901 to 1924 by Martin Bach, Sr., in Queens, New York. Other glassware by other firms, such as Loetz, Steuben, and Tiffany, resembles this gold-colored iridescent glass. Martin Bach died in 1921. His son-in-law, Conrad Vahlsing, Jr., went to work at the Lustre Art Company about 1920 and his son, Martin Bach, Jr., worked at the Durand Art Glass division of the Vineland Flint Glass Works after 1924.

Basket, Green, White Pulled Feather, Gold Chain, Pinched Sides, Twisted Handle, Pontil, 8 x 7½ In. 5405.00
Basket, Ivorene, Pulled Feathers, Gold Iridescent Chain, Trim & Handle, 8 x 7½ In. *illus* 7188.00
Bowl, Gold Iridescent, Cream Ground, Overlapping Pulled Feather, Pontil, Signed, 10 In. 345.00
Compote, Gold Aurene, Purple Highlights, Flared Rim, 5 x 8 In. *illus* 300.00
Compote, Gold Iridescent, Applied Blue Coil, 3¼ In. 345.00
Compote, White Iridescent, Opal Pulled Feather, Ribbed Gold Iridescent Foot, Ruffled Edge, 7 In. 2817.00
Knife Rest, Twisted, Square Ends, Gold Iridescent, Signed, 3⅞ In. 520.00
Lamp, 11-Light, Flower-Form Shades, Brass, 26½ In. 3600.00
Lamp, Gold Iridescent Lily Shades, Patinated Metal Base, c.1920, 18 In. 3120.00
Salt, Gold, Magenta Highlights, Ribbed, Silver Repousse Spoon, 2½ In. 185.00 to 230.00
Shade, Bell Shape, Green & Gold Pulled Feathers, White Ground, 5½ In., 4 Piece 1560.00
Shade, Bell Shape, Opal, Gold, Iridescent, Green Pulled Feathers, Signed, 5¼ In. 1175.00
Shade, Bell Shape, White & Green Pulled Feather, Gold Ground, 5¾ x 10 In. 1200.00
Shade, Gold, 5 Green Pulled Leaves, Bell Shape, Opal Coils, 6⅝ x 6 In. 1150.00
Shade, Gold, Rhythmic Pattern, Ribbed, Antique Ivory, Emerald Green, 4⅞ In. 546.00
Shade, Gold Iridescent, Yellow Pattern, Cream Ground, Flared, 9 In. 1370.00
Shade, Green & Gold Pulled Leaf, 6¼ In., Pair 1080.00
Shade, Morning Glory, Green Pulled Feathers, Ruffled Edge, Gold Iridescent, 6¼ In. 633.00
Shade, Morning Glory, Ribbed, Ribbons, Ivory Ground, Gold Interior, 4¾ In. 748.00
Shade, Snakeskin, Ribbed, Opal, Magenta Blue, Honey Gold, 4 In. 690.00
Shade, Snakeskin, Zipper, Ribbed, Wavy, Scalloped Rim, Multicolored Iridescent, 5 In. 2530.00
Shade, Tulip, Green Leaves, Gold Tips, Magenta, Opal Body, 4½ In. 805.00
Vase, Flower Form, Insert, Gold Iridescent, Flared, Ruffled, Green & Red Highlights, 6 In. 1840.00
Vase, Gold & Green Iridescent Pulled Feathers, Folded Rim, 8½ In. *illus* 2739.00
Vase, Gold Iridescent, Flowers, Silver Overlay, Blue Iridescent Foot, 6¼ In. 1800.00
Vase, Gold Iridescent, Green & White Pulled Feather, White Ground, Ruffled Edge, 6 In. 2243.00
Vase, Gold Iridescent, Silver Overlay, Flowers, Leaves, Ruffled Edge, 7 In. 3360.00
Vase, Gold Iridescent, Squat, Bulbous Base, c.1915, 6½ In. 2760.00
Vase, Gold Iridescent, Yellow & White Hooked Feather, Cream, Swirled Border, 9 In. 5405.00
Vase, Gold Pulled Feathers, Gold Iridescent Rim & Shoulder, c.1925, 12 In. 2820.00
Vase, Green, White Iridescent, Ruffled Edge, c.1915, 6⅛ In. 1800.00
Vase, Jack-In-The-Pulpit, Gold Iridescent, Green Pulled Feather, Alabaster, Bulbous, 13 x 8 In. 13225.00
Vase, Jack-In-The-Pulpit, Gold Iridescent, Green Pulled Feather, King Tut Border, 11 In. 36800.00
Vase, Jack-In-The-Pulpit, Gold Iridescent, Green Pulled Feathers, Wide Base, 8½ In. 3622.00
Vase, Jack-In-The-Pulpit, Green Iridescent, Pulled Leaves, c.1915, 10½ In. 9000.00
Vase, King Tut, Blue Iridescent Coils, Gold Iridescent Ground, Shouldered, 4⅜ In. *illus* 1035.00
Vase, Opal, Blue & Yellow Iridescent Hooked Feathers, Swirls, Flared Rim, 6 In. 1610.00
Vase, Opal, Blue Iridescent Coils, Gold Interior, Cylindrical, Inward Rolled Rim, 6¾ In. 1035.00
Vase, Opal, Green Pulled Feather, Flowers Over Gold Hearts & Vines, Shouldered, 13 In. 575.00
Vase, Swirled Colors, Bulbous, Long Neck, Ruffled Edge, Signed, 6⅜ In. *illus* 3450.00
Vase, Trumpet, Gold Iridescent, Flared, Applied Inverted Saucer Foot, Pontil, Signed, 8 In. 805.00
Vase, Trumpet, Golden Cast Blue, Magenta, 16 Ribs, Green Interior, Flared Rim, 5½ In. 1610.00

QUILTS have been made since the seventeenth century. Early textiles were very precious and every scrap was saved to be reused. A quilt is a combination of fabrics joined to a filler and a backing by small stitched designs known as quilting. An appliqued quilt has pieces stitched to the top of a large piece of background fabric. A patchwork, or pieced, quilt is made of many small pieces stitched together. Embroidery can be added to either type.

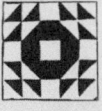

Amish, Appliqued, Block, Pink Ground, Black Diamond Sashing, Embroidered, 66 x 75 In. 144.00
Amish, Center Star, Green, Purple, Blue Ground, Hanging Bar, 40 x 40 In. 240.00

Amish, Diamond, Square, Sawtooth, Green, Red, Initials, A.M.C., c.1880, 78 x 78½ In.	605.00
Amish, Diamond In The Square, Gray, Purple, Late 19th Century, 69½ x 72 In.	245.00
Amish, Joseph's Coat, 7 Color Stripes, Diagonal Edges, 73½ x 72 In.	413.00
Amish, Joseph's Coat, Brown, Yellow, Orange, Green, Brown Back, 82 x 86 In.	403.00
Amish, Joseph's Coat, Multicolored, 68 x 72	770.00
Amish, Patchwork, Alternating Diamonds, Blue, Green, Black, 68 x 80 In.	518.00
Amish, Stripes, Red, Mustard, White, Blue, Green Ground, 84 x 85 In.	385.00
Amish, Trip Around The World, Gray & Purple, Twill Weave, Cottons, 1910, 82 x 83 In.	1045.00
Amish, Triple Irish Chain, Blue, Purple, Borders, Purple Binding, Amish, Cotton, 40 x 52 In.	575.00
Appliqued, 4 Cockscombs, Urns, Flowers, Vines, Hearts, Red Binding, Pencil Lines, 79 x 84 In.	805.00
Appliqued, 6 Blocks, Green & Yellow Roses, Flower & Vine Border, 93 x 79 In. . . . . *illus*	1150.00
Appliqued, 9 Blocks, Hands, Red & Gray Sashing, Borders, Sarah M. Taylor, 84 x 65 In.	1093.00
Appliqued, 12 Sunflowers, In Wreath Panels, 84 x 66 In.	83.00
Appliqued, 20 Blocks, Animals, Red & Black Sashing, Borders, Adkins, 1991, 92 x 77 In.	2760.00
Appliqued, 20 Blocks, Half Round & x Design, Initials, 19th Century, 78 x 64 In.	374.00
Appliqued, Acorn & Oak Leaf, Green, Red, Brown Prints, White Ground, c.1844, 93 x 96 In.	2300.00
Appliqued, Album, 25 Squares, Flowers, Vine Border, Red, Green, White, c.1843, 102 x 100 In.	5750.00
Appliqued, Amish Farm Scene, A Smith Harvestore 1976, 91 x 104 In.	316.00
Appliqued, Baskets, Red, Yellow, Tape Signature, c.1900, 85 x 86 In.	440.00
Appliqued, Cherry Trees, Yellow Birds, Cherry Vine, Embroidered, 80 x 92 In.	575.00
Appliqued, Dark Blue Eagle, Red & White Ground, 1885, 80 x 80 In.	910.00
Appliqued, Eagles, Spread Wing, Red, White, Tan, Orange, Sawtooth Border, 77 x 83 In.	1430.00
Appliqued, Flower, White Ground, Tulips, Red Circles, Stars, 74 x 67 In.	150.00
Appliqued, Flowers, Red, Beige, Green Leaves, White Ground, 79 x 88 In.	77.00
Appliqued, Flowers, Red, Green, White Ground, 74 x 93½ In.	220.00
Appliqued, Flowers, Red, Green Leaves, White Ground, Double Green Border, 78½ x 76 In.	33.00
Appliqued, Green Printed Circles, Red Hearts, Green Calico, 66 x 83 In.	240.00
Appliqued, Lady Of The Lake, Tester Bedpost Cut, 1848, 69 x 77 In.	595.00
Appliqued, Medallions, Washington, Cleveland, Presidential Centennial, 78 x 82 In. . . . *illus*	1404.00
Appliqued, Oak Leaf, Red, Green, Border Stripe, c.1890, 78 x 66½ In.	495.00
Appliqued, Pink & Red Flowers, Green Leaves, Scalloped Red Border, 71 x 85 In.	230.00
Appliqued, Princess Feather, Green, Brown Print, Floral & Swag Border, 83 x 81 In.	440.00
Appliqued, Princess Feather, Red, Green, Sawtooth Border, C.H. Wagner, 90 x 89 In.	523.00
Appliqued, Princess Feather, Red, Green, Yellow, Double Border, Flying Geese, 92 x 96 In.	770.00
Appliqued, Red, Green, Mustard Ground, Holly Leaf, Berry Border, 78 x 80 In.	715.00
Appliqued, Red, Green, Orange Ground, Double Border, Printed Backing, 74 x 80 In.	605.00
Appliqued, Red & Green Flowers, White Ground, Vine Border, Lehigh Co., Pa., 103 x 104 In.	187.00
Appliqued, Red Flowers, Bud, Oak Leaves, White Ground, Swag & Bow Border, 90 x 90 In.	748.00
Appliqued, Red Flowers, Green Leaves, White Ground, Flower & Vine Border, 77 x 81 In.	198.00
Appliqued, Star, Multicolored, Double Border, Lancaster County, Pa., 1900s, 82 x 82 In. *illus*	634.00
Appliqued, Star Of Bethlehem, Blue, Sawtooth Border, Edna O. Landes 1933, 80 x 78 In.	978.00
Appliqued, Starburst, Spread Wing Eagles, Sawtooth Border, Earth Tones, 88 x 77 In. . . *illus*	1430.00
Appliqued, Sunflower, Flowers Baskets, Chickens, Butterflies, Cow, 88 x 90 In.	10350.00
Appliqued, Tulip, Calico, Yellow Ground, Triangle Border, 80 x 82 In.	605.00
Appliqued, Tulip, Four-Poster Bed, c.1860, 88 x 92 In.	295.00
Appliqued, Tulip, Red, Yellow, Green, White Ground, Red Border, 84¼ x 84 In.	330.00
Appliqued, Turkey Tracks, c.1930, 80 x 83 In.	472.00
Appliqued, Urn & Basket, Signed, 1857, 79½ x 78¾ In.	531.00
Appliqued, Wreath, Tan, Pink, White Ground, Triple Border, 78 x 80 In.	220.00
Bar, Variation Patchwork, 4 Square Design On Stripes, Printed Fabric, 85 x 76 In. . . . . *illus*	605.00
Bear Track, 9 Blocks, Orange, Green Brown, Sawtooth Border, 1855, 81 x 94 In.	880.00
Bride's, Patchwork, Star, Pineapple & Feather Design, Swag Border, 1920s, 73 x 80 In.	2645.00
Bride's, White, Trapunto, Center Medallion, Flowers, Urn, c.1810, 109 x 97 In.	16800.00
Bride's, White On White, 77 x 74 In.	230.00
Bride's, White On White, Circle Center, Lancaster, Pa., c.1770, 85 x 78 In.	247.00
Cat, 4 Kittens, Glass Bead Eyes, Flowers, Black, Red, Striped Border, c.1870, 82 x 85 In.	27500.00
Crazy, Asian Figures, Fans, Flowers, Animals, Silk, Velvet, Tassels, Late 1880s, 60 x 60 In.	4313.00
Crazy, Embroidered, Silk, Velvet, c.1894, 80 x 78 In.	353.00
Crazy, Flowers, Black, Rust, Yellow, Gray, & White, Wool, Dated 1918, 69 x 85 In.	440.00
Embroidered, Stars On Stars, Multicolored, Diamonds, Feathered Wreaths, 88 x 90 In.	604.00
Mennonite, Patchwork, Yellow Star Medallions, Initials, Red, Lancaster, Pa., c.1880 . . . *illus*	470.00
Patchwork, 5-Point Stars, 10 Rows Of 10 Stars, Printed Fabrics, 86½ x 87 In. . . . . *illus*	660.00
Patchwork, 6-Point Star, Cotton Seeds In Batting, c.1930, 78 x 64 In.	295.00
Patchwork, 8-Point Stars, Paisley Borders, Calico, Cotton, Mid 19th Century, 85 x 73 In.	705.00
Patchwork, 25 Blocks, Center Sunburst, 1850, 88 x 89 In.	1135.00

Quezal, Vase, King Tut, Blue Iridescent Coils, Gold Iridescent Ground, Shouldered, 4⅜ In. $1035.00

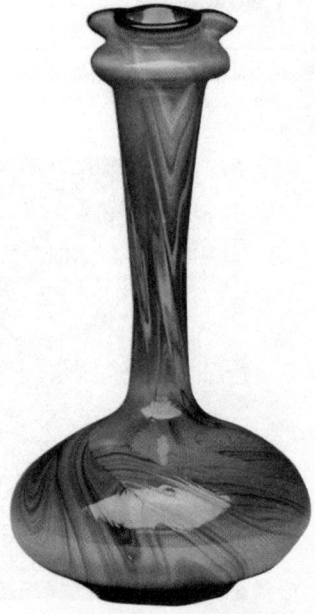

Quezal, Vase, Swirled Colors, Bulbous, Long Neck, Ruffled Edge, Signed, 6⅜ In. $3450.00

Q

Quilt, Appliqued, 6 Blocks, Green & Yellow Roses,
Flower & Vine Border, 93 x 79 In.
$1150.00

Quilt, Appliqued, Medallions, Washington, Cleveland, Presidential
Centennial Bandanna, 78 x 82 In.
$1404.00

Quilt, Appliqued, Star, Multicolored, Double Border,
Lancaster County, Pa., 1900s, 82 x 82 In.
$634.00

Quilt, Appliqued, Starburst,
Spread Wing Eagles, Sawtooth Border, Earth Tones, 88 x 77 In.
$1430.00

Quilt, Bar, Variation Patchwork,
4 Square Design On Stripes, Printed Fabric, 85 x 76 In.
$605.00

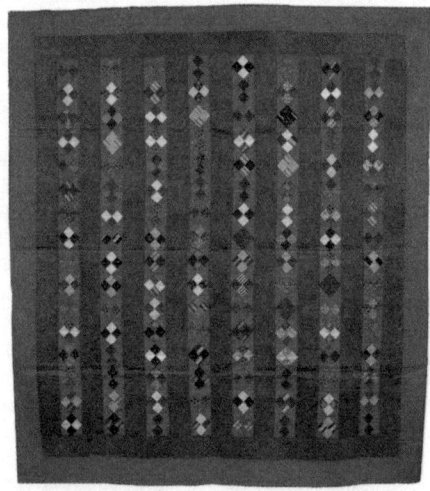

Quilt, Mennonite, Patchwork, Yellow Star Medallions,
Initials, Red Ground, Lancaster, Pa., c.1880
$470.00

Patchwork, 30 Blocks, Crosses, Light Blue Binding, 58 x 82 In. ....*illus*	259.00
Patchwork, 1000 Pyramids, Printed & Plain Fabric, Double Sawtooth Border, 85 x 82 In. ..	605.00
Patchwork, Album, Squares, Red & White Borders, Lancaster County, Pa., c.1885, 80 x 78 In. . *illus*	350.00
Patchwork, Basket, Multicolored, Tan Ground, Red, Green, Double Sawtooth Border, 84 x 86 In.	605.00
Patchwork, Basket, Red, Green, Wide Green Border, 87½ In.	720.00
Patchwork, Bear Track, Calico, On Pink, Sawtooth Border, 86 In.	154.00
Patchwork, Carpenter's Wheel, Red, Green, Yellow, White Ground, Cotton, 76 x 86 In.	460.00
Patchwork, Diamonds, Maroon Floral Print Back, Pennsylvania, 1890s ....*illus*	350.00
Patchwork, Double Wedding Ring, White Ground, 77 x 90 In.	518.00
Patchwork, Drunkard's Path, Red On White, Scalloped Edge, 1940, 73 x 81 In.	355.00
Patchwork, Flower Basket Variation, Blocks On Point, Pineapple, Flowers, 60 x 74 In.	630.00
Patchwork, Fox & Geese, c.1930, 73 x 88 In.	531.00
Patchwork, Friendship, Embroidered, Lydia Brandy, Rolling Stone, 83 x 80 In.	358.00
Patchwork, Grandma's Fan, Blue, Pink, Red, Mustard, Printed Fabric Back, 88½ x 90 In. ..	303.00
Patchwork, Irish Chain, Blue, Pink, On White Ground, Triple Border, 86 x 74 In.	88.00
Patchwork, Log Cabin, 36 Blocks, Triple Border, 84 x 82 In.	1045.00
Patchwork, Log Cabin, Purple, On White Ground, 86 x 87 In.	165.00
Patchwork, Log Cabin, Red, White, Blue, Calico Back, c.1896, 69 x 67 In.	489.00
Patchwork, Lone Star, 19th Century, 86¾ x 85½ In.	189.00
Patchwork, Lone Star, Blue, Pink, White Ground, 80½ x 70 In.	121.00
Patchwork, Lone Star, Blue Ground, Sawtooth Border, 77 x 80 In.	440.00
Patchwork, Lone Star, Bricker Family, Lancaster County, Pa., c.1900, 77 x 77 In. .....*illus*	702.00
Patchwork, Lone Star, Double Border, Printed Backing, Machine Stitched, 45 x 45 In.	44.00
Patchwork, Lone Star, Earth Tone Fabrics, Double Borders, 80 x 80 In.	275.00
Patchwork, Lone Star, Green Border, Printed Backing, 42 x 42 In.	275.00
Patchwork, Lone Star, Multicolored, Black Ground, Red Border, Paisley Backing, 83 x 84 In. ...	2420.00
Patchwork, Lone Star, Red, Yellow, White, Pink, Green, 86 x 82 In.	385.00
Patchwork, Lone Star, Yellow Ground, Sawtooth Border, 84 x 84 In.	303.00
Patchwork, Mariner's Compass, Calico, Lancaster County, c.1885, 72 x 73 In. ....*illus*	527.00
Patchwork, Mariner's Compass, Red, Green, Blue, Brown, Pink, White, Signed, 1844, 99 x 100 In. ..	660.00
Patchwork, Mennonite, Split Bar, Orange, Pink, Red, Green, Print Border, 69 x 80 In.	288.00
Patchwork, Ohio Star, Printed & Plain Fabric, Wide Checked Border, 77½ x 78 In.	495.00
Patchwork, Ohio Star, Yellow Calico Ground, Triple Border, Bucks Co., Pa., 83½ x 86 In. ...	110.00
Patchwork, Oval Medallion, Washington, Liberty Bell, Paisley Border, Striped, 90 x 88 In. *illus*	5300.00
Patchwork, Red & Blue Star, White Field, Miss Bender, 73 x 75 In.	805.00
Patchwork, Sampler, Baskets, Plain & Printed Fabric, Double Sawtooth Border, 84 x 86 In. *illus*	605.00
Patchwork, Signature, 25 Blocks, Red & Green, Calico, White Field, 94 x 94 In.	1495.00
Patchwork, Star, Red, Pink, White & Blue, Leah Souders, 80 x 81 In.	605.00
Patchwork, Star Of Bethlehem, Blue Calico, Wide Blue Border, Lancaster Co., 92 x 92 In. ...	275.00
Patchwork, Star Of Bethlehem, c.1840, 80 x 80 In.	325.00
Patchwork, Star Of Bethlehem, Madder Red, Pink, Green, Yellow, 91 x 92 In.	489.00
Patchwork, Star Of Bethlehem, Yellow, Red, & Green, 1880s, 96 x 72 In.	1650.00
Patchwork, Star Variant, Red, Yellow, Green Ground, Sawtooth Border, 90 x 90 In.	523.00
Patchwork, Star Variation, Printed Red Ground, Squares In Corners, 41 x 41 In.	132.00
Patchwork, Sunshine & Shadow, Amish, Lancaster, Pa., c.1930, 79 x 80 In. ....*illus*	936.00
Patchwork, Triangle, Sawtooth Borders, Paisley Border, Cotton, Mid 1800s, 92 x 76 In.	1175.00
Patchwork, Triangles, Double Zigzag Border, Floral Print Back, Crib, 38 x 38 In. .....*illus*	819.00
Patchwork, Trip Around The World, Blue Calico Border, Yellow & Pink Bar Back, 84 x 82 In. .	1045.00
Patchwork, Trip Around The World, Multicolored, Green & Red Border, Lancaster Co., 77 x 77 In.	2420.00
Patchwork, Trip Around The World, Outlined Border, Multicolored, c.1890, 82 x 83 In.	1045.00
Patchwork, Trip Around The World, Rainbow Colors, Lancaster, Pa., c.1890, 82 x 83 In. *illus*	1112.00
Patchwork, Trip Around The World, Red, Blue, Yellow, Green, Red Border, Lancaster Co., 90 x 90 In.	1100.00
Patchwork, Trip Around The World, Red, Yellow, Sawtooth Borders, 69½ x 71 In.	523.00
Patchwork, Tulip, Vine Border, White Ground, Charity Whickkar, Cotton, 1851, 82 x 82 In. .	470.00
Patchwork, Turkey Tracks, 5 Rows, Calico, 90 x 92 In.	385.00
Patchwork, Turkey Tracks, Sawtooth Border, Pink & Green, 1890, 73 x 69 In.	325.00
Patchwork, Wild Goose Chase, Brown, Yellow, Green Ground, Printed Backing, 76 x 88 In. ..	495.00
Patchwork, Wild Goose Variation, Green, White Ground, Double Border, 76½ x 84 In.	88.00
Patchwork, Windmill Variation, Hand Sewn, Machine Bound, Cotton, 94 x 80 In.	402.00
Patchwork & Appliqued, Autumn Oaks, Red, Green, 70 x 68 In.	495.00
Patchwork & Appliqued, Flowers, Sawtooth, Triple Green & White Border, 77½ In.	1650.00
Patchwork & Appliqued, Friendship, 16 Squares, Oak Leaves, 1850, 90 x 90 In.	775.00
Patchwork & Appliqued, Palama Mission, Crest, Hawaiian Flags, Cotton, 84 x 88 In.	13200.00
Patchwork & Appliqued, Whig Rose, White Ground, Red, Orange Flowers, Cotton, 81 x 85 In. .	1058.00
Whig Rose, Scalloped Border, c.1850, 82 x 83 In.	590.00

Quilt, Patchwork, 5-Point Stars, 10 Rows Of 10 Stars, Printed Fabrics, 86½ x 87 In.
$660.00

Quilt, Patchwork, 30 Blocks, Crosses, Light Blue Binding, 58 x 82 In.
$259.00

Quilt, Patchwork, Album, Squares, Red & White Borders, Lancaster County, Pa., c.1885, 80 x 78 In.
$350.00

Q

Quilt, Patchwork, Diamonds,
Maroon Floral Print Back,
Pennsylvania, 1890s
$350.00

Quilt, Patchwork, Lone Star, Bricker Family,
Lancaster County, Pa., c.1900,
77 x 77 In.
$702.00

Quilt, Patchwork, Mariner's Compass,
Calico, Lancaster County, Pa.,
c.1885, 72 x 73 In.
$527.00

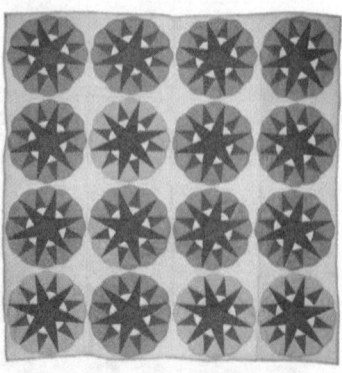

Quilt, Patchwork, Oval Medallion,
George Washington, Liberty Bell,
Paisley Border, Striped, 90 x 88 In.
$5300.00

Quilt, Patchwork, Sampler, Baskets,
Plain & Printed Fabric, Double Sawtooth
Border, 84 x 86 In.
$605.00

Quilt, Patchwork, Sunshine & Shadow, Amish, Lancaster, Pa.,
c.1930, 79 x 80 In.
$936.00

Quilt, Patchwork, Triangles,
Double Zigzag Border, Floral
Print Back, Crib, 38 x 38 In.
$819.00

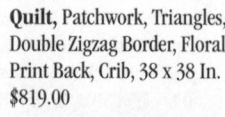

Quilt, Patchwork, Trip Around The World,
Rainbow Colors, Lancaster, Pa.,
c.1890, 82 x 83 In.
$1112.00

Q

QUIMPER pottery has a long history. Tin-glazed, hand-painted pottery has been made in Quimper, France, since the late seventeenth century. The earliest firm, founded in 1685 by Jean Baptiste Bousquet, was known as HB Quimper. Another firm, founded in 1772 by Francois Eloury, was known as Porquier. The third firm, founded by Guillaume Dumaine in 1778, was known as HR or Henriot Quimper. All three firms made similar pottery decorated with designs of Breton peasants and sea and flower motifs. The Eloury (Porquier) and Dumaine (Henriot) firms merged in 1913. Bousquet (HB) merged with the others in 1968. The group was sold to a United States family in 1984. The American holding company is Quimper Faience Inc., located in Stonington, Connecticut. The French firm has been called Societe Nouvelle des Faienceries de Quimper HB Henriot since March 1984.

HR. Quimper

Butter Chip, Octagonal, 2 In.	95.00
Cake Plate, Pedestal, Scalloped Edge, Henriot, c.1930, 9½ x 4½ In.	155.00
Creamer, Man Smoking, 5¼ In.	250.00
Creamer, Panels, Red Croiselle, Flower Sprays, Woman, 4¼ x 3 x 4 In.	85.00
Cup & Saucer, Tan Underglaze, Multicolored Flowers, Art Deco Shape, Square Handle	40.00
Eggcup, Wood Fired Glaze, c.1900	20.00
Jardiniere, Boat Shape, Man, Flower, 1930, 6 x 3 x 2 In.	225.00
Oyster Plate, 6 Wells, Man Center, c.1930	195.00
Oyster Plate, Signed, 8¾ In.	395.00
Pitcher, White Tin Glaze, Tricorner Shape, Religious Scene, Faience, 5½ In.	95.00
Plate, Cobalt Blue, Scalloped Rim, Faience, c.1880, 8 In.	125.00
Plate, Dinner, French Revolution, Henriot, c.1940	75.00
Salt, Double, Man, Flower, Spongeware Blue Handle	47.00
Serving Bowl, Blue Flowers, 10¾ x 8 x 2 In.	60.00
Soup, Dish, c.1890, 9½ x 1½ In.	200.00
Soup, Dish, Sponge Blue, Flowers, Scalloped Rim, c.1930, 10 x 1¾ In., Pair	140.00
Tea Set, Blue Hexagonal, Flesh Colored Glaze, Geometric, 25 Piece	1025.00
Tray, Butter, Mistral, Blue Pattern, Woman In Center, 1 Lb.	50.00
Tray, Flower, Ruffled Edge, 11½ x 9 In.	95.00
Vase, Bud, Horn Shaped, Woman Holding Flower, c.1890, 5 In.	110.00
Vase, Dolphin Tail Arms, Men Playing Flute, Bagpipes, Flowers, Henriot, 13 x 9½ In.	895.00
Vase, Wall, Double Cornet, Man Smoking Pipe, Flowers, c.1900, 10½ x 7½ x 3½ In.	475.00

RADFORD pottery was made by Alfred Radford in Broadway, Virginia; Tiffin and Zanesville, Ohio; and Clarksburg, West Virginia, from 1891 until 1912. Jasperware, Ruko, Thera, Radura, and Velvety Art Ware were made. The jasperware resembles the famous Wedgwood ware of the same name. Another pottery named Radford worked in England and is not included here.

RADURA.

Vase, Black Berries & Leaves, Dark Green Ground, Bottle Shape, Albert Haubrick, 11 In.	*illus*	540.00
Vase, White Relief Cherubs, Eagles, Clouds, Light Olive Ground, Shouldered, 9⅜ In.	*illus*	180.00

RADIO broadcast receiving sets were first sold in New York City in 1910. They were used to pick up the experimental broadcasts of the day. The first commercial radios were made by Westinghouse Company for listeners of the experimental shows on KDKA Pittsburgh in 1920. Collectors today are interested in all early radios, especially those made of Bakelite plastic or decorated with blue mirrors. Figural advertising radios and transistor radios are also collected.

Addison, Model 5, Catalin, Tube, Marbleized Brown & Butterscotch, 1940	800.00
Advertising, KCFI, Microphone Shape, Fixed Reception For 1250AM, c.1950, 14 In.	118.00
Arvin, Clock, AM, Alarm, Appliance Outlet, Cream Color, Plastic Case, 1960s, 13½ x 7 In.	73.00
Barbie, Transistor, AM, Carrying Strap, c.1980, 7 In.	30.00
Bendix, Model 0526C, Bakelite, Marbleized Case, 11 x 7 In.	550.00
Bendix, Model 526MC, Green Swirl, 2 Knobs, Bakelite, 7 x 10½ In.	550.00
Bulova, Model 208, White, Modern Design, 1955	30.00
Champion Spark Plug, Plastic, AM, FM, 14½ In.	77.00
Dog, Transistor, Long-Haired, Original Cardboard Tag, Japan, 6½ x 8 In.	45.00
Emerson, Model BT-245, Tombstone, Catalin, Red Marble, White Accent, 1939, 10 In.	4245.00
Emerson, 5 Plus 1, Raised Bakelite Grill, Decal, 9¼ x 6¾ In.	1760.00
Emerson, Model 522, Bakelite, Mottled Brown, Carry Handle, c.1946, 11 x 7 In.	65.00
Fada, Bakelite, Cloth Mesh Grill, Marbleized Blue Case, Green Patina, 6¾ x 10¾ In.	1870.00
Fada, Model 711, Orange, Red, Luggage Style, Handle, 2 Knobs, 8 x 11 In.	440.00
Fada, Model 845, Bakelite, Green, Red Knobs, 1947, 10½ x 6½ In. *illus*	990.00
Fada, Model 1000, Bakelite, Red, Orange, 10½ x 6½ In. *illus*	880.00
Fada, Model 1000, Bullet, Superheterodyne, Art Deco, Red, Amber, Catalin Case, 1947, 10 In.	705.00
Fada, Model 1000, Temple, Blue Marbleized Case, Handle, Cloth Mesh Grill, 6 x 10 In.	1760.00
Grand Old Parr Scotch Whiskey, Bottle Shape, 2¾ x 5½ In.	42.00

Radford, Vase, Black Berries & Leaves, Dark Green Ground, Bottle Shape, Albert Haubrick, 11 In. $540.00

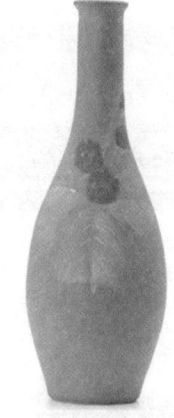

Radford, Vase, White Relief Cherubs, Eagles, Clouds, Light Olive Ground, Shouldered, 9⅜ In. $180.00

Radio, Fada, Model 845, Bakelite, Green, Red Knobs, 1947, 10½ x 6½ In. $990.00

Radio, Fada, Model 1000, Bakelite, Red, Orange, 10½ x 6½ In. $880.00

R

Radio, Grundig, World's Finest Radio, Wood Grain Case, West Germany, 1940s, 24 x 13 x 9 In. $165.00

Radio, Reico, Model W 206, Long & Medium Wave, Wood Case, Double Doors, 5 Valves, c.1933 $351.00

Radio, Siemens, Model 62W, Gentleman In Tail Coat, Bakelite Case, 3 Valves, c.1930 $204.00

Clock Radios

There were clock radios in the 1950s. Peter Max added decoration to clock radios made by General Electric in the 1960s. A clock radio was cased with a tiny television set in the 1980s.

Grundig, World's Finest Radio, Wood Grain Case, West Germany, 1940s, 24 x 13 x 9 In. *illus*	165.00
Majestic, Charlie McCarthy, Brown Bakelite, Metal Figure Of Charlie, 1940s, 6 x 7 In.	675.00
Novelty, Campbell's, Tomato Soup Can, Original Box, c.1996	45.00
Novelty, Freshlike Vegetables Green Beans & Sweet Corn Can, 1991	50.00
Novelty, Tweety Bird, Telephone, Clock, Talking Alarm, Telemania, 16 x 9½ In.	45.00
RCA Victor, Bakelite, Marbleized, Louvered Grill, Original Label, 8¼ x 5¼ In.	1650.00
RCA Victor, Model 563, Bakelite, Police Band, Woven Fabric Grill, 9½ x 6 In.	1100.00
Reico, Model W 206, Long & Medium Wave, Wood Case, Double Doors, 5 Valves, c.1933 *illus*	351.00
Siemens, Model 62W, Gentleman In Tail Coat, Bakelite Case, 3 Valves, c.1930 *illus*	204.00
Silvertone, Model 4486, Cloth Grille, 1937, Floor Model	99.00
Smurf, Transistor, Blue, Belt Clip, Nasta, Hong Kong, 1981, 5 x 2¾ In.	30.00
Sony Transistor, Model ICR 200, AC Power, Battery Charger, Leather Case, Integrated Circuit	245.00
Spartan, Model 557, Mirror, Blue, Wood, Chromed Metal, 1936, 9 In.	7800.00
Stewart Warner, Bakelite, Shortwave Band, Marbleized, 13 x 8 In.	523.00
Zenith, Art Deco Style, Floor Model, 1938, 42 x 27 x 15 In. *illus*	885.00
Zenith, Model K-518, Clock, Alarm, Bakelite, Maroon, 1960s	45.00
Zenith, Model L-600, Shortwave, Black Stag, Sliderule Dial, Trans-Oceanic, c.1954, 17 x 11 In.	285.00

RAILROAD enthusiasts collect any train memorabilia. Everything is wanted, from oilcans to whole train cars. The Chessie system has a store that sells many reproductions of their old dinnerware and uniforms.

Bank, Brotherhood Of Locomotive Engineers, Trust Company, Celluloid, Round, c.1940	275.00
Bell, Number Plate, Steam Locomotive, Rutland, Brass, Cast Iron, c.1937, 14 In.	2938.00
Bowl, B & O, Carrolton Viaduct, Lamberton China, Scammells, Blue, White, 1 x 5¼ In.	24.00
Celery Dish, Milwaukee Road Traveler, Syracuse China, 1947, 9 x 5 In.	175.00
Lantern, Nickel Plate Housing, Glass Shade, Pierce Vent, Patd. 1866, 16½ In.	118.00
Paperweight, Bear, Walking, Chicago, Milwaukee & St. Paul Railway, Bronze Finish, 3 x 5 x 2¾ In.	242.00
Pin, Brotherhood Of Locomotive Firemen & Enginemen, 1900-12, 1 In.	122.00
Pin, Put Me Off At Buffalo, Black Porter, 1905, 1¼ In.	405.00
Sign, Bound Brook Route, 2 Hour Express, Train, Cardboard Lithograph, 10⅝ x 8⅝ In.	578.00
Stamp Holder, Texas & Pacific Railway, Stick To Old Reliable, Horse, Celluloid, 2¼ x 1¼ In.	126.00
Stock, Nickel Plate Route, New York Chicago & St. Louis Railroad, 1950s, 3 Piece	12.00
Tape Measure, Dorfan Electric Trains, Newark, N.J., Celluloid, Round, 1½ In.	126.00
Tape Measure, Hamler Boiler & Tank Co., Celluloid, Round, 1905, 2 In.	153.00
Tape Measure, Texas & Pacific Railway, Celluloid, Round	139.00
Timetable, Great Northern, Passenger, Oct. To Dec., c.1948	20.00
Tumbler, Pennsylvania Railroad 4902, 4⅜ In.	25.00

RAZORS were used in ancient Egypt and subsequently wherever shaving was in fashion. The metal razor used in America until about 1870 was made in Sheffield, England. After 1870, machine-made hollow-ground razors were made in Germany or America. Plastic or bone handles were popular. The razor was often sold in a set of seven, one for each day of the week. The set was often kept by the barber who shaved the well-to-do man each day in the shop.

Collins, Safety, Round Head, Blades, Silver Plated, Instructions, Leather Pouch	250.00
Gem Micromatic, Single Edge Blades, 1930, 3½ In.	24.00
Gillette, Double Edge, Goldtone, 1904	22.00
Gillette, Double Edge, Goldtone, 1960s	15.00
Keen Kutter, Straight Edge, Model 1150, Bakelite Handle, 3-Inch Blade	35.00
Pin, Marlin Blades, 20 For 25 Cents, Late 1930s, 3½ In.	216.00
Schick, Injection, Goldtone Head, Beige Bakelite Handle, 1940s	18.00
Star, Flip Top, 6-Sided, Notches, Silvertone	8.00
Straight, Bakelite Handle, Black	50.00
Straight, Bakelite Handle, White	30.00
Straight, Horse's Head On Ivory Handle	60.00
Strop, U.S. Navy, Sailor Standing By Ship's Capstan, J.R. Torrey Razor Co., 14 In.	285.00
Strop, Valet, Goldtone, Semi Disposable Blades, 1937	25.00
Universal, Safety, Case, Attachments, Extra Blade, Celluloid Handle	36.00
Valet, Single Edge, 20th Century	18.00

REAMERS, or juice squeezers, have been known since 1767, although most of those collected today date from the twentieth century. Figural reamers are among the most prized.

Ceramic, Clown, 1940s	85.00
Ceramic, Frog	33.00

Ceramic, Ivory, 8 x 1¾ In.	20.00
Ceramic, White, Sunkist, 8 x 1½ In.	30.00
Crisscross, Loop Handle, Twisted Cone, Hazel Atlas, 1938	27.00
Glass, 2 Sections, Base Has Pour Spout & Handle, 6 x 7¾ x 4 In.	28.00
Glass, Amber, Ribs, Loop Handle, 6 In.	9.00
Glass, Apple Green, 7 x 8½ In.	33.00
Glass, Chaline Blue, Sunkist ....*illus*	260.00
Glass, Clear, Tab Handle, Spout, Anchor Hocking, 6 x 2¾ In.	18.00
Glass, Deep Dish, Paneled Sides, Finger Loop Handle, Ridged	24.00
Glass, Green, 8½ x 2¼ In.	35.00
Glass, Green, Embossed, Sunkist, 1920s	41.00
Glass, Green, Hocking, 3¾ x 6 In.	6.00
Glass, Green, Tab Handle, 5 In.	18.00 to 28.00
Glass, Hand Blown, Pink, 8½ x 6 x 2 In.	35.00
Glass, Jade, 2 Sections	48.00
Glass, Jadite, Mixer Attachment, Embossed, 1930s	25.00
Glass, Loop Handle, Ribbed Panels	20.00
Glass, Manny's, 1889	20.00
Glass, Onyx, Handle, Sunkist ....*illus*	410.00
Glass, Opalescent, Embossed Sunkist, McKee Glass, 8 In.	54.00
Glass, Opalescent Blue, 6 x 2¼ In.	48.00
Glass, Pearl, Tab Handle, 6¼ x 2⅜ In.	35.00
Glass, Red, Amberina, 4½ In.	33.00
Glass, Ribbed, 8½ In.	15.00
Glass, Ribbed, Flower Center, 12 Sections, Tab Handle, 2 x 8 In.	18.00
Glass, Ribbed, Looped Handle, Raised Lip	20.00
Glass, Swirled Cone, 10 Seed Dams, Tab Handle, Hazel Atlas	20.00
Glass, Top, Jadeite, Jeannette, 6 x 3½ In.	45.00
Glass, Vaseline, Edna Barnes, 2 Piece	250.00
Glass, Vertical Ribbing, Ribbed Handle, 1950s, 2¼ x 7¾ In.	15.00
Glass, Vertical Ribbing, Ring Handle, Foot	15.00
Milk Glass, Embossed, Sunkist	35.00
Plastic, Pink, Lustroware, 6 In.	8.00
Plastic, Red, Westland Plastics, Inc., 6 In.	8.00
Plastic, White, Quikut, 5¼ x 4 In.	7.00
Pottery, Ables, Matte, Glossy Glaze, 9½ x 7½ x 3¼ In.	25.00
Pottery, Medallion, Ivory Glaze	175.00
Vaseline Glass, 2 Sections, Edna Barnes, 1980s	250.00
Vaseline Glass, 3¾ x 8½ In.	25.00

RECORDS have changed size and shape through the years. The cylinder-shaped phonograph record for use with the early Edison models was made about 1889. Disc records were first made by 1894, the double-sided disc by 1904. High-fidelity records were first issued in 1944, the first vinyl disc in 1946, the first stereo record in 1958. The 78 RPM became the standard in 1926 but was discontinued in 1957. In 1932, the first 33⅓ RPM was made but was not sold commercially until 1948. In 1949, the 45 RPM was introduced. Compact discs became available in the U.S. in 1982 and many companies began phasing out the production of phonograph records.

Arthur Godfrey, What Is A Boy, What Is A Girl, Columbia Records, 78 RPM	10.00
Basie In London, Hi-Fi Mono Recording, Verve Records, LP, 1957	70.00
Beach Boys, Spirit Of America, Capitol Records, LP, c.1975, 2 Records	20.00
Bing Crosby, Favorite Hawaiian Songs, Booklet, 1946, 78 RPM, 5 Records	24.00
Captain Kangaroo, The Horse In Striped Pajamas, 45 RPM, Golden Record, 1959	30.00
Del Shannon, Hey Little Girl, Big Top Records, 1961, 45 RPM	35.00
Eileen Farrell Soprano, Irish Songs, Columbia Masterworks, 78 RPM, 1947	16.00
Elvis Presley, Blue Christmas, Santa Claus Is Back In Town, Paper Sleeve, 45 RPM	35.00
Huck, Yogi & Quick Draw Safety Song, Hanna Barbera, 45 RPM, Golden Record, 1961	39.00
Huddie Lead Belly Leadbetter, Negro Sinful Songs, Pamphlet, 5 Records, 1940s, 78 RPM	274.00
Jane & Judy Jetson, Songs Of The Jetsons, Hanna Barbera, 45 RPM, Golden Record	45.00
Jane Mansfield, Music For Bachelors, RCA Victor, 1956, 33⅓ RPM	35.00
Kiss, Picture Disc, 1984	10.00
Otis Redding, Live In Europe, Volt Records, LP, 1967	50.00
Peter Frampton, Picture Disc, 1976	8.00
Shadow, Transcription Disc, Traffic In Death, Black Abbot, Paper Sleeve, 16 In.	504.00
Shangri-Las, Leader Of The Pack, What Is Love, Red Bird Records, 45 RPM, 1960s	15.00
Sweet Marie, Stella's Candy Store, Another Feelin', Yard Bird Records, 45 RPM, 1972	10.00

Radio, Zenith, Art Deco Style, Floor Model, 1938, 42 x 27 x 15 In. $885.00

Reamer, Glass, Chaline Blue, Sunkist $260.00

Reamer, Glass, Onyx, Handle, Sunkist, $410.00

Early Phonograph Needles
Early phonographs had no volume control, and the sound depended on the needle. Sapphire heads were durable. Steel needles had to be changed frequently. Needles made of wood, bamboo, and other materials could be sharpened and reused. Needles were stored in small, collectible tins that have lithographed designs.

R

Eva Zeisel

Eva Zeisel (1906–present) is a Hungarian-born designer and ceramicist. She worked in factories in Budapest, Germany, Russia, Austria, and England before coming to the United States in 1938. She designed for many companies and is best known for her dinnerware. She made *Stratoware* (Sears, Roebuck, 1942), all-white *Museum* dinnerware (Museum of Modern Art, 1942, made by Castleton China Company), *Town and Country* (Red Wing Pottery, 1947 to 1954), *Tomorrow's Classic* (Hall China, 1952), and *Century* (Hall China, 1956). These modern solid-white dinnerware shapes were sometimes decorated. In the late 1990s and early 2000s, she designed for Zsolnay and Kispester-Granit in Hungary and KleinReid in the United States.

Redwing, Bob White, Gravy Boat, Cover $35.00

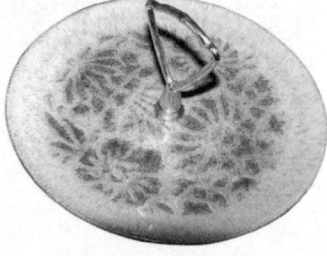

Redwing, Damask, Tidbit Tray, 7⅜ In. $26.00

The Knack, My Sharona, Let Me Out, Capitol Records, 45 RPM, c.1979	8.00
TV Bozo, The World's Most Famous Clown, 45 RPM, Golden Record	34.00
Voices From The Moon, Moon Landing, Apollo 11, Philco-Ford, 33⅓ RPM, 1969	30.00
Woody Woodpecker, Picture Disc	25.00
Zombies, Tell Her No, Leave Me Be, Parrot Records, 45 RPM, 1960s	25.00

RED WING Pottery of Red Wing, Minnesota, was a firm started in 1878. The company first made utilitarian pottery, including stoneware jugs and canning jars. In the 1920s art pottery was introduced. Many dinner sets and vases were made before the company closed in 1967. Rumrill pottery made by the Red Wing Pottery for George Rumrill is listed in its own category. For more information, see *Kovels' Depression Glass & Dinnerware Price List*.

Advertising, Ashtray, To Popa, Love Sanford, Child's Artwork	55.00
Advertising, Baking Dish, Compliments Of C.A. Habergarten & Co., Waconia, Minn.	95.00
Advertising, Bean Pot, Fred Haar Farm Machinery, 1882-1932, 50th Anniversary, Freeman, S.D.	100.00
Advertising, Beater Jar, Compliments Of Frank J. Martin, Ackley, Iowa	240.00
Advertising, Beater Jar, Compliments Of P. Mohrbacher & Sons, Cologne, Minn., Double Mark	200.00
Advertising, Beater Jar, Compliments Of Rieke Bros., Kingsley, Iowa, Blue Band	285.00
Advertising, Beater Jar, George Chamberlain, 3rd Street Grocer, We Deliver, Blue Band	90.00
Advertising, Bowl, Compliments Of Martinson & Johnson, New Richland, Minn., Greek Key, 8 In.	165.00
Advertising, Bowl, It Pays To Mix With E.M. Weiser, Elmwood, Wis., Sponge, 6 In.	215.00
Advertising, Bowl, It Pays To Mix With Hoecks Grocery, Sibley, Iowa, Sponge, 7 In.	155.00
Advertising, Bowl, It Pays To Mix With Nelson Anderson Co., Yankton, S.D., Greek Key, 9 In.	85.00
Advertising, Bowl, It Pays To Mix With Wm. F. Christel Inc., Valders, Wis., Sponge, 7 In.	45.00
Advertising, Bowl, Trade At The Big L Store, Sumner, Iowa, Sponge, 7 In.	235.00
Advertising, Butter Pail, Lid, Jensen Merc. Co., Satisfaction Our Aim, Wis., 5 Lb.	165.00 to 375.00
Advertising, Carrier, Butter, A Square Deal For All, Meysembough's Almena, 3 Lb.	225.00
Advertising, Casserole, Cover, Compliments Of Pitts Brothers, Alexandria, S.D.	45.00
Advertising, Crock, Butter, Charles Zoller Cash Grocer, Fort Plain, N.Y., 2 Lb.	85.00
Advertising, Crock, Butter, Crescent Creamer Co., Sioux Falls, S.D., 3 Lb.	165.00
Advertising, Crock, Butter, Fresh Butter Model Dairy, Inc., 3 Lb.	55.00
Advertising, Crock, Butter, Goodhue County Co-Operative Company, 5 Gal.	400.00
Advertising, Crock, Butter, Lid, Ev-Re-Day Oloemargarine, Milwaukee, 5 Lb.	50.00
Advertising, Crock, Butter, Return To Rhinelander Creamer, 3 Lb.	230.00
Advertising, Crock, Butter, Willow Farm Churned, Oak, La Grange, Ill., 3 Lb.	10.00
Advertising, Crock, Carl J. Schneider Dealer In General Merchandise, Schneider, Neb., Gal.	975.00
Advertising, Crock, Drink 3 Star Coffee, C. Shenkberg Co., Sioux City, Iowa, ½ Gal.	165.00
Advertising, Jar, Lid, We Trade With M. Hakes & Sons, Laurens & Havelock, 5 Lb.	575.00
Advertising, Jar, Pantry, Lid, Wing, Pitts Bros., Alexandria, S.D.	1350.00
Advertising, Jar, Storage, Pitts Bros., Alexandria, S.D., No Lid	525.00
Advertising, Jug, E.E. Bruce & Co., Wholesale Druggist, Omaha, Neb., ½ Gal.	225.00
Advertising, Jug, Excelsior Springs, Mo., Mineral Waters, Bail Handle, Qt.	325.00
Advertising, Jug, John Coates Liquor Co., Wholesale Whiskies, Brainerd, Minn., ½ Gal.	525.00
Advertising, Jug, Shoulder, Brion & Weaverling, Ewing, Neb., Gal.	275.00
Advertising, Jug, Shoulder, Julius Sieler Wholesale Liquors, Tripp, S.D., 2 Gal.	205.00
Advertising, Jug, Who Will Win, Minnesota Michigan, Miniature	215.00
Advertising, Pail, Refrigerator, Herman Fleer Daylight Store, Bail Handle, No Lid	140.00
Advertising, Pitcher, Compliments Of Fairway Market, Cambridge, Minn, Sponge, Large	355.00
Advertising, Pitcher, Everything To Eat & Wear At Home Department Store, Springfield, Minn.	250.00
Advertising, Pitcher, Jensen Merc. Co., Satisfaction Our Aim, Milltown, Wis., Cherry Band, Medium	400.00
Advertising, Pitcher, Merry Christmas Andrew Westin & Co., Cherry Band, Medium	85.00
Advertising, Pitcher, Neosha Co-Operative Co., Neosha, Wisconsin, Sponge, Large	300.00
Advertising, Refrigerator Jar, Harrison Merc. Co., Swift Falls, Minn., Blue & White, 3 Lb.	130.00
Advertising, Snuff Jar, Bowers 3 Thistles Snuff, Large	550.00
Advertising, Sugar, Frederic Farmers Co-Operative Exchange, White, Embossed Flower	50.00
Bob White, Gravy Boat, Cover	*illus* 35.00
Damask, Tidbit Tray, 7⅜ In.	*illus* 26.00
Lexington Rose, Bowl, 9¼ In.	*illus* 40.00
Lute Song, Cup & Saucer	*illus* 15.00
Pepe, Casserole, Sections, 12½ In.	*illus* 41.00
Random Harvest, Plate, Dinner, Futura Shape, 1961, 10 In.	*illus* 18.00
Stoneware, Bean Pot, Cover, Albany Slip	30.00
Stoneware, Bowl, Blue, White, Marked, 5 In.	125.00
Stoneware, Bowl, Burgundy, White, 9 In.	85.00
Stoneware, Bowl, Burgundy, White, Marked, 6 In.	105.00
Stoneware, Bowl, Shoulder, 10 In.	85.00
Stoneware, Bowl, Shoulder, 15 In.	155.00

R

Stoneware, Bowl, Shoulder, Blue, 7 In.		115.00
Stoneware, Bowl, Shoulder, Blue, 9 In.		85.00
Stoneware, Bowl, Shoulder, Blue, Marked, 12 In.		450.00
Stoneware, Bowl, Sponge Panel, 8 In.		60.00
Stoneware, Bowl, Sponge Panel, 9 In.		70.00
Stoneware, Bowl, White, Sponge, 9 In.		90.00
Stoneware, Bowl, White, Sponge, 10 In.		80.00
Stoneware, Butter Churn, Tornado Design, Salt Glaze, 4 Gal.		425.00
Stoneware, Butter Pail, Wood Lid, 3 Lb.		55.00
Stoneware, Chamber Pot, Lid, Marked		235.00
Stoneware, Churn, Birch Leaf, Ski Oval, 6 Gal.		145.00
Stoneware, Churn, Cover, Molded Handles, Union Oval, 5 Gal.		775.00
Stoneware, Churn, Cover, Wing & Ski Oval, 8 Gal.		3300.00
Stoneware, Churn, Cover, Wing & Oval, 2 Gal.		270.00
Stoneware, Churn, Cover, Wing & Oval, 3 Gal.		155.00
Stoneware, Churn, Cover, Wing & Oval, 4 Gal.		185.00
Stoneware, Churn, Cover, Wing & Oval, 6 Gal.		500.00
Stoneware, Churn, Leaf, Salt Glaze, 4 Gal.		600.00
Stoneware, Churn, Ribcage, Salt Glaze, 3 Gal.		675.00
Stoneware, Crock, Birch Leaf, Ski Oval, 2 Gal.		50.00
Stoneware, Crock, Birch Leaf, Ski Oval, 4 Gal.		65.00 to 75.00
Stoneware, Crock, Birch Leaf & Union Oval, Blue Markings, 10 Gal.		135.00
Stoneware, Crock, Birch Leaf & Union Oval, Blue Markings, 12 Gal.		145.00
Stoneware, Crock, Birch Leaves, No Oval, 2 Gal.		30.00
Stoneware, Crock, Butter, 10 Lb.		15.00
Stoneware, Crock, Butter, Blue, 3 Lb.		30.00
Stoneware, Crock, Butter, Lid, Sponge, Tall		400.00
Stoneware, Crock, Butterfly, Salt Glaze, 6 Gal.		900.00
Stoneware, Crock, Leaf, Salt Glaze, 10 Gal.		700.00
Stoneware, Crock, Molded Handles, Minnesota Oval, 3 Gal.		100.00
Stoneware, Crock, Molded Handles, No Oval, 2 Gal.		80.00
Stoneware, Crock, Molded Handles, No Oval, 6 Gal.		175.00
Stoneware, Crock, Molded Handles, No Oval, 10 Gal.		220.00
Stoneware, Crock, Molded Handles, Transition, Handwritten 8, Albany Slip Interior, 8 Gal.		600.00
Stoneware, Crock, Molded Handles, Transition, Handwritten 10, Albany Slip Interior, 10 Gal.		425.00
Stoneware, Crock, Molded Handles, Transition, Handwritten 20, Albany Slip Interior, 20 Gal.		500.00
Stoneware, Crock, Molded Handles, Transition, Stamped 5, Albany Slip Interior, 5 Gal.		325.00
Stoneware, Crock, Molded Handles, Union Oval, 5 Gal.		285.00
Stoneware, Crock, Molded Handles, Union Oval, 6 Gal.		65.00
Stoneware, Crock, Molded Handles, Union Oval, 10 Gal.		275.00
Stoneware, Crock, Ribcage, Salt Glaze, 4 Gal.		125.00
Stoneware, Crock, Target, Salt Glaze, Marked, 3 Gal.		165.00
Stoneware, Crock, Transition, Leaf, 6 Gal.		900.00
Stoneware, Crock, Wing, 2 Gal.		105.00
Stoneware, Crock, Wing, No. 6 Oval, 10 Gal.		95.00
Stoneware, Crock, Wing, No. 6 Oval, 12 Gal.		115.00
Stoneware, Crock, Wing, No. 6 Oval, 30 Gal.		235.00
Stoneware, Crock, Wing & Oval, 2 Gal.		20.00 to 45.00
Stoneware, Crock, Wing & Oval, 3 Gal.		40.00
Stoneware, Crock, Wing & Oval, 5 Gal.		60.00
Stoneware, Crock, Wing & Oval, 6 Gal.		75.00
Stoneware, Crock, Wing & Oval, 8 Gal.		95.00
Stoneware, Crock, Wing & Oval, 10 Gal.		105.00 to 155.00
Stoneware, Crock, Wing & Oval, 12 Gal.		175.00
Stoneware, Crock, Wing & Oval, 20 Gal.		245.00
Stoneware, Crock, Wing & Ski Oval, 3 Gal.		95.00
Stoneware, Crock, Wing & Ski Oval, 5 Gal.		205.00
Stoneware, Filter Bottom, Success, Wing		245.00
Stoneware, Filter Bottom, Success		105.00
Stoneware, Filter Top, Success		215.00
Stoneware, Jar, Ball Lock, Wing & Oval, 3 Gal.		35.00
Stoneware, Jar, Ball Lock, Wing & Oval, 5 Gal.		195.00
Stoneware, Jar, Canning, Lid, ½ Gal.		55.00
Stoneware, Jar, Canning, Lid, Gal.		23.00
Stoneware, Jar, Canning, Lid, 2 Gal.		55.00
Stoneware, Jar, Pantry, Lid, 5 Lb.		255.00

Redwing, Lexington Rose,
Bowl, 9¼ In.
$40.00

Redwing, Lute Song,
Cup & Saucer
$15.00

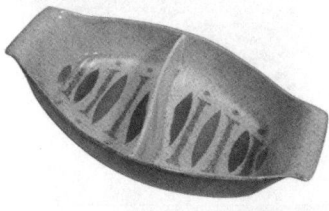

Redwing, Pepe, Casserole,
Sections, 12½ In.
$41.00

Redwing, Random Harvest,
Plate, Dinner, Futura Shape,
1961, 10 In.
$18.00

R

Redwing, Town & Country,
Casserole, Forest Green, 13¾ In.
$100.00

Redwing, Town & Country, Pitcher, 7 In. $275.00

Redware, Bean Pot, Cover, Manganese Splashes, Strap Handle, 7½ In. $250.00

Redware, Charger, Yellow Slip, Bird, Pennsylvania, 11¼ In. $550.00

Redware, Crock, Pudding, Manganese Splotches, Incised Lines, Rolled Rim, 5 In. $578.00

Stoneware, Jar, Pantry, Lid, Gal.	220.00
Stoneware, Jar, Pantry, Lid, Lb.	375.00
Stoneware, Jug, Bail Handle, ½ Gal.	30.00
Stoneware, Jug, Beehive, Birch Leaves, No Oval, 4 Gal.	525.00
Stoneware, Jug, Beehive, Birch Leaves, Union Oval, Black Markings, 3 Gal.	400.00
Stoneware, Jug, Beehive, Birch Leaves, Union Oval, Black Markings, 5 Gal.	350.00
Stoneware, Jug, Beehive, Elephant Ears & Union Oval, 3 Gal.	3500.00
Stoneware, Jug, Beehive, Leaf, Salt Glaze, 5 Gal.	4650.00
Stoneware, Jug, Beehive, Salt Glaze, 2 Gal.	175.00
Stoneware, Jug, Beehive, Salt Glaze, Bee Sting Design, 3 Gal.	650.00
Stoneware, Jug, Beehive, Salt Glaze, Bee Sting Design, 4 Gal.	850.00
Stoneware, Jug, Beehive, Salt Glaze, Bee Sting Design, 5 Gal.	750.00
Stoneware, Jug, Beehive, Wing & Oval, 3 Gal.	375.00
Stoneware, Jug, Beehive, Wing & Oval, 4 Gal.	275.00 to 625.00
Stoneware, Jug, Beehive, Wing & Oval, 5 Gal.	125.00 to 225.00
Stoneware, Jug, Shoulder, Marked, Qt.	25.00
Stoneware, Jug, Shoulder, North Star, Salt Glaze, Marked	145.00
Stoneware, Lamp, Kerosene	155.00
Stoneware, Lily, Slop Jar, No Lid	50.00
Stoneware, Nappy, Blue & White, 10 In.	210.00
Stoneware, Water Cooler, Lid, 3 Gal.	275.00
Stoneware, Water Cooler, Lid, 5 Gal.	200.00
Stoneware, Water Cooler, Lid, 8 Gal.	100.00
Stoneware, Water Cooler, Wing & Oval, Molded, 3 Gal.	265.00
Stoneware, Water Cooler, Wing & Oval, Molded, 5 Gal.	85.00
Teapot, Rooster, Yellow	65.00
Town & Country, Casserole, Forest Green, 13¾ In. ....*illus*	100.00
Town & Country, Pitcher, 7 In. ....*illus*	275.00
Vase, Cranes Wading, Brushware, Marked, Ink Stamp, 8 In.	61.00
Vase, Lady & Deer, Turquoise, White Crackle Glaze, 1942, 8 In.	80.00
Wall Pocket, Banjo, 4 Copper Wire Strings, Stamped, Red Wing USA 908, 15¼ In.	125.00
Western Colonial, Beater Jar	425.00
Western Colonial, Bowl, 5 In.	250.00
Western Colonial, Butter, Lid, Bail Handle, Small	275.00
Western Colonial, Butter, No Lid, Bail Handle, Large	205.00
Western Colonial, Butter, No Lid, Bail Handle, Small	95.00
Western Colonial, Butter, No Lid, Large	625.00
Western Colonial, Custard	350.00
Western Colonial, Pitcher, Water	500.00
Western Colonial, Salt, Lid, Hanging	325.00

REDWARE is a hard, red stoneware that originated in the late 1600s and continues to be made. The term is also used to describe any common clay pottery that is reddish in color.

Bank, Beehive, Seated Dog, White Slip Glaze, Leaf Shapes, Manganese Splotches, 5½ In.	6600.00
Bank, Black Face, Multicolored, Decorated, Southern, 3½ In.	1725.00
Bank, Cylinder Shape, Mushroom Finial, Manganese Splotch Glaze, 3¼ In.	193.00
Bank, Dog, Spaniel, Seated, Mottled Manganese Glaze, Molded 2 On Base, 9¾ In.	1093.00
Bank, Jug, Applied Loop Handle, Old Red Surface, 4½ In.	83.00
Bank, Jug, Bluebird On Branch, Hand Painted, 4½ In.	165.00
Bank, Jug, Old Gold Paint, 2½ In.	110.00
Bank, Penny, Jug Shape, Pointed Vertical Striping, 3⅝ In.	44.00
Bean Pot, Cover, Manganese Splashes, Strap Handle, 7½ In. ....*illus*	250.00
Bowl, Applied Bouquets, Manganese Splotches, Christian Schutter, 5½ x 9 In.	1540.00
Bowl, Applied Flower, Rosettes, Scroll Handles, Manganese Speckles, 4 x 5⅜ In.	2640.00
Bowl, Applied Rope Twist Handles, Squiggled Line, Green Slip, Stripes, 5 x 13½ In.	7150.00
Bowl, Brown Glaze, Interior Green Band, Ruffled Rim, Openwork Handles, 5 x 14 In.	605.00
Bowl, Coggled Rim, 3-Line Slip, Stamped, J. McCully, 6½ In.	1320.00
Bowl, Serpentine Slip Band, Flared Rim, 4¼ x 12 In.	72.00
Bowl, Slip Trailed Squiggle Band, Flared Rim, Impressed 6, 10¼ In.	358.00
Bowl, Yellow Slip Designs, Scallops, Rings, Central Flower, Pennsylvania, 10 x 3 In.	230.00
Bowl, Yellow Slip Loops, 8 x 12 In.	2160.00
Bust, Man, Cigar In Mouth, Manganese Splotches, Incised Hair Lines, 3½ x 5¼ In.	2640.00
Candlestick, Butterfly, Flowers, Loop Handle, Left-Handed, Russell Henry, 4¾ In.	110.00
Charger, Coggled Rim, Yellow Slip Wavy Lines, Green Speckles, 11½ In.	863.00

Charger, Yellow Slip, Bird, Pennsylvania, 11¼ In. . . . .*illus*	550.00
Creamer, Brown Glaze, c.1850, 4½ In.	176.00
Creamer, Lid, Deep Orange Glaze, Mushroom Finial, Pinched Spout, Ear Handle, 4¾ In. . . .	248.00
Creamer, Lid, Short, Squat, Pinched Spout, Ear Handle, 4¼ In.	495.00
Creamer, White House, Trees, Left-Handed, Signed, Russell Henry, 25688, 3¼ In.	61.00
Crock, Batter, Pour Spout, Glazed Interior, 7 x 14 In.	83.00
Crock, Glazed Interior, 2⅝ In.	39.00
Crock, Manganese Design Over Brown Slip Glaze, 5¾ In.	83.00
Crock, Manganese Glaze, 1⅞ In.	143.00
Crock, Manganese Splotches, Incised Lines C-Scroll Handle, 5½ In.	204.00
Crock, Orange Glaze, 2½ In. . . . . 72.00 to 165.00	
Crock, Orange Glaze, Handle, 7½ In.	105.00
Crock, Pudding, Manganese Splotches, Incised Lines, Rolled Rim, 5 In. . . . .*illus*	578.00
Crock, Storage, Incised Line Around Shoulder, Bulbous, 6½ In.	55.00
Cup, Slip, Bottle Shape, Pinched Sides, Manganese Glaze, 3 In.	198.00
Cup, Slip, Jug Form, Flat Sides, Pinched Indents, 3 In.	176.00
Cuspidor, Concave Center, Pierced Drain Hole, 1 x 2 In.	154.00
Cuspidor, Orange To Green Glaze, Manganese Splotches, Serpentine Lines, 4 x 8¼ In.	358.00
Dish, Glazed, Slip, Coggled Rim, 4⅛ In.	908.00
Dish, Slip, 4 Line Waves & Quill Marks, Coggled Rim, 14¼ x 8¼ In.	1210.00
Dish, Slip, Beef, White Script, Squiggle Lines, Flared, 12½ x 10¼ In.	880.00
Doorstop, Lamb, Lying Down, Incised Woolen Coat, Slab Base, 10 In.	143.00
Eggcup, Green, White & Orange, 2⅞ In.	935.00
Figurine, Bird, Slab Base, Pinched Rim, Incised Wing & Tail, 4 x 7½ In.	6875.00
Figurine, Cat, Seated, Multicolored Glaze, Slab Base, Signed, R.R. Stahl, 1951, 4 In.	77.00
Figurine, Deer, Slab Base, Incised Accents, Signed, S. Singer, 6½ x 5 In.	550.00
Figurine, Dog, Seated, Orange & Yellow Glaze, Manganese Splotches, Breininger, 1971, 4 In.	341.00
Figurine, Dog, Seated, Slab Base, Incised Accents, John Bell, 4½ x 3¾ In.	2860.00
Figurine, Dog, Spaniel, Seated, Raised Paw, Brown Luster Glaze, 8⅞ In.	1175.00
Figurine, God, Slab Base, Incised Body, Green, Brown Glaze, 4 x 5 In.	1980.00
Figurine, Lion, Reclining, Buff Glaze, Lorenzo Johnson, Newstead, N.J., c.1880, 9 In.	748.00
Figurine, Rabbit, Manganese Splotches, Molded Base, 1¾ x 2¼ In.	880.00
Figurine, Rocking Chair, Scroddleware, Applied Initials BR, Beaded Border, 6½ In.	110.00
Figurine, Rooster, Dark Manganese Glaze, 4⅜ In.	209.00
Figurine, Rooster, Incised Feather, Open Mouth, Incised Design Around Edge, 14 In.	275.00
Figurine, Rooster, Manganese Splotches, Round Base, Gadrooned Rim, 5¼ In.	990.00
Flask, Flower Emerging From Heart, Multiglaze Design, 7⅝ In.	275.00
Flask, Horse, Man, Incised Decoration, Flattened Oval, Inscriptions, 7⅝ In. . . . .*illus*	441.00
Flask, Pig, Reclining, Molded, Incised, Slip Glazed, Hole In Rear, c.1880, 7½ In.	7638.00
Flowerpot, Coggled Wheel Band, Scalloped Rim, 2¾ In.	1155.00
Flowerpot, Incised Shoulder Line, 2⅛ In.	83.00
Flowerpot, Manganese Splotches, Attached Undertray, 6 In.	495.00
Flowerpot, Manganese Splotches, Double Incised Band, Incised, 8, 5⅛ In.	358.00
Flowerpot, Manganese Splotches, Incised Lines, Ruffled Rim, 5½ In.	165.00
Flowerpot, Undertray, Applied Ruffled Bands, Flowers, Manganese Glaze, 8¼ In.	330.00
Flowerpot, Undertray, Green, Brown, Black Glazes, Pinched Edges, 5 In. . . . .*illus*	2090.00
Flowerpot Undertray, Orange To Green Glaze, Ruffled Rim, Applied Band, 2¼ x 7 In.	550.00
Fuddling Cup, Slipware, West Country, Triple, Yellow Glaze, Spattered Green, c.1730, 7 In. . .	4406.00
Jar, Basket Shape, Applied Ribbed Handle, Running Manganese Glaze, 7½ In.	2530.00
Jar, Brown Glaze, Incised Line Around Shoulder, Bulbous, 9¾ In.	105.00
Jar, Bulbous, Brown Glaze, 7 In.	61.00
Jar, Canning, Manganese Daubs, Faint Green, 7 x 11 In.	144.00
Jar, Cover, Cylindrical, Brown Manganese, 9¾ In. . . . .*illus*	1293.00
Jar, Cylindrical, Dark Brown Manganese, Brushstrokes, 8¾ In.	235.00
Jar, Manganese Glaze, Dark Splotches, Flared Lip, 1850-70, 7 In.	112.00
Jar, Mottled Glaze, Bulbous, 8½ In.	44.00
Jar, Oval, Flared Neck, Applied Lug Handles, Brown Manganese, 9⅝ In.	353.00
Jar, Oval, Glossy Gold & Olive Green Glaze, Dark Brown Streaks, 9 In.	1998.00
Jar, Oval, Olive, Brown Glaze, Raised Flared Rim, Beaded Neck, Applied Lug Handles, 8 In. . .	470.00
Jar, Oval, Raised Flared Rim, Green, Golden Brown Glaze, 7⅞ In.	470.00
Jar, Storage, Albany Slip Glaze, Bulbous, 8 In.	50.00
Jar, Storage, Albany Slip Glaze, Straight Sides, 7 In.	55.00
Jar, Storage, White Slip Dots, 8¾ In.	193.00
Jug, Albany Slip Glaze, Bulbous, Ear Handle, 4¼ In.	303.00
Jug, Albany Slip Glaze, Bulbous, Molded Shaped Handle, 6¼ In.	110.00
Jug, Albany Slip Glaze, Ear Handle, 6½ In.	110.00

Redware, Flask, Horse, Man, Incised Decoration, Flattened Oval, Inscriptions, 7⅝ In. $441.00

Redware, Flowerpot, Undertray, Green, Brown, Black Glazes, Pinched Edges, 5 In. $2090.00

Redware, Jar, Cover, Cylindrical, Brown Manganese, 9¾ In. $1293.00

R

Redware, Jug, Vinegar, Oval, Incised Lines, Applied Strap Handle, Olive Glaze, Orange Halos, 7 In. $1058.00

Redware, Pitcher, Yellow, Green, Orange, Agate Ware Glaze, 7 In. $2160.00

Redware, Plate, Coggled Rim, Slip Decorated, 3 Wavy Quill Lines, Stylized Tree Shapes, 9 In. $3080.00

Richard, Vase, Flowers, Pink, Magenta Overlay, Elongated Cylindrical Neck, 7½ In. $130.00

Jug, Albany Slip Glaze, Incised Lines, Applied Handle, Oval, 6 In.	193.00
Jug, Albany Slip Glaze, Incised Lines, Applied Handle, Oval, 8 In.	220.00
Jug, Albany Slip Glaze, Incised Lines, Applied Handle, Oval, 10 In.	248.00
Jug, Black Glaze, Bulbous, 13 In.	83.00
Jug, Brown Glaze, Incised Line Around Shoulder, Bulbous, Handle, 7½ In.	143.00
Jug, Brown Speckled Glaze, Olive Green, Straight Side, Applied Strap Handle, 5⅜ In.	294.00
Jug, Bulbous, Brown Glaze, 9¾ In.	83.00
Jug, Bulbous, Handle, Green & Manganese, Mottled Glaze, 4 In.	105.00
Jug, Bulbous, Olive Glaze, 10½ In.	110.00
Jug, Harvest, Unglazed, Center Loop Handle, Spigot, Air Spout, 10¾ In.	17.00
Jug, Orange Glaze, Pinched Spout, Applied Handle, 7¼ In.	220.00
Jug, Oval, Applied Reeded Strap Handle, Incised, Brown Manganese, 8⅞ In.	1880.00
Jug, Oval, Applied Strap Handle, Mottled Green, Brown, 7 In.	441.00
Jug, Oval, Green Glaze, Applied Reeded Strap Handle, Orange, Brown Manganese, 8¾ In.	1116.00
Jug, Oval, Olive Green Glaze, Golden Brown Halos, Applied Strap Handle, 7⅝ In.	999.00
Jug, Teardrop, Forest Green Glaze, Handle, c.1820, 6 In.	24000.00
Jug, Teardrop, Light Green Glaze, Incised Lines, Handle, 8½ In.	12500.00
Jug, Vinegar, Oval, Incised Lines, Applied Strap Handle, Olive Glaze, Orange Halos, 7 In. *illus*	1058.00
Jug, Vinegar, Oval, Ribbed Strap Handle, Incised, Olive Green, Brown Glaze, 4¾ In.	353.00
Jug, White Slip Dots, Burnt Orange Slip Sprays, Squiggled Slip Lines, Handle, 8¼ In.	1100.00
Jug, Yellow, Orange, Green Glaze, Center Handle, Spout, Air Stem, Shenandoah Valley, 6½ In.	1870.00
Mug, Manganese Splotches, Incised Lines Around Upper Rim, 4½ In.	110.00
Mug, Mother Goose Rhyme, Applied Ear Handle, Left-Handed, Russell Henry, 3½ In.	38.00
Mug, Slip Trailed Pinstripes, White Interior Glaze, Ear Handle, 3¾ In.	50.00
Mug, Yellow Band, Ground Upper Rim, 3 In.	522.00
Pan, Milk, Wavy Pale Yellow Slip Designs, 12¾ In.	374.00
Pie Plate, Abstract Squiggles, Yellow Slip, Red Ground, 12½ In.	1200.00
Pie Plate, Coggled Rim, Yellow Slip Design, Stylized Flags, Wavy Lines, 8 In.	604.00
Pie Plate, Coggled Rim, Yellow Slip Liner, 8 In.	345.00
Pie Plate, Yellow & Green Slip, 8¾ In.	4914.00
Pie Plate, Yellow Slip, Coggled Rim, 10¼ In.	258.00
Pitcher, Agate Glazed, Ceramic, 7¼ In.	2280.00
Pitcher, Applied Ear Handle, Pinched Spout, Orange Glaze, Manganese Speckles, 2¼ In.	578.00
Pitcher, Applied Reeded Handle, Brown Splotch Stripes, Early 19th Century, 6½ In.	176.00
Pitcher, Applied Strap Handle, Yellow Spot Slip Decoration, Early 1800s, 6½ In.	470.00
Pitcher, Cream Glaze, Orange, Green Squiggle, Stripe, 3¾ In.	1080.00
Pitcher, Glaze, Dark Brown Splotches, 6 In.	2280.00
Pitcher, Manganese & Green Glaze, Incised, Applied Strap Handle, 6½ In.	259.00
Pitcher, Manganese Glaze, Corrugated Handle, 1840-60, 2¾ In.	44.00
Pitcher, Manganese Splotches, Bulbous, Ear Handle, 8¾ In.	138.00
Pitcher, Milk, Incised Lines Around Rim, C-Scroll Handle, Black Albany Slip Glaze, 6 In.	193.00
Pitcher, Orange, Brown, Yellow, Black Dots, Bulbous, 4¼ In.	1200.00
Pitcher, Orange, Green, Brown, Agate Ware, Glaze, 6 In.	1440.00
Pitcher, Orange Glaze, Incised Lines Around Shoulder & Rim, Ear Handle, 8⅜ In.	248.00
Pitcher, Red, Green, Orange Glaze, Tall Neck, Bulbous, 6½ In.	840.00
Pitcher, Red, Green, Yellow Slip, Glaze, Bulbous, 5 In.	960.00
Pitcher, Syrup, Applied Handle, Pinched Spout, Manganese Splotches, 6½ In.	660.00
Pitcher, Yellow, Green, Orange, Agate Ware Glaze, 7 In. *illus*	2160.00
Pitcher, Yellow Glaze, Slip, Dotted Diamond, Green Splotches, 4½ In.	1200.00
Pitcher, Yellow Glaze, Slip, Tic-Tac-Toe, 4 In.	1440.00
Plate, 2 Trail Lines, Squiggle Lines & Dashes, White Slip, Impressed, 5, 9⅝ In.	248.00
Plate, 3 Bands Of Quill Marks, Slip, 8¼ In.	105.00
Plate, 3-Line Slip, 6½ In.	132.00
Plate, Coggled Rim, 3 Squiggle Lines, 2 Intersecting Lines With 3 Squiggles, Slip, 9¾ In.	248.00
Plate, Coggled Rim, 3 Squiggle Lines & Dash, Slip, 8¾ In.	303.00
Plate, Coggled Rim, 3 Trail Lines, Squiggle Lines & Dash, White Slip, 11½ In.	605.00
Plate, Coggled Rim, 3-Line White Slip, 6 White Squiggle Bands, 10¾ In.	155.00
Plate, Coggled Rim, 4 Quill Design, Slip, Impressed, 8 In., 4 Piece	495.00
Plate, Coggled Rim, 5 Bands Of Squiggle Lines, 9 In.	110.00
Plate, Coggled Rim, Alternating Pinstripe & Squiggle Band Slip, J. McCully, 11½ In.	1320.00
Plate, Coggled Rim, Slip Decorated, 3 Wavy Quill Lines, Stylized Tree Shapes, 9 In. *illus*	3080.00
Plate, Coggled Rim, Slip Decorated, Yellow Slip Wavy Line Decoration, 9 In.	823.00
Plate, Coggled Rim, Stylized Squiggle Lines, 14 In.	853.00
Plate, Coggled Rim, Stylized White Slip Lines, 11 In.	303.00
Plate, Coggled Rim, Stylized Yellow Slip, 8¾ In.	403.00
Plate, Coggled Rim, Tulip, Brown & Green Slip, Dryville, 7¾ In.	3080.00
Plate, Coggled Rim, Wavy Line Slip, Impressed E, Pennsylvania, 19th Century, 9 In.	230.00

R

Plate, Coggled Rim, Yellow Slip, 11 In.	1115.00
Plate, God Bless This House & All Within, Doves, Crimped Rim, Russell Henry, 1971, 8⅜ In.	468.00
Plate, Manganese Design Surrounding Rim With Center X, 7¾ In.	303.00
Plate, Slip Decorated, 4 Quill Lines, Groups Of Dashes, Coggled Rim, 9¼ In.	330.00
Plate, Slip Decorated, White Pine Tree, Coggled Rim, 4 In.	550.00
Plate, Slip Decorated, White Squiggled & Straight Lines, 6½ In.	121.00 to 253.00
Plate, Small Dot Slip, 6½ In.	358.00
Plate, Squiggle Line Surround Rim, Slip, 1787, 10¾ In.	1320.00
Plate, White Slip Dots, 8¾ In.	110.00
Platter, Comb Design, Coggled Rim, 11 x 9 In.	2310.00
Pot, Decorated, Side Handle, Glazed, Incised Notched Shoulder, Early 1800s, 5¾ In.	690.00
Rattle, Bird, Manganese Splotches, Incised, Slab Base, Pressed Circles, 2¾ x 3¾ In.	9350.00
Rattle, Bird, Manganese Splotches, Slab Base, Pressed Snowflakes, 2⅛ x 3¼ In.	2860.00
Rattle, Cat, Slab Base, Round Stamped Edge, 5 x 4½ In.	1100.00
Salt, Bulbous, Manganese Splotches, 1½ In.	193.00
Salt, Double, Central Finial Handle, Slip Glaze, Schofield, 2 x 5 x 3 In.	209.00
Storage Jar, Thick Forest Green Glaze, c.1820, 9½ In.	21000.00
Sugar, Green Glaze, Manganese Sponges, Handles, 2⅝ x 5 In.	495.00
Sugar, Marbleized, Green, Brown, Black, Applied Handles, Marked, Bethlehem, Pa., 1⅝ x 3⅜ In.	1320.00
Sugar & Creamer, Yellow Band On Upper Half, 3 In.	1018.00
Tray, 6-Line White Slip, 4 x 5 In.	715.00
Wall Pocket, Tree Trunk Form, Old Paint, 10¾ In.	55.00
Washbowl, Interior Glaze, 10½ x 21¼ In.	303.00

REGOUT, *see Maastricht category.*

RICHARD was the mark used on acid-etched cameo glass vases, bowls, night-lights, and lamps made by the Austrian company Loetz after 1918. The pieces were very similar to the French cameo glasswares made by Daum, Galle, and others.

Toothpick, Yellow Glass, Green Stemmed Foliage Decoration, Cameo, 3¼ In.	201.00
Vase, Baluster, Footed, Pink Design, Green Deco Flowers, Cameo, Signed, 9 In.	316.00
Vase, Flowers, Pink, Magenta Overlay, Elongated Cylindrical Neck, 7½ In. ....*illus*	130.00
Vase, Oval, Pink, Amethyst Flowers, Footed, Cameo, Signed, 5 In.	403.00

RIDGWAY pottery has been made in the Staffordshire district in England since 1808 by a series of companies with the name Ridgway. The transfer-design dinner sets are the most widely known product. They are still being made. Other pieces of Ridgway are listed under Flow Blue.

Bowl, Etruscan Festoon, Pink, Black, 1835, 2¾ x 5½ In.	175.00
Bowl, Vegetable, Lorraine, Blue, White, 9 x 3 In.	345.00
Butter, Cover, Blue, Green Flowers, Leaves, Scrolls, 4 x 8¼ In.	58.00
Creamer, Flower, Green Stripe	22.00
Cup, Pink, Yellow Flowers, Green Leaves, White Ground, Scalloped, 2¾ In.	20.00
Cup & Saucer, Green, 5⅞ & 2¼ In.	14.00
Cup & Saucer, Handleless, Log Cabin, Columbia Star Border, 1840, Blue Transfer .....*illus*	316.00
Cup & Saucer, Pink, Flower Spray, Gold Trim	32.00
Cup & Saucer, White, Gold Trim, Green Plaid, Purple Thistles, 1950s, 3 x 4¾ In.	50.00
Jug, Bundle Of Faggots, Green, 5½ x 4 In.	95.00
Mug, Girls, Silver Luster Handle	69.00
Pitcher, Coaching Days, 5½ x 5½ In.	55.00
Pitcher, Coaching Days, 5¾ x 6¼ In.	65.00
Pitcher, Pewter Cover, Beige, Figures, Tam O'Shanter, 1835, 9 In.	295.00
Plate, Bread & Butter, Green, 6 In.	10.00
Plate, Daffodil, Mottled Beige Ground, 10 In.	19.00
Plate, Etruscan Festoon, Pink, Black, 1835, 9½ In.	250.00
Plate, Well & Tree, Oval, Molded Reservoir, Chinoiserie Transfer, c.1895, 19½ x 16 In.	316.00
Platter, Dark Mulberry, 13 x 11 In.	475.00
Platter, Flowers, 17 x 14 In.	75.00
Platter, Rhine, Slate Blue, 12¾ x 10½ In.	165.00
Soup, Dish, Octagon Church, Boston, Flower Border, Medium Blue Transfer, 9¾ In.	230.00
Tankard, Racing The Mall, Winter Day's Amusement Scene, c.1900s, 4¾ x 4⅜ In.	35.00
Tea Tin, 5 O'Clock, 4 x 3½ x 2 In.	20.00
Tureen, Blue, White, Octagonal Top, 8 x 8 In.	125.00

RIFLES *that are firearms are not listed in this book. BB guns and air rifles are listed in the Toy category.*

Ridgway, Cup & Saucer, Handleless, Log Cabin, Columbia Star Border, 1840, Blue Transfer $316.00

1940s Tableware

In the 1940s, entertaining became less formal. Groups talked, played games like bridge, canasta, and Scrabble, and munched snacks from the new chip 'n' dip sets. Progressive dinners, going from house to house, each hostess serving a course, were the popular dinner party. After World War II in 1945, returning servicemen and their families wanted to buy new houses and furnishings. Tract homes were one-story houses with a living-dining area, and little woodwork and unadorned walls. This type of home and lack of servants led to buffet dinners. Ceramic and metal casseroles were used to cook and serve food. New shapes were created. Rimless plates that stacked and easy-to-hold cups became popular. Solid-color patterns like Fiesta and Riviera were made in mix-and-match colors.

R

Rockingham, Coffeepot, Yellowware, Shaped Handle, Footed $290.00

Rookwood, Ashtray, Clown, Seated On Rim, Yellow, Black, Purple, Sallie Toohey, 1930, 4 In. $288.00

Rookwood, Bookends, Eagle, Blue Gray Over Tan Matte Glaze, Louise Abel, 1934, 5¼ In. $2530.00

Rookwood, Bowl, Blue & White Persian Style Decoration, Flared Rim, Hentschel, 1921, 4 x 8 In. $920.00

RIVIERA dinnerware was made by the Homer Laughlin Co. of Newell, West Virginia, from 1938 to 1950. The pattern was similar in coloring and in mood to Fiesta and Harlequin. The Riviera plates and cup handles were square. For more information, see *Kovels' Depression Glass & Dinnerware Price List.*

Blue, Bowl, Dessert, 5¼ In.	14.00
Blue, Bowl, Vegetable, 8¼ In.	17.50
Blue, Plate, Bread & Butter, 6¼ In.	9.00
Blue, Plate, Dinner, 9 In.	8.00 to 13.50
Blue, Teapot, Cover	105.00
Blue, Tumbler	75.00
Green, Creamer	25.00
Green, Cup	9.00
Green, Pitcher, Lid	70.00
Green, Plate, Bread & Butter, 6¼ In.	7.95
Green, Plate, Dinner, 9 In.	12.50 to 19.00
Green, Plate, Salad, 7 In.	10.50
Green, Platter, 11 In.	26.50
Green, Shaker	9.50
Green, Soup, Dish, 8 In.	27.00
Green, Sugar, Cover	19.00 to 20.00
Ivory, Butter, Cover	65.00
Ivory, Platter, 11 In.	19.50
Ivory, Platter, 15 In.	31.00
Ivory, Sugar	15.00
Red, Baker	19.00
Red, Bowl, Cereal, 6 In.	33.00
Red, Bowl, Oval, 9⅛ In.	19.00
Red, Bowl, Vegetable, 8¼ In.	28.00
Red, Butter, Cover	55.00
Red, Casserole, Cover	80.00
Rose, Plate, Dinner, 9 In.	12.00
Yellow, Casserole, No Cover	60.00
Yellow, Creamer	12.50
Yellow, Plate, Dinner, 9 In.	8.00 to 12.50
Yellow, Plate, Salad, 7 In.	14.50
Yellow, Saucer	5.50
Yellow, Shaker	11.50
Yellow, Teapot, Cover	170.00
Yellow, Tumbler	55.00

ROBLIN Art Pottery was founded in 1898 by Alexander W. Robertson and Linna Irelan in San Francisco, California. The pottery closed in 1906. The firm made faience with green, tan, dull blue, or gray glazes. Decorations were usually animal shapes. Some red clay pieces were made.

Vase, Brown Drips, Celadon Flambe Ground, Squat, 2¼ x 3¼ In.	1920.00

ROCKINGHAM, in the United States, is a pottery with a brown glaze that resembles tortoiseshell. It was made from 1840 to 1900 by many American potteries. Mottled brown Rockingham wares were first made in England at the Rockingham factory. Other types of ceramics were also made by the English firm. Related pieces may be listed in the Bennington category.

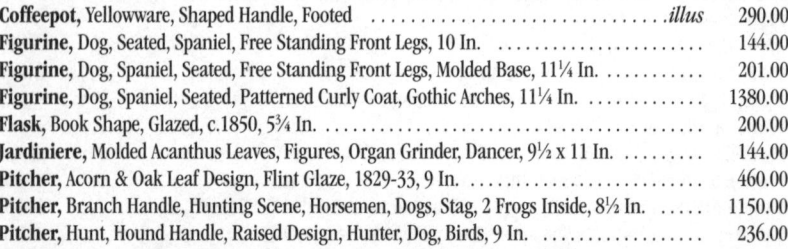

Coffeepot, Yellowware, Shaped Handle, Footed *illus*	290.00
Figurine, Dog, Seated, Spaniel, Free Standing Front Legs, 10 In.	144.00
Figurine, Dog, Spaniel, Seated, Free Standing Front Legs, Molded Base, 11¼ In.	201.00
Figurine, Dog, Spaniel, Seated, Patterned Curly Coat, Gothic Arches, 11¼ In.	1380.00
Flask, Book Shape, Glazed, c.1850, 5¾ In.	200.00
Jardiniere, Molded Acanthus Leaves, Figures, Organ Grinder, Dancer, 9½ x 11 In.	144.00
Pitcher, Acorn & Oak Leaf Design, Flint Glaze, 1829-33, 9 In.	460.00
Pitcher, Branch Handle, Hunting Scene, Horsemen, Dogs, Stag, 2 Frogs Inside, 8½ In.	1150.00
Pitcher, Hunt, Hound Handle, Raised Design, Hunter, Dog, Birds, 9 In.	236.00
Pitcher, Protection To American Industry, Scattergood Hightstown N.J., 9 In.	1840.00
Pitcher, Toby, Grape Decorated Handle, Flat Bottom, 6½ In.	210.00

ROGERS, *see John Rogers category.*

ROOKWOOD pottery was made in Cincinnati, Ohio, from 1880 to 1960. All of this art pottery is marked, most with the famous flame mark. The R is reversed and placed back to back with the letter P. Flames surround the letters. After 1900, a Roman numeral was added to the mark to indicate the year. The name and some of the molds were purchased in 1984. A few new pieces were made, but these were glazed in colors not used by the original company.

Ashtray, Blue Matte Glaze, 1914, 4⅛ In. 690.00
Ashtray, Car, Dog, Red, Walter E. Schott Willys Dealership, Woodburn, 1949, 6⅜ In. 230.00
Ashtray, Clown, Seated On Rim, Yellow, Black, Purple, Sallie Toohey, 1930, 4 In. ...... *illus* 288.00
Bookends, 2 Boys Reading Book, Tan Matte Glaze, 1921 .... 345.00
Bookends, 2 Penguins, 1923, 5¾ x 4¾ In. 518.00
Bookends, 2 Penguins, Black, White, Pale Green, 1931, 5¾ In. 1060.00
Bookends, Basset Hound, Dark Brown Matte Glaze, 1927 .... 805.00
Bookends, Blue Rooks On Blue Matte Glaze, 1939, 5½ In. 320.00
Bookends, Buddha, Tan Matte Glaze, Blue Crystals, 1922 .... 920.00
Bookends, Dutch Boy & Girl, Brick Wall, Tulips, High Glaze, Toohey, 1928, 6 In., Pair 715.00
Bookends, Eagle, Blue Gray Over Tan Matte Glaze, Louise Abel, 1934, 5¼ In. .... *illus* 2530.00
Bookends, Eagle, Spread Wings, Brown High Glaze, 1945, 6 In. 288.00
Bookends, Elephant, 1924 .... 175.00
Bookends, Elephant, Walking, Ivory Matte Glaze, 1927, 4¾ In. 345.00
Bookends, Elephants, Trunks Up, Coromandel Glaze, 1937, 7 In. 2990.00
Bookends, Female Court Figures, White Matte Glaze, 1940, 6 In. 288.00
Bookends, Horse's Head, Bronze Glaze, 1927, 6¼ In. 345.00
Bookends, Little Boy, Sitting, Brown Matte Glaze, 1920 .... 250.00
Bookends, Nude Woman Kneeling On Plinth, Cream Uncrazed High Glaze, 7 In. 1840.00
Bookends, Owl, Butterscotch High Glaze, 1946, 6 In. 288.00
Bookends, Owl, Green Glossy Glaze, No. 2655, 6 In. 374.00
Bookends, Panther, Reclining, 1945 .... 345.00
Bookends, Polar Bear, Sitting, Ivory Matte Glaze, 1965 .... 850.00
Bookends, Rook, Green Matte Glaze, 1922, 5 In. 230.00
Bookends, Rook, Ivory Matte Glaze, Small, William McDonald, 1948 .... 105.00
Bookends, Sailing Ships, Light Blue Matte Glaze, William McDonald, 1929, 5 In. 257.00
Bookends, St. Francis, Animals, Brown, Gray, Flesh Tones, 1945, 7½ In. 530.00
Bookends, St. Francis, With Dog, Brown, Gray, Flesh Tone, 1945, 7½ In. 288.00
Bowl, Birds, Blooming Branches, Round, 1929, 5¼ x 6¼ In. 1440.00
Bowl, Blue & White Persian Style Decoration, Flared Rim, Hentschel, 1921, 4 x 8 In. ... *illus* 920.00
Bowl, Nude Woman, Trees, Flowers, 8 Panels, Jens Jensen, 1944, 3 x 8⅜ In. 1389.00
Bowl, Square, Yellow, Handles, Footed, 1926, 3¾ In. 175.00
Box, Cover, Flower Medallion, Lattice Border, Green Glaze, 2⅜ x 6⅜ In. 264.00
Box, Cover, Ivory Matte Glaze, Turquoise High Glaze Interior, 1922, 2¾ x 7 In. 289.00
Box, Cover, Mandarin Duck Finial, White, 5½ In. 184.00
Brush Pot, Rook, Tree, Panels In Relief, 5-Sided, Blue Matte Glaze, 1920, 4½ In. 353.00
Candlestick, Orange, 6-Sided, 1923, 8⅜ In., Pair 142.00
Charger, Butterfly, Moon, Oriental Tree, Limoges Glaze, Matt Daly, 1885, 8¾ In. 1320.00
Cigarette Lighter, 5 Birds Perched On Branch, Blue Shading, J Sacksteder, 1946, 2¾ In. ... 138.00
Clock, Panther, Ivory Glossy Glaze, c.1950, 7¾ In. 294.00
Cornucopia, Glossy Tan Glaze, Shirayamadani, 6 In. 81.00
Ewer, Berries, Leaves, Standard Glaze, Shaped Handle, Irene Bishop, 1902, 8¾ In. 235.00
Ewer, Dahlias, Gold, Brown & Green Standard Glaze, Ruffled, Matthew Daly, 1892, 14 In. ... 353.00
Ewer, Flower Sprays, Standard Glaze, Katharine Hickman, 1897, 6½ In. 345.00
Ewer, Grasses, Gold Threading On Neck, Anna Marie Bookprinter, 1886, 8½ In. ...... *illus* 460.00
Ewer, Roses, Standard Glaze, Matt Daly, 1892, 9½ In. 910.00
Ewer, Yellow Roses, Brown Shading, Standard Glaze, Shirayamadani, 1890, 12¼ In. 1725.00
Figurine, Cardinal On Branch, 1946 .... 518.00
Figurine, Dog, Boxer, 1945, 10¼ In. 700.00
Figurine, Elephant, 1928, 5 x 6 In. 293.00
Figurine, Jay Bird, Branch, Blue, Brown, Multicolored, 1946, 7 In. 285.00
Figurine, Kingfisher, Multicolored, 1942, 5¼ x 6 In. 690.00
Figurine, Mermaid, Light Green Matte Glaze, 1886, 16½ In. .... *illus* 489.00
Figurine, Spanish Dancer, Maiden Wearing Turquoise Gown, Black Jacket, 1953, 10⅞ In. ... 345.00
Figurine, Squirrel, Multicolored, Sallie Toohey, 1928, 4¼ x 4 In. 288.00
Flower Frog, 2 Nudes Kneeling, Ivory Matte Glaze, Chester Beach, 1927, 6 In. 348.00
Flower Frog, Flowers, Buds, Pink, Blue, Green, Shirayamadani, 1926, 4½ In. 465.00
Flower Holder, Frog On Lily Pads & Flowers, Blue Matte Glaze, 1927, 3¾ In. .... *illus* 460.00
Inkwell, Rook, Cover, Insert, Blue Matte Glaze, 7¼ In. 675.00
Jar, Cover, Apple Blossom Band, Blue Stems, Yellow Centers, Initials ETH, 3⅞ In. 235.00

Rookwood, Ewer, Grasses, Gold Threading On Neck, Anna Marie Bookprinter, 1886, 8½ In.
$460.00

Rookwood, Figurine, Mermaid, Light Green Matte Glaze, 1886, 16½ In.
$489.00

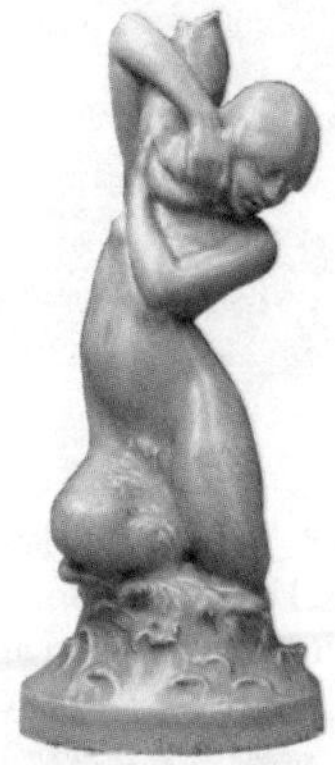

Rookwood, Flower Holder, Frog On Lily Pads & Flowers, Blue Matte Glaze, 1927, 3¾ In.
$460.00

Rookwood, Temple Jar, Blue High Glaze, Flowers & Rabbits, Pink Interior, Conant, 1920, 14 In.
$633.00

Rookwood, Trivet,
Dutch Mother & Child At Lake,
Footed, c.1927, 5¾ In.
$235.00

Rookwood, Trivet, Southern Belle,
Blue & Green Dress, High Glaze,
White Ground, 1922, 5¾ In.
$259.00

Rookwood, Vase, Band Of Flowers,
Brown Speckled Glaze On Top,
William Hentschel, 1925, 7¼ In.
$1265.00

Rookwood, Vase, Blue Flowers,
Green Leaves, Gray, Cream, Yellow,
Blue, Ed Diers, 1929, 8¾ In.
$920.00

Mug, Daffodil, Blue Matte Glaze, Vellum Glaze, Rose Fechheimer, 1905, 5⅝ In.	1620.00
Paperweight, 2 Geese, Brown Matte Glaze, 1912, 4 In.	489.00
Paperweight, Bunny, Orange, 1961	489.00
Paperweight, Burro, Pink, Red, Blue, On White Ground, 6 In.	175.00
Paperweight, Cat, Crouching, White, Pink Flowers, Green Leaves, 1946	465.00
Paperweight, Cat, Seated, Black High Glaze, Louise Abel, 1947, 6¾ x 4¾ In.	725.00
Paperweight, Cat, Seated, Medium Blue Matte Glaze, Arthur Conant, 1964, 4½ In.	405.00
Paperweight, Chick, 1934, 3¾ In.	489.00
Paperweight, Chick, Yellow, Louise Abel, 1934, 3¾ In.	484.00
Paperweight, Clipper Ship, Blue Matte Crystalline Glaze, 1930, 3¾ In.	345.00
Paperweight, Dog, Ivory Matte Glaze, 1928, 4¾ In.	920.00
Paperweight, Dog, Lying Down, Nubian Black Glaze, 1934, 2¼ x 4½ In.	620.00
Paperweight, Dog, Terrier, Ivory Matte Glaze, 1934, 4½ In.	399.00
Paperweight, Donkey, White, Louise Abel, 1932, 6 x 4½ In.	207.00
Paperweight, Elephant, Seated, Blue Matte Glaze, 1934, 4 In.	315.00
Paperweight, Elephant, Walking, Ivory Matte Glaze, William McDonald, 1927, 3 In.	290.00
Paperweight, Elephant, With Clowns, Brown, Tan, William McDonald, 1922	575.00
Paperweight, Goat, Light Green, Louise Abel, 1945, 6¼ In.	138.00
Paperweight, Kitten, On Back, Blue High Glaze, 1945, 3 In.	465.00
Paperweight, Lamb, Reclining, 1938, 2¾ x 5 In.	978.00
Paperweight, Lamb, Standing, White, 1945, 5 In.	185.00
Paperweight, Monkey, On Book, Mottled Dark Blue Matte Glaze, 1925, 3½ In.	620.00
Paperweight, Monkey, Sitting On Book, Gray Green Matte Glaze, 1929, 3½ In.	460.00
Paperweight, Nude, Ivory Matte Glaze, Louise Abel, 1932, 4 In.	267.00
Paperweight, Nude, Seated, c.1938, 4¼ In.	206.00
Paperweight, Nude Woman, Seated, 1928, 4¼ In.	374.00
Paperweight, Parrot, Louise Abel, 1931, 8 In.	1380.00
Paperweight, Penguin, White, Shirayamadani, 1934, 5 In.	575.00
Paperweight, Rabbit, Green Matte Glaze, 1931, 3 In.	400.00
Paperweight, Rabbit, Light Green, Louise Abel, 1951, 3¼ In.	748.00
Paperweight, Rook, Blue, Tan, 1925, 3 x 4 In.	690.00
Paperweight, Rook, On Pedestal, Green Matte Glaze, 1925, 3 In.	374.00
Paperweight, Rook, Standing Near Acorn, Blue, 1930, 4 In.	1020.00
Paperweight, Rook, Tan Matte Glaze, 1922	290.00
Paperweight, Rook With Acorn, 1924, 4 x 5 In.	1380.00
Paperweight, Rooster, Multicolord, Base, 1946, 5 In.	220.00
Paperweight, Rooster, Red, Yellow, Brown, Green Matte Glaze, William McDonald, 1943, 5 In.	550.00
Pencil Holder, Rooks, Trees, 5-Sided, Black Over Blue Matte Glaze, 1923, 4⅝ In.	450.00
Pin Tray, Nude Woman Wrapped Around Edge, Ivory Matte Glaze, 1930	219.00
Pitcher, Falling Leaves, Amelia Sprague, 1891, 8⅞ In.	431.00
Pitcher, Pink Glaze Rim, Green Matte Glaze, c.1904, 5¾ In.	264.00
Pitcher, Tricorner, Yellow Matte Glaze, Orange, 1905, 5 In.	345.00
Pitcher, Water, White Flowers, Green Stems, Limoges Green Glaze, Round, Cylindrical, 5 In.	201.00
Plaque, A Calm Evening, Vellum Glaze, Frame, Fred Rothenbusch, 1920, 11 x 8 In.	5100.00
Plaque, Birch Trees, Vellum Glaze, Frame, E.T. Hurley, 1912, 8 x 4 In.	3150.00
Plaque, Carl Malery Portrait, Hand On Chest, Dull Finish, Frame, Grace Young, 1902, 10 x 7 In.	2640.00
Plaque, Dry Creek, Vellum Glaze, Frame, Lorinda Epply, 1918, 8 x 5 In.	3500.00
Plaque, Fritz Van Houten Raymond & Bride, Profiles, Round, Louise Abel, 1942, 8 x 5 In.	400.00
Plaque, Landscape, River, Mountains, Vellum Glaze, Frame, Fred Rothenbusch, 10 x 12 In.	9200.00
Plaque, Mountain, Trees, Vellum Glaze, Sara Sax, 1915, 12⅛ x 9 In.	12000.00
Plaque, Mountains, Trees, Road, Vellum Glaze, Frame, Ed Diers, 1925, 9¾ x 11¾ In.	9850.00
Plaque, Pine Trees, Stream, Vellum Glaze, Frame, Lenore Asbury, 1929, 11 x 6¾ In.	7400.00
Plaque, Trees, River, Mountains, Vellum Glaze, Frame, E.T. Hurley, 1927, 8 x 10 In.	7100.00
Plaque, Woodland, Lake, Trees, Sunlit Mountain, Frame, C. McLaughlin, 1915, 4 x 6 In.	4140.00
Plate, Spider, Piecrust Edge, Limoges Glaze, Albert Humphreys, 1888, 6¾ In.	115.00
Potpourri Jar, Cutout Lid, Blue, 4¼ In.	115.00
Potpourri Jar, Reticulated Lid, Medium Blue Glaze, 1922, 2½ In.	175.00
Rose Bowl, Molded Ferns, Reticulated Rim, Green Matte Glaze, 1908, 2¾ x 8 In.	930.00
Sculpture, Nude Woman, Sitting, Louise Abel, 1941, 14 In.	3000.00
Tankard, Carved, Apple Branches, C.S. Todd, c.1912, 12 x 7 In.	900.00
Tea Set, Ship Border, White, Cornflower Blue Glaze, Impressed Mark, 24 Piece	558.00
Teapot, Flowers, Standard Glaze, Ed Diers, 7 In.	230.00
Temple Jar, Blue High Glaze, Flowers & Rabbits, Pink Interior, Conant, 1920, 14 In. . . . *illus*	633.00
Tile, Blue, Brown Matte Ground, Quatrelobed, Faience, 5⅞ In.	178.00
Tile, Brown Cross, Purple, Yellow, Faience, Impressed, Frame, 1941, 6 In.	188.00
Tile, Cat, White, Stripes, Gold Eyes, Oak Frame, 6 In.	725.00

Tile, Ducks At Edge Of Pond, Oak Frame, 1 x 10 x 5¾ In.	1380.00
Tile, Faience, Stylized Yellow Rose, Green Leaves, Pink Ground, Frame, 4 x 4 In.	360.00
Tile, Griffins, Birds, Matte, Gloss Glaze, Faience, 12 x 12 In.	1093.00
Tile, Magnolia Blooms, Pin, Yellow Matte, Green Leaf, Faience, 5⅞ In.	374.00
Tile, Woman, Hand On Tree, Green, Blue, Purple, Faience, 12 In.	1500.00
Tile, Woman, Picking Apples, Green, Blue, Purple, Brown, Faience, 12 In.	960.00
Tray, Bengal Brown Glaze, 1949, 4½ x 7 In.	748.00
Tray, Frog, Green Matte Glaze, 1922, 3 In.	978.00
Tray, Owl, Brown, Purple, Light Gray, 1952, 4¼ In.	140.00
Tray, Owl Perched On Limb, Black Matte Glaze, Green Highlights, 1929, 6 In.	127.00
Tray, Rook, Violet Gray Bird, Claire De Lune Glaze, 1954, 4⅜ In.	2630.00
Trivet, 2 Seagulls, Flying Above Waves, Blue, White, Green, Yellow, Round, 1921, 5½ In.	95.00
Trivet, 2 Seagulls, Flying Above Waves, Blue Matte Glaze, Round, 1916, 5½ In.	395.00
Trivet, 3 Geese, Pond, No. 3207, Frame, 1925, 5½ In.	1150.00
Trivet, 3 Geese, White, Green, Tan, 1930, 5⅞ In.	430.00
Trivet, Bluebird On Tree Branch, Blue Ground, Round, 1922, 6 In.	385.00
Trivet, Dutch Mother & Child At Lake, Footed, c.1927, 5¾ In. *illus*	235.00
Trivet, Grapes, Leaves, Vines, Blue, Green, Brown, 1920, 5⅞ In.	257.00
Trivet, Parrot, On Perch, Blue, Green, Yellow, 5½ In.	370.00
Trivet, Southern Belle, Blue & Green Dress, High Glaze, White Ground, 1922, 5¾ In. *illus*	259.00
Umbrella Stand, Warty, Thick Green Matte Glaze, Flared, 1902, 23⅞ In.	3030.00
Vase, 2 Peacocks, Seated On Branches, Carved, Matte Glaze, Charles Todd, 1912, 21¾ In.	7000.00
Vase, 3 Monkey, 3 Panels, Geometrics, Blue Matte Glaze, Flared, 1937, 10⅝ In.	790.00
Vase, 4 Leaves, Flowers, Maroon, 1912, 7⅝ In.	374.00
Vase, 4 Rooks Perched On Branches, Moon, Iris Glaze, 2 Handles, J.D. Wareham, 1897	1150.00
Vase, 6 Molded Leaves, Pink Matte Glaze, Green Glaze Highlights, 1920, 5 In.	142.00
Vase, American Indian, Maroon Matte Glaze, Blue Accents, Squat, 4¾ x 9 In.	189.00
Vase, American Indian, Sea Green, Squat, 3⅜ In.	259.00
Vase, Baluster, Amber Oak Leaves, Standard Glaze, Painted, 1903, 7¾ x 5 In.	600.00
Vase, Band Of Flowers, Brown Speckled Glaze On Top, William Hentschel, 1925, 7¼ In. *illus*	1265.00
Vase, Band Of Rooks Around Bottom, Pink, Gray, Production, 1922, 6⅝ In.	415.00
Vase, Birds, Clouds, Grasses, Green, Blue, Black, Standard Glaze, Humphreys, 10½ In.	1528.00
Vase, Birds On Branches, Purple, Leaves, Flowers, Vellum Glaze, Sara Sax, 1918, 9 In.	1380.00
Vase, Blossoms, Carved Mat, Wavy Ground, W. Hentschel, 1913, 11 x 4¾ In.	2280.00
Vase, Blue Daisies Border, White Ground, Katherine Van Horne, 1914, 6¼ In.	633.00
Vase, Blue Flowers, Green Leaves, Gray, Cream, Yellow, Blue, Ed Diers, 1929, 8¾ In. *illus*	920.00
Vase, Blue Leaves, Flowers, White Ground, Elizabeth Barrett, 1935, 8⅛ In.	1150.00
Vase, Bud, 3 Tiers, Crystalline Blue Matte Glaze, 1932, 7½ In.	230.00
Vase, Butterfly, Pink Matte Glaze, Cylindrical, c.1929, 6¾ In.	118.00
Vase, Catfish, Jumping Out Of Water, Sea Green Glaze, Silver Rim, Hurley, 1903, 10¼ In.	9750.00
Vase, Cattails, Blue High Glaze, 1946, 4¾ In.	88.00
Vase, Cherries, Green & Magenta Glaze, No. 837, Elizabeth Lincoln, 1918, 10½ In. *illus*	805.00
Vase, Cherry Blossoms, Mauve To Yellow Ground, Vellum Glaze, 15½ In.	2875.00
Vase, Cherry Boughs, Blossoms, White Band, Vellum Glaze, E. McDermott, 1916, 7⅝ In.	748.00
Vase, Chestnuts, Incised, Painted, Green Vellum, Marianne Mitchell, 1905, 5¼ In.	2580.00
Vase, Chrysanthemum, Embossed, Painted Matte, Indigo Ground, 1901, 8½ x 3½ In.	5100.00
Vase, Circles, Raised, Painted, Hi-Glaze, Bulbous, Flared, Loretta Holtkamp, 1951, 7¼ In.	550.00
Vase, Conifers, Tree Panels, Dark Blue Matte Glaze, Hexagonal, 4½ In.	345.00
Vase, Daisies, Gray, Vellum Glaze, Fred Rothenbusch, 1907, 9 x 3¾ In.	1140.00
Vase, Dark Green Matte Glaze, Light Green Interior, Melon Lobes, 1926, 5 In. *illus*	207.00
Vase, Dogwood, Sterling Silver Overlay, Long Neck, Shaded Ocher To Olive, 9½ In.	1440.00
Vase, Dragon, Brown Ground, c.1885, 10 In.	3107.00
Vase, Ducks, Trees, Lagoon, Purple Mountains, Blue Ground, Conant, 1920, 13¼ In.	10800.00
Vase, Embossed, Poppies, Green Matte Glaze, c.1907, 9¾ x 4 In.	780.00
Vase, Fish, Turquoise To Cream, Vellum Glaze, Edith Noonan, 1909, 6½ In.	748.00
Vase, Flowers, Bell Shaped, Pink, Carved, Brown, 1915, 7 x 4 In.	1440.00
Vase, Flowers, Blue Matte, 1924, 11½ In.	975.00
Vase, Flowers, Incised, Around Bottom, Speckled Brown Glaze Top, Hentschel, 1925, 7¼ In.	1265.00
Vase, Flowers, Leaves, Art Deco, Blue Vellum Glaze, Ed Diers, 1930, 6 In.	1500.00
Vase, Flowers, Blue Matte, Vellum, Shouldered, No. 1925, Margaret McDonald, 1919, 6⅝ In. *illus*	431.00
Vase, Flowers, Pink, Blue, Green, Orange, Vellum Glaze, Elizabeth McDermott, 1919, 13 In.	1950.00
Vase, Flowers, Vellum Glaze, Blue, Pink, Yellow, 12¾ x 6½ In.	5100.00
Vase, Flowers, Vines, Red, Green, White Ground, Hand Colored, 1946, 6¾ In., Pair	230.00
Vase, Flying Geese, Vellum Glaze, Indigo Ground, 1916, 8 x 4½ In.	1920.00
Vase, French Red, Roses, Cylindrical, Sara Sax, 1918, 10⅛ In.	3565.00

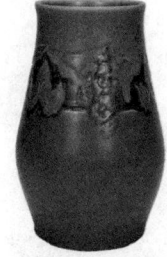

Rookwood, Vase, Cherries, Green & Magenta Glaze, No. 837, Elizabeth Lincoln, 1918, 10½ In. $805.00

Rookwood, Vase, Dark Green Matte Glaze, Light Green Interior, Melon Lobes, 1926, 5 In. $207.00

Rookwood, Vase, Flowers, Blue Matte, Vellum, Shouldered, No. 1925, Margaret McDonald, 1919, 6⅝ In. $431.00

Rookwood, Vase, Green Clover, Red Flowers, Yellow Matte Ground, K. Shirayamadani, 1928, 8 In. $2300.00

R

TIP
A matte glazed pottery piece can be rubbed with olive oil, then wiped clean.

Rookwood, Vase, Lilies Of The Valley, Vellum Glaze, Carl Schmidt, 1914, 10⅞ In.
$1093.00

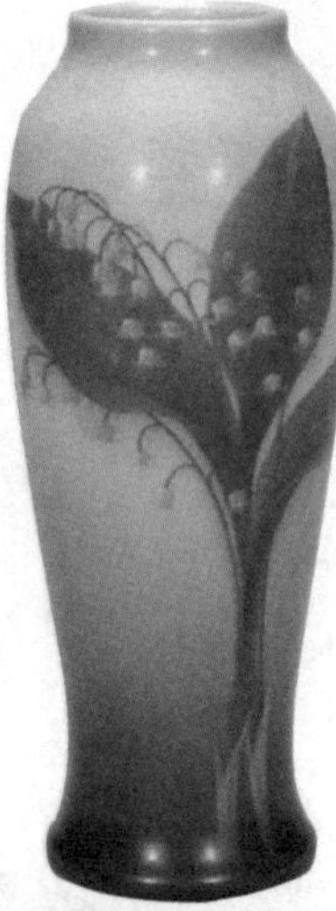

Rookwood, Vase, Morning Glories, Red, Pink, Blue, Black Opal, Swollen Neck, Harriet Wilcox, 1929, 8 In.
$5175.00

Rookwood, Vase, Ombroso, Carved & Painted Flowers, William Hentschel, 1914, 5⅝ x 6 In.
$2415.00

Vase, French Red, Sara Sax, 1917, 4⅝ In. 1050.00
Vase, Ginkgo Leaf, Nut Band, Squat, Vellum Glaze, E. Lincoln, c.1908, 4¼ x 4½ In. 1020.00
Vase, Grapes, Leaves, Purple, Green, Blue Ground, 1920, 13 x 8 In. 2760.00
Vase, Green Clover, Red Flowers, Yellow Matte Ground, K. Shirayamadani, 1928, 8 In. *illus* 2300.00
Vase, Green Holly Leaves, Red Berries, Black Ground, Black Iris, Sara Sax, 1906, 6¼ In. 6750.00
Vase, Hawthorne Flowers, Pink, Vellum Glaze, Fred Rothenbusch, 1931, 5⅝ In. 1580.00
Vase, Hydrangeas, Bottle Form, Flared Neck, Amelia B. Sprague, 12½ In. 546.00
Vase, Incised & Painted Shoulder, Pink, Purple, Tan Matte Glaze, Charles Todd, 1919, 6 In. 795.00
Vase, Iris, Blue, 1935, 5¼ In. 210.00
Vase, Iris, Lenore Asbury, 1904, 8½ In. 308.00
Vase, Irises, Yellow, Dark Yellow Ground, Harriet Wilcox, 1903, 10 In. 19000.00
Vase, Jewel, Bird In Peony Garden, Arthur Conant, 1921, 8 x 4 In. 2280.00
Vase, Jewel, Painted, Blue Ground, Big Flowers, Leaves, Jens Jensen, 1934, 4¾ In. 192.00
Vase, Lake, Pine Trees, Snow Tipped Mountains, Green Vellum Glaze, 1911, 7¾ In. 6900.00
Vase, Lanceolate Leaves, Turquoise Crystalline Glaze, Shouldered, Earl Menzel, 1936, 6 In. 790.00
Vase, Landscape, Vellum Glaze, Cylindrical, Fred Rothenbusch, 1920, 9⅝ x 4¼ In. 2703.00
Vase, Leaves, Berries, Blue Ground, Elizabeth Barrett, 1929, 5½ In. 748.00
Vase, Leaves, Cylindrical, Green Glaze, 1921, 7¼ In. 385.00
Vase, Leaves, Squeezebag, Brown, Turquoise, E.T. Hurley, c.1927, 9 x 7 In., Pair 2160.00
Vase, Lilies, Cornflowers, Black Opal Glaze, Harriet Wilcox, 13 In., Pair 8050.00
Vase, Lilies, White & Yellow, Bulbous, Kataro Shirayamadani, 1945, 5⅜ In. 1580.00
Vase, Lilies Of The Valley, Vellum Glaze, Carl Schmidt, 1914, 10⅞ In. *illus* 1093.00
Vase, Lotus Blossoms, White, Green, 1906, 6½ x 5 In. 1560.00
Vase, Magnolia, Mottled Pink To Green Matte Ground, M. McDonald, 1936, 6½ In. 705.00
Vase, Magnolia, White, Indigo Ground, 9 x 5 In. 1920.00
Vase, Molded Leaves, Blue High Glaze, 1932, 6¼ In. 142.00
Vase, Moresque, Maroon, Blue, Lavender, Green, McLaughlin, 1919, 5⅜ In. 1093.00
Vase, Morning Glories, Blue, Green Leaves, Brown Tendrils, Yellow Ground, Ley, 1945, 4¾ In. 465.00
Vase, Morning Glories, Red, Pink, Blue, Black Opal, Swollen Neck, Wilcox, 1929, 8 In. *illus* 5175.00
Vase, Narrow Mouth, Widening Cylindrical Shape, Pink Glaze, c.1920, 6¾ In. 176.00
Vase, Nude Figures, Gray Green Matte Glaze, Louise Abel, 1922, 4⅞ In. 465.00
Vase, Ombroso, Carved & Painted Flowers, William Hentschel, 1914, 5⅝ x 6 In. *illus* 2415.00
Vase, Painted Flower Poppies, Bugs, Shaded Ground, M.L. Perkins, 1894, 9¾ In. 690.00
Vase, Peach Matte Stippled Glaze, Tapering, c.1917, 10¾ In. 264.00
Vase, Pinecones, Carved Matte, Brown, Red Ground, Bulbous, 1906, 6 x 5 In. 1800.00
Vase, Pink Carnations, Green Leaves, Double Vellum, L. Epply, 1931, 4¾ In. 690.00
Vase, Pink Flower, Leafy Stem, Vellum Glaze, Edward Diers, c.1908, 8½ In. 436.00
Vase, Pink Matte Glaze, 2 Shaped Handles, Footed, 1928, 7½ In. *illus* 115.00
Vase, Pink Matte Glaze, Pale Green, 1920, 3 In. 150.00
Vase, Poppies, Cylindrical, Earth Tones, c.1900, 10½ In. 588.00
Vase, Poppies, Lavender, Iris Glaze, 1908, 8¾ x 3¾ In. 1560.00
Vase, Portrait, Actress Sarah Siddons, Painted, Standard Glaze, 8¾ x 4¼ In. 3120.00
Vase, Purple & Blue High Glaze, Shouldered, Tapered, 1938, 5½ x 4½ In. 420.00
Vase, Purple Glaze, Brown Matte Glaze, Shirayamadani, 4½ In. 403.00
Vase, Red Flowers, Green Leaves & Stems, Cylindrical, Sallie Coyne, c.1906, 8¼ In. 940.00
Vase, Red Nasturtiums, Buds, Green Ground, Iris Glaze, 7⅝ In. 1380.00
Vase, Rook, Trees, 5-Sided, Tan, Blue, 4⅝ In. 345.00
Vase, Rooks, Black, Carved, Painted, Sea Green Glaze, Matt Daly, 1899, 11½ In. 30000.00
Vase, Sculpted & Applied Morning Glories, Bulbous, 1882, 13 x 13 In. 800.00
Vase, Sparrows, Blooming Branch, Emerald Green Ground, 1920, 9½ x 3¾ In. 2280.00
Vase, Strawberry Plants, Cylindrical, Brown, c.1891, 12¾ In. 837.00
Vase, Swan Band, Water Lily Pond, Vellum Glaze, Ed Diers, c.1907, 8¾ x 4¾ In. 1560.00
Vase, Tan Matte Glaze, 1924, 17½ In. 460.00
Vase, Trumpet Shape, Amethyst Glossy Finish, c.1921, 10¾ In. 235.00
Vase, Trumpet Vines, Orange Flowers, Swirled, Ruffled Rim, J. Zettel, 1893, 5½ In. 748.00
Vase, Tulips, Leaves, Chocolate Brown Over Turquoise, Elizabeth Barrett, 1943, 5⅝ In. 615.00
Vase, Violets, Shaded Ground, Vellum Glaze, Bulbous, F. Rothenbusch, 1905, 8 x 4½ In. 1140.00
Vase, Waves Crashing Against Shoreline, Stormy Sky, Vellum Glaze, 9¼ In. 4485.00
Vase, Wax Matte, Birds, Sunflowers, Elizabeth Lincoln, c.1925, 17¼ x 8 In. 5400.00
Vase, Wax Matte, Flowers, Jewel Tone, Purple Ground, Squat, Louise Abel, 1923, 4 x 7 In. 1560.00
Vase, Wax Matte, Painted, Purple, Ivory Hollyhocks, Shirayamadani, 1939, 10 x 5½ In. 3900.00
Vase, White Calla Lilies, Blue Ground, Butterfat Glaze, William Hentschel, 1931, 13 In. 10000.00
Vase, White Flowers, Green Matte, Bulbous, Constance Baker, 5¼ In. *illus* 690.00
Vase, White Poppies, Iris Glaze, Katherine Van Horne, 1909, 6½ In. 1380.00
Vase, White Star Lilies, Yellow Centers, Shaded Lavender To Cream, Iris Glaze, 7½ In. 1150.00

Vase, Wild Roses, Standard Glaze, Irene Bishop, 1900, 5 In.	489.00
Vase, Windmills, Green Frothy Matte Glaze, 1901, 7½ x 5½ In.	1080.00
Vase, Woman Standing By Prunus Tree, Standard Glaze, Shirayamadani, 1896, 7 In.	7188.00
Vase, Woodsy Trillium, Standard Glaze, Jeanette Swing, 1902, 6¾ In.	575.00
Vase, Yellow Daffodils, Standard Glaze, Josephine Zettel, 12¼ In.	1035.00
Vase, Yellow Daffodils, Standard Glaze, Painted, Bulbous, 1896, 8 x 5½ In.	600.00
Vase, Yellow Flower, Green Leaves, Earth Tones, 7⅛ In.	294.00
Vase, Yellow Jonquils, Standard Glaze, Baluster, Mary Nourse, 1897, 9½ In. ....*illus*	920.00
Vase, Yellow Nasturtiums, Vellum Glaze, Painted, Pink, Blue Ground, Ed Diers, 7 x 5½ In.	780.00
Wall Pocket, Irises, Molded, Purple, 1923, 12½ In.	1900.00
Water Jug, Flying Owls, Bats, Full Moon, Berry Branches, M.L. Nichols, 1882	4485.00

RORSTRAND was established near Stockholm, Sweden, in 1726. By the nineteenth century Rorstrand was making English-style earthenware, bone china, porcelain, ironstone china, and majolica. The company is still working. The three crown mark has been used since 1884.

Baking Dish, Handle, Picknick Pattern, 11½ In.	85.00
Board, Tile, Picknick Pattern, 11 x 10 In.	150.00
Bowl, Nesting, Picknick Pattern, 1950s, 8½ In.	55.00
Bowl, Nesting, Picknick Pattern, 1950s, 10½ In.	25.00
Cup & Saucer, Set Of 4	125.00
Plate, Dessert, Astoria Pattern, White Ground, Steel Blue Lines, 1960s, 7 In.	4.00
Plate, Flow Blue Style, East Indies, Sweden Ship Logo, 10¾ In.	50.00
Plate, Mother's Day, 1971, Happy Collecting, 8¼ In.	35.00
Platter, Purple, Landscape Scene, Scalloped Rim, c.1790, 12 x 10 In.	450.00
Pot, Street Crowns Union, c.1910, 8¼ x 9½ In.	475.00
Vase, Brown Glaze, Marked, 7¼ In.	65.00
Vase, Brown Mottled Glaze, Style Band On Shoulder, Marked, c.1920, 12 In.	365.00
Vase, Storks In Flight, High Relief, Pale Blue Ground, Marked, c.1900, 32¼ In.	9000.00
Vase, Tan & Blue Crystalline Glaze, Tapered, Marked, 7½ x 3½ In.	510.00

ROSALINE, *see Steuben category.*

ROSE BOWLS were popular during the 1880s. Rose petals were kept in the open bowl to add fragrance to a room, a popular idea in a time of limited personal hygiene. The glass bowls were made with crimped tops, which kept the petals inside. Many types of Victorian art glass were made into rose bowls.

Opalescent, Green Stripes, Enameled Lilies, Orange Belt, Folded Over Rim, 5 In.	12.00
Opaque, Yellow, Footed, Egg Shape, Multicolored Scrolling, Late 1800s, 6½ In.	94.00
Satin Glass, Egg Shape, Turquoise To Cream, Late 1800s, 3¼ In.	176.00

ROSE CANTON china is similar to Rose Mandarin and Rose Medallion, except no people or birds are pictured in the decoration. It was made in China during the nineteenth and twentieth centuries in greens, pinks, and other colors.

Garden Seat, Drum Shape, 19 In., Pair	5405.00
Pitcher, 3¼ In.	155.00
Plate, 10¾ In.	300.00
Plate, 19th Century, 10 In.	125.00
Plate Warmer, 3 x 10 In.	400.00
Teapot, Strawberry Finial, c.1800, 6 x 9 In.	750.00
Vase, Iron Red Ground, Chinese Export, 12 In.	266.00

ROSE MANDARIN china is similar to Rose Canton and Rose Medallion. If the panels in the design picture only people and not birds, it is Rose Mandarin.

Basin, 19th Century, 5 x 16 In.	823.00
Cup & Saucer, c.1840, 2½ x 4 x 4¾ & 6 In.	295.00
Plate, 5 Scenes, Fluted, Square, Notched Corners, 19th Century	448.00
Plate, Porcelain, Chinese, c.1830, 8¼ In., 5 Piece	590.00
Plate, Soup, Courtly Figures, Armorial, Round Reserve, Early 1800s, 10 In., Pair	1410.00
Punch Bowl, Courtiers In Butterfly Border, 19th Century	2988.00
Punch Bowl, Courtiers Outside, Trellis & Scrolls Inside, 1800s, 10¼ In. Diam.	1016.00
Razor Box, Center Divider, c.1800, 8½ x 4½ x 3 In.	1650.00
Serving Dish, Oval, Enameled Courtyard Figures, Footed, 3¼ x 11 In., Pair	2233.00

Rookwood, Vase, Pink Matte Glaze,
2 Shaped Handles, Footed,
1928, 7½ In.
$115.00

Rookwood, Vase, White Flowers,
Green Matte, Bulbous,
Constance Baker, 5¼ In.
$690.00

Rookwood, Vase, Yellow Jonquils,
Standard Glaze, Baluster,
Mary Nourse, 1897, 9½ In.
$920.00

R

How Old is Your Famille Rose

Famille Rose (rose family) porcelain is a five-color Chinese porcelain. Collectors have named three patterns of Famille Rose: Rose Medallion, Rose Mandarin, and Rose Canton.

Age can be told by color and glaze. Early pieces had a thick, opaque, muddy mauve pink glaze. By the 1730s, the glaze was opaque rose pink, often mixed with white. By 1800 the rose glaze was thin and almost translucent. Late eighteenth-century pieces are more valuable than later brilliantly colored and carelessly painted late nineteenth-century pieces.

Rose Mandarin, Vase, Raised Serpent, Foo Dog Handles, 24 In., Pair
$4025.00

Rose Medallion, Cadogan, Pot, Shaped Spout & Handle, 5½ In.
$390.00

Tureen, Sauce, Oval, Panels, Double Handles, 6 x 8 In.	1265.00
Vase, Blue Greek Key, Foo Dog Handles, 12¼ x 4½ In.	850.00
Vase, Green Cartouche, Foo Dog Handles, 7¾ x 3¾ In.	575.00
Vase, Qilins, Foo Dog Handles, 13 In.	354.00
Vase, Raised Serpent, Foo Dog Handles, 24 In., Pair .....*illus*	4025.00

ROSE MEDALLION china was made in China during the nineteenth and twentieth centuries. It is a distinctive design with four or more panels of decoration around a central medallion that includes a bird or a peony. The panels show birds and people. The background is a design of tree peonies and leaves. Pieces are colored in greens, pinks, and other colors. It is similar to Rose Canton and Rose Mandarin.

Bowl, Black Border Cartouches, 6 x 15 In.	1035.00
Bowl, Cut Corner, 19th Century, 4¾ x 9¼ In.	353.00
Bowl, Porcelain, Cut Corner, Gilt Monogram, 4⅝ x 10 In.	588.00
Bowl, Round, Late 19th Century, 4¼ x 10⅝ In.	558.00
Cadogan, Pot, Shaped Spout & Handle, 5½ In. .....*illus*	390.00
Candlestick, Mid 19th Century, 7¾ In., Pair	418.00
Chamber Pot, Cover, 19th Century, 7 x 11½ In.	470.00
Dish, 4 Panels, Figures, Flowers, Birds, Gilt Bronze Rim & Handles, 12 In.	528.00
Dish, Figures, Leaves, Butterflies, Reserve Panels, Late 1800s, 13½ In.	440.00
Oil Lamp Stand, Removable Font, Urn Shape, Chinese Export, c.1860, 13 In., Pair	575.00
Plate, Chinese Export, 9½ In., 6 Piece	374.00
Plate, Enamel, Gilt, 9¼ In., 6 Piece	588.00
Platter, Figures, Chinese Export, 14½ In.	112.00
Platter, Figures, Patio, Oval, Mid 19th Century, 12 x 9½ In.	175.00
Platter, Oval, Canton, 12 x 9 x 1 In.	300.00
Platter, Oval, Late 19th Century, 13⅜ In.	206.00
Punch Bowl, 19th Century, 14½ In.	472.00
Punch Bowl, c.1830, 16 In.	3910.00
Punch Bowl, Flowers, Central Medallion, Reserve Panels, 19th Century, 13¾ In.	1920.00
Punch Bowl, Panels, 19th Century, 6 x 15 In.	1668.00
Punch Bowl, People, Butterflies, 13½ In.	1645.00
Punchbowl, Panel Decoration, 19th Century, 6¼ x 14½ In.	1380.00
Teapot, Basketry Holder, Drum Shape Pot, Handles, Flat Lid, 5½ In.	144.00
Teapot, Cover, Flared Body, Dome Lid, 1900s, 8 In.	360.00
Tureen, Cover, Figures, Scenes, 8-Sided, c.1875, 4 x 7 x 8 In.	80.00
Umbrella Jar, Chinese, c.1840, 25 x 9 In.	2633.00
Umbrella Stand, Porcelain, Chinese, 20th Century, 18 In.	153.00
Vase, Baluster Shape, Dragon Handles, Court Figures, Flowers, Butterflies, 24½ In.	1527.00
Vase, Flared Rim, Urn Shape, Gilt Salamander, c.1920, 18 In.	230.00
Vase, Oval, Brocade, Gilt, Lion Head Ring Handles, 10 In.	472.00
Warming Dish, 5 Scenes, Handles, 19th Century	329.00

ROSE O'NEILL, *see Kewpie category.*

ROSE TAPESTRY porcelain was made by the Royal Bayreuth factory of Tettau, Germany, during the late nineteenth century. The surface of the porcelain was pressed against a coarse fabric while it was still damp, and the impressions remained on the finished porcelain. It looks and feels like a textured cloth. Very skillful reproductions are being made that even include a variation of the Royal Bayreuth mark, so be careful when buying.

Basket, Pink Rose, Royal Bayreuth, 5¼ In.	150.00
Basket, White & Lavender, Japanese Chrysanthemums, Royal Bayreuth, 6¾ In.	575.00
Basket, White Rose, Royal Bayreuth, 4 In.	125.00
Bowl, Royal Bayreuth, 10¾ In.	300.00
Box, Cover, Violets, Royal Bayreuth, 4 In.	200.00
Box, Pink, Yellow, White Roses, Buckle Shape Cover, Royal Bayreuth, 2 x 4¾ In.	175.00
Chocolate Pot, Roses, Pink, Yellow, White, Royal Bayreuth, 8½ In.	800.00
Creamer, Pink, Yellow, White Roses, Pinched Spout, Royal Bayreuth, 4 In.	100.00
Creamer, Pink, Yellow & White Roses, Blue Mark, Royal Bayreuth, 3¼ In.	425.00
Creamer, Pink Roses, Yellow Roses, 3½ In.	160.00
Dish, Leaf, Roses, 4¼ x 5 In.	175.00
Dresser Box, Royal Bayreuth, 3¼ x 2¼ In.	245.00
Hair Receiver, Peach, Pink Roses, Muted Daisies	379.00
Hair Receiver, Pink Rose, Cover, Royal Bayreuth, 4 In.	75.00
Hair Receiver, Pink Roses, Misty Green Ground	195.00

Hatpin Holder, Pink Rose, Royal Bayreuth, 4½ In.	200.00
Powder Box, Cover, Pink, Yellow & White, Royal Bayreuth, 4 In.	20.00
Relish, Pink Roses, Handle, Royal Bayreuth, 7¾ In.	125.00
Saltshaker, Roses, Pink, Yellow, White, Royal Bayreuth, 3½ In.	40.00
Shoe, Woman's, High Heel, Pink Rose, Royal Bayreuth, 3½ In.	375.00
Sugar, Cover, 3 Roses, Pink, White & Yellow, Blue Mark, 3½ In.	210.00
Sugar, Wild Flower, Handles, Royal Bayreuth	70.00
Vase, Gold Rim, Royal Bayreuth, 6 In.	350.00

ROSEMEADE Pottery of Wahpeton, North Dakota, worked from 1940 to 1961. The pottery was operated by Laura A. Taylor and her husband, R.I. Hughes. The company was also known as the Wahpeton Pottery Company. Art pottery and commercial wares were made.

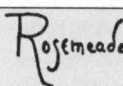

Bell, Pink Rose, Green Leaves, 3½ In.	165.00
Figure, Moccasin, Maroon, Black, Signed	65.00
Figure, Pheasant, Marked, 3 In.	50.00
Figure, Seal, 1¾ In. Tallest Seal, 3 Piece	74.00
Flower Holder, Heron, 1950s, 6¾ In.	87.00
Salt & Pepper, Bear, Brown, Seated, 3¼ In.	77.00
Salt & Pepper, Bears, 1950s, 3½ In.	75.00
Salt & Pepper, Cat, Black, 3 In.	89.00
Salt & Pepper, Coyote, Howling, 3¼ In. & 2¾ In.	275.00
Salt & Pepper, Duck, Black, 2½ In. & 2¼ In.	82.00
Salt & Pepper, Flamingo, 4½ In.	37.50
Salt & Pepper, Mice, 1¾ In. & 1 In.	95.00
Salt & Pepper, Pheasant, Squat, 1½ x 5¼ In.	99.00
Salt & Pepper, Pheasant, Tail, 4 In.	129.00
Salt & Pepper, Pheasant, Tail Down, 2¾ In.	72.00
Salt & Pepper, Prairie Rose, 2½ In.	65.00
Salt & Pepper, Siamese Cat, 2¾ In.	65.00
Vase, Green, Ruffled Rim, Flared, Marked, 4¼ x 3 In.	68.00

ROSENTHAL porcelain was made at the factory established in Selb, Bavaria, in 1880. The factory is still making fine-quality tablewares and figurines. A series of Christmas plates was made from 1910. Other limited edition plates have been made since 1971. In 1998 Rosenthal was acquired by the Waterford Wedgwood Group.

MARKE

Bowl, Vegetable, Summerwind, Round, 9½ In.	69.00
Centerpiece, Pedestal Base, Upright Arms Emerging From Bowl, 1980, 22½ In.	472.00
Coffeepot, Sansoucci, Mini, 3 Cup, 9 In.	100.00
Coffeepot, Summerwind, Platinum Trim	99.00
Creamer, Maria, 5½ x 5 In.	25.00
Cup & Saucer, Demitasse, Footed, Peonies, Roses, Blue, Yellow & Purple Flowers	39.00
Cup & Saucer, Dignity, Cobalt Blue, Gold Wheat, 4⅛ & 5⅞ In.	35.00
Dinner Service, Allegorical Figures In Center, Gilt Border, Austria, 20 Piece	263.00
Dinner Service, Eminence Pattern, White, Dark Blue Rim, Gold Edge, 1970s, 47 Piece	2351.00
Eggcup, Moss Rose, Sterling Silver Base, 2¾ x 2¼ In.	25.00
Figurine, Ballerina, Light Green Costume, Aqua Slippers, Signed, 1940s, 9 x 9½ In.	650.00
Figurine, Dog, Springer Spaniel, Impressed M. Fritz, c.1939, 5¼ x 9 In.	450.00
Figurine, Fawn, Lying Down, Heidenreich, Green Mark, 5 x 11 In.	450.00
Figurine, Flapper, Arm Outstretched, White, Stepped Octagonal Base, 13 In.	264.00
Figurine, Horse, Gray Dapple, Oval Base, 20th Century, 7 In.	118.00
Figurine, Laughing Rabbit, White, 6½ In.	60.00
Figurine, Reclining Nude, White, Fritz Klimsch, 20th Century, 16 In.	392.00
Gravy Boat, Chrysanthemum Floral, Purple & Yellow, Green Leaves	65.00
Gravy Boat, Quince, 4½ x 4⅛ x 3½ In.	28.00
Gravy Boat, Underplate, Summerwind	75.00
Group, Dancing Twins, White, Art Deco, Lore Friedrich-Gronau, 11 x 8 In.	595.00
Group, Little Boy Holding Baby Lamb, Karl Himmelstoss, 1948, 6 x 4½ In.	350.00
Group, Young Man On Bent Knee, Offering Heart To Girl, R. Peynet, 9½ In. ......*illus*	235.00
Plate, Annette, Gold Trim, 9¾ In.	26.00
Plate, Bread & Butter, Rosenthal Rose, 6¼ In.	10.00
Plate, Dessert, Cobalt Blue, Gold Wheat, 6 In.	25.00
Plate, Salad, Louis XIV, Marked, 7½ In.	24.00
Plate, Salad, Vienna, Center Flowers, 7½ In.	26.00
Plate, Wild Violets, Pink, Yellow, Green, Orange, Signed, Kimmel, 6⅞ In.	25.00

Rosenthal

Rosenthal made dishes to use in the dining room in the early 1900s. In 1916 they introduced a white, angular shape, Maria, with pomegranates in relief. In the 1920s and 1930s, figurines of theatrical characters and people in everyday clothes were best-sellers. In the 1950s, rimless plates, straight-sided teapots, and cups were combined in sets. Decorations were usually geometric shapes in muted colors or bold designs in black or maroon. Pastel-colored vases had tall necks, cylinder or egg shapes, or abstract shapes with off-center flower holes. More abstract shapes and designs were created in the 1970s and '80s. Studio-Line tableware, introduced in 1961, is still being made.

Rosenthal, Group, Young Man On Bent Knee, Offering Heart To Girl, R. Peynet, 9½ In. $235.00

R

Roseville, Apple Blossom, Planter, Underplate, Pink Matte Glaze, Flared, 6 x 8 In.
$100.00

Roseville, Clematis, Candlestick, Yellow Flower, Striated Blue & Green Ground, Waisted, 5 In., Pair
$134.00

Roseville, Columbine, Vase, Peach Flowers, Pink, Cylindrical, Swollen, Handles, Footed, 10 In.
$162.00

Roseville, Jonquil, Vase, Textured Ground, Bulbous, Tapered, Handles, 6¾ In.
$125.00

Platter, Ceres, Gray Trim, 13 x 8½ In.	32.00
Platter, Summerwind, 13¼ In.	99.00
Saucer, Donatello, Marked, 5¾ In.	24.00
Server, Footed, Floral Center, Blue Scalloped Border, Gold Trim, 9½ In.	175.00
Sugar, Cover, Ceres, Gray Trim, 2⅞ x 3½ In.	26.00
Sugar, Cover, Maria, 6½ x 3½ In.	28.00
Sugar, Cover, Quince, Gold Trim, 2¾ In.	26.00
Sugar, Cover, Summerwind	55.00
Sugar, Pompadour Style, Orange Poppies, Cream, Ruffled Top, Lid, Gold Finial, 4 In.	55.00
Teapot, Summerwind	99.00
Vegetable, Cover, Summerwind	115.00

ROSEVILLE Pottery Company was organized in Roseville, Ohio, in 1890. Another plant was opened in Zanesville, Ohio, in 1898. Many types of pottery were made until 1954. Early wares include Sgraffito, Olympic, and Rozane. Later lines were often made with molded decorations, especially flowers and fruit. Most pieces are marked *Roseville*. Many reproductions made in China have been offered for sale the past few years.

Apple Blossom, Jardiniere, Pedestal, Base, Pink, 10 x 21¾ In.	173.00
Apple Blossom, Planter, Underplate, Pink Matte Glaze, Flared, 6 x 8 In. .... *illus*	100.00
Azurean, Candlestick, Clover, Blue, White, Impressed, 9 In.	465.00
Baneda, Vase, Green, 2 Handles, Footed, 6⅛ In.	465.00
Baneda, Vase, Green, 2 Handles, Footed, 7⅛ In.	575.00
Baneda, Vase, Pink, 2 Handles, Footed, 6 In.	221.00 to 295.00
Baneda, Vase, Pink, Bulbous, 10¼ x 7½ In.	510.00
Baneda, Vase, Pink, Footed, Handles, 12 In.	1150.00
Baneda, Vase, Pink, Globular Shape, 1933, Gold Foil Label, 5 x 6 In.	855.00
Bittersweet, Tea Set, Blue, Branch Handles, 3 Piece	230.00
Carnelian I, Bowl, Rose Matte, Flared, Handles, Drainage Hole In Base, 14½ In.	90.00
Carnelian I, Vase, Geometric Design, Mottled Green & Blue Matte, Handles, 8½ x 10 In.	605.00
Carnelian I, Vase, Multitoned Rose Matte, Shouldered Form, Paper Label, 9 In.	240.00
Carnelian I, Vase, Rose Matte, Double Gourd, Handles, 7 In.	290.00
Carnelian II, Vase, Pink, 2 Handles, 5 In.	368.00
Checkerboard, Jardiniere, Bowl, Footed, Spade Shape Buttresses, 10¼ x 12½ In.	360.00
Chloron, Umbrella Stand, Flowers, Long Stem, Raised, Green Matte Glaze, 22½ x 11 In.	1000.00
Clemana, Flower Frog, 4¼ x 3¼ In.	88.00
Clematis, Candlestick, Yellow Flower, Striated Blue & Green Ground, Waisted, 5 In., Pair *illus*	134.00
Clematis, Console, Blue, 3½ x 6½ In.	70.00
Clematis, Jardiniere, Brown, 6¼ x 9 In.	147.00
Columbine, Basket, Blue, Shaped Handle, Footed, 12½ In.	316.00
Columbine, Vase, Peach Flowers, Pink, Cylindrical, Swollen, Handles, Footed, 10 In. ...... *illus*	162.00
Creamware, Bowl, 6 Puppies, 2⅛ In.	378.00
Creamware, Breakfast Set, Sun Bonnet Girls, Bowl, Mug, Creamer, Cup, Saucer, Baby Bowl	275.00
Creamware, Creamer, Puppy, 2 Handles Mug, Bowl, Plate	267.00
Creamware, Plate, Fancy Cat, Stamped, 7½ In.	625.00
Creamware, Stein Set, Elk, 6 Mugs, 11½ x 6 In. Pitcher	267.00
Cremo, Vase, Stylized Flowers, Grapes, Vines, Pink, Yellow, Green, 7½ In.	2020.00 to 2500.00
Cremona, Vase, Pink, Footed, Flared Rim, 12 In.	400.00
Dahlrose, Jardiniere, Pedestal, Bulbous, Ivory Flowers, Mottled Orange Ground, 30 In.	400.00 to 705.00
Dawn, Ewer, Green, White, Square Footed, Impressed, 15⅝ In.	220.00
Donatello, Powder Jar, 1930, 2 x 5 In.	88.00
Donatello, Vase, Green, Fluted, Flared, Footed, 5¾ In.	259.00
Egypto, Lamp, 3 Figural Elephants, Riders, Encircle Base, 10¼ In.	3070.00
Falline, Vase, Blue, 2 Handles, Footed, 6⅛ In.	420.00
Falline, Vase, Brown, Gourd, Handles, 7½ In.	690.00
Ferella, Bowl, Brown, Built-In Flower Frog, 3½ x 9⅜ In.	180.00
Ferella, Console, Brown, 13 In.	845.00
Freesia, Tea Set, Green Ground, White & Lavender Flowers, 3 Piece	410.00
Freesia, Teapot, Green, 7¼ In.	144.00
Fuchsia, Basket, Brown, 10 In.	431.00
Fuchsia, Urn, Green, Double Handle, 4 In.	70.00
Futura, Jardiniere, Leaf Design, Orange Ground, Handles, 9 x 13 In.	500.00
Futura, Planter, Hanging, Conical, Ribbed Rim, Gray Glaze, 1900s, 6½ x 8¾ In.	235.00
Futura, Vase, Candlestick, Triangular, Pedestal Foot, Blue Glaze, 8¼ & 2½ In.	353.00
Futura, Vase, Graduated Opening, Square Body, Yellow Glaze, Brown, Green, 6 In.	264.00
Futura, Vase, Green, Stepped Base, Buttresses, 12¼ x 5 In.	960.00
Futura, Vase, Mauve Thistle, Footed, 8⅛ In.	935.00

R

Futura, Vase, Mottled Orange & Green, Telescope Shape, 2 Handles, 7⅛ In. 323.00
Futura, Vase, Pink Twist, 8⅛ In. 433.00
Imperial I, Vase, Pink, Blue & Green Drip, Shouldered, 8½ In. 1060.00
Imperial I, Vase, Yellow & Green Drip, Blue Glaze, Swollen, Paper Label, 11 In. 1800.00
Imperial II, Vase, Runny Yellow, Brown & Blue Matte Glaze, 8½ In. 1065.00
Iris, Vase, Blue, Flat Sides, 2 Handles, 1930s, 8 In. 235.00
Jonquil, Vase, Brown, 2 Handles, 7⅛ In. 257.00
Jonquil, Vase, Textured Ground, Bulbous, Handles, 6¾ In. *illus* 125.00
La Rose, Vase, Cream, Raised Flowers, Flared Rim, Handles, c.1930, 4½ In. 120.00
Magnolia, Bowl, Orange & Green Matte Glaze, Footed, 2 Handles, 10 In. *illus* 66.00
Ming Tree, Vase, Blue High Glaze, Gnarled Branch Handles, 8½ In. *illus* 179.00
Mock Orange, Jardiniere, Pedestal, Flowers, Pink, Marked, 24¾ In. 345.00
Morning Glory, Vase, Green, 2 Handles, Footed, 9¼ In. 405.00
Morning Glory, Vase, Green, Ball Shape, Handles, 6 x 7 In. 575.00
Morning Glory, Vase, Green, Gourd, 2 Handles, 6⅛ In. 320.00
Morning Glory, Vase, Green, Trumpet Form, 2 Handles, 8¼ In. 465.00
Morning Glory, Vase, Green Ground, Footed, 2 Handles, 9⅜ x 7½ In. 470.00
Morning Glory, Vase, Ivory, Gourd, 2 Handles, 6⅛ In. 295.00
Morning Glory, Wall Pocket, Green, Double, 8½ In. 480.00
Moss, Vase, Pink, 2 Handles, Footed, Marked, 7¼ In. 405.00
Mostique, Basket, Hanging, Stylized Flowers, Leaves, Brown, Green, Lilac, 5½ x 8¾ In. 147.00
Mostique, Jardiniere, Gray, Geometric Design, Glossy Glaze, 9 x 11 In. 147.00
Mostique, Vase, Tan, Cylindrical, Green Flowers, 6 In. 345.00
Mostique, Vase, Tan, Cylindrical, Green Leaves, 10 In. 320.00
Mostique, Vase, Tan, Cylindrical, White Flowers, 7¾ In. 378.00
Mostique, Vase, Tan, White Flowers, Green Leaves, Bulbous, 11⅝ In. 487.00
Pine Cone, Bowl, Brown, 9 In. 88.00
Pine Cone, Jardiniere, Stand, Blue, 32 x 13½ In. 1645.00
Pine Cone, Planter, Green, Brown Matte Glaze, Branch Handle, 8½ In. *illus* 100.00
Pine Cone, Tray, 2 Sections, Open Arched & Looped Handle, 6½ x 13 In. 316.00
Pine Cone, Vase, 2 Handles, Footed, Impressed, 10¼ In. 433.00
Pine Cone, Vase, Brown, Flat Form, Handles, Marked, 8½ x 9 In. 620.00
Pine Cone, Vase, Tapered, Footed, Branch Handles, 10¼ In. 294.00
Pine Cone, Vase, Twig Handles, 10 In. 330.00
Pine Cone, Wall Pocket, Blue, Double, 8 In. 420.00
Pitcher, Basin, Colonial, Blue, Early, 4½ x 15½ In. 150.00
Pitcher, Man With Horn, Jester With Stein, Raised, Green, Brown, Cream, Early, 7⅜ In. 320.00
Pitcher, Owl Sitting In Tree, Brown, Green, Cream Ground, Early, 6⅝ In. 285.00
Pitcher, Teddy Bears Dressed As Boy & Girl, Brown, Green, Yellow, Blue, Cream, Early, 6 In. 1015.00
Pitcher, Tulip, Painted, Early, 8 x 8 In. 76.00
Poppy, Ewer, Pink, 10¾ In. 173.00
Poppy, Vase, Yellow Flowers, Green Leaves, Pink & Green Ground, 2 Low Handles, 6 In. *illus* 87.00
Raymor, Bun Warmer, Brown Matte Glaze, 6 x 12 In. 1265.00
Rozane, Pitcher, Egypto, Raised Geometrics, Green Matte Glaze, Handle, Mark, 11 x 5 In. 330.00
Rozane, Vase, Boat, Lake, Mountains, Blue, Handles, Ruffled Rim, Pillow Form, 9 x 12 In. 3625.00
Rozane, Vase, Dog With Woodcock, Brown Glaze, Ruffled Rim, Handles, 9 x 12 In. 1430.00
Rozane, Vase, Old Tuttle Homestead, Brown, Ruffled Rim, Pillow, Handles, 9 x 12 In. 460.00
Rozane, Vase, Portrait, Shakespeare, Brown To Green Glaze, Loop Handles, 13 x 7 In. 633.00
Rozane Royal, Pitcher, Light, Currants, Sprigs, Cream, Gray, Marked, 5¾ In. 395.00
Rozane Royal, Vase, Brown, Spaniel, Pheasant, Pillow, Handles, Signed, Timberlake, 11 In. 1840.00
Russco, Vase, Green, Footed, Flared Lip, Marked, 8¼ In. 378.00
Sign, Roseville, Rose Matte Glaze, 2 x 6¼ In. 1485.00
Sunflower, Vase, Bulbous, Brown & Green, 8⅛ In. 1015.00
Sunflower, Vase, Gourd, Green, 2 Handles, 9⅛ In. 1250.00
Sunflower, Vase, Green, 10⅛ In. 1700.00
Teasel, Vase, Ivory To Terra-Cotta, Cutout Around Rim, 2 Handles, 6 In. 109.00
Tourist, Vase, Lady Driving Car, Flared Rim, 9¼ In. 1600.00
Tourist, Window Box, Motor Car Being Pulled By Horses, 7 x 13 x 8 In. 1990.00
Tourmaline, Vase, Blue, Ocher Highlights, 2 Handles, Footed, 8¼ In. 131.00
Tourmaline, Vase, Blue, Twisted Form, Marked, 8¼ In. 171.00
Tourmaline, Vase, Mottled Green, Flared, Footed, 8¼ In. 267.00
Tourmaline, Vase, Powder Blue, 2 Handles, 12¼ In. 625.00
Tourmaline, Vase, Turquoise, Bulbous, Flared, 10¼ In. 230.00
Tourmaline, Vase, Turquoise, Cornucopia Shape, Footed, 9¼ In. 208.00
Victorian Art, Vase, Brown, Band Of Leaves, 6⅛ In. 489.00
Vintage, Planter, Brown, Liner, Marked, 5½ x 12 In. 555.00
Vista, Jardiniere, Pedestal, Trees, Blue, Green, Purple, 36½ In. 1300.00

Roseville, Magnolia, Bowl, Orange & Green Matte Glaze, Footed, 2 Handles, 10 In.
$66.00

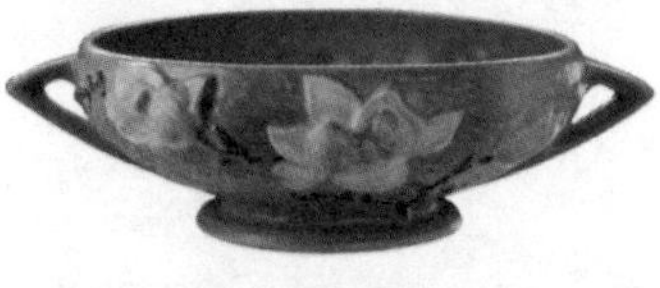

Roseville, Ming Tree, Vase, Blue High Glaze, Gnarled Branch Handles, 8½ In.
$179.00

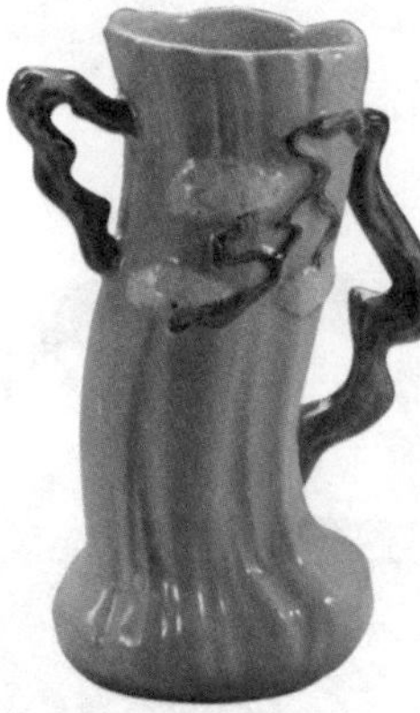

Roseville, Pine Cone, Planter, Green, Brown Matte Glaze, Branch Handle, 8½ In.
$100.00

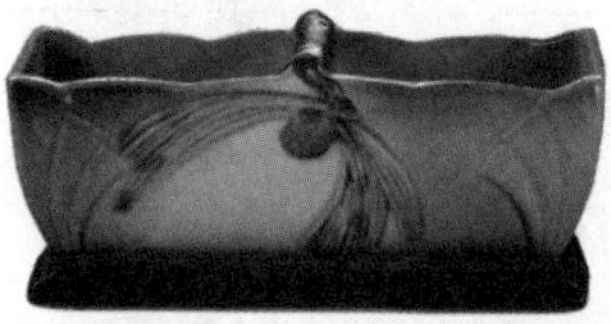

Roseville, Poppy, Vase, Yellow Flowers, Green Leaves, Pink & Green Ground, 2 Low Handles, 6 In.
$87.00

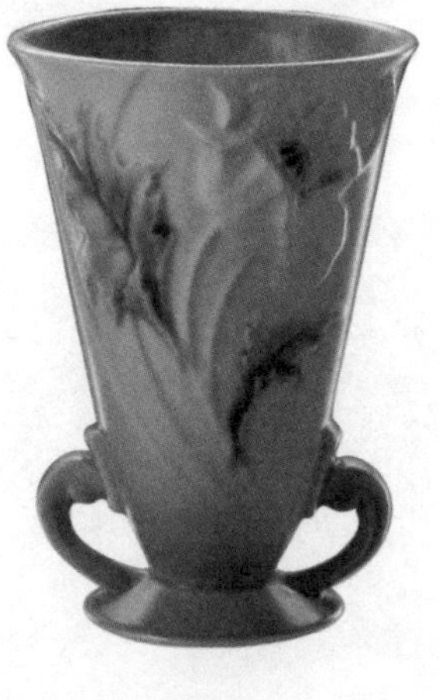

Roseville, Zephyr Lily, Basket, Pink & Yellow Flowers, Green Ground, Arched Handle, 7½ In. $75.00

Royal Bayreuth, Pitcher, Green Leaves, Free-Form Mold, Gold Twig Handle, c.1900, 7 In. $294.00

Vista, Jardiniere, Trees, Green, Gray Ground, 10¼ x 12 In.	588.00
Vista, Vase, Palm Trees, Marked, 17¾ In.	1500.00
Vista, Vase, Trees, Green, Gray, Purple, 2 Handles, 14⅝ In.	1090.00
Vista, Vase, Trees, Green, Gray Ground, Handles, Marked, 9½ In.	795.00
Windsor, Vase, Blue, Flared, 2 Handles, 7¼ In.	328.00
Wisteria, Vase, Blue, 2 Handles, Footed, Marked, 8⅛ In.	575.00
Wisteria, Vase, Blue, Squat, 2 Handles, 4 In.	345.00
Wisteria, Vase, Brown, 2 Handles, Footed, 8¼ In.	257.00
Wisteria, Vase, Brown, Flared, Lower Handles, Kiln Mark, 9 In.	600.00
Wisteria, Vase, Brown, Gourd, 2 Handles, 6½ In.	489.00
Wisteria, Vase, Brown & Blue, Footed, Lower Handles, 8 In.	575.00
Wisteria, Vase, Oval, Stand-Up Rim, 2 Handles On Shoulder, 6 In.	288.00
Zephyr Lily, Basket, Pink & Yellow Flowers, Green Ground, Arched Handle, 7½ In. ....*illus*	75.00
Zephyr Lily, Vase, Green, 1946, 7½ In.	82.00 to 146.00

ROWLAND & MARSELLUS Company is part of a mark that appears on historical Staffordshire dating from the late nineteenth and early twentieth centuries. Rowland & Marsellus is the mark used by an American importing company in New York City. The company worked from 1893 to about 1937. Some of the pieces may have been made by the British Anchor Pottery Co. of Longton, England, for export to a New York firm. Many American views were made. Of special interest to collectors are the plates with rolled edges, usually blue and white.

Plate, American Poets, Portraits, Roses, Banner, Cobalt Blue, 10 In.	85.00
Plate, Views Of Niagara Falls, Rolled Edge, Blue Transfer, 10 In.	86.00
Plate, Soup, Pocahontas, Green Transfer, c.1893	32.00
Plate, Soldier's Monument At Seaside Park, Bridgeport, Conn., Blue & White, 10 In.	86.00
Plate, View Of Denver, Blue & White, 10 In.	100.00
Plate, Mrs. Robinson, Signed Sir Joshua Reynolds P.R.A., 10¼ In.	235.00

ROY ROGERS was born in 1911 in Cincinnati, Ohio. In the 1930s, he made a living as a singer; in 1935, his group started work at a Los Angeles radio station. He appeared in his first movie in 1937. From 1952 to 1957, he made 101 television shows. The other stars in the show were his wife, Dale Evans, his horse, Trigger, and his dog, Bullet. Roy Rogers memorabilia is collected, including items from the Roy Rogers restaurants.

Ashtray, Cast Metal, Copper Luster, Trigger, Best Wishes Roy Rogers, 1950s, 4 x 6½ In.	574.00
Badge, Deputy, 5-Point Star, Tin, Embossed, Premium, c.1950, 2¼ In.	39.00
Belt, Roy Rogers, Trigger, Plastic, Metal Buckle, Hickok, Package, 1950s, 28 In.	234.00
Book, Paint, Whitman, No. 668, 1944, 11 x 8½ In., 130 Pages	84.00
Book, Punch-Out, Whitman, c.1952, 15 x 10 In.	140.00
Cereal Box, Quick Quaker Oats, Photograph Premium Offer, Canada, 1950s, 10 In.	252.00
Crayon Set, Stencils, Pictures, Unused, Standard Toycraft Products, Original Box	440.00
Display, Dale Evans, Kool-Aid, Die Cut, c.1950s, 18 x 18 In.	1192.00
Figure, Trigger, Plaster, Painted, E. Zerbini Regd., 1940s, 16 In.	280.00
Flashlight, USAlite, Signal Siren, U.S. Electric Mfg., Box, 1950s	133.00
Gun, Cap, Long Tom, Unfired, Kilgore, 1950s, 10 In.	1008.00
Lantern, Ranch, Tin Lithograph, Battery Operated, Ohio Art, Box, 1950s, 7½ In.	400.00
Lunch Box, Dale & Roy, Bar Ranch, Metal, Wood Grain, American Thermos, 1953	252.00
Lunch Box, Metal, Double R Bar Ranch, Bottle, Decal Sheet, American Thermos Co., 1953	739.00
Lunch Box Thermos, Roy, Trigger, Dale Evans, Bullet, American Thermos, 1950s	50.00
Newsletter, Double-R-Bar Ranch News, October, 1943, 12 x 9¼ In., 12 Pages	168.00
Nodder, Composition, 6½ In.	138.00
Paper Dolls, Roy Rogers & Dale Evans, Whitman, Uncut, c.1952, 13 x 10½ In., 8 Pages	134.00
Pencil, Unused, 7½ In.	10.00
Pin, King Of The Cowboys, Red Hat, Bandanna, Australia, 1950s, 1¾ In.	101.00
Poster, Movie, Heldorado, Republic, 1946, 27 x 41 In.	230.00
Poster, Movie, Twilight In Sierras, Re-Release, 1956, 22 x 28 In.	123.00
Poster, Movie, Under Western Stars, Republic, 1938, 27 x 41 In.	1680.00
Program, Rodeo, The Singing Cowboy, Boston Garden, 1942, 36 Pages	60.00
Ring, Microscope, Brass, Red Plastic, Quaker Cereals, 1949	101.00
Ring Toss & Horseshoes, Tin Lithograph, 2 Rope Rings, 4 Horseshoes, Ohio Art, 1950s	85.00
Schoolbag, Roy Rogers King Of The Cowboys, Leatherette, Strap, 1950s, 10 x 13 In.	123.00
Toy, Ring Toss & Horseshoes, Lithograph, Tin Bases, Rope Rings, Horseshoes, Ohio Art, 1950s	85.00
Toy, Stagecoach, Fix-It, Catalog, Unopened, Ideal, Box, 5 x 6½ x 15 In.	496.00
Wristwatch, Dale Evans, Bradley, Box, 1950s, 2¼ x 5½ x 4 In.	271.00
Wristwatch, King Of Cowboys, For Boys, Bradley Time, Box, 1951, 8½ x 3¼ In.	493.00
Wristwatch, Roy & Trigger, Green Ground, Expansion Band, Ingraham, Box, 1957	645.00

ROYAL BAYREUTH is the name of a factory that was founded in Tettau, Bavaria, in 1794. It has continued to modern times. The marks have changed through the years. A stylized crest, the name *Royal Bayreuth,* and the word *Bavaria* appear in slightly different forms from 1870 to about 1919. Later dishes may include the words *U.S. Zone,* the year of the issue, or the word *Germany* instead of *Bavaria.* Related pieces may be found listed in the Rose Tapestry, Sand Babies, Snow Babies, and Sunbonnet Babies categories.

Ashtray, Fox Hunt Scene, Horseshoe Shape, 4½ In.	160.00
Basket, Pink Rose, White & Green Luster, Oval, 5 In.	25.00
Basket, White Rose, White Ground, 5¼ In.	25.00
Basket, Woman Portrait, Green & Brown, 5 In.	120.00
Bowl, Grape, Yellow, Red, Vintage Mold, 10½ In.	75.00
Bowl, Peacock Scene, 10¾ In.	1100.00
Cake Plate, Polar Bear Scene, Handles, 10½ In.	1700.00
Creamer, Elk, Blue Mark, 4¼ In.	325.00
Creamer, Gray & White, Blue Mark, 4½ In.	460.00
Creamer, Lobster, Red, Blue Mark, 4 In.	395.00
Ewer, Nymph Sitting On Rock, Green, Handle, 8½ In.	325.00
Hatpin Holder, Yellow Rose, Light Brown, 4¾ In.	125.00
Humidor, Ship, Swan & Flower Border, Enamel Jewels, Gray Ground, Green Mark, 7 In.	173.00
Humidor, Women & Lamb Scene, 8 In.	225.00
Inkwell, Elk, Matte Finish, Original Glass Insert	350.00
Mug, Devil & Cards, Devil Handle, 5 In.	227.00
Mustard Pot, Lobster, Cover, Open Claw Handled Spoon, Green Mark, 4½ In.	250.00
Pitcher, Green Leaves, Free-Form Mold, Gold Twig Handle, c.1900, 7 In. *illus*	294.00
Pitcher, Landscape, Castle On Lake, Snowtopped Mountains, Gold Trim, 5⅞ In. *illus*	288.00
Plate, Coral, Blue, Yellow & Green Leaves, Brown Branches, Floral Rim, 10 In.	25.00
Plate, Man, Shooting At Ducks, Dog, Marshland, 9½ In.	77.00
Plate, Yellow Rose, Pink, Blue, Green Tones, Pierced Border, 9¾ In.	80.00
Plate, Yellow Rose, Yellow & Rose Ground, 8½ In.	30.00
Relish, Girl Holding Flower Basket, Handle, 7¾ In.	125.00
Shoe, Black, Lady's, High Heel, 3½ In., Pair	125.00
Shoe, Gray & Black, Lady's, High Heel, 3½ In., Pair	200.00
Shoe, Lady's Slipper, Rose Tapestry, Pink Rose, 2½ In.	150.00
Sugar, Scuttle, Woman & Horse, 3 In.	275.00
Tea Set, Tomato Shape, c.1900, 8-In. Teapot, 3 Piece *illus*	147.00
Teapot, Apple, Figural, Blue Mark	450.00
Vase, Christmas, Tapestry, 4¼ In.	125.00
Vase, Nymph Sitting On Bench, Green, 6½ x 5 In.	400.00
Vase, Nymph Sitting On Bench, Green, 7¼ In.	375.00
Vase, Nymph Sitting On Rock, Cobalt Blue, 4½ In.	375.00
Vase, Nymph Sitting On Rock, Cobalt Blue Bands, Iridescent & Gold Stencils, Bulbous, 5 x 5 In.	400.00
Vase, Nymph Sitting On Rock, Green, Reticulated Rim, 7½ In.	300.00
Vase, Polar Bear Scene, 4½ In.	650.00
Vase, Polar Bear Scene, 5½ In.	1000.00
Vase, Scenic, c.1900, 5¾ In.	105.00
Vase, Woman & Horse, Blue, Green, 4¼ In.	75.00

ROYAL BONN is the nineteenth- and twentieth-century trade name used by Franz Anton Mehlem, who had a pottery in Bonn, Germany, from 1836 to 1931. Porcelain and earthenware were made. The factory was purchased by Villeroy & Boch in 1921 and closed in 1931. Many marks were used, most including the name *Bonn,* the initials *FM,* and a crown.

Cheesekeeper, Transferware, Marked	189.00
Clock, Ansonia, La Marne, 8-Day, Strike Movement, 12 x 13 In.	800.00
Clock, Ansonia, La Nord, 8-Day, Time & Strike, Porcelain, c.1904, 12 In.	1073.00
Clock, Ansonia, La Savoie, 8-Day, Time & Strike, Porcelain, c.1914, 11 In.	303.00
Clock, Ansonia, La Tosca, Porcelain, Yellow, Pink, Flowers, c.1905, 15 In.	1375.00
Clock, Mantel, Ansonia Open Escapement, Pink, Yellow, Blue Flowers, Brown, 11 x 14 In.	800.00
Clock, Mantel, La Vendee, Flowers, Shaped Green Case, Ansonia Works, c.1900, 15 In. *illus*	529.00
Creamer, Wildrose, Flow Blue, 3½ In.	40.00
Dish, Flow Blue Twigs, Fluting, Scalloped Rim, 6½ x 3 In., 4 Piece	95.00
Ewer, Bird Claws, c.1880, 11 In.	275.00
Ewer, Roses, 9 In.	395.00
Jardiniere, Roses, Dark Green, Embossed Rim, 1896-1920, 11 x 8¼ In.	150.00
Serving Bowl, 13½ x 8¼ In.	65.00
Umbrella Stand, White Art Nouveau Flowers, Majolica Glazes, 21¾ x 10 In. *illus*	570.00

Royal Bayreuth, Pitcher, Landscape, Castle On Lake, Snowtopped Mountains, Gold Trim, 5⅞ In. $288.00

Royal Bayreuth, Tea Set, Tomato Shape, c.1900, 8-In. Teapot, 3 Piece $147.00

Royal Bonn, Clock, Mantel, La Vendee, Flowers, Shaped Green Case, Ansonia Works, c.1900, 15 In. $529.00

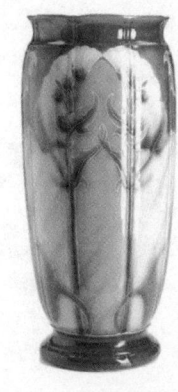

Royal Bonn, Umbrella Stand, White Art Nouveau Flowers, Majolica Glazes, 21¾ x 10 In. $570.00

R

Royal Copenhagen, Bowl, Cover, Flora Danica, Polygonum Nodosum Pers., Branch Handle, Rim, 15 x 7 In. $3346.00

Royal Copenhagen, Bowl, Vegetable, Flora Danica, Ajuga Reptans, Gold Beaded Rim, 7 x 9½ In. $1793.00

Royal Copenhagen, Figurine, Wave & Rock, 2 Lovers On Rock, Cresting Wave, T. Lundberg, 1897, 18½ In. $690.00

Vase, Castle Scene, Flowers, Ormolu Bronze Handles, Tapestry, c.1850, 17½ In.	3000.00
Vase, Cover, Flowers, Leaves, Handles, 5½ In.	695.00
Vase, Flowers, Leaves, Gold Leaf Handles, Lid, 11 x 5½ In.	695.00
Vase, Flowers, Pink, Rose, Lavender, Blue, 5 x 4 In.	60.00
Vase, Flowers, Portrait, Woman, 14½ x 10 In.	2500.00
Vase, Painted Flowers, 8 In.	125.00
Vase, Painted Roses, Dark Green, Embossed Rim, 11 x 8¼ In.	150.00
Vase, Portrait, Cavalier, Wishing Well, Red, Gold, Blue, c.1900, 8 x 3 In.	350.00
Vase, Portrait, Woman, 14½ x 10 In.	2500.00
Vase, Portrait, Woman, Painted, Flowers, Signed, 14½ x 10 x 6 In.	3250.00
Vase, Scenic Design, Gilt Leaves Around Rim, Grass Bottom, 8 In.	379.00
Vase, Squat, Celadon Bachelor's Buttons, Green, Brown Volcanic Ground, 6 x 9 In.	720.00
Vase, Thistle, Blue, Gray, Ivory Ground, c.1880, 11 In.	95.00

ROYAL COPENHAGEN porcelain and pottery have been made in Denmark since 1775. The Christmas plate series started in 1908. The figurines with pale blue and gray glazes have remained popular in this century and are still being made. Many other old and new style porcelains are made today.

Bowl, Cover, Flora Danica, Polygonum Nodosum Pers., Branch Handle, Rim, 15 x 7 In. *illus*	3346.00
Bowl, Vegetable, Flora Danica, Ajuga Reptans, Gold Beaded Rim, 7 x 9½ In. ....*illus*	1793.00
Cup & Saucer, White Diamond	12.00
Dessert Set, Blue Half Lace, Plate, Coffeepot, Cup & Saucer, 31 Piece	702.00
Dish, Golden Clover, 4 In.	45.00
Figurine, Fat Robin, 3 In.	85.00
Figurine, Polar Bear, Roaring, On Haunches, 13 In.	263.00
Figurine, Poultry Seller, Woman Holding Chicken, Egg Basket, Triple Wave Mark, c.1785, 6⅞ In.	1440.00
Figurine, Wave & Rock, 2 Lovers On Rock, Cresting Wave, T. Lundberg, 1897, 18½ In. ..*illus*	690.00
Inkwell, 2 Bottles, Square, Lid, Tray, c.1920, 3 x 9 x 5½ In.	70.00
Plaque, Education Of Cupid, Biscuit Porcelain, Relief, Signed, 5 x 12 In.	240.00
Plate, Christmas, 1919, In The Park, 7 In.	135.00
Plate, Christmas, 1961, Training Ship, Denmark, 7 In.	125.00
Plate, Christmas, 1962, Little Mermaid At Wintertime, 7 In.	225.00
Plate, Christmas, 1969, Old Farmyard, 7 In.	40.00
Plate, Christmas, 1970, Rose & Cat, 7 In.	64.00
Plate, Christmas, 1976, Vibaek Mill, 7 In.	40.00
Plate, Christmas, 1978, Greenland Scenery, 7 In.	40.00 to 60.00
Plate, Christmas, 1979, Choosing The Christmas Tree, 7 In.	44.00 to 60.00
Plate, Christmas, 1983, Merry Christmas, 7 In.	40.00
Plate, Christmas, 1987, Christmas Eve At The White House, 5⅓ In.	18.00
Plate Set, Bread & Butter, Flora Danica, Raised Rim, 5½ In., 4 Piece	956.00
Plate Set, Fish, White, Gold Border, 10 In., 12 Piece	633.00
Soup, Cream, Underplate, Golden Clover, Handles, 5 x 6½ In.	46.00
Vase, Faience, Stoneware, Nils Thorsson, 1950s, 7 In.	123.00
Vase, Sailboat, Blue Ground, 8½ In.	88.00
Vase, Stylized Leaves & Flowers, Faience, Johanne Gerber, 1969 ....*illus*	106.00

ROYAL COPLEY china was made by the Spaulding China Company of Sebring, Ohio, from 1939 to 1960. The figural planters and the small figurines, especially those with Art Deco designs, are of great collector interest.

Bank, Pig, 4⅝ In. ....*illus*	45.00
Planter, Cocker Spaniel, Tan, Brown, 8 In.	32.00
Planter, Ivy, 3 x 4¾ x 5½ In.	5.00
Planter, Philodendron, 3 x 7½ x 6½ In.	12.00
Planter, Rib & Cornice, Yellow, White, 5 x 3¼ In.	7.00
Vase, Flowers, Cream Ground, Rope Border, Marked, c.1940-50	20.00
Vase, Flowers, Urn Form, Handles, Marked, 6¼ In.	12.00
Wall Pocket, Flowers, 7¾ x 4 In.	85.00
Wall Pocket, Pirate, Face, Embossed, 8½ x 6 In.	95.00

ROYAL CROWN DERBY Company, Ltd., was established in England in 1890. There is a complex family tree that includes the Derby, Crown Derby, and Royal Crown Derby porcelains. The Royal Crown Derby mark includes the name and a crown. The words *Made in England* were used after 1921. The company is now a part of Royal Doulton Tableware Ltd.

Box, Cover, Imari, c.1918, 2½ In., Pair	372.00
Cake Plate, Oval, Derby Japan Pattern, c.1892, 10¼ x 8 In.	450.00

Candlestick, Bone China, Imari Pattern, 10½ In., Pair	819.00
Cup & Saucer, Demitasse, Derby Japan Pattern, 3 x 5 In.	70.00
Cup & Saucer, Demitasse, Imari, Can Shape Cup, c.1930s, 2 x 4⅛ In.	60.00
Cup & Saucer, Imari, Fluted, Gold Trim, 2½ x 5¾ In.	78.00
Cup & Saucer, Imari Pattern, c.1930, 8 Piece	196.00
Dish, Octagonal, Derby Japan Pattern, Gilding, 1890-1940, 9 In., Pair	250.00
Dish, Shell, Kings Pattern, 3 Sections, c.1895, 10½ In.	167.00
Earring & Brooch Set, Floral, ⅝ In.	75.00
Eggcup, Derby Posies, Fluted Rim, Gilding, 1¾ In.	27.00
Knife Set, Ceramic Handles, Stainless Steel Blades, Box, 7 In., 6 Piece	75.00
Napkin Ring, Floral Transfer, Gold Banding, c.1935, Pair	55.00
Paperweight, Armadillo, Gold Stopper, Box, 1996-99	126.00
Paperweight, Baby Rabbit, Gold Stopper, Box, 1990	63.00
Paperweight, Barn Owl, Gold Stopper, Box, 1995	105.00
Paperweight, Beaver, Gold Stopper, Box, 1994-97	74.00
Paperweight, Derby Ram, Gold Stopper, Box, 1998-99	200.00
Paperweight, Dragon Of Happiness, Gold Stopper, Limited Edition, Box, 1999	210.00
Paperweight, Honey Bear, Gold Stopper, Box, 1994-97	126.00
Paperweight, Koala & Baby, Australian Collection, John Ablitt, 1999, 3¾ In.	190.00
Paperweight, Little Owl, Gold Stopper, Box, 1998	95.00
Paperweight, Millennium Bug, Scarab, John Ablitt, 1¼ In.	95.00
Paperweight, Millennium Dove, Gold Stopper, Limited Edition, Box	168.00
Paperweight, Panda, Seated, Gold Stopper, Box, 1994-2001	137.00
Paperweight, Penguin, Chick, Gold Stopper, Box, 1998	105.00
Paperweight, Santa & Sleigh, John Ablitt, 1999-2004, 3½ In.	160.00
Paperweight, Sleeping Piglet, John Ablitt, 1999-2002, 2½ In.	100.00
Paperweight, Starlight Hare, Gold Stopper, Collectors Guide, Box	148.00
Paperweight, Teddy Bear, Gold, White Ground, Cobalt Blue Paws, c.1964, 5 In.	1150.00
Paperweight, Teddy Bear, No. 06851, 1997, 5 In.	115.00
Pin, Floral, Hand Painted, England, ½ x 2 In.	45.00
Planter, Auricula, Without Gold Band, 4¼ In.	275.00
Plate, Blue Mikado, 1920s, 6¼ In.	35.00
Plate, Floral Medallion, Cobalt Blue, Gold, c.1890, 9⅛ In.	495.00
Plate, Japan Pattern, Gilt, 8-Sided, 9 In.	250.00
Plate, Sandwich, Scalloped, Lobed, Gold Festoons, Medallions, c.1891, 9 In.	68.00
Plate Set, Dinner, Pale Blue Body, Gilt Birds, Flowers, 10¼ In., 12 Piece	1062.00
Platter, Gold Vine, Oval, 13½ In.	135.00
Platter, Imari, 10¾ In.	399.00
Platter, Imari, 18th Century, 13 In.	475.00
Platter, Imari, 18th Century, 16¼ In.	500.00
Platter, Imari, 18th Century, 19¾ In.	525.00
Soup, Cream, Underplate, Gold Vine, Handles, 4¾ In.	40.00
Stopper, Guppy Fish, Gold, Limited Edition, Certificate, Box	148.00
Tea Strainer, Bowl, 3¾ x 1¼ & 5 x 2¾ In.	275.00
Tureen, Cover, Vine Pattern	275.00
Vase, Cover, Cobalt Blue, Enameled Roses, Bees, Dragonflies, Gilt Reticulated Handles, 11 In. *illus*	1725.00
Vase, Reticulated, Gilded, Openwork, Scrolling Leaves, Flowers, 11¼ In.	2000.00
Vase, Yellow Ground, Gilt Foo Dogs, Shouldered Handles, c.1850, 6 In.	395.00

ROYAL DOULTON is the name used on Doulton and Company pottery made from 1902 to the present. Doulton and Company of England was founded in 1853. Pieces made before 1902 are listed in this book under Doulton. Royal Doulton collectors search for the out-of-production figurines, character jugs, vases, and series wares. Some vases and animal figurines were made with a special red glaze called flambe. Sung and Chang glazed pieces are rare. The multicolored glaze is very thick and looks as if it were dropped on the clay. Royal Doulton was acquired by the Waterford Wedgwood Group in 2005.

Animal, Cow, Charolais Cow & Calf, DA 33, 7¼ In.	215.00
Animal, Dog, Cairn Terrier, Seated, K 11, 2½ In.	56.00
Animal, Dog, Cocker Spaniel With Pheasant, HN 1029, 3½ In.	181.00
Animal, Dog, Cocker Spaniel With Pheasant, HN 1062, 3½ In.	192.00
Animal, Dog, English Setter With Pheasant, HN 2529, 1938-46, 8 In.	433.00
Animal, Dog, Great Dane, Ch. Rebeller Of Ouborough, HN 2561, 6 In.	315.00
Animal, Elephant, Trunk Down, Flambe, HN 1121, 1938-68	4500.00
Animal, Horse, Black Beauty Foal, Black, Box, DA 66, 5¾ In.	45.00
Animal, Horse, Black Bess, DA 179, 7¾ In.	56.00
Animal, Horse, Brown, Head Tucked, Leg Up, DA 51, 7½ In.	56.00

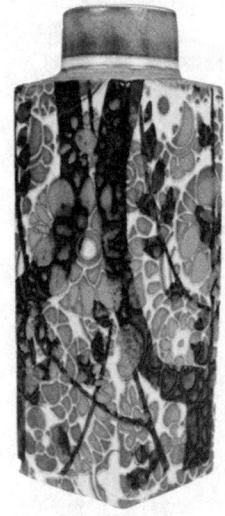

Royal Copenhagen, Vase,
Stylized Leaves & Flowers, Faience,
Johanne Gerber, 1969
$106.00

Royal Copley, Bank,
Pig, 4⅝ In.
$45.00

Royal Crown Derby, Vase,
Cover, Cobalt Blue, Enameled Roses,
Bees, Dragonflies, Gilt Reticulated
Handles, 11 In.
$1725.00

R

Character Jugs

Royal Doulton started making character jugs in 1934. Early jugs were three-dimensional portraits of famous English characters of history, literature, and song. By the 1980s, movie, television, and political figures from many countries were included. The jugs had figural handles: Long John Silver's handle was a parrot, Clark Gable's was a movie camera. A few rarities like the Granny with no teeth (the common jug has one tooth) or the Red-Headed Clown have sold for thousands of dollars each.

Royal Doulton, Character Jug, Jockey, D 6625, 1971-75, Large $74.00

Royal Doulton, Character Jug, Sairey Gamp, D 5528, 1935-86, Small $94.00

Animal, Horse, Desert Orchid, Wood Plinth Base, DA 184, 1994-Present	203.00
Animal, Horse, Gude Gray Mare, HN 2570, 1941-67, 3¾ In.	165.00
Animal, Horse, Horse Of The Year, Chestnut, DA 193A, 8¼ In.	93.00
Animal, Horse, Lipizzaner, DA 243, 11 In.	282.00
Animal, Horse, New Forest Pony, Brown, DA 244, 6 In.	56.00
Animal, Horse, Shetland Pony, Dapple Gray, DA 185, 5¼ In.	56.00
Animal, Horse, Spirit Of Love, Wood Plinth Base, DA 225, 6½ In.	102.00
Animal, Horse, Spirit Of Peace, Matte Brown, DA 63B, 5¾ In.	102.00
Animal, Horse, Spirit Of The Wild, Matte White, DA 183, 12 In.	83.00 to 102.00
Animal, Horse, Spirit Of Youth, Wood Plinth Base, Brown, DA 59B, 8 In.	79.00
Animal, Horse, Stocky Jogging Mare, Gloss Black, DA 44, 6 In.	74.00
Animal, Penguin, Flambe, HN 846 In.	129.00
Animal, Tiger On Rock, HN 2639, 1952-92, 12 In.	644.00
Bowl, Flambe, Asian Scene, Building, Trees, 8 In.	88.00

Royal Doulton character jugs depict the head and shoulders of the subject. They are made in four sizes: large, 5¼ to 7 inches; small, 3¼ to 4 inches; miniature, 2¼ to 2½ inches; and tiny, 1¼ inches. Toby jugs portray a seated, full figure.

Character Jug, Aladdin's Genie, Flambe, D 6971, 1994, Large	234.00
Character Jug, Anne Boleyn, Ax Handle, D 6644, Large	59.00
Character Jug, Antique Dealer, D 6807, 1988, Large	137.00
Character Jug, 'Ard Of 'Earing, D 6591, 1964-67, Small	324.00
Character Jug, Athos, D 6452, 1956-91, Small	57.00
Character Jug, Auctioneer, World Series, Certificate, D 6838, 1988, Large	113.00 to 158.00
Character Jug, Bill Sikes, D 6981, 1994, Large	166.00
Character Jug, Bonnie Prince Charlie, D 6858, 1990-94, Large	74.00
Character Jug, Buffalo Bill, D 6735, 1985-89, Large	65.00
Character Jug, Cap'n Cuttle, D 5842, 1948-60, Small	46.00
Character Jug, Capt Ahab, D 6500, 1959-84, Large	83.00
Character Jug, Capt Hook, D 6947, 1994, Large	74.00
Character Jug, City Gent, D 6815, 1988-91, Large	68.00
Character Jug, Collector, D 6796, 1988, Large	169.00
Character Jug, Confucius, Flambe, D 7003, Large	234.00
Character Jug, Dick Whittington, D 6375, 1953-60, Large	124.00
Character Jug, Elephant Trainer, D 6841, 1990-93, Large	204.00
Character Jug, Elizabeth I, D 6992, 1994, Tiny	139.00
Character Jug, Falconer, D 6533, 1960-61, Large	56.00
Character Jug, Farmer John, D 5788, 1938-60, Large	46.00
Character Jug, Fat Boy, D 5840, 1948-60, Small	111.00
Character Jug, Fortune Teller, D 6874, 1991, Large	102.00
Character Jug, Francis Rossi, D 6961, 1993, Mid	74.00
Character Jug, Gardener, D 6634, 1973-81, Small	65.00
Character Jug, General Custer, D 7079, 1997-99, Large	82.00
Character Jug, George Washington, D 6669, 1982-94, Large	79.00
Character Jug, Glen Miller, D 6970, 1994-98, Large	200.00
Character Jug, Golfer, D 6623, 1971-95, Large	57.00
Character Jug, Golfer, D 6623, 1990-95, Small	62.00
Character Jug, Gondolier, D 6595, 1964-69, Miniature	203.00
Character Jug, Guy Fawkes, D 6861, 1990-96, Large	74.00
Character Jug, Henry V, D 6671, 1982-84, Large	181.00
Character Jug, Jane Seymour, D 6646, 1979-90, Large	79.00
Character Jug, Jarge, D 6288, 1950-60, Large	169.00 to 179.00
Character Jug, Jockey, D 6625, 1971-75, Large	*illus* 74.00
Character Jug, John Barley Corn, D 5327, 1934-39, Large	68.00
Character Jug, John Doulton, D 6656, 1981-94, Small	42.00
Character Jug, Johnny Appleseed, D 6372, 1953-69, Large	192.00
Character Jug, Little Mester Museum Piece, D 6819, 1988, Large	90.00
Character Jug, Long John Silver, D 6386, 1952-98, Small	23.00
Character Jug, Louis Armstrong, D 6707, 1984-88, Large	65.00
Character Jug, Mephistopheles, Verse, D 5758, 1937-48, Small	648.00
Character Jug, Mikado, D 6507, 1959-69, Small	139.00
Character Jug, Mine Host, D 6468, 1958-82, Large	37.00
Character Jug, Monty, D 6202, 1946-91, Large	74.00
Character Jug, Mr. Pickwick, D 5839, 1938-48, Mid	56.00 to 74.00

Character Jug, Neptune, D 6548, 1961-91, Large	68.00
Character Jug, Old Charley, D 5420, 1934-83, Large	55.00
Character Jug, Oliver Twist, D 6677, Tiny	83.00
Character Jug, Parson Brown, D 5529, 1935-60, Small	813.00
Character Jug, Paul McCartney, D 6724, 1984-91, Mid	139.00
Character Jug, Pearly King, D 6760, 1987-91, Large	63.00
Character Jug, Queen Mary I, D 7188, 2004, Large	65.00 to 148.00
Character Jug, Red Queen, D 6777, 1987-91, Large	102.00
Character Jug, Regency Beau, D 6562, 1962-67, Small	407.00
Character Jug, Rick Parfitt, D 6962, 1993, Mid	74.00
Character Jug, Robin Hood, 1947-60, Miniature	25.00
Character Jug, Robinson Crusoe, D 6546, Miniature	41.00
Character Jug, Sairey Gamp, D 5528, 1935-86, Small ....*illus*	94.00
Character Jug, Sam Weller, D 5841, 1948-60, Small	56.00
Character Jug, Santa Claus, Doll Handle, D 6668, 1981, Large	179.00
Character Jug, Santa Claus, Teddy Handle, D 7060, 1997, Tiny	68.00
Character Jug, Scaramouche, D 6558, 1962-67, Large	497.00
Character Jug, Sir Thomas Moore, D 6792, 1988-91, Large	113.00
Character Jug, Vice Admiral Lord Nelson, D 6932, 1993, Large	139.00
Character Jug, Viking, D 6496, 1959-75, Large	102.00
Character Jug, Walrus & Carpenter, D 6600, 1965-80, Large	74.00
Character Jug, Winston Churchill, D 6907, 1992, Large	352.00
Character Jug, Witch, Flambe, D 7239, 2005, Large	240.00
Character Jug, Wizard, Flambe, D 7240, 2005, Large	240.00
Character Jug, Yachtsman, D 6820, 1989-91, Large	65.00
Coffeepot, Coppice Pattern, D 5803, 9½ In.	28.00
Cup & Saucer, Dickens Ware, Fat Boy & Barkis	140.00
Figurine, A Good Catch, HN 2258, 1966-86	230.00
Figurine, A La Mode, HN 2544, 1974-79	65.00
Figurine, A Victorian Lady, HN 728, 1925-52	120.00
Figurine, Affection, HN 2236, 1962-94	37.00
Figurine, Alexandra, HN 3286, 1990-2000	146.00
Figurine, Anne Boleyn, HN 3232, 1990	271.00
Figurine, Anniversary, HN 3625, 1994-98	116.00
Figurine, Aragorn, HN 2916, 1981-84	105.00
Figurine, Ascot, HN 2356, 1968-95	117.00
Figurine, Auctioneer, HN 2988, 1986	148.00
Figurine, Autumn Breezes, HN 1911, 1939-76	117.00
Figurine, Autumn Breezes, HN 1913, 1939-71	172.00
Figurine, Autumn Breezes, HN 1934, 1940-97	79.00
Figurine, Ballerina, HN 2116, 1953-73	206.00
Figurine, Balloon Girl, HN 2818, 1982-97	248.00
Figurine, Balloon Man, HN 1954, 1940-Present	82.00
Figurine, Barliman Butterbur, HN 2923, 1987-84	421.00
Figurine, Bell O' The Ball, HN 1997, 1947-79	168.00 to 176.00
Figurine, Belle, HN 3703, 1996	146.00
Figurine, Biddy Penny Farthing, HN 1843, 1938-Present	71.00
Figurine, Bilbo, HN 2914, 1980-84	95.00
Figurine, Blacksmith, HN 2782, 1987-91	215.00
Figurine, Bon Voyage, HN 3866, 1998-2001	82.00
Figurine, Bonnie Lassie, HN 1626, 1934-53	248.00
Figurine, Boromir, HN 2918, 1981-84	126.00
Figurine, Bride, HN 2166, 1956-76 ....*illus*	353.00
Figurine, Bunnykins, Artist, Box, DB 13, 1975-82, 3¾ In.	158.00
Figurine, Bunnykins, Ballerina, DB 176, 1998-2001, 3½ In.	65.00
Figurine, Bunnykins, Bedtime, DB 55, 1987-98, 3¼ In.	23.00
Figurine, Bunnykins, Captain Cook, Box, DB 251, 2001, 5 In.	53.00
Figurine, Bunnykins, Cavalier, Box, DB 179, 1998, 4½ In.	105.00
Figurine, Bunnykins, Collector, DB 54, 1987, 4¼ In.	222.00
Figurine, Bunnykins, Day Trip, DB 260, 2002	102.00
Figurine, Bunnykins, Downhill, DB 31, 1985-88, 2½ In.	84.00
Figurine, Bunnykins, Easter Surprise, DB 225, 2000	37.00
Figurine, Bunnykins, Father, Mother & Victoria, DB 68, 1988-96, 4½ In.	65.00
Figurine, Bunnykins, Fortune Teller, DB 240, 2002-03	56.00
Figurine, Bunnykins, Gymnast, DB 207, 2000	37.00

Bunnykins

Bunnykins children's dishes have been popular—and in production—since Royal Doulton introduced them in 1934. The bunny characters on the dishes were based on drawings by Sister Barbara Vernon, a nun whose father was manager of the Royal Doulton Pottery in Stoke-on-Trent, England.

The success of Bunnykins dishes led to the introduction of six Bunnykins earthenware figurines in 1939. Production of the figurines stopped during World War II. It started up again in 1972. Royal Doulton has made more than 200 Bunnykins figurines. Some were commissioned for special events, such as the 1984 Summer Olympics (Olympic Bunnykins, DB 28), or made in limited editions for collectors. The figurines are still being made.

Royal Doulton, Figurine, Bride, HN 2166, 1956-76
$353.00

R

Royal Doulton, Figurine, Lisa,
HN 2310, 1969-82
$71.00

Royal Doulton, Figurine, Christine,
HN 2792, 1978-94
$94.00

Transmutation Glazes
Potters at Royal Doulton created *transmutation* glazes during the early 1890s. Copper oxide and other chemicals were applied to the pottery, then the flow of oxygen to the kiln was reduced. This made an unpredictable glaze of reds, yellows, blues, and greens. Rouge flambé, first made in 1904, is still made.

Figurine, Bunnykins, Ice Hockey, DB 282, 2003	56.00
Figurine, Bunnykins, Lawyer, DB 214, 2000	37.00 to 56.00
Figurine, Bunnykins, Little Jack Horner, DB 221, 2000-03	28.00
Figurine, Bunnykins, Minstrel, DB 211, 2000	46.00
Figurine, Bunnykins, Olympic, DB 28, 1984-88, 3¾ In.	80.00
Figurine, Bunnykins, On Line, Box, DB 238, 2001, 2¾ In.	63.00
Figurine, Bunnykins, Parisian, Box, DB 317, 2005	79.00
Figurine, Bunnykins, Samurai, Box, DB 280, 2003	80.00 to 90.00
Figurine, Bunnykins, Sandcastle Money Box, DB 228, 2002	46.00
Figurine, Bunnykins, Sands Of Time, DB 229, 2001	56.00
Figurine, Bunnykins, Santa's Helper, DB 192, 1999	56.00
Figurine, Bunnykins, Schoolmaster, DB 60, 1987-96, 4 In.	46.00
Figurine, Bunnykins, Seaside, DB 177, 1998, 3 In.	46.00
Figurine, Bunnykins, Sleigh Ride, DB 81, 1989, 3½ In.	41.00
Figurine, Bunnykins, Statue Of Liberty, DB 198, 1999, 5 In.	65.00
Figurine, Bunnykins, Swimmer Bunnykins, DB 206, 2000	37.00
Figurine, Bunnykins, Town Crier, Box, DB 259, 2002	90.00 to 93.00
Figurine, Bunnykins, Trumpet Player, Box, DB 210, 2001	68.00
Figurine, Bunnykins, Witch's Cauldron, Box, DB 293, 2004	89.00 to 102.00
Figurine, Camellias, HN 3701, 1995-98	117.00
Figurine, Captain, HN 2260, 1965-82	316.00
Figurine, Captain Cook, HN 2889, 1980-84	339.00
Figurine, Catherine Howard, HN 3449, 1992	316.00
Figurine, Centurion, HN 2726, 1982-84	83.00 to 158.00
Figurine, Charity, HN 4243, 2000-01	82.00
Figurine, Charlotte, HN 2421, 1972-86	94.00
Figurine, Charmian, HN 1948, 1940-73	117.00
Figurine, Chloe, HN 1479, 1931-49, 5½ In.	407.00
Figurine, Christine, HN 2792, 1978-94 *illus*	94.00
Figurine, Christine, HN 3767, 1996-98	95.00
Figurine, Christine, HN 3905, 1998	71.00
Figurine, Cobbler, HN 1706, 1935-69	130.00
Figurine, Country Maid, Milk Maid, HN 4305, 2001-02	59.00
Figurine, Courtney, Chic Trends, HN 4762, 2005	74.00
Figurine, Daddy's Girl, HN 3435, 1993-98	65.00
Figurine, Daydreams, HN 1731, 1935-96	146.00
Figurine, Deborah, HN 3644, 1995	82.00
Figurine, Debutante, HN 2210, 1963-67	102.00
Figurine, Diana, HN 3266, 1990	74.00
Figurine, Dragon, Flambe, HN 3552, 1993-95	205.00
Figurine, Drummer Boy, HN 2679, 1976-81	147.00
Figurine, Dulcinea, HN 1343, 1929-36	1626.00
Figurine, Eleanor, HN 3906, 1998	71.00
Figurine, Elephant, Flambe, HN 891, 1926-50	205.00
Figurine, Elizabeth Bennett, HN 3845, 1998	146.00
Figurine, Enchantment, HN 2178, 1957-82	71.00
Figurine, Fair Lady, HN 2193, 1963-96	82.00 to 88.00
Figurine, Fair Maid, HN 4222, 2000-02	59.00
Figurine, Faith, HN 4151, 1999-2000	70.00
Figurine, Farmer's Wife, HN 3164, 1988-91	293.00
Figurine, Feeding Time, Box, HN 3373, 1991	84.00
Figurine, Fleur, HN 2368, 1968-95	46.00
Figurine, Flower Seller's Children, HN 1342, 1929-93	102.00 to 293.00
Figurine, Foaming Quart, HN 2162, 1955-92	71.00 to 86.00
Figurine, Forget-Me-Nots, HN 3700, 1995-98	117.00
Figurine, Forty Winks, HN 1974, 1945-73	130.00
Figurine, Frodo, HN 2912, 1980-84	95.00
Figurine, Galadriel, HN 2915, 1981-84	116.00
Figurine, Gamekeeper, HN 2879, 1984-92	158.00
Figurine, Gandalf, HN 2911, 1980-84	95.00
Figurine, Geisha, Flambe, HN 3229, 1989	234.00
Figurine, Genie, Flambe, HN 2999, 1990-95	176.00
Figurine, Genie, HN 2989, 1983-90	148.00
Figurine, Geraldine, HN 2348, 1972-76	234.00
Figurine, Gimli, HN 2922, 1981-84	105.00

Figurine, Gollum, HN 2913, 1980-84	148.00
Figurine, Good Catch, HN 2258, 1966-86	137.00
Figurine, Good Companion, HN 3608, 1994-99	59.00
Figurine, Gossips, HN 2025, 1949-67	206.00
Figurine, Grand Manner, HN 2723, 1975-81	118.00
Figurine, H.M. Queen Elizabeth, The Queen Mother, HN 4086, 2000	146.00
Figurine, His Holiness Pope John-Paul II, HN 2888, 1982-92	94.00
Figurine, Hope, HN 4097, 1998-99	82.00
Figurine, Hornpipe, HN 2161, 1955-62	700.00
Figurine, HRH Prince Philip, HN 2386, 1981	195.00
Figurine, Huckleberry Finn, HN 2927, 1982-85	124.00
Figurine, Invitation, HN 2170, 1956-75	74.00
Figurine, Isabella, Countess Of Sefton, HN 3010, 1991	193.00
Figurine, Jane Eyre, HN 3842, 1997	293.00
Figurine, Jane Seymour, HN 3349, 1991	587.00
Figurine, Janice, HN 2022, 1949-55	234.00
Figurine, Jessica, HN 3850, 1997	82.00 to 146.00
Figurine, Jessie, HN 4763, 2005	74.00
Figurine, Jester, HN 2016, 1949-97	226.00
Figurine, Jester, Mask, HN 1609, 1998	678.00
Figurine, Jovial Monk, HN 2144, 1954-76	59.00
Figurine, Judge, HN 2443, 1972-76	158.00
Figurine, June, HN 1691, 1935-49	227.00
Figurine, Kate Hannigan, HN 3088, 1989	56.00
Figurine, Kathleen, HN 3100, 1986	93.00
Figurine, Katie, HN 3360, 1992-97	146.00
Figurine, Kimberly, HN 3379, 1992-97	117.00
Figurine, Lady April, HN 1965, 1941-49	497.00
Figurine, Lady Charmian, HN 1948, 1940-73	82.00
Figurine, Lady Diana Spencer, HN 2885, 1982	347.00
Figurine, Lady From Williamsburg, HN 2228, 1960-83	46.00
Figurine, Lady Jane Grey, HN 3680, 1995	384.00
Figurine, Last Waltz, HN 2315, 1967-93	94.00 to 117.00
Figurine, Laura, HN 3136, 1988	65.00
Figurine, Lauren, HN 3975, 1999	94.00
Figurine, Lavender Rose, HN 3481, 1993-95	88.00
Figurine, Legolas, HN 2917, 1981-84	95.00
Figurine, Lily, HN 3902, 1998	71.00
Figurine, Lisa, HN 2310, 1969-82 ....*illus*	71.00
Figurine, Little Bridesmaid, Lavender, Pink, HN 1433, 1930-51	113.00
Figurine, Loretta, HN 2337, 1966-81	59.00
Figurine, Love Everlasting, HN 4280, 2000-Present	45.00
Figurine, Lucy, HN 3858, 1997-99	88.00
Figurine, Lynne, HN 3740, 1995	117.00
Figurine, Madonna Of The Square, HN 1969, 1941-49	825.00
Figurine, Making Friends, Box, HN 3372, 1991	179.00
Figurine, Margery, HN 1413, 1930-49	187.00
Figurine, Maria, HN 3381, 1993-99	59.00
Figurine, Marietta, HN 1341, 1929-40	433.00
Figurine, Mary, HN 3903, 1998	82.00
Figurine, Mask Seller, HN 2103, 1953-95	158.00
Figurine, Memories, HN 1855, 1938-49	215.00
Figurine, Mendicant, HN 1365, 1929-69	88.00
Figurine, Miss Demure, HN 1402, 1930-75	117.00
Figurine, Moll Flanders, HN 3849, 1999 ....*illus*	146.00
Figurine, Mrs. Hugh Bonfoy, HN 3319, 1992	146.00
Figurine, Musicale, HN 2756, 1983-85	52.00
Figurine, Newsvendor, HN 2891, 1986	237.00
Figurine, Nicola, HN 2804, 1987	83.00
Figurine, Nicole, HN 4112, 1999	117.00
Figurine, Nina, HN 2347, 1969-76	71.00
Figurine, Ninette, HN 2379, 1971-97	106.00
Figurine, Ninette, HN 3417, 1992	146.00
Figurine, Old Balloon Seller, HN 1315, 1929-98	144.00 to 240.00
Figurine, Open Road, HN 4161, 1999-2001	88.00

Royal Doulton, Figurine, Moll Flanders, HN 3849, 1999 $146.00

Royal Doulton, Figurine, Santa Claus, HN 2725, 1982-93 $234.00

R

Royal Doulton Figurines

Figurines were made at the end of the nineteenth century. From 1909 and 1914 small figurines were made. Royal Doulton figurines have been made every year since. They were realistic models of people, like the *Old Balloon Seller* or *Top o' the Hill.* Royal Doulton artists were making more contemporary figurines by 1978 and figurines like the Images line of streamlined white figures were created.

Royal Doulton, Figurine, Victoria, HN 2471, 1973-2000
$235.00

Royal Doulton, Vase, Flambe, Painted, Gourd Shape, C.J. Noke, 7½ x 7 In.
$780.00

Figurine, Orange Lady, HN 1759, 1936-75		88.00
Figurine, Orange Lady, HN 1953, 1940-75		148.00
Figurine, Paige, HN 4767, 2005		74.00
Figurine, Paisley Shawl, HN 1987, 1946-59		235.00
Figurine, Paisley Shawl, HN 1988, 1946-75		176.00
Figurine, Paisley Shawl, M 4, 1932-45		235.00
Figurine, Pantalettes, HN 1362, 1929-42		293.00
Figurine, Patchwork Quilt, HN 1984, 1945-59		240.00
Figurine, Patricia, HN 1431, 1930-49		413.00
Figurine, Patricia, HN 3907, 1998		70.00
Figurine, Penelope, HN 1901, 1939-75		92.00
Figurine, Primrose, HN 3710, 1996-98		146.00
Figurine, Prized Possessions, HN 2942, 1982		361.00
Figurine, Punch & Judy Man, HN 2765, 1981-90		384.00
Figurine, Puppy Love, Box, HN 3371, 1991		148.00
Figurine, Rachel, HN 2936, 1985-97		88.00
Figurine, Rebecca, HN 2805, 1980-96		264.00
Figurine, Rebecca, HN 4041, 1998		205.00
Figurine, Repose, HN 2272, 1972-79		294.00
Figurine, Reverie, HN 2306, 1964-81		106.00
Figurine, Rose, HN 3709, 1996-2000		117.00
Figurine, Rosebud, HN 1983, 1945-52		382.00
Figurine, Samwise, HN 2925, 1982-84		421.00
Figurine, Santa Claus, HN 2725, 1982-93	*illus*	234.00
Figurine, Sara, HN 2265, 1981-2000		88.00
Figurine, Sarah, HN 3852, 1996-99		146.00
Figurine, Sir Walter Raleigh, HN 1751, 1936-49		475.00
Figurine, Sir Winston Churchill, HN 3057, 1985-Present		158.00
Figurine, Skater, HN 2117, 1953-71		165.00
Figurine, Solitude, HN 2810, 1977-83		176.00
Figurine, Sophie, HN 3257, 1990-92		82.00
Figurine, Spring Flowers, HN 1807, 1937-59		227.00
Figurine, Springtime, HN 3033, 1983		102.00
Figurine, Stop Press, HN 2683, 1977-81		59.00
Figurine, Summertime, HN 3137, 1987		83.00
Figurine, Susan, HN 2952, 1982-93		205.00
Figurine, Suzette, HN 2026, 1949-59		205.00
Figurine, Sweet & Twenty, HN 1298, 1928-69		148.00
Figurine, Sweet Anne, HN 1318, 1929-49		140.00
Figurine, Sweet Seventeen, HN 2734, 1975-93		147.00
Figurine, Sweet Sixteen, HN 3648, 1994-98		59.00
Figurine, Sweeting, HN 1935, 1940-73		147.00
Figurine, Tess Of The D'urbervilles, HN 3846, 1998		146.00
Figurine, Thank You, HN 2732, 1983-86		158.00
Figurine, Thanks Doc, HN 2731, 1975-90		206.00
Figurine, Tiffany, HN 4771, 2005		74.00
Figurine, Tinsmith, HN 2146, 1962-67		169.00
Figurine, Tom Bombadil, HN 2924, 1982-84		421.00
Figurine, Town Crier, HN 2119, 1953-76		120.00
Figurine, Toymaker, HN 2250, 1959-73		210.00
Figurine, Valerie, HN 2107, 1953-95		83.00
Figurine, Valerie, HN 3904, 1998		71.00
Figurine, Veronica, HN 1517, 1932-51		323.00
Figurine, Victoria, HN 2471, 1973-2000	*illus*	235.00
Figurine, Vivienne, HN 2073, 1951-67		206.00
Figurine, Wedding Morn, HN 3853, 1966-99		117.00
Figurine, Wintertime, HN 3060, 1985		83.00
Figurine, Wizard, Flambe, HN 3121, 1990-95		205.00
Figurine, Young Master, HN 2872, 1980-89		74.00
Flask, Moon, Simeon, Toby, Enamel, 7¾ In.		411.00
Inkwell, Hinged Top, Woman, Votes For Women, Crossed Arms, Green Dress, 3½ In.		1554.00
Jug, Dickens Ware, Fagin, Square, c.1925, 5¼ In.		96.00
Jug, Dickens Ware, Mr. Micawber, 8 In.		150.00
Jug, Merry Wives Of Windsor, No. 1126, 7¾ In.		56.00
Lamp, 2-Light, Landscape, Blue Trees, Yellow Fruit, 1935, 30 In.		1115.00
Loving Cup, Admiral Lord Nelson, 1935, 10½ In.		1626.00

Loving Cup, Commemorative, Queen Elizabeth II, Coronation, 1953, 10 In.	310.00
Loving Cup, Regency Coach, 1931, 10 In.	858.00
Napkin Ring, Tony Weller	407.00
Panel, Tile, Oriental Style, Prophet, Long Robe, Headdress, F. Pilter, 42 x 18 In., 21 Piece	2160.00
Pitcher & Bowl, Aubrey, Flow Blue Wash, Gilt Highlights, 16 In.	500.00
Pitcher & Bowl, Earthenware, Green Ground, River Landscape Border	235.00
Plaque, Horse Head, In Horseshoe, Facing Right, No. 806	93.00
Plate, Bunnykins, Raft, 1959-98, 7½ In.	30.00
Plate, Dickens Ware, Fat Boy, 8 In.	99.00
Plate, Dickens Ware, Mr. Pickwick, 10½ In.	59.00
Plate, Dinner, Carolyn, 10½ In., 15 Piece	176.00
Plate, Dinner, Fruit Urns, Black Ground, Blue Border, Gold Trim, 10 In., 8 Piece	978.00
Plate, Dinner, White, Gold Floral Border & Rim, Early 1900s, 10 In., 6 Piece	206.00
Plate, Gnomes Living Among Tree Roots, Gold Trim, Scalloped Edge, 9½ In.	288.00
Plate, Parson, D 6280, Series Ware, 10½ In.	24.00
Platter, Madras, Flow Blue, Oval, 21½ x 17½ In.	200.00
Platter, Turkey, Flow Blue, Gilt Trim, 22 x 18 In.	1725.00
Stein, Fox Hunting, Stoneware, Metal Top Ring, No. 5520, ½ Liter	80.00
Tankard, Dickens Ware, Sairey Gamp, Green Rim, 5½ In.	185.00
Toby Jug, King Henry VIII, Box, D 7047, 1996, Small	42.00
Trivet, Life In The Forest Of Sherwood, 6½ In.	106.00
Vase, Blue Green Glaze, Molded Grapevine Bands, E. Beard, c.1903, 13¼ In., Pair	700.00
Vase, Chang, Multicolor, C.J. Noke, Fred Moore, c.1930, 3 In.	1282.00
Vase, Flambe, Cobalt Blue Flowers, Green Leaves, 17 x 6½ In.	1560.00
Vase, Flambe, Painted, Gourd Shape, C.J. Noke, 7½ x 7 In. *illus*	780.00
Vase, Grapes, Striated Blue Ground, Bulbous, Flared Rim, 6¾ In.	173.00
Vase, Heart Designs, Blue, Green & Brown Glaze, Signed BN, 9½ In.	450.00
Vase, Stick, Flambe, Asian Landscape Scene, HN 1612, 8 x 3 In.	117.00
Vase, Stoneware, Green, Gold, Red Scroll Coration, Gilt Trim, Francis Pope, c.1905, 7 In.	229.00
Vase, Sung, Arthur Eaton, C.J. Noke, c.1930, 9 In.	5335.00
Washbowl Set, Aubrey, Flow Blue, Gold Trim, 16-In. Bowl *illus*	499.00

ROYAL DUX is the more common name for the Duxer Porzellanmanufaktur, which was founded by E. Eichler in Dux, Bohemia (now Duchov, Czech Republic), in 1860. By the turn of the century, the firm specialized in porcelain statuary and busts of Art Nouveau–style maidens, large porcelain figures, and ornate vases with three-dimensional figures climbing on the sides. The firm is still in business.

Bust, Woman, Ruffled Bonnet & Dress, Flowers, Marked, Triangle E, 19½ x 13 In.	2000.00
Figurine, Abudanza, Maiden Brings Fruit, Incised, Hampet, 22 x 10 In.	1300.00
Figurine, Arab Man Riding Camel, Another Boy, Czechoslovakia, 18 x 14 x 6 In.	480.00
Figurine, Bird, Fantail, Incised, 7 x 5½ In.	95.00
Figurine, Bust, Art Nouveau Woman, Flowing Hair, Applied Daisies, 12¼ In.	1035.00
Figurine, Clock, Art Nouveau, Beige & Pink Flowers, Gold Trim, Handles, Marked, 13 In.	97.00
Figurine, Crane, Cream, Tan, Marked, 7¾ In.	112.00
Figurine, Dancing Couple, Marked, 13 x 8 In.	1200.00
Figurine, Dog, Boxer, Pink Triangle Mark, 6½ In.	45.00
Figurine, Dog, Bulldog, No. 6, Pink Triangle Mark, 6 In.	55.00
Figurine, Dog, German Shepherd, Marked, 2¼ x 6 In.	18.00
Figurine, Dog, Russian Wolfhound, White, Brown	125.00
Figurine, Elephant, Raised Trunk, White, Green Stamp Mark, 5¾ x 7½ In.	1300.00
Figurine, Fish, Black, Gray, Pink, Wave Base, 20 In.	58.00
Figurine, Fish, Grayling, Wave Base, 14 In.	29.00
Figurine, Flamenco Dancers, Gold Trim, Pink Triangle Mark, 15 x 9½ x 4½ In.	1250.00
Figurine, Girl, Basket, Wood, Bisque, c.1900, 24 In.	1117.00
Figurine, Girl, Looking In Mirror, Brushing Hair, Pink Triangle Mark, 7½ In.	55.00
Figurine, Grecian Maiden, Arm Holding Scarf, Flowing Gown, Pot, Signed, 24 In.	900.00
Figurine, Maiden At The Well, Red Dress, Green Jug, Tree, Pool Of Water, 17 x 9 In.	720.00
Figurine, Man, Shoulder Bag, Net, Woman, Apples In Apron, Jug, 22 & 20 In., Pair	720.00
Figurine, Mockingbird, Pink Triangle Mark, 6¼ x 8½ x 3½ In.	80.00
Figurine, Nature Nymph, Lilies, Trumpets, Art Nouveau, 20 x 18 x 8 In.	2500.00
Figurine, Nude, Bather, Dangles Foot Into Water, Marked, Art Nouveau, 15 x 6 x 7 In.	2200.00
Figurine, Nude, On Rock, Washing Foot, Marked, 12 x 5 In.	950.00
Figurine, Nude, Winged, Seated, Butterfly, Marked, 20 x 7 In.	3000.00
Figurine, Pan Flutist, Shepherdess, Organic Nouveau, Marked, 16 x 7 x 8 In.	1200.00
Figurine, Peacock, Black, Pink Triangle Mark, 10½ x 7 In.	85.00

Royal Doulton, Washbowl Set, Aubrey, Flow Blue, Gold Trim, 16-In. Bowl
$499.00

Royal Dux, Vase, Figural, Conch Shell, 2 Maidens, On Flowery Trunk, Pink Lotus Blossom, 17 x 14 In.
$978.00

Royal Dux, Vase, Woman, Bird, Light Gold, Trellis Handles, Flowers, Art Nouveau, 24½ In., Pair
$1200.00

R

Royal Flemish, Ewer, 6 Shields,
Black Enamel Dots, Gold Scrolls,
Flowers, Gold Rope Handle, 8¾ In.
$4371.00

Royal Flemish, Ewer,
Rampant Lion, Crown & Lance,
Stylized Flower Medallion,
Twist Handle, 12 In.
$4600.00

Royal Flemish, Vase,
2 Egyptian Men, Camel, Pyramids,
Stars, Raised Gold Decoration,
Handles, 13 In.
$28175.00

Figurine, Pierrot & Princess, Pink Triangle Mark, 12 x 12 In.	700.00
Figurine, Pig, Beige, Pink Triangle Mark, 1¾ x 3¾ In.	66.00
Figurine, Pig, White, Pink Triangle Mark, 1¾ x 3¾ In.	66.00
Figurine, Polar Bear, Pink Triangle Mark, 10 x 13 In.	240.00
Figurine, Sea Lion, Gray, Stamped, 8½ In.	55.00
Figurine, Seal, Gray, White, Pink Triangle Mark, 5 x 7½ In.	40.00
Figurine, Seminude, Eunuch, Boy In Green, Offering Gift, Stamped, 21 In.	650.00
Figurine, Stallion, Twisted, White, Pink Triangle Mark, 6¼ In.	85.00
Figurine, Tango Girl, Cobalt Blue, Gilt, E Mark, 14 x 6 x 4 In.	1100.00
Figurine, Tropical Bird, Triangle Mark, 13 In.	250.00
Figurine, Woman, Carrying Urn, 14 In.	867.00
Figurine, Woman, Caught In Wind, Stamped, 12 x 8 In.	250.00
Figurine, Woman, Nude, With Urn, Marked, 6 x 8½ In.	80.00
Figurine, Woman, Sheep, Art Nouveau, Pink Triangle Mark, c.1920, 21 x 8 In.	850.00
Figurine, Woman, Sitting, With Mirror, Pink Triangle Mark, 6¼ In.	140.00
Mug, Cherries, Triangle With Acorn	15.00
Vase, Drapery, Grapes, Vines, Cream, Gold, Handles, 17 In.	575.00
Vase, Figural, Conch Shell, 2 Maidens, On Flowery Trunk, Pink Lotus Blossom, 17 x 14 In. . . *illus*	978.00
Vase, Flowers, White, Dusted Black Finish, Gold Trim, Art Nouveau Style, 21 x 12 In.	518.00
Vase, Maidens, Seminude, Sitting, Conch Type Shell, Lotus Blossom, Marked, 17½ x 4 In. . . .	978.00
Vase, Ocean Sprites, Green & White Matte Glaze, Art Nouveau, Marked, Late 1800s, 19½ x 11 In. .	510.00
Vase, Sprite, Clinging To Leaves, Celadon & White Matte Glaze, Early 1900s, 26 x 7 In.	660.00
Vase, Woman, Bird, Light Gold, Trellis Handles, Flowers, Art Nouveau, 24½ In., Pair . . . *illus*	1200.00
Vide Poche, Change Receiver, Cockatiels, Earthenware, c.1930, 15¾ In.	449.00

ROYAL FLEMISH glass was made during the late 1880s in New Bedford, Massachusetts, by the Mt. Washington Glass Works. It is a colored satin glass decorated with dark colors and raised gold designs. The glass was patented in 1894. It was supposed to resemble stained glass windows.

Biscuit Jar, Raised Panels, Spider Mums, Turquoise Leaves, Shaped Handle, 10 In.	3013.00
Bowl, Citrine, Frosted, Diamond Quilted, Bramble Flowers, Rectangular, 2¾ In.	575.00
Castor, Frosted, White & Yellow Stemmed Mums, Pairpoint Reticulated Holder, 10 In.	3163.00
Ewer, 6 Shields, Black Enamel Dots, Gold Scrolls, Flowers, Gold Rope Handle, 8¾ In. . . *illus*	4371.00
Ewer, Rampant Lion, Crown & Lance, Stylized Flower Medallion, Twist Handle, 12 In. . *illus*	4600.00
Jar, Cover, Raised Gold Panels, Romanesque Medallions, Leafy Scrolls, Crown Finial, 10 In. .	6325.00
Jug, Cover, Raised Gold Panels, Medallion, Lions, Scrolls, Crimson Rim, Gold Finial, 14 In. . .	6325.00
Toothpick, Amber, White & Yellow Mums, Melon Ribbed, Beaded Border, 1½ In.	863.00
Vase, 2 Egyptian Men, Camel, Pyramids, Stars, Raised Gold Decoration, Handles, 13 In. *illus*	28175.00
Vase, Raised Gold Panels, Roman Medallions, Squat, Pinched Rim, Crimson Scrolls, 8 In. . .	3163.00
Vase, Snow Geese In Flight, Gold Sun, Raised Gold Trim, Cylindrical, Tapered, 14 In.	3335.00

ROYAL HAEGER, *see Haeger category.*

ROYAL HICKMAN designed pottery, glass, silver, aluminum, furniture, lamps, and other items. From 1938 to 1944 and again from the 1950s to 1969, he worked for Haeger Potteries. Mr. Hickman operated his own pottery in Tampa, Florida, during the 1940s. He moved to California and worked for Vernon Potteries. The last years of his life he lived in Guadalajara, Mexico, and continued designing for Royal Haeger. Pieces made in his pottery listed here are marked *Royal Hickman* or *Hickman*.

Figurine, Swan, Peach Agate, 20 In.	195.00
Planter, Light Turquoise, Petty Crystal Glaze, Oblong, 8 x 3½ In.	75.00
Vase, Deep Red, Blue Overtones, Petty Crystal Glaze, Round, 5 In.	75.00
Vase, Double Shell, Mauve Agate, Cream Interior, Marked, 6½ In.	50.00
Vase, Lavender, Blue, Pink, Petty Crystal Glaze, 8 In.	175.00
Vase, Nautilus Shell Form, Mauve Agate, 7¾ In.	45.00
Vase, Petty Crystal Glaze, 7 In.	250.00
Vase, Rose, Blue, Petty Crystal Glaze, Bulbous, Bottleneck, Signed, 11 In.	150.00
Vase, Swan, Mauve Agate, Marked, 8½ x 6¼ x 3½ In., Pair	120.00
Salt, Divided, Bombe, Bird In Tree, Scrolled Edge, 4-Footed, Oval, Shield, c.1765, 3½ In.	840.00

ROYAL OAK *pieces are listed in the Northwood category by that pattern name.*

ROYAL RUDOLSTADT, *see Rudolstadt category.*

ROYAL VIENNA, *see Beehive category.*

R

ROYAL WORCESTER is a name used by collectors. Worcester porcelains were made in Worcester, England, from about 1751. The firm went through many different periods and name changes. It became the Worcester Royal Porcelain Company, Ltd., in 1862. Today collectors call the porcelains made after 1862 "Royal Worcester." In 1976, the firm merged with W. T. Copeland to become Royal Worcester Spode. Some early products of the factory are listed under Worcester.

Bowl, Elephant, Cream, Gold Highlights, Footed, 5 x 7¾ In.	350.00
Bowl, Floral Bouquets, Gilt Highlights, Swag, Tassel Base, Paw Feet, 16 In.	863.00
Bracket, Rockwork Backplate, Seated Figures, Winter, Spring, 9 x 7 In., Pair	978.00
Cup & Saucer, Huntsman, H.R. Millais, Large	19.00
Dinner Service, Embassy Pattern, 12 Settings, 60 Piece	1170.00
Ewer, Fern, Cream Ground, Flower Shape Handle, 8 In.	100.00
Figurine, Bathtime, Katie's Day Series, Box, 7 In.	105.00
Figurine, Bedtime, Katie's Day Series, Box, 4¾ In.	84.00
Figurine, Caroline, Prince Regent, Special Edition	93.00
Figurine, Chinese Man, White, 6¾ In.	188.00
Figurine, Monday's Child Is Fair Of Face, 6¾ In.	84.00
Figurine, Only Me, F. Doughty Puce Mark, 6 In.	149.00
Figurine, Playtime, Katie's Day Series, Box, 6¼ In.	105.00
Figurine, Polly Put The Kettle On, F. Doughty Black Mark, 5¾ In.	112.00
Figurine, Rose Of Camelot, Limited Edition	84.00
Figurine, Schooltime, Katie's Day Series, Box	74.00
Figurine, Sleepy Boy, Margaret Can Puce Mark	224.00
Figurine, Storytime, Katie's Day Series, Box, 4¼ In.	116.00
Figurine, Tarpon, 11 x 9 In.	293.00
Figurine, Tea Time, Katie's Day Series, Box, 5¾ In.	74.00
Figurine, Young Horse, Eric Aumonier, c.1932, 6½ In.	144.00
Pitcher, Water, Flowers, Cream Ground, Bulbous, 9 In.	275.00
Plate Set, Dinner, Different Color Grounds, Painted, Gilt Flowers, 9 In., 12 Piece	529.00
Plate Set, Green Design On White, c.1910, 10½ In., 12 Piece	99.00
Potpourri, Pierced Cover, Porcelain, Multicolored, Enameled, Ferns, 1899, 13 In.	235.00
Vase, Bird & Flower, Cream Ground, Swirl Mold, 4¼ In.	425.00
Vase, Cover, Potpourri, Flying Swans, Swallows, Celadon Ground, c.1906, 8¼ In.	5390.00
Vase, Cover, Potpourri, Painted, Pheasants, Gilt, James Stinton, c.1919, 5 In.	1135.00
Vase, Floral Sprays, Hand Painted, Molded, Gilded Handles, Long Neck, c.1885, 11⅜ In.	490.00
Vase, Pink & Yellow Roses, Cream & Green Panels, Gold Stencil, Pedestal, 10½ In.	450.00

ROYCROFT products were made by the Roycrofter community of East Aurora, New York, in the late nineteenth and early twentieth centuries. The community was founded by Elbert Hubbard, famous philosopher, writer, and artist. The workshops owned by the community made furniture, metalware, leatherwork, embroidery, and jewelry. A printshop produced many signs, books, and the magazines that promoted the sayings of Elbert Hubbard. Furniture by the Roycroft community is listed in the Furniture category.

Ashtray, Copper, Hammered, Patina, 4½ In.	125.00
Bell, Copper, Hammered, Original Patina, Impressed Mark, 3 x 1¾ In.	240.00
Bookends, Copper, Hammered, Applied Ring, Patina, Mark, 4 x 5 In.	320.00
Bookends, Copper, Hammered, Chased Design, Red, Green, c.1910, 5 x 3¾ In.	295.00
Bookends, Copper, Hammered, Poppy, Orb & Cross Mark, 5¼ x 5 In.	540.00
Bookends, Copper, Hammered, Riveted, 6½ x 4¼ In.	450.00
Bookends, Copper, Hammered, Rose, 6 x 8½ x 3½ In.	400.00
Bookends, Copper, Hammered, Tooled & Applied Poppies, Patina, Mark, 6 x 5½ In.	600.00
Bookends, Copper, Hammered, Tooled Flowers, Cutout Center, Patina, Mark, 9 x 6 In.	290.00
Bookends, Copper, Hammered, Tooled Owl, Patina, Mark, 4 x 6½ In.	500.00
Bookends, Copper, Hammered, Tooled Ship, Patina, Mark, 5½ x 5 In.	210.00
Bookends, Copper, Hammered, Trillium, Patina, Mark, 5 x 3½ In.	325.00
Bookends, Mahogany, Roycroft Seal, Molded Edge, Rectangular Base, 7½ x 7 In. . . . . . *illus*	259.00
Box, Copper, Brass, Hammered, Wood Insert, 4 x 5½ In.	395.00
Candelabrum, 6-Light, Copper, Hammered, Original Brass Patina, Mark	460.00
Candlestick, Copper, Hammered, 3 Curved Legs, Domed Foot, 9 In., Pair	7200.00
Candlestick, Copper & Silver, Secessionist, Dard Hunter, 8¼ x 5 In., Pair . . . . *illus*	21600.00
Desk Set, Copper, Hammered, Brass Washed, Woodgrain, Orb & Cross Mark, 10 Piece	1220.00
Desk Set, Copper, Hammered, Calendar, Inkwell, Blotter Corners, Letter Rack, 7 Piece . . *illus*	390.00
Firestarter, Copper, Hammered, Spill Tray, Impressed Head, Heart & Hand, 12 x 10 In. . *illus*	1300.00
Lamp, Copper, Hammered, Square Base, Cone Shades, Pull Chain, Electric, 22 x 8 In., Pair .	4200.00

Roycroft, Bookends, Mahogany, Roycroft Seal, Molded Edge, Rectangular Base, 7½ x 7 In. $259.00

Roycroft, Candlestick, Copper & Silver, Secessionist, Dard Hunter, 8¼ x 5 In., Pair $21600.00

Roycroft, Desk Set, Copper, Hammered, Calendar, Inkwell, Blotter Corners, Letter Rack, 7 Piece $390.00

R

Down with the Lusitania Roycroft founder Elbert Hubbard and his second wife, Alice, died on the British ocean liner *Lusitania* when it was sunk by a German submarine in 1915. The Roycroft shops were managed by Elbert Hubbard II until they closed in 1938.

Roycroft, Firestarter, Copper, Hammered, Spill Tray, Impressed Head, Heart & Hand, 12 x 10 In. $1300.00

Roycroft, Vase, Copper, Hammered, Silver Overlay, 4-Sided, Pierced Squares, 6¾ x 2½ In. $9600.00

Lamp, Copper, Hammered, Wood Grain Pattern, Helmet Shade, 4 Mica Panels, Electric, 14 x 6 In.	3240.00
Tray, Copper, Hammered, Octagon, 2 Handles, 10 In.	300.00
Vase, Bud, Copper, Hammered, Glass Holder, Patina, Silver Finish, Orb Mark, 8¼ x 3¾ In.	175.00
Vase, Bud, Copper, Hammered, Glass Holder, Patina, Orb Mark, 8 x 3¾ In.	260.00
Vase, Copper, Hammered, 4-Sided, Tapered, Pierced Squares, 7 x 2½ In.	7200.00
Vase, Copper, Hammered, American Beauty, 22 x 8 In.	5100.00
Vase, Copper, Hammered, Flower-Form Top, Dark Patina, Orb & Cross Mark, 9 x 4 In.	1200.00
Vase, Copper, Hammered, Gourd, Patina, Mark, 5¼ x 2½ In.	265.00
Vase, Copper, Hammered, Shouldered, Patina, Orb Mark, 5 x 5½ In.	340.00
Vase, Copper, Hammered, Shouldered, Patina, Ring On Neck, Flared, Orb Mark, 12 x 6½ In.	2620.00
Vase, Copper, Hammered, Silver Overlay, 4-Sided, Pierced Squares, 6¾ x 2½ In. ....*illus*	9600.00

ROZANE, *see Roseville category.*

ROZENBURG worked at The Hague, Holland, from 1890 to 1914. The most important pieces were earthenware made in the early twentieth century with pale-colored Art Nouveau designs.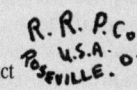

Jar, Cover, Flowers, Yellow, Red, Green, Blue, Marked, 6 In.	725.00
Vase, Cover, Frogs, Lily Pads, Green On White, Marked, c.1915, 7 In.	2468.00
Vase, Flowers, Multicolored, Squat, Marked, 3¾ x 5 In.	186.00
Vase, Stylized Irises, Multicolored, Marked, 4⅛ In.	230.00
Vase, Yellow Lizard, Stylized Flowers, Egg Shell Glaze, 4-Sided, 3 In.	748.00

RRP, or RRP Roseville, is the mark used by the firm of Robinson-Ransbottom. It is not a mark of the more famous Roseville Pottery. The Ransbottom brothers started a pottery in 1900 in Ironspot, Ohio. In 1920, they merged with the Robinson Clay Product Company of Akron, Ohio, to become Robinson-Ransbottom. The factory is still working.

Birdbath Frog, 7 In.	125.00
Crock, Amish Children, 5½ x 5 In.	33.00
Crock, Pink Heart, Navy Blue, Signed, Alan Merrick, Qt.	34.00
Dish, Pizza, 12 In.	45.00
Jardiniere, Majolica Style, c.1979, 10 x 8¾ In.	120.00
Jardiniere, Pedestal, c.1910, 12½ x 11 In.	765.00
Jardiniere, Raised Design, White Matte, c.1937, 6 x 7 In.	39.00
Jardiniere, Raised Flower, White Matte, c.1952	79.00
Kitty Dish, 6 x 3 In.	36.00
Mug, Dog 4 x 3¾ In.	33.00
Mug, Tan, Brown Drip Glaze, 4½ x 3¾ x 4½ In.	20.00
Planter, 8½ x 2½ In.	25.00
Planter, Aqua Glaze, 1950	29.00
Vase, Aqua Gloss, Deer Insert, 5½ x 7¾ In.	28.00
Vase, Cream, Green Leaves, Rose Flowers, 6 x 4 In.	34.00
Vase, Ribs, White, Glossy, 11 x 8 In.	95.00

RS GERMANY is part of the wording in marks used by the Tillowitz, Germany, factory of Reinhold Schlegelmilch from 1914 until about 1945. The porcelain was sold decorated and undecorated. The Schlegelmilch families made porcelains marked in many ways. See also ES Germany, RS Poland, RS Prussia, RS Silesia, RS Suhl, and RS Tillowitz.

Basket, Green, Bird, Flowers, 4¼ x 5¼ In.	125.00
Bowl, 10⅛ x 3⅛ In.	350.00
Bowl, Art Deco Decoration, Square, Reticulated Pedestal Base, 4¾ In. ....*illus*	71.00
Bowl, Harvest, Green, Daylilies, Green Leaves, 10 In.	48.00
Bowl, Strawflowers, 2 Handles, Oval, 7¾ x 6 In.	100.00
Cup, Peonies, Translucent Green, Pink, Gold Trim	25.00
Demitasse Pot, Pink & White Roses, Yellow Tones, 8½ In.	20.00
Hair Receiver, Pink, Light Green, Flowers, c.1917	80.00
Hatpin Holder, Pink Flowers	100.00
Hatpin Holder, Poppies, 4½ In.	115.00
Pitcher, Cider, Pink Rose, Green Tones, 6½ In.	40.00
Plate, Flowers, 10½ In.	250.00
Plate, Orchid, Gold Trim, c.1915, 8½ In.	80.00
Plate, Pink Peonies, Daisy, Purple, Orange Rim, Handles, 9¾ In.	20.00
Toothbrush, Pink Roses	75.00
Toothpick, Pink & White Flowers, Marked	145.00

R

Toothpick, Pink Roses, Lavender, Blue Leaves, 3 Handles, Gold Trim	65.00
Toothpick, White Flower, Marked	195.00
Vase, Bud, Roses, 6 In.	60.00
Vase, Children, Pink Luster, 3¼ In.	35.00

RS POLAND

RS POLAND (German) is a mark used by the Reinhold Schlegelmilch factory at Tillowitz from about 1946 to 1956. After 1956, the factory made porcelain marked *PT Poland*. This is one of many of the RS marks used. See also ES Germany, RS Germany, RS Prussia, RS Silesia, RS Suhl, and RS Tillowitz.

Biscuit Jar, Lid, Peach & Cream Flowers, White To Purple Ground, 7 x 7 In.	325.00
Bowl, Footed, White & Lavender Flowers, Gold Trim, 7 x 3¼ In.	350.00
Bowl, Mayonnaise, Footed, Saucer, White Hydrangeas, Gilt, Double Mark	125.00 to 175.00
Centerpiece, Pedestal, Blown-Out Panels, Roses Inside & Out, Fire Gold Rim	675.00
Vase, Woodland Scene, Chinese Pheasant Pair, 11 In.	1295.00

RS PRUSSIA

RS PRUSSIA appears in several marks used on porcelain before 1917. Reinhold Schlegelmilch started his porcelain works in Suhl, Germany, in 1869. See also ES Germany, RS Germany, RS Poland, RS Silesia, RS Suhl, and RS Tillowitz.

Bowl, Flower, Gold Stenciled, 10 In.	1600.00
Bowl, Flower Border, Double Mold, c.1900, 10½ In.	294.00
Bowl, Flowers, 9¼ In.	125.00
Bowl, Flowers, Blown-Out Scalloped & Ruffled Rim, Footed, 8 In.	*illus* 118.00
Bowl, Flowers, c.1900, 10½ In.	353.00
Bowl, Flowers, c.1900, 11 In.	176.00 to 235.00
Bowl, Hanging Basket Scene, White Ground, Gold Highlights, Satin Finish, 10 In.	175.00
Bowl, Madame Recamier, Green Iridized Tiffany Finish, 10½ In.	6000.00
Bowl, Madame Recamier, Lily Mold, Tiffany Finish, Gold Trim, 10 In.	2000.00
Bowl, Red Star Mark, c.1900, 2¾ x 11 In.	176.00
Bowl, Snowbird, Medallions, Old Man In The Mountain, Sheepherder, Black, 10½ In.	2900.00
Bowl, Willow Tree, Medieval Building, Footed, 6¼ In.	400.00
Cake Plate, Old Man In The Mountain, Cameo Scenes, Medallions, Black, 10 In.	2600.00
Cake Plate, Pink Flowers, Pierced Handles, c.1900, 11 In.	94.00
Celery Dish, Cream, Peach, Beige Ground, 2 Handles, 10½ In.	125.00
Charger, Woman, Silesia, 11½ In.	275.00
Cheese Server, Pink Roses	145.00
Chocolate Pot, Apple Blossoms, 9¾ In.	225.00
Chocolate Pot, Autumn Portrait, Iridescent Lavender, Gold Stencil, 9¼ In.	2900.00
Chocolate Pot Set, Poppy, Carnation Mold, Satin Finish, 4 Cups & Saucers, 11½ In. Pot	1250.00
Cracker Jar, Old Man In The Mountain, Swans, Handles, Cover, Black Finish, 5½ In.	7000.00
Creamer, Flowers, Gold Rim	65.00
Cup & Saucer, Hand Painted, Red Star Mark, 6 x 3½ In.	35.00
Demitasse Pot, Spring Portrait, Gold Trim, 9½ In.	2250.00
Dish, Hand Painted, Flowers, Pink, White Ground, c.1900, 6 x 11 In.	94.00
Hatpin Holder, 6-Sided, Embossed Flowers	100.00
Jam Jar, Underplate, Rosebuds, 4 x 5½ In.	145.00
Pitcher, Cider, Pink Poppy, Green, Gold Highlights, Carnation Mold, 9 In.	*illus* 550.00
Pitcher, Hand Painted, Gold Trim, White, Yellow, Peach Roses, 4 In.	75.00
Pitcher, Lemonade, Old Man In The Mountain Scene, Black Finish, 6¼ In.	10250.00
Pitcher, White, Yellow, Peach Roses, Gold Trim, 4 In.	75.00
Plate, Admiral Peary Arctic Scene, 9 In.	3000.00
Plate, Parrot, Blue, White, Flowers, Branch, 3 Handles, 7⅞ In.	125.00
Plate, Poppies, Silver Scrolls, Gold Trim, 8½ In.	80.00
Plate, Winter Scene, Gold & Light Blue Border, Keyhole, 9 In.	1400.00
Powder Jar, Cover, Melon Eaters, 4 x 3 In.	350.00
Syrup, Plate, Cover, Leaf, Shaded Ground	125.00
Syrup, Underplate, Flowers, Gold Border, Melon Ribbed, Scalloped Rim, 4½ In.	*illus* 147.00
Tankard, Green Leaves, Red Berries, Columnar Shape, 13 In.	275.00
Tankard, Winter Season, 13 In.	2800.00
Teapot, Sugar, Red Star, c.1900	94.00
Toothbrush Holder, 6 Holes, Pink Roses	75.00
Toothpick, White Pearl Finish, 3 Handles, Marked	225.00
Tray, Yellow Roses, 12¾ In.	110.00
Vase, Greek Key, Lebrun Gold Dots, Round, 5 x 4½ In.	500.00
Vase, Melon Eaters, 5 In.	675.00
Vase, Pink, Yellow Flowers, Blue Ground, 8 In.	525.00

RS Germany, Bowl, Art Deco Decoration, Square, Reticulated Pedestal Base, 4¾ In.
$71.00

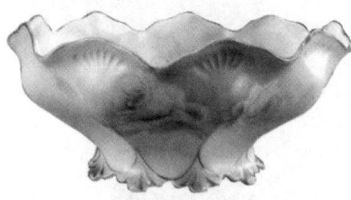

RS Prussia, Bowl, Flowers, Blown-Out Scalloped & Ruffled Rim, Footed, 8 In.
$118.00

RS Prussia, Pitcher, Cider, Pink Poppy, Green, Gold Highlights, Carnation Mold, 9 In.
$550.00

RS Prussia, Syrup, Underplate, Flowers, Gold Border, Melon Ribbed, Scalloped Rim, 4½ In.
$147.00

R

Rubina Verde, Lamp, Pink, Crimped & Ruffled Edges, Burner, 9½ In. $2588.00

Rudolstadt, Vase, Flowers, Cream, Gold Trim, Pinched Waist, Scrolled & Pierced Handles, Footed, 17¾ In. $288.00

Vase, Pink, Yellow Roses, Castle, 4½ In.		450.00
Vase, Woman Cartouche, Greek Key Band, Green, 8¼ In.		500.00

RS SILESIA appears on porcelain made at the Reinhold Schlegelmilch factory in Tillowitz, Germany, from the 1920s to the 1940s. The Schlegelmilch families made porcelains marked in many ways. See also ES Germany, RS Germany, RS Poland, RS Prussia, RS Suhl, and RS Tillowitz.

Plate, Roses, White Flowers, Green Ground, Gold Floral Stenciling, 1930s, 6⅜ In.		38.00
Tray, Roses, Old Ivory, 6¼ In.		75.00

RS SUHL is a mark used by the Reinhold Schlegelmilch factory in Suhl, Germany, between 1900 and 1917. The Schlegelmilch families made porcelains in many places. See also ES Germany, RS Germany, RS Poland, RS Prussia, RS Silesia, and RS Tillowitz.

Biscuit Jar, 3-Footed, Floral, Rose & Pink, Blue Green, Lavender, Gilt Accents.		185.00
Tea Set, Teapot, Creamer, Sugar, Lids, Scalloped Handles, Gold Trim, Roses, 7 In.		175.00

RS TILLOWITZ was marked on porcelain by the Reinhold Schlegelmilch factory at Tillowitz from the 1920s to the 1940s. Table services and ornamental pieces were made. See also ES Germany, RS Germany, RS Poland, RS Prussia, RS Silesia, and RS Suhl.

Plate, Hanging Fuchsia Flowers, Transfer, 6¼ In.		14.00
Salt Set, Plate, 2 Salts, Green, Gold Leaves, 3 Piece, 6½ & 3 In.		75.00
Syrup, Underplate, 3¾ x 4¾ In.		30.00

RUBINA is a glassware that shades from red to clear. It was first made by George Duncan and Sons of Pittsburgh, Pennsylvania, about 1885. This coloring was used on many types of glassware. The pressed glass patterns of Royal Ivy and Royal Oak are listed under Northwood.

Pitcher, Optic Ribbed, White & Blue Flowers, Octagonal Bottom, Applied Clear Handle, 9 In.		145.00
Pitcher, Yellow & White Flowers, Egg Shape, Tricornered Rim, Clear Reeded Handle, 8¾ In.		230.00

RUBINA VERDE is a Victorian glassware that was shaded from red to green. It was first made by Hobbs, Brockunier and Company of Wheeling, West Virginia, about 1890.

Creamer, Coin Spot, Enameled Flower, 4 In.		173.00
Cruet, Coin Spot, Teepee Shape, Faceted Vaseline Stopper & Applied Handle, 6¾ In.		460.00
Lamp, Pink, Crimped & Ruffled Edges, Burner, 9½ In.	*illus*	2588.00
Pitcher, Hobnail, Bulbous, Square Rim, Applied Vaseline Handle, Hobbs, Brockunier, 8 In.		460.00
Pitcher, Water, Coin Spot, Square Rim, Applied Vaseline Handle, Hobbs, Brockunier, 8 In.		201.00
Vase, Optic Ribbed, Rigaree Vaseline Collar, Acanthus Leaves, Tri-Leaf Foot, 4½ In.		230.00

RUBY GLASS is the dark red color of a ruby, the precious gemstone. It was a popular Victorian color that never went completely out of style. The glass was shaped by many different processes to make many different types of ruby glass. There was a revival of interest in the 1940s when modern-shaped ruby table glassware became fashionable. Sometimes the red color is added to clear glass by a process called flashing or staining. Flashed glass is clear glass dipped in a colored glass, then pressed or cut. Stained glass has color painted on a clear glass. Then it is refired so the stain fuses with the glass. Pieces of glass colored in this way are indicated by the word *stained* in the description. Related items may be found in other categories, such as Cranberry Glass, Pressed Glass, and Souvenir.

Candy Dish, Textured, Diamond Quilted Pattern, 3 x 3½ In.		28.00
Cup, Acid Etched Flowers, Forget-Me-Not, Applied Handle, Pontil, 3½ x 2½ In.		30.00
Sugar, Cover, Galleried Rim, Short Stem, Applied Foot, Knop, 7 x 3¼ In.		605.00

RUDOLSTADT was a faience factory in the Thuringia region of Germany from 1720 to about 1791. In 1854, Ernst Bohne began working in the area. From about 1887 to 1918, the New York and Rudolstadt Pottery made decorated porcelain marked with the RW and crown familiar to collectors. This porcelain was imported by Lewis Straus and Sons of New York, which later became Nathan Straus and Sons. The word *Royal* was included in their import mark. Collectors often call it "Royal Rudolstadt." Most pieces found today were made in the late nineteenth or early twentieth century. Additional pieces may be listed in the Kewpie category.

Bowl, Fruit, Pink Roses, Gold Trim, Ribs, 2 Handles, c.1900-18, 12¾ x 8½ x 2½ In.		65.00
Cake Plate, Roses, Pierced Handles, 10 In.		65.00
Celery Tray, White, Yellow, Cream Ground, 12 x 5½ In.		65.00

Creamer, Ivory, Gold Leaf	90.00
Figurine, Cakewalker, Black Man & Woman Dressed Up, Marked, c.1900, 7¼ In.	359.00
Jug, Rococo Mold, Hand Painted Flowers, c.1900, 14 In.	264.00
Lamp, Lesbian Love, 9½ x 5½ x 5½ In.	450.00
Pitcher, Flow Blue, Flower, 4 In.	55.00
Plate, Fern, 6 In.	10.00
Plate, Roses, Yellow, White Ground, Gold Trimmed, 8¼ In.	10.00
Vase, Bulbous, Flower Bouquet, Cream Ground, Leaf Scrolled, Flower, 18 In.	230.00
Vase, Burgundy, Sage Green Leaves, Gold Sprig, Bisque, 7¼ In.	125.00
Vase, Flowers, Cream, Gold Trim, Pinched Waist, Scrolled & Pierced Handles, Footed, 17¾ In. *illus*	288.00
Vase, Oval, Ewer Shape, Cream Flowers, 10½ In.	195.00
Vase, Peach Leaves, Bird In Flight, Ewer Shape, Copper Handles, 10 In.	120.00
Vase, Pink Flowers, Dark Green, Pastel Green Ground, Bisque, 1887-1918, 8½ In.	175.00
Vase, Yellow, Pink, Blue Mums, Gold Stenciled, 10 In.	120.00

RUGS have been used in the American home since the seventeenth century. The oriental rug of that time was often used on a table, not on the floor. Rag rugs, hooked rugs, and braided rugs were made by housewives from scraps of material.

Afghan Bokhara, 10 Black Guls, Red Ground, Wide Geometric Border, 8 Ft. 4 In. x 4 Ft. 9 In.	413.00
Agra, Allover Boteh Cream, Tan Flowers, Mauve Ground, 10 x 14 Ft.	2714.00
Akstafa, Prayer, Browns, c.1890, 5 Ft. 1 In. x 2 Ft. 11 In.	2400.00
Anatolian, Esparta, Ivory, Blue, Red, Green, Flowerhead Medallion, 20 Ft. x 12 Ft. 6 In.	3000.00
Anatolian, Prayer, Blue Field, Ivory Ground, Serrated Mihrab, 5 Ft. 5 In. x 3 Ft. 6 In.	240.00
Art Deco, Nichols, Flowers, Maroon Ground, Blue Border, Mauve Border, 9 Ft. 10 In. x 9 Ft.	411.00
Art Deco, Tan Ground, Flowers, Lanterns, Bird, Landscape, Mauve Border, 9 Ft. 10 In. x 8 Ft. 11 In.	294.00
Aubusson, Blue, Gray Ground, Garland Trellis, Borders, 16 Ft. 2 In. x 10 Ft. 3 In.	6000.00
Aubusson, Center & Border Cartouches, Floral Garlands, Ivory Ground, 9 x 12 Ft.	2937.00
Aubusson, Louis Philippe, Brown, Burgundy, Border, Mid 19th Century, 10 Ft. 6 In. x 9 Ft.	7200.00
Aubusson, Louis Philippe, Multicolored, Black Ground, 6 Ft. 4 In. x 7 Ft. 3 In.	8400.00
Aubusson, Louis Philippe, Multicolored, Border, 12 Ft. 3 In. x 13 Ft. 10 In.	4200.00
Aubusson Style Oushak, Open Center Field, Green, Amber, Ivory, 13 Ft. 6 In. x 20 Ft.	863.00
Bagface, Afshar, South Persia, Late 19th Century, 2 Ft. 2 In. x 1 Ft. 9 In.	558.00
Bagface, Kurdish, Northwest Persia, Late 18th Century, 2 Ft. x 1 Ft. 8 In.	558.00
Baluchi, Coral, Orange, Blue Allover Geometric, Banding, c.1970, 3 x 6 Ft.	165.00
Bidjar, Green, Blue, Red Center Ground, Red Border, 10 Ft. 11 In. x 14 Ft. 6 In.	1380.00
Bidjar, Green, Orange, Blue Ground, Blue Border, 7 Ft. 8 In. x 10 Ft. 10 In.	1380.00
Bidjar, Kurdish, North Persia, Blue & Orange Medallions, Red Ground, c.1890, 10 x 5 Ft. 7 In.	600.00
Bidjar, North Persia, c.1880, 18 Ft. 8 In. x 11 Ft. 3 In. *illus*	10200.00
Bidjar, North Persia, Flat Weave, Browns, Red, Ivory Medallion, c.1896, 20 Ft. 5 In. x 7 Ft. 2 In.	4500.00
Bidjar, Open Field, Red Ground, Blue & Red Borders, 19 Ft. x 15 Ft. 10 In.	17600.00
Bidjar, Persia, Blue Ground, Red Border, Flower Motifs, c.1880, 15 Ft. x 5 Ft. 10 In.	4200.00
Bidjar, Red Ground, Floral, Red Border, 22 Ft. 5 In. x 12 Ft. 1 In.	15400.00
Bidjar, Red Ground, Tan Border, Flowers, 3 Ft. 6 In. x 6 Ft. 4 In.	633.00
Bokhara, Black, Cream, Red Guls, Red Ground, Black Geometric Border, 2 Ft. 11 In. x 5 Ft.	106.00
Bokhara, Cream, Brown Guls, Geometric Border, c.1950, 3 Ft. 1 In. x 4 Ft.	236.00
Bokhara, Pakistani, Rows Of Guls, Star & Cross Motif, Cream Ground, 12 Ft. 4 In. x 9 Ft.	472.00
Braided, Brown, Beige, Orange, White, Gray, 29¼ In. Diam.	302.00
Braided, Gray, Black, Red, Brown, Round, 29¼ In. *illus*	303.00
Braided, Printed & Plain Fabrics, Mat, 12 In. Diam.	121.00
Caucasian, 6 Center Medallions, Coarse Weave, 2 Ft. 9 In. x 8 Ft. 4 In.	1610.00
Caucasian, Borders, Geometrics, Brown Field, Animals, Runner, 10 Ft. x 3 Ft. 7 In.	863.00
Caucasian, Center Medallions, Burgundy Field, Blue, Flowers, Borders, 5 Ft. 4 In. x 8 Ft.	1380.00
Caucasian, Center Panel, Flower Bands, Geometric & Flower Borders, 3 Ft. 5 In. x 7 Ft. 3 In.	3910.00
Caucasian, Ivory Field, 4 Center Medallions, 3 Ft. 8 In. x 5 Ft. 6 In.	431.00
Caucasian, Kazak, Ivory Center Medallion, Hook Designs, 6 Ft. 3 In. x 7 Ft. 3 In.	1840.00
Caucasian, Red Field, Geometric, Red, Brown, Rust, Center Borders, 3 Ft. 9 In. x 7 Ft. 3 In.	305.00
Caucasian, Red Ground, 3 Medallions, 4 Ft. 7 In. x 2 Ft. 11 In.	398.00
Caucasian, Red Ground, Floral Border, c.1940, 6 Ft. 7 In. x 3 Ft. 7 In.	310.00
Caucasian, Repeating Flowers, Dark Blue Field, 3 Ft. 11 In. x 5 Ft. 1 In.	460.00
Chinese, Art Deco, Green Ground, Asymmetrical Floral Border, 8 Ft. 6 In. x 11 Ft. 4 In.	1920.00
Chinese, Blue Ground, Birds, Flowers, 10 Ft. x 17 Ft. 4 In.	235.00
Chinese, Cream Medallion, Border, Green Ground, Asian Motifs, 10 Ft. 6 In. x 17 Ft. 6 In.	590.00
Chinese, Flower Sprigs, Navy Ground, Tan Border, c.1900, 2 Ft. 11 In. x 5 Ft.	118.00
Chinese, Flowering Plants, Peach Blossoms, Blue Ground, Floral Border, Oval, 7 Ft. x 8 Ft. 5 In.	325.00
Chinese, Flowers, Blue Field, Ivory & Blue Floral Border, 1920s, 8 Ft. 9 In. x 11 Ft. 8 In. *illus*	4600.00

Rug, Bidjar, North Persia, c.1880, 18 Ft. 8 In. x 11 Ft. 3 In. $10200.00

Rug, Braided, Gray, Black, Red, Brown, Round, 29¼ In. $303.00

Braided Rugs

The *braided rug* was first popular from the 1820s to the 1850s. It was made from braided strips of worn fabric that were sewn together, round and round, until a circular rug was made. This type of rug was back in style in the 1890s Colonial Revival rooms and is still popular today.

R

Rug, Chinese, Flowers, Blue Field, Ivory & Blue Floral Border, 1920s, 8 Ft. 9 In. x 11 Ft. 8 In. $4600.00

Oriental Rugs

Oriental rugs were used in the eighteenth-century home and afterward. The name "Oriental rug" usually refers to the hand-knotted rugs made in southeastern Europe, Turkey, North Africa, Iran, Pakistan, India, or China. The designs have symbolic meanings and are part of geometric patterns. Seventeenth- and eighteenth-century portraits sometimes show an Oriental rug on a table.

Chinese, Flowers, Vases, Navy Ground, Beige & Ivory Border, c.1910, 10 Ft. 4 In. x 17 Ft.	826.00
Chinese, Medallion, Flowers, Navy Ground, Sprigs, Spandrels, c.1900, 2 Ft. 6 In. x 4 Ft.	304.00
Chinese, Needlepoint, 10 Monkeys, Fruit, Leaves, Garland Border, 8 Ft. 11 In. x 5 Ft. 10 In.	472.00
Chinese, Nichols, Vine, Leaf, Cinnamon Field, Blue Border, 3 Ft. 2 In. x 5 Ft. 9 In.	288.00
Chinese, Phoenix, Flowers, Ivory Field, Blue & Rose Border, Sunburst, 1920s, 4 Ft. 2 In. x 7 Ft.	805.00
Chinese, Pictorial, Bird In Tree, Blue, Olive Green, Beige Field, 3 Ft. 4 In. x 7 Ft. 4 In.	173.00
Dagestan, Borders, Blue, Ivory, Red Ground, Roosters, People, Horses, 4 Ft. 3 In. x 5 Ft. 3 In.	7188.00
Donegal, Ireland, Wool, Hand Knotted, c.1905, 14 Ft. 11 In. x 11 Ft. 6 In.	9000.00
Donegal, Ireland, Wool, Hand Knotted, Green, 1920s, 14 Ft. 7 In. x 14 Ft. 8 In.	9000.00
Donegal, Ireland, Wool, Hand Knotted, Green, Red Border, c.1900, 15 Ft. 5 In. x 9 Ft. 10 In.	13200.00
Donegal, Ireland, Wool, Hand Knotted, Red, 1920s, 9 Ft. 7 In. x 7 Ft. 8 In.	11400.00
Drugget, Beige Ground, Arrowheads, Rust, Green, Blue Border, 8 Ft. 10 In. x 11 Ft. 4 In.	300.00
Drugget, Geometric, Red, Green, Brown, Beige Ground, Wool, 3 Ft. 11 In. x 6 Ft. 8 In.	720.00
Feraghan, North Persia, Blue, Black, Herati Field, Vine, Multicolored, 13 Ft. 3 In. x 3 Ft. 6 In.	1560.00
Feraghan Sarouk, Center Medallion, Ivory Field, 4 Ft. 6 In. x 6 Ft. 11 In.	5060.00
Feraghan Sarouk, Center Medallion, Red Ground, Corner Spandrels, 4 Ft. 1 In. x 6 Ft. 2 In.	633.00
Feraghan Sarouk, Medallion, Brown, Black Field, Floral Border, 3 Ft. 4 In. x 4 Ft. 10 In.	1610.00
Gorevan, Blue Spandrels, Salmon Red Ground, Blue, Ivory Borders, 5 Ft. 8 In. x 8 Ft. 4 In.	3565.00
Hamadan, Allover Flowers, Red Field, Blue Borders, 4 Ft. 5 In. x 6 Ft. 3 In.	374.00
Hamadan, Beige Center Medallion, Interlocking Diamonds, 4 Ft. 2 In. x 6 Ft. 11 In.	10350.00
Hamadan, Black Medallion, Pendants, Red Ground, Black Flower Border, 4 Ft. 10 In. x 8 Ft.	118.00
Hamadan, Blue, Red, Multiple Borders, Mid 1900s, 6 Ft. 2 In. x 3 Ft. 6 In.	633.00
Hamadan, Blue, Red, Orange Medallion, Red Ground, 20th Century, 4 Ft. 2 In. x 6 Ft.	189.00
Hamadan, Diamond Medallion, Blue, Black, Red Field, Flowers, 6 Ft. 8 In. x 5 Ft. 3 In.	345.00
Hamadan, Diamond Medallion, Pendants, Red, Black Bands, 17 Ft. 2 In. x 4 Ft. 5 In.	236.00
Hamadan, Iran, Cream, Diamond Medallion, Spandrels, 9 Ft. 9 In. x 6 Ft. 2 In.	189.00
Hamadan, Northwest Persia, Early 20th Century, 6 Ft. x 3 Ft. 8 In.	529.00
Hamadan, Plum Ground, Blue Border, 6 Ft. 5 In. x 9 Ft. 3 In.	805.00
Hamadan, Red, Blue Curvilinear, Geometric, Red Ground, Blue Band, 6 Ft. 1 In. x 3 Ft. 7 In.	142.00
Hamadan, Red Ground, Black Border, White Banding, 16 Ft. 8 In. x 2 Ft. 8 In.	212.00
Hamadan, Repeating Geometric Designs, Blue Field, 3 Ft. 7 In. x 17 In.	633.00
Hamadan, Tan Medallion, Blue, Orange Allover Geometric, Red, Blue Border, 4 Ft. 7 In. x 6 Ft.	266.00
Hereke, Prayer, Pastel, Ivory, Embossed Medallions, Silk, 2 Ft. 10 In. x 3 Ft. 10 In.	1035.00
Hereke, Rust Border, Tan Ground, Signed, Silk, 4 Ft. 6 In. x 3 Ft. 2 In.	2124.00
Heriz, Blue & Red Center Medallions, Red Field, Blue Corners, 7 Ft. x 9 Ft. 7 In.	1150.00
Heriz, Center Lobed Medallion, Red Ground, Ivory, Blue, Mid 1800s, 8 Ft. 9 In. x 6 Ft. 6 In.	1250.00
Heriz, Diamond Medallion, Flowers, Red Ground, Dark Border, 8 Ft. x 10 Ft. 7 In.	649.00
Heriz, Geometric Medallions, Red Field, Camel Border, Runner, 11 Ft. 8 In. x 3 Ft. 3 In.	690.00
Heriz, Ivory Spandrels, Red Ground, Dark Blue Border, 9 Ft. 8 In. x 17 Ft. 4 In.	2875.00
Heriz, Medallion, Diamond & Rectangle, Pendants, Spandrels, Navy Border, 10 x 8 Ft.	885.00
Heriz, Northwest Persia, Browns, Greens, Fringe, c.1880, 12 Ft. 3 In. x 10 Ft. 6 In.	20400.00
Heriz, Northwest Persia, Late 19th Century, 9 Ft. 10 In. x 6 Ft. 10 In.	1116.00
Heriz, Northwest Persia, Mid 20th Century, 11 x 8 Ft.	1763.00
Heriz, Northwest Persia, Mid 20th Century, 12 Ft. 8 In. x 9 Ft. 10 In.	1763.00
Heriz, Red Field, Blue Flowerhead Medallion, Palmettes, Spandrels, Vines, 10 Ft. 6 In. x 6 Ft. 8 In.	3000.00
Heriz, Row Of 9 Medallions, Brick Red Field, Runner, 3 Ft. 3 In. x 13 Ft. 7 In.	1725.00
Hooked, 2 Boys, You Been Farming Long, Beige, Black, Initials, RL, 21 x 38 In.	88.00
Hooked, 2 Farmers, Oxen & Plow, 2 Houses, Pine Trees, Initials, RL, 21 x 38 In.	55.00
Hooked, 2 Reindeer In Center, Flowers & Oak Leaves Red Border, Wool, 1800s, 31 x 64 In.	1875.00
Hooked, 3 Bears, Holding Bowls Of Porridge, Mounted On Board, 34 x 18 In.	825.00
Hooked, 3 Rabbits Eating Carrots, Gray Ground, 38 x 21 In. ....*illus*	121.00
Hooked, 4 Children, Holding Hands, Rear View, Tan Ground, Gray Border, Initials, RL, 21 x 38 In.	22.00
Hooked, 4 Petal Red Flower Heads, Yellow Scrolls, 33 x 58 In.	2640.00
Hooked, 5 Wide-Eyed Cats In Silhouette, Cream Ground, 41 x 60 In.	23627.00
Hooked, 15 Squares, Multicolored, Late 19th Century, 39½ x 25 In.	239.00
Hooked, 17 Chicks, Surrounding Water Dish, Brown Ground, Initials, RL, 21 x 38 In.	44.00
Hooked, 117 Squares, Objects, Flower Sprig, 108 x 144 In.	5975.00
Hooked, 177 Squares, Flowers, Shields, Birds, Multicolored, Bullard, 1946, 108 x 144 In.	5975.00
Hooked, Barnyard, Pig, Sheep, Chicken, Dog, Blue Ground, Swag Border, RL, 21 x 38 In.	44.00
Hooked, Beaver Floating On Log, Red & Black Maple Leaf Corners, Initials, RL, 21 x 38 In.	143.00
Hooked, Black Pony, Beige, Yellow, Brown, Vine Border, On Stretcher, 36 x 41 In.	2100.00
Hooked, Boston Terrier, Brown, Tan, Black, Striped Border, Wool On Burlap, 31 x 50 In.	550.00
Hooked, Calico Cat, Spandrels, Morning Glories, Petunias, On Stretcher, 1800s, 33 x 57 In.	3300.00
Hooked, Cat, Reclining, Brown Rug, Orange Bow & Flowers, 45 x 28 In.	193.00
Hooked, Cats, White Cat, Yellow Ribbon, Bird, Leaves, Scroll, Cotton, Wool, 16½ x 32 In.	529.00

R

Hooked, Centennial, Shield, Stars, Arrows, Star Border, Wool, c.1876, 24 x 36 In.	1763.00
Hooked, Center Pinwheel, Pink, Blue, Yellow, Tan, Wool, Mounted, 52 x 26 In.	546.00
Hooked, Cheshire Cat, Large Grin, Blue Eyes, Gray Ground, 1948, 28 x 18 In.	535.00
Hooked, Clamshells, Black Ground, c.1890, 31 x 65 In.	3800.00
Hooked, Cottage Scene, Oval Center, Brown, Tan, Red Chimney, Flowers, 27 x 53 In.	173.00
Hooked, Cow, Spotted, Blue Ground, Trees, Borders, 25 x 45 In.	1840.00
Hooked, Cow, Spotted, Diamond Border, Burlap, 39 x 20½ In.	275.00
Hooked, Dog, German Shepherd & Lad, Tan, Black, Pink & Blue, Wool & Cotton, 24 x 36 In.	115.00
Hooked, Dog, Irish Setter, Multicolored, 42½ x 36 In.	83.00
Hooked, Dog, Spaniel, Reclining, Wool, Cotton, Rayon Strips, Burlap, 20½ x 34 x ¾ In.	235.00
Hooked, Eagle, Spread Wing, Blue Ground, Clutching Oak Leaf, Arrows, Shield, 37 x 24 In.	330.00
Hooked, Fall Leaves, Tan, Gold, Brown, Wool & Cotton On Burlap, 14½ x 79 In.	374.00
Hooked, Farm, Horse, Rail Fence, Bird, Flower Garden, Brown Border, Initials, RL, 21 x 38 In.	110.00
Hooked, Floral, Rectangular, Stylized Flowers, Early 20th Century, 25 x 36½ In.	206.00
Hooked, Floral Wreath, Greek Key Border, 35 x 50 In.	403.00
Hooked, Flower, Potted, Rectangular Block Border, 38 x 45 In.	154.00
Hooked, Flower, Potted In Pitcher, Red, Blue, White, Tan, Dentil Border, 47 x 36 In.	28.00
Hooked, Flowers, Pink & Red, Green Leaves, Multicolored Border, 50 x 26 In.	33.00
Hooked, Garden, Navy Blue, Cranberry, Red Green, Beige, 1945-51, 120 x 72½ In.	7200.00
Hooked, Geometric, Crisscross X, Red, Green, Blue, 30 x 53 In.	2640.00
Hooked, Geometric, Stepped Zigzag, Red, Brown, Green, Rust, Black, 73 x 52½ In.	558.00
Hooked, Geometric Pastels, 31 x 56 In.	443.00
Hooked, Grapevine, Gray, Green, Mustard Black, Wool, 43 x 25 In.	86.00
Hooked, Grenfell, Labrador, Seagulls, Blue Ground, 19 x 22 In.	1000.00
Hooked, Grenfell, Polar Bear, Woven Seal Fur, Frame, 11½ x 10½ In.	748.00
Hooked, Hawaiian Design, Gold Loops, Abstract Border, 1820, 42 x 51 In.	3500.00
Hooked, Horse, Multicolored Ground, Red, Brown, Gray, Black, Brown, 48 x 36 In.	6600.00
Hooked, Horse, Red, Leaves In Corners, Multicolored Border, 45 x 35¾ In.	2970.00
Hooked, House, Mat, 8 x 16 In.	403.00
Hooked, Hunt Scene, Man On Horse, Dogs, Raccoon In Tree, Multicolored, Frame, 51 x 27 In.	660.00
Hooked, Indian In Canoe, On River, Teepee, Cotton, Wool, 19th Century, 26 x 39½ In.	6000.00
Hooked, Kazak Design, Red Field, Flowers, Fringe, Germany, 72 x 104 In.	546.00
Hooked, Kitten, Geometric Border, Cotton & Wool On Burlap, 26 x 43 In.	8500.00
Hooked, Layered Squares, Rosette Border, 22 x 39¼ In.	176.00
Hooked, Leaves, Flowers, Wool, Gray, Blue Ground, 6 Narrow, Wide Borders, 29½ x 51½ In.	529.00
Hooked, Lighthouse With Sailboat, Brown Border, 38 x 21 In. *illus*	44.00
Hooked, Lion, Bird On Branch, Leaves & Branches On Corners, 29 x 53 In.	1150.00
Hooked, Lion, Reclining, Black Ground, Leafy Vine Corners, 31½ x 77 In.	770.00
Hooked, Lion, Reclining, Brown, Black Mane, Gray Ground, Initials, RL, 21 x 38 In.	110.00
Hooked, Lion, Reclining, Cream Ground, Striped Border, 25½ x 39 In.	743.00
Hooked, Log Cabin Pattern, Grays, Tans, Black, Orange, c.1890, 33 x 68 In.	2400.00
Hooked, Mallard Ducks In Flight, Rayon, Silk, Burlap, 52¾ x 39¾ In.	5581.00
Hooked, Moose, Water, Pine Trees, Birds In Flight, Green Border, Initials, RL, 21 x 38 In.	88.00
Hooked, Multicolored Diamonds, Gray Ground, Navy Border, Wool On Burlap, 27 x 53 In.	316.00
Hooked, Multicolored Stripe Crisscross Cube, Geometric, Red, Yellow, Gray, Beige, 32 x 64 In.	1200.00
Hooked, National Road, Commemorative, Multicolored, c.1953, 36 x 59½ In.	3600.00
Hooked, Nude Woman, Butterflies, Trees, Tan Ground, Border, Initials, ERS, 38 x 21 In.	330.00
Hooked, Oak Leaf Branches, Maroon, Yellow, Pink, Black, Brown, 30 x 53 In.	1200.00
Hooked, Oak Leaf Branches, Red, Yellow, Green, Brown, 32 x 45 In.	960.00
Hooked, Parrot On Branch, Date 1896, Black Border, Salmon Scrolls, 24½ x 39½ In.	374.00
Hooked, Patchwork Squares, Stars, Cats, Birds, Horse, Rooster, Flowers, c.1860, 24 x 39½ In.	24000.00
Hooked, Redheaded Bird, Black & White Stripe Wings, Wool, On Burlap, Mat, 18½ x 19 In.	259.00
Hooked, Red House, Blue Sky, Duck On Pond, Sunrise, Mounted, 17 x 23½ In.	144.00
Hooked, Rider On Horseback, Hunting Dogs, Critter In Tree, 27 x 51 In.	660.00
Hooked, Roosters, Oval Center, Leaf & Flower Borders, Cotton, Wool, 37 x 61 In.	2468.00
Hooked, Running Horse, White, Black Mane, Tail, Mottled Ground, 29 x 39½ In.	353.00
Hooked, Scottie Dog, Brown Ground, Swag Edge, Flower Corners, Fringed, 21 x 33 In.	413.00
Hooked, Scottie Dog, Multicolored, Gray Ground, 1930, 22 x 36 In.	235.00
Hooked, Squirrel Center, Cats, Eagles, Horses, 35 x 33 In.	2530.00
Hooked, Stag, Center Medallion, Mauve, Flowers, Scroll, Mounted To Frame, 34 x 27 In.	247.00
Hooked, Stained Glass Design, Multicolored, Beige Border, 20th Century, 35 x 35½ In.	191.00
Hooked, Stepped Striped, Red, Brown, Black, 47 x 41 In.	3000.00
Hooked, Striped, Black Border, Many Colors, 57½ x 33 In.	863.00
Hooked, Stripes, Blue, Purple, Tans, Black Border, Shag, 22 x 38 In.	86.00
Hooked, Stylized Commas, Concentric Oval Field, 35 x 57½ In.	468.00

Hooked Rugs

Hooked rugs were used in America by 1700. A hook was used to pull narrow strips of cloth through a coarse fabric backing. The colored strips made designs of flowers, animals, scenes, and geometric patterns. An artistic housewife might draw her own patterns; the less talented would buy a pattern from designers like Edward Frost. He sold thousands of patterns from about 1870 to 1900. Cheap factory-made rugs appeared in the 1840s.

Rug, Hooked, 3 Rabbits Eating Carrots, Gray Ground, 38 x 21 In. $121.00

Rug, Hooked, Lighthouse With Sailboat, Brown Border, 38 x 21 In. $44.00

R

Rug, Hooked, Urn, Flowers, Leafy Branches, Salmon, Multicolored, 20 x 34 In. $5288.00

Button Rugs

Button rugs wwere canvas-backed homemade rugs that used round, button-shaped pieces of cloth. The backing fabric of the rug showed between the circles that were stitched to it. The button rug was fashionable during the 1820s. A few late examples, sometimes called *penny rugs*, were made from blue and gray pieces cut from old Civil War uniforms in the 1870s.

Rug, Kazak, Karachopt, Original Macrame Fringe, c.1890, 7 Ft. 7 In. x 4 Ft. 4 In. $3900.00

R

Tongue Rugs

Some early rugs in America were made from fabric scraps. *Tongue rugs* were made from tongue-shaped pieces of cloth overlapped and sewn to the backing. The tongues completely covered the backing.

Hooked, They Had To Leave, Adam, Eve, Satan's Expulsion From Eden, c.1930, 37 x 48 In.	1680.00
Hooked, Three Bears, Papa, Mama, Baby, Carrying Steaming Bowl, 28½ x 43 In.	850.00
Hooked, Tree Of Life, Flowers, Gray, Blue, Green-Black Border, Wool On Burlap, 1929, 34 x 59 In.	150.00
Hooked, Tulip & Heart, Blue Ground, 42½ x 30 In.	303.00
Hooked, Urn, Flowers, Leafy Branches, Salmon, Multicolored, 20 x 34 In. ....*illus*	5288.00
Hooked, Village, Landscape, Green, Yellow, Tan, Orange, Black, 24 x 37½ In.	288.00
Indo-Aubusson, Green, Ivory Border, Ivory Center Medallion, 9 Ft. 10 In. x 17 Ft. 9 In.	115.00
Indo-Kerman, Repeating Flowers, Burgundy Field, 13 Ft. 11 In. x 22 Ft. 9 In.	14900.00
Isfahan, Flower Medallion, Blue, Red Field, Flowers, Blue Border, 9 Ft. 6 In. x 13 Ft. 5 In.	575.00
Isfahan, Medallion, Red Ground, Flowers, Scrolling Vines, Blue Border, 10 Ft. x 14 Ft. 5 In.	1121.00
Isparta, Turkish, Red Ground, Geometric Border, 3 Ft. 11 In. x 6 Ft. 6 In.	180.00
Karabagh, 3 Seated Figures, Water Pipe, Flower & Vine Border, 5 Ft. 4 In. x 6 Ft. 5 In.	1265.00
Karabagh, Blue Ground, Green Border, 3 Ft. 3 In. x 6 Ft. 3 In.	259.00
Karabagh, Medallions, Ivory, Red, Blue, Ivory Border, 3 Ft. 8 In. x 6 Ft. 5 In.	460.00
Karagashli, Northeast Caucasus, Browns, c.1910, 5 Ft. 9 In. x 3 Ft. 8 In.	2100.00
Karaja, 4 Center Medallions, Burgundy Field, 2 Ft. 11 In. x 10 Ft. 11 In.	460.00
Karaja, Blue Field, Multicolored Medallions, Guls, Rosettes, Runner, 10 Ft. 9 In. x 2 Ft. 10 In.	4200.00
Kashan, Center Medallion, Burgundy Field, 9 Ft. 6 In. x 12 Ft. 1 In.	633.00
Kashan, Flowers, Navy Ground, Border, Blue Banding, 4 Ft. 4 In. x 6 Ft.	354.00
Kashan, Iran, Navy, Cream, Blue, Diamond Medallion, 12 Ft. 8 In. x 9 Ft. 6 In.	354.00
Kashan, Navy Diamond Medallion, Spandrels, Border, Allover Flowers, 3 Ft. 3 In. x 4 Ft.	236.00
Kashan, Plum Ground, Blue Borders, Signed, 9 Ft. 1 In. x 17 Ft. 11 In.	3450.00
Kasvin, Red Ground, Blue Center Medallion, Border, 12 Ft. x 21 Ft. 1 In.	4140.00
Kazak, 3 Center Medallions, Ivory, Salmon Field, Hand Woven, 3 Ft. 6 In. x 6 Ft. 3 In.	748.00
Kazak, 3 Medallions, Blue Ground, Red, Borders, Early 19th Century, 8 Ft. 5 In. x 5 Ft. 3 In.	575.00
Kazak, 3 Medallions, Red Ground, c.1900, 9 Ft. 3 In. x 5 Ft. 7 In.	774.00
Kazak, 4 Center Medallions, Blue Field, 3 Ft. 9 In. x 4 Ft. 9 In.	575.00
Kazak, 5 Multicolored Lozenge Medallions, Blue Field, Runner, 19th Century, 9 Ft. x 3 Ft.	2040.00
Kazak, Caucasus, Blue Field, Ivory, Red, Hooked Vines, Chalice Border, 9 Ft. 6 In. x 3 Ft. 8 In.	1800.00
Kazak, Center Medallions, Blue Field, 3 Ft. 2 In. x 4 Ft. 7 In.	1725.00
Kazak, Geometric, Border, Red Ground, 7 Ft. 11 In. x 4 Ft.	944.00
Kazak, Karachopt, Original Macrame Fringe, c.1890, 7 Ft. 7 In. x 4 Ft. 4 In. ....*illus*	3900.00
Kazak, Karachopt, Southwest Caucasus, Browns, c.1880, 7 Ft. 5 In. x 5 Ft. 6 In.	10200.00
Kazak, Prayer, Geometric Borders, Blue Medallions, Red Ground, 3 Ft. 8 In. x 4 Ft. 7 In.	1495.00
Kazak, Rust Ground, Blue, Black Ground, Cream, Red Borders, 3 Ft. 10 In. x 7 Ft. 3 In.	1100.00
Kazak, Southwest Caucasus, Browns, Runner, c.1890, 14 Ft. 4 In. x 3 Ft. 6 In.	4200.00
Kazak, Southwest Caucasus, Late 19th Century, 9 Ft. 5 In. x 5 Ft.	588.00
Kerman, Center Shaped Medallion, Red Field, Blue, White, Tan Border, 9 Ft. 10 In. x 12 Ft. 6 In.	634.00
Kerman, Cream Diamond Medallion, Scrolling Flowers, Tan, Blue Spandrels, 10 x 12 Ft.	325.00
Kerman, Ivory Ground, Runner, c.1920, 17 Ft. x 2 Ft. 3 In.	1135.00
Kerman, Pastel, Blue Field, Medallion, Broken Border, Flowers, 11 Ft. 7 In. x 8 Ft. 11 In.	345.00
Kerman, Pink Field, Mint Green, Cream Borders, Flowers, Mid 1900s, 9 x 12 Ft.	944.00
Kerman, Repeating Flowers, Burgundy Field, 12 Ft. 7 In. x 19 Ft. 10 In.	748.00
Kilim, Allover Rust, Beige, Cream Diamond Pattern, Geometric Border, 9 Ft. 3 In. x 12 Ft.	187.00
Kuba, Northeast Caucasus, Blue Ground, Diamond Rows, Ivory Gul Border, 4 Ft. x 3 Ft. 4 In.	3900.00
Kuba, Repeating Flowers, Blue Field, Green, Blue Borders, 3 Ft. 10 In. x 5 Ft. 4 In.	460.00
Kurdish, Northwest Persia, Red Field, 3 Ft. 5 In. x 8 Ft.	1393.00
Kurdish, Red Border, Blue Ground, Runner, 3 Ft. 2 In. x 9 Ft. 8 In.	1093.00
Lavar Kerman, Center Medallion, Ivory Field, Corner Work, 9 Ft. 5 In. x 13 Ft. 8 In.	2530.00
Lavar Kerman, Tree Of Life, 4 Ft. 7 In. x 7 Ft. 11 In.	857.00
Lilihan, Persian, Turquoise, Red, Blue Arabesques, Geometric, Runner, 2 Ft. 10 In. x 15 Ft.	4583.00
Mahal, Allover Flowers, Black Ground, Red Border, 6 Ft. 11 In. x 9 Ft. 8 In.	590.00
Mahal, Ivory Field, Rust, Blue, Brown Geometrics, 7 Ft. 1 In. x 10 Ft. 5 In.	1725.00
Mahal, Navy Diamond Medallion, Pendants, Salmon Ground, Spandrels, 5 x 6 Ft.	266.00
Mahal, Salmon Medallion, Allover Flowers, Navy Ground, Spandrels, 4 Ft. 2 In. x 6 Ft.	295.00
Malayer, Blue Ground, Border, c.1920, 12 Ft. 4 In. x 5 Ft. 3 In.	2167.00
Malayer, Persia, Blue Field, Allover Palmettes, Blue Rosette Border, c.1910, 20 x 12 Ft.	10200.00
Malayer, Red Ground, Floral Border, c.1920, 6 Ft. 2 In. x 4 Ft. 10 In.	387.00
Malayer, Repeating Designs, Blue Field, 5 Ft. 8 In. x 16 Ft. 3 In.	1840.00
Meshed, Blue & Red Ground, Allover Flowers, 10 x 11 Ft.	235.00
Meshed, Center Cartouche, Blue, White, Red Ground, Herati Border, 8 Ft. 3 In. x 11 Ft. 3 In.	499.00
Meshed, Navy Diamond Medallion, Pendants, Corners, Border, Red Ground, 9 x 12 Ft.	472.00
Mogan, Geometric Medallions, Brown Field, Diamond Borders, Runner, 3 Ft. 7 In. x 11 Ft. 9 In.	1495.00
Needlepoint, Allover Flowers, Geometric Bandings, 9 Ft. 9 In. x 16 Ft. 2 In.	472.00
Northwest Persia, Blue Field, Geometric, Red, Blue, Green Borders, 6 Ft. 1 In. x 17 Ft.	6435.00

Northwest Persia, Blue Field, Medallion, Flowers, Red, Blue Borders, 3 Ft. 5 In. x 5 Ft. 2 In.	300.00
Northwest Persia, Browns, Flowers, Geometric, Red Borders, c.1810, 13 Ft. 4 In. x 6 Ft. 9 In.	10800.00
Northwest Persia, Red Field, Flowers, Borders, Red, Blue, Green, Cream, 4 Ft. x 6 Ft. 2 In. ..	88.00
Penny, Applied Brown & Orange, Scalloped Edge, Blue Ground, Gray Back, Wool, 40 x 26 In. *illus*	173.00
Penny, Brown, Navy & Olive Green, Circles, Plaid Ground, 1900s, 36 x 31 In.	315.00
Penny, Dove Motifs, Blue, Yellow, White, Lavender, Wool, Cotton, 30¼ x 46 In.	235.00
Penny, Green, Red, Mustard, Black Disks, 6-Point Star, Yellow Ground, Wool, 73 x 43 In.	920.00
Persian, 10 Stepped Diamond Medallion, Beige Field, Runner, 3 Ft. 6 In. x 15 Ft. 4 In.	920.00
Persian, Abrash Plum Ground, Green Spandrels, Blue Borders, Runner, 3 Ft. 1 In. x 12 Ft. ..	230.00
Persian, Allover Design, Gold & Olive Field, Ivory Border, Runner, 3 Ft. 4 In. x 8 Ft. 4 In.	1265.00
Persian, Allover Flowers, Beige, Red, Blue Ground, Floral Border, 9 Ft. 2 In. x 12 Ft. 3 In. ...	480.00
Persian, Allover Flowers, Red Ground, Blue Border, 8 Ft. 10 In. x 11 Ft. 8 In.	1293.00
Persian, Blue, Red Ground, Repeating Motif, Runner, 3 Ft. 3 In. x 8 Ft. 10 In.	900.00
Persian, Brown Ground, Red, Orange, Yellow, Runner, 16 Ft. 4 In. x 6 Ft. 5 In.	1880.00
Persian, Concentric Diamond, Center Medallion, Ivory Field, 2 Ft. 8 In. x 4 Ft. 4 In.	115.00
Persian, Floral Center, Dark Blue & Red Leaf Border, 6 Ft. 11 In. x 9 Ft. 4 In.	780.00
Persian, Geometric, Rectangular Block, Trees, Flowers, 11 Ft. 10 In. x 14 Ft. 10 In.	2990.00
Persian, Hamadan, Medallion, Red Ground, Floral & Geometric Border, 4 Ft. 9 In. x 10 Ft. 7 In. .	300.00
Persian, Hamadan, Red Ground, 3 Ft. 6 In. x 13 Ft. 4 In.	708.00
Persian, Heriz, Medallion, Leaf Ground, Geometric Border, Red, Blue, 8 Ft. 3 In. x 11 Ft. 2 In.	840.00
Persian, Mahal, Repeating Designs, Dark Blue Field, 10 Ft. 3 In. x 13 Ft.	2300.00
Persian, Rust Ground, Green Spandrels, Ivory Border, Runner, 3 Ft. 8 In. x 10 Ft. 9 In.	690.00
Persian, Sarouk, Red Ground, Allover Floral & Urns, Runner, 7 Ft. 3 In. x 10 Ft. 3 In.	528.00
Persian, Serapi, Center Turquoise Teardrop Medallion, Geometric, 14 Ft. x 16 Ft. x 4 In.	11456.00
Persian, Serapi, Multicolored Ground, Serrated, Floral Medallions, 16 x 21 In.	15275.00
Persian, Shiraz, Ivory Medallions, Quadrupeds, Barber Pole Kilim, 5 Ft. 9 In. x 9 Ft. 8 In. ...	1840.00
Rag, Gray, Tan, Blue, Yellow Stripes, 3 Panels, Cotton, Wool, 8 Ft. 9 In. x 11 Ft.	144.00
Sarouk, Blue, Ivory, Orange, Early 20th Century, 15 Ft. 9 In. x 10 Ft. 10 In.	3220.00
Sarouk, Broken Border Design, Allover Flowers, Blue, Ivory, Red, 11 Ft. 10 In. x 9 Ft.	1495.00
Sarouk, Center Blue Medallion, Serrated Border, Brick Red Field, 3 Ft. 7 In. x 5 Ft. 3 In.	1035.00
Sarouk, Center Diamond Medallion, Flowers, Burgundy Field, Blue Border, 6 Ft. 6 In. x 4 Ft. 2 In.	805.00
Sarouk, Center Medallion, Red Field, Multiple Borders, Flower Field, 6 Ft. 6 In. x 5 Ft. 1 In. .	240.00
Sarouk, Center Red Medallion, Allover Flowers, 11 Ft. 10 In. x 2 Ft. 9 In.	403.00
Sarouk, Feraghan, Salmon Ground, Medallion, Floral Border, c.1890, 6 Ft. 3 In. x 4 Ft. 1 In. .	754.00
Sarouk, Flowers, Red Field, Black Border, Runner, 2 Ft. 8 In. x 7 Ft. 10 In.	345.00
Sarouk, Flowers, Trailing Vines, Blue Field, 3 Floral Borders, 6 Ft. 7 In. x 4 Ft. 3 In.	3565.00
Sarouk, Red Field, Allover Flowers, Runner, 6 Ft. 5 In. x 2 Ft. 6 In.	518.00
Sarouk, Red Ground, Allover Flowers, 3 Ft. 4 In. x 4 Ft. 11 In.	240.00
Sarouk, Red Ground, Allover Flowers, Multiple Broken Borders, 11 Ft. 10 In. x 9 Ft. 2 In. ...	1208.00
Sarouk, Red Ground, Allover Flowers, Red, Blue Border, 9 x 12 Ft.	2633.00
Sarouk, Red Ground, Blue Border, Yellow Bands, c.1940, 6 Ft. 6 In. x 4 Ft. 1 In.	767.00
Sarouk, Repeating Flowers, Burgundy Field, 3 Ft. 4 In. x 4 Ft. 10 In.	920.00
Sarouk, Repeating Flowers, Salmon Field, 10 Ft. 11 In. x 13 Ft. 10 In.	3910.00
Sarouk, Salmon Field, Brown, Blue, Geometric Designs, 1920s, 2 Ft. 7 In. x 5 Ft. 2 In.	460.00
Sarouk, Salmon Ground, Navy Border, Tan Bands, 6 Ft. 6 In. x 7 Ft. 11 In.	354.00
Saruok, Flower Vase, Blue Field, Signature Panels, 10 Ft. x 13 Ft. 5 In.	920.00
Senneh, Geometric, Brown, Beige, Black, Rust Field, 5 Borders, 4 Ft. 6 In. x 3 Ft. 5 In.	485.00
Serapi, Central Medallion, Salmon Field, Blue Corners, 9 Ft. 4 In. x 12 Ft. 8 In.	3910.00
Shirvan, East Caucasus, Browns, c.1880, 4 Ft. 6 In. x 3 Ft. 6 In.	2400.00
Shirvan, Red Field, Multicolored, Hooked Lozenge, Medallions, Guls, 9 Ft. 4 In. x 4 Ft. 8 In. .	2400.00
Shirvan, Red Ground, Blue Corner Medallions, Ivory Border, 4 Ft. x 5 Ft. 4 In.	288.00
Shirvan, Repeating Geometric Medallion, Salmon Field, 3 Ft. 8 In. x 6 Ft. 5 In.	518.00
Shirvan, Serrated Central Medallion, Blue Field, c.1800s, 5 Ft. 9 In. x 4 Ft. 4 In.	1265.00
Shirvan, Terra-Cotta Ground, Medallions, Geometric Floral Border, c.1900, 4 Ft. 8 In. x 3 Ft.	258.00
Soumak, Grid, Stylized Roosters, White, Red Borders, Silk, Cotton, 6 Ft. 4 In. x 4 Ft.	561.00
Soumak, Multicolored, 4 Pointed Stars, Beige, Diamonds, Geometric, 6 Ft. 6 In. x 3 Ft. 5 In. ..	189.00
Soumak, Repeating Diamond Medallions, Cream, Blue, Rust Ground, 7 Ft. 7 In. x 9 Ft. 9 In. ..	1680.00
Soumak, Russian, Red To Rust Ground, Geometric Border, Black, 9 Ft. 11 In. x 7 Ft. 4 In. ...	558.00
Southeast Caucasian, Late 19th Century, 10 Ft. 4 In. x 3 Ft. 8 In.	940.00
Tabriz, Medallion, Urns, Flower Vines, Red Field, Blue Border, 9 Ft. 9 In. x 12 Ft. 8 In.	633.00
Tibetan, Lotus Pattern, Russet Field, 1 Ft. 2 In. x 2 Ft. 3 In.	857.00
Tibetan, Tan Ground, Blue, Green, Red Geometric Design, c.1930, 4 Ft. 10 In. x 3 Ft.	671.00
Turkeman, Black, White, Red Guls, Red Ground, Geometric Border, c.1960, 4 Ft. 4 In. x 5 Ft.	118.00
Turkish, Red Medallion, Green Ground, Blue Border, c.1920, 25 x 18 Ft.	568.00
Turkish, Rust Red Ground, Blue Border, 1 Ft. 8 In. x 1 Ft. 6 In.	345.00

Floorcloths

Floorcloths were used in England by 1680 and the idea spread to the colonies.

Nathan Smith started a factory in Knightsbridge, England, in 1754. He made floorcloths from resin, pitch, beeswax, linseed oil, and Spanish brown that were pressed into a canvas. Then it was painted or printed with a pattern.

In 1844 a new product was developed by Elijah Galloway, who used rubber cork dust and coloring on canvas. In 1860 Frederick Walton invented a way to use oil in place of rubber. It was the first inexpensive linoleum.

Rug, Penny, Applied Brown & Orange, Scalloped Edge, Blue Ground, Gray Back, Wool, 40 x 26 In. $173.00

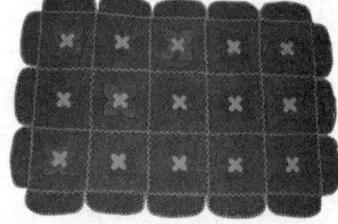

Rug, Wool, Yellow, White Sunburst, Gerhardt, 101 x 102 In. $270.00

Ruskin, Vase, Blue & Green Glaze, Shouldered, Flared Rim, 4½ In. $210.00

Ruskin, Vase, Grape Leaf, Vine & Cluster Design, Mottled Yellow, Luster Glaze, Marked, 6¼ In. $115.00

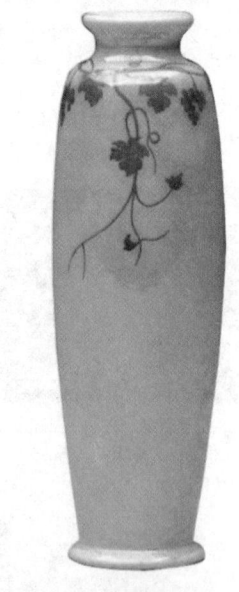

R

Russel Wright, Imperial Pinch, Tumbler, Juice, 3¼ In. $15.00

Vine Scroll, Dark Blue Ground, Oak Leaf Border, Dusty Rose, 9 Ft. 1 In. x 12 Ft.	1100.00
William Morris, Allover Poppies, Leaves, Rose Ground, Vine Border, 9 x 12 Ft.	1800.00
William Morris, Vine Scroll, Green, Cream, Blue, Rust Ground, Leaf Border, 9 x 12 Ft.	1020.00
Wool, Yellow, White Sunburst, Gerhardt, 101 x 102 In. ....*illus*	270.00
Yomud, West Turkestan, Flatweave, Red & Blue Bands, Geometric, c.1890, 9 Ft. 1 In. x 5 Ft. 5 In.	1080.00
Yuruk, East Anatolia, Prayer, Green Field, Hourglass Shapes, c.1900, 5 Ft. 6 In. x 4 Ft. 2 In.	480.00
Zenjan, Red Hexagonal Medallion, Navy, Red Ground Geometric Border, 4 Ft. 3 In. x 6 Ft. ...	295.00
Ziegler Mahal, Central Persia, Pastels, Early 20th Century, 12 Ft. 7 In. x 8 Ft. 2 In.	8400.00

RUMRILL Pottery was designed by George Rumrill of Little Rock, Arkansas. From 1933 to 1938, it was produced by the Red Wing Pottery of Red Wing, Minnesota. In January 1938, production was transferred to the Shawnee Pottery in Zanesville, Ohio. It was moved again in December of 1938 to Florence Pottery Company in Mt. Gilead, Ohio, where Rumrill ware continued to be manufactured until the pottery burned in 1941. It was then produced by Gonder Ceramic Arts in South Zanesville until early 1943.

RumRill

Jug, Ball, Blue Sponge, Matte Finish, Ivory Inside, Red Wing Pottery Co., 7½ x 6 In.	299.00
Planter, Bulb, Green, Sage, Scalloped, 3¼ x 6¾ In.	32.00
Vase, Blue, No. 311, Stoneware, 5 In.	25.00
Vase, Blue Matte, Deco Shaped, 8 In.	400.00
Vase, Blue Speckled, Handles, 7¾ In.	65.00
Vase, Fan, Blue, Mottled, 8 x 6 In.	60.00
Vase, Fan, Desert Rose Matte, Red Wing, c.1938, 9½ x 6½ In.	50.00
Vase, Fan, Dutch Blue Matte, Mottled, Stippled, 6 x 6 In.	80.00
Vase, Green, 3 Swan Handles, 7½ x 4½ In.	250.00
Vase, Green, 4¼ In.	100.00
Vase, Ivory Semimatte, White, Green, Handles, Red Wing, 5⅜ In.	100.00
Vase, Off-White, Pink, Urn Shape, 5½ x 9 In.	148.00

RUSKIN is a British art pottery of the twentieth century. The Ruskin Pottery was started by William Howson Taylor and his name was used as the mark until about 1899. The factory, at West Smethwick, Birmingham, England, stopped making new pieces in 1933 but continued to glaze and sell the remaining wares until 1935. The art pottery is noted for its exceptional glazes.

RUSKIN POTTERY WEST SMETHWICK

Vase, Blue, Incised, c.1925, 6¼ In.	1054.00
Vase, Blue & Green Glaze, Shouldered, Flared Rim, 4½ In. ....*illus*	210.00
Vase, Blue & Green Mottled Glaze, Shouldered, Pottery, Signed, 4½ In.	195.00
Vase, Bronze Luster Glaze, High Shoulder, Flared Base & Rim, 11 In.	1665.00
Vase, Flambe, White, Squat, 6¼ In.	1581.00
Vase, Grape Leaf, Vine & Cluster Design, Mottled Yellow, Luster Glaze, Marked, 6¼ In. ..*illus*	115.00
Vase, High Fired, Signed, William Howson Taylor, c.1913, 13 In.	7182.00
Vase, Kingfisher Blue Luster Glaze, Cylindrical, Flared Rim, 8¼ In.	925.00
Vase, Lavender, Green & Black Over Red Kiln, Shouldered, Flared, 1914, 14 In.	8338.00
Vase, Luster, Classic Shape, Signed, 1914, 9 x 4 In.	1495.00
Vase, On Stand, Mottled Green & Blue, 8½ In.	738.00
Vase, Orange High Glaze, Tan Ground, Bulbous, Flattened, Cylindrical Neck, 6¾ In.	1480.00
Vase, Orange Luster, 9 In.	168.00
Vase, Orange Luster Glaze, Purple, Red, Green Iridescence, Round Foot, Tapered Neck, 5 x 5 In.	117.00
Vase, Red Flambe Lilly, 9¾ In.	1792.00
Vase, Speckled Orange High Glaze, Cream Ground, Flared Rim, 1933, 6 In.	1480.00

RUSSEL WRIGHT designed dinnerwares in modern shapes for many companies. Iroquois China Company, Harker China Company, Steubenville Pottery, and Justin Tharaud and Sons made dishes marked *Russel Wright*. The Steubenville wares, first made in 1938, are the most common today. Wright was a designer of domestic and industrial wares, including furniture, aluminum, radios, interiors, and glassware. Dinnerwares and other pieces by Wright are listed here. For more information, see *Kovels' Depression Glass & Dinnerware Price List.*

Russel Wright MFG. BY STEUBENVILLE

American Modern, Bowl, Coral	25.00
American Modern, Bowl, Seafoam Blue, 7 x 2½ In.	34.00
American Modern, Bowl, Vegetable, Cedar Green, 2 Sections, Handle Slots	35.00
American Modern, Cocktail, Smoke, 3 Oz., 3 In.	12.00
American Modern, Cup, Chartreuse, 2 x 3 In.	12.00
American Modern, Goblet, Granite Gray, 10 Oz., 4⅛ In.	10.00
American Modern, Gravy Boat, Coral	25.00
American Modern, Gravy Boat, Granite Gray	20.00

American Modern, Plate, Coral, 10 In.	24.00
American Modern, Plate, Dinner, Gray, 10 In.	15.00
American Modern, Salt & Pepper, Coral, 2 In.	25.00
Imperial Pinch, Tumbler, Juice, 3¼ In. ....*illus*	15.00
Imperial Twist, Goblet, 6½ x 3⅜ In.	10.00
Iroquois Casual, Platter, Aqua, Square 13 In.	60.00
Iroquois Casual, Platter, Avocado Yellow, 13 In.	40.00
Iroquois Casual, Platter, Nutmeg Brown, 13 In.	20.00
Iroquois Casual, Platter, Nutmeg Brown, 15 In.	40.00
Iroquois Casual, Platter, Pink Sherbet, 10 In.	35.00
Iroquois Casual, Platter, White, 13¼ In.	25.00
Iroquois Casual, Platter, White, Oval, 12⅝ x 9⅝ In.	30.00
Iroquois Casual, Soup, Dish, Avocado Yellow, 5⅜ x 2¾ In.	30.00
Iroquois Casual, Soup, Dish, Nutmet Brown, 5⅜ x 2¾ In.	30.00I
Iroquois Casual, Sugar & Creamer, Ripe Apricot, 5¾ In.	10.00
Iroquois Casual, Sugar & Creamer, Stacking, Brown Drip, 5¾ In.	10.00

SABINO glass was made in the 1920s and 1930s in Paris, France. Founded by Marius-Ernest Sabino (1878–1961), the firm was noted for Art Deco lamps, vases, figurines, and animals in clear, colored, and opalescent glass. Production stopped during World War II but resumed in the 1960s with the manufacture of nude figurines and small opalescent glass animals. The new pieces are a slightly different color and can be recognized.

Sabino France

Bowl, Opalescent, Raised Figures, 20th Century, 4¼ x 9½ In.	335.00
Box, Gold, Suspended In Glass, 4¾ x 1⅞ In.	265.00
Dish, Clam Shape, Embossed Handle, 7 x 4 In.	125.00
Figurine, Bird, Opalescent, 1¼ x 2 In.	40.00
Figurine, Cat, Seated, 4 In.	176.00
Figurine, Dove, Head Up, Opalescent, Art Deco, 2 x 2 In.	85.00
Figurine, Turkey, Opalescent, Signed, 2 In.	66.00
Knife Rest, Poodle Pattern, 3½ In.	38.00
Vase, Cockatoo, Amber, 20th Century, 8 In.	374.00
Vase, Wide Mouth, Tapered Cylinder, Border, Birds, Female Nudes, 9⅛ In.	940.00

SALOPIAN ware was made by the Caughley factory of England during the eighteenth century. The early pieces were blue and white with some colored decorations. Another ware referred to as Salopian is a late nineteenth-century tableware decorated with color transfers.

Salopian

Plate, Ferry Bridge, 8-Sided, Brown Pearlware, c.1820	475.00
Plate, White Ground, Blue Flowers & Edge, c.1780, 8 In., 4 Piece	413.00
Teapot, Pheasant & Rose, c.1820	475.00

SALT AND PEPPER SHAKERS in matched sets were first used in the nineteenth century. Collectors are primarily interested in figural examples made after World War I. Huggers are pairs of shakers that appear to embrace each other. Many salt and pepper shakers are listed in other categories and can be located through the index at the back of this book.

Aunt Jemima & Uncle Mose, Plastic, 1950s, 5 In.	56.00
Barrels, Old McDonald's Farm, Gold Trim, Regal China, 4 In.	125.00
Bear, Nodder, Japan, 1940s	95.00
Bell, Blue Specks, Stoneware, 2⅜ In.	275.00
Big Boy, Large Check Pattern Overalls, Brown Hair, 1960s, 4 In.	140.00
Big Boy, Small Check Pattern Overalls, Black Hair, Japan, 1960s, 4 In.	154.00
Binoculars, Joan Of Arc, Porcelain, Gold Trim, c.1965, 3⅛ In.	24.00
Birds & Nest, Nodder, Japan, 1940s	195.00
Black River & Western Railroad, Japan, 4¼ In.	56.00
Borden, Beulah & Beauregard, Elsie Holder, Ceramic, 1950s, 5 In.	140.00
Borden, Elsie & Elmer, Ceramic, 1950s, 3¾ x 4 In.	136.00
Boy & Girl, Fat Cheeked Kids, Boy In Overalls, Girl In Dress & Apron, 4 In.	14.00
Boy & Girl, Old McDonald's Farm, Regal China, 3½ In.	120.00
Budweiser Beer, Bud Man, Ceramic, 1960s, 3½ In. ....*illus*	246.00
Dairy Queen, Girl, Ceramic, Japan, 3¾ In.	112.00
Dean Martin & Jerry Lewis, Guess Who?, Ceramic, Napco, 3¼ In. ....*illus*	560.00
Eskimo Boy & Girl, Alaska, 1½ x 1¾ x 3¼ In.	40.00
Farmwell Feeds, 1960s, 3½ In.	56.00
Kangaroo, Nodder, Japan, 1950s	145.00

American Modern
The American Modern dinnerware designed by Russel Wright (1905–1976) was made by Steubenville Pottery Company of Steubenville, Ohio, from 1939 to 1959. During the 1950s, American Modern outsold all other dinnerware patterns marketed in the United States. American Modern was made in colors that were then unfamiliar for dinner sets—muted tones called Seafoam Blue, Cedar Green, and Chutney. The dish shapes were different, too. The dinner plate has no rim; the celery dish is a curved free-form cross between a bowl and a plate; the cups turn in at the rim.

Salt & Pepper, Budweiser Beer, Bud Man, Ceramic, 1960s, 3½ In.
$246.00

Salt & Pepper,
Dean Martin & Jerry Lewis, Guess Who?, Ceramic, Napco, 3¼ In.
$560.00

Salt & Pepper, Lantern, Street, New York City, Flowers, Buildings, Wood, Japan, 5 In.
$5.00

S

Salt & Pepper, Luzianne Mammy, Red Plastic, Painted Accents, Plastic Stoppers, 1950s, 5 In. $90.00

Salt & Pepper, Piel's Beer Brothers, Bert & Harry, Ceramic, 1960s, 4-In. Harry, 3-In. Bert $186.00

Salt Glaze, Ewer, Animal Head Spout, Round Center, Grapes & Birds, Lion Heads, Stamped, 19 In. $230.00

Salt Glaze, Stein, Figural, Bearded Gentleman, Hands On Belly, Hinged Hat, Plaque Center, 13½ In. $288.00

Ladies' Heads, Iron Shape, Japan	65.00
Lantern, Street, New York City, Flowers, Buildings, Wood, Japan, 5 In. *illus*	5.00
Laurel & Hardy, Ceramic, Beswick, England, c.1940, 4-In. Laurel, 3-In. Hardy	284.00
Lennox Furnace Co., Lennie Lennox, Ceramic, 4½ In.	92.00
Li'l Abner, Shmoo, Green Bowtie, Red Bowtie, Painted, Plaster, No Stoppers, 3 In.	196.00
Luzianne Mammy, Red Plastic, Painted Accents, Plastic Stoppers, 1950s, 5 In. *illus*	90.00
Maggie & Jiggs, 3¼ In.	95.00
Nikolai, Caviar Of Vodkas, Russian Man, Dancing, 1960s, 4½ In.	67.00
Phonograph, Victrola, With Horn, Napco, 1950s, 3¼ In.	19.00
Piel's Beer Brothers, Bert & Harry, Ceramic, 1960s, 4-In. Harry, 3-In. Bert *illus*	186.00
Sailor Elephant, Twin Winton, 5 x 3½ In.	28.00
Shmoo, Blue, Pink, China, 1940s, 2¼ In.	277.00
Shmoo, Canfield Speedway	80.00
Shmoo, Pink, Blue, Heart Necklaces, Ceramic, 2½ In.	217.00
Sourdough Jake, Gold Miners, c.1960s, 4 In.	168.00
Tomato & Red Pepper, Red, Green Leaves, 1¾ In.	6.00
Waddles Restaurant, Duck, Stamped, Occupied Japan, 1940s, 2½ In.	95.00
Windmill, Occupied Japan, 2½ In.	38.00
Woodsy Owl, Give A Hoot, Don't Pollute, Japan, 1970s, 4 In.	84.00

SALT GLAZE has a grayish white surface with a texture like an orange peel. It is a method of decoration that has been used since the eighteenth century. Salt-glazed pieces are still being made.

Crock, Self Handles, Brown Mottled Glaze, 13¼ x 15¼ In.	45.00
Ewer, Animal Head Spout, Round Center, Grapes & Birds, Lion Heads, Stamped, 19 In. *illus*	230.00
Jug, Milk, Cherubs, Blue Gray, c.1820, 6¼ x 5¾ In.	95.00
Jug, Stoneware, 9⅝ x 3½ In.	45.00
Jug, Translucent, Fluted, Ribs, 6 In.	325.00
Pitcher, Pewter Cover, Pale Green, Embossed, 8 In.	288.00
Soup, Dish, Seed, c.1760, 8¾ x 1⅛ In.	495.00
Stein, Figural, Bearded Gentleman, Hands On Belly, Hinged Hat, Plaque Center, 13½ In. *illus*	288.00
Teapot, Pewter Cover, Melon Shape, Embossed, 10 x 6 x 6 In.	328.00

SAMPLERS were made in America from the early 1700s. The best examples were made from 1790 to 1840. Long, narrow samplers are usually older than square ones. **ABCDE** Early samplers just had stitching or alphabets. The later examples had numerals, borders, and pictorial decorations. Those with mottoes are mid-Victorian. A revival of interest in the 1930s produced simpler samplers, usually with mottoes.

Adam & Eve, Alphabets, 10 Commandments, Verse, Frame, Early 1800s, 24 x 22 In.	1528.00
Adam & Eve, Apple, Tree, Serpent, Mary Chandler, 1809, Linen, Green Silk, 8 x 16 In.	1035.00
Alphabet, Detailed Bands, Anna Holyoak, Oct. 6 1744, Silk, On Linen, Frame, 9 x 9½ In.	920.00
Alphabet, Flower Rows, Hearts, Geometric Shapes, Tiger Maple Frame, 14½ x 14 In.	990.00
Alphabet, Lucinda Clark, Aged 11, House, Trees, Crisscross Border, c.1853, 23 x 20 In.	1650.00
Alphabet, Matilda Werner, Penn, Ebonized Frame, 9 x 7¼ In.	275.00
Alphabet, Numbers, Brick Building, Peacocks, Flowers, Strawberry Vines, 1825, 17 x 17 In. *illus*	460.00
Alphabet, Numbers, Eliza Hollister, Age 7, Blue, Silk, Linen, Gold, Black, Frame, 9 x 11 In.	259.00
Alphabet, Numbers, School, Flowers, Bird, Tree, Forget-Me-Not, Frame, 12 x 15 In.	1045.00
Alphabet, Numbers, Schoolhouse, Ann Jane G. Boggs, 1826, Walnut Frame, Carved, 15 x 15 In.	1175.00
Alphabet, Over Stylized Potted Flowers, Tree, Easter C. Dukcher, 1800, Frame, 12½ x 9 In.	110.00
Alphabet, Sarah Ann Root, 1816, Signature Inscription, 12¼ x 17 In.	649.00
Alphabet, Verse, Baskets Of Flowers, Joanna Scott Armstrong, Frame, 17 x 15½ In.	288.00
Alphabet, Verse, Flowers, Mary Barker, Wool, On Linen, Frame, c.1828, 12 x 15½ In.	575.00
Alphabet, Verse, Rebeckah M. Locke, Mass., Silk, Linen, Wool, Early 1800s, 16 x 16 In.	900.00
Alphabet, Verse, Vines, Flowers, Baskets, Amy S. Peirce, 1827, Silk On Linen, 17 x 14 In.	1840.00
Alphabets, Flowers, Heart Center, Sunburst, Hannah Schell, 1820, 8 x 9 In.	285.00
Alphabets, Flowers, Trees, Biblical Subject, England, 1850s, 12 x 16 In.	445.00
Alphabets, Monograms, Jannet Lidsy, Aged 10 Years, Collinsburg, 1807, 17 x 13 In.	7050.00
Alphabets, Numbers, Lucia Carpenter, Age 12 Years, Strafford, Frame, c.1822, 18 x 13 In.	3819.00
Alphabets, Prayer For Wisdom, Catherine Egan, Aged 9, Frame, c.1814, 17 x 13½ In.	294.00
Alphabets, Verse, Mary Cynthia Mitchell, 1809, Bridgewater, 15½ x 15½ In.	500.00
Alphabets, Verse, Peggy Meloon, Aged 12 Years, 1797, Linsey-Woolsey, Frame, 17 x 7 In.	1880.00
Baskets Of Fruit, House, Blue Ground, Mary Evans Born Ohio 1815, Verse, 16 x 13 In.	1300.00
Family Record, Alphabets, Pious Verses, Isabella Thompson, April 1832, 16 x 16 In.	1998.00
Flower Urn, Strawberries, Fruit Bowl, Initials, CT & DT, Maple Frame, c.1815, 8 x 8 In.	264.00

S

Sampler, Alphabet, Numbers, Brick Building, Peacocks, Flowers, Strawberry Vines, 1825, 17 x 17 In.
$460.00

Early Samplers

Most early samplers were made from smooth or coarse linen, muslin, or canvas found at home. Loosely woven material was easier to embroider. Early samplers were narrow (eight to nine inches wide) because looms were not very wide. Later samplers were wider because the fabric was woven on larger looms. By the late eighteenth and early nineteenth century, the sampler was wider than it was high.

Eighteenth-century samplers were usually made with wool thread. Silk was used after the 1770s.

Sampler, Map Of England & Wales, Mt. Melick Boarding School, 1796, Oval, Frame, 20½ x 18½ In.
$1150.00

Dating Samplers

Look for the maker's name and a date as part of the design. Early samplers were decorated with the alphabet, examples of types of stitching, a maker's name, and a motto. Alphabets in several styles were used after 1720. Mourning and memorial samplers were popular in the early 1800s. In England, maps embroidered on linen were common. Nineteenth-century samplers had pictures of military campaigns, historical events, hobbies, family portraits, and simple geometric designs. Cross-stitch samplers were first made in the early 1800s. They were popular again in the 1930s.

Sampler, Verse, Acorns, Trees, Ann Jones, Philadelphia, 1772, Silk, Linen Ground, 5¼ x 4¼ In.
$7800.00

S

Samson, Perfume Bottle, Pink, Baroque Scene In Cartouche, Enameled, 3½ In. $441.00

Samson, Teapot, Lowestoft Style, Crest, Lions, Flowers, Ribbed, Twig Finial & Handle, 9 In. $115.00

Sandwich Glass, Candlestick, Dolphin, Canary, Double Stepped Base, 10 In., Pair $288.00

Flowers, Birds, Wreath, Urn, Building, Well, Man, Christian Stormfelt, 1843, Frame, 15 x 18 In.	330.00
Flowers, Stars, Vine Border, Initials, E.J., E.M., A.W., 1843, Frame, Silk On Linen, 24 x 15 In. .	518.00
House, Trees, Fruit Basket, Alphabet, Initials MC, Penn., c.1807, 16½ x 17 In.	8400.00
Lord's Prayer, Figures, Trees, Frame, Ann Nobes, Age 7, 1772, Silk On Linen, 15 x 12 In.	2645.00
Manor House, Sheep, Vines, Signed Elizabeth Smith 1836, Linen, Frame, 14 x 13 In.	525.00
Map Of England & Wales, Mt. Melick Boarding School, 1796, Oval, Frame, 20½ x 18½ In. *illus*	1150.00
Mourning, Woman In Black, Tomb, Willow Tree, 1800, Gilt Frame, 22 x 20 In.	77.00
Pictorial, Cross-stitch, Susanah Mathem, Ontario, Linen, c.1840, 15¼ x 15¼ In.	100.00
Rowena Sargent, Age 10 Years, 1849, Ohio, Silk On Linen, 15 x 17 In.	3335.00
Scenic, Sarah Greaves, Aged 14, Penn., Linen, Wool, Frame, c.1818, 10¼ x 8 In.	960.00
Scenic, Silk, Watercolor, Ink, Rebecca Johns, Aged 10, Penn., Linen, c.1808, 17 x 13 In.	1800.00
Strawberry Vine, Flower Sprigs, Inscription, 1826, 22 x 23 In.	1673.00
Tulip Tree, Fanny Nissly's, Sawtooth Border, 1847, Mahogany Frame, 8¼ x 9 In.	330.00
Verse, 2 Women With Flowers, Urn, House, 1839, Frame, 18 x 18½ In.	359.00
Verse, Acorns, Trees, Ann Jones, Philadelphia, 1772, Silk, Linen Ground, 5¼ x 4¼ In. . . *illus*	7800.00
Verse, Against Slavery, Cowper, Sarah Gilbert, Age 8, c.1804, 17 x 12 In.	1404.00
Verse, Alphabet, Julia, 1, 7, 09, Church, Get One Friend, Be Content, Chain Border, 18 x 9 In.	920.00
Verse, Alphabet, Mary Reeve, November 1834, Linen, 19 x 17 In.	527.00
Verse, Alphabet, Sarah Laycock, 13 Year Of Her Age, 1787, Frame, 13 x 12 In.	588.00
Verse, Bible, Cherubs, Potted Flowers, Stag, Dog, People, Squirrels, 1823, Frame, 16 x 12 In. .	303.00
Verse, Cherubs, Friendship, Vine Borders, H. Bradshaw, 1813, Silk, On Linen, 10 x 13 In. . .	515.00
Verse, Flowers, Tree, Mullavilla School, 1823, Wool, Silk, Linen, 18 x 20 In.	460.00
Verse, House, Trees, Julia Sargeant, Age 9 Years, 1829, Linen, Frame, 21¼ x 20¾ In.	9000.00
Verse, Needlework, Sarah E. Sanford, Age 8, Flower Wreath, 1818, 20 x 18 In.	1015.00
Verse, Red House, Sarah Ann Crick, 1833, Silk On Linen, 12¼ x 13 In.	1150.00
Verse, Rose Vine Border, Man, Flower Border, Elizabeth Bradley, c.1856, 16½ x 23 In.	275.00
Verse, Wrought By The Hands Of Jane Bailey, Silk, On Silk, c.1823, 14¼ In.	7800.00
Verse, Young Christian Prayer, Eliza B. Hammond, 16 Aug, 1824, Frame, 16 x 21 In.	22000.00
Village Scene, House, Lawn, Flowers, Bird, Elizabeth Shrivers, 1838, 15½ x 16½ In.	3600.00
Woman, Kneeling, Urn & Column, Draped In Flowers, Walnut Frame, 11½ x 9½ In.	110.00

SAMSON and Company, a French firm specializing in the reproduction of collectible wares of many countries and periods, was founded in Paris in the early nineteenth century. Chelsea, Meissen, Famille Verte, and Chinese Export porcelain are some of the wares that have been reproduced by the company. The firm uses a variety of marks on the reproductions. It is still in operation.

Cachepot, Compagnie Des Indes, Painted Flowers, Gilt Border, c.1900, 7 In., Pair	229.00
Cup & Saucer, Scalloped Flower Form, Raised Leaves, 1898	75.00
Figurine, Man, Woman Carrying Flower Basket, 18th Century Dress, c.1900, 6 In., Pair	118.00
Figurine Set, Allegorical, The Elements, Late 19th Century, 9 In., 4 Piece	310.00
Inkwell, Bronze Fittings, Painted, Flower Closure, Chinese Style, c.1890, 3¼ x 9 In.	325.00
Perfume Bottle, Pink, Baroque Scene In Cartouche, Enameled, 3½ In. . . . . *illus*	441.00
Plate, Bowl, Armorial, 9½ In., 4 Piece	590.00
Plate, Cabinet, Enameled, Reticulated, Cutout, Gold Border, c.1880, 9½ In.	200.00
Snuffbox, Painted Flowers, Scale Design, Hinged Lid, Clasp, 2½ x 1 In.	220.00
Tea Caddy, Square, Round Neck, White Ground, Wharf Scene, Late 1800s, 4½ In.	450.00
Tea Service, Lidded Teapot, Sugar, Creamer, Cups & Saucers, 1800s, 15 Piece	345.00
Teapot, Lowestoft Style, Crest, Lions, Flowers, Ribbed, Twig Finial & Handle, 9 In. . . . . . *illus*	115.00

SANDWICH GLASS is any of the myriad types of glass made by the Boston and Sandwich Glass Works in Sandwich, Massachusetts, between 1825 and 1888. It is often very difficult to be sure whether a piece was really made at the Sandwich factory because so many types were made there and similar pieces were made at other glass factories. Additional pieces may be listed under Pressed Glass and in related categories.

Bowl, Loop, Fiery Opalescent, Scalloped Rim, Short Hexagonal Stem, Domed Foot, 4¾ In. . .	242.00
Candlestick, Acanthus Leaf, Clambroth, 6-Sided, Cornflower Blue Socket, 9¼ In.	316.00
Candlestick, Canary, Columnar, Stepped Base, Tooled Rim, Pontil, 9⅜ In., Pair	1008.00
Candlestick, Dolphin, Canary, Double Stepped Base, 10 In., Pair . . . . *illus*	288.00
Candlestick, Medium Blue, Columnar Base, Petal Socket, 9⅛ In.	345.00
Cigar Holder, Pink To White, Oval, Crosshatch Cutting, 3⅛ In.	88.00
Claret, Cranberry To Clear, Engraved, Flower Swag, 4¾ In.	55.00
Claret, Cranberry To Clear, Engraved, Fly & Grass, 3 Piece, 4¾ In.	242.00
Claret, Cranberry To Clear, Engraved, Grape Band, Cut Panels, Hollow Stem, 5⅛ In.	44.00
Claret, Cranberry To Clear, Engraved, House, Trees, Hollow Stem, 5 In.	66.00
Cologne, 8-Sided, Pinched Waist, Cobalt Blue, Inward Rolled Flared Mouth, 1840-60, 5¾ In.	1456.00

Cologne, 12-Sided, Amethyst, 1860-80, 7 In. 1232.00
Cologne, 12-Sided, Amethyst, Flared Mouth, 1860-80, 7½ In. 420.00
Cologne, 12-Sided, Teal Blue, Flared Mouth, 1860-80, 11 In. 840.00
Cologne, Cobalt Blue, Heart M, Stopper, 1840, 6 In. 3850.00
Cologne, Dark Sky Blue, Applied Lip, Pontil, 1840-60, 10½ In. 130.00
Cologne, Elongated Ovals, Bull's-Eye, Amber, Bevel Pointed Stopper, 5¼ In. ....*illus* 210.00
Cologne, Horn Of Plenty, Embossed H.E. Swan On Panel, 5¾ In. 77.00
Cologne, Opaque White, Beaded, Fluted, Tooled Lip, 6½ In. 99.00
Cologne, Steel Blue, Purple, Pinched Waist, 8 Panels., 4 In. .... 198.00 to 440.00
Compote, Loop, Fiery Opalescent, Scalloped Rim, Hexagonal Stem, Domed Foot, 9 x 9 In. .. 220.00
Compote, Morning Glory, Faceted Hexagonal Stem, 6½ x 9 In. 209.00
Compote, Morning Glory, Shaped Rim, Domed Foot, 9½ x 10⅜ In. 187.00
Compote, Scalloped Rim, Applied Baluster & Base, Pontil, Flint, 1830-40, 10 x 12 In. 198.00
Compote, Star, 6-Lobe Stem, Scalloped Rim, Round Foot, 9½ x 11¾ In. 385.00
Creamer, Flowered Oval, Applied Handle, Footed, 5¾ In. 358.00
Decanter, Bull's-Eye & Fleur-De-Lis, Pewter Lip, Cork, Qt., 12 In. 253.00
Decanter, Sapphire Blue, Bar Lip, Pontil, 10¾ In. 358.00
Dish, Fiery Opalescent, Flowers, Openwork Edge, 2¼ In. 1320.00
Dish, Hen On Nest Cover, Blue, Molded Straw Rim, Draped Panel Sides, 5¾ x 7 In. 4950.00
Drapery Rod Finial, Green Hobnail Bulb, Milk Glass Stem, Brass, 1840-70, 7⅜ In., Pair ... 246.00
Eggcup, Diamond Point, Alabaster, Clambroth Base, 5⅝ In. 468.00
Lamp, Camphene, Cobalt Blue, Burners, Caps, Loop Pattern, 12 In., Pair 8750.00
Paperweight, Star, Faceted Finial, Rayed Base, Variant, 3½ x 2⅜ In. 121.00
Pomade Jar, Bear, Amethyst, 3¾ In. 550.00
Pomade Jar, Bear, Black Amethyst, 4 In. .... 253.00 to 345.00
Pomade Jar, Bulbous, Clambroth, Cap Like Cover, Ring On Top, 2⅝ In. 66.00
Pomade Jar, Cavalier, Translucent Blue, Hat Crown, Plume, 3¾ In. 825.00
Pomade Jar, Drum, Shield, Crossed Drumsticks, 3⅝ In. 4070.00
Salt, Basket Of Flowers, Beaded Scroll, Fiery Opalescent, Footed, 1⅞ x 1⅞ x 3¼ In. 143.00
Salt, Basket Of Flowers, Clambroth, Mottling, Footed, 2⅛ x 1⅞ x 3 In. 198.00
Salt, Basket Of Flowers, Clear, Moonstone Tint, Footed, 2 x 1⅞ x 3 In. 55.00
Salt, Basket Of Flowers, Fiery Opalescent To Opaque, Footed, 2⅛ x 1⅞ x 3 In. 22.00
Salt, Basket Of Flowers, Peacock Green, Footed, 2 x 1¾ x 3⅛ In. 1100.00
Salt, Chariot, Clear, Scallop & Point Rim, 1⅝ x 2⅛ x 2⅞ In. 187.00
Salt, Chariot, Silvery Opaque White, Scallop & Point Rim, 1⅞ x 2⅛ x 2⅞ In. 143.00
Salt, Clear, Complex Rim, Scroll Feet, Divided, 2 x 1¾ x 3¼ In. 66.00
Salt, Clear, Flat Rim, Rectangular, Divided, 1½ x 2⅛ x 3¼ In. 231.00
Salt, Clear, Shaped Rim, Stippled Ovals, Waffle Base, 1¾ x 2 x 3 In. 55.00
Salt, Cornucopia & Scroll, Mottled, Translucent Blue Opalescent, 1⅜ x 2⅜ In. 9075.00
Salt, Cornucopia & Scroll, Serrated Scalloped Rim, Clear, 1½ x 2⅜ x 3⅜ In. 33.00
Salt, Diamond Rosette & Swag, Scalloped Rim, Red Amber, 1½ x 2⅛ x 3¼ In. 1320.00
Salt, Eagle, Clear, Scallop & Point Rim, 1⅞ x 2⅛ x 2⅞ In. .... 55.00 to 88.00
Salt, Eagle, Clear, Scallop Rim, Octagonal, 1½ x 2¾ x 3⅞ In. 154.00
Salt, Eagle & Shield, Clear, Footed, 2⅛ x 2 x 3⅛ In. .... 77.00 to 100.00
Salt, Eagle & Ship, Clear, Leaf Chain Rim, 1⅞ x 3 In. 1100.00
Salt, Gothic Arch, Violet Blue, Opalescent Scalloped Rim, 1¾ x 2 x 2¾ In. 440.00
Salt, Gothic Arch & Heart, Blue, Scalloped Rim, 1¾ x 2 x 2¾ In. 88.00
Salt, Gothic Arch & Heart, Clear, Scalloped Rim, 1¾ x 2 x 2¾ In. 77.00
Salt, Lafayet, Steamboat, Clear, 1½ x 3⅝ x 1⅞ In. ....*illus* 165.00
Salt, Lafayette Steamboat, Fiery Opalescent, 1⅝ x 1⅞ x 3¼ In. 231.00
Salt, Lafayette Steamboat, Sapphire Blue, 1⅝ x 1⅞ x 3⅝ In. 1430.00
Salt, Lyre, Clear, Scrolled, Footed, 1⅞ x 2⅛ x 3⅛ In. 88.00
Salt, Lyre, Opaque Lavender Blue, Mottled, Scrolled, Footed, 1⅞ x 2 x 3⅛ In. 7700.00
Salt, Lyre, Opaque Violet Blue, Variant Cover, Pinecone Finial, 2 x 3⅛ In. ....*illus* 34100.00
Salt, Lyre, Peacock Blue, Shaped Rim, 1½ x 1⅞ x 3 In. 44.00
Salt, Peacock Eye, Sapphire Blue, Scalloped Rim, Oval, 1½ x 2⅞ x 3¾ In. 4290.00
Salt, Peacock Eye, Scalloped Rim, Rayed Base, Oval, 1¼ x 2¾ x 3¾ In. ...... 88.00 to 121.00
Salt, Peacock Eye, Violet Blue, Serrated Scallop, Point Rim, Pedestal, 2 x 3⅛ In. 358.00
Salt, Peacock Eye Medallion, Acanthus Leaf, Sapphire Blue, Footed, Rays, 1⅞ x 3¼ In. 8525.00
Salt, Sapphire Blue, Bubbles, Pleated Rim, Octagonal, 1½ x 2⅜ x 3½ In. 264.00
Salt, Scroll & Beaded, Medium Amber, Footed, 1¾ x 2 x 3⅛ In. 1760.00
Salt, Shell, Clear, Shaped Rim, 1⅝ x 2 x 3 In. 33.00
Salt, Shell, Peacock Green, Scrolled Feet, 1¾ x 2 x 3¼ In. .... 66.00 to 121.00
Salt, Shell & Hairpin, Purple Blue, Scrolled Feet, 1⅝ x 2 x 3⅛ In. 121.00
Salt, Stag's Horn, Amber, 20-Ray Base, 1¾ x 1⅞ x 3 In. 88.00
Salt, Stag's Horn, Clambroth, 32-Ray Base, 1⅝ x 1⅞ x 3⅛ In. 99.00

Sandwich Glass, Cologne, Elongated Ovals, Bull's-Eye, Amber, Bevel Pointed Stopper, 5¼ In. $210.00

Sandwich Glass, Salt, Lafayet, Steamboat, Clear, 1½ x 3⅝ x 1⅞ In. $165.00

Sandwich Glass, Salt, Lyre, Opaque Violet Blue, Variant Cover, Pinecone Finial, 2 x 3⅛ In. $34100.00

Sandwich Glass, Salt, Star In Diamond, Medium Amethyst, Oval, Scalloped High-Point Rim, 1¾ x 3⅜ x 2¼ In. $198.00

S

Sandwich Glass, Sugar, Cover, Gothic Arch, Electric Blue, 6-Sided, 1840-50, 5¼ In.
$2090.00

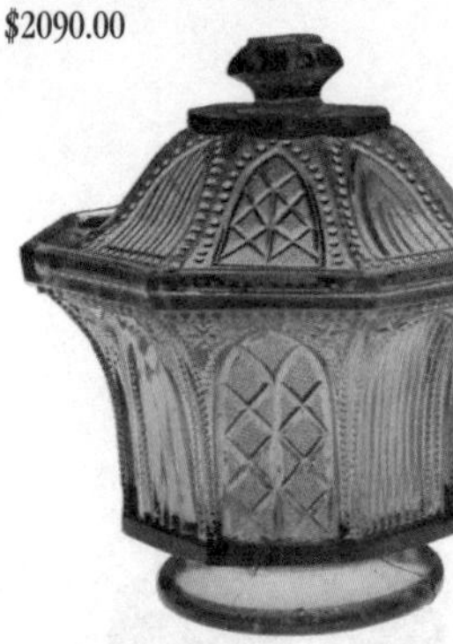

Sandwich Glass, Vase, Excelsior, Canary, Fluted Top, Octagonal Base, 7¼ In., Pair
$660.00

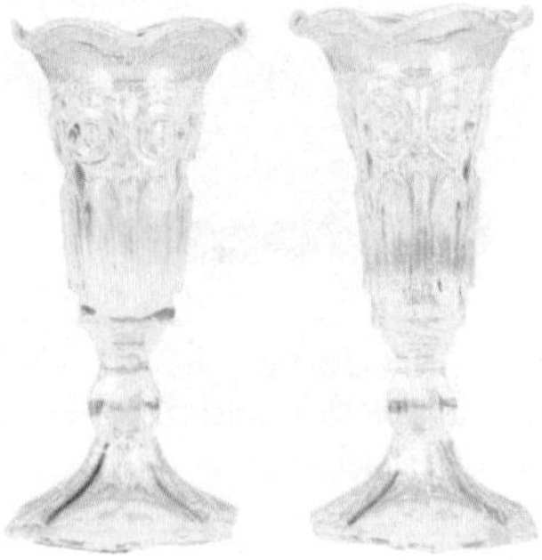

Sascha Brastoff, Dish, Alaska Series, Igloo Scene, Gold Trim, Tab Handles, Marked, 7⅛ In.
$15.00

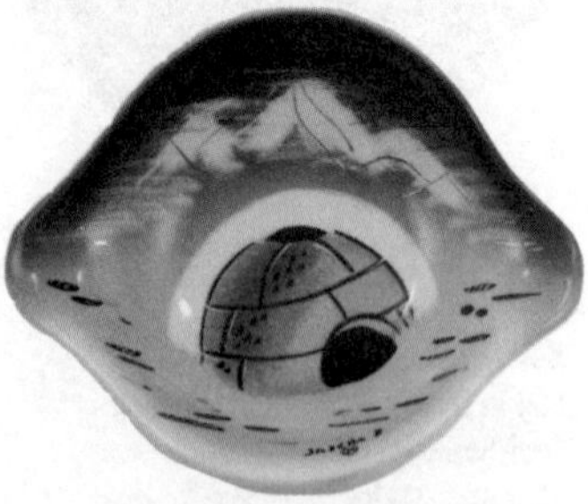

TIP
A mixture of flour and olive oil can sometimes remove a dull film from a lacquered piece. Rub on the paste, then wipe and polish with a soft cloth.

Salt, Stag's Horn, Clear, 16 Spaced Rays, Overlaid Ovals, 1¾ x 2 x 3⅛ In. 33.00
Salt, Stag's Horn, Gray Blue, 20-Ray Base, 1¾ x 1⅞ x 3 In. 154.00
Salt, Star In Diamond, Medium Amethyst, Oval, Scalloped High-Point Rim, 1¾ x 3⅜ x 2¼ In. *illus* 198.00
Salt, Strawberry-Diamond, Beaded, Purple Blue, High & Low Point Rim, 1¾ x 2 x 3½ In. ... 165.00
Salt, Strawberry-Diamond, Clear, Paw Feet, Scalloped Rim, 30-Ray Base, 2 x 2⅜ x 3¼ In. ... 77.00
Salt, Strawberry-Diamond, Fan, Clear, Serrated Rim, Corner Ovals, 1½ x 2 x 3½ In. 176.00
Salt, Strawberry-Diamond, Fan, Scalloped Rim, Clear, Serrated Points, 2 x 3⅜ In. 100.00
Salt, Strawberry-Diamond, Fan, Scalloped Rim, Serrated Points, Paw Feet, 2 x 3⅜ In. 88.00
Salt, Wagon, Clear, Wheels, 2 x 2 x 3 In. 253.00
Salt Cover, Clear, Pinecone Finial, Beads, 1⅝ x 1 7/16 x 2 7/16 In. .... 1045.00 to 1210.00
Saltshaker, Christmas, Cranberry, Bulbous, Metal Lid, Salt Breaker, 2⅝ In. 616.00
Spooner, Grapevine, Green, Brown & Gold Enameled, Stepped Foot, 5 In. .... 110.00 to 143.00
Sugar, Cover, Clambroth, Gothic Arch, 6-Sided, Round Foot, 1835-45, 5¼ In. 385.00
Sugar, Cover, Gothic Arch, Electric Blue, 6-Sided, 1840-50, 5¼ In. .... *illus* 2090.00
Sugar, Cover, Heart With Diamond Point Center, Hexagonal, Footed 66.00
Vase, Arch, Left Twist To Center, Amethyst, Gauffered Rim, Hexagonal Stem, Base, 11¾ In. .. 1980.00
Vase, Arch, Sapphire Blue, Gauffered Rim, Hexagonal Stem, Base, 11¼ In. 2420.00
Vase, Bull's-Eye & Fleur-De-Lis, Scalloped Rim, Hexagonal Baluster Stem, 9½ In. 330.00
Vase, Canary, 9 In., Pair 920.00
Vase, Circle & Ellipse, Canary, Gauffered Rim, 6-Sided Base, c.1850, 7¼ In. 475.00
Vase, Excelsior, Canary, Fluted Top, Octagonal Base, 7¼ In., Pair .... *illus* 660.00
Vase, Eye & Scale, Citron, Gauffered Rim, Hexagonal Base, 9¼ In. 770.00
Vase, Tulip, Amethyst, Panels, Peg Extension, Octagonal Base, 9¾ In. 3850.00
Vase, Tulip, Emerald Green, Milky White Streaks, Panels, Octagonal Base, 5½ In. 2530.00
Vase, Tulip, Peacock Green, Panels, Peg Extension, Octagonal Base, 9¾ In. 3740.00
Vase, Twisted Loop, Cobalt Blue, Flared Rim, Octagonal Foot, 10½ In. 3410.00
Whimsy, Pen, Amethyst, Amber, Cobalt Blue, Ruby Finial, Beads, Ribbed Nib, 8 In. 413.00
Wine, Horn Of Plenty, 12 Piece 1315.00

SARREGUEMINES is the name of a French town that is used as part of a china mark. Utzschneider and Company, a porcelain factory, made ceramics in Sarreguemines, Lorraine, France, from about 1775. Transfer-printed wares and majolica were made in the nineteenth century. The nineteenth-century pieces, most often found today, usually have colorful transfer-printed decorations showing peasants in local costumes.

Dessert Set, Fruit, Majolica, Platter, Plates, 7 Piece 600.00
Fish Set, Stylized Fish Shape, White, Scale Border, 21-In. Platter, 11-In. Plate, 11 Piece 518.00
Oyster Plate, Majolica, Signed, 1920s, 9½ In. 55.00
Plate, Fruit, Basket Weave Edge, Teal, Majolica, 7 In. 55.00

SASCHA BRASTOFF made decorative accessories, ceramics, enamels on copper, and plastics of his own design. He headed a factory, Sascha Brastoff of California, Inc., in West Los Angeles, from 1953 until about 1973. He died in 1993. Pieces signed with the signature *Sascha Brastoff* were his work and are the most expensive. Other pieces marked *Sascha B.* or with a stamped mark were made by others in his company.

Ashtray, Blue Flowers, Green Notched Edges, Enamel, 8 In. 15.00
Ashtray, Chi-Chi Bird Eggs On Nest 40.00
Ashtray, Gray Mottled, Matte, Figure Kneeling, Signed, 7½ In. 125.00
Ashtray, Mushrooms, Copper, Enamel, 3 Cigarette Slots, Signed, 7 In. 30.00
Ashtray, Orange, Gold, Green, Free-Form, Copper, Enamel, Signed, 1950s 59.00
Ashtray, Rooftops, White Ground, 10½ x 7¾ In. 50.00
Ashtray, Rooster, 17 x 9 In. 55.00
Ashtray, Round, Gold Matte, Brocade Figures, Signed, 11⅛ In. 60.00
Ashtray, Star Steed, Dark Green Ground, Free-Form, Signed, 8½ In. 55.00
Ashtray, Triangular, 8 x 8 x 8 In. 65.00
Box, Cover, Fruit, Leaf, Signed, 5 In. 60.00
Charger, Purple Stylized Flowers, Green, Blue Leaves, Marked, 12 In. 58.00
Cigarette Set, Rooftops, Ashtray, Lighter, Cigarette Container, 1958, 3 Piece 125.00
Dish, Alaska Series, Blue, Gold, Black, Elongated, Signed, 10 x 5½ In. 65.00
Dish, Alaska Series, Igloo Scene, Gold Trim, Tab Handles, Marked, 7⅛ In. .... *illus* 15.00
Dish, Aztec, Gold Bird, 7 In. 49.00
Dish, Free-Form, 7 x 6½ In. 35.00
Dish, Grapes, Green Ground, Enamel, 8 In. 40.00
Dish, Jewel Bird, Free-Form, Signed, 10 In. 85.00
Dish, Rooftops, Oval, 7 In. 50.00
Dish, Yellow, Citrus Fruit, Blue, Gold, Black Leaves, 10½ In. 45.00

Nut Dish, Aztec, 7 In.	45.00
Planter, Star Steed, Gray, Black Ground, Signed, 4½ x 4¾ In.	55.00
Plate, Ivory, Gold Circles, Signed, 10⅞ In.	200.00
Platter, Alaska Series, Tray Seal, White Ground, Blue Sky, Signed, c.1962, 13¾ x 8 In.	125.00
Vase, Alaska Series, Eskimo Girl, Blue, White, Signed, 8 In.	45.00
Vase, Alaska Series, Totem Pole, Gold Metallic Eyes, Marked, 6 In.	66.00
Vase, Horizontal Bands, Blue, Green, Gold, Marked, Tapered, 8¼ In. ....*illus*	35.00

SATIN GLASS is a late-nineteenth-century art glass. It has a dull finish that is caused by hydrofluoric acid vapor treatment. Satin glass was made in many colors and sometimes has applied decorations. Satin glass is also listed by factory name, such as Webb, or in the Mother-of-Pearl category in this book.

Basket, Black, Bird & Flower Design, Late 1940s, 10½ In.	225.00
Basket, Blue, 11½ x 6 In.	115.00
Basket, Pink, Cane Bottom, Lancaster Glass, 4½ x 4¾ In.	25.00
Basket, Pink, Layered, Applied Handle, Viking Glass Co., 7½ x 7¼ In.	50.00
Berry Bowl, Shell Shape, Shaded Pink, Opaque White Shell Handle, c.1920, 5⅜ x 4¾ In. ...	125.00
Bottle, Genie, Shaded Pink, 1920s, 9½ x 4¾ In.	125.00
Bowl, Enameled, 3-Footed, 7¾ x 3½ In.	30.00
Bowl, Green, Footed, Ruffled Edge, Pot Metal Base, 6½ x 10 In.	45.00
Box, Cover, Figural, Colonial Woman, Cobalt Blue, 1930s	30.00
Candleholder, Blue, 2½ x 2¼ In., Pair	35.00
Candleholder, Cobalt Blue, Pedestal, 4 x 3 In.	28.00
Candlestick, Celeste Blue, 1920s, 9 In.	40.00
Candlestick, Figural, Kneeling Lady, Cachepot, Pink, Late 1930s, 6¾ In., Pair	195.00
Candlestick, Pink, 3-Footed, Scalloped Edge, 3 x 5 In.	15.00
Candy Dish, Cover, Conical, Art Deco Style, Green, Diamond-Quilted, 6 In.	35.00
Candy Dish, Cover, Grape Pattern, Green, Jeannette	38.00
Candy Dish, Octagonal, Pink, 2 Handles, 1¼ x 7 In.	25.00
Candy Dish, Pink, Handles, Ruffled Edges, 7½ x 2⅜ In.	49.00
Cigar Holder, Enameled Smoking Cigar, 4½ In.	295.00
Compote, Cover, Green, Grape Pattern, 10 In.	23.00
Console, Orange, 9 In.	60.00
Dish, Shell Shape, Footed, Sterling Silver Overlay, Rocaille Design, c.1900	190.00
Epergne, 4-Lily, Blue, Threading, Ruffled Edge, 18 In. ....*illus*	147.00
Ewer, Enameled, Blown, Green, Melon Ribbed, Blue, Tangerine Enamel, 9½ x 4 In.	325.00
Figure, Show Horse, Lavender, 6½ In.	125.00
Jar, Cover, Ball Finial, Ribbed, White	20.00
Pin Tray, Pink Swirl, 10½ x 3 In.	20.00
Pitcher, Blue, Violet, Pink, Lime, 5¾ In.	40.00
Pitcher, Pink, Florette, Camphor Handle, 7½ In.	144.00
Pitcher, Shaded Pink, Egyptian Scene, Shaped Blue Satin Handle, 6 In.	2070.00
Powder Jar, Lid, Green, Taussaunt, 4¾ In.	28.00
Rose Bowl, Cased, Pink, 4½ x 4 In.	45.00
Rose Bowl, Diamond-Quilted, Aqua, Cased White, 6 x 5½ In.	160.00
Rose Bowl, Pink, 3-Footed, 4½ x 3½ In.	45.00
Rose Bowl, Pink, Cased White, Crimped Rim, 4½ x 3¾ In.	45.00
Rose Bowl, Shaded Pink, Cased White, Ruffled Rim, 5 In.	295.00
Salt & Pepper, Pink, 3½ In.	34.00
Sandwich Server, Pink, Octagonal, Center Handle, 12 In.	35.00
Vase, Blue, Gold Bands, 11½ x 4 In.	33.00
Vase, Bottle Shape, Green, Gold Enameled Peony, 7½ In.	32.00
Vase, Double Gourd, Butterscotch Shaded To Peach, Cased, Late 1800s	185.00
Vase, Pink Interior, Crimped Rim, 6 x 3½ In.	225.00
Vase, Yellow, 7 x 4½ In.	25.00

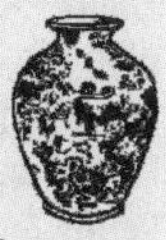

SATSUMA is a Japanese pottery with a distinctive creamy beige crackled glaze. Most of the pieces were decorated with blue, red, green, orange, or gold. Almost all Satsuma found today was made after 1860, especially during the Meiji Period, 1868–1912. During World War I, Americans could not buy undecorated European porcelains. Women who liked to make hand-painted porcelains at home began to decorate plain Satsuma. These pieces are known today as "American Satsuma."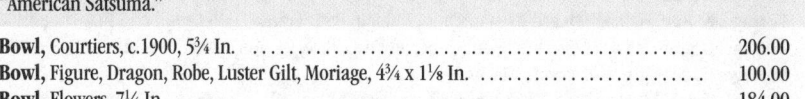

Bowl, Courtiers, c.1900, 5¾ In.	206.00
Bowl, Figure, Dragon, Robe, Luster Gilt, Moriage, 4¾ x 1⅛ In.	100.00
Bowl, Flowers, 7¼ In.	184.00

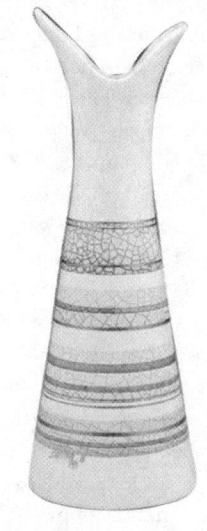

Sascha Brastoff, Vase, Horizontal Bands, Blue, Green, Gold, Marked, Tapered, 8¼ In. $35.00

Satin Glass, Epergne, 4-Lily, Blue, Threading, Ruffled Edge, 18 In. $147.00

Satsuma, Incense Burner, Painted Figures, 2 Handles, 4-Footed, Foo Dog Finial, 5½ In. $153.00

S

Marks on Japanese Ceramics

In 1890 the United States government passed a law that the country of origin be written on all imports to the United States. The Japanese word for Japan, *Nippon*, was added to imports from 1891. In 1921 the United States required the English word *Japan* or *Made in Japan*.

The United States was part of the Allied occupying force in Japan after World War II. The words *Occupied Japan* or *Made in Occupied Japan* were required on pottery and porcelain. Occupied Japan era was from 1945 to 1952. Often the mark was on a removable paper label.

Satsuma, Vase, Samurai Warriors, Gilt Trim, Baluster, Ring Handles At Neck, c.1890, 12 In.
$394.00

Scale, Balance, Toledo, Cast Iron, Child's, 6 x 5 In.
$410.00

Bowl, Peacock & Wisteria Center, 5 Lobes, Wisteria Exterior, Gilt, Signed, c.1900, 5 In.	340.00
Bowl, Samurai, Leaf Edge, Early 20th Century, 6 In.	323.00
Charger, Men, Vases, Trees, Fired Gold Accents, c.1920, 16 In.	380.00
Dish, 19th Century, 2 x 5 In.	231.00
Dish, Birds, Flowers, Rectangular, 5½ x 7 In.	70.00
Dish, Court Scene, Square, Reticulated Rim, Painted, 2 x 6½ In.	690.00
Egg, Gilt, Lacquered Fruit Wood Stand, Enameled, Moriage, c.1910	60.00
Figurine, Welcome Cat, Paw Up, Enamel, Early 1900s, 23 x 14 In.	1528.00
Flask, 7 Gods Of Luck, 100 Poets, 9½ In.	529.00
Incense Burner, Painted Figures, 2 Handles, 4-Footed, Foo Dog Finial, 5½ In. ......*illus*	153.00
Jardiniere, Stand, Painted, c.1900, 8 x 14 In.	293.00
Plate, Earthenware, Painted, c.1890, 7½ In., 2 Piece	53.00
Tea Set, Earthenware, Satsuma Crest, Gilt Highlights, 23 Piece	384.00
Tea Set, Gilt Dragon Handles & Spout, Signed, 9 Piece	374.00
Teapot, Dragon Spout, Geese In Water, Mt. Fuji, Black & Gold Chop Mark, 7 In.	1006.00
Teapot, Warriors, Brocade, c.1900	588.00
Urn, Cover, Porcelain, Pedestal Base, 20 x 16 In., Pair	205.00
Vase, Beautiful Woman, Earthenware, Painted, 20th Century, 7½ In., Pair	189.00
Vase, Buddhist Saint, 31 In., Pair	944.00
Vase, Chrysanthemums, Tan Glaze, Tied Money Bag Shape, 5¾ In.	176.00
Vase, Dragon, Landscape, Molded, Urn Shape, Painted, c.1910, 12½ In.	173.00
Vase, Dragons In Landscape, Heavy Gilt Trim, Baluster Shape, 10 In., Pair	660.00
Vase, Figures, Fan Shaped Reserves, Early 20th Century, 5 In.	147.00
Vase, Figures, Flowers, Axe Head Form, 7½ In.	230.00
Vase, Flowers, Butterflies, Late 19th Century, 14 In.	382.00
Vase, Flowers, Earthenware, 10½ In., Pair	177.00
Vase, Immortals, Trees, Flowering Plants, Cartouches, Gilt, Flared, c.1900, 7 In.	1500.00
Vase, Samurai Warriors, Gilt Trim, Baluster, Ring Handles At Neck, c.1890, 12 In. .....*illus*	394.00
Vase, Women, Ruffled Trumpet, Foo Dog Handles, 29 In.	147.00

SATURDAY EVENING GIRLS, *see Paul Revere Pottery category.*

SCALES have been made to weigh everything from babies to gold. Collectors search for all types. Most popular are small gold dust scales and special grocery scales.

Apothecary, Christian, Walnut, Glass Panes, 2 Doors, Drawerbecker, New York, 18 x 18 In. ..	374.00
Apothecary, Schaar & Co., Glass Panes, Lift Door, Wood Case, Chicago, 17 x 16¾ In.	144.00
Balance, Apothecary, Ash & Metal, c.1880, 7 x 5½ x 12½ In.	64.00
Balance, Apothecary, Twin Nickel Plated Pans, Marble Platform, Cherry Case, 13 In.	71.00
Balance, Beam, Brass, Pat. 29876, Vase Shape Pillar, Scrolling Bracket, Final, 13 In.	206.00
Balance, Beam, Brass Pillar, Finial, Pans, Mahogany Case, 17½ In.	235.00
Balance, Brass, c.1920, 3½ x 8½ In.	35.00
Balance, Cast Iron, Red Paint, Brass Pan & Handles, 10 Kg.	114.00
Balance, Coin, Holt, Steel Beam, Brass Pans, Case, Pocket, 7 In.	441.00
Balance, Crystal, Brass, Marble, 22 In.	95.00
Balance, Fairbanks, China Tray, Blind Justice, Painted, Green, Red, Case Weights, 6 x 13 In. ..	118.00
Balance, Fairbanks, Cast Iron Base, Ceramic White Trays, Marked, No. 4, c.1930	90.00
Balance, Griffin & George, Analytical, Micrometer Wheel, Brass, 16½ In.	147.00
Balance, Howe Jewelers, Model No. 6433, Stencil, Pinstripes, 9½ x 5½ In.	236.00
Balance, Iron Base, Brass Trays, Marked Force 25 Kilog, France, 1900s, 29¾ In.	118.00
Balance, S. Mordan & Co. Of London, Weights, Brass, c.1900, 3¾ x 8½ x 11 In.	117.00
Balance, Shaker, Walnut, Cherry, Poplar, Weight Holders, Union Village, Oh, c.1850, 11 x 36 In.	468.00
Balance, Toledo, Cast Iron, Child's, 6 x 5 In. ......*illus*	410.00
Balance, W & T Avery, Brass, Wooden Base, 5 Weights, 22 In.	258.00
Balance, Wooden, Shaker, Mustard Paint, Tin Ruler Nailed At Base, 13 In.	546.00
Candy, National Scale Co., Pennsylvania, Brass Pan, 2 Lb. Version, 10 x 11 In.	715.00
Coin, Brass, Fitted Wood Case, France, 19th Century	293.00
Jewelry, Howe Jewelers, Black Paint, Stenciled, Striped, Model No. 6433, 9½ x 5½ In.	236.00
Penny, Hanson Scale Co., Black Tin Case, 5 Metal Cups, 1930s, 9 x 6½ In.	155.00
Penny, National Novelty Co., Iron, Embossed, American Shield, Minn., 71 In.	4200.00
Postage, Bronze, Bust, Winged Woman, Scrolls, Dolphin Base, France, 19th Century, 9 In. ..*illus*	441.00
Postage, Bronze, Figural, Winged Woman's Bust, Dolphin Base, France, 19th Century, 15 In.	646.00
Postage, Degrave & Co., Mahogany, Brass, Canadian Post Office, London, 1800s, 23¾ In. ...	321.00
Postage, Howe Mfg. Co., Cast Iron, Weighs 0-4 Lbs., Rates For Mar. 26, 1944, 20 x 8 In.	285.00
Postage, Matchless Letter Scale, Mail Carrier, Tin Lithograph, Hand Held, Cast Iron, 6⅛ x 3⅜ In.	820.00

Postage, Selector, Grabner Bros., Norwalk, Celluloid Face, White, Blue, Black, 5½ x 3½ In. . .	248.00
Postage, Triner, Mail Rates, First Class, 5 x 8 x 4 In.	165.00
Postage, Triner, Ounces, 3 Cents, 5 x 9 x 4 In.	165.00
Weighing, Butcher, Toledo, No. 498789, Enamel	79.00
Weighing, Coin-Operated, Campbell & Nicholls, Cast Iron, Art Deco Design, 72 In.	3850.00
Weighing, Coin-Operated, National, Cast Iron, Marquee, Porcelain Face Plate, 78 In.	1870.00
Weighing, Coin-Operated, National Cash Register, Cast Iron, 70 In.	4950.00
Weighing, Columbia, Black, 24 Pounds By Ounces Family Scale, Stamped, Pat. Sep. 17, '06	30.00
Weighing, Egg, Hart Tru-Way, Metal, 3¾ x 9 x 2½ In.	95.00
Weighing, Egg, Wood, Painted, Hens Best, Egg Grading, Salesman Sample, 6 x 9 x 3 In.	195.00
Weighing, Fairbanks, Globe Logo, Ceramic Tiles, Cast Iron, 5 x 14 x 6⅛ In.	310.00
Weighing, Salters Household Scale, No. 46, 28 Lb., Green Paint, Cast Iron Base, 12 In.	105.00
Weighing, Stimpson, Cast Iron, Glass Tray, 33 In.	55.00
Weighing, Universal Household, Metal, Green Paint, 24 Pound, 8 In.	50.00
Weighing, Wrigley's Spearmint Pepsin Gum, Brass, Painted Metal, Embossed, 7¾ x 10 In.	852.00

SCHAFER & VATER, makers of small ceramic items, are best known for their amusing figurals. The factory was located in Volkstedt-Rudolstadt, Germany, from 1890 to 1962. Some pieces are marked with the crown and R mark, but many are unmarked.

Box, Dome Lid, Angel, Youths In Garden, Wreath, Cherubs, Jasperware, 3¾ x 7 In.	225.00
Box, Lid, Blue, White, Jasperware, Germany, c.1900, 5 In.	195.00
Candlestick, 8 In.	170.00
Match Holder, Man In Top Hat, Open Mouth, Match Holes, 4 In. . . . . *illus*	180.00

SCHNEIDER Glassworks was founded in 1917 at Epinay-sur-Seine, France, by Charles and Ernest Schneider. Art glass was made between 1917 and 1930. The company still produces clear crystal glass. See also the Le Verre Français category.

Charger, Brown & Green Swirls, Orange Rim, Signed, 15½ In.	235.00
Compote, Mottled Yellow, Amethyst, Signed, 14 In.	353.00
Compote, Orange Shaded To Purple, Clear Stem, Berry Foot, Signed, 7 In.	2115.00
Compote, Spattered Opaque White & Clear, Footed, 1908, 5 x 14 In.	470.00
Pitcher, Red, Blue Mottling At Base, Yellow Spout, Black Handle, 12¼ In.	441.00
Vase, Amber Glass, Etched, Flared Rim, Footed, 1925-30, 7½ In.	481.00
Vase, Amethyst, Amber, Mottled Green, Flared & Flattened Rim, Pedestal Base, 9¾ In. . . *illus*	250.00
Vase, Blue, Internally Decorated, Amethyst Stem, Wrought Iron Foot, 10 x 9½ In. . . . . . *illus*	1840.00
Vase, Egg Shape, Purple Design, Geometric Pattern, Stamped, 4 In.	325.00
Vase, Green, Bubbles, Internal Decoration, Blue, Stylized Elephant, 8¾ In.	441.00
Vase, Mottled Blue, Aubergine Spots, Oval, Lobed, Wrought Iron Holder, c.1925, 12¼ In. *illus*	2390.00
Vase, Olive Green, Controlled Bubbles, Mottled Sea Green Handles, Footed, Signed, 15 In. . . .	1495.00
Vase, Padded Grapes, Inlaid Vines, Mottled Orange, Red, Footed, Flared, Cameo, Signed, 15¼ In. . .	12000.00
Vase, Textured Purple, Geometric, Art Deco, Oval, Signed, 4 In.	374.00

SCIENTIFIC INSTRUMENTS of all kinds are included in this category. Other categories such as Barometer, Binoculars, Dental, Medical, Nautical, and Thermometer may also price scientific apparatus.

Air Compressor, Sorensen, Tankless, Model 220, No. 5329, 9-In. Flywheel	235.00
Alidade, Surveyor's, W. & L.E. Gurley, Troy, N.Y., Carrying Case	275.00
Armillary Sphere, Brass, 17 In.	410.00
Armillary Sphere, France, Mounted, Ebonized Fruitwood Base, 20¾ In.	2223.00
Barograph, Clockwork, Drum, Pressure Discs, Recording Arm, Case, 12 In.	470.00
Cipher Machine, Enigma Type A, 3 Rotors, Wood Case, 1941 . . . . *illus*	27408.00
Compass, Brinton, London, Round, Folds Shut, Mirror	59.00
Compass, Cased Brass, Paper Dial, Removable Protractor, Walnut Case	115.00
Compass, Eagle Pencil Co., Floral Vine Pattern, c.1894	105.00
Compass, Engraved Initial On Cover, 2¾ In.	35.00
Compass, Military, Plastic Case, Mirror, c.1930, 2 x ½ In.	125.00
Compass, Pocket, Engraved Dial, 32-Point Rose, Fleur-De-Lis North, 3 x 3 In.	235.00
Compass, R.A. Tibbets, Box, 7 In.	201.00
Compass, Surveyor's, Bernier, Brass, William Young, No. 3472, 10 x 16 In.	881.00
Compass, Surveyor's, Brass, H.M. Pool, 5-In. Dial, 9¾ x 15 In.	823.00
Compass, Surveyor's, David Rittenhouse, Brass, 8⅜ x 14½ In.	19975.00
Compass, Surveyor's, Gurley, Cased Brass, Silvered Dial, 10½ x 15½ In.	518.00
Compass, Surveyor's, Vernier, Stancliffe & Draper, Brass, 16 x 10 In.	1116.00
Compass, Wrist, Waltham Watch Co., Plastic Cover, U.S. Model 1949	15.00

Scale, Postage, Bronze, Bust, Winged Woman, Scrolls, Dolphin Base, France, 19th Century, 9 In.
$441.00

Schafer & Vater, Match Holder, Man In Top Hat, Open Mouth, Match Holes, 4 In.
$180.00

Schneider, Vase, Amethyst, Amber, Mottled Green, Flared & Flattened Rim, Pedestal Base, 9¾ In.
$250.00

S

Schneider, Vase, Blue,
Internally Decorated, Amethyst Stem,
Wrought Iron Foot,
10 x 9½ In.
$1840.00

Schneider, Vase, Mottled Blue,
Aubergine Spots, Oval, Lobed, Wrought
Iron Holder, c.1925, 12¼ In.
$2390.00

Scientific Instrument,
Cipher Machine, Enigma Type A,
3 Rotors, Wood Case, 1941
$27408.00

Drafting Set, J. Halden & Co., Burl Veneer Case, Ivory Handles, 9 x 7 In.	748.00
Hydrometer, Sike's, No. 6674, Thermometer, Brass Bulb, Brass Weights, 5 In.	176.00
Microscope, Andrew Pritchard, London, Brass, Fitted Case, 13 x 9 In.	1840.00
Microscope, Bausch & Lomb, Cast Iron, Oak Case, Pat. 1915, 11½ In.	145.00
Microscope, Bausch & Lomb, Spencer, 11 In.	175.00
Microscope, Binocular, Gary, London, Brass, Wood Box, c.1880, 15¾ In. .... *illus*	768.00
Microscope, Binocular, R. & J. Beck, No. 8906, Wenham Body Tube, 15 In.	646.00
Microscope, C. Reichert Wein VIII Bennogasse, Brass, Engraved, Case	230.00
Microscope, Chain Focus, T.H. McAllister, Brass, 11 In.	235.00
Microscope, Compound, Lietz, No. 136694, Brass Tube, 10 In.	294.00
Microscope, Culpepper Type, Brass, Vertical Rack & Pinion Focus, 11 In.	823.00
Microscope, Dissecting, Watson & Sons, London, Brass, Mahogany Case, 7 In.	575.00
Microscope, Dolland, London, Brass, Fitted Case, 10½ x 7¾ x 7 In.	587.00
Microscope, Dolland, London, Brass, Wood Case, Early 19th Century	2530.00
Microscope, Dru, Martin-Pattern, Brass, Rackwork Focus, Slides, 11 In.	353.00
Microscope, R. & G. Beck, London, Brass, Mahogany Case, 19½ In.	4715.00
Microscope Lamp, Bockett, Collins, Brass, Oil, Glass Font, London, 17 In.	402.00
Motor, Electric, Diehl, AC, No. 206136, 100 Volt, 60 Cycles, 1893, 13 In.	176.00
Orrery, Delamarche, France, 22 In.	3510.00
Orrery, Tellurian, Cast Iron, Brass Globe, 12 Chromolithed Gores, 21 x 27 In.	2350.00
Pocket Coin Balance, Weights, Measures, Cased, Protractor, Rule, Case	176.00
Sighting Scope, Compass, Keuffel & Esser Co., 10-In. Telescope, 10¼ In.	176.00
Slide Rule, Acumath, No. 400, Case, c.1935, 12⅛ x 1¾ In.	25.00
Slide Rule, Keuffel & Esser, Model No. N4053.5, N.Y., Oak, Case, 1900, 20 In.	150.00
Slide Rule, Keuffel & Esser, Pat. June 5, 1900, 20 In.	150.00
Spyglass, Telescoping, Brass Shaft, Engraved, Open 33¼ In.	353.00
Staff Level, Surveyor's, Adie & Son, 7-In. Telescope, Compass, 7½ In.	206.00
Steam Gauge, Crosby, A.H. Moulton, No. 542407, Silvered Dial, Brass Bezel	235.00
Telegraph Apparatus, Siemens & Halske, Brass Fittings, Mahogany Base	1293.00
Telegraph Key, Vibroplex Lightning Bug, Bakelite Knobs, 1952, 7 x 4 In.	285.00
Telegraph Receiver Box, 7 x 5 x 4 In.	125.00
Telescope, G. Bradford, London, Brass, Leather Cover, 36 In.	288.00
Telescope, Gilbert, Wright & Hooke, London, Brass, 4 Eyepieces, Case, 31 In.	575.00
Telescope, Reflecting, Lacquered Brass, 9-In. Tube, Mahogany Case, 12 In.	2350.00
Telescope, Refracting, Spencer & Son, Brass, 3 In., 37-In. Tube, Tripod	1410.00
Telescope, Refractor, Discoverer Model, Sears, Wood Case, c.1950, 38 In.	59.00
Telescope, Reverse Taper, 1 In., 37-In. Octagonal Faceted Mahogany Tube	999.00
Telescope, Richard Harris, Gilt Brass, Tripod Base, 404, Strand, 33½ In.	705.00
Telescope, Table, Brass, Rosewood, Stand, 16¾ x 10¼ x 21¾ In.	190.00
Telescope, Terrestrial, Veri Power, Broadhurst Clarkson & Co., 33 In.	154.00
Telescope Lens, Brashear, Brassbound, Achromatic, 9 In., F/15.36, Case	1528.00
Theodolite, Benjamin Cole, 4-In. Dial, 8 Points, Mahogany Box, 9 In.	823.00
Theodolite, Surveying, Warren-Knight, Slide Board Mount, 14 x 7 In.	345.00
Transformer, Kinetoscope, Edison Home, UW Model No. 1, Ser. 1031, 7 In.	323.00
Transit, Solar, Vernier, 10-In. Brass Telescope, Vertical Circle, Case, 10 In.	1058.00
Transit, Vernier, Queen & Co., Anodized Finish, Brass Fittings, No. 6342, 15 In.	646.00
Transit, W. & L.E. Gurley, Brass Light, Mountain, No. 171074, 11½ In.	499.00
Vacuum Pump, Milvay, Cast Iron, Blown Glass Bell Jar, 26 In.	345.00
Wantage Rod, Spirits, U.S. Standard, Brass, Ivory Mounted, 36 In.	489.00
Wye Level, Gurley, Teledyne, Model 100a, No. 570003, 10-In. Telescope	235.00
Wye Level, Surveyor's, Jas. W. Queen & Co., Reversible Telescope, Tripod	470.00
Wye Level, W. & L.E. Gurley, No. 28685, 19-In. Telescope, Mahogany Case	176.00

SCRIMSHAW is bone or ivory or whale's teeth carved by sailors and others for entertainment during the sailing-ship days. Some scrimshaw was carved as early as 1800. There are modern scrimshanders making pieces today on bone, ivory, or plastic. Other pieces may be found in the Ivory and Nautical categories.

Bodkin, Incised Lines, Turned Handle, c.1850, 3¾ In.	345.00
Bodkin, Remember Me When I Am Far Away 1839, Incised Lines, Turned Handle, 3¾ In.	695.00
Bodkin, Whale, Turned Designs, Incised, Red Wax Inset, c.1850, 3¾ In.	345.00
Bodkin, Whalebone, Arched Top, Open Scrollwork, Inset Baleen Dots, 6½ In.	450.00
Box, Dominoes, Whalebone, Carved, Sliding Lid, Painted, Neptune, 1800s, 1 x 1¼ x 3 In.	470.00
Box, Whalebone, Jewelry, Drawer, Dovetailed Corners, Hinged Lid, 8⅝ x 4¾ In.	12500.00
Box, Whale's Tooth, Couple, Ship, Flower Border, Mother-Of-Pearl Inlaid Lid, Raised Panels, 5⅝ In.	1434.00
Busk, Bone, Incised, Flowers, Stars, Hearts, Altar Platform & Harp, 14 In.	805.00

Busk, Whalebone, Carving, Hearts, Flowers, Stars, Pinwheels, c.1840, 13½ In. 1750.00
Busk, Whalebone, Colored Ink, Inscribed, Potted Plants, Tree, Building, Steeple, Shield, 13 In. 1495.00
Busk, Whalebone, Polychrome, 9 Scenic Sections, c.l840, 13½ x 1⅜ In. 1750.00
Busk, Whalebone, Polychrome, Carved, 3 Panels, c.1850, 2 x 14¼ In. 4250.00
Cane, Eagle Handle, Black Inset Eyes, Tapered Ebony Shaft, Ivory Tip, 34½ In. 1675.00
Clamp, Table, Whalebone, G-Shape, Turned Cup End, Turn Screw, Carved Diamonds, c.1845 1850.00
Clamp, Whale, Turned Cup, Carved Diamonds, c.1850, 5 x 2 In. 1850.00
Clothespin, Whalebone, Rectangular, Chamfered Details, c.1860, 4¼ In. 145.00
Cribbage Board, Raised Diamond Center, Holes Around Border, 9¾ x 3 In. 1150.00
Cribbage Board, Walrus Ivory, Carved, Alaska, 19th Century, 14¾ In. 750.00
Cribbage Board, Walrus Task, Relief Carving, 6 Panels, Walrus, Polar Bear, Eskimo, 25 In. .. 19500.00
Cup, Whale's Tooth, Hollowed Out, Carved Flowers, Scalloped Edge, Turned Wood Base, 6 In., Pair .. 3275.00
Dipper, Coconut, Whalebone, Wood, Ebony, 19th Century, 17 In. 1985.00
Dipper, Rum, Coconut Cup, Ivory Tip, 17¼ In. 920.00
Dirk, Whale Penis Bone, Portrait Of Woman, Man & Shield, Soldier, 18 In. 3565.00
Ditty Box, Baleen, Carved, Building, Church, Palm Trees, Leaf Border, 6½ x 4½ x 3 In. 750.00
Ditty Box, Whalebone, Ships, Lighthouse, Finger Joints, c.1840, 7⅞ x 3½ In. 8250.00
Fid, Whalebone, Carved Top, Ball Final, Tapered Octagonal Section, 1800s, 7 x 1¾ In. 350.00
Fid, Whalebone, Tapered Shaft, Turned End, Incised, c.1840, 5¼ x ¾ In. 235.00
Food Chopper, Panbone Blade & Tang, Tapered Handle, 8 Incised Lines, c.1850, 6¾ x 5 In. .. 2100.00
Food Chopper, Whalebone, Tapered Handle, Incised Lines, c.1850, 6¾ x 5 In. 2100.00
Jewelry Box, Whalebone, Drawer, Interior Shelf, Dovetailed, Hinged, 8⅝ x 4¾ In. 12500.00
Measuring Stick, Whale, Leaf, Vine, Willow, Diamond, 19th Century, 31 x ¾ In. 875.00
Pie Crimper, Whalebone, 3-Tine Fork, Ebony, Mahogany, c.1850, 2 x 7¾ In. 825.00
Pie Crimper, Whale's Tooth, 3-Tine Fork, 6 In. 1150.00
Pie Crimper, Whale's Tooth, Ebony, Heart Cutouts, 7½ In. 2185.00
Riding Crop, Whale's Tooth Handle, Wood Shaft, c.1840, 25 In. 485.00
Rolling Pin, Ivory Handles, Hard Wood Spacers, Teak, c.1840, 20 x 4¼ In. 1875.00
Rolling Pin, Teak Center Section, Whalebone Handles, c.1835, 20 In. 1875.00
Swordfish Bill, Mounted, Mahogany, Eagle, Shield, Whaling Scene, Whale, 37 In. 1150.00
Walrus Tusk, Victorian Woman & Man, c.1950 .... 2070.00
Whalebone, Painted Whaling Scene, Men In Rowboats, Whaling Boat, 26 In. 173.00
Whale's Tooth, Dancing Woman, Couple Verso, Multicolored, c.1850, 5½ x 2¼ In. 3450.00
Whale's Tooth, Engraved, King Richard & Robin Hood, Canary's Nest, 6¾ In. 2585.00
Whale's Tooth, Engraved Panel, Man Giving A Woman A Painting On Locket, 5¾ In. 978.00
Whale's Tooth, Engraved, Woman With Flag, Word Liberty, 6¼ In. 8775.00
Whale's Tooth, Figure Of Neptune, Reverse Side Has Cape Horn & Ship, 7¾ In. 4025.00
Whale's Tooth, Girl's Portrait, Emma On Banner, Woman's Portrait On Reverse, 5 In. 2650.00
Whale's Tooth, Incised, Young Mother & Daughter In Ringlets, 6⅝ In. 230.00
Whale's Tooth, Inscribed, My Brother Lost At Lizzo, 19th Century, 6 In. 2530.00
Whale's Tooth, Man, Woman, Mid Victorian Dress 1705.00
Whale's Tooth, Man & Woman, Shield, 6 Flags, Stars & Stripes, Initials, 4½ In. ......*illus* 2760.00
Whale's Tooth, Navel Vessels Engaged In Battle, 6¼ x 2⅛ In. 11500.00
Whale's Tooth, Pipe Smoking Man, Whaling Scene, Signed Frank, 8¾ In. 4700.00
Whale's Tooth, Ship, H.M.S. Victory, Banner, Nelson's Ship Victory, 5¼ In. 1150.00
Whale's Tooth, Sperm Whaling Scene, 19th Century, 8¼ x 2¼ In. 14500.00
Whale's Tooth, Starboard View Of English Barque, Intaglio Style, 8 x 3¼ In. 4750.00
Whale's Tooth, The Lady Alice, Victorian Woman Smelling Flower, 7 In. ....*illus* 9775.00
Whale's Tooth, Urn, Leaves, Sunburst, Inlaid Mother-Of-Pearl, Engraved, 1800s, 7¼ x 2¾ In. 2640.00
Whale's Tooth, Whaling Scene, Longboat, Boats Passing Lighthouse On Reverse, 8 x 2¼ In. 14500.00

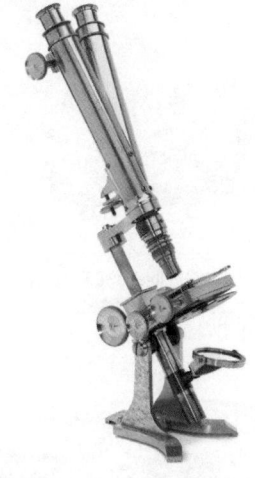

Scientific Instrument, Microscope, Binocular, Gary, London, Brass, Wood Box, c.1880, 15¾ In.
$768.00

Scrimshaw, Whale's Tooth, Man & Woman, Shield, 6 Flags, Stars & Stripes, Initials, 4½ In.
$2760.00

Scrimshaw, Whale's Tooth, The Lady Alice, Victorian Woman Smelling Flower, 7 In.
$9775.00

SEBASTIAN MINIATURES were first made by Prescott W. Baston in 1938 in *Prescott W. Baston* Marblehead, Massachusetts. More than 400 different designs have been made and collectors search for the out-of-production models. The mark may say *Copr. P.W. Baston U.S.A.,* or *P. W. Baston, U.S.A.,* or *Prescott W. Baston.* Sometimes a paper label was used.

Bob Cratchett & Tiny Tim, 3½ In. 20.00
Boy & Pelican, Box, 3½ In. 21.00
Coronado & Senora, Box, 3 In. 24.00
Cranberry Picker, Box, 2 In. 24.00
Donald McKay, Box, 3½ In. 21.00
Family Reads Aloud, Box, 2½ In. 22.00
First House, Box, 3 x 3¾ In. 30.00
George Washington, Mason, Gray Label, 3¾ In. 28.00
Gibson Girl At Home, Box, 3 In. 24.00
Glassblower, Colonial, 3 In. 49.00

S

Sevres, Bowl, Cover, Flowers, 4 Paw Feet, Ring Finial, Blue Mark, 11 x 6½ In. $173.00

Sevres, Salt, Double, Oval Panels, Flowers, Scroll, Gilt, Marked, c.1760, 4⅞ In. $4500.00

Sewer Tile, Umbrella Stand, Redware, Embossed Tree Trunk Decoration, Bird On Branch, 22 In. $44.00

S

Sewing, Bird, Red Velvet, Pincushion Top, Wood Beak, Wire Legs, 6¾ In. $187.00

Ichabod Crane, Box, 3¼ x 2½ In.	20.00
Kite First, 3¼ In.	18.00
Lincoln Memorial, 3½ x 3½ x 2⅞ In.	45.00
Michigan Millers 75th Year, Paperweight, 2 In.	199.00
Rip Van Winkle, 3¼ In.	20.00
Shoemaker, Paperweight, First County National Bank, 3½ In.	199.00
Toll House, Town Crier, Marblehead Label, 3½ In.	62.00
Williamsburg Couple, 3 In.	24.00

SEG, *see Paul Revere Pottery category.*

SEVRES porcelain has been made in Sevres, France, since 1769. Many copies of the famous ware have been made. The name originally referred to the works of the Royal Porcelain factory. The name now includes any of the wares made in the town of Sevres, France. The entwined lines with a center letter used as the mark is one of the most forged marks in antiques. Be very careful to identify Sevres by quality, not just by mark.

Bowl, Birds, Blue, Gilt Trellis & Flower Border, 10-Sided, Flared, Rim, 1700s 10½ In.	2000.00
Bowl, Cover, Flowers, 4 Paw Feet, Ring Finial, Blue Mark, 11 x 6½ In. *illus*	173.00
Bowl, Gilt, Enamel, Antelope, Leaping, Jean Mayodon, 1957, 4¾ In.	3120.00
Box, Rectangular, Gilt Bronze Mounted, Enamel, Cherubs, Jeweled Border, 9 x 7 x 5 In.	3408.00
Charger, Battle Scene, Count Maurice De Saxe, Signed, L Moreau, Marked, 19¾ In.	2400.00
Coffee & Chocolate Service, Louis Philippe, Coffeepot 10 In., 14 Piece	1053.00
Cup & Saucer, Acanthus Leaves, Husk Garland, Powder Blue Ground, Gilt, c.1765-70	1080.00
Cup & Saucer, Birds, Landscape, Blue, Gold, Red Circle Dot Ground, Dentil Border, c.1767	3900.00
Cup & Saucer, Birds In Branches, Green Ground, Gilt, Marked, 18th Century	480.00
Cup & Saucer, Boy Playing Pipe, Dog, Shepherdess, Blue, Gilt, Marked, c.1780	2880.00
Cup & Saucer, Cover, Trembleuse, Turquoise, Scenic, Early 19th Century, 5¼ In.	1039.00
Cup & Saucer, Lapis Border, Center Bird Design, Late 18th Century, 4 In.	304.00
Dish, Oval, Turquoise, Floral Reserves, Late 18th Century, 8¾ In.	413.00
Dresser Box, Floral Decoration, 3 x 5 In.	193.00
Inkstand, Gilt Bronze, France, 19th Century, 4½ x 8½ In.	234.00
Jewelry Box, Allegorical Scene, Hinged, Painted, 6 x 8 x 13 In.	234.00
Plate, Dinner, Apple Green & Black Floral Reserve Panels, Gilt Trim, 9½ In., 6 Piece	2585.00
Plate, Portrait, Courting Scene, 19th Century, 9½ In., Pair	53.00
Plate Set, Chateau De St. Cloud, Courting Scenes, 8¼ In.	468.00
Plate Set, Signed Bord, France, 19th Century, 9¾ In., 4 Piece	527.00
Salt, Double, Oval Panels, Flowers, Scroll, Gilt, Marked, c.1760, 4⅞ In. *illus*	4500.00
Teapot, Cover, Flower Sprays, Green Ground Border Edge, Gilt, Marked, 1757-58, 5 In.	5400.00
Teapot, Empire Style, Painted, Gilt, Portrait Bust, Josephine, 8 In.	1695.00
Teapot, Flower Scrolls, Garland, Green Ground, Gilt, Fruit Form Knop, Silver Chain, 1780, 5¾ In.	4200.00
Trinket Box, Turquoise, Scenic, Signed, Ch. Fritz, c.1900, 7 In.	298.00
Tureen, Sauce, Cover, Gilt Bleu Du Ciel, Neoclassical Style, Oval, c.1832, 1 In.	600.00
Urn, Cover, Couple Under Tree, Green, Gold, Bronze Base, Signed, 17 In., Pair	1650.00
Urn, Palace, Louis XVI, Military Scene, H. Depres, 19th Century, 39 In.	9360.00
Urn, Potpourri, Gilt Bronze Mounted, Flowers, Basket, Dome Lids, 10¾ In., Pair	940.00
Vase, Black & Silver Glazed, 7½ In.	175.00
Vase, Bronze Mounted, France, 20th Century, 39 In.	2925.00
Vase, Panels, Couple, Sheep, Landscape, Turquoise, Gilt Borders, Stand, Marked, 7½ In.	3840.00
Vase, Red High Glaze, Black Accents, Stepped Rim, Paul Milet, Egg Shape, 7⅛ In.	138.00

SEWER TILE figures were made by workers at the sewer tile and pipe factories in the Ohio area during the late nineteenth and early twentieth centuries. Figurines, small vases, and cemetery vases were favored. Often the finished vase was a piece of the original pipe with added decorations and markings. All types of sewer tile work are now considered folk art by collectors.

Bank, Pig, Stamped Jim, Summit County, Ohio, 12½ In.	4945.00
Bust, American Indian, Barberton, Ohio, 10 In.	3220.00
Bust, Statue Of Liberty, 1918, 9½ In.	3738.00
Figure, Cat Family, Father, Mother, Kitten, Glass Eyes, Molded Slab Base, 17½ x 18¾ In.	1540.00
Figure, Dog, Seated, Incised Fur, Ohio, 11 In.	920.00
Figure, Dog, Spaniel, Flathead, Incised Collar, Features, 11½ In.	2415.00
Figure, Dog, Spaniel, Seated, Crisscross Design On Base, Incised Initials, 8½ In.	173.00
Figure, Eagle, Incised Feathers, Inscribed, For Dave Marten, By W. Frederick, 1925, 8⅛ In.	288.00
Figure, Frog, Tooled Smiling Face, Ohio, 9 In.	546.00
Figure, Lion, Reclining, Smiling, Rectangular Base, 9 x 7 In.	316.00
Pitcher, Molded, Applied Liberty & 13 Stars, Spurred C-Scroll Handle, 7 In.	345.00

Planter, Tree Stump, Lions, Hollow, Hand Formed, Green Glaze, 8 In.	230.00
Planter, Tree Trunk, Simulated Bark, Uhrichsville Fire Clay Co., Ohio, 38 x 14 In.	460.00
Roof Adornment, Rooster, Redware, Incised, Porcelain Eyes, 19 In.	990.00
Umbrella Stand, Redware, Embossed Tree Trunk Decoration, Bird On Branch, 22 In. ....illus	44.00

SEWING equipment of all types is collected, from sewing birds that held the cloth to tape measures, needle books, and old wooden spools. Sewing machines are included here. Needlework pictures are listed in the Picture category.

Basket, Brass Coins, Glass Beads, Blue, Green, Silk, Gold Tassels, Chinese, 7½ x 3 In.	95.00
Basket, Needles, Thread, Darner, Scissors, Buttons, Dritz, 8 x 6 x 5 In.	38.00
Basket, Oak, Splint, God's-Eye Wrap, Double Lift Lid, Fixed Handle, 7¼ x 8¼ In.	138.00
Basket, Splint, Woven, Carved Wood Handles, Yellow, Dark Blue, 7¼ x 7 x 13¼ In.	176.00
Basket, Travel, Sweet Grass, Gold Silk, Quilted Lining, Brass Handle, 1850s	350.00
Bird, Clamp, Pincushion, Burled Walnut, Cylinder, Turned Wood Screw, 5¼ In.	138.00
Bird, Pincushion, Silver Plate Over Brass, Screw End, Clamp, 10 In.	798.00
Bird, Red Velvet, Pincushion Top, Wood Beak, Wire Legs, 6¾ In. ....illus	187.00
Bird, Stylized Body Over Shaped Clamp Platform, Thumbscrew, Steel, 4⅛ In.	77.00
Bobbin, Pillow Lace, Black Glass Button, Amethyst, Amber Weight, Wood, England, 3½ In.	30.00
Bobbin, Pillow Lace, Blue Spangle Glass Weight, England, 19th Century, 4⅛ In.	47.00
Bobbin, Pillow Lace, Tiger Pattern, 3 Bands, Glass Weight, Wood, England, 19th Century, 4⅝ In.	48.00
Box, Mahogany, Pincushion Knob, Needle Mounts, Mirror, Early 1900s, 8 x 7 In.	316.00
Box, Needlework, Stumpwork, Trapunto, Walnut Frame, Oak, Beech, Fitted Interior, 16 x 12 In.	6210.00
Box, Oak, Excelsior Machine, 7 x 19 x 12 In.	82.00
Box, Softwood, Brown Sponge Over Yellow Paint, Finger Jointed, Lift-Out Tray, 3⅝ x 9¾ x 7 In.	132.00
Box, Softwood, Painted, Brass Bail Handle, Paper Lined Tray, Lithograph, 6½ x 11 In.	358.00
Box, Straw, Multicolored, Round, 9 x 3¾ In.	20.00
Box, Walnut, Eagle, Ivory, Bone Hearts, Leaves, Arrows, Hinged Lid, 1864, 4 x 13 x 9 In.	1200.00
Box, Walnut, Inlaid, Veneer, Slant Lid, Molded Frame & Base, Heart Pincushion, 1700s	359.00
Box, Wood, Blond, c.1950s, 6 x 11½ x 10¼ In.	25.00
Buttonhole Cutter, Large & Small, Twisted Loop Shaft, Whitesmithed, 3 x 2⅜ In. ....illus	303.00
Cabinet, Spool, see also the Advertising category under Cabinet, Spool.	
Cabinet, Spool, 5 Glass Drawers, 2 Solid Drawers, 17 x 19½ x 16 In.	330.00
Cabinet, Spool, Georgian, Mahogany, 2 Sections, 2 Doors, Marlboro Legs, 29 x 15 In. ..illus	354.00
Cabinet, Spool, Oak, Spools On Swivel Base, 23 x 16 In.	192.00
Cabinet, Spool, Walnut, 6 Drawers, Paneled Construction, c.1900, 17 x 29 In.	411.00
Caddy, Square, 4-Footed, Dovetail Drawer, Turned Post Supports Pincushion, 6½ x 9 In.	489.00
Darner, Lady's Leg Form, Walnut, Early 1800s	350.00
Darner, Sock, Wood, Black Lacquer, Needle & Thread Storage In Ball, 1920s, 7 In.	14.00
Etui, Case, Egg Shape, Palais Royal, Mother-Of-Pearl, Ormolu Mounts, Chain, 2⅜ x 1 In.	145.00
Kit, Bisque, Dove, Thread, Scissors, Tape Measure, 4½ x 4¾ In.	18.00
Kit, Leather, Wallet, Black, White Stripes, Thread, Thimble, Tape Measure, 3½ x 3 In.	5.00
Kit, Needles, Thread, Thimble, World War II, W. Crowley & Sons, England, 5 In.	15.00
Kit, Pincushion, Drawers, Threads, Thimble, Round, Painted, Japan, 3 In.	18.00
Kit, Vinyl, Gold Lame, Gold Tone Hardware, 2-Sided, 2½ x 3½ In.	5.00
Lamp, Lace Maker, Pewter, 15 In.	523.00
Machine, Grover & Baker, No. 10574, Flywheel, Gilt, Rosewood Case, c.1856, 13 In.	881.00
Machine, Singer, Featherweight	325.00
Machine, Singer, No. 221-1, Feather Weight, Portable, Electric, Case, 10 In.	147.00
Machine, Tiny Tailor, Needle, Bobbin, AC Adaptor, Free Arm, 10½ x 8½ In.	165.00
Needle Case, Art Nouveau, Silver Bodkin, Embossed, Ribbon & Scroll, Germany, 2½ In.	149.00
Needle Case, Bakelite, Green Marble, White Screw Top, Tassel, Darning Needles, 3¾ In.	45.00
Needle Case, Bee, On Leaf, Gilt, Metal, Wm. Avery & Son, Late 19th Century, 4¼ In.	588.00
Needle Case, Birds, Flowers, 5 x 2½ In.	45.00
Needle Case, Brass, 2¼ x ⅝ In.	30.00
Needle Case, Cross Fox Metal, Graphics	45.00
Needle Case, Plastic Top, Gold Colors, Threader, Pins, Bobbins, Scissors	5.00
Needle Case, Porcupine Quills, Gilt Metal, Hinged Lid, Embossed, Late 1800s, 3¾ In.	411.00
Needle Case, Sterling Silver, Art Nouveau	22.00
Needle Case, Sterling Silver, Repousse Flower	24.00
Needle Case, Wood, Carved, Screw Cap, 2 In.	70.00
Needle Case, Wood, Paper Covered, c.1870	115.00
Needle Case, Wood, Pedestal Base, 2½ x ¾ In.	65.00
Needle Case, Wood, Push On Cap, 2 In.	13.00
Niddy Noddy, Carved Central Shaft, Oriental Writing, 20 x 11 In.	345.00
Niddy Noddy, Chip Carved Central Shaft, Red Paint, 19 x 11 In.	115.00

Sewing, Buttonhole Cutter, Large & Small, Twisted Loop Shaft, Whitesmithed, 3 x 2⅜ In. $303.00

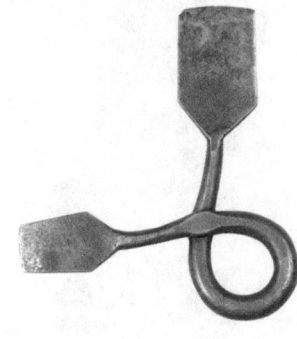

Sewing, Cabinet, Spool, Georgian, Mahogany, 2 Sections, 2 Doors, Marlboro Legs, 29 x 15 In. $354.00

Sewing, Pincushion, Chicken, Black & White Velvet, Button Eyes, Spool Base, 5 In. $88.00

S

Sewing, Tape Measure, Baseball Player, Celluloid, 3 In. $29.00

Sewing, Yarn Winder, Oak, Standard & Double Tusk Through Tenon, 3 Legs, 42 x 30 x 19 In. $92.00

Niddy Noddy, Mortised, Wooden, 19¼ In.	77.00
Pattern, Costume, Dazian's, N.Y., c.1940	22.00
Pin Cube, Glass Head Pins, Victorian, 1¼ x 1¼ In.	35.00
Pincushion, Ball, Color Creating Star On Ends, Diamond In Square Interior, 2½ In.	220.00
Pincushion, Boyles Bennett & New, King, N.C., Celluloid, 2½ In.	33.00
Pincushion, Chicken, Black & White Velvet, Button Eyes, Spool Base, 5 In. *illus*	88.00
Pincushion, Dutch Wooden Shoe, England	15.00
Pincushion, Footstool, Velvet, Metal Legs, Victorian, 2 x 3 In.	95.00
Pincushion, Indian Chief By Drum, 3 In.	8.00
Pincushion, Mountain Climbing Shoe, Victorian, 3 x 2½ In.	95.00
Pincushion, Needlework, Flower, Wreath, Hand Holding Stem, Blue Chintz, Beads, 7 x 6¼ In.	550.00
Pincushion, Needlework, Multicolored Flowers, Bead Rope Work, 8 x 8 In.	33.00
Pincushion, Needlework, Round, Orange & Purple Flower, Openwork Edge, Blue Silk, 4¾ In.	138.00
Pincushion, Needlework, Starburst, Flower, Wreath, Blue Silk, Green Beads, 6½ In.	440.00
Pincushion, Needlework, Starburst, Yellow Flower, Sprays, Light Blue, Beads, 4¾ In.	55.00
Pincushion, Needlework, Strawberry, Beads, Tassels, 3 In.	39.00
Pincushion, Needlework, Turtle Form, Flower, Wreath, Hand, Brown Chintz, Beads, 7½ x 5 In.	880.00
Pincushion, Shoe, Applied Flowers, Ceramic	12.00
Pincushion, Shoe, Dutch Wooden, Gingham, Painted, Thimble Holder, 6 In.	32.00
Pincushion, Silk, Crocheted Lace Trim, 1890-1910, 5 x 2½ In.	28.00
Pincushion, Squirrel, Pink, Embroidered Accents, 7⅜ In.	11.00
Pincushion, Turtle, Nods, Wags Tail, Rhinestone Eyes, Blue Velveteen, Florenza, 3 x 2 In.	58.00
Pincushion Dolls are listed in their own category.	
Pins, Straight, Black Porcelain Head, Original Box, Morralls-Cross Fox Brand, 1¾ In.	15.00
Spool Cabinets are listed here or in the Advertising category under Cabinet, Spool.	
Spoolholder, Turned, 2 Tiers, Pincushion Top, 6 Lift Wire Spool Supports, 6½ In.	330.00
Tape Loom, English Pine, Through Mortises, 19th Century, 19 x 24 In.	46.00
Tape Measure, Abbott's Ice Cream, Serve It Tonight, Waitress, Celluloid, Round, 2 In.	368.00
Tape Measure, Altoona, Pa., City Hall, Horseshoe Curve, Celluloid, Round, c.1910, 2 In.	46.00
Tape Measure, Arlington Skirt Mfg. Co., Petticoats, Celluloid, Round, 2 In.	168.00
Tape Measure, Asbury Park, Casino, Boardwalk, Celluloid, Round, 1½ In.	29.00
Tape Measure, Baseball Player, Celluloid, 3 In. *illus*	29.00
Tape Measure, Brass, Iron, Winding Handle, Germany	70.00
Tape Measure, Cawston's Ostrich Farm, So. Pasadena, Ca., Celluloid, Round, c.1900, 2 In.	85.00
Tape Measure, Chr. Hansen's Laboratory, Have Some Junket, Celluloid, Round, 2 In.	62.00
Tape Measure, Colgate Fab's Laundry Detergent, Celluloid, 1913-18, 1½ In.	30.00
Tape Measure, De Bevoise Brassiere, Newark, N.J., Celluloid, Round, 2 In.	103.00
Tape Measure, Elmer Elephant, Celluloid, Japan, 1930s, 2½ In.	574.00
Tape Measure, Gold Shield Coffee, Girl, Can, Schwabacker Bros., Celluloid, 1¾ In.	130.00
Tape Measure, H.P. Hood & Sons Milk, Hood's Dairy Products, Cow, Celluloid, Round, 2 In.	76.00
Tape Measure, Hoover Vacuums, 1960	35.00
Tape Measure, Iron Shape	400.00
Tape Measure, Ko-Ko-Mar, Oleomargarine, Nut Butter, Celluloid, Round, 2 In.	29.00
Tape Measure, Leather, Metallic, Lufkin Rule Co.	35.00
Tape Measure, McCormick Harvesting Machine Co., Celluloid, Round, 2 In.	153.00
Tape Measure, McKibbin Driscoll & Dorsey, St. Paul, Minn., Celluloid, Round, 2 In.	204.00
Tape Measure, Minnie Mouse, Celluloid, England, 1930s, 4¼ In.	585.00
Tape Measure, Northfield Milk, Peninsular Grocery, Tampa, Fla., Celluloid, Round, 2 In.	85.00
Tape Measure, One Man, Hook On End, Crogan Manufacturing Co., 1915.	170.00
Tape Measure, Philadelphia Knitting Mills, Full Fashioned Hosiery, Celluloid, Round, 2 In.	226.00
Tape Measure, Pneumatic Dress Form, Pneu Form Company, N.Y., Celluloid, Round	103.00
Tape Measure, Pocket, Keen Kutter	375.00
Tape Measure, Raybone, Metal, Leather Covered Case, 100 Ft., 1920	110.00
Tape Measure, S&H Green Stamps, Red Border, Celluloid, Round, 2 In.	85.00
Tape Measure, Singing Tower, Lake Wales, Fla. Metal, Cloth, Retracting, Germany, 1½ In.	38.00
Tape Measure, Standard Shoe House, Plattsburgh, N.Y., Woman On Stairs, Celluloid, Round, 2 In.	33.00
Tape Measure, Sterling Silver, Crank Handle, Embossed Flower Case, 1 x 1 In.	68.00
Tape Measure, Sterling Silver, Scroll Border, Repousse, Cloth, 1¼ x ½ In.	50.00
Tape Measure, Wooden Barrel, Handle, Treenware, 2¾ In.	125.00
Thimble, Bone China, Painted, Thatched Cottage, Garden, Gold Trim, 1970s, 1 x 1 In.	18.00
Thimble, Cloisonne, Cobalt Blue Ground, Flowers	15.00
Thimble Holder, Egg Shape, Wood, Carved	140.00
Work Box, Black Lacquered, Multicolored, Lift-Out Tray, Winged Paw Feet, 6 x 14 In.	1320.00
Work Box, Parcel Gilt, Black Lacquer, Octagonal, Paw Feet, 11 x 7½ In.	660.00
Yarn Winder, Oak, Standard & Double Tusk Through Tenon, 3 Legs, 42 x 30 x 19 In. *illus*	92.00

Yarn Winder, Poplar, Walnut, Pine, Adjustable Wheels, Heart, Pinwheels, 42 x 17½ In.	115.00
Yarn Winder, Wood, 30 In.	165.00

SHAKER items are characterized by simplicity, functionalism, and orderliness. There were many Shaker communities in America from the eighteenth century to the present day. The religious order made furniture, small wooden pieces, and packaged medicines, herbs, and jellies to sell to "outsiders." Other useful objects were made for use by members of the community. Shaker furniture is listed in this book in the Furniture category.

Abacus, Maple, Varnish, Red, White, Blue Beads, Handle, Scribe Lines, Ma., c.1870, 15 x 12 In. ..	1989.00
Awl & Holder, Maple, Natural Varnish, Apple Core Shaped Holder, Steel Awl, N.Y., 4½ In.	1345.00
Awl & Holder, Maple, Red Paint, Apple Core Shaped Holder, Handle, Steel Awl, N.H., 5 In. ...	1813.00
Basket, Berry, Kitten Head, Handle, Gray Wash, 7¼ x 5⅝ In.	1540.00
Basket, Berry, Tin Rim, Base Band, 3⅞ In.	325.00
Basket, Fixed Handle, Push-Up Bottom, Footed Round Base, 7½ x 13½ In.	120.00
Basket, Gathering, Black Ash, Red Paint, Cat's Head Arched Base, 10 x 15¾ In.	877.00
Basket, Gathering, Black Ash, Wrapped Rim, Heart Handles, Inverted Base, Patina, 15 x 21 In. ..	585.00
Basket, Gathering, Black Ash, Wrapped Rim, Loop Handle, 2 Runners, 14 x 19 In.	819.00
Basket, Sewing, Ash, Kitten Head, Handles, Openwork, Pincushion, N.Y., c.1890, 4 x 6 In.	2950.00
Basket, Sewing, Black Ash, Cat's Head, Splint, Heart Handles, 9 Interior Baskets, 5 x 16 In. ..	2032.00
Basket, Sewing, Open Weave, 6-Sided, Ribbon On Lid, Sister Hatch, Ma., c.1880, 3 x 6 In. ...	1053.00
Basket, Sewing, Swallowtail Fingers, Copper Tacks, Handle, Silk Liner, No Lid, 2 x 7 In.	230.00
Basket, Splint, Round, Domed Base, Carved Wooden Handles, 7⅞ x 14 In.	2585.00
Basket, Swing Handle, Push-Up Bottom, 7 x 2 In.	345.00
Basket, Work, Black Ash, Carved Handles, Wrapped Rim, Brown Patina, 3 Runners, 34 x 21 In. .	1521.00
Basket, Work, Black Ash, Splint, Wrapped Rim, Carved Handles, Interior Shelf, 17 x 13 In. ..	439.00
Basket, Work, Black Ash, Wrapped Rim, Carved Handles, Patina, 3 Runners, c.1850, 17 x 22 In. .	526.00
Basket, Work, Black Ash, Wrapped Rim, Ticking Lined, Handle, Tag, E. Canterbury, 17 x 22 In.	2691.00
Berry Bucket, Dark & Light Stained Staves, Tin Bands, Wire Handle, Wood Grip, 3 x 4 In. ..	275.00
Berry Bucket, Green Paint, Tin Bands, Wire Bail Handle, Wood Hand Grip, 3 x 4¾ In.	825.00
Berry Bucket, Yellow, Tin Bands, Wire Bail Handle, Wood Grip, 3½ x 4½ In. .... *illus*	880.00
Bonnet, Sisters, Poplar, Purple Silk, Black Dots, Taffeta, Round Head Pins, Ribbons, 7 x 8 In. .	1404.00
Box, 3-Finger, Maple, Pine, Dark Ocher Finish, Pincushion Top, 2⅜ x 3 x 2 In.	2808.00
Box, 3-Finger, Maple, Pine, Mustard Yellow Stain, Dated, August 1, 1862, 3¾ x 2½ In.	1755.00
Box, 3-Finger, Oval, Maple, Pine, Chrome Yellow Finish, 1½ x 3⅝ x 2⅜ In.	8190.00
Box, 3-Finger, Oval, Maple, Pine, Gray Green Paint Over Red, c.1840, 8 x 5¾ In.	1521.00
Box, 3-Finger, Oval, Maple, Pine, Mustard Yellow Paint, 1¾ x 4½ In.	2457.00
Box, 3-Finger, Oval, Maple, Pine, Ocher Stain, Pincushion, Elizabeth Durgin, 1793, 2 x 3 In. .	1989.00
Box, 3-Finger, Oval, Maple, Pine, Original Light Red Paint, 3½ In.	2691.00
Box, 3-Finger, Oval, Maple, Pine, Varnish, Copper Tacks, Canterbury, c.1850, 1⅝ x 3⅝ In. .	585.00
Box, 3-Finger, Oval, Pine, Maple, Copper Tacks, Brown Paint, 2 x 6⅛ In.	323.00
Box, 3-Finger, Oval, Pine, Maple, Copper Tacks, Gray Paint, 2⅞ x 7⅞ In.	1410.00
Box, 3-Finger, Oval, Pine, Maple, Copper Tacks, Natural, 1⅝ x 3¾ In.	881.00
Box, 4-Finger, Band, Oval, Old Yellow Paint, Stamped, A.H., 3⅝ x 9⅜ x 6⅞ In.	4400.00
Box, 4-Finger, Band, Oval, Varnished, 3½ x 9 x 6 In.	605.00
Box, 4-Finger, Band, Oval, Yellow Wash, 5 x 11¾ x 8¾ In.	1100.00
Box, 4-Finger, Maple, Pine, Brown Paint Over Red, Copper Tacks, c.1840, 5 x 11½ In.	761.00
Box, 4-Finger, Maple, Pine, Red Cherry Stain, Inscribed, Sara From Mabel, 12 x 8 In.	1872.00
Box, 4-Finger, Oval, Cover, Maple, Copper Tacks, Pine Top, Bottom, 4 x 10⅜ In.	588.00
Box, 4-Finger, Oval, Maple, Pine, Copper Tacks, Bittersweet, 2½ x 6⅜ In.	4700.00
Box, 4-Finger, Oval, Maple, Pine, Copper Tacks, Blue, Green Paint, 3⅜ x 8⅞ In.	1998.00
Box, 4-Finger, Oval, Maple, Pine, Copper Tacks, Green Paint, 4⅝ x 11⅜ In.	2233.00
Box, 4-Finger, Oval, Maple, Pine, Copper Tacks, Natural, 4⅝ x 11⅜ In.	353.00
Box, 4-Finger, Oval, Maple, Pine, Copper Tacks, Natural, 5½ x 13⅜ In.	2115.00
Box, 4-Finger, Oval, Maple, Pine, Copper Tacks, Red Brown Stain, 4 x 10⅜ In.	705.00
Box, 4-Finger, Oval, Maple, Pine, Light Red Stain, Copper Tacks, c.1860, 8 x 5⅜ In.	761.00
Box, 4-Finger, Oval, Maple, Pine, Original Cherry Red Paint, 3⅜ x 8⅝ In.	9360.00
Box, 4-Finger, Oval, Maple, Pine, Original Orange Varnish, Copper Tacks, 4⅝ x 3 In.	1521.00
Box, 4-Finger, Oval, Maple, Pine, Pumpkin Red Stain, Canterbury, N.H., c.1850, 4 x 10 In. ...	4095.00
Box, 4-Finger, Oval, Maple, Pine, Red Paint, Yellow Paint Interior, c.1825, 8½ x 5⅝ In.	1287.00
Box, 4-Finger, Oval, Maple, Pine, Red Stain, Pincushion, Canterbury, N.H., c.1840, 8 x 5 In. .	3050.00
Box, 4-Finger, Oval, Maple, Pine, Yellow Paint Over Blue, Canterbury, c.1855, 3 x 10 In.	1287.00
Box, 4-Finger, Pine, Maple, Green Paint, Paper Label, Maine, c.1830, 10½ x 7½ In.	1872.00
Box, 5-Finger, Maple, Pine, Sky Blue Paint, Copper Tacks, c.1845, 5⅜ x 13 In.	4388.00
Box, 5-Finger, Oval, Maple, Pine, Original Cherry Red Paint, Copper Tacks, 5¾ x 13 In.	7313.00
Box, 5-Finger, Oval, Pine, Maple, Copper Tacks, Brown Stain, 6 x 14⅞ In.	1645.00

Who Were the Shakers?
The Shakers were a religious sect that came to America from England in 1774. The Shaker religion stressed honesty, integrity, goodness, trust, hard work, equality, and celibacy. The members of the sect made their own nails; wove strips of fabric for chair seats; invented the flat broom, circular saw, and clothespin. Some helped Mr. Borden can evaporated milk. Shakers believed dedication to work and perfection were a part of their dedication to God. They sold chairs, herbs, medicine, and other products to outsiders. Over six thousand Shakers lived in nineteen settlements about 1850. By 1942 most of the communities were empty and today only a few Shakers remain.

Shaker, Berry Bucket, Yellow, Tin Bands, Wire Bail Handle, Wood Grip, 3½ x 4½ In.
$880.00

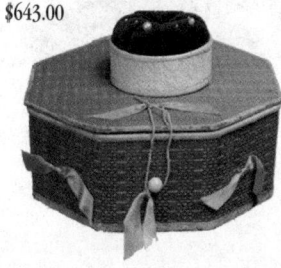

Shaker, Box, Sewing, Poplar, Kid Trim, 8-Sided, Pincushion, Silk, Sabbathday Lake, 6¾ In.
$643.00

S

Shaker, Carrier, 3-Finger, Oval, Maple, Pine, Yellow Paint, Copper Nails, Arched Handle, 7 x 9 x 6½ In. $105300.00

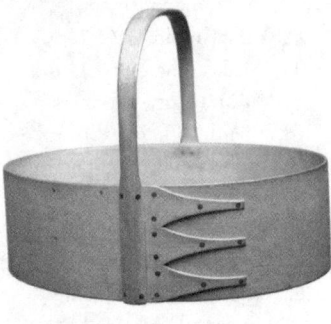

Shaker, Sewing Set, Bag, Silk, Beeswax Ball, Emery, Pincushions, Needle Book, 4 Piece $293.00

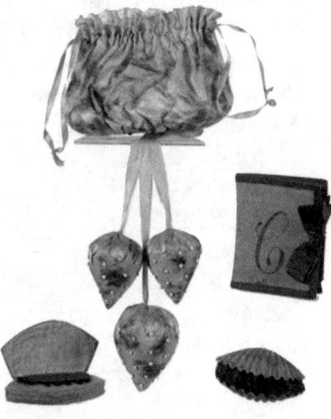

Shaker, Spool Holder, Cherry, Knob Top, 4 Hooks, 13 Spools, Betsey Hastings, Died May 15, 1844, 9 In. $4329.00

Box, Bonnet, Poplar, Bittersweet Paint, Straps, Hinged Lid, 4-Peg Interior, 20 x 18 In.	2223.00
Box, Bonnet, Poplar, Walnut Stain, Lid, Dovetailed, 3-Peg Interior, c.1850, 20 x 20½ In.	1638.00
Box, Cover, Red Paint, Oval, 9 x 7 x 3½ In.	690.00
Box, Harvard Type, Opposing Fingers, Copper Tacks, Label, B. Sprague, 5½ In.	978.00
Box, Pine, Red Paint, Cast Iron & Birch Handle, Iron Bail Plates, c.1845, 20 x 20 x 14 In.	1170.00
Box, Pine, Sectioned, Dovetailed, Arched Feet, Canterbury, c.1850, 26 x 40 x 16 In.	1170.00
Box, Pine, Varnish, Red Stain, Sections, Handles, Dovetailed, Initialed, c.1850, 16 x 9 In.	819.00
Box, Pipe, Salmon Red Stain, Pine, Drawer, Fishtail Back, Hole For Peg, 14¼ x 4¼ In.	468.00
Box, Sewing, 4-Finger, Maple, Pine, Varnish, Satin Lined, 11¾ In.	351.00
Box, Sewing, Butternut, Brass Handle, Dovetailed, Liner, N.H., c.1860, 6 x 3 In.	2574.00
Box, Sewing, Poplar, Kid Trim, 8-Sided, Pincushion, Silk, Sabbathday Lake, 6¾ In. *illus*	643.00
Box, Spit, 4-Finger, Maple, Pine, Red-Orange Stain, Iron Bail Plates, Round, 13 In.	3802.00
Box, Storage, Pine, Mustard, Dovetailed, Tin Hinges, Clasp, Canterbury, c.1850, 29 x 9 In.	2223.00
Box, Walnut, Cutout Leaf & Star Design, Pin Hinged Lid, 4½ x 11½ x 8 In.	147.00
Box, Walnut, Varnish, 2 Drawers, Dovetailed, Medial Slides, Knob Top, c.1870, 6 x 8¾ In.	1053.00
Bucket, Ash, Pine, Brown, Carved Swing Handle, Extended Ears, 3 Hoops, 14½ x 11 In.	819.00
Bucket, Oak, White Paint, Corn In Black Script, Extended Ears, Rope Handle, 12½ x 12 In.	3978.00
Bucket, Pine, Red Paint, Wire & Wood Bail Handle, NF Shakers, Enfield, N.H., 13 x 9½ In.	644.00
Bucket, Pine, Red-Ocher Stain, Bent Hickory Swing Handle, Iron Bands, 15 x 11¼ In.	1521.00
Butter Stamp, Maple, 2-Part, Cylindrical Holder, Deep Cut 5, 5¾ x 3 In.	644.00
Carrier, 3-Finger, Oval, Maple, Pine, Yellow Paint, Copper Nails, Arched Handle, 7 x 9 x 6½ In. *illus*	105300.00
Carrier, 4-Finger, Oval, Maple, Red Varnish, Swing Handle, Lotte Byrdsall, 9 x 11¾ In.	234.00
Carrier, 4-Finger, Pine, Maple, Light Stain Varnish, Swing Handle, c.1880, 7 x 9¼ In.	526.00
Carrier, Carpenter's, Pine, Gray, Cutout Handle, Tin Bands, New Lebanon, N.Y., 33 x 11 In.	702.00
Carrier, Herb, Poplar, Brown Stain, Fixed Handle, Copper, Watervliet, N.Y., 10¾ x 11 In.	3570.00
Carrier, Sewing, 3-Finger, Maple, Swing Handle, Silk, Pincushion, Needle Case, Emery, 8 In.	205.00
Carrier, Sewing, 4-Finger, Maple, Swing Handle, Sewing Pieces, Sabbathday Lake, 7 x 9 In.	819.00
Carrier, Utensil, Maple, Varnish, Dovetailed, Heart Handle, c.1850, 5 x 13¾ x 7 In.	1404.00
Cloak, Sister's, Black, Wool, Hooded, Labeled, Dorothy, E. Canterbury, Hart & Shepard, 48 In.	468.00
Cloak, Wool, Red, Satin Ribbons, Hood, 53 In.	410.00
Drying Rack, Cherry, Birch, 4 Turned Ladders, Arched Feet, Watervliet, N.Y., 45 x 17 In.	819.00
Drying Rack, Pine, 3 Sections, 4 Rails, Carved, Round Tops, Canterbury, 1850, 66 x 108 In.	293.00
Drying Rack, Pine, White Paint, 4 Bars, 3 Sections, Signed, James M. Upton	527.00
Fan, Feather, Turkey Feathers, Silk Ribbon, Shirley, Ma., c.1880, 20 In.	176.00
Fan, Poplar, Quatrefoil Center, Maple Handle, 2 Scribe Lines, 11½ x 8 In.	1989.00
Herb Dryer, Cherry, 8 Poles, Rivets, Iron Hook, Harvard, Mass., c.1860, 56 x 42 In.	351.00
Ladder, Cheese Basket, Oak, Ash, Red, 20 Spokes, Latticework, New Lebanon, c.1850, 6 x 33 In.	2223.00
Peg Rack, Maple, 4 Turned Pegs, Old Red Paint, 41½ x 3 In.	105.00
Sconce, Wall, Candle, Tin, Yellow Paint, Rectangular Back, N.Y., c.1850, 12 x 4 In.	2340.00
Scoop, Maple, Carved, Shaped Handle, Formed Hook On End, 12 In.	1521.00
Seat Pad, Hooked, Red, Blue, Gray, Orange, Border, Mottled Green, Braid Ties, 16 x 20 In.	117.00
Seed Box, Pine, Lid, Red Paint, 6-Section Interior, Mt. Lebanon, N.Y., c.1860, 23 x 11 In.	468.00
Sewing Set, Bag, Silk, Beeswax Ball, Emery, Pincushions, Needle Book, 4 Piece *illus*	293.00
Spinning Wheel, Flax, Maple, Oak, Old Finish, Patina, Stamped, SRAL, 34 x 37½ In.	526.00
Spinning Wheel, Flax, Maple, Tiger Maple, Oak, Natural Varnish, Me., 43 x 34 In.	644.00
Spinning Wheel, Wool, Standing, Maple, Gray, Pewter Collar, Marked, JH, 58½ x 45 In.	526.00
Spool Holder, Cherry, Knob Top, 4 Hooks, 13 Spools, Betsey Hastings, Died May 15, 1844, 9 In. *illus*	4329.00
Spool Holder, Walnut, Revolving, 2 Tiers, 15 Holders, Strawberry Emery, Pincushion, 11 x 8½ In.	550.00
Tub, Pine, Ash, Red, White Interior, Interlocking Bands, Cutout Handles, c.1850, 12 x 18 In.	1053.00
Wall Box, Pine, Red Ocher, Carved, Hole For Peg, Pocket, Mt. Lebanon, N.Y., c.1835, 24 x 7 In.	234.00

SHAVING MUGS were popular from 1860 to 1900. Many types were made, including occupational mugs featuring pictures of men's jobs. There were scuttle mugs, silver-plated mugs, glass-lined mugs, and others.

Aug. Fehr, Gold, Blue, White Shield, Label Under Glass, 1885-1925, 3⅞ In.	190.00
Fraternal, Elk, C. Hargo, Porcelain, Enamel, Gold Trim, 3¾ In.	160.00
Fraternal, Indian In Headdress, R.R. Ryan, Allentown, Pa., 1885-1925, 3⅝ In.	253.00
Fraternal, Junior Order Of United American Mechanics, A.G. Lyngen, 1885-1925, 3⅝ In.	232.00
Fraternal, Knights Of Pythias, Order Of Forester Of America, 1885-1925, 3⅞ In.	258.00
Fraternal, Redmen Lodge, Improved Order Of Red Men, 1885-1925, 3⅝ In.	420.00
Fraternal, Shriner, Ceramic, Kansas City, Regnier & Shoup Co., 1930s, 3½ In.	38.00
Hunting Scene, Hunter, Dog, 1885-1925, 3⅞ In.	123.00
Occupational, Baker, Putting Bread In Oven, W.H.S., 1885-1925, 3⅝ In.	302.00
Occupational, Baseball, 12 Players, Grandstand, R.R. Tinney	7475.00
Occupational, Baseball, Catcher & Batter, 1885-1925, 4 In.	2016.00

Occupational, Blacksmith, Anvil, Tongs, Hammer, Henry Stimes, 3¼ In.	....	187.00
Occupational, Blacksmith, Hitting Anvil Brick, Wm. Weller, 3⅞ In.	....	176.00
Occupational, Blacksmith, Shoeing Horse, Chas. Wickert, Stamped, T & V France, 3⅞ In.	..	198.00
Occupational, Blacksmith, Shoeing Horse, Wm. Breckenridge, 1885-1925, 3¾ In.	....	385.00
Occupational, Blacksmiths, Anvil, Flowers, T & V Limoges, 1885-1925, 4 In.	....	504.00
Occupational, Boilermaker, Hammering On Side Of Boiler, Edward Rice, 3⅝ In.	....	303.00
Occupational, Boot, Sprig Of Flowers, L. Friesner, 1885-1925, 3½ In.	....	467.00
Occupational, Boxcar, G.W. Albert, 1885-1925, 3⅜ In.	....	440.00
Occupational, Buggy, J.F. Lash, 1885-1925, 3¾ In.	....	330.00
Occupational, Butcher, Chopping Block, D & Co., 1885-1925, 3½ In.	....	672.00
Occupational, Butcher, Steer's Headtools, J.F. Fuchs, 1885-1925, 3½ In.	....	90.00
Occupational, Caboose, Man Holding Flag, B. & R.R.T., Smith Barber Supplies, 3½ In.	....	132.00
Occupational, Caboose, Red, T & V Limoges, France, 1885-1925, 3⅝ In.	....	420.00
Occupational, Camera, Black Wrap, G.W. Priest, T & V France, 1885-1925, 3⅝ In.	....	302.00
Occupational, Carpentry Tools, Sherman B. Gilbert, 1885-1925, 3½ In.	....	67.00
Occupational, Chickens, Building, T. Miranda & D. Fontano, T & V Limoges, France, 3⅝ In.		990.00
Occupational, Coal Wagon, Driver, Horse, H.H. Cope, 3½ In.	....	560.00
Occupational, Dentures, Black Ground, D. & Co., France, 1885-1925, 3⅝ In.	....	616.00
Occupational, Electrical Lineman, Marked, Heckle Bros., Kansas City, Mo.	.....*illus*	2645.00
Occupational, Farmer, Plowing Field, 2-Horse Team, Buildings, L.W. Dodds, 3⅞ In.	....	143.00
Occupational, Florist, Luther A. Schuller, Allover Flowers & Leaves, Footed, 3¾ In.	....*illus*	336.00
Occupational, Flywheel Generator, J.C. Ross, 4 In.	....	132.00
Occupational, Football Players, Tackling, B.H.S. 04, Chas. A Donachy	....	5290.00
Occupational, Furniture, Victorian, L.P. Goos, 1885-1925, 4 In.	....	1870.00
Occupational, Grocery Store Scene, H. Keller, 1885-1925, 4 In.	....	440.00
Occupational, Harley Davidson Motorcycle, N. Beltz, Germany, 3½ In.	....	240.00
Occupational, Hearse, Horse Drawn, 1885-1925, 3⅝ In.	....	1064.00
Occupational, Horse Breeder, Ben Nickerson, Horse, Standing, 3½ In.	.............*illus*	168.00
Occupational, Locomotive & Tender, Engineer, M. Dockins, 3⅞ In.	....	165.00
Occupational, Locomotive & Tender, J.C. Stephens, 1885-1925, 3½ In.	....	146.00
Occupational, Lumberjack, Tree Stump, Adolph Kritzman, 1916, 3⅝ In.	....	121.00
Occupational, Man, Driving Horse Drawn Buggy, H.S. Provost, 1885-1925, 4 In.	....	198.00
Occupational, Man, Driving Horse Drawn Coal Wagon, J. Tansosch, 1885-1925, 3⅝ In.	....	385.00
Occupational, Man, Horse Drawn Stake Wagon, J.J. Cassioy, T & V Limoges, 1900, 3⅝ In.	...	605.00
Occupational, Man, Horse Drawn Stake Wagon, O.A. Peacock, Geo. F. Wagner & Co., 1900, 4 In.		385.00
Occupational, Man, Operating Printing Press, Chas. Drooman, 1885-1925, 3½ In.	....	198.00
Occupational, Man, Waving Flag At Train, B.M. Curry, Marked, KPM	....	880.00
Occupational, Man, Working At Lathe, P. Germany, 1885-1925, 3¾ In.	....	364.00
Occupational, Man Installing Iron Gate & Fence, O.R. Schellenberger, Limoges	....	4680.00
Occupational, Mason's Tools, E.Z. Jackson, Limoges W.G. & Co., 1885-1925, 4 In.	....	143.00
Occupational, Milk Wagon, Horse Drawn, 1885-1925, 3¾ In.	.... 532.00 to 672.00
Occupational, Pig & Steer Head, L.W. Butlerheckel Bros., K-C, Mo., 1825-1925, 4 In.	....	121.00
Occupational, Printers Block, Claude Wallis, Leonard Vienna Austria, 1885-1925, 4⅛ In.	...	88.00
Occupational, Printing Press, O.S. Dunham, 1885-1925, 3⅝ In.	....	522.00
Occupational, Sewing Machine, Singer, G.A. Ziemendorf, 1885-1925, 4 In.	....	715.00
Occupational, Stake Wagon, Horse Drawn, T & V Limoges, 1885-1925, 3⅝ In.	....	168.00
Occupational, Steam Dynamo, R.H. Heckman, 1885-1925, 3⅞ In.	....	330.00
Occupational, Tailor Shop Scene, 6 People, C.F. Theidel, T & V France, 1885-1925, 3½ In.	..	412.00
Occupational, Ticket Punch, Sprig Of Flowers, Skipps Sirs, 1885-1925, 3½ In.	....	415.00
Pennsylvania State Seal, 1885-1925, 3¾ In.	....	308.00
Rebus, Sheep & The Word Bros., Flowers, M.R. France, 1885-1925, 3⅝ In.	....	187.00

Shaving Mug, Occupational, Electrical Lineman, Marked, Heckle Bros., Kansas City, Mo. $2645.00

Shaving Mug, Occupational, Florist, Luther A. Schuller, Allover Flowers & Leaves, Footed, 3¾ In. $336.00

Shaving Mug, Occupational, Horse Breeder, Ben Nickerson, Horse, Standing, 3½ In. $168.00

SHAWNEE POTTERY was started in Zanesville, Ohio, in 1937. The company made vases, novelty ware, flowerpots, planters, lamps, and cookie jars. Three dinnerware lines were made: Corn, Lobster Ware, and Valencia (a solid color line). White Corn pattern utility pieces were made in 1945. Corn King was made from 1946 to 1954; Corn Queen, with darker green leaves and lighter colored corn, from 1954 to 1961. Shawnee produced pottery for George Rumrill during the late 1930s. The company closed in 1961.

Shawnee USA

Bowl, Corn King, 8⅞ In.	....	44.00
Bowl, Soup, Corn King, 6 In.	....	75.00
Butter, Cover, Corn King	....	90.00
Candlestick, White Matte, Scalloped Rim, 3¼ In., Pair	....	18.00
Casserole, Cover, Corn King, 10¾ In.	....	50.00
Chop Plate, Valencia, Green, 13 In.	....	38.00
Cookie Jar, Muggsy, Blue Neckerchief, 11 In.	....	450.00

Shawnee, Cookie Jar,
Puss 'N Boots, 10¼ In.
$295.00

Shawnee, Creamer, Cat,
Yellow, Green Herringbone Wrap,
No. 85, 4¾ In.
$40.00

Sheet Music Value

Age, popularity, rarity, condition, fame of artist, and category determine the price of sheet music. Music picturing special categories, like automobiles or political events, bring more money than earlier examples.

To be valuable, sheet music must have all pages in good condition. Be sure the page is not trimmed. Sheet music sold before the 1930s was often too wide to store in a piano bench, so musicians cut it to fit.

Cookie Jar, Puss 'N Boots, 10¼ In. ....*illus*	295.00
Creamer, Cat, Yellow, Green Herringbone Wrap, No. 85, 4¾ In. ....*illus*	40.00
Creamer, Puss 'N Boots, Gold Trim, 4¾ In.	300.00
Creamer, Smiley Pig	165.00
Dish, Fruit, Corn King, 6 In.	98.00
Figurine, Chinese Boy	18.00
Figurine, Dog, Pekingese, Foil Label, 2⅜ In.	33.00
Figurine, Dog, Terrier, Curly Hair, 6¼ In.	45.00
Figurine, Donkey, Spots, 6¼ x 4½ In.	69.00
Figurine, Puppy Dog, 3½ x 2½ In.	29.00
Figurine, Tumbling Bear, Flax Blue, 3 In.	95.00
Mixing Bowl, Corn King, 6¼ In.	35.00
Planter, Daisy, Lime Green, 2¾ x 9½ In.	12.50
Planter, Dog, White Matte, 6½ In.	20.00
Planter, Donkey & Cart, White Matte, 5 x 8 In.	20.00
Planter, Green, Scalloped Rim, Marked, USA 2001, 2¾ x 11 In. ...	18.00
Planter, Lamb & Cart	9.00
Planter, Sea Shell, 2¼ x 6 In.	22.00
Planter, Swan, White Matte, 5 x 7½ In.	20.00
Planter, Train Engine, Blue, 6 In.	24.00
Plate, Corn King, 10 In.	59.00
Salt & Pepper, Duck, 3¼ In.	51.00
Salt & Pepper, Dutch Boy & Girl, 5 In.	70.00
Salt & Pepper, Muggsy, 5 In.	100.00
Salt & Pepper, Owls, Gold Trim, 3 In.	65.00
Salt & Pepper, Puss 'N Boots	68.00
Salt & Pepper, Smiley & Winnie Pig, 5 In.	245.00
Teapot, Granny Ann	165.00
Vase, Bud, Fawn, Handles, 8 x 2½ In.	12.00
Vase, Cornucopia, Aqua, Fluted, Footed	36.00
Vase, Diamond, Sunshine Yellow, Handles, 6⅞ In.	35.00
Vase, Peach, Pedestal Base, 8 x 5½ In.	30.00
Wall Pocket, Wheat, 5 In.	35.00
Window Box, Platinum Gray, Textured Finish, Ruffled Edge, Cameo, 4 x 14 In.	23.00

SHEARWATER pottery is a family business started by Mr. and Mrs. G.W. Anderson, Sr., and their three sons. The local Ocean Springs, Mississippi, clays were used to make the wares in the 1930s. The company is still in business.

SHEARWATER

Bowl, Alkaline Blue, Impressed, 1930-40, 2¼ x 9¼ In.	360.00
Bowl, Black & White Scroll Design, Stamped, 3½ x 9 In.	3525.00
Bowl, Cover, Fish, Black, Ivory, Tan, Stamped, Signed, 1982, 5½ x 8 In.	5040.00
Bowl, Dancing Blacks, Yellow Ground, Signed, 1986, 9¼ In.	4560.00
Bowl, Fish, Yellow, Black, White, Stamped, Signed, 1987, 3½ x 8¼ In.	3840.00
Bowl, Mottled Ocher, Taupe, Pink Glazes, Jim Anderson, 1960s, 5 x 8¼ In.	264.00
Figurine, Lion, Walking, Antique Green, Impressed, 5½ x 4 x 12¾ In.	420.00
Figurine, Seagull, Resting, White Enamel Glaze, Impressed, 5½ x 4¼ x 10½ In.	570.00
Lamp, Pelican, Brown Glaze, Cobalt Blue Shade, Impressed, 7½ In.	420.00
Lamp Base, Equestrienne, Brown, White, Impressed, 10 x 10¼ In.	480.00
Lamp Base, Wisteria, Baluster Form, Impressed, 9½ x 3¾ In.	210.00
Pitcher, Alligator Form, Lid, White, Blue, Green, Brown, Signed, c.1935-40, 9 x 15 In.	2880.00
Pitcher, Bird Form, White Ground, Blue Green, Brown, Incised, c.1940, 15 In.	3360.00
Vase, Antique Green, Matte Glaze, Long Neck, Impressed, 11 x 4½ In.	420.00
Vase, Cast, Blue Alkaline Glaze, c.1928, 3½ x 2½ In.	88.00
Vase, Incised Cats, Green Matte Glaze, Bulbous, Impressed Mark, 4½ In.	6800.00
Vase, Yellow, Ivory, Lavender, Impressed, 1983, 3¼ x 2¾ In.	300.00
Wall Pocket, Cicada Form, Gray, Brown, Black, Signed, 1987, 15½ In.	3120.00

SHEET MUSIC from the past centuries is now collected. The favorites are examples with covers featuring artistic or historic pictures. Early sheet music covers were lithographed, but by the 1900s photographic reproductions were used. The early music was larger than more recent sheets, and you must watch out for examples that were trimmed to fit in a twentieth-century piano bench.

Annabelle, L. Brown & R. Henderson, Brooke Johns Photo, Flapper, 1923, 9 x 12 In.	6.00
Bringing Up Father, Jiggs, 1920	112.00
Buttons & Bows, Movie Paleface, Bob Hope & Jane Russell, 1948	55.00

Come To Baby Do, Les Brown & Doris Day On Cover, Copyright 1945	10.00
Comin' In On A Wing & A Prayer, Harold Adamson Lyrics, Jimmy McHugh Music, 1943	4.00
Honolulu Hulu Girl, Sonny Cunha, Picture Of Hawaiian Woman, 1909	24.00
Millionaires March, Two-Step, Baseball Team, C.D. Henninger, 1908	187.00
Miss Columbia March, Two-Step, Woman Wrapped In American Flag, Osborne, 1908	14.00
Mr. & Mrs. Is The Name, From Movie Flirtation Walk, 1934	9.00
My One & Only Highland Fling, By Ira Gershwin & Harry Warren, 1949	25.00
Rum & Coca-Cola, Andrews Sisters, By Morey Amsterdam, 1944, 2 Pages	12.00
Sh-Boom, Life Could Be A Dream, Crew Cuts On Cover, 1954	30.00
Torch, Dorothy Dainty Scott Lyric & Music, War Time Edition	12.00

SHEFFIELD *items are listed in the Silver Plate and Silver-English categories.*

SHELLEY first appeared on English ceramics about 1912. The Foley China Works started in England in 1860. Joseph Ball Shelley joined the company in 1862 and became a partner in 1872. Percy Shelley joined the firm in 1881. The company went through a series of name changes and in 1910 the then Foley China Company became Shelley China. In 1929 it became Shelley Potteries. The company was acquired in 1966 by Allied English Potteries, then merged with the Doulton group in 1971. The name Shelley was put into use again in 1980. A trio is the name for a cup, saucer, and cake plate set.

Ashtray, Blue, Dainty, 3½ In.	25.00
Candleholder, Bird, Grapes, Frederick Rhead, 3½ x 7 In.	188.00
Candleholder, Luster Bird, Grapes, 3¼ In.	188.00
Candleholder, Purple, Dainty, Gilt, 2¼ x 4½ In.	50.00
Candy Dish, Begonia, Oleander, 1945-66	48.00
Candy Dish, Rambler Rose, Dainty, Brass Colored Handle, 7 In.	38.00
Creamer, Rose, Red Daisies, Dainty, 6 Flutes, Pink Handle, Rim, 5 In.	54.00
Cup & Saucer, Black, Gold, Dainty, 1930	175.00
Cup & Saucer, Blue Rock Flower, Dainty, White Ground, 6 Deep Flutes, c.1945	75.00
Cup & Saucer, Campanula, Purple, Green, Violet, White Ground, 1½ x 2 In.	375.00
Cup & Saucer, Gold Gilt Leaf, Yellow Scalloped Rim, Cream Ground, Demitasse	69.00
Cup & Saucer, King Edward VIII Coronation, Oxford	148.00
Cup & Saucer, Oleander, Yellow, Summer Glory, Pink, Purple, Blue, White	230.00
Cup & Saucer, Pansies, Roses, Purple, Pink, White Ground	185.00
Cup & Saucer, Rock Garden, Chintz, Petals, Pink, Yellow, Blue, White, Footed Oleander	260.00
Cup & Saucer, Rock Garden, Oleander, Yellow, Footed, c.1940	260.00
Cup & Saucer, Summer Glory, Oleander, Footed, c.1940s	230.00
Cup & Saucer, Summer Glory, Oleander, Mauve, Pink, Purple, Blue, Footed, c.1940	225.00
Cup & Saucer, Thistle, Dainty, Lavender, Purple, White Ground, 6 Deep Flutes, Scalloped	115.00
Cup & Saucer, Thistle, Dainty, Leaf Transfer, Pink Edges, Fluted, Scalloped, Handle, c.1966	115.00
Cup & Saucer, Thistle, Dainty, White Ground, Blossom, 6 Flutes, Scalloped, c.1940-66	115.00
Dish, Rosebud, 2 x 3¼ In.	20.00
Eggcup, White, Dainty, Gold Trim, Footed, 2 In.	20.00
Gravy Boat, Underplate, Blue, Dainty, White Ground	200.00
Pin Tray, Bridge Scene, Purple, Heather, Round, 4 In.	50.00
Pin Tray, Fruit Basket, Dainty, c.1930, 4 x 4 In.	50.00
Pin Tray, Red Roof Cottage, Dainty, 1930s, 5 x 4 In.	60.00
Plate, Cottage, Village, Ocher Border, Signed, Eric Slater, 8 x 8 In.	132.00
Plate, Primulas, Green Leaf, Pink Ribbon Edge, 6 In.	17.00
Sugar & Creamer, Royalty, Pink Rose	55.00
Teapot, Underplate, Art Deco, Banded *illus*	265.00
Trio, Blue, Dainty, White Ground	190.00
Trio, Blue Iris, Queen Anne, 1927	190.00
Trio, Campanula, White Ground, Lavender, Purple, Flower, Deep Flutes, 8 In.	205.00
Trio, Melody, Richmond, Semi-Scalloped	165.00 to 185.00
Trio, Primrose Chintz, Richmond, Pink Trim	140.00
Trio, Wallflower, Oxford Shape *illus*	125.00
Vase, Carnations, Black Ground, 3¾ x 3½ In.	78.00

SHIRLEY TEMPLE, the famous movie star, was born in 1928. She made her first movie in 1932. Thousands of items picturing Shirley have been and still are being made. Shirley Temple dolls were first made in 1934 by Ideal Toy Company. Millions of Shirley Temple cobalt blue glass dishes were made by Hazel Atlas Glass Company and U.S. Glass Company from 1934 to 1942. They were given away as premiums for Wheaties and Bisquick. A bowl, mug, and pitcher were made as a breakfast set. Some pieces were decorated with the

English Registry Mark

One of the most common marks found on English ceramics is the English registry mark. The mark records the year the ceramic piece was designed. The diamond-shaped mark has a letter or number in each corner and the letters Rd in the center. From 1842 to 1867 there was a letter in the top corner of the diamond. From 1868 to 1883 there was a numeral in the top corner. In 1884 the diamond-shaped mark was replaced by a mark made of letters and numbers in a straight line. It said *Rd. No.* and then a numeral.

Rd Nº 821205.

Many books and online sites have tables of information that explain how to find the exact date indicated by each mark.

Shelley, Teapot, Underplate, Art Deco, Banded
$265.00

Shelley, Trio, Wallflower, Oxford Shape
$125.00

Shirley Temple, Doll, Composition, Sleep Eyes, 5-Piece Body, Dress Tag, 11 In.
$144.00

Shirley Temple, Stringholder, Chalkware, Painted, String Hole At Mouth, Wire Hanger, 6 x 7 In.
$58.00

Silver Deposit, Dresser Bottle, Scrolls, Leaves, Clear Glass, Tapered, Stopper, Monogram, c.1900, 7 In.
$460.00

picture of a very young Shirley, others used a picture of Shirley in her 1936 *Captain January* costume. Although collectors refer to a cobalt creamer, it is actually the 4½-inch-high milk pitcher from the breakfast set. Many of these items are being reproduced today.

Bank, Celluloid, Real Photo Image Of Shirley, 1930s, 2 x 4 In. 84.00
Button, Black, White Photo, Red, My Friend Shirley Temple, 1930s, 1¼ In. 34.00
Doll, Composition, Sleep Eyes, 5-Piece Body, Dress Tag, 11 In. .... *illus* 144.00
Doll, Ideal, Composition, Flirty Eyes, 26 In. 147.00
Doll, Ideal, Composition, Jointed, Vintage Clothes, c.1930, 18 In. 86.00
Doll, Ideal, Composition, Original Pin, Dress, Shoes, 20 In. 147.00
Doll, Ideal, Hazel Sleep Eyes, Blond Mohair Wig, Cowboy Outfit, 1936-37 .... 1960.00
Doll, Ideal, Playpal, Plastic, Rooted Wig, Sleep Eyes, Box, 1960, 17 x 36 x 9 In. 3696.00
Doll, Ideal, Rooted Hair, Sleep Eyes, Purse, Tag, 1950s, 19 In. 185.00
Doll, Ideal, Tagged, Red Dress, Socks, Shoes, 27 In. 764.00
Fan, Advertising, R.C. Cola 35.00
Lobby Card, Baby Take A Bow, Fox, 1934, 11 x 14 In. 184.00
Lobby Card, Captain January, 1936, 11¼ x 8 In. 196.00
Lobby Card, Our Little Girl, Fox, 1935, 11 x 14 In. 748.00
Mirror, Pocket, Dog, Celluloid, Label, Japan, 1930s, 2 In. 76.00
Movie Poster, Captain January, 20th Century Fox, 1936, 27 x 41 In. 1140.00
Movie Poster, Little Miss Broadway, 20th Century Fox, 1938, 81 x 40 In. 6325.00
Movie Poster, Littlest Rebel, Fox, 1935, 27 x 41 In. 2990.00
Ring, Puckered Lips Photograph, Silver Luster, Plastic, Octagonal, Japan, 1930s 73.00
Stringholder, Chalkware, Painted, String Hole At Mouth, Wire Hanger, 6 x 7 In. .... *illus* 58.00
Window Card, Susannah Of The Mounties, 1939, 11¼ x 8 In. 216.00

SHRINER, *see Fraternal category.*

SILVER DEPOSIT glass was first made during the late nineteenth century. Solid sterling silver is applied to the glass by a chemical method so that a cutout design of silver metal appears against a clear or colored glass. It is sometimes called silver overlay.

Bottle, Opaque Blue Glass, Flowers Overlay, Screw Crown Stopper, 2½ In. 88.00
Claret Jug, Duck Form, Crystal & Sterling Silver, Handle, c.1880, 9½ x 6 In. 13500.00
Dresser Bottle, Scrolls, Leaves, Clear Glass, Tapered, Stopper, Monogram, c.1900, 7 In. .... *illus* 460.00
Vase, Amethyst Glass, Blue Luster, Sterling Silver Scrolls, Austria, 4¼ In. .... *illus* 575.00
Vase, Emerald Green Glass, Wild Rose Overlay, Flared, Footed, 1¾ In. .... *illus* 1610.00
Vase, Peacock Branches, Funnel Neck, Urn Shape, 12¾ In. 176.00
Vase, Portrait Of Woman, Red, Porcelain, Gorham, c.1895, 8½ In. 1170.00
Vase, Trumpet, Green Glass, Flower & Vine Overlay, Medallion, Monogram, 14 In. .... *illus* 690.00
Vase, Wind God Faces, Flowers, Red, Spherical Body, Lenox, 5¼ x 5 In. 852.00

SILVER FLATWARE includes many of the current and out-of-production silver and silver-plated flatware patterns made in the past eighty years. Other silver is listed under Silver-American, Silver-English, etc. Most silver flatware sets that are missing a few pieces can be completed through the help of one of the many silver matching services that advertise in many of the national publications.

SILVER FLATWARE PLATED

Always, Tablespoon, Oneida, 1958 .... 9.00 to 10.00
Beethoven, Gravy Ladle, Oneida, 1971, 7¾ In. 15.00
Berkeley, Bread Knife, Wm. A. Rogers, 1929, 9⅞ In. 20.00
Berkeley, Salad Spoon, Wm. A. Rogers, 1929, 8¾ In. 20.00
Caprice, Cold Meat Fork, Oneida Nobility, 8½ In. 24.00
Carloina, Pickle Fork, Holmes & Edwards, 1914, 6¼ In. 18.00
Cordova, Cream Ladle, Rogers Silver, 1898 .... 12.00
Coronation, Serving Spoon, Community, 1936, 8½ In. 35.00
Coronation, Spoon, Community, 1936, 8½ In. 16.00
Daffodil, Baby Spoon, Rogers, 1950, 5¼ In. 12.50
Daisy, Meat Fork, Rogers Bros., 1910, 7¾ In. 20.00
Eternally Yours, Service For 8, Rogers, 56 Piece .... *illus* 82.00
Eudora, Ladle, Towle Silversmiths, 1888, 10½ In. 54.00
Evening Star, Olive Fork, Oneida, 1950, 6⅜ In. 19.95
Fairoaks, Berry Spoon, Wm. Rogers, 1909, 9¾ In. 14.50
First Love, Youth Spoon, 1847 Rogers, 1937 .... 29.00
Flirtation, Spoon, Slotted, 1881 Rogers, 1959, 8¼ In. 12.00
Floral, Dinner Fork, Wallace, 1902 .... 15.00

Forever, Tomato Server, Community, 1939, 7⅞ In.	21.00 to 22.00
Fortune, Pie Server, Oneida, 1939, 8½ In.	15.50
Garland, Meat Fork, Oxford, Oneida, 1910, 8¼ In.	24.50
Garland, Pickle Fork, Oxford, Oneida, 1910	20.00
Grape, Carving Set, Rogers Bros., 3 Piece	75.00
Grosvenor, Serving Spoon, Community, 1921, 8¼ In.	11.50
Harmony, Baby Spoon, Oneida, 1958, 5¹³⁄₁₆ In.	12.50
Her Majesty, Butter Knife, Rogers, 1931	12.00
Heritage, Cheese Scoop, 1847 Rogers Bros., 1953, 6 In.	20.00
Italian, Youth Knife, Reed & Barton, 1885	30.00
Jennifer, Dessert Server, Oneida, 1959, 8⅝ In.	16.50
King James, Sugar Shell, Rogers, 1881, 1985	15.00
La Vigne, Citrus Spoon, Rogers, 1908	25.00
Longfellow, Olive Fork, Rogers Bros., 1919, 6 In.	17.50
Louis XVI, Gravy Ladle, Oneida, Community, 1911, 6½ In.	30.00
Mayfair, Serving Fork, Wm. Rogers, 1923, 8¼ In.	15.00
Milady, Cake Fork, Oneida, Community, 1940, 9⅜ In.	24.00
Milady, Cucumber Server, Oneida, Community, 1940, 4½ In.	18.00
Modern Baroque, Baby Spoon, Community, 1969	18.00
Morning Star, Butter, Master, Oneida, Community, 1948	12.00
Narcissus, Spoon, Oxford Silver Plate, 1908, 5¾ In.	18.00
Narcissus, Teaspoon, National, 1935	4.00
Norwood, Sugar Shell, Towle, 1884, 6⅛ In.	14.50
Old Colony, Dessert Spoon, 1847 Rogers, 1911	15.00
Old Colony, Gravy Ladle, 1847 Rogers, 1911	15.00
Old Colony, Soup Ladle, Rogers Brothers, 1911	25.00
Orleans, Meat Fork, International, 1964, 8¾ In.	7.50
Patrician, Cold Meat Fork, Oneida, Community, 1914	14.00
Precious Mirror, Serving Spoon, Wm. Rogers, 1954, 8½ In.	14.00
Princess Royal, Pie Server, National, 1930	15.00
Puritan, Fruit Knife, 1847 Rogers Bros., 1912, 6½ In.	15.50
Queen Bertha, Dessert Spoon, Glastonbury, Oneida, 1910, 6 Piece	30.00
Queen Bess, Pie Server, Oneida, 1946, 9½ In.	30.00 to 55.00
Rialto, Olive Fork, Aurora, 1894	35.00
San Diego, Sauce Ladle, Rogers Bros., 1889, 6¼ In.	17.50
Silver Flowers, Pie Server, Oneida, 1960, 9⅜ In.	14.00
Silver Shell, Dinner Knife, Community, 1978, 9½ In.	9.00
Silver Tulip, Cake Server, International, 1956, 8³⁄₁₆ In.	15.50
Silver Tulip, Cold Meat Fork, International, 1956, 7¾ In.	12.00
Silver Tulip, Luncheon Fork, International, 1956	3.50
Silver Tulip, Pie Server, International, 1956, 8⅝ In.	12.00
South Seas, Youth Fork, Community, 1955, 4⅞ In.	15.00
Sovereign, Oyster Cocktail Fork, 5⅝ In., Set Of 4	25.00
Starlight, Meat Fork, International, 1939, 8¾ In.	15.50
Sweep, Pie Server, Rogers Bros., 1958, 9⅞ In.	15.00
Tiger Lily, Soup Spoon, Reed & Barton, 7⅛ In.	16.00
Tipped, Spoon, J & G Silver Co., 1900	15.00
Tuxedo, Olive Spoon, 1847 Rogers Bros., 1890, 5¾ In.	15.00
Windsong, Salad Server, Nobility, 1955	38.00
Windsong, Tomato Server, Nobility, 1955, 7¾ In.	22.00
Woodsong, Serving Fork & Spoon, Holmes & Edwards, 1958	30.00

SILVER FLATWARE STERLING

Acanthus, Cheese Slice, Georg Jensen, 8 In.	205.00
Acorn, Server, Johan Rohde, For Georg Jensen, Post 1945, 9 In., 2 Piece	195.00
Arlington, Ice Cream Spoon, Repousse Handle, Vermeil Bowl, Towle, 1884, 5⅜ In., 12 Piece	378.00
Burgundy, Serving Fork, Reed & Barton, 8¼ In., 2 Piece	176.00
Cactus, Pastry Server, Georg Jensen, 9¼ In.	400.00
Cactus, Server, Gundorph Albertus, For Georg Jensen, Post 1945, 9 In., Pair	226.00
Chrysanthemum, Serving Spoon, Durgin, 9½ In.	500.00
Engaged Medallion, Macaroni Spoon, Krider, c.1890, 9¼ x 2¼ In.	1434.00
Fairfax, Teaspoon Set, Durgin Division, Gorham, c.1910, 12 Piece	234.00
Frontenac, Carving Set, Art Nouveau Flowers, International, 3 Piece	176.00
Hepplewhite, Tea Strainer, Over Cup Style, Reed & Barton, 1920s, 8 In.	250.00
Lily, Fork & Spoon Set, Serving, Whiting Division, Gorham, 9 In., 2 Piece	40.00
Louis XV, Spoon Set, Engraved Initials, Whiting Mfg. Co., c.1890, 6 Piece	35.00

Silver Deposit, Vase, Amethyst Glass, Blue Luster, Sterling Silver Scrolls, Austria, 4¼ In.
$575.00

Silver Deposit, Vase, Emerald Green Glass, Wild Rose Overlay, Flared, Footed, 1¾ In.
$1610.00

Silver Deposit, Vase, Trumpet, Green Glass, Flower & Vine Overlay, Medallion, Monogram, 14 In.
$690.00

S

Silver Flatware Plated,
Eternally Yours, Service For 8,
Rogers, 56 Piece
$82.00

Silver Flatware Sterling, Medallion,
Ladle, Gilt Wash, Gorham, 1864, 14 In.
$436.00

Silver Flatware Sterling,
Medallion, Macaroni Server,
J.B. & S.M. Knowles, 9 In.
$1434.00

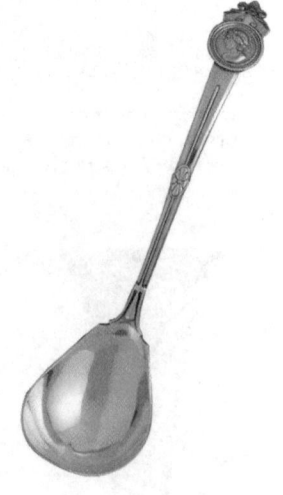

Love Disarmed, Serving Spoon & Fork, Reed & Barton, 1899, 10½ In.		600.00
Maryland, Punch Ladle, Gorham, c.1896, 12½ In.		108.00
Medallion, Ladle, Gilt Wash, Gorham, 1864, 14 In.	*illus*	436.00
Medallion, Macaroni Server, J.B. & S.M. Knowles, 9 In.	*illus*	1434.00
Old French, Asparagus Tongs, Pierced Blades, Gorham, 1905, 9½ In.	*illus*	717.00
Prelude, Carving Set, International Silver, 1960s, 13-In Fork, 11-In. Knife		88.00
Queen Bess, Pie Server, Oneida, 1946, 9½ In.		55.00
Raphael, Cold Meat Fork, Art Nouveau Woman & Flower, Alvin, c.1902, 7¾ In.	*illus*	685.00
Raphael, Cucumber Server, Alvin, c.1902, 6 In.		144.00
Rose, Asparagus Fork, Monogram R, Wallace, Patent 1898, 9½ In.		350.00
Rose, Youth Knife & Fork, J.B. & S.M. Knowles, c.1881, 7 In.		108.00
Salad Server, Esther Variant, Frank M. Whiting Co., c.1900, 9 In., Pair		5400.00
Sunset, Salad Servers, Spoon, Fork, Gourd Shape, Allan Adler, 12¾ In.		591.00
Swedish Modern, Knives, Forks, Spoons, Allan Adler, 76 Piece		6600.00
Violet, Ladle, Wallace, c.1910, 12½ In.		177.00

SILVER PLATE is not solid silver. It is a ware made of a metal, such as nickel or copper, that is covered with a thin coating of silver. The letters *EPNS* are often found on American and English silver-plated wares. Sheffield is a term with two meanings. Sometimes it refers to sterling silver made in the town of Sheffield, England. Sometimes it refers to an old formal plated silver.

Basket, Handle, Thomas Bradbury & Son, Late 19th Century, 11¼ In.		109.00
Bell, Hotel, Filigree, Windup, 4 x 4 In.		145.00
Biscuit Box, Floral Finial, Oval Hinged Cover, Decorated, Handles, c.1900, 8 x 9 In.		259.00
Biscuit Box, Georgian Style, Oval, Lion Head Ring Handles, 8 x 7½ In.		245.00
Biscuit Box, Renaissance Revival, Round, Hinged Lid, c.1870, 6 x 8 In.		240.00
Biscuit Warmer, Arched, Lobed, Folds Out, 3 Sections, Marked G & L, England, 9½ In.	*illus*	470.00
Bottle Caisson, Regency Style, Detailed Spokes, Wheels, Bottle Rest, Chain		1998.00
Bowl, Center, Flower Arranger, Wallace, 8 x 9 In.		117.00
Bowl, Center, Round, Floral Border, Putti Playing Horns, Monogram, 7 x 9 In., Pair		460.00
Bowl, Cover, WMF, Cut Green Glass, c.1900, 10 In.		307.00
Bowl, Hemispherical, Repousse Waves, 4 Ball Feet, Dragon Handles, Derby, 5 x 10 In.		146.00
Bowl, Monteith, Liner, England, 4 x 5 In.		35.00
Bowl, Shell Shape, Raised Relief, c.1940, 3 x 14 x 16 In.		29.00
Bucket, Stand, Sheffield, c.1900, 10 & 21 In.		176.00
Butter, Triple Plate, Cover, Rogers, Late 19th Century, 6½ x 8 In.		47.00
Candelabra are listed in the Candelabrum category.		
Candlesnuffer, Scissor, Seated Lion, 7⅛ In.		39.00
Candlesticks are listed in their own category.		
Carving Set, Horn Handle, 3-Piece, Silver Tips, England, c.1920		75.00
Carving Set, Knife & Fork, Carbon Steel Blade, c.1930		50.00
Carving Set, Knife & Fork, Celluloid Handles, Original Box, c.1900		95.00
Centerpiece, Figural, Cherubs, Playing Instruments, 13½ In.	*illus*	443.00
Centerpiece, Vultures, Perched On Balls, Connecting Chains, Dragons, c.1870, 19 In.		518.00
Chafing Dish, Dome Cover, Scrolled Feet, Oval, Removable Liner, Plate, 17¼ In.		443.00
Cocktail Shaker, Penguin Shape, Handle, Emil A. Schuelke, c.1936, 12¼ In.		960.00
Cocktail Shaker, Tray, 6 Goblets, Keystone Silver Co., 12½ x 16½ In.		70.00
Cocktail Tray, Countess, On Copper, International, Hand Chased Relief, 14 In.		176.00
Coffee Set, Hammered, Tapered, Shaped Handle, WMF, 4 Piece	*illus*	940.00
Coffee Urn, Meriden Britannia Co., Victorian, c.1870, 19½ In.		152.00
Coffee Urn, Sheffield, England, J. Watson & Son, c.1830, 15½ x 13 In.		575.00
Coffeepot, Pear Shape, Gooseneck Spout, C-Scroll Handle, Domed Foot, George III, 11 In.		540.00
Compote, Fruit, Nickel Silver, Electroplate, Meriden Silver Co., c.1870, 7 x 9½ In.		23.00
Compote, Glass Bowl, Blue Rim, Ruffled Edge, Handles, Openwork Base, 10¾ In.		351.00
Cover, Meat, Graduated Sizes, Victorian, Elkington & Co., Late 1800s, Pair		619.00
Cruet Stand, Sheffield, England, 19th Century, 9 x 5 x 9½ In.		88.00
Cup, 2 Handles, Filigree Pedestal, Van Bergh S.P. Co., c.1900, 12½ In.		125.00
Decanter Set, Colored Glass, 3 Decanters, Silver Plate Mounts, 1800s, 13 x 9 In.		717.00
Dessert Knife & Fork Set, Mother-Of-Pearl Handles, John Round & Son, 24 Piece		326.00
Dish, Cover, Ivory Knob, Harrods, England, c.1900, 8 In.		41.00
Dish, Entree, Rectangular, Oak Branch Handle, Sheffield, William IV, 14 In., Pair		1680.00
Dispenser, Soda Fountain, Pat. No. 1128, Philadelphia Soda Fountain, 1880s, 19 x 26 In.		2230.00
Egg Coddler, William Hutton & Sons, England, c.1900, 8½ x 4¼ In.	205.00 to 527.00	
Entree Cover, Elkington, From R.M.S. Queen Mary, 1930s, 2½ x 8½ In., Pair		147.00
Entree Warming Dish, Sheffield, 9 x 14½ In.		146.00

Epergne, 4-Arm Cut Crystal Bowl, Scalloped Rim, Decorated Stand, 8½ x 19½ In.	748.00
Epergne, Victorian, Cut Glass, Paw Footed Central Stem, 3 Small Bowls, 19 In.	1880.00
Ewer, Vase Shape, Greek Key Band, Monogram, George IV, c.1820, 12½ x 7 In.	646.00
Fish Serving Set, Ivory Handles, Engraved, England, c.1900, 11¾ In.	84.00
Flask, Fish Shape, Stopper In Mouth, Towle, 6 In.	288.00
Flask, Twist Cap, Engraved B & B, Art Nouveau Flowers, Oval Body, 5 x 2¾ In.	115.00
Fork Set, Old Sheffield, Rounded Handles, Beaded Borders, 3 Tines, 7 In., 12 Piece	575.00
Fruit Set, 6 Fruit Spoons, 6 Fruit Forks, Serving Spoon, 1940	75.00
Fruit Set, Engraved Blades & Tines, Mother-Of-Pearl Handles, Fitted Case, 24 Piece	230.00
Goblet Set, Wine, Electroplate, 4½ In., 12 Piece	105.00
Hot Water Urn, Baluster Shape, Ebony Finial, Reed & Barton, c.1900, 15¾ In.	104.00
Ice Bucket, Sky Scraper, Handles, c.1928, 7⅝ In.	6600.00
Ice Bucket, Stand, R.M.S. Queen Mary, Elkington For Cunard White Star Line, 18 In. *illus*	764.00
Inkwell, Glass, Openwork Plated Frame, Lid, Tapazio Casquinha, Portugal, 1½ x 3 In.	201.00
Kettle, Hot Water, Hoop Finial, Dome Lid, Urn Shape, Ivory Cap Spigot, 19 x 13 In.	748.00
Kettle, Hot Water, On Stand, Reed & Barton, 19th Century, 16 In.	176.00 to 293.00
Kettle, Stand, Sheffield, England, Early 19th Century, 13¼ In.	234.00
Kettle, Stand, Spherical, Flat Surface, Beaded Borders, Flower Finial, 14¾ In.	235.00
Knife Set, Mother-Of-Pearl, Plain Handles, Classical Ferrule Decoration, 10 In., 12 Piece	176.00
Lazy Susan, Sheffield, Revolving, Fitted With Serving Pieces, 18 x 26 In.	700.00
Letter Opener, St. Paul, Depicts State Capitol, Indian In Headdress, 6½ In.	125.00
Mirror, Art Nouveau, Shell Shape, Pierced, c.1900, 13¾ x 9½ In.	205.00
Mug, Canterbury Tales, Sheffield, England, 7 x 6¼ In.	47.00
Napkin Rings are listed in their own category.	
Pin Tray, Nude Woman, 8¼ x 4 In.	90.00
Pitcher, Floral Scrolls, Bird Finial, R. Martin, Ebenezer Hall & Co., Sheffield, 12 x 7 In. *illus*	288.00
Plate Set, Service, Gorham, Gadroon Serpentine Rim, c.1902, 10 In., 8 Piece	1534.00
Plateau, 3 Sections, Round Rectangle, Gadroon Border, Mid 1800s, 16 x 50 In.	1495.00
Plateau, Edwardian, Round, Vintage Motif, Grapes, Vines, Scroll Feet, 3¾ x 15½ In.	323.00
Plateau, Mirror, Beaded Rim, Molded Body, Scrolling Feet, Round Mirror, 3 x 13 In.	460.00
Platter, Sheffield, Raised Relief, 2 x 10 x 13 In.	234.00
Punch Bowl, Tray, Cups, Ladle, England, 15 Piece	1053.00
Samovar, Undertray, Waste Bowl, Aesthetic Movement Patterning, Poland, 28 In.	6125.00
Sauceboat, Engraved Vines, Gadroon Edge, Leaves, Mappin & Webb, Prince's Plate, 5 x 9 In. *illus*	115.00
Savory Dish, Rectangular, Dome Lid, Sheffield Plate, c.1800, 3½ x 6½ x 9 In.	205.00
Server, Revolving, Reeded, Paw Feet, Handles, William Hutton & Sons, 8 x 13 In.	58.00
Shaker, Cocktail, Early 20th Century, 7 In.	23.00
Shield, Lion, Medallions, Battle, Maidens, Relief, Marked, Kunstanstalt, 29½ x 19½ In.	1265.00
Spoon, Repousse Bowl, Rose, Shaped Finial, Pairpoint, 6¼ In.	26.00
Spoon, Souvenir, see Souvenir category.	
Spoon Holder, Bulldog, Holder On Back, 6 In.	207.00
Stein, Sculpted Body, Cherub Finial Holding Cup, Inscribed, 1901, 1 Liter, 14 In.	322.00
Sugar & Creamer, Old Sheffield, England, c.1840, 8 In.	18.00
Sugar Spoon, Fluted Bowl, Pairpoint, 6 In.	8.00
Tazza, Fold Over Rim, Chevron Pattern, Acme Silver Co., Late 1800s, 3 x 9¾ In.	155.00
Tea & Coffee Set, Classistic Pattern, Barbour, 10½-In. Coffeepot, 5 Piece *illus*	235.00
Tea & Coffee Set, Danish Pattern, Meriden International, c.1940, 5 Piece	176.00
Tea Caddy, Sheffield, Hinged Lid, Urn Finial, Fluted Sided, Ring Handles, 6 x 7 In.	200.00
Tea Set, Melon Shape, Scroll Handles, Stepped Base, J. Dixon & Sons, 6 Piece	1265.00
Tea Set, Teapot, Sugar, Cover, Creamer, Tray, Bakelite, Gene Theobald, c.1928	5700.00
Teakettle, Burner Stand, Squat, Round, Plum Finial, William IV, c.1835, 15¾ In.	413.00
Teapot, Rectangular, Mushroom Finial, Wooden Handle, Pedestal, Old Sheffield, 8 x 11 In.	403.00
Teapot, Ribbed Bottom Half, Wood Handle & Finial, Sheffield, 5½ x 10¾ In. *illus*	115.00
Teapot, Warming Stand, Duke Of Wellington Horse Show Trophy, TW & Co., 11 In.	35.00
Tray, Footed, Hand Chased, Birmingham Silver Co., 17 x 28 In.	117.00
Tray, Footed, Oval, Reticulated Rim, Grapevine Border, Handles, 27½ x 17½ In.	293.00
Tray, Gallery, England, 10 x 15 In.	59.00
Tray, Octagonal, Gallery, Cast Handles, 8-Footed, Engraved, 27 x 18 In.	5750.00
Tray, Old Sheffield, Rounded Rectangle, Gadroon Border, Handles, 30 x 19 In.	748.00
Tray, Oval, Grapevines, Bacchus Masks, Handles, W. Wheatcroft Harrison, c.1885, 21 x 27 In.	470.00
Tray, Over Copper, Round, Grape Design, 16 In.	117.00
Tray, Reticulated Gallery, 2 Handles, Oval, Flat Surface, Gadroon Borders, 22 x 15 In.	240.00
Tray, Rope Twist Border, Reed & Rope Handles, Oval, Elkington & Co., 1877, 33 x 23 In.	1116.00
Tray, Serving, 2 Handles, Engraved, Victorian, 19th Century, 28½ In.	435.00
Tray, Serving, Chippendale, Wallace, 14 x 18 In.	35.00
Tray, Stacking, Lapis Lazuli, Triangular, Gucci, c.1965, 10 x 8¼ In.	6000.00

Silver Flatware Sterling, Old French, Asparagus Tongs, Pierced Blades, Gorham, 1905, 9½ In.
$717.00

Silver Flatware Sterling, Raphael, Cold Meat Fork, Art Nouveau Woman & Flower, Alvin, c.1902, 7¾ In.
$685.00

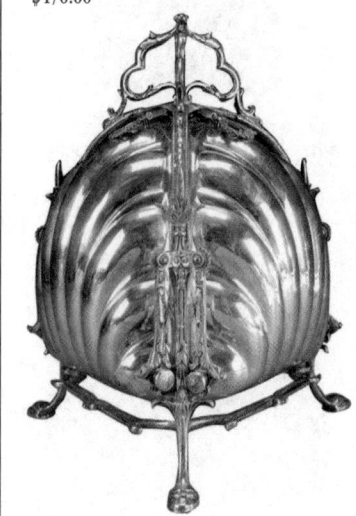

Silver Plate, Biscuit Warmer, Arched, Lobed, Folds Out, 3 Sections, Marked G & L, England, 9½ In.
$470.00

S

Quick Tips for Identifying Old Sheffield

Scratch your fingernail underneath the border of the silver dish. If it is old Sheffield silver, a thin sheet of silver was rolled over copper and your fingernail will catch the edge of this sheet of silver.

If the silver layer has worn off and copper is showing through, it is called "bleeding."

Hold the dish and huff at the engraving so your breath clouds the silver. Old Sheffield has an inset piece of solid silver for the engraving. The block of silver should be faintly outlined by your breath.

Silver Plate, Centerpiece, Figural, Cherubs, Playing Instruments, 13½ In. $443.00

Silver Plate, Coffee Set, Hammered, Tapered, Shaped Handle, WMF, 4 Piece $940.00

Tureen, Oval Bowl, Gadroon Rim, Scrolled Handles, Sheffield, 13¼ x 16¼ In.	165.00
Tureen, Revolving Dome Lid, Embossed, Paw Foot Supports, 9½ x 14 In.	810.00
Tureen, Round, Gadroon Shell & Scroll Border & Handles, Paw Feet, Dome Lid, 12 In.	780.00
Tureen, Soup, Cover, Elkington & Co., Oval, Footed, Reed Handles, 1885, 11 x 15 In.	998.00
Urn, Ice Water, 2 Horned Bull Handles With Rings, Garrett & Sons, Phila., 22 In. _illus_	489.00
Urn, Repousse, Continental Style, c.1900, 8 x 10 In.	146.00
Vase, Wirework, Trumpet, Tapered Frame, Stepped Round Base, 18½ In., Pair	1116.00
Warming Dish, Cover, Continental, Round, 2 Handles, Shell Border, 16 x 24 In., Pair	3819.00
Wine Bottle Holder, Jugenstil, WMH, 2 Handles, Reticulated Frame, c.1900, 8 x 4 In.	353.00
Wine Coaster, Magnum, Plain Body, Floral & Scrolled Flared Rim, 5 x 9 In., Pair	470.00
Wine Coaster, Sheffield, Serpentine Edges, Turned Treen Base, George III, c.1810, Pair	354.00
Wine Cooler, Campana Shape, Removable Liner, England, 20th Century, 10 x 9 In.	1763.00
Wine Cooler, Handles, Sheffield, Early 19th Century, 12 In.	304.00
Wine Funnel, Round Bowl, Clip, Gadroon Edge, Sheffield, 5 x 3¼ In.	470.00

SILVER, SHEFFIELD, see Silver Plate; Silver-English categories.

SILVER-AMERICAN. American silver is listed here. Coin and sterling silver are included. Most of the sterling silver listed in this book is subdivided by country. There are also other pieces of silver and silver plate listed under special categories, such as Candelabrum, Napkin Ring, Silver Flatware, Silver Plate, Silver-Sterling, and Tiffany Silver. For information about makers and marks, see Kovels' American Silver Marks: 1650 to the Present.

SILVER-AMERICAN

Basket, Oval, Hinged Handle, Acanthus Border, Theodore Evans, c.1850, 10 x 11 In.	1495.00
Basket, Oval, Reticulated, Hinged Handle, Lebkuecher & Co., c.1900, 9 x 10 In.	418.00
Basket, Reticulate Open Scroll, Plate Liner, 20th Century, Gorham, 14½ In.	1763.00
Basket, Sugar, Cobalt Blue Liner, Dominick & Haff, 3 x 4¾ In.	303.00
Beaker, Round, Tapering Sides, Gold Rim, Coin, Andrews, Norfolk, 3½ x 3 In.	3450.00
Beaker Set, Barrel Shape, Engraved, 3⅜ In., 4 Piece	7800.00
Bonbon Scoop, Embossed Leaves & Berries, Round Bowl, Handle, Gorham, 10¾ In. _illus_	657.00
Bowl, Celtic Knot Band, Arthur Stone, Footed, 5½ In.	1058.00
Bowl, Cloverleaf, Reed & Barton, 7 In.	70.00 to 82.00
Bowl, Copper, Brass, Cherries, Leaves, Butterflies, Hammered, 3-Footed, 8 In.	7800.00
Bowl, Domed, Scroll Border, Chased, Pierced Strawberries, Leaves, Lebolt, 17 In.	3600.00
Bowl, Engraved Wriggle Border, Circular, c.1815, 7 In.	1920.00
Bowl, Floral Repousse, Commemoration, Whiting Mfg., 3¼ x 8 In.	478.00
Bowl, Francis I Pattern, Reed & Barton, 1950, 2½ x 11 In. _illus_	518.00
Bowl, Francis I Pattern, Scalloped Panels, Reed & Barton, 1907, 2½ x 12 In.	585.00
Bowl, Giraffe, Hemispherical, Chased Ribs, Flared Rim, Carnelian Balls, Gorham, 4 In.	4800.00
Bowl, Gorham, c.1947, 10 x 13 In.	293.00
Bowl, Grape & Vine, Frosted Bowl, Benjamin Smith, c.1846, 18 In.	8200.00
Bowl, Hammered, Copper, Pedestal, Gebelein, c.1910, 8¼ In.	720.00
Bowl, Hammered, Grapevine Border, Tab Feet, Barbour, c.1910, 9¾ In.	720.00
Bowl, Hammered, Round, Karl Leinonen, Boston, 7⅜ In.	294.00
Bowl, Hemispherical, Flared Rim, Pedestal Foot, 12½ In.	1920.00
Bowl, International, c.1920, 2¼ x 10¼ In.	176.00
Bowl, J. Wagner & Son, c.1965, 1¼ x 7 In.	47.00
Bowl, Joel Hewes, Titusville, Penn., c.1930, 8 In.	246.00
Bowl, Lobed, Oval, Leafy Openwork Pedestal, Stepped Base, Randahl, 6 In.	235.00
Bowl, Normandie Pattern, Wallace, 7½ In.	117.00
Bowl, Oval, 4 Ball Feet, Die Roll Wrigglework Border, c.1819, 7 In.	2280.00
Bowl, Oval, Double Handled, Applied Gooseberries, Cockatiels, Gorham, 5 x 10 In.	872.00
Bowl, Oval, Flared Rim, Scrolls, Flower Swags, Roger Williams, 8⅛ In.	1116.00
Bowl, Oval, Floral Repousse, 3 Letter Monogram, Gorham, 1899, 10 In.	405.00
Bowl, Oval, Turned Rim, Embossed, Applied Border, Paw Feet, c.1895, 18 In.	8400.00
Bowl, Pierced, Chased Flowers, Scrolls, Oval, Gorham, 1884, 18½ In.	2400.00
Bowl, Reed & Barton, c.1941, 7 x 10 In.	117.00
Bowl, Reeded Base, Lobes, Reeded Rim, Monogram, 7 x 4⅝ In.	1680.00
Bowl, Reeded Rim, Ribbed, Pedestal Foot, c.1920, 14⅝ In.	2400.00
Bowl, Repousse, Flowers & Leaves, Footed, S. Kirk & Son, Baltimore, c.1900, 9 In.	1507.00
Bowl, Repousse, Garden Scene, Flowers, Footed, Kirk & Son, c.1900, 9¼ In.	2233.00
Bowl, Repousse, Lobed, Round, Open Scrollwork, R. Wallace & Sons, 13 In.	429.00
Bowl, Ribbed, Reed & Barton, c.1949, 3 x 9¾ In.	146.00 to 205.00
Bowl, Rogers, Lunt & Bowlen, Mid 20th Century, 6 In.	82.00
Bowl, Rose Bouquet Pattern, Fisher, 2⅜ x 9 In.	88.00 to 94.00

Bowl, Sauce, On Stand, Redlich & Co., 3½ x 5¼ In.	117.00
Bowl, Scroll Border, Monogram, Frank Smith Silver Co., Late 1800s, 3 x 15 In.	1058.00
Bowl, Shaped, Lobed, Round Foot, Arthur Stone, 12 In.	1116.00
Bowl, Shaped Rim, Monogram, A.M. Soffel Co., c.1930, 2¼ x 9 In.	123.00
Bowl, Square, Gorham, c.1948, 2½ x 9 In.	234.00
Bowl, Towle, 7½ x 9 In.	117.00
Bowl, Upswept Rim, Round Base, Schultz, 3¼ x 10¼ In.	316.00
Bowl, Wedgwood, International, 2½ x 8 In.	146.00
Bowl, Windsor Pattern, Reed & Barton, 9 In.	176.00
Bowl Set, Carmel, Oval, Rims, Hammered Band, Trefoils, Wallace, 12 Piece	1293.00
Bowl Set, Reticulated, Scrolling, Pierced, Gorham, c.1873, 2½ x 5 In., 7 Piece	2185.00
Box, Heart Shape, Repousse, Gorham, c.1892, 5 x 4¾ In.	351.00
Box, Hinged Lid, CLW Monogram, c.1940, 1 x 3¼ x 5⅞ In.	47.00
Box, Mauser Mfg. Co., c.1900, 1½ x 2½ In.	176.00
Bread & Butter Dish, Gorham, 12 x 7 In.	1638.00
Bread Tray, Scalloped Border, Chased Poppies, Leaves, Rectangular, Gorham, 13 In.	1320.00
Butter, Cover, Double Handle, Elk Finial, Black & Co., 5 x 9½ In.	990.00
Butter, Dome Top, Medallion, Female Supports, Soldier Finial, Wood & Hughes, 8 x 6 In.	1265.00
Cake Basket, Reticulated Border, Flower Repousse, Oval Foot, Gorham, 11¼ In., Pair	885.00
Cake Knife, Hand Wrought, Hammered, Pineapple, F. Porter, c.1925, 8½ In.	147.00
Candelabra are listed in the Candelabrum category.	
Candlestick, Hexagonal, Raised Stepped Base, Arthur Stone, 10½ In., 4 Piece	10575.00
Candy Dish, Francis I, Reed & Barton, 8 In., Pair	585.00
Candy Dish, Richard Dimes Co., Watrous & Alvin, 6 In., 4 Piece	70.00
Cann, Cup, Baluster, Molded Base, Scroll Handle, Benjamin Burt, c.1760, 5 In.	3600.00
Cann, Cup, Baluster, Molded Foot, Leaf Scroll Handle, Detachable Cover, c.1805, 7½ In., Pair	9600.00
Cann, Cup, Baluster, Molded Foot, Leaf Scroll Handle, Detachable Cover, c.1805, 8¼ In., Pair	4800.00
Cann, Cup, Baluster, Molded Foot, Scroll Handle, Leaf Join, c.1750, 4¾ In.	3360.00
Card Case, Bridge Scene, Engine Turned, Leonard & Wilson, Penn., c.1850, 3½ In. *illus*	329.00
Card Case, Enameled, Chrysanthemums, Leaves, Green Ground, Chain, c.1885, 4 In.	8400.00
Card Case, Fountain, Grapevine, Flip Lid, H.L. Webster & Co., R.I., c.1840, 3¾ In. *illus*	508.00
Card Tray, Hammered, Chevrons, Acanthus Scroll Supports, Arts & Crafts, 5 x 8 In.	480.00
Charger, Marie Antoinette, Flower Swags, Leafy Scrolls, Acanthus, 10½ In., 8 Piece	3918.00
Charger, Molded Edge, Inner Beaded Rim, Husks, Acanthus Leaf Tip, 11⅛ In., 12 Piece	8225.00
Child's Set, Bowl, Underplate, Nursery Rhymes, Early 1900s, 7 In.	529.00
Cigar Light, Applied Saddle, Crop, Pipe, Pedestal Base, Square Foot, Gorham, 1913, 6 In. *illus*	287.00
Cigarette Case, Fishing Scene, Gold Inlay, Fuller & Mayer, c.1897, 3 x 2½ In.	157.00
Cocktail Shaker, Hawkes, Crystal, 8 x 4 In.	176.00
Coffee Set, Engraved, Ball Tompkins & Black, N.Y., c.1850, 3 Piece	1413.00
Coffee Set, Flowers, Leaves, Matte Ground, Jacobi & Jenkins, 3 Piece, c.1900	1320.00
Coffee Set, Pilgrim Pattern, Reed & Barton, Round Tray, 4 Piece	295.00
Coffee Set, Pot, Sugar, Creamer, Water Kettle On Stand, Arthur Stone, 6 Piece	3819.00
Coffeepot, Baluster, Domed Foot, Twig Border, Grapes, c.1861, 13 In.	960.00
Coffeepot, Baluster, Leaf Spout, Wood Handle, Shell, Lozenge, c.1775, 12¼ In.	9000.00
Compote, Chantilly-Duchess Pattern, Gorham, Mid 1900s, 10½ x 4½ In.	108.00
Compote, Floral Repousse, Monogram, International Silver, 5½ x 10 In.	224.00
Compote, Floral Repousse Rim, 3 x 6 In., Pair	239.00
Compote, Francis I, Footed, Reed & Barton, c.1907, 11½ x 5½ In.	1560.00
Compote, Francis I, Reed & Barton, 4½ x 8¾ In.	468.00 to 527.00
Compote, Hammered, Round, Tapered Foot Stem, Crimped Rim & Foot, Whiting, 6 x 10 In.	558.00
Compote, Hexagonal, Pedestal Base, Gorham, 9¼ In., Pair	540.00
Condiment Jar, Drum Shape, Red Crystal, R. Blackinton & Co., 3 x 3 In.	117.00
Creamer, Coin, Campbell & Donigan, Nashville, Tenn., 5½ In. *illus*	23000.00
Creamer, Coin, G.A. Baker, 6½ In.	230.00
Creamer, Helmet Form, Square Foot, Beaded Border, Upswept Handle, c.1790, 7 In.	1140.00
Creamer, Helmet Form, Square Foot, Upswept Loop Handle, 7 In.	1320.00
Creamer, Oval, Reeded Foot, Urn Shape, Wriggle Work, Geometric, 7¼ In.	1200.00
Creamer, Pear Shape, 3 Pad Feet, Shell Joins, Double Scroll Handle, c.1830, 4 In.	4800.00
Cruet Stand, Rectangular, Ball Feet, Wire Frame, Angular Handle, c.1811, 8 In.	2640.00
Crumber, Undertray, Black, Starr & Frost, Engraved, Leafy Scroll Borders, c.1900	499.00
Cup, Handles, Beaded Borders, Square Base, Monogram, J.E. Caldwell, 4½ x 5 In.	35.00
Cup, Octagonal, Round Foot, Scroll Handle, Engraved, John Mood, 1849, 3¾ In.	2280.00
Cup, Tapering, Cylindrical, Engraved Monogram, c.1780, 1⅝ In.	3600.00
Desk Tray, Crichton & Co., New York, 8 x 14 In.	263.00
Dish, Cover, Lord Robert, Gadroon Rim, Scroll Handle, International, 12 x 9 In.	413.00
Dish, Entree, Cover, Chippendale, Gorham, 20th Century, 10½ In.	304.00

Silver Plate, Ice Bucket, Stand, R.M.S. Queen Mary, Elkington For Cunard White Star Line, 18 In. $764.00

Silver Plate, Pitcher, Floral Scrolls, Bird Finial, Martin, Ebenezer Hall & Co., Sheffield, 12 x 7 In. $288.00

Silver Plate, Sauceboat, Engraved Vines, Gadroon Edge, Leaves, Mappin & Webb, Prince's Plate, 5 x 9 In. $115.00

Silver Plate, Tea & Coffee Set, Classistic Pattern, Barbour, 10½-In. Coffeepot, 5 Piece $235.00

S

Silver Plate, Teapot, Ribbed Bottom Half, Wood Handle & Finial, Sheffield, 5½ x 10¾ In.
$115.00

Silver Plate, Urn, Ice Water, 2 Horned Bull Handles With Rings, Garrett & Sons, Phila., 22 In.
$489.00

Silver-American, Bonbon Scoop, Embossed Leaves & Berries, Round Bowl, Handle, Gorham, 10¾ In.
$657.00

Silver-American, Bowl, Francis I Pattern, Reed & Barton, 1950, 2½ x 11 In.
$518.00

Dish, Open, Handles, Parcel Gilt, Bracket Feet, Scrolls, Chased Flowers, c.1880, 11 In.	2700.00
Dish, Oval, Frank W. Smith Co., Gardner, Mass., Early 20th Century, 10 In.	117.00
Dresser Set, Powder Jar, Jewelry Box, Pincushion Cover, Brushes, Mirror	13200.00
Dresser Set, Wm. B. Kerr & Co., c.1920, 7 Piece	322.00
Drinking Set, Tray, Copper, Horn Handles, Hammered, c.1890, 8¾ In., 8 Piece	6000.00
Ewer, Cloisonne Enamel, Exotic Bird, Flowers, Orange Ground, Baluster, 6¾ In.	7800.00
Ewer, Inverted Baluster, Stepped Round, Stebbins, c.1835, 13½ In.	1920.00
Ewer, Japanese Style, Spirals, Elephants, Leaves, Dragon Handle, c.1883, 14 In.	36000.00
Ewer, Repousse Flowers, Swan, Butterfly, Ram's Head, Kirk, c.1830, 16 In. ......*illus*	4481.00
Finger Bowl Set, Round, Straight-Sided, Molded Foot, Chased, S. Kirk & Son, 5 In., 16 Piece	5100.00
Fish Fork, Charleston, Monogram, Theodore Evans & Co., c.1860, 6¾ In.	403.00
Fish Fork, Fiddle Thread Pattern, Coin, Hyde & Goodrich, New Orleans, c.1850, 8 In.	212.00
Fish Server, Hollow Handle, Oval Openwork Blade, Coin, Forbes, c.1820, 12¾ In.	1380.00
Fish Set, Bright Cut, Fitted Case, Gorham, c.1880	850.00
Fork Set, Coin, Round Upturned Tip, Fiddle Handles, Monogram, 8 In., 6 Piece	1955.00
Fork Set, Fiddle Handles, Coin, Hyde & Goodrich, 7½ In., 8 Piece	690.00
Fruit Bowl, Monogram, 1½ In.	410.00
Goblet, Liqueur, Monogram, Early 1900s, Randahl Shop, 4 In.	203.00
Goblet, Presentation, Inscription, Engraved, Coin, c.1860, 6¾ x 3¼ In.	695.00
Goblet, Urn Shape Body, Shield, Scrollwork, Coin, Gorham, c.1850, 3¾ In.	748.00
Gravy Boat, Undertray, Stylized Flower Bud Loop Handle, Karl F. Leinonen, 7⅞ In.	646.00
Hand Mirror, Hand, Love's Dream, Unger Brothers, 10 In.	275.00
Hand Mirror, International, Monogram, 6½ x 9½ In.	105.00
Ice Bucket, Baroque, Raised Relief, Wallace, 9 x 10 In.	1872.00
Ice Serving Spoon, Applied Stag, Monogram B, Gorham, c.1885, 9¾ In.	975.00
Inkwell, Cut Glass, Yachting Flags, Flower Sprays, Dome Shape, 6¾ In.	14400.00
Julep Cup, Tapered, Molded Rim, Incised Lines 3½ In., 12 Piece	2333.00
Julep Cup, Tapered Sides, Beaded Top, Bottom, Coin, S. Simpson, 1857, 3½ In.	7480.00
Julep Cup, Tapered Sides, Thread & Dot Border, Bellanger, c.1827, 3¼ x 3 In.	1265.00
Julep Cup, Tapered Sides, Thread Borders, c.1863, 3½ In., 4 Piece	3335.00
Kettle, Hot Water, Stand, Scrolls, Lobed, Bun Feet, Theodore B. Starr, 13½ In. ......*illus*	1135.00
Kettle, Stand, Coffeepot, Teapot, Cream Jug, Sugar, c.1865, 17 In.	7200.00
Knife Set, Fiddle Thread, Coin, Wm. Gale & Sons, 1850, 7¾ In., 10 Piece	650.00
Ladle, Fiddle Handle, Engraved Monogram, John Delarue, c.1825, 15 In.	4800.00
Ladle, Fiddle Handle, Pointed Fins, Monogram VCW G.C. Johnson, 12 In.	316.00
Ladle, Fiddle Handle, Pointed Fins, Oval Bowl, Coin, Wilson & Klein, 14 In.	3910.00
Ladle, Fiddle Handle, Pointed Fins, Oval Bowl, Kentucky, Coin, Marked Kitts, 13 In.	650.00
Ladle, Fiddle Handle, Pointed Fins, Wilson McGrew, 13¼ In.	548.00
Ladle, Fiddle Handle, Shell, Rounded Fins, Coin, Savannah, 12¾ In.	3220.00
Ladle, Leafy Decoration, Monogram, Dominick & Haff	234.00
Ladle, Monogram, J.E. Caldwell, Late 19th Century, 11½ In.	199.00
Ladle, Oval Bowl, Tapered Handle, Marked, Allan Adler, 1900s, 9⅝ In.	147.00
Ladle, Round Bowl, Bright Cut Handles, Bellflowers, c.1795, 15¾ In.	3600.00
Letter Opener, Applied Beetle, Engraved Characters, Whiting, c.1885, 8¼ In. ......*illus*	1315.00
Marrow Scoop, 2-Sided, Leaf & Band Decoration, Coin, J. Conning, c.1825, 9 In.	978.00
Marrow Scoop, Leaf Engraving, 9⅞ In.	180.00
Medal, Peace, Chester A. Arthur, 1881	97750.00
Medal, Peace, George Washington, U.S. Mint Issue Of 1910	1725.00
Medal, Peace, James Garfield, 1881	52900.00
Medal, Peace, Thomas Jefferson, 1801, Large Size	189750.00
Medal, Peace, Zachary Taylor, 1849	29000.00
Milk Jug, Watermelon Finial, Scalloped Hinged Cover, Bulbous, Coin, c.1850, 6½ In.	3910.00
Muffineer, Silver Gilt Mounted, Baluster Shape, Chased, c.1890, 8½ In.	2160.00
Mug, C-Scroll Handle, Coin, William Gale, New York, 1867, 4¼ In. ......*illus*	1380.00
Mug, Racehorse Engraving, Tapered, Concentric Incised Lines, Inscription, 1822, 4 In.	700.00
Mug, Repousse Flowers & Scrolls, Beaded Border, Coin, Marked G & H, 4 In. ......*illus*	863.00
Mug, Round, Beaded Border, C-Scroll Handle, Repousse, Coin, 3¾ x 4¾ In.	863.00
Mug, Round, Hollow C-Scroll Handle, Vine Decoration, Applied Detail, 3½ In.	2070.00
Mug, Tongue & Dart Border, Scroll Handle, Geradus Boyce, 3 x 4 In. ......*illus*	201.00
Mug, Urn Shape, C-Scroll Handle, Applied Borders, Engraved, 4¼ In.	316.00
Napkin Rings are listed in their own category.	
Nut Dish, Calla Lily, Pedestal Foot, Handle, Musician, Whiting, c.1880, 14½ In.	1200.00
Nut Dish, Floral Repousse, S. Kirk & Son, Late 1800s, 1½ x 4½ In., Pair	179.00
Nut Dish, Francis I, Reed & Barton, c.1907, 4 Piece	330.00
Nut Dish, Francis I, Reed & Barton, c.1910, 3½ In.	120.00
Nut Set, Scrolling Rim, Oval Reticulated Body, Gorham, 8 Piece	690.00

S

Silver-American, Card Case, Bridge Scene, Engine Turned, Leonard & Wilson, Penn., c.1850, 3½ In.
$329.00

Silver-American, Card Case, Fountain, Grapevine, Flip Lid, H.L. Webster & Co., R.I., c.1840, 3¾ In.
$508.00

Silver-American, Cigar Light, Applied Saddle, Crop, Pipe, Pedestal Base, Square Foot, Gorham, 1913, 6 In.
$287.00

Silver-American, Ewer, Repousse Flowers, Swan, Butterfly, Ram's Head, Kirk, c.1830, 16 In.
$4481.00

Silver-American, Kettle, Hot Water, Stand, Scrolls, Lobed, Bun Feet, Theodore B. Starr, 13½ In.
$1135.00

Silver-American, Creamer, Coin, Campbell & Donigan, Nashville, Tenn., 5½ In.
$23000.00

Silver-American, Letter Opener, Applied Beetle, Engraved Characters, Whiting, c.1885, 8¼ In.
$1315.00

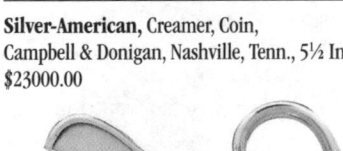

S

Silver-American, Mug, C-Scroll Handle, Coin, William Gale, New York, 1867, 4¼ In. $1380.00

Silver-American, Papboat, Thread Decoration, Monogram, Strap Handle, Coin, Charleston, 2¼ x 5¾ In. $1840.00

Silver-American, Mug, Repousse Flowers & Scrolls, Beaded Border, Coin, Marked G & H, 4 In. $863.00

Silver-American, Pitcher, Helmet Shape, Flower & Scroll Band, Acanthus Border, Scroll Handle, Coin, 14 In. $2760.00

Silver-American, Pitcher, Water, Grapevine, Salamander, Bird Handle, R. & W. Wilson, Phila., 1845, 13 In. $9000.00

Silver-American, Mug, Tongue & Dart Border, Scroll Handle, Geradus Boyce, 3 x 4 In. $201.00

Silver-American, Nutmeg Grater, Fluted Nut Shape, Monogrammed K, Hinged Steel Grater, 2 In. $747.00

Silver-American, Pitcher, Water, 8-Sided, Hammered, Monogram, EE, Kalo Shop, 1912, 7 In. $5290.00

Silver-American, Pitcher, Water, Shells & Seaweed, Copper Crab, Hammered, Whiting, c.1880, 7¼ In. $10800.00

Nutmeg Grater, Fluted Nut Shape, Monogrammed K, Hinged Steel Grater, 2 In.	*illus*	747.00
Olive Dish, Oval, Hammered Surface, Flared Rim, Chased, Martele, c.1898, 7 In.		3120.00
Olive Fork, Parcel Gilt, Narragansett, Shell Shape Bowl, Gorham, c.1890, 11 In.		3600.00
Open Salt, Monogram, Wood & Hughes, Late 1800s, 1¾ x 2½ In.		448.00
Papboat, Thread Decoration, Monogram, Strap Handle, Coin, Charleston, 2 x 5¾ In.	*illus*	1840.00
Papboat, c.1770, 4½ In.		1800.00
Papboat, Engraved Monogram, c.1800, 3⅝ In.		2160.00
Pitcher, Bucket Shape, Waisted Collar, C-Scroll Handle, Ogee Domed Foot, Watson, 9 In.		440.00
Pitcher, George B. Sharp, Scenic Repousse, Commemoration, Mid 1800s, 11 In.		3884.00
Pitcher, Hammered, Egg Shape, Loop Handle, Rolled Rim, 1918, 9¼ In.		588.00
Pitcher, Hammered, Monogram, 4 Pints, Kalo, 8¼ x 7 In.		4200.00
Pitcher, Helmet Shape, Flower & Scroll Band, Acanthus Border, Scroll Handle, Coin, 14 In.	*illus*	2760.00
Pitcher, Oval, Short Neck, Spout, Ear Handle, Boston, Late 19th Century, 6¼ In.		646.00
Pitcher, Square Foot, Script Monogram, Elevated Handle, J.E. Caldwell, 8½ In.		323.00
Pitcher, Water, 8-Sided, Hammered, Monogram, EE, Kalo Shop, 1912, 7 In.	*illus*	5290.00
Pitcher, Water, Baluster, Faceted, Die Rolled Border, Angular Handle, c.1830, 7¼ In.		5040.00
Pitcher, Water, Baluster, Round Base, Repousse, Scroll Handle, 12 In.		2280.00
Pitcher, Water, Baluster, Scroll Handle, Hammered Surface, c.1930, 8 In.		720.00
Pitcher, Water, Grapevine, Salamander, Bird Handle, R. & W. Wilson, Phila., 1845, 13 In.	*illus*	9000.00
Pitcher, Water, Leafy & Scroll Etched Decoration, Monogram, Gorham, 10 In.		671.00
Pitcher, Water, Navarre Pattern, Watson Co., Attleboro, Mass., 10¾ In.		1020.00
Pitcher, Water, Royal Danish Pattern, International Silver Co., 8½ In.		390.00
Pitcher, Water, Shells & Seaweed, Copper Crab, Hammered, Whiting, c.1880, 7¼ In.	*illus*	10800.00
Plate, Downturned Rim, Waterfall Border, W.W. Dodge, Asheville, N.C., 10¾ In.		978.00
Plate, Sandwich, Martele, Chased Leaf & Flowers, Gorham, c.1911, 11½ In.		2390.00
Plate Set, Carmel, Hammered Band, Trefoils, Wallace, 6 In., 12 Piece		1645.00
Plate Set, Flower Swags, Leafy Scrolls, Acanthus, Monogram, 6⅜ In., 8 Piece		1528.00
Plate Set, Leaf Tip, Flower Rims, Chased Borders, Swags, Rosettes, c.1910, 12 Piece		3300.00
Plate Set, Manchester Silver Co., 6 In., 7 Piece		176.00
Plate Set, Renaissance Revival Strapwork, Gorham, c.1890, 11½ In., 10 Piece		6600.00
Plate Set, Scalloped Border, Chased Flowers, Scrolls, Gorham, c.1900, 12 Piece		6000.00
Platter, Oval, Shaped Convex Molding, Engraved, 20¼ In.		2700.00
Platter, Round, Leafy Scroll, Flower Border, C-Scroll, Roger Williams Co., 15⅝ In.		1528.00
Porringer, 3-Hold Tab Handle, Engraved, c.1740, 7½ In.		4200.00
Porringer, Copper Fish, Frog, Lily Pads, Round, Gorham, 1881, 5⅛ In.		1800.00
Porringer, Keyhole Handle, Engraved, c.1730, 7¼ In.		2880.00
Porringer, Keyhole Handle, Engraved, c.1815, 8 In.		1440.00
Porringer, Openwork Handle, Flared Rim, 5¼ In.		518.00
Porringer, Pierced Keyhole Handle, Engraved, c.1753, 7⅜ In.		7800.00
Punch Bowl, Art Deco, Incised Rim, Pedestal Foot, Engraved, 12½ In.		3600.00
Punch Bowl, Ladle, Tray, Shreve, Crump & Low, c.1885, 9¾ x 14 In.		7800.00
Punch Bowl, Presentation, Adam Style, Pedestal, Whiting, c.1906, 21 In.		6000.00
Punch Ladle, Fiddle, Scalloped Bowl, Engraved Stem, c.1840, 11½ In.		540.00
Punch Ladle, Upturned Fiddle Tipped Handle, Elliptical Bowl, Coin, 13 In.		368.00
Salad Set, Hammered, Monogram, Lebolt & Co., 20th Century, 9¾ In.		335.00
Salt & Pepper, Open Salt, Footed, Fisher, 4½ In., 3 Piece		53.00
Salver, Boat Shape, Serpentine Rim, Poppies, 4 Scroll Feet, Martele, Gorham, 12 In.		3360.00
Sauceboat, Kalo Shop Tray, Fluted Foot, Handwrought, Falick Novick, 4 In.		881.00
Sauceboat, Oval, 3 Ball & Claw Feet, Lion's Head Joins, c.1850, 9 In., Pair		2400.00
Sauceboat, Oval, 3 Hoof Feet, Leafy Joints, Scroll Handle, 1760, 7½ In.		960.00
Saucepan, Side Wood Handle, Engraved, Monogram, Dome Lid, c.1810, 15 In.		4560.00
Serving Dish, Durham, Mid 20th Century, 9 x 15½ In., Pair		1404.00
Serving Dish, Francis I, 4-Footed, Shaped Oval, Reed & Barton, c.1956, 15 In., Pair		4800.00
Serving Plate, Floral & Scroll Designs, Wallace, 14 In.		322.00
Serving Plate, Lunt Silversmiths, c.1940, 9¾ In.		293.00
Serving Spoon, Ephraim Brasher, Engraved Initials, c.1780, 9 In.		2328.00
Serving Spoon, Pierced, Whiting Mfg. Co., 8½ In.		146.00
Shaker, Pepper, Footed, Handles, Engraved, Early 20th Century, 6¼ In.		418.00
Slice, Scrolling Vine, Ivory Handle, Whiting, New York, c.1900, 12¼ In.		582.00
Soup Ladle, Old English, Engraved Stem, Script Monogram, c.1780, 13¾ In.		840.00
Spoon, Coffin Handles, Monogram, Selph & Pyle, N.C., 5⅜ In., 5 Piece		2070.00
Spoon, Condiment, French Thread Pattern, Engraved Initials, Coin, 3¾ In., 4 Piece		115.00
Spoon, Downturned Fiddle Handles, Pointed Fins, Shells, Coin, 6¼ In., 12 Piece		2300.00
Spoon, Fiddle Handle, Oval Bowl, Monogram, Coin, A. Blanchard, 8¾ In.		633.00
Spoon, Fiddle Handle, Pointed Fins, Coin, Monogram, 1800s, 3½ In., 6 Piece		374.00
Spoon, Fiddle Handle, Pointed Fins, Coin, Monogram, Elliston, c.1856, 8½ In.		2185.00

Silver-American, Tea & Coffee Set, Shaped Scroll Handles, Dome Lids, Fisher Silversmiths, 5 Piece
$1912.00

Silver-American, Tea Set, 8-Sided, Fluted, Paneled, Cartouches, John Sayre, N.Y., c.1800, 7¾-In. Teapot, 4 Piece
$7200.00

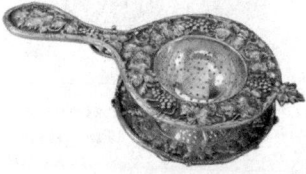

Silver-American, Tea Strainer, Stand, Chased Grapes, Vine, F. Fuchs & Bros., Shreve, Crump & Low, c.1885
$478.00

Silver-American, Toy, Whistle, Chased, Rococo, 4 Rows Of Bells, Coral Teether, Marked PS, Phila., 5 In.
$4200.00

S

Silver-American, Tureen, Cover,
Embossed, Flowers, Berries,
Dominick & Haff, N.Y., 1883, 12¼ In.
$2700.00

Silver-American, Vase, Leaves,
Applied Copper & Brass Bird & Leaves,
Dominick & Haff, 1¾ In.
$418.00

Silver-Austrian, Tea Set, Secessionist,
Ribbons, Crown Finial, V. Mayer & Sohne,
c.1910, 5 Piece
$777.00

Silver-Chinese, Card Case,
Reticulated Bamboo, Heart,
Chinese Characters, Gilt Trim, 3¼ In.
$263.00

Spoon, Fluted Handle, Upturned Terminal, Oval Bowl, Flattened Drop, 15 In.	960.00
Spoon, Fruit Design Handle, Pattern Back Bowl, Engraved, Coin, 7 In.	345.00
Spoon, Scalloped Shell, Initials, AL, Marked, JE, 18th Century, Coin, 4¾ In.	300.00
Spoon, Upturned Tipt Handles, Thomas You, Charleston, S.C., c.1786, 8 In., Pair	1840.00
Spoon Set, Demitasse, Serving, Hammered, Applied Copper, Gorham, 7 Piece	837.00
Spoon Set, Down Turned Fiddle Ends, Monogram, Coin, W. Mannerback, 6¾ In., 12 Piece	385.00
Spoon Set, Round Fiddle Tip Handles, Monogram, Coin, 6 In., 13 Piece	1840.00
Spoon Set, Shaped Tip Fiddle Handles, Monogram, Coin, 7¼ In., 9 Piece	920.00
Spoon Set, Stanley Pattern, Coin, 6 Piece	117.00
Strainer, Punch, Pierced Leaves, Geometric Crosses, Side Ring Handle, c.1745, 4¼ In.	5040.00
Stuffing Spoon, Bright Cut Engraved Wrigglework Border, c.1775, 13 In.	6000.00
Sugar, Cover, Urn Shape, Garlands, Bead Border, Baluster Knop, Schanck, c.1795, 9¾ In.	2640.00
Sugar, Urn Shape, Reeded Foot, Engraved, Wrigglework, Cartouche, c.1800, 7 In.	1920.00
Sugar, Vase Shape, Square Base, Engraved Cartouche, c.1790, 9½ In.	2400.00
Sugar & Creamer, Coin, James Ball & Poor, Boston, 6½ x 8 In.	460.00
Sugar & Creamer, Scroll Handles, Paneled, Monogram, Cooper & Fisher, 8¾ In.	187.00
Sugar Shaker, Kirk & Sons, Inc., 1900, 7½ In.	370.00
Sugar Shaker, Repousse, Rococo, Dome Lid, Dominick & Haff, 6⅜ In., Pair	1527.00
Sweetmeat, Pierced Acanthus, Serpentine Rim, Oval, Hinged Handle, Lebkuecher, 9 In.	510.00
Table, Japanese Style, Barley Twist Legs, Claw, Ball Feet, Square, 1880, 30½ In.	9000.00
Tablespoon, Engraved Initials, Marked Revere, 8¾ In.	8625.00
Tablespoon, Georgian, Old English Bright Cut, George Smith, 8¾ In., Pair	180.00
Tankard, Tapered Cylinder, Dome Lid, Thomas Edwards, Boston, 1770, 8¼ In.	8400.00
Tankard, Yacht, Cylindrical, Shells, Seaweed Borders, Mermaid Handle, 13 In.	16800.00
Tazza, Bakelite Stem Inset, Rim, Grogan Company, Pittsburgh, c.1930, 7 In., Pair	2700.00
Tazza, Cover, Hammered, Curls, Joel F. Hewes, 9¼ x 7 In.	3900.00
Tazza, Round, Openwork, Engraved Scrolling Flowers, c.1900, 13 In., Pair	2160.00
Tea & Coffee Set, Classical Urn Shape, Greek Key Band, International, 5 Piece	973.00
Tea & Coffee Set, Diamond, Gio Ponti, Reed & Barton, c.1960, 5 Piece	2160.00
Tea & Coffee Set, Diamond Pattern, Angular Form, Reed & Barton, 4 Piece	1645.00
Tea & Coffee Set, Medallion Pattern, Gorham, c.1868, 5 Piece	9600.00
Tea & Coffee Set, Neo-Classical, Gorham, 1914, 6 Piece	6000.00
Tea & Coffee Set, Plymouth, Gorham, c.1958, 5 Piece	1800.00
Tea & Coffee Set, Shaped Scroll Handles, Dome Lids, Fisher Silversmiths, 5 Piece ..... *illus*	1912.00
Tea & Coffee Set, Vase Shape, Oval Base, Leaf Capped Handle, Gorham, 5 Piece	5400.00
Tea Caddy, Crichton Brothers, N.Y., 1916, 4 x 3 x 3½ In.	322.00
Tea Caddy, Tapering Square, Hairy Paw Feet, Hinged, Dome Lid, c.1835, 5¾ In.	6600.00
Tea Set, 8-Sided, Fluted, Paneled, Cartouches, John Sayre, N.Y., c.1800, 7¾-In. Teapot, 4 Piece . *illus*	7200.00
Tea Set, Bachelor's, Initials, Ball, Black & Co., 1860s, 4½ In., 3 Piece	670.00
Tea Set, Engraved Leaf Borders, Goose Neck Spout, Monogram, c.1815, 3 Piece	4200.00
Tea Set, Francis I, Renaissance Tray, Reed & Barton, 5 Piece	6440.00
Tea Set, Lids, Repousse, Oval Teapot, Sugar, Geometric, St. Louis, Mo., 4 Piece	2350.00
Tea Set, Neoclassical Style, Gale & Willis, 10 In., 4 Piece	2160.00
Tea Set, Oval Paneled Bodies, International, 5 Piece	920.00
Tea Set, Plymouth, Gorham, 5 Piece	1232.00
Tea Set, Pot, Creamer, Sugar, Covers, Hammered, Flowers, Insects, 3 Piece	3600.00
Tea Set, Pot, Cups, Saucer, Tray, Creamer, Sugar, Waste Bowl, 6 Piece	15600.00
Tea Set, Repousse, 6 Piece, 1894-1908	5520.00
Tea Set, Strasbourg Pattern, Footed, Scroll Handles, 9¼-In. Teapot, 3 Piece	546.00
Tea Set, Teapot, Creamer, Sugar, Bombe Oval, Ribbon, Wreaths, Foliage Bands, 3 Piece	3000.00
Tea Set, Towle, 3 Piece	468.00
Tea Set, Tray, Cocktail Shaker, Royal Danish, International, c.1930, 5 Piece	527.00
Tea Set, Urn Finials, C-Scroll Handle, Monograms, Tray, Gorham, 4 Piece	460.00
Tea Strainer, Stand, Chased Grapes, Vine, F. Fuchs & Bros., Shreve, Crump & Low, c.1885 *illus*	478.00
Tea Strainer, Stand, Hemispherical Shape, Pierced, Wide Lip, Chased, c.1891	478.00
Teapot, Oval, Beaded, Engraved Borders, Cartouche, Monogram, 12 In.	4560.00
Teapot, Shaped Oval, Engraved Flowers, Wriggle, Laurel Wreath, c.1815, 13½ In.	1320.00
Teapot, Stand, Oval, Straight Spout, Wood Handle, Dome Lid, Urn Finial, 12 In.	2400.00
Teapot, Vase Shape, Square Base, Domed Plinth, Wiltberger, c.1790, 11 In.	4560.00
Teapot, Vase Shape, Stepped Circular Foot, Beaded, Gadroon, c.1815, 10 In.	3600.00
Teaspoon Set, Floral, Fruit Handles, 6 Styles, Gilt Wash, c.1880, 5½ In., 12 Piece	149.00
Toast Rack, Coin, Marked John B Jones & Co., Boston, c.1838, 6½ x 6¾ In.	4500.00
Toy, Whistle, Chased, Rococo, 4 Rows Of Bells, Coral Teether, Marked PS, Phila., 5 In. . . *illus*	4200.00
Tray, 2 Handles, Floral Repousse, Monogram, Dominick & Haff, 15 x 9¾ In.	1245.00
Tray, Border Shells, Scrolls, Flowers, Round, Dominick & Haff, 17 In.	1200.00
Tray, Oval, Gadroon Border, Hoop Handles, Stephen Richard, c.1820, 30 In.	12000.00

Tray, Oval, Scalloped Reeded Rim, Engraved Wreath, Monogram, 1830, 27¼ In.	6600.00
Tray, Pompeian Adam, Oval, Old English Monogram, Towle, c.1921, 12 x 7 In.	108.00
Tray, Preisner Silver Co., Mid 20th Century, 1¼ x 13¼ In.	146.00
Tray, Rectangular, Cutout Handles, Hammered, Blossoms, Leaves, 1915, 20½ In.	9600.00
Tray, Scalloped Edge, Handles, Gorham, c.1909, 26½ In.	1989.00
Tray, Scalloped Rim, Kalo, Inscribed, c.1919, 8 In.	431.00
Tray, Serving, Plymouth, 2 Handles, Oval, Gorham, 1914, 24 x 18 In.	3055.00
Tray, Shreve, Crump & Low, c.1900, 11¼ x 15½ In.	1521.00
Tray, Woodside Sterling Co., c.1920, ⅞ x 12¼ In.	117.00
Tureen, Cover, Branch Shape Handles, Scroll Feet, S. Kirk & Son, c.1883, 14 x 11 In.	6600.00
Tureen, Cover, Embossed, Flowers, Berries, Dominick & Haff, N.Y., 1883, 12¼ In. ..... illus	2700.00
Urn, Royal Danish, International, 3 x 2¼ In., Pair	59.00
Urn, Winged Figural Handles, Masks, Grape & Scroll, Dixon & Sons, 20 x 12 In.	805.00
Vanity Set, Hand Mirror, Brush, Scissors, Nail File, 1920	51.00
Vase, Art Nouveau, Spreading Round Foot, Baluster Stem, George W. Shiebler, 14 In.	9988.00
Vase, Fluted Rim, Band Edge, Monogram, Arthur Stone, c.1923, 6 In.	1293.00
Vase, Bud, Aquatic Scene, Fish, Lily Pads, Rockscape, Butterflies, Gorham, 1880, 8 In.	960.00
Vase, Crystal, Reed & Barton, 8 x 7¼ In.	702.00
Vase, Inverted Ball, Leaf Wrapped Reeded Borders, Corsair, 1898, 6 In., Pair	2700.00
Vase, La Paglia Design, International, 9¼ In., Pair	1416.00
Vase, Leaves, Applied Copper & Brass Bird & Leaves, Dominick & Haff, 1¾ In. .... illus	418.00
Vase, Round Base, Repousse Flowers, Kirk & Son, c.1907, 10 In.	1680.00
Vase, Trumpet, Hand Chased, Pierced, J.E. Caldwell & Co., c.1916, 13½ In.	936.00
Waste Bowl, Applied Beading, Monogram, John David, c.1875, 4½ x 6 In.	2990.00
Wine Siphon, U-Shape Tube, Cylindrical Pump, c.1825, 15 In.	4800.00

SILVER-AUSTRIAN

Basket, Oval, Grid, Reticulated Squares, Handle, J. Hoffmann, 10 In.	1763.00
Box, Patch, 18th Century, 2⅓ x 1½ In.	146.00
Cachepot, Vienna, Early 20th Century, 5 In.	707.00
Salt Shovel, French Thread Pattern, Engraved, Crown Crest, c.1846, 4 In., Pair	288.00
Tea Set, Secessionist, Ribbons, Crown Finial, V. Mayer & Sohne, c.1910, 5 Piece .... illus	777.00

SILVER-CANADIAN

Basket, Pierced, Henry Birks & Sons, Montreal, Early 1900s, 6¼ In.	333.00
Bowl, Footed, 2 Round Handles, Poul Petersen, Montreal, 1935-1953, 13 In.	3420.00
Bowl, Ladle, Poul Petersen, Montreal, c.1953, 3 In.	430.00
Candy Dish, Poul Petersen, Montreal, c.1953, 4 In., Pair	246.00
Chalice, Laurent Amiot, Quebec, c.1830, 9½ In.	1869.00
Coaster Set, Raised Rim, Monogram, Poul Petersen, 1935-1953, 12 Piece	385.00
Plate, Douglas Boyd, Toronto, c.1942, 10 In.	246.00
Porringer, Inscribed, Henry Birks & Sons, Montreal, c.1900, 6 In.	141.00
Rose Bowl, Henry Birks & Sons, Montreal, c.1929, 10½ In.	877.00
Rose Bowl, Henry Birks & Sons, Montreal, c.1935, 9½ In.	619.00
Salt Cellar, Poul Petersen, Montreal, c.1953, 4 In., Pair	185.00
Salver, Presentation, Savage & Lyman, Montreal, c.1868, 8 In.	1858.00
Tablespoon, Fiddle Pattern, Robert Hendery, Montreal, c.1860, 6 Piece	227.00
Tea Set, Henry Birks & Sons, Montreal, c.1901, 3 Piece	289.00
Tray, Serving, Inscribed, Roden Bros., Toronto, c.1929, 28 In.	1445.00

SILVER-CEYLON

Box, Humidor, Anglo Indian, Ebony, c.1840, 10 x 5½ In.	399.00

SILVER-CHINESE

Basket, Handle, 6½ In.	250.00
Bowl, Openwork, Repousse, Dragon, Early 20th Century, 2¾ x 5¼ In.	568.00
Bowl, Repousse, Court Scenes, Tripod Wood Stand, 29 x 17 In.	3304.00
Candy Dish, Pierced Flowers, Bamboo, Footed Caddy, 10 In.	550.00
Card Case, Reticulated Bamboo, Heart, Chinese Characters, Gilt Trim, 3¼ In. .... illus	263.00
Censer, Gold, Reticulated Floral, Cranes Wading In Water, Early 1900s, 4 x 6 In.	1650.00
Condiment, Figural, Cart With Pole, Balanced Salt Basket, Pepper Castor, 3¼ In.	440.00
Cup, Cover, Hawk Finial, Duck, Flower, c.1900, 9 In.	650.00
Fan, c.1840-50, 8⅜ In.	4500.00
Jewelry Box, Pierced Dragon, Phoenix Bird, 2¾ In.	750.00
Nutmeg Grater, Urn Shape, Bands At Shoulder, Hinged Cover, Steel Grater, 3 In. ..... illus	956.00
Pot, Wine, 19th Century, 7½ In.	450.00

Silver-Chinese, Nutmeg Grater, Urn Shape, Bands At Shoulder, Hinged Cover, Steel Grater, 3 In. $956.00

Silver-Chinese, Wine Cooler, Dragon, Ring Handles, Pail Form, Luen Hing, Shanghai, 8 In. $6600.00

Silver-Continental, Chocolate Pot, Rooster Form, Beak Spout, Claw Foot Legs, France, 9 In. $4600.00

S

Silver Numbers

Numbers, 800 or 900, are used to tell the quality of the silver in some European countries. Silver dishes marked 800 are considered solid silver and are usually German, Italian, or Russian. In the United States or England at least 925 parts out of 1,000 must be silver to be considered solid or sterling silver.

Silver-Danish, Spoon, Serrated Edge, Curved Handle, Loop & Beaded End, Georg Jensen, Pair
$460.00

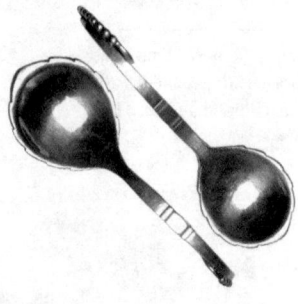

Silver-English, Basket, Cherub Medallions, Pierced & Beaded Rim, Handle, W. Hall, 1780, 14 x 10 In.
$1725.00

TIP
To clean silver, gold, or diamond jewelry, soak it in a glass of vodka overnight. But remember, discard the vodka after using it; don't drink it.

Tea Caddy, Round, Branch Decoration, Low Relief, 5½ In.	590.00
Tea Set, Bamboo Shape Handles, Spout, Finial, Marked, 5 Piece	1180.00
Trophy, 3 Handles, Iris Flower, 19th Century, 4¼ In.	675.00
Trophy, Cherry Blossom, Birds, 19th Century, 14 In.	4500.00
Wine Cooler, Dragon, Ring Handles, Pail Form, Luen Hing, Shanghai, 8 In. . . . . *illus*	6600.00

SILVER-CONTINENTAL

Beaker, Parcel Gilt, Conical, Engraved, Coat Of Arms, 1744, 7⅜ In.	5581.00
Bowl, Oval, Reclining Maiden, Grape & Leaf Edges, Late 1800s, 11¼ In.	374.00
Box, Oval, Repousse Motif, Cherubs, Floral Basket, 7½ In.	266.00
Chalice, Hammered, Enameled Medallions, Knop Stem, Arts & Crafts, c.1910, 7 In.	1150.00
Chocolate Pot, Rooster Form, Beak Spout, Claw Foot Legs, France, 9 In. . . . . *illus*	4600.00
Cigarette Case, Rectangular, Engraved Fern, Early 1900s, 4¾ x 3¼ In.	657.00
Dish, Shallow, Round, Reed & Tie Border, Early 1800s, 12½ In.	147.00
Dish, Silver Vine Lead, 19th Century, 11½ In.	333.00
Etui, Needle Case, Hardstone Mount, 19th Century, 3¾ In.	406.00
Ewer, Bombe Helmet, Heart Shape Punch, Cast Scroll Rim, 8½ In.	1058.00
Figurine, Garnitures, Pheasant, Movable Wings, Head, 13 In., Pair	1440.00
Figurine, Partridge, Removable Head, c.1925, 6½ x 4½ x 2¼ In.	550.00
Frame, Rectangular, Shell, Scroll, Flowers, Dragon Decorations, 15 x 11 In.	288.00
Gravy Boat, Lobed Lower Bowl, Gadroon Borders, Lion Mask, 5 x 9 In.	440.00
Muffineer, Urn Shape, Pierced Lid, Finial, 4 Legs, Shell Feet, 8¼ In.	470.00
Pepper Shaker, Owl, Figural, Removable Head, 3 x 3¼ In.	600.00
Serving Spoon, Oval Bowl, 1840, 14 In.	88.00
Spoon, Figural, Man With Fish, Grotesque Griffin, Scrolls, Swags, 8⅜ In.	88.00
Sugar Castor, Turned Baluster, Swirled Ribs, Eagle, 1793, 9 In.	294.00
Tray, Round, c.1930, 13 In.	234.00
Wine Coaster, Initials, Czechoslovakia, 5½ In., 4 Piece	598.00

SILVER-DANISH

Bowl, Flared Rim, Leaf & Ball Stem, Circular Foot, Georg Jensen, 5⅛ In.	999.00
Box, Georg Jensen, Copenhagen, c.1930, 1 In.	195.00
Compote, Hammered, Leaf Style Stem, Georg Jensen, Early 1900s, 5 x 5½ In.	1315.00
Cup, Cover, Pedestal, Georg Jensen, 6 x 4⅞ In., Pair	3738.00
Jug, Water, Johan Rohde, For Georg Jensen, Copenhagen, c.1944, 6½ In.	3693.00
Spoon, Jam, Curled Handle, Blossom At End, Georg Jensen, 5¼ In.	316.00
Spoon, Leaf-Shaped Bowl, Curled Beaded Handle, Georg Jensen, 7¾ In.	230.00
Spoon, Serrated Edge, Curved Handle, Loop & Beaded End, Georg Jensen, Pair . . . . . . *illus*	460.00
Spoon Set, Demitasse, Sterling, Enamel, Case, 3¾ In., 6 Piece	176.00
Table Bell, Cactus Pattern, Gundorph Albertus, Georg Jensen, Post 1945, 3 In.	324.00
Toddy Ladle, Wood Handle, Ivory Finial, Silver Gilt, Grapes, 1830, 17 In.	177.00

SILVER-DUTCH

Barge, Tow Horse, Miniature, 20th Century, 7½ In.	186.00
Basket, Pierced, Oval, Bonebakker & Zoon, c.1916, 9½ In.	350.00
Figure, Pheasant, c.1900, 24½ In.	1413.00
Kettle, Miniature, Arnoldus Van Geffen, Amsterdam, c.1742, 1½ In.	676.00
Nutmeg Grater, 19th Century, 2½ In.	416.00
Salt, Trencher, Miniature, Frederik Van Strant, Amsterdam, c.1742, 1 In.	499.00
Soup Ladle, Fiddle & Thread Pattern, c.1907, 13 In.	249.00
Vinaigrette, Sabot Shape, Animals, Birds, Flowers, 2½ x 1⅛ In.	316.00

SILVER-ENGLISH.

English sterling silver is marked with a series of four or five small hallmarks. The standing lion mark is the most commonly seen sterling quality mark. The other marks indicate the city of origin, the maker, and the year of manufacture. These dates can be verified in many good books on silver.

Basket, Charles Aldridge & Henry Green, London, 1772, 3¾ x 13 In.	819.00
Basket, Cherub Medallions, Pierced & Beaded Rim, Handle, W. Hall, 1780, 14 x 10 In. . . *illus*	1725.00
Basket, Handle, London, Georgian, 1799, 15 x 10 x 7½ In.	1800.00
Basket, Reticulated Oval, Swing Handle, Peter & Ann Bateman, George III, 6 x 6 In.	863.00
Basket, Reticulated Scroll Work, Sheffield, 1930, 8½ In.	382.00
Bell, Table, Chased & Engraved Design, Ball Finial, George II, 1734, 4¾ In.	1725.00
Bowl, 3 Handles, Charles Boyton & Son, Sheffield, Edwardian, c.1908, 10 In.	520.00
Bowl, Oval, Scroll Handles, Pedestal Base, Sheffield, Edward VII, 1905, 7 x 11 In.	633.00
Bowl, Reeded Rim, Foot, George III, 1780, 7 x 4 In.	2233.00
Bowl, Round, Scalloped Sides, Applied Scroll, Gadroon Border, c.1831, 3¾ In.	3335.00

S

Box, Heart Shape, Repousse, London, 2½ x 2½ In.	351.00
Breakfast Dish, Oval, William & George Sissons, Victorian, 1874, 11¾ In.	3262.00
Candelabra are listed in the Candelabrum category.	
Candlesticks are listed in their own category.	
Cann, Cup, Double-Scroll Handle, Engraved, George III, 1763, 3½ x 3½ In.	460.00
Card Case, Reticulated, Hinged, Swan Hallmarks, c.1845, 2½ x 3½ In.	568.00
Castor, Baluster Shape, 1914, 6⅛ In.	250.00
Castor, Baluster Shape, 1926, 6 In.	250.00
Castor, Crest, Initialed, Robert Preston, London, George III, c.1770, 5½ In.	395.00
Chatelaine, Flower Repousse, 6 Implements, CM Maker, 1896, 12 In.	1293.00
Cigar Cutter, Bakelite Cigar Holder, Compass, 3 In.	197.00
Cigar Lighter, Desk Shape, Victorian, Hubert Thornhill, c.1890, 4 In.	2683.00
Cigarette Box, Hinged Lid, Engine Turned Decor, W.H. Manton, c.1955, 2 x 3½ x 5¼ In.	323.00
Cigarette Box, Hinged Lid, Engine Turned Decor, Adie Bros., c.1956, 1¾ x 3½ x 4 In.	264.00
Cigarette Box, Hinged Lid, Engine Turned Decor, c.1939, 1½ x 3½ In.	146.00
Cigarette Box, Hinged Lid, Engine Turned Decor, Charles S. Green, c.1935, 1¼ x 6 In.	293.00
Claret Jug, Cut Glass, Repousse Scenic Mount, 11½ In.	999.00
Claret Jug, Engraved, Moorish Flowers, Geometric, 1881, 11 x 4½ x 4 In.	1495.00
Claret Jug, Lid, Vasiform, Beaded Rim, Rattan Wrapped Loop Handle, 1778, 13¼ In.	9988.00
Claret Jug, Mounted, Cut Glass, Charles Boyton, c.1898, 8¼ In.	333.00
Claret Jug, Richard Martin & Ebenezer Hall, c.1874, 11½ In.	1032.00
Coffeepot, Dome Lid, Lighthouse Form, George II, 1736, 9½ In.	4994.00
Coffeepot, Dome Lid, Tapered Cylindrical, Urn Finial, George II, 1753, 10 In.	1645.00
Coffeepot, Francis Pages, London, George II, c.1730, 8¼ In.	1871.00
Coffeepot, Tapered Cylindrical Shape, Acanthus Spout, Sheffield, 10 In.	176.00
Coffeepot, Wood Scroll Handle, Engraved, London, George II, 1748, 9½ In.	2233.00
Compote, Victorian, Messrs. Barnard, London, c.1856, 6¾ In.	291.00
Creamer, Faceted Body, Ribbed Bandwork, Basket Weave Rim, George III, c.1810	236.00
Creamer, Helmet Shape, Trumpet Foot, Square Base, Loop Handle, George III, 1796, 5 In.	206.00
Creamer, Melon Form, Scroll Bud Finial, Scroll Handle, Family Crest, Jos. Angell, 1865, 6 In.	748.00
Creamer, Pear Shape, Scroll Handle, Drake Feet, George II, 1750, 4 x 3¾ In.	259.00
Cruet Frame, Peter, Ann, Wm. Bateman, London, George III, c.1802, 10½ In.	585.00
Cup, 2 Handles, Engraved Family Armorial, James Smith, George II, 1733, 6 In.	3800.00
Cup, Caudle, Crested, Marker's Mark, Monogram, William & Mary, c.1694, 4 In.	1740.00
Cup, Vining Handles, Pedestal, c.1930, 10 x 10½ In.	627.00
Desk Set, Chased, 2 Cut Glass Inks, Candle Socket, Snuffer, London, JC NC, 1853	1092.00
Dish Entree, Cover, William Pitts & Joseph Preedy, George III, 1799, 10 In., Pair	4783.00
Ewer, Baluster, Loop Handle, Renaissance Revival, 1874, 14½ In., Pair	813.00
Fish Slice, Pointed Blade, Reticulated, Threaded Handle, George III, 11¾ In.	235.00
Flagon, Makers, Round, Repousse, W. & J. Priest, George III, c.1764, 7½ In.	1872.00
Fork, 3-Prong, Hanoverian Pattern, Crested, George II, c.1740, 7½ In., 6 Piece	883.00
Fork Set, Hester Bateman, Round Upturned Handles, Crest, George III, 12 Piece	1610.00
Goblet, Round, Bulbous, Repousse, John Angell, George III, c.1818, 5 In.	527.00
Goblet, Round, Gilded Interior, Mappin & Webb, Edward VII, c.1902, 6½ In.	176.00
Goblet, Round, Open Handle, Pedestal, Border, George III, c.1816, 7¾ In.	720.00
Hot Water Urn, George Tweedie, London, c.1778, 23 x 10½ In.	1760.00
Jug, Hot Water, Cover, Cylindrical, Reeding To Base, Flaring Foot, George IV, 1821, 9⅛ In.	940.00
Jug, Hot Water, Fluted Vase Form, Pineapple Finial, Pedestal Foot, George III, 14¾ In.	3000.00
Jug, Hot Water, Sheffield, Edwardian, c.1901, 9 In.	330.00
Ladle, Downturned Tipt Back, Rounded Handle, George III, 1700s, 12¾ In.	201.00
Letter Rack, Pierced, Birmingham, Edwardian, c.1904, 4½ In.	1247.00
Marrow Scoop, Hester Bateman, George III, 9 In. *illus*	748.00
Marrow Spoon, Double, Pattern Back Design, George II, c.1756, 8¼ In.	230.00
Mug, James Charles Edington, London, c.1852, 3¾ In.	520.00
Mug, Thomas Rush, London, George II, c.1739, 4 In.	624.00
Napkin Rings are listed in their own category.	
Nipple Shield, Round, Upturned, Thomas & James Phipps II, 1¼ x 2¼ In.	460.00
Pitcher, Pear Shape, Cast Scroll Handle, Coat Of Arms, George II, 1749, 8 In.	9988.00
Pitcher, Round Foot, Bulbous Body, Flaring Rim, Elizabeth II, c.1962, 12½ In.	767.00
Place Card Holders, Owl Shape, S. Mordan & Co., Ltd., c.1910, 8 Piece	1287.00
Punch Bowl, Dragon, Banner, Straps & Daggers, Domed Base, George IV, 7 x 10 In.	6900.00
Rose Bowl, Engraved, Birmingham, c.1937, 9 In.	330.00
Salt, Crested, John Eames, London, George III, c.1804, 5¼ In., Pair	395.00
Salt, London, George III, c.1772, 3 In., Pair	206.00
Salt Cellar, Shell Form, 3-Footed, Marked Birmingham, 1897, 2 In.	525.00
Salt Set, Shell Shape, 3 Ball Feet, Fitted Case, M. Boulton, Birmingham, 2 In., 4 Piece	528.00

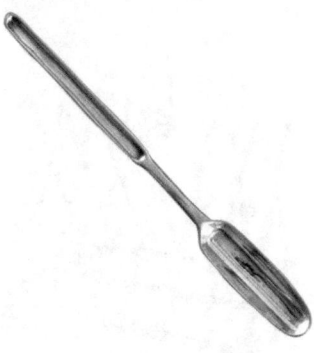

Silver-English, Marrow Scoop, Hester Bateman, George III, 9 In.
$748.00

Silver-English, Salver, Lion, Cartouche, Shell Piecrust Rim, 3-Footed, E. Coker, London, 1763, 7¼ In.
$1035.00

Silver-English, Sauceboat, Shell Shape, C.F. Kandler, London, George II, 1747, 7 In., Pair
$15535.00

Silver-English, Teapot, Hinged Lid, Wood Finial & Handle, Henry Chawner, London, 1810, 5¾ In.
$538.00

S

Silver-English, Toast Rack,
Crossed Croquet Mallets,
Angular Handle, Ball Feet, 6 x 6 In.
$110.00

Silver-English, Vinaigrette,
Barrel Shape, 2 Compartments,
Knob & Chain, S. Mordan,
London, 1¾ In.
$508.00

Silver-English, Vinaigrette,
Bright Cut Scrolls, Pierced Gilt Floral
Grill, John Shaw, Birmingham, 1 In.
$237.00

Salver, Birmingham, c.1930, 11¾ In.	410.00
Salver, Chester, Engraved, c.1924, 13½ In.	475.00
Salver, Crested, Edward Hutton, London, c.1889, 8 In.	499.00
Salver, Double Sunburst Mark, Chased, Engraved, Piecrust Rim, Sheffield, Georgian, 21 In.	1528.00
Salver, Engraved Crest, Floral, Scrollwork, Ball & Claw Feet, George II, 1780, 8 In.	546.00
Salver, Lion, Cartouche, Shell Piecrust Rim, 3-Footed, E. Coker, London, 1763, 7¼ In. *illus*	1035.00
Salver, Martin Hall & Co., Ltd, Sheffield, Edwardian, c.1904, 14½ In.	728.00
Salver, Octagonal, Walker & Hall, Sheffield, c.1925, 7¾ In.	354.00
Salver, Reeded Rim, Flower Swag Rim, 1782, 12 In.	1880.00
Salver, Robert Rogers, Maker, Round, 3 Ball & Claw Feet, George III, c.1774, 8 In.	936.00
Salver, Round, Scallop & Shell Border, Dennis Langton, George II, 1738, 6¼ In.	748.00
Salver, S.C. Younge & Co., Sheffield, George IV, c.1824, 10½ In.	924.00
Sauce Ladle, Geo. Baskerville, London, George III, c.1782, 6½ In.	117.00
Sauceboat, Crested, Paul Crespin, London, George II, c.1744, 9¼ In.	5653.00
Sauceboat, Gadroon Edge, S-Scroll Handle, George III, c.1763, 4 x 8½ In., Pair	2645.00
Sauceboat, Oval, Shaped Rim, Flared Spout, Scroll Handles, George III, 7½ In., Pair	1680.00
Sauceboat, Shell Shape, C.F. Kandler, London, George II, 1747, 7 In., Pair *illus*	15535.00
Saucepan, Wood Handle, Edward Fernell, London, George III, c.1784, 12¼ In.	924.00
Service Plate, Engraved Armorial, Serpentine Rim, George V, 11½ In., 2 Piece	708.00
Serving Spoon, Fiddle & Thread, William Eaton, c.1845, 12½ In.	326.00
Serving Spoon, Old English, Thomas Chawner, George III, c.1776, 11¼ In.	196.00
Skewer, Meat, Initialed, Mary Chawner, London, William IV, 1835, 13 In.	239.00
Spoon, Seal Top, Leopard's Head Hallmark In Bowl, London, c.1600	1200.00
Spoon Set, Coffee, Wakely & Wheeler, c.1896, 4⅝ In., 12 Piece	117.00
Spoon Set, Rounded Down Turned Handles, Bateman, George III, 12 Piece	1840.00
Stuffing Spoon, Old English Pattern, P., W. & A. Bateman, London, Pair	180.00
Sugar, Dome Lid, Drapery Swags, Glass Liner, Edward VII, 1905, 6 In., Pair	323.00
Sugar, Gilt Sterling Lid, Rim, Joseph Willmore, c.1817, 6 x 5¾ In.	108.00
Sugar & Creamer, Ball Feet, Gilt Interior, Engraved Border, c.1808, 4 x 8 In.	274.00
Sugar Basket, Urn Shape, Beaded Swing Handle, Cobalt Blue Liner, 5¾ In.	1880.00
Sugar Castor, Vase Shape, J. Rodgers & Sons, Edwardian, 1907, 7½ In.	174.00
Sugar Tongs, Cymric, Liberty & Co., London, 1899, 3½ In.	92.00
Tankard, Dome Lid, Serpentine Handle, Trefoil Thumbpiece, George III, 1800, 7¼ In.	1763.00
Tankard, Tapered, C-Scroll Handle, Dome Lid, Engraved Crest, George II, 7½ In.	690.00
Tea & Coffee Set, Kettle, Stand, Birmingham, c.1920, 6 Piece	1521.00
Tea & Coffee Set, Pear Shape, Swan Neck Spouts, Dome Lids, R. Comyns, c.1950, 6 Piece	7200.00
Tea Caddy, Crested, Initials, George I, c.1715, 5 In.	2392.00
Tea Caddy, Dome Lid, Oval, Fruitwood Finial, Reeded Rims, George III, 1795, 4¾ In.	764.00
Tea Caddy, Oval, Beaded Border, Engraved Floral Bands, William Abdy, 1788, 5½ x 6 In.	2990.00
Tea Caddy Spoon, Fiddle Shell, J. Taylor & S. Knight, Georgian, 3½ In., 2 Piece	998.00
Tea Set, Gadroon, Acanthus Paw Feet, Naphtali Hart, 1821, 3 Piece	2950.00
Tea Set, Neoclassical Style, Engraved, Monogram, George III, 3 Piece	978.00
Teapot, Armorial, Oval, Reed Foot, Ebonized Handle, Finial, Georgian, 5¼ In.	117.00
Teapot, Elongated Oval, Ebony Handle, Mappin & Webb, Sheffield, c.1951, 5¾ In.	333.00
Teapot, Flat Lid, Oval, Straight Spout, Fruitwood Ear Handle, Finial, George III, 4½ In.	382.00
Teapot, Fluted Baluster Shape, Wood Handle, George III, 1819, 6½ In.	359.00
Teapot, George Baskerville, Maker, Oval, Fluted, George II, c.1818, 6½ In.	468.00
Teapot, George III, Digby Scott & Benjamin Smith II, London, c.1803, 10 In.	5612.00
Teapot, Hinged Lid, Wood Finial & Handle, Henry Chawner, London, 1810, 5¾ In. *illus*	538.00
Teapot, Monogram, Goddehere & Wigan, Georgian, c.1793, 5 x 3½ In.	468.00
Teapot, Victorian, Augustus George Piesse, London, 1865, 4½ In.	385.00
Teaspoon Set, Old English Pattern, Bateman, George III, c.1785, 4¾ In., 6 Piece	312.00
Toast Rack, Crossed Croquet Mallets, Angular Handle, Ball Feet, 6 x 6 In. *illus*	110.00
Toast Rack, John Emes, London, George III, 1802, 6½ In.	435.00
Toast Rack, Robert Harper, London, Victorian, c.1860, 6½ In.	676.00
Toast Rack, Round, Wire Form, Rectangular Base, Scroll Feet, 5 x 6¼ In.	920.00
Toddy Ladle, Coin Inset, Baleen Handle, George III, 14 In.	200.00
Tray, Gadroon Rim, Greek Key Band, Reeded Handle, Oval, George III, 1804, 18½ In.	3290.00
Tray, Gadroon Rim, Handles, Wreath Engraved, Oval, George III, 9¾ In.	2938.00
Tray, Gadroon Rim, Scroll Handles, Robert Hennell II, George IV, 29 x 17 In.	3840.00
Tray, Scalloped Rim, Nasturtiums, Art Nouveau, Comyns & Sons, 1903, 7 x 11 In.	176.00
Tray, Serving, Crested, Inscribed, Barker Brothers, Ltd., c.1889, 24¾ In.	1455.00
Tray, Tea, Pierced Rim, 2 Handles, London, Oval, Edwardian, 1905, 28 x 16 In.	3055.00
Tureen, Cover, Dolphin Form Finial, Coat Of Arms, George III, 15 In.	8225.00
Tureen, Sauce, Oval, Footed, 1800, Pair	4140.00
Urn, Cover, William IV, Gilt, Floral Finial, Oystershell Cover, c.1837, 17 x 11 In.	6900.00

Vinaigrette, Barrel Shape, 2 Compartments, Knob & Chain, S. Mordan, London, 1¾ In. *illus*   508.00
Vinaigrette, Bright Cut Scrolls, Pierced Gilt Floral Grill, John Shaw, Birmingham, 1 In. *illus*   237.00
Vinaigrette, Gold Vermeil, Raised Flowers, c.1814, 1¼ x 1½ In. 657.00
Vinaigrette, Pierced, Fire Gilded, Hinge Grille, Birmingham, Jos. Wilmore, 1833, 1¼ In. 245.00
Waiter, J.B. Chatterley & Sons, Birmingham, c.1914, 14½ In. 457.00
Wine Coaster, Ball & Claw Feet, George III, 1767, 2⅜ x 5½ In. 975.00
Wine Coaster, Crested, Edward Leapidge, London, George III, 1777, 5 In. 870.00
Wine Coaster, Gadroon Rim, Turned Wooden Base, Sheffield, 5¹¹⁄₁₆ In. 90.00
Wine Coaster, Pierced, Crested, Hester Bateman, George III, c.1777, 4½ In. 832.00
Wine Funnel, Crested, Hester Bateman, London, George III, 1782, 5¼ In. 1033.00
Wine Funnel, Elizabeth Morley, London, George III, c.1810, 6½ In. 1143.00

SILVER-FRENCH

Basket, Decorative Strawberries, Vermeil, Cartier, 3 x 2 In., Pair 878.00
Basket, Reticulated, Footed, Scalloped Edge, 1800s, 3½ x 12½ In. 311.00
Box, Daphnis Et Chloe, After Pillet, c.1900, 3 In. 413.00
Box, Rounded Rectangular, Engraved, Musical Instrument & Fire, Scrolls, c.1825, 3 x 2 In. .   546.00
Bread Basket, Ram's Head, Garland Swags, Embossed Landscape, 12 x 6½ x 2½ In. 800.00
Cordial Set, Hemispherical Bowl, Acanthus Stem, Round Base, 3¾ In., 12 Piece 403.00
Cup, Bell Shape, Embossed, Stars, Domed Foot, Louis XV/XVI, 3⅜ In. 323.00
Dish, Leaf Shape, 3 Ball Feet, Cartier, 3¾ x 4¼ In., Pair 230.00
Dish, Meat, Oval, Running Anthemion Border, c.1838, 18 x 12 In. 1116.00
Goblet, Crested, Odiot, Paris, 19th Century, 6 In., Pair 191.00
Holder, Shopping Bag Shape, 2 Rope Twist Handles, Cartier, 3¾ In. ....*illus*   179.00
Jug, Hot Water, Turned Wood Handle, Paris, Late 19th Century, 7 In. 500.00
Knife, Folding, 2 Blades, Fruit Hallmarked, Steel Blade, Pearl Panels, 1700s 285.00
Money Clip, Pocket, Sundial, Compass, c.1850, 1½ x 2 In. 250.00
Sauce, Oval, Short Spout, Cattail Ear Handle, Louis XV, Paris, c.1745, 5⅜ x 9 In., Pair 6463.00
Tea & Coffee Set, Coffeepot, Teapot, Covered Sugar, Creamer, Tray, Puiforcat, 4 Piece 9560.00
Vase, Chevrons, Stylized Leaves, Oval, Stepped Neck & Base, Christofle, c.1935, 9¾ In. ..*illus*   1315.00
Vase, Marble Base, Triangular, Adolphe Truffier, c.1925, 8½ In. 4200.00
Vinaigrette, Engraved, Chased, 3 Vermeil Birds, Hinged Front, 1800s, 1½ x 1 In. 717.00
Wine Taster, Inscribed Georget Ronot Alox, c.1875, 4¼ x 3¼ In. 201.00
Wine Taster, Snake Form Handle, 5 Franc Coin Base, 3¼ x 4 x 1 In. 350.00

SILVER-GERMAN

Basket, Reticulated Border, Scrolls, Grapevines, 4-Footed, 7¾ In. 224.00
Bowl, Acanthus Feet, Flared Rim, 9½ In. 384.00
Bowl, Inscribed, c.1935, 10¾ In. 395.00
Bowl, Pierced, Early 20th Century, 2½ x 10 In. 234.00
Bowl, Square, Engraved, Dresden, Late 19th Century, 12 x 12 In. 227.00
Cigarette Case, Enameled, Early 20th Century, 3½ In. 676.00
Cruet Stand, Rococo Revival, Etched Glass Bottles, Figures, Putti, c.1875, 11½ In. 1998.00
Figure, Pheasant, Early 20th Century, 18¾ In. 924.00
Nautilus Shell, Silvered Metal Mount, 16th Century, 11¾ In., Pair 600.00
Planter, Round, 3 Horn Handles, 3 Ball Feet, Wilhelm Binder, 8½ x 10½ In. 2990.00
Platter, Oval, Engraved, Munich, 1768, 17¾ In. 1528.00
Trophy Cup, Gothic Revival, Gilt, Lobed, Tall Finial, Lobed Foot, c.1888, 19 In. 764.00
Wedding Cup, Lady, Removable Head, Touchmarks, c.1850, 10¼ In. 1150.00

SILVER-IRISH

Bowl, Crested, David King, Dublin, George I, 1723, 6¾ In. 9785.00
Cream Jug, Crested, John Hamilton, George II, c.1740, 4 In. 1740.00
Creamer, Helmet Shape, Dublin, 1750, 5 In. 1440.00
Dish Ring, Crested, Edmond Johnson Jr., Dublin, Edwardian, c.1905, 8¼ In. 1848.00
Fruit Basket, Basket Weave, Rope Twist Rim, Openwork Swing Handle, 13 In. 1645.00
Ladle, Shell Shape Bowl, Engraved Handle, Mid 18th Century, 14½ In. ....*illus*   274.00
Sauceboat, 3-Footed, Dimensional Faces, Late 19th Century, 3¼ x 8 In., Pair 1494.00
Skewer, Meat, Crested, Samuel Neville, Dublin, George III, c.1802, 11¾ In. 436.00
Stuffing Spoon, Engraved Family Crest, Samuel Neville, 1799-1800, 12 In. 275.00
Sugar, Basket, Crested, Initialed, Dublin, George III, c.1790, 7 In. 624.00
Tablespoon Set, Hanoverian Pattern, Crested, George III, c.1780, 8 Piece 815.00

SILVER-ITALIAN

Salt & Pepper, Buccellati, Mushroom Shape, 3 x 4 In. 1638.00
Salt Cellar, Spoon, Fish Shape, Gilt Shell Bowl, Tiffany, 1900s, 3 In., Pair 660.00

Silver-French, Holder, Shopping Bag
Shape, 2 Rope Twist Handles,
Cartier, 3¾ In.
$179.00

Silver-French, Vase, Chevrons,
Stylized Leaves, Oval,
Stepped Neck & Base, Christofle,
c.1935, 9¾ In.
$1315.00

Silver-Irish, Ladle,
Shell Shape Bowl, Engraved Handle,
Mid 18th Century, 14½ In.
$274.00

S

Silver-Japanese, Cocktail Shaker, Hammered, Applied Dragons, Cylindrical, Tapered, Bisansha, 8 In. $508.00

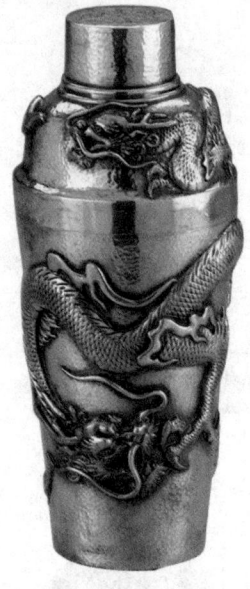

Silver-Mexican, Coffee Set, William Spratling, c.1965, 8¼-In. Pot, 5 Piece $4500.00

Silver-Mexican, Pitcher, Shouldered, Chased Rim, Handle & Foot, 20th Century, 11 In. $448.00

SILVER-JAPANESE

Box, Embossed, Hammered, Dragon, 1868-1926, 3 x 9 In.	1998.00
Cocktail Shaker, Hammered, Applied Dragons, Cylindrical, Tapered, Bisansha, 8 In. . . *illus*	508.00
Koro, Enamel, Ivory, Shibayama Style, Dragon Handles, Flower Finial, 8¼ In.	4130.00
Punch Bowl, Sterling, Iris Floral Relief, Signed, Kakitsubaki, 12 x 6 In.	4388.00
Rose Bowl, Miyamoto, Tokyo, 1920s, 8½ In., Pair	1351.00
Tea Set, Lid, Pot, Creamer, Sugar, Waste Bowl, Kettle, Lampstand, Tray, Asahi, 6 Piece	1860.00

SILVER-LAOTIAN

Bowl, Stem, Repousse Reserves, Figures, 9¾ x 9¾ In.	224.00

SILVER-MEXICAN

Ashtray, Round, 3 Scrolled Feet, Hallmark, Spratling, c.1963, 4 In.	294.00
Bowl, Charger, Sterling, Lobed Center, Repousse Roses, Serpentine Edge, 17 In.	944.00
Box, Casket Form, Hinged, William Spratling, c.1942, 2⅜ x 3⅜ In.	705.00
Candlestick, Flared Holder, Petal Foot, William Spratling, c.1942, 2 In., Pair	2880.00
Cockerel, Gilt, Inset Ruby Cabochon Eyes, 20th Century, 16 In.	1298.00
Coffee Set, William Spratling, c.1965, 8-¼ In. Pot, 5 Piece . *illus*	4500.00
Coffee Set, Wood Side Handle, Open Sugar, William Spratling, c.1967, 3 Piece	3900.00
Coffeepot, Fluted, 8 x 12 In.	220.00
Dish, Lid Rectangular, Scalloped Edge, 2 Handle Lid, Sanborns, 11 x 7 In.	690.00
Dish, Rectangular, Scalloped Rim, L. Maciel, 14¼ In.	489.00
Ice Bucket, Baroque Style, Sterling, Parcel Gilt, Octagonal, Tane, 1900s, 8 In.	1770.00
Pitcher, Shouldered, Chased Rim, Handle & Foot, 20th Century, 11 In. . *illus*	448.00
Pitcher, Water, Lobed Pear Shaped Body, Reticulated Scroll Supports, 8 In.	521.00
Punch Cup Set, Scrolling Band, C-Scroll Handle, Tray, 11½ In., 7 Piece	206.00
Salad Set, Rope Design, Split Curl Ends, Hector Aguilar, 8⅝ x 8¾ In.	529.00
Service Plate, Serpentine Corners, 20th Century, 12 In., 12 Piece	3658.00
Serving Dish, Open, Oval, Scalloped Rim, Sanborns, 12¾ In.	345.00
Serving Fork, Handwrought, 4-Tine, Reticulated Scrollwork, 11 In.	59.00
Sugar & Creamer, C-Shape Hardwood Handles, Ball Finial, Spratling, Taxco, c.1935	2938.00
Tea Set, Scrolled Band, Shaped Handle, Liceves, 9-In. Pot, 3 Piece . *illus*	687.00
Tray, Floral Repousse Edge, Center, L. Maciel, 20th Century, 16 In.	448.00
Tray, Round, Rope Turned Edge, Spratling, Taxco, 3½ In.	59.00

SILVER-MIDDLE EASTERN

Dog Collar, Handwrought, Wirework, Flower Clasp, 1 x 11 In.	411.00

SILVER-NORWEGIAN

Pepperettes, Penguin Shape, David Andersen, 1920s, 2 In., Pair	431.00

SILVER-PERUVIAN

Charger, Shaped Border, Center Repousse, Coat Of Arms, 1900s, 16½ In.	295.00
Vase, Man's Head, Repousse, Handwrought, c.1935, 10¼ In.	3000.00

SILVER-PORTUGUESE

Basket, Fruit, Oval, Navettes Border, Reeded Band, Low Foot, Swing Handle, 1886, 12 In.	176.00
Bowl, 2 Handles, Crested, Tottenham Green, c.1700, 12 In.	6088.00
Oval, Pointed Scallop Rim, Shells, Swags, Shell-Shaped Trim, 1886, 11 In.	264.00
Pitcher, Water, Baluster Form, S-Scroll Rim, Loop Handle, Classical Style, 10¾ In.	881.00
Platter, Oval, Raised Ridge, 4 Scrolls, 20th Century, 16 In.	206.00
Salver, Round, Overlapping Daisies, Leafy Scroll Feet, 1836, 11¾ In.	118.00
Tea Set, Lid, Pear Shape Teapot, S-Scrolls, Acanthus, Acorn Finials, 5 Piece	2468.00

SILVER-RUSSIAN. Russian silver is marked with the Cyrillic, or Russian, alphabet. The numbers 84, 88, or 91 indicate the silver content. Russian silver may be higher or lower than sterling standard. Other marks indicate maker, assayer, or city of manufacture. Many pieces of silver made in Russia are decorated with enamel. Faberge pieces are listed in their own category.

Belt, Niello, Mounted, St. Petersburg, c.1900	310.00
Biscuit Jar, Hinged Cover, Barrel Form, Engraved, Swing Handle, 1856, 7½ In.	1645.00
Bowl, Flared Rim, Trumpet Foot, Beaded Rims, Crest, Motto, c.1785, 7 In.	881.00
Box, Cover, Medallion, Sunburst, Laurel, Niello, Gilt, Marked, 3⅜ In. Diam.	2700.00
Box, Raised Relief, Birds In Leaves, 1 x 4 x 6¼ In.	380.00
Cigarette Box, Gold Inscription, S.N. Matusovski, 4½ In.	354.00

S

Cigarette Case, Cigar Band Lid Cover, Oblong, Engraved Shoulders, 4¾ x 2¾ In.	441.00
Cigarette Case, Cloisonne, Swan Swimming In Pond, Flowers Scroll, 4 x 3 In.	233.00
Cigarette Case, Engraved Flower Stem, Cartouches, Egyptian Revival, 4¾ In.	200.00
Cigarette Case, Warrior & Blacksmith, Cyrillic Writing, 4¼ x 3¼ In.	377.00
Creamer, Melon Ribbed, Flared, Scroll Edges, Leaves Around Base, Twig Handle, 1855 *illus*	777.00
Crucifix, Embossed Scenes, Life Of Christ, Cherubs, Domed Foot, 1854, 13¾ In.	2233.00
Decanter Stand, Oval Tray, Shaped Border, Circular Grapevine, 11¼ In.	1298.00
Ladle, Enameled, Bulbous Bowl, Reeded Panels, Shaped Handle, c.1900, 7 In.	6900.00
Salt Cellar, Bands, Flowers, Cyrillic Script, Nazarov, Moscow, 1873, 3 x 3 In. ....*illus*	717.00
Spoon, Gilt, Painted Enamel, Moscow, c.1900, 5½ In. .... 197.00 to 261.00	
Sugar, Cloisonne Enameled, Scroll Filled Teardrops, Squat Oval, Swing Handle, 3⅝ In.	1410.00
Sugar & Creamer, Cloisonne, Green, Purple, Swing Handle, Gold Wash, 2⅛ In.	4406.00
Tablespoon, Spiral Fluted Stem, Teardrop Shaped Bowl, Engraved, Enameled, ⅞ In.	176.00
Tankard, Cylindrical, Peaked Domed, Lobed Lid, Raised Diamonds, Moscow, 1851, 8½ In. ..	4700.00
Teapot, Neoclassical, Palmette & Shell Band, Ivory Handle & Finial, I.S. Gubkin, Moscow, 1837 *illus*	1075.00

SILVER-SCANDINAVIAN

Bowl, Center, Pedestal, Greek Key, E. Fleming, Atelier Borgila, Stockholm, 1937, 4 x 9 In. *illus*	1725.00

SILVER-SCOTTISH

Quaich, Provincial, Initialed, Donald Fraser, Inverness, c.1820, 5 In.	4365.00
Salver, Serpentine Border, Engraved Flowers, Scrolls, George III, c.1765, 8 In.	885.00
Spoon Set, Rounded Downturned Handles, c.1785, 8½ In., 4 Piece	316.00
Stuffing Spoon, Script Monogram, Edinburgh, 1800, 14 In.	402.00
Teapot, Paneled, Chased Scrolls, Openwork Foot, William Marshall & Sons, 1881, 7 In. .*illus*	400.00

SILVER-SIAMESE

Box, Presentation, Niello, Hinged Lid, Scenic Landscape, 1900s, 8 x 5 In.	148.00

SILVER-SPANISH

Pheasants, 20th Century, 13 In., Pair	330.00
Stirrup, Colonial, Engraved, 19th Century, 9¼ In.	391.00

SILVER-STERLING. Sterling silver is made with 925 parts silver out of 1,000 parts of metal. The word *sterling* is a quality guarantee used in the United States after about 1860. The word was used much earlier in England and Ireland. Pieces listed here are not identified by country. Other pieces of sterling quality silver are listed under Silver-American, Silver-English, etc.

Bowl, Center, Round, Overlapping Border, Pierced, Flowers, 12 & 16 In., 2 Piece	3600.00
Bread & Butter Plate, Scalloped Rim, Chased, Floral Swags, c.1900, 6 In., 13 Piece	2415.00
Caddy Spoon, Fiddle & Thread Handle, Shell Shape Bowl, 3¼ In.	259.00
Candelabra are listed in the Candelabrum category.	
Candlesticks are listed in their own category.	
Candy Dish, Footed, Round, 3¼ x 6 In.	60.00
Chalice, Chased, Latin Motto, Hallmark, S & Co., Lion, Shepheard & Co., 4 x 4½ In.	2280.00
Cigar Cutter, Golf Bag Shape, 5½ In.	430.00
Cigarette Box, Cut Glass, Rectangular, Vertical Navette, Early 1900s, 6¼ In.	570.00
Cigarette Case, Art Deco, 14K Gold, Engraved, Rose, Gold Bands, 4 In.	60.00
Cigarette Case, Bakelite, Oriental Design, Seal, 1920	234.00
Cigarette Case, Graf-Und-Stift, Car, Hinged, Push Button, 1923, 3⅛ x 4⅞ x ⅜ In.	974.00
Cigarette Case, Mythical Figures, Ocean, Shell, c.1884, 4½ x 3¼ In.	310.00
Coaster, Bottle, George III, Ball & Claw Feet, England, 1767, 2⅜ x 5½ In.	975.00
Coaster, Round, Scrolled Border, Openwork Sides, Raised Detail, 7½ In., Pair	173.00
Cocktail Shaker, Round, Handle, Pouring Spout, Monogram, 10½ In.	585.00
Compote, Grape Bunch Decoration, Monogram, 6⅜ x 6¼ In.	300.00
Cup, Commemorative, St. Patrick's Day, Enameled Shamrock, 1901, 2½ In.	259.00
Cup, Cover, 2 Handles, Urn Shape, Domed, Round Base, Bead Border, c.1902, 16 In.	1800.00
Dish, Entree, Georgian Style, Reeded Edge, Removable Leaf & Scroll Handle, 12½ In.	1495.00
Fish Set, Carved Mother-Of-Pearl Handles, Ferrules, HG, Box, 1895	245.00
Fish Set, Ivory, Silver Ferrules, Plain Handles, Engraved Tines, Blade, Case, 24 Piece	450.00
Flask, Floral Design, Hammered, c.1930, 6 x 3 In.	82.00
Goblet, Water, Bell Shape, Pedestal Base, 20th Century, 7 In., 12 Piece	1175.00
Gravy Boat, Undertray, Oval, Floral Repousse Sprays, Mid 20th Century, 4 x 8 In.	499.00
Honey Jar, Amethyst Glass, Beehive Shape, Etched, c.1925, 3 x 3¾ In.	558.00
Jar, Dresser, Crystal, 2 x 3¼ In. & 6¾ x 4¾ In., 2 Piece	146.00

Silver-Mexican, Tea Set, Scrolled Band, Shaped Handle, Liceves, 9-In. Pot, 3 Piece
$687.00

Silver-Russian, Creamer, Melon Ribbed, Flared, Scroll Edges, Leaves Around Base, Twig Handle, 1855
$777.00

Silver-Russian, Salt Cellar, Bands, Flowers, Cyrillic Script, Nazarov, Moscow, 1873, 3 x 3 In.
$717.00

Silver-Russian, Teapot, Neoclassical, Palmette & Shell Band, Ivory Handle & Finial, I.S. Gubkin, Moscow, 1837
$1075.00

Silver-Scandinavian, Bowl, Center, Pedestal, Greek Key, E. Fleming, Atelier Borgila, Stockholm, 1937, 4 x 9 In. $1725.00

Silver-Scottish, Teapot, Paneled, Chased Scrolls, Openwork Foot, William Marshall & Sons, 1881, 7 In. $400.00

Silver-Sterling, Nutmeg Grater, Chased Scrolls & Flowers, Vase Shape, Screw Cover, Steel Grater, 2 In. $1673.00

Sinclaire, Vase, Cover, Allover Engraved Flowers & Leaves, Signed, 14½ In., Pair $115.00

Meat Cover, Tray, Round, Reeded Borders, Applied 18K Gold Monogram	920.00
Mustard Pot, Glass, Reticulated Round Frame, Scroll Handle, Hinged, 2½ In.	47.00
Nail File, American Indian Handle, 5 In.	55.00
Napkin Rings are listed in their own category.	
Nutmeg Grater, Chased Scrolls & Flowers, Vase Shape, Screw Cover, Steel Grater, 2 In. *illus*	1673.00
Pastry Server, Art Nouveau Style, 9⅞ In.	351.00
Porringer, Celtic Knot On Handle, Raised Lip, Arts & Crafts, 1921, 4 x 2 In.	382.00
Salt, Figural Supports, Gilt Interior, 6 Oz., Pair	212.00
Skimmer, Wood Handle, 18th Century, 18¼ In.	165.00
Spoon, Souvenir, see Souvenir category.	
Stuffing Spoon, Fiddle Pattern, Engraved, Initials MW, c.1846, 12 In.	230.00
Table Ornament, Pheasant, 20th Century, 18 In., Pair	2360.00
Tablespoon, Fiddle Pattern, Engraved TBA, Pseudo Hallmarks, 8½ In., 3 Piece	288.00
Tea & Coffee Set, Jack Shepard, Fisher, 4 Piece	420.00
Teapot, Art Deco, Cabochon Agate Finial, c.1930	212.00
Teaspoon Set, Upturned Fiddle Ends, Monogram, G. Heller, 5⅝ In., 5 Piece	165.00
Toothpick, Salt, Pepper, Damask, Gadroon, 4 Piece	35.00
Tray, Serving, 2 Handles, Chased, Ornate Rim, Oval, Flower Heads, 32 x 22 In.	3290.00
Tray, Tea, Presentation, Oval, Applied Leaves, Angular Handles, Engraved, 1906, 33 In.	6600.00
Trophy, State Fair, Bronze, Decorated, Silver Crest, 7 x 13 In.	205.00
Vase, Stand, Round, Pierced, Cornucopia, Flowers Baskets, Tapering, 17 In.	5040.00
Vase, Trumpet, Weighted Base, 2½ x 11 In.	263.00
Wine Coaster, Raised Bacchanalia Decoration, 5 x 5 In.	439.00

SILVER-THAI

Bowl, Rice, Jataka Theme, Repousse, Northern Thailand, 1900s, 10½ In.	300.00

SINCLAIRE cut glass was made by H.P. Sinclaire and Company of Corning, New York, between 1904 and 1929. He cut glass made at other factories until 1920. Pieces were made of crystal as well as amber, blue, green, or ruby glass. Only a small percentage of Sinclaire glass is marked with the S in a wreath.

Salt & Pepper, Pressed Glass, Diamond Quilted, Tin Plate Brass Cap, c.1929, 1¾ In.	22.00
Vase, Celeste Blue, Floral, Intaglio Cut, Silver Band, Rolled Rim, c.1929, 7½ x 3¼ In.	495.00
Vase, Cover, Allover Engraved Flowers & Leaves, Signed, 14½ In., Pair *illus*	115.00

SKIING, *see Sports category.*

SLAG GLASS resembles a marble cake. It can be streaked with different colors. There were many types made from about 1880. Caramel slag is the incorrect name for Chocolate glass. Pink slag was an American product made by Harry Bastow and Thomas E.A. Dugan at Indiana, Pennsylvania, about 1900. Purple and blue slag were made in American and English factories in the 1880s. Red slag is a very late Victorian and twentieth-century glass. Other colors are known but are of less importance to the collector. New versions of chocolate glass and colored slag glass are being made.

Blue, Toothpick, 3 Kittens, 2 In.	14.95
Caramel Slag is listed in the Imperial Glass category.	
Green, Vase, 12 In.	135.00
Purple, Box, Cover, Bee Finial, 5½ In.	125.00
Purple, Compote, Cover, Early 20th Century, 9 In.	71.00
Purple, Cruet, Stopper, 1970s, 7 In.	65.00
Purple, Platter, Raindrop, Notched Rim	150.00
Purple, Pokal, Cover, 9½ In.	150.00
Purple, Syrup	100.00

SLEEPY EYE collectors look for anything bearing the image of the nineteenth-century Indian chief with the drooping eyelid. The Sleepy Eye Milling Co., Sleepy Eye, Minnesota, used his portrait in advertising from 1883 to 1921. It offered many premiums, including stoneware and pottery steins, crocks, bowls, mugs, and pitchers, all decorated with the famous profile of the Indian. The popular pottery was made by Western Stoneware, Weir Pottery Company, and other companies long after the flour mill went out of business in 1921. Reproductions of the pitchers are being made today. The original pitchers came in only five sizes: 4 inches, 5¼ inches, 6½ inches, 8 inches, and 9 inches. The Sleepy Eye image was also used by companies unrelated to the flour mill.

Cookbook, Loaf Of Bread	105.00
Crock, Butter, Blue & Cream, Old Sleepy Eye, 5 x 6½ In.	605.00
Letter Opener, Sleepy Eye Mill Co., Bronze, 8 In.	413.00
Mug, Blue & White, 4¼ In.	120.00 to 145.00
Mug, Brown Chestnut, 1952, 22 Oz.	110.00
Mug, Indian, Blue & Yellow, Old Sleepy Eye, 4⅜ In.	110.00
Paperweight, Commemorative, Brown, 1979	33.00
Paperweight, Indian Bust, Copper Flashed, Old Sleepy Eye, 3 In.	330.00
Pitcher, Blue & Gray, No. 5, 9 In.	475.00
Pitcher, Blue & White, No. 2, 5¼ In.	110.00 to 325.00
Pitcher, Blue & White, No. 3, 6½ In.	140.00 to 150.00
Pitcher, Blue & White, No. 3, Marked, WSCO	325.00
Pitcher, Blue & White, No. 4, 8 In.	*illus* 145.00
Pitcher, Blue & White, No. 5, 9 In.	250.00
Pitcher, Blue & White, Old Sleepy Eye, No. 1, 4¼ In.	110.00 to 113.00
Pitcher, Blue & White, Old Sleepy Eye, No. 4, 8 In.	236.00
Pitcher, Blue & White, Old Sleepy Eye, No. 5, 9 In.	236.00
Pitcher, Blue Rim, No. 5, 9 In.	475.00
Pitcher, Indian Profile, Blue & White, White On Handle & Base, Old Sleepy Eye, 5½ In.	3850.00
Pitcher, Indian Profile, Brown & Gold, Old Sleepy Eye, 7¾ In.	2200.00
Pitcher, Indian Standing, Blue & Yellow, Old Sleepy Eye, No. 4, 8 In.	275.00
Pitcher, Weir, No. 4, 8 In.	275.00
Pitcher, White, No. 3, 6½ In.	375.00
Ruler, Old Sleepy Eye	650.00
Salt Crock, Stoneware	240.00
Sign, Flour, Embossed, Cardboard, Easel Back, 12 x 7¼ In.	1155.00
Spoon, Indian	28.00
Spoon, Rose	80.00
Stein, Brown & Gold, 7¾ In.	675.00
Stein, Brown & White, 7¾ In.	550.00 to 825.00
Stein, Directors, 1972	45.00
Stein, Indian, Brown & White, Old Sleepy Eye, 7½ In.	550.00
Stein, Yellow & Green, 7½ In.	385.00
Sugar, Blue & White, 3 In.	350.00 to 600.00
Thimble	200.00
Vase, Dragonfly, Green Glaze, 8½ In.	1375.00
Vase, Old Sleepy Eye, Cattails, Dragonfly, Light & Dark Blue, Cylindrical, 8½ In.	*illus* 176.00
Vase, Old Sleepy Eye, Dragonfly, Brown & Cream, Cylindrical, 8¼ In.	767.00
Vase, Old Sleepy Eye, Dragonfly, Green, Cylindrical, 8¼ In.	1375.00
Vase, Old Sleepy Eye, Profile, Cattails, Dragonfly, Blue & Gray, Cylindrical, 8¾ In.	83.00
Vase, Old Sleepy Eye, Profile, Cattails, Dragonfly, Blue & White, Cylindrical, 8½ In.	176.00

SLOT MACHINES *are included in the Coin-Operated Machine category.*

SMITH BROTHERS glass was made after 1878. Alfred and Harry Smith had   *Smith Bros. Co.* worked for the Mt. Washington Glass Company in New Bedford, Massachusetts, for seven years before going into their own shop. They made many pieces with enamel decoration.

Biscuit Jar, Enameled Pansy, Silver Plate Lid, Late 1800s, 6¾ x 4½ In.	550.00
Bowl, Cream, Yellow & Pink Pansies, White & Gold Beaded Rim, Signed, Lion, 5½ In.	213.00
Bowl, Melon Ribbed, Silver Plate Rim, Acorn & Leaf, Gilt Trim, 4 x 8½ In.	750.00
Box, Cover, Pink & Lilac Carnations, Gold Trim, Melon Ribbed, 3½ x 5½ In.	*illus* 259.00
Castor Set, White Satin, Melon Ribbed, Pansies, Silver Plate Mount, Signed, 4 In.	550.00
Rose Jar, Melon Ribbed, Mold Blown, Amber, Flowers, Gold Outline, Lion Mark, 9 In.	403.00
Sweetmeat Jar, Ivory, Polychrome Pansies, Lid, Stamped Lion Mark, 7 In.	201.00
Vase, Cylindrical, Opal Glass, Double Ring, Marsh Reeds, Stork, c.1885, 8 In.	110.00

SNOW BABIES, made from bisque and spattered with glitter sand, were first manufactured in 1864 by Hertwig and Company of Thuringia. Other German and Japanese companies copied the Hertwig designs. Originally, Snow Babies were made of candy and used as Christmas decorations. There are also Snow Babies tablewares made by Royal Bayreuth. Copies of the small Snow Babies figurines are being made today and can easily confuse the collector.

Figurine, Snow Baby, Skiing, Bisque, Painted Features, Snow Crusted Suit, Pair, 4½ In.	825.00

SNUFF BOTTLES *are listed in the Bottle category.*

Sleepy Eye, Pitcher, Blue & White, No. 4, 8 In. $145.00

Sleepy Eye, Vase, Old Sleepy Eye, Cattails, Dragonfly, Light & Dark Blue, Cylindrical, 8½ In. $176.00

Smith Brothers, Box, Cover, Pink & Lilac Carnations, Gold Trim, Melon Ribbed, 3½ x 5½ In. $259.00

Snuffbox, 14K Gold, Ruby,
Bands Of Flowers, Etched Diamonds,
Rectangular, 3 In.
$1912.00

Snuffbox, Cowrie Shell,
Silver Hinged Lid,
Sweden, c.1856, 3 In.
$657.00

Snuffbox, Papier-Mache,
Military Officer On Horseback,
Oficier Der Krakhuser, 3⅛ In.
$165.00

Snuffbox, Papier-Mache, Painted,
Orange & White Compass Star,
Blue Ground, Round, 2 In.
$99.00

SNUFFBOXES held snuff. Taking snuff was popular long before cigarettes became available. The gentleman or lady would take a small pinch of the ground tobacco or snuff in the fingers, then sniff it and sneeze. Snuffboxes were made of many materials, including gold, silver, enameled metal, and wood. Most snuffboxes date from the late eighteenth or early nineteenth centuries.

14K Gold, Ruby, Bands Of Flowers, Etched Diamonds, Rectangular, 3 In. . . . .*illus*	1912.00
Carnelian, Stone, Reeded, 6 Panels, Leaves, Silver, Gilt Mount, Mark JOL, Paris, c.1830, 2⅞ In. . .	3300.00
Coconut Shell, Hand Carved, 18th Century, 2¼ x 3½ In.	1850.00
Cowrie Shell, Silver Hinged Lid, Sweden, c.1856, 3 In. . . . . *illus*	657.00
Gold, Basketwork, Waved Borders, Oval Medallion On Lid, Base, LB, France, 1733, 2¾ In. . . .	24000.00
Horn, Brass Pegs, 2½ x 1½ In.	125.00
Horn, Tortoiseshell, Round, Stamped Medallion, Washington Profile, Morel Fils Fecit, 3¼ In. . .	345.00
Metal, Riverside Village Scene, Flower Sprays, South Staffordshire, c.1775, 3 In.	4500.00
Painted, Star In Stripes & Dots, Burnt Orange, 19th Century, 2¾ In.	239.00
Papier-Mache, Military Officer On Horseback, Oficier Der Krakhuser, 3⅛ In. . . . .*illus*	165.00
Papier-Mache, Painted, Orange & White Compass Star, Blue Ground, Round, 2 In. . . .*illus*	99.00
Papier-Mache, Robert Fulton Esq., Portrait Medallion, c.1810, 3¼ In. Diam.	837.00
Silver, Engraved, Commemorative, Gilt Interior, Late 1800s, 2¾ x 2 In.	263.00
Silver, Gilt Interior, R. Steele, Birmingham, England, c.1826, 2½ x 1½ In.	418.00
Silver, Hinged Lid, Engraved, Inset Agate Quatrefoil, George V, 1922	259.00
Silver, Moses Basket, Hooded, Infant, c.1895, 2 In. . . . . *illus*	478.00
Silver, Musical, Sectional Comb, Monogram, 3½ In.	2703.00
Silver, Niello, France, 19th Century, 3 In.	413.00
Silver, Pastoral Scene, Signed, Italy, 1⅛ x ½ In.	275.00
Sterling Silver, Whaling Scene, Hinged Lid, 2¾ x 2 In.	1250.00
Tinplate, Musical, Flower Frieze, Lakeside Image, Transfer Case, 2¾ In.	705.00
Tortoiseshell, Gilt Silver Mount, 19th Century, 2½ In. *illus*	329.00
Wood, Carved Scenes, Coat Of Arms, Mirror, Patina, England, 3¼ x 1¾ In.	450.00

SOAPSTONE is a mineral that was used for foot warmers or griddles because of its heat-retaining properties. Soapstone was carved into figurines and bowls in many countries in the nineteenth and twentieth centuries. Most of the soapstone seen today is from China or Japan. It is still being carved in the old styles.

Box, Carved, Leaf Shape, Lacquer, Chinese, 4½ In.	5900.00
Buddha, Seated, Wooden Base, Chinese, 20th Century, 8 x 6 In.	117.00
Figurine, Carved, Immortal, Seated, Goats, Chinese, 20th Century, 6½ x 9 In.	316.00
Figurine, Female Immortal, Chinese, 19th Century, 11¾ In.	139.00
Figurine, Immortal, Dragon, Chinese, 6½ x 10 In.	165.00
Figurine, Man, Foo Dog, Chinese, 2 In.	118.00
Figurine, Meiren, Flowers, Fungus, Crane, Chinese, Early 20th Century, 15¾ In.	364.00
Figurine, Pagoda, 7 Tier, Bird Finial, Carved Bells, Original Wood Case, 28¼ In.	316.00
Figurine, Scholar, Seated, Carved, Chinese, 19th Century, 6 x 4½ In.	105.00
Guanyin, Holding Scroll, Lotus Throne, Rock Crystal, 20th Century, 10¼ x 6 In.	115.00

SOFT PASTE is a name for a type of pottery. Although it looks very much like porcelain, it is a chemically different material. Most of the soft-paste wares were made in the early nineteenth century. Other pieces may be listed under Gaudy Dutch or Leeds.

Basket, Pink Glaze, Encrusted Flowers, Gilt Trim, Oval, 10 In., Pair . . . .*illus*	287.00
Cup & Saucer, Red Flowers, Green Leaves, Pink Geometric Border	28.00

SOUVENIRS of a trip—what could be more fun? Our ancestors enjoyed the same thing and souvenirs were made for almost every location. Most of the souvenir pottery and porcelain pieces of the nineteenth century were made in England or Germany, even if the picture showed a North American scene. In the twentieth century, the souvenir china business seems to have gone to the manufacturers in Japan, Taiwan, Hong Kong, England, and America. Another popular souvenir item is the souvenir spoon, made of sterling or silver plate. These are usually made in the country pictured on the spoon. Related pieces may be found in the Coronation and World's Fair categories.

Apron, California, State Map, White, Cotton, 1960s, 20 x 22 In.	26.00
Ashtray, Alaska, Land Of The Midnight Sun, 49th State, 7 x 5 In.	15.00
Ashtray, Florida, Flamingos, Gold Trim, Palm Trees, Japan, 11 x 7 In.	24.00
Ashtray, Old Oregon Trail, Conestoga Wagon, White, Yellow Shading, Moriage, 4¾ In.	16.00
Ax, Capitol, Souvenir Of Washington D.C., 7,000 Macerated Money, 8¼ In.	173.00
Basket, Sea Shell, Florida, Palm Tree Decal, 2½ x 4¾ In.	18.00

Basket, Wells Fargo, Porcelain, Pink Luster, Applied Flowers, c.1900, 6¼ In. ....*illus*	118.00
Bobble Head, Canadian Mountie, Resin, High Gloss Finish, Paper Label, Giftcraft, 7½ In. ..	25.00
Bookmark, Montana, Brass, Enamel, Crest In Center, Original Case, 3½ x 1½ In.	17.50
Bookmark, Prospect Point, Niagara Falls, Shield Shape, Engraved, Laurel Wreath	20.00
Box, Island Of Manhattan, Tin, c.1920, 6 x 10 In.	53.00
Box, Midwinter Fair, San Francisco, c.1894, 3¼ x 1¾ In.	59.00
Coaster Set, Florida, Flamingo, Palm Tree, Wooden, Rack, Japan, 3½ In., 6 Piece	24.00
Cup, Demitasse, Niagara Falls, Maroon & 24K Gold Band, Germany, 1940s, 2¼ In.	28.00
Cup, Nashville Music City, USA, Red Guitar, Gold Trim, Music Notes, Foil Label	7.00
Custard Mug, North Anson Maine, Glass, Gold Decoration, 3¼ In.	55.00
Dish, Miles Canyon Yukon, Gold Fluted Edge, Duchess Bone China, 5 In.	8.00
Dish, Sea Shell, Florida, Palm Tree, Plastic Flamingo, 3½ x 3 In.	18.00
Fob, Pioneer Days Of California, The Days Of 49, Eureka Facsimile, 1850, 2 x 2 In.	425.00
Handkerchief, Florida, State Map, Cotton, Red, Black, Palm Trees, 1950s, 13 x 12½ In.	22.00
Handkerchief, Panama, American Flag, Silk, 1950s, 15½ x 15 In.	9.00
Horseshoe, Florida, Thoroughbred Racehorse, Good Luck, 7½ x 5 In.	18.00
Jug, Crest Of Pembroke Dock, 19th Century	18.00
Mug, Kennedy Space Center, Space Shuttle	10.00
Mug, Seaside Oregon, Handle, Custard Glass, Jefferson, c.1912	77.00
Nightlight, Crest Of Tenby, 2⅜ In.	39.00
Pennant, Lookout Mt., Colo., Buffalo Bill Cody, Green, White, Felt, 13 x 28 In.	165.00
Pennant, Monkees Fan Club, Felt, Chicago Chapter 170, 13 In.	123.00
Pennant, Pennsylvania Turnpike, Purple, White Lettering, Kittatinny Tunnel, 1952, 27 In. ..	15.00
Pin, Alaska Yukon Pacific Exposition, Clock Face, Hour, Second Hands, Month, 1¾ In.	246.00
Pin, Aviation Contest, Los Angeles, 1910, Crowd Watching, Celluloid, 6 In. ....*illus*	1494.00
Pin, Dayton, City Of A Thousand Factories, 1911, 2⅛ In.	49.00
Pin, Grand Rapids 60th Anniversary, 1910, Welcome Home, 2¹⁄₁₆ In.	99.00
Pin, Let The World Hear From Gary, Lithograph, 1⅛ In.	60.00
Pin, Movie, Ralph Bellamy, FDR, Sunrise At Campabello	27.00
Pin, New England Exhibit, Yankee, Photo, 1¼ In.	49.00
Pin, RCA Victor, Television Convention, Celluloid, 2 In.	52.00
Pin, Ringling Bros., World's Greatest Shows, 5 Men, 1900-10, 1¼ In.	137.00
Pin, The Who Concert, New York, Lithograph, 1976, 2¼ In.	41.00
Pin, Worldwide Radio Amateur Convention, ⅞ In.	73.00
Plate, Alaska Kodak Bear Sitka Navy Dutch Harbor	47.00
Plate, Arkansas, 1943	34.95
Plate, Atlantic City, Fluted Edge, Casinos, Slot Machine, Cards, Dice	7.00
Plate, Birmingham Alabama, 8½ In.	28.00
Plate, Bits Of The Old Northwest Log Jam, 8½ In.	107.00
Plate, Carlsbad Caverns, Flow Blue, Hall Of Giants, Road Runner, Cave Man, 10 In.	40.00
Plate, Delaware The First State, 8½ In.	25.00
Plate, Eau Galle, Wisconsin, Strawberries, Wm. Brunt Pottery Co., 8¼ In.	38.00
Plate, Emma Sweeny Train Railroad Ticket To Tomahawk	58.00
Plate, Florida, Flamingo, Palm Tree, Painted, Open Weave Design, Gold Trim, 8 In.	24.00
Plate, Historic Saint Augustine Florida, 1940s, 8½ In.	25.00
Plate, Kentucky, 10¾ In.	24.00
Plate, Los Angeles, 1950s, 10½ In.	28.00
Plate, Marine Series, Porthole Gale Turnbull, 10½ In.	107.00
Plate, Mt. Rushmore, South Dakota, Flow Blue, Johnson Bros., 10 In.	40.00
Plate, Niagara Falls, Luster Finish, c.1900, 7½ x 4¼ In.	32.00
Plate, Old Faithful Geyser, Yellowstone Park Centennial, Flow Blue, c.1972, 10 In.	40.00
Plate, Quebec, Canada, Openwork Edge, Giftcraft, Toronto, 8½ In. ....*illus*	10.00
Plate, Samoset Hotel, Rockland, Maine, 10-Sided, Reticulated Border, Germany, 8 In.	287.00
Plate, Seattle, Mt. Rainier Boeing Airplane Ferry Kalakala, 10½ In.	58.00
Plate, Seattle, University Of Washington Mt. Rainier	64.00
Plate, Townsend, Washington, 10½ In.	56.00
Salt & Pepper, Alligators, Florida Spelled Out On Tail, Eau Gallie, Fla., 1¼ x 4 In.	20.00
Soap Dish, KPM, City Of Nurenberg, Germany	15.00
Spoon, Pike's Peak, Sterling Silver, Wooded Scene, Garden Of The Gods, 5 In.	40.00
Spoon, Portland, Ore., Art Nouveau, Mermaid, Nude, Sterling Silver, c.1905, 4⅞ In.	145.00
Spoon, Royal Canadian Mounted Police, Engraved Bowl, Nickel Silver	8.50
Spoon, Stockbridge, Massachusetts, Sterling Silver, American Indian, 4¼ In.	44.00
Sugar & Creamer, Weymouth Coat Of Arms, Ribbed, Shell Like, Pearl Luster Glaze	26.00
Table Cover, Hawaii, Aloha, Hula Girl, Rayon, 29 x 29 In.	22.00
Tablecloth, Alaska, State Map, 49th State, Red, Blue, Yellow, Cotton, 50 x 54 In.	90.00
Tape Measure, Florida, Plastic, Red, White, Beach, Flying Flamingos, 1⅓ x ½ In.	12.00

Snuffbox, Silver, Moses Basket, Hooded, Infant, c.1895, 2 In.
$478.00

Snuffbox, Tortoiseshell, Gilt Silver Mount, 19th Century, 2½ In.
$329.00

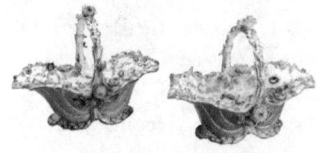

Soft Paste, Basket, Pink Glaze, Encrusted Flowers, Gilt Trim, Oval, 10 In., Pair
$287.00

Souvenir, Basket, Wells Fargo, Porcelain, Pink Luster, Applied Flowers, c.1900, 6¼ In.
$118.00

S

Souvenir, Pin, Aviation Contest, Los Angeles, 1910, Crowd Watching, Celluloid, 6 In. $1494.00

Souvenir, Plate, Quebec, Canada, Openwork Edge, Giftcraft, Toronto, 8½ In. $10.00

Is It Spatterware or Spongeware?

It's easy to tell if it is spatterware or spongeware. Spatterware dishes are decorated with drops of glaze that look like paint spatters. Spongeware looks as if paint was dabbed on with a sponge. Authors and collectors have jumbled the names until many of the similar spatter and sponge decorations are lumped under the name spatterware. It is correct today to use the terms "design spatter," "stick spatter," and "cut sponge." They are all old-fashioned names for types of spatterware and spongeware.

Tea Towel, Atlantic City, New Jersey State Map, 28 x 16 In.	32.00
Teapot, Florida, White Lusterware, Gold Trim, 1950s, 7 In.	24.00
Toothpick, Jug Shape, Gatlinburg, Tennessee, Paden City Pottery	4.50
Torch, Olympics, 1984, Los Angeles, Summer Games	1592.00
Vase, Prospect Point At Niagara Falls, Silver, Blue Iridescent, Dragon, Japan, 1950	8.00
Wall Pocket, Florida, 2 Flamingos, 3 Palm Trees, 5¾ Diam.	59.00

SPANGLE GLASS is multicolored glass made from odds and ends of colored glass rods. It includes metallic flakes of mica covered with gold, silver, nickel, or copper. Spangle glass is usually cased with a thin layer of clear glass over the multicolored layer. Similar glass is listed in the Vasa Murrhina category.

Bride's Basket, Blue, Ruffled Edge, Silver Frame, Pierced, 4-Footed, Ornate Handle	750.00
Bride's Bowl, Pink To Light Pink Interior, Silver Flakes, Ruffled Edge, Footed, Late 1800s	185.00
Jam Jar, Turquoise, Gold Speckles, Melon Form, Silver Frame & Lid, Twisted Bail Handle	95.00
Pitcher, Ruby, 8¾ In.	395.00
Sugar & Creamer, Light Cranberry To White, Silver Flakes, Silver Plated Carrier	550.00
Tumbler, White, Oxblood, Gold Mica Flakes, 1880s	240.00
Vase, Aventurine, Tapered, Global Body, Cylindrical Neck, 4¾ In.	225.00
Vase, Opaque, Blue, Yellow, Silver, Gourd Shape, Ribbed, c.1900, 8 In.	195.00
Vase, Pink, Green, White, Bulbous, Ruffled Edge, 9 In.	65.00
Vase, Pink, White Interior, Bulbous, Ruffled Edge, 1880s	225.00

SPANISH LACE *is listed in the Opalescent category as Opaline Brocade.*

SPATTER GLASS is a multicolored glass made from many small pieces of different colored glass. It is sometimes called End-of-Day glass. It is still being made.

Basket, Fluted Edge, Pink, Amber, Cased White, Ground Pontil, 6½ x 6 In.	100.00
Basket, Green, Yellow, Clear Handle, 6½ In.	100.00
Basket, Red, Pink, Yellow, Blue, Rectangular, Crimped Top, Thorn Handle, 5¾ In.	120.00
Bowl, Red, White, Gold, 10 In.	375.00
Celery Vase, Blue, Side Handle, Resilvered Frame	550.00
Cruet, Ruby, Applied Reeded Handle, Iron Pontil Scar	29.00
Dish, Coppertone Mica, Controlled Bubbles, Blown, 8¼ x 5½ In.	32.00
Perfume Stopper, Gold, White Painted Flowers, 4½ x 2⅛ In.	125.00
Pickle Castor, Silver Plate, Inverted Thumbprint, End Of Day, Victorian	1200.00
Pitcher, Blue, Burgundy, Ribbed, Clear Handle, 9 x 5 In.	101.00
Pitcher, End Of Day, Cased White Interior, Clear Handle	160.00
Rolling Pin, White, Blue	195.00
Rose Bowl, Crimped Edge, Pink, White, Yellow, Mold Blown, 5¾ x 4¼ In.	25.00
Sugar Shaker, Cranberry, Ribbed, Northwood, Victorian, 1800s, 4½ In.	275.00
Sugar Shaker, Cranberry, Ring Neck, Hobbs, Brockunier, 4¾ In.	160.00 to 270.00
Toothpick, Cranberry, 2¼ x 1½ In.	200.00
Vase, Bud, Multicolored, White Cased, Bohemian, 8 In.	332.00
Vase, Bulbous Base, Pink, Green, White, Ruffled Edge, 9 In.	65.00
Vase, Clear, Multicolored, Baluster Form, Crimped Rim, Disc Foot, 6 In.	605.00
Vase, Cranberry, Applied Flowers, 6-Footed, 12 In.	200.00
Vase, Cranberry, Artichoke Mold, Victorian, 5 In.	100.00
Vase, Enameled, Blown, 1960s, 7 In.	85.00
Vase, Mold Blown, Cased, Applied Handles, 4¾ x 3½ In.	32.00
Vase, Mold Blown, Enameled, Victorian, 6 x 3⅛ In.	45.00
Vase, Pink, Applied Thorny Handle, Victorian, 6½ In., Pair	400.00
Vase, Pink, Green, White, Ruffled Edge, 5⅜ x 4¾ In., Pair	54.00
Vase, Purple, Pink, Ruffled Edge, Applied Foot, Pink, Blue, Lavender, 7 x 4 In.	420.00
Vase, Stretched Neck, Ruffled Edge, 7⅛ x 3 In.	15.00

SPATTERWARE is the creamware or soft paste dinnerware decorated with colored spatter designs. The earliest pieces were made in the late eighteenth century, but most of the spatterware found today was made from about 1800 to 1850, or it is a form of kitchen crockery with added spatter designs, made in the late nineteenth and twentieth centuries. The early spatterware was made in the Staffordshire district of England for sale in America. The later kitchen type is an American product.

Basket, Green, Yellow Leaves, Berries	100.00
Bowl, Rose, Blue, 11⅜ In.	220.00
Bowl, Star, Blue, Paneled, Sunburst Border, 9½ In.	385.00

Bowl, Stick, Red & Green Bands, Spiral Handles, Shell Terminals, 6¾ x 7¼ In.	358.00
Bowl, Vegetable, Thistle, Yellow, Open, 2 x 9¼ In.	7425.00
Coffeepot, Peafowl, Blue, Paneled, Gooseneck Spout, 8¾ In.	193.00
Creamer, 8-Point Star, Blue, Purple Rim, 4½ In.	468.00
Creamer, Blue Clusters Of Buds, Brown, Green Ground	28.00
Creamer, Bud Cluster, Red, Green Leaves, Red Sponge, 4¼ In.	176.00
Creamer, Columbine, Yellow, Ear Handle, Elongated Spout, 3⅝ In.	1045.00
Creamer, Cow, 2-Tone, Green Base, Milkmaid In Green Dress, 5½ In.	175.00
Creamer, Peafowl, Blue, Applied Ear Handle, 3½ In.	55.00
Creamer, Peafowl, Green, Applied Ear Handle, Shell Terminals, 3½ In.	187.00
Creamer, Peafowl, Red, Applied Ear Handle, Shell Terminals, 3½ In.	110.00
Creamer, Rainbow, 3 Colors, Bulbous, Ribbed Body, Scalloped Rim, 6½ In.	13200.00
Creamer, Rainbow, Red & Green Vertical Bands, Leaf Terminals, 5¼ In.	358.00
Creamer, Rose, Black & Brown Bands, 3¾ In. ....*illus*	440.00
Creamer, Strawberry Thumbprint & Crisscross, Blue, Child's, 3½ In.	523.00
Creamer, Thistle, Yellow, Applied Ear Handle, Elongated Spout, 3½ In.	5500.00
Cup, Parrot, Red, Handleless, 2⅜ x 6 In.	550.00
Cup, Peafowl, Blue, 1½ x 2¼ In.	50.00
Cup, Peafowl, Purple, Green & Yellow, Red Spatter, Handleless, Child's .....*illus*	440.00
Cup, Rooster, Mustard, Blue, Red, Blue Ground, Handleless, Child's	193.00
Cup, Tree, Green, Black Highlights, Center Dot, Purple, Handleless	66.00
Cup & Saucer, 4-Color Peafowl, Yellow, Handleless, 1⅞ x 4½ In.	1760.00
Cup & Saucer, Buds, Red, Green Leaves, Blue Border, Handleless	61.00
Cup & Saucer, Bull's-Eye, Rainbow, Red & Green Bands, Handleless, 2⅝ x 5⅝ In.	110.00
Cup & Saucer, Bull's-Eye, Red & Blue Rainbow Border, Handleless, Child's	110.00
Cup & Saucer, Castle, Blue, Handleless, 2¾ x 5¾ In.	220.00
Cup & Saucer, Dot, Blue & Purple Stripes, Handleless, 2½ x 5¾ In.	715.00
Cup & Saucer, Dot, Red & Blue, Handleless, 2¼ x 6 In.	1980.00
Cup & Saucer, Dot, Red & Purple Vertical Bands, 2½ x 5¾ In.	633.00
Cup & Saucer, Dot, Teal, Handleless	165.00
Cup & Saucer, Dove, Red, Handleless, 2½ x 5⅝ In.	550.00
Cup & Saucer, Festoon, Blue, Lavender, Olive Green	165.00
Cup & Saucer, Fort, Blue, Handleless, 2½ x 6 In. .... 165.00 to 358.00
Cup & Saucer, Holly Berry, Red, Green, Purple Border, Handleless	27.00
Cup & Saucer, Peafowl, Blue, 2½ x 5⅞ In.	413.00
Cup & Saucer, Peafowl, Blue, Yellow, Green, Red Ground, Handleless	143.00
Cup & Saucer, Peafowl, Green, Leaves, Handleless, 2½ x 5¾ In.	440.00
Cup & Saucer, Peafowl, Red, Handleless, 2½ x 5⅞ In.	220.00
Cup & Saucer, Rainbow, Red, Blue & Green Bands, Handleless ....*illus*	209.00
Cup & Saucer, Rooster, Green, Handleless, 1¾ x 3⅜ In.	440.00
Cup & Saucer, Rooster, Mustard, Blue, Red, Purple Border, Handleless	715.00
Cup & Saucer, Rooster, Mustard, Red, Blue, Red Ground	303.00
Cup & Saucer, Rooster, Peafowl, Red, 2½ x 5¾ In.	935.00
Cup & Saucer, Rose, Blue, Rainbow, Vertical Blue Bands, 2½ x 5¾ In.	440.00
Cup & Saucer, Rose, Purple, 2¼ x 5⅞ In.	220.00
Cup & Saucer, Rose, Red & Blue Bands, Rainbow, Handleless, 2½ x 5¾ In.	275.00
Cup & Saucer, Rose, Red, Green, Blue Spatter Border, Handleless ....*illus*	132.00
Cup & Saucer, School House, Handleless ....*illus*	260.00
Cup & Saucer, Star, Red & Blue, Alternating Colors, Handleless, 2½ x 5¾ In.	138.00
Cup & Saucer, Thistle, Mulberry, Handleless, 2½ x 5⅞ In.	385.00
Cup & Saucer, Thistle, Rainbow, Red & Yellow Vertical Bands, 2½ x 6 In. ...... 578.00 to 880.00
Cup & Saucer, Thistle, Rainbow, Red & Yellow Vertical Bands, 3 x 6 In.	660.00
Cup & Saucer, Thistle, Red, Green Leaves, Blue Ground, Handleless	248.00
Cup & Saucer, Thistle, Red, Green Leaves, Mulberry Border, Handleless	1045.00
Cup & Saucer, Thistle, Yellow, 2½ x 6 In. .... 660.00 to 770.00
Cup & Saucer, Tic-Tac-Toe, Red, Green, White Spatter	605.00
Cup & Saucer, Tulip, Blue & Red, Green Leaves, Blue Border, Handleless	165.00
Cup & Saucer, Tulip, Blue & Red, Green Leaves, Red Border, Handleless	138.00
Cup & Saucer, Tulip, Open, Red, Blue, Green, Yellow Border, Handleless	990.00
Cup & Saucer, Tulip, Red, Green Leaves, Red Border, Handleless	660.00
Jug, Blue, Glazed, Mid 19th Century, 6½ In.	186.00
Jug, Blue, Late 19th Century, 3½ In.	131.00
Nappy, Blue, White Spatter, Applied Handle, 4 x 5 x 2 In.	18.00
Pepper Pot, Peafowl, Blue, 4½ In.	1320.00
Pitcher, Blue, White, Applied Handle, Pontil, Ruffled Spout, 6 x 5 In.	50.00
Pitcher, Blue Crisscross & Strawberry Thumbprint, Child's, 3½ In. ....*illus*	523.00

Spatterware, Creamer, Rose, Black & Brown Bands, 3¾ In.
$440.00

Spatterware, Cup, Peafowl, Purple, Green & Yellow, Red Spatter, Handleless, Child's
$440.00

Spatterware, Cup & Saucer, Rainbow, Red, Blue & Green Bands, Handleless
$209.00

Spatterware, Cup & Saucer, Rose, Red, Green, Blue Spatter Border, Handleless
$132.00

Spatterware, Cup & Saucer, School House, Handleless
$260.00

S

Spatterware, Pitcher, Blue Crisscross & Strawberry Thumbprint, Child's, 3½ In. $523.00

Spatterware, Plate, School House, Red & Yellow, Green & Brown Tree, Blue Spatter, Paneled, 8½ In. $1430.00

Spatterware, Plate, Soup, Thistle, Red, Green Leaves, Yellow Paneled Border, 9¾ In. $10450.00

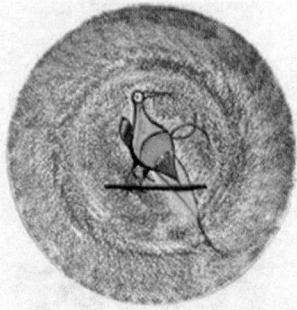

Spatterware, Saucer, Peafowl, Yellow, Blue, Red, Green, Red Ground, 6 In. $192.00

Pitcher, Peafowl, Red, Rope Twist Applied Handle, 8 In.	853.00
Pitcher, Rainbow, 5-Color, Bulbous, Paneled Body, Scroll Handle, 12½ In.	4950.00
Pitcher, Rainbow, 5-Color, Embossed Swag, Scalloped Rim, Scroll Handle, 8¾ In.	4675.00
Pitcher, Rainbow, Bulbous, Embossed Swag Shoulder, Scalloped Rim, Scroll Handle, 9¾ In.	5775.00
Pitcher, Rainbow, Paneled, Alternating Red & Blue Vertical Bands, 12¼ In.	468.00
Planter, Half Moon, Red, Peafowl, 2¼ x 3⅛ In.	440.00
Plate, Acorn, Red, Paneled, 6 In.	2970.00
Plate, Acorn, Red, Paneled, 8½ In.	3410.00 to 4510.00
Plate, Bull's-Eye, Blue, Purple, Rainbow, 8½ In.	385.00
Plate, Bull's-Eye, Rainbow, Blue, Green, 8¼ In.	880.00
Plate, Bull's-Eye, Red & Green, Rainbow Border, 7¼ In.	187.00
Plate, Castle, Purple, 5⅛ In.	55.00
Plate, Dahlia, Blue & Red, Green Sprigs, Blue, Paneled, 8¼ In.	193.00
Plate, Dahlia, Blue & Red, Green Sprigs, Purple, Paneled, 8¼ In.	83.00
Plate, Dahlia, Red & Blue, Green Leaves, Blue Ground, Paneled, 9⅛ In.	61.00
Plate, Double Acorn, Brown, Green Leaves, Blue Border, Paneled, 8¼ In.	770.00
Plate, Fort, Blue, Paneled, 9½ In.	121.00 to 248.00
Plate, Fort, Gray & Brown, Green Trees, Blue Border, Paneled, 8¾ In.	220.00
Plate, Morning Glory, Yellow, Paneled, 8½ In.	990.00
Plate, Peafowl, Blue, 9½ In.	193.00
Plate, Peafowl, Blue, Black & White Stripe, Green, Red Ground, Paneled, 8½ In.	275.00
Plate, Peafowl, Blue, Feather Edge, Green Grass, 8⅝ In.	330.00
Plate, Peafowl, Blue, Paneled, 9⅜ In.	220.00 to 578.00
Plate, Peafowl, Blue, Yellow, Green, Red Around Bird & Border, 9¾ In.	468.00
Plate, Peafowl, Blue, Yellow, Green, Red Ground, 7½ In.	110.00
Plate, Peafowl, Blue, Yellow, Green, Red Ground, 8¼ In.	220.00
Plate, Peafowl, Blue, Yellow, Red, Blue Spatter, 8¼ In.	110.00
Plate, Peafowl, Green, 9⅛ In.	550.00
Plate, Peafowl, Green, Yellow, Red, 14-Sided Cobalt Blue Border, 7½ In.	297.00
Plate, Peafowl, Green, Yellow, Red, Blue Spatter, 7½ In.	137.00
Plate, Peafowl, Red, 5¼ In.	61.00
Plate, Peafowl, Red, 8½ In.	330.00 to 413.00
Plate, Peafowl, Red, Feather Edge, 6¼ In.	165.00
Plate, Peafowl, Red, Paneled, 8⅜ In.	1100.00
Plate, Peafowl, Red, Yellow, Green, Light Blue Ground, 7½ In.	83.00
Plate, Pineapple, Blue, 8 In.	3575.00
Plate, Pomegranate, Blue, Maker's Name, 6⅝ In.	165.00
Plate, Rainbow, Dot, Blue, Red, 8¼ In.	605.00
Plate, Rose, Blue, 4⅛ In.	55.00
Plate, Rose, Blue, Paneled, 6⅞ In.	110.00
Plate, Rose, Red, Green Leaves, Red, Blue, Green Border, 9½ In.	248.00
Plate, School House, Red, 4¾ In.	110.00
Plate, School House, Red, Red Roof, Green Grass & Tree Top, Brown Ground, 10⅜ In.	121.00
Plate, School House, Red & Yellow, Green & Brown Tree, Blue Spatter, Paneled, 8½ In. *illus*	1430.00
Plate, Soup, Rose, Red, Blue Bud, Green Leaves, Purple Paneled Border, 10½ In.	990.00
Plate, Soup, Thistle, Red, Green Leaves, Yellow Paneled Border, 9¾ In. *illus*	10450.00
Plate, Stick, Flow Blue Leaves, Red Rosettes, Red & Green Scrolls, 9⅛ In.	55.00
Plate, Thistle, Purple, 6⅜ In.	853.00
Plate, Thistle, Rainbow, Red & Green Vertical Bands, 7⅛ In.	605.00
Plate, Thistle, Yellow, Paneled, 9¾ In.	2200.00
Plate, Tulip, Blue & Red, Green Leaves, Blue, Paneled, 9¼ In.	138.00
Plate, Tulip, Blue & Red, Green Leaves, Purple Border, Paneled, 8 In.	248.00 to 358.00
Plate, Tulip, Blue & Red, Green Leaves, Red Border, Paneled, 9¼ In.	440.00
Plate, Tulip, Mulberry, Blue Tipped, Green Leaves, 8½ In.	275.00
Plate, Tulip, Red, Green Leaves, Blue Sponge Border, 8¾ In.	66.00
Plate, Tulip, Red, White, Blue, Green Leaves, Black Stem, Blue, Paneled, 8⅜ In.	110.00
Platter, Blue, Octagonal, 19⅛ x 13½ In.	345.00
Platter, Bull's-Eye, Blue, 8-Sided, 16⅞ In.	83.00
Platter, Holly, Red Buds, Green Leaves, Blue Border, 16⅜ In.	193.00
Platter, Peafowl, Blue, 15⅝ In.	990.00
Platter, Peafowl, Blue, Red Green, Blue Ground, 15¾ In.	1540.00
Relish, Shell, Blue, Scalloped Rim, Embossed Flowers, 9 x 5 In.	220.00
Salt, Master, Blue, Footed, 2¼ In.	165.00
Sauce, Peafowl, Blue, Green, Brown, Red Border, 5 In.	55.00
Sauce, Peafowl, Feather Edge, Red, 5 In.	33.00
Saucer, Deer, Red Border, 6 In.	192.00

Saucer, Parrot, Red, Green, On Branch, Red Border, 5⅝ In.		248.00
Saucer, Peafowl, 4-Color, Red, Blue, Green Splotched Ground, 5½ In.		358.00
Saucer, Peafowl, Teal, Child's, 4⅝ In.		44.00
Saucer, Peafowl, Yellow, Blue, Red, Green, Red Ground, 6 In.	*illus*	192.00
Saucer, Rose, Red, Green Leaves, Red & Green Border, 5⅝ In.		99.00
Saucer, Sailboat, Green Border, 6 In.		935.00
Saucer, Stick, Green Bowtie, Red Rosettes, 4⅛ In.		44.00
Soup, Dish, Blue & Purple Flowers, Red Drapes & Border, Stick Spatter, 9¾ In.	*illus*	143.00
Soup, Dish, Thistle, Red, Green Leaves, Yellow Spatter Border, Paneled, 9¾ In.	*illus*	10450.00
Sugar, Blue & Green, Flared Rim, Bulbous Body, Footed Base, 5½ In.		72.00
Sugar, Castle, Brown, 4¾ In.		193.00
Sugar, Chinese Transfer, Paneled, Applied Shell Handles, Blue, 7½ In.		440.00
Sugar, Cluster Of Buds, Blue, 3⅝ In.		99.00
Sugar, Cockscomb, Blue, Paneled, Applied Shaped Handles, 8¼ In.		193.00
Sugar, Cover, Blue Flowers, Red Ground, Bulbous, 4¼ In.		358.00
Sugar, Cover, Cluster Of Buds, Red, Green Leaves, Blue Ground, 4 In.		165.00
Sugar, Cover, Peafowl, Blue, Yellow, Green, Red Ground		110.00
Sugar, Cover, Peafowl, Blue, Yellow, Red, Blue Border		330.00
Sugar, Cover, Peafowl, Green, Red, Blue, Ring & Shell Embossed Handles, Blue Ground		1430.00
Sugar, Cover, Peafowl	*illus*	117.00
Sugar, Cover, Rainbow, 3-Color, Yellow, Red, Green, Festoon, 5¼ In.		2750.00
Sugar, Cover, Rainbow, Blue, Red, 5¼ In.		330.00
Sugar, Cover, Rooster, Red Band & Rim, Molded Finial, 4½ x 5⅛ In.		575.00
Sugar, Cover, Thistle, Red, Rainbow, Green Leaves, 3¾ In.		1320.00
Sugar, Fort, Red, Lid, Green, Button Finial, 4¼ In.		385.00
Sugar, Peafowl, Blue, Paneled, Open Handles, 6¾ In.		55.00
Sugar, Peafowl, Yellow, 4 In.		990.00
Sugar, Primrose, Blue, Paneled, Applied Embossed Scroll Handles, 7¼ In.		220.00
Sugar, Rainbow, Alternating Red & Green Vertical Bands, 5¼ In.		138.00
Sugar, Rooster, Red, Lid, Embossed Flower Finial, 4½ In.		550.00
Sugar, Rose, Brown, 6 In.		330.00
Sugar, Rose, Rainbow, 3-Color, Gooseneck Spout, Mushroom Finial, 8½ In.		4400.00
Sugar, Rose, Red, 4½ In.		132.00
Sugar & Creamer, Golden, 1940-50s, 2½ In.		13.00
Teapot, Cockscomb, Red Flower, Green Leaves, Blue Ground, Bulbous, 5¾ In.	*illus*	350.00
Teapot, Peafowl, Blue, Paneled, Gooseneck Spout, Scrolled Handle, 7 In.		110.00
Teapot, Peafowl, Blue, Yellow, Red, Brown Border		220.00
Teapot, Rose, Purple, Applied Ear Handle, Gooseneck Spout, 6 In.		110.00
Teapot, Rose, Red, Applied Ear Handle, Gooseneck Spout, 5¾ In.		193.00
Vase, Pink, Green, White, Bulbous, Ruffled Top, 9 In.		65.00
Vase, Sunny Yellow, Scalloped Edge, Diamond, Multicolored, c.1940, 5 In.		75.00
Vase, Yellow, White, Orange, Gold Flowers, 5½ In.		14.00
Washbowl & Pitcher, Peafowl, Red, Mustard, Green, Blue Ground, 10¼-In. Pitcher		880.00
Waste Bowl, Peafowl, Blue, Mustard, Red, 3½ x 6⅛ In.		110.00
Waste Bowl, Rainbow, Red, Green, 3⅜ x 6⅜ In.		330.00

SPELTER is a synonym for a zinc alloy. Figurines, candlesticks, and other pieces were made of spelter and given a bronze or painted finish. The metal has been used since about the 1860s to make statues, tablewares, and lamps that resemble bronze. Spelter is soft and breaks easily. To test for spelter, scratch the base of the piece. Bronze is solid; spelter will show a silvery scratch.

Figure, Children, On Stump, Fish Head Protruding From Water, 16¾ In.		201.00
Figure, Fawn, Lying Down, Marble Base, c.1930, 5 x 8 In.		47.00
Figure, Mercury, Marble Base, c.1900, 12 In.		88.00
Figure, Penelope, c.1880, 12 In.		410.00
Figure, Putti, With Musical Instruments, Cement Loaded, 24¾ In.		510.00
Figure, Stags, Head-To-Head Combat, Bronze Patinat, Marble Base, Art Deco, 11 x 35 In.		1527.00
Figure, Woman, Wearing Ball Gown, Marble Base, Germany, c.1920, 7 x 6 In.		117.00

SPINNING WHEELS in the corner have been symbols of earlier times for the past 100 years. Although spinning wheels date back to medieval days, the ones found today are rarely more than 200 years old. Because the style of the spinning wheel changed very little, it is often impossible to place an exact date on a wheel.

Blue, Salmon, Yellow & Green Paint, Leather Strap, Child's, 20¾ x 24 In.		688.00
Canted Spool Turned Legs, Yellow Paint, Tulip Feet, 35½ In.		275.00

Spatterware, Soup, Dish, Blue & Purple Flowers, Red Drapes & Border, Stick Spatter, 9¾ In.
$143.00

Spatterware, Soup, Dish, Thistle, Red, Green Leaves, Yellow Spatter Border, Paneled, 9¾ In.
$10450.00

Spatterware, Sugar, Cover, Peafowl
$117.00

Spatterware, Teapot, Cockscomb, Red Flower, Green Leaves, Blue Ground, Bulbous, 5¾ In.
$350.00

S

Spinning Wheel, Turned Spindles, 19th Century, 31 In.
$147.00

Spongeware, Plate, Rabbits, Virginia Rose, Conductor, Doctor, Family, Dancers, 9¼ In.
$715.00

Spongeware, Plate, Rabbits Playing Baseball, Virginia Rose, 9 In.
$1870.00

TIP
Early plates often have no rim on the bottom.

Fruitwood, Ebonized Wheels, Finial Uprights, Continental, 48 x 31 In.	206.00
Gold & White Paint, Signed, E.G. Nicodemus, Aug. 14, 1897, Waterloo, Oh., 63 In.	345.00
Maple, Oak, Distaff, 19th Century, 41 x 32 In.	118.00
Turned Spindles, 19th Century, 31 In. ......*illus*	147.00

SPODE pottery, porcelain, and bone china were made by the Stoke-on-Trent factory of England founded by Josiah Spode about 1770. The firm became Copeland and Garrett from 1833 to 1847, then W.T. Copeland or W.T. Copeland and Sons until 1976. It then became Royal Worcester Spode Ltd. The word *Spode* appears on many pieces made by the factories. Most collectors include all the wares under the more familiar name of Spode. Porcelains are listed in this book by the name that appears on the piece. Related pieces may be listed under Copeland, Copeland Spode, and Royal Worcester.

Bowl, Open, Gilt Rim, Flowers, England, 8½ x 11 In.	410.00
Cup & Saucer, Asian Style Design, Exotic Birds, Flowers, 2¾ x 5½ In., 24 Piece	173.00
Cup & Saucer, Seashell Pattern, Transfer Print, Gold Bands, Cylindrical Cup, c.1813, Pair	352.00
Dinner Service, Camilla Pattern, Blue & White, 60 Piece	293.00
Plate, Blue, Tower Pattern, Spode, c.1820, 9¾ In.	175.00
Plate, Blue & White Transfer, Caramanian, City Of Corinth, c.1825, 10 In.	375.00
Plate, Blue Bowpot, England, c.1940, 10⅜ In., 8 Piece	117.00
Plate, Crescent Shape, Blue & White, 18th Century, 6¼ x 12⅝ In., 4 Piece	59.00
Plate, Soup, Etruscan Vases, Transfer, Urns, Palmette, Scroll Border, 10½ In., Pair	118.00
Plate, Soup, Tower Pattern, Pearlware, c.1820, 9½ In.	225.00
Platter, Floral, Bluebells, Roses, Blue Transfer, Pearlware, c.1835, 17 x 13 In.	675.00
Platter, Grapes, Blue & White, Transfer, Pearlware, c.1825, 15 In.	950.00
Platter, Mandarin's Garden, Octagonal, Ironstone, 21 x 16 In.	1410.00
Platter, Roasted Meats, New Stone, Flowers, Octagonal, Oblong, Wrought Iron, 21 In.	210.00
Tray, Pastry, Maritime Rose, Multicolored Flower Sprays, 11 x 9½ In.	293.00

SPONGEWARE is very similar to spatterware in appearance. The designs were applied to the ceramics by daubing the color on with a sponge or cloth. Many collectors do not differentiate between spongeware and spatterware and use the names interchangeably. Modern pottery is being made to resemble the old spongeware, but careful examination will show it is new.

Bowl Set, Vegetable, Peafowl, Yellow, Open, Octagonal, 9¼, 10¼ & 11¼ In.	50.00
Charger, Rabbits & Frog In Meadow Center, Virginia Rose Border, 12⅞ In.	825.00
Charger, Tulip Center, Virginia Rose Border, 4 Brown Panels, Rabbit Scenes, 12⅞ In.	523.00
Charger, Virginia Rose, Running Rabbit Border, 12½ In.	825.00
Cooler, 3 Parts, Molded Panel, c.1880, 23½ In.	303.00
Cup & Saucer, Handleless, 2¾ x 5¼ In., 4 Piece	11.00
Cup & Saucer, Rainbow, Blue, Red, Green Circles, Ear Handles, 1¾ x 4⅜ In.	83.00
Dish, Blue Accent Bands, 2 x 6 In.	121.00
Mug, Virginia Rose, Rabbits & Frog Rim, Running Rabbits On Bottom, 5⅜ In.	2310.00 to 2420.00
Mug, Virginia Rose, Rabbits In Meadow, 5⅜ In.	467.00
Mug, Virginia Rose, Rabbits Playing Cricket, Flowers, Multicolored, 4½ In.	2200.00
Pitcher, Blue, White, Blue Accent Bands, 7 In.	275.00
Pitcher, Utility, 7¼ In.	55.00
Pitcher, Virginia Rose, Rabbits Golfing, Flowers, Multicolored, Stamped, 8½ In.	7700.00
Pitcher, Water, Peafowl, Yellow, Footed, Scroll Handle, Elongated Spout, 10¼ In.	55.00
Plate, Peafowl, Blue, 8¾ In.	770.00
Plate, Peafowl, Green, 3¾ In.	83.00
Plate, Rabbits, Adam's Rose, Hayfield, Split Rail Fence, Adams, 9¼ In.	495.00
Plate, Rabbits, Sporting Scene, Golf, Virginia Rose, Adams, 9¼ In.	468.00
Plate, Rabbits, Virginia Rose, Conductor, Doctor, Family, Dancers, 9¼ In. ......*illus*	715.00
Plate, Rabbits, Virginia Rose Border, 4 Blue Panels, 9¼ In.	358.00
Plate, Rabbits, Virginia Rose Border, 4 Brown Panels, 9¼ In.	209.00
Plate, Rabbits & Frog In Meadow, Virginia Rose Border, 9¼ In.	275.00
Plate, Rabbits & Frog In Meadow, Virginia Rose Border, Red, Blue, Green Rim, 9 In.	248.00
Plate, Rabbits & Frog In Meadow, Virginia Rose Border, Red Rim, 9¼ In.	330.00
Plate, Rabbits Driving Car, Flowers, Virginia Rose, Multicolored, 9¼ In.	2200.00
Plate, Rabbits Golfing, Flowers, Virginia Rose, Multicolored, 9⅛ In.	1980.00
Plate, Rabbits In Field, Virginia Rose Border, 9¼ In.	330.00
Plate, Rabbits In Meadow, Red, Blue, Green Border, Red Rim, 9¼ In.	176.00
Plate, Rabbits Playing Baseball, Virginia Rose, 9 In. ......*illus*	1870.00
Plate, Rabbits Playing Croquet, Flowers, Virginia Rose, Multicolored, Stamped, 9 In.	1870.00
Plate Set, Peafowl, Yellow, Paneled, 9⅜ In.	11.00
Platter, Peafowl, Yellow, Octagonal, 14⅝ x 11½ In.	39.00

Platter, Rabbits & Frog In Meadow, Red, Blue Flowers, Green Leaves Border, 14⅝ In.	330.00
Platter, Rabbits & Frog In Meadow, Virginia Rose Border, 14⅝ In.	1100.00
Sugar & Creamer, Applied Ear Handles, Elongated Spout, 4½ In.	28.00
Teapot, Tulip, Blue, Gooseneck Spout, Applied Scroll, 5¾ In.	330.00

SPORTS equipment, sporting goods, brochures, and related items are listed here. Items are listed by sport. Other categories of interest are Bicycle, Card, Fishing, Sword, Toy, and Trap. Kentucky Derby glasses are listed in the Decorated Tumblers category.

Auto Racing, Button, Indianapolis Speedway Concession, 1931, 2½ In.	139.00
Auto Racing, Program, International Speed Trials, Daytona Beach, 1935	249.00
Auto Racing, Tie Bar, Johnny Parsons, Indianapolis 500 Winner, Wynn's Oil, 1950, 3 In.	76.00
Baseball, Ashtray, Brooklyn Dodgers, 10 In A Row, Round, 1955	595.00
Baseball, Ball, Autographed, Al Kaline, Official American League Ball	25.00
Baseball, Ball, Autographed, Babe Ruth, c.1925	1928.00
Baseball, Ball, Autographed, Bill Castro, Official Pacific Coast League Baseball	18.00
Baseball, Ball, Autographed, Clemente, Mays, Cepeda, Marichal	1315.00
Baseball, Ball, Autographed, Ernie Banks, Official National League Baseball	120.00
Baseball, Ball, Autographed, Harmon Killebrew	45.00
Baseball, Ball, Autographed, Jackie Robinson, Gil Hodges, Pee Wee Reese, Dodgers, 1947	1000.00
Baseball, Ball, Autographed, Jackie Robinson	2122.00
Baseball, Ball, Autographed, Johnny Mize, Official National League Baseball	65.00
Baseball, Ball, Autographed, Lefty O'Doul, 1934	2335.00
Baseball, Ball, Autographed, Max Bishop	342.00
Baseball, Ball, Autographed, Nolan Ryan, Rawlings Official	60.00
Baseball, Ball, Autographed, Pee Wee Reese, Dizzy Dean	342.00
Baseball, Ball, Autographed, Pittsburgh Pirates, 1926, 23 Signatures ....*illus*	418.00
Baseball, Ball, Autographed, Ralph Kiner, Official Major League Baseball	60.00
Baseball, Ball, Autographed, Reggie Jackson, Official A.L. Lee MacPhail Baseball	65.00
Baseball, Ball, Autographed, Riggs Stephenson	555.00
Baseball, Ball, Autographed, Sandy Koufax, Cy Young Winner	897.00
Baseball, Ball, Autographed, Satchel Paige	2122.00
Baseball, Ball, Autographed, Ted Lyons	1086.00
Baseball, Bat, Autographed, Duke Snider, 1950-60	1195.00
Baseball, Bat, Autographed, Harvey Kuenn, 1950-60	174.00
Baseball, Bat, Autographed, Marty Marion, 1943-49	282.00
Baseball, Bat, Autographed, Ralph Kiner, 1946-49	1195.00
Baseball, Bat, Autographed, Ted Williams, 1950-60	814.00
Baseball, Bat Rack, Hillerich & Bradsby, c.1940	1752.00
Baseball, Bat Rack, Wilson, 1950	458.00
Baseball, Booklet, Autographed, Joe DiMaggio, Dodge Advertising, 1938	504.00
Baseball, Button, Cleveland Indians Knothole Club, Van Lane, WERE, 1⅝ In.	75.00
Baseball, Button, Leroy Satchel Paige, Ball, Ribbon, c.1948, 1¾ In.	493.00
Baseball, Button, Mickey Mantle, Suspended Glove, Photo, c.1955, 1¾ In.	277.00
Baseball, Button, Pepper Martin, St. Louis Cardinals, Red, 1¼ In.	115.00
Baseball, Button, Robin Roberts, Philadelphia Phillies, Whiz Kids, 1950s, 1¾ In.	83.00
Baseball, Button, Wrigley Field Usher 126, Chicago Cubs, c.1950, 1¾ In.	152.00
Baseball, Comic Book, Pride Of The Yankees, Life Of Lou Gerhig, c.1949 ....*illus*	78.00
Baseball, Figure, Babe Ruth, Plastic, Hartland, 8 In.	110.00
Baseball, Figure, Bat Boy, Plastic, Hartland, 6 In.	55.00
Baseball, Figure, Don Drysdale, Plastic, Hartland, 8 In.	138.00
Baseball, Figure, Duke Snider, Plastic, Hartland, Tag, 8 In.	385.00
Baseball, Figure, Ed Mathews, Plastic, Hartland, Tag, 8 In.	275.00
Baseball, Figure, Hank Aaron, Plastic, Hartland, Tag, 8 In.	330.00
Baseball, Figure, Harmon Killebrew, Plastic, Hartland, Tag, 8 In.	550.00
Baseball, Figure, Mickey Mantle, Plastic, Hartland, 8 In.	220.00
Baseball, Figure, Mickey Mantle, Plastic, Hartland, Tag, Box, 8 In.	1315.00
Baseball, Figure, Nellie Fox, Plastic, Hartland, 8 In.	55.00
Baseball, Figure, Rocky Colavito, Plastic, Hartland, 8 In.	165.00
Baseball, Figure, Roger Maris, Plastic, Hartland, 8 In.	220.00
Baseball, Figure, Stan Musial, Plastic, Hartland, 8 In.	28.00
Baseball, Figure, Ted Williams, Plastic, Hartland, Tag, 8 In. ....*illus*	385.00
Baseball, Figure, Warren Spahn, Plastic, Hartland, 8 In.	55.00
Baseball, Figure, Willie Mays, Plastic, Hartland, 8 In.	165.00
Baseball, Figure, Yogi Berra, Plastic, Hartland, String Tag, 8 In. ....*illus*	330.00
Baseball, Glove, Fielder's, Walter Johnson, Model, 1920s	504.00

Sports, Baseball, Ball, Autographed, Pittsburgh Pirates, 1926, 23 Signatures
$418.00

Sports, Baseball, Comic Book, Pride Of The Yankees, Life Of Lou Gerhig, c.1949
$78.00

Sports, Baseball, Figure, Ted Williams, Plastic, Hartland, Tag, 8 In.
$385.00

Sports, Baseball, Figure, Yogi Berra, Plastic, Hartland, String Tag, 8 In.
$330.00

S

Sports, Baseball, Program,
1947 All-Star Game,
Wrigley Field, Chicago
$132.00

Sports, Baseball, Silk, Joe Tinker,
Chicago Nationals, Old Mill Cigarettes,
S-74, 1910
$57.00

Sports, Basketball, Nodder,
Harlem Globetrotter, Composition,
Square Base, 1962, 6½ In.
$193.00

Baseball, Model Kit, Babe Ruth, Greatest Moments In Sports, Box, Sealed, 9 x 14 In.	448.00
Baseball, Nodder, Anaheim Angel, Composition, 1961-63, 6½ In.	83.00
Baseball, Nodder, Baltimore Oriole, Black Face, Composition, Box, 1963-65, 7 In.	880.00
Baseball, Nodder, Cleveland Indian, Green Base, 1963-65, 7 In.	185.00
Baseball, Nodder, Mickey Mantle, Composition, 1961-62, Miniature, 4½ In.	1430.00
Baseball, Nodder, Mickey Mantle, Composition, 7 In.	495.00
Baseball, Nodder, Roberto Clemente, Composition, Pirates Decal, 1961-63, 6½ In.	660.00
Baseball, Nodder, Roger Maris, Composition, 1961-62, Miniature, 4½ In.	495.00
Baseball, Nodder, Roger Maris, Composition, 1961-63, 6½ In.	495.00
Baseball, Nodder, Roger Maris, New York Yankees, Box	550.00
Baseball, Nodder, Willie Mays, Composition, 1961-63, 6½ In.	248.00
Baseball, Pen & Pencil Set, Mickey Mantle, Card, Late 1950s, 9¼ x 3½ In.	67.00
Baseball, Pencil Box, Bob Feller, Simulated Leather, Willard Mullin Images, 1950s, 8 x 3¼ In.	168.00
Baseball, Pencil Box, Spectators Watching Game, Keyhole, Enamel, c.1880	390.00
Baseball, Pencil Clip, Bill Veeck, ⅞ In.	249.00
Baseball, Pencil Clip, Bob Lemon, Cleveland Indians, Celluloid, ⅞ In.	59.00
Baseball, Pencil Clip, Luke Easter, Cleveland Indians, Celluloid, ⅞ In.	52.00
Baseball, Pennant, Cleveland Indians, Team Roster, Felt, 1954, 29 In.	123.00
Baseball, Pennant, Joe DiMaggio, Felt, 1940	458.00
Baseball, Pennant, Milwaukee Braves, Team Photo, Felt, 1957, 29 In.	84.00
Baseball, Photograph, Autographed, Mickey Mantle & Willie Mays, Sepia, 16 x 20 In.	611.00
Baseball, Postcard, Forbes Field, Pittsburgh Pirates, Opening Day, Fold-Out, 1909	264.00
Baseball, Postcard, Grover Cleveland Alexander, House Of David, Donkeys, Photo, 1930s	522.00
Baseball, Postcard, Toledo Mud Hens, Real Photo, 1909	168.00
Baseball, Program, 1947 All-Star Game, Wrigley Field, Chicago ....*illus*	132.00
Baseball, Ring, Tex Carleton, St. Louis Cardinals, World Champion, 1934	6573.00
Baseball, Salt, Ball Shape, 3 Crossed Bats Base, Tassels On Cover, 5 In.	495.00
Baseball, Scorer, El Paso Morning Times, Rio Grande Baseball Ass'n., Celluloid, Strap	334.00
Baseball, Seat, Crosley Field, Cincinnati, Double, Figural Side, Orange, 1935	2200.00
Baseball, Seat, Crosley Field, Cincinnati, Triple, Figural Side, Orange, 1935	1554.00
Baseball, Seat, Yankee Stadium, New York, Double, Blue, Nos. 3, 4, 1930s	3884.00
Baseball, Shoes, Joe DiMaggio, Unused, Tag, Box, Size 9	410.00
Baseball, Silk, Joe Tinker, Chicago Nationals, Old Mill Cigarettes, S-74, 1910 ....*illus*	57.00
Baseball, Trophy, Silver, Reed & Barton	212.00
Baseball, Tumbler, N.Y. Yankees, Johnny Blanchard, 5 In.	92.00
Baseball, Yankee Suitcase, Billy Martin, 1950-57	416.00
Basketball, Jersey, Autographed, Grant Hill, Detroit Pistons, 1997-98	377.00
Basketball, Nodder, Harlem Globetrotter, Composition, Square Base, 1962, 6½ In. ....*illus*	193.00
Basketball, Ring, Marques Haynes, Legends, Harlem Globetrotters	1434.00
Basketball, Watch, Lew Alcindor's, Los Angeles Basketball Classic, 1967	611.00
Bowling, Medal, Best Record Single Game, Coughlin's Stars, 1907, 5½ x 1½ In.	177.00
Boxing, Button, Be Lucky With Joe Louis, c.1940, ⅞ In.	162.00
Boxing, Button, Fitzsimmons-Corbett Fight, Arm, Don't Get In The Way Of This, 1897, ⅞ In.	150.00
Boxing, Button, Joe Louis Milk Co., Pride You Can Pour, Yellow, 1940s, 2¼ In.	274.00
Boxing, Button, Muhammad Ali, I Am King, Promotional, 1975, 2¼ In.	308.00
Boxing, Clock, Joe Louis, Figural, c.1940	256.00
Boxing, Glove, Muhammad Ali, Joe Frazier, Promotional, January 28, 1974, 12 In.	410.00
Boxing, Plaque, Jack Dempsey & Friend, In Swim Suits, Celluloid, Tin Cover, 1920s, 6 x 8 In.	187.00
Boxing, Poster, Louis-Schmeling Fight, Martin's V.V.O. Whiskey, 1938, 22 x 13½ In.	179.00
Boxing, Poster, World Champions & Past Greats Of The Prize Ring, 21 x 28 In.	55.00
Boxing, Ring, Joe Louis Portrait, Nickel Plated, Facsimile Autograph, 1940s	2740.00
Canoe Paddle, Tulip, Leaves, Signed, GP, 1825, 11½ In.	269.00
Canoe Seat, Wicker, Leather Straps, Compartment Under Seat, Leather-Wrapped Legs	92.00
Exercise, Dumb Bells, Maple, Black Stripes, Lowe & Campbell, 1½ & 3 Lbs., 2 Pair	39.00
Exercise, Indian Clubs, Black, Green, Red, No. 6, 18 In., Pair	325.00
Exercise, Indian Clubs, Green, Black, Red, Lady's, No. 2, 17 In., Pair	472.00
Exercise, Indian Clubs, Green, Black, Red, Lady's, No. 6, 21 In., Pair	303.00
Fencing, Mask, Body Protector, c.1911	106.00
Football, Bank, Baltimore Colts, Football Player, Ceramic, Fred Kail, 1960s, 9½ In.	112.00
Football, Button, Baltimore Colts, 1¼ In.	62.00
Football, Button, Chicago Bears, Celluloid, 1940s, 1¼ In.	25.00
Football, Button, Gator Bowl, Celluloid, 1949, 1¼ In.	31.00
Football, Button, Green Bay Packers, Green, Yellow, c.1950, 1¾ In.	151.00
Football, Button, I'm For The Colts, Football Player On Horse, Blue, White, Celluloid, 1 In. ..	22.00
Football, Cleats, Pads, Padded Pants, Glove, Headgear, 1920s	885.00

Football, Figure, John Arnett, Running With Ball, Plastic, Hartland, 8 In. . . . . *illus*	193.00
Football, Helmet, Andre Reed, Buffalo Bills, Game Used	611.00
Football, Helmet, Chicago Bears, Game Used, Wilson, 1974-1982 . . . . *illus*	162.00
Football, Jersey, Autographed, Brett Favre, Green Bay Packers, 2002	2826.00
Football, Pennant, 1939 Rose Bowl, USC, Brown Ground, Gold Lettering, 19 x 39 In.	315.00
Football, Pennant, Green Bay Packers, Felt, 1950s, 29 In.	140.00
Football, Poster, Gale Sayers, I Don't Smoke Cigarettes, 1971, 16 x 12 In.	140.00
Football, Program, Dallas Texans Vs. Oakland Raiders, 1960, 44 Pages	355.00
Football, Ring, John Riggins, 1983 Washington Redskins, NFC Champions	2569.00
Football, Watch, Pocket, Green Bay Packers, NFL Champion, 1929	9560.00
Golf, Bag, Leather, Tooled Indian Chief, 1940	975.00
Golf, Bag, Louis Vuitton, Leather, Brass Mounts, Strap, 34 In.	1725.00
Horse Racing, Jockey Scale, Brass, Mahogany, Green Leather, Brass Guards, 26 x 26 In.	2415.00
Horse Racing, Trophy, Silver, Jockey Boot Toe Caps, Engraved, 1884, 1904, 1914	148.00
Lacrosse, Stick, Bentwood, Carved, Leather Netting, Kapucha, c.1925, 26 x 2¼ In., Pair	230.00
Pool, Cue Rack & Billiard Board, Edwardian, Inlay, Gothic Pediment, 13 x 42½ In.	2070.00
Pool, Table, ABT Dutch, Walnut, Lithographed Face, Coin-Operated, 30 In.	2750.00
Rowing, Medal, Bismarck Regatta, Lawrence, Kansas, Gold, c.1882, 2¾ x 2 In.	110.00
Rowing, Medal, Crossed Oars, Flags, Gold Center, c.1885, 2¾ x 1¼ In.	83.00
Rowing, Medal, Northwestern Amateur Rowing Assn., Gold, c.1880, 4 x 1½ In.	165.00
Rowing, Medal, Relief Roman Figure, c.1883, 3¾ x 2 In.	165.00
Rowing, Scull Racing, Stickpin, Single Shell, Gold, Red Stone, 1890s, 3 x 2¾ In.	275.00
Skating, Ice Skates, Goose Neck, c.1880, 12 In.	8990.00
Skating, Ice Skates, Iron Runners, Brass Acorn Ends, Red, Leather Straps, 13½ In. . . . *illus*	385.00
Skating, Ice Skates, Wood, Iron Front Curve, Stamped P, Late 19th Century, 4½ x 14 In. . . .	480.00
Snowshoes, Bear Paw, Military Style, C.A. Lund, 28 In., Pair	58.00
Snowshoes, Leather Straps, L.L. Bean, Maine, 48 In.	127.00
Table Tennis, Button, National Championship, Chicago, Gray, Metal Backing, 1933, 1¾ In. . .	73.00
Tennis, Trophy, Rackets & Ball On Base, Silver Plate, Handles, Toronto Silver Plate Co., 11 In.	92.00
Trap Shooting, Trophy, Silver Plate, 3 Double-Barrel Shotguns, Dog, Toronto, 1886	384.00

STAFFORDSHIRE, England, has been a district making pottery and porcelain since the 1700s. Hundreds of kilns are still working in the area. Thousands of types of pottery and porcelain have been made in the many factories that worked and still work in the area. Some of the most famous factories have been listed separately, such as Adams, Davenport, Ridgway, Rowland & Marsellus, Royal Doulton, Royal Worcester, Spode, Wedgwood, and others. Some Staffordshire pieces are listed under categories like Fairing, Flow Blue, Mulberry, Shaving Mug, etc.

Baking Dish, Cream Ground, Piecrust Rim, Brown Slip Lines, 18th Century, 18 In.	5400.00
Basket, Blue & White Pastoral Scene, Cattle, Sheep, River, 1802, 10 In.	850.00
Bowl, Government Building, 2 Men, Embossed Flower Handles, Blue, 3 x 12¼ In.	330.00
Bowl, Multicolored, Floral, 4½ x 10 In.	39.00
Bowl, Upper Ferry Bridge Schuylkill River, Eagle & Flower Border, Blue, 4 x 12 In.	230.00
Bowl, Vegetable, Alpine Amusement, Blue Transfer, Oval, Shaped Rim, 9½ x 12¾ In. . . . *illus*	176.00
Bowl, Vegetable, Blue, States Arms Of North Carolina, Marked, 9 x 12 In.	5175.00
Bowl, Vegetable, Cover, Manor House, Flowers, Grapevine Border, Handles, Blue, 7¾ x 10 In.	1035.00
Bust, Earthenware, Green Glaze, Classical Male Figure, 19th Century, 20 In.	3173.00
Bust, George Washington, c.1850, 8½ In. . . . . *illus*	468.00
Candlestick, Flower Sprays, Baluster Turned Stem, Domed Scalloped Foot, 11 In. . . . . . *illus*	382.00
Coffeepot, Cover, Enameled, Salt Glazed, Stoneware, Baluster, c.1765, 9¼ In.	4200.00
Coffeepot, Flowering Vines, Green, Ocher, Crabstock Handle, c.1760, 6½ In. . . . . *illus*	960.00
Cream Jug, Agateware, Silver Shape, Baluster, Low Relief, c.1760, 3¾ In.	4800.00
Cup & Saucer, Pink Luster, 2⅛ x 5⅝ In., Pair	75.00
Dish, Slipware, Press Molded, Stag In Center, Brown Slip, c.1750, 11¼ In.	45000.00
Figurine, Bear, Standing, Earthenware, Buff Ground, Applied Cream, Brown Chips, 10 In. . .	1116.00
Figurine, Ben Franklin, Standing, Holding Hat & Scroll, 14¾ In. . . . . *illus*	1093.00
Figurine, Benjamin Franklin, Full-Length, Mislabeled As Washington, 15 In.	1035.00
Figurine, Bonnie Prince, c.1860, 12¼ In.	468.00
Figurine, Boy With Monkey, c.1850, 7 In.	293.00
Figurine, Bull & Serpent, Obadiah Sherratt, Early 19th Century, 6 In.	722.00
Figurine, Castle, c.1850, 6¼ x 5¼ In.	351.00
Figurine, Cat, Seated, Agate, Mottled Brown To White, 18th Century, 4¼ In.	646.00
Figurine, Cat, Seated On Blue Pillows, Gilt Trim, Yellow Ribbon At Neck, 7 In., Pair	430.00
Figurine, Cockatoo, White, Yellow Combs, 13½ x 14 In., Pair	705.00
Figurine, Couple Under Umbrella, c.1850, 6⅓ In.	176.00

Sports, Football, Figure, John Arnett, Running With Ball, Plastic, Hartland, 8 In.
$193.00

Sports, Football, Helmet, Chicago Bears, Game Used, Wilson, 1974-1982
$162.00

Sports, Skating, Ice Skates, Iron Runners, Brass Acorn Ends, Red, Leather Straps, 13½ In.
$385.00

Staffordshire, Bowl, Vegetable, Alpine Amusement, Blue Transfer, Oval, Shaped Rim, 9½ x 12¾ In.
$176.00

Staffordshire, Bust,
George Washington,
c.1850, 8½ In.
$468.00

Staffordshire, Candlestick,
Flower Sprays, Baluster Turned Stem,
Domed Scalloped Foot, 11 In.
$382.00

Staffordshire, Coffeepot,
Flowering Vines, Green, Ocher,
Crabstock Handle, c.1760, 6½ In.
$960.00

Figurine, Dick Turpin On Horseback, c.1850, 8¾ In.	146.00
Figurine, Dog, King Charles Cavalier Spaniel With Basket, c.1850, 6½ In.	527.00
Figurine, Dog, King Charles Spaniel, Brown, Cream, Locked Collar, Draped Chain, 8½ In., Pair	646.00
Figurine, Dog, Poodle, Seated, Pups, Oval Cobalt Blue Base, Coleslaw Trim, 8 In.	248.00
Figurine, Dog, Pug, Seated, White, Black, Gilt Collar, Early 20th Century, 12½ In.	375.00
Figurine, Dog, Spaniel, Seated, Facing Each Other, Black Spots, Gilt, 9¼ In.	258.00
Figurine, Dog, Spaniel, White, Gold, 19th Century, 13 In., Pair	206.00
Figurine, Dog, Spaniel, White Coat, Iron Red Patches, 10 In., Pair .....*illus*	502.00
Figurine, Dog, Spaniel, White Crackle Glaze, Green Luster Glaze, Late 1800s, 10 x 7 In., Pair	323.00
Figurine, Dog, Whippet, Carrying Dead Hare In Mouth, Stump Base, 11 In., Pair	1057.00
Figurine, Eagle With Dog, c.1860, 6½ In.	351.00
Figurine, Elephant, c.1880, 8 x 10 In.	1053.00
Figurine, Girl, Barefoot, Basket Of Fruit, Walton On Banner, 7 In.	402.00
Figurine, Girl On Goat, Russet & Burnt Orange, 13 In.	293.00
Figurine, Girl On Goat With Falcon, c.1850, 5 In.	234.00
Figurine, Gleaner, c.1850, 12¾ In. .....*illus*	234.00
Figurine, Highland Hunter & His Dog, Multicolored, 15 In.	411.00
Figurine, Hunter & His Dog, 23½ In. .....*illus*	161.00
Figurine, Lion, Glass Eyes, Marked, Made In England, L & Sons Ltd., 11 x 13½ In., Pair	316.00
Figurine, Lion, Standing, Glass Eyes, 10 In., Pair	443.00
Figurine, Markswoman, Bow & Arrow, Straw Target, Tree, Walton On Banner, 8 In.	288.00
Figurine, Milk Boy, c.1840, 9½ x 11 In.	468.00
Figurine, Princess Royal On Horseback, 19th Century, 7 In.	109.00
Figurine, Queen Victoria, c.1870, 13½ In.	819.00
Figurine, Ram & Lamb, Coleslaw Vegetation, Walton On Banner, 6¾ In.	431.00
Figurine, Royal Dancers, 19th Century, 9½ x 5½ In.	293.00
Figurine, Samson & Lion, 12 In.	403.00
Figurine, Scottish Bagpiper With King Charles Spaniel, c.1850, 17 x 7½ In.	293.00
Figurine, Scottish Couple, c.1860, 14 In.	117.00
Figurine, Scottish Girl On King Charles Spaniel, 6½ x 7 In.	1404.00
Figurine, Scottish Girl On Pony, c.1870, 9¼ In.	176.00
Figurine, Stanfield Hall, Norfolk Country House, Double Murder Site, c.1849, 5½ In.	88.00
Figurine, Tom King On Horseback, c.1850, 8¼ x 7 In.	205.00
Figurine, Violinist, Reclining On Couch, 7 x 6½ In.	230.00
Figurine, Winter's Tale, c.1860, 12 x 6½ In.	410.00
Group, Auld Lang Syne, 3 Men, c.1840, 8 x 7½ In.	410.00
Group, Courting Highland Couple, With Bird, On Draped Sofa, Multicolored, 10½ In.	235.00
Group, Damsel, Bird, Cat, Seated Next To Beehive, Tulip Shape Vase, 7½ In.	88.00
Group, Gypsy Couple, Flanking Classical Column, Wreath, Salt Glaze, 8½ In.	235.00
Group, Man & Woman, Seated Under Leaf & Grape Garland, 13¾ In. .....*illus*	173.00
Group, Married Couple, c.1850, 9¼ In.	205.00
Group, Miller & His Wife, Mill With 2 Arches, Ducks, 9¼ In.	176.00
Group, New Marriage Act, 19th Century, 6 In.	473.00
Group, Robin Hood, With 2 Members Of His Merry Band & Dog, Stump Spill Holder, 14 In.	381.00
Group, The Widow, Multicolored Bocage, 10 In.	411.00
Jug, Flowers, Bamboo Figural Handle, Orange Peel Ground, 6¾ In.	65.00
Jug, White Salt Glazed, Stoneware, Pecten Shell, Strap Handle, c.1750, 3 In.	4200.00
Knife Rest, Romantic Purple Transfer, c.1835, 3¾ x 1 In., Pair	375.00
Milk Jug, Russet, Baluster Shape, Mask & Paw Feet, Loop Handle, c.1750, 3½ In.	1920.00
Mug, Motto, Dr. Franklin's Poor Richard Maxims, Black Transfer, Child's, 2¾ In.	92.00
Pepper Pot, Man In Field With Cows, Castle, Village, Blue Transfer, Bulbous	105.00
Pepper Pot, Red Flower, Green Leaves, Running Pattern, Bulbous, Cylindrical	61.00
Pitcher, Highland Fling, Pink Sunderland Luster, c.1860, 8⅓ In.	117.00
Pitcher, Peace, Plenty, Independence, Off-White, Silver Glaze, c.1820, 8½ x 4¾ In.	1770.00
Pitcher, Spaniel, Seated, Black & White, Spotted, Red Bow, Early 1800s, 8 In.	294.00
Plate, Basket Of Flowers, Red, Blue, Green, Pink Border, 9⅞ In.	165.00
Plate, Black, Purple & Green Flowers, 7⅞ In.	44.00
Plate, Boston State House, Flower Border, Medium Blue, 9¾ In.	115.00
Plate, Cabbage Rose, Red, Yellow, Green, 9⅛ In.	61.00
Plate, Commodore MacDonnough's Victory, Shell Border, Dark Blue Transfer, Wood, 9 In.	488.00
Plate, Constitutional Grievances, Blue Transfer, c.1850, 7 In.	435.00
Plate, Franklin's Proverbs, Man Plowing, Embossed Flowers & Wheat, J & G Meakin, 7 In.	61.00
Plate, Girl Sitting On Log, Bird On Leaf Hand, Transfer, Impressed, Wood, 3¾ In.	44.00
Plate, Landing Of General Lafayette, Castle Garden, c.1836, 7¾ In.	235.00
Plate, Landing Of General Lafayette, Clews, 10 In., Pair	345.00

S

Staffordshire, Figurine, Ben Franklin, Standing, Holding Hat & Scroll, 14¾ In. $1093.00

Staffordshire, Figurine, Hunter & His Dog, 23½ In. $161.00

Staffordshire, Group, Man & Woman, Seated Under Leaf & Grape Garland, 13¾ In. $173.00

Staffordshire, Figurine, Dog, Spaniel, White Coat, Iron Red Patches, 10 In., Pair $502.00

Staffordshire, Platter, Fishing Scene, 2 Men, Mother, Child, Church, Flowers, 14½ x 19 In. $840.00

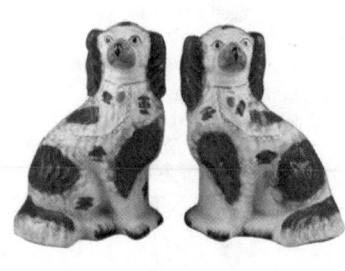

Staffordshire, Figurine, Gleaner, c.1850, 12¾ In. $234.00

Staffordshire, Teapot, Cover, Lead Glazed, Cream Colored, Apple Shape, c.1765, 3½ In. $10800.00

Staffordshire, Teapot, Cover, Salt Glazed, Stoneware, Littler's Blue, Globe Shape, c.1755, 5 In. $8400.00

S

Staffordshire, Tureen, Sauce, Cover, Underplate, Cambridge Pattern, Shell Handles, 6½ x 7½ In. $316.00

Staffordshire, Tureen, Sauce, Cover, Underplate, Ladle, Canova, White, Red Transfer, Thomas Mayer, 8¼ In. $558.00

Stangl Birds

Stangl Pottery birds were first made in 1939. Over sixty different birds were made before 1978. The figurines are based on pictures in James Audubon's *Birds of America* and Alexander Wilson's *American Ornithology.*

Plate, Lead Glazed, Cream Colored, Sponged, Seeded Diaper Border, c.1760, 8 In.	600.00
Plate, Luncheon, Crown, Yellow Center, Flower Border, 9¾ In., 12 Piece	117.00
Plate, Multicolored, Flowers, Scalloped Rim, 9⅛ In., Pair	94.00
Plate, Multicolored, Flowers, Scalloped Rim, 10 In., Pair	127.00
Plate, Multicolored, Pomegranate, Scalloped Rim, 10½ In.	105.00
Plate, Napoleon Bonaparte, Transfer, 10 In.	138.00
Plate, Philadelphia Library, Flower Border, Medium Blue Transfer, 8¼ In.	230.00
Plate, Scenic, Verse, Walk In Garden By Moon Light, Embossed, Transfer, 7½ In.	138.00
Plate, Soup, Romantic View, Castle Ruin Scene, Blue Transfer, 10 In. Diam.	55.00
Plate, State Arms Of North Carolina, Marked, Transfer Eagle, 7¼ In.	460.00
Plate, Strawberry, Running Rose & Vine, 8⅞ In.	121.00
Plate, Winter View Of Pittsfield, Mass., Scalloped Edge, Dark Blue Transfer, Clews, 8¾ In.	316.00
Platter, Blue, Printed Flowers, Flower Border, Oval, c.1820, 20½ In.	641.00
Platter, Blue & White, Well & Tree, Castle, Water Buffalo, People, 1920s, 16 In.	1435.00
Platter, Castle, Water Bridge, Vignette Pattern, Wood Stand, 19¾ x 16 In.	920.00
Platter, Customs House, Banner Edge, 15 States Named, Clews, 18½ In.	1840.00
Platter, Fishing Scene, 2 Men, Mother, Child, Church, Flowers, 14½ x 19 In. *illus*	840.00
Platter, Florentine Villas, Scalloped Edge, Blue Transfer, Jackson Warranted, 14 x 18 In.	110.00
Platter, Green, Brown Transfer, Landscape, Buildings, Flower Border, 20 x 7 In.	690.00
Platter, Landing Of General Lafayette At Castle Garden, New York, Blue, c.1825, 19½ In.	1793.00
Platter, Multicolored, Eagle With Olive Branch, 15 x 11⅝ In.	248.00
Platter, Multicolored, Flowers, 14⅞ x 11⅝ In.	275.00
Platter, Multicolored, Flowers, Eagle Clutching Olive Branch, 14 x 11 In.	275.00
Platter, Multicolored, Flowers, Scalloped Rim, 10⅝ x 8⅜ In.	110.00
Platter, Port Scene, Sail Ship, Blue, Shell & Flower Border, 14⅞ x 11¾ In.	1045.00
Platter, Post Office Of Dublin, Blue, Tams Pottery, 18¼ x 14⅝ In.	523.00
Platter, Regenta Quadrant, London, Blue, 17⅜ x 13½ In.	495.00
Platter, Vegetable, Blue, State Arms Of North Carolina, 9¾ x 12¼ In.	5175.00
Platter, Winter View Of Pittsfield, Mass., Blue Transfer, Oval, Scalloped Edges, 18 x 15 In.	1553.00
Punch Bowl, Flared Foot, Capitol Building, Flower, Leaf Border, 10¾ In.	2749.00
Sauce, Cover, Underplate, Ladle, Canova, White, Red Transfer, Thomas Mayer, 8¼ In. *illus*	558.00
Sauceboat, Agateware, Silver Shape, Bulbous, Scalloped, Reeded Rim, c.1760, 8 In.	9000.00
Sauceboat, Flower Finial, Blue Transfer, 4-Footed, Scrolls, Roses, Bee Skeps, c.1810, 6 x 8 In.	299.00
Sauceboat, Red Agateware, Double Lipped, Swirling Striations, c.1740, 6¼ In.	5100.00
Sauceboat, Woman, Vase, Prunus Blossoms, Trellis & Flower Band, Scalloped Edge, 7 In.	1800.00
Soup, Dish, Fruit & Flowers, Embossed, 8¼ In.	50.00
Soup, Dish, Men Fishing At Water's Edge, Seated Ladies, Blue, 9¾ In.	138.00
Soup, Dish, Old Ivory Border, Gold Trim, 10 In., 8 Piece	450.00
Soup, Dish, Oriental Man By Water, Pagoda, Blue, 10⅝ In.	220.00
Soup, Dish, Woman, Man, Donkey, Church, Blue, 10 In.	193.00
Spill Holder, Dog, Seated, Gilt Accents, 13⅜ In.	690.00
Spill Vase, Figural, Cow, Milkmaid, Oval Base, Early 1800s, 8¼ In.	411.00
Spill Vase, Red Fox, Goose, England, 9 x 7 In.	146.00
Stirrup Cup, Fox Head, 5 x 3½ In., Pair	605.00
Stirrup Cup, Fox Head, Red Spattered, Black Collar, 19th Century, 5 x 3 x 3¼ In.	805.00
Tea Bowl, Saucer, Lead Glazed, Cream Colored, Earthenware, c.1755, 4⅝ In.	900.00
Tea Canister, Agateware, Combed Surface, Brown, Cream, Green Band, c.1800, 4⅞ In.	1410.00
Teapot, 3 Houses, Trees, Bridge, Salt Glaze, Crabstock Finial, Spout & Handle, 4 In.	960.00
Teapot, Canova, Green & Red Transfer, Thomas Mayer, 1826-35, 11 In.	1116.00
Teapot, Cover, Agateware, Globe Shape, Brown, Buff, Rust Enamels, Green Trim, 4½ In.	4113.00
Teapot, Cover, Agateware, Globular, Loop Handle, Curved Spout, c.1760, 4 In.	10800.00
Teapot, Cover, Agateware, Shell, Lion Finial, Scroll Handle, c.1740, 6½ In.	5760.00
Teapot, Cover, Blue, White Salt Glaze, Stoneware, Crabstock Handle, Spout, 4 In.	881.00
Teapot, Cover, Enameled, Salt Glazed, Stoneware, Kakiemon Style, c.1750, 5½ In.	15600.00
Teapot, Cover, Enameled, Salt Glazed, Stoneware, King Of Prussia, c.1757, 4 In.	2160.00
Teapot, Cover, Glazed Redware, Seated Camel, Howdah, c.1745, 5½ In.	7200.00
Teapot, Cover, Lead Glazed, Cream Colored, Apple Shape, c.1765, 3½ In. *illus*	10800.00
Teapot, Cover, Lead Glazed, Cream Colored, Earthenware, c.1760, 3½ In.	1440.00
Teapot, Cover, Lead Glazed, Cream Colored, Hexagonal, c.1765, 4½ In.	4800.00
Teapot, Cover, Littler's, Blue Ground, Salt Glaze, Stoneware, Globe Shape, 1700s, 3¾ In.	999.00
Teapot, Cover, Pear Shape, Enameled, Salt Glazed, Stoneware, c.1760, 5¼ In.	2160.00
Teapot, Cover, Salt Glazed, Stoneware, Littler's Blue, Globe Shape, c.1755, 5 In. *illus*	8400.00
Teapot, Cover, Salt Glazed Stoneware, House Shape, Serpent Spout, c.1750, 5 In.	2160.00
Teapot, Cover, White Salt Glaze, Globe Shape, Lion Mask, Paw Feet, 18th Century, 5 In.	823.00
Teapot, Multicolored, Floral, Gooseneck Spout, Ear Handle, 6 In.	11.00

Teapot, Oriental Design, Stepped Lid, 8-Sided, Bulbous, Blue Transfer, Footed, Early 1800s ..	203.00
Toby Jugs are listed in their own category.	
Tray, Canova, Green & Red Transfer, c.1950, 13½ In.	999.00
Tureen, Canova, Green & Red Transfer, Thomas Mayer, 1826-35, 13 In.	2820.00
Tureen, Cover, Chicks On Nest, Painted, England, 7½ x 10 In.	2091.00
Tureen, Cover, Oriental Pattern, 2 Shell Form Handles, Footed, 8½ x 13 x 8 In.	403.00
Tureen, Cover, Woman, Man, Donkey, Church, Blue, Flower & Leaf Border, 7 x 10 In.	165.00
Tureen, Cover, Women & Children By Stream, Scroll Border, Blue, 6¼ x 12½ In.	110.00
Tureen, Cover, Underplate, Figures, Man On Horse, Early 19th Century, 6 x 14 x 9 In.	625.00
Tureen, Sauce, Cover, Underplate, Cambridge Pattern, Shell Handles, 6½ x 7½ In. ....*illus*	316.00
Vase, Chimney, Burns & His Mary, Scottish Attire, 12 In., Pair	115.00
Vase, Garniture, Oriental Flowers Pattern, Paneled, Cinnabar Dragon Handles, 19 In.	382.00
Vase, Tulip Shape, Red Striated Blossom & Bud, Leafy Mound Base, c.1925, 6¼ In., Pair	2400.00
Washbowl, Multicolored, Flowers, Paneled Flared Rim, 4 x 12¼ In.	61.00
Washbowl & Pitcher, Flowers, Birds, Gilt, Green, Charles Barlow, c.1900, 13 In.	147.00
Waste Bowl, Lafayette & Franklin's Tomb, Blue Transfer, 5½ x 3 In.	374.00

STANGL Pottery traces its history back to the Fulper Pottery of New Jersey. In 1910, Johann Martin Stangl started working at Fulper. He left to work at Haeger Pottery from 1915 to 1920. Stangl returned to Fulper Pottery in 1920, became president in 1926, and changed the company name to Stangl Pottery in 1929. Stangl acquired the firm in 1930. The pottery is known for dinnerware and a line of bird figurines. Martin Stangl died in 1972 and the pottery was sold to Frank Wheaton, Jr., of Wheaton Industries. Production continued until 1978, when Pfaltzgraff Pottery purchased the right to the Stangl trademark and the remaining inventory was liquidated. A single bird figurine is identified by a number. Figurines made up of two birds are identified by a number followed by the letter *D* indicating Double.

Bachelor's Button, Bowl, Vegetable, 8 In.	8.00
Bachelor's Button, Tidbit, Handle, 10 In.	10.00
Bird, Bluebird, No. 3276, 5⅛ In.	55.00
Bird, Chat Or Carolina Wren, No. 3590, 4½ In. ....*illus*	60.00
Bird, Cockatoo, Double, No. 3405D, 9⅜ In.	143.00
Bird, Cockatoo, No. 3405, 6⅛ In.	95.00
Bird, Golden Crowned Kinglet, No. 3848, 4⅛ In.	63.00
Bird, Key West Quail Dove, No. 3454, 9¼ In.	176.00
Bird, Kingfisher, No. 3406S, 3½ In. ....*illus*	72.00
Bird, Oriole, No. 3402S, 3¼ In.	110.00
Bird, Parula Warbler, No. 3583, 4¼ In.	60.00
Bird, Penguin, No. 3274, 6 In. ....*illus*	100.00
Bird, Yellow Warbler, No. 3447, 5⅛ In.	55.00
Golden Blossom, Cup & Saucer	8.00
Golden Blossom, Plate, 6 In.	6.00
Golden Blossom, Plate, 10 In.	9.00
Golden Blossom, Platter, Oval, 14¾ In.	25.00
Golden Harvest, Bowl, Vegetable, 8 In.	30.00
Golden Harvest, Casserole, Skillet Shape, 6 In.	18.00
Golden Harvest, Plate, 6¼ In.	10.00
Golden Harvest, Plate, 10¼ In.	10.00
Magnolia, Relish	24.00
Orchard Song, Bowl, Fruit, 5½ In.	9.00
Orchard Song, Platter, Oval, 14¾ In.	35.00
Sculptured Fruit, Plate, 6 In.	9.00
Sculptured Fruit, Plate, 10 In.	10.00
Sculptured Fruit, Tidbit, 10⅛ In.	10.00
Sunburst, Vase, Fan, Stepped Sides, Orange, Brown, Green & Blue High Glaze, 6¼ In.	259.00
Terra Rose, Bowl, Light Pink, Mauve Striated, Ruffled Rim, 2½ x 11 x 7 In.	30.00
Terra Rose, Vase, Leaf Wrapped Sides, Blue, 4 In.	45.00
Thistle, Plate, 6 In.	5.00
Town & Country, Plate, Blue, 8 In.	28.00
Town & Country, Saltshaker, Blue, 5 x 3 In.	10.00
Tulip, Creamer, Yellow Flowers	10.00
Tulip, Salt, Yellow Flower, No Cork	10.00
Tweed, Vase, Bud, Gold, 6 In.	9.00
White Dogwood, Creamer, 4¼ In.	20.00
White Dogwood, Cup, 2¾ In.	10.00
White Dogwood, Plate, 10 In.	10.00

Stangl, Bird, Chat Or Carolina Wren, No. 3590, 4½ In. $60.00

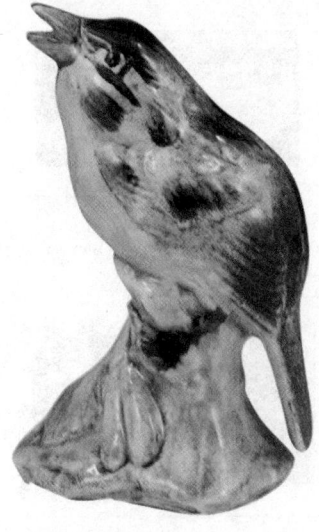

Stangl, Bird, Kingfisher, No. 3406S, 3½ In. $72.00

Stangl, Bird, Penguin, No. 3274, 6 In. $100.00

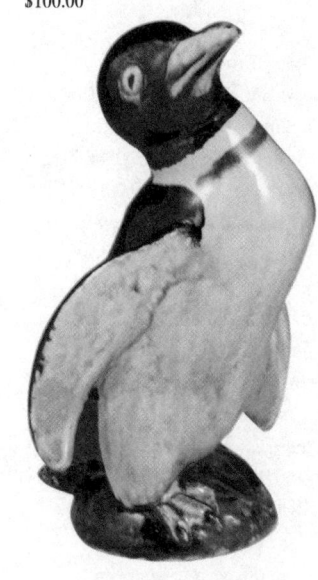

S

Star Trek, Toy, Playset,
USS Enterprise Bridge, Decals, 8 Figures,
Box, Mego, 12 x 24 In.
$115.00

Star Trek, Toy, USS Enterprise,
Die Cast Metal, No. 358, Box, Dinky,
1975, 5 x 9 x 3 In.
$115.00

Star Wars, Figure, Luke Skywalker,
On Card, Kenner, 1978-79, 3¾ In.
$170.00

Space Toys

Two of the earliest space toys are Buck Rogers' 25th Century Rocket Ship and Flash Gordon's Rocket Fighter, produced by Marx in the 1930s and 1940s. Television shows *Space Patrol* and *Tom Corbett, Space Cadet* and the movie *Forbidden Planet* licensed a variety of toys in the 1950s. Television's six *Star Trek* series (1966–2005), the ten *Star Trek* motion pictures (1979–2002), and the six *Star Wars* movies (1977–2005) licensed even more space-related toys that are popular with collectors.

STAR TREK AND STAR WARS collectibles are included here. The original *Star Trek* television series ran from 1966 through 1969. The series spawned an animated series, three sequels, and a prequel, which is still in production. The first Star Trek movie was released in 1979 and nine others followed, the most recent in 2002. The movie *Star Wars* opened in 1977. Sequels were released in 1980 and 1983; prequels in 1999, 2002, and 2005. Other science fiction and fantasy collectibles can be found under Batman, Buck Rogers, Captain Marvel, Flash Gordon, Movie, Superman, and Toy.

STAR TREK

Comic Art, Sunday, Divono & Harris, December 13, 1981, 12½ x 18 In.	101.00
Figure, Captain Kirk, First Issue, 5-Picture Back, Mego, Blister Card, 1974, 8 In.	123.00
Lunch Box, Metal, Dome, Aladdin, 1968	308.00
Toy, Flashlite Ray Gun, Plastic, Larami Corp., On Card, 1968, 7½ x 10¾ In.	547.00
Toy, Playset, USS Enterprise Bridge, Decals, 8 Figures, Box, Mego, 12 x 24 In. ....*illus*	115.00
Toy, USS Enterprise, Die Cast Metal, No. 358, Box, Dinky, 1975, 5 x 9 x 3 In. ....*illus*	115.00

STAR WARS

Box, Empire Strikes Back Cards, Series 3, Contents, Topps, c.1980, 6 x 7½ x 3 In.	56.00
Comic Book, No. 1, August, 1977	239.00
Figure, C-3PO, Jointed, Plastic, 1978, 12 In.	110.00
Figure, Luke Skywalker, On Card, Kenner, 1978-79, 3¾ In. ....*illus*	170.00
Movie Poster, Empire Strikes Back, 20th Century Fox, 1980, 40 x 30 In.	510.00
Movie Poster, Revenge Of The Jedi, 1983, 27 x 41 In.	448.00
Movie Poster, Revenge Of The Jedi, Advance, 20th Century Fox, 1982, 1 Sheet	978.00
Movie Poster, Star Wars, Style C, 20th Century Fox, England, 1978, Quad, 30 x 40 In.	546.00
Pencil Sharpener, Episode 1, Tin, Unopened	7.00
Pin, Official Star Wars Fan Club, Rebel Recruiter, c.1978, 2½ In.	34.00
Teapot, Luke Skywalker On Taun Taun, Sigma, Early 1980s, 10 x 10 In.	280.00

STEINS have been used by beer and ale drinkers for over 500 years. They have been made of ivory, porcelain, stoneware, faience, silver, pewter, wood, or glass in sizes up to nine gallons. Although some were made by Mettlach, Meissen, Capo-di-Monte, and other famous factories, most were made by less important German potteries. The words *Geschutz* or *Musterschutz* on a stein are the German words for "patented" or "registered design," not company names. Steins are still being made in the old styles. Lithophane steins may be found in the Lithophane category.

Brewery, Erstes Kulmacher, Transfer, Enamel, Stoneware, Pewter Lid, L. Hohlwein, ½ Liter	290.00
Brewery, Lowenbraubraukeller Munchen No. 81510, Hand Engraved, Pewter Lid, 1 Liter	241.00
Brewery, Mathaserbrau Munchen, Etched, MB, Pewter Lid, 1 Liter	418.00
Brewery, Pschorr-Brau Munchen, Schutze-Marke, Etched, Stoneware, 1 Liter	145.00 to 241.00
Character, Acorn, Pottery, Lid, No. 1235, ½ Liter	207.00
Character, Alligator, Porcelain, Lid, Schierholz, ½ Liter	445.00
Character, Alligator, Wrap Around, Porcelain, Inlaid Lid, E. Bohne & Sohne, ½ Liter	558.00
Character, Artillery Shell, Stoneware, Pewter Lid, J. Reinemann, Munchen, ½ Liter	374.00
Character, Automobile, Chauffer, Family, Road, Glass, Transfer, Enamel, Pewter Lid, ½ Liter	1207.00
Character, Barmaid, Porcelain Lid, Schierholz, ½ Liter	4660.00
Character, Beehive, Pottery, Inlaid Lid, No. 1384, Reinhold Merkelbach, ½ Liter	348.00
Character, Bismarck, Blue, Porcelain, Lid, Schierholz, ½ Liter	1012.00
Character, Bismarck, Blue & White, Porcelain, Lid, Schierholz, ½ Liter	1012.00
Character, Bismarck, Porcelain, Lid, Schierholz, ½ Liter	603.00
Character, Bismarck Radish, Porcelain, Inlaid Lid, Schierholz, ⅓ Liter	603.00
Character, Cat, Sitting On Back Legs, Porcelain, Inlaid Lid, Schierholz, ½ Liter	552.00
Character, Clown, Pottery, Diesinger, 4¼ In.	99.00
Character, Devil, Porcelain, Inlaid Lid, E. Bohnes & Sohne, ⅓ Liter	518.00
Character, Drunken Monkey, Porcelain, Inlaid Lid, Schierholz, ½ Liter	495.00
Character, Fox, Stoneware, Inlaid Lid, No. 148, Marked, Reinhold Merkelbach, ½ Liter	255.00
Character, Hanswurst, Stoneware, Inlaid Lid, Marked, J. Reinemann, F. Ringer, ⅓ Liter	784.00
Character, Hops Lady Face, Pottery, Pewter Lid, ½ Liter	435.00
Character, Iron Maiden, Stoneware, Inlaid Lid, Marked, TW, ½ Liter	472.00
Character, Man Holding 2 Geese, Porcelain, Inlaid Lid, E. Bohne & Sohne, ½ Liter	845.00
Character, Man Riding High Wheel Bicycle, Pewter Lid, ½ Liter	3278.00
Character, Man Smoking Pipe, Pottery, Inlaid Lid, Majolica Glaze, ½ Liter	345.00
Character, Man's Face, Bug On Forehead, Pottery, Pewter Lid, ½ Liter	250.00
Character, Monk, Pottery, Pewter Lid, Stylized Bee, No. T74/1, Goebel, c.1950, ½ Liter	230.00
Character, Monkey Holding Boot, Pottery, Inlaid Lid, No. 888, Gerz, ½ Liter	356.00
Character, Munich Child, Cobalt Blue, Stoneware, Inlaid Lid, No. 298, ¼ Liter	319.00
Character, Munich Child, Holding Stein, Pottery, Porcelain Inlaid Lid, No. 117, ½ Liter	400.00

S

Character, Munich Child, On Barrel, Porcelain, Lid, Marked, Schierholz, 1 Liter	785.00
Character, Munich Child, Pointed Hood, Porcelain, Inlaid Lid, ½ Liter	241.00
Character, Munich Child, Porcelain, Inlaid Lid, ½ Liter	170.00
Character, Munich Child, Pottery, Lid, No. 5162, ½ Liter	483.00
Character, Newspaper Lady, Blue, Porcelain, Lid, Schierholz, ½ Liter	483.00
Character, Nun, Holding Bible, Porcelain, Inlaid Lid, Lithophane, ½ Liter	218.00
Character, Nurnberg, VIII Deutsches Sangerbundesfest 1912, Pottery, Lid, F & N, 5¾ In.	241.00
Character, Nurnberg Tower, Pottery, Pewter Lid, No. 1190, 5¾ In.	86.00
Character, Orangutan, Porcelain, Inlaid Lid, E. Bohne & Sohne, ½ Liter	2415.00
Character, Owl, Blue & Purple Salt Glaze, Stoneware, Inlaid Lid, Hauber & Reuther, ½ Liter	603.00
Character, Owl, Yellow Eyes, Beak, Porcelain, Inlaid Lid, E. Bohne & Sohne, ½ Liter	3795.00
Character, Pig, Cards On Breastplate, Pottery, Inlaid Lid, No. 116, ½ Liter	338.00
Character, Pig, Holding Cards, Pottery, Inlaid Lid, No. 1116, Reinhold Merkelbach, ½ Liter	483.00
Character, Pig, Smoking, Porcelain, Inlaid Lid, Schierholz, ½ Liter	288.00
Character, Skull, Snake Handle, Porcelain, Inlaid Lid, E. Bohne & Sohne, ½ Liter	490.00
Character, Skull On Book, Porcelain, Inlaid Lid, E. Bohne & Sohne, ¼ Liter	518.00
Character, Tower, Pewter, Lid, Engraved, Tir Cantonal Neuchatel 1906, ½ Liter, 9¾ In.	278.00
Character, Umbrella Men, Porcelain, Pewter Lid, Schierholz, ½ Liter	646.00
Character, Woman's Head, Pottery, Inlaid Lid, No. 702, ½ Liter	551.00
Faience, Horse, Leaping, Multicolored, Pewter Lid, Crown Thumblift, 8¼ In.	440.00
Glass, Blown, Amber, Munich Child, Enamel, Pewter Lid, ½ Liter	303.00
Glass, Blown, Clear, Engraved Scene, Fluted, I. Zittau, Glass Inlaid Lid, c.1850, 4¾ In.	313.00
Glass, Blown, Clear, Red Stain, Rabbit In Forest, Glass Inlaid Lid, c.1850, ½ Liter	218.00
Glass, Blown, Green, Ribbed, Pewter Base & Lid, ½ Liter	106.00
Glass, Blown, Purple Overlay, Cut On Body, Base, Handle, Relief Pewter Lid, 2 Dogs, ½ Liter	2028.00
Glass, Blown, Stag, Enamel, Fluted, Pewter Lid, Horn Finial, ½ Liter	93.00
Glass, Pressed, Lalique Style, Inlaid Lid, Bock Thumblift, ⅓ Liter	165.00
Mettlach Steins are listed in the Mettlach category.	
Military, Boy As Husar, Wilhelm II, Frederick III, Transfer, Enamel, Porcelain, Inlaid Lid, ½ Liter	845.00
Military, Medical Scene, Transfer, Enamel, Stoneware, Pewter Lid Marked Georg Mayer, ½ Liter	460.00
Occupational, Brewer, 2 Scenes, Karl Bernhardt, Transfer, Porcelain, Pewter Lid, ½ Liter	230.00
Occupational, Blacksmith, Lassalle, Woman, Torch, Porcelain, Enamel, Pewter Lid, ½ Liter	443.00
Occupational, Butcher, Porcelain, F. Huber, ½ Liter	230.00
Occupational, Okonomie Farming, Porcelain, Enamel, Pewter Lid, Soldier, ½ Liter	200.00
Occupational, Teamsters, Grain Bags, Xavier Moelle, Lithophane, Pewter Lid, 10 In. *illus*	230.00
Pewter, 2 Headed Eagle, Scenes, Pewter Lid, Siegburg Style, 1573, 1 Liter, 12 In.	345.00
Pewter, Scenes, Urfeld, Relief, Pewter Lid, 6½ In.	110.00
Porcelain, 2 Young Girls, Hand Painted, Pewter Lid, Flowers & Initials, c.1850, ½ Liter	461.00
Porcelain, Bayerische Erziehung, Baby Drinking Beer, Transfer, Enamel, Pewter Lid, ½ Liter	184.00
Porcelain, Blue Onion Design, Hand Painted, Lithopone, Inlaid Lid, ½ Liter	130.00
Porcelain, Crocodile, 3 Babies, 3 Eggs, Hand Painted, Pewter Lid, ½ Liter	604.00
Porcelain, Man, Woman, Flowers, Hand Painted, Silver Lid, Gold Wash, 1 Liter, 8½ In.	1150.00
Porcelain, Musik Und Gesangverein 1896, Transfer, Enamel, Glass Inlaid Lid, ½ Liter	194.00
Pottery, 20 Coins, Relief, Inlaid Lid, No. 1262, ½ Liter	392.00
Pottery, 3 Scenes, Herman, Falstaff, Student, Etched, Pewter Lid, ½ Liter	302.00
Pottery, Bird, Post Telegraph, Post Horn Handle, Relief, No. 1265, Pewter Lid, ½ Liter	310.00
Pottery, Lohengrins Abschid, Etched, Inlaid Lid, No. 906, JWR, ½ Liter	145.00
Pottery, Man Serenading Woman, Etched, Inlaid Lid, No. 439, Thewalt, ½ Liter	120.00
Pottery, Musicians, Relief, Pewter Lid, No. 802, 1 Liter	170.00
Pottery, People Drinking & Dancing, Transfer, Relief, Pewter Lid, No. 635, 2½ Liter	287.00
Pottery, Shooting Festival, 3 Bundesschiessen 1894, Transfer, Enamel, Pewter Lid, ½ Liter	302.00
Pottery, Student Society, S.L. LBF. Karl Schmidt Al. Rest. 1913-14, Pewter Lid, ½ Liter	170.00
Regimental, 1 Abt. Feld Artillerie Regt. No 24 Gustrow, Scene, Pottery, Pewter Lid, ¼ Liter	194.00
Regimental, 3 Inf.-Rgt., Prinz Karl Von Bayern, 12. Comp Augsburg 1908, 12 In. *illus*	259.00
Regimental, Roster, 2 Bayr Jager Batl. 3 Comp. Aschaffenburg 1898-1900, ½ Liter	632.00
Regimental, Roster, 2 Cp. Konigl. Bayr. II Fuss Artillery Regt. Metz 1901-03, Res. Pausch, ½ Liter	604.00
Regimental, Roster, Porcelain, 2 Side Scenes, Eagle Thumblift, ½ Liter, 10¾ In.	465.00
Regimental, Roster, Porcelain, 2 Side Scenes, Lion Thumblift, ½ Liter, 11½ In.	604.00
Regimental, Roster, Stoneware, 4 Side Scenes, Eagle Thumblift, ½ Liter, 10 In.	634.00
Stoneware, 2 Women In Musical Design, Etched, Inlaid Lid, No. 1258, KB, Girmscheid, ¾ Liter	152.00
Stoneware, 4 Scenes Of Men, Etched, Pewter Lid, No. 938, Girmscheid, 1 Liter	129.00
Stoneware, Cavaliers Drinking, Etched, Stoneware Lid, No. 1084a, Girmscheid, ½ Liter	150.00
Stoneware, Deer & Flowers, Hand Engraved, Pewter Lid, Westerwald, 1 Liter, 10 In.	739.00
Stoneware, Dwarfs, Figural Dwarf Lid, Etched, No. 171, Girmscheid, ¾ Liter	253.00
Stoneware, Dwarfs, Speaking With King Dwarf, Etched, Figural Lid, No. 172, Girmscheid, ½ Liter	145.00
Stoneware, Falstaff, Etched, Pewter Lid, No. 930, Girmscheid, ½ Liter	133.00
Stoneware, Festive Scene, Etched, Pewter Lid, No. 743, Girmscheid, 1 Liter	163.00

Stein, Occupational, Teamsters, Grain Bags, Xavier Moelle, Lithophane, Pewter Lid, 10 In.
$230.00

Stein, Regimental, 3 Inf.-Rgt., Prinz Karl Von Bayern, 12. Comp Augsburg 1908, 12 In.
$259.00

Stein, Tankard, Woman Churning Butter, Talking To Man, c.1900, 16 In.
$176.00

Steuben, Candlestick, Topaz, Applied Celeste Blue Rims On Bobeche & Foot, 12 In. $690.00

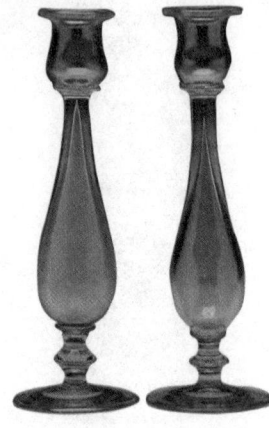

Steuben, Figurine, Cheese & Mouse, Crystal, Metal Gold Mouse, Presentation Box, 4 x 3½ In. $1725.00

Steuben, Figurine, Owl, 10¾ In. $1955.00

Stoneware, Flowers, Engraved, Pewter Lid, 1½ Liter	218.00
Stoneware, Flowers, Hand Engraved, Pewter Lid, Westerwald, 1 Liter, 10¼ In.	622.00
Stoneware, Gambrinus, Etched & Relief, Pewter Lid, No. 963, Girmscheid, 1 Liter	153.00
Stoneware, Kolner Billiard-Klub, Alstadt, 1932, H. Mehls Klubmeister, Painted, Pewter Lid, ½ Liter	244.00
Stoneware, Man Bowling, Etched, Stoneware Lid, No. 1087, Girmscheid, 1 Liter	217.00
Stoneware, Man Falling Off High Wheel Bike, Relief, Pewter Lid, ½ Liter	241.00
Stoneware, Man In Yellow Jacket, Pewter Lid, Transfer, Enamel, F. Ringer, ½ Liter	271.00
Stoneware, Man Stealing Beer, Etched, Stoneware Lid Of Knight, No. 1088, Kb, Girmscheid, 1 Liter	167.00
Stoneware, Men Drinking, Cat, Etched, Bead Design, Pewter Lid, ½ Liter	205.00
Stoneware, Men Drinking, Pewter Lid, No. 843, Girmscheid, ½ Liter	133.00
Stoneware, Munich Child, Munchen Skyline, Transfer, Enamel, Pewter Lid, F. Ringer, ½ Liter	303.00
Stoneware, Woman, Art Nouveau, Etched, Pewter Lid, No. 931, Girmscheid, ½ Liter	170.00
Stoneware, Woman, Art Nouveau, Pewter Lid, No. 932, Girmscheid, ½ Liter	138.00
Tankard, Woman Churning Butter, Talking To Man, c.1900, 16 In. ....*illus*	176.00

STEREO CARDS that were made for stereoscope viewers became popular after 1840. Two almost identical pictures were mounted on a stiff cardboard backing so that, when viewed through a stereoscope, a three-dimensional picture could be seen. Value is determined by maker and by subject. These cards were made in quantity through the 1930s.

Captain Jack, Chief Of Modocs, No. 320, Weitfle, Central City, Colorado	650.00
Clipper Ship, Great Republic, George Stacy	161.00
Colorado Scene, 7 Buff Views, Alex Martin	115.00
Dorothea Dix, Great Reformer	220.00
Drawing Wood In Winter, 3 Men, Dog, Horse Drawn Sleigh, F. & F.J. Taylor	69.00
Evening Shadows In The Fish-Ponds, Hastings	50.00
Farmstead, Bennington, Vt., D.H. Cross	58.00
Horse-Shoe Falls, Canada Side, Artist At Niagara, London Stereoscopic Co.	65.00
Isle Of Shoals, Maine, Davis Brothers	81.00
Lawrence Street, Denver, Pioneer Beer Hall, Buildings, Signs, Wagon, Alex Martin	121.00
New England Kitchen, W.E. James, 1864	1725.00
Savannah, Ga., Ladies Seated On Ground, Photographer Stands With Equipment	322.00
Shadow Of Man With Camera Under Donkey Head, No. 3524 W.H. Jackson	276.00
State St. Leadville, Boys & Men Pose On Unpaved Street, No. 208, Alex Martin	121.00
Steamboat Wharf, Bar Harbor, Mt. Desert, Me., No. 179, Bradley	110.00
Tenting In Old Santa Monica, No. 214, A.C. Varela, Los Angeles	85.00
View From Foot Of Beale Street, Ship, No. 334, Muybridge	207.00
Views, Burma, Underwood, Boxed, Book Shape Volume, c.1907, 50 Slides	264.00
Views, Chicago, Great Fire, 1871, 40 Views	294.00
Views, Colorado, Landmarks, Boxed Set, Keystone, 36 Views	382.00
Views, Switzerland, Underwood, Book Shape Volume, Cloth Binding, 100 Slides	264.00
Views, United States, Travel Co., Book Shape Volume, c.1909, 100 Views	558.00
Views, Utah, C.R. Savage, Missouri River To Pacific Ocean, 7 Views	323.00
Yellowstone, 30 Views, N.A. Forsythe, Box	480.00

STEREOSCOPES were used for viewing stereo cards. The hand viewer was invented by Oliver Wendell Holmes, although more complicated table models were used before his was produced in 1859. Do not confuse the stereoscope with the stereopticon, a magic lantern that used glass slides.

Brewster Pattern, Ogee Mahogany Body, Bone Fittings, Brassbound Lenses, 6 In.	441.00
J. Andrieu, Ebonized, Incised Decoration, Ivory, Europe Views, 23 Slides	294.00
Keystone, Oak Cabinet, 400 Cards, c.1900, 19½ In.	646.00
Keystone, Views, Tour Of The World, Double Book Shape Volumes, 800 Slides	1410.00
Stanhope, Monocular, Ivory, ⅝ In.	47.00

STERLING SILVER, see *Silver-Sterling category.*

STEUBEN glass was made at the Steuben Glass Works of Corning, New York. The factory, founded by Frederick Carder and T.G. Hawkes, Sr., was purchased by the Corning Glass Company. Corning continued to make glass called Steuben. Many types of art glass were made at Steuben. The firm is still making exceptional quality glass but it is clear, modern-style glass. Additional pieces may be found in the Aurene, Cluthra, and perfume bottle categories.

Basket, Clear, Open Latticework, Applied Berry Prunts, Oval, 10 In.	288.00
Bottle, Bath Salts, Clear, Ruby Threads, Flower Finial Stopper, 4¾ In.	288.00

Bottle, Bath Salts, Wisteria, Square, Swirls, Mushroom Stoppers, 4⅞ x 5 In.	570.00
Bowl, Centerpiece, Blue Calcite, Low, Rolled Over Rim, 14 In.	748.00
Bowl, Centerpiece, Blue Jade, Flared Rim, 11 In.	690.00
Bowl, Centerpiece, Pomona Green, Topaz Base, Optic Ribbed, Fleur-De-Lis, 5⅝ x 11⅝ In.	863.00
Bowl, Centerpiece, Rosa, Bubbles, Threaded Rim, Flared & Flattened Rim, 14 In.	230.00
Bowl, Clear, Ball Feet, John Dreves, Signed, c.1939, 6 x 8¾ In.	480.00
Bowl, Footed, John Dreves, c.1942, 10¾ In.	176.00
Bowl, Grotesque, Amber, Flared & Ruffled Rim, 6¾ x 12½ In.	173.00
Bowl, Grotesque, Clear Shaded To Amethyst, Flared & Ruffled Rim, 6 In.	230.00
Bowl, Grotesque, Clear Shaded To Cranberry, Ruffled Rim, 4-Footed, 11 In.	546.00
Bowl, Grotesque, Ivory, 5¼ x 7 In.	176.00
Bowl, Leafy Base, James McNaughton, 1937, 8½ In.	176.00
Bowl, Pink Swirl, Underplate, Pedestal Foot, Signed, 3 x 6 In.	125.00
Bowl, Rosaline, Pedestal, 4¼ x 7½ In.	150.00
Bowl, Snail-Shaped Handle, 3½ x 5 In.	293.00
Bowl, Spiral, Arnold Pollard, c.1954, 6¾ In.	146.00
Bowl, Talisman, Donald Pollard, 1954, 3½ x 7¼ In.	300.00
Bowl, Yellow Jade, Wide Flared Rim, Footed, 9½ In.	460.00
Box, Presentation, Pan-Am, Etched Building, 1⅞ x 4⅜ x 3⅜ In.	175.00
Candlestick, Amber, Blue, c.1920, 12 In., Pair	2280.00
Candlestick, Amber, Celeste Blue Rim, Double Bulbous Stem, Flared Cup & Bobeche, 15 In.	748.00
Candlestick, Gold Ruby Cabochons, Squared Sockets, Threading, Twisted Stem, 12 In., Pair	978.00
Candlestick, Gold Ruby Socket & Foot, Clear Baluster Stem, Flattened Rim, 10 In., Pair	920.00
Candlestick, Teardrop, 3¾ In., Pair	527.00
Candlestick, Teardrop, 8¾ In., Pair	580.00
Candlestick, Topaz, Applied Celeste Blue Rims On Bobeche & Foot, 12 In., Pair ......*illus*	690.00
Cocktail, Teardrop, George Thompson, 3⅝ In., 12 Piece	300.00
Cocktail, Trumpet, Tangerine Swirl Body, Blue Foot, 6½ In.	90.00
Cologne, Cranberry, Swirled, Square, Threading, Flattened Ball Stopper, Signed, 4 In.	230.00
Compote, Blue Calcite, Everted Rim, 6¼ In.	633.00
Compote, Clear Dimpled Bowl & Foot, Bristol Yellow Twist Stem, Blue Threading, 6¾ In.	201.00
Compote, Cyprian, Celeste Blue Rims & Ring Handles, Flared Foot, 10 In.	1725.00
Compote, Pomona Green Bowl & Foot, Knopped Topaz Stem, Optic Ribbed, 8 In.	489.00
Compote, Rosaline, Petal Shape, Alabaster Stem & Wafer, Rosaline Domed Foot, 8 In., Pair	1150.00
Cruet, Rosaline, Stopper, 6 In.	125.00
Cup, White, Blue Applied Handle, 2¼ x 3 In.	129.00
Decanter, Clear, Eagle Finial, 10½ In.	410.00
Figurine, Banana, 6¼ In.	460.00
Figurine, Beaver, Cranberry Eyes, Signed, 3¾ In.	315.00
Figurine, Cheese & Mouse, Crystal, Metal Gold Mouse, Presentation Box, 4 x 3½ In. ...*illus*	1725.00
Figurine, Eagle, 5½ In.	410.00
Figurine, Fig, 3 In.	351.00
Figurine, Grapes, 7 In.	351.00
Figurine, Kangaroo, 10¼ In.	644.00
Figurine, Owl, 10¾ In. ...*illus*	1955.00
Figurine, Polar Bear, 5 x 7½ In.	702.00
Figurine, Trout, Crystal, James Houston, c.1966, 8 In.	2340.00
Figurine, Water Bird, 10 x 11 In.	527.00
Finger Bowl, Underplate, Gold Calcite, 2½ x 6 In.	300.00
Goblet, Amethyst Bowl & Foot, Optic Rib, Celeste Blue Stem, 7½ In.	1265.00
Goblet, Oriental Jade, Opalescent Twist Stem, 8¼ In.	633.00
Goblet, Oriental Poppy Swirl, Clear Stem, Opalescent Knob, 8¼ In.	403.00
Goblet, Rosaline, Intaglio Flower Swags, Flared Rim, Alabaster Stem & Foot, 6½ In., Pair	345.00
Goblet, Teardrop, 7½ In., 12 Piece	585.00
Goblet, Yellow, Signed, 6 In.	25.00
Jam Jar, Cover, Topaz Bowl & Foot, Celeste Blue Stem & Ball Finial, 6⅝ In. ....*illus*	518.00
Lamp Base, Acid Cut Back, Wheat, Green Cintra, Embossed Green Metal Fittings, 34 In.	1725.00
Martini Set, Cocktail Shaker, Goblets, 13 Piece	1076.00
Paperweight, Apple, 4¾ In.	205.00
Perfume Bottle, Blue Jade, Bell Shape, Alabaster Stopper, Signed, 5 In.	259.00
Perfume Bottle, Celeste Blue, Optic Ribs, Footed, Teardrop Stopper, 7½ In.	345.00
Perfume Bottle, Clear, Black Threading, Oval, Black Flattened Stopper, 3 In.	431.00
Perfume Bottle, Ruby, Flattened Melon Shape, Teardrop Stopper, 4½ In.	403.00
Pitcher, Green Jade, Swirled, Shouldered, Applied Alabaster Handle, 9½ In.	345.00
Plate, Canape, Clear, Lloyd Atkins, c.1953, 10½ In.	146.00
Plate, Green Jade, Signed, 8⅝ In., Pair	144.00

Steuben, Jam Jar, Cover,
Topaz Bowl & Foot,
Celeste Blue Stem & Ball Finial, 6⅝ In.
$518.00

Steuben, Vase, Acid Cutback,
Sherwood, French Blue Flowers,
Textured Alabaster, 6⅝ In.
$3335.00

Steuben, Vase, Acid Cutback Oriental
Tree, Green Jade, Bulbous, 7 In.
$920.00

Steuben, Vase, Moss Agate,
Shouldered, Rolled Rim, 10½ In.
$14400.00

S

Steuben Glassware
Steuben made Cluthra, Cintra, Verre de Soie, and other types of glass. Aurene, an iridescent glass, is the most popular of the early glass. It was often combined with Calcite (white) or Ivrene (ivory) opaque glass and then decorated with swirled and feathered designs.

Steuben, Vase, Tree Trunk, 3 Prong, Footed, Pomona Green, Signed, 5⅝ In.
$288.00

Stevens & Williams, Ewer, Cranberry, White & Yellow, Metal Handle, Spout & Lid, 10½ In.
$316.00

Plate, Oriental Poppy, Alternating Pink & Opalescent Panels, Scalloped Rim, 8 In. 173.00

Plate, Owls, One On Branch, One In Flight, Intaglio, 9¾ In., Pair 201.00

Rose Bowl, Rosaline Shaded To White, Flowers, 7 In. 529.00

Sherbet, Clear, Engraved Flowers, Leaves, Beaded Swags, Frosted, Green Threads, 3⅜ In. ... 138.00

Sherbet, Rosaline, Alabaster Stem, 4 In. 86.00

Sugar, Pomona Green, Optic Ribbed, Amber Foot & Handles 230.00

Tumbler, Iced Tea, Cintra, Mottled Orange & Clear, Cone Shape, Spread Foot, 6¼ In. 403.00

Tumbler, Rosaline, 3⅞ In. 60.00

Tumbler, Selenium Red, Reeded, Signed, 5⅞ In. 115.00

Vase, Acid Cutback, Leaves, Rose Quartz, Mottled Rose Design, Flared, Signed, 8 In. 920.00

Vase, Acid Cutback, Sherwood, French Blue Flowers, Textured Alabaster, 6⅝ In. ...... *illus* 3335.00

Vase, Acid Cutback Oriental Tree, Green Jade, Bulbous, 7 In. .... *illus* 920.00

Vase, Acid Cutback, Chang, Plum Jade, Oriental Medallions & Floral Scrolls, Stalagmite Foot, 8 In. .. 8050.00

Vase, Alabaster, 8½ x 7½ In. 702.00

Vase, Amber, c.1900, 5 In. 322.00

Vase, Aquamarine, Footed, Urn Shape, 7 In. 264.00

Vase, Calcite, Gold Aurene Hearts, Pinched Waist, Spread Foot, 6¼ In. 431.00

Vase, Calcite, Gold Iridescent, Wavy Bands, Tapered Oval, Signed, c.1925, 6⅛ In. 1998.00

Vase, Clear, Round, Tapered, 8 Heavy Ribs Around Base, Signed, 10 In. 173.00

Vase, Clear, Scroll Handles, 10½ In. 351.00

Vase, Cornucopia, Ivrene, Ribbed, Round Base, 5⅛ In. 159.00

Vase, Fan, Amber, Fluted, Pomona Green Foot, Signed, 8 In. 173.00

Vase, Fan, Bristol Yellow, Ribbed, 8 In. 275.00

Vase, Fan, Clear, Ruby Threading On Base, Footed, Signed, 8¼ In. 230.00

Vase, Fan, Green, Optic Ribbed, Knopped Stem, Footed, Signed, 8½ In. 201.00

Vase, Fan, Pomona Green, Optic Ribbed, Etched Spanish Galleon, 8½ In. 240.00

Vase, Flower Shape, Gold Calcite, Scalloped Rim, 10½ In. 546.00

Vase, Flower Shape, Ivrene, Optic Ribbed, Squat, Scalloped Rim, Signed, 4½ x 6 In. 316.00

Vase, French Blue, Spiral Ribs, Oval, Flared Rim, Footed, Signed, 7½ In. 230.00

Vase, Gold Ruby, Urn Shape, Swirled Body, Cupped Rim, 9 In. 425.00

Vase, Green Jade, Alabaster, Flared Rim, Tapered, Round Foot, Etched, 8¾ In. 999.00

Vase, Green Jade, c.1910, 3 x 6 In. 205.00

Vase, Green Jade, Handles, 9½ In. 403.00

Vase, Green Jade, Optic Ribbed, Signed, Fleur-De-Lis, 5 In. 403.00

Vase, Grotesque, Amethyst Shaded To Clear, Signed, 4¾ x 9 In. 290.00

Vase, Grotesque, Ivory, 9 In. 230.00

Vase, Ivory, Cylindrical, Bulging Ribs, Footed, 9½ In. .... 350.00 to 403.00

Vase, Ivrene, Ribbed, Flared & Ruffled Rim, Signed, 8 In. 431.00

Vase, Jack-In-The-Pulpit, Ivrene, Ribbed, Signed, 6½ In. 316.00

Vase, Lavender Stripes, Amber, Gourd Shape, Signed, 15½ In. 25.00

Vase, Moss Agate, Shouldered, Rolled Rim, 10½ In. .... *illus* 14400.00

Vase, Selenium Red, Optic Ribbed, Double Bulbous Shape, Flared, 6 In. 345.00

Vase, Silverina, Amethyst, Silver Aventurine, Urn Shape, Flared, Footed, 7 In. 575.00

Vase, Stick, Green Jade, Bulbous Base, Alabaster Foot, 20th Century, 13 In. 294.00

Vase, Swirl Design, Green, c.1900, 6½ In. 819.00

Vase, Thorn, Black, 3-Sided, Disc Foot, 19 In. 1380.00

Vase, Topaz, Urn Shape, Buttressed M-Shaped Handles, Footed, 12 In. 575.00

Vase, Tree Trunk, 3 Prong, Celeste Blue, 6 In. 865.00

Vase, Tree Trunk, 3 Prong, Clear, Signed, 6 In. .... 185.00 to 429.00

Vase, Tree Trunk, 3 Prong, Footed, Pomona Green, Signed, 5⅝ In. .... *illus* 288.00

Vase, Tree Trunk, 3 Prong, Honey Amber, 6 In. 315.00

Vase, Tree Trunk, 3 Prong, Pink, On Clear Base, 6⅛ In. 1399.00

Vase, Trumpet, Rosaline, Alabaster Disc Foot, 6 In. .... 115.00 to 230.00

Vase, Wisteria, Optic Ribbed, Bulbous, Flared Rim, 6 In. 1150.00

Wine, Clear, Reeded, c.1900, 6½ In., 4 Piece 351.00

Wine, Dark Lavender Bowl & Foot, Light Blue Stem, Signed, 5¾ In. 200.00

Wine, Green Jade, Calcite Stem & Foot, 4¾ In. 50.00

Wine, Oriental Jade, Opalescent Twist Stem, 7 In., Pair 604.00

STEVENGRAPHS are woven pictures made like fancy ribbons. They were manufactured by Thomas Stevens of Coventry, England, and became popular in 1862. Most are marked *Woven in silk by Thomas Stevens* or were mounted on a cardboard that tells the story of the Stevengraph. Other similar ribbon pictures have been made in England and Germany.

Bookmark, Remember Me, Silk, Thomas Stevenson Of Coventry, 1870s 65.00

Bookmark, Star Spangled Banner	144.00
Bookmark, The Crystal Palace, 1893, 5½ x 2½ In.	550.00
Bookmark, The Final Spurt, 1900, 6 x 2 In.	395.00
Picture, First Point, Fox Hunt Scene, Silk, Walnut Frame, 3½ x 6½ In.	83.00
Picture, Good Old Days, Horsedrawn Coach, Frame, 1890s, 5¼ x 8½ In.	142.00 to 395.00
Picture, Lady Godiva Procession, Frame, 1890s, 5¼ x 8½ In.	133.00
Picture, Last Lap, 5 High-Wheel Bicycles, Frame, 1890s, 5¼ x 8½ In.	430.00

STEVENS & WILLIAMS of Stourbridge, England, made many types of glass, including layered, etched, cameo, and art glass, between the 1830s and 1930s. Some pieces are signed *S & W*. Many pieces are decorated with flowers, leaves, and other designs based on nature.

Decanter, Green Cut To Clear, Trees, Butterflies, 1890, 7½ In.	1080.00
Ewer, Cranberry, White & Yellow, Metal Handle, Spout & Lid, 10½ In. ....*illus*	316.00
Ewer, Mother-Of-Pearl, Pink, Swirls, Melon Ribbed, Camphor Thorny Handle, 12 In.	805.00
Goblet, Amethyst Jade, Alabaster Stem & Foot, 6¼ In., Pair	58.00
Perfume Bottle, Amber, Swirl, Cream Interior, Satin, Bulbous, 6 In.	745.00
Rose Bowl, Applied Pears, Plums & Blossoms, Peachblow, Cased, 10¼ In.	275.00
Rose Bowl, Basket Shape, Peachblow, Frosted Thorn Handle, Acorn, Leaves, Footed, 14 In.	450.00
Rose Bowl, Translucent Green, Zipper Ribs, 2½ In.	86.00
Vase, Amethyst, Silver & Green, Green Threading, Bulbous, Pinched Sides, 6½ In.	4888.00
Vase, Amethyst Cut To Clear, Grapevines, Flared, Footed, 5⅛ In. ....*illus*	219.00
Vase, Blue Cut To Clear, Stemmed Flowers & Leaves, 7½ In.	374.00
Vase, Citron, Branch & Blooming Flowers, Gourd Shape, 8½ In.	690.00
Vase, Clear, Pinched, Ribbed, Pink Rim, Amber Apple, Rigaree Feet, Handles, 10 In.	690.00
Vase, Gourd Shape, Frosted Red Ground, Christmas Roses, Cameo, 12 In.	2585.00
Vase, Pink, Applied Flowers, Leaves, Amber, Ruffled Edge, Signed, 9¼ In. ....*illus*	173.00
Vase, Pink, Mother-Of-Pearl Stripes, Leafy Camphor Base, 4¼ In. ....*illus*	546.00
Vase, Posy, Mother-Of-Pearl, Peppermint Stripe, 3-Footed Metal Holder, 6 In., Pair ....*illus*	441.00
Vase, Red Rolled Rim, Flower Sprays, Moorish Banded, Bulbous, Cameo, 10 In.	2588.00
Vase, Stick, Diamond Quilted, Mother-Of-Pearl, Flowers, Bulbous, Cameo, 8½ In.	3105.00

STIEGEL TYPE glass is listed here. It is almost impossible to be sure a piece was actually made by Stiegel, so the knowing collector refers to this glass as Stiegel type. Henry William Stiegel, a colorful immigrant to the colonies, started his first factory in Pennsylvania in 1763. He remained in business until 1774. Glassware was made in a style popular in Europe at that time and was similar to the glass of many other makers. It was made of clear or colored glass and was decorated with enamel colors, mold blown designs, or etching.

Bottle, 20 Diamonds, Amethyst, Flattened Bulbous, Sheared Mouth, Pontil, 1763-75, 5⅜ In.	2375.00
Bottle, Bride's, Clear, Enameled Flowers, Bird, Flared Lip, Pontil, 5¼ In.	55.00
Bottle, Bride's, Clear, Enameled Flowers, Bird, Pewter Collar, Screw Cap, 5¾ In.	187.00
Bottle, Bride's, Clear, Enameled Flowers, Pewter Collar, Threads, 7¼ In.	242.00
Bottle, Cobalt Blue, Enameled Flowers, Half Post Shape, Pewter Top, 5½ In. ....*illus*	360.00
Bottle, Enameled Daisies, Flowers, 5¼ In.	110.00
Bottle, Enameled Daisies, Flowers, Pewter Screw Top, 7¼ In.	275.00
Bottle, Enameled Flowers, Bird, White, Fitted Top, Half Post Neck, 7 In.	115.00
Bottle, Enameled Flowers, Bird, White & Pastel Blue, Fitted Top, Half Post Neck, 4¾ In.	115.00
Bottle, Enameled Flowers, Cobalt Blue, Pewter Top, 5½ In.	230.00
Bottle, Enameled Flowers, Cobalt Blue, Pewter Top, Half Post Neck, 5½ In.	360.00
Bottle, Enameled Flowers, Cobalt Blue, Pewter Top, Half Post Neck, 6 In.	230.00
Bottle, Enameled Urn, Flowers, Squiggle Line, 6½ In.	330.00
Bottle, White, Enameled Flowers & Birds, Half Post Shape, Fitted Top, 7 In. ....*illus*	115.00
Bowl, Cobalt Blue, Footed, Flint, 3 In.	220.00
Flask, Amethyst, Diamond Daisy, Flattened Bulbous, Sheared Mouth, Pontil, 4⅜ In.	1344.00
Flask, Spirits, Amethyst, 18-Ribs, Swirled To Left, 1780-1810, 5¾ In.	1064.00
Flask, Spirits, Enamel, Rabbit, Playing Drum, Germany, 1770-1810, 4¾ In.	1232.00
Mug, Engraved, Clear, Flared Lip, Strap Handle, Pontil, 5½ In.	187.00
Salt, Cobalt Blue, Flint, Footed, 3 In.	220.00
Sugar, Cover, 11-Diamond Pattern, Cobalt Blue, Footed, Pontil, 6½ x 4¼ In.	7280.00
Sugar, Cover, 16-Diamond Pattern, Cobalt Blue, Trumpet Foot, Ribbed Finial, 6 In. ....*illus*	3640.00
Tumbler, Enameled Bird & Flower, Pontil, 1750-1800, 3¼ In.	240.00
Tumbler, Enameled Flowers, Bird, Heart, 3¼ In.	358.00
Tumbler, Fiery Opalescent, Enameled, Flowers, 1750-1800, 3½ In.	208.00
Tumbler, Flip, Clear, Pontil, 5½ In.	33.00

Stevens & Williams, Vase,
Amethyst Cut To Clear, Grapevines,
Flared, Footed, 5⅛ In.
$219.00

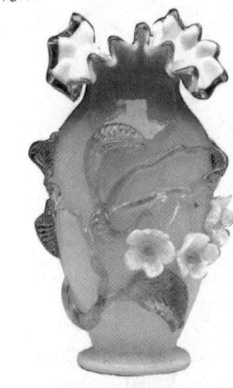

Stevens & Williams, Vase, Pink,
Applied Flowers, Leaves, Amber,
Ruffled Edge, Signed, 9¼ In.
$173.00

Stevens & Williams, Vase,
Pink, Mother-Of-Pearl Stripes,
Leafy Camphor Base, 4¼ In.
$546.00

Stevens & Williams, Vase, Posy,
Mother-Of-Pearl, Peppermint Stripe,
3-Footed Metal Holder, 6 In., Pair
$441.00

S

Stiegel Type Bottles

Stiegel Type, Bottle, Cobalt Blue, Enameled Flowers, Half Post Shape, Pewter Top, 5½ In.
$360.00

Stiegel Type, Bottle, White, Enameled Flowers & Birds, Half Post Shape, Fitted Top, 7 In.
$115.00

Stiegel Type, Sugar, Cover, 16-Diamond Pattern, Cobalt Blue, Trumpet Foot, Ribbed Finial, 6 In.
$3640.00

Stone, Planter, Hardstone, Floral Panels, Wood Base, Elephant Head Handles, Chinese, 9½ In.
$106.00

STOCKTON Terra Cotta Company was started in Stockton, California, in 1891. The art pottery called Rekston was made there after 1897. The factory burned in 1902 and never reopened.

Jardiniere, Square, Brown, Mottled Green Glaze, 8⅞ x 10 In.		1395.00
Pitcher, Tree Branch Shape Handle, Standard Glaze, 7 In.		495.00
Vase, Floral Decoration, Ruffled Rim, 10½ In.		850.00

STONE includes those articles made of stones, coral, shells, and some other natural materials not listed elsewhere in this book. Micro mosaics, (small decorative designs made by setting pieces of stone into a pattern), urns, vases, and other pieces made of natural stone are listed here. Stoneware is pottery and is listed in the Stoneware category. Alabaster, Jade, Malachite, Marble, Soapstone are in their own categories.

Box, Micro Mosaic, London, 18K Yellow Gold, c.1815, 1¼ x 1¾ In.	3803.00
Box, Micro Mosaic, St. Peter's Square, Enameled Glass, Italy, Late 19th Century, 2½ In.	320.00
Bust, Roman Emperor, Laurel Crown, Carved, Signed, E. Reed, 11 In.	1035.00
Bust, Young Girl, Laurel Leaf Crown, Sandstone, Carved, Signed, E. Reed, 8½ In.	690.00
Duck, Sandstone, Carved, Green Glass Eyes, Signed, E. Reed, 14 In.	690.00
Duck, Sandstone, Carved, Signed, E. Reed, 12¼ In.	575.00
Figure, Bull, Chinese, 20th Century, 8 x 10 In.	105.00
Figure, Elder, With Staff, Rose Quartz, Chinese, 14 x 6½ In.	351.00
Figure, Elephant, Raised Trunk, Spelter, Onyx, Marble Base, Continental, c.1920, 7 x 9½ In.	117.00
Figure, Foo Dog, Amethyst, Rock Crystal, 19th Century, 4½ In.	330.00
Figure, Foo Dog, Hardstone, Carved, Plinth, Chinese, 9 x 3½ In., Pair	657.00
Figure, Guanyin & Attendant, Coral, Chinese, 5¾ In.	295.00
Figure, Head, Lohan, Chinese, 7 In.	1003.00
Figure, Head, Woman, Eskimo, 8 In.	531.00
Figure, Indian Chief, Headdress, Bear Claw Necklace, Tomahawk, E. Reed, Ohio, 8½ In.	920.00
Figure, Indian Warrior, Sandstone, Signed, Ernest Popeye Reed, 34 x 12¾ In.	2185.00
Figure, Man Holding Peach Branch, Peacock, Rose Quartz, 12 In.	323.00
Figure, Mountain Man, Rifle, Knife, Sandstone, Signed, E.R., 13¾ In.	1035.00
Figure, Phoenix, Salmon, Silver Inlaid Stand, Coral, Chinese, 12 In.	6463.00
Figure, Snake, Tree, House, River Stone, Raymond Coins, 39 x 15 In.	3335.00
Frieze, Gray Schist, Gandharan, Carved, Column, Figures Wrestling, 10½ In.	1180.00
Fruit, Grapes, Walnut, Plum, Avocado, Orange, Pears, Apples, Peaches, Multicolored, 13 Piece	345.00
Fruit, Oranges, Peaches, Apples, Lemon, Multicolored, Basket, 14 x 8½ In., 8 Piece	201.00
Mounting Step, Limestone, Carved, 25 x 17 x 26 In.	3680.00
Planter, Hardstone, Floral Panels, Wood Base, Elephant Head Handles, Chinese, 9½ In. . . . . *illus*	106.00
Plaque, Micro Mosaic, Pliny's Doves, Round, Late 19th Century, Italy, 2½ In.	3633.00
Plaque, Pietra Dura, Flower, Bird, Butterfly, Brass Frame, Semiprecious Stones, 5½ x 4½ In.	350.00
Scholar's Stone, Wood Base, Chinese, 10¾ x 13½ In.	561.00
Table Screen, Painted, Figural Landscape, Inscription On Reverse, 12½ x 12½ In.	392.00
Tree, Cloisonne Planter, Chinese, 13 x 9½ In.	12870.00
Urn, Quartz, Green, Metal Base, Chinese, c.1900, 13¾ x 6 In.	702.00
Vase, Limestone, Carved, Ring Turned Exterior, Rounded Rim, 27 In.	345.00
Vase, Rose Quartz, Cover, Carved, Rose Blossoms, Foliage, Wood Stand, 10 x 7½ In.	191.00

STONEWARE is a coarse, glazed, and fired potter's ceramic that is used to make crocks, jugs, bowls, etc. It is often decorated with cobalt blue decorations. In the nineteenth and early twentieth centuries, potters often decorated crocks with blue numbers indicating the size of the container. A *2* meant 2 gallons. Stoneware is still being made. American stoneware is listed here.

Baker, Mix With Roelofs & Vanderbok, Rock Valley, Iowa, Blue	35.00
Basket, Strainer, Brown Glaze, Pierced Base & Body, 8 In.	55.00
Batter Pail, Blue Accents, Bail Handle, c.1860, 4 Qt., 8 In.	275.00
Batter Pail, Blue Accents, Clay Line, c.1860, Gal., 7½ In.	176.00
Batter Pail, Flower, Brush, Bail Handles, c.1870, Gal., 10 In.	715.00
Batter Pail, Flower, Drooping, Blue, Handles, c.1870, Gal., 9½ In.	248.00
Batter Pail, Lid, Tin, Bird, Wire Bail Handle, c.1870, 1½ Gal., 11½ In.	578.00
Batter Pail, Running Bird, Wire Bail Handle, c.1870, 4 Qt., 10¼ In.	523.00
Bean Pot, Buckingham, Debossed, Gar, Nov. 21, 1883, Post No. 12, Brown Glaze, 3 x 3 In.	150.00
Beater Jar, 9th Annual Greetings, J. Yepsen & Son, Kanawha, Iowa, Blue Band	115.00
Beater Jar, Colonial	275.00
Beater Jar, Compliments Of F.C. Smith, Fort Atkinson, Iowa, Blue Band	215.00
Beater Jar, E.J. Schwingle & Co., Muscoda, Wisconsin, Blue Band	150.00
Beater Jar, J.A. Rutherford General Merchandise, Gray, Iowa, Blue Band	155.00

Beater Jar, Mix With Us & Save Dough, E.E. Kirkhart, Lorimore, Iowa, Blue Band	165.00
Beater Jar, When Beating Think Of Eating Pure Food Groceries From Satterlee, Blue Band .	85.00
Birdfeeder, Cobalt Blue Flowers, 5⅞ In.	4183.00
Birdhouse, Attached Snake, Olive, Gray Alkaline Glaze, B.B. Craig, 5¾ x 9 In.	288.00
Birdhouse, Face, Tapered Body, Bulging Eyes, Olive Alkaline Glaze, B.B. Craig, 9 In.	374.00
Birdhouse, Snake, Swirled Clay Body, Hole Perch, B.B. Craig, 8½ In., Pair	748.00
Bottle, Figural, Man In Nightcap, Mug, Rockingham Glaze, England, c.1880, 8¾ In. .. *illus*	258.00
Bottle, Green, Tan Alkaline Glaze, c.1850, 11 In.	132.00
Bowl, A. Zabolio Co., General Merchandise & Furniture, Genoa, Wis., Rust Band	775.00
Bowl, Blue Accents, Impressed, Ears, 1832, 6½ In.	1485.00
Bowl, Cover, Leaves, Grapes, Salt Glaze, 7 x 3½ In.	295.00
Bowl, Deichmann, Erica & Kjeld Deichmann, c.1950, 8½ In.	1052.00
Bowl, Flower, Blue c.1833, Gal., 6 x 10½ In.	358.00
Bowl, Flowers, Drop Swag Around Rim, Blue, Applied Handles, Solomon Bell, Va., 6 x 11 In. .	1320.00
Bowl, Karatsu Style, Nuka Glaze, Iron Glaze Leaf, Japan, 9 In.	1080.00
Bowl, Milk, Spout, Blue Accent, J. Mantell, c.1860, Gal., 9½ In.	715.00
Bowl, St. Ives, Impressed Mark, c.1960, 3½ In.	103.00
Bowl, Stylized Flower, Blue, H.B. Pfaltzgraff, 5¼ x 11 In.	605.00
Bowl, Wedding Ring, Blue & White, 5 In.	33.00
Bucket, Sugar, Stamped, 2 Maple Leaves, Cobalt Blue, Gray, No Lid, Bail Handle, 10½ In. ...	24.00
Butter, Cover, Colonial, Large	1200.00
Butter Carrier, Colonial, Lid, Bail Handle, Small	250.00
Butter Carrier, Compliments Of L.H. Cohen, Blue & White, No Lid	55.00
Butter Pail, Lid, Colonial, Bail Handle, Large	375.00
Cane Holder, Dog & Tree Stump, Molded, Maker's Mark, Late 1800s, 24 x 13½ In.	4700.00
Canister, Lid, Wildflowers, Sago & Coffee, Blue & White	90.00
Canister, Tea, Incised Flowers, Elizabeth Woodley, 1769, Salt Glaze, Bovey Tracey, 5 In. . *illus*	1320.00
Carpet Ball, Blue Stripes, 3 In.	85.00
Carpet Ball, Green Snowflakes, 3½ In.	90.00
Carpet Ball, Green Stripes, 2½ In.	65.00
Carpet Ball, Red Flowers, 3 In.	85.00
Carpet Ball, Red Spots, 2½ In.	60.00
Casserole, Cover, Colonial, Large	155.00
Chicken Feeder, Leaves, Hooded Opening, Blue, 11¾ In.	935.00
Chicken Feeder, Union Oval	125.00
Chicken Waterer, Alkaline Glaze, Incised Shoulder, B.B. Craig, Vale, N.C., 11½ In.	633.00
Chicken Waterer, Coggle Wheel Design Around Shoulder, Russ Fountain, Blue, 13 In.	110.00
Chicken Waterer, Coggle Wheel Line Around Shoulder, Russ Fountain, Blue, 9 In.	165.00
Chicken Waterer, Flowers On Shoulder, Blue, 10¼ In.	2530.00
Chocolate Pot, Applied Vines, Red, Offset Crabstock Handle, Twig Finial, c.1750, 7⅜ In. *illus*	960.00
Churn, Bird, Leaf, Cobalt Blue, 5, Lid, Dasher, Impressed Haxstun & Co., 17 In.	661.00
Churn, Brown, Gal.	75.00
Churn, Cobalt Blue, 6, Cherries, Branches, Handles, 18 x 10¼ In.	489.00
Churn, Cobalt Blue, 3 Flowers, c.1850, 3 Gal., 15 In.	578.00
Churn, Face, Lug Handles, Applied Ears, Bulging Eyes, B.B. Craig, 14¾ In.	1093.00
Churn, Flower, Wavy Line, Cylinder Shape, c.1860, 3 Gal., 14½ In.	385.00
Churn, Flower Filled Vase, M. Woodruff Cortland, c.1870, 6 Gal.	4400.00
Churn, Flower Sprays, Accents On Handles, Blue, Stamped 2, 14½ In.	248.00
Churn, Flowers, Blue Accent, c.1870, 6 Gal., 19 In.	4400.00
Churn, Lid, Flower, c.1870, 6 Gal., 18 In.	798.00
Churn, Maple Leaf, Lid, Western, Gal.	700.00
Churn, Mottled Olive Alkaline Glaze, Blue Rutile Highlights, B.B. Craig, 18½ In.	400.00
Churn, Ribbed Oak Leaf, T. Harrington, Lyons, c.1850, 5 Gal., 18½ In.	2035.00
Churn, Scrolls, Serpentine Lines, Wood Lid, Dasher, Hamilton & Jones, 17½ In.	303.00
Churn, Stenciled, Flower, Star, Hamilton & Co., Shield, 9¼ In.	330.00
Churn, Stylized Flower, Leaves, Blue, Chart & Son, Sherburne, 15¼ In.	220.00
Churn, Swags, Tulips, 5 Gal.	690.00
Churn, Upside Down Leaf, Lid, Western, Gal.	2100.00
Churn, Wind & Union Oval, Bail Handles, 3 Gal.	125.00
Churn, Wreath, Starburst, Blue Accents, E.W. Farrington & Co., c.1890, 8 Gal., 18 In.	3410.00
Cream Pot, Blue Script, Squiggled Frame, c.1850, ½ Gal., 6 In.	209.00
Cream Pot, Cobalt Blue, c.1820, 2 Gal., 8 In.	303.00
Cream Pot, Fish, Incised, Oval, c.1790, 2 Gal., 12 In.	1705.00
Cream Pot, Flower, Double, Blue, Oval, c.1847, 2 Gal., 10½ In.	688.00
Cream Pot, Flower, Spray, Dotted, Blue, Haxstun Ottman & Co., N.Y., c.1870, 4 Gal., 13 In. ..	770.00
Crock, 2 Flowers, Cobalt Blue, Stamped 2, Wm. Moyer, Harrisburg, Pa., Handles, 12¾ In. ...	880.00

Stoneware, Bottle, Figural,
Man In Nightcap, Mug,
Rockingham Glaze, England,
c.1880, 8¾ In.
$258.00

Stoneware, Canister, Tea,
Incised Flowers, Elizabeth Woodley,
1769, Salt Glaze, Bovey Tracey, 5 In.
$1320.00

Stoneware, Chocolate Pot,
Applied Vines, Red, Offset Crabstock
Handle, Twig Finial, c.1750, 7⅜ In.
$960.00

Stoneware, Crock, 2 Flowers, Stems, Blue, Bulbous, D.P. Hobart, Williamsport, Pa., 2, 9½ In. $880.00

Stoneware, Crock, Bird On Branch, Cobalt Blue, F.B. Norton & Co., Worcester, Mass., 4 Gal., 11 In. $468.00

Stoneware, Crock, Cake, Cover, Stylized Swag, Flowers, Incised Bands, Applied Ear Handles, 5½ In. $413.00

Stoneware, Crock, Flowers, Cobalt Blue, N. Clark Jr., Athens, N.Y., 2 Gal., 9½ x 10 In. $322.00

Crock, 2 Flowers, Stems, Blue, Bulbous, D.P. Hobart, Williamsport, Pa., 2, 9½ In. .....*illus*	880.00
Crock, 3 Bunches Of Grapes, Cobalt Blue, No. 5, Oval, 2 Handles, 15¼ In.	460.00
Crock, Bird, Blue, c.1870, 3 Gal., 10½ In.	275.00
Crock, Bird, Blue, Flack & Van Arsdale Cornwall, c.1870, 3 Gal., 10 In.	523.00
Crock, Bird, Blue, West Troy, N.Y., 2 Gal.	403.00
Crock, Bird, Dots, Dashes, Branch, Cobalt Blue, Handles, 2, W. Roberts, Bingham, N.Y., 9½ In.	385.00
Crock, Bird, Facing Right, Impressed Mark, Open Top, 2 Handles, 10½ x 5½ In.	173.00
Crock, Bird, On Berry Branch, Blue, Impressed, 5, 11½ In.	385.00
Crock, Bird, On Branch, Cobalt Blue, 3, New York Stoneware, Fort Edward, Handles, 16 In. ..	385.00
Crock, Bird, On Branch, Cobalt Blue, 4, Handles, New York Stoneware, Fort Edward, 11½ In.	308.00
Crock, Bird, On Branch, Cobalt Blue, B. Norton Sons, Worcester, Mass., Handles, 9 In.	138.00
Crock, Bird, On Branch, Cobalt Blue, F.B. Norton & Co., Worcester, Mass., 4 Gal., 11 In. .*illus*	468.00
Crock, Bird, On Branch, Flowers, Cobalt Blue, 2, Handles, W.H. Farrar, Geddes, N.Y., 10¾ In. .	4950.00
Crock, Bird, On Branch, Flowers, Cobalt Blue, 3, N.A. White & Co., Handles, 12¼ In.	1265.00
Crock, Bird, On Branch, Open Top, Side Handles, 4 Gal., 11 x 11¾ In.	575.00
Crock, Bird, On Stump, Cobalt Blue, Stamped 4, Handles, 11 In.	193.00
Crock, Bird, On Stylized Branch, Blue, Stamped 2, 9 In.	348.00
Crock, Bird, On Tree Stump, Blue, Stamped 4, 11¾ In.	330.00
Crock, Bird, Running, Trophy Frame, White's, Utica, N.Y., c.1865, 5 Gal., 13 In.	1540.00
Crock, Bird, Salt Glaze, 13¼ In.	1150.00
Crock, Birds, Squiggled Frame, Cobalt Blue, Pail Shape, c.1840, 3 Gal., 10 In.	440.00
Crock, Blue Decoration, Leaf Spray, Utica, N.Y., 9 x 10½ In.2 Gal.	210.00
Crock, Blue Decoration, Stenciled, Williams & Reppert, Greensboro, Pa., 10¾ In.	99.00
Crock, Brown Glaze, A.L. Hyssong, Bloomsburg, Pa., Handles, 7¾ In.	17.00
Crock, Butter, A. Moll Grocer Co., St. Louis, Mo., 10 Lb.	90.00
Crock, Butter, Bowman Dairy, Blue, 2 Lb.	75.00
Crock, Butter, Bowman Dairy, Blue, Lb.	15.00
Crock, Butter, Boyda Dairy Co. Fresh Butter, Chicago, Ill., 3 Lb.	120.00
Crock, Butter, Double Leaf, Blue Decoration, 2 Handles, 2 Gal., 5¾ x 1 In.	316.00
Crock, Butter, Enjoy Kennedy Creamery Butter, 2 Lb.	85.00
Crock, Butter, Lambrechts, Lb.	50.00
Crock, Butter, S.P. & S., Whitehall, Lb.	60.00
Crock, Butter, Western, Maple Leaf, 20 Lb.	750.00
Crock, Butterfly, Back Stamped Minnesota, Split Oval, 20 Gal.	2700.00
Crock, Cake, Cover, Stylized Swag, Flowers, Incised Bands, Applied Ear Handles, 5½ In. .*illus*	413.00
Crock, Cake, Flower Sprays, Blue, Applied Handles, 6¾ x 12¼ In.	440.00
Crock, Cake, Flower Swag On Rim, Blue, Applied Handles, 4¼ x 8 In.	358.00
Crock, Cake, Leaf Swag, Snowflake, Blue, Stamped Circled 1, 5 x 10½ In.	468.00
Crock, Cake, Lid, Leaf, Repeated, Blue, c.1850, 4½ In.	1265.00
Crock, Chicken Pecking Corn, c.1870, 3 Gal., 10 In.	358.00
Crock, Chicken Pecking Corn, c.1880, 4 Gal., 11½ In.	853.00
Crock, Chicken Pecking Corn, Poughkeepsie, N.Y., c.1870, 3 Gal., 10½ In.	495.00
Crock, Cobalt Blue 4 In Wreath, Impressed, Applied Handles, 14½ In.	805.00
Crock, Cobalt Blue Decoration, Straight-Sided, Applied Lug Handles, 2 Gal., 8⅞ In.	441.00
Crock, Cobalt Blue Pecking Chicken, 2 Handles, Impressed 2, Lid, 11 In.	575.00
Crock, Cobalt Blue Polka Dot Flower, ½ Gal., 8½ In.	345.00
Crock, Commemorative, J. Nicholson, Blue Vine Frame, c.1871, 6 Gal., 13½ In.	1705.00
Crock, Dancing Man, Cobalt Blue, James River, c.1840, 9½ In.	7500.00
Crock, Drooping Flowers, Blue, Applied Handles, 14 In.	275.00
Crock, Eagle, Clutching Banner, Spread Wings, Union, Liberty, Salt Glaze, c.1870, 11½ In. ..	4200.00
Crock, Elephant Ear, Bottom Marked, 2 Gal.	90.00
Crock, Family, Branches, Flowers, Blue, White Swan Inn, Uniontown, Handles, c.1825, 16 In. ..	16500.00
Crock, Flower, Blue Oval, M. Tyler & Co., Albany, N.Y., c.1840, Gal., 9 In.	275.00
Crock, Flower, Cobalt Blue, Stamped 2, A.O. Whittemore, Havana, N.Y., Handles, 9¼ In.	94.00
Crock, Flower, Cobalt Blue, Salt Glaze, Baluster Form, Handles, 10 Gal.	1680.00
Crock, Flower, Double, Blue, Riedinger & Caire, Poughkeepsie, N.Y., c.1870, 4 Gal., 11 In. ...	99.00
Crock, Flower, Leafy Stem, Blue, Stamped, Moyer Harrisburg, 10 In.	853.00
Crock, Flower, Leaves, Blue, 4, Evan R. Jones, Pittston, Pa., 12 In.	358.00
Crock, Flower, Vine, Blue, Applied Handles, c.1820, 2½ Gal., 13 In.	4400.00
Crock, Flower & Leaf Band, Surrounding Shoulder, Blue, 7½ In.	689.00
Crock, Flower Bowtie, Blue, Stamped 2, Applied Handles, Cowden & Wilcox, 10¼ In.	358.00
Crock, Flower Sprays, Layered, Blue, Stamped 3, Applied Handles, Cowden & Wilcox, 12 In. .	485.00
Crock, Flowers, Blue, Stenciled, T.F. Reppert, Greensboro, Pa., 10⅛ In.	209.00
Crock, Flowers, Cobalt Blue, 2 Handles, Impressed, 10½ In.	316.00
Crock, Flowers, Cobalt Blue, N. Clark Jr., Athens, N.Y., 2 Gal., 9½ x 10 In. ....*illus*	322.00
Crock, Flowers, Drooping, Repeated Around Shoulder, Cobalt Blue, Stamped 3, 13 In.	330.00

Crock, Flowers, Leaf Band, Blue, Stamped 5, Remmy, Philadelphia, 14 In.	523.00
Crock, Flowers, Leafy Vine On Shoulder, Applied Handles, Impressed 5, 15¾ In.	330.00
Crock, Flowers, Leaves, Blue, Salt Glaze, Albany Slip, Ear Handles, c.1875, 3 Gal., 10¼ In.	142.00
Crock, Flowers, Leaves, Cobalt Blue, Applied Handles, Stamped, John Bell, 13 x 16 In.	4950.00
Crock, Flowers, Stenciled Hamilton & Jones, H&J, Greensboro, Pa., 9⅞ In.	138.00
Crock, Flying Chicken, Cobalt Blue, N.Y. Stoneware Co., Fort Edward, N.Y., 4 Gal., 14¼ In. *illus*	854.00
Crock, Holly, Blue, Impressed 1, Applied Handles, 9 In.	440.00
Crock, Humboldt Dairy Products Co., Chicago, Ill., 10 Lb.	255.00
Crock, Incised Fish, Blue Accents, Applied Handles, 11⅝ In.	2090.00
Crock, Jas. Hamilton, 5½ In.	288.00
Crock, Leaf, Incised, Blue, Oval, Loop Handles, c.1790, 2 Gal., 11½ In.	1815.00
Crock, Lid, Bail Handle, 12 Gal.	255.00
Crock, Lid, Bail Handle, 15 Gal.	145.00
Crock, Lid, Bird, On Leafy Branch, Cobalt Blue, 2, New York Stoneware, Handles, 11¼ In.	467.00
Crock, Man, Top Hat, Outstretched Arms, Tulip, Blue, 1½ Gal., 11¼ In.	3850.00
Crock, Man In Moon, Long Nose, Blue, Moore, Nichols & Co., Williamsport, Pa., 8 In.	6600.00
Crock, Morning Glory, Stylized 5S, Blue, Applied Handles, 13 In.	385.00
Crock, Oval, Blue Decoration, N. Clark & Co., Lyons, c.1852, 9½ In.	144.00
Crock, Oval, Flower, Cobalt Blue, 2, AG, Handle, Austin Graves, 10½ In.	431.00
Crock, Oval, Handles, Brown Running Glaze, Impressed, 12½ In.	115.00
Crock, Parrot, Blue, 2 Handles, Oval, 7½ In.	270.00
Crock, Peach, Elongated Stem, Blue, 9¼ In.	220.00
Crock, Potted Flower, Cobalt Blue, Impressed 4, 2 Applied Handles, 12 In.	316.00
Crock, Royal Crown, Flower Wreath, N.A. White & Son, Utica, N.Y., c.1870, 3 Gal., 10½ In.	275.00
Crock, Sailing Ship, Closed Handles, Goodwin & Webster, 1820-40, 12⅝ In.	8960.00
Crock, Sailing Ship, Don't Give Up The Ship, Salt Glaze, c.1850, 4 Gal.	7200.00
Crock, Salt Glaze, 2 Ear Handles, Stamped, Goodwin & Webster, 8¾ x 8¼ In.	115.00
Crock, Salt Glaze, Applied Handled, Cobalt Blue Lettering, 2 Gal., 13½ In.	235.00
Crock, Sanford's Ink, Paste, 10 In.	330.00
Crock, Scallop Design, Blue Accents, Applied Looped Handles, c.1790, 2 Gal., 11½ In.	1155.00
Crock, Spitting Flower, Cobalt Blue, 2, F.H. Cowden Harrisburg, 1881-88, 2 Gal., 11¼ In.	157.00
Crock, Squiggled Line, Upper & Lower Bands, Blue, 6½ In.	330.00
Crock, Squiggles, Leaves, Blue, 3, Salt Glaze, Ear Handles, 1860-80, 13 In.	153.00
Crock, Stag, Fence, Trees, Bulbous, Flared Rim, Ear Handles, Edmands & Co., 10½ In. *illus*	6050.00
Crock, Stenciled Cobalt, C.H. Torsch & Co., 12½ In.	373.00
Crock, Stylized Flower, Cobalt Blue, Straight-Sided, Ear Handles, C. Hart & Son, 11 In. *illus*	154.00
Crock, Stylized Flowers, Leaves, Blue, Applied Handles, John Bell, Waynesboro, 13 x 16 In.	8950.00
Crock, Sunflowers, Cobalt Blue, 2 Handles, 9¼ In.	115.00
Crock, Swan, Blue, Salt Glaze, Ear Handles, Semi-Oval Form, 1850-65, 11 In.	112.00
Crock, Tornado, Slip Blue, J. Burger, Jr., Rochester, N.Y., c.1885, 2 Gal., 9 In.	413.00
Crock, Tulips, Cobalt Blue, No. 3, 2 Applied Handles, Incised Rings, 13½ In.	345.00
Crock, Wood Lid, Stylized Bird, Looking Back, On Branch, 3, White's, Utica, Blue, 10 In.	523.00
Cuspidor, Scrolled Flowers, Blue, T.H. Wilson & Co., 3¼ x 6¾ In.	5610.00
Figurine, Dog, Dachshund, Brown Glaze, Grenzhausen, 8¾ In.	460.00
Figurine, Lamb, Laying Down, Blue Face, Hooves, Pfaltzgraff, 8¾ In.	193.00
Figurine, Rooster, Applied Snake, Green, Blue Glaze, Edwin Meaders, 1990, 16 In.	1495.00
Figurine, Rooster, Cobalt Blue Glaze, Marked, Edwin Meaders, 15½ In.	1093.00
Figurine, Rooster, Green & Brown Glaze, Red, Yellow, Applied Eyes, Marked, M. Bailey, 23½ In.	546.00
Figurine, Rooster, Green Matte & Glossy Glaze, Stamped, R Armfield, 10¾ In.	316.00
Figurine, Rooster, Incised Feathers, Glossy Red Glaze, Incised, Charles Moore, 8½ In.	265.00
Figurine, Rooster, Incised Feathers, Red, Marked, Charles Mills, Ram Pottery, 17¾ In.	805.00
Figurine, Rooster, Incised Feathers, Runny Blue, Gray, Red, Orange, Marked, C. West, 18 In.	748.00
Figurine, Rooster, Mottled Green & Orange Glaze, Round Base, 14 In.	440.00
Figurine, Rooster, Mottled Olive Glaze, Edwin Meaders, 1989, 14 In.	2415.00
Figurine, Rooster, Runny Gray & Olive Glaze, Incised, Clete Meaders, 13 In.	259.00
Figurine, Shoe, Lady's, Buckle, Blue, 3 x 5⅞ In.	248.00
Figurine, Turkey, Foamy & Runny Red Glaze, Applied Turkey Beard, M. Hanning, 14 In.	748.00
Flask, Blue, Reeded Neck, c.1830, 1¼ x 8½ In.	198.00
Flask, Brown Alkaline Glaze, c.1830, 8½ In.	99.00
Flask, Portrait Of Man, Sideburns, Blue, 6½ In.	11000.00
Flask, Salt Glaze, Cobalt Blue, Oval, Incised, C.H. Smith, 1860, 7¾ In.	7200.00
Flowerpot, Cylinder Base, Flower, Unglazed, Tanware, c.1880, 6 In.	413.00
Humidor, Lid, Relief Rope Handles, c.1870, ½ Gal., 7 In.	110.00
Jar, 2 Drooping Flower Swags, Blue, 8½ In.	413.00
Jar, 3 Flowers, Leafy Sprays, Blue, 10¾ In.	303.00
Jar, Black Glaze, Oval, Shoulders, 2 Loop Handles, Chinese, 7½ In.	236.00

Stoneware, Crock, Flying Chicken, Cobalt Blue, N.Y. Stoneware Co., Fort Edward, N.Y., 4 Gal., 14¼ In. $854.00

Stoneware, Crock, Stag, Fence, Trees, Bulbous, Flared Rim, Ear Handles, Edmands & Co., 10½ In. $6050.00

Stoneware, Crock, Stylized Flower, Cobalt Blue, Straight-Sided, Ear Handles, C. Hart & Son, 11 In. $154.00

Stoneware, Jug, Bird, Paddletail, Cobalt Blue, N.A. White & Son, Utica, N.Y., 2 Gal., 14¼ In. $380.00

S

Stoneware, Jug, Face,
Broken China Teeth,
Wavy Lines On Shoulders,
B.B. Craig, N.C., 7¼ In.
$690.00

Stoneware, Jug, Face,
Devil Monkey, Ceramic Teeth,
Eyes, Runny Olive Glaze,
Steve Abee, 13 In.
$173.00

Stoneware, Jug, Face, Double,
Stone Teeth, Runny Olive Glaze,
Lanier Meaders, 10 In.
$5750.00

Jar, Blue Decoration, Stenciled, Scroll Accents, Hamilton & Jones, 6⅝ In.	165.00
Jar, Brown Bands, Albany Slip Glaze Interior, Salt Glaze, Oval, Boston, 10⅞ In.	558.00
Jar, Brown Splotches On Shoulder, Stamped, Soloman Blee, Strasburg, Va., 8¾ In.	303.00
Jar, Canning, Bull's-Eye Flower, Lehman & Riedinger, N.Y., c.1855, 2 Gal., 11 In.	853.00
Jar, Canning, Flower, Blue, Drape Accents, Leaf, c.1841, 2 Gal., 13 In.	468.00
Jar, Canning, Flower, Blue Accents, M. Tyler, Albany, N.Y., c.1840, 2 Gal., 11½ In.	220.00
Jar, Canning, Lid, Crowning Rooster, Impressed Mark, C.W. Braun, c.1860, 2 Gal.	34650.00
Jar, Canning, Lid, Excelsior Pure Preserves, H.A. Johnson & Co., Boston, Mass., Qt.	85.00
Jar, Canning, Lid, Flower Bouquet, Dots, c.1860, 2 Gal., 11½ In.	1265.00
Jar, Canning, Lid, Snowflake, Double 2's, Lyons, c.1860, 2 Gal., 11 In.	2035.00
Jar, Canning, Maple Leaf, Brown Top, Western, ½ Gal.	55.00
Jar, Canning, North Star, ½ Gal.	65.00
Jar, Canning, North Star, Gal.	20.00
Jar, Canning, Vine, Ship, Blue Ribbed, c.1860, ½ Gal., 8½ In.	248.00
Jar, Cobalt Blue, Decoration, Seymour & Bosworth Hartford, c.1890, 2 Gal., 11¾ In.	353.00
Jar, Demuth's Celebrated Snuff, Blue, Lancaster, c.1770, 7 In.	330.00
Jar, Drape Design, Incised, Blue, Oval, Loop Handles, c.1790, 3 Gal., 14 In.	4840.00
Jar, Drop Flower Decoration, Leaf Swags, Blue, 8 In.	242.00
Jar, Drop Flowers, Blue, 10¾ In.	165.00
Jar, Fan, c.1860, Gal., 9 In.	209.00
Jar, Flower, Oval, c.1840, 2 Gal., 10 In.	303.00
Jar, Grape Bunch, Vine, Blue, A.K. Ballard, Burlington, Vt., Applied Handles, No. 6	1045.00
Jar, Horse, Cobalt Blue, Salt Glaze, Wide Mouth, 2 Gal., 11 In.	3643.00
Jar, Leaf Sprays, Blue, 8½ In.	275.00
Jar, Leaf Swag, Shoulder Stamp, Blue, T.H. Wilson, Harrisburg, 9½ In.	3630.00
Jar, Lid, 2 Inchworm Swatches, Blue, 6¼ In.	910.00
Jar, Mottled Tan, Brown Glaze, Cylinder, c.1811, ½ Gal., 9¼ In.	3520.00
Jar, Narrow Neck, Impressed Wm. Hare Wilmington, Del., 9 In.	172.00
Jar, Olive Oil, Amphora Form, Amber To Ocher, Spout, 19th Century, 50 In.	1180.00
Jar, Plume, Brush, Oval, J.F. Brayton & Co., N.Y., c.1835, 2 Gal., 12 In.	220.00
Jar, Runny Brown Alkaline Glaze, Ear Stamp, Nelson Bass, 17½ In.	1495.00
Jar, Tooled Flower, Sawtooth Design, Ribbon Handle, c.1810, Qt., 5¼ In.	578.00
Jardiniere, Stylized Flower, Applied Handles, c.1840, 2 Gal., 10½ In.	303.00
Jug, 3 Flowers, Blue, 8¼ In.	193.00
Jug, 3 Leafy Stems, Blue, 8 In.	770.00
Jug, 10 Faces In Relief, Broken China Teeth, Green Glaze, 3 Loop Handles, B. Ferguson, 14 In.	518.00
Jug, Applied Handle, Impressed Mark, Fisher, Lyons, N.Y., 11 In.	230.00
Jug, Band Of Flowers, Blue, 8¼ In.	303.00
Jug, Batter, Flower, Leaf Stem, Blue, Evan R. Jones, 10 In.	1375.00
Jug, Bearded Face, Impressed, Iron, Oxide Slip, Bellarmine, c.1760, 8 x 5 In.	944.00
Jug, Beehive, Blue, c.1880, 11½ In.	413.00
Jug, Beehive, Brown Bros., c.1860, 2 Gal., 12 In.	385.00
Jug, Beehive, Colfax Mineral Water Co., Colfax, Iowa, Macomb, 5 Gal.	450.00
Jug, Beehive, Fort Dodge Salt Glaze, Cobalt Blue Design, Stamped, 4 Gal.	7750.00
Jug, Bird, Cobalt Blue, Handles, W. Roberts, Binghampton, N.Y., 10½ In.	330.00
Jug, Bird, Flower Branch, Blue, White's, Utica, N.Y., c.1865, 2 Gal., 13½ In.	495.00
Jug, Bird, On Branch, Blue, 14 In.	523.00
Jug, Bird, On Branch, Blue, Applied Ear Handle, 2⅞ In.	1320.00
Jug, Bird, On Branch, Blue, Applied Handle, Cowden & Wilcox, Harrisburg, Pa., 17 In.	3300.00
Jug, Bird, On Flower Branch, Cobalt Blue, Stamped 2, Handle, 14 In.	193.00
Jug, Bird, Paddletail, Cobalt Blue, N.A. White & Son, Utica, N.Y., 2 Gal., 14¼ In. ...... *illus*	380.00
Jug, Bird, Singing, c.1870, 2 Gal., 13 In.	578.00
Jug, Blue Decoration, c.1840, Gal., 11½ In.	275.00
Jug, Blue Decoration, Incised Bird, Leafy Vine, Oval, 12 In.	8525.00
Jug, Blue Decoration, John Horting, Lancaster, Pa., 11 In.	1870.00
Jug, Blue Decoration, O.L. & A.K. Ballard, Burlington, Vt., 5 Gal.	1725.00
Jug, Blue Decoration, Oval, c.1835, Gal., 10½ In.	413.00
Jug, Blue Decoration, Oval, Handle, c.1820, 2 Gal., 13½ In.	165.00
Jug, Brown Glaze, A.L. Hyssong, Bloomsburg, Pa., Handles, 10 In.	39.00
Jug, Bull's-Eye Flower, Cobalt Blue, Reeded Neck, c.1800, 2 Gal., 12 In.	853.00
Jug, Cinnamon Clay, Oval, Marks, Gal., c.1835, 10 In.	1045.00
Jug, Cobalt Blue, Bird, Brady & Ryan, 14 In.	316.00
Jug, Cobalt Blue 2 In Design, HF Phillips & Stein, Richmond, Va., 13 In.	288.00
Jug, Cobalt Blue Decoration, Egg Shape, Late 19th Century, 2 Gal., 14 In.	235.00
Jug, Cobalt Blue Inscription, William Kelly, Scranton, Pa., 4 Gal.	1650.00
Jug, Diamond Ink, Original Label & Cork, 13 In.	385.00

Jug, Dog, Rabbit, Stippled, Incised, Applied 2-Hole Handles, Georgia Blizzard, 11 x 9 In.	748.00
Jug, Double Flower, Drooping, Leaves, Blue, Applied Handle, 2, D.P. Shenfelder, 13 In.	688.00
Jug, Double Flower, Leaves, Blue, Round Stamp 2, N. Clark Jr., 13½ In.	303.00
Jug, Drooping Tulip, Blue, Applied Handle, Cowden & Wilcox, 11 In.	440.00
Jug, Eagle & Cannon, Tooled Bands, c.1830, 3 Gal., 16 In.	935.00
Jug, Face, 4 Teeth, Olive Alkaline Glaze, Inscribed, Lanier Meaders, 8 In.	4370.00
Jug, Face, Broken China Teeth, Albany Slip Glaze, Stamped, Brown Pottery, 5¼ In.	1300.00
Jug, Face, Broken Chain Teeth, Handles, Olive Alkaline Glaze, B.B. Craig, 19½ In.	3105.00
Jug, Face, Broken China Teeth, Impressed, BB Craig, 10¼ In.	546.00
Jug, Face, Broken China Teeth, Incised Mustache, Beard, Brown Glaze, Charles Lisk, 12 In. . .	200.00
Jug, Face, Broken China Teeth, Mottled Olive Alkaline Glaze, B.B. Craig, 12¾ In.	546.00
Jug, Face, Broken China Teeth, Olive Alkaline Glaze, B.B. Craig, 11 In.	489.00
Jug, Face, Broken China Teeth, Wavy Lines On Shoulders, B.B. Craig, 16½ In.	1150.00
Jug, Face, Broken China Teeth, Wavy Lines On Shoulder, B.B. Craig, N.C., 7¼ In. . . . . . *illus*	690.00
Jug, Face, Bulging Eyes, Broken China Teeth, Brown Alkaline Glaze, Brown's, 12 In.	460.00
Jug, Face, Candelabrum, 4 Socket, Double, Runny Olive Glaze, Meaders, 11 In.	748.00
Jug, Face, Ceramic Eyes, Teeth, Runny Olive Glaze, Cleater & Billie Meaders, 11 In.	288.00
Jug, Face, Ceramic Teeth, Runny Olive Glaze, Lanier Meaders, 9½ In.	1840.00
Jug, Face, Devil, Glazed Eyes, Teeth, Runny Olive Glaze, Cleater & Billie Meaders, 10¼ In. . .	546.00
Jug, Face, Devil Monkey, Ceramic Teeth, Eyes, Runny Olive Glaze, Steve Abee, 13 In. . . . . *illus*	173.00
Jug, Face, Devil, Open Mouth, Teeth, Olive Alkaline Glaze, Steve Abee, 16½ In.	690.00
Jug, Face, Devil's Head, Brown Glaze, Strap Handle, Albert Hodge No. 15, Newton, N.C., 13 In. .	115.00
Jug, Face, Double, Broken China Teeth, Bulging Eyes, Snake, Chester Hewell, 10½ In.	259.00
Jug, Face, Double, Stone Teeth, Runny Olive Glaze, Lanier Meaders, 10 In. . . . . *illus*	5750.00
Jug, Face, Head Of Napoleon, Eagle Head On Handle, Stephen Green, c.1840, 8¾ In.	646.00
Jug, Face, Incised Eyebrows, Ceramic Teeth, Olive Glaze, A.G. Meaders, 10¼ In.	230.00
Jug, Face, Pinched Expression, Alkaline Glaze, Ceramic Eyes, Inscribe, L. Meaders, 9¼ In. . . .	3000.00
Jug, Face, Runny Blue Glaze, China Teeth, Pottery, Marked, Bill Flowers N.C., 10½ In.	398.00
Jug, Face, Smiling, No Teeth, Inscribed, Lanier Meaders, 8½ In.	3220.00
Jug, Fancy Tulip, Cobalt Blue, 3, Applied Handle, 15½ In.	230.00
Jug, Fish Design, 9¼ In.	6050.00
Jug, Flower, Blue, Ball Shape, Oval, Cinnamon, J.F. Brayton & Co., N.Y., 2 Gal., 13 In.	413.00
Jug, Flower, Blue, Bulbous Body, Applied Handle, Stamped 3, 13 In.	275.00
Jug, Flower, Blue, Chollar Darby & Co., c.1840, 3 Gal., 14½ In.	523.00
Jug, Flower, Blue, J.M. Harris, Easton, Pa., 14 In.	330.00
Jug, Flower, Blue, Stylized No. 2, Applied Handle, Burger & Lang, Rochester, N.Y., 14 In.	220.00
Jug, Flower, Blue, Weston & Gregg, Ellenville, N.Y., c.1869, Gal., 10½ In.	110.00
Jug, Flower, Blue Accents, Ball Shape, Tyler & Dillon, c.1825, 2 Gal., 13 In.	550.00
Jug, Flower, Blue Oval, S.S. Perry, c.1830, Gal., 11 In.	413.00
Jug, Flower, c.1880, 3 Gal., 15 In.	385.00
Jug, Flower, Cobalt Blue, 2, Applied Handle, W.H. Farrar & Co., Geddes, N.Y., 13 In. . . . . *illus*	805.00
Jug, Flower, Cobalt Blue, Applied Handle, Cowden & Wilcox, 13½ In.	440.00
Jug, Flower, Cobalt Blue, Strap Handle, F.B. Norton & Co., Worchester, Mass., 2 Gal.	201.00
Jug, Flower, Dotted, Incised, c.1860, 3 Gal., 16 In.	248.00
Jug, Flower, Dotted, Oval, J.G. Ball & Co., c.1836, 3 Gal., 15½ In.	743.00
Jug, Flower, Dotted, Ribbed, H. Becker, c.1870, 2 Gal., 14½ In.	880.00
Jug, Flower, Leafy Stem, Blue, Handle, Stamped 3, 16½ In.	385.00
Jug, Flower Burst, Leaves, Blue, J. Heiser, Buffalo, N.Y., No. 3, 13¾ In.	770.00
Jug, Flowers, Blue, Applied Handle, F.H. Cowden, 10¾ In.	330.00
Jug, Flowers, Blue, J.B. Cartwright & Co., Montreal, 1800s, 5 Gal., 19 In.	109.00
Jug, Flowers, Blue, Stamped 2 On Shoulder, Applied Handle, 13½ In.	358.00
Jug, Flowers, Dancing, Blue, Harrington & Burger, Rochester, N.Y., c.1853, 2 Gal., 13½ In. . .	330.00
Jug, G. Nagle III, Haverhill St., Boston, Blue Slip, 2, Applied Handle, Ottman Bros., 14 In. . .	132.00
Jug, Grape Bunch, Blue, Applied Handle, Sipe, Nichols & Co., Williamsport, Pa., 10¾ In.	165.00
Jug, Handle, Stamped Lyons, 10½ x 8 In.	17.00
Jug, I. Seymour & Co., Troy, Oval, c.1825, 2 Gal., 16 In.	468.00
Jug, John M. Connelly, Elmira, N.Y., Cone Top, Gal.	25.00
Jug, Leaf, Cobalt Blue, Impressed, L. & B.C. Chace, Somerset, Strap Handle, 11½ In.	374.00
Jug, Leaf Spray, Blue, Stamped 4 On Shoulder, 16¼ In.	578.00
Jug, Long Neck Bird, Cobalt Blue, Impressed, White's Utica 3, Handle, 16 In.	575.00
Jug, Man's Profile, Top Hat, Goatee, Mustache, Blue, 3, 15¼ In.	7975.00
Jug, Memory, Applied Trinkets, Applied Porcelain Plate, Gold Paint, 8½ In.	193.00
Jug, Monkey, Maple Leaf, Brown Top, Western, Gal.	95.00
Jug, Olive Alkaline Glaze, Incised 4, 2 Handles, Signed, Michael Crocker, 17½ In.	460.00
Jug, Oval, Brown Alkaline Glaze, Incised 3, Strap Handle, 16 In.	805.00
Jug, Oval, Handles, Runny Olive Glaze, Cleater Meaders, c.1987, 13½ In.	144.00

Stoneware, Jug, Flower, Cobalt Blue, 2, Applied Handle, W.H. Farrar & Co., Geddes, N.Y., 13 In. $805.00

Stoneware, Mug, Large Y, Blue, Incised, Elise Garr Henry, Allan M. Hirsh, 1901, 3⅝ In. $2200.00

Stoneware, Pitcher, Stylized Branch, Cobalt Blue, Northwest Ohio, 12¾ In. $259.00

S

Stoneware, Pitcher Pump, Spitting Tulips, Blue Bands, Cover, Slot Center, Stepped Rim, 20 In. $22100.00

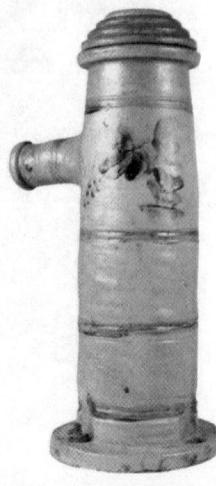

Jug, Portrait Of Man, Large Upturned Nose, Blue, 12¼ In.	523.00
Jug, Primitive Flowers Around Shoulder, Blue, 16 In.	132.00
Jug, Puzzle, Pierced Neck, 5 Spouts, Gentleman Now Try Your Skill, c.1837, 8¼ In.	206.00
Jug, Salt Glaze, Cobalt Blue, Straight-Sided, Applied Strap Handle, 1872, 10 In.	558.00
Jug, Shoulder, Maple Leaf, Brown Top, Western, ½ Gal.	15.00
Jug, Shoulder, Maple Leaf, Brown Top, Western, 2 Gal.	10.00
Jug, Shoulder, Maple Leaf, Brown Top, Western, Gal.	10.00
Jug, Snowflake, Blue, H.M. Whitman, Havana, N.Y., Stamped, 15½ In.	715.00
Jug, Soldier On Horse, Dog, Inscripted Fremont, Cobalt Blue, c.1856, 10 Gal., 21½ In.	35000.00
Jug, Stenciled, J.W. McKie, Blue Point Saloon, Goshen, Ind., Miniature	1450.00
Jug, Stenciled 4 ES & B, New Brighton, Pa., 15 In.	688.00
Jug, Stylized Bird, Plume, Branch, Blue, O.L. & A.K. Ballard, 14½ In.	413.00
Jug, Syrup, Birds, Trees, Fences, Edmands & Co., c.1870, 3 Gal.	11000.00
Jug, Tomato, Maple Leaf, Brown Top, Gal.	20.00
Jug, Tree Of Life, Blue, Oval, c.1830, 3 Gal., 14½ In.	688.00
Jug, Tulip, Dotted Leaves, Blue, Decorated Handle, 11¼ In.	7975.00
Jug, Wavy Line Shoulder Decoration, Glaze Runs, Oval, B.B. Craig, 12¾ In.	546.00
Jug, Wreath, Blue, Burger & Lang, Rochester, N.Y., c.1870, 2 Gal., 14½ In.	187.00
Mug, Barrel Shape, Cobalt Blue Glaze	10.00
Mug, Flower, Stem, 2 Incised Lines At Shoulder & Base, Blue, Applied Ear Handle, 5 In.	990.00
Mug, Gray, Blue Bands, Incised, Atlantic Garden 50 Bonery, 1840-60, Jersey, 5 In.	440.00
Mug, Large Y, Blue, Incised, Elise Garr Henry, Allan M. Hirsh, 1901, 3⅜ In. *illus*	2200.00
Mug, Pure Test Malt & Hops Co., Chicago, Western	85.00
Mug, Seattle Extract Co., Chicago, Ill., Blue & White Bands	90.00
Pan, Milk, Formed Spout, Leaf, c.1850, Gal., 4¼ x 10 In.	330.00
Pitcher, 2 Branch Flowers, Accents On Spout & Rim, Blue, Applied Handle, 9 In.	1430.00
Pitcher, Applied Grapes, Vines, Alkaline Glaze, Edwin Meaders, 1988, 9½ In.	748.00
Pitcher, Blue Gray, Applied Ear Handle, Pinched Spout, 4½ In.	99.00
Pitcher, Bobwhite, 14 In.	55.00
Pitcher, Butterfly, Blue Slip, c.1870, ½ Gal., 8½ In.	303.00
Pitcher, Cattails, Blue & White, 9 In.	105.00
Pitcher, Compliments Of C.W. Davenport Co., Gladbrook, Iowa, Scroll Handle, Blue, White	85.00
Pitcher, Cows, Blue & White, Blue Borders, Oval, 8 In.	230.00
Pitcher, Double Flower, Single Stem, Incised Line Around Shoulder, Blue, 9¼ In.	523.00
Pitcher, Fish Scale & Wild Rose, Blue & White, 7 In.	95.00
Pitcher, Flower, Blue, Cowden & Wilcox Stamp, Applied Handle, 8 In.	2090.00
Pitcher, Flower, Blue, Stamped 1½, Frank B. Norton, 11 In.	440.00
Pitcher, Flower, Leaf Swags Around Rim, Blue, P. Herman, 10 In.	2530.00
Pitcher, Flower, Slip Blue, Long Stem, Mottled Clay Color, c.1850, Gal., 11 In.	358.00
Pitcher, Flower Bouquet, Cobalt Blue, c.1870, 2 Gal., 13 In.	825.00
Pitcher, Flowers, Incised, Crosshatched Bloom, Blue, 8¼ In.	330.00
Pitcher, Flowers, Leaves, Blue, Applied Handle, 7½ In.	1210.00
Pitcher, Flowers & Swags, Blue, 8½ In.	1155.00
Pitcher, Glazed, Globular, Loop Hand, 7½ In.	600.00
Pitcher, Matthews Harris & Co., Cider Vinegar, Glazed, 6¾ x 5½ In.	805.00
Pitcher, Pine Tree, Blue & White	65.00
Pitcher, Plume, c.1870, 1½ Gal., 11½ In.	176.00
Pitcher, Poppy Flower, Blue, c.1860, Gal., 9½ In.	578.00
Pitcher, Red, Brown Alkaline Glaze, c.1809, ½ Gal., 8 In.	6050.00
Pitcher, Seattle Extract Co., Chicago, Ill., Blue & White Rivets, Bands	90.00
Pitcher, Stylized Branch, Cobalt Blue, Northwest Ohio, 12¾ In. *illus*	259.00
Pitcher, Swirl, Alternating Bands, Blue, Green, Ivory Alkaline Glaze, B.B. Craig, 12 In.	546.00
Pitcher, Tall Flower Branches, Leaves Surrounding Rim & Handle, Blue, 10½ In.	1540.00
Pitcher, Tree Trunk, Incised, Miss Maria Murphy, 1881, 8½ In.	44.00
Pitcher Pump, Spitting Tulips, Blue Bands, Cover, Slot Center, Stepped Rim, 20 In. *illus*	22100.00
Pot, Effigy, Hand Formed, Incised Rim, Just A Little Pebble, Georgia Blizzard, 4 x 6 In.	920.00
Punch Bowl, Drinking Scenes, Grapes, Vines, Blue, Early 1900s, 12 x 31 In.	863.00
Rolling Pin, Compliments Of B.B. Witmer, Flowers, Leaves, Blue, No Handles, 7¼ In.	330.00
Rolling Pin, Compliments Of Pierz Mercantile Co., Pierz, Minn., Wildflower, Blue & White	675.00
Rolling Pin, Rhodes Burford House Furnishing Co., Complete On Easy Terms, Blue Band	625.00
Rolling Pin, Trade With Zwigkl & Save Dough, Blue Band	500.00
Salt Box, Hanging, Wildflower	40.00
Salt Box, Lid, Colonial, Hanging	200.00
Soap Dish, Wildflower, Blue & White	255.00
Stove Foot, Paw Form, Blue, Flowers, Vines, 4½ In.	110.00
Strainer, Basket Shape, Pierced Body, 11½ In.	605.00

Teapot, Cover, Chinese Yixing, Red, Hexagonal, 6 Panels, Early 1700s, 3¾ In.	2700.00
Vase, Adam & Eve In Paradise Garden, Hand Painted, Sgraffito, c.1938, 14¼ In.	4800.00
Vase, Blue, Gray, Cream Matte Glaze, Oval Panels, Body, 17¼ In.	4200.00
Vase, Daisy Design, Bottom Marked, 7½ In.	85.00
Vase, Double Eagle Ring Handles, Blue & White, Germany, 19th Century, 19 In.	205.00
Vase, Figure Holding Shawl, When I'm Moaning, Georgia Blizzard, 9 x 6½ In.	1610.00
Vase, Oxblood Raku Glaze, Walter Dexter, 1980s, 7½ In.	192.00
Water Cooler, 4 Blue Bands, Lid, Chrome Spout, Crown Mark, c.1930, 2 Gal., 13½ In.	105.00
Water Cooler, 10 Blue Bands, Gray, Lid, Black Rubber Spout, c.1940, 2 Gal., 12 In.	50.00
Water Cooler, Embossed Stag In Forest, Blue Glaze, Cover, Pinecones, Needles, 12 In. *illus*	330.00
Water Cooler, Flowers, Salt Glaze, 17½ In.	2400.00
Water Cooler, Flowers, Scroll, Blue, Jas. Hamilton & Co., Handles, 16½ In.	440.00
Water Cooler, Flowers, Sway Around Spigot Hole, Applied Handles, Blue, 14½ In.	2520.00
Water Cooler, Iced Tea, Lid, 2 Gal.	210.00
Water Cooler, Lid, Trees, Blue Accent Bands, Northwind Face, c.1885, 2 Gal., 13 In.	688.00
Water Cooler, Man, Well, Cornucopia, Cobalt Blue, Robinson Clay Products, c.1900, 12¼ In.	202.00
Water Cooler, Sunflowers, Eagle, Banner, E Pluribus Unum, Dots, Blue, Handles, 20 In.	2200.00
Water Pig, Flowers, Leaves, Blue, Applied Feet, 9¼ x 12 In.	468.00
Whistle, Bird, Cobalt Blue, Mulberry Wings, Beak, 2½ In.	403.00

 STORE fixtures, cases, cutters, and other items that have no advertising as part of the decoration are listed here. Most items found in an old store are listed in the Advertising category in this book.

Cabinet, Hardware, Softwood, Stencil, Octagonal Case, 10 Vertical Drawers, 56 x 31 In.	990.00
Cabinet, Pine, Octagonal, Swivels, 80 Drawers, American Bolt & Screen Case Co., 34 In. *illus*	995.00
Cabinet, Tobacco, P. Lorillard, Glass Doors, 1880s, 32 x 36 x 18 In.	3850.00
Case, Oak, Pyramid Shape Top, Country, 23 x 21 x 49 In.	110.00
Case, Ribbon, Oak, Henrich Exhibition Co., Late 1800s, 47 x 19 x 23 In. *illus*	3803.00
Case, Swan Fountain Pen, Etched Glass, Countertop, 16 x 10 x 17 In.	275.00
Case, Walnut, Glass Panels, Sloping Top, Mirrored Back Door, Countertop, 36 x 20 In.	345.00
Case, Walnut, Oak Columns, Molded Base, 3 Glass Sides, 15 x 15 x 34 In.	345.00
Cigar Cutter, Beer Keg, Horse Rearing, Cast Iron, No. 11, 3½ x 5 x 3 In.	180.00
Cigar Cutter, Novelty, Erotic, Reclining Woman, Gilt Brass, Russia, Early 1900s, 5½ In.	797.00
Cigar Cutter, Zeppelin Shape, 1918 Patent, 1½ In.	88.00
Cigar Cutter & Holder, Abercrombie & Co., Wood & Iron, Barrel Form, Pat. 1891, 6½ In.	825.00
Coffee Bin, Stenciled, Fresh Roasted Coffee, Painted, Red Ground, 17 x 18 In.	248.00
Coffee Grinders are listed in their own category.	
Cutter, Tobacco Plug, Flat Iron Shape, Assorted Flat Iron Tobacco Tags	1300.00
Dispenser, Cigar, Wood, Guillotine Style, 8 In.	335.00
Dispenser, Ice Cream Cone, Glass, Marble Base, 32 In.	303.00
Dispenser, Koffee Bean, Tin, White Ground, Black Lettering, Gilt Accents, 24½ In.	154.00
Malt Mixer, Hand Crank, Cast Iron, Red Paint, 50 In.	1540.00
Millinery Head, Papier-Mache, Hand Painted, France, 20 x 7 In.	322.00
Mold, Boot, Carved, Painted, Wood, Iron, 19th Century, 20 x 12½ In.	1800.00
Mold, Boot, Carved, Wood, 19th Century, 27 x 10¾ In.	4800.00
Sign, 10 Cents Counter, Black, Gold, Reverse Glass, Chain Hung, 5 x 11 In.	160.00
Sign, Anchor, Wood, Dark Bluegreen Paint, Hanging Bracket, Late 19th Century, 53 x 40 In.	1560.00
Sign, Catfish Shape, Catfish Painted On Side, Wooden, Tin Fins & Whiskers, 1900s, 48 In.	690.00
Sign, Cobbler, Boot, 25¼ In.	1348.00
Sign, Glasses, Red & Blue Lenses, Glass, Cast Iron, 8½ x 17½ In.	187.00
Sign, Hand Saw Shape, Filed & Set Painted On Blade, Weathered Patina, 7½ x 30¼ In.	945.00
Sign, No Smoking, Red, White, 2-Sided, Porcelain, 6 Grommets, 6 x 20 In.	70.00
Sign, No Spitting On Sidewalk, Embossed, Tin Lithograph, 4¾ x 7 In.	330.00
Sign, Optometrist, Eyes Tested, Free, Wood, Painted, 19th Century, 8 x 30 In.	2400.00
Sign, Restroom, Colored, Men, Ladies, Porcelain, 2 x 10 In.	660.00
Sign, Saddlery, Molded Zinc, Horseshoe Surrounding Horse Head, 21 x 17 In.	1175.00
Sign, Shoe, Wood, Old Green Paint, Carved, 18 In.	230.00
Sign, Spices, Welcome, Soap, Gilt Lettering, Black Smalt Ground, Gilt, 6½ x 23 In.	881.00
Sign, Trade, Chinese Calligraphy, 61 x 9 In., Pair	146.00
Sign, Whale, Showing Teeth, Carved, Painted, Iron Chain, Early 1800s, 17¼ x 32 In.	24000.00
Stringholder, Cast Iron, Claw Feet, 7 x 5 In.	236.00
Stringholder, Cast Iron, Pedestal Base, 6 x 4 In.	33.00
Stringholder, SSS For The Blood, Kettle Form, Red Paint, Footed, 4¾ x 5 In.	83.00
Tobacco Cutter, Little Imp, Figural, Cast Iron, Old Red Paint, Brighton, 10 x 7 In.	575.00

Stoneware, Water Cooler, Embossed Stag In Forest, Blue Glaze, Cover, Pinecones, Needles, 12 In. $330.00

Store, Cabinet, Pine, Octagonal, Swivels, 80 Drawers, American Bolt & Screen Case Co., 34 In. $995.00

Store, Case, Ribbon, Oak, Henrich Exhibition Co., Late 1800s, 47 x 19 x 23 In. $3803.00

S

Stove, Parlor, Coal, House Shape, Temple Stove Co., Avon, N.Y., c.1854 $575.00

Sunderland, Bowl, Pink Luster, Transfer, Pictures The Ship Caroline, 10½ In. $702.00

Sunderland, Pitcher, Black Transfers, View Of Cast Iron Bridge, Ship, R's Verse, 8 In. $230.00

STOVES have been used in America for heating since the eighteenth century and for cooking since the nineteenth century. Most types of wood, coal, gas, kerosene, and even some electric stoves are collected.

Cast Iron, Tapered Rounded Sides, Hinged Door, Penny Feet, Shaker, 34 x 20 In.	374.00
Glazier Stove Co., Kerosene, Brightest & Best, Chelsea, Mich.	20.00
Model, Paragon, Brass, 1920s	98.00
Parlor, Andirons, Hand Forged, Cast Iron, E. & C. Gurney, Hamilton, Pat. 1864, 41 In.	207.00
Parlor, Coal, House Shape, Temple Stove Co., Avon, N.Y., c.1854 ....*illus*	575.00
Shaker, Canted Sides, Lipped Base, 4 Peg Legs, Cast Iron, Watervliet, N.Y., c.1830, 20 x 29 x 12 In.	1404.00
Stove Plate, Iron, Good For Evil 1758, Tulips, Verse, Thomas Pots, 23½ x 23¼ In.	605.00
Stove Plate, Iron, Thomas Pots, Double Arch, Tulips, Hearts, c.1758, 23¾ x 23¾ In.	633.00
Stove Plate, Tulip & Heart, Cast Iron, Colebrookdale Furnace, 25¾ x 24 In.	770.00
Stove Plate, Tulip & Heart, Tombstone, Henrich Wilhelm Elizabeth, 25 x 23 In.	550.00 to 715.00
Stove Plate, Tulips & Pinwheels, Cast Iron, Amos Geret, 1752, 28¼ x 26½ In.	1210.00
Stove Plate, Vines, Leaves, Cast Iron, Steigel, 1769, 23¼ x 19½ In.	550.00
Wood Knob, Lipped Front, Stepped Down Back, Cast Iron, New Lebanon, N.Y., 1830, 17 x 29 x 13 In.	1872.00

SUMIDA is a Japanese pottery that was made from about 1895 to 1941. Pieces are usually everyday objects—vases, jardinieres, bowls, teapots, and decorative tiles. Most pieces have a very heavy orange-red, blue, brown, black, green, purple, or off-white glaze, with raised three-dimensional figures as decorations. The unglazed part is painted red, green, black, or orange. Sumida is sometimes mistakenly called *Sumida gawa*, but true Sumida gawa is a softer pottery made in the early 1800s.

Bowl, 5 Figures, Ryosai, Signed, c.1900, 8 In.	195.00
Bowl, 7 Comic Figures, Brown Phosphatic Glaze, Vertical Sides, Early 1900s, 8 In.	350.00
Bowl, Woman Looking Over Edge, Ruffled Rim, Gawa, Encrustation, c.1900, 5 x 3½ In.	495.00
Jar, Cover, Iris, c.1890, 4¾ x 3¼ In.	295.00
Jar, Figural Cover, Man, Violet, 4 x 3½ x 2½ In.	175.00
Mug, Old Man, Early 20th Century, 3¼ x 4¾ In.	350.00
Mug, Oni Devil & Child, Early 20th Century, 3¼ x 4¾ In.	350.00
Vase, Japanese Figure, Relief, Red Ground, Bulbous, 3½ In.	250.00
Vase, Relief Figures, Grooved Body, Red Stain, Phosphatic Brown Glaze, 8½ In.	350.00

SUNBONNET BABIES were first introduced in 1900 in the book *The Sunbonnet Babies*. The stories were by Eulalie Osgood Grover, illustrated by Bertha Corbett. The children's faces were completely hidden by the sunbonnets. The children had been pictured in black and white before this time, but the color pictures in the book were immediately successful. The Royal Bayreuth China Company made a full line of children's dishes decorated with the Sunbonnet Babies. Some Sunbonnet Babies plates have been reproduced, but are clearly marked.

Book, Mother Goose Land, Eulalie Osgood Grover, Hardback, 1942, 6½ x 6 In.	20.00
Bowl, Tuesday, Ironing, Large	65.00
Cream Pitcher, Cleaning	55.00
Figurine, Monday, Washing	50.00
Figurine, Tuesday, Ironing	150.00
Pitcher, All Days	120.00
Plate, Friday, Molly & Mae Walking, China Pewter, Wilton Columbia, 11 In.	75.00
Plate, Friday, Sweeping, 6 In.	110.00
Plate, Friday, Sweeping, 7¼ In., 7 Piece	199.00
Plate, Molly & Mae, Playing Catch, Kern Collectible Plate, Box, 1982, 7 In.	225.00
Sugar & Creamer	525.00
Table Linen, Embroidered, Appliqued, 34 x 34 In.	22.00
Teapot, Tuesday, Ironing, Folding	110.00

SUNDERLAND luster is a name given to a special type of pink luster made by Leeds, Newcastle, and other English firms during the nineteenth century. The luster glaze is metallic and glossy and appears to have bubbles in it. Other pieces of luster are listed in the Luster category.

Bowl, Pink Luster, Transfer, Pictures The Ship Caroline, 10½ In. ....*illus*	702.00
Pitcher, Black, Sailor's Poem, Cast Iron Bridge, To John & Elizabeth Cillock, 1796, 8 In.	230.00
Pitcher, Black Transfers, View Of Cast Iron Bridge, Ship, R's Verse, 8 In. ......*illus*	230.00
Plaque, Ship, American Flag, Pink Luster, Transfer, No Poem, 7¾ x 8¾ In.	311.00
Salt, Master, Copper Luster Foot, Rim, 2¾ x 2¼ In.	65.00
Vase, Posy, Pink Luster, Ruffled Lip, c.1820, 7¼ In.	450.00

SUPERMAN was created by two seventeen-year-olds in 1938. The first issue of *Action* comics had the strip. Superman remains popular and became the hero of a radio show in 1940, cartoons in the 1940s, a television series, and several major movies.

Advertisement, Newspaper, St. Louis Post Dispatch, Nov. 2, 1939, 16½ x 21 In.	4312.00
Bank, Ceramic, Pink, Nat. Com. Pub. Inc., c.1949, 9½ In.	746.00
Bicycle Ornament, Hood, Gold Luster, Action Pose, Box, L W. Lee Mfg. Co., 1946, 5½ In.	4312.00
Bottle, Bubble Bath, Superman Upper Body, Bronze Color, c.1970, 4½ In.	250.00
Bottle, Bubble Bath Soaky, 9½ In.	25.00
Coloring Book, Superman World Without Water, 1980	15.00
Comic Book, No. 34, May 6, 1945, Jack Burnley Cover Art ....*illus*	520.00
Comic Book, Sticker, Cut Out, Whitman Book, 1977, 8½ x 12 In.	19.00
Cookie Jar, Escaping From Chains, Warner Bros., Box, 1997, 12 x 9¼ In.	65.00
Cookie Jar, In Phone Booth, Square, California Originals, 1978, 13 x 5¼ In.	650.00
Dental Set, Giveaway, Comic Book, Py-Co-Pay Tooth Powder, Toothbrush, c.1942	1092.00
Doll, Wood, Composition, Jointed, Ideal, 1940, 13 In.	1170.00
Figure, Arms & Legs Move, Jointed Knees, Copyright DC, 1984, 4¾ In.	10.00
Figure, Posable, Window Box, Mego, 1972, 8 In.	168.00
Figure, Superman, Bend-Em, 5½ In.	15.00
Figure, Superman, Rubber, 1973, 7 In.	44.00
Figure, Wood, Jointed, Composition Head, Painted Features, Cloth Cape, Ideal, c.1940, 13 In. . *illus*	558.00
Game, Calling Superman, Board, Cardboard Figures, Transogram, 1954	125.00
Magic Kit, Official, Bar Zim, Box, 1956, 12¼ x 15¼ In.	610.00
Movie Poster, Superman & Mole Men, Lipperty, 1951, 27 x 41 In.	3600.00
Movie Poster, You'll Believe A Man Can Fly, 1978, 27 x 41 In.	72.00
Ornament, Christmas, Hallmark, Flying Over Metropolis, Robert Chad, Box, 1993	12.00
Pin, Superman Film Serial, Hoyts Suburban Theatres, Australia, c.1948, 1 In.	328.00
Poster, Superman Breaking Kryptonite Chains, G & F Posters, 27 x 40 In.	112.00
Poster, Trifold, Superman Flies Again, 20th Century Fox, 30 x 14 In.	374.00
Puppet, Cloth Body, Vinyl Head, Cape, Peter Puppet Playthings, c.1954, 10 In.	168.00
Salt & Pepper, Tin Container, Black & White, Drawings On Side, Vandor, 6¼ x 4 In.	20.00
Shirt, Image Of Superman In Front, Norwich National Comics, 1950s, Child's	1232.00
Sign, Superman Bread, King Arthur Markets, Early 1940s, 5½ x 16¼ In.	847.00
Sign, Superman Bread, King Arthur Markets, Early 1940s, 6 x 4 In.	448.00
Socks, Red, Green, City Skyline, Superman, Design, Sport Wear Hosiery, c.1949, 12 In.	728.00
Watch, Pocket, Superman On Dial, Black & Yellow Border, Metal, 2 In. ....*illus*	205.00
Wrapper, Super Bubble Gum, Waxed Paper, c.1940, 6 x 4½ In.	298.00
Wristwatch, Fossil, Box, 1993, 7 x 4 In.	142.00
Wristwatch, Superman Standing, Chrome Plated Case, Supertime, Ingraham, Box, 1950s, 8 In.	3850.00

SUSIE COOPER began as a designer in 1925 working for the English firm A.E. Gray & Company. In 1932 she formed Susie Cooper Pottery, Ltd. In 1950 it became Susie Cooper China, Ltd., and the company made china and earthenware. In 1966 it was acquired by Josiah Wedgwood & Sons, Ltd. The name Susie Cooper appears with the company names on many pieces of ceramics.

Bouillon, Handles, 2 x 6½ In.	25.00
Bouillon, Wedding Band, Turquoise	40.00
Bowl, Lotus, White, 7 In.	120.00
Bowl, Mariposa, Footed, 4½ In.	15.00
Bowl, Vegetable, Oval, 2½ x 7¾ In.	38.00
Creamer, Bone, 5½ x 2¾ In.	20.00
Creamer, Sepia Rose	95.00
Cup, Demitasse, Wedding Band, 3¼ x 2½ In.	15.00
Cup, Tea, Rust, Brown, Green Flowers	77.00
Cup, Wedding Band	25.00
Cup & Saucer, Sepia Rose	50.00
Dessert Set, Spiral Fern, Cup, Saucer	55.00
Gravy Boat, Sepia Rose, Gold Trim	160.00
Plate, Dinner, Art Deco, c.1930, 10 In.	23.00
Plate, Dinner, Dresden Spray, 1930s, 10 In.	22.50
Plate, Dinner, Sepia Rose, 10⅝ In.	65.00
Plate, Salad, Bone, 8¼ In.	20.00
Plate, Salad, Fruit Center, Blue Border, 1930s, 8¾ In., 12 Piece	192.00
Plate, Salad, Wedgwood, 8½ In.	15.00
Platter, Ashet, Oval, 14 x 11 In.	75.00
Platter, Bone, 13¼ x 10½ In.	45.00

Superman, Comic Book, No. 34, May 6, 1945, Jack Burnley Cover Art $520.00

Superman, Figure, Wood, Jointed, Composition Head, Painted Features, Cloth Cape, Ideal, c.1940, 13 In. $558.00

Superman, Watch, Pocket, Superman On Dial, Black & Yellow Border, Metal, 2 In. $205.00

S

Viktor Schreckengost

Viktor Schreckengost (1906-present) is a man a creative genius. He designed printing presses, oscillating fans, steam buses, metal chairs, lawn mowers, cab-forward trucks, bicycles, pedal cars, and even worked on radar for pilots during World War II. He is best known for his ceramics. His Cowan pottery *Jazz Bowl* is probably the most famous example of American art deco ceramic design. The punch bowl, decorated with streetlights, abstract signs, and skyscrapers, was ordered by Eleanor Roosevelt in 1930.

Viktor worked for Cowan Pottery, Leigh Potters, Limoges China Company, Onondaga Pottery, Salem China Company, and Sebring Pottery.

Manhattan (1935) was one of the first modern American modern dinnerware designs. Viktor's other designs included: *Flower Shop* (1935), *Primitive* (1955) with animal pictures that looked like cave drawings, and *Christmas Eve* (1950-1999), one of the first Christmas sets.

Syracuse, Avalon, Plate, Dinner, 10¼ In. $29.00

Platter, Hazelwood, 12 In.	40.00
Saucer, Cornpoppy	15.00
Saucer, Endon, 4⅞ In.	77.00
Saucer, Yellow Swirl With Pink, Mauve	28.00
Sugar, Cover, Sepia Rose, Handles	115.00
Sugar, Sepia Rose, Gold Trim	95.00
Teapot, Wedding Ring	50.00
Tureen, Vegetable, Cover, Clematis, 5½ x 10½ In.	82.00

SWANKYSWIGS are small drinking glasses. In 1933, the Kraft Food Company began to market cheese spreads in these decorated, reusable glass tumblers. They were discontinued from 1941 to 1946, then made again from 1947 to 1958. Then plain glasses were used for most of the cheese, although a few special decorated Swankyswigs have been made since that time. A complete list of prices can be found in *Kovels' Depression Glass & Dinnerware Price List*.

Antique No. 1, Black, 3¾ In.	6.00
Antique No. 1, Blue, 3¾ In.	7.00
Band No. 2, 3⅜ In.	8.00
Bicentennial Tulip, Red, 3¾ In.	28.00 to 35.00
Bustlin' Betsy, Blue, 1930s, 3¾ In.	7.00
Bustlin' Betsy, Brown, 3¾ In.	7.00
Kiddie Kup, Red, 3¾ In.	7.00
Posy, Tulip, Red, 3½ In.	8.00
Posy, Violet, 3½ In.	10.00

SWORDS of all types that are of interest to collectors are listed here. The military dress sword with elaborate handle is probably the most wanted. A *tsuba* is a hand guard fitted to a Japanese sword between the handle and the blade. Be sure to display swords in a safe way, out of reach of children.

Bayonet, Plug, Forged Blade, Wrought Iron, Revolutionary War, c.1776, 17 In.	767.00
Calvary, Saber, Gilt Brass Mounts, Shagreen Hilt, Leather Scabbard, Mid 1800s, 36 In.	705.00
Cavalry, Saber, Scabbard, Roby, US, 1864	665.00
Continental, Medieval Style, Steel, Cylindrical Grip, 42½ In.	176.00
Double Edge Blade, Pitting, Facet Cut Grip, Pommel, Knuckle Bow, 18 Century, 30 In.	354.00
England, Whites London, Curved Blade, Silver Plated Hilt, Wire Grip, c.1800, 32 In.	413.00
Japan, Leather Covered Wood Handle, 41 In.	206.00
Katana, Japan, Papers, Signed, c.1941, 28¼ In.	5310.00
Katana, Japan, Signed, 17th Century, 31 In.	5310.00
Katana, Japan, Wavy Temper Line, Brass Cuff, Wood Handle & Scabbard, 31 In.	633.00
Katana, Signed, 16th Century, 37½ In.	2006.00
Matador's, Spain, Wrapped Handle, Etched Blade, Leather Covered End, c.1940, 38 In.	48.00
Musician's, Emerson, Brass-Wrapped Grip & Guard, Nickel-Plated Scabbard, 1863, 39 In.	230.00
Naval, Cutlass, Figure 8, Straight Blade, Forged Iron Grip, c.1790, 27 In.	1550.00
Naval, France, Cutlass, Curved, Single Blade, Solid Grip, Cup, 1842, 26½ In.	472.00
Naval Officer's, U.S. Model 1852, Hilburn Hamburger, Etched, Scabbard, 33 In.	374.00
Non-Commissioned Officer's, Brass Grip, Scabbard, Ames, Chickopee, Mass., 1861, 39 In.	431.00
Officer's, Saber, Artillery, Brass Mounted, 37¾ In.	145.00
Rapier, Continental, Wooden Grip, Spherical Pommel, Arched Hand Guards, 54 In.	646.00
Rapier, Mexico, Double Edge Blade, Pierced Iron Cup, Brass Ball Ends, 1800s, 31 In.	531.00
Samurai, Black Enamel, Scabbard, Brass, Braided Wrapped Handle, 43 & 29 In.	133.00
Samurai, Cord Wrapped Over Sharkskin Hilt, Wooden Scabbard, 34¼ In.	767.00
Silver Mounted, Charles Boehme, Wrought Metal, Wood Handle, Mid 1800s, 30½ In.	3680.00
Steel, Fluted Grip, Guard, Vasiform Pommel, Engraved, France, 18th Century, 37 In.	499.00
Steel, Wire Wrapped Grip, Oval Pommel, Continental, 33¾ In.	705.00
Triangular Blade, Brass Cast Hilt, Pitting, 18th Century, 33 In.	354.00
U.S. Officer's, H.V. Allen & Co., N.Y., Eagle, Wire-Wrapped Grip, Scabbard, 1880, 32-In. Blade	460.00
Victoria, Double Edge, Straight Blade, Brass Hilt, Leather Bound Grip, 19th Century, 31 In.	472.00
Wakizashi, Iron Tsuba, Mon Handle, Black Lacquered Wood Scabbard, Japan, 19 In.	1416.00

SYRACUSE is a trademark used by the Onondaga Pottery of Syracuse, New York. The company was established in 1871. It is still working. The name became the Syracuse China Company in 1966. It is known for fine dinnerware and restaurant china.

SYRACUSE
China

Adobe, Bouillon, Econo Rim, Orange Trim	4.00
Advertising, Ashtray, Wright Company, Atlanta, Ga., 3 Holders, 5¼ In. Diam.	18.00
Angelica, Plate, Dinner, Staffordshire Shape, Ivory, 9 In.	5.00

Appleton, Sugar, Cover, Federal Shape	25.00
Avalon, Plate, Dinner, 10¼ In. . . . . *illus*	29.00
Baroque, Saucer, Berkeley Shape, c.1966	5.00
Black Lace, Plate, Bread & Butter, 6½ In.	3.50
Black Platinum, Plate, Bread & Butter, 6½ In.	3.00
Blue Grass, Platter, Carefree Shape, 12½ In.	20.00
Bombay, Bowl, Fruit, Winthrop Shape, 4½ In.	4.00
Bracelet, Saucer, After Dinner, Virginia Shape, Gold Band	5.00
Briarcliff, Bowl, Vegetable, Oval, Gold Trim, 10¾ x 8 In.	38.00
Briarcliff, Cup & Saucer, Federal Shape	18.00
Camellia, Plate, Square, 8¼ In.	12.00
Canterbury, Plate, Dinner, Mayflower Shape, 9¾ In.	18.00
Captain's Table, Plate, Luncheon, American Shape, 9 In.	5.00
Cardinal, Cup & Saucer, Econo Rim, 3⅞ x 2½ In.	10.00
Castaways, Plate, 7¼ In.	29.00
Chevy Chase, Cup, California Shape	12.00
China Spring, Plate, Salad, Berkeley Shape, 8 In.	18.00
Colonial, Plate, Dessert, 7¼ In.	4.00
Concord, Cup, Green	24.00
Concord Rose, Bowl, Vegetable, Divided, 10 In.	30.00
Concord Rose, Cup & Saucer	70.00
Concord Rose, Plate, Bread & Butter, 6¼ In.	7.00
Concord Rose, Plate, Dinner, 10⅛ In.	10.00
Concord Rose, Platter, Oval, 12 In.	18.00
Concord Rose, Saucer	3.00
Coralbel, Cup, 1960s	10.00
Coralbel, Plate, Salad, 7½ In.	10.00
Coralbel, Platter, 12 In.	30.00
Coventry, Gravy Boat, Attached Underplate . . . . *illus*	35.00
Debonair, Bonbon, Footed, Gold Trim, 3⅜ x 6 In.	28.00
Debonair, Bowl, Vegetable, Oval, 10 x 7⅝ In.	45.00
Debonair, Platter, Gold Trim, 14⅛ x 10 In.	45.00
Debutante, Sugar, Cover	25.00
Dogwood, Cup & Saucer, After Dinner	20.00
Dorado, Platter, Winthrop Shape, 10⅞ In.	7.50
Dorian, Cup & Saucer, California Shape	15.00
Ducks In Flight, Cup & Saucer, Airbrushed, Gray & White	12.00
Embassy, Bowl, Vegetable, Morwel Shape, 8¾ In.	8.00
Evening Star, Gravy Boat, Underplate	100.00
Falling Leaves, Cup & Saucer, Winthrop Shape	6.50
Festival, Bowl, Fruit, Winthrop Shape, 4¾ In.	3.00
Finesse, Sugar & Creamer . . . . *illus*	22.00
Flame Lily, Bowl, Vegetable, Divided, 10 In.	50.00
Flame Lily, Creamer	26.00
Flame Lily, Platter, 12½ In.	50.00
Flame Lily, Sugar, Cover	28.00
Fleur-De-Lis, Gravy Boat, Underplate	28.00
Fleur-De-Lis, Platter, Oval, 14¼ x 10¼ In.	28.00
Fusan, Creamer	40.00
Fusan, Sugar, Cover	35.00
Gardenia, Plate, Luncheon, Mayflower Shape, c.1925, 8¾ In.	10.00
Gibraltar, Soup, Dish, Tab Handle	5.00
Gourmet, Plate, Dessert, Winthrop Shape, Gold Trim, 7¼ In.	4.00
Graymont, Creamer	28.00
Green Leaf, Butter	12.00
Greyson, Plate, Bread & Butter, 6¼ In.	3.00
Haddon, Plate, Dinner, Winchester Shape, 9¾ In.	23.00
Harvest Gold, Platter, 11½ x 10 In.	24.00
Highland, Plate, Salad, Morwel Shape, c.1952, 7 In.	4.00
Indian Tree, Plate, Dinner, Mayflower Shape, 9¾ In.	24.00
Iroquois, Celery Dish, Oval, 1950s, 10 In.	10.00
Jefferson, Plate, Dinner, 10 In. . . . . *illus*	27.00
Jubilee, Sugar, Cover, Green, Brown, Yellow Diamonds	18.00
Juno, Casserole, Gold Trim, 12 x 7 In.	18.00
King's Inn, Cup, Olympus Shape	4.00
Lilac Rose, Platter, Gold Trim, 12 x 8⅝ In.	40.00

Syracuse, Coventry, Gravy Boat, Attached Underplate
$35.00

Syracuse, Finesse, Sugar & Creamer
$22.00

Syracuse, Jefferson, Plate, Dinner, 10 In.
$27.00

S

Syracuse, Rose Marie, Plate, Salad, Winchester Shape, c.1952, 8 In. $15.00

Dating Dinnerware by Design

Designs used on dinnerware, vases, figurines, and other decorative arts for much of the twentieth century were influenced by themes found in movies, books, and television. They give a clue to an item's age. Naturalistic patterns and muted colors were popular in the Arts and Crafts era. Colonial scenes and people in period costume were popular in the 1930s because of the restoration of Colonial Williamsburg. When Mexican and Hawaiian themes were trendy in the late 1930s and 1940s, hand-painted and decal designs of cactus or hula dancers were common. Disney-inspired designs were popular by the 1940s. Rustic-looking, California-inspired, mix-and-match pottery was "in" for young marrieds. At the same time, western designs seemed to follow the popularity of movie cowboys like Tom Mix and Hopalong Cassidy. By the 1950s, stars, planets, and other space-related patterns were in. A peasant look gained favor in the 1960s. In the 1960s and 1970s, op art patterns, wild colors, and huge flowers were popular. Fruit and flowers in more natural colors decorated dinnerware in the 1980s and '90s.

Lynnfield, Coffeepot, 9¼ In.	20.00
Madame Butterfly, Bowl, Dessert, 5 In.	8.00
Mayfair, Platter, Green, Oval, 11 In.	40.00
Memory Lane, Casserole, Cover, Royal China	110.00
Mesa Grande, Platter, Morwel Shape, 11 In.	6.00
Mistic, Creamer, Mayflower Shape	24.00
Monticello, Plate, Salad, Winchester Shape, 8 In.	18.00
Nimbus, Bowl, Vegetable, Virginia Shape, Platinum Trim, 9 In.	48.00
Olympia, Plate, Dinner, Olympus Shape, 9¼ In.	5.00
Orchard, Plate, Salad, Federal Shape, 8 In.	18.00
Oriental, Casserole, Cover, Mayflower Shape, 8½ In.	25.00
Orleans, Plate, Dinner, Mayflower Shape, 9¾ In.	20.00
Palomino, Plate, Dinner, Econo Rim, 9 In.	5.00
Pine Cone, Plate, Green Border, c.1960, 9¾ In.	12.00
Pink Shell Edge, Platter, Oval, 13 In.	10.00
Plymouth, Plate, Dinner, 9¾ In.	9.00
Puritan, Bowl, Fruit, Pink & Green Flower Border, 5¼ In.	5.00
Rosbury, Plate, Luncheon, Purple, Econo Rim, 9½ In.	8.50
Rose Marie, Plate, Salad, Winchester Shape, c.1952, 8 In. .....*illus*	15.00
Roslyn, Plate, Bread & Butter, Mayflower Shape, 6¼ In.	7.50
Roxbury, Soup, Dish, Econo Rim, c.1946, 6 In.	10.00
Sherwood, Soup, Dish, 8¾ In. .....*illus*	10.00
Stansbury, Platter, 12 x 9 In.	28.00
Stansbury, Sugar, Cover	28.00
Victoria, Bowl, Vegetable, Oval, Gold Trim, 10½ x 8 In.	35.00
Virginia, Soup, Dish, Black Flowers, 8⅞ In.	12.00
Wintergreen, Cup & Saucer	10.00

TAPESTRY, PORCELAIN, *see Rose Tapestry category.*

TEA CADDY is the name for a small box made to hold tea leaves. In the eighteenth century, tea was very expensive and it was stored under lock and key. The first tea caddies were made with locks. By the nineteenth century, tea was more plentiful and the tea caddy was larger. Often there were two sections, one for green tea, one for black tea.

Bird's-Eye Maple, Black Stenciled Scallops, Coffin Shape, Brass Bun Feet, 6 x 10 In.	660.00
Black Lacquer, Chinoiserie, Chinese, Late 19th Century, 5¼ x 8 x 5 In.	1520.00
Black Lacquer, Gilt Mandarin, Winged Paw Feet, 2 Pewter Containers, 5 x 8 In.	3055.00
Black Lacquer, Gilt Mandarin Reserves, 8-Sided, Dragon Masque Feet, 5 x 8 In.	2585.00
Black Lacquer, Mandarin Design, Mother-Of-Pearl Inlaid Robes, Overhanging Lid, 10 In.	450.00
Black Lacquer, Mandarin's Garden, Gilt, Octagonal, Domed Lid, Chinese, 9 x 6 In.	2160.00
Black Lacquer, Multicolored, Gilt, Chinese Export, c.1915, 5½ x 8¾ In.	1645.00
Bone Inlaid, Oval, Satinwood, Double Compartment, Georgian, 5 x 7½ In.	720.00
Burl, Silver Plate Mount, Tortoiseshell Block Front, England, 6¼ x 8 x 5 In.	1465.00
Ebony, Macassar, Mother-Of-Pearl Escutcheon, 3 Compartments, George IV, 7 x 13 In.	763.00
Ebony, Paper, Filigree, Gilt, Scrolls, Georgian, Early 19th Century, 5 x 6½ In.	940.00
Elm Burl, Ebonized Fruitwood Edges, Disc Feet, Coffin Shape, William IV, 6 x 10 In.	528.00
Fruitwood, Pear Shape, Hinged Lid, Georgian, 6 x 4½ In. .....*illus*	2070.00
Fruitwood, Pear Shape, Lid, Early 20th Century, 5¾ In., Pair	633.00
George III Style, Mahogany, Fruitwood, Turned, Ebonized, 6 x 3½ In.	500.00
Horn, Rose & Black-Tinted, Inlaid Bone Strips, Conforming Lid, 8-Sided, 4 x 4 In.	4080.00
Inlaid Satinwood, Mahogany, Band, Inlay, Scrolled Patera, 1800s, 6 x 12 In.	288.00
Mahogany, Bombe, Brass Mounted & Inlaid, Ringed Lion's Mask Handles, 7 x 9 In.	1057.00
Mahogany, Brass Mounted, Interior Compartments, Secret Drawer, 9 x 5 In., Pair	1610.00
Mahogany, Coffin Shape, Ball Footed, England, Early 19th Century, 8 In.	217.00
Mahogany, Crossbanded, England, Late 18th Century, 10 In.	389.00
Mahogany, Cut Brass, Inlaid, Gilt Tooled, Leather Border, Georgian, 6½ x 4¾ In.	840.00
Mahogany, Ebonized Fruitwood, Pear Shape, Turned, England, c.1885, 6 x 3½ In.	499.00
Mahogany, Inlaid, 2 Lidded Interior Compartments, Georgian, 5 x 9 In.	374.00
Mahogany, Inlaid, Banded, 8-Sided, Georgian, Sheraton, 4½ In.	1200.00
Mahogany, Inlay, 3 Compartments, Ring Handles, Coffin Shape, Brass Ball Feet, 8 x 15 In.	881.00
Mahogany, Satinwood Inlay, Dome Lid, Brass Handle, 3 Compartments, 6 x 11 In. ....*illus*	598.00
Mahogany Veneer, Inlay, Patera, Diamond Keyhole Escutcheon, Brass Ball Feet, 4 x 6 In.	488.00
Nickel Silver, Tortoiseshell, Serpentine Front, Mother-Of-Pearl Grips, 1800s, 5¼ x 8 In.	2880.00
Olivewood, Double, Mother-Of-Pearl Escutcheon, 2 Compartments, 4 x 7 In.	489.00
Porcelain, Cover, Rectangular, Blue & White, Chinese, c.1850, 5½ x 2 In.	117.00

Rosewood, Brass Inlay, Ebonized Fruitwood Button Grips, 4½ x 8 In.	210.00
Rosewood, Geometric Inlay, Star Escutcheon, Compartments, 6¾ x 12¾ In.	165.00
Rosewood, Mother-Of-Pearl Inlay, Rosewood Disc Feet, Coffin Shape, William IV, 6 x 9 In. ..	558.00
Satinwood, Inlay, Canted Corners, 2 Lidded Interior, Regency, 5 x 7 In.	374.00
Tortoiseshell, Blond, Rectangular, Rounded Corners, Button Grips, Brass Ball Feet, 5 x 12 In.	2640.00
Tortoiseshell, Bone, Serpentine Edge, England, c.1865, 5¾ x 6 In.	4700.00
Tortoiseshell, Bow Front, Canted Lid, Bone Button Grips & Feet, 4 x 5½ In.	1800.00
Tortoiseshell, Canted Corners, Silver Wire & Mother-Of-Pearl Inlay, Bone Ball Feet, 6 x 7 In. .	1920.00
Tortoiseshell, Ivory, Velvet Lining, 2 Compartments, Regency, 1800s, 7 x 4 x 5 In.	3900.00
Tortoiseshell, Lidded Interior, Brass Ball Feet, George III, c.1800, 6½ x 7 In.	1762.00
Tortoiseshell, Mother-Of-Pearl, Alternating Panels, Flared Bottom, 4½ x 7 In.	4800.00
Tortoiseshell, Mother-Of-Pearl Medallion, Silver, 8-Sided, Regency, 4½ x 6⅜ In.	3450.00
Tortoiseshell, Nickel Silver Mounted, Bombe Shape, Brass Ball Feet, 6 x 6 x 4 In.	5288.00
Tortoiseshell, Serpentine Front, Silver Wire Inlay, England, c.1835, 5¼ x 7 In.	4935.00
Tortoiseshell, Silver, Wire Inlaid, 8-Sided, Georgian, 4 x 4¼ In.	1800.00
Tortoiseshell, Silver Wire Inlay, Radiant Fan Lid, 8-Sided, 4-Bone Paw Feet, 4 x 7 In.	1560.00
Tortoiseshell, Wire & Bone Inlay, 8-Sided, Ball Finial & Feet, 2 Compartments, 7 x 7 In.	5405.00
Tortoiseshell Veneer, Ivory, Double, Hinged, Compartments, Ball Feet, 1800s, 5 x 7 In.	764.00
Trombly Ware, Erih Castle, Hinged Lid, Cut Crystal Mixing Bowl, c.1880, 5½ x 11½ In.	585.00
Tunbridge Marquetry, Square, Brass Lock, Paktong Lining, Fitted, 4½ x 5¼ In.	570.00
Walnut Burl, Bombe, Coffin Shape, String Inlay, Burlwood Lid, Bone Grips, Paw Feet, 6 x 9 In. .	881.00
Wood, Apple Shape, Lock, Inset Stem, 4½ x 5 In.	3680.00
Wood, Pewter, Black Lacquer, Gilt, Octagonal, 2 Parts, Chinese, 6 x 8 x 7 In.	1645.00

TEA LEAF IRONSTONE dishes are named for their decorations. There was a superstition that it was lucky if a whole tea leaf unfolded at the bottom of your cup. This idea was translated into the pattern of dishes known as "tea leaf." By 1850 at least twelve English factories were making this pattern, and by the 1870s it was a popular pattern in many countries. The tea leaf was always a luster glaze on early wares, although now some pieces are made with a brown tea leaf. There are many variations of tea leaf designs, such as Teaberry, Pepper Leaf, and Gold Leaf. The designs were used on many different white ironstone shapes, such as Bamboo, Lily of the Valley, Empress, and Cumbow.

Bowl, Mush, Plain, Meakin	140.00
Bowl, Vegetable, Cover, Brocade, Meakin	60.00 to 100.00
Bowl, Vegetable, Cover, Cable, Shaw	120.00
Bowl, Vegetable, Cover, Daisy Chain, Wilkinson	45.00 to 70.00
Bowl, Vegetable, Cover, Fishhook, Meakin	40.00
Bowl, Vegetable, Cover, Lily Of The Valley, Shaw	180.00
Bowl, Vegetable, Cover, Lions Head, Mellor Taylor	50.00
Bowl, Vegetable, Cover, Maiden Hair Fern, Wilkinson Maid	25.00
Bowl, Vegetable, Cover, Quartered Rose	110.00
Bowl, Vegetable, Cover, Victory, Edwards	35.00
Brush Box, Fanfare, Elsmore & Forester	675.00
Brush Vase, Fishhook, Meakin	110.00
Brush Vase, Scalloped, Meakin	70.00
Brush Vase, Shaw	110.00
Butter, Chinese, Shaw	275.00
Butter, Heavy, Square, Clementson	900.00
Cake Plate, Brocade, Meakin	120.00
Cake Plate, Cable, Shaw	90.00
Cake Plate, Grindley Favorite	190.00
Cake Plate, Hexagon, Shaw	90.00
Chamber Pot, Niagara Fan, Walley	1050.00
Chamber Pot, Peerless, Edwards	300.00
Coffeepot, Bamboo, Meakin	50.00
Coffeepot, Chinese, Clementson	300.00
Coffeepot, Fanfare, Elsmore & Forester	300.00
Coffeepot, Fig Cousin, Davenport	150.00
Coffeepot, Fishhook, Meakin	50.00
Coffeepot, Grindley Favorite	42.00
Coffeepot, Luster Band, Meakin	80.00
Coffeepot, Niagara Fan, Shaw	170.00
Coffeepot, Wheat, J. Furnival	250.00
Coffeepot, Wheat Meadow, Powell & Bishop	325.00
Creamer, Bamboo, Meakin	60.00 to 70.00

Syracuse, Soup, Dish, 8¾ In.
$10.00

Tea Caddy, Fruitwood, Pear Shape, Hinged Lid, Georgian, 6 x 4½ In.
$2070.00

Tea Caddy, Mahogany, Satinwood Inlay, Dome Lid, Brass Handle, 3 Compartments, 6 x 11 In.
$598.00

Tea Leaf Ironstone, Teapot, Morning Glory, Portland Shape, Elsmore & Forster, 12 In.
$25.00

T

Tea Leaf Ironstone,
Washbowl & Pitcher, Bamboo, Meakin
$225.00

TIP

When storing a sugar bowl with a cover on a high shelf, be sure to fasten the top with string or tape. The lid could fall off if you tip the bowl when you try to take it off the shelf. This applies to any piece of china or glass with a cover.

Teco, Plant Stand, Green Matte Glaze, Tapered Top, Open Skirt, 3 Legs, 20¾ x 11 In.
$1150.00

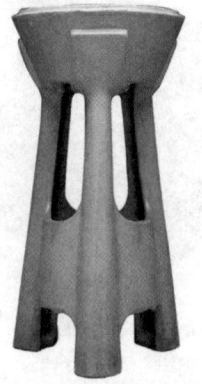

Teco, Vase, Green Matte Glaze, Charcoal Highlights, 2 Buttressed Handles, Gates, 8 x 6 In.
$2400.00

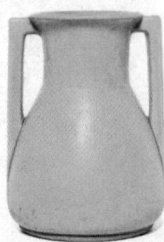

Creamer, Blanket Stitch, Alcock	170.00
Creamer, Bullet, Shaw	140.00
Creamer, Cable, T. Furnival	140.00
Creamer, Chelsea, Meakin	100.00
Creamer, Chinese, Shaw	410.00
Creamer, Crystal, Clementson	190.00
Creamer, Fig Cousin, Davenport	270.00
Creamer, Grindley Favorite	310.00
Creamer, Lions Head, Mellor Taylor	220.00
Creamer, Wheat Meadow, Powell & Bishop	300.00
Eggcup, Empress, Adams	90.00
Ewer, Acanthus, Johnson Bros.	525.00
Ewer, Bamboo, Grindley	185.00
Ewer, Hexagon, Shaw	275.00
Ewer, Pagoda, Burgess	210.00
Gravy Boat, Basketweave, Shaw	160.00
Gravy Boat, Bullet, Shaw	130.00
Gravy Boat, Chelsea, Johnson Bros.	15.00
Gravy Boat, Empress, Adams	10.00
Gravy Boat, Grindley Favorite	120.00
Gravy Boat, Peerless, Edwards	90.00
Gravy Boat, Scroll, Meakin	110.00
Gravy Boat, Sunburst, Wilkinson	30.00
Gravy Boat, Sydenham, Walley	250.00
Gravy Boat, Victory, Edwards	130.00
Jar, Waste, Ginger, T. Elsmore	1300.00
Jug, Water, Chinese, Shaw	150.00
Ladle, Soup, Gold Leaf, Iona Shape, Powell & Bishop	150.00
Pitcher, Chelsea, Meakin	200.00
Pitcher, Fishhook, Meakin	70.00 to 130.00
Pitcher, Golden Scroll, Powell & Bishop	70.00
Pitcher, Hot Water, Cable, Shaw	1200.00
Pitcher, Milk, Bamboo, Grindley	50.00
Plate, Meakin, 10 In.	35.00
Platter, Gothic, Walley	50.00
Platter, Grindley Favorite	10.00
Platter, Niagara Fan, Shaw	13.00
Relish, Cable, Shaw	40.00
Relish, Chinese, Shaw	220.00
Shaving Mug, Bamboo, Grindley	200.00
Shaving Mug, Basketweave, Shaw	625.00
Shaving Mug, Cable, Shaw, Large	275.00
Shaving Mug, Chinese, Shaw	80.00
Shaving Mug, Gothic, Livesley, Powell & Co.	100.00
Shaving Mug, Grindley Favorite	1050.00
Shaving Mug, Pagoda, Burgess	300.00
Shaving Mug, Sayer	30.00
Shaving Mug, Shaw, Extra Large	350.00
Soap Dish, Bamboo, Grindley, 2 Piece	40.00
Soap Dish, Brocade, Meakin, 3 Piece	360.00
Soap Dish, Cable, Shaw, 3 Piece	180.00
Sugar, Wheat Meadow, Powell & Bishop	70.00
Teapot, Bamboo, Meakin	65.00
Teapot, Morning Glory, Portland Shape, Elsmore & Forster, 12 In. ....*illus*	25.00
Teapot, Scroll, Meakin	160.00
Tureen, Cover, Gold Leaf, Iona Shape, Powell & Bishop	20.00
Washbowl & Pitcher, Bamboo, Meakin ....*illus*	225.00
Waste Bowl, Lily Of The Valley, Shaw	130.00

TECO is the mark used on the art pottery line made by the American Terra Cotta and Ceramic Company of Terra Cotta and Chicago, Illinois. The company was an offshoot of the firm founded by William D. Gates in 1881. The Teco line was first made in 1885 but was not sold commercially until 1902. It continued in production until 1922. Over 500 designs were made in a variety of colors, shapes, and glazes. The company closed in 1930.

Chamberstick, Angular Handles, Green Matte Glaze, Fray Highlights, 4½ x 5 In., Pair 585.00

Lamp Base, Tapered Base, Embossed, Leaves, Green Matte Glaze, 2 Socket, 20¾ x 9½ In. . . .	2640.00
Pitcher, Aventurine, Stamped, 4 x 5 In.	300.00
Plant Stand, Green Matte Glaze, Tapered Top, Open Skirt, 3 Legs, 20¾ x 11 In. . . . . . *illus*	1150.00
Plant Stand, Tapered, Cylindrical, Openwork Lugs, Green Matte Glaze, 20 x 10½ In.	748.00
Vase, 2 Lobes, Green Matte Glaze, Charcoal, 18 x 5½ In.	10200.00
Vase, 4 Buttressed Handles, Brown Frothy Glaze, 14 x 10 In.	3000.00
Vase, 4 Buttressed Handles, Buff Matte Glaze, 7 x 4¼ In.	1560.00
Vase, 4 Buttressed Handles, Bulbous, Green Matte Glaze, 6½ In.	2530.00
Vase, 4 Handles, Flared, Green Matte Glaze, Charcoal Highlights, Impressed Mark, 7 x 4½ In. .	1900.00
Vase, Bulbous, Green Matte Glaze, 9¼ x 9¼ In.	1680.00
Vase, Calla Lilies, Ferns, Embossed, Green Matte Glaze, 13 x 5½ In.	3000.00
Vase, Columbine Flowers, Overlapping Leaves, Charcoal, Impressed, 8¾ In.	2480.00
Vase, Egyptian, Bulbous Top, Flared Base, Green Matte Glaze, Impressed Mark, Mundie, 9 x 4¾ In. .	1300.00
Vase, Green Matte Glaze, Charcoal, Embossed, 4-Footed, 17 x 6½ In.	9600.00
Vase, Green Matte Glaze, Charcoal Highlights, 2 Buttressed Handles, Gates, 8 x 6 In. . . . *illus*	2400.00
Vase, Lobes, Blue Matte Glaze, Stamped, 5¼ x 3½ In.	900.00
Vase, Lobes, Scalloped Base, Green Matte Glaze, Impressed Mark, 9 x 4 In.	1790.00
Vase, Openwork Handles, Green Glaze, Stamped, 5½ x 8½ In.	863.00
Vase, Organic Shape, Water Lilies, Green, Charcoal Matte Glaze, Hugh Garden, 9 x 11½ In. *illus*	57000.00
Vase, Oval, Flared Rim, Brown Matte Glaze, 3¾ In.	345.00
Wall Pocket, Round Medallion, Embossed, Asian Pattern, Green Matte Glaze, 6½ x 5 In.	1080.00

TEDDY BEARS were named for a president of the United States. The first teddy bear was a cuddly toy said to be inspired by a hunting trip made by Teddy Roosevelt in 1902. Morris and Rose Michtom started selling their stuffed bears as "teddy bears" and the name stayed. The Michtoms founded the Ideal Novelty and Toy Company. The German version of the teddy bear was made about the same time by the Steiff Company. There are many types of teddy bears and all are collected. The old ones are being reproduced. Other bears are listed in the Toy section.

Bride & Groom, Mohair, Humpback, Elongated Limbs, Shoebutton Eyes, 14 In., Pair	385.00
Chiltern, Hug-A-Me, Mohair, Champagne, Square Face, Jointed, England, 1950s, 18 In.	448.00
Chiltern, Hug-A-Me, Mohair, Tan, Swivel Head, Jointed, England, c.1950, 25 In.	504.00
Diem, Mohair, Champagne, Curly Coat, Disc Jointed, Germany, c.1950, 23 In.	532.00
Diem, Mohair, Golden, Curly, Embroidered Nose, Jointed, Germany, 1940s, 26 In.	448.00
Diem, Mohair, Golden, Swivel Head, Jointed Limbs, Germany, c.1950, 19 In.	448.00
Diem, Mohair, Tan, Curly Coat, Jointed Arms & Legs, Germany, c.1950, 22 In.	308.00
Diem, Mohair, White, Swivel Head, Embroidered Nose, Mouth, Germany, c.1940, 14 In.	504.00
Ideal, Mohair, Golden, Glass Eyes, Swivel Head, Straw, Humpback, 1910, 32 In.	1635.00
Mohair, Beige, Felt Pads, Long Arms, Shoebutton Eyes, c.1910, 20 In.	690.00
Mohair, Beige, Oversized Head, Shaved Muzzle, Jointed, Button Eyes, 1940s, 19 In.	336.00
Mohair, Blond, Large Ears, Felt Pads, Glass Eyes, 26 In.	115.00
Mohair, Brown, Curly, Jointed, Amber Eyes, Excelsior Filling, Germany, 1950s, 19 In.	280.00
Mohair, Brown, Swivel Head, Square Face, Round Muzzle, Jointed, England, c.1940, 16 In. . .	280.00
Mohair, Champagne, Curly, Embroidered Nose, Mouth, Jointed, Glass Eyes, c.1950, 20 In. . . .	644.00
Mohair, Champagne, Curly, Shaved Muzzle, Embroidered Nose, Disc Jointed, 1950s, 21 In. . .	504.00
Mohair, Golden, Character Expression, Swivel Head, Jointed, England, c.1940, 16 In.	392.00
Mohair, Golden, Long Curly Coat, Swivel Head, Jointed, England, 1930s, 22 In.	728.00
Mohair, Golden, Long Torso, Flattened Snout, Jointed, England, 1940s, 24 In.	308.00
Mohair, Golden, Straw Stuffed, Jointed, Glass Eyes, 6 In.	66.00
Mohair, Russet Brown, Swivel Head, Embroidered Nose, Mouth, 1940s, 20 In.	392.00
Mohair, Rust, Curly Coat, Embroidered Nose & Mouth, Jointed, c.1940, 24 In.	504.00
Mohair, Tan, Swivel Head, Shaved Muzzle, Embroidered Nose, Jointed, 1940s, 20 In.	336.00
Mohair, White, Felt Paws, Embroidered Nose Tip, Disc Jointed, Glass Eyes, 11 In.	1320.00
Mohair, White, Humpback, Stitched Claws, Jointed, Glass Eyes, U.S. Zone Germany, 12 In. . .	440.00
Mohair, White, Polar, Velvet Pads, Button Eyes, Open Mouth, Stitched Nose, France, 16 In. . .	288.00
Panda, Mohair, Embroidered Nose, Mouth, Googly Eyes, England, 1940s, 20 In.	448.00
Panda, Plush Fur, Jointed, White Glass Eyes, Stitched Nose, Velvet Pads, 24 In. . . . . *illus*	345.00
Plush, Paddington, Tan, Blue Felt Coat, Hooded, Yellow Hat, Eden Toy Co., c.1980, 20 In. . . .	75.00
Plush, White, Polar, Wool, Pointy Muzzle, England, 1940s, 18 In.	336.00
Steiff, Mohair, Beige, Long Arms, Narrow Snout, Shoebutton Eyes, 15 In.	2530.00
Steiff, Mohair, Blond, Tan Felt Pads, Blue Gingham Outfit, Button Eyes, c.1905, 17 In.	2938.00
Steiff, Mohair, Brown, Seated, Open Mouth, Jointed, Button & Tag, c.1950, 11 In.	420.00
Steiff, Mohair, Honey Color, Shoebutton Eyes, Felt Pads, 18 In. . . . . *illus*	1955.00
Steiff, Zotty, Mohair, 2 Color Curly Coat, Swivel Head, Jointed, c.1950, 21 In.	448.00
Steiff Style, White, Jointed Arm & Leg, Button Eyes, Needlework Nose, 15 In.	863.00

Teco, Vase, Organic Shape, Water Lilies, Green, Charcoal Matte Glaze, Hugh Garden, 9 x 11½ In. $57000.00

Teddy's Bear
Theodore Roosevelt refused to shoot a bear cub when on a hunting trip in Smedas, Mississippi, in 1902. Clifford Berryman, a newspaper cartoonist, drew a cartoon, "Drawing the Line in Mississippi." It inspired Morris Michtom, founder of the Ideal Novelty Toy Company, to name his toy bears Teddy's Bears.

Teddy Bear, Panda, Plush Fur, Jointed, White Glass Eyes, Stitched Nose, Velvet Pads, 24 In. $345.00

Teddy Bear, Steiff, Mohair, Honey Color, Shoebutton Eyes, Felt Pads, 18 In. $1955.00

T

Telephone, Ader, Wood, Carbon Rod Microphone, Metal Bullring Receivers, France, c.1880 $7830.00

Telephone, Automatic Electric Co., Stick, Chrome Finish, Dial, Chicago, 13 In. $2588.00

Teplitz, Compote, Art Nouveau Woman Emerging From Sea, Flowing Hair, Amphora, 20 In. $6900.00

TELEPHONES are wanted by collectors if the phones are old enough or unusual enough. The first telephone may have been made in Havana, Cuba, in 1849, but it was not patented. The first publicly demonstrated phone was used in Frankfurt, Germany, in 1860. The phone made by Alexander Graham Bell was shown at the Centennial Exhibition in Philadelphia in 1876, but it was not until 1877 that the first private phones were installed. Collectors today want all types of old phones, phone parts, and advertising. Even recent figural phones are popular.

Ader, Wood, Carbon Rod Microphone, Metal Bullring Receivers, France, c.1880 ......*illus*	7830.00
Automatic Electric Co., Stick, Chrome Finish, Dial, Chicago, 13 In. ....*illus*	2588.00
Kellogg, Art Deco, Ivory Polymer, c.1940	206.00
Kellogg, Wall, Ringer, Early 20th Century, 19 In.	106.00
Leich, Crank, Convertible, Generator, Rust Colored, Plug-In Cord, 1930-60	30.00
Mickey Mouse, Animated, Cordless, 900 MHz, Speed Dial, Memory, Redial, Box	150.00
Pin, Pioneer Long Distance Telephone, Celluloid, Early 1900s, 1¾ In.	164.00
Sign, AT&T, Booth, Porcelain, Flange, 12 x 17 In.	468.00
Sign, Bell System, Telephone, Business Office, New England, Porcelain, c.1935, 25 x 42 In. ..	2090.00
Sign, Bell System, Telephone Office, Blue, White, 2-Sided, Porcelain, 44 x 35 In.	1320.00
Sign, Bell System Public Telephone, Porcelain, 2-Sided, 1950s, 11 x 11 In.	250.00
Sign, Bell Telephone, 2-Sided, Porcelain, Flange, 12 x 16¼ In.	440.00
Sign, C.N. Cox & Co., Deep River, Ia., c.1907	30.00
Western Electric, Doughnut, Rotary Dial	65.00

TELEVISION sets are twentieth-century collectibles. Although the first television transmission took place in England in 1925, collectors find few sets that pre-date 1946. The first sets had only five channels, but by 1949 the additional UHF channels were included. The first color television set became available in 1951.

Philco, Predicta, Stand, 21-In. Screen, Box, 44½ In.	1485.00

TEPLITZ refers to art pottery manufactured by a number of companies in the Teplitz-Turn area of Bohemia during the late nineteenth and early twentieth centuries. Two of these companies were the Alexandra Works and The Amphora Porcelain Works, run by Reissner, Stellmacher, and Kessel. Ernst Wahliss, connected with the RS & K wares, started his own factory after 1900.

Bust, Girl In Victorian Dress, Applied Flowers, Berries, Tree Trunk, 1884-94, 14 In.	1750.00
Bust, Woman, Large Headdress, Art Nouveau, 18 x 18 In.	2250.00
Chamberstick, Organic Shape, Multicolored Matte Glaze, Amphora, Daschel, 11 x 6 In.	945.00
Compote, Art Nouveau Woman Emerging From Sea, Flowing Hair, Amphora, 20 In. ...*illus*	6900.00
Ewer, Flowers, Gold Raised Outlines, c.1905	150.00
Figurine, Cherubs, Flowers, Grapes, Austria, 21 x 13 In.	585.00
Figurine, Dancing Figures, Amphora, 17 x 15 In.	850.00
Figurine, Woman In Classic Dress, 17 In.	600.00
Humidor, Arab Horseman, Oak Green, Gold, Raised Sword, Headdress, 6½ x 6½ In.	750.00
Jug, Hand Painted, Flower Mold, Art Nouveau, c.1900, 9¼ In.	176.00
Jug, Purple Art Nouveau Flowers, Floral Mold, 9¼ In. ....*illus*	176.00
Pitcher, Leaves, Flowers, Overglaze Enamel, c.1891-1915, 10 x 6¼ In.	35.00
Planter, Seascape, Boats, Incised Ovals, Egg Shape, Dragon Head Handles, Amphora, 7 x 16 In. .	940.00
Rose Bowl, Ruby Red, Crimped, Opal Netting, Wilhelm Habel, 4 In.	173.00
Urn, Cupid In Cartouche, Raised Scrolls, Cobalt Blue Ground, Pedestal Base, 10 In. ...*illus*	173.00
Vase, Applied Chestnuts & Leaves, 2 Leaf Handles, Amphora, 6¼ In.	345.00
Vase, Applied Leaves, Sculpted, Gourd Form, Handles, Amphora & Turn Teplitz, 7 x 6½ In. ..	745.00
Vase, Applied Pomegranates, Reticulated Leaves, Pinched Waist, Amphora, 9½ In.	173.00
Vase, Arab Warrior, Holding Spear, Enameled, Handles, Mottled Bronze, Gold, 1905-06	350.00
Vase, Art Nouveau, Poppy, Cream, Gold Glazes, 16½ x 7½ In.	900.00
Vase, Art Nouveau Maiden, Flowing Hair, Oval, Flared Petal Rim, Amphora, 5½ In. ....*illus*	1265.00
Vase, Birch Trees, Landscape, Turn Teplitz, Signed, Daschel, Amphora, 8½ x 5½ In.	980.00
Vase, Blue, Applied Cherries & Leaves, Branch Handles, Pedestal Base, Amphora, 13½ In. *illus*	345.00
Vase, Blue & Green Matte Glaze, Double Gourd Shape, Paul Daschel, 14 x 8½ In. .....*illus*	1200.00
Vase, Burgundy, Milk Chocolate Glaze, 2 Handles, Amphora, 12 x 10 x 10 In.	950.00
Vase, Double Gourd, Blue, Green Matte Glaze, Handles, Spouts, Daschel, Amphora, 14 x 8 In. .	1200.00
Vase, Dragon, Sculpted, Applied, Ruffled Rim, Marked, Amphora, Czechoslovakia, 13 x 5 In. .	7000.00
Vase, Figural, Wall, Mailbox Attached, Girl Depositing Letter, Amphora, 10 x 9 x 5 In. . .*illus*	300.00
Vase, Grape Leaf Design, Cylindrical, 2 Handles, Impressed, Amphora, 11½ In.	148.00
Vase, Grapevine, Serpent Handles, Amphora, 8½ x 5 In.	500.00
Vase, Green Matte Glaze, Bulbous, Rim, 4 Handles, Signed, Stellmacher, 7 x 11 In.	750.00
Vase, Holly, Green, 4½ In.	85.00

Vase, Jeweled, Stamens, Flowers, Green, Raised Spider Web Slip, Egg Shape, Amphora, 10 In.	2300.00
Vase, Long Neck, Bulbous Base, Grapes, Vines, Leaves, Gray, Cream, Amphora, 11 In.	353.00
Vase, Molded Scarabs At Rim, Green Matte Glaze, Art Nouveau Design On Foot, 13 In.	230.00
Vase, Open Petaled Flowers, Long Stems, Gold, Tapered Loop Handles, Amphora, 14 In.	235.00
Vase, Organic Shape, Green, Brown Metallic Glaze, Double Handles, Amphora, Daschel, 11 In.	3750.00
Vase, Oval, Vines, Gilded Fruit, Modeled Sage Green Ground, Marked, c.1915, 7¾ In.	118.00
Vase, Portrait, Woman, Landscape, Bulbous, Flared, Turn Teplitz Bohemia, Amphora, 15 x 6 In.	15000.00
Vase, Portrait, Woman, Landscape, Double Bulbous, Turn Teplitz Bohemia, Amphora, 6 x 4 In.	4000.00
Vase, Portrait, Woman, Landscape, Turn Teplitz Bohemia, Amphora, 7½ x 4½ In.	4000.00
Vase, Troubadour, 7 In.	365.00

TERRA-COTTA is a special type of pottery. It ranges from pale orange to dark reddish-brown in color. The color comes from the clay, which is fired but not always glazed in the finished piece.

Bowl, Glazed, 2¾ x 5¼ In.	35.00
Bust, Boy, Multicolored, 11½ x 9¾ In.	351.00
Figurine, Bear, Mottled Finish, Black, Sweden, 1950s, 5 In.	82.00
Figurine, Fox Head, Inset Paste Glass Eyes, Trophy Salver Frame, 13 x 14 In.	1410.00
Figurine, General Andrew Jackson, New Orleans, 1890s, 34 x 44 In.	3575.00
Figurine, Great Dane, Glazed, Plinth Base, 39 In.	999.00
Figurine, Lion, Reclining, Early 20th Century, 18 x 22 In., Pair	924.00
Figurine, Satyr, Seated, Eating Grapes, Painted, France, 24 In.	600.00
Fountain Figure, 2 Children, Sheet Metal Umbrella, Galloway & Gray, c.1875, 50 In.	4700.00
Jar, Betrothal, Green Gloss Glaze, Applied Heart, 3 Handles, Spout, 16 x 13 In.	560.00
Jar, Storage, Baluster Shape, Swan Neck Handle, Glazed Interior, 31 x 18 In.	235.00
Mannequin Head, Glass Eyes, Natural-Looking Teeth, 1950s	5460.00
Panel, Classical Maiden, Euterpe, Muse Of Music, Holding Violin & Flute, Relief, 40 x 18 In.	1175.00
Plaque, American Shield, Red, White Blue, Green Bannerette, 1800s, 22½ In. Diam., Pair	1016.00
Plaque, Madonna & Child, 32 x 20 In.	825.00
Plaque, Putti Playing With Ribbon, Louis XVI Style, Oval, Cast, Tinted, 19 x 23 In.	480.00
Urn, Mosaic, White, California Terra-Cotta, c.1920, 35 x 27 In., Pair	675.00
Vase, Light Blue Crystalline Glaze, Tan Ground, Norweta, 8⅜ In.	1150.00

TEXTILES listed here include many types of printed fabrics and table and household linens. Some other textiles will be found under Clothing, Coverlet, Rug, Quilt, etc.

Altar Cover, Figural Decoration, Silk, Chinese, 46 x 246 In.	6195.00
Bed Curtain, 3 Panels, Franklin & Washington, c.1785	8963.00
Bedcover, Crewel Work, Chain Lock Stitch, Allover Stylized Art Deco Leaves, c.1925 ....*illus*	425.00
Blanket, Acadian, Homespun, Brown Cotton Warp, Natural Cotton Weft, c.1900, 82 x 56 In.	720.00
Blanket, Wool, Embroidered, Flowers, Stems, Blue, Brown, Yellow, 68 x 72 In.	1680.00
Collar, Silk, Embroidered, Chinese, 14½ x 15 In.	236.00
Crewelwork, Linen Panel, Elongated, Meandering Flowers, Wool Yarn, 5 x 54½ In.	1528.00
Curtain, Wool, Maroon With Pink Flowers, Satin Stitched, 1912, 26 x 56 In.	305.00
Doily, Battenburg Lace, 12 In. Diam.	20.00
Doily, Battenburg Lace, Ecru, c.1890, 11 In. Diam.	18.00
Doily, Pinwheel Design, 9 In.	8.00
Doorway Curtains, Stenciled, Stylized Pink Rose Band, Celadon Ground, 84 x 35 In., Pair	840.00
Flag, American, 13 Stars, Sesquicentennial, Wool, 1932, 57 x 35 In.	551.00
Flag, American, 26 Stars, Silk, Frame, c.1837, 31½ x 35 In.	6100.00
Flag, American, 38 Stars, Centennial, 1876, 16 x 24 In.	1760.00
Flag, American, 39 Stars, Dakota Territory Into Statehood, 1889, 28 x 46 In.	675.00
Flag, American, 39 Stars, North Dakota, Silk, 1889, 33 x 46½ In.	1715.00
Flag, American, 45 Stars, Blue Field, 13 Bars & Stripes, Frame, c.1908, 7¾ x 12¼ In.	518.00
Flag, American, 48 Stars, Cotton, Whipple Pattern Stars, 1910, 14 x 23 In.	2550.00
Flag, Louisiana State Secession, Pelican On Star, Silk, Frame, c.1861, 5 x 7½ In.	3877.00
Flag, Parade, U.S., Starred Numerals In Canton, Centennial, Cotton, Linen, Frame, 1886, 38 x 46 In.	4560.00
Handkerchief, Cotton, Flowers, Blue, Red & White Ground, Sears Roebuck, 1960s, 4 Piece	25.00
Mattress Cover, Blue & White, Checked, Cotton, String Tag, 68 x 58 In.	77.00
Mattress Cover, Blue & White, Plaid, Cotton, 67 x 50 In.	11.00
Mirror Case, Green & White Check, Pink & Red Wool Overstitch, New England, c.1825	225.00
Napkins, Nicholas II, Coronation Dinner, Damask, Linen, Eagles, 34 x 27½ In., 9 Piece	2350.00
Needlework, Eagle On Shield, Banner, Sailor Portrait, Watercolor Of Ship, 46 x 26 In. *illus*	1725.00
Needlework, Ship, Fully Rigged, Flying British Red Ensign, Frame, 22 x 30 In.	1495.00
Panel, Burlap, Cotton, 5 Appliqued Cats, Brown, Black, 24½ x 55 In.	940.00

Teplitz, Jug, Purple Art Nouveau Flowers, Floral Mold, 9¼ In.
$176.00

Teplitz, Urn, Cupid In Cartouche, Raised Scrolls, Cobalt Blue Ground, Pedestal Base, 10 In.
$173.00

Teplitz, Vase, Art Nouveau Maiden, Flowing Hair, Oval, Flared Petal Rim, Amphora, 5½ In.
$1265.00

Teplitz, Vase, Blue, Applied Cherries & Leaves, Branch Handles, Pedestal Base, Amphora, 13½ In.
$345.00

Teplitz, Vase, Blue & Green Matte Glaze, Double Gourd Shape, Paul Daschel, 14 x 8½ In.
$1200.00

Teplitz, Vase, Figural, Wall, Mailbox Attached, Girl Depositing Letter, Amphora, 10 x 9 x 5 In.
$300.00

Textile, Bedcover, Crewel Work, Chain Lock Stitch, Allover Stylized Art Deco Leaves, c.1925
$425.00

Panel, Children Playing, Chinese, 19th Century, 19 x 80 In.	2468.00
Panel, Embroidered, Dragons, Metallic Thread, Waves, Flower Borders, Frame, 60 x 47 In.	1035.00
Panel, India, Painted, 5 Woman, Krishna, Radha, Cow Herd, Lotus, Early 1900s, 70 x 43 In.	144.00
Panel, Needlework, Gros Point, Petit Point, Fox & Dog Under Tree, 1800s, 23½ In.	403.00
Panel, Needlework, Multicolored, Flowers, Black Ground, 9 Ft. 2 In. x 3 Ft. 9 In.	5100.00
Panel, Silk, Applique, Black Silk Ground, Cherubs, Flowers, Butterflies, Frame, 26 x 14 In.	450.00
Panel, Silk, Embroidered, Beautiful Woman, Lion, Chinese, c.1900, 56¾ x 27½ In.	188.00
Panel, Silk, Embroidered, Bird, On Flowering Spray, Frame, Chinese, 27½ x 12½	47.00
Panel, Silk, Embroidered, Metallic Thread, Scrolls, Lovebirds, Frame, 41¾ x 41 In.	411.00
Panel, Silk, Embroidered, Red, Flower Filled Vase, Frame, 17 x 19 In.	94.00
Panel, Silk, Embroidered, Samurai, Dragon, Japan, Early 20th Century, 30 x 25¼ In.	374.00
Panel, Silk, Flowers, Frame, 29 x 29½ In.	413.00
Pillow, Tapestry, Aubusson, Bronze Silk, Songbird, Flowers, Double Tassel Edges, 22 x 22 In.	470.00
Pocket, Embroidered, Silk, On Linen, Blue, Gold, Tan, Stylized Flowers, Cross-Stitch, 15 In.	1035.00
Ribbon, Silk, Centennial, Declaration Of Independence, Mat, Frame, c.1876, 10¼ In.	472.00
Roundel, Silk, Rust, Embroidered Figure, Chinese, Frame, 19th Century, 22½ x 22½ In.	165.00
Seat Cover, Needlepoint, Figures, Landscape, 17th Century, 15¾ x 19½ In.	6000.00
Table Cover, Embroidered, Hand Stitched, Mirrored Inserts, Persian, 30 x 33 In.	53.00
Tablecloth, Cotton, Blue & White, Plaid, Hemmed Fringe Edges, 60 x 58 In.	33.00
Tablecloth, Fruits, Leaves, Green, Pink, Tan, 68 x 106 In.	32.00
Tablecloth, Silk, La Contessina, Embroidered, Appliqued, Scrolling Designs, 65 x 65 In.	720.00
Tapestry, 2 Dogs Stag Hunting, Noblemen, Wool, Silk, Late 17th Century, 99½ x 64 In.	16100.00
Tapestry, Aubusson Style, Oriental Pagoda On Mound, Temple, Birds, Trees, 89 x 115 In.	460.00
Tapestry, Aubusson Style, Summer, Rose Ground, Garlands, Figures In Medallion, 40 x 92 In.	4700.00
Tapestry, Aubusson Style, Wool, 3 Women In Garden, Lambs, Birds, Flower Border, 92 x 64 In.	1293.00
Tapestry, Cartoon, Month Of February, Figures, Satyr Parade, 13½ x 119 In.	3290.00
Tapestry, Cotton, Samuel Slater, Old Slater Mill, Red, White, Blue, 14¼ x 26 In.	354.00
Tapestry, Flemish Style, Romans Enjoying Feast, Fruit, Flowers, Trophy Borders, 84 x 64 In.	1528.00
Tapestry, Woodland Scene, Flemish, 18th Century, 81 x 96 In.	5290.00
Tapestry, Woven, Medieval Scene, Woman, 2 Men, Castle, Soldiers, Border, 117 x 71 In.	2185.00
Tea Cloth, Embroidered, Pansies, Green Leaves, Ann MacBeth, Arts & Crafts, 34 x 34 In.	2160.00
Towel, Show, Central Flower, Initials, Elizabeth Bransteterin, c.1809, 48 x 17 In.	121.00
Towel, Show, Cross-Stitch Designs, Linen, Blue, Pink, Openwork, Christina, 1812, 52 x 14 In.	431.00
Towel, Show, Elisabet Schenk, Sawtooth Frame, c.1829, 50 x 17¾ In.	121.00
Towel, Show, Elisabeth Bener, Initials, E.B., c.1820, 50 x 14½ In.	38.00
Towel, Show, Embroidered, Gentleman, Long Tailed Coat, Peaked Hat, c.1836, 52 x 17 In.	770.00
Towel, Show, Embroidered, Leaping Stags, Tulip In Urn, Hearts, c.1846, 50 x 17 In.	88.00
Towel, Show, Silk, Cotton, On Linen, Pulled Thread, Barbara Miller, Aug. 8 1808, 62 x 17 In.	431.00

THERMOMETER is a name that comes from the Greek word for heat. The thermometer was invented in 1731 to measure the temperature of either water or air. All kinds of thermometers are collected, but those with advertising messages are the most popular.

7Up, Black, White, Red, Metal, 20 x 5 In.	84.00
Abbotts Bitters, Flavors, Cocktails, Beverages, Fruits, Blue, White, Porcelain, 27 x 6 In.	1100.00
Alta Crest Farms, Certified Milk, Cow, Stork, Baby, Celluloid, 6 x 2 In.	95.00
B-1 Lemon-Lime Soda, Metal Frame, Glass Front, Mounting Hooks, 12 In. *illus*	81.00
Bakelite, Black, Round Chrome Dial, Art Deco, 3½ x 4 In.	176.00
Bentzinger Bros. Inc., Quality Brush At A Price, Paint Brush, 25½ x 9¾ In.	60.00
Bradley & Currier Co., Mantels, Tiles, Grates, Wood, 21 x 5½ In.	295.00
Calumet Baking Powder, Wood, 27 x 7¼ In.	880.00
Camel, Have A Real Cigarette, Tin, Embossed, 1950s, 13½ x 5½ In.	216.00
Denby Cigars, Denby, Cigar You Want, Made Right, Blue, White, Porcelain, 27 x 7 In.	385.00
Doan's Kidney Pills, Wood, 21 x 5 In.	385.00
Dr. Caldwell's Syrup Pepsin, Cures Constipation, Wood, 21 x 5½ In.	295.00
Dr. Swett's Root Beer, Bottle Cap, Metal, 17⅛ x 5 In.	220.00
Dubble Bubble, Boat Steering Wheel Shape, Brass, 5 x 5 In.	80.00
Eagle Pencil, 75th Anniversary, Wood, 1856-1931, 14 In.	575.00
Eagle Pencil Co., Pencil, 75th Anniversary, Wood, Rubber Eraser, 14¼ x 1¼ In.	580.00
Ed Pinaud Hair Tonic, Barber Pole, Barber, Tin, 9 x 26 In.	1375.00
Esso Atlas Anti-Freeze, Red, White, Blue, Dial, Aluminum, Glass, 17 x 17 In.	275.00
Ex-Lax, Chocolated Laxative, Porcelain, 37 In.	83.00
Ex-Lax, Keep Regular, Safe Chocolated Laxative, Blue, Yellow, White, Porcelain, 36 x 8 In.	275.00
Flowers, White, Green, Cast Iron, Signed, Candlestick Co., 6 In.	280.00
Ford Tractor Dealer, E.M. Barth, Yellow, Wood, Yuba & Sutter, Marysville, Calif., 10 x 2 In.	80.00
Gall Cure Horse Collars, J.W. Murray, Wood, Tin Lithograph, 10⅝ x 3 In.	330.00

Gulf, No-Nox Gasoline & Gulfpride Oil, Yellow, Black, Red, Metal, 26½ x 7 In.	300.00
Hills Bros. Coffee, Man In Nightshirt Drinking Coffee, Porcelain, 1915, 21 x 9 In. ....*illus*	770.00
Honest Scrap Chewing Tobacco, Porcelain, 27¼ x 7 In.	385.00
Kickapoo Oil Pain Cure, Weather Predicting Tube, Wood, Tin Lithograph, 9 x 3 In.	176.00
Kirk's Jap Rose Soap, Toilet, Bath, Shampoo, Blue, White, Yellow, Porcelain, 1915, 27 x 7 In.	177.00
London Free Press, White, Blue, Red, Porcelain, 30 x 8 In.	138.00
Mail Pouch, Treat Yourself To The Best, Blue, White, Yellow, Porcelain, 38½ x 8 In.	198.00
Milo Coffee, Right Blend For The Perfect Cup, Red, White, Enameled, 11 x 4 In.	115.00
Montana Tobacco, State Seal, Old Style Smokers, White, Blue, Porcelain, 27 x 7¼ In.	495.00
National Canners Assoc. Convention, Can Shape, American Can, 1907, 4 x 2¾ In. Diam.	385.00
Nature's Remedy Tablets, Come In, If You Get It Here It's Good, Porcelain, 27 x 7 In.	358.00
Nesbitt's, Don't Say Orange Say Nesbitt's, Yellow, Orange, Tin Lithograph, 1950s, 27 x 7 In.	330.00
NuGrape, Twin Bottles, Tin, 16 In.	440.00
Old Dutch Beer, Wood, 15 x 4 x ½ In.	198.00
Park & Pollard's, Lay Or Bust Poultry Feed, Yellow, Red, Black, Porcelain, 27 x 7 In.	3198.00
Peanuts, Plastic Key, Cardboard Gauge, Box, 8⅜ x 2¾ In.	908.00
Peter's Shoes, Solid Leather, We'll Put Together, Blue, White, Yellow, Porcelain, 19 x 6 In.	715.00
Pine Island, Florida, Lucite Cube, Shells, Water, Sea Grass, 3¾ x 2 In.	18.00
Prestone, You're Safe & You Know It, Porcelain, 36 In.	83.00
Pureoxia Ginger Ale, For Sale Here, Wood, 21 x 8¾ In.	550.00
Pureoxia Ginger Ale, Wood, Image Of Early Bottles, 21 x 8¾ In.	550.00
Red Seal Dry Battery, Beach Company, Ohio, Porcelain, 1915, 7 x 17 In.	265.00
Royal Pancake, Just Try It Today, Wood, 15 x 4 In.	242.00
Sauer's Vanilla Extract, Wood, 1919, 8 x 3¾ In.	475.00
Tums, Nature's Remedy All Vegetable Laxative, Red, White, Blue, Porcelain, 27 x 7 In.	385.00
Valentine's Valspar Enamel Paints, Red, White, Blue, Porcelain, 1915, 72½ x 17 In.	2750.00
Varsity Ginger Ale, 12 x 3 In.	99.00
Vess Soda, Billion Bubble Beverages, All Your Favorite Flavors, Chalkware, c.1945, 16 x 12 In.	198.00
Walter I. Keeler, Optician, Eyes Examined, Glasses Fitted, Painted, Wood, 15 x 4 In.	77.00
Ward's Vitovim Bread, Keeps Him Smiling, Boy Holding Bread, Porcelain, 1920-30	1900.00
Waterman's Ideal Fountain Pen, Clip Cap, Die Cut, Tin Lithograph, 19½ x 3¾ In.	1600.00

TIFFANY is a name that appears on items made by Louis Comfort Tiffany, the American glass designer who worked from about 1879 to 1933. His work included iridescent glass, Art Nouveau styles of design, and original contemporary styles. He was also noted for stained glass windows, unusual lamps, bronze work, pottery, and silver. Other types of Tiffany are listed under Tiffany Glass, Tiffany Pottery, or Tiffany Silver. The famous Tiffany lamps are listed in this section. Tiffany jewelry is listed in the jewelry and wristwatch categories. Some Tiffany Studio desk sets have matching clocks. They are listed here. Clocks made by Tiffany & Co. are listed in the Clock category. Reproductions of some types of Tiffany are being made.

Louis C. Tiffany

Ashtray, Bronze, Gold Dore, Ribbed Handles, Signed, 1 x 4 In.	150.00
Ashtray, Match Holder, Adam, Bronze, Gold Dore, Marked, 2¾ x 6 x 3½ In.	450.00
Ashtray, Match Holder, Grapevine, Green Slag Glass, Bronze, Signed	750.00
Ashtray, Match Holder, Pine Needle, Green Glass, Bronze, Marked, 4½ In.	650.00
Ashtray, Match Holder, Pine Needle, Green Slag Glass, Bronze, Marked, 5¼ x 4½ In.	700.00
Basket, Blue Iridescent, Pulled Feathers, Flared, Bronze Enameled Holder, Favrile, 7 In.	2875.00
Basket, Enamel, Red & Gold Iridescent, Bronze, Gold Dore, Pedestal Base, Marked, 8 In.	2000.00
Bill File, Paperweight, Pine Needle, Green Slag Glass, Bronze, Spindle, 7½ x 3 In.	1500.00
Bill File, Pine Needle, Green Slag Glass, Bronze, Marked, 7½ x 3 In.	1500.00
Bill File, Venetian, Bronze, Gold Dore, Round Bottom, Spindle, Marked, 7 In.	2000.00
Bill File, Zodiac, Bronze, Dark Patina, 8-Sided Base, Curved Spindle, Marked, 7½ In.	650.00
Blotter, American Indian, Bronze, Dark Patina, 5½ x 3 In.	350.00
Blotter, Grapevine, Green Slag Glass, Bronze, Marked, 6 In.	240.00 to 250.00
Blotter, Hand, Gold Dore, Knob Handle, 5½ x 2¾ x 1½ In.	350.00
Blotter, Pine Needle, Green Slag Glass, Bronze, Dark Patina, Signed	650.00
Blotter Ends, Adam, Bronze, Gold Dore, Marked, 19 x 2 In., Pair	350.00
Blotter Ends, American Indian, Bronze, Dark Patina, Marked, 19 x 2 In., Pair	400.00
Blotter Ends, Bronze, Dark Patina, 5¾ x 5¾ x 8 In., 4 Piece	650.00
Blotter Ends, Graduate, Bronze, Gold Dore, Marked, 12¼ x 2¼ In., Pair	173.00
Blotter Ends, Graduate, Bronze, Gold Dore, Marked, 19 x 2¼ In., Pair	350.00
Blotter Ends, Pine Needle, Bronze, Dark Patina, 4 Corners, Marked, 6 x 6 x 8 In.	650.00
Blotter Ends, Pine Needle, Bronze, Marked, 12 In.	86.00
Bookend, Single, Bookmark, Bronze, Gold Dore, Marked, 6 x 4¾ In. ....*illus*	518.00
Bookends, Abalone, Iridescent Discs, Bronze, Gold Dore, 5½ x 5½ In.	3000.00
Bookends, Bookmark, Bronze, Gold Dore, Marked, 5 x 6 In.	2200.00 to 2500.00

Textile, Needlework, Eagle On Shield, Banner, Sailor Portrait, Watercolor Of Ship, 46 x 26 In.
$1725.00

Thermometer, B-1 Lemon-Lime Soda, Metal Frame, Glass Front, Mounting Hooks, 12 In.
$81.00

Thermometer, Hills Bros. Coffee, Man In Nightshirt Drinking Coffee, Porcelain, 1915, 21 x 9 In.
$770.00

T

Tiffany, Bookend, Single, Bookmark, Bronze, Gold Dore, Marked, 6 x 4¾ In. $518.00

Tiffany, Box, Pine Needle, Green Slag Glass, Bronze, Wood Lining, 2 Compartments, 6 x 9 In. $1610.00

Tiffany, Candelabrum, 4-Light, Bronze, Curved Arms, Stylized Leaves, Green Glass Jewels, 12¼ In. $4313.00

Tiffany, Candlestick, Bronze, Bocheche Stem, Root Feet, Marked, 12½ In. $1898.00

Bookends, Ninth Century, Blue & Green Glass Cabochons, Bronze, Gold Dore, Marked, 6 In.	2760.00
Bookends, Venetian, Enameled, Bronze, Gold Dore, Marked, 5 x 6 In. . . . . 2500.00 to	3000.00
Bookrack, Grapevine, Amber Slag Glass, Bronze, 14 x 23 In.	3000.00
Bowl, Bronze, Gold Dore, Enameled, Green, Burgundy, Glass Inset, Marked, 1 x 8 In.	264.00
Bowl, Bronze, Out-Turned Edge, Marked, 1¾ x 5½ In.	350.00
Bowl, Centerpiece, Bronze, Gold Dore, Enameled, Footed, Favrile Glass Inset, 4½ x 8 In.	2500.00
Bowl, Centerpiece, Gold Iridescent, Green, Blue Highlights, Bronze, Flared, Footed, 4½ x 8 In. . . .	2500.00
Bowl, Centerpiece, Tray, Bronze, Gold Dore, Entwined Lines, Marked, 12 x 15 In.	1500.00
Box, Abalone, Bronze, Gold Dore, Ball Feet, Cedar Lining, Marked, 2½ x 6½ x 4½ In.	2500.00
Box, Card, Hinged Cover, Grapevine, Green Slag Glass, Bronze, 2 Sections, 3 x 4½ In.	2500.00
Box, Card, Hinged Cover, Pine Needle, Green Slag Glass, Bronze, 3 x 4½ In. . . . . 2500.00 to	2875.00
Box, Glove, Grapevine, Green Slag Glass, Bronze, Dark Patina, Marked, 3 x 4 x 13 In.	4000.00
Box, Grapevine, Green Slag Glass, Bronze, Beading, Ball Feet, 1¾ x 4½ x 3 In.	850.00
Box, Handkerchief, Grapevine, Amber Slag Glass, Bronze, Beading, Ball Feet, 8 In.	3500.00
Box, Handkerchief, Grapevine, Caramel Slag Glass, Marked, Bronze, 8 x 8 In.	1035.00
Box, Handkerchief, Grapevine, Green Slag Glass, Bronze, Marked, 2½ x 8 x 8 In.	3000.00
Box, Hinged Cover, Bookmark, Bronze, Gold Dore, 5 x 3¼ x 1¾ In.	950.00
Box, Hinged Cover, Bookmark, Bronze, Gold Dore, Trees, Cedar Lining, 6 x 5½ x 2½ In.	3000.00
Box, Hinged Cover, Gold Iridescent, 6-Sided, Ribbed, Bronze Border, 6 x 2 In.	4500.00
Box, Hinged Cover, Medallion, Bronze, Gold Dore, 4½ x 3¼ x 1½ In.	750.00
Box, Hinged Cover, Medallion, Enamel, Bronze, Ball Feet, 6¼ x 4 x 2 In.	1500.00
Box, Hinged Cover, Pine Needle, Bronze, Caramel Slag Glass, Ball Feet, 4 x 3 x 1 In.	720.00
Box, Hinged Cover, Pine Needle, Green Slag Glass, Bronze, Ball Feet, 4 x 3 x 1½ In.	850.00
Box, Hinged Cover, Zodiac, Bronze, Gold Dore, 3 Sections, Marked, 3¾ x 2¼ x 1 In.	600.00
Box, Pine Needle, Green Slag Glass, Bronze, Wood Lining, 2 Compartments, 6 x 9 In. . . *illus*	1610.00
Box, Stamp, Hinged Cover, Grapevine, Caramel Slag Glass, Bronze, 5½ x 4½ In.	382.00
Box, Stamp, Hinged Cover, Zodiac, Bronze, Dark Patina, 3 Compartments, Marked, 3¾ x 2¼ In. .	650.00
Box, Zodiac, Bronze, Gold Dore Patina, No. 810, Tiffany Studios N.Y., 1 x 5½ x 3½ In.	600.00
Calendar, Adam, Bronze, Gold Dore, Easel Back, Marked, 6½ x 6 In.	1200.00
Calendar, American Indian, Bronze, Dark Patina, Easel Back, Marked, 6 x 7½ In.	1500.00
Calendar, Bookmark, Bronze, Gold Dore, Easel Back, Marked, 5½ x 6 In.	1200.00
Calendar, Bronze, Gold Dore, Flower, Sunburst, Easel Back, 6½ In.	1200.00
Calendar, Zodiac, Symbols, Enamel, Bronze, Easel Back, Marked, 8 x 7 In.	1500.00
Candelabrum, 2-Light, Bronze, 12½ x 5¾ In.	2510.00
Candelabrum, 4-Light, Bronze, Curved Arms, Stylized Leaves, Green Jewels, 12¼ In. . . *illus*	4313.00
Candelabrum, 4-Light, Bronze, Glass Shades, Favrile, c.1910, 14½ x 13½ In.	5760.00
Candelabrum, 6-Light, Leaf Arms, Bronze, Gold Dore, Bobeches, 10 x 5 In., Pair	4000.00
Candelabrum, Bronze, Twisted Stem, Oval Base, 9 x 7½ In.	3240.00
Candle Holder, Bronze, Cast Column, 4-Prong Shade Holder, 10½ In.	1755.00
Candlestick, Bronze, Bocheche Stem, Root Feet, Marked, 12½ In. . . . . *illus*	1898.00
Candlestick, Bronze, Gadrooned Cups, Medallions, Tripod Base, 8 x 5 In.	1560.00
Candlestick, Bronze, Gold Dore, Bulbous Cup, Stick Stem, 3 Prong Feet, 18½ In., Pair	1645.00
Candlestick, Bronze, Gold Dore, Round Candle Cups, Tapered Stem, c.1920, 12½ In., Pair . .	1528.00
Candlestick, Bronze, Green Glass Inserts, Beaded Nozzle, Arts & Crafts, c.1900, 17½ In.	1853.00
Candlestick, Bronze, Opaque Green Glass Inserts, c.1900, 17½ In.	1704.00
Candlestick, Bronze, Queen Anne's Lace, Round Base, Green Glass Inserts, 18 In., Pair	7080.00
Canister, Cover, Bronze, Gold Dore, Sailboat, Marked, 3½ x 3 In.	450.00
Card Box, Hinged Lid, Green Slag Glass, Bronze, 2 Compartments, Marked, 4½ x 3 x 2 In. . .	2500.00
Chamberstick, Bronze, Gold Dore, Enameled Disc, Attached Bobeche, 3½ In., Pair	2500.00
Chandelier, 5-Light, Bronze, Favrile Glass Shades, Ribbed, c.1910, 27 In.	2115.00
Charger, Bronze, Gold Dore, 14 In.	259.00
Clip, Chinese, Bronze, Patina, Marked, 3½ x 2½ In.	240.00
Clip, Pine Needle, White & Caramel Slag Glass, Bronze, Patina, Marked, 3¾ x 2½ In.	260.00
Clip, Zodiac, Bronze, Patina, Marked, 4 x 2½ In.	240.00
Compote, Bronze, Gold Dore, Enameled Flower Border, 5 x 3 In.	1500.00
Compote, Bronze, Gold Dore, Enameled Flowers, Rondels, 10 x 5 In.	1500.00
Compote, Bronze, Impressed Stylized Triangles On Rim, Marked, 6¼ In. . . . . *illus*	173.00
Desk Set, Adam, Bronze, Gold Dore, 8 Piece . . . . *illus*	4313.00
Desk Set, Bookmark, Bronze, Marked, 10 Piece	5175.00
Desk Set, Grapevine, 9 Piece	4313.00
Desk Set, Pine Needle, Bronze, Gold Dore, Slag Glass, c.1920, 10 Piece	2160.00
Desk Set, Pine Needle, Rocker Blotter, Toothpick, Inkwell, 3 Piece	1560.00
Desk Set, Zodiac, Bronze, Gold Dore, c.1925, 7 Piece . . . . *illus*	1725.00
Frame, Adam, Bronze, Gold Dore, Easel Back, Marked, 12 x 8⅞ In.	3163.00
Frame, Adam, Bronze, Gold Dore, Marked, 12 x 9 In.	2500.00
Frame, Bronze, Etched, Gold Favrile Glass, Marked, 10½ x 7 In.	3600.00

Frame, Bronze, Gold Dore, Blue, Textured Decoration, Marked, 7½ x 6¼ In.		1500.00
Frame, Grapevine, Caramel Slag Glass, Bronze, Marked, 9 x 7½ In.		1380.00
Frame, Grapevine, Green Slag Glass, Bronze, Marked, 6½ x 7½ In.		3000.00
Frame, Grapevine, Green Slag Glass, Bronze, Oval Opening, Marked, 4 x 5½ In.		3500.00
Frame, Grapevine, Slag Glass, Bronze, Easel Back, 8 x 10 In.		3500.00
Frame, Grapevine, Yellow Glass, Beaded Border, Oval Opening, Tiffany Studios, 10 x 8 In.		1495.00
Frame, Heraldic, Bronze, Gold Dore, Shields, Swords, Helmet, Marked, 10 x 12 In.		3000.00
Frame, Pine Needle, Caramel Slag Glass, Bronze, Gold Dore, Marked, 9¼ x 7¾ In.		1150.00
Frame, Pine Needle, Green Slag Glass, 9⅛ x 7¾ In.		1035.00
Frame, Pine Needle, Green Slag Glass, Bronze, Easel Back, 8½ x 7 In.		3000.00
Frame, Venetian, Bronze, Gold Dore, 9 x 12 In.		3000.00
Frame, Zodiac, Bronze, Patina, Marked, 14 x 12 In.		5700.00
Frame, Zodiac, Gold Dore, Marked, 11 x 9 In.		2000.00
Goblet, Bronze, Gold Dore, Embossed Thistle, 7¾ x 4¼ In.		900.00
Inkwell, Grapevine, Green Slag Glass, Bronze, Ball Feet, Square 3½ x 4 In.		950.00
Inkwell, Grapevine, Green Slag Glass, Bronze, Round, Marked, 2¼ x 3¾ In.		650.00
Inkwell, Hinged Cover, Abalone, Bronze, Gold Dore, 8-Sided, Marked, 3½ In.	750.00 to 850.00	
Inkwell, Hinged Cover, American Indian, Bronze, Glass Insert, Marked, 5½ In.		950.00
Inkwell, Hinged Cover, Bookmark, Bronze, Gold Dore, 8-Sided, Glass Insert, Marked, 2½ x 4½ In.		1200.00
Inkwell, Hinged Cover, Chinese, Bronze, Glass Insert, 6¼ In.		1200.00
Inkwell, Hinged Cover, Graduate, Bronze, Gold Dore, Marked, 3 x 3 In.		510.00
Inkwell, Hinged Cover, Pine Needle, Caramel Slag Glass, Bronze, 4-Sided, Marked, 4 In.		690.00
Inkwell, Hinged Cover, Pine Needle, Green Slag Glass, Bronze, Round, 3 x 7 In.	2000.00 to 2500.00	
Inkwell, Hinged Cover, Pine Needle, Green Slag Glass, Bronze, Round, Marked, 3 x 7 In.		2500.00
Inkwell, Hinged Cover, Venetian, Chain Latch, 2 Glass Inserts, 5 x 3 x 2 In.		1500.00
Inkwell, Hinged Cover, Zodiac, Bronze, Glass Insert, 6½ x 4 In.		950.00
Inkwell, Hinged Cover, Zodiac, Bronze, Patina, 8-Sided, Marked, 4 In.	420.00 to 550.00	
Inkwell, Pine Needle, Bronze, Gold Dore, Glass Insert, Marked, c.1920, 4 x 8 In.		382.00
Inkwell, Tray, Zodiac, Bronze, Dark Patina, 8-Sided Inkwell, Marked, 10¾-In. Tray		2500.00
Inkwell, Venetian, Double, Bronze, Gold Dore, Chain Latch, Links, 5 x 3 x 2 In.		1500.00
Jewelry Box, Byzantine, Bronze, Gold Dore, Patina, Casket, Claw Feet, 3 x 5½ In.		2200.00
Jewelry Box, Grapevine, Slag Glass, Bronze, Velvet Drawers, 3⅜ x 9½ In.		1645.00
Jewelry Box, Hinged Cover, Grapevine, Amber Slag Glass, Bronze, Ball Feet, 3 x 6½ x 4 In.		2500.00
Jewelry Box, Hinged Cover, Pine Needle, Amber Slag Glass, Bronze, Beaded		2500.00
Jewelry Box, Pine Needle, Green Slag Glass, Bronze, Ball Feet, Marked, 3 x 6½ x 4 In.		2500.00
Ladle, Fiddle Thread Pattern, Monogram, Mid 1800s, 11½ In.		150.00
Lamp, 2-Light, Bronze, Pull Chain, c.1920, 24½ In.		6000.00
Lamp, Abalone Shade, Fluted Bronze Base, Stamped, 13 x 7 In.		9600.00
Lamp, Acorn Shade, Bronze, Green & Yellow Slag Glass, Tripod Base, 55 In.		9667.00
Lamp, Acorn Shade, Green Tiles, Pink Border, Bronze Base, 3 Arms, 17 x 12½ In.		14455.00
Lamp, Acorn Shade, Yellow & Green Slag Glass, Bronze, Gold Dore, Spread Foot, 21 x 16 In.		11450.00
Lamp, Apple Blossom Shade, Opalescent Glass, Bronze Urn Base, c.1910, 16 In.	*illus*	38240.00
Lamp, Balance, Damascene Shade, Round Foot, 9¾ In.		11750.00
Lamp, Base, Bronze, Patinated, Harp Shape, Ball Feet, 16 x 6¼ In.		1195.00
Lamp, Candlestick, Bronze, 9 Jewels, Spread Foot, Gold Iridescent Ribbed Shade, 13 In.		8625.00
Lamp, Candlestick, Bronze, Gold Iridescent, Ruffled Edge, Spiral Ribs, 14 In.	*illus*	2070.00
Lamp, Candlestick, Bronze, Green Glass, Tulip Shade, Tripod Base, 16⅝ In.		7800.00
Lamp, Candlestick, Bronze, Twisted Base, Gold Favrile Shade, Ruffled Rim, 13 x 7 In.		1800.00
Lamp, Candlestick, Gold, Honeycomb, Ruffled Shade, Ribbed, Favrile, 13 In.	1175.00 to 1410.00	
Lamp, Candlestick, Gold Favrile Base, Silver Iridescent Shade, Pulled Feathers, c.1905, 12½ In.		1175.00
Lamp, Candlestick, Gold Iridescent, Green Pulled Feathers, Favrile, Marked, 14 In.		1800.00
Lamp, Candlestick, Twisted Stem, Peacock Blue, Diamond Quilted Shade, Favrile, 14 In.		6000.00
Lamp, Colonial Shade, Bronze, Gold Dore, 12 Paneled Sides, Mottled Glass, 16 x 22 In.		9988.00
Lamp, Desk, 2-Light, Bronze, Gold Dore, Domed Shade, Fluted Base, 18¼ In.		1680.00
Lamp, Desk, Adam, Caramel Slag Glass, Pierced Bronze, 17½ x 13 In.	*illus*	12075.00
Lamp, Desk, Etched Leaves, Amber Slag Glass, Domed Shade, Marked, 15 In.		6000.00
Lamp, Desk, Scarab, Iridescent Beetle Shade, Bronze, Marked, 9 In.		12390.00
Lamp, Desk, Zodiac, Iridescent Turtleback Tile Shade, Bronze Base, 14 x 10 x 6 In.	*illus*	14340.00
Lamp, Dogwood Shade, Bronze Base, Twisted, Stylized Leaves, 4-Footed, 23 x 18 In.	*illus*	39600.00
Lamp, Dragonfly Shade, Leaded Glass, Bronze Base, c.1910, 21¼ x 17 In.		42000.00
Lamp, Favrile Glass Shade, Bronze, Patina, Tripod Base, 55 In.		7605.00
Lamp, Fleur-De-Lis, Green & Amber Blown Glass, Bronze, 20 x 16 In.	*illus*	47800.00
Lamp, Flower Shaped Shade, Gold Pulled Feathers, Veined Leaves On Base, 19 In., Pair		2938.00
Lamp, Geometric Shade, Dichroic, Leaded Glass, Bronze Base, c.1920, 22¼ x 16½ In.		16800.00
Lamp, Gold Favrile Shade, Stretched Rim, Spiral Turned Base, Marked, 12½ In.		1410.00
Lamp, Green & Caramel Slag Glass, Feathers, Amber & Green Jewels, Bronze Base, 21 x 16 In.	*illus*	13800.00

Tiffany, Compote, Bronze, Impressed Stylized Triangles On Rim, Marked, 6¼ In.
$173.00

Tiffany, Desk Set, Adam, Bronze, Gold Dore, 8 Piece
$4313.00

Tiffany, Desk Set, Zodiac, Bronze, Gold Dore, c.1925, 7 Piece
$1725.00

Tiffany, Lamp, Apple Blossom Shade, Opalescent Glass, Bronze Urn Base, c.1910, 16 In.
$38240.00

T

Tiffany, Lamp, Candlestick, Bronze, Gold Iridescent, Ruffled Edge, Spiral Ribs, 14 In. $2070.00

Tiffany, Lamp, Desk, Adam, Caramel Slag Glass, Pierced Bronze, 17½ x 13 In. $12075.00

Tiffany, Lamp, Desk, Zodiac, Iridescent Turtleback Tile Shade, Bronze Base, 14 x 10 x 6 In. $14340.00

Lamp, Hanging, Fir Branches, Glass, 6-Sided Shades, c.1914, 14½ x 6½ In.	1680.00
Lamp, Leaf & Vine Shade, Dichroic, Leaded Glass, Bronze Base, c.1910, 16¼ x 12 In.	21600.00
Lamp, Lily, 3-Light, Blue Iridescent Shades, Bronze, Gold Dore Base, 13½ In.	9400.00
Lamp, Lily, 3-Light, Gold Favrile Shade, Bronze, 8½ x 5 In.	2390.00
Lamp, Linenfold Shade, Panels, Amber, Bronze Base, Ribbed, 5 Ball Feet, 22 x 19 In. *illus*	20700.00
Lamp, Linenfold Shade, 3-Light, Bronze, Candlestick Base, 20 x 14½ In.	16450.00
Lamp, Linenfold Shade, Green, Bronze Harp Base, Patina, 54¾ x 15 In.	4200.00
Lamp, Mosque, Green Shade, Feather Pulled, Bronze Base, Gold Dore Finial, 8½ In.	5500.00
Lamp, Mosque, Pulled Green Feather, Ivory Opalescent, Bronze, Gold Dore, Wood Base, 8½ In.	5500.00
Lamp, Peony Shade, Leaded Glass, Bronze Base, c.1910, 26 x 18¼ In.	90000.00
Lamp, Pine Needle, Domed Shade, Green Slag Glass, Bronze Base, 3 Arms, 17 x 10 In.	4800.00
Lamp, Poinsettia Shade, 26 In.	99450.00
Lamp, Pomegranate Shade, Hampshire Pottery Base, Green, Melon Ribbed, 19 In. *illus*	12000.00
Lamp, Poppy Shade, Mottled Yellow Ground, Bronze Base, Art Nouveau, 22 x 17 In. *illus*	66125.00
Lamp, Sconce, Bronze, c.1914, 8½ In.	1080.00
Lamp, Spider Shade, Bronze, 3 Arms, Center Shaft, Ribbed Legs, Petal Circular Base, 12 In.	1116.00
Lamp, Turtleback Tile Shade, Dichroic Yellow Ground, Bronze, Marked, 14-In. Shade	28600.00
Lamp, Weight-Balance, Bronze, Favrile Glass Shade, c.1910, 16½ x 6½ In.	8400.00
Lamp, Zodiac, Bronze, Gold Dore, 6-Sided Base, Marked, 13½ In.	5500.00
Lamp, Zodiac, Harp Arm, Bronze, 18 In.	5500.00
Letter Holder, Abalone, Bronze, Gold Dore, 2 Sections	1500.00
Letter Holder, Adam, Bronze, Gold Dore, 2 Sections, Marked, 6 x 9¼ x 2¼ In.	900.00
Letter Holder, American Indian, Bronze, Dark Patina, 2 Sections, Marked, 6 x 11 x 3 In.	1500.00
Letter Holder, Bookmark, Gold Dore, 14K Gold Plate, 2 Sections, Marked, 5½ x 9 x 2 In.	1500.00
Letter Holder, Chinese, 3 Sections, 8 x 12 x 3½ In.	2000.00
Letter Holder, Grapevine, Caramel Slag Glass, Bronze, Gold Dore, 2 Sections, Marked, 6¼ x 10 In.	748.00
Letter Holder, Grapevine, Green Slag Glass, Bronze, 12½ x 8½ x 3½ In.	2500.00
Letter Holder, Grapevine, Green Slag Glass, Bronze, Dark Patina, 10 x 5 x 2¼ In.	1500.00
Letter Holder, Pine Needle, Bronze, Green Slag Glass, 3 Sections, 4 Ball Feet, 5 In.	575.00
Letter Holder, Pine Needle, Green Slag Glass, Bronze, 2 Sections, Marked, 5½ x 6¼ In.	1500.00
Letter Holder, Venetian, Bronze, Gold Dore, Sculptured Minks, 2 Sections, 10 x 6 x 2¾ In.	1800.00
Letter Opener, Adam, Bronze, Gold Dore, Curved Handle, Marked, 9 In.	600.00
Letter Opener, American Indian, Bronze, Patina, 10 In.	650.00
Letter Opener, Chinese, Bronze, Gold Dore, Marked, 11 In.	600.00
Letter Opener, Graduate, Bronze, Gold Dore, Handle, Marked, 9 In.	500.00
Letter Opener, Grapevine, Amber Slag Glass, Bronze, Gold Dore, Marked, 9¼ In.	650.00
Letter Opener, Grapevine, Green Slag Glass, Bronze, Patina, 9¼ In.	650.00
Letter Opener, Pine Needle, Amber Slag Glass, Bronze, Gold Dore, Marked, 9¼ In.	650.00 to 750.00
Letter Opener, Pine Needle, Green Slag Glass, Bronze, Patina, Marked, 9¼ In.	650.00 to 750.00
Letter Opener, Scissors, Chinese, Bronze, Dark Patina, Leather Case, Marked, 10¾ In.	2300.00
Magnifying Glass, Abalone, Bronze, Gold Dore, Marked, 9 x 4 In.	1800.00
Magnifying Glass, American Indian, Bronze, Gold Dore, Marked, 8¼ x 4 In.	1500.00
Magnifying Glass, Bookmark, Bronze, Gold Dore, Marked, 8¾ x 4 In.	1500.00
Magnifying Glass, Grapevine, Bronze, Gold Dore, Slag Glass, Marked, 8 x 3½ In.	1800.00
Magnifying Glass, Venetian, Bronze, Gold Dore, Marked, 9 x 4 In.	1500.00
Magnifying Glass, Zodiac, Bronze, Dark Patina, Marked, 8¾ x 4 In.	1500.00
Notepad Holder, Bookmark, Bronze, Gold Dore, 4½ x 7½ In.	950.00
Notepad Holder, Grapevine, Caramel Slag Glass, Bronze, Partial 1925 Calendar, 7½ x 4½ In.	480.00
Notepad Holder, Indian Mask, Bronze, Dark Patina, Marked, 7½ x 4½ In.	550.00
Paper Clip, Grapevine, Green, Slag Glass, Bronze, Dark Patina, 2½ x 3¼ In.	650.00
Paper Clip, Zodiac, Bronze, Dark Patina, Marked, 2½ x 4 In.	650.00
Paper Clip, Zodiac, Bronze, Gold Dore, 2½ x 3¾ In.	550.00
Paperweight, Dog, Bulldog, Reclining, Bronze, Brown Patina, Tiffany Studios, 2 In.	748.00
Paperweight, Dog, Bulldog, Standing, Bronze, Marked, 2 x 3½ x 2 In.	805.00
Paperweight, Dog, Bulldog's Head, Bronze, Gold Patina, Marked, 1¾ In.	978.00
Paperweight, Dog, Retriever's Head, Bronze, Gold Dore, Marked, 2 x 3½ In.	720.00
Paperweight, Grapevine, Green Glass, Bronze, Marked, 3¾ In.	345.00
Paperweight, Grapevine, Green Slag Glass, Bronze, Dark Patina, 3½ In.	650.00
Paperweight, Tiger, Reclining, Bronze, Gold Dore, Marked, 5 In.	540.00
Paperweight, Turtleback Tile, Blue Iridescent, 4-Footed, Bronze Mount, 6 In.	1495.00
Paperweight, Turtleback Tile, Bronze Mount, Footed, 6 x 5 In.	1434.00
Paperweight, Venetian, Bronze, Gold Dore, Sculptured Minks, Marked, 4 x 2 x ¾ In.	950.00
Pen Brush, Bookmark, Bronze, Gold Dore, 2½ x 3 In.	750.00
Pen Brush, Pine Needle, Green Slag Glass, Bronze, Marked, 2¼ x 1½ In.	650.00
Pen Tray, American Indian, Bronze, Dark Patina, 2 Sections, Marked, 4 x 11 In.	450.00
Pen Tray, Grapevine, Green Glass, Bronze, Ball Feet, 9½ x 3½ In.	550.00

T

Tiffany, Lamp, Dogwood Shade, Bronze Base, Twisted, Stylized Leaves, 4-Footed, 23 x 18 In.
$39600.00

Tiffany, Lamp, Green & Caramel Slag Glass, Feathers, Amber & Green Jewels, Bronze Base, 21 x 16 In.
$13800.00

Tiffany, Lamp, Fleur-De-Lis, Green & Amber Blown Glass, Bronze, 20 x 16 In.
$47800.00

Tiffany, Lamp, Linenfold Shade, Panels, Amber, Bronze Base, Ribbed, 5 Ball Feet, 22 x 19 In.
$20700.00

T

Tiffany, Lamp, Pomegranate Shade, Hampshire Pottery Base, Green, Melon Ribbed, 19 In. $12000.00

Tiffany, Lamp, Poppy Shade, Mottled Yellow Ground, Bronze Base, Art Nouveau, 22 x 17 In. $66125.00

Record Prices for Tiffany Lamps

In 1998 a Tiffany Peacock centerpiece lamp sold for $1,875,500 and a Tiffany Magnolia leaded glass and gilt-bronze floor lamp sold for $1,762,500. A Tiffany Poinsettia floor lamp sold in 2004 for $321,100, setting a record for that design.

Penholder, Grapevine, Green Slag Glass, Bronze, Easel Back, 3 Hooks, 5 x 4 In.	450.00
Penholder, Pine Needle, Green Slag Glass, Bronze, Dark Patina, Easel Back, 3 Hooks, 4 x 5 In. . .	550.00
Planter, Pine Needle, Amber Slag Glass, Bronze, Gold Dore, Marked, 8½ x 10½ In.	2500.00
Plate, Abalone, Bronze, Gold Dore, 9 In.	115.00
Plate, Peacock Eye & Trailing Borders, Bronze, Gold Dore, Marked, 6½ In.	520.00
Platter, Bronze, Gold Dore, Marked, 12 In.	460.00
Platter, Geometric Border, Bronze, Gold Dore, Marked, 9 x 1¼ In.	400.00
Postage Scale, Grapevine, Green Slag Glass, Bronze, Marked, 1½ x 3 x 3 In.	1500.00
Postage Scale, Pine Needle, Green Slag Glass, Bronze, Marked, 3 x 2 x 3 In. . . . . . . 1380.00 to 1800.00
Postage Scale, Zodiac, Bronze, Dark Patina, Marked, 3¼ x 3 x 1½ In.	650.00
Serving Bowl, Bronze, Turned Edge, Marked, 5½ x 1¾ In.	350.00
Smoking Set, Geometric, Red & Black Enamel, Bronze, Gold Dore, Marked, 4 Piece	3500.00
Smoking Stand, Bronze, Ribbed, 2 Rests, Removable Liner, Marked, 28 In.	2200.00
Smoking Stand, Matchbox Holder, Staghorn Rim, Round Leaf Base, 27 In.	1540.00
Tazza, Enameled, Bronze, Gold Dore, Heart Shape, Favrile, 7 x 6½ In.	3500.00
Tazza, Enameled, Gold Iridescent, Bronze, Gold Dore, Heart Shape, 6½ x 4 In.	3500.00
Thermometer, Bookmark, Bronze, Gold Dore, Marked, 9 x 2½ In.	3000.00
Thermometer, Pine Needle, Bronze, c.1900, 8½ x 4 In.	1434.00
Thermometer, Pine Needle, Green Slag Glass, Bronze Beading, 8½ x 4 In.	3500.00
Thermometer, Venetian, Bronze, Gold Dore, Sculptured Minks, Easel Back, Marked, 8 x 4 In. . . .	3000.00
Thermometer, Zodiac, Easel Back, Bronze, Dark Patina, Marked, 8 x 4 In.	2000.00
Tile, Geometric Squares, Green, Red, Celadon, Favrile, 4 x 4 In., 25 Piece	2520.00
Tray, Bronze, Art Deco, Enameled, Marked, 11½ In.	1200.00
Tray, Bronze, Gold Dore, Enameled, Peacock Feather Border, 6½ In.	550.00
Vase, Bronze, Curved Wreath, Raised Berries & Leaves, Fluted Rim, 3½ x 4½ In.	1500.00
Vase, Bronze, Gold Dore, Bulbous, Flared Rim, Marked, 6 In.	863.00
Vase, Bronze, Incised Lines, Tapered, Flared Rim, Footed, 15 In.	861.00
Vase, Geometric, Bronze, Art Nouveau, c.1925, 15 In.	1136.00
Vase, Gold Iridescent, Green Pulled Vines, Bulbous, Bronze Base, 13 x 12 In.	1116.00

TIFFANY GLASS

Bonbon, Gold Iridescent, Silver, Violet, Ruffled Edge, Favrile, 5½ x 2 In.	400.00
Bowl, Blue Iridescent, Diagonal Ribs, Low, Scalloped Edge, Favrile, Marked, 6 In.	469.00
Bowl, Blue Iridescent, Optic Ribbed, Scalloped Edge, Marked, 8 In.	353.00
Bowl, Blue Iridescent, Rolled Rim, Favrile, c.1919, 6½ In.	518.00
Bowl, Centerpiece, Attached Flower Frog, Blue Iridescent, Green Lily Pads, 11½ In.	4000.00
Bowl, Centerpiece, Attached Flower Frog, Gold Iridescent, Lily Pads, Vines, Favrile, 9½ In. . . .	2588.00
Bowl, Centerpiece, Attached Flower Frog, Green Leaves & Vines, Gold Iridescent, Favrile, 12⅝ In. *illus*	1520.00
Bowl, Centerpiece, Blue Iridescent, Ruffled Edge, Folded Rim, Ribbed, Marked, 2 x 4½ In. . . .	1500.00
Bowl, Centerpiece, Floral, Pulled Hearts & Vines, 2-Tiered Flower Frog, Favrile, 4 x 10½ In. .	2032.00
Bowl, Centerpiece, Gold & Blue Iridescent, Deep Well, Shell Feet, Favrile, Marked, 2½ In. . . .	2500.00
Bowl, Centerpiece, Gold Highlights, Blue Iridescent, Footed, 2½ In.	2500.00
Bowl, Centerpiece, Gold Iridescent, Footed, Favrile, c.1910, 9½ In.	705.00
Bowl, Centerpiece, Gold Iridescent, Opalescent Underside, Flower Shape, 12 In.	1013.00
Bowl, Centerpiece, Green Opalescent, Diamond Quilted, Flared, Gold Foot, Favrile, 9¾ In. . .	2038.00
Bowl, Flower Shape, Gold Iridescent, White Opalescent, Favrile, Marked, 12 In.	705.00
Bowl, Gold Iridescent, Bulbous, 4 Pulled Feet, Favrile, Marked, c.1920, 4 x 3 In.	470.00
Bowl, Gold Iridescent, Bulbous, Pinched & Scalloped Edge, 3½ In.	1035.00
Bowl, Gold Iridescent, Inward Folded Scalloped Edge, Favrile, c.1910, 7¾ In.	1095.00
Bowl, Gold Iridescent, Leaves, 16 Molded Ribs, 2⅝ x 6 In.	690.00
Bowl, Gold Iridescent, Lily Pads, Vines, Folded Rim, Favrile, Marked, 10 In.	470.00
Bowl, Gold Iridescent, Pulled Feathers, 3-Sided, Favrile, 4 In.	450.00
Bowl, Gold Iridescent, Ribbed, Crimped Rim, Favrile, 4½ In.	441.00
Bowl, Gold Iridescent, Ribbed, Favrile, 7¾ In.	588.00
Bowl, Gold Iridescent, Ruffled Edge, Intaglio Cut, Leaf & Vine, Favrile, 7 x 2½ In.	1500.00
Bowl, Low, Scalloped Edge, Gold Iridescent, Favrile, c.1915, 4⅞ In.	235.00
Bowl, Peacock Blue Iridescent, Favrile, 1½ x 1½ In.	4000.00
Candlestick, Blue Iridescent, Twisted Stem, Flared Foot, Favrile, 5½ In.	633.00
Candlestick, Blue Pastel, Opalescent Stem, Spread Rim, Onionskin Edge, Favrile, 1927, 5 In. . .	380.00
Candlestick, Gold Iridescent, Ribbed Ring, Base, Flanged Cup, Favrile, 7 In., Pair	1000.00
Candlestick, Gold Iridescent, Twisted Ribs, Favrile, Marked, 5 In.	978.00
Candlestick, Green & White Opalescent Stem, Favrile, Marked, 3⅜ In., Pair	1175.00
Compote, Blue & Green Iridescent, Opalescent Optic Diamond, Footed, Favrile, 5¼ x 2 In. . .	950.00
Compote, Blue Iridescent, Green Stretched Edge, Opalescent Rim, 5¼ x 2¼ In.	950.00
Compote, Blue Iridescent, Intaglio Flowers, Ribbed Base, Favrile, 1900, 5 In.	2935.00
Compote, Blue Iridescent, Pedestal Base, Marked, 4½ x 8 In.	3000.00

Compote, Blue Iridescent, Purple, Pedestal Base, Favrile, 4 x 4½ In.	3000.00
Compote, Flower Shape, Gold Iridescent, Pink, Blue, Flared Rim, Pedestal Base, 7 x 3¾ In.	2500.00
Compote, Gold Iridescent, 4½ x 5⅝ In.	460.00
Compote, Gold Iridescent, Band Of Intaglio-Cut Leaves & Grapes, Favrile, 3½ x 4½ In.	920.00
Compote, Gold Iridescent, Footed, 10 In.	975.00
Compote, Gold Iridescent, Optic Ribbed, Footed, Marked, c.1900, 2¼ In.	345.00
Compote, Gold Iridescent, Ribbed, Pedestal Base, 3¾ In.	750.00
Compote, Green Iridescent Rim, Opalescent Base, Favrile, Marked, 6 In.	1920.00
Compote, Leaves, Vines, Trailings, Footed, Favrile, Marked, 2 x 7 In.	820.00
Compote, Pastel Green, Stretched Rim, Opalescent Stem & Foot, Favrile, 4⅜ In.	575.00
Compote, Pink Pastel, Opalescent Leaves, Stretch Border, Opalescent Foot, Favrile, 3 In.	575.00
Compote, Rose Iridescent, Opalescent Diamond, Gold Highlights, 8 x 2½ In.	1500.00
Compote, Yellow Opalescent, Folded Out Rim, Footed, c.1900, 6 In. *illus*	176.00
Cordial, Blue Iridescent, Green Damascene, Green Interior, Pinched Sides, Favrile, 1½ In.	2358.00
Cordial, Gold Iridescent, Favrile, 5½ In., Pair	529.00
Cordial, Gold Iridescent, Magenta & Blue Highlights, Pigtail Prunts, Ribbed, Marked, 1¾ In.	460.00
Cordial, Gold Iridescent, Pigtail Prunts, Favrile, 2 In., 6 Piece	2013.00
Cordial, Gold Iridescent, Pinched Sides, Marked, 1¾ In.	174.00 to 370.00
Decanter, Gold Iridescent, Favrile, 9¾ x 3½ In.	2340.00
Decanter, Yellow Amber, Carved Swirls, Gold Iridescent Foot & Stopper, 11¼ In. *illus*	1725.00
Dish, Pink Pastel, Opalescent Rays, Favrile, Marked, 7½ In.	288.00
Epergne, Blue Iridescent, Purple Highlights, Rolled Rim, 11½ x 1½ In.	4000.00
Finger Bowl, Underplate, Earl, Gold Iridescent Red Highlights, Stretched, Ruffled, 6 In. *illus*	920.00
Finger Bowl, Underplate, Gold Iridescent, Ruffled Edge, Favrile, Marked, 6 In.	750.00
Finger Bowl, Underplate, Scalloped Edge, Gold Iridescent, Favrile, Marked, 6 In., 3 Piece	1440.00
Goblet, Green Bowl, Ribbed Opalescent Stem & Foot, Favrile, 8¾ In.	805.00
Goblet, Opalescent, Green Interior, Yellow Green Opalescent Stem & Foot, Favrile, 6 In. *illus*	518.00
Goblet, Pastel Yellow, Opalescent Leaves, Optic Ribbed, Twisted Stem, Flared, 8 In.	805.00
Humidor, Gold Iridescent, Cylindrical, Flattened Folded Out Rim, Ball Finial, Favrile, 8 In.	1093.00
Jar, Cover, Gold Iridescent, Enameled, Squat, Favrile, 3½ x 2 In.	1200.00
Loving Cup, Gold Iridescent, Green Trailing Leaves & Vines, 3 Handles, Marked, 5 x 3 In.	2200.00
Ornament, Rondel, Gold Iridescent, Favrile, 2 In.	325.00
Parfait, Pastel Green Opalescent Foot, Favrile, Marked, 5¼ In.	345.00
Plate, Flower Shape, Pastel, Turquoise & Opalescent, Favrile, 11 In.	1020.00
Plate, Pastel Green, Scalloped Opalescent Onionskin Edge, 10½ In.	460.00
Plate, Pastel Green & Opalescent Alternating Panels, Scalloped Edge, Favrile, 11 In.	431.00
Plate, Wisteria, Pastel Iridescent, Stretched Border, 8⅞ In. *illus*	403.00
Powder Box, Hinged Cover, Gold Iridescent, Bronze Edge, Favrile, 4¼ x 1¾ In.	3000.00
Powder Jar, Yellow, White Ribs, Pink Swirls, Bronze Cover, Enameled Flowers, 5½ In. *illus*	6900.00
Rose Bowl, Blue Iridescent, Royal Blue Hearts & Vines, Favrile, Marked, 2½ In.	1495.00
Salt, Blue & Gold Iridescent, Spiral Pods, 1⅛ x 2 In.	377.00
Salt, Gold Iridescent, Ribbed, 4 Pulled Feet, 1½ In. *illus*	161.00
Salt, Gold Iridescent, Ruffled Edge, Favrile, 1 x 2½ In.	100.00 to 351.00
Salt, Spirals & Ridges, Blue & Magenta Iridescent, Master, 1⅜ x 2¾ In.	315.00
Salt, Spoon, Blue & Gold Iridescent, Ribbed, Scalloped Edge, 2¾ In.	184.00
Shade, Gold Iridescent, Ruffled Edge, Stretched, Favrile, 6 x 2½ In.	705.00
Shade, Swirling Leaf, Orange, Yellow, Green, Marked, 18 In.	16675.00
Sherbet, Pink Iridescent, Opalescent Diamond Optic, Footed, Favrile, 2½ x 3 In.	1500.00
Tumbler, Gold, Threading, Favrile, Marked, 5½ In.	259.00
Tumbler, Whiskey, Gold Iridescent, Pinched Sides, 2 In.	294.00
Vase, Agate Green, Gilt Bronze Mount, Favrile, c.1904, 9½ In.	5400.00
Vase, Black, Platinum Pulled Zipper, Bulbous, Rolled Rim, Favrile, 3 In. *illus*	3738.00
Vase, Blue & Green Iridescent, Bulbous, Elongated Neck, Favrile, c.1919, 11¼ In.	7200.00
Vase, Blue & Purple Iridescent, Favrile, c.1900, 3⅛ In.	7200.00
Vase, Blue Iridescent, Favrile, c.1913, 3¾ x 6¼ In.	2223.00
Vase, Blue Iridescent, Pulled Leaves, Cobalt Blue Base, Marked, 8 In.	978.00
Vase, Blue Iridescent, Urn Shape, Reeded Handles, Footed, Favrile, c.1913, 6½ In. *illus*	823.00
Vase, Blue Iridescent, White Interior, Ribbed, Favrile, Marked, c.1915, 5¾ In.	1763.00
Vase, Bronze, Feather, Flower Form, Favrile, 14½ x 5 In.	1195.00 to 1315.00
Vase, Bud, Gold Iridescent, Green Leaf Vine, Favrile, 10½ x 3¾ In.	2000.00
Vase, Bud, Gold Iridescent, Green Pulled Leaves, Bronze Foot, Favrile, Marked, 12 In.	1140.00
Vase, Bud, Gold Iridescent, Ribbed, Favrile, 6 In.	650.00
Vase, Bud, White Opalescent, Gold Pulled Feathers, Footed, Favrile, c.1910, 10 In.	1980.00
Vase, Corona, Blue & Green Iridescent, Pulled Feathers, Favrile, 5 In.	1725.00
Vase, Cypriote, Flat Back, Gold Iridescent, Favrile, 8¾ In. *illus*	12000.00
Vase, Cypriote, Gold, Iridescent, Coiled Snake, Metal Mount, Favrile, 1901	6600.00

Tiffany Glass, Bowl, Centerpiece,
Attached Flower Frog,
Green Leaves & Vines, Gold Iridescent,
Favrile, 12⅝ In.
$1520.00

Tiffany Glass, Compote,
Yellow Opalescent, Folded Out Rim,
Footed, c.1900, 6 In.
$176.00

Tiffany Glass, Decanter,
Yellow Amber, Carved Swirls,
Gold Iridescent Foot & Stopper, 11¼ In.
$1725.00

Tiffany Glass, Finger Bowl, Underplate,
Earl, Gold Iridescent Red Highlights,
Stretched, Ruffled, 6 In.
$920.00

Tiffany Glass, Goblet, Opalescent,
Green Interior, Yellow Green Opalescent
Stem & Foot, Favrile, 6 In.
$518.00

T

Tiffany Glass, Plate, Wisteria,
Pastel Iridescent, Stretched Border, 8⅞ In.
$403.00

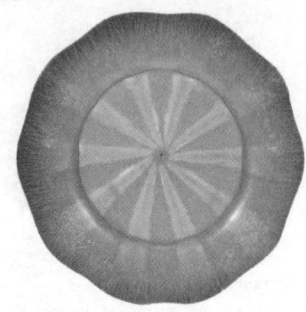

Tiffany Glass, Powder Jar, Yellow, White Ribs,
Pink Swirls, Bronze Cover, Enameled Flowers,
5½ In.
$6900.00

Tiffany Glass, Salt, Gold Iridescent,
Ribbed, 4 Pulled Feet, 1½ In.
$161.00

Tiffany Glass, Vase, Black, Platinum Pulled
Zipper, Bulbous, Rolled Rim, Favrile, 3 In.
$3738.00

Tiffany Glass, Vase, Blue Iridescent,
Urn Shape, Reeded Handles, Footed,
Favrile, c.1913, 6½ In.
$823.00

Tiffany Glass, Vase, Cypriote, Flat Back,
Gold Iridescent, Favrile, 8¾ In.
$12000.00

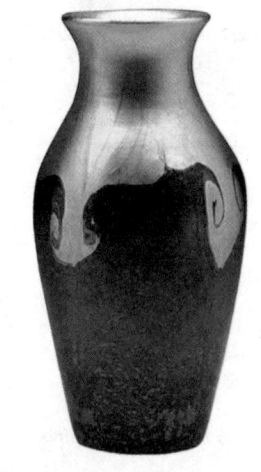

Tiffany Glass, Vase, Egyptian Shape,
Gold Iridescent, Shouldered, Wide Mouth,
Footed, Favrile, 4¾ In.
$460.00

Tiffany Glass, Vase, Gold Iridescent,
Gourd Shape, Pinched Sides,
Silver Iridescent Rim, 9½ In.
$748.00

Tiffany Glass, Vase, Jack-In-The-Pulpit,
Gold Iridescent, Onionskin Edge,
Rolled Foot, 16½ In.
$6931.00

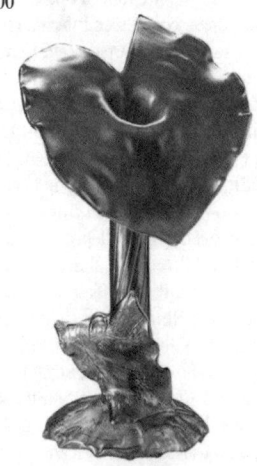

Tiffany Glass, Vase, Millefiori, Green,
Purple To Charcoal Iridescent, 3 In.
$7475.00

Vase, Cypriote, Green & Cream, Gold & Blue Iridescent Flashes, 5 In.	1840.00
Vase, Egyptian Chain, Bronze Iridescent Collar, Favrile, c.1913, 6¾ In.	6000.00
Vase, Egyptian Shape, Gold Iridescent, Shouldered, Wide Mouth, Footed, Favrile, 4¾ In. *illus*	460.00
Vase, Flower Shape, Gold Iridescent, 5-Fold Flared Out Rim, 5½ x 3 In.	1800.00
Vase, Flower Shape, Gold Iridescent, Irregular Sides, 10 Ribs, Scalloped Edge, 7 In.	1495.00
Vase, Flower Shape, Gold Iridescent, Raised Leaves, Vines, 6⅛ In.	2415.00
Vase, Flower Shape, Gold Iridescent, Ribbed, Flared & Ruffled Edge, 11¼ In.	7480.00
Vase, Flower Shape, Gold Iridescent, Ribbed, Scalloped Edge, Footed, Marked, 3½ In.	709.00
Vase, Gold Iridescent, 6 Raised Lily Pads, 3 Trailing Stems, Reeded Center, Marked, 3⅝ In. . .	497.00
Vase, Gold Iridescent, 18 Vertical Ribs, Flared, Gilt Bronze Base, Inset Green Glass Beads, 17⅞ In.	5000.00
Vase, Gold Iridescent, Amethyst, Blue Highlights, Ribbed, Marked, 2⅛ In.	739.00
Vase, Gold Iridescent, Bulbous, Inward Folded Rim, Pedestal Base, Favrile, Marked, 6½ In. . .	950.00
Vase, Gold Iridescent, Cylindrical, c.1925, 8¼ In.	529.00
Vase, Gold Iridescent, Gourd Shape, Pinched Sides, Silver Iridescent Rim, 9½ In. . . . . . *illus*	748.00
Vase, Gold Iridescent, Green Hearts, Vines, Round, 2½ In.	2200.00
Vase, Gold Iridescent, Green Heart-Shaped Leaves, Favrile, Marked, 6¼ In.	6000.00
Vase, Gold Iridescent, Green Leaves, Trailing Vines, Bulbous, Long Neck, Favrile, 5¾ In.	2200.00
Vase, Gold Iridescent, Green Pulled Feathers, Long Ribbed Neck, Favrile, 12¾ In.	1058.00
Vase, Gold Iridescent, Optic Ribbed, Urn Shape, Footed, 2 Handles, Favrile, Marked, 5½ In. . .	863.00
Vase, Gold Iridescent, Optic Ribbed, Waisted, Inward Folded Rim, Favrile, c.1900, 3½ In.	403.00
Vase, Gold Iridescent, Pedestal Base, Favrile, 7½ In.	1058.00
Vase, Gold Iridescent, Pink, Violet, Ribbed, Tapered, Pedestal, Favrile, 3 x 2 x 1½ In.	750.00
Vase, Gold Iridescent, Platinum, Favrile, 3¼ x 2 x ½ In.	750.00
Vase, Gold Iridescent, Pulled Feathers, Stretched Edge, Footed, Favrile, 4½ In.	1410.00
Vase, Gold Iridescent, Pulled Vines & Leaves, Favrile, Marked, 6¼ In., Pair	2925.00
Vase, Gold Iridescent, Rainbow Highlights, Teardrop Shape, 4 In.	546.00
Vase, Gold Iridescent, Raised Zipper, Bulbous, Favrile, 4 x 6 In.	1800.00
Vase, Gold Iridescent, Ruffled Edge, Undulating Rim, Melon Ribbed, Favrile, 11¼ In.	1880.00
Vase, Gold Iridescent, Threading, Marked, 3⅛ In.	635.00
Vase, Green, Intaglio Cut, Flowers, Favrile, c.1915, 7⅞ In.	9600.00
Vase, Jack-In-The-Pulpit, Gold Iridescent, Onionskin Edge, Rolled Foot, 16½ In. . . . . . *illus*	6931.00
Vase, Millefiori, Gold Iridescent, Squat, Favrile, 3 In.	5700.00
Vase, Millefiori, Green, Purple To Charcoal Iridescent, 3 In. . . . . *illus*	7475.00
Vase, Paperweight, Yellow Flowers, Leaves, Button Pontil, Marked, 10¼ In. . . . . *illus*	18400.00
Vase, Pastel Pink, Morning Glory, Opal Stems, 5½ In.	1333.00
Vase, Peacock Blue, Ribbed, Dimples, Flared Rim, Footed, Favrile, 6 In.	1293.00
Vase, Peacock Eye, Amethyst, Cobalt Blue, Pinched Waist, Favrile, 14¾ In.	9200.00
Vase, Red, Gold Swirls, Marked, c.1905, 5¾ In.	1763.00
Vase, Stick, Gold Iridescent, Green Vines & Tendrils, Favrile, 6⅛ In. . . . . *illus*	2300.00
Vase, Tapered Body, Footed, Pulled Feathers & Swirls On Base, Label, 7¼ In.	4113.00
Vase, Tel El Amarna, Red, Cylindrical Neck, Black Applied Foot, Favrile, 11¾ In.	9600.00
Vase, Trumpet, Gold Iridescent, Favrile, c.1905, 13¾ In.	2115.00
Vase, Trumpet, Gold Iridescent, Green & White Pulled Feathers, c.1910, 12 In.	2040.00
Vase, Trumpet, Incised Butterfly, Bronze Mount, Favrile, 17½ In.	1016.00
Vase, Trumpet, Knopped Stem, Flared Rim, Optic Ribbed Foot, 15 In.	2350.00
Vase, Trumpet, Knopped Stem, Footed, Favrile, c.1917, 18 In.	1880.00
Vase, Trumpet, Ribbed, Gilt Bronze Petal Base, Favrile, 14 In.	1434.00
Vase, Yellow, Brown, Leaves, Favrile, c.1906, 5½ In.	5400.00
Vase, Yellow Opalescent, Flowers, Leaves, Amethyst Pulled Vines, Oval, Footed, 4¾ In.	5980.00
Window, Leaded Glass, Landscape, Water, Sailboat, Flowers, 5 Sections, Frame, 60 x 48 In. . .	96900.00
Window, Leaded Glass, Trophy Center, Crest, Ribbons, Oak Leaves, 16 x 28 In.	8400.00
Window, Leaded Glass, Wisteria, Blue, Lavender, Mauve, Copper Foil, 26 x 35½ In.	43650.00

TIFFANY POTTERY

Vase, Spring Green Matte Glaze, White Ground, 7¾ In.	765.00

TIFFANY SILVER

Basket, Fruit, Reticulated, Oval, Scalloped, Swing Handle, 13½ x 9 In.	2820.00
Bell, Dinner, Gothic Decoration, Squat Button Handle, 1927, 2½ x 2 In.	470.00
Berry Bowl, Pierced & Chased Branch Border, Folded Out Rim, 9½ In.	426.00
Berry Spoon, 3 Strawberries, 9¼ In.	518.00
Berry Spoon, Olympian, Pierced, 9 Wells, Marked, 7¼ In.	575.00
Bonbon, Gold Wash, 4 x 7 In.	275.00
Bowl, c.1960, 3½ x 6 In.	245.00
Bowl, Centerpiece, Applied Leaves, Pierced Border, Round, Turned Out Rim, 12¼ In.	1440.00
Bowl, Centerpiece, Chased & Pierced Clover Border, 10¼ In.	861.00

Tiffany Glass, Vase, Paperweight, Yellow Flowers, Leaves, Button Pontil, Marked, 10¼ In. $18400.00

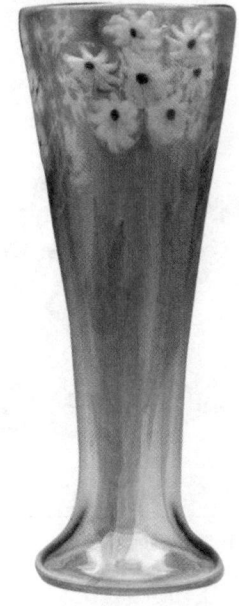

Tiffany Glass, Vase, Stick, Gold Iridescent, Green Vines & Tendrils, Favrile, 6⅛ In. $2300.00

T

Tiffany Silver, Kettle, Hot Water, Stand, Hammered, Japanese Style, Ivory Accents, 1881, 12¾ In. $10158.00

Tiffany Silver, Pitcher, Classical Hunters, Dogs, Boar, Chased, Embossed, c.1890, 8¼ In. $14400.00

Tiffany Silver, Serving Fork, Persian Pattern, Engraved, Pierced, 1872, 9¾ In. $1434.00

Bowl, Centerpiece, Flared & Turned In Beaded Rim, c.1915, 3 x 13 In.	1265.00
Bowl, Centerpiece, Flowers, Brass Flower Frog, c.1913, 3½ x 15 In.	2151.00
Bowl, Centerpiece, Molded & Pierced Clover Border, Flared, 12¾ In.	1410.00
Bowl, Centerpiece, Oval, Embossed, Chased, Molded Rim, Ball Feet, c.1878, 14 In.	7200.00
Bowl, Cover, Repousse Flowers, Squat, Ribbed, Mushroom Finial, Gold Wash Interior, 2¾ In.	1093.00
Bowl, Flower, Pierced C-Scrolls & Shells, Round Wide Deeply Turned Out Rim, 13½ In.	960.00
Bowl, Flower, Rococo Cartouches, Acanthus Border, Turned Out Rim, Round, 14 In.	1560.00
Bowl, Fruit, Oval, Serpentine Border, Shell & Leaf Molded Handles, 1875-91, 17 In.	3819.00
Bowl, Fruit, Pierced Wild Rose Rim, Crowned Monogram, 10 In.	881.00
Bowl, Hammered, Etched Horse Racers, 4 Pod Feet, Round, c.1891, 12 In.	6600.00
Bowl, Monogram, c.1925, 2½ x 12 In.	448.00
Bowl, Ogee Sides, Spiral Gadrooning, Wide Acanthus Scrolled Rim & Foot, c.1900	2820.00
Bowl, Rectangular, Rounded Corners, Banded Edge, 9 x 7 In.	403.00
Bowl, Round, Chippendale Style Border, 2⅜ x 12 In.	633.00
Bowl, Vegetable, Acanthus Scrolls, Shellwork Scrolled Feet, 14½ In.	1528.00
Bowl, Vegetable, Cover, Chrysanthemum, 2 Handles, Engraved, c.1885, 12¾ In.	9400.00
Box, Trinket, Round, Stylized Border, Repousse Cover, c.1902, ⅝ x 1⅞ In.	294.00
Bread Tray, Boat Shape, Pierced Rondel, Bellflowers, Reticulated Rim, 11⅞ In.	353.00
Bread Tray, Rectangular, Convex Sides, Openwork Flowers, Leaf Scrolled Handles, 6 x 14 In.	1762.00
Bread Tray, Rectangular, Early 20th Century, 1½ x 11¼ In.	227.00
Candlestick, Baluster Stem, Flared Nozzle, Stepped Foot, 6¼ In., Pair	1013.00
Candy Dish, Pierced, Footed, c.1902	263.00
Card Case, Japanese Style, Lacquer Trim, Lift-Off Cover, Red Ribbon Bow, c.1910, 4 In.	44400.00
Cigarette Box, Rectangular, Wood Lining, 5⅞ In.	382.00
Claret Jug, Etched Garland & Leaves, Squat Baluster Shape, Hinged Cover, 10½ In.	4200.00
Coffee Set, Paneled, Urn Shape, Monogram, 4 Piece	767.00
Coffee Set, Parcel Gilt, Embossed, Flowers, Scrolls, Putti, c.1891, 3 Piece	4560.00
Coffeepot, After Dinner, Ogee, Molded Lighthouse Shape, Serpentine Handle, Spout, 8½ In.	648.00
Compote, Round, Bulbous Base, Winged Paw Feet, Turned Out Rim, 9 In., Pair	5040.00
Compote, Round, Shell & Thread Pattern, Marked, 3¾ x 8¾ In.	748.00
Condiment Jar, Apple Shape, Tongs, Gold Wash, 2½ x 1½ In.	146.00
Crumber, Chrysanthemum Pattern, c.1880, 13 In.	777.00
Dish, Vermeil, Leaf Shape, 4 x 6 In.	117.00
Ewer, Woman's Head, Ivy Crown, Scrolled Leaf & Flower Handle & Rim, Marked, 20 In.	8050.00
Fish Set, Fork, Slice, Electroplate, c.1900, 2 Piece	176.00
Fish Slice, Persian Pattern, Engraved, Pierced Bowl, c.1872, 9¾ In.	1434.00
Flask, Bacchic, Nymphs, Pan, Grapevine, Etched, c.1895, 7¾ In.	4500.00
Flatware Set, English King Pattern, Monogram, Early 20th Century, 330 Piece	33000.00
Flatware Set, Olympian Pattern, 129 Piece	10800.00
Flatware Set, Persian Pattern, Serving Pieces, Engraved, 7 Piece	881.00
Flatware Set, Shell & Thread, J Monogram, Box, 104 Piece	21600.00
Fork, Cold Meat, Chrysanthemum Pattern, 2 Tines, Sterling Silver, Marked, 7½ In.	345.00
Frame, Early 20th Century, 12½ x 9¾ In.	347.00
Fruit Set, Olympian Pattern, Forks, Knives, c.1878, 24 Piece	1840.00
Grape Shears, Japanese Style, Hammered, Pierced Clouds, c.1800, 8 In.	3840.00
Inkstand, Rectangular, Cherubs, Satyr Mask Handles, Edward Moore, c.1865, 10 In.	3600.00
Jug, Hot Milk, Hinged Cover, Hammered, Poppies, Leaves, Baluster Shape, 7¼ In.	3840.00
Kettle, Hot Water, Stand, Hammered, Japanese Style, Ivory Accents, 1881, 12¾ In. . . . . .*illus*	10158.00
Knife Rest, Palmette Terminals, Paw Feet, 3¼ In., Pair	480.00
Lamp, Fluid, Sterling, Spiral Form, 3 In., Pair	215.00
Loving Cup, Engraved, Grapevines, Scrolled Serpentine Handles, 1907-38, 6⅝ In.	1645.00
Loving Cup, Presentation, 3 Handles, Marked, 8¼ Pts., 9 In.	1763.00
Martini Set, Pitcher, 8 Goblets, Organic Shape, Spreading Stem, c.1965, 9 Piece	2880.00
Muffin Server, Flared, Leaf Scroll Border, Domed Cover, Acanthus Finial, 9 In.	759.00
Napkin Ring, Repousse, HBL Monogram, c.1900, 1⅞ In.	245.00
Nut Cup, Shell Shape, Molded Turtle, Back Tipt Handles, 6½ In., 8 Piece	8813.00
Nut Dish, Pierced, Footed, c.1891, 3 x 4 x 7 In.	527.00
Pitcher, Applied Grapevine, Woven Wood Handle, 7½ In.	2360.00
Pitcher, Classical Hunters, Dogs, Boar, Chased, Embossed, c.1890, 8¼ In. . . . .*illus*	14400.00
Pitcher, Cocktail, Scroll Handle, Stirrer, Rooster Tip, c.1955, 8-In. Pitcher	863.00
Pitcher, Die-Rolled Floral Bands, Gadroon Border, Baluster Shape, c.1891, 7 In.	1920.00
Pitcher, Hammered, Applied Dragonflies, Baluster Shape, 1878-91, 7½ In.	9600.00
Pitcher, Helmet Shape, Molded, Acanthus Leaf, Gadroon Base, 10 In.	4800.00
Plate, Bread & Butter, Round, Reeded Rim, 6⅛ In., 8 Piece	1440.00
Powder Box, Repousse Garlands, Flowers, Monogram, c.1901, 2¼ x 3¾ In.	717.00
Punch Bowl, 5 x 10⅜ In.	410.00

T

Rattle, Bar Bell, 1¼ x 2¾ In.	82.00
Ring Holder, Hand Shape, 3 x 3 In., Pair	527.00
Salt, Gilt, Applied Chrysanthemum, Leaf Feet, Rectangular, 1907, 4¼ In., Pair	1920.00
Salt Spoon, Lap-Over-Edge Pattern, Hammered, c.1879, 2¾ In., Pair	4302.00
Salver, Chrysanthemum, Leaves, Shaped Rim, Engraved Coat Of Arms, 14¼ In.	7050.00
Salver, Embossed Flower Heads, Leaf Scrolls, Paw Feet, 11¼ In.	1528.00
Salver, Round, Stylized Acanthus, 3 Tree Of Life Feet, Monogram, 10¼ In.	3360.00
Salver, Scalloped, Gadroon Border, Footed, Marked, c.1867, 1¼ x 10¾ In.	403.00
Sauceboat, Chrysanthemum, Fluted, Flared Rim, 8½ In., Pair	7200.00
Scent Bottle, Flower Form, Jeweled, Gold Enamel, Late 1800s, 2⅞ In.	10200.00
Serving Dish, Oval, Shell & Scroll Border, 4¾ x 11¼ In.	403.00
Serving Fork, Persian Pattern, Engraved, Pierced, 1872, 9¾ In. ....*illus*	1434.00
Shaker, Pepper, Lap-Over-Edge Pattern, Hammered, c.1877, 3 In., Pair	3884.00
Spoon, Olympian Pattern, c.1878, 7 In.	75.00
Sugar Sifter, Vines, Flowers, Openwork, 1875-91, 6⅜ In.	382.00
Tazza, Raspberry Clusters, Reticulated Rim, Trumpet Foot, 1891-1902, 3½ x 7¼ In.	823.00
Tea & Coffee Set, Ivy Pattern, Scroll Handles, c.1870, 6 Piece	8400.00
Tea Caddy, Bird's Nest Pattern, Scrolling Vines, Edward Moore, c.1869, 4½ In.	9600.00
Teapot, Flower Basket Finial	518.00
Teapot, Hammered, Applied Leaves, Beetles, Round, c.1880, 5 In.	15600.00
Teaspoon, Wave Edge Pattern, 1875-91, 6 In., 11 Piece	118.00
Tray, Chippendale Style, Oval, C Monogram, Marked, 18 x 13½ In.	1150.00
Tray, Flower Border Plated, Monogram, 20th Century, 26¼ x 19½ In.	1076.00
Tray, Japanese Style, Frog, Oak Leaf, Baskets, Folded Up Corners, 1881, 17 In.	6000.00
Tray, Oval, Scrolled Edge, 12½ x 8¼ In.	460.00
Tray, Presentation, Oval, Molded Border, Handles, Engraved, c.1970	2950.00
Tray, Round, Indented Center, Scrolled Edge, Marked, 13 In.	690.00
Trophy, Punch Bowl, Applied Reeded Rim Bands, Engraved, 1931-37, 11⅜ In.	23055.00
Trophy, Yachting, Tureen, Cover, Oval, Rope Twist Border, Sailor Finial, 1874, 18 In.	14400.00
Vase, Campana Shape, Pedestal Base, Acanthus Leaf Handles, c.1902, 15 In.	13200.00
Vase, Hammered, Chased Floral Bands, Waisted Neck & Foot, 6¾ In.	2640.00

TIFFIN Glass Company of Tiffin, Ohio, was a subsidiary of the United States Glass Co. of Pittsburgh, Pennsylvania, in 1892. The U.S. Glass Co. went bankrupt in 1963, and the Tiffin plant employees purchased the building and the inventory. They continued running it from 1963 to 1966, when it was sold to Continental Can Company. In 1969, it was sold to Interpace, and in 1980, it was closed. The black satin glass, made from 1923 to 1926, and the stemware of the last twenty years are the best-known products.

Ball & Swirl, Compote, 6⅞ x 8¼ In.	40.00
Bouquet, Lamp, Flower Basket, 1920s, 8½ In. ....*illus*	425.00
Byzantine, Cocktail, 5⅜ In.	13.50
Canterbury, Vase, Copen Blue, 8 In.	85.00
Cherry Rose, Oyster Cocktail, 5¼ In.	30.00
Cherry Rose, Tumbler, Iced Tea, Footed, 12 Oz.	40.00
Chipperfield, Tray, Dresser, Geometric, 3 Sections	135.00
Compote, Ruby Flashed	22.00
Diamond Optic, Champagne, 5⅜ In.	25.00
Empress Modern, Basket, Light Blue, 13 In.	125.00
Flanders, Cordial, Yellow, Clear Stem, 1½ Oz., 5 In.	82.00
Flanders, Plate, Pink, 8 In.	32.00
Flanders, Vase, Pink, Flared Rim, 8 In.	675.00
Fuchsia, Champagne, 5⅜ In.	18.00
Horn Of Plenty, Vase, 9 In.	495.00
June Night, Bowl, 3¾ x 11 In.	68.00
June Night, Goblet, 10 Oz., 8 In.	30.00
June Night, Sherbet, 5½ Oz., 4 In.	16.00
June Night, Sherbet, Stem, 6 Oz., 4¾ In.	18.50
June Night, Tumbler, Iced Tea, Footed, 10½ Oz., 6¼ In.	22.50
June Night, Tumbler, Iced Tea, Footed, 11 Oz., 5½ In.	30.00
Jungle Assortment, Candy Jar, Cover, Green Satin, 7½ In.	75.00
King's Crown, Compote, Ruby Stained	75.00
King's Crown, Cordial, 3¾ In.	20.00
King's Crown, Cup, 2½ In.	8.00
King's Crown, Glass, Juice, 4 Oz.	13.00
King's Crown, Goblet, Cranberry Flashed, 9 Oz., 5½ In.	30.00

Tiffin, Bouquet, Lamp, Flower Basket, 1920s, 8½ In.
$425.00

Tiffin, Modern, Bowl, Twilight, 10-Lobed Base, 4½ x 8 In.
$155.00

Tiffin, No. 310, Vase, Fan, Black Satin, 8½ In.
$95.00

Tiffin, Rockwell, Vase, Blue Satin, Cupped, Silver Overlay, Dahlia, 6½ In.
$85.00

T

Tile, Frieze, Classical Warrior,
Green Glaze, Kensington Tile Works,
3-Tile, Frame, 18 In., Pair
$920.00

Tile, Purple, Lavender & White
High Glaze, Art Nouveau,
Oak Frame, 5⅞-In. Tile
$85.00

Tile, Rabbit, White, Blue Ground,
Flint Michigan Tile Co.,
Frame, 2⅞ In.
$374.00

T

King's Crown, Goblet, Water, Ruby Stained, 9 Oz., 5⅓ Oz.	8.00
King's Crown, Salad Bowl, Underplate, Amber Stained	28.00
King's Crown, Sherbet, Cranberry Flashed	15.00
King's Crown, Tumbler, Juice, Ruby Flashed, 4¼ In.	13.00
King's Crown, Wedding Bowl, Footed, 10 In.	75.00
King's Crown, Wine, Ruby Flashed, 3½ In.	15.00
Milrose, Tumbler, Juice, Footed, Green, 6 Piece	195.00
Modern, Bowl, Twilight, 10-Lobed Base, 4½ x 8 In. .....*illus*	155.00
Moonglow, Goblet, 7½ In.	35.00
No. 310, Vase, Fan, Black Satin, 8½ In. .....*illus*	95.00
Oneida, Bonbon, Cover, Low Foot	85.00
Princess, Sherbet, 6 Oz.	12.50
Princess, Tumbler, Whiskey, 2¹⁄₁₆ In.	17.50
Rockwell, Vase, Blue Satin, Cupped, Silver Overlay, Dahlia, 6½ In. .....*illus*	85.00
Sweet Pea, Candleholder, No. 10	60.00
Thistle, Champagne, 4¾ In.	15.00
Thistle, Goblet, 3⅝ In.	10.00

TILES have been used in most countries of the world as a sturdy building material for floors, roofs, fireplace surrounds, and surface toppings. The cuerda seca (dry cord) technique of decoration uses a greasy pigment to separate different glaze colors during firing. In cuenca (raised line) decorated tiles, the design is impressed, leaving ridges that separate the glaze colors. Many of the American tiles are listed in this book under the factory name.

Art Nouveau, Flower, Oak Frame, 6-In. Square Tile, 12-In. Frame	176.00
Art Nouveau, Purple, Lavender, White Glaze, Mission Frame, 6-In. Tile, 11¾-In. Frame	94.00
Bird Hunter, Dancing Dog, Hand Painted, France, 19th Century, 8 x 8 In.	35.00
Dog Head, Green & Cream, Hamilton, Ohio, 6 x 6 In., Pair	234.00
Floor, Encaustic, Belgium, Frame, 27¼ x 24 In., 2 Piece	192.00
Flower, Stylized, Yellow, Iridescent Glaze, Marked, Lewis F. Day, England, Frame, 6 In.	115.00
Flowers, Blue, Green, High Glaze, Arts & Crafts, Marked, A.M. Ltd., England, Frame, 6 In.	40.00
Flowers, Embossed, Multicolored Glaze, Majolica, Arts & Crafts Frame, 6 x 6 In., 11 Piece	540.00
Fox Head, Green, American, 6 x 6 In.	205.00
Frieze, Cereus, Turquoise, White Blossoms, Black, Mirror Border, Harris Strong, 30 x 18 In.	230.00
Frieze, Classical Warrior, Green Glaze, Kensington Tile Works, 3-Tile, Frame, 18 In., Pair *illus*	920.00
Frieze, Houses On Hill, Multicolored, Harris G. Strong, 4-Tile, Frame	230.00
Girl In Profile, Garland In Hair, Rose Pink High Glaze, Cambridge Tile Works, Frame, 6 In.	173.00
Goddess, Playing Lute, Blue Glaze, Vertical, Marked, Isaac Broome, Frame, 18 x 6 In.	540.00
Goose, By Pond, Cuenca, Green Matte Glaze Ground, Vertical, Owens, 11¾ x 8¾ In.	1800.00
Lily, Purple, Yellow, Brown, Green, High Glaze, Hasselt, Belgian, Frame, 6 In.	115.00
Macintosh Style, Ellison, Stamped, 3½ x 3½ In.	35.00
Mission Courtyard, Fountain, Palms, Matte Glaze, Claycraft, Frame, 8½ x 16½ In.	1560.00
Owl, Holding Egg, Arts & Crafts, Matte Glaze, Wood Hartford Faience, Frame, 13 x 13 In.	16800.00
Panel, Nude, Reclining, Ceramic, Krystyna Sadowska, Frame, 12 x 24 In.	299.00
Panels, Hand Painted, Garden Theme, Late 1800s, 60 x 18 In., 33 Panels	2900.00
Peacock, Deer Hunt, Cuenca, De Porceleyne Fles, Arts & Crafts Frame, 4¾ x 17 In., Pair	1320.00
Pirates, On Ship Deck, Multicolored Matte Glaze, Claycraft, Arts & Crafts Frame, 12 x 16 In.	1080.00
Portrait, Man, Banner, Goldsmith, Hand Painted, Daniel Cottier, 1880s, 8 x 8 In.	600.00
Portrait, William E. Gladstone, British Prime Minister, Aquamarine, c.1890	165.00
Profile, Woman With Curly Hair, Brown Glaze, Kensington Tile Works, Frame, 6 In., Pair	219.00
Purple, Lavender & White High Glaze, Art Nouveau, Oak Frame, 5⅞-In. Tile .....*illus*	85.00
Rabbit, White, Blue Ground, Flint Michigan Tile Co., Frame, 2⅞ In. .....*illus*	374.00
Waterfowl, Cuenca, Richard E. Bishop, Mosaic Tile Co., 6 x 6 In., 18 Piece	1440.00
White Rabbit, Blue Ground, Square, Flint Michigan Tile Co., Frame, 3 In.	374.00
Windblown Pine, Mission On Coast, Porcelain, Muresque, 8 x 16 In.	2880.00

TINWARE containers for household use have been made in America since the seventeenth century. The first tin utensils were brought from Europe, but by 1798, tin plate was imported and local tinsmiths made the wares. Painted tin is called *tole* and is listed separately. Some tin kitchen items may be found listed under Kitchen. The lithographed tin containers used to hold food and tobacco are listed in the Advertising category under Tin.

Beaker, Cylindrical, Rolled Rim, Painted, Green, White, Swags, Tassels, c.1830, 2¾ In.	1320.00
Box, Fish Shape, Ribbed, Tripod Wire Legs, Hinged Lid, 12⅝ In.	770.00
Candle Snuffer, Scissor Shape, 6 In.	8.00
Coffeepot, Ear Handle, S. Culver, Miller Cronise & Co., Newark, Dec. 1858, 20 x 13 In.	1090.00
Coffeepot, Elongated Spout, Scroll Handle, 10½ In.	275.00

Coffeepot, Flowers, Leaves, Black Ground, Turned Wood Finial, 10½ In.	598.00
Coffeepot, Punched, Gooseneck Spout, Mid 19th Century, 11 In.	2195.00
Coffeepot, Punched, Peafowl, Sunbursts, Gooseneck Spout, Dome Top, 1945, 11 In.	2860.00
Coffeepot, Punched, Potted Tulip, Medallions, Rosettes, Gooseneck Spout, Ear Handle, 11 In.	467.00
Cup, 3 Children Feeding Kittens, Cottage, Fence, Lithograph, c.1920, 3 x 3 In.	308.00
Cup, Fox Stalking 3 Ducks, Flowers, Rattles, Embossed, Lithograph, c.1900, 3 x 3½ In.	336.00
Ink Sander, For Pen & Pencil, Japanned, 3 x 3 In.	250.00
Mold, Candle, 1 Tube, 18 In.	138.00
Mold, Candle, 2 Tube, Crimped, 10½ In.	198.00
Mold, Candle, 2 Tube, Rectangular Base & Top, 3½ In.	297.00
Mold, Candle, 4 Tube, 10 In.	88.00
Mold, Candle, 8 Tube, 24 Holes, Wood, 7¾ x 8 In.	55.00
Mold, Candle, 12 Tube, 6½ In.	770.00
Mold, Candle, 12 Tube, Handles, 10 In.	66.00
Reflector, Iron, Crimped, 33 In.	908.00
Rooster, Sheet Iron, Cutout, Black Paint, Molded Wood Frame, 16½ x 16¼ In.	264.00
Rooster, Silhouette, Cutout, Wing Detail, 24½ In.	230.00
Sconce, Candle, Arched Back, Tulips, Wavy Lines, Handle On Back, 8 In., Pair	2070.00
Stencil, 3 Stars, Over H.K. Dillinger, 7-Sided, Sporting Hill, Pa., 9 x 10 In.	220.00
Suit Of Armor, Child's Size, c.1930, 48 In.	468.00
Trinket Box, Painted, Blossoms, Leaves, Pinstriping, Hinged Cover, c.1835, 2 x 3 In.	2160.00

TOBACCO CUTTERS *may be listed in either the Advertising or Store categories.*

TOBACCO JAR collectors search for those made in odd shapes and colors. Because tobacco needs special conditions of humidity and air, it has been stored in special containers since the eighteenth century.

Anchor Hocking, Star Stamped, Ribbed, Loose Fitting Lid, 7¼ x 4½ In.	18.00
Building, Brass, Finial, England, 18th Century, 7½ In.	450.00
Devil, Porcelain, E. Bohne & Sohne, 5 In.	223.00
Grape & Cable, Colonial Orange, Fenton, 1970	119.00
Humidor, Black Man In Top Hat, Holding Matchbox, Painted, 7½ In.	725.00
Humidor, Portrait Of Man, Bagdad, Blue, Green, Ceramic, 6½ In.	150.00
Man, Holding Beer Stein, Terra-Cotta, Marked, 12½ In.	845.00
Man, Holding Document, Terra-Cotta, Marked, 12 In.	725.00
Man, Holding Pipe & Cigars, Amber, Plastic Liner, 10 x 5 In.	15.00
Man, Leaning On Table, Terra-Cotta, Marked, 9½ In.	345.00
Man, Sitting On Box, Terra-Cotta, Marked, 10¾ In.	460.00
Man, Sitting On Cigars, Terra-Cotta, Marked, 10½ x 7 In.	718.00
Man, Sitting On Leather Chair, Terra-Cotta, Marked, 10 In.	690.00
Man, Wearing Lederhosen, Terra-Cotta, Marked, 11½ In.	665.00
Man, With Writing Board, Terra-Cotta, Marked, 11 In.	725.00
Prince Albert, Sun Colored Amethyst Glass Lid, c.1914	85.00
Woman, Binoculars In Case, Terra-Cotta, Marked, 12¾ In.	782.00

TOBY JUG is the name of a very special form of pitcher. It is shaped like the full figure of a man or woman. A pitcher that shows just the top half of a person is not correctly called a toby. More examples of toby jugs can be found under Royal Doulton and other factory names.

Creamware, Seated Figure, With Empty Jug, Blue, Yellow, Staffordshire, c.1800, 10 In.	588.00
Creamware, Seated Figure, With Empty Jug, Blue Sponging, Staffordshire, c.1800, 10 In.	646.00
Game Keeper, Tankard, Dog, Branch Handle, Staffordshire, England, 10 In. ....*illus*	23500.00
Gentleman, Seated, Holding Lantern, Spout In Back Of Chair, England, Late c.1790, 9 In.	390.00
Johnnie Walker, Limited Edition, Marked, Percy Metcalf, Ashtead, 11¼ In.	1054.00
Man, Blue Coat, Yellow Britches, Tricornered Hat, Mid 19th Century, 11¼ In.	315.00
Man, Purple Face, Blue Frock Coat, Holding Jug, Snake-Coiled Pipe, Yorkshire, 10 In. ..*illus*	2115.00
Man, Seated, Blue Coat, Brown Britches, Tricorner Hat, Impressed, Copeland, 10 In.	345.00
Man, Seated, Blue Coat, White Tricornered Hat, England, 19th Century, 10 In.	920.00
Man, Seated, Brown & Red Coat, Tan Britches, Tricornered Hat, Pearlware, 10½ In.	1010.00
Man, Seated, Brown Coat, Striped Vest, Green Britches, Banner, Walton, 10¼ In.	1125.00
Man, Seated, Holding Ale Jug, Cup, Pratt Type, Dr. Johnson, Staffordshire, 6½ In.	1293.00
Man, Seated, Holding Ale Jug, Pipe, Pratt Type, Staffordshire, 7 In.	705.00
Man, Seated, Holding Ale Jug, Yorkshire Type, Pearlware, 7¼ In.	588.00
Man, Seated, Holding Pitcher, Green Coat, Yellow Britches, Tricornered Hat, Staffordshire, 9 In.	515.00
Man, Seated, Holding Pitcher, Red Coat, Yellow Britches, England, 19th Century, 9 In.	730.00
Man, Seated On Barrel, Holding Jug, Cup, Home Brewed Ale, Staffordshire, 11 In.	353.00

Toby Jug, Game Keeper, Tankard, Dog, Branch Handle, Staffordshire, England, 10 In. $23500.00

Toby Jug, Man, Purple Face, Blue Frock Coat, Holding Jug, Snake-Coiled Pipe, Yorkshire, 10 In. $2115.00

Toby Jug, Martha Gunn, Holding Cup, Ale Jug, Staffordshire, England, 10¼ In. $1116.00

Toby Jug, Sailor, Seated On Sea Chest, Dollars, Staffordshire, England, 12 In. $8225.00

Tole, Box, Document, Dome Lid, Cherries, Black, Red, Green, Mustard, Bail Handle, 7 x 9 x 5 In. $480.00

Tole, Box, Document, Dome Lid, Red & White Flowers, Fern, Wire Handle, 7¾ x 9⅝ x 6 In. $2090.00

Tole, Coffeepot, Multicolored Fruit & Flowers, Black, Gooseneck Spout, Ear Handle, 10 In. $2640.00

Man, Standing, Holding Ale Jug, Pipe, Pratt Type, Staffordshire, c.1800, 6½ In.	4113.00
Martha Gunn, Holding Cup, Ale Jug, Staffordshire, England, 10¼ In. *illus*	1116.00
Pearlware, Martha Gunn, Brown, Blue Glazes, Staffordshire, Late 1700s, 11 In.	5288.00
Sailor, Seated On Sea Chest, Dollars, Staffordshire, England, 12 In. *illus*	8225.00
Sandra Kuck, Hearty Good Fellow, Kevin Francis, Limited Edition	127.00
Seated Man, Orange Jacket, Red Pitcher, Figural Handle, Staffordshire, 10 In.	230.00
William McKinley, On Throne, Holding Money, Protection & Prosperity, 9 In.	1434.00

TOLE is painted tin. It is sometimes called japanned ware, pontypool, or toleware. Most nineteenth-century tole is painted with an orange-red or black background and multicolored decorations. Many recent versions of toleware are made and sold. Related items may be listed in the Tinware category.

Basket, Hunter Green Finish, Flowers, Deer Shape Handles, 11 x 5¼ x 5 In.	21.00
Box, Document, Dome Lid, Cherries, Black, Red, Green, Mustard, Bail Handle, 7 x 9 x 5 In. *illus*	480.00
Box, Document, Dome Lid, Fern, Fruit, Leaves, Flowers, Red, Gold, White Band, Black, 7¾ x 9⅝ In.	2090.00
Box, Document, Dome Lid, Fruit, Red, Smoked White Band, Yellow Swags, Japanned, 9 x 5 In.	748.00
Box, Document, Dome Lid, Leafy Pinwheels, Red, Yellow, Black Ground, 8 x 4¾ In.	230.00
Box, Document, Dome Lid, Red & White Flowers, Fern, Wire Handle, 7¾ x 9⅝ x 6 In. *illus*	2090.00
Box, Document, Dome Lid, Swags, Bands, Pinwheel Sides, Japanned, Wire Handle, 9 x 6 In.	920.00
Box, Dome Lid, Red & Yellow Flower Sprays, Multicolored, Black Ground, 4¾ x 8 In.	220.00
Bread Tray, Fruit, Yellow Swag Border, Black Ground, Flared Sided, 13½ x 7 In.	132.00
Candlestick, Yellow Ground, Flared Rim, Loop Carry Handle, Saucer Base, 1½ In.	138.00
Canister, Brown Commas, Black Ground, Lid, 9½ x 5 In.	110.00
Centerpiece, 5 Tiers, Graduating Taper, Round, Painted, Gilt Strip, Greek Key, 14 In.	1116.00
Coal Bin, Tapered, Oval, Side Handles, Hinged Lid, Hunting Scene, Green, 1900, 19 In.	2100.00
Coal Bucket, Red, Flared, Footed Base, Swing Handle, 1½ In.	50.00
Coffeepot, Dome Lid, Red, Yellow, Tulips, Flowers, Fruit, Brass Finial, 10 In.	517.00
Coffeepot, Dome Lid, Red, Yellow Leaves, Scrolled Finial, 10¼ In.	3105.00
Coffeepot, Flowers, Leaves, Swag Wreath, Black Ground, Ear Handle, 9 In.	908.00
Coffeepot, Flowers, Stars, Swags, Sawtooth Border, Embossed, Footed, C-Shaped Handle, 11½ In.	770.00
Coffeepot, Handle, Straight Spout, Eagle, Snake, American Flag, 8¾ In.	3163.00
Coffeepot, Lighthouse Shape, Black Painted, Gooseneck Spout, Hinged Cover, c.1835, 11 In.	2400.00
Coffeepot, Lighthouse Shape, Fruit, Flowers, Black Ground, Brass Lift, 10½ In.	413.00
Coffeepot, Multicolored Fruit & Flowers, Black, Gooseneck Spout, Ear Handle, 10 In. *illus*	2640.00
Coffeepot, Punched, Tulips, Leaves, Hearts, Red, Blue, Green, Yellow, Gooseneck Spout, 14 In.	110.00
Coffeepot, Red, Flower, Fruit, Swag Rim, Scalloped Loop Lift, Ear Handle, 9 In.	2640.00
Coffeepot, Red, Fruit, Leaves, Bands, Brass Finial, Strap Handle, 10½ In.	3105.00
Coffeepot, Red, Fruit, Leaves, Swags, Starburst On Lid, Brass Finial, Pennsylvania, 10 In.	8337.00
Coffeepot, Red, Yellow & Red Fruit, Flowers, Brass Finial, Pennsylvania, 10 In.	2300.00
Coffeepot, Red, Yellow Leaves, Fruit, Red Berries, Brass Finial, 10 In.	1380.00
Coffeepot, Tulip, Flowers, Chain Band, Gooseneck Spout, Mushroom Finial, 11 In.	330.00
Coffeepot, Tulip Tree, Scalloped Swag, Sawtooth, Ear Handle, 10¾ In.	770.00
Cooler, Bottle, Dome Lid, Putto Masques & Leaves, Pottery Finial, Germany, 17 In.	352.00
Creamer, Green, Yellow & Red Flowers, Ear Handle, 3¾ In.	275.00
Cup, Red & Yellow Swag, Black Ground, 3¾ In.	303.00
Jardiniere, Tapered Box Shape, Wrought Iron Strapwork, Finials At Corners, 31 x 27 In., Pair	1292.00
Mug, Painted, Leaves, Pinstripe, Applied Strap Handle, Child's, c.1830, 1¾ In.	1920.00
Mug, Yellow Swags, Flowers, Bands, 5⅞ In.	374.00
Planter, Green, Gilt, Footed, Stand, 19th Century, 7¾ x 20½ In.	825.00
Sconce, Candle, Flowers, Black Ground, Crimped Arch Crest, Half Moon Base, 13¾ In., Pair	88.00
Shaker, Brown Flowers, Yellow Ground, Loop Handle, 3 In.	275.00
Snuffbox, Red, Pink Bud, Leaves, Scallops, Asphaltum Ground, Hinged Cover, c.1830, 2 x 3 In.	4800.00
Sugar, Lid, Red Flower, Swag, Flowers, Black Ground, Double Scroll Line, 3½ In.	193.00
Tea Bin, Labeled Oolong, J. Hall Rohrman & Son, 13½ x 9½ In.	240.00
Tea Caddy, Berries, Leaves, Yellow Swags, White Band, Red Ground, 4⅛ In.	920.00
Tea Caddy, Flowers, Red, Green, Yellow Swags, Japanned, 8 In.	518.00
Tea Caddy, Red & Yellow Flowers, Black Ground, 5¼ In.	330.00
Tray, 3 Roosters, Hand Painted, Georges Briard, 20th Century, 22½ x 28 In.	29.00
Tray, Apple, Outward Scroll, Lobed Sides, White Border, Berries, Leaves, 1¼ x 4½ In.	2400.00
Tray, Apple, Red, Yellow, Pink Bands, Center, Leaves, 7½ x 12¾ x 2⅝ In.	2875.00
Tray, Battle Scene, British & Dutch Fleets, Octagonal, Pierced Handles, 1700s, 30 x 20 In.	1410.00
Tray, Beehives, Girl, Dog, Painted, Stenciled, 14 x 10¼ In.	717.00
Tray, Cherries, Leaves, Feathers, Scalloped, Black Asphaltum, Stand-Up Rim, 1900, 3 x 12 In.	5400.00
Tray, Flower Spray In Center, Red, 17 x 12 In.	16500.00
Tray, Flower Wreath, Combed Center, Black Ground, Octagonal, 12⅝ x 9 In.	28.00

Tray, Flowers, Fruit, Red, Green, Yellow, Japanned, Octagonal, 8½ x 12¼ In.	5750.00
Tray, Flowers, Leaves, Wide Flower Band, Brown Ground, Flared, 12⅞ x 7⅞ In.	83.00
Tray, Flowers, Swag Border, Red, Flared, Rolled Rim, Octagonal, 17½ x 12 In., 2 Piece	16500.00
Tray, Flowers & Leaves, Multicolored, Yellow Band, Brown Pinstripe, Flared, 12½ x 8 In.	689.00
Tray, Fruit, Flowers, Black Ground, Flared Rim, Octagonal, 12⅜ x 8¾ In.	935.00
Tray, Fruit, Flowers, Crystallized Center, Black Ground, Octagonal, 12¼ x 8¾ In.	385.00
Tray, Fruit, Leaves, Pinstripe, Black Paint, Black Asphaltum, Octagonal, Stand-Up Rim, 9 In.	5700.00
Tray, Fruit, Leaves, Pinstripe, Rope Twist, Black Paint, Oval, Stand-Up Rim, 2 x 7 In.	4200.00
Tray, Fruit, Yellow, Green Leaves, Black Paint, Octagonal, Stand-Up Rim, 8 In.	6000.00
Tray, Gilt Flower Bands, Leaves, Black Ground, Finger Holds, c.1830, 29½ In.	588.00
Tray, Man, Smoking Pipe, Yoked Water Boy, Black, Gilt Stencil Border, Oval, 24 x 19 In.	660.00
Tray, Pastoral Scene, Oval, 19th Century, 23½ In.	283.00
Tray, Red & Green Flowers, Yellow Band Border, Oval, 8½ x 13¼ In.	55.00
Tray, Red Berries, Green Leaves, Crystallized Center, Coffin Ends, 8-Sided, 8½ x 12½ In.	1495.00
Trinket Box, Dome Lid, Flowers, Leaves, White Band, Black Ground, 1¾ x 3 In.	121.00
Vase, Garniture, Restoration, Reserve With Ruins, Red Ground, Flared, Square, 11 In., Pair	450.00
Watering Can, Flowers, Black, Gold, 12 In.	117.00

TOM MIX was born in 1880 and died in 1940. He was the hero of over 100 silent movies from 1910 to 1929, and 25 sound films from 1929 to 1935. There was a Ralston Tom Mix radio show from 1933 to 1950, but the original Tom Mix was not in the show. Tom Mix comics were published from 1942 to 1953.

Badge, Siren, Sheriff, Dobie County, Whistle, Embossed, 1946	62.00
Book, Big Little Book, Tom Mix Plays A Lone Hand, Wilton West, 1935	35.00
Film Viewer, Miracle Rider, Mechanical, Cardboard, Instructions, 1935, 6½ In.	123.00
Film Viewer, RCA Victor, 5 Films, Original Mailer	150.00
Film Viewer, Rustlers' Roundup, Mechanical, Cardboard, Instructions, 1935, 6½ In.	196.00
Lobby Card, Destry Rides Again, Universal, 1932	690.00
Movie, Poster, For Big Stakes, Fox, 1922, 41 x 27 In.	2990.00
Movie, Poster, Just Tony, Linen Mounted, 1922, 41 x 27 In. ....*illus*	493.00
Movie, Poster, Miracle Rider, Mascot, 1933, 41 x 27 In.	748.00
Movie, Poster, No Man's Gold, Insert, Fox, 1926, 36 x 14 In.	748.00
Movie, Poster, Rustlers' Roundup, Tom Mix, Universal, 1933, 41 x 27 In.	1955.00
Pin, From Tom Mix & Tony, Paramount Theatre, Toledo, 1½ In.	224.00
Puzzle, Tom Mix & His New Horse Tony Jr., Rexall Toothpaste, 1930s, 10 x 13 In.	84.00
Ring, Siren, Steel, Brass Plating, Ralston, 1944	191.00
Telescope, Enamel, Black, Advertisement, 1938, 2½ In. ....*illus*	123.00

TOOLS of all sorts are listed here, but most are related to industry. Other tools may be found listed under Iron, Kitchen, Tinware, and Wooden.

Adze, Cooper's, Integral Hammer Poll, 6-In. Cutting Edge, France, 9 In.	83.00
Auger Bit, Countersink, Winchester Repeating Arms Co., As Good As The Gun	33.00
Ax, Broad, O.R. Bartchall, Goose Wing Blade, Wood Handle, Marked, Rochester, N.Y., 17½ In.	52.00
Ax, Broad, Wooden Haft, Black Paint, Partial Stamp, Baltimore, 32½ In.	115.00
Ax, Chisel, C. Valsechy	170.00
Ax, Cooper's, Guyot, Single Bevel Blade, Round Finial, France, 15 In.	385.00
Ax, Medieval Pattern, 12 In.	39.00
Beader, Coach Maker's, Dual Wooden Handles, Multiple Blades, 12 In.	358.00
Bed Smoother, Maple, Painted Flowers & Geometrics, Horse Handle, 25 x 5 In.	489.00
Bed Smoother, Pine, Initialed, Dated 1724	275.00
Bevel, Brass, Ebony, Sandwich Pattern, 11 In.	72.00
Book Press, Mahogany, Dovetailed Case, Threaded Wooden Screw, Platform Base, 21 In.	431.00
Boring Machine, Upright, Cast Frame Arms, c.1881, 22½ In.	143.00
Brace, Bit, Brass Mounted, Ivory Inlay, 16½ In.	288.00
Brace, Bit, C. & T. Pilkington, Sheffield, Applied Frame, Pedigor & Storrs Patent, 1857-64	660.00
Brace, Bit, James Holley, Turret Head, Bits Attached, November 24, 1903	5500.00
Brace, Bit, Stanley, Boxed Ratchet, Rosewood Handles, No. 813, 16 In.	132.00
Brace, Folding, Undertaker's, Frame Mounted, Closes Casket, 12 In.	440.00
Branding Iron, 165 Brand, Handmade, Fruit Of Maguey, Tequila, 1920s, 19½ In.	115.00
Branding Iron, Heart Shape, Hand Forged, c.1900, 23 In.	138.00
Branding Iron, Wrought, Tapered, Ring Terminal, Copper End, Raised Lettering, 12¾ In.	1650.00
Caliper, Double, Pocket, Folding, Inside & Outside Arms, 4½ In.	165.00
Cart, Wood Frame, Handles, Old Bicycle Wheel, 30 x 27 x 52 In.	259.00
Chest, Wood, Raised Panel, Removable Sections, Figural Center, Mahogany	1540.00
Clamp, Floor, H.E. Hatch, Dexter, Maine, Patent, 1884	209.00

Toleware

The earliest toleware was dark brown or black with hand-painted designs. By 1820 stencils were used. Toleware was painted with scenes, fruits, flowers, and birds. Decorations became simpler, less realistic, and more peasant-like during the late 1800s.

Toleware made in New England, New York, and Pennsylvania had similar designs. Most had black or dark brown backgrounds, but pieces made in Pennsylvania had a red background and brighter decorations.

Tom Mix, Movie, Poster, Just Tony, Linen Mounted, 1922, 41 x 27 In. $493.00

Tom Mix, Telescope, Enamel, Black, Advertisement, 1938, 2½ In. $123.00

Tool, Hayfork, Wood, Carved, 5 Tines, Mid To Late 19th Century, 69 x 30 In. $176.00

Tool, Level, Davis Level & Tool Co., Inclinometer, Cast Iron, Springfield, Mass., c.1867, 12 In. $138.00

Tool, Plane, Dado, Stanley, No. 39, Cast Iron, Japanned, ¼-In. Width, 8 In. $132.00

Early Construction Tools

Early construction tools include axes, adzes, saws, planes, chisels, drills, turning tools, hammers, vises, wrenches, screwdrivers, rules, and much more. Some nineteenth- and twentieth-century tools can be dated by the marks, usually the name of the company or person that made them.

Cobbler's Bench, Dovetailed Drawers, Brass Tacks, Cast Iron Mounts, 45 x 51 In.	546.00
Cobbler's Bench, Shaker, Drawer, Signed, Erastus Rude For Benjamin Snow, 1819, 24 x 27 In.	2925.00
Cobbler's Last, Woman's Shoe, Oak, Carved, Scallops, Flowers, 1793	550.00
Compass, Wheelwright's Wing, Square Nail	135.00
Cranberry Picker, Wooden, Patina, Early 1900s, 16 x 21 x 10 In.	110.00
Croze, Cooper's, Benjamin F. Horn, Cast Brass, Ill., Lignum Vitae, 14½ In.	116.00
Croze, Cooper's, Screw Adjustable, Triple Blade, Continental, 8 In.	110.00
Cutter, Benjamin F. Horn, Barrel Top, Cooper's, Stag Logo, Ill., 28½ In.	358.00
Divider, Wooden, Fitted Joint, Rosewood Hinge Pin, 13½ In.	248.00
Drawing Knife, Peck, Stow & Wilcox, Metal Caps, Ferrule, Wood Handles, 8 In.	45.00
Drawing Knife, Peck, Stow & Wilcox Co., Lineman's, Angle Guide, 23 In.	61.00
Drill Brace, Samson, Forward, Reverse, Wood Handle	85.00
Flax Hackle, Wood Base, Iron Spikes, Tin Floor, Punched Initials, Wood Cove, 13¼ In.	154.00
Froe, Riving, 15½ In.	88.00
Funnel, Candle Mold, 4 Tubes, 3½ In.	94.00
Garden Dibber, Bulb Planter, England, 16 In.	25.00
Gauge, Rotary, Brass, 3 Serpentine Spokes, Calibrated To 24 In., 13 In.	374.00
Hacksaw, Edison Steel Works, Triangular Frame, Steel Blade, Ohio, 18 In.	220.00
Hammer, Bill Poster's, A.R. Robertson, 2 Sections, Boston, 36 In.	143.00
Hammer, Claw, Belknap Hardware Co., Bluegrass, Louisville, 7 Oz., 11¼ In.	55.00
Hammer, Jeweler's, Turned Handle, Nickel Plated Head, 8¼ In.	248.00
Hammer, Log Marking, Fawn Foot Handle, Minnesota, 13 In.	143.00
Hammer, Watchmaker, Turned Handle, Stylized Imprints, 18th Century, 5 In.	275.00
Hatchet, GFSM, Tooled Circle, Scrolled Line, Intaglio Stamp, Wood Handle, 5⅝-In. Blade	165.00
Hayfork, Wood, Carved, 5 Tines, Mid To Late 19th Century, 69 x 30 In. *illus*	176.00
Holder, Scythe Stone, Carved Serpent, Folk Art, 19th Century, 10½ In.	220.00
Jack, Wagon, Iron Post, c.1770, 21 x 11 x 8 In.	374.00
Jack, Wagon, Old Red Paint, Initialed, C.B., 1873, 24 In.	303.00
Jointer, Pinwheel Design, Continental	688.00
Level, Carpenter's, Davis Level & Tool Co., Japanned, May 29, 1877, 6 In.	770.00
Level, Corey Chatburn, Rosewood, Brass, England, 9 In.	220.00
Level, Davis Level & Tool Co., Inclinometer, Cast Iron, Springfield, Mass., c.1867, 12 In. *illus*	138.00
Level, Keen Kutter, Cast Iron, 6 In.	3200.00
Level, L.L. Davis, Iron, Filigree, 12 In.	80.00
Level, L.L. Davis, Iron, Inclinometer, Filigree, 18 In.	180.00
Level, Sheffield, Inclinometer, Mahogany, Brass, Semicircular Brass Blade, 6 In.	413.00
Motor, Electric, General Electric Co., Iron Frame, Continuous Current, Pat. 1890 & 1903	375.00
Mouse Trap, Ketch-All, Kness Mfg. Co.	40.00
Needle Case, Shoemaker's, Brass, Prick Wheel, 18th Century	185.00
Padlock, Key, Steel, Pierced Brass Design, 18th Century, 6½ x 3¾ x ⅝ In.	880.00
Pitchfork, Wrought Iron, 3 Curved Tines, French Provincial, 78 In.	660.00
Plane, Carpenter, Wood, 1774	250.00
Plane, Compass, Blade, Rosewood, 1700s	200.00
Plane, Dado, Stanley, No. 39, Cast Iron, Japanned, ¼-In. Width, 8 In. *illus*	132.00
Plane, Jack, Bronze, Scalloped Edges, Pilot Wheel Adjustment Screw	2750.00
Plane, Jessop's, Best Wood Plane, Engraved Label, 8 x 2¾ In.	38.00
Plane, Jointer, E.E. Carpenter, Double Wedge, Penn., 22 In.	176.00
Plane, Millers Falls, No. 95	120.00
Plane, Molding, Davis Lamb & Co., Hollow, Petersburg, Va., c.1850, 9½ In.	220.00
Plane, Molding, E. Baldwin, Sash Coping, New Orleans, 9½ In.	248.00
Plane, Norris, No. 1., Rosewood, c.1935, 16½ In.	3950.00
Plane, Plow, Gleave, Wedge Arm, Handle, Oldham St., Manchester, England, 10 In.	132.00
Plane, Plow, Z.J. M'Master & Co., Ivory Tipped Screw Arms, Brass Thumb Screw, N.Y., 9 In.	660.00
Plane, Rabbet, Cabinet Maker's, Stanley, No. 94, Shoulder, Cast Iron, Nickel Plated, 1902, 7½ In.	358.00
Plane, Rabbet, Cast Iron, 3-Finger Grip, 1½ In.	105.00
Plane, Rabbet, George Weaver, Iron, Patented	900.00
Plane, Rabbet, Molding, E.W. Carpenter, Ship, Lancaster, Penn., 22½ In.	468.00
Plane, Rabbet, Stair Builder's, Ebony Handle, 5½ In.	413.00
Plane, Scraper, Stanley, No. 11½, Adjustable, Black Jappaned, 7½ In.	468.00
Plane, Smoothing, Brass Cutout Cap, Shield Shape, Scotland, 2¼ In.	198.00
Plane, Smoothing, Ellis H. Morris, Metallic, Diamond Pattern Sole, Nov. 9, 1870	3000.00
Plane, Smoothing, Ohio Tool Co., Cast Iron, Grain Painted Handles, 9 In.	44.00
Plane, Smoothing, Ohio Tool Company, No. 1C	11330.00
Plane, Smoothing, Tower & Lyon, No. 1205, Chaplin's Patent, N.Y., 9 In.	83.00
Plumb Bob, Brass, Screw In Keeper, Winding Reel, String, 3½ In.	165.00
Plumb Bob, Brass, Turnip Shape, Engraved Decoration, Iron Point, 19th Century, 9 In. *illus*	374.00

T

Polishing Wheel, Treadle Operated, Cast Iron, Oak Top, 19th Century, 44 In.	198.00
Rake Tooth Maker, Harry Wehler, Wood, Dover, Penn., 8½ In.	143.00
Reamer, Bung Hole, Cooper's, Brass, Removable Cutting Iron, 16 In.	165.00
Router, Brass Face Plate, Wing Nut, 7 In.	44.00
Rule, Folding, 6-Fold, Bone, Hand Engraved, Original Shagreen Case, England, c.1740	550.00
Rule, Folding, E.C. Simmons Hardware Co., Brass Bound, St. Louis, Mo., 24 In.	55.00
Rule, Folding, Stanley, No. 83C, 4-Fold, Caliper, 24 In.	110.00
Rule, Rope Gauge, J.D. Ainsley, Boxwood, Imprinted Scales, Brass Caliper, England, 3½ In.	105.00
Rule, Stanley, No. 212, Boxwood, Brass Slide, 5 In.	66.00
Saw, Bow, Model, Rosewood Stretcher, Swan Neck Finials, 9 In.	330.00
Saw, Bow, Turned Arms & Fittings, Carved Ivory Finial On Stretcher, 18th Century	1870.00
Saw, Hand, Richardson Bros., Universal Depth Gauge, Attached 1922 Patent	280.00
Saw, Hand, Winchester, No. 40, Old Trusty, Wood Handle, 26 In.	70.00
Saw, Pattern Maker's, E.C. Atkins & Co., Indiana, 7½-In. Cutting Edge, 11 In.	193.00
Saw, Tenon, Sargent & Company, Conn., 12 In.	143.00
Scraper, Chair Makers, Rosewood, Bone Wear Plates, 12 In.	66.00
Screwdriver, H.D. Smith Company, Triple Lever, Perfect Handle Brand, Conn., 9 In.	358.00
Shaving Horse, Oak, Fitted Round Legs, 19th Century, 60 In.	121.00
Shears, Tailor's, T. Wilkinson & Son, Brass, Knurled Adjustment Screws, Sheffield, 14 In.	99.00
Shovel, Brass, Hardwood Handle, 3¼ x 12 In.	60.00
Slick, B. Arnold, 392 Madison St., N.Y., 4 In.	125.00
Slide Rule, Caliper, Ebony, English & Metric Graduations, 11 In.	66.00
Snuffer, Scissor, Pickwick, Silver Plated, 9½ In.	330.00
Spokeshave, Stanley, No. 76, Razor Edge, Cast Iron, Nickel Plated, 1905, 11 In.	154.00
Square, Try, Stanley, Hand-Y Feature, Machinist's, Rosewood Frame, 11½ In.	50.00
Tape Measure, Car Shape, Red, Gold Color, 1920s, 2½ In.	153.00
Tire Repair Kit, Michelin, Trepan, Sliding Lid, Wood Box, France, c.1920, 9 x 2¼ x 3 In.	321.00
Tobacco Slicer, Cupples Co., Arrow, 18 In.	88.00
Tongs, Blacksmith's, Handwrought Iron, 1780s, 35 In.	50.00
Trammel, Steel, Wheat Basket, Animals, Pierced Crest, Brass, Adjustable, 1790, 34½ x 16 In.	1035.00
Trammel, Wrought Iron, Brass, Ratchet Mechanism, Pinwheel, Openwork, 1700s, 36½ In.	43.00
Trimmer, Wick, Scissors, Cast Iron, 5¹³⁄₁₆ In.	19.00
Wagon Ax Holder, Fish Shape, Conestoga, 9¾ In.	3276.00
Wagon Jack, Conestoga, Punch Work Decoration, Orange Painted Shaft, c.1812, 22 In.	220.00
Wagon Jack, Conestoga, Punch Work Decoration, Painted Shaft, c.1893, 22 In.	121.00
Wagon Jack, Conestoga, Punch Work Decoration, Red Painted Shaft, c.1804, 22 In.	275.00
Wagon Jack, Red Paint, Marked 1770, 21 x 11 In. ....*illus*	575.00
Wagon Jack, Punch Work Decoration, Painted Shaft, Marked Tobias Stove, c.1790, 22 In.	495.00
Wheel Traveler, Bronze, Rapson Mfg., Bad Axe, Mich., 12¾ In.	523.00
Workbench, Engraver's, Pine, Maple, Mahogany, 4 Drawers, Lidded Section, 40 x 42½ In.	460.00
Wrench, Combination, Pipe, Nut, Bemis & Call Company, S-Shaped Handle, Mass., 6 In.	385.00
Wrench, Keen Kutter, Crescent Type, Adjustable, 4 In.	175.00
Wrench, Nut, Canuck Tool Company, Pivot Head Self Adjustable, Toronto, 10 In.	204.00
Wrench, Nut, Yemco, Quick Adjust, Push Button Release, Penn., 8 In.	88.00
Yoke, Oxen, Painted, Carved, Iron Tack Eyes, String Tails, 5 In., Pair	411.00

TOOTHBRUSH HOLDERS were part of every bowl and pitcher set in the late nineteenth century. Most were oblong covered dishes. About 1920, manufacturers started to make children's toothbrush holders shaped like animals or cartoon characters. A few modern toothbrush holders are still being made.

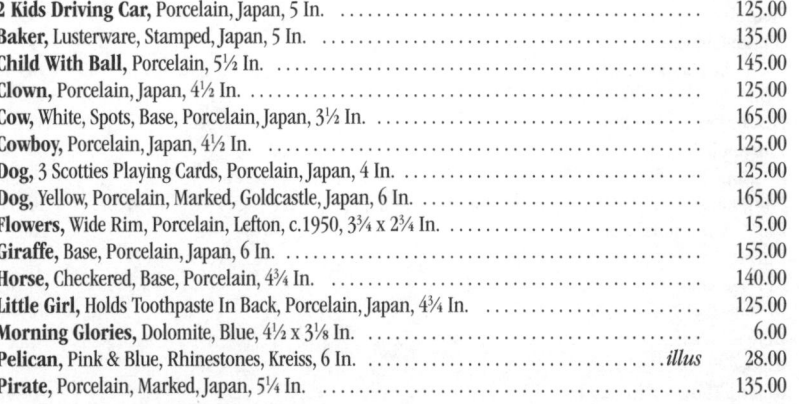

2 Kids Driving Car, Porcelain, Japan, 5 In.	125.00
Baker, Lusterware, Stamped, Japan, 5 In.	135.00
Child With Ball, Porcelain, 5½ In.	145.00
Clown, Porcelain, Japan, 4½ In.	125.00
Cow, White, Spots, Base, Porcelain, Japan, 3½ In.	165.00
Cowboy, Porcelain, Japan, 4½ In.	125.00
Dog, 3 Scotties Playing Cards, Porcelain, Japan, 4 In.	125.00
Dog, Yellow, Porcelain, Marked, Goldcastle, Japan, 6 In.	165.00
Flowers, Wide Rim, Porcelain, Lefton, c.1950, 3¾ x 2¾ In.	15.00
Giraffe, Base, Porcelain, Japan, 6 In.	155.00
Horse, Checkered, Base, Porcelain, 4¾ In.	140.00
Little Girl, Holds Toothpaste In Back, Porcelain, Japan, 4¾ In.	125.00
Morning Glories, Dolomite, Blue, 4½ x 3⅛ In.	6.00
Pelican, Pink & Blue, Rhinestones, Kreiss, 6 In. ....*illus*	28.00
Pirate, Porcelain, Marked, Japan, 5¼ In.	135.00

Stanley Tools
Before 1920 there were two companies using the Stanley name. Stanley's Bolt Manufactory in New Britain, Connecticut, founded in 1843 by brothers Frederick and William Stanley. The company was incorporated in 1852 as The Stanley Works.

Augustus, Timothy, and Gad Stanley and Thomas Conklin founded A. Stanley & Company in New Britain in 1854.

After mergers they became The Stanley Works in 1920. It is now The Stanley Tools Division of The Stanley Work in New Britain, Connecticut.

Tool, Plumb Bob, Brass, Turnip Shape, Engraved Decoration, Iron Point, 19th Century, 9 In.
$374.00

Tool, Wagon Jack, Red Paint, Marked 1770, 21 x 11 In.
$575.00

T

Toothbrush Holder, Pelican, Pink & Blue, Rhinestones, Kreiss, 6 In.
$28.00

Toothbrush Holder, Skippy, Bisque, 6 In.
$225.00

Toothpick Holders and Other Small Containers

Toothpick holders can be confused with other small vaselike containers, such as match holders, shot glasses, unlidded mustard pots, tiny rose bowls, individual open sugars or salt dips, small vases, or even toy spoon holders.

- If a toy-set pattern was also made in a full-sized table setting, then the mold for the toy spooner would be used for the full-sized toothpick holder.
- Small match holders are often figurals; toothpicks are not. Match holders usually have a corrugated surface area for striking matches and are usually shorter.

Rabbit, Standing, Holding 2 Carrots, Marked, Goldcastle, 6⅜ In.	145.00
Rush Flowers, Peaches, Magenta, Purple, Blue, 3 Bay, RS Prussia, 4 x 4 In.	125.00
Satin Glass, Hand Painted, Violet Leaves	20.00
Scholar, Porcelain, Marked, Japan, 5¾ In.	125.00
Skeezix, Listerine, Tin, Box, 1930s	350.00
Skippy, Bisque, 6 In. ....*illus*	225.00
Wild Bill Hickok, Die Cut, 2 Brushes, Aluminum Holsters, 1950s, 5 In.	185.00

TOOTHPICK HOLDERS are sometimes called "toothpicks" by collectors. The variously shaped containers used to hold small wooden toothpicks are made of glass, china, or metal. Most of the toothpick holders are Victorian. Additional items may be found in other categories, such as Bisque, Silver Plate, Slag Glass, etc.

Amberina, 3-Sided	195.00
Amberina, Coin Spot, Hat Shape, 2¼ In.	978.00
Amberina, Diamond Quilted, Trifold Rim	299.00
Beaded Ovals, Sand	135.00
Beatty Waffle, Blue Opalescent	30.00
Beveled Star, Green	125.00
Bohemian, Gold Trim, Cranberry Glass	319.00
Bull's-Eye & Star, Rose Stain On Rim	30.00
Burmese Glass, Art Deco Decoration, 6-Point Piecrust Rim, Webb	399.00
Burmese Glass, Bulbous, Square Rim, Mt. Washington	329.00
Burmese Glass, Bulbous, Square Rim, Webb	379.00
Burmese Glass, Diamond Quilted, Glossy, Trifold Rim	399.00
Carnation	35.00
Carnival Glass, Green, Fluted	35.00
Carnival Glass, Marigold, Fluted	25.00
Cased Glass, Rose, Rigaree Trim	225.00
Chrysanthemum Leaf, Clear, Gold Trim	175.00
Colonial Ware, Delft, Hat Shape, Mt. Washington	475.00
Columbian Coin, Pressed Glass, Clear, Ruby Stain	150.00
Delaware, Green, Gold Trim	55.00
Devil, Footed	75.00
Essex, Clear, Alternating Frosted Panels	55.00
Green Opaque, Gold & Amethyst Staining, Gold Scalloped Band, Pinched Waist, 2 In.	230.00
Heavy Drape, Clear, Gold Trim	100.00
Heisey, Prison Stripe, Clear	225.00
Heisey, Queen Anne, Clear	550.00
Heisey, Sunburst, Clear, Gold Trim	60.00
Horse With Cart, Blue	155.00
Idyll, Apple Green	175.00
Indian Chief, Custard ....*illus*	18.00
Intaglio Sunflower, Green, Gold Trim	95.00
Kittens, Blue Slag Glass, 2 x 1¾ In.	15.00
Kittens, Carnival Glass, Marigold	65.00
Kittens, Carnival Glass, Purple	150.00
Lacy Medallion, Green	25.00
Madame Bovary, Ruby Stain	230.00
Man With Basket, Silver Plate, James Tufts	200.00
Manila, Wreath & Shell, Blue Opalescent	235.00
Meander, Blue, Opalescent, 2 In.	52.50
Opaline, Blue, 3¾ In.	95.00
Pairpoint, Buffalo	160.00
Pansy, Pink	150.00
Peachblow, Square Rim	399.00
Pineapple & Fan	99.00
Pleating, Ruby Stain	95.00
Pomona, Frosted, Amber Tricornered Rim, 2nd Grind	169.00
Punty & Diamond Point	280.00
Purple, Carnival Glass, Fluted	35.00
Reverse Amberina, Diamond Quilted, 2 In.	259.00
Reverse Swirl, Blue, Speckled	129.00
Ribbed Drape, Flowers	95.00
Ribbed Spiral, Opalescent	100.00
Ribbed Thumbprint, Custard	89.00

T

Royal Doulton, Welsh Ladies	105.00
RS Prussia, Flowers, Ribbed, Flared, 3 Handles	135.00
RS Prussia, Lily, White, Green, Ribbed, Flared & Scalloped Rim, 2 Handles	145.00
Rubina, Royal Ivy ....*illus*	59.00
Scalloped Skirt, Cranberry, Enameled Decoration	100.00
Shoshone, Clear, Ruby Stain	180.00
Squirrel On Stump, 3½ x 2¼ In.	50.00
Sterling Silver, Umbrella	45.00
Tokyo, Green Opalescent	210.00
Tramp's Shoe, Milk Glass, 1890	45.00
Urn, Fiery Opalescent	55.00
Vermont, Ivory Opaque	59.00
Victoria, Ruby Stain	220.00
Wave Crest, Flowers, Petal Rim	135.00
White, Amber Overlay, Ruffled Rim, Silver Openwork Stand	235.00
Wreath Shell, Blue Opalescent	245.00

TORTOISESHELL is the shell of the tortoise. It has been used as inlay and to make small decorative objects since the seventeenth century. Some species of tortoise are now on the endangered species list, and old or new objects made from these shells cannot be sold legally.

Box, Brass, England, 19th Century, ¾ x 1⅝ In.	234.00
Box, Lid, Red Amber, Coiled Dragon, Engraved, Felt Lined, Late 18th Century	135.00
Calendar, Desk, Silver Mounted, Marked, London, 1922, 3¾ In.	171.00
Comb, Spanish Style, Faux, Green Rhinestones	75.00
Glasses, Wood Case, 4½ & 5¼ In.	350.00
Glove Stretcher, Gold Monogram	200.00
Prayer Book, Missal, Gold Edged Pages, In Spanish, 1800s, 5 x 3¾ x 1¼ In.	550.00
Shoehorn, 4¼ x 1⅞ In.	27.00
Tatting Shuttle, 2 In.	18.00

TOY collectors have special clubs, magazines, and shows. Toys are designed to entice children, and today they have attracted new interest among adults who are still children at heart. All types of toys are collected. Tin toys, iron toys, battery operated toys, and many others are collected by specialists. Dolls, Games, Teddy Bears, and Bicycles are listed in their own categories. Other toys may be found under company or celebrity names.

Accident Reconstruction Set, Chalkboard Base, Magnetic, Wood Case, 1952, 35 Piece	135.00
Acrobat Marvel, Metal, Windup, USA, 1930s, 13 In.	225.00
Acrobatic Monkeys, Windup, Wyandott, 10 In.	295.00
Action Figure, Alan Carter, Space:1999, Red Suit, Boots, Mego	49.00
Action Figure, Alien, Plastic, Kenner, Box, 1979, 18 In.	399.00
Action Figure, Aquaman, Yellow & Green Outfit, Mego, 1979, 8 In.	4480.00
Action Figure, Ben Cartwright, American Character, Box, 1966, 8 In.	277.00
Action Figure, Cylon Centurion, Mattel, Blister Card, 1978, 4¼ In.	45.00
Action Figure, Doug Davis, Posable, Mattel, On Card, 1968, 6 In.	136.00
Action Figure, James Bond, 7, Thunderball, Unopened, A.C. Gilbert, Box, 1965, 12 In.	928.00
Action Figure, Janice West, Accessories, Marx, Box, c.1967, 9 In.	84.00
Action Figure, Oddjob, Karate Outfit, James Bond, Unopened, A.C. Gilbert, Box, 1965, 10½ In.	468.00
Aerial Derrick, Pressed Steel, Buddy L, 1930s, 43 In.	605.00
Aero Circus, Cast Iron Blimp, Wood Planes, Newton Mfg., Box, c.1931, 36 In.	825.00
Aero Swing, Tin, Lever, 4 Litho Cars, Child Riders, Music Plays, Chein, Box, 12 In.	440.00
Air Combat Squadron, 5 Airplanes, Hubley, Box, 1958, 12 x 21 x 3 In.	708.00
Air Control Tower, Tin, Battery Operated, Chrome Plate Plane, Helicopter, Box, 30 In.	248.00
Airliner, Viscount Capital, 4 Engine, Battery Operated Remote, Linemar, Box, 14 In.	220.00
Airplane, 3 Motors, Pressed Steel, Metalcraft, 14-In. Wingspan	132.00
Airplane, 4 Engine, Cast Iron, Silver, Red Props, Rubber Tires, Hubley, 5½ In.	165.00
Airplane, Aero Dawn, Spirit Of St. Louis, Tootsietoy, c.1928, 3¾-In. Wingspan	150.00
Airplane, Air Cruiser, Pressed Steel, Red & White, 4 Engine, Buddy L, 26 In.	403.00
Airplane, Airliner, Red, Nickeled Wings, Wingspan, Hubley, 5¾ In.	250.00
Airplane, Airmail, Single Engine, Opening Side Door, Yellow, Red, Keystone, 1920s, 25 In.	690.00
Airplane, Airmail, Sit-N-Ride, Pressed Steel, White & Red, Side Door, Keystone, 1930s, 24 In.	1955.00
Airplane, American Airlines, Electra, Friction, Tin Litho, Battery Operated, 21-In. Wingspan	77.00
Airplane, American Airlines, Tin Lithograph, Battery Operated, 16-In. Wingspan	66.00
Airplane, American Airlines, Tin Lithograph, Plastic, Battery Operated, 19-In. Wingspan	339.00
Airplane, Amphibian, Wing Mounted Props, Pontoons, Clockwork, Bing, 16-In. Wingspan	1480.00
Airplane, Army Scout, Orange & Green, Decals, Steelcraft, 1920s, 22 In.	375.00

Toothpick,
Indian Chief, Custard
$18.00

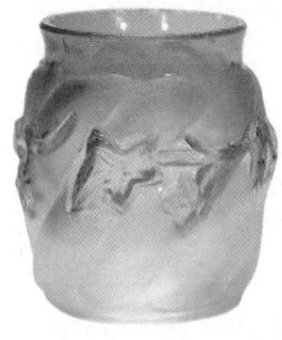

Toothpick, Rubina,
Royal Ivy
$59.00

Toy, Airplane, Bremen Junker, Ribbed
Fuselage, Embossed Wings,
Cast Iron, Green, 10 In.
$6325.00

Toy, Airplane, Dox, 6 Engines
On Ribbed Wing, Nickel-Plated Tires,
Hubley, 7½ In.
$9200.00

Toy, Airplane, Fighter, Navy,
American Eagle, Blue & Red, Hubley,
Box, 10½ In.
$115.00

Toy, Airplane, Lindy, Cast Iron,
Gray Paint, Embossed Wings,
Disc Wheels, Hubley, 10 In.
$978.00

Toy, Airplane, Spirit Of St. Louis,
Felt-Covered Pilot, Tin, Friction,
Schuco, 4 In.
$995.00

Toy, Airplane, Tat, Cast Iron, Ribbed
Wings, Green & Yellow Paint, Embossed,
Kilgore, 13½ In.
$3450.00

Airplane, Army Scout, Steelcraft, Pressed Steel, 1930s, 22½ In.	303.00
Airplane, Big Boy, Tin, Katz No. 337, 27 In.	144.00
Airplane, Biplane, Aero Dawn, Tootsietoy, c.1928	115.00
Airplane, Bremen Junker, Ribbed Fuselage, Embossed Wings, Cast Iron, Green, 10 In. . . *illus*	6325.00
Airplane, Cast Iron, Pressed Steel, Wood Wheels, 1941, 10-In. Wingspan	300.00
Airplane, Constellation, Silver, White, Metal, Tootsietoy	100.00
Airplane, Dox, 6 Engines On Ribbed Wing, Nickel-Plated Tires, Hubley, 7½ In. . . . . . *illus*	9200.00
Airplane, Fighter, Navy, American Eagle, Blue & Red, Hubley, Box, 10½ In. . . . . *illus*	115.00
Airplane, Ford Trimotor, Tin Friction, Nomura, Box, 14¾ In.	1485.00
Airplane, Ford Trimotor Airliner, Silver, Tootsietoy	275.00
Airplane, Gyroplane, Red, Rubber Tires, Hubley, 4½ In.	275.00
Airplane, Junker, Bremen, D1167, Passengers, Props Spin, Iron, Hubley, 10-In. Wingspan	2800.00
Airplane, Lady Luck, Pressed Steel, Green & Orange, 17 In.	259.00
Airplane, Lindy, Cast Iron, Gray Paint, Embossed Wings, Disc Wheels, Hubley, 10 In. . . . *illus*	978.00
Airplane, Lockheed Siris, Tin Wing, Purple Wheels, Prop, Tootsietoy	125.00
Airplane, Looping Plane, Man In Cockpit, Windup, Tin Lithograph, Marx, Box, 7½ In.	385.00
Airplane, Loopo, Tin, Windup, Flips, Japan	225.00
Airplane, Military Transport, C-124, Lights, Doors Open, Vehicle Inside, Japan, 7 Co., 20 In.	775.00
Airplane, Mono Coupe, Cast Iron, Pressed Steel, Nickel Plated Propeller, 7-In. Wingspan	495.00
Airplane, Mono Coupe, Cast Iron, Pressed Steel, Nickel Plated Propeller, 10½-In. Wingspan	825.00
Airplane, Navy, Landing Gear, Rubber Tires, Red, Green, Blue Over Silver, Hubley, 5 In.	115.00
Airplane, Night, Tin Plate, No. 220, Schieble, 29 x 27 In.	411.00
Airplane, P-47 Thunderbolt, Turning Prop, Cap Firing, Tin, Friction, Frankonia, Box, 5½ In.	72.00
Airplane, Pan American World Airways, Metal, Friction, Gama, Germany, 20-In. Wingspan	225.00
Airplane, Pressed Steel, White Rubber Tires, Wyandotte, 10½-In. Wingspan	50.00
Airplane, Seaplane, Sea Gull, Cream, Green, Cast Iron, Kilgore, 4¼-In. Wingspan	735.00
Airplane, Silver Eagle, Windup, Automatic Toy Co., Box, 1930, 13-In. Wingspan	295.00
Airplane, Sirius, Pressed Steel, Dark Red & Cream, Steelcraft Lockheed, 1920s, 22 In.	1035.00
Airplane, Sky Bolt, Tin Litho, Trigger Action, Plastic Rockets, Cragstan, Box, Japan, 1960s	92.00
Airplane, Spirit Of St. Louis, Felt-Covered Pilot, Tin, Friction, Schuco, 4 In. . . . . *illus*	995.00
Airplane, Spirit Of St. Louis, Tin, Windup, Lithograph, Chein, 6½ In.	330.00
Airplane, Stratocruiser, Silver, White, Metal, Tootsietoy	135.00
Airplane, Tat, Cast Iron, Ribbed Wings, Green & Yellow, Embossed, Kilgore, 13½ In. . . . *illus*	3450.00
Airplane, Transport, 4 Engine, Pressed Steel, Black, Yellow Body, Buddy L, 1940s, 27 In.	260.00
Airplane, U.S. Army, Blue, Silver, Folding Wheels, Metal, Hubley, 1939, 8-In. Wingspan	150.00
Airplane, U.S. Army Stars, No. NX 130, Steelcraft, 24 x 23 In.	382.00
Airplane, U.S. Mail, Tri-Motor, Black & Orange, Steelcraft, 24 In.	920.00
Airplane, U.S. Mail, Tri-Motor, White, Side Door, Pressed Steel, Steelcraft, 26 In.	1035.00
Airplane, United-Boeing Airliner, Green, Nickel Plate, Arcade, 5-In. Wingspan	275.00
Airplane, UX166, Cast Iron, Hubley, 6 In.	195.00
Airport, Wood, Cast Iron Flag, Airplanes, Arcade, 12 In.	990.00
Airport Set, Doepke, Die Cast, Pressed Steel, Rubber Tires, 1950s, 27½ In.	468.00
Airship, Silver, Nickeled Wheels, Dent, 4½ In.	175.00
Alabama Coon Jigger, Lehmann, 1912, 9 In.	475.00
Alabama Roof Dancer, Tombo, Tin, Windup, Strauss	1380.00
Alley Alligator, Rubber, Battery Operated, Marx, 18 In.	475.00
Alligator, Native Boy On Top, Windup, Tin Lithograph, Chein, 15 In.	165.00
Alligator, Wood, Jointed, Ball Socket Tail & Head, Carved Mouth, Schoenhut, 12¾ In.	220.00
Ambulance, 2 Horses, Tin Lithograph, Meier, Germany, Penny, 4¾ In.	403.00
Ambulance, Ford, Tin, Friction, Japan, 1959, 9 In.	145.00
Ambulance, Mercedes, White, Labels, Stretcher, Matchbox, Box	17.00 to 51.00
Ambulance, Nickel Plating, Multicolored, Painted, Motorized, Kenton, 10 In.	805.00
Ambulance, Savoye, 4 In.	235.00
Ambulance, Steel, Opening Rear Door, Wood Wheels, Decals, Wyandotte, 11¼ In.	149.00
Ambulance, Tin, Friction, Lupor, 1950s, 7 In.	120.00
Ambulance, White, Red Crosses, Tin, Friction, Bandai, Japan, Box, 1960s, 7 In.	125.00
American Circus, Tin, Windup, Monkey Riders Move, Japan, 5¾ In.	303.00
Amos 'N' Andy, Walker, To-Night, In Person, Tin, Windup, Box, 12 In., 2 Piece	3300.00
Amos 'N' Andy, Walker, Windup, Marx	850.00
Animals, Man In Straw Hat, Jointed Bodies, 8 Animals, Schoenhut, 4½ In. To 8 In.	633.00
Armoire, Doll's, Wood, Green, Cream Painted, Shelves, Lace, Linens, France, 18 In.	840.00
Army Helmet, Prussian, Tootsietoy, 1909, 3½ In.	500.00
Astronaut, Super, Rotate-O-Matic, Battery Operated, Tin Litho, Horikawa, Box, 1960s, 11½ In.	140.00
Atomic Rocket, Woodette, Print-O-Matic, Plastic, Windup, Rocket Roar, Sparks, Box, 14½ In.	88.00
Auto Road 1000, Tin, Electric, Driving Toy, Plastic, Autobahn 1001, Box, 15 x 18 In.	248.00
Bake Set, Mother's Little Helper, A & J, Box, c.1920	75.00

Baler, Pressed Steel, John Deere, Box, 7 x 11 In.	353.00
Balky Mule, Clown, Cart, Tin, Windup, Lehmann, Germany, Box, 8 In.	385.00
Ballet Dancer, Tin Lithograph, Windup, Marx, Box, 6 In. *illus*	250.00
Balloon Vendor, Plastic, Tin, Clown, Rings Bell, Frankonia, Box, Japan, 1961, 10½ In. *illus*	230.00
Balloon Vendor, Tin, Windup, Distler, 6½ In.	650.00
Barn, Open, Wood, Animals, 12¾ In.	66.00
Barn, Open, Wood, Animals, Converse, 10½ In.	55.00
Barn, Red Robin, Wood, Accessories, Weather Vane, Converse, 19½ In.	495.00
Barn, Wood, Painted, Lithograph Cardboard Animals, 22 x 26½ x 18 In.	269.00
Barn, Wood, Ramp, Weather Vane, Animals, Converse, 20 In.	1650.00
Barnacle Bill, Floor Puncher, Tin, Windup, Celluloid Bag, Chein, 7 In.	935.00
Barnacle Bill, In Barrel, Tin, Windup, Chein, 7 In.	550.00
Barnacle Bill, Tin, Windup, Shuffles, Body Moves, Lithograph, Chein, 6 In.	165.00
Barnacle Bill, Walker, Tin, Windup, Chein, Box, 6 In.	660.00
Barney Google, On Wheeled Platform, Tin, Pull, 1920s	850.00
Barney Google, Riding Sparkplug, Red Wheels, Tin, Push, Nifty, Germany, 1924, 8 In.	450.00
Baseball Player, Mr. Baseball, Battery Operated, Japan, 7 In. *illus*	175.00
Bat, Eric, Mohair, Beige, Yellow, Excelsior Stuffed Body, Steiff, 1960s, 7 x 14½ In.	382.00
Bathtub, Doll's, Porcelain, Cast Iron, Speckled Blue, Handles, 17 In.	288.00
Bear, Barber, Battery Operated, Tin, Plush Heads, Linemar, Box, 8 In. *illus*	470.00
Bear, Blacksmith, Battery Operated, Box	350.00
Bear, Brown, Jointed, Leather Ears, Rope Tail, Glass Eyes, Neck, Schoenhut, 7½ In.	1210.00
Bear, Ironing, White, Mechanical, Windup	40.00
Bear, Jumping Jack, Carved, Glass Eyes, 8 In.	11.00
Bear, On Skis, Cloth Suit, Legs Move, Windup, 7 In.	195.00
Bear, Pa Pa Bear, Smokes, Walks, Remote Control, Japan, Box, 1930s	145.00
Bear, Panda, Smoking, Shoe Shining, Battery Operated, Alps, Box	275.00
Bear, Picnic Bear, Eyes Light-Up, Alps Of Japan, Box, 1950s	250.00
Bear, Smokey The Bear, In Jeep, Tin Lithograph, Battery Operated, TN, Japan, Box, 1950s	1123.00
Bear, Smokey The Bear, Talker, Pull Toy, Knickerbocker, 1960s	75.00
Bear, Smoking & Shoe Shining Bear, Battery Operated, Alps, Box, 10 In.	275.00
Bear, Somersaults, Celluloid, Windup, Occupied Japan, 6 In.	125.00
Bear, Spanking, 6 Actions, Noise, Battery Operated, Box, c.1950	285.00
Bear, The Shoemaker, Battery Operated, Box	350.00
Bear, Walks On 4 Legs, Head Moves, Fuzzy, Windup, Japan, 6 In.	95.00
Bear, Yes-No, Plush, Mohair, Jointed, Schuco, c.1930, 19 In. *illus*	440.00
Bears Are Also Listed In The Teddy Bears category.	
Bebop The Jiving Jigger, Marx, 10 In.	400.00
Bed, Doll's, Applied Hearts & Stars, Red Stripes, 18½ x 22 x 15 In.	120.00
Bed, Doll's, Fruitwood, Stencils, Sleigh Style, Charles X, France, c.1840, 19 In.	385.00
Bed, Doll's, Poster, Canopy, Shaped Headboard, Square Legs, Feet, 28 x 16½ x 27 In.	345.00
Bed, Doll's, Softwood, Arched Headboard, Footboard, Coverlet, Pillow, 11 x 10½ In.	132.00
Bee, Crawling, Lehmann, Box, 1900	250.00
Beetle, Crawling, Clockwork, Tin Litho, Moving Legs, Wings, Lehmann, EPL 431, Box	529.00
Bell Ringer, Harold Lloyd, Hat, Eyeglasses, Tin Lithograph, Germany, 6 In.	248.00
Bicycles That Are Large Enough To Ride are listed in their own category.	
Big Joe Chef, Tin, Windup, Japan, Box	165.00
Billiards Player, Blue Jacket, Holes In Table, Green, Red, Yellow, Windup, Germany, 6 In.	825.00
Billiards Player, Shooting Pool, Windup, Kico Co., Germany, 1920s, 6 In.	375.00
Billiards Player, Tin, Pool Shooter, Plaid Suit, Germany, 1920s, 7½ In.	440.00
Bird, Caged, Blue, Orange, Flocked, Mounted On Perch, Wire, Wood Cage, Squeak, 7¼ In.	500.00
Bird, Pik-Pik, Cloth Covered, Mechanical, Hops, Windup, Key, Schuco, Germany, Early 1900s	85.00
Black Man Playing Banjo, Painted, Tin, Windup, Gunthermann, Germany, 9 In.	305.00
Blocks, Alphabet, Pictures, Paper On Wood, Nesting, Germany, 6 Blocks, 2¾ In. Largest	303.00
Blocks, Baby Bunting ABC, Pictures, Paper On Wood, Germany, 5 Blocks, 4¼ In. Largest	220.00
Boat, 2 Masts, Flag, Tin, Windup, G & K, Germany, 12 In. *illus*	878.00
Boat, B-619, Tin, Crank, B Japan, 1950	175.00
Boat, Battleship, USS Washington, Gun Sparks, Tin, Windup, Marx, 15 In.	265.00
Boat, Big Wood, Flying Yankee, Windup, USA, 1920, 18 In.	575.00
Boat, Cabin Cruiser, Princess Pat, Tin, Windup, Deck Litho, Chein, Box, 15 In.	138.00
Boat, Celluloid, Clockwork, Windup, Fairy Craft, 18½ In.	215.00
Boat, Cruise Ship, Windup, Fleischmann, U.S. Zone, Germany, 20½ In.	495.00
Boat, Excursion, M-1024, Sun Roof, Tin, Crank, Japan, 1950s, 10 In.	145.00
Boat, Fly Wheel Driven, Germany, c.1915, 7 In.	185.00
Boat, Flying Yankee, Seaworthy, 1920, 20 In.	600.00
Boat, Motor, Diamond, Electric, Tin, Battery Operated, 50s Colors, Yonezawa, Box, 8 In.	110.00

Toy, Ballet Dancer, Tin Lithograph, Windup, Marx, Box, 6 In. $250.00

Toy, Balloon Vendor, Plastic, Tin, Clown, Rings Bell, Frankonia, Box, Japan, 1961, 10½ In. $230.00

Toy, Baseball Player, Mr. Baseball, Battery Operated, Japan, 7 In. $175.00

T

Toy, Bear, Barber, Battery Operated, Tin, Plush Heads, Linemar, Box, 8 In. $470.00

Toy, Bear, Yes-No, Plush, Mohair, Jointed, Schuco, c.1930, 19 In. $440.00

Boat, Ocean Liner, 2 Stacks, Flags, Rudder, Tin, Windup, Marklin, 1920s, 16 In. . . . . . .*illus*	2475.00
Boat, Ocean Liner, Red, Black, White, Yellow, Tin, Windup, Fleischmann, Germany, 14 In. . . .	225.00
Boat, Pop Pop, Metal, TK Japan, Box, 1950, 4½ In.	55.00
Boat, Putt Putt, Metal, Windup, Box, USA, 1930s, 5 In.	75.00
Boat, Putt Putt, PT 10, Marx, Box, 9½ In.	425.00
Boat, Rowboat, Painted, Man, Cloth, Fabric, Mustache, Clockwork Mechanism, 11 In.	1208.00
Boat, Sail, Wood Hull, Cass, 1930-40, 16 In.	110.00
Boat, Speed, Metal, Battery Operated, M.S.K., Japan, 16½ In.	475.00
Boat, Speedboat, Battery Operated, 2 Engines, Black, Red, Wood, Japan, c.1950, 18 In.	295.00
Boat, Speedboat, Battery Operated, Zoom, Japan, 1950s, 10 In.	145.00
Boat, Speedboat, Driver, A-35, Crank, Tin, San Japan, 1950s, 10½ In.	95.00
Boat, Speedboat, Driver, No. 36, Metal, Crank, Japan, 1950s, 10 In.	245.00
Boat, Speedboat, Sea Bear, Battery Operated, Japan, 1950s, 10 In.	225.00
Boat, Speedboat, Tin, Battery Operated Remote, Nikko Toy, Box, 7 In.	110.00
Boat, Torpedo, Remote Control, Tin, Linemar, Japan, 1950s, 11½ In.	175.00
Boat, Tugboat, Battery Operated, Engine Sound, Turning Prop, Puffs Smoke, Box, 12½ In. . .	178.00
Boat, Wood, Pressed Steel, Battery Operated, Motor, Box, 12 In.	303.00
Boat Pilot, Harbor Department, Tin Crank, Litho Driver, Bandai, Box, 10½ In.	220.00
Boob McNutt, Walker, Black Jacket, Red Pants, Yellow Hat, Tin, Windup, Strauss, 9 In.	385.00
Bop Bag, Kukla, Inflatable, Vinyl, Burr Tillstrom, 1954, 20 In.	112.00
Bowling Alley, Pressed Tin, Felt Top, 12 In.	11.00
Boxer, Knockout Champs, Celluloid, Windup, Metal Ring, Box, 1930s	750.00
Boxer Rebellion, 4 Chinese Figures, Canopy, Clockwork, Lehmann, Germany, 1900s, 5 In. . .	19040.00
Boy, Being Bitten On Seat By Dog, Celluloid, Windup, Occupied Japan	350.00
Boy On Bicycle, Enameled, White Tires, Blue Spokes, Chain Driven Motor, Gunthermann, 8 In. .	978.00
Boy Riding Pig, Composition, Boy Has Celluloid Head, Goes Up & Down, Germany, 7 In. *illus*	878.00
Bozo, Tin, Windup, Rocks Back & Forth, Alps, Box, 8 In.	387.00
Bucket Loader, Pressed Steel, Buddy L, 24 In.	495.00
Buffalo, Wood, Jointed, Cloth Mane, Leather Ears, Glass Eyes, Style I, Schoenhut, 8 In.	285.00
Bull, Papier-Mache, Pull, Germany, Early 1900s, 31 In.	3200.00
Bulldozer, Climbing, Sparkling, Tin, Windup, Rubber Treads, Marx, Box, 10½ In.	220.00
Bullwinkle Magic Color Kit, Gold Medal Flour Premium, 1962, 5½ x 7½ In., 8 Pages	199.00
Bullwinkle Super Slate, Unused, Ward, Saalfield, c.1960, 14 x 8½ In.	93.00
Bump Ball, Milton Bradley, Box, 1968	35.00
Burro, Wood, Jointed, Leather Ears, Rope Tail, Painted Eyes, Schoenhut, 7 In. . . . .*illus*	248.00
Bus, 7 Figures On Top, Green, Red, White Tires, Kenton, 1927, 12 In.	3360.00
Bus, Airporter, Lights, Battery Operated, Linemar, Box, 10 In.	145.00
Bus, Camping, Volkswagon, Tin, Friction, Yonezawa, Box, 9 In.	358.00
Bus, Cast Iron, Painted Red, Fageol, A.C. Williams, Ravenna, Oh., c.1930, 7¾ In.	196.00
Bus, Coast To Coast, Orange, Silver, Rubber Ties, 2 Piece, Barclay, c.1938, 2⅛ In.	95.00
Bus, Double-Decker, Cast Iron, 7½ In.	39.00
Bus, Double-Decker, Cast Iron, Arcade, 1939, 8 In. . . . . 450.00 to 595.00
Bus, Double-Decker, City, Red, Kenton, 6½ In.	650.00
Bus, Double-Decker, Driver, Yellow, Green, Gold Trim, Coach, Arcade, 14 In.	3500.00
Bus, Double-Decker, London, Green, Gold Radiator, Matchbox	7055.00
Bus, Double-Decker, London, Plastic Wheels, Players Please, No. 5B, Matchbox, Box . . .*illus*	216.00
Bus, Double-Decker, Staircase, Strauss, Box, 11 In.	1265.00
Bus, Dream, Avenue Bus, Tin, Friction, Daiya, Box, 9½ In.	110.00
Bus, Driver, Bus De Luxe, No. 105, Light Blue, Tin, Strauss, 13 In.	672.00
Bus, Fageol, Arcade, 8 In.	495.00
Bus, G.M. Coach Passenger, Tin, Battery Operated, Mystery Action, Yonezawa, Box, 16 In. . . .	193.00
Bus, Glacier Park Transportation, Retro Toy Company, Pressed Steel, 30 In.	523.00
Bus, GMC, Coast To Coast, Arcade, 9 In.	350.00
Bus, Greyhound, Blue, White, Tootsietoy, 9 In.	135.00
Bus, Greyhound, Cruiser Coach, Silversides, Arcade, 1941, 9¼ In.	475.00
Bus, Greyhound, Metal, Battery Operated, Japan, 1950s, 7 In.	95.00
Bus, Greyhound, New York, Tin, Friction, Cragstan, 9 In.	135.00
Bus, Greyhound, Tin Litho, Door Opens, Driver, Cragstan, Japan, Box, 1960s, 11½ In.	213.00
Bus, Greyhound, World's Fair, Arcade, 1939, 7 In.	375.00
Bus, Greyhound Lines, Tin, Friction, Black Passenger In Back, Marusan, 12½ In.	248.00
Bus, Greyhound Super Coach, Arcade, c.1937, 9 In. . . . . 385.00 to 425.00
Bus, Inter-State, Driver, Green, Yellow, Red, Tin, Windup, Strauss, 10 In.	385.00
Bus, Inter-State Bus, Tin Lithograph, Windup, Strauss, 10 In. . . . .*illus*	410.00
Bus, Magic Greyhound, Tin Lithograph, KTS, Japan, Box, 1950s, 10¾ In.	290.00
Bus, Metal, Friction, Argentina, 1950s, 12 In.	295.00
Bus, National Park Excursion Bus, Bluebird, Tin, Friction, Tin Litho, Daiya, Box, 14 In.	154.00

Bus, Red, A.C. Williams, 5 In.	155.00
Bus, School Bus System, No. 15, Metal, Friction, Japan, 11 In.	75.00
Bus, Sightseeing, Runs On Zigzag Highway, Metal, Windup, T.P.S., Japan, Box	75.00
Bus, Super Coach, Tin, Friction, GM Super Scenicruiser, Lithograph, Nomura, 21 In.	193.00
Bus, Tin, Windup, No.590, Steerable Front Wheels, Tin Wheels, Lehmann, 8 In.	1150.00
Bus, Volkswagen, Tin, Battery Operated, Vinyl Driver, Bandai, Box, 9½ In.	633.00
Bus, Wolverine Express, Metal, Push Down Action, Box, 1950s, 14 In.	275.00
Bus, Yellow Coach, Green & Gold, Arcade, 14 In.	3500.00
Busy Bridge, Cars Move On Bridge, Tin, Windup, Marx, 24 In.	275.00
Buttercup, Crawls, Red Shirt, Blue Shorts, Tin Litho, Windup, Germany, Box, 1925, 8 In.	1792.00
Buttercup & Spareribs, Buttercup Hits Sparerib With Broom, Platform, Tin, Chein, 8 In.	724.00
Cabinet, Kitchen, Arcade Boone, Cast Iron, Pressed Steel, 8 In.	770.00
Cabinette, Hubley, Cast Iron, Pressed Steel, 7½ In.	330.00
Call Me Baby, Infant, Crawls, Talks, Battery Operated, Rosko Toy *illus*	71.00
Calvaryman, Mounted, With Cannon, Carrying Sword, Tin, Windup, T.P.S., Box, 5 In.	330.00
Camel, Arabian, Hump, Wood, Jointed, Leather Ears, Rope Tail, Glass Eyes, Schoenhut, 9 In.	550.00
Camel, Bactrian, 2 Humps, Wood, Jointed, Rope Tail, Painted Eyes, Schoenhut, 7 In.	330.00
Camel, Mohair, Brown, 2-Humps, Pull, Cast Iron Wheels, Steiff, 10 x 13 In.	385.00
Camera, Brenda Starr Cub Reporter, Plastic, Seymore Products Co., 1950s, 5 x 2½ In.	375.00
Camper, 5th Wheel, Tonka, Box, 1960s	375.00
Campus Queen, Girl Driving Tractor, Marx, 5¼ In.	350.00
Canary Cage, Canary Peeks, Lever, 4 Colors, Tin Litho, Penny Toy, Meier, Germany, 3 In.	83.00
Cannon, Bronze, 19th Century, 31 In.	5378.00
Cannon, Bronze, 19th Century, 34 In.	5975.00
Cannon, Howitzer, Mounted For Field Service, 2 Loader, Shells, Britains, Box, 18 In.	112.00
Cap Gun, 0.45, Ric-O-Shay, Die Cast, Engraved Nickel Finish, Hubley, Box, c.1959, 12 In.	138.00
Cap Gun, Bulldog, Figural, Embossed, Cast Iron, June 21 1887 Patent, 2½ x 4½ In.	132.00
Cap Gun, Duck, Figural, Cast Iron, 4½ x 3¾ In.	550.00
Cap Gun, Jet Jr., Die Cast, Radiant Silver Finish, Automatic, Stevens, Box, 6 In.	688.00
Cap Gun, Kit Carson, 50 Shot, Kilgore, 1950s, 8 In.	131.00
Cap Gun, Lion, Figural, Embossed, Cast Iron, 2¾ x 5¼ In.	140.00
Cap Gun, Mule & Clown, Figural, Mule Kicks Clown, Cast Iron, 5¼ x 5½ In.	230.00
Cap Gun, Punch & Judy, Punch Springs Into Judy, Japanned, Iron, Ives, c.1882, 5 In.	605.00
Cap Gun, Ranger, Cast Iron, Nickel Plated, Red Grips, 1940s, 8½ In.	154.00
Cap Gun, Shoot The Hat, Man Puts Hat On Seated Man, Cast Iron, 4½ x 4¾ In.	330.00
Cap Gun, Top Hand 250, Cast Metal, Nichols, On Card, 1960s, 9 In.	123.00
Cap Gun, Top Hand Twins, Cameo Grips, Kilgore, Box, 1960s, 10 x 16 In., Pair	440.00
Capitol Hill Racer, USA, Box, 1930s, 18 In.	195.00
Captain America, Vinyl, Windup, Mechanical, Marx, Box, 1968, 5 In.	149.00
Captain Video Rocket Launcher, Lido Toy Co., Box, 1950s, 6 x 8 x 5¾ In.	451.00
Car, 700, Driver, Blue, Red, Yellow, White, Green, Tin, Windup, Lehmann, 4 In.	880.00
Car, Andy Gump, Hand Crank, License Plate, Multicolored Driver, 7½ In.	460.00
Car, Balky Mule, Crazy, Tin, Windup, Driver Rocks, Marx, Box, 8½ In.	193.00
Car, Bear Driver, Clown Face On Hood, No. 3, Tin, Friction, Japan, 1950s, 5 In.	35.00
Car, Bugatti, No. 3, Driver, France, SLF, 1930s, 8 In.	475.00
Car, Buick, Convertible, Gold, B-Japan, 1958, 8½ In.	175.00
Car, Buick, Convertible, Tin Lithograph, Hood Emblem, 11 In.	308.00
Car, Buick, Coupe, Driver, Nickel Plated, 5 Windows, Iron, Rubber Tires, Arcade, 1927, 8½ In.	3750.00
Car, Buick, Patrol, Metal, Friction, Japan, 1959, 11 In.	195.00
Car, Buick, Roadmaster, Fat Car, Friction, Yoshiya, 11 In.	350.00
Car, Buick, Sedan, Electric Mobile, Battery Operated, Instructions, Box, Japan, 1954, 10¼ In.	575.00
Car, Bumper, Pop-Up Clown Driver, Metal, Japan, 1950s	225.00
Car, Bumper, Pressed Steel, Tin Litho Riders, Rubber Bumper, Grille, Lights, Wyandotte, 9 In.	355.00
Car, Cabriolet, Plastic, White, Wiking, 4 In.	225.00
Car, Cad Mobile, Tin, Battery Operated, Tricolor Wheel Covers, Nomura, Box, 8½ In.	182.00
Car, Cadillac, 1929 Model, Coupe, Driver, Windup, Marx, 12 In.	475.00
Car, Cadillac, 1952 Model, Convertible, Tin, Friction, Alps, Box, 11½ In.	2200.00
Car, Cadillac, 1959 Model, Convertible, Tin, Friction, 4 Door, Bandai, 11½ In.	358.00
Car, Cadillac, 1960 Model, 2 Door, Hardtop, Tin, Friction, Marusan, Box, 11½ In.	1870.00
Car, Cadillac, Blue, Cream, Battery Operated, 1960s, 10 In.	185.00
Car, Cadillac, Convertible, Tin, Friction, Purple, Bandai, 12 In.	165.00
Car, Cadillac, Metal, TN, Japan, 1965, 25 In.	495.00
Car, Cadillac, Tin Lithograph, Friction, Masudaya, Japan, Box, 1950s, 5 In.	166.00
Car, Cadillac Stunt, Battery Operated, Japan, 1960s, 11 In.	145.00
Car, Captain Marvel, Windup, Automatic Toy Company	100.00
Car, Captain Scarlet & Mysterious Spectrum Maximum Security, Dinky Toy, Box, 5¼ In.	96.00

Toy, Boat, 2 Masts, Flag, Tin, Windup, G & K, Germany, 12 In.
$878.00

Toy, Boat, Ocean Liner, 2 Stacks, Flags, Rudder, Tin, Windup, Marklin, 1920s, 16 In.
$2475.00

Toy, Boy Riding Pig, Composition, Boy Has Celluloid Head, Goes Up & Down, Germany, 7 In.
$878.00

Toy, Burro, Wood, Jointed, Leather Ears, Rope Tail, Painted Eyes, Schoenhut, 7 In.
$248.00

T

Lithographed Tin Toys

Most lithographed tin toys were made between 1870 and 1915, although some were made later. Collectors like animated groups of animals or people, toys that make noise or music, or toys that move. Makers of special interest include Lehmann, Marx, Chein, Unique, Wolverine, and Strauss.

Toy, Bus, Double-Decker, London, Plastic Wheels, Players Please, No. 5B, Matchbox, Box
$216.00

Toy, Bus, Inter-State Bus, Tin Lithograph, Windup, Strauss, 10 In.
$410.00

Toy, Call Me Baby, Infant, Crawls, Talks, Battery Operated, Rosko Toy
$71.00

TIP

Don't store a rubber doll in a plastic bag. Wrap it in a white cotton pillowcase.

Car, Chevrolet, 1954 Model, Tin, Friction, 2 Door Sedan, Litho, Chrome, Marvsan, 11 In.	825.00
Car, Chevrolet, Cabriolet Roof, Spare Tire, Emblem, Cast Iron, Nickel Plated Wheels, Arcade, 18 In.	863.00
Car, Chevrolet, Convertible, Tin, Friction, Lithograph, Masudaya, Box, 11 In.	634.00
Car, Chevrolet, Corvair, 1960 Model, 4 Door, Hardtop, Tin, Friction, Yonezawa, Box, 11 In.	330.00
Car, Chevrolet, Corvair, 1960 Model, Tin, Friction, 4 Door Tri Tone, Sedan, Ichiko, 9¼ In.	138.00
Car, Chevrolet, Corvair, Sports Wagon, Tin, Friction, Tatsuya, Box, 8 In.	138.00
Car, Chevrolet, Coupe, Black, Gray, Cast Iron, Arcade, 8 In.	1265.00
Car, Chevrolet, Coupe, Cast Iron, Nickel Plated Driver, Rubber Tires, Arcade, 1925, 7 In.	605.00
Car, Chevrolet, Friction, Japan, 1954, 11 In.	750.00
Car, Chevrolet, Hood Ornament, Friction, Linemar, 1954, 11 In.	750.00
Car, Chevrolet, Impala, 007 Secret Agent, 5 Actions, Tin, Joy Toy Co., Japan, Box, 1963, 15 In.	595.00
Car, Chevrolet, Impala, 1961 Model, Tin, Friction, 4 Door, Lithograph, Bandai, Box, 11 In.	303.00
Car, Chevrolet, Impala, 1963 Model, Tin, Battery Operated, 4 Door, Bump & Go, 13 In.	193.00
Car, Chevrolet, Impala, Sedan, Tin, Friction, 1963, 11 In.	195.00
Car, Chevrolet, Metal, Musical, Friction, Ichiko, Japan, 1956, 10 In. ....*illus*	245.00
Car, Chevrolet, Red, Yellow Top, Friction, Metal, Linemar, 1955, 3½ x 11 In.	880.00
Car, Chevrolet, Secret Agent, Blue, Tin, Battery Operated, Yonezawa, Box, 1962, 14½ In.	485.00
Car, Chevrolet, Sedan, Cast Iron, White Rubber Tires, Nickel Driver, Arcade, 1925, 7 In.	550.00
Car, Chevrolet, Sedan, Touring, Iron, Nickel Driver, Arcade, 1925, 7 In.	935.00
Car, Chief Car, Rubber Tires, Pressed Steel, Buddy L, 1930s, 22 In.	1320.00
Car, Chrysler, Airflow, Coupe, Salmon, Cast Iron, 4½ In.	275.00
Car, Chrysler, Airflow, Sedan, Red, Cast Iron, 1934, 6 In.	375.00
Car, Chrysler, Saratoga, Friction, Chrome, Tin Litho, Lights, Wheel Covers, 1952, 10 In.	493.00
Car, Circus, Windup, Germany, 3½ In.	245.00
Car, Convertible, Red, Cream, Plastic, Windup, Clinford, 9 In.	155.00
Car, Coo Coo, Tin, Windup, Marx, c.1920s, 8 x 3 x 5¾ In.	895.00
Car, Coupe, Airflow, Olive Green, Hubley, 4½ In.	225.00
Car, Coupe, Cast Iron, Green, Rubber Wheels, Arcade, 3½ In.	225.00
Car, Coupe, Convertible, Green, Maroon, 8 In.	350.00
Car, Coupe, Doctor's, Cast Iron, Nickel Driver, Wheels, Arcade, 1924, 7 In.	187.00
Car, Coupe, Red, Blue, Rumble Seat, Jumbo Tires, Kilgore, 5 In.	550.00
Car, Coupe, Red, Cast Iron, Champion, 5 In.	275.00
Car, Coupe, Red, Cast Iron, Hubley, 6 In.	200.00
Car, Coupe, Red, Driver, Cast Iron, Nickel Wheels, Arcade, 7 In. ....*illus*	440.00
Car, Coupe, Red Paint, Cast Iron, Champion, 4½ In.	275.00
Car, Coupe, Tin, Windup, Germany, 1920s, 5½ In.	225.00
Car, Crash, Motorcycle, Policeman Drives, Hose Reel, Bottles, Medical Kit, Hubley, 11 In.	1380.00
Car, Crazy Cowboy, Tin Lithograph, Driver, Plastic Hat, Great Britain, 6 In.	235.00
Car, DeSoto, Airflow, Green, Cast Iron, Hubley, 4½ In.	350.00
Car, DeSoto, Airflow, Sedan, Green, Arcade, 4 In.	295.00
Car, Dizzie Lizzie, Tin Lithograph, Windup, Strauss, Box, 1930s, 8 In.	728.00
Car, Driver, Red, Push, 1920, 6 In.	275.00
Car, Driver Training, Tin, Plastic, Marx, Box, 6¾ In.	193.00
Car, Edsel, Station Wagon, Tin, Friction, 2 Door, Opening Rear Gate, Nomura, 10½ In.	220.00
Car, Ferrari, 813, 1960s Model, Tin, Friction, Bandai, Box, 8 In.	440.00
Car, Ferrari, SuperAmerica, Tin Lithograph, Bandai, Box, 1960s, 11 In.	370.00
Car, Ferrari, SuperAmerica, 1960s Model, Tin, Friction, 2 Door Coupe, Bandai, 11½ In.	193.00
Car, Ferrari Berlinetta 250 Lemans, Tin, Battery Operated, Asahi, Box, 11 In.	165.00
Car, Fire Bird, Driver, No. 7, Tin, Friction, Japan, 1950s, 6½ In.	195.00
Car, Fire Chief, American National, Pressed Steel, Pull Toy, Rubber Tires, 1930s, 29 In.	2310.00
Car, Fire Chief, Cadillac, Red, White, Friction, 1960s, 9 In.	135.00
Car, Fire Chief, Cast Iron, White Rubber Tires, Arcade, 1932, 5 In.	176.00
Car, Fire Chief, Metal, Battery Operated, Y Japan, Box, 1950s, 10 In.	295.00
Car, Fire Chief, Pressed Tin Lithograph, Friction, Courtland, 7 In.	28.00
Car, Fire Chief, Pull, Tin, c.1940, 8 In.	185.00
Car, Fire Chief, Red & Black, Siren, Windup, Headlights, Decals, Hoge, 1935, 14½ In.	450.00
Car, Fire Chief, Tin, Friction, Advances With Siren, Courtland, Box, 7 In.	110.00
Car, Fire Chief, Tin, Friction, Marx USA, 1950s, 7½ In.	95.00
Car, Fire Chief, Tin, Windup, Courtland, USA, 1950s, 7¼ In.	75.00 to 95.00
Car, Fire Chief, Tin, Windup, Lupor, 1950s, 7 In.	145.00
Car, Flivver Coupe, Pressed Steel, Buddy L, 1927, 11 In. ....*illus*	819.00
Car, Ford, 1934 Model, Coupe, Tootsietoy, 3 In.	85.00
Car, Ford, 1934 Model, Sedan, Green, Tootsietoy, 3 In.	115.00
Car, Ford, 1935 Model, Roadster, Silver, Tootsietoy, 3 In.	60.00 to 65.00
Car, Ford, 1935 Model, Sedan, Blue & Silver, Tootsietoy, 3 In.	65.00
Car, Ford, 1952 Model, 2 Door Hardtop, Tin, Friction, Marusan, 10¼ In.	275.00

Car, Ford, 1961 Model, Station Wagon, Country Squire, Tin, Friction, Ichimura, Box, 10 In.	143.00
Car, Ford, Color TV News, Metal, Friction, Japan, 1959, 9½ In.	275.00
Car, Ford, Coupe, Aqua, Hubley, 1935, 5½ In.	40.00
Car, Ford, Coupe, Purple, Cast Iron, No. 404, Hubley, 1936, 5½ In.	65.00
Car, Ford, Coupe, Separate Grill, Tootsietoy, 1934-35	125.00
Car, Ford, Coupe, Yellow Top, Green, Cast Iron, Nickel Wheels, Box, 1936, 4½ In.	132.00
Car, Ford, Fairlane, 1964 Model, Tin, Friction, 2 Door, License Plate Series, Box, 8 In.	94.00
Car, Ford, Fairlane 500, 1959 Model, Tin, Friction, 2 Door, Litho, Masudaya, Box, 8½ In.	550.00
Car, Ford, Falcon, 1961 Model, Tin, Battery Operated, Marusan, 8¾ In.	121.00
Car, Ford, Falcon, 1962 Model, Highway Patrol, Station Wagon, Alps, Tin, Friction, Box, 9 In.	94.00
Car, Ford, Falcon, Sedan, Tin, Friction, Japan, 8½ In.	95.00
Car, Ford, Galaxie 500, Windup, Friction, Japan, 1965, 10 In.	145.00
Car, Ford, Light Beige, Battery Operated, Japan, 1950s, 7½ In.	95.00
Car, Ford, Maroon, Steering, Tin, Metal, Battery Operated, Gunthermann, 1951, 10½ In.	475.00
Car, Ford, Model A, Coupe, Driver, Blue, A.C. Williams, 3¾ In.	250.00
Car, Ford, Model A, Coupe, Iron, Nickel Wheels, Arcade, 1928, 5 In.	154.00
Car, Ford, Model A, Phaeton, 1929 Model, Beam Decanter	125.00
Car, Ford, Model A, Tudor, Cast Iron, Nickel Driver, Wheels, Arcade, 1929, 6¾ In.	248.00
Car, Ford, Model T, 4 Door, Cast Iron, Nickel Driver, Arcade, 1924, 6½ In.	220.00
Car, Ford, Model T, 4 Door, Cast Iron, Nickel Wheels, Arcade, 5 In.	176.00
Car, Ford, Model T, Coupe, Cast Iron, Nickel Driver, Arcade, 1922, 6½ In.	385.00
Car, Ford, Model T, Coupe, Cast Iron, Nickel Driver, Rubber Tires, Arcade, 1924, 6½ In.	413.00
Car, Ford, Model T, Coupe, Cast Iron, Nickel Wheels, Arcade, 1924, 5 In.	154.00
Car, Ford, Model T, Coupe, Doctor's, Cast Iron, Nickel Wheels, Arcade, 1927, 5 In.	143.00
Car, Ford, Model T, Coupe, Driver, Black, Gold Stripe, High Top, Arcade, c.1923, 6½ In.	650.00
Car, Ford, Model T, Sedan, 4 Door, Black, Arcade, 6½ In.	650.00
Car, Ford, Model T, Sedan, Black, Gold, Arcade, 6½ In.	575.00
Car, Ford, Model T, Sedan, Green, Green Trim, Gold, Black Fenders, Orobr, Box, 6 In.	795.00
Car, Ford, Model T, Sedan, Stripe, Black, Gold, Arcade, 6½ In.	650.00
Car, Ford, Model T, Sedan, Touring, Cast Iron, Nickel Wheels, Driver, Arcade, 1924, 6½ In.	209.00
Car, Ford, Model T, Touring, Driver, Black, Gold Stripe, Arcade, 6½ In.	1500.00
Car, Ford, Model T, Touring, Tin, Windup, License Plate 242242, Germany, 7½ In.	413.00
Car, Ford, Mustang, Boss Hoss, The Spoilers, No. 7 Sticker, Hot Wheels, Mattel, 1969, Box *illus*	805.00
Car, Ford, Mustang, Door Opens, Battery Operated, Japan, 1965, 13 In.	375.00
Car, Ford, Mustang, Orange, Red Interior, Black Tires, No. 8E, Matchbox *illus*	196.00
Car, Ford, Mustang, Retractable Top, Tin, Battery Operated, Yonezawa, Box, 13½ In.	138.00
Car, Ford, Open & Close Top, Battery Operated, Japan, 1962, 11 In.	195.00
Car, Ford, Station Wagon, 2 Door, Chrome, Tin Lithograph, Friction, 1956, 12 In.	280.00
Car, Ford, Station Wagon, Tin Lithograph, Friction, Ichimura, Japan, Box, 1960s, 10¼ In.	84.00
Car, Ford, Zodiac, Teal Blue, Metal Wheels, No. 33A, Matchbox, Box *illus*	942.00
Car, Ford Type, Sedan, Driver, License Plate, Black, Tin, Windup, Bing, Germany, Box, 6 In.	385.00
Car, Formula Racing, Plastic, Battery Operated, Yonezawa, Box, 13 In.	193.00
Car, G Man, Tin, Friction, Machine Gun On Hood, Masudaya, Box, 5 In.	94.00
Car, Gerard, Coupe, Headlights Light-Up, Pressed Steel, Windup, 15 In.	450.00
Car, Green, Black, Push, 6½ In.	145.00
Car, Hercules Roadster, Tin, Rumble Seat, Luggage Rack, Tin Tires, Chein, 17½ In.	440.00
Car, Horse Trailer, Horse, Jumbo, Tootsietoy, On Card, 1960s, 7 x 10½ In.	56.00
Car, Hot Rod, Sparkling, Plastic, Friction, Straight 8 Engine, Marx, Box, 7½ In.	138.00
Car, Hudson Terraplane, Convertible, Yellow, Cast Iron, Hubley, 1936, 4½ In.	565.00
Car, Hudson Terraplane, Coupe, Blue, Cast Iron, Hubley, 1936, 4½ In.	565.00
Car, Jaguar, Light Blue, Doepke, 1955, 18 In.	495.00
Car, Jaguar, MK, Rally Car, 1950s, Tin Litho Interior, Rubber Tires, Ichiko, 8¼ In.	220.00
Car, Jaguar, Pace, Tritone Blue, 1956, 6 In.	385.00
Car, Jaguar, SKE Coupe, 1960s, Tin Litho, Friction, Wire Wheel Covers, Nomura, 11½ In.	407.00
Car, Jaguar, Tin, Friction, Japan, 1950s, 9½ In.	195.00
Car, Jaguar, XK 120, Convertible, 1950s, Tin, Friction, Alps, Box, 6½ In.	248.00
Car, Jaguar, XK 120, Convertible, 1950s, Tin, Friction, Japan, Box, 11¼ In.	990.00
Car, Jaguar, XKE GTX-753, Tin, Battery Operated Remote, 2 Door, Takatoku, Box, 11 In.	303.00
Car, Jaguar XKE, Tin Lithograph, Bandai, Box, 1950s, 8¼ In.	164.00
Car, Karmann Ghia, Coupe, Plastic, White, Wiking, Box, 4 In.	150.00
Car, King Racer, Driver, Windup, Marx, 9 In.	450.00
Car, Kojak's Buick, Corgi, Box, 1976, 6 In. *illus*	123.00
Car, Limousine, 4 Light, Tin, Black, White Roof, Red Seats, Friction Motor, Japan	94.00
Car, Limousine, Carette, 2 Door, Litho, Beveled Windshield, Windows, Nickel Plate, 16 In.	5581.00
Car, Limousine, Flywheel Drive, Red, Republic, 1932, 12 In.	225.00
Car, Limousine, Karl Bubb, 14 In.	2250.00

Toy, Car, Chevrolet, Metal, Musical, Friction, Ichiko, Japan, 1956, 10 In. $245.00

Toy, Car, Coupe, Red, Driver, Cast Iron, Nickel Wheels, Arcade, 7 In. $440.00

Toy, Car, Flivver Coupe, Pressed Steel, Buddy L, 1927, 11 In. $819.00

Rules for Dating Most Cars by the Wheels

Before World War II, toy car wheels were open-spoked metal wheels, solid metal disc wheels, solid metal disc wheels with embossed spokes, white rubber tires with metal rims, or solid white rubber tires mounted directly on the axles. The rule is that white rubber tires were used before World War II, black tires after. Since the 1960s, black plastic wheels have been used.

T

Toy, Car, Ford, Mustang, Boss Hoss, The Spoilers, No. 7 Sticker, Hot Wheels, Mattel, 1969, Box $805.00

Hot Wheels

The number on the base of a Hot Wheels car is the year it was copyrighted, not the year the car was made.

Toy, Car, Ford, Mustang, Orange, Red Interior, Black Tires, No. 8E, Matchbox $196.00

Toy, Car, Ford, Zodiac, Teal Blue, Metal Wheels, No. 33A, Matchbox, Box $942.00

Toy, Car, Kojak's Buick, Corgi, Box, 1976, 6 In. $123.00

Car, Limousine, Policeman, Safety First, Square, Tin, Windup, Distler, Prewar, Box, 8½ In.	550.00
Car, Limousine, Tin Litho, Cream, Spoked Tin Wheels, Beveled Glass, Hans Ebo, 10½ In.	900.00
Car, Limousine & Driver, Carl Bubb, Windup, 1920s, 11 In.	1350.00
Car, Limping Lizzie, Driver, Windup, Marx, Box, 1930	495.00
Car, Lincoln, 1956 Model, Tin, Friction, Rubber Tires, Tin Litho, Kanto, Box, 10½ In.	72.00
Car, Lincoln, 1957 Model, Tin, Friction, 4 Door, Hardtop, Siren, Chrome, Ichiko, 12½ In.	825.00
Car, Lincoln, Dog Head Out The Window, Metal, Japan, 1954, 7½ In.	175.00
Car, Lincoln, Honk-Along, 1957, Tin, Friction, Horn Sound Advancement, Ichiko, Box, 7 In.	110.00
Car, Lincoln, Town Car, Battery Operated, 1964, 10 In.	450.00
Car, Lincoln Continental MK III, 1958 Model, Tin, Friction, Hardtop, Bandai, Box, 11½ In.	385.00
Car, Lotus, Hi Speed Racer, Tin, Plastic, Battery Operated, Mystery Action, Box, 12½ In.	110.00
Car, Man From U.N.C.L.E. Gun-Firing T.H.R.U.S.H. Buster, Die Cast, Corgi, Box, c.1966, 4¼ In.	410.00
Car, Marx Stutz Style, Tin Lithograph, Coupe, Windup, Driver, Painted Wheels, 1920s, 9 In.	370.00
Car, Mercedes-Benz, 219, Convertible, Tin, Friction, Bandai, 1950s, 8 In.	166.00
Car, Mercedes-Benz, 220, Convertible, Tin, Friction, M, Japan, Box, 1960s, 8 In.	165.00
Car, Mercedes-Benz, 300, Adenauer Limo, Tin, Battery, Alps, 1950s, 9½ In.	1238.00 to 1430.00
Car, Mercedes-Benz, 220S, Automatic Jack, Tin, Battery Operated, 4 Door Sedan, 1960s, 12 In.	220.00
Car, Mercedes-Benz, 220SE, Coupe, Red, Matchbox, Box	2550.00
Car, Mercedes-Benz, 300SE, Tin Lithograph, Friction, 24 In.	250.00
Car, Mercedes-Benz, 300SL Coupe, Tin Lithograph, Bandai, Box, 1950s, 8 In.	203.00
Car, Mercury, Cougar, Metallic Green, Red Interior, No. 62, Superfast, Matchbox, Box	98.00
Car, MG, Plastic, Right Hand Drive, 3-Speed Gear Shift, Ideal, Box, 9 In.	88.00
Car, MG Midget, 1955, Overland Race Winner, Tin, Friction, Dual Windscreens, Bandai, 8½ In.	248.00
Car, MG Midget, 1955, Overland Race Winner, Tin, Windup, Bandai, 8¼ In.	165.00
Car, MGA, Convertible, Tin, Friction, Folding Windshield, Masudaya, 1950s, 8½ In.	138.00
Car, Nash, Sedan, Wipers, Tin, Friction, Japan, 1950s	95.00
Car, Nash, Windshield Wipers, Blue, Japan, 8 In.	110.00
Car, Nash Rambler, Station Wagon, Tin, Friction, 4 Door Convertible, Bandai, 1959, 8¼ In.	121.00
Car, Oho, Driver, Green, White, Tin, Windup, Lehmann, Germany, 4 In.	385.00
Car, Oho, Tin Lithograph, Lehmann, 1906-16, 4 In.	336.00
Car, Old Jalopy, Crazy, Tin, Windup, Driver Jumps Out Of Seat, Marx, c.1931, 8 In.	440.00
Car, Old Jalopy, Driver, Blue, Tin, Friction, Japan, 1950s, 5 In.	95.00
Car, Old Jalopy, Driver, Hop Inn, Blue, Tin, Friction, Linemar, Japan, 1950, 5 In.	120.00
Car, Old Jalopy, Driver, Red, Tin, Friction, Japan, 1950s, 5 In.	95.00
Car, Oldsmobile, 1952 Model, Tin, Friction, 4 Door, Siren Sound, Yonezawa, Box, 10½ In.	193.00
Car, Oldsmobile, Station Wagon, Super 88, Tin, Friction, Japan, 7½ In.	95.00
Car, Oldsmobile Toronado, 1967 Model, Tin, Battery Operated, Bump & Go, Bandai, Box, 11 In.	165.00
Car, Onkel, 3 Wheels, Driver, Passenger With Umbrella, Tin, Windup, Lehmann, 5 In. *illus*	385.00
Car, Opel, Diplomat, Gold, Gray Plastic Motor, Black Base, No. 36, Box, 1966	27.00
Car, Opel, Sedan, Red, Friction, 1960s, 11 In.	365.00
Car, Opel Olympia Rekord, Sedan, 2-Door, Tin, Battery Operated, Yonezawa, 1956, 11½ In.	633.00
Car, Packard, 1913 Model, Brown, Cream, Friction, Box, 6 In.	85.00
Car, Packard, Coupe, Red, Distler, Lithograph, Box, 10 In.	675.00
Car, Plymouth, Coupe, Red, Cast Iron, Arcade, 4¾ In.	485.00
Car, Plymouth, Fury, 1965 Model, Hardtop, Tin, Friction, 2-Tone Combo, Litho, Bandai, 8 In.	94.00
Car, Police, Bentley, Battery Operated, Box, 1950s, 8½ In.	195.00
Car, Police, Broderick Crawford Back, 10-4, Metal, Friction, Great Britain	375.00
Car, Police, Highway Patrol, Driver, Battery Operated, Bandai, Japan, Box, 10½ In.	145.00
Car, Police, Mystery, Tin, Battery Operated, Siren, Hood Light Blinks, Nomura, Box, 10 In.	165.00
Car, Police, Savoye, 3⅞ In.	235.00
Car, Police, State, Tin, Wood Wheels, Courtland, 7 In.	72.00
Car, Police, Tin, Friction, Siren, Hood Mounted Gun Moves, Nomura, Box, 7 In.	138.00
Car, Pontiac, Convertible, Brown, Rosko Toy, Y Japan, Box, 1962, 8½ In.	245.00
Car, Pontiac, Convertible, Cream & Green, Cast Iron, Kilgore, 10 In. *illus*	1045.00
Car, Pontiac, Convertible, Green, Rosko Toy, Y Japan, Box, 1962, 8½ In.	245.00
Car, Pontiac, GTO, 1970, Red, Prize Code, Plastic, Box, 8¼ In.	112.00
Car, Pontiac, Sedan, Red, Arcade, 4 In.	295.00
Car, Pontiac, Sedan, Red, Nickeled Grille, Arcade, 1934, 4¼ In.	375.00
Car, Pontiac Firebird III Concept, 1950s, Tin, Battery Operated, Mystery Action, 11½ In.	248.00
Car, Porsche, 914, 1960s Model, Tin, Battery Operated, 2 Door Hardtop, Daiya, Box, 8¾ In.	303.00
Car, Pull Toy, Metal, U.S.A., Cohn, N.Y., 9 In.	275.00
Car, Pull Toy, Wood, Metal, Cast Iron Driver, Mason & Parker, 9 In.	330.00
Car, Racing, Alpha Romeo, Red, No. 232, Dinky Toys, Box, 1954	85.00
Car, Racing, Champion, Tin, Friction, No. 8, Shooting Star, Box, 8½ In.	275.00
Car, Racing, Condor, Blue, Tin, Windup, JNF, Box, Germany U.S. Zone, 7 In. *illus*	275.00
Car, Racing, Dick Dastardly, Cast Metal, Plastic, Corgi Comics, Mettoy, Box, c.1973, 5 In.	211.00

T

Car, Racing, Driver, Boat Tail, Cast Iron, 8½ In.		235.00
Car, Racing, Driver, Indianapolis, Maroon, Rubber, Auburn, c.1948, 6½ In.		75.00
Car, Racing, Driver, Metal, Windup, England, 1930s, 7½ In.		175.00
Car, Racing, Driver, No. 4, Tin, Windup, Marx, 1950s, 5½ In.		110.00
Car, Racing, Driver, Silver, Red Trim, No. 2299, Hubley, 5⅜ In.		250.00
Car, Racing, Fire Bird, Tin, Windup, Japan, 1950s, 9 In.		325.00
Car, Racing, Fire Bird III, Cockpits, Lights Flash, Battery, Cragstan, Box, 11½ In.	*illus*	575.00
Car, Racing, Ford, Formula 1, Tyrrell, Key & Wrench, Blue, Orange, Plastic, Tin, Schuco, 9½ In.		235.00
Car, Racing, Golden Racer, Driver, Tin, Friction, Japan, 1960s, 11 In.		95.00
Car, Racing, H.W.M., Green, No. 23J-G, Dinky Toys, Box, 1953		115.00
Car, Racing, Jaguar, Tin, Friction, Japan, 1950s, 8 In.		175.00
Car, Racing, Metal, Windup, Marx, England, 1950s, 8 In.		175.00
Car, Racing, Midget Special, Blue, Yellow, Marx, 5 In.		295.00
Car, Racing, No. 3, Pressed Steel, Friction, U.S.A., 1920s, 10½ In.		295.00
Car, Racing, No. 3, Tin, Windup, Open Wheel, Litho Driver, Chein, 6¼ In.		248.00
Car, Racing, No. 4, Driver, Tin, Windup, Marx, 1950s, 5½ In.		110.00
Car, Racing, No. 410, Driver, Metal, Windup, England, 1940s, 10½ In.		195.00
Car, Racing, Red, Yellow, Green Grill, Blue Wheels, Marx, 5 In.		295.00
Car, Racing, Rocket Racer, Driver, Metal, Windup, Marx, 1930s, 16 In.		225.00
Car, Racing, Silver, Red Trim, Hubley, 5⅜ In.		250.00
Car, Racing, Speed Champion, Driver, Battery Operated, Box		200.00
Car, Racing, Tether, Electric, Orange, Shark, Remco, Box, 1960s, 15½ In.		95.00
Car, Racing, Thimbledrome, No. 88, Gas, Red, Roy Cox, 1940s, 9½ In.		350.00
Car, Racing, Tin, Friction, ATC, Japan, 1950s		275.00
Car, Racing, Tin, Windup, GT Britain, Marx, 7½ In.		195.00
Car, Racing, Tin Friction, Japan, 1950s, 8½ In.		325.00
Car, Racing, Tin Lithograph, Green, Blue, Red Grill, Orange Stripes, 5 In.		275.00
Car, Racing, Tornado, No. 8, Red, Silver, Air Powered, Woodette, 1950s, 12 In.		110.00
Car, Racing, USA, Metal, Windup, 1950s, 11½ In.		95.00
Car, Racing, Vanwall Grand Prix, No. 239, Dinky Toys, Box, c.1950s		110.00
Car, Racing, Volkswagen, Windup, Tin Lithograph, Ichiko, Japan, Box, 1960s, 7½ In.		351.00
Car, Racing, White, Aluminum, Cast Iron, No. 22, Hubley, c.1940		175.00
Car, Racing, Windup, England, 1950s, 11½ In.		225.00
Car, Racing, Windup, Gescha, Metal, Germany, 5 In.		395.00
Car, Racing, Windup, Marx USA, 1930s, 16 In.		245.00
Car, Roadster, Austin Hot Rod, Blue, Rubber Tires, Arcade, 3¾ In.		275.00
Car, Roadster, Bing Model T, Tin, Windup, 6½ In.		176.00
Car, Roadster, Built-In Key, Blue, Convertible, Tin, Marx, Box, 1950, 11 In.		348.00
Car, Roadster, Cast Iron, No. If-2867, A.C. Williams, c.1932, 3⅝ In.		165.00
Car, Roadster, Cast Iron, Red, Chassis, Yellow, Kilgore, 4 In.		150.00
Car, Roadster, Driver, Blue, Kilgore, 6¼ In.		500.00
Car, Roadster, Driver, Red, Kilgore, 8 In.		650.00
Car, Roadster, Driver, Rumble Seat, Cast Iron, Kilgore, 5 In.		300.00
Car, Roadster, Lasalle, Jade Blue, Green, Marx, 11 In.		175.00
Car, Roadster, Mechanical, Windup, Yellow, Marx, Box, 6¾ In.		375.00
Car, Roadster, Pressed Steel, Rubber Tires, Schieble, 18 In.		248.00
Car, Roadster, V8, Tin, Battery Operated, Mystery Action, Fan Blade Turns, Daiya, Box, 11¼ In.		209.00
Car, Rolls-Royce, Silver Cloud, Dark Green, White Top, Tin, Cragstan, 1960s, 12 In.		230.00
Car, Rolls-Royce, Silver Cloud, Tin, Friction, Yonezawa, Box, 1960s, 8½ In.		220.00
Car, Sedan, 4 Door, Cast Iron, No. 2232, Hubley, c.1930		175.00
Car, Sedan, 4 Door, Driver, Yellow, Green, Red, Chein, 7 In.		325.00
Car, Sedan, 5 Wheel, Red, Rubber Tires, Champion, 5¼ In.		375.00
Car, Sedan, Blue, Hubley, 1930s, 5 In.		230.00
Car, Sedan, Cast Iron, Blue Chassis, Red, Kilgore, 4¾ In.	170.00 to 195.00	
Car, Sedan, Cast Iron, Rubber Tires, Clicker, Arcade, 1941, 8½ In.		303.00
Car, Sedan, Electromobile, Cream, Red Trim, Battery Operated, 8 In.		295.00
Car, Sedan, Green, Orange, Cream, A.C. Williams, 2 Piece, 4½ In.		195.00
Car, Sedan, Metal, Battery Operated, Japan, 1950s, 14 In.		295.00
Car, Sedan, Old Tune, Windup, Metal, Marx, 1950s, 7 In.		175.00
Car, Sedan, Open, Orange, Black, Chein No. 221, 8½ In.		350.00
Car, Sedan, Pierce Arrow, Cast Iron, 1935, 7 In.		1100.00
Car, Sedan, Plastic, Green, Box, 4 In.		125.00
Car, Sedan, Red, Black Bumpers, Wyandotte, 1930, 6½ In.		150.00
Car, Sedan, Steel, Radiator, Bumpers, Tin Litho, Tires, Wyandotte, c.1937, 9 In.		550.00
Car, Sedan, Steel, Schieble, c.1920, 17½ In.		352.00
Car, Sheriff, Tin, Battery Operated, Siren, Hood Light Blinks, Nomura, Box, 10 In.		220.00

Toy, Car, Onkel, 3 Wheels, Driver, Passenger With Umbrella, Tin, Windup, Lehmann, 5 In. $385.00

Toy, Car, Pontiac, Convertible, Cream & Green, Cast Iron, Kilgore, 10 In. $1045.00

Toy Cars

Most toy cars made before 1940 were cast iron, aluminum, stamped steel, or metal alloys. Inexpensive cars were made of a zinc alloy or a white metal alloy called pot metal.

Some toy cars were made of hard rubber. Collectors aren't as interested in these cars because rubber hardens, cracks, and ages badly.

Plastic wasn't used for toys until the late 1930s. Makers tried Bakelite, but it was too fragile. It was replaced by Butyrate in the 1940s, which melted. So manufacturers switched to polystyrene, a plastic invented in 1927. Modern car models are made of metal, plastic, or a combination of the two.

Toy, Car, Racing, Condor, Blue,
Tin, Windup, JNF, Box,
Germany U.S. Zone, 7 In.
$275.00

Toy, Car, Racing, Fire Bird III,
Cockpits, Lights Flash, Battery, Cragstan,
Box, 11½ In.
$575.00

Toy, Carnival Ride, Hot Air Balloon,
Zeppelin, Tin Lithograph,
Germany, 4 In.
$3300.00

Toy, Carriage, Doll's, Early American
Stenciled Flowers On Sides, Wood,
Iron Wheels, 9 In.
$117.00

Car, Soap Box Derby Racer, Wood Wheels, Tin, Wyandotte, 8 In.		248.00
Car, Speedcar, Playboy, Pressed Steel, Yellow, Black Wheels, 1914, 33 x 16 In.		230.00
Car, Speedster, Boxed Set, Metal, Box Converts To Garage, 4 In.		1000.00
Car, Studebaker, Avanti, Metallic Blue, Friction, Bandai, 1960s, 8 In.		225.00
Car, Studebaker, Convertible, Cast Iron, Green, Hubley, 5 In.		400.00
Car, Studebaker, Coupe, Cast Iron, Blue, Hubley, 5 In.		425.00
Car, Studebaker, Sedan, Cast Iron, Blue, Hubley, 5 In.		450.00
Car, Stuffed, Black Velvet, Embroidered Nose, Mouth, 6¼ x 10 In.		147.00
Car, Taxi, American Yellow Cab Co., Driver, Windup, Lenox 530, Germany, 1920s, 7 In.		550.00
Car, Taxi, Yellow, Driver, Windup, 1930s		475.00
Car, Tin, 4 Gear, Windup, Distler, 9½ In.		339.00
Car, Tin, Windup, Germany, 1920s, 5½ In.		225.00
Car, Tin, Windup, Germany, 1920s, 7 In.		325.00
Car, Touring, Canvas Style Roof, Driver, Goggles, Woman, Kenton, c.1910, 9 In.		1495.00
Car, Touring, Chauffeur, Hand Crank, Windup, Lithograph, Germany, 10 In.		863.00
Car, Touring, Tin, 4 Door, Metal Bumper, Rubber Tires, Schieble, 18 In.		413.00
Car, Traffic, Indian, Orange, Nickel Wheels, Hubley, c.1931, 4¾ In.		375.00
Car, U.S. Army, Anti-Tank, Tin, Friction, Courtland, Box, 7 In.		248.00
Car, Uncle Wiggily, Crazy, Tin, Windup, Head Spins, Marx, c.1935, 7 In.		660.00
Car, Uncle Wiggily, Crazy, Tin, Windup, Marx, Box, 7 In.		1210.00
Car, Volkswagen, 1600, Tin Lithograph, Friction, Ichimura, Japan, Box, 1960, 7¼ In.		81.00
Car, Volkswagen, Metallic Silver Blue, Green Windows, Matchbox, Box		1598.00
Car, Volkswagen Micro-Bus, Tin Lithograph, Bandai, Box, Early 1960s, 7¾ In.		511.00
Car, Waddles Family Car, Head Moves, Battery Operated, Japan, 1950		145.00
Car, Wells, Tin Litho Wheels, Tires, Key, Driver On Right, Windup, England, 1930s, 8½ In.		370.00
Car, Woman Driver, License, Spare Tire, Red, Black, Tin, Windup, Bing, Germany, BW, 7 In.		1045.00
Car, Wonder MG, Tin, Windup, Passengers, Umbrella, Marusan, Box, 5 In.		413.00
Car, Wrecker, Green, Hubley, 5 In.		225.00
Car & House Trailer, Friction, Red, Yellow, Japan, 8 In.		110.00
Car & Trailer Set, Ford, 1957 Model, Convertible, Boat, Speedo, Tin, Friction, Haji, Box, 16 In.		385.00
Car Carrier, Die Cast, 3 Plastic Cars, Hubley, Box, 14 In.		165.00
Car, Racing, Auburn, Rubber, Red, Silver, 1940s, 10½ In.		95.00
Carnival Ride, Hot Air Balloon, Zeppelin, Tin Lithograph, Germany, 4 In. *illus*		3300.00
Carousel, Gilt Metal Trim, Pewter Figures, c.1920, 32 x 36 In.		1638.00
Carousel, Swans, Airplanes, Windup, Wyandotte, 1930s, 6 In.		325.00
Carpenter Set, Nickel Plated, Arcade, 1941		99.00
Carriage, Doll's, Cast Iron, Nickel Plated Wheels, Handle, 4¼ In.		99.00
Carriage, Doll's, Cast Iron, Nickel Plated Wheels, Handle, Bonnet, 5½ In.		22.00
Carriage, Doll's, Early American Stenciled Flowers On Sides, Wood, Iron Wheels, 9 In. *illus*		117.00
Carriage, Doll's, Metal, Green Paint, Metal Wheel Rims, Rubber Tires, 1920s, 14 x 15 In.		100.00
Carriage, Doll's, Natural Finish, Adjustable Hood, Serpentine Roll, c.1900, 28 x 16 In.		795.00
Carriage, Doll's, Reeding, Star Shape Crest, Turned Spool Work, 1890s, 25 x 32 In.		1250.00
Carriage, Doll's, Wicker, Green, Gold, Sage Wing, Upholstery, Round Windows, 32 x 16 In.		295.00
Carriage, Doll's, Wicker, Green, Upholstery, Window, Swivel Body, Hard Rubber Tires, 31 x 32 In.		295.00
Carriage, Doll's, Wicker, Pink, Metal Spring Frame, Painted White, 18 x 25 In.		145.00
Carriage, Horse, Tin Lithograph, Meier, Germany, Penny Toy, 4¾ In.		288.00
Carriage, Milk Float, Horse Drawn, White Driver, Crates, Metal Wheels, Matchbox, Box		38.00
Cart, Boy Sits On Ostrich, Tin Lithograph, Meier, Germany, Penny Toy, 4 In.		720.00
Cart, Chester Gump, Pulled By Horse, Cast Iron, 1900		385.00
Cart, Goat Drawn, 2 Wheels, Original Paint, Cast Iron, Pressed Steel, 7¾ In.		61.00
Cart, Horse Drawn, Doctor's, Driver, Silver Paint, Yellow Wheels, Cast Iron, 5¼ In.		50.00
Cart, Horse Drawn, Doctor's, Driver In Long Coat & Derby, Original Paint, Cast Iron, 10 In.		330.00
Cart, Horse Drawn, Driver, Tin, Windup, Mark, Marx		165.00
Cart, Horse Drawn, Milk, Borden's Farm Products, Wood, Metal, Rice Toy Co., 8 x 19 In.		412.00
Cart, Horse Drawn, Tin, Blue Litho Horse, Painted Cart, Driver, 8½ In.		138.00
Cart, Horse Drawn, Tin, Windup, Marx		145.00
Cart With Yellow Kid, Pulled By Donkey, Cast Iron, Nickel Wheels, Harris, 9 In. *illus*		470.00
Casper The Friendly Ghost, Nods, Hops, Tin, Windup, Linemar		625.00
Castle, Lithographed Paper On Wood & Cardboard, Gottschalk, 14 In. *illus*		375.00
Cat, Brown, Cloth, Button Eyes, Red Bow, Stuffed, Handmade, Amish, 6 In.		305.00
Cat, Drinking, Licking, Battery Operated, Tin, Play, Box		275.00
Cat, Felix, Driving Car, Tin, Windup, Ingap, Italy, 6 In.		4025.00
Cat, Felix, Figure, Wood, Jointed, Schoenhut, 8 In. *illus*		55.00
Cat, Felix, Jointed, Wood, Rubber Head, K.E.S. Co., 9 In.		475.00
Cat, Felix, On Scooter, Tin, Windup, Spring Tail, Ingap, Italy, 6 In. *illus*		3510.00
Cat, Felix, Push & Pull, Wood, Felix On Chest, 13 In. *illus*		248.00

T

Cat, Felix, Sparkler, Black & White, Pointed Ears, Nifty, Germany, Marked, 5½ In.	385.00
Cat, Felix, Speedy, Racer, Mechanical Wood, Nifty, Germany, 12 In.	750.00
Cat, Felix, Wood, Vinyl, Jointed, King Features, 9½ In.	204.00
Cat, Gray, Cream, Striped, Flocked Papier-Mache Body, Kidskin Bellows, Squeak, 7 In.	1410.00
Cat, Kitty Cat, Metal, Windup, Montgomery Ward, USA Marx, Box, 1930s	175.00
Cat, Pip-Squeak, Brown, Black, Open Mouth, Mouth Moves, 7 In.	719.00
Cat, Vines On Cloth, Stuffed, Handmade, Amish, 7 x 8 In.	55.00
Cat, Wood, Jointed, Painted Whiskers & Eyes, Molded Ears, Leather Tail, Schoenhut, 9 In. ...	880.00
Cat & Dog, Doghouse, Cat Rears Back, Tin Lithograph, Penny Toy, Meier, Germany, 4 In. ...	715.00
Cat Dozer, Yellow, Doepke, 1952, 15 In.	450.00
Cement Mixer, Jaeger, Pressed Steel, Doepke, 1950s, 15 In.	339.00
Cement Mixer, Wonder, Portable Model, Red & Nickel Plate, Hubley, 3¼ In.	125.00
Chair, Doll's, Hoop Back, Vasiform Splat, Stretcher, Yellow Paint, 16¾ In.	385.00
Chair, Doll's, Maple, Bamboo-Turned Spindles, Arms, France, c.1890, 14 In.	275.00
Chair, Doll's, Plank Seat, Yellow Paint, Pennsylvania, 16 In.	2808.00
Chariot, Black Horse, Paper On Wood, Embossed Interior, Bliss, 15½ x 23 In.	3575.00
Chariot, Clown, Burro, Glass Eyes, Papier-Mache, Wood Frame, Schoenhut	5225.00
Charleston Trio, Roof Dancing, Tin, Windup, Marx, 9 In. .... 660.00 to 840.00	
Chick Mobile, Peter Rabbit, Red Vest, Clockwork, Yellow Hand Cart, Lionel Corp., 20½ In. ..	499.00
Chimp, Touchdown, Tin, Windup, Somersaults, Technofix, Box, 4½ In.	385.00
Circus Animal Car, Iron Driver, Mechanical, Friction, Dayton Toy Co., 15 In.	350.00
Circus Parade, Tin, Windup, T.P.S., Box, 11 In.	395.00
Circus Parade Truck, Lions, Tin, Elephant Pulls Trailer, Lithograph, Courtland, 11¾ In. ..	202.00
Clown, Beats Drum, Hits Cymbals, Walker, Tin, Cloth, Windup, Germany, c.1900, 9 In.	950.00
Clown, Boxer, Tin, Windup, Celluloid Punching Bag, Head Moves, Chein, 8¼ In.	935.00
Clown, Celluloid, Cloth, Windup, Cragston, 9 In.	295.00
Clown, Charlie, Plays Drums, Nose Lights Up, Battery Operated, Japan, 1950s, Box	195.00
Clown, Dandy Jim, Strauss	595.00
Clown, Horn, Figural, Tin Lithograph, Germany, 7 In.	140.00
Clown, Metal, Windup, Japan, 1950s, 9 In.	75.00
Clown, On Cart, Dog Pushing, Original Flag, Tin, Windup, Germany, 8 In.	880.00
Clown, On Donkey, Moves Back & Forth, Windup, Gama, Germany, 1920s	395.00
Clown, On Drum, Plays Clarinet, Ballerina Dances, Windup, Music, Gunthermann, 8½ In. ..	920.00
Clown, On Horse, Bounces Up & Down, Wheels, Windup	350.00
Clown, On Platform, Strums Guitar, Head Bobs, Litho, Windup, Distler, Germany, 8½ In. ...	475.00
Clown, On Roller Skates, Tin, Windup, Skating Motion Advance, T.P.S., Box, 6¼ In. . 248.00 to 375.00	
Clown, Papier-Mache, Germany, 5½ In.	85.00
Clown, Pinky, Juggles, 5 Actions, Whistle, Battery Operated, 1950s	250.00
Clown, Pinky, Tin, Blows Whistle, Juggles, Balances Pole, Battery Operated, Japan, c.1950, 19 In.	153.00
Clown, Playing Violin, Sitting On Wheel, Musical, Windup, 1900, 9 In.	850.00
Clown, Riding Horse, Bounces Up & Down, Windup, Germany, 1900, 8 In.	475.00
Clown, Riding Lion, Wheels, Windup, Painted, Germany, 10 In.	1070.00
Clown, Roller, Burro, Moves Up & Down, Metal Spoke Wheels, Chimes, Pull Toy, 12 x 14½ In. ...	1870.00
Clown, Rolls Over, Celluloid, Windup, Japan, 1950s	95.00
Clown, Roly Poly, Composition, Noma, c.1930	95.00
Clown, Roly Poly, Composition, Schoenhut, 1920s, 5½ In.	165.00
Clown, Roly Poly, Multicolored, Composition, Schoenhut, 15 In.	295.00
Clown, Walks On Hands, Windup, Tin Lithograph, Distler, Germany, 7 In.	336.00
Clown, Windup, Germany, 10 In.	165.00
Coal Cart, Mule, Driver, Dent, 1900s, 13½ In.	850.00
Coast Defense Gun, Wood, Steel, Crank Operated, Wood Shells, Baldwin, Box, 5½ In.	72.00
Coney Island, Plastic, Tin Base, 2 Windup Cars, Key, Technofix, Box, 21 x 15 In.	200.00
Construction Set, Bridge, 2 Tootsietoys, Cardboard, Parker Bros., 1961	135.00
Construction Set, No. 3, Nickel Pieces, Manual, Meccano, 2 Tiers Box, 1919 ....*illus*	177.00
Construction Set, No. 8, Red & Green Pieces, Manual, Meccano, Box, 1940s ....*illus*	177.00
Cow, Platform, Brown, Horns, Legs, Metal Wheels, Papier-Mache, Pull Toy, 5½ In.	330.00
Cow, Wood, Jointed, Leather Horns & Ears, Rope Tail, Glass Eyes, Bell, Schoenhut, 8½ In. ...	660.00
Cowboy, Horse, Tin, Windup, Japan, 1960s	95.00
Cowboy, In Cart, Jumps Up & Down, Pulled By Zebra, Windup, Lehmann, 1954	350.00
Cowboy, On Horse, Jumps, Metal, Windup, Japan, 5 In.	75.00
Cowboy, On Horse, Lasso, Marx, Box	395.00
Cowboy, Walks Sideways, Cloth Pants, Windup, 1900	475.00
Cowboy & Indian, Tin, Windup, Japan, 1960s	145.00
Cradle, Doll's, Hooded, Pine, Footboard, Rocker, 17 x 10½ In.	403.00
Cradle, Doll's, Poplar, Dovetailed, Cut Nails, 19th Century, 7 x 26½ x 8½ In.	58.00
Cradle, Doll's, Softwood, Red Wash, Square Nails, Cheese Cutter Rockers, 6¾ x 13⅝ x 7 In. .	55.00

Toy, Cart With Yellow Kid, Pulled By Donkey, Cast Iron, Nickel Wheels, Harris, 9 In.
$470.00

Toy, Castle, Lithographed Paper On Wood & Cardboard, Gottschalk, 14 In.
$375.00

Toy, Cat, Felix, Figure, Wood, Jointed, Schoenhut, 8 In.
$55.00

Toy, Cat, Felix, On Scooter, Tin, Windup, Spring Tail, Ingap, Italy, 6 In.
$3510.00

Toy, Cat, Felix, Push & Pull, Wood, Felix On Chest, 13 In. $248.00

Toy, Construction Set, No. 3, Nickel Pieces, Manual, Meccano, 2 Tiers Box, 1919 $177.00

Toy, Construction Set, No. 8, Red & Green Pieces, Manual, Meccano, Box, 1940s $177.00

Toy, Cycle Car Delivery, Motorcycle Base, Bell, Windup, Tin, Hoge Mfg. Co., N.Y., Box, 11 In. $6600.00

Cradle, Doll's, Walnut, Dovetailed, Shaped Rockers, 5½ x 8½ x 6¼ In.	39.00
Crane, Tin, Push, Crank Operated Bucket, Chein, 9 In.	138.00
Crayons, Little Lulu, Blue Box, Smiling Lulu At Easel Writing Name, Milton Bradley, 1948	70.00
Creamer, Cobalt Blue, Applied Pale Blue Handle, Crosshatch, Pontil, 1850-80, 2½ In.	112.00
Crow, Wood, Black Paint, Pull, 20th Century, 14½ x 15 x 8 In.	1560.00
Cycle Car Delivery, Motorcycle Base, Bell, Windup, Tin, Hoge Mfg. Co., N.Y., Box, 11 In. *illus*	6600.00
Dancer, Checkered Coat, Dance On Box, Windup, 1920, Pair	365.00
Dancer, Irish, Clockwork Mechanism, 2 Part, Ives, 12 In.	1760.00
Dancing Black Man, Top Hat, Red Shirt, Dancing Platform, Long Handle, Polychrome, 15 In.	338.00
Dancing Couple, Celluloid, Windup, Occupied Japan, 4½ In.	125.00
Dancing Dan, Plastic, Battery Operated, Dances While Speaking, Bell Product, Box, 14 In.	358.00
Dancing Men, 2 Black Men On Springboard, Articulated Joints, Windup, Painted, 15½ In.	604.00
Dandy, Tin, Windup, Walking Movement Advances, Tips Hat, Mikuni, Box, 6 In.	138.00
Dandy Jim, 2 Clowns On Top Of Circus Tent, Tin, Windup, Unique Art, 9 In.	330.00
Dandy Jim, Roof Dancer, Plays Cymbals, On & Off Switch, Unique Art, 10 In.	137.00
Dapper Dan Coon Porter, Dances, Tin, Windup, Marx, 8 In.	385.00
Datsun Fairlady, Tin, Friction, Ichiko, Japan, Box, 11½ In.	138.00
Derrick, Pressed Steel, Buddy L, 26 In.	358.00
Dinner Set, Glass, Delft, Cups, Saucers, Bowls, Jeanette Jr, 10 Piece	110.00
Dinnerware, Doll's, Soft Paste, Urn, Tureens, Casserole, Compote, Gravy Boat, Plates, Bowls	715.00
Dirigible, Tin, Painted, Windup, 1930s, 10½ In.	246.00
Dizzy Donkey, Pop-Up Kritter, Fisher-Price	95.00
Dog, Brown, Cloth, Button Eyes, Holding Wood Spool, Stuffed, Handmade, Amish, 6½ In.	305.00 to 495.00
Dog, Brown, Cloth, Button Eyes, Stuffed, Handmade, Amish, 7 In.	137.00
Dog, Bulldog, Papier-Mache, Glass Eyes, Growls, Head Moves, 4 Wheels, 10 x 19 In. *illus*	1035.00
Dog, Cloth, Holding Spool, Button Eyes, Stitched Mouth, Stuffed, Handmade, Amish, 6 In.	55.00
Dog, Dinky, Cloth, Kellogg's Premium From Canada, 13 x 16 In.	60.00
Dog, Flippo, Metal, Windup, Linemar, Japan	95.00
Dog, Fur, Button Eyes, Red Stitched Mouth, Stuffed, Handmade, Amish, 7 In.	165.00
Dog, Fur Covered, Squeaker, Barks When Cord Is Pulled, Glass Eyes, Germany, 9 In. *illus*	260.00
Dog, Mohair, White, Brown, Glass Eyes, Pull, Cast Iron Wheels, Steiff, 18 x 21 In.	880.00
Dog, Plush, Mohair, Push & Pull, Iron Wheels, Button In Ear, Steiff, 16 x 12 In. *illus*	3575.00
Dog, Poodle, White, Wood, Jointed, Cloth Mane, Rope Tail, Glass Eyes, Schoenhut, 7½ In.	165.00
Dog, See-Em-Walk, Noma, Box, 7 x 10 In.	11.75
Dog, Sniffing, Ears, Nose & Tail Moves, Windup, TN, Japan, Box, 1950s	95.00
Dog, Space Dog, Windup, KO, Box	550.00
Dog, Velvet, Painted Spots, Seated, Carries Basket With Pincushion, Steiff, c.1910, 4 In.	2530.00
Dog, Wee Scottie, Metal, Windup, Marx, 5¼ In.	110.00
Dollhouse, 2 Rooms, Brick & Stone, Cardboard, Paper Lithograph, Folds, McLoughlin Bros.	230.00
Dollhouse, 2 Rooms, Chimney, Garden, Lithographed, McLoughlin, Early 1900s, 9 x 17 x 7 In.	118.00
Dollhouse, 2 Story, 4 Rooms, Victorian, Applied Details, Mica Windows, Furniture, 56 x 29 In.	431.00
Dollhouse, 2 Story, 6 Rooms, Wood, Mansard Roof, Wallpaper, Late 1800s, 44 x 42 x 26 In.	5225.00
Dollhouse, 2 Story, Open Window & Door, Lithograph, Bliss, 9¾ x 7¾ x 4¾ In.	468.00
Dollhouse, 2 Story, Tudor, Wood, Attic, England, 19th Century, 52 x 44 x 27 In.	11000.00
Dollhouse, 2 Story, Wood, Open Porch, Steps, 2 Ladder Back Chairs, Green Roof, 14½ In.	176.00
Dollhouse, 2 Story, Wood, Paper Lithograph, Cobblestone, 8¾ In.	143.00
Dollhouse, 2 Story, Wood, Paper Lithograph, Green Roof, Converse, 13¼ In.	154.00
Dollhouse, 2 Story, Wood, Reed Paper Lithograph, 8¾ In.	100.00
Dollhouse, 2 Story, Wraparound Porch, Gutters, Balcony, Paper Litho, 4 Dolls, Germany, 20 In.	1093.00
Dollhouse, 3 Story, Wood, Windows, Staircase, Fireplace, Furniture, Dolls, 43 x 37 In.	6775.00
Dollhouse, Cardboard, Metal, Tootsietoy, 16 x 21 In.	220.00
Dollhouse, Cardboard, Paper Lithograph, Folding, Brick, Stone Facade, McLoughlin Bros.	230.00
Dollhouse, Lady, Molded Curly Hair, Baby, Carriage, Shoulder Head, Cloth Body, 4¾ In.	118.00
Dollhouse, Walnut, Natural Finish, Clock Tower, England, 1800s, 44 x 30 x 16 In.	10450.00
Dollhouse, Wood, Bay Windows, Steps, Converse, 15 In.	154.00
Dollhouse Furniture, Baby Carriage, Pink, Blue, Acme Thomas Industries, 1¾ In.	9.00
Dollhouse Furniture, Bookcase, Glass Door, Drawer, Miniature Books, 6 x 4 In. *illus*	480.00
Dollhouse Furniture, Buffet, Ormolu, Gallery, Doors Open, 6 x 4 In. *illus*	748.00
Dollhouse Furniture, Cabinet, Biedermeier, 3 Shelves, Mirrored Back, Drawer, 6 x 4 In.	470.00
Dollhouse Furniture, Chaise, Biedermeier, Red Tooled Leather Upholstery, 6½ In.	588.00
Dollhouse Furniture, Chandelier, 3-Arm, Console Mirror, Ormolu, Eckhart & Shone, 4 In.	705.00
Dollhouse Furniture, Curio Cabinet, Sconces, Ormolu, Art Nouveau, Mirror, Glass, 3 x 5 In.	588.00
Dollhouse Furniture, Etagere, Bone, Turned Supports, 3 Shelves, Dishes, 3¾ In. *illus*	144.00
Dollhouse Furniture, Grand Piano, Wood, Strombecker, 1930s	13.00
Dollhouse Furniture, Patio, Wood, Chairs, Table, Swing Set, Strombecker, Box, c.1950	201.00
Dollhouse Furniture, Salon, Piano, Table, Fireplace, Mirror, Clock, Chandeliers, Settee, Chairs	1430.00

Dollhouse Furniture, Squirrel, Bird Cages, Ormolu, Revolving, Footed, 1½ x 1¾ In.	1116.00
Dollhouse Furniture, Stool, Walnut, Floral Upholstered Seat, Turned Legs, 7¼ In.	99.00
Dollhouse Furniture, Vanity, Biedermeier Gothic, Mirrored, Stenciled, 5 x 5½ In.	764.00
Dolls are listed in their own category.	
Dolly Seamstress, Tin, Moves Material, Turns Head While Sewing, Nomura, Box, 8 In.	220.00
Dolly's Washing Machine, Tin Lithograph, Crank Operated Agitator, Chein, Box, 8 In.	165.00
Dolphin, Moves Tail While Floating, Windup, France, 1890s, 15½ In.	450.00
Donkey, Wood, Jointed, Leather Ears, Rope Tail, Cloth Mane, Felt Blanket, Schoenhut, 9 In.	55.00
Dr. Duck, Duck Holding Medical Bag, Wood, Pull, No. 100, Fisher-Price, Prewar, 10 In.	495.00
Dracula, Walker, Plastic, 5⅜ In.	280.00
Dredge, Pressed Steel, Buddy L, 30 In.	660.00
Drive Set, Tin, Friction, Ford Fairlane, Gas Pump, Road Signs, Masudaya, Box, 8 Piece	358.00
Drum, Barney Google, Sparkplug, Tin Lithograph, 10 In.	280.00
Drum, Mutt & Jeff, Mutt Hits Jeff With Baseballs, Tin Lithograph, Converse, 13 In.	308.00
Drum, Tin, World War II Battle Scenes, 7½ In.	125.00
Drum Major, Plays Drum, Windup, Wolverine, Box, 13 In.	350.00
Drum Major, Tin, Windup, Chein, Box, 8¾ In.	303.00
Drum Major, Wolverine, Tin, Windup, Round Base, Box, 13¼ In.	385.00
Drummer, Mechanical, Tin, Cloth, Windup, Stepping Motion, Japan, Box, 8½ In.	165.00
Drummer Boy, Windup, Japan, Box, 1930s, 11¾ In.	195.00
Duck, Head Bobs, Bill Opens & Closes, Wood, Painted, 3 Wheels, Pull Toy, 4 In.	275.00
Duck, Skiing, Tin, Windup, Arms Move, Linemar, Box, 3¾ In.	303.00
Duck, Walks, Wings Move, Makes Sound, Metal, Windup, Japan, Box, 1950s	75.00
Ducky Ducklings, Mom Duck Pulling Babies, Tin, Windup, Wyandotte, Box, 1950s, 16 In.	195.00
Dustpan, 2 Children, Tray Lifts When Handle Pressed, Tin Lithograph, Penny Toy, 4¼ In.	193.00
Earth Mover, Euclid, Pressed Steel, Rubber Tires, Doepke, 27 In.	154.00
Elephant, Jumbo, Bubble Blowing, Y Co. Of Japan, Box	125.00
Elephant, Sunshine Animal Crackers, Cloth, Cardboard Base, 7 x 5½ x 2 In.	358.00
Elephant, Wood, Jointed, Leather Ears, Tusk, Rope Tail, Glass Eyes, Drum, Schoenhut, 11 In.	66.00
Elf, Pushing Wheelbarrow, Tin, Windup, Painted, Germany, 7 In.	550.00
Elf, Windup, Musical, 11 In.	95.00
Elmer Fudd, Tips Hat, Rubber, Metal Crank, Plastic Base, 1950s, 2 In.	156.00
Engine, Ignitionless, CO2 Powered, For Model Airplanes, Herkimer Tool Co., 1930s	125.00
Engineer Set, Army, Pressed Steel, Plastic Tires, Structo, 1950s, 6 Piece	468.00
Erector Set, No. 7, The Toy That Builds The Steam, Red Wood Box, c.1927, 21½ In. *illus*	100.00
Erector Set, Pressed Steel, Motors, Box	88.00
Express Silver Star, Tin, Friction, Chrome Plate, Daiya, Box, 9¾ In.	110.00
Ferdinand The Bull, Horns, Flower, Butterfly, Tin, Windup, Marked, Marx, Box, 1938, 7 In.	495.00
Ferris Wheel, Metal, Windup, USA, Box, 16 In.	295.00
Ferris Wheel, Tin, Windup, Hercules, 6 Gondolas, Entrance Sign, Chein, 16 In.	235.00 to 253.00
Figure, California Raisins, Hardee's Kids Meal Premium, 1987, Set Of 5	6.00
Figure, Full Cry, Mounted Huntsmen, Dogs, Fox, Britains, 21 Piece	353.00
Figure, Mickey McGuire, Toonerville Character, Fontaine Fox, Wood, Painted, Movable Limbs, 7 In.	125.00
Figure, Poured Wax, Gentleman, Glass Eyes, Muslin Body, England, c.1875, 20 In.	2820.00
Filling Station, Electric Lighted, Roadside Rest, Pressed Steel, Marx, Box, 14 In. *illus*	819.00
Finnegan The Porter, Drives Luggage Cart, Windup, Unique Art, 13½ In.	195.00
Fire Hydrant, Cast Iron, Eddy Prescott, 1925, 3¼ In.	110.00
Fire Pumper, 2 Horses, Removable Driver, Cast Iron, 12 In.	33.00
Fire Pumper, 2 White Galloping Horses, Yellow, Gold, Driver, Kenton, 26½ In.	3738.00
Fire Pumper, 3 Horses, Cast Iron, Driver, Boiler, 23 In.	33.00
Fire Pumper, 3 Horses, Cast Iron, Wilkins, c.1900, 19 In.	529.00
Fire Pumper, 3 Horses, Driver Holding Reins, Painted, Wilkins, 21 In.	900.00
Fire Pumper, Cast Iron, Red, Nickel Plate, Hubley, 1930s, 5 In.	150.00
Fire Pumper, Driver, Cast Iron, Nickel Plated Boiler, Kenton, 14 In.	495.00
Fire Pumper, Horses Gallop, Tin, Steel, Wood, 17 In.	925.00
Fire Pumper, Pontiac, Arcade, c.1936, 4½ In.	140.00
Fire Pumper, Steam, Nickeled Bumper, Kenton, 12 In.	500.00
Fire Pumper, Steam, Red, Silver, Nickel Grill, Hubley, 8½ In.	650.00
Fire Pumper, White Horses, Driver, Cast Iron Eagle, Wood Gas Bag, Brown, 19 In.	575.00
Fire Station, Red Roof, No. MF1, Matchbox *illus*	157.00
Fire Truck, Aerial Ladder, Pressed Steel, Buddy L, 1930s, 40 In.	935.00
Fire Truck, Aerial Ladder, Windup, Siren, Doepke American, 32 In.	275.00
Fire Truck, Battery Operated, Japan, 1950s, 12 In.	175.00
Fire Truck, Dump, Fixed Bed, Pressed Steel, Rubber Tires, Spoke Wheels, Buddy L, 25 In.	935.00
Fire Truck, Extension Ladder Trailer, GMC, Buddy L, 28 In.	118.00
Fire Truck, Hook & Ladder, Fire Dept., Steel, Art Deco, Crank Ladder, Wyandotte, 23 In.	385.00

Toy, Dog, Bulldog, Papier-Mache, Glass Eyes, Growls, Head Moves, 4 Wheels, 10 x 19 In. $1035.00

Toy, Dog, Fur Covered, Squeaker, Barks When Cord Is Pulled, Glass Eyes, Germany, 9 In. $260.00

Toy, Dog, Plush, Mohair, Push & Pull, Iron Wheels, Button In Ear, Steiff, 16 x 12 In. $3575.00

Toy, Dollhouse Furniture, Bookcase, Glass Door, Drawer, Miniature Books, 6 x 4 In. $480.00

T

Toy, Dollhouse Furniture, Buffet, Ormolu, Gallery, Doors Open, 6 x 4 In. $748.00

Toy, Dollhouse Furniture, Etagere, Bone, Turned Supports, 3 Shelves, Dishes, 3¾ In. $144.00

Toy, Erector Set, No. 7, The Toy That Builds The Steam, Red Wood Box, c.1927, 21½ In. $100.00

Toy, Filling Station, Electric Lighted, Roadside Rest, Pressed Steel, Marx, Box, 14 In. $819.00

Fire Truck, Ladder, Cast Aluminum, Red, Nickel Plating, Kiddy Toy, Hubley, 1950s, 12 In. ...	65.00
Fire Truck, Ladder, GMC, Buddy L, Box, 26 In.	395.00
Fire Truck, Ladder, Pull & Ride, Red, White, Buddy L, 1949, 30 In.	325.00
Fire Truck, Ladder, Tonka, 1980s, 34 In.	50.00
Fire Truck, Mack, Tootsietoy, Package, 10 In.	150.00
Fire Truck, No. 6, Extension Ladders, Buddy L, 1950s	94.00
Fire Truck, Red, Separate Chassis, A.C. Williams, 7½ In.	1650.00
Fire Truck, Reel, Ladder, Pressed Steel, Buddy L, 26 In.	990.00
Fire Truck, Tin, Friction, Japan, Early 1950s, 5¼ In.	149.00
Fire Wagon, Hook & Ladder, 2 Horses, 2 Ladders, 2 Firemen, Cast Iron, Hubley, 1910, 24 In. ..	825.00
Fire Wagon, Hook & Ladder, 2 Horses, Firemen, Copper Wash, 1880s, 25 In.	1795.00
Fire Wagon, Hook & Ladder, 2 Horses, Phoenix, Yellow Frame, Ives, 1880s, 26 In.	1595.00
Fire Wagon, Hook & Ladder, 3 Horses, 3 Ladders, 2 Firemen, Dent, 1905, 26 In.	1195.00
Fire Wagon, Hook & Ladder, Horses, Figures, Jones & Bixler, 1908, 31 In.	2795.00
Fire Wagon, Hook & Ladder, Horses, Figures, Kenton, 1910, 16¾ In.	650.00
Fire Wagon, Patrol, 2 Horses, Driver, 6 Firemen, Phoenix, Ives, c.1885, 21 In.	2350.00
Fire Wagon, Pumper, 3 Horses, Driver, Iron, Spokes, Gold Boiler, Kenton, 12¾ In. ..... *illus*	288.00
Fire Wagon, Red Paint, Mustard Highlights, Slat Supports, Ladder, Barrel, 40 x 20 In.	1035.00
Firehouse, 2 Ladder Fire Trucks, Flag, Buddy L, 1947	2500.00
Firehouse, General Alarm, 2 Garages, 2 Vehicles, Marx	1095.00
Firehouse, Wood, Nickel Plated Bell, Arcade, 12 In.	880.00
Fireman, Smokey Joe The Climbing Fireman, Windup, Tin, Marx, Box, 20 In. .... *illus*	495.00
Flintstones, Dino, On Tricycle, Tin, Windup, Celluloid, Marx	585.00
Flintstones, Dino-The-Dinosaur, Battery Operated, 18 x 12 In.	988.00
Flintstones, Dino-The-Dinosaur, Tin Lithograph, Windup, Linemar, Box, 1961, 5½ In.	588.00
Flintstones, Flivver, Fred Flintstone Driving Car, Friction, Marx, Japan, 7 In.	495.00
Flintstones, Tricycle, Dino, Tin, Celluloid, Windup, Marx, Box, 4¼ In.	750.00
Flip The Frog, Velveteen, Stuffed, Wire For Posing, Dean's Rag Book, 1930s, 8 In.	335.00
Flippo Dog, Windup, Linemar, Japan	110.00
Flying Jeep, Tin Lithograph, Friction, Spark, Linemar, Box, 1950s, 6 In.	484.00
Flying Saucer, Metal Toys, Tin, Battery Operated, Mystery Action, Cragston, Box, 9½ In.	358.00
Food Grinder, Wood, Doepke, 1957	95.00
Foodini & Friends, Pop-Up, Canister, Tin Lithograph, c.1951, 5 In.	252.00
Forklift, Tin, Plastic, Battery Operated, Blinking Engine Light, KY, Japan, Box, 10½ In.	110.00
Fox, Dressed As Master-Of-The-Hounds, Pink Jacket, Black Boots, Chocolate Plush, 29 In. ...	176.00
Fox The Magician, Tin, Fabric, Plush, Windup, Box	475.00
Frankenstein, Tin, Vinyl, Walks, Pants Drop, Face Turns Red, Nomura, Box, 13 In.	193.00
Frankenstein, Mechanical, Walks, Windup, Tin, Plastic, Marx, Box, 5 In. .... *illus*	770.00
Frankenstein, Plastic, Remote Control, Battery Operated, Marx, 1963, 5¼ In.	1172.00
Frankenstein, Walker, Plastic, Universal Pictures, 1960s, 5½ In.	820.00
French Trapeze, Les Voltigeurs, Composition, Metal, France, Box, 14 In.	110.00
Funland Cup Ride, Tin, Plastic, Cups Spin, Battery Operated, Kanto, Box, 7 In.	286.00
Funny Face, Harold Lloyd, Marx, Box, 11 In.	995.00
Funny Face, Walker, Tin, Windup, Marx, Box, 10½ In.	784.00
G.I. Joe & His Jouncing Jeep, Tin Lithograph, Windup, Unique Art, Box, c.1950, 7 In.	277.00
G.I. Joe & K-9 Pups, Tin Lithograph, Windup, Unique Art, c.1950, 9 In.	246.00
G.I. Joe Shave 'N Shine Kit, Hasbro, 1967, 9¾ x 10¼ In.	373.00
Games are listed in their own category.	
Garage, Wood, 2 Doors, Green Roof, Arcade, 15 In.	825.00
Garage, Wood, 5 Stalls, Doors Open, Arcade, 16 In.	1980.00
Garage, Wood, Pressed Steel Door, Green Roof, Arcade, 12¾ In.	825.00
Garage, Yellow, Red Roof, Gas Pump Island, Tin, Lithographed Paper, 15 In. .... *illus*	403.00
Gas Pump, Cast Iron, Arcade, 7 In.	385.00
Gas Pump, Cast Iron, Rope Hose, A.C. Williams, 4¾ In.	165.00
Gas Pump, Cast Iron, Rope Hose, Arcade, 1934, 6 In.	303.00
Gas Pump, Cast Iron, Rope Hose, Nickel Crank, A.C. Williams, 6½ In.	440.00
Gas Pump, Cast Iron, Stencil, Decal, Arcade, 6¼ In.	275.00
Gas Pump, Pressed Steel, Red, Woven Cord Hose, Arcade, 6¾ In. .... *illus*	265.00
Gas Station, Mobil Oil, Tin, 2 Cars, Japan, 1950s	145.00
Gas Station, Roadside Rest Service Station, Pumps, Car, Diner, Metal, Marx, 1950s, 13½ In.	345.00
Gazelle, Wood, Jointed, Leather Ears & Horns, Painted Eyes, Schoenhut, 6 In.	660.00
General Butler, Walker, Blue Jacket, Red Pants, Crank, Ives, 19th Century, 9½ In.	3360.00
George The Drummer Boy, Tin, Windup, Fixed Eye, Marx, Box, 9 In.	193.00
Giraffe, Button In Right Ear, Pull, Cast Iron Wheels, Steiff, 20 In.	385.00
Giraffe, Wood, Jointed, Leather Ears, Rope Tail, Glass Eyes, Schoenhut, 9½ In.	523.00
Goat, On Platform, Fur, Painted, Composition, Glass Eyes, Metal Wheels, Pull Toy, 6 In.	138.00

Goat, Wood, Jointed, Gray & White, Leather Horns, Beard & Tail, Glass Eyes, Schoenhut, 7¾ In.	138.00
Go-Cart, Driver, No. 7, Tin, Friction, Japan, 1950s, 7½ In.	145.00
Go-Cart, Driver, Tin, Light-Up, Battery Operated, Japan, 1950s, 10 In.	125.00
Go-Cart, Tin, Driver, Friction, Japan, 1950s, 7 In.	145.00
Golfer, On Stick, Metal Arms, Club, Molded Wood Head & Body, Ratchet Action, Schoenhut, 27 In.	440.00
Good Time Charlie, Mixed Material, Windup, Bends At Knees, Twirls Cane, Alps, 13 In.	220.00
Gorilla, Mechanical, Mixed Material, Windup, Walking Motion, Beats Chest, Marx, Box, 8 In.	248.00
Grandpa Bear, In Rocker, Battery Operated, Alps, Box, 9 In.	325.00
Graphoscope, Stereo, Hand Held Lens Viewer, Turned Wooden Handle, 8¾ In. ......*illus*	115.00
Grasshopper, Green, Cast Iron, Aluminum Legs, Rubber Tires, Hubley, 10 In.	605.00
Greenhouse, Wood, Glass Windows, Paper Litho Base, Work Tables, Plants, c.1890, 24 In.	3080.00
Grocery Shop, Wood, Open Front, Shelves, Drawers, Counter, Food, 10 x 25 x 11 In.	441.00
Guided Missile Launcher, Platform Turns, Lever Fires Missiles, Yonezawa, Box	275.00
Guitar, Doctor Dolittle, Image Of Rex Harrison, Turn Crank, Mattel, 1962	65.00
Gun, Astro Fleet Flying Saucer, Plastic, Parker Plastics, Box, 1950s, 8¾ x 9 In.	31.00
Gun, BB, Jr. Shooters Outfit, Target, Accessories, Unopened, Daisy, Box, 1960s, 12 x 23½ In.	524.00
Gun, Deputy Pistol, Die Cast Nickel, Plastic Badge, Hubley, Box, c.1960, 4½ x 10½ In.	1007.00
Gun, Lost In Space Roto Jet, Plastic, Mattel, Box, 1966, 7 x 13½ x 4 In.	2587.00
Gun, Machine, Double Barrel, Sparks, Noise, Friction, Tin Litho, Metal, TN Of Japan, Box	85.00
Gun, Sambo, Cast Iron, Figural, 2½ x 4¾ In.	495.00
Gun, Smoke Ring, Plastic, Nu-Age Production, Box, 1950s, 9 In.	299.00
Gun & Holster, Bat Masterson, Cane, Vest, Carnell Roundup, Box, c.1958, 18 x 13 In.	678.00
Gun & Holster, Civil War Centennial, Model 61, Keystone, Nichols, Box, 1961, 7 x 11 In.	438.00
Gun & Holster, Double, 6-Gun, Lone Star, England, 1950s, 11½-In. Guns	1568.00
Gun & Holster, Shoulder Holster, I Spy, Plastic Gun, Ray Plastic, On Card, 1966, 13 x 11 In.	168.00
Gun & Holster, Swivel Shot Trick, Mattel, Box & Instructions	300.00
Gunboat, Hillclimber, Green, Flywheel, Schiebel, 10½ In.	140.00
Ham & Sam, Minstrel Team, Tin, Windup, Strauss, 7 In.	330.00
Handcar, Easy Rider, No. 500, Pressed Steel, Advertising Tag, Buddy L, c.1931, 36 x 29 In. *illus*	7700.00
Handcar, Moon Mullins, Kayo Standing On Dynamite, Black, Tin, Windup, Marx, Box, 6 In.	110.00
Hansel & Gretel, Gingerbread House, Forest, Fence, Witch, Cat, Crow, 18¼ In.	2880.00
Hansom Cab, Horse Drawn, Driver In Back, Lady Passenger, Tin Litho, Penny, Meier, 3½ In.	303.00
Hansom Cab, White Horse, Cast Iron, Kenton, 13 In. ......*illus*	410.00
Happy Band Trio, Battery Operated, Modern Toys, Box	650.00
Happy Bunny, Comic Fold-Up Car, Bunny Driver, Tin Friction, Japan, 6 In.	195.00
Happy Hooligan, Dancing On Drum, Crank, Kiddies Metal Toy Co., 1930s	1450.00
Happy Hooligan, Roly Poly, Schoenhut, 1910, 4¼ In.	195.00 to 225.00
Happy Hooligan, Walker, Windup, Chein, 1930s	475.00
Happy Hooligan, Wood, Lithograph Paper, Movable Limbs, 14 In.	145.00
Happy Jack, Black Minstrel Dances, Crank Turn, Kellerman Co., Germany	550.00
Harlem Dancer, Lenox Ave. & 125 St., Tin, Windup, 1940s	133.00
Haunted House, Skeleton, Spooky Sounds, Winds, Ghost, Battery Operated, Marx, 11 In.	540.00
Helicopter, Battle, Tin, Plastic, Windup, Army, Soldiers, Litho, Alps, Box, 13½ In.	204.00
Helicopter, Evacuation, Tin Lithograph, Marx, Box, 1966, 10 In.	84.00
Helicopter, Sky Patrol, Metal, Plastic, 2 Propellers, Korea, Box, 1960, 8 In.	75.00
Helmet, Texaco Fire Chief, Box, 14 In.	118.00
Henry & Henrietta Travelers, Walker, Tin Suitcases, Celluloid, Windup, Japan, Box, 7 In.	3300.00
Henry & His Swan, Swan Pulls Henry Sitting On Cart, Celluloid, Windup, Japan, Box, 8 In.	2090.00
Henry On Elephant, Black Boy On Top, White Boy On Trunk, Celluloid, Windup, Japan, 9 In.	660.00
Hey-Hey Chicken Snatcher, Tin, Windup, Marx, 9 In.	1650.00
Highway Transport Set, Semi, Gas Truck, Dump Truck, Tin, Friction, Harusame, Box	300.00
Hippo, Wood, Sleep Eyes, Schoenhut	375.00
Hoky Poky, Metal, Windup, 2 Clowns, Wyandotte, 1950s, 6½ In.	195.00
Honeymoon Special, Tin, Windup, Key, Red Bridge, Litho Leaves, Marx, 6 In.	121.00
Horse, Black, Cloth, Fur Mane, Tail, Button Eyes, Stitched Mouth, Handmade, Amish, 16 x 13 In.	110.00
Horse, Black, Fur, White Stitched Mouth, Stuffed, Handmade, Amish, 15 x 13 In.	55.00
Horse, Brown, Saddle, Blue, Red, Cloth, Button Eyes, Handmade, Amish, 9 x 10 In.	4675.00
Horse, Cab, Tin Lithograph, Logos, Fischer, Germany, Penny, 4¾ In.	300.00
Horse, Carousel, Jumping, Glass Eyes, Saddle Jewels, Leather, Metal Stirrups, 58 x 40½ In.	1208.00
Horse, Carousel, Rearing, Rockers, Multicolored, Glass Eyes, 58 x 52 In.	1265.00
Horse, Cast Iron, Metal, Windup, Wolverine, 1922	175.00
Horse, Hide Covered, Platform, Iron Wheels, Leather Bridle, Blanket, Pull, 14½ x 12½ In.	232.00
Horse, Mohair, Leather Ears, Saddle, Horsehair Tail, Platform, Iron Wheels, Pull, 11 x 11 In.	275.00
Horse, Pulling Green Sleigh, Woman Driver, Cast Iron, 14 In.	86.00
Horse, Ride On, On Wheels, Painted, Saddle Seat, Wood, 12 x 12 In.	210.00
Horse, Rocking, Brown Felt, Fur Mane, Horsehair Tail, Carved Muzzle, Hooves, 30 x 43 In.	316.00

Toy, Fire Station, Red Roof, No. MF1, Matchbox
$157.00

Toy, Fire Wagon, Pumper, 3 Horses, Driver, Iron, Spokes, Gold Boiler, Kenton, 12¾ In.
$288.00

Toy, Fireman, Smokey Joe The Climbing Fireman, Windup, Tin, Marx, Box, 20 In.
$495.00

Toy, Frankenstein, Mechanical, Walks, Windup, Tin, Plastic, Marx, Box, 5 In.
$770.00

Toy, Garage, Yellow, Red Roof, Gas Pump Island, Tin, Lithographed Paper, 15 In. $403.00

Toy, Gas Pump, Pressed Steel, Red, Woven Cord Hose, Arcade, 6¾ In. $265.00

Toy, Graphoscope, Stereo, Hand Held Lens Viewer, Turned Wooden Handle, 8¾ In. $115.00

Toy, Handcar, Easy Rider, No. 500, Pressed Steel, Advertising Tag, Buddy L, c.1931, 36 x 29 In. $7700.00

Horse, Rocking, Carved, Painted, Pinstriped Rockers, 53 In.	748.00
Horse, Rocking, Cutout Head, Pine, Seat On Platform, Stenciling, Cloth Seat, 46 x 21 In.	1265.00
Horse, Rocking, Dapple Gray, Wood, Leather Ears, Horsehair Mane & Tail, Tack Eyes, 52 In.	1840.00
Horse, Rocking, Wood, Dapple Gray Paint, Red Rocker, Straw Stuffed Saddle, 43 x 22½ In.	1121.00
Horse, Spring, Rearing, Painted, Scrolled Spring Support, Shaped Base, 44½ x 57 In.	935.00
Horse, Spring Base, Galloping Noise, Painted, Papier-Mache, Wood Base, 7 In.	44.00
Horse & Sleigh, Open Sleigh, Victorian Woman Driver, Cast Iron, Hubley, 15 In.	750.00
Horse & Wagon, 2 Horses, Weber, Cast Iron, Arcade, 12 In.	295.00
Horse & Wagon, Ride On, Wood, Glass Eyes, Spoked Metal Wheels, c.1875, 60 In.	3520.00
Horse & Wagon, Sand & Gravel, Driver, 2 Horses, Green, Red Wheels, Kenton, 15 In.	325.00
Horse & Wagon, U.S. Mail, Mail Pouch, Tin & Wood, Gibbs Toy Co., 12 In.	880.00
Horse & Wagon, U.S. Mail, White Horse, Pulling Tin Wagon, Paint, Cast Iron, 11 In.	198.00
Horse Racing, 3 Horses & Riders, Bell, Tin, Windup, Japan	110.00
Hot Mammy, Wood Head, Lead Feet, No. 810, Fisher-Price, Box, 6 In.	880.00
Hound Dog, Dressed As Man, Dachshund, Wheeled Base, Tin, Gesch, Germany, 4 In. *illus*	605.00
House Trailer, 1961 Ford Convertible, Tin, Friction, Haji, Box, 16¾ In.	825.00
Humphrey Mobile, Joe Palooka, Comic Strip, Tin, Windup, Wyandotte, Box, 7 x 10 In.	616.00
Humphrey Mobile, Windup, Wyandotte, Box, 1940s	750.00
Hungry Chicks, Spins, Bells Ring, Chickens Pop Out, Celluloid, Windup, Japan	125.00
Hyena, Wood, Jointed, Leather Ears, Rope Tail, Glass Eyes, Carved Mouth, Schoenhut, 6 In.	2475.00
I.C.B.M. Launching Station, Tin, Friction, Crank, 2-Stage Rocket, Horikawa, Box, 18½ In.	523.00
Ice Box, Alaska, Pressed Steel, Cast Iron, Hubley, 5 In.	121.00
Ice Box, Cast Iron, Pressed Steel, Leonard, Arcade, 5¾ In.	154.00
Ice Cream Vendor, Tin, Plastic, Windup, Monkey Vendor, Pushes Cart, Yone, Box, 5 In.	193.00
Ice Cream Vendor, Windup, Masudaya, Japan, Box, 4 In.	295.00
Indian, Horse, Tin, Windup, Japan, 1960s	95.00
Indian, Jumping Jack, Feather Headdress, String Pull, Multicolor, 9⅝ In.	39.00
Indian, On Horse, Windup, Haji, Japan, 9 In.	130.00
Indian, Walker, Metal, Windup, Marx, Japan, 1950s, 4 In.	75.00
Irish Mail Cart, Child's, Self-Propelled, Handle, Wood Seat, 4 Spoke Wheels	600.00
Iron, Plastic, My Little Steam Iron, Cord, Musical	10.00
Iron, Play At Home, Musical, Water Spray, Box	5.00
Iron-Jawed Lady, Trapeze Artist, Wood, Carved, Painted, Wire, Flags, Feathers, 24 x 12 x 5 In.	1035.00
Jack Sprat & His Wife, Painted, Tin, Windup, Gunthermann, 7 In. *illus*	322.00
Jambo Jin, With Fiddler, 1920s, 9 In.	600.00
James Bond 007 Spy Tricks, A.C. Gilbert, Box, 1965, 13¾ x 20¼ In.	493.00
Jazzbo Jim, Roof Dancer, Tin, Windup, Linemar, 7 In.	1725.00
Jazzbo Jim, Roof Dancer, Tin, Windup, Unique Art, 10 In.	460.00
Jeep, Commander, Tin Lithograph, Hadson, Japan, Box, 1950s, 9¼ In.	166.00
Jeep, G.I. Joe & His Bouncing Jeep, Windup, Unique Art, Box, 1940s, 7 In.	263.00
Jeep, Jumpin', Tin, Windup, 4 Soldiers, Lithograph, Crazy Car, Marx, Box, 1947, 6 In.	220.00
Jeep, Jumpin' Jeep, 4 People, Windup, Marx, 6 In.	125.00
Jeep, M38, Radio, Battery Operated, Mystery Action, Articulated Driver, Nomura, Box, 11 In.	165.00
Jeep, Radar, Nomura, Tin, Battery Operated, Radar Dish Turns, Box, 11 In.	165.00
Jeep, U.S. Air Force Radio, Marx, Box, 1940s	475.00
Jeep, United Airlines, Tin, Friction, Driver Waving Advances, Litho, Yoshiya, Box, 7 In.	88.00
Jeep, Willys, Pressed Steel, Marx, 11 In.	195.00
Jigger, Black, Hat, Green Tie, Coattails, Wood Carved, Wishbone Shape Handle, c.1900, 16 In.	353.00
Joe Penner, Walker, Tin, Windup, Marx, 8½ In.	385.00
Jumping Racer, Tin, Friction, 2 Card, Ramp, Lithograph, Marusan, Box, 24½ In.	605.00
Jungle Trio, 2 Monkeys, Elephant, Playing Instruments, Battery Operated, Japan, Box, 8 In.	440.00
Jungle Trio, Whistle, Battery Operated, Linemar, Box	1125.00
Junior Jack, For Pedal Cars, Pressed Steel, Box, 6 In.	44.00
Kaleidoscope, Brass, Marble Stand, 16 In.	440.00
Kaleidoscope, Parlor, Bush, Paper Covered Tube, Brass Object Box, Walnut Base, 14½ In.	999.00
Kangaroo, Baby In Pouch, Moves Up & Down, T.P.S., Japan, 1950s, 6½ In.	95.00
Kangaroo, Wood, Jointed, Leather Ears, Carved Mouth, Glass Eyes, Schoenhut, 7 In.	935.00
Kid Samson, Hits Mallet, Rings Bell, Tin, Windup, B & R, 9 In.	550.00
Kitty Cat, Metal, Windup, Marx, Montgomery Ward, 1930s	175.00
Knights, Crescent Toys, England, Box, 1950s, 3 x 14 x 1 In., 6 2-In. Figures	135.00
Knights, Crescent Toys, England, Box, 1950s, 6½ x 14½ x 1½ In., 12 2-In. Figures	952.00
Knock-Out Prize Fighters, Red Mike, Battling Jim, Tin, Windup, Strauss, Box, 1920s	392.00
Knock-Out Prize Fighters, Wood Figures, Tin Base, Rope, Windup, Strauss, 5 In.	987.00
Kool-Aid Dispenser, Glass Jar Stand, 2 Packages Kool-Aid, c.1950, 11 In.	246.00
Krazy Kat, On Scooter, Tin, Windup, Nifty, Germany, c.1920s, 7½ In.	625.00
Lamb, Lamb's Wool Fleece, Papier-Mache, Wheels, Felt, Glass Eyes, France, c.1890, 17 In.	1265.00

T

Lamb, Wool, Jointed, Leather Ears, Glass Eyes, Red Fabric Collar, Bell, Schoenhut, 7 In.	468.00
Landing Of Columbus, Bell, Cast Iron, c.1900	650.00
Lantern Robot, Tin, Battery Operated Remote, Tettering Walking, Linemar, 7¾ In.	1650.00
Lawnmower, Reel, Cast Iron, Nickel Plated Wheels, Kilgore, 3¾ In.	523.00
Leopard, Wood, Jointed, Yellow, Spots, Rope Tail, Glass Eyes, Drum, Schoenhut, 7¼ In.	990.00
Li'l Abner Dogpatch Band, Tin, Windup, Unique Art, Box, c.1945	523.00
Lion, Wood, Jointed, Carved Mane, Ball Jointed, Circus Pedestal, Schoenhut, 7¼ In.	660.00
Lion, Wood, Jointed, Cloth Mane, Open Mouth, Circus Pedestal, Style I, Schoenhut, 7 In.	1045.00
Lion & Clown, Lion Chases Clown Up Pole, Battery Operated, TN, Japan, 1950s	375.00
Log Trailer, Cast Metal, 5 Wood Logs, Structo, Box, 1950s, 18½ In.	327.00
Magic Slate, Rin Tin Tin, Stylus, Whitman, 1950s, 14 x 9¼ In.	101.00
Main Street, Tin Lithograph, Windup, Marx, Box, c.1929, 3½ x 24 x 3 In.	949.00
Mama Duck Pulling 2 Babies, Wheels, Wood, Push Pull, No. 101, Fisher-Price, 9 In. . . *illus*	2340.00
Mammy, Tin, Windup, Litho, Apron, Kerchief, Lindstrom, 7¾ In.	275.00
Man, Shooting, From Mars, Windup, Irwin, 11½ In.	246.00
Man Da Rin, Chinese Men Toting Carriage, Tin, Lehmann, 7 In. . . . . *illus*	2633.00
Man In Barrel, Black, Moves Side To Side, Polychrome Paint, Handle, 7 In.	66.00
Man Pushing Wheelbarrow, Tin, Windup, Black Figure, Girard, 5¾ In.	204.00
Map, Weber City, Amos 'N' Andy, Pepsodent Premium, Original Letter, Mailer, 1935	120.00
Marionette, Jambo The Jiver, Wood, Painted, Jointed, Box, 13½ In.	50.00
Marky Mapo, Sitting, Vinyl, Squeak, 1960s, 9 In.	142.00
Mary & Lamb, Wood, Glass Eyes, Jointed, Schoenhut, 8 In. *illus*	550.00
Mechanic Set, Nickel Plated, Showcase, Arcade, 1941	66.00
Mercury Explorer, Tin, Plastic, Battery Operated, Mystery Action, Lighted, T.P.S., Box, 8 In. .	248.00
Merry Cockyolly See-Saw, 2 Roosters, Windup, Masuya, Japan, Box, 7 In.	325.00
Merry-Go-Round, Playland, Tin, Windup, Swans, Children Riding Horses, Chein, Box, 10 In.	457.00
Merry-Go-Round, Tin, Windup, Horses, Wire Hung Airplanes, Wolverine, Box, 11 In.	330.00
Merrymakers Band, 4 Mice, Play Instruments, Dances, Art Deco, Marx, 9½ In.	920.00
Merrymakers Band, Tin, Windup, Violin Player, Marx, 9 In.	920.00
Merrymakers Band, Violin Player, Piano, Drums, Tin, Windup, Marx, 10 In.	825.00
Mice, Playing, 2 Mice Race Down Spiral Rod, Lehmann, 1926, 14 In.	125.00
Military Set, Tin, Friction, Tank, Jet Plane, Helicopter, Truck, Trailer, Hayashi, Box, 10 Piece	330.00
Minstrel, Black Man Seated, Chair, Uses Arms & Legs To Play Instruments, Windup, Painted	1250.00
Minstrel, Black Man, Checkered Coat, Jumps Up & Down On Base, American Co., 1930s	195.00
Mobile, Metal, Humphrey, 9½ In.	445.00
Model Kit, Airplane, Spirit Of St. Louis, Instructions, Metalcraft, Box, 1930s, 11½ In. . . *illus*	115.00
Model Kit, American Astronaut, Unused, Aurora, Box, 1967	56.00
Model Kit, Dracula, Aurora, Canada, Box, 1964	168.00
Model Kit, King Kong, Unopened, Aurora, Box, 1972	388.00
Model Kit, Land Of The Giants, No. 816-150, Plastic, Box	333.00
Model Kit, Mummy, Aurora, Box, 1963	224.00
Model Kit, Voyage To The Bottom Of The Sea, Seaview, Aurora, Box, 1966	328.00
Monkey, Bisque, Mask Face, Painted, Pin-Jointed, Germany, c.1900, 3½ In.	633.00
Monkey, Drinking, Windup, Linemar, Japan, Box, 6 In.	175.00
Monkey, Fishing On Whale, T.P.S., Box	365.00
Monkey, Irish Mail Cart, Bellows, Pull Toy, Steiff, 10½ In.	450.00
Monkey, Perfume, Green Mohair, Schuco, c.1920	850.00
Monkey, Playing Guitar, Sitting On Stump, Tin, Celluloid, Windup, Musical, 7½ In.	275.00
Monkey, Playing Violin, Schuco	150.00
Monkey, Roly Poly, Tin, Weighted Base Wobbles, Chein, 6½ In.	165.00
Monkey, String-Jointed, Bent Arms, Voice Box, Button Ears, Steiff, 1903, 32 In.	6610.00
Monkeys, Acrobatic, Tin, Windup, Clown On Motorcycle, Wyandotte, 10 In.	193.00
Monoplane, Tin, Windup, Chein, 6½ In.	165.00
Monoplane, Tin, Windup, Litho, Chein, 6¾-In. Wingspan	193.00
Monster, Creature From Black Lagoon, Action Aerating, Penn-Plax, Box, 1971, 5¾ In.	1607.00
Moon Explorer, Tin, Battery Operated, Lights Flash, Pistons Move, Alps, 17½ In.	2200.00
Moon Rocket, Tin, Battery Operated, Flashing Lights, Sound, Masudaya, Box, 9½ In.	300.00
Moon Rocket, Tin, Battery Operated, Non Fall Action, Flashing Lights, Masudaya, 9½ In. . . .	171.00
Moon Traveler, Apollo Z, Tin Lithograph, Plastic, Nomura, Box, c.1969, 11½ In.	224.00
Mother Goose, Cat, Goose, Tin, Windup, Marx, 9 In.	660.00
Motorcycle, Acrocycle, Circus Clown, Tin Lithograph, Key, Windup, 1950s, 6¼ In.	375.00
Motorcycle, Blue, Rubber Tires, Champion, 7¼ In.	475.00
Motorcycle, Delivery, Easter Bunny, Sidecar, Tin Lithograph, Wyandotte, 1930s, 9½ In.	163.00
Motorcycle, Driver, Battery Compartment For Light Bulb, Cast Iron, Hubley, 6 In.	350.00
Motorcycle, Driver, Echo, Spokes, Windup, Tin Lithograph, Lehmann, Germany, 8½ In. *illus*	2875.00
Motorcycle, Driver, No. 3, Tin, Friction, MC, Japan, 1950s	75.00

Toy, Hansom Cab, White Horse,
Cast Iron, Kenton, 13 In.
$410.00

Toy, Hound Dog, Dressed As Man,
Dachshund, Wheeled Base, Tin,
Gesch, Germany, 4 In.
$605.00

Toy, Jack Sprat & His Wife, Painted,
Tin, Windup, Guntherman, 7 In.
$322.00

Toy, Mama Duck Pulling 2 Babies,
Wheels, Wood, Push Pull, No. 101,
Fisher-Price, 9 In.
$2340.00

T

Toy, Man Da Rin, Chinese Men Toting Carriage, Tin, Lehmann, 7 In. $2633.00

Toy, Mary & Lamb, Wood, Glass Eyes, Jointed, Schoenhut, 8 In. $550.00

Toy, Model Kit, Airplane, Spirit Of St. Louis, Instructions, Metalcraft, Box, 1930s, 11½ In. $115.00

Toy, Motorcycle, Driver, Echo, Spokes, Windup, Tin Lithograph, Lehmann, Germany, 8½ In. $2875.00

Motorcycle, Indian, Policeman, Sidecar, Cast Iron, Hubley, 9 In.	750.00
Motorcycle, MAC 700, Red, Tin, Windup, Rider Gets On & Off, Arnold, Box, 8 In.	1073.00
Motorcycle, Police, Blue, Rubber Tires, Champion, 7¼ In.	475.00
Motorcycle, Police, Sidecar Passenger, Red, Blue, Hubley, 4 In.	295.00
Motorcycle, Police, Siren, Windup, Marx, 1930s, 8 In.	325.00
Motorcycle, Police, Tin Lithograph, Windup, Key, Policeman, Unique Art, 1930s, 8½ In.	336.00
Motorcycle, Policeman, Cast Iron, Champion, 7 In.	250.00
Motorcycle, Policeman, Cast Iron, Hubley, 4¼ In.	145.00
Motorcycle, Policeman, Cast Iron, Hubley, 6½ In.	250.00
Motorcycle, Policeman, Cast Iron, Nickel Wheels, Champion, 7 In. ....*illus*	585.00
Motorcycle, Policeman, Cast Iron, Red, White Rubber Tires, Hubley, 1930s	125.00
Motorcycle, Policeman, Red, Rubber Tires, Cast Iron, 1940s, 4 x 6¼ In.	77.00
Motorcycle, Sidecar, Driver, Orange, Cast Iron, Hubley, 4 In.	150.00
Motorcycle, Sidecar, Driver, Rider, Red, Blue, Cast Iron, Hubley, 4 In.	275.00
Motorcycle, Sidecar, Policemen, Cast Iron, Hubley, 9 In.	750.00
Motorcycle, Sidecar, Triumph, Metallic Silver, Blue, Knobbly, Plastic Tires, Matchbox, Box	102.00
Motorcycle, Speedboy, Tin, Windup, Marx, 10 In.	660.00
Motorcycle, Tin, Rubber Tires, Tin Spoke Wheels, Rider, Friction Motor, Japan, 11½ In.	1438.00
Motorcycle, Tin, Windup, Wheels Turn, Sparks Fly, Gunthermann, 6¾ In.	2280.00
Motorcycle, Tricky, Tin, Windup, Police, Runs In Circle, Marx, Box, 4¼ In.	248.00
Mouse, Gray, Windup, Schuco, 1940s, 6 In.	75.00
Movie Viewer, Land Of The Giants, 2 Rolls Of Film, Kent, Chemtoy, On Card, 1969	56.00
Mr. & Mrs. Potato Head & Pets, Box, 1950s, 10½ x 15 x 1½ In.	154.00
Mr. Mercury, Tin, Plastic, Walking Motion, Linemar, Box, 13 In.	633.00 to 825.00
Mr. Strong Pup, Lifts Weights Over Head, Battery Operated, Box	350.00
Mule & Cart, Jenny The Balking Mule, Clown Driver, Strauss	325.00
Myriopticon, Panorama, Rebellion, Fort Sumter, Crank Advanced, Box, 8¼ In.	529.00
Native On Alligator, Tin, Windup, 15 In.	150.00
Noah's Ark, Hinged Lid, 72 Carved Wooden Animals, Painted, Stenciled, 10 x 6¾ x 24 In.	2350.00
Noah's Ark, Simulated Log Sides, Roof, Animals, Painted, Wood, Germany, 14 x 23 In.	1980.00
Nodder, Happy Hooligan, Red Shirt, Hat, Papier-Mache, 9 In.	138.00
Noisemaker, Couple Dancing, Handle, Gene Bosch, Chein	145.00
Noisemaker, Wizard Of Oz, Metal, Lithograph, U.S. Metal Toy, 10 In.	247.00
Oil Can, Buddy L, 4 Piece	425.00
Old Kentucky Home, 6 Black Figures Dance, Crank, Paper Lithograph, 15 x 10 In.	2475.00
Orbit Explorer, Astronaut Advances, Spark Lighting, Tin, Friction, Yoshiya, Box, 4¾ In.	248.00
Ostrich, Wood, Jointed, Rope Tail, Glass Eyes, Open Mouth, Schoenhut, 8 In.	1045.00
Our Gang, Painted, Bisque, Box, 9 Piece	92.00
Our Gang Color Culture Set, 9 Plaster Figures, Box, 8¼ x 13 x 2½ In.	799.00
Outboard Motor, Mercury 55, Battery Operated, c.1955, 5½ In.	176.00
Oven, Quick-Meal, Cast Iron, Tin, 6 Burners, 26 In.	323.00
Owl, Jumping Jack, Carved, Applied Glass Eyes, Ear Tufts & Beaks, String Pull, 10 In.	22.00
Paddy's Dancing Pig, Tin, Windup, Lehmann, Germany, Box, 6 In.	1050.00 to 2475.00
Pail, Animals, Battleships, T Bros., c.1900, 4 In.	195.00
Pail, Children, Gathering Shells, Lily Pads, Tin, Wire Bail, Wood Handle, T. Bros., 6 x 5¾ In.	140.00
Pail, Children, Goat Cart, At Beach, Wire Bail, Wood Handle, Embossed, c.1900, 5⅝ In.	168.00
Pail, Children, On Path, Beach, Woman & Child, Handle, Germany, c.1900, 6 x 6¼ In.	616.00
Pail, Children, Zeppelin, Airplane, Beach, Red, Yellow, Blue, Tin, Handle, c.1930, 6 x 5¾ In.	392.00
Pail, Duck Pond, Cartoon Animals All Around, 8 x 8 In.	209.00
Pail, Duck Pond, Tin Lithograph, Cartoon Ducks Driving In Car, Chein, 8 x 8 In.	210.00
Pail, Eagle Over Flag Crest, Seaside, Red, White, Blue, Handle, Tin Lithograph, 3½ In.	546.00
Pail, Gun Boat, World War I, Half-Moon Shape, Stock Package Co., c.1930, 4 x 9 In.	784.00
Pail, Mary & Little Lamb, Children Feeding Sheep, Signed, Germany, c.1900	168.00
Pail, Present From The Seaside, Children Playing In Sand, Red, Blue Interior, Handle, 4 In.	173.00
Pail, Shovel, Clowns, Circus Animals, Tin Lithograph, T. Cohn, c.1930, 5¾ In.	175.00
Panda Bear, Smoking Shoe Shine, Battery Operated, Mixed Material, Alps	275.00
Pan-Gee, Funny Dancer, Tin, Windup, Carter, 9½ In.	392.00
Pedal Car, Airplane, Air Mail, Pressed Steel, Steelcraft, 48 x 30 In.	2090.00
Pedal Car, Airplane, Pursuit, Pressed Steel, Propeller, Steelcraft, 1940s, 36 In.	880.00
Pedal Car, Boat, White, Yellow, Red, Murray, 1950s, 41 In.	550.00
Pedal Car, Fire Chief, Metal Wheels, Rubber Tires, Pressed Steel, 35 In.	275.00
Pedal Car, Murray, Ranch Wagon, Pressed Steel, Green, 1950s, 48 In.	275.00
Pedal Car, Pioneer Hummer, Red, Yellow Trim, Steering Wheels, 1914, 33 x 16 In.	2070.00
Pedal Car, Pontiac, Pressed Steel, Rubber Tires, Garton, 44 In.	1210.00
Pedal Car, Roadster, Convertible, Blue Paint, Red Pin Stripe, Triang, England, 41 In.	936.00
Pedal Car, Skippy, Pressed Steel, Rubber Tires, 37 In.	1210.00

Pedal Car, Spirit Of St. Louis, Painted, Wood, Tin, Steelcraft, c.1927, 53 In.	823.00
Pedal Car, Wrecker, Mack, 5 Ton, Pressed Steel, Blue, Steelcraft, 1940s, 70 In.	1760.00
Pedal Car, Yellow, AMF, Never Assembled, Box, 1960s, 36 In.	220.00
Performing Seal & Monkey, Fish, Tin, Windup, Rocks, Box, 7¾ In.	332.00
Periscope, Space Patrol, Cardboard, Ralston Premium, Envelope, 9¼ x 14 In.	542.00
Pete The Pup, Jointed, Cameo Company, Box, 1930s, 9 In.	295.00
Pete The Pup, Wood, Jointed, Composition Head, Cameo, 1930s, 10 In.	585.00
Phonograph, 2-Note Music, Crank, Multicolor, Gold, Penny Toy, Meier, Germany, 2 x 2 x 3 In.	275.00
Piano, Baby Grand, Bench, Cast Iron, Decal, Sticker, Arcade, 5½ In.	605.00
Piano, Hand Crank, Music Box, Schoenhut, c.1900, 10½ In.	395.00
Picnic Bear, Drinks, Tin, Plush, Alps, Box	275.00
Pig, Wood, Jointed, Leather Ears, Curly Tail, Glass Eyes, Carved Mouth, Trough, Schoenhut, 7 In.	220.00
Pig Acrobat, Pig & Ladders Move, Painted, Tin, Windup, Gunthermann, Germany, 9 In.	305.00
Pile Driver, On Track, Pressed Steel, Buddy L, 1930s, 24 In.	1540.00
Pink Panther One-Man Band, Plastic, Tin, Plush, Box	195.00
Playset, Captain Gallant, Plastic, Bagged, Marx, c.1955, 11 x 6 In., 22 Piece	336.00
Playset, How The West Was Won, H-G Toys, Box, 19½ x 15 In.	68.00
Playset, Interplanetary Rocket Base, Plastic Rockets, 8 x 14 In.	275.00
Playset, Rin Tin Tin Cavalry, Plastic, Bagged, Marx, 1957, 11 x 6 In., 26 Piece	561.00
Playset, Safety First, Tin, Windup, Distler, Germany, Box, 9 x 9 In. *illus*	2633.00
Playset, Westgate Auto Center, Tin Litho, Plastic, Unopened, Box, 1968, 16 x 28 x 2½ In.	678.00
Pool Player, Tin Lithograph, Windup, 11 In.	605.00
Pool Players, 2 Men Playing Billiards, Tin, Windup, Ranger Steel, 14 In.	247.00
Pop-Eyed Pete & Comical Clara, T.P.S. Japan, Pair	650.00
Porky Pig, Cowpuncher, Tin, Windup, Marx, 1949, 8 In.	285.00
Porky Pig, With Umbrella, Windup, Leon Schlesinger, Marx, 1939, 8 In. *illus*	260.00
Porter, Black Man Carries Luggage, Red Cap, Windup, Box	750.00
Power Shovel, Tin, Diesel, Lever & Push Button Control Box, Sss, 13½ In.	138.00
Powerful Katrinka, Holding Up Jimmy, Tin, Windup, Nifty, Germany, 5 In.	825.00 to 990.00
Powerful Katrinka, Jimmy In Wheelbarrow, Tin Lithograph, Windup, Nifty, Germany, 6 In.	1904.00
Powerful Katrinka, Pulling Jimmy Up By Shirt, Tin Litho, Windup, Nifty, Germany, 6 In.	1680.00
Praxinoscope Theater, Wood, Paper, Candle, 5 Animations, E. Reynaud, France, c.1879 *illus*	2875.00
Projector Set, Juniors Television, c.1950	95.00
Pump Car, Skudder, Red, Spoke Wheels, 1900s, 46 x 39 In.	316.00
Quack Quack, Mama Duck, 3 Ducks In Cart, Tin, Windup, Lehmann, Germany, Box, 8 In.	1430.00
Rabbit, Brown, Cloth, Button Eyes, Blue Bow, Stuffed, Handmade, Amish, 9 In.	220.00
Rabbit, In Cart, Tin Lithograph, Steering, Fischer, Germany, Penny Toy, 3 In.	900.00
Rabbit, Mohair, Dressed, Brown Glass Eyes, Jointed, Cotton Skirt, Steiff, 1950s, 11 In.	176.00
Rabbit, On Wheels, Windup, Tin, Box, Occupied Japan	90.00
Rabbit, Pulling Cart, White, Purple, Metal, Embossed, Silver Spoke Wheels, Stanley, 7¼ In.	193.00
Railroad Hand Car, Tom & Dick, Metal, Windup, Japan, Box, 1950s, 5 In.	120.00
Railroad Porter Cart, Wood Frame, Crates, 3 Metal Wheels, Nord, France, c.1887, 14 In.	3520.00
Railway, Elevated, Iron, Steam Locomotive, Trestles, Windup, Hubley, c.1895, 30 In. *illus*	9520.00
Ramp Walker, Camel, 2 Humps, Ornate Saddle	95.00
Ramp Walker, Captain Flint The Parrot, Premium From Long John Silver's, 1980s	45.00
Ramp Walker, Circus Horse, Red With Yellow Legs	35.00
Ramp Walker, Clown Riding On Dinosaur, Red Hat & Green Shirt, Yellow Pants, Marx	75.00
Ramp Walker, Cow, Brown, Black Spots, Holding Head In Mooing Position	45.00
Ramp Walker, Cow, Brown, White Spots, Pink Underbelly, Gray Horns, Marx, 5 In.	50.00
Ramp Walker, Cowboy On Horseback, Reddish Brown, Cereal Premium, 1950s	40.00
Ramp Walker, Giggles Woman, Premium, Grins, Giggles & Smiles Cereal, 1978	50.00
Ramp Walker, Goofy Riding Hippo, Marx, 1950s	110.00
Ramp Walker, Jollie Ollie, Orange, Premium, Pillsbury's Funny Face Drink, 1960s	95.00
Ramp Walker, Maid, Blue & White Apron, Peasant Woman, Wilson, 1939	85.00
Ramp Walker, Monkey Riding On Dinosaur, Red Fez & Green Scarf, Brown Dino, Marx	65.00
Ramp Walker, Mother Goose, 3 Goslings, Red & Yellow, Marx	35.00
Ramp Walker, Nurse, Brown Hair, Closed Mouth, Arms Swing, Wilson, 1939	85.00
Ramp Walker, Pig, White, Marx	39.50
Ramp Walker, Soldier, Wearing Khaki Canvas Overcoat, Private's Cloth Hat	75.00
Ramp Walker, Sydney The Dinosaur, Premium, Long John Silver's, 1980s	45.00
Ramp Walker, Spacemen, Yellow, Space Suit, Orange Feet, 1970s	40.00
Ramp Walker, Turtle, Green, Yellow Undershell, Premium, Long John Silver's, 1980	45.00
Rattle, Clown Head, Red, White, Blue, Tin, Prewar, Marked, DRGM, 6½ In.	92.00
Refrigerator, G.E., Electric, Iron, Pressed Steel, Nickel Plated Ice Tray, Hubley, 7 In.	1100.00
Refrigerator, G.E., Electric, Iron, Pressed Steel, Nickel Plated Ice Trays, Hubley, 9½ In.	715.00
Rhino, Wood, Jointed, Leather Ears, Rope Tail, Glass Eyes, Schoenhut, 8½ In.	303.00

Toy, Motorcycle, Policeman, Cast Iron, Nickel Wheels, Champion, 7 In.
$585.00

Toy, Playset, Safety First, Tin, Windup, Distler, Germany, Box, 9 x 9 In.
$2633.00

Toy, Porky Pig, With Umbrella, Windup, Leon Schlesinger, Marx, 1939, 8 In.
$260.00

Toy, Praxinoscope Theater, Wood, Paper, Candle, 5 Animations, E. Reynaud, France, c.1879
$2875.00

T

Toy, Railway, Elevated, Iron, Steam Locomotive, Trestles, Windup, Hubley, c.1895, 30 In. $9520.00

Toy, Robot, Great Garloo, Battery Operated, Necklace, Serving Tray, Instructions, Box, 20 In. $644.00

Toy, Robot, Non-Stop Robot, Lavender, Battery Operated, Tin, Japan, Repro Box, 15 In. $5500.00

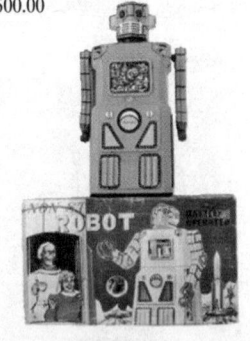

Toy, Robot, Planet Robot, Tin, Windup, Box, Japan, 9 In. $193.00

Rin Tin Tin, Vinyl Head, Plush Stuffed Body, Ideal, 1950s, 20 x 7 In.		500.00
Ring, Rin Tin Tin, Magic Ring, Premium		225.00
Ring-A-Ling Circus, Ringmaster, Elephant, Monkey, Tin, Windup, Marx, 8 In.		990.00
Road Roller, Keystone, Pressed Steel, 1930s, 20 In.		88.00
Robot, Cosmic Raider Force, Lights, Sounds, Bump & Go, Plastic, Taiwan, Box, 1970s, 14½ In.		144.00
Robot, Excavator, Plastic, Battery Operated, Horikawa, Box, 1970s, 10 In.		172.00
Robot, Flying Man, Tin, Windup, Box		725.00
Robot, Great Garloo, Battery Operated, Necklace, Serving Tray, Instructions, Box, 20 In. *illus*		644.00
Robot, Great Garloo, Bends, Grabs, Plastic, Metal, Battery Operated, Marx, Box, 1962, 23 In.		233.00
Robot, Non-Stop Robot, Lavender, Battery Operated, Tin, Japan, Repro Box, 15 In. *illus*		5500.00
Robot, Planet Robot, Tin, Windup, Box, Japan, 9 In. *illus*		193.00
Robot, Robby, Bulldozer, Tin, Friction, Battery Operated, Bump & Go, Marusan, Box, 6½ In.		7425.00
Robot, Robby, Piston Action Pug, Battery Operated, Remote, Walking Motion, Nomura, 9 In.		660.00
Robot, Space Commando, Windup, Tin, Original Dome, 8 In.		275.00
Robot, Sparky, Tin, Windup, Yoshiya, Japan, Box, 1950s, 7¾ In.		392.00
Robot, Swinging Baby, Tin, Windup, Yonezawa, Box, 12 In.		750.00
Robot, Thunder Robot, Tin, Plastic, Battery Operated, Asakusa, Box, Japan, 12 In. *illus*		3025.00
Robot, Tin, Block Base, Ratchet Arms, Battery Operated, KO, Japan, 12 In. *illus*		323.00
Robot, Tractor, Tin, Battery Operated, Lighted Pistons, Nomura, Box, 9¾ In.		478.00
Rocket Ride, Twirly Whirly, Tin, Windup, Alps, Box, 13½ In.		798.00
Rocketman, Tin, Plastic, Walking Motion, Turning Wheels, Remote, Alps, Box, 16 In.		2750.00
Rocketship, Tom Corbett, Tin Lithograph, Windup, Marx, 1952, 3¾ x 12 x 3½ In.		336.00
Rocking Horse, White Paint, Horse Hair Mane & Tail, Leather Saddle, Bridle, 41 x 70 In.		1870.00
Rocking R Ranch, Girl & Boy On Seesaw, Tin, Windup, Courtland, Box, 18 In.		192.00
Rodeo Joe Crazy Car, Tin, Windup, Unique Art, 7½ In.		193.00
Roly Poly, Clown, Schoenhut, 1920s, 5½ In.		165.00
Roly Poly, Foxy Grandpa, Papier-Mache, 1900s, 9½ In.		485.00
Roly Poly, Indian Baby, Papier-Mache, 4 In.		95.00
Roly Poly, Keystone Kop, Papier-Mache, 4 In.		125.00
Roly Poly, Punch & Judy, Spectators, Cardboard, Wood, Musical, c.1884, 8 x 6 In.		413.00
Roly Poly, Rabbit, Clown Suit, Red, Green, Blue, Brown, Composition, 10¼ In.		275.00
Rooster, Composition, Multicolor, Canted Base, Linen Bellows, Squeak, 6⅝ In.		143.00
Roundabout, Carnival, Passengers, Wire Suspension, Windup, Germany, 14 In.		750.00
Rudy The Ostrich, Pink, Blue, White, Tin, Windup, Nifty, Germany, 9 In.	385.00 to	448.00
Sailboat, Goes Up & Down, Wheeled Base, Tin Lithograph, Gesch, Germany, 4 In. *illus*		2200.00
Sailboat, Peggy Ann, Tin, Steerable Rudder, Chein, 12 In.		149.00
Sailor, Dancing, Tin Body, Cloth Suit, Columbia On Hat, Lehmann, 7¼ In. *illus*		518.00
Sambo, Mixed Material, Windup, Monkey, Composition Face, Ukulele, Alps, Box, 9½ In.		248.00
Scale, Orange, Silver, Cast Iron, Toledo, Child's, 28 x 15 In.		385.00
Schoolroom, Desks, Benches, Blackboard, 10 Students, Desk Shape Box, Wood, 20 x 13 In.		2530.00
Schoolroom, Teacher, 10 Bisque Dolls, Desks, Mechanical, Wood, 11 x 18 In.		3808.00
Scooter, Benteco Coffee Company Logo On Side, Yellow, 1920s, 37 x 32 In.		345.00
Scooter, Bonzo, Tin, Push-Pull Advance, Pull String, Green Vase, Chein, 7¼ In.		688.00
Scooter, Chief Scooting, Art Deco, Red, Foot Brake, Rubber Pad, 1930s, 40 x 33 In.		460.00
Scooter, Hard Plastic, Friction, Motoneta Gran Sport, Argentina, Box, 1950s, 8½ In.		245.00
Scooter, Kick & Go, Pressed Steel, Rubber Tires, Honda, 30 In.		66.00
Scooter, Skippy, Racer, Pressed Steel, Red Paint, Foot Brake, 1920s, 44 x 32 In. *illus*		460.00
Scooter, Smitty On Scooter, Striped Shirt, Black Shorts, Tin, Windup, Marx, 8 In.		2200.00
Scooter, Torpedo, Red, 2-In. Wheels, 1930s, 23 x 26 In.		288.00
Sea Lion, Wood, Jointed, Whiskers, Glass Eyes, Leather Flippers & Ears, Ball, Schoenhut, 8 In.		1980.00
Seaplane, Cast Iron, Arcade, 1939, 4¼-In. Wingspan		440.00
Seaplane, Tin, Windup, Blue, Red, Yellow, Chein, 1950s, 7½ In.		121.00
Secretary, Doll's, Rosewood, Maitrise Model, Drop Front, France, c.1840, 17 In.		1980.00
Seesaw, Merry Cockolly, Tin, Windup, Chickens Move, Yoneya, Box, 6 In.		165.00
Service Station, 16 Building Parts, 2 Pump Islands, 2 Tootsietoys, Sunnyville, 3½ In.		225.00
Service Station, Cardboard, Cars, Light Bulbs, Keystone, 22 In.		100.00
Service Station, Wood, Cast Iron Gas Pumps, Car, 12 In.		1870.00
Settee, Doll's, Wood, Gilded, Spindled Back, Silk Upholstery, Curved Arms, c.1880, 15 In.		2530.00
Sewing Machine, American Girl, White, Wood Base, National Sewing Machine Co., c.1930		80.00
Sewing Machine, Casige, Fairy On Front, Marked, 121, Germany, 6 In.		70.00
Sewing Machine, Casige, Marked, 125, Germany, 8 In.		105.00
Sewing Machine, Casige, Western Germany British Zone, Box, c.1956, 6 x 20 In.		147.00
Sewing Machine, Pony, Cast Iron, Flowers, Black Enamel, Wood Base		110.00
Sewing Machine, Sew-O-Matic, Ivory, Red Base, Senior, Straco		75.00
Sewing Machine, Singer, Black, Gold Letters, 6 In.		200.00
Sewing Machine, Singer, Black, White, Marked, 6 In.		110.00

Sewing Machine, Treadle, Iron, Tin Cover, Swivel Spindle Back Chair, Child's, 32 In. 4840.00
Sharp Shooter, Makes Noise, Head Turns, Moves Forward, Celluloid, Windup, Japan, Box .. 210.00
Sheep, White, Pull, Cast Iron Wheels, Steiff, 9 x 14 In. 825.00
Shoot The Moon, Heavy Tin, Moon Face, Hole In Mouth, Original Decal, 15 In. ......*illus* 250.00
Shooting Gallery, Rubber Ball, Revolver, Clowns, Backdrop, Marquee, Paper Litho, 13 x 13 In. 385.00
Showboat, Cast Iron, White Rubber Tire, Bell, Arcade, 1928, 11 In. 880.00
Shutter Bug, Boy Turns Head, Raises Camera, Flash, Battery Operated, TN Co., 9 In. 475.00
Sign, Go, Cast Iron, Arcade, 1925, 5¼ In. 385.00
Sign, Highway, Curve, Cast Iron, Arcade, 1934, 5 In. 110.00
Sign, Hill, Cast Iron, Arcade, 1934, 5 In. 275.00
Sign, Stop & Go, Cast Iron, Arcade, 1924, 3¾ In. 198.00
Skillet, Child's, Hammered, Nickel Plated, 4¾ In. 50.00
Skip Rope Animals, Tin, Windup, Dog, Squirrel, Twirl, Bear Jumps, T.P.S., Box, 8½ In. 193.00
Skip Rope Animals, Tin, Windup, T.P.S., Box, 4¾ In. 295.00
Skittles, Camel & Arab, Papier-Mache Camel, Iron Wheels, 9 Figures, c.1900, 19 In. ...*illus* 27500.00
Sky Patrol, Tin, Battery Operated, Mystery Action, Nomura, Box, 13 In. 495.00
Sky Rangers, Prop Plane, Tin Dirigible, OAW, Tin, Windup, Unique Art, 23 In. 385.00
Skybird Flyer, Plane, Dirigible, Tin, Windup, Marx, Box, Prewar, 10 x 26 In. 413.00
Sled, 3-Runner, Lightning, Wood Platform & Handle, Metal Runners, 1920s, 40 x 33 In. 115.00
Sled, Bentwood Seat Back, Green Paint, Iron Runners, Spindles, 32 x 16 In. 115.00
Sled, Black Beauty, Wood, Steel Runners, Painted, 44 In. 550.00
Sled, Cannon Ball, Cast Iron, Wood Platform & Steering Handle, Double Runners, 1920s ... 115.00
Sled, Flexible Flyer, Patent Model, Walnut, Samuel Leeds Allen, Patented 1888, 13½ In. 460.00
Sled, Flexible Flyer, Wood, Cast Iron, 59 In. 39.00
Sled, Flexible Flyer, Wood & Steel, 4-Man, 102 In. 600.00
Sled, Oak, Carved, Bentwood Runners, Wood Peg Construction, Mid 1800s, 25 x 13½ In. 176.00
Sled, Oak & Iron, Painted Steamboat, c.1900, 39 In. 460.00
Sled, Painted, Shaped Maple Seat Panel, Painted, Oak Runners, Iron, Columbia, 7 x 12 In. .. 823.00
Sled, Pine, Metal Rails, Painted, King Of The Hills, Landscape, Late 1800s, 34 x 18 In. 230.00
Sled, Wood, Multicolored Finish, Swan Head Iron Finials, Victorian, 35 In. 265.00
Sled, Wood, Painted, V.R.D., Cut Nails, 1837, 27 In. 518.00
Sleigh, Cast Iron, Horse, Woman Driver, Hubley, 15 In. 850.00
Sleigh, Wood, Blue Painted, 12 In. 695.00
Sleigh, Wood, Flowers, Painted, Green, Red, Wire Runners, 13½ In. 660.00
Sleigh, Wood, Iron Reinforced Runners, Child's, c.1900, 36 In. 588.00
Slipping Sam The Climbing Fireman, Tin Lithograph, Windup, Marx, Box, 1930s, 22 In. . 659.00
Smokey Joe, Climbing Fireman, Tin, Windup, Marx, Box, 23 In. 385.00
Smokey The Bear, Talker, Pull String, Knickerbocker, 1960s 75.00
Snail, Rocking, Beige, On Rocker, Mobo, 1930s, 28 x 11 In. 345.00
Snik Snak, Man Walking 2 Dogs, Clockwork, Tin Litho, Lehmann, Germany, 8 x 16 In. 6720.00
Solar X Space Rocket, Tin, Plastic, Battery Operated, Flashing Nose, Nomura, Box, 15 In. .. 100.00
Soldier Playing Drum, Push Pull, 3 Wheel, Original Stick, Fisher-Price, No. 520, 12 In. *illus* 2925.00
Soldier Set, 10th Hussars, Set 315, Prewar, Britains, Box 411.00
Soldier Set, 12th Lancers, Set 128, Prewar, Britains, Box, 4 Piece 147.00
Soldier Set, Armies Of The World, 7th Rajput, Prewar, No. 1342, Britains, Box, 8 Piece 140.00
Soldier Set, Band Of 1st Life Guards, Set 101, Prewar, Britains, Box, 12 Piece 529.00
Soldier Set, Bikanir Camel Corps., Indian Army, Prewar, No. 123, Britains, Box, 3 Piece 560.00
Soldier Set, Body Guard, Abyssinia, Emperor, Prewar, No. 1424, Britains, Box, 8 Piece 336.00
Soldier Set, British Infantry Firing, Prewar, No. 1260, Britains, Box, 9 Piece 112.00
Soldier Set, Devonshire Regiment, No. 110, Britains, Box, c.1914, 8 Piece .... 336.00 to 728.00
Soldier Set, Duke Of Cornwall's Light Infantry, Postwar, No. 2088, Britains, Box, 8 Piece 112.00
Soldier Set, Egyptian Cavalry, Movable, Prewar, No. 115, Britains, Box, c.1901, 5 Piece 616.00
Soldier Set, French Cuirassiers, Standing Life Guards, Yeoman, No. 138, Britains, 14 Piece . 106.00
Soldier Set, Gordon Highlander, Legs Together, 1st Version, No. 118, Britains, Box, 10 Piece . 196.00
Soldier Set, Infanteria Argentina, Prewar, No. 216, Britains, Box, 8 Piece 336.00
Soldier Set, Infanteria Espanola, Spanish Infantry, Prewar, No. 92, Britains, Box, 8 Piece ... 560.00
Soldier Set, Infantry, Austro-Hungarian Army, Prewar, No. 177, Britains, Box, 8 Piece 1008.00
Soldier Set, King's African Rifles, Prewar, No. 225, Britains, Box, 8 Piece 112.00
Soldier Set, North American Indians, Prewar, No. 208, Britains, Box, c.1935, 8 Piece 504.00
Soldier Set, Pipes Of The Scot's Guards, No. 69, Prewar, Britains, 8 Piece 147.00
Soldier Set, Regiments Of All Nations, Soldiers, Postwar, No. 2072, Britains, Box, 8 Piece ... 56.00
Soldier Set, Royal Welch Fusiliers, Prewar, No. 2124, Britains, Box, 4 Piece 112.00
Soldier Set, Seaforth Highlanders, Prewar, No. 112, Britains, Box, 8 Piece 140.00
Soldier Set, Seven Regiment Display, Britains, Box, c.1962, 37 Piece 4200.00
Soldier Set, Turcos, Types Of The French Army, Prewar, No. 191, Britains, Box, 8 Piece 140.00
Soldier Set, U.S.A. Forces Infantry, Prewar, No. 227, Britains, Box, 8 Piece 112.00

Toy, Robot, Thunder Robot, Tin,
Plastic, Battery Operated, Asakusa,
Box, Japan, 12 In.
$3025.00

Toy, Robot, Tin, Block Base, Ratchet
Arms, Battery Operated, KO, Japan, 12 In.
$323.00

Toy, Sailboat, Goes Up & Down,
Wheeled Base, Tin Lithograph, Gesch,
Germany, 4 In.
$2200.00

Toy, Sailor, Dancing, Tin Body,
Cloth Suit, Columbia On Hat,
Lehmann, 7¼ In.
$518.00

T

Toy, Scooter, Skippy, Racer, Pressed Steel, Red Paint, Foot Brake, 1920s, 44 x 32 In. $460.00

Toy, Shoot The Moon, Heavy Tin, Moon Face, Hole In Mouth, Original Decal, 15 In. $250.00

Toy, Skittles, Camel & Arab, Papier-Mache Camel, Iron Wheels, 9 Figures, c.1900, 19 In. $27500.00

Toy, Soldier Playing Drum, Push Pull, 3 Wheel, Original Stick, Fisher-Price, No. 520, 12 In. $2925.00

Soldier Set, United Nations Infantry, Prewar, No. 2155, Britains, Box, 8 Piece	196.00
Soldier Set, West India Regiment, 1st Version, No. 19, Britains, Box, c.1901, 8 Piece	448.00
Soldiers, With Rifles, Lunge At Each Other, Tin, Gesch, Germany, 4 In. ....*illus*	385.00
Space Blazer, Fisher-Price, 1940	345.00
Space Capsule, Friendship 7, Tin, Friction, Spark, Noise, Horikawa, Box, 6½ In.	210.00
Space Dog, Tin, Battery Operated, Remote, Ears Flap, Mouth Opens, Light Flashes, Yoshiya, 7½ In.	275.00
Space Explorer, Bump & Go, Tin, Crank, Astronaut Driver, Pistons Move, Yoshiya, Box, 6 In.	385.00
Space Explorer, Tin, Friction, S-61 Space Train, Astronaut Drivers, Nomura, Box, 12½ In.	385.00
Space Patrol, Tin, Friction, NASA Markings, Plastic, Masudaya, Box, 7 In.	193.00
Space Port, Tin, Plastic, Building, Fence, 10 Alien Figures, Launcher, Superior, Box	506.00
Space Radar Scout Pioneer, Turning Plastic Discs, Friction, Masudaya, Box, 6¾ In.	310.00
Space Ranger, Sparking, Tin, Friction, Lithographed Canopy, Pilot, Box, 6½ In.	2420.00
Space Rocket Pistol, Tin, Battery Operated, Noise, Spark, Nomura, Box, 10 In.	440.00
Space Satellite, Lever Action, Tin Lithograph, Niedermeier, Box, 1960s, 4 x 13 x 5½ In.	168.00
Space Surveillant X-07, Tin, Battery Operated, Lights Flash, Masudaya, Box, 4¾ In.	193.00
Space Surveyor X-12, Tin, Battery Operated, Sound, Lights Flash, Masudaya, Box, 8 In.	1045.00
Spaceman, Mechanical, Tin, Windup, Sparking Chest Panel, Noguchi, Box, 5½ In.	138.00
Spaceship, Robot, Tom Corbett, Shoots Sparks, Tin Litho, Windup, Marx, Box, 12 In. ..*illus*	1900.00
Speedway, Daredevil Jump, 2 Windup Race Cars, Plastic Track, Marx, Box	88.00
Spic & Span, Hams What Am, 2 Musicians, Red Hats, Tin, Windup, Marx, 10 In.	2200.00
Squirrel, Mother & Baby, Metal, Windup, Japan, 1950s	95.00
Stable, Wood, Farm Animals, 31½ x 17 In.	358.00
Stage Coach, Santa Fe, Tin, Plastic, Friction, Horses Gallop, Frankonia, Box, 11½ In.	165.00
Stamp Set, Brownie, No. 1401, Baumgarten & Company, Early 1900s	150.00
Steam Shovel, Pressed Steel, Buddy L, 1930s, 20 x 14 In.	77.00
Steam Shovel, Pressed Steel, Buddy L, 26 In.	176.00
Stick Dancer, Jointed Limbs, Painted, Green Jacket, Stockings, Mustard Pants, Tin, Steel Rod, 17 In.	115.00
Stove, Blue Bird, Grey Iron, Cast Iron, Pressed Steel, 6½ In.	88.00
Stove, Blue Bird, Grey Iron, Cast Iron, Pressed Steel, 10½ In.	1187.00
Stove, Blue Eagle, Cast Iron, Pressed Steel, Hubley, 8 In.	198.00
Stove, Cast Iron, 3-Footed, Internal Grate, No. 9, 2 Fire Bricks, Geometrics, Flowers, 23 In.	275.00
Stove, Cast Iron, Nickel Plated, Coal Hod, Scoop, Kenton, 9½ In.	303.00
Stove, Cast Iron, Nickel Plated, Pressed Steel, Kent, Kenton, 7¾ In.	330.00
Stove, Detroit Stove Works, Silver Paint, Cast Iron, 17 In.	2090.00
Stove, Eagle, Cast Iron, Pressed Steel, Adjustable Flame, Eagle, 5 In.	110.00
Stove, Eagle, Cast Iron, Pressed Steel, Hubley, 9¼ In.	143.00
Stove, Empire, Child's, Pressed Steel, Electric, 10 In.	88.00
Stove, Engman-Matthews, Black, Cast Iron, Nickel Trim, Warmer Shelf, 30½ x 18 In.	2090.00
Stove, Globe, Cast Iron, Child's, Kenton, 18 In. ....*illus*	936.00
Stove, Ideal, No. 5, Cast Iron, 6 Burner, Reservoir, Kettle, Pan, Dutch Oven, Sadiron, 17 In.	1410.00
Stove, Little Darling, Pressed Steel, Nickel Plated, Electric, 15 x 16½ In.	132.00
Stove, Nickel Plated, Pressed Steel, Accessories, Kenton, 12½ x 12½ In.	1045.00
Stove, Peninsular, Cast Iron, Nickel Plated, Pressed Steel, Arcade, 7 In.	468.00
Stove, Roper, Cast Iron, Pressed Steel, Arcade, 4½ In.	121.00
Stove, Royal Esther, Cast Iron, Child's, 16 In. ....*illus*	1755.00
Stove, Stevens, Nickel Plated, Embossed, 11¾ In.	248.00
Stove, Stevens, Nickel Plated, Pressed Steel, 12½ In.	240.00
Stove, Stevens Queen, Cast Iron, Pots, Pans, 13¼ In.	248.00
Stove, Tin, Brass, Claw Feet, Paneled Sides, Chimney, Utensils, Germany, 12 x 7 x 8 In.	825.00
Stove, Vindex, Cast Iron, Pressed Steel Inserts, Nickel Plated, 15 In.	1870.00
Stove, W.J. Loth Co., Fuel Saver, Cast Iron, 5½ In.	825.00
Street Sweeper, Cast Iron, Elgin, Hubley, 8¾ In. ....*illus*	3803.00
Super Space Capsule, Horikawa, Tin, Plastic, Battery Operated, Stop 'N' Go, Box, 9 In.	110.00
Surrey, 2 Horses, Man, Woman, Fringed Top, Kenton, 1940s, 13 In.	475.00
Susie Lovable Slinky Worm, Pull Toy, Plastic, James Industries Inc., 1955, 5½ In.	58.00
Suzy, Bouncing Ball, Windup, T.P.S., Japan, Box, 1950s	95.00
Sweeping Mammy, I Dance As I Sweep, Tin, Windup, Lindstrom, Box, 1930s, 8 In.	395.00
Table, 2 Chairs, Wood, Enameled ABC Top, 2 Chairs, Child's, 18 x 20 In.	99.00
Table, Doll's, 2 Chairs, Cast Iron, Arcade, 4¾ & 4 In.	154.00
Tank, Destroyer, German Hanomag, No. 694, Dinky Toy, Box	95.00
Tank, Sparks, Recoiling Cannon, Metal, Marx, 5½ In.	195.00
Tank, Sparks, Windup, Movable Barrel, Gama Of Germany, 1936, 7½ In.	395.00
Tank, Sparks, Windup, No. 703, Gama Of Germany, Box, 5½ In.	100.00
Tank, U.S. Tank Division, Sparks, Recoiling Cannon, Metal Lithograph, Marx, Box, 5 x 9 In.	198.00
Tanker, Gulf Oil, Original Box, Plastic, 27 In.	28.00
Taxi, Amos 'N' Andy, Cardboard Figures, Tin Litho, Windup, Box, 1930s, 8 In.	1344.00

T

Taxi, Amos 'N' Andy, Fresh Air, Driver & Dog, Man In Back, Tin Litho, Windup, 5½ x 8 In. . . .	632.00
Taxi, Amos 'N' Andy, Fresh Air, Tin Lithograph, Windup, 5½ x 8 x 4 In.	635.00
Taxi, Amos 'N' Andy, Fresh Air Taxicab Co., Windup, Tin, Marx, Box, 8 In. . . . .*illus*	770.00
Taxi, Amos 'N' Andy, Taxi Hat, Tin, Windup, Marx, 9 In.	605.00
Taxi, Cast Iron, Flat Top, Rubber Tires, Nickel Driver, Headlights, Arcade, 1929, 8½ In.	1210.00
Taxi, Electromobile, Tin, Battery Operated, Buick, Headlights, Mizuno, Box, 1950, 8¼ In. . . .	94.00
Taxi, Free Roller, Pressed Steel, Black Fenders, Roof, Yellow Body, Marx, 9½ In.	185.00
Taxi, Yell-O-Taxi, Tin Lithograph, Built-In Key, Strauss, 1930s, 8½ In. . . . . 650.00 to 801.00
Taxi, Yellow, Black, Tin, Windup, Marked, BW, Bing, Germany, 8 In.	2750.00
Taxi, Yellow, Cast Iron, Rubber Tires, Clicker, Arcade, 1941, 8½ In.	468.00
Taxi, Yellow, Cast Iron, Stenciled Phone Number, Yellow Cab, Arcade, 1929, 5¼ In.	468.00
Taxi, Yellow, Driver, Windup, No. 316, Mohawk, 7 In.	450.00
Taxi, Yellow, Tin, Push, N.Y. License Plate, Chein, 1923, 7½ In.	275.00
Taxi, Yellow Cab, Driver, Black, Orange, No. 311, Cast Iron, Arcade, 9 In.	1250.00
Tea Set, Barbie, Purple, Plastic, Worcester Toy Co., Box, 1961, 27 Piece	175.00
Tea Set, Doll's, Teapot, Cups, Saucers, Tray, Napkins, Spoons, Cakes, Box	550.00
Tea Set, Krazy Kat, Tin, Teapot, Sugar, Creamer, 4 Cups & Saucers, Plates, Tray, Chein	138.00
Teapot, Child's, Cast Iron, 4 In.	100.00
Teapot, Child's, Nickel Plated, 4 In.	248.00
Teddy Bears Are Also Listed In The Teddy Bear category.	
Telephone Linemen Maintenance Set, No. 5679, Metal & Plastic, Buddy L, Box	660.00
Tent, Humpty Dumpty Circus, Rope, Props, Acrobat Wings, Canvas, Schoenhut, 34 x 55 In. . .	8250.00
Theater, Marionette, Figures, Windup, Box, 1930s, 11 In.	895.00
Theater, Ombres Chinoises, Stage, Backdrops, Rollers, Sheets, Paper Litho, France, 15 In. . . .	440.00
Tidy Tim The Clean Up Man, White Uniform, Pushes Wheelbarrow, Marx, 8 x 8½ In.	575.00
Tiger, On Tricycle, Bell, Windup, Marx	95.00
Tiger, Wood, Jointed, Leather Ears, Rope Tail, Glass Eyes, Circus Drum, Schoenhut, 8½ In. . .	1100.00
Timmy Turtle, Pull, Musical, Green Plastic Shell, Lithograph, Wood, Fisher-Price, 12 x 6 In.	75.00
Tool Set, Garage, Nickel Plated, Arcade, 1941	154.00
Tool Set, Nickel Plated, Wood Handles, Pressed Steel, Yankee, Arcade, Box, 1923	220.00
Toonerville Trolley, Bisque, Painted, Borgfeldt, Japan, 1920s, 3½ In.	225.00
Toonerville Trolley, Conductor, Tin, Windup, Nifty, Germany, 1922, 5 x 7 In. . . . . . . 495.00 to 1250.00
Toonerville Trolley, Set, Trolley, Depot, C & M Enterprises, Box	440.00
Top, 3 Bears & 3 Pigs, Tin, Fern Bisel Peat, Ohio Art, 1930s	75.00
Top, 3 Little Pigs, Tin Lithograph, Blackie Pig's House, Wolf, Chein, 9 In.	88.00
Top, Gulliver's Travels, Tin Lithograph, Chein, 1939, 9 In.	196.00
Top, Musical, Clown, Tin Lithograph, Wood Hat, Chein, Box, 7 In.	116.00
Totem Head, Space Patrol, Man-From-Mars, Cardboard, Die Cut, Chex Cereal, Envelope, 1954 . .	111.00
Touchdown Pete, Tin, Windup, Running Motion, Advances, Linemar, 5½ In. . . . . . 200.00 to 300.00
Toyland Seesaw, 2 Elephants Playing Instruments, Windup, Masuya, Japan, 7 In.	325.00
Tractor, Cast Iron, Avery, Box, 5 In. . . . .*illus*	550.00
Tractor, Caterpillar, Silver Plastic Rollers, Green Rubber Tracks, Matchbox, Box . . . . 153.00 to 255.00
Tractor, Driver, Minneapolis-Moline, Rubber, Auburn, 7½ In.	115.00
Tractor, Driver, Windup, Kingsbury, 8 In.	600.00
Tractor, Ford, Selecto Speed, Steering, Die Cast, Red, Gray, Cardboard Base, Hubley, 10 In. . .	250.00
Tractor, Ford 600, Plastic, 1950s, 9 In.	175.00
Tractor, Ford 8N, Plastic, 1950s, 9 In.	175.00
Tractor, Fordson, Driver, Green, Cast Iron, Arcade, 3½ In.	55.00
Tractor, Fordson, Driver, Red, Green, Cast Iron, Arcade, 5¾ In.	900.00
Tractor, High Lift, Marx, Box, 17 In.	225.00
Tractor, John Deere, Cast Aluminum, Arcade, 7½ In. . . . .*illus*	188.00
Tractor, John Deere, Green, Yellow Plastic Hubs, Grey Tires, Matchbox, Box	51.00
Tractor, Massey Harris, Driver, Grey Plastic Wheels, Rounded Axles, Matchbox, Box	162.00
Tractor, Mechanical, Tin, Windup, Lithograph, Rubber Tires, Courtland, Box, 6½ In.	193.00
Tractor, Motor Express, Red, Silver, Hubley, 7½ In.	500.00
Tractor, Trac-Tractor, Driver, Nickel Plated, Cast Iron, Rubber Tracks, Arcade, 1941, 7½ In. . .	950.00
Tractor Set, Climbing, Sparking, Windup, Tin Litho, Painted Trailer, Marx, Box, 16½ In. . . .	165.00
Trailer, Circus, Tin, Friction, American Circus, Rear Gate Opens, Yoshi, Box, 11 In.	385.00
Train, Buddy L, Wrecking Crane	2000.00
Train, Climber, Black Paint, Red, Yellow Pin Stripes, Wood, Iron Wheels, 12½ In.	154.00
Train, Cor-Cor, Locomotive, Tender, Freight, Red, Black, 1930s	275.00
Train, Daiya, Bullet, Tin, Friction, Litho, Box, 20½ In.	138.00
Train, Elenee Toys Inc., Spirit Of 1776, Tin Litho, Pull Screw Type, Windup, 1940s, 18 In. . .	163.00
Train, Marx, Honeymoon Express, Windup, Box, 1966, 7 x 7 x 2½ In.	142.00
Train, Tiger, Whistles, Metal, Battery Operated, Japan, Box, 1950s	125.00
Train, TM, Western Special Locomotive, Puffing Noise, Whistle, Battery, Japan, Box, 1950s, 14 In.	75.00

Toy, Soldiers, With Rifles,
Lunge At Each Other, Tin, Gesch,
Germany, 4 In.
$385.00

Toy, Spaceship, Robot, Tom Corbett,
Shoots Sparks, Tin Litho,
Windup, Marx, Box, 12 In.
$1900.00

Toy, Stove, Globe, Cast Iron,
Child's, Kenton, 18 In.
$936.00

Toy, Stove, Royal Esther, Cast Iron,
Child's, 16 In.
$1755.00

Toy, Street Sweeper, Cast Iron,
Elgin, Hubley, 8¾ In.
$3803.00

Toy, Taxi, Amos 'N' Andy,
Fresh Air Taxicab Co., Windup,
Tin, Marx, Box, 8 In.
$770.00

Toy, Tractor, Cast Iron, Avery,
Box, 5 In.
$550.00

Toy, Tractor, John Deere,
Cast Aluminum, Arcade, 7½ In.
$188.00

Toy, Train Car, Ives, Locomotive,
No. 3242, Gray, Brass Plates,
Standard Gauge
$288.00

Train, TN, Cable Express, Battery Operated, Japan, Box, 1950s	65.00
Train, Wood, 4 Cars, Grandad's Toy Shop, North Hertford, Vermont, 72 In.	489.00
Train Accessory, Buddy L, Railroad Trestle, Outdoor, Pressed Steel, 14½ In.	1430.00
Train Accessory, Buddy L, Water Tower, Outdoor, 24 In.	275.00
Train Car, Buddy L, Caboose, Outdoor, Pressed Steel, 19 In.	303.00
Train Car, Buddy L, Gondola, Outdoor, Pressed Steel, 22 In.	193.00
Train Car, Buddy L, Locomotive, Tender, Outdoor, Pressed Steel, 42 In.	1210.00
Train Car, Buddy L, Lumber, Outdoor, Pressed Steel, 21 In.	303.00
Train Car, Buddy L, Steam Shovel, Outdoor, Pressed Steel, 30 In.	1430.00
Train Car, Buddy L, Tank, Red, Outdoor, Pressed Steel, 19 In.	358.00
Train Car, Ives, Locomotive, No. 3242, Gray, Brass Plates, Standard Gauge _illus_	288.00
Train Car, Lionel, No. 392E, Engine, Black, Copper Trim, Tender, Standard Gauge _illus_	920.00
Train Set, Bandai Toys, Zephyr, 4 Cars, Tin, Battery Operated, 1960s	75.00
Train Set, Marx, Steam Line, Electrical, Engine, Tender, Caboose, 4 Cars, Transformer, Track	147.00
Train Set, Marx, Steam Line, Electrical, Engine, Tender, Caboose, Wabash Car, Penn. Car	88.00
Train Set, Marx, Streamlined Train, Box, 1930s, 10 x 14½ x 2½ In.	404.00
Train Set, Marx, Streamlined Train, Box, 1950s, 10 x 14½ x 2½ In.	295.00
Train Set, Mechanical, Marx, Tin, Plastic, Windup, Engine, Tender, Gondola, Caboose, Track	72.00
Train Set, Overland Express, Tin Lithograph, Battery Operated, Japan, Box, 1960s, 17 In.	70.00
Train Set, Spears Games, Tiny Town, Locomotive, 3 Cars, Station, Tunnel, People, 10 x 7 In.	100.00
Travel Chiks, Tin Lithograph, Windup, Strauss, Box	985.00
Trencher, Cletrac, Pressed Steel, Retro Toy Company, Box, 14 In.	550.00
Tricycle, Boy Rider, Metal, Windup, Unique Art, 1950s, 8 In.	275.00
Tricycle, Cast Iron, Nickel Wheels, Seat, Kilgore, 5 In.	1100.00
Tricycle, Monkey, Crank, Marx, 1930s, 6 In.	495.00
Trolley, Broadway, Tin, No. 270, Chein, 8 In.	138.00
Trolley, Lionel, No. 100, Electric Rapid Transit, 4 Wheel, Standard Gauge _illus_	748.00
Trolley, Metal, Windup, SG, Germany, 1930s, 12 In.	295.00
Trolley, Pressed Steel, Yellow, Open Sides, City Hall Park, Union Depot, Converse, 15 In. _illus_	489.00
Trolley, Red, Raised Roof, Enameled Driver, Silver Horse, Harness, Wilkins, 13 In.	3105.00
Trolley, San Francisco Streetcar, Metal, Friction, Japan, Box, 1950s, 10 In.	175.00
Trolley, Tin, Windup, Germany, 1950s, 10 In., 2 Piece	295.00
Trolley, Tin Lithograph, Windup, Marx, Box, c.1930, 9 In.	672.00
Truck, 2 Door, Metal Toys, Tin, Friction, Celluloid Drive, Lithograph, 1960s, 12½ In.	385.00
Truck, 3 Seats, Doors Open, Metal, Friction, Japan, 1950s, 19 In.	395.00
Truck, Air Express, Tonka, 1959	395.00
Truck, Allied Van, Tonka, 1951	350.00
Truck, Arctic Ice Cream, Iron, Blue & Orange, Embossed, Disc Wheels, Kilgore, 8 In. _illus_	489.00
Truck, Army Cannon, Tin, C Cab, Bulldog Mac, Canvas Back, Chein, 8 In.	165.00
Truck, Army Transport, Pressed Steel, Retro Toy Company, Box, 28 In.	248.00
Truck, Army Transport, Tin, 6 Shells, Soldiers, 7½-In. Cannon, Marx, Box, 13 In.	352.00
Truck, Artillery, Pressed Steel, Paint, Trim & Turret, Driver, Friction, Dayton, 12 In. _illus_	2300.00
Truck, Bell Telephone, Cast Iron, Crank Handle, Pull Cord, Olive Green, Hubley, 9½ In.	650.00
Truck, Bell Telephone, Olive Green, White Letters, Tools, Red Flag, Metal, Hubley, 12 In.	335.00
Truck, Big Show Circus, Lion & Lion Tamer, Driver, Mechanical, Windup, Strauss, 1920s	375.00
Truck, Borden's Dairy, Pressed Steel, Rubber Tires, Windup, Kingsbury, 9 In.	220.00
Truck, Cannon, Olive Green, Cannon Shoots, Windup, Kingsbury, 1939, 15 In.	200.00
Truck, Canvas, Tin, Japan, 1950s, 10 In.	95.00
Truck, Car Carrier, 2 Cars, SSS, Japan, Box	275.00
Truck, Car Carrier, 4 Cars, 1949 Cadillacs, Hubley, Box	475.00
Truck, Car Carrier, Dark Red & Gold, Flywheel Drive, Schiebel, 1920s, 11 In.	150.00
Truck, Car Carrier, Orange, Pressed Steel, Wood Wheels, Wyandotte, c.1932, 21½ In.	200.00
Truck, Car Carrier, Tonka, Box, 1963	495.00
Truck, Carousal, Friction, Japan, c.1950s, 8¼ In.	295.00
Truck, Cattle, Dodge, Blue Back, Matchbox, Box	34.00
Truck, Cement Mixer, Custom Built, 13 In.	1200.00
Truck, Cement Mixer, Jaeger, Red, Nickel Drum, Kenton, 7 In.	1675.00
Truck, Cement Mixer, Orange Metal Wheels, Matchbox	30.00
Truck, Chemical, Ladder, Red Nickel Wheels, Kilgore	500.00
Truck, Chevrolet, Pickup, 1956, Tin, Friction, 2 Door, Opening Tail Gate, Bandai, 9¾ In.	385.00
Truck, Chevrolet, Pickup, Apache, Japan, 1955, 7½ In.	475.00
Truck, Chevrolet, Tin, Friction, Asahi, Box, 7 In.	138.00
Truck, Circus, Cast Iron, Custom Built, 13 In.	975.00
Truck, Circus, Tin, Friction, Japan, 1960s, 9½ In.	95.00
Truck, Circus Roll, Windup, Courtland, 9 In.	175.00
Truck, Coal, Hy Lift, Red, Arcade, 10 In.	1350.00

Truck, Coal, Mack, Nickel Plated Driver, Rubber Tires, Crank, Painted, Arcade, 9¾ In.	748.00
Truck, Cowdery, Ice, Pressed Steel, Black, Yellow, Box, 16 In.	1320.00
Truck, Crane, Plastic, Tin, Pressed Steel, Wood Hubs, Rubber Tires, Wyandotte, 14 In.	245.00
Truck, Crane, Tin Friction, Japan, c.1950s, 7½ In.	110.00
Truck, Daihasu, Midget, 3 Wheel, Tin, Friction, Nomura, 6¾ In.	3356.00
Truck, Dairy, Van Graham, Cream, Black, Tootsietoy	250.00
Truck, Delivery, Dairy, Tin, Glass Milk Bottle, Marx, Box, 11 In.	688.00
Truck, Delivery, Express Delivery, Inc., Metal, Friction, Japan, 1960s, 7 In.	95.00
Truck, Delivery, Express Line, Nickel Wheels, Buddy L, Early 1930s, 25 In.	1870.00
Truck, Delivery, Kraft, Box, 1950s	2850.00
Truck, Delivery, Marshall Field's, Tonka	1500.00
Truck, Delivery, Meadow Gold Butter, Metalcraft, Box	2750.00
Truck, Delivery, Parcel Post, Pressed Steel, Sonny, 25½ In.	495.00
Truck, Delivery, Red, Yellow, White, Metal Wheels, Marx, 10½ In.	145.00
Truck, Delivery, Rival Dog Food, Buddy L, 1956, 15 In.	225.00
Truck, Delivery, Rival Dog Food, Steel, Opening Rear Doors, Buddy L, Box, 14½ In.	660.00
Truck, Delivery, Tin, Prewar Japan, 7 In.	330.00
Truck, Dodge, Salerno Crackers, Tin, 1950s, 11 In.	175.00
Truck, Dugan's Baker, Metal, Divco, Japan, 1950s, 7½ In.	295.00
Truck, Dump, Bottom, Doepke, 1950, 27 In.	175.00
Truck, Dump, Bottom, Doepke, 25 In.	195.00
Truck, Dump, Cast Iron, Blue, Yellow Cab, Green, Kilgore, 6 In.	225.00
Truck, Dump, Ford, Model T, Red, Green, Nickel Wheels, Arcade, 6 In.	475.00
Truck, Dump, Ford, Red, Blue, Tin, Marked, Gabriel, Japan, Box, 8 In.	90.00
Truck, Dump, Heavy Duty, Tin, Battery Operated, Mystery Action, Yonezawa, Box, 15 In. . . .	165.00
Truck, Dump, Hydraulic, Pressed Steel, Buddy L, 25 In.	468.00
Truck, Dump, International, Driver, Arcade, 10 In.	600.00
Truck, Dump, Mack, Driver, Hydraulic Pump, Cast Iron, Arcade, 12 In.	650.00
Truck, Dump, Mack, Driver, Spoke Wheels, Red, Painted, Cast Iron, Nickel, Arcade, 8½ In. . .	358.00
Truck, Dump, Orange, Wyandotte, 1930s, 10 In.	225.00
Truck, Dump, Pickup, Pressed Steel, Red, Black, Buddy L, 1930s, 24 In.	1210.00
Truck, Dump, Plastic, Tin, Battery Operated, GMC, 12 In.	100.00
Truck, Dump, Pressed Steel, England, 1940s, 16 In.	195.00
Truck, Dump, Pressed Steel, Rubber Tires, Wyandotte, 13 In.	143.00
Truck, Dump, Ratchet, Pressed Steel, Buddy L, 1930s, 25 In.	385.00
Truck, Dump, Red, Black, Electric Headlights, Wyandotte, 1930s	250.00
Truck, Dump, Red Baby, Cast Iron, Arcade, 10½ In.	475.00
Truck, Dump, Red Baby, Driver, Cast Iron, Rubber Tires, Arcade, 10½ In.	385.00
Truck, Dump, Ride 'Em, Pressed Steel, Rubber Tires, Seat, Keystone, 27 In.	770.00
Truck, Dump, Rubber Tires, Hydraulic, Buddy L, 1940s, 26 In.	1100.00
Truck, Dump, Sand & Gravel, 4⅓ In.	450.00
Truck, Dump, Sand & Gravel, Green, Yellow, Buddy L, 1949, 13 In.	135.00
Truck, Dump, Sand & Gravel, Red, Marx, 1940s, 9 In.	85.00
Truck, Dump, Sand Load, Tin, Steel, Hand Operated Bed, Wood Wheels, 16 In.	138.00
Truck, Dump, Side, Red, Green, Wyandotte, 1940s, 17 In.	120.00
Truck, Dump, Tin, Blue, Red, Chein, 9 In.	125.00
Truck, Dump, Tin, Windup, Minic, 6 In.	50.00
Truck, Dump, Tin Bed, Black, Silver Rubber Tires, Painted, Green, 11 In.	300.00
Truck, Dump, Tonka, 1955, 13 In.	195.00
Truck, Dumper, Driver, Gold Trim, Green Metal Wheels, Matchbox	51.00 to 94.00
Truck, Earth Hauler, Euclid, Army Green, Firestone Tires, Doepke, 1940s	525.00
Truck, Easter, Tin Lithograph, Chein, 8½ In.	495.00
Truck, Emergency Rescue, Tin, Plastic, Windup, Spring Loaded Ladder, Courtland, 13 In. . . .	110.00
Truck, Express Line, Screenside, Pressed Steel, Buddy L, 24 In. . . . . *illus*	1989.00
Truck, Express Transport, Cream, Green, Red, Wells, 7 In.	175.00
Truck, Farm, Plastic, Battery Operated, Tricky Action, Marx, Box, 1965, 11 In.	123.00
Truck, Federal Van, Jermyn Brothers Toys, Yellow, Tootsietoy, c.1928	785.00
Truck, Flat Bed, Tin, Friction, Movable Rear Gate, Bandai, Box, 13 In.	149.00
Truck, Florist, Federal Van, Dark Green, Cast Iron, Tootsietoy, c.1924	400.00
Truck, Ford, Model A, Cast Iron, White Rubber Tires, Nickel Wheels, Red, 7 In.	44.00
Truck, Ford, Model A, Stake, Arcade, c.1932, 4¾ In.	295.00
Truck, Ford, Refuse, Cut Outs, Tow Slot, Matchbox, Box	13.00
Truck, GMC, Rexall Drug Company, Smith-Miller, Box	2895.00
Truck, GMC, Silver Streak, Polished Aluminum, Simth-Miller, 1951, 24 In.	260.00
Truck, Graham Dairy, Cream, Black, Tootsietoy	250.00
Truck, Gravel, Marx, c.1940, 10 In.	145.00

Toy, Train Car, Lionel, No. 392E, Engine, Black, Copper Trim, Tender, Standard Gauge
$920.00

Toy, Trolley, Lionel, No. 100, Electric Rapid Transit, 4 Wheel, Standard Gauge
$748.00

Toy, Trolley, Pressed Steel, Yellow, Open Sides, City Hall Park, Union Depot, Converse, 15 In.
$489.00

Toy, Truck, Arctic Ice Cream, Iron, Blue & Orange, Embossed, Disc Wheels, Kilgore, 8 In.
$489.00

Toy, Truck, Artillery, Pressed Steel, Paint, Trim & Turret, Driver, Friction, Dayton, 12 In.
$2300.00

T

Toy, Truck, Express Line, Screenside, Pressed Steel, Buddy L, 24 In. $1989.00

Toy, Truck, Merry-Go-Round, Carousel, Animals Revolve, Buddy L, c.1967, 14 In. $104.00

Toy, Truck, Tow, Ford, Red Cab, Amber Windows, White Body, Decal, Esso, No. 71, Matchbox $39.00

Toy, Uncle Sam On Bicycle, String Operated, Painted, Tin, 12 In. $234.00

Truck, Grocery, Red, Cast Iron, Hubley, c.1910, 3¾ In.	175.00
Truck, Handyman's Repair, Friction, Japan, 1950, 15 In.	145.00
Truck, Heinz Pickle, Bulbs, Spare Tire, Electric Lights, Metalcraft, 10 x 29 In.	750.00 to 850.00
Truck, Hercules Motor Express, Tin Lithograph, Chein, 15½ In.	578.00
Truck, Hi Way Cattle, Tin, Friction, Alps, 1950s, 12 In.	110.00
Truck, Hino, Bakery, Yellow, White, Friction, Marusan, 1950s, 9 In.	295.00
Truck, Hino, Suburban Cleaners, Yellow, Friction, Marusan, 9 In.	295.00
Truck, Home Town Laundry, Driver, Metal, Friction, Japan, 1950s, 13 In.	275.00
Truck, Ice, Black Cab, Frame, Yellow Bed, Step, Buddy L, 25 In.	510.00
Truck, Ice, Cast Iron, Nickel Wheels, Driver, Ice Tongs, Ice Block, Arcade, 1931, 8½ In.	660.00
Truck, Ice, White Rubber Tires, Nickel Grill, Ice, Tongs, Arcade, 1941, 6¾ In.	358.00
Truck, Ice Cream, Howard Johnson's, Tin, Friction, Japan, 1950s, 8½ In.	225.00
Truck, Ice Cream, Volkswagen, Friction, Japan, 1950s, 9 In.	395.00
Truck, Insurance Patrol, Pressed Steel, Buddy L, 25½ In.	880.00
Truck, International Harvester, Pressed Steel, Opening Doors, Accessories, Buddy L, 25 In.	605.00
Truck, International Harvester, Red Baby Prototype, Pressed Steel, Lou Racioppo, 96 In.	5500.00
Truck, International Railway Express, Olive, Red, White Lettering, Tootsietoy	85.00
Truck, Ladder, Pressed Steel, Keystone, 28 x 17¾ In.	431.00
Truck, Laundry, Metal Friction, Japan, 1950s, 11½ In.	375.00
Truck, Livestock, Metal, Lithograph, Friction, Japan, Box, 1950s, 13 In.	120.00
Truck, Loft Candy, Wood, Plastic Tires, Courtland, 11½ In.	402.00
Truck, Log, Orange, Hubley, 7½ In.	250.00
Truck, Log, Tin, Chein, 8½ In.	138.00
Truck, Low Boy, Pressed Steel, Retro Toy Company, 53 In.	880.00
Truck, Low Boy, Shovel, Pressed Steel, Tonka, 27 In.	358.00
Truck, Mack, Champion Gas & Oil, Cast Iron, 8 In.	550.00
Truck, Mack, Ice, Cast Iron, Nickel Driver, Ice Tongs, Ice Blocks, 1931, 10¾ In.	1320.00
Truck, Mack, Ice, Cast Iron, White Rubber Tires, Ice, 1931, 6⅞ In.	303.00
Truck, Market Delivery, Motor, Steel, Stake Bed, Decals, Marx, 17 In.	165.00
Truck, McHenry Concrete Company, Pressed Steel, Retro Toy Company, 25 In.	1045.00
Truck, Mechanical, Tin, Windup, Plastic Wheels, Courtland, Box, 8½ In.	94.00
Truck, Mercedes, Mint Green, Orange Canopy, No. 1, Box, 1968	42.00
Truck, Merry-Go-Round, Carousel, Animals Revolve, Buddy L, c.1967, 14 In. ....*illus*	104.00
Truck, Merry-Go-Round, Tin, Friction, 3 Horses, Riders, Bell Rings, Nomura, Box, 8¼ In.	385.00
Truck, Metro, Box, 7 In.	175.00
Truck, Milk, Pressed Steel, Triang, England, 1960s, 13 In.	145.00
Truck, Milk, Studebaker, White, 4 In.	120.00
Truck, Milk, Tin, Friction, Japan, 1950s, 7 In.	110.00
Truck, Milk & Cream, White Paint, Cast Iron, Hubley, 3¾ In.	550.00
Truck, Mortuary, M.L. Grimm, Pressed Steel, Black, White Wall Tires, Casket, 24 In.	468.00
Truck, Motor Express, Red, Silver, Cast Iron, Hubley, 7½ In.	500.00
Truck, Moving Van, Allied Moving, Buddy L, Box, 1940s	4695.00
Truck, Moving Van, Mayflower, Product Miniature Co., 1953, 18½ In.	350.00
Truck, Moving Van, Metalcraft, c.1930, 5 x 11 In.	264.00
Truck, Moving Van, North American Van Lines, Steel, Windup, Gate Opens, Marx, 13½ In.	248.00
Truck, Open, Courtland Lines, Tin, Plastic, Windup, Courtland, 13 In.	138.00
Truck, Panel, White Rubber Tires, Nickel Plated Driver, Back Door Opens, Arcade, 9 In.	900.00
Truck, Panel, White Rubber Tires, Painted Red, Nickel Plated Grill, Bumper, Arcade, 9 In.	1560.00
Truck, Pay Loader, Ny-Lint, 1950s	375.00
Truck, Rabbit, Easter Greetings, Tin, Lithograph, Courtland, 8½ In.	275.00
Truck, Red, Green, Metalcraft, 1930s, 11½ In.	95.00
Truck, Refuse, Dennis, Silver Grill, Decals, Knobbly Black Plastic Wheels, Matchbox, Box	128.00
Truck, Repair, Pressed Steel, Buddy L, 1950s, 25½ In.	132.00
Truck, Robotoy, Pressed Steel, Rubber Tires, Buddy L, 1930s, 22 In.	165.00
Truck, Robotoy, Rubber Tires, Electric Headlights, Buddy L, 1940s, 22 In.	715.00
Truck, Roller, Circus, Metal, Windup, Courtland, 1948, 9½ In.	210.00
Truck, Roller Chime, Tin, Windup, Animals On Roller, Courtland, Box, 9½ In.	88.00
Truck, Sand & Gravel, Tin, Plastic, Windup, Lever Operated, Courtland, 13 In.	377.00
Truck, Sanitary Service, Blue, White, Tonka, 1969, 16 In.	145.00
Truck, Semi-Trailer, Rubber Tires, Pressed Steel, Buddy L, 40 In.	413.00
Truck, Semi-Trailer, Western Auto, Steel, Plastic Tires, Rear Doors Open, Marx, Box, 25 In.	550.00
Truck, Semi-Trailer, White 3000, Plastic, Engine, Tilt Cab, Liner, Inserts, Topping, 13½ In.	1250.00
Truck, Side Tipper, Tin, Plastic, Windup, We Move The Earth, Courtland, 13 In.	88.00
Truck, Spearmint, Pressed Steel, Buddy L, 1950s, 14½ In.	395.00
Truck, Stake, GMC, Tin, Friction, Lithograph, Yonezawa, 1954, 10 In.	248.00
Truck, Stake, Jeep, 1960s Model, Tin, Friction, 2 Door, Rear Gate Opens, Bandai, Box, 7½ In.	138.00

Truck, Stake, Mack, Driver, Spoke Wheels, Red, Painted, Cast Iron, Nickel, Arcade, 8¾ In. . . .	605.00
Truck, Stake, Mack, Green, Champion, 7½ In.	425.00
Truck, Stake, Red, Black, Wood Wheels, No. 325, Wyandotte, 10 In.	110.00
Truck, Stake, Red, Blue, Pressed Steel, Marx, 1940s, 20 In.	225.00
Truck, Stake, Red & Black, Cast Iron, Arcade, 3½ In.	200.00
Truck, Stake, Studebaker, Mobil Gas, Condor, Tin, Friction, Marusan, 1950s, 13½ In.	413.00
Truck, Stake, Studebaker, Red, Blue, Wood Wheels, 6 In.	140.00
Truck, Stake, Tin, Friction, Battery Operated Headlights, Linemar, Box, 15 In.	220.00
Truck, Tanker, Fuel, Aviation, Blue Paint, Nickel Plated, Iron Wheels, Kilgore, 12¼ In.	1955.00
Truck, Tanker, Fuel, Dark Red, Windup, Penny Toy, Germany, 1930s	150.00
Truck, Tanker, Gasoline, Cast Iron, Gray, Rubber Tires, Mack Decals, Driver, Arcade, 13 In.	690.00
Truck, Tanker, Gasoline, Embossed Mack, Green, Rubber Tires, Silver Rims, Arcade, 12½ In.	1438.00
Truck, Tanker, Gasoline, Mack, Hose, Driver, Cast Iron, Arcade, 1926, 12½ In.	1550.00
Truck, Tanker, Gasoline, Mack, Hose, Driver, Cast Iron, Arcade, 1929, 12½ In.	1450.00
Truck, Tanker, Gasoline, Pressed Steel, Germany, 8½ In.	175.00
Truck, Tanker, Gasoline, Shell, Pressed Steel, Triang, England, 17 In.	695.00
Truck, Tanker, Gasoline, Shell, Triang, England, Minic Toy, 7½ In.	295.00
Truck, Tanker, Gasoline, Standard Oil Co., Custom Built, 12 In.	1075.00
Truck, Tanker, Gasoline, Texaco, Red, Semi, Kenton, 9½ In.	2650.00
Truck, Tanker, GMC, Pressed Steel, Rubber Tires, 26 In.	385.00
Truck, Tanker, International Fuel, Metal, Japan, 1950s, 9½ In.	145.00
Truck, Tanker, Red Lion, Gilmore, Pressed Steel, Yellow, Red, 28 In.	385.00
Truck, Tanker, Shell, Pressed Steel, Orange, Side Mirror, Grill, Emblem, Buddy L, 24 In.	185.00
Truck, Tanker, Texaco, Buddy L, 1959, 24 In.	130.00
Truck, Tow, Blue, Red, Green, Marx, 12 In.	275.00
Truck, Tow, Checker Cab Co., Green Roof, Fenders, Yellow, 12 In.	180.00
Truck, Tow, Cities Service, Tin, Hand Operated Hook, Wood Wheel, Marx, 21 In.	248.00
Truck, Tow, Emergency Service, Tin, Friction, Plastic Boom, Battery Operated, Marx, 14 In.	138.00
Truck, Tow, Ford, 1934 Model, Green, Tootsietoy, 3 In.	135.00
Truck, Tow, Ford, Red Cab, Amber Windows, White Body, Decal, Esso, No. 71, Matchbox *illus*	39.00
Truck, Tow, Ford, Tin, Friction, Crank Operated Tow Hook, Daito, Box, 1959, 12½ In.	193.00
Truck, Tow, Goodrich Silvertown Tires, Art Deco, Metalcraft, 13 In.	695.00
Truck, Tow, Green, Cast Iron, Arcade, 3½ In.	200.00
Truck, Tow, Pressed Steel, Plastic Tires, Structor, 11½ In.	33.00
Truck, Tow, Red, Nickel Spoke Wheels, Arcade, 8½ In.	400.00
Truck, Tow, Repair-It, Auto Service, Pressed Steel, Buddy L, 21 In.	295.00
Truck, Tow, Retro, Pressed Steel, 24 In.	1210.00
Truck, Tow, Rubber Tires, Pressed Steel, Sturdi Toy, 30 In.	2200.00
Truck, Transport, Metal, Battery Operated, Japan, 1950s, 16½ In.	295.00
Truck, U.S. Mail, No. 52375, Metal, Banner, 1950s, 12 In.	110.00
Truck, U.S. Mail, Use Zip Code, Tin, Friction, Japan, 1950s, 9 In.	145.00
Truck, U.S.A. Army, Canvas Top, Windup, Marx, 10½ In.	250.00
Truck, Water, Tank Line, Pressed Steel, Buddy L	16000.00
Truck Set, Semi-Trailer, Aluminum, Windup, Tin Litho Driver, Marx, Box, 16½ In.	220.00
Trumpet Player, Tin Lithograph, Vinyl, Fabric, Windup, Nomura, Japan, 1960s, 9 In.	246.00
Trunk, Doll's, Blue, Hats, Shoes, Stockings, Lithographed Paper, Interior Tray, 10 x 7 x 7 In.	940.00
Trunk, Doll's, Pine, Paper Cover, Tin Edges, 16 x 9 x 9 In.	173.00
Tut Tut, Man Driving Car, Blowing Horn, Tin, Windup, Lehmann, Germany, 7 In.	1650.00
TV Space Patrol, Futuristic Car, Tail Fins, Astronaut Driver, Tin, Friction, Asahi, Box, 9 In.	9350.00
Typewriter, Light & Dark Blue, No. 200, Buddy L, Box, 1976	45.00
Typewriter, Simplex 100, Mailing Box, Child's	47.00
U.S. Destroyer, Plastic, 8 Depth Charges, 2 Torpedoes, Ideal, Box, 15 In.	110.00
Uncle Sam On Bicycle, String Operated, Painted, Tin, 12 In. . . . . *illus*	234.00
Unit Crane, Construction, On Wheels, Doepke, 1940s, 19 x 20 In.	154.00
Unit Crane, Construction, On Wheels, Stickers, Doepke, 1940s, 19 x 20 In.	165.00
Unit Crane, Pressed Steel, Doepke, 28 In.	176.00
Vehicles, Dime Store, Manoli, Soup Kitchen, Water Wagon, Tractor, Tank, Gas Truck, 7 Piece	206.00
Velocipede, 3 Cast Iron Spoke Wheels, 2 Pedals, T Bar Steering, Velvet Seat, 39 x 25 In.	549.00
Velocipede, 3 Spoked Wheels, Pedal, Upholstered Seat Cushion, 19th Century, 38 In.	323.00
Waffle Iron, Child's, Cast Iron, 5½ In.	110.00
Waffle Iron, Child's, Nickel Plated, 4 In.	66.00
Wagon, ABC, Tin Lithograph, Ohio Art, 1920s, 6½ In.	195.00
Wagon, Band, Humpty Dumpty Circus, 4 Horses, Musicians, Driver, Schoenhut, 40 In.	44000.00
Wagon, Black Horses, Drivers, Leather Harness, Paint, Wood, Cloth, Plywood Base, 7 x 20 In.	58.00
Wagon, Blue Paint, Yellow Pinstripes, Red Undercarriage, Wheels, Wood, 6¾ x 23 x 7 In.	176.00

Toy, Wagon, Hay, Donkey, Driver, Tin Lithograph, Georg Fischer, Germany, Penny, 6 In.
$201.00

Toy, Wagon, Humpty Dumpty Circus, Cage, Marquee, Red, Wood, Schoenhut, 12 In.
$1045.00

Toy, Wagon, Milk, Horse Drawn, Sheffield Farms Company, Wood, Rich Toys, 22 In.
$585.00

TIP

Don't repaint a metal doll head no matter how worn. Painting destroys the collector value.

Toy, Walker, Superhero, Super Kun No. 1, Japanese Characters, Tin, Battery, Nomura, 12 In.
$205.00

Toy, Windmill, Holland, Cast Iron, Pressed Steel, Nickel Plated, 1923, 15 In. $358.00

Toy, Zeppelin, Graf, Pressed Steel, Paint, Disc Wheels, Rubber Tires, Steelcraft, 29 In. $575.00

Toy, Zilotone, Clown Plays Xylophone, 6 Records, Tin, Windup, Wolverine, 6 In. $585.00

Tramp Art, Box, Chip Carved, Pincushion Top, Drawer, Square, 7 x 5½ In. $165.00

Wagon, Bread, Driver, Celluloid, Japan, 4 In.	95.00
Wagon, Cement, Horse, Driver, 14 In.	2415.00
Wagon, Circus, Band, Cast Iron, Horses, Driver, Riders, Kenton, 16 In.	695.00
Wagon, Circus, Overland Circus Bandwagon, Kenton, 1940s, 15 In.	1050.00
Wagon, Coaster, Wood, 4 Wood Runners, 32-Inch Pull Handle, Sherwood, 43 x 17 In.	145.00
Wagon, Conestoga, Blue, Red Paint, Linen Cover, Lancaster, Pa., c.1910, 38 x 69 x 23 In.	4675.00
Wagon, Express Flyer, Cast Iron, Nickel Plated, Kilgore, 6¾ In.	88.00
Wagon, Hay, Donkey, Driver, Tin Lithograph, Georg Fischer, Germany, Penny, 6 In. *illus*	201.00
Wagon, Hercules, Wood, Side Rack, 28-Inch Pull Handle, 1938, 52 x 21 x 24 In.	175.00
Wagon, Humpty Dumpty Circus, Cage, Marquee, Red, Gray Bars, Wood, Schoenhut, 10 In.	1210.00
Wagon, Humpty Dumpty Circus, Cage, Marquee, Red, Wood, Schoenhut, 12 In. *illus*	1045.00
Wagon, Milk, Horse Drawn, Sheffield Farms Company, Wood, Rich Toys, 22 In. *illus*	585.00
Wagon, Milk, Sheffield Farms, Wood Folk Art, Horse Drawn, 9 x 21 x 6 In.	880.00
Wagon, Milk, Tin, Windup, Marx, 10 In.	165.00
Wagon, Milk & Horse, Tin, Windup, Marx, 4½ x 10 In.	94.00
Wagon, Rough Rider, Metal, Spoke Wheels, Undercarriage, Wood Floor, Handle, 15 x 26 In.	280.00
Wagon, Wood, Painted Yellow, Red, Black Accents, 9¼ x 15 In.	358.00
Wagon, Wood, Spoke Wheels, Handle, Metal Axle, Wheel Rims, Hand Grip, 14 x 32 In.	392.00
Wagon, World's Fair, Lindy Flyer, Red, Pressed Steel, Front Bumper, Electric Lights, 1933	1035.00
Walker, Superhero, Super Kun No. 1, Japanese Characters, Tin, Battery, Nomura, 12 In. *illus*	205.00
Wallet, Dracula, Mummy, Vinyl, Mirror, Universal Pictures, 1963, 3½ x 4½ In.	410.00
Wallet, Marshall Wyatt Earp, Vinyl, Identification Card, Badge, c.1957, 3 x 4 In.	84.00
Wallet Kit, Space Ranger, Deluxe, Simulated Leather, 1950s, 3 x 8½ In.	112.00
Warehouse, Wood, Windup, Elevator, Converse, 9 In.	165.00
Washing Machine, Busy Betty, Pressed Steel, Depression Glass, Hoge Mfg. Co., 10¼ In.	790.00
Washing Machine, Pressed Tin, Glass, Wolverine, 10 In.	88.00
Washing Machine, Pressed Tin, Glass Insert, 10¾ In.	132.00
Water Pump, Cast Iron, Green, Arcade, 1900s, 4¾ In.	60.00
Water Pump, Cast Iron, Red Tank, Decal, Arcade, 1900s, 8 In.	132.00
Watering Can, Flying Gull, Ducks, Oval, Signed, Germany, c.1900, 6½ In.	196.00
Watering Can, Girl, Flowers, Goose, Chein, 1930s, 6¾ In.	165.00
Watering Can, Girl In Flower Garden, Tin, Chein, 1950s, 9¾ In.	125.00
Wheelbarrow, Metal, Spoke Wheel, Legs, Wood Undercarriage, Handles, Child's, 12 x 36 In.	504.00
Wheelbarrow, Pressed Steel, Blue, Yellow, Marx, 9 In.	45.00
Wheelbarrow, Sam The City Gardener, Tools, Marx, 9 In., Box	350.00
Whistle, Squirrel In Wheel, Red, Blue, Gold, Tin Litho, Penny Toy, France, c.1925, 5 In.	110.00
Whistle, Squirrel Moves On Rotating Cage, Penny Toy	145.00
Whoopee Car, Cowboy, Tin Lithograph, Windup, Marx, c.1932, 8 In.	336.00
Windmill, Holland, Cast Iron, Pressed Steel, Nickel Plated, 1923, 15 In. *illus*	358.00
Windmill, Pressed Steel, Cast Iron Base, Arcade, 1902, 5 In.	385.00
Windmill, Pressed Steel, Nickel Plated, Arcade, Box, 1923, 26 In.	248.00
Wolf, Brown, Wood, Jointed, Leather Ears, Carved Mouth, Glass Eyes, Schoenhut, 6½ In.	1430.00
Woman, Pushing Baby Carriage, Tin, Windup, Walking Motion, Haji, 6½ In.	149.00
Woman, With Baby Carriage, Cream, Blue, Pink, Windup, 6¼ In.	385.00
Wonder Cyclist, Boy Riding Tricycle, Tin, Windup, Marx, 9 In.	605.00
Woodchopper, Cast Lead Head, Brass Hat, Wood Body, Windup, 7¼ x 4¼ In.	3738.00
Woodsy-Wee Zoo, Elephant, Bear, Lion, Giraffe, Camel, Pull Toy, No. 487, Fisher-Price, Box, 1931	785.00
Yellow Kid, Bell Ringer, Metal Head & Hands, Spring Loaded, c.1896, 9 In.	2300.00
Yeti, Abominable Snowman, Tin, Plush, Battery Operated Remote, Marx, Box, 11 In.	825.00
Zebra, Wood, Jointed, Yellow, Brown, Leather Ears, Glass Eyes, Mohair Mane, Schoenhut, 8½ In.	550.00
Zebu, Wood, Jointed, Leather Horns & Ears, Painted Eyes, Schoenhut, 8 In.	605.00
Zeppelin, Graf, Pressed Steel, Paint, Disc Wheels, Rubber Tires, Steelcraft, 29 In. *illus*	575.00
Zeppelin, Propeller, Penny Toy, 1930s, 3 In.	145.00
Zigzag, Rolls, Lehmann, c.1907	1050.00
Zilotone, Clown Plays Xylophone, 6 Records, Tin, Windup, Wolverine, 6 In. *illus*	585.00

TRAMP ART is a form of folk art made since the Civil War. It is usually made from chip-carved cigar boxes. Examples range from small boxes and picture frames to full-sized pieces of furniture.

Box, Chip Carved, Pincushion Top, Drawer, Square, 7 x 5½ In. *illus*	165.00
Box, Stepped Pyramid, Drawer, Applied Leaves, Birds, Gold Paint, 6½ x 8½ In.	1610.00
Cabinet, Sewing, Tambour Doors, Pivoting 2-Tier Spool Rack, Drawer, Painted, 9½ x 5 In.	144.00
Crucifix, Carved, Interlocking Wood Pieces, 16½ x 8½ In.	98.00
Fern Stand, Straw, Woven, Twisted, Pine Top, Square, 30 x 16 In. *illus*	141.00
Frame, 10 Panes, Chip Carved, Leaves, Flowers, Gold Paint, 15 x 12½ In.	373.00

T

Frame, 12 Panes, Carved Tiers, Applied Scrolled Vine, Heart Corners, 24 x 21⅝ In.	220.00
Frame, Carved, Painted, 12 x 16 In.	403.00
Frame, Chip Carved, Scalloped Edge, Star Corners, Brass Rosettes, 14 x 21 In.	83.00
Frame, Crown Of Thorns, 10¼ x 7 In. ....*illus*	303.00
Frame, Geometric Lapped Hearts, Dark Red Paint, 22½ x 19 In.	1058.00
Frame, Mirror, Chip Carved, Sawtooth Borders, X-Forms, Gold, Silver Paint, 19 x 15½ In.	235.00
Frame, Mirror, Tiered Pyramids, 19¼ x 12¼ In.	248.00
Frame, Porcelain Button Corners, Indian Maiden Print, 11¼ x 9¼ In.	99.00
Frame, Wood, Chip Carved, Stacked Hearts, Triangles, Rounds, Teardrops, 31 x 28 In.	2703.00
Frame, Wood, Gnarled, Entwined Tree Roots, 39 x 47 In.	4818.00
Pyramids, Chip Carved, 18 In.	370.00

TRAPS for animals may be handmade. One of the most unusual is the mousetrap made  so that when the mouse entered the trap, it was hit on the head with a mallet. Other traps were commercially manufactured and often are marked with the name of the manufacturer. Many traps were designed to be as humane as possible, and they would trap the live animal so it could be released in the woods.

Fly, Glass Blown, Apple Green, 14 Vertical Ribs, 3 Applied Feet, 1890-1920, 7 In.	224.00
Fly, Hornet, Wasp, Purple-Blue, Mold Blown, Controlled Bubbles, Embossed SJ	100.00
Gopher, Steel Wire, 10 x 3 In.	23.00
Minnow, McSwain Glass Co., Embossed, Wire Handle, Jonesboro, Ark., 12 In.	150.00
Mouse, Choker, Victor Animal Trap Co., Wood, 4 x 4 In.	45.00
Mouse, Ketch-All, No. 2, Glavanized Steel, Kness Mfg. Co., Albia, Iowa	40.00
Mouse Gum, Hollowed Out Log, Wire, Wood, Steel Door, 8½ In.	104.00
Roach, Redware, Interior Glaze, 6⅛ In.	33.00
Shrimp, Reed, Handwoven, Veracruz, 1950s, 20 x 14 In.	58.00

TREEN, *see Wooden category.*

TRENCH ART is a form of folk art made by soldiers. Metal casings from bullets and mortar shells were cut and decorated to form useful objects, such as vases.

Ashtray, Bullets, World War II, 1942	75.00
Lighter, 50 Caliber Shell Casing, Wood Base	85.00
Lighter, Bullet, Brass Shell, Granite Base, 8¼ In.	125.00
Vase, Shell, Hammered Casing, Bronze Patina, AEF, Argonne, 1918, 13½ In.	125.00
Vase, Shell, Hand Hammered, World War I, Signed, E.J. Cuery, 9 x 3½ In.	70.00

TRIVETS are now used to hold hot dishes. Most trivets of the late nineteenth and early twentieth centuries were made to hold hot irons. Iron or brass reproductions are being made of many of the old styles.

Brass, Concentric Hearts, Steel Center Heart, England, 6½ x 4 In.	173.00
Brass, G.R. Lever, Footed, Pierced Scrolls, Heart, Diamond, Star, c.1825, 10¾ In.	173.00
Brass, Iron, Openwork, Turned Wood Handle, Tripod Base, Fender Hooks, 8½ x 6½ In.	201.00
Brass, Openwork Top, Frieze, Hearts, Scrolls, 19th Century, 12 x 17 In.	144.00
Heart, Flattened Spear Point Feet, 1½ x 6¾ In.	121.00
Iron, Flat Handle, Rattail Terminal, Hand Forged, 14½ In. ....*illus*	88.00
Iron, Heart, Spear Point Terminals, Flat Handle, Pierced End, Scroll Feet, Hand Forged, 10 In.	143.00
Iron, Running Wheel & Star, Openwork, 10 In.	33.00
Iron, Y Post Handle, Rattail, Tall Legs, Flat Feet, Hand Forged, 18 In.	193.00
Sterling Silver, Glass, Circle With Squares In Center, 7 In.	110.00
Sterling Silver, Glass, Flowers, Vines, 6 In.	83.00

TRUNKS of many types were made. The nineteenth-century sea chest was often handmade of unpainted wood. Brass-fitted camphorwood chests were brought back from the Orient. Leather-covered trunks were popular from the late eighteenth to mid-nineteenth centuries. By 1895, trunks were covered with canvas or decorated sheet metal. Embossed metal coverings were used from 1870 to 1910. By 1925, trunks were covered with vulcanized fiber or undecorated metal. Suitcases are listed here.

Blanket, Painted, Locking Key, c.1940, 38 x 24 x 26 In.	325.00
Box, Turkish, Glass, 1900-40, 12¾ x 5⅝ x 6½ In.	495.00
Box, Turkish, Glass, 1900-40, 17¼ x 8½ x 10 In.	795.00
Camphorwood, Brass Key Hole, Escutcheon, 22 x 12⅜ x 14 In.	695.00

Tramp Art, Fern Stand, Straw, Woven, Twisted, Pine Top, Square, 30 x 16 In.
$141.00

Tramp Art, Frame, Crown Of Thorns, 10¼ x 7 In.
$303.00

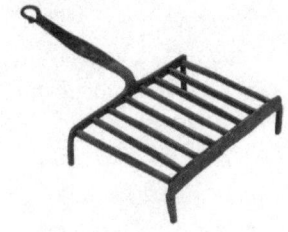

Trivet, Iron, Flat Handle, Rattail Terminal, Hand Forged, 14½ In.
$88.00

Trunk, Immigrant's, Pine, Grain Painted, Iron Straps, H. Peppler, Germany, 22 x 33 x 19 In.
$259.00

T

Trunk, Steamer, Dome Top, Embossed Tin Panels, c.1900, 25 x 32 x 18 In. $47.00

Trunk, Steamer, Leather, Brass Strap Corners, 3 Graduated Drawers, c.1900, 24 x 34 In. $35.00

Camphorwood, Brass Mounts, Lock, Handles, 42 x 23 x 21 In.	2400.00
Dome Top, Hand Forged Iron Strapping, 42½ x 22 x 22 In.	6500.00
Dome Top, Leather, Red, Black, Inlaid Card Suites, Patchwork Interior, 28 x 17 In.	230.00
Dome Top, Leather, Secret Lid Compartments, France, c.1900, 24 x 32 In.	3000.00
Dome Top, Metal, Faux Alligator Panels, Hardwood Ribs, Leather Handles, 21 x 30 x 17 In.	165.00
Dome Top, Pine, Dovetailed, Carved Reeded Squares, Light Blue Paint, 24 x 12 In.	460.00
Dome Top, Pine, Smoke Grain On Yellow, Dovetailed, Wire Hinge, 24 x 12 x 10 In.	345.00
Dutch Style, Wrought Iron, Painted, Handmade Hinges, 70 x 46 In.	322.00
Gothic, Walnut, Patinated, Carved, Iron, France, 18th Century, 26 x 70 In.	11000.00
Hardwood, Iron Strapwork, Paneled Top, Hinged, Finials, Coffered Front, India, 35 x 52 In.	470.00
Hermes, Set, Handbag, Toiletry Case, Carry-On Bag, Ostrich, Cadillac Series	1404.00
Hermes, Set, Overnight, Carry-On Bag, Briefcase, Ostrich, Cadillac Series	1053.00
Immigrant's, Pine, Grain Painted, Iron Straps, H. Peppler, Germany, 22 x 33 x 19 In. ...*illus*	259.00
Leather, Wallpaper Lining, Tray, c.1880-1910, 33 x 19 x 17½ In.	250.00
Louis Vuitton, Document Box, Leather Straps, Brass, Early 1900s, 8½ x 16 x 15½ In.	840.00
Louis Vuitton, Fold-Down Interior Section, 22 x 26 In.	1840.00
Louis Vuitton, Footlocker, Double Yellow Stripe, Monogram, 21¼ x 40¼ In.	23500.00
Louis Vuitton, Footlocker, Leather Trim, Brass Nail Heads, Monogram, c.1900, 22 x 40 In.	19500.00
Louis Vuitton, Footlocker, Wood, Brass Mounted, Monogram, 15 x 29 x 15 In.	2640.00
Louis Vuitton, Leather Trim, Vuitinite Fabric, c.1900, 22 x 43½ In.	11000.00
Louis Vuitton, Pet Carrier, Leather Trim, 14¼ In.	192.00
Louis Vuitton, Pet Carrier, Leather Trim, 16 In.	470.00
Louis Vuitton, Pet Carrier, Leather Trim, 18 In.	214.00
Louis Vuitton, Steamer, Wood, Leather, Brass Mounted, Early 1900s, 25 x 36 x 22 In.	4800.00
Louis Vuitton, Toilette Case, Traveling, 8¼ x 9 x 16 In.	695.00
Louis Vuitton, Travel Case, Wood, Brass, Leather Handle, Labels, 21 x 24 x 18½ In.	3840.00
Louis Vuitton, Wardrobe, Leather Trim, Monogram, Opens Length Wise, 22 x 45 In.	22000.00
Marriage, Paint Decorated, Lift Top, Applied Beaded Edge, 10½ x 21 In.	2350.00
Oak, Recessed Panels, Fluted Pilasters, Ribbed, 27¼ x 48½ x 20¾ In.	502.00
Pine, Grain Painted, Mustard & Brown Vinegar Decoration Over Red, 24 x 12 In.	546.00
Poplar, Diamond Panels, Escutcheon, Flowers, c.1680, 27½ x 47 x 21 In.	2120.00
Stage Coach, Jenny Lind, Leather Covered, Bread Loaf Shape, c.1875, 28 x 16 x 15¼ In.	465.00
Steamer, Dome Top, Embossed Tin Panels, c.1900, 25 x 32 x 18 In. ...*illus*	47.00
Steamer, Leather, Brass Strap Corners, 3 Graduated Drawers, c.1900, 24 x 34 In. ...*illus*	35.00
Storage, Walnut, Railroad, Mid 1800s, 30 x 26½ x 42 In.	975.00
Suitcase, Cross, Leather, Stand, 18¼ In. & 14 x 22¼ In.	234.00
Tilt Top, Elm, Bird & Branch, Metal Hardware, Handles, Germany, 27 x 45 x 26 In.	3186.00
Valascoli, Carry-On Bag, Briefcase, Ostrich, Italy, 2 Piece	1404.00
Walnut, Carved, Stucco Facade, Turned Columns, France, c.1890, 26 x 57½ x 16½ In.	2086.00
Wedding, Painted, Lovebirds, Hearts, Flowers, France, 18th Century, 19 x 12 In.	2200.00
Wood, Multicolored, Figures, Chinese, 27 x 40¾ x 24 In.	1003.00

TUTHILL Cut Glass Company of Middletown, New York, worked from 1902 to 1923. Of special interest are the finely cut pieces of stemware and tableware.

Vase, Brilliant Cut, Ruffled, Elongated Star Border, Feathers, c.1900, 9 In.	530.00

TYPEWRITER collectors divide typewriters into two main classifications: the index machine, which has a pointer and a dial for letter selection, and the keyboard machine, most commonly seen today. The first successful typewriter was made by Sholes and Glidden in 1874.

American, No. 5834, Indicator Style, Curved Index, Metal Cover	510.00
American, No. 6836, Indicator Style, Curved Index, Wood Base	450.00
Blickensderfer, No. 133618, Model 8, Tabulator Keys	240.00
Blickensderfer, No. 182570, Aluminum, Folding Space Bar	180.00
Calligraph, No. 23087, Keyboard, Wrist Rest, Wood Cover	540.00
Corona, Portable, Folding, Patent Date 1917, 6 x 11 x 10 In. ...*illus*	92.00
Corona, Portable, Model No. 10778, Creampica Type, 1927	60.00
Crandall, No. 7730, 2 Rows, Curved Keyboard, Type Sleeve, Oak Case, c.1900	8400.00
Daugherty, No. 1778, 4 Rows, Keyboard, Front Stroke, Mahogany Base	960.00
Edelmann, Shift & Space Key, Wooden Base & Case, 1897	1017.00
Franklin, No. 7, Curved Ideal Keyboard, Rectangular Wood Base, 1898 ... 1017.00 to 1080.00
Frolio 5, German, Gundka Werke, 1920s, Original Case	150.00
Gundka, No. 2639, Index, Selector, Oak Base, Metal Cover, 1920s	90.00
Hall, Model 1, Square Index, Selector, Ink, Accessories, Walnut Base, 15 x 9 In.	660.00
Hall, No. 7555, Portable, 1881 ...*illus*	1097.00

Hammond, Model 1, No. 11421, Curved 2-Row Keyboard, Twin Typeshuttles	1440.00
Lambert, No. 171, Index, Round Letter Dial, Shaped Base, 1896	1329.00
Mignon, Model 4, No. 71257, Type Sleeve, Pointer, Index, Oak Case	210.00
National, No. 3209, Curved Keyboard, 3 Rows, Upstroke, Mahogany, Metal Lid	3600.00
Odell's, Index, Round Scrolled Base, T-Shaped Mechanism, 1889	964.00
Olivetti, Studio 44, Red Leather Case, 1950s	85.00
People's, No.4609, Brass Type Wheel, Curved Index, Gilt Lined, Mahogany Case	500.00
Pittsburg, Model 10, No. 11008, Platen, Basket, Oak Base, Metal Cover, 19 In.	1440.00
Rem-Blick, Original Wooden Case, 12 In. ....*illus*	175.00
Remington, Black, Gold Lettering, Decoration, 1900s, 11 x 13 x 14 In.	120.00
Remington, New York, Early 1900s, 10¾ x 15 x 14½ In.	100.00
Royal, Deluxe, Portable, Black, Case, c.1936, 6 x 12⅔ x 12 In.	350.00
Salter, Standard, No. 10, 1908	1063.00
Simplex, No. 300, Original Box, Instructions, Simplex Typewriter Co. Inc., N.Y.	55.00
Smith, Premier, No. 1, 1889	281.00
Williams, No. 6, No. 39008, Grasshopper Action, Wood Base, Metal Cover	570.00
World, No. 13450, Index Wheel, Typewriter Improvement Co., c.1886, 12 In.	382.00
World, Upper, Lower Case, Semicircular Index, Oak Base, Walnut Case	540.00

TYPEWRITER RIBBON TINS are now being collected. The lithographed tin containers have been used since the 1870s. Most popular with collectors are tins with pictorial graphics.

Allied, Art Deco, Allied Carbon & Ribbon Mfg., N.Y.	20.00
Amneco, Square	75.00
Bar Brand, L.C. Smith Corona Typewriters Inc	14.00
Carter's Midnight, Carter's Ink Company	12.00
Ditto, Art Deco, Underwood Typewriter, Purple, Red	10.00
Hallmark, Cameron Mfg. Co., Texas, 2½ In.	20.00
Royal Typewriter Co., Vogue, Green, Blue Flowers, Art Deco, 2½ In.	13.00
Thorobred Typewriter, Underwood Corp., Burlington, N.J.	20.00
Webster Star Brand, Non-Filling, F.S. Webster Co., Boston	18.00

UHL pottery was made in Evansville, Indiana, in 1854. The pottery moved to Huntingburg, Indiana, in 1908. Stoneware and glazed pottery were made until the mid-1940s.

Coffee Set, Cobalt Blue	1200.00
Cookie Jar, Flowers, White Interior, Hand Painted, Ransburg, 9 x 9 In.	64.00
Crock, Hand Turned, c.1930, 36 x 13½ In.	800.00
Jug, Tan, No. 125, c.1940	20.00
Mug, Barrel Form, 4½ x 5½ In.	21.00
Pitcher, Flowers, Blue, Hand Painted, Ransburg, 6 In.	65.00
Washboard, Stoneware Wash Surface, Wood Frame, 14 x 20 In.	1000.00

UMBRELLA collectors like rain or shine. The first known umbrella was owned by King Louis XIII of France in 1637. The earliest umbrellas were sunshades, not designed to be used in the rain. The umbrella was embellished and redesigned many times. In 1852, the fluted steel rib style was developed and it has remained the most useful style.

Bakelite Handle, Pearlized, Pink Flower	7.00
Bamboo, Folding, Purple Fabric, Flowers, Pink Threading	30.00
Gold Handle, Scrolling, Mother-Of-Pearl, Victorian, Multicolored, 1800s, 35 x 30 In.	295.00
Handle, Ivory, Louis XV Motifs, Carved, Quadrille, Rocaille, French Dieppe, 1800s, 11 In.	450.00
Parasol, Pink, Wood, Metal Handle, Lavender, Mauves, Loop Chain, 33 x 36 In.	34.00
Parasol, Walking Stick, Silk Taffeta, Floral, 1910, 44 In.	105.00
Plastic Handle, Leaf Design, Rose Red Tip, Deep Red	35.00
Red Hats, Purple Panels, 42 In.	12.00
Rolled Gold Handle, Flower Scroll, Mother-Of-Pearl, Victorian, 1800s, 46 x 36 In.	300.00

UNION PORCELAIN WORKS was established at Greenpoint, New York, in 1848 by Charles Cartlidge. The company went through a series of ownership changes and finally closed in the early 1900s. The company made a fine quality white porcelain that was often decorated in clear, bright colors.

Match Holder, Advertising For UPW	375.00

UNIVERSITY OF NORTH DAKOTA, *see North Dakota School Of Mines category.*

Louis Vuitton
Watch for luggage by Louis Vuitton. The company has been in business since 1854, and its trunks sell for hundreds and even thousands of dollars. Vuitton made the first flat, stackable trunks. They were made of canvas. The name "Louis Vuitton" is on clasps and locks and the trademark "LV" monogram, introduced in 1896, on the canvas. Watch for fakes, especially pieces with LV fabric.

Typewriter, Corona, Portable, Folding, Patent Date 1917, 6 x 11 x 10 In.
$92.00

Typewriter, Hall, No. 7555, Portable, 1881
$1097.00

Typewriter, Rem-Blick, Original Wooden Case, 12 In.
$175.00

Val St. Lambert, Paperweight, Cut To Clear, Printies, Diamond Panels, Facets, Red, 4 In. $374.00

Val St. Lambert, Vase, Brown, Frosted, Stylized Leaves & Tendrils, Oval, Rolled Rim, 10 In. $685.00

Vallerysthal, Vase, Pink, Enameled Roman Decoration, Elongated Neck, Cameo, 12 In. $3738.00

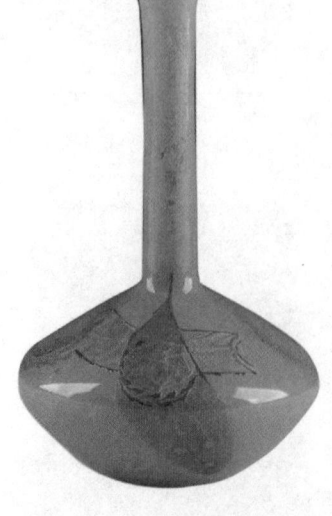

VAL ST. LAMBERT Cristalleries of Belgium was founded by Messieurs Kemlin and Lelievre in 1825. The company is still in operation. All types of table glassware and decorative glassware have been made. Pieces are often decorated with cut designs.

Ashtray, 6¼ In. Diam.	75.00
Atomizer, Frosted, Textured Design, Crimson Flower Swags, Signed, 10½ In.	575.00
Bowl, Centerpiece, Cranberry, Original Tag, 16 In.	250.00
Bowl, Cranberry To Clear, 8 In.	300.00
Cocktail, Stylized, Pulled Stem, 4½ In.	25.00
Goblet, Louise, 6⅞ In.	6.00
Paperweight, Cut To Clear, Printies, Diamond Panels, Facets, Red, 4 In. ....*illus*	374.00
Paperweight, Egg Shape, Art Nouveau, Signed, 3¼ In.	495.00
Vase, Brown, Frosted, Stylized Leaves & Tendrils, Oval, Rolled Rim, 10 In. ...*illus*	685.00
Vase, Bumble Bee, Pussy Willows, Slender, Footed, Cameo, Signed, 14¾ In.	3730.00
Vase, Campagna Form, Inverted Bell Shape, Square Base, Etched, 7 x 6¾ In.	395.00
Vase, Imperial, Diamond Facets, Marked, 7 x 5 In.	25.00
Vase, Lavender Flowers, Frosted Ground, Cameo, Signed, 16½ In.	850.00
Vase, Twisting & Stylized Foliage, 7¾ x 6½ In.	175.00

VALLERYSTHAL Glassworks was founded in 1836 in Lorraine, France. In 1854, the firm became Klenglin et Cie. It made table and decorative glass, opaline, cameo, and art glass. A line of covered, pressed glass animal dishes was made in the nineteenth century. The firm is still working.

Candlestick, Dolphin, Marked, PV, 5½ In.	60.00
Dish, Alligator, Blue Milk Glass, Marked	2800.00
Dish, Elephant & Rider, Blue Milk Glass, Marked	200.00
Dish, Fish, Blue Milk Glass, Marked	200.00
Dish, Mouse On Toadstool, Milk Glass	325.00
Salt, Hen On Nest, 2⅜ x 1⅞ In.	10.00
Vase, Enamel Dragonfly, Vines, Ruby Ground, Gilt Fence On Foot, 4 x 6½ In.	3450.00
Vase, Green, Bees, Beehive, Leafy Branches, Cylindrical, Tapered, 7½ In.	460.00
Vase, Green, Turquoise, Amethyst Iris, Butterflies, Gold Trim, Bulbous, Footed, 13 In.	2645.00
Vase, Pink, Enameled Roman Decoration, Elongated Neck, Cameo, 12 In. ....*illus*	3738.00

VAN BRIGGLE pottery was started by Artus Van Briggle in Colorado Springs, Colorado, after 1901. Van Briggle had been a decorator at Rookwood Pottery of Cincinnati, Ohio. He died in 1904 and his wife took over managing the pottery. The wares usually had modeled relief decorations and a soft, dull glaze. The pottery is still working and still making some of the original designs.

Bookends, Owl, Mulberry Glaze, c.1928	115.00
Bowl, Acorn & Leaf, Ming Turquoise Glaze, Marked, 6½ In.	72.00
Bowl, Butterfly, Ming Turquoise, 3¼ x 3½ In.	65.00
Bowl, Centerpiece, Mermaid, Blue & Turquoise, Footed, 9 x 14½ In. ....*illus*	480.00
Bowl, Flower Frog, Dragonflies, Green & Brown Matte Glaze, 2½ x 9 In.	374.00
Bowl, Flower Frog, Tulips, Turquoise, 20th Century, 8½ In.	147.00
Bowl, Green, 1916, 8 In.	275.00
Bowl, Ming Turquoise, 3¼ x 2½ In.	60.00
Bowl, Molded Leaves, Purple, Blue, 20th Century, 4½ In.	206.00
Bowl, Pinecone, Rose Matte Glaze, 3 x 5½ In.	295.00
Bowl, Tulip, Blue Green, 6 x 3 In.	75.00
Candleholder, Black, Blue Tip, 5 x 7 In., Pair	84.00
Candleholder, Green, Brown Gloss Glaze, c.1958, 3 x 5½ In.	34.00
Dish, Turtle, Cover, Brown & Green Glaze, Anna Van Briggle, 6¾ In.	66.00
Ewer, Mauve Glaze, Flowing Design, Signed, 11½ In.	115.00
Ewer, Purple & Violet Matte Glaze, 11 In. ....*illus*	212.00
Figurine, Blushing Rabbit, Cream, Blue, Pink, 3¾ x 3¾ In.	65.00
Figurine, Elephant, Brown Gloss Glaze, c.1970, 3¼ In.	120.00
Figurine, Hopi Maiden, Grinding Corn, Blue Matte Glaze, 6 In.	201.00
Figurine, Rabbit, Ming Turquoise, Marked, 3½ x 2⅞ In.	50.00
Flower Frog & Bowl, Tulips, Crimson, 20th Century, 8½ In.	147.00
Jardiniere, Embossed, Morning Glories, Raspberry, Yellow Glaze, 1905, 6½ x 8 In.	1200.00
Night-Light, Curved Leaf Shape, Brown Matte Glaze, Handle, 5½ In.	138.00
Pitcher, Low Handle, 5⅞ x 3⅜ In.	75.00
Pitcher, White Drip Over Black Glaze, Marked, 11¼ In.	28.00
Planter, Shell Shape, 9 x 5 In.	55.00

Sugar & Creamer, Persian Rose, Marked, 2 In.	39.00
Tile, Blue Bird On Branch, Cuenca, 6 x 6 In.	1800.00
Tile, Logo, Glazed Grasses, Leaves, 6 x 6 In.	45.00
Tile, Mountain Landscape, Trees, Cuenca, 6¼ x 6¼ In.	2640.00
Tile, Purple Kingfisher On Branch, Cuenca, 6 x 6 In.	1800.00
Tile, Sailboats On Lake, Blue, Green, White, Cuenca, 6 x 6 In.	1440.00
Tray, Leaf, Deep Green, c.1984, 14½ x 9¼ In.	125.00
Vase, Blue, Gray To Brown Matte Glaze, Feathers, 1905, 8½ x 4 In.	1640.00
Vase, Brown Clay, Peacock Feathers, Gray Green Glaze, 1911, 9 x 4 In.	1680.00
Vase, Bud, Black, Seafoam Rim, 6⅞ In.	18.00
Vase, Bulbous, Leaf & Stem Decoration, Rose Glaze, 2½ In.	88.00
Vase, Carved Stem, Flower, Red, Blue Matte Glaze, c.1912, 2½ In.	495.00
Vase, Carved Stem & Flower, Red & Blue Glaze, 2½ In.	500.00
Vase, Dark Mulberry Matte Glaze, Tapered, 4½ x 7½ In.	161.00
Vase, Dragonflies, Turquoise Matte Glaze, Swollen Top, 6⅝ In.	173.00 to 219.00
Vase, Flowers, Mulberry Glaze, Swollen Neck, 1918, 5 In.	184.00
Vase, Indian Heads, Maroon, Blue Matte Glaze, Late 1920s, 12 x 5¼ In.	595.00
Vase, Jonquils, Green & Rose Matte Glaze, 1905, 10½ x 4 In.	2040.00
Vase, Leaf, Blue, Green Drip Glaze, 1950s, 5¾ In.	60.00
Vase, Lorelei, Celadon Glaze, 11 x 4½ In.	235.00
Vase, Lorelei, Ming Turquoise, Marked, 11 In.	308.00
Vase, Melon Shape, Brown Matte Glaze, 2¾ In.	75.00
Vase, Morning Glories, Raspberry Glaze, Green Accents, 1905, 7 x 4 In.	1320.00
Vase, Navy Blue, Flower Shape, 6 In.	95.00
Vase, Oval, Leaves, Purple Matte Glaze, 1920s, 5 x 3¾ In.	395.00
Vase, Peacock Feathers, Blue & White Glaze, 1904, 10¾ x 3¾ In.	1440.00
Vase, Peacock Feathers, Persian Rose Glaze, 4 Short Handles, 13½ In.	1320.00
Vase, Peacock Feathers, White Glaze, Cylindrical, 2 Handles At Top, 6⅞ In.	863.00
Vase, Persian Rose Glaze, Early 20th Century, 10 In.	294.00
Vase, Poppies, Yellow Matte Glaze, Swollen Neck, 1915, 7⅛ In.	748.00
Vase, Poppy Pods, Leaves, Purple, Light Green Frothy Glaze, 10 x 4¾ In.	5760.00
Vase, Repeating Leaves, Mulberry Glaze, Blue Highlights, Swollen Neck, 5 In.	173.00
Vase, Triple, Green Matte, 7 In.	95.00
Vase, Trumpet Shape, Handles, Crimson Shading To Blue, 1900s, 15½ In.	353.00
Vase, Yucca, Aspen Sunrise, 17½ x 7 In.	300.00
Vase, Yucca, Semimatte Turquoise Glaze, Marked, 4⅜ x 5½ In.	44.00

VASA MURRHINA is the name of a glassware made by the Vasa Murrhina Art Glass Company of Sandwich, Massachusetts, about 1884. The glassware was transparent and was embedded with small pieces of colored glass and metallic flakes. The mica flakes were coated with silver, gold, copper, or nickel. Some of the pieces were cased. The same type of glass was made in England. Collectors often confuse Vasa Murrhina glass with aventurine, spatter, or spangle glass. There is uncertainty about what actually was made by the Vasa Murrhina factory. Related pieces may be listed under Spangle Glass.

Basket, Rose Aventurine, Green, 1960s, 7 In.	50.00
Creamer, Rose Mist	115.00
Dish, Sweetmeat, Cranberry, Yellow Spatter, Gold Aventurine, Ribbed, 6½ In.	316.00
Perfume Bottle, Black Amethyst, 19th Century	350.00
Vase, Fan, Rose Mist, 7 In.	145.00
Vase, Magnolia, Amethyst, Black, Shouldered, Flared Foot, Cameo, 8 In.	1320.00
Vase, Yellow, Brown Streaks, Gold Aventurine, Double Gourd, Ruffled Edge, 11 In.	115.00

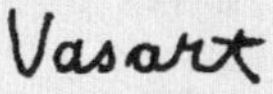

VASART is the signature used on a late type of art glass made by the Streathearn Glass Company of Scotland. Pieces are marked with an engraved signature on the bottom. Most of the glass is mottled or shaded.

Vasart

Vase, Blue, Cluthra, Mottled, Wide Rim, Pontil, c.1940-50, 2½ In.	195.00

VASELINE GLASS is a greenish-yellow glassware resembling petroleum jelly. Pressed glass of the 1870s was often made of vaseline-colored glass. Some vaseline glass is still being made in old and new styles. Additional pieces of vaseline glass may also be listed under Pressed Glass in this book.

Ashtray, Pipe Holder, Green, 6½ x 4 In.	56.00
Ashtray, Translucent, Daisy Pattern, 1920s, 5¼ In.	25.00
Bowl, 4-Leaf Clovers, 3 Sections, Silver-Plate Holder, 7 In.	30.00

Van Briggle, Bowl, Centerpiece, Mermaid, Blue & Turquoise, Footed, 9 x 14½ In.
$480.00

Van Briggle, Ewer, Purple & Violet Matte Glaze, 11 In.
$212.00

Van Briggle Pottery and Marks

The *AA* mark (for Artus Van Briggle and his wife, Anne) is usually in a rectangle or trapezoid. Some pottery is marked only *Van Briggle*. Some, made from 1955 to 1968 with a glossy finish, are marked *Anna Van*. Pieces made between 1900 and 1907 and from 1912 to 1919 are marked with the date. Many marks include the words *Colorado Springs* or *Colo Sprgs.*

U
V

Vaseline Glass, Lamp, Kerosene, Petal Topped Shade, Optic Panel Base, Burner, 9¾ In. $575.00

Verlys, Bowl, Orchard, Satin, Signed, 14 In. $193.00

Verlys, Vase, Gems, Opalescent, 6½ In. $71.00

Bowl, Basket Weave, 2½ In.	20.00
Bowl, Centerpiece, c.1930, 2 x 14 In.	55.00
Bowl, Diamond & Button, Star Shaped, 8½ In.	39.00
Bowl, L.G. Wright, 1960s, 6 x 4 In.	80.00
Bowl, Leaf Shape, 5½ x 1½ In.	35.00
Bowl, Star & Arch, 6½ In.	59.95
Bucket, Daisy, Handle, 4 x 3 In.	22.00
Butter, Cover, Eye Winker, 4¾ x 7½ In.	39.00
Butter, Cover, Queens, Scalloped Edge, Mosser, 5½ x 7½ In.	33.00
Butter, Dome Cover, Croesus, 7½ x 5½ In.	68.00
Candlestick, Open Pontil, Victorian, Miniature, Pair	325.00
Candlestick, Swirl Tops, Octagonal Stem, Flint, 8¼ In., Pair	121.00
Celery Vase, Mikado Pattern, Daisy & Button Base	75.00
Coaster, Furniture Leg, Cross Shape Interior, 3 In., 5 Piece	25.00
Compote, Daisy & Leaf, 4½ x 5½ In.	60.00
Compote, Inverted Thistle, 6½ In.	33.00
Compote, Lattice Edge, Challinor & Taylor, 9 x 7 In.	165.00
Compote, Thistle, 6½ x 6 In.	65.00
Custard Cup, Tufglas, 2½ x 3½ In., Pair	15.00
Dish, Banner, Higbee Glass Co., 1909, 5 x 7 In.	38.00
Dish, Footed, Hobnail, 3 x 4 In.	10.00
Dish, Thumbprint, 6½ In.	45.00
Dish, Vanity, Rosebud, 4½ x 2½ In.	20.00
Epergne, 4 Lily, Opalescent Rim, Brass Mounts, 17 In.	200.00
Fairy Lamp, Holly, Mosser, 5½ x 5 In.	40.00
Figure, Dolphin, Leaping, Gibson Glass Co., 4 In.	20.00
Jar, Pickle, Moon & Stars	79.00
Lamp, Kerosene, Petal Topped Shade, Optic Panel Base, Burner, 9¾ In. ....*illus*	575.00
Mayonnaise Ladle, 5 In.	15.95
Pitcher, 6 Glasses, Columnar Fluting, Bulbous Bottom, 9½ & 5⅝ In.	795.00
Plate, Spider Web, 7½ In.	45.00
Salt & Pepper, Holder, Blown, 5½ x 6¼ In.	46.00
Shaker, Mitre Diamond	75.00
Spooner, Basket Weave	55.00
Spooner, Mule Shoe	48.00
Vase, Bud, Green, Scalloped Edge, 7 x 2¼ In.	45.00
Vase, Bud, Green, Scalloped Edge, 8¼ x 2½ In.	38.00
Vase, Enameled Flowers, 12 In.	850.00
Vase, Fan, Hobnail, 7½ In.	285.00
Vase, Iris, 6½ In.	68.00
Vase, Iris, Satin, 6¼ In.	68.00
Vase, Satin, 13½ x 4½ In.	75.00
Vase, Swung, 3 In.	50.00
Vase, Twisted Optic, Rolled Edge, Handles, Footed, 7⅛ In.	35.00
Votive Holder, 3¼ x 2⅝ In.	8.00
Whimsy, Whiskbroom, Victorian	95.00

VENETIAN GLASS, *see Glass-Venetian category.*

VENINI GLASS, *see Glass-Venetian.*

VERLYS glass was made in Rouen, France, by the Société Holophane Français, a company that started in 1920. It was made in Newark, Ohio, from 1935 to 1951. The art glass is either blown or molded. The American glass is signed with a diamond-point-scratched name, but the French pieces are marked with a molded signature. The designs resemble those used by Lalique.

Bowl, Centerpiece, Birds & Bees, 13 In.	86.00
Bowl, Kingfisher, Satin, c.1950, 13 In.	71.00
Bowl, Orchard, Satin, Signed, 14 In. ....*illus*	193.00
Bowl, Pine Cone, Satin, 3-Footed, 6¼ x 1¾ In.	66.00 to 175.00
Bowl, Wild Duck, Smoke, Signed, 13¼ In.	80.00
Vase, Frosted, Opalescent, Raised Flowers, c.1920, 6½ In.	478.00
Vase, Gems, Opalescent, 6½ In. ....*illus*	71.00
Vase, Pine Cone, Satin, 9¾ x 7 In.	595.00
Vase, Thistle, 9¾ In.	575.00

Vernon Kilns, Desert Bloom,
Sauceboat, Fast Stand
$42.00

The company VERNON KILNS was the name used by Vernon Potteries, Ltd. The company, which started in 1931 in Vernon, California, made dinnerware and figurines until it went out of business in 1958. The molds were bought by Metlox, which continued to make some patterns. Collectors search for the brightly colored dinnerware and the pieces designed by Rockwell Kent, Walt Disney, and Don Blanding. For more information, see *Kovels' Depression Glass & Dinnerware Price List*.

Arcadia, Plate, Dinner, 10½ In.	50.00
Barkwood, Mug	12.00
Beverly, Bowl, Chowder, Lug Handles, 6 In.	17.00
Brown Eyed Susan, Bowl, Vegetable, 9 In.	15.00
Brown Eyed Susan, Teapot	95.00
Casual California, Creamer, Mocha Brown	15.00
Casual California, Creamer	15.00 to 18.00
Casual California, Plate, Serving	13.00
Casual California, Sugar, Cover, Mocha Brown	18.00
Casual California, Sugar, Cover	18.00
Casual California, Tumbler, Mahogany Brown, 5⅜ In.	30.00
Chintz, Bowl, Vegetable, Oval, 9½ In.	29.00
Chintz, Plate, Salad, 7½ In.	5.00
Chintz, Sugar & Creamer	50.00
Commemorative, Plate, Will Rogers, 1935, 10½ In.	37.00
Commorative, Plate, Our West, Maroon, Cream, c.1942, 10½ In.	48.00
Coronado, Bowl, Fruit, 5½ In.	10.00
Coronado, Cup	15.00
Coronado, Plate, Dinner, 10½ In.	10.00 to 25.00
Coronado, Plate, Salad, 7½ In.	10.00 to 15.00
Coronado, Saucer	10.00
Desert Bloom, Bowl, Vegetable, 9 In.	26.00
Desert Bloom, Sauceboat, Fast Stand *illus*	42.00
Desert Bloom, Sugar, Cover	49.00
Dessert Bloom, Creamer	26.00
Dolores, Plate, Dinner, 10½ In.	18.00
Dolores, Salt & Papper, 3 In., Pair	10.00
Early California, Bowl, Salad, 13 In.	55.00
Early California, Chop Plate, 12 In.	35.00
Early California, Creamer	7.50
Early California, Platter, Oval, 12 In.	24.00
Early California, Saltshaker	15.00
Early Days, Sauceboat, Fast Stand	26.00
Early Days, Soup, Dish, Rim, 8½ In.	10.00
Figurine, Bette Davis, Blue Gown, Janice Pettee, c.1940, 10½ In. *illus*	1150.00
Fruitdale, Plate, Salad, 7½ In.	15.00
Gingham, Bowl, Vegetable, 9 In.	25.00
Gingham, Carafe, 10 Cup	50.00
Gingham, Pitcher, Qt. *illus*	40.00
Gingham, Plate, Bread & Butter, 6½ In.	5.00
Gingham, Plate, Dinner, 10½ In.	15.00
Gingham, Plate, Luncheon, 9½ In.	12.00
Gingham, Saucer	3.00
Gingham, Soup, Dish, Handles, Rim, 8½ In.	12.00
Hawaiian, Sugar & Creamer	25.00
Hawaiian Flowers, Cup & Saucer	12.00
Hawaiian Flowers, Sauceboat	20.00
Heavenly Days, Pitcher, Qt.	7.00
Heyday, Cup & Saucer	10.00
Homespun, Bowl, Vegetable, 9 In.	19.00
Homespun, Carafe, Lo Cup	28.00
Homespun, Casserole, Cover, 8 In.	45.00
Homespun, Chop Plate, 13¾ In.	35.00
Homespun, Plate, Luncheon, 8½ In.	7.50
Homespun, Platter, 10½ In.	23.00
May Flower, Cup & Saucer	15.00
May Flower, Plate, Bread & Butter, 6½ In.	15.00
May Flower, Plate, Dinner, 10½ In.	15.00 to 27.00
May Flower, Salt & Pepper	20.00

Vernon Kilns, Figurine,
Bette Davis, Blue Gown, Janice Pettee,
c.1940, 10½ In.
$1150.00

Vernon Kilns, Gingham,
Pitcher, Qt.
$40.00

U
V

TIP
Never put a modern collector plate in a dishwasher or microwave oven. The glaze may be damaged.

Popular Vernon Kilns Patterns

Brown Eyed Susan (1946 to 1958), yellow flowers and a brown border.

Casual California (1947 to 1956), Acacia Yellow, Dawn Pink, Duck Gray, Lime Green, Mahogany Brown, Mocha Brown, Pine Green, Sno-white and Turquoise Blue.

Raffia (c.1950), green brushed with brownish red to give a textured effect.

Plaid patterns include:

Gingham (1949 to 1958), green and yellow plaid with a dark green border.

Homespun (1949 to 1958), green and yellow plaid with a dark green border.

Organdie (1940s and '50s), brown and yellow.

Tam O'Shanter (1949 to 1958), rust, chartreuse, and dark green.

Tweed (1950 to 1955), yellow and gray blue

Vernon Kilns, Organdie, Soup, Dish, 8½ In. $8.00

U V

May Flower, Saucer	8.00
Modern California, Plate, Dinner, 10½ In.	15.00
Montecito, Bowl, Chowder, Lug Handles, 6 In.	13.00
Monterey, Creamer	15.00
Monterey, Saucer	4.00
Native California, Plate, Salad, 7½ In.	15.00
Organdie, Butter	35.00
Organdie, Chop Plate, 12 In.	10.00
Organdie, Chop Plate, 14 In.	12.00
Organdie, Cup, Tea	5.00
Organdie, Cup & Saucer	12.00
Organdie, Mixing Bowl, 9 In.	45.00
Organdie, Plate, Bread & Butter, 6½ In.	8.00
Organdie, Plate, Dinner, 10½ In.	7.50
Organdie, Platter, 14 In.	18.00
Organdie, Soup, Dish, 8½ In. ......*illus*	8.00
Organdie, Salt & Pepper	18.00
Raffia, Bowl, Vegetable, Divided, 11¾ In.	30.00
Raffia, Butter, Base Only, ¼ Lb.	10.00
Raffia, Butter, Cover	35.00
Raffia, Creamer	12.00
Raffia, Cup & Saucer	8.00
Raffia, Cup	6.00
Raffia, Plate, Bread & Butter, 6 In.	3.00 to 3.75
Raffia, Plate, Dinner, 10 In.	8.50 to 10.00
Raffia, Plate, Salad, 7½ In.	6.00
Rose-A-Day, Plate, Dinner, 10 In.	6.00
Sherwood, Pitcher, 2 Qt.	38.00
Sierra Madre, Chop Plate, Blue, 12 In.	12.00
Souvenir, Ashtray, Tombstone, Arizona, Maroon, Ivory, 5½ In.	6.00
Souvenir, Plate, Arkansas, Brown, White, 1943, 10½ In.	35.00
Souvenir, Plate, Bedloes Island, N.Y., Statue Of Liberty, N.Y. Skyline On Rim, 10 In.	40.00
Souvenir, Plate, Carlsbad Caverns, New Mexico, 10½ In.	15.00
Souvenir, Plate, Colorado, 10½ In.	22.00
Souvenir, Plate, Colorado Springs, Colorado, Maroon, White, 10½ In.	15.00
Souvenir, Plate, Massachusetts, 10½ In.	12.00
Souvenir, Plate, New Orleans, 1930s, 10½ In.	33.00
Souvenir, Plate, Santa Fe, New Mexico, Maroon, 10½ In.	35.00
Souvenir, Plate, Statue Of Liberty, Blue, Cream, 10½ In.	33.00
Souvenir, Plate, Wyoming, Map, Maroon, Cream, 10½ In.	45.00
Tam O'Shanter, Bowl, Vegetable, 9 In.	22.00
Tam O'Shanter, Carafe, Cover, 10 Cup	60.00
Tam O'Shanter, Cup & Saucer	9.00
Tam O'Shanter, Plate, Bread & Butter, 6½ In.	4.00
Tam O'Shanter, Shaker, Pepper	7.50
Tam O'Shanter, Teapot	75.00
Tickled Pink, Gravy Boat	20.00 to 22.00
Tweed, Bowl, Vegetable, 9 In.	24.00
Tweed, Chop Plate, 12 In.	28.00
Tweed, Plate, Bread & Butter, 6½ In.	4.00
Tweed, Saucer	8.00
Tweed, Sugar	15.00
Woodleaf, Gravy Boat	30.00
Woodleaf, Plate, Dinner, 10 In.	7.50 to 8.00
Woodleaf, Saucer	2.00
Woodleaf, Tumbler, 4½ In.	9.00

VERRE DE SOIE glass was first made by Frederick Carder at the Steuben Glass Works from about 1905 to 1930. It is an iridescent glass of soft white or very, very pale green. The name means "glass of silk," and it does resemble silk. Other factories have made verre de soie, and some of the English examples were made of different colors. Verre de soie is an art glass and is not related to the iridescent, pressed, white carnival glass mistakenly called by its name. Related pieces may be found in the Steuben category.

Bowl, Centerpiece, Spreading Rim, Celeste Blue Lip Wrap, Footed, 14 In.	232.00
Compote, c.1910, 3¼ x 8 In.	105.00
Perfume Bottle, Cone Shape, Raspberry Colored Stopper, 3¾ In.	259.00

Perfume Bottle, Green Threading, Flattened Stopper, Oval, Steuben, 3½ In.	368.00
Perfume Bottle, Green Threading, Round Dabber, 3¾ In.	713.00
Perfume Bottle, Melon Ribbed, Flame Stopper, Steuben, 7 x 3½ In.	650.00
Perfume Bottle, Melon Ribbed, Green Teardrop Stopper, Signed, Steuben, 4½ In.	288.00
Perfume Bottle, Onion Shape, Melon Ribbed, Celeste Blue Stopper, Steuben, 4½ In.	230.00
Perfume Bottle, Onion Shape, Melon Ribbed, Rose DuBarry Stopper, Steuben, 4½ In.	345.00
Perfume Bottle, Ribbed, Rose DuBarry Over Calcite Flame Stopper, 5 In.	115.00
Sherbet, Underplate, Steuben, 3¼ & 6 In.	295.00
Sugar & Creamer, Cut Swags & Drops, Steuben, 4 In.	748.00
Torchere, Gold Aurene Shade, Flared, Embossed Pierced Metal Stand, Footed, 8¼ In., Pair	690.00
Tumbler, Etched, Letter D, Steuben, 4 In.	125.00
Vase, Applied Green Rigaree, 3¾ In.	110.00
Vase, Celeste Blue Rim, Shouldered, Steuben, 12 In.	288.00
Vase, Ribs, Iridescent Green Branch, Applied Purple Plums, Ribbed, 10⅝ In.	104.00
Vase, Gold Ruby Threading, Tapered, Optic Ribbed, Ruffled Edge, 4 In.	144.00

VIENNA, *see Beehive category.*

VIENNA ART plates are round metal serving trays produced at the turn of the century. The designs, copied from Royal Vienna porcelain plates, usually featured a portrait of a woman encircled by a wide, ornate border. Many were used as advertising or promotional items and were produced in Coshocton, Ohio, by J. F. Meeks Tuscarora Advertising Co. and H.D. Beach's Standard Advertising Co.

Plate, Goddess Artemis Amusing Cupids In Forest, Art Nouveau, c.1900, 10 In.	49.00
Plate, Goddess In Garden Surrounded By Birds, Art Nouveau, c.1900, 10 In.	39.00
Plate, Poesie, Milwaukee, Wisconsin, Advertisement	38.00
Plate, Portrait Of Woman In Center, Susanne M.	75.00
Plate, Woman With Vase, Season Greetings, Empire Bottling Co., Denver, 1909, 10 In.	152.00

VILLEROY & BOCH Pottery of Mettlach was founded in 1836. The firm made many types of wares, including the famous Mettlach steins. Collectors can be confused because although Villeroy & Boch made most of its pieces in the city of Mettlach, Germany, they also had factories in other locations. The dating code impressed on the bottom of most pieces makes it possible to determine the age of the piece. Additional items, including steins and earthenware pieces marked with the famous castle mark or the word *Mettlach,* may be found in the Mettlach category.

Bowl, Monkey Holding Bowl, Marked, Villeroy & Boch Merzig, 5 x 8 In.	194.00
Box, Candy, Lid, Courting Scene, Transfer	75.00
Coffeepot, Lid, Scene	100.00
Dish, Cover, 3-Sided, Marked, Saar-Basin, 1½ x 6 In.	125.00
Dish, Cover, Flowers, Oval, Handles, 6 In.	68.00
Paperweight, Dwarf Pushing On Wax Seal, 5 x 5 In.	342.00
Plaque, Cavalier, Hand Painted, Relief, Dresden, No. 1501, 13 In.	368.00
Plate, Dinner, Amapola, Poppies, 10½ In.	60.00
Plate, Dinner, Basket Of Fruit, Green Rope, Basket Weave Border, 10½ In.	25.00
Plate, Dinner, Parkland, Seedling, Leaf, Blossom, Wide Rim	36.00
Plate, French Country, Plums, Yellow Border, Rust, Golden Band, 10½ In.	25.00
Plate, Leaf, Majolica, 7¾ In.	175.00
Plate, Russian Fairy Tales, 8⅝ In., 8 Piece	234.00
Plate, Salad, Jardin D'Alsace Fleur, Flowers, Blue, Yellow, Pink Band, 8½ In.	36.00
Punch Bowl, Oriental Transfer, Houses, Trees, Blue & White, Footed, 10 x 19 In.	55.00
Soup, Dish, Arco Weiss, Large Rim, 9⅜ In.	46.00
Soup, Dish, French Country, Flowering Lemon, Green Leaves, Large Rim, Marked	40.00
Vase, Courting Couple, Applied Decoration, Flared, Footed, 6½ In. ....*illus*	94.00
Vase, Lions, Tan, Blue, Brown, Luxembourg Matte Glaze, Bulbous, 9 In.	1840.00
Vase, Jugendstil Style, Mushrooms, 4 Buttress Feet, Marked, 21 In. ....*illus*	1170.00
Wash Set, Bosna Pattern, Bowl, Pitcher, Soap Dish, Early 20th Century, 3 Piece	117.00

VOLKSTEDT was a soft-paste porcelain factory started in 1760 by Georg Heinrich Macheleid at Volkstedt, Thuringia. Volkstedt-Rudolstadt was a porcelain factory started at Volkstedt-Rudolstadt by Beyer and Bock in 1890. Most pieces seen in shops today are from the later factory.

VOLKMAR Corona N.Y

Box, Cover, Footed, Cloud Scene, c.1920, 2½ In.	225.00
Box, Hinged, Flowers, Gilt, 2½ x 2 In.	175.00
Figurine, Anthony & Cleopatra, Early 20th Century, 13 x 12 In.	2500.00

Villeroy & Boch
Villeroy & Boch began to make ceramics in contemporary shapes, designs, and colors in the 1960s. Important designers included Paloma Picasso and Keith Haring. In the 1980s, the company made tiles and sanitary wares, tableware and crystal.

Villeroy & Boch, Vase, Courting Couple, Applied Decoration, Flared, Footed, 6½ In. $94.00

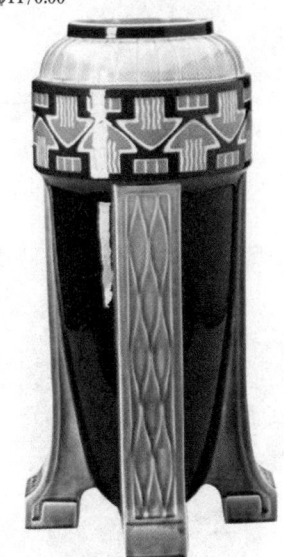

Villeroy & Boch, Vase, Jugendstil Style, Mushrooms, 4 Buttress Feet, Marked, 21 In. $1170.00

U
V

Wade, Figurine, Dog,
Norwich Terrier, 2½ In.
$20.00

Wall Pocket, Cornucopia Shape,
Wallpaper Covered, Brown Ground,
Flower, Leaves, 9 In.
$646.00

Wall Pocket, Peacock,
Flowers, Luster Ware,
Japan, 8 In.
$55.00

Figurine, Bird Loving Maiden, Art Deco, 10 x 10 In.	850.00
Figurine, Cherubs, Flowers, c.1915, 6⅝ x 5 In.	695.00
Figurine, Man, Fancy Dress, Lace Jabot, Muller Co., 4½ In.	195.00
Figurine, Pheasant Birds, Painted, 19th Century, 6⅛ In., Pair	600.00
Group, Man With Harp, Woman With Flowing Hair, c.1800	600.00
Jar, Potpourri, Raised Rocailles, Painted Flowers	649.00

WADE pottery is made by the Wade Group of Potteries started in 1810 near Burslem, England. Several potteries merged to become George Wade & Son, Ltd. early in the twentieth century, and other potteries have been added through the years. The best known Wade pieces are the small figurines given away with Red Rose Tea and other promotional items. The Disney figures are listed in this book in the Disneyana category.

WADE figures c.1936+

Cookie Jar, Tetley Tea Truck, England, 1980s, 5½ In.	196.00
Dish, Bramble, Raised Purple Berries, Green Leaves, 5⅛ In.	19.00
Figurine, 3 Bears, Red Rose Tea Premium, No. 217, 1⅜ In.	20.00
Figurine, African Elephant, World Of Survival Series, 1978, 6 x 10 In.	140.00
Figurine, American Brown Bear, World Of Survival Series, 1980, 4 x 5½ In.	243.00
Figurine, Bambi, Blow Up, Walt Disney Series, 1960s, 4½ In.	116.00
Figurine, Chimpanzee, Beige Face, Gray Body, 1½ In.	25.00
Figurine, Circus, Set, 15 Piece	50.00
Figurine, Dog, Norwich Terrier, 2½ In. .... *illus*	20.00
Figurine, Mary Had A Little Lamb, 3 In.	38.00
Figurine, Shire Horse, Whimsey, Farm Yard Set, White	148.00
Figurine, Si & Am, Blow Up, Walt Disney Series, 1960s, 5¾ In., Pair	221.00
Figurine, Swan, Whimsey, Farm Yard Set	137.00
Figurine, Thumper, Blow Up, Walt Disney Series, 1960s, 5 In.	253.00
Figurine, Trusty, Blow Up, Walt Disney Series, 1960s, 5¼ x 3 In.	148.00
Figurine, Widda Cafferty, Bill Harper, Ireland, 6 In.	190.00
Napkin Ring, Sweetpea, 2¾ x 2¼ In.	15.00
Pin Tray, Angel Fish, Aqua, Pair	19.00
Plaque, Mallard Drake, In Flight, Peter Scott, 9½ In.	52.00
Salt & Pepper, Pots, Marked, Irish Porcelain, c.1950, 2½ In.	35.00

WAHPETON POTTERY, *see Rosemeade category.*

WALL POCKETS were popular in the 1930s. They were made by many American and European factories. Glass, pottery, porcelain, majolica, chalkware, and metal wall pockets can be found in many fanciful shapes.

Blue Glass, 8½ In.	17.00
Canary, Yellow, On Curved Flower Petal, 5½ x 4½ In.	28.00
Cloisonne, Bronze, c.1800, 10½ In.	325.00
Cornucopia Shape, Wallpaper Covered, Brown Ground, Flower, Leaves, 9 In. .... *illus*	646.00
Floral Chintz, Mayfair Pattern, Crocus Shape, Lobed Body, Royal Winton, 8½ x 5 In.	850.00
Flowers, Red, Green, Yellow Lustre Ware, Japan, 5½ In.	25.00
Half Flower, Blue, Orange, Gold Design, Black Wash, c.1930-40, 6 x 2 In.	25.00
Mallard Duck, Green Ring Neck, In Flight, Gilt, 4 x 8¼ In.	15.00
Milk Glass, Butterfly Shape, Coralene, 5 In.	295.00
Peacock, Flowers, Luster Ware, Japan, 8 In. .... *illus*	55.00
Pear, Lacey Edge, Plastic, 7 In. Diam.	15.00
Rooster & Roses, Early Provincial, Hand Painted, Japan, 7 In.	115.00
Rose, Leaves, Marked F On Back, 6 x 5 In.	29.00

WALLACE NUTTING *photographs are listed under Print, Nutting. His reproduction furniture is listed under Furniture.*

WALRATH was a potter who worked in New York City; Rochester, New York; and at the Newcomb Pottery in New Orleans, Louisiana. Frederick Walrath died in 1920. Pieces listed here are from his Rochester period.

Walrath Pottery

Bowl, Crouching Nude Center	400.00
Flower Frog, Swan, White, Sitting On Bed Of Greenery, Signed Walrath, 3½ x 4 x 3 In.	245.00

WALT DISNEY, *see Disneyana category.*

WALTER, *see A. Walter category.*

WARWICK china was made in Wheeling, West Virginia, in a pottery working from 1887 to 1951. Many pieces were made with hand painted or decal decorations. The most familiar Warwick has a shaded brown background. The name *Warwick* is part of the mark and sometimes the mysterious word *IOGA* is also included.

Creamer, Restaurant Ware, White Ground, Flowers, Marked 5.00
Creamer, Straight Sides, Off White Ground, Band, Gray, Rust, Wide, Art Deco, Marked 15.00
Mug, American Indian Brave, Long Black Hair, 5 In. 236.00
Mug, American Indian Chief, Side Profile, Feather Headdress, 4¼ In. 226.00
Pitcher, Flowers, Transfer, Gold Trim 75.00

WATCH pockets held the pocket watch that was important in Victorian times because it was not until World War I that the wristwatch was used. All types of watches are collected: silver, gold, or plated. Watches are listed here by company name or by style. Wristwatches are a separate category.

Agassiz, Art Deco, Platinum, Diamond, Open Face, Goldtone Dial, Plain Case, Pocket 1175.00
E. Ingraham, Sentinel, Chrome, Black Enamel, Art Deco Style, 2 In. .... *illus* 25.00
Elgin, Art Deco, Enameled, Chrome Stand, Mid 20th Century, Pocket, 3 In. 59.00
Elgin, Inset Ruby, Raised Decoration, Inscription, 14K Yellow Gold, c.1886 .... 780.00
Elgin, Open Face, Thin, 14K Gold, Multicolor Hunting Case, Size 12 .... 850.00
Elgin, White Enamel Dial, Arabic, 17 Jewel, 14K Tri-Color Gold, Hunting Case, Pocket 940.00
Enamel, Quarter Hour Repeating, Open Face, Goldtone Dial, 18K Gold Case, Pocket 1645.00
Hamilton, Hunting Case, Hinged, Multicolored Gold, Late 1800s 2200.00
Hunting Case, Scenes, Art Nouveau, Black Enamel, Arabic Numerals, c.1900, 2 In. .... *illus* 249.00
Hunting Case, White Enamel Dial, Roman Numerals, Diamond, 18K Gold 529.00
Jacques Roulet, White Enamel Dial, Scalloped, 15 Jewel, 18K Gold, Hunting Case, Pocket .. 1410.00
Longines, Stop, Split Second, 21 Jewel Fast Beat Movement, Stainless Steel Case, c.1951 .... 139.00
Omega, Grand Prix Paris 1906, Golfers, Engraved, Open Face, Square Case, 2 In. ..... *illus* 658.00
Patek Philippe, Enamel, Arabic Numerals, Jeweled Lever, Monogram, 18K Gold, Pocket 3290.00
Pendant, Enamel, Seed Pearl, Open Face, White Enamel Dial, Roman, Arabic Numerals 705.00
R.P. Cramber, Enameled Face, Regiment Of British Infantry, English 489.00
Railroad, Roman Numerals, Extended Stem, Pocket, Signed, Morton, England 649.00
Ravene, Berlin, Open Face, Verge Fusee Quarter-Hour Repeater, 18K Red Gold, 2¼ In. 1500.00
Rolex, President Oyster, Perpetual Day & Date Movement, 18K Yellow Gold, 7¾ In. 7480.00
Rolex, Woman's, Silver & Enameled Case, c.1915, Pocket 375.00
Sheffield, Open Face, Key Wind Movement, 18K Yellow Gold, 1800s, Pocket, 1⅝ In. 649.00
Tiffany & Co., Art Deco, Platinum, Open Face, 19 Jewel, 7 Adjustment, Meylan, Pocket 1763.00
Tiffany & Co., Open Face, Silvertone Dial, Zenith 17 Jewel, 14K Gold, Pocket 323.00
Waltham, 15 Jewel Movement, 14K Yellow Gold Box, Model 1883, c.1887, Pocket 1496.00
Waltham, Howard Gold, Fob Seals, Pocket Knife, Diamond, 1899, Pocket, 1⅜ x 1¾ In. 1200.00

WATCH FOBS were worn on watch chains. They were popular during Victorian times and after. Many styles, especially advertising designs, are still made today.

Bulldog Tobacco, Metal, Celluloid, 1¾ x 1⅝ In. 275.00
Circle, Silver Leaves, Aventurine Center, Swivel End, Grosgrain Ribbon 55.00
Compass, Swivel, 9K Yellow Gold 300.00
Elks Club, Chain, 14 & 1 x 1¼ In. 135.00
Hires Root Beer, Embossed, Metal, 1⅝ x 1½ In. 121.00
Mack Truck, Bulldog, Leather Strap 112.00
Savage Rifles, Savage Arms Co., Utica, N.Y., Indian In Headdress, Bronze, 1½ In. 168.00
Shells, Horse Head, Mother-Of-Pearl, Brass Wire, c.1910 .... 135.00
Shield, Sterling Silver, Molded, 1935-36, England 78.00
Ship Compass, Brass, Swivel End, Grosgrain Ribbon 55.00
Silver, Harley-Davidson Motorcycles, 1920s, 1½ In. 59.00
Tooth, Mother-Of-Pearl, Butterscotch, Goldtone Wire, Prong Set Stones, 1¼ x ½ In. 45.00
Victorian, 18K Yellow Gold, Mine Diamond, Christmas 1898 Presentation 210.00

WATERFORD type glass resembles the famous glass made from 1783 to 1851 in the Waterford Glass Works in Ireland. It is a clear glass that was often decorated by cutting. Modern glass is being made again in Waterford, Ireland, and is marketed under the name Waterford. Waterford merged with Wedgwood in 1986 to form the Waterford Wedgwood Group.

Candlestick, Gemini, 8 In., Pair 122.00
Chess Set, 4-Part Glass Board, Mahogany Base, Storage Compartment, 15 x 15 In. 4406.00
Clock, Grecian 85.00

Watch, E. Ingraham, Sentinel, Chrome, Black Enamel, Art Deco Style, 2 In.
$25.00

Watch, Hunting Case, Scenes, Art Nouveau, Black Enamel, Arabic Numerals, c.1900, 2 In.
$249.00

Watch, Omega, Grand Prix Paris 1906, Golfers, Engraved, Open Face, Square Case, 2 In.
$658.00

W

Finger Bowl, Diamond Band, Star Bottom, 4 x 2¼ In.	32.00
Goblet, Lismore, 4 x 7 In., 4 Piece	146.00
Honey Jar, Cover, 3½ x 2½ In.	125.00
Tumbler, Lismore, 20th Century, 5 In., 12 Piece	289.00
Vase, Overture, 14 In.	288.00

WATT family members bought the Globe pottery of Crooksville, Ohio, in 1922. They made pottery mixing bowls and tableware of the type made by Globe. In 1935 they changed the production and made the pieces with the freehand decorations that are popular with collectors today. Apple, Starflower, Rooster, Tulip, and Autumn Foliage are the best-known patterns. Pansy, also called Rio Rose, was the earliest pattern. Apple, the most popular pattern, can be dated from the leaves. Originally, the apples had three leaves; after 1958 two leaves were used. The plant closed in 1965. For more information, see *Kovels' Depression Glass & Dinnerware Price List*.

Acorn, Crock, Brown Top, Stoneware, 2 Gal.	105.00
Acorn, Crock, Stoneware, 3 Gal.	10.00
Acorn, Crock, Stoneware, 8 Gal.	65.00
Acorn, Jug, Brown Top, Stoneware, 5 Gal.	30.00
Advertising, Keg, 5th Ave Iced Tea, Dark Brown, Lid	65.00
Advertising, Keg, Bernice Iced Tea, Dark Brown, Lid	20.00
Advertising, Keg, Confederate Iced Tea, Lid, Gal.	1000.00
Advertising, Keg, Golden Flow Iced Tea, Light Brown, Lid	35.00
Advertising, Keg, Haserots Iced Tea, Dark Brown, Lid	50.00
Advertising, Keg, Hendersons Iced Tea, Brown, Lid	10.00
Advertising, Keg, Ireland Iced Tea, Light Brown, Lid	60.00
Advertising, Keg, Kennys Iced Tea, Light Brown, Lid	20.00
Advertising, Keg, Ko-We-Ba Iced Tea, Dark Brown, Lid	25.00
Advertising, Keg, Lacas Iced Tea, Dark Brown, Lid	35.00
Advertising, Keg, Maxwell House Iced Tea, Light Brown	50.00
Advertising, Keg, Neffco Iced Tea, Light Brown, Lid	50.00
Advertising, Keg, Old Reliable Iced Tea, Light Brown, Lid	25.00
Advertising, Keg, Stewarts Iced Tea, Light Brown, Script, Lid	70.00
Advertising, Keg, Superior Iced Tea, Lid	30.00
Advertising, Keg, Tetley Iced Tea, Light Brown, Lid	40.00
Apple, Baker, Cover, 2-Leaf, Wire Stand, No. 67, 6½ x 8½ In.	65.00
Apple, Baker, Cover, Ribbed, No. 600, 7¾ In.	55.00
Apple, Baker, Cover, Ribbed, No. 601, 6½ x 8¾ In.	55.00 to 75.00
Apple, Baker, Rectangular, Tab Handles, No. 85, 9 x 5½ In.	1150.00
Apple, Bank, Barrel Shape	25.00
Apple, Bean Cup, No. 75, 2¼ x 3½ In.	105.00 to 325.00
Apple, Bean Pot, 2-Leaf, No. 76, 2½ Qt., 6½ x 5½ In.	50.00
Apple, Bean Pot, 3-Leaf, Cover, 6½ In.	150.00
Apple, Bean Pot, Cover, No. 76, 6½ In.	85.00
Apple, Bean Pot, Cover, No. 502, 4 Qt., 7½ x 6½ In.	1300.00
Apple, Bowl, 2-Leaf, Deep, No. 63, 6½ In.	45.00
Apple, Bowl, 2-Leaf, Deep, No. 64, 7½ In.	45.00
Apple, Bowl, 2-Leaf, Deep, No. 65, 8½ In.	40.00
Apple, Bowl, 2-Leaf, No. 8, 5½ In.	30.00
Apple, Bowl, 2-Leaf, No. 64, 7½ In.	145.00
Apple, Bowl, 3-Leaf, Cover, 9 x 6½ In.	110.00
Apple, Bowl, Cereal, No. 23, 5¾ In.	45.00
Apple, Bowl, Cereal, No. 74, 5½ In.	30.00 to 55.00
Apple, Bowl, Cover Only, No. 67, 8½ In.	15.00
Apple, Bowl, No. 63, 6½ In.	100.00
Apple, Bowl, Salad, No. 24, 11 In.	60.00
Apple, Bowl, Spaghetti, 2-Leaf, No. 39, 13 In.	50.00
Apple, Canister, Cover, 2-Leaf, No. 72, 9 In.	205.00
Apple, Casserole, Cover, 8½ In.	115.00
Apple, Casserole, Cover, No. 73, 6 x 9½ In.	85.00
Apple, Casserole, Cover, Square, No. 84, 8 In.	550.00
Apple, Casserole, Cover, Stick Handle, Individual, No. 18, 5 In.	110.00
Apple, Casserole, Tab Handles, Individual, 5½ In.	95.00
Apple, Chip & Dip, Wire Holder, No. 120 & 96	65.00 to 125.00
Apple, Chop Plate, No. 49, 12 In.	305.00
Apple, Cookie Jar, No. 503, 8 x 6½ In.	145.00

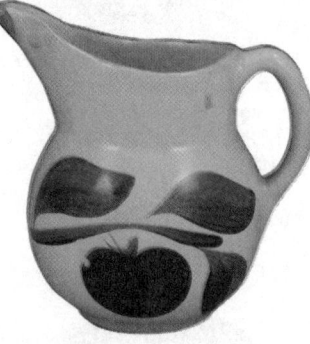

Watt, Apple, Pitcher, 3-Leaf, No. 15, 5¼ In.
$165.00

Watt, Pansy, Berry Bowl, Master, 5½ In.
$5.00

Watt, Rooster, Crock, Cheese, No. 80, 5¾ x 8¾ In.
$800.00

W

Apple, Creamer, No. 62	80.00
Apple, Cruet Set, Oil, Vinegar, Lids, No. 126, 7 In., 2 Piece	950.00
Apple, Grease Jar, No. 47, 4½ In.	225.00
Apple, Ice Bucket, Cover, 2-Leaf, No. 59, 7 x 7½ In.	95.00
Apple, Ice Bucket, Cover, No. 59, 7 x 7½ In.	245.00
Apple, Mixing Bowl, 2-Leaf, No. 5, 5 In.	30.00
Apple, Mixing Bowl, 2-Leaf, No. 6, 6 In.	30.00
Apple, Mixing Bowl, 2-Leaf, No. 7, 7 In.	30.00
Apple, Mixing Bowl, No. 6, 6 In.	85.00
Apple, Mixing Bowl, No. 7, 7 In.	85.00
Apple, Mixing Bowl, Ribbed, No. 7, 7 In.	110.00
Apple, Mixing Bowl, Ribbed, No. 9, 9 In.	40.00
Apple, Mug, Beer Barrel, No. 501, 4½ In.	225.00
Apple, Nappy, Ribbed, 2 x 4¼ In.	85.00
Apple, Pie Plate, Kenyon, Minn., No. 33, 9¼ In.	75.00
Apple, Pitcher, 3-Leaf, No. 15, 5¼ In. ....illus	165.00
Apple, Pitcher, Anderson, S.C., No. 15, 5¼ In.	30.00
Apple, Pitcher, Compliments Of Hjalmer, Marian, Fred & Lavonne Lindberg, No. 15, 5¼ In.	35.00
Apple, Pitcher, Compliments Of River Falls Lumber Co., No. 15, 5¼ In.	65.00
Apple, Pitcher, Diamond Oil Co., Ivanhoe, Minn., No. 15, 5¼ In.	65.00
Apple, Pitcher, No. 17, 8 In.	325.00
Apple, Pitcher, Wilmont, Minn., No. 16, 6½ In.	65.00
Apple, Plate, Dinner, Coons Corner, Oxford, Jct., No. 29, 9½ In.	205.00
Apple, Plate, Dinner, No. 29, 9½ In.	400.00
Apple, Salt & Pepper, Hourglass, No. 117 & 118, 4¾ In.	135.00
Apple, Sugar, Cover, Mr. & Mrs. Myers PC, Junction, Iowa, No. 98	185.00
Apple, Teapot, Cover, No. 112, 6 Cup	1150.00
Autumn Foliage, Bowl, Salad, No. 94, 6 In.	8.00
Double Apple, Creamer, No. 62, 4¼ In.	175.00
Dutch Tulip, Saltshaker, 4 In.	575.00
Eagle, Churn, Stoneware, Bail Handles, 5 Gal.	65.00
Eagle, Crock, Stoneware, 2 Gal.	25.00
Eagle, Crock, Stoneware, 4 Gal.	20.00
Eagle, Crock, Stoneware, 5 Gal.	25.00
Eagle, Jug, Brown Top, Stoneware, 5 Gal.	25.00
Esmond, Bowl, Cereal, Apple, No. 74, 5½ In.	85.00
Esmond, Bowl, Salad, Apple & Pear, No. 73, 9½ In.	105.00
Kitch-N-Queen, Mixing Bowl, Ribbed, Green & White Bands, 6 In.	59.00
Pansy, Berry Bowl, Master, 5½ In. ....illus	5.00
Pansy, Bowl, Cereal, Bullseye, 5½ In.	25.00
Pansy, Casserole, Cover, Individual, 5 In.	30.00
Pansy, Casserole, Handles, Raised, Individual, Marked, 5 x 9 In.	145.00
Pansy, Plate, Luncheon, Bullseye, 8¾ In.	30.00
Pansy, Plate, Salad, Bullseye, 7½ In.	40.00
Rio Rose, see Pansy.	
Rooster, Baker, Cover, No. 66, 7¼ In.	105.00
Rooster, Crock, Cheese, No. 80, 5¾ x 8¾ In. ....illus	800.00
Rooster, Nappy, Cover, Ribbed, Hershey, Pa., No. 05, 5¼ In.	175.00
Rooster, Pitcher, Refrigerator, Square, Ice Lip, No. 69, 8 In.	300.00
Starflower, Baker, No. 68, 5¼ In.	22.00
Swirl, Pitcher, Yellow, No. 15, 5¼ In. ....illus	15.00
Tear Drop, Baker, Cover, Oval, Tab Handles, No. 86, 10 In.	275.00
Tear Drop, Baker, Rectangular, Tab Handles, No. 85, 9 In.	145.00
Tear Drop, Bowl, Cereal, No. 74, 5½ In.	10.00
Tear Drop, Pitcher, No. 15, 5¼ In.	40.00
Tulip, Bowl, Salad, No. 73, 9½ In.	39.00
Tulip, Creamer, No. 62	75.00
Tulip, Mixing Bowl, Deep, No. 64, 7½ In.	175.00
Tulip, Mixing Bowl, Deep, No. 65, 9 In.	190.00
Tulip, Pitcher, No. 15, 5½ In. ....illus	750.00

Watt, Swirl, Pitcher, Yellow, No. 15, 5¼ In. $15.00

Watt, Tulip, Pitcher, No. 15, 5½ In. $750.00

Wave Crest, Biscuit Jar, Scrolls, Molded, Pink, Blue Flowers, Cover, c.1900, 8 In. $353.00

WAVE CREST glass is an opaque white glassware manufactured by the Pairpoint Manufacturing Company of New Bedford, Massachusetts, and some French factories. It was decorated by the C.F. Monroe Company of Meriden, Connecticut. The glass was painted in pastel colors and decorated with flowers. The name Wave Crest was used after 1898.

WAVE CREST WARE

Wave Crest, Dresser Box, Flowers, Shaded Brown, Beaded Top, Mirror, 3½ x 5 In. $826.00

Wave Crest, Photo Receiver, Egg Crate Mold, Yellow Flowers, Green, Brass Rim, 4 x 5½ In. $225.00

Wave Crest, Whiskbroom Holder, Flowers, Light Blue, White, Brass Fittings, Banner Mark, 10 In. 4800.00

W

Biscuit Jar, Helmschmied Swirl, Mauve, White Flowers, Arched Handle, 10 In.	4043.00
Biscuit Jar, Scrolls, Molded, Pink, Blue Flowers, Cover, c.1900, 8 In. *illus*	353.00
Biscuit Jar, Spring Blossoms, White, Blue, Leaves, Antique White, Handle, Cover, 9 In.	230.00
Bonbon, Sunflower, Pink, White, Silver Plate Lid & Bail, 5¼ In.	225.00
Box, Chrysanthemum, Hinged Cover, 5½ x 3 In.	895.00
Box, Collars & Cuffs, Blown-Out Drapery, Flowers, Footed, Marked, 7½ x 8 In.	1485.00
Box, Collars & Cuffs, Blown-Out, Flowers, 4-Sided, 6 x 6½ In.	1760.00
Box, Collars & Cuffs, Blown-Out Flowers, Blue Ground, 6 x 7½ In.	1210.00
Box, Collars & Cuffs, Light Blue Flowers, Honeycomb Pattern, Square, 7½ x 5 In.	880.00
Box, Egg Crate Mold, Flowers, Tapestry, Cream & Green, Hinged Cover, 3½ x 6 In.	375.00
Box, Glove, Scroll Mold, Roses, Yellow, Hinged Cover, Metal Base, 5 x 9½ In.	1200.00
Box, Rococo Mold, Pink Flowers, Light Blue Ground, Scroll Mold, Hinged Cover, 4 In.	150.00
Box, Rococo Mold, Venetian Canal Scene, Hinged Cover, Beaded Collar, 3 x 4 In.	288.00
Carafe, Water, Pink Blossoms, White, 8 In.	350.00
Cigarette Holder, Pink Ground, Metallic Pink Outline, Flowers, Handles, 4 x 4 In.	200.00
Condiment Set, Mushroom Pattern, Sugar, Creamer, Spoon Jar, Swirled Glass, 3 Piece	660.00
Creamer, Ivory, Lavender, Yellow Flowers, Green Leaves, 5 In.	175.00
Dresser Box, 2 Women In Field, Cream Ground, Square, Hinged Cover, 6½ In.	275.00
Dresser Box, Blown-Out Flower Cover, Moss Green, Satin Lining, Marked, 3 x 4 In.	743.00
Dresser Box, Cut Glass, Sterling Silver Rim, Marked, C.F.M., 8 In. Diam.	1210.00
Dresser Box, Egg Crate Mold, Amethyst Medallion, Blue Daisies, 6½ In.	374.00
Dresser Box, Egg Crate Mold, Black, Gold Flecks, Medallion, Metal Feet, 5¼ In.	1265.00
Dresser Box, Egg Crate Mold, Daisies, Blue & Cream Ground, Hinged Cover, 6½ In.	325.00
Dresser Box, Ferns, Red Flowers, Helmschmied Swirl, 5½ In.	173.00
Dresser Box, Flowers, Green Serpentine, Helmschmied Swirl, Hinged Cover, 7 In.	250.00
Dresser Box, Flowers, Recessed Flower Lid, Satin Lining, 3 x 4 In.	580.00
Dresser Box, Flowers, Shaded Brown, Beaded Top, Mirror, 3½ x 5 In. *illus*	826.00
Dresser Box, Spider Web, Forget-Me-Nots, Blue, 3 x 5¼ In.	2880.00
Dresser Box, Yellow, Flowers, Rope Mold, Round, Hinged Cover, Banner Mark, 7 In.	200.00
Dresser Jar, Blues, Brown, Flowers, Ormolu Mounts, Footed, 4 In.	300.00
Ewer, Lavender Flowers, Metal Spout & Base, 15 In.	105.00
Fernery, Egg Crate Mold, Blue Mums, Pink & White, Outline, Metal Insert, 6½ In.	175.00
Fernery, Lake, Scene, Light Blue, Brass Rim, 5½ In.	125.00
Fernery, Light Yellow, 7½ In.	150.00
Fernery, Pink Blossoms, Blue Ground, Pine Tree Mold, 6-Sided, 7 In.	200.00
Fernery, Pink Flowers, Light Blue Ground, Round, 7 In.	175.00
Humidor, Cigar, Flowers, Cigars, Yellow, Blown-Out Seashell Cover, 6 x 4 In.	1416.00
Humidor, Cigar, Opal Ware, Cigar In Gold, Brass Ormolu Rims, 1892, 7 x 5 x 7 In.	800.00
Humidor, Tobacco, Blown-Out Flowers, White, 4-Sided, 4¼ x 5 In.	1320.00
Humidor, Tobacco, Blue Flowers, Light Green, Banner Mark, 5 In.	300.00
Jam Jar, Handle, Flowers, Leaves, White, Spoon, Marked, 7½ x 3½ In.	531.00
Jewelry Box, Bishops Hat Shape, Mill, Light Green, Hinged Cover, 4½ x 5½ In.	200.00
Jewelry Box, Blown-Out Mold, Niagara Falls, White Ground, Hinged Cover, 7 In.	400.00
Jewelry Box, Blue, Flowers, White, Hinged Cover, Metal Finial, Square, 4½ In.	100.00
Jewelry Box, Pansy, Cobalt Blue, Hinged Cover, 4½ In.	700.00
Jewelry Box, Pink Blown-Out Flowers, White, Blue, Round, Hinged Cover, 4 x 5½ In.	275.00
Jewelry Box, Rope Mold, Pink Flowers, White, Green, Hinged Cover, Round, 5 x 7½ In.	350.00
Jewelry Box, Seafoam Mold, Round, Green, Venice Scene, Hinged Cover, 4 In.	200.00
Jewelry Box, Seafoam Mold, Tree & Creek, Yellow & Pink, Hinged Cover, 4 In.	300.00
Jewelry Box, Shell Mold, Pink Rose, Pink & White Ground, Hinged Cover, 4 In.	250.00
Jewelry Box, Spray Of Cornflowers, Roped Border, Hinged Cover, 4 x 6¾ In.	264.00
Jewelry Box, Swirl Mold, Sailboat, Cream Ground, Enamel, Hinged Cover, 5 In.	250.00
Jewelry Box, Venice Scene, Cream, Hinged Cover, 4½ In.	200.00
Jewelry Box, Yellow, Woman Picking Flowers, 4-Sided, Hinged Cover, 4 In.	250.00
Jewelry Box, Zinnia Mold, Pink, Emerald Green, Hinged Cover, 5 In.	200.00
Mustard, Cover, Pink Flowers, Green Leaves, 3½ x 1½ In.	330.00
Photo Receiver, Egg Crate Mold, Fern, Light Pink, Brass Rim, 4 x 5½ In.	150.00
Photo Receiver, Egg Crate Mold, Yellow Flowers, Green, Brass Rim, 4 x 5½ In. *illus*	225.00
Pin Dish, Hanging, Scroll Mold, Blue, Pink Roses, Brass Frame, 4 In.	800.00
Pin Tray, Flowers, Yellow, Brass Rim & Foot, 3¼ In.	50.00
Plate, Cherub, Blossom, Fairy, 8 In.	150.00
Powder Box, Brown, Yellow, Blown-Out Yellow Chrysanthemum Cover, 3 x 5 In.	935.00
Salt & Pepper, Green & White Flowers, 2¾ x 2 In.	220.00
Sugar, Cover, Pink Blossoms, Yellow, Metal Handles, 4¾ In.	230.00
Sugar & Creamer, Cupids, 4½ x 3 & 3½ x 4 In.	165.00
Sugar & Creamer, Ferns, Embossed Metal Fittings, 3 In.	173.00
Sugar Shaker, Fern, Yellow, Silver Plated Top, 6¼ In.	125.00

Syrup, Ferns, White, Yellow, Silver Plated Spout, 5½ In.		150.00
Tray, Helmschmied Swirl, Flower, Oval, 4¼ In.		35.00
Tray, Pink Flowers, Cobalt Blue, Handles, 5½ In.		100.00
Vase, Bud, Blue Flowers, Pink Ground, Handles, 4 In.		275.00
Vase, Pink & White Flowers, Green Leaves, 8 x 3¼ In.		440.00
Vase, Pink Flowers, Green Ground, Footed, Handles, 8 In.		200.00
Vase, Pink Mums, Green Ground, 8 In.		70.00
Vase, Scroll Mold, Pink Thistle, Cream Ground, Gilt Metal, 10¼ In.		275.00
Vase, Stick, Scroll Mold, Pink Flowers, Light Green, 7 In.		200.00
Whiskbroom Holder, Flowers, Light Blue, White, Brass Fittings, Banner Mark, 10 In. . . *illus*		800.00

WEAPONS listed here include instruments of combat other than guns, knives, rifles, or swords. Firearms are not listed in this book. Knives and Swords are listed in their own categories.

Crossbow, Walnut, Bone, Leaves, Lady, Cornucopia, Iron Bow, Trigger, 1600s, 27 In.		1725.00
Dueling Pistols, Derringer, 6-In. Faceted Top Barrels, Walnut Grips, Engraved, c.1830		19975.00
Hand Grenade, Iron, Hollow Ball, Fuse, Revolutionary War, c.1775, 3 In.		602.00

WEATHER VANES were used in seventeenth-century Boston. The direction of the wind was an indication of coming weather, important to the seafaring and farming communities. By the mid-nineteenth century, commercial weather vanes were made of metal. Today's collectors often consider weather vanes to be examples of folk art, even though they may not have been handmade.

2 Owls & Crow, Iron, 31 x 42 In.		358.00
Airplane, Wood, Metal, Painted, 2 Red Props, Blue Wings, Yellow Directionals, 32 In.		1293.00
Banner, Copper, Leafy Quatrefoil, Late 19th Century, 18¼ x 44 In.		1058.00
Banner, Copper, Wood, Weathered Wooden Spire, 23¾ x 34½ In.		2115.00
Bull, Wooden, Flat, Full-Bodied, Arrow, Iron Strap, Metal Stand, 21¾ x 54½ In.		3525.00
Cow, Copper, Iron Face, 16 x 26½ In.		6325.00
Cow, Copper, Molded, Horns, Square Paint Design, Late 19th Century, 17½ x 28 In.		26400.00
Cow, Horns, Arrow, Zinc, Gilt, 50½ x 49½ In.		9600.00
Dog, Copper, Flat, Full-Bodied, 2 Rods, Black Metal Stand, 18 x 27¾ In.		4994.00
Dragon, Cast Zinc, Original Paint, From Cincinnati Zoo, 1875, 31 In.		75000.00
Eagle, Arrow, Directional Support, Gilded Copper, 27 In.		2242.00
Eagle, Copper, 20th Century		359.00
Eagle, Copper, Gilded, Mounted, Wrought Iron Stand, Late 1800s, 49 In.		4425.00
Eagle, Copper, Painted, Mounted On Ball & Arrow, 18½ In.		239.00
Eagle, Copper, Weathered Patina, 24 x 20 In.		460.00
Eagle, Flying, Full-Bodied, Molded Feathers, Talons, Tin, Gold Paint, 25 x 38 In.		5778.00
Eagle, On Ball & Arrow, Ready To Fly, Copper, Gilt, Full Body, Fiske, 24 x 27 In.		3163.00
Eagle, Spread Wings, Mounted On Ball, Arrow, Copper, 22 x 19 In.		518.00
Eagle, Spread Wings, On Half-Ball, Copper, Gold Paint, 18½ x 37 In.		2185.00
Farmer Leading 2 Oxen, Pulling Wagon, Copper, c.1930, 56 x 22 In.		4800.00
Fighting Cock, Bell, Copper, Molded, Zinc Head, Feet, Cushing & White, c.1865, 23 In.		19500.00
Fish, Copper, 24 In.		4183.00
Fish, Copper, Gilt, Molded, Cushing & White, Mass., Late 1700s, 19 x 42 In.		24000.00
Fish, Wood, Incised Gill & Tail, Applied Tin Fins, Metal Tack Eyes, Stand, 47¼ In.		1320.00
Fox, Running, Original Black Paint, 1930s		330.00
Gabriel, Lyre, Wood, Cutout, White & Red Paint, 26¼ In.		4600.00
Gamecock, Copper, Molded, Zinc Legs, Flattened, Full Body, 23 In.		5580.00
Gentleman, Country, Copper, Painted, Embossed, Cutout, 19th Century, 26 In.		588.00
Heart, Scrolled Wire, Curled Accents, Tin, Ball Finial, Baluster Shaft, 57½ In.		935.00
Horse, Cast, Sheet Iron, Rochester Iron Works, N.H., c.1875, 19 x 25 In.		19200.00
Horse, Cast Zinc, Copper, Blue, Gray Verdigris, Swelled Body, 1900, 14 x 19 In.		16800.00
Horse, Cast Zinc, Molded Copper, Wood Base, c.1860, 19½ x 27 In.		52875.00
Horse, Hackney, Copper, Molded, 25 x 24½ In.		9200.00
Horse, Prancing, Copper, Molded, Cast Zinc, J. Howard, Mass., c.1850, 15 x 25 In.		32500.00
Horse, Prancing, Hollow Body, Copper, 44 x 53 In.		40000.00
Horse, Rider, Gentleman, Stovepipe Hat, Copper, Molded, c.1863, 23 x 19 In.		17625.00
Horse, Running, Cast Zinc, Verdigris, Gilding, Swelled Body, 1900, 19 x 40 In.		12000.00
Horse, Running, Copper, 19th Century, 25 In.		1554.00
Horse, Running, Copper, 19th Century		1870.00
Horse, Running, Copper, Black Hawk, Flat, Full Body, Molded, 17¼ x 22¾ In.		4406.00
Horse, Running, Copper, Flat, Full-Bodied, Rod, Black Metal Stand, 16½ x 28½ In.		5581.00
Horse, Running, Copper, Full-Bodied, J. Harris & Son, Boston, 15 x 32 In.		770.00
Horse, Running, Copper, Full-Bodied, 40 In.		3738.00

Weather Vane, Rooster, Standing, Copper, Light Green Patina, Wood Stand, 24 x 18 In. $2040.00

Weather Vane, Stag, Leaping, Copper, Molded, Cast Iron Head, Antlers & Ears, 18 x 27 In. $10175.00

Record-Breaking Prices for Weather Vanes

An October 2006 auction included four Indian-shaped weather vanes from a single collection. The almost-unbelievable record price was $5.8 million, for a molded copper Indian chief weather vane attributed to J. L. Mott Iron works, c.1900. The other Indian weather vanes sold for $72,000, $192,000, and $716,000. The $5.8 million Indian, the highest-priced piece of American folk art ever auctioned, was on top of a previous owner's house for years. Previous 2006 record prices for an auctioned weather vane were $1,080,000 in January, and $1,216,000 in August.

W

Webb, Lamp, Boudoir, Fuchsia, Leaves, White Over Red Over Citron, Camphor Feet, 7½ In. $10925.00

Webb, Plate, Leaves, Flowers, Seed Pods, Aqua Blue Ground, Flower Rim, Cameo, 7¼ In. $6038.00

Webb, Vase, 3 Windows, Ivy, Bricks, White & Gray On Green, Cameo, 6¾ x 4¾ In. $28750.00

Horse, Running, Copper, Gilt, Cast Ears, W.F. Fiske, 30 In.	5175.00
Horse, Running, Copper, Gilt, Directionals, Rhode Island, 44 In.	17250.00
Horse, Running, Copper, Iron Ears, Full-Bodied, Contemporary Stand, 19 x 30½ In.	1320.00
Horse, Running, Copper, Zinc, 20½ x 53 In.	7200.00
Horse, Running, Copper Body, Cast Head, Gold Paint, 19th Century, 15 x 30 In.	805.00
Horse, Running, Half Round, Iron, 21¾ x 31¾ In.	1815.00
Horse, Running, White Paint, Iron, 19 x 29 In.	330.00
Horse, Trotting, Copper, Molded, Zinc Head, Late 19th Century, 25 x 25½ In.	10800.00
Horse, Trotting, Wood, Carved, Painted, Somerville, Maine, 13 In.	1438.00
Horse & Sulky, Copper, 20th Century, 16 x 34 In.	239.00
Horse & Sulky, Driver, Aluminum, 20th Century, 25 x 22 In.	58.00
Horse & Sulky, Driver, Red & Yellow Paint, Tin, 32½ In.	660.00
Horse & Sulky, Old Ocher Paint, L.W. Cushing & Sons, Massachusetts	33500.00
Huntress Diana, On Horse, Killing Tiger, Molded Copper, Mid 1800s, 23 x 30 In.	168000.00
Indian, Drawn Bow, Sheet Iron, 1800s, 37½ x 22½ In.	9500.00
Indian, Holding Bow & Arrow, Copper, 38½ In.	7170.00
Indian, Kneeling, Shooting Arrow, Sheet Iron, Original Paint, c.1880, 36 x 30 In.	19500.00
Liberty, American Flag, Copper, Painted, Cushing & White, c.1865, 22 x 10 In.	464000.00
Lightning Rod, Copper, 5 Twig, Amethyst Stained Glass, 35 x 21 In.	325.00
Lightning Rod, Horse, Diddie, Blitzen Ball, Cast Iron, Copper Rod, c.1800	295.00
Locomotive, Steel, Flat, Open Back Compartment, 13 x 23¼ In.	288.00
Love Bird, Flying, Copper, Green Patina, Iron Spear Point, 33¼ x 36 In.	935.00
Owls, Iron, Silhouettes, Perched On Branch, 18 x 14 In.	374.00
Pattern, Horse, Prancing, Tin, Pierced Eye, 17½ x 22 In.	165.00
Peacock, Copper, Swelled Body, Repousse, c.1930, 20 x 26 In.	8400.00
Pig, Silhouette, Sheet Metal, Wooden Base, 10½ x 16¾ In.	382.00
Pigeon, Standing On Ball, Zinc, Hollow, 24 In.	374.00
Quill, Ball Top, Molded Copper, Gilt, Late 19th Century, 79¼ x 50 In.	8400.00
Quill, Molded, Sheet Copper, Gilt, Late 19th Century, 30 x 49 In.	8400.00
Rooster, Cast Zinc, Copper Legs & Tail, 12¾ x 14½ x 3 In.	9775.00
Rooster, Copper, Black Metal Base, 19th Century, 23 x 29 In.	5100.00
Rooster, Copper, Molded, Full-Bodied, Brass Ball, 26 x 17 In.	1880.00
Rooster, Copper, Molded, Full-Bodied, Embossed Comb, Wattle, Tail, 39 x 33¼ In.	8813.00
Rooster, Copper, Molded, Gilt, Late 19th Century, 26½ x 16 In.	8400.00
Rooster, Copper, Molded, Painted, Late 19th Century, 29⅝ x 25¾ In.	10800.00
Rooster, Cutout Head, Brass Tail	8500.00
Rooster, On Arrow, Copper, Old Gold Paint, 26 x 30 In.	2300.00
Rooster, Serrated Tail, Wings, Comb, Molded Sheet Metal, Wood Stand, 32 In.	1888.00
Rooster, Sheet Copper, Molded, Verdigris, 27½ x 22 In.	657.00
Rooster, Sheet Iron, Wood Base, 19th Century, 29½ x 18 In.	4200.00
Rooster, Silhouette, Sheet Metal, Red Paint, Riveted To Post, 30 In.	374.00
Rooster, Standing, Copper, Light Green Patina, Wood Stand, 24 x 18 In. *illus*	2040.00
Rooster, Wood, Carved, Painted Comb, Lead Wattle, Conn., 14 In.	2013.00
Rooster, Zinc, Full-Bodied, Copper Tail, J. Howard	17000.00
Sailboat, Copper, Hollow Molded, Early 20th Century, 26 x 18½ In.	840.00
Schooner, 3-Masted, 2 Lifeboats, Wood, Metal, Wire, Painted, Late 1800s, 21 x 38 In.	805.00
Scroll Banner, Letter Directional, Scrolled Supports, Rod, Tin, Iron, 62½ In.	330.00
Sea Captain, Peg Leg, Telescope, Sheet Metal, Mounted On Pole, 28 x 17 In.	345.00
Seahorse, Wood, 18½ x 23½ In.	3565.00
Sheep, Copper, Molded, Gilt, Late 19th Century, 14½ x 19 In.	19200.00
Ship, 3-Masted, Wooden, Painted, Tin, Green, White, Early 1900s, 22 x 25 In.	558.00
Ship, Mast, Flag, Copper, Molded, Late 19th Century, 27 x 14 In.	8200.00
Snake, Sheet Iron, Cut, Painted, 19th Century, 45¼ x 56¼ In.	14400.00
Sperm Whale, Copper, Verdigris, Patina, McQuarry, 20th Century, 36 In.	431.00
Stag, Leaping, Cast Zinc, Brass, Full-Bodied, Fiske, Wood Base, 29 x 27 In.	7475.00
Stag, Leaping, Copper, Gilt, Late 19th Century, 32¾ x 28 In.	13200.00
Stag, Leaping, Copper, Molded, Cast Iron Head, Antlers & Ears, 18 x 27 In. *illus*	10175.00
Steer, Copper, Zinc, Gilt, Jonathan Howard, Mass., c.1860, 28 In.	55000.00
Tulip, Sheet Iron, Arrow Head, Baluster Knop, 74 In.	4500.00
Whale, Copper, Wood, Red Paint, Early 19th Century, 11 x 36 In.	31200.00

WEBB glass was made by Thomas Webb & Sons of Ambelcot, England. Many types of art and cameo glass were made by them during the Victorian era. Production ceased by 1991 and the factory was demolished in 1995. Webb Burmese and Webb Peachblow are special colored glasswares of the Victorian era. They are listed at the end of this section. Glassware that is not Burmese or Peachblow is included here.

Webb

Bowl, Clear & Frosted, Spiral Flutes, Rolled Foot, Pinched Waist, Cameo, c.1890, 9½ In. 10781.00
Bride's Basket, Wisteria, Yellow Interior, Ribbed, Ruffled Edge, Apricot, Tarrington, 14 In. .. 1265.00
Celery Vase, Pink Satin, Enameled Beetle, Flowers, 6 In. 275.00
Chalice, Coronation, Engraved, Monogram Of Queen Elizabeth, Intaglio Thistles, 8 In. 106.00
Epergne, Pink Over White, Blue Interior, Enameled Flowers, 17 x 11 In. 2468.00
Finger Bowl, Alexandrite, Oval, Piecrust Rim, 5 In. 1035.00
Lamp, Boudoir, Fuchsia, Leaves, White Over Red Over Citron, Camphor Feet, 7½ In. ... *illus* 10925.00
Lemonade Set, Opaline, Floral, Butterfly, Raised Enamel, Gold, 5 Piece 275.00
Peachblow, Vase, Enameled Butterfly, Gold Berries, 1800s, Pair 2000.00
Peachblow, Vase, Flowered Branches, Enameled, 5½ x 2¾ In. 375.00
Peachblow, Vase, Rose To Rose Pink, White Interior, c.1885, 8 x 6½ In., Pair 1000.00
Peachblow, Vase, Salmon To White Base, Victorian, 8½ In. 400.00
Peachblow, Vase, Shaded Rose Pink, Creamy White, Glossy, c.1885, 8 x 6½ In. 1000.00
Perfume Bottle, Clear, Hallmarked Sterling Silver Lid, Laydown, 11 In. 403.00
Perfume Bottle, Clear, White & Red Spatter, Gold Ferns, Laydown, Embossed Lid, 5 In. 288.00
Perfume Bottle, Flowers, Butterfly, Blue, Teardrop Shape, Cameo, Silver Flip Lid, 4 In. 1333.00
Perfume Bottle, Leaves, White Over Red, Teardrop Shape, Laydown, Metal Lid, 3½ In. 1495.00
Perfume Bottle, Teardrop, Red Body, Gold Flowers, Silver Lid, 6 In. 374.00
Pitcher, Gold Apple Blossoms, Water, Peach Shaded To Teal, Frosted Reeded Handle, 8 In. ... 345.00
Planter, Rose, Butterfly, Briar Decoration, White Over Cranberry, Round, 7¾ x 9 In. 690.00
Plate, Leaves, Flowers, Seed Pods, Aqua Blue Ground, Flower Rim, Cameo, 7¼ In. ..... *illus* 6038.00
Punch Set, Palmate & Star Design, Signed, 13-In. Bowl, 8 Piece 150.00
Scent Bottle, Flowers, Buds, Leaves, Branch, White, Cameo, Sterling Silver Lid, 2¾ In. 1495.00
Vase, 3 Windows, Ivy, Bricks, White & Gray On Green, Cameo, 6¾ x 4¾ In. .... *illus* 28750.00
Vase, Acanthus, Textured Golden Amber, Cameo, Bulbous, Elongated Neck, Stamped, 13 In. . 14000.00
Vase, Alexandrite, Cylindrical, Ruffled Edge, 2½ In. 1093.00
Vase, Allover Stemmed Flowers, Holly Border, Textured Amber, Baluster, Cameo, 3¼ In. 7480.00
Vase, Bird, Branch, Butterfly, Fern, Pink Satin, Gourd Shape, 10 In., Pair 650.00
Vase, Blue, Satin, Ruffled Edge, Gold Highlights, 11¼ In. 595.00
Vase, Branch, Butterfly, Citron, White Over Red, Cameo, Stamped, 5¼ In. 1380.00
Vase, Buds, Butterfly, Blue, Rose, Waisted Neck, Oval, Cameo, c.1890, 7⅞ In. 10781.00
Vase, Butterfly, White, Light Blue Leaves, Azure Ground, Flared, Footed, Cameo, 7½ In. 3738.00
Vase, Cascading Branches, 6 Insects, Ivory, Cameo, Signed, 4¼ In. 345.00
Vase, Cascading Flowering Branch, Butterflies, Frosted Red, Bulbous, Clover Rim, 4 In. 1093.00
Vase, Daffodil, Butterfly, Citron, Pinched Neck, Flared Rim, Cameo, 5½ In. 575.00
Vase, Dahlias, Crimson Ground, Egg Shape, Tapered, Cameo, Signed, 8 In. .... *illus* 3738.00
Vase, Double-Stemmed Branch, Butterfly, Crimson, Bulbous, Cylindrical Neck, 6½ In. 978.00
Vase, Fish, Acid Etched, Cylindrical, 8 In. 71.00
Vase, Flower Blossoms, Enameled, Yellow Satin, 13 In., Pair 250.00
Vase, Flower Blossoms On Branch, Yellow Green Ground, Bulbous Base, Cameo, 5 In. 487.00
Vase, Flower Spray, Insect, Clear Satin, Pink, Opaque White, Oval, Cameo, c.1885, 11 In. 4043.00
Vase, Flower Sprays, Grass, Butterflies, Turquoise, Blue, Slender Neck, Cameo, 9¾ In. 7008.00
Vase, Flowers, Branches, White Over Blue, White Bands, Squat, Flared, Cameo, 3 x 5 In. 1437.00
Vase, Iridescent, 12½ In. 588.00
Vase, Ivory, Gold Serpentine Handles, Gold Stem, Footed, Shouldered, Signed, 6½ In. 920.00
Vase, Lilies & Stems, Waisted, Cameo, Signed, c.1920, 11⅜ In. 881.00
Vase, Morning Glories, Butterflies, Cinnamon, Waisted Neck, Cameo, c.1890, 7¼ In. 2695.00
Vase, Stick, Lovebirds Sitting On Fence, White Interior, Bulbous Base, Signed, 9⅝ In. 345.00
Vase, White & Blue Leaves, Branches & Butterfly, Blue Ground, Cameo, 7½ In. .... *illus* 3738.00

WEBB BURMESE is a colored Victorian glass made by Thomas Webb & Sons of Stourbridge, England, from 1886.

Biscuit Jar, Stemmed Flowers & Buds, Silver Lid, Hinged Handle, 8½ In. 431.00
Condiment Set, Melon Ribbed, Mustard, 4-In. Shaker, 3 Piece .... *illus* 176.00
Cruet, Stopper, c.1885-95 .... 245.00
Epergne, 1 Lily, 2 Fairy Lamps, 2 Posy Vases, Cricklite, c.1887, 10½ In. 2013.00
Epergne, 1 Lily, 3 Posy Vases, Mirrored Base, c.1890, 10 In. 823.00
Fairy Lamp, 3-Light, Prunus Blossoms, Ruffled Base, S. Clarke, Signed, 6 In. 2530.00
Fairy Lamp, Clear Base, S. Clarke, c.1890, 4 In. 147.00
Fairy Lamp, Maple Leaves, Enameled, Clear Base, S. Clarke, c.1890, 4 In. 411.00
Fairy Lamp, Oak Leaves, Enameled, Clear Inserts, Ruffled Base, 6¼ In. .... *illus* 1116.00
Fairy Lamp, Prunus, Enameled, Clear Base, Scalloped Rim, 6½ In. 1380.00
Fairy Lamp, Red Berries, Green Leaves, Enameled, 2 Inserts, Crimped Base, 7 In. 2185.00
Jam Jar, Pine Cones & Branches, Silver Lid, Shaped Handle, 6 In. 489.00
Rose Bowl, Blue, White Flowers, Rust Leaves 450.00

Webb, Vase, Dahlias, Crimson Ground, Egg Shape, Tapered, Cameo, Signed, 8 In.
$3738.00

Webb, Vase, White & Blue Leaves, Branches & Butterfly, Blue Ground, Cameo, 7½ In.
$3738.00

Webb Burmese, Condiment Set, Melon Ribbed, Mustard, 4-In. Shaker, 3 Piece
$176.00

W

Webb Burmese, Fairy Lamp, Oak Leaves, Enameled, Clear Inserts, Ruffled Base, 6¼ In.
$1116.00

Webb Peachblow, Bride's Basket, Silver Plated Holder, Masks, Scrolled Handles, 8½ In.
$125.00

Webb Peachblow, Jar, Cover, Glossy, Cylindrical, Clear Ball Finial, c.1890, 7½ In.
$118.00

TIP

If you have a lightweight vase that tips easily, fill it with sand.

Rose Bowl, c.1885-90	245.00
Vase, Bird, Yellow Flowers, 3 Red Roses, Butterfly, Bulbous, 8 In.	920.00
Vase, Bulbous, Green, Brown, Yellow Prunus Flowers, Square Top, 3 In.	525.00
Vase, Crimped Rim, Pedestal Foot, 6½ In.	275.00
Vase, Posy, Oak Leaves, Berries, Enameled, 3½ In.	403.00
Vase, Stick, Yellow & Orange Flowers, Green Leaves, Bulbous Base, 10½ In.	1150.00

WEBB PEACHBLOW is a colored Victorian glass made by Thomas Webb & Sons of Stourbridge, England, from 1885.

Bride's Basket, Silver Plated Holder, Masks, Scrolled Handles, 8½ In. ...*illus*	125.00
Jar, Cover, Glossy, Cylindrical, Clear Ball Finial, c.1890, 7½ In. ...*illus*	118.00
Perfume Bottle, Raised Gold Ginko Flowers, Silver Lid, Teardrop Shape, Laydown, 4 In.	748.00
Pitcher, Applied Vine Handle, Pontil, 5 x 5 x 2½ In.	395.00
Pitcher, Milk, Applied Vine, Ground Pontil, 5 x 5 In.	395.00
Vase, Amber To Rose, Flowing Flowers, Butterfly, Cupped Rim, Cameo, 9¼ In.	4025.00
Vase, Bulbous Stick, Gold Enameled Mums, 3 Insects, Gold Rim, 13 In.	719.00
Vase, Coralene, 5¼ In.	525.00
Vase, Crimped Rim, White Interior, 5½ In.	125.00
Vase, Enameled, Butterfly, 8½ In.	400.00
Vase, Enameled, c.1910, 3¾ x 2½ In.	250.00
Vase, Gold Fleur-De-Lis, 8 In.	500.00
Vase, Stick, Gold, Enameled Flowers, c.1880, 8⅞ In.	425.00
Vase, Stick, Gold, Enameled Insect, Flowers & Branches, Bulbous Base, 15 In.	2350.00
Vase, Thistle, Gold Enameled, 10½ In.	300.00

WEDGWOOD, one of the world's most successful potteries, was founded by Josiah Wedgwood, who was considered a cripple by his brother and was forbidden to work at the family business. The pottery was established in England in 1759. A large variety of wares has been made, including the well-known jasperware, basalt, creamware, and even a limited amount of porcelain. There are two kinds of jasperware. One is made from two colors of clay, the other is made from one color of clay with a color dip to create the contrast in design. The firm is still in business. Other Wedgwood pieces may be listed under Flow Blue, Majolica, Tea Leaf Ironstone, or in other porcelain categories. In 1986 Wedgwood and Waterford Crystal merged to form the Waterford Wedgwood Group.

WEDGWOOD

Basin, Pearlware, Blue Transfer, Corinth Pattern, Floral Border, 1800s, 17½ In.	411.00
Basket, Creamware, Orange, Footed, Scalloped Edge, Top Handle, c.1900, 11½ In.	299.00
Basket, Jasperware, Gray, White, 5½ x 3½ In.	40.00
Beaker, Presentation, Black Basalt, c.1929, 3½ & 4⅛ In., 2 Piece	382.00
Biscuit Jar, Cover, Jasper Dip, Dark Blue, Classical Figures, Finial, 5 x 8¼ In.	288.00
Biscuit Jar, Cover, Jasper Dip, Dark Blue, Classical Figures, Globe Shape, 5½ In.	328.00
Bonbon, Jasperware, White, Lilac, 1960, 2¾ x 2 In.	49.00
Bottle, Jasper Dip, Green, Classical Figures, Grapevine Band, Silver Rim, 7¼ In.	881.00
Bottle, Scent, Jasperware, Oval, Blue, Ram & Cart, Sphinx, 4 In.	460.00
Bowl, Black Basalt, Drapery Swags, High Relief, Acanthus, Footed, 1800s, 17¼ In.	5288.00
Bowl, Bone China, Blue Ground, Mice, White Inside, c.1915, 5 In.	823.00
Bowl, Butterfly Luster, Footed, Daisy Makeig-Jones, 1920s, 8½ In.	226.00
Bowl, Butterfly Luster, Scalloped Rim, Orange, Chinese Ornaments, Mottled, 7 In.	470.00
Bowl, Cover, Annular Ware, Green Matte Glaze, Keith Murray, c.1935, 11⅜ In.	194.00
Bowl, Cover, Queen's Ware, Orange, Scrolled Bands, Flowers, Mark, c.1879, 11¾ In.	1763.00
Bowl, Fairyland Luster, Dancing Fairies In Garden, Green, Blue, Purple, Gilt, 13 In.	5405.00
Bowl, Fairyland Luster, Daventry, Dana Band, Copper Ground, c.1925, 10 In.	17625.00
Bowl, Fairyland Luster, Dragons, 8 Panels, Jade, Cobalt Blue, 4¾ In.	294.00
Bowl, Fairyland Luster, Dragons, Pagodas, 8 Panels, Jade, Emerald Green, 7 In.	705.00
Bowl, Fairyland Luster, Lahore, Melba Center, Elephants, Camels, Footed, 5½ x 8 In.	8050.00
Bowl, Fairyland Luster, Melba Center, Garden Of Paradise Exterior, c.1920, 8⅛ In.	441.00
Bowl, Fairyland Luster, Octagonal, Dana, Castle On Road, Fairy In Cage, 5 x 9 In. ...*illus*	5975.00
Bowl, Fairyland Luster, Octagonal, Woodland Elves VI, Fiddler, Ship, Mermaid, 8 In.	5175.00
Bowl, Fruit, Bone China, c.1822, 11¾ In.	437.00
Bowl, Jasper Dip, Yellow, Footed, Black Classical Relief, Oak Leaf Border, 6½ In.	1175.00
Bowl, Jasperware, Green, Classical Design, 1979, 2½ x 5 In.	108.00
Bowl, Salad, Majolica, Argenta Ware, Vegetable, Panels, Spoon, Forks, c.1878, 10 In.	294.00
Bowl, Salad, Majolica, Seafood, Lobsters, Garnishes, Lobed Sides, Painted, 10¾ In.	1058.00
Bulb Stand, Black Basalt, 2 Tiers, 3 Wells, Cupids Holding Festoon, c.1800, 7 In.	3819.00
Bust, Abraham Lincoln, Parian, 19 x 11 In.	2800.00
Bust, Aristotle, Black Basalt, Round Pedestal, Impressed Tile, Mark, 1800s, 12 In.	1175.00
Bust, George II, Black Basalt, Laurel Wreath, Armor, Medallion, c.1775, 9½ In.	4042.00

Bust, Horace, Black Basalt, Waisted Round Pedestal, Impressed Mark, 14¾ In.	....	1880.00
Bust, Lord Palmerston, Black Basalt, Round Pedestal, Tile, Mark, c.1865, 10 In.	....	705.00
Bust, Marcus Aurelius, Black Basalt, Round Pedestal, Tile, Mark, c.1775, 15 In.	....	4406.00
Bust, Roman Soldier, Black Basalt, Turned Pedestal, Marked England, 19 x 11 In.	....	2350.00
Bust, Seneca, Black Basalt, Round Pedestal, Impressed Tile, Mark, c.1877, 10⅛ In.	....	823.00
Bust, Socrates, Black Basalt, Round Pedestal, Iron Red Enamel, Mark, 19¾ In.	....	4406.00
Bust, William Shakespeare, Black Basalt, 10 In.	....	168.00
Butter, Cover, Luster, Gaudy Willow Pattern, Colorful, Child's, 5 x 2½ In.	...........*illus*	230.00
Candlestick, Earthenware, Ivory Glaze, Columnar Shape, Green Trim, c.1861, 9 In.	......	323.00
Charger, Pearlware, Painted, Blue Leaf, J.B. Evans, c.1880, 15¼ In.	....	176.00
Charger, Queen's Ware, Leaf Border, Persian Pattern, 16 In.	....	1880.00
Charger, Queen's Ware, Painted, Yellow Rim, Foliage, Angels, Medallion, c.1863, 12 In.	.....	176.00
Creamer, Jasperware, Light Blue, Greek Mythology, 2⅝ In.	....	95.00
Cup, Fairyland Luster, Melba, Elves On Branch, Flowers, Footed, Marked, 3 x 4½ In.	....	2300.00
Cup, Saucer, Black Ground, Silver Luster, Alfred Powell, Deer, c.1935, 4¼ In., Pair	....	118.00
Dessert Service, Majolica, Strawberry, c.1880, 9 Piece	....	272.00
Dessert Service, Proverbs, Late 19th Century, 9½ In., 11 Piece	....	619.00
Dish, Creamware, Painted, Shaped, c.1770, 26½ In.	....	1145.00
Dish, Jasperware, Light Blue, Sir Winston Churchill, 3¼ In.	....	45.00
Dish, Queen's Ware, Pink Luster, Red Enamel, Geometric Border, 18 In.	....	1175.00
Dish, Queen's Ware, Scalloped Oval Shape, Etruria School, Emile Lessore, 12 In.	....	881.00
Dish, Redware, Glazed, Black Transfer, Enameled, Fretwork Border, 11⅝ In.	....	206.00
Dish, Serving, Caneware, 2 Loop Handles, Raised Foot, c.1830, 12¼ In.	....	881.00
Ewer, Black Basalt, Satyr, Bacchus, Neptune, Fluted Stem, Square Base, 15½ & 15¾ In., Pair .. *illus*		8400.00
Ewer, Wine, Cobalt Blue Glaze, Gilt Trim, Satyr, On Ram's Head, c.1860, 16½ In.	......	1528.00
Figurine, Bulldog, Black Basalt, Glass Eyes, c.1915, 4⅞ In.	....	558.00
Figurine, Fawn, Bacchantes, Queen's Ware, Round Plinth, Late 1800s, 17¾ In., Pair	....	881.00
Figurine, Finding Moses, Parian, Signed, 18½ x 15½ In.	....	1762.00
Figurine, Flicker, Bone China, Bird, Branch, H.W. Palliser, A.D. Holland, c.1940, 9½ In.	....	353.00
Figurine, Kingfisher, Black Basalt, Pierced, Reed Molded Mound, 1900s, 7⅜ In.	....	999.00
Figurine, Psyche, Seated On Rock, Holding Bow, Queen's Ware, 1800s, 8½ In.	....	176.00
Figurine, Raven, Black Basalt, Glass Eyes, c.1915, 4¼ In.	....	323.00
Figurine, Summer, Lady, Wreath, Grain, Black Basalt, Round Base, Late 1800s, 10 In.	......	499.00
Figurine, Venus, Atop A Wave, Rocky Base, Black Basalt, Tile, Mark, c.1900, 12¾ In.	......	1293.00
Figurine, Winter, Lady, Cloak, Berries, Black Basalt, Round Base, Mark, c.1900, 9½ In.	.....	1528.00
Game Set, Turkeys, Flow Blue, Platter, 12 Plates, 18 x 13 In., 10-In. Plates	....	2357.00
Inkstand, Moonlight Luster, 3 Dolphin Feet, Insert Pot, c.1810, 4½ In.	....	1645.00
Jar, Biscuit, Cover, Jasperware, Green, Scrolled Handles, Dancing Hours, 7½ In.	....	558.00
Jar, Canopic, Cover, Caneware, Applied Hieroglyphs, Zodiac Symbols, 1800s, 10 In.	....	1528.00
Jar, Potpourri, Cover, Earthenware, Ivory Glaze, Globular, Loop Handles, 1885, 9 In.	....	382.00
Jardiniere, Jasper Dip, Blue, White, Garlands, Late 19th Century, 8 In.	....	304.00
Jardiniere, Jasper Dip, Green, Medallions, Franklin, Washington, Lafayette, 6½ In.	....	382.00
Jardiniere, Majolica, Argenta Ware, Paneled Sides, Branches, c.1862, 14⅝ In.	....	235.00
Jelly Mold Cone, Pearlware, Wedge Shape, Multicolored Enamel, Flowers, 5 In.	....	2468.00
Jug, Cover, Jasper Dip, Olive Green, Washington, Franklin, Oval Frames, 8⅜ In.	....	294.00
Jug, Earthenware, Barrel Shape, Black Ground, Stag, c.1925, 5½ In.	....	264.00
Jug, Jasper Dip, Crimson, Barrel Shape, Classical Figures, Leaf Frame, Border, 4⅜ In.	......	1175.00
Jug, Jasper Dip, Crimson, Twisted Handle, Classical Figure, c.1920, 3¾ In.	....	353.00
Jug, Pearlware, Water, Globular, Brown Trim, Transfer, Support Handle, 12¼ In.	....	235.00
Jug, Poet, Blue Transfer, Mottos From Chaucer, Doric Shape, Male Mask, 1878, 12 In.	......	176.00
Jug, Queen's Ware, Harvest, Silver Luster, Black Transfer, 1959, 8 In.	....	823.00
Jug, Rosso Antico, Egyptian, Black, White, Iron Red, Encaustic, c.1880, 8 In.	....	823.00
Jug, Rosso Antico, Rope Twist Handle, Gold Chinoiserie Pagoda, 7½ In.	....	470.00
Medallion, Black Basalt, Portrait, Shakespeare, Agrippa, Domitian, 2¾ In., 4 Piece	....	558.00
Medallion, Jasper Dip, Blue, White Relief, Frame, c.1780, 2⅝ x 3¼ In.	....	705.00
Medallion, Jasper Dip, Blue, White Relief, Mourning Maiden, c.1780, 2½ x 3¼ In.	....	764.00
Medallion, Jasperware, White, Portrait, Oval, Queen Charlotte, 3 x 4¼ In.	....	588.00
Medallion, Portrait, Trial, Dr. Johnson, Inscribed, Late 18th Century, 3½ In.	....	676.00
Mold, Vase, Queen's Ware, Handles, Oval, Scalloped Rim, Mark, Late 1700s, 11¼ In.	....	1058.00
Mug, Jasper Dip, Yellow, 3 Handles, White Classical Relief, Leaf Frames, 5 In.	....	1116.00
Napkin Ring, Jasperware, Blue & White, 1¼ x 5 In.	....	35.00
Pie Dish, Cover, Caneware, Oval, Fruiting Grapevines, Relief, Pastry Design, 8 In.	....	323.00
Pitcher, Doris Pattern, Blue Transfer, Scrolls, Flowers, Gilt, 14½ In.	....	115.00
Pitcher, Jasperware, Blue, 6¼ In., Pair	....	234.00
Pitcher, Jasperware, Blue, White Classical Scene, 9 In.	....	146.00
Plaque, Black Basalt, Relief, Biblical Scene, Self-Framed, 19th Century, 5¾ x 9 In.	....	1410.00

Wedgwood, Bowl, Fairyland Luster, Octagonal, Dana, Castle On Road, Fairy In Cage, 5 x 9 In.
$5975.00

Wedgwood, Butter, Cover, Luster, Gaudy Willow Pattern, Colorful, Child's, 5 x 2½ In.
$230.00

Wedgwood, Ewer, Black Basalt, Satyr, Bacchus, Neptune, Fluted Stem, Square Base, 15½ & 15¾ In., Pair
$8400.00

Wedgwood, Punch Bowl, Fairyland Luster, Poplar Trees, Woodland Bridge Interior, 5 x 10 In.
$14375.00

W

Wedgwood, Teapot, Basalt, Classical Figures, Animals, Reeded Lower Border, 4⅝ x 9 In. $403.00

Weller, Blossom, Vase, Blue Matte Glaze, Cornucopia Shape, Scrolled Foot, c.1935, 8 In. $54.00

Weller, Dickens Ware, Vase, Indian, Headdress, Yellow Shaded To Brown Ground, 11½ In. $785.00

Plaque, Blue, White Relief, Endymion On Rock Latmos, 10 x 13 In.	1293.00
Plaque, Earthenware, Mistress Ford, Round, Raised Gilt Leaves, c.1881, 15 In.	353.00
Plaque, Impasto, Sailing Ship, Monogram, c.1888, 8 x 12 In.	999.00
Plaque, Jasper Dip, Black, Oval, White Relief Female, Cymbals, Early 1800s, 12⅝ In.	1410.00
Plaque, Jasper Dip, Black, Oval, White Relief Hercules, 1800s, 7¼ In.	1293.00
Plaque, Jasper Dip, Green, White Relief, Psyche Bound, Shot By Cupid, 5½ x 12 In.	646.00
Plaque, Majolica, Green Glaze, Relief Nereids, c.1870, 7¾ x 14½ In.	588.00
Plaque, Majolica, Green Glaze, Relief Nereids, Frame, c.1870, 7¾ x 10½ In.	382.00
Plaque, Queen's Ware, Enameled, Diana At Bath, Emile Lessore, c.1870, 12 x 16 In.	3819.00
Plate, Christmas, 1970, Jasperware, Blue, Trafalgar Square	38.00
Plate, Christmas, 1982, Jasper, Blue, Box	42.00
Plate, Christmas, Jasperware, Winchester Cathedral, 7¼ In.	65.00
Plate, Jasperware, Light Blue, 1960	50.00
Plate, Jasperware, Sacrifice To Cupid, 9½ In.	68.00
Plate, Pheasant Transfer, Marked, England, 8⅞ In., 12 Piece	143.00
Plate, Queens Ware, Hound Portrait, Brown Transfer, Impressed Mark, c.1878, 12 In.	176.00
Plate, Soup, Darwin Service, Water Lily Pattern, c.1810, 9¾ In.	354.00
Plate, Water Lily, Blue & White Transfer, Pearlware, c.1820	350.00
Plate Set, Harvard, Scenic, Blue & White, c.1927, 10¼ In., 18 Piece	1416.00
Plate Set, Majolica, Cabbage Leaf, Green, Raised Rim, 1950s, 8 In., 7 Piece	278.00
Plate Set, Porcelain, Wide Blue & White Floral Band, 11 In., 12 Piece	205.00
Platter, Queen's Ware, Red Transfer, Exotic Birds, c.1810, 15 In.	1890.00
Platter, Transferware, Nankin, Deep Blue, Flowers, c.1880, 16½ x 13¾ In.	200.00
Plinth, Jasperware, Blue, Square, Paneled, Applied White Figures, Festoons, 6 In.	1998.00
Pot, Malfrey, Cover, Lahore, Pattern Z5266, c.1925, 8⅜ In.	6443.00
Potpourri Vase, Jasperware, Tricolor, Fixed Pedestal, c.1810, 6⅝ In.	780.00
Powder Box, Carousel Cover, Grape, Leaf Border, Spiked Nob, 4⅞ x 2⅛ In.	50.00
Punch Bowl, Fairyland Luster, Poplar Trees, Woodland Bridge Interior, 5 x 10 In. ...*illus*	14375.00
Salt & Pepper, Flow Blue, Chusan	1210.00
Salt & Pepper, Jasperware, Blue, White, 3⅞ x 2⅛ In.	65.00
Tankard, Jasperware, Blue, Huntsmen, Dogs, Hound, Horse, 4 x 3¼ In.	38.00
Tea Set, Jasperware, Lilac, 19th Century, 4 Piece	70.00
Teapot, Basalt, Classical Figures, Animals, Reeded Lower Border, 4⅝ x 9 In. ...*illus*	403.00
Teapot, Caneware, Basket Weave, Wheat Sheaf Finial, c.1817, 6¼ x 4½ In.	295.00
Teapot, Cover, Creamware, Oval, Red, Astrologer, Fortune Teller, c.1770, 5½ In.	1800.00
Teapot, Cover, Jasper Dip, Crimson, Classical Relief, Leaf Borders, c.1920, 3¾ In.	999.00
Tile, Dog, Blue, White, Victorian, 6 x 6 In.	205.00
Tile, Jasperware, 7 White Classical Figures, Brown Ground, 6 x 17½ In.	403.00
Tile, Majolica, Portrait, Brown Glaze, Relief Male Portrait, c.1860, 8¼ x 13 In.	353.00
Tray, Breakfast, Bone China, Cut Corners, Gilt Trim, Leaves, c.1880, 17 12 In.	88.00
Tray, Caneware, Oval, c.1830, 13½ In.	470.00
Tray, Fairyland Luster, Lily, Gondola, Daylight Sky, Flying Geese, c.1920, 13 In.	7638.00
Tray, Imari Flowers, Octagonal, 12½ In.	264.00
Tray, Majolica, Ice Cream, Cut Corners, Scalloped Rim, Fans, c.1880, 10½ In.	118.00
Tray, Serving, Shell Shape, Impressed Marks, Pink, Titled, Mid 19th Century, 4 Piece	1527.00
Trowel, Queen's Ware, Fish, Pierced Blade, Leaf Molded Handle, 1800s, 11¾ In.	1175.00
Tureen, Cover, Underplate, Ladle, 14 x 13 In, 4 Piece	528.00
Umbrella Jar, Etruria, Blue Underglaze, 21 x 10 In.	82.00
Urn, Black Basalt, Relief Grapes & Leaves On Neck, Classical Scenes, 10½ In.	1175.00
Urn, Jasper Dip, Blue, Classical Muses, Wreaths, Leaves, 2 Handles, 8 x 3½ In., Pair	646.00
Urn, Jasperware, Blue, Classical Figures, 3½ In.	45.00
Vase, 2 Handles, Multicolored, Enamel, Silver Luster, c.1925, 9¼ In.	1528.00
Vase, Black Basalt, Encaustic, Classical Figures, Iron Red, 17 In., Pair	2585.00
Vase, Black Basalt, Flared Rim, Footed, Impressed Tile, Mark, Early 1800s, 13¼ In.	1645.00
Vase, Blue, Keith Murray, 6½ In.	527.00
Vase, Bud, Jasperware, Light Blue, 2 Seasons, Spring, Fall, Flower Vine, 5¼ In.	85.00
Vase, Caneware, Glazed, Copper Luster, Flowers, Leaves, c.1930, 8 In.	558.00
Vase, Cover, Agate, Gilded Laurel, Berry Handles, Woman Mask Head, c.1775, 12 In.	2703.00
Vase, Cover, Ivory Glaze, Bronze, Gilt Trim, Scrolled Leaves, Late 1800s, 10 In.	294.00
Vase, Cover, Porphyry, Gilded Cream, Palmette Border, Swags, c.1775, 9 In., Pair	3055.00
Vase, Cover, Victoria Ware, Blue, Salmon Border, Medallions, Zodiac, 12 In., Pair	2350.00
Vase, Cream Matte Glaze, Horizontal Ribs, Flared, Footed, Keith Murray, c.1945, 7 In.	403.00
Vase, Dragon Luster, Gilt, Magenta Ground, 9 In.	450.00
Vase, Dragon Luster, Trumpet, Mottled Orange, Red Exterior, c.1920, 8 In.	411.00
Vase, Earthenware, Grapes, Leaves, 2 Handles, 10 x 11 In.	293.00
Vase, Earthenware, Ivory Glaze, Bottle Shape, Banded Border, Flowers, 10½ In.	176.00

Vase, Earthenware, Ivory Glaze, Iron Red Ground, Gilded Leaves, c.1885, 9⅝ In.	147.00
Vase, Earthenware, Sang De Boeuf, Wine Red Glaze, Late 19th Century, 9¾ In.	206.00
Vase, Fairyland Luster, Baluster, Imps On Bridge, 2 Black Goblins, Green Bird, 12 In.	16675.00
Vase, Fairyland Luster, Candlemas, 4 Panels, Queen's Head, Signed, 8 In.	20125.00
Vase, Fairyland Luster, Candlemas, Daisy Makeig-Jones, 1920s, 8½ In.	2702.00
Vase, Fairyland Luster, Dragon King, Pattern Z4968, Turquoise Sky, c.1920, 23 In.	48825.00
Vase, Fairyland Luster, Firbolgs, Red Ground, c.1920, 7½ In.	823.00
Vase, Fairyland Luster, Willow, Candle Lighthouse, Gnomes, Marked, 10¼ In.	8625.00
Vase, Golconda Ware, Buff Ground, Gilded, Enameled Slip Leaves, c.1885, 10 In.	118.00
Vase, Jasper Dip, Black, Classical Figures, Laurel Border, Trophies, 10 In., Pair	2115.00
Vase, Jasper Dip, Blue, White Flowers, Foliage, Loop Handle, 10½ In., Pair	9988.00
Vase, Jasper Dip, Dark Blue, Muses, 2 Arched Handles, Footed, 7¾ In., Pair	2040.00
Vase, Jasperware, Black, White, Phrygian Head, c.1870, 10½ In.	9600.00
Vase, Jasperware, Blue, Classical Figures, 1976, 5 In.	28.00
Vase, Jasperware, Blue, Scrolled Snake Handles, White Relief, Late 1700s, 15½ In.	9988.00
Vase, Jasperware, Green, Cherubs, 3½ x 3½ In.	78.00
Vase, Lindsay Ware, Enamel, Bottle Shape, Loop Handles, 9¾ In.	2585.00
Vase, Luster, Butterflies, Dragons, Red, Blue, Green Interior, Gilt, 4-Sided, Flared, 7 In.	2587.00
Vase, Majolica, Cherub, Basket Shape, Oval Base, 1866, 6¾ In., Pair	940.00
Vase, Marsden Art Ware, Yellow, Orange Ground, Flowers, Leaves, c.1890, 9½ In.	411.00
Vase, Pearlware, Painted, Coiled Snake Handles, Gilt, Bronze Trim, c.1870, 14¾ In.	1293.00
Vase, Potpourri, Stoneware, White Glaze, Loop Handles, Vine Border, c.1830, 10 In.	294.00
Vase, Queen's Ware, Scrolled Snake Handles, Buff Ground, Speckling, c.1775, 15 In.	2468.00
Vase, Queen's Ware, Transfer Printed, Puce, Scrolled Leaf Handles, Birds, 10⅛ In.	1410.00
Vase, Single Handle, Applied Classical Relief, Leaf Borders, 8½ In., Pair	1116.00
Vase, White Matte Glaze, Art Deco Telescoping Body, Shouldered, 1933, 11 In.	863.00
Vase, Yellow Matte Glaze, Oval, Telescoping Bands, Keith Murray, 1930s, 7 In.	431.00

WELLER pottery was first made in 1872 in Fultonham, Ohio. The firm moved to Zanesville, Ohio, in 1882. Artwares were introduced in 1893. Hundreds of lines of pottery were produced, including Louwelsa, Eocean, Dickens Ware, and Sicardo, before the pottery closed in 1948.

LOUWELSA
WELLER

Ardsley, Bowl, Cattails, Fish Flower Frog, Stamped, Weller Pottery, 3⅜ x 12¼ In.	378.00
Ardsley, Flower Holder, Kingfisher, Marked, Ink Stamp, 8⅜ In.	352.00
Art Nouveau, Vase, Rose, Incised, Painted, Shouldered Form, Impressed Mark, 10½ In.	600.00
Aurelian, Ewer, Ruffled Rim, Amber, Yellow Nasturtium, T.J. Wheatley, 13 x 6 In.	720.00
Baldin, Jardiniere, Pedestal, 38¼ In.	523.00
Barcelona, Vase, Flower, Hand-Thrown Form, Handles, Marked, 11 In.	570.00
Blossom, Vase, Blue Matte Glaze, Cornucopia Shape, Scrolled Foot, c.1935, 8 In. ....*illus*	54.00
Bonito, Vase, Blue Lilies-Of-The-Valley, Green Leaves, Handles, Marked, 5¾ In.	70.00
Bonito, Vase, Pansy & Bud, Green Leaves, 2 Handles, Wavy Rim, Marked, EC, 6 In.	175.00
Brighton, Figurine, Parrot, Perched, Multicolored, Impressed Mark, 12¼ In.	1900.00
Brighton, Figurine, Pheasant, Multicolored, 5 x 7 In.	260.00
Brighton, Flower Frog, Kingfisher, On Tangled Roots, Impressed, 5¾ In.	330.00
Burnt Wood, Vase, 4 Birds, Flowers Blooming On Leafy Branches, 11 In.	196.00
Chengtu, Urn, Cover, Orange, Footed, Stamp Mark, 12 In.	260.00
Claywood, Bowl, Fish, 3½ x 2¼ In.	44.00
Claywood, Vase, Relief Flowers, Tan, Brown, Stippled, 5 In.	115.00
Clinton Ivory, Jardiniere, Molded Flowers, 7¾ x 6¼ In.	44.00
Cookie Jar, Black Mammy, Holding Watermelon, White Dress & Hair Band, 12 x 7 In.	585.00
Coppertone, Bowl, Applied Frog, Water Lilies, Stamp Mark, 3½ x 15½ In.	615.00
Coppertone, Figurine, Frog, Script Mark, 3⅝ In.	422.00
Coppertone, Figurine, Frog With Water Lily, Green Glaze, Marked, 3¾ x 4½ In.	88.00
Coppertone, Flower Frog, Frog In A Lotus Pod, Ink Stamp, 4⅝ In.	378.00
Coppertone, Garden Ornament, Frog, Painted, Marked, 6 x 6 In.	489.00
Coppertone, Lawn Ornament, Frog, Bronze, Green, Tan, Marked, 6 In.	550.00
Coppertone, Vase, Applied Frog, Carved Leaf, Marked, 7 x 7 In.	1150.00
Coppertone, Vase, Applied Frog, Flared, Footed, Marked, 9 In.	487.00
Coppertone, Vase, Bronze & Verde Green Overlay Glaze, Footed, Incised, 8½ In.	430.00
Coppertone, Vase, Frog & Water Lily, Marked, 4 x 5 In.	240.00
Delta, Vase, Raspberries On Thorn Branch, Cylindrical, Impressed, Louwelsa, 6½ In.	810.00
Dickens Ware, Humidor, Turk, Marked, 7½ In.	685.00
Dickens Ware, Mug, Monk Drinking From Stein, Green & Tan Ground, 5½ In.	210.00
Dickens Ware, Pitcher, Jester, Tapered, Marked, 11½ In.	955.00
Dickens Ware, Pitcher, Man In Turban, Profile, Blue, Brown, Yellow, Gray, 10¾ In.	150.00

Weller, Forest, Vase, Low Relief, Forest, River, Matte Brown, Green & Blue Glaze, 8 In.
$199.00

Weller, Novelty Line, Planter, Rabbit & Duck, Glossy Yellow Glaze, Black Trim, 6⅝ In.
$70.00

Weller, Roma, Vase, Tan, Floral Swags, Square, 6 In.
$49.00

W

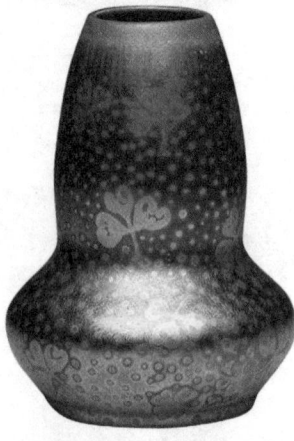

Weller, Sicardo, Vase, Allover Clover Leaf & Dots, Bulbous, 6½ In. $460.00

Weller, Velva, Vase, Relief Flower Panel, Tan, Green Matte Glaze, Applied Handles, Footed, 5 In. $75.00

Dickens Ware, Vase, Baluster, Cavalier Portrait, 14 x 5 In.	360.00
Dickens Ware, Vase, Duck, Pond, Flat Form, Impressed Mark, 5 x 6 In.	375.00
Dickens Ware, Vase, Indian, Headdress, Yellow Shaded To Brown Ground, 11½ In. ....*illus*	785.00
Dickens Ware, Vase, Tear Shape, Portrait Of Woman, 12¾ x 8½ In.	420.00
Eocean, Mug, 2 Claret Plums, Black, Green Ground, Marked, 5¾ In.	185.00
Eocean, Vase, Border Collie Portrait, Signed, Elizabeth Blake, 12¼ In.	2000.00
Eocean, Vase, Cherries & Leaves, Shouldered, Impressed Mark, 10¼ In.	790.00
Eocean, Vase, Lotus Blossom, Impressed, 15 In.	5875.00
Etna, Vase, Daffodils, Tapered, No. 315, Impressed Mark, 11¼ In.	530.00
Etna, Vase, Grapes, Marked, Signed, 15 In.	489.00
Etna, Vase, Roses, Raised, Painted, Green To White To Pink Ground, Signed, 14 In.	489.00
Flemishware, Umbrella Stand, 23 x 11 In.	819.00
Fleron, Vase, Green, Hand-Thrown Form, Handles, Marked, 9½ In.	140.00
Forest, Jardiniere, Pedestal, 18½ x 8½ In.	1053.00
Forest, Vase, Low Relief, Forest, River, Matte Brown, Green & Blue Glaze, 8 In. ....*illus*	199.00
Fru Russet, Vase, Blue Flowers, Green Ground, Embossed, 2 Handles, 3⅛ In.	1600.00
Fru Russet, Vase, Flowers, Blue Ground, Gourd Form, Impressed Mark, 5¼ x 4½ In.	308.00
Fru Russet, Vase, Flowers, Green, Double Gourd Form, Handles, Impressed Mark, 3 x 5 In.	230.00
Garden Ornament, Cat, White, Blue Eyes, Signed, 9 x 14 In.	7800.00
Garden Ornament, Pelican, White, Yellow, 20 x 17 In.	4825.00
Garden Ornament, Rabbit, Mottled Brown Matte Glaze, Marked, 7½ In.	1150.00
Glendale, Candlestick, Yellow Bird, Egg Filled Nest, Berry Tree, Marked, 5 In.	220.00
Glendale, Vase, Bird, Nest, Eggs, Blue Ground, Footed, 6¼ x 5 In.	680.00
Glendale, Vase, Bird, Nest, Eggs, Daisies, Flared Rim, 6½ x 4 In.	459.00
Glendale, Vase, Bird Flying, Tapered, Paper Label, 6½ x 4 In.	170.00
Glendale, Vase, Brown Bird On Forest Floor, Marked, 5 In.	230.00
Glendale, Vase, Double Bud, Bluebird On Nest, Raspberries, Dragonfly, Marked, 7¼ In.	315.00
Glendale, Vase, Gray & Brown Matte Glaze, Experimental, Impressed Mark, 5½ In.	420.00
Glendale, Wall Pocket, Mother & 3 Baby Birds In Nest, Marked, 12 In.	465.00
Greora, Vase, Pillow, Molded Vines, 2 Handles, Footed, Label, 7⅜ In.	230.00
Hudson, Dogwood Blossoms, Blue, Purple, Gray Ground, Shoulder, Impressed Mark, 9 In.	295.00
Hudson, Vase, 2 Field Daisies, Incised, Dorothy England, 6 In.	267.00
Hudson, Vase, 4 Birds In Flight, Shouldered, Impressed Mark, 10 In.	3190.00
Hudson, Vase, Blue Daisies, Pink Ground, Marked, 6⅛ In.	735.00
Hudson, Vase, Daffodils, Gray, Blue, White, Cylindrical, Impressed Mark, 9½ In.	415.00
Hudson, Vase, Flowers, Marked, Signed, Hood, 11½ x 6½ In.	1650.00
Hudson, Vase, Flowers, Multitoned Green Ground, Shouldered, 9 In.	480.00
Hudson, Vase, Forest Landscape, Cylindrical, Stamped, Signed, 9¼ In.	3120.00
Hudson, Vase, Geraniums, Pink, Gray & Ivory Ground, Shouldered, C.L.L., 10 In.	290.00
Hudson, Vase, Grapes & Vines, Flared, Marked, 17 In.	849.00
Hudson, Vase, Gray & White Persian Cat, Impressed, 9⅛ In.	2680.00
Hudson, Vase, Iris, Stamped, Signed, Sarah Timberlake, 9½ In.	298.00
Hudson, Vase, Perfecto, Signed, EF, 4⅜ In.	506.00
Hudson, Vase, Roses, Gray Ground, High Glaze, 13 x 7 In.	900.00
Hudson, Vase, Ships At Sea, Bulbous, Impressed Mark, 9½ In.	4780.00
Hudson, Vase, White Lilies-Of-The-Valley Sprays, 2 Handles, Hester Pillsbury, 7 In.	910.00
Jap Birdimal, Jardiniere, Pedestal, House & Trees, 31 x 13 In.	489.00
Jap Birdimal, Mug, Squeezebag, Geisha, Cat, Blue Green Ground, 5¼ x 5 In.	600.00
Jardiniere, Stand, Blue & White, Flowers, Leaves, Mask Faces, 32 x 14½ In.	240.00
Juneau, Vase, Red, Tan, Blue Dripping Over Pink Ground, Bulbous, Marked, 5½ In.	131.00
Knifewood, Jardiniere, Pedestal, Daisies & Butterflies, 21½ x 11 In.	1010.00
Knifewood, Vase, Canaries, Marked, 5 x 4 In.	345.00
Knifewood, Wall Pocket, Daisies, 5½ x 4 In.	200.00
Knifewood, Wall Pocket, Daisies, Marked, 8 x 5 In.	257.00
Lorber, Vase, Peacocks, Leaves, 9 x 4½ In.	175.00
Lorber, Vase, Squirrels, Leaves, 11½ x 6 In.	510.00
Louwelsa, Jardiniere, Pansies, 3⅜ x 4¼ In.	105.00
Louwelsa, Vase, American Indian Portrait, Impressed, 7 x 6¾ In.	1500.00
Louwelsa, Vase, c.1920, 15 In.	585.00
Mug, Trunk Shape, Oak Leaves, 3 Fox, Double Twig Handle, Brown, Green, 6 In.	322.00
Muskota, Flower Frog, Boy Kneeling, 4¼ x 4 In.	260.00
Muskota, Flower Frog, Swan, Marked, 2⅝ x 8¼ In.	252.00
Muskota, Incense Burner Lid, Foxy Grandpa, Marked, 3½ x 3 In.	340.00
Muskota, Vase, Bud, Girl With Doll, Tree, Marked, 8 x 4 In.	615.00
Novelty Line, Planter, Rabbit & Duck, Glossy Yellow Glaze, Black Trim, 6⅝ In. ....*illus*	70.00
Panella, Vase, Yellow & Pink Nasturtiums, Green Leaves, Gray Matte Ground, 10¾ In.	323.00

W

Parian, Vase, Stylized Flower, 8¾ In.	90.00
Roma, Vase, Double Bud, Marked, 8½ x 5 In.	50.00
Roma, Vase, Tan, Floral Swags, Square, 6 In. ....*illus*	49.00
Sabrinian, Pitcher, Seashells, Sea Horse Handle, Stamped, 10⅝ In.	208.00
Scandia, Bowl, Low, 6 In.	50.00
Selma, Vase, Birds Feeding On Berry Vines, Foxes, 9⅞ In.	1800.00
Selma, Vase, Daisies, Cylindrical, Impressed, 7¼ In.	115.00
Sicardo, Lamp Base, Flowers, Twisted Form, Metallic Glaze, Wood Base, Signed, 13½ In.	520.00
Sicardo, Vase, Allover Clover Leaf & Dots, Bulbous, 6½ In. ....*illus*	460.00
Sicardo, Vase, Flowers, 4-Sided, Metallic Glaze, Signed, 4½ In.	368.00
Sicardo, Vase, Flowers, Stems, Metallic Luster, Iridescent Burgundy Ground, 15¾ In.	8200.00
Sicardo, Vase, Stylized Chrysanthemums, Maroon & Purple Iridescent Glaze, 13 In.	1380.00
Silvertone, Vase, Flowers, Branches, Pink, White, Green, Brown, Handles, Marked, 9¼ In. ..	290.00
Silvertone, Vase, Jonquil Sprays, Purple, Green, Yellow, 2 Handles, Marked, 7½ In.	310.00
Silvertone, Vase, White Lilies, Green & Purple Ground, Bulbous, Flared, Marked, 11 In.	529.00
Souevo, Vase, Geometric Design, Impressed Mark, 8½ In.	195.00
Souevo, Vase, Geometric Figures & Design, Squat, 5 In.	175.00
Tutone, Vase, 3-Sided, Green & Purple, 7½ In.	83.00
Vase, Birds, Berries & Branches, Cream Ground, Stamped, 8 In.	1305.00
Velva, Vase, Relief Flower Panel, Tan, Green Matte Glaze, Applied Handles, Footed, 5 In. *illus*	75.00
Woodcraft, Flower Frog, Frog Emerging From Water Lily Blossom, 4½ In.	310.00
Woodcraft, Flower Frog, Swan, 2½ x 5½ In.	139.00
Woodcraft, Jardiniere, Woodpecker & Mushrooms, Handles, Impressed Mark, 6 x 12 In.	415.00
Woodcraft, Planter, Branches, Tree Trunk, Den Of Foxes, c.1925, 4½ x 8 In.	294.00
Woodcraft, Vase, Foxes, In Tree Stump, Impressed Mark, 7 x 5½ In.	175.00
Woodcraft, Vase, Squirrel, Oak Leaves, Acorns, Marked, 5 x 10 In.	175.00
Woodcraft, Vase, Trunk, 5 Openings, Earthtone Glazes, 20th Century, 10 In.	118.00
Woodcraft, Wall Pocket, Branch, Apple, Early 20th Century, 11½ In.	235.00
Woodrose, Jardiniere, Bucket Shape, 2 Handles, 8 In.	71.00
Xenia, Vase, Clematis, Pastel Colors, Bulbous, Impressed, 11 In.	1350.00
Zona, Jardiniere, Pedestal, Cattails, Kingfishers, 30½ In.	2040.00
Zona, Pitcher, Kingfisher, On Perch, Aged Tree, Marked, 8⅜ In.	205.00

WEMYSS ware was made by Robert Heron in Kirkaldy, Scotland, from 1850 to 1929. It is a colorful peasant-type pottery that is occasionally found in the United States.

Figurine, Cat, White, Pink Clover, Green Glass Eyes, Joe Nekola, c.1930, 12¼ In. ......*illus*	4679.00
Figurine, Pig, Painted, Thistles, 1930s, 16 In. ....*illus*	2880.00
Figurine, Pig, Seated, Pink, Roses, Leaves, 9½ In.	550.00

WESTMORELAND GLASS was made by the Westmoreland Glass Company of Grapeville, Pennsylvania, from 1890 to 1984. They made clear and colored glass of many varieties, such as milk glass, pressed glass, and slag glass.

Animal Dish, Doves, Cover, Basket Weave, Green, Satin Base, 1980s	62.00
Animal Dish, Fox, Cover, Lacy Base, Milk Glass	38.00
Animal Dish, Hen On Nest, Cover, Basket Weave Base, Milk Glass	8.00
Animal Dish, Hen On Nest, Cover, Pink, Opaque, Basket Weave Base, 8 In.	2.00
Animal Dish, Lion Cover, Lacy Base, Blue Milk Glass, 6⅜ x 8 In. ....*illus*	40.00
Della Robbia, Bowl, Belled, Ruby Flashed, Footed, 12 In.	125.00
Della Robbia, Bowl, Heart Shape, Dark Stain, 8 In.	125.00
English Hobnail, Bonbon, Amber, 6½ In.	11.00
English Hobnail, Bonbon, Handle, Hexagonal, 6½ In.	15.00
English Hobnail, Candlestick, Green, Round, 3½ In.	22.00
English Hobnail, Candlestick, Green, Square, 5¾ In.	35.00
English Hobnail, Coaster	8.00
English Hobnail, Cologne Bottle, Stopper, Green, 5 Oz.	50.00
English Hobnail, Cologne Bottle, Stopper, Ice Blue, 5 Oz.	100.00
English Hobnail, Console, Amber, Rolled Edge, 11 In.	30.00
English Hobnail, Cordial, Oz., 3¼ In.	15.00
English Hobnail, Creamer, Green, Square Foot	55.00
English Hobnail, Creamer, Hexagonal Foot	10.00
English Hobnail, Cup, After Dinner	15.00
English Hobnail, Lamp, Candlestick	36.00
English Hobnail, Nut Dish, Fired-On Blue, Footed, 2 In.	10.00
English Hobnail, Nut Dish, Green, Footed, 2 In.	14.00
English Hobnail, Plate, 8 In.	10.00 to 13.00

Wemyss, Figurine, Cat, White, Pink Clover, Green Glass Eyes, Joe Nekola, c.1930, 12¼ In. $4679.00

Wemyss, Figurine, Pig, Painted, Thistles, 1930s, 16 In. $2880.00

Westmoreland Glass, Animal Dish, Lion Cover, Lacy Base, Blue Milk Glass, 6⅜ x 8 In. $40.00

W

Westmoreland Glass, Figurine, Bulldog, Emerald Green, 2¾ In. $28.00

Westmoreland Glass, Old Quilt, Dish, Mayonnaise, Canary, Footed, 4½ In. $29.00

Westmoreland Glass, Ring & Petal, Bowl, Blue, Footed, 10 In. $29.00

Wheatley, Vase, Green Matte, Bulbous, Collared Rim, 11½ x 9¾ In. $390.00

English Hobnail, Plate, Amber, 8 In.	15.00
English Hobnail, Plate, Amber, 10½ In.	18.00
English Hobnail, Plate, Sherbet, 6½ In.	6.00
English Hobnail, Sugar, Hexagonal Foot	10.00
English Hobnail, Tumbler, Round Foot, 5 Oz.	9.00
English Hobnail, Tumbler, Square Foot, 11 Oz.	12.00
English Hobnail, Wine, 2 Oz., 4½ In.	9.00
Figurine, Bird, Pink Satin, Rectangular Base, 3¼ x 2½ In.	20.00
Figurine, Bulldog, Emerald Green, 2¾ In. *illus*	28.00
Figurine, Swan, Raised Wing, Milk Glass	15.00
Hat, Uncle Sam, 2½ In.	35.00
Old Quilt, Dish, Mayonnaise, Canary, Footed, 4½ In. *illus*	29.00
Paneled Grape, Ashtray, Milk Glass, Large	1.00
Paneled Grape, Basket, Milk Glass	25.00
Paneled Grape, Basket, Oval, Milk Glass	4.00
Paneled Grape, Basket, Oval, Yellow Satin Glass	95.00
Paneled Grape, Berry Set, Milk Glass, 10 Piece	20.00
Paneled Grape, Butter, Cover, Milk Glass	4.00
Paneled Grape, Candlestick, Milk Glass, Pair	2.00
Paneled Grape, Compote, Milk Glass, Deep	6.00
Paneled Grape, Cruet, Stopper, Milk Glass	3.00
Paneled Grape, Cup & Saucer, Milk Glass	5.00
Paneled Grape, Decanter, Stopper, Milk Glass	35.00
Paneled Grape, Gravy Boat, Milk Glass	4.00
Paneled Grape, Pitcher, Milk, Milk Glass	6.00
Paneled Grape, Plate, Milk Glass, 6 In.	1.00
Paneled Grape, Plate, Milk Glass, 9 In.	1.00
Paneled Grape, Plate, Milk Glass, 15 In.	55.00
Paneled Grape, Sandwich Server, Handle, Milk Glass	6.00
Paneled Grape, Sugar & Creamer, Milk Glass	2.00
Paneled Grape, Toothpick, Milk Glass	3.00
Paneled Grape, Tumbler, Milk Glass, 4½ In.	1.00
Paneled Grape, Tumbler, Milk Glass, 6 In.	1.00
Paneled Grape, Vase, Milk Glass, Footed, 6 In.	1.00
Paneled Grape, Vase, Milk Glass, Footed, 11 In.	10.00
Ring & Petal, Bowl, Blue, Footed, 10 In. *illus*	29.00
Thousand Eye, Plate, Peacock Blue, 18 In.	60.00

WHEATLEY Pottery was established in 1880. Thomas J. Wheatley had worked in Cincinnati, Ohio, with the founders of the art pottery movement, including M. Louise McLaughlin of the Rookwood Pottery. Wheatley Pottery was purchased by the Cambridge Tile Manufacturing Company in 1927.

Lamp Base, Milkweed Pods, Crusty Green Matte Glaze, 15 In.	978.00
Plate, 2 Lily Stalks, Hand Painted, Barotine, Incised, 11 In.	1200.00
Tile, 4 Conjoined Circles, Curdled Matte Green, Self-Framed Edge, Brown Glaze, 4¼ In.	300.00
Tile, 4-Petal Design, Diamond Shapes, Blue, Yellow, Brown, Pink, Incised, c.1915-20, 4 In.	210.00
Tile, Carved, Faience, Multicolored, Marked, c.1915	450.00
Tile, Cross, Blue, Yellow, Brown Gold, Incised, c.1915-20, 4⅛ In.	135.00
Tile, Grapes, Stylized Leaves, Cream, Green & Dark Blue Matte, Incised, c.1920, 4 In.	325.00
Tile, Pink, Yellow, Gray Matte, Incised, c.1920, 4 In.	245.00
Tile, Shield, Gun Metal Black Iridescent, Gold Green Ribbon, Beige, Orange, c.1925, 4 In.	230.00
Vase, Bulbous, Green Matte Glaze, 11½ x 9½ In.	840.00
Vase, Green Matte, Bulbous, Collared Rim, 11½ x 9¾ In. *illus*	390.00

WHIELDON was an English potter who worked alone and with Josiah Wedgwood in eighteenth-century England. Whieldon made many pieces in natural shapes, like cauliflowers or cabbages.

Cake Plate, Flowers, Blue, Pink, Rust, Gold Rim, 8-Sided, 9¾ In.	12.00
Plate, Oriental, Transfer, Multicolored, 8-Sided, 8¾ In.	15.00
Plate Set, Pink Border, Flower Center, Square Bowl, Luncheon Plates, 8¾ In., 13 Piece	59.00

WILLETS Manufacturing Company of Trenton, New Jersey, began work in 1879. The company made belleek in the late 1880s and 1890s in shapes similar to those used by the Irish Belleek factory. They stopped working about 1912. A variety of marks were used, all including the name Willets.

W

Mug, Flowers, Leaves, Dragon Handle, Signed, E. Meier	110.00
Mug, Grape Clusters, Purple, Green, Red, Marked, Belleek, 4¼ In.	120.00
Pitcher, Milk, Grapes, Belleek, Initialed, Marked, 7 In.	295.00
Plate, Flowers, Pink, Blue, Purple, Gilt Leaves, Belleek, c.1880-1904	195.00
Tankard, Dragon Handle, Signed, Belleek, 9¼ In.	425.00
Vase, Mums, Belleek, 16 In.	1700.00
Vase, Roses, Hand Painted, Cylindrical, Marked, Belleek, 16 In.	995.00

WILLOW pattern has been made in England since 1780. The pattern has been copied by factories in many countries, including Germany, Japan, and the United States. It is still being made. Willow was named for a pattern that pictures a bridge, birds, willow trees, and a Chinese landscape. Most pieces are blue and white.

Bowl, 2 Sections, 2 x 10 In.	25.00
Bowl, Cover, Flower Border, 1900s, 9½ x 4½ x 2 In.	40.00
Bowl, Fruit, Herringbone, Flowers, House, Boat, Trees, Birds, 3 Men, c.1920	16.00
Bowl, Vegetable, 8½ In.	15.00
Bowl, Vegetable, 9¼ In.	25.00
Cake Server, 10¾ In.	17.00
Coffeepot, 10 x 9 In.	40.00
Crumber Brush, 7¾ In.	15.00
Cup & Saucer, Japan, 3½ x 2½ & 6 In.	16.00
Drawer Pull Set, 4 In., 2 Piece	15.00
Gravy Boat, 7¾ x 4⅛ In.	18.00
Grill Plate, Red, Japan, 10¼ In.	16.00
Plate, Dinner, 9 In., 3 Piece	18.00
Plate, Salad, Herringbone, c.1920, 7¾ In.	24.00
Platter, Blue Printed, Oval, Staffordshire, Early 19th Century, 14½ In.	166.00
Salt & Pepper, Japan, 1940s, 3 In.	95.00
Saucer, 6⅛ In., Pair	15.00
Saucer, Herringbone, c.1920, 5¾ In.	16.00
Soap Dish, 5½ In.	15.00
Soap Holder, Bathtub, 3 x 5 In.	17.00
Soup, Dish, c.1902-26, 8 In.	16.00
Sugar, 4 In.	18.00
Teapot, Pink, Flat Spout	75.00
Thimble	4.00
Tumbler, 5⅛ In.	40.00

WINDOW glass that was stained and beveled was popular for houses during the late nineteenth and early twentieth centuries. The old windows became popular with collectors in the 1970s; today, old and new examples are seen.

Leaded, Arrow, Green, Yellow, Gold Leaf, 46 x 22 In., Pair	5400.00
Leaded, Glass, Ecclesiastical, White Lilies, Cross, Slag Glass Border, Frame, 34 x 29 In.	705.00
Leaded, Glass, Fruiting Trees, Multicolored, Opalescent Ground, Frame, 15 x 9 In., Pair	4200.00
Leaded, Glass, Landscape, Multicolored Slag Glass Sky, Frame, 48¾ x 34 In.	382.00
Leaded, Stained Glass, Diamonds, Blue Ground, Pennsylvania, c.1890, 20½ x 40 In.	425.00
Leaded, Stained Glass, Green Border, Wood Frame, Early 20th Century, 21 x 28 In.	106.00
Leaded, Stained Glass, Roses, 31 x 23 In., Pair	293.00
Pediment, Oak, Chestnut, Carved, Angelic Head, 19th Century, 7 x 34 In., Pair	1058.00
Stained Glass, 3 Sections, Orange Ground, Red Flowers, Green Stems, c.1940, 68 x 21 In.	351.00
Stained Glass, Abstract Design, Primary Colors, 29½ x 18 In., Pair	384.00
Stained Glass, Arched, 4 Panels, Geometric, Wood Frame, 1800s, 65 x 34 In., Pair	472.00
Stained Glass, Beveled, Flowers, Vining, Blue, Green, Red, White, 69 x 41 In.	527.00
Stained Glass, Hesperiden, Pre-Raphaelite, England, c.1890, 24 x 13½ In. ....*illus*	1410.00
Stained Glass, Leaded, Caramel Slag Glass, Wood Frame, 23 x 28 In., Pair ....*illus*	294.00
Stained Glass, Leaded, Sailing Ship, Jan Piefer, c.1900, 8 x 6 In.	146.00
Stained Glass, Leaded, Woman, Frame, Riordan & Co., 12 x 16 In. ....*illus*	4200.00
Stained Glass, Virgin & Child Jesus, 19th Century, 33 x 14½ In. ....*illus*	3760.00
Stained Glass, Wood Frame, c.1920, 34 x 24 In., 2 Piece	88.00
U.S. Post Office, Steel, Iron, Tin, Decal, Postmasters Supply Co., 22 x 48 x 23 In.	385.00

WOOD CARVINGS and wooden pieces are listed separately in this book. Many of the wood carvings are figurines or statues. There are also wooden pieces found in other categories, such as Kitchen.

Alligator, 7 Ft. 3½ In.	850.00

Window, Stained, Hesperiden, Pre-Raphaelite, England, c.1890, 24 x 13½ In. $1410.00

Window, Stained Glass, Leaded, Caramel Slag Glass, Wood Frame, 23 x 28 In., Pair $294.00

Window, Stained Glass, Leaded, Woman, Frame, Riordan & Co., 12 x 16 In. $4200.00

W

Window, Stained Glass, Virgin & Child Jesus, 19th Century, 33 x 14½ In. $3760.00

Wood Carving, Humidor, 2 Bears Carrying Stump-Shaped Pipe Rack, Black Forest, 11¼ x 14½ x 9 In. $1265.00

Wood Carving, Jardiniere, Black Forest, Vine Covered Basket, Branch Tripod Base, 32 In. $1175.00

Angel, Multicolored, Deep Folds, Curly Hair, 12 In.	529.00
Angels, Carved, Painted, Distressed White Paint, 21 x 6½ In, Pair	460.00
Antelope, On Rocks, Black Forest, 6¾ x 4⅜ In.	275.00
Archangel, Wearing Soldier's Tunic, Boots, Tin Wings, 1800s, 13½ In.	322.00
Arhat, Shaved Head, Inverted Lotus Base, Painted, Gilt, Japan, 1700s, 28 In.	2400.00
Bear, Carrying Log, Rectangular Base, Black Forest, 7⅛ x 4¾ In.	440.00
Bear, Cub At Side, Cub On Shoulder, Frog On Ground, Black Forest, 20 In.	1725.00
Bear, Seated, Cross-Legged, Open Mouth, Black Forest, 10¾ In.	575.00
Bear, Standing, Holding Shield, Glass Eyes, Haslital, Black Forest, c.1910, 14¼ In.	2070.00
Bear, Standing On Hind Legs, Mouth Open, Square Base, Black Forest, 14½ x 6 In.	523.00
Bird, Notched Carved Wing & Tail, Black Paint, Relief Base, Wood Block, 4 x 5 In.	6050.00
Bird, Painted, Driftwood, 3½ In.	176.00
Bird, Robin, Inset Glass Eyes, Brown, Red, Bark Plank Fence, 7 x 12¼ x 3¾ In.	353.00
Bird, Robin, Wire Legs, Painted, Wooden Feet, Oval, Green Pine Base, 5 x 7¾ In.	264.00
Bird, Tern, In Flight, Painted, Glass Eyes, Wood Base, 7¾ x 14 In.	118.00
Bird Tree, 8 Polychrome Birds, On Drooping Branches, Log Base, Strawser, 25 In.	715.00
Bluebirds, Pine, Blue, Brown, Feathered, Carved Wings, Wire Feet, 7½ In., Pair	4200.00
Boots, Pine, Painted, Red, Black, Incised Heart, 5 In., Pair	2400.00
Bowl, Formed From Hollowed-Out Log, Beech, 19th Century, 12 x 37½ In.	805.00
Bowl, Kava, 6 Cylindrical Legs, Animal Head, Polynesia, 6 x 17½ In.	588.00
Buddha, Reclining, One Hand Propping Head, Burmese, 25½ In.	381.00
Buddha, Seated, Gilt Wood, Chinese, Ming Dynasty, 16½ In.	826.00
Buddha, Seated On Double Lotus Base, Chinese, 11½ In.	443.00
Bust, Bird, Openwork Beak, Pronounced Ears, Black Forest, 6 x 7 In.	198.00
Bust, Mountain Goat, Black Forest, 11 x 4½ In.	132.00
Bust, Wolf, Black Forest, 7½ x 5¾ In.	468.00
Canoe, Fishermen, Pole, Paddle, Net, Fish Basket, Mahogany, 14 x 48 In.	2070.00
Case, Pocket Watch, Hinged Lid, Applied Acorn & Leaf, Velvet Lining, 3¾ x 2 In.	198.00
Cat, Seated, Glass Eyes, Leather Ears, Gray Tabby Paint, 14 In.	690.00
Cherub, Baroque Carved, Silvered, Multicolored, Germany, 8 x 8 In., Pair	1645.00
Christ, Late 19th Century, South America, 42 In.	531.00
Christ, Polychrome, Painted, Guatemala, 18th Century, 20½ In.	620.00
Christ, Spain, 17th Century, 36 In.	2596.00
Coconut Shell, Windsor Arms, Bridgewater City, Castle, Monkey Face, 5¾ In.	230.00
Deity, Holding Pearl, Glass Eyes, Painted, Multicolored, Chinese, 27 In.	2115.00
Divine, Religious, On Throne, Continental, 9 x 6 x 5 In.	29.00
Dog, Cross-Hatched Body, Knob Tail, 4⅛ x 5½ In.	523.00
Dog, Hunting, Standing, Post Fence, 5½ x 6 x 1¾ In.	206.00
Dog, Seated, Painted Black, White, 7⅞ In.	470.00
Dog, Shoulder Marks, Germany, 5 x 6¼ In.	11.00
Dog, Spaniel, Docked Tail, Feathered Legs, Brown, Black, White Paint, 5½ In.	345.00
Dog, Spaniel, Pine, Reclining, White, Dark Brown, 3⅝ x 9 In.	235.00
Dove, Gray & Yellow Paint, Pink Highlights, Glass Eyes, 11½ x 9¾ In.	144.00
Doves, Holy Spirit, Multicolored, Latin America, 14 x 29 In., Pair	881.00
Duck, Mallard, Tree Trunk Base, 2 Flying Ducks, Male, Female, 6 x 7 In., Pair	58.00
Duck, Standing, Screw Eyes, Signed In Pencil, E. Reed, 13½ x 8½ In.	345.00
Eagle, Painted Banner, Don't Give Up The Ship, 28½ In.	546.00
Eagle, Pilot House, Ballamy Style, Carved, Spread Wings, 28 x 28 In.	3450.00
Eagle, Spread Wings, Carved Wings, Hatch Marks, 6 x 12½ In.	44.00
Eagle, Spread Wings, Flag, Multicolored, Late 19th Century, 19 x 37 In.	18000.00
Eagle, Spread Wings, On Ball, Hooked Beak, Metal Rod, Cross Base, 28 x 18 In.	1495.00
Eagle, Spread Wings, Open Beak, Incised Feathers, 50½ x 30 In.	1430.00
Eagle, Spread Wings, Walnut, Dark Patina, Late 1800s, 13 x 19½ In.	3680.00
Eagle, Wings Up, Relief Carved Feathers, 16 x 9 In., Pair	489.00
Eagle Head, Hardwood, Incised Feathers, Plaque, 2½ x 4¼ In.	40.00
Egret, Inset Glass Eyes, Wire Legs, Painted White, Yellow Bill, 22⅝ In.	1763.00
Elephant, Rosewood, Trunk Lowered, 12 x 13 In., Pair	380.00
Female, Dressmaker's Form, Walnut, Late 19th Century, 36 In.	1840.00
Finial, Regency, Giltwood, Carved, Eagles, Spread Wings, 13 x 14 In., Pair	960.00
Fish, Flying, 10 x 20 In.	3190.00
Foo Dog, Giltwood, Chinese, 16 In., Pair	325.00
Foo Dog, Teakwood, Carved, Chinese, 10 x 11 In., Pair	35.00
Friar, Book In Hand, Round Base, 10½ In.	587.00
Gaming Horse, Jockey On Horse, Painted, Stand, Marked, 1890-1910, 13 In.	1093.00
Griffin, Walnut, Seated, Continental, 12 x 6 x 15 In., Pair	1058.00
Guardian, Gilt Wood, Chinese, 12 In.	118.00

Hat Rack, Fox Head, Glass Eyes, Clenching Branch, 2 Loops, Black Forest, 12½ In.	1175.00
Head, Buddha, Burmese, Gilt, 19th Century, 29½ In.	1180.00
Head, Guanyin, Wearing High Chignon, Headdress, Polychrome, Chinese, 16¾ In.	531.00
Head Of Saint, Polychrome, Inset Glass Eyes, Spanish Colonial, 11½ In.	395.00
Headrest, Elongated, Round Feet, Woman Head, Stylized Hair, Africa, 2¾ x 30 In.	1528.00
Hearse Curtain, 34 x 30 In., Pair	690.00
Holder, Pocket Watch, Falcon, On Rock, Tree Branch Hook, Black Forest, 6½ x 4 In.	248.00
Horse, Rearing, Painted, Italy, 19th Century, 42 In.	995.00
Horse, Standing, Applied Fur Mane & Tail, Brown Paint, 6¾ In.	747.00
Humidor, 2 Bears Carrying Stump-Shaped Pipe Rack, Black Forest, 11¼ x 14½ x 9 In. *illus*	1265.00
Humidor, Owl, Feathers, Glass Eyes, Base, Late 19th Century, 13 In.	1610.00
Hunter, Chamois At Feet, Hat With Feather, Holding Stick, Swiss, c.1900, 34 In.	4025.00
Immortals, Boxwood, Chinese, 4 In., Pair	142.00
Jardiniere, Black Forest, Vine Covered Basket, Branch Tripod Base, 32 In. *illus*	1175.00
Kwan Yin, Giltwood, Standing, Praying, Lotus Base, Cambodia, 31 x 10 In.	1080.00
Lamb, Lying Down, Book With Cross, Flag, 16 x 19 In.	143.00
Lion, Cub, Japan, 16 In.	411.00
Lion, Incised Mane, Gold Paint, 12 In.	132.00
Lion, Lioness, Cub, Glass Eyes, Bone Teeth, Japan, 16½ In.	235.00
Madonna & Child, Gesso, Polychrome, 20½ In.	146.00
Man, Black Suit, Movable Head, Multicolored, 5⅜ In.	33.00
Man, Holding 2 Geese, Nurnberg, Germany, c.1950, 4½ In.	110.00
Man, Religious, Beard, Beaded Man, Holding House, Crosier, 37 In.	330.00
Man, Waving Club, Craggy Rock Shape Base, Chinese, 7 In.	1062.00
Man & Woman, German Outfits, Trestle Bench, Gesso, Multicolored, 39 x 26 In.	1552.00
Man's Head, Eyes Closed, Protruding Chin, Long Beard, Mustache, 12 x 13 In.	403.00
Monk, Japan, 19½ In.	325.00
Monk, St. Bernard Dog, Searching For Lost Traveler, Black Forest, 20 In. *illus*	4700.00
Moose, Iron Tack Eyes, Brown, Black Hooves, 9 In.	118.00
Neck Rest, Animal Form, Africa, 24½ x 8½ x 5¼ In.	472.00
Ornament, Beechwood, Putti, Fruit, Flower Swag, Blanc-De-Trianon, 38 In., Pair	1440.00
Owl, Balsa, Sleep Eyes, Stand, 15 In.	4180.00
Owl, Northwest Arkansas, 24 In.	335.00
Owl, On Rock Formation, Over Molded Base, 35¼ In.	3850.00
Owl, Plaster Legs, Wire Feet, Original Paint, Tree Stump Base, 7½ In.	690.00
Owls, On Knotted Log, Brown & Gold Paint, Turned Wood Base, 14½ x 7½ In.	2300.00
Ox, Applied Ears & Horns, Brown Paint, 5¼ x 7½ In., Pair	440.00
Panel, Oak, St. George Slaying Dragon, Half Round, Multicolored, 24½ x 18 In.	705.00
Panel, Plaque, Mother Holding Baby, Figures, Pierced, 41 x 14½ In.	374.00
Panel, Religious, Giltwood, Sunburst Frame, Painted, Angels, 12 x 11 In.	518.00
Parrot, Multicolored, Incised Wing, Painted Beads, Stepped Base, 17¾ In.	468.00
Parrot, Painted, Multicolored Plumage, Wire Legs, Domed Base, 12½ x 7⅜ In.	1175.00
Parrot, Stepped Pedestal Base, Carved Wing, Tail, Feet, Painted, 12 In.	550.00
Peacock, Multicolored, Stepped Pedestal Base, Keith Collis, 22¾ In.	550.00
Penguin, Carved, Painted, Tack Eyes, Beak, Applied Flippers, 6½ x 3 In.	2350.00
Penguin, Tack Eyes, Applied Flippers, Black, White Paint, 1936, 5 x 1¾ In.	1880.00
Penguin, Tack Eyes, Applied Flippers, Black, White Paint, c.1935, 6⅞ x 2¾ In.	3525.00
Pheasant, Multicolored, Applied Wings, Painted, Iron Wire Legs, 18 x 21 In.	220.00
Pig, Grooved Feet, Painted, 13 x 22 x 12 In.	978.00
Pine Tree, 1 Side With Bark, Chainsaw Carved, Oak, 78 In.	275.00
Pipe Head, Uncle Sam, Multicolored, Gilt, Early 1900s, 5½ x 2 x 2½ In.	1850.00
Plaque, 2 Fish, Rope Stringer, Flowers, Leaves, Burl, Walnut Frame, 15 x 16 In.	248.00
Plaque, 2 Sisters, Flowers, Leaf Border, Bow, Gilt, Green, 19th Century, 24 x 20 In.	33600.00
Plaque, Angel, Germany, 10 x 9½ In.	640.00
Plaque, Eagle, Spread Wings, Arrows, Shield, Painted, Red, Gold, White, Blue	508.00
Plaque, Eagle, Spread Wings, Flags, Banner, Motto, Gilt, Red, Blue, 25 x 42½ In.	3450.00
Plaque, Eagle & Flag, Shield & Arrows, Painted, Delaware Valley, 24 x 40 In.	55000.00
Plaque, Figural, Whale, Single Plank, V-Shaped Tail, 86½ x 10½ In.	3738.00
Plaque, Man, Woman, Open Hands, Tasseled Drapery, Birds, Red Brown, 15 x 14 In.	7200.00
Plaque, Our Lady Of Sorrows, Multicolored, Deep Folds, Germany, 27 x 21 In.	2350.00
Plaque, Stag & Bird, Walnut Relief, Germany, c.1900, 20 x 35 In.	990.00
Plaque, Wall, White Eagle On Branch, Maple, Inset Glass Eyes, 10½ x 31¼ In.	470.00
Plaque, Walnut, Grouse, Black Forest, 19th Century, 28 x 19 In.	2400.00
Possums, Mama & 2 Babies, Painted, Lonnie & Twyla Money, Ky.	633.00
Protractor, Multicolored Decoration, Chinese, 9 In., Pair	350.00
Putto, Flying, Cornucopia, Giltwood, Iron Suspension Bracket, Italy, 19 x 12 In.	705.00

Wood Carving, Monk, St. Bernard Dog, Searching For Lost Traveler, Black Forest, 20 In. $4700.00

Wood Carving, Woman, Colorful Dress, Painted, Paneled Plinth Base, 83 In., Pair $5750.00

W

Wooden, Bucket, Sugar, Green Paint, Sapling Bands, Extended End Staves, Flat Lid, 12 x 9 In.
$358.00

Wooden, Firkin, Cover, Interlocking Finger Bands, 11⅜ x 10¼ In.
$44.00

Rat, Seat, Holding Foot In Paws, 3½ x 8 In.	110.00
Rooster, Dragon, Chinese, 16 In.	235.00
Rooster, Fan Tail, Original Paint, 5 In.	288.00
Rooster, Painted, Detailed Feathers, Tail, 25 x 19½ In.	1650.00
Saint, Male, Robed, Polychrome, Parcel Gilt, French Provincial, 19½ In.	1080.00
Santo, Figure Of Bishop, Bishop's Miter & Robes, 19th Century, 18 In.	234.00
Santo, Painted, White Robe, Continental, 19th Century, 31¾ x 9½ In.	92.00
Santo, Saint San Antonio D. Padua, Holding Child, New World, 1800s, 19 In.	164.00
Santo, Standing, Black Cloth, Polychrome, 19th Century, 16 In.	660.00
Sheep, White Paint, Standing On Green Hill, 19th Century	108.00
Shelf, Walnut, Stag Support, Wreath, Leaf Drop, 13½ In.	11.00
Shrine, 3 Apostles, Carved, Beech Wood, c.1960	105.00
Spoon, Luba Wood, 23 In.	142.00
Spoon, Serrated Edge, Bone Inlaid Heart, Rattail Terminal, Annie 1924, 10 In.	121.00
Squirrel, Flat, Eating Nut, Brown & Green Paint, 6½ In.	538.00
St. Vincent, Blue Mantle, Multicolored, Continental, 24 x 15 In.	617.00
Statue, St. Christopher, Carrying Christ Child, 18½ In.	499.00
Tabernacle, Walnut, 2 Pillars, Angel, 19½ x 15 x 13 In.	1528.00
Torso, Male, Pine, Movable Parts, France, c.1860	2800.00
Toy, Cow, Painted, Green Platform Base, 4 Wheels, 15½ x 20 In.	805.00
Vase, Textured, Turned Olivewood, Marked, Phil Pratt, 8 x 7 In.	145.00
Virgin & Christ Child, Pine, 19th Century, 19½ In.	246.00
Virgin Mary, Ivory, Deep Folds, 17 In.	1998.00
Virgin Of The Rosary, Flowing Robes, Deep Folds, Multicolored, 14¾ In.	353.00
Watch Hutch, Maple, Tall Case Clock Shape, Punch Work, 13¾ x 3⅜ In.	143.00
Whimsy, Book Shape, Slide Lid Edge, Painted Snake, Nail Fangs, 4 x 2¾ In.	55.00
Woman, Colorful Dress, Painted, Paneled Plinth Base, 83 In., Pair ....*illus*	5750.00
Woman With Urn, Crane, Chinese, Late 19th Century, 39 In.	353.00
Woman's Head, Birch, 12½ In.	460.00

WOODEN wares were used in all parts of the home. Wood was used for many containers and tools. Small wooden pieces are called *treenware* in England, but the term *woodenware* is more common in the United States. Additional pieces may be found in the Advertising, Kitchen, and Tool categories.

Barrel, Oak, 6 Brass Hoops, Georgian, 24 In.	940.00
Barrel, Oval, Wood Banding, 1 Open Handle, 27½ In.	259.00
Barrel, Stave Construction, Red Paint, Vines, Stencil Label, S&R, Portland, 15 x 22 In.	402.00
Basin, Round, Exterior Turned Edges, Treen, 18th Century, 3 x 17½ In.	323.00
Basket, Burl, 2 Handles, Dark Patina, 18½ x 12½ In.	518.00
Basket, Vegetable, Swing Handles, Picket Type, Wire Banding, 8½ x 13 x 20 In.	300.00
Berry Bucket, Tin Bands, Wire Swing Handle, Wood Hand Grip, 3¼ x 4¾ In.	66.00
Boat, Great Lakes Steam Freighter, Carved, Metal Fittings, Multicolored, 18½ In.	1528.00
Boat, Screw Steamer, Carved, Painted, 20¼ x 28½ In.	2350.00
Bowl, Ash Burl, Shaped Rim, Foot Ring, 19th Century, 3 x 11¾ In.	3335.00
Bowl, Blue Gray Paint, Treen, Patina, 6½ x 19½ In.	862.00
Bowl, Burl, 2⅛ x 6¾ In.	138.00
Bowl, Burl, Carved, 2 Carved Stylized Horse Heads, Oblong, 16¼ In.	1725.00
Bowl, Burl, Carved, Round, 19th Century, 5⅞ x 19½ In.	3525.00
Bowl, Burl, Dark, Steep Sided, Flat Base, 6½ x 15¾ In.	345.00
Bowl, Burl, Molded Rim, 6¾ x 14 In.	1320.00
Bowl, Burl, Native American, TIPBurl Ladle, 18th Century, 18-In. Bowl, 15-In. Ladle	3600.00
Bowl, Burl, Tapered, 4 x 9 In.	341.00
Bowl, Burl, Treen, Molded Lip & Base, 3 Incised Bands Around Center, 7⅞ x 19 In.	2530.00
Bowl, Burl, Treen, Molded Rim, 15¼ In.	9350.00
Bowl, Burl, Treen, Patina, 3 x 11¾ In.	1265.00
Bowl, Burl, Worn Rim, Old Lead Repair To Hole In Bottom, 12½ In.	1980.00
Bowl, Burl Maple, Molded Rim, Late 18th Century, 5 x 14¾ In.	2300.00
Bowl, Cover, Sponged Vinegar Seaweed, Red & Mustard, 8¼ x 7 In.	1035.00
Bowl, Oval, Carved, Exterior Geometric Design, 8¼ x 12 In.	2300.00
Bowl, Robin's-Egg Blue, Treen, Indented Rim, 5½ x 18½ In.	173.00
Bowl, Salmon Painted, Treen, Round, Incised Rim Band, Early 1800s, 7⅞ x 24 In.	1000.00
Bowl, Small Rock Maple, Melvin Lindquist, c.1973, 3¾ In.	767.00
Bowl, Trencher, Old Blue Paint, 25 x 14 In.	1380.00
Bowl, Tulipwood, Ed Moulthrop, 1970s, 12 x 18¾ In.	7800.00
Box, Saffron, Cover, Salmon, Strawberries, Flowers, Mushroom Finial, Lehn, 3½ x 2 In.	3850.00

Bucket, Georgian, Brass Bound, Oval, Navette Shape, 1800s, 14 x 13 & 13 x 15 In., Pair	1057.00
Bucket, Lid, Old Yellow Paint, Hatched Handle, Tin Bands, Wire Bail Handle, 10 x 10 In.	110.00
Bucket, Lid, Polychrome, Flowers, White, Bail, Mushroom Finial, Tin Bands, 7½ x 10 In. ...	1650.00
Bucket, Mahogany, Brassbound, Country English, Staves, Brass Handle, 18 x 17 In.	420.00
Bucket, Mahogany, Brassbound, Liner, Dutch, 19th Century, 14 In.	988.00
Bucket, Old Yellow Paint, Tin Bands, White Washed Interior, 4¼ x 10 In.	165.00
Bucket, Painted, Stave Construction, Bentwood Handle, Interlocking Bands, 9 x 7½ In.	805.00
Bucket, Red Paint, Stave Construction, Wrought Iron Bands, Wood Handle, 12 x 13 In.	345.00
Bucket, Red Paint, Vines, Multicolor, White Interior, Iron Bands, Bail, Lehnware, 7 x 9 In. ...	5775.00
Bucket, Red Paint, Vines, Multicolor, White Interior, Iron Bands, Bail, Lehnware, 8 x 10 In. .	2860.00
Bucket, Sugar, Concentric Bands, White, Red Vines, Stripes, Finial, Iron Bands, 9 x 7 In. ...	1155.00
Bucket, Sugar, Green Paint, Sapling Bands, Extended End Staves, Flat Lid, 12 x 9 In. ..*illus*	358.00
Bucket, Sugar, Lid, Red Paint, Vines, Multicolor, Iron, Porcelain Finial, Lehnware, 10 x 7 In.	2970.00
Bucket, Tar, Conestoga, Wood Lid, Leather Strap Handle, 10 In.	66.00
Bucket, Well, 4 Iron Bands, Swivel Handle, Hook Eye, 14 x 9 In.	330.00
Busk, Landscape Panels, Hearts, Gold Ground, 14 In.	403.00
Candle Dipping Frame, 12 Arm, Wood, Leather Strap Handle, 6⅞ x 13½ In.	330.00
Candle Dipping Ladder, Mortised, Pinned, 10¼ x 25¼ In.	605.00
Candle Dipping Rack, 36 Tubes, 10½ x 17 In.	880.00
Canteen, Cap, Leather Strap, Concentric Circles, c.1775, 10 In.	1298.00
Canteen, Red Paint, Keg Shape, 7 x 4 In.	300.00
Card Case, Ebony, Anglo Egyptian, Inlaid Bone, Geometric Design, 4 x 3 In.	59.00
Casket, Writing, Silver, Shagreen, Velvet Lined Interior, Bottles, Pen, Nibs, Leather Pouch ...	1410.00
Cheese Coaster, Mahogany, Early 19th Century, 16 In.	491.00
Cheese Trolley, Regency, Mahogany, Interior Divider, Brass & Leather Casters, 7 x 18 In. ...	920.00
Chest, Feed, Softwood, Slant Lid, Doweled Blocks, Ball Feet, Red Wash, 14¼ x 19 In.	605.00
Chest, Spice, 12 Drawers, Painted Green, 9 x 19 x 13 In.	345.00
Chopping Block, Oak Slab, Chamfered Legs, Early 20th Century, 32 x 16 In.	345.00
Churn, Cedar, Ash, Old Red & Blue Paint, Wooden Bands, 15½ In.	147.00
Churn, Red Paint, Stave Construction, 4 Wooden Bands, Tacks, 17 In.	288.00
Cigar Chest, Humidor, Black Forest, Carved, Lovebirds Tending Nest, 12 x 10½ In.	895.00
Clock Hands, Tower Clock, 52 In.	288.00
Coaster Set, Painted Flowers, Butterflies On Lid, Carved, Oriental Houses, 2 x 2½ In., 6 Piece .	16.00
Coat Hook, Black Forest, Carved, Terrier, Cap, Jacket, Rifle, Curved Hooks, 15½ In.	2115.00
Coffer, Marriage, Pine, Painted, Floral, Geometric Panels, Hinged Lid, Bun Feet, 29 x 44 In. .	822.00
Column Cover, Chinese Calligraphy, Painted, 100 x 10 In., Pair	585.00
Container, Turned Lid, Finial, Red Over Mustard Vinegar Decoration, 6½ x 7 In.	805.00
Cooler, Exotic Wood Bands, Black Trim, Footed, 13¾ x 16½ In.	585.00
Cornucopia, Carved, Multicolored, 20 In.	2233.00
Cup, Cream Ground, Flowers, Stepped Pedestal Base, Treen, Lehnware, 4 In.	358.00
Cup, Footed, Poplar, Pink, Strawberries, Leaves, Vines, Lehnware, c.1870, 3 In.	3300.00
Cup, Footed, Poplar, Pink, Yellow Interior, Stylized Tulips, Buds, Lehnware, c.1870	3600.00
Cup, Footed, Poplar, Tulip Form, Flared Lip, Strawberries, Leaves, Lehnware, c.1870, 2 In. ...	1200.00
Cup, Footed, Poplar, Tulip Form, Flared Rim, Pansies, Leaves, Lehnware, c.1870, 2¾ In.	3000.00
Cup, Saffron, Cover, Salmon, Multicolored, Fruit, Blue Finial, Footed, Lehnware, 5 x 2 In. ...	1100.00
Cup, Saffron, Cover, Salmon, Multicolored, Strawberry, Vine, Footed, Lehnware, 6 x 2½ In. ..	3300.00
Cup, Saffron, Salmon Ground, Flowers, Leafy Vines, Red Shaft, Flared, Footed Base, 3⅛ In. ..	3300.00
Cup, Saffron, Salmon Ground, Flowers, Vines, Red Shaft, Flare, Footed, Polychrome, 3 In. ...	1485.00
Cup & Saucer, Poplar, Mauve, Strawberries, Leaves, Blue, White Rim, Lehnware, c.1870	2400.00
Drying Rack, Cypress, Folding, 3 Sections, Cast Iron Hardware, 50 In.	940.00
Dumbbells, Mahogany, Turned Centerpiece, Ball Shape Weights, Early 1900s, 14½ In.	173.00
Eggcup, Salmon Ground, Strawberry & Vine, Multicolored, Footed, Lehnware, 2⅝ x 2 In. ..	1210.00
Firkin, Cover, Interlocking Finger Joints, 11⅜ x 10¼ In. ....*illus*	44.00
Firkin, Cover, Interlocking Finger Joints, Carved Initials, Swing Handle, 11 x 10 In. ...*illus*	165.00
Firkin, Green Paint, Overlapping Fingers, Swing Handle, It's Our Centennial Best, 1876, 17 In. .	220.00
Firkin, Old Brown Paint, Swing Handle, 12 In.	83.00
Firkin, Old Green Blue Paint, Overlapping Fingers, Brass Brads, Swing Handle, 20 In.	330.00
Firkin, Old Mustard Paint, Overlapping Finger Joint Bands, Staples, Swing Handle, 14 In. ...	248.00
Firkin, Old Yellow Paint, Wood Finger Jointed Bands, Swing Handle, 9¼ x 9 In.	523.00
Firkin, Yellow Grain Paint, Overlapping Fingers, Brass Brads, Swing Handle, 16½ In.	248.00
Firkin, Yellow Grained Paint, Finger Jointed Bands, Swing Handle, 12 x 11¾ In.	248.00
Frame, Walnut, 10 Heart Terminals, 7½ x 8½ In.	495.00
Hat Block, Adjustable, 2-Way	270.00
Hourglass, Blown Glass, Carved, Olive Green Paint, 19th Century, 6½ In.	2468.00
Humidor, Oak, Nickel Plate, Railroad, 2-Part Interior, Ash Tray, Match Holder, 13 x 8 In. ...	1438.00
Jar, Burl, Treen, Lid, Mushroom Finial, Pedestal Base, 8½ x 5⅛ In.	303.00

Wooden, Firkin, Cover, Interlocking Finger Joints, Carved Initials, Swing Handle, 11 x 10 In. $165.00

Wooden, Towel Holder, Jiggs, Painted, Black, Gray, White, c.1930, 12½ In. $47.00

TIP

To remove the odor from a wooden bowl, try washing it with baking soda or vinegar and then airing it in sunlight. As a last resort, use diluted household bleach. Soak the bowl for about 15 minutes, then rinse with full-strength vinegar, then clear water. If this does not remove the odor, repeat the process with a stronger solution of bleach.

W

Worcester, Urn, Oval Panels, Flowers, Jeweled, Cobalt Blue, Gilt Trim, Flight & Barr, 9¾ In.
$1955.00

World War I, Feed Bag, U.S. Cavalry, Green, Straps, Stenciled U.S., P.B. & Co.
$60.00

World War I, Pillow, Cover Only, Silk, Flag Of Nation At War With Germany, 1912, Frame
$25.00

Jar, Cover, Beehive Shape, Incised Ring Turnings On Side, Painted Brown, 8½ In.	235.00
Jar, Goblet Form, Carved, Flowers, Leaves, Acanthus Finial, 8½ In.	121.00
Jar, Lid, Incised Concentric Circles, Treen, Ball Finial, Pedestal Base, 10¼ x 4½ In.	209.00
Jar, Lid, Treen, 2-Piece Vase Shape Finial, Pedestal Base, 13½ In.	357.00
Jar, Lid, Treen, Ball Finial, Footed, 8 In.	165.00
Jar, Tapered, Old Gray Paint, Sapling Bands, Lid, 6¼ x 4½ In.	176.00
Jewelry Chest, Oriental, Rosewood, Inner Drawers, Brass, Inlay, c.1950, 11 x 8 In.	35.00
Jug, Wine, Stave Construction, Oak, Copper Rivets, France, 1800s, 11½ x 6 In.	395.00
Keg, Gunpowder, Oak, Brass, Hazard Kentucky Rifle Gunpowder	385.00
Keg, Water, Oak, Green Paint, Marked, R & R, Stamped, Iron Bands, Leather, Cork, 9 x 6 In.	880.00
Liquor Case, Brass Mounted, Hinged Lid, Iron Latch, Handles, 12 Bottles, 11 x 16 In.	1058.00
Log Cabin, Model, 1 Room, Porch, Logs On Tongue & Groove Pine Base, 21 x 25 x 22 In.	1150.00
Log Cabin, Model, Fence, Stone, Lichen, Painted, Metal Gable Roof, 2 Chimneys, 19 x 28 In.	490.00
Log Cabin, Model, Porch, Stacked Log Fireplace, 15½ x 24 x 15½ In.	345.00
Niddy Noddy, Wood, Green & White Paint, 17¾ In.	88.00
Noisemaker, Walnut, Box Form, Tiered Posts, Toothed Cog, Iron Handle, 11 x 9½ x 5½ In.	110.00
Pail, Green Painted, Pine Staves, Iron Hoop Construction, Wire Bail, 4⅝ In.	529.00
Patent Model, Fence, September 14th 1858, 6⅛ x 1½ x 17¼ In.	588.00
Pedestal, Multicolored, Pair, 31½ In.	1528.00
Plate, Treen, Molded Lip, 10½ In. Diam.	715.00
Plate Rack, Wall Mounted, Pine, Cutouts, 18 Slots, 3 Bar Top, Soap Holder, 22 In.	431.00
Rack, Tobacco & Pipe, Wall Mount, Pine, 2-Tier Shelf, 19 Slots, Drawers, 22 x 17¾ In.	29.00
Rooster, Crowing, Cutout, L Shaped Surround, Polychrome, Plywood, 29 x 24 In.	400.00
Salt, Salmon, Multicolored, Strawberry & Vine, Footed, Lehnware, 2 x 1¾ In.	248.00
Scoop, Burl, Tab Handle, 2 x 7 In.	2115.00
Scoop, Grain, Pine, Bentwood Oak Handles, Wrought & Cut Nails, 1800s, 28 x 55 In.	201.00
Scoop, Wire Bail Handle, Nailed Construction, 20¼ x 11¼ In.	138.00
Shelf, Brown Painted, 2 Shelves, Cutout Scrolled Ends, 32½ x 23½ x 5½ In.	1645.00
Shelf, Leaves, Roots, Carved, Germany, 1900s, 12½ x 23½ x 8¾ In.	447.00
Shoeshine Stand, Turkish, Brass, Teakwood, Dome Box, Fitted Bottles, 20 x 32½ In.	294.00
Spoon Rack, Shaped Crest, Flowers, 2 Pierced Shelves, 6 Pewter Spoons, 12 x 6½ In.	220.00
Tool Chest, Birch, Walnut, Mahogany, False Bottom, Sliding Tops, Drawers, 20 x 37⅜ x 21 In.	3500.00
Towel Holder, Jiggs, Painted, Black, Gray, White, c.1930, 12½ In. ....*illus*	47.00
Towel Rack, Pine, Carved Fan, Tulips, Blue, Green Paint, 15½ x 19½ x 4½ In.	1175.00
Tray, Lacquered, Handmade, Quail In Landscape, 18 x 24 In.	64.00
Tray, Mother-Of-Pearl Inlay, Bird Perched On Flowering Tree, Chinese, 22 x 15¼ In.	153.00
Tray, Pine, Beveled Corners, Green Paint, Cutout Handles, 3½ x 26 x 17½ In.	115.00
Trencher, Carved, Painted, 18 In.	345.00
Trencher, Hand Hewn, Blue Paint Exterior, 12½ x 22 In.	460.00
Trencher, Painted Red, 26 In.	316.00
Trencher, Red Paint, 19th Century, 5½ x 27¼ In.	825.00
Trencher, Yellow Paint, Openwork Handle, 6¾ x 26 x 19 In.	220.00
Tub, Lid, Treen, Ebonized Rings, Slotted Staves, 4 x 4¼ In.	132.00
Urn, Cutlery, Mahogany, Georgian Style, Telescoping Lid, Late 1800s, 27 In., Pair	3995.00
Vase, 2 Quails Next To Tree Trunk Vase, Black Forest, 4¾ x 4⅜ In.	44.00
Vase, Game Bird Next To Tree Trunk Form Vase, Black Forest, 3¾ x 4¼ In.	44.00
Vase, Tree Form, Flowers, Leaves, Prancing Mountain Goats, Black Forest, 17⅝ x 10 In.	220.00
Wagon Hatchet, Conestoga, Punches Above, Along Length, Marked, c.1813, 13 In.	105.00
Wheelbarrow, Red & Blue Paint, Spoke Wheel, Iron Rim, Child's, 12½ x 42 x 17 In.	490.00

WORCESTER porcelains were made in Worcester, England, from 1751. The firm went through many name changes and eventually, in 1862, became The Royal Worcester Porcelain Company Ltd. Collectors often refer to Dr. Wall, Barr, Flight, and other names that indicate time periods or artists at the factory. It became part of Royal Worcester Spode Ltd. in 1976. Related pieces may be found in the Royal Worcester category.

Bowl, Dr. Wall, Late 18th Century, 6⅝ In., Pair	117.00
Bowl, Footed, Precipice, Blue & White, c.1770, 8 In.	150.00
Butter, Underplate, Blue Chinoiserie, Flower Finial, Flared Handles, 6⅛ In. Underplate	717.00
Dessert Set, Imari Pattern, Flight, Barr & Barr, England, 18 Piece	3554.00
Dish, Butterflies, Blue Border, 4 Scroll Edge Panels, Gilt, Scallop Edge, c.1770, 11¾ In.	780.00
Dish, Junket, Central Roundel, Cartouches, Flowers, Basket Molded, Yellow, c.1765, 9 In.	3600.00
Dish, Junket, Pinecone, Blue Printed, Scalloped Edge, c.1775, 10 In.	1603.00
Figurine, Warblers, Cerulean, Dorothy Doughty, 1965, 9¼ x 5 x 4⅞ In., Pair	1950.00
Jug, Painted, Multicolored, Flowers, c.1770, 3½ In.	146.00
Mug, Marquis Of Granby, Transfer, Portrait, Fame With Trumpet, Mars, c.1760, 3⅜ In.	3840.00

Plate, Blue Printed Gilliflower, c.1780, 9¾ In.	187.00
Plate, Dessert, Bengal Tiger, Scalloped Edge, c.1770, 4 Piece	720.00
Plate, Dinner Set, Japan Pattern, c.1811-20, 6 Piece	660.00
Plate, Rich Queens, Armorial, Earl Of Errol, Crest, Imari Border, Flower Panels, 9½ In.	3840.00
Plate Set, Botanical Fern, Goldware, c.1890, 9 In., 4 Piece	186.00
Platter, Imari Pattern, Oval, Flight, Barr & Barr, England, 16¼ In.	2039.00
Platter, Oval, Painted, Center Flower, Edge Decoration, Flight, Barr & Barr, c.1840, 23 In.	467.00
Tea Bowl & Saucer, Mother & Child, Blue Printed, c.1780, 5 In.	257.00
Teapot, Fluted Ball Shape, Flowers, Straight Spout, Loop Handle, Finial, 1700s, 6 In.	717.00
Urn, Oval Panels, Flowers, Jeweled, Cobalt Blue, Gilt Trim, Flight & Barr, 9¾ In. . . . . . .*illus*	1955.00
Vase, Grainger, Reticulated, Cover, c.1800, 7 In.	109.00

WORLD WAR I and World War II souvenirs are collected today. Be careful not to store anything that includes live ammunition. Your local police will tell you how to dispose of the explosives. See also Sword and Trench Art.

WORLD WAR I

Bag, 112th Infantry Division, Flag, Pockets, Original Ties	150.00
Bowl, Nation's Peace, Blue & Red Edge Stripe, 5 Country Flags, Dove, 6 In.	10.00
Bowl, Patriotic, Flags, Field Marshall Paul Von Hindenburg, German, 1916	85.00
Buttons, Brass, 112th Infantry Division, 2 Large, 2 Small	150.00
Canteen, U.S. Army, Aluminum	12.00
Dog Tags, Shirely Stealey, 112th Infantry Division	80.00
Feed Bag, U.S. Cavalry, Green, Straps, Stenciled U.S., P.B. & Co. . . . .*illus*	60.00
Medal, Army, British, Private D.R. Saunders, Royal Sussex Regiment, King George V	125.00
Pillow, Cover Only, Silk, Flag Of Nation At War With Germany, 1912, Frame . . . .*illus*	25.00
Pin, All Hell Can't Stop Us, Berlin Via America, ⅞ In.	45.00
Pin, If We Cannot Go, Let Us Help Those Who Can, ⅞ In.	31.00
Plate, Dinner, Nation's Peace, Blue & Red Edge Stripe, 5 Country Flags, Dove, 9¼ In.	24.00
Poster, 4th Liberty Loan, Sweep Them Out Of France, German Soldiers, Cardboard, 12 x 22 In.	255.00
Poster, Don't Waste Food While Others Starve, c.1914, 29½ x 19½ In.	708.00
Poster, Hun Or Home, Buy More Liberty Bonds, 30 x 20 In.	582.00
Puttees, Wool, U.S. Army	18.00

WORLD WAR II

B 29 Airplane, 100 Dollar War Bond, 1¼ In.	106.00
Badge, Douglas Aircraft, 3 Planes Flying, Bond-A-Month, Silvered Brass, ⅞ In.	42.00
Belt, Web, Khaki, Brass Officer's Buckle, U.S. Army, Size 36	14.00
Blanket, Wool, Eggshell Color, U.S.N. Medical	45.00
Bombsight, Sperry, S-1 Precision	1121.00
Booklet, Health For Victory Club Meal Planning, Westinghouse, 1943, 71 Pages	8.00
Bucket, U.S. Army, Canvas, Lined, Olive Drape, 8 In.	15.00
Canteen, German Officers', Leather Straps, Wool Cover, Plastic Cap, 10 x 7 In.	55.00
First Aid Pouch, Web, Khaki, U.S. Army	8.00
Leggings, White, 7 Hooks, U.S. Navy, Size 16, Pair	12.00
Matchbox Holder, In The Allies Grip, Hitler, Celluloid, England, 1½ x 2¼ x 1 In.	111.00
Mess Kit, Pan, Plate, U.S. Army	13.00
Pillow Cover, Fort Benning Georgia, Airplanes, Tank, Soldiers, Mother, 16 x 16 In.	18.00
Pin, Brass, Over The Top, Portland, Oregon, 1917, Eagle, Cannons, 1⅛ In.	25.00
Pin, Dentistry To Victory, Make It Gold, May, 1942, 1¾ In.	43.00
Pin, Food For Freedom, V, Pig On Hind Legs, 1¼ In.	112.00
Pin, Gen. MacArthur, 1¼ In.	45.00
Pin, Gen. MacArthur, 2½ In.	43.00
Pin, Hitler Hates Me, I've Pledged 10 Percent For Bonds, ⅝ In.	73.00
Pin, On To Victory, Soldier, Sailor, Marine, Letter V, 1942, 1⁹⁄₁₆ In.	42.00
Pin, Pabst Breweries, War Bond Man, 1¼ In.	54.00
Pin, Remember (Mounted Pearl) Harbor, Brass Luster, Die Cut, 1⅜ In. . . . .*illus*	52.00
Pin, Remember Pearl Harbor, Flag, 1¼ In.	62.00
Pin, Remember Pearl Harbor, Red Border, 1 In.	28.00
Pin, Victory, Bakelite Plastic, Ribbon Accent, Curled Ends, Letter V, 2 In.	43.00
Pin, Victory, Hand Holding V, Brass Luster, White Metal, Rhinestones On Cuff, 2¾ In. . . .*illus*	190.00
Pin, Victory, Morse Code Brass Accents, Plastic, 2 x ¼ In.	37.00
Pin, Victory, V, Red Rhinestones, Brass Luster Mount, 2½ In. . . . .*illus*	51.00
Pin, Victory, V, Sterling Silver, On Card, Guaranteed Indian Made, 1½ In. . . . .*illus*	95.00
Pin Back, Anti-War, Keep Us Out Of War, Philadelphia Badge Co., 1939, ⅞ In.	9.50
Puzzle, Put Hitler In The Dog House, Cardboard Tiles, Box, 3½ x 4½ In.	144.00

World War II, Pin, Remember (Mounted Pearl) Harbor, Brass Luster, Die Cut, 1⅜ In. $52.00

World War II, Pin, Victory, Hand Holding V, Brass Luster, White Metal, Rhinestones On Cuff, 2¾ In. $190.00

World War II, Pin, Victory, V, Red Rhinestones, Brass Luster Mount, 2½ In. $51.00

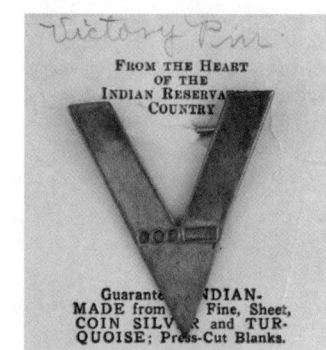

World War II, Pin, Victory, V, Sterling Silver, On Card, Guaranteed Indian Made, 1½ In. $95.00

W

World's Fair, Bottle, 1934, Chicago, Marking Repeal Of Prohibition, Silver Lip & Stopper, 10 In. $120.00

World's Fair, Figurine, 1893, Chicago, Dog, Porcelain, 6 In. $155.00

World's Fair, Lamp, 1901, Buffalo, Milk Glass, North, South America Map, Nutmeg Burner, 8½ In. $1610.00

World's Fair, Pitcher, 1893, Chicago, Machinery Hall & Japan's Expo Building, Satsuma, 7¼ In. $359.00

Ration Book, Office Of Price Administration, Enes W. Cole, Partially Used, USA	24.00
Seaman's Cap, Navy Wool, U.S. Navy, Size 6¾	20.00
Sewing Kit, Oil Cloth, Olive Drab, Snap Closure, U.S. Army, Civilian Mfg.	12.00
Sleeping Bag, Wool, Olive Drab, With Case, U.S. Army	65.00
Stickpin, Churchill With Cigar, Brass Luster, c.1940, 1¾ In.	54.00
Stickpin, Mop Up Japan, Mop Shape, Sterling Silver, 1⅝ In.	101.00
Tablecloth, FDR, Hitler, Mussolini, 50 x 50 In.	202.00
Tool, Entrenching, U.S. Army	25.00
Trousers, Officer, Wool Gabardine, Green, U.S. Marine Corps, 32 x 30 In.	30.00
Trousers, Wool, 13 Buttons, Flap Front, Enlisted Man, U.S. Navy, 28 x 31 In.	25.00
Vest, Ammo, Military, Khaki OD, 1942, Size 38 Or 40 Chest	16.00

WORLD'S FAIR souvenirs from all of the fairs are collected. The first fair was the Great Exhibition of 1851 in London. Some other important exhibitions and fairs include Philadelphia, 1876 (Centennial); Chicago, 1893 (World's Columbian); Buffalo, 1901 (Pan-American); St. Louis, 1904 (Louisiana Purchase); San Francisco, 1915 (Panama-Pacific); Philadelphia, 1926 (Sesquicentennial); Chicago, 1933 (Century of Progress); Cleveland, 1936 (Great Lakes); San Francisco, 1939 (Golden Gate International); New York, 1939 (World of Tomorrow); Seattle, 1962 (Century 21); New York, 1964; Montreal, 1967; New Orleans, 1984; Tsukuba, Japan, 1985; Vancouver, B.C., 1986; Brisbane, Australia, 1988; Seville, Spain, 1992; Genoa, Italy, 1992; Seoul, South Korea, 1993; and Lisbon, Portugal, 1998. Memorabilia of fairs include directories, pictures, fabrics, ceramics, etc. Memorabilia from other similar celebrations may be listed in the Souvenir category.

Mug, 1901, Pan-American Exposition, Drinking Scene, Bristol Glaze, 5 In.	165.00
Badge, 1939, New York, Junior Police, Shield Shape	88.00
Badge, 1962, Seattle, Security Officer, Century 21, Nickel Plated, 3 In.	168.00
Bank, 1964, New York, Silver Luster, Metal, 10½ In.	305.00
Bank, 1939 New York, U.S. Royal Giant Tire, Battery Operated, Box, 7 x 13 x 11 In.	339.00
Banner, 1892, Columbian Exposition, Christopher Columbus, Stars, Cotton, 21 x 36 In.	216.00
Banner, 1937, Paris, Airplanes, Buildings, 18½ x 45 In.	162.00
Bookends, 1939, New York, Marble	321.00
Bookends, 1939, New York, Syroco, Metal Base, 6 x 4½ In.	85.00
Bottle, 1893, Chicago, Columbian Exposition, Patent Medicine, Columbus, 6¼ In.	225.00
Bottle, 1934, Chicago, Marking Repeal Of Prohibition, Silver Lip & Stopper, 10 In. ....*illus*	120.00
Bust, 1893, Chicago, Columbian Exposition, Pressed Glass, Satin, Embossed, 5¼ In.	66.00
Change Holder, 1964, New York, Vinyl, Triangle, Orange, Child's	30.00
Clock, 1893, Chicago, Columbian Expostition, Burnett's Extracts, 30½ In.	4183.00
Coffee Set, 1939, New York, Porcelier, 8-In. Pot, 3 Piece	476.00
Compact, 1939, New York, Blue, Square, 3½ In.	88.00
Compact, 1939, New York, Helena Rubinstein, Flags, White Ground, Plastic, Round, 3 In.	126.00
Compact, 1939, New York, Trylon & Perisphere, Round, Plastic, Metal Rim, 3 In.	88.00
Desk, 1939, Art Deco, Walnut Veneer, 8 Stacked Drawers, 1 Central Drawer	1853.00
Figurine, 1893, Chicago, Dog, Porcelain, 6 In. ....*illus*	155.00
Flag, 1939, New York, Cotton, Pole, 30½ x 21½ In.	212.00
Handkerchief, 1876, Philadelphia International Exhibition, Frame, 20 x 33 In.	270.00
Handkerchief, 1939 New York, Purple, Red, Blue, Green, Costumes, 9 x 9 In.	15.00
Hat, Guide, 1934, Chicago, Khaki Cloth, Mann Uniform	300.00
Lamp, 1901, Buffalo, Milk Glass, North, South America Map, Nutmeg Burner, 8½ In. ..*illus*	1610.00
Lamp, 1939, New York, Frosted Glass, Chrome Base, Battery Operated, 5½ In.	110.00
License Plate, 1939, New York, Embossed	320.00
Match Dispenser, 1933, Chicago, Elephant, 6 x 8 In.	247.00
Match Safe, 1901, Buffalo, Pan-American, Copper Colored Metal, 3½ x 2 In.	108.00
Medal, 1893, Chicago, Columbian Exposition, Columbus Arrival, Saint-Gaudens, Case	335.00
Medal, 1939, New York, Trylon & Perisphere, World Of Tomorrow, Today, Yesterday, 3 In.	65.00
Mustard Pot, 1893, Chicago, Columbian Exposition, Pressed Glass, King's Crown, 4 In.	88.00
Napkin Ring, 1939, New York, Catalin, Green, Orange, Fair Symbols, 2 Piece	168.00
Pencil, 1934, Chicago, Century Of Progress, Marbleized, Avon, 5 In.	49.00
Pencil Sharpener, 1939, New York, Trylon & Perisphere, Catalin, Yellow, Red, Black	70.00
Pennant, 1915, San Francisco, 24½ x 58 In.	311.00
Pin, 1893, Columbian Exposition, Half Dollar, Beaded Frame, Bar Pin, Silver Luster, 1⁵⁄₁₆ In.	91.00
Pin, 1904, St. Louis, Gen. Cronje, Hero Of Paardeberg, Boer War, Celluloid, 1½ In.	168.00
Pin, 1915, Panama-Pacific, San Francisco, Red, Yellow Cross, Blue, Celluloid, 1½ In.	42.00
Pin, 1915, Panama-Pacific International Expo, 1½ In.	37.00
Pin, 1931, Chicago, Employee, Clerk, Welcome Visitors, 2¹⁄₁₆ In.	92.00
Pin, 1939, New York, Flower, California	217.00

Pin, 1939, New York, Flower, Connecticut 147.00
Pin, 1939, New York, Flower, Pennsylvania 88.00
Pin, 1939, New York, Ford, 37th Anniversary, August 22, Round 103.00
Pin, 1939, New York, Guernsey's, Round, 1¼ In. 76.00
Pin, 1939, New York, Ice, Peter & Penelope Rabbit, Red Ground, Round, 2 In. 51.00
Pin, 1939, New York, Lady's Hand Holding Medal, Trylon & Perisphere, Brass, 2½ In. 22.00
Pin, 1939, New York, Odd Fellows Day, 37854, Round, Celluloid, 3¼ In. 153.00
Pin, 1939, New York, Puerto Rico Pavilion, Celluloid, 1¼ In. 17.00
Pin, 1939, New York, Wonder Bread Day, Celluloid, 2¼ In. 204.00
Pin, 1964, New York, Napa Convention, 2 In. 31.00
Pin Tray, 1904, St. Louis, Antikamnia Chem., Insomnia, Nervousness, Tin Litho, 3 x 5 In. ... 80.00
Pitcher, 1893, Chicago, Machinery Hall & Japan's Expo Building, Satsuma, 7¼ In. ....*illus* 359.00
Pitcher & Bowl, 1876, Philadelphia, Centennial, Ironstone, 9¼-In. Pitcher, 14-In. Bowl ... 747.00
Plate, 1893, Chicago, Columbia Exposition, Horticultural Building, Pink Transfer, 8 In. 60.00
Plate, 1904, St. Louis, Goofus Glass, Festival Hall, Cascade Gardens, 7¼ In. 50.00
Pocket Knife, 1939, New York, 2 Blades, Trylon & Perisphere In Handle, 3⅛ In. 5.00
Postcard, 1904, St. Louis, Louisiana Purchase Expo, Palace Of Education, Woven Silk   *illus* 59.00
Pouch, 1939, New York, Trylon & Perisphere, Red, Green, Blue On Tan, Zippered, 4 x 6 In. .. 15.00
Purse, 1964, New York, Vinyl, Metal Snap, Strap, Unisphere, Child's, 7 x 5½ In. 45.00
Ring, 1939, New York, Enameled Logo, Trylon & Perisphere, Blue & Orange 52.00
Scale, 1876, Philadelphia, Centennial, Fairbanks, Painted, Metal, 5 x 9½ In. 360.00
Spoon, 1915, San Francisco Panama-Pacific, Various Pictures 24.00
Spoon, 1493-1893, Scenic, 4¼ In., 4 Piece 39.00
Stickpin, 1901, Pan American Exposition, Buffalo, 1½ x ⅞ In. 33.00
Tankard, 1901, Buffalo, Pan-American, 7½ In. 514.00
Tape Measure, 1901, Buffalo, Pan-American, Flag, Celluloid, Whitehead & Hoag Co. 56.00
Teapot, 1939, New York, Porcelier, 5½ x 8 In. ....*illus* 71.00
Thermometer, 1939, New York, Trylon & Perisphere, Bakelite, 2¼ In. 24.00
Thermometer, 1939, New York, Trylon & Perisphere, Key Shape, Celluloid, 8 x 3 In. 9.00
Tie Rack, 1939, New York, Trylon & Perisphere, Syroco, 5¾ In. 31.00
Tip Tray, 1915, San Francisco, A-Best-O Electric Iron, Safety Always, Saves Current, 4¼ In. .. 130.00
Toy, Bus, 1933, Century Of Progress, G.M.C., Arcade, 10½ In. 315.00
Toy, Tractor & Trailer, 1939, New York, Cast Iron, Tin Roof, Decals, Arcade, 7 In. ......*illus* 525.00
Tumbler, 1939, New York, Hall Of Shelter, 5¼ In. 10.00
Vase, 1893, Chicago, Columbian Exposition, Ruby Band, Annie Griffiths, Flared, 4 In. ..*illus* 16.00
Vase, 1904, St. Louis, Palace Of Machinery, Blue & White, Handles, Roland & Marcellus, 9 In. .. 530.00
Wallet, 1939, New York, Trylon & Perisphere, Coney Island, Suede, 4 x 8 In. 31.00

WPA is the abbreviation for Works Progress Administration, a program created by executive order in 1935 to provide jobs for millions of unemployed Americans. Artists were hired to create murals, paintings, drawings, and sculptures for public buildings. Pieces are marked *WPA* and may have the artist's name on them.

Book, Bundle Of Troubles & Other Tarheel Tales, North Carolina, 1943, 206 Pages 80.00
Book, Mississippi, Guide To The Magnolia State, Federal Writers' Project, 1938 .... 35.00
Handbook, Our Job With The WPA, Workers Handbook, 8 x 5½ In., 1936 .... 10.00
Panel, Masonite, Pencil, Guache, Watercolor, 9 Historical Scenes, 9 Panels, 1935, 15 x 5 In. .. 1800.00
Poster, Pennsylvania, Amish Costumes & Handicrafts, Tulip, Frame, 18½ x 15½ In. 440.00
Poster, Pennsylvania, Amish Family, Rooster, Katherine Milhous, Frame, 21 x 17 In. 605.00
Poster, Pennsylvania, Amish Life Vignettes, Katherine Milhous, Frame, 20 x 16 In. 413.00
Poster, Pennsylvania, Amish School Children, Katherine Milhous, Frame, 23 x 19 In. 550.00
Poster, Pennsylvania, Little Red Schoolhouse, Children, Katherine Milhous, 20 x 16 In. 440.00
Print, Big Maple Tree, A.G. Arnold, Federal Art Project, Frame, 1936, 21 x 16 In. 138.00
Watercolor, San Francisco, California, Cityscape, c.1930-40, 31 x 20 In. 2025.00

WRISTWATCHES came into use during World War I. Wristwatches are listed here by manufacturer or as advertising or character watches. Wristwatches may also be listed in other categories. Pocket watches are listed in the Watch category.

Advertising, Budweiser Beer, Bullwinkle & Others, Jay Ward, Original Strap, 1971 .... 225.00
Ardath, 2 Round Dials, Gold Flexible Band, 17 Jewel, 1935, 9¾ x 1¼ In. ....*illus* 132.00
Audiguet, Platinum, Diamond, Ivorytone Dial, Manual, Art Deco, 18K Gold, 17 Jewel 1293.00
Baume & Mercier, Woman's, 18K Gold, Diamond, Goldtone Dial, Braided Links, 6 In. 1000.00
Baume & Mercier, Woman's, Lapis Dial, 18K White Gold Case, Diamonds, Sapphires 962.00
Bulova, Woman's, 3 Diamonds, 17 Jewel, Leather Band, c.1949, 8¾ In. ....*illus* 199.00
Cartier, Must 21, Quartz Movement, Stainless Steel Case, Band, Gold Crown, Trim 598.00

World's Fair, Postcard, 1904, St. Louis, Louisiana Purchase Expo, Palace Of Education, Woven Silk
$59.00

World's Fair, Teapot, 1939, Porcelier, 5½ x 8 In.
$71.00

World's Fair, Toy, Tractor & Trailer, 1939, New York, Cast Iron, Tin Roof, Decals, Arcade, 7 In.
$525.00

World's Fair, Vase, 1893, Chicago, Columbian Exposition, Ruby Band, Annie Griffiths, Flared, 4 In.
$16.00

Wristwatch, Ardath, 2 Round Dials, Gold Flexible Band, 17 Jewel, 1935, 9¾ x 1¼ In.
$132.00

Wristwatch, Bulova, Woman's, 3 Diamonds, 17 Jewel, Leather Band, c.1949, 8¾ In. $199.00

Wristwatch, Elgin, Woman's, Diamonds, Elliptical Face, 14K White Gold, c.1950 $560.00

Wristwatch, Glycine, Woman's, Oval Face, Diamond Surround, 14K Gold, Integral Links, c.1960 $299.00

Wristwatch, Lewitt & Co., Diamonds, Emeralds, 18K White Gold, 17 Jewel, Art Deco Style $353.00

Yellowware, Creamer, Rolled Rim, 8 In. $29.00

Cartier, Stainless Steel, Silvertone, Dial, Roman, Baton Numerals	880.00
Character, Bugs Bunny, Carrot Hands, New Haven Clock & Watch Co., Box, c.1951	2800.00
Character, Space Explorer, Bradley, Case, Late 1960s, 1 x 6 In.	191.00
Character, Tom Corbett Space Cadet, Chrome Case, Leather Bands, Ingraham, c.1951	300.00
Character, Wonder Woman, Leather Band, Dabs, Plastic Case, 1977, 1⅜-In. Dial	185.00
Elgin, Woman's, Diamonds, Elliptical Face, 14K White Gold, c.1950 ....*illus*	560.00
Elgin, Woman's, Platinum, Diamond, Arabic, Abstract Numerals, 19 Jewel, 6⅜ In.	1763.00
Enigma, Bulgari, Quartz Movement, Mother-Of-Pearl Dial, Stainless Steel Case, Date	534.00
Geneve, Woman's, Quartz Movement, 14K Yellow Gold Case, Band	652.00
Georg Jensen, Woman's, Stainless Steel Case, Integral Bangle Band, No. 227	511.00
Glycine, Woman's, Oval Face, Diamond Surround, 14K Gold, Integral Links, c.1960 ...*illus*	299.00
Gruen, Rectangular Case, 14K White Gold, Embossed Bezel, 1920s, 1 x 1½ In.	300.00
Hamilton, Platinum, Diamond Melee, Ivory Tone Dial, 17 Jewel, 6½ In.	1175.00
IWC, Da Vinci, Rattrapante, Perpetual Calendar, 43 Jewel, Leather Band	15480.00
Lewitt & Co., Diamonds, Emeralds, 18K White Gold, 17 Jewel, Art Deco Style ....*illus*	353.00
Longines, Woman's, Stainless, Gold	122.00
Movado, Sapphire, Diamond, Silvertone Dial, Roman Numerals, 14K Gold, 17 Jewel	880.00
Omega, Speedmaster Automatic Chronograph, Commemorating 1969 Moon Landing	700.00
Omega, Woman's, Oval, Goldtone Dial, 14K Gold, Interwoven Bracelet, 6¾ In.	236.00
Oscar Heyman & Bros., Woman's, Diamond Melee, Sapphire, 1944	6463.00
Patek Philippe, Woman's, Goldtone Dial, Abstract Numbers, 18K Gold, 7¼ In.	2350.00
Patek Philippe, Woman's, Goldtone Dial, Arabic Numerals, 18K Gold	2233.00
Rolex, 14K Yellow Gold, 15 Jewel, Arabic Numerals, Lizard Skin Band	717.00
Rolex, No. 5513, Oyster, Perpetual, Submariner, 17 Jewel, Automatic Wind, c.1962	2993.00
Rolex, Oyster Perpetual, Gold Tone Dial, Fluted Bezel, 14K Gold, Papers, Box	3173.00
Rolex, Woman's, No. 2616, 18 Jewel, 18K Yellow Gold Case, Mesh Band	495.00
Rolex, Woman's, Oyster, Perpetual Datejust, 29 Jewel, 18K Yellow Gold Case, c.1984	5716.00
Rolex, Woman's, Oyster, Perpetual, Stainless, Yellow Gold	936.00
Tiffany & Co., Art Deco, Platinum, Diamond Melee, Grosgrain Bracelet, Box, 6 In.	1000.00
Tiffany & Co., Art Deco, Platinum, Sapphire, Diamond Melee, 17 Jewel, 6¼ In.	1880.00
Vacheron & Constantin, Triple-Date, 17 Jewel, 18K Yellow Gold Case, c.1945	5779.00

YELLOWWARE is a heavy earthenware made of a yellowish clay. It varies in color from light yellow to orange-yellow. Many nineteenth- and twentieth-century kitchen bowls and jugs were made of yellowware. It was made in England and in the United States. Another form of pottery that is sometimes classed as yellowware is listed in this book in the Mocha category.

Baker, Signed, 3 x 12 x 9 In.	27.00
Bank, Figural, Bulldog, 5⅛ In.	72.00
Bank, Pig, 5 x 2½ In.	155.00
Bank, Pig, Sponged, Green & Brown, 6 x 3 In.	110.00
Batter Bowl, Spout, 6½ x 14 In.	55.00
Bean Pot, Handles, c.1880, 2 In.	303.00
Bowl, Blue Bands, 10 In.	40.00
Bowl, Brown Band, 12 In.	60.00
Bowl, Mocha Caramel Glaze, 8¼ x 3¼ In.	154.00
Bowl, Pink & Blue Bands, 7 In.	20.00
Bowl, Rolled Lip, 10 Tall Columns, Round Top, 4 In.	174.00
Bowl, Vegetable, Rim, 9½ In.	110.00
Chamber Pot, c.1880, 1¾ In.	176.00
Creamer, Cover, 8 In.	27.00
Creamer, Pewter Lid, Thumblift, Applied Ear Handle, 5 In.	330.00
Creamer, Rolled Rim, 8 In. ....*illus*	29.00
Cup, Caramel Spongework, Applied Handle, 1880, 8 Oz.	155.00
Dish, Corncob Mold, Fluted Interior, Rim, 4 x 8½ In.	92.00
Flowerpot, 8 In.	27.00
Jug, Harvest, Keg Shape, Spout, Loop Handles, Incised Lines, 7 In.	358.00
Mixing Bowl, 6½ x 14¼ In.	110.00
Pie Plate, c.1880, 10½ In.	125.00
Pitcher, Game, 9½ In.	127.00
Pitcher, Slip Decorated, Light Blue Band, 8 Black Bands, Early 1800s, 7 In.	650.00
Pitcher, Sponge, Green & Brown, 9½ In.	92.00
Rolling Pin, Turned Handles, 15 In.	374.00
Rolling Pin, Wood Handles, 14 In.	385.00

W

Teapot, Rockingham Glaze, Branch Handle		275.00
Washboard, Pine Frame, Brass Screws, 23 x 12½ In.		1195.00
Water Cooler, Band Decoration, Metal Spigot, 15½ In.		94.00
Window Props, Lions Pride, c.1820, 5½ x 4 In., Pair		395.00

ZANESVILLE Art Pottery was founded in 1900 by David Schmidt in Zanesville, Ohio. The firm made faience umbrella stands, jardinieres, and pedestals. The company closed in 1962. Many pieces are marked with just the words *La Moro*.

LA MORO

Basket, White Glossy Glaze, 8¾ In.	40.00
Bowl, Bulb, Black Glossy Glaze, 6½ In. Diam.	45.00
Flowerpot, Homespun, Green, Marked, 1008, 9½ x 11½ In.	100.00
Jardiniere, Aqua, 5½ x 5½ In.	69.00
Jardiniere, Aqua, Flared, 5 x 6½ In.	32.00
Jardiniere, Homespun, 7 x 8¾ In.	50.00
Planter, Pig, Green Glossy Glaze, Large	45.00
Planter, Pig, Green Glossy Glaze, Small	45.00
Vase, Blue Glossy Glaze, Yellow Clay Bottom, 4 x 6 In.	36.00
Vase, Carved Female Figure, Purple Matte Glaze, Stoneware, 11 x 6½ In. ....*illus*	240.00
Vase, Green Matte, Marked, 8½ In.	121.00
Vase, Homespun, White Drip Over Brown Ring, Cylindrical, Marked, 17¾ In.	100.00

ZSOLNAY pottery was made in Hungary after 1862 and was characterized by Persian, Art Nouveau, or Hungarian motifs. A series of new Zsolnay figurines with green-gold luster finish is available in many shops today. Early Zsolnay was not marked, but by 1878 the tower trademark was used.

Bowl, Centerpiece, 4 Cherubs With Bowl, Fruit Edges, Blue Iridescent Glaze, 7½ x 13 In. *illus*	1495.00
Box, Cover, Egyptian Figures, Carved, Round, Signed	395.00
Ewer, Handle, Woman, Drinking From Fountain, Luster Gold, Green Glaze, 1900, 16½ In. ..	9600.00
Ewer, Pierced, Blue & Red Enamel, Dragon Head Handle, Marked, 9½ In. ....*illus*	1265.00
Figurine, Bear, Reclining, 8½ x 12½ In.	351.00
Figurine, Chicken Little, Green Blue Luster	40.00
Figurine, Dog, Boxer, Purple, Marked, Pecs, 5½ In.	295.00
Figurine, Dog, Cocker Spaniel, Green, Signed, 5 In.	75.00
Figurine, Frog, 2¾ x 3 In.	41.00 to 117.00
Figurine, Frog, Red, Standing, Marked, Hungary, 3 In.	325.00
Figurine, Nude Undressing, Water Urn, Iridescent Turquoise, Cathedral Mark, 10½ In.	230.00
Figurine, Snail, Red, PECS, 2½ x 4¾ In.	289.00
Jardiniere, Flowers, Art Nouveau, Marked, No. 505, c.1890, 15 In. Wide	650.00
Perfume Bottle, City Scene, Footed, Handles, Hungary, 2¹⁵⁄₁₆ In.	24.00
Tankard, Oak Branches, Beetles, Luster Glazes, 15½ x 7 In.	22800.00
Tile, Green, Central Flower Design, Raised, Eosin, Marked, K2, 9 In.	585.00
Vase, Birds, Branches, Iridescent Glaze, Pierced, c.1906, 7½ In.	2400.00
Vase, Flowers, Gold Trim, Marked, 10 In.	95.00
Vase, Green & Blue Metallic Glaze, Red Beads, Cream Ground, Art Deco, 8 In. ....*illus*	4830.00
Vase, Iridescent Blue On Gold, Tapered, Fluted, Ruffled Rim, 8 In.	201.00
Vase, Iridescent Turquoise, Stemmed Flowers, Cylindrical, Cathedral Mark, 11 In.	345.00
Vase, Landscape, Iridescent Glaze, c.1898, 11 In.	9600.00
Vase, Landscape, Iridescent Glaze, c.1909, 10⅝ In.	20400.00
Vase, Pheasants, Crouching, Luster Green, Gold Glaze, c.1930, 14 In.	6000.00
Vase, Poppies, Luster Red Ground, c.1900, 13⅜ In.	4800.00
Vase, Red, Pink Geraniums, Green Leaves, Luster Aqua Ground, 9 x 5¾ In.	10800.00
Vase, Silver, Black, Red, Flared, Signed, 17 In.	3300.00

Zanesville, Vase, Carved Female Figure, Purple Matte Glaze, Stoneware, 11 x 6½ In.
$240.00

Zsolnay, Bowl, Centerpiece, 4 Cherubs With Bowl, Fruit Edges, Blue Iridescent Glaze, 7½ x 13 In.
$1495.00

Zsolnay, Ewer, Pierced, Blue & Red Enamel, Dragon Head Handle, Marked, 9½ In.
$1265.00

Zsolnay, Vase, Green & Blue Metallic Glaze, Red Beads, Cream Ground, Art Deco, 8 In.
$4830.00

INDEX

This index is computer-generated, making it as complete and accurate as possible. References in uppercase type are category listings. Those in lowercase letters refer to additional pages where pieces can be found. There is also an internal cross-referencing system used in the main part of the book, so if you look for a Kewpie doll in the Doll category, you will be told it is in its own category. There is additional information at the end of many paragraphs about where to find prices of pieces similar to yours.

HOW TO GET ANTIQUE PRICING
INFORMATION THAT CHANGES MONTHLY

Some markets are more volatile than others.
Auctions, trends, and collections impact prices in some categories dramatically.

If you're a dealer or a collector who NEEDS to know what is happening, SUBSCRIBE NOW to our award-winning monthly newsletter, *Kovels on Antiques and Collectibles.*

This is THE SOURCE that helps COLLECTORS and DEALERS keep up with the fast-changing world of antiques and collectibles.

- Learn about auction prices at the latest sales and auctions
- Spot tomorrow's emerging trends so you can cash in TODAY
- Discover the true value of dozens of collectibles as prices change month to month
- Find out how to avoid fakes and frauds and what is being faked right now!
- Accurately assess the quality of antiques and collectibles every month

For a FREE sample copy of the newsletter, just fill in your name and address on the back of this form and mail it to:

Kovels on Antiques and Collectibles
P.O. Box 420349
Palm Coast, Florida 32142-9656

The Kovels (collectors for more than 40 years, authors of 95 books, and stars of the show "Flea Market Finds with the Kovels" on HGTV) will clue you in so you can identify treasures that might be disguised as trash. Become a more informed, successful collector.

Don't wait! Mail the form on the back of this page now,
and we'll rush you a FREE issue of Kovels.